Th

8th Annual
COMPUTER
INDUSTRY
ALMANAC

Karen Petska-Juliussen
and
Dr. Egil Juliussen

The
8th Annual COMPUTER INDUSTRY ALMANAC

Manufactured in the United States of America

10 9 8 7 6 5 4 3 2 1

ISBN 0-942107-07-1 Paperback
ISBN 0-942107-08-X Hardcover

ISSN 0893-0791

Hardcover distributed by:
The Reference Press, Inc.
1033 LaPosada Drive, #250
Austin TX 78752
512/374-4500, Fax 512/374-4501
To order call (800) 486-8666

Distribution to the book trade:
International Thomson Publishing
Kentucky Distribution Center
7625 Empire Drive
Florence KY 41042
800/842-3636, Fax 606/525-7778

Disclaimer

Computer Industry Almanac has made its best effort in preparing this book and the information contained in it. Computer Industry Almanac makes no representation or warranties with respect to the accuracy or completeness of the contents hereof and specifically disclaim any implied warranties of merchantability or fitness for any particular purpose. Computer Industry Almanac is not responsible for errors in articles reprinted by permission from other sources.

Trademarks

Most computer hardware and software brand names have trademarks or registered trademarks. Since Computer Industry Almanac lists thousands of product and company names, the individual trademarks have not been listed.

Dedication

For Kåre Øgreid

Acknowledgment

The editors wish to thank the contributors to Computer Industry Almanac. Without the hard work and support of the individuals listed below, this book would not have been completed:

Krista Juliussen-Bauer
Peter Bartelme: Cover design

The 8th Annual Computer Industry Almanac was Prepared Using:

Hardware:
Compaq Deskpro 486/25
CTI 486DX2 desktop PC w/4X CD-ROM
Epson ActionNote 486SLC noteboook PC
HP LaserJet 4 Plus
Pentium 133 desktop PC w/8X CD-ROM
Yamaha and Bose speakers

Cornerstone Technology XL full-page monitor
DFI 486/50 desktop PC
HP Colorado Trakker tape backup
IBM LaserPrinter 4019
Portrait Display Labs Portrait/15 full-page monitor

Software:
Adobe FrameMaker 5.0
America Online 3.0
CompuServe WinCim 2.01
CyberMedia FirstAid 95
Micrografx Charisma 4.0
Microsoft DOS 6.2 and Windows 3.1
Microsoft Windows 95 and Plus
Quarterdeck CleanSweep 95

Adobe Type Manager 2.0
Borland Paradox 4.0
Computer Support's Arts & Letters Express 5
Intuit Quickbooks 3.0 for Windows
Microsoft Access 2.0
Microsoft Excel 6.0
Microsoft Word 6.0

Comments, Suggestions, Your Information and Orders

Omissions are inevitable due to the scope and dynamic nature of the computer industry and the thousands of decisions the editors had to make for inclusion or exclusion. If your information is not in and you'd like it to be, please phone, E-mail or fax info to us and we'll try to include it. We apologize in advance for any oversights or omissions.

Users of Computer Industry Almanac are encouraged to submit comments and suggestions for inclusion in subsequent editions. Orders for the Computer Industry Almanac or databases therein can be made to the following address:

Computer Industry Almanac, Inc.; (800) 377-6810 Pacific time
FAX 702/749-5864; CompuServe 73543,3506; cialmanac@aol.com

Sources

Adscope, Inc.
1601 Oak Street, Ste. B, Eugene OR 9740 U.S.; 503/687-1519
Business Communications Co.
25 Van Zant St, Norwalk CT 06855 U.S.; 203/853-4266, Fax 203/853-0348
CIO Communications/IDG Communications
492 Old Connecticut Path, Framingham MA 01701 U.S.; 508/872-0080, Fax 508/879-7784
Computer Ethics Institute
11 Dupont Circle NW #900, Washington DC 20036 U.S.; 202/939-3707
Computer Industry Almanac Inc.
P.O. Box 600, Glenbrook NV 89413-0600 U.S.; 702/749-5053, Fax 702/749-5864
Computer Press Association
3 Floyd Drive, Mt. Arlington NJ U.S.; 201/398-7300, Fax 201/398-3888
Computer Reseller News/CMP Publications
1 Jericho Plaza, Wing A, Jericho NY 11753 U.S.; 800/521-3463, Fax 516/733-8636
Computer Retail Week/CMP Publications
2800 Campus Drive, San Mateo CA 94403 U.S.; 415/525-4300
Computerworld/CW Publishing
P.O. Box 9171, Framingham MA 01701 U.S.; 508/879-0700, Fax 508/875-8931
Consumer Electronics Manufacturers Association
2500 Wilson Boulevard, Arlington VA 22201 U.S.; 703/907-7600, Fax 703/907-7601
CreaTECH
91 Highland Road, Scarsdale NY 10583 U.S.; 800/273-2832
Data Analysis Group
5100 Cherry Creek Rd, Cloverdale CA 95425 U.S.; 707/539-3009, Fax 707/486-5618
Datamation/Cahners Publishing Assoc.
275 Washington St., Newton MA 02158 U.S.; 617/964-3030, Fax 617/558-4506
Disk/Trend, Inc.
1925 Landings Dr., Mountain View CA 94043 U.S.; 415/961-6209, Fax 415/969-2560
Electronic Business Today/Cahners Publishing
275 Washington St., Newton MA 02158 U.S.; 617/964-3030
Forbes
60 Fifth Ave., New York NY 10011 U.S.; 212/620-2200
Forward Concepts
1575 W. University Avenue #111, Tempe AZ 85281 U.S.; 602/968-3759, Fax 602/968-7145
Freeman Associates
311 East Carillo Street, Santa Barbara CA 93101 U.S.; 805/963-3853, Fax 805/962-1541
Frost & Sullivan
2525 Charleston Road, Mountain View CA 94043 U.S.; 415/961-9000, Fax 415/961-5042
Giga Information Group
One Longwater Circle, Norwell MA 02061 U.S.; 617/982-9500
HLS Associates
19 Halifax Court, #200, Sterling VA 20165 U.S.; 703/444-7037, Fax 703/406-9298

Infomart
1950 Stemmons Fwy., Dallas TX 75207 U.S.; 214/746-3500, Fax 214/749-3501
Information Technology Industry Council
311 First St. NW, #500, Washington DC 20001 U.S.; 202/737-8888, Fax 202/638-4922
Machover Associates
152-A Longview Avenue, White Plains NY 10605 U.S.; 914/949-3777, Fax 914/949-3851
Macworld Communications
501 Second St, San Francisco CA 94107 U.S.; 415/243-0505, Fax 415/442-0766
Multimedia PC Systems
3104 Canyon Creek Drive, Richardson TX 75080-1507 U.S.
NewMedia
901 Mariner Island Blvd. #365, San Mateo CA 94404 U.S.; 415/573-5170, Fax 415/573-5170
Pacific Media Associates
1121 Clark Avenue, Mountain View CA 94049 U.S.; 415/948-3080, Fax 415/948-3092
PC Magazine/Ziff-Davis Publishing
One Park Ave., New York NY 10016-5255 U.S.; 212/503-5255, Fax 212/503-5519
PC World/PCW Communications
501 Second St., #600, San Francisco CA 94107 U.S.; 415/243-0500, Fax 415/442-1891
Positive Support Review
2500 Broadway, #320, Santa Monica CA 90404 U.S.; 310/453-6100, Fax 310/453-6253
Romtec
Vanall Road, Maidenhead Berks, UK SL6 4UB; 1628-770-077, Fax 1628-785-433
Soft•letter
17 Main Street, Watertown MA 02172 U.S.; 617/924-3944, Fax 617/924-7288
Software Magazine/Sentry Publishing
1900 W Park Drive, Westborough MA 01581 U.S.; 508/366-2031, Fax 508/366-8104
Software Publishers Association
1730 M St. NW, #700, Washington DC 20036 U.S.; 202/452-1600, Fax 202/223-8756
Source Edp
P.O. Box 809030, Dallas TX 75380 U.S.; 800/840-8090
Source Engineering
P.O. Box 809032, Dallas TX 75380 U.S.; 800/840-8090
U.S. Department of Labor
Washington DC 20212 U.S.
Upside/Upside Publishing Co.
2015 Pioneer Court, San Mateo CA 94403 U.S.; 415/377-0950, Fax 415/377-1962
VLSI Research
1754 Technology Drive #117, San Jose CA 95110 U.S.; 408/453-8844, Fax 408/436-0608
Voice Information Associates
14 Glen Road South, P.O. Box 625, Lexington MA 02173 U.S.; 617/861-6680, Fax 617/863-8790

About the Authors

Karen Petska-Juliussen

Karen Petska Juliussen is Chairman and Editor-in-Chief of Computer Industry Almanac, Inc. which compiles and publishes the book and CD-ROM versions of the Computer Industry Almanac. The 1992 Computer Industry Almanac received the Computer Press Association Computer Press Runner-up award in the nonfiction computer book category. Previously, Karen was Vice President of Marketing for Workstation Laboratories Inc., which specializes in benchmark performance testing of PCs and workstations. Karen was also a co-founder of StoreBoard Inc. and left in 1987 to dedicate full-time to the Almanac. StoreBoard was sold to Computer Intelligence in August, 1989. Prior to this Karen was with Future Computing, Inc. from 1984 to 1986. Future Computing was an information service company specializing in the personal computer industry. Karen was born in Chicago Illinois and grew up in Manitowoc Wisconsin, U.S. where this book was done.

Egil Juliussen

Dr. Egil Juliussen is President of Computer Industry Almanac, Inc. which creates the Computer Industry Almanac and does computer industry consulting. Previously he was also Chairman of Workstation Laboratories Inc., which specializes in performance testing of workstations and personal computers. Egil was a member of the advisory board of Corporate Computing magazine, COMDEX and Sunworld. In 1986 he was a co-founder of StoreBoard Inc. which tracks the sales of personal computer products through computer specialty stores. Prior to this, Dr. Juliussen was President, Chairman, and Co-founder of Future Computing, which was an information service company that specialized in product testing, market research, for the personal computer industry. In 1984, Future Computing was sold to McGraw-Hill. Previously, Dr. Juliussen was with Texas Instruments Inc. where he was a strategic and product planner for microprocessors, minicomputers and personal computers. Dr. Juliussen was also employed by Norden, a division of United Technologies, where he designed graphics systems. He regularly writes columns and papers for computer publications and makes presentations, seminars and lectures in the U.S., Japan and Europe. He received B.S., M.S., and Ph.D. degrees in electrical engineering from Purdue University. Egil is a native of Norway and grew up in Stavanger.

Contents

Chapter 1

Computer Industry Overview

Overview

Thirty years ago computers were mainly a curiosity and only large companies could afford one. In 1965 there were only 25,000 computers in the U.S. Even by 1975 there were less than 200,000 computers in the U.S. Then came the personal computer and the world changed forever. By 1980 the number of computers in the U.S. surpassed one million units. In 1990 the number of computers in the U.S. exceeded 50M units and in 1996 the installed base surpassed 100M units. Today over 35% of U.S. households have a computer at home and over 50% of U.S. workers use a PC. In the office a significant portion of the computer users do not have just one desktop PC, but also a notebook or subnotebook computer for use on the road or wherever they may go. In 1994 the computers sold in the U.S. surpassed the number of automobiles sold. The value of PCs sold to homes exceeded the value of all TVs sold in the U.S. in 1995. The U.S. computer industry has now surpassed the $400B mark or nearly 6% of the gross domestic product (GDP).

The amazing thing is that the computer is at most at its half-way point in its impact on our world. If anything, the next ten years will be even more exciting than the last ten years. By the turn of the century the average PC will be more powerful than the 1995 supercomputer. In year 2000 the number of computers sold in the U.S. will surpass 30M units and the installed base will be in the 160M range or over one computer for every two people. Worldwide the numbers are even more impressive--120M computers may be sold in the year 2000 and over 550M computers may be in use. By the year 2000, the U.S. computer industry will approach $700B and may contribute over 7% of the GDP.

The computer industry is also exciting and glamorous. There are many visionary and colorful people. Fortunes are made and fortunes are lost. There are thousands of people in the computer industry that have become millionaires from their stock ownership in rapidly growing computer companies. There are now eight computer executives who have a net worth exceeding one billion dollars, up from four in 1989: Bill Gates, Paul Allen, Larry Ellison, Steve Ballmer, William Hewlett, Gordon Moore, Ross Perot and Ted Waitt. Bill Gates is currently ranked first in the Forbes 400 of America's richest people and the richest man in the world in the Forbes ranking of the world's billionaires. Paul Allen also has the distinction of owning the Portland Trailblazers professional basketball team. There were 41 individuals or families from the computer and related industries listed in the 1995 Forbes 400 worth over $60B. The 1993 Forbes 400 had 25 computer-related executives worth $30B.

High growth is the norm in the computer industry. The growth of the computer industry has slowed due to its sheer size and is no longer immune to economic cycles. However, compared to other large industries, the computer industry moves many times faster no matter how the speed is measured: market growth rate, product life cycle, distribution channel change, market segment evolution or technological change. Even though the overall computer industry is growing less than 10% per year there are segments that grow 50% to 100% per year.

Computer technology growth has been phenomenal in the last 40 years. In this time span, the performance of the fastest computers has increased over a million times. The price of an entry-level computer has decreased by a factor of over 1,000, and there is no end in sight. The performance and price/performance of computers will continue to improve at breakneck speeds. A quote from Intel's Gordon Moore says it best: "If the auto industry had moved at the same speed as our industry, your car today would cruise comfortably at a million miles an hour and probably get a half a million miles per gallon of gasoline. But it would be cheaper to throw your Rolls Royce away than to park it downtown for an evening."

The continued computer advances are impacting and overlapping other industries. For instance, microcomputer chips and boards have replaced electromechanical or other control systems in nearly all types of equipment ranging from microwave ovens, TVs, stereo systems, automobiles, cash registers, copiers, telephones, toys, oscilloscopes and sewing machines to military weapon systems. The number of microprocessors sold with such equipment far exceeds the number of computers sold per year. For instance, the typical car today has several microcomputers and the automotive industry's yearly consumption of microprocessors is as large as the computer industry. However, the microprocessors used in cars are not as powerful as those used in computers.

With such diversity and rapid change it is helpful to have a common framework of the computer industry. The next sections explain the structure of the computer industry--primarily from a product viewpoint. This product structure is used throughout the Computer Industry Almanac.

What is a Computer?

A computer is an electronic machine that performs high-speed mathematical or logical calculations or that assembles, stores, correlates or otherwise processes and prints information derived from coded data in accordance with a predetermined program[1] Today most computers are built from microprocessors. A microprocessor is a semiconductor central processing unit (CPU) usually contained on a single integrated circuit chip[1] A chip is a minute square of semiconducting material, such as silicon or germanium, doped and otherwise processed to have specified electrical characteristics, especially such a square before attachment of electrical leads and packaging as an electronic component or integrated circuit[1] A microcomputer is a small computer built around a microprocessor[1].

What is a Computer?

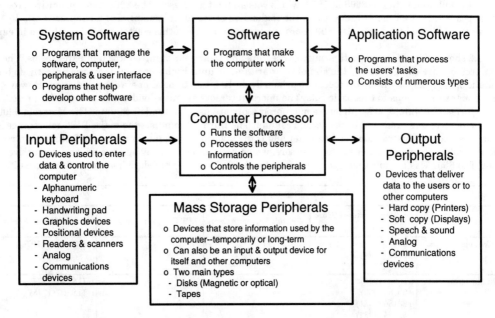

Figure 1.1

Figure 1.1 shows the elements of a computer and gives a short explanation of each category. The computer processor or central processor unit is the actual computer. Computer Industry Almanac divides the computers into nine categories. Software consists of two main types: system software and application software. System software, such as the operating system, manages the computer system or provides tools for developing software. Application software accomplishes the users tasks.

There are three types of computer auxiliary devices that are called peripherals. Mass storage peripherals such as disks and tapes keep the data and programs that computers use. These devices may store the data temporarily or permanently.

Output devices show the results from the computers' calculations and information processing. There are two types of output peripherals: hard-copy devices provide a permanent copy (i.e., printed paper) and soft-copy devices show the information only temporarily (i.e., display).

1American Heritage Dictionary, Second College Edition

Input devices are used for two purposes: to enter data and to control the operation of the computer. Keyboards, graphics tablets and scanners are examples of data input devices. Positional or pointing devices such as mouse devices, trackballs and light pens are input devices that control how the software and computer operate.

In this edition we added a fourth peripheral category--communications peripherals. Communications peripherals are both input and output peripherals, but are getting so important that a separate listing seems appropriate. We also added a section on microprocessors to give you an idea of their evolution and status.

Microprocessor Categories

When mainframe computers appeared in the 1950s and minicomputers in the 1960s, the processors were built from hundreds of semiconductor chips. In the early 1970s, the semiconductor technology had advanced enough to make the processor portion of a computer on a single or a few chips. The first microprocessor chip was the Intel 4004, which appeared in 1971. It was a 4-bit processor and was used for calculators and similar functions. Intel quickly followed with the 8008 in 1972, which was an 8-bit processor. The 8008 was a primitive processor, but its appearance raised the awareness and the realization of the future potential of microprocessors. In 1974 both the Intel 8080 and the Motorola 6800 microprocessors arrived and this started the PC revolution in earnest.

Figure 1.2 shows most of the important microprocessors and their year of introduction in parenthesis. The microprocessors are categorized by the size of their arithmetic unit. Eight-bit microprocessors mostly do 8-bit arithmetic operations, 16-bit microprocessors primarily do 16-bit arithmetic operations and so on. However, there are many exceptions to this basic rule. The microprocessors are also divided into four vendor or architecture categories. The Intel x86 architecture microprocessors are listed in the left column. The Motorola 6800 and 68000 microprocessors are listed in the second column. The third column lists the major RISC microprocessors. RISC means Reduced Instruction Set Computer and is the favorite technique for designing fast microprocessors. The fourth column includes other microprocessors, which have all faded away and are no longer in active development. The 6502 was the most important because the Apple II and Commodore home computers used it.

Figure 1.2: Microprocessor Categories				
	Intel Architecture Microprocessors	Motorola Microprocessors	RISC Microprocessors	Other Microprocessors
8-Bit Microprocessors	o 8008 (1972) o 8080 (1974) o Zilog Z80 (1976)	o 6800 (1974)		o MOS 6502 (1976)
16-Bit Microprocessors	o 8086 (1978) o 8088 (1980) o 80186 (1981) o 80286 (1982)			o TI 9900 (1977) o TI 9980 (1978)
32-Bit Microprocessors	o 80386DX (1985) o 80386SX (1988) o 80386SL (1990) o 80486DX (1989) o 80486SX (1991) o 80486SL (1993) o 80486DX2 (1993) o 80486DX4 (1994) o Pentium (1993) o Pentium Pro (1995) o Pentium P55C (1997)	o 68000 (1979) o 68010 (1981) o 68020 (1984) o 68030 (1987) o 68040 (1989)	o SPARC (1987) o MIPS Rx000 (1986) o Motorola 88000 (1989) o Intel I860 (1989) o IBM RS/6000 (1990) o HP PA (1991) o PowerPC 601 (1993) o PowerPC 603 (1995) o PowerPC 604 (1994) o PowerPC 620	o National 32000 o Fairchild Clipper
64-Bit Microprocessors	o P7 (1997-98) o P8 (2000-01)		o DEC Alpha (1993) o MIPS R8000 (1994) o MIPS R10000 (1994) o UltraSPARC (1995) o HP PA (1996) o PowerPC	

The Intel architecture is the most important microprocessor family and its members are shown in the most detail--including potential future members. Some of the Intel compatible microprocessors from AMD, Cyrix and

IBM are not listed. Motorola has stopped developing additional microprocessors in the 68000 family and is supporting the PowerPC processor instead.

The main competition to the Intel microprocessors are the five RISC processor families. SPARC is used by Sun Microsystems and is the leading microprocessor in the workstation market. The MIPS family microprocessors are used by Silicon Graphics and others and also in Nintendo's latest video game machine. Digital Equipment's Alpha was the first 64-bit microprocessor, but today all the RISC processors have 64-bit processors. Hewlett-Packard's Precision Architecture (PA) is one of the performance leaders. The PA architecture is likely to merge with the Intel architecture in the P7 microprocessor at the end of this decade because HP and Intel are jointly developing this microprocessor. The PowerPC microprocessor is the volume leader among the RISC processors, because it is replacing the 68000 family in the Macintosh.

Computer Categories

The three main types of computers and their subtypes are summarized in Figure 1.3. The microcomputer started with an 8-bit microprocessor in the mid 1970s and used primarily the 16-bit microprocessor in the 1980s. The 32-bit microprocessor emerged in 1987 and has now overtaken the 16-bit microprocessor. The 64-bit microprocessor is now starting to emerge. The use of the 32-bit microprocessor has already narrowed the performance gap between the microcomputer and midrange computer. Microcomputers using 64-bit processors have the potential to revolutionize the midrange computer and mainframe segments in the next five years.

The microcomputer is the lowest-priced computer. Prices start at under $1,000 for the personal computer and range up to $100,000 for workstations and desktop supercomputers. The microcomputer is normally configured in a desktop computer, tower or minitower form factor. The minitower form factor is primarily used for consumer PCs. The portable computer has gotten so small in the last few years that the typical version now is the size of a thick notebook, fits inside a briefcase and runs for hours on batteries.

Figure 1.3: Computer Product Categories		
Microcomputers o 16-, 32- & 64-bit processors o Typical price from $1K to $100K o Desktop, tower or portable form factor	Midrange Computers o 32-bit & 64-bit processors o Typical price from $10K to $1M o Tower, rack or cabinet form factor	Large Computers o 32-bit & 64-bit processors o Typical price from $0.5M to $10M o May require special cooling
Personal Computers o Computers used by individuals o Primary use is office productivity tasks o Recreation, education & work-at-home	PC Servers o Serves multiple users on LANs o Provides information for the Internet o Web server for Internet & intranets	Mainframe Computers o Computers for large companies o Primary use is enterprise applications o Large staffs run system 24 hours a day
Workstation Computers o High-performance computer for individuals o 3D graphics capability is key feature o Favored by scientists & engineers	Workstation Servers o High-performance server o Serves multiple users on networks o Web server for Internet & intranets	Supercomputers o Used for large computer problems o Mostly scientific applications o Emerging commercial applications
Desktop Supercomputers o Small supercomputer for individuals o Mostly scientific applications o Multiple processors	Minicomputers o Computers for medium & large companies o Primarily multiuser systems o Used in industrial & scientific applications	Massively Parallel Computers o Used for special applications o Data mining an emerging application o Hundreds of microcomputers

The personal computer is the most popular computer and accounts for over 90% of all computers in use. In the U.S. nearly 100M PCs are in use and worldwide there are over 250M PCs. At the high end, PCs compete with workstations and midrange computers.

The home PC is used for recreation, office work and school work. Today most home PCs are compatible with the PCs used in businesses. Office PCs are used to improve productivity of individual tasks such as writing, calculating, filing and drawing. The PC is rapidly becoming a communication device used to send and receive electronic mail, fax and retrieving information from the Internet and online services. An important trend in the office is to structure the workflow around computer capabilities which shows a potential for large productivity increases. This trend is usually called reengineering.

The workstation is also a computer designed for use by individuals. Its strength is graphics capabilities and performance in scientific calculations. Workstations were originally used primarily by engineers and scientists and are often called technical workstations. The workstation is becoming increasingly popular to any person who does graphic design work or has complex calculation needs. The workstation is common as a server in local area networks (LANs) and as web information servers on the Internet.

In the 7th edition of the Computer Industry Almanac multiuser microcomputers were included as a separate category. Multiuser microcomputers use PC or workstation technology and add the capability of serving more than one user at a time. This requires more sophisticated software and a display terminal or PC for each user. Business operations such as accounting and database management are the most common applications for the multiuser microcomputer. Usually, these systems serve 8 to 16 users, but may handle over 100 users simultaneously. The multiuser microcomputer competes with the minicomputer and has been included in this category. Both minicomputers and multiuser microcomputers now use the UNIX operating system. In the past the minicomputer used proprietary operating systems that were different for each minicomputer manufacturer. Both categories are fading and will be extinct in a few years.

The desktop supercomputer is a recent category. It uses multiple high-performance microprocessors and some may even have hundreds of microprocessors. Its peak performance approaches the low-end supercomputer's performance. The desktop supercomputer is also called microsupercomputer or personal supercomputer. In many ways the desktop supercomputer has characteristics similar to the massively-parallel computer.

The minicomputer started with an 8-bit processor in the mid-1960s and went to a 16-bit processor in the early 1970s. By the late 1970s, the 32-bit processor appeared and is now prevalent. The 64-bit processor is also used. Prices of low-end minicomputers start at $10,000 while high-end or superminis may cost hundreds of thousands of dollars. The minicomputer is traditionally used for scientific and engineering applications and for industrial and automation tasks. Business applications such as accounting are also popular. The minicomputer may be single-user system, but is normally a multiuser computer. The minicomputer typically serves 16 to 64 users while a supermini can handle over 100 users. The high-end supermini has a performance similar to the low-end mainframe computer and competes with such products. In the next few years most minicomputers will fade away.

The previous edition of the Almanac listed minisupercomputers as a separate category. The minisupercomputer is a mixture of minicomputer and supercomputer technology. Prices of a few hundred thousand dollars are common. It often uses multiple processors to achieve its high performance. Minisupercomputers are being squeezed by the increasing power of workstations and PCs and the category has been deleted.

The PC and workstation server categories have been added to the midrange computer spectrum. Both provide information to users on LANs, corporate networks, intranets and to the Internet. Intranets are internal corporate networks that use Internet standards and technology. They also provide extra storage capabilities, expensive peripheral functions, distribute electronic mail and run workgroup applications.

The mainframe computer was the first commercial computer that appeared in the 1950s. It is still room size, but today its the peripherals that require most of the room. Mainframes are now referred to as legacy systems. The mainframe and the supercomputer are the two largest and most powerful computers. As a system, they cost millions of dollars and in the past required special cooling--either air conditioning or liquid cooling. Today the special cooling is going away as mainframes are built using microprocessors. Traditional mainframe computers are multiuser systems that can handle hundreds or thousands of users. They are normally operated by a staff who runs the system around the clock to get maximum use of such an expensive resource.

The supercomputer is used for large-scale scientific calculations. It has a special purpose vector processor and often consists of multiple processors. Vector processors can do many arithmetic calculations in parallel or simultaneously. The first supercomputer appeared in the mid-1960s.

Massively-parallel computers are used for special applications and consist of hundreds and even thousands of microprocessors. These computer systems are only effective on problems that can be split into many parallel segments. The performance of massively-parallel computers is very high and exceeds supercomputer performance when all the processors are utilized.

Figure 1.4 shows the spectrum of personal computers. The majority of PCs are fixed location computers during their operation. The server PC normally has a tower form factor and is used as a server on a local area network and as Internet and intranet web servers. Only about 4% to 5% of PCs are server PCs, but the percentage will probably double in the next five years due to Internet/intranet growth. Most desktop PCs sold today have both a hard disk and a floppy disk and in the last three years CD-ROMs have also become standard. Ten years ago only a small fraction of PCs came with a hard disk. Floppy disk-based PCs were the norm in the early 1980s, but PCs using only floppy disks are now extinct.

Diskless PCs are a result of the increasing popularity of LANs. LAN servers have a large amount of mass storage and can provide mass storage for diskless PCs. The diskless PC can also replace the terminal in multiuser systems. The diskless PC is a niche market and will remain a small segment.

There are three types of portable PCs that are defined by their physical size and weight. All portable PCs have about a 20% share of the PC market and are expected to surpass 30% by the late 1990s. The luggable, AC-powered PC was the original portable PC and was the target of many jokes due to its 25 to 35 pound weight. Today the luggable PC is almost extinct and is no longer included in these figures.

The portable PC segments have been the most dynamic and fast-changing in the computer industry. The laptop PC was the main category a few years ago, but declined rapidly and is no longer included in the battery PC categories. Instead the notebook PC has taken control and the subnotebook PC is emerging.

Figure 1.4: Personal Computer Categories		
Fixed Location PCs	Portable PCs	Application Specific PCs
o AC-powered	o Battery-powered	o Simpler user interface than today's PCs
o No mobility while running	o Light-weight	o Inexpensive: $200-$700
o Desktop PC is largest category	o Small physical size	o Emerging categories
Server PCs	Notebook PCs	Network Computers
o Single or multiple processors (SMP)	o 5-10 lbs, 9"x12"x 2"	o Used to access Internet
o Mass storage centric	o PC Card slots	o Receive programs & data from Internet
o Network operating system	o May have CD-ROM	o Uncertain success potential
Desktop PCs	Subnotebook PCs	Information Appliances
o Graphical user interface (GUI)	o 3-5 lbs, 6"x10"x1"	o Very simple user interface
o Office focused PCs	o PC card slots	o Dedicated to one or more applications
o Consumer focused PCs	o Limited peripherals	o Uncertain success potential
Diskless PCs	Pocket PCs	Personal Digital Assistants (PDAs)
o No disks	o 1-2 lbs, 4"x8"x1"	o Dedicated to one or more applications
o Used as stations on LANs	o PC Card slots	o Pocket PC form factor & features
o Terminal replacement	o Keyboard and/or pen	o Limited success so far

The notebook PC capability leapt forward in 1990 as Compaq and other vendors sold book-size PCs with both floppy disks and hard disks. In 1991 the notebook PC proliferated and went to the 386SX and 386SL microprocessors. The first pen-based notebook PCs were also introduced in 1991. In 1992 notebook PCs with 486 microprocessors appeared. Now the Pentium has invaded the notebook segment. Today notebook PCs have nearly the full capabilities of desktop PCs. Even CD-ROMs are rapidly becoming a standard peripheral.

The subnotebook PC is now appearing due to the need for a smaller PC for computer users on the go. It is lighter than a notebook PC, has longer battery life, but less capabilities. It may only have one mass storage device--usually a hard disk. Other peripherals are available via a PC card slot. The PC card or PCMCIA is a peripheral interface standard for memory cards, small disk drives, modems and other peripherals.

The smallest full-function PC category is the pocket or handheld PC. The size constraints of fitting into a large pocket dictates a keyboard with small keys that are close together, making touch-typing difficult, and a display that folds over the keyboard. Currently, there is no room for a mass storage device and removable PC cards are used for additional programs, data storage and peripherals. The battery life for the pocket PC is up to 100 hours.

The application-specific computer is a new category of personal computers. The reason for their emergence is that even though the PC user interface has been simplified in the last 10 years, there is a large portion of potential users that find PCs too hard to use. Even some Macintosh users--fresh out of school--find Windows PCs hard to use as they have not been educated in basic concepts of computers. Add to that the $1,000 plus price of a PC is out of reach for a significant portion of the U.S. population and there is a market opportunity for low-cost, simple-to-use computers. The international market also has potential--especially if the price is lowered significantly.

The personal digital assistant (PDA) was the first application-specific PC when it appeared in 1993, but has had limited success so far. It differs from the pocket PC in its ease of use and by being dedicated to specific functions. The pen and/or keyboard are likely to be the most common user interfaces, but may be challenged by speech recognition. There will be many different types of PDAs with a spectrum of prices. Initially the prices will range from $500 to $3,000 depending on capabilities. In a few years the price points will range from $100 to $1,000 for the most commonly used PDAs.

The network computer (NC) or Internet computer has received much interest in 1996. Its main function is to access the Internet. Numerous companies including IBM, Oracle, Netscape and Sun Microsystems are supporting a standard definition for NCs. The first NCs are now appearing.

Several companies are working on other application-specific, simple-to-use computers. Such devices are being called information appliances. Most of these products are aimed at the home market and the consumer electronics companies are interested in entering this market. The first information appliances are starting to appear. Time will tell which application-specific computers will be most successful.

Figure 1.5 shows the many computer product segments and how they overlap. The horizontal axis plots computer system price and the vertical axis shows relative computer performance. It is a qualitative picture and is not for quantitative comparisons. This picture has changed significantly in the last five years and will see more changes in the future. A projection of changes in the next few years is shown in Chapter 4: Future Product Trends.

1997 Computer Product Segments

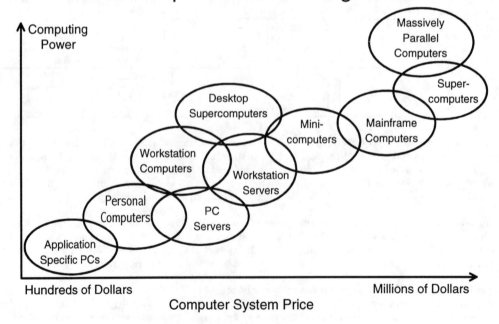

Figure 1.5

Software Categories

There are numerous types of software. There are also several ways of categorizing software. Computer Industry Almanac is using the categories and subcategories shown in Figure 1.6. Most categories have both vertical and horizontal software. Horizontal software is used by a wide variety of people. Vertical software is used by narrow segments of customers. For instance, most word processing programs are horizontal and are used across industries and job functions. However, a word processing program aimed toward scientists is a vertical program.

There are two types of system software. Operating system (OS) software is required for every computer. It is a program that manages the operation of a computer. The operating system can be relatively simple, as it was for the PC in the early 1980s, or very complex, as it is for mainframe computers. The operating system is the most important program because nearly all application programs use the capabilities of the operating system and must adhere to its interfacing conventions.

Figure 1.6: Computer Software Categories					
o Horizontal software is used by a wide spectrum of customers across many industries o Vertical software is used by a narrow segment of customers, usually in specific industries					
System Software -Programs that manage computer operation -Programs that develop software	Business Operation -Programs that manage company-wide or divisional activities	Office Automation -Programs that improve individual or workgroup productivity	Communications -Programs that let people/computers communicate with other people/devices	Educational Software -Programs that teach subjects or tasks -Programs that train or improve skills	Recreation Software -Programs used for entertainment -Programs used for recreation
o Operating systems o Graphical user IF o Languages o Middleware o Security software o CASE o Utilities	o Accounting o Inventory mgmt. o Sales mgmt. o Manufacturing o CAD o Simulation o Data warehousing	o Word processing o Database mgmt. o Spreadsheets o Graphics o Desktop publishing o Project mgmt. o Decision making	o Terminal emulation o File transfer o Faxing o Email o Online access o Web browser o Video conferencing	o Computer literacy o Training software o Testing software o Courseware o Help desk software o Reference software o Edutainment	o Music software o Genealogy software o Collector software o Video games o Simulation games o Fantasy games o Learning games

Operating environment or software is a category that has become very important. It is a program that gives the application software a graphical user interface (GUI). Such a program may be a separate program such as Microsoft Windows 3.1 or part of the operating system as in the Apple Macintosh and Microsoft Windows 95. The advantage of having an operating environment program is the user interface commands become more similar between people and the PC is much easier to learn for novices and people that are afraid of PCs.

The other type of system software is the software development tool that helps construct new programs and maintain old programs. Examples are high-level compiled languages such as Cobol, Fortran, C and Pascal. Basic and Java are interpretive languages. Language compilers and interpreters translate the higher level languages into binary machine code that computers can understand. Languages that use object technology are becoming very important because they make it easier to manage complex programs. Smalltalk and C++ are examples of object-oriented languages. The emerging Java is based on C++.

Utilities are various types of programs that simplify software development or computer operation. Examples of utility software that help the computer operation are disk-management programs, screen savers, performance monitors and backup programs.

Recently we have added a new category of software: security software. It was previously included in utility software, but is becoming important enough to be listed by itself. Anti-virus software is the best-known example of security software. Software that protects against unwanted intrusion is growing in importance--especially for online and networking operations.

Computer Aided Software Engineering (CASE) consists of sophisticated software development tools that are useful for large software development projects. CASE is very important because it improves the productivity of computer programmers.

Business operation software is a category of programs that manage company-wide activities. These applications usually have a centralized database that is used by multiple divisions and by many people. Examples are accounting, inventory management and computer aided design (CAD). Most of the manufacturing processes and product design activities also fall in this class. Many business operation programs are vertical software. Examples of vertical software are: accounting for medical offices, sales management for home products dealers, design for mechanical engineers and circuit design simulation for electronic engineers.

Office automation software became feasible as the price of computers could be justified for small groups and then for individuals. These programs can help with common tasks such as writing, calculating, filing, drawing, managing, decision making and communicating with others. Office automation software is primarily horizontal, but there are some vertical programs. The majority of this software is for personal computers and, to a lesser degree, for workstations and multiuser computers. Groupware is a term that has crept into the software vocabulary. It means software for use by workgroups. Much groupware development is taking place and major products will appear in the next few years. Lotus Notes is the leading example of this category. Groupware may not be a separate product class, but can be a network version of existing office automation software.

Communications software has become so important and widespread that a separate category is needed. Terminal emulation and file transfer software have been around for a long time. Web browsers and video conferencing are new and rapidly growing applications.

Educational software teaches specific subjects or tasks to people. Such educational programs are called computer-aided instruction (CAI) and computer-based training (CBT). Educational programs that teach computer skills are called computer literacy software. Nearly all educational programs are vertical software. Examples are mathematics for fifth grade, SAT training programs and high school physics. Computer-based training software also has a large variety. CBT software ranges from relatively simple tasks such as learning Windows 95 to complex multimedia software to learning the operation of military weapons systems. Multimedia capabilities are starting to improve educational software quality and more is expected in the future.

Recreational software became popular when personal computers appeared. The large installed base of home PCs created a large market for recreational software such as games and music programs. There is now a large variety of computer games ranging from the classical board games such as Chess and Monopoly to card games and simulation games. New classes of games, such as flight simulators, are not possible without computers. Often game programs overlap the educational software category or visa versa. PC-game software is increasingly overlapping with video-game software.

Multimedia software is a popular term. It means software that uses not just a text and graphics display to interact with the user, but may have sound, speech and video. Any software may become multimedia software. For instance a word processing program that generates documents that have text, graphics, voice message and still images is multimedia software. Or a database program that stores text, charts, speech messages and images is multimedia software. But before multimedia software can be prevalent we must have inexpensive computer hardware that can store, process and handle input and output functions for multimedia. This is now happening as all the multimedia pieces are now in place and outstanding multimedia software is starting to appear.

Peripherals Categories

There are three main types of peripherals: mass storage, output and input. Mass storage devices store the programs and data used by computers. Output peripherals provide the computer user with results from information processing and for control purposes in computer automation applications. Input peripherals feed the computers with programs and data--either directly from computer users or from other computers and equipment and also control the operation of a computer system. The next three sections explain the peripheral classes in more detail.

Mass Storage Peripherals

Mass storage devices are the most important peripherals in deciding the overall capabilities of computers. Figure 1.7 is an overview of mass storage and memory devices. Mass storage technologies have more varieties in capacity, performance and price than any other peripheral category. The storage capacity differs by a factor of over 1,000--from a fraction of a megabyte for low-end floppy disks to many gigabytes stored on the large mainframe disks. The performance characteristics vary even more--by over a million times in access time between tapes and semiconductor memory boards. Data transfer rates differ by a factor of 1,000 between low-performance tapes and high-speed disks. Price variations are also substantial--a factor of over 10,000 between large automated tape library systems or fault tolerant disk arrays and low-cost floppy disks or tape devices.

Figure 1.7: Computer Mass Storage Peripherals			
Magnetic Disks -Data stored on magnetic platters -Platter diameter & number vary	Magnetic Tapes -Data stored on long strip of tape -Length, width & package vary	Optical Disks -Laser read data stored on platter -Platter diameter varies	Semiconductor Memory -Data stored in electronic chips -Mounted on boards or cards
Floppy Disks o Flexible magnetic media o Interchangeable media o High-capacity version emerging	3M Cartridge o Developed by 3M o Several cartridge sizes o QIC types are standards	Read-Only Disks (CD-ROM) o Bits prestored as small pits o Same disk as music CD o Becoming standard on PCs	Read Only Memory (ROM) o Bits stored as permanent electronic circuitry in factory o Bits stored in field (PROM)
Hard Disks o Mostly fixed-media disks o Removable media is reappearing o Most important product	Digital Audio Tape (DAT) o Based on music DAT o Large storage capacity o Used for backup	Write-Once Disks o Bits stored by making pits o Data becomes permanent o Used as masters for CD-ROMs	Electrically Alterable Memory o Bits stored as semi-permanent electronic circuitry o Bits can be erased & restored
Disk Arrays (RAID) o Multiple disk drives o Fault-tolerant o Mostly used on servers	Other Tapes o Automated tape library systems o Cassettes, reel-to-reel tapes o VCR and many others	Erasable Disks o Bits stored by laser o Bits read by laser o Bits can be erased	Random Access Memory (RAM) o Bits stored & read rapidly o In Dynamic RAM bits must be restored or refreshed periodically

Magnetic disks are the most important and most common of the mass storage devices. Each data bit is stored as individual magnets on magnetically coated platters. The platters spin under a movable read-write head (a magnetic coil). The operation is similar to a record player, except there is no contact between the platter and the read-write head. The data organization is also different from the spiral traced by the pickup of a record player. The data on disks is stored along many concentric circles--one inside the other (called tracks). The diameter of the disks varies; the most popular sizes today are 3.5 inch and 5.25 inch. Larger 8 inch and 14 inch disk drives are rapidly disappearing. The number of platters ranges from 1 to 10. The mainframe computer used disks with many large platters, but are now moving to disk arrays consisting of many small disk drives. The personal computer uses a disk with small size platters and just one or a few platters. Even smaller-sized disks have appeared recently: 1.8 inch and 2.5 inch disks for use with notebook and subnotebook computers.

The floppy disk is a common mass storage device for the small computer. It is also the distribution media for software, but it is now getting serious competition from CD-ROMs. Most floppy disks store only up to a few megabytes or less. The most common diskette size was 5.25 inch, but the 3.5 inch floppy disk has now overtaken its larger cousin. There are high-capacity floppy disks that can store up to 100 MBytes, and they are now gaining in popularity.

The hard or rigid disk has much higher performance than the floppy disk. Nearly all computers have hard disks. Most hard disks are fixed and do not have removable media. Some medium- and large-size hard disks have a removable media called a disk cartridge or disk pack. The removable disk was prevalent in the 1970s, and is making a comeback. The removable disk is increasingly being used with the PC and is especially popular in the Macintosh market.

Arrays of small hard disks, usually called Redundant Arrays of Inexpensive Disks (RAID), is a recent mass storage category. It was originally developed to compete with the large disk used with the mainframe computer. But it is also very popular with PC servers and workstation servers. The main advantages of the RAID is its fault-tolerant features and price-performance.

The magnetic tape stores data on a long strip of magnetic media. Individual bits are reached by pulling the tape past a magnetic read-write head. The width and length of the tape and the number of tracks of data stored on the tape determine the storage capacity. Diverse methods are used to package the tape, ranging from reel-to-reel tapes, cartridges and cassettes to automated cartridge library systems that use robot arms to retrieve any one of many cartridges.

Optical storage is an emerging technology that shows great future promise. The optical disk is now entering the marketplace in force. There are three types of optical disks, as shown in Figure 1.7.

The read-only disk has pre-recorded information, where data is stored as individual microscopic pits in the disk surface. A laser detects the presence or absence of such pits. These disks are called CD-ROMs because they are based on the compact digital audio disks used in the music industry (4.77-inch diameter) and are read only memory devices. There are disk drives that will read both music CDs and CD-ROMs. In the last three years the CD-ROM started to take off in the PC market and will soon be as common as the hard and floppy disks. An improved version of the CD-ROM will be available soon. It is called the Digital Video Disk (DVD) and will be used to store movies, music and computer data. The technical specifications for the DVD have been set and products are expected in late 1996 or early 1997.

The write-once disk has no pre-recorded information. A laser writes data on the disk by burning small pits in the disk surface. Once written, these pits are not erasable. Disk sizes of 5.25 inch, 8 inch and 12 inch are used. Write-once optical disks are also called DRAW (Direct Read After Write) or WORM (Write Once, Read Many).

The erasable optical disk can both be written and erased. Drives using the 12-inch diameter disk were first available. The smaller size disks (5.25 inch and 3.5 inch) were introduced a few years ago. Erasable optical disks have lower performance than magnetic disks, but use removable media which is an advantage for data backup.

The semiconductor memory board is used primarily as main memory. Main memory or random access memory (RAM) is the fastest memory available and it stores the programs and data while the computer processes the users tasks. The memory board is also used as mass storage. When random access memory is used as a mass storage device it is called an electronic disk because it simulates a very fast disk.

The use of the removable semiconductor memory card in handheld or pocket computers is growing. These PCs are so small there is currently no room for disk drives. Standards for the memory card were agreed upon in 1990 and updated in 1992 to include other peripheral devices. The result will be increased usage of the semiconductor memory card with small computers. Notebook and subnotebook PCs are also likely to use these memory cards and desktop PCs may not be far behind. The updated PC Card standard also allows small disks and communication devices to be implemented as PC Card devices. The PC Card will also be used in other computer and electronic devices such as laser printers, fax machines, test equipment and scanners.

Output Peripherals

As shown in Figure 1.8, many different output peripherals exist. There are, however, two basic types of output devices. Hard-copy peripherals such as printers and plotters leave a permanent copy of the data. Soft-copy peripherals such as displays and sound devices leave only temporary images--unless recorded by some means.

The printer is the most important hard-copy output peripheral. There are three main printer categories. The page printer prints one page at a time and use non-impact technology based primarily on copiers. The prices of page printers range from $400 for low-end products to $100,000 for high-speed mainframe laser printers. The page printer is used with all types of computers and is the largest printer revenue segment. In the PC industry laser printers account for about 30% of the units sold and over 50% of the revenue.

The line printer prints one line at a time. The technology is mostly impact printing (one line of characters strike the paper simultaneously). The line printer is a popular printer for mainframes and minicomputers, but is rarely used with microcomputers. The line printer has peaked in importance and is losing market share to other printers.

Figure 1.8: Computer Output Peripherals				
Printers & Plotters (Hard-Copy)	Other Hard Copy	Displays (Soft Copy)	Speech & Sound	Computer-Controlled Activators
Page Printers o Print a page at a time o Uses copier technology	Cameras o Picture of display output o Digital cameras emerging	Display Controller Boards o Creates images & text of varying resolution	Speech Synthesizers o Generate speech from digital data	Digital Actuators o Programmable controllers o Relays & others

Figure 1.8: Computer Output Peripherals				
Printers & Plotters (Hard-Copy)	Other Hard Copy	Displays (Soft Copy)	Speech & Sound	Computer-Controlled Activators
Line Printers o Print a line at a time o Use impact technology	Microfiche (COM) o Text & graphics stored on sheets of film	Color CRTs o Varying resolution o Use TV technology	Music Synthesizers o Generate music from digital data	Analog Actuators o Motors o Others
Character Printers o Print a character at a time o Impact & non-impact	Fax o Fax software sends output to a fax machine	Flat Displays o LCD is prevalent o EL, plasma & others	Speakers o Reproduce music, sound & speech	D/A Converters o Translate digital data to analog data
Plotters o Make drawings o Use one or more pens	Others o Punched cards o Punched tapes	Display Projectors o Project computer output to a large screen		

printing technologies are available. There are two types of impact printers: the fully-formed character printer and the dot matrix character printer. Fully-formed characters mounted on a thimble or daisy wheel is a computer printer technology similar to that used in the electronic typewriter. These printers are called letter-quality printers. This technology peaked in importance 10 years ago due to the growth and improvement in the matrix printer. The dot matrix impact printer uses a matrix of dots to form the characters--usually 9 or 24 dots.

The non-impact character printer may use regular paper or specially treated paper. Printers using special paper (i.e. thermal and electrostatic printers) are niche products. Non-impact character printers using regular paper such as the thermal transfer and the inkjet printer are increasing in popularity. The inkjet printer has grown dramatically in the last couple of years and is now the leading PC printer category. This is due to its low price, silent operation and color capability.

The color printer can use most of the above technologies. It was too expensive for widespread use a few years ago, but the prices have decreased dramatically. The color inkjet printer is now available starting at under $300 and still going down. Sales of inkjet color printers have recently become the unit leader among all printers.

The plotter is the choice when a hard copy of complex drawings and other graphics is needed. Plotter prices range from a few hundred dollars to tens of thousands of dollars. Plotter applications are primarily in the scientific and engineering field.

There are many other hard-copy output devices. Cameras record the image of displays. Slide camera sales are increasing due to the popularity of slide presentations and the ease of creating business graphics with PCs.

Computer output microfiche (COM) store large amounts of data generated by mainframe computers. COM or microfiche can replace books and reports. A special viewer is needed to look at the pictures.

Other output devices which are rapidly increasing in popularity are the fax machine when used with computer fax hardware and software. Punched card and punched tape were important in the past, but have faded away except for special applications.

The display is the most popular soft-copy output device. The monochrome and color CRT (which are based on TV technology) are very important peripherals. The display controller board that creates the images is also crucial. A variety of new display technologies are now used (flat displays are desirable). The liquid crystal display (LCD) is popular with low-power products such as the notebook computer. The quality of LCD is now acceptable for most applications and is improving rapidly. The color LCD became prevalent on notebook PCs as their price premium declined. Plasma and electroluminescence (EL) are also flat displays but require more power than LCD. They are also more expensive but have better display quality than LCD. Both have future potential and are used on portable computers. The display projector controlled by a computer is becoming popular. Some use overhead projectors and others use expensive optical projectors.

Speech and sound synthesizers are also output peripherals. The speech synthesizer generates speech but has seen limited use. Speech quality is improving and prices are reasonable. Multimedia requirements will increase the importance of speech synthesis. The music synthesizer is used for recreational and entertainment purposes.

The capability of the computer as a music synthesizer is improving rapidly. Multimedia will also make the music synthesizer more common. Speakers are required to hear the sound and music.

The computer-controlled actuator is important in industrial automation applications. These output devices vary from relays and programmable controllers to motors and digital-to-analog (D/A) converters that control analog devices.

Input Peripherals

As depicted in Figure 1.9, there are numerous input devices. The input peripheral is segmented into five categories. The alphanumeric input devices include the keyboard and the punched card reader. The keyboard is used with nearly all computers. The punched card was important in the past but has limited use today. The handwriting pad and pen with software that recognizes handwriting is in its infancy.

The graphics and pointing devices are increasing in importance. These devices can enter data but are even more important as control devices for selecting and using software (usually called the graphics user interface--GUI). The mouse is the most important input controller due to its prevalent use with Macintosh and Windows operating environments. Some users prefer the trackball instead of the mouse due to better ergonomics of the trackball and less arm and wrist motion when heavily used.

The graphic tablet has been used for years to create drawings, primarily for engineering applications but also for artistic uses. The introduction of software that recognizes handwriting may make the graphic tablet an important input device. Handwriting recognition software is limited in functionality and is currently used mostly in "clipboard-jobs" (i.e. tasks where people enter data using paper and clipboards). The handwriting pad and graphics tablet segments will overlap and may merge into one product category.

Figure 1.9: Computer Input Peripherals				
Alphanumeric Input Devices	Graphics & Positional Devices	Readers & Scanners	Speech Input Systems	Computer-Controlled Sensors
Keyboards o Sends text & numbers in coded form to computer	Mouse Devices o Positional devices rolling on a flat surface	Optical Character Readers o Read & recognize special character fonts	Speech Recognition o Recognizes spoken words o Vocabulary size varies	Digital Sensors o Switches & relays o Clocks & calendars
Handwriting Pads & Pens o Records writing strokes & recognize text	Trackballs o Stationary devices with a rolling ball	Image Scanners o Scan & digitize text & graphics images	Speaker Verification o Verifies speaker identity from recorded voice	Analog Sensors o Temperature & pressure o Acceleration & light
Punched Card/Tape o Reads cards or paper tape coded with data	Graphics Tablets o Record drawings made by a stylus or pen	Cameras o Capture images or video in analog or digital form	Microphones o Translate speech to analog data	A/D Converters o Translate analog data to digital data
	Others o Joysticks & light pens o Touch tablets & others	Other Readers o Bar code o Optical mark		

There are several types of readers and scanners that input information to the computer. The optical character reader normally uses a laser to read and recognize printed text and the use of special character fonts minimizes potential errors. The bar-code reader recognizes bar-codes and are similar to the bar-code readers used in grocery stores. The image scanner digitizes pictures regardless of whether the original is text or graphics. This scanner is also used with pattern recognition software to recognize any printed text as an alternative to keyboard data entry.

Cameras can also be used as input devices. The video camera and the emerging digital video camera are used for desktop video conferencing, a rapidly growing application. The video cameras are also used to input images for multimedia applications. The new digital cameras used in digital photography are also providing computer image inputs.

Speech input to the computer has been a research goal for over 25 years. The technology is improving fast but still has a way to go. The size of the vocabulary that is recognized depends on the speech recognition product price. Products used with the PC recognize a few thousand words and the system is trained for each speaker (i.e., store the voice pattern of key words to increase accuracy). The high-end system is more capable but costs more. The speaker verification system is used to control the physical access to sensitive areas such as military installations or restricted laboratories.

There are numerous computer-controlled sensors that input information to the computer. Digital sensors range from switches to clock and calendar boards. Analog sensors include those for temperature, pressure, humidity, light and acceleration. The data from analog sensors is translated to digital form by using an analog-to-digital (A/D) converter.

Communications Peripherals

Computer communications have been around for over 30 years. The terminal was the first communications peripheral as millions of terminals were connected to mainframes by the early 1980s. The terminal had a built-in modem to communicate with host computers over telephone lines. Most mainframes and minicomputers used different or proprietary communications protocol that the terminals had to match. A modem is a device that converts data from a form usable in computers to a form usable in phone or other analog signal transmission. Modem is an abbreviation of modulator and demodulator. As modem use grew with PCs, modem standards were established resulting in lower prices and faster acceptance. The growth of online services in the early 1990s increased the use of modems. The popularity of the Internet has further increased the sales and use of modems. Over 35% of PCs in the U.S. now have modems.

The other major computer communications peripheral is the local area network (LAN) interface card. A LAN is a group of computers that are connected together via a high-speed communications link. One of the computers on the LAN is the server and usually has extra mass storage and other capabilities that can be shared by the connected computers. A typical LAN has about 8 to 10 PCs connected, but may have as many as 20 to 25 PC clients. LANs emerged in the mid 1980s and have grown dramatically since then. Today nearly 50% of all office PCs are connected to LANs. The communications speed for LAN connections is a few megabits per second for low-end LANs and 10Mbits per second for high-end LANs. In the future LAN communication speed will go to 100Mbits per second. Several LAN standards are used but the Ethernet is the clear leader.

The communications peripherals are determined by the communications link and the devices at each end. There are now numerous established and emerging computer communications peripherals as shown in Figure 1.10. As the PC is becoming a major communications tool there will undoubtedly be additional future communications peripherals.

The growth of the Internet has highlighted a major problem for computer communications: It can be slow if you are on a LAN and it is agonizingly slow without a LAN. Unfortunately, there is no easy fix at a reasonable price for the next few years. For large corporations that can afford internetworking equipment there are solutions that will deliver the necessary speed. For the rest of us, we have to keep our fingers crossed and hope that some of the emerging technologies will do better than expected.

For the majority of computer communications users, most of the information is flowing to the user (downstream) and little data is flowing the other way (upstream). Hence the phone modem can be used to send data in the low bandwidth direction. This is an opportunity to broadcasting stations, which have extra bandwidth available on their normal broadcast signals. Information is currently delivered via FM and TV signals to PCs, but they are niche markets and tend to be information that can be used by many people. Examples are stock prices and financial news.

An interesting idea is to send computer information during the blanking interval of the TV signal. This is the time when the CRT beam intensity is turned off to move from one side of the screen to the other side to start drawing another line. A few of these blanking lines have reserved usage, but most are available for data transmission. The technology is similar to the teletex and viewdata that are used in many European countries to send information to TV viewers. The potential transmission speed is much higher than for phone modems.

The use of satellite transmission has even more potential--especially the direct satellite broadcast (DSB) signals. Data transmission via DSB will soon be available to computer users at a reasonable price.

Figure 1.10: Computer Communications Peripherals			
Broadcast Receivers o Usually 1-way communications o Receive information included in normal broadcast signals	Analog Communication o 2-way communications o Use existing & emerging analog telecom network	Digital Communication o 2-way communications o Use existing & emerging digital telecom network	Internetworking o 2-way communications o Use existing & emerging high-speed digital telecom network
TV Receiver o Receive information from TV broadcast signals	Terminal Emulation o Used with legacy systems o Phone modem included	LAN Interfaces o Only high-speed connection to large portion of computers	Gateways o Connect & translate between very different networks
FM Receivers o Receive information from FM broadcast signals	Phone Modems o Leading product category o 28.8Kb/sec is close to max	Wireless LAN Interfaces o Emerging technology for easier implementation of LANs	Routers o Connect dissimilar networks
Radio Receivers o Receive information from AM radio broadcast signals	Cellular Modems o Only wireless option o Slower than phone modem	ISDN Interfaces o Use modified phone lines o 64K to 128Kb/sec	Bridges o Connect similar networks
Satellite Receivers o Receive information from satellite broadcast signals	Cable Modems o Uses cable TV system o 10X-100X phone modem speed	ADSL Interfaces o High-speed via phone lines o Trial stage, available in 2-3 years	

The cable modem has good potential to send data to the computer user, but has limited capacity to receive data from computer users. The cable modem has received a lot of publicity lately as an Internet connection media, but so far there is mostly future promise and little concrete results. The problem is that most cable TV systems have to undergo expensive equipment upgrades to deliver the data transmission promise. It will be at least 2-3 years until cable modems will see widespread use.

ISDN is currently the best bet for delivering higher transmission speeds than phone modems. In the last year ISDN has made strides forward, but still has a long way to go. ISDN is now available in most communities and the price is reasonable in most places. The main drawback is difficult installation and it is especially hard to find competent support from the phone companies. A long term drawback and potential fatal characteristic is that ISDN is only 2 to 4 times faster than phone modems.

The sleeper technology is ADSL or asymmetrical digital subscriber loop. The technology is just entering the testing stage, but has some impressive advantages. ADSL is based on the regular phone line and is likely to cost less than ISDN lines. ADSL can handle up to 8Mbits per second downstream to the user and 640Kbits per second upstream. The main current drawback is that it only works up to 12,000 feet or two plus miles without repeaters.

The internetworking market has grown dramatically in the last five years. Internetworking products transfers large amounts of data at high speeds between LANs, large computers and corporate networks. Internetworking products and their high-speed communications links are primarily used by large and medium-size companies. Small companies have to wait for one of the emerging high-speed communications technologies to be successful to afford to ship lots of data between networks.

Client/Server Computing

The client/server or C/S is a hot topic and has become such a buzzword that it needs an explanation. Client/server is a term that is over used, is confusing, is poorly defined and means different things to different people. On the other hand, client/server is gaining momentum and there is no question it will happen, but when will it be prevalent. Client/server is a framework or strategy for changing yesterday's stand-alone PC, technical workstation, departmental computer and centralized mainframe into a cooperative, distributed network of powerful client computers and server computers. The client computer will primarily be PCs of all form factors, but workstations, X-terminals, network computers and even PDAs may be client computers. Server computers will range from high-end PCs to workstations, midrange computers, mainframes and supercomputers.

The concept of client/server is straight forward, but the implementation is quite complex. This is due to the immaturity of the client/server marketplace. A big problem is too many competing standards and it is too early to tell which ones will become dominant. A second problem is the low availability of client/server software development tools. However, substantial effort is directed at this problem and the development tools are appearing at a rapid pace. The third problem is that there is a shortage of knowledge on how to develop client/server systems because few have implemented such systems. Another complicating factor is that often a reengineering project is part of the goal and complicates the implementation of a client/server system.

There are usually numerous near-term and long-term goals for client/server computing. The goals will vary from one organization to another. Here are some of the most common goals:

o Integrate the PCs and LANs into the corporate MIS structure.
o Preserve investments in legacy systems (i.e. mainframe computers) by using them on the network.
o Enable centralized enforcement of business rules, security and integrity.
o Provide users with wider choices and timely availability of corporate data.
o Avoid new mainframe applications due to high development and support costs.
o Downsize existing mainframe applications.
o Upsize existing PC/LAN applications (for growing companies).
o Improve application development productivity via desktop computer tools and price-performance.
o Improve application performance.
o Improve information technology productivity.
o Improve information technology price-performance.

In many ways the Internet is a large client/server system. The rapidly growing intranets are also client/server systems. Intranets are much simpler to implement than traditional client/server systems. An intranet is a small Internet used by a corporation to distribute information to their employees and sometimes to their suppliers. Tremendous intranet growth started in 1995 and is continuing in 1996 and into 1997.

This is the new battleground for the computer industry. All major vendors are trying to set key standards and to become the leaders of this next generation computer industry. The PC and workstation vendors are upsizing from their LANs and leveraging their experience in open systems. The mainframe and midrange vendors are downsizing and leveraging their experience in systems integration and building complex computer systems.

In every previous computer generation, a few start-up companies have grown to become giants in the computer industry. We are likely to see a few success stories in the client/server industry as well by the end of this decade.

Accessories and Supplies

The many supply and accessory categories are shown in Figure 1.11. Supplies are the consumable products needed to operate computer systems. Supplies include all types of storage media (i.e. diskettes), paper products, printer ribbons, inkjet and laser printer cartridges and cleaning supplies. The laser and inkjet printer cartridges are the two largest supply market segments.

Accessories are products that help make computer systems run smoother and products that lessen the user's efforts. Some accessories protect the computer against dust, static electricity, electrical surges and power outages. Other products protect users from printer noise (acoustical covers), cut down the amount of low-frequency radiation from the display or help users avoid back pain (ergonomic furniture). Accessories may also help the user and equipment by storing the supplies in an organized manner.

Figure 1.11: Computer Supplies and Accessories	
Supplies Consumable products used to operate the computers	**Accessories** Products that improve the user and/or computer operation
<u>Storage Media</u> o Diskettes o Disk cartridges o Optical disks o Tape cartridges o Tape reels	<u>Electrical Accessories</u> o Uninterruptible power supplies (UPS) o Surge protectors & cables o Multiplexers & T-switches o Cooling devices o Batteries
<u>Paper Products</u> o Computer paper o Computer forms o Mailing labels o Diskette mailers o Diskette labels o Other labels	<u>Mechanical Accessories</u> o Computer furniture o Equipment racks, stands & enclosures o Sheet feeders o Acoustical covers o Magnetic media storage o Lock & security products
<u>Other Supplies</u> o Laser printer cartridges o Inkjet printer cartridges o Printer ribbons, wheels, bands etc. o Plotter pens o Cleaning supplies	<u>Other Accessories</u> o Carrying cases & dust covers o Ergonomic accessories o Antiglare screen covers o Antistatic products o Antiradiation filters

Supplies and accessories usually receive little attention, but having the right products will greatly improve the computer user's life and will prolong the equipment's useful life. Ergonomic products are especially important as they can literally take away the pain in the neck, the pain in the butt, the pain in the wrists, eyes and head.

Computer Services

The computer services segment is a vibrant and growing industry. There are three major computer service categories shown in Figure 1.12: processing services, professional services and information services. Companies that offer processing services normally use their own hardware and software to process large volumes of transactions for customers. Transaction processing and timesharing are the two sub-segments in processing services. In timesharing a vendor sells a slice of time from their computers to clients. Timesharing proliferated in the 1960s and 1970s when computers were expensive. By spreading the high cost among many users, timesharing offered an economic means for small companies to use the resources of a large computer center. As the small computer became affordable in the late 1970s and early 1980s, timesharing became less attractive and started declining.

Transaction processing service vendors offer sophisticated vertical market applications that process large volumes of transactions. The applications primarily address the back office functions, such as payroll, healthcare claims, insurance claims and other accounting and record-keeping functions.

Professional service vendors offer data-processing consulting, system design, development, custom software, systems integration, implementation, documentation, training, facilities management, maintenance and disaster recovery services. The vendors offer one or more of these services. Systems integration is becoming the most important segment. A systems integrator is responsible for planning, designing and implementing computer systems and networks. The federal government is the largest systems integration customer. Computer facilities management, where a service company does on-site management of a company's computer operation has been available for a long time. This trend has gone one step further with outsourcing, where the service company may take on all or major parts of a company's information services. The outsourcing service company uses its own employees, owns the computer equipment and may locate the data center on its own premises.

Figure 1.12: Computer Services Categories		
Processing Services Uses large computer facilities & proprietary software to process data & transactions for customers	Professional Services Provides services to plan, design, purchase, integrate, document, train, manage, operate & maintain computer systems	Information Services Provides access to large & mostly proprietary databases--either online or off-line
o Timesharing o Transaction processing o Payroll processing o Financial services o Healthcare processing	o Data processing consulting o Contract programming o Systems integration o Maintenance service o Disaster recovery o Computer facilities management o Outsourcing	o Marketing information o Direct mail marketing o Product sales information o Financial information o Economic information o Stock quotations o News retrieval o Abstract retrieval o Communications services

An information service provider collects, manipulates and disseminates information about specific topics. The information is stored in large databases and distributed via communications links, by magnetic media (disks or tapes) or in paper form. A rapidly emerging method is to use the CD-ROM to distribute large volumes of information. The type of information varies from stock quotations, abstracts of technical articles to monthly sales data for consumer or business products. Information services have a bright future since competitive industries require accurate and timely information and because technological changes will allow new and better products and distribution methods.

Computer Industry Structure

As seen in Figure 1.13, the computer industry overlaps considerably with six other industries. The biggest overlap is with the electronics industry which provides most of the components used to build computers. The electronics industry also uses computers in many of its systems such as factory automation, measurement and test equipment. Microcomputer boards are an example of products that are in both industries.

The biggest overlap with the consumer electronics industry is the home computer. The home computer or home PC is included in the computer industry. The CD-ROM is also an overlapping product and is based on the music CD. The CD-ROM is now an important computer peripheral and is included in the computer industry. Future optical disks used in the consumer electronics industry, such as the computer video disk (CVD), are almost certain to be used in the computer industry. A few years down the road the TV will add computer capabilities, most likely Internet access, and many PCs will have built-in digital TV reception capabilities. The software side is also starting to overlap. Computer games are based on movies and movies are starting to be based on computer games. Eventually computer entertainment software and movies/TV programs will have a considerable overlap. It is also likely that the PC will become a delivery vehicle for entertainment, news and information similar to TVs and movie theaters.

The computer and telecommunications industries are also overlapping. Examples are modems, internetworking, online services and video conferencing. These products are included in the computer industry. ISDN (Integrated Services Digital Network) and other emerging telecom technologies are important for the computer industry. As telecom products increasingly use digital technology the overlap with the computer industry will increase. The Personal Digital Assistant (PDA) will often have communications capabilities and is an overlapping product. As the Internet grows in capabilities and importance, the computer and communications industries will get more and more tangled.

With the introduction of desktop publishing in the mid-1980s, the computer industry is also overlapping the printing industry. As the resolution of laser printers increase and color printers for computers proliferate, the overlap with the printing industry will grow, especially in the pre-press segments.

Computer and Related Industries

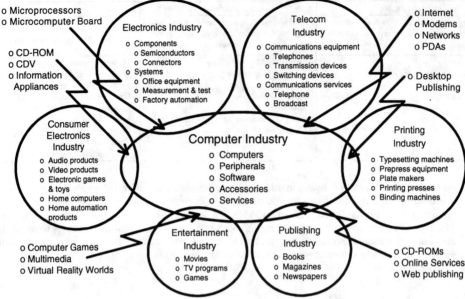

Figure 1.13

The computer industry certainly has provided new opportunities for the publishing industry. Just look at the publications directory in Chapter 12 of the Computer Industry Almanac where over 1,100 computer-related publications are listed. The number of magazines, newspapers, newsletters and books on computer topics is phenomenal. However, computer technologies are also providing alternative media for publishing and distributing information. Newsletters and books on diskettes and CD-ROM are rapidly gaining in importance. Online services and the Internet's web are also showing strong growth. Up until now, the computer industry has expanded the publishing industry without changing it. As the installed base of computers increases, the CD-ROM becomes prevalent and Internet access grows, the computer industry started to impact the publishing industry dramatically.

The overlap between the entertainment and computer industries is small today--primarily computer games and the increasing usage of computers for special effects in producing TV programs and movies. Already the impact of desktop video PCs is being felt and lowers the video production costs dramatically. Tomorrow's multimedia-based software will mix movie video techniques and computer software technology and has the potential to impact and drastically change the entertainment industry. The nature of the impact is hard to predict, but should manifest itself in the late 1990s.

The computer industry structure is depicted in Figure 1.14 as a flow of products. The main product categories are the four blocks near the top of the figure. The products are sold directly to the computer customers or are distributed via the many types of computer resellers. A conservative estimate of the number of vendors is shown in each block. The bottom of Figure 1.14 shows the computer customer segments. A rapidly growing segment is the home-office business. Today about 35% of U.S. households have one or more computers.

The large computer category consists mostly of mainframe computers which have been dominated by IBM for over 30 years. There are less than 20 mainframe vendors worldwide. Several mainframe vendors such as Amdahl and Hitachi make IBM-compatible mainframes. The mainframe computer market is declining as networks of PCs and workstations are taking over many mainframe applications.

Figure 1.14: Computer Industry Structure			
Computer Product Manufacturers and Service Providers			
Peripherals Manufacturers	Computer Manufacturers	Software Publishers & Authors	Computer Service Firms
o Mass storage devices	o Large computers	o System software	o Processing services
o Input devices	o Midrange computers	o Application software	o Professional services
o Output devices	o Microcomputers	o Client/server software	o Information services
o Communications devices	o Information appliances	o Over 5,000 publishers	o Supplies & accessories
o Over 1,400 vendors	o Over 450 vendors	o Over15,000 authors	o Over 2,000 firms
Computer Distribution Channels			
Direct Marketing Channels (Over 400 firms)	Primary Computer Resellers (Over 16,000 resellers)		Secondary Computer Resellers (Over 28,000 resellers)
o Direct sales force	o Computer dealers	o Computer superstores	o Consumer superstores
o Direct marketing	o VARs and systems integrators	o Local assemblers	o Mass merchants
o Mail order/catalog	o Computer distributors	o Software stores	o Distributors
Customers Using Computers			
o Government agencies	o Large corporations	o Small businesses	o Consumers
o Educational institutions	o Medium size companies	o Home offices	

The minicomputer and midrange computer market has been led by Digital Equipment, IBM and Hewlett-Packard for over 20 years. There are less than 40 minicomputer vendors worldwide. The minicomputer industry is also declining due to PC, workstation and network growth.

There are hundreds of microcomputer vendors worldwide and the number is still growing. In a few years the microcomputer industry will be the whole computer industry.

There are thousands of software publishers and many more software authors that are trying to write the next hit program. The author-publisher relationship in the computer industry is similar to the book industry. The growth in the software industry is coming in the Internet and client/server segments, ranging from software development tools and applications to system management tools.

There are hundreds of computer services companies. They range from small local companies that perform computer installations, maintenance or custom programming to multi-billion dollar corporations that design, build, manage and maintain worldwide networks. The computer services market is on a growth path.

Product and service vendors sell their products directly to computer users or via a variety of computer resellers. Computer dealers and computer superstores focus their energies on selling personal computers and related products and are the most important sales channel for such computers. Workstations are also trying to establish a foothold in the computer dealers. Software stores specialize in selling software, supplies, accessories and some peripherals. Value added resellers (VARs) specialize in specific narrow-market segments (usually called vertical markets). A distributor is primarily a middleman between the manufacturer and the reseller and usually does not sell to computer users. Other stores such as office product superstores, consumer electronics stores, department stores, discount stores, warehouse clubs and toy stores have recently added computers to their product selection. All of these resellers, as well as catalog, mail order and many other resellers, are important sources of computer products. Computer resellers are explained in the next sections.

Computer Distribution Channels

Computer distribution channels or how computer products are sold is a major factor in determining how successful computer vendors will become. In the early days of the computer industry when computers were quite expensive, the main distribution channel was a direct sales force. As the mainframe computer industry grew in the 1960s, the direct sales force grew as well and became a entry barrier to new competitors.

When the minicomputer emerged in the mid 1960s, a direct sales force also became a primary distribution channel as the price of computers still remained quite high. But as minicomputer sales grew resellers emerged to sell minicomputers or products based on minicomputers. These resellers became the basis for the value added resellers and systems integrators that are now prevalent for the midrange computer, workstation and client/server computing system.

When the personal computer evolved in the mid 1970s, its price was too low to afford a direct sales force and new distribution channels were necessary for PCs to sell in large volume. The key distribution channel in the late 1970s and early 1980s was the computer specialty store or computer dealer. The first computer store was opened in 1975. By 1980 there were 500+ computer stores and by 1985 there were nearly 4,600 computer stores. In the mid 1980s, the computer store/computer dealer was the dominant PC distribution channel and key chains such as ComputerLand, MicroAge, InaCom and Businessland had a major impact on which vendors were successful.

As the PC sales grew, other distribution channels also became important and today there is a plethora of computer resellers as shown in Figure 1.15. Fifteen distinct computer distribution channels are listed with examples of the leading chains, the leading vendors or a short description when there are no chains. The "Other Reseller Categories" lists a variety of reseller types that sell computer hardware or software products to some extent.

Figure 1.15: Computer Resellers			
Primary Computer Resellers o Computers are the only or the primary business o Computer sales contribute more than 50% of revenue		Secondary Computer Resellers o Computers are one of many product lines o Computer sales contribute less than 50% of revenue	
VARs/Systems Integrators o Sell systems or networks to vertical markets	Computer Dealers o CompuCom o ComputerLand	Office Product Superstores o Office Club o OfficeMax	Department Stores o Sears o Montgomery Ward
Direct Sales Force o IBM o Hewlett-Packard	o InaCom o Intelligent Electronics o MicroAge	Consumer Electronics Superstores o Best Buy o Circuit City	Other Reseller Categories o Appliance stores o Bookstores
Direct Marketing o Dell Computer o Gateway 2000	Computer Superstores o CompUSA o Computer City	Consumer Electronics Stores o Radio Shack o Regional chains	o Catalog showrooms o Drug stores o Furniture stores o Mail order/catalogs
Mail Order/Catalog o Micro Warehouse o PC Connection	Local Assemblers o Sell low-cost, no-brand PCs in a local region	Warehouse Clubs o Price-Costco o Sam's	o Music stores o Office product stores o Online resellers
Online Resellers o Sell computer products via online services or web servers	Software Stores o Egghead o Babbage's	Discount Stores o Target o Wal-Mart	o Toy stores o Video stores

There are basically two classes of computer resellers--the primary computer reseller which depends on computer products for the majority of its business and the secondary computer reseller which gets the majority of its business from products other than computers. The primary computer reseller gets 50% to 100% of its revenue from computer products and is the most important distribution channel for the computer vendors. Computer products range in importance for the secondary computer resellers. Computer products contribute 10% of sales to as high as 30% for the office product and consumer electronics superstore. For the warehouse club, department store and discount store, computer products may contribute less than one percent of sales up to a few percentage points.

The mainframe, midrange computer and workstation are primarily sold via two distribution channels: the manufacturers' direct sales force and VAR/systems integrator. The remaining distribution channels shown in Figure 1.15 are for PC-related products. The low-end workstation and a few midrange computers are starting to appear in the computer dealer and via direct marketing/mail order distribution channels.

Since the PC has very complicated sales operations, the next section profiles the trends and current status of PC distribution channels.

PC Distribution Channel Trends

When the personal computer was born in 1975 there were no distribution channels and the manufacturers had to be innovative and use whatever was available.

Personal computer distribution channels have changed substantially in the last 20 years and will probably change as much in the next 10 years. In the early 1980s there were primarily three channels--the computer specialty store/computer dealer, VAR and manufacturers' direct sales force--that dominated sales to the office segment. Additionally, some mass merchants were selling home PCs, low-end computers such as Commodore and Atari, to the consumer market.

By 1990 there were five important distribution channels for the business PC market--the computer specialty store/computer dealer, VAR, direct sales force, direct marketing/mail order and the computer superstore. Direct marketing was pioneered by Dell Computer and became a major force in the early 1990s as numerous vendors successfully copied Dell's strategy. The computer superstore also became important by 1990 due to its impact on other computer resellers even though their overall market share remained low. By 1990 some mass merchants were selling MS-DOS and Windows-based computers and became a competitor to the computer dealer.

By 1990 another channel that received little attention was also emerging--the local assembler. These "mom and pop" operations assemble PCs from sub-systems and sell in a local region. Local assemblers tend to have the lowest prices, but due to their low profitability, their margin of error is small and many go out of business. Even today, this channel receives little attention and is difficult to quantify and forecast.

In the last few years, three more channels have risen and are becoming important--the office product superstore, consumer electronics superstore and warehouse club. These three channels were emerging independent of the PC, but as the personal computers became a commodity product it is natural for these channels to add PC products. The PC is now a major category for the office product superstore and consumer electronics superstore.

Today a variety of consumer distribution channels are selling PC products--ranging from department and discount stores to toy stores, furniture stores and TV/appliance stores. The number and variety of stores selling PC products continues to increase.

Why did the PC distribution channels change? There are several reasons ranging from different buyer dynamics, limited shelf space in existing channels to the ease of making Windows-based computers. The most important reason is the change in buyer dynamics. In the early 1980s the PC buyers needed lots of handholding as they were cautiously trying out this new product. By the late 1980s most PC buyers and users were experienced and felt comfortable with PCs and were buying their second or third PC. Hence the repeat PC buyer was driving the PC industry by 1990. The amount of information available from all the computer magazines that were testing, rating and recommending brands made it possible even for novices to buy intelligently.

In the late 1980s and early 1990s it became increasingly simple to make MS-DOS and Windows-based computers, and the number of PC vendors grew dramatically. However, the existing distribution channels had no shelf space for new brands and these vendors had to find new ways of reaching the PC buyers. The increasing proportion of knowledgeable repeat buyers made additional PC distribution channels feasible. The direct marketing channel emerged first because it required minimal start-up capital and did not need other infrastructures. Initially, repeat buyers had low expectations of direct marketing vendors' support capabilities. But they were pleasantly surprised and coupled with low prices this made the direct marketing channel grow rapidly.

The computer superstore evolved next. This channel initially focused on filling a void that existed for software and PC aftermarket products. In the mid-1980s there were no good distribution channels for PC aftermarket products. The first computer superstores capitalized on this opportunity. They quickly added PCs to their product selection as customers also wanted to buy low-priced computers. It is no coincidence that the leading superstore was called Softwarehouse until it changed its name to CompUSA. The computer superstore growth will be very strong and it will have a major impact on other distribution channels. The computer superstore will limit the growth of the computer dealer and will also slow the growth of direct marketing vendors. But the superstore will not dominate the market as long as continued technology advancements are taking place in the computer industry.

PC Distribution Channels Characteristics

Figure 1.16 shows the 3Q 1996 characteristics of the most important computer reseller categories. There are large varieties in some channels due to differences in the major chains or differences in reseller segments. For instance, the independent computer dealers are usually different from company-owned chains and franchised chains. Similarly, the Radio Shack consumer electronics stores are quite different from the independent and regional consumer electronics chains. The "Other Mass Merchants" category includes discount stores (i.e. K-Mart, Target and Wal-Mart), department stores (i.e. Sears, Macy's and Dillard), catalog showrooms (i.e. Service Merchandise) and other stores that sell PCs--ranging from home furnishing stores to military stores.

Figure 1.16: Computer Reseller Characteristics								
3Q 1996 Statistics	VARs & Systems Integrators	Computer Dealers	Computer Superstores	Office Product Superstores	Consumer Electronics Superstores	Consumer Electronics Stores	Warehouse Clubs	Other Mass Merchants
Est. Locations (#)	6,290	3,500	400	1,470	1,330	10,800	840	11,600
Store Size, sq ft (#K)	N/A	2 - 5	25 - 40	15 - 20	15 - 20	1 - 4	80 - 120	30 - 100
Revenue/Store ($M)	0.5 - 3	1 - 10	30 - 80	5 - 8	10 - 20	0.4 - 5	50 - 90	10 - 50
PC Share of Rev. (%)	70 - 80	70 - 80	70 - 80	8 - 25	10 - 40	5 - 20	0.3 - 3	0.1 - 1
PC Revenue/Store ($M)	0.3 - 2.5	0.7 - 4	23 - 60	0.5 - 1.8	1 - 10	0.05 - 0.8	0.3 - 1.5	0.05 - 0.5
PCs/Store/Month (#)	5 - 50	30 - 180	350 - 750	25 - 95	20 - 250	4 - 30	25 - 90	3 - 35
PC Gross Margin (%)	20 - 35	15 - 25	11 - 15	14 - 20	15 - 20	15 - 25	8 - 15	15 - 25

There are over 6,000 PC VARs which vary greatly in size, product mix and customer focus. Yearly revenue varies from a few hundred thousand dollars to several million dollars with an average of about $1M. Computer dealers have less diversity than VARs, but still have large differences--ranging from small independent stores with retail focus to large chain sales offices with a Fortune 1000 customer focus. Average sales per computer dealer location is over $3M. The computer superstore has a very large sales volume--up to 10X the sales of a computer dealer, but operates on much tighter margins.

Currently PC products account for 8% to 25% (average about 16%) of office product superstores' revenue and the average will grow to over 20% of their sales by the late 1990s. Typical annual revenue per office product superstore is about $5M to $8M. The consumer electronics superstore has annual revenues of around $10M to $20M and the PC portion ranges from 10% to 40%. The regular consumer electronics store is much smaller than its superstore cousin. The average Radio Shack store has annual revenues of only $0.6M with less than 11% coming from PC products. The regional consumer electronics store chains have annual revenues in the $2M to $5M range and PC revenues are about 15% if they sell PCs. The warehouse club or wholesale club has annual revenues of $50M to $90M and computer revenue is a small portion--only 0.3% to 3%, but the average may grow to 3% to 5% by 2000.

Figure 1.17 shows the growth of the computer resellers and lists the leading chains or categories of resellers. In some of the PC distribution channels there are a few major chains that dominate their segment. In other channels there are a few chains that are trendsetters and constitute a significant portion of the total sales volume.

Figure 1.17: PC Reseller Categories and Growth				
PC Reseller Categories	Number of Stores/Locations			Leading Chains or categories
	1990	1994	1996	
Computer Dealers (formerly called Computer Specialty Stores)	4,600	4,000	3,500	CompuCom, ComputerLand, Entex Information, InaCom, MicroAge, Intelligent Electronics
Value Added Resellers & Systems Integrators	6,150	6,200	6,230	Computer vendors, computer services firms, accounting firms, telecom firms, computer dealers, national VARs, local VARs
Local Assemblers	3,500	5,040	5,000	Not applicable
Computer Superstores	30	230	390	CompUSA, Computer City, MicroCenter, Fry's, Elek-Tek
Office Product Superstores	290	1,060	1,420	Office Depot, OfficeMax, Staples
Consumer Electronics Superstores	630	1,150	1,420	Best Buy, Circuit City, YES/Fretter, Good Guys
Consumer Electronics Stores	9,700	11,200	10,800	Radio Shack, many regional chains
Warehouse Clubs	350	720	840	Sam's, Price-Costco, BJ's Wholesale Club
Discount Stores	850	3,000	3,500	Wal-Mart, K-Mart, Target, Venture

PC Reseller Categories	Number of Stores/Locations			Leading Chains or categories
	1990	1994	1996	
Department Stores	700	2,150	2,600	Sears, JC Penney, Montgomery Ward, May, Dillard, Merwin's
Other Mass Merchants	2,200	2,950	3,600	Catalog showrooms, TV/appliance stores, toy stores, furniture/ home improvement stores, bookstores, video stores, etc.
Software Stores	800	1,200	1,600	Egghead, Babbage's, Electronics Boutique, Software Etc.
All Other Computer Resellers	3,200	4,100	4,600	Office product dealers, office supply stores, distributor direct, military stores, mail order/catalog, etc.
Total PC Resellers	33,000	43,000	45,500	

Figure 1.17: PC Reseller Categories and Growth

The computer dealer remains the leading PC distribution channel. The number of locations are not as important as before as most of their sales come from an out-bound sales force. ComputerLand is now owned by Merisel while ComputerLand's systems integration/VAR business is a separate business called Vanstar. These six chains had 1995 revenues of about $13B or about 60% of the total computer dealer channel.

The VARs and systems integrators have a tremendous range--from the major computer vendors with international reach to small local value added resellers. Most major computer vendors such has IBM, Digital Equipment, Hewlett-Packard and Unisys have systems integration divisions. The major computer services firms such as EDS and Computer Sciences are among the largest systems integrators. The big accounting firms such as Andersen Consulting, Ernst & Young, Price Waterhouse, KPMG Peat Marwick, Deloitte & Touche and Coopers & Lybrand are major players in the systems integration business. The telecom vendors such as AT&T and MCI are also systems integrators with emphasis on the computer network market. The computer dealers such as Ina-Com, Entex Information and MicroAge are also among the top 25 systems integrators.

The computer superstore has grown dramatically. The store count is the average for the year. There are currently numerous independent computer superstores which consist of single location stores and regional chains such as CDW Computer Discount Warehouse, Computer Attic, Computer Express, NCA Computer and J&R Computer. Many of these superstores also have significant mail order operation.

The leading office product superstores have embraced PC products and are particularly important for printer sales. This channel is dominated by three chains which account for over 90% of the total store locations.

The top two consumer electronics superstore chains--Computer City and Best Buy-- account for over 50% of the consumer electronics superstores that are selling PCs. Best Buy is the most aggressive PC retailer and its PC revenue portion is much larger than Circuit City and others.

The leading warehouse clubs added PCs in the early 1990s. In 1993 there were four chains that dominated the warehouse segment and accounted for nearly 90% of the total. Now there are only two major chains left. Costco and Price Club have merged and K-Mart sold its Pace warehouse clubs to Sam's which is owned by Wal-Mart.

Today there are about 45,500 computer resellers, up from 33,000 in 1990 and about 18,000 in 1985. The number of computer resellers will continue to climb and their diversity will expand. The impact of electronic commerce via the Internet and other online services will be interesting to watch. Electronic commerce is likely to have a large impact on current distribution channels over the next decade. Software products will be sold, distributed and supported via the Internet and online networks. Other computer products will be sold and supported via the Internet. The question is what market share will electronic commerce gain in the next decade and beyond.

Computer Industry Almanac: Further Reading

There are hundreds of good computer books that explain how computers are designed, how they work, how specific software programs are used and so on. Here are a few sources we can recommend for further reading:

1. Nathan Shedroff et al. "Understanding Computers", Sybex (ISBN 0-7821-1060-6)
   A small book that explains a lot in few pages.

2. Julia S. Lacy et al. "How to Survive Your Computer Workstation", CRT Services, P.O. Box 1525, Linden, TX
   Ergonomic information that is useful for any computer user.

3. "Understanding Computers", Time-Life Books
   A series of 8 books that explains most aspects of computers.

4. Lawrence J. Magid, "The Little PC Book", Peachpit Press (ISBN 0-938151-54-1)
   Basic information to get started with MS-DOS and Windows computers.

5. Joan Stigliani, "The Computer User's Survival Guide", O'Reilly & Associates (ISBN 1-56592-030-9)
   Information on how to stay healthy in a high tech world.

Chapter 2

Companies

Company Rankings

Computer Retail Week: Top 100 Retailers

"This list was compiled by the staff of Computer Retail Week with the support of industry analyst, suppliers and the retailers themselves. All the data in this report is presented as Computer Retail Week estimates based on data available from both public and private sources.

'In addition, all the numbers in this report reflect calendar year 1995 sales and are updates from sales estimates originally published in January. In most cases, the store counts were obtained directly from the retailers and represent the actual or estimated number of stores with computer-related merchandise as of December 31, 1995 and June 1, 1996.

'Some of the numbers have been updated from previous Computer Retail Week reports based on new information. All numbers refer to U.S. stores and U.S. sales. All sales figures exclude office machines, telephones and video-game hardware and software. Per-store sales figures were calculated using fractional amounts for new stores reflecting the length of time they were open."--Computer Retail Week

Rank	Retailer	Headquarters	# PC Stores 6/96	# PC Stores 12/95	'95 Total Sales ($M)	Retail Only Sales ($M)	Hardware Sales ($M)	Software Sales ($M)	Pre-Store Retail Sales ($M)
1	CompUSA	Dallas, TX	105	95	3,235.0	2,480.0	2,375.0	545.0	29.4
2	Best Buy	Minneapolis, MN	259	251	2,771.0	2,771.0	2,371.0	286.0	12.7
3	Computer City	Fort Worth, TX	90	88	1,750.0	1,310.0	1,415.0	210.0	19.2
4	Office Depot	Delray Beach, FL	489	476	1,600.0	1,420.0	988.0	122.0	3.4
5	Circuit City	Richmond, VA	386	378	1,570.0	1,570.0	1,482.0	30.0	4.8
6	Micro Center	Columbus, OH	11	11	930.0	789.0	697.9	157.8	80.5
7	Egghead Software	Issaquah, WA	162	168	890.0	495.0	90.0	735.0	3.0
8	Staples	Framingham, MA	450	380	718.0	645.0	350.0	78.0	2.5
9	Sears	Hoffman Estates, IL	810	803	700.0	700.0	629.0	35.0	0.9
10	OfficeMax	Shaker Heights, OH	475	449	671.0	671.0	476.0	75.0	1.6
11	CDW Computer Warehouse	Chicago, IL	2	2	630.0	61.6	500.7	72.6	30.8
12	Sam's Club	Bentonville, AR	433	434	622.0	575.0	320.0	115.0	1.3
13	Wal-Mart	Bentonville, AR	2,200	2,200	585.0	535.0	360.0	110.0	0.3
14	Fry's Electronics	Palo Alto, CA	9	8	414.0	373.0	310.0	85.0	57.4
15	Creative Computers	Los Angeles, CA	4	4	400.0	75.0	340.0	52.0	18.8
16	PriceCostco	Kirkland, WA	197	192	397.0	375.0	268.0	97.0	2.0
17	NeoStar	Dallas, TX	837	817	354.7	354.7	32.5	228.1	0.4
18	Elek-Tek	Skokie, IL	7	7	335.0	161.0	257.0	50.0	23.0
19	Radio Shack	Fort Worth, TX	6,782	6,782	330.0	330.0	293.5	8.5	0.05
20	Montgomery Ward	Chicago, IL	375	375	324.3	324.3	305.0	9.5	0.9
21	PC Warehouse	Rochelle Park, NJ	87	87	321.0	250.0	288.5	3.5	2.9
22	Army/Air Force Exchange	Dallas, TX	142	142	258.0	258.0	224.0	32.0	1.8
23	Catalink Direct	Bristol, PA	2	2	233.0	29.0	202.7	23.3	14.5
24	J&R Computer World	New York, NY	1	1	230.0	180.0	126.0	63.8	1.8
25	Nobody Beats the Wiz	Carteret, NJ	56	54	187.0	187.0	155.0	4.0	3.5
26	Sun TV & Appliances	Columbus, OH	47	46	186.0	186.0	175.0	6.0	4.4
27	Incredible Universe	Fort Worth, TX	16	17	182.0	185.0	128.0	38.5	16.8
28	Electronics Boutique	West Chester, PA	425	395	176.0	176.0	10.1	131.1	0.5
29	Lechmere	Woburn, MA	28	28	161.0	161.0	125.0	20.0	5.8
30	Good Guys	Burlingame, CA	70	70	136.0	136.0	130.0	0.0	2.2
31	Future Shop	Burnaby, BC	16	16	132.0	132.0	101.0	24.6	8.3

Rank	Retailer	Headquarters	# PC Stores 6/96	# PC Stores 12/95	'95 Total Sales ($M)	Retail Only Sales ($M)	Hardware Sales ($M)	Software Sales ($M)	Pre-Store Retail Sales ($M)
32	Whole Earth Access	Emoryville, CA	3	5	98.0	85.0	75.5	10.5	15.5
33	Computer Express	Miami, FL	1	1	90.0	27.0	85.3	2.0	27.0
34	ComputerWare	Palo Alto, CA	10	10	88.0	48.0	71.0	13.0	4.8
35	NCA Computer Products	Sunnyvale, CA	5	5	78.0	54.0	55.0	19.0	12.0
36	SBI Computer Warehouse	Sacramento, CA	6	6	75.0	52.0	62.5	4.0	8.7
37	Computer Town	Salem, NH	5	5	73.0	66.0	66.9	2.7	12.0
38	Computer Attic	Redwood City, CA	1	1	62.5	29.4	47.0	10.4	29.4
39	Campo	Harahan, LA	31	31	61.0	61.0	59.1	0.8	2.1
40	BJ's Wholesale Club	Natick, MA	72	72	57.1	57.1	41.0	10.2	0.8
41	Kmart	Troy, MI	2,100	2,100	56.4	55.4	1.0	32.0	0.03
42	Fretter	Brighton, MI	7	50	54.0	54.0	49.0	1.3	0.4
43	Media Play (Musicland)	Minneapolis, MN	86	89	52.0	52.0	0.0	52.0	0.5
44	Lucky Computer	Richardson, TX	5	5	51.2	34.0	47.0	1.5	2.4
45	American TV	Madison, WI	8	8	51.0	51.0	42.0	4.0	6.4
46	Service Merchandise	Brentwood, TN	412	412	48.0	48.0	40.0	0.0	0.1
47	Office 1 Superstore	Chicago, IL	35	35	48.0	48.0	24.0	6.0	1.6
48	P.C. Richard & Son	Hauppauge, NY	34	32	47.2	47.2	45.0	0.0	1.5
49	Target Stores	Minneapolis, MN	635	635	44.8	44.8	8.0	32.0	0.1
50	BrandsMart U.S.A.	Miami, FL	3	3	44.0	44.0	43.1	0.4	14.7
51	Computer Expo	Houston, TX	3	3	40.0	20.5	30.0	3.0	6.8
52	Navy Resale & Services	Richmond, VA	39	39	39.9	39.9	34.9	3.5	1.0
53	Specialty Retail Group	Fort Worth, TX	58	57	39.0	39.0	34.0	1.0	0.7
54	Soundtrack/Ultimate	Denver, CO	18	18	38.9	38.9	36.4	0.0	2.2
55	RCS	New York, NY	1	1	38.2	28.0	33.1	3.4	28.0
56	Software City	Englewood, NJ	31	31	36.5	18.4	14.0	21.4	0.6
57	Computize	Houston, TX	17	17	36.0	23.0	33.0	1.5	1.4
58	47th St. Photo	Brooklyn, NY	1	2	35.7	35.7	28.7	5.1	17.9
59	Fred Meyer	Portland, OR	98	95	35.6	35.6	22.5	7.7	0.4
60	Computer Stores Northwest	Corvallis, OR	5	6	32.0	32.0	26.0	2.0	5.3
61	ABC Warehouse	Pontiac, MI	29	29	31.1	31.1	28.4	0.0	1.1
62	HD Computers	Sunnyvale, CA	5	5	30.5	30.5	27.3	3.0	6.1
63	PC Club	City of Industry, CA	5	5	30.0	28.5	29.0	0.0	6.0
64	May Company, The	St. Louis, MO	192	192	29.8	29.8	23.4	2.0	0.2
65	Dillard Department Stores	Little Rock, AR	154	154	29.0	29.0	25.5	2.0	0.2
66	Hastings	Dallas, TX	109	109	28.4	28.4	0.0	26.0	0.3
67	H.H. Gregg Appliance	Indianapolis, IN	16	16	28.0	28.0	26.3	0.2	1.8
68	Tops Appliance City	Edison, NJ	8	8	25.0	25.0	21.6	2.0	3.1
69	Nebraska Furniture Mart	Omaha, NE	1	1	25.0	25.0	21.5	2.5	25.0
70	CW Electronics	Denver, CO	1	1	23.6	21.0	21.8	1.0	21.0
71	Laptop Superstore	Natick, MA	8	8	22.3	10.6	21.2	0.5	1.7
72	Access Technologies	Santa Clara, CA	2	2	19.5	15.1	13.8	0.3	7.6
73	R.C. Willey Home Furnishings	Salt Lake City, UT	5	5	19.0	19.0	18.5	0.3	3.8
74	Alpha Computers	Portland, OR	2	3	18.7	9.8	16.0	1.7	2.5
75	Doppler Computer	Seattle, WA	1	1	18.0	15.8	16.5	1.0	15.8
76	Fedco	Santa Fe Springs, CA	10	10	16.8	16.8	15.5	0.4	1.7
77	Toys'R'Us	Paramus, NJ	650	650	16.5	16.5	0.5	15.0	0.03
78	Boscov's	Reading, PA	25	26	16.0	16.0	14.0	0.8	0.6
79	Roberd's	Dayton, OH	22	22	15.0	15.0	13.7	0.5	0.7

Rank	Retailer	Headquarters	# PC Stores 6/96	# PC Stores 12/95	'95 Total Sales ($M)	Retail Only Sales ($M)	Hardware Sales ($M)	Software Sales ($M)	Pre-Store Retail Sales ($M)
80	DataVision	New York, NY	1	1	15.0	2.8	11.2	3.0	2.8
81	Rex Stores	Dayton, OH	97	97	14.4	14.4	14.2	0.0	0.2
82	Dayton Hudson	Minneapolis, MN	40	40	14.2	14.2	13.0	1.0	0.4
83	AMS Computer Stores	Walker, MI	9	6	14.0	12.5	11.8	2.0	1.4
84	Barnes & Nobles	New York, NY	1,006	1,002	13.5	13.5	0.0	8.0	0.01
85	State Street Discount	Portsmouth, NH	1	1	9.1	9.1	9.0	0.0	9.1
86	ACP Superstore	Santa Ana, CA	1	1	8.0	4.5	6.8	1.0	4.5
87	American Appliance	Pennsauken, NJ	35	28	8.0	8.0	6.5	0.5	0.3
88	Kay-Bee Toys	Pittsfield, MA	1,148	1,148	7.5	7.5	0.0	7.5	0.01
89	Ekos Computers	Flint, MI	1	1	7.5	7.5	5.3	0.7	7.5
90	Caldor	Norwalk, CT	166	166	7.2	7.2	2.2	1.9	0.04
91	Atlantic Computer Systems	Toms River, NJ	1	1	7.0	7.0	6.4	0.3	7.0
92	Foley's	Houston, TX	48	46	6.5	6.5	6.1	0.0	0.1
93	Borders	Ann Arbor, MI	18	NA	6.3	6.3	0.0	3.6	0.4
94	Baillio's	Albuquerque, NM	2	2	6.0	6.0	4.8	0.2	3.0
95	Steinberg's	Cincinnati, OH	18	18	5.8	5.8	4.1	0.6	0.3
96	Computer Warehouse of Nevada	Las Vegas, NV	1	1	5.2	5.2	3.4	1.1	5.2
97	Meijer	Grand Rapids, MI	99	86	5.2	5.2	0.0	3.0	0.1
98	Virgin Megastores	Los Angeles, CA	5	5	4.8	4.8	0.0	4.8	1.0
99	Apex Department Store	Pawtucket, RI	3	3	4.0	4.0	3.5	0.3	1.3
100	Great Buys Plus	Evansville, IA	2	2	3.7	3.7	2.8	0.0	1.8

Excerpted with permission, Computer Retail Week 6/3/96, p 47. Copyright © 1996, CMP Publications, 600 Community Dr., Manhasset NY 11030 U.S.

Datamation: Datamation 100

"You'd think Datamation 100 companies just couldn't get enough of each other last year--through acquisition that is. It was a year that demanded vigilance from buyers and sellers alike, as many of the largest and some of the smallest on our list bought competitors in an attempt to beef up product lines and marketing muscle. And they did. On this, the 20th anniversary of the Datamation 100, a dozen companies joined the billionaire's club, bringing the roster to 75, up from 63 in 1994, 52 five years ago and 31 a decade ago.

Rank	Companies, Revenue ($M)	Total IS Revenue	Large Sys Revenue	Server Revenue	Desktop Revenue	Software Revenue	Datacom Revenue	Svc & Support Rev	Peripheral Revenue
1	IBM	71,940	6,475	6,475	12,949	12,949	2,878	20,143	10,072
2	Fujitsu	26,798	5,092	2,144	8,843	4,020	536	3,752	2,412
3	Hewlett-Packard	26,073	-	3,650	5,475	782	1,304	6,258	8,604
4	NEC	19,350	3,870	2,516	5,225	2,322	387	2,516	2,516
5	Hitachi	16,208	4,376	486	1,621	1,297	648	2,917	4,862
6	Compaq Computer	14,800	-	3,256	9,176	-	296	1,036	1,036
7	Digital Equipment	14,440	43	1,689	2,599	1,300	578	6,498	1,733
8	EDS	12,422	-	-	-	-	-	12,422	-
9	AT&T	11,384	-	3,529	1,025	569	3,244	3,017	-
10	Toshiba	11,380	-	2,048	6,259	-	-	-	3,073
11	Apple Computer	11,378	-	569	8,534	455	-	683	1,138
12	Siemens Nixdorf	8,951	770	1,226	1,396	1,226	-	2,757	1,575
13	Seagate Technology	8,200	-	-	-	410	-	-	7,790
14	Microsoft	7,418	-	-	-	7,418	-	-	-

Rank	Companies, Revenue ($M)	Total IS Revenue	Large Sys Revenue	Server Revenue	Desktop Revenue	Software Revenue	Datacom Revenue	Svc & Support Rev	Peripheral Revenue
15	Matsushita	7,026	-	-	1,827	-	1,757	422	3,021
16	Sun Microsystems	6,500	-	650	3,965	325	-	845	715
17	Unisys	6,202	1,116	-	806	744	-	3,535	-
18	Olivetti	6,035	127	296	1,672	1,279	181	1,575	905
19	Acer	5,700	-	114	2,736	-	-	1,254	1,596
20	Canon	5,616	-	-	-	-	-	-	5,616
21	Groupe Bull	5,300	795	424	1,272	530	-	1,484	795
22	Dell Computer	5,296	-	159	4,555	-	-	-	583
23	NTT Data	5,287	-	-	-	-	3,172	2,115	-
24	Xerox	4,668	-	-	-	98	-	1,816	2,754
25	Packard Bell	4,300	-	-	4,300	-	-	-	-
26	Andersen Consulting	4,220	-	-	-	422	-	3,798	-
27	Quantum	4,174	-	-	-	-	-	-	4,174
28	Mitsubishi	4,145	290	870	539	-	1,078	-	1,368
29	Computer Sciences	4,100	-	-	-	205	-	3,895	-
30	Cap Gemini	3,785	-	-	-	170	-	3,614	-
31	Gateway 2000	3,676	-	-	3,676	-	-	-	-
32	Intel	3,240	-	-	-	648	648	648	1,296
33	Computer Associates	3,196	-	-	-	2,461	-	735	-
34	ADP	3,157	-	-	-	-	-	3,157	-
35	Oki	3,071	-	92	154	215	522	276	1,812
36	Motorola	2,974	-	773	744	-	1,457	-	-
37	Oracle	2,707	-	-	-	1,527	-	1,180	-
38	Cisco Systems	2,668	-	-	-	-	2,668	-	-
39	Silicon Graphics	2,541	254	610	1,397	-	-	279	-
40	AST	2,349	-	-	2,349	-	-	-	-
41	Western Digital	2,340	-	-	-	-	-	-	2,340
42	KPMG Peat Marwick	2,300	-	-	-	-	-	2,300	-
43	Tandem	2,285	-	1,846	-	-	-	439	-
44	Lockheed Martin	2,057	-	-	-	1,234	-	206	617
45	Novell	2,040	-	-	-	1,897	-	143	-
46	Seiko Epson	2,026	-	-	912	-	-	-	1,114
47	Ricoh	1,966	-	-	511	334	118	236	767
48	3Com	1,963	-	-	-	-	1,963	-	-
49	Storage Technology	1,929	-	-	-	-	289	-	1,640
50	EMC	1,921	-	-	-	-	-	-	1,921
51	SAP	1,887	-	-	-	1,349	-	538	-
52	Entex	1,785	-	-	-	-	-	1,785	-
53	Bay Networks	1,700	-	-	-	-	1,700	-	-
54	Amdahl	1,516	758	76	-	76	-	606	-
55	Lexmark	1,478	-	-	-	-	-	-	1,478
56	SAIC	1,401	-	-	-	911	-	490	-
57	Samsung	1,400	-	161	336	28	-	-	875
58	Texas Instruments	1,313	-	-	302	249	-	144	617
59	Kingston Technology	1,300	-	-	-	-	195	130	975
60	Coopers & Lybrand	1,260	-	-	-	-	-	1,260	-
61	Maxtor	1,230	-	-	-	-	-	-	1,230
62	Data General	1,205	-	458	84	-	-	398	265
63	Stream International	1,200	-	-	-	-	-	1,200	-

Rank	Companies, Revenue ($M)	Total IS Revenue	Large Sys Revenue	Server Revenue	Desktop Revenue	Software Revenue	Datacom Revenue	Svc & Support Rev	Peripheral Revenue
64	Alcatel	1,156	-	-	-	-	1,156	-	-
65	LM Ericsson	1,107	-	-	-	-	885	221	-
66	Finsiel	1,103	-	-	-	66	-	1,037	-
67	Cabletron	1,100	-	-	-	-	990	110	-
68	Intergraph	1,098	-	-	714	-	-	384	-
69	Wang	1,095	-	304	-	35	-	712	44
70	U.S. Robotics	1,092	-	-	-	-	1,092	-	-
71	Sema Group	1,067	-	-	-	85	-	982	-
72	Mitac	1,062	-	-	797	-	-	-	266
73	General Electric	1,050	-	-	-	-	-	1,050	-
74	Nomura	1,042	94	94	94	83	52	573	52
75	Tatung	1,032	52	-	454	52	93	52	330
76	MCI	992	-	-	-	-	-	992	-
77	Memorex Telex	981	-	-	49	-	481	334	118
78	Sybase	957	-	-	-	641	-	316	-
79	Alltel	927	-	-	-	-	-	927	-
80	Price Waterhouse	880	-	-	-	-	-	880	-
81	Sony	847	-	-	398	-	-	-	449
82	British Telecom	838	-	-	-	-	377	461	-
83	Micron Electronics	833	-	-	833	-	-	-	-
84	Sligos	778	-	-	-	16	-	762	-
85	Adobe	762	-	-	-	762	-	-	-
86	First International Computer	725	-	-	537	-	-	7	181
87	Informix	714	-	-	-	714	-	-	-
88	Fiserv	703	-	-	-	42	-	661	-
89	Cray Research	676	412	-	-	27	-	210	27
90	Comparex	670	214	-	-	-	-	194	261
91	Ceridian	667	-	133	-	133	-	400	-
92	Ernst & Young	653	-	-	-	-	-	653	-
93	Shared Medical	651	-	-	-	-	-	651	-
94	PRC	648	-	-	-	-	-	648	-
95	Newbridge Networks	641	-	-	-	32	545	64	-
96	Intec	637	-	-	-	-	-	637	-
97	American Management Systems	632	-	-	-	57	-	575	-
98	Sterling Software	610	-	-	-	244	-	366	-
99	Racal	604	-	-	-	-	513	91	-
100	Deloitte & Touche	600	-	-	-	-	-	600	-
	Total	443,804	24,7368	34,649	99,112	50,4401	31,802	118,050	85,011

Top Large-Scale System Suppliers

'The mainframe is back. Contrary to predictions that client/server applications would drain away demand for enterprise systems, client/server growth actually increases demand for mainframes.

Rank	Company	100 Rank	Country	Large System Revnue ($M)	Total IT Revenue ($M)	Large Sys/Total IT Revenue (%)	Net Income ($M)
1	IBM	1	United States	6,474.6	71,940.0	9.0	4,178.0
2	Fujitsu	2	Japan	4,823.6	26,798.0	19.0	900.0
3	Hitachi	5	Japan	4,376.2	16,208.1	27.0	NA

Rank	Company	100 Rank	Country	Large System Revnue ($M)	Total IT Revenue ($M)	Large Sys/Total IT Revenue (%)	Net Income ($M)
4	NEC	4	Japan	3,870.0	19,350.0	20.0	700.0
5	Unisys	17	United States	1,116.4	6,202.3	18.0	-624.6
6	Groupe Bull	21	France	795.0	5,300.0	15.0	61.0
7	Siemens Nixdorf	12	Germany	769.8	8,951.0	8.6%	16.1
8	Amdahl	54	United States	758.0	1,516.0	50.0	29.0
9	Cray Research	89	United States	412.4	676.0	61.0	-226.4
10	Mitsubishi	28	Japan	290.2	4,145.2	7.0	NA
11	Silicon Graphics	39	United States	254.1	2,540.8	10.0	237.0
12	Sequent	-	United States	237.7	540.3	44.0	35.1
13	Comparex	90	Germany	214.4	670.0	32.0	42.0
14	Olivetti	18	Italy	126.7	6,035.0	2.1	NA

'Large-system growth over the last two years has been spectacular. IBM reports that it shipped 41% more System 390 MIPS in 1994 than in 1993 and 60% more MIPS in 1995 than the previous year. Analysts predict 40 to 60% gains will continue over the next five years as users continue to shift from older water-cooled ECL technology to newer, cheaper complementary CMOS machines.

Top Server Suppliers

'Microsoft's Windows NT Advanced Server operating system took over the low end of the server market last year as corporate buyers transformed it into the de facto standard for LAN and departmental application server environments.

Rank	Company	100 Rank	Country	Server Revenue ($M)	Total IT Revenue ($M)	Server/Total IT Revenue (%)	Net Income ($M)
1	IBM	1	United States	6,474.6	71,940.0	9.0	4,178.0
2	Hewlett-Packard	3	United States	3,650.2	26,073.0	14.0	2,433.0
3	AT&T	9	United States	3,529.1	11,384.1	31.0	139.0
4	Compaq Computer	6	United States	3,256.0	14,800.0	22.0	789.0
5	NEC	4	Japan	2,515.5	19,350.0	13.0	700.0
6	Tandem	43	United States	1,846.2	2,285.0	80.8	107.5
7	Toshiba	10	Japan	1,820.8	11,380.3	16.0	850.0
8	Digital Equipment	7	United States	1,689.4	14,439.5	11.7	431.0
9	Fujitsu	2	Japan	1,607.9	26,798.0	6.0	671.0
10	Siemens Nixdorf	12	Germany	1,226.3	8,951.0	13.7	16.1
11	Mitsubishi	28	Japan	870.5	4,145.2	21.0	NA
12	Motorola	36	United States	773.3	2,974.1	26.0	1,781.0
13	Sun Microsystems	16	United States	650.0	6,500.0	10.0	447.0
14	Silicon Graphics	39	United States	609.8	2,540.8	24.0	237.0
15	Apple Computer	11	United States	568.9	11,378.0	5.0	167.0
16	Hitachi	5	Japan	486.2	16,208.1	3.0	NA
17	Data General	62	United States	457.9	1,205.0	38.0	-66.2
18	Groupe Bull	21	France	424.0	5,300.0	8.0	61.0
19	Wang Laboratories	69	United States	304.4	1,095.0	27.8	-81.4
20	Olivetti	18	Italy	295.7	6,035.0	4.9	NA
21	Stratus Computer	-	United States	276.4	588.0	47.0	17.0
22	Samsung	57	Korea	161.0	1,400.0	11.5	NA
23	Dell Computer	22	United States	159.0	5,300.0	3.0	272.0
24	Sequent	-	United States	156.7	540.3	29.0	35.1
25	Control Data	-	United States	155.0	455.0	34.0	9.0

'The server category includes the PC servers, Unix servers, IBM AS/400, DEC VAX and other proprietary mid-range and minicomputers.

Top Desktop Suppliers

'Pentium sales, already skyrocketing in 1994, just kept zooming along last year, as Intel continued its aggressive price/performance push. Over the last year, Intel introduced a faster Pentium chip approximately every three months; each new version came in at a price similar to its predecessor's. Intel's actions caused a ripple effect among PC makers whose price/performance curve just keep getting better.

Rank	Company	100 Rank	Country	Desktop Revenue ($M)	Total IT Revenue ($M)	Desktop/Total IT Revnue (%)	Net Income ($M)
1	IBM	1	United States	12,949.2	71,940.0	18.0	4,178.0
2	Compaq Computer	6	United States	9,176.0	14,800.0	62.0	789.0
3	Apple Computer	11	United States	8,533.5	11,378.0	75.0	167.0
4	Fujitsu	2	Japan	6,431.5	26,798.0	24.0	671.0
5	Toshiba	10	Japan	5,690.1	11,380.3	50.0	850.0
6	Hewlett-Packard	3	United States	5,475.3	26,073.0	21.0	2,433.0
7	NEC	4	Japan	5,224.5	19,350.0	27.0	700.0
8	Dell Computer	22	United States	4,558.0	5,296.0	86.0	272.0
9	Packard Bell	25	United States	4,300.0	4,300.0	100.0	NA
10	Sun Microsystems	16	United States	3,965.0	6,500.0	61.0	447.0
11	Gateway 2000	31	United States	3,676.0	3,676.0	100.0	173.0
12	Acer	19	Taiwan	2,736.0	5,700.0	48.0	NA
13	Digital Equipment	7	United States	2,599.1	14,439.5	18.0	431.0
14	AST Research	40	United States	2,348.5	2,348.5	100.0	-263.2
15	Matsushita	15	Japan	1,826.8	7,026.2	26.0	1,017.0
16	Olivetti	18	Italy	1,671.7	6,035.0	27.7	NA
17	Hitachi	5	Japan	1,620.8	16,208.1	10.0	NA
18	Silicon Graphics	39	United States	1,397.4	2,540.8	55.0	237.0
19	Siemens Nixdorf	12	Germany	1,396.4	8,951.0	15.6	16.1
20	Groupe Bull	21	France	1,272.0	5,300.0	24.0	61.0
21	AT&T	9	United States	1,024.6	11,384.1	9.0	139.0
22	Seiko Epson	46	Japan	911.6	2,025.7	45.0	NA
23	Micron Electronics	83	United States	833.3	833.3	100.0	43.4
24	Unisys	17	United States	806.3	6,202.3	13.0	-624.6
25	Mitac	72	Taiwan	796.5	1,062.0	75.0	5.8

'The desktop category includes personal computers, workstations and all portable computers--from notebook to handheld units.

Top Software Suppliers

'Ask just about any software company executive what the biggest IT trend of 1997 will be, and you'll get a single answer: corporate intranets. Intranets are the hottest communication technology to hit corporations since email. Intranets are increasingly viewed either as an improvement on, or an extension to, client/server applications, distributing information to an ever wider and increasingly amorphous group of employees working from remote offices, their homes and the back seats of taxis.

Rank	Company	100 Rank	Country	Software Revenue ($M)	Total IT Revenue ($M)	Software/Total IT Revenue (%)	Net Income ($M)
1	IBM	1	United States	12,949.2	71,940.0	18.0	4,178.0
2	Microsoft	14	United States	7,418.0	7,418.0	100.0	1,838.0
3	Fujitsu	2	Japan	6,431.5	26,798.0	24.0	671.0

Rank	Company	100 Rank	Country	Software Revenue ($M)	Total IT Revenue ($M)	Software/Total IT Revenue (%)	Net Income ($M)
4	Computer Associates	33	United States	2,460.9	3,196.0	77.0	700.0
5	NEC	4	Japan	2,322.0	19,350.0	12.0	700.0
6	Novell	45	United States	1,897.2	2,040.0	93.0	338.0
7	Oracle	37	United States	1,526.9	2,707.3	56.4	423.4
8	SAP	51	Germany	1,349.2	1,887.0	71.5	283.0
9	Digital Equipment	7	United States	1,299.6	14,439.5	9.0	431.0
10	Hitachi	5	Japan	1,296.7	16,208.1	8.0	NA
11	Olivetti	18	Italy	1,279.4	6,035.0	21.2	NA
12	Lockheed Martin	44	United States	1,234.1	2,056.8	60.0	683.0
13	Siemens Nixdorf	12	Germany	1,226.3	8,951.0	13.7	16.1
14	SAIC	56	United States	910.8	1,401.2	65.0	57.3
15	Hewlett-Packard	3	United States	782.2	26,073.0	3.0	2,433.0
16	Adobe Systems	85	United States	762.3	762.3	100.0	93.5
17	Unisys	17	United States	744.3	6,202.3	12.0	-624.6
18	Informix Software	87	United States	714.0	714.0	100.0	97.6
19	Intel	32	United States	648.1	3,240.4	20.0	3,556.0
20	Sybase	78	United States	640.9	956.6	67.0	-19.5
21	AT&T	9	United States	569.2	11,384.1	5.0	139.0
22	Autodesk	-	United States	546.9	546.9	100.0	87.8
23	SAS Institute	-	United States	534.3	562.4	95.0	NA
24	Groupe Bull	21	France	530.0	5,300.0	10.0	61.0
25	Apple Computer	11	United States	455.1	11,378.0	4.0	167.0
26	Andersen Consulting	26	United States	422.0	4,220.0	10.0	NA
27	Symantec	-	United States	418.0	418.0	100.0	-37.3
28	Seagate Technology	13	United States	410.0	8,200.0	5.0	NA
29	SSA	-	United States	405.0	405.0	100.0	35.2
30	BMC Software	-	United States	396.9	396.9	100.0	70.2
31	Compuware	-	United States	388.7	580.1	67.0	41.2
32	Ricoh	47	Japan	334.1	1,965.5	17.0	NA
33	Attachmate	-	United States	331.5	390.0	85.0	NA
34	Sun Microsystems	16	United States	325.0	6,500.0	5.0	447.0
35	D&B Software	-	United States	315.0	350.0	90.0	NA
36	Cadence	-	United States	290.7	548.4	53.0	97.3
37	Texas Instruments	58	United States	249.4	1,312.8	19.0	1,088.0
38	Sterling Software	98	United States	244.2	610.4	40.0	92.2
39	Octel	-	United States	236.0	236.0	100.0	31.0
40	Platinum Technology	-	United States	234.5	275.9	85.0	-112.5
41	Software AG	-	Germany	231.8	552.0	42.0	NA
42	Candle	-	United States	230.0	230.0	100.0	NA
43	J.D. Edwards	-	United States	228.3	340.8	67.0	NA
44	Information Builders	-	United States	216.8	255.0	85.0	NA
45	Oki	35	Japan	215.0	3,071.2	7.0	343.0
46	PeopleSoft	-	United States	211.6	227.5	93.0	29.4
47	Borland International	-	United States	208.0	208.0	100.0	-45.0
48	Computer Sciences	29	United States	205.0	4,100.0	5.0	133.0
49	Marcam	-	United States	204.7	204.7	100.0	-36.3
50	JBA International	-	United States	196.9	196.9	100.0	13.7

'Software includes all system software, networking software, applications software and other software not embedded in hardware.

Top Datacom Equipment Suppliers

'In the datacom hardware market, the division between LANs and WANs is crumbling like the Berlin Wall. The increasing homogeneity of communications technologies and the consolidation of key industry players are combining to remake the networked landscape.

Rank	Company	100 Rank	Country	Datacom Equip Revenue ($M)	Total IT Revenue ($M)	Datacom/Total IT Revenue (%)	Net Income ($M)
1	AT&T	9	United States	3,244.5	11,384.1	28.5	139.0
2	NTT Data	23	Japan	3,172.0	5,286.7	60.0	80.9
3	IBM	1	United States	2,877.6	71,940.0	4.0	4,178.0
4	Cisco System	38	United States	2,667.8	2,667.8	100.0	634.0
5	3Com	48	United States	1,962.8	1,962.8	100.0	176.4
6	Matsushita	15	Japan	1,756.6	7,026.2	25.0	1,017.0
7	Bay Networks	53	United States	1,700.0	1,700.0	100.0	221.0
8	Motorola	36	United States	1,457.3	2,974.1	49.0	1,781.0
9	Hewlett-Packard	3	United States	1,303.7	26,073.0	5.0	2,433.0
10	Alcatel Business Systems	64	France	1,155.6	1,155.6	100.0	-5,000.0
11	U.S. Robotics	70	United States	1,091.6	1,091.6	100.0	89.2
12	Mitsubishi	28	Japan	1,077.7	4,145.2	26.0	NA
13	Cabletron Systems	67	United States	990.0	1,100.0	90.0	202.0
14	LM Ericsson	65	Sweden	885.5	1,106.8	80.0	761.8
15	Hitachi	5	Japan	648.3	16,208.1	4.0	NA
16	Intel	32	United States	648.1	3,240.4	20.0	3,556.0
17	Digital Equipment	7	United States	577.6	14,439.5	4.0	431.0
18	Ascom	-	Switzerland	560.0	560.0	100.0	NA
19	Newbridge Networks	95	Canada	544.9	641.0	85.0	138.0
20	Fujitsu	2	Japan	536.0	26,798.0	2.0	671.0
21	Oki	35	Japan	522.1	3,071.2	17.0	343.0
22	Racal Electronics	99	UK	513.4	604.0	85.0	66.0
23	Memorex Telex	77	United States	480.7	981.0	49.0	NA
24	Madge Networks	-	United States	423.4	423.4	100.0	-2.0
25	NEC	4	Japan	387.0	19,350.0	2.0	700.0

'Datacom equipment includes any products used to send data over local or wide-area networks such as bridges, hubs, routers, terminals, servers and modems.

Top Service and Support Suppliers

'Services include outsourcing, facilities management, systems integration, IT consulting, contract programming and disaster recovery.

Rank	Company	100 Rank	Country	Services Revenue ($M)	Total IT Revenue ($M)	Services/Total IT Revenue (%)	Net Income ($M)
1	IBM	1	United States	20,143.2	71,940.0	28.0	4,178.0
2	EDS	8	United States	12,422.1	12,422.1	100.0	938.9
3	Digital Equipment	7	United States	6,497.8	14,439.5	45.0	431.0
4	Hewlett-Packard	3	United States	6,257.5	26,073.0	24.0	2,433.0
5	Computer Sciences	29	United States	3,895.0	4,100.0	95.0	133.0
6	Andersen Consulting	26	United States	3,798.0	4,220.0	90.0	NA

Rank	Company	100 Rank	Country	Services Revenue ($M)	Total IT Revenue ($M)	Services/Total IT Revenue (%)	Net Income ($M)
7	Fujitsu	2	Japan	3,751.7	26,798.0	14.0	671.0
8	Cap Gemini Sogeti	30	France	3,614.2	3,784.5	95.5	NA
9	Unisys	17	United States	3,535.3	6,202.3	57.0	-624.6
10	ADP	34	United States	3,156.7	3,156.7	100.0	422.0
11	AT&T	9	United States	3,016.8	11,384.1	26.5	139.0
12	Hitachi	5	Japan	2,917.5	16,208.1	18.0	NA
13	Siemens Nixdorf	12	Germany	2,756.9	8,951.0	30.8	16.1
14	NEC	4	Japan	2,515.5	19,350.0	13.0	700.0
15	KPMG Peat Marwick	42	United States	2,300.3	2,300.3	100.0	NA
16	NTT Data	23	Japan	2,114.7	5,286.7	40.0	80.9
17	Xerox	24	United States	1,815.7	4,667.7	38.9	-472.0
18	Entex Information Services	52	United States	1,785.0	1,785.0	100.0	NA
19	Olivetti	18	Italy	1,575.1	6,035.0	26.1	NA
20	Groupe Bull	21	France	1,484.0	5,300.0	28.0	61.0
21	General Electric	73	United States	1,050.0	1,050.0	100.0	6.6
22	Coopers & Lybrand	60	United States	1,260.0	1,260.0	100.0	NA
23	Acer	19	Taiwan	1,254.0	5,700.0	22.0	NA
24	Stream International	63	United States	1,200.0	1,200.0	100.0	NA
25	Oracle	37	United States	1,180.4	2,707.3	43.6	423.4

Top Peripherals Suppliers

'Peripherals include disks drives, tape and other storage devices, printers, monitors, add-in boards and all input/output devices."--Datamation

Rank	Company	100 Rank	Country	Peripherals Revenue ($M)	Total IT Revenue ($M)	Peripherals/ Total IT Rev (%)	Net Income ($M)
1	IBM	1	United States	10,071.6	71,940.0	14.0	4,178.0
2	Hewlett-Packard	3	United States	8,604.1	26,073.0	33.0	2,433.0
3	Seagate Technology	13	United States	7,790.0	8,200.0	95.0	NA
4	Canon	20	Japan	5,615.7	5,615.7	100.0	429.0
5	Hitachi	5	Japan	4,862.4	16,208.1	30.0	NA
6	Quantum	27	United States	4,174.0	4,174.0	100.0	56.0
7	Fujitsu	2	Japan	3,215.8	26,798.0	12.0	671.0
8	Matsushita	15	Japan	3,021.3	7,026.2	43.0	1,017.0
9	Xerox	24	United States	2,753.9	4,667.7	59.0	-472.0
10	Toshiba	10	Japan	2,731.3	11,380.3	24.0	850.0
11	NEC	4	Japan	2,515.5	19,350.0	13.0	700.0
12	Western Digital	41	United States	2,430.0	2,430.0	100.0	90.7
13	EMC	50	United States	1,921.3	1,921.3	100.0	365.4
14	Oki	35	Japan	1,812.0	3,071.2	59.0	343.0
15	Digital Equipment	7	United States	1,732.7	14,439.5	12.0	431.0
16	Storage Technology	49	United States	1,639.7	1,929.0	85.0	-142.0
17	Acer	19	Taiwan	1,596.0	5,700.0	28.0	NA
18	Siemens Nixdorf	12	Germany	1,575.4	8,951.0	17.6	16.1
19	Lexmark	55	United States	1,478.1	1,478.1	100.0	32.4
20	Mitsubishi	28	Japan	1,367.9	4,145.2	33.0	NA
21	Intel	32	United States	1,296.2	3,240.4	40.0	3,556.0
22	Maxtor	61	United States	1,230.0	1,230.0	100.0	-81.8
23	Apple Computer	11	United States	1,137.8	11,378.0	10.0	167.0

Rank	Company	100 Rank	Country	Peripherals Revenue ($M)	Total IT Revenue ($M)	Peripherals/ Total IT Rev (%)	Net Income ($M)
24	Seiko Epson	46	Japan	1,114.1	2,025.7	55.0	NA
25	Compaq Computer	6	United States	1,036.0	14,800.0	7.0	789.0

Excerpted with permission from Datamation, June 15, 1996, p. 32. Copyright © 1996, The Cahners Publishing Company, Newton MA 02158 USA.

Electronic Business Today: Top 200 Electronics Companies

"In 1995, the growth of the U.S. electronics industry far outpaced that of the economy overall. While economic growth was lack luster, the electronics industry was enjoying one of its best years in two decades. Sales of components and systems by the Top 200 U.S. electronics companies rose 15%, to $549.3B.

'Many companies took advantage of their strong sales to improve efficiency, rather than expanding staff. Revenues per employee rose an impressive 24%, to $264,808. Still, the cost of sales as a percentage of sales rose to 66.3%, compared with 63.3% the previous year. Sales, general and administrative costs increased to 19.5%, up from 15.3%. At the same time, the Top 200 companies were readying themselves for the future: spending on research and development rose to 6.8% of sales from 4.9% in 1994."--Electronic Business Today

Rank 1995	Rank 1994	Company	Electronics Sales ($M)	Total Sales ($M)	Net Profits ($M)	Profits (% of Sales)	ROA (%)	Cost of Sales (% of Sales)	SG&A Costs (% of Sales)	R&D Spending (% Sales)	Sales per Employee ($K)
1	1	IBM	71,940.0	71,940.0	4,178.0	5.8	5.2	58	23	8	323
2	3	Hewlett-Packard	33,503.0	33,503.0	2,621.0	7.8	11.1	64	18	7	314
3	2	AT&T	31,867.4	79,609.0	139.0	0.2	0.2	62	32	5	264
4	4	Motorola	27,037.0	27,037.0	1,781.0	6.6	8.8	65	17	8	197
5	8	Intel	16,202.0	16,202.0	3,566.0	22.0	22.8	48	11	8	437
6	6	Hughes Electronics	14,771.8	14,771.8	948.3	6.4	6.2	77	8	5	181
7	10	Compaq	14,755.0	14,755.0	789.0	5.3	11.3	77	11	2	939
8	7	Digital Equipment	14,439.0	14,439.0	431.0	3.0	1.2	68	24	8	198
9	11	Texas Instruments	13,128.0	13,128.0	1,088.0	8.3	13.4	71	13	7	227
10	5	Xerox	12,201.0	16,611.0	-472.0	NM	-1.8	80	29	6	192
11	12	Apple Computer	11,378.0	11,378.0	167.0	1.5	7.4	74	14	6	904
12	9	Lockheed Martin	10,078.3	22,853.0	1,372.0	6.0	7.7	91	NA	3	137
13	18	Microsoft	7,419.0	7,419.0	1,838.0	24.8	23.1	15	36	15	359
14	14	General Electric	6,972.5	70,028.0	6,573.0	9.4	3.2	44	8	3	316
15	15	Honeywell	6,731.3	6,731.3	333.6	5.0	6.7	68	19	5	133
16	17	Sun Microsystems	6,389.8	6,389.8	446.5	7.0	11.0	58	25	9	425
17	13	Unisys	6,202.3	6,202.3	-624.6	NM	-8.7	74	30	7	165
18	16	Loral	6,178.9	6,178.9	339.2	5.5	5.8	90	10	4	178
19	19	Merisel	5,957.0	5,957.0	-49.2	NM	-4.1	78	5	0	1,881
20	21	Arrow Electronics	5,919.4	5,919.4	202.5	3.4	8.5	83	10	0	877
21	20	Rockwell International	5,904.8	13,420.0	769.0	5.7	6.6	77	13	5	168
22	23	Seagate Technology	5,493.5	5,493.5	394.0	7.2	8.3	80	5	5	77
23	24	Raytheon	5,346.0	11,715.6	792.5	6.8	9.2	78	10	3	176
24	28	Dell Computer	5,296.0	5,296.0	272.0	5.1	14.5	80	11	2	716
25	26	AMP	5,227.2	5,227.2	427.3	8.2	9.9	68	19	11	140
26	25	GTE	5,093.5	19,957.0	2,538.0	12.7	6.4	38	19	1	184
27	27	Avnet	4,616.6	4,797.6	171.5	3.6	7.2	81	12	0	506
28	31	TRW	4,393.6	10,172.0	446.0	4.4	7.7	81	7	4	156
29	33	Quantum	4,174.0	4,174.0	55.5	1.3	7.0	83	5	5	693

Rank 1995	Rank 1994	Company	Electronics Sales ($M)	Total Sales ($M)	Net Profits ($M)	Profits (% of Sales)	ROA (%)	Cost of Sales (% of Sales)	SG&A Costs (% of Sales)	R&D Spending (% Sales)	Sales per Employee ($K)
30	35	Gateway 2000	3,676.3	3,676.3	173.0	4.7	18.3	83	10	1	499
31	56	Micron Technology	3,603.5	3,603.5	1,013.3	28.1	39.2	45	7	4	438
32	57	Applied Materials	3,596.4	3,596.4	560.0	15.6	19.5	54	13	11	360
33	30	Harris	3,526.2	3,526.2	164.8	4.7	5.6	67	7	17	127
34	-	Eaton	3,517.6	6,822.0	399.0	5.8	8.2	74	14	3	132
35	47	SCI Systems	3,513.9	3,513.9	62.3	1.8	4.8	97	1	1	212
36	42	Oracle	3,479.1	3,479.1	477.1	13.7	22.0	26	43	9	204
37	29	Ford	3,428.4	137,137.0	4,139.0	3.0	1.8	74	4	5	401
38	32	Eastman Kodak	3,383.7	15,269.0	1,252.0	8.2	8.5	52	27	6	158
39	38	Computer Associates	3,196.2	3,196.2	-108.6	NM	15.0	NA	40	9	363
40	-	Emerson Electric	3,088.2	10,294.1	934.8	9.1	10.2	65	19	3	131
41	40	Tech Data	3,068.6	3,068.6	21.6	0.7	2.4	93	5	0	1,255
42	36	Pitney Bowes	2,767.2	3,554.7	407.7	11.5	5.3	40	35	2	117
43	46	Johnson Controls	2,736.2	8,659.0	201.6	2.3	4.8	85	10	2	146
44	39	Allied Signal	2,710.0	14,346.0	919.0	6.4	7.7	80	10	2	163
45	66	Cisco Systems	2,667.8	2,667.8	633.9	23.8	30.0	33	22	8	491
46	45	National Semiconductor	2,651.6	2,651.6	291.5	11.0	13.0	58	17	12	106
47	53	Northrop Grumman	2,588.0	6,818.0	252.0	3.7	4.4	78	14	2	171
48	58	Silicon Graphics	2,497.2	2,497.2	252.7	10.1	13.1	46	28	11	405
49	50	General Instrument	2,432.0	2,432.0	123.8	5.1	5.6	70	9	6	198
50	54	Western Digital	2,430.4	2,430.4	73.5	3.0	16.4	82	6	6	299
51	49	Advanced Micro Devices	2,429.7	2,429.7	300.5	12.4	11.0	53	16	16	201
52	44	AST Research	2,348.5	2,348.5	-263.2	NM	-9.8	90	13	1	460
53	61	Solectron	2,249.5	2,249.5	88.7	3.9	9.3	90	4	0	225
54	48	Tandem Computers	2,151.1	2,151.1	34.4	1.6	5.4	50	30	14	271
55	51	Litton Industries	2,041.0	3,413.0	144.0	4.2	5.6	80	10	2	114
56	52	Novell	1,985.9	1,985.9	320.3	16.1	15.4	24	36	18	252
57	65	Storage Technology	1,929.5	1,929.5	-128.0	NM	-6.3	44	23	10	187
58	70	EMC	1,921.3	1,921.3	326.8	17.0	21.3	52	17	8	514
59	68	Corning	1,771.7	5,313.1	-37.1	NM	-0.6	64	21	3	127
60	74	Bay Networks	1,727.9	1,727.9	221.3	12.8	20.2	45	22	10	371
61	73	Medtronic	1,713.6	2,089.7	400.2	19.2	16.5	31	33	11	198
62	81	3Com	1,698.3	1,698.3	221.6	13.0	20.1	46	24	10	482
63	72	Tektronix	1,651.4	1,651.4	96.2	5.8	7.4	55	27	11	182
64	64	Chrysler	1,595.9	53,195.0	4,245.0	8.0	8.2	78	8	3	475
65	63	Varian Associates	1,580.8	1,580.8	144.0	9.1	14.2	65	19	6	210
66	59	ITT Industries	1,559.0	8,884.0	612.0	6.9	7.2	86	8	5	105
67	62	Amdahl	1,516.4	1,516.4	81.8	5.4	2.9	63	24	12	220
68	82	DSC Communications	1,422.0	1,422.0	192.7	13.6	12.3	52	15	13	252
69	77	Molex	1,336.5	1,336.5	139.1	10.4	9.6	58	25	7	136
70	-	Micron Electronics	1,304.2	1,304.2	70.1	5.4	24.4	82	7	0	512
71	109	Mark IV Industries	1,302.6	2,038.5	89.3	4.4	5.0	67	18	2	133
72	67	Zenith Electronics	1,273.9	1,273.9	-90.7	NM	-13.5	94	9	3	64
73	88	LSI Logic	1,267.7	1,267.7	238.1	18.8	15.3	53	13	10	334
74	89	Maxtor	1,230.0	1,230.0	-92.0	NM	-20.7	94	9	7	116
75	83	Vishay Intertechnology	1,224.4	1,224.4	92.7	7.6	6.4	74	13	1	71
76	-	DuPont	1,214.0	42,163.0	3,293.0	7.8	8.9	56	7	3	398

Rank			Calendar Year 1995					Fiscal Year 1995			
1995	1994	Company	Electron- ics Sales ($M)	Total Sales ($M)	Net Profits ($M)	Profits (% of Sales)	ROA (%)	Cost of Sales (% of Sales)	SG&A Costs (% of Sales)	R&D Spending (% Sales)	Sales per Employee ($K)
77	108	Teradyne	1,191.0	1,191.0	164.9	13.8	18.5	54	15	10	246
78	97	Cirrus Logic	1,187.1	1,187.1	71.1	6.0	10.7	58	14	19	425
79	84	Thermo Electron	1,168.2	2,207.4	140.1	6.3	4.1	55	22	4	179
80	85	Scientific-Atlanta	1,140.1	1,140.1	33.9	3.0	8.9	72	13	7	273
81	80	McDonnell Douglas	1,125.5	14,300.0	1,422.0	9.9	12.5	84	5	2	221
82	90	Marshall Industries	1,113.8	1,113.8	48.1	4.3	10.3	81	12	0	714
83	79	Perkin-Elmer	1,113.6	1,113.6	75.3	6.8	7.5	53	30	9	180
84	78	Intergraph	1,098.0	1,098.0	-45.4	NM	-5.4	61	33	10	125
85	94	Wang Laboratories	1,094.7	1,094.7	12.1	1.1	0.9	69	24	3	169
86	145	U.S. Robotics	1,091.7	1,091.7	123.1	11.3	19.4	59	20	6	371
87	101	Read-Rite	1,082.2	1,082.2	146.6	13.5	15.7	74	4	4	48
88	76	Raychem	1,079.4	1,601.5	64.4	4.0	-1.3	50	32	8	151
89	96	Wyle Laboratories	1,077.5	1,077.5	36.2	3.4	9.7	83	12	0	NA
90	75	Data General	1,024.7	1,024.7	-64.0	NM	-5.6	67	29	7	215
91	112	Lam Research	1,018.0	1,018.0	119.2	11.7	16.8	52	18	16	259
92	100	Cabletron Systems	999.5	999.5	202.5	20.3	27.2	41	19	10	190
93	103	Sensormatic Electronics	992.4	992.4	-19.7	NM	5.4	40	43	3	137
94	102	Pioneer-Standard	965.0	965.0	24.9	2.6	9.1	81	13	0	751
95	106	Sybase	956.6	956.6	4.5	0.5	0.6	25	57	16	179
96	95	Analog Devices	955.5	955.5	119.3	12.5	13.1	49	20	14	165
97	-	3M	948.6	13,460.0	1,428.0	10.6	10.5	57	26	7	173
98	91	Beckman Instruments	930.1	930.1	76.6	8.2	8.8	46	32	10	160
99	93	EG&G	907.3	1,419.6	68.0	4.8	8.5	74	17	3	51
100	105	Tracor	886.9	886.9	27.9	3.1	6.1	80	12	1	93
101	114	Dover	873.5	3,745.9	278.3	7.4	11.7	68	20	3	155
102	99	Diebold	863.4	863.4	76.2	8.8	10.8	66	17	5	174
103	111	General Signal	800.5	1,863.2	36.1	1.9	2.4	70	19	3	148
104	107	Amphenol	783.2	783.2	62.9	8.0	9.2	65	15	2	146
105	116	Adobe Systems	762.3	762.3	110.4	14.5	13.8	17	32	18	391
106	115	Pittway	754.0	945.7	40.4	4.3	6.5	62	30	2	166
107	104	GTECH	737.4	737.4	12.0	1.6	0.1	66	13	4	178
108	117	VLSI Technology	720.0	720.0	46.0	6.4	6.3	60	17	12	252
109	134	Informix	709.0	709.0	105.3	14.9	18.8	18	48	11	310
110	147	Jabil Circuit	686.1	686.1	10.7	1.6	3.2	94	3	0	268
111	87	Cray Research	676.2	676.2	-226.4	NM	-21.0	65	25	18	149
112	121	Shared Medical Systems	650.6	650.6	39.8	6.1	9.8	51	39	7	142
113	118	Andrew	647.9	647.9	72.3	11.2	15.0	57	22	4	195
114	151	Integrated Device Tech.	645.0	645.0	123.3	19.1	17.2	43	15	19	151
115	126	Tellabs	635.2	635.2	115.6	18.2	39.4	43	19	13	236
116	155	Atmel	634.2	634.2	113.7	17.9	15.6	51	12	11	276
117	132	ADC Telecommunications	627.0	627.0	61.0	9.7	11.8	52	22	11	208
118	98	Premier Industrial	620.0	849.3	112.7	13.3	20.6	55	24	0	190
119	140	Kemet	613.8	613.8	55.1	9.0	8.0	71	8	3	56
120	127	Sterling Software	610.4	610.4	92.1	15.1	4.8	32	38	11	176
121	146	Cypress Semiconductor	596.1	596.1	120.3	20.2	18.4	46	12	12	363
122	139	Adaptec	593.5	593.5	92.3	15.6	23.5	44	18	13	284
123	119	Stratus Computer	587.9	587.9	17.3	2.9	2.8	52	28	14	221

Rank		Company	Calendar Year 1995					Fiscal Year 1995			
1995	1994		Electron-ics Sales ($M)	Total Sales ($M)	Net Profits ($M)	Profits (% of Sales)	ROA (%)	Cost of Sales (% of Sales)	SG&A Costs (% of Sales)	R&D Spending (% Sales)	Sales per Employee ($K)
124	133	Compuware	580.1	580.1	41.2	7.1	15.7	32	39	6	185
125	113	Anacomp	569.6	569.6	-210.8	NM	-39.2	75	18	0	148
126	173	KLA Instruments	569.3	569.3	102.0	17.9	13.5	46	19	10	317
127	135	Symbol Technologies	555.2	555.2	46.5	8.4	9.2	51	25	8	227
128	143	Cadence Design Systems	548.4	548.4	97.3	17.7	26.5	21	41	16	200
129	136	Autodesk	546.9	546.9	87.8	16.1	17.6	12	47	14	297
130	138	Sequent Computer Sys.	540.3	540.3	35.1	6.5	7.5	55	29	8	269
131	122	Augat	534.8	534.8	26.3	4.9	6.9	79	14	4	129
132	169	Silicon Valley Group	534.3	534.3	50.1	9.4	10.1	60	20	9	306
133	130	Electronic Arts	521.5	521.5	45.7	8.8	18.1	53	18	15	439
134	-	Xilinx	520.3	520.3	87.4	16.8	22.6	39	22	13	456
135	153	American Power Conversion	515.3	515.3	69.5	13.5	22.7	55	22	3	238
136	149	Komag	512.2	512.2	106.8	20.9	19.2	61	9	5	185
137	128	Ceridian	509.5	1,333.0	97.5	7.3	9.3	60	23	4	135
138	-	Volt	509.5	950.6	16.6	1.7	6.7	89	5	5	34
139	120	Computervision	507.1	507.1	30.7	6.1	12.0	48	28	9	230
140	157	International Rectifier	501.1	501.1	52.6	10.5	9.5	65	19	5	134
141	141	Octel Communications	501.0	501.0	36.9	7.4	8.7	39	31	15	197
142	-	United Technologies	485.5	22,624.0	750.0	3.3	4.7	78	12	4	132
143	-	Danaher	481.8	1,486.8	108.3	7.3	8.4	70	18	2	145
144	131	Dynatech	481.4	481.4	13.2	2.7	7.5	47	33	11	172
145	129	Polaroid	469.7	2,236.9	-140.2	-6.3	-6.1	58	38	7	188
146	142	California Microwave	465.8	465.8	-6.5	NM	-1.3	74	16	6	207
147	148	Bell Industries	463.1	564.3	11.9	2.1	5.5	77	17	0	383
148	124	Tyco	460.0	4,842.8	273.0	5.6	7.8	73	16	1	156
149	174	Logicon	456.7	456.7	24.3	5.3	13.8	82	9	1	92
150	137	Esco Electronics	455.4	455.4	5.2	1.1	1.4	78	17	3	125
151	123	Control Data Systems	454.8	454.8	8.9	2.0	3.4	73	25	2	193
152	154	Telxon	443.6	443.6	12.9	2.9	3.4	59	27	9	215
153	192	Parametric	440.9	440.9	90.6	20.5	28.1	9	47	6	242
154	150	Reynolds & Reynolds	430.4	935.6	81.1	8.7	11.3	52	32	2	158
155	-	Intuit	426.4	490.1	-4.5	NM	-21.1	30	31	13	145
156	144	Audiovox	425.6	500.7	-9.3	NM	-3.4	86	16	0	530
157	176	Symantec	418.0	418.0	-1.5	NM	18.6	18	49	19	253
158	156	Fluke	412.7	412.7	20.3	4.9	5.7	49	35	10	150
159	175	Cherry	408.6	408.6	13.9	3.4	6.5	71	16	6	102
160	166	System Software Associates	404.8	404.8	35.2	8.7	13.0	38	22	10	208
161	-	Altera	401.6	401.6	86.9	21.6	18.7	40	19	8	464
162	159	Advanced Technology Labs	399.4	399.4	12.0	3.0	3.6	54	30	12	156
163	172	BMC Software	396.9	396.9	70.2	17.7	16.8	9	26	16	319
164	160	Liuski	395.1	395.1	-1.1	NM	-1.4	93	7	0	681
165	179	VeriFone	387.0	387.0	32.5	8.4	9.2	52	25	12	176
166	170	Watkins-Johnson	387.0	387.0	31.4	8.1	12.0	57	20	12	176
167	164	Mentor Graphics	384.5	384.5	49.9	13.0	11.6	29	39	20	186
168	168	Exide Electronics	382.2	382.2	12.5	3.3	6.0	73	18	3	252
169	152	Exabyte	374.1	374.1	-12.4	NM	-5.0	83	13	10	296
170	-	Novellus	373.7	373.7	82.5	22.1	26.2	42	16	11	473

Rank		Company	Calendar Year 1995					Fiscal Year 1995			
1995	1994		Electronics Sales ($M)	Total Sales ($M)	Net Profits ($M)	Profits (% of Sales)	ROA (%)	Cost of Sales (% of Sales)	SG&A Costs (% of Sales)	R&D Spending (% Sales)	Sales per Employee ($K)
171	162	Hubbell	370.5	1,143.1	121.9	10.7	11.6	70	15	1	154
172	181	Gerber Scientific	362.2	362.2	21.4	5.9	5.9	56	30	8	201
173	171	Boeing	362.0	19,515.0	393.0	2.0	1.8	95	5	6	171
174	180	BancTec	353.8	353.8	-58.4	NM	4.3	71	17	3	126
175	158	Standard Microsystems	350.1	350.1	-7.4	NM	11.6	57	24	7	469
176	198	PictureTel	346.8	346.8	19.6	5.7	7.8	50	29	13	329
177	199	Bell Microproducts	346.3	346.3	4.0	1.2	2.9	88	9	0	852
178	-	Maxim	345.3	345.3	76.1	22.0	17.9	41	19	17	162
179	-	Kent Electronics	340.0	340.0	22.8	6.7	10.8	74	17	0	265
180	186	Ametek	338.6	837.5	44.5	5.3	8.7	77	9	2	134
181	-	DII Group	335.4	335.4	17.0	5.1	7.7	83	9	0	96
182	194	Measurex	335.2	335.2	26.9	8.0	8.9	60	23	6	151
183	193	Applied Magnetics	331.9	331.9	22.5	6.8	0.7	86	3	12	53
184	-	StrataCom	331.7	331.7	52.5	15.8	21.7	38	21	18	350
185	-	Tencor Instruments	330.2	330.2	65.3	19.8	22.5	37	21	10	263
186	163	Acuson	328.9	328.9	7.1	2.2	2.3	47	32	20	198
187	-	Network Equipment Tech.	328.9	328.9	39.6	12.0	12.9	50	29	12	258
188	-	Linear Technology	327.9	327.9	112.5	34.3	26.6	31	14	9	208
189	-	Iomega	326.2	326.2	8.5	2.6	5.0	72	18	6	256
190	197	Hutchinson Technologies	319.8	319.8	21.6	6.8	12.3	75	10	5	64
191	189	Ball	315.8	2,591.7	99.6	3.8	5.9	90	4	1	256
192	-	Teledyne	304.6	2,567.8	162.0	6.3	10.5	74	17	2	143
193	196	Methode Electronics	301.4	301.4	30.2	10.0	14.8	73	13	5	98
194	188	CTS	300.2	300.2	17.2	5.7	7.9	75	13	3	74
195	200	Thomas & Betts	297.9	1,236.8	80.9	6.5	6.6	66	21	2	154
196	-	Genicom	294.1	294.1	6.2	2.1	4.3	74	18	3	146
197	183	Executone	293.4	293.4	-36.9	NM	-20.7	59	34	5	123
198	-	Plexus	289.1	289.1	6.3	2.2	5.4	92	4	0	120
199	195	Becton Dickinson	276.9	2,759.0	262.7	9.5	8.2	53	27	5	148
200	187	Group Technologies	273.6	273.6	-17.7	NM	-15.0	98	7	1	125

Forbes: Ranking the Forbes 500

"Big companies are getting bigger. When the first Forbes 500s Directory came out 27 years ago, it took $255M to get on the sales lists, $14M for profits, $416M for assets and $280M for market value. Corresponding minimums for this year's rankings: $2.2B, $122M, $3.3B and $2.3B. Back out inflation and you still have a near doubling of what it means to be big.

'The ranking table that follows shows where to find a company on each of the four 500-company rankings. There are 275 companies that make all four of the lists. The other 512 appear three or fewer times."--Forbes

Computer Industry Almanac has listed only the computer, electronics and telecommunications-related companies in this table.

Where They Rank: 1995				Company	Sales ($M)	Net Profits ($M)	Assets ($M)	Mkt Value ($M)	Cash Flow ($M)	Empl (#K)
Sales	Net Prfts	Assets	Mkt Val							
-	-	-	464	Adobe Systems	762	93.5	885	2,520	153.9	1.9
471	234	-	498	Advanced Micro Devices	2,430	300.5	3,031	2,328	563.0	12.3
-	472	337	76	AirTouch Communications	1,619	131.9	5,648	15,089	347.7	6.5
381	200	374	220	Alltel	3,110	354.6	5,073	5,773	764.4	16.1
-	-	-	424	Altera	402	86.9	716	2,785	99.8	0.8
-	-	-	268	America Online	713	4.4	694	4,708	108.3	2.5
77	25	101	37	Ameritech	13,428	2,007.6	21,943	30,115	4,184.7	64.5
239	171	411	132	AMP	5,227	427.3	4,505	9,349	788.7	37.4
-	463	-	359	Analog Devices	1,014	135.7	1,309	3,376	202.1	5.7
100	397	305	380	Apple Computer	11,378	167.0	6,553	3,200	297.9	15.9
331	130	-	202	Applied Materials	3,596	559.9	3,243	6,213	657.2	8.5
204	342	-	493	Arrow Electronics	5,919	202.5	2,701	2,354	237.7	6.8
-	-	-	229	Ascend Communications	150	30.6	335	5,573	32.7	0.2
484	-	-	-	AST Research	2,348	-262.1	1,056	262	-235.3	6.6
5	454	26	3	AT&T	79,609	139.0	88,884	98,122	4,984.0	301.9
-	-	-	457	Atmel	634	113.7	920	2,562	172.6	2.4
371	173	457	100	ADP	3,166	422.0	3,728	11,690	610.1	25.0
379	443	-	413	Avery Dennison	3,114	143.7	1,964	2,918	251.6	15.5
263	383	-	-	Avnet	4,798	171.5	2,462	2,068	212.2	9.0
-	323	-	180	Bay Networks	1,728	218.3	1,429	6,824	282.2	4.1
76	30	86	39	Bell Atlantic	13,430	1,861.8	24,157	26,919	4,488.9	67.1
44	40	67	26	BellSouth	17,886	1,564.0	31,880	36,033	5,019.0	89.8
184	-	-	-	Best Buy	6,589	56.3	2,758	779	108.2	18.6
-	-	-	408	BMC Software	397	70.2	542	2,946	99.3	1.3
-	405	-	253	Cabletron Systems	1,070	164.4	942	5,066	190.4	5.3
-	-	-	355	Cascade Communications	135	25.4	112	3,404	30.9	0.3
182	369	-	409	Circuit City Stores	6,686	181.0	3,150	2,944	258.6	31.0
442	118	-	41	Cisco Systems	2,668	633.9	2,366	26,861	703.8	3.3
500	-	377	-	Comdisco	2,246	106.0	5,058	1,064	1,131.0	2.1
65	90	269	111	Compaq Computer	14,755	789.0	7,818	10,613	1,003.0	15.7
378	-	-	-	CompUSA	3,135	39.8	882	1,034	63.2	7.2
369	-	386	64	Computer Associates	3,196	-108.6	4,882	17,570	249.9	7.6
291	469	-	320	Computer Sciences	4,100	133.3	2,536	3,976	362.8	32.9
233	259	-	390	Dell Computer	5,296	272.0	2,148	3,117	309.2	8.1
66	169	223	124	Digital Equipment	14,440	430.5	10,015	9,859	937.4	61.7
492	358	-	325	Dow Jones	2,284	189.6	2,599	3,897	395.6	10.7
-	352	-	357	DSC Communications	1,422	192.7	1,865	3,381	295.5	5.6
224	222	345	117	Dun & Bradstreet	5,415	320.8	5,516	10,121	795.3	48.3
63	50	159	43	Eastman Kodak	14,980	1,252.0	14,477	25,293	2,168.0	96.5
-	218	-	266	EMC	1,921	326.8	1,746	4,770	380.5	3.5
112	72	231	62	Emerson Electric	10,294	934.8	9,733	17,896	1,358.5	78.9
293	-	194	72	First Data	4,081	-84.2	12,218	15,743	262.6	36.5
-	-	-	401	FORE Systems	198	24.0	398	3,000	26.3	0.9
-	440	-	259	Frontier	2,144	144.8	2,109	4,922	314.5	7.0
322	377	-	-	Gateway 2000	3,676	173.0	1,124	2,087	211.1	6.9
7	2	6	1	General Electric	70,028	6,573.0	228,035	126,238	8,154.0	219.0
469	495	-	372	General Instrument	2,432	123.8	2,301	3,240	233.9	12.3

Where They Rank: 1995				Company	Sales ($M)	Net Profits ($M)	Assets ($M)	Mkt Value ($M)	Cash Flow ($M)	Empl (#K)
Sales	Net Prfts	Assets	Mkt Val							
35	17	58	22	GTE	19,957	2,537.9	37,019	40,475	6,213.3	108.6
339	401	-	454	Harris	3,507	164.8	3,007	2,578	338.8	26.6
-	-	-	330	HBO & Co.	496	-25.2	535	3,854	5.0	3.0
16	16	82	13	Hewlett-Packard	33,503	2,621.0	25,753	50,929	3,776.0	102.0
-	-	-	254	Informix	709	105.3	674	5,020	141.3	2.7
56	7	130	15	Intel	16,202	3,566.2	17,504	48,336	4,936.3	40.5
342	-	-	-	Intelligent Electronics	3,475	-19.0	894	216	-2.9	1.2
6	5	30	8	IBM	71,940	4,178.0	80,292	65,664	9,780.0	222.6
-	-	-	497	Intuit	490	-4.5	510	2,334	57.8	2.7
-	-	-	351	Linear Technology	328	112.5	448	3,439	122.4	1.4
27	113	129	75	Lockheed Martin	22,853	682.0	17,648	15,094	1,603.0	169.0
-	295	-	342	LSI Logic	1,268	238.1	1,850	3,653	373.3	3.9
409	309	-	293	McGraw-Hill	2,935	227.1	3,104	4,453	458.5	15.4
61	134	118	59	MCI Communications	15,265	548.0	19,301	19,294	1,915.0	43.1
213	-	-	-	Merisel	5,802	-9.2	1,469	80	9.3	3.2
-	-	-	321	MFS Communications	583	-267.9	1,867	3,975	-125.4	3.2
392	-	-	-	MicroAge	3,047	-1.1	583	135	14.4	1.9
299	65	468	184	Micron Technology	3,972	1,018.0	3,642	6,754	1,293.9	6.8
159	31	244	10	Microsoft	7,419	1,838.0	9,106	60,811	2,121.0	18.0
21	34	96	32	Motorola	27,037	1,781.0	22,801	32,897	3,712.0	137.0
441	272	-	-	National Semiconductor	2,681	257.5	2,602	2,031	480.7	20.8
-	-	-	348	Netscape Communications	81	-3.4	228	3,483	-3.4	0.4
-	-	349	334	Nextel Communications	178	-263.2	5,467	3,780	-263.2	2.1
-	223	-	278	Novell	1,986	320.3	2,355	4,571	416.4	7.5
79	60	79	55	Nynex	13,407	1,069.5	26,220	21,080	3,636.3	68.2
231	471	-	384	Office Depot	5,313	132.4	2,531	3,178	197.2	22.0
457	490	-	-	OfficeMax	2,543	125.8	1,588	2,007	167.0	14.5
310	144	-	51	Oracle	3,777	518.6	2,763	21,275	706.1	19.2
131	62	143	105	Pacific Telesis Group	9,042	1,048.0	15,841	11,289	2,912.0	50.2
-	-	-	460	Paging Network	646	-44.2	1,228	2,535	104.8	4.3
-	-	-	270	Parametric Technology	441	90.6	497	4,702	101.6	1.7
-	-	-	441	Paychex	311	48.4	216	2,689	61.2	3.4
-	-	-	432	PeopleSoft	228	29.4	314	2,731	44.4	1.0
334	127	268	170	Pitney Bowes	3,555	583.1	7,845	7,310	854.8	30.3
-	-	-	442	Premier Industrial	866	114.8	570	2,682	124.3	4.5
-	-	-	476	Qualcomm	457	34.3	961	2,449	70.7	2.5
286	-	-	-	Quantum	4,174	55.5	1,894	1,027	145.3	7.3
-	435	-	-	Read-Rite	1,083	146.6	944	882	226.2	20.8
78	92	197	94	Rockwell International	13,420	769.3	12,027	12,410	1,366.0	77.3
88	28	100	34	SBC Communications	12,670	1,889.3	22,003	31,142	4,059.2	59.1
338	-	-	-	SCI Systems	3,514	62.3	1,269	1,047	116.5	13.2
222	184	452	209	Seagate Technology	5,493	394.0	3,830	5,888	650.5	64.3
461	304	-	323	Silicon Graphics	2,497	231.4	2,265	3,943	350.8	6.3
468	-	-	-	Solectron	2,435	98.3	1,229	2,169	164.8	8.8
-	390	-	465	S. New England Telecom	1,839	168.8	2,724	2,513	514.8	9.4
86	70	150	95	Sprint	12,765	946.1	15,089	12,407	2,412.5	48.5
388	-	-	393	Staples	3,068	73.7	1,403	3,063	117.3	8.2
-	-	-	462	StrataCom	332	52.5	295	2,523	76.2	0.8
189	165	-	144	Sun Microsystems	6,390	446.5	3,268	8,409	725.7	14.5

Where They Rank: 1995				Company	Sales ($M)	Net Profits ($M)	Assets ($M)	Mkt Value ($M)	Cash Flow ($M)	Empl (#K)
Sales	Net Prfts	Assets	Mkt Val							
495	-	-	-	Tandem Computers	2,263	74.3	1,801	1,042	254.5	8.4
209	329	-	417	Tandy	5,839	212.0	2,722	2,886	304.0	44.4
384	-	-	-	Tech Data	3,087	21.5	1,044	574	38.9	2.4
452	411	-	-	Teledyne	2,568	162.0	1,606	1,621	232.4	18.0
-	-	486	429	Telephone & Data Systems	954	104.0	3,469	2,765	305.0	5.8
-	-	-	305	Tellabs	635	115.6	552	4,174	139.3	2.7
83	59	243	121	Texas Instruments	13,128	1,088.0	9,215	9,943	1,844.0	58.0
-	396	-	171	3Com	1,792	167.1	1,254	7,297	230.1	3.1
-	-	-	451	360° Communications	834	-1.7	1,973	2,597	113.0	3.1
126	51	137	81	U.S. West, Comm. Grp.	9,484	1,184.0	16,585	14,566	3,226.0	51.1
194	-	292	-	Unisys	6,202	-624.6	7,113	1,114	-229.0	41.9
-	-	-	216	U.S. Robotics	1,092	95.7	746	5,858	109.9	2.4
470	-	-	-	Western Digital	2,430	90.8	906	852	140.6	7.6
192	-	136	166	Westinghouse Electric	6,296	15.0	16,752	7,524	233.0	77.8
325	264	306	149	WorldCom	3,640	267.7	6,552	8,198	578.9	7.5
51	-	80	83	Xerox	16,611	-472.0	25,969	14,423	188.0	86.4
-	-	-	447	Xilinx	520	87.4	671	2,617	99.7	1.0

Soft•letter: Soft•letter 100

"The Soft•letter 100, published annually since 1984, is defined formally as 'a ranking of the top 100 personal computer software companies in the U.S., based on calendar year revenues.' That definition (which continues to evolve with the industry itself) helps explain why some companies appear on our list and why others are excluded.

'Our basic eligibility rules are simple: To be ranked, a company must be an independent, U.S-based company (subsidiaries do not qualify) that generates at least 50% of its revenues from personal computer software development or publishing. For the great majority of the companies we review, eligibility is a straightforward issue.

'In determining eligibility, we now look at several issues: pattern of use (does the user perform personal tasks or function as part of a workgroup or enterprise-wide system?), pricing (is the price level appropriate for an individual purchase?), distribution channels (in particular, is the product marketed to individual end users or to MIS departments?) and the local computing environment (does the product function in an open, multi-product world or only as part of a closed and centralized system?).

'On another front, we currently don't include companies that create software for dedicated or single-purpose hardware platforms. This rule applies primarily to the videogame segment, where the basic platforms as yet don't support general purpose applications.

'Finally, it's important to note that our rankings only include companies that supply data on the record. To insure accountability, we don't accept estimates from analysts or other outside sources; thus, a few privately-held companies do not appear in our rankings because they declined to provide us with on-the-record revenue data."--Soft•letter

1996 Rank	Company	1995 Revenues ($K)	Ownership	Stock Symbol	# of 1995 Employees	% International	1995 Rank	% Growth from 1995	1994 Revenues ($K)
1	Microsoft	7,419,000	Public	(MSFT)	19,641	44	1	41	5,266,000
2	Novell	1,901,547	Public	(NOVL)	7,272	47	2	-5	2,003,024
3	Adobe Systems	762,300	Public	(ADBE)	2,192	32	4	13	675,617

1996 Rank	Company	1995 Revenues ($K)	Ownership	Stock Symbol	# of 1995 Employees	% International	1995 Rank	% Growth from 1995	1994 Revenues ($K)
4	Autodesk	534,167	Public	(ACAD)	1,894	63	5	17	454,612
5	Intuit	502,557	Public	(INTU)	2,733	11	8	73	290,000
6	Symantec	437,800	Public	(SYMC)	2,200	35	7	3	423,100
7	Attachmate	415,000	Private		2,000	40	6	6	390,000
8	SoftKey International	254,664	Public	(SKEY)	850	26	12	110	121,287
9	Borland International	207,847	Public	(BORL)	913	33	9	-17	249,609
10	GT Interactive Software	204,135	Public	(GTIS)	590	n/a		140	85,176
11	Santa Cruz Operation	199,329	Public	(SCOC)	1,034	55	10	5	190,409
12	Brøderbund Software	189,500	Public	(BROD)	575	10	11	43	132,068
13	Cheyenne Software	157,600	Public	(CYE)	690	54	13	50	104,761
14	Davidson & Associates	147,226	Public	(DAVD)	669	8	18	58	93,171
15	Sierra On-Line	144,764	Public	(SIER)	950	30	20	48	97,879
16	FTP Software	136,376	Public	(FTPS)	740	46	15	46	93,245
17	NetManage	125,400	Public	(NETM)	625	30		104	61,606
18	Walker Richer & Quinn	111,569	Private		425	40	16	25	89,280
19	Wall Data	110,741	Public	(WALL)	641	28	14	9	101,240
20	Interplay Productions	99,646	Private		365	20	23	75	56,999
21	Macromedia	96,897	Public	(MACR)	358	41	28	119	44,172
22	Bentley Systems	95,000	Private		450	55		239	28,000
23	Quarterdeck Corp.	93,016	Public	(QDEK)	670	20	38	103	45,850
24	McAfee Associates	90,065	Public	(MCAF)	275	30	36	174	32,900
25	Netscape Communications	80,700	Public	(NSCP)	550	20		5652	1,403
26	Micrografx	64,467	Public	(MGXI)	243	57	22	11	58,238
27	SPSS	63,029	Public	(SPSS)	439	55	25	22	51,757
28	Spectrum HoloByte	57,313	Public	(SBYT)	400	46	17	-35	87,970
29	Platinum Software	56,150	Public	(PSQL)	400	32	24	5	53,400
30	Insignia Solutions	55,095	Public	(INSGY)	265	23	30	40	39,361
31	Phoenix Technologies	53,066	Public	(PTEC)	364	52	19	-31	77,177
32	Maxis	52,221	Public	(MXIS)	193	18	32	40	37,357
33	Caere	51,939	Public	(CAER)	217	30	21	-12	59,130
34	Connectix	48,000	Private		90	18		243	14,000
35	Stac	46,362	Public	(STAC)	150	10	34	29	35,973
36	Activision	46,345	Public	(ATVI)	216	25	31	22	38,132
37	State of the Art	46,118	Public	(SOTA)	371	1	33	24	37,340
38	ON Technology	44,121	Public	(ONTC)	329	14	40	71	25,828
39	INSO Corp.	43,387	Public	(INSO)	176	13	44	85	23,463
40	MapInfo	40,666	Public	(MAPS)	305	30	37	24	32,765
41	Visio	39,400	Public	(VSIO)	150	25	46	70	23,200
42	Datastorm Technologies	39,000	Private		322	7	29	-8	42,402
43	Best Programs	38,168	Private		280	5	35	15	33,334
44	Softdesk	35,608	Public	(SDSK)	231	21	43	48	24,021
45	XcelleNet	34,100	Public	(XNET)	246	10	39	27	26,900
46	MECC	33,815	Public	(MECC)	220	5	41	37	24,634
47	Edmark	31,524	Public	(EDMK)	178	10	56	88	16,807
48	Primavera Systems	29,968	Private		205	32	42	22	24,584
49	Expert Software	27,638	Public	(XPRT)	140	10	52	40	19,727
50	Timberline Software	24,819	Public	(TMBS)	295	6	49	15	21,641
51	SystemSoft	24,590	Public	(SYSF)	150	25		58	15,590
52	Software Publishing Corp.	24,001	Public	(SPCO)	110	35	26	-53	51,195

1996 Rank	Company	1995 Revenues ($K)	Ownership	Stock Symbol	# of 1995 Employees	% International	1995 Rank	% Growth from 1995	1994 Revenues ($K)
53	Living Books	23,473	Private		53	5		13	20,781
54	Traveling Software	23,244	Private		120	24	48	7	21,812
55	IQ Software Corp.	21,855	Public	(IQSW)	160	28	51	9	20,097
56	Pro CD	21,674	Private		100	20		173	7,951
57	IMSI	20,539	Public	(IMSI)	122	37	47	-6	21,966
58	Asymetrix	20,000	Private		210	40		43	14,000
59	Systems Plus	19,750	Private		75	0	53	12	17,600
60	Persoft	19,450	Private		135	32	58	21	16,100
61	Eagle Point Software	18,909	Public	(EGPT)	265	9	62	62	11,660
62	Fractal Design	18,764	Public	(FRAC)	61	38		71	10,958
63	MathSoft	18,094	Public	(MATH)	140	31	45	-17	21,687
64	Globalink	17,600	Public	(GNK)	93	42	54	2	17,300
65	MicroHelp	17,209	Private		61	14	55	14	15,096
66	WizardWorks	17,000	Private		32	6		70	10,000
67	SBT Accounting Systems	16,666	Private		140	3	59	19	13,971
68	DataWatch	16,633	Public	(DWCH)	84	20		44	11,521
69	ViaGrafix	16,500	Private		132	10		143	6,800
70	Syncronys Software	16,410	Public	(SYCR)	15	5		1285	1,185
71	Accolade	16,200	Private		108	5		-67	49,533
72	Id Software	15,595	Private		14	1		103	7,690
73	Blyth Software	14,706	Public	(BLYH)	115	25	57	-10	16,252
74	Citrix Systems	14,568	Public	(CTXS)	77	18	66	44	10,086
75	Now Software	13,542	Private		73	22	65	33	10,181
76	MySoftware Company	13,399	Public	(MYSW)	69	1		45	9,224
77	DataEase International	12,700	Private		60	67	50	-40	21,000
78	7th Level	12,161	Public	(SEVL)	203	18	92	196	4,103
79	CE Software	11,997	Public	(CESH)	109	24	61	-6	12,762
80	Formgen	11,929	Private		32	20	67	19	10,015
81	ConnectSoft	11,631	Private		130	5	78	47	7,900
82	FutureSoft	11,100	Private		88	25	73	25	8,894
83	Spyglass	10,350	Public	(SPYG)	84	7		185	3,629
84	Cosmi	9,560	Private		48	5	76	17	8,169
85	Healthcare Communications	9,500	Private		112	0	69	-4	9,900
86	Touchstone	9,356	Public	(TSSW)	57	14	81	30	7,202
87	Dantz Development	9,262	Private		51	31	72	11	8,317
88	Algor	9,120	Private		67	25	80	17	7,798
89	Campbell Services	8,828	Private		85	4	75	6	8,360
90	RealWorld	8,823	Private		110	3	63	-22	11,300
91	MultiGen	8,222	Private		59	39		31	6,278
92	Jandel Scientific	8,011	Private		68	39	77	-1	8,096
93	Starfish Software	8,000	Private		60	10		n/a	0
94	Ray Dream	7,700	Private		40	37	86	44	5,343
95	Pinnacle Publishing	6,700	Private		32	10	82	3	6,500
96	Campbell Software	6,500	Private		62	0	99	86	3,500
97	Visual Software	6,400	Private		35	10		178	2,300
98	Micro Star Software	6,200	Private		78	10	85	3	6,000
99	Individual Software	6,100	Private		40	10	88	18	5,150
100	Data Access Corp.	6,000	Private		44	61	74	-29	8,400

Software Magazine: Software 100

"The Software 100 methodology: Software Magazine's annual Software 100 ranking is based on total worldwide packaged software revenue for 1995, not total corporate revenue. Software revenue includes license fees, maintenance and support. Revenue from professional services/consulting, custom programming, training and hardware sales is excluded. Figures are based on the calendar year so that all firms are measured over the same period.

'Only independent software companies are ranked among the Software 100. If a company is owned by a parent company, it must operate independently and report its revenue separately from the parent company. For a company to be considered, revenue from the sales and support of packaged software must constitute 50% of the company's total corporate revenue. Therefore, hardware manufacturers are excluded, as are professional services providers that have software revenue of less than 50% of total corporate revenue."--Software Magazine

1995 Rank	1994 Rank	Company	Packaged Software Revenue ($M)				Total Corporate Revenue ($M)	# 1995 Employees	% Revenue on R&D
			1995 WW	1994 WW	WW % Growth	U.S. 1995			
1	1	Microsoft	7,271.0	5,044.0	44	4,581.0	7,419.0	20,000	15
2	2	Computer Associates Int'l.	3,196.0	2,455.0	30	1,611.0	3,196.0	9,000	9
3	4	Oracle	2,558.0	1,736.0	47	1,074.4	3,479.1	19,945	9
4	3	Novell	1,900.0	1,900.0	0	1,007.0	2,041.2	7,000	18
5	6	SAP AG	1,350.0	914.0	48	460.0	1,887.0	6,857	17
6	7	Sybase	786.1	720.4	9	487.4	956.6	5,865	14
7	8	Adobe Systems	762.3	675.6	13	442.1	762.3	2,319	18
8	12	Informix	536.0	363.8	47	225.1	709.0	3,693	12
9	9	SAS Institute	534.3	472.4	13	256.5	562.4	3,683	31
10	15	Symantec	437.8	423.1	3	280.3	437.8	2,194	16
11	14	BMC Software	396.9	328.7	21	233.0	396.9	1,331	16
12	19	Sterling Software	390.0	299.0	30	237.0	610.4	3,600	11
13	13	Compuware	388.7	352.6	10	195.6	580.1	4,710	8
14	11	Software AG	376.0	364.0	3	95.0	552.0	2,800	25
15	17	Attachmate	347.0	312.0	11	191.0	412.0	2,200	18
16	18	Dun & Bradstreet Software	285.0	265.0	8	199.5	365.0	2,000	25
17	21	System Software Associates	280.3	243.1	15	126.1	404.8	2,400	10
18	24	J.D. Edwards & Co.	236.6	190.2	24	146.7	340.8	2,312	10
19	42	Platinum Technology	230.4	170.6	35	175.1	275.9	2,700	34
20	22	Candle	230.3	213.0	8	133.6	230.3	1,213	35
21	23	Information Builders	225.0	204.0	10	146.0	240.0	1,750	NA
22	34	PeopleSoft	211.0	108.0	95	177.0	227.6	1,341	16
23	20	Borland International	208.0	250.0	-17	98.0	208.0	894	24
24	26	Claris	183.8	157.3	17	93.7	183.8	700	15
25	25	Santa Cruz Operation, The	178.1	169.5	5	75.9	199.3	1,034	16
26	32	Progress Software	168.4	123.7	36	79.5	180.1	1,105	14
27	37	Cheyenne Software	157.6	104.8	50	67.8	157.6	685	12
28	27	Cincom Systems	157.0	151.0	4	60.0	157.0	979	12
29	28	Boole & Babbage	150.4	134.5	12	53.1	155.9	760	12
30	35	Intersolv	138.7	106.5	30	88.8	146.0	835	16
31	-	Intentia International	137.0	91.0	51	9.6	137.0	874	17
32	52	Baan Co. N.V., The	131.8	70.9	86	38.6	216.2	1,500	9
33	33	Cognos	131.3	109.3	20	61.2	151.3	1,019	13
34	47	FileNet	127.0	85.6	48	86.3	215.5	1,126	9
35	55	NetManage	125.4	71.5	75	87.8	125.4	700	19
36	46	FTP Software	123.0	86.2	43	65.2	136.4	740	22

1995 Rank	1994 Rank	Company	Packaged Software Revenue ($M)				Total Corporate Revenue ($M)	# 1995 Employees	% Revenue on R&D
			1995 WW	1994 WW	WW % Growth	U.S. 1995			
37	45	Hyperion Software	122.1	86.7	41	81.6	158.1	990	19
38	-	McDonnell Info. Sys. Group	122.0	107.0	14	36.0	234.0	1,850	14
39	29	Banyan Systems	118.4	130.9	-10	81.0	129.7	762	16
40	30	Micro Focus Group	114.2	130.8	-13	62.8	122.0	708	28
41	43	WRQ	111.6	89.3	25	66.9	111.6	525	NA
42	38	Wall Data	110.7	101.2	9	85.3	110.7	783	18
43	41	Marcam	100.8	92.0	9	53.4	204.7	1,100	20
44	60	Tibco	95.0	50.4	88	35.0	130.0	327	NA
45	72	Macromedia	95.0	43.3	119	56.0	96.9	358	18
46	44	Software Engineering of America	94.6	88.4	7	65.4	94.6	325	20
47	39	Comshare	94.1	82.1	15	42.3	117.4	711	15
48	94	Quarterdeck	93.0	45.8	103	74.0	93.0	700	13
49	83	McAfee Associates	90.1	52.9	70	63.9	90.1	280	10
50	49	JBA Holdings Plc.	76.7	73.5	4	36.4	196.9	1,600	14
51	51	Softlab	74.0	71.0	4	14.0	132.0	875	24
52	-	Netscape Communications	73.2	1.1	6,637	60.1	80.7	500	31
53	56	Lawson Software	69.5	57.7	20	61.2	84.6	705	17
54	57	Rational Software	68.6	56.6	21	50.7	85.0	530	17
55	50	Interleaf	68.1	71.8	-5	50.4	91.5	627	24
56	48	Ross Systems	64.6	74.0	-13	42.6	65.6	500	17
57	-	Micrografx	64.5	58.2	11	27.1	64.5	250	8
58	58	Seer Technologies	60.8	52.9	15	17.0	112.5	841	12
59	62	SPSS	56.8	45.9	24	25.6	63.0	439	14
60	97	Business Objects S.A.	56.1	27.5	104	21.6	60.6	350	13
61	96	Hummingbird Communications	54.3	28.0	94	37.0	54.3	235	10
62	71	VMark Software	53.9	55.6	-3	39.9	68.4	456	15
63	84	Systems Union Group	49.4	32.7	51	7.8	59.3	425	15
64	69	Software 2000	48.7	42.0	16	44.2	65.3	470	26
65	-	Thomson Software Products	48.2	NA	NA	28.6	61.3	470	NA
66	-	Insignia Solutions Plc.	47.9	30.8	56	35.4	55.1	265	18
67	63	Landmark Systems	46.9	44.9	4	24.1	46.9	225	27
68	79	Visual Edge Software	45.5	35.0	30	32.0	65.0	70	80
69	76	Apertus Technologies	44.2	38.8	14	41.6	53.2	370	23
70	68	American Software	44.1	43.3	2	33.2	80.1	619	16
71	66	Synon	43.9	43.6	1	17.2	72.0	430	11
72	85	Computron Software	43.5	29.1	49	38.3	55.5	431	17
73	-	Inso	43.4	23.5	85	37.7	43.4	176	17
74	104	Tivoli Systems	43.3	24.9	74	36.4	49.6	278	16
75	-	Pure Software	43.3	21.4	102	30.9	44.0	288	17
76	61	Caere	41.7	45.1	-8	29.6	51.9	220	15
77	-	Antares Alliance Group	40.8	34.0	20	20.6	55.0	400	27
78	-	PC Docs Group International	40.5	21.7	87	36.5	44.4	395	16
79	87	Manugistics	40.0	31.9	25	29.9	58.7	500	17
80	75	Macro 4 Plc.	39.9	38.8	3	13.5	39.9	210	10
81	95	Project Software & Development	39.6	28.1	41	22.3	50.2	264	13
82	82	Group 1 Software	39.6	33.3	19	35.6	42.3	215	5
83	80	BGS Systems	39.4	34.0	16	25.5	41.1	230	31
84	86	Platinum Software	39.0	38.4	1	29.0	51.0	400	31

1995 Rank	1994 Rank	Company	Packaged Software Revenue ($M)				Total Corporate Revenue ($M)	# 1995 Employees	% Revenue on R&D
			1995 WW	1994 WW	WW % Growth	U.S. 1995			
85	98	Coda Group Plc., The	38.9	26.4	47	13.8	52.5	394	20
86	92	Wind River Systems	38.6	28.7	35	25.3	44.0	208	15
87	119	Mercury Interactive	37.5	22.6	66	26.6	39.5	296	36
88	81	InterSystems	37.4	33.5	12	28.8	38.2	165	12
89	125	Atria Software	36.2	19.0	90	28.6	40.1	217	20
90	93	New Dimension Software	35.7	28.2	27	19.0	35.7	299	19
91	73	Cadre Technologies	35.6	41.0	-13	16.2	39.5	205	21
92	102	Programart	33.6	26.0	29	21.6	34.3	176	21
93	101	LBMS Plc.	33.6	25.8	30	25.2	42.3	310	21
94	70	Walker Interactive Systems	33.6	42.2	-20	23.7	58.9	388	29
95	88	Cyborg Systems	33.2	31.6	5	22.4	41.5	350	20
96	-	Object Design	32.0	25.0	28	24.0	35.0	220	25
97	108	Symix Systems	31.6	24.5	29	24.9	43.2	297	12
98	-	CheckPoint Software Technologies	31.0	10.0	210	15.5	31.0	70	NA
99	-	Remedy	30.4	16.2	88	20.1	40.1	226	18
100	106	Consilium	30.3	24.6	23	20.8	35.4	220	32
		Totals	28,750.2	22,381.8	28	15,739.4	33,144.0	150,583	18.5

Upside: Hot Private Technology Companies

"How Upside Compiled the List: Identifying hot private technology companies is an inexact science. In May, the Upside 200 ranked publicly traded technology companies on the basis of gain in market cap, but private companies don't generally disclose details that would allow us to rank them in any quantifiable, verifiable fashion. Thus, we surveyed those who work most closely with private companies--venture capitalists, investment banks and consultants--in coming up with a list. We did not define 'hot'--it is not dependent on sales or growth--but left it to the judgment of our respondents. We did insist that VCs limit their selection of their own portfolio companies to three and then nominate up to five companies outside their portfolios.

'The resulting list is, admittedly, somewhat subjective and arbitrary. It is weighted toward venture-backed companies, especially those in hot new areas like the Internet and future IPO candidates. Bootstrapped firms and those determined to remain private probably got left out. We invite our readers to write or e-mail us about other hot companies that we missed. No doubt there were many. But at least this represents an attempt to introduce our readers to 100 entrepreneurial companies that might be in tomorrow's Upside 200."--Upside

Rank	Company	CEO; Founder(s) (* Denotes CEO who is also a Founder)	Rev Last FY ($M)	Profitable	# Empl.	Founded
1	AccessLine Tech.	Daniel Kranzler; Robert M. Fuller, Fred Epler	NA	NA	150	1983
2	Accom	Junaid Sheikh; Luigi Gallo, Ian Craven, Lance Kelson	NA	Yes	80	1987
3	Advanced Fibre Comm.	Donald Green; John Webley, Jim Hoeck, Henri Sulzer	NA	NA	140	1992
4	Airnet Comm.	Bernie Smedley	NA	No	50	1994
5	Airsoft	Jagdeep Singh	NA	NA	15	1992
6	Answersoft	Jeanne Bayless; Gary Young	NA	No	26	1993
7	Arbor Software	James Dorrian; Robert Earle	12.0	Yes	80	1991
8	Ashtech	Chuck Bosenburg; Javad Asjaee	32.0	Yes	280	1987
9	Aspect Dev.	Romesh Wadhwani	8.5	Yes	140	1991
10	Attachmate	Frank Pritt	**391.0	Yes	2,200	1982

Rank	Company	CEO; Founder(s) (* Denotes CEO who is also a Founder)	Rev Last FY ($M)	Prof-itable	# Empl.	Found ed
11	Avail Sys.	Robert Wight; David Dodd, Ronald Blickenstaff	NA	NA	45	1991
12	Brio Tech.	Yorgen Edholm; Katherine Edholm-Glassey	NA	Yes	45	1984
13	Catapult Ent.	Adam Grosser; Lynn Heublein, Steve Perlman, Steve Roskowski	NA	No	50	1994
14	Cayman Sys.	S. Bradley Noblet*; Ted Stabler	NA	NA	50	1987
15	Centerview Software	Mark Douglas	.415	No	16	1993
16	Centillion Networks	Bobby Johnson; Earl Ferguson	NA	No	40	1993
17	Citrix Sys.	Roger W. Roberts; Edward Iacobucci	10.0	Yes	85	1989
18	Collabra Software	Eric Hahn	NA	NA	40	1993
19	Combinet	Thomas Williams; Lou Cole, Edward Jordan, Ron Roybal	6.0	Yes	87	1988
20	Commquest Tech.	Hussein El-Ghoroury; Dale McNeill, Mark Lindsey, Harry Van Trees	NA	Yes	90	1991
21	Connect	Thomas Kehler	NA	NA	30	1989
22	Cybercash	Bill Melton; Dan Lynch	NA	NA	25	1994
23	DaVinci Time & Space	Carol Peters; Jeff Apple	NA	No	25	1993
24	Dazel	Bob Fabbio	1.0	No	40	1991
25	Dendrite Int'l.	John Bailye	39.0	Yes	400	1986
26	Digital Express Grp.	Doug Humphrey; Mike Doughney	2.0	Yes	45	1992
27	DocuMagix	Al Sisto; Steve Leung, Sam Hahn	NA	No	18	1993
28	Documentum Inte.	Jeff Miller; Howard Shao, John Newton	10.0	Yes	110	1990
29	Enterprise Inte.	Jay M. Tenenbaum; Jeff Pan, Jay Glicksman	NA	NA	45	1990
30	Escalade	K. Larry La (President); Min-Yu Hsueh	NA	NA	40	1993
31	Evolutionary Tech.	Katherine Hammer; Robin Curle	NA	Yes	95	1991
32	Fastech Inte.	James Pecusi; Hans Bukow	12.1	Yes	95	1986
33	First Virtual	Ralph Ungermann; Jeff Leffingwell, Allwyn Sequeira, Marlis Rossetta	NA	No	31	1993
34	First Virtual Holdings	Lee Stein; Nathaniel Borenstein, Marshall T. Rose, Einar A. Strefferud	NA	NA	NA	1994
35	Forté Software	Martin Sprinzen; Paul Butterworth, Rich Scheffer, Peter Schmitz, Joe Cortopassi, Neil Goodman, Steve Langley	10.0	No	130	1991
36	Frontier Tech.	Prakash Ambegaonkar	14.0	Yes	85	1983
37	Grand Junction Networks	Howard Charney*; Larry Birenbaum, Jack Moses	NA	Yes	60	1992
38	GT Interactive Software	Ron Chaimowitz; Joe Cayre	80.0	Yes	50	1993
39	Illustra Information Tech.	Dick Williams*; Gary Morgenthaler, Michael Stonebraker	NA	NA	75	1992
40	Infinity Financial Tech.	Roger Lang; Tejbir Sidhu	12.6	Yes	75	1989
41	Infoseek	Steve Kirsh; Vickie Blackeslee, Andrew Newton, Zara Haimo, Ed Miller, Andy Bensky, Todd Gonz	None	No	12	1993
42	InSoft	Daniel Harple; Richard Pizzarro	NA	Yes	63	1991
43	International Network Svcs.	Donald K. McKinney	NA	NA	160	1991
44	International Wireless Comm.	John Lockton; Hugh McClung	NA	No	512	1991
45	ISOCOR	Andrew DeMari; Bjorn Ahlen, Raomal Perera	10.0	Yes	130	1991
46	Knowledge Adventure	Bill Gross (Chairman), Ruth Otte	NA	NA	130	1991
47	Legato Sys.	Louis C. Cole	16.3	Yes	110	1988
48	Logic Works	Ben Cohen	12.0	Yes	130	1988
49	Maxm Sys.	John J. Reis*; Jim Anderson, Dixon Doll	23.2	NA	125	1987
50	Mergent Int'l.	John Worthen*; Alain Dube, Tom Costello	NA	Yes	100	1985
51	Nabnasset	Greg Borton; Brian Sherman	NA	NA	30	1990
52	Netedge Sys.	Albert Vender	6.6	No	120	1993
53	NETpower	Robert Miller; Walt Pienkos, Skip Stritter, Ed Frank, Jorge Titinger	6.0	No	65	1993
54	Netscape Comm.	James Barksdale*; James Clark, Marc Andreessen	NA	NA	130	1994
55	Network Appliance	Daniel Warmenhoven*; James Lau, David Hitz, Michael Malcolm	Mid-10s	No	70	1992
56	Nvidia	Jen-Hsun Huang; Curtis Priem, Chris Malachowsky	None	No	40	1994
57	Object Design	Kenneth Marshall; Thomas Atwood	25.0	NA	275	1988
58	Omnicell Tech.	Sheldom Asher; Randall Lipps	NA	NA	130	1992

Rank	Company	CEO; Founder(s) (* Denotes CEO who is also a Founder)	Rev Last FY ($M)	Prof-itable	# Empl.	Founded
59	ON Tech.	Chris Risley; Mitch Kapor	NA	Yes	215	1987
60	Open Market	Shikhar Ghosh; David Gifford	NA	No	60	1994
61	Pacific Monolithics	Christopher J. Weseloh; Allen Podell	20.0	Yes	155	1984
62	Pagemart Nationwide	John D. Beletic; Roger D. Lindquist	110.0	No	1,206	1989
63	Physicians' Online	Sheryle Bolton (President); Christian Mayaud, William Greenberg	NA	NA	110	1991
64	Pinnacle Multimedia	Michale Mermmott	NA	No	110	1991
65	Polycom	Brian Hinman; Jeffrey C. Rodman	NA	NA	50	1992
66	Power Computing	Steven Kahng; Enzo Torresi	NA	NA	30	1993
67	Premenos	Dan Sederman*; Lou Jenkins	NA	NA	150	1986
68	Primary Rate	Mark Galvin	4.8	No	75	1989
69	Princeton Financial Sys.	Will Mayhall; Jerry Finsen	15.5	Yes	125	1989
70	Prism Solutions	Jim Ashbrook; W.H. Inmon, Ed Young, Cynthia Schmidt	8.3	Yes	100	1991
71	Pro CD	Jim Bryant; Scott Beatty	9.5	Yes	62	1992
72	Pure Software	Reed Hastings	20.0	Yes	150	1990
73	Quicklogic	Thomas Hart*; H.T. Chua, Andrew Chan, John Birkner	8.0	No	75	1988
74	RadioLAN	Dave Cooper; Bob Stillman, Jessie Cable	NA	NA	30	1993
75	Rambus	Geoff Tate*; Mike Farmwald, Mark Horowitz	NA	No	70	1990
75	Red Brick Sys.	Christopher G. Erickson*; Ralph Kimball	NA	Yes	125	1986
77	Red Pepper Software	Monte Zweben; Daniel Doles	5.0	No	25	1993
78	Rocket Science Games	Steve Blank; Peter Barrett, Ron Cobb, Mike Backes	NA	NA	75	1993
79	Rogue Wave Software	Tom Keffer	5.0	Yes	90	1989
80	Saros	Wayne Carpenter; Mike Kennewick	NA	Yes	115	1986
81	Scopus Technology	Ori Sasson; Bahram Nour-Omid, Sharam Sasson, David Shwab, Aaron Omid	12.1	Yes	120	1991
82	Seer Tech.	Gene Bedell	84.2	Yes	700	1990
83	Showcase	Ken Holec*; David C. Wenz, Barbara Regnier, Dave Youngers	9.0	NA	108	1989
84	Softbridge	Drew Hannah*; Mark Eisner	5.0	Yes	30	1983
85	Spyglass	Doug Colbeth*; Tim Krauskopf	NA	Yes	56	1990
86	Summit Design	Larry J. Gerhard*; Zamir Paz	NA	Yes	118	1994
87	Sundisk	Eli Harari	35.0	Yes	150	1988
88	Teleos Comm.	Michael Caglarkin*; Rod Randall	20.0	No	115	1987
89	Thinking Tools	John Hiles	NA	NA	18	1994
90	Travelnet	Ken Grunzweig*; John Shoolery	None	No	30	1991
91	Treasury Svcs.	John Dorman; Krista Foley	14.0	Yes	135	1983
92	Trilogy Dev.	Joe Liemandt	NA	Yes	65	1989
93	Vantive	John Luongo*; Steve Goldsworthy, Roger Sippl, William Davidow	10.2	Yes	110	1990
94	Verity	Philippe Courtot; Phil Nelson	20.0	Even	150	1988
95	Visio	Jeremy Jaech (President); Dave Walter, Ted Johnson	20.0	Yes	130	1990
96	Visioneer	Michael A. McConnell*; David A. Brown, Pierre-Alain Cotte	NA	Yes	60	1992
97	Vivo Software	Staffan Ericsson; Anthony Antonuccio, Oliver Jones, Daud Power, Bernd Girod	NA	NA	40	1993
98	Wildfire Comm.	William Warner; Nick d'Arbeloff, Rich Miner, Anthony Lovell	None	No	25	1991
99	Wire Networks	Marlene McDaniel*; Nancy Rhine, Ellen Pack	NA	No	15	1992
100	Xylan	Steve Kim; Yuri Pikover	100.0	Yes	120	1993

** Merged with Digital Communications Asso. in 1994/combined revenue.

NA: Not Available

Upside: Upside 200

"The telcos are back! After a one-year hiatus from the heights of the Upside 200, our annual ranking of companies based on value creation, seven of the top 12 in 1995 were telecommunications companies, including several RBOCs. Big, bad Microsoft may have gotten the bulk of the media attention, but it was bigger, badder AT&T that created the most value for shareholders in 1995.

'Last year's top gun, Microsoft, slipped to fifth place, indicating that the market was less than thrilled with the software giant's tardy entry into the Internet. The Internet is the future, and Netscape Communications seems to have captured precious mind share in that area. But the bubbly reception that Internet companies, such as Netscape, got from Wall Street last year wasn't reflected in our list, since most of these firms went public too late to qualify."--Upside

Rank	Company	'95 Value ($M)	Mrkt Val 12/ 31/95 ($M)	% Tot Shrhldr Retn	Last 4Qs Sales ($M)	% Sls Grth Last 4Q	Last 4Qs R&D ($M)	Last 4 Qs EPS ($)
1	AT&T	22,750.6	101,593.1	31	78,588	6	3,460	8.92
2	Intel	20,495.5	46,875.5	78	14,850	46	1,229	13.66
3	Hewlett-Packard	17,232.9	42,683.5	69	29,473	28	2,220	16.23
4	BellSouth	16,314.5	43,173.1	66	17,516	6	-	8.11
5	Microsoft	15,469.1	50,982.8	44	5,609	28	766	8.76
6	GTE	13,028.6	42,343.1	51	19,744	2	-	10.38
7	IBM	10,505.3	53,702.0	26	69,916	9	4,040	28.31
8	SBC Communications	10,278.3	34,869.9	46	12,435	12	-	11.75
9	Ameritech	10,202.0	32,467.3	51	13,077	7	-	13.59
10	Cisco Systems	10,179.0	19,230.6	112	1,719	54	234	5.41
11	Bell Atlantic	7,469.7	29,169.9	40	13,762	-6	-	14.89
12	Nynex	7,307.0	22,874.2	53	13,494	-2	-	9.05
13	EDS	6,563.2	25,048.4	37	11,711	22	-	7.45
14	Computer Associates	5,895.2	13,661.8	76	3,196	39	1,598	-
15	Oracle	5,615.4	18,363.5	44	3,676	20	-	-
16	MCI Communications	5,270.0	17,765.0	42	14,529	13	-	4.07
17	Sun Microsystems	5,232.2	8,563.9	157	5,657	26	504	5.84
18	Ericsson North Dakota	4,969.3	16,943.9	43	13,514	45	-	-
19	Digital Equipment	4,393.1	9,124.2	93	13,986	6	1,126	(44.60)
20	Sprint	4,179.6	13,801.4	47	13,248	4	-	10.53
21	Micron Technology	3,579.3	8,075.6	81	2,416	79	117	12.39
22	Ascend Communications	3,395.0	3,882.6	696	103	289	10	0.72
23	Applied Materials	3,069.8	6,623.2	86	2,547	104	273	7.67
24	3Com	2,886.1	6,455.8	81	1,928	30	-	-
25	Texas Instruments	2,606.8	9,546.3	39	12,307	33	838	19.49
26	Worldcom	2,524.4	5,627.4	81	3,266	64	-	-
27	Cabletron Systems	2,465.7	5,789.0	74	999	31	108	-
28	Compaq Computer	2,218.8	12,529.8	22	13,305	27	250	12.95
29	Automatic Data Processing (ADP)	2,216.0	10,446.9	28	2,759	18	184	5.21
30	Pacific Telesis Group	2,120.3	14,206.2	25	9,116	-2	-	10.32
31	First Data	2,099.0	7,198.6	41	-	-	-	-
32	Bay Networks	1,988.9	3,811.8	109	1,269	27	-	2.19
33	Adobe Systems	1,972.1	3,791.3	109	727	53	-	2.95
34	Informix	1,825.2	3,928.4	87	642	55	85	2.56
35	Parametric Technology	1,821.3	3,785.0	93	344	77	42	4.92
36	Tele-Communications	1,782.2	14,311.6	14	6,454	37	-	-
37	Intuit	1,716.8	3,000.8	134	440	203	-	-

Rank	Company	'95 Value ($M)	Mrkt Val 12/ 31/95 ($M)	% Tot Shrhldr Retn	Last 4Qs Sales ($M)	% Sls Grth Last 4Q	Last 4Qs R&D ($M)	Last 4 Qs EPS ($)
38	Seagate Technology	1,711.6	3,459.5	98	4,248	30	202	13.14
39	C-Cube Microsystems	1,632.0	1,924.5	558	88	187	-	-
40	Cadence Design Systems	1,606.3	2,388.2	205	506	28	-	4.77
41	U.S. Robotics	1,563.9	2,075.3	306	728	75	43	4.08
42	Cascade Communications	1,476.9	2,315.6	176	109	140	16	2.50
43	LSI Logic	1,435.8	3,742.9	62	1,174	38	113	6.07
44	Stratacom	1,365.6	2,607.0	110	301	115	54	4.23
45	Glenayre Technologies	1,365.6	2,323.6	143	271	101	21	3.74
46	America Online	1,362.1	2,173.5	168	283	244	60	(1.58)
47	HBO & Co.	1,342.4	2,434.6	123	455	51	-	(1.55)
48	MFS Communications	1,315.1	3,416.1	63	514	73	-	-
49	Altera	1,238.3	2,138.1	138	335	122	54	4.23
50	Macromedia	1,224.5	1,619.8	310	97	144	-	-
51	Maxim Integrated Products	1,204.3	2,207.9	120	219	64	38	1.99
52	Cincinnati Bell	1,170.6	2,291.7	109	1,316	5	-	0.03
53	PeopleSoft	1,155.8	2,060.1	128	190	103	-	1.68
54	Adtran	1,136.4	1,963.3	137	168	49	18	2.75
55	Dell Computer	1,121.0	2,747.8	69	4,790	60	89	-
56	Computer Sciences	1,062.0	3,875.8	38	4,100	34	-	-
57	Linear Technology	1,052.9	2,850.2	59	244	32	22	3.85
58	Madge Networks NV	1,005.8	1,366.5	279	347	179	-	2.98
59	Qualcomm	978.2	2,213.9	79	344	39	73	1.46
60	PictureTel	956.1	1,324.7	259	319	42	48	-
61	Analog Devices	899.9	2,662.0	51	888	25	128	3.40
62	Adaptec	897.9	2,118.8	74	594	43	-	-
63	Total System Services	864.4	1,971.2	79	232	38	-	1.55
64	Iomega	840.3	900.5	1,397	216	138	17	0.18
65	Tellabs	796.5	3,229.7	33	602	23	76	4.36
66	Xilinx	754.9	2,141.9	54	520	58	-	-
67	Paging Network	747.9	2,471.8	43	598	32	-	(1.20)
68	BMC Software	722.8	2,158.9	50	397	31	-	-
69	Electronics For Imaging	719.3	1,049.0	218	174	49	12	4.72
70	Structural Dynamics	693.5	848.8	447	187	19	-	(0.47)
71	ECI Telecom	692.0	1,718.3	69	436	12	51	4.42
72	Solectron	686.6	1,822.5	60	1,937	42	5	6.61
73	Fore Systems	668.2	1,544.1	76	145	125	-	-
74	Ceridian	652.7	1,872.8	53	1,273	5	-	6.10
75	Frontier	649.3	2,194.8	46	1,967	36	-	4.38
76	ADC Telecommunications	641.4	2,035.8	46	541	30	59	3.41
77	Conner Peripherals	603.3	1,101.7	121	2,532	23	135	5.44
78	Comcast	597.6	4,347.4	17	2,718	152	-	-
79	Teradyne	595.3	1,826.7	48	1,030	107	108	6.24
80	Synopsys	576.1	1,357.6	74	247	34	-	2.48
81	EG&G	558.1	1,336.8	76	1,382	7	50	0.84
82	Computervision	550.7	738.3	294	514	-8	-	1.65
83	Gandalf Technologies	550.6	599.0	1,136	115	-5	-	-
84	Safeguard Scientifics	540.6	704.2	330	1,478	7	-	-
85	McAfee Associates	532.0	768.4	225	102	82	-	-
86	Sterling Software	527.5	1,284.0	70	547	30	-	(0.43)

Rank	Company	'95 Value ($M)	Mrkt Val 12/ 31/95 ($M)	% Tot Shrhldr Retn	Last 4Qs Sales ($M)	% Sls Grth Last 4Q	Last 4Qs R&D ($M)	Last 4 Qs EPS ($)
87	International Rectifier	524.1	1,017.6	106	399	33	19	2.67
88	Cirrus Logic	515.0	1,196.7	76	1,187	29	-	-
89	Pairgain Technologies	514.7	695.8	284	91	94	9	0.85
90	Atmel	510.5	2,030.8	34	542	71	61	3.70
91	Security Dynamics Tech.	504.1	608.0	485	29	107	4	1.55
92	Shared Medical Systems	496.1	1,247.5	69	624	22	-	6.45
93	Quarterdeck	487.7	550.3	780	59	121	-	(1.65)
94	Cheyenne Software	480.0	1,013.3	90	112	26	-	3.83
95	Harris Corp.	476.5	2,146.7	32	3,442	1	-	13.90
96	Advanced Semiconductor	471.7	520.6	965	322	11	-	-
97	Cambridge Technology	468.7	764.5	158	119	46	-	2.57
98	Tektronix	467.7	1,544.4	45	1,712	12	-	-
99	Komag	458.0	1,056.3	77	457	35	23	6.51
100	System Software Associates	455.5	880.7	108	377	22	-	2.21
101	American Mobile Satellite	443.3	759.5	140	6	51	-	(6.00)
102	Diebold	434.1	1,686.7	37	827	15	42	9.31
103	BBN	432.0	676.8	176	204	7	25	6.50
104	LCI International	422.4	1,215.4	53	600	45	-	0.74
105	Comdisco	396.8	1,245.4	49	2,195	9	-	4.33
106	Cognos	359.6	599.9	150	141	22	21	-
107	S3	355.4	642.5	124	257	175	33	2.04
108	Electronic Arts	349.7	1,328.8	36	521	10	-	-
109	Atria Software	347.6	549.5	172	35	96	8	1.28
110	Sungard Data Systems	347.2	1,069.7	48	499	20	-	4.85
111	Intergraph	341.5	705.4	94	1,093	6	120	(6.04)
112	Aspect Telecommunications	340.5	680.9	100	179	29	21	3.95
113	Applied Magnetics	333.8	411.0	432	265	14	30	(6.16)
114	Fiserv	332.8	1,174.7	40	664	23	-	1.83
115	Shiva	329.8	729.8	82	103	36	-	0.35
116	Arrow Electronics	328.9	1,985.2	20	5,614	26	0	-
117	National Semiconductor	322.4	2,717.0	13	2,774	16	-	-
118	Mitel	317.3	687.6	86	420	-9	-	-
119	Avnet	315.1	1,819.5	23	4,042	25	-	11.68
120	Medic Computer Systems	313.4	642.7	95	133	34	7	4.78
121	Kent Electronics	313.3	572.4	121	340	55	-	-
122	C Tec	305.3	850.8	56	306	21	-	2.19
123	Acxiom	302.7	613.8	97	248	35	-	-
124	Excalibur Technologies	301.7	358.2	535	16	61	4	-
125	Lattice Semiconductor	299.9	616.3	95	185	42	-	-
126	Microchip Technology	299.7	1,215.6	33	272	44	-	-
127	CompUSA	297.5	574.3	108	2,697	30	0	0.21
128	Vicor	296.0	830.9	55	138	24	10	2.53
129	Inso	289.9	494.1	142	36	88	-	1.46
130	Borland International	284.3	452.2	169	208	-2	-	-
131	American Management Systems	281.6	785.9	56	587	37	-	-
132	Octel Communications	278.0	779.5	55	454	18	71	3.32
133	Brøderbund	274.7	1,192.2	30	162	40	20	5.21
134	Auspex Systems	263.3	417.9	170	101	40	14	1.60
135	Computer Horizons	258.9	339.3	322	187	32	-	2.13

Rank	Company	'95 Value ($M)	Mrkt Val 12/31/95 ($M)	% Tot Shrhldr Retn	Last 4Qs Sales ($M)	% Sls Grth Last 4Q	Last 4Qs R&D ($M)	Last 4 Qs EPS ($)
136	Newbridge Networks	257.1	3,403.4	8	654	14	-	-
137	Clearnet Communications	249.7	491.7	103	25	29	-	
138	Siliconix	245.3	368.5	199	229	28	18	6.69
139	GRC International	243.3	345.8	237	134	16	-	2.33
140	GTECH Holdings	243.3	1,124.4	28	737	10	31	-
141	Hummingbird Communications	240.3	483.5	99	40	129	3	3.96
142	Veritas Software	239.9	311.6	334	22	103	6	3.51
143	Burr-Brown	236.8	366.0	183	249	43	25	4.83
144	Stac	232.1	360.8	180	42	43	21	(0.30)
145	Progress Software	230.1	463.4	99	167	33	27	4.42
146	Cray Research	229.2	627.2	58	677	-23	124	(23.51)
147	VLSI Technology	224.7	664.9	51	685	24	86	3.67
148	Symbol Technologies	221.8	1,016.0	28	535	15	51	-
149	FileNet	221.7	520.9	74	205	28	-	-
150	Dialogic	220.6	566.3	64	156	37	27	-
151	Alantec	218.6	485.0	82	45	116	5	3.19
152	CompuCom Systems	214.8	320.1	204	1,384	13	0	1.89
153	Symantec	213.8	864.3	33	418	0	-	-
154	Read-Rite	211.3	1,047.9	25	911	49	33	6.99
155	Kulicke & Soffa Industries	210.3	383.6	121	254	114	27	5.81
156	Gateway 2000	208.1	1,773.7	13	3,255	38	-	7.31
157	Wang Laboratories	207.9	531.7	64	870	23	-	(3.85)
158	Park Electrochemical	207.4	377.7	124	294	26	-	-
159	Project Software & Development	200.6	275.7	267	43	44	7	2.46
160	PC DOCS Group	200.0	215.1	1,330	28	107	-	(2.23)
161	LAM Research	200.0	1,076.4	23	703	72	106	9.92
162	Sanmina	197.1	415.3	90	149	54	-	1.55
163	Davidson & Associates	196.8	752.9	35	133	58	19	-
164	Rational Software	193.3	280.2	223	85	29	-	-
165	Integrated Systems	192.3	370.3	108	66	36	12	-
166	Sierra On-Line	191.7	474.0	68	141	53	-	-
167	Wyle Electronics	190.5	428.3	82	1,003	34	-	8.76
168	Checkpoint Systems	190.0	391.7	94	179	56	-	3.13
169	Heartland Wireless Comm.	188.9	330.5	133	10	869	-	-
170	Wind River Systems	186.7	265.2	238	41	40	6	-
171	HADCO	186.2	273.9	213	252	14	-	6.17
172	Applix	184.1	241.8	319	28	78	5	1.19
173	Control Data Systems	176.0	270.9	185	498	-7	-	(18.97)
174	Henry (Jack) & Associates	175.1	288.9	156	42	18	-	2.41
175	Continuum	172.2	755.6	30	379	11	-	-
176	Flextronics	171.1	348.1	97	389	106	-	-
177	Optical Data Systems	169.3	400.0	73	111	39	8	2.96
178	Logicon	168.8	371.4	85	454	51	-	-
179	Network General	167.8	728.6	30	175	37	-	-
180	Affiliated Computer Services	166.4	390.0	74	294	17	-	4.99
181	Computer Products	165.0	233.5	241	180	27	15	1.80
182	Microcom	162.4	288.8	129	127	73	-	-
183	Comverse Technology	161.7	398.1	68	124	25	-	-
184	Itron	161.2	402.9	67	148	23	-	3.14

Rank	Company	'95 Value ($M)	Mrkt Val 12/31/95 ($M)	% Tot Shrhldr Retn	Last 4Qs Sales ($M)	% Sls Grth Last 4Q	Last 4Qs R&D ($M)	Last 4 Qs EPS ($)
185	IMP	160.1	204.9	358	70	27	-	-
186	Mentor Graphics	154.1	937.1	20	373	15	-	2.90
187	Physician Computer Network	153.8	307.6	100	30	81	2	-
188	Coherent Communications Sys.	152.9	264.6	137	41	35	5	1.63
189	Global Village Communications	151.7	286.8	112	123	81	-	-
190	Health Management Systems	148.9	344.9	76	83	22	-	2.11
191	VeriFone	147.7	663.4	29	362	31	43	5.19
192	Boca Research	147.4	223.3	194	121	82	-	-
193	Identix	146.8	206.6	245	25	28	1	(0.28)
194	TCA Cable TV	144.4	678.8	30	178	20	-	4.55
195	Trident Microsystems	141.9	272.2	109	95	54	12	1.58
196	Tencor Instruments	140.7	669.2	27	293	82	31	6.78
197	Telxon	138.7	353.5	65	444	33	-	-
198	Geoworks	137.9	213.9	181	5	145	-	-
199	Electroglas	136.3	427.3	47	149	54	13	6.79
200	Lincoln Telecommunications	133.4	683.4	28	214	25	-	4.42

Leading Computer Users

CIO: CIO 100

"Consultants, authors and business scholars searched the world over to find the 1996 CIO 100 winners, a diverse collection of companies that have distinguished themselves in the global marketplace. The 30 judges, each with an expertise in global business, selected the 100 World Leaders in a two-step judging process. First, panelists individually nominated a total of nearly 250 organizations with reputations for excelling in some aspect of global business. CIO editors compiled ballots listing all nominees and returned them to the judges, along with descriptions of the companies' global operations and the rationales for the nominations. In the second round of voting, judges evaluated whether organizations qualified as global business leaders, considering business and IT practices contributing to success."--CIO

Company, Location	Executives, Titles	Rev. ($)	# Empl.	Business
3M St. Paul, MN	L.D. DeSimone, Chmn & CEO David P. Drew, Staff VP, IT	13.5B	70,687	Manufacturing
ABB Asea Brown Boveri Zurich, Switzerland	Percy Barnevik, Chmn & CEO Jean A. Egan, VP, IT	34.0B	210,000	Manufacturing
Allen-Bradley Milwaukee, WI	Jodie K. Glore, Pres. & COO Mike Sloan, VP, IT	NA	25,000	Industrial automation
Allied Signal Morristown, NJ	Lawrence A. Bossidy, Chmn & CEO Larry Kittelberger, VP & CIO	14.3B	77,500	Manufacturing
Aluminum Company of America Pittsburg, PA	Paul H. O'Neill, Chmn & CEO G. Keith Turnbull, EVP Strategic Analysis	12.5B	72,000	Aluminum production
American Express New York, NY	Harvey Golub, Chmn & CEO Allan Z. Loren, EVP & CIO	15.8B	70,347	Financial services
American International Group New York, NY	M.R. Greenberg, Chmn & CEO William C. Vinck, VP & CIO	25.9B	32,000	Financial services
Amoco Chicago, IL	H. Laurance Fuller, Chmn & CEO Carl Williams, VP, IT	31.0B	42,689	Petrochemicals
Andersen Consulting Chicago, IL	George T. Shaheen, Mng Partner Charles M. Paulk, CIO	4.22B	38,000	Tech consulting
Applied Communications Omaha, NE	David C. Russell, Pres & COO Jon L. Howe, CTO	NA	NA	Software
AT&T Basking Ridge, NJ	Ron Ponder, EVP Oper & Svcs Mgmt Allan Jones, VP & GM	50.0B	110,000	Telecommunications
BankAmerica San Francisco, CA	David A. Coulter, CEO Martin A. Stein, Vice Chmn	20.4B	94,100	Financial services
Bankers Trust New York, NY	Frank N. Newman, Chmn, Pres & CEO Carmine Vona, Mng Dir	8.5B	14,000	Banking
Bank of Montreal Toronto, Canada	Matthew J. Barrett, Chmn & CEO Lloyd F. Darlington, CTO & GM Oper Group	8.8B	33,000	Financial services
Bata Shoe Organization Don Mills, Canada	T.G. Bata, Chmn Tim Jude, Dir Finance & Int'l IS	NA	60,000	Footwear
Benetton Group Ponzano Veneto, Italy	Carlo Gilardi, Mng Dir Bruno Zuccaro, Dir IS	2.0B	6,300	Apparel manufacturing
Berkeley Systems Berkeley, CA	Wes Boyd, Chmn & CEO -	28.0M	120	Software
Body Shop International West Sussex, UK	Gordon Roddick, Chmn Nick Eastwood, Head Corp Svcs	340.5M	14,500	Cosmetic products
Boeing Seattle, WA	Phillip M. Condit, Pres & CEO John D. Warner, Pres Info & Support Svcs	19.7B	105,000	Aerospace
British Petroleum London, England	John Browne, Group CEO John Cross, GM, IT	57.0B	56,650	Petroleum & Petrochemicals
Cable News Network (CNN) Atlanta, GA	Tom Johnson, Pres Elahe Hessamfar, VP & CIO	NA	2,800	News & features reporting

Company, Location	Executives, Titles	Rev. ($)	# Empl.	Business
Canadian Imperial Bank of Commerce Toronto, Canada	A.L. Flood, Chmn & CEO David Marshall, EVP & CIO	182.0B	40,000	Commercial investment & corp banking
Canon Tokyo, Japan	Fujio Mitaraii, Pres & Rep Dir Hiroshi Tanaka, Vice Chmn & Rep Dir	21.0B	20,261	Business machines, photo & optical prod
Carrier Farmington, CT	John R. Lord, Pres John W. Owens, VP, IS	5.4B	30,000	Air conditioning, heating & ventilating
Chase Manhattan New York, NY	Walter Shipley, CEO Denis O'Leary, CIO	8.2B	74,000	Banking
Chicago Mercantile Exchange Chicago, IL	William J. Brodsky, Pres & CEO Michael Kelly, SVP & CIO	164M	1,000	Futures & options exchange
Cigna Philadelphia, PA	Wilson H. Taylor, Chmn & CEO J. Raymond Caron, SVP	18.9B	44,707	Health care, insurance, & financial services
Citicorp New York, NY	John S. Reed, Chmn & CEO Colin Crook, Sr Tech Officer	256.9B	80,000	Financial services & bank- ing
Coca-Cola Atlanta, GA	Roberto C. Goizueta, Chmn & CEO Hugh H. Switzer, VP & Dir, IS Div	18.0B	32,000	Beverages
Compaq Computer Houston, TX	Eckhard Pfeiffer, Pres & CEO John W. White, VP & CIO	14.8B	17,000	Computers
CS First Boston New York, NY	John M. Hennesey, Chmn & CEO Frank J. Fanzilli, Mng Dir, Head Global IS	2.2B	5,200+	Investment banking & securities
Dow Chemical Midland, MI	William S. Stavropoulos, Pres & CEO David T. Buzzelli, VP & Corp Dir	20.2B	39,500	Chemical, plastics, & agricultural products
DuPont Merck Pharmaceutical Wilmington, DE	Kurt M. Landgraf, Pres & CEO Stephen E. Thompson, CIO, VP Info Svcs	1.3B	4,200	Pharmaceuticals
Eastman Chemical Kingsport, TN	Earnest W. Deavenport Jr., Chmn & CEO A. Jack Spurgeon, VP, Dir Comp Svcs	5.04B	17,709	Chemical manufacturing
Eastman Kodak Rochester, NY	George M.C. Fisher, Chmn, Pres & CEO Edith W. Martin, VP, IS & CIO	14.9B	96,600	Manufacturing & imaging
Eaton Cleveland, OH	Stephen R. Hardis, Chmn & CEO Derek R. Mumford, VP, IT	6.8B	54,000	Manufacturing
Eli Lilly & Co. Indianapolis, IN	Randall L. Tobias, Chmn & CEO Thomas Trainer, VP, IT & CIO	6.8B	26,800	Pharmaceuticals
Emerson Electric St. Louis, MO	Charles F. Knight, Chmn, Pres & CEO -	10.0B	78,900	Electronics & electrical products & systems
EMI Music Publishing Worldwide New York, NY	Martin Bandier, Chmn & CEO -	NA	NA	Music publishing
Federal Express Memphis, TN	Frederick W. Smith, Chmn, Pres & CEO Dennis H. Jones, CIO & SVP	9.4B	120,000	Express transportation service
Fidelity Investments Boston, MA	Edward C. Johnson III, Chmn & CEO Albert Aiello Jr., Pres	4.28B	18,000	Financial services
Ford Motor Co. Dearborn, MI	Alex Trotman, Chmn, Pres & CEO Charles W. Szuluk, VP Process Leadership	137.1B	346,990	Automotive
GE Capital Services Stamford, CT	Gary C. Wendt, Chmn, Pres & CEO John A. McKinley, VP & CTO	2.4B	37,000	Financial services
General Electric Fairfield, CT	John F. Welch, Chmn & CEO Gary Reiner, SVP & CIO	70.0B	222,000	Technology, manufactur- ing & service
Georgia-Pacific Atlanta, GA	A.D. Corell, Chmn & CEO Carl Wilson, VP Info Resources	14.3B	47,000	Paper & wood products
Halliburton Energy Services Houston, TX	Ken R. LeSuer, Pres & CEO H.D. Teel Jr., VP & CIO	2.6B	20,000	Oil field services
Hewlett-Packard Palo Alto, CA	Lewis E. Platt, Chmn, Pres & CEO Robert R. Walker, VP & CIO	31.5B	105,200	Computers, comm & measurement equip
Hoechst Frankfurt, Germany	Jurgen Dormann, CEO Utz-Hellmuth Felcht, Board of Mgmt Member	7.8B	161,000	Pharmaceuticals, indus- trial chemicals
IKEA Home Furnishings Almhult, Sweden	Anders Moberg, Pres Goran Astrand, IS Mgr	5.1B	30,500	Retail home furnishings

Company, Location	Executives, Titles	Rev. ($)	# Empl.	Business
ING Group Amsterdam, Netherlands	Aad G. Jacobs, CEO, Exec Board Mem Marinus Minderhoud, Exec Board Mem	25.7B	50,000	Integrated financial services
Intel Santa Clara, CA	Andrew Grove, Pres & CEO Carlene Ellis, VP, IT	16.2B	41,600	Computer products
Intrados Group Washington, DC	Margaret Ghadar, Pres & CEO Scott Lamb, Dir Capital Mkts	10M	100	Securities & capital markets
J.P. Morgan & Co. New York, NY	Douglas Warner, Chmn & CEO; Martha Gallo, Head Corp Tech; Peter Miller, Head Corp Tech	5.9B	15,500	Financial services
Kyocera Kyoto, Japan	Kazuo Inamori, Chmn -	5.7B	26,000	Tech ceramic mtrls, components, info equip
LG Group Seoul, South Korea	Bon-Moo Koo, Chmn -	38.0B	NA	Chemicals, energy, electronics, machinery
Loctite Hartford, CT	David Freeman, Pres & CEO Richard C. Parker, VP Corp Controller	785.1M	4,339	Ind, elec, medical, auto & consumer prod
McDonald's Oak Brook, IL	Michael R. Quinlan, Chmn & CEO Carl F. Dill Jr., SVP	30.0B	600,000	Restaurants
MCI Communications Washington, DC	Bert C. Roberts Jr., Chmn & CEO Lance B. Boxer, CIO	15.0B	45,000	Telecom
Merck & Co. Whitehouse Station, NJ	Raymond V. Gilmartin, Chmn, Pres & CEO Charles Popper, VP Corp Comp Res	16.7B	45,200	Pharmaceuticals
Microsoft Redmond, WA	William H. Gates III, Chmn & CEO Chris Gibbons, CIO Worldwide	5.9B	20,000	PC software
Mitsubishi International New York, NY	Motohiko Numaguchi, Pres, CEO & Dir Mitsuru Hashimoto, SVP Info & Telecom	9.9B	710	Trading company
Morgan Stanley and Co. New York, NY	John J. Mack, Pres Kevin Parker, CIO	4.3B	9,200	Investment banking
Motorola Schaumburg, IL	Gary L. Tooker, Vice Chmn & CEO -	27.0B	142,000	Electronics manufacturing
NEC Technologies Boxborough, MA	Kenjiro Nitta, Chmn & CEO David L. Thomae, Strategic Sys VP & CIO	2.4B	7,000	Computers
Nestle Vevey, Switzerland	Helmut Maucher, Chmn & CEO J.C. Dispaux, SVP	48.6M	212,000	Food & beverages
Netscape Communications Mountain View, CA	Jim Barksdale, Pres & CEO Larry Geisel, CIO	80M	750	Internet/intranet software
Nike Beaverton, OR	Philip H. Knight, Chmn & CEO Ron Edwards, CIO	4.7B	14,800	Footwear & apparel manufacturing
Nokia Group Helsinki, Finland	Jorma Ollila, Pres & CEO Tapio Kuusisto, MIS Manager	8.4B	34,000	Mobile telephone manufacturing
Northern Telecom (Nortel) Mississauga, Canada	Jean C. Monty, Pres & CEO Keith Powell, VP, IS & CIO	10.6B	63,000	Telecommunications
Nucor Charlotte, NC	John D. Correnti, Vice Chmn, Pres & CEO -	3.4B	6,200	Steel products manufacturing
Osram Sylvania Danvers, MA	Dean T. Langford, Pres William Schwidder, VP Info Tech	NA	13,250	Electrical lighting products & service
Otis Elevator Farmington, CT	Jean-Pierre van Rooy, Pres -	5.3B	68,000	Elevators & escalators
Owens Corning Toledo, OH	Glen H. Hiner, Chmn & CEO Michael Radcliff, VP & CIO	3.6B	18,000	Glass components & building material sys
Pacific Gas and Electric San Francisco, CA	Stanley T. Skinner, Chmn & CEO John C. Danielsen, VP Comp & Telecom	9.6B	20,800	Energy utility
PepsiCo Purchase, NY	Roger A. Enrico, CEO & Vice Chmn Allan B. Deering, VP Mgmt Info	30.0B	480,000	Snacks, beverages & restaurants
Pfizer New York, NY	William C. Steere Jr., Chmn & CEO Cathleen A. O'Connor, VP Corp IT	10.0B	44,000	Pharmaceuticals
Phillips Petroleum Bartlesville, OK	Wayne Allen, Chmn & CEO N.F. Barbee, Mgr IT	13.5B	17,400	Petroleum

Company, Location	Executives, Titles	Rev. ($)	# Empl.	Business
Port of Singapore Authority Singapore	Khoo Teng Chye, CEO Eric Lui, Dir IS	NA	7,500	Transportation terminal operation
PPG Industries Pittsburgh, PA	Jerry E. Dempsey, Chmn & CEO David W. Smith, VP IT	7.1B	31,200	Mfr of coatings, fiberglass & chemicals
Procter & Gamble Cincinnati, OH	John E. Pepper, Chmn & CEO Frank R. Caccamo, VP Mgmt Sys	34.4B	99,200	Mfr of laundry, paper, cleaning etc products
Project Software and Development Cambridge, MA	Dean Goodermote, Pres Jack Young, VP R&D	61M	385	Client/server maintenance mgmt SW
RSA Data Security Redwood City, CA	D. James Bidzos, Pres & CEO -	NA	45	Encryption tech & cryptographers' toolkits
Samsung Electronics Seoul, South Korea	Kwang-Ho Kim, Vice Chmn & CEO Sukkoo D. Kim, Dir Info Strategy Team	21.0B	70,000	High-tech electronics
SBC Warburg London, England	Marcel Ospel, CEO Craig Heimark, Global Head of IT	NA	9,461	Investment banking
S.C. Johnson & Son Racine, WI	William D. George Jr., Pres & CEO David J. Spurlock, CIO	NA	13,000	Chemical specialty products
Seagram Co. Ltd. New York, NY	Edgar Bronfman Jr., Pres & CEO Judy Shapiro, SVP, MIS	11.0B	30,000	Beverages, entertainment & comm
Shell Oil Houston, TX	P.J. Carroll, Pres & CEO M.C. Bone, Dir Tech	24.6B	21,050	Oil and gas
Siemens New York, NY	Heinrich V. Pierer, Pres & CEO	7.33B	47,200	Electrical & electronic products
Singapore Airlines Singapore	Cheong Choong Kong, Mng Dir Cheong Kai Mun, Dir Mgmt Svcs	4.9B	25,358	Air transportation
SmithKline Beecham Philadelphia, PA	Jan Leschly, Chief Exec John Parker, VP & Dir Info Resources	11.0B	53,000	Health care
Sonoco Products Hartsville, SC	C.W. Coker, Chmn & CEO Bernard Campbell, VP & CIO	2.7B	19,000	Package manufacturing
Sony Tokyo, Japan	Norio Ohga, Chmn & CEO Hitashi Nara, Sr General Mgr	44.8B	138,000	Electronics
Sprint Westwood, KS	William T. Esrey, Chmn & CEO George N. Fuciu, Pres, Tech Svcs	12.8B	48,000	Communications
Texas Instruments Software Plano, TX	J.R. McLendon, Pres Jodie N. Ray, CIO	250M	1,500	Client/server application dev tools
Toyota Motor Sales, USA Torrance, CA	Shinji Sakai, Pres & CEO Doug Plescia, VP, IS	23.0B	6,650	Automotive sales & marketing
UPS Atlanta, GA	Kent C. Nelson, Chmn & CEO Frank Erbrick, CIO	21.0B	335,000	Package distribution & logistics
VeriFone Redwood City, CA	Hatim A. Tyabji, Chmn, Pres & CEO Kathy Cruz, CIO & VP MIS	387M	2,500	Secure electronic payment systems
Wal-Mart Stores Bentonville, AR	David Glass, CEO Randall D. Mott, SVP & CIO	93.6B	675,000	Discount retail merchandising
Whirlpool Benton Harbor, MI	David R. Whitwam, Chmn & CEO Bob Jones, VP Corp Info Sys	8.35B	45,435	Mfg & mktng home appliances
Xerox Stamford, CT	Paul A. Allaire, CEO Patricia M. Wallington, VP & CIO	16.6B	85,200	Document processing products & systems

Computerworld: Premier 100

"How we rank the Premier 100: Computerworld's ranking of the Premier 100 is based on a three-year moving average of IS Consultant Paul Strassmann's Information Productivity Index (IPI). A more refined measure than IT spending or installed base, the IPI measures a company's effectiveness at managing information. The IPI is like any productivity measure in that it has an output in the numerator and an input in the denominator. The output measures management's contribution to the company, namely its economic value-added (EVA); either Stern, Stewart & Co.'s EVA or the numerator in the formula below. The input represents the management cost of doing business. Unlike last year, this year's denominator included research and development costs because R&D is considered a significant management cost of doing business.

'Also new this year, Computerworld used a three-year moving average of the IPI to rank the Premier 100 instead of a single-year figure. This is because some firms show wide swings in profit from year to year. Any company with a significant negative IPI in fiscal year 1992, 1993 or 1994 was excluded from consideration as was any company that reported both favorable operating profits after taxes and large accounting write-offs. In addition, to qualify for the list, companies had to have a fiscal year 1994 IPI of 0.20 or greater. Computerworld considered companies with sales of more than $100M for inclusion. However, if a company was unwilling to provide detailed IS information, Computerworld reserved the right to exclude it from consideration. All data used to calculate the IPI are publicly available.

$$\frac{\text{Operating Profit after tax} - (\text{Shareholder equity} \times \text{Cost of capital*})}{\text{Sales, general and administrative costs} + \text{Research and development expenses}}$$

* Cost of Capital: 1992: 11.3%, 1993: 10.4%, 1994: 11.8%"--Computerworld

The High-Tech Top 10		
Rank	Company	Info Productivity Index
1	Cisco Systems	.833
2	Gateway 2000	.754
3	Intel	.468
4	Cabletron	.412
5	Micron Technology	.341
6	Microsoft	.329
7	Newbridge	.305
8	EMC	.302
9	Adaptec	.201
10	Compaq	.155

"Computer hardware, software and office equipment companies are excluded from the Premier 100 because of their unique position as developers of information systems and related technologies."--Computerworld

Rank	Company	3-Year IPI '92-'94	Total Revenue ($M)	Total IS Budget '95 (Range)	% Chg IS Bdgt '94-'95	Client/Server % IS Budget	Outsourcing % IS Budget
1	Superior Industries	1.41	456	1-4.9	25	NA	0
2	AES	1.26	533	<1	0	0	0
3	Destec Energy	1.01	727	1-4.9	-45	3	3
4	UST	.98	1,223	10-24.9	14	1	3
5	Carnival	.94	1,806	10-24.9	5	15	5
6	Chase Brass & Copper	.93	260	<1	52	4	50
7	United HealthCare	.91	3,768	100-249.9	14	25	2
8	California Energy	.91	154	1-4.9	15	0	0
9	Outback Steakhouse	.91	451	<1	25	58	42
10	Alza	.84	260	NA	NA	NA	NA
11	Mercury Finance	.84	252	NA	NA	NA	NA
12	Arnold Industries	.83	302	NA	NA	NA	NA
13	King World Productions	.82	480	<1	0	50	NA
14	Adams Resources & Energy	.80	634	<1	20	20	5
15	Western National	.79	615	1-4.9	36	48	0
16	International Game Tech.	.77	674	5-9.9	-8	10	3

Rank	Company	3-Year IPI '92-'94	Total Revenue ($M)	Total IS Budget '95 (Range)	% Chg IS Bdgt '94-'95	Client/Server % IS Budget	Outsourcing % IS Budget
17	U.S. Healthcare	.77	2,974	NA	NA	NA	NA
18	John Nuveen Co.	.76	220	5-9.9	13	50	0.1
19	Medusa	.67	276	NA	NA	NA	NA
20	BMC Industries	.66	219	<1	-30	10	10
21	Louisiana-Pacific	.63	3,039	NA	NA	NA	NA
22	Illinois Central	.62	593	10-24.9	0	0	25
23	Wabash National	.61	561	<1	20	20	5
24	Green Tree Financial	.60	497	NA	NA	NA	NA
25	Wausau Paper Mills	.57	426	1-4.9	7	10	2
26	Great Lakes Chemical	.56	2,065	NA	NA	NA	NA
27	Mylan Laboratories	.56	251	NA	NA	NA	NA
28	HealthCare Compare	.55	186	10-24.9	9	40	0
29	Morgan Keegan	.55	231	1-4.9	13	15	20
30	Clark Equipment	.54	946	NA	NA	NA	NA
31	Topps	.52	268	NA	NA	NA	NA
32	Galey & Lord	.52	451	1-4.9	3	5	1
33	Bear Stearns	.44	3,441	100-249.9	7	17	3
34	Caraustar Industries	.44	456	1-4.9	12	20	0
35	Dairy Queen	.44	340	1-4.9	27	38	0
36	Cooper Tire & Rubber	.43	1,403	10-24.9	7	20	5
37	Marvel Entertainment	.43	514	NA	25	33	33
38	Equitable of Iowa Cos.	.42	651	5-9.9	10	35	0
39	Southern Energy Homes	.42	188	>1	50	23	0
40	Amgen	.41	1,549	50-99.9	45	3	5
41	TBC	.40	551	1-4.9	5	0	1
42	WMS Industries	.40	358	1-4.9	5	3	2
43	Boston BanCorp	.40	147	1-4.9	7	17	84
44	Breed Technologies	.40	277	1-4.9	6	10	10
45	Fossil	.39	161	1-4.9	25	1	10
46	First Data	.36	1,471	NA	NA	NA	NA
47	Kinetic Concepts	.34	269	5-9.9	50	40	0
48	Abbott Laboratories	.34	9,156	NA	NA	NA	NA
49	International Flavors & Fragrances	.34	1,315	5-9.9	5	40	5
50	Merck & Co.	.34	14,969	100-249.9	16	39	16
51	A.G. Edwards	.32	1,278	NA	NA	NA	NA
52	CBS	.32	3,711	NA	-2.3	10	NA
53	CMI	.32	128	1-4.9	20	25	0
54	Electroglas	.31	112	<1	15	5	7
55	T. Rowe Price Associates	.31	382	25-49.9	29	33	8
56	Arrow International	.30	178	1-4.9	0	0	0
57	American Home Products	.29	8,966	100-249.9	7.5	7	5
58	Valley National Bancorp	.29	265	NA	15	NA	NA
59	Morgan Stanley Group	.29	9,176	>500	15	25	8
60	Health Management Associates	.29	438	1-4.9	6	30	NA
61	Coca-Cola	.28	16,172	NA	NA	NA	NA
62	Worthington Industries	.28	1,285	NA	NA	NA	NA
63	Ethyl	.27	1,174	5-9.9	0	90	NA
64	Norfolk Southern	.27	4,581	50-99.9	10	5	5
65	Masland Industries	.27	429	NA	NA	NA	NA

Rank	Company	3-Year IPI '92-'94	Total Revenue ($M)	Total IS Budget '95 (Range)	% Chg IS Bdgt '94-'95	Client/Server % IS Budget	Outsourcing % IS Budget
66	Progressive	.27	2,415	50-99.9	24	26	8
67	Schering-Plough	.27	4,657	NA	NA	NA	NA
68	Charles Schwab	.26	1,064	100-249.9	30	20	NA
69	Nine West Group	.26	652	5-9.9	15	15	0
70	Vicor	.24	115	1-4.9	30	20	0
71	Gannett	.23	3,824	50-99.9	5	5	2
72	Charter One Financial	.23	423	NA	NA	NA	NA
73	Vencor	.23	396	25-49.9	20	14	50
74	Chromcraft Revington	.23	134	1-4.9	-10	20	20
75	Express Scripts	.23	384	10-24.9	30	40	20
76	Rubbermaid	.22	2,169	NA	14	1	10
77	Ellett Brothers	.22	160	1-4.9	15	20	5
78	Bristol-Myers Squibb	.22	11,984	NA	NA	NA	NA
79	Wm. Wrigley Jr. Co.	.21	1,596	10-24.9	9	6	1
80	St. John Knits	.21	127	1-4.9	19	12	15
81	Equifax	.20	1,421	100-249.9	9	8	42
82	Martin Marietta Materials	.20	501	1-4.9	10	5	NA
83	Cagles'	.18	312	NA	NA	NA	NA
84	Stewart & Stevenson Services	.18	1,138	1-4.9	0	5	5
85	Champion Enterprises	.18	615	<1	5	15	NA
86	Toll Brothers	.18	501	1-4.9	70	0	0
87	Sunbeam-Oster	.18	198	NA	NA	NA	NA
88	Rollins Truck Leasing	.17	450	1-4.9	10	16	4
89	McDonald's	.17	8,320	50-99.9	13	6	4
90	Arthur J. Gallagher & Co.	.16	356	10-24.9	0	30	20
91	Solectron	.15	1,456	10-24.9	30	60	5
92	Royal Caribbean Cruises	.15	1,171	10-24.9	NA	5	0
93	Supreme Industries	.15	136	<1	0	0	2.5
94	Anheuser-Busch	.15	12,053	NA	NA	NA	NA
95	ARCO Chemical	.14	3,267	10-24.9	0	10	5
96	Applebee's International	.13	208	1-4.9	20	40	NA
97	Eli Lilly & Co.	.12	5,711	250-499.9	2.5	3	0
98	Swift Transportation	.11	365	1-4.9	0	10	90
99	Audiovox	.11	486	1-4.9	5	20	10
100	Campbell Soup	.11	6,690	100-249.9	20	40	40

Company Directory

01 Communique Laboratory Inc. 1450 Meyerside Dr #500, Mississauga Ontario L5T 2N5 Canada; 905/795-2888, 800/668-2185 Fax: 905/795-0101, Co Email: 72762.53@compuserve.com, Web URL: 01.ca, Focus: Software for fax capabilities for networks and PCs, Prdts: 01/FAX for Windows, 01/FAXCOM, Ownrshp: PVT, Founded: 1991, Andrew Cheung, Pres, S.C. Cheung, Chmn, Brian J. McElwain, VP Sales & Mktng

1-800 Service Partners 11002 Metric Blvd, Austin TX 78758 USA; 512/719-9335, 800/860-7390 Fax: 512/836-1864, Focus: Technical support for computer hardware and software, Linda Bush-over, Pres

100VG-AnyLAN Forum (VGF), PO Box 1378, N Highlands CA 95660 USA; 916/348-0212, Co Email: vgf@anylan.win.com, Focus: Interoperability testing, certification and implementation of IEEE 802.12, Ownrshp: Nonprofit, Kenneth R. Hurst, Chmn

1394 Trade Assoc. c/o Skipstone, 3925 W Breaker Ln, #425, Austin TX 78759 USA; 512/305-0202, Fax: 512/305-0212, Co Email: ipra@netcom.com, Web URL: firewire.org, Focus: Promote IEEE 1394 high-speed serial bus, Ownrshp: Nonprofit, Founded: 1994, Empl: 25+, Gary A. Hoffman, Chmn, Email: gary@skipstone.com; James Snider, Vice Chair, Myles Suer, Dir Mktng

1776 Inc. 8632 S Sepulveda Blvd, #203, Los Angeles CA 90045 USA; 310/215-1776, Fax: 310/217-1107, Co Email: 1776@cup.portal.com, Focus: Disk array management software, Ownrshp: PVT, Founded: 1987, Rob Kramarz, Pres

1st Tech Corp. 12201 Technology Blvd, #130, Austin TX 78727-6101 USA; 512/258-3570, 800/533-1744 Fax: 512/258-3689, Focus: Memory products, Ownrshp: PVT, Founded: 1993, Empl: 70, Sales ($M): 41, Fiscal End: 12/94; Gary Pankonien, Chmn, Chris Efstathiou, VP Materials, Mike Moreland, VP Sales & Ops, Karl Baumbach, Dir Bus Dev, Don Turner, CFO

2-Lane Media 1575 Westwood Blvd, #301, Los Angeles CA 90024 USA; 310/473-3706, Web URL: launchonline.com, Focus: Interactive multimedia, Ownrshp: PVT, Founded: 1994, Empl: 30, David Goldberg, CEO

20/20 Software Inc. 8196 SW Hall Blvd #200, Beaverton OR 97008 USA; 503/520-0504, Fax: 503/520-9118, Co Email: info@twenty.com, Web URL: twenty.com/~twenty, Focus: Software utility products, Prdts: PC-Install, Ownrshp: PVT, Joe Wang, Pres

360°Communications 8725 W Higgins Rd, Chicago IL 60631 USA; 312/399-2500, Fax: 312/399-3805, Web URL: 360c.com, Focus: Telecom services, Ownrshp: OTC, Sales ($M): 834, Fiscal End: 12/95; Dennis E. Foster, CEO

3Com Corp. 5400 Bayfront Plaza, PO Box 58145, Santa Clara CA 95052-8145 USA; 408/764-5000, 800/638-3266 Fax: 408/764-5001, Web URL: 3com.com, Focus: LAN products, Ownrshp: OTC, Stk Sym: COMS, Founded: 1979, Empl: 5,190, Sales ($M): 2,327.1, Fiscal End: 5/96; Eric A. Benhamou, Pres & CEO, Robert J. Finocchio Jr., EVP, Christopher B. Paisley, VP & CFO, Janice M. Roberts, VP Mktng, Sandra L. Sully, VP MIS, David J. Abramson

3D Systems Corp. 26081 Ave Hall, Valencia CA 91355 USA; 805/295-5600, Fax: 805/257-1200, Focus: Imaging software, Ownrshp: OTC, Stk Sym: TDSC, Founded: 1986, Empl: 200, Sales ($M): 62.6, Fiscal End: 12/95; Charles W. Hull, Pres & COO, Arthur B. Sims, Chmn & CEO, Robert E. Horrell, VP Ops, Richard P. Fedchenko, VP Mkt Dev, Gordon L. Almquist, VP & CFO

3D/Eye Inc. 700 Galleria Pkwy, Atlanta GA 30339 USA; 770/937-9000, Fax: 770/937-0700, Co Email: @eye.com, Focus: 3D software, Ownrshp: PVT, Founded: 1981, Samir L. Hanna, Pres & CEO, Mark Walton, VP Mktng & Sales, Email: mawa@eye.com; Shaun Murphy, Mktng Mgr, Angie Ciarloni, Comm Mgr, Email: angiec@eye.com; Sela Missirian, Com Coord

3DO Co. (3DO), 600 Galveston Dr, Redwood City CA 94063-4746 USA; 415/261-3000, Fax: 415/261-3120, Co Email: @3do.com, Web URL: 3do.com, Focus: Hardware and software standards for interactive CD-ROM platform, Ownrshp: OTC, Stk Sym: THDO, Founded: 1991, Empl: 300, Sales ($M): 37.9, Fiscal End: 3/96; Trip Hawkins, Pres & CEO, D. Rex Golding, VP & CFO, Diane R. Hunt, PR Mgr, Email: diane.hunt@3do.com

3DTV Corp. PO Box Q, San Rafael CA 94913-4316 USA; 415/479-3516, Fax: 415/479-3316, Web URL: stereospace.com, Focus: 3D hardware and software for PCs and TVs, Prdts: 3D MAGIC, Ownrshp: PVT, Michael Starks, Pres, Email: starks@stereospace.com

3G Graphics Inc. 23632 Hwy 99 #F407, Edmonds WA 98026-9206 USA; 206/774-3518, Fax: 206/771-8975, Focus: Desktop publishing clip art, Ownrshp: PVT, Founded: 1986, Empl: 7, Gail Giaimo, Pres, Glenn Giaimo, VP

4-Sight LC 1801 Industrial Cr, PO Box 65340, W Des Moines IA 50265-5557 USA; 515/221-3000, Fax: 800/224-0802, Web URL: 4sight.com, Focus: Network fax and ISDN software, Prdts: 4-Sight Fax, 4-Sight ISDN Manager, 4-Sight ISDN Broadcast, Ownrshp: PVT, Founded: 1992, Empl: 20, Sales ($M): 6, Fiscal End: 9/95; Lyndon Stickley, Pres, Jason Taylor, Prod Mktng Mgr, Scott Regnier, Reg Sales Mgr, Peter Chapman, Tech Svs Mgr, Heidi Bobzin, Email: heidi_bobzin@cesoft.com

4Home Products One Computer Associates Plaza, Islandia NY 11788-7000 USA; 516/342-2000, 800/773-5445 Fax: 516/342-6854, Focus: Lifestyle software products, Ownrshp: Sub. Computer Associates Int'l, Sue Rizzi

4i Solutions Inc. 9800 Muirlands Blvd, Irvine CA 92718-2515 USA; 800/228-1416 Focus: Image processing software, Prdts: 4Site, 4Most, Ownrshp: PVT, Founded: 1991, Empl: 10, Douglas J. Russo, EVP & COO, Khoi Turner, VP Prod Dev, Craig Curtner, Dir Mktng

5th Wave by Rich Tennant, The 16 Rowe Point, Rockport MA 01966 USA; 508/546-2448, Fax: 508/546-7747, Co Email: the5wave@tiac.net, Focus: Syndicated computer cartoons, Prdts: The 5th Wave, Ownrshp: PVT, Founded: 1983, Rich Tennant, Debbie Clark

7th Level Inc. 5225 San Fernando Rd, W Los Angeles CA 90039 USA; 818/547-1955, Fax: 818/246-5198, Web URL: 7thlevel.com, Focus: Interactive multimedia software, Ownrshp: PVT, Founded: 1993, Empl: 200, Sales ($M): 12.2, Fiscal End: 12/95; George Grayson, Chmn, Pres & CEO, Robert Ezrim, EVP & Co-Chmn, Scott Page, EVP, Jeff Croson, VP Sales, David Craig, CFO

@Home Network 385 Ravendale Dr, Mountain View CA 94043 USA; 415/944-7367, Fax: 415/944-8500, Co Email: @home.com, Web URL: home.net, Focus: Constant Internet connection, real-time delivery and updating of content via coaxial cable, Ownrshp: PVT, Founded: 1995, Empl: 45, William R. Hearst III, Chmn, Thomas A. Jermoluk, Pres & CEO

a/Soft Development Inc. 24 Eastman Ave, Bedford NH 03110-6703 USA; 603/666-6699, Fax: 603/666-6460, Co Email: @asoft-dev.com, Web URL: asoft-dev.com/asoft-dev, Focus: Text utility software, Prdts: nu/TPU, Ownrshp: PVT, Founded: 1989, Empl: 8, Ken Graf, VP Dev, Email: support@asoft-dev.com; James Graf, VP Sales, Email: sales@asoft-dev.com; Debbie Cote, Mktng PR

Abacus Accounting Systems Inc. 9707 110 St, #488, Edmonton Alberta T5K 2L9 Canada; 403/488-8100, 800/665-6657 Fax: 403/488-8150, Co Email: abacus-group.com, Focus: Accounting software, Prdts: Abacus, Ownrshp: FO, Founded: 1983, Empl: 20, Dwayne Kushniruk, Pres & CEO, Terry Orletsky, VP, Peter Pellatt, CFO, Tom Dawson, Dir Sales & Mktng, Email: tomd@abacus-group.com

Abacus Concepts Inc. 1918 Bonita Ave, Berkeley CA 94704-1014 USA; 510/540-1949, 800/666-7828 Fax: 510/540-0260, Co Email: info@abacus.com, Web URL: abacus.com, Focus: Statistical and graphics software for the Macintosh, Prdts: StatView, SuperA-NOVA, Ownrshp: PVT, Founded: 1984, Empl: 30, Daniel S. Feldman Jr., Pres, Jim Gagnon, CTO, Robin Rafferty, VP Mktng, Email: marketing@abacus.com; Bob McCall, VP Sales, Email: sales@abacus.com; Gregory S. Galliford, VP Fin, Will Scoggin, EVP Business Dev, Email: wills@abacus.com

ABCO Distributors 400 Rt 59, Monsey NY 10952 USA; 914/368-1930, Fax: 914/368-1271, Focus: Microcomputer product distributor, Ownrshp: PVT, B.P. Slome, Pres, Dominick Pagnozzi, VP, Roz Slome, VP, Richard Greenbaum, VP Sales & Mktng

ABL Engineering Inc. 6111 Heisley Rd, Mentor OH 44060 USA; 216/974-8585, Fax: 216/974-0089, Focus: Multimedia technologies, Prdts: SW1616 Broadband Switch

Abra Cadabra Software 888 Executive Cntr. Dr W #300, St Petersburg FL 33702 USA; 813/527-1111, Fax: 813/528-2178, Focus: Human resource software, Ownrshp: Sub. Best Programs, Founded: 1985, Empl: 96, Sales ($M): 10, Jim Foster, Pres, Joe Bailey, VP Sales, David Thuma, Dir Mktng, Ken Schild, MIS Admin, Linda Miller

Absolute Software Corp. 101-1001 W Broadway Dept. 121, Vancouver BC V6H 4B1 Canada; 604/730-9851, Fax: 604/730-9581, Co Email: trace@absolute.com, Focus: Computer theft retrieval system, Prdts: Computrace TRS, Ownrshp: PVT, Christian Cotichini, Pres, John Livingstone, CEO

AbTech Corp. 1575 State Farm Blvd #1-2, Charlottesville VA 22911-8611 USA; 804/977-0686, Fax: 804/977-9615, Co Email: abtech@compuserve.com, Focus: AI software, Prdts: StatNet, PredictNet, Ownrshp: PVT, Founded: 1988, Empl: 18, Gerard Montgomery, Pres & CEO, Michael Araiza, VP Mktng, Keith Drake, Dir R&D, Amy Edwards, Dir Mktng, Email: amy@abtech.com

Academic Systems 444 Castro St, #1200, Mountain View CA 94041 USA; 415/694-6850, Fax: 415/694-6830, Web URL: academic.com, Focus: Interactive learning system for colleges, Ownrshp: PVT, Founded: 1992, Empl: 95, John Gottsman, CEO

ACC Technology Group 7 Whatney, Irvine CA 92718 USA; 714/454-2441, Fax: 714/454-8527, Co Email: @acctechnology.com, Focus: PC peripherals, Ownrshp: Sub. Lam Soon, Singapore, Founded: 1994, Empl: 100, Mike Zachan, Pres, Sunny Lum, VP Ops, Kit Tan, CFO, Satish Trikha, VP Sales, Christa Judson, Sales & Mktng

Accelerated Technology Inc. 720 Oak Cr Dr E, Mobile AL 36685 USA; 334/661-5770, Fax: 334/661-5788, Co Email: @atinucleus.com, Web URL: atinucleus.com, Focus: Embedded software products & support tools, Prdts: Nucleus C++, Neil Henderson, Pres, Michelle Anderson, Dir Mktng, Email: manderson@atinucleus.com

Accent Software Int'l. Ltd. 1401 Dove St #470, Newport Beach CA 92660 USA; 714/223-0620, 800/535-5256 Fax: 714/223-0629, Co Email: 73251.2535@compuserve.com, Focus: Multilingual word processor, Prdts: LanguageWare, Ownrshp: OTC, Stk Sym: ACNTF, Robert Rosenschein, Pres, Mitchell Joelson, EVP, Herbert Zlotogorski, COO, Jeffrey Rosenschein, VP R&D, Norman Kreger, Dir Corp Com, Email: normank@accent.co.il

Access Graphics Inc. 1426 Pearl St, 4th Floor, Boulder CO 80302 USA; 303/938-9333, 800/733-9333 Fax: 303/938-8210, Web URL: access.com, Focus: Channel integrator for Unix-based distributed computing solutions, Ownrshp: PVT, Founded: 1988, Empl: 425, Sales ($M): 840.0, Fiscal End: 12/95; John Ramsey, Pres & CEO, Email: Jramsey@access.com; Thomas Carson, VP & CFO, Email: tomc@access.com; Ross Churchill, VP Sales & Mktng, Email: ross@access.com; Laurie Carlson, VP Mkt Dev, Email: Lcarlson@access.com; Geoff Cooper, VP Info Tech, Email: geoffc@access.com; Julann Velvin, PR Mgr, Email: julannv@access.com

Access Software Inc. 4750 Wiley Post Way, #200, Salt Lake City UT 84116 USA; 801/359-2900, 800/800-4880 Fax: 801/359-2968, Web URL: accesssoftware.com, Focus: Entertainment software, Ownrshp: PVT, Founded: 1982, Empl: 126, Bruce Carver, Pres, Susan Dunn

Acclaim Entertainment Inc. 70 Glen St, Glen Cove NY 11542-2708 USA; 516/624-8888, Fax: 516/624-2884, Focus: Entertainment software, Ownrshp: OTC, Stk Sym: AKLM, Founded: 1987, Empl: 800, Sales ($M): 480.8, Fiscal End: 11/94; Gregory Fischbach, Chmn & CEO, James Scoroposki, EVP, Robert Holmes, Pres & COO, Anthony Williams, EVP & CFO, Allyne Mills, Mgr PR

ACCO USA Inc. 770 S ACCO Plaza, Wheeling IL 60090-6070 USA; 847/541-9500, 800/222-6462 Fax: 800/247-1317, Focus: Office products, Prdts: Swingline, Wilson Jones, Day-Timer, Ownrshp: Sub. American Brands, Bruce Gescheider, Pres, Andrew Roth, VP Mktng

Accolade Inc. 5300 Stevens Creek Blvd, San Jose CA 95129 USA; 408/985-1700, Fax: 408/246-0885, Web URL: accolade.com, Focus: Entertainment software, Prdts: Hardball, Star Control, Bubsy, Jack Nicklaus Golf, Ownrshp: PVT, Founded: 1984, Empl: 110, Sales ($M): 16.2, Fiscal End: 12/95; James Barnett, Chmn & CEO, Stan Roach, EVP Sales & Mktng, David Grenewetzki, EVP Prod Dev, Jill Anderson, CFO, Erica Olson, Mgr PR & Comm, Email: accolpr@aol.com

Acculogic Inc. 7 Whatney, Irvine CA 92718 USA; 714/454-2441, 800/234-7811 Fax: 714/454-8527, Focus: IDE and SCSI controller products, Ownrshp: Sub. Lam Soon Group, Singapore, Founded: 1988, Empl: 100, Michael P. Zachan, Pres, Sunny Lum, VP Ops, Kit Tan, CFO, Satish Trikha, VP Sales, Christa Judson, Sales & Mktng

Accurate Research Inc. 762 Palomar Ave, Sunnyvale CA 94086-2914 USA; 408/523-4788, 800/799-8802 Fax: 408/523-4789, Web URL: drcdrom.com, Focus: CD-ROM software, Prdts: Dr. CD-ROM, CD Mate, MPEG Titles, Ownrshp: PVT, Founded: 1993, Empl: 10, Sales ($M): 2.5, Fiscal End: 9/95; Eric Ho, Mng Dir, Email: eric.ho@drcdrom.com; Cathy Wang, Mktng Mgr, Email: cathy.wang@drcdrom.com

Acecad Inc. 791 Foam St, PO Box 431, Monterey CA 93940 USA; 408/655-1900, 800/676-4223 Fax: 408/655-1919, Web URL: acecad.com, Focus: PC graphics tablets and digitizers, Prdts: ACE-CAT II, Ownrshp: PVT, Founded: 1988, Todd Waldman, Pres, Bryn Stephens, Sales Mgr, Rhonda Sturgill, Ops Mgr, David Preller, MIS Mgr

Acer America Corp. 2641 Orchard Pkwy, San Jose CA 95134 USA; 408/432-6200, Fax: 408/922-2949, Co Email: @acer.com, Web URL: acer.com, Focus: PCs and peripherals, Ownrshp: Sub. Acer Group, Taiwan, Founded: 1976, Empl: 1,150, Sales ($M): 1,440, Fiscal End: 12/95; Ronald Chwang, Pres & CEO, Steve Tsui, VP Sales, Robert Marks, VP Mfg, Olend King, VP Cust Scvs, Michael Tung, VP Fin, Jessica Kersey

Acer Inc. 6F, 156 Min Sheng E Rd Sec. 3, Taipei TW-105 Taiwan ROC; 2-545-5288, Fax: 2-545-5308, Focus: PCs and peripherals, Ownrshp: FO, Empl: 11,000, Sales ($M): 5,700, Fiscal End: 12/95; Stan Shih, Chmn & CEO

ACI US Inc. (ACI), 20883 Stevens Creek Blvd, Cupertino CA 95014 USA; 408/252-4444, Fax: 408/252-4829, Co Email: @acius.com, Focus: Macintosh productivity software, Prdts: 4th Dimension, 4D Server, Ownrshp: Sub. ACI, France, Founded: 1987, Empl: 230, Sales ($M): 40, Fiscal End: 12/94; Mark Vernon, Pres, Dominique Hermsdorff, VP Eng, Marilyn Guerrieri, CFO, Suzanne Whitney-Smedt, Mktng Mgr, Michele Landry, Marcom Mgr, Email: michele@acius.com

ACL Inc. 1960 E Devon Ave, Elk Grove IL 60007 USA; 708/981-9212, Fax: 708/981-9278, Focus: Anti-static and computer cleaning products, Ownrshp: PVT, Founded: 1969, Stuart Blankstein, Pres, Lori Jacobson

Acquired Knowledge Inc. 3655 Nobel Dr, #380, San Diego CA 92122 USA; 619/587-4668, Fax: 619/587-4669, Focus: Computer software training, Ownrshp: PVT, Founded: 1990, John Deubert, Pres, Todd Donahue, VP

ACT Networks Inc. 188 Camino Ruiz, Camarillo CA 93012-6712 USA; 805/388-2474, Fax: 805/388-3504, Co Email: ir@acti.com, Focus: Manufactures and sells network access products, Ownrshp: OTC, Stk Sym: ANET, Founded: 1987, Empl: 120, Sales ($M): 28.4, Fiscal End: 6/96; Martin Shum, Chmn, Pres & CEO, H. Peter Staab, VP Eng, John W. Tucker, VP Sales & Mktng, Andre de Fusco, VP Bus Dev, Melvin L. Flowers, VP & CFO

Action Technologies Inc. 1301 Marina Village Pkwy #100, Alameda CA 94501 USA; 510/521-6190, Fax: 510/769-0596, Focus: E-mail and workflow software, Prdts: Action Workflow System, Ownrshp: PVT, Founded: 1983, Empl: 70, Bill Welty, Chmn, Terry McGowan, Pres & CEO, Chuck Pendell, VP Sales, Sumi Shohara, VP Mktng, Mike Bendel, Marcom Specialist

ActionTec Electronics Inc. 750 N Mary Ave, Sunnyvale CA 94086 USA; 408/739-7000, Fax: 408/739-7001, Focus: Plug 'n' play compatible PC cards, Ownrshp: PVT, Founded: 1993, Dean Chang, Pres, Minsiu Huang, VP Ops, Michael Halloran, VP Sales & Mktng, Jack H. Peterson, Dir Strategic Planning

Activision Inc. 11601 Wilshire Blvd, #300, Los Angeles CA 90025 USA; 310/473-9200, Fax: 310/479-9409, Co Email: ir@activision.com, Web URL: activision.com, Focus: Entertainment software, Prdts: Mech Warrior 2, Pitfall, Earthworm Jim, Ownrshp: OTC, Stk Sym: ATVI, Founded: 1979, Empl: 319, Sales ($M): 61.4, Fiscal End: 3/96; Robert A. Kotick, Chmn & CEO, Eric Johnson, VP Mktng, Howard E. Marks, EVP Studios, Steve Crane, VP Tech, Brian G. Kelly, CFO & COO

Acucobol Inc. 7950 Silverton Ave, #201, San Diego CA 92126 USA; 619/689-7220, 800/262-6585 Fax: 619/566-3071, Co Email: info@acucobol.com, Web URL: acucobol.com, Focus: Portable Cobol compilers and database interfaces, Prdts: Acucobol-85, Acu 4GL, AcuServer, AcuScreens, Ownrshp: PVT, Founded: 1988, Sales ($M): 10.0, Pamela Coker, Pres, Email: pamela@acucobol.com; Drake Coker, Chief Scientist, Email: drake@acucobol.com; Cameron Jenkins, VP Mktng, Email: cameron@acucobol.com; Derryl Rodgers, Dir Tech Ops, Email: derryl@acucobol.com; Susan P. Boyer, Mgr Marcom

Acxiom Corp. 301 Industrial Blvd, PO Box 2000, Conway AR 72032-7103 USA; 501/336-1000, 800/922-9466 Fax: 501/450-1414, Co Email: info@acxiom.com, Web URL: acxiom.com, Focus: Marketing information services, Ownrshp: OTC, Stk Sym: ACXM, Founded: 1969, Empl: 3,098, Sales ($M): 269.9, Fiscal End: 3/96; Charles D. Morgan, Jr., Chmn, Pres & CEO, Rodger S. Kline, EVP & COO, James T. Womble, EVP, Robert S. Bloom, CFO, C. Alex Dietz, VP & CIO

Ada Information Clearinghouse (AdaIC), PO Box 1866, Falls Church VA 22041 USA; 800/232-4211 Fax: 703/681-2869, Co Email: adainfo@sw-eng.falls-church.va, Web URL: sw-eng.falls-church.va.us, Focus: Information on the Ada community

ADAM Software 1600 RiverEdge Pkwy #800, Atlanta GA 30328 USA; 404/980-0888, Fax: 404/955-3088, Co Email: 74431.1605@compuserve.com, Focus: Surgery simulation software, Ownrshp: PVT, Founded: 1990, Empl: 86, Robert S. Kramer, Chmn, Gregory M. Swayne, Pres, Curtis A. Cain, CEO

Adaptec Inc. 691 S Milpitas Blvd, Milpitas CA 95035 USA; 408/945-8600, Fax: 408/262-2533, Co Email: goadaptec@compuserve.com, Web URL: adaptec.com, Focus: PC peripherals controllers, Prdts: SCSI Master, EZ-SCSI, AIRport, Ownrshp: OTC, Stk Sym: ADPT, Founded: 1981, Empl: 2,000, Sales ($M): 659.3, Fiscal End: 3/96; John G. Adler, Chmn, F. Grant Saviers, Pres & CEO, Bob Stephens, COO, Sam Kazarian, VP Ops, Paul G. Hansen, VP & CFO, Bruce Frymire, PR Dir, Email: bfrymire@corp.adaptec.com

Adaptiv Software Inc. 125 Pacifica, #250, Irvine CA 92718-9601 USA; 714/789-7300, Fax: 714/789-7320, Web URL: adaptiv.com, Focus: People scheduling software, Prdts: PeopleScheduler, Ownrshp: PVT, Founded: 1989, Kenneth S. Forbes III, Pres, Email: kforbes@adaptiv.com; Richard D. Barker, VP, Email:

barker@adaptiv.com

Adaptive Solutions Inc. 1400 NW Compton Dr, #340, Beaverton OR 97006 USA; 503/690-1236, Fax: 503/690-1249, Co Email: @asi.com, Web URL: asi.com, Focus: Parallel processing applications and systems, Prdts: CNAPS, Ownrshp: OTC, Stk Sym: ADSO, Founded: 1988, Empl: 64, Sales ($M): 10.7, Fiscal End: 12/95; John J. Migliore, Pres & CEO, Dan Hammerstrom, CTO, Wendell Henry, VP Eng, Robert Anundson, VP Mktng, John C. Carveth, VP Fin

ADC Telecommunications 4900 W 78th St, Minneapolis MN 55435 USA; 612/938-8080, 800/468-9716 Fax: 612/946-3292, Focus: Communications products and services, Ownrshp: OTC, Stk Sym: ADCT, Founded: 1953, Empl: 2,984, Sales ($M): 586.2, Fiscal End: 12/95; William J. Cadogen, Chmn, Pres & CEO, Lynn J. Davis, SVP, Lawrence D. Asten, VP Sales, William C. Hamer, VP & CTO, Robert E. Switz, VP & CFO

Addison-Wesley Publishing Co. 1 Jacob Way, Reading MA 01867 USA; 617/944-3700, Fax: 617/944-7273, Co Email: @aw.com, Focus: Publisher of books and software, Ownrshp: PVT, Founded: 1942, Empl: 1,000, Don Hammonds, Chmn & CEO, Warren Stone, Pres & COO

ADFlex Solutions Inc. 2001 W Chandler Blvd, Chandler AZ 85224 USA; 602/963-4584, Fax: 602/786-8280, Focus: Circuit-based interconnect solutions, Ownrshp: OTC, Stk Sym: AFLX, Founded: 1993, Empl: 3,530, Sales ($M): 101.2, Fiscal End: 12/95; Rolando C. Esteverena, Pres & CEO, Michael L. Pierce, EVP Ops, Robert G. Pape, CFO, Greg H. Nelson, VP App & Sales

ADI Systems Inc. 2115 Ringwood Ave, San Jose CA 95131 USA; 408/944-0100, Fax: 408/944-0300, Web URL: adi-online.com, Focus: Monitors, Prdts: MicroScan series, Ownrshp: Sub. ADI, Taiwan, Founded: 1979, Empl: 1,800, Sales ($M): 500 WW, Raymond Hou, Pres, Email: rhou@adiusa.com; Vincent Lin, Dir Mktng, Email: vlin@adiusa.com; Karen Mar, Sr Mktng Specialist, Email: kmar@adiusa.com

AdLib MultiMedia Inc. 580 Grande-Allee est, #40, Quebec Quebec G1R 2K2 Canada; 418/522-6100, Fax: 418/522-4919, Focus: PC audio products, Ownrshp: PVT, Christoph Klein, Pres & CEO, Mark Pickering, Tech Dir, Daniel-Victor Tremblay, Sales Dir

Adobe Systems Inc. 1585 Charleston Rd, PO Box 7900, Mountain View CA 94039-7900 USA; 415/961-4400, Fax: 415/961-3769, Co Email: @adobe.com, Web URL: adobe.com, Focus: Software to print integrated text and graphics, Prdts: PostScript, Illustrator, Ownrshp: OTC, Stk Sym: ADBE, Founded: 1983, Empl: 1,584, Sales ($M): 762.3, Fiscal End: 11/95; John E. Warnock, Chmn & CEO, Charles M. Geschke, Pres & COO, Stephen A. MacDonald, SVP, David B. Pratt, SVP, M. Bruce Nakao, SVP & CFO, LaVon Peck

Adonis Corp. 11130 NE 33rd Place, #250, Bellevue WA 98004-1448 USA; 800/234-9497 Fax: 206/869-0252, Focus: E-mail software, Ownrshp: PVT, Mitchell B. London, Pres & CEO, Email: 75540.3170@compuserve.com

Adra Systems Inc. 2 Executive Dr, Chelmsford MA 01824-2558 USA; 508/937-3700, Fax: 508/453-2462, Web URL: adra.com, Focus: Scientific software, Ownrshp: PVT, Founded: 1983, Empl: 110, Sales ($M): 20, William Mason, Pres & CEO, James Blaschke, VP Mktng, Mark O'Connell

adRem Technologies 354 Eisenhower Pkwy, Livingston NJ 07039 USA; 201/740-0337, Fax: 201/740-0270, Prdts: Project ToolBox, Jerry Cohen, Pres

ADSL Forum 303 Vintage Park Dr, Foster City CA 94404-1138 USA; 415/378-6680, Fax: 415/525-0182, Co Email: adslforum@adsl.com, Focus: Promote use of Asymmetric Digital Subscriber Line technology, Ownrshp: Nonprofit, Founded: 1994, Gretta Tierney, Assoc Coord, Kim Maxwell, Chmn & Pres, Email: adslforum@aol.com; Greg Whelan, VP, Email: greg.whelan@analog.com

Adtran Inc. 901 Explorer Blvd, Huntsville AL 35806 USA; 205/

971-8000, Fax: 205/971-8699, Focus: Telecom products, Ownrshp: OTC, Stk Sym: ADTN, Founded: 1986, Empl: 483, Sales ($M): 72.4, Fiscal End: 12/93; Marc C. Smith, Chmn, Pres & CEO, Howard A. Thrailkill, EVP & COO, John A. Jurenko, VP Sales & Mktng, Lonnie S. McMillian, VP Eng, Irwin O. Goldstein, VP & CFO, Stacy Thomas, PR Coord

Advanced Archival Products Inc. (AAP), 10949 E Peakview Ave, Englewood CO 80111-6804 USA; 303/792-9700, Fax: 303/792-2465, Focus: Mass storage management software, Ownrshp: Sub EMASS, Founded: 1988

Advanced Concepts Inc. 4129 N Port Washington Ave, Milwaukee WI 53212-1029 USA; 414/963-0999, 800/222-6736 Fax: 414/963-2090, Co Email: 72623.3273@compuserve.com, Focus: Wholesale and retail distribution software, sales automation, Prdts: Order Plus, SalesCTRL, Ownrshp: PVT, Founded: 1980, Empl: 10, Sales ($M): 1, Fiscal End: 12/90; Jeffrey Wohlfahrt, Pres

Advanced Digital Information Corp. 10201 Willows Rd, Redmond WA 98052 USA; 206/881-8004, 800/336-1233 Fax: 206/881-2296, Co Email: info@adic.com, Web URL: adic.com, Focus: LAN storage peripherals, Stk Sym: INTP, Founded: 1983, Empl: 120, Fiscal End: 10/95; Chuck Stonecipher, COO, Bill Britts, VP Mktng & Sales, Kari Matheny, PR Coord

Advanced Digital Systems (ADS), 13909 Bettencourt St, Cerritos CA 90703 USA; 310/926-1928, 800/888-5244 Fax: 310/926-0518, Web URL: ads-mm.com, Focus: PC to video converter, Prdts: Game Zapper, Ownrshp: PVT, Founded: 1991, Empl: 12, Sales ($M): 2, Mike McCoy, Pres, Scott Anderson, Reg Sales Mgr

Advanced Electronic Support Products Inc. 1810 NE 144th St, N Miami FL 33181 USA; 305/944-7710, Fax: 305/652-8489, Focus: LAN cabling products, Ownrshp: PVT, Founded: 1983, Empl: 40, Sales ($M): 6, Roman Briskin, Dir Int'l. Sales

Advanced Gravis Computer Technology Ltd. 101-3750 N Fraser Way, Burnaby BC V5J 5E9 Canada; 604/431-5020, Fax: 604/431-5155, Co Email: @gravis.com, Focus: Peripherals and security software, Ownrshp: Public, Stk Sym: GRVS-F, Founded: 1982, Empl: 160, Sales ($M): 23.5, Fiscal End: 1/94; Grant N. Russell, CTO, K. Michael Cooper, Pres & CEO, David T. Reid, VP Sales, Dennis Scott-Jackson, VP Dev, Bryan Del Rizzo, Marcom Exec

Advanced Hardware Architecture 2365 NE Hopkins Ct, Pullman WA 99163-5601 USA; 509/334-1000, Fax: 509/334-9000, Co Email: @aha.com, Web URL: aha.com, Focus: Data compression and error correction semiconductors, Ownrshp: PVT, Founded: 1988, Empl: 50, John Overby, Pres & CEO, Gordon Scott, CFO

Advanced Input Devices W 250 AID Dr, Coeur d'Alene ID 83814 USA; 208/765-8000, 800/444-5923 Fax: 208/772-7613, Web URL: advanced-input.com, Focus: Keyboards & data entry devices, Prdts: PanelKey, ErgoKey, MicroKey, Ownrshp: PVT, Founded: 1979, Empl: 300, Sales ($M): 32, Fiscal End: 10/95; Frederic Zucker, Pres & CEO, Tim Teich, VP Sales & Mktng, Crawford Byxbee, VP Prod Eng, Bradley Garrett, VP Ops, Michael Wilson, VP Fin & CFO

Advanced Integration Research Inc. (AIR), 2188 Del Franco St, San Jose CA 95131 USA; 408/428-0800, Fax: 408/428-0950, Focus: PC motherboards and adapter boards, Ownrshp: PVT, Founded: 1988, Jimmy Lee, Pres, Thomas Nguyen, VP Eng, Chuck Brush, VP Sales & Mktng

Advanced Logic Research (ALR), 9401 Jeronimo Rd, Irvine CA 92718 USA; 714/581-6770, 800/444-4257 Fax: 714/581-9240, Web URL: alr.com, Focus: PCs and LAN servers, Ownrshp: OTC, Stk Sym: AALR, Founded: 1984, Empl: 475, Sales ($M): 192.4, Fiscal End: 9/95; Gene Lu, Chmn, Pres & CEO, Ronald J. Sipkovich, VP & CFO, David G. Kirkey, VP Sales & Mktng, David L. Kelly, VP HW Eng, Vic Sangveraphunsiri, VP Syst Eng

Advanced Matrix Technology Inc. (AMT), 747 Calle Plano, Camarillo CA 93012-8556 USA; 805/388-5799, Fax: 805/484-

5282, Focus: PC printers, Ownrshp: PVT, Founded: 1982, Empl: 75, Joseph Eichberger, Pres

Advanced Micro Devices Inc. (AMD), 1 AMD Place, PO Box 3453, Sunnyvale CA 94088-3453 USA; 408/732-2400, Web URL: amd.com, Focus: Integrated circuits, Ownrshp: NYSE, Stk Sym: AMD, Founded: 1969, Empl: 11,800, Sales ($M): 2,429.7, Fiscal End: 12/95; Jerry Sanders III, Chmn & CEO, Richard Previte, Pres & COO, Gene Conner, SVP Ops, Stephen Zelencik, SVP & CMO, Joseph Proctor, VP Info Syst, John Wilkinson, Email: john_wilkinson@amd.com

Advanced Processing Labs Inc. 5871 Oberlin Dr, San Diego CA 92121-3745 USA; 619/546-8626, Fax: 619/546-0278, Focus: Real-time systems, Ownrshp: PVT, Founded: 1985, Empl: 80, Sales ($M): 10, Douglas A. Giese, Pres

Advanced RISC Machines (ARM), 985 University Ave, #5, Los Gatos CA 95030 USA; 408/399-5199, Fax: 408/399-8854, Web URL: arm.com, Focus: ARM RISC processors, Ownrshp: Sub ARM, UK, Founded: 1990, Empl: 130, Tim O'Donnell, Pres

Advanced Software Development Corp. 203 Westside Blvd, Houma LA 70364 USA; 504/851-6600, 800/859-6607 Focus: Business and accounting automation software, Prdts: U.A. Accounting, Founded: 1993

Advanced Visual Systems Inc. 300 Fifth Ave, Waltham MA 02154 USA; 617/890-4300, 800/728-1600 Fax: 617/890-8287, Web URL: avs.com, Focus: Visualization software, Prdts: Application Visualization System (AVS), Developers AVS, Ownrshp: PVT, Founded: 1992, Empl: 110, John W. Poduska, Chmn, George F. Brandt, Pres & CEO, David Kamins, VP Eng, David Craig, VP Sales, Christopher B. Andrews, VP & CFO

Advantage kbs Inc. (AKBS), 1 Ethel Rd, #106B, Edison NJ 08817 USA; 908/287-2236, 800/252-7937 Fax: 908/287-3193, Co Email: info@akbs.com, Web URL: akbs.com, Focus: Problem resolution software and customer support automation services, Prdts: IQSupport Application Suite, Ownrshp: PVT, Founded: 1988, Empl: 42, Sales ($M): 5.0, Fiscal End: 12/95; DeJean Melancon Jr., Pres, Email: dmelancon@akbs.com; Eileen Lynch Weinstein, VP Eng, Email: eweinstein@akbs.com; Dina Barr, Dir Mktng, Email: dbarr@akbs.com; Bill Lund, Sys Admin, Email: blund@akbs.com

AEC Software Inc. 22611-113 Markey Ct, Sterling VA 22170 USA; 703/450-1980, 800/346-9413 Fax: 703/450-9786, Focus: Project management software, Prdts: FastTrack, Ownrshp: PVT, Founded: 1986, Empl: 12, Dennis Bilowus, Pres, Kurt D. Wyckoff, Dir Sales & Mktng

Aeon Systems Inc. 8401 Washington Place NE, Albuquerque NM 87113 USA; 505/828-9120, Fax: 505/828-9115, Focus: Alpha single-board computers, Ownrshp: PVT, Steve Kadner, Pres, Mark Bronson

AER Energy Resources Inc. 4600 Highlands Pkwy #G, Smyrna GA 30082 USA; 404/433-2127, Fax: 404/433-2286, Focus: Batteries for portable computers, Ownrshp: OTC, Stk Sym: AERN, Founded: 1989, Sales ($M): 48.5, Fiscal End: 12/94; Jon A. Lindseth, Chmn, David W. Dorheim, Pres & CEO, M. Beth Donley, VP & CFO, Frank M. Harris, VP Mktng & Sales, Email: 74164.2372@compuserve.com

AG Communication Systems Corp. PO Box 52179, Phoenix AZ 85072-2179 USA; 602/582-7000, Focus: Digital communication switches and network products, Prdts: GTD-5 Switching Systems, INgage Advanced Intelligent Network Products, Ownrshp: Sub. AT&T & GTE, Founded: 1891, Empl: 1,900, Sales ($M): 320, Fiscal End: 12/95; W.M. Applegate, Pres & CEO, J.W. Seigel, VP Mktng

Ag Group Inc., The 2540 Camino Diablo, #200, Walnut Creek CA 94596 USA; 510/937-7900, 800/466-2447 Fax: 510/937-2479, Co Email: info@aggroup.com, Web URL: aggroup.com, Focus: Network products, Prdts: EtherPeek, Skyline/Satellite, Netmeter, Ownrshp: PVT, Founded: 1990, Mahboud Zabetian, Pres &

CEO, Janice Spampinato, VP Sales & Mktng

AGE Logic Inc. 12651 High Bluff Dr, San Diego CA 92130 USA; 619/755-1000, Fax: 619/755-3998, Focus: X Window software, Prdts: Xoftware, Ownrshp: PVT, Founded: 1984, Empl: 60, Peter J. Shaw, Pres & CEO, Robert S. Alford, VP, Robert E. Astley, VP Sales, Charles B. Rice, VP & Tech Dir, Charles F. Kimmel, VP & CFO, Susan Eppel

Agfa 208 Ballardvale St, Wilmington MA 01887 USA; 508/658-5600, Fax: 508/658-4193, Focus: Imaging products, Ownrshp: Sub. Miles, Founded: 1960

aha!software corp. 1685 Plymouth St, Mountain View CA 94043 USA; 415/988-2080, 800/242-7638 Fax: 415/988-2081, Co Email: 426.2752@mcimail.com, Focus: Electronic ink software, Prdts: InkWriter, Ownrshp: PVT, Gregory Stikeleather, Pres & CEO, Email: 426.2752@mcimail.com

AIB Software Corp. 46030 Manekin Plaza, #160, Sterling VA 22170 USA; 703/430-9247, Fax: 703/450-4560, Co Email: info@aib.com, Focus: Unix software tools, Prdts: Sentinel, Ownrshp: PVT, Founded: 1993, Empl: 20, Adam C. Joseph, Pres, Email: adam.joseph@aib.com; Stan Joseph, CEO, Email: stan.joseph@aib.com; Michael S. Simon, VP Sales, Email: mike.simon@aib.com; Conor P. Cahill, VP Eng, Email: conor.cahill@aib.com

Aim Technology 4699 Old Ironsides Dr, #400, Santa Clara CA 95054-1828 USA; 408/748-8649, Fax: 408/748-0161, Co Email: @aim.com, Focus: Unix performance measurement, system management, network file management, Ownrshp: PVT, Founded: 1981, Empl: 18, Jim Geers, Pres, Email: jim@aim.com; Paul V. Farr, VP & GM, Email: paul@aim.com; Tammy L. Bauer, Dir, Email: tammy@aim.com; Melanie Deane, Mgr Corp Admin, Email: melanie@aim.com

Aimnet Corp. 2350 Mission College Blvd, #600, Santa Clara CA 95054-1542 USA; 408/257-0900, Fax: 408/257-5452, Co Email: info@aimnet.co, Web URL: aimnet.com, Focus: Internet access, tools and services, Ownrshp: PVT, Founded: 1994, Empl: 16, Hong Chen, CEO, Stuart Froman, Dir Mktng

AimTech Corp. 20 Trafalgar Sq., #300, Nashua NH 03063-1987 USA; 603/883-0220, 800/289-2884 Fax: 603/883-5582, Focus: Multimedia software, Prdts: IconAuthor, Ownrshp: PVT, Founded: 1984, Empl: 75, Sales ($M): 6.1, Andrew J. Huffman, Pres & CEO, Elaine LeBlanc, SVP, Leo Lucas, CTO, Jack Slavin, VP Sales, David Conti, Dir Marcom

AIQ Systems Inc. PO Drawer 7530, Incline Village NV 89450 USA; 702/831-2999, Fax: 702/831-6784, Focus: Expert system software for financial industry, Prdts: MarketExpert, StockExpert, TradingExpert, Ownrshp: PVT, Founded: 1984, Empl: 24, Sales ($M): 3, Fiscal End: 12/93; Mitch R. Legarza, CEO, Sandy Junell, VP Finance

Aironet Wireless Communications Inc. 367 Ghent Rd, #300, Fairlawn OH 44333 USA; 330/665-7900, Fax: 330/665-7922, Co Email: sales@aironet.com, Focus: Wireless LAN products, Ownrshp: Sub Telxon, Founded: 1982, Roger J. Murphy, Pres & CEO, William D. Huhn, EVP & COO, William J. Brodnick, CFO

Airsoft Inc. 20833 Stevens Creek Blvd, #200, Cupertino CA 95014 USA; 408/777-7500, 800/708-4247 Fax: 408/777-7527, Co Email: info@airsoft.com, Web URL: airsoft.com, Focus: Networking software, Prdts: Powerburst, Ownrshp: PVT, Founded: 1993, Empl: 18, Jagdeep Singh, Pres & CEO, Email: jagdeep@airsoft.com; Gary Krall, VP Mktng, Email: gary@airsoft.com; Kent Jarvi, CFO, Email: jarvi@airsoft.com; Don Oestreicher, VP Eng, Email: dono@airsoft.com

AirTouch Communications 1 California St, 30th Fl., San Francisco CA 94111 USA; 415/658-2000, Fax: 415/658-2034, Focus: Cellular, paging and wireless services, Ownrshp: NYSE, Stk Sym: ATI, Founded: 1994, Empl: 4,700, Sales ($M): 1,590.3, Fiscal End: 12/95; Sam Ginn, Chmn & CEO, C. Lee Cox, Pres & COO, Arun Sarin, SVP Corp Dev, F. Craig Farrill, VP Tech Plng & Dev, Mohan

Gyani, EVP & CFO

AirWorks Media One Thornton Ct #700, Edmonton Alberta T5J 2E7 Canada; 403/424-9922, 800/525-5962 Fax: 403/424-9993, Co Email: airworks@supernet.ab.ca, Web URL: tunebldr@supernet.ab.ea, Focus: Auto-editing music software, Prdts: TuneBuilder, Founded: 1987, Empl: 39, Darryl Goede, Chmn, Pres & CEO, Nancy Goede, VP Corp Affairs, Harland Kirby, VP Mktng, Steve Fleming, Mgr Ops, Marlene Davis, Mgr Comm

AITech International Corp. 47971 Fremont Blvd, Fremont CA 94538-6508 USA; 510/226-8960, 800/882-8184 Fax: 510/226-8996, Web URL: aitech.com, Focus: Desktop video and multimedia products, Ownrshp: PVT, Founded: 1987, Empl: 53, Sales ($M): 4, Michael Chen, Chmn & Pres, Mark Wodyka, VP Sales & Mktng, Jerry Huang, Prod Mktng Mgr

AIWA America 800 Corporate Dr, Mahwah NJ 07430 USA; 201/512-3600, Fax: 201/512-3704, Focus: Electronics, tape drives and data products, Prdts: AIWA/Core LightningArray, Ownrshp: Div. AIWA Japan, Nario Nagano, VP Sales & Mktng

Aladdin Knowledge Systems 350 Fifth Ave, #6614, New York NY 10118 USA; 212/564-5678, 800/223-4277 Fax: 212/564-3377, Focus: Software security products, Prdts: HASP, Ownrshp: OTC, Stk Sym: ALDNF, Founded: 1985, Empl: 60, Yanki Margalit, Pres, David Glassman, VP Mktng & Sales, Shai Saul, VP Bus Dev

Aladdin System Inc. 165 Westridge Dr, Watsonville CA 95076 USA; 408/761-6200, Fax: 408/761-6206, Co Email: info@aladdin.com, Web URL: aladdinsys.com, Focus: Macintosh utilities and development tools, Prdts: StuffIt, SITcomm, Installermaker, Ownrshp: PVT, Founded: 1988, Empl: 90, Marco A. Gonzalez, Pres, Email: marco@aladdinsys.com; Darryl Lovato, Dir Dev Tech, Email: dlovato@aladdinsys.com; Jonathan Kahn, Dir Sales & Mktng, Email: jonkahn@aladdinsys.com; Jennifer Lyng, PR, Email: jennifer@aladdinsys.com

Alantec Corp. 2115 O'Nel Dr, San Jose CA 95131-2032 USA; 408/955-9000, 800/252-6832 Fax: 408/955-9500, Co Email: powerhub@alantec.com, Web URL: alantec.com, Focus: LAN switches, Prdts: PowerHub, PowerBits, PowerSight, PowerCell, Ownrshp: OTC, Stk Sym: ALTC, Founded: 1987, Empl: 200, Sales ($M): 25.1, Fiscal End: 12/94; George Archuleta, Pres & CEO, Email: arch@alantec.com; John Wakerly, EVP & CTO, Email: jfw@alantec.com; Patrick Klein, VP Sales, Email: aklein@alantec.com; Allen Sadler, VP Ops, Email: sadler@alantec.com; Patrick Royan, VP & CFO, Email: royan@alantec.com; Barbara Reichert, Acct Exec, Email: barbarar@alantec.com

Alaras Corp. 1910 Sedwick Rd, #300-D, Research Triangle Pk NC 27709-4562 USA; 919/544-1228, Fax: 919/544-7772, Focus: Pre-press and graphics software, Ownrshp: PVT, Founded: 1991, Michael Hoffman, Pres

Alaris Inc. 47338 Fremont Blvd, Fremont CA 94538 USA; 510/770-5700, Fax: 510/770-5769, Web URL: alaris.com, Focus: PCs, motherboards and peripherals, Prdts: QuickVideo, Ownrshp: PVT, Founded: 1991, Raymond Yu, Pres, Philip Lau, VP, Johnny Lee, VP, Don Dea, VP, David Todd, Mktng Mgr

Aldridge Company, The 2500 CityWest Blvd, #575, Houston TX 77042 USA; 713/953-1940, 800/548-5019 Fax: 713/953-0806, Co Email: aldridgeco@aol.com, Focus: Utility software, Prdts: PreCursor, Tree86, Cache86, Ownrshp: PVT, Founded: 1984, Empl: 10, David L. Aldridge, Pres, Valerie Burson, VP, Terry Canup, VP Mktng, Valerie Burson

Alexander Communications Inc. 400 Colony Square, #980, Atlanta GA 30361 USA; 404/897-2300, Fax: 404/897-2311, Web URL: alexander-pr.com, Focus: PR and marketing communications, Ownrshp: PVT, Empl: 40, Pam Alexander, Pres

Algor Inc. 150 Beta Dr, Pittsburgh PA 15238 USA; 412/967-2700, Fax: 412/967-2781, Web URL: algor.com, Focus: Graphics and CAD software, Ownrshp: PVT, Founded: 1982, Empl: 67, Sales ($M): 9.1, Fiscal End: 12/95; Michael L. Bussler, Pres, Virginia A. Goebel, CFO

AliMed Inc. 297 High St, Dedham MA 02026 USA; 617/329-2900, Fax: 617/329-8392, Focus: Ergonomics products, Prdts: Keyboard wrist rest, Ownrshp: PVT, Julian Cherubini, Pres, Barry Nyer, Mktng Dir

Aliroo America Inc. 151 Woodlake Dr, #608, Woodbury NY 11797 USA; 516/496-3599, Fax: 516/496-4666, Focus: Scrambling/descrambling software, Prdts: PrivaSoft, Ownrshp: PVT

Allegiant Technologies Inc. 9740 Scranton Rd, #300, San Diego CA 92121-1745 USA; 619/587-0500, 800/255-8258 Fax: 619/587-1314, Co Email: info@allegiant.com, Web URL: allegiant.com, Focus: Multimedia authoring tools, Prdts: SuperCard, Marionet, Ownrshp: OTC, Stk Sym: ALGT, Founded: 1993, Empl: 30, Joel Staadecker, Pres & CEO, Email: staad@allegiant.com; Stuart Henigson, VP Mktng, Email: stuart_henigson@allegiant.com; Kevin La Rue, Dir Mkt Dev, Email: kevin_larue@allegiant.com; Bill Gordon, Dir WW Sales, Email: bill_gordon@allegiant.com

Allen Communication 5 Triad Ctr 5th Fl., Salt Lake City UT 84180-1102 USA; 801/537-7800, 800/325-7850 Fax: 801/537-7805, Co Email: info@allencomm.com, Web URL: allencomm.com, Focus: Multimedia software and custom development, Prdts: Quest Multimedia Authoring System, Designer's Edge, Ownrshp: Sub. Times Mirror, Founded: 1981, Empl: 110, Steven W. Allen, CEO, Email: sallen@allencomm.com; Ron Johnson, Prod Dev, Email: rjohnson@allencomm.com; Rex Allen, Pres, Email: rallen@allencomm.com; Larry Cleary, VP Sales & Mktng, Britta Glade, PR Mgr, Email: bglade@allencomm.com

Allen Systems Group (ASG), 750 11th St S, Naples FL 33940 USA; 941/435-2200, 800/932-5536 Fax: 941/263-3692, Web URL: allensysgroup.com, Focus: Enterprise system management, Web development tools, Prdts: ASG-IMPACT, Webgalaxy, Ownrshp: PVT, Founded: 1986, Empl: 200, Arthur Allen, Pres & CEO, Fred Roberts, VP & CFO, Brian Bisa, VP Mktng, Larry Goddard, VP Sales, Ellen Snelling, Dir Marcom

Allerion Inc. 10 Bloomfield Ave, Pine Brook NJ 07058-9724 USA; 201/877-1000, Fax: 201/887-5981, Focus: Network integration, Ownrshp: NYSE, Stk Sym: ALI, Founded: 1978, Empl: 300, Sales ($M): 84, Fiscal End: 4/94; Michael J. O'Donnell, Chmn, Pres & CEO, Alexander W. Giles Jr., EVP & CFO

Alliance Manufacturing Software Inc. 18 Anacapa St, PO Box 2009, Santa Barbara CA 93120-2009 USA; 805/965-3000, 800/490-2520 Fax: 805/957-4555, Focus: Single & multi-user material resource planning software, Prdts: E-Z-MRP, Ownrshp: PVT, Founded: 1983, William Urschel, Chmn, William Urschel, Pres, Jim Diamond, Dir Dev, Locke Urschel, Dir Sales

Alliance Semiconductor 3099 N First St, San Jose CA 95134 USA; 408/383-4900, Fax: 408/383-4999, Focus: Memory products and memory-intensive logic products, Prdts: ProMotion, Ownrshp: OTC, Stk Sym: ALSC, Sid Agrawal, VP Mktng, Spencer Greene, Email: sgreene@nimbus.com

AllMicro Inc. 18820 US Hwy 19 N #215, Clearwater FL 34616 USA; 813/539-7283, 800/653-4933 Fax: 813/539-7283, Co Email: allmicro@ix.netcom.com, Web URL: allmicro.com, Focus: Disk data recovery software, Prdts: Rescue Data Recovery, Troubleshooter PC Diagnostics, LAN Designer, Ownrshp: PVT, Founded: 1991, Empl: 80, Sales ($M): 5.5, Michael Kaplan, Pres, Jamie Sene, VP Mktng, Joe Webb, VP Sales, Rick Gertsen, GM

Allodyne Inc. 47000 Warm Springs Blvd, #505, Fremont CA 94539-7467 USA; 510/770-1101, Fax: 510/770-1102, Focus: Disk arrays, Ownrshp: PVT, Founded: 1991, Empl: 14, Yin So, Pres

AllPen Software 51 University Ave, #J, Los Gatos CA 95030 USA; 408/399-8800, Fax: 408/399-4395, Web URL: allpen.com, Focus: PDA software, Prdts: NetHopper, Ownrshp: PVT, Wayne Yurtin, Co-Founder

AlltelCorp. 1 Allied Dr, Little Rock AR 72202 USA; 501/661-8000, Fax: 501/661-8487, Web URL: alltel.com, Focus: Telephone service, information and communication products, Ownrshp: NYSE, Stk Sym: AT, Founded: 1960, Empl: 16,300, Sales ($M): 3,109.7, Fiscal End: 12/95; Joe T. Ford, Chmn, Pres & CEO, Dennis J. Ferra, SVP, John E. Steuri, CEO Alltel Info Svcs, Michael T. Flynn, Pres Com Group, Tom T. Orsini, SVP Fin & Dev, Ronald D. Payne, VP Corp Com

ALOS Micrographics Corp. 118 Bracken Rd, Montgomery NY 12549-2604 USA; 914/457-4400, 800/431-7105 Fax: 914/457-9083, Co Email: 75052.2760@compuserve.com, Focus: Image software, Prdts: DocuWare, Ownrshp: PVT, Founded: 1977, Empl: 30, Urs B. Kopp, Pres, Gregory J. Schloemer, VP

Alpha Microsystems 2722 S Fairview St, Santa Ana CA 92704 USA; 714/957-8500, Fax: 714/957-8705, Web URL: alphamicro.com, Focus: Information technology products & services concentrating on vertical markets, Ownrshp: OTC, Stk Sym: ALMI, Founded: 1977, Empl: 369, Sales ($M): 38.8, Fiscal End: 2/94; Clark E. Reynolds, Chmn, Douglas J. Tullio, Pres & CEO, Email: dtullio@alphamicro.com; John F. Glade, VP Eng & Mfg, Email: jfglade@alphamicro.com; Michael J. Lowell, VP & CFO

Alpha Systems Lab Inc. (ASL), 2361 McGaw Ave, Irvine CA 92714-5831 USA; 714/252-0117, Fax: 714/252-0887, Focus: PCs and multimedia products, Prdts: Transformer, Cyber Audio, Ownrshp: PVT, Founded: 1990, Empl: 60, Sales ($M): 40, Fiscal End: 12/94; Rose Hwang, Pres & CEO, Mitchell Phan

Alpha Technologies 3767 Alpha Way, Bellingham WA 98226-8302 USA; 360/647-2360, 800/421-8089 Fax: 360/671-4936, Web URL: alpha-us.com, Focus: Power protection and back-up power products, Prdts: XM Cable UPS, BPS Broadband Power Systems, CFR UPS, Ownrshp: PVT, Founded: 1975, Empl: 700, Sales ($M): 100, Fiscal End: 12/95; Richard Williams, CFO, James Clark, VP & GM, Dale Jones, VP Sales & Svc, William Campbell, VP Mktng, Eric Wentz, Marcom Mgr

AlphaBlox Corp. 168 Middlesex, Burlington MA 01803 USA; 617/229-2924, Focus: Global component software, Prdts: OfficeBlox, Ownrshp: Div. Alpha Software Corp., Michael Skok, Chmn, Selwyn Rabins, Co-Chmn, Mary Regan

ALPS America 3553 N First St, San Jose CA 95134-1898 USA; 408/432-6000, 800/825-2577 Fax: 408/432-6035, Focus: Printers, plotters and scanners, Ownrshp: Sub. Alps Electric USA, Founded: 1985, Harvey Labban, Dir Mktng

Alta Research Corp. 600 S Federal Hwy, Deerfield Beach FL 33441 USA; 305/428-8538, 800/423-8535 Fax: 305/428-8678, Focus: PC network cards, Ownrshp: PVT, Founded: 1992, Fred Thiel, VP Mktng & Sales

Altec Lansing Consumer Products Rt 6 & 209, Milford PA 18337-0277 USA; 717/296-2818, Focus: Computer speaker systems, Founded: 1927, Andrew Bergstein, Email: axb35@email.psu.edu

Altera Corp. 2610 Orchard Pkwy, San Jose CA 95134-2020 USA; 408/894-7000, Fax: 408/248-6924, Web URL: altera.com, Focus: User configured ICs, Ownrshp: OTC, Stk Sym: ALTR, Founded: 1983, Empl: 667, Sales ($M): 401.6, Fiscal End: 12/95; Rodney Smith, Chmn, Pres & CEO, Erik Cleage, VP Mktng, James Sansbury, VP Tech, Peter Smyth, VP Sales, Thomas J. Nicoletti, VP & CFO

Alternative Resources Corp. (ARC), 75 Tri-State Int'l. #100, Lincolnshire IL 60069-4435 USA; 708/317-1000, Focus: Technical staffing services, Ownrshp: OTC, Stk Sym: ALRC, Founded: 1988, Empl: 1,200, Sales ($M): 53.1, Fiscal End: 12/93; Larry I. Kane, Pres & CEO, Daniel J. Weinfurter, EVP, Michael E. Harris, VP & CFO

Altima Systems Inc. 2440 Stanwell Dr, Concord CA 94520-4811 USA; 800/356-9990 Fax: 415/356-2408, Focus: Laptop and notebook PCs, Ownrshp: PVT, Founded: 1989, Go Sugiura, Chmn, Steve Hagman, VP Ops, Rene Lopas, Nat'l. Sales Mgr

Alydaar Software Corp. 6701 Carmel Rd, #302, Charlotte NC 28226-3983 USA; 704/544-0092, Fax: 704/544-0260, Co Email: alydaar@vnet.net, Focus: Software reengineering services, Year 2000 conversion services, artificial intelligence, Ownrshp: Public,

Stk Sym: ALYD, Founded: 1982, Empl: 15, Sales ($M): 10, Fiscal End: 12/95; Robert F. Gruder, Pres, Frank W. Bachinsky, VP, E. Rust Muirhead, Secretary

AM International Inc. 9399 W Higgins Rd, #900, Rosemont IL 60018 USA; 847/818-1294, Fax: 847/818-3499, Focus: Graphics equipment, Ownrshp: NYSE, Stk Sym: AM, Founded: 1924, Empl: 2,900, Sales ($M): 509.5, Chmn, Pres & CEO, Richard J. Bonnie, Pres AM Graphics, Steven R. Andrews, VP, Thomas D. Rooney, VP & CFO

Amcom Corp. 6205 Bury Dr, Eden Prairie MN 55346 USA; 612/949-9400, 800/328-7723 Fax: 612/949-0750, Focus: Software, reseller and service for midrange computers, Ownrshp: PVT, Founded: 1983, Empl: 120, Sales ($M): 18.7

Amdahl Corp. 1250 E Arques Ave, PO Box 3470, Sunnyvale CA 94088-3470 USA; 408/746-6000, 800/538-8460 Fax: 408/773-0833, Web URL: amdahl.com, Focus: Hardware, software and service for IBM-compatible and open systems computing environments, Prdts: Millennium, Spectris, Huron Object Star, UTS, Ownrshp: AMEX, Stk Sym: AMH, Founded: 1970, Empl: 8,000, Sales ($M): 1,516.4, Fiscal End: 12/95; John C. Lewis, Chmn, E. Joseph Zemke, Pres & CEO, Bruce J. Ryan, EVP & CFO, David L. Anderson, EVP, Tama H. Olver, VP Info Svcs, A. William Stewart, Dir Fin & PR

America Online Inc. 8619 Westwood Ctr Dr, Vienna VA 22182-2285 USA; 703/448-8700, 800/827-6364 Fax: 703/883-1509, Web URL: blue.aol.com, Focus: Online services for over 3M subscribers, Prdts: America Online, Ownrshp: OTC, Stk Sym: AMER, Founded: 1985, Empl: 3,000, Sales ($M): 1,093.9, Fiscal End: 6/96; Ted Leonsis, SVP & Pres. AOL Svcs Co, Stephen M. Case, Chmn & CEO, Michael M. Connors, SVP & Pres. AOL Technologies, John L. Davies, SVP & Pres. AOL Int'l, David Cole, SVP & Pres. AOL Enterprise Sol, Jean N. Villanueva, VP Corp Comm

American Advantech Corp. 750 E Arques Ave, Sunnyvale CA 94086 USA; 408/245-6678, Fax: 408/245-8368, Focus: I/O boards, Ownrshp: PVT, Founded: 1982, Empl: 300, Y.M. Hwang, Pres, Thomas Chen, VP Mktng

American Business Systems Inc. 315 Littleton Rd, Chelmsford MA 01824 USA; 508/250-9600, 800/356-4034 Fax: 508/250-8027, Focus: Business management software, Prdts: ABS Accounting Systems, ABS Point of Sale System, Ownrshp: PVT, Founded: 1978, Empl: 18, James O. Hamilton, Pres, Jim Hanlon, Mktng Mgr, Richard Martin, Nat'l Sales Mgr

American Computer Resources 155 Research Dr, Stratford CT 06497 USA; 203/380-4600, Fax: 203/380-4622, Co Email: sales@the-acr.com, Web URL: the-acr.com, Focus: International PC distributor, Ownrshp: PVT, Founded: 1983, Empl: 30, Sales ($M): 65, Hubert A. Bowen Jr., Pres, Email: bbowen@the-acr.com; Steven A. Bowen, COO, Ronald J. Verrilli, CFO, Richard T. Kenny, Tech/Svc Mgr, Email: rkenny@the-acr.com; Leslie A. Kenny, Mktng Coord, Email: lkenny@the-acr.com

American Electronics Assoc. (AEA), 5201 Great America Pkwy, #520, Santa Clara CA 95054 USA; 408/987-4200, Fax: 408/970-8565, Co Email: @aeanet.org, Web URL: aeanet.org, Focus: Serves and represents the nation's electronics industry, Ownrshp: Nonprofit, Founded: 1943, Empl: 3,500

American Facsimile Assoc. (AFA), 2200 Ben Franklin Pkwy #N-108, Philadelphia PA 19130 USA; 215/981-0292, Fax: 215/981-0295, Focus: Information for fax industry, Ownrshp: Nonprofit, Founded: 1986, Gerard Brodsky, Pres

American Healthware Systems Inc. 4522 Fort Hamilton Pkwy, Brooklyn NY 11219 USA; 718/435-6300, Fax: 718/435-0275, Focus: Computer services to the health care industry, Prdts: Eagle 2000, Ownrshp: PVT, Founded: 1988, Empl: 70, Sales ($M): 16, Fiscal End: 9/95; George Weinberger, Pres, Daniel J. Malcolm, SVP & COO

American Internet Corp. 4 Preston Ct, Bedford MA 01730 USA; 617/276-4500, Fax: 617/275-4930, Web URL: ameri-can.com, Focus: Software for Web site construction for Novell NetWare, Ownrshp: PVT, Founded: 1995, Empl: 32, Brad Parket, Founder, Throop Wilder, Founder & CEO

American Management Systems (AMS), 4050 Legato Rd, Fairfax VA 22033 USA; 703/267-8000, Fax: 703/267-5067, Web URL: amsinc.com, Focus: Systems integration and consulting services, Prdts: Advanced Consumer Lending System, BureauLink, Strata, Ownrshp: OTC, Stk Sym: AMSY, Founded: 1970, Empl: 6,000, Sales ($M): 460, Fiscal End: 12/94; Paul A. Brands, CEO, Frank A. Nicolai, EVP & CFO, Charles O. Rossotti, Chmn, Patrick W. Gross, Vice Chmn, Philip Giuntini, Pres, Charlene Baldwin, Mgr Corp PR

American Megatrends Inc. 6145-F Northbelt Pkwy, Norcross GA 30071-2972 USA; 770/263-8181, 800/828-9264 Fax: 770/263-9381, Web URL: aim.com, Focus: PC motherboards and BIOS, Ownrshp: PVT, Founded: 1985, Empl: 120, Subramonian Shanker, Pres, Pat Sarma, EVP, Joe P. Leader, Mktng Mgr, Email: joel@american.megatrends.com

American Mobile Telecommunications Assoc. (AMTA), 1150 18th St, #250, Washington DC 20036 USA; 202/331-7773, Fax: 202/331-9062, Focus: Association for wireless industry, Ownrshp: Nonprofit

American Power Conversion (APC), 132 Fairgrounds Rd, PO Box 278, W Kingston RI 02892 USA; 401/789-5735, 800/877-4080 Fax: 401/789-3710, Co Email: apcc.com, Web URL: apcc.com, Focus: Uninterruptible power supplies, Prdts: Back-UPS, Back-UPS Pro, Smart-UPS, Matrix-UPS, Surge Arrest, Ownrshp: OTC, Stk Sym: APCC, Founded: 1981, Empl: 2,400 WW, Sales ($M): 378.2, Fiscal End: 12/94; Roger B. Dowdell Jr., Chmn, Pres & CEO, David P. Vieau, VP WW Mkt Dev, Edward W. Machala, VP Ops, Darrell Lucente, VP Sales, Neil M. Rasmussen, VP, Aaron Davis, VP Corp Comm

American Small Business Computers Inc. 1 American Way, Pryor OK 74361-8801 USA; 918/825-4844, Fax: 918/825-6359, Co Email: 70131.200@compuserve.com, Focus: CAD software, Prdts: DesignCAD, Ownrshp: PVT, Founded: 1980, Empl: 35, Sales ($M): 13.5, Bruce M. Taylor, Pres, Robert E. Webster, VP, Keith Campbell, VP Mktng, Craig Hendrickson, VP

American Society for Information Science (ASIS), 8720 Georgia Ave, #501, Silver Spring MD 20910 USA; 301/495-0900, Fax: 301/495-0810, Focus: Improve access to information through policy, technology and research, Ownrshp: Nonprofit, Founded: 1937, Empl: 3,700, Clifford Lynch, Pres

American Software Inc. 470 E Paces Ferry Rd, Atlanta GA 30305 USA; 404/264-5296, Fax: 404/264-5206, Web URL: amsoftware.com, Focus: Business application software, Ownrshp: OTC, Stk Sym: AMSWA, Founded: 1971, Empl: 600, Sales ($M): 77.6, Fiscal End: 4/96; Thomas L. Newberry, Chmn, James C. Edenfield, Pres & CEO, J. Michael Edenfield, EVP & COO, Lawrence A. Mueller, SVP WW Ops, Joseph L. Wiley, VP & CFO, Carla W. Myer

American Software Users Group (ASUG), 401 N Michigan Ave, Chicago IL 60611-4267 USA; 312/644-6610, Fax: 312/321-6869, Focus: Users of American Software's products, Ownrshp: Nonprofit, Founded: 1981, Empl: 2,000

AmeriQuest Technologies Inc. 2722 Michelson Dr, Irvine CA 92715 USA; 714/222-6000, Fax: 714/549-4004, Focus: Distributor of PC products, Ownrshp: NYSE, Stk Sym: AQS, Founded: 1983, Empl: 190, Sales ($M): 87.6, Fiscal End: 6/94; Harry Krischik, Chmn

Ameritech Corp. 30 S Wacker Dr, Chicago IL 60606 USA; 312/750-5000, 800/275-0902 Fax: 312/207-0016, Co Email: @ameritech.com, Web URL: ameritech.com, Focus: Regional Bell operating company (RBOC), Ownrshp: NYSE, Stk Sym: AIT, Founded: 1983, Empl: 65,345, Sales ($M): 13,427.8, Fiscal End: 12/95; Richard C. Notebaert, Chmn & CEO, W. Patrick Campbell, EVP Bus Dev, Oren G. Shaffer, EVP & CFO, John E. Vaughn, Pres Info

Ind Svcs, Joel S. Engel, VP Tech, Rita P. Wilson, SVP Corp Com

Amiable Technologies Inc. Scott Plaza 2, #625, Philadelphia PA 19113 USA; 800/668-1920 Focus: CAD software, Prdts: Flexi-CAD, FlexiSign, Ownrshp: PVT, Founded: 1987, Faith Boyle

AMP Inc. PO Box 3608, Harrisburg PA 17105-3608 USA; 717/564-0100, 800/522-6752 Fax: 717/780-6130, Web URL: amp.com, Focus: Electronic connectors and peripherals, Ownrshp: NYSE, Stk Sym: AMP, Founded: 1941, Empl: 42,000, Sales ($M): 5,227.2, Fiscal End: 12/95; James E. Marley, Chmn, William J. Hudson, Pres & CEO, Ted L. Dalrymple, VP Global Mktng, Dean Hooper, VP US Sales & Mktng, Robert Ripp, VP & CFO, Merrill A. Yohe, VP Pub Affairs

Amquest Corp. 705 Olde Hickory Rd, Lancaster PA 17601 USA; 717/569-8030, Fax: 717/569-8530, Focus: Modems and fax/modems, Ownrshp: PVT, Robert A. Norman, Pres

Amrel Technology Inc. 11801 Goldring Rd, Arcadia CA 91006 USA; 818/303-6688, Fax: 818/303-8538, Focus: Modular notebook computers, Prdts: ROCKY, Dana O'Donnell, Mkt Dev Mgr

Amtex Software Corp. PO Box 572, Belleville Ontario K8N 5B2 Canada; 613/967-7900, 800/810-7345 Fax: 613/967-7902, Web URL: trlos.ca/.ca, Focus: Entertainment software, Prdts: Gone Fishin', Tristan, Eight Ball Deluxe, Royal Flush, Ownrshp: PVT, Founded: 1991, Empl: 22, Peter Zuuring, Pres & CEO, Shawn Kehoe, CFO, Lisa Moore, PR Mgr

Anacomp Inc. 11550 N Meridian St, PO Box 40888, Indianapolis IN 46240 USA; 317/844-9666, 800/350-3044 Co Email: @anacomp.com, Web URL: anacomp.com, Focus: Micrographic equipment for banking industry, Ownrshp: NYSE, Stk Sym: AAC, Founded: 1968, Empl: 3,600, Sales ($M): 591.2, Fiscal End: 9/95; Lang Lowrey, Pres & CEO, Paul G. Roland, Chmn, Jack R. O'Donnell, EVP & CFO, Michael H. Riley, VP Mktng, William C. Ater, VP & CAO, Jeff Withem

Analog and Digital Peripherals Inc. (ADPI), PO Box 499, Troy OH 45373 USA; 513/339-2241, 800/758-1041 Fax: 513/339-0070, Focus: PC tape and optical disk systems, Prdts: All on One, One for All Series, Read Runner, Ownrshp: PVT, Founded: 1978, Empl: 23, Lyle Elliott, Pres, May Keller, EVP, Jerry Davis, GM, Mickey Deitrick, Eng Mgr, May Keller, PR Coord

Analog Devices Inc. 1 Technology Way, PO Box 9106, Norwood MA 02062-9106 USA; 617/329-4700, Fax: 617/329-1241, Co Email: @analog.com, Web URL: analog.com, Focus: ICs and systems, Ownrshp: NYSE, Stk Sym: ADI, Founded: 1965, Empl: 5,400, Sales ($M): 941.5, Fiscal End: 10/95; Ray Stata, Chmn & CEO, Jerald G. Fishman, Pres & COO, Brian McAloon, VP Sales, Donald D. French, VP & GM Computer Prod, Joseph E. McDonough, VP & CFO, Al Haun, Mgr Marcom

Analogic Corp. 8 Centennial Dr, Peabody MA 01960 USA; 508/977-3000, Fax: 508/977-6811, Focus: Data conversion and signal processing products, Ownrshp: OTC, Stk Sym: ALOG, Founded: 1969, Empl: 1,400, Sales ($M): 208.8, Fiscal End: 7/95; Bernard M. Gordon, Chmn & CEO, Bruce R. Rusch, Pres & COO, M. Ross Brown, VP, Michael Rasmussen, VP SW Eng, John A. Tarello, SVP & Treasurer

Analysts International Corp. 7615 Metro Blvd, Minneapolis MN 55439-3050 USA; 612/835-5900, 800/800-5044 Fax: 612/835-4924, Web URL: analysts.com, Focus: Contract programming and software services, Ownrshp: OTC, Stk Sym: ANLY, Founded: 1966, Empl: 3,670, Sales ($M): 329.5, Fiscal End: 6/96; Frederick W. Lang, Chmn & CEO, Victor C. Benda, Pres & COO, Gerald M. McGrath, VP & CFO, George R. Zak, VP Mktng

ANDATACO 10140 Mesa Rim Rd, San Diego CA 92121-2914 USA; 619/453-9191, 800/334-9191 Fax: 619/453-9294, Co Email: inquire@andataco.com, Web URL: andataco.com, Focus: Designs and manufactures of network storage solutions, Ownrshp: PVT, Founded: 1986, Empl: 200, Sales ($M): 100, W. David Sykes, Pres, Email: dave@andataco.com; Matt Westover, Nat'l. Sales Mgr, Email: matt.westover@andataco.com; Frank Berry, Dir

Mktng, Email: frankb@andataco.com; Daryl Beeson, Mgr MIS, Email: daryl@andataco.com; Emily Ospenson, Marcom Mgr, Email: emily.ospenson@andataco.com

Andersen Consulting 69 W Washington St, Chicago IL 60602 USA; 312/372-7100, Web URL: ac.com, Focus: Consulting and system integration, Ownrshp: PVT, Founded: 1920, Empl: 22,500, Sales ($M): 4,220, Fiscal End: 12/95

Anderson Soft-Teach 983 University Ave, Los Gatos CA 95030 USA; 408/399-0100, 800/338-4336 Fax: 408/399-0500, Co Email: @teach.com, Focus: Training software, Prdts: SmartTrainer HelpDesk, Warren Anderson, Pres

Andor Communications Inc. 6130 Blue Circle Dr, Minnetonka MN 55343 USA; 612/932-4000, Web URL: ancor.com, Focus: Network communications products, Ownrshp: OTC, Stk Sym: ANCR, Founded: 1986, Empl: 49, Sales ($M): 4.8, Fiscal End: 12/94; Dale C. Showers, Chmn, Stephen C. O'Hara, Pres & CEO, Tim Donaldson, VP Sales & Mktng, Lee B. Lewis, VP & CFO, Doug Anderson, Email: douga@ancor.com

Andrea Electronics Corp. 11-40 45th Rd, Long Island City NY 11101 USA; 800/442-7787 Fax: 718/729-8500, Web URL: andrea_electronics.com, Focus: Audio communications equipment, Prdts: Andrea Anti-Noise, Active Noise Cancellation Technology, Ownrshp: AMEX, Stk Sym: AND, Founded: 1934, Empl: 85, Sales ($M): 3.3, Fiscal End: 12/94; Patrick D. Pilch, CFO, Douglas Andrea, Co-Pres, John Andrea, Co-Pres, Frank Andrea, CEO & Chmn, Thomas Norton, Daisy Guadalupe, VP Corp Comm

Andrew Corp. 10500 W 153rd St, Orland Park IL 60462 USA; 708/349-3300, Fax: 708/349-5943, Focus: Communication products, Ownrshp: OTC, Stk Sym: ANDW, Founded: 1937, Empl: 3,370, Sales ($M): 626.5, Fiscal End: 9/95; Floyd L. English, Chmn, Pres & CEO, John B. Scott, VP R&D & Mktng, Thomas E. Charlton, Group VP, Alan J. Rossi, Group VP, Charles R. Nicholas, EVP & CFO

Andromeda Interactive Inc. 1050 Marina Village Pkwy, #107, Alameda CA 94501 USA; 510/769-1616, 800/769-1616 Fax: 510/769-1919, Co Email: androm@netcom.com, Focus: Electronic and online publishing, Ownrshp: Sub Andromeda, Debbie Cook, Sales Admin

Angia Communications 441 E Bay Blvd, Provo UT 84606 USA; 801/371-0488, 800/877-9159 Fax: 801/373-9847, Web URL: angia.com, Focus: Data and fax modems, Ownrshp: PVT, Founded: 1992, Empl: 135, Richard D. McCloskey Jr., Pres & CEO, James Western, VP & GM, Robert A. Sorensen, CFO, Dale R. Erling, Dir Mktng, Ryan Smith, IS Mgr, Paul Stout, Dir Com

Ansel Communications 8711-148th Ave NE, Redmond WA 98052 USA; 206/869-4928, 800/341-7978 Fax: 206/869-5015, Co Email: ansel.com, Focus: Network hardware and software, Prdts: AnseLink, PrintWiz, Ownrshp: PVT, Founded: 1991, Empl: 20, Patrik Edenholm, Pres, Radu Tomescu, EVP, Email: tomescu@ansel.com; Adam Childers, Controller, Alyson Robin, Proj Controller, Email: robin@ansel.com

Ansys Inc. (SASI), Johnson Rd, PO Box 65, Houston PA 15342-1300 USA; 800/937-3321 Fax: 412/746-9494, Co Email: ansys.info@ansys.com, Web URL: ansys.com, Focus: Finite element analysis software, Prdts: Ansys, Ownrshp: PVT, Founded: 1970, Empl: 200, Peter J. Smith, Pres & CEO, Laura Carrabine, PR Mgr, Email: lcarrabine@ansys.com

Antares Alliance Group 17304 Preston Rd, #1200, Dallas TX 75252 USA; 972/447-5500, Web URL: antaresalliance.com, Focus: Legacy and C/S software, Ownrshp: EDS & Amdahl, Founded: 1993, Empl: 395, Sales ($M): 55, Fiscal End: 12/95; John Cavalier, Pres & CEO

Antec Inc. 2859 Bayview Dr, Fremont CA 94538-6520 USA; 510/770-1200, Fax: 510/770-1288, Co Email: @antec-inc.com, Web URL: antec-inc.com, Focus: PC cases and power supplies, Ownrshp: PVT, Founded: 1985, Empl: 25, Andrew Lee, Pres, Rene Buhay, Dir Sales & Mktng, Karen Janes Powers, Mgr Marcom

Antex Electronics Corp. 16100 S Figueroa St, Gardena CA 90248 USA; 310/532-3092, 800/338-4231 Fax: 310/532-8509, Co Email: antexsales@aol.com, Web URL: antex.com, Focus: PC digital audio products, Ownrshp: PVT, Founded: 1983, Empl: 55, Sales ($M): 5, James Antrim, Pres, Richard Gross, VP, Robert Bird, VP

Anthro Corp. 10450 SW Manhasset Dr, Tulatin OR 97062 USA; 503/691-2556, 800/325-3841 Fax: 503/691-2409, Co Email: @anthro.com, Focus: Computer furniture, Ownrshp: PVT, Founded: 1984, Karen Baker, PR Dir, Email: karen@anthro.com

Apertus Technologies Inc. 7275 Flying Cloud Dr, Eden Prairie MN 55344 USA; 612/828-0300, Web URL: apertus.com, Focus: Terminals and communications products, Ownrshp: OTC, Stk Sym: APTS, Founded: 1979, Empl: 210, Sales ($M): 49.3, Fiscal End: 3/96; Robert D. Gordon, Chmn, Pres & CEO, Don C. McIlwain, VP Ops, Martin Hahn, GM Internet Group, Lizabeth Converse-Wilson, GM Enterprise Syst, Sue Hogue, CFO

Apex Computer 4500 150th Ave NE, Redmond WA 98052 USA; 206/867-1900, Fax: 206/883-4910, Co Email: info@apex.com, Focus: Computer maintenance, education and hardware, Ownrshp: Sub. Cerplex, Founded: 1985, Empl: 70, Clint Morse, Pres, Rich Shockley, EVP, Lynly Schambers, Marcom

Apex Data Inc. 6624 Owens Dr, Pleasanton CA 94588 USA; 510/416-5656, Fax: 510/416-0909, Focus: PCMCIA peripherals, Ownrshp: Sub Smart Modular Tech., Founded: 1992, Sales ($M): 44, Fiscal End: 12/94; John Chess, GM, Becky Takeda, Dir Mktng, Wayne Eisenberg, Dir Sales, Theresa Elam, Distr Sales Mgr, Derek Maloney, Prod Mktng Mgr

Aplet Warehouse 326 Pacheco Ave, #200, Santa Cruz CA 95062-1233 USA; 408/426-4400, Fax: 408/426-4411, Co Email: findus@apletware.com, Web URL: apletware.com, Focus: Software warehouse for web developers, Ownrshp: PVT, Founded: 1996, Robert Aston, Pres

Apogee Software Ltd. PO Box 496389, Garland TX 75049 USA; 214/271-1765, 800/276-4331 Fax: 214/278-4670, Web URL: apogeel.com, Focus: Software developing and publishing, Prdts: Wolfenstein 3D, Rise of the Triad, Terminal Velocity, Blood, Ownrshp: PVT, Founded: 1987, Empl: 30, Sales ($M): 68.3, Fiscal End: 12/95; Scott Miller, Partner, George Broussard, Partner, Steven Blackburn, COO, Dennis Scarff, VP Intl Dist, Terry Nagy, Ops Mgr

Apple Computer Inc. 1 Infinite Loop, Cupertino CA 95014-2084 USA; 408/996-1010, Fax: 800/227-5329, Web URL: apple.com, Focus: PCs and peripherals, Prdts: Macintosh, Ownrshp: OTC, Stk Sym: AAPL, Founded: 1977, Empl: 11,287, Sales ($M): 11,062.0, Fiscal End: 9/95; A.C. Markkula Jr., Vice Chmn, Gilbert F. Amelio, Pres & CEO, Jeanne Seeley, VP Finance, David C. Nagel, SVP R&D, Joseph D. Riera, VP Info Syst, Frank O'Mahony

Apple Dealers Association (ADA), 450 E 22nd St, #230, Lombard IL 60148-6158 USA; 630/268-1818, Fax: 630/240-1384, Focus: Association for Apple resellers, Ownrshp: Nonprofit, Empl: 500, Elizabeth G. Berglund, Dir Marcom

Application Partners Inc. 100 Wood Ave S, Iselin NJ 08830 USA; 908/549-5464, 800/603-7732 Fax: 908/549-4435, Web URL: application-partners.com, Focus: Software for Lotus Notes, Ownrshp: PVT, Founded: 1991, Empl: 15, Richard Wilson, Pres, Gordon Smith

Application Techniques Inc. 10 Lomar Park Dr, Pepperell MA 01463 USA; 800/433-5201 Focus: Screen capture and conversion software, Prdts: Pizazz Plus, WinDings, Pizazz 5, Ownrshp: PVT, Founded: 1980, Carol Case, VP Ops

Applicon 4251 Plymouth Rd, Ann Arbor MI 48106-0986 USA; 313/995-6000, 800/367-2728 Fax: 313/995-6171, Focus: CAD/CAM systems, Prdts: Bravo, Ownrshp: Sub. Gores Enterprises, Founded: 1969, Empl: 650, Vance Diggins, Pres & CEO

Applied Magic Inc. 2649 Vista Way #837, Oceanside CA 92054-6389 USA; 619/599-2626, Focus: Digital editing and image compression systems, Ownrshp: PVT, Robert Wallin, Pres, Eric Gilliatt, VP Mktng

Applied Magnetics Corp. 75 Robin Hill Rd, Goleta CA 93117 USA; 805/683-5353, Fax: 805/967-8227, Focus: Magnetic heads, Ownrshp: NYSE, Stk Sym: APM, Founded: 1957, Empl: 5,500, Sales ($M): 292.6, Fiscal End: 9/95; Craig D. Crisman, Chmn, Pres, CEO & CFO, John Ross, GM, Peter T. Altavilla, Controller

Applied Micro Circuits Corp. (AMCC), 6195 Lusk Blvd, San Diego CA 92121-2793 USA; 619/450-9333, 800/755-2622 Fax: 619/450-9885, Co Email: compinfo@amcc.com, Web URL: amcc.com, Focus: Standard and ASIC for computer and communications markets, Ownrshp: PVT, Sales ($M): 46, Fiscal End: 3/95; David M. Rickey, Pres & CEO, John Grosse, VP Ops, Joel Holiday, CFO, Monica Lawrence, Ad/PR Mgr

Applied Resources Inc. 9821 Widmer Rd, Lenexa KS 66215-1239 USA; 913/492-8888, Fax: 913/492-0492, Focus: Image display products, interactive kiosk development, micrographics products, Prdts: Information Station, ARIS Micrographics Image Kit, Ownrshp: PVT, Founded: 1988, Empl: 15, E. Brooks Lilly, Pres, Kevin Quirk, Prod Mgr, Meredith Lilly, Dir Corp Comm, Robert Ayers, Chief Eng

Applix Inc. 112 Turnpike Rd, Westboro MA 01581 USA; 508/870-0300, 800/827-7549 Fax: 508/366-9313, Co Email: info@applix.com, Web URL: applix.com, Focus: Unix support software, Prdts: Applixware, Applix Builder, Stk Sym: APLX, Founded: 1983, Empl: 230, Sales ($M): 32.3, Fiscal End: 12/95; Jit Saxena, Pres & CEO, Richard Davis, EVP, Abe Hirsch, VP Mktng, Email: ahirsch@applix.com; Craig Cervo, VP R&D, Richard Fanwell, Dave Gayman, Mgr PR, Email: dgayman@applix.com

Appoint 1324 Vendels Cr #101, Paso Robles CA 93446-3801 USA; 510/803-8850, Fax: 510/803-1995, Focus: Computer input devices, Prdts: MousePen, Thumbelina, Gulliver, Gliffic, Ownrshp: PVT, Founded: 1989, Empl: 55, Jack Barrett, CEO

APS America Ltd. #200-6816 Morrison Blvd, Charlotte NC 28211-3579 USA; 704/364-3346, Fax: 704/364-5676, Focus: Multifunction PC software, Prdts: Ability Plus, Ownrshp: Sub. NA Productivity SW, Founded: 1991, Empl: 4, Gordon N. Lewchuk, Pres & CEO, Alice Llorens, PR Mgr

APS Technologies 6131 Deramus, PO Box 4987, Kansas City MO 64120-0087 USA; 816/483-1600, 800/325-6316 Fax: 816/483-3077, Co Email: sales@apstech.com, Focus: Portable storage products, Ownrshp: PVT, Paul Mandel, Pres, Paul McGraw, EVP, Karen F. Saper, Dir Marcom

Apsylog Inc. 1900 Embarcadero Rd, #209, Palo Alto CA 94303 USA; 415/812-7700, Fax: 415/812-7707, Co Email: 7563.3614@compuserve.com, Focus: Asset management software, Prdts: Cabling System Manager, Apsylog Asset Manager, Ownrshp: PVT, Founded: 1986, Empl: 75, Sales ($M): 9, Bruno Paulet, Pres, Cassanora Bailey, Sales Mgr

Arbor Image Corp. 5651 Plymouth Rd, Ann Arbor MI 48105-9586 USA; 313/741-8700, Focus: Image processing software, Ownrshp: PVT, Founded: 1988, Empl: 7, Tom Gray, Pres, Chuck Krapf, VP Dev

Arbor Software Corp. 1325 Chesapeake Terrace, Sunnyvale CA 94089 USA; 408/727-5800, Fax: 408/727-7140, Web URL: arborsoft.com, Focus: C/S software, Prdts: eSSbase Data Server, Ownrshp: OTC, Stk Sym: ARSW, Founded: 1991, Empl: 130, Sales ($M): 25.1, Fiscal End: 3/96; Jim Dorrian, Pres & CEO, Kirk A. Cruikshank, VP Mktng, John M. Dillon, VP Sales, Stephen V. Imbler, VP & CFO, Joanna McMillan, Email: jmcmillan@arborsoft.com

ArborText Inc. 1000 Victors Way, #400, Ann Arbor MI 48108 USA; 313/996-3566, Fax: 313/996-3573, Co Email: @arortext.com, Web URL: arbortext.com, Focus: Editing and publishing software, Prdts: ADEPT-Editor, ADEPT-Publisher, Ownrshp: PVT, Founded: 1982, James J. Sterken, Pres & CEO, John M. Ford, EVP, George B. Underwood, VP Sales, P.G. Bartlett, VP Mktng,

Paul B. Grosso, VP Res, Violeta Kellersohn, Marcom Mgr, Email: vik@arbortext.com

ARC International Corp. 4000 Chesswood Dr, Downsview Ontario M3J 2B9 Canada; 416/630-0200, Fax: 416/630-4414, Focus: Electronic products, Ownrshp: FO, Empl: 349, Sales ($M): 74.0, Fiscal End: 12/95; Arnold S. Tenney, Pres & CEO, Jeffrey D. Chelin, VP, Richard W. Noble, Controller US Ops.

Arc Media Inc. 238 Davenport Rd, #306, Toronto Ontario M5R 1J6 Canada; 416/410-4429, Fax: 416/410-9651, Co Email: arc@io.org, Focus: CD-ROM software, Prdts: Cards & Close-Ups, Table Magic, Ownrshp: PVT, Oliver Huang, Pres, Anthony Lindan, Mktng Dir

Arcada Software Inc. 37 Skyline Dr, #1101, Lake Mary FL 32746 USA; 407/333-7500, 800/327-2332 Fax: 407/333-7770, Co Email: @arcada.com, Focus: Storage management software, Ownrshp: Sub. Conner Peripherals, Founded: 1994, Kevin Azzouz, Pres & COO, Joseph W. Seebach, VP Bus Dev, Chris Gibson, VP Ops, Don Flanagan, VP Sales, David Hallmen, VP Mktng, Steve Coppock, Dir Marcom, Email: scoppock@arcada.com

ArcanaTech 120 S Whitfield St, Pittsburgh PA 15206 USA; 412/441-6611, 800/364-4677 Fax: 412/361-5103, Focus: Wireless handheld pointing device, Prdts: IMP, Ownrshp: PVT, Founded: 1991, Empl: 6, Jack Copper, Pres, Randell L. Urban, CFO

Archetype Inc. 100 Fifth Ave, Waltham MA 02154 USA; 617/890-7544, Fax: 617/890-3661, Web URL: atype.com, Focus: Publishing software, Prdts: InterSep, Ownrshp: PVT, Founded: 1992, Paul Trevithick, Pres & CEO, Sue Robertson, EVP, George Farnham, Dir Sales, Rick Mohr, Dir Dev

Arcland 7 Great Valley Pkwy E, #330, Malvern PA 19355 USA; 610/993-9904, Fax: 610/993-9908, Co Email: @arcland.com, Focus: Diagramming and data modeling software, Prdts: Flow-Model, Ownrshp: PVT, Founded: 1992, Donald A. Ramsey, Pres & CEO, Kim Shah, VP Mktng, Greg Mathews, Dir Sales, Gordon Sellers, Dir Mktng, Email: gsellers@arcland.com

ARCNET Trade Assoc. (ATA), 2460 Wisconsin Ave, Downers Grove IL 60515 USA; 630/960-5130, Fax: 630/963-2122, Web URL: arcnet.org, Focus: Arcnet LAN vendor association, Ownrshp: Nonprofit, Founded: 1987, Empl: 50

ArcSys 1208 E Arques Ave, Sunnyvale CA 94086 USA; 408/738-8881, Focus: IC design software, Ownrshp: OTC, Stk Sym: ARCS, Founded: 1991, Empl: 59, Sales ($M): 6.2, Fiscal End: 12/94; Gerald C. Hsu, Pres & CEO, Yuh-Zen Liao, VP Tech.

ARDIS 300 Knightsbridge Pkwy, Lincolnshire IL 60069 USA; 708/913-1215, Fax: 708/913-1453, Web URL: ardis.com, Focus: Wireless data communications network, Ownrshp: PVT, Walt Purnell, Pres & CFO, Mary Jane Grinstead, SVP Dist & Ops, Daniel Croft, SVP Mktng Ops, Michael Woodruff, Dir Ops, Naomi Yeransian

Area Electronics Systems Inc. 950 Fee Ana St, #B, Placentia CA 92670-6755 USA; 714/993-0300, Fax: 714/993-0087, Focus: PC and workstation products, Ownrshp: PVT, Founded: 1986, Empl: 25, Sales ($M): 15.0, Fiscal End: 2/91; William Huang, Pres

Ares Software Corp. 565 Pilgrim Dr, #A, Foster City CA 94404 USA; 415/578-9090, 800/783-2737 Fax: 415/378-8999, Co Email: 70253.3164@compuserve.com, Focus: Font and graphics software, Ownrshp: PVT, Founded: 1990, Russell F. McCann Jr., Pres & CEO, Larry Applegate, VP, Ernie Brock, VP, Robin Henson, VP, Rob Friedman

Argus Systems Group Inc. 1405 E Florida Ave #A, Urbana IL 61801-6009 USA; 217/384-6300, Fax: 217/384-6404, Co Email: argus.cu-online.com, Focus: Enhanced security modules for Solaris 2.4x86 and SPARC and secure networking products, Prdts: C2 with an Attitude, B1/CMW, Advanced Secure Networking, Ownrshp: PVT, Founded: 1992, Empl: 20, Randall J. Sandone, Pres & CEO, Email: sandone@argus.cu-online.com; Paul A. McNabb, VP, Email: mcnabb@argus.cu-online.com; Kevin Reeks, VP Govt Sys, Mary P. Sandone, Office Mgr

Ariel Corp. 433 River Rd, Highland Park NJ 08904 USA; 908/

249-2900, Fax: 908/249-2123, Co Email: ariel@ariel.com, Web URL: ariel.com, Focus: PC boards, Stk Sym: ADSP, Founded: 1982, Empl: 80, Anthony Agnello, Pres, Steve Curtin, Marcom, Email: steve.curtin@ariel.com

Aries Technology Inc. 900 Chelmsford St, Lowell MA 01851-5198 USA; 508/453-5310, Fax: 508/458-2541, Focus: Mechanical CAE software, Ownrshp: PVT, Larry McArthur, Pres & CEO

Aristo-Soft Inc. PO Box 1629, Pleasanton CA 94566-0162 USA; 510/426-5355, Fax: 510/426-6703, Focus: PC utility software, Ownrshp: PVT, Founded: 1986, Ernest Priestly, Pres & CEO, Bessie Essex, VP

Arix Corp. 1024 Morse Ave, Sunnyvale CA 94089 USA; 408/541-8700, Focus: Unix-based computer systems, Ownrshp: OTC, Stk Sym: ARIX, Founded: 1982, Empl: 140, Sales ($M): 24, Fiscal End: 6/92; Eugene Manno, Chmn, Pres & CEO

Arizona Software Assoc. 3900 E Camelback, #200, Phoenix AZ 85018 USA; 602/912-5351, Fax: 602/957-4828, Focus: Organization for software companies in Arizona, Ownrshp: Nonprofit

Arlington Industries 1001 Technology Way, Libertyville IL 60048 USA; 800/323-4147 Focus: Distributes PC and office products

Armor Systems Inc. 1626 W Airport Blvd, Sanford FL 32773-4814 USA; 407/323-9787, Fax: 407/330-0442, Web URL: armor-net.com, Focus: Accounting software, Prdts: Premier, Ownrshp: PVT, Founded: 1978, Empl: 75, Sales ($M): 15, Nick Barth, Pres & CEO, Steve Nelson

Arnet Corp. 618 Grassmere Park Dr, #6, Nashville TN 37211 USA; 615/834-8000, 800/366-8844 Fax: 615/834-5399, Co Email: @arnet.com, Focus: Multi-user microcomputer expansion products, Ownrshp: Sub. Digi Int'l., Founded: 1983, Ken Luttrell, VP & GM, Fred Berry, Dir Mktng, Rick Hill, Dir Eng, Nancy Matthews, Dir Sales, Susan Massey, Email: susan@arnet.com

Around Technology Inc. 6777 Engle Rd, Unit J, Cleveland OH 44130 USA; 216/234-6402, Fax: 216/234-2233, Co Email: us@aroundtech.com, Web URL: aroundtech.com, Focus: CD-ROM networking sharing software, CD towers and servers, Prdts: CD-ACCESS, Datahouse, Ownrshp: PVT, Founded: 1988, Lel F. Somogyi, Pres, Email: lsomogyi@aroundtech.com; Julie Burgess, Controller, Steve Mihalic, Tech Mgr

Arrow Electronics Inc. 25 Hub Dr, Melville NY 11747 USA; 516/391-1300, Fax: 516/391-1640, Focus: Distributes electronic and computer products, Ownrshp: NYSE, Stk Sym: ARW, Founded: 1946, Empl: 3,800, Sales ($M): 5,919.4, Fiscal End: 12/95; John C. Waddell, Chmn, Stephen P. Kaufman, Pres & CEO, Robert J. McInerney, Pres Commercial Syst, Don E. Burton, VP, Robert E. Klatell, SVP & CFO

Art & Logic PO Box 56465, Sherman Oaks CA 91413 USA; 818/501-6990, Fax: 916/272-5085, Co Email: info@artlogic.com, Web URL: artlogic.com, Focus: Develops complex custom applications for Mac, OS and Microsoft Windows, Ownrshp: PVT, Justin Souter, CEO, Paul Hershenson, CFO, Laura Tolladay, Mktng Dir

Artbeats Software Inc. 2611 S Myrtle Rd, Myrtle Creek OR 97457 USA; 503/863-4429, Fax: 503/863-4547, Focus: Background art for desktop publishing & multimedia, Prdts: Marble & Granite, WebTools, Ownrshp: PVT, Founded: 1989, Phil Bates, Pres, Lenny Kissell, Mktng Mgr

Artecon PO Box 9000, Carlsbad CA 92018-9000 USA; 619/931-5500, 800/872-2783 Fax: 619/931-5527, Web URL: artecon.com, Focus: Computer storage devices, Ownrshp: PVT, Founded: 1984, Empl: 130, James L. Lambert, Pres & CEO, Dana Kammersgard, VP Mktng, Gerry MacDonald

Artek Computer Systems 47709 Fremont Blvd, Fremont CA 94538 USA; 510/490-8402, Focus: PCs and peripherals, Ownrshp: PVT

Artel Software Inc. PO Box 1877, Brookline MA 02146 USA; 617/566-0870, Fax: 617/731-6787, Co Email: artel@tiac.com, Web URL: tiac.net/artel, Focus: Video effects software, Prdts:

Boris Effects, Ownrshp: PVT, Founded: 1995, Boris Yamnitsky, Pres, David Kagan, VP Mktng

Articulate Systems Inc. 600 W Cummings Park, #4500, Woburn MA 01801 USA; 617/935-5656, Fax: 617/935-0490, Web URL: artsys.com, Focus: Voice dictation products, Prdts: Power Secretary Series, Ownrshp: PVT, Founded: 1986, Ivan Mimica, Pres & CEO

Artisoft Inc. 2202 N Forbes Blvd, Tucson AZ 85745 USA; 520/670-7100, 800/233-5564 Fax: 520/670-7101, Co Email: @artisoft.com, Web URL: artisoft.com, Focus: LAN hardware and software, Prdts: LANtastic, Ownrshp: OTC, Stk Sym: ASFT, Founded: 1982, Empl: 500, Sales ($M): 61.0, Fiscal End: 6/96; William C. Keiper, Chmn & CEO, Gary Acord, VP & CFO, Joel J. Kocher, Pres & COO, William T. Peterson, VP Mktng, Terri Childs, Mgr Corp Com, Email: tchilds@artisoft.com

Artistic Visions 2075 Winchester Blvd, #107, Campbell CA 95008-3432 USA; 408/378-1435, Fax: 408/378-3480, Co Email: info@cdworld.com, Web URL: cdworld.com, Focus: Internet discount music store, Ownrshp: PVT, Bruce Pettyjohn, Pres, Branca Alvernaz, Email: branca@cdworld.com

ASA International Ltd. 10 Speen St, Framingham MA 01701-4661 USA; 508/626-2727, Fax: 508/626-0645, Co Email: webmaster@asaint.com, Web URL: asaint.com, Focus: Vertical market software, Prdts: Mozart, SmartTime, Ownrshp: OTC, Stk Sym: ASAA, Founded: 1969, Empl: 200, Sales ($M): 31.0, Fiscal End: 12/95; Alfred C. Angelone, Chmn & CEO, Christopher J. Crane, Pres, Eli Szklanka, VP

Asante Technologies Inc. 821 Fox Ln, San Jose CA 95131-1593 USA; 408/435-8388, Fax: 408/432-1117, Co Email: @asante.com, Focus: Macintosh network products, Prdts: NetStacker, AsanteHub, Ownrshp: OTC, Stk Sym: ASNT, Founded: 1988, Empl: 175, Sales ($M): 60.9, Fiscal End: 9/95; Jeff Lin, Pres & CEO, Wilson Wong, VP & Co-Chmn, Paul Smith, VP Mktng, William C. Leung, VP Ops, Steven A. Hess, VP & CFO

ASAP Software Express Inc. 850 Asbury Dr, Buffalo Grove IL 60089-4557 USA; 847/465-3710, 800/248-2727 Fax: 847/465-3277, Web URL: asapsoftware.com, Focus: Reseller PC software and add-on hardware, Ownrshp: PVT, Founded: 1984, Empl: 150, Scott Wald, Pres & CEO, Stanley Owens, Chmn, Paul Jarvie, VP Mktng, Rick Gunther, VP Sales, Bob Lewandowski, VP Sys, Sheri Rosenbaum-Kinnavy, Marcom Mgr, Email: sxrosenbaum@mci-mail.com

Ascend Communications Inc. 1701 Harbor Bay Pkwy, One Ascend Plaza, Alameda CA 94502-3002 USA; 510/769-6001, 800/621-9578 Fax: 510/747-2300, Co Email: info@ascend.com, Web URL: ascend.com, Focus: ISDN and network products, Ownrshp: OTC, Stk Sym: ASND, Founded: 1988, Empl: 115, Sales ($M): 149.6, Fiscal End: 12/95; Mory Ejabat, Pres & CEO, Anthony Stagno, VP Ops, Curtis N. Sanford, VP Sales, Bernie Schneider, VP Mktng, Robert K. Dahl, VP & CFO

Ascent Solutions Inc. (ASI), 10460 Miamisburg-Springboro Pike, Dayton OH 45342 USA; 513/885-2031, Fax: 513/885-2032, Focus: Compression utilities, Prdts: PKZIP UNIX, Shannon Wendel

ASCII Entertainment Software Inc. 900 Veterans Blvd, #600, Redwood City CA 94063-1744 USA; 415/780-0800, Fax: 415/780-0855, Co Email: @asciient.com, Web URL: asciient.com, Focus: Entertainment software, Prdts: King's Field, asciiPad PS, asciiStick PS, Fighter Pad SG-6, Ownrshp: PVT, Founded: 1990, Empl: 17, Sales ($M): 5, Hide Irie, Pres, Email: hide.irie@asciient.com; Sal Estrada, VP Ops, Email: sal.estrada@asciient.com; Jane Cowley, Mktng Mgr, Email: jane.cowley@asciient.com; John Creel, Reg Sales Mgr, Email: john.creel@asciient.com

ASCII Group Inc., The 7475 Wisconsin Ave, #350, Bethesda MD 20814-3412 USA; 301/718/2600, Fax: 301/718-0435, Web URL: ascii.com, Focus: Chain of over 1,200 computer resellers in USA, Canada, Mexico & Europe, Ownrshp: PVT, Founded: 1984, Empl: 20, Sales ($M): 5,100 WW, Alan Weinberger, Chmn, Pres &

CEO, Jill L. Kerr, VP Sales & Mktng, Tim Butts, VP Reseller Mktng, Dan Corrigan, PR Officer

ASD Software Inc. 4650 Arrow Hwy, #E-6, Montclair CA 91763 USA; 909/624-2594, Fax: 909/624-9574, Co Email: 102404.3630@compuserve.com, Focus: Macintosh software, Prdts: FileGuard, WindoWatch, FileDuo, TrashGuard, WizTools, Achive Memory, Ownrshp: PVT, Founded: 1989, Empl: 10, Sales ($M): 2, Francine Dubois, GM, Wes Wason, Sales & Mktng Mgr

Ashlar Inc. 1290 Oakmead Pkwy, Sunnyvale CA 94086 USA; 408/746-1800, Fax: 408/746-0749, Web URL: ashlar.com, Focus: Design and drafting software, Prdts: Vellum, Drawing Board, Ownrshp: PVT, Founded: 1988, Empl: 25, Martin Newell, CTO, Jack Hendren, Pres & CEO

ASI Int'l. 111 Pine St, #950, San Francisco CA 94111 USA; 415/421-8191, Fax: 415/391-0326, Focus: Real estate management software, Ownrshp: PVT, Lisa S. Levine

askSam Systems 119 Washington St, PO Box 1428, Perry FL 32347 USA; 904/584-6590, 800/800-1997 Fax: 904/584-7481, Co Email: info@asksam.com, Web URL: asksam.com, Focus: PC text retrieval and database software, Prdts: askSam, Ownrshp: PVT, Founded: 1985, Empl: 20, Phil Schnyder, Pres & CEO, Michael H. McKinney, Chmn, Bea McKinney, VP, Michael J. McKinney, EVP & CFO

ASL LCD Inc. 1099 Wall St W, #396, Lyndhurst NJ 07071 USA; 201/896-8888, 800/275-5231 Fax: 201/896-0012, Focus: LCD display projectors, Ownrshp: Sub Tandberg Data, Norway, Gary Plavin, VP & GM

Aspec Technology Inc. 830 E Arques Ave, Sunnyvale CA 94086-4519 USA; 408/774-2199, Fax: 408/522-9450, Web URL: aspec.com, Focus: ASIC design tools, Ownrshp: PVT, Founded: 1991, Empl: 95, Sales ($M): 8, Conrad J. Dell'Oca, Pres & CEO, Robert Grossman

Aspen Systems Inc. 4026 Youngfield St, Wheat Ridge CO 80033-3862 USA; 303/431-4606, Fax: 303/431-7196, Co Email: aspen@aspsys.com, Web URL: aspsys.com, Focus: Single board computers and systems, Prdts: Alpine, Telluride, Timberline and Summit Power Workstations & Servers, Ownrshp: PVT, Founded: 1978, Empl: 18, Steve Spring, Pres, Alan Kahn, VP Sales, Email: alank@aspsys.com; Severen Pedersen, Dir Sales, Email: severenp@aspsys.com; Randy Perry, Sales Mgr, Email: randyp@aspsys.com; Amy Sterk, PR Dir, Email: amys@aspsys.com

Aspen Technology Inc. 10 Canal Park, Cambridge MA 02141 USA; 617/577-0100, Fax: 617/577-0303, Co Email: info@aspentec.com, Focus: Computer-aided chemical engineering software, Prdts: Polymers Plus, Ownrshp: OTC, Stk Sym: AZPN, Empl: 410, Sales ($M): 103.6, Fiscal End: 6/96; Larry Evans, Chmn & CEO, Alan McKee, VP Dev, Mary Dean Palermo, SVP & CFO, Mary K. Deery, Dir Marcom, Email: deery@aspentec.com

Associated Research Services Inc. 4320 N Beltline, #A202, Irving TX 75038 USA; 214/570-7100, Fax: 214/570-4201, Web URL: arso.com, Focus: Marketing and promotion data on PCs, printers and workstations, Ownrshp: PVT, Founded: 1987, Empl: 17, Phil Magney, Pres, Mike Hagan, VP Sales & Mktng

Association for Computing Machinery (ACM), 1515 Broadway, 17th Floor, New York NY 10036-5701 USA; 212/869-7440, Fax: 212/944-1318, Co Email: @acm.org, Web URL: acm.org, Focus: Educational and scientific society for computer professionals, Ownrshp: Nonprofit, Founded: 1947, Empl: 80,000, Joseph S. DeBlasi, Exec Dir, Lillian Israel, Dir Memb, Lisa Ernst, Dir Conf, John A. Osmundsen, Assoc Dir Pub Affairs

Association for Educational Communications and Technology (AECT), 1025 Vermont Ave NW, #820, Washington DC 20005 USA; 202/347-7834, Fax: 202/347-7839, Web URL: aect.org, Focus: Educational technology such as computerized instruction, Ownrshp: Nonprofit, Stanley Zenor, Exec Dir, Shannon Gordon, Dir Fin, Marry Kavalier, Dir Pubs

Association for Information and Image Management

(AIIM), 1100 Wayne Ave, #1100, Silver Spring MD 20910 USA; 301/587-8202, Fax: 301/587-2711, Web URL: aiim.org, Focus: Advancing technology for capture, storage and retrieval of image documents, Prdts: AIIM Show, Ownrshp: Nonprofit, Founded: 1945, Empl: 9,000, John Mancini, Exec Dir

Association for Services Management Int'l. (AFSM), 1342 Colonial Blvd, #25, Ft. Myers FL 33907 USA; 941/275-7887, 800/444-9786 Focus: Association for high-tech services and support, Ownrshp: Nonprofit, Joseph R. Trpik, EVP, Robert M. Steele, Exec Dir, Joanna L. Baker, Dir Membership, Leonard Mafrica, Dir Ed Svcs

Association for Systems Management (ASM), 1433 W Bagley Rd, PO Box 38370, Cleveland OH 44138-0370 USA; 216/243-6900, Fax: 216/234-2930, Focus: Continuing education for information systems professional, Ownrshp: Nonprofit, Founded: 1947, Empl: 6,000, Robert C. La Prad, Exec Dir, Ross A. Flaherty, Pres

Association for Women in Computing 41 Sutter St, #1006, San Francisco CA 94104 USA; 415/905-4663, Co Email: awc@acm.org, Web URL: halcyon.com/monih/awc, Focus: Association for women in the computer industry, Ownrshp: Nonprofit, Founded: 1978

Association for Women in Science (AWIS), 1200 New York Ave NW, #650, Washington DC 20005 USA; 202/326-8940, Fax: 202/326-8960, Co Email: awis@awis.org, Focus: Expanding educational and career opportunities for women in the sciences, Ownrshp: Nonprofit, Empl: 5,000, Catherine Didion, Exec Dir

Association for Work Process Improvement 185 Devonshire St, Boston MA 02110 USA; 617/426-1167, Fax: 617/521-8675, Co Email: tawpi@aol.com, Focus: Data capture, document, remittance and electronic processing applications, Ownrshp: Nonprofit, Founded: 1970, Empl: 1,000, Linda Cooper, Exec Dir, Kerry Stackpole, Pres

Association of Color Thermal Transfer Technology Inc. (ACT), 310 Commerce Dr, #228, Amherst NY 14228-2396 USA; 716/691-5817, Fax: 716/691-3395, Focus: Promote color thermal transfer printer technology, Ownrshp: Nonprofit, Founded: 1993, Rick W. Wallace, Exec Dir

Association of Database Developers (ADD), 3165 16th St, San Francisco CA 94103 USA; 415/281-5638, Focus: Organization for software developers using Xbase, Ownrshp: Nonprofit, Founded: 1982, Empl: 160, Joann Castillo, Pres

Association of Desk-Top Publishers (AD-TP), 3401-A 800 Adams Ave, San Diego CA 92116 USA; 619/563-9714, Fax: 619/280-3778, Focus: Trade association for desktop publishers, Ownrshp: Nonprofit, Founded: 1986, Norman Paddock, Exec Dir

Association of Information and Dissemination Centers (ASIDIC), PO Box 8105, Athens GA 30603 USA; 706/542-6820, Focus: Organization for database producers and users, Ownrshp: Nonprofit, Founded: 1968, Empl: 80, Bill Bartenbach, Pres, Taissa Kusma, Past Pres, Jeanette Webb, Email: jwebb@arches.uga.edu

Association of Online Professionals 6010 Burdon Ct, #302, Alexandria VA 22315 USA; 703/924-9594, Fax: 703/924-9594, Focus: Organization for online users, Ownrshp: Nonprofit, Empl: 200, David McClure, Exec Dir

Association of Personal Computer Users Group (APCUG), 1730 M St NW, #700, Washington DC 20036 USA; Focus: Helping user groups worldwide, Empl: 425, Tom Heffernan, Pres, Eagan Foster, VP, Charles Kelly, Sec, Maralyn Henry, Treas

Association of Shareware Professionals (ASP), 545 Grover Rd, Muskegon MI 49442-9427 USA; 616/788-5131, Fax: 616/788-2765, Co Email: @asp-shareware.org, Web URL: asp-shareware.org, Focus: Association for shareware software vendors and authors, Ownrshp: Nonprofit, Founded: 1987, Empl: 1,500, George Campbell, Chmn, Richard Harper, Pres, Jan Abbott, Exec Dir

Association of the DEC Marketplace (DDA), 107 S Main St, Chelsea MI 48118 USA; 313/475-8333, 800/DDA-1130 Fax: 313/475-4671, Web URL: dda.org, Focus: Serves vendors and consumers of the open Digital marketplace, Founded: 1982

Association of the Institute of Certification of Computer Prof. (AICCP), 2200 E Devon Ave, #247, Des Plaines IL 60018 USA; 847/299-4227, Fax: 847/299-4280, Focus: Certification of computer professionals, Ownrshp: Nonprofit

AST Research Inc. (AST), 16215 Alton Pkwy, PO Box 57005, Irvine CA 92619-7005 USA; 714/727-4141, Fax: 714/727-9355, Web URL: ast.com, Focus: PCs and peripherals, Prdts: AST Premium, AST Bravo, Ownrshp: OTC, Stk Sym: ASTA, Founded: 1980, Empl: 6,006, Sales ($M): 2,348.5, Fiscal End: 12/95; Kug-Ho Kim, Chmn, Young-Soo Kim, Pres, Gerald T. Devlin, SVP, Gary D. Weaver, SVP Mfg, Bruce C. Edwards, EVP & CFO

Astea Int'l. 100 Highpoint Dr, Chalfont PA 18914 USA; 215/822-8888, Fax: 215/997-9060, Co Email: info@astea.com, Web URL: astea.com, Focus: Enterprise-wide customer interaction software, Prdts: ACES, Ownrshp: OTC, Stk Sym: ATEA, Founded: 1979, Empl: 350, Sales ($M): 43, Zack Bergreen, Pres & CEO, Michael Vail, SVP Sales, Keith Larson, VP Mktng, Avner Schneur, CTO, Leonard W. von Vital, CFO

Asymetrix Corp. 110 110th Ave NE, #700, Bellevue WA 98004-5840 USA; 206/637-5859, Fax: 206/637-1650, Web URL: asymetrix.com, Focus: Multimedia software development tools, Prdts: ToolBook, Ownrshp: PVT, Founded: 1985, Empl: 210, Sales ($M): 20, Fiscal End: 12/95; Paul Allen, Chmn, Jim Billmaier, Pres, Chuck Ellison, SVP Sales & Mktng, Shabbir Dahod, VP, John Atherly, VP Fin, Ann Bagley, Media Relations, Email: annb@asymetrix.com

Asyst 48761 Kato Rd, Fremont CA USA; 510/661-5023, 800/345-7643 Focus: Material management systems for semiconductor companies, Prdts: Asyst-SMIF, Ownrshp: OTC, Stk Sym: ASYT, Founded: 1984, Mihir Parikh, CEO, Doug McCutcheon, CFO

AT&T CommVault Systems 1 Industrial Way, Eatontown NJ 07724 USA; 908/935-8000, 800/331-6207 Fax: 908/935-8040, Co Email: info@abars.att.com, Focus: Network storage management systems, Ownrshp: Sub. AT&T, Scotty R. Neal, Pres, Kim I. Ciapka, Marcom Mgr

AT&T Corp. 32 Ave of the Americas, New York NY 10013-2412 USA; 212/387-5400, Fax: 212/387-5347, Web URL: att.com, Focus: Communications and networking products and service, Ownrshp: NYSE, Founded: 1885, Empl: 304,500, Sales ($M): 79,609.0, Fiscal End: 12/95; Robert E. Allen, Chmn & CEO, Marilyn Laurie, SVP PR

AT&T Global Product Compliance Laboratory 101 Crawford Corners Rd, Rm 11C-196, Holmdel NJ 07733-3030 USA; 908/834-1800, Fax: 908/834-1830, Focus: Testing, certification & education for phone, computer and electronics products, Ownrshp: PVT, Carolann Nicholas

AT&T Multimedia Software Solutions 2701 Maitland Ctr Pkwy, Maitland FL 32751 USA; 800/448-6727 Fax: 407/662-7117, Focus: Multimedia presentation tools, Ownrshp: Sub. AT&T

AT&T Paradyne 8545 126th Ave N, Largo FL 34649-2826 USA; 813/530-2000, 800/482-3333 Focus: Modems and data communication products, Ownrshp: Sub. AT&T, Founded: 1969, Randy Hawks, VP & GM Multimedia

AT&T Software Solutions Group (AT&T SSG), 10 Independence Blvd, PO Box 4911, Warren NJ 07059-6799 USA; 908/580-6444, 800/462-8146 Fax: 908/580-6355, Focus: C/S software, Ownrshp: Sub. AT&T, Larry Isley, Dir, Paul Fillinich, Mktng Mgr

AT&T Wireless Services 5400 Carrillon Point, PO Box 97060, Kirkland WA 98083 USA; 206/827-4500, Focus: Cellular telephone services, Ownrshp: OTC, Stk Sym: MCAWA, Empl: 5,800, Sales ($M): 2,194.8, Fiscal End: 12/93; Steve M. Hooper, Pres & CEO, Keith Grinstein, Pres Cellular Div, Nicolas Kauser, EVP & CTO, Peter L.S. Currie, EVP, Bob Ratliffe, VP Corp Com

Athena Design Inc. 332 Congress St, 5th Floor, Boston MA 02210-1217 USA; 617/617-6372, Fax: 617/426-7665, Co Email:

info@athena.com, Focus: Spreadsheet software, Prdts: Mesa 2, Ownrshp: PVT, Founded: 1989, David Pollak, Pres, Sarah Garnsey

ATI Technologies Inc. 33 Commerce Valley Dr E, Thornhill Ontario L3T 7N6 Canada; 905/882-2600, Fax: 905/882-2620, Web URL: atitech.ca, Focus: Graphics and communication products, Ownrshp: FO, Stk Sym: ATY, Founded: 1985, Empl: 650, Sales ($M): 359, Fiscal End: 8/95; K.Y. Ho, Pres & CEO, Henry Quan, VP Mktng, Lance McIntosh, VP Fin, Lee Lau, VP Strat Plng, Adrian Hartzog, VP Eng, Terry Wildman, Corp Com Mgr

Atlantic Cable Technology 45 Rt 125, Kingston NH 03848 USA; 800/642-8816 Fax: 603/642-8826, Co Email: peerless1@aol.com, Focus: Cables, network products and accessories, Ownrshp: PVT, Founded: 1989, Empl: 8, Sales ($M): 2.0, Jon Bowers, Pres, Keith Dias, VP Sales & Mktng

ATM Forum (ATM), 2570 W El Camino Real, #304, Mountain View CA 94040-1313 USA; 415/949-6700, Fax: 415/949-6705, Co Email: info@atmforum.com, Web URL: atmforum.com, Focus: Speed development of Asynchronous Transfer Mode products, Ownrshp: Nonprofit, Founded: 1991, Empl: 580, Steve Walters, Chmn & Pres, Anne M. Ferris, Exec Dir, Sanjay Uppal, VP Mktng

Atmel Corp. 2325 Orchard Pkwy, San Jose CA 95131 USA; 408/441-0311, Fax: 408/436-4200, Focus: Semiconductor chips, Ownrshp: OTC, Stk Sym: ATML, Founded: 1984, Sales ($M): 634.2, Fiscal End: 12/95; George Perlegos, Chmn, Pres & CEO, B. Jeffrey Katz, VP Mktng, Tsung-Ching Wu, EVP Tech, Ralph Bohannon, VP Mfg, Kris Chellam, VP & CFO

Atomic City Electronics Inc. 1247 Central Ave #D, Los Alamos NM 87544-3215 USA; 505/662-7059, Fax: 505/662-6647, Co Email: atomic_city@unix.nets.com, Web URL: adpages.com/website/atomic, Focus: High performance PCs, PC parts and memory, Founded: 1993, Empl: 10, Harrison K. Millard III, Chmn & Pres, Jack L. Johnson, Secretary, James Potter

Atria Software 20 Maguire Rd, Lexington MA 02173-3104 USA; 617/676-2400, Fax: 617/676-2550, Co Email: info@atria.com, Web URL: atria.com, Focus: CASE programs, Prdts: ClearCase, Ownrshp: OTC, Stk Sym: ATSW, Founded: 1990, Empl: 75, Sales ($M): 40.1, Fiscal End: 12/95; Paul H. Levine, Pres & CEO, David Leblang, CTO, Robert G. Parker, VP Mktng, Howard Spilke, VP R&D, Elliot Katzman, CFO, Email: elliot@atria.com; John E. Brewer, Dir Marcom

Attachmate Corp. 3617 131st Ave SE, Bellevue WA 98006-1332 USA; 206/644-4010, 800/426-6283 Fax: 206/747-9924, Co Email: @attachmate.com, Web URL: attachmate.com, Focus: Micro-to-mainframe connectivity products, Prdts: Extra!, Now!, Rally, ZIP!, Ownrshp: PVT, Founded: 1982, Empl: 2,000, Sales ($M): 415, Fiscal End: 12/95; James D. Lidner, Pres & CEO, Larry Zito, EVP, Barry Horn, EVP Sales & Mktng, Paul Rodwick, EVP, William E. Bolsvert, CFO, Dennis L. Sullivan, Dir PR

Attack Systems Int'l. (ASI), 111 Pine St, #950, San Francisco CA 94111 USA; 415/421-8191, Fax: 415/391-0326, Focus: Real estate management software, Ownrshp: PVT, Founded: 1993, Empl: 15, Mark Lambourne, CEO, John McCrocklin, Sr Advisor, Lisa L. Lavine, Mktng Mgr, Lisa L. Levine

Attain Corp. 48 Grove St, Somerville MA 02144-2500 USA; 617/776-1110, 800/925-5615 Fax: 617/776-1626, Co Email: info@attain.com, Web URL: attain.com, Focus: Macintosh work organizing software, Prdts: In Control, Ownrshp: PVT, Founded: 1990, Empl: 20, Alan Albert, Chmn & VP Mktng, Email: aalbert@qm.attain.com; Dan Chadwick, Pres, Email: dan_chadwick@qm.attain.com; Jeff Hulton, VP Sales, Email: jeff_hulton@qm.attain.com; Karen Dunne

ATTO Technology Inc. 40 Hazelwood Dr, #106, Amherst NY 14228 USA; 716/691-1999, Fax: 716/691-9353, Co Email: atto@aol.com, Focus: Disk caching products, Prdts: SiliconDisk, SiliconCache, Ownrshp: PVT, Founded: 1988, Empl: 50, Timothy Klein, Pres & CEO, David Snell, VP Eng, David J. Aillo, Dir Marcom

Audio Digital Imaging 511 W Golf Rd, Arlington Heights IL 60005 USA; 708/439-1335, Fax: 708/430-1533, Web URL: adi.net, Focus: Data compression products, Prdts: Apogee Series Chips, Ownrshp: OTC, Stk Sym: ADH, Founded: 1989, Empl: 20, Sales ($M): 0.16, Fiscal End: 12/94; Jean Monroe, Chmn & CEO, John S. Helmer, VP, Kevin Monroe, GM Corp Secretary, Mutahir Kazmi, Controller

Audits & Surveys 650 Ave of the Americas, New York NY 10011 USA; 212/627-9700, Fax: 212/627-2034, Web URL: surveys.com, Focus: PC sales tracking data, Ownrshp: PVT, Carl Ravitch, EVP, Bill Liebman, SVP

Auravision Corp. 47865 Fremont Blvd, Fremont CA 94538 USA; 510/252-6800, Fax: 510/438-9350, Co Email: @auravision.com, Focus: ICs for multimedia, Ownrshp: PVT, Founded: 1992, Empl: 50, Steven Chan, Pres & CEO, Email: steve@auravision.com; Wayne Ricciardi, VP Sales & Mktng, Email: wricciardi@auravision.com; Mark E. Hopper, Dir Sales, Steve Recht, CFO, Email: srecht@auravision.com

Aurora Technologies Inc. 176 Second Ave, Waltham MA 02154 USA; 617/290-4800, Fax: 617/290-4844, Co Email: info@auratek.com, Web URL: auratek.com, Focus: Workstation peripherals, Prdts: Aurora SPARC Terminal Servers, Aurora HP Workstation Terminal Servers, Ownrshp: PVT, Founded: 1988, Empl: 30, Sales ($M): 5, Fiscal End: 12/95; Dennis Daudelin, Pres, Kim Kinnear, VP Eng, Ralph Cafiero, VP Sales, Michael Tanner, VP Ops, Mark Sandman, Mktng Mgr

Aurum Software Inc. 3385 Scott Blvd, Santa Clara CA 95054-3115 USA; 408/562-6370, Fax: 408/562-6195, Web URL: aurum.com, Focus: Customer resource planning software, Prdts: TeleTrak, SupportTrak, QualityTrak, Ownrshp: PVT, Founded: 1990, Empl: 160, Mary Coleman, Pres, David Buchanan, EVP, Susan Buchanan, CFO

Auspex Systems Inc. 5200 Great American Pkwy, Santa Clara CA 95054 USA; 408/986-2000, Fax: 408/986-2020, Focus: Network servers, Ownrshp: OTC, Stk Sym: ASPX, Founded: 1987, Empl: 400, Sales ($M): 162.6, Fiscal End: 6/96; Laurence B. Boucher, CEO, Bruce Moore, Pres & COO, James H. Lawson, VP WW Sales, Joe Brown, VP Mktng, Esther W. Lee, VP & CFO

Austin Software Council 8920 Business Park Dr, Austin TX 78759 USA; 512/794-9994, Fax: 512/794-9997, Focus: Organization for Austin software companies, Ownrshp: Nonprofit

Auto F/X Corp. 189 Water St, PO Box 112, Exeter NH 03933 USA; 603/772-4725, Fax: 603/772-4644, Focus: Image editing software, Prdts: Photo/Graphic Edges, Ownrshp: PVT

Autodesk Inc. 111 McInnis Pkwy, San Rafael CA 94903 USA; 415/507-5000, Fax: 415/507-5100, Co Email: @autodesk.com, Web URL: autodesk.com, Focus: CAD software, Prdts: AutoCAD, 3D Studio, Ownrshp: OTC, Stk Sym: ADSK, Founded: 1982, Empl: 1,894, Sales ($M): 534.2, Fiscal End: 1/96; Carol Bartz, Chmn, Pres & CEO, James D'Arezzo, VP Mktng, Godfrey Sullivan, VP Americas, Richard Cuneo, VP US Sales, Eric Herr, VP & CFO

Autologic 1050 Rancho Conejo Blvd, Thousand Oaks CA 91320 USA; 805/498-9611, Fax: 805/499-1167, Web URL: autologic.com, Ownrshp: PVT

Automated Computer Business Systems PO Box 1555, Morgantown WV 26507 USA; 304/296-0290, Fax: 304/296-0292, Focus: Software for resellers and distributors, Prdts: Onex, Ownrshp: PVT, Founded: 1993, Daren J. Bieniek, Pres & CEO, Kenneth Vance, Co-Founder, Jimmy Chester, Co-Founder, Jennifer Robinson

Automated Imaging Association (AIA), 900 Victors Way, PO Box 3724, Ann Arbor MI 48106 USA; 313/994-6088, Fax: 313/994-3338, Focus: Productive use of image processing and machine vision, Ownrshp: Nonprofit, Jeff Burnstein, Mngng Dir

Automatic Data Processing Inc. (ADP), One ADP Blvd, Roseland NJ 07068 USA; 201/994-5000, Fax: 201/994-5495, Focus: Computer services, Prdts: AutoPay, PC Payroll to Personnel, FS

Partner, Ownrshp: NYSE, Stk Sym: AUD, Founded: 1961, Empl: 25,000, Sales ($M): 2,893.7, Fiscal End: 6/95; Josh S. Weston, Chmn & CEO, Arthur F. Weinbach, Pres & COO, Gary C. Butler, Group Pres, Robert J. Casale, Group Pres, Fred D. Anderson Jr., VP & CFO

AutoTester Inc. 8150 N Central Expwy, #1300, Dallas TX 75206 USA; 214/363-6181, Fax: 214/750-9668, Focus: Software testing tools, Prdts: AutoTester, Ownrshp: PVT, Founded: 1985, Empl: 75, Sales ($M): 7, Fiscal End: 9/93; Jerry Levine, Pres & CEO, K. Patrick Lee, VP Sales, Kyle Carper, VP Mktng, Randy Jesberg, New Bus Dev, Ellen Tarry, Dir Mktng

Autotime Corp. 6605 SW Macadam Ave, Portland OR 97201 USA; 503/452-8577, Fax: 503/452-8495, Co Email: info@autotime.com, Focus: Memory board, Ownrshp: PVT, Founded: 1985, Empl: 21, Michael Faunce, Pres, Bill Matson, Sales Mgr

Autumn Technologies 11705 69th Way N, #C, Largo FL 34643 USA; 813/530-0626, 800/837-8551 Fax: 813/538-0928, Co Email: autumn@intnet.net, Focus: PC testing products, Prdts: Test Bed, Test Bed Pro, Ownrshp: PVT, Founded: 1990, Empl: 8, Lisa K. Augustyniak, Pres, Peter G. Augustyniak, VP

Avail Systems Corp 4760 Walnut St, Boulder CO 80301 USA; 303/444-4018, 800/962-8245 Fax: 303/546-4219, Web URL: avail.com, Focus: Storage management software, Prdts: NetSpace, Ownrshp: PVT, Founded: 1991, Robert Wight, Pres, Greg Mangold, VP Mktng, Risa Wight

Avalan Technology Inc. PO Box 6888, Holliston MA 01746-6888 USA; 508/429-6482, Fax: 508/429-3179, Co Email: avalan@avalan.com, Web URL: avalan.com, Focus: Remote control software for Windows & DOS, Prdts: Remotely Possible, Ownrshp: PVT, Founded: 1989, Empl: 10, Anthony Amundson, Pres

Avanti Corp. (ISS), 1208 E Arques Ave, Sunnyvale CA 94086 USA; 408/738-8881, Fax: 408/738-8508, Co Email: info@avanticorp.com, Focus: IC CAD software, Prdts: ArcCell, VeriCheck, Ownrshp: OTC, Stk Sym: AVNT, Founded: 1985, Empl: 207, Sales ($M): 38, Fiscal End: 12/95; Gerald C. Itsu, Chmn, Pres & CEO, Eric Cho, VP Sales, John P. Huyett, VP & CFO

Avantos Performance Systems Inc. 5900 Hollis St, #A, Emeryville CA 94608 USA; 510/654-4600, 800/282-6867 Fax: 510/654-1276, Co Email: 525.0776@mcimail.com, Focus: Job enhancement software, Prdts: GoalTender, Ownrshp: PVT, Founded: 1991, Empl: 15, W. Norman Wu, Pres & CEO, Email: 615.6237@mcimail.com; Gerald B. Huff, VP Dev, Marti Pozzi, VP Sales, Darlene K. Mann, VP Mktng, Jennifer Klatt, Dir Fin

Avatar Systems Corp. 1455 McCarty Blvd, Milpitas CA 95035-7433 USA; 408/321-0110, Fax: 408/321-0115, Co Email: avatar4000@aol.com, Web URL: avatarltd.com, Focus: Removable cartridge disk drives, Prdts: AR2170NI (Remington)IDE, HD-170 Hardiskette, Ownrshp: PVT, Founded: 1991, Empl: 400, Robert E. Martell, Pres & CEO, Tom Maher, EVP WW Ops, Gailen Vick, VP Mktng & Sales, Email: gailenvic@aol.com; Rex Hamilton, Electric Eng, Aki Kumano, Mech Eng, Brian Ramos, Marcom Mgr, Email: ramosba@aol.com

AVerMedia Inc. 47923A Warm Springs Blvd, Fremont CA 94539 USA; 510/770-9899, 800/863-2332 Fax: 510/770-9901, Co Email: @aver.com, Web URL: aver.com, Focus: Video editing software, Prdts: VideoEditor, Ownrshp: PVT, Founded: 1991, Empl: 20, Michael Kyo, Pres, Amy S. Wong, CFO, Email: amyw@aver.com; Kathy Shih

Avery Dennison 150 N Orange Grove Blvd, Pasadena CA 91103 USA; 818/304-2000, Fax: 818/792-7312, Co Email: @averydennison.com, Focus: Labeling software and hardware, Ownrshp: NYSE, Stk Sym: AVY, Founded: 1977, Empl: 15,500, Sales ($M): 3,113.9, Fiscal End: 12/95; Charles D. Miller, Chmn & CEO, Philip M. Neal, Pres & COO, Alan J. Gotcher, SVP Mfg & Tech, R. Gregory Jenkins, SVP & CFO, Johan J. Goemans, VP MIS, Tina Ortiz-Burns

Avid Technology Inc. One Park W, Tewksbury MA 01876 USA; 508/640-6789, Fax: 508/640-1366, Focus: Digital media on multi-

ple platforms, Prdts: Media Composer, AudioVision, NewsCutter, AirPlay, Media Spectrum, Ownrshp: OTC, Stk Sym: AVID, Founded: 1987, Empl: 1,476, Sales ($M): 406.7, Fiscal End: 12/95; William J. Miller, Chmn & CEO, Dan Keshian, Pres, C. Edward Hazen, VP Finance, Eric C. Peters, VP Tech, Jonathan H. Cook, VP & CFO, Patrice Burkett, Corp Com Mgr

Avnet Inc. 80 Cutter Mill Rd, Great Neck NY 11021 USA; 516/466-7000, Fax: 516/466-1203, Web URL: avnet.com, Focus: Distributes electronic components and computer products, Ownrshp: NYSE, Stk Sym: AVT, Founded: 1955, Empl: 8,000, Sales ($M): 4,798, Fiscal End: 6/95; Leon Machiz, Chmn & CEO, Roy Vallee, Pres & COO, Stanley Benerofe, SVP, Raymond Sadowski, SVP & CFO, Anthony DeLuca, SVP & CIO

Award Software Int'l. Inc. 777 E Middlefield Rd, Mountain View CA 94043-4023 USA; 415/968-4433, Fax: 415/968-0274, Web URL: award.com, Focus: PCMCIA and BIOS software, Prdts: CardWare, Ownrshp: Sub. GCH, Founded: 1983, Empl: 85, George C. Huang, Chmn & CEO, M. Greg Paley, GM & SVP, Ann Shen, VP Sales & Mktng, John P. McCraken, Int'l. Acct Mgr, Jeffrey Flink, Mktng Dir

Axent Technologies 2440 Research Blvd, Rockville MD 20850 USA; 301/258-2620, Fax: 301/330-5756, Focus: C/S security software and services, Ownrshp: Sub Raxco, Founded: 1994, Richard A. Lefebvre, Pres & CEO, John C. Becker, EVP, Pete Privateer, SVP Ops, Brett Jackson, SVP Sales & Mktng

Axis Communications Inc. 4 Constitution Way, Woburn MA 01801-1030 USA; 617/938-1188, 800/444-2947 Fax: 617/938-6161, Co Email: info@axisinc.com, Focus: Printer controllers, Ownrshp: Sub. Axis Com., Sweden, Founded: 1988, Sales ($M): 7, Stephen Gurdon, Pres, Mikael Karlsson, Chmn

Axonix Corp. 844 S 200 E, Salt Lake City UT 84111-4203 USA; 801/521-9797, 800/866-9797 Fax: 801/521-9798, Focus: Laptop PC peripherals, Prdts: MilWrite, LapStation, Ownrshp: PVT, Founded: 1983, Empl: 30, Sales ($M): 6, Fiscal End: 8/92; Michael K. Hickey, Pres, David L. Cox, VP Sales & Mktng, Kevin Snyder, Controller

Axxon Computer Corp. 3979 Tecumseh Rd E, Windsor Ontario N8W 1J5 Canada; 519/974-0163, 800/361-1913 Fax: 519/974-0165, Co Email: axxon@netcore.ca, Web URL: netcore.ca/~axxon, Focus: I/O peripherals, Arthur Yanamoto, Ops Mgr

Aydin Corp. 700 Dresher Rd, Horsham PA 19044 USA; 215/657-7510, Fax: 215/657-3830, Focus: Monitors, displays and electronic products, Ownrshp: NYSE, Stk Sym: AYD, Founded: 1967, Sales ($M): 140.6, Fiscal End: 12/95; Ayhan Hakimoglu, Chmn & CEO, Donald S. Taylor, Pres, John Vanderslice, EVP, John Wong, VP, Gary T. Boswell, GM Computer & Monitors

Azalea Software Inc. PO Box 16745, Seattle WA 98116 USA; 206/932-4030, 800/482-7638 Fax: 206/937-5919, Co Email: @azela.com, Focus: Bar code software, Prdts: VampireXT, Ownrshp: PVT, Founded: 1992, Jerry Whiting, Pres

Azeena Technologies Inc. PO Box 92169, Long Beach CA 90809 USA; 310/981-2771, Fax: 310/988-7607, Focus: Windows graphics software, Ownrshp: PVT, Founded: 1992, John Housten, Pres

Azerty Inc. 13 Centre Dr, Orchard Park NY 14127 USA; 716/662-0200, Fax: 716/662-7616, Focus: Wholesaler of peripherals and supplies, Founded: 1983, Empl: 270, William Dueger, GM, Kevin Bowman, Dir Sales & Mktng, Jeff Peager, Advertising Mgr

Aztech Labs Inc. 47811 Warm Spring Blvd, Fremont CA 94539-7400 USA; 510/623-8988, Fax: 510/623-8989, Focus: Multimedia and sound products, Prdts: Sound Galaxy, Ownrshp: Sub. Aztech Group, Hong Kong, Founded: 1992, Empl: 2,100 WW, Sales ($M): 210 WW, Fiscal End: 12/94; Michael Mun, Pres, Loh Ngiang Guan, VP Tech Div, Patricia Ng, VP Sales & Mktng, Peter Teo, Dir Ops, Karen Klimas

B-Plan USA 245 Pegasus Ave, Northvale NJ 07647 USA; 201/784-0900, Fax: 201/767-7227, Co Email: 100274.360@compuserve.com, Web URL: elron.net:80/bplan, Focus: Business planning software, Ownrshp: PVT, Jack Lahav

B.C. Software Inc. 11965 Venice Blvd, #405, Los Angeles CA 90066 USA; 310/636-4711, 800/231-4055 Fax: 310/636-4688, Co Email: info@bcsoftware.com, Focus: Information management software, Prdts: Final Draft, Three by Five, Ownrshp: PVT, Founded: 1986, Ben Cahan, Pres, Email: cahan@bcsofware.com; Marc Madnick, EVP, Email: madnick@bcsoftware.com; Eric Cohen, VP Ops, Email: cohen@bcsoftware.com

Baan Co. 4600 Bohannon Dr, Menlo Park CA 94025 USA; 415/462-4949, Web URL: baan.com, Focus: Resource planning software, Prdts: Triton, Ownrshp: OTC, Stk Sym: BAANF, Founded: 1981, Empl: 1,500, Sales ($M): 216.2, Fiscal End: 12/95; Jan Baan, Chmn & CEO, Tom Tinsley, Pres, David C. Cairns, CFO

Baker & Taylor Software 8501 Telfair Ave, Sun Valley CA 91352-3928 USA; 805/522-9800, Focus: Software distributor, Ownrshp: Sub. Baker & Taylor, Founded: 1983, Empl: 200, Sales ($M): 130, Jim Warburton, Pres, Marty Brandtner, CEO

Ballard Synergy 1223 NW Finn Hill Rd, Poulsbo WA 98370 USA; 360/697-9260, 800/692-0492 Fax: 360/598-2450, Web URL: ballardsynergy.com, Focus: CD-ROM accelerators, Prdts: d-Time Office, Ownrshp: PVT, Founded: 1987, Clint Ballard, CEO, Daniel Kerber

Balt Inc. 201 N Crockett, Cameron TX 76520 USA; 817/697-4953, 800/749-2258 Fax: 817/697-6258, Focus: Computer furniture, Ownrshp: PVT, Founded: 1985, Empl: 15, Sales ($M): 3, Lorraine Moore, Co-Owner, Ernest Moore, Co-Owner, Kathy Terry, VP Corp, Holly Roberts, Dir Advertising

BancTec Inc. 4435 Spring Valley Rd, Dallas TX 75244 USA; 214/450-7700, Web URL: banc-tec.com, Focus: Financial transaction computer systems, Ownrshp: NYSE, Stk Sym: BTC, Founded: 1972, Empl: 3,560, Sales ($M): 297.5, Fiscal End: 3/95; Grahame N. Clark, Jr., Chmn, Pres & CEO, John G. Guthrie, SVP, William E. Bassett, EVP, Raghavan Rajaji, SVP & CFO, Gordon F. Kipp, VP Info Serv, John E. Moss, Dir Corp Comm

Bansai 24 Coast Oak Way, San Rafael CA 94903 USA; 415/492-3307, 800/566-6832 Fax: 415/492-9655, Co Email: @bansai.com, Web URL: bansai.com, Focus: Portable scanner/fax, Prdts: MicroFax, Ownrshp: Sub Dietrich & Streicher

Banyan Systems Inc. 120 Flanders Rd, Westboro MA 01581 USA; 508/898-1000, Fax: 508/898-1755, Web URL: banyan.com, Focus: Network products, Prdts: Vines, Ownrshp: OTC, Stk Sym: BNYN, Founded: 1983, Empl: 859, Sales ($M): 129.7, Fiscal End: 12/95; David C. Mahoney, Chmn, Pres & CEO, A. Peter Hamilton, COO, C. James Schaper, SVP WW Sales & Mktng, Lawrence R. Floryan, VP & CTO, Jeffrey D. Glidden, VP & CFO

Barco Chromatics 2558 Mountain Industrial Blvd, Tucker GA 30084-3893 USA; 770/493-7000, Fax: 770/493-1314, Co Email: @barco.com, Focus: Graphics products for command and control, Prdts: IVS4000 Series, Megacalibrator, Ownrshp: Sub. Barco, Belgium, Founded: 1976, Empl: 100, Sales ($M): 15, Luc Van den Broucke, Pres, H. David Scott, EVP & GM, Email: scott@barco.com; Tom Burdette, VP Ops, Robert Creasy, Dir Sales, Luc Fobry, Marcom Mgr, Email: fobry@barco.com

Baron, McDonald & Wells 6292 Lawrenceville Hwy NW, #C, Tucker GA 30084 USA; 770/492-0373, Fax: 770/492-0374, Co Email: bmwpr@bmwpr.com, Web URL: mindspring.com/~bm&w/bmwhome, Focus: PR and marketing strategies, Ownrshp: PVT, Founded: 1992, Peter Baron, Pres, Email: pbaron@bmwpr.com; Beverly McDonald, Principal, Email: bmcdonald@bmwpr.com; Terry L. Wells, Principal, Email: twells@bmwpr.com; Sharon Cuppett, VP & Mgng Dir, Email: scuppett@bmwpr.com

Barr Systems Inc. 4131 NW 28 Ln, Gainesville FL 32606-6681 USA; 904/371-3050, 800/227-7797 Fax: 904/491-3141, Co Email: @barrsys.com, Focus: PC-to-mainframe communications, Prdts: BARR/GATE, Ownrshp: PVT, Founded: 1978, Empl: 65,

Sales ($M): 11, Fiscal End: 12/94; Anthony J. Barr, Pres, Kay Barr, VP, Paul B. Firth, Dir Mktng, Email: paul@barrsys.com

Barra Inc. 1995 University Ave, #400, Berkeley CA 94704 USA; 510/548-5442, Fax: 510/548-4374, Web URL: barra.com, Focus: Financial and investment software, Ownrshp: OTC, Stk Sym: BARZ, Founded: 1975, Empl: 371, Sales ($M): 61.0, Fiscal End: 3/96; Andrew Rudd, Chmn & CEO, Robert L. Honeycutt, COO, Edward D. Baker, SVP, C.E. Beckers, SVP, Daniel Beck, VP

BASF Corp. 8 Campus Dr, Parsippany NJ 07054 USA; 201/397-2700, 800/669-2273 Fax: 201/397-4525, Focus: Computer tape and floppy disks, Ownrshp: Sub. BASF, Germany, Stk Sym: BASF, Founded: 1956, Empl: 16,000, Sales ($M): 5,201.8, Fiscal End: 12/93; J. Ditter Stein, Pres & CEO, Manfred Buller, EVP, Werner Burgert, EVP, R. Wayne Godwin, EVP, Gerard de Beuckelaer, SVP Info Syst, James H. Murphy, VP Corp Com

BASIS Inc. 5758 Hollis St, Emeryville CA 94608-2514 USA; 510/547-5900, Fax: 510/547-5061, Web URL: basisinc.com, Focus: Open system integration - UNIX, Prdts: BIS/System, Ownrshp: PVT, Founded: 1981, Patricia Shanks, Pres, Michael Denney, VP Mktng

Basis Int'l. 5901 Jefferson St NE, Albuquerque NM 87109 USA; 505/345-5232, Fax: 505/345-5082, Web URL: basis.com, Focus: Software development tools, Prdts: Visual PRO/5 Series, BASIS ODBC Drr, BBx, TAOS Series, Ownrshp: PVT, Founded: 1985, Empl: 51, George Hight, Pres, Joe Rose, VP Fin, Maile Foster, Dir Mktng, Email: mfoster@basis.com; John Schroeder, Mgr Eng, Email: jfs@basis.com; Jill Salva, Mgr Marcom, Email: jsalva@basis.com

BateTech Software Inc. 7550 W Yale Ave, #B-130, Denver CO 80227 USA; 303/763-8333, Fax: 303/763-2783, Co Email: @batetech.com, Web URL: batetech.com, Focus: C/S software, Prdts: iWay-One, Customer-One, Ownrshp: Sub Workgroup Systems, Kevin Smith, VP Mktng, Email: kevins@batetech.com; Eric Peterson, Email: ericp@batetech.com

Battery Technology Inc. 5700 Bandini Blvd, Commerce CA 90040 USA; 213/728-7874, Fax: 213/728-7996, Web URL: batterytech.com, Focus: Portable computer accessories, Ownrshp: PVT, Christopher Chu, SVP Mktng & Sales

Bay Networks Inc. 4401 Great America Pkwy, Santa Clara CA 95052-8185 USA; 408/988-2400, Fax: 408/988-5525, Web URL: baynetworks.com, Focus: Network products, Ownrshp: OTC, Stk Sym: BNET, Founded: 1989, Empl: 5,758, Sales ($M): 2,057, Fiscal End: 6/96; Paul J. Severino, Chmn, Andrew K. Ludwick, Pres & CEO, Ronald V. Schmidt, EVP & CTO, William J. Ruehle, EVP & CFO

BayStone Software 18809 Cox Ave, #250, Saratoga CA 95070 USA; 408/370-9301, Fax: 408/370-9301, Co Email: info@baystone.com, Web URL: baystone.com, Focus: Customer interaction software solutions, Prdts: SupportCenter, Ownrshp: PVT, Founded: 1995, Robert Lux, Pres & CEO, Email: bob@baystone.com; Warren Teitelman, VP Eng, Craig Olson, VP Mktng, Email: craig@baystone.com

Bayware Inc. 1660 S Amphlett Blvd, #128, San Mateo CA 94402 USA; 415/286-4480, Fax: 415/578-1884, Web URL: bayware.com, Focus: Language tutorial software, Prdts: Power Japanese, Kanji Moments, Power Spanish, Ownrshp: PVT, Founded: 1989, Empl: 12, Sales ($M): 1.3, Andrew Wang, Pres, Norman Donald, VP, Kathy Chin, Mktng & Sales Mgr, Email: kathy@bayware.com

BBN Planet Corp. 150 Cambridge Park Dr, Cambridge MA 02140-9955 USA; 617/873-8730, Fax: 617/873-5620, Co Email: @bbnplanet.com, Web URL: bbnplanet.com, Focus: Internet access provider, Ownrshp: Sub BBN, Founded: 1993, Paul R. Gudonis, CEO

BBN Software Products Corp. 150 CambridgePark Dr, Cambridge MA 02140 USA; 617/873-5000, 800/331-2266 Focus: Data analysis software, Ownrshp: Sub Bolt Beranek and Newman, Jeffrey

H. Palmer, VP

BCB Holdings Inc. 418 Hanlan Rd, #4, Woodbridge Ontario L4L 4Z1 Canada; 905/850-8266, Fax: 905/850-8276, Web URL: bcb!.org, Focus: PC-based digital dictation systems, Prdts: PC-DART, Courtroom-DART, Multiple User Recording Facility (MURF), Stk Sym: BIV, Founded: 1992, Empl: 17, Fiscal End: 9/95; Kenneth G. Murton, Pres & CEO, Zev Hershtal, EVP & COO, Daryl R. Duda, VP Sales, Leo Halpern, VP Systems

BCE Inc. 1000, rue de La Gauchetiere Ouest, Bureau 3700 Montreal H3B 4Y7 Canada; 514/397-7267, Fax: 514/397-7157, Co Email: bcecomms@bce.ca, Web URL: bce.ca, Focus: Telecom products and services, Sales ($M): 24,624.0, Fiscal End: 12/95; L.R. Wilson, Chmn, Pres & CEO, Derek H. Burney, EVP Int'l., Charles A. Labarge, VP Corp. Svcs., Ronald W. Osborne, EVP & CFO

BDM Int'l. 1501 BDM Way, McLean VA 22102 USA; 703/848-5000, Fax: 703/848-5221, Co Email: bdmit@bdm.com, Web URL: bdm.com, Focus: Systems integration, Ownrshp: OTC, Stk Sym: BDMI, Empl: 2,800, Sales ($M): 890.0, Fiscal End: 12/95; Philip A. Odeen, Pres & CEO, David N. Walker, VP & Controller, Andrew E. Bilinski, Group VP, Lowell R. Smith, Corp VP, Roger A. Young, VP & CFO

BEA Systems Inc. 385 Moffett Park Dr, #105, Sunnyvale CA 94089-1208 USA; 408/743-4000, Fax: 408/734-9234, Co Email: @beasys, Web URL: beasys.inter.net, Focus: Enterprise middleware solutions, Prdts: TUXEDO, Founded: 1995, Empl: 335, Sales ($M): 35, Fiscal End: 12/95; William Coleman, Chmn & CEO, Edward Scott Jr., EVP Ops, Alfred Chuang, EVP & CTO, Jay Fry, Email: jayfry@aol.com

Beame & Whitside Software Ltd. 706 Hillsborough St, Raleigh NC 27603-1655 USA; 919/831-8989, 800/463-5697 Fax: 919/831-8990, Co Email: sales@bws.com, Focus: Connectivity software, Prdts: BW-Services, BW-Server, Ownrshp: Sub Hummingbird, Canada, Founded: 1987, Carl Beame, Chmn & CTO, Paul Rasmussen, Pres & CEO, Graham Wright, VP Tech, Fred Whiteside, Mgr R&D, Terry Stanfield, Email: terrys@bws.com

Bedini Electronics Inc. 2619 Seltic Way, Coeur d'Alene ID 83814 USA; 208/667-8300, Fax: 208/667-5300, Focus: Multimedia audio products, Ownrshp: PVT, John Bedini, Pres

BeInfinite Inc. 455 Vallejo St, #P5, San Francisco CA 94133 USA; 800/554-6624 Co Email: beinfinite@aol.com, Focus: Adobe Illustrator add-on products, Ownrshp: PVT, Keith McGreggor, Pres

Belkin Components 1303 Walnut Park Way, Compton CA 90220 USA; 310/898-1100, 800/223-5546 Fax: 310/898-1111, Focus: Printer sharing devices and cables, Ownrshp: PVT, Founded: 1983, Empl: 80, Chester Pipkin, Pres, Stephen Bellow, VP Sales & Mktng

Bell Atlantic Corp. 1717 Arch St, Philadelphia PA 19103 USA; 215/963-6000, 800/235-5595 Web URL: bell-atl.com, Focus: Regional Bell operating company (RBOC), Ownrshp: NYSE, Stk Sym: BEL, Founded: 1983, Empl: 61,800, Sales ($M): 13,429.5, Fiscal End: 12/95; Raymond W. Smith, Chmn & CEO, James G. Cullen, Pres, John F. Gamba, SVP, Joseph T. Ambrozy, VP Strat Plng, William O. Albertini, EVP & CFO

Bell Industries Inc. 11812 San Vicente Blvd, Los Angeles CA 90049-5022 USA; 310/826-2355, Fax: 310/447-3265, Web URL: bellind.com, Focus: Distributes electronic components and PCs, Ownrshp: NYSE, Stk Sym: BI, Founded: 1952, Empl: 1,600, Sales ($M): 564.3, Fiscal End: 12/95; Theodore Williams, Chmn & CEO, Bruce M. Jaffe, Pres & COO, Paul F. Doucette, SVP, Tracy A. Edwards, VP & CFO, D.J. Hough, VP & CIO

Bellcore (Bellcore). 445 South St, Morristown NJ 07960-6438 USA; 201/829-2000, 800/521-2673 Web URL: bellcore.com, Focus: Telecom consulting and software, Ownrshp: Bell telephone companies, Founded: 1984, Empl: 6,100, Sales ($M): 1.1, Fiscal End: 12/94; George H. Heilmeier, Pres & CEO, Robert W. Lucky, Corp VP Applied Res, George C. Via, EVP Customer Solutions, N.

Michael Grove, VP Gen Counsel, Rodney L. Everhart, SVP & CFO, Barbara McClurken, Dir External Comm, Email: bsm@cc.bellcore.com

BellSouth Corp. 1155 Peachtree St NE, Atlanta GA 30309-3610 USA; 404/249-2000, Fax: 404/249-5597, Web URL: bell-south.com, Focus: Regional Bell operating company (RBOC), Ownrshp: NYSE, Stk Sym: BLS, Founded: 1983, Empl: 87,600, Sales ($M): 17,886.0, Fiscal End: 12/95; John L. Clendenin, Chmn, F. Duane Ackerman, Pres & CEO, C. Sidney Boren, SVP Strag Plng, Mark L. Feidler, VP Corp Dev, Ronald M. Dykes, EVP & CFO

Benchmark Laboratories Inc. 7600 Parklawn, #408, Minneapolis MN 55435 USA; 612/897-3505, Fax: 612/897-3524, Focus: Software testing for MS-DOS, Windows, OS/2, Macintosh, LANs and Unix, Ownrshp: PVT, Founded: 1987, Empl: 15, Larry Decklever, Pres, Chuck Le Count, Project Mgr

Bendata Management Systems 1125 Kelly Johnson Blvd, #100, Colorado Springs CO 80920-3961 USA; 719/531-5007, 800/776-7889 Fax: 719/536-9623, Web URL: bendata.com, Focus: Help desk, asset tracking and cost accounting software, Prdts: HEAT, Ownrshp: Sub. Astea International, Founded: 1982, Empl: 115, Sales ($M): 2.3, Ron Muns, Chmn & CEO, Randall Casto, Pres

Bentley Systems Inc. 690 Pennsylvania Dr, Exton PA 19341 USA; 610/458-5000, Fax: 610/458-1060, Co Email: @bentley.com, Web URL: bentley.com, Focus: CAD software, Prdts: MicroStation, Ownrshp: PVT, Empl: 450, Sales ($M): 95, Fiscal End: 12/95; Greg Bentley, Pres, Paul Lamparski, CFO

Berkeley Software Design Inc. (BSDI), 5575 Tech Ctr Dr, #110, Colorado Springs CO 80918 USA; 719/593-9445, 800/800-4223 Fax: 719/598-4238, Co Email: info@bsci.com, Focus: Internet software, Prdts: BSDI Internet Server, Ownrshp: PVT, Founded: 1991, Empl: 30, Rob Kolstad, Pres, Email: kolstad@bsdi.com; Mike Karels, Chief Syst Arch, Email: karels@bsdi.com; Gary Johnson, VP Sales & Mktng, Email: garyj@bsdi.com; Frank Orasin, CFO, Email: orasin@bsdi.com

Berkeley Systems Inc. 2095 Rose St, Berkeley CA 94709 USA; 510/540-5535, 800/344-5541 Fax: 510/549-3978, Co Email: cs@berksys.com, Web URL: berksys.com, Focus: Entertainment software, Prdts: AfterDark, Star Trek, Disney Collection Screen Savers, Ownrshp: PVT, Founded: 1987, Empl: 120, Sales ($M): 25+, Fiscal End: 6/96; Wesley Boyd, Chmn & CEO, Julie Wainwright, Pres & COO, Nicholas Rush, VP Prod, Phil Duncan, VP Int'l Sales, DeEtte Christie, PR Coord, Email: dchristie@berksys.com

Bernstein and Associates 5 Dunwoody Park, #118, Atlanta GA 30338 USA; 770/392-1488, Fax: 770/671-1618, Focus: Computer training software, Prdts: Design-A-Course, Founded: 1986, Louis Bernstein, Developer

Best Buy Co. Inc. PO Box 9312, 7075 Flying Cloud Dr, Minneapolis MN 55440-9312 USA; 612/947-2000, Fax: 612/947-2422, Focus: Consumer electronics and PC reseller, Ownrshp: NYSE, Stk Sym: BBY, Founded: 1966, Empl: 15,200, Sales ($M): 7,217.4, Fiscal End: 2/96; Richard M. Schulze, Chmn & CEO, Bradbury H. Anderson, Pres & COO, Wade R. Fenn, SVP Sales, Lee H. Schoenfeld, SVP Mktng, Steven R. Anderson, SVP MIS

Best Data Products Inc. 21800 Nordhoff St, Chatsworth CA 91311 USA; 818/773-9600, Fax: 818/773-9619, Co Email: admin@bestdata.com, Web URL: bestdata.com, Focus: Modems and fax modems, Prdts: Smart One, Ownrshp: PVT, Founded: 1983, Bruce Zaman, Pres, Danny Horowitz, Mktng Mgr, Email: danny@bdp.mhs.compuserve.com; Lauren Finkelman, Email: 76225.2253@compuserve.com

Best Power Technology Inc. PO Box 280, Hwy 80 S, Necedah WI 54646 USA; 608/565-7200, 800/356-5794 Fax: 608/565-2221, Co Email: info@bestpower.com, Web URL: best-power.com, Focus: Uninterruptible power supplies, Prdts: FER-RUPS, Ownrshp: Sub General Signal, Founded: 1977, Empl: 846, Sales ($M): 149.4, Fiscal End: 12/94; Gurcharn Dang, Pres, John A.

Lombardi, VP Sales & Mktng, Fred Stich, CTO, Brian Crowe, VP Sales, Louhon Tucker, VP Finance, Larry Bobrowski

Best Programs Inc. 11413 Isaac Newton Square, Reston VA 22090-9721 USA; 703/709-5200, 800/368-2405 Fax: 703/318-0499, Web URL: bestprograms.com, Focus: Accounting and financial software, Ownrshp: PVT, Founded: 1982, Empl: 280, Sales ($M): 38.2, Fiscal End: 12/95; James F. Petersen, Chmn, Melody Ranelli, CFO, Dorothy Webb, SVP

Best!Ware 300 Roundhill Dr, Rockaway NJ 07866 USA; 201/586-8986, Fax: 201/586-9344, Co Email: @bestprog.com, Focus: Accounting software, Prdts: MYOB, Ownrshp: Sub. Best Programs, Founded: 1982, Empl: 75, Sales ($M): 5.1, Fiscal End: 3/95; Christopher P. Lee, Pres, Barry Reicherter, PR Mgr, Email: barry_reicherter@bestprog

Best-Seller Inc. 3300 Cote-Vertu, #303, Montreal Quebec H4R 2B8 Canada; 514/337-3000, Fax: 514/337-7629, Co Email: @bestseller.com, Web URL: bestseller.com, Focus: Web database software, Prdts: BestWeb, Shirley Kieran, Pres

BGS Systems Inc. 128 Technology Ctr, Waltham MA 02254-9111 USA; 617/891-0000, Fax: 617/890-0000, Co Email: best1@bgs.com, Web URL: bgs.com, Focus: Computer performance measurement software, Ownrshp: OTC, Stk Sym: BGSS, Founded: 1975, Empl: 185, Sales ($M): 41.1, Fiscal End: 1/96; Harold S. Schwenk Jr., Chmn, Pres & CEO, James S. McGuire, COO, Jeffrey P. Buzen, SVP, Normand Bilodeau, CFO

Big Island Communications Inc. 10161 Bubb Rd, Cupertino CA 95014 USA; 408/342-8300, Fax: 408/257-7306, Co Email: info@big-island.com, Web URL: big-island.com, Focus: Telephone management software, Prdts: YoYo, Ownrshp: PVT, Founded: 1995, Empl: 20, Derrick Miley, CEO, Buz Roberts, Dir Eng, Larry Becker, CFO, David L'Heureux, Dir Mktng, Email: david@big-island.com; Todd Cone, Dir Info Syst

Big Software Inc. 2111 Grant Rd, Los Altos CA 94024-6954 USA; 415/919-0200, Fax: 415/919-0205, Co Email: @bigbusiness.com, Web URL: bigbusiness.com, Focus: Business management software, Ownrshp: PVT, Founded: 1993, Ted Helvey, Pres, Eric Herzog, VP Mktng, Email: herzog@bigbusiness.com; Ellen Akunda, Mktng Mgr, Email: ellen@bigbusiness.com

Big Top Productions Inc. 548 Fourth St, San Francisco CA 94107 USA; 415/978-5363, Fax: 415/978-5353, Web URL: bigtop.com, Focus: Multimedia educational software, Ownrshp: PVT, Founded: 1994, Empl: 30, Jim Myrick, Co-founder, Jake Myrick, Co-founder, Lisa Van Cleef, VP, Erica Eusebio, PR Mgr

Binar Graphics Inc. 30 Mitchell Blvd, San Rafael CA 94903-2034 USA; 415/491-1565, Fax: 415/491-1164, Co Email: binar@crl.com, Web URL: crl.com/~binar, Focus: Windows and OS/2 utility software, Prdts: AnyView Professional, SkyScraper: Desktop Manager for OS/2, Ownrshp: PVT, Founded: 1989, Empl: 25, Scott Vouri, Pres, Paul King, GM

Binuscan Inc. 505 5th Ave, New York NY 10017 USA; 212/681-0600, 800/881-2352 Fax: 212/681-0603, Focus: Image management software, Prdts: binuscan, Ownrshp: Sub Binuscan, Monaco, Lisa Morris

Bionic Buffalo Corp. 2533 N Carson St, #1884, Carson City NV 89706-0147 USA; 702/882-1842, Fax: 702/882-6047, Prdts: Tatanka ORB, Michael Marking

Biscom Inc. 321 Billerica Rd, Chelmsford MA 01824-4100 USA; 508/250-1800, 800/477-2472 Fax: 508/250-4449, Co Email: @biscom.com, Web URL: biscom.com, Focus: Fax servers, Prdts: FAXCOM, Ownrshp: PVT, Founded: 1986, Empl: 40, S.K. Ho, Pres & CEO, Stephen M. Pytka, EVP, Chris MacKenze, Dir Mktng

Bit 3 Computer Corp. 8120 Penn Ave S, Minneapolis MN 55431-1393 USA; 612/881-6955, Fax: 612/881-9674, Co Email: info@bit3.com, Web URL: bit3.com, Focus: Add-in boards and peripherals, Prdts: VMEbus System, Ownrshp: PVT, Founded: 1979, Phil Vukovic, Pres, Larry Larsen, VP, Jerry Medley, Dir Sales

BitWise Designs Inc. Technology Ctr, Rotterdam Industrial Park,

Schenectady NY 12306 USA; 518/356-9741, 800/683-7022 Fax: 518/356-9749, Focus: Portable computers, Prdts: ScreenStar, DocSTAR, Ownrshp: OTC, Stk Sym: BTWS, Founded: 1985, Empl: 17, Sales ($M): 23.9, Fiscal End: 6/95; John T. Botti, Chmn, Pres & CEO, Email: jbotti@docstar.com; Ira C. Whitman, SVP R&D, Dennis H. Bunt, CFO

Black & White Software 2155 S Bascom Ave, #210, Campbell CA 95008 USA; 408/369-7400, Fax: 408/369-7406, Focus: Unix application software tools, Ownrshp: PVT, Founded: 1991, Julia Miller, CEO & Dir Bus Dev, Charles White, Pres, Don Middleton, Dir Strategic Sales, Andrew Sacks, Dir Sales, Todd Scallan, Dir Corp Partnership

Black Box Corp. 1000 Park Dr, Lawrence PA 15055 USA; 412/746-5500, Fax: 412/746-0746, Co Email: info@blackbox.com, Web URL: blackbox.com, Focus: Communications and connectivity products, Stk Sym: BBOX, Founded: 1977, Empl: 650, Sales ($M): 165, Fiscal End: 3/95; Jeff Boetticker, CEO, Fred C. Young, CFO

Black Data Processing Associates (BDPA), 1250 Connecticut Ave NW, #700, Washington DC 20036 USA; 202/775-4301, 800/727-2372 Fax: 202/637-9195, Focus: Educational opportunities and information sharing, Ownrshp: Nonprofit, Founded: 1975, Empl: 2,000, Margaret E. Johnson, Exec Dir, Diane L. Davis, Pres

Black Sun Interactive Inc. 50 Osgood Place, #330, San Francisco CA 94133 USA; 415/273-7000, Fax: 415/273-7001, Web URL: blacksun.com, Focus: Multiuser VRML browser, server and VRML/Java authoring software, Ownrshp: PVT, Founded: 1995, Empl: 25, Franz Buchenberger, CEO

Blackship Computer Systems Inc. 2031 O'Toole Ave, San Jose CA 95131 USA; 408/432-7500, 800/531-7447 Fax: 408/432-1443, Co Email: sales@blackship-computers.com, Web URL: blackship-computers.com, Focus: PCs, peripherals and multimedia software, Prdts: Blackship Atlantis 486DX2/66, Aquarius 486DX4/100, Ownrshp: PVT, Founded: 1980, Empl: 26, Sales ($M): 6.5, Fiscal End: 9/92; Saroj Gupta, Pres, Rajeev Kumar, GM, Don Sales, VP Sales, Belinda Richardson, Admin

Blast Software Inc. PO Box 808, 49 Salisbury St W, Pittsboro NC 27312 USA; 919/542-3007, 800/242-5278 Fax: 919/542-0161, Co Email: @blast.com, Web URL: blast.com, Focus: Communication software, Prdts: Blast, Ownrshp: PVT, Founded: 1993, Tamy Schwerin, Dir Sales & Ops, Melinda Pfeiffer, Email: melinda@blast.com

Blenheim Group USA Inc. Fort Lee Exec Park, One Exec Dr, Ft. Lee NJ 07024 USA; 201/346-1400, 800/829-3976 Fax: 201/346-1532, Web URL: shownet.com, Focus: Computer tradeshows, Prdts: PC Expo, Networks Expo, UNIX Expo, DB/Expo, Ownrshp: Public, Steve Ianuzzi, CEO, Mark Dineen, VP, Email: mdineen@blenheim.com; Tom Portesy, VP, Email: tportesy@blenheim.com; Don Berey, VP, Email: dberey@blenheim.com; Annie Scully, PR Director, Email: ascully@blenheim.com

BLOC Development Corp. 1 Datran Ctr, 15th Fl, 9100 S Dadeland Blvd, Miami FL 33156 USA; 305/445-0903, Fax: 305/529-2931, Focus: Reseller, Ownrshp: OTC, Stk Sym: BDEV, Gilbert Fiorentino, Pres & CEO

Blue Lance 1700 W Loop S, #1100, Houston TX 77027 USA; 713/680-1187, 800/856-2583 Fax: 713/622-1370, Focus: Network security software, Prdts: LT Auditor, Ownrshp: PVT, Founded: 1985, Umesh K. Verma, Pres & CEO

Blue Ribbon SoundWorks Ltd. 1605 Chantilly Dr, #200, Atlanta GA 30324 USA; 404/315-0212, Fax: 404/315-0213, Focus: Music and multimedia products, Ownrshp: PVT, Melissa Jordan Grey, Pres, Todor Fay, CTO

Blue Sky Software Corp. 7777 Fay Ave, #201, La Jolla CA 92037 USA; 619/459-6365, 800/677-4946 Fax: 619/459-6366, Co Email: 71052.1641@compuserve.com, Web URL: bluesky.com, Focus: Windows utility software, Prdts: WindowsMAKER, Ownrshp: PVT, Founded: 1989, Leslie Lazareck, Pres,

Jorgen Lien, Founder, Marylin Guarino, PR Mgr, Email: maryling@blue-sky.com

Bluebird Systems 5900 LaPlace Ct, Carlsbad CA 92008 USA; 619/438-2220, 800/669-2220 Fax: 619/438-4560, Focus: Document management/imaging, Prdts: SuperDOS/Image ABLE, Ownrshp: PVT, Founded: 1982, Empl: 75, Sales ($M): 25, Fiscal End: 10/93; Hal Tilbury, Pres & CEO, Desmond Crain, VP Imaging Sales, Alfred Riedler, CFO, Kay Sakata, VP Int'l. Sales, Gail Karon, Mgr Prof Svs, Tom Toperczer, Marcom Mgr

Bluestone Inc. 1000 Briggs Rd, Mount Laurel NJ 08054-4101 USA; 609/727-4600, Fax: 609/778-8125, Focus: Unix software, Ownrshp: PVT, Founded: 1989, Mel Baiada, Pres, Robert W. Bickel, Dir Prod, Email: bluestone!bickel@uunet.uu; Ron Guide, Dir Prof Svcs, Art Liggio, Dir Training, Chuck Patrick, Dir Dev

Blyth Software Inc. 989 E Hillsdale Blvd, #400, Foster City CA 94404 USA; 415/571-0222, 800/346-6647 Fax: 415/571-1132, Web URL: blyth.com, Focus: C/S software, Prdts: OMNIS, Ownrshp: OTC, Stk Sym: BLYH, Founded: 1983, Empl: 115, Sales ($M): 14.7, Fiscal End: 3/96; Stephen R. Lorentzen, Pres & COO, David R. Seaman, CTO, Michael J. Minor, CEO, Thomas C. Meyer, SVP Ops, William Glynn, CFO, Shannon Titus, Mgr Mktng Programs, Email: shannon_titus@blyth.com

BMC Software Inc. (BMC), 2101 CityWest Blvd, Houston TX 77042-2827 USA; 713/918-8800, 800/841-2031 Fax: 713/918-8000, Web URL: bmc.com, Focus: Mainframe software, Ownrshp: OTC, Stk Sym: BMCS, Founded: 1980, Empl: 1,185, Sales ($M): 428.9, Fiscal End: 3/96; Max P. Watson, Chmn, Pres & CEO, Douglas J. Erwin, EVP & COO, Richard Gardner, SVP NA Sales, Leland D. Putterman, VP WW Mktng, David A. Farley, VP & CFO, Marcy Burchett

BMUG Inc. (BMUG), 1442A Walnut St, #62, Berkeley CA 94709-1496 USA; 510/549-2684, Fax: 510/849-9026, Co Email: bmuginfo@bmug.org, Web URL: bmug.org, Focus: PC users group, Ownrshp: Nonprofit, Founded: 1984, Empl: 12,000, Ann Wrixon, Exec Dir

Boca Research Inc. 1377 Clint Moore Rd, Boca Raton FL 33487-2722 USA; 407/997-6227, Fax: 407/997-0918, Focus: PC peripheral boards, Ownrshp: OTC, Stk Sym: BOCI, Founded: 1985, Empl: 250, Sales ($M): 143.0, Fiscal End: 12/95; Tim Farris, Chmn, Pres & CEO, David B. Farris, VP R&D, Lawrence F. Steffann, VP Ops, Kenneth L. Wyrick, VP Sales & Mktng, R. Michael Brewer, VP Fin, Gale Blackburn, PR Mgr

Boeing Computer Services Co. 7755 E Marginal Way S, Seattle WA 98108 USA; 206/655-2121, Focus: Computer services and system integration, Ownrshp: Sub. Boeing, Stk Sym: BA, Founded: 1916, Empl: 13,000, Sales ($M): 407, Fiscal End: 12/93; John D. Warner, Pres

Bohle Company, The 1999 Ave of the Stars, #550, Los Angeles CA 90067 USA; 310/785-0515, Fax: 310/286-9551, Co Email: @bohle.com, Focus: PR and marketing communications, Ownrshp: PVT, Empl: 14, Sue Bohle, Pres, Lee McEnany, VP

Bolt Beranek & Newman Inc. (BBN), 150 Cambridge Park Dr, Cambridge MA 02140 USA; 617/873-4000, Fax: 617/873-5011, Co Email: info@bbn.com, Focus: Contract R&D, software, ATM networks, Internet services & SI, Ownrshp: NYSE, Stk Sym: BBN, Founded: 1953, Empl: 2,000, Sales ($M): 215.0, Fiscal End: 6/95; Stephen R. Levy, Chmn, George H. Conrades, Pres & CEO, David M. Campbell, SVP, Julie D. Donahue, VP, Ralph A. Goldwasser, SVP & CFO

BookMaker Corp. 2470 El Camino Real, #108, Palo Alto CA 94306 USA; 415/345-8160, 800/766-8531 Fax: 415/856-4734, Focus: Booklet printing software, Prdts: ClickBook, Ownrshp: PVT, Founded: 1993, Martin Mazner, Pres, Email: 228.2035@mcimail.com; Stan Otani, Email: stanotan@aol.com

Books That Work 2300-100 Geng Rd, #10230, Palo Alto CA 94303-0930 USA; 415/326-4280, Fax: 415/326-9165, Focus: Interactive multimedia software, Prdts: Design & Build Your Deck,

Ownrshp: PVT, Founded: 1992, Empl: 15, Stuart Gannes, CEO, Dan Levin, Pres & CFO

Boole & Babbage Inc. 3131 Zanker Rd, San Jose CA 95134-1933 USA; 408/526-3000, 800/222-6653 Fax: 408/526-3053, Web URL: boole.com, Focus: System software for IBM mainframe and networks, Ownrshp: OTC, Stk Sym: BOOL, Founded: 1967, Empl: 645, Sales ($M): 154.4, Fiscal End: 9/95; Paul E. Newton, Pres & CEO, Johannes S. Bruggeling, EVP Int'l Ops, Arthur F. Knapp Jr., SVP & CFO, Email: aknapp@boole.com; Saverio Merlo, SVP Mktng, James E.C. Black, SVP Eng

Border Network Technologies Inc. 1 Yonge St, #1400, Toronto Ontario M5E 1J9 Canada; 416/368-7157, 800/334-8195 Fax: 416/368-7789, Co Email: info@border.com, Web URL: border.com, Focus: Internet firewall software, Prdts: BorderWare Firewall Server, Ownrshp: PVT, Founded: 1994, Empl: 55, Steven Lamb, Pres & CEO, Richard Earle, VP Mktng, Deborah Brooks, Mgr Marcom, Email: deborah@border.com

Borland Int'l. 100 Borland Way, PO Box 660001, Scotts Valley CA 95066-3249 USA; 408/431-1000, Fax: 408/439-7800, Co Email: @wpo.borland.com, Web URL: borland.com, Focus: Database and programming tool software, Prdts: Paradox, dBase, Turbo Pascal, Ownrshp: OTC, Stk Sym: BORL, Founded: 1983, Empl: 1,100, Sales ($M): 215.2, Fiscal End: 3/96; William Miller, Chmn, Whitney Lynn, Pres & CEO, Robert H. Kohn, SVP, Richard L. Schwartz, SVP & CTO, David Mullen, VP & CFO, Tim Casey, PR Mgr, Email: tcasey@wpo.borland.com

Boston Business Computing Ltd. 13 Branch St, Methuen MA 01844-1955 USA; 508/725-3222, Fax: 508/725-3229, Co Email: bbc@bbc.com, Focus: VMS to Unix migration software, Prdts: Vbackup, Vmail, EDT+, VCL, Ownrshp: PVT, Founded: 1983, Empl: 8, Sales ($M): 1.5, David Pikcilingis, Pres, Email: dcpik@bbc.com

Boundless Technologies 9430 Research Blvd, #IV-200, Austin TX 78759-6543 USA; 512/346-2447, Fax: 512/346-7062, Focus: Multi-user PC products and terminals, Ownrshp: Sub. All-Quotes Inc., Founded: 1986, Empl: 350, Gerald Youngblood, Pres, William Long, EVP, Anthony Giovaniello, COO, Craig Parks, Dir Mktng

Boxer Software PO Box 3230, Peterborough NH 03458-3230 USA; 603/924-6602, Fax: 603/924-4471, Co Email: 70242.2126@compuserve.com, Web URL: boxersoftware.com/users/dhamel, Focus: Text editing software, Prdts: Boxer Text Editor, Ownrshp: PVT, Founded: 1991, David R. Hamel, Pres, Email: 74777.170@compuserve.com

Brand X Software 3228 C W Cary St, Richmond VA 23221 USA; 804/355-0374, Fax: 804/358-3847, Focus: Macintosh software, Ownrshp: Sub. MacXperts, Founded: 1989, Empl: 30, William Tyler, Pres & CEO, Russ LaValle, VP Ops, Robert M. Solomon, Dir Mktng, Scott Laing, Dir Dev

Breakthrough Productions 210 Park Ave, Nevada City CA 95959 USA; 916/265-0911, Fax: 916/265-8036, Co Email: mktmaster@aol.com, Focus: Sales management and education software, Prdts: MarketMaster, Ownrshp: PVT, Founded: 1980, Empl: 5, Marla Robinson, Pres

British Telecommunications Plc. (BT), 81 Newgate St, London EC1 7AJ UK; 71-356-5000, Focus: Telecom services, Ownrshp: FO, Empl: 200,000, Sales ($M): 20,942, Fiscal End: 12/95

Broadview Associates 1 Bridge Plaza, Ft. Lee NJ 07024 USA; 201/461-7929, Fax: 201/346-9191, Web URL: broadview.com, Focus: Statistics on mergers and acquisitions in the information technology industry, Ownrshp: PVT, Founded: 1973, Empl: 85, Gilbert Mintz, Founding Partner, Harvey Poppel, Partner

Broadvision Inc. 333 Distel Cr, Los Altos CA 94022 USA; 415/943-3600, Web URL: broadvision.com, Focus: Internet marketing and electronic commerce application system, Ownrshp: OTC, Stk Sym: BVSN, Founded: 1993, Empl: 80, Sales ($M): 0.5, Fiscal End: 12/95; Pehong Chen, CEO

Brøderbund Software Inc. 500 Redwood Blvd, PO Box 6121,

Novato CA 94948-6121 USA; 415/382-4400, 800/521-6263 Fax: 415/382-4582, Web URL: broderbund.com, Focus: Productivity, education and entertainment software, Prdts: Printshop, Carmen Sandiego, Myst, Ownrshp: OTC, Stk Sym: BROD, Founded: 1980, Empl: 563, Sales ($M): 186.2, Fiscal End: 8/96; Douglas G. Carlston, Chmn, Joe Durrrett, CEO, Harry R. Wilker, SVP, Jan L. Gullett, SVP Mktng & Sales, Albert Sonntag, VP Ops, Eric Winkler, PR Mgr

Brodeur & Partners Inc. 9 Hillside Ave, Waltham MA 02154 USA; 617/622-2869, Fax: 617/622-2828, Co Email: @brodeur.com, Focus: PR and marketing communications, Ownrshp: PVT, Empl: 60, John Brodeur, Pres

Brooklyn North Software Works Inc. 1969 Upper Water St, #1703, Box 55, Halifax NS B3J 3R7 Canada; 902/493-6080, Fax: 902/835-2600, Co Email: @brooknorth.com, Web URL: brooknorth.com, Focus: Hybertext tools for the World Wide Web, Prdts: HTML Assistant Pro, Howard Harawitz, Pres

Brooks Power Systems 1400 Adams Rd, #E, Bensalem PA 19020 USA; 215/244-0264, 800/523-1551 Fax: 215/241-0160, Focus: Power protection products, Ownrshp: PVT, Founded: 1981, Empl: 10, Joseph G. Brooks, Pres

Brooks/Cole Publishing Co. 511 Forest Lodge Rd, Pacific Grove CA 93950-5098 USA; 408/373-0728, Fax: 408/375-6414, Co Email: @brookscole.com, Focus: Educational software, Ownrshp: Sub. Int'l. Thomson, Sales ($M): 35, Fiscal End: 12/93; William M. Roberts, Pres, Bob Evans, Dir Electr Pub, Email: bobevans@brookscole.com; Adrian Perenon, Dir Mktng, Email: adrianperenon@brookscole.com; Margaret Parks, Dir Marcom, Email: margaretparks@brookscole.com

Brooktree Corp. 9868 Scranton Rd, San Diego CA 92121-3707 USA; 619/452-7580, 800/228-2777 Fax: 619/452-1249, Co Email: apps@brooktree.com, Web URL: brooktree.com, Focus: ICs for computer graphics and imaging, Ownrshp: OTC, Stk Sym: BTREE, Founded: 1981, Empl: 625, Sales ($M): 137.7, Fiscal End: 9/95; James A. Bixby, Chmn, Pres & CEO, Phillip DenAdel, VP Ops, Jeffrey R. Teza, VP Tech & Bus Dev, Pete R. Fowler, VP Sales & Mktng, David H. Russian, VP & CFO

Brooktrout Technology Inc. 410 First Ave, Needham MA 02194 USA; 617/499-4100, Fax: 617/449-9009, Web URL: brooktrout.com, Focus: Electronic messaging products, Prdts: TruFax, TR Series, Quadra Fax, Fax Router, Ownrshp: OTC, Stk Sym: BRKT, Founded: 1984, Empl: 93, Sales ($M): 34.4, Fiscal End: 12/95; Eric Giler, Pres, Email: erg@brooktrout.com; David W. Duehren, VP R&D, Email: dwd@brooktrout.com; Robert C. Leahy, VP Fin & Ops, Email: bcl@brooktrout.com; David B. Lowe, VP Sales, Email: dbl@brooktrout.com; R. Andrew O'Brien, VP Mktng & Bus Dev, Email: aob@brooktrout.com; Heather Magliozzi, Mgr Marcom, Email: hjm@brooktrout.com

Brother International Corp. 200 Cotton Tail Ln, Somerset NJ 08875-6714 USA; 908/356-8880, Fax: 908/356-4085, Focus: Printers and electronic typewriters, Ownrshp: Sub. Brother Industries, Founded: 1954, Empl: 555, Sales ($M): 350, Hiromi Gunji, Pres & CEO, Dean F. Shulman, SVP Mktng, John Wandishin, Dir Mktng

BSG Corp. 11 Greenway Plaza, #900, Houston TX 77046-1102 USA; 713/965-9000, Fax: 713/993-9249, Focus: Systems integration, Ownrshp: PVT, Founded: 1987, Empl: 600, Sales ($M): 43, Fiscal End: 12/94; Steven G. Papermaster, Chmn & CEO, Don Baker, Pres, David Lundeen, CFO, Beth Miller

BTG Inc. 1768 Old Meadow Rd, McLean VA 22102-4303 USA; 703/641-1200, 800/449-4228 Fax: 703/876-1920, Web URL: btg.com, Focus: Alpha-based PCs, Ownrshp: OTC, Stk Sym: BTGI, Founded: 1984, Sales ($M): 150

Bull HN Information Systems Inc. 300 Concord Rd, Billerica MA 01821-4199 USA; 508/294-6000, Web URL: bull.com, Focus: Mainframes, microcomputers, UNIX systems, software systems and technologies integration, Ownrshp: Sub. Groupe Bull, France,

Founded: 1955, Empl: 3,600, Sales ($M): 5,400 WW, Fiscal End: 12/95; Robert Kelly, Pres & CEO, J. Patrick Mansfield, Pres US Sales, Thomas Gallagher, EVP Chief Legal Counsel, Peter Stavropulos, Dir Comm, Bruce MacDonald, Dir, Email: b.macdonald@ma30p.bull.com

Burr-Brown Corp. 6730 S Tucson Blvd, PO Box 11400, Tucson AZ 85734-1400 USA; 602/746-1111, 800/548-6132 Fax: 602/889-1510, Focus: Microcomputer boards, modems, multiplexers and electronic products, Ownrshp: OTC, Stk Sym: BBRC, Founded: 1956, Empl: 1,928, Sales ($M): 269.2, Fiscal End: 12/95; Thomas R. Brown Jr., Chmn, Syrus P. Madavi, Pres & CEO, John L. Carter, EVP & CFO, Michael M. Pawlik, VP Mktng, Robert E. Reynolds, VP Ops

Burton Group, The 7040 Union Park Ctr, Midvale UT 84047 USA; 801/566-2880, Fax: 801/566-3611, Co Email: info@tbg.com, Web URL: tbg.com, Focus: Research, market analysis and consulting on network computing, Ownrshp: PVT, Founded: 1989, Empl: 12, Craig Burton, Principal, Jamie Lewis, Pres, Doug Allinger, VP Sales

Business Applications Performance Corp. (BAPC), 2200 Mission College Blvd, RNB4-21, Santa Clara CA 95051 USA; 408/988-7654, Fax: 408/765-4920, Co Email: john_peterson@bapco.com, Web URL: bapco.com, Focus: Develop applications-based industry standard benchmarks, Ownrshp: Nonprofit, Founded: 1991, Empl: 19, John Sammons, Pres, John E. Peterson, Admin of Ops

Business Objects Inc. 20813 Stevens Creek Blvd, #100, Cupertino CA 95014 USA; 408/973-9300, Fax: 408/973-1057, Co Email: @busobj.com, Web URL: businessobjects.com, Focus: Network database software, Prdts: BusinessObjects, Ownrshp: Sub Business Objects, France, Stk Sym: BOBJY, Founded: 1990, Empl: 300, Sales ($M): 60.6, Fiscal End: 12/95; Bernard Liautaud, Pres & CEO, Denis Payre, COO, William B. Binch, VP Sales, Matthew DiMaria, VP Mktng, Robert P. Verheecke, CFO, Tracy Eiler, Email: teiler@busobj.com

Business Printing Center 8195 166th Ave NE, Redmond WA 98052 USA; 206/869-6319, Fax: 206/882-4312, Focus: Online store for purchase of custom business printing, Ownrshp: PVT, Empl: 32, Joe Verschueren, CEO, Email: joev@parallelcomm.com; Jack Hooper, CFO, Cory Klatt, CTO, John Jerome, Chief Mktng Officer

Business Products Industry Assoc. (BPIA), 301 N Fairfax St, Alexandria VA 22314 USA; 703/549-9040, Fax: 703/683-7552, Web URL: recyclefurn.org, Focus: Association for resellers of office products, Ownrshp: Nonprofit, Founded: 1904, Empl: 7,000, Daniel Scott, Pres

Business Resource Software 2013 Wells Branch Pkwy #301, Austin TX 78728 USA; 512/251-7541, 800/473-1228 Fax: 512/251-4401, Co Email: info@brs-inc.com, Web URL: brs-inc.com, Focus: Business management software, Prdts: Business Insight, Quick Insight, Plan Write for Business, Ownrshp: PVT, Founded: 1984, Empl: 12, Fiscal End: 12/95; Kent Ochel, Pres, James Brawner, Dir Mktng, Email: jeb@brs-inc.com

Business Software Alliance 2001 L St NW, #400, Washington DC 20036 USA; 202/872-5500, Fax: 202/872-5501, Co Email: software@bsa.org, Focus: Prevention of software piracy, Ownrshp: Nonprofit, Founded: 1988, Robert Holleyman, Pres, Diane Smiroldo

Business Technology Assoc. (BTA), 12411 Wornall Rd, Kansas City MO 64145 USA; 816/941-3100, Fax: 816/941-4838, Web URL: btanet.org, Focus: Association for resellers of office automation equipment and LANs, Ownrshp: Nonprofit, Founded: 1926, Empl: 6,000, Keith Anderson, Exec Dir, Jan Kitta, Marcom Mgr

BusinessVision Management Systems Inc. 2600 Skymark Ave, Bldg. 3, Mississauga Ontario L4W 5B2 Canada; 905/629-3233, 800/537-4296 Fax: 905/399-5093, Co Email: @businessvision.com, Focus: PC accounting software, Prdts: BusinessVision II, BusinessVision Turbo, BusinessVision Delta, Ownrshp: PVT,

Founded: 1987, Empl: 30, Murray Aston, Pres & CTO, Jeremy Martin, VP R&D, Kevin Hollis, Dir Sales

BusLogic Inc. 4151 Burton Dr, Santa Clara CA 95054 USA; 408/492-9090, Fax: 408/492-1542, Web URL: buslogic.com, Focus: I/O host adapters, Prdts: FlashPoint, Ownrshp: Sub. Mylex Corp., Founded: 1988, Jesse Chen, Pres, Peter Harvey, Chmn, Donald Pate, VP Sales, George Koestner, CFO, Elyse Phillips, Marcom Mgr

ButtonWare Inc. 13800 Montfort Dr, #100, Dallas TX 75240-4345 USA; 214/713-6370, Focus: Database software, Prdts: PC-File, button:File, Ownrshp: PVT, Founded: 1982, Empl: 15, Sales ($M): 2.1, Fiscal End: 12/92; Jim Button, CEO, Steve Wilson, Pres, Suzanne Faith, VP Sales

Buyers Laboratory Inc. 20 Railroad Ave, Hackensack NJ 07601 USA; 201/488-0404, Fax: 201/488-0461, Focus: Office product testing and specification guides, Ownrshp: PVT, Founded: 1961, Empl: 40, Anthony Polifrone, Pres, Marion Davidowicz, VP

Byron Preiss Multimedia Co. Inc. 24 W 25th St, New York NY 10010 USA; 212/989-6252, Fax: 212/989-6550, Focus: Multimedia software, Prdts: Will Eisner's The Spirit, Robot City, Hard Hat, The Ultimate Einstein, Ownrshp: OTC, Stk Sym: CDRM, Founded: 1992, Empl: 60, Sales ($M): 6.3, Fiscal End: 12/95; Byron Preiss, Chmn, Pres & CEO, Jim Dellomo, CFO, Jackie Snyder, Mktng Dir

Byte by Byte Corp. 3925 W Baker Ln #329, Austin TX 78759-5321 USA; 512/795-0150, Fax: 512/795-0021, Focus: 3D graphics software, Prdts: Sculpt, Ownrshp: PVT, Founded: 1985, Empl: 10, Scott A. Peterson, Pres, Vernon C. Peterson, CFO, Eric Graham, Chief Scientist

C-Cube Microsystems Inc. 1778 McCarthy Blvd, Milpitas CA 95035 USA; 408/944-6300, Fax: 408/944-6314, Co Email: @c-cube.com, Focus: Digital video ICs, Ownrshp: OTC, Stk Sym: CUBE, Founded: 1988, Empl: 254, Sales ($M): 124.6, Fiscal End: 12/95; William J. O'Meara, Pres & CEO, Alexandre A. Balkanski, EVP & COO, James G. Burke, VP & CFO, Brian T. Connors, VP Sales, Sai-Wai Fu, VP Eng, Mary Sharpless, Email: mary.sharpless@c-cube.com

C3 Inc. 460 Herndon Pkwy, Herndon VA 22070-5201 USA; 703/471-6000, Focus: Systems integration, Ownrshp: PVT, Founded: 1968, Empl: 1,900, Sales ($M): 211.2, Fiscal End: 12/93; Joseph P. Beninatii, Chmn, John B. Wood, Pres & CEO, Lorenzo Tellez, VP & CFO, Robert J. Marino, SVP Fed Ops

Ca$hGraf 2901 58th Ave N, St Petersburg FL 33714 USA; 813/528-2477, 800/872-0405 Fax: 813/528-2671, Web URL: cash-graf.com, Focus: Single solution business software, Prdts: Ca$hGraf Appointments Plus, Ownrshp: PVT, Founded: 1992, Richard Pearce, Pres

CabiNet Systems Inc. 900 Corporate Dr, Mahwah NJ 07430 USA; 201/512-1040, Fax: 201/512-1650, Co Email: 74563.2367@compuserve.com, Web URL: cabinet-sys.com, Focus: Document management software, Prdts: CabiNet, Ownrshp: Sub. CabiNet, Israel, Founded: 1994, Empl: 31, Vadim Shur, VP NA Sales, Email: vadim@cabinet-sys.com; Ami Grynberg, Pres, Email: ami@cabinet-sys.com; William Sheer, Email: william@cabinet-sys.com

Cable Television Laboratories Inc. (CableLabs), 400 Centennial Pkwy, Louisville CO 80027-1208 USA; 303/661-9100, Fax: 303/661-9199, Web URL: cablelabs.com, Focus: R&D consortium for the cable TV industry, Ownrshp: Nonprofit, Donald Frazier

Cable/Information Technology Convergence Forum c/o CableLabs, 400 Centennial Pkwy, Louisville CO 80027-1208 USA; 303/661-9100, Fax: 303/661-9199, Focus: Communications between computer and cable TV companies, Ownrshp: Nonprofit, Founded: 1994

Cables To Go 1501 Webster St, Dayton OH 45404 USA; 513/224-8646, 800/826-7904 Focus: Computer cables and connectors, Ownrshp: PVT

Cabletron Systems 35 Industrial Way, PO Box 5005, Rochester NH 03867-0505 USA; 603/332-9400, Fax: 603/332-4616, Web

URL: cabletron.com, Focus: LAN connectivity products, Ownrshp: NYSE, Stk Sym: CS, Founded: 1983, Empl: 5,377, Sales ($M): 1,069.7, Fiscal End: 2/96; S. Robert Levine, Pres & CEO, Craig R. Benson, Chmn & COO, David Kirkpatrick, CFO, Christopher J. Oliver, Dir Eng

CACI International Inc. (CACI), 1100 N Glebe Rd, #3, Arlington VA 22201-4714 USA; 703/841-7800, Fax: 703/841-7882, Focus: Computer systems and services, Ownrshp: OTC, Stk Sym: CACIA, Founded: 1962, Empl: 3,069, Sales ($M): 244.6, Fiscal End: 6/96; Jack P. London, Chmn, Pres & CEO, Ray J. Oleson, Pres CACI Inc., Joseph S. Annino, Pres CACI Prod Co, Samuel R. Strickland, EVP & CFO, John J. Davis, EVP

Cadec Systems Inc. 8 E Perimeter Rd, Londonderry NH 03053 USA; 603/668-1010, 800/252-2332 Fax: 603/668-0820, Focus: On board computers for transportation & distribution industries, Ownrshp: Sub. Cummins Engine, Founded: 1976, Empl: 85, Sales ($M): 18.9, Fiscal End: 12/95; R. Cimino, GM, R.D. Wilkins, VP Sales, J.R. Quarles, VP Prod Plng, Topher Neumann, Mgr Special Mktng Programs

Cadence Design Systems Inc. 555 River Oaks Pkwy, San Jose CA 95134 USA; 408/943-1234, Fax: 408/943-0513, Focus: IC, CAE and PCB design automation software, Prdts: Opus, Ownrshp: OTC, Stk Sym: CDNC, Founded: 1988, Empl: 2,449, Sales ($M): 548.4, Fiscal End: 12/95; Joseph B. Costello, Pres & CEO, Leonard Y.W. Liu, COO, M. Robert Leach, SVP Consulting, Scott W. Sherwood, SVP Human Resources, H. Raymond Bingham, EVP & CFO

Cadix International Inc. 1200 Ashwood Pkwy #135, Atlanta GA 30338 USA; 404/804-9951, Fax: 404/804-9949, Focus: Signature verification systems, Ownrshp: PVT, Founded: 1980, Ben Lee, Pres, Steve Hollingsworth, Dir Mktng, George Tryfon, Sales Mgr, Joel M. Levine, Tech Mktng Mgr

Cadre Technologies Inc. 222 Richmond St, Providence RI 02903 USA; 401/351-5950, Fax: 401/455-6800, Co Email: info@cadre.com, Focus: Software development solutions, Prdts: Teamwork, Ensemble, Ownrshp: PVT, Founded: 1982, Empl: 205, Sales ($M): 39.5, Fiscal End: 12/95; Larry Sutter, Chmn, Email: lsutter@cadre.com

Caere Corp. 100 Cooper Ct, Los Gatos CA 95030 USA; 408/395-7000, Fax: 408/354-2743, Co Email: @caere.com, Web URL: caere.com, Focus: Optical character recognition software and systems, Prdts: Omnipage, PageKeeper, Ownrshp: OTC, Stk Sym: CAER, Founded: 1976, Empl: 223, Sales ($M): 51.9, Fiscal End: 12/95; Steven C. Humphreys, Pres, Robert Teresi, Chmn & CEO, Chad Kinzelberg, VP Mktng, Dan Duke Borozan, VP Ops, Blanche M. Sutter, VP & CFO, Patrick Crisp, PR Mgr, Email: patrick.crisp@caere.com

CAF Technology Inc. 1315 Johnson Ave, City of Industry CA 91745 USA; 818/369-3690, Fax: 818/369-3692, Focus: PCs and notebook computers, Ownrshp: Sub. CAF, Taiwan, Founded: 1989, Empl: 30, Sales ($M): 10, Joe Lee, Pres, David Zung, Sales Dir, Sigun Kuang, Purchaser

Cahners Publishing Co. 275 Washington St, Newton MA 02158 USA; 617/558-4565, Fax: 617/558-4228, Focus: 20+ computer and high-tech magazines, Prdts: Datamation, Design News, Digital News & Review, EDN, TWICE, GCN, Ownrshp: PVT, Bruce Barnett, Pres & CEO, Stephen A. Thompson, SVP, Jackie Daya, EVP & CFO

CalComp Inc. 2411 W La Palma Ave, Anaheim CA 92801 USA; 714/821-2000, 800/932-1212 Fax: 714/821-2832, Focus: Computer graphics peripherals, Prdts: DrawingMaster, Solos 4, DrawingBoard, ScanPlus, Ownrshp: Sub. Lockheed Martin, Founded: 1958, Empl: 1,150, Gary R. Long, Pres, Ernest J. Baessler, EVP Fin, Mark C. Lewis, Prod Mgr, Richard Tippett, VP Mfg, Hal Simerath, VP Prod Dev, Richard Stehr, PR Mgr

Caldera 931 W Center St, Orem UT 84057 USA; 801/229-1675, Fax: 801/229-1579, Web URL: caldera.com, Focus: Linux-based operating system, Ownrshp: PVT, Founded: 1995, Bryan Sparks,

Pres, Ransom Love, VP Mktng

California Software Products Inc. 525 N Cabrillo Park Dr, Santa Ana CA 92701-5017 USA; 714/973-0440, 800/841-1532 Fax: 714/558-9341, Co Email: 74644.3140@compuserve.com, Focus: Systems software, Prdts: Baby/36, 400 Developer Desktop, 400 Enterprise System, Ownrshp: PVT, Founded: 1975, Empl: 40, Sales ($M): 5.1, Peter Warkenton, Pres, Elizabeth Richell, VP Mktng, Bill Holmes, VP Mktng, Alicia Mutchins

Caligari Corp. 1955 Landings Dr, Mountain View CA 94043 USA; 415/390-9600, 800/351-7620 Fax: 415/390-9755, Focus: 3D graphics software, Prdts: trueSpace, Ownrshp: PVT, Roman Ormandy, Pres, Jack Strange, VP Sales & Mktng

Calluna Technology Inc. 1762 Technology Dr, #223, San Jose CA 95110 USA; 408/453-4753, Fax: 408/453-0427, Focus: Disk drive PC cards, Ownrshp: Sub Calluna, UK, Founded: 1991, Bruce Serpa, US Sales Mgr

CallWare Technologies 2323 Foothill Dr, Salt Lake City UT 84109 USA; 801/486-9922, Fax: 801/486-8294, Co Email: @callware.com, Focus: Communications software, Ownrshp: PVT, R. Craig Hansen, Chmn & CEO, Alec Belfer, EVP Mktng

Calyx Corp. 16745 W Bluemound Rd, #200, Brookfield WI 53005-9935 USA; 414/782-0300, Fax: 414/782-3182, Focus: Medical and dental software, Ownrshp: Sub. Flagship Group, Founded: 1982, Empl: 20, Sales ($M): 4.5, Mike Goodspeed, GM, Mark Seely, VP Dev, Mike Wallace, VP Tech Support, Helene Cavataio, Admin Mgr, Paul Stamas, Prod Analyst

Cambex Corp. 360 Second Ave, Waltham MA 02154 USA; 617/890-6000, Fax: 617/890-2899, Focus: Memory products, Ownrshp: OTC, Stk Sym: CBEX, Founded: 1968, Empl: 140, Sales ($M): 35.2, Fiscal End: 8/95; Joseph F. Kruy, Chmn, Pres & CEO, Robert Norton, EVP, Fay Elassy, VP Eng, Sheldon M. Schenkler, VP & CFO, Rose M. Curran

Cambridge Parallel Processing 16755 Von Karman Ave, #120, Irvine CA 92714-4918 USA; 714/261-8901, 800/995-8879 Fax: 714/724-8399, Co Email: info@cppus.com, Focus: Massively parallel processing computer systems, Prdts: Gamma II, Founded: 1986, Empl: 25, Sales ($M): 10, Philip Buckley, Pres, Bruce Alper, VP Bus Dev, Email: bruce@cppus.com; Gordon Pacey, VP Ops, Email: gordon@cppus.com; Josy Ruth, VP Eng, Email: josy@cppus.com; Michele Herbel, Dir Admin & Marcom, Email: michele@cppus.com

Cambridge Software Group Inc. 101 Rogers St, #214, Cambridge MA 02142 USA; 617/577-0600, 800/792-7248 Fax: 617/577-0602, Co Email: @csgnotes@notes.net, Focus: Software for Lotus Notes, Prdts: Formula Editor, Application Outliner, Chart Object, Ownrshp: PVT, Founded: 1992, Empl: 10, Eric Peterson, Pres, Email: ericpeterson@csgnotes@notes.net; Katie Donovan, Mgr, Email: katiedonovan@csgnotes@notes.net

Cambridge Technology Partners 304 Vassar St, Cambridge MA 02139 USA; 617/374-9800, Web URL: ctp.com, Focus: C/S distribution applications, Founded: 1991

Camelot Corp. 17770 Preston Rd, Dallas TX 75252 USA; 214/733-3005, Fax: 214/733-4308, Web URL: planeteers.com, Focus: CD-ROM Software, Prdts: Digiphone, Digiphone Deluxe, Mr. CD-ROM Stores, Ownrshp: OTC, Stk Sym: CAML, Empl: 40, Daniel Wettreich, Chmn & CEO, Carla R. Kienast, Corp Rel Mgr, Email: ckienast@camelotcorp.com

Camintonn Z-RAM Corp. 22 Morgan, Irvine CA 92718-2022 USA; 714/454-1500, Fax: 714/830-4726, Focus: PC and workstation memory products, Ownrshp: PVT, Founded: 1981, Empl: 50, Bosco Sun, Pres & CEO, Carolyn Aliotta, Mgr Marcom

Campbell Services Inc. 21700 NW Hwy, #1070, Southfield MI 48075 USA; 810/559-5955, Fax: 810/559-1034, Co Email: ontime.com, Focus: Time management software for PCs, Prdts: OnTime, Ownrshp: PVT, Founded: 1971, Empl: 85, Sales ($M): 8.8, Fiscal End: 12/95; Anik Ganguly, Pres, Jennifer Konitsney, CFO

Campbell Software 1603 Orrington Ave, Evanston IL 60201 USA; 847/328-3200, Fax: 847/328-3459, Focus: Time and attendance software, Ownrshp: PVT, Founded: 1989, Empl: 62, Sales ($M): 6.5, Fiscal End: 12/95; Michael H. Campbell, Pres, David B. Menzel, CFO

Canadian Information Processing Society 430 King St W, #106, Toronto Ontario M5V 1L5 Canada; 416/593-4040, Focus: Association for Canadian computer professionals, Ownrshp: Nonprofit, Founded: 1958, Empl: 5,000

Canary Communications Inc. 1851 Zanker Rd, San Jose CA 95112-4213 USA; 408/453-9201, Fax: 408/453-0940, Focus: Network and storage products, Ownrshp: PVT, Founded: 1987, Vinh Tran, Pres, S. Ted Sanford, VP Sales & Mktng, Roland Yamaguchi, VP Ops

Candle Corp. 2425 Olympic Blvd, Santa Monica CA 90404 USA; 310/829-5800, 800/843-3970 Fax: 310/582-4287, Web URL: candle.com, Focus: Systems management software for the enterprise, Prdts: Candle Command Center, OMEGAMON, Ownrshp: PVT, Founded: 1976, Sales ($M): 230.3, Fiscal End: 12/95; Aubrey Chernick, Chmn & CEO, Philip Little

Canon Computer Systems Inc. 2995 Redhill Ave, Costa Mesa CA 92626 USA; 714/438-3000, Fax: 714/438-3099, Focus: PCs, printers and scanners, Ownrshp: Sub. Canon, Founded: 1992, Sales ($M): 800, Fiscal End: 12/95; Yasuhiro Tsubota, Pres & CEO, Peter Bergman, VP Mktng, John Arnos, VP Sales, Mike Rusert, VP Ops, Carolyn Perrier, Dir Peripheral Mktng, Sherri Snelling

Canon Inc. 30-2, Shimomaruko 3-chome, Ohta-ku, Tokyo 146 JP-146 Japan; 3-33758-2111, Web URL: canon.co.jp, Focus: Printers, PCs, fax machines and photographic products, Ownrshp: FO, Founded: 1937, Empl: 67,672, Sales ($M): 19,333, Fiscal End: 12/94; Hajime Mitarai, Pres, Ryuzaburo Kaku, Chmn, Hiroshi Tanaka, EVP, Giichi Marushima, Chief R&D

Canon USA Inc. One Canon Plaza, Lake Success NY 11042-1198 USA; 516/488-6700, Fax: 516/328-5069, Web URL: usa.canon.com, Focus: PCs, peripherals, office and consumer electronics products, Ownrshp: Sub Canon, Japan, Founded: 1955, Empl: 8,000+, Sales ($M): 6,100, Fiscal End: 12/94; Haruso Murase, Pres & CEO, Robert Bryson, SVP & GM, Seymour Liebman, SVP & GM, Farr David, SVP & GM, Marchetta Russell, Mgr

CAP Automation (CAP), 3737 Ramona Dr, Ft. Worth TX 76116-7001 USA; 817/560-7007, 800/826-5009 Fax: 817/560-8249, Web URL: capauto.com, Focus: Software for POS accounting, Prdts: Quick Check, CAP POS, SellWise, Cash'n Carry, CAP Accountant, Ownrshp: PVT, Founded: 1978, Empl: 12, Sales ($M): 1.0, Fiscal End: 12/95; Chuck Atkinson, Pres, Jan Atkinson, VP

CAP Gemini Sogeti 11 Rue de Tilsitt, Paris F-75017 France; 1-4754-5000, Web URL: cgs.fr, Focus: Computer services and system integration, Ownrshp: FO, Stk Sym: CAPGSO, Founded: 1975, Empl: 18,919, Sales ($M): 1,776, Fiscal End: 12/91

Capcom 475 Oakmeadow Pkwy, Sunnyvale CA 94086-4709 USA; 408/727-0500, Web URL: capcoment.com, Focus: Entertainment software, Prdts: Super St Fighter, Mega Man, Dark Stalkers, Resident Evil, Ownrshp: PVT, Founded: 1985, Empl: 65, Fiscal End: 3/96; Ryuichi Hirata, Pres, Capcom USA, Greg Ballard, Pres, Capcom Ent., Steve Hanawa, Pres, Capcom Digi. Studio, Rich Moore, VP R&D, Capcom Digital Studios, Melinda Mongelluzzo

Capital Network Inc. 3925 W Braker Ln, #406, Austin TX 78759-5321 USA; 512/305-0826, Fax: 512/305-0836, Co Email: david@ati.utexas.edu, Focus: Economic development organization for high-tech companies, Ownrshp: Nonprofit, Founded: 1989, David Gerhardt, Exec Dir

Capital Relations Inc. 2801 Townsgate Rd, #121, Westlake Village CA 91361-3003 USA; 805/494-0830, Fax: 805/494-0780, Co Email: @caprel.com, Focus: PR and marketing communications

Capsoft Dev. Corp. 732 E Utah Valley Dr, #400, American Fork UT 84003-9773 USA; 801/763-3915, Fax: 801/763-3999, Focus: Document management tools, Prdts: CAPS Author, CAPS User,

HotDocs, Ownrshp: PVT, Founded: 1983, Marshall Morrise, Pres, Kent Lundin, VP Mktng, Nancy Groll, PR Mgr

Caravelle Networks Corp. 210 Colonnade Rd S, #301, Nepean Ontario K2E 7L5 Canada; 613/225-1172, Fax: 613/225-4777, Co Email: @caravelle.com, Web URL: caeavelle.com, Focus: Network management software, Prdts: Watcher, Ownrshp: PVT, Empl: 20, Don Pare, Pres & CEO, Email: dpare@caravelle.com; Dan Shipley, Dir Prod Mktng, Debbie Parkhill, Mktng & Media Rel, Email: dparkhill@caravelle.com

Carbela Tek Inc. 1210 San Mateo Ave, S San Francisco CA 94080 USA; 415/873-6484, Fax: 415/873-6486, Focus: Multimedia software, Ownrshp: PVT, Michael S. Rabette, COO, John Sanfillippo, Dir Ops, Sean Williams, Dir Mktng, Mark Kennedy, Dir Sales, Charles McKelvie, Dir Fin

Cardiff Software Inc. 1782 La Costa Meadows Dr, San Marcos CA 92069 USA; 619/761-4515, 800/659-8755 Fax: 619/761-5222, Co Email: @cardiffsw.com, Web URL: cardiffsw.com, Focus: Fax management and OCR software, Prdts: TeleForm, Ownrshp: PVT, Founded: 1991, Empl: 14, Joseph C. Larson, Pres, Dennis E. Clerke, VP Mktng & Sales, Mark Seaman, VP, J. Joel Faul, VP Eng, Tim Dubes, PR Mgr, Email: tdubes@cardiffsw.com

Cardinal Business Media Inc. 1300 Virginia Dr, #400, Ft. Washington PA 19034 USA; 215/643-8000, Fax: 215/643-8099, Web URL: cardinal.com, Focus: 10+ magazines, newsletters and computer books on midrange computers, Prdts: DEC Professional, HP Professional, LAN Computing, Midrange System, Ownrshp: PVT, Robert N. Boucher, Pres & CEO, Thomas C. Breslin, CFO

Cardinal Technologies Inc. 1827 Freedom Rd, Lancaster PA 17601 USA; 717/293-3000, Fax: 717/293-3055, Web URL: cardtech.com, Focus: Modems, Prdts: Cardinal 288 Fax Modems, Ownrshp: PVT, Founded: 1987, Empl: 250, Sales ($M): 35, Wolfgang Hausen, Pres & CEO, Email: whausen@cardtech.com; John Rose, CFO, Email: johnr@cardtech.com; Dean Tucker, VP Sales, Email: deant@cardtech.com; Robert Young, VP Mktng, Email: byoung@cardtech.com; Jeff Murphy, VP Mfg, Email: jeffm@cardtech.com; Tom Ransom, Dir Corp Comm, Email: tomr@cardtech.com

Carina Software 12919 Alcost Blvd, #7, San Ramon CA 94583-1340 USA; 510/355-1266, Fax: 510/355-1268, Focus: Scientific software, Prdts: Voyager, Ownrshp: PVT, Founded: 1988, Empl: 5, Thomas Mathis, Pres

Carroll Touch Inc. 811 Paloma Dr, PO Box 1309, Round Rock TX 78680 USA; 512/244-3500, 800/386-8241 Fax: 512/244-7040, Focus: Touch panels, Prdts: Smart-Frame, Add-Touch, Ownrshp: Sub, AMP, Founded: 1973, Empl: 115, Sales ($M): 15, David Martin, VP & GM, John Ashall, VP Sales & Mktng, Wayne Wehrer, Dir Eng, Carol Roberts, Dir Fin

Casady & Greene Inc. 22734 Portola Dr, Salinas CA 93908-1119 USA; 408/484-9228, Fax: 408/484-9218, Co Email: casady@aol.com, Web URL: casadyg.com, Focus: Utility, font and game software, Prdts: Info Genie, Snap Mail, Ownrshp: PVT, Founded: 1984, Empl: 45, Charles R. Fulweiler, CEO, Terry Kunysz, Pres, Laura Kunysz, EVP, Beth Miller, CFO, Judith Frey, Dir PR, Email: judythecootie@casadyg.com

Cascade Communications 5 Carlisle Rd, Westford MA 01886 USA; 508/692-2600, Web URL: casc.com, Focus: Telecom services, Ownrshp: OTC, Empl: 300, Sales ($M): 135, Fiscal End: 12/95; Daniel Smith, CEO

Cascade Systems Inc. 1 Corporate Dr, Andover MA 01810-2447 USA; 508/794-8000, Fax: 508/794-0005, Focus: Publishing software and systems integration, Ownrshp: PVT, Founded: 1993, Malcolm McGrory, Pres, Brian Gorman, VP Sales, Sandra Kynes, Marcom Mgr

Casio Inc. 570 Mt. Pleasant Ave, Dover NJ 07801 USA; 201/361-5400, Focus: Digital cameras, peripherals and organizers, Ownrshp: Sub. Casio, Japan

Castelle Corp. 3255-3 Scott Blvd, Santa Clara CA 95054 USA;

408/496-0474, Fax: 408/496-0502, Focus: LAN print servers, Ownrshp: PVT, Founded: 1987, Empl: 65, W. Charles Hazel, Chmn, Peter Stolinsky, VP Mktng

Cayenne Software 8 New England Executive Park, Burrlington MA 01803 USA; 617/273-9003, Fax: 617/229-9904, Focus: CASE software, Ownrshp: OTC, Stk Sym: BACH, Founded: 1983, Empl: 341, Sales ($M): 32.0, Fiscal End: 6/96; Charles W. Bachman, Chmn, Peter J. Boni, Pres & CEO, Curt Bloom, VP Field Ops, Joan Cohen, VP Mktng & Bus Dev, Paul K. McGrawth, VP & CFO, David Smith

CBIS Inc. 5805 State Bridge Rd #G303, Duluth GA 30155-6427 USA; 770/446-1332, Fax: 770/446-9164, Focus: LAN operating systems and CD-ROM drives, Prdts: Desk to Desk, CD Connection, Ownrshp: PVT, Founded: 1978, Empl: 35, Robert C. Smith, Pres, Tim Fearney, Marcom Mgr

CD ROM-USA Inc. 1301 Arapahoe St #7, Golden CO 80401-1855 USA; 303/384-3922, Fax: 303/384-3926, Co Email: cdrom-inc.com, Focus: CD-ROM hardware and software, Ownrshp: PVT, Founded: 1988, Empl: 10, Roger Hutchison, Pres & CEO, Lisa Weber, VP Mktng

CD Solutions Inc. 111 Speen St, #202, Framingham MA 01701-9107 USA; 508/879-0006, 800/285-3821 Fax: 508/820-4396, Co Email: info@cdsolutions.com, Web URL: cdsolutions.com, Focus: Instructional CD-ROMs for Internet usage, Prdts: Using the Internet for Profit, Ownrshp: PVT, Empl: 1992, Paul H. Earl, Pres, Email: phearl@cdsolutions.com; Colleen Hurley, Bus Mgr, Email: cvhurley@cdsolutions.com

CD-ROM Strategies Inc. 6 Venture, #208, Irvine CA 92718 USA; 714/453-1702, Fax: 714/453-1311, Focus: Multimedia products, Ownrshp: PVT, Founded: 1989, Ash Pahwa, Pres

CDPD Forum Inc. (CDPD), 401 N Michigan Ave, Chicago IL 60611 USA; 800/335-2373 Focus: Support development of nationwide CDPD network, Ownrshp: Nonprofit, Founded: 1994, Empl: 57

CE Software Inc. 1801 Industrial Cr, PO Box 65580, W Des Moines IA 50265 USA; 515/221-1801, 800/523-7638 Fax: 515/221-2258, Co Email: @cesoft.com, Web URL: cesoft.com, Focus: E-mail and LAN software, Prdts: QuickMail, QuicKeys, Ownrshp: OTC, Stk Sym: CESH, Founded: 1982, Empl: 110, Sales ($M): 11.5, Fiscal End: 9/95; Ford H. Goodman, Pres & CEO, Christian Gurney, VP, Curtis W. Lack, CFO, Paul Cogdale, Dir Sales, Duane Varnum, Dir Prod Mktng, Jessica Dunker, Marcom Mgr

CED Research Triangle Software Developers Roundtable PO Box 13353, Research Triangle Pk NC 27709 USA; 919/460-5355, Fax: 919/460-3861, Focus: High-tech organization for N Carolina, Ownrshp: Nonprofit

Cegelec ESCA 11120 NE 33rd Place, Bellevue WA 98004 USA; 206/822-6800, Fax: 206/889-1700, Co Email: electra@esca.com, Web URL: esca.com, Focus: Software and systems for energy management, Prdts: Energy Management Platform, HABITAT, SCADA, Ownrshp: PVT, Founded: 1978, Empl: 200, Sales ($M): 28, Fiscal End: 12/91; Alain Steven, Pres, J.D. Hammerly, Dir Sales & Mktng, D.J. Beatenbough, Dir Finance, Lindsay von Ulm Paulson, Mgr Marcom

Celeritas Technologies Ltd. 26300 La Alameda, #385, Mission Viejo CA 92691 USA; 714/367-8650, Fax: 714/367-1190, Focus: Communications software, Ownrshp: PVT, Glenn R. Ray, Pres & CEO, P. Steven Rodriguez, VP Mktng & Sales, Michael G. Dolan, VP R&D

Center for Multimedia 3240 118th Ave SE, #100, Bellevue WA 98005 USA; 206/643-9039, Fax: 206/643-9032, Web URL: fmm.com, Focus: Multimedia services, Ownrshp: PVT, Founded: 1992, Empl: 9, Eric Dawes, Pres, Patrick Boyd, VP, Patrick Dooley, Jennifer Pearson, Mktng PR

Center for Software Development (CSD), 111 W St John, #200, San Jose CA 95113 USA; 408/494-8378, Fax: 408/494-8383, Co Email: info@center.org, Web URL: center.org/csd,

Focus: Self-service software testing and porting lab, Ownrshp: Nonprofit, Marnie Rice, Office Mgr, Bill McCarty, Dir, Email: mccarty@center.org

CenterLine Software Inc. 10 Fawcett St, Cambridge MA 02138-1110 USA; 617/498-3000, Fax: 617/868-6655, Co Email: @centerline.com, Web URL: centerline.com, Focus: Software development tools, Prdts: CodeCenter, ObjectCenter, Ownrshp: PVT, Founded: 1985, Sales ($M): 20+, Fiscal End: 12/94; James Meehan, Chmn, Pres & CEO, Stephen Kaufer, VP R&D, Paul Henderson, VP Mktng, John J. Bingenheimer, VP & CFO, Jill Godett, Dir Marcom, Email: godett@centerline.com

Centigram Communications Corp. 91 E Tasman Dr, San Jose CA 95134 USA; 408/944-0250, Fax: 408/428-3732, Focus: Voice processing systems, Ownrshp: OTC, Stk Sym: CGRM, Founded: 1980, Empl: 319, Sales ($M): 79.2, Fiscal End: 10/94; George H. Sollman, Pres & CEO, Anthony R. Muller, SVP Ops, Robert M. Nugent, SVP Sales, David M. Weinstein, VP Mktng

Centon Electronics Inc. 20 Morgan, Irvine CA 92718 USA; 714/855-9111, 800/234-9292 Fax: 714/855-1144, Focus: PC memory boards, Ownrshp: PVT, Founded: 1978, Empl: 150, Sales ($M): 250, Gene Miscione, Pres & CEO, John Bui, VP Finance, Gary Clark, VP Purchasing, Rick Webb, Dir Sales

Central Data Corp. 1602 Newton Dr, Champaign IL 61821-1098 USA; 217/359-8010, Fax: 217-359-6904, Co Email: info@cd.com, Web URL: cd.com, Focus: Computer connectivity hardware, Prdts: SCSI Terminal Servers, Ownrshp: PVT, Founded: 1975, Empl: 65, Jeffrey Roloff, Chmn, Earl Jacobsen, Pres, Mark Decker, Dir Mktng

Centron Software Technologies Inc. 300 American Legion Ln, #4, Pinehurst NC 28374 USA; 910/215-5708, 800/848-2173 Fax: 910/692-2173, Focus: Entertainment software, Prdts: Puzzle Power, Ownrshp: PVT, Ron Centner, Pres

Centura Software Corp. 1060 Marsh Rd, Menlo Park CA 94025 USA; 415/321-9500, Fax: 415/321-5471, Web URL: centurasoft.com, Focus: Database and LAN software, Prdts: SQLBase Server, SQLWindows, SQLNetwork, Ownrshp: OTC, Stk Sym: GPTA, Founded: 1984, Empl: 406, Sales ($M): 56.1, Fiscal End: 12/93; Umang P. Gupta, Chmn, Pres & CEO, Nicolas Birtles, EVP, Richard J. Heaps, VP Bus Dev, Clark W. Catelain, SVP Eng, Stephen V. Imbler, SVP & CFO

Century Software 5284 S Commerce Dr, #C134, Salt Lake City UT 84107 USA; 801/268-3088, 800/877-3088 Fax: 801/268-2772, Co Email: @censoft.com, Web URL: censoft.com, Focus: Connectivity software, Prdts: TinyTERM Series, Ownrshp: PVT, Founded: 1985, Empl: 50, Tom McFarland, Pres, Greg Haerr, CEO, Jon Gibbs, Dir Sales & Mktng, Kevin VanMondfrans, Mktng Mgr, Melissa Clyne, PR Consultant

CERFnet PO Box 85608, San Diego CA 92186-9784 USA; 619/455-3900, 800/876-2373 Fax: 619/455-3990, Co Email: info@cerf.net, Web URL: cerf.net, Focus: Internet service provider, Ownrshp: Aff General Atomics, Founded: 1989, Karsten Blue, Pres, Pushpendra Mohta, Exec Dir, Email: pushp@cerf.net; Fred Parker, Dir Mktng, Email: fparker@cerf.net; Pushpendra Mohta, Exec Dir, Email: pushp@cerf.com

Ceridian Corp. 8100 34th Ave S, Minneapolis MN 55425-1640 USA; 612/853-8100, Web URL: ceridian.com, Focus: Computer services, Ownrshp: NYSE, Stk Sym: CEN, Founded: 1992, Empl: 7,600, Sales ($M): 1,333.0, Fiscal End: 12/95; Lawrence Pearlman, Chmn, Pres & CEO, Glenn W. Jeffrey, EVP, James D. Miller, VP Strategy, Loren D. Gross, VP, Linda J. Jadwin, VP Com

Cerner Corp. 2800 Rockcreek Pkwy, #601, Kansas City MO 64117-2551 USA; 816/221-1024, Fax: 816/474-1742, Web URL: cerner.com, Focus: Information systems for the medical industry, Ownrshp: OTC, Stk Sym: CERN, Founded: 1980, Empl: 1,091, Sales ($M): 186.9, Fiscal End: 12/95; Neal L. Patterson, Chmn & CEO, Clifford W. Illig, Pres & COO, David M. Marguiles, EVP, Charles S. Runnion III, EVP Sales & Mktng

Cerplex Group Inc. 1382 Bell Ave, Tustin CA 92680 USA; 714/258-5151, 800/272-2007 Fax: 714/258-5161, Co Email: cerplex.com, Web URL: cerplex.com, Focus: Computer maintenance and logistics service, Ownrshp: OTC, Stk Sym: CPLX, Founded: 1990, Empl: 2,000, Sales ($M): 170, Fiscal End: 12/95; Bruce A. Klein, Chmn, Email: wklein@cerplex.com; James T. Schraith, Pres & CEO, Email: jschraith@cerplex.com; Richard C. Davis, Pres Intl Ops, Email: rdavis@cerplex.com; Alan L. Weaver, SVP, Email: aweaver@cerplex.com; Bruce D. Nye, VP CFO, Email: bnye@cerplex.com; Bonni L. Parsons, Mgr Marcom

Cerprobe Corp. 531 E Elliot Rd, #120, Chandler AZ 85225-1118 USA; 602/497-4200, Fax: 602/497-4242, Focus: Printed circuit board interfaces and probe cards for the ATE industry, Stk Sym: CRPB, Founded: 1976, Empl: 300, Sales ($M): 18.0, Fiscal End: 12/95; Zane Close, Pres & CEO, Bob Bench, CFO, Jacque Stewart, Mktng Dir

CF2GS 1008 Western Ave, Seattle WA 98104 USA; 206/223-6464, Fax: 206/223-2765, Focus: PR and marketing communications, Ownrshp: PVT, Empl: 40, Bill Fritsch, Pres, Ron Christiansen, Principal

CH Products 970 Park Center Dr, Vista CA 92083 USA; 619/598-2518, Fax: 619/598-2524, Co Email: @chproducts.com, Web URL: chproducts.com, Focus: PC input devices, Prdts: F-16 Series, Throttle Line, Ownrshp: PVT, Founded: 1977, Empl: 300, Chuck Hayes, Pres, Greg Stearns, CEO, Brenda Hayes-Curtis, VP Sales & Mktng, Alison A. Evans, Dir Marcom

Champion Business Systems Inc. 6726 S Revere Pkwy, Englewood CO 80112 USA; 303/792-3606, 800/243-2626 Fax: 303/792-0255, Focus: Accounting software, Prdts: Champion System 5, Champion Desktop, Ownrshp: PVT, Founded: 1981, Empl: 37, Sales ($M): 3.4, Charles Hager, Pres, Rusty Fraser, EVP, Jim Long, COO, Jack Zoellner, VP Ops, Bill McCabe, Trade Show Mgr

Chancery Software Ltd. 4170 Still Creek Dr, #450, Burnaby BC V5C 6C6 Canada; 604/294-1233, 800/999-9931 Fax: 604/294-2225, Focus: Macintosh school administration software, Prdts: MacSchool Student Information System, CSL Thesis, Ownrshp: PVT, Founded: 1985, Empl: 90, Lee Wilson, VP Mktng, Barbara Vanjoff, VP Sales

Charles Babbage Institute (CBI), 103 Walter Library, Univ. of Minnesota, Minneapolis MN 55455 USA; 612/624-5050, Fax: 612/624-8054, Co Email: cbi@vx.cis.umn.edu, Web URL: cbi.itdean.umn.edu/cbi, Focus: Archival collection and researches history of information processing and computing, Ownrshp: Nonprofit, Founded: 1978, Robert W. Seidel, Dir, Email: rws@maroon.tc.umn.edu

Charles River Analytics Inc. 55 Wheeler St, Cambridge MA 02138 USA; 617/491-3474, 800/913-3535 Fax: 617/868-0780, Co Email: sesame@cra.com, Web URL: opensesame.com, Focus: Learning agent software, Prdts: Open Sesame, Ownrshp: PVT, Founded: 1983, Empl: 30, Alper Caglayan, Pres, Greg Zacharias, VP, Robin Jones, Mktng Dir

Charles River Media Inc. PO Box 417, Rockland MA 02370 USA; 800/382-8505 Co Email: chrivmedia@aol.com, Focus: Publisher of books, software tools and other materials, Prdts: HTML TemplateMaster CD, David Fickes, Email: david@advice.com

Chase Research Inc. 545 Marriott Dr, #100, Nashville TN 37210 USA; 615/872-0770, Fax: 615/872-0771, Focus: Communication software, Ownrshp: Sub. Chase Research, England, Founded: 1986, Empl: 50, Jeff Pack, Pres, David Gumbs, Sales Mgr

Chatham Township Data Corp. (CTDATA), 31 Birchwood Rd, Denville NJ 07834-1224 USA; 201/586-0700, Fax: 201/586-1837, Co Email: info@ctdata.com, Web URL: ctdata.com/ctdata, Focus: Mac & PC software and systems integration, Prdts: dBinterface Rapid, Ownrshp: PVT, Founded: 1989, Empl: 5, Sales ($M): 1.0, Fiscal End: 12/95; David E. Aiello, Pres, David Plaut, VP Sales

Chatsworth Products Inc. 31425 Agoura Rd, Westlake Village CA 91361 USA; 818/735-6100, Fax: 818/735-6199, Focus: LAN/WAN rack and cable management systems, Ownrshp: PVT,

Founded: 1991, Empl: 200, Joseph Cabral, Chmn & Pres, Richard Jones, VP Mktng & Sales, Jerry Rice, Dir IS, James Dorsett, Mktng Mgr

Check Point Software Technologies Ltd. 400 Seaport Ct, #105, Redwood City CA USA; 617/859-9051, 800/429-4391 Fax: 617/863-0523, Co Email: info@checkpoint.com, Web URL: checkpoint.com, Focus: Internet security products, Prdts: FirWall-1, Ownrshp: Sub Check Point, Israel, Founded: 1993, Empl: 50+, Sales ($M): 31, Fiscal End: 12/95; Gil Shwed, Chmn, Deborah Triant, Pres & CEO

Checkfree Corp. 8275 N High St, Columbus OH 43235-1497 USA; 614/825-3000, Focus: Personal finance software, Ownrshp: OTC, Founded: 1981, Empl: 370, Sales ($M): 49.3, Fiscal End: 12/95; Peter Kight, CEO, Mark Johnson, EVP Bus Dev, Mark Phelan, EVP Sales & Mktng, Michael Sapienza, VP Mktng, Howard Baulch, EVP & CTO

Chem USA 2368 W Winton Ave, Hayward CA 94545 USA; 510/785-8080, Fax: 510/785-1010, Focus: Notebook PCs, Ownrshp: Sub Chung-Hsin Electronic, Founded: 1991, Vicki Chen, Pres, Richard Liu, VP Sales & Mktng

Cherry Corp. 3600 Sunset Ave, Waukegan IL 60087-3298 USA; 847/662-9200, Fax: 847/360-3508, Focus: Keyboards, displays and switches, Ownrshp: OTC, Stk Sym: CHER, Founded: 1953, Empl: 4,399, Sales ($M): 424.7, Fiscal End: 2/96; Peter B. Cherry, Chmn, Pres & CEO, Alfred S. Budnick, VP, Klaus D. Lauterback, VP, Keith E. Huebner, Marcom Mgr

Cheyenne Software Inc. 3 Expwy. Plaza, Roslyn Heights NY 11577 USA; 516/484-5110, 800/243-9462 Fax: 516/484-3446, Web URL: cheyenne.com, Focus: C/S and LAN management software, Ownrshp: AMEX, Stk Sym: CYE, Founded: 1983, Empl: 690, Sales ($M): 174.1, Fiscal End: 6/96; Eli Oxenhorn, Chmn, ReiJane Huai, Pres & CEO, Alan W. Kaufman, VP Sales, James P. McNiel, VP Bus Dev, Elliot Levine, CFO, Robin Lutchansky

Chicago Software Assoc. 2 N Riverside Plaza, #2400, Chicago IL 60606 USA; 708/358-0567, Fax: 708/358-0586, Focus: Association for Chicago area software developers, Ownrshp: Nonprofit, Ed Dennison, Exec Dir

Chinon America Inc. 615 Hawaii Ave, Torrance CA 90503-9747 USA; 310/533-0274, Fax: 310/533-1727, Focus: Peripherals and electronic equipment, Ownrshp: PVT, Founded: 1984, Empl: 40, Sales ($M): 25, Ken Matsui, Pres, Michael T. Bilous, EVP Sales & Mktng, David M. Cole, EVP Prod Dev, Cynthia Marin, Mktng Mgr, Pat Petrocelli, CFO

Chips & Technologies Inc. 2950 Zanker Rd, San Jose CA 95134 USA; 408/434-0600, Fax: 408/894-2082, Focus: Chips for PCs, Ownrshp: OTC, Stk Sym: CHPS, Founded: 1984, Empl: 200, Sales ($M): 150.8, Fiscal End: 6/96; James F. Stafford, Pres & CEO, Lee J. Barker, VP Ops, Scott E. Cutler, VP SW, Keith Angelo, VP Mktng

Choreo Systems Inc. 112 Kent St, #1300, Tower B, Place de Ville, Ottawa Ontario K1P 5P2 Canada; 613/238-1050, 800/565-8649 Fax: 613/238-4453, Web URL: choreo.ca, Focus: Interoperable networking, messaging and communications security software, Founded: 1987, Stephen P. Spence, VP Sales, Email: steves@choreo.ca

Chorus Systems Inc. 1999 S Bascom Ave, #400, Campbell CA 95008-2203 USA; 408/879-1350, 800/972-4678 Fax: 408/879-4102, Focus: Operating system software, Ownrshp: Sub. Chorus, France, Founded: 1986, Hubert Zimmermann, Chmn & CEO, Michael Gien, VP Mktng & Tech, David Robinson, EVP Sales, Janet Cardwell, Marcom Mgr

Chroma ATE Inc. 1620 Oakland Rd, #D105, San Jose CA 95131 USA; 408/437-0798, Fax: 408/437-0799, Focus: PC peripherals, Ownrshp: Sub. Chroma, Taiwan, Ming H. Chang, Pres, Joe Wu, VP

Chromatic Research 615 Tasman Dr, Sunnyvale CA 94089 USA; 408/752-9100, Focus: Multimedia microprocessors, Prdts: Mpact, Ownrshp: PVT

Chronologic Corp. 4925 N Camino Antonio, Tucson AZ 85718-6005 USA; 602/293-3100, Fax: 602/293-0709, Focus: Personal information management software, Ownrshp: PVT, Founded: 1987, Empl: 10, Robert Weed, Pres, Robert Humphrey, VP Dev

Chronologic Simulation 5150 El Camino Real, #E-30, Los Altos CA 94022 USA; 415/965-3312, Fax: 415/965-2705, Focus: Verilog simulation software, Prdts: VCS, VMC, Ownrshp: Sub. Viewlogic Systems, Founded: 1984, David Burow, Group VP, Ghulam Nurie, Dir Mktng, Karen Wills, Email: kwills@viewlogic.com

CIBER, Inc. 5251 DTC Pkwy, #1400, Englewood CO 80111-2742 USA; 303/220-0100, Fax: 303/220-7100, Web URL: ciber.com, Focus: Information technology services, Ownrshp: OTC, Stk Sym: CIBR, Founded: 1974, Empl: 1,650, Sales ($M): 109.0, Fiscal End: 6/95; Bobby G. Stevenson, Chmn, Pres & CEO, Mac J. Slingerlend, EVP & CFO, William E. Storrison, SVP Ops, David G. Durham, VP Finance, Kara Kennedy, Investor Relations, Email: kkennedy@ciber.com

CIMLINC Inc. 1222 Hamilton Pkwy, Itasca IL 60143 USA; 708/250-0090, Fax: 708/250-8513, Focus: Software for CIM and mechanical CAD, Ownrshp: PVT, Founded: 1981, Empl: 225, John West, Pres & CEO

Cincinnati Bell Inc. 201 E Fourth St, PO Box 2301, Cincinnati OH 45202 USA; 513/397-9900, 800/345-6301 Web URL: cinbell-linc.com, Focus: Telecom services and products, Ownrshp: NYSE, Stk Sym: CSN, Founded: 1873, Empl: 15,100, Sales ($M): 1,336.1, Fiscal End: 12/95; Dwight H. Hibbard, Chmn, John T. LaMacchia, Pres & CEO, David S. Gergacz, EVP, Brian C. Henry, EVP & CFO, Wayne E. Buckhout

Cincinnati Bell Information Systems (CBIS), 600 Vine St, Cincinnati OH 45202 USA; 513/784-5900, Focus: Network and systems integration, Ownrshp: Sub. Cincinnati Bell, Empl: 4,000, Sales ($M): 343.8, Fiscal End: 12/94; James F. Orr, Pres & CEO, Charles J. Del Riesgo, SVP Tech, David F. Stelzer, Pres Com Solutions, Thomas E. Smaldrone, Pres Mktng Group, William R. Coleman, SVP Fin

Cincinnati Milacron Inc. 4701 Marburg Ave, Cincinnati OH 45209 USA; 513/841-8100, Focus: Factory automation products, Ownrshp: NYSE, Stk Sym: CMZ, Founded: 1983, Empl: 11,701, Sales ($M): 1,649.3, Fiscal End: 12/95; Daniel J. Meyer, Chmn & CEO, Raymond E. Ross, Pres & COO, Richard L. Kegg, VP Tech, Ronald D. Brown, VP & CFO

Cincom Systems Inc. 2300 Montana Ave, Cincinnati OH 45211-3899 USA; 513/662-2300, Fax: 513/481-8332, Web URL: cincom.com, Focus: Database, LAN, office and manufacturing automation software, Prdts: Total, Ownrshp: PVT, Founded: 1968, Empl: 1,000, Sales ($M): 157, Fiscal End: 9/95; Thomas M. Nies, Pres & CEO, Jerry Shawhan, VP, Ron Hank, Dir Corp Rel

Cinemar Corp. 10700 SW Beaverton-Hillsdale Hwy, #2-470, Beaverton OR 97005 USA; 503/646-2800, 800/203-8502 Fax: 503/626-5610, Co Email: @cinemar.com, Focus: Multimedia training software, Ownrshp: PVT, Founded: 1994, Andy Leonard, Pres, Phil Seder, Email: phils@cinemar.com

Ciprico Inc. 2800 Campus Dr, Plymouth MN 55441 USA; 612/551-4000, Fax: 612/551-4002, Co Email: @ciprico.com, Web URL: ciprico.com, Focus: Disk array products, Prdts: Rimfire, Ownrshp: OTC, Stk Sym: CPCI, Founded: 1978, Empl: 80, Sales ($M): 16.0, Fiscal End: 9/95; Ronald B. Thomas, Chmn, Robert H. Kill, Pres & CEO, Cory J. Miller, VP & CFO

Circle Inc., The 5600 Ayala Ave, Irwindale CA 91706 USA; 800/635-8558 Fax: 800/359-3306, Focus: Toner cartridges, Ownrshp: PVT, Founded: 1988, H. Lee Ashby, Pres, Al Brown, Sales Mgr

Circle Systems Inc. 1001 Fourth Ave, #3200, Seattle WA 98154 USA; 206/682-3783, Fax: 206/328-4788, Co Email: @circlesys.com, Focus: Spreadsheet utility software, Ownrshp: PVT, Founded: 1986, Steven Dubnoff, Pres, Marian Lowe, Email: mlowe@circlesys.com

Circuit City Stores Inc. 9950 Maryland Dr, Richmond VA

23233-1464 USA; 804/527-4000, Fax: 804/527-4164, Focus: Chain of consumer electronics superstores, Ownrshp: NYSE, Stk Sym: CC, Empl: 33,000, Sales ($M): 7,029.1, Fiscal End: 2/96; Richard L. Sharp, Chmn, Pres & CEO, Richard S. Birnbaum, EVP Ops, Michael T. Chalifoux, SVP & CFO, W. Augustine Ligon, SVP Corp Plng, Raymond M. Albers, VP & CIO

Circuit Research Corp. 5 Northern Blvd, #12, Amherst NH 03031-2330 USA; 603/880-4000, Fax: 603/880-8297, Focus: Fax modems, Ownrshp: PVT, Founded: 1980, Empl: 6, Jeffrey Perkins, Pres

Cirque Corp. 433 W Lawndale Dr, Salt Lake City UT 84115 USA; 801/467-1100, 800/454-3375 Fax: 801/467-0208, Focus: Pointing devices, Prdts: GlidePoint, Ownrshp: PVT, Founded: 1991, George Gerpheide, Pres, James O'Callaghan, EVP, Kristiana Ellis, Marcom Mgr

Cirrus Logic Inc. 3100 W Warren Ave, Fremont CA 94538-6423 USA; 510/623-8300, Fax: 510/226-2240, Co Email: @corp.cirrus.com, Web URL: cirrus.com, Focus: ICs for peripheral control, Ownrshp: OTC, Stk Sym: CRUS, Founded: 1984, Empl: 1,809, Sales ($M): 1,146.9, Fiscal End: 3/96; Michael L. Hackworth, Pres & CEO, Suhas S. Patil, Chmn & EVP, George N. Alexy, SVP Mktng, Thomas F. Kelly, EVP & CFO, Tom Rigoli, VP Corp Com

Cisco Systems Inc. 170 W Tasman Dr, San Jose CA 94134-1706 USA; 408/526-4000, 800/553-6387 Fax: 408/526-4100, Co Email: @cisco.com, Web URL: cisco.com, Focus: Internetworking computer systems, Prdts: Catalyst, Ownrshp: OTC, Stk Sym: CSCO, Founded: 1984, Empl: 5,000, Sales ($M): 4,096.0, Fiscal End: 7/96; John P. Morgridge, Chmn, Ed Kozel, CTO, Dan LeBeau, SVP WW Sales, Frank J. Marshall, VP & GM, Larry Carter, VP & CFO, Bob Michelet, Dir Corp Com

Citadel Computer Systems 2950 N Loop W, #1080, Houston TX 77092 USA; 713/686-6400, 800/962-0701 Fax: 713/686-6495, Co Email: contact@citadel.com, Web URL: citadel.com, Focus: Netware software utilities, Prdts: NetOff, Ownrshp: PVT

Citizen America Corp. 2450 Broadway, #600, Santa Monica CA 90411-4003 USA; 310/453-0614, Fax: 310/453-2814, Focus: Peripherals and microcomputers, Ownrshp: Sub. Citizen Watch, Japan, Founded: 1984, Empl: 90

Citrix Systems Inc. 210 University Dr, #700, Coral Springs FL 33071-9908 USA; 305/340-2246, Fax: 305/341-6880, Web URL: citrix.com, Focus: Business software, Ownrshp: OTC, Stk Sym: CTXS, Founded: 1989, Empl: 75, Sales ($M): 14.6, Fiscal End: 12/95; Edward E. Iacobucci, Chmn, Roger Roberts, Pres & CEO, Jim Felcyn, CFO

Clarify Inc. 2702 Orchard Pkwy, San Jose CA 95134-9963 USA; 408/428-2000, Fax: 408/428-0633, Co Email: info@clarify.com, Web URL: clarify.com, Focus: C/S software, Prdts: Clear Support, Clear Quality, Clear Helpdesk, Clear Logistics, Ownrshp: OTC, Stk Sym: CLFY, Founded: 1990, Empl: 150, Sales ($M): 20.9, Fiscal End: 12/95; David Stamm, Pres & CEO, James L. Patterson, Chmn, Donna J.H. Novitsky, VP Mktng, Bob A. Spinner, VP Sales, Ray M. Fritz, CFO, Anne Morrissey, PR & Marcom Mgr

Claris Corp. 5201 Patrick Henry Dr, PO Box 58168, Santa Clara CA 95052-8168 USA; 408/987-7000, Fax: 408/987-7440, Co Email: @claris.com, Web URL: claris.com, Focus: Mac & PC software, Prdts: ClarisWorks, FileMaker Pro, Ownrshp: Sub. Apple, Founded: 1987, Empl: 700, Sales ($M): 183.8, Fiscal End: 9/95; Guerrino De Luca, Pres & CEO, Steve Pollock, VP Prod Mktng, Steve Ruddock, PR Dir, Email: steve_ruddock@claris.com

Clarity Software Inc. 2700 Garcia Ave, Mountain View CA 94043 USA; 415/691-0320, Fax: 415/964-4383, Co Email: info@clarity.com, Web URL: clarity.com, Focus: Cross-platform communication and interoperability, Prdts: Rapport, Ownrshp: PVT, Founded: 1990, Empl: 20, Howard J. Smith, Pres & CEO, Gwen Peterson, VP Mktng, Email: info@.clarity.com

Clary Corp. 1960 S Walker Ave, Monrovia CA 91016 USA; 818/359-4486, 800/442-5279 Fax: 818/305-0254, Focus: UPS, Prdts:

OnGuard, Ownrshp: PSE, Stk Sym: CLYP, Founded: 1939, Empl: 80, Sales ($M): 8.9, Fiscal End: 12/93; John G. Clary, Chmn, Donald G. Ash, Pres & CEO, Dina Deryan, Marcom Mgr

ClassAct Multimedia 1121 S Orem Blvd, Orem UT 84058-6976 USA; 801/221-9400, 800/235-3276 Fax: 801/221-9942, Focus: Software training CD-ROMs, Ownrshp: PVT, Teresa Crowell, PR Dir, Email: tcrowell@itsnet.com

Classic PIO Partners 87 E Green St, #309, Pasadena CA 91105 USA; 818/564-8106, 800/370-2746 Fax: 818/564-8554, Focus: Clip art, Ownrshp: PVT

Clear Software Inc. 385 Elliot St, Newton MA 02164 USA; 617/965-6755, Fax: 617/965-5310, Focus: Diagramming and flowcharting software, Prdts: allCLEAR, Ownrshp: PVT, Founded: 1987, Empl: 17, Vadim Yasinovsky, Pres, Colleen Terry, VP Sales & Mktng

CMD Technology Inc. 1 Vanderbilt, Irvine CA 92718 USA; 714/454-0800, 800/426-3832 Fax: 714/455-1656, Co Email: @cmd.com, Focus: SCSI and RAID controllers, Ownrshp: PVT, Founded: 1987, Empl: 85, Simon Huang, Pres & CEO, Thomas Chen, VP Ops, Bob Rudy, VP Sales & Mktng, Robert Wang, VP R&D, Robert Leondis

CMP Publications Inc. 600 Community Dr, Manhasset NY 11030-3847 USA; 516/562-5000, Fax: 516/562-5055, Co Email: @cmp.com, Web URL: techweb.cmp.com, Focus: 15+ computer magazines, Prdts: CommunicationsWeek, CRN, CRW, EET, InformationWeek, Windows, Ownrshp: PVT, Sales ($M): 380, Fiscal End: 12/95; Michael S. Leeds, Pres & CEO, Grace Monahan, EVP, Jeffrey L. Strief, SVP, Kenneth D. Cron, Pres Publishing, Joseph E. Sichler, CFO, Barbara Kerbel

CMR Publishing Inc. 448 S E St, #201, Santa Rosa CA 95404 USA; 707/575-4652, 800/551-3564 Fax: 707/575-4710, Focus: Project management software, Prdts: DailyLog, Ownrshp: PVT, Founded: 1983, Kenji P. Hoshino, Pres

CMS Enhancements Inc. 1051 S East St, Anaheim CA 92805 USA; 714/517-0915, Fax: 714/956-8156, Focus: Mass storage products, Ownrshp: PVT, Ken Burke, SVP & GM

Coast Manufacturing Co. 200 Corporate Blvd S, Yonkers NY 10701 USA; 914/376-1500, 800/333-6282 Fax: 914/376-0400, Focus: Computer carrying cases and accessories, Ownrshp: PVT, Founded: 1946, William Mooar, Pres & CEO, Floyd Barker, EVP, Richard Flashenberg, VP, Seth Hochman, Sales Mgr

Cobalt Blue 555 Sun Valley Dr, #K4, Roswell GA 30076-1465 USA; 770/518/1116, Fax: 770/640-1182, Focus: Fortran maintenance and conversion tools; VR consulting, Prdts: FOR-STRUCT, FOR-C, FOR-STUDY, Ownrshp: PVT, Founded: 1985, Clyde Lightfoot, Software Dev Mgr, Beverley Lightfoot, Mktng Dir

Cobb Group, The, 9420 Bunsen Pkwy, #300, Louisville KY 40220 USA; 502/491-1900, Fax: 502/491-4200, Web URL: cobb.com, Focus: 40+ computer software newsletters, books and software, Ownrshp: Sub. Ziff-Davis, John Jenkins, Pres

Cobotyx Corp. 0 Miry Brook Rd, Danbury CT 06810-7409 USA; 203/282-0010, 800/288-6342 Focus: Voice processing systems, Ownrshp: Sub. Farmstead Telephone, George J. Taylor Jr., Chmn & CEO, Peter S. Buswell, Pres, Tom Williams, CTO

Coconut Computing Inc. 565 Pearl St, La Jolla CA 92037-5051 USA; 619/456-2002, Co Email: info@coconut.com, Focus: Software for online interactive services, Prdts: COCONET, CocoTalk, CocoMedia, Ownrshp: PVT, Founded: 1990, Brian Dear, Pres

Coda Inc. 1155 Elm St, Manchester NH 03101 USA; 603/647-9600, Focus: Accounting software, Prdts: OAS, Ownrshp: Sub. Coda, UK, Founded: 1988, Empl: 394, Sales ($M): 52.5, Fiscal End: 12/95; Rodney Potts, Chmn, Robert Brown, Pres

Coda Music Technology 6210 Bury Dr, Eden Prairie MN 55436 USA; 612/937-9611, Fax: 612/937-9760, Focus: Music software, Prdts: Finale, MusicProse, Vivace Personal Accompanist, Ownrshp: OTC, Stk Sym: COMT, Founded: 1985, Empl: 40, Sales ($M): 4.9, Fiscal End: 12/95; Ron Raup, Pres, Bill Hinely, SVP Sales & Mktng,

Nancy Cohen, Marcom Spec

Cogent Data Technologies Inc. 640 Mullis St, Friday Harbor WA 98250 USA; 360/378-2929, Fax: 360/378-2882, Co Email: @cogentdata.com, Web URL: cogentdata.com, Focus: Ethernet adapters and hubs, Ownrshp: PVT, Founded: 1982, Charles R. Anderson, Pres, Email: chuck@cogentdata.com; Deanna Anderson, EVP, Email: deanna@cogentdata.com; John Pageler, VP Sales, Email: john@cogentdata.com; Dan Wittkopp, VP Fin & Admin, Troy Emmerson, Network Admin, Email: Troy@cogentdata.com; Hendrik Wacker, Dir Corp Com, Email: Hendrik@cogentdata.com

Cogent Electronics Inc. (CEI), 210A Twin Dolphin Dr, Redwood City CA 94065 USA; 415/591-6617, Fax: 415/591-8310, Focus: Multimedia products, Prdts: Media-V, Video Clipper, PC PrimeTime, Video Wizard, Ownrshp: Sub. CEI, Hong Kong, Founded: 1992, Empl: 700, Sales ($M): 50, K.H. Tan, Pres, Eugene Tan, Dir Mktng

Cogent Technologies Inc. 375 Pierce St, Kingston PA 18704 USA; 717/283-2257, Focus: Trial balance/workpaper software, Prdts: Workpapers, Ownrshp: PVT, Edward A. Wielage

Cognex Corp. 1 Vision Dr, Natick MA 01760-2059 USA; 508/650-3000, Web URL: krl.com/cognex, Focus: Machine vision systems, Prdts: Cognex 4000, Cognex 5000, Checkpoint, Ownrshp: OTC, Stk Sym: CGNX, Founded: 1981, Empl: 300, Sales ($M): 104.5, Fiscal End: 12/95; Robert J. Shillman, Chmn, Pres & CEO, Patrick Alias, EVP Sales & Mktng, Richard Snyder, EVP Ops, John Rogers, EVP & CFO, Sam Scheider, Dir IS, Kathy Bedrosian, Corp Comm Mgr

Cognitive Systems Inc. 880 Canal St, Stamford CT 06902 USA; 203/356-7756, Fax: 203/356-7760, Focus: AI-based software, Ownrshp: OTC, Stk Sym: CSAI, Founded: 1979, Sales ($M): 0.8, Fiscal End: 11/94; Stephen Craig Mott, Pres & CEO

Cognitronics Corp. 3 Corporate Dr, Danbury CT 06810-4130 USA; 203/830-3400, Focus: Voice response products, Ownrshp: AMEX, Stk Sym: CGN, Founded: 1962, Empl: 80, Sales ($M): 17.5, Fiscal End: 12/95; Brian J. Kelley, Pres & CEO, Kenneth G. Brix, VP Sales, Michael N. Keefe, VP Eng, Garrett Sullivan, CFO, Harold F. Mayer, VP Admin

Cognos Corp. 67 S Bedford St, #200W, Burlington MA 01803-5164 USA; 617/229-6600, 800/426-4667 Fax: 617/229-1839, Focus: CASE and database programs, Ownrshp: Sub. Cognos, Canada, Stk Sym: COGNF, Founded: 1969, Empl: 1,000, Sales ($M): 150.1, Fiscal End: 2/94; Patrick O'Leary, VP Mktng, Terry Hall, SVP WW Sales, Roberta Carlton, PR Mgr, Email: 345.6507@mciamail.com

Cognos Inc. 3755 Riverside Dr, Ottawa Ontario K1G 4K9 Canada; 613/738-1440, 800/267-2777 Fax: 613/738-0002, Web URL: cognos.com, Focus: CAD and database software, Ownrshp: OTC, Stk Sym: COGNF, Founded: 1969, Empl: 1,005, Sales ($M): 207.6, Fiscal End: 2/96; Michael U. Potter, Chmn & CEO, Renato Zambonini, Pres & COO, Neal Hill, VP Mktng, Alan Rottenberg, SVP, Donnie M. Moore, SVP & CFO

Coleman Computer Association 7380 Parkway Dr, La Mesa CA 91942-1532 USA; 619/465-4063, Focus: Association for computer professionals, Ownrshp: Nonprofit, Founded: 1967

Colorado Advanced Software Institute 1898 S Flatirons Ct, #5A, Boulder CO 80301 USA; 303/440-3695, Fax: 303/440-4083, Focus: Organization for Colorado software companies, Ownrshp: Nonprofit

Colorado Software Assoc. 190 E 9th Ave, #300, Denver CO 80203 USA; 303/220-2000, Fax: 303/220-2120, Focus: Association for Colorado software developers, Ownrshp: Nonprofit, Ray Meuller, Chmn

Coloray 1045 Mission Ct, Fremont CA 94539 USA; 510/623-3300, Fax: 510/623-3399, Focus: Digitizers and flat panel displays, Ownrshp: Sub Scriptel, Stk Sym: SCRH, M. Kathy Vieth, Pres & COO

Colorbus Inc. 18261 McDurmott W, Irvine CA 92714 USA; 714/852-1850, Fax: 714/852-1909, Co Email: @colorbus.com, Focus: Print server software and hardware, Prdts: Cyclone, Ownrshp: PVT, Founded: 1990, Worth Probst, Chmn, Paul Peffer, Pres & CEO, Cameron Altenhof-Long, VP & CTO, Ann Selbe, VP Sales, Dean Trojan, VP Fin, Barbara Stange, Email: stange@colorbus.com

Colorgraphic Communications Corp. 5980 Peachtree Rd, Atlanta GA 30341-1602 USA; 770/455-3921, Fax: 770/458-0616, Web URL: colorgfx.com, Focus: PC multi-screen graphics boards, Prdts: Pro Lightning, Mega Lightning, Voyager VGA for PCMCIA, Ownrshp: PVT, Founded: 1980, Empl: 25, Ezra Mintz, Pres, Elyse Mintz, VP Mktng, Claudia Shaw, VP Sales

Colossal Graphics Inc. 2666 E Bayshore Rd, Palo Alto CA 94303 USA; 415/858-2993, Fax: 415/858-2994, Focus: Printer supplies, Ownrshp: PVT, Ron L. Jones, Pres & CEO

COM&DIA PO Box 97487, Raleigh NC 27624-7487 USA; 919/848-0001, Fax: 919/848-7779, Co Email: info@com-dia.com, Web URL: com-dia.com, Focus: PC security software, Prdts: Dia-Lock Boot, SecurED, Ownrshp: PVT, Founded: 1994, Doug Kendrick, Pres, Email: dkendric@aol.com

Combinet Inc. 333 W El Camino Real, #320, Sunnyvale CA 94087 USA; 408/522-9020, Fax: 408/732-5479, Focus: Network products, Ownrshp: PVT, Founded: 1988, Tom Williams, Pres

Comdisco Inc. 6111 N River Rd, Rosemont IL 60018 USA; 847/698-3000, Fax: 847/518-5060, Web URL: comdisco.com, Focus: Computer leasing and disaster recovery services, Ownrshp: NYSE, Stk Sym: CDO, Founded: 1969, Empl: 1,875, Sales ($M): 2,240, Fiscal End: 9/95; Jack Slevin, Pres & CEO, Robert A. Bardagy, EVP, William N. Pontikes, EVP, Alan J. Andeini, EVP, John J. Vosicky, EVP & CFO, Mary C. Moster, VP Corp Com

Comfy Inc. 1054 Saratoga-Sunnyvale Rd, #102, San Jose CA 95129 USA; 408/865-1777, 800/992-6639 Fax: 408/865-1877, Focus: Education and entertainment software, Ownrshp: Sub Comfy, Israel, Karrie Jo Lace, Pres, Cynthia Colmenares, VP Sales & Mktng

Command Software Systems Inc. 1061 E Indiantown Rd, #500, Jupiter FL 33477 USA; 407/575-3200, 800/423-9147 Fax: 407/575-3026, Co Email: command@mcimail.com, Web URL: commandcom.com, Focus: PC and network security software, Prdts: Security Guardian, Langard, Ownrshp: PVT, Founded: 1983, Empl: 17, Dyan Dyer, Pres, Therese G. Padilla, Prod Mgr, Email: padilla@commandcom.com

Command Technology Corp. 1040 Marina Village Pkwy, Alameda CA 94501 USA; 510/521-5900, 800/336-3320 Fax: 510/521-0369, Co Email: ctcinquiry@aol.com, Focus: Mainframe class software for PCs, Prdts: SPF/PC, Ownrshp: PVT, Founded: 1984, Empl: 10, Tim Tetiva, Pres & CEO, Pamela Curtis, Controller, Sabrina Schultz, Mgr Mktng & Sales

Commax Technologies Inc. 2031 Concourse Dr, San Jose CA 95131 USA; 408/435-5000, 800/526-6629 Fax: 408/435-5005, Focus: Notebook PCs and peripherals, Ownrshp: PVT, Founded: 1983, Empl: 30, Sales ($M): 40, Henry Chen, Pres, Daphne Chen, VP Ops, Patrick Lawlor, Sales Mgr

Commcrypt Inc. 12211 Distribution Way, Beltsville MD 20705-1443 USA; 301/470-2500, Fax: 301/470-2507, Focus: Security software, Ownrshp: PVT, Founded: 1984, Empl: 15, William Landgraf, Pres

Commerce Direct International Inc. (CDI), 205-591 Bernard Ave, Kelowna BC V1Y 6N9 Canada; 604/861-3217, Fax: 604/861-3266, Co Email: canada@cdi.net, Focus: Business solutions for the electronic distribution marketplace, Toby Tobaccowala, CEO

CommerceNet 800 El Camino Real, Menlo Park CA 94025 USA; 415/617-8790, Fax: 415/617-1516, Co Email: info@commerce.net, Web URL: commerce.net, Focus: Consortium to create an Internet electronic marketplace, Ownrshp: Nonprofit, Founded: 1994, Empl: 135, Cathy Medich, Exec Dir

Commercial Internet eXchange Assoc. (CIX), 1035 Sterling Rd, #201, Herndon VA 22071 USA; 703/318-7218, Fax: 703/

904-0646, Co Email: @cix.org, Web URL: cix.org/cixhome, Focus: Association for internet information providers, Ownrshp: Nonprofit, Empl: 180, Susan Fitzgerald, Exec Dir, Email: sfitzger@cix.org; Robert D. Collet, Chmn & Pres, Email: rcollet@cix.org; Barbara Dooley, Managing Ed, Email: imasters@pipeline.com

Commercial Software Inc. PO Box 648, Edison NJ 08818-0648 USA; 908/985-8966, Fax: 908/819-7321, Focus: Application software generator, Prdts: Casegen, Ownrshp: PVT, Founded: 1981, Empl: 4, Sales ($M): 0.8, Fiscal End: 9/95; Bob Hoffman, Pres

Commix SP Inc. 8300 Boone Blvd #700, Vienna VA 22182-2626 USA; 703/356-9858, Fax: 703/356-6148, Focus: Image management software, Prdts: MultiMaster, Ownrshp: PVT, Founded: 1992, Stephen Giordano, Pres & CEO

Common Grounds Software Inc. 1301 Shoreway Rd, #220, Belmont CA 94002-4106 USA; 415/802-5800, 800/598-3821 Fax: 415/593-6868, Co Email: info@commonground.com, Web URL: commonground.com, Focus: Electronic document distribution software, Prdts: DigitalPaper, Ownrshp: PVT, Founded: 1991, Richard T. Preston, Pres & CEO, Email: rpreston@commonground.com; Nick Gault, VP Eng, Robert Gronski, VP Sales, Steve McConaughey, Dir Mktng

CommTouch Software Inc. 298 S Sunnyvale Ave, #209, Sunnyvale CA 94086 USA; 408/245-8682, Focus: E-mail software, Ownrshp: PVT, Founded: 1991, Nahum Sharfman, Pres, Amir Lev, VP R&D, Ronny Gorlicki, VP Mktng

Communications Managers Assoc. (CMA), 1201 Mt. Kemble Ave, Morristown NJ 07960 USA; 201/425-1700, Fax: 201/425-0777, Web URL: cma.org, Focus: Information sharing, education and enhancement of the telecommunications profession, Ownrshp: Nonprofit, Founded: 1948, Empl: 500, Matt O'Brien, Pres, Katherine Pakacs, Managing Dir

Communications Specialties Inc. 89A Cabot Ct, Hauppauge NY 11788 USA; 516/273-0404, Fax: 516/273-1638, Co Email: csimail@marist.edu, Focus: VGA & Mac to video scan converters, Prdts: Scan Do, Ownrshp: PVT, Founded: 1983, Empl: 17, John Lopinto, Pres, Email: john@commspecial.com; Norman Weingart, VP, Email: normanw@commspecial.com; Paul Seiden, Sales Mgr, Email: pseiden@commspecial.com; Krista Demaria, Media Relations, Email: krista@commspecial.com

COMNET Corp. 4200 Parliament Place, #600, Lanham MD 20706-1860 USA; 301/918-0400, 800/368-5806 Fax: 301/918-0430, Focus: Specialized marketing and mail management software, Ownrshp: OTC, Stk Sym: CNET, Empl: 256, Sales ($M): 45.9, Fiscal End: 3/96; Robert S. Bowen, Pres & CEO, Charles A. Crew, EVP & CFO, Ronald F. Friedman, Dir

Compact Flash Assoc. (CFA), PO Box 51537, Palo Alto CA 94303 USA; 415/843-1220, Fax: 415/493-1871, Co Email: info@compactflash.org, Web URL: compactflash.org, Focus: Association for compact flash card vendors, Prdts: Compact Flash Specification Standard, Ownrshp: Nonprofit, Founded: 1995, Empl: 30, Bill Frank, Exec Dir, Email: billfrank@compactflash.org

Compaq Computer Corp. 20555 SH 249, PO Box 692000, Houston TX 77269-2000 USA; 713/370-0670, 800/888-5858 Fax: 713/374-4583, Co Email: @compaq.com, Web URL: compaq.com, Focus: Desktop and notebook PCs, Ownrshp: NYSE, Stk Sym: CPQ, Founded: 1982, Empl: 14,372, Sales ($M): 14,755, Fiscal End: 12/95; Eckhard Pfeiffer, Pres & CEO, Ross Cooley, SVP NA, Gregory E. Petsch, SVP Corp Ops, Daryl J. White, SVP & CFO, John W. White, VP & CIO, Debra Globe

Comparex Informations Systeme Gmbh Gottlieb Daimler Strasse 10, Mannheim 1 D-68165 Germany; 49-621-40090, Focus: Mainframe computers, Ownrshp: FO, Sales ($M): 670, Fiscal End: 12/95

Compass Design Automation 1865 Lundy Ave, San Jose CA 95131 USA; 408/433-4880, Fax: 408/434-7820, Web URL: compass-da.com, Focus: Electronic design automation tools and librar-

ies, Prdts: Passport, Dieter Mezger, Pres, Ken Brock, Bus Dev Mgr, F. Taylor Scanlon, VP WW Mktng

Compatible Systems Corp. 4730 Walnut St, #102, Boulder CO 80301 USA; 303/444-9532, 800/356-0283 Fax: 303/444-9595, Co Email: info@compatible.com, Web URL: compatible.com, Focus: LAN and internetworking products, Ownrshp: PVT, Founded: 1985, Empl: 22, Sales ($M): 4, Matt McConnell, Pres & CEO, Email: matt@compatible.com; Tim Schultz, VP Eng, Email: tim@compatible.com; Tom Ferrell, Tech Mktng Mgr, Email: tom@compatible.com; Brenda Holt-Harris, Marcom Mgr

CompLink Ltd. 175 Community Dr, Great Neck NY 11021 USA; 516/829-1883, Fax: 516/829-5001, Co Email: @complink.com, Focus: Notes utility software, Ownrshp: OTC, Stk Sym: CLNK

Component Integration Laboratories (CI Labs), PO Box 61747, Sunnyvale CA 94088-1747 USA; 408/864-0300, Fax: 408/0380, Co Email: cilabs@cil.org, Focus: Develop object technology standards-OpenDoc, Ownrshp: Nonprofit, Jed Harris, Pres, Email: jed@cil.org; Andrew Poupart, VP Ops, Michael Barton, VP Mktng

Comprehend Franchise Corp. 3200 N 29th Ave, Hollywood FL 33020 USA; 954/921-6040, 800/601-5876 Fax: 954/923-0126, Co Email: comped1@aol.com, Focus: Franchised PC education centers, Ownrshp: PVT, Founded: 1991, Dean Snow, Pres, Mark Miller, VP, Jim Mendoza, Dir Training

Compression Labs Inc. (CLI), 2860 Junction Ave, San Jose CA 95134-1900 USA; 408/435-3000, Fax: 408/922-5429, Focus: Video communications products, Ownrshp: OTC, Stk Sym: CLIX, Founded: 1987, Empl: 549, Sales ($M): 113.0, Fiscal End: 12/95; Arthur G. Anderson, Chmn, Gary Trimm, Pres & CEO, Wen-hsiung Chen, SVP Res, John J. Walsh, SVP Plng & Strat, William A. Berry, SVP & CFO, Joyce Strand

Comptek Research Inc. 2732 Transit Rd, Buffalo NY 14224 USA; 716/677-4070, Fax: 716/677-0014, Focus: Systems, software and services to the military, Ownrshp: AMEX, Stk Sym: CTK, Founded: 1968, Empl: 661, Sales ($M): 55.2, Fiscal End: 3/96; John R. Cummings, Chmn, Pres & CEO, James D. Morgan, VP & Chief Scientist, Christopher A. Head, EVP, John J. Sciuto, Pres & CEO Fed Syst, George J. Barry, VP & CFO

Compton's NewMedia Inc. 2320 Camino Vida Roble, Carlsbad CA 92009 USA; 619/929-2500, Fax: 619/929-2555, Focus: Education, edutainment, infotainment and reference software, Prdts: Compton's Interactive Encyclopedia, Ownrshp: Sub. Softkey International, Founded: 1983, Empl: 150, Jim Longson, Pres & CEO, Bob Bellack, VP Ops, Bill Perrault, VP Mktng & Sales, Jim Till, VP Sales, Keith Motte, Network Admin Mgr, Ernie Clark, Dir PR

Comptronix Corp. 3 Maryland Farms, #140, Brentwood TN 37027 USA; 615/377-3330, Co Email: comptron@comptronix.com, Focus: Contract manufacturing, Ownrshp: OTC, Stk Sym: CMPX, Founded: 1984, Empl: 900, Sales ($M): 92.2, Fiscal End: 12/95; E. Townes Duncan, Chmn & CEO, Michael C. Thompson, VP Ops, Joseph G. Andersen, CFO, Kristi Hester

Compu-Design Group Inc. (CDG), 233 W Central, 1st Fl., Natick MA 01760 USA; 508/655-1177, Fax: 508/655-1440, Focus: C/S management solutions, Prdts: PCDuo, Ownrshp: PVT, Michelle Drolet, Pres

CompuAdd Corp. 12337 Technology Blvd, Austin TX 78727 USA; 512/250-1489, 800/627-1961 Fax: 512/250-3494, Focus: Direct marketing of PCs, Ownrshp: PVT, Founded: 1982, Sales ($M): 233.4, Fiscal End: 12/93; Rick Krause, Pres, Dania Buchanan, Mgr Mktng & Advertising

CompuCom Systems 10100 N Central Expwy, Dallas TX 75231 USA; 214/265-3600, Fax: 214/265-5220, Web URL: compucom.com, Focus: Chain of computer stores, Ownrshp: OTC, Stk Sym: CMPC, Founded: 1981, Empl: 1,060, Sales ($M): 1,441.6, Fiscal End: 12/95; Edward R. Anderson, Pres & CEO, Michael V. Wise, VP Ops, Daniel F. Brown, EVP Sales, Jack D. Dowling, VP & CIO, Robert J. Boutin, SVP & CFO

Compulink Management Center Inc. 370 S Crenshaw Blvd,

#E106, Torrance CA 90503-1701 USA; 310/212-5465, Fax: 310/212-5064, Co Email: imaging@ix.netcom.com, Web URL: laserfiche.com, Focus: Image and text processing systems; document storage and retrieval, Prdts: LaserFiche Series, Ownrshp: PVT, Founded: 1975, Empl: 40, Nien-Ling Wacker, Pres & CEO, Christopher Wacker, VP Mktng & Sales, Lance Wayman, VP Ops, Gregg Schaeberle, Sales Dir, Art Smith, Email: 75162.2305@compuserve.com; John Case, Tech Coord

CompUSA Inc. 14951 N Dallas Pkwy, Dallas TX 75240 USA; 214/982-4000, 800/278-4685 Fax: 214/982-4276, Web URL: compusa.com, Focus: Chain of computer superstores, Ownrshp: OTC, Stk Sym: CUSA, Founded: 1984, Empl: 6,426, Sales ($M): 3,829.8, Fiscal End: 6/96; Giles H. Batesman, Chmn, James F. Halpin, Pres & CEO, Harold F. Compton, EVP COO, Ronald J. Gilmore, SVP Mktng & Adv, James L. Infinger, VP & CIO

Compusearch Software Systems Inc. 7926 Jones Branch Dr, #260, McLean VA 22102 USA; 703/893-7200, Fax: 703/893-7499, Co Email: @compusearch.com, Focus: Electronic document management software, Prdts: Image Fast, Ownrshp: PVT, Founded: 1984, Empl: 45, Sales ($M): 5, Fiscal End: 12/95; Henry Frain, Pres, Cynthia O'Connell, VP R&D, Patrick Devlin, Dir Prod Mktng, Glenn Spring, Email: gspring@compusearch.com

CompuServe Inc. 5000 Arlington Ctr Blvd, Columbus OH 43220 USA; 614/457-8600, 800/433-0389 Fax: 614/457-0348, Web URL: compuserve.com, Focus: On-line services and communication software, Prdts: CompuServe Information Service, Ownrshp: OTC, Stk Sym: CSRV, Founded: 1969, Empl: 1,500, Sales ($M): 793.2, Fiscal End: 4/96; Bob Massey, Pres & CEO, Debra Young

CompuServe Internet Div. 316 Occidental Ave S, #200, Seattle WA 98104 USA; 206/447-0300, 800/777-9638 Fax: 206/447-9008, Co Email: info@spry.com, Web URL: spry.com, Focus: Internet access software, Prdts: Internet In A Box, Sprynet, Ownrshp: Sub CompuServe, Founded: 1987, Empl: 100, David Pool, Pres, Tim Gelinas, VP Eng, Lisa Thorell, VP Mktng, Bo Wandell, VP Sales, Stuart White, VP Svcs & Support, Deanna Leung, PR Mgr, Email: deanna@spry.com

Computer 2000 Baierbrunner Strasse 31, Munich 70 D-8000 Germany; 89-724-90276, Focus: Distribution of PC products in Europe, Ownrshp: FO, Sales ($M): 650, Jochen Tschunke, Chmn

Computer Access Technology Corp. (ABIG), 3375 Scott Blvd, #410, Santa Clara CA 95054 USA; 408/727-6600, Fax: 408/727-6622, Focus: USB products, Ownrshp: PVT, Dan Wilnai, Pres, Dorothy Brown

Computer Aid Inc. (CAI), 901 Market St, #1200, Wilmington DE 19801 USA; 302/888-5444, Fax: 302/888-5443, Focus: Support services

Computer and Communications Industry Assoc. (CCIA), 666 Eleventh St NW, 6th Fl, Washington DC 20001 USA; 202/783-0070, Fax: 202/783-0534, Focus: Association for computer and communications industry, Ownrshp: Nonprofit, Founded: 1972, Empl: 65, Edward Black, Pres

Computer Applications America Co. Ltd. (CAC America), 30 Rockefeller Plaza, #4528, New York NY 10112 USA; 212/332-2580, Fax: 212/332-2595, Focus: Systems integration, Ownrshp: Sub. CAC, Japan, Founded: 1989, Yoichi Wada, Pres

Computer Assistance Inc. 82277 Weiss Rd, Creswell OR 97426 USA; 503/895-3347, Fax: 503/895-3999, Co Email: 73650.444@compuserve.com, Focus: Automotive repair software, Prdts: GarageKeeper, Motive Power, Ownrshp: PVT, Founded: 1979, Empl: 4, Sales ($M): 0.5, Fiscal End: 12/92; Myles Swift, Pres, Patricia Swift, VP

Computer Associates Int'l. Inc. (CA), One Computer Associates Plaza, Islandia NY 11788-7000 USA; 516/342-5224, Fax: 516/342-5329, Web URL: cai.com, Focus: Software for mainframes, midrange and PCs, Ownrshp: NYSE, Stk Sym: CA, Founded: 1976, Empl: 6,900, Sales ($M): 3,504.6, Fiscal End: 3/96; Charles B. Wang, Chmn & CEO, Russell M. Artzt, EVP R&D, Peter A.

Schwartz, SVP & CFO, Sanjay Kumar, Pres & COO

Computer Association of N America (CANA), 136-21 Rosevelt Ave, 3rd Floor, Flushing NY 11354 USA; 718/460-9770, Fax: 718/460-9771, Ownrshp: Nonprofit, Founded: 1991, Arrina Chang, Admin. Secretary

Computer Concepts Corp. 80 Orville Dr, Bohemia NY 11716 USA; 516/244-1500, Fax: 516/563-8085, Focus: PC software, Ownrshp: OTC, Stk Sym: CCEE, Founded: 1989, Sales ($M): 16.3, Fiscal End: 12/95; Daniel DelGiorno, Pres

Computer Data Systems Inc. (CDSI), One Curie Ct, Rockville MD 20850-4389 USA; 301/921-7000, Fax: 301/948-9328, Focus: Computer services, Ownrshp: OTC, Stk Sym: CDSI, Founded: 1968, Empl: 3,400, Sales ($M): 251.1, Fiscal End: 6/96; Clifford M. Kendall, Chmn, Peter A. Bracken, CEO, Thomas A. Green, EVP, Mary Ann Mayhew, EVP Bus Dev, Dennis Conley, CIO, Donald E. Ziegler

Computer Discount Warehouse 1020 E Lake Cook Rd, Buffalo Grove IL 60089 USA; 847/465-6000, 800/305-4239 Fax: 847/465-6800, Web URL: cdw.com, Focus: Mail order sales of computer products, Ownrshp: OTC, Stk Sym: CDWC, Empl: 400+, Sales ($M): 628.7, Fiscal End: 12/95; Michael Krasny, Chmn & CEO, Greg Zeman, Pres, Daniel B. Kass, VP Ops, Harry J. Harczak Jr., CFO

Computer Dynamics 1905 Wisteria, Denton TX 76205 USA; 817/566-5515, Fax: 817/382-5089, Web URL: iglobal.net/cd, Focus: Single board computers, flat displays and touch panels, Ownrshp: PVT, Founded: 1981, Empl: 100, Sebastian Ernest, Pres

Computer Easy Int'l. Inc. 414 E Southern Ave, Tempe AZ 85281 USA; 800/522-3279 Fax: 602/829-9616, Focus: Macintosh utility software, Ownrshp: PVT

Computer Economics Inc. 5841 Edison Place, Carlsbad CA 92008 USA; 619/438-8100, Fax: 619/431-1126, Co Email: custserv@compecon.com, Focus: Mainframe, workstations and midrange computers; forecast of residual value, new products, Ownrshp: PVT, Founded: 1979, Empl: 25, Bruno Bassi, Pres, Mark McManus, Editor-in-Chief, Email: mmcmanus@compecon.com

Computer Emergency Response Team Coordination Center (CERT), CMU Software Eng Institute, Pittsburgh PA 15213 USA; 412/268-7090, Co Email: cert@cert.org, Focus: Respond to computer security incidents on the Internet, Ownrshp: Nonprofit

Computer Expressions Inc. 4200 Mitchell St, Philadelphia PA 19128-3593 USA; 215/487-7700, Fax: 215/487-7728, Focus: Computer accessories, Ownrshp: PVT, Founded: 1986, Empl: 60, Sales ($M): 6, Bennett J. Beer, Pres, Chris Franke

Computer Fun 8250 Valdosta Ave, San Diego CA 92126-2130 USA; 619/271-9090, 800/521-8484 Fax: 619/271-9291, Co Email: @computerfun.com, Web URL: computerfun.com, Focus: Computer accessories, Prdts: Animal & Classic Car Mouse Pads, Powercover & Happy Face! Dust Covers, Ownrshp: PVT, Founded: 1988, Gary O'Mary, Co-founder, Email: garyo@computerfun.com

Computer Group Inc., The 4455 Reynolds Dr, Hilliard OH 43026 USA; 614/876-8600, 800/466-4076 Fax: 614/777-2361, Focus: Software duplication services, Ownrshp: PVT, Sandy Seago, VP Sales & Mktng

Computer Horizons Corp. 49 Old Bloomfield Ave, Mountain Lakes NJ 07046-1495 USA; 201/402-7400, Focus: Year 2000 conversion, Prdts: Signature 2000, CHAMPS, Ownrshp: OTC, Stk Sym: CHRZ, Founded: 1969, Empl: 3,000, Sales ($M): 200.0, Fiscal End: 12/95; John J. Cassese, Chmn & Pres, David Reingold, VP, Email: dreingold@msn.com

Computer Identics Corp. 5 Shawmut Rd, Canton MA 02021 USA; 617/821-0830, Fax: 617/828-8942, Web URL: tiac.net/users/cmptrid, Focus: Bar code and scanner products, Prdts: Starnode Data Collection Network, Data Collection Terminals, Ownrshp: Sub. Robotic Vision Systems, Founded: 1968, Empl: 135, Sales ($M): 27.7, Fiscal End: 12/95; Richard C. Close, Pres & CEO, Jeffrey A. Weber, VP Ops & Fin, Stephen L. Abbey, VP NA Sales &

Mktng, Thomas J. Chisholm, VP R&D, Elizabeth Payne, Bus Admin

Computer Intelligence/InfoCorp 3344 N Torrey Pines Ct, La Jolla CA 92037 USA; 619/450-1667, Fax: 619/452-7491, Focus: Database of computer installations--including mainframe, mini, PC & telecom, Ownrshp: PVT, Founded: 1969, Robert G. Brown, Pres

Computer Language Research Inc. 2395 Midway Rd, Carrollton TX 75006 USA; 214/250-7000, Web URL: clr.com, Focus: Tax processing services, Prdts: FastTax, Ownrshp: OTC, Stk Sym: CLRI, Founded: 1964, Empl: 946, Sales ($M): 110.7, Fiscal End: 12/95; Francis W. Winn, Chmn, Stephen T. Winn, Pres & CEO, M. Brian Healy, Group VP & CFO, Douglas H. Gross, VP

Computer Law Assoc. (CLA), 3028 Javier Rd, #500E, Fairfax VA 22031 USA; 703/560-7747, Fax: 703/207-7028, Focus: Information for attorneys in computer law, Ownrshp: Nonprofit, Founded: 1971, Empl: 1,300, Barbara Fieser, Exec Dir

Computer Learning Foundation (CLF), 2431 Park Blvd, PO Box 60007, Palo Alto CA 94306-0007 USA; 415/327-3347, Fax: 415/327-3349, Co Email: clf@legal.com, Focus: Effective and ethical use of technology among educators, parents and youth, Ownrshp: Nonprofit, Founded: 1987, Empl: 200+, Sally Bowman Alden, Exec Dir

Computer Leasing & Remarketing Assoc. Inc. (CDLA), 401 N Michigan Ave, Chicago IL 60611-4267 USA; 312/644-6610, Fax: 312/321-6869, Focus: Represents companies that buy, sell, lease and broker computers and high-tech equipment, Ownrshp: Nonprofit, Founded: 1981, Empl: 260, Douglas B. McAllister, Dir Com

Computer Measurement Group Inc. (CMG), 414 Plaza Dr, #209, Westmont IL 60559 USA; 630/655-1812, Fax: 630/655-1813, Web URL: cmg.cs.csi.cuny.edu, Focus: Performance, planning and management of computer systems, Ownrshp: Nonprofit, Founded: 1975, Judith K. Keel, Exec Dir

Computer Network Technology Corp. (CNT), 605 N Hwy 169, #800, Minneapolis MN 55441 USA; 612/797-6000, 800/638-8324 Fax: 612/797-6813, Web URL: cnt.com, Focus: Channel extension and legacy-to-open systems connectivity, Prdts: CHANNELink, Ownrshp: OTC, Stk Sym: CMNT, Founded: 1983, Empl: 400, Sales ($M): 78.8, Fiscal End: 12/95; John Rollwagen, Chmn, Bruce Coleman, Pres & CEO, Kathleen E. Brush, VP Mktng, Richard Helgeson, VP Sales, John R. Brintnall, VP & CFO, Ilyssa Greene, PR Mgr, Email: ilyssa_greene@cnt.com

Computer Outsourcing Services Inc. (COSI), 360 W 31st St, New York NY 10001 USA; 212/564-3730, Fax: 212/947-7458, Focus: Outsourcing and computer services, Ownrshp: OTC, Stk Sym: COSI, Founded: 1984, Empl: 418, Sales ($M): 22.1, Fiscal End: 10/95; Zach Lonstein, Chmn, Pres & CEO, Jeffrey Millman, EVP, Roger Kaufman, CFO

Computer Peripherals Inc. (CPI), 7 Whatney, Irvine CA 91718 USA; 714/454-2441, Fax: 714/454-8527, Focus: Telecom products, Prdts: VIVA, Ownrshp: Lamsoon, Singapore, Founded: 1982, Empl: 100, Mike Zachan, Pres, Sunny Lum, VP Ops, Satish Trikna, VP Sales, Kit Tan, CFO, Christa Judson, Sales & Mktng

Computer Press Association (CPA), 631 Henmar Dr, Landing NJ 07850 USA; 201/398-7300, Fax: 201/398-3888, Co Email: 102751.1445@compuserve.com, Focus: Promotes excellence in computer journalism, Ownrshp: Nonprofit, Founded: 1983, Empl: 350, Jeff Yablon, Pres, Michael Desmond, VP, Heidi Wagner, Admin

Computer Product Testing Services Inc. 2329 Hwy 34 S, #201, Manasquan NJ 08736 USA; 908/223-5700, Fax: 908/223-5744, Focus: PC compatibility, performance, functionality and quality assurance testing, Mac testing, Ownrshp: PVT, Founded: 1983, Empl: 15, Tom Benford, Pres & CEO, Email: benfordtom@aol.com; Elizabeth Benford, EVP Mktng, Lawrence Withrow, VP Sales, Peter Clark, Evaluation Mgr, Nehib Conrad, Admin Assist

Computer Recruiters Inc. 22276 Buenaventura St, Woodland Hills CA 91364-5006 USA; 818/704-7722, Fax: 818/704-7724, Focus: Computer employment agency, Ownrshp: PVT, Founded:

1980, Empl: 3, Bob Moore, Pres, Email: b.moore@ix.netcom.com

Computer Research Inc. Cherrington Ctr, Bldg. 200, Coraopolis PA 15108-3100 USA; 412/262-4430, Focus: Data processing services and CAD/CAM products, Ownrshp: OTC, Stk Sym: CORE, Founded: 1963, Empl: 50, Sales ($M): 6.2, Fiscal End: 8/95; James L. Schultz, Pres & CEO, David J. Vagnoni, EVP

Computer Sciences Corp. (CSC), 2100 E Grand Ave, El Segundo CA 90245 USA; 310/615-0311, Fax: 310/322-9805, Web URL: csc.com, Focus: Computer services and system integration, Ownrshp: NYSE, Stk Sym: CSC, Founded: 1959, Empl: 32,900, Sales ($M): 4,242.4, Fiscal End: 2/96; William R. Hoover, Chmn, Van B. Honeycutt, Pres & CEO, Milton E. Cooper, Pres Systems Group, Lawrence Parkus, VP Corp Dev, Leon J. Level, VP & CFO, C. Bruce Plowman, VP Corp & Marcom

Computer Security Institute (CSI), 600 Harrison St, San Francisco CA 94107 USA; 415/905-2626, Fax: 415/905-2218, Co Email: csi@mfi.com, Web URL: gosci.com/csi, Focus: Information for protecting an organization's information assets, Prdts: Network Security, CSI Annual Conference, Ownrshp: Nonprofit, Founded: 1974, Empl: 3,100, Patrice Rapalus, Dir, Email: prapalus@mfi.com; Nancy Baer, Mktng Mgr, Peter Allen, Managing Ed

Computer Service Technology Inc. 2336 Lu Field Rd, Dallas TX 75229 USA; 214/241-2662, Fax: 214/241-2661, Focus: Test equipment, SIMM memory tester, Founded: 1985, Cathy Cheung, Mktng Coord

Computer Software Industry Assoc. (CSIA), 101 First St, #324, Los Altos CA 94022 USA; 415/948-9192, Focus: Educates members on California and federal software legislation, Ownrshp: Nonprofit, Founded: 1982, Empl: 125, Kaye Caldwell, Pres

Computer Support Corp. 15926 Midway Rd, Dallas TX 75244 USA; 214/661-8960, Fax: 214-661-5429, Focus: Graphics software, Prdts: Arts & Letters, Ownrshp: PVT, Founded: 1970, Empl: 70, Fred Schoeller, Pres, Gail Campbell, VP Ops, Keith Magee, VP Sales & Mktg

Computer Systems Advisers Inc. (CSA), 300 Tice Blvd, Woodcliff Lake NJ 07675-8405 USA; 201/391-6500, Fax: 201/391-2210, Focus: C/S development tools, Ownrshp: Sub. CSA, Singapore, Founded: 1970, Empl: 800, Anthony C. De Taranto, Pres

Computer Systems Policy Project (CSPP), 1001 G St NW, #900E, Washington DC 20001 USA; 202/393-1010, Web URL: cspp.org, Focus: Promotes creation of national information infrastructure, Ownrshp: Nonprofit, Founded: 1989, Ken Kay, Exec Dir

Computer Task Group Inc. (CTG), 800 Delaware Ave, Buffalo NY 14209-2094 USA; 716/887-7424, 800/992-5350 Fax: 716/887-7246, Web URL: ctg.com, Focus: Information technology services, Ownrshp: NYSE, Stk Sym: TSK, Founded: 1966, Empl: 5,100, Sales ($M): 339.4, Fiscal End: 12/95; Gale S. Fitzgerald, Chmn & CEO, Email: gale.fitzgerald@ctg.com; Steve Hoffman, VP Ops, Email: steve.hoffman@ctg.com; Joe Makowski, VP Support Svcs, Email: joseph.makowski@ctg.com; Tracey Eastman, Mgr Corp Comm

Computer Technology Research Corp. (CTR), 6 N Atlantic Wharf, Charleston SC 29401-2115 USA; 803/853-6460, Fax: 803/853-7210, Co Email: ctrreports@aol.com, Web URL: sims.net/ctr, Focus: Mainframe, midrange, microcomputers & telecom information, Ownrshp: PVT, Founded: 1979, Empl: 25, Edward Wagner, Pres, Brian Lindgren, Editor, Stacey C. Evangelist, Mngng Editor

Computer Television Network (CTVN), 12242 Business Park Dr, Studio 31, Truckee CA 96161 USA; 916/582-5083, 800/365-5055 Fax: 916/582-0410, Co Email: ctvn@sierra.net, Web URL: ctvnet.com, Focus: 24-hour television network focusing on personal computers, Ownrshp: dba of PC NET, LLC, Duane E. Evans, Pres & CEO, William J. Horton, EVP Ops, John J. Doran, EVP, Terry Crosby, Exec Producer

ComputerPREP 410 N 44th St, #600, Phoenix AZ 85008 USA;

602/275-7700, 800/228-1027 Fax: 602/275-1603, Co Email: computerprep@computerprep.com, Web URL: computer-prep.com, Focus: Personal computer courseware for business software training, Prdts: PREP Web@ssessor, Founded: 1983, Michael Holliday, Pres

Computervision Corp. 100 Crosby Dr, Bedford MA 01730-1480 USA; 617/275-1800, Fax: 617/275-2670, Web URL: cv.com, Focus: CAD/CAM systems, Prdts: CADDS, Medusa, EDM, Theda, Ownrshp: NYSE, Stk Sym: CVN, Founded: 1969, Empl: 2,300, Sales ($M): 507.1, Fiscal End: 12/95; Russell E. Planitzer, Chmn & CEO, Kathleen A. Cote, Pres & COO, Anthony N. Fiore Jr., VP Bus Dev, Patrick L. Clark, VP Sales & Mktng, Douglas P. Smith, VP & CFO

Computing Research Association Inc. (CRA), 1875 Connecticut Ave NW, #718, Washington DC 20009 USA; 202/234-2111, Fax: 202/667-1066, Web URL: cra.org, Focus: Promote computing technology research, Ownrshp: Nonprofit, Founded: 1972, Empl: 150, William Asprey, Exec Dir, Dave Patterson, Chmn

Computing Technology Industry Assoc. (CTIA), 450 E 22nd St, #230, Lombard IL 60148-6156 USA; 630/268-1818, Fax: 630/268-1384, Co Email: comptiahq@aol.com, Web URL: comp-tia.org, Focus: Association for computer resellers and vendors, Ownrshp: Nonprofit, Founded: 1982, Empl: 500, John A. Venator, EVP & CEO, Jeffrey Masich, Pres

Computone Corp. 1100 Northmeadow Pkwy, #150, Roswell GA 30076 USA; 770/475-2725, 800/241-3946 Fax: 770/664-1510, Co Email: @computone.com, Web URL: computone.com, Focus: Microcomputer communications boards, Prdts: IntelliServer, Intelli-Port, IntelliCluster, Ownrshp: OTC, Stk Sym: CMPT, Founded: 1984, Empl: 75, Sales ($M): 14.6, Fiscal End: 4/94; John D. Freitag, Chmn, Thomas J. Anderson, Pres & COO, Brian Kretschman, Dir Sales, Email: brian@computone.com; Erik R. Myrmo, VP Eng, Email: erik@computone.com; Gregg Alba, Controller, Daphne Shi, Mktng Mgr, Email: daphnes@computone.com

CompuTrac Inc. 222 Municipal Dr, Richardson TX 75080-3583 USA; 214/234-4241, Fax: 214/234-6280, Web URL: ctinc.com, Focus: Computer systems for the legal profession, Ownrshp: AMEX, Stk Sym: LLB, Founded: 1977, Empl: 52, Sales ($M): 5.3, Fiscal End: 1/96; Harry W. Margolis, Chmn & CEO, George P. McGraw, Pres & GM, Email: georgem@ctinc.com; Lynda K. Thomas, VP Admin, Cheri L. White, VP & CFO, Deborah S. Greening, VP Ops

CompuTrend Systems 1306 John Reed Ct, City of Industry CA 91745 USA; 818/333-5121, 800/677-6477 Fax: 818/369-6803, Co Email: @premiopc.com, Web URL: premiopc.com, Focus: PCs, motherboards and add-in boards, Prdts: PREMIO, PREMIO Triton, Ownrshp: PVT, Founded: 1989, Empl: 85, Sales ($M): 76, Fiscal End: 12/94; Thomas F. Bayens, Mktng Mgr, Email: tbayens@premiopc.com

Computron Software Inc. 301 Rt 17 N, Rutherford NJ 07070 USA; 201/935-3400, Web URL: ctronsoft.com, Focus: Financial management software, Ownrshp: OTC, Founded: 1978, Empl: 430, Sales ($M): 55.5, Fiscal End: 12/95; Andreas Typaldos, Chmn & CEO, Joe Esposito, Pres

Compuware Corp. 31440 Northwestern Hwy, Farmington Hills MI 48334-2564 USA; 810/737-7300, Fax: 810/737-2718, Web URL: compuware.com, Focus: Computer services and systems integration, Ownrshp: OTC, Stk Sym: CPWR, Founded: 1973, Empl: 4,844, Sales ($M): 614.4, Fiscal End: 3/96; Peter Karmanos Jr., Chmn & CEO, Joseph A. Nathan, Pres & COO, Thomas Thewes, Vice Chmn, W. James Prowse, SVP Mktng, Ralph A. Caponigro, SVP & CFO, Chris Norris, Dir Corp Com

Comshare Inc. 555 Briarwood Cr, Ann Arbor MI 48108 USA; 313/994-4800, Fax: 313/994-5895, Web URL: comshare.com, Focus: Executive information systems, Ownrshp: OTC, Stk Sym: CSRE, Founded: 1966, Empl: 1,045, Sales ($M): 119.0, Fiscal End: 6/96; Richard Crandall, Chmn, T. Wallace Wrathall, Pres & CEO,

Kathryn A. Jehle, SVP & CFO

Comtech Publishing Ltd. PO Box 12340, Reno NV 89510 USA; 702/825-9000, 800/456-7005 Fax: 702/825-1818, Co Email: 70724.561@compuserve.com, Web URL: accutek.com.comtech, Focus: Database utility software, Prdts: dSALVAGE PROFESSIONAL, Ownrshp: PVT, Founded: 1985, Empl: 3, Paul Heiser, Pres, Taeko Nikaido, VP Mktng

Comtrade 1215 Bixby Dr, Hacienda Heights CA 91745-1708 USA; 818/961-6688, Fax: 818/369-1479, Focus: PCs, Ownrshp: PVT, Founded: 1989, Empl: 110, Sales ($M): 130, Christopher Luke, Pres, Allen Chang, VP, Rachel Luke, Acct Mgr

Comtronic Systems Inc. 205 N Harris Ave, Cle Elum WA 98922 USA; 509/674-7000, Fax: 509/674-2383, Co Email: comtron@eburg.com, Focus: Property management, debt collection and loan servicing software, Prdts: Property Manager, Debtmaster, Contract Collector, Ownrshp: PVT, Founded: 1980, Empl: 14, Sales ($M): 1.1, Jeffrey Dantzler, Pres, Marc Zimmerman, Sales Mgr

Concentra Corp. 21 North Ave, Burlington MA 01803-3305 USA; 617/229-4600, Fax: 617/229-4700, Focus: Knowledge-based software, Prdts: The ICAD System, Selling Point, Stk Sym: CTRA, Founded: 1984, Empl: 130, Sales ($M): 20.2, Fiscal End: 3/95; Larry Rosenfeld, Pres & CEO, David Lemount, VP & COO, Gerald Schimmoeller, VP & CFO

Concentric Data Systems Inc. 110 Turnpike Rd, Westboro MA 01581 USA; 508/366-1122, 800/325-9035 Fax: 508/366-2954, Co Email: 71601.1465@compuserve.com, Focus: Data access & report writing tools, Prdts: R&R Report Writer, Ownrshp: Sub. of Wall Data, Founded: 1979, Empl: 30, Fiscal End: 9/93; Barry Gerken, VP, Vincent Femia, VP Dev, Rob Hershfield, Mgr Prod Mktng, Email: 70474.3674@compuserve.com; Stephanie Smith, Mktng Assist

Concord Communications Inc. 33 Boston Post Rd W, #400, Marlboro MA 01752-1829 USA; 508/460-4646, 800/851-8725 Fax: 508/481-9772, Co Email: info@concord.com, Web URL: concord.com, Focus: Automated network reporting software, Prdts: Network Health, Ownrshp: PVT, Founded: 1992, Empl: 60, Jack Blaeser, Pres, Dan Phillips, VP Sales, Kevin Conklin, VP Mktng, Fred Engel, VP Eng

Concurrent Computer Corp. 2 Crescent Place, Oceanport NJ 07757 USA; 908/870-4500, Fax: 908/870-5967, Co Email: @acpt.ccur.com, Focus: Superminicomputers, Ownrshp: OTC, Stk Sym: CCUR, Founded: 1966, Empl: 800, Fiscal End: 6/95; John T. Stihl, Chmn, Pres & CEO, Rick Maule, VP Mktng, Roger Mason, VP & CFO, C. Dennis McWatters, VP Sales, David Bopp, Dir IS, Ronald Baker, Dir Corp & Marcom, Email: bakerr@ocpt.ccur.com

Concurrent Controls Inc. 880 Dubuque Ave, S San Francisco CA 94080 USA; 415/873-6240, 800/487-2243 Fax: 415/873-6091, Co Email: info@conctrls.com, Web URL: conctrls.com, Focus: Multiuser system software for PCs, Prdts: Multiuser DOS 7 Gold, WinNET Networking System, CCI Concurrent DOS, Ownrshp: PVT, Founded: 1986, Empl: 30, Sales ($M): 3, Fiscal End: 6/93; Dawn J. DeBruyn, Pres, Email: ddebruyn@conctrls.com; Raymond C. Novarina, VP Eng, Email: rnovarina@conctrls.com; Ken Warner, Mktng, Email: kwarner@conctrls.com

Conextions Inc. 1545 Osgood St, #108, N Andover MA 01845 USA; 508/689-3570, Fax: 508/689-2450, Co Email: info@conextions.com, Focus: Network software, Prdts: 3270Vision, 3270Builder, 5250 Builder, 5250 Vision, QS Vision, Ownrshp: PVT, Founded: 1989, Ed Kodinsky, Pres, Scott Opitz, Sales & Mktng Dir

Connect Inc. 515 Ellis St, Mountain View CA 94043-2242 USA; 415/254-4000, Fax: 415/254-4800, Co Email: info@connect-inc.com, Web URL: connectinc.com, Focus: Online information management software, Ownrshp: PVT, Founded: 1987, Empl: 88, Thomas P. Kehler, Pres & CEO, Michael Muller, Chmn, Kenneth M. Ross, EVP Dev, Edward A. Forman, VP Mktng, Email: edfor-

man@connectinc.com; Henry Morgan, EVP & CFO
Connect Tech Inc. 727 Speedvale Ave W, Guelph Ontario N1K
1E6 Canada; 519/836-1291, Fax: 519/836-4878, Co Email: @con-
necttech.com, Web URL: connecttech.com, Focus: PC add-in
boards, Prdts: Intellicon, DFLEX, Ownrshp: PVT, Founded: 1985,
Empl: 18, David Worthen, Pres, Email: djw@connecttech.com;
Michael Powers, Treas, Email: mike@connecttech.com
Connectivity Systems 531 E Elliot Rd, Chandler AZ 85225 USA;
602/813-3288, Fax: 602/545-0439, Focus: Portable CD-ROM
drives, Prdts: CyberManCD, Ownrshp: Sub DataCal, Founded:
1994, George Everett, Prod Mgr, Email: georgee@datacal.com
Connectix Corp. 2655 Campus Dr, San Mateo CA 94403 USA;
415/571-5100, 800/950-5880 Fax: 415/571-5195, Co Email:
@connectix.com, Web URL: connectix.com, Focus: Mac & Win-
dows utilities, Ownrshp: PVT, Founded: 1988, Empl: 90, Sales
($M): 48, Fiscal End: 12/95; Roy K. McDonald, Pres & CEO,
Jonathan F. Garber, VP Tech, Bonnie E. Fought, VP & CFO, Debbie
Degutis, Mktng Mgr
ConnectSoft 11130 NE 33rd Place, #250, Bellevue WA 98004
USA; 206/827-6467, Fax: 206/822-9095, Web URL: connect-
soft.com, Focus: Telecom software, Prdts: E-mail Connection, Font
Connection, Clip-Art Connection, Ownrshp: PVT, Founded: 1988,
Empl: 130, Sales ($M): 11.6, Fiscal End: 12/95; Mitchell B. Lon-
don, Pres & CEO, Email: 75540.3170@compuserve.com; Robert
D. Dickinson, VP Sales & Mktng, Stephen M. Teglovic, VP Eng, J.
Thomas Young, VP Ops
Connectware Inc. 1301 E Arapaho Rd, Richardson TX 75081-
2444 USA; 214/907-1093, Fax: 214/907-1594, Focus: Network
and telecom software, Ownrshp: Sub. AMP, Founded: 1993, Empl:
200, Tim Sullivan, Pres & CEO, James Helm, VP Ops, Dick Ln, VP
Sales & Mktng, Alan Leverett, Mgr Bus Dev, Tom Hyatt, VP &
CFO, Cynthia Stine
Conner Peripherals Inc. 3081 Zanker Rd, San Jose CA 95134-
2128 USA; 408/456-4500, Fax: 408/456-4501, Focus: Winchester
disk drives, Ownrshp: OTC, Stk Sym: CNNR, Founded: 1986,
Empl: 10,290, Sales ($M): 2,716.6, Fiscal End: 12/95; Finis F.
Conner, Chmn & CEO, David T. Mitchell, Pres & COO, Peter
Knight, VP Bus Dev, P. Jackson Bell, EVP & CFO, Mike Workman,
SVP & CTO, Kevin Burr
Connexperts 2626 Lombardy, #107, Dallas TX 75220 USA; 214/
233-8800, Fax: 214/239-6490, Focus: PC networking & connectiv-
ity: peripheral sharing, file transfer & e-mail software, Prdts: Net
Solution, Systemizer, Ownrshp: Sub. Applied Creative Techn.,
Founded: 1982, Timothy Wilde, Pres & CEO
Connors Communications 45 Belden Place, San Francisco CA
94104-2808 USA; 415/217-7500, Fax: 415/217-7503, Co Email:
webmaster@connors.com, Web URL: connors.com, Focus: PR and
marketing communications, Ownrshp: PVT, Empl: 30, Connie
Connors, Pres, Email: connie@connors.com; Shari Haber, SVP,
Email: shari@connors.com; Wendy Handler, VP, Email:
wendy@connors.com; Dean Kephatt, VP
Consilium Inc. 485 Clyde Ave, Mountain View CA 94043 USA;
415/691-6100, Web URL: consilium.com, Focus: Manufacturing
software, Ownrshp: OTC, Founded: 1978, Empl: 220, Sales ($M):
35.4, Fiscal End: 12/95; Jonathan J. Golovin, Chmn, Thomas
Tomasetti, Pres & CEO
**Consortium for Advanced Manufacturing-International
Inc.** (CAM-I), 3301 Airport Fwy, #324, Bedford TX 76021 USA;
817/860-1654, Fax: 817/275-6450, Co Email: @cam-i.com,
Focus: Cooperative R&D in Computer Integrated Manufacturing
(CIM), Ownrshp: Nonprofit, Founded: 1972, Empl: 80, Woody
Noxon, Pres
Continuum Company Inc., The 9500 Arboretum Blvd, Austin
TX 78759-6399 USA; 512/345-5700, Fax: 512/338-7041, Focus:
Software for insurance industry, Ownrshp: NYSE, Stk Sym: CNU,
Founded: 1968, Empl: 4,300, Sales ($M): 499.5, Fiscal End: 3/96;
Ronald C. Carroll, Chmn, W. Michael Long, Pres & CEO, Neil R.

Cullimore, EVP, Robert S. Maltempo, EVP, John L. Westerman III,
VP & CFO
Continuus Software Corp. 108 Pacifica, Irvine CA 92718 USA;
714/453-2200, Fax: 714/453-2276, Web URL: continuus.com,
Focus: Configuration management software, Ownrshp: PVT,
Founded: 1987, Empl: 80, Sales ($M): 13.1, Fiscal End: 12/95;
John R. Wark, Pres & CEO, Robert Chamberlain, SVP Sales, Martin
Cagan, VP R&D, Jennifer Arme, VP NA Sales, Kay Church, CFO
Contour Design Inc. 101 Rock St, Lowell MA 01854 USA; 508/
937-2422, 800/977-1000 Fax: 508/937-2422, Co Email: con-
tour@usa.net, Focus: Input devices, Ownrshp: PVT, Founded:
1995, Steve Wang, Pres, Carol J. Gilliland, VP Sales & Mktng,
Email: 102747.1244@compuserve.com
Control Concepts Inc. 8500 Executive Park Ave, Fairfax VA
22031 USA; 703/876-6444, 800/922-9259 Fax: 703/876-6416,
Co Email: presearch.com, Focus: SCSI and I/O controllers, Prdts:
Black Lightning, Multi I/O Controllers, Ownrshp: Sub. Presearch,
Founded: 1963, Empl: 220, Sales ($M): 25, Michael L. Gollobin,
Pres, Email: gollobim@presearch.com; Glenn Taube, VP, Email:
taubeg@presearch.com; Laurin Ajer, Controller, Email: ajerl@pre-
search.com; Rebecca Holmes, Office Mgr, Email: holmesb@pre-
search.com
Control Data Systems Inc. 4201 N Lexington Ave N, Arden
Hills MN 55126-6198 USA; 612/482-2401, 800/257-6736 Web
URL: cdc.com, Focus: Systems integration, Ownrshp: NYSE, Stk
Sym: CDAT, Founded: 1957, Empl: 1,800, Sales ($M): 454.8, Fis-
cal End: 12/95; James E. Ousley, Pres & CEO, Michael W. Dub-
yak, VP NA Syst, Arnold Rutgers, VP Mktng, Michael G.
Eleftheriou, VP Ops & Plng, Joseph F. Killoran, VP & CFO
Convex Computer Corp. 3000 Waterview Pkwy, PO Box
833851, Richardson TX 75083-3851 USA; 214/497-4000, Focus:
Minisupercomputers, Ownrshp: Sub HP, Founded: 1982, Empl:
1,000, Sales ($M): 144.2, Fiscal End: 12/94; Robert J. Paluck,
Chmn & CEO, Terrence L. Rock, Pres, Steven J. Wallach, SVP
Tech, James A. Balthazar, VP Mktng, David W. Craig, VP & CFO
Coopers & Lybrand 1251 Aves of the Americas, New York NY
10020 USA; 212/536-2000, Web URL: colybrand.com, Focus: Sys-
tem integration and management consulting, Ownrshp: PVT, Empl:
66,000, Sales ($M): 5,600, Fiscal End: 12/93; Eugene M. Freed-
man, Chmn
Copia International Ltd. 1342 Avalon Ct, Wheaton IL 60187
USA; 708/682-8898, 800/689-8898 Fax: 708/665-9841, Web
URL: copia.com, Focus: PC utility software, Prdts: FaxFacts, Acc-
Sys for xBase, AccSys for Paradox, Ownrshp: PVT, Founded: 1987,
Empl: 10, Steve Hersee, Pres, Terry Flanagan, VP, Dorothy K.
Gaden, VP Mktng
Copithorne & Bellows 100 First St, #2600, San Francisco CA
94105-2634 USA; 415/284-5200, Fax: 415/495-3992, Co Email:
@sf.cbpr.com, Focus: PR and marketing communications, Ownr-
shp: PVT, David Copithorne, Partner, Bill Bellows, Partner
CopyPro Inc. 1590 Solano Way, Concord CA 94520-5300 USA;
510/689-1200, 800/887-9906 Fax: 510/689-1263, Web URL:
copypro.com, Focus: Automatic diskette duplication, labelers, CD-
ROM and PC card duplicators, Prdts: CopyPro 2000, CopyPro LA
2002, CopyPro PC3000, Ownrshp: PVT, Founded: 1994, Empl:
25, Sales ($M): 3.0, Fiscal End: 12/95; David B. Miller, Pres &
CEO, Lori Mankin, Mktng Dir, Howard Ensler, Sales Mgr, William
Hess, Prod Mgr
Core Int'l. 6500 E Rogers Cr, Boca Raton FL 33487-2699 USA;
407/997-6055, Fax: 407/997-6009, Focus: PC mass storage sys-
tems, disk arrays, backup products, Prdts: CoreTape, Micro Array,
Ownrshp: PVT, Founded: 1979, Empl: 150, Sales ($M): 40, Fiscal
End: 12/93; Makomoto Takazawa, Pres & CEO, Gerry Smith, EVP
& COO
Core Technology Corp. (CTC), 7435 Westshire Dr, Lansing MI
48917-9764 USA; 517/627-1521, 800/338-2117 Fax: 517/627-
8944, Co Email: @ctc-core.com, Web URL: ctc-core.com, Focus:

Computer support services, Robert M. Bessette, Pres & CEO

Corel Corp. 1600 Carling Ave, Ottawa Ontario K1Z 8R7 Canada; 613/728-8200, Fax: 613/761-9350, Web URL: corel.com, Focus: Graphics and SCSI control software, Prdts: CorelDraw, Ownrshp: FO, Stk Sym: COS, Empl: 275, Sales ($M): 196.4, Fiscal End: 11/95; Michael C.J. Cowpland, Chmn, Pres & CEO, Charles A. Norris, CFO, Eid Eid, Dir Graphics SW, Patrick R. Beirne, Chief Eng, Arlen Bartsch, Dir SAles & Mktng

Corion Industrial Corp. 2272 Calle Del Mundo, Santa Clara CA 95054 Canada; 408/980-8988, Fax: 408/980-8999, Focus: PC monitors and peripherals, Ownrshp: PVT, Founded: 1985

Corollary Inc. 2802 Kelvin, PO Box 18977, Irvine CA 92714 USA; 714/250-4040, Fax: 714/250-4043, Co Email: @corollary.com, Web URL: corollary.com, Focus: PC multiprocessor hardware and software, Ownrshp: PVT, Founded: 1985, Empl: 57, George P. White, Pres, Alan Slipson, VP, Thomas DeMarchi, VP Sales & Mktng, James Gula, VP Eng, Gail Michelsen, Email: gailm@corollary.com

Corporate Association for Microcomputer Professionals (CAMP), 950 Skokie Blvd, #310, Northbrook IL 60062 USA; 847/291-1360, Fax: 847/291-1360, Focus: Association of corporate MIS director, Ownrshp: Nonprofit, Founded: 1984, Empl: 4,000+, Julian Horwich, Exec Dir

Corporate Solutions 116-T Edwards Ferry Rd NE, Leesburg VA 20176 USA; 800/622-4686 Fax: 703/777-3652, Co Email: cs@corpsol.com, Web URL: corpsol.com, Focus: Training software, Prdts: Intranet Based Training, Dawn Perusse, Pres

Corporate Sources 26071 Merit Cr, #108, Laguna Hills CA 92653 USA; 714/582-1946, 800/722-7748 Fax: 714/582-3706, Focus: Input devices, Prdts: Star-Track, Ownrshp: PVT, Sonny Burkett, GM

Corporate Visions Inc. 8908 S Yale, #360, Tulsa OK 74137 USA; 918/488-0301, 800/720-2842 Fax: 918/492-2560, Focus: Sales and demo training for computer-industry companies, Prdts: Samurai Selling System, Power Demos Seminars, Ownrshp: OTC, Stk Sym: CVIA, Founded: 1986, Chuck Laughlin, Pres, Karen Sage, EVP

Cosmi Corp. 2600 Homestead Place, Rancho Dominguez CA 90220-5610 USA; 310/833-2000, Fax: 310/886-3500, Web URL: cosmi.com, Focus: Home/office productivity & entertainment software, Prdts: Paint Plus, Desktop Publisher Plus, Label Publisher, PC Attorney, Ownrshp: PVT, Founded: 1982, Empl: 33, Sales ($M): 9.6, Fiscal End: 12/95; George Johnson, Pres, Jeff Fryer, CFO

CoSystems Inc. 1263 Oakmeadow Pkwy, Sunnyvale CA 94086-4032 USA; 408/522-0500, Fax: 408/720-9114, Web URL: cosystems.com, Focus: Data communication products, Prdts: CoALM, CoALM-S, CoSECURE, CoPOP, CoPIO, CoISDN, Webxplorer, Ownrshp: PVT, Founded: 1981, Empl: 23, Shirish Patel, Pres, Email: shirish@cosystems.com

Cougar Mountain Software 7180 Potomac Dr, #D, Boise ID 83704 USA; 208/375-4455, Fax: 208/375-4460, Focus: POS, accounting and not-for-profit accounting software, Ownrshp: PVT, Founded: 1982, Empl: 40, Sales ($M): 3, Robert Gossett, Pres, David Bassari, GM, Chris Macaw, Sales Mgr, Teresa Reeder, Sr Tech Writer

Courtland Group Inc. 10500 Little Patuxent Pkwy, #300, Columbia MD 21044 USA; 410/730-7668, Fax: 410/730-8271, Focus: Electronic filing software, Prdts: Courtland Augusta, Ultra Win/DOS Document Management Software, Ownrshp: PVT, Founded: 1986, Empl: 13, George J. Trigilio, Jr., Pres & CEO, Philip J. Gerolstein, VP Sales & Mktng, J. Perry McGahan, VP Prod Dev, Bonnie Trigilio, VP Admin

CPLEX Optimization Inc. 930 Tahoe Blvd, Bldg. 802,#279, Incline Village NV 89451 USA; 702/831-7744, Fax: 702/831-7755, Co Email: info@cplex.com, Web URL: cplex.com, Focus: Linear optimization software & services, Prdts: CPLEX Linear Optimizer, CPLEX Callable Library, Ownrshp: PVT, Founded: 1988,

Empl: 10, Todd Lowe, Pres, Email: tlowe@cplex.com; Janet Lowe, VP, Email: janet@cplex.com

Cranel Inc. 8999 Gemini Pkwy, Columbus OH 43240 USA; 614/431-8000, 800/288-3475 Fax: 614/431-8388, Web URL: cranel.com, Focus: Workstation scanning and mass storage products, Ownrshp: PVT, Founded: 1985, Empl: 100, Sales ($M): 60, Fiscal End: 12/95; James Wallace, Pres, Carl Reichert, EVP

Cray Research Inc. 655A Lone Oak Dr, Eagan MN 55121 USA; 612/452-6650, Fax: 612/683-7198, Web URL: cray.com, Focus: Supercomputers, peripherals and software, Prdts: Cray T3E, Cray T90, Cray J90, Cray CS6400, Ownrshp: Sub Silicon Graphics, Founded: 1972, Empl: 4,225, Sales ($M): 676.2, Fiscal End: 12/95; J. Phillip Samper, Chmn & CEO, Robert H. Ewald, Pres & COO, Carl W. Dungworth, SVP Sales & Mktng., Email: mickd@cray.com; Laurence L. Betterly, CFO, Patrick J. Tullo, EVP Sales, Steve Conway, Sr Dir Corp Com, Email: conways@cray.com

Cray Research Super Servers Inc. 3601 SW Murray Blvd, Beaverton OR 97005 USA; 503/641-3151, 800/765-2774 Fax: 503/641-4497, Focus: High performance servers, Ownrshp: Sub. Cray Research, Founded: 1970, Empl: 465, Sales ($M): 58.5, Fiscal End: 10/91; Martin Buchanan, GM

Creative Data Movers Inc. 28 W 38th St 4W, New York NY 10018 USA; 212/730-5245, Fax: 212/921-2065, Focus: Training in client/server, PC and mainframe application development & sys support tools

Creative Digital Research (CDR), 7291 Coronado Dr, San Jose CA 95129 USA; 408/255-0999, Fax: 408/255-1011, Co Email: info@cdr1.com, Focus: CD-ROM publishing software, Ownrshp: PVT, Founded: 1992, Paul Ling, Pres & CEO, K.C. Garrigan

Creative Interaction Technologies Inc. 800 Eastowne Dr, #111, Chapel Hill NC 27514 USA; 919/419-1694, 800/545-2442 Fax: 919/489-1063, Focus: System software for Windows and NT, Prdts: AshWin, Ownrshp: PVT, Founded: 1992, Empl: 20, Robbie Hardy, Pres, Robert Dale, Chief Architect, David Neal, CFO, Deb Lovig

Creative Labs Inc. 1901 McCarthy Blvd, Milpitas CA 95035-7442 USA; 408/428-6600, 800/998-1000 Fax: 408/428-6611, Focus: Sound boards and peripherals, Prdts: Sound Blaster, Ownrshp: OTC, Stk Sym: CREAF, Founded: 1981, Empl: 1,800, Sales ($M): 1,308.1, Fiscal End: 6/96; W.H. Sim, Chmn & CEO, K.S. Chay, Pres & COO, Patrick Verderico, CFO, Theresa Pulidd, PR Coord

Creative Solutions Inc. 7509 Connelley Dr #D, Hanover MD 21076-1664 USA; 410/766-4080, Fax: 410/766-4087, Co Email: csi@applelink.com, Focus: PC peripherals, Prdts: Hurdler, Huster, Ownrshp: PVT, Founded: 1976, Empl: 5, Sales ($M): 0.8, John Credle, Pres, Juernene Bass, Prod Mgr, Jim McDonald, Eng Mgr, Anne McDermaid, Sales & Mktng Mgr

Creative Strategies 4010 Moorpark Ave, #212, San Jose CA 95117-1843 USA; 408/985-1110, Fax: 408/985-1114, Focus: Computers, CAD/CAM, AI, office automation and telecom, Ownrshp: PVT, Founded: 1969, Empl: 12, Tim Bajarin, Pres

Cresta Systems Inc. 20245 Stevens Creek Blvd, #200, Cupertino CA 95014 USA; 408/342-9000, Fax: 408/342-9009, Co Email: @cresta.com, Focus: Conferencing products, Prdts: MediaModem, Ownrshp: PVT, Founded: 1993, Alessandro Gatti, Pres, Email: alessandro_gatti@cresta.com

CrossComm Corp. 450 Donald Lynch Blvd, Marlboro MA 01752 USA; 508/481-4060, 800/388-1200 Fax: 508/229-5535, Co Email: marcom@crosscomm.com, Web URL: crosscomm.com, Focus: High-performance networking solutions, Ownrshp: OTC, Stk Sym: XCOM, Founded: 1987, Empl: 300, Sales ($M): 44.3, Fiscal End: 12/95; Tad Witkowicz, Pres & CEO, Allan Kline, CFO

CrossWind Technologies Inc. 1505 Ocean St, #1, Santa Cruz CA 95060-2867 USA; 408/469-1780, Fax: 408/469-1750, Co Email: info@crosswind.com, Web URL: crosswind.com, Focus: Time management software, Prdts: Synchronize, Ownrshp: PVT,

Founded: 1989, David Wellington, Pres, Email: david@cross-wind.com; Chris L. Knudsen, VP Mktng, Email: chris@cross-wind.com; Kevin Colgate, VP Sales, Email: kevin@crosswind.com

Crystal Group Inc. 1165 Industrial Ave, Hiawatha IA 52233-1120 USA; 319/378-1636, 800/378-1636 Fax: 319/393-2338, Focus: Industrial PC accessories, Craig Jensen, Pres, Curtis Nelson, VP Sales & Mktng

Crystal Inc. 1095 W Pender St, 4th Floor, Vancouver BC V6E 2M6 Canada; 604/681-3435, 800/877-2340 Fax: 604/681-2934, Web URL: seagate.com/software/crystal, Focus: Windows reporting software, Prdts: Crystal Report, Ownrshp: Sub. Seagate, Founded: 1984, Terry Cunningham, CEO, Greg Kerfoot, Pres, Warren Bell, Dir Sales, Heather MacKenzie, Dir Mktng, Armanda Padwick, Dir Fin, Matt Dion, Email: mattd@crystalinc

CrystalGraphics Inc. 3350 Scott Blvd, Bldg 14, Santa Clara CA 95054 USA; 408/496-6175, 800/867-2733 Fax: 408/496-0970, Focus: Graphics and animation software, Prdts: Crystal Flying Fonts Pro, Crystal 3D Designer, Crystal Kaleidoscope, Ownrshp: PVT, Founded: 1986, Ray Noorda, Chmn, Dennis Ricks, Pres & CEO, Roma Marwick, Mktng Mgr, Richard Ballard, Dir Sales, Deborah Derana, Dir Customer Relations, Email: dderana@aol.com

CSPI 40 Linnell Cr, Billerica MA 01821 USA; 508/663-7598, Fax: 508/663-0150, Focus: Array processors and software, Ownrshp: OTC, Stk Sym: CSPI, Founded: 1968, Sales ($M): 19.6, Fiscal End: 8/94; Samuel Ochlis, Chmn, David S. Botten, Pres & CEO, Michael M. Stern, VP Ops, Donald E. Johansen, VP Bus Dev, Gary W. Levine, VP & CFO

CTX International Inc. 20530 Earlgate St, Walnut CA 91789 USA; 909/598-8094, Fax: 919/594-1236, Focus: Monitors and notebook PCs, Ownrshp: Sub. Chuntex, Taiwan, Founded: 1986, Empl: 1,700 WW, Y.C. Liu, Pres, Robert S. Luke, EVP, Bradfield Hunter, SVP Sales, Tom LaRocca, Dir Mktng

Cubix Corp. 2800 Lockheed Way, Carson City NV 89706-0719 USA; 702/888-1000, 800/829-0550 Fax: 702/888-1001, Web URL: cubix.com, Focus: LAN communications products, Prdts: ERS/FT II, SAFESTOR/FT, ERS II, CMS, World Desk, Ownrshp: PVT, Founded: 1975, Empl: 200, Jim Zakzeski, VP Sales & Mktng, Denise Jones, Marcom, Email: denisejones@cubix.com

Cunningham Communication Inc. 3945 Freedom Cr, 9th Fl, Santa Clara CA 95054 USA; 408/982-0400, Fax: 408/982-0403, Web URL: ccipr.com, Focus: PR and marketing communications, Ownrshp: PVT, Empl: 90, Andrea Cunningham, Pres, Ron Ricci, Principal New Bus

Currid & Co. 11000 Richmond Ave, #140, Houston TX 77042 USA; 713/789-5995, Fax: 713/789-5994, Web URL: currid.com, Focus: Technology assessment for Fortune 500 companies and computer industry clients, Ownrshp: PVT, Founded: 1991, Empl: 16, Cheryl Currid, Pres, Email: cheryl@currid.com; Diane Bolin, Ops Mgr

Cway Software 30 E Lincoln Ave, Hatfield PA 19440 USA; 215/368-9494, Co Email: cway@ix.netcom.com, Focus: Personnel management software, Prdts: Sway Improve, Cway Personnel, Cway Skills, Ownrshp: PVT, Founded: 1983, Empl: 10, Bill Dipietro, Pres, Joanne Truesdell, VP Dev, Chris Ager, Mktng

Cyber-Safe 3200 Wilcrest, #370, Houston TX 77042-3366 USA; 713/784-2374, Focus: Data encryption software, Ownrshp: PVT, Arnold R. Vobach, Chmn, Carl R. Rose, Pres, Email: carl@da.com

Cyberflix Inc. 4 Market Square, Knoxville TN 37902 USA; 615/546-1157, Fax: 615/546-0866, Co Email: cyberflix@aol.com, Focus: CD-ROM entertainment software, Prdts: Jump Raven, Ownrshp: PVT, Founded: 1993, Empl: 13, Bill Appleton, Pres, Email: cyberflix@aol.com; Andrew Nelson, Creative Dir, Email: cyberflix@aol.com; Erik S. Quist, GM, Email: cyberflix@aol.com; Ben Calica, Dir Production, Email: cyberflix@aol.com; David Haynes, Email: cyberflix@aol.com

Cyberian Outpost Inc. 27 N Main St, Kent CT 06757-0358 USA; 203/927-2050, 800/856-9800 Fax: 203/927-2055, Co Email: info@cybout.com, Web URL: cybout.com, Focus: Internet virtual computer store, Ownrshp: PVT, Founded: 1994, Darryl Peck, Pres, Email: dpeck@cybout.com; Bob Rathbun, VP Mktng, Email: rdr@cybout.com; Christopher Madesre, Sales Mgr, Email: cdm@cybout.com; Bill Reichle, Purchasing Mgr

CyberMedia Inc. 3000 Ocean Park Blvd, #2001, Santa Monica CA 90405 USA; 310/843-0800, 800/721-7824 Fax: 310/843-0120, Co Email: @cybermedia.com, Focus: PC utility software, Prdts: First Aid, PC 911, Ownrshp: PVT, Founded: 1991, Empl: 75, Unni Warrier, Pres, Sri Chari, VP Mktng, Email: 75460.32@compuserve.com; Anne Lam, VP Bus Dev, Email: 74044.3466@compuserve.com; Brad Kingsbury, VP Tech, Jeffrey Beaumont, CFO, Giselle Bisson, PR Mgr, Email: gisellemb@aol.com

Cybermedix Inc. 8230 Old Court House Rd, #300, Vienna VA 22182 USA; 703/917-6600, Fax: 703/917-6606, Focus: Expert information systems for emergency medicine, Prdts: Cliniplex, Ownrshp: PVT, Founded: 1985, Empl: 15, Randall B. Case, Pres & CEO, Richard T. Howe, Sales, Gordon R. Stauffer, VP Dev

Cybernetics Tera One, Yorktown VA 23693 USA; 804/833-9100, Fax: 804/833-9300, Focus: Mass storage, Ownrshp: PVT, Founded: 1978, Monique Jackson, Mktng Assist

Cybersource Corp. 550 S Winchester Blvd, #301, San Jose CA 95128 USA; 408/556-9306, Fax: 408/241-8270, Web URL: cybersource.com, Focus: Electronic distribution of software, Ownrshp: PVT, Founded: 1994, Empl: 15, Sales ($M): 1, Fiscal End: 12/95; William McKiernan, CEO

Cybex Corp. 4912 Research Dr, Huntsville AL 35805-5906 USA; 205/430-4000, Fax: 205/430-4030, Focus: PC peripherals, Ownrshp: OTC, Stk Sym: CBXC, Empl: 125, Sales ($M): 20, Fiscal End: 12/95; Stephen F. Thornton, Chmn, Pres & CEO, R. Byron Driber, SVP & COO, Remigius G. Shatas, SVP & CTO, Robert R. Asprey, SVP Eng, Doyle C. Weeks, SVP & CFO

Cyborg Systems Inc. 2 N Riverside Plaza, 12th Fl, Chicago IL 60606 USA; 312/454-1865, Web URL: cyborg.com, Focus: Human resource management software, Ownrshp: PVT, Founded: 1974, Empl: 350, Sales ($M): 41.5, Fiscal End: 12/95; Michael D. Blair, Chmn & CEO, Gary M. Tarr, Pres

CyCare Systems Inc. 7001 N Scottsdale Rd, #1000, Scottsdale AZ 85253-3644 USA; 602/596-4300, Focus: Computer services to healthcare industry, Ownrshp: NYSE, Stk Sym: CYS, Founded: 1969, Empl: 486, Sales ($M): 62.9, Fiscal End: 12/95; Jim H. Houtz, Chmn, Pres & CEO, David H. Koeller, Pres Group Practice, Peg S. Hafkemeyer, VP, Randy L. Skemp, SVP, Mark R. Schonau, CFO, Jeff E. Cramer, VP Mktng

Cyco Int'l. 1908 Cliff Valley Way, Atlanta GA 30329 USA; 404/634-3302, Fax: 404/633-0154, Co Email: 71722.273@compuserve.com, Focus: Document management software, Prdts: AutoManager, Ownrshp: PVT, Founded: 1988, Empl: 25, Ken Shain, Pres, Trent Fox, VP Bus Dev, Hillman Lentz, VP Sales, Greg Peay, Marcom Mgr

CyData Inc. 7001 N Scottsdale Rd, #1000, Scottsdale AZ 85253-3628 USA; 800/336-4018 Fax: 602/596-4466, Focus: Physician's claims processing, Ownrshp: Sub. CyCare Systems, Founded: 1992, Sales ($M): 15.2, Fiscal End: 12/94; Carolyn S. Haupert, SVP & GM, Jeffrey L. Schlueter, VP

Cygnus Support 1937 Landings Dr, Mountain View CA 94043 USA; 415/903-1400, Fax: 415/903-0122, Co Email: info@cygnus.com, Focus: Software development tools and network security, Ownrshp: PVT, Founded: 1989, Empl: 50, Kaz Hasimoto, Pres, Christine Russell, CFO, Rolf Brauchler, VP Mktng, Samuel Drucker, GM, Jacqueline Carter, PR Mgr

Cylink Corp. 910 Hermosa Ct, Sunnyvale CA 94086 USA; 408/735-5800, Fax: 408/735-6643, Focus: Wireless modems and security products, Ownrshp: PVT, Founded: 1984, Empl: 190, Lewis C. Morris, Pres, Bill Lattin, VP Mktng, Arlene Lightford, Corp Com Dir

Cyma Systems Inc. 2330 W University Dr #7, Tempe AZ 85281-7237 USA; 602/831-2607, Fax: 602/345-5743, Focus: Accounting and vertical market software, Ownrshp: PVT, Founded: 1980, Empl: 60, Sales ($M): 4.8, Michael L. Glaser, Pres, Greg Vokoun, VP Prod Dev

CyNet Inc. 12777 Jones Rd, #400, Houston TX 77070 USA; 713/897-8317, Fax: 713/890-6213, Web URL: cynet-fax.com, Focus: Network for fax and data transmissions for business & fax software, Prdts: CyNet Digital Network, Ownrshp: PVT, Ray Davis, CEO

Cypress Research Corp. 240 E Caribbean Dr, Sunnyvale CA 94089-1007 USA; 408/752-2700, Fax: 408/752-2735, Co Email: @cypressres.com, Web URL: cypressr.com, Focus: Macintosh fax and communications products, Prdts: MegaPhone, PhonePro, Ownrshp: PVT, Founded: 1987, Empl: 30, Edward M. Cluss, Pres & COO, W. Martin Wingren, Chmn, John C. Hurley, VP, Carl Linhardt, VP Mktng, John Sommerfield, PR Mgr, Email: johns@cypressres.com

Cypress Semiconductor Corp. 3901 N First St, San Jose CA 95134-1599 USA; 408/943-2600, Fax: 408/943-2796, Web URL: cypress.com, Focus: Integrated circuits, Ownrshp: NYSE, Stk Sym: CY, Founded: 1982, Empl: 1,850, Sales ($M): 596.1, Fiscal End: 12/95; Pierre Lamond, Chmn, T.J. Rodgers, Pres & CEO, Emmanuel Hernandez, CFO, J. Daniel McCranie, VP Mktng & Sales, Antonio Alvarez, VP R&D, John Hamburger, Dir Corp Com

Cyrix Corp. 2703 N Central Expwy, PO Box 850118, Richardson TX 75085-0118 USA; 214/968-8388, Fax: 214/699-9857, Co Email: @cyrix.com, Web URL: cyrix.com, Focus: Microprocessors and peripheral chips, Ownrshp: OTC, Stk Sym: CYRX, Founded: 1988, Empl: 389, Sales ($M): 228.0, Fiscal End: 12/95; Gerald D. Rogers, Pres & CEO, Tom Brightman, VP Bus & Tech, Kevin C. McDonough, SVP Eng, James N. Chapman, SVP Sales, Timothy W. Kinnear, VP Fin, Michelle Moody, PR Mgr, Email: moody@cyrix.com

D & D Computers Inc. 1405 SW 107th Ave, #301D, Miami FL 33174 USA; 305/220-6848, 800/816-6848 Fax: 305/220-3368, Focus: Contact management software, Prdts: Magic Merge, Ownrshp: PVT, David Hall

D&H Distributing Co. 2525 N 7th St, PO Box 5967, Harrisburg PA 17110 USA; 800/340-1001 Focus: Microcomputer distributor, Founded: 1918, Empl: 300, Sales ($M): 400, Izzy Schwab, Pres, Mark Greenwald, VP Mktng, Email: ejcv47a@prodigy.com

D-Link Systems Inc. 5 Musick, Irvine CA 92718 USA; 714/455-1688, 800/326-1688 Fax: 714/455-2521, Co Email: sales@irvine.dlink.com, Focus: LAN products, Prdts: LANsmart, LANmagic, Ownrshp: PVT, Founded: 1986, Empl: 220, Sales ($M): 27, Fiscal End: 12/92; Roger Kao, Pres, Steven Joe, Dir Ops, Email: sjoe@irvine.dlink.com; Henry Ngai, VP Eng, Steven Moore, PR, Email: smoore@irvine.dlink.com

DacEasy Inc. 17950 Preston Rd, #800, Dallas TX 75252 USA; 214/732-7500, Fax: 214/930-8824, Focus: Accounting and productivity software, Prdts: DacEasy Accounting & Payroll, Ownrshp: Sub. Sage Group, UK, Founded: 1985, Empl: 200, Kevin Howe, Pres & CEO, Allen Walker, VP R&D, Dan Goodwin, Controller, Bobby Crawford, MIS Mgr, Dorsey Jennings, PR Mgr

Dallas Digital Corp. 624 Krona, #160, Plano TX 75074 USA; 214/424-2800, Fax: 214/422-4842, Focus: Storage product distributor, Ownrshp: Sub Tripac Systems, Founded: 1981, John Gamradt, Chmn, Roger Scott, Pres, Phil Van Guilder, VP Sales & Mktng, Mark Behrens, VP Ops, Carol Polasky, CFO

Dallas Semiconductor Corp. 4401 S Beltwood Pkwy, Dallas TX 75244-3292 USA; 214/450-0400, Co Email: @dalsemi.com, Web URL: dalsemi.com, Focus: ICs, Ownrshp: NYSE, Stk Sym: DS, Founded: 1984, Empl: 1,078, Sales ($M): 233.3, Fiscal End: 12/95; C.V. Prothro, Chmn, Pres & CEO, Chao C. Mai, SVP, Michael L. Bolan, VP Mktng, F.A. Scherpenberg, VP Computer Prod, Alan P. Hale, VP Fin

Damark International Inc. 7101 Winnetka Ave N, PO Box 29900, Minneapolis MN 55429-0900 USA; 612/531-0066, 800/729-9000 Fax: 612/531-0281, Web URL: internetmci.com, Focus: Direct marketing of PC products and electronics, Ownrshp: OTC, Stk Sym: DMRK, Founded: 1986, Empl: 1,937, Sales ($M): 500.0, Fiscal End: 12/95; Mark A. Cohn, Chmn & CEO, Jeff G. Palkovich, VP Ops, Mike Moroz, VP Retail Mktng, Arlyn Lomen, VP & CFO, Kent Arett, VP Sys & Ops, Marquita Matthes, Dir Fin Planning

Dantz Development Corp. 4 Orinda Way, Bldg C, Orinda CA 94563 USA; 510/253-3000, Fax: 510/253-9099, Co Email: @dantz.com, Web URL: dantz.com, Focus: Macintosh backup software, Prdts: Retrospect, DiskFit Pro, DiskFit Direct, Ownrshp: PVT, Founded: 1984, Empl: 42, Sales ($M): 8.9, Larry Zulch, Pres & Co-Founder, Craig Isaacs, VP Sales & Mktng, Email: craig_isaacs@dantz.com; Richard Zulch, VP Eng & Co-Founder, Walt Hays, VP Prod, Kerry MacInnes, Mktng Mgr, Email: kerry_macinnes@dantz.com

DAP Technologies 14502 N Dale Mabry Hwy #227, Tampa FL 33618 USA; 813/969-3271, 800/229-2822 Fax: 813/969-3334, Focus: MS-DOS handheld computers, Ownrshp: PVT, Founded: 1980, Empl: 100, Sales ($M): 15, Michel Lapointe, Pres, Gerald Rodts, VP & GM, Yves Larocque, VP Fin & GM

Data Access Corp. 14000 SW 119th Ave, Miami FL 33186-6017 USA; 305/238-0012, 800/451-3539 Fax: 305/238-0017, Co Email: godaccess@compuserve.com, Web URL: daccess.com, Focus: Application development systems, Prdts: DataFlex, FlexQL, WinQL, Ownrshp: PVT, Founded: 1976, Empl: 45, Sales ($M): 6, Fiscal End: 12/95; Charles Casanave III, Co-Pres, Cory Casanave, Co-Pres, Stephen Meeley, Prod Mgmt, Email: stephen-m@daccess.com; Doug Goldner, Dir Tech Sup, Email: doug-g@daccess.com; Donna Gruberg, Comm Mgr, Email: donna-g@daccess.com

Data Administration Management Assoc. (DAMA), PO Box 6096, Chesterfield MO 63006-6096 USA; 314/878-3372, Fax: 314/878-4016, Focus: Information management issues, Ownrshp: Nonprofit, Founded: 1986, Empl: 3,000, Carol Mugas, Pres, Joe Daniclewicz, VP Com

Data Critical Corp. 22733 152nd Ave NE, Redmond WA 98053 USA; 206/885-3500, Co Email: @datacrit.com, Web URL: datacrit.com, Focus: Wireless communication software, Ownrshp: PVT, Jeff Brown, Pres, Craig Kairis, VP Bus Dev

Data Entry Systems Inc. 1035 Putnam Dr, #B, Huntsville AL 35816 USA; 205/430-3023, Fax: 205/430-0989, Focus: Pen-based computers, Prdts: ScriptsWriter, Ownrshp: PVT, Founded: 1986, John C. Coyne, Pres, Thomas Scott, EVP, Rick Lynch, National Sales Mgr, E.T. Beasley Jr., Dir Tech

Data Fellows Inc. 2465 E Bayshore Rd, #301, Palo Alto CA 94303 USA; 415/354-0233, Fax: 415/424-0860, Co Email: info@datafellowes.fi, Focus: Anti-virus software, Ownrshp: Sub. Data Fellows, Finland, Founded: 1988, Risto Siilasmaa, Pres & CEO, Ari Hypponen, Dir Dev, Ismo Bergroth, Dir Tech

Data General Corp. 4400 Computer Dr, Westboro MA 01580 USA; 508/898-5000, Co Email: @dg.com, Web URL: dg.com, Focus: Minicomputers and workstations, Ownrshp: NYSE, Stk Sym: DGN, Founded: 1968, Empl: 5,800, Sales ($M): 1,205, Fiscal End: 9/95; Ronald L. Skates, Pres & CEO, J. Thomas West, SVP, Arthur W. DeMelle, VP & CFO, Robert C. Hughes, VP WW Sales, James J. Ryan, VP Info Mgmt

Data I/O Corp. 10525 Willows Rd NE, Redmond WA 98052 USA; 206/881-6444, Fax: 206/882-1043, Focus: Systems to program and test programmable ICs, Ownrshp: OTC, Stk Sym: DAIO, Founded: 1969, Empl: 401, Sales ($M): 66.0, Fiscal End: 12/95; William C. Erxleben, Pres & CEO, Neil G. Mathieson, VP Sales, Steve M. Gordon, VP & CFO, William J. Haydamack, VP & GM Des SW

Data International Inc. 613 Hillcrest Ave, Westfield NJ 07090 USA; 908/232-3485, Fax: 908/789-2406, Co Email: milind@intac.com, Focus: Document management software, Prdts: ICARSYS, Ownrshp: PVT, Founded: 1989, Empl: 4, Mukund Satwalekar

Data Pro Accounting Software Inc. 5439 Beaumont Ctr Blvd, #1050, Tampa FL 33634 USA; 813/885-9459, Fax: 813/882-8143, Focus: Accounting software, Prdts: Infinity, StageSoft, Ownrshp: PVT, Founded: 1985, Empl: 45, Sales ($M): 4, Fiscal End: 12/92; Joel Brock, Pres, Scott Fenimore, VP Mktng & Sales, Waldo Bibb, Mktng Mgr

Data Processing Management Assoc. (DPMA), 505 Busse Hwy, Park Ridge IL 60068-3191 USA; 708/825-8124, Fax: 708/825-1693, Focus: Broader understanding of the methods and principles of data processing systems, Ownrshp: Nonprofit, Founded: 1951, Empl: 30,000, George Eggert, Exec Dir

Data Race 11550 IH-10 W, #395, San Antonio TX 78230 USA; 210/558-1900, Fax: 210/558-1929, Focus: Data communications products, Ownrshp: OTC, Stk Sym: RACE, Founded: 1983, Empl: 260, Sales ($M): 17.2, Fiscal End: 6/96; Herbert T. Hensley, Pres & CEO, Garrick C. Colwell, VP Sales & Mktng, Walter D. Warren, SVP Ops, Steven W. Riebel, VP & CFO

Data Systems & Software Inc. (DSSI), 200 Rt 17, Mahwah NJ 07430-1296 USA; 201/529-2026, Fax: 201/529-3163, Focus: Computer services, Ownrshp: OTC, Stk Sym: DSSI, Founded: 1986, Empl: 815, Sales ($M): 129.8, Fiscal End: 12/95; George Morgenstern, Chmn, Pres & CEO, Schmuel Fogel, VP, Sanford L. Kane, VP, David Weldler, VP

Data Systems Network Corp. 34705 W 12 Mile Rd, #300, Farmington Hills MI 48331 USA; 810/489-7117, 800/544-2086 Fax: 810/489-1007, Web URL: dsnc.com, Focus: Systems integration, Stk Sym: DSYS, Founded: 1986, Empl: 65, Sales ($M): 30.5, Fiscal End: 12/95; Michael Grieves, Pres, Greg Cooke, VP Sales, Barbara Hanswirth, Mktng Mgr

Data Technology Corp. (DTC), 1515 Centre Pointe Dr, Milpitas CA 95035-8010 USA; 408/942-4006, Fax: 408/942-4027, Web URL: datatechnology.com, Focus: Hard disk controllers, Byron Smythe, Prod Mktng Mgr

Data Translation Inc. 100 Locke Dr, Marlboro MA 01752-1192 USA; 508/481-3700, Fax: 508/481-8620, Web URL: datx.com, Focus: Data acquisition and image processing products, Ownrshp: OTC, Stk Sym: DATX, Founded: 1973, Empl: 347, Sales ($M): 72.4, Fiscal End: 11/95; Alfred Molinari, Chmn & CEO, Peter J. Rice, CFO, John A. Molinari, VP & GM Multimedia, Lori Dustin, Dir Bus Dev

DataBeam Corp. 3191 Nicholasville Rd, Lexington KY 40503 USA; 606/245-3500, 800/877-2325 Fax: 606/245-3528, Co Email: fs_win@databeam.com, Web URL: databeam.com, Focus: Data conferencing technology/application software, Ownrshp: PVT, Founded: 1983, Empl: 62, Lee T. Todd, Pres & CEO, Email: ltodd@databeam.com; Neil Starkey, EVP & CTO, Email: nstarkey@databeam.com; Dave Panos, VP Mktng, Email: dpanos@databeam.com; Adam Hannah, VP Eng, Email: ahannah@databeam.com; Barry Ruditsky, VP OEM Sales, Email: bruditsky@databeam.com; Becky Taylor, Mktng Mgr, Email: btaylor@databeam.com

Databook Inc. 99 Rosewood Dr, #140, Danvers MA 01923 USA; 508/762-9779, Fax: 508/762-9758, Co Email: @databook.com, Focus: PCMCIA controller ICs, Prdts: Thin Card Integrated Controller, Patriot Controller IC, Ownrshp: PVT, Founded: 1987, Empl: 25, Sales ($M): 15, Fiscal End: 12/95; Jeffrey Grammer, Pres & CEO, Email: jhg@databook.com; Patrick Chiumiento, VP Sales & Mktng, Email: patc@databook.com; William Junkemeier, VP & CFO

DataCal Corp. 531 E Elliot Rd, #145, Chandler AZ 85225-1152 USA; 602/831-3100, 800/223-0123 Fax: 602/545-8090, Focus: Keyboard templates and overlays, Prdts: WorldFont, Ownrshp: PVT, Founded: 1982, Empl: 85, E. James Lunt, Chmn & CEO, A. Brent Payne, Pres, Lars P. Nielson Jr., Nat'l. Sales Mgr, Email:

74111.3420@compuserve.com; Cindy Ziegler

Datacap Systems Inc. 212A Progress Dr, Montgomeryville PA 18936 USA; 215/699-7051, Fax: 215/699-6779, Web URL: datacap.com, Focus: POS equipment and credit payment processing peripherals, Prdts: DataTran, Dataceptor, DC Series, SSDE, Ownrshp: PVT, Founded: 1983, Empl: 40, Terry Zeigler, Pres, Leon Morsillo, VP Prod Eng & Tech, Gale Peters, VP Sales & Mktng

DataEase International Inc. 7 Cambridge Dr, Trumbull CT 06611 USA; 203/374-8000, Fax: 203/365-2317, Focus: Database, graphics and image software, Ownrshp: PVT, Founded: 1982, Empl: 250, Sales ($M): 12.7, Fiscal End: 12/95; Arun Gupta, Chmn & CEO, Jim Falanga, Pres

DataFocus Inc. 12450 Fair Lakes Cr, #400, Fairfax VA 22033-3831 USA; 703/631-6770, 800/637-8034 Fax: 703/818-1532, Web URL: datafocus.com, Focus: Systems integration and UNIX to Win 32 migration tools, Prdts: NutCRACKER, Ownrshp: Sub KTI, Stk Sym: KTIE, Founded: 1983, Empl: 8090, Sales ($M): 12, Fiscal End: 12/95; Patrick B. Higbie, Chmn & CEO, Email: pat@datafocus.com; Thomas A. Bosanko, EVP, Email: tab@datafocus.com; Mitch Lindenfelder, Dir Fin & Admin, Email: mitch@datafocus.com; Wendy Mades, Dir Marcom, Email: wendy@datafocus.com

DataGrant Internet Services PO Box 101, Newport Beach CA 92662-0101 USA; 714/645-7716, Co Email: ggrant@wowi.com, Web URL: ni.net/wowi.com/pressrom, Focus: Internet web site of press releases, Prdts: The Press Room, Ownrshp: PVT, Gerry Grant, Founder

DataHand Systems Inc. 2923 N 33rd Ave, Phoenix AZ 85017 USA; 602/860-8584

Datalight Inc. 18810 59th Ave NE, Arlington WA 98223-8763 USA; 206/435-8086, Fax: 206/435-0253, Focus: Software development tools, Prdts: ROM-DOS, Ownrshp: PVT, Empl: 11, Sales ($M): 1.2, Roy L. Sherrill, Pres, Drew Gislason, VP R&D

Datalogix Int'l. 100 Summit Lake Dr, Valhalla NY 10595 USA; 914/747-2900, Fax: 914/747-2987, Focus: Manufacturing planning software, Ownrshp: OTC, Stk Sym: DLGX, Founded: 1981, Empl: 223, Sales ($M): 49.2, Fiscal End: 6/96; Richard Giodanella, Chmn, Pres & CEO, John F. Cingari, VP Mktng, Joseph McDermott, VP & CTO, Peter B. Sobiloff, VP Ops, Rick L. Smith, VP & CFO

Datamark Inc. 43 Butterfield Cr, El Paso TX 79906 USA; 915/778-1944, 800/477-1944 Fax: 915/778-1988, Focus: Data entry services, Ownrshp: PVT, Founded: 1989, Empl: 1,000+, William J. Holmes, Pres & CEO, Rebecca L. Holmes, EVP, William F. Randag Jr, VP Sales & Mktng, Anne M. Garcia, Dir IS

Datametrics Corp. 21135 Erwin St, Woodland Hills CA 91367 USA; 818/598-6200, Fax: 818/598-6290, Focus: Ruggedized computers and peripherals, Ownrshp: AMEX, Stk Sym: DC, Founded: 1962, Sales ($M): 20.0, Fiscal End: 10/95; Sidney E. Wing, Pres & CEO, Gerald A. Horwitz, SVP, Carl C. Stella, SVP, James D. Sturgeon Jr., VP Ops, John J. Van Buren, SVP & CFO

DataPak Software Inc. (DSI), 11815 NE 99th St, #1200, Vancouver WA 98682 USA; 360/891-0542, 800/327-6703 Fax: 360/891-0743, Co Email: marketing@datapak.com, Focus: Software development tools and contract software, Prdts: Paige, Ownrshp: PVT, Founded: 1983, Empl: 10, Sales ($M): 1.0, Christopher D. Nulph, Pres, Email: D0142@applelink.com; Gary Crandall, VP R&D, Email: D0142@applelink.com; Mark A. Nulph, VP Sales & Mktng, Dennis McNannay, Prod Mgr, Bruce Kyle, MIS Dir

Datapro Information Services Group 600 Delran Pkwy, Delran NJ 08705-9904 USA; 609/764-0100, Fax: 609/764-8953, Co Email: datapro@mgh.com, Web URL: datpro.com, Focus: 40+ loose-leaf publications on technology, products and management, Ownrshp: Sub McGraw-Hill, Founded: 1971, Empl: 450, Sales ($M): 55, Stephen Thomas, Pres, Martin Levine, VP Tech

Dataquest 1290 Ridder Park Dr, San Jose CA 95131-2398 USA; 408/437-8000, Fax: 408/437-0292, Co Email: @dataquest.com, Focus: PC, workstation, supercomputer, mass storage, printer &

semiconductor information, Ownrshp: Sub Gartner Group, Founded: 1971, Judy Hamilton, Pres & CEO, Robert J. Steinerd, VP, Paul Wheaton, Media Rel Mgr

Dataram Corp. Princeton Rd, PO Box 7528, W Windsor Township NJ 08543-7528 USA; 609/799-0071, 800/328-2726 Fax: 609/799-6734, Focus: Memory boards, Ownrshp: AMEX, Stk Sym: DTM, Founded: 1967, Empl: 151, Sales ($M): 107.6, Fiscal End: 4/96; John J. Cahill, Chmn, Robert V. Tarantino, Pres & CEO, Carmen J. Marchionni, VP Mktng, Carl B. Anderson, VP Sales, Bernard L. Riley, VP & CFO

Datasonix Corp. 5700 Flatiron Pkwy, Boulder CO 80301 USA; 303/545-9500, 800/328-2779 Fax: 303/545-9249, Co Email: @datasonix.com, Web URL: datasonix.com, Focus: Mobile computer products, portable tape backup, Prdts: Pereos, Ownrshp: PVT, Founded: 1992, Empl: 35, Juan Rodriguez, Chmn, Lew Frauenfelder, Pres, Kelly Beavers, EVP Eng, Michael Rosol, VP Sales & Mktng, Patty Serlis, Marcom Mgr

Datasouth Computer Corp. 4216 Stuart Andrew Blvd, Charlotte NC 28217 USA; 704/523-8500, Fax: 704/523-9298, Focus: Printers, Ownrshp: OTC, Stk Sym: DSCC, Founded: 1977, Empl: 123, Sales ($M): 16.9, Fiscal End: 12/93; James W. Busby, Pres

Datastorm Technologies Inc. 2401 Lemone Industrial Blvd PO Box 1471, Columbia MO 65205 USA; 573/443-3282, 800/474-1573 Fax: 573/875-0595, Web URL: datastorm.com, Focus: Internet, fax and data communications software, Prdts: PROCOMM PLUS, Ownrshp: PVT, Founded: 1985, Empl: 325, Sales ($M): 39, Fiscal End: 12/95; Bruce Barkelew, Pres, Tom Smith, EVP, Stephen Monaco, VP Mktng, Chris Force, CFO, Matt Basta, PR Coord

Datastream Systems Inc. 1200 Woodruff Rd, #C-40, Greenville SC 29607 USA; 803/297-6775, Fax: 803/627-7227, Focus: Computerized maintenance systems, Ownrshp: OTC, Stk Sym: DSTM, Empl: 120, Sales ($M): 20.3, Fiscal End: 12/95; Larry G. Blackwell, Chmn, Pres & CEO, John M. Sterling, VP Sales, John F. Christ, VP Prod Dev, Russell A. Wagner, VP, Daniel H. Christie, CFO, Diane Ustanik, PR Mgr

Datasym Inc. 435 Elgin St, Brantford Ontario N3T 5Y6 Canada; 519/758-5800, 800/265-9930 Fax: 519/758-5600, Focus: PC-based POS products, Prdts: Symposium, Ownrshp: PVT, Founded: 1984, Empl: 40, Sales ($M): 6, Rick Sterne, Pres, Frank Hader, VP Sales, Rick Cole, Mktng Mgr

DataTech Software 6360 Flank Dr, #300, Harrisburg PA 17112 USA; 717/652-4344, Fax: 717/652-3222, Focus: Sports software, Ownrshp: PVT, Paul Endress, Pres

DataTimes Corp. 14000 Quail Springs Pkwy, #450, Oklahoma City OK 73134 USA; 405/751-6400, 800/642-2525 Fax: 405/755-8028, Co Email: datatime@datatimes.com, Web URL: enews.com:80/clysters/datatime, Focus: Business information services, Prdts: EyeQ, News EyeQ, EyeQ Publishers, DataTimes Online, Ownrshp: PVT, Founded: 1981, Allen Paschal, Pres & CEO, Doug Stussi, CFO, Wes Crews, VP Corp Dev, John M. Paschal, Pres. DataTimes Info Partner., John Buckman, Dir Comm, Email: jbuckman@datatimes.com

Datatrac Corp. 8601 Dunwoody Place, Atlanta GA 30350 USA; 770/552-3866, Fax: 770/552-3870, Web URL: ilcnet.com/~datatrac, Focus: Software for package delivery industry, Prdts: Courier Order Processing System, Ownrshp: PVT, Founded: 1977, Empl: 30, Henry D. Dixon, Pres, David F. Patterson, VP Sales & Mktng, Andrew S. Pardue, VP Ops

DataViews Corp. 47 Pleasant St, Northampton MA 01060 USA; 413/586-4144, Fax: 413/586-3805, Co Email: info@dvcorp.com, Focus: Graphics user interface software, Prdts: DataViews, Ownrshp: Sub. Dynatech Corp., Founded: 1986, Empl: 90, Irwin Jacobs, Pres & CEO, Alan C. Morse, VP R&D & CTO, Roger Howard, VP Sales & Mktng, Shana Corby, Marcom, Email: scorby@dvcorp.com

DataViz Inc. 55 Corporate Dr, Trumbull CT 06611 USA; 203/268-0030, 800/733-0030 Fax: 203/268-4345, Co Email: d0248@applelink.apple.com, Web URL: dataviz.com, Focus: Connectiv-

ity software, Prdts: MacLink Plus, Ownrshp: PVT, Founded: 1984, Empl: 30, Richard Fontana, Pres, Ray Nicholl, Co-founder, Stacey Graham, Prod Mktng

Dataware Technologies Inc. 222 3rd St, #3300, Cambridge MA 02142-1188 USA; 617/621-0820, 800/229-8055 Fax: 617/621-0307, Co Email: info@dataware.com, Web URL: dataware.com, Focus: Software and services for information providers, Prdts: Net Answer BRS/Search, Total Recall, CD Author/CD Answer, Ownrshp: OTC, Stk Sym: DWTI, Founded: 1988, Empl: 294, Sales ($M): 41.1, Fiscal End: 12/95; Kurt Mueller, Chmn & CEO, Jeff Nyweide, Pres & COO, Mead Wyman, CFO, David Wilcox, SVP, Charlie Rabie, VP Prod Mgmt, Ann Hawkins, PR Dir, Email: ahawkins@dataware.com

Datawatch Corp. 234 Ballardvale St, Wilmington MA 01887 USA; 508/988-9700, 800/988-4739 Fax: 508/988-0697, Focus: Virus and support software, Prdts: Virex, Q-Support, Ownrshp: OTC, Stk Sym: DWCH, Founded: 1985, Empl: 69, Sales ($M): 16.6, Fiscal End: 12/95; Thomas R. Foley, Pres & CEO, Bruce R. Gardner, EVP & CFO, Andrew W. Mathews, VP Sales, Marco D. Peterson, VP Mktng

Dauphin Technology Inc. 3100 Dundee Rd #704, Northbrook IL 60062-2442 USA; 847/971-3400, Fax: 847/971-8443, Focus: Portable PCs, Ownrshp: OTC, Stk Sym: DNTK, Founded: 1988, Empl: 20, Sales ($M): 23.6, Fiscal End: 12/93; Alan Yong, Chmn, Pres & CEO, John R. Trimderger, COO & CFO, Lucy Young, Exec Dir, Colleen Burke, Dir Corp Com

Davenport Group c/o O'Reilly, 101 Morris St, #A, Sebastopol CA 95472 USA; 707/829-0515, Fax: 707/829-0104, Focus: Establish common interchange format among UNIX software vendors, Ownrshp: Nonprofit, Founded: 1992, Dale Dougherty, Chmn

Davidson & Associates Inc. 19840 Pioneer Ave, Torrance CA 90503 USA; 310/793-0600, 800/545-7677 Fax: 310/793-0601, Web URL: davd.com, Focus: Educational and entertainment software, Prdts: Math Blaster, English Express, Kid Works, Your Personal Trainer, Ownrshp: OTC, Stk Sym: DAVD, Founded: 1982, Empl: 679, Sales ($M): 147.2, Fiscal End: 12/95; Jan Davidson, Pres, Bob Davidson, Chmn & CEO, John Goodman, VP Ops, John Patrick, VP Mktng, Jack Allewaert, CFO, Linda L. Duttenhaver, Corp Com Dir, Email: lduttenhaver@davd.com

Davox Corp. 6 Technology Park Dr, Westford MA 01886 USA; 508/952-0200, 800/480-2299 Fax: 408/952-0201, Focus: Call center management systems, Prdts: Unison, Ownrshp: OTC, Stk Sym: DAVX, Founded: 1981, Empl: 170, Sales ($M): 37.6, Fiscal End: 12/95; Alphonse M. Lucchese, Chmn, Douglas Smith, VP Sales & Mktng, James F. Mitchell, SVP & CTO, John Connolly, VP & CFO, Stepehen M. Wallace, Dir Marcom

Dayna Communications Inc. 849 W Levoy Dr, Salt Lake City UT 84123-2544 USA; 801/269-7200, Fax: 801/269-7363, Co Email: daynacomm@aol.com, Web URL: dayna.com, Focus: Networking and communication software and hardware, Prdts: Blue Streak Fast Ethernet, CommuniCard PC Cards, EtherPrint, Ownrshp: PVT, Founded: 1984, Empl: 75, Brad Romney, Pres & CEO, Email: bromney@dayna.com; Mark Seethaler, CFO, Email: mseethaler@dayna.com; Tom Hogan, VP Mktng & Sales, Email: thogan@dayna.com; Suzanne Kimball, Dir Corp Com, Email: skimball@dayna.com

DayStar Digital Inc. 5556 Atlanta Hwy, Flowery Branch GA 30542 USA; 770/967-2077, Fax: 770/967-3018, Co Email: @daystar.com, Web URL: daystar.com, Focus: Multi-processor Macintoshes and peripherals, Prdts: Genesis MP, PowerPro 601, Turbo 040, PhotoMatic, Ownrshp: PVT, Founded: 1983, Empl: 100, Sales ($M): 35, Andrew Lewis, Pres & CEO, Bill Heys, COO, Frank Cook, VP Ops, Paul Barber, VP Sales, David Methven, Prod Mgr, Email: dmethven@daystar.com

Dazel Corp. 6034 W Courtyard Dr, #210, Austin TX 78730-5014 USA; 512/328-6977, Fax: 512/328-2789, Web URL: dazel.com, Focus: Information distribution software, Prdts: Dazel, Ownrshp:

PVT, Founded: 1991, Empl: 90, Robert Fabbio, Pres, Doug Miller, VP Mktng, Dale Howe, VP Sales, Gary Epple, VP Dev, Gary Neill, CFO

Dearborn Publishing Group 155 N Wacker Dr, Chicago IL 60606-1719 USA; 312/836-4400, Fax: 312/836-1021, Focus: Personal productivity CD-ROMs, Ownrshp: PVT, Founded: 1967, Empl: 250+, Dennis Blitz, Pres, Robert C. Kyle, CEO, Anita A. Constant, SVP, Timothy Honaker, SVP

Decisive Technology Corp. 1020 Corporate Way, #100, Palo Alto CA 94303 USA; 415/528-4300, 800/987-9995 Fax: 415/528-4321, Co Email: info@decisive.com, Web URL: decisive.com, Focus: Desktop survey applications, Prdts: Decisive Survey Internet, Ownrshp: PVT, Empl: <20, John Chisholm, Pres, Email: jchisholm@decisive.com; Harvey Yap, CFO, David Peranich, Dir Sales

Dell Computer Corp. 2214 W Braker Ln, #D, Austin TX 78758-4053 USA; 512/338-4400, Fax: 512/728-3653, Web URL: dell.com, Focus: PCs and peripherals, Prdts: Latitude, OptiPlex, Dimension, PowerEdge, Ownrshp: OTC, Stk Sym: DELL, Founded: 1984, Empl: 7,100, Sales ($M): 5,296.0, Fiscal End: 1/96; Michael S. Dell, Chmn & CEO, Morton L. Topfer, Vice Chmn, Thomas J. Meredith, CFO, Eric F. Harslem, SVP

Deloitte & Touche 10 Westport Rd, Wilton CT 06897 USA; 203/761-3000, Web URL: dttus.com, Focus: Consulting and systems integration, Ownrshp: PVT, Empl: 56,000, Sales ($M): 5,000, J. Michael Cook, CEO

DeLorme Mapping Lower Main St, PO Box 298, Freeport ME 04032 USA; 207/865-1234, 800/452-5931 Fax: 207/865-9291, Co Email: webmaster@delorme.com, Web URL: delorme.com, Focus: Mapping software: CD-ROM maps, GPS and GIS software, Prdts: St Atlas USA, Phone Search USA, Map 'n' Go, Ownrshp: PVT, Founded: 1975, David DeLorme, Pres, Stu Richards, Mktng Dir, Email: richards@delorme.com

Delphax Systems 5 Campanelli Cr, Canton MA 02021 USA; 617/828-9917, 800/952-3278 Fax: 617/828-9962, Focus: High-speed printers, high speed on-press printing systems, print management software, Prdts: ImageFast, Presidax, VISTA, Ownrshp: PVT, Founded: 1980, Empl: 400, Sales ($M): 68, Roger B. Parsons, Pres & CEO, John Buchanan, EVP & CFO, Paul Coletta, VP Sales, David Crowley, Dir Mktng Prog, Email: dcrowley@ccmail.delphax.com; Karin Boyd, Mgr Mktng Prog, Email: kboyd@ccmail.delphax.com

Delrina Corp. 895 Don Mills, 500-2 Park Centre, Toronto Ontario M3C 1W3 Canada; 416/441-3676, Fax: 416/441-0333, Co Email: info@delrina.com, Web URL: delrina.com, Focus: Forms processing and fax/modem software, Ownrshp: Sub Symantec, Founded: 1988, Empl: 440, Sales ($M): 101.1, Fiscal End: 6/94; Dennis Bennie, Chmn & CEO, Mark Skapinker, Pres, Albert Amato, EVP & CTO, Lou Ryan, EVP Sales, Michael Cooperman, CFO, Josef Zankowicz, Dir PR

Delta Products Corp. 3225 Laurelview Ct, Fremont CA 94538 USA; 510/770-0660, Fax: 510/770-0122, Focus: Hi-res PC monitors

DeltaPoint Inc. 2 Harris Ct, #B-1, Monterey CA 93940 USA; 408/648-4000, 800/446-6955 Fax: 408/648-4020, Co Email: deltapoint@aol.com, Web URL: deltapoint.com, Focus: Graphics and word processing software, Prdts: DeltaGraph, Drag 'n Draw, Ownrshp: OTC, Stk Sym: DTPT, Founded: 1989, Empl: 35, Sales ($M): 4.0, Fiscal End: 12/95; John A. Ambrose, CEO, Donald Witmer, COO & CFO, Email: don_witmer@deltapoint.com; Spencer Leyton, EVP Mktng & Sales, Bill Pryor, VP R&D, Amy McManus, PR Mktng Coord

Deltec Corp. 2727 Kurtz St, San Diego CA 92110 USA; 619/291-4211, 800/854-2658 Fax: 619/296-8039, Co Email: info@deltecpower.com, Web URL: deltecpower.com, Focus: UPS, Prdts: PowerRite, Ownrshp: Sub. Exide Electronics, Founded: 1972, Empl: 600, Ray Meyer, Pres, Jeff Frank, SVP Sales, Susan Connell, VP Mktng, Email: sconnell@deltecpower.com; Shawn A. Shepard, Tech Com Mgr

Deneba Software 7400 SW 87th Ave, Miami FL 33173 USA; 305/596-5644, Fax: 305/273-9069, Co Email: deneba@applelink.com, Focus: Graphics software for Macintosh, Prdts: Canvas, UltraPaint, Ownrshp: PVT, Founded: 1984, Empl: 32, Manny Menendez, Pres, Joaquin de Soto, VP, Joe Curley, Dir Sales, Doug Levy, VP Corp Com, David Hawkins

Denon Electronics 222 New Rd, Parsippany NJ 07054 USA; 201/575-7810, Fax: 201/808-1608, Focus: Electronics for professional, broadcast, multimedia and consumer audio markets, Ownrshp: PVT

Design Science Inc. 4028 Broadway, Long Beach CA 90803 USA; 310/433-0685, 800/827-0685 Fax: 310/433-6969, Co Email: mtinfo@mathtype.com, Web URL: mathtype.com/mathtype, Focus: Mathematical equation editing software, Prdts: MathType, Ownrshp: PVT, Founded: 1986, Empl: 14, Paul R. Topping, Pres, Email: pault@mathtype.com; Bruce A. Virga, VP Sales & Mktng, Email: brucev@mathtype.com

Design Technology 11489 Woodside Ave, Santee CA 92071-4724 USA; 619/448-2888, 800/945-7367 Fax: 619/448-3044, Co Email: 73650.443@compuserve.com, Focus: Input devices, Ownrshp: Sub Microspeed, Founded: 1978, Empl: 40, Tim Barry, Pres, Peggy Jonas, COO, Starr Ownby, Sales Mgr

Desktop Data Inc. 80 Blanchard Rd, Burlington MA 01803 USA; 617/229-3000, 800/255-3343 Fax: 617/229-3030, Web URL: desktopdata.com, Focus: Text retrieval and news capture software, Prdts: NewsEDGE, Ownrshp: OTC, Stk Sym: DTOP, Founded: 1988, Empl: 45, Sales ($M): 23.2, Fiscal End: 12/95; Donald McLagam, Pres & CEO

Desktop Management Task Force (DMTF), 2111 NE 25th St, Hillsboro OR 97209-4023 USA; 503/264-9300, Fax: 503/264-9027, Co Email: @dmtf.org, Focus: Open, standard for managing desktop systems, Ownrshp: Nonprofit, Founded: 1992, Empl: 300, Edward Arrington, Chairperson

Destiny Technology Corp. 521 Almanor Ave, Sunnyvale CA 94086-3512 USA; 408/562-1000, Fax: 408/562-1010, Focus: Laser printer controllers, Prdts: PageStyler, LaserAct, WinStyler, RIDA, Ownrshp: PVT, Founded: 1986, Empl: 125, Gary Cheng, Pres & CEO, David Larrimore, VP Mktng, Lou Yang, VP Eng, James Lung, VP Eng

Devcom Mid-America Inc. 2603 W 22nd St, #23, Oak Brook IL 60521 USA; 708/574-3600, Fax: 708/572-0508, Co Email: info%devcom@uunet.uu.net, Focus: Fax management software, Prdts: FaxFX, Ownrshp: PVT, Founded: 1980, Ronald G. Diener, Pres, Email: uunet!devcom.com!rgd

Development Technologies Inc. 308 Springwood Rd, Forest Acres SC 29206-2113 USA; 803/790-9230, Fax: 803/738-0218, Focus: OS/2 software utilities, Ownrshp: PVT, Founded: 1985, Noel J. Bergman, Pres, Evan Bergman, VP, Eileen Tognini, VP Sales & Mktng

DFI 100 Huan-Ho St, Hsi-Chih Town, Taipei TW Taiwan ROC; Focus: PCs, motherboards, peripherals & scanners, Ownrshp: FO

DH Technology Inc. (DH), 15070 Ave of Science, San Diego CA 92128 USA; 619/451-3485, Fax: 619/451-3573, Focus: Matrix print heads and printers, Ownrshp: OTC, Stk Sym: DHTK, Founded: 1983, Empl: 611, Sales ($M): 98.9, Fiscal End: 12/95; William H. Gibbs, Chmn, Pres & CEO, David T. Ledwell, VP & GM DHTech, Bernard Masson, VP & GM DHPrint, Richard L. Strautman, VP, Janet W. Shanks, CFO

Di-An Controls Inc. 16 Jonathon Dr, Brockton MA 02401 USA; 508/559-8000, 800/878-3134 Fax: 508/559-8658, Focus: Printers for tags, tickets and labels and POS systems for food service, Prdts: Concession/Master System, Ownrshp: OTC, Stk Sym: DICC, Founded: 1958, Sales ($M): 0.4, Fiscal End: 12/92; Robert D. Kodis, Pres

DiagSoft Inc. 5615 Scotts Valley Dr, #140, Scotts Valley CA 95066 USA; 408/438-8247, 800/348-4163 Fax: 408/438-7113, Focus: PC diagnostic software, Ownrshp: PVT, Founded: 1987,

Gordon H. Kraft, Chmn & CEO, Jon Gordon, Pres, Ed Merrifield, CFO, Carl Snedaker, VP Eng, Melvyn Brodie, SVP

Dialogic Corp. 1515 Rt 10, Parsippany NJ 07054 USA; 201/993-3000, 800/755-4444 Fax: 201/993-3093, Web URL: dialogic.com, Focus: PC-based call processing systems, Ownrshp: OTC, Stk Sym: DLGC, Founded: 1983, Empl: 600, Sales ($M): 168.7, Fiscal End: 12/95; Nicholas Zwick, Chmn, Howard G. Bubb, Pres & CEO, Kenneth J. Burkhardt Jr., EVP Bus Dev, John Landau, VP Mktng, Edward B. Jordan, VP & CFO, Athena J. Mandros, PR Writer, Email: a.mandros@dialogic.com

Diamond Flower Electric Instrument Co. Inc. (DFI), 135 Main Ave, Sacramento CA 95838-2041 USA; 916/568-1234, Fax: 916/568-1233, Focus: PCs, motherboards, peripherals & scanners, Ownrshp: Sub DFI, Taiwan, Founded: 1981, Empl: 200, Sales ($M): 300, Fiscal End: 7/94; Y.C. Lu, Pres & CEO, David Lu, Pres DFI-USA, Megan McKenzie

Diamond Multimedia Systems Inc. 2880 Junction Ave, San Jose CA 95134-1922 USA; 408/325-7000, Fax: 408/325-7070, Co Email: @diamondmm.com, Focus: Multimedia hardware, Ownrshp: OTC, Founded: 1982, Empl: 500+, Sales ($M): 467.6, Fiscal End: 12/95; William J. Schroeder, Pres & CEO, Hyung Hwe Huh, CTO, Ken Wirth, VP MKtng, C. Scott Holt, VP Sales, Jack Kister, VP Eng, Kimberley Stowe, Marcom Specialist, Email: kims@diamondmm.com

Diamond Optimum Systems 22801 Ventura Blvd, #105, Woodland Hills CA 91364 USA; 818/224-2010, 800/862-8271 Fax: 818/224-2009, Co Email: diamondos@aol.com, Web URL: diamondos.com, Focus: Software configuration management tools, Prdts: Verson Control System, Ownrshp: PVT, Founded: 1982, Empl: 20, Sales ($M): 2.0, Fiscal End: 4/95; Igor Yasno, Pres

Diaquest Inc. 1440 San Pablo Ave, Berkeley CA 94702 USA; 510/526-7167, Fax: 510/526-7073, Co Email: diaquest@crl.com, Focus: Video animation products, Prdts: Animaq, Ownrshp: PVT, Founded: 1984, Dan Lindheim

Diba 3355 Edison Way, Menlo Park CA 94025 USA; 415/482-3300, Fax: 415/482-3400, Web URL: diba.com, Focus: Information appliances, Ownrshp: PVT, Founded: 1995, Empl: 40, Farzad Dibachi, Pres, Farid Dibachi, Chmn & CTO, Joe Gillach, COO, Mark Moore, VP Eng, David Thatcher, CFO

DIC Digital Supply Corp. 500 Frank W Burr Blvd, Teaneck NJ 07666-6802 USA; 201/692-7700, Fax: 201/692-7757, Co Email: ddigital@pipeline.com, Focus: Optical disks and backup tape drives, Ownrshp: Sub. Dainippon, Japan, Founded: 1987, Joseph Martinez, Pres, Kevin Kennedy, VP Mktng

Diebold Inc. 818 Mulberry Rd SE, PO Box 8230, Canton OH 44711-8230 USA; 216/489-4000, Focus: ATMs and electronic security equipment, Ownrshp: NYSE, Stk Sym: DBD, Founded: 1859, Empl: 4,731, Sales ($M): 863.4, Fiscal End: 12/95; Robert W. Mahoney, Chmn, Pres & CEO, Gregg A. Searle, EVP, William T. Blair, EVP, Albert W. Warf, Group VP, Gerald F. Morris, EVP & CFO, Donald E. Eagon Jr., VP Corp Com

DieHard Computer Corp. 4815 W Braker Ln #502-182, Austin TX 78759-5616 USA; 512/328-3322, Fax: 512/327-3330, Focus: Ruggedized PCs, Ownrshp: PVT, Founded: 1993

Digi Int'l. 6400 Flying Cloud Dr, Eden Prairie MN 55344 USA; 612/943-9020, Fax: 612/943-5398, Co Email: @digibd.com, Focus: PC communications boards, Ownrshp: OTC, Stk Sym: DGII, Founded: 1985, Empl: 450, Sales ($M): 130.9, Fiscal End: 9/94; John P. Schinas, Chmn, Ervin F. Kamm Jr., Pres & CEO, Dana R. Nelson, VP Sales & Mktng, Joseph A. Diodati, VP Mktng, Gerald A. Wall, VP & CFO, Donna Burke, PR Mgr, Email: donnab@digibd.com

Digicom Systems Inc. (DSI), 188 Topaz St, Milpitas CA 95035 USA; 408/262-1277, Fax: 408/262-1390, Focus: Modems and fax modems, Ownrshp: PVT, Founded: 1987, Empl: 75, Gwong-Yih Lee, Pres & CEO, Jason Blazensky, VP Mktng, Sean Cheng, VP Fin, Clifford Gard, Dir Sales, Nan-Sheng Lin, EVP Eng, Sonia Duenas

Digital Animation Corp. 24445 Northwestern Hwy, #105, Southfield MI 48075 USA; 810/354-0890, 800/572-0098 Fax: 810/354-0796, Focus: Animation software, Ownrshp: PVT, Tom Hammill, Pres, Stephen D. Smith, Dir Mktng

Digital Communications Associates Inc. (DCA), 1000 Alderman Dr, Alpharetta GA 30202-4199 USA; 770/442-4000, Fax: 770/442-4346, Focus: Communication and software products, Prdts: Irma, Crosstalk, Ownrshp: PVT, Founded: 1972, Empl: 1,100, Sales ($M): 209.4, Fiscal End: 6/92; James A. Lidner, Chmn, Pres & CEO

Digital Directory Assistance Inc. 6931 Arlington Rd, #405, Bethesda MD 20814-5231 USA; 301/657-8548, 800/284-8353 Fax: 301/652-7810, Co Email: 74774.1537@compuserve.com, Web URL: dda-inc.com, Focus: CD-ROM phone directory software, Prdts: PhoneDisc, Ownrshp: PVT, Founded: 1986, Claude Schoch, CEO, Email: claudes@dda-inc.com; Joe Molino, CFO, Email: joem@dda-inc.com; Eric Schoch, VP Mktng, Email: erics@dda-inc.com

Digital Equipment Corp. (DEC), 111 Powdermill Rd, Maynard MA 01754-2571 USA; 508/493-5111, Fax: 508/493-8780, Co Email: @digital.com, Web URL: digital.com, Focus: Minicomputers, mainframes, workstations and PCs, Prdts: Alpha, VAX, Ownrshp: NYSE, Stk Sym: DEC, Founded: 1957, Empl: 61,700, Sales ($M): 14,562.8, Fiscal End: 6/96; Robert B. Palmer, Pres & CEO, Charles F. Christ, VP, William Strecker, VP & CTO, Vincent J. Mullarkey, VP & CFO

Digital Frontiers 1019 Asbury Ave, Evanston IL 60202 USA; 847/328-0880, 800/328-7789 Fax: 847/869-2053, Co Email: info@digfrontiers.com, Web URL: digfrontiers.com, Focus: Software tools for web and multimedia graphics designers, Prdts: HVS Color, Ownrshp: PVT, Founded: 1995, Richard Bruno, Chmn, Email: rjbrunoc@aol.com; Chuck Duff, Pres, Email: cduff@digfrontiers.com; Doug Frohman, VP Bus Dev, Email: douglasf@digfrontiers.com

Digital Impact 6506 S Lewis, #250, Tulsa OK 74136 USA; 918/742-2022, 800/775-4232 Fax: 918/742-8176, Focus: Edutainment software, Ownrshp: PVT, Empl: 28, Louise Short, Pres & CEO, Jerry Short, VP Bus Dev, Michael Reynolds, VP Sales, Diane Crockett, VP Mktng, Holly Rankin, Media Rel Mgr

Digital Media Int'l. 3916 State St, #2B, Santa Barbara CA 93105 USA; 805/563-9490, Fax: 805/563-9480, Focus: Multimedia software, Prdts: Digital Meteor, Ownrshp: PVT, Founded: 1990, Marco Pinter, Pres, Michael Pugh, VP Bus Dev, Email: mikeadmi&aol.com; Matt Hummel, Creative Dir, David Douglas, Tech Dir

Digital Playground 21630 Marilla St, Chatsworth CA 91311 USA; 818/773-4999, Focus: Adult CD-ROM software, Ownrshp: PVT, Founded: 1993, Ray Nieto

Digital Products Inc. (DPI), 411 Waverly Oaks Rd, Waltham MA 02154 USA; 617/647-1234, 800/243-2333 Fax: 617/647-4474, Co Email: info@digprod.com, Web URL: digprod.com, Focus: Printer sharing and LAN products, Prdts: NetPrint, JetxPrint, PrintDirector, Ownrshp: PVT, Founded: 1984, Empl: 107, Sales ($M): 20, Fiscal End: 12/95; Cornelius Peterson, Pres & CEO, William Peisel, VP Eng, George Simmons, CFO, Marilyn Peterson, Dir Sales Support

Digital Systems Int'l. 6464 185th Ave NE, Redmond WA 98052-6736 USA; 206/881-7544, Fax: 206/869-4530, Focus: Communications products, Prdts: Voicelink, Ownrshp: OTC, Stk Sym: DGTL, Founded: 1984, Empl: 329, Sales ($M): 68.0, Fiscal End: 12/95; Pat Howard, Pres & CEO, Thomas J. Edwards, VP & CTO, Mark C. Perrin, SVP Bus Dev, John J. Flavio, SVP & CFO, W. Bradford Weller

Digital Theater Inc. 5805 State Bridge Rd #G303, Duluth GA 30155-6427 USA; 770/446-3580, Fax: 770/446-9164, Focus: LAN products, Prdts: Desk To Desk, Ownrshp: PVT

Digital Tools Inc. 10351 Bubb Rd, Cupertino CA 95014 USA;

408/366-6920, Fax: 408/446-2140, Co Email: info@digit.com, Focus: Project management software, Prdts: AutoPLAN, Ownrshp: PVT, Founded: 1989, Empl: 100, Mohan Uttarwar, Pres, Vinay Deshpanande, VP Eng, Vijay Uttarwar, VP Fin, Diana Nelson, Marcom Mgr, Email: diana@digit.com

Digital Video Arts Ltd. (DVA), 715 Twining Rd, #107, Twining Ctr, Dresher PA 19025 USA; 215/576-7920, Fax: 215/576-7932, Co Email: @dval.com, Focus: Digital video technology, Prdts: NewWorld products, Ownrshp: PVT, Founded: 1991, George Breen, Pres, Email: george@dval.com; Stephen Kraiman, VP Prod Dev

Digital Vision Inc. 270 Bridge St, Dedham MA 02026 USA; 617/329-5400, Fax: 617/329-6286, Web URL: digvis.com/digvis, Focus: Video digitizers, Prdts: Computer Eyes, TelevEyes, Ownrshp: PVT, Founded: 1984, Empl: 21, Sales ($M): 2, David Pratt, Pres, John R. Pratt, VP Mktng, Steve Sarsfield, Prod Mgr, Email: sarsfld@tiac.net

Digital Wisdom Inc. 300 Jeanette Dr, PO Box 2070, Tappahannock VA 22560-2070 USA; 804/443-9000, Fax: 804/443-3632, Co Email: 72673.3360@compuserve.com, Focus: CD-ROM software, Ownrshp: PVT, David Broad, Pres, Alastair Campbell, Co-founder

Digitran Corp. 399 Thornall St #3, Edison NJ 08837-2238 USA; 800/828-7115 Fax: 800/336-0835, Web URL: faxsav.com, Focus: Fax products and services, Prdts: faxSAV, Ownrshp: PVT, Founded: 1989

Direct Technology 10 E 21st St, #1106, New York NY 10010 USA; 212/475-2747, Fax: 212/529-4941, Co Email: info@dtl.com, Web URL: dtl.com, Founded: 1981, Mike Palmer, Pres, Mark Murray, Dir SW Dev, Richard Turner, Dir Sales & Mktng, Douglas M. Turner, Dir Sales & Mktng

DISC Distributing Corp. 19430 S Van Ness Ave, Torrance CA 90501 USA; 310/787-6800, Fax: 310/787-6810, Focus: PC product distributor, Ownrshp: PVT, Founded: 1985, Dan Hoffman, Pres, Carrie Pollare, EVP

Disc Manufacturing Inc. 1409 Foulk Rd, #102, Wilmington DE 19803 USA; 302/479-2500, Fax: 302/479-2527, Co Email: 517.1444@mcimail.com, Focus: CD and CD-ROM manufacturing, Ownrshp: Sub. Quixote, Sales ($M): 90, Fiscal End: 6/95; Myron R. Shain, Pres, Rushton Capers, VP

Discovery Channel, The 7700 Wisconsin Ave, Bethesda MD 20814-3579 USA; 301/986-1999, Fax: 301/986-4828, Focus: Multimedia software, Founded: 1985, Empl: 270, John S. Hendricks, Chmn & CEO, Thomas A. Porter, Publisher & GM, Eric Eggleton, VP, Tom Burke, VP, Jim Boyle, VP Com, Email: jboyle@discovery.com

Disk Technologies Corp. (Disctec), 925 S Semoran Blvd #114, Winter Park FL 32792-5313 USA; 407/671-5500, Fax: 407/671-6606, Focus: Removable hard disks, Ownrshp: PVT, Founded: 1990, C. Allen Amos, Pres & CEO, Douglas Caldes, EVP, Thomas J. Hunt, VP Sales & Mktng, Email: tom-hunt@radiomail.net

DISK/TREND Inc. 1925 Landings Dr, Mountain View CA 94043 USA; 415/961-6209, Fax: 415/969-2560, Co Email: dtinfo@disk-trend.com, Focus: Publishes annual Disk/Trend reports on rigid, disk drive arrays and optical disk drives, Ownrshp: PVT, Founded: 1977, Empl: 4, James N Porter, Pres, Robert H. Katzive, VP

Distributed Processing Technology 140 Candace Dr, Maitland FL 32751 USA; 407/830-5522, Fax: 407/260-5366, Co Email: @dpt.com, Focus: Peripheral controllers, Prdts: SmartCache, Ownrshp: PVT, Founded: 1977, Empl: 200, Steve Goldman, Pres, Jim Campbell, VP Mktng, David Race, VP Strat Plng, Johnny Cardosi, VP, Woody Whitchurch, CFO, Christina Hardison, PR Spec, Email: hardison@dpt.com

Distributed Systems Solutions Int'l. (DSSI), 31255 Cedar Valley Dr, #319, Westlake Village CA 91362-4037 USA; 818/991-0200, Fax: 818/991-4606, Co Email: @dssi.com, Focus: Software for Lotus Notes

Ditek Int'l. 2800 John St, #15, Markham Ontario L3R 0E2 Canada; 416/479-1990, Fax: 416/479-1882, Co Email: goditek@compuserve.com, Focus: CAD software, Ownrshp: PVT, Founded: 1984, Oren Asher, Pres & CEO

DiviCom Inc. 1708 McCarthy Blvd, Milpitas CA 95035-7417 USA; 408/944-6700, 800/286-1600 Fax: 408/944-6705, Co Email: @divi.com, Web URL: divi.com, Focus: Digital compression and broadcast products, Ownrshp: PVT, Founded: 1993, Nolan Daines, Pres & CEO, Tom Lookabaugh, VP R&D, Brian Johnson, VP Adv Dev, Bob Natwick, VP Sales

Division Inc. 400 Seaport Ct, #101, Redwood City CA 94063 USA; 415/364-6067, Fax: 415/364-4663, Web URL: division.com, Focus: Virtual reality systems and software, Prdts: dVISE, dVS, Ownrshp: Sub. Division Group, Plc, Founded: 1989, Empl: 100, Charles Grimsdale, CEO

DK Multimedia 95 Madison Ave, New York NY 10016 USA; 212/213-4800, Fax: 212/213-5240, Focus: Eduational multimedia software, Ownrshp: Sub DK Publishing, UK, Founded: 1991, Cheri Grand, Email: dkcheri@aol.com

DK&A Inc. 1010 Turquoise St, #300, San Diego CA 92109 USA; 619/488-8118, Fax: 619/488-4021, Focus: Publishing software, Prdts: INposition, Ownrshp: PVT, Founded: 1987, Empl: 17, David King, Pres & CEO, Robert Kline, COO

DMCD Interactive Design Services 245 Mill St, Greenwich CT 06830 USA; 203/531-4007, Fax: 203/531-4010, Focus: Interactive multimedia design and programming, Ownrshp: Sub DMCD, Founded: 1963, Michael deMartin, Dir

Docucon Inc. 7461 Callaghan Rd, San Antonio TX 78229 USA; 210/525-9221, Fax: 210/525-9484, Focus: Optical disks, scanning and conversion, Ownrshp: OTC, Stk Sym: DOCU, Founded: 1986, Empl: 100, Sales ($M): 11.0, Fiscal End: 12/95; Edward P. Gistaro, Chmn & CEO, Allan H. Hobgood, Pres & COO, Jim Feuerstein, SVP & CTO

DocuMagix Inc. 2880 Zanker Rd, #204, San Jose CA 95134-2122 USA; 408/434-1138, Fax: 408/434-0915, Web URL: documagix.com, Focus: Document management software, Prdts: PaperMaster, Ownrshp: PVT, Founded: 1993, Steve Leung, Chmn, Al Sisto, Pres & CEO, Sam Hahn, VP Eng, George Skaff, VP Mktng, Hedy Breakfield, CFO

Document Imaging Systems Corp. (DISC), 541 Weddell Dr, Sunnyvale CA 94089 USA; 408/734-5287, Fax: 408/734-2692, Focus: Optical disk libraries, Ownrshp: OTC, Stk Sym: DCSR, Sales ($M): 4.3, Fiscal End: 12/94; J. Richard Ellis, Pres & CEO, David C. Harder, Mktng Mgr

Documentum Inc. 5671 Gibraltar Dr, Pleasanton CA 94588-8547 USA; 510/463-6800, Fax: 510/463-6850, Focus: Document management software, Prdts: Documentum Server, Workspace, Ownrshp: PVT, Founded: 1990, Empl: 60, Jeffrey A. Miller, Pres & CEO

Dolch Computer Systems 3178 Laurelview Ct, Fremont CA 94538 USA; 510/661-2220, Fax: 510/490-2360, Co Email: @dolch.com, Focus: Portable and ruggedized PCs, Ownrshp: PVT, Founded: 1976, Empl: 100+, Sales ($M): 17.3, Fiscal End: 3/94; Volker Dolch, Pres, Marco Gallo, Marcom Specialist, Email: marco@dolch.com

Dolphin Inc. 3625 E Thousand Oaks Blvd, #216, Westlake Village CA 91362-3626 USA; 805/371-9493, Fax: 805/371-9785, Co Email: knal@netcom.com, Focus: SCI and ATM products, Ownrshp: Sub. Dolphin, Norway, Founded: 1992, Empl: 25, Martyn Albert, Pres, Knut Alnes, VP Mktng

Dotronix Inc. 160 First St SE, New Brighton MN 55112-7894 USA; 612/633-1742, 800/720-7218 Fax: 612/633-7025, Web URL: dotronix.com, Focus: OEM of video CRT displays, Ownrshp: OTC, Stk Sym: DOTX, Founded: 80, Empl: 165, Sales ($M): 14.6, Fiscal End: 6/96; William S. Sadler, CEO & Pres, Michael Hopkins, VP Sales & Mktng, Steve Sims, Corp Com

Dow Jones & Company Inc. (DJ), World Financial Ctr, 200

Liberty St, New York NY 10281 USA; 212/416-2000, Fax: 212/416-3299, Web URL: dowjones.com, Focus: Publishing and information services, Prdts: Dow Jones News/Retrieval, Wall St Journal, Ownrshp: NYSE, Stk Sym: DJ, Founded: 1882, Empl: 9,600, Sales ($M): 2,283.8, Fiscal End: 12/95; Peter R. Kann, Chmn & CEO, Kenneth L. Burenga, Pres & COO, Dorothea Coccoli Palsho, Pres Info Serv, Bernard T. Flanagan, VP Mktng, Kevin J. Roche, VP & CFO

DP-Tek Inc. 9920 E Harry, Wichita KS 67207 USA; 316/687-3000, Fax: 316/687-0489, Focus: Desktop publishing and imaging products, Ownrshp: PVT, Founded: 1979, Empl: 40, Allen Frazier, Chmn & CEO, Robert Harbison, Pres

Dragon Systems Inc. 320 Nevada St, Newton MA 02160 USA; 617/965-5200, Fax: 617/527-0372, Co Email: @dragonsys.com, Focus: Speech recognition hardware and software, Ownrshp: PVT, Founded: 1982, James K. Baker, Chmn & CEO, Janet M. Baker, Pres, Chris Gardner, Corp Com Mgr

Drake Training & Technologies 2601 W 88th St, Bloomington MN 55431 USA; 612/896-7000, Fax: 612/896-7010, Focus: Computer-based certification, licensing and assessment testing, Ownrshp: PVT, Founded: 1990, Empl: 150, William H. Dorman, Pres & CEO, Charles B. Johnston, VP Tech, Alan W. Hupp, VP Mktng, Pamela Cabalka, VP Sales, Sherry Reid, VP Ops

Dream IT Inc. 2620 7th St, Boulder CO 80304 USA; 303/417-9313, Fax: 303/473-9670, Co Email: @dreamit.com, Web URL: dreamit.com, Focus: Mobile computing, wireless communications, pens, digitizers and consulting, Ownrshp: PVT, Founded: 1991, Empl: 3, Sales ($M): O.6, Portia Isaacson, Pres, Email: portia@dreamit.com

DreamWorks Interactive 640 N Sepulveda, Belle Air CA 90049 USA; 310/234-7070, Fax: 310/234-7089, Focus: Interactive entertainment software, Ownrshp: Microsoft & DreamWorks, Founded: 1994, Empl: 560, Glenn Entis, CEO

Dresselhaus Computer Products 10241B Trademark St, Rancho Cucamonga CA 91730 USA; 909/945-5600, 800/368-7737 Fax: 909/989-2436, Focus: Printer accessory products, Prdts: SmartPrint, Ownrshp: PVT, Founded: 1982, Empl: 15, Sales ($M): 3+, Fiscal End: 12/94; Daniel Dresselhaus, Pres

Driftwood Systems Inc. 2361 214th Pl. SW, Brier WA 98036 USA; 206/775-6495, Fax: 206/774-8564, Co Email: info@driftwood.com, Focus: Product development and consulting for Magic Cap & Telescript, Prdts: Telescript based Information Service, Ownrshp: PVT, Founded: 1993, Steve Knox, Pres, Email: fortknox@driftwood.com

Drive Savers Inc. 400 Bel Marin Keys Blvd, Novato CA 94949 USA; 415/382-2000, 800/440-1904 Fax: 415/883-0780, Web URL: drivesavers.com, Focus: Data recovery services, Ownrshp: PVT, Founded: 1989, Empl: 12, Scott Gaidano, Pres, Jay Hagan, VP, Karen Stange, MIS Mgr, Scott Gaidano, Mktng Mgr

Droege Computing Services Inc. 20 W Colony Place, #120, Durham NC 27705-5590 USA; 919/403-9459, Fax: 919/403-8199, Co Email: 71333.3015@compuserve.com, Focus: Database software, Prdts: Camera Ready Auction Management Sys, Media Management Information Sys, Ownrshp: PVT, Founded: 1985, Empl: 8, Tom Droege, Pres, Paula Droege, CFO, Stephen Scott, Dir Sales & Mktng

DSC Communications Corp. (DSC), 1000 Coit Rd, Plano TX 75075-5813 USA; 214/519-3000, Fax: 214/519-4289, Web URL: dsccc.com, Focus: Telecom systems, Ownrshp: OTC, Stk Sym: DSC, Founded: 1976, Empl: 5,860, Sales ($M): 1,422.0, Fiscal End: 12/95; James L. Donald, Chmn, Pres & CEO, Kenneth R. Vines, VP Finance, Charles H. Ansley, SVP, Allen R. Adams, Group VP, Gerald F. Montry, SVP & CFO, Terry Adams

DSP Development Corp. 1 Kendall Square, Bldg. 100, 3rd Floor, Cambridge MA 02139 USA; 617/577-1133, 800/777-5151 Fax: 617/577-8211, Co Email: dspdev@world.std.com, Web URL: dadisp.com, Focus: Data analysis software, Prdts: DADISP, Ownr-

shp: PVT, Founded: 1984

DSP Group Inc. 3120 Scott Blvd, Santa Clara CA 95054 USA; 408/986-4300, Fax: 408/986-4323, Co Email: @dspg.com, Focus: DSP and speech products, Ownrshp: OTC, Stk Sym: DSPG, Founded: 1987, Empl: 64, Sales ($M): 50.4, Fiscal End: 12/95; Igal Kohaui, Chmn, Eli Porat, Pres & CEO, Cohen Yuval, VP Mktng, Sylvia Shirely, Mgr Investor Relations, Email: sshirely.dspg.com

DST Systems Inc. 1055 Broadway, 9th Fl., Kansas City MO 64105 USA; 816/435-1000, Fax: 816/435-8630, Focus: Software for mutual fund industry, Ownrshp: OTC, Stk Sym: DST, Empl: 5,000, Sales ($M): 404.3, Fiscal End: 12/94; Thomas A. McDonnell, Pres & CEO, Kenneth V. Hager, VP & CFO, Robert C. Canfield, SVP, Thomas A. McCullough, EVP, James P. Horan, CIO, Rod Weirick

DTC Data Technology Corp. (DTC), 1515 Centre Pointe Dr, Milpitas CA 95035 USA; 408/942-4000, Fax: 408/942-4052, Web URL: datatechnology.com, Focus: Computer peripherals, Ownrshp: OTC, Stk Sym: DTEC, Founded: 1979, Empl: 29, Sales ($M): 16.6, Fiscal End: 2/95; James T. Koo, Pres, W. Morris Chubb, CFO, Stephanie J. Forsythe, CFO

DTK Computer Inc. 770 Epperson Dr, City of Industry CA 91748 USA; 818/810-0098, Fax: 818/810-0090, Co Email: @dtk-computer.com, Web URL: dtkcomputer.com, Focus: PCs and motherboards, Ownrshp: Sub. Datatech, Taiwan, Founded: 1981, Empl: 300, Sales ($M): 190, Duke Liao, Pres, Dan Tsuei, CFO, Michelle Nguyen, Mktng Mgr

Dun & Bradstreet Corp., The (D&B), 187 Danbury Rd, Wilton CT 06897 USA; 203/834-4200, Fax: 203/834-4262, Web URL: dnb.com, Focus: Information services and market research to the computer industry, Ownrshp: NYSE, Stk Sym: DNB, Founded: 1930, Empl: 49,500, Sales ($M): 5,415.1, Fiscal End: 12/95; Robert E. Weissman, Chmn & CEO, William G. Jacobi, EVP, Volney Taylor, EVP, Robert J. Lievense, EVP, Nicholas L. Trivisonno, EVP & CFO

Dun & Bradstreet Software Services Inc. (D&B Software), 3445 Peachtree Rd NE, Atlanta GA 30326 USA; 404/239-2000, Fax: 404/290-7374, Co Email: @dbsoftware.com, Web URL: dbsoftware.com, Focus: Mainframe software, Ownrshp: Sub. Dun & Bradstreet, Founded: 1990, Empl: 2,675, Sales ($M): 365, Fiscal End: 12/95; Doug MacIntyre, Pres & CEO, Jim Schaper, EVP & COO, Peter F. Sinisgalli, EVP & CFO, Jeff Scherb, SVP & CTO, Craig Richards, VP Mktng, Randy Renbarger, Email: rrenb@dbsoftware.com

Duracell Int'l. Berkshire Industrial Park, Bethel CT 06801 USA; 203/791-3010, Fax: 203/796-4096, Web URL: duracell.com, Focus: Batteries, Ownrshp: OTC, Empl: 3,700, Sales ($M): 2,180, Fiscal End: 12/95; Charles R. Perrin, CEO, J. Norman Allen, SVP New Prod, Harry Taylor, VP, Mark S. Bertolami, Group Prod Mgr, Paul B. Stratton, VP Mktng, Jill Fallon

Duracom Computer Systems 1425 Greenway Dr, Irving TX 75038 USA; 214/518-1200, Fax: 214/518-1090, Focus: PCs and workstations, Ownrshp: PVT, Founded: 1989, Sales ($M): 15, Tom Dodson, Pres, Brian Burke, Mktng Mgr

Durand Communications Network Inc. 147 Castilian Dr, Santa Barbara CA 93117 USA; 805/961-8700, Fax: 805/961-8701, Web URL: durand.com, Focus: C/S software and development tools for the Internet community, Prdts: MindWire, Ownrshp: PVT, Founded: 1991, Empl: 30, Andre Durand, Pres & CEO, Randall Green, VP Bus Dev, Bryan Elliot, CTO, Craig Wirths, COO, Charlie Colquhoun, VP Prod Dev, Jennifer C. Slavin, Dir Mktng, Email: jennslavin@durand.com

Dux Software Corp. 201 San Antonio Cr, C 250, Mountain View CA 94040 USA; 415/948-6200, Web URL: dux.com, Focus: Workstation graphics software, Founded: 1990, Robert B. Adams, Pres & CEO, Bill Feeley, VP Sales

Dycam Inc. 9414 Eton Ave, Chatsworth CA 91311 USA; 818/998-8008, Fax: 818/998-7951, Focus: PC imaging hardware, Stk Sym: DYC, John Edling, Chmn & Pres

Dynamic Graphics Inc. 6000 N Forest Park Dr, PO Box 1901, Peoria IL 61656-1901 USA; 309/688-8800, 800/255-8800 Fax: 309/688-3075, Co Email: dyngraphic@aol.com, Focus: Clip art software and services, Prdts: clipper, Print Media Service, Designer's Club, Volk, Ownrshp: PVT, Founded: 1964, Empl: 150, Jayne Mueller, Pres, Peter T. Force, VP Sales & Mktng, Charlene L. Dixon

Dynapro Systems Inc. 800 Carleton Ct, New Westminster BC V3M 6L3 Canada; 604/521-3962, Fax: 604/521-4629, Focus: Computer interface products, Ownrshp: PVT, Founded: 1981, Empl: 450, Sales ($M): 52, Karl H. Brackhaus, Pres & CEO, Tom E. Dodd, VP Mktng, Robert J. Mielcarski, VP R&D, Neil McDonnell, VP Sales & Mktng, Lloyd E. Kearl, VP Fin

Dynasty Technology 650 Warrenville Rd #300, Lisle IL 60532-4314 USA; 708/355-8300, Fax: 708/355-9345, Focus: Object-oriented software, Ownrshp: PVT, Founded: 1990, Empl: 30, Michael Lyons, CEO

Dynatech Corp. 3 New England Exec Park, Burlington MA 01803-5087 USA; 617/272-6100, Fax: 617/272-2304, Focus: Telecom and electronic products, Ownrshp: OTC, Stk Sym: DYTC, Founded: 1959, Empl: 3,100, Sales ($M): 488.8, Fiscal End: 3/95; John F. Reno, Pres & CEO, Roger C. Cady, VP Bus Dev, George A. Merrick, VP Display Bus, John R. Peeler, VP, Allan M. Kline, CFO, Steve Cantor, Mgr Corp Com

DynaTek Automation Systems Inc. 200 Bluewater Rd, Bedford NS B4B 1G9 Canada; 902/832-3000, Fax: 902/832-3010, Co Email: @dynatek.ca, Focus: RAID and mass storage systems, Ownrshp: PVT, Founded: 1988, Empl: 130, Sales ($M): 75, Sam Gur, Pres, Howard Goldberg, VP Ops, Howard Phee, CFO, Alex Kosarow, Dir Export Sales, Andrew Clarke, Corp Com Mgr, Email: aclarke@dynatek.ca

Dynaware USA Inc. 111 Anza Blvd, #115, Burlingame CA 94010-1932 USA; 415/349-5700, Fax: 415/349-5879, Focus: Graphics and music software, Prdts: DynaPerspective, DynaDuet, Ballade, Ownrshp: Sub. Dynaware Corp., Founded: 1987, Empl: 25, Ken Hayashi, GM, Robert Howard, VP Sales & Mktng

E Corp. 950 Green Tree Rd, Pittsburgh PA 15220 USA; Fax: 412/937-2820, Co Email: @e-corp.com, Web URL: e-corp.com, Focus: Email software, Prdts: email complete, Michael Wittlen, Pres, John Iannucci, CEO

E-Lock Software 1978 Virginia St, Medford OR 97501 USA; 503/734-2412, Fax: 503/779-7429, Co Email: elock@mind.net, Web URL: mind.ne/elock, Focus: Online security software, Ownrshp: PVT

E-Net Corp. 505 Sansone St, 20th Floor, San Francisco CA 94111 USA; 415/433-3800, Fax: 415/433-3881, Co Email: @enet.com, Focus: Disaster recovery software, Ownrshp: PVT, Founded: 1984, Empl: 25, Sales ($M): 4, James de Remer, Pres, Tom Flesher, EVP, Jennifer L. Campbell, Mktng Coord

E-Systems Inc. 6250 LBJ Freeway, PO Box 660248, Dallas TX 75266-0248 USA; 214/661-1000, Fax: 214/661-8508, Focus: Electronic products, Ownrshp: NYSE, Stk Sym: ESY, Founded: 1964, Empl: 16,700, Sales ($M): 2,028.3, Fiscal End: 12/94; A. Lowell Lawson, Chmn & CEO, Brian D. Cullen, SVP, J. Robert Collins, VP Strat Plg & Dev, Harry L. Thurman, VP Bus Dev, James W. Pope, VP & CFO

E.E.S. Companies Inc. 2 Vernon St, #404, Framingham MA 01701 USA; 508/653-6911, Fax: 508/650-1872, Co Email: sales@eesco.com, Focus: Macintosh POS and business software, Prdts: POS/OE, Merchant's Edge, Credit Card DB, Ownrshp: PVT, Founded: 1988, Hank Szretter, Pres, June Szretter, VP Mktng

E.M.M.E. Interactive 1200 Summer St, Stamford CT 06905 USA; 203/406-4041, Fax: 203/406-4043, Focus: CD-ROM software on cultural, art and history, Founded: 1994, Philippe Guttieres-Lasry, Pres, Stephen Smith, VP Sales & Mktng

EA Research Inc. 2420 Camino Ramon, #212, San Ramon CA 94583 USA; 510/867-0967, Fax: 510/867-0684, Focus: Macintosh

graphics and multimedia products, Ownrshp: PVT, Founded: 1992, David B. Evans, Pres, Karen E. Evans, CFO, Richard Sutton, Dir Eng, Scott Rafer, Dir Sales & Mktng

Eagle Point Softwa
re 4131 Westmark Dr, Dubuque IA 52002 USA; 319/556-8392, 800/678-6565 Fax: 319/556-5321, Co Email: 73457.433@compuserve.com, Web URL: netins.net/showcase/eaglewww, Focus: Land planning and design software, Prdts: Civil Applications Advantage Series, Structural Expert Series, Ownrshp: OTC, Stk Sym: EGPT, Founded: 1983, Empl: 260, Sales ($M): 19.2, Fiscal End: 6/96; Rod Blum, CEO, Dennis George, CFO, John Biner, VP, Ed Graham, VP, Brent Straka, Dir Mktng

Eagle Software Inc. 123 Indiana Ave, Salina KS 67401 USA; 913/823-7257, 800/477-5432 Fax: 913/823-6185, Co Email: info@eaglesoft.com, Web URL: eaglesoft.com, Focus: Disk management software and backup solutions, Prdts: Disk-Pak for UNIX, Alexandria Backup Librarian, Spectra 4000 & 9000, Ownrshp: PVT, Founded: 1981, Empl: 13, Sales ($M): 1.5, Fiscal End: 9/95; David J. Hiechel, Pres & CEO, Email: dave@eaglesoft.com; Dale Swindler, VP Sales, Email: dale@eaglesoft.com; Andy Kratzer, Sr SW Eng, Email: andy@eaglesoft.com; Shelly Chenoweth, VP Mktng, Email: shelly@eaglesoft.com

EarthLink Network Inc. 3100 New York Dr, Pasadena CA 91107 USA; 818/296-2400, 800/395-8425 Fax: 818/296-2470, Co Email: sales@earthlink.net, Web URL: earthlink.com, Focus: Internet service provider, Ownrshp: PVT, Founded: 1994, Empl: 400, Sky Dayton, Chmn & CEO, Charles G. Betty, Pres & COO, Tiare Widmaier, Dir PR, Email: tiarew@earthlink.net

EAS Technologies Inc. 4345 Security Pky., New Albany IN 47150-9366 USA; 812/941-9360, Focus: Time and attendance software, Ownrshp: PVT, Kimberly Charlet, Dir Mktng

East-West Foundation 23 Drydock Ave, 3rd Fl, Boston MA 02210 USA; 617/261-6699, Fax: 617/261-6644, Co Email: ewedf@ix.netcom.com, Focus: Donations of surplus computers for use in Eastern-Europe, Ownrshp: Nonprofit, Founded: 1990, Stephen C. Farrell, Exec Dir

Eastman Kodak Co. 343 State St, Rochester NY 14650 USA; 716/724-4000, 800/785-6325 Fax: 716/726-3758, Web URL: kodak.com, Focus: Photographic products, diskettes and peripherals, Ownrshp: NYSE, Stk Sym: EK, Founded: 1880, Empl: 110,400, Sales ($M): 14,980.0, Fiscal End: 12/95; George M.C. Fisher, Chmn, Pres & CEO, Leo J. Thomas, Group VP, Harry L. Kavetas, SVP & CFO, John J. Chiazza, CIO

EasySpooler 5327 N Central Expwy, Dallas TX 75205 USA; 214/522-2324, Fax: 214/522-1306, Focus: Print spooler software, Ownrshp: Sub Seay Systems, Founded: 1976, Bob Fazen, VP, Karen Garver

ECC International Corp. 175 Strafford Ave, #116, Wayne PA 19087-3377 USA; 610/687-2600, Fax: 610/254-9268, Focus: Computer-based training, simulation and interactive learning systems, Ownrshp: NYSE, Stk Sym: ECC, Founded: 1969, Empl: 951, Sales ($M): 117.2, Fiscal End: 6/96; George W. Murphy, Pres & CEO, Ajit W. Hirani, VP & GM, James B. Conyers Jr., VP Bus Dev, Patrick M. Donohue, VP Mktng

ECCS Inc. One Sheila Dr, Bldg. 6A, Tinton Falls NJ 07724 USA; 908/747-6995, 800/322-7462 Fax: 908/747-6542, Focus: Mass storage for open systems, Prdts: Synchronix, RAID MicroDFT-IE, RAID Micro-DFT1, Ownrshp: OTC, Stk Sym: ECCS, Founded: 1980, Empl: 100, Sales ($M): 44, Michael E. Faherty, Chmn & CEO, Gregg M. Azcuy, Pres & COO, Priyan Gunerame, VP Ops, Louis J. Altieri, VP Finance & Admin, Patricia M. Aberle, Asst to CEO

Eclipse Systems Inc. 2770 De La Cruz Blvd, Santa Clara CA 95050-2624 USA; 800/278-7197 Focus: PC fax software, Ownrshp: PVT, Victor H. Schiller, Chmn & CEO, Gary MacDougal, Pres & COO

Eden Systems Corp. 9302 N Meridian St, #350, Indianapolis IN

46260-1820 USA; 317/848-9600, 800/288-9510 Fax: 317/843-2271, Co Email: @edensys.com, Web URL: edensys.com/eden-sys/eden, Focus: Cobol and electronic meeting software, Prdts: Q/Auditor, Q/Artisan, Q/Executive, Ownrshp: PVT, Founded: 1985, Richard P. Nashleanas, CEO, Email: ricknash@edensys.com; Patricia Nashleanas, Pres, Email: patnash@edensys.com; S. Brad Schweibold, Dir Sales, Email: essales@edensys.com

Edify Corp. 2840 San Thomas Expwy, Santa Clara CA 95051 USA; 408/982-2000, Fax: 408/982-0777, Co Email: info@edify.com, Web URL: edify.com, Focus: Interactive services, Prdts: Electronic Workforce, Ownrshp: PVT, Founded: 1990, Empl: 140, Jeffrey Crowe, Pres, Email: jcrowe@edify.com; Thomas Glassanos, VP Mktng, Email: tglassanos@edify.com; Terry Shough, VP Sales, Email: terrys@edify.com

Edmark Corp. 6727 185th Ave NE, PO Box 97021, Redmond WA 98073-9721 USA; 206/556-8400, 800/426-0856 Fax: 206/556-8430, Web URL: edmark.com, Focus: Educational software and hardware, Prdts: TouchWindow, Kid Desk, Ownrshp: OTC, Stk Sym: EDMK, Founded: 1970, Empl: 121, Sales ($M): 32.2, Fiscal End: 6/96; Sally G. Narodick, Chmn & CEO, John R. Moore, VP Ops, Daniel P. Vetras, VP Cons Sales, Donna G. Stanger, VP Prod Dev, Paul Bialek, CFO, Sue Whitcomb, PR Mgr, Email: 73363.3672@compuserve.com

EDS 5400 Legacy Dr, Plano TX 75024-6000 USA; 214/604-6000, Web URL: eds.com, Focus: Information technology services, Ownrshp: NYSE, Stk Sym: GME, Founded: 1962, Empl: 80,000, Sales ($M): 12,422, Fiscal End: 12/95; Lester M. Alberthal Jr., Chmn, Pres & CEO, Gary J. Fernandes, SVP, Joseph M. Grant, SVP & CFO, Paul J. Chiapparone, SVP, Tony Good, Dir PR

EDUCOM 1112 16th St NW, #600, Washington DC 20036 USA; 202/872-4200, Fax: 202/872-4318, Focus: Consortium of universities regarding computer and communication in higher education, Ownrshp: Nonprofit, Founded: 1964, Kenneth King, Pres, Steven Gilbert, VP, Roger Smith, DB/Pub MIS Manager, Windy Rickard Bollentin, PR/Pub

Effective Management Systems (EMS), 12000 W Park Place, Milwaukee WI 53224 USA; 414/359-9800, 800/962-1279 Fax: 414/359-9011, Web URL: execpc.com/emsinc, Focus: CIM and business management software, Prdts: Time Critical Manufacturing, NCM-EMS Enterprise Management Software, Ownrshp: OTC, Stk Sym: EMSI, Founded: 1978, Empl: 200, Sales ($M): 29.0, Fiscal End: 11/95; Michael D. Dunham, Pres & CEO, Thomas M. Dykstra, VP R&D, Robert E. Weisenberg, VP Ops & GM, Thomas G. Allen, VP Sales & Mktng, Jeffrey J. Fossum, CFO

Egghead Inc. 22705 E Mission, Liberty Lake WA 99019 USA; 509/922-7031, Fax: 800/773-9359, Focus: Chain of software stores, Ownrshp: OTC, Stk Sym: EGGS, Founded: 1984, Empl: 2,300, Sales ($M): 403.8, Fiscal End: 3/96; Terence M. Strom, Pres & CEO, George P. Orban, Chmn, Ronald C. Foster, VP Ops, Brian W. Bender, VP & CFO

Eicon Technology Corp. 14755 Preston Rd, #620, Dallas TX 75240 214/239-3270, Fax: 214/239-3304, Co Email: sales@eicon.com, Web URL: eicon.com, Focus: PC and workstation network products, Ownrshp: FO, Stk Sym: EIC, Founded: 1984, Empl: 365, Sales ($M): 99.2, Fiscal End: 6/95; Peter Brojde, Pres, Maks Wulkan, EVP, Jeff Paine, VP Mktng, Harald Mueller, VP Ops, Francois Campeau, VP & CFO

Eiger Labs Inc. 1237 Midas Way, Sunnyvale CA 94086 USA; 408/774-3456, 800/653-4437 Fax: 408/774-3444, Co Email: headon@slip.net, Web URL: eiger.labs.com, Focus: Mobile computing products, Prdts: HeadOn DSVD, Ownrshp: PVT, Founded: 1994, Tom Wolf, VP Sales & Mktng

Eiki Int'l. 26794 Vista Terrace Dr, Lake Forest CA 92630 USA; 714/457-0200, Fax: 714/457-7878, Focus: Portable personal computer and video LCD projector, Prdts: LC-4200, Susan Frease, Mktng Assist

EJ Bilingual Inc. 2463 Torrance Blvd, #1, Torrance CA 90501

USA; 310/320-8139, Fax: 310/320-3228, Web URL: ejbilingual.com, Focus: English/Japanese translation software, Prdts: EZ JapaneseWriter, Reader, Speaker, Ownrshp: PVT, Founded: 1990, Empl: 6, Ryozo Kimihira, EVP

Elan Computer Group Inc. 888 Villa St, 3rd Floor, Mountain View CA 94041 USA; 415/964-2200, Fax: 415/964-8588, Co Email: sales@elan.com, Web URL: elan.com, Focus: Software licensing tools, Prdts: License Manager, Ownrshp: PVT, Founded: 1984, Ken Greer, Pres, Janett K. Peace, Marcom Mgr, Email: janett@elan.com

Elastic Reality Inc. 6400 Enterprise Ln #201, Madison WI 53719-1138 USA; 608/273-6585, Fax: 608/271-1988, Focus: Imaging and special effects software, Ownrshp: PVT, Founded: 1986, Perry Kivolowitz, Pres, Dan Esenther, VP

Electrohome Ltd. 809 Wellington St N, Kitchener Ontario N2G 4J6 Canada; 519/744-7111, Fax: 519/749-3139, Focus: Large screen displays and monitors, Ownrshp: FO, Stk Sym: EL.X, Founded: 1907, Empl: 825, Sales ($M): 186, Fiscal End: 8/95; John Pollock, Chmn & CEO, David Lowafer, Pres & COO Visual Comm Group, Bruce Cowie, Pres & COO Broadcast Group, Dan Wright, VP & CFO, Bill Alguire, Secretary

Electronic Arts 1450 Fashion Island Blvd, San Mateo CA 94404 USA; 415/571-7171, Fax: 415/571-5137, Web URL: ea.com, Focus: Entertainment software, Ownrshp: OTC, Stk Sym: ERTS, Founded: 1982, Empl: 1,500, Sales ($M): 531.9, Fiscal End: 3/96; Lawrence F. Probst, Chmn, Pres & CEO, Bing Gordon, EVP Mktng, E. Stanton McKee JR, SVP & CFO, Mark S. Lewis, SVP, Patricia Becker, Dir Corp Com

Electronic Book Technologies Inc. (EBT), 1 Richmond Square, Providence RI 02906 USA; 401/421-9550, Fax: 401/421-9551, Co Email: info@ebt.com, Web URL: ebt.com, Focus: Electronic publishing for Internet and CD-ROM, Prdts: DynaText, DynaWeb, DynaTag, DynaPage, FIGleaf, CADleaf, Ownrshp: PVT, Founded: 1989, Empl: 150, Louis R. Reynolds, Pres & CEO, Yvonne Dahl, VP Sales, Email: ymd@ebt.com; Kent Summers, Dir Mktng, Email: kjs@ebt.com; Jeff Vogel, Dir Eng, Email: jlv@ebt.com; Paul Lamoureux, PR Mgr, Email: pcl@ebt.com

Electronic Commerce World 380 St Antoine, #3280W, Montreal Quebec H2Y 3X7 Canada; 514/288-3555, Fax: 514/288-4199, Co Email: institute@ecworld.org, Web URL: ecworld.org, Focus: Research, education and information on EDI, Ownrshp: Nonprofit, Founded: 1992, Empl: 15, Andre Vallerand, Pres, Sylvie Labreche

Electronic Document Systems Foundation 24238 Hawthorne Blvd, Torrance CA 90505-6505 USA; 310/373-3633, 800/669-7567 Fax: 310/375-4240, Co Email: info@xplor.org, Web URL: xplor.org, Focus: Electronic document systems industry and society, Ownrshp: Nonprofit, Ray Simonson, Chmn

Electronic Form Systems 1555 Valwood Pkwy, #150, Carrollton TX 75006 USA; 214/243-4343, Fax: 214/488-8680, Co Email: @efs.com, Focus: Forms processing systems, Prdts: Electronic Form Software, Ownrshp: Sub. of Vanier, Founded: 1981, Empl: 65, Wendell Wheeler, Pres, Jerry Elmore, Dir Sales, Bruce Fisher, Dir Mktng & Bus Dev, Carol Hohmann, Sr Mktng Specialist, Email: carol_hohmann@efs.com

Electronic Industries Assoc. (EIA), 2500 Wilson Blvd, Arlington VA 22201-3834 USA; 703/907-7500, Fax: 703/907-7501, Co Email: @eia.org, Web URL: eia.org, Focus: Trade organization of computer, communications and electronics manufacturers, Ownrshp: Nonprofit, Founded: 1924, Empl: 1,000, Peter F. McCloskey, Pres, John J. Kelly, VP & Gen Counsel, T. Glyn Finley, VP Mkt Res, Kevin G. Richardson, VP Gov Rel, Mark V. Rosenker, VP Pub Aff

Electronic Messaging Assoc. 1655 N Fort Meyer Dr #850, Arlington VA 22209 USA; 703/524-5550, Fax: 703/524-5558, Web URL: ema.org, Focus: Association for electronic messaging users & vendors, Ownrshp: Nonprofit, Founded: 1983, Empl: 400, Victor Parra, Pres, Mark Rockwell, PR Mgr

Electronic Systems Technology Inc. 415 N Quay St, Kennewick WA 99336-7735 USA; 509/735-9092, Fax: 509/783-5475, Focus: Wireless modem, Prdts: Esteem, Ownrshp: OTC, Stk Sym: ELST, Founded: 1982, Empl: 11, Sales ($M): 1.3, Fiscal End: 12/94; Tom Kirchner, Pres, Robert Southworth, Treas

Electronic Technology Group Inc. (ETG), 10640 Lyndale Ave S, Bloomington MN 55420 USA; 612/948-3100, Fax: 612/948-3106, Focus: Rackmount PC enclosures and systems, Prdts: Rackmaster, Founded: 1992, Empl: 55, Patrick Buehl, Pres, Richard Swedburg, Eng Mgr

Electronics for Imaging Inc. (EFI), 2855 Campus Dr, San Mateo CA 94403 USA; 415/286-8600, Fax: 415/286-8686, Co Email: @efi.com, Focus: Graphics and imaging products, Prdts: Fiery Color Server, Cachet, EfiColor, Ownrshp: OTC, Stk Sym: EFII, Founded: 1989, Empl: 200, Sales ($M): 190.5, Fiscal End: 12/95; Efi Arazi, Chmn, Dan Avida, Pres & CEO, Jeffrey J. Lenches, EVP, Fred Rosenzweig, VP Mfg, G. Michael Maciag, Dir Mktng, Email: maciag@efi.com

Electronics Representatives Assoc. (ERA), 20 E Huron St, Chicago IL 60611 USA; 312/649-1333, Fax: 312/649-9509, Co Email: info@era.org, Web URL: era.org, Focus: Networking for manufacturers to find sales representatives to carry their product lines, Ownrshp: Nonprofit, Founded: 1935, Empl: 2,200, Ray Hall, EVP & CEO

Elek-Tek 7350 N Linder Ave, Skokie IL 60077 USA; 847/677-7660, 800/395-1000 Fax: 847/677-7168, Web URL: elektek.com, Focus: Chain of computer stores, Ownrshp: OTC, Stk Sym: ELEK, Founded: 1979, Empl: 732, Sales ($M): 338.0, Fiscal End: 12/95; Richard L. Rodriguez, Pres & COO, Miguel A. Martinez Jr, VP & CFO, Rory K. Zaks, VP Retail

Elektroson USA 10 Presial Blvd, #125, Bala Cynwyd PA 19004 USA; 610/617-0850, Fax: 610/617-0856, Co Email: @elektroson.com, Focus: Software for recordable CDs, Ownrshp: Sub. Elektroson, Netherlands, Founded: 1986, Henk J. Noorderhaven, Pres, Steve Sullivan, VP Sales, Jiren Parikh, GM, Email: jparikh@elektroson.com

Elgin Interactive Software Inc. 104 Joslyn Dr, Elgin IL 60120 USA; 847/697-9654, Fax: 847/697-9689, Co Email: elgin@mcs.com, Web URL: mcs.net/~elgin, Focus: Multimedia and virtual reality entertainment, Prdts: Virtual Encounter, William Bravos, Pres

Elite Software PO Box 11224, Pittsburgh PA 15238-0224 USA; 800/745-8491 Fax: 412/795-8492, Web URL: eliteinc.com/soft, Focus: Entertainment & business software, Ownrshp: PVT, Founded: 1981, John Waclo, Pres, Email: johnw@eliteinc.com

Elixir Technologies Corp. PO Box 1559, Ojai CA 93024 USA; 805/641-5900, Fax: 805/641-5920, Co Email: elixir@elixir.com, Focus: Desktop publishing software, Ownrshp: PVT, Founded: 1985, Empl: 50, Basit Hamid, Chmn, Email: basit_hamid@notes.elixir.com; Bill McInroy, Pres, Email: bill_mcinroy@notes.elixir.com; Feroz Zaidi, Co-Chmn, Email: feroz-zaidi@notes.elixir.com; Frank McGee, VP Dev, Email: frank_mcgee@notes.elixir.com; Kevin Laracey, VP Mktng, Email: kevin_laracey@notes.elixi.com; Naveed Vardak, Mktng Prog Coord, Email: naveed_vardak@notes.elixi.com

Elo TouchSystems Inc. 105 Randolph Rd, Oak Ridge TN 37830 USA; 615/482-4100, Fax: 615/482-4943, Focus: Touch screen monitors, Prdts: IntelliTouch, AccuTouch, Touchscreens, Ownrshp: Sub. Raychem Corp., Founded: 1971, Empl: 300, Robert R. Roeser, Pres & CEO, John Carlson, VP Mktng, Joseph A. Barresi, VP Sales, Donald B. Armstrong, Dir Bus Dev, Stephen A. DeLateur, VP Tech, Debbie S. Maxie, Marcom Mgr

ELSA Inc. 2041 Mission College Blvd, #165, Santa Clara CA 95054 USA; 408/565-9669, 800/272-3572 Fax: 408/565-9650, Web URL: elsa.com, Focus: Windows graphics accelerators and telecom products, ISDN and video conferencing, Prdts: WINNER 1000 AVI, ElSAmotion, MicroLink ISDN, ELSAvision, Ownrshp:

Sub. ELSA GmbH, Germany, Founded: 1980, Empl: 245, Sales ($M): 80.0, Fiscal End: 12/95; Theo Busch, Pres & CEO, Thomas Neubert, VP & GM, Email: thomasn@elsa-usa.mhs

ELSNER Technologies Company 5020 Mark IV Pkwy, Ft. Worth TX 76106 USA; 817/626-4110, 800/243-2228 Fax: 817/626-5330, Co Email: 75457.1377@compuserve.com, Focus: Remote systems management solutions for mainframe, client/server and LAN environments, Founded: 1994, Edgar Elsner, Pres, Kris McHam, Dir Ops

Eltron International Inc. 41 Moreland Rd, Simi Valley CA 93065-1692 USA; 805/579-1800, 800/344-4003 Fax: 805/579-1808, Co Email: eltron@eltron.com, Focus: Label printers and software, Prdts: TLP Series Printers, Ownrshp: OTC, Stk Sym: ELTN, Founded: 1991, Empl: 300, Sales ($M): 75.0, Fiscal End: 12/95; Donald K. Skinner, Chmn & CEO, Hugh K. Gagnier, Pres & COO, Daniel C. Toomey Jr., VP & CFO, Linda Broderick, Mgr Inv Rel

Embedded Systems Products Inc. 10450 Stancliff Raod, #110, Houston TX 77099-4383 USA; 713/561-9990, Fax: 713/561-9980, Co Email: sales@esphou.com, Focus: Embedded system software, Prdts: RTXC, Ownrshp: PVT, Founded: 1978, Tom Barrett, Pres, Email: atb@esphou.com; Ron Hodge, Sales, Bill Dittmann, Eng, Email: support@esphou.com; Barbara Patterson, Email: barbara@patterson.com

EMC Corp. 171 South St, Hopkinton MA 01748-9103 USA; 508/435-1000, Fax: 508/435-7954, Web URL: emc.com, Focus: Mass storage and peripherals, Ownrshp: NYSE, Stk Sym: EMCS, Founded: 1979, Empl: 2,452, Sales ($M): 1,921.3, Fiscal End: 12/95; Richard J. Egan, Chmn, Michael C. Ruettgers, Pres & CEO, John R. Egan, EVP Sales & Mktng, Harold P. Ano, SVP Mktng, W. Paul Fitzgerald, SVP & CFO

EMD Enterprises 73 E Forrest Ave, #20, Shrewsbury PA 17361 USA; 717/235-4423, 800/898-9363 Fax: 717/227-9746, Co Email: emd@emdent.com, Focus: Computer security and antivirus products, Prdts: EMD Trakker Lite, Ownrshp: PVT

Emerson Electric Co. 8000 W Florissant Ave, PO Box 4100, St Louis MO 63136 USA; 314/553-2000, Fax: 314/553-3527, Focus: Electronic systems and products, Ownrshp: NYSE, Stk Sym: EMR, Founded: 1890, Empl: 73,900, Sales ($M): 10,294.1, Fiscal End: 9/95; Charles F. Knight, Chmn & CEO, Albert E. Suter, Sr Vice Chmn & COO, J.J. Adorjan, Pres, W.J. Galvin, SVP & CFO, S.L. Rieves, VP Info Syst, P.A. Roberts, VP Pub Affairs

EMIS Software Inc. 900 NE Loop 410, #D-214, San Antonio TX 78209-1407 USA; 210/822-8499, Fax: 210/822-8509, Prdts: S3, EMIS, Ownrshp: PVT, Edward P. Stevens, Pres

EmmaSoft Software Co. Inc. PO Box 238, Lansing NY 14882 USA; 607/533-4685, Co Email: 71333.1577@compuserve.com, Web URL: execpc.com/~emmasoft, Focus: Shareware software, Prdts: Catalog-On-A-Disk, EmmaSetup for Windows, Darn! Don't Forget!, Ownrshp: PVT, Founded: 1989, Daniel Veaner, Pres, Karen M. Veaner, VP

Empac International Corp. 47560 Seabridge Dr, Fremont CA 94538 USA; 510/683-8800, Fax: 510/683-8662, Focus: PCs and peripheral boards, Ownrshp: PVT, Founded: 1986, Empl: 50, Sales ($M): 27, Allen Yu, Pres

Empress Software Inc. 6401 Golden Triangle Dr, #220, Greenbelt MD 20770 USA; 301/220-1919, Fax: 301/220-1997, Co Email: @empress.com, Web URL: empress.com, Focus: Database software, Prdts: Empress RDBMS, Empress DBServer, Empress GUIBuilder, Empress 4GL, Ownrshp: PVT, Founded: 1979, Empl: 50, John Kornatowski, Pres, Email: jkornatowski@empress.com; Ivor Ladd, VP Tech, Email: iladd@empress.com; Njai Wong, VP Prod Dev, Email: nwong@empress.com; Jim Sweeney, Mktng Mgr, Email: jsweeney@empress.com; Michele Phair, Mktng Coord, Email: mphair@empress.com

Emulex Corp. 3535 Harbor Blvd, Costa Mesa CA 92626 USA; 714/662-5600, 800/854-7112 Fax: 714/241-0792, Focus: Storage and connectivity products, Ownrshp: OTC, Stk Sym: EMLX,

Founded: 1978, Empl: 298, Sales ($M): 51.3, Fiscal End: 6/96; Paul F. Folino, Pres & CEO, Walter J. McBride, SVP & CFO, Jay R. O'Donald, VP Eng, Michael A. Peitler, VP WW Sales

ENCAD Inc. 6059 Cornerstone Ct W, San Diego CA 92121-3734 USA; 619/452-0882, 800/356-2808 Fax: 619/452-0891, Focus: Inkjet plotters and printers, Ownrshp: OTC, Stk Sym: ENCD, Founded: 1981, Empl: 114, Sales ($M): 65.5, Fiscal End: 12/95; David A. Purcell, Chmn & CEO, Richard A. Plante, Pres & COO, Serge Drobatschewsky, VP Ops, Jiri Modry, VP Mktng & Sales, Carol Giesecke, VP & CFO

Endpoint Marketing Information Systems 20813 Stevens Creek Blvd #250, Cupertino CA 95014-2107 USA; 408/725-4200, 800/725-4255 Co Email: 71641.1376@compuserve.com, Focus: Sales automation software, Prdts: LEADS!, Ownrshp: PVT, Founded: 1986, Empl: 15, Matt Cobb, Chmn, Neal Amsden, Pres

Energizer Power Systems Hwy 441N, PO Box 147114, Gainesville FL 32614-7114 USA; 904/462-3911, Fax: 904/462-4726, Focus: Batteries, Ownrshp: Sub. Eveready, Founded: 1993, George Meffert, EVP, Joe McClanathan, VP & GM, Darrell Musick, VP Mktng & Sales, Ralph A. Millard, Dir Bus Dev, Randy Benz, VP Fin, Alan Bracken

Engineered Software 615 Guilford-Jamestown Rd, PO Box 18344, Greensboro NC 27419-8344 USA; 910/299-4843, Fax: 910/852-2067, Co Email: engsw@aol.com, Focus: Macintosh CAD software, Prdts: PowerDraw, PowerCADD, Ownrshp: PVT, Founded: 1983, Empl: 16, W. L. Stanley Jr., Pres & CEO, Susan Stanley, VP, Mike Martin

Engineering Animation Inc. (EAI), 2625 N Loop Dr, Ames IA 50010-8615 USA; 515/296-9908, 800/324-6777 Fax: 515/296-7025, Web URL: vislab.eai.com, Focus: 3D animation software, Prdts: VisiLab, Ownrshp: PVT, Founded: 1990, Empl: 58, Matthew M. Rizai, Pres & CEO, Martin J. Vanderploeg, EVP, Jeff D. Trom, VP, Michael Jablo, VP SW Sales & Mktng, Lana Rushing

Enteractive Inc. 110 W 40th St, New York NY 10018 USA; 212/221-6559, Fax: 212/730-6045, Focus: Interactive educational software, Ownrshp: PVT, Founded: 1993, Andrew Gyenes, Chmn & CEO, John Ramo, Pres & COO, Ken Gruber, VP & CFO, Margaret Tuttle, VP Mktng & Dist

Enterprise Computer Telephony (ECTF), 303 Vintage Park Dr, Foster City CA 94404 USA; 415/578-6852, Fax: 415/378-6692, Focus: Open forum on interoperability in computer telephony industry, Ownrshp: Nonprofit, Founded: 1995, Lisa Winkler, Exec Dir, Tom Zenisek, Pres & Chmn

Enterprise Corporation International (ECI), 2113 Landings Dr, Mountain View CA 94043 USA; 415/691-4466, 800/842-5788 Fax: 415/691-4460, Web URL: eciusa.com, Focus: Multimedia quality assurance software and technical support service, Prdts: eCi Inspector Series, Founded: 1988

Enterprise Integration Technologies (EIT), 800 El Camino Real, Menlo Park CA 94025 USA; 415/617-8000, Fax: 415/617-8019, Co Email: info@eit.com, Web URL: eit.com, Focus: Internet software, consulting and services, Ownrshp: PVT, Empl: 35, Steven L. Harari, Pres

Enterprise Solutions Ltd. 2900 Townsgate Rd, #210, Westlake Village CA 91361-3001 USA; 805/449-4181, Fax: 805/449-4186, Focus: E-mail and messaging software, Ownrshp: PVT, Founded: 1991, Empl: 100, Karl Klessig, Pres & CEO, Richard Shirley, SVP, Jeff Drake, Sales Dir, Brenda Barnetson, Marcom Mgr

Enterprising Service Solutions Co. (ESSC), 1 Solutions Way, Waynesboro VA 22980-1999 USA; 888/367-3772 Fax: 540/949-1500, Focus: Network services, network integration & multivendor services

Entex Information Services 6 Int'l. Dr, Rye Brook NY 10573 USA; 914/935-3600, Web URL: entex-is.com, Focus: Computer reseller and systems integrator, Ownrshp: PVT, Founded: 1982, Sales ($M): 1,785, Fiscal End: 12/95; John McKenna, Pres & CEO, Fred Rubin, VP, Robert Auray, VP & CFO, John Lyons, VP Mktng

Prog

Envelope Manager Software 247 High St, Palo Alto CA 94301-1041 USA; 800/576-3279 Fax: 415/321-0356, Focus: Mail management software, Prdts: Envelope Manager Software, Dazzle, Ownrshp: Sub. PSI Assoc., Founded: 1989, Empl: 15, Sales ($M): 1.3, Harry T. Whitehouse, Pres, Lee Kennedy, Dir Sales & Mktng, Scott Montgomery, VP Prod Dev

Environmental Systems Research Institute Inc. (ESRI), 380 New York St, Redlands CA 92373-8100 USA; 909/793-2853, 800/447-9778 Fax: 909/793-5953, Co Email: info@esri.com, Web URL: esri.com, Focus: Mapping and GIS software, Prdts: ARC/Info, ArcCAD, ArcView, BusinessMAP, Ownrshp: PVT, Founded: 1969, Empl: 1,400, Jack Dangermond, Pres, Laura Dangermond, VP

Envisions Solutions Technology Inc. 822 Mahler Rd, Burlingame CA 94010 USA; 800/365-7226 Fax: 415/692-9064, Co Email: @envisions.com, Focus: CAD/CAM software and scanner products, Prdts: 47400 Seabridge, Ownrshp: PVT, Founded: 1989, Empl: 27, Sales ($M): 57, Jerry Gradbois, Dir Ops, Hugh Bethell, Mktng Mgr, Email: hugh-bethell@envisions.com

Epic Data Inc. 7280 River Rd, Richmond BC V6X 1X5 Canada; 604/273-9146, Fax: 604/273-1830, Focus: Designs, manufacturers, integrates and supports automated data collection systems, Founded: 1975, Empl: 200

Epoch Inc. 171 South St, Hopkinton MA 01748-2208 USA; 508/435-1000, Focus: LAN storage management systems, Prdts: Epoch-1, Ownrshp: Sub. EMC Corp., Founded: 1986, Empl: 100, Kenneth Holberger, Chmn, Chris Robert, Pres & CEO, Daniel J. Cronin, VP Mktng

Epson America Inc. 20770 Madrona Ave, Torrance CA 90509-2842 USA; 310/782-0770, 800/289-3776 Fax: 310/782-5220, Web URL: epson.com, Focus: Printers, scanners, PCMCIA cards and PCs, Ownrshp: Sub. Seiko Epson, Japan, Founded: 1975, Empl: 700, Norio Niwa, Pres & CEO, John Lang, COO, Shosuke Kawai, EVP, Ron Prather, VP Sales & Mktng, Akihiko Sakai, VP, Jan Marciano, Mgr PR

Equilibrium 475 Gate Five Rd, #225, Sausalito CA 94965 USA; 415/332-4343, Fax: 415/332-4433, Co Email: first_last@equil.com, Web URL: equilibrium.com, Focus: Graphics software, Prdts: DeBabelizer, Ownrshp: PVT, Founded: 1989, Sean B. Barger, Chmn, Bob Eige, VP Ops, Michael Ross, Dir Sales, Wanda Meloni

Equinox Systems Inc. One Equinox Way, Sunrise FL 33351-6709 USA; 305/746-9000, 800/275-3500 Fax: 305/746-9101, Co Email: @equinox.com, Focus: I/O communications products, Ownrshp: OTC, Stk Sym: EQNX, Founded: 1983, Empl: 76, Sales ($M): 20.2, Fiscal End: 12/95; William A. Dambrackas, Pres & CEO, Robert F. Gintz, VP Dev, Mark Kacer, VP & CFO, Mark L. Cole, VP, David Forsch, Email: davidf@equinox.com

Ergotron Inc. 1181 Trapp Rd, Eagan MN 55121 USA; 612/681-7600, Focus: Computer suspension and ergonomic furniture, Ownrshp: PVT, Founded: 1980, Empl: 35, Sales ($M): 4.2

Ericsson Stockholm S-12625 Sweden; 468-719-0000, Fax: 468-719-1976, Web URL: ericsson.com, Focus: Telecom products and services, Ownrshp: FO, Empl: 76,000, Sales ($M): 13,836, Fiscal End: 12/95; Lars Ramquist, Pres & CEO, Carl W. Ros, EVP & CFO, Lennart Grabe, SVP Bus Dev, Bo Landin, SVP Mktng, Hakon Jansson, SVP Tech, Nils I. Lundin, SVP Corp Rel

Ericsson Inc. 45C Commerce Way, Totowa NJ 07512-1154 USA; 201/890-3600, Fax: 201/256-8768, Focus: Communications products, Ownrshp: Sub. Ericson & GE, Founded: 1989, Henrik Holgberg, VP & GM, Barbara Pistilli, Dir Marcom, Email: bpistilli@wynd.net

Ernst & Young 787 Seventh Ave, New York NY 10019 USA; 212/773-3000, Fax: 212/489-1838, Web URL: ey.com, Focus: Systems integration and consulting, Ownrshp: PVT, Founded: 1989, Empl: 64,000, Sales ($M): 6,870, Fiscal End: 12/95; Ray J. Groves,

CEO, Howard Bailen

Escalade 2475 Augustine Dr, Santa Clara CA 95054-3002 USA; 408/654-1600, Fax: 408/654-1616, Web URL: edac.org/escalade.com, Focus: Design software, Prdts: DesignBook, Ownrshp: PVT, Founded: 1993, Empl: 35, Fiscal End: 12/95; Min-Yu Hsueh, Chmn, K. Larry Lai, Pres, Mark Miller, VP Sales & Mktng, Steve Carlson, VP Design Methodology, Sabrina Merrill, Dir Marcom, Email: sabrinam@escalade.com

ESS Technology Inc. 46107 Landing Pkwy, Fremont CA 94538 USA; 510/226-1088, Fax: 510/226-1098, Co Email: @esstech.com, Focus: Audio compression products, Ownrshp: OTC, Stk Sym: ESST, Founded: 1984, Empl: 60, Sales ($M): 105.7, Fiscal End: 12/95; Fred S.L. Chan, Pres & CEO, Albert Mak, VP Mktng, Nicholas Aretakis, VP Sales, Bill Windsor, Strategic Mktng Mgr, Email: bill.windsor@esstech.com

Essex Interactive Media (ESX), 560 Sylvan Ave, Englewood Cliffs NJ 07632 USA; 201/894-8700, Fax: 201/894-1479, Focus: Brings budget and midline products to the interactive media market, Ownrshp: PVT, Founded: 1994, Richard Greener, Mngng Partner, Sam Goff, Mngng Partner

Etak Inc. 1430 O'Brien Dr, Menlo Park CA 94025 USA; 415/328-3825, Fax: 415/328-3148, Focus: Map software, Prdts: Etamap, Ownrshp: Sub. News Corp. America, Founded: 1983, Empl: 270, George Bremser Jr., Chmn, John E. Rehfeld, Pres & CEO, Howard Koch, VP Mktng, Bruce Harders, VP Sales

ETC Computer Inc. 2917 Bayview Dr, Fremont CA 94538-6520 USA; 510/226-6250, Fax: 510/226-6252, Focus: PC monitors, Ownrshp: Sub. ETC Group, Taiwan, Founded: 1991, Kent Huang, Pres, Frank Yang, Dir Sales, April Huang, Fin Mgr, Tim Tseng, Tech Mgr

Eurom Flashware Inc. 4655 Old Ironsides Dr, #290, Santa Clara CA 95054-1808 USA; Co Email: eurom@ix.netcom.com, Focus: Solid state mass storage, Prdts: Disk on Chip, Voice Chip, Ownrshp: Sub. Eurom, Israel, Founded: 1992, Empl: 20, Richard Iorillo, Pres, David Dietcher, VP Eng

Evans & Sutherland Computer Corp. 600 Komas Dr, PO Box 58700, Salt Lake City UT 84108 USA; 801/588-1000, Fax: 801/588-4500, Web URL: es.com, Focus: Graphics computers and software, Ownrshp: OTC, Stk Sym: ESCC, Founded: 1968, Empl: 754, Sales ($M): 113.2, Fiscal End: 12/95; Stewart Carrell, Chmn, James R. Oyler, Pres & CEO, Email: joyler@es.com; Gary E. Meredith, SVP, Email: gmeredith@es.com; John T. Lemley, VP & CFO, Email: jlemley@es.com; Robert A. Schumacker, Pres Simulation Div, Jayne Anderson, PR, Email: jlanderson@es.com

Eventus Software 220 Sansome St, 3rd Fl., San Francisco CA 94104 USA; 415/477-3700, 800/871-4871 Fax: 415/477-3737, Focus: Oracle database tool developer, Prdts: ADHAWK, Ownrshp: PVT, Mike Burkland, Pres, Charman Weidenbach, Int'l Sales Mgr, Email: charmanw@miti.com

Everex Systems Inc. 5020 Brandin Ct, Fremont CA 94538 USA; 510/498-1111, Fax: 510/683-2186, Focus: PCs, peripherals & network servers, Prdts: Step, Tempo, Ownrshp: Sub. FPG, Taiwan, Founded: 1983, Peter Ow, EVP, Robert Morrison, Email: rmorrisn@ix.netcom.com

Evergreen International Technology Inc. 930 W 1st St, #102, N Vancouver BC V7P 3N4 Canada; 604/986-6121, 800/667-4340 Fax: 604/980-7121, Co Email: 73762.2745@compuserve.com, Focus: Concurrency technology software, Prdts: JOT-IT!, Ownrshp: VSE, Stk Sym: EGN, Founded: 1984, Anthony Bird, VP Sales

Evergreen Systems Inc. 120 Landings Ct, Novato CA 94945 USA; 415/897-8888, Fax: 415/897-6158, Focus: Remote LAN access products, Ownrshp: PVT, James J. Mulholland, VP Sales & Mktng, Vince Conroy, VP Prod Dev

Evergreen Technologies Inc. 915 NW 8th St, Corvallis OR 97330-6211 USA; 541/757-0934, 800/667-4340 Fax: 541/757-7350, Co Email: @evertech.com, Web URL: evertech.com, Focus:

PC processor upgrades, Ownrshp: Sub Evergreen, Canada, Founded: 1989, Empl: 10, Kenneth Magee, Pres, Stan Harbaugh, VP Ops, Steven Johnson, VP Mktng, Email: stevenj@evertech.com; Jeff Weger, MIS Mgr

EveryWare Development Corp. 7145 W Credit Ave, Bldg 1, Mississauga Ontario L5N 6J7 Canada; 905/819-1173, 888/819-2500 Fax: 905/819-1172, Co Email: info@everyware.com, Web URL: everyware.com, Focus: Mac SQL database and cross platform internet related software, Prdts: ButlerSQL, TANGO, Bolero, Enterprise Document Management, Ownrshp: PVT, Dan McKenzie, Pres & CEO, Henry J. Lach, VP Mktng, Email: hlach@everyware.com; Stephen Whiteside, Mgr Enterprise Solutions, Jeff Hendry, Mktng Assoc, Email: jhendry@everyware.com

Ex Machina Inc. 11 E 26th St, Floor 16R, New York NY 10010-1402 USA; 212/843-0000, Co Email: info@exmachina.com, Web URL: exmachina.com, Focus: Messaging software, Prdts: Notify, Ownrshp: PVT, David S. Rose, Chmn & CEO, John Payne, Pres

Exabyte Corp. 1685 38th St, Boulder CO 80301 USA; 303/442-4333, 800/392-2983 Fax: 303/447-7170, Focus: Data storage products, Ownrshp: OTC, Stk Sym: EXBT, Founded: 1985, Empl: 880, Sales ($M): 374.1, Fiscal End: 12/95; Peter D. Behrendt, Chmn, Pres & CEO, Dave L. Riegel, EVP & COO, Mark W. Canright, VP Sales & Mktng, William L. Marriner, EVP & CFO, Susan L. Merriman, Mgr PR

Excalibur Technologies Corp. 1959 Palomar Oaks Way, #100, Carlsbad CA 92009 USA; 619/438-7900, 800/788-7758 Fax: 619/438-7979, Co Email: @excalib.com, Web URL: excalib.com, Focus: Image management software, Ownrshp: OTC, Stk Sym: EXCA, Founded: 1980, Empl: 125, Sales ($M): 18, Pat Condo, Pres & CEO, Edwin Addison, EVP, Jim Bechanan, CFO, Darrell Atkin, Dir Marcom

Excel Software PO Box 1414, Marshalltown IA 50158 USA; 515/752-5359, Fax: 515/752-2435, Co Email: casetools@aol.com, Focus: CASE tools, Prdts: MacAnalyst, MacDesigner, Ownrshp: PVT, Harold Halbleib

ExcellNet Communications 6754 Daryn Dr, W Hills CA 91307 USA; 818/340-6430, Fax: 818/343-1436, Focus: Ethernet network solution products, Prdts: ExcellentConnection Adapters, Ownrshp: PVT, Abe Queller, Prod Mgr

Executive Software Int'l. 701 N Brand Blvd, 6th Floor, Glendale CA 91203-1242 USA; 818/547-2050, 800/829-4357 Fax: 818/545-9241, Co Email: infodesk@executive.com, Web URL: execsoft.com, Focus: VAX/VMS and Windows NT system software, Prdts: Diskeeper, Frag Guard, Ownrshp: PVT, Founded: 1981, Empl: 125, Sales ($M): 15.2, Craig Jensen, Chmn & CEO, Email: cjensen@executive.com; Pat Boyers, Exec Dir, Email: pboyers@executive.com; Peter Mead, VP Mktng, Email: pmead@executive.com; Dawn Chaban, VP Field Svcs, Email: dchaban@executive.com

Executive Technologies Inc. 2120 16th Ave S, Birmingham AL 35205 USA; 205/933-5494, Focus: Document imaging software, Prdts: SearchExpress, Ownrshp: PVT, Founded: 1984

Executone Information Systems Inc. 478 Wheelers Farm Rd, Milford CT 06460 USA; 203/876-7600, Focus: Voice and data communications equipment, Ownrshp: OTC, Stk Sym: XTON, Founded: 1935, Empl: 2,300, Sales ($M): 292.0, Fiscal End: 12/94; Alan Kessman, Chmn, Pres & CEO, Michael W. Yacenda, EVP, Anthony R. Guarascio, VP & CFO, Andrew Kontomerkos, SVP, John T. O'Kane, VP MIS

Exide Electronics Group 8521 Six Forks Rd, Raleigh NC 27615 USA; 919/872-3020, 800/554-3448 Fax: 919/870-3450, Focus: Power protection systems, Ownrshp: OTC, Stk Sym: XUPS, Founded: 1962, Empl: 1,400, Sales ($M): 326.6, Fiscal End: 9/94; James A. Risher, Pres & CEO, Mark A. Ascolese, VP & GM Svcs, Marty R. Kittrell, VP & CFO, Warren J. Johnson, VP Corp Dev, William J. Raddi, SVP & CTO, Karin K. Cram, Corp Com Spec

Exite Inc. 1091 N Shoreline Blvd, Mountain View CA 94043 USA;

415/934-3611, Fax: 415/943-1299, Web URL: architext.com, Focus: Internet navigation software, Prdts: Excite, Ownrshp: Non-Profit, Founded: 1993, Empl: 60, George Bell, CEO

Exodus Communications Inc. 948 Benencia Ave, Sunnyvale CA 94086 USA; 408/522-8450, 800/263-8872 Fax: 408/736-6843, Co Email: sales@exodus.com, Focus: Internet access provider, Ownrshp: PVT, Founded: 1994, Chandra Sekhar, Pres & CEO, Fred Sibayan, VP Sales & Mktng, B.V. Jagadeesh, VP Eng, Kathryn Weakley

Experience In Software Inc. 2000 Hearst Ave, #202, Berkeley CA 94709-2176 USA; 510/644-0694, 800/678-7008 Fax: 510/644-3823, Focus: Decision support software, Prdts: Idea Generator, Project KickStart, Art of Negotiating, Ownrshp: PVT, Founded: 1983, Empl: 5, Roy A. Nierenberg, Pres

Expert Choice Software 4612 Trail W, Austin TX 78735 USA; 512/422-1622, Fax: 512/892-5453, Focus: Productivity software, Prdts: Executive Desk, Letter Writer, Ownrshp: PVT, Founded: 1991, Empl: 3, Harold Gregg, Pres, Email: 70034.227@compuserve.com

Expert Graphics Inc. 1908 Cliff Valley Way, #2010, Atlanta GA 30329 USA; 404/320-0800, Fax: 404/315-7645, Web URL: expertg.com, Focus: Graphics boards and document management software, Prdts: RASTEREX, Ownrshp: PVT, Founded: 1989, Empl: 8, Sales ($M): 1, Fiscal End: 6/92; Darrell Knight, Pres, Email: darrell@expertg.com; Cyndee Nielsen, VP Mktng, Email: cyndee@expertg.com

Expert Software Inc. 800 Douglas Rd, 7th Floor, Coral Gables FL 33134-3128 USA; 305/567-9990, 800/759-2562 Fax: 305/443-0786, Web URL: icanect.net/exp, Focus: Personal, business productivity and hobbyist software, Prdts: Home Design 3D, Landscape Design 3D, Astronomer, Greeting Card Maker, Ownrshp: OTC, Stk Sym: XPRT, Founded: 1992, Empl: 84, Sales ($M): 27.6, Fiscal End: 12/95; Kenneth Currier, CEO, Sue Currier, Pres, Tim Leary, VP Sales, Ken Tarolla, VP Dev, Joshua Schainbaum, Comm Mgr

ExperVision Inc. 930 Thompson Place, Sunnyvale CA 94086-4517 USA; 408/523-0900, 800/732-3897 Fax: 408/523-0909, Web URL: expervision.com, Focus: OCR software, Prdts: TypeReader, Ownrshp: PVT, Founded: 1987, Empl: 16, Steve Hui, Pres & CEO, Qing Ren Wang, CTO, Dave Summers, CFO, Clarence Lam, Prod Mgr, Shuh Hai Wong, Network Mgr, Email: shuhhai@pebble.expervision.com; Jorge Borges, Mktng Assoc, Email: marketing@expervision.com

Express Systems Inc. 2101 4th Ave, #303, Seattle WA 98121-2314 USA; 206/728-8300, Fax: 206/728-8301, Co Email: info@express-systems.com, Web URL: express-systems.com, Focus: Network license management software, Prdts: Express Metce, Enterprise Optimization Module, Windows Express, Ownrshp: PVT, Founded: 1986, Empl: 24, Brian Conte, CEO, Email: brian@express-systems.com; Paul Davis, Dir Sales & Mktng, Email: paul@express-systems.com; Arthel Burkland, Dir Ops, Pam Vaughn, Dir Fin & Mfg, Email: pam@express-systems.com; Patti Burke, Marcom Consultant, Email: patti@express-systems.com

EXSYS Inc. 1720 Louisiana Blvd #312, Albuquerque NM 87110-7019 USA; 505/256-8356, Fax: 505/256-8359, Co Email: tnexsys@pop.nm.org, Web URL: nm.org/~exsys, Focus: Expert system development software, Ownrshp: PVT, Founded: 1984, Empl: 12, Sales ($M): 1.1, Dustin Huntington, Pres, Michael Eskew, Sales Mgr, Nancy Clark, Mktng Dir

Extech Instruments Corp. 335 Bear Hill Rd, Waltham MA 02154 USA; 617/890-7440, Fax: 617/890-7864, Focus: Portable printers, Ownrshp: PVT, Jerry Blakeley, Pres

Extend Inc. 4847 Hopyard Rd, #3218, Pleasanton CA 94588 USA; 510/484-0395, 800/943-8883 Fax: 510/484-0153, Co Email: 74024.3574@compuserve.com, Focus: Windows 95 utilities, Prdts: WinZones, Ownrshp: PVT, Founded: 1993, Lorraine Ling, Pres & CEO, Paul Ling, Dir Bus Dev

Extended Systems 5777 N Meeker Ave, Boise ID 83704 USA; 800/235-7576 Fax: 208/377-1906, Focus: Printer networking and sharing devices, Ownrshp: PVT, Founded: 1984, Raymond A. Smelek, Pres & CEO, Gary Atkins, Chmn, Fred Roehm, Mktng Mgr, Holmes Lundt

Extensis Corp. 55 SW Yamhill St, 4th Floor, Portland OR 97204 USA; 503/274-2020, Fax: 503/274-0530, Co Email: info@extensis.com, Focus: Utility software, Ownrshp: PVT, Founded: 1993, Greg Barnes, Pres, John Chaffee, Dir Mktng, Craig Keudell, Dir Sales

Extron Electronics 1230 S Lewis St, Anaheim CA 92805-6428 USA; 714/491-1500, 800/633-9876 Co Email: @extron.com, Web URL: extron.com, Focus: Large screen display products, Prdts: Super Emotia, Inertia, Ownrshp: PVT, Founded: 1983, Andrew Edwards, Pres, Gary Kayye, VP Sales, Jay Hitz, Apps Eng, Ivan Perez, Marcom Mgr

EZ Image Inc. PO Box 73284, Puyallup WA 98373 USA; 206/840-2004, 800/677-8333 Fax: 206/840-0877, Web URL: ezimage@aa.net, Focus: Data warehousing software, Prdts: EZ Archive, EZ Recall, Ownrshp: PVT, Founded: 1992, Craig Goodwill, CEO, John Hall, VP, Craig Goodwin

F3 Software Corp. 129 Middlesex Turnpike, Burlington MA 01803 USA; 617/270-0001, Fax: 617-270-0007, Co Email: @f3forms.com, Web URL: f3forms.com, Focus: Intelligent electronic forms technology, Prdts: F3 Forms, Ownrshp: PVT, Geoffrey D. Cronin, Pres & CEO, Miles R. Greenberg, VP & CFO, William P. McHale, VP Sales & Mktng, David Grabel, VP Prod Dev, Stephanie Fox, Mktng Mgr, Email: sfox@f3forms.com

Factura Kiosks Inc. 882 Linden Ave, Rochester NY 14625 USA; 716/264-9600, Fax: 716/264-9575, Focus: Interactive kiosks, Ownrshp: Sub MicroTouch, Founded: 1986, Gregory Swistak, Pres, William Graham, Dir Ops, Paul Swistak, Dir Sales & Mktng, Michael Thayer, Dir Eng, Donald Plant, Controller

Fairstone Technologies Corp. 229 Laurel Rd, E Northport NY 11731 USA; 516/261-0023, Fax: 516/261-0108, Focus: UPS, Ownrshp: Sub Fairstone, Taiwan, Founded: 1992, Patrick Lin, Pres, Dan Rothman, Dir Sales & Mktng

Fakespace Inc. 4085 Campbell Ave, Menlo Park CA 94025 USA; 415/688-1940, Fax: 415/688-1949, Co Email: fakespce@well.com, Web URL: fakespace.com, Focus: Stereoscopic displays, Ownrshp: PVT, Founded: 1989, Empl: 20, Mark Bolas, Pres, Email: bolas@well.comm; Ian E. McDowall, VP, Eric R. Lorimer, VP & CFO, David M. Eggleston, VP

Falco Data Products 1176 Aster Ave #H, Sunnyvale CA 94086-6803 USA; 408/745-7123, Fax: 408/745-7860, Focus: Terminals and terminal repair, Prdts: Falco Terminals, Ownrshp: PVT, Founded: 1979, Empl: 100, Joseph D'Alessandro, Pres & CEO, Chris Perry, Dir Mktng

Falcon Systems Inc. 1417 N Market Blvd, Sacramento CA 95834-1936 USA; 916/928-9255, Fax: 916/928-9355, Web URL: falcons.com, Focus: Workstation peripherals, Prdts: Falcon RAID, FalconServer, Ownrshp: PVT, Founded: 1986, Empl: 50, Sales ($M): 30, Craig Caudill, Pres, Email: craig@falcons.com; Jim Kangas, Ops Mgr, Email: kangas@falcons.com; Jenna Lim, Nat'l. Sales Mgr, Email: jenna@falcons.com; Vicki Vance, Dir Mktng, Email: vicki@falcons.com; Patti Thomas, CFO, Email: patti@falcons.com

Farallon Computing Inc. 2470 Mariner Square Loop, Alameda CA 94501-1010 USA; 510/814-5100, Fax: 510/814-5020, Co Email: info@farallon.com, Web URL: farallon.com, Focus: Macintosh and PC network and internet products, Prdts: Timbuktu, EtherWave, Netopia, Ownrshp: PVT, Founded: 1986, Empl: 230, Reese Jones, Chmn, Alan B. Lefkof, Pres & CEO, Richard Maslana, VP Ops, Steve Solomon, VP SW Prod, Jim Clark, CFO, Amal Abed, PR Mgr, Email: amal@farallon.com

Fargo Electronics Inc. 7901 Flying Cloud Dr, Eden Prairie MN 55344-9606 USA; 612/941-9470, 800/327-4694 Fax: 612/941-7836, Co Email: webmaster@fargo.com, Web URL: fargo.com,

Focus: Color page printers and ID card printers, Ownrshp: PVT, Founded: 1978, Mark D. Strobel, VP Sales & Mktng, Harley Jergensen, VP

FarPoint Communications 104 E Ave K-4, #F, Lancaster CA 93535 USA; 805/726-4420, Fax: 805/726-4438, Web URL: fapo.com, Focus: Enhanced parallel port products, IEEE 1284 ports and cables, Prdts: F/Port, F/Port Plus, 1284 Port, All/IO, F/Port IDE, Express Port, Ownrshp: PVT, Founded: 1992, Larry A. Stein, Pres

Fast Electronic U.S. Inc. 393 Vintage Park Dr, Foster City CA 94404 USA; 415/295-3500, Fax: 415/345-3447, Co Email: @fastusa.com, Web URL: fast-multimedia.com, Focus: Multimedia and desktop video, Prdts: AV Master, Ownrshp: Sub. Fast, Germany, Founded: 1985, Empl: 260, Sales ($M): 50, William P. Mountanos, Pres & CEO, Bob Hatton, PR Mgr, Email: bob_hatton@fastusa.com

FastComm Communications Corp. 45472 Holiday Dr, Sterling VA 20166 USA; 703/318-7750, Fax: 703/787-4625, Focus: Data compression products, Ownrshp: OTC, Stk Sym: FSCX, Empl: 57, Sales ($M): 10.0, Fiscal End: 4/96; Peter C. Madsen, Pres & CEO, Robert N. Dennis, Chmn, Robert C. Abbott, VP Eng, William Flanigan, VP Mktng, Mark H. Rafferty, VP & CFO

Faulkner Information Services 114 Cooper Ctr, 7905 Browning Rd, Pennsauken NJ 08109-4319 USA; 609/662-2070, 800/843-0460 Fax: 609/662-3380, Web URL: faulkner.com, Focus: Information services on computer and communications products, Ownrshp: PVT, Founded: 1985, Empl: 90, Martin Murphy, Pres, Barbara Forkel, VP Sales & Mktng

FaxBack Inc. 1100 NW Compton Dr, 2nd Floor, Beaverton OR 97006 USA; 503/690-6357, 800/873-8753 Fax: 503/690-6377, Co Email: @faxback.com, Focus: Fax-on-demand products, Ownrshp: PVT, Founded: 1990, Art King, Pres, Ron Ares, Marcom Mgr, Email: rares@faxback.com

Faximum Software Inc. 1497 Marine Dr, #300, W Vancouver BC V7T 1B8 Canada; 604/925-3600, Fax: 604/926-8182, Web URL: faximum.com, Focus: Fax software, Ownrshp: PVT, George Pajari, Pres, Carolanne Reynolds, VP

FDP Corp. 2140 S Dixie Hwy, Miami FL 33133 USA; 305/858-8200, Focus: Software for life insurance and employee benefit industries, Ownrshp: OTC, Stk Sym: FDPC, Founded: 1968, Empl: 237, Sales ($M): 19.4, Fiscal End: 11/95; Michael C. Goldberg, Pres & CEO, Douglas Kennedy, EVP, Kathy Muro, VP, Ed Pick, VP, Beverly Price, VP

Federal Filings Inc. 601 Pennsylvania Ave NW, #700, Washington DC 20004-2601 USA; 202/393-2098, Fax: 202/393-5439, Focus: News and financial information management software, Prdts: NewsManager, Ownrshp: Sub. Dow Jones

Feith Systems & Software Inc. 425 Maryland Dr, Ft. Washington PA 19034 USA; 215/646-8000, Fax: 215/540-5495, Co Email: info@feith.com, Web URL: feith.com, Focus: Electronic document management software, Ownrshp: PVT, Founded: 1979, Empl: 49, Sales ($M): 12, Donald Feith, Pres & CEO, Email: don@feith.com, Len Herman, VP West Reg, Email: len@feith.com; Robert Spitz, VP Ops, Cary Tye, VP, John Wehle, VP Eng, Dushianthi Edrisingh, PR Mgr, Email: dushy@feith.com

Fellowes Manufacturing Co. 1789 Norwood Ave, Itasca IL 60143-1095 USA; 708/893-1600, 800/945-4545 Fax: 708/893-1648, Focus: Computer accessory products, Ownrshp: PVT, Founded: 1917, Empl: 1,100, Sales ($M): 200, John E. Fellowes, Chmn & CEO, Jim Fellowes, Pres & COO, Peter Fellowes, EVP, Park Owens, VP Mktng, Jill Schmidt, SVP

Fiber & Wireless Inc. 370 Amapola Ave, #100, Torrance CA 90501 USA; 310/787-7097, Fax: 310/787-7099, Co Email: fiberwire@aol.com, Focus: Digital video transmission software, Prdts: Mediafone, Fonewatch, Ownrshp: PVT, Founded: 1991, Chris P. Cladis, CEO & GM, Raymond Felton, Dir Sales & Mktng, Leslie J. Haigh, Dir Fin, Anthony M. Harvey, Dir Strat Plng

Fibre Channel Assoc. (FCA), 950 Westbank Dr, #207, Austin TX 78746 USA; 512/328-8422, Fax: 512/328-8423, Co Email: fca@fibrechannel.com, Web URL: fibrechannel.com, Focus: Promotion of Fibre Channel technology, Ownrshp: Nonprofit, Founded: 1993, Brenda Chritiensen, Chair

Fibre Channel Loop Community (FCLC), PO Box 2161, Saratoga CA 95070 USA; 408/867-6630, Web URL: tachyon.rose.hp.com/fclc, Focus: Promote Fibre Channel-Arbitrated Loop as serial interface standard, Ownrshp: Nonprofit, Founded: 1995, Empl: 40

Fibronics International Inc. 16 Esquire Rd, N Billerica MA 01862-2590 USA; 508/671-9440, Fax: 508/667-7262, Co Email: @fibusa.com, Focus: Networking products, Prdts: GigaHub, InterView NMS, Ownrshp: OTC, Stk Sym: FBRX, Empl: 400, Sales ($M): 47.6, Fiscal End: 12/93; Joe Parini, Pres, Email: joeparine@fibusa.com; Ed Flannery, VP & GM, Email: edflannery@fibusa.com; Lynne Spugnardi, Mktng Mgr, Email: lspugnar@fibusa.com

Fidelity International Technologies (FIT), 215 Campus Plaza, Edison NJ 08837-3939 USA; 908/417-2230, Fax: 908/417-5994, Focus: Portable mass storage products, Prdts: Handie Disk, Ownrshp: PVT, Founded: 1992, Empl: 16, Don Chu, VP

FieldWorks Inc. 9961 Valley View Rd, Eden Prairie MN 55344 USA; 612/947-0856, 888/343-5396 Fax: 612/947-0859, Focus: Ruggedized laptop and notebook computer for field professionals, Gary Beeman, Pres, Vincent Dipas, Comm Mgr

FileNet Corp. 3565 Harbor Blvd, Costa Mesa CA 92626-1420 USA; 714/966-3400, 800/345-3638 Co Email: @filenet.com, Web URL: filenet.com, Focus: C/S work management and document-imaging software, Ownrshp: OTC, Stk Sym: FILE, Founded: 1982, Empl: 1,126, Sales ($M): 215.5, Fiscal End: 12/95; Theodore J. Smith, Chmn, Pres & CEO, Fred H. Selby, SVP Sales, Jordan M. Libit, VP Mktng, William J. Kreidler, VP Ops, Mark S. St Clare, SVP & CFO, Email: mstclare@filenet.com; Robin Tanchum, Dir Corp Com, Email: rtanchum@filenet.com

Finsiel Spa Via Isonso 21/B, Rome I-00198 Italy; 39-6-84311, Focus: Software and services, Ownrshp: FO, Empl: 5,400, Sales ($M): 1,103, Fiscal End: 12/95

Firefly Software Corp. PO Box 782, Jericho NY 11753 USA; 516/935-7060, Fax: 516/932-7905, Co Email: 73354.2672@compuserve.com, Focus: Screen saver software, Prdts: PhotoGenix, Ownrshp: PVT, Paula Rosenthal, VP, Howard Rosenthal

Firefox Inc. 2841 Junction Ave, #103, San Jose CA 95134-1921 USA; 408/321-8344, 800/230-6090 Fax: 408/321-8311, Focus: Communications servers, Prdts: NOV*IX, Ownrshp: Sub. Firefox, UK, Founded: 1989, Frank M. Richardson, Pres & CEO, Victor Woodward, VP Ops, Victor Woodward

FirePower Systems Inc. 190 Independence Dr, Menlo Park CA 94025 USA; 415/462-3000, Fax: 415/462-3051, Co Email: @firepower.com, Focus: PowerPC computers, Ownrshp: PVT, Founded: 1993, Empl: 85, Hideyo Kondo, CEO, Jon Rubinstein, COO, Glen Miranker, VP HW Eng, Keiichi Uno, VP Bus Dev, Phil Schiller

First Byte 19840 Pioneer Ave, Torrance CA 90503-1660 USA; 310/793-0610, Fax: 310/793-0611, Co Email: info@first-byte.davd.com, Web URL: firstbyte.davd.com, Focus: Speech synthesis software, Prdts: ProVoice, Monologue, Ownrshp: Sub. Davidson & Assoc., Founded: 1981, Empl: 11, Ken Kucera, Pres, Linda Duttenhaver, Dir Corp Com, Email: duttenhaver@davd.com

First Data Corp. 401 Hackensack Ave, Hackensack NJ 07601 USA; 201/525-4700, Fax: 201/342-0402, Focus: Computer services, Ownrshp: NYSE, Stk Sym: FDC, Empl: 36,000, Sales ($M): 4,186.2, Fiscal End: 12/95; Henry C. Duques, Chmn & CEO, Lee Adrean, EVP & CFO, Robert J. Levenson, EVP, Edward C. Nafus, EVP

First Financial Management Corp. (FFMC), 5660 New Northside Dr, #1400, Atlanta GA 30328 USA; 770/857-0001, 800/735-3362 Focus: Computer services to financial industry, Ownrshp:

NYSE, Stk Sym: FFM, Founded: 1971, Empl: 15,000, Sales ($M): 2,207.5, Fiscal End: 12/94; Patrick H. Thomas, Chmn, Pres & CEO, Richard D. Jackson, Vice Chmn & COO, Robert J. Amman, Vice Chmn & COO, Stephen D. Kane, Vice Chmn & CAO, M. Tarlton Pittard, Vice Chmn & CFO, Donald Y. Sharp, SVP Corp Com

First Floor Inc. 444 Castro St, #200, Mountain View CA 94041 USA; 415/968-1101, Fax: 415/968-1193, Co Email: @firstfloor.com, Focus: Workgroup information management software, Ownrshp: PVT, Founded: 1992, David J. Cardinal, Pres & CEO, Rod G. March, VP, David Gang, VP Sales & Mktng, Byron Ryono, Dir Bus Dev, Mike Ouye, VP Eng, Mark Bonacorso, Dir Mktng, Email: markb@firstfloor.com

First International Computer Inc. (FIC), 6F, 201 Tung Hwa N Rd, Taipei Taiwan ROC; 2-717-4500, Fax: 2-718-2782, Web URL: fic.com, Focus: PCs, motherboards and peripherals, Ownrshp: Sub FPG, Taiwan, Sales ($M): 725, Fiscal End: 12/95; Ming Chien, Chmn, Charlene Wang, Pres, Peter Ow, EVP, Ernest Chen, VP PC Div, Richard Brown

First International Computer USA 980A Mission Ct, Fremont CA 94539-8202 USA; 510/252-8888, 800/342-2636 Fax: 510/252-8888, Co Email: @fica.com, Web URL: fica.com, Focus: PCs and LAN products, Ownrshp: Sub FIC, Taiwan, Founded: 1980, Ernest Chen

Fischer International Systems Corp. 4073 Mercantile Ave, PO Box 9107, Naples FL 33942 USA; 941/643-1500, Fax: 941/643-3772, Focus: Communication and security software, Ownrshp: PVT, Founded: 1982, Empl: 142, Addison M. Fischer, Chmn, Ron Kaplan, CFO, Michael S. Battaglia, Pres & CEO, Art Burton, VP Sales & Mktng

Flserv Inc. PO Box 979, 255 Flserv Dr, Brookfield WI 53045 USA; 414/879-5000, 800/872-7882 Focus: Computer services to financial industry, Ownrshp: OTC, Stk Sym: FISV, Founded: 1984, Empl: 6,300, Sales ($M): 703.4, Fiscal End: 12/95; George D. Dalton, Chmn & CEO, Leslie M. Muma, Pres & COO, Kenneth R. Jensen, Sr EVP & CFO, Dean C. Schmelzer, EVP Mktng & Sales

Fitnesoft Inc. 11 E 200 N, #204, Orem UT 84057 USA; 801/221-7777, 800/607-7637 Fax: 801/221-7707, Focus: Personal health management software, Prdts: Life Form, Ownrshp: PVT, Founded: 1994, Pete Peterson, D. Clive Winn, Pres

Flextronics Int'l. 2241 Lundy Ave, San Jose CA 94131-1822 USA; 408/428-1300, Fax: 408/428-0420, Co Email: @flextronics.com, Focus: Electronics manufacturing, Ownrshp: Sub. Flextronics, Singapore, Empl: 1,700, Sales ($M): 448.3, Fiscal End: 3/96; Michael E. Marks, Chmn & CEO, Tsui Sung Lam, Pres & COO, Daniel P. Stradford, SVP Sales & Mktng

Fluke Corp. 6920 Seaway Blvd, Everett WA 98203 USA; 206/347-6100, 800/443-5853 Co Email: fluke-info@tc.fluke.com, Web URL: fluke.com, Focus: Test equipment, Ownrshp: NYSE, Stk Sym: FLK, Founded: 1947, Empl: 2,100, Sales ($M): 413.5, Fiscal End: 4/96; William G. Parzybok, Chmn & CEO, George M. Winn, Pres & COO, Elizabeth J. Huebner, VP & CFO, Ronald R. Wambolt, SVP WW Sales

Focus Computer Products Inc. 35 Pond Park Rd, Hingham MA 02043 USA; 617/741-5008, Fax: 617/740-2071, Focus: Anti-glare glass screen filters for VDTs, Ownrshp: PVT, Kimberly A. Cimetti

Focus Electronics Corp. 21078 Commerce Pointe Dr, Walnut CA 91789 USA; 909/468-5533, Fax: 909/468-5525, Focus: Keyboards, Ownrshp: PVT, Founded: 1981, R.E. Frazier, Dir Mktng

Focus Enhancements Inc. 800 W Cummings Park, Woburn MA 01801 USA; 617/938-8088, Fax: 617/938-7741, Co Email: focusenhan@eworld.com, Focus: Graphics and networking products for PC and Mac platforms, Ownrshp: OTC, Stk Sym: FCSE, Founded: 1992, Empl: 50, Sales ($M): 18, Fiscal End: 12/95; Thomas Massie, Chmn & CEO, William Coldick, Vice-Chmn, Jeremiah Cole Jr., VP Finance, Stauros Cademenos, VP Int'l Sales, Rick O'Connell, Dir Sales, Jim Gargas, Dir Mktng

Folio Corp. 5072 N 300 W, Provo UT 84604-5652 USA; 801/

344-3700, 800/543-6546 Fax: 801/374-5753, Co Email: sales@folio.com, Web URL: folio.com, Focus: Electronic publishing software, Prdts: Folio VIEWS, Ownrshp: Sub. Reed Elsevier plc, Founded: 1986, Empl: 150, Bill Bennett, Pres, Email: bbennett@folio.com; Curt D. Allen, EVP, Email: callen@folio.com; Bruce E. Brown, VP Dev, Email: bbrown@folio.com; Mark Rogers, VP, Email: mrogers@folio.com; Ron Hocutt, VP Support Svcs, Email: rhocutt@folio.com; Mike Judson, Sr Dir Marcom, Email: mjudson@folio.com

Fore Systems Inc. 174 Thorn Hill Rd, Warrendale PA 15086-7586 USA; 412/772-6600, 800/884-0040 Fax: 412/772-6500, Co Email: info@fore.com, Web URL: fore.com, Focus: Asynchronous Transfer Mode products, Ownrshp: OTC, Stk Sym: FORE, Founded: 1990, Empl: 977, Sales ($M): 235.2, Fiscal End: 3/96; Eric C. Cooper, Chmn & CEO, Onat Menzilcioglu, Pres, Francois J. Bitz, VP Eng, Michael I. Green, VP Mktng & Sales, Thomas J. Gill, VP & CFO, Don Reckles, Mgr PR, Email: reckles@fore.com

Foresight Software Six Concourse Pkwy, #2200, Atlanta GA 30328 USA; 770/206-1000, Fax: 770/206-1100, Web URL: foresight-esp.com, Focus: Integrated customer service mgmt. sys. built on a advanced client/server dev. platform, Prdts: Service Management System, Ownrshp: Sub. Marcam Corp., Founded: 1995, Empl: 100, Kent LaRoque, Pres, Jeffrey Fisher, EVP, Frank Orchard, VP Dev, Jerry Goldstein, VP Mktng, Graham Wood, CFO

FormalSoft PO Box 495, Springville UT 84663 USA; 801/489-3102, Focus: Genealogy products: Family Origins, Ownrshp: PVT, Founded: 1986, Bruce Buzbee, Pres

Formgen 15649 Greenway-Hayden Loop, Scottsdale AZ 85260 USA; 602/443-4109, Fax: 602/951-6810, Web URL: formgen.com, Focus: Entertainment software, Ownrshp: PVT, Founded: 1987, Empl: 35, Sales ($M): 11.9, Fiscal End: 12/95; Jim Perkins, Pres, Randy MacLean, CEO, Dale Newman, VP Sales & Mktng, Peter Gibson, CFO, Mark Shander, Comm Mgr, Email: shander@cis.compuserve.com

Forminco 9610-A Ignace, Brossard Quebec J4Y 2R4 Canada; 514/444-9488, Fax: 514/444-9378, Focus: Ergonomic computer accessories, Ownrshp: PVT, Michael Levy, Pres

Forrester Research Inc. 1033 Massachusetts Ave, Cambridge MA 02138 USA; 617/497-7090, Fax: 617/868-0577, Web URL: forrester.com, Focus: Analysis of PCs, LANs, software and network management for Fortune 1000 market, Ownrshp: PVT, Founded: 1983, Empl: 17, George F. Colony, Pres

Forte Software Inc. 1800 Harrison, 15th Floor, Oakland CA 94612 USA; 510/869-3400, Fax: 510/869-3480, Web URL: forte.com, Focus: C/S development software, Ownrshp: PVT, Founded: 1991, Empl: 221, Sales ($M): 30.0, Fiscal End: 3/96; Marty Sprinzen, Chmn, Pres & CEO, Richard Scheffer, VP Mktng, Rodger Weismann, VP & CFO

Forte Technologies Inc. 1057 E Henrietta Rd, Rochester NY 14623 USA; 716/427-8595, Fax: 716/292-6353, Web URL: fortevr.com, Focus: Virtual reality peripherals and head mounted displays, Prdts: VFXI Headgear Virtual Reality System, Cyber Puck, Ownrshp: PVT, Founded: 1994, Empl: 105, Paul Travers, Pres, Email: ptravers@fortevr.com; Pete Matthews, VP Mktng, Email: pmatthews@fortevr.com; Brad Craig, VP Mkt & Bus Dev, Email: bcraig@fortevr.com; Steve McGowan, VP Eng, Email: sbm@servtech.com; Irwin J. Metzger, CFO, Bryan Del Rizzo, PR Mgr, Email: fortevfxi@aol.com

Fortner Research LLC 100 Carpenter Dr, #203, Sterling VA 20164-4464 USA; 703/478-0181, 800/252-6479 Fax: 703/689-9593, Co Email: info@fortner.com, Web URL: langsys.com/langsys, Focus: Compiler and visualization software, Prdts: LS Fortran, PLOT, Transform, Slicer, Ownrshp: PVT, Founded: 1984, Empl: 16, Brand Fortner, Chmn, Email: brand@fortner.com; Guy McCarthy, Pres & CEO, Email: guy@fortner.com; Lisa Jones, Mktng Dir, Email: lisa@fortner.com; Lynn Foster, Sales Mgr, Email: lynn@fortner.com; Enrico Santos, CFO, Email: rico@fortner.com

Fortran Users Group (FUG), PO Box 4201, Fullerton CA 92634 USA; 714/441-2022, Fax: 714/441-2022, Web URL: fortran.com, Focus: Updates Fortran users on standards, programming trends and reviews products, Ownrshp: Nonprofit, Founded: 1987, Charles Ritz, Co-Editor, Walter Brainerd, Co-Editor

Fortress Systems Inc. 1150 N 1st St, #206, San Jose CA 95112-4923 USA; 408/955-9888, Fax: 498/955-9895, Focus: Text-to-speech software, Prdts: SounText, Ownrshp: PVT, Founded: 1988

Forvus Research Inc. 5205 Capital Blvd, Raleigh NC 27604 USA; 919/954-0063, Fax: 919/954-9254, Focus: Communication software and hardware, Ownrshp: PVT, Founded: 1990, Carl McLawhorn, Pres

Four Season Software 2025 Lincoln Hwy, Edison NJ 08817 USA; 908/248-6667, Fax: 908/248-6675, Focus: Operating software, Prdts: SuperNOVA, Ownrshp: PVT, Founded: 1988, Sales ($M): 10+, Fiscal End: 12/94; Joseph Gil, Chmn, Ron Bassin, Pres, Ed Ott, VP

Four11 Corp. 200 Middlefield Rd, #102, Menlo Park CA 94087 USA; 415/617-2000, Fax: 415/617-2005, Web URL: four11.com, Focus: Free e-mail directory service for Internet, Ownrshp: PVT, Founded: 1994, Empl: 8, Michael Santullo, CEO

FourGen Software Inc. 115 NE 100th St, Seattle WA 98125-8013 USA; 206/522-0055, 800/333-4436 Fax: 206/672-4950, Co Email: @fourgen.com, Focus: Accounting software, Prdts: FourGen Supply Chain Management, Ownrshp: PVT, Founded: 1983, Empl: 170, Gary Gagliardi, Pres, Gordon Schaeffer, VP Mktng, Mike Jacobsen, CFO, Jim Robb, VP WW Sales, Daren Kloes, Comm Dir, Email: darenk@fourgen.com

Fourth Shift Corp. 7900 Int'l. Dr, Minneapolis MN 55425 USA; 612/851-1900, 800/342-5675 Fax: 612/851-1560, Co Email: info@fs.com, Web URL: fs.com, Focus: Software for manufacturing & financial management, Prdts: Manufacturing Software System, Ownrshp: OTC, Stk Sym: FSFT, Founded: 1985, Empl: 420, Sales ($M): 37.2, Fiscal End: 12/95; M.M. Stuckey, Chmn & CEO, Jim Caldwell, Pres & COO, David Latzke, VP & CFO, Allen Peterson, EVP, Karen Klimas, Dir Marcom

Fox Electronics 5570 Enterprise Pkwy, Ft. Myers FL 33905 USA; 941/693-0099, Fax: 941/693-1554, Focus: Electronics products, Ownrshp: PVT, Founded: 1979, Empl: 97, Sales ($M): 38.0, Fiscal End: 12/92; Edward L. Fox, Pres, Eugene Trefethen, GM, Edward L. Fox Jr., VP Sales & Mktng, Jerry Hogan, Nat'l Sales Mgr, Barry Hamilton, IS Mgr

Fractal Design Corp. 335 Spreckels Dr, #F, Aptos CA 95003 USA; 408/688-5300, 800/297-2665 Fax: 408/688-8836, Web URL: fractal.com, Focus: Graphics software, Prdts: Painter, Ownrshp: OTC, Stk Sym: FRAC, Founded: 1991, Sales ($M): 21.8, Fiscal End: 3/96; Mark Zimmer, Pres & CEO, Tom Hedges, Chmn & VP R&D, Stephen Manousos, VP Sales, Steve Guttman, VP Mktng, Leslie Wright, VP & CFO

Frame Relay Forum (FRF), 303 Vintage Park Dr, Foster City CA 94404 USA; 415/578-6980, Fax: 415/525-0182, Co Email: frf@sbexpos.com, Web URL: frame-relay.indiana.edu, Focus: Promotion of frame relay technology usage, Ownrshp: Nonprofit, Founded: 1991, Vivian Beaulieu, Exec Dir, Andrew Greenfield, Chmn & Pres

Franklin Datacom Inc. 733 Lakefield Rd, Westlake Village CA 91361 USA; 805/373-8688, 800/372-6556 Fax: 805/373-7373, Co Email: fwp@ftel.com, Web URL: ftel.com, Focus: Communications and networking products, Prdts: UltraFast Hurrican/155 LAN, D-Mark Channel Bank, Ownrshp: OTC, Stk Sym: FTCO, Founded: 1981, Empl: 22, Sales ($M): 26, Fiscal End: 6/91; Frank Peters, Pres, Colin Paterson, Secretary

Franklin Electronic Publishers Inc. 1 Franklin Plaza, Burlington NJ 08016-4907 USA; 609/386-2500, Focus: Electronic reference products, Ownrshp: OTC, Stk Sym: FDOS, Founded: 1980, Empl: 216, Sales ($M): 83.3, Fiscal End: 3/95; Morton E. David, Chmn, Pres & CEO, Michael R. Strange, EVP, Gregory J. Winsky,

SVP, Gary M. Schwartz, EVP & GM Cons Div, Kenneth H. Lind, VP Fin

Franklin Quest Co. 2200 W Parkway Blvd, Salt Lake City UT 84119 USA; 801/975-9992, Fax: 801/975-9995, Focus: PIM and contact management software, Prdts: Ascend, Ownrshp: NYSE, Stk Sym: FNQ, Founded: 1983, Empl: 2,000, Hyrum W. Smith, CEO, Arlen B. Crouch, Pres, Todd Simons, Mktng Dir

Franz Inc. 1995 University Ave, Berkeley CA 94704 USA; 510/548-3600, 800/333-7260 Fax: 510/548-8253, Co Email: info@franz.com, Web URL: franz.com, Focus: Lisp compilers, Ownrshp: PVT, Founded: 1984, Fritz Kunze, Chmn & Pres, Hanoch Eiron, VP & GM, Sheng-Chuan Wu, VP Bus Dev, Jim Veitch, VP Tech, Jack Kemp, CFO, Michael Schuster, Marcom Mgr, Email: michaels@franz.com

Fraser/Young Inc. 100 Wilshire Blvd #440, Santa Monica CA 90401 USA; 310/451-0300, Fax: 310/451-0903, Focus: PR, marketing communications and advertising, Ownrshp: PVT, Founded: 1995, Empl: 20, Agnes Huff, SVP, John Dillon, VP PR, Robyn Barnett, PR Coordinator

FreeMail Inc. 2504 W Main St, #K, Bozeman MT 59771-1656 USA; 406/586-4200, Fax: 406/586-4336, Co Email: freemail@aol.com, Focus: E-mail and telecom software, Prdts: FreeMail, Ownrshp: PVT

Freeman Associates Inc. 311 E Carrillo St, Santa Barbara CA 93101 USA; 805/963-3853, Fax: 805/962-1541, Co Email: freemaninc@aol.com, Web URL: freemaninc.com, Focus: Market analysis and consulting on tape and optical storage; Co-sponsors DataStorage conf., Ownrshp: PVT, Founded: 1977, Empl: 8, Raymond C. Freeman, Jr., Pres, Email: ray@freemaninc.com; Robert C. Abraham, VP

Friesen, Kaye and Associates 3448 Richmond Rd, Ottawa Ontario K2H 8H7 Canada; 613/829-3410, Fax: 613/829-0845, Co Email: fka@magi.com, Focus: Software tools, Prdts: Instructional Systems Design

Frontier Technologies Corp. 10201 N Port Washington Rd, Mequon WI 53092 USA; 414/241-4555, 800/929-3054 Fax: 414/241-7084, Co Email: info@frontiertech.com, Web URL: frontiertech.com, Focus: Network communication software, Prdts: Super-X.25, Super-TCP, Ownrshp: PVT, Founded: 1982, Empl: 150, Prakash Ambegaonkar, Pres, Geoffrey Hibner, CFO

Frontline Systems Inc. PO Box 4288, Incline Village NV 89450 USA; 702/831-0300, Fax: 702/831-0314, Co Email: info@frontsys.com, Web URL: frontsys.com, Focus: PC productivity software, Ownrshp: PVT, Founded: 1987, Daniel Fylstra, Pres & CEO, Email: dfylstra@frontsys.com

Frost & Sullivan Inc. 2525 Charleston Rd, Mountain View CA 94043 USA; 415/961-9000, Fax: 415/961-5042, Focus: Telecom, computers, office automation, ICs & electronics information, Ownrshp: PVT, Founded: 1960, Empl: 250, Sales ($M): 26, David Frigstad, Pres & CEO, Barry Bartlett, VP Research, David Miller, Dir Mktng, Email: dmiller@frost.com

Frye Computer Systems Inc. 31 St James Ave, 2nd Fl., Boston MA 02116-4101 USA; 617/451-5400, Fax: 617/451-6711, Focus: Network systems integration, Ownrshp: PVT, Founded: 1988, Russell H. Frye, Pres

FSA Corp. 1011 First St SW, #508, Calgary Alberta T2R 1J2 Canada; 403/264-4822, Fax: 403/264-0873, Co Email: info@fsa.com, Web URL: fsa.ca, Prdts: PowerBroker, Robyn M. Porter, Sr Acct Exec

FTG Data Systems 8381 Katella Ave, #J, Stanton CA 90680 USA; 714/995-3900, 800/962-3900 Fax: 714/995-3989, Co Email: 74774.3142@compuserve.com, Focus: Light pens, Ownrshp: PVT, Founded: 1976, Empl: 34, Douglas E. Lippincott, Pres & CEO, Email: 70444.66@compuserve.com; Bernard J. Weir, VP Prod Dev, Toni L. Foster, Sales Mgr, Ron Zayas, Dir Mktng, Email: ronzayas@aol.com

FTP Software Inc. (FTPS), 100 Brickstone Square, 5th Floor,

Andover MA 01810 USA; 508/685-4000, Fax: 508/794-4488, Co Email: (@ftp.com, Web URL: ftp.com, Focus: TCP/IP networking products, Prdts: PC/TCP, OnNet, Ownrshp: OTC, Stk Sym: FTPS, Founded: 1986, Empl: 320, Sales ($M): 136.4, Fiscal End: 12/95; David H. Zirkle, Pres & CEO, David B. Fowler, VP Sales & MKtng, Bartel H. Broussard, VP Mktng, Dean Carmeris, VP Cust Svcs, John J. Warnock, SVP & CFO, Karen A. Wharton, Dir Inv Rel, Email: kwharton@ftp.com

Fuji Photo Film USA Inc. 555 Taxter Rd, Elmsford NY 10523 USA; 914/789-8100, Focus: Imaging and information products, Ownrshp: Sub Fuji, Japan, Osamu Inoue, Pres, T.E. McGrath, SVP Imaging Grp, Stan Bauer, VP & GM Magnetic Div, Rod King, VP Mktng, Ron Dubner, VP Sales

Fujitsu Active Information 3055 Orchard Dr, San Jose CA 95134-2022 USA; 800/240-1378 Fax: 408/456-7041, Co Email: @activeinfo.com, Web URL: activeinfo.com, Focus: Internet solutions, Ownrshp: Sub Fujitsu America, Empl: 120, Roger Connolly, Dir, Email: connolly@activeinfo.com; Jasper Rose, Mgr Bus Dev, Email: jrose@activeinfo.com; Rhonda Tordsen, Sales Mktng Support, Email: rtordsen@activeinfo.com

Fujitsu Computer Products 2904 Orchard Pkwy, San Jose CA 95134-2022 USA; 408/432-6333, 800/626-4686 Fax: 408/894-1706, Web URL: fujitsu.com, Focus: Data storage, printers and scanners, Ownrshp: Sub. Fujitsu America, Founded: 1968, Empl: 850, Fiscal End: 3/91; Larry Sanders, Pres & CEO, Steve Butterfield, SVP, Doug May, VP Mktng, Wayne Simmons, VP Sales, David Brinkley, Dir, Mary Medeiros, PR Mgr, Email: mme-deiros@fcpa.fujitsu.com

Fujitsu Ltd. 6-1 Marunochi, 1-chome, Chiyoda-ku, Tokyo 100 JP-100 Japan; 3-3216-3211, Web URL: fujitsu.co.jp, Focus: Computers, peripherals, semiconductors and telecom products, Ownrshp: FO, Stk Sym: FUJITS, Empl: 51,000, Sales ($M): 39,974, Fiscal End: 3/96

Fujitsu Microelectronics Inc. (FMI), 3345 N First St, San Jose CA 95134-1804 USA; 408/922-9000, 800/637-0683 Fax: 408/432-9044, Focus: SPARC microprocessors and ICs, Ownrshp: Sub Fujitsu, Japan, Founded: 1979, Empl: 1,100, Sales ($M): 916, Fiscal End: 3/94; Ken Katashiba, Pres & CEO, Vincent Sollitto, VP & GM, John Herzing, VP Sales & Mktng, Kiyoshi Miyasaka, VP Spec Proj, Tom Miller, VP Corp Plng, Emi Igarashi

Fujitsu Personal Systems Inc. 5200 Patrick Henry Dr, Santa Clara CA 95054 USA; 408/982-9500, 800/831-3183 Fax: 408/496-0575, Focus: Portable computers, Prdts: Stylistic Series, Poquet Pad Plus, Ownrshp: Sub. Fujitsu, Japan, Founded: 1988, Akio Hanada, Pres, Louis Panetta, EVP

Fujitsu Systems Business of America Inc. 5200 Patrick Henry Dr, Santa Clara CA 95054 USA; 408/988-8012, Fax: 408/492-1982, Focus: Data conferencing and service support software, Prdts: LiveHelp, Ownrshp: Sub. Fujitsu Ltd., Takashi Matsutani, Pres, Tac Misumi, Mktng Mgr, Denise Lejardi

Fulcrum Technologies Inc. 785 Carling Ave, Ottawa Ontario K1S 5H4 Canada; 613/238-1761, 800/385-2786 Fax: 613/238-7695, Co Email: info@fulcrum.com, Web URL: fulcrum.com, Focus: Information retrieval software, Prdts: Search Server, Surfboard, Ownrshp: OTC, Stk Sym: FULCF, Founded: 1983, Empl: 250, Sales ($M): 42.9, Fiscal End: 12/95; Eric R. Goodwin, Pres & CEO, David Keys, VP Corp Dev, E. Peter Eddison, VP Mktng, Michael Laginski, COO, Peter C. Reid, VP & CFO, Gillian Brouse, Mgr PR, Email: gillianb@fulcrum.com

Full Circle Technologies Inc. PO Box 4316, Mountain View CA 94040-0316 USA; 415/691-1044, Fax: 415/968-3459, Co Email: 74040.1042@compuserve.com, Focus: Anti-virus and fax-to-scanner software, Prdts: Fax-2-Scan, VirusWeb, VirusBlaster, Ownrshp: PVT, Mark O'Deady

Funk Software Inc. 222 Third St, Cambridge MA 02142 USA; 617/497-6339, Fax: 617/547-1031, Focus: Networking and remote access software, Prdts: WanderLink, Proxy, Ownrshp:

PVT, Founded: 1983, Empl: 25, Sales ($M): 5.5, Paul Funk, Pres, Joseph D. Ryan, VP

Future Domain Corp. 2801 McGaw Ave, Irvine CA 92714 USA; 714/253-0400, Fax: 714/253-0913, Focus: Mass storage controllers, Ownrshp: PVT, Founded: 1982, Empl: 90, Jack A. Allweiss, Pres & CEO, Mark A. Robertson, VP Ops, Patricia A. Allweiss, VP & CFO, Ervin A. Hauck, VP Eng, Laura Brandlin, Marcom Mgr

Future Labs Inc. 5150-E21 El Camino Real, Los Altos CA 95022 USA; 408/254-9000, Fax: 408/254-9010, Web URL: futurelabs.com, Focus: E-mail and electronic meeting software, Prdts: TalkShow, Vis-A-Vis, Ownrshp: PVT, John H.C. Chua, Pres & CEO, Email: jchua@futurelabs.com; Min Zhu, VP & CTO, Richard Vieth, VP Sales & Mktng, Email: rvieth@futurelabs.com; June Ping, Sales & Mktng Mgr, Email: jping@futurelabs.com

Future Now 8044 Montgomery Rd, #601, Cincinnati OH 45236 USA; 513/792-4500, Web URL: tfn-in.com, Focus: PC reseller, Ownrshp: OTC, Stk Sym: FNOW, Founded: 1975, Empl: 1,900, Sales ($M): 795.7, Fiscal End: 12/94; Terry L. Theye, Chmn & CEO, Lewis E. Miller, Pres & COO, David L. Durham, VP & CFO, Norma Skoog, VP

Future Pirates Inc. 228 Main St, #A, Venice CA 90291 USA; 310/396-6788, Fax: 310/396-0898, Focus: Multimedia entertainment software, Ownrshp: PVT, Founded: 1993, Tsuyoshi Takashiro, Pres

Future Trends Software Inc. PO Box 1213, DeSoto TX 75123-1213 USA; 214/224-3288, Fax: 214/224-3328, Focus: Educational software, Prdts: EzSound, EZShopper, languageWiz, Geography-Wiz, Ownrshp: PVT, Founded: 1987, Empl: 7, Monty Shelton, Pres

Future Vision Multimedia 300 Airport Exec Park, Nanuet NY 10954 USA; 914/426-0400, Fax: 914/426-2606, Focus: CD-ROM reference software, Prdts: InfoPedia, Ownrshp: PVT

FutureSoft 12012 Wickchester Ln #600, Houston TX 77079-1222 USA; 713/496-9400, 800/989-8908 Fax: 713/496-1090, Co Email: info@fse.com, Web URL: fse.com, Focus: PC terminal emulation software, Prdts: DynaComm, Ownrshp: PVT, Founded: 1982, Empl: 90, Sales ($M): 11.1, Fiscal End: 12/95; Tim Farrell, Chmn & CEO, Warren White, Pres, Mike Karaffa, VP Sales & Mktng, Eric Grayson, VP Intl Sales, Lisa Crofton, Mgr Mktng Activities

FutureTel Inc. 1092 E Arques Ave, Sunnyvale CA 94086 USA; 408/522-1400, Fax: 408/522-1439, Web URL: ftelinc.com, Focus: Audio and video compression products, Prdts: Primeview II, MPEG-publisher, MPEGworkshop, MPEGworks, MPEGtools, Ownrshp: PVT, Founded: 1993, Empl: 50, Mark Koz, CTO, Masato Hata, Pres, Franco Franca, VP Mktng, Thomas Gilley, SVP, Tom Rice, CEO, Cindy Hammond, Dir Corp Comm

Futuretouch Corp. 2030 E 4th St, #152, Santa Ana CA 92705 USA; 714/558-6824, Fax: 714/558-4889, Co Email: 71441.2207@compuserve.com, Focus: Multimedia control accessories, Prdts: Multimedia Soundpad, Soundpad Remote, Ownrshp: PVT, Founded: 1994, Kenneth M. Woog, Pres, Dale E. Buscaino, VP Eng, Scott C. Daniel, VP Bus Dev

FutureWave Software Inc. 8305 Vickers St, #200, San Diego CA 92111-2111 USA; 619/637-6190, 800/619-6193 Fax: 619/637-9032, Co Email: futurewav@aol.com, Web URL: future-wave.com, Focus: Graphics software, Prdts: SmartSketch Series, Ownrshp: PVT, Founded: 1993, Charlie Jackson, Chmn, Jonathan Gay, VP Dev, Email: 71562.2726@compuserve.com; Michelle Welsh, VP Mktng, Email: 73124.3426@compuserve.com

FWB Inc. 1555 Adams Dr, Menlo Park CA 94025 USA; 415/325-4392, Fax: 415/833-4657, Co Email: info@fwb.com, Web URL: fwb.com, Focus: Storage subsystems and software, Prdts: Hammer, Ownrshp: PVT, Founded: 1984, Empl: 15, Eric Herzog, VP Mktng, David X. Lamont, Dir Mktng, James C. Nelson, Marcom Mgr, Email: fwbjcn@aol.com

Galileo Electro-Optics Corp. Galileo Park, PO Box 550, Sturbridge MA 01566 USA; 508/347-9191, Fax: 508/347-3849, Web URL: galileocorp.com, Focus: Fiberoptic and electro-optic components, Ownrshp: OTC, Stk Sym: GAEO, Founded: 1959, Sales ($M): 34.0, Fiscal End: 9/95; William T. Hanley, Pres & CEO, Josef W. Rokus, VP & CFO, David W. Skiles, VP Sales & Mktng

Gallium Software Inc. 303 Moodie Dr, #4000, Nepean Ontario K2H 9R4 Canada; 613/721-0902, Fax: 613/721-1278, Focus: Font software for Unix computers, Prdts: FontTastic, Ownrshp: PVT, Founded: 1985, Empl: 45, Jack Prior, Pres & CEO, Email: jprior@gallium.com; Peter Hanschke, Dir Mktng, Email: phanschke@gallium.com; Barry Sullivan, Dir SW Components Div, Email: bsullivan@gallium.com; Bernadette Vezina, Marcom, Email: bvezina@gallium.com

GameNet Corp. 611 Broadway, #428, New York NY 10012 USA; 212/254-5300, Fax: 212/979-2999, Co Email: realperson@gamenet.com, Focus: Online gaming service for the Macintosh, Ownrshp: PVT, Founded: 1995, Empl: 3, Marc H. Bell, Pres, Email: mhb@pfm.net; Marc Jaffe, SVP, Email: marc@pfmc.net; Ronnie Schultz, SysOp, Email: ronnie_schultz@gamenet.com

GameTek Inc. 2999 NE 191st St, #500, N Miami Beach FL 33180 USA; 305/935-3995, 800/927-4263 Fax: 305/932-8651, Web URL: gametek.com, Focus: Entertainment and educational software, Prdts: Jeopardy, Wheel of Fortune, Ownrshp: OTC, Stk Sym: GAME, Founded: 1987, Empl: 50, Sales ($M): 50, Fiscal End: 7/94; James D. Harris, Chmn, Kelly Sumner, COO, R. Lynn Anderson, CFO, Thomas Reuterdahl, VP Prod Dev

Gandalf Technologies Inc. 130 Colonnade Rd S, Nepean Ontario K2E 7M4 Canada; 613/274-6500, Fax: 613/226-1717, Focus: Communications and network products, Ownrshp: OTC, Stk Sym: GANDF, Founded: 1971, Empl: 900, Sales ($M): 116.5, Fiscal End: 3/96; Thomas A. Vassiliades, Chmn, Pres & CEO, Walter R. MacDonald, CFO, Wendy Burgess, VP Comm, Maureen Kelly, Dir MIS

Gartner Group 56 Top Gallant Rd, PO Box 10212, Stamford CT 06904-2212 USA; 203/964-0096, Fax: 203/967-6143, Web URL: gartner.com, Focus: Information on mainframe, mini and PCs, LANs, software, office automation & telecom, Ownrshp: OTC, Stk Sym: GART, Founded: 1979, Empl: 1,175, Sales ($M): 229.2, Fiscal End: 9/95; Manny Fernandez, Pres & CEO, William T. Clifford, EVP & COO, E. Follett Carter, EVP Sales & Mktng, David G. Familiant, EVP Int'l Ops, John F. Halligan, EVP & CFO, Kate Berg, Mgr Media Rel

Gasper Corp. 1430 Oak Ct, #314, Dayton OH 45430 USA; 513/427-5200, Fax: 513/427-5201, Focus: Automatic Teller Machine software management systems, Prdts: Gasper 4, Ownrshp: PVT, Founded: 1983, David Gasper, Pres, Gary L. Harrison, Marcom Mgr

Gateway 2000 610 Gateway Dr, PO Box 2000, N Sioux City SD 57049-2000 USA; 605/232-2000, 800/846-2000 Fax: 605/232-2023, Web URL: gw2k.com, Focus: PCs and peripherals, Ownrshp: OTC, Stk Sym: GATE, Founded: 1985, Empl: 8,000+, Sales ($M): 3,676.3, Fiscal End: 12/95; Theodore W. Waitt, Chmn & CEO, Richard D. Snyder, Pres & COO, Michael Hammond, VP, Todd S. Osborn, VP Sales, Robert M. Spears, VP

GBC Technologies 100 GBC Ct, Berlin NJ 08009 USA; 609/767-2500, Fax: 609/753-1123, Focus: Microcomputer distributor, Ownrshp: OTC, Founded: 1981, Empl: 183, Sales ($M): 318.8, Fiscal End: 12/94; Norman M. Some, Chmn & CEO, Harvey S. Kane, Pres & COO

GCC Technologies Inc. 209 Burlington Rd, PO Box 9143, Bedford MA 01730-9143 USA; 617/275-5800, 800/422-7777 Fax: 617/275-1115, Web URL: gcctech.com, Focus: Macintosh peripherals, Ownrshp: PVT, Founded: 1981, Empl: 150, Kevin Curran, Pres & CEO, Douglas Macrae, Chmn, Eli Fuchs, VP Eng, Eric Grodziski, WW Com Mgr

GDT Softworks 4664 Lougheed Hwy, #188, Burnaby BC V5C 6B7 Canada; 604/291-9121, 800/663-6222 Fax: 604/291-9689,

Co Email: 72137.3246@compuserve.com, Focus: Printer driver software, Ownrshp: PVT, Founded: 1984, Empl: 36, Jim McIntosh, Pres, Craig Scott, VP Sales & Mktng, Mike Blackstock, VP Dev, Gord Scott, Dir Fin, Steven Gully, Prod Mktng Mgr

GE Information Services 401 N Washington St, Rockville MD 20850 USA; 301/340-4000, Co Email: info@geis.geis.com, Web URL: geis.com, Focus: Electronic commerce and business productivity solutions, Ownrshp: Sub. General Electric, Hellene S. Runtagh, Pres & CEO

Gemstone Systems Inc. 15400 NW Greenbriar Pkwy, #280, Beaverton OR 97006-9813 USA; 800/243-9369 Focus: Object-oriented database software, Prdts: GemStone, Ownrshp: PVT, Founded: 1982, Empl: 80, Sales ($M): 8, Bryan Grumman, Pres & CEO, Ron Brown, VP Eng, Karen Wood, VP Blackstock, Christopher J. Moore, Controller, Brian Edwards

Genasys II Inc. 1501 S Lemay Ave, Genasys Bldg., Ft. Collins CO 80524-4263 USA; 970/493-0035, Fax: 970/493-0966, Web URL: genasys.com, Focus: GIS products, Prdts: GenaMap, GenaCell, Digit, Spatial Viewer, Ownrshp: PVT, Founded: 1986, Empl: 183, Sales ($M): 25, Carl Reed, CTO, Email: carlr@genasys.com; Michael Fields, COO, Email: mikef@genasys.com; Greg Stecher, CFO, Email: gregs@genasys.com; Jennifer Freeman, Marcom Coord, Email: jennif@genasys.com

General Computer Corp. 2045 Midway Dr, Twinsburg OH 44087 USA; 216/425-3241, Fax: 216/425-3249, Focus: Computers for pharmacy and medical offices, Ownrshp: OTC, Stk Sym: GCCC, Founded: 1970, Empl: 215, Sales ($M): 16.6, Fiscal End: 5/94; Carol A. Dragan, Pres & CEO, Sidney Dworkin, Chmn

General DataComm Industries Inc. 1579 Straits Turnpike, Middlebury CT 06762-1299 USA; 203/574-1118, 800/777-4005 Fax: 203/758-9468, Web URL: gdc.com, Focus: Communications and network equipment, Ownrshp: NYSE, Stk Sym: GDC, Founded: 1969, Empl: 1,780, Sales ($M): 221.2, Fiscal End: 9/95; Charles P. Johnson, Chmn & CEO, Ross A. Belson, Pres & COO, Michael C. Thurk, SVP Mktng, Robert S. Smith, VP Bus Dev, William S. Lawrence, VP & CFO

General Electric Co. (GE), 3135 Easton Turnpike, Fairfield CT 06431 USA; 203/373-2211, 800/626-2004 Co Email: geinfo@www.ge.com, Web URL: ge.com, Focus: Automation and electronic products, Prdts: GENIE, MSNBC, NBC Desktop Video, EDI, Ownrshp: NYSE, Stk Sym: GE, Founded: 1892, Empl: 216,000, Sales ($M): 70,028.0, Fiscal End: 12/95; John F. Welch Jr., Chmn & CEO, Paolo Fresco, Vice Chmn, Lewis E. Edelheit, SVP R&D, John Opie, Vice Chmn, Joyce Hergenhan, VP PR

General Instrument Corp. 8770 W Bryn Mawr Ave, Chicago IL 60631 USA; 312/695-1000, Fax: 312/695-1001, Web URL: gi.com, Focus: Broadband communications products, Ownrshp: NYSE, Stk Sym: GIC, Founded: 1923, Empl: 9,700, Sales ($M): 2,432.0, Fiscal End: 12/95; Richard S. Friedland, Chmn & CEO, Thomas A. Dumit, VP & CAO, Charles T. Dickson, VP & CFO, Mark Borman

General Magic Inc. 420 N Mary Ave, Sunnyvale CA 94086 USA; 408/774-4000, Fax: 408/774-4010, Co Email: info@genmagic.com, Web URL: genmagic.com, Focus: Personal communication software, Prdts: Telescript, Magic Cap, Ownrshp: Apple, AT&T, Sony & others, Stk Sym: GMGC, Founded: 1990, Empl: 161, Sales ($M): 2.5, Fiscal End: 12/94; Steve Markman, Chmn, Pres & CEO, Bob Kelsch, EVP & COO, Lucia Hicks-Williams, VP Strat Plng, Andrew Hertzfeld, VP & SW Wizard, Jane Anderson, Dir PR

General Parametrics Corp. 1250 Ninth St, Berkeley CA 94710 USA; 510/524-3950, Fax: 510/524-9954, Focus: Desktop graphics presentation systems, Ownrshp: OTC, Stk Sym: GPAR, Founded: 1981, Empl: 41, Sales ($M): 9.5, Fiscal End: 10/95; Gerard M Jacobs, Co-Chmn, T. Benjamin Jennings, Co-Chmn, Daniel B. Burgess, EVP Sales & Mktng, James C. Cogan, SVP Ops, William A. Spazante, CFO

General Signal Corp. 1 High Ridge Park, PO Box 10010, Stamford CT 06904 USA; 203/329-4100, Focus: Electronics and telecom products, Ownrshp: NYSE, Stk Sym: GSX, Founded: 1904, Empl: 15,000, Sales ($M): 1,863.2, Fiscal End: 12/95; Michael D. Lockhart, Chmn, Pres, CEO & COO, Joel S. Friedman, SVP Ops, Philip A. Goodrich, VP Corp Dev, Terence D. Martin, EVP & CFO, Nino J. Fernandez, VP Investor Rel

Genesis Technology 3400 Arden Rd, Hayward CA 94545-3906 USA; 510/782-4800, Fax: 510/782-4842, Focus: Printer accessories, Ownrshp: PVT, Andrew Bernard, Prod Mktng Mgr

Geneva Group of Cos. Inc. 7109 31st Ave N, Minneapolis MN 55427-2848 USA; 612/546-5620, 800/358-5600 Fax: 612/546-0933, Focus: Computer accessories, Ownrshp: PVT, Ed Griffin, Pres

GENICOM Corp. 14800 Conference Ctr Dr, #400, Chantilly VA 22021-3806 USA; 703/802-9200, 800/436-4266 Fax: 703/802-9039, Focus: Printers and accessories, Ownrshp: OTC, Stk Sym: GECM, Founded: 1983, Empl: 2,400, Sales ($M): 294.1, Fiscal End: 12/95; Don E. Ackerman, Chmn, Paul T. Winn, Pres & CEO, Raymond D. Stapleton, SVP, W. Allen Surber, SVP, James C. Gale, SVP & CFO, Cynthia J. Green, Sr Marcom Spec

Genova 709 E Walnut St, Carson CA 90746 USA; 310/538-4102, Fax: 310/538-1754, Focus: Monitors and graphics peripherals, Ownrshp: PVT, Founded: 1994, S.H. Jong, Pres, William Park, EVP Mktng, Jay Kang, Dir Tech Sup

Genovation Inc. 17741 Mitchell N, Irvine CA 92714-9676 USA; 714/833-3355, 800/822-4333 Fax: 714/833-0322, Co Email: mail@genovation.com, Web URL: genovation.com, Focus: PC input devices, Ownrshp: PVT, Founded: 1989, Sales ($M): 3.0, Fiscal End: 3/95; Leonard Genest, Pres, Joseph Meshi, EVP & CFO

Geoworks 960 Atlantic Ave, Alameda CA 94501 USA; 510/814-1660, Fax: 510/814-4250, Co Email: @geoworks.com, Web URL: geoworks.com, Focus: Operating systems for consumer computing devices, Prdts: GEOS operating system, Ownrshp: PVT, Founded: 1983, Empl: 125, Sales ($M): 5.0, Fiscal End: 3/96; Brian P. Dougherty, Chmn, Gordon E. Mayer, Pres & CEO, Dennis H. Rowland, VP & CFO, Clive G. Smith, VP Bus Dev, Craig S. Taylor, VP Eng, Deborah Dawson, Dir Mktng

Gerber Scientific Inc. 83 Gerber Rd W, S Windsor CT 06074 USA; 860/644-1551, Fax: 860/643-7039, Web URL: gerberscientific.com, Focus: Factory automation systems, Ownrshp: NYSE, Stk Sym: GRB, Founded: 1945, Empl: 1,700, Sales ($M): 359.1, Fiscal End: 4/96; George M. Gentile, Chmn & CEO, Gary K. Bennett, VP Fin & CFO, Fredric K. Rosen, SVP

Gessler Publishing Company 10 E Church Ave, Roanoke VA 24011 USA; 540/345-1429, 800/456-5825 Fax: 540/342-7172, Web URL: gessler.com/gessler, Focus: Foreign language software, Ownrshp: PVT, Founded: 1932, Empl: 17, Seth Levin, Pres, Richard Kursham, CEO, Bobbi Kursham, VP, Bob Delzell, VP R&D

GetC Software Inc. PO Box 52069, N Vancouver BC V7J 3T2 Canada; 604/254-5521, 800/663-8066 Fax: 604/254-5571, Co Email: jlowe@unixg.vbc.ca, Focus: File utility software, Prdts: File Shuttle, Lazy Susan, Ownrshp: PVT, Founded: 1983, Empl: 3, Art Bayne, Pres

GfxBase Inc. PO Box 360814, Milpitas CA 95036-0814 USA; 408/262-1469, Fax: 408/262-8276, Focus: Graphics and network products, Prdts: XII, Motif, Boing! Mouse, Ownrshp: PVT, Founded: 1987, Empl: 1, Dale Luck, Pres, Email: d.luck@ieee.org

Giga Information Group One Kendall Square, Bldg. 1400W, Cambridge MA 02139 USA; 617/577-9595, 800/874-9988 Fax: 617/577-1649, Co Email: @gigasd.com, Web URL: gigaweb.com, Focus: Electronic imaging, information processing and telecom data, Ownrshp: Sub Giga Information, Founded: 1979, Empl: 300, Sales ($M): 28, Gideon Gartner, Chmn & CEO, Jeff Swartz, SVP Mktng, Richard Goldman, SVP & CFO, Andrew Jennings, SVP WW Sales, Martha Popoloski

GigaTrend Inc. 2234 Rutherford Rd, Carlsbad CA 92008 USA; 619/931-9122, 800/743-4442 Fax: 619/931-9959, Co Email: backup@gigatrend.com, Web URL: gigatrend.com, Focus: Tape storage solutions, Prdts: MasterDat, MasterSafe, ServerDat, Ownrshp: Sub. DPC, Founded: 1988, Empl: 21, Sales ($M): 5, Fiscal End: 3/95; Peter T. Fei, CEO

Gigatron Software Corp. (GSC), 2382 Morse Ave, Irvine CA 92714 USA; 714/261-1777, Fax: 714/261-5147, Co Email: gsc_info@gsclion.com, Web URL: gsclion.com, Focus: Computer-aided transcription products for legal applications, Prdts: StenoCAT, Founded: 1993, Tariq Chaudhary, Pres, Susan Sawyer, Dir Mktng, Email: s_sawyer@gsclion.com

Gilmore Corp. #200-880 Wellington St, Ottawa Ontario K1R 6K7 Canada; 613/237-7770, 800/795-6661 Fax: 613/237-6351, Co Email: global@doculink.com, Focus: Digital printing, offset printing & distribution services, online training documentation, Richard Weedmark, VP Bus Dev

Gimpel Software 3207 Hogarth Ln, Collegeville PA 19426-1506 USA; 610/584-4261, Fax: 610/584-4266, Focus: Debugging software, Prdts: PC-lint, FlexeLint, C-Vision, C Shroud, Ownrshp: PVT, Founded: 1984, Empl: 5, James F. Gimpel, Pres

Glare/Guard 310 Sutton Place, Santa Rosa CA 95407 USA; 800/545-6254 Fax: 707/525-7595, Focus: Anti-glare and anti-radiation filters, Ownrshp: Sub OCLI, Laurence D. Parson, VP & GM, Jeffrey C. Foster, Dir Mktng

Glenco Engineering Inc. 270 Lexington Dr, Buffalo Grove IL 60089-6930 USA; 847/808-0300, Fax: 847/808-0313, Focus: Computer protection and security products, Ownrshp: PVT, Founded: 1979, Empl: 18, Sales ($M): 1.2

Global Knowledge Network Inc. 129 Parker St, Maynard MA 01754 USA; 508/493-3862, Focus: Computer related training services, Prdts: Mentys International

Global Turnkey Systems Inc. 20 Waterview Blvd, 3rd Fl., Parsippany NJ 07054-1219 USA; 201/445-5050, Focus: Computers for book and magazine publishing, Ownrshp: Sub. Devers Group, Founded: 1969, Empl: 75, Robert Farina, Pres & CEO

Global Village Communication 1144 E Arques Ave, Sunnyvale CA 94086 USA; 408/523-1000, 800/948-4547 Fax: 408/523-2287, Co Email: @globalvillage.com, Web URL: globalvillage.com, Focus: Macintosh modems, Prdts: TelePort, Ownrshp: OTC, Stk Sym: GVIL, Founded: 1989, Empl: 125, Sales ($M): 80.0, Fiscal End: 3/95; Leonard A. Lehmann, Chmn, Neil Selvin, Pres & CEO, Charlie Oppenheimer, VP & GM Mac Div, Rex Cardinale, VP & GM Internet Div, James M. Walker, VP & CFO, Kathy A. Bower, Dir Marcom, Email: kathy_bower@globalvillage.com

Globalink Inc. 9302 Lee Hwy, 12th Floor, Fairfax VA 22031-1208 USA; 703/273-5600, 800/255-5660 Fax: 703/273-3866, Co Email: info@globalink.com, Web URL: globalink.com, Focus: Language translation software and services, Prdts: Language Assistant, Power Translator, Translate Direct, Ownrshp: AMEX, Stk Sym: GNK, Founded: 1990, Empl: 95, Sales ($M): 17.6, Fiscal End: 12/95; Jim Lewis, Pres, Email: jlewis@globalink.com; Ronald W. Johnston, CFO, Ronald Johnston, COO, Jeff Gray, VP Ind Mktng, Email: jgray@globalink.com; Kelly Mullins, PR Mgr, Email: kmullins@globalink.com

Globetrotter Software 300 Orchard City Dr, #131, Campbell CA 95008-2946 USA; 408/370-2800, Fax: 408/370-2884, Co Email: info@globes.com, Web URL: globetrotter.com, Focus: Remote support and license management software, Prdts: Flexadmin, FLEXlm, Ownrshp: PVT, Founded: 1982, Empl: 29, Matt Christiano, Pres, Richard Mirabella, VP Sales & Mktng, Sallie Calhoun, VP Finance, Liz Naughton, Marcom Mgr, Email: liz@globes.com

Gold Disk Inc. 2475 Augustine Dr, Santa Clara CA 95054-3002 USA; 408/982-0200, Fax: 408/982-0298, Focus: Presentation software, Ownrshp: PVT, Founded: 1984, Empl: 63, Kailash Ambwani, Pres & CEO

Gold Standard Multimedia Inc. 235 S Main St, #206, Gainesville FL 32601-6585 USA; 904/373-1100, Fax: 904/373-7124, Co Email: @gsm.com, Web URL: gate.net/gsm, Focus: Medical reference software, Ownrshp: PVT, Jonathan Seymour, Pres, James Lowry, CEO, Bill Bradley, PR Dir, Email: bradley.b@gsm.com

GoldMine Software Corp. 17383 Sunset Blvd, #101, Pacific Palisades CA 90272 USA; 310/454-6800, 800/654-3526 Fax: 310/454-4848, Co Email: 74431.1624@compuserve.com, Web URL: goldminesw.com, Focus: Contact management software, Prdts: GoldMine, GoldSync, Ownrshp: PVT, Founded: 1989, Empl: 55, Elan Susser, Pres, Jon V. Ferrara, EVP, Brenda Christensen, PR Dir, Email: 73053.2571@compuserve.com

Good Guys Inc., The 7000 Marina Blvd, Brisbane CA 94005-1840 USA; 415/615-5000, Focus: Chain of consumer electronics superstores, Ownrshp: OTC, Stk Sym: GGUY, Founded: 1976, Empl: 4,000, Sales ($M): 889.2, Fiscal End: 9/95; Ronald A. Unkefer, Chmn, Robert A. Gunst, Pres & CEO, Thomas A. Hannah, SVP Ops, Robert E. Baird, VP Mktng, William C. Curley, VP MIS & Ops

Gradco USA Inc. 39 Parker, Irvine CA 92718-1605 USA; 714/206-6100, Fax: 714/206-6110, Focus: Paper handling systems, Ownrshp: Sub Gradco, Japan, Founded: 1973, Empl: 93, Masakazu Takeuchi, Pres & CEO

Gradient Technologies 5 Mt Royal Ave, Marlboro MA 01752 USA; 508/624-9600, 800/525-4343 Fax: 508/229-0338, Co Email: info@gradient.com, Web URL: gradient.com, Focus: Unix development software, Ownrshp: PVT, Dave Fowler, VP Sales & Mktng, Dave Zwicker, VP Sales, Derek Brink, Dir Bus Dev

Grand Junction Networks Inc. 47281 Bayside Pkwy, Fremont CA 94538 USA; 510/252-0726, Fax: 510/252-0915, Focus: Networking products, Prdts: FastSwitch, HastHub, Ownrshp: PVT

Graphic Development Int'l. 20A Pimental Ct, #B, Novato CA 94949 USA; 415/382-6600, Fax: 415/382-0742, Focus: Electronic forms processing application, Ownrshp: PVT, Founded: 1985, Empl: 10, Sales ($M): 1, Fiscal End: 3/94; Christophe Meneau, Pres

Graphic Enterprises of Ohio Inc. 3874 Highland Park NW, N Canton OH 44720 USA; 216/494-9694, Fax: 216/494-5481, Focus: Laser printers, Ownrshp: PVT

Graphic Utilities Inc. 2149 O'Toole Ave, #L, San Jose CA 95131 USA; 408/577-0334, Fax: 408/577-0348, Focus: Printer accessories, Ownrshp: PVT, Founded: 1985, Richard Crystal, Pres & CTO, Jack Marks, EVP, Jacob Levy, EVP Ops, Marge Buck, Dir Mktng

Graphics Performance Characterization Committee (GPC), 10754 Ambassador Dr, #201, Manassas VA 22111 USA; 703/331-0180, Fax: 703/331-0181, Co Email: info@specbench.org, Web URL: specbench.org/gpc, Focus: Defines standard benchmarks for measuring graphics performance, Ownrshp: Nonprofit, Founded: 1987, R. Willisobert, Project Mgr, Rodney Sanford, Project Admin

Graphsoft Inc. 10270 Old Columbia Rd, Columbia MD 21046 USA; 410/290-5114, Fax: 410/290-8050, Co Email: @graphsoft.com, Web URL: graphsoft.com, Focus: PC CAD software, Prdts: MiniCad, Blueprint, Azimuth, Ownrshp: OTC, Stk Sym: DIEG, Founded: 1985, Empl: 32, Sales ($M): 5.2, Fiscal End: 5/95; Richard Diehl, Pres & CEO, Dan Monaghan, VP Mktng, Email: dan@graphsoft.com; Don Webster, VP Ops, Sean Flahertly, VP Eng, Laura Maron

Gray Matter Design 300 Brannan St, #210, San Francisco CA 94107 USA; 415/243-0394, Fax: 415/243-0396, Web URL: mediabooks@aol.com, Focus: Multimedia development software, Prdts: MediaBook, Ownrshp: PVT, Karyn Scott, GM, Terry R. Schussler, Principle, Email: schussler@aol.com

Great Plains Software 1701 SW 38th St, Fargo ND 58103 USA; 701/281-0550, 800/456-0025 Fax: 701/281-3700, Co Email: info@gps.com, Web URL: gps.com, Focus: Accounting software, Prdts: Great Plains Accounting, Dynamics, Dynamic C/S+, Ownrshp: PVT, Founded: 1981, Empl: 500, Douglas Burgum, Pres & CEO, Jodi Uecker-Rust, VP Employee Svcs, Robin Pederson, SVP

WW Sales & Mktng, Ray August, CTO, Mike Slette, VP Bus Dev, Michael Olsen, VP Corp Comm

Great Wave Software 5353 Scotts Valley Dr, Scotts Valley CA 95066 USA; 408/438-1990, Fax: 408/438-7171, Focus: School and home education software, Ownrshp: PVT, Founded: 1984, Empl: 15, Stacy McKee Mitchell, CEO, Chad L. Mitchell, CTO, Roberta Sosbee, Sales Dir, Elia Surran, Mktng Dir

GreenSpring Computers Inc. 1204 O'Brien Dr, Menlo Park CA 94025 USA; 415/327-1200, Fax: 415/327-3808, Co Email: @gspring.com, Focus: Industrial computer boards, Ownrshp: Sub. of SBS Tech., Founded: 1984, Empl: 30, Sales ($M): 3, Joe Zabkar, Pres, Email: joe@gspring.com; Fred Trevor, VP Ops, Email: fred@gspring.com; Kim Rubin, VP Eng, Email: kim@gspring.com

Greystone Peripherals Inc. 130-A Knowles Dr, Los Gatos CA 95030 USA; 408/866-4739, Fax: 408/866-8328, Co Email: grystone@ix.netcom.com, Focus: Mass storage products, Ownrshp: PVT, Founded: 1992, John Usher, Pres

Grolier Electronic Publishing Inc. Sherman Turnpike, Danbury CT 06816 USA; 203/797-3500, 800/285-4534 Fax: 203/797-3197, Focus: CD-ROM software, Ownrshp: Sub. Lagardere Group, David Arganbright, Pres, Joseph Szczepaniak, VP Sales, Maryanne Piazza, Dir Mktng

Group 1 Software 4200 Parliament Place, #600, Lanham MD 20706-1844 USA; 301/731-2300, 800/368-5806 Fax: 301/731-0360, Web URL: g1.com, Focus: Database marketing and mailing software, Prdts: CODE-1 Plus, Mail Stream Plus, Ownrshp: OTC', Stk Sym: GSOF, Founded: 1986, Empl: 286, Sales ($M): 45.9, Fiscal End: 3/96; Robert S. Bowen, Chmn & CEO, Ronald F. Friedman, Pres & COO, Alan P. Slater, EVP, Charles A. Crew, VP & CFO, B. Scott Miller, VP Prod Dev, Suzanne Porter-Kuchay, Mgr PR

Group Technologies Corp. 10901 Malcolm McKinley Dr, Tampa FL 33612 USA; 813/972-6477, Fax: 813/972-6715, Co Email: @grtk.com, Focus: Communication products and contract manufacturing, Ownrshp: OTC, Stk Sym: GRTK, Founded: 1989, Empl: 2,100, Sales ($M): 273.6, Fiscal End: 12/95; Carl McCormick, Pres & CEO, Email: c.mccormick@grtk.com; Jack Calderon, VP Intl Ops, Email: j.calderon@grtk.com; Hardie Harris, Domestic Ops, Email: h.harris@grtk.com

Gryphon Software Corp. 7220 Trade St, #120, San Diego CA 92121 USA; 619/536-8815, Fax: 619/536-8932, Co Email: gryphonsw@aol.com, Focus: Children's software, Prdts: Morph, Ownrshp: PVT, Founded: 1991, Michael Malone, Pres, Anne L. Hutchinson, Dir Mktng

GT Interactive Software 16 E 40th St, New York NY 10016 USA; 212/726-6500, Fax: 212/726-4202, Web URL: gtinteractive.com, Focus: Entertainment software, Prdts: Doom, Hexen, Ownrshp: OTC, Stk Sym: GTIS, Founded: 1992, Empl: 700, Sales ($M): 204.1, Fiscal End: 12/95; Ron Chaimowitz, Pres, Andy Gregor, CFO

GTCO Corp. 7125 Riverwood Dr, Columbia MD 21046 USA; 410/381-6688, Fax: 410/290-9065, Focus: Digitizers, Prdts: Ultima, Roll-Up, AccuTab, QuikRuler, Ownrshp: PVT, Founded: 1975, Empl: 66, B.J. Fadden, Pres & CEO, Steve Kaye, GM, Paul Warkentin, Dir Mktng

GTE Corp. One Stamford Forum, Stamford CT 06904 USA; 203/965-2000, Fax: 203/965-2520, Web URL: gte.com, Focus: Telecom and electronic products, Ownrshp: NYSE, Stk Sym: GTE, Founded: 1935, Empl: 106,000, Sales ($M): 19,957, Fiscal End: 12/95; Charles R. Lee, Chmn & CEO, Kent B. Foster, Pres, Nicholas L. Trivisonno, EVP Strat Plng, Thomas F. Lysaugh, VP Mktng, J. Michael Kelly, SVP Fin, Bruce Redditt, VP Com

GTE Government Systems, Information Systems Div. 15000 Conference Ctr Dr, Chantilly VA 22021 USA; 703/818-4000, Fax: 703/818-5484, Web URL: gtefsd.com, Focus: Systems integration, Ownrshp: Sub. GTE, Founded: 1979, Empl: 1,450, Irving Zaks, VP & GM Govt Sys, Giles Sinkewiz, VP & GM Integrated Cust Sol, Joel

Katz, VP & GM Info Enterprise Sys, Robert D. Bishop, Dir Com

GTE Personal Communications Services (GTE PCS), 245 Perimeter Ctr Pkwy, Atlanta GA 30346 USA; 404/391-8000, Focus: Wireless communications, Ownrshp: Sub. GTE, C.J. Waylan, EVP, Charles M. Parrish, GM Mobile Data, Jay Sheeth, Dir Mktng, John Strickling

GTECH Corp. 55 Technology Way, PO Box 4001, W Greenwich RI 02817 USA; 401/392-1000, Fax: 401/392-1234, Focus: On-line computer lottery products, Ownrshp: OTC, Stk Sym: GTCH, Founded: 1980, Empl: 4,300, Sales ($M): 744.1, Fiscal End: 2/96; Guy B. Snowden, Co-Chmn & CEO, Victor Markowicz, Co-Chmn, William Y. O'Conner, Pres & COO, Donald L. Stanford, SVP Tech, Joseph J. Pietropaolo, VP & CFO

GTM Software 293 E 950 S, Orem UT 84058-5004 USA; 801/235-7000, Fax: 801/235-7099, Focus: Windows utility, accounting, and foreign language software, Prdts: Q-DOS, Collect-A-Debt, Let's Speak (German, French, Italian & Spanish), Ownrshp: PVT, Founded: 1985, Empl: 3, Sales ($M): 1.0, Richard Knapp, CEO

GVC Technologies Inc. 400 Commons Way, Rockaway NJ 07866-2027 USA; 201/579-3630, Fax: 201/579-2702, Focus: Modems and LAN products, Ownrshp: PVT, Founded: 1978, Empl: 1,000

Gyrus Systems Inc. 620 Moorefield Park Dr, Richmond VA 23236 USA; 804/320-1414, 800/328-2829 Fax: 804/320-2323, Web URL: gyrus.com, Focus: Human resource software, Prdts: Training Administrator, Training Wizard, Ownrshp: PVT, Founded: 1982, Empl: 30, Robert Dust, Pres, Email: bobdust@ix.netcom.com; Robert Minteer, VP, Email: rminteer@ix.netcom.com; Connie Frudden, VP Tech Svcs, Email: frudden@ix.netcom.com; Gary Graham, Sales Mgr, Email: graham@ahaynet.com

H&R Block Inc. 4410 Main St, Kansas City MO 64111 USA; 816/753-6900, Fax: 816/753-8628, Focus: Tax preparation and owner of CompuServe, Ownrshp: NYSE, Stk Sym: HRB, Founded: 1955, Empl: 4,100, Sales ($M): 1,528, Fiscal End: 4/96; Richard H. Brown, CEO

H.A. Technical Solutions Inc. 2500 Minnesota World Trade Ctr, 30 E Seventh St, St Paul MN 55104-4901 USA; 612/221-1661, Fax: 612/221-1699, Focus: High availability software, Prdts: H.A.-Internet, LeRoy D. Earl, VP Sales & Mktng

Hadron Inc. 9990 Lee Hwy, Fairfax VA 22030 USA; 703/359-6404, Fax: 703/359-6409, Focus: Software and telecom consulting services, Ownrshp: OTC, Stk Sym: HDRNC, Founded: 1964, Empl: 500, Sales ($M): 18.5, Fiscal End: 6/94; C.W. Gilluly, Chmn & CEO

Halskar Systems 47000 Warm Springs Blvd, #301, Fremont CA 94539 USA; 510/656-5157, Fax: 510/656-7279, Focus: PCs and industrial control systems, Prdts: Halskar Systems, Ownrshp: PVT, Founded: 1983, Empl: 7, Sales ($M): 0.9, Fiscal End: 10/92; Henry Chen, Pres, Nelson Hung, GM, Nai-Ling Chen, MIS Mgr

Hand Held Products 7510 E Independence Blvd, #100, Charlotte NC 28227-9411 USA; 704/541-1380, Fax: 704/541-1333, Focus: Bar code scanners, Prdts: Micro-Wand, Ownrshp: PVT, Founded: 1992, Scott Cardais, Pres & CEO, John Dreibelbis, Dir Mktng, Dwain Kinsinger, VP Sales, Kevin Ahearn, VP Eng

Hands-On Technology 577 Airport Blvd, #450, Burlingame CA 94010 USA; 415/579-7755, Fax: 415/579-7739, Co Email: info@hot.sf.ca.us, Focus: Interactive expert software, Prdts: Hot Mentor Series, Ownrshp: PVT, Regis McKenna, Chmn, Michael Mellin, Pres & CEO, Rick Davis, VP Mktng & Sales, Kent Daniel, VP & COO, Susan Korade, Dir Marcom

Harbinger EDI Services Inc. 1055 Lenox Park Blvd, Atlanta GA 30319 USA; 800/367-4272 Fax: 404/841-4364

Hard Dr Associates Inc. (HDA), 3318 SW 16th Ave, Portland OR 97202 USA; 503/233-2821, Fax: 503/233-2911, Focus: Computer repair and data recovery, Ownrshp: PVT, Empl: 36, Marti Granmo, Pres, Steve Granmo, VP, Robb Bauer, GM

Harlequin Inc. 1 Cambridge Ctr, Cambridge MA 02142 USA; 617/374-2400, Fax: 617/252-6505, Co Email: @harlequin.com, Web URL: harlequin.com, Focus: Pre-press and electronic publishing software, Prdts: ScriptWorks, Ownrshp: PVT, Founded: 1986, Empl: 250, Jo Marks, Chmn, Dodie Bump, Email: dbump@harlequin.com

Harmonic Lightwaves 3005 Bunker Hill Ln, Santa Clara CA 95054 USA; 408/970-9880, 800/788-1380 Fax: 408/970-8543, Co Email: @harmaonic-lightwaves.com, Focus: Fiber optics communications systems, Prdts: MAXLink, PWRLink, VAGLink, Network Management System, Stk Sym: HLIT, Founded: 1988, Empl: 160, Tony Ley, Pres & CEO, John Dahlquist, VP Mktng, Robin Dickson, CFO, Catlin Walker, Marcom Mgr, Email: catlin.walker@harmonic-lightwaves.c

Harmonic Vision 906 University Place, Evanston IL 60201 USA; 847/467-2395, Fax: 847/467-3008, Focus: Music education software, Prdts: Music Ace, Ownrshp: PVT, Founded: 1991, Joel A. May, Pres, Philip C. Rockenbach, CEO, Michelle Labrador

Harris Computer Systems Corp. 2101 W Cypress Creek Rd, Ft. Lauderdale FL 33309-1892 USA; 305/973-5100, Fax: 305/977-5580, Co Email: @hcsc.com, Web URL: hcsc.com, Focus: Realtime computers, Ownrshp: Sub Harris Corp., Founded: 1967, Empl: 430, Sales ($M): 58.9, Fiscal End: 6/94; E. Courtney Sigel, Chmn, Pres & CEO, Robert T. Menzel, CP & GM, Katherine K. Hudson, Dir Mktng, Rick A. Siebenaler, Dir SW Dev, Robert E. Chism, Dir Prod Ops, Lisa Thornhill Jones, Email: lisa.thornhill@mail.hcsc.com

Harris Corp. 1025 W NASA Blvd, Melbourne FL 32919 USA; 407/727-9100, Fax: 407/727-9344, Web URL: harris.com, Focus: Electronic systems, ICs, communications and office products, Ownrshp: NYSE, Stk Sym: HRS, Founded: 1926, Empl: 28,200, Sales ($M): 3,699.3, Fiscal End: 6/96; John T. Hartley, Chmn & CEO, Phillip W. Farmer, Pres & COO, Bryan R. Roub, SVP & CFO, Robert E. Sullivan, SVP Admin, Herbert N McCauley, VP Info Mgmt, W. Peter Carney, VP Corp Rel

Hayes Microcomputer Products Inc. 5835 Peachtree Corners E, Norcross GA 30092-3405 USA; 770/840-9200, Fax: 770/441-1238, Co Email: @hayes.com, Focus: Modems, LAN and ISDN products, Ownrshp: PVT, Founded: 1978, Empl: 800, Dennis C. Hayes, Chmn & CEO, Daniel Aghion, VP Mktng, Willis Young, VP & CFO, Andrew W. Dod, Dir Corp Com, Email: adod@hayes.com

Haynes Group 1301 Dove St, #680, Newport Beach CA 92660 USA; 714/250-8630, Fax: 714/250-8836, Co Email: haynes@earthlink.com, Focus: Advertising design & marketing communications, Ownrshp: PVT, Robert L. Haynes, Owner, Dian Mellus, Dir Acct Svcs

HBO & Co. 301 Perimeter Ctr N, Atlanta GA 30346 USA; 770/393-6000, Fax: 770/393-6092, Web URL: hboc.com, Focus: Healthcare software, Ownrshp: OTC, Stk Sym: HBOC, Founded: 1974, Empl: 2,383, Sales ($M): 495.6, Fiscal End: 12/95; Charles W. McCall, Pres & CEO, Michael W. McCarty, EVP Sales, Michael L. Kappel, VP, Russell G. Overton, SVP Bus Dev, Jay P. Gilbertson, VP & CFO

Healthcare Communications Inc. 210 Gateway Mall #200, Lincoln NE 68505-2481 USA; 402/466-8100, 800/888-4344 Fax: 402/466-9044, Web URL: healthcc.com, Focus: Medical and dental software, Ownrshp: PVT, Founded: 1983, Empl: 110, Sales ($M): 9.5, Fiscal End: 12/95; Michael Edwards, Chmn, Edward Brown, Pres

HEI Inc. 1495 Steiger Lake Ln, Victoria MN 55386-0738 USA; 612/443-2500, Fax: 612/443-2668, Focus: Microelectronic devices, scanners and light pens, Ownrshp: OTC, Stk Sym: NMS, Founded: 1968, Empl: 143, Sales ($M): 20.7, Fiscal End: 8/96; Eugene W. Courtney, Pres & CEO, Jerald H. Mortenson, VP & CFO

Heizer Software 1941 Oak Park Blvd, PO Box 232019, Pleasant Hill CA 94523 USA; 510/943-7667, Fax: 510/943-6882, Focus:

Spreadsheet templates and hypermedia products, Ownrshp: PVT, Founded: 1982, Empl: 11, Sales ($M): 1.1, Fiscal End: 12/92; Ray Heizer, Pres

Helix Software Co. Inc. 803 East St, Frederick MD 21701 USA; 800/469-4572 Fax: 800/899-3457, Focus: PC utility software, Prdts: Headroom, Netroom, Hurricane, Ownrshp: PVT, Founded: 1986, Empl: 15, Michael L. Spilo, Pres

Helix Technologies 744 Pinecrest Dr, Prospect Heights IL 60070 USA; 847/465-0242, 800/364-3549 Fax: 847/465-0252, Web URL: mcs.net/~hxtech, Focus: Macintosh workgroup information management software, Prdts: Helix Express, Helix Client/Server, Ownrshp: Sub. Albara Corp., Robert L. Shumate, Pres, Richard M. Wilhelm, VP Mktng, Mark Bosko, VP Dev

Help Desk Institute (HDI), 1755 Telstar Dr, #101, Colorado Springs CO 80920-1017 USA; 719/531-5138, Fax: 719/528-4250, Web URL: helpdeskinst.com, Focus: Training and education for help desk professionals, Ownrshp: PVT, Founded: 1989, Empl: 25, Dennis Privitera, Exec Dir

Help Desk Technology Corp. 1370 Hurontario St, Mississauga Ontario L5G 3H4 Canada; 905/891-9100, Fax: 905/823-7156, Web URL: helpstar.com, Focus: Help desk support software, Prdts: HelpSTAR, Ownrshp: PVT

Henning Associates 1710 Allied St, #36, Charlottesville VA 22903 USA; 804/295-0554, 800/823-6896 Co Email: 72176.2507@compuserve.com, Web URL: users.aol.com/mikerh1053, Focus: Windows utilities, Prdts: Rolodeck, Mike Henning, Founder

Hercules Computer Technology Inc. 3839 Spinnaker Ct, Fremont CA 94538 USA; 510/623-6030, 800/532-0600 Fax: 510/623-1112, Co Email: sales@hercules.com, Web URL: hercules.com, Focus: Graphics boards, Prdts: Dynamite and Stingray/Video families, Terminator Professional, Ownrshp: PVT, Founded: 1982, Empl: 65, Van Suwannukul, Chmn, John Edeleanu, Pres & CEO, Hon P. Sit, VP Eng, Catherine Driscoll, Dir Mktng, Peggy Fong, CFO, Wendy Bulawa, Sr Acct Exec, Email: wendy_bulawa@mcimail.com

Hergo Ergonomic Support Systems Inc. 321 Fifth Ave, New York NY 10016-5015 USA; 212/684-4666, 800/434-3746 Fax: 212/684-6853, Focus: Ergonomic computer accessories, Prdts: Modular Computer Racks, Ownrshp: Aff. Hertz Tech., Founded: 1992, Eli Hertz, Pres, Daniel R. Schar, VP, Wendy Freid, Mktng Mgr, Wendy M. Freid

Hertz Computer Corp. 325 Fifth St, New York NY 10016 USA; 212/684-4141, 800/232-8737 Fax: 212/684-3658, Focus: PCs and LAN servers, Prdts: Hertz PCs, Workstations, Servers and Notebooks, Ownrshp: PVT, Founded: 1981, Eli Hertz, Pres, Marilyn Hertz, VP, Barry Goldsammler, VP Ops, Wendy Freid, Mktng Mgr

Hewlett-Packard Co. (HP), 5201 Stevens Creek Blvd, Santa Clara CA 95052-8059 USA; 408/553-4300, Fax: 800/333-1917, Co Email: @hp.com, Web URL: hp.com, Focus: Instruments, computers and peripherals, Ownrshp: PVT, Stk Sym: HWP, Founded: 1939, Empl: 102,300, Sales ($M): 31,519, Fiscal End: 10/95; Lewis E. Platt, Chmn, Pres & CEO, Robert P. Wayman, EVP & CFO, Willem P. Roelandts, SVP & GM Comp Syst, Richard E. Belluzzo, EVP Computer Org, Joel S. Birnbaum, SVP R&D, Mrlene Somsak, Mgr Corp PR

Hi Resolution Inc. 12 Federal St, #46, Newburyport MA 01950 USA; 508/463-6953, Fax: 508/463-9619, Co Email: hi.res.us@applelink.com, Focus: Macintosh software, Ownrshp: PVT, Donna MacDonald, Mktng Mgr

High Performance Systems Inc. 45 Lyme Rd, #300, Hanover NH 03755 USA; 603/643-9636, 800/332-1200 Co Email: support@hps-inc.com, Web URL: hps-inc.com, Focus: Business simulation and management software, Prdts: ithink, Ownrshp: PVT, Founded: 1985, Empl: 30, Barry Richmond, Pres, Nancy Maville, VP Fin & Admin

High Technology Software Corp. (HiTecSoft), 3370 N Hayden

Rd, #123-175, Scottsdale AZ 85251-6695 USA; 602/970-1025, Fax: 602/970-6323, Co Email: @hitecsoft.mhs.compuserve.com, Web URL: hitecsoft.com, Focus: NetWare software development tools, Prdts: ManageWare, Ownrshp: PVT, Founded: 1991, Empl: 8, Sean Moshir, Pres, Karen Handwork

Hilgraeve Inc. 111 Conant Ave, #A, Monroe MI 48161 USA; 313/243-0576, Fax: 313/243-0645, Co Email: @hilgraeve.com, Web URL: hilgraeve.com, Focus: Communication software, Prdts: HyperACCESS, Ownrshp: PVT, Founded: 1980, Empl: 10, Matthew H. Gray, Pres, Email: mgray@hilgraeve.com; Robert Everett, EVP, John Hile, VP R&D, Jeff Beamsley, VP Sales

Hitachi America Computer Div. 2000 Sierra Point Pkwy, MS 500, Brisbane CA 94005-1835 USA; 415/589-8300, 800/448-2244 Fax: 415/244-7647, Web URL: hitachi.com, Focus: Computers and peripherals, Ownrshp: Sub. Hitachi Ltd., Japan, Founded: 1910, Cynthia Huey, Marcom Sup

Hitachi America Ltd. 50 Prospect Ave, Tarrytown NY 10591-4698 USA; 914/332-5800, Fax: 914/332-5555, Focus: Peripherals, computers and semiconductors, Ownrshp: Sub. Hitachi, Japan, Founded: 1959, Empl: 6,000, Sales ($M): 4,000, Fiscal End: 3/95; Korchi Uemo, Pres, Manabu Kuwae, VP & GM, Gerard F. Corbett, Dir Corp Comm

Hitachi Data Systems (HDS), 750 Central Expwy, PO Box 54996, Santa Clara CA 95056-0996 USA; 408/970-1000, Fax: 408/727-8036, Co Email: @hdshq.com, Web URL: hdshq.com, Focus: Mainframe computers and peripherals, Ownrshp: Hitachi & EDS, Empl: 2,400, Sales ($M): 1,720, Fiscal End: 3/95; John Staedke, Pres & CEO, Mark Mickelson, VP, Mark Lewis, Email: lewis@hdshq.com

Hitachi Home Electronics Inc. 3890 Steve Reynolds Blvd, Norcross GA 30093-3012 USA; 800/241-6558 Focus: PC and workstation peripherals, Ownrshp: Sub. Hitachi, Japan, Peter Nitale

Hitachi Ltd. 6 Kanda-Surugadai, 4-chome, Chiyoda-ku, Tokyo 101 JP-101 Japan; 3-3258-1111, Web URL: hitachi.co.jp, Focus: Computer, communications and electronic products, Ownrshp: NYSE, Stk Sym: HIT, Founded: 1910, Empl: 331,673, Sales ($M): 76,640.0, Fiscal End: 3/96; Katsushige Mita, Chmn, Tsutomu Kanai, Pres

Hitachi Office Automation Systems 110 Summit Ave, Montvale NJ 07645 USA; 201/573-0774, Focus: Monitors, CD-ROMs and printers, Ownrshp: Sub. Hitachi, Japan, Founded: 1984, Amy Edmonds

Hitachi PC Corp. 2520 Junction Rd, Bldg D, San Jose CA 95134 USA; 408/321-5000, Fax: 408/321-5100, Focus: Notebook PCs, Ownrshp: Sub. Hitachi, Japan, Founded: 1995, Empl: 100, Ryuichi Otsuki

Hitachi Semiconductor & IC Div. 2000 Sierra Point Pkwy, Brisbane CA 94005-1835 USA; Focus: ICs, Ownrshp: Sub. Hitachi, Japan, Jeff Muscatine

Hitachi Telecom USA Inc. 3617 Parkway Ln, Norcross GA 30092-2829 USA; 770/446-8820, Fax: 770/242-1414, Focus: Telecom products, Prdts: AMS 5000, Ownrshp: Sub. Hitachi Ltd., Japan, Founded: 1987, Empl: 200, Makoto Suzuki, Pres, Peter Westafer, Marcom Mgr, Email: pwest@hitel.com

HNC Software Inc. 5930 Cornerstone Ct W, San Diego CA 92121-3728 USA; 619/546-8877, Fax: 619/452-6524, Focus: Neural network-based credit card fraud detection system, Ownrshp: OTC, Stk Sym: HNCS, Founded: 1986, Empl: 152, Sales ($M): 25.2, Fiscal End: 12/95; Robert L. North, Pres & CEO, Michael A. Thieman, EVP Sales & Mktng, Todd W. Gutschow, VP Tech, Allen P. Jost, VP Bus Dev, Raymond V. Thomas, VP & CFO, Fran DuCharme, Marcom

Hogan Systems Inc. 5080 Spectrum Dr, #400E, Dallas TX 75248 USA; 214/386-0020, Fax: 214/386-0315, Focus: Banking software, Ownrshp: OTC, Stk Sym: HOGN, Founded: 1977, Empl: 600, Sales ($M): 92.6, Fiscal End: 3/95; Michael H. Anderson, Chmn, Pres & CEO, David R. Bankhead, SVP & CFO, Paul J.

Zoukis, SVP Sales & Mktng, W. Daniel Johnson, SVP Corp Dev

Home Recording Rights Coalition (HRRC), PO Box 33576, 1145 19th St NW, Washington DC 20033 USA; 800/282-8273 Co Email: hrrc@access.digex.com, Web URL: digex.net/hrrc, Focus: Protect consumer's fair use right of electronic/computer products, Ownrshp: Nonprofit, Founded: 1981, Ruth Rodgers

Home Systems 1500 K Oliver Rd, #114, Fairfield CA 94533 USA; 707/422-6625, Fax: 707/422-1936, Focus: Personal inventory software, Prdts: Collect-On, Ownrshp: PVT

Honeybee Software Inc. 245 Victoria Ave, #800, Westmount Quebec H3Z 2M6 Canada; 514/989-5030, Fax: 514/989-8167, Focus: Vertical accounting software, Ownrshp: PVT, Founded: 1988, Jeff Klein, Pres, Mike Kreaden, VP Eng, Mark Jourdenais, Info Syst Mgr

Honeywell Inc. Honeywell Plaza, PO Box 524, Minneapolis MN 55440-0524 USA; 612/951-1000, Fax: 612/951-2294, Web URL: honeywell.com, Focus: Automation products, Prdts: Space and Aviation Control, Home and Building Control, Ownrshp: NYSE, Stk Sym: HON, Founded: 1885, Empl: 50,100, Sales ($M): 6,731.3, Fiscal End: 12/95; Michael R. Bonsignore, Chmn & CEO, D. Larry Moore, Pres & COO, William M. Hjerpe, VP & CFO, Edward D. Grayson, VP Gen Counsel, William L. Sanders, VP Info Syst, Meta Gaertnier, Dir Corp PR

Horizons Technology Inc. (HTI), 3990 Ruffin Rd, San Diego CA 92123-1873 USA; 619/292-8331, 800/828-3808 Fax: 619/292-7321, Co Email: info@horizons.com, Web URL: horizons.com, Focus: Network management, desktop mapping and multimedia software, Prdts: Interactive Marketing, Ownrshp: PVT, Founded: 1977, Empl: 450, Sales ($M): 43, James T. Palmer, Chmn & CEO, Pat Boyce, Pres & COO, Cynthia Mordaunt, VP Mktng, Kari Guentner, Email: kguentner.com

Houghton Mifflin Interactive 222 Berkeley St, Boston MA 02116-3764 USA; 617/351-5000, Co Email: @hmco.com, Web URL: hmco.com, Focus: Multimedia software, Prdts: Kids' Summer Clubhouse, Ownrshp: Sub Houghton Mifflin, Founded: 1995, Doug Eisenhart, Dir Dev & Licensing

Houston Area Apple Users Group (HAAUG), PO Box 610150, Houston TX 77208-0150 USA; 713/522-2179, Fax: 713/956-9049, Focus: Apple II, Macintosh and Newton users, Ownrshp: Nonprofit, Empl: 1,000, Ken Martinez, Pres, Mark Jacob, Past Pres

Howtek Inc. 21 Park Ave, Hudson NH 03051 USA; 603/882-5200, Fax: 603/880-3843, Focus: Color scanners, Ownrshp: AMEX, Stk Sym: HTK, Founded: 1984, Empl: 116, Sales ($M): 20.6, Fiscal End: 12/95; Robert Howard, Chmn, David Bothwell, CEO, M. Russell Leonard, EVP & COO, Robert Dusseault, VP Sales & Mktng, Robert J. Lungo, VP & CFO

HP Home Products Div. 5301 Stevens Creek Blvd, Santa Clara CA 95052 USA; 408/246-4300, Fax: 408/246-7293, Focus: Home PCs, Ownrshp: Sub. Hewlett-Packard, Harry W. McKinney, GM, Greg Jones, Mktng Mgr, Byron Connell, Prod Line Mgr, Dona Rozhin, Mkt Dev Mgr, John Romano, R&D Mgr

Hughes Network Systems-DirecPC 11717 Exploration Ln, Germantown MD 20876 USA; 301/428-5500, 800/347-3272 Fax: 301/428-1868, Co Email: info@direcpc.com, Web URL: direcpc.com, Focus: Multimedia satellite broadcast for PCs, Ownrshp: Sub. Hughes Electronics, Thomas R. McPherson, VP & GM

Human Code Inc. 1411 West Ave, #100, Austin TX 78710 USA; 512/477-5455, Fax: 512/477-5456, Co Email: @humancode.com, Web URL: humancode.com, Focus: Multimedia software, Ownrshp: PVT, Founded: 1993, Empl: 55, Chipp Walters, Pres & CEO, Liz Walters, COO, Lloyd Walker, VP Dev, Cindy Taylor, Dir PR, Email: cindy@humancode.com

Hummingbird Communications Ltd. 1 Sparks Ave, N York Ontario M2H 2W1 Canada; 905/470-1203, Fax: 905/470-1207, Web URL: hummingbird.com, Focus: X-server software, Ownrshp: OTC, Stk Sym: HUMCF, Founded: 1985, Empl: 235, Sales ($M): 54.3, Fiscal End: 12/95; Fred Sorkin, Pres, Jan Adamek, SVP Sales

& Mktng, Barry Litwin, VP R&D

Humongous Entertainment 16932 Woodinville-Redmond Rd NE, #204, Woodinville WA 98072 USA; 206/487-9258, 800/499-8386 Fax: 206/486-9494, Co Email: @humongous.com, Web URL: humongous.com, Focus: Entertainment and education software, Prdts: Freddi Fish, Putt-Putt, Ownrshp: PVT, Founded: 1992, Empl: 93, Shelley Day, Pres & CEO, Ron Gilbert, Co-founder, Ralph Giuffre, EVP Mktng, Alex Brown, VP Sales, John Uppendahl, Comm Dir

Hunter Digital 11999 San Vicente Blvd #440, Los Angeles CA 90049 USA; 310/471-5852, 800/576-6873 Fax: 310/471-1669, Focus: Input devices, Prdts: NoHands Mouse, Ownrshp: PVT, Aaron H. Sones, Pres

Hutchinson Technology Inc. 40 W Highland Park, Hutchinson MN 55350-9784 USA; 612/587-3797, 800/689-0755 Fax: 612/587-1810, Focus: Hard disk components, Ownrshp: OTC, Stk Sym: HTCH, Founded: 1965, Empl: 4,575, Sales ($M): 299.9, Fiscal End: 9/95; Wayne M. Fortun, CEO, Richard C. Myers, VP Admin, John A. Ingleman, VP & CFO, Richard J. Penn, VP Sales & Mktng

Hybrid Networks Inc. 10161 Bubb Rd, Cupertino CA 95014-4167 USA; 408/725-3250, Fax: 408/725-2439, Co Email: @hybrid, Web URL: hybrid.com, Focus: Cable modems, Ownrshp: PVT

Hyperion Software 900 Long Ridge Rd, Stamford CT 06902-1247 USA; 203/703-3000, Fax: 203/595-8500, Web URL: hys-oft.com, Focus: C/S business software, Ownrshp: OTC, Stk Sym: IMRS, Empl: 554, Sales ($M): 172.8, Fiscal End: 6/96; James A. Perakis, Pres & CEO, Peter F. DiGiammarino, Pres, David M. Sample, SVP, John N. Adinolfi, VP Mktng, Lucy Rae Ricciardi, VP & CFO

HyperLogic Corp. 1855 E Valley Pkwy, #210, Escondido CA 92027 USA; 619/746-2765, Fax: 619/746-4089, Co Email: prod-info@hyperlogic.com, Web URL: hyperlogic.com/hl, Focus: Fuzzy logic and neural network software, Prdts: CubiCalc, OWL Neural Network Library, Ownrshp: PVT, Founded: 1990, Fred Watkins, Pres, Email: fwatkins@hyperlogic.com; Bonnie Packert, EVP, Email: bpackert@hyperlogic.com

Hyundai Digital Media 510 Cottonwood Dr, Milpitas CA 95035 USA; 408/232-8000, Fax: 408/232-8131, Co Email: @hea.com, Focus: MPEG-2 decoders, Ownrshp: Sub. Hyundai Electronics, Founded: 1993, Empl: 62, Anvil Sawe, VP & GM, Vahe Akay, VP Mktng & Sales, Lit Lam, Sr Mktng Mgr, David Tahmassebi, Sr Mktng Mgr, Email: dtahmassebi@hea.com

Hyundai Electronics America 510 Cottonwood Dr, Milpitas CA 95035 USA; 408/232-8000, Fax: 408/232-8131, Co Email: @hea.com, Focus: PCs, peripherals and ICs, Ownrshp: Sub. Hyundai, Korea, Founded: 1983, Sales ($M): 1,400+, Y.H. Kim, Pres & CEO, I.B. Jeon, VP, Dennis McKenna, SVP Sales & Mktng

I-Kinetics Inc. 1 New England Exec Park, Burlington MA 01803-5005 USA; 617/661-8181, Fax: 617/661-8625, Focus: C/S software, Ownrshp: PVT, Founded: 1991, Bruce H. Cottman, Pres

I-O Data Devices Inc. 2005 Hamilton Ave, #220, San Jose CA 95125 USA; 408/377-7062, Fax: 408/377-7085, Focus: Multimedia products, Ownrshp: Sub. I-O Data, Japan, Founded: 1976, Akio Hosono, Pres, Haruo Kosugi, VP, Finney Gilbert, Mktng Mgr

I/O Software Inc. 1533 Spruce St #300, Riverside CA 92507-2427 USA; 909/222-7600, 800/800-7970 Fax: 909/222-7601, Co Email: info@iosoftware.com, Web URL: iosoftware.com, Focus: Software localization for Far-East market, Prdts: Stereolusions, Ownrshp: PVT, Founded: 1986, Tas Diens

i2 Technologies Inc. 909 E Las Colines Blvd, 16th Fl., Irving TX 75039 USA; 214/860-6000, Fax: 214/860-6060, Co Email: @i2.com, Focus: Planning and scheduling of supply chain, Ownrshp: PVT, Founded: 1988, Empl: 24, Sanjiv Sidhu, Pres, Email: sanjiv_sidhu@i2.com; Ken Sharma, Sr Partner, Email: ken_sharma@i2.com; Greg Brady, Pres Field Ops, Email: greg_brady@i2.com; Karen Johnson, Email:

karen_johnson@i2.com

Ibex Technologies Inc. 4921 RJ Matthews Pkwy, El Dorado Hills CA 95762 USA; 916/939-8888, Fax: 916/939-8899, Web URL: ibex.com, Focus: Fax-on-demand products, Prdts: Fax-It-Back, Ownrshp: PVT, Founded: 1989, Empl: 10, Ney Grant, Pres & CEO, Zoe Ann Meegan, Marcom Dir

IBM Credit Corp. 290 Harbor Dr, Stamford CT 06904 USA; 203/973-7000, Co Email: financing@vnet.ibm.com, Web URL: financing.hosting.ibm.com, Focus: Financing and leasing of information technology, Ownrshp: Sub. IBM Corp., Founded: 1981, Empl: 1,350, W. Wilson Lowery Jr., Chmn, Robert Braun, Dir Comm

IBM Personal Computer Co. (IBM PC), Rt 100, Sommers NY 10589 USA; 914/766-3700, 800/426-3333 Web URL: ibm.com, Focus: PCs, Ownrshp: Sub. IBM Corp., Founded: 1992, Empl: 10,000, Sales ($M): 9,000, William McCracken, GM Fullfillment

IBM Personal Software Products (IBM PSP), 11400 Burnet Rd, Austin TX 78758-3493 USA; 512/823-3176, Focus: PC software, Ownrshp: Sub. IBM Corp., John W. Thompson, GM PSP Div., John V. Harrison, VP Dev, David L. Harrington, Dir Strategy, John G. Schwarz, VP Mktng, Joseph L. Stunkard, Mgr PR

IC Systems 473 Roland Way, Oakland CA 94621-2014 USA; 510/339-3480, Fax: 510/339-0391, Focus: Credit card verification software, Prdts: ICVerify, Ownrshp: PVT, Founded: 1983, Steve Elefant, Pres, Merrell Sheehan

ICEM Technologies 4201 Lexington Ave N, Arden Hills MN 55126-6198 USA; 800/597-3094 Focus: CAD software, Ownrshp: Sub Control Data, Sales ($M): 50, Fiscal End: 12/94

ICL Inc. 11490 Commerce Park Dr, Reston VA 22091 USA; 703/648-3300, Fax: 703/648-3350, Web URL: icl.com, Focus: Software for enterprise-wide distributed computing, Prdts: Access Manager, Ownrshp: Sub. ICL, UK, Founded: 1968, Empl: 24,000, Sales ($M): 4,000, Fiscal End: 12/95; Anthony J. Cancelosi, VP & GM, Anne Prine, Marcom, Email: aprine@earthlink.net

ICONIX Software Engineering Inc. 2800 28th St, #320, Santa Monica CA 90405 USA; 310/458-0092, Fax: 310/396-3454, Co Email: iconix@eworld.com, Web URL: biap.com/iconix, Focus: Software engineering tools, Prdts: PowerTools, Ownrshp: PVT, Founded: 1984, Doug Rosenberg, Pres, Hunter Deane, VP Sales & Mktng, Andrea Lee, Marcom Mgr

Iconovex Corp. 7900 Xerxes Ave, #550, Bloomington MN 55431 USA; 612/896-5100, 800/943-0292 Fax: 612/896-5101, Co Email: fyi@iconovex.com, Web URL: iconovex.com, Focus: Indexing software, Prdts: Indexicon, AnchorPage, Ownrshp: Sub. Innovex, Stk Sym: INVX, Empl: 26, Thomas Haley, Chmn, Steve Waldron, Pres, Jeff Burkhardt, VP Sales, Bart Davis, Prod Mktng Mgr, Bernardo Sotomayor, VP & GM, Marcie Pietrs, Mktng Mgr

ICOT Corp. 3801 Zanker Rd, PO Box 5143, San Jose CA 95150-5143 USA; 408/433-3300, Fax: 408/433-0260, Focus: Network products, Ownrshp: OTC, Stk Sym: ICOT, Founded: 1968, Empl: 46, Sales ($M): 8.2, Fiscal End: 6/94; Arnold N. Silverman, Chmn, Aamer Latif, Pres & CEO, David J. Bivolcic, SVP

ICVerify Inc. 473 Roland Way, Oakland CA 94621 USA; 510/553-7500, Fax: 510/553-7553, Co Email: info@icverify.com, Focus: Credit card verification software, Prdts: ICVerify, Ownrshp: PVT, Founded: 1988, Empl: 40, F. Thomas Aden, Pres, Email: taden@icverify.com; Andrea R. Skov, VP Mktng, Email: askov@icverify.com; John F. Sauerland, CFO, Email: jsauerland@icverify.com

Id Software 18601 LBJ Fwy. #615, Mesquite TX 75150 USA; 214/613-3589, Fax: 214/686-9288, Web URL: idsoftware.com, Focus: Entertainment software, Prdts: Doom, Ownrshp: PVT, Founded: 1990, Empl: 14, Sales ($M): 15.6, Fiscal End: 12/95; John Carmakk, Pres, Email: John@idsoftware.com; Jay Wilbur, CEO, Email: Jay@idsoftware.com; Kevin Cloud, Secretary, Email: kevin@idsoftware

IDC Government 3110 Fairview Park Dr, #1100, Falls Church VA 22042-4503 USA; 703/876-5055, Fax: 703/876-5077, Web URL: idcg.com, Focus: Information technology data and consulting, Ownrshp: PVT, Matthew Mahoney, Research Dir

IDC/LINK 2 Park Ave #1420, New York NY 10016 USA; 212/726-0900, Fax: 212/696-8096, Web URL: idcresearch.com, Focus: Electronic information svcs, education market data, mass market computing & telecom, Ownrshp: IDC, Founded: 1976, Empl: 45, Andy Bose, Group VP, Email: bose@idcresearch.com; Mark Winther, VP, Email: mwinther@idcresearch.com; Julia Blelock, VP, Email: jblelock@idcresearch.com; Simon Salamon, VP, Email: ssalamon@idcresearch.com; June Wallach, VP, Email: jwallach@idcresearch.com; Elleen Zimber, Grp Op Mgr, Email: ezimbler@idcresearch.com

IdeaFisher Systems Inc. 2222 Martin St, #110, Irvine CA 92715 USA; 714/474-8111, Fax: 714/757-2896, Focus: Creativity software tools, Prdts: IdeaFisher, Writer's Edge, Ownrshp: PVT, Founded: 1988, Marshall Fisher, Chmn & CEO

IDG Communications (IDG), 1 Exeter Plaza, 15th Fl, Boston MA 02116 USA; 617/534-1200, Fax: 617/859-8642, Focus: Over 200 computer magazines in 60+ countries, Prdts: CIO, Computerworld, InfoWorld, Macworld, Network World, PC World, Ownrshp: PVT, Empl: 5,000, Sales ($M): 1,400, Fiscal End: 12/95; Patrick J. McGovern, Chmn, Kelly Conlin, Pres, Jim Casella, COO

IDOC Inc. 10474 Santa Monica Blvd, #404, Los Angeles CA 90025 USA; 310/446-4666, 800/336-9898 Fax: 310/446-4661, Co Email: @idocinc.com, Focus: Software and documentation translation services, Ownrshp: PVT, Founded: 1980, Empl: 75, Claudio Pinkus, Pres, Email: claudio@idocinc.com; Ruben Servi, Mktng Dir, Email: ruben@idocinc.com

IEEE Computer Society (IEEE-CS), 1730 Massachusetts Ave NW, Washington DC 20036-1992 USA; 202/371-0101, Fax: 202/728-9614, Web URL: computer.org, Focus: Association for computer professionals, Ownrshp: Nonprofit, Founded: 1951, Empl: 100,000, T. Micahel Elliott, Exec Dir, Anneliese von Mayrhauser, VP Conf & Tutorials

IEM Inc. PO Box 1889, Ft. Collins CO 80522 USA; 970/221-3005, Fax: 970/221-1909, Focus: Mass storage for HP computers, Founded: 1981, Empl: 35, Anita Sayed, Pres, Hushi Sayed, CEO

Iiyama North America 650 Louis Dr, #120, Warminster PA 18974 USA; 215/957-6543, 800/914=9264 Fax: 215/957-6651, Web URL: iiyama.com, Focus: Monitors, Ownrshp: Sub. Iiyama Electric Co. Ltd., Founded: 1981, Mike Omaru, Pres, Kent Petersen, VP, Dave Cameron, VP

Ikos Systems Inc. 19050 Pruneridge Ave, Cupertino CA 95014 USA; 408/255-4567, Fax: 408/366-8699, Focus: Simulation systems for ASIC and system design, Prdts: Voyager, Ownrshp: OTC, Stk Sym: IKOS, Founded: 1984, Empl: 113, Sales ($M): 28.6, Fiscal End: 9/95; Gerald S. Casilli, Chmn, Ramon A. Nunez, Pres & CEO, Lawrence A. Meling, VP Mktng, William B. Fazakerly, CTO, Joseph W. Rockom, VP & CFO

ILT Systems Inc. 2 Penn Plaza, New York NY 10121 USA; 212/629-5790, Fax: 212/629-0690, Focus: Imaging managing products, Ownrshp: PVT, Michael Kelly, Dir Sales, Ella Nyc

Image Axis Inc. 38 W 21st St, New York NY 10010 USA; 212/989-5000, Fax: 212/989-5444, Co Email: kgo@applelink.com, Focus: Digital imaging and pre-press services, Ownrshp: PVT, Founded: 1993, Kevin O'Neill, Co-founder, Paul Foley, Co-founder, Nicola Foley

Image Smith Inc. 1313 W Sepulveda Blvd, Torrance CA 90501 USA; 310/325-1429, Fax: 310/539-9784, Focus: Multimedia education software, Ownrshp: PVT, Founded: 1991, Dominique Claessens, Pres, Jake Myrick, VP Ops, Jim Myrick, VP Mktng, Deborah K. Berland, Com Mgr

IMAGE Society Inc. PO Box 6221, Chandler AZ 85246 USA; 602/839-8709, Co Email: image@acvax.inre.asu.edu, Focus: Advancing real-time visual simulation technology and applications, Ownrshp: Nonprofit, Founded: 1987, Empl: 600, Eric Monroe, Chmn & Pres, VP

IMAGE-X 5765 Thornwood Dr, Goleta CA 93117-3801 USA; 805/964-3537, Fax: 805/683-8525, Co Email: @imagexx.com, Web URL: imagexx.com, Focus: Image storage systems, Prdts: IMAGEVIEW, Ownrshp: PVT, Founded: 1985, Empl: 35, Sales ($M): 1.5, Fiscal End: 12/95; Mohammed Shaikh, Chmn, Email: mohammed@imagexx.com; Saleem Meeran, Pres, Email: saleem@imagexx.com; George Jacob, VAR Mgr, Email: george@imagexx.com; Mark Wilkinson, Acct Mgr, Email: mark@imagexx.com

ImageMind Software Inc. 5 Triad Ctr, #600, Salt Lake City UT 84180 USA; 801/350-9461, 800/321-5933 Fax: 801/355-5008, Co Email: @imagemind.com, Web URL: imagemind.com, Focus: Video and audio software, Prdts: Video Express Viewer

Imagina Inc. 510 Oregon Pioneer Bldg, 320 SW Stark St, Portland OR 97204 USA; 503/224-8522, Fax: 503/224-8505, Web URL: imagina.com, Focus: Macintosh based Usenet news server, Prdts: Newstand, Ownrshp: PVT, Brian Caldwell, Pres, Email: bcaldwell@imagina.com

Imagine That Inc. 6830 Via Del Oro, #230, San Jose CA 95119 USA; 408/365-0305, Fax: 408/629-1251, Co Email: extend@imaginethatinc.com, Web URL: imaginethatinc.com, Focus: Software development, Prdts: Extend, Extend BPR, Ownrshp: PVT, Founded: 1987, Empl: 50, Bob Diamond, Pres, Pat Diamond, CFO, Steve Jamperti, Dir Research

Imaging Technologies Assoc. (ITA), 25 Mid-Tech Dr #C, W Yarmouth MA 02673 USA; 508/775-3433, Fax: 508/790-4778, Focus: Association of printer supplies manufacturers, Ownrshp: Nonprofit, Founded: 1922, Chuck Sabatt, Exec Secretary, Chuck Sabatt, Exec Secretary

Imagraph Corp. 11 Elizabeth Dr, Chelmsford MA 01824 USA; 508/256-4624, Fax: 508/250-9155, Focus: Imaging and graphics controllers, Ownrshp: Sub. Microfield Graphics, Founded: 1985, Sheldon Liebman, Marcom Mgr

Imateq Systems Corp. 108 Scandia Rise NW, Calgary Alberta T3L 1V6 Canada; 403/285-9551, Focus: Educational and training software, Prdts: Puzzle Maker, Teach & Test, Ownrshp: PVT, Founded: 1985, Empl: 2, Jerry Pelletier, Pres

IMC Networks Corp. 16931 Millikan Ave, Irvine CA 92714 USA; 714/724-1070, 800/624-1070 Fax: 714/724-1020, Co Email: sales@imcnetworks.com, Web URL: imcnetworks.com, Focus: Ethernet hubs and repeaters, Ownrshp: PVT, Founded: 1988, Empl: 40, Jerry Roby, Pres & CEO, Email: jroby@imcnetworks.com; Michael Schleider, VP Sales & Mktng, Email: mschleider@imcnetworks.com; Jan Morrison, Dir Marcom, Email: jmorrison@imcnetworks.com

IMP Inc. 2830 N First St, San Jose CA 95134-2071 USA; 408/432-9100, Fax: 408/434-0335, Web URL: impweb.com, Focus: Mixed analog & digital CMOS ASICs, Ownrshp: OTC, Stk Sym: IMPX, Founded: 1981, Empl: 400, Sales ($M): 76.8, Fiscal End: 3/96; David A. Laws, Pres & CEO, Moiz B. Khambaty, VP Tech, Russ Almand, VP WW Sales, David Laws, SVP Mktng, Charles S. Isherwood, SVP & CFO

Improve Technologies 345 E 800 S, Orem UT 84058 USA; 801/224-6550, Fax: 801/224-0355, Co Email: itsales@transera.com, Web URL: transera.com/improve, Focus: PC processor upgrades, Ownrshp: PVT, Founded: 1976, Empl: 25, Ron Wilson, CEO, Ralph Wilson, EVP, David Washburn, Dir Sales & Mktng, Email: davidw@transera.com; Nick Mecham, Mgr, Email: nickm@transera.com

In Focus Systems Inc. 27700-B SW Pkwy Ave, Wilsonville OR 97070-9215 USA; 503/685-8888, 800/294-6400 Fax: 503/685-8887, Web URL: infs.com, Focus: LCD projection devices, Ownrshp: OTC, Stk Sym: INFS, Founded: 1986, Empl: 391, Sales ($M): 202.8, Fiscal End: 12/95; John V. Harker, Chmn, Pres & CEO, Lyle W. Jordan, VP Ops, Mark E. Reed, VP Sales & Mktng, Allen H. Alley, VP Prod Dev, Michael D. Yonker, VP IS & CFO

In-Stat Inc. PO Box 14667, Scottsdale AZ 85260-2418 USA; 602/483-4440, Fax: 602/483-0400, Web URL: instat.com, Focus: Information services on semiconductor, computer and communications industries, Prdts: In-Stat Electronics Report, Ownrshp: PVT, Founded: 1981, Empl: 17, Sales ($M): 2.5, Jack Beedle, Founder, John Abram, Pres, Morry Marshall, Dir Analysts

InaCom Corp. 10810 Farnam Dr, #200, Omaha NE 68154 USA; 402/392-3900, 800/843-2762 Web URL: inacom.com, Focus: Computer store franchisor and operator, Ownrshp: OTC, Stk Sym: INAC, Founded: 1976, Empl: 1,400, Sales ($M): 2,200.3, Fiscal End: 12/95; Bill L. Fairfield, Pres & CEO, Rick Inatome, Chmn, David C. Guenthner, EVP & CFO, Mike Steffan, Pres Distribution, Larry Fazzini, VP Corp Resources, Geri Michelic, VP Marcom, Email: gmichelic@inacom.com

Inchcape Inc. 1 Tech Dr, Andover MA 01810 USA; 508/689-9355, Fax: 508/689-9353, Web URL: worldlab.com, Focus: Independent testing, inspection and certification, Prdts: ETL Listed, WH Listed, Ownrshp: PVT, Eric N. Birch, Pres, Glen R. Dash, VP R&D, Alan B. Dittrich, Dir Mktng, Patrick Sweeney, VP & CFO, Cheri Hart, Marcom Mgr

Inchcape Testing Services 593 Massachusetts Ave, Boxborough MA 01719 USA; 508/263-2662, Fax: 508/263-7086, Focus: FCC compliance, product safety and international compliance testing, Ownrshp: PVT, Founded: 1983, Chuck Kolifrath, GM

Inclination Software Inc. PO Box 8668, Incline Village NV 89452-8668 USA; 702/831-5595, Fax: 702/831-4979, Co Email: @isiinc.com, Web URL: isiinc.com, Focus: C development tools, Prdts: SpeedEdit, Quick-E, Ownrshp: PVT, Founded: 1978, Russ Bradford, Pres, Email: russ@isiinc.com; Sandra K. Bradford, VP Sales & Mktng, Email: sales@isiinc.com

Incomnet Inc. 21031 Ventura Blvd #1100, Woodland Hills CA 91364 USA; 818/887-3400, Fax: 818/587-5697, Focus: Networking and communication services, Ownrshp: OTC, Stk Sym: ICNT, Founded: 1974, Empl: 30, Sales ($M): 46.8, Fiscal End: 12/94; Melvyn Rednick, Pres & CEO, Stephen Caswell, VP Mktng & Sales

InContext Systems Corp. 2 St Clair Ave W, 16th Floor, Toronto Ontario M4V 1L5 Canada; 416/922-0087, Fax: 416/922-6489, Web URL: incontext.ca, Focus: SGML software, Prdts: InContext 2, Ownrshp: VSE, Stk Sym: INI, Founded: 1991, Sales ($M): 1.5, Fiscal End: 3/95; Robert Arn, Chmn & Pres, Ian Hembery, VP Mktng & Sales

Independence Technologies Inc. 42705 Lawrence Place, Fremont CA 94538 USA; 510/438-2000, Fax: 510/438-2034, Focus: Middleware, Ownrshp: PVT, Dan Carnese, Dir Eng

Independent Computer Consultants Assoc. (ICCA), 933 Gardenview Office Pkwy, St Louis MO 63141 USA; 314/997-4633, Fax: 314/567-5133, Co Email: 70007.1407@compuserve.com, Focus: Association for computer consultants, Ownrshp: Nonprofit, Founded: 1976, Empl: 2,100, Glenn Koenen, Exec Dir, Deborah Sampson, Chmn, Email: 70007.4250@compuserve.com; Ray Rauth, Pres, Email: 70007.4251@compuserve.com

Indiana Cash Drawer Co. (ICD), 1315 S Miller St, Shelbyville IN 46176 USA; 317/398-6643, 800/227-4379 Fax: 317/392-0958, Focus: POS products, Prdts: POShoe, SLD, Ownrshp: PVT, Founded: 1921, Empl: 80, Randy Boone, VP Finance, Phil Stephens, VP Ops, Robert Benavides, VP Sales & Mktng, Catherine Woods, Marcom Mgr

Individual Inc. 8 New England Exec Park W, Burlington MA 01803 USA; 617/273-6000, Fax: 617/273-6060, Co Email: info@individual.com, Web URL: newspage.com, Focus: Software agent to search for information, Prdts: HeadsUp, Ownrshp: PVT, Founded: 1989, Yosi Amran, Chmn & Pres, Jacques Bouvard, VP Eng, Annette Lissauer, VP Sales, Richard Vancil, VP Mktng, Bruce Glabe, VP & CFO, Joseph Zahner

Individual Software Inc. 5870 Stoneridge Dr, #1, Pleasanton CA 94588 USA; 510/734-6767, 800/822-3522 Fax: 510/734-8337, Co Email: 76366.3213@compuserve.com, Focus: Training and productivity software, Prdts: Individual Training series, Individual Productivity & Lifestyle series, Ownrshp: PVT, Founded: 1981, Empl: 45, Sales ($M): 6.1, Fiscal End: 11/95; Jo-L Hendrickson, Pres & CEO, Diane Dietzler, VP Mktng & Sales, Bill Riley, VP Sales, Gary Jose, VP New Bus Dev, Kathleen Turnball, PR Mgr, Email: 76366.3213@compuserve.com

Industrial CPU Systems Inc. 111-D W Dyer Rd, Santa Ana CA 92707 USA; 714/957-2815, 800/832-4274 Fax: 714/957-3128, Co Email: 102172.722@compuserve.com, Focus: PCs, Ownrshp: PVT, Founded: 1989, Mehrdad Ayati, Pres

Inference Corp. 100 Rowland Way, Novato CA 94945 USA; 415/899-0100, 800/332-9923 Fax: 415/899-9080, Co Email: info@inference.com, Web URL: inference.com, Focus: AI software, Ownrshp: OTC, Stk Sym: INFR, Founded: 1979, Empl: 200, Sales ($M): 29.4, Fiscal End: 1/96; Peter R. Tierney, Chmn, Pres & CEO, Michael Thoma, SVP Mktng, Alan P. Patty, SVP Sales, John Binns, VP Prod Dev, William D. Griffin, SVP & CFO

Influence Online Systems 6633 Portwest Dr, #100, Houston TX 77024-8001 USA; 713/789-4808, Fax: 713/789-4662, Focus: Online operating software, Prdts: I-Online, Ownrshp: PVT

InfoAccess Inc. 2800 156th Ave SE, #205, Bellevue WA 98007 USA; 206/747-3203, 800/344-9737 Fax: 206/641-9367, Co Email: @infoaccess.com, Web URL: infoaccess.com, Focus: Interactive electronic publishing software, Prdts: Guide Professional Publisher, Guide Author, HTML Transit, Ownrshp: PVT, Founded: 1985, Empl: 30, Richard Dillhoff, CEO, W. James Culbertson, Pres, Michael New, Dir Mktng, Brian Pavicic, Dir Sales, Frances Bigley, Email: fbigley@infoaccess.com

InfoBusiness Inc. 887 S Orem Blvd, #B, Orem UT 84058-5009 USA; 801/221-1100, 800/657-5300 Fax: 801/221-1194, Web URL: infobusiness.com, Focus: Multimedia CD-ROMs, Prdts: Information USA, Mega Movie Guide, Getting Business to Come to You, Ownrshp: PVT, Founded: 1991, Empl: 15, Bryan Barron, Pres, Matthew Tippetts, VP Prod Dev, Dennis Riley, VP Mktng

Infodata Systems Inc. 12150 Monument Dr, #400, Fairfax VA 22033 USA; 703/934-5205, Fax: 703/934-7154, Focus: Database and text management software, Prdts: Inquire/Text, Ownrshp: OTC, Stk Sym: INFD, Empl: 170, Sales ($M): 7.0, Fiscal End: 12/95; Richard T. Bueschel, Chmn, Harry Kaplowitz, Pres, David Van Daele, SVP, Richard M. Tworek, SVP

Infographix Technologies Inc. 250 Williams St, #1120, Atlanta GA 30303 USA; 404/523-4944, Fax: 404/523-4882, Focus: Multimedia and digital printing products, Ownrshp: PVT, Founded: 1991, Empl: 40, Ken O. Lipscomb, Pres, Brian Bernier, EVP, Genevieve Tondi, Dir Sales & Mktng, Richard Robinson, Dir SW Dev, Raviv Laor, CFO, Michelle Comrie, Dir PR

Infogrip Inc. 1141 E Main St, Ventura CA 93001 USA; 805/652-0770, 800/397-0921 Fax: 805/652-0880, Co Email: infogrip@infogrip.com, Web URL: infogrip.com/infogrip, Focus: Compact ergonomic keyboards for one hand use, Prdts: BAT, Ownrshp: PVT, Founded: 1986, Elizabeth W. Jacobs, Pres, Email: 76106.430@compuserve.com; Aaron Gaston

InfoImaging Technologies Inc. 3977 E Bayshore Rd, Palo Alto CA 94303 USA; 415/960-0100, 800/966-1140 Fax: 415/960-0200, Co Email: info@infimaging.com, Web URL: infoimaging.com, Focus: Fax software, Prdts: 3D Fax, Ownrshp: PVT, Doug Wathor, VP Sales & Mktng, Doug Wathor

Infomart 1950 Stemmons Fwy, Dallas TX 75207-3199 USA; 214/746-3500, Fax: 214/746-3501, Web URL: infomartusa.com, Focus: Permanent product showroom for computer companies, Ownrshp: PVT, Founded: 1985, Empl: 110, Tom Jones, Pres & GM

Inforite Corp. 1670 S Amphlett Blvd #100, San Mateo CA 94402-2511 USA; 415/571-8766, Fax: 415/571-7547, Focus: Pen data entry products, Ownrshp: Sub. Moore Bus. Forms, Founded: 1982, Kiroku Kato, Pres & CEO, Mike McFarland, SVP Sales & Mktng, Steve Melnicki, VP Ops, Bill Alex, Dir Sales, Edward Murray, VP Eng, Peter Wickman, Dir Mktng

Information Access Co. 362 Lakeside Dr, Foster City CA 94404

USA; 415/378-5200, Fax: 415/378-5369, Focus: CD-ROM with text of over 110 computer magazines, Prdts: Computer Select, Ownrshp: Sub Thomson Corp., Founded: 1976, Empl: 600, Morris Goldstein, Pres, Robert Howell, EVP & GM

Information Builders Inc. 1250 Broadway, 37th Floor, New York NY 10001-3782 USA; 212/736-4433, Fax: 212/268-7470, Web URL: ibi.com, Focus: Database software, Prdts: Focus, Ownrshp: PVT, Founded: 1975, Empl: 1,700, Sales ($M): 240, Fiscal End: 12/95; Gerald D. Cohen, Pres, David Kemler, VP Mktng & Sales, Timothy Benthall, VP Int Com, Martin Slagowitz, VP Prof Svcs, Harry Lerner, VP Fin, Pamela Haas

Information Dimensions Inc. (IDI), 5080 Tuttle Crossing Blvd, Dublin OH 43017-3569 USA; 614/761-8083, Fax: 614/761-7290, Web URL: idi.oclc.org, Focus: Document management and retrieval, Prdts: ZyIndex, Ownrshp: Sub OCLC, Founded: 1986, Empl: 230, Sales ($M): 26.5, Bill Forquer, Pres & CEO, Bruce Duff, VP Mktng, George Shemas, VP Prod Dev, Barbara Johnson, PR Mgr, Email: bjohnson@idi.oclc.org

Information Industry Association (IIA), 1625 Massachusetts Ave NW, #700, Washington DC 20036 USA; 202/986-0280, Fax: 202/638-4403, Web URL: infoindustry.org, Focus: Association for companies that create, use or distribute information electronically, Ownrshp: Nonprofit, Founded: 1968, Empl: 550, Ronald Dunn, Exec Dir

Information Management Associates Inc. (IMA), 1 Corporate Dr, #414, Shelton CT 06484-6210 USA; 203/925-6800, 800/776-0462 Fax: 203/925-1170, Co Email: imainfo@ima-inc.com, Focus: Call center management software, Prdts: Telemar, Edge TeleBusiness Software, Ownrshp: PVT, Founded: 1984, Empl: 225, Sales ($M): 21, Albert Subbloie, Pres & CEO, Gary Martino, VP & CFO, James Aufdemberge, VP Sales & Mktng, David Caldeira, VP Prod, Andrei Poludnewycz, EVP Prod, Kathy Corry, Marcom Coord, Email: corryk@ima-inc.com

Information Management Research Inc. 5660 Greenwood Plaza Blvd, #210, Englewood CO 80111 USA; 303/689-0022, Fax: 303/689-0055, Co Email: imrgold@aol.com, Focus: Indexing/retrieval software, Ownrshp: PVT, Dan Lucarini, Dir Mktng, LeAnne Troutman

Information Presentation Technologies Inc. 994 Mill St, #200, San Luis Obispo CA 93401 USA; 805/541-3000, Fax: 805/541-3037, Co Email: info@iptech.com, Web URL: iptech.com, Focus: Mac to NFS connectivity products, Prdts: uShare, Partner, uPrint, CanOPI, TurboTalk, LessTalk, PrintQMgr, Ownrshp: PVT, Founded: 1983, Empl: 45, Jonathan Simonds, Pres, Olivia Favela, VP Sales & Mktng, Kerstin Barr, Marcom, Email: kerstinb@iptech.com

Information Resources Inc. (IRI), 150 N Clinton St, Chicago IL 60661 USA; 312/726-1221, Focus: Decision support software and services, Prdts: Express, Ownrshp: OTC, Stk Sym: IRK, Founded: 1969, Empl: 4,087, Sales ($M): 399.9, Fiscal End: 12/95; Thomas W. Wilson Jr., Chmn, Gian M. Fulgoni, CEO, Jeffrey P. Stamen, Pres SW Group, Randall S. Smith, Pres Info Svcs, George Garrick, Pres NA Group

Information Storage Devices Inc. 2045 Hamilton Ave, San Jose CA 95125 USA; 408/369-2400, 800/825-4473 Fax: 408/369-2422, Focus: Voice storage/playback ICs, Ownrshp: OTC, Stk Sym: ISDI, Founded: 1987, Sales ($M): 55.5, Fiscal End: 12/95; David L. Angel, Pres & CEO, Scott Owen, VP & COO, Trevor Blyth, VP Dev, Stephan Stephansen, VP Mktng & Sales, Felix Rosengarten, VP & CFO, Karin Bootsma, Mktng Dir

Information Systems Audit & Control Assoc. (ISACA), 3701 Algonquin Rd, #1010, Rolling Meadows IL 60008 USA; 847/253-1545, Fax: 847/253-1443, Web URL: isaca.org, Focus: Advancement of information system audit and control, Ownrshp: Nonprofit, Founded: 1969, Empl: 13,500, Susan M. Caldwell, Exec Dir

Information Systems Security Assoc. Inc. (ISSA), 1926 Waukegan Rd, #1, Glenview IL 60025 USA; 847/657-6746, Co

Email: issa@mcs.com, Web URL: uhsa.uh.edu/issa, Focus: Association for information security professionals, Ownrshp: Nonprofit, Founded: 1981, Empl: 2,000, Carl A. Wangman, Exec Dir

Information Technologies Research Inc. PO Box 3166, Hallandale FL 33008-3166 USA; 407/852-9919, Fax: 407/962-1181, Focus: Image compression and processing software, Founded: 1987, Empl: 10, Sales ($M): 2.0, Fiscal End: 12/92; Gregory Kisor, Pres & CEO

Information Technology Association America (ITAA), 1616 N Forth Myer Dr, #1300, Arlington VA 22209-9998 USA; 703/522-5055, Fax: 703/525-2279, Web URL: itaa.com, Focus: Trade association for software & services firms, Ownrshp: Nonprofit, Founded: 1960, Empl: 650, Harris Miller, Pres, Olga Grkavaz, SVP

Information Technology Foundation 1616 N Forth Myer Dr, #1300, Arlington VA 22209-9998 USA; 703/522-5055, Fax: 703/525-2279, Focus: Information technologies to benefit disabled persons, Ownrshp: Nonprofit, Founded: 1986

Information Technology Industry Council (ITI), 1250 Eye St NW, #200, Washington DC 20005 USA; 202/737-8888, Fax: 202/638-4922, Web URL: itic.com, Focus: Association for information technology industry, Ownrshp: Nonprofit, Founded: 1916, Empl: 28, Oliver Smoot, EVP

Informative Graphics 706 E Bell Rd, #207, Phoenix AZ 85022 USA; 602/971-6061, Fax: 602/971-1714, Focus: Document management software, Ownrshp: PVT

Informer Computer Systems Inc. 12833 Monarch St, Garden Grove CA 92641-3921 USA; 714/891-1112, Fax: 714/898-2624, Focus: Portable terminals, 9-1-1 terminals and call tracking systems, Ownrshp: PVT, Founded: 1972, Empl: 20, Sales ($M): 5, Fiscal End: 3/94; Ed Dailey, CEO, Tien Van, Pres, Will Little, SVP, Janet Yi, Dir Marcom

Informix Software Inc. 4100 Bohannon Dr, Menlo Park CA 94025 USA; 415/926-6300, Fax: 415/926-6593, Web URL: informix.com, Focus: Database software, Ownrshp: OTC, Stk Sym: IFMX, Founded: 1980, Empl: 2,212, Sales ($M): 709.0, Fiscal End: 12/95; Phillip E. White, Chmn, Pres & CEO, Edwin C. Winder, SVP Sales, Stephen E. Hill, SVP Corp Dev, Steven R. Sommer, VP Mktng, Howard H. Graham, SVP & CFO, Brenda Hansen, Mgr PR

Infosafe Systems Inc. 342 Madison Ave, #622, New York NY 10173 USA; 212/867-7200, Fax: 212/867-7227, Co Email: @infosafe.com, Web URL: infosafe.com, Prdts: Design Palette, Ownrshp: OTC, Stk Sym: ISFEU, Founded: 1992, Empl: 22, Fiscal End: 7/95; Thomas H. Lipscomb, Pres, Email: tom@infosafe.com; Charlton H. Calhoun, EVP Mktng, Robert H. Nagel, EVP Tech, Alan Alpern, CFO, Cathleen Cogswell, Corp Comm Dir, Email: execoffice@infosafe.com

Infoseek Corp. 2620 Augustine Dr, #250, Santa Clara CA 95054 USA; 408/567-2700, Web URL: infoseek.com, Focus: Internet search software, Prdts: Infoseek, Ownrshp: OTC, Stk Sym: SEEK, Founded: 1994, Empl: 57, Sales ($M): 1.0, Fiscal End: 12/95; Robin Johnson, CEO

InfoSource Inc. 6947 University Blvd, Winter Park FL 32792 USA; 407/677-0300, 800/393-4636 Fax: 407/677-9226, Co Email: isisale@istraining.com, Web URL: istraining.com, Focus: Personal computing training software, Ownrshp: PVT, Founded: 1983

InfoStructure Services & Technologies Inc. Iowa State Univ Research Park, Ames IA 50010 USA; 515/296-6903, Fax: 515/296-9910, Focus: Network security software, Ownrshp: PVT, Greg Shanon, Pres

Infotel Distributing 6990 US Rt 36E, Fletcher OH 45326 USA; 513/368-3753, 800/528-4504 Focus: PC product distributor, Ownrshp: PVT, Empl: 680

Infrared Data Assoc. (IrDA), PO Box 3883, Walnut Creek CA 94598 USA; 510/934-6546, Fax: 510/943-5600, Co Email: info@irda.org, Web URL: irda.org, Focus: Interoperable IR data interconnection standard, Ownrshp: Nonprofit, Empl: 130, John

LaRoche, Exec Dir, Email: jlaroche@netcom.com

Ingram Laboratories 1395 S Lyon St, Santa Ana CA 92705 USA; 714/566-1000, Focus: Benchmark, acceptance, comparison, compatibility, usability, software and custom testing, Ownrshp: PVT, Founded: 1982, Empl: 18, Karman Stick

Ingram Micro Inc. 1600 E St Andrew Place, PO Box 25125, Santa Ana CA 92799-5125 USA; 714/566-1000, Fax: 714/566-7815, Focus: Distributes microcomputer products, Ownrshp: Sub. Ingram Industries, Founded: 1983, Empl: 1,600, Sales ($M): 4,000, Fiscal End: 12/93; Jerre Stead, CEO

Initio Corp. 2901 Tasman Dr, #201, Santa Clara CA 95054 USA; 408/988-1919, Fax: 408/988-3254, Focus: Peripheral controllers, Ownrshp: PVT, Founded: 1993, S Chris Chen, Pres & CEO, Larry Ko, VP HW Dev, Winston Hung, VP SW Dev, Ali H. Zadeh, VP Sales & Mktng, Email: aliz@initio.com; Robert A. Robinson, Dir Sales

Inland Assoc. 15021 W 117th St, Olathe KS 66062 USA; 913/746-7977, 800/888-7800 Focus: Computer hardware distribution, Ownrshp: PVT, Founded: 1969, Empl: 50, Sales ($M): 27.0, Peggy Meader, Pres, Chuck Floyd, CFO, Michele Grabber, Mktng Dir

Inmac Corp. 2465 Augustine Dr, Santa Clara CA 95052-8031 USA; 408/727-1970, Fax: 408/727-4131, Focus: Mail order of computer peripherals, accessories and supplies, Ownrshp: OTC, Stk Sym: INMC, Founded: 1975, Empl: 925, Sales ($M): 349.4, Fiscal End: 7/95; Kenneth A. Eldred, Chmn, Jeffrey A. Heimbuck, Pres & CEO, Bennet R. Goldberg, EVP Mktng, Margo M. Hart, VP Human Res, Raymond E. Nystrom, VP & CFO

Innovative Tech Systems Inc. 444 Jacksonville Rd #200, Warminster PA 18974 USA; 215/441-5600, Focus: Computer integrated facilities management software, Ownrshp: OTC, Stk Sym: ITSY, Founded: 1986, Empl: 34, Sales ($M): 1.7, Fiscal End: 1/94; William M. Thompson, Pres & CEO, John M. Thompson, COO, John R. Smart, VP Mktng

Input 1881 Landings Dr, Mountain View CA 94043-0848 USA; 415/961-3300, Fax: 415/961-3966, Co Email: @input.com, Focus: Market research on information service, networks, software, SI and electronic commerce, Ownrshp: PVT, Founded: 1974, Empl: 70, Sales ($M): 8, Peter Cunningham, Pres & CEO, Email: pac@input.com; Bob Goodwin, VP Sales & Mktng, Email: bob_goodwin@input.com

Insight Development Corp. 2420 Camino Ramon, #205, San Ramon CA 94583-4207 USA; 510/244-2000, 800/825-4115 Fax: 510/244-2020, Focus: Software utilities for printers, Prdts: Render-Print, PrintAPlot Pro, Squiggle, Ownrshp: PVT, Founded: 1985, Empl: 11, Steve Haber, Chmn, Pres & CEO

Insights Software 8405 Pershing Rd, #400, Playa del Rey CA 90293 USA; 310/577-1185, Fax: 310/577-1189, Co Email: info@successware.com, Focus: Motivational software, Ownrshp: PVT, Andrew Maltin, Co-founder, Gary Thomas, Co-founder, Matthew Stasior

Insignia Solutions Inc. 2200 Lawson Ln, Santa Clara CA 95054 USA; 408/327-6000, 800/848-7677 Fax: 408/327-6105, Co Email: isinc@insignia.com, Web URL: insignia.com, Focus: PC software emulator for Macintosh and workstations, Prdts: SoftWindows for Power Mac and Unix, NTrigue, Ownrshp: Sub. Insignia Solutions, UK, Stk Sym: INSGY, Founded: 1986, Empl: 260, Sales ($M): 55.1, Fiscal End: 12/95; Robert P. Lee, Chmn, Pres & CEO, Roger D. Friedberger, SVP & CFO, David Gibbs, VP Mac Sales, John H. Chang, VP Prod Mktng, George Buchan, SVP Eng, Joanne Hartzell, PR Mgr, Email: jhartzell@isinc.insignia.com

Inso Corp. 31 St James Ave, #11, Boston MA 02116-4101 USA; 617/753-6500, Fax: 617/753-6666, Co Email: @inso.com, Web URL: inso.com, Focus: Information retrieval software, Prdts: IntelliScope, Quick View Plus, Ownrshp: OTC, Stk Sym: INSO, Founded: 1982, Sales ($M): 43.4, Fiscal End: 12/95; Steven R. Vana-Paxhia, Pres & CEO, Kirby A. Mansfield, VP Mktng, Jeffrey J. Melvin, VP Sales, Betty J. Savage, VP & CFO, Robert Heywood,

Mgr IS, Meryl Flanzman, PR Mgr, Email: mfranzman@inso.com

Insoft Inc. 4718 Old Gettysburg Rd, Mechanicsburg PA 17055 USA; 717/730-9501, Fax: 717/730-9504, Co Email: info@insoft.com, Web URL: insoft.com, Focus: Multimedia, conferencing and digital video software, Prdts: Communique!, INTV!, Ownrshp: PVT, Founded: 1991, Empl: 64, Daniel L. Harple Jr., Chmn & CEO, Richard Pizzarro, Chief Eng, Keith Wimberley, Dir Mktng, William J. Conners Jr., VP Strategic Bus Dev, Joe Sander, VP WW Sales

Inspiration Software Inc. 2920 SW Dolph Ct, #3, Portland OR 97219 USA; 503/245-9011, Fax: 503/246-4292, Focus: Brainstorming, diagraming and writing software, Prdts: Inspiration, Ownrshp: PVT, Founded: 1982, Empl: 10, Mona Westhaver, Pres, Donald J. Helfgott, VP R&D, Chuck Nakell, Dir Mktng, Email: cnakell@mcimail.com

Institute for Certification of Computing Professionals (ICCP), 2200 E Devon Ave, #247, Des Plaines IL 60018 USA; 847/299-4227, Fax: 847/299-4280, Co Email: 74040.3722@compuserve.com, Focus: Certification of computer professionals, Ownrshp: Nonprofit, Founded: 1973, Perry Anthony, Exec Dir, Email: 74040.3722@compuserve.com, Carolyn DuShane, Com Dir

Institute of Electrical and Electronics Engineers Inc. (IEEE), 345 E 47th St, New York NY 10017-2394 USA; 212/705-7900, Fax: 212/752-4929, Web URL: ieee.org, Focus: Association for electrical and computer engineers, Ownrshp: Nonprofit, Founded: 1884, Empl: 320,000, John H. Powers, Exec Dir, William Cook, Dir Info Svcs

Instrument Data Communications 7101 Hwy 71 W, #200, Austin TX 78735 USA; 512/288-7355, 800/324-4244 Fax: 512/288-6645, Focus: High-tech workshops for engineers and scientists

Instruments Specialties Co. Inc. Shielding Way, Delaware Water Gap PA 18327 USA; 717/424-8510, Fax: 717/424-6213, Focus: RFI/EMI shielding, EMC and FCC 15J compliance testing, Ownrshp: PVT, Founded: 1938, Empl: 330, Frank J. Rushen, Pres

Intec Inc. 2-11 Okudamachi, Toyama, Toyama 930 JP-930 Japan; 764-344-1111, Web URL: intec.co.jp, Focus: Computer and telecom services, Sales ($M): 637, Fiscal End: 12/95

Integral Peripherals Inc. 5775 Flatiron Pkwy, Boulder CO 80301 USA; 303/449-8009, Fax: 303/449-8089, Web URL: integralnet.com, Focus: 1.8-inch and 2.5-inch winchester disk drives, Prdts: Viper Series, Platinum Series, Ownrshp: PVT, Founded: 1990, Empl: 440, Steven B. Volk, Chmn & CEO, Larry Birtzer, Pres & COO, William J. Almon Jr., VP Sales & Mktng, Nancy Miller, Dir Corp Com

Integrated Business Computers (IBC), 2685-C Park Center Dr, Simi Valley CA 93065-6210 USA; 805/527-8792, 800/896-5320 Fax: 805/527-6362, Co Email: ibc@ibc.com, Web URL: ibc.com, Focus: Video on demand, Internet, network and application servers, Prdts: Enterprise Galaxy, Enterprise Voyager, Ownrshp: PVT, Founded: 1979, Empl: 25, Sales ($M): 4, Allan Allal, Chmn, Randy Huddleston, Pres

Integrated Computer Solutions Inc. (ICS), 201 Broadway, Cambridge MA 02139 USA; 617/621-0060, Fax: 617/621-9555, Co Email: info@ics.com, Web URL: ics.com, Focus: X-Windows related products, Prdts: Database Xcessory, Ownrshp: PVT, Founded: 1987, Peter Winston, Pres & CEO, Email: winston@ics.com; Mark Hatch, VP Mktng, Email: mhatch@ics.com; Linda Musmon, Marcom Mgr, Email: musmon@ics.com

Integrated Device Technology Inc. (IDT), 2975 Stender Way, Santa Clara CA 95054-3090 USA; 408/727-6116, Fax: 408/492-8674, Focus: CMOS VLSI circuits, Ownrshp: OTC, Stk Sym: IDTI, Founded: 1980, Empl: 2,765, Sales ($M): 236.3, Fiscal End: 3/93; D. John Carey, Chmn, Leonard Perham, Pres & CEO, Larry Jordan, VP Mktng, Bill Snyder, CFO, Caroline Phillips, Mgr PR

Integrated Information Technology Inc. 2445 Mission College Blvd, Santa Clara CA 95054 USA; 408/727-1885, Fax: 408/980-0432, Co Email: @iit.com, Web URL: iit.com, Focus: Video

conferencing codecs & MPEG 1&2 processors, Prdts: VCP, MPP, MEP, LVP, Ownrshp: PVT, Founded: 1987, Empl: 110, Sales ($M): 41, Fiscal End: 3/93; Joseph L. Parkinson, Chmn, Pres & CEO, Larry Barber, COO, Sandy Abbott, CFO, Y.W. Sing, Vice Chmn, Bryan Martin, CTO, Robin Chirico, Marcom Mgr, Email: robinc@iit.com

Integrated Micro Products Inc. (IMP), 14180 N Dallas Pkwy, #600, Dallas TX 75240 USA; 214/980-2771, Fax: 214/980-2806, Focus: Computer systems for telecommunications, Ownrshp: Sub. IMP, UK, Stk Sym: IMPTY, Founded: 1982, Empl: 150, Sales ($M): 11.5, Fiscal End: 9/95; Stephen Mark I'Anson, Pres & CEO, David Lonsdale, VP WW Sales, Al Dei Maggi, VP Field Ops, Margaret Pacheco, Dir Corp & Marcom, Email: mmp@impltd.com

Integrated Micro Solutions Inc. 2085 Hamilton Ave, 3rd Floor, San Jose CA 95125 USA; 408/3698282, Fax: 408/369-0128, Focus: PC chipset ICs, Ownrshp: PVT, Founded: 1991, Douglas J. Yokoyama, VP Sales & Mktng

Integrated Systems Inc. 201 Moffett Park Dr, Sunnyvale CA 94089 USA; 408/542-1500, Fax: 408/542-1950, Co Email: @isi.com, Focus: Real-time control, Prdts: Matrix X, pSOSystem, Ownrshp: Public, Stk Sym: INTS, Founded: 1980, Empl: 416, Sales ($M): 84.4, Fiscal End: 2/96; Narendra K. Gupta, Chmn, David P. St Charles, Pres & CEO, Moses Joseph, VP Mktng, Joseph Addiego, VP Sales, Steven Sipowicz, CFO, Email: ssipowicz@isi.com; Jennifer Martin, Dir Corp Commun

Integrated Systems Solutions Corp. (ISSC), Rt 100, Somers NY 10589 USA; 800/873-4772 Web URL: issc.ibm.com, Focus: Outsourcing and systems integration, Ownrshp: Sub. IBM Corp., Founded: 1991, Empl: 15,000, Dennie Welsh, Chmn, Sam J. Palmisano, Pres & CEO, Ken Neal

Integrix Inc. 1200 Lawrence Dr, #150, Newbury Park CA 91320 USA; 805/375-1055, Fax: 805/375-2799, Focus: SPARC workstations and peripherals, Ownrshp: PVT, Founded: 1990, Jason Lo, Pres, Jonathan Kong, VP Eng

Intel Corp. 2200 Mission College Dr, Santa Clara CA 95052-8119 USA; 408/765-8080, Fax: 408/765-1774, Web URL: intel.com, Focus: Microprocessors, microcomputers and parallel computers, Ownrshp: OTC, Stk Sym: INTC, Founded: 1968, Empl: 32,600, Sales ($M): 16,202, Fiscal End: 12/95; Gordon E. Moore, Chmn, Andrew S. Grove, Pres & CEO, Craig R. Barrett, EVP & COO, David L. House, SVP, Leslie L. Vadasz, SVP Bus Dev

Intelecsis Inc. 1312 E Upas Ave #A, McAllen TX 78501-5619 USA; 210/682-0649, Fax: 210/682-5602, Co Email: inteleinc@aol.com, Focus: PCs, printers and bilingual software, Prdts: Enteia, Ownrshp: PVT, Founded: 1985, Empl: 2, Sales ($M): 0.5, Fiscal End: 10/95; Manuel Rivero, Pres

InteliSys Inc. 12015 Lee Jackson Hwy, Fairfax VA 22033 USA; Focus: PCs, Ownrshp: PVT, Sales ($M): 5.0, Hsin Yen, CEO

Intell.X 1100 Wilson Blvd, #950, Arlington VA 22209 USA; 703/524-7400, 800/718-7180 Fax: 703/524-7401, Focus: Information for LAN and e-mail systems, Ownrshp: Sub DataTimes, Founded: 1995, David Hoppmann, Pres & CEO, Art Bushnell, SVP Sales, Jeff Massa, SVP Bus Dev, Catherine Michela, VP Mktng

IntelliCorp Inc. 1975 El Camino Real W, Mountain View CA 94040-2216 USA; 415/965-5500, Fax: 415/965-5647, Focus: AI software, Prdts: Kappa, KEE, Kappa-PC, Object Management Workbench (OMW), Ownrshp: OTC, Stk Sym: INAI, Founded: 1980, Empl: 106, Sales ($M): 11.0, Fiscal End: 6/96; Kenneth H. Haas, Pres & CFO, Paul Sutton, VP WW Sales

Intelligence At Large Inc. 3508 Market St, #230, Philadelphia PA 19104-3316 USA; 215/387-6002, Fax: 215/387-9215, Co Email: @beingthere.com, Web URL: beingthere.com, Focus: Macintosh and PC development software, Prdts: Being There, Ownrshp: PVT, Founded: 1991, Cartwright Reed, Pres, Philip D. Hagerty, Dir Sales, Email: phil.hagerty@beingthere.com

Intelligent Computer Solutions (ICS), 9350 Eton Ave, Chatsworth CA 91311 USA; 818/998-5805, Fax: 818/998-3190, Web

URL: scsn.net/~ics, Focus: PC testing systems, Ownrshp: PVT, Founded: 1990, Gonen Ravid, Pres, Meir Sharony, VP Sales & Mktng, Ezra Kohavi, VP Ops

Intelligent Electronics Inc. 411 Eagleview Blvd, Exton PA 19341 USA; 610/458-5500, Fax: 610/458-8217, Focus: Franchisor of computer stores, Ownrshp: OTC, Stk Sym: INEL, Founded: 1982, Empl: 1,162, Sales ($M): 3,588.1, Fiscal End: 1/96; Richard D. Sanford, Chmn & CEO, Gregory A. Pratt, Pres & COO, Mark R. Briggs, SVP, Timothy D. Cook, SVP, Edward A. Melzer, VP & CFO

Intelligent Light 1099 Wall St W #387, Lyndhurst NJ 07071-3617 USA; 201/460-4700, 800/887-8500 Fax: 201/460-0221, Co Email: sgk@ilight.com, Focus: Visualization software, Prdts: Field-view, Ownrshp: PVT, Founded: 1984, Empl: 15

Intelligent Micro Software Ltd. (IMS), 2115 Palm Bay Rd NE, #7, Palm Bay FL 32905 USA; 407/726-0024, Fax: 407/951-7292, Co Email: ims@lii.com, Web URL: lii.com/imshome, Focus: Multi-tasking and multiuser system software, Prdts: REAL/32, IMS Multiuser DOS, Ownrshp: Sub. IMS, UK, Founded: 1985, Empl: 20, David Crocker, Chmn, Email: 71333.3555@compuserve.com; Andrew Freeman, Sales & Mktng Dir, Email: 100012.1270@compuserve.com; Tony Sprague, Tech Mgr, Email: 100066.517@compuserve.com

Intelligent Network Forum (IN Forum), 11312 LBJ Fwy, #600-1114, Dallas TX 75238 USA; Web URL: inf.org, Focus: Association for the intelligent network industry, Ownrshp: Nonprofit, Founded: 1996, Cathy Horn, Exec Dir, Email: chorn@ballistic.com

IntelliLink Corp. 1 Tara Blvd, #210, Nashua NH 03062 USA; 603/888-0666, Fax: 603/888-9817, Focus: Connectivity software for PDAs, Prdts: Magic Xchange, Ownrshp: PVT, Founded: 1990, Keith Crozier, CEO

Intellimation 130 Cremona Dr, Santa Barbara CA 93117 USA; 805/968-2291, Fax: 805/968-8899, Co Email: intelllfm@aol.com, Focus: Educational software, Ownrshp: PVT, Founded: 1986, Empl: 20, Ron Boehm, Pres, Guy Smith, VP, Becky Snyder, Publisher, Rebecca Garrett, Educational Media Rep

IntelliPower Inc. 15520 Rockfield Blvd, #J, Irvine CA 92718-2717 USA; 714/587-0155, Fax: 714/587-0230, Focus: UPS, Ownrshp: PVT, Founded: 1988, G. William Shipman, Pres, J. Robert Hashbarger, VP Sales

IntelliQuest 1250 Capital of Texas Hwy S, Bldg 2, Plaza 1, Austin TX 78746 USA; 512/329-2424, Fax: 512/329-0888, Co Email: @intelliquest.com, Web URL: intelliquest.com, Focus: Custom research for technology products and services, Ownrshp: PVT, Founded: 1985, Empl: 150, Sales ($M): 15, Peter Zandan, CEO, Brian Sharples, Pres, James Schellhase, CFO

IntelliTools 55 Leveroni Ct, #9, Novato CA 94949-5751 USA; 415/382-5959, 800/899-6687 Fax: 415/382-5950, Co Email: intellitool@aol.com, Focus: Keyboards and software for disability, Prdts: IntelliKeys, IntelliTalk, IntelliPics, Overlay Maker, Click It!, Ownrshp: PVT, Founded: 1979, Empl: 22, Steve Gensler, Founder, Arjan Khalsa, Pres, Joan Cunningham, Dir Sales & Mktng, Dave Schmitt, Dir Prod Dev

Intentia Int'l. 10255 W Higgins Rd, #200, Rosemont IL 60018 USA; 847/768-1300, Focus: Business software, Ownrshp: Sub Intentia, Sweden, Founded: 1984, Empl: 870, Sales ($M): 137, Fiscal End: 12/96; William J. Lyons, Pres

Interact Accessories Inc. 10945 McCormick Rd, Hunt Valley MD 21031 USA; 410/785-5661, Fax: 410/785-5725, Focus: Joysticks, Ownrshp: Sub STD, Hong Kong, Kathy Blecker

Interactive Catalog Corp. (iCat), 1420 Fifth Ave #1800, Seattle WA 98101 USA; 206/623-0977, Fax: 206/623-0477, Co Email: moreinfo@icat.com, Web URL: icat.com, Focus: Technology and tools for interactive catalogs, Prdts: iCat Electronic Commerce Toolkit, Ownrshp: PVT, Founded: 1993, Craig Danuloff, Pres & CEO, C. Rowland Hanson, Vice Chmn, Jamie Miller, CFO & Dir Ops, Brian Welter, VP Eng

Interactive Design Consultants (IDC), 12721 Wolf Rd, Geneseo IL 61254 USA; 309/944-8108, Fax: 309/944-6532, Co Email: @idc.geneseo.com, Web URL: geneseo.com, Focus: Utility software and CAD software distributor, Prdts: UV, Ownrshp: PVT, Founded: 1986, Sales ($M): 1, Tom Zwica, Pres, Email: tomz@idc.geneseo.com

Interactive Development Environments Inc. (IDE), 595 Market St, 10th Floor, San Francisco CA 94105 USA; 415/543-0900, 800/888-4331 Fax: 415/543-0145, Co Email: @ide.com, Focus: CASE tools for workstations, Ownrshp: PVT, Founded: 1983, Empl: 150, Sales ($M): 22.7, Fiscal End: 12/91; Chris Kenber, Pres & CEO, Anthony I. Waserman, Chmn, John Kirsten, VP WW Sales, Mark Coggins, VP Prod Dev, Chris Lalli, Marcom PR Mgr, Email: lalli@ide.com

Interactive Educational Systems Design Inc. 310 W 106 St, #16D, New York NY 10025 USA; 212/769-1715, Fax: 212/769-0909, Focus: Educational technology consulting services, Ownrshp: PVT, Founded: 1984, Empl: 2, Ellen Bialo, Pres, Jay Sivin-Kachala, VP

Interactive Image Technologies Ltd. 111 Peter St, #801, Toronto Ontario M5V 2H1 Canada; 416/977-5550, Fax: 416/977-1818, Web URL: interactive.com, Focus: Electronics simulation software for use in engineering and education, Prdts: Electronics Workbench, Ownrshp: PVT, Founded: 1982, Empl: 27, Joseph Koenig, Pres, Email: jkoenig@omteractiv.com; Roy Bryant, VP, Email: rbryant@interactiv.com

Interactive Multimedia Assoc. (IMA), 48 Maryland Ave, #202, Annapolis MD 21401 USA; 410/626-1380, Fax: 410/263-0590, Co Email: info@ima.org, Web URL: ima.org, Focus: Association for multimedia industry, Ownrshp: Nonprofit, Founded: 1987, Empl: 280, Philip Dodds, Pres

Interactive Services Assoc. (ISA), 8403 Colesville Rd, #865, Silver Spring MD 20910 USA; 301/495-4955, Fax: 301/495-4959, Co Email: isa@isa.net, Web URL: isa.net/isa, Focus: Online services and interactive information, Ownrshp: Nonprofit, Robert L. Smith Jr., Exec Dir

Interactive Software Engineering Inc. 270 Storke Rd, #7, Goleta CA 93117 USA; 805/685-1006, Fax: 805/685-6869, Web URL: eiffel.com, Focus: Object-oriented development environments & components, Prdts: Eiffel, ArchiText, Ownrshp: PVT, Founded: 1986, Empl: 15, Sales ($M): 10, Bertrand Meyer, Pres, Email: bertrand@eiffel.com; Darcy Harrison, Mktng Dir, Email: darcy@eiffel.com

Interactive Solutions Inc. 5776 Stoneridge Mall Rd, #333, Pleasanton CA 94588 USA; 510/734-0730, Fax: 510/734-0758, Web URL: interactivesol.com, Focus: Multimedia production software, Prdts: MovieWorks, Ownrshp: PVT, Founded: 1987, Bill LaCommare, Pres, Steve LaCommare, VP Sales

Interactive Television Assoc. (ITA), 1030 Fifteenth St NW, #1053, Washington DC 20005 USA; 202/408-0008, Fax: 202/408-0111, Co Email: intertv@aol.com, Focus: Association to advance interactive TV, Ownrshp: Nonprofit, Founded: 1993, Empl: 13, Andy Sernovitz, Pres, Peter Waldheim, EVP, Yasha Harari, Dir Membership, Matthew Laurencelle, Dir Member Svcs, Philip Strohl, Dir Res & Pubs

Interactive Training Inc. 111 Speen St, #202, Framingham MA 01701-9107 USA; 508/879-0006, Fax: 508/820-4396, Co Email: info@trainingforum.com, Focus: Interactive training products, Founded: 1996, Paul Earl, CEO

InterApps Inc. 1414 Pacific Coast Hwy, #C, Hermosa Beach CA 90254 USA; 310/374-4125, Fax: 310/374-7971, Web URL: interapps.com, Focus: Help desk customer service software, Prdts: Dominion, Ownrshp: PVT, Founded: 1991, Empl: 10, Mark Hripko, VP Prod Dev, Email: mhripko@aol.com; Thom Stoughton, VP Cust Support Svcs, Email: tstoughton@aol.com; Jeff Yarrington, VP Sales, Email: jeffyarr@aol.com

Intercim Corp. 501 E Hwy 13, Burnsville MN 55337-2877 USA;

612/894-9010, 800/445-7785 Fax: 612/894-0399, Focus: Manufacturing software, Ownrshp: Sub. Effective Management Sys., Founded: 1983, Empl: 58, Sales ($M): 4.5, Fiscal End: 6/94; Michael R. Viola, Pres & CEO, Chester L. Moutrie, VP Eng, Richard J. Keller, VP & CFO, Mary Franzen

Interex 8447 E 35th St N, Wichita KS 67226 USA; 316/524-4747, Fax: 316/524-4636, Focus: Computer accessories, Ownrshp: PVT, Founded: 1983, Gregory W. Menas, Pres, M. Lance Chastain, EVP, Michael R. Ross, VP Sales & Mktng, Bryan Distefano, Dir Sales, Gary L. Pember, Dir Mktng

Interface Systems Inc. 5855 Interface Dr, Ann Arbor MI 48103 USA; 313/769-5900, Fax: 313/769-1047, Focus: Printers, data communication and industrial computers, Ownrshp: OTC, Stk Sym: INTF, Founded: 1967, Empl: 210, Sales ($M): 70.2, Fiscal End: 9/95; Carl L. Bixby, Pres & CEO, David O. Schupp, VP, George W. Perrett, VP

Intergraph Corp. Huntsville AL 35894-0001 USA; 205/730-8302, Fax: 205/730-8300, Web URL: intergraph.com, Focus: Computer graphics and CAD/CAM systems, Ownrshp: OTC, Stk Sym: INGR, Founded: 1969, Empl: 9,600, Sales ($M): 1,098.0, Fiscal End: 12/95; James Meadlock, Chmn & CEO

InterGroup Technologies Inc. 14205 SE 36th St, #100, Bellevue WA 98006 USA; 206/643-8089, Fax: 206/643-6977, Focus: Tools for Visual Basic, Prdts: VisualWare, Ownrshp: PVT, Tom McKenna, Pres, Email: tomm@connected.com

Interleaf Inc. Prospect Place, 9 Hillside Ave, Waltham MA 02154 USA; 617/290-0710, Fax: 617/290-4943, Co Email: i-direct@ileaf.com, Web URL: ileaf.com, Focus: Document management software solutions, Prdts: Interleaf, Cyberleaf, RDM, WorldView, Ownrshp: OTC, Stk Sym: LEAF, Founded: 1981, Empl: 650, Sales ($M): 88.6, Fiscal End: 3/96; David Boucher, Chmn, Ed Koepfler, Pres & CEO, Email: ekoepfler@ileaf.com; Bob Maher, VP Eng, Email: bmaher@ileaf.com; Gordon M. Large, SVP & CFO, Email: glarge@ileaf.com

Interlink Computer Sciences Inc. 47370 Fremont Blvd, Fremont CA 94538 USA; 510/657-9800, Fax: 510/659-6381, Focus: TCP/IP network products, Ownrshp: PVT, Founded: 1982, Empl: 100, Sales ($M): 21, Charles W. Jepson, Pres & CEO, Barbara Booth, VP R&D, Gloria M. Purdy, CFO, Linda Nixon, Marcom Mgr, Email: lnixon@interlink.com

Interlink Electronics 546 Flynn Rd, Camarillo CA 93012 USA; 805/484-8855, Fax: 805/484-8989, Co Email: support@interlinkelec.com, Web URL: interlinkelec.com, Focus: Input devices, Prdts: VersaPoint, RemotePointPlus, DuraPoint, Ownrshp: OTC, Stk Sym: LINK, Empl: 55, Sales ($M): 10.7, Fiscal End: 12/95; E. Michael Thoben, Chmn, Pres & CEO, David Arthur, SVP Mfg, William A. Yates, SVP Sales & Mktng, Stuart I. Yaniger, VP R&D, Keith M. Roberts, Dir Corp Com, Email: kroberts@interlinkelec.com

Intermec Corp. 6001 36th Ave, PO Box 4280, Everett WA 98203 USA; 206/348-2600, 800/347-2636 Fax: 206/355-9551, Co Email: info@intermec.com, Web URL: intermec.com, Focus: Automated data collection systems, Ownrshp: Sub. Western Atlas, Founded: 1966, Empl: 1,850, Michael Ohanian, Pres, Gregory L. Tannheimer, EVP, Keith Everett, VP Mktng, Michael E. Callahan, VP Sales, Joan Scoll, Dir MIS, Christine Goetz, PR Mgr

Intermetrics Inc. 733 Concord Ave, Cambridge MA 02138-1002 USA; 617/661-1840, Fax: 617/547-3879, Focus: Systems software and military applications software, Ownrshp: OTC, Stk Sym: IMET, Founded: 1969, Empl: 588, Sales ($M): 54.0, Fiscal End: 2/95; John E. Miller, Chmn, Joseph A. Saponaro, Pres & CEO, Nicholas A. Pettinella, VP & CFO

International Association for Computer Systems Security 6 Swarthmore Ln, Dix Hills NY 11746 USA; 516/499-1616, Focus: Association for computer security, Ownrshp: Nonprofit, Robert Wilk, Pres

International Association for Management Automation (IAMA), 1342 Colonial Blvd, #25, Ft. Myers FL 33907 USA; 941/

275-7887, 800/333-9786 Fax: 941/275-0794, Web URL: afsmi@afsmi.org, Focus: Management automation, Empl: 5,000+, Bob Steele, Mgng Dir

International Association of Science and Tech. (IAST), 4500 16th Ave NW, #80, Calgary Alberta K3B 0M6 Canada; 800/995-2161 Fax: 403/247-6851, Co Email: iasted@orion.oac.uci.edu, Ownrshp: Nonprofit, Nadia Hamza, Conf Planner

International Business Machines Corp. (IBM), Old Orchard Rd, Armonk NY 10504 USA; 914/765-1900, 800/426-3333 Web URL: ibm.com, Focus: Mainframes, minis, workstations, PCs, peripherals, software and microelectronic technology, Prdts: IBM 3090, IBM AS/400, IBM PC, OS/2, RS/6000, Ownrshp: NYSE, Stk Sym: IBM, Founded: 1914, Empl: 220,000, Sales ($M): 71,940.0, Fiscal End: 12/95; Louis V. Gerstner, Chmn & CEO, G. Richard Thoman, SVP & CFO, J. Thomas Bouchard, SVP, HR, Nicholas Donofrio, SVP Server Grp, L.R. Ricciardi, SVP, David Kalis, VP Comm

International Communications Assoc. (ICA), 12750 Merit Dr, #710, LB-89, Dallas TX 75251-1240 USA; 214/233-3889, 800/422-4636 Fax: 214/233-2813, Web URL: icanet.com, Focus: Major user organization for voice, data and image telecom, Prdts: ICA Expo, Ownrshp: Nonprofit, Founded: 1948, Empl: 700, Robert Eilers, Exec Dir, Lawrence Gessini, Pres, Michael Case

International Communications Industries Assoc. (ICIA), 11242 Wapless Mill Rd, Fairfax VA 22030 USA; 703/273-7200, Fax: 703/278-8082, Web URL: usa.net/icia, Focus: Association for firms selling video, audio-visual and computer products, Ownrshp: Nonprofit, Founded: 1949, Empl: 950, Walter G. Blackwell, EVP

International Compliance Corp. 802 N Kealy, Lewisville TX 75057 USA; 817/491-3696, Fax: 817/491-3699, Focus: Compliance testing for FCC, UL, CSA, IEC, TUV, VDE and European CE, Ownrshp: PVT, Founded: 1986, Empl: 7, Val E. Erwin, Pres, Kurt Fischer, VP

International Council for Computer Communication (ICCC), PO Box 9745, Washington DC 20016 USA; 703/836-7787, Focus: Advance R&D, applications and education of computer communication, Ownrshp: Nonprofit, Founded: 1972, Empl: 100

International Data Corp. (IDC), 5 Speen St, Framingham MA 01701 USA; 508/872-8200, 800/343-4935 Fax: 508/935-4015, Co Email: info@idcresearch.com, Web URL: idcresearch.com, Focus: Market research on computer hardware, software, workgroup applications, PC & services, Ownrshp: PVT, Founded: 1964, Empl: 500, Sales ($M): 130, Fiscal End: 12/95; Kirk Campbell, Pres & CEO, Email: kcampbell@idcresearch.com; Philippe de Marcillac, SVP, WW Research, Email: pdemarcillac@idcresearch.com; David Vellante, SVP, Email: dvellante@idcresearch.com; John Gantz, SVP, Email: jgantz@idcresearch.com; Gigi Wang, SVP, Email: gwang@idcresearch.com; Chris Whelan, Marcom Mgr, Email: cwhelan@idcresearch.com

International Engineering Consortium 303 E Wacker Dr, #740, Chicago IL 60601-5212 USA; 312/938-3500, Fax: 312/938-8787, Ownrshp: Nonprofit, Founded: 1944

International Information Management Congress (IMC), 1650 38th St, #205W, Boulder CO 80301-2623 USA; 303/440-7085, Fax: 303/440-7234, Web URL: iimc.org, Focus: Document and electronic imaging, Ownrshp: Nonprofit, Founded: 1963, Empl: 85, Lynn Pontcher, Admin Dir, John A. Lacy, Pres & CEO, Lase Low

International Interactive Communications Society (IICS), 14657 SW Teal Blvd, #119, Beaverton OR 97007 USA; 503/579-4427, Fax: 503/579-6272, Focus: Advancement of multimedia and interactive technologies, Ownrshp: Nonprofit, Founded: 1983, Empl: 3,000, Debra Palm, Managing Dir, Brian Blum, Pres

International Management Services Inc. (IMS), 363 E Central St, Franklin MA 02038-1300 USA; 508/520-1555, Fax: 508/420-3338, Co Email: imstrain@ix.netcom.com, Focus: Ergonomic keyboards (Maltron keyboard), Ownrshp: PVT, Founded: 1973, Empl:

15, Sales ($M): 2, Raymond Wenig, Pres, Email: rwening@delphi.com; Terry Pardoe, EVP, Sandra Wenig, VP

International Microcomputer Software Inc. (IMSI), 1895 E Francisco Blvd, San Rafael CA 94901 USA; 415/257-3000, Fax: 415/257-3565, Focus: Productivity and graphics software, Prdts: TurboCAD, VirusCure, Ownrshp: OTC, Stk Sym: IMSI, Founded: 1983, Empl: 106, Sales ($M): 25.7, Fiscal End: 6/96; Martin Sacks, Pres & CEO, Geoffrey Koblick, Chmn, Robert Mayer, VP Sales, Rob Halligan, Dir Mktng, Mark Cosmez, VP & CFO, Haskin

International Network of Women in Technology (WITI), 4641 Burnet Ave, Sherman Oaks CA 91403 USA; 800/334-9484 Co Email: info@witi.com, Web URL: witi.com, Focus: Organization for women in the technology field, Ownrshp: Nonprofit, Founded: 1989, Empl: 3,000, Carolyn Leighton, Exec Dir

International Parallel Machines Inc. 50 Conduit St, New Bedford MA 02745-6016 USA; 508/990-2977, Fax: 508/990-2772, Focus: Industrial computers, Ownrshp: PVT, Founded: 1980, Empl: 30, Sales ($M): 2.0, Robin Chang, Pres, Robert Nolley, Dir, Raymond Chang, VP, Email: raychang@ici.net; Peter Erkkinen, PR Admin

International Power Technologies 538 S 1400 W, Orem UT 84058 USA; 801/224-4828, Fax: 801/224-5872, Focus: UPS, Ownrshp: PVT, Bob Mount, Pres & CEO

International Society for Technology in Education (ISTE), 1787 Agate St, Eugene OR 97403-1923 USA; 541/346-4414, Fax: 541/346-5890, Focus: Supports computer use and technology in the classroom, Ownrshp: Nonprofit, Founded: 1979, Empl: 13,000, David Moursund, CEO, Anita Best, Editor

International Society of Certified Electronics Technicians (ISCET), 2708 W Berry St, #3, Ft. Worth TX 76109 USA; 817/921-9101, Fax: 817/921-3741, Focus: Certifies electronics technicians, Ownrshp: Nonprofit, Founded: 1970, Empl: 2,000, Clyde W. Nabors, Exec Dir, Barbara Rubin, Bus Mgr, George Brownyard, Chmn

International Software Group Inc. 67 S Bedford St, Burlington MA 01803-5152 USA; 617/221-1450, 800/237-1875 Fax: 617/272-2531, Focus: Application generator software, Prdts: CorVision, Ownrshp: OTC, Stk Sym: SISGF, Founded: 1977, Empl: 100, Steven M. Fisch, Pres & CEO, Theodore Chimiklis, VP Sales, Paul Yanakakis, VP Fin, Jim Warner, Dir Dev, Nina Giovannelli, Dir Marcom

International Software Services Inc. (ISSI), PO Box 32149, Fridley MN 55432-0149 USA; 612/935-9339, Focus: PC software and hardware, Ownrshp: PVT, Founded: 1993, Donald W. Cartwright, Pres

International TechneGroup Inc. (ITI), 5303 DuPont Cr, Milford OH 45150 USA; 513/576-3900, 800/787-9199 Fax: 513/576-3994, Co Email: info@iti-oh.com, Web URL: iti-oh.com, Focus: CAD/CAM/CAE/PDM translation software, Prdts: PDE/Lib., IGES/Works, STEP/Works, Ownrshp: PVT, Founded: 1984, Empl: 245, Jason Lemon, CEO, Don Hemmelgarn, VP Prod Data Integration, Email: dmh@iti-oh.com; Ed Carl, VP, Email: ejc@iti-oh.com; Robert Farrell, Marcom Coord, Email: farrell@iti-oh.com

International Teleconferencing Assoc. (ITCA), 1650 Tysons Blvd #200, McLean VA 22102 USA; 800/360-4822 Fax: 703/506-3266, Focus: Teleconferencing industry, Ownrshp: Nonprofit, Tom Gibson, Exec Dir

International Television Assoc. (ITVA), 6311 N O'Connor Rd, #230, Irving TX 75039 USA; 214/869-1112, Fax: 214/869-2980, Co Email: itvahq@ix.netcom.com, Web URL: itva.org, Focus: Visual communications

Internet Group Inc. 305 S Craig St, Pittsburgh PA 15213 USA; 412/688-9696, Fax: 412/688-9697, Co Email: info@tig.com, Web URL: tig.com, Focus: Internet publishing and marketing systems and services, Prdts: Market Manager, Ownrshp: PVT, Founded: 1993, Empl: 14, Michael Bauer, Pres, Email: bauer@tig.com; Kurt Lorence, Project Mgr, Email: kurt@tig.com;

Michael Provance, Bus Mgr, Email: pra@tig.com; Todd Kaufmann, Email: tad@tig.com, Paul Buter, Mktng Mgr, Email: paul@tig.com

Internet Profiles Corp. (I/PRO), 785 Market St 13th Fl., San Francisco CA 94103-2003 USA; 415/322-9600, Fax: 415/322-9818, Co Email: info@ipro.com, Web URL: ipro.com, Focus: Internet software and services, Ownrshp: PVT, Founded: 1994, Empl: 50, Ariel Poler, Pres, Mark Ashida, CEO

Internet Security Systems Inc. (ISS), 41 Perimeter Ctr E, #660, Atlanta GA 30346 USA; 770/395-0150, Fax: 770/395-1972, Co Email: iss@iss.net, Web URL: iss.net, Focus: Commercial computer attack simulation and security audit tools, Ownrshp: PVT, Founded: 1994, Empl: 35, Christopher Klaus, CEO

Internet Shopping Network (ISN), 3475 Deer Creek Rd, Bldg C, Palo Alto CA 94304-1316 USA; 415/842-7400, 800/677-7467 Fax: 415/842-7415, Web URL: shop.internet.net, Focus: Internet shopping mall with 40,000 products, Ownrshp: PVT, Founded: 1993, Empl: 40, Randy Adams, Pres, Email: randy@internet.net; Bill Rollinson, VP Mktng, Email: bill@internet.net

Internet Society 12020 Sunrise Valley Dr, #270, Reston VA 22091 USA; 703/648-9888, Fax: 703/648-9887, Web URL: isoc.org, Focus: Association for users of the Internet, Ownrshp: Nonprofit, Empl: 5,000, Anthony M. Rutkowski, Exec Dir, Vinton Cerf, Pres

InterNex Information Services 2348 Walsh Ave, Santa Clara CA 95131-2013 USA; 408/327-2355, Fax: 408/496-5485, Co Email: info@internex.net, Web URL: internex.net, Focus: Hispeed Internet connectivity, Internet infrastructure and Web server hostings, Prdts: ISDN Internet Connectivity, WebFarm, Ownrshp: PVT, Founded: 1993, Empl: 65, Sales ($M): 5, Ken Tai, CEO, Email: ktai@internex.net; Gloria Wahl, Pres, Email: gwahl@internex.com; Robert Berger, Founder & CTO, Email: rberger@internex.com; Frank Chan, VP Ops, Email: ftchan@internex.com; William Chen, Dir MIS, Email: wchen@internex.com; Susan Cooney, Dir Marcom, Email: smcooney@internex.net

Interphase Corp. 13800 Senlac Dr, Dallas TX 75234-8823 USA; 214/919-9000, Fax: 214/919-9200, Focus: Network products, Ownrshp: OTC, Stk Sym: INPH, Founded: 1974, Empl: 190, Sales ($M): 47.4, Fiscal End: 10/95; R. Stephen Polley, Chmn & CEO, Ernest E. Godsey, VP Bus Dev, Robert L. Drury, VP & CFO, Gregory R. Iverson, VP Mktng, James C. Gleason, VP Ops

Interplay Productions Inc. 17922 Fitch Ave, Irvine CA 92714 USA; 714/553-6655, Fax: 714/252-2820, Web URL: interplay.com, Focus: Entertainment and education software, Ownrshp: PVT, Founded: 1983, Empl: 365, Sales ($M): 99.6, Fiscal End: 12/95; Brian Fargo, Pres & CEO, Chuck Camps, CFO

Interpretive Software Inc. 1932 Arlington Blvd, #107, Charlottesville VA 22903 USA; 804/979-0245, Fax: 804/979-2454, Co Email: 70401.2062@compuserve.com, Web URL: execpc.com/~isi, Focus: Business education software, Prdts: AutoSim, PharmaSim, Ownrshp: PVT

INTERSOLV Inc. 9420 Key West Ave, Rockville MD 20850 USA; 301/838-5000, 800/547-4000 Fax: 301/838-5064, Co Email: idsinfo@intersolv.com, Web URL: intersolv.com, Focus: Computer-aided software engineering products, Ownrshp: OTC, Stk Sym: ISLI, Founded: 1983, Empl: 877, Sales ($M): 145.3, Fiscal End: 4/96; Kevin J. Burns, Chmn & CEO, Gary G. Greenfield, Pres & COO, Thomas P. Costello, SVP Res & Dev, Michael J. Duffy, VP Ops, Kenneth A. Sexton, VP & CFO, Larry Death, Mgr PR

Interstar Technologies Inc. 1242 Peel St, #300, Montreal Quebec H3B 2T6 Canada; 514/875-6710, Fax: 514/875-9360, Co Email: interstar@ranmar.qc.ca, Focus: Fax server software, Prdts: Lightning Fax, Ownrshp: PVT, Founded: 1991, Walter J. Huber, VP Mktng, Email: w.huber@ranmar.qc.ca

InterSystems Corp. 1 Memorial Dr, Cambridge MA 02142 USA; 617/621-0600, Fax: 617/494-1631, Web URL: intersys.com, Focus: Database application software generator, Prdts: Open M/

SQL, Ownrshp: PVT, Founded: 1978, Empl: 165, Sales ($M): 38.2, Fiscal End: 12/95; Phillip T. Ragon, Pres, Jayne Giarrusso

InterTan Inc. 201 Main St, #1805, Ft. Worth TX 76102 USA; 817/348-9701, Focus: Distributes Tandy's products in international markets, Ownrshp: NYSE, Stk Sym: ITN, Founded: 1986, Empl: 5,660, Sales ($M): 506.4, Fiscal End: 6/96; John A. Capstick, Chmn & CEO, James B. Williams, Pres & COO, James G. Gingerich, SVP & CFO

IntraCorp Inc. 501 Brickell Key Dr, Miami FL 33131-2608 USA; 305/591-5900, Fax: 305/591-1561, Focus: Entertainment software, Prdts: Trump Castle, Grandmaster Chess, BridgeMaster, Home Alone, Dark Half, Ownrshp: PVT, Founded: 1985, Empl: 40, Leigh M. Rothschild, Pres & Publisher

Intuit Inc. 2535 Garcia Ave, Mountain View CA 94043 USA; 415/944-6000, Web URL: intuit.com, Focus: Personal/business accounting software, Prdts: Quicken, QuickBooks, TurboTax, Ownrshp: OTC, Stk Sym: INTU, Founded: 1983, Empl: 2,732, Sales ($M): 552.9, Fiscal End: 7/96; Scott D. Cook, Chmn, William V. Campbell, Pres & CEO, Jim Heeger, VP & CFO, William H. Harris Jr., EVP, Alan A. Gleicher, VP Sales

Invisible Software Inc. 939 Longdale Ave, Longwood FL 32750-3284 USA; 800/982-2962 Focus: LAN software, Prdts: Invisible-LAN

InVision Interactive 2445 Faber Place, #102, Palo Alto CA 94303-3316 USA; 415/812-7380, Fax: 415/812-7386, Co Email: info@cybersound.com, Web URL: cybersound.com, Focus: Audio and music synthesizer products, Prdts: CyberSound, Ownrshp: PVT, Founded: 1989, Empl: 13, G. Scott France, CEO, Mitch Richman, COO, Denny Mayer, VP Sales, Candice Denton, Email: candiced@cybersound.com

InVision Systems Corp. 2655 Campus Dr, San Mateo CA 94403-2519 USA; 800/847-1662 Focus: Desktop video conferencing products, Prdts: InVision, Ownrshp: PVT, James J. Geddes Jr., Pres & CEO

Ioline Corp. 12020 113th Ave NE, Kirkland WA 98034 USA; 206/821-2140, 800/598-0029 Fax: 206/823-8898, Focus: Pen plotters, Prdts: Summit 910, Summit 2200, Studio 8/40A, Ownrshp: PVT, Founded: 1985, Empl: 60, Frank Schimicci, Pres & CEO, Gregg Roberts, VP Fin, Heidi Weston, HR Mgr

Iomega Corp. 1821 W Iomega Way, Roy UT 84067 USA; 801/778-1000, 800/697-8833 Fax: 801/778-3450, Focus: Removable disk drives, Ownrshp: OTC, Stk Sym: IOMG, Founded: 1980, Empl: 900, Sales ($M): 326.2, Fiscal End: 12/95; Kim B. Edwards, Pres & CEO, Leon J. Staciokas, SVP & COO, Edward D. Briscoe, VP Sales, Timothy L. Hill, VP Mktng, Leonard C. Purkis, SVP & CFO, A. Cory Maloy, Mgr PR, Email: acmaloy@aol.com

Iona Technologies 55 Fairbanks Blvd, Marlboro MA 01752 USA; 508/460-6888, 800/672-4948 Fax: 508/460-6099, Co Email: @iona.com, Web URL: iona.com, Focus: Object software, Prdts: Orbix, Ownrshp: PVT, Founded: 1991, Annrai O'Toole, VP Dev

IPC Technologies Inc. 10300 Metric Blvd, Austin TX 78758 USA; 512/339-3500, 800/752-1577 Fax: 512/454-1357, Co Email: @ipctechinc.com, Web URL: ipctechinc.com, Focus: PCs, Ownrshp: Sub. IPC, Singapore, Founded: 1984, Empl: 240, Sales ($M): 90, David J. Scull, Pres & CEO, Greg Block, VP Logistics, Rusty Johnson, VP Sales, Jack Hall, VP Mktng, Benny Galloway, CFO, Don E. Gross, Media Rel Mgr

Ipsilon Networks Inc. 2191 E Bayshore Rd, Palo Alto CA 94303 USA; 415/846-4600, Fax: 415/855-1414, Web URL: ipsilon.com, Focus: TCP/IP switches for routing with high-speed, high-capacity ATM & frame-relay switching HW, Ownrshp: PVT, Founded: 1994, Empl: 39, Brian Nesmith, Pres & CEO, Larry Blair, VP Mktng, Tom Lyons, CTO

IQ Engineering (IQE), PO Box 60955, Sunnyvale CA 94088-0955 USA; 408/733-1161, Fax: 408/733-2585, Focus: Laser font cartridges, Ownrshp: PVT, Founded: 1988, Empl: 12, Michael Gardner, Pres

IQ Software Corp. 3295 River Exchange Dr, #550, Norcross GA 30092-4220 USA; 770/446-8880, 800/458-0386 Fax: 770/448-4088, Co Email: info@iqsc.com, Web URL: iqsc.com, Focus: Data analysis software, Prdts: Intelligent Query, WordMARC, Ownrshp: OTC, Stk Sym: IQSW, Founded: 1984, Empl: 100, Sales ($M): 21.9, Fiscal End: 1/96; Charles R. Chitty, Pres & CEO, Matthew C. Reedy, Chmn & VP Dev, Robert W. Ott, VP Sales, Michael J. Casey, VP Fin

ISDN Executive Council c/o COS, 8260 Willow Oaks Corp. Dr #700, Fairfax VA 22031 USA; 703/205-2700, Fax: 703/896-8590, Ownrshp: Nonprofit, Elizabeth Schrock, Dir

ISDN*tek PO Box 3000, San Gregorio CA 94074 USA; 415/712-3000, Fax: 415/712-3003, Co Email: info@isdntek.com, Web URL: isdntek.com, Focus: ISDN products, Ownrshp: PVT, Founded: 1987, Ed Klingman, Pres, Susan Wolbrueck, Email: susanw@isdntek.com

Island Software Corp. 90 Digital Dr, Novato CA 94949-5704 USA; 415/491-1000, Fax: 415/491-0402, Focus: Graphics software, Ownrshp: Sub Dainippon, Japan, Founded: 1981, Empl: 40, Daniel Remer, Pres, Paul Remer, GM, David Newman, Mktng Dir

ISODE Consortium 3925 W Braker Ln, Austin TX 78759 USA; 512/305-0280, Fax: 512/305-0285, Web URL: isode.com, Focus: Promote and develop the ISODE package of OSI applications, Ownrshp: Nonprofit, Founded: 1992, Steve Kille, CEO

ISTR Inc. 360 Delaware Ave, #300, Buffalo NY 14202-1610 USA; 716/855-0295, Fax: 716/855-0299, Co Email: inkwell@istr.com, Focus: Professional services, Prdts: Magic Inkwell, Magic Separator, Wacom Tablet Drr, Ownrshp: PVT, Founded: 1988, Empl: 10, Sales ($M): 2.0, Alan Stout, Pres, Joseph A. Rosati Jr., VP, Dan Bryndle, Dir Mktng, David J. Aiello, Dir Com

IT Design USA Inc. 15732 Los Gatos Blvd, #117, Los Gatos CA 95032 USA; 408/995-3019, Fax: 408/358-8751, Co Email: itdesign@aol.com, Web URL: itdesign.ie, Focus: Information retrieval software, Prdts: Viper Instant-Access, Ownrshp: PVT

IT Solutions Inc. 500 W Madison St, #2210, Chicago IL 60661 USA; 312/474-7700, 800/394-4487 Fax: 312/474-9361, Co Email: @its.com, Web URL: its.com, Focus: World Wide Web authoring system, Prdts: Neticity, Ownrshp: PVT, Founded: 1990, Ted Shelton, Pres & CEO, Lisa Glick, Ops Mgr

ITA (ITA), 182 Nasau St, #209, Princeton NJ 08542 USA; 609/279-1700, Fax: 609/279-1999, Co Email: ita@bccom.com, Focus: Trends and innovations in magnetic and optical media, Ownrshp: Nonprofit, Founded: 1970, Empl: 450, Charles Van Horn, Exec Dir

ITAC Systems Inc. 3121 Benton St, Garland TX 75042 USA; 214/494-3073, 800/533-4822 Fax: 214/494-4159, Co Email: @moustrak.com, Web URL: mousetrak.com, Focus: User interface hardware, Prdts: Mouse-Trak, Ownrshp: PVT, Founded: 1977, Empl: 26, Sales ($M): 5, Donald P. Bynum, Pres & CEO, Email: bynum@moustrak.com; John Ernsberger, Chmn, Email: johne@moustrak.com; Douglas Miller, VP Ops, Email: miller@moustrak.com; JoAnne Ross, Controller, Email: joanne@moustrak.com; Lori Morris, Corp Comm Mgr, Email: lori@moustrak.com

Itautec America 586 Main St, Dennis MA 02638 USA; 508/385-8181, Fax: 508/385-8176, Co Email: itautec@aol.com, Focus: C/S development software, Prdts: GRIP, Ownrshp: Sub. Itautec, Brazil

Iterated Systems Inc. 5550-A Peachtree Pkwy #650, Norcross GA 30092 USA; 770/840-0310, Fax: 770/840-0806, Focus: Image compression, Prdts: ColorBoy, VideoBox, Ownrshp: PVT, Founded: 1987, John R. Festa, Pres & CEO, Michael F. Barnsley, CTO, Alan D. Sloan, EVP, Neal W. McEwen, VP & CFO

Itron Inc. 2818 N Sullivan Rd, Spokane WA 99216-1897 USA; 509/924-9900, Fax: 509/928-1465, Focus: Data acquisition and wireless communication products, Ownrshp: OTC, Stk Sym: ITRI, Founded: 1978, Empl: 712, Sales ($M): 155.4, Fiscal End: 12/95; Johnny M. Humphreys, Pres & CEO, Paul A. Redmond, Chmn, Robert D. Neilson, VP Mktng, Richard G. Geiger, VP Prod Dev,

James F. Thompson, VP & CFO, Jemima Scarpelli, Treas

IVI Publishing Inc. 7500 Flying Cloud Rd, Minneapolis MN 55344-3739 USA; 612/996-6000, 800/432-1332 Fax: 612/996-6001, Co Email: info@ivi.com, Web URL: ivi.com, Focus: Multimedia software, Prdts: Mayo Clinic Series, Ownrshp: OTC, Stk Sym: IVIP, Founded: 1991, Empl: 100, Ron Buck, CEO, Joy Solomon, GM, Tom Skiba, CFO

IXI Corp. 324 Encinal St, Santa Cruz CA 95060-2101 USA; 408/427-7700, Fax: 408/427-5407, Focus: Motif and X Window software, Ownrshp: Sub. SCO, Founded: 1991, Raymond Anderson, Chmn

J-Mark Computer Corp. 13111 Brooks Dr, #A, Baldwin Park CA 91706 USA; 818/856-5800, Fax: 818/960-5937, Focus: Motherboards and fax/data modems, Ownrshp: PVT, Alfred Yau, Pres

J. Feuerstein Systems (JFS), 1055 Parsippany Blvd, 3rd Floor, Parsippany NJ 07054 USA; 201/402-7779, Fax: 201/402-7681, Focus: Litigation support software, Ownrshp: Sub Docucon, Jim Feuerstein, CTO

J.D. Edwards & Co. 8055 E Tufts Ave, Denver CO 80237 USA; Web URL: jdedwards.com, Focus: Midrange and C/S software, Ownrshp: PVT, Founded: 1977, Sales ($M): 340.8, Fiscal End: 12/95; C. Edward McVaney, Pres & CEO

J.D. Power & Associates 30401 Agoura Rd, Agoura Hills CA 91301 USA; 818/889-6330, Fax: 818/889-3719, Focus: Customer satisfaction research for automobiles, PCs and consumer electronics, Ownrshp: PVT, Founded: 1968, Empl: 200, Dave Power, Chmn, Steve Goodall, Pres, Patti Patono, Dir Spec Projects

J3 Learning 10729 Bren Rd E, Minneapolis MN 55343 USA; 612/930-0330, 800/532-7672 Fax: 612/930-0560, Focus: Computer learning software, Ownrshp: PVT, Empl: 120, Chuck J. Gorman, Pres & CEO, Chad Worcester, Dir Multimedia, Shel Mann, Dir Consumer Prod

Jabra Corp. 9191 Towne Centre Dr, #330, San Diego CA 92122 USA; 619/622-0764, Fax: 619/622-0353, Co Email: @jabra.com, Focus: Telecom software and hardware, Prdts: EarPhone, JabraNet, DocTel, Ownrshp: PVT, Founded: 1993, Randy Granovetter, Pres & CEO, Lisa A. Heller, Dir Mktng, Email: lheller@jabra.com

Jandel Scientific Inc. 2591 Kerner Blvd, San Rafael CA 94901 USA; 415/453-6700, 800/452-6335 Fax: 415/453-7769, Co Email: sales@jandel.com, Web URL: jandel.com, Focus: Scientific software, Ownrshp: PVT, Founded: 1982, Empl: 68, Sales ($M): 8.0, Fiscal End: 12/95; John J. Osborn, Chmn, Joseph Osborn, Pres, Email: joe@jandel.com; Richard Mitchell, Dir Res, Walter Feigenson, Dir Mktng, Email: walterf@jandel.com; Ross Garofolo, CFO

Janna Systems Inc. 15951 Los Gatos Blvd, #6, Los Gatos CA 95032 USA; 408/356-6647, 800/268-6107 Co Email: info@janna.com, Web URL: janna.com, Focus: Contact and document management software, Ownrshp: PVT, Founded: 1990, Bill Tatham, Pres & CEO, Steven Cherry, VP Sales & Mktng, Email: stevec@janna.com; Stephen Kaplan, VP Fin & Ops

Janus Interactive 1600 NW 167th Place, #320, Beaverton OR 97006 USA; 503/629-0587, 800/766-0835 Fax: 503/690-6690, Focus: CD-ROM software, Prdts: License to Dr, Ownrshp: Sub Sirius Enterprises, Founded: 1995, Steve Thyggersen, Pres, Wade Brooks, VP, Dennis Kambury, VP Dev

Japan Digital Laboratory Co. Ltd. 4770 Calle Quetzal, Camarillo CA 93012 USA; 805/588-8709, Fax: 805/588-8708, Focus: Distributes plotters for Japanese parent company, Prdts: Express-Plotter II, Ownrshp: FO, Founded: 1984, Empl: 23, Sales ($M): 8, Goro Narisawa, GM, Bryan Doherty, Sr Mgr, Email: jdl-doherty@aol.com; Mike Sherick, Nat'l. Sales Mgr, Pat Caminiti, Ad/PR Spec, Email: jdlpat@aol.com

JASC Inc. 5610 Rowland Rd #125, Minnetonka MN 55343 USA; 612/930-9800, 800/622-2793 Fax: 612/930-9172, Co Email: @jasc.com, Focus: Windows graphics and multimedia software products, Prdts: Illuminatus, Chris Anderson, VP Sales & Mktng

Jasmine Multimedia 6746 Valjean Ave, #100, Van Nuys CA 91406 USA; 818/780-3344, Fax: 818/780-8705, Focus: Multimedia software, Ownrshp: PVT, Jay A. Smith, Pres

Jawai Interactive Inc. 501 E Fourth St #511, Austin TX 78701 USA; 512/469-0502, 800/469-0502 Web URL: jawai.com, Focus: Music and art for PC, Prdts: Screen Caffeine Pro, Java Beat

Jazz Multimedia 1040 Richard Ave, Santa Clara CA 95050 USA; 408/727-8900, Fax: 408/727-9092, Focus: Graphics accelerator and MPEG video, Prdts: 3D Magic, Ownrshp: PVT, Barry J. Lebu, Pres & CEO, Michael Yang

Jazz Speakers 1217 John Reed Ct, City of Industry CA 91745 USA; 818/336-2689, Fax: 818/336-2489, Focus: PC speakers, Ownrshp: PVT, Founded: 1981, Empl: 600, Sales ($M): 81, Fiscal End: 12/94; Jazz Hsu, Pres & CEO, Tony Hsu, VP, Stuart Garb, National Sales Mgr, Vincent Lukas, Mktng Mgr, Elizabeth Huang, CFO

JBA Int'l. 3701 Algonquin Rd, #1000, Rolling Meadows IL 60008 USA; 847/590-0299, Fax: 847/590-0049, Web URL: jba.co.uk, Focus: C/S software, Ownrshp: Sub JBA Holdings, UK, Empl: 1,500, Sales ($M): 196.9, Fiscal End: 12/95; Rich Halperin, Pres & CEO

JetForm Corp. 7600 Leesburg Pike, #430, Falls Church VA 22043 USA; 703/448-9544, 800/538-3676 Fax: 703/448-9543, Web URL: jetform.com, Focus: Forms software, Prdts: JetForm, Ownrshp: OTC, Stk Sym: FORMF, Founded: 1982, Empl: 60, Sales ($M): 43.5, Fiscal End: 4/96; John Kelly, Pres & CEO, John Gleed, EVP & CTO, Phil Weaver, SVP Sales & Mktng, Brownell Chalstrom, VP Mktng, Lynne Boyd, SVP Gov Ops

Jian Tools for Sales Inc. 1975 W El Camino Real, #301, Mountain View CA 94040-2218 USA; 415/254-5600, 800/346-5426 Fax: 415/254-5640, Web URL: jianusa.com, Focus: Business management software, Prdts: BizPlanBuilder, MarketingBuilder, LoanBuilder, AgreementBuilder, Ownrshp: PVT, Founded: 1986, Burke Franklin, Pres, Email: burke@jianusa.com; David Shohfi, VP Sales & Mktng, Email: shohfi@jianusa.com; Shelley Beban, VP Fin & Admin, Email: sbeban@jianusa.com; Neal Novotny, VP Prod R&D, Email: nnovotny@jianusa.com; Alicia Parnell, Media Rel Mgr

JMR Electronics Inc. 20400 Plummer St, Chatsworth CA 91311 USA; 818/993-4801, Fax: 818/993-9173, Focus: Computer peripheral enclosures, Ownrshp: PVT, Founded: 1982, Joseph Rabinowitz, CEO, Charles O'Reilly, EVP, V. Steven Arnaudoff, VP Mktng & Sales, Lee R. Mannheimer, Dir Sales, Debra Ciaramella, Mktng Mgr

JobShop Software Solutions 1900 Sources Blvd, Pointe-Claire Quebec H9R 4Z3 Canada; 514/697-8621, Fax: 514/697-8621, Focus: CAD/CAE/CAM software, Prdts: AutoCAM, Ownrshp: PVT, John Nassr Jr., Bus Mgr

Jones Computer Network (JCN), 9697 E Mineral Ave, PO Box 3309, Englewood CO 80155-3309 USA; 303/792-3111, 800/226-6788 Fax: 303/792-5608, Co Email: jcninfo@meu.edu, Web URL: meu.edu, Focus: Computer TV programming, Prdts: Digital Gurus, New Media News, Home Computing, Computer Kids, Ownrshp: Sub. Jones Int'l., Founded: 1993, Empl: 50, Glenn R. Jones, Pres & CEO, Wally Griffin, Grp Pres, John Cooke, VP & GM, Jerry Czuchna, VP Advertising, Andy Holdgate, VP PR, Email: ahold-gate@meu.edu

Jones Futurex Inc. 3715 Atherton Rd, Rocklin CA 95765 USA; 916/632-3456, 800/251-5112 Fax: 916/632-3445, Focus: Security products and electronic manufacturing services, Prdts: SentryLine, Ownrshp: Sub Jones Intercable, Founded: 1981, Bryon D. Axt, COO, Gerald R. Scott, VP, Robert Norton, Sales Mgr, Email: snorton@meu.com

Jostens Home Learning 9920 Pacific Heights Blvd #500, San Diego CA 92121-4330 USA; 619/587-0087, 800/521-8538 Fax: 619/622-7873, Focus: Home educational software, Ownrshp: Sub Jostens Learning, Harriett Perry, VP, Maggie Sherrod, Mktng Mgr, Kaaren Webb, Dir Prod Dev

JourneyWare Media 550 Center St #123, Moraga CA 94556-1636 USA; 510/254-4520, Fax: 510/284-2619, Co Email: info@jorneyware.com, Web URL: journeyware.com, Focus: Multimedia books, Prdts: Virtual Seminar Series, Ownrshp: PVT, Founded: 1993, Empl: 7, David Marshall, Pres & CEO, Email: dpmars@ix.netcom.com; David Goldsmith, VP Tech Svcs, Email: david.goldsmith@pobox.com; Mark Pierce, VP Sales, Email: 73052.73@compuserve.com

JSB Corp. 108 Whispering Pines Dr, #115, Scotts Valley CA 95066-4785 USA; 408/438-8300, Fax: 408/438-8360, Co Email: info@jsb.com, Web URL: jsb.com, Focus: Graphical user interface software, Prdts: MultiView, Ownrshp: Sub. JSB Computer, England, Founded: 1981, Steve Jones, Chmn, Rob Barrow, CEO, Kevin Blakeman, GM

Jupiter Communications Co. 627 Broadway 2nd Fl., New York NY 10012-2612 USA; 212/780-6060, 800/488-4345 Fax: 212/780-6075, Co Email: jup5@aol.com, Web URL: jup.com/jupiter, Focus: Telecom, information services and videotex information, Ownrshp: PVT, Founded: 1986, Empl: 6, Joshua Harris, Pres, Gene DeRose, Ed Dir

JVC Information Products Co. 17811 Mitchell Ave, Irvine CA 92714 USA; 714/261-1292, Fax: 714/261-9690, Focus: PC peripherals, Ownrshp: Sub. JVC, Japan, Founded: 1926, Richard Young, Pres, Jack Moran

JYACC Inc. 116 John St, New York NY 10038 USA; 212/267-7722, Fax: 212/608-6753, Co Email: @jyacc.com, Web URL: jyacc.com, Focus: C/S development software, Prdts: JAM, Ownrshp: PVT, Founded: 1978, Empl: 229, Robert Ismach, Pres, Frank Vafier, EVP, Mark Jaffe, VP Mktng, Darryl Zack, VP Sales, Peter Stoll, VP Fin, Eric Block, Email: eblock@jyacc.com

K-12 MicroMedia Publishing Inc. 16 McKee Dr, Mahwah NJ 07430-2117 USA; 201/529-4500, 800/292-1997 Fax: 201/529-5282, Focus: Educational software, Prdts: Dicipline Pro, SportsPro:Hoops, SportsPro:Diamond, Ownrshp: PVT, Founded: 1985, Empl: 10, Anthony Schweiker, Pres, Lori McCaughey, VP, Michael Dolce, Prod Mgr

K.I.O. Corp. 43 Butterfield Cr, #C-5, El Paso TX 79906 USA; 915/774-5355, 800/870-6737 Fax: 915/774-5353, Focus: Data entry software, Prdts: Keying on Image, Ownrshp: PVT, Founded: 1993, Empl: 10, Bill Holmes, Pres & CEO, Becky Holmes, EVP, Bill Randag, VP Sales & Mktng, Quent Quiner, Sales Mgr

Kaetron Software Corp. 25211 Grogans Mill Rd #260, The Woodlands TX 77380-2924 USA; 713/298-1500, 800/938-8900 Fax: 713/298-2520, Co Email: kaetron@neosoft.com, Focus: Graphics software, Prdts: TopDown, FlowChart Express, Org Chart Express, Ownrshp: PVT, Founded: 1986, Wendy Sternick, Pres, Wendy S. Sternick

Kalman Technologies Inc. 1188 W Georgia St, #650, Vancouver BC V6E 4A2 Canada; 604/684-3118, Fax: 604/684-2324, Focus: Fax and telephony software, Ownrshp: PVT, Andrew Loui, Dir Mktng & Sales

Kanesmen Corp. 546 Valley Way, Milpitas CA 95035-4106 USA; 408/263-9881, Fax: 408/263-9883, Co Email: info@kansmen.com, Web URL: kansmen.com, Focus: Windows development tools, Ownrshp: PVT, Founded: 1991, Kanhom Ng, Pres, Susan Ng, Mktng Dir, Email: susan_ng@kansmen.com

KASEWORKS Inc. 1 Meca Way #150, Norcross GA 30093-2919 USA; 770/448-4240, Fax: 770/448-4163, Focus: GUI development tools, Prdts: KASE:VIP, Ownrshp: PVT, Founded: 1988, Joseph Richburg, Chmn & CEO, Joseph Trino, Pres & COO

KCS&A Public Relations 820 Second Ave, New York NY 10017-4504 USA; 212/682-6300, Fax: 212/697-0910, Co Email: kcsa@aol.com, Web URL: kcsa.com, Focus: PR and marketing communications, Ownrshp: PVT, Empl: 40, Henry Feintuch, Managing Partner

Keane Inc. 10 City Square, Boston MA 02129 USA; 617/241-9200, Web URL: keane.com, Focus: Software services, Ownrshp:

AMEX, Stk Sym: KEA, Founded: 1965, Empl: 1,400, Sales ($M): 382.7, Fiscal End: 12/95; John F. Keane, Pres & CEO, Raymond W. Paris, VP, Wallace A. Cataldo, VP Fin, Edward H. Longo Jr., SVP Info Svcs, Larry Vale, Dir Marcom

Keithly MetraByte 440 Myles Standish Blvd, Taunton MA 02780-9904 USA; 508/880-3000, 800/348-0033 Fax: 508/880-0179, Focus: Data acquisition hardware and software, Ownrshp: Sub Keithly Instruments

Kelly Micro Systems Inc. 2400 S Micro Age Way #MS4, Tempe AZ 85282-1824 USA; 800/854-3900 Focus: PC memory upgrades, Ownrshp: Sub. MicroAge, Founded: 1985, Rick Scherle, Pres, Alexx Wood

Kenan Systems Corp. One Main St, Cambridge MA 02142-1517 USA; 617/225-2224, Fax: 617/225-2291, Co Email: info@kenan.com, Web URL: kenan.com, Focus: Decision support and transaction software, Prdts: Acumate, Arbor/BP, Ownrshp: Sub. Kenan Systems, Founded: 1982, Kenan Sahin, Pres, John O'Rourke, CMO, Email: johno@kenan.com; Bob Crowley, Sales Mgr, Brian McGill, Dev Mgr

Kent Electronics Corp. 7433 Harvin Dr, Houston TX 77036-2015 USA; 713/780-7770, Focus: Distributor of electronics products, Ownrshp: NYSE, Stk Sym: KNT, Empl: 808, Sales ($M): 372.0, Fiscal End: 3/96; Morrie K. Abramson, Chmn, Pres & CEO, Randy J. Corporron, EVP, Larry D. Olson, EVP Sales, Mark A. Zerbe, EVP Ops, Duane Davis, VP MIS

Kent Marsh Ltd. 3260 Sul Ross St, Houston TX 77098-1930 USA; 713/522-5625, Fax: 713/522-8965, Focus: Computer security products, Prdts: FolderBolt NightWatch, QuickLock, MacSafe, Ownrshp: PVT, Founded: 1984, Vance Nesbitt, Chmn & CEO, Robert Wesolek, COO

Kentek Information Systems Inc. 2945 Wilderness Place, Boulder CO 80301 USA; 303/440-5500, Focus: LED-based page printers, Prdts: IBM 3816, Ownrshp: PVT, Founded: 1982, Empl: 200, Sales ($M): 13.1, Fiscal End: 6/96; Philip Shires, Pres & CEO, Bob Parks, VP Mktng, Craig Lamdoun, VP Fin & Admin

Ketchum Public Relations 55 Union St, San Francisco CA 94111-1266 USA; 415/984-6100, Fax: 415/982-0505, Focus: PR and marketing communications, Ownrshp: PVT, Empl: 45, Dianne Snedacker, Pres, Betsy Gullickson, SVP & GM

Key Tronic Corp. N 4424 Sullivan Rd, Spokane WA 99216 USA; 509/928-8000, Fax: 509/927-5248, Focus: Keyboards and input devices, Ownrshp: OTC, Stk Sym: KTCC, Founded: 1969, Empl: 3,056, Sales ($M): 201.0, Fiscal End: 6/96; Stanley Hiller Jr., Chmn, Fred Wenninger, Pres & COO, Glenford F. Griffin, VP Sales & Mktng, Jim Chapman, Dir Sales, Ronald F. Klawitter, VP Fin

Keyfile Corp. 22 Cotton Rd, Nashua NH 03063 USA; 603/883-3800, 800/453-9345 Fax: 603/889-9259, Co Email: @keyfile.com, Focus: Document management software, Prdts: Keyfile, Ownrshp: PVT, Founded: 1989, Empl: 68, Christopher D. Robert, Pres & CEO, Email: chrisrobert@keyfile.com; John Matera, VP WW Sales, Email: johnmatera@keyfile.com; Roger Sullivan, VP Mktng, Email: rogersullivan@keyfile.com; Irene O'Donnell, VP Admin, Email: ireneodonnell@keyfile.com

Keyspan 3095 Richmond Pkwy, #207, Richmond CA 94806 USA; 510/222-0131, Fax: 510/222-0323, Web URL: keyspan.com, Focus: Macintosh communications products, Ownrshp: Sub Inno-Sys, Mike Ridenhour, Pres

Khoral Research Inc. 6001 Indian School Rd NE, #200, Albuquerque NM 87110 USA; 505/837-6500, Fax: 505/881-3842, Co Email: info@khoral.com, Web URL: khoral.com, Focus: Object-based application development software system, Tom Sauer

Kinetic Systems Corp. 900 N State St, Lockport IL 60441 USA; 815/838-0005, 800/328-2669 Co Email: mkt-info@kscorp.com, Web URL: kscorp.com, Focus: Hardware and software for high speed data acquisition, Prdts: LabVIEW, Ownrshp: PVT, Founded: 1970, Empl: 88, Sales ($M): 10.0, Fiscal End: 9/95; James M. Stephenson Jr., Chmn & Pres, Robert T. Cleary, CEO, Arun P.

Sheth, VP Sales, Philippe Roy, Dir Mktng, Jenifer Cochran, Marcom Spec, Email: jcochran@kscorp.com

Kingston Technology Corp. 17600 Newhope St, Fountain Valley CA 92708 USA; 714/435-2600, 800/337-8410 Fax: 714/435-2699, Co Email: info@kingstone.com, Web URL: kingston.com, Focus: Memory boards, processor upgrades and mass storage, Ownrshp: PVT, Founded: 1987, Empl: 450, Sales ($M): 1,300, Fiscal End: 12/95; John Tu, Pres, David Sun, VP Eng, Peggy Kelly, Email: peggy_kelly@kingston.com

KL Group Inc. 260 King St E, 3rd Floor, Toronto Ontario M5A 1K3 Canada; 416/594-1026, 800/663-4723 Fax: 416/594-1919, Co Email: info@klg.com, Web URL: klg.com, Focus: 3D graphics software for X Windows, Ownrshp: PVT, Founded: 1989, Greg Kiessling, Pres, Edward Lycklama, Co-founder, Giovanna Artuso, Dir Mktng, Email: gba@klg.com; Bradley Moseley-Williams, Dir PR, Email: bmw@klg.com

Klynas Engineering PO Box 499, Simi Valley CA 93062-0499 USA; 805/583-1133, Fax: 805/583-1457, Co Email: streets_info@klynas.com, Web URL: klynas.com, Focus: Rd mapping software, Prdts: Sts on a Disk, Ownrshp: PVT, Founded: 1985, Scott Klynas, Pres

Knowledge Access Int'l. 2685 Marine Way, #1305, Mountain View CA 94043 USA; 415/969-0606, 800/252-9273 Fax: 415/969-1405, Focus: Document management software, Prdts: CD-Rchiver, Ownrshp: Sub Rimage, Matilda Butler, Pres, William Paisley, EVP

Knowledge Garden Inc. 127 Wilderness Rd, St James NY 11780-9726 USA; 516/862-0600, Fax: 516/862-0644, Co Email: info@kgarden.com, Web URL: kgarden.com, Focus: PC software development tools, Prdts: KPWin, WRAP, KPDOS, Ownrshp: PVT, Founded: 1986, Empl: 8, John Slade, Pres, Email: jslade@kgarden.com

Knowledge Media 436 Nunneley Rd, #B, Paradise CA 95969 USA; 916/872-7487, Fax: 916/872-3826, Web URL: km-cd.com, Focus: Consumer multimedia software, Ownrshp: PVT, Founded: 1984, Paul A. Benson, Pres, Sigmund Hartman, CEO

Knowledge Quest 310 Broadway, Laguna Beach CA 92651 USA; 714/376-8150, Fax: 714/497-6502, Co Email: 102671.3661@compuserve.com, Focus: Computer-based interactive training products, Prdts: QuickSuccess, Ownrshp: PVT, Mark Dawson, Pres

Knowledge Revolution 66 Bovet Rd, #200, San Mateo CA 94402 USA; 415/574-7777, 800/766-6615 Fax: 415/574-7541, Co Email: info@krev.com, Web URL: krev.com, Focus: Mechanical simulation software, Prdts: Working Model, Ownrshp: PVT, Founded: 1988, David Baszucki, Pres, Paul Baszucki, Chmn, Umberto Milletti, Dir Prod Dev, Greg Baszucki, VP Sales, Connie Wal, Mktng Coord, Email: connie@krev.com

KnowledgeBroker Inc. (KBI), 13295 Mira Loma Rd, Reno NV 89511 USA; 702/852-5711, 800/829-4524 Web URL: kbi.com, Focus: Computer support services, Prdts: HelpNet, Ownrshp: OTC, Stk Sym: KBIZ, Founded: 1992, Brad Stanley, Pres, Gail Wetmore, Dir Mktng

KnowledgePoint 1129 Industrial Ave, Petaluma CA 94954-1141 USA; 707/762-0333, 800/727-1133 Fax: 707/762-0802, Focus: Personnel management software, Prdts: Performance Now, Descriptions Now, Policies Now, Ownrshp: PVT, Founded: 1987, Empl: 30, Michael Troy, Pres & CEO, Rudy Lacoe, VP, Greg Tognoli, VP Sales & Mktng, Diane Pratt, Dir Prod Dev, Judy Segner, PR Dir, Email: jjsegner@aol.com

KnowledgeSet Corp. 555 Ellis St, Mountain View CA 94043-2205 USA; 415/254-5400, Web URL: kset.com, Focus: Text management software, WWW programming, Prdts: Knowledge Retrieval System, Ownrshp: PVT, Founded: 1984, Empl: 26, Peter Hepburn, Pres, Email: phepburn@kset.com; Ione Ishii, VP Ops, Email: iishii@kset.com; Robert L. Smith, VP Eng, Email: rlsmith@kset.com; Bruce Kusch, VP Sales, Email:

bkusch@kset.com

KnowledgeSoft Inc. 5000 Ritter Rd, Mechanicsburg PA 17055 USA; 800/366-2381 Web URL: knowledgesoft.com, Focus: Knowledge management software, Prdts: Learning Organization Information System, Founded: 1986

Knozall Systems Inc. 375 E Elliot Rd, #10, Chandler AZ 85225-1130 USA; 602/545-0006, Fax: 602/545-0008, Web URL: indirect.com/www/knozall, Focus: Network utility software, Prdts: FileWizard, NLMAuto, NLMErlin, File Auditor, Ownrshp: PVT, Founded: 1990, Empl: 7, Donald R. Lundell, Pres, Email: donl@tesi.com; John C. Lucas, EVP, Email: johnl@tesi.com; Gail A. Lundell, Dir Marcom, Email: gaill@tesi.com

Kodak Digital Science 901 Elmgrove Rd, Rochester NY 14653-5245 800/235-6325 Co Email: kodak@aol.com, Web URL: kodak.com, Focus: Imaging products and PC cards, Ownrshp: Sub Eastman Kodak

Kolvox Communications Inc. 4100 Young St, #607, N York Ontario M2P 2B5 Canada; 416/221-2400, Fax: 416/218-3110, Web URL: kolvox.com, Focus: Speech recognition software, Prdts: Office Talk, Law Talk, Voice Companion, Ownrshp: FO, Stk Sym: KOL, Founded: 1990, Empl: 40, Isaac Raichyk, Pres, Kurt Lynn, VP Sales & Mktng, Martin Tuori, VP Tech, Email: mtuori@kolvox.com; Mary McDermott, Exec Assist

Komag Inc. 275 S Hillview Dr, Milpitas CA 95035 USA; 408/946-2300, Fax: 408/946-1126, Focus: Thin film media and disk heads, Ownrshp: OTC, Stk Sym: KMAG, Founded: 1983, Empl: 2,635, Sales ($M): 512.2, Fiscal End: 12/95; Stephen C. Johnson, Pres & CEO, Will Kauffman, SVP & COO, T. Hunt Payne, SVP Sales & Mktng, James E. Opfer, Group VP R&D

Konexx 5550 Oberlin Dr, San Diego CA 92121-1717 USA; 619/622-1400, 800/275-6354 Fax: 619/550-7330, Co Email: sales@konexx.com, Web URL: konexx.com, Focus: Computer-phone connection accessories, Prdts: Konexx, Ownrshp: PVT, Founded: 1987, Empl: 28, Howard Gutzmer, Pres & CEO, William Sopp, VP Sales & Mktng, Email: bsopp@konexx.com; Jason Treiber, Finance Mgr, Barssra Asler, Acct Exec

Konica Business Machines USA Inc. 500 Day Hill Rd, Windsor CT 06095 USA; 203/683-2222, 800/456-6422 Fax: 203/285-7617, Focus: Laser printers, copiers and fax machines, Ownrshp: Sub. Konica, Japan, Founded: 1986, Empl: 485, Terry Kawaura, Chmn & Pres, Cyrus L. Tyler, VP Corp Com

Koss Corp. 4129 N Port Washington Ave, Milwaukee WI 53212 USA; 414/964-5000, Focus: Computer audio products, Sales ($M): 36.4, Fiscal End: 6/96; John C. Koss, Chmn, Michael J. Koss, Pres & CEO, Cameryne Roberts

KPMG Peat Marwick (KPMG) 3 Chestnut Ridge Rd, Montvale NJ 07645 USA; 201/307-7000, Web URL: kpmg.com, Focus: Management consulting and network integration, Ownrshp: PVT, Founded: 1800, Empl: 76,000, Sales ($M): 7,500, Fiscal End: 12/95; Stephen G. Butler, Chmn & CEO, Roger S. Siboni, Deputy Chmn

Kubota Pacific Computer Inc. 2880 Lakeside Dr, #131, Santa Clara CA 95054-2814 USA; 408/727-8100, Fax: 408/727-9301, Co Email: @kpc.com, Focus: 3D graphics accelerators, Ownrshp: Sub. Kubota, Japan, Empl: 235, Ben Wegbreit, Chmn & CEO, Ronald Curtis, VP Sales, Email: rcurtis@kpc.com; Email: scece.kpc.com

Kurzweil Applied Intelligence 411 Waverly Oaks Rd, Waltham MA 02154 USA; 617/893-5151, Fax: 617/893-6525, Web URL: kurz-ai.com, Focus: Voice recognition systems, Ownrshp: OTC, Stk Sym: KURZ, Founded: 1982, Sales ($M): 9.4, Fiscal End: 1/96; Mark D. Flanagan, EVP

Kurzweil Technology Group 625 S Church St, Murfreesboro TN 37130 USA; 615/848-5321, Fax: 615/848-5322, Co Email: @musicpro.com, Web URL: musicpro.com, Focus: Multimedia audio/music synthesizer, Prdts: MASS, SASH, Ownrshp: PVT

KYE International Corp. 2605 E Cedar St, Ontario CA 91761

USA; 909/923-3510, Fax: 909/923-1469, Focus: Handheld scanners, mice, trackballs and digitizer tablets, Ownrshp: PVT, Chris Ho, Pres

Kyocera Electronics Inc. 100 Randolph Rd, Somerset NJ 08875 USA; 908/560-3400, 800/232-6797 Fax: 908/560-8380, Focus: Printers, Ownrshp: Sub. Kyocera, Japan, Mike Okuno, Pres, Gerry Rittenbery, VP, Glenn Gruber, Dir Mktng, Steve Petix

KyTek Inc. 28 Duck Pond Rd, Weare NH 03281 USA; 603/529-2512, Fax: 603/529-2015, Co Email: sales@kytek.com, Focus: Page layout software, Prdts: Autopage, Ownrshp: PVT, Keith Erf, Pres

L.I.S.T. Inc. 320 Northern Blvd, Great Neck NY 11021 USA; 516/482-2345, Fax: 516/487-7721, Co Email: info@l-i-s-t.com, Web URL: l-i-s-t.com, Focus: High-tech company mailing list, Prdts: Top 750 CIOs, Glenn Freedman, Pres

LA SOUND International 14508 S Garfield Ave, Paramount CA 90723 USA; 310/602-0572, 800/874-3436 Fax: 310/602-1390, Focus: Manufacture and sale of multimedia products

Labtec Enterprises Inc. 3801 109th Ave, #J, Vancouver WA 98682 USA; 360/896-2000, Fax: 360/896-2020, Focus: Speakers, headphones and sound accessories, Ownrshp: PVT, Founded: 1983, Richard James, CEO, Gary Savadove, SVP Mktng, David Dietz, SVP Sales, Mark Zadeh, SVP Intl Sales, Debbie DeFreece, Mktng Mgr

Lachman Technology Inc. 2400 Cabot Dr, Lisle IL 60532-3621 USA; 708/505-9100, Fax: 708/505-9133, Focus: Open system and network software, Ownrshp: Sub. Legent, Founded: 1977, Empl: 60, Sales ($M): 8, Ron Lachman, Pres & CEO

LADDIS Group, The 10754 Ambassador Dr, #201, Manassas VA 22110 USA; 703/331-0181, Fax: 703/331-0181, Co Email: info@specbench.com, Web URL: specbench.com, Focus: Develop benchmarks for comparing NFS file server performance, Ownrshp: Nonprofit, Founded: 1990

Lahey Computer Systems Inc. 865 Tahoe Blvd, PO Box 6091, Incline Village NV 89450 USA; 702/831-2500, Fax: 702/831-8123, Co Email: 71333.2000@compuserve.com, Focus: Fortran language systems, Ownrshp: PVT, Founded: 1967, Empl: 35, Thomas M. Lahey, Pres & CEO, Bob Runyan, EVP, Guy C. Ceragioli, VP Mktng

LAN Support Group Inc. 3355 W Alabama St, #1200, Houston TX 77098-1718 USA; 713/789-0881, Fax: 713/977-9111, Focus: LAN management software, Ownrshp: PVT, Founded: 1990, Empl: 52, Eric Pulaski, Pres

LANCAST 12 Murphy Dr, Nashua NH 03062-1918 USA; 603/880-1833, 800/952-6227 Fax: 603/881-9888, Co Email: lancast1@aol.com, Focus: LAN products, Ownrshp: PVT, Founded: 1981, Empl: 51, Sales ($M): 9.3, Fiscal End: 9/95; Hong Yu, Pres & CEO, Asbjorn Sorhaug, EVP & COO, Email: asbjorns@aol.com; Mike Ongarato, VP Sales & Mktng, Email: mikeong@aol.com; Yeh-Tsong Wen, VP Eng, Tonya McMurray, Mktng Mgr, Email: tmlancast1@aol.com

Landmark Graphics Corp. 15150 Memorial Dr, Houston TX 77079-4304 USA; Ownrshp: OTC, Stk Sym: LMRK, Sales ($M): 187.3, Fiscal End: 6/96; Sam K. Smith, Chmn, Robert P. Peebler, Pres, CEO & COO, William H. Seippel, VP & CFO, S. Rutt Bridges, VP & CTO, Denese D. Van Dyne, VP Corp Com

Landmark Systems Corp. 8000 Towers Crescent Dr, Vienna VA 22182 USA; 703/902-8000, Fax: 703/893-5568, Web URL: landmark.com, Focus: Mainframe software, Ownrshp: PVT, Founded: 1982, Empl: 225, Sales ($M): 46.9, Fiscal End: 12/95; Katherine K. Clark, Pres & CEO, Patrick H. McGettigan, Chmn

Language Automation Inc. 1806 Parkwood Dr, San Mateo CA 94403-3954 USA; 415/571-7877, 800/571-4685 Fax: 415/571-6294, Co Email: info@lai.com, Web URL: lai.com/lai, Focus: Internet-based foreign language translation software and services, Prdts: Web Plexer Intelligent Language Server, Ownrshp: PVT, David Lakritz, Pres & CEO, Email: dave@lai.com

Language Publications Interactive (LPI), 121 W 27th St,

#801, New York NY 10001 USA; 212/620-3193, 800/882-6700 Fax: 212/620-3806, Focus: Language instruction software, Prdts: Who is Oscar Lake, Founded: 1993, Robert L. Miller, Chmn & CEO

Lanop Corp. 310 E 44th St, New York NY 10017 USA; Focus: Test preparation centers for Novell CNE certification, Ownrshp: PVT, Founded: 1992, John Goodfriend, VP

LanQuest Group 47800 Westinghouse Dr, Fremont CA 94539-7469 USA; 510/354-0940, Fax: 510/354-0950, Co Email: info@lanquest.com, Web URL: lanquest.com, Focus: Network testing and analysis, Prdts: Framethrower, NET/WRx, Ownrshp: PVT, Founded: 1986, Ron Kopeck, Pres & CEO, Paul Czarnik, VP Dev

Lansafe Network Services Inc. 31 E 28th St, 8th Floor, New York NY 10016 USA; 212/889-8100, Fax: 212/889-8146, Focus: LAN management hardware and help desk, Prdts: NETLink, Ownrshp: PVT, Founded: 1991, Empl: 21, Sales ($M): 1.5, Alan Cooper, Pres, Victor Abrahamsen, VP

LANSource Technologies Inc. 221 Dufferin St, #310A, Toronto Ontario M6K 3J2 Canada; 416/535-3555, 800/677-2727 Fax: 416/535-6225, Co Email: @lansource.com, Focus: Network fax and data communications software, Prdts: FAXport LAN, Marc Bisnaire, Pres, Andrea Quesnelle, Email: andrea@lansource.com

Lante Corp. 35 W Wacker Dr, #3200, Chicago IL 60601 USA; 312/236-5100, Fax: 312/236-0664, Co Email: @lante.com, Focus: Microcomputer services, Ownrshp: PVT, Mark A. Tebbe, Pres, Email: mtebbe@lante.com; Jeff Alvis, Dir, Email: jalvis@lante.com; Eugene Riden, Dir Bus Relations, Email: eriden@lante.com; John Meyer, Dir Tech, Email: jmeyer@lante.com; Lisa Dalton, Comm Specialist, Email: ldalton@lante.com

Lanworks Technologies Inc. 2425 Skymark Ave, Mississauga Ontario L4W 4Y6 Canada; 905/238-5528, 800/808-3000 Fax: 905/238-9407, Co Email: @lanworks.com, Focus: LAN management software, Prdts: BootWare, BootWare Manager, Ownrshp: PVT, Founded: 1985, Empl: 30, George Kostiuk, Pres, Email: george@lanworks.com; Gilbert Yeung, SW Dev Mgr, Email: gilbert@lanworks.com; Ron McNab, VP Sales & Mktng, Email: ran@lanworks.com; Elizabeth Williams, Marcom Mgr, Email: liz@lanworks.com

Laptop Solutions Inc. (LSI), 16000 Barkers Point Ln, Houston TX 77079-4023 USA; 713/556-5051, Fax: 713/556-5035, Focus: Laptop notebook upgrade products, Ownrshp: Sub. Enhance Services Co., Ken Duckman, Pres, Harry Ameen, VP Sales & Mktng, Email: hameen@lsi-tx.com

Large Storage Configurations (LSC), 4211 Lexington Ave N, St Paul MN 55126-6164 USA; 612/482-4535, 800/831-9482 Fax: 612/482-4595, Co Email: info@lsci.com, Web URL: lsci.com, Focus: Mass storage management software, Prdts: SAM-FS, IDS, Ownrshp: PVT, Founded: 1985, Empl: 15, Paul G. Miller, Chmn, Email: pgm@lsci.com; James Murdakes, Pres & CEO, Email: jmurdaks@lsci.com; Don Crouse, SVP, Email: don@lsci.com; Harriet Coverston, VP SW Dev, Email: hgc@lsci.com; Gregg Juettner, VP Mktng, Email: gregg@lsci.com

Lari Software Inc. 207 S Elliott Rd, #203, Chapel Hill NC 27514 USA; 919/968-0701, 800/933-7303 Fax: 919/968-0801, Co Email: sales@larisoftware.com, Web URL: larisoftware.com, Focus: Illustration software, Prdts: LightningDraw, Ownrshp: PVT, Founded: 1994, Humayun Lari, Pres

Laser Communications Inc. 1848 Charter Ln, #F, Lancaster PA 17601 USA; 717/394-8634, 800/527-3740 Fax: 717/396-9831, Co Email: lasercomm@epix.net, Web URL: lasercomm.com/lasercomm, Focus: Communications systems, Prdts: LACE, OmniBeam, Ownrshp: PVT, Founded: 1983, Empl: 12, Sales ($M): 3, Richard Guttendorf, Pres & CEO, John Jutila, VP Intl Sales, Timothy Grotzinger, VP Eng

LaserCard Systems Corp. 2644 Bayshore Pkwy, Mountain View

CA 94043 USA; 415/969-4428, Focus: Optical memory cards, Ownrshp: PVT

Lasergate Systems Inc. (LSI), 28050 US 19 N, #502, Clearwater FL 34621 USA; 813/725-0882, Fax: 813/724-8489, Focus: Bar code products, Prdts: GATEPAS, Ownrshp: OTC, Stk Sym: LSGT, Founded: 1985, Empl: 16, Sales ($M): 1.1, Fiscal End: 12/94; Jacqueline E. Soechtig, Chmn, Pres & CEO, John Warnick, CFO, William I. Fenner, VP & COO, Fred R. Maglione, VP Sales & Mktng

LaserMaster Corp. 7090 Shady Oak Rd, Eden Prairie MN 55344 USA; 612/941-8687, 800/477-7714 Fax: 612/941-8652, Focus: Page printers for PCs and LANs, Prdts: TurboRes, ThermalRes, Ownrshp: OTC, Stk Sym: LMTS, Founded: 1985, Empl: 500, Sales ($M): 93.6, Fiscal End: 6/96; Melvin L. Masters, Chmn, Pres & CEO, Larry J. Lukis, EVP & CTO, Robert J. Wenzel, COO, Randall L. Ruegg, CFO, David Noah, Dir PR, Email: 73124.222@compuserve.com

LaserScan Systems Inc. 5310 NW 33rd Ave, #115, Ft. Lauderdale FL 33309 USA; 305/777-1300, Fax: 305/739-7845, Co Email: paclid@ibm.net, Focus: Imaging and DBMS systems, Prdts: DORIAN Imaging System, Ownrshp: PVT, Founded: 1985, Empl: 22, Sales ($M): 2.4, Fiscal End: 5/96; Leonard Fox, Pres & CEO, Salvatore F. Patalano, COO, Terrence J. Goodwin, CIO

LaserVend Inc. 12215 S 900 E, Draper UT 84020 USA; 801/553-9080, 800/909-6077 Fax: 801/553-8780, Focus: Software vending machines, Ownrshp: PVT, David J. Griffiths, Pres, Jeff L. Peery, Dir PR

Lattice Inc. 3020 Woodcreek Dr, #D, Downers Grove IL 60515 USA; 800/444-4309 Fax: 708/769-4083, Focus: Programming tools and pen software, Prdts: PenPoll, PenTalk, PenBase, Ownrshp: PVT, Founded: 1981, Empl: 15, Peter Muzzy, Pres

Lattice Semiconductor Corp. 5555 Northeast Moore Ct, Hillsboro OR 97124-6421 USA; 503/681-0118, Fax: 503/681-0347, Web URL: lscc.com, Focus: CMOS programmable logic devices, Ownrshp: OTC, Stk Sym: LSCC, Founded: 1983, Empl: 263, Sales ($M): 198.2, Fiscal End: 4/96; Cyrus Y. Tsui, Chmn, Pres & CEO, Steven A. Laub, VP & GM, Jonathan K. Yu, VP Ops, Rodney F. Sloss, VP Fin

Lava Computer Mfg. Inc. 28A Dansk Ct, Rexdale Ontario M9W 5V8 Canada; 416/674-5942, 800/241-5282 Fax: 416/674-8262, Focus: Modems, Ownrshp: PVT, Roman Wynnyckyj, Pres, Mike Wynnyckyj, VP Sales & Mktng, Email: 75662.110@compuserve.com

Lawrence Productions 1800 S 35th St, Galesburg MI 49053-9687 USA; 616/665-7075, Fax: 616/665-7060, Focus: Entertainment and educational software, Prdts: McGee, Katie's Farm, Nigel's World, The Lost Tribe, Ownrshp: PVT, Founded: 1980, Empl: 45, John Lawrence, Chmn, Tim Knapper, VP, Email: tknapper@aol.com

Lawson Software 1300 Godward St, Minneapolis MN 55413-3004 USA; 612/379-2633, 800/477-1357 Fax: 612/379-7141, Co Email: @lawson.com, Web URL: lawson.com, Focus: Enterprisewide, client/server business application solutions, Prdts: Open Enterprise Financial System, Ownrshp: PVT, Founded: 1975, Empl: 725, Sales ($M): 101.8, Fiscal End: 5/96; Richard Lawson, Pres & CEO, Email: richard.lawson@lawson.com; John Cerullo, Chmn, Email: john.cerullo@lawson.com; Ken Behrendt, CFO, Email: ken.behrendt@lawson.com; Daniel Metzger, VP Mktng, Email: daniel@metzger@lawson.com; William Lawson, Dir MIS & COO, Email: william.b.lawson@lawson.com; Terry Plath, Marcom Mgr, Email: terry.plath@lawson.com

LBMS 1800 W Loop S, 6th Fl, Houston TX 77027 USA; 713/625-9300, Web URL: lbms.com, Focus: C/S software, Ownrshp: OTC, Founded: 1977, Empl: 310, Sales ($M): 42.3, Fiscal End: 12/96; Rainer Brchett, Chmn, John T. Bantleman, Pres & CEO

LCS Industries Inc. 120 Brighton Rd, Clifton NJ 07012-1694 USA; 201/778-5588, Fax: 212/947-3351, Focus: Services for direct marketing companies, Ownrshp: OTC, Stk Sym: LCSI,

Founded: 1969, Empl: 1,000, Sales ($M): 62.7, Fiscal End: 9/94; Arnold J. Scheine, Pres & CEO, Mitchell Goldklank, SVP Sales & Mktng, Marvin Cohen, SVP, Pat R. Frustaci, VP Fin, Kathryn Barber, VP

LDI Open Software (LDI) 3 Summit Park Dr, #300, Cleveland OH 44131-2582 USA; 216/498-5500, Fax: 216/498-4646, Focus: Software and systems integration, Ownrshp: Sub. LDI Corp., Michael T. Joseph, Pres

LEAD Technologies Inc. 900 Baxter St, Charlotte NC 28204 USA; 704/332-5532, 800/637-4699 Fax: 704/372-8161, Web URL: leadtools.com, Focus: Image compression software, Prdts: LEADVIEW, Ownrshp: PVT, Founded: 1990, Rich Little, Pres, Moe Daher, VP Eng, Jeanne Desrosiers

Leadtek Research Inc. 46721 Fremont Blvd, Fremont CA 94538 USA; 510/490-8076, Fax: 510/490-7759, Focus: Manufactures graphics and video graphics products, Prdts: WINFast S510, Ownrshp: PVT, Founded: 1986

Leaf Systems Inc. 8 Technology Dr, #100, Westboro MA 01581-1751 USA; 508/460-8300, Fax: 508/460-6470, Focus: Scanners and digital cameras, Ownrshp: Sub. Scitex, Founded: 1985, Empl: 100, Robert A. Caspe, Pres, Chanoch Biran, EVP

Learning Company, The 6493 Kaiser Dr, Fremont CA 94555 USA; 510/792-2101, Fax: 510/792-9628, Focus: Children's educational software, Ownrshp: OTC, Stk Sym: LRNG, Founded: 1979, Empl: 238, Sales ($M): 53.2, Fiscal End: 6/95; William A. Dinsmore III, Pres & CEO, Les Schmidt, COO, John M. Stacy, VP Mktng & Sales, David L. Scanlin, VP Sales, Stephen A. Joseph, VP R&D

Learning Services Inc. PO Box 10636, 3895 E 19th, Eugene OR 97440 USA; 541/683-3827, Fax: 541/484-7499, Co Email: @ls.learnserv.com, Web URL: learnserv.com, Focus: Educational software, Ownrshp: PVT, Founded: 1985, Empl: 45, Sales ($M): 8.9, Fiscal End: 7/95; John Crowder, Pres, Email: john@ls.learnserv.com; K. Ray Barnes, Secretary, Email: ray@ls.learnserv.com; Steve Christensen, Treas, Email: steve@ls.learnserv.com

Learning Tree Int'l. 1805 Library St, Reston VA 22090-9919 USA; 703/709-9019, Fax: 703/709-6405, Focus: Computer technology training seminars, Ownrshp: Public, Founded: 1974, Sales ($M): 78.8, Fiscal End: 9/95; Alan B. Salisbury, Pres

LearningWare Inc. 855 Village Ctr Dr, #321, N Oaks MN 55127 USA; 612/636-6244, Fax: 612/332-2046, Focus: Educational software, Prdts: Quiz Factory, Founded: 1994

Learningways Inc. 10 Fawcett St, 4th Fl., Cambridge MA 02138-1110 USA; 617/234-5800, Fax: 617/234-5801, Focus: Educational software, Ownrshp: Sub. Davidson & Associates, Founded: 1980, Empl: 35, Chuck Olson, Pres, Louise Dube, CFO

LearnIT Corp. 2407 NW 15th Place, Gainesville FL 32605 USA; 904/375-6655, 800/352-4806 Fax: 904/376-0022, Co Email: learnit@msn.com, Prdts: Interactive Training for Windows 95, Paul Firth, Pres

Ledge Multimedia One Canal Park, 2nd Fl., Cambridge MA 02141 USA; 617/494-0090, Fax: 617/577-2343, Web URL: ledgemm.com, Focus: Internet and CD-ROM multimedia software products, Ownrshp: Sub. Dataware Technologies, Founded: 1992, Dana Lewis, Email: dana@ledgemm.com

Legato Systems Inc. 3145 Porter Dr, Palo Alto CA 94304-1213 USA; 415/812-6000, Fax: 415/812-6032, Web URL: legato.com, Focus: Network backup and recovery software, Prdts: NetWorker, Ownrshp: OTC, Stk Sym: LGTO, Founded: 1989, Empl: 170, Sales ($M): 30.0, Fiscal End: 12/95; Louis C. Cole, Pres & CEO, Kent D. Smith, EVP Customer Ops, Edward Cooper, VP Mktng, Gilbert Wai, SVP Prod Dev, Gary Thompson, CFO, Suzan Woods, Dir Mkt Relations

Legend Entertainment Co. 14200 Park Meadow Dr, PO Box 10810, Chantilly VA 22021-0810 USA; 703/222-8500, Fax: 703/222-3471, Co Email: legendentr@aol.com, Focus: Adventure games, Prdts: Mission Critical, Shannara, Ownrshp: PVT, Founded:

1988, Empl: 26, Robert Bates, Pres, Mike Verdu, Chmn, Peggy Oriani, Dir Mktng, Kathy Frazier, PR Mgr, Email: kathyfraz@aol.com

Legent Corp. 575 Herndon Pkwy, Herndon VA 22070-5226 USA; 703/708-3000, Fax: 703/708-3209, Focus: Data, system and network management software, Ownrshp: OTC, Stk Sym: LGNT, Founded: 1973, Sales ($M): 501.7, Fiscal End: 9/94; Joe M. Henson, Chmn, David F. Wetmore, EVP & COO, Robert Yellin, SVP & CTO, Franchon M. Smithson, SVP & CFO

Lernout & Hauspie Speech Products 20 Mall Rd, Burlington MA 01803 USA; 617/238-0960, Fax: 617/238-0986, Focus: Speech software and hardware, Ownrshp: OTC, Stk Sym: LHSPF, Founded: 1987, Empl: 100, Sales ($M): 3.3, Fiscal End: 12/95; Jo Lernout, Managing Dir, Yacov Levy, CEO, Bart Verhaeghe

Level Five Research 1335 Gateway Dr, #2005, Melbourne FL 32901 USA; 407/729-6004, 800/444-4303 Fax: 407/727-7615, Co Email: @l5r.com, Web URL: l5r.com, Focus: Development software for knowledge-based systems and intelligent agents, Prdts: Level 5 Object, Ownrshp: sub. Information Builders, Founded: 1984, Ron Hencin, VP Sales & Mktng, Doug Taylor, Mktng Mgr, Email: doug@l5r.com

Leverage Software Inc. 2241-R Tackett's Mill Dr, Woodbridge VA 22192 USA; 703/494-0818, 800/344-2322 Fax: 703/551-4924, Focus: Office automation software/Federal acquisitions regulations, Prdts: PDQFAR Database Retrieval System, Ownrshp: PVT, Founded: 1982, Empl: 15, Clancy McQuigg, Pres, Robert B. Andrews, CEO & Dir

Lexicus Corp. 490 California Ave, #300, Palo Alto CA 94306 USA; 415/462-6800, 800/539-4287 Fax: 415/323-4772, Co Email: info@lexicus.mot.com, Web URL: mot.com/lexicus, Focus: Handwriting recognition software, Prdts: Longhand Professional, QuickPrint, LexiPen, Ownrshp: Sub. Motorola, Founded: 1992, Ronjon Nag, GM, Elton Sherwin, VP Mktng, Email: eltons@lexicus.mot.com; Denise Brosseau, Mgr US Bus Dev, Email: deniseb@lexicus.mot.com; Brenda Scariot, Assist Mktng Mgr, Email: brendas@lexicus.mot.com

Lexmark International Inc. 55 Railroad Ave, Greenwich CT 06836 USA; 606/232-2000, 800/358-5835 Co Email: @lexmark.com, Web URL: lexmark.com, Focus: Printers, electronic typewriters, Prdts: MarkVision, Ownrshp: PVT, Founded: 1991, Empl: 6,600, Sales ($M): 2,158.0, Fiscal End: 12/95; Marvin L. Mann, Chmn, Paul Curlander, VP & GM Printing Syst, Rick Scott

LG Electronics 1000 Sylvan Ave, Englewood Cliffs NJ 07632 USA; 201/816-2000, Fax: 201/816-0636, Focus: Monitors, CD-ROM drives and modems, Ownrshp: Sub. LG Group, Founded: 1958, Empl: 35,000

Liant Software Corp. 959 Concord St, Framingham MA 01701-4613 USA; 508/872-8700, 800/818-4754 Fax: 508/626-2221, Web URL: liant.com, Focus: Language compilers, Prdts: RM/COBOL, LPI-C, LPI-C++, LPI-FORTRAN, LPI COBOL, Ownrshp: PVT, Founded: 1990, Empl: 135, Sales ($M): 20, Fiscal End: 9/93; Ed Lucente, Pres & CEO, John M. Bradley, SVP Bus Dev, Robert M. Lapides, VP LPI, Bruce Flory, Dir Mktng, Kenneth J. Guerra, VP Fin, Lauren Langevin, Dir Prod Mktng

Library & Information Technology Assoc. (LITA), 50 E Huron St, Chicago IL 60611 USA; 312/280-4270, Fax: 312/280-3257, Co Email: lita@ala.org, Focus: Information technologies for libraries, Ownrshp: Nonprofit, Jacqueline Mundell, Exec Dir

Liebert Corp. 1050 Dearborn Dr, PO Box 29186, Columbus OH 43229 USA; 614/888-0246, Fax: 614/841-6973, Focus: UPS and computer cooling systems, Ownrshp: Sub Emerson Electric, Wally O'Dell, Pres WW, Edward Feeney, Pres NA, James Good, VP Sales

Life Change Productions PO Box 433, Sedro Woolley WA 98284 USA; 800/490-0055 Focus: Software to add romance to your life, Prdts: Romantic Adventures, Ownrshp: PVT, Kevin Benedict, Pres

LifeTime Media Inc. 17205 Vashon Hwy, Bldg. C2, Vashon WA

98070 USA; 206/567-5500, 800/567-7741 Focus: Training software, Prdts: Training Planner

Ligature Software Inc. 25 Burlington Mall Rd, #300, Burlington MA 01803 USA; 617/238-6734, Fax: 617/272-3085, Focus: OCR software solutions for desktop systems, business environments and embedded application, Prdts: CharacterEyes, FormReader, Founded: 1989, Gideon Ben-Zvi, Pres & CEO, Jonathan Eran Kali, Mgr R&D, Noam Shanny, EVP Eng, Jacob Shaya, EVP & Chief Scientist, Barry Braunstein, Email: 75104.516@compuserve.com

Light Source Inc. 17 E Sir Francis Drake Blvd #100-4, Larkspur CA 94939-1727 USA; 415/461-8000, Fax: 415/461-8011, Co Email: lightsource@applelink.com, Focus: Graphics software, Prdts: Colortron Color System, Ownrshp: PVT, Founded: 1989, Phillip Moffitt, Chmn & CEO, Robert Cook, Pres, Steven Miller, VP Mktng, Edward Granger, Principal Scientist

Lighthouse Design Ltd. 2929 Campus Dr, #250, San Mateo CA 94403-2534 USA; 415/570-7736, 800/366-2279 Fax: 415/570-7787, Co Email: info@lighthouse.com, Web URL: lighthouse.com, Focus: Project management software, Prdts: TaskMaster, Ownrshp: PVT, Founded: 1989, Jonathan Schwartz, Pres & CEO, Angela Grady

Linear Technology Corp. 1630 McCarthy Blvd, Milpitas CA 95035-7487 USA; 408/432-1900, Fax: 408/434-0507, Focus: Linear ICs, Ownrshp: OTC, Stk Sym: LLTC, Founded: 1981, Empl: 1,350, Sales ($M): 377.8, Fiscal End: 6/96; Robert H. Swanson Jr., Pres & CEO, Clive B. Davies, VP & COO, Sean T. Hurley, VP Ops, Thomas D. Recine, VP Mktng, Paul Coghlan, VP & CFO

Linguistic Technology Corp. PO Box 309, Newton Square PA 19073-9509 USA; 610/325-7500, 800/425-8200 Fax: 610/325-7506, Focus: Speech-based database utility software, Ownrshp: PVT

Link Technologies Inc. 3471 N 1st St, Bldg M/S 615-3, San Jose CA 95134-1801 USA; 408/473-1200, Focus: Terminals, Prdts: MAX Series, MC Series, Ownrshp: Sub. Wyse, Founded: 1983, Charlet T. Comiso, Pres, Larry Schuster, VP Sales & Mktng, Farhad Kashani, VP Ops, David Brooks, Dir Eng, Jeff Wolf, VP Fin

Linker Systems Inc. 13612 Onkayha Cr, Irvine CA 92720 USA; 714/552-1904, Fax: 714/552-6985, Co Email: linker@linker.com, Focus: Animation and paint software, Prdts: Animation Stand, Ownrshp: PVT, Founded: 1983, Empl: 5, Sales ($M): 1, Toni Poper, Pres, Email: tmp@linker.com; Sheldon Linker, VP, Email: sol@linker.com

Linkpro Inc. PO Box 6044, Irvine CA 92716-6044 USA; 714/854-3322, 800/449-7963 Fax: 714/854-3312, Focus: Windows utility software, Ownrshp: PVT, Frank Reinhart, Pres & CEO, Al Alcala, VP Mktng & Sales

LinkStar Communications Corp. 662 S. Military Trail, Deerfield Beach FL 33442 USA; 954/426-5465, Fax: 954/426-1350, Co Email: info@linkstar.com, Web URL: linkstar.com, Focus: Web directory, Prdts: LinkStar directory, Stewart Padveen, Pres, Bridgette King, Dir PR, Email: bridget@linkstar.com

Linksys 17401 Armstrong Ave, Irvine CA 92714 USA; 714/261-1288, 800/546-5797 Fax: 714/261-8868, Focus: PC peripheral controllers, Ownrshp: Sub. DEW Int'l., Founded: 1988, Empl: 100, Sales ($M): 40, Janie C. Tsao, Pres, Scott Wichmann, VP Fin, Donella Cecrle, Dir Mktng, Greg LaPolla, Dir R&D, Victor Tsao, Dir Ops

Linotype-Hell Co. 425 Oser Ave, Hauppauge NY 11788 USA; 516/434-2000, 800/842-9721 Fax: 516/233-2166, Co Email: @linotype.com, Web URL: linotype.com, Focus: Prepress products and systems, Ownrshp: Sub Linotype-Hell, Germany, Dani Herzka, VP Mktng, Helene C. Smith, Email: helene@linotype.com

Lion Optics Corp. 1751 McCarthy Blvd, Milpitas CA 95035 USA; 408/954-8089, Fax: 408/954-8138, Focus: CD-ROMs and mass storage, Ownrshp: Sub. Lion Group, Malaysia, Founded: 1993, Empl: 60, Austin Jieh, Chmn, Chen-Hwa Shin, Pres & CEO, Jerry Fu, VP Mfg, Jerome N. Harris, VP Strategic Planning

LitleNet 2 Manor Pkwy, Salem NH 03079-2841 USA; 603/894-

9000, Fax: 603/894-9121, Co Email: info@litle.net, Web URL: litle.net, Focus: Network that monitors vendor performance, Prdts: Direct Commerce Network, Ownrshp: PVT, Founded: 1995, Thomas J. Litle, Chmn & Pres

Litronics Information Systems 43088 Wintergrove Dr, Ashburn VA 22011 USA; 703/729-1700, Fax: 703/729-1896, Co Email: @litronic.com, Focus: Communication and computer security products, Ownrshp: PVT, Founded: 1971, Empl: 100

Litton Industries Inc. 21240 Burbank Blvd, Woodland Hills CA 91367 USA; 818/598-5000, Fax: 818/598-3322, Web URL: littoncorp.com, Focus: Electronics products, Ownrshp: NYSE, Stk Sym: LIT, Founded: 1953, Empl: 49,500, Sales ($M): 3,412, Fiscal End: 7/95; Robert H. Swanson, CEO

Liuski International Inc. 6585 Crescent Dr, Norcross GA 30071 USA; 770/447-9454, 800/454-8754 Fax: 770/368-8095, Focus: Microcomputer distributor, Ownrshp: OTC, Stk Sym: LSKI, Founded: 1984, Empl: 375, Sales ($M): 395.1, Fiscal End: 12/95; Manuel C. Tan, Pres & COO, Morries Liu, Chmn & CEO, Shirley Lee, EVP, Mike Hong, SVP Sls & Mktng, Mark Rafuse, VP & CFO

Living Books 160 Pacific Ave Mall, San Francisco CA 94111 USA; 415/352-5200, Fax: 415/352-5238, Focus: Education software, Ownrshp: Random House & Broderbund, Founded: 1993, Empl: 55, Sales ($M): 23.5, Fiscal End: 12/95; Jeffrey Schon, CEO, Rambabu Yariagadda, CFO, Kim Dempster

Livingston Enterprises Inc. 6920 Koll Ctr Pkwy, #220, Pleasanton CA 94566 USA; 510/426-0770, 800/458-9966 Fax: 510/426-8951, Co Email: info@livingston.com, Web URL: livingston.com, Focus: LAN-LAN connectivity products, Prdts: Livingston PortMaster series, Ownrshp: PVT, Founded: 1986, Steven Willens, Pres & CEO, Joseph Sasek, VP WW Sales, Ronald Willens, EVP, Bruce Byrd, Dir Mktng, Email: byrd@livingston.com

Localization and Consulting Services (LCS), 2001 6th Ave, #2308, Seattle WA 98121 USA; 206/443-5627, Fax: 206/443-5642, Co Email: 102021.1353@compuserve.com, Focus: Software localization, Ownrshp: PVT, Founded: 1979, Empl: 11, Olivier Redon, Bus Mgr, Nadja Honeywell, Program Mgr, Martin Guttinger, Program Mgr

Lockheed Martin 6801 Rockledge Dr, Bethesda MD 20817 USA; 301/897-6000, Fax: 301/897-6083, Web URL: lmco.com, Focus: Aerospace systems and computer services, Ownrshp: NYSE, Stk Sym: LK, Founded: 1932, Empl: 73,000, Sales ($M): 22,853.0, Fiscal End: 12/95; Norman R. Augustine, CEO

Lockheed Martin Information Sciences 6801 Rockledge Dr, Bethesda MD 20817 USA; 301/897-6000, Web URL: lockheed.com, Focus: Computer services, Ownrshp: Sub Lockheed Martin, Founded: , Empl: 6,000, Sales ($M): 2,057, Fiscal End: 12/95

Locus Computing Corp. 9800 La Cienega Blvd, Inglewood CA 90301-4440 USA; 310/670-6500, Fax: 310/670-2980, Focus: Connectivity software, Prdts: PC-Interface, Ownrshp: PVT, Founded: 1983, Empl: 250, Gerald J. Popek, Chmn, Martin C. Waters, Pres & CEO, Mike Smith, GM Connectivity Group, Bob Peterson, Dir Merge Prod, Email: bobp@locus.com

Logic Devices Inc. 628 E Evelyn Ave, Sunnyvale CA 94086 USA; 408/737-3300, Fax: 402/733-7690, Co Email: litreq@logicd.mhs.compuserve.com, Focus: CMOS integrated circuits, Ownrshp: OTC, Stk Sym: LOGC, Founded: 1983, Empl: 49, Sales ($M): 16.6, Fiscal End: 12/95; William J. Volz, Pres, Todd J. Ashford, CFO, Anthony G. Bell, VP Tech, William L. Jackson, VP Mfg, Cecelia Kong, Marcom, Email: cecelia@logicd.mhs.compuserve.com

Logic Works Inc. 111 Campus Dr, University Square at Princeton, Princeton NJ 08540 USA; 609/514-1177, Fax: 609/514-1175, Web URL: logicworks.com, Focus: PC database utilities, Ownrshp: OTC, Stk Sym: LGWX, Empl: 200, Sales ($M): 30.7, Fiscal End: 12/95; Benjamin Cohen, Pres & CEO, Shelley Perry, Dir Mktng, Mark Finkel, CFO, Jeffrey Whitney

Logical Decisions Inc. 1014 Wood Lily Dr, Golden CO 80401 USA; 303/526-7536, 800/355-6452 Fax: 303/526-7537, Focus: Decision support software, Prdts: Logical Decision, Ownrshp: PVT, Gary Smith

Logical Operations 500 Canal View Blvd, Rochester NY 14623 USA; 716/240-7500, 800/456-4677 Fax: 716/240-7760, Co Email: lo_sales_information@zd.com, Web URL: logicalops.com, Focus: Training products and services, Ownrshp: Sub Ziff-Davis, Founded: 1982, Empl: 230, William A. Rosenthal, Pres, Todd Husted, VP Support Prod, Tary Simizon

Logicode Technology Inc. 1380 Flynn Rd, Camarillo CA 93012 USA; 805/388-9000, 800/735-6442 Fax: 805/388-8991, Co Email: logicode@aol.com, Focus: Modems and multimedia peripherals, Prdts: Quicktel, TVideo, TVideo + MPEG, QuickWave, Ownrshp: Sub. Inductotherm, Founded: 1989, Empl: 80, Moe Hadaegh, Pres & CEO, Elliot Hadaegh, VP Mktng & Sales, Allen Gharapetian, Mktng Mgr, Susan J. Laury, Mktng Admin

Logicom Inc. 23-00 Rt 208, Fair Lawn NJ 07410 USA; 201/703-1188, Fax: 201/703-1830, Co Email: logicom@panix.com, Prdts: Appointment TeleManager

Logicon Inc. 3701 Skypark Dr, Torrance CA 90505-4794 USA; 310/373-0220, Web URL: logicon.com, Focus: Computer and electronic systems to the military, Ownrshp: NYSE, Stk Sym: LGN, Founded: 1961, Empl: 4,986, Sales ($M): 476.1, Fiscal End: 3/96; John R. Woodhull, Pres & CEO, Frank T. Cummings, VP, Ralph L. Webster, VP & CFO, James E. Dalton, VP, Dan B. Wallace, VP

Logicraft Information Systems 22 Cotton Rd, Nashua NH 03063 USA; 603/880-0300, 800/880-5644 Fax: 603/880-7229, Co Email: @logicraft.com, Web URL: logicraft.com, Focus: CD-ROM networking solutions, Prdts: LanCD, CD Executive XF Server Series, Omni-Wave, Omni-Access, Ownrshp: Sub. IHS, Founded: 1975, Empl: 100, Sales ($M): 20, William Thomasmeyer, Pres & CEO, Chris Caggiula, VP Mktng, Email: ccaggiula@logicraft.com; Chris Rowen, VP Eng, Kristina M. O'Connell, Mktng Mgr, Email: koconnell@logicraft.com

Logitech Inc. 6505 Kaiser Dr, Fremont CA 94555 USA; 510/795-8500, 800/231-7717 Fax: 510/792-8901, Focus: Input devices and software for PCs, Prdts: MouseMan, TrackMan, MouseWare, MouseKey, Ownrshp: FO, Founded: 1981, Empl: 2,000, Sales ($M): 302.8, Fiscal End: 3/95; Daniel Borel, Chmn & CEO, Pierluigi Zappacosta, Pres, Barak Berkowitz, VP Sales & Mktng, George Moore, VP Plng, Thom Weatherford, VP & CFO

Longshine Microsystems Inc. 10400-9 Pioneer Blvd, Santa Fe Springs CA 90670 USA; 310/903-0899, Fax: 310/944-2201, Focus: PC peripherals, Ownrshp: PVT, Founded: 1987

Looking Glass Software Inc. 11222 La Cienga Blvd #305, Inglewood CA 90304 USA; 310/348-8240, Fax: 310/348-9786, Focus: 3D and hypermedia software, Prdts: Cheetah 3D, ViperWrite, MediaVerse, Ownrshp: PVT, Founded: 1991, Samuel B. Covington, CEO, Chris van Hamersveld, Pres

Looking Glass Technologies Inc. 100 Cambridge Park Dr, #300, Cambridge MA 02140 USA; 617/441-6333, Fax: 617/441-3946, Web URL: lglass.com, Focus: Entertainment and simulation software, Prdts: Flight Unlimited, Terra Nova, Ownrshp: PVT, Founded: 1992, Empl: 60, Paul Neurath, Principal, Ned Lerner, Principal

Loox Software Inc. 4962 El Camino Real, #206, Los Altos CA 94022-1410 USA; 415/903-0942, Fax: 415/903-9824, Co Email: info@loox.com, Web URL: loox.com, Focus: Unix graphic software development tools, Prdts: Loox, Looxmaker, Looxlib, BXLoox, Loox ++, Ownrshp: PVT, Peter Meehan, Pres & CEO, Email: peter@loox.com

Lotus Development Corp. 55 Cambridge Pkwy, Cambridge MA 02142 USA; 617/577-8500, Fax: 617/693-1779, Co Email: @lotus.com, Web URL: lotus.com, Focus: PC productivity software, Prdts: Lotus 1-2-3, Notes, Freelance, Ami Pro, Approach, SmartSuite, Ownrshp: OTC, Stk Sym: LOTS, Founded: 1982, Empl: 5,500, Sales ($M): 971, Fiscal End: 12/94; Michael Zisman,

EVP & CEO
LSI Logic Corp. 1551 McCarthy Blvd, Milpitas CA 95035 USA; 408/433-8000, Fax: 408/433-7715, Web URL: lsilogic.com, Focus: ASICs and RISC microprocessors, Ownrshp: NYSE, Stk Sym: LSI, Founded: 1980, Empl: 3,870, Sales ($M): 1,267.7, Fiscal End: 12/95; Wilfred J. Corrigan, Chmn & CEO, Cyril F. Hannon, EVP Ops, Albert A. Pimentel, SVP & CFO, Cindy E. Johnson, VP Info Sys, Bruce L. Entin, VP Corp Com

LTX Corp. LTX Park at University Ave, Westwood MA 02090 USA; 617/461-1000, Focus: Semiconductor test systems, Ownrshp: OTC, Stk Sym: LTXX, Founded: 1985, Empl: 944, Sales ($M): 210.3, Fiscal End: 7/95; Graham C.C. Miller, Chmn, Roger W. Blethen, Pres, Martin F. Francis, Pres, Kenneth E. Daub, SVP, John J. Arcari, CFO

Lucas Management Systems 3702 Pender Dr, #300, Fairfax VA 22030-6066 USA; 703/222-1111, Fax: 703/222-8203, Focus: Project planning software, Ownrshp: PVT, Founded: 1979

LucasArts Entertainment Co. PO Box 10307, San Rafael CA 94912 USA; 415/472-3400, 800/985-8227 Fax: 415/444-8240, Web URL: lucasarts.com, Focus: Entertainment software, Prdts: Rebel Assault II, Dark Forces, Full Throttle, Ownrshp: PVT, Founded: 1982, Empl: 200, Jack Sorensen, Pres, Steve Dauterman, Dir Dev, Mary Bihr, Alex Gerson, Sr Mgr Info, Tom Sarris, PR Specialist

Lucent Technologies 600-700 Mt. Ave, Murray Hill NJ 08974 USA; 908/582-8500, Fax: 908/508-2577, Web URL: lucent.com, Focus: Telecom equipment, Ownrshp: NYSE, Empl: 131,000, Sales ($M): 21,400, Fiscal End: 12/95; Henry Schacht, Chmn & CEO

Luminex Software Inc. 6840 Indiana Ave, 130, Riverside CA 92506 USA; 909/781-4100, Fax: 909/781-4105, Co Email: @luminex.com, Focus: CD-ROM products, Prdts: Fire Series, LSX-SCSI Expander, Ownrshp: PVT, Founded: 1994, Empl: 8, Brian Hawley, Pres, Michael Saunders, VP, Arthur R. Tolsma

Lundeen & Associates 909 Marina Village Pkwy, #595, Alameda CA 94501 USA; 510/521-5855, Fax: 510/522-6647, Web URL: lundeen.com, Focus: Personal productivity and network software products, Prdts: Web Crossing, Founded: 1986, Tim Lundeen, Pres

LXE 303 Research Dr, #144, Norcross GA 30092 USA; 770/447-4224, Fax: 770/447-4405, Focus: Wireless communications products, Ownrshp: Public, Stk Sym: LXEI, Founded: 1983, Empl: 370, Sales ($M): 45.7, Fiscal End: 12/93; John E. Pippin, Chmn & CEO, Jack Farrell, Pres, Don T. Scartz, VP Fin, Steve Flemig, Prod Mktng Mgr, Gary Davis

Lycos Inc. 293 Boston Post Rd W, Marlboro MA 01752 USA; 508/229-0717, Web URL: lycos.com, Focus: Internet search software, Ownrshp: OTC, Founded: 1995, Empl: 30, Sales ($M): 5.3, Fiscal End: 7/96; Robert Davis, CEO

Lynx Real-Time Systems Inc. 2239 Samaritan Dr, San Jose CA 95124-4407 USA; 408/879-3900, Fax: 408/879-3920, Web URL: lynx.com, Focus: Real time operating system, Prdts: PosixWorks, Founded: 1985, Inder Singh, Pres & CEO, Derek Taylor

LYSIS Corp. 740 W Peachtree St, Atlanta GA 30308-1139 USA; 404/892-3301, Fax: 404/892-3313, Co Email: @lysis.com, Focus: Help desk software, Prdts: Answer Base Management System, Founded: 1988, Richard A. Heller, Pres & CEO, Joe Cox, Email: jcox@lysis.com

M Technology Assoc. (MTA), 1738 Elton Rd, #205, Silver Spring MD 20903-1725 USA; 301/431-4070, Fax: 301/431-0017, Co Email: mta1994@aol.com, Web URL: members.aol.com/mta1994, Focus: Provides a forum for the exchange of information and knowledge for MUMPS computer language, Ownrshp: Nonprofit, Founded: 1971, Empl: 1,800, John Covin, Chmn, Maureen Lilly, Admin Dir

M-USA Business Systems Inc. 15806 Midway Rd, Dallas TX 75244 USA; 214/386-6100, Fax: 214/404-1957, Focus: Accounting software, Prdts: Pacioli 2000, Mondial, Perfect Time, Ownrshp: PVT, Founded: 1987, Empl: 40, Jose Hurtado, Pres & CEO, Martha

R. Craig

M4 Solutions Inc. 4451 Enterprise Ct #B, Melbourne FL 32934-9228 USA; 407/639-6487, Fax: 407/639-9800, Focus: 9-track streaming tape drives, Ownrshp: FO, Founded: 1986, Empl: 160, Sales ($M): 25, Duke Ebenezer, CEO

Ma Labs Inc. 1972 Concourse Dr, San Jose CA 95131 USA; 408/954-8188, Focus: PC motherboards and peripherals, Ownrshp: PVT

Mac McIntosh Co., The 1739 Havemeyer Ln, Redondo Beach CA 90278-4716 USA; 310/376-1221, 800/944-5553 Fax: 310/376-7722, Co Email: mac4leads@aol.com, Focus: Sales lead and inquiry management consulting, Ownrshp: PVT, Mac McIntosh

MacAcademy 100 E Granada Blvd, Ormond Beach FL 32176-1712 USA; 904/677-1918, 800/527-1914 Fax: 904/677-6717, Web URL: macacademy.com, Focus: Macintosh computer training, Ownrshp: PVT, Founded: 1987, Empl: 40, Sales ($M): 5.9, Fiscal End: 12/92; Donald M. Crabb, Pres & CEO, Clair Crookston, EVP, Keith Kiel, VP, Bonnie Saliba, VP, Bruce Couch, VP

MacNeal-Schwendler Corp., The (MSC), 815 Colorado Blvd, Los Angeles CA 90041-1777 USA; 213/258-9111, Fax: 213/259-3838, Web URL: macsch.com, Focus: CAE software, Prdts: MSC/NASTRAN, Ownrshp: NYSE, Stk Sym: MNS, Founded: 1963, Empl: 300, Sales ($M): 130.5, Fiscal End: 1/96; Richard H. MacNeal, Chmn, Thomas C. Curry, Pres & CEO, Dennis A. Nagy, SVP Sales, Ken Blakely, VP Mktng, Louis A. Greco, CFO

Macola Inc. 333 E Center St, Marion OH 43302 USA; 614/382-5999, 800/468-0834 Fax: 614/382-0239, Co Email: response@macola.usa.com, Focus: Accounting, distribution and manufacturing software for PC & LANs, Prdts: Macola Progression Series, Macola Horizon Series, Ownrshp: PVT, Founded: 1971, Empl: 23, Fiscal End: 9/95; Bruce A. Hollinger, Pres & CEO, Mark Mewhorter, VP Progression Sys Dev, Dave Shirk, VP Sales & Mktng, Dale Haddod, VP Fin & Ops, Dave Reisch, Mgr MIS, Phyllis Butterworth, PR Coord, Email: psb@macola.usa.com

Macro 4 Plc 35 Waterview Blvd, PO Box 292, Parsippany NJ 07054 USA; 201/402-8000, Web URL: macro4.com, Focus: Mainframe and C/S software, Ownrshp: Sub Macro 4, UK, Founded: 1968, Empl: 210, Sales ($M): 39.9, Fiscal End: 12/95; Terence P. Kelly, Chmn, Bob Hess, CEO

Macromedia Digital Arts Group 269 W Renner Pkwy, Richardson TX 75080 USA; 214/680-2060, Fax: 214/680-0537, Focus: Graphics and font software, Prdts: Freehand, Fontographer, Virtuoso, Ownrshp: Sub Macromedia, Founded: 1984, Empl: 65, Sales ($M): 7.6, James Von Ehr, VP & GM, Kevin Crowder, VP Prod Integration, Martha Harry, PR Mgr

Macromedia Inc. 600 Townsend 310W, San Francisco CA 94103 USA; 415/252-2000, 800/288-4797 Fax: 415/626-0554, Co Email: macropr@macromedia.com, Web URL: macromedia.com, Focus: Multimedia software, Prdts: Authorware, Director, Freehand, Fontographer, Ownrshp: OTC, Stk Sym: MACR, Founded: 1984, Empl: 150, Sales ($M): 116.7, Fiscal End: 3/96; John C. Colligan, Pres & CEO, Joseph D. Dunn, VP Prod Dev, Richard B. Wood, VP & CFO, Miles Walsh, VP Mktng, Mary Leung, Mgr PR, Email: mleong@macromedia.com

Macronix America Inc. 1348 Ridder Park Dr, San Jose CA 95131 USA; 408/453-8088, Fax: 408/453-8488, Focus: PC peripherals, Ownrshp: PVT, Founded: 1983

MACSCITECH Assoc. 49 Midgley Ln, Worcester MA 01604 USA; 508/755-5242, Fax: 508/795-1636, Web URL: macscitech.org, Focus: Enhance scientific and engineering use of Apple Macintosh, Ownrshp: Nonprofit, Founded: 1991, Empl: 1,500, Shari Worthington, Exec Dir

MAG Innovision Inc. 2801 S Yale St, Santa Ana CA 92704 USA; 714/751-2008, Fax: 714/751-5522, Co Email: @maginnovision.com, Focus: PC and workstation monitors, Ownrshp: Sub. MAG Technology, Taiwan, Founded: 1987, Sales ($M): 450, Fiscal End: 12/94; William Wang, Pres, J.L. Aguirre, VP, Ron Shiroke, Dir Sales, Kay Rinas, Dir Bus Dev, Ken Lowe, Eng Mgr, Kelli Baker,

PR Mgr, Email: kbaker@maginnovision.com

Magee Enterprises Inc. 2909 Langford Rd, #A600, Norcross GA 30071-1506 USA; 770/446-6611, 800/662-4330 Fax: 770/368-0719, Co Email: 76004.1541@compuserve.com, Web URL: magee.com, Focus: Utility software, Prdts: Automenu, Rosebud, Network H.Q., Ownrshp: PVT, Founded: 1983, Empl: 25, Marshall Magee, Pres & CEO, Judy Pancoast, VP Sales & Mktng

Magellan Geographix 6464 Hollister Ave, Santa Barbara CA 93117 USA; 805/685-3100, 800/929-4627 Fax: 805/685-3330, Co Email: go magellan@compuserve.com, Focus: 2-D and 3-D digital maps, J. Douglas Crawford, Pres & CEO

Magic Quest Inc. 1825 Grant St #410, San Mateo CA 94402-2661 USA; 415/321-5838, Fax: 415/321-8560, Focus: Educational software, Ownrshp: PVT, Founded: 1989, Bob Stevens, Pres, David Smith, Chmn, Robert Bierman, VP Eng

Magic Software Enterprises Inc. (MSE), 1200 Main St, Irvine CA 92714 USA; 714/250-1718, Fax: 714/250-7404, Focus: Database development tools, Ownrshp: OTC, Stk Sym: MGICF, Founded: 1986, Empl: 100, Sales ($M): 25.4, Fiscal End: 12/95; David Assia, Chmn, Pres & CEO, David Wegman, COO, Basil W. Maloney, Dir Mktng, Lisa Parkhurst

Magic Solutions Inc. 10 Forest Ave, Paramus NJ 07652-5238 USA; 201/587-1515, 800/966-2442 Fax: 201/587-8005, Web URL: magicsolutions.com, Focus: Help desk, asset and service management software, Prdts: ServiceMagic, SupportMagic, Ownrshp: PVT, Founded: 1988, Empl: 140, Sales ($M): 12.1, Fiscal End: 4/95; Igal Lichtman, Pres & CEO, Mike Pallatta, VP Sales, Andrew Rawson, VP Mktng, John Von Lintig, VP & CFO, Florenic Schlanger, VP Client Svcs

MagicRAM 1850 Beverly Blvd, Los Angeles CA 90057 USA; 213/413-9999, 800/272-6242 Fax: 213/413-0828, Co Email: magicram@pacificnet.net, Focus: PCMCIA products and DRAM memory upgrades, Ownrshp: PVT, Founded: 1988, Empl: 18, Sales ($M): 6.0, Fiscal End: 4/95; Eddie Mirarooni, Chmn & CEO, Mike Navid, CFO, Allen Nouray, VP Ops

Magni Systems Inc. 9500 SW Gemini Dr, Beaverton OR 97008 USA; 503/626-8400, 800/237-5964 Fax: 503/626-6225, Focus: Video graphics boards and monitoring products, Prdts: VGA Producer Pro, Ownrshp: PVT, Founded: 1984, Empl: 35, Victor L. Kong, Chmn & CEO, David J. Jurgensen, SVP, Gary M. Thomas, Dir Sales

MAI Systems Corp. 9600 Jeronimo Rd, Irvine CA 92718 USA; 714/580-0700, 800/854-8032 Fax: 714/580-2391, Focus: Multiuser microcomputer systems, Ownrshp: AMEX, Stk Sym: NOW, Founded: 1984, Empl: 646, Sales ($M): 66.3, Fiscal End: 12/95; George G. Bayz, Pres & COO, Richard S. Ressier, Chmn & CEO, Richard W. Gooding, Pres MAI NA, W. Brian Kretzmer, VP & CFO

Mailer's Software 970 Calle Negocio, San Clemente CA 92673-6201 USA; 714/492-7000, Fax: 714/492-7086, Focus: Direct marketing and mailing list software, Prdts: Mailer's +4, Mailer's LookUp, Ownrshp: PVT, Founded: 1985, Empl: 30, Raymond F. Melissa, Pres, Philip Maitano, Mgr SW Dev, Samantha G. Dobyns, Sales Mgr, John Kirwan, Tech Svcs Mgr, Kathy L. Eyre, Controller, Jonathan Boswell, Email: jonathan@800mail.com

Maine Software Developers Assoc. 17 Oak St, PO Box 492, Orono ME 04473-0492 USA; 207/866-0496, Fax: 207/866-0362, Focus: Association for software developers in Maine, Ownrshp: Nonprofit, George Markowsky, Pres

Mainsoft Corp. 1270 Oakmead Pkwy, #310, Sunnyvale CA 94086 USA; 408/774-3400, Fax: 408/774-3404, Co Email: info@mainsoft.com, Web URL: mainsoft.com, Focus: Cross-platform development tools with Windows API, Prdts: OLE, Jeff Elpern, Pres & CEO, Jose Luu, VP Eng, Celeste Baldi, Email: celeste@mainsoft.com

Mainstay 591-A Constitution Ave, Camarillo CA 93012-9106 USA; 805/484-9400, Fax: 805/484-9428, Co Email:

76004.1525@compuserve.com, Focus: Macintosh software, Prdts: MacFlow, WinFlow, Plan & Track, Phyla, Mark Up, Captivate, Ownrshp: PVT, Founded: 1982, Empl: 21, Sales ($M): 3.7, Tom Nalevanko, Pres, Lance Merker, Sales & Mktng Mgr

Make Systems 201 San Antonio Cr, #225, Mountain View CA 94040 USA; 415/941-9800, Fax: 415/941-5856, Web URL: makesys.com/makesys, Focus: Network management software, Prdts: Netmaker XA, Ownrshp: PVT, Founded: 1986, Empl: 65, Stephen M. Howard, CEO, Walt Brown, VP Field Ops, Richard Wood, CFO & VP Fin, Ed Sykes, VP R&D, Beverly Dygert, Corp Comm

Man & Machine 3706 West St, Landover MD 20785-2326 USA; 301/277-3760, Fax: 301/779-1455, Focus: Service and sales of portable computers, Ownrshp: PVT, Founded: 1983, Empl: 12, Sales ($M): 2.5, Clifton Broumand, Pres

Management Graphics Inc. 1401 E 79th St, Minneapolis MN 55425 USA; 612/854-1220, Fax: 612/851-6159, Co Email: @mgi.com, Web URL: mgi.com, Focus: Image and graphics products, Prdts: Solitaire, Sapphire & Opal Digital Film Recorders, JetStream, Ownrshp: PVT, Founded: 1981, Empl: 80, James Teter, Pres, Robert Helsing, VP, Torben E. Holm, VP Intl Sales, Bill Hansen, Mktng Mgr, Tom Peterson, Nat'l Sales Mgr, Kristin Bergren, Marcom, Email: bergren@mgi.com

Management Software Assoc. (TMSA), 35 Gardner Rd, Brookline MA 02146 USA; 617/232-4111, Fax: 617/734-3308, Focus: Promote growth of business management software, Ownrshp: Nonprofit, Founded: 1993, Empl: 10, Michael Shirer, Pres

Mannesmann Tally Corp. 8301 S 180th St, PO Box 97018, Kent WA 98032 USA; 206/251-5500, Fax: 206/251-5520, Co Email: @tally.com, Web URL: tally.com, Focus: Printers, Ownrshp: Sub. Mannesmann AG, Germany, Founded: 1948, Empl: 1,480, Sales ($M): 250, William Munro, Pres, Alan Pinsonneault, VP Ops, Richard Waddell, Dir Mktng, Zong Luo, VP R&D, Scott Dombrowski, Mgr Corp Com

ManTech Solutions Corp. 8000 Corporate Ct, Springfield VA 22153 USA; 703/913-2400, Focus: PCs and monitors, Ownrshp: Sub. ManTech Int'l., Founded: 1968, Kevin Kilroy, Pres

Manufacturing and Consulting Services Inc. (MCS), 7560 E Redfield Rd, Scottsdale AZ 85260 USA; 602/991-8700, Fax: 602/991-8732, Web URL: anvil5k.com, Focus: Mechanical design & engineering software, Prdts: ANVIL-5000, Ownrshp: PVT, Founded: 1971, Empl: 80, Patrick J. Hanratty, Pres & CEO, Brian J. Hanratty, EVP, Scott M. Hanratty, SVP Mktng & Sales, Email: scotth@anvil5k.com; or Vic Dawson, VP Sales

Manugistics Inc. 2115 E Jefferson St, Rockville MD 20852 USA; 301/984-5000, Fax: 301/984-5370, Web URL: manugistics.com, Focus: Supply chain management software, Prdts: Manugistics, Statgraphics, APL*Plus, Ownrshp: OTC, Stk Sym: MANU, Founded: 1969, Empl: 499, Sales ($M): 62.3, Fiscal End: 2/96; William M. Gibson, Chmn, Pres & CEO, Peter Q. Repetti, VP & CFO, Thomas A. Skelton, EVP & COO, Keith J. Enstice, SVP Field Ops, Carole Anne Hardy, Marcom Writer

MapInfo Corp. 1 Global View, Troy NY 12180-8399 USA; 518/285-6000, Fax: 518/285-6060, Co Email: @mapinfo.com, Web URL: mapinfo.com, Focus: Desktop mapping software, Prdts: MapInfo, MapBasic, Ownrshp: OTC, Stk Sym: MAPS, Founded: 1986, Empl: 305, Sales ($M): 41.1, Fiscal End: 9/95; Michael D. Marvin, Chmn, Brian D. Owen, Pres & CEO, Matthew J. Szulik, SVP Sales & Mktng, John F. Haller, VP Tech, D. Joseph Gersuk, VP & CFO, Randy Drawas, Marcom

MapLinx Corp. 5720 Lyndon B Johnson Fwy #180, Dallas TX 75240-6328 USA; 214/231-1400, Fax: 214/248-2690, Focus: PC database utilities, Ownrshp: PVT, Kenneth Eaken, VP & GM

Marasys Inc. 2615 N 4th St, #755, Coeur d'Alene ID 83814 USA; 208/772-0248, Fax: 208/772-0248, Focus: Productivity software, Ownrshp: PVT, Founded: 1990, William Meng, Pres

Marcam Corp. 95 Wells Ave, Newton MA 02159 USA; 617/965-0220, 800/962-7226 Fax: 617/965-7273, Web URL: marcam.com, Focus: Inventory, distribution and manufacturing software, Ownrshp: OTC, Stk Sym: MCAM, Founded: 1980, Empl: 1,040, Sales ($M): 202.3, Fiscal End: 9/95; Paul A. Margolis, Chmn, Michael Quinlan, Pres & CEO, David M. Stoner, EVP Ops, Thomas D. Ebling, SVP Prod Dev, George A. Chamberlain, CFO, Patricia Foye, VP Mktng

Marcus Technology Inc. 243 Riverside Dr, #103, New York NY 10025 USA; 212/678-0406, Fax: 212/222-7322, Focus: Publishing and prepress systems, Ownrshp: PVT, Founded: 1980, Sales ($M): 2+, Irwin Marcus, Pres, Edward Fleiss, Tech Sales Mgr, Todd Eckler, Dir R&D

Marin Research 100 Larkspur Landing Cr #220, Larkspur CA 94939-1703 USA; 415/389-5444, Fax: 415/389-5448, Focus: Project management software, Ownrshp: PVT, Founded: 1989, Gary M. Cole, Pres, Lee A. Davis, VP

Maris Multimedia 4040 Civic Ctr Dr, #200, San Rafael CA 94903 USA; 415/492-2819, Fax: 415/492-2867, Web URL: maris.com/maris, Focus: Multimedia software, Prdts: Solar System Explorer, Ownrshp: Sub Maris, UK, Founded: 1992, Nick Maris, Chmn, Jeneane Harter, VP Sales & Mktng, Email: 100443.3121@compuserve.com

Mark IV Industries 501 John James Audubon Pkwy, 1 Towne Centre, Amherst NY 14226-0810 USA; 716/689-4972, Ownrshp: NYSE, Stk Sym: IV, Sales ($M): 2,088.5, Fiscal End: 2/96; Sal S. Alfiero, Chmn & CEO, Clement R. Arrison, Pres, John J. Byrne, VP Finance, William P. Montague, EVP & CFO

Marsh Software Systems (MSS), 1020-A Central Dr, Concord NC 28027 USA; 704/788-9335, Fax: 704/788-4775, Focus: Financial and job costing software for multiple industries, Prdts: Axiom Project Manager, Project Management 2000, Ownrshp: PVT, Founded: 1984, Empl: 12, Donald H. Marsh, Pres & CEO, Sarah T. Marsh, VP, Anthony J. Eury, Mktng Dir

Marshall Industries 9320 Telstar Ave, El Monte CA 91731-2895 USA; 818/307-6000, 800/432-2223 Co Email: info@marshall.com, Web URL: marchall.com, Focus: Distributes semiconductor and computer products, Ownrshp: NYSE, Stk Sym: MI, Founded: 1954, Empl: 1,454, Sales ($M): 822.5, Fiscal End: 5/94; Gordon S. Marshall, Chmn, Robert Rodin, Pres & CEO, Richard D. Bentley, EVP, Henry W. Chin, VP & CFO

MasPar Computer Corp. 749 N Mary Ave, Sunnyvale CA 94086 USA; 408/736-3300, Fax: 408/736-9560, Focus: Massively parallel computers, Ownrshp: PVT, Founded: 1988, Empl: 110, Kenneth W. Simonds, Chmn, John Harte, Pres & CEO

Mass Optical Storage Technologies (MOST), 11205 Knott Ave, #B, Cypress CA 90630 USA; 714/898-9400, 800/233-6104 Fax: 714/373-9960, Focus: Erasable optical disk drives, Prdts: Jupiter 1, Ownrshp: PVT, Founded: 1990, Yas Yamazaki, Chmn, James Conway, VP & GM, James Kaufmann, VP Sales & Mktng

Massachusetts Software Council Inc. 1 Exeter Plaza, #200, Boston MA 02116 USA; 617/437-0600, Fax: 617/437-9686, Web URL: swcouncil.org, Focus: Promotes Massachusetts software industry, Ownrshp: Nonprofit, Founded: 1985, Empl: 350, Joyce Plotkin, Exec Dir, Carol Greenfield, Program Dir

Mastech Corp. 1004 McKee Rd, Oakdale PA 15071 USA; 412/787-2100, Fax: 412/787-7460, Focus: Software, Ownrshp: PVT

Mastersoft Inc. 8737 E Via de Commercio, Scottsdale AZ 85258 USA; 602/948-4888, Fax: 602/948-8261, Co Email: @mastersoft.com, Focus: File conversion utility software, Prdts: Word for Word, Ownrshp: PVT, Founded: 1986, Empl: 18, Sales ($M): 3, Kent C. Mueller, Pres & CEO, Email: kent@mastersoft.com; Sue Scheen, VP Channel Sales, Email: sue@mastersoft.com; Karl Forster, VP SW Dev, Email: karl@mastersoft.com; Trine Tobias, Sales & Mktng Assist, Email: trine@mastersoft.com

MathSoft Inc. 101 Main St, Cambridge MA 02142-1521 USA; 617/577-1017, Fax: 617/577-8829, Web URL: mathsoft.com, Focus: Vertical market software, Prdts: WebStore, Ownrshp: OTC, Stk Sym: MATH, Founded: 1984, Empl: 118, Sales ($M): 20.8, Fis-

cal End: 6/96; Steven Vana-Paxhia, Chmn & CTO, Charles J. Digate, Pres & CEO, Donald F. Boudreau, SVP Ops, Paul F. Guerin, VP Sales, Robert P. Orlando, VP & CFO, Tina Hong

MathWorks Inc., The 24 Prime Park Way, Natick MA 01760-9889 USA; 508/653-1415, Fax: 508/653-2997, Co Email: info@mathworks.com, Focus: Scientific computational software, Prdts: MathLab, Simulink, Ownrshp: PVT, Founded: 1984, Empl: 300

Matrox Graphics Inc. 1055 St Regis Blvd, Dorval Quebec H9P 2T4 Canada; 514/685-2630, Fax: 514/685-2853, Co Email: @matrox.com, Focus: Video display systems and controllers, Ownrshp: PVT, Founded: 1974, Empl: 620, Sales ($M): 80, Branko Matic, Chmn, Lorne Trottier, Pres

Matsushita Consumer Electronics Co. 1 Panasonic Way, Secaucus NJ 07094 USA; 201/348-7000, Focus: Consumer electronics and computer products, Ownrshp: Sub. Matsushita, Japan, Michelle Camerlengo

Matsushita Electric Industrial Co. Ltd. 1006 Oaza Kadoma, Kadoma-shi, Osaka 571 JP-571 Japan; 6-908-0447, Web URL: mei.co.jp, Focus: Video, audio, computer and telecom equipment, Ownrshp: NYSE, Stk Sym: MC, Empl: 193,000, Sales ($M): 78,069, Fiscal End: 3/96

Maxell Corp. of America 22-08 Rt 208, Fair Lawn NJ 07410 USA; 201/794-5900, Fax: 201/796-8790, Focus: Magnetic media and memory cards, Ownrshp: Sub. Maxell, Japan, Michael Golacinski, EVP Sales & Mktng

Maxi Switch Inc. 2901 E Elvira Rd, Tucson AZ 85706 USA; 520/294-5450, Fax: 520/294-6890, Focus: Keyboard and input devices, Prdts: Maxi Sound Multimedia Keyboard, Maxi Mouse, Ownrshp: PVT, Founded: 1968, Empl: 100, Syed Hasan, Pres, Mark A. Griffin, VP Sales & Mktng, Rocky Iman, Sales Mgr, Nick Hyrka, Prod Mktng

Maximum Computer Technologies Inc. 1000 Cobb Place Blvd Bldg 200, #240, Kennesaw GA 30144-3684 USA; 770/428-5000, 800/582-9337 Fax: 770/428-5009, Web URL: maxtech.com, Focus: System management software, Prdts: Doublevision, Ownrshp: PVT, Founded: 1985, Vincent Frese, Pres, Email: vince@maxtech.com; John P. Jarrett, VP SW Eng, Charlotte Canup, Email: ccanup@maxtech.com

Maximum Strategy Inc. 801 Buckeye Ct, Milpitas CA 95035-7408 USA; 408/383-1600, Fax: 408/383-1616, Co Email: @maxstrat.com, Focus: RAID disk storage products, Ownrshp: PVT, Founded: 1986, Del W. Masters, Pres & CEO, Wes E. Meador, EVP, Kenneth Katai, VP Dev, Ed Calkins, VP Mktng, Nadine Wiley Priestley, CFO, Sandy Staufenbiel, Mgr Marcom, Email: sandys@maxstrat.com

Maxis 2121 N California Blvd, Walnut Creek CA 94596 USA; 510/933-5630, Fax: 510/927-3736, Web URL: maxis.com, Focus: Entertainment and education software, Prdts: SimCity, Simisle, Ownrshp: OTC, Stk Sym: MXIS, Founded: 1987, Empl: 152, Sales ($M): 55.4, Fiscal End: 3/96; Jeff Braun, Chmn & CEO, Sam Poole, Pres, Robin Harper, VP Mktng, Joe Scirica, VP Prod Dev, Fred M. Gerson, VP & CFO, Sally Vandershaf, PR Coord

Maxoptix Corp. 3342 Gateway Blvd, Fremont CA 94538-6525 USA; 510/353-9700, 800/848-3092 Fax: 510/353-1845, Co Email: @maxoptix.usa.com, Focus: Optical disk drives and media, Ownrshp: Sub. Kubota, Founded: 1989, Empl: 100, Gary Potts, Pres & CEO, Howard Wing, VP Sales & Mktng, Gordon Knight, CTO, Koshi Kokubo, VP Bus Dev, Mitch Cipriano, GM, Email: cipriano@maxoptix.usa.com

Maxpeed Corp. 1120 Chess Dr, Foster City CA 94404 USA; 415/345-5447, 800/877-7998 Fax: 415/345-6398, Co Email: @maxpeed.com, Web URL: maxpeed.com, Focus: Multiconsole products and multiport controllers, Prdts: VGA MaxStation, SS Intelligent Multiports, Ownrshp: PVT, Founded: 1988, Wei Ching, Pres, Chu Nei, VP Eng, Athol M. Foden, Mktng Dir, Email: afoden@maxpeed.com

Maxsoft-OCRON Inc. 47400 Seabridge Dr, Fremont CA 94538-6548 USA; 510/252-0200, 800/933-1399 Fax: 510/252-0202, Co Email: @maxsoft-ocron.com, Web URL: maxsoft-ocron.com, Focus: OCR software, Prdts: Recore, Perceive, Wordlinx, Business Card Reader, Ownrshp: PVT, Founded: 1988, Empl: 20, Ding-Yuan Tang, Pres, Email: ding@maxsoft-ocron.com; Joe G. Budelli, VP Sales

MaxTech Corp. 400 Commons Way, Rockaway NJ 07866 USA; 201/586-3008, Fax: 201/586-5330, Co Email: maxtech@aol.com, Web URL: maxcorp.com, Focus: Data communication, connectivity and PC products, Prdts: Multimedia Pentium YESBOOK, Ownrshp: PVT, Founded: 1978, Gary Schultz, Mktng Dir, Email: gary_schultz@maxcorp.com; George Zhu, Dir Prod Dev, Email: george_zhu@maxcorp.com; Jeff Geis, Mktng Mgr, Email: jeff_geis@maxcorp.com

Maxtek Components Corp. 13335 SW Terman Rd, Beaverton OR 97075 USA; 503/627-4133, Fax: 503/627-4651, Co Email: technology@maxtek.com, Focus: Analog ICs and multichip modules, Ownrshp: Tektronix & Maxim, Founded: 1994, Empl: 250, Peter Guest, Pres & CEO, Brian Durwood, Dir Bus Dev, Richard Sasaki, Dir Fin, Vadya Kale, Dir Tech, Scott Jansen, Dir Eng

Maxtor Corp. 211 River Oaks Pkwy, San Jose CA 95134 USA; 408/432-1700, 800/262-9867 Fax: 408/432-4510, Co Email: @maxtor.com, Web URL: maxtor.com, Focus: Winchester and optical disk drives, Ownrshp: OTC, Stk Sym: MXTR, Founded: 1982, Empl: 7,200, Sales ($M): 1,230, Fiscal End: 3/96; M.H. Chung, Chmn, C.S. Park, Pres & CEO, Richard Balanson, EVP & CTO, Gary Galusha, SVP Mktng, Katherine C. Young, SVP Ops

Maxum Development Corp. 820 S Bartlett Rd, #104, Streamwood IL 60107 USA; 708/830-1113, Fax: 708/830-1262, Co Email: info@maxum.com, Web URL: maxum.com, Focus: Software development and services, Prdts: NetCloak, Ownrshp: PVT, Founded: 1991, John O'Fallon, Pres, Dean Dahlgren, Dir Sales & Mktng, Email: dean@maxum.com; Michael Clark, Dir Eng

Maxvision 47400 Seabridge Dr, Fremont CA 94538 USA; 510/252-0267, Fax: 510/252-0536, Focus: Scanning-related and document imaging software, Prdts: Presto! Series, ViewOffice Power-Suite, Ownrshp: Sub. Maxsoft-Ocron, Founded: 1994, Empl: 20, Ding-Yuan Tang, Pres, Joe G. Budelli, VP Sales, John Dixon, Prod Mgr

McAfee Assoc. 2710 Walsh Ave, #200, Santa Clara CA 95051-0963 USA; 408/988-3832, Fax: 408/970-9727, Co Email: @mcafee.com, Web URL: mcafee.com, Focus: LAN management and security software, Ownrshp: OTC, Stk Sym: MCAF, Founded: 1989, Empl: 33, Sales ($M): 90.1, Fiscal End: 12/95; John McAfee, Chmn & CTO, Bill Larson, Pres & CEO, Email: larson@mcafee.com; Rick Kreysar, VP Mktng, Bob Chappelear, VP Eng, Dan McCammon

McDonald and Associates 2544 156th Cr, Omaha NE 68130 USA; 402/691-8248, 800/338-1581 Fax: 800/242-5751, Focus: Memory component distribution, Carol L. McDonald, Pres

McDonnell Douglas Corp. PO Box 516, St Louis MO 63166-0516 USA; 314/232-0232, Fax: 314/234-3826, Focus: Electronic systems and information services, Ownrshp: NYSE, Stk Sym: MD, Founded: 1921, Empl: 63,612, Sales ($M): 14,332.0, Fiscal End: 12/95; John F. McDonnell, Chmn, Harry C. Stonecipher, Pres & CEO, Kenneth A. Francis, EVP, Robert L. Brand, VP Controller, Herbert J. Lnse, EVP & CFO

McDonnell Information Systems Group 5310 Beethoven St, Los Angeles CA 90066 USA; 310/306-4000, Web URL: mdis.com, Focus: Financial software, Ownrshp: Sub McDonnell, UK, Empl: 1,800, Sales ($M): 234, Fiscal End: 12/95; Ian Hay Davidson, Chmn, John Klein, Pres

McGraw-Hill Inc. 1221 Ave of the Americas, New York NY 10020-1095 USA; 212/512-2000, Fax: 212/512-3511, Web URL: mcgraw-hill.com, Focus: Numerous computer and telecom magazines, Prdts: BYTE, Data Communications, LAN Times, Open

Computing, Ownrshp: NYSE, Founded: 1925, Empl: 15,004, Sales ($M): 2,935.3, Fiscal End: 12/95; Joseph L. Dionne, Chmn & CEO, Harold McGraw III, Pres & COO, Robert N. Landes, Sr EVP, Robert E. Evanson, EVP Corp Dev, Robert J. Bahash, EVP & CFO

MCI Business Markets 3 Ravinia Dr, Atlanta GA 30346-2102 USA; 404/698-8000, Focus: Telecom and information services, Ownrshp: Sub MCI, Timothy F. Price, Pres, Richard G. Ellenberger, SVP, John G. Donoghue, VP Mktng, Brian A. Brewer, VP

MCI Communications Corp. (MCI), 1801 Pennsylvania Ave NW, Washington DC 20006 USA; 202/872-1600, 800/765-2115 Fax: 202/887-2967, Co Email: 640.5834@mcimail.com, Web URL: mci.com, Focus: Voice and data communications services, Ownrshp: OTC, Stk Sym: MCIC, Founded: 1968, Empl: 36,235, Sales ($M): 15,265.0, Fiscal End: 12/95; Bert C. Roberts Jr., Chmn & CEO, Gerald H. Taylor, Pres & COO, Richard T. Liebhaber, EVP & CTO, Susan Mayer, SVP Corp Dev, Douglas L. Maine, CFO

McKenna Group Inc. 1755 Embarcadero Rd, Palo Alto CA 94303 USA; 415/494-2030, Fax: 415/494-8660, Focus: PR and marketing communications, Ownrshp: PVT, Empl: 100, Regis McKenna, Chmn, Elizabeth Chaney, Managing Partner

Measurex Corp. 1 Results Way, Cupertino CA 95014-5991 USA; 408/255-1500, Fax: 408/864-7570, Focus: Computer integrated manufacturing products, Ownrshp: NYSE, Stk Sym: MX, Founded: 1968, Empl: 2,360, Sales ($M): 335.2, Fiscal End: 11/95; David A. Bossen, Chmn & CEO, John C. Gingerich, Pres & COO, Glenn R. Wienkoop, EVP, William J. Weyand, EVP Sales, Robert McAdams Jr., EVP & CFO

Mecklermedia Corp. 20 Ketchum St, Westport CT 06880 USA; 203/226-6967, Fax: 203/454-5840, Co Email: info@mecklermedia.com, Web URL: iworld.com, Focus: Internet publications, tradeshows and consulting, Prdts: Internet World, Web Week, Web Developer, Ownrshp: OTC, Stk Sym: MECK, Founded: 1971, Empl: 87, Sales ($M): 14.5, Fiscal End: 9/95; Alan M. Meckler, Chmn & CEO, Email: ameck@mecklermedia.com; David Egan, Pres & COO Mag Grp, Email: degan@mecklermedia.com; Carl S. Pugh, Pres & COO Tradeshow Grp, Email: cpugh@mecklermedia.com; Paul A. Stanton, VP Mktng, Email: stanton@mecklermedia.com; Christopher S. Cardell, SVP & CFO, Email: scardell@mecklermedia.com; Francie Coulter, Dir PR, Email: fcoulter@mecklermedia.com

Mecom Software PO Box 1578, Snellville GA 30278 USA; 404/564-0473, Fax: 404/564-0473, Co Email: postmast@spshb.donetsk.ua, Focus: Education and entertainment software, Prdts: Christmas Singalong, Little Painter, Formula One, Ownrshp: PVT, Founded: 1992, Empl: 24, Stanislaw Sapunov, Pres, Alexander Makarenko, EVP & GM

MEDE America Corp. 2045 Midway Dr, Twinsburg OH 44087 USA; 216/425-3241, 800/521-4548 Fax: 216/963-7726, Focus: Computers for pharmacy and medical offices, Ownrshp: PVT, Founded: 1970, Empl: 450, Sales ($M): 22, Fiscal End: 6/95; Thomas P. Staudt, Pres & CEO, Elias Nemnom, CFO, Lewis H. Titterton, EVP Sales, Jim Stinton, CIO, Jerome C. Mizer, Dir Corp Mktng

Media Cybernetics L.P. 8484 Georgia Ave, #200, Silver Spring MD 20910 USA; 301/495-3305, 800/992-4256 Fax: 301/495-5964, Web URL: mediacy.com, Focus: Graphics and imaging analysis software, Prdts: Image Pro Plus, Gel-Pro Analyzer, Prints-Pro, Ownrshp: PVT, Founded: 1981, Empl: 41, Sales ($M): 3.6, Michael Galvin, Chmn & Pres, Gerard Fleury, CFO, Email: gerard@mediacy.com; Jean-Paul Martin, VP Eng, Caroline Cho, Mktng Admin, Email: caroline@mediacy.com

Media Depot 209 Erie St, Pomona CA 91768 USA; 909/629-2597, Fax: 909/629-7084, Co Email: mediadpt@lightside.com, Web URL: lightside.com/mediadpt, Focus: Multimedia software and hardware, Prdts: Media Mouse, SSS-170W Surround Sound System, Ownrshp: PVT, Founded: 1994, Empl: 25, Sales ($M): 5, Fiscal End: 6/95; Jimmy Chen, Pres, Rita Chen, CFO, Kevin Lin,

Nat'l Mktng Mgr
Media Logic 310 S St, PO Box 2258, Plainville MA 02762 USA; 508/695-2006, Fax: 508/695-8593, Focus: Magnetic media testing, Ownrshp: OTC, Sales ($M): 3.6, Fiscal End: 3/96; David Lennox, Pres

Media Synergy 260 King St E, #403, Toronto Ontario M5A 1K3 Canada; 416/369-1100, Fax: 416/369-9037, Focus: 3D tools, Prdts: VR Workshop+, Paul Chen, Pres, Mina Chen, VP

MediAlive 762 San Aleso Ave, Sunnyvale CA 94086 USA; 408/752-8500, Fax: 408/752-8501, Focus: Multimedia software, Prdts: America Alive, Ownrshp: Sub CD Technology, Founded: 1987, Empl: 5, Sales ($M): 2, Fiscal End: 12/95; William W. Liu, Pres

MediaLogic ADL Inc. 4999 Pearl E Cr, Boulder CO 80301 USA; 303/939-9780, Fax: 303/939-9745, Co Email: adlinc@aol.com, Web URL: adlinc.com/adlinfo, Focus: Automated data storage library solutions, Prdts: Scalable Library Architecture, Ownrshp: Sub Media Logic Inc., Lee H. Elizer, Pres & CEO, Scott DeWall, VP Sales

MediaMap 215 First St, 3rd Floor, Cambridge MA 02142-1293 USA; 617/374-9300, Fax: 617/374-9345, Web URL: mediamap.com, Focus: Computer publications and tradeshows information, Ownrshp: PVT, Founded: 1985, John Pearce, CEO

MediaShare Corp. 5927 Priestly Dr #101, Carlsbad CA 92008-8813 USA; 619/931-7171, Fax: 619/431-5752, Focus: Multimedia software, Prdts: Prism, Ownrshp: PVT, Founded: 1990, Empl: 38, Sales ($M): 6, Richard Byrne, Pres & CEO

Medic Computer Systems 8601 Six Forks Rd, #300, Raleigh NC 27615 USA; 919/847-8102, Fax: 919/846-1555, Focus: Medical software, Ownrshp: OTC, Founded: 1982, Empl: 370, Sales ($M): 143.2, Fiscal End: 12/95; John McConnel, Pres

Medicus Systems Corp. One Rotary Ctr, #400, Evanston IL 60201-4802 USA; 847/570-7500, Fax: 847/570-7518, Focus: Healthcare software, Ownrshp: OTC, Stk Sym: MECS, Founded: 1985, Empl: 306, Sales ($M): 31.1, Fiscal End: 5/96; Richard C. Jelinek, Chmn, Pres & CEO, James M. Alland, EVP & COO, Susan P. Dowell, EVP & COO, William W. Cowan, VP & CFO

Medio Multimedia Inc. 1904 3rd Ave, #326, Seattle WA 98101-1126 USA; 206/867-5500, Fax: 206/885-4142, Focus: Multimedia information and software, Ownrshp: PVT, Founded: 1993, Steven Podradchik, Pres

Mega Dr Systems Inc. 489 S Robertson Blvd, Beverly Hills CA 90211 USA; 310/247-0006, Fax: 310/247-8118, Co Email: @megadrive.com, Focus: Portable and removable Winchester disks, Ownrshp: PVT, Founded: 1988, Empl: 22, Sales ($M): 5, Alex K. Bouzari, Co-Chmn & Pres, Paul S. Bloch, Co-Chmn & CEO, Derrek J. Michael, Dir Ops, Chris Aarons, Mktng Dir, Erin Poole, Mgr PR, Email: epoole@megadrive.com

Megahertz Corp. 605 N 5600 W, PO Box 16020, Salt Lake City UT 84116-0020 USA; 801/320-7000, Fax: 801/320-6010, Co Email: salesinfo@mhz.com, Web URL: megahertz.com, Focus: PC data/fax modems, Ownrshp: Sub US Robotics, Founded: 1985, Empl: 750, Spencer F. Kirk, Pres, Tod W. Frohen, SVP Ops, Steven B. Smith, VP Mktng, Michael D. Keough, SVP Sales, Paul Nagel, SVP Eng, Karleen Broadwater, PR Mgr, Email: kbroadwater@mhz.com

Melita International 5051 Peachtree Corners Cr, Norcross GA 30092 USA; 770/446-7800, Fax: 770/409-4444, Focus: Telecom products, Prdts: PhoneFrame, MAGELLAN, PowerPACT, Ownrshp: PVT, Founded: 1979, Aleksander Szlam, Chmn & CEO, J. Neil Smith, Pres, Steve Dmetruk, VP Sales & Mktng, Diane Bates, Dir Mktng, Ginny Fisher, Email: gfisher@melita.com

Melson Technologies 707 Skokie Blvd #700, Northbrook IL 60062-2842 USA; 847/291-4000, Fax: 847/291-4022, Focus: Real estate software, Prdts: Skyline, Project C, Ownrshp: PVT, Founded: 1982, Empl: 160, James Melson, Chmn

Memorex Telex Corp. 545 E John Carpenter Fwy., Irving TX 75062 USA; 214/444-3500, Fax: 214/444-3501, Web URL: mtc.com, Focus: Enterprise network, storage and service solutions, Ownrshp: Sub. Memorex Telex, Stk Sym: MEMXY, Founded: 1936, Empl: 4,000, Sales ($M): 843.1, Fiscal End: 12/95; Marcelo Gumucio, Pres & CEO, Brad Sowers, VP WW Mktng, George Bennett, VP Sales, David J. Faulkner, Vice Chmn & CFO, Laura Ster, Mgr Corp Comm

Memory Experts Int'l. 7750 Henri Bourassa W, #102, Montreal Quebec H4S 1W3 Canada; 514/333-5010, 888/422-6726 Fax: 514/333-5020, Co Email: @canram.com, Web URL: canram.com, Focus: Memory cards, Prdts: CANRAM, Guadalupe Reusing, Pres

Memory Masters Inc. 4950 Keller Springs Rd, #480, Addison TX 75248 USA; 214/392-3726, 800/463-6679 Focus: Computer memory distribution, Ownrshp: PVT

Mentalix Inc. 1700 Alma, #110, Plano TX 75075 USA; 214/423-9377, Fax: 214/423-1145, Co Email: info@pfx.com, Web URL: pfx.com, Focus: Scanning & image manipulation software for UNIX, Prdts: Pixel!FX, Ownrshp: PVT, Founded: 1986, Empl: 11, Paul Siegert, Pres, Bill Cave, Dir Mktng, Brian Gross, VP Eng

Mentor Graphics Corp. 8005 SW Boeckman Rd, Wilsonville OR 97070-7777 USA; 503/626-7000, Fax: 503/685-7707, Focus: Electronic Design Automation software, Ownrshp: OTC, Stk Sym: MENT, Founded: 1981, Empl: 2,100, Sales ($M): 384.5, Fiscal End: 12/95; Thomas H. Bruggere, Chmn, Walden C. Rhines, Pres & CEO, Frank S. Delia, VP & CAO, Waldo R. Richards, SVP, R. Douglas Norby, SVP & CFO

Mercury Computer Systems Inc. 199 Riverneck Rd, Chelmsford MA 01824 USA; 508/256-1300, Fax: 508/256-3599, Co Email: info@mc.com, Web URL: mc.com, Focus: Real-time embedded multi-computers, Prdts: Race Series, Ownrshp: PVT, Founded: 1983, Empl: 260, Sales ($M): 55.5, Fiscal End: 6/95; Jay Bertelli, Pres, Leigh McLeod, PR, Mktng Spec, Email: mcleod@mc.com

Mercury Interactive Corp. 470 Potrero Ave, Sunnyvale CA 94086 USA; 408/523-9900, Fax: 408/523-9911, Web URL: mercint.com, Focus: Testing systems for software development, Prdts: XRunner, WinRunner, LoadRunner, Ownrshp: OTC, Stk Sym: MERQ, Founded: 1989, Empl: 270, Sales ($M): 39.5, Fiscal End: 12/95; Aryeh Finegold, Chmn & CEO, Amnon Landan, COO, Ken Klein, VP Sales, Jayaram Bhat, VP Mktng, Sharlene Abrams, VP & CFO, Sue Ann Murray, PR Mgr

Merex Corp. 140 S Ash Ave, Tempe AZ 85281 USA; 602/921-7077, 800/383-5636 Fax: 602/967-8267, Focus: Word processing software, Prdts: MerexEdit, Ownrshp: PVT, Founded: 1987, Ray Karesky, Pres, Lynda B. Bowman, VP

Mergent Int'l. 70 Inwood Rd, Rocky Hill CT 06067 USA; 860/257-4223, 800/688-1199 Fax: 860/257-4245, Web URL: mergent.com, Focus: PC and LAN security software, Prdts: CSM/ISM, SmartPass, Ownrshp: PVT, Founded: 1985, Empl: 81, John D. Worthen, Pres & CEO, Ross Curns, VP WW Sales, Email: rcurns@mergent.com; Al Dube, CFO & Co-Founder, Email: adube@mergent.com; Stephanie Mitchell, PR Specialist, Email: smitchell@mergent.com

Meridian Data Inc. 5615 Scotts Valley Dr, Scotts Valley CA 95066-3424 USA; 408/438-3100, 800/767-2537 Fax: 408/438-6816, Web URL: meridian-data.com, Focus: Fault-tolerant LAN servers, Prdts: CD Net Software, CD Net Servers, Ownrshp: OTC, Stk Sym: MDCD, Founded: 1986, Empl: 100, Sales ($M): 25.3, Fiscal End: 12/95; Charlie Bass, Chmn, Gianluca Rattazzi, Pres & CEO, Erik Miller, VP & CFO, Richard Krueger, VP Mktng

Merisel Inc. 200 Continental Blvd, El Segundo CA 90245-0984 USA; 310/615-3080, Fax: 310/615-6819, Web URL: merisel.com, Focus: Distributes microcomputer products worldwide, Ownrshp: OTC, Stk Sym: MSEL, Founded: 1980, Empl: 3,263, Sales ($M): 6,000, Fiscal End: 12/95; Dwight A. Steffensen, Chmn & CEO, Ronald Rittenmeyer, Pres & COO, James E. Illson, SVP & CFO, John Connors, Pres US Ops, Paul M. Lemerise, SVP MIS

Merriam-Webster Inc. 47 Federal St, PO Box 281, Springfield

MA 01102 USA; 413/734-3134, Fax: 413/731-5979, Co Email: merriam@aol.com, Focus: Dictionary software, Ownrshp: PVT, Founded: 1831, Thomas E. Stanley, SVP & Publisher, Alicia di Leo, Email: adileo@m-w.com

Merrin Information Services Inc. 2275 E Bayshore Rd, #101, Palo Alto CA 94303 USA; 415/493-5050, Fax: 415/493-5480, Focus: PC product marketing and distribution data and consulting, Ownrshp: PVT, Founded: 1988, Empl: 11, Seymour Merrin, Pres

Mesa Group 29 Crafts St, Newton MA 02160 USA; 617/964-7400, Fax: 617/964-4240, Co Email: info@mesa.com, Focus: Workgroup solutions, Prdts: Conference+, Ownrshp: PVT, Founded: 1989, Eric V. Schultz, Chmn & CEO, Michel A. Yazbek, SVP Sales & Mktng, Michael Barrow, VP & CTO, John Paglierani, VP Prod Dev, Ben Shelton, Dir Mktng, Email: bens@mesa.com

META Group 208 Harbor Dr, Stamford CT 06912 USA; 203/973-6700, Fax: 203/354-8066, Co Email: info@metagroup.com, Web URL: metagroup.com, Focus: Consulting and information on computer technology impact on business, Ownrshp: OTC, Stk Sym: METG, Founded: 1989, Empl: 200, Sales ($M): 29.6, Fiscal End: 12/95; Dale Kutnick, Pres, Marc Butlein, Chmn, Joe Gottlieb, EVP Sales & Mktng, Heather Whiteman, Mktng Mgr, Email: heatherw@metagroup.com

Metatec Corp. 7001 Discovery Blvd, Dublin OH 43017 USA; 614/761-2000, Fax: 614/766-3146, Web URL: metatec.com, Focus: Multimedia software on CD-ROM, Prdts: Nautilus, Ownrshp: OTC, Stk Sym: META, Founded: 1986, Empl: 325, Sales ($M): 39.3, Fiscal End: 12/95; Jeffrey M. Wilkins, Chmn & CEO, Gregory T. Tillar, Pres & COO, William H. Largent, EVP & CFO, Alex Deak, VP CIO, John Kompa, Mgr Corp Comm, Email: kompa@metatec.com

MetaTools Inc. 6303 Carpinteria Ave, Carpinteria CA 93013 USA; 805/566-6200, Fax: 805/566-6385, Co Email: kptsupport@metatools.com, Web URL: metatools.com, Focus: Imaging and multimedia software, Prdts: Kai's Power Tools, KPT Convolver, KPT Bryce, KPT Vector Effects, Ownrshp: OTC, Founded: 1987, Sales ($M): 16.7, Fiscal End: 12/95; John Wilczak, Chmn, Pres & CEO, Kai Krause, Co-Founder, Terry Kinninger, CFO, Michael Tchong, VP Mktng, Kristin Keyes, Email: kkeyes@aol.com

Methode Electronics Inc. 7444 W Wilson Ave, Chicago IL 60656 USA; 708/867-9600, Fax: 708/867-3288, Focus: Electronic products, Ownrshp: OTC, Stk Sym: METHA, Founded: 1946, Empl: 2,500, Sales ($M): 307.5, Fiscal End: 4/96; William J. McGinley, Chmn, William T. Jensen, Pres, Kevin J. Hayes, CFO, Michael G. Andre, Sr EVP

Metra Information Systems Inc. 45395 Northport Loop W, Fremont CA 94538-6417 USA; 510/226-9188, Focus: PC motherboards, Ownrshp: PVT, Founded: 1988, Empl: 10, Wun-Yann Liao, Pres, Sam Shieh, VP Eng

Metrica Inc. 8 Winchester Place, Winchester MA 01890 USA; 617/756-0022, Fax: 617/756-0023, Focus: Technical data management software for workstations, Prdts: Metrica, Ownrshp: PVT, J.M. Berman, Pres & CEO, M. Carley

Metricom Inc. 980 University Ave, Los Gatos CA 95030 USA; 408/399-8200, Fax: 408/354-1024, Co Email: info@metricom.com, Web URL: metricom.com, Focus: Wireless digital communication networks, Prdts: Ricochet, UtiliNet, Ownrshp: OTC, Stk Sym: MCOM, Founded: 1985, Empl: 200, Sales ($M): 5.8, Fiscal End: 12/95; Robert P. Dilworth, Pres & CEO, Gary M. Green, EVP & COO, LeRoy D. Nosbaum, EVP UtiliNet Div, Donald F. Wood, EVP Ricochet Div, William D. Swain, CFO, Megan O'Reilly-Lewis, Corp Commun, Email: moreillylewis@wmc.com

Metrologic Instruments Inc. Coles Rd at Rt 42, Blackwood NJ 08012 USA; 609/228-8100, 800/436-3876 Fax: 609/228-6673, Focus: Manufacturer laser bar code scanners, Prdts: ScanGlove, ScanPal, Mini-Slot, Scan Key, MS900 Series, Ownrshp: OTC, Stk Sym: MTLG, Founded: 1968, Empl: 300, Sales ($M): 36, C. Harry Knowles, Pres & CEO, Janet Knowles, VP Admin, Dale Fischer, VP

Intl Sales, Mel Fiehler, MIS/DP Mgr, Betty Williams, PR/Adv Mgr

Metropolis Software Inc. 100 Hamilton Ave, #100, Palo Alto CA 94301 USA; 415/462-2200, Fax: 415/617/5978, Web URL: metropolis.com, Focus: Sales force automation software for PC, Prdts: Metropolis Sales 4.0, Founded: 1988, Empl: 45, Craig Jorasch, Pres, Thomas McGannon, VP

mFactory Inc. 1440 Chapin Ave, #200, Burlingame CA 94010 USA; 415/548-0600, Fax: 415/548-9249, Focus: Multimedia software development tools, Ownrshp: PVT, Founded: 1992, R. Hamish Forsyth, Pres, Anu Shukla, COO, Norm Gudmundson, VP Eng, Hal Steger, VP, Chris Krook, VP Fin

MFS Communications 3555 Farnan St, Omaha NE 68131 USA; 402/977-5300, Fax: 402/977-5325, Web URL: mfsdatanet.com, Focus: Telecom services, Ownrshp: OTC, Stk Sym: MFST, Empl: 700, Sales ($M): 583.2, Fiscal End: 12/95; James Q. Crowe, CEO

Michigan Technology Council 2005 Baits Dr, Ann Arbor MI 48109 USA; 313/763-9757, Fax: 313/936-2746, Focus: High-tech organization for Michigan, Ownrshp: Nonprofit

Micom Communications Corp. 4100 Los Angeles Ave, Simi Valley CA 93063-3397 USA; 805/583-8600, 800/642-6687 Fax: 805/583-1997, Co Email: info@micom.com, Web URL: micom.com, Focus: Data/voice integration and communications network products, Prdts: Marathon Integration Multiplexer, NetRunner Integration Router, Ownrshp: OTC, Stk Sym: MICM, Founded: 1973, Empl: 420, Sales ($M): 88.3, Fiscal End: 3/95; Barry Phelps, Chmn, Gil Gabral, Pres & COO, Fran Good, VP CFO, Dwight Olson, VP Ops, Ken Guy, VP Mktng, Email: keng@micom.com; Sharon Porter, PR, Email: sporter@micom.com

Micro 2000 Inc. 1100 E Broadway, #301, Glendale CA 91205 USA; 818/547-0125, Fax: 818/547-0397, Focus: PC diagnostic software, Ownrshp: PVT, Founded: 1990, Robert McFarlane, CEO, Paul Buzby, Media Liason

Micro Central PO Box 1009, Old Bridge NJ 08857-1009 USA; 908/360-0300, 800/836-4276 Fax: 908/360-0303, Focus: Microcomputer software and hardware product distributor, Ownrshp: PVT, Founded: 1985, Empl: 95, Jay Lopatin, Pres & GM, Charlotte Woodland, Sales Mgr, David Levine, Dir Mktng, Matt Lopatin, Vendor Acq

Micro Channel Developers Assoc. (MCDA), 2280 N Bechelli Ln, #B, Redding CA 96002 USA; 916/222-2262, 800/438-6232 Fax: 916/222-2528, Web URL: microchannel.inter.net, Focus: Promote Micro Channel compatible products, Ownrshp: Nonprofit, Founded: 1990, Empl: 66, Steve Petracca, Chmn, Ramiz H. Zakhariya, Pres, Email: rzakhari@interserv.com

micro Computer Inc. 955 Commercial St, Palo Alto CA 94303 USA; 415/855-0940, Focus: PC graphics and video, Prdts: microCrystal, Ownrshp: Sub. micro Computer, Germany, Founded: 1982, Sales ($M): 60 WW, Randall L. Stickrod, Exec Dir

Micro Computer Systems Inc. 2300 Valley View Ln, #800, Irving TX 75062 USA; 214/659-1624, Fax: 214/659-1514, Focus: NetBIOS software, Ownrshp: PVT, Founded: 1980, Wendell Alumbaugh, Pres, Jerry Presley, VP, Gary Phillips, Mktng Dir

Micro Design Int'l. Inc. (MDI), 6985 University Blvd, Winter Park FL 32792 USA; 407/677-8333, 800/228-0891 Fax: 407/677-8365, Co Email: info@microdes.com, Web URL: microdes.com, Focus: Optical mass storage devices, Prdts: SCSI Express, CD-Express Library, EZ Express, Ownrshp: PVT, Founded: 1978, Empl: 125, Sales ($M): 31, Fiscal End: 1994; M. Geoffrey Legat, Pres, Daniel Pieplow, VP Fin & Ops, Arnold Jones, Dir R&D, Shelly Smith, Prod Mktng Mgr, Email: ssmith@microdes.com

Micro Dynamics Ltd. 8555 Sixteenth St, #701, Silver Spring MD 20910 USA; 301/589-6300, Fax: 301/589-3414, Co Email: info@mdl.com, Web URL: mdl.com, Focus: Image management systems, Prdts: Micro Dynamics MARS, MARS/NT, Ownrshp: PVT, Founded: 1985, Empl: 50, Bill Newell, Pres & CEO, Email: bill_newell@mdl.com; Charles Abod, CFO, Email:

charles_abod@mdl.com; Melany Smith, Mktng Dir, Email: melany_smith@mdl.com; Mike Sebeck, Sales Dir, Email: mike_sebeck@mdl.com; Alice Jones, Mgr Corp Comm, Email: alice_jones@mdl.com; Marlee Margopoulos, Marcom Mgr, Email: marlee_margopoulos@mdl.com

Micro Exchange Corp. 682 Passaic Ave, Nutley NJ 07110 USA; 201/284-1200, Fax: 201/284-1550, Focus: Sale and service of used and liquidated computers, Ownrshp: PVT

Micro Express Inc. 1811 Kaiser Ave, Irvine CA 92714-5707 USA; 714/852-1400, Fax: 714/852-1225, Focus: Laptop, notebook and desktop PCs, Ownrshp: PVT, Founded: 1986, Empl: 75, Sales ($M): 25, Art Afshar, GM

Micro Focus Inc. 2465 E Bayshore Dr, #400, Palo Alto CA 94303 USA; 415/856-4161, 800/872-6265 Fax: 415/856-6134, Web URL: microfocus.com, Focus: Enterprise application software, Prdts: COBOL/2 Workbench, Ownrshp: OTC, Stk Sym: MIFGY, Founded: 1976, Empl: 710, Sales ($M): 122, Fiscal End: 1/96; Paul O'Grady, Chmn & CEO, Email: pog@mfltd.co.uk; John Beggs, Pres WW Sales, Email: jnb@mfltd.co.uk; Paul Adams, Pres Prod & Bus Dev, Email: pa@mfltd.co.uk; Ron Forbes, CFO, Email: rhf@mfltd.co.uk; Peter Katz, VP Mktng, Email: pek@mfltd.co.uk

Micro Format Inc. 830-3 Seton Ct, Wheeling IL 60090-5772 USA; 847/520-4699, 800/333-0549 Fax: 847/520-0197, Web URL: sendit.com/mformat, Focus: Printer paper, Prdts: Ink Jet Banner Band, Steve Singer, Pres

Micro Perfect Corp. 225 W 34th St, New York NY 10122 USA; 212/629-6082, Fax: 212/629-8578, Focus: Vertical market software, Ownrshp: PVT

Micro Star Software 2245 Camino Vida Roble, Carlsbad CA 92009 USA; 800/777-4228 Fax: 619/931-4950, Ownrshp: PVT, Founded: 1986, Empl: 78, Sales ($M): 6.2, Fiscal End: 12/95; Stephen H. Benedict, Pres, Chris Burnett, CFO

Micro Warehouse 535 Connecticut Ave, Norwalk CT 06854 USA; 203/899-4000, Focus: Mail order of microcomputer products, Ownrshp: OTC, Stk Sym: MWHS, Empl: 720, Sales ($M): 1,308.0, Fiscal End: 12/95; Peter Godfrey, Chmn, Pres & CEO, Adam Schaffer, VP Mktng, Melvin Seiler, EVP & COO, Powell Crowley, VP Bus Dev, Steven Purcell, VP & CFO

Micro-Integration Corp. (MI), 1 Science Park, Frostburg MD 21532 USA; 301/689-0800, 800/832-4526 Fax: 301/689-0808, Web URL: miworld.com, Focus: Communication and micro-mainframe software, Ownrshp: OTC, Stk Sym: MINT, Founded: 1978, Empl: 75, Sales ($M): 7.8, Fiscal End: 3/96; John A. Parsons, Chmn & Pres, William L. Shomo, VP Prod Research, P. Edward Fisher, VP Prod Dev, Mark A. Proudfoot, VP Mktng, Chris J. Burgess, VP Fin, Donna Dice, Mktng Rep

MicroAge Inc. 2400 S MicroAge Way, Tempe AZ 85282-1896 USA; 602/804-2000, Fax: 602/966-7339, Co Email: @microage.com, Web URL: microage.com, Focus: Computer stores franchisor and microcomputer product distributor, Ownrshp: OTC, Stk Sym: MICA, Founded: 1976, Empl: 2,088, Sales ($M): 2,941.1, Fiscal End: 9/95; Jeffrey D. McKeever, Chmn & CEO, Alan Hald, Vice Chmn, Kenneth R. Waters, Pres, James R. Daniel, SVP & CFO, Lawrence J. Szambelan, VP Info Syst

MicroBiz Corp 300 Corporate Dr, Mahwah NJ 07430-3605 USA; 201/512-0900, Focus: Point of sale software, Ownrshp: PVT, Founded: 1987, Empl: 85, Sales ($M): 9, Fiscal End: 6/93; Craig L. Aberle, Pres, Ken Phelan, CEO

MicroClean Inc. 2050 S 10th St, San Jose CA 95112 USA; 408/995-5062, 800/326-4881 Fax: 408/995-0814, Focus: Computer cleaning products, Prdts: QIC Data Cartridge Cleaners, CD Lens Cleaner, CD-ROM Radial Cleaner, Ownrshp: PVT, Founded: 1981, Empl: 30, Jim Taylor, VP Mktng Sales, Yvette Moss, Sales Admin

Microcom Inc. 500 River Ridge Dr, Norwood MA 02062-5028 USA; 617/551-1000, 800/822-8224 Fax: 617/551-1968, Web URL: microcom.com, Focus: Modems and communication soft-

ware, Ownrshp: OTC, Stk Sym: MNPI, Founded: 1980, Empl: 400, Sales ($M): 146.0, Fiscal End: 3/96; Roland D. Pampel, Pres & CEO, Lewis A. Bergins, EVP, Peter J. Minihane, EVP & CFO, William Andrews, VP Sales & Mktng

Microcomputer Managers Assoc. Inc. (MMA), PO Box 4615, Warren NJ 07059 USA; 908/585-9091, Focus: Organization focused on technology management issues, Ownrshp: Nonprofit, Founded: 1982, Empl: 1,000, Alex Kask, Exec Dir, Email: 418.5392@mcimail.com; Leonard Steinbach, Pres, Email: lstein@nln.org; Dana Tate, VP, Email: 70272.154@compuserve.com

MicroDesign Resources Inc. 874 Gravenstein Hwy S #14, Sebastopol CA 95472 USA; 707/824-4004, 800/527-0288 Fax: 707/823-0504, Web URL: chipanalyst.com, Focus: Consulting & conferences on microprocessors, semiconductor, workstation and PC technology, Ownrshp: PVT, Founded: 1987, Empl: 12, Michael Slater, Pres

Microdyne Corp. 3601 Eisenhower Ave, Alexandria VA 22304-6439 USA; 703/739-0500, Fax: 703/739-0558, Focus: LAN products, Ownrshp: OTC, Stk Sym: MCDY, Founded: 1984, Empl: 400, Sales ($M): 78.2, Fiscal End: 9/93; Philip T. Cunningham, Chmn, Pres & CEO, Lizanna Stahnke, SVP, Chris Maginniss, EVP & CFO, R. Dale D'Alessio, SVP Sales, Neal H. Sanders, VP Corp Com

Microelectronics & Computer Technology Corp. (MCC), PO Box 200195, Austin TX 78720 USA; 512/343-0978, Fax: 512/338-3892, Focus: Cooperative R&D organization with focus on application-driven information technology, Ownrshp: Nonprofit, Founded: 1982, Craig Fields, Pres & CEO, Alan Salisbury, COO

Microfield Graphics Inc. 9825 SW Sunshine Ct, #A1, Beaverton OR 97005 USA; 503/626-9393, Fax: 503/641-9333, Co Email: @mfg.com, Web URL: softboard.com, Focus: Graphics controllers, Prdts: SoftBoard, Ownrshp: OTC, Stk Sym: MICG, Founded: 1984, Empl: 37, Sales ($M): 5.3, Fiscal End: 12/95; John B. Conroy, Pres & CEO, Samuel W. Mallicoat, Chmn & VP R&D, Peter F. Zinsli, VP Mktng, Michael W. Stansell, VP Ops, Randall R. Reed, CFO, Karl Damhave, Mgr Marcom, Email: karld@mfg.com

MicroFrontier Inc. 3401 101st, #E, Des Moines IA 50322 USA; 515/270-8109, Fax: 515/278-6828, Co Email: mfrontier@aol.com, Focus: Graphics software, Ownrshp: PVT, Founded: 1987

Micrografx Inc. 1303 Arapaho Rd, Richardson TX 75081 USA; 214/234-1769, 800/676-3110 Fax: 214/994-6227, Web URL: micrografx.com, Focus: Graphics software, Prdts: Designer, Charisma, Picture Publisher, ABC Graphics Suite, Ownrshp: OTC, Stk Sym: MGXI, Founded: 1982, Empl: 251, Sales ($M): 72.9, Fiscal End: 3/96; J. Paul Grayson, Chmn & CEO, Herman DeLatte, COO, Larry G. Morris, Acting CFO, John Dearborn, VP Sales, Robert Lytton, Dir Info Tech, Margaret Turbeville, Mgr PR, Email: margt@micrografx.com

MicroHelp Inc. 4211 JVL Industrial Park Dr NE, Marietta GA 30066 USA; 770/516-0899, 800/777-3322 Fax: 770/516-1099, Focus: Windows programming tools, Ownrshp: PVT, Founded: 1985, Empl: 60, Sales ($M): 17.2, Fiscal End: 12/95; Tim O'Pry, Pres & CEO, John A. Lamb, VP R&D, Tom Lynch, VP Sales & Mktng, Janet Van Pelt, CFO

Microlytics Inc. 2 Tobey Village Office Park, Pittsford NY 14534 USA; 716/248-9150, Fax: 716/248-3868, Co Email: info@microlytics.com, Web URL: microlytics.com, Focus: Electronic directory software and solutions, Prdts: Micro Pages, Smart Directory, Stk Sym: MYCX, Founded: 1985, Empl: 40, Sales ($M): 5.9, Fiscal End: 3/95; Roy W. Haythorn, Pres & CEO, Gregory J. Gordon, EVP & CFO, Email: ggordon@microlytics.com

MicroMedium Inc. 2 Davis Dr, PO Box 14506, Research Triangle Pk NC 27709-4506 USA; 919/558-9225, Co Email: @micromedium.com, Web URL: micromedium.com, Focus: Multimedia training software, Prdts: Digital Trainer, Founded: 1992, Alfred J. Heyman, Dir Dev, Martin Renkis, Email: mar@micromedium.com

Micron Electronics 900 E Karcher Rd, Nampa ID 83687 USA; 208/893-3434, 800/515-9197 Fax: 208/893-3424, Web URL: mei.micron.com, Focus: Manufactures electronic products for computing and digital applications, Prdts: Millennia TransPort, Ownrshp: OTC, Stk Sym: MUEI, Empl: 1,370, Sales ($M): 1,764.9, Fiscal End: 8/96; Joseph M. Daltoso, Chmn, Pres & CEO, T. Erik Oaas, VP & CFO, Gregory D. Stevenson, EVP Ops, Kenneth C. Birch, VP PC Eng

Micron Technology Inc. 8000 S Federal Way, PO Box 6, Boise ID 83707-0006 USA; 208/368-4400, Fax: 208/368-4435, Web URL: micron.com, Focus: Memory chips, boards and PCs, Ownrshp: NYSE, Stk Sym: MU, Founded: 1978, Empl: 5,400, Sales ($M): 3,653.8, Fiscal End: 8/96; Steve Appleton, Chmn & CEO, Wilbur Stover, VP & CFO, Tyler Lowrey, Vice Chmn & COO, Nancy M. Self, VP Admin, Kipp Bedard

MicroNet Technology Inc. 80 Technology, Irvine CA 92718 USA; 714/453-6000, Fax: 714/453-6001, Co Email: @micronet.com, Web URL: micronet.com, Focus: Mass storage peripherals, Founded: 1988, Empl: 60, Morris Taradalsky, Pres & CEO, Meryl Cook, PR Mgr, Email: meryl@micronet.com

Micronics Computers Inc. 232 E Warren Ave, Fremont CA 94539-7085 USA; 510/651-2300, 800/577-0977 Fax: 510/651-9635, Co Email: @mcrn.com, Focus: Motherboards and cache memory boards, Ownrshp: OTC, Stk Sym: MCRN, Founded: 1986, Empl: 263, Sales ($M): 234.1, Fiscal End: 9/95; Shanker Munshani, Pres, David J. Nealon, VP WW Ops, Chuang Li, VP Eng, Larry Lummis, VP WW Sales, Robert Campbell, VP & CFO, Julie Dibene, Corp Rel Mgr

Microplex Systems Ltd. 8525 Commerce Ct, Burnaby BC V5A 4N3 Canada; 604/444-4232, 800/665-7798 Fax: 604/444-4239, Co Email: info@microplex.com, Web URL: microplex.com, Focus: Data communications equipment, Prdts: M208 Workgroup Server, Ownrshp: PVT, Gerry Sawkins, Email: gas@microplex.com

Micropolis Corp. 21211 Nordhoff St, Chatsworth CA 91311 USA; 818/709-3300, 800/395-3748 Fax: 818/709-3396, Co Email: @micropolis.com, Focus: Disk drives, Prdts: SuperCapacity, RAIDION, Ownrshp: OTC, Stk Sym: MLIS, Founded: 1976, Empl: 3,000, Sales ($M): 211.3, Fiscal End: 12/95; J. Larry Smart, Pres & CEO, Barbara V. Scherer, VP & CFO, Holly Sacks, VP MKtng, Ericson M. Dunstan, SVP Corp Eng, Peggy L. Garcia, PR Mgr, Email: peggy_garcia@microp.com

Microport Inc. 108 Whispering Pines Dr, Scotts Valley CA 95066 USA; 408/438-8649, 800/367-8649 Fax: 408/438-7560, Web URL: mport.com, Focus: LAN software, Prdts: TotalNet, NetMark 1000, Ownrshp: PVT, Founded: 1986, Empl: 12, Pete Holstrom, VP & GM, Mark Ryan, Eng Mgr, Email: mark@mport.com; Mike Grinder, Ops Mgr, Email: mike@mport.com; Scott Engmann, Mktng Dir, Email: scott@mport.com

MicroQuest 11142 Thompson Ave, Lenexa KS 66219 USA; 913/438-2155, 800/345-3950 Fax: 913/888-6928, Web URL: microquest.com, Focus: Personal and business software, Prdts: Inside Track, Founded: 1993, Thomas Harris, VP

Microrim Inc. 15395 SE 30th Place, Bellevue WA 98007-6537 USA; 206/649-9500, 800/628-6990 Fax: 206/649-2785, Web URL: microrim.com, Focus: Database software and web database software, Prdts: R:BASE, R:WEB, Ownrshp: Sub Abacus Accounting, Founded: 1981, Empl: 75, Art Miller, Pres & CEO, Email: artm@microrim.com; Rufe Vanderpool, COO & VP, Email: rufev@microrim.com; Jonathin Couse, Dir Dev, Email: jonathinc@microrim.com; Fred Antrobus, MIS Mgr, Email: freda@microrim.com; Jessica Leber, PR Coord, Email: jessical@microrim.com

Micros Systems Inc. 12000 Baltimore Ave, Beltsville MD 20705-1291 USA; 301/210-6000, Fax: 301/490-6699, Focus: Point-of-sale systems and software, Ownrshp: OTC, Stk Sym: MCRS, Founded: 1977, Empl: 300, Sales ($M): 112.0, Fiscal End: 6/95; A.L. Giannopoulos, Pres & CEO, Ronald J. Kolson, EVP & COO,

Daniel G. Interlandi, SVP Sales & Mktng, T. Paul Armstrong, VP, Gary C. Kaufman, VP & CFO

Micros-To-Mainframes Inc. (MTM), 614 Corporate Way, Valley Cottage NY 10989 USA; 914/268-5000, 800/468-6782 Fax: 914/268-9695, Focus: Systems integration, Ownrshp: OTC, Stk Sym: MTMC, Founded: 1986, Empl: 47, Sales ($M): 47.3, Fiscal End: 3/96; Howard Pavoney, Pres, Stephen H. Rothman, Co-CEO, Frank T. Wong, VP Fin

Microsemi Corp. 2830 S Fairview St, PO Box 26890, Santa Ana CA 92704 USA; 714/979-8220, Fax: 714/966-5989, Focus: Semiconductors and surface mount assemblies, Ownrshp: OTC, Stk Sym: MSCC, Founded: 1960, Empl: 1,591, Sales ($M): 133.9, Fiscal End: 10/95; Philip Frey Jr., Chmn, Pres & CEO, Jiri Sandera, VP Eng, Andy T.S. Yuen, VP Int'l Ops, James M. Thomas, VP, David R. Sonksen, VP & CFO

MicroSlate Inc. 9625 Ignace St, #D, Brossard Quebec J4Y 2P3 Canada; 514/444-3680, Fax: 514/444-3683, Focus: Mobile communications computers, Prdts: MicroSlate, Founded: 1989, Empl: 35, William A. Clough, Pres, Nicholas Kohras, EVP, Jan Rowinski, VP Ops, Daniel Ovelleyye, VP Eng, Peter Hilton, VP Sales

Microsoft Corp. One Microsoft Way, PO Box 97017, Redmond WA 98052-6399 USA; 206/936-4400, 800/285-7772 Fax: 206/936-8000, Co Email: msft@microsoft.com, Web URL: microsoft.com, Focus: PC system and application software, Prdts: Windows 95, Windows NT, Excel, Word, Works, Ownrshp: OTC, Stk Sym: MSFT, Founded: 1975, Empl: 19,700, Sales ($M): 8,671, Fiscal End: 6/96; William H. Gates, Chmn & CEO, Steven A. Ballmer, EVP, Michael J. Maples, EVP, Robert J. Herbold, COO, Jeffrey S. Raikes, SVP

MicroSolutions Inc. 132 W Lincoln Hwy, DeKalb IL 60115 USA; 815/756-3411, 800/890-7227 Fax: 815/756-2928, Co Email: @micro-solutions.com, Web URL: micro-solutions.com, Focus: PC mass storage products, Prdts: Backpack, Ownrshp: PVT, Founded: 1980, Empl: 100, Ronald Proesel, Pres, Jack Moloney, EVP & GM, Patrick Barron, VP Sales, Debbie Armstrong, Mktng Mgr, Email: debbiea@micro-solutions.com

MicroSpeed Inc. 5005 Brandin Ct, Fremont CA 94538 USA; 800/438-7733 Co Email: mspeed@microspeed.com, Web URL: microspeed.com, Focus: Input devices: mice, keyboards, trackballs and joysticks, Prdts: WinTRAC 95, PC TRAC Deluxe, Mouse Deluxe, Keyboard Deluxe, Ownrshp: PVT, Founded: 1985, Empl: 50, Timothy C. Barry, Pres & CEO, John J. Cahill, VP Mktng, Daniel J. Mertens, VP Ops, Ronald P. Petralia, VP Sales, Julianne Whitelaw, Mktng Support Mgr

Microspot USA Inc. 12380 Saratoga-Sunnyvale Rd, #6, Saratoga CA 95070 USA; 408/253-2000, 800/622-7568 Fax: 408/253-2055, Co Email: microspot@aol.com, Web URL: microspot.inter.net, Focus: Macintosh software, Prdts: MacPlot, MacPalette, MacInteriors, PhotoFix, 3D World, Ownrshp: PVT, Founded: 1964, Empl: 30, Robert Coulling, Pres, Autumn Moore, Dir Sales & Mktng, Cindy Johnson, Mktng Mgr

Microsystems Engineering Co. (MEC), 2500 Highland Ave, #350, Lombard IL 60148 USA; 630/261-0111, Fax: 630/261-9520, Co Email: info@microsystems.com, Focus: Software and services, Prdts: SysDraw, John Rigas, Pres

MicroTech Conversion Systems Inc. 940 Industrial Ave, Palo Alto CA 94303 USA; 415/424-1174, Fax: 415/424-1176, Focus: Media conversion and duplication systems, Ownrshp: PVT, Founded: 1980, Empl: 15, Sales ($M): 3, Fiscal End: 12/93; Corwin L. Nichols, Pres, Steven L. Shray, VP & COO, Richard D. Wilson, VP Sales, Steve Shray

Microtek Lab Inc. 3715 Doolittle Dr, Redondo Beach CA 90278-1226 USA; 310/297-5000, Fax: 310/297-5050, Focus: Scanners for PCs and Macs, Prdts: Scan Maker III, Scan Maker E-3, Scan Maker 35T, PageWiz, Ownrshp: Sub. Microtek Int'l., Taiwan, Founded: 1980, Empl: 75, Shih-Chi Lee, Pres, Doug Summers, Sales Dir, Mary Ann Whitlock, Mktng Dir, Kai Lam, VP R&D

Microtest Inc. 4747 N 22nd St, Phoenix AZ 85016-4708 USA; 602/952-6400, 800/526-9675 Fax: 602/952-6401, Focus: LAN equipment, Ownrshp: OTC, Stk Sym: MTST, Founded: 1984, Empl: 143, Sales ($M): 52.5, Fiscal End: 12/95; Richard G. Meise, Pres & CEO, Ray M. Healy, VP Sales, Mark W. Johnston, VP Prod Mktng, Carl E. Strain, VP Ops & CFO

MicroTouch Systems Inc. 300 Griffin Brook Dr, Methuen MA 01844 USA; 508/659-9000, Fax: 508/659-9100, Co Email: touch@mts.mhs.compuserve.com, Web URL: microtouch.com, Focus: Touch screens and input devices, Prdts: TruePoint, ClearTek, Ownrshp: OTC, Stk Sym: MTSI, Founded: 1982, Empl: 425, Sales ($M): 76.7, Fiscal End: 12/95; James D. Logan, Chmn, Wes Davis, Pres & CEO, Joel Blenner, VP Sales, James J. Waldron, VP Bus Dev, Geoffrey P. Clear, VP Fin & Admin, Annette M. Burak, Marcom Mgr, Email: aburak@mts.mhs.microtouch.com

MicroVideo Learning Systems 250 Park Ave S, New York NY 10003 USA; 212/777-9595, 800/231-4021 Fax: 212/777-9597, Co Email: info@microvideo.com, Focus: Computer-based training products, Prdts: Windows 95 CD-ROM Learning System, Ownrshp: PVT, Founded: 1982, Empl: 50, Sales ($M): 5, Eric Sternbach, Pres, Email: eric_sternbach@microvideo.com; Travis Hudelson, EVP, Email: travis_hudelson@microvideo.com; Eli Amdur, Corp Sales Mgr, Email: eli_amdur@microvideo.com; Ken Gellerman, VP Govt Sales, Email: ken_gellerman@microvideo.com; Jordan Serlin, Mktng Dir, Email: Jordan@microvideo.com

Microvitec Inc. 4405 Mall Blvd, #340, Union City GA 30291-2044 USA; 404/964-9288, Focus: Monitors, terminals and graphics cards, Ownrshp: OTC, Founded: 1984, Empl: 15, Al Melkerson, Pres

Microware Systems Corp. 1900 NW 114th St, Des Moines IA 50325-7077 USA; 515/224-1929, 800/475-9000 Fax: 515/224-1352, Co Email: info@microware.com, Web URL: micro-wave.com, Focus: Real-time operating systems, Prdts: OS-9, DAVID, FasTrak, Ownrshp: PVT, Founded: 1977, Empl: 200, Ken Kaplan, Pres & CEO, George Barry, CFO, Steve Johnson, EVP New Media, Mike Burgher, EVP Core Technologies, Steve Simpson, Marcom Mgr, Email: steves@microwave.com

Microworks Corp. PO Box 415, Butler NJ 07405-0415 USA; 201/492-1691, Fax: 201/492-1692, Co Email: mworks@microworx.com, Web URL: microworx.com/microworx, Focus: Multimedia, music and graphics software, Prdts: CAMPS, Ownrshp: PVT, Jai Salvatroi, Mgr Ops

MIDI Land Inc. 440 S Lone Hill Ave, San Dimas CA 91773 USA; 909/592-1168, Fax: 909/592-6159, Focus: MIDI sequencing software and sound cards, Founded: 1991

Midisoft Corp. 1605 NW Sammamish Rd #205, Issaquah WA 98027 USA; 206/391-3610, 800/PRO-MIDI Fax: 206/391-3422, Co Email: salesinfo@midisoft.com, Web URL: midisoft.com, Focus: PC music software, Ownrshp: OTC, Stk Sym: MIDI, Founded: 1986, Empl: 45, Sales ($M): 5.4, Fiscal End: 12/95; Larry Foster, Chmn, Pres & CEO, Melinda A. Bryden, CFO, Jon L. Scherrer, VP, Chuck Robb, Dir Mktng

Milkyway Networks Corp. 2055 Gateway Place, #400, San Jose CA 95110 USA; 408/467-3868, Fax: 408/441-9152, Co Email: info@milkyway.com, Web URL: milkyway.com, Focus: Internet and intranet security solutions, Prdts: Black Hole, Ownrshp: PVT, Founded: 1994, Hung Vu, Pres & CEO, Roberto Medrano, VP WW Mktng, David Della-Maggiore, Email: ddella@milkyway.com

Miller Freeman Inc. 600 Harrison St, San Francisco CA 94107 USA; 415/905-2200, 800/829-2505 Fax: 415/905-2389, Web URL: mfi.com, Focus: Computer and high-tech magazines and tradeshows, Prdts: DBMS, OS/2, CADENCE, AI Expert, LAN, STACKS, UNIX Review, Ownrshp: PVT, Graham J.S. Wilson, Chmn, Marshall W. Freeman, Pres & CEO, Thomas L. Kemp, EVP & COO

Miltope Corp. 500 Richardson Rd S, Hope Hull AL 36043-4022 USA; 334/284-8665, 800/645-8673 Fax: 334/613-6302, Focus: Ruggedized computers & peripherals, Prdts: Prowler, Super Bobcat, Vixen, Ownrshp: OTC, Stk Sym: MILT, Founded: 1975, Empl: 350, Sales ($M): 65.7, Fiscal End: 12/95; George K. Webster, Pres & CEO, Bob Kaseta, VP Eng, John Dautel, VP Programs, John Cochran, VP Bus Dev, Greg Myers, Mgr Marcom

Mind Path Technologies 12700 Park Central Dr, #400, Dallas TX 75251 USA; 214/233-9296, 800/634-7424 Fax: 214/233-9308, Co Email: mindpath@aol.com, Focus: Wireless remotes for computer presentations, Prdts: Remote Control for Windows 95, Ownrshp: sub. Proxima Corp., Founded: 1985, Alex T. Tsakiris, Pres, Peter Whitney, VP & GM, Email: pwhitney@aol.com

Mind The Store Inc. 121 Willowdale Ave, #100, N York Ontario M2N 6A3 Canada; 416/226-9520, Fax: 416/226-9527, Web URL: mindthestore.com, Focus: Integrated retail sales management, inventory and fulfillment software apps, tools & svcs, Prdts: Mind the VIRTUAL Store, Ownrshp: PVT, Founded: 1982, Empl: 14

Mindcraft Inc. 410 Cambridge Ave, Palo Alto CA 94306 USA; 415/323-9000, Fax: 415/323-0854, Focus: Testing for POSIX conformance, Ownrshp: PVT, Founded: 1985, Empl: 15, Bruce Weiner, Pres, Email: bruce@mindcraft.com; Charles Karish, VP, Email: karish@mindcraft.com

Minden Group Inc. 236 N Santa Cruz Ave, #237A, Los Gatos CA 95030 USA; 408/399-6645, 800/800-9600 Focus: Memory enhancement solutions, Prdts: SIMMexpander, Michael E. Spencer, VP Mktng & Sales

Mindflight Technology Inc. 1480 Gulf Rd, Point Roberts WA 98281 USA; 604/294-6465, 800/263-3888 Fax: 604/294-1301, Focus: Mass storage devices and CD-ROM readers and recorders, Prdts: M3, HARDPAC, Michael Volker, CEO

Mindscape Inc. 60 Leveroni Ct, Novato CA 94949 USA; 415/883-3000, Fax: 415/883-3303, Focus: Education and entertainment software, Ownrshp: OTC, Stk Sym: TWRX, Founded: 1982, Empl: 335, Sales ($M): 119.6, Fiscal End: 3/93; Robert E. Lloyd, Chmn & CEO, M. Robert Goldberg, EVP & GM, Gordon A. Landies, SVP Comp Prod, James P. Maslyn, SVP & CFO, Nancy Van Natta, Dir Marcom

Mindshare User Group Program 1 Microsoft Way, Redmond WA 98052 USA; 206/882-8080, 800/228-6738 Fax: 206/936-2483, Co Email: mindshar@microsoft.com, Web URL: microsoft.com/mindshar, Focus: Umbrella organization for Microsoft local and special interest groups, Ownrshp: Nonprofit

Minerva 2933 Bunker Hill Ln, #202, Santa Clara CA 95054 USA; 408/970-1780, Fax: 408/982-9877, Focus: Video compression and video publishing systems, Prdts: Minerva Compressionist, Ownrshp: PVT, Founded: 1992, Empl: 50, Mauro Bonomi, CEO

Minnesota Educational Computing Corp. (MECC), 6160 Summit Dr N, Minneapolis MN 55430-4003 USA; 612/569-1500, 800/685-MECC Fax: 612/569-1551, Web URL: mecc.com, Focus: Educational software, Ownrshp: OTC, Stk Sym: MECC, Founded: 1973, Empl: 197, Sales ($M): 33.8, Fiscal End: 3/96; Charles L. Palmer, Chmn, Dale E. LaFrenz, Pres & CEO, Susan L. Schilling, SVP Dev, William P. Wilde, VP Sales & Mktng, Donald W. Anderson, SVP & CFO

Minnesota Mining & Manufacturing (3M), 3M Ctr, St Paul MN 55144-1000 USA; 612/733-1110, 800/364-3577 Fax: 612/736-7775, Co Email: innovation@mmm.com, Web URL: mmm.com, Focus: Magnetic media and electronic devices, Ownrshp: NYSE, Stk Sym: MMM, Founded: 1902, Empl: 85,166, Sales ($M): 13,460, Fiscal End: 12/95; L.D. DeSimone, Chmn & CEO, Lawrence E. Eaton, EVP, Giuliu Agostini, SVP Fin, Ronald A. Mitsch, EVP, David P. Drew, VP Info Tech, D. Drew Davis, VP Pub Affairs

Minnesota Software Assoc. 1200 Washington Ave S, Minneapolis MN 55415 USA; 612/338-4631, Fax: 612/337-3400, Focus: Organization for Minnesota software companies, Ownrshp: Nonprofit

Minolta Corp. 101 Williams Dr, Ramsey NJ 07446-1293 USA; 201/825-4000, Fax: 201/423-0590, Focus: Copiers and laser printers, Ownrshp: Sub Minolta, Japan, Founded: 1959, Sam Kusumoto, Chmn, Hiro Fujii, Pres, Kirk Goto, SVP & GM BED

Minuteman 1455 LeMay Dr, PO Box 815188, Carrollton TX 75007 USA; 214/446-7363, 800/238-7272 Fax: 214/446-9011, Web URL: minuteman-ups.com, Focus: UPS, Prdts: Pro 200, Ownrshp: PVT, Founded: 1982, Steve Lam, CEO, Les Robertson, VP Sales & Mktng, Bill Allen, Dir Mktng, Rick Hunteman, Dir Sales, Pat Ledvig, VP Fin, Judson Rogers, Marcom Mgr

Miramar Systems Inc. 121 Gray Ave, #200B, Santa Barbara CA 93101 USA; 805/966-2432, Fax: 805/965-1824, Co Email: miramar@pacrain.com, Focus: Windows-Mac connectivity software, Prdts: Maclan, Ownrshp: PVT, Founded: 1989, Neal Rabin, Pres

miro Computer Products Inc. 955 Commercial St, Palo Alto CA 94303 USA; 415/855-0940, 800/249-6476 Fax: 415/855-9004, Focus: Multimedia products, Ownrshp: Sub miro, Germany, Bob Butchko, Pres, Mark Gullans, VP Fin, Brenda Connery, VP Sales, John Roman, Dir Mktng, Michael Kuehn, CEO, Marsha Adams, Sr Marcom Mgr

Miros Inc. 572 Washington St, #18, Wellesley MA 02181 USA; 617/235-0330, Fax: 617/235-0720, Web URL: miros.com, Focus: Pattern recognition software, Prdts: TrueFaceR CyberWatch, Founded: 1994, Michael Kuperstein, Pres

Mirror Technologies Inc. PO Box 188, Hopkins MN 55343-0188 USA; 612/270-2718, Focus: Macintosh peripherals, Ownrshp: OTC, Stk Sym: MIRR, Founded: 1985, Empl: 34, Sales ($M): 20.7, Steve Schewe, Pres & CEO, Tom Burke, EVP

Mirror World Inc. 511 Sir Francis Drake Blvd, #201, Greenbrae CA 94904 USA; 415/461-6696, Fax: 415/461-6690, Focus: Visual programming software, Ownrshp: PVT

Mirus Industries Corp. 3350 Scott Blvd Bldg 48, Santa Clara CA 95054-3123 USA; 408/980-6600, Fax: 408/980-6601, Co Email: mirus@applelink.com, Focus: Desktop presentation systems, Ownrshp: PVT, Founded: 1985, Empl: 16, Bruce A. MacKay, Pres & CEO, Duncan Mackay, Chief Eng

Mission Research Corp. 1720 Randolph Rd SE, Albuquerque NM 87106-4245 USA; 505/768-7727, Fax: 505/768-7601, Focus: Scientific simulation software for Power Mac, PC workstations and parallel computers, Prdts: SimCad, IVORY, IPROP, SPHINX, LSP, Magic, SOS, Ownrshp: PVT, Founded: 1970, Empl: 425, Bruce Goplen, VP Advanced Technologies, Email: goplen@mrcwdc.com; Michael A. Mostrom, Div Mgr Plasma Sciences, Email: mmostrom@rt66.com

Mita Copystar America Inc. 225 Sand Rd, PO Box 40008, Fairfield NJ 07004-0008 USA; 201/808-8444, Focus: Copiers and fax machines, Ownrshp: Sub Mita, Japan, Founded: 1973, Empl: 5,500 WW

Mitac International Corp. 75 Ming Sheng E Rd, 8th Floor, Taipei TW Taiwan ROC; 2-501-8231, Fax: 2-501-4265, Web URL: mitac.mic.com, Focus: PCs and peripherals, Ownrshp: PVT, Founded: 1974, Empl: 1,500, Sales ($M): 550, Fiscal End: 12/94; Matthew Miau, CEO, C.S. Ho, Pres, Jerry Woo

Mitek Systems Inc. 6225 Nancy Ridge Dr, San Diego CA 92121 USA; 619/587-9157, 800/367-5660 Fax: 619/587-0825, Focus: Forms processing software, Prdts: QuickStrokes, Ownrshp: PVT, Larry Shiohama, Sales Mgr

Mitel Corp. 350 Legget Dr, PO Box 13089, Kanata Ontario K2K 1X3 Canada; 613/592-2122, 800/267-6244 Fax: 613/592-4784, Focus: Telecom equipment, Ownrshp: NYSE, Stk Sym: MLT, Founded: 1971, Empl: 3,761, Sales ($M): 496.4, Fiscal End: 3/94; Gordon S. Byrn, Chmn, John B. Millard, Pres & CEO, E. Terrell Atwood, VP, Ian Munns, SVP Mktng & Tech, Jean-Jacques Carrier, VP & CFO

MITEM Corp. 640 Menlo Ave, Menlo Park CA 94025 USA; 415/323-6164, Fax: 415/322-8607, Co Email: sales@mitem.com, Web URL: mitem.com, Focus: C/S development tools, Ownrshp: PVT,

Founded: 1985, Aurel Kleinerman, CEO, Gale R. Aguilar, Pres & COO

MITI (MITI), 1080 Marsh Rd, Menlo Park CA 94025 USA; 415/326-5000, Fax: 415/326-5100, Co Email: info@miti.com, Focus: Database tools and utilities, production report writer for relational databases, Prdts: SQL*C++, RPT2C andSQR Workbench, SQR3 Workbench, Ownrshp: PVT, Founded: 1985, Ofir Kedar, Pres, Email: ofirk@miti.com; Larry Pinalto, CFO, Email: larryp@miti.com; Gadi Yedwab, VP Eng, Email: gadiy@miti.com; Bruce Mitchell, VP Mktng, Email: brucem@miti.com; Candice Tuttle, Marcom Dir, Email: candicet@miti.com

Mitsubishi Electric Corp. 2-2-3 Marunouchi, 2-chome, Chiyoda-ku, Tokyo 100 JP-100 Japan; 3-3218-2111, Focus: Computers, peripherals and semiconductors, Ownrshp: FO, Stk Sym: MITSUB, Founded: 1921, Empl: 102,700, Sales ($M): 34,543, Fiscal End: 3/96; Yasuo Endo, EVP

Mitsui Comtek Corp. 12980 Saratoga Ave, Saratoga CA 95070 USA; 408/725-8525, Fax: 408/725-0442, Co Email: @mitsuicomtek.com, Focus: Color LCDs, Empl: 50, Sales ($M): 332.1, Fiscal End: 12/95; Toshihiro Soejima, Pres & CEO, Masaaki Miura, VP & GM, Tadashi Abe, VP & GM, Hironori Furukawa, VP & GM, Koji Matsuo, Mkt Analyst, Email: kmatsuo@mitsuicomek.com

Mobile Insights Inc. 2001 Landings Dr, Mountain View CA 94043 USA; 415/390-9800, Fax: 415/919-0930, Web URL: mobileinsights.com, Focus: Market research and conferences for the mobile computing and communications industry, Ownrshp: PVT, J. Gerry Purdy, Pres & CEO, Email: gpurdy@mobileinsights.com; Michael French, Dir Mkt Res, Email: mfrench@mobileinsights.com; Vanessa Vla-Koch, VP Ops, Email: vvlay@mobileinsight.com

Mobile Products Inc. 1200 E Orangeburg Ave, Modesto CA 95350-4625 USA; 209/526-7119, Fax: 209/526-0328, Focus: Software for peripherals, Prdts: QuickLink, Founded: 1994, Michael P. Zagaris, CEO

Mobile Security Communications 1000 Holcomb Woods Pkwy #210, Roswell GA 30076 USA; 770/594-0424, Fax: 770/594-0697, Focus: Products that incorporate GPS and cellular technologies, Prdts: CarCop, FleetWatch, Ownrshp: PVT, Founded: 1993, Malcolm M. Bibby, Pres & CEO, Sam Johnson, VP, James P. Nickless, VP Ops, William A. Tolhurst, VP Eng

Mobile Telecommunications Technologies Corp. (MTEL), 200 S Lamar, Jackson MS 39201 USA; 601/944-1300, Focus: Wireless paging and text services, Ownrshp: OTC, Sales ($M): 246.0, Fiscal End: 12/95; Bernard Puckett, CEO

MobileComm 1800 E County Line Rd, #300, Ridgeland MS 39157 USA; 601/966-0888, 800/685-5555 Fax: 601/977-1779, Focus: Paging and voice messaging services, Ownrshp: Sub MobileMedia, Founded: 1962, Sales ($M): 250, Fiscal End: 12/94; Steve Pazian, Pres & CEO, Mark Witsaman, SVP Tech, Santo J. Pittsman, VP & CFO, Jean H. Coppenbarger, Mgr Marcom

MobileWare Corp. 2425 N Central Expwy. #1001, Dallas TX 75080-2748 USA; 214/952-1200, 800/260-7450 Fax: 214/690-6185, Co Email: @mobilware.com, Web URL: mobileware.com, Focus: Network connection software for mobile computers, Ownrshp: PVT, Founded: 1991, Jack Blount, Pres & CEO, Peggy Burt, VP Mktng, Email: pburt@mobileware.com

Mobius Computer Corp. 5627 Stoneridge Dr, #312, Pleasanton CA 94588-4037 USA; 510/460-5252, Fax: 510/460-5249, Web URL: mobius.com, Focus: Personal UNIX workstations, Prdts: Protege Series of Unix Servers, Alantra Series of Groupware Servers, Ownrshp: PVT, Founded: 1988, Fiscal End: 12/95; Jeff Webber, Pres, Henry Montgomery, CFO, Craig Stouffer, Dir Prod Mktng

Modgraph Inc. 6-F Gill St, Woburn MA 01801-1721 USA; 617/938-4488, 800/327-9962 Fax: 617/938-4455, Focus: Rugged portable PCs, CRT and LCD monitors, Prdts: Guardian Portable, Guardian-Lite Portable, Ownrshp: PVT, Founded: 1981, Empl: 20, Donald Berman, Pres, Michael Berman, VP Mktng, John Malin, VP

Ops

Molloy Group Inc., The (TMG), 4 Century Dr, Parsippany NJ 07054 USA; 201/540-1212, Fax: 201/292-9407, Co Email: molloy@molly.com, Web URL: molloy.com, Focus: Help desk software, Prdts: Top of Mind, Ownrshp: PVT, Founded: 1985, Empl: 8, Bruce G. Molloy, Chmn & CEO, Peter Dorfman, Dir Mktng, Email: pdorfman@molloy.com

Monarch Avalon 4517 Harford Rd, Baltimore MD 21214 USA; 410/254-9200, Fax: 410/254-0991, Focus: Entertainment software, Prdts: Avalon Hill, Ownrshp: OTC, Stk Sym: MAHI, Founded: 1958, Empl: 175, Sales ($M): 7.6, Fiscal End: 4/91; Jackson Dott, Pres, Phyllis Opolko, VP Mktng

Monotype Typography Inc. 985 Busse Rd, Elk Grove Village IL 60007 USA; 847/718-0400, Fax: 847/718-0500, Co Email: 71333.2361@compuserve.com, Web URL: monotype.com, Focus: Font software, Ownrshp: Sub. Monotype, UK, Founded: 1897, Steve Kuhlman, VP Sales & Mktng, Email: stevek@monotype-usa.com; Steve Kuhlman, Dir Sales

Montage Graphics 2730 Scott Blvd, Santa Clara CA 95050 USA; 408/654-0700, Fax: 408/654-0704, Maria Owen, CEO, James Creede, VP Ops

Moore Information Systems 22276 Buenaventura St, Woodland Hills CA 91364-5006 USA; 818/704-7722, Fax: 818/704-7724, Focus: PC software for employment agencies, Prdts: EASI, Ownrshp: PVT, Founded: 1987, Empl: 3, Bob Moore, Pres, Email: b.moore@ix.netcom.com

Morris Media 2707 Plaza Del Amo, #601, Torrance CA 90503 USA; 310/533-4800, 800/843-3606 Fax: 310/533-1993, Focus: Computer training and Internet access software, Prdts: Internet Connection, Ownrshp: PVT, Founded: 1984, Empl: 30, George Morris, Chmn & CEO, Dawn Morris, Pres, Roger Casas, VP Mktng, Kandra Inga, VP Sales

MorseMcFadden Communications Inc. 610 Market St, #100, Kirkland WA 98033 USA; 206/889-0528, Fax: 206/889-0917, Web URL: morsepr.com, Focus: PR and marketing communications, Ownrshp: PVT, Bob Moore, CEO, Dave McFadden, Pres

Mortice Kern Systems Inc. (MKS), 185 Columbia St W, Waterloo Ontario N2L 5Z5 Canada; 519/884-2251, Fax: 519/884-8861, Co Email: @mks.com, Focus: Software development tools, Prdts: MKS Source Integrity, MKS Toolkit, MKS Code Integrity, Ownrshp: PVT, Founded: 1984, Empl: 112, Sales ($M): 14, Randall Howard, Chmn, Ruth Songhurst, Pres, Ellyn Winters-Robinson, Mgr PR, Email: ellyn@mks.com

Moscom Corp. 3750 Monroe Ave, Pittsford NY 14534 USA; 716/381-6000, Focus: Computer-based telecommunications management systems, Ownrshp: OTC, Stk Sym: MSCM, Founded: 1983, Empl: 157, Sales ($M): 17.6, Fiscal End: 12/95; Albert J. Montevecchio, Chmn, Pres & CEO

Moses Computers 15466 Los Gatos Blvd #201, Los Gatos CA 95032 USA; 408/358-1550, Fax: 408/356-9049, Focus: LAN products, Prdts: ChosenLAN, Ownrshp: PVT, Founded: 1988, Frank Berko, Chmn & CEO, Ted E. Lewis, VP & COO, David McCallen, Email: 632.5150@mcimail.com

Motion Pixels 7320 E Butherus Dr, #100, Scottsdale AZ 85260 USA; 602/951-3288, Fax: 602/951-2683, Co Email: @motionpixels.com, Web URL: motionpixels.com, Focus: Video compression, Ownrshp: Sub. Sirius Corp., William Fidler, EVP SW Dev, Phillip Lowry, VP Bus Dev, Darrell Smith, VP Prod Dev, Jim Matney, Corp Com, Email: jmatney@motionpixels.com

Motorola Computer Group 2900 S Diablo Way, Tempe AZ 85282 USA; 602/438-3000, Focus: Unix computers and VMEbus boards, Ownrshp: Sub. Motorola, Edward F. Staiano, Pres & GM

Motorola Inc. 1303 E Algonquin Rd, Schaumburg IL 60196 USA; 847/576-5000, 800/262-8509 Fax: 847/576-7653, Web URL: mot.com, Focus: Semiconductor, telecommunication and computer products, Ownrshp: NYSE, Stk Sym: MOT, Founded: 1928, Empl: 142,000, Sales ($M): 27,037, Fiscal End: 12/95; Gary L. Tooker,

Vice-Chmn & CEO, Christopher B. Galvin, Pres & COO, Robert W. Galvin, Chmn, John F. Mitchell, Vice Chmn, Carl F. Koeneman, EVP & CFO

Mountain Network Solutions Inc. 360 El Pueblo Dr, Scotts Valley CA 95066-4268 USA; 408/438-6650, Fax: 408/461-3047, Focus: Mass storage systems and software, Ownrshp: Sub. Nakamichi Peripherals, Founded: 1977, Empl: 55, William E. Kunz, Pres & CEO, Joseph Taglia, SVP, Mitchell Cipriano, VP Mktng

MountainGate Data Systems Inc. 9393 Gateway Dr, Reno NV 89511 USA; 702/851-9393, 800/556-0222 Fax: 702/851-5533, Co Email: @mntgte.lockheed.com, Focus: Removable mass storage, Prdts: DataShuttle, IncreMeg, Ownrshp: Sub. Lockheed, Founded: 1970, Empl: 500, Glen T. Williamson, Pres, Ed Wilkes, Dir Sales & Mktng, Dave Challis, Dir Bus Dev, Chris Stone, Dir Bus Dev, Terese Parrish, Marcom Mgr, Email: teresep@mntgte.lockheed.com

Mouse Products Inc. 6211 W Northwest Hwy, #253D, Dallas TX 75225 USA; 214/363-8326, Fax: 214/363-3097, Co Email: teammice@aol.com, Focus: Electronic products and computer accessories, Prdts: Team Mouse, Marc Andres, Pres, David Zoller

Mpath Interactive Inc. 10455-A Bandley Dr, Cupertino CA 95015 USA; 408/342-8800, Fax: 408/342-8822, Co Email: @mpath.com, Web URL: mpath.com, Focus: Software platform for interactive applications, Ownrshp: PVT, Founded: 1995, Empl: 50, Paul Matteucci, CEO

MPSI Systems Inc. (MPSI), 8282 S Memorial Dr, Tulsa OK 74133 USA; 918/250-9611, 800/727-6774 Fax: 918/254-8764, Focus: Decision support systems and software, Ownrshp: OTC, Stk Sym: MPSI, Founded: 1970, Empl: 240, Sales ($M): 23.4, Fiscal End: 9/95; Ronald G. Harper, Chmn, Pres & CEO, Roger A. Finn, VP & COO, Bryan D. Porto, VP

MTI Technology Corp. 4905 E La Palma Ave, Anaheim CA 92807 USA; 714/970-0300, 800/999-9684 Fax: 714/693-2256, Web URL: mti.com, Focus: System storage solutions, Prdts: Fail-Safe, CIQBA, StingRay, Liberator, Infinity, Ownrshp: OTC, Stk Sym: MTIC, Founded: 1987, Empl: 600, Sales ($M): 131.9, Fiscal End: 4/96; Steve Hamerslag, Vice Chmn, Earl Pearlman, Pres & CEO, Bob P. Goetz, SVP Sales, Richard T. Hicksted, CTO, Bob L. Corey, EVP & CFO, Jean Hamerslag, VP Marcom

Multi-Tech Systems Inc. 2205 Woodale Dr, Mounds View MN 55112 USA; 612/785-3500, 800/328-9717 Fax: 612/785-9874, Web URL: multitech.com, Focus: Communications and LAN products, Prdts: MultiCom Tower, Ownrshp: PVT, Founded: 1970, Empl: 373, Sales ($M): 132.0, Fiscal End: 12/95; Raghu Sharma, Pres, Jan Hubbard, Int'l Sales Mgr, Paul Kraska, Prod Mktng Mgr

Multicom Publishing Inc. 188 Embarcadero, 5th Fl., San Francisco CA 94105 USA; 415/777-5300, Fax: 415/777-4729, Co Email: @multicom.com, Web URL: multicom.com, Focus: Multimedia CD-ROM software, Ownrshp: PVT, Founded: 1991, Tamara L. Attard, Chmn & CEO, Paul G. Attard, Pres & COO, Kelly D. Conway, VP Sales & Mktng, Kurt E. Rolland, CTO & VP Res, Joan M. Murray, Mktng Assoc, Email: jmurray@multicom.com

MultiGen 550 S Winchester Blvd, San Jose CA 95128 USA; 408/261-4100, Fax: 408/261-4101, Web URL: multigen.com, Focus: Software, Prdts: MultiGen, GameGen, Ownrshp: PVT, Founded: 1986, Empl: 59, Sales ($M): 8.2, Fiscal End: 12/95; Joe Fantuzzi, Pres, Kevin Rains, CFO

MultiLing International Inc. 40 S 100 W, #300, Kress Bldg, Provo UT 84601 USA; 801/377-2000, Fax: 801/377-7085, Focus: Translation and localization, Prdts: TranslationManager, Ownrshp: PVT, Founded: 1988, Daniel Oswald, Pres

Multimedia Development Group (MDG), 2601 Mariposa St, San Francisco CA 94110 USA; 415/553-2300, Fax: 415/553-2403, Co Email: mdgoffice@aol.com, Focus: Promote multimedia industry growth, Ownrshp: Nonprofit, Empl: 300, Susan Worthman, Exec Dir

Multimedia Telecommunications Assoc. (MMTA), 1820 Jefferson Place NW, #100, Washington DC 20036 USA; 202/296-9800, Fax: 202/296-9810, Web URL: mmta.org, Focus: Protects and expands competitive markets (domestic/foreign) for telecommunications and com, Ownrshp: Nonprofit, Founded: 1970, Empl: 650, William Moroney, Pres, Mary I. Bradshaw, Dir Ind Rel

Multiwave Innovation Inc. 747 Camden Ave, #D, Campbell CA 95008-4147 USA; 408/379-2900, Fax: 408/379-3292, Focus: PC sound cards, Ownrshp: Sub NatSteel, Singapore, James Tan, Pres

MultiWriter Software 763 Stelton St, Teaneck NJ 07666 USA; 201/837-0420, Fax: 201/837-1470, Focus: Multilingual PC software, Ownrshp: PVT, Founded: 1978, Empl: 1, Fiscal End: 12/95; Israel M. Yaker, Pres

Murata Electronics North America Inc. 2200 Lake Park Dr, Smyma GA 30080-7604 USA; 404/436-1300, Fax: 404/436-3030, Focus: Manufactures electronic components, Ownrshp: Sub. Murata, Japan, Founded: 1950, Empl: 1,452 US, Fred Chanoki, Chmn, Tom Yamamoto, Pres, Chris Conlin, VP Mktng, George Beylouny, SVP Ops, Chris Dunlap

Musicware 8654 154th Ave NE, Redmond WA 98052 USA; 206/881-9797, Fax: 206/881-9664, Web URL: halcyon.com/musicware, Focus: Music education software, Ownrshp: PVT, Founded: 1993, Empl: 15, Sales ($M): 1, Daniel S. Peterson, Pres, Thomas L. Peterson, VP, Roger McRea, VP, Dan Santos, Dir Mktng

Musitek 410 Bryant Cr, #K, Ojai CA 93023 USA; 805/646-8051, Fax: 805/646-8099, Focus: Music reading software, Prdts: Midiscan, Ownrshp: PVT, Founded: 1991, Christopher Newell, Pres

Mustang Software Inc. (MSI), 6200 Lake Ming Rd, PO Box 2264, Bakersfield CA 93306 USA; 805/873-2500, 800/999-9619 Fax: 805/873-2599, Co Email: @mustang.com, Web URL: mustang.com, Focus: Communication software, Prdts: Wildcat BBS, Qmodem, Ownrshp: OTC, Stk Sym: MSTG, Founded: 1986, Empl: 50, Sales ($M): 4.8, Fiscal End: 12/95; Jim Harrer, Pres & CEO, Email: jim.harrer@mustang.com; Rick Heming, VP Ops, Email: rick.heming@mustang.com; Scott Hunter, VP Eng, Donald Leonard, VP & CFO, Rod Braly, Dir Sales & Mktng, Email: rod.braly@mustang.com

Mustek Inc. 1702 McGaw Ave, Irvine CA 92714-5732 USA; 714/247-1300, Focus: Scanners and imaging products, Prdts: One-Pass, Ownrshp: PVT, Founded: 1988, Empl: 30, Peter Chen, Pres, Mike Feng, VP, John Blair, Prod Mgr, David Hsieh, Mktng Coord

My Software Co. 2197 E Bayshore Rd, Palo Alto CA 94303 USA; 415/473-3600, Fax: 415/325-0873, Co Email: @mysoftware.com, Web URL: mysoftware.com, Focus: PC productivity software, Ownrshp: OTC, Stk Sym: MYSW, Founded: 1986, Empl: 69, Sales ($M): 13.4, Fiscal End: 12/95; David P. Mans, Pres & CEO, Jim Willenborg, Chmn & VP Mktng, Mike Thoma, VP Prod Dev, Denis J. Squeri, VP Sales, Tim Goode, PR Mgr, Email: timg@mysoftware.com

Mylex Corp. 34551 Ardenwood Blvd, PO Box 5035, Fremont CA 94537-5035 USA; 510/796-6100, 800/776-9539 Fax: 510/745-7654, Web URL: mylex.com, Focus: Disk arrays, motherboards and peripheral boards, Ownrshp: OTC, Stk Sym: MYLX, Founded: 1983, Empl: 140, Sales ($M): 100.4, Fiscal End: 12/95; Ismael Dudhia, Chmn, Al Montross, Pres & CEO, Barry Waxman, VP Sales, Sherman W. Tom, VP Ops, Colleen Gray, VP & CFO, Biz Loscalzo, Marcom Mgr

Mystic River Software Inc. 125 Cambridge Park Dr, Cambridge MA 02140 USA; 617/497-1585, Fax: 617/864-7747, Focus: Visual programming software, Ownrshp: PVT, Jerry Bedrick, Pres, Mary Babic

n th degree software 312 Dorla Ct, PO Box 10430, Zephyr Cove NV 89448 USA; 702/588-4900, 800/428-9797 Fax: 702/588-4901, Co Email: nthdegree@sierra.net, Web URL: nthzone.com, Focus: Software for cost-optimized magazine and newspaper makeup, Prdts: Proteus, The Magazine Architect, Ownrshp: PVT, Founded: 1992, Bill Guttman, CEO, Frank Stock, VP Dev, Woody

Ligget, VP Sales, Carla Scheland, Dir Client Svcs

Nada Chair 771 NE Harding St, Minneapolis MN 55413 USA; 612/623-4436, Fax: 612/331-1613, Focus: Ergonomic accessories, Prdts: Back-Up, Ownrshp: PVT, Victor Toso, Pres

NAFT Computer Service Corp. 611 Broadway, #430, New York NY 10012 USA; 212/982-9800, Fax: 212/979-2999, Focus: Computer service and training, Ownrshp: PVT, Founded: 1994, Empl: 14, Marc H. Bell, Pres, Email: mhb@pfm.net; Marianne McCormack, Service Mgr

NAFT International Ltd. 611 Broadway, #415, New York NY 10012 USA; 212/982-0800, Fax: 212/979-2999, Co Email: naft@applelink.apple.com, Focus: Value added reseller, Ownrshp: PVT, Founded: 1991, Empl: 30, Sales ($M): 6, Fiscal End: 12/94; Marc H. Bell, Pres, Email: mhb@pfm.net; Jennifer Spain, Dir Ops, Email: jen_spain@naft.com; William Jahnke, Sales Mgr, Email: william_jahnke@naft.com

Nakamichi America Corp. 955 Francisco St, Torrance CA 90502 USA; 310/538-8150, Focus: CD-ROM and multimedia products, Ownrshp: Sub Nakamichi, Japan

Nanao USA Corp. 23535 Telo Ave, Torrance CA 90505 USA; 310/325-5202, Fax: 310/530-1679, Focus: PC and Mac monitors, Prdts: FlexScan, Ownrshp: Sub. Nanao, Japan, Founded: 1985, Empl: 30, Sales ($M): 35, Dan Makino, EVP, Chris Ota, Mktng Mgr, Craig Sloss, Prod Mktng Mgr, Pamela K. Hashimoto, Marcom Coord, Email: phashimoto@aol.com

Napersoft Inc. 40 Shuman Blvd, Naperville IL 60563-8466 USA; 708/420-1515, Web URL: napersoft.com, Focus: Software tools for automating correspondence in mainframe environments, Prdts: WinMerge, Bart Carlson, CEO

Nashua Corp. 44 Franklin St, PO Box 2002, Nashua NH 03061-2002 USA; 603/880-2323, Fax: 603/880-5671, Focus: Diskettes and magnetic media, Ownrshp: NYSE, Stk Sym: NSH, Founded: 1904, Empl: 3,100, Sales ($M): 452.1, Fiscal End: 12/95; Joseph A. Baute, Chmn, Gerald G. Garbacz, Pres & CEO, Robin J.T. Clabburn, VP & CTO, Bruce T. Wright, VP, Daniel M. Junius, VP & CFO

National Association of Computer Consultants Businesses 10255 W Higgins, #800, Rosemont IL 60019 USA; 847-297-5607, Focus: Organization for computer consultants

National Association of Desktop Publishers (NADTP), 462 Old Boston St, #62, Topsfield MA 01983 USA; 800/874-4113 Fax: 508/887-6117, Focus: Association for desktop publishing users, Ownrshp: Nonprofit, Founded: 1986, Empl: 13,000, Barry Harrigan, Pres, Susan Sigel, VP

National Center for Education Statistics 555 New Jersey Ave NW, Washington DC 20208 USA; 202/219-1828, Fax: 202/219-1736, Focus: Analyzes data on the performance of the US educational system, Ownrshp: Nonprofit

National Center for Supercomputing Applications (NCSA), 605 E Springfield Ave, Champaign IL 61820 USA; 217/244-3049, Fax: 217/244-9195, Focus: High-performance computing research, Prdts: NCSA Mosaic, Ownrshp: Nonprofit, Founded: 1985, John R. Melchi, Pub Info Officer, Email: jmelchi@ncsa.uiuc.edu

National Commission on Library & Information Sciences 1110 Vermont Ave NW, #820, Washington DC 20005-3522 USA; 202/606-9200, Fax: 202/606-9203, Focus: Independent federal agency advising Pres & Congress on library and information policy, Ownrshp: Nonprofit, Founded: 1970, Peter R. Young, Exec Dir

National Computer Security Assoc. (NCSA), 10 S Courthouse Ave, Carlisle PA 17013 USA; 717/258-1816, Fax: 717/243-8642, Co Email: @ncsa.com, Web URL: ncsa.com, Focus: Microcomputer security and computer viruses, Ownrshp: Nonprofit, Founded: 1989, Empl: 1,600, Robert C. Bales, Exec Dir, Michel E. Kabay, Dir Ed, David M. Harper, Dir Mktng, Peter S. Tippett, Pres, Larry Teien, PR Mgr

National Computer Systems Inc. 11000 Prairie Lakes Dr, PO Box 9365, Minneapolis MN 55344 USA; 612/829-3000, Fax: 612/

829-3186, Focus: Computer-based optical mark reading systems, Ownrshp: OTC, Stk Sym: NLCS, Founded: 1962, Empl: 2,700, Sales ($M): 336.9, Fiscal End: 1/95; Charles W. Oswald, Chmn, Russell A. Gullotti, Pres & CEO, Robert C. Bowen, SVP, Donald J. Gibson, SVP, Jeffrey W. Taylor, VP & CFO

National Computers Plus (NCP), 4610 S 101st E Ave, PO Box 470123, Tulsa OK 74147 USA; 918/664-0690, 800/522-2910 Fax: 918/664-7350, Focus: Workstations, Prdts: Viper 300 Series, Viper 100 Series, Ownrshp: PVT, Founded: 1994, James O. Sutton II, Chmn & CEO

National Cristina Foundation (NCF), 591 W Putnam Ave, Greenwich CT 06830 USA; 203/622-6000, 800/274-7846 Fax: 203/622-6270, Co Email: ncfnasd@gteens.com, Focus: Obtains used or surplus microcomputers for free distribution to groups serving disabled an, Ownrshp: Nonprofit, Founded: 1985, Dr. Yvette Marrin, Pres

National Data Corp. National Data Plaza, Atlanta GA 30329-2010 USA; 404/728-2000, Fax: 404/728-2551, Focus: On-line financial, telemarketing and health care services, Ownrshp: NYSE, Stk Sym: NDC, Founded: 1967, Empl: 1,900, Sales ($M): 325.8, Fiscal End: 5/96; Robert A. Yellowlees, Chmn & CEO, J. David Lyons, EVP Mktng & Sales, Jerry W. Braxton, EVP & CFO, Donald B. Graham, SVP Ops, Joe A. Rose, EVP Info Serv

National Education Training Group (NETG), 1751 W Diehl Rd, 2nd Fl., Naperville IL 60563-9099 USA; 708/369-3000, Fax: 708/983-4863, Focus: Technology-enhanced learning products, Prdts: Precision Learning, Ownrshp: Sub. National Education Corp., Founded: 1969, Sales ($M): 54.o, Chuck Moran, Pres, Jerry Nine, VP Sales & Mktng, Jim L'Allier, VP Prod Dev, Mark Townsend, VP Adv Tech, Tom McDonald, VP & CFO

National Electronics Service Dealers Assoc. (NESDA), 2708 W Berry St, Ft. Worth TX 76109-2356 USA; 817/921-9061, Fax: 817/921-3741, Focus: Association for computer and electronic service industry, Ownrshp: Nonprofit, Founded: 1963, Empl: 900, Clyde W. Nabors, Exec Dir, Barbara Rubin, Bus Mgr, Ln H. Norman, Pres

National Federation of Abstracting & Information Services (NFAIS), 1518 Walnut St, #307, Philadelphia PA 19102-3403 USA; 215/893-1561, Fax: 215/893-1564, Co Email: nfais@hslc.org, Focus: Information for producers, distributors and corporate users of information, Ownrshp: Nonprofit, Founded: 1958, Empl: 70, Ann Marie Cunningham, Exec Dir

National Instruments Corp. 6504 Bridge Point Pkwy, Austin TX 78730-5039 USA; 512/794-0100, 800/433-3488 Fax: 512/794-8411, Co Email: info@natinst.com, Web URL: natinst.com, Focus: Data acquisition, instrument control, hardware and software, Prdts: LabView, LabWindows, Ownrshp: OTC, Stk Sym: NATI, Founded: 1976, Empl: 1,062, Sales ($M): 164.8, Fiscal End: 12/95; James Truchard, Chmn, Pres & CEO, Carsten Thomsen, VP Eng, Donald J. Nadon, VP Sales, Timothy R. Dehne, VP Mktng, Joel B. Rollins, VP & CFO, Tad Driart, Media Rel Spec

National Power Laboratory PO Box 280, Necedah WI 54646 USA; 608/565-7200, Fax: 608/565-2929, Focus: Nationwide power quality testing, Ownrshp: PVT, Founded: 1988, Robert E. Jurewicz, Dir

National Semiconductor Corp. 2900 Semiconductor Dr, PO 58090, Santa Clara CA 95020-8090 USA; 408/721-5000, Fax: 408/739-9803, Web URL: natsemi.com, Focus: Semiconductors, Ownrshp: NYSE, Stk Sym: NSM, Founded: 1967, Empl: 22,300, Sales ($M): 2,623.1, Fiscal End: 5/96; Brian L. Halla, Pres & CEO, Patrick J. Brockett, EVP Sales & Mktng, Donald Macleod, EVP & CFO, Mike Bereziuk, SVP, Charles P. Carinalli, SVP & CTO

National Software Testing Laboratories Inc. 625 Ridge Pike, Bldg. D, Conshohocken PA 19428-1180 USA; 610/941-9600, 800/257-9402 Fax: 610/941-9952, Focus: Comparison, compatibility and usability testing of PC products, Ownrshp: PVT, Founded: 1983, Empl: 75

National Systems Programmers Assoc. (NaSPA), 4811 S 76th St, #210, Milwaukee WI 53220-9933 USA; 414/423-2420, Fax: 414/423-2433, Focus: Association for corporate computing professionals, Ownrshp: Nonprofit, Founded: 1986, Empl: 29,000, Scott Sherer, Pres, Emit Hurdelbrink, VP

National Technical Information Service (NTIS), 5285 Port Royal Rd, Springfield VA 22161 USA; 703/487-4650, Fax: 703/321-8547, Focus: Central source for sale of government-sponsored scientific & technical reports including f, Ownrshp: Nonprofit, Founded: 1945, Donald R. Johnson, Dir NTIS, Renee Edwards, Pub Aff Dir

National Venture Capital Assoc. 1655 N Fort Myer Dr, #700, Arlington VA 22209 USA; 703/351-5267, Fax: 703/351-5268, Focus: Venture capital industry trends, Ownrshp: Nonprofit, Empl: 300, Daniel Kingsley, Exec Dir

Natural Language Inc. (NLI), PO Box 5729, Walnut Creek CA 94596-1729 USA; 510/814-0500, Fax: 510/814-9983, Co Email: info@nli.com, Focus: Natural language front-end for database software, Prdts: ICon, Ownrshp: PVT, Founded: 1984, Empl: 55, John Manferdelli, Pres, Betty Bloom, Dir Client Svcs

Natural MicroSystems Corp. 8 Erie Dr, Natick MA 01760-1339 USA; 508/650-1300, Fax: 508/650-1352, Focus: Voice processing products, Ownrshp: OTC, Stk Sym: NMSS, Founded: 1983, Empl: 47, Sales ($M): 32.8, Fiscal End: 12/95; Robert Schechter, Pres, David Levi, Chmn & CEO, Ronald J. Bleakney, VP Sales & Mktng, George D. Kontopidis, VP Eng, R. Brough Turner, SVP Ops

Navision Software US Inc. 1 Meca Way, Norcross GA 30093 USA; 770/564-8000, Fax: 770/564-8010, Co Email: 75057.2155@compuserve.com, Focus: Accounting software, Prdts: Financials' C/SIDE, Ownrshp: Sub PC&C, Denmark, Founded: 1993, Rene Stockner, GM, Dave Vitak, Dir Prod Mktng

NaviSoft Inc. 8619 Westwood Ctr Dr, Vienna VA 22182-2285 USA; 703/448-8700, Focus: Internet publishing software, Prdts: NaviPress, NaviServer, Ownrshp: Sub America Online, David C. Cole, Pres, Lydia Dobyns, VP & GM, Linda Dozier, VP & CTO

NCI Information Systems Inc. 8260 Greensboro Dr, #400, McLean VA 22102 USA; 703/893-8623, Focus: Computer services and systems integration, Ownrshp: PVT, Empl: 350, Sales ($M): 24.0, Fiscal End: 12/94; Charles K. Narang, Pres

NCL America Computer Products Inc. 1031 E Duane Ave, #H, Sunnyvale CA 94086 USA; 408/737-2496, Fax: 408/730-1621, Focus: Systems integration, Ownrshp: Sub. National Computer, Japan, Founded: 1986, Sales ($M): 68, Mike Kirby, Chmn & CEO, Mark Miyakawa, Pres & COO, Karen Trifari, VP & CFO

NCR Corp. 1700 S Patterson Blvd, Dayton OH 45479 USA; 513/445-5000, Focus: Mainframes, minicomputers, microcomputers and peripherals, Ownrshp: Sub. AT&T, Founded: 1884, Empl: 41,100, Sales ($M): 8,200, Fiscal End: 12/95; Lars Nyberg, Chmn & CEO, Alice Lusk, SVP & CIO, Richard Evans, SVP

nCUBE Corp. 110 Marsh Dr, Foster City CA 94404 USA; 415/593-9000, Fax: 415/508-5408, Focus: Interactive media servers, Ownrshp: PVT, Founded: 1983, Empl: 170, Ron Dilbeck, Pres & CEO, Anne Banta, Dir Corp Com

Neal Nelson & Associates 330 N Wabash Ave, Chicago IL 60611-3604 USA; 312/755-1000, Fax: 312/755-1010, Co Email: office@nna.com, Web URL: nna.com, Focus: Performance tests of multiuser systems, networks, web software, databases & other hardware, Ownrshp: PVT, Founded: 1973, Empl: 11, Neal Nelson, Pres

NEBS Software & Computer Forms 20 Industrial Park Dr, Nashua NH 03062 USA; 603/880-5100, Fax: 603/880-5102, Focus: Software and computer forms, Prdts: One-Write Plus, Paper Magic, Ownrshp: Sub. NEBS, Empl: 200, Jerry Kokos, GM, Joe Dugan, Dir Mktng, John Vasil, Dir Sales, Chuck McGonagle, Sr Prod Mgr

NEC America 8 Corporate Ctr Dr, Melville NY 11747 USA; 516/753-7000, Ownrshp: Sub NEC, Japan, Mineo Sugiyama, Pres & CEO, Kotaro Kato, SVP

NEC Corp. 7-1 Shiba 5-chome, Minkato-ku, Tokyo 108-01 JP-108-01 Japan; 3-3454-1111, Fax: 3-3798-1510, Web URL: nec.co.jp, Focus: Computers, telecommunication, semiconductors and consumer electronic products, Ownrshp: OTC, Stk Sym: NIPNY, Founded: 1899, Empl: 147,910, Sales ($M): 41,095, Fiscal End: 3/96; Dr. Tadahiro Sekimoto, Chmn, Hisashi Kaneko, Pres, Akira Kabayashi, Sr EVP, Tadashi Suzuki, Sr EVP, Ken Fukuchi, Mgr PR

NEC Electronics Inc. 475 Ellis St, PO Box 7241, Mountain View CA 94039-7241 USA; 415/960-6000, Fax: 415/965-6130, Focus: ICs and electronic components, Ownrshp: Sub NEC, Japan, Founded: 1981, Empl: 2,900, Sales ($M): 1,200, Fiscal End: 3/94; Kunisho Saito, Pres & CEO, Allison C. Niday, Corp Com, Email: aniday@mcimail.com

NEC Technologies Inc. 1414 Massachusetts Ave, Boxborough MA 01719-2298 USA; 508/264-8000, 800/632-4636 Fax: 508/264-8488, Web URL: nec.com, Focus: PCs, minicomputers and peripherals, Ownrshp: Sub. NEC, Japan, Founded: 1989, Empl: 1,800, Sales ($M): 1,500, Jerry Benson, Pres, Dale L. Fuller, VP, Jan Rasmussen, Dir PR

Nelco Inc. 3130 S Ridge Rd, PO Box 10208, Green Bay WI 54307-0208 USA; 414/337-1000, Fax: 414/336-5130, Focus: Tax preparation and accounting software, Prdts: Directronic Electronic Filing Software, Stk Sym: DELUX, Founded: 1952, Empl: 200, Joseph Langer, Pres, Cary Parker, VP Mktng, Tom Reader, Marcom

Nelson's Computer Services PO Box 2601, Glenview IL 60025 USA; 708/965-7325, Co Email: 70274.1772@compuserve.com, Focus: Software and database of 7,600 motels, Prdts: National INNdex, Ownrshp: PVT, Greg Nelson, Pres

Neon Software Inc. 3685 Mt. Diablo Blvd #203, Lafayette CA 94549-3736 USA; 510/283-9771, Fax: 510/283-6507, Web URL: neon.com, Focus: Network software tools, Prdts: NetMinder, LANsurveyor, RouterCheck, TrafficWatch II, Ownrshp: PVT, Founded: 1989, Michael J. Swan, Pres, Dwight G. Barker, Sales Dir, Email: dwight@neon.com

NeoSoft Corp. 354 NE Greenwood Ave, #108, Bend OR 97701-4631 USA; 541/389-5489, 800/545-1392 Fax: 541/388-8221, Co Email: sysadmin@neosoftware.com, Web URL: neosoftware.com/~neosft, Focus: PC utility software, Prdts: QuikMenu, NeoPaint, NeoShow, Phantom Screen, NeoBook, NeoSoft Viewer, Ownrshp: PVT, Founded: 1990, Empl: 15, David Riley, Pres & CEO, Kevin N. Daniel, Dir Mktng, Email: knd@neosoftware.com; T.W. Martin, Dir Sales, Email: twm@neosoftware.com; Robert Brittsan, Dir Applied Tech

Neostar Retail Group Inc. 10741 King William Dr, Dallas TX 75220-2414 USA; 214/401-9000, Fax: 214/401-9002, Focus: A chain of 740+ software specialty stores, Ownrshp: OTC, Stk Sym: NEOS, Founded: 1983, Empl: 1,400, Sales ($M): 513.5, Fiscal End: 2/96; James B. McCurry, Chmn & CEO, Daniel A. DeMatteo, Pres & COO, Opal P. Ferraro, CFO, Roxanne M. Koepsell, VP Mktng, Patrick D. McCullough, VP Info Syst

net.Genesis 56 Rogers St, Cambridge MA 02142-1119 USA; 617/577-9800, Fax: 617/577-9850, Co Email: info@netgen.com, Web URL: netgen.com, Focus: Internet software and services, Ownrshp: PVT, Bradley A. Feld, Chmn, Rajat Bhargava, Pres & CEO, Matthew J. Cutler, Dir Bus Dev, Matthew K. Gray, CTO, Eric R. Richard, VP Eng

NetCom On-Line Communications Services Inc. 3031 Tisch Way, San Jose CA 95128-2541 USA; 408/345-2600, 800/353-6600 Fax: 408/241-9145, Web URL: netcom.com, Focus: TCP/IP network and internet services, Ownrshp: OTC, Stk Sym: NETC, Founded: 1988, Sales ($M): 52.4, Fiscal End: 12/95; Robert J. Rieger, Chmn & CEO, David W. Garrison, Pres & COO, Warren J. Kaplan, EVP & CFO, Donald Hutchison, VP Sales & Mktng, Robert Tomasi, VP Ops, Jeannie Slone, Email: jslone@ix.netcom.com

NetCon 53 Knightsbridge Rd, Piscataway NJ 08854-3925 USA; 908/756-3200, Fax: 908/756-9220, Focus: DOS to Unix connectivity, Ownrshp: PVT

NetCorp 8 Place du Commerce, bureau 200, Brossard Quebec J4W 3H2 Canada; 514/923-4040, Fax: 514/923-4882, Co Email: info@netcorp.qc.ca, Focus: Network products, Prdts: WINswitch, OPENswitch, Founded: 1992

NetDynamics 185 Constitution Dr, Palo Alto CA 94025 USA; 415/969-6665, Fax: 415/617-5920, Web URL: w3spider.com, Focus: Web/database tools, Ownrshp: PVT, Founded: 1995, Empl: 31, Zack Rinat, CEO

NetFrame Systems Inc. 1545 Barber Ln, Milpitas CA 95035 USA; 408/474-1000, Fax: 408/474-4190, Web URL: netframe.com, Focus: LAN servers, Ownrshp: OTC, Stk Sym: NETF, Founded: 1987, Empl: 284, Sales ($M): 76.4, Fiscal End: 12/95; Robert L. Puette, Pres & CEO, Carl Amdahl, Chmn & CTO, Marty C. DiPietro, VP Ops, John W. Van Siclen, VP Mktng & Sales, David S. Dury, VP & CFO

NetManage Inc. 10725 N De Anza Blvd, Cupertino CA 95014-2030 USA; 408/973-7171, Fax: 408/257-6405, Co Email: sales@netmenage.com, Web URL: netmanage.com, Focus: PC network and Internet access software, Prdts: Chameleon, ECCO, Ownrshp: OTC, Stk Sym: NETM, Founded: 1990, Empl: 600, Sales ($M): 125.4, Fiscal End: 12/95; Zvi Alon, Chmn, Pres & CEO, Amatzia Ben-Artzi, VP Bus Dev, Larry Hootnick, COO, Robert Williams, VP Mktng, Walter Amaral, SVP & CFO, Donna Loughlin, PR Mgr, Email: donna@netmanage.com

NetPro Computing Inc. 7150 E Camelback Rd, #100, Scottsdale AZ 85251-1240 USA; 602/941-3600, 800/998-5090 Fax: 602/941-3610, Co Email: info@netpro.com, Web URL: info@netpro.com, Focus: Network software, Prdts: Admin ToolBox, DS Expert NetWare, SpaceGuard, Founded: 1991, Empl: 30, Randy Bradley, Chmn & CTO, Joanne Carthey, Pres & CEO, Edward F. Gannon, Dir Mktng & Sales, Jason Lamb, Prod Mgr, Email: jasonl@netpro.com

Netrix Corp. 13595 Dulles Technology Dr, Herndon VA 22071 USA; 703/742-6000, Fax: 703/742-4048, Web URL: netrix.com, Focus: Network products, Ownrshp: OTC, Stk Sym: NTRX, Founded: 1985, Empl: 192, Sales ($M): 48.2, Fiscal End: 12/95; Charles W. Stein, Pres & CEO, J. Gerard Cregan, VP Ops, John K. Mullaney, VP Sales & Mktng, Lynn C. Chapman, VP Prod Dev, Richard G. Tennant, VP & CFO, Renate Neely, Dir Corp Com, Email: rneely@netrix.com

Nets Inc. 639 Alpha Dr, Pittsburgh PA 15238 USA; 412/967-3500, 800/569-9789 Fax: 412/967-3504, Co Email: info@industry.net, Web URL: industry.net, Focus: Online services and publications, Prdts: Industry.Net Report, Ownrshp: PVT, Founded: 1990, Empl: 150, Donald H. Jones, Chmn, Email: donjones@industry.net; Jim Manzi, Pres & CEO, Email: jimmanzi@industry.net; David Mawhinney, VP Adv Apps, Email: davemawhinney@industry.net; Cutch Moore, VP Sales, Email: cutchmoore@industry.net; Tom Jones, VP Mktng, Email: tomjones@industry.net; Autumn J. Jones, Email: autumn@industry.net

Netscape Communications Corp. 501 E Middlefield Rd, Mountain View CA 94043-4042 USA; 415/254-1900, Fax: 415/528-4124, Co Email: info@mcom.com, Web URL: netscape.com, Focus: Internet navigation software, Ownrshp: OTC, Stk Sym: NSCP, Founded: 1994, Empl: 600+, Sales ($M): 80.7, Fiscal End: 12/95; James H. Clark, Chmn, James Barksdale, Pres & CEO, Marc Andreessen, SVP Tech, Rosanne M. Siino, Dir Com

NetSoft 31 Technology Dr, #200, Irvine CA 92718-2322 USA; 714/789-8000, Fax: 714/753-0810, Focus: PC connectivity software, Ownrshp: PVT, Founded: 1980

NetStream Inc. 101 W Mall Plaza, 1st Fl., Carnegie PA 15106 USA; 412/276-9600, Fax: 412/276-6005, Co Email: info@netstream.com, Focus: Mobile computing for PCs, Prdts: NETGAIN, Ownrshp: PVT, Founded: 1993, Empl: 7, Bruce J. DaCosta, Pres & CEO, Stephen Davis, Dir Mktng

NETSYS Technologies Inc. 100 Hamilton Ave, #175, Palo Alto CA 94301 USA; 415/833-7500, Fax: 415/833-7597, Web URL:

netsystech.com, Focus: Enterprise network problem solving and planning software tools, Founded: 1991, Herbert Madan, Pres & CEO, Joel Evanier, VP Sales & Mktng, Elise Raphael

NetWare Users Int'l. (NUI), 122 E 1700 S, Provo UT 84606 USA; 801/222-6000, 800/638-9273 Focus: Umbrella organization of over 220 worldwide Novell NetWare user groups, Ownrshp: Nonprofit, Founded: 1985, Empl: 90,000

Network Appliance Corp. 295 N Bernardo Ave, Mountain View CA 94043 USA; 415/428-5100, Fax: 415/428-5151, Co Email: info@netapp.com, Focus: File server, Prdts: FAServer, Ownrshp: PVT, Founded: 1992, Empl: 70, Sales ($M): 2, Fiscal End: 3/94; Daniel J. Warmenhoven, Pres & CEO, Michael Malcolm, SVP Strategic Dev, James Lau, VP Eng, Email: jlau@netapp.com; Tom Mendoza, VP NA Sales, Email: tmendoza@netapp.com; Ray G. Myers, VP Quality, Email: rgm@netapp.com; Chad Davies, Mgr Marcom, Email: chad@netapp.com

Network Computing Devices Inc. (NCD), 350 N Bernardo Ave, Mountain View CA 94043-3514 USA; 415/694-0650, Fax: 415/961-7711, Co Email: info@ncd.com, Web URL: ncd.com, Focus: X-terminals and X-server software, Ownrshp: OTC, Stk Sym: NCDI, Founded: 1988, Empl: 406, Sales ($M): 142.0, Fiscal End: 12/95; Edward Staiano, Chmn, Edward Marinaro, Pres & CEO, Lorraine Hariton, VP Bus Dev, Michael D. Harrigan, VP, Jack A. Bradley, VP & CFO, Carey Mitchell, PR Mgr, Email: carey@ncd.com

Network Connection Inc., The (TNCi), 1324 Union Hill Rd, Alpharetta GA 30201 USA; 770/751-0889, 800/327-4853 Fax: 770/751-1884, Web URL: tnc.www.com, Focus: Media file servers and digital video solutions, Prdts: HiPer Cheetah Servers, Wil Riner, Chmn & CEO, Allan Regenbauma, VP Sales, Email: regenbauma@tnc.www.com; Jennifer Riner, Mktng, Email: rinerjl@tnc.www.com

Network Equipment Technologies Inc. (NET), 800 Saginaw Dr, Redwood City CA 94063-4740 USA; 415/366-4400, Fax: 415/780-5160, Web URL: net.com, Focus: Network products, Ownrshp: NYSE, Stk Sym: NWK, Founded: 1983, Empl: 1,164, Sales ($M): 338.9, Fiscal End: 3/96; John B. Arnold, Chmn, Joseph J. Francesconi, Pres & CEO, Craig M. Gentner, SVP & CFO, Raymond E. Peverell, SVP Sales & Mktng, David P. Owen, VP Corp Dev & Strat

Network General Corp. 4200 Bohannon Dr, Menlo Park CA 94025 USA; 415/473-2000, 800/764-3337 Fax: 415/321-0855, Co Email: support@ngc.com, Web URL: ngc.com, Focus: Network fault and performance management software, Prdts: Expert Sniffer Network Analyzer, Foundation Manager, Ownrshp: OTC, Stk Sym: NETG, Founded: 1986, Empl: 700, Sales ($M): 188.8, Fiscal End: 3/96; Harry Saal, Chmn, Leslie G. Denend, Pres & CEO, Jim Richardson, VP & CFO, Richard H. Lewis, VP WW Sales, Jim Whitacker, CIO, Erin Bergamo, PR Specialist, Email: erinb@ngc.com

Network Long Distance Inc. 525 Florida St, Baton Rouge LA 70801-1708 USA; 504/343-3125, Focus: Telecom services, Ownrshp: OTC, Stk Sym: NTWK, Empl: 23, Sales ($M): 4.5, Fiscal End: 3/93; Michael M. Ross, Pres & CEO, Joseph M. Edelman, VP

Network Management Forum 1201 Mt. Kimble Ave, Morristown NJ 07960-6628 USA; 201/425-1900, Fax: 201/425-1515, Web URL: mnf.org, Focus: Association for network interoperability, Ownrshp: Nonprofit, Elizabeth Adams, Managing Dir

Network Music Inc. 15150 Ave of Science, San Diego CA 92128 USA; 619/451-6400, 800/854-2075 Fax: 619/451-5619, Focus: Music, sound effects and production elements for Windows, Prdts: Presentation Audio, Founded: 1979, Bruce Tucker, VP Bus, Larry Anderson, PR Dir

Network Peripherals 1371 McCarthy Blvd, Milpitas CA 95035 USA; 408/321-7300, Fax: 408/321-9218, Co Email: @npix.com, Web URL: npix.com, Focus: Network products, Ownrshp: OTC, Stk Sym: NPIX, Founded: 1989, Empl: 104, Sales ($M): 47.1, Fiscal

End: 12/95; Pauline L. Alker, Pres & CEO, Truman Cole, CFO, Gordon L. Stitt, VP & GM Spec Prod, Mark S. Smith, VP Sales, John P. Chan, VP Ops, Don Morrison

Network Professional Assoc. (NPA), 151 E 1700 S, Provo UT 84606 USA; 801/379-0330, Fax: 801/379-0331, Focus: Organization for network computing service professionals, Ownrshp: Nonprofit, Founded: 1991, Empl: 11,000, Berkeley Geddes, Pres, Bruce Law, Dir Mktng, Keith Parsons, Tech Mgr, Gerry Dye, Dir Int'l Rel

Network TeleSystems (NTS), 550 Del Rey Ave, Sunnyvale CA 94086 USA; 408/523-8100, Fax: 408/523-8118, Focus: TCP/IP software, Prdts: TCP Pro, Ownrshp: PVT, John Davidson, Pres, Mike Homer, VP Mktng, Peter Manzo

Network Translation Inc. 1901 Embarcadero Rd, Palo Alto CA 94303 USA; 415/494-6387, Fax: 415/424-9110, Co Email: info@translation.com, Focus: Internet security products, Prdts: PIX, Ownrshp: PVT, John Mayes, Pres, Rebecca Jepsen

Network-1 Software & Technology PO Box 8370, Long Island City NY 11101 USA; 718/932-7599, 800/638-9751 Fax: 718/545-3754, Focus: Internet security software, Prdts: Net1-FireWall, Ownrshp: PVT, Brian J. Wade, VP Sales & Mktng, Bill Hancock, EVP

Networks Northwest Inc. 15379 NE 90th St, Redmond WA 98052-3562 USA; 206/391-0618, Fax: 206/391-0834, Focus: Communication hardware and software, Prdts: Bridges, Routers, Ownrshp: PVT, Founded: 1990, Empl: 25, Sales ($M): 4, Fiscal End: 12/93; John J. Hansen, Pres & CEO, Email: jhansen@networksnw.com

NeuralWare Inc. 202 Parkwest Dr, Pittsburgh PA 15275-1002 USA; 412/787-8222, Fax: 412/787-8220, Co Email: @neuralware.com, Web URL: neuralware.com, Focus: Neural network software, training, services, Prdts: NeuralWorks, Ownrshp: PVT, Founded: 1987, Empl: 30, Jane Klimasauskas, Pres & CEO, Tim Graettinger, VP Prod Dev, David Spitzer, VP & CFO, Tiffeny Lee, Mktng Mgr, Dan Ketelaar, Email: dan@neuralware.com

New Dimension Software 1 Park Plaza, 11th Fl, Irvine CA 92717 USA; 714/757-4300, Web URL: ddddf.com, Focus: C/S software, Ownrshp: Sub New Dimension, Israel, Founded: 1983, Empl: 300, Sales ($M): 35.7, Fiscal End: 12/95; Roni Einav, Chmn, Dan Barnea, CEO, Dalia Prahsker, Pres

New England Business Service Inc. (NEBS), 500 Main St, Groton MA 01471-9811 USA; 508/448-6111, Fax: 800/234-4324, Web URL: nebs.com, Focus: Business forms, software and supplies, Prdts: One-Write Plus, Paper Magic, Ownrshp: OTC, Founded: 1954, Empl: 2,014, Sales ($M): 255.0, Fiscal End: 6/96; Robert J. Murray, Chmn, Pres & CEO, Kenneth R. Kaisen, VP Info Syst, Edward M. Bolesky, VP Ops, Russell V. Corsini Jr., VP & CFO

New Era Systems Services Ltd. 425 First St SW, # 710, Calgary Alberta T2P 3L8 Canada; 403/231-9800, 800/531-7111 Fax: 403/266-6767, Co Email: @newera.ab.ca, Focus: Software to distribute, backup and archive distributed data, Prdts: Harbor, Ownrshp: PVT, Founded: 1988, Empl: 50, Ben Dulley, Pres, John Eddy, VP Fin, Al Saurette, VP Bus Dev

New Hampshire High Tech Council PO Box 10308, Bedford NH 03110-0308 USA; 603/647-8324, Fax: 603/668-3906, Focus: High-tech organization for New Hampshire, Ownrshp: Nonprofit

New Horizons Computer Learning Centers Inc. 1231 E Dyer Rd, #140, Santa Ana CA 92705-5605 USA; 714/556-1220, Fax: 714/556-4612, Focus: Computer training centers, Prdts: Computer Training, Stk Sym: HAND, Founded: 1982, Empl: 400, Tom Bresman, CEO, Chuck Kinch, COO, Bob McMillan, CFO, Gene Longobardi, VP Ops

New Information Industry Cooperative Endeavor (NIICE), c/o X/Open, 1010 El Camino Real, #380, Menlo Park CA 94025 USA; 415/323-7992, Fax: 415/323-8204, Co Email: @xopen.co.uk, Focus: Database software interoperability, Ownrshp: Nonprofit, Founded: 1995

New Machine Publishing 350 Main St, Venice CA 90291-2524

USA; 310/581-3600, Fax: 310/581-3644, Co Email: @newma-chine.com, Focus: Adult CD-ROM software, Ownrshp: PVT, Rob Neason, Pres, Email: neason@newmachine.com

New Media Corp. (NMC), 1 Technology Dr, #A, Irvine CA 92718-2339 USA; 714/453-0100, 800/453-0550 Fax: 714/453-0550, Focus: PCMCIA peripherals, Ownrshp: PVT, Founded: 1992, Carl C. Perkins, Pres & CEO, Rodney J. Corder, VP Eng, Eric A. McAfee, CFO, Jay Kerutis, VP Mktng & Sales, Saundy Morrison Hill

Newbridge Microsystems 603 March Rd, Kanata Ontario K2K 2M5 Canada; 613/599-3600, 800/267-7231 Fax: 613/592-1320, Web URL: newbridge.com/microsystems, Focus: Semiconductor interface components, Prdts: Universe, LIFE, Trooper, Spanner, Ownrshp: Sub. Newbridge Networks Corp., Stk Sym: NNC, Founded: 1985, Empl: 40, Adam Chowaniec, Pres, Jim Roche, VP & GM

Newbridge Networks Corp. 3665 Kingsway, #350, Vancouver BC V5R 5W2 Canada; 604/430-3600, Fax: 604/435-8181, Web URL: newbridge.com, Focus: Network products, Ownrshp: OTC, Stk Sym: NNCXF, Sales ($M): 921.2, Fiscal End: 4/96; Terry Matthews, Chmn

NewCom Inc. 31166 Via Colinas, Westlake Village CA 91362 USA; 818/597-3200, Fax: 818/597-3210, Focus: Communications and multimedia products, Ownrshp: Sub. Aura Systems, Founded: 1994, Sonia Kiarashi

Newer Technology 7803 E Osie, #105, Wichita KS 67207 USA; 316/685-4904, 800/678-3726 Fax: 316/685-9368, Co Email: info@newertech.com, Web URL: newertech.com, Focus: Memory and mass storage, Prdts: GURU, Ownrshp: PVT, Founded: 1984, James Wiebe, Pres, Roger Kasten, VP Tech, Gene Hildebrandt, VP Sales & Mktng

NewGen Systems Corp. 3345 Cadillac Ave, #A, Costa Mesa CA 92626-1401 USA; 714/641-8600, 800/756-0556 Fax: 714/641-2800, Focus: Laser printers, Ownrshp: PVT, Founded: 1987, Bernard Girma, Pres & CEO, Robin Poei, Dir Ops, Don Cason, Dir Sales, Jackie Rieck

Newpoint Corp. 6370 Nancy Ridge Dr, San Diego CA 92121-3212 USA; 619/677-5700, Fax: 619/558-1408, Focus: Surge protection and power control products, Prdts: Home Office-Grade, Personal Computer-Grade, Network-Grade, Ownrshp: Sub. Proxima Corp., Founded: 1982, Empl: 150, Mary June Makoul, PR Marcom Mgr

Newport Systems Solutions Inc. 2569 McCabe Way, Irvine CA 92714-6243 USA; 714/752-1511, Fax: 714/752-8389, Focus: Internetworking products, Ownrshp: PVT, Founded: 1988, Larry J. Stephenson, Pres & CEO, Robert Grice, VP & CFO

Newton-Evans Research Co. Inc. 10176 Baltimore National Pike, #204, Ellicott City MD 21042 USA; 410/465-7316, Fax: 410/750-7429, Focus: Supercomputers, microcomputers, datacom, control systems & vertical market data, Ownrshp: PVT, Founded: 1978, Empl: 6, Sales ($M): 1, Charles Newton, Pres, Loretta Smolenski, Mgr Ops

Nexar Technologies Inc. 182 Turnpike Rd, Westboro MA 01581 USA; 508/836-8700, Fax: 508/836-8729, Focus: PCs, Prdts: Nexar ISPA, Ownrshp: Sub. Palomar Medical Tech., Albert J. Agbay, Chmn & CEO, Bob Hamirani, Pres, Michael Paciello, SVP, James P. Lucivero, VP Sales

NexGen Microsystem 1623 Buckey Dr, Milpitas CA 95035-7423 USA; 408/435-0202, Fax: 408/435-0262, Focus: High-performance microprocessors, Prdts: Nx586, Ownrshp: Sub AMD, Founded: 1986, Empl: 90, S. Atiq Raza, Chmn, Pres & CEO, Vinod Dham, EVP & COO, David I. Epstein, VP Eng, Dana B. Krelle, VP Sales & Mktng, Anthony S. Chan, VP & CFO, David Kulbarsh

NeXT Inc. 900 Chesapeake Dr, Redwood City CA 94063 USA; 415/366-0900, 800/879-6398 Fax: 415/780-3914, Web URL: next.com, Focus: NEXTSTEP/OPENSTEP software and web objects software, Prdts: NEXTSTEP, OPENSTEP, Enterprise

Objects Framework, Webobjects, Ownrshp: PVT, Founded: 1985, Empl: 310, Sales ($M): 49.7, Fiscal End: 12/94; Steven P. Jobs, Chmn & CEO, Jean-Marie Hullot, CTO, Mitchell Mandich, VP NA Sales, Avadis Tnanian, VP Eng, Dominique Trempont, CFO, Kindle Digiusto, Email: kindle_digiusto@next.com

Nextel Communications 201 Rt 17 N, Rutherford NJ 07070 USA; 201/438-1400, Fax: 201/939-4888, Focus: Telecom services, Ownrshp: OTC, Sales ($M): 178, Fiscal End: 12/95; Daniel Akerson, CEO

Nichols Research Corp. 4040 S Memorial Pkwy, Huntsville AL 35802-1326 USA; 205/883-1140, Fax: 205/882-3422, Focus: Aerospace electronics and computers, Ownrshp: OTC, Stk Sym: NRES, Founded: 1976, Empl: 1,336, Sales ($M): 24.3, Fiscal End: 8/96; Chris H. Horgen, Chmn & CEO, Michael J. Mruz, Pres & COO, Michael W. Solley, VP SI, Roy J. Nichols, SVP & CTO, Darrell B. McIndoe, VP Info Syst

NickleWare PO Box 393, Orem UT 84059 USA; 801/785-4507, 800/250-3988 Fax: 801/785-7897, Co Email: 72730.1002@com-puserve.com, Focus: Genealogical database software, Prdts: Parents

Nihon Unisys Ltd. 1-1-1 Toyosu, Koto-ku, Tokyo 135 JP-135 Japan; 3-5546-4111, Focus: Mainframe computers, PCs and software, Empl: 8,200, Sales ($M): 2,528, Fiscal End: 3/92

Nikon Electronic Imaging 1300 Walt Whitman Dr, Melville NY 11747-3064 USA; 516/547-4355, Fax: 516/547-0305, Focus: Film scanners, color printers and image systems, Ownrshp: Sub. Nikon, Japan, Founded: 1989, Douglas E. Howe, GM, Richard LoPinto, VP

Niles & Associates Inc. 800 Jones St, Berkeley CA 94710 USA; 510/559-8592, 800/554-3049 Fax: 510/559-8683, Co Email: @niles.com, Web URL: niles.com, Focus: Scientific software, Prdts: EndNote, EndLink, Ownrshp: PVT, Founded: 1985, Empl: 10, Richard Niles, Pres, Emanuel Rosen, VP Mktng, Email: manu@niles.com; Kimberly Mattingly, Dir Mktng Dev, Email: kimberly@niles.com; Alison Hamilton, Dir Channel Mktng, Email: alison@niles.com

Nimax Inc. 7740 Kenamar Ct, San Diego CA 92121 USA; 619/566-4800, Fax: 619/566-2551, Focus: POS and barcode product distributor, Ownrshp: PVT, Founded: 1984, Empl: 75, Sales ($M): 50, Fiscal End: 12/93; Steve Hsieh, Pres, Kevin Su, COO, Vickie Wolf, CFO, Peter Wu, Dir Eng, Dorinda Hoffland, Mktng

Nintendo of America Inc. 4820 150th Ave NW, Redmond WA 98052 USA; 206/882-2040, Fax: 206/882-3585, Web URL: nintendo.com, Focus: Entertainment software, Ownrshp: Sub. Nintendo, Japan, Stk Sym: NTDOY, Founded: 1980, Empl: 1,000, Howard Lincoln, Chmn

Nissei Sangyo America Ltd. 100 Lowder Brook Dr, #2400, Westwood MA 02090-1124 USA; 617/461-8300, Focus: PC & Mac monitors, Prdts: SuperScan, Ownrshp: Sub. Nissei Sangyo, Japan, Founded: 1969, Empl: 157, Sales ($M): 448, Akihiko Nozaki, Pres, Junjiro Kanno, VP, Kevin Bowler, Assist VP, Kathleen Murphy, Marcom Mgr, Email: kathy@halsic/hitachi.com

Nisus Software Inc. 107 S Cedros Ave, PO Box 1300, Solana Beach CA 92075-1900 USA; 619/481-1477, Fax: 619/481-6154, Co Email: @nisus-soft.com, Web URL: nisus-soft.com, Focus: Word processing software, business productivity software, Prdts: Nisus Writer, Mailkeeper, Ownrshp: PVT, Founded: 1984, Empl: 25, Jerzy Lewak, Pres, Email: jerzy@nisus-soft.com; Edwina Riblet, Dir Mktng, Email: edwina@nisus-soft.com

NMB Technologies Inc. 9730 Independence Ave, Chatsworth CA 91311 USA; 818/341-3355, Fax: 818/341-8207, Focus: Peripherals and ICs, Ownrshp: Sub. Minebea, Japan, Founded: 1988, Empl: 120, Sales ($M): 150, Myron D. Jones, Pres, Jeff Miller, Dir Prod Mgmt, Susan Shippey, Sr Mktng Admin

Nokia Group PO Box 226, Helsinki Fin-00101 Finland; 3580-18071, Fax: 3580-656388, Focus: Telecom products, Ownrshp: NYSE, Stk Sym: NOK.A, Founded: 1865, Empl: 34,000, Sales ($M): 8,444.6, Fiscal End: 12/95; Jorma Ollila, Chmn, Pres & CEO, Matti Alahuhta, Pres Nokia Telecom, Pekka Ala-Pietila, Pres

Mobil Phones, Sari Baldauf, Pres Cellular Syst, Olli-Pekka Kallas-vuo, EVP &CFO

Nomura Research Institute Ltd. Edobashi Bldg II, 1-10-1 Nihonbashi, Chuo-ku, Tokyo 103 JP-103 Japan; 3-5255-1800, Web URL: ni.co.jp, Focus: Computer services and systems integration, Ownrshp: FO, Sales ($M): 1,042, Fiscal End: 3/96

NoRad Corp. 1160 E Sandhill Ave, Carson CA 90746-1315 USA; 310/605-0808, 800/262-3260 Fax: 310/605-5051, Focus: Monitor radiation/glare shields, Prdts: NoRad Shield, Ultra Glass, ELF Pro-Tech, Jitter Box, Ownrshp: PVT, Founded: 1985, Michelle C. Hartzell, Pres & CEO, Morton M. Winston, Chmn, Bruce Sperka, Dir Mktng

Norand Corp. 550 Second St SE, Cedar Rapids IA 52401 USA; 319/369-3100, Fax: 319/369-3453, Co Email: @norand.com, Web URL: norand.com, Focus: Data collection systems and hand-held terminals, Ownrshp: OTC, Stk Sym: NRND, Founded: 1968, Empl: 927, Sales ($M): 193.0, Fiscal End: 8/94; N. Robert Hammer, Chmn, Pres & CEO, Thomas O. Miller, VP Mobile Syst, Greg L. Reyes, VP RF Syst, Alan G. Bunte, VP Strat Plng, Gerald J. Sweas, VP & CFO, Katherine Wacker, Dir Com

Norman Data Defense Systems Inc. 3040 Williams Dr, 6th Fl, Fairfax VA 22031 USA; 703/573-8802, Fax: 703/573-3919, Web URL: norman.com, Focus: Anti-virus software, Ownrshp: PVT, George Dreyer, Pres

North American ISDN Users' Forum (NIU), c/o NTIS, Rt I-270 & Quince Orchard Rd, Gaithersburg MD 20899-0001 USA; 301/975-4858, Focus: Implementation of ISDN applications, Ownrshp: Nonprofit, Founded: 1988, Anne Enright Shepherd

North Carolina Electronics & Information Technologies Assoc. (NCEITA), 3203 Woman's Club Dr, #220, Raleigh NC 27612 USA; 919/787-8818, Fax: 919/783-9058, Focus: Association for NC's electronics and information companies, Ownrshp: Nonprofit, Betsy Justus, Exec Dir

North Shore Systems Inc. PO Box 8687, Incline Village NV 89452-8687 USA; 702/831-1108, Fax: 702/831-8553, Focus: PC utility software, Prdts: CursorPower, Ownrshp: PVT, Founded: 1989, Empl: 4, Richard K. Stouffer, Pres

Northeast Software Assoc. c/o Hyperion Software, 777 Long Ridge Rd, Stamford CT 06902 USA; 203/321-3711, Fax: 203/968-2932, Focus: Association for software developers in Connecticut and New York, Ownrshp: Nonprofit, Les Trachtman, Chmn

Northeast Technical Assoc. (NTA), c/o ProLine Communications, 13 Crescent Rd, Livingston NJ 07039 USA; 201/716-9457, Fax: 201/533-0463, Focus: Organization for computer companies in the northeast, Ownrshp: Nonprofit, Bruce Freeman, Pres

Northern Telecom Ltd. 3 Robert Speck Pkwy, Mississauga Ontario L4Z 3C8 Canada; 905/566-3178, Fax: 905/566-3058, Focus: Telecom products, Ownrshp: NYSE, Stk Sym: NT, Founded: 1884, Empl: 58,000, Sales ($M): 10,672.0, Fiscal End: 12/95; Paul G. Stern, Chmn, Jean C. Monty, Pres & CEO

Northern Virginia Technology Council 8391 Old Courthouse Rd, #300, Vienna VA 22182 USA; 703/734-9500, Fax: 703/734-2836, Focus: Organization for Virginia high-tech companies, Ownrshp: Nonprofit

Notable Technologies Inc. 411 108th Ave SE, #1000, Bellevue WA 98004 USA; 206/455-4040, 800/814-4214 Fax: 206/455-4440, Co Email: @notable.com, Web URL: notable.com, Focus: Wireless information products for media professionals, Prdts: AirNote Wireless Messaging System, Ownrshp: PVT, Founded: 1991, Empl: 30, Steve Wood, Pres & CEO, Email: swood@notable.com; Jim Rulfs, VP Bus Dev, Email: jrulfs@notable.com; Michael Scheaffer, Dir Fin, Email: mscheaffer@notable.com; Marina Hardy, Dir Mktng, Email: mhardy@notable.com; Curt Miller, Dir Eng, Email: cmiller@notable.com

NovaLink Technologies Inc. 48511 Warm Springs Blvd #208, Fremont CA 94539 USA; 510/249-9777, 800/668-2546 Fax: 510/249-9666, Co Email: info@novatech.com, Web URL: novat-

ech.com, Focus: Communications products for mobile PCs, Prdts: GoAnyWhere Modem, Ownrshp: PVT, Founded: 1993, G.A. Keyworth, Chmn, Baldev Krishan, Pres & CEO, Robert B. Fultz, Dir Sales & Mktng, Kaylan V. Krishnan, VP SW Prod, Demonder Chan, Dir Eng

NovaLogic Inc. 26010 Mureau Rd, #200, Calabasas CA 91302 USA; 818/880-1997, Fax: 818/880-1998, Co Email: @novalogic.com, Web URL: novalogic.com, Focus: Interactive entertainment software, Prdts: Comanche, Armored Fist, Werewolf vs Comanche, Ownrshp: PVT, Founded: 1985, Empl: 44, John A. Garcia, Pres & CEO, Email: jgarcia@novalogic.com; James T. Lamorticelli, VP Mktng, Email: jlamorticelli@novalogic.com; Lee Milligan, CFO, Email: lmilligan@novalogic.com; Michael Markin, Prod Mktng Mgr, Email: mmarkin@novalogic.com

NovaStor Corp. 80-B W Cochran St, Simi Valley CA 93065 USA; 805/579-6700, 800/668-2786 Fax: 805/579-6710, Co Email: @novastor.com, Web URL: novastor.com, Focus: C/S data management software and systems, Prdts: NovaBack, Ownrshp: PVT, Founded: 1987, Empl: 40, Sales ($M): 4, Fiscal End: 7/95; Peter Means, Pres, Email: peter@novastor.com; Shaun Walsh, VP OEM Sales, Email: shaun@novastor.com; Keith Murphy, VP Dist Sales, Email: keith@novastor.com

Novell Inc. 155 N Technology Way, Orem UT 84057 USA; 801/222-6000, 800/453-1267 Fax: 801/228-7077, Co Email: @novell.com, Web URL: novell.com, Focus: LAN operating system, Ownrshp: OTC, Stk Sym: NOVL, Founded: 1983, Empl: 7,272, Sales ($M): 2,041.2, Fiscal End: 10/95; John Young, Chmn, Joseph Marengi, Pres, James R. Tolonen, SVP & CFO, Richard W. King, EVP Netware Group, Steven Markman, EVP Info Access, Terri S. Holbrooke, VP Corp Com

Now Software Inc. 921 SW Washington, #500, Portland OR 97205-2823 USA; 503/274-2800, Fax: 503/274-0670, Co Email: info@nowsoft.com, Web URL: nowsoft.com, Focus: Utility software, Prdts: NOW Utilities, NOW Up-to-Date, NOW Contact, Ownrshp: PVT, Founded: 1990, Empl: 73, Sales ($M): 13.5, Fiscal End: 12/95; Duane Schulz, Pres & CEO, Timothy A. Marcotte, VP Ops & CFO, Dan Meub, VP Mktng & Sales, P. Shelton Virden, VP Sales, Steve Frison, VP Dev, Deb Catello, PR Mgr, Email: catello@nowsoft.com

NPES The Association for Suppliers of Printing & Publishing Tech. (NPES), 1899 Preston White Dr, Reston VA 20191-4367 USA; 703/264-7200, Fax: 703/620-0994, Co Email: npes@npes.org, Web URL: npes.org, Focus: Association for companies in the printing, publishing and graphic communications, Ownrshp: Nonprofit, Founded: 1933, Empl: 300, Regis J. Delmontagne, Pres

NSM Jukebox America Inc. 1158 Tower Ln, Bensenville IL 60106 USA; 708/860-5100, 800/238-4676 Fax: 708/860-5144, Focus: CD-ROM jukeboxes, Prdts: Mercury Net, Mercury 31, Ownrshp: Sub NSM, Germany, Armin Frank, GM, Philip Vena, Mktng Mgr

Ntergaid Inc. 60 Commerce Park, Milford CT 06460 USA; 203/783-1280, 800/254-9737 Fax: 203/882-0850, Co Email: 75160.3357@compuserve.com, Focus: Hypermedia and multimedia authoring software, Prdts: HyperWriter, AutoLinker/WEB, Ownrshp: PVT, Founded: 1987, Empl: 12, Sales ($M): 2.1, J. Scott Johnson, Pres

NTT Data Communications Systems Corp. 3-3-3 Toyosu, 3-chome, Koto-ku, Tokyo 135 JP-135 Japan; 3-5546-8202, Focus: System integration and communications networks, Ownrshp: Sub NTT, Japan, Empl: 7,000, Sales ($M): 5,287, Fiscal End: 3/96

NTT Soft 595 Market St, #2040, San Francisco CA 94105 USA; 415/908-0200, Fax: 415/908-0220, Focus: Software for information systems, communications systems and network service systems, Prdts: CyberCampus, Ownrshp: Sub. NTT, Japan, Founded: 1985

Nu Horizons Electronics Corp. 6000 New Horizons Blvd, Amityville NY 11701 USA; 516/226-6000, Focus: Electronics distributor, Ownrshp: OTC, Stk Sym: NUHC, Founded: 1982, Sales ($M): 202.8, Fiscal End: 2/96; Irving Lubman, Chmn, Arthur Nadata, Pres & Treasurer, Paul Durando, VP Fin, Paul Kline, VP Sales, Ben Schwartz, VP Mktng

Nu-Mega Technologies Inc. PO Box 7780, Nashua NH 03060-7780 USA; 603/889-2386, 800/468-6342 Fax: 603/889-1135, Co Email: info@numega.com, Web URL: numega.com, Focus: Software utilities, Prdts: Bounds Checker, Soft-ICE, Ownrshp: PVT, Founded: 1989, Franklin Grossman, Pres, James Moskun, Chmn

NuIQ Software Inc. 415-A Richbell Rd, Larchmont NY 10538 USA; 914/833-3479, 800/844-6526 Fax: 914/833-3623, Co Email: info@nuiq.com, Web URL: nuiq.com, Focus: Software that helps companies develop their own online service, Prdts: Powerboard BBS, NetBBS, Ownrshp: PVT, Founded: 1991, Empl: 8, Scott W. Brown, Pres & CEO, Email: scott@nuiq.com; Janet Brown, VP Ops & COO, Email: janet@nuiq.com; Roland A. Baroni III, EVP, Email: roland@nuiq.com; Douglas B. Vermes, VP Software Dev, Email: doug@nuiq.com

nuLogic 475 Hillside Ave, Needham MA 02194 USA; 617/444-7680, Fax: 617/444-2803, Co Email: info@nulogic.com, Focus: Real-time control products, Prdts: FlexMotion, pcControl, pcStep, Ownrshp: PVT, Founded: 1988, Empl: 12, Jeffrey S. Seiden, Pres, Jonathan R. Leehey, VP Eng, Rob Luschemat, Sales Mgr, Scott D. MacMillan, Marcom

Number Nine Visual Technology Corp. 18 Hartwell Ave, Lexington MA 02173-3103 USA; 617/674-0009, 800/438-6263 Fax: 617/674-2919, Co Email: @nine.com, Web URL: nine.com, Focus: Graphics accelerator boards, Prdts: Imagine 128 Series2, Ownrshp: OTC, Stk Sym: NINE, Founded: 1982, Empl: 115, Sales ($M): 116.8, Fiscal End: 12/95; Andrew Najda, Pres & CEO, Stanley Bialek, Co-founder, William Frentz, EVP, Greg McHale, VP Mktng, Kevin M. Hanks, CFO, Phil Parker, Email: pparker@nine.com

Numera Software Corp. 1501 Fourth Ave, #2880, Seattle WA 98101 USA; 206/622-2233, 800/956-2233 Fax: 206/622-5382, Co Email: info@numera.com, Web URL: numera.com, Focus: CAD software, Prdts: Visual CADD, Ownrshp: PVT, Founded: 1993, Empl: 23, Kevin M. Cable, Pres & CEO, Email: kevinc@numera.com; Peter C. Acker, EVP, Email: petera@numera.com; Randy Anderson, VP Mktng, Email: randya@numera.com; Carl Ransdell, VP New Tech, Email: carlr@numera.com; Matthew Brown, VP R&D, Email: mattb@numera.com; Ed Petersen, PR Mktng Specialist, Email: edp@numera.com

Numerical Algorithms Group Inc. (NAG), 1400 Opus Place, #200, Downers Grove IL 60515-5702 USA; 630/971-2337, Fax: 630/971-2706, Co Email: naginfo@nag.com, Web URL: nag.com, Focus: Scientific and engineering software, Prdts: NAG Fortran Libraries, IRIS Explorer, Axiom, Ownrshp: PVT, Founded: 1968, Empl: 120, Sales ($M): 15, Fiscal End: 3/93; Brian Ford, Pres, David Benco, EVP, Email: benco@nag.com; Tony Nilles, Sales Mgr, Email: nilles@nag.com; Kierith Ferrara-Kurth, Mktng Mgr, Email: ferrara@nag.com

Numetrix Ltd. 101 Merritt 7, Norwalk CT 06851 USA; 203/847-3452, 800/555-2173 Fax: 203/846-3537, Focus: Logistic planning and scheduling software, Prdts: Linx, Planx, Schedulex, Ownrshp: PVT, Founded: 1977, Empl: 200, Joseph Schengili, Pres, Veerle Schengili, VP Ops, Hoon Chung, VP Consulting, Ed Sitarski, VP R&D, Gary Brown, VP Fin, Jeff Miller, Dir Mktng

Numonics Corp. 101 Commerce Dr, PO Box 1005, Montgomeryville PA 18936 USA; 215/362-2766, Fax: 215/361-0167, Focus: Digitizers and plotters, Ownrshp: PVT, Founded: 1969, Empl: 80, Sales ($M): 8, Fiscal End: 12/92; Al Basilicato, Pres & CEO, Phillip L. Henderson, VP Eng, Carol S. Dabrowski, Marcom Mgr

nView Corp. 860 Omni Blvd, Newport News VA 23606 USA; 804/873-1354, Fax: 804/873-2153, Focus: Projection displays for PCs, Prdts: ViewFrame, Ownrshp: OTC, Stk Sym: NVUE,

Founded: 1987, Empl: 96, Sales ($M): 32.9, Fiscal End: 12/95; Angelo Guastaferro, Chmn, Robert D. Hoke, Pres & CEO, Charles L. Ball, VP Sales, Jerry W. Stubblefield, VP & CFO, Cassie Hagan, Mgr PR

Nynex Corp. 1095 Ave of the Americas, New York NY 10036 USA; 212/395-2121, Fax: 212/921-2917, Web URL: nynex.com, Focus: Regional Bell Operating Company (RBOC), Ownrshp: NYSE, Stk Sym: NYN, Founded: 1983, Empl: 65,400, Sales ($M): 13,407, Fiscal End: 12/95; William C. Ferguson, Chmn, Frederic V. Salerno, Vice Chmn, Ivan G. Seidenberg, Pres & CEO, Raymond F. Burke, EVP, Alan Z. Senter, SVP & CFO, Patrick F.X. Mulhearn, VP PR

O'Neil Electronics 8 Mason, Irvine CA 92718-2705 USA; 714/727-1234, Fax: 714/727-4350, Focus: Portable printers and software, Prdts: microFlash, OutBack, Ownrshp: PVT, Founded: 1981, Empl: 61, Tim O'Neil, Pres, Zeke Lopez, VP Sales & Mktng, David Holt, Mgr SW Dev, Joy Anthony, Email: eyxx21a@prodigy.com

O'Reilly & Associates Inc. 103 Morris St, #A, Sebastopol CA 95472 USA; 707/829-0515, 800/998-9938 Fax: 707/829-0104, Co Email: order@ora.com, Web URL: ora.com, Focus: Software, books on Unix, Internet and Worldwide Web Journal, Prdts: Website, The Whole Internet User's Guide & Catalog, WWW Journal, Ownrshp: PVT, Founded: 1978, Empl: 140, Tim O'Reilly, Pres, Brian Erwin, Dir Sales & Mktng, Richard Peck, VP Bus Dev, Sara Winge, PR Dir, Email: sara@ora.com

Oberon Software Inc. 222 3rd St, #3100, Cambridge MA 02142-1188 USA; 617/494-0990, Fax: 617/494-0414, Focus: Software development tools, Prdts: Prospero, Ownrshp: PVT, Founded: 1989, Empl: 20, Masaharu Kawamata, Pres & CEO, Mike McMahon, EVP, Hiroaki Nishimoto, VP Bus Dev, Bill Clark, Dir Sales & Mktng

Object Database Management Group 14041 Burnhaven Dr, #105, Burnsville MN 55337 USA; 612/953-7250, Fax: 612/397-7146, Co Email: info@odmg.com, Web URL: odmg.com, Doug Barry, Pres, Email: dbarry@odmg.org

Object Design Inc. (ODI), 25 Mall Rd, Burlington MA 01803-4100 USA; 617/674-5000, Web URL: odi.com, Focus: Database software, Ownrshp: PVT, Founded: 1988, Empl: 220, Sales ($M): 35, Fiscal End: 12/95; Robert Goldman, Chmn, Pres & CEO

Object Management Group (OMG), 492 Old Connecticut Path, Framingham MA 01701 USA; 508/820-4300, Fax: 508/820-4303, Web URL: omg.org, Focus: Industry standard object-oriented application integration environment, Ownrshp: Nonprofit, Founded: 1989, Empl: 250, Christopher Stone, Pres, Richard Soley, VP

Objectivity 301B E Evelyn, Mountain View CA 94041 USA; 415/254-7100, Fax: 415/254-7171, Co Email: info@objy.com, Web URL: objectivity.com, Focus: Object database software, Prdts: Objectivity/DB, Ownrshp: PVT, Founded: 1988, Empl: 50, David Caplan, CEO, Ralph Reda, VP Sales, Bill Evans, VP Mktng, Vickie Clements, Marcom Spec, Email: vickie@objy.com

ObjectSpace Inc. 14881 Quorum Dr, #400, Dallas TX 75240 USA; 214/934-2496, 800/625-3281 Fax: 214/663-9100, Web URL: objectspace.com, Focus: Object technology services and products, Prdts: ObjectCatalog, ObjectMetrics, Ownrshp: PVT, Graham W. Glass, Co-founder, David L. Norris, VP & Co-founder, Heather Drake, Mktng Mgr Prod Div, Email: hdrake@objectspace.com

Objx Inc. 10033 Morgan Trace Dr, Loveland OH 45140-8924 USA; 513/398-0300, Fax: 513/398-0998, Focus: Software development tools, Ownrshp: PVT, Founded: 1993, Thomas C. Hammergren, Pres

Ocean Microsystems Inc. 11235 Knott Ave, #A, Cypress CA 90630 USA; 714/898-1340, Fax: 714/891-8484, Focus: Optical mass storage, Ownrshp: Sub. MOST, Betty Yamanka

Octel Communications Corp. 1001 Murphy Ranch Rd, Milpitas CA 95035-7912 USA; 408/321-2000, 800/444-5590 Co Email: @octel.com, Web URL: octel.com, Focus: Voice information processing systems, Ownrshp: OTC, Stk Sym: OCTL, Founded: 1982,

Empl: 2,700, Sales ($M): 563.6, Fiscal End: 6/96; Robert Cohn, Chmn, Pres & CEO, David Ladd, EVP, W. Michael West, EVP, Margaret Norton, VP, Gary A. Wetsel, EVP & CFO

OCTuS Inc. PO Box 232397, San Diego CA 92193-2397 USA; 619/268-5140, Fax: 619/268-5175, Focus: Networking & personal communication software, Prdts: Subway, Ownrshp: OTC, Stk Sym: OCTS, Founded: 1983, Empl: 4, Sales ($M): 1.2, Fiscal End: 12/94; John C. Belden, Chmn, Pres & CEO

Odetics Inc. 1515 S Manchester Ave, Anaheim CA 92802-2907 USA; 714/774-5000, Fax: 714/774-9432, Focus: Automatic tape library systems, Ownrshp: OTC, Stk Sym: ODETA, Founded: 1969, Empl: 603, Sales ($M): 84.2, Fiscal End: 3/94; Joel Slutzky, Chmn & CEO, Crandall Gudmundson, Pres, Tom Bartholet, VP Corp Dev

Odyssey Development Inc. 8775 E Orchard Rd, #811, Greenwood Village CO 80111 USA; 303/689-9998, Fax: 303/689-9997, Co Email: isys@dash.com, Web URL: isysdev.com, Focus: Information retrieval software, Prdts: ISYS, Ownrshp: Sub. Odyssey, Australia, Founded: 1988, Empl: 30, Martin Steinberg, Pres, Diana Paty, Dir Sales, Anna-Maria Evangelista-Frace, Dir Tech Support, Kathy Perkins, Dir Mktng

Office Depot Inc. 2200 Old Germantown Rd, Delray Beach FL 33445 USA; 407/278-4800, Fax: 407/279-3239, Focus: Office product and PC reseller chain, Ownrshp: NYSE, Stk Sym: ODP, Founded: 1986, Empl: 20,000, Sales ($M): 5,313.2, Fiscal End: 12/95; David I. Fuente, Chmn & CEO, Mark D. Begelman, Pres & COO, Gary D. Foss, EVP Mktng, Richard M. Bennington, EVP Ops, Barry J. Goldstein, EVP & CFO

OfficeMax Inc. 3605 Warrensville Ctr Rd, Shaker Heights OH 44122-5203 USA; 216/921-6900, Fax: 216/283-3365, Web URL: officemax.com, Focus: Office product and PC reseller chain, Ownrshp: NYSE, Stk Sym: OMX, Empl: 10,212, Sales ($M): 2,542.5, Fiscal End: 1/96; Michael Feuer, Chmn & CEO, Edward L. Cornell, EVP & CFO, George H. Luckey, EVP, John C. Martin, Pres Retail Stores, Robert E. Danielson, SVP Info Sys, Juris Pagrabs, Dir Corp Com

Oki America Inc. 3 University Plaza, Hackensack NJ 07601 USA; 201/646-0011, Fax: 201/646-9229, Focus: Telecom, computer and semiconductor products, Ownrshp: Sub. Oki, Japan, Founded: 1962, Empl: 1,718, Sales ($M): 1,100, Fiscal End: 3/95; Tetsujii Bruno, EVP, Tokihiko Shimomura, GM, Jay Mehta, VP Finance, Takeshi Sato, Chief Rep

Oki Electric Industry Co. Ltd. 7-12 Toranomon 1-chome, Minato-ku, Tokyo 105 JP-105 Japan; 3-3501-3111, Fax: 3-3581-5522, Web URL: oki.co.jp, Focus: Telecom, computer and semiconductor products, Ownrshp: FO, Stk Sym: OKIEIC, Founded: 1881, Empl: 22,585, Sales ($M): 6,980, Fiscal End: 3/96; Shiko Sawamura, Pres & CEO, Minoru Imai, EVP, Tadao Higashi, EVP, Yasunori Nishizawa, Sr Managing Dir

Oki Semiconductor 785 N May Ave, Sunnyvale CA 94086-2909 USA; 408/720-1900, Fax: 408/720-1918, Focus: ICs and memory cards, Ownrshp: Sub. Oki, Japan, Founded: 1977, Joe Baranowski, VP Mktng

Okidata 532 Fellowship Rd, Mt. Laurel NJ 08054 USA; 609/235-2600, 800/654-3282 Fax: 609/778-4184, Web URL: okidata.com, Focus: Printers and fax machines, Prdts: MicroLine, OkiFax, Okijet, Pacemark, Ownrshp: Sub. Oki Electric Ind., Japan, Founded: 1972, Empl: 700, Dennis P. Flanayan, Pres & CEO, Joseph O'Malley, SVP Sales, Jim Butterworth, SVP Bus Dev, Bill Fabian, VP, Elissa LiVecchi

Olicom USA 900 E Park Blvd #180, Plano TX 75074-5465 USA; 214/423-7560, Fax: 214/423-7261, Co Email: olicom-us.com, Focus: Network solutions, Ownrshp: Sub. Olicom, Denmark, Stk Sym: OLCMF, Founded: 1985, Empl: 200, Sales ($M): 113.6, Fiscal End: 12/94; Max Jensen, Pres & CEO, Email: maxj@smtpgwy.olicom-us; Peter Haslam, GM, Email: peterh@smtpgwy.olicom-us; Wilson Prokosch, VP NA Sales,

Email: wilsonp@smtpgwy@olicom-us.com; Tonya McMurray, PR & Fin Mgr, Email: tonyam@smtpgwy.olicom-us.com

Olivetti & Co. Via G. Jervis, 77, Ivrea I-10015 Italy; 39-125-5200, Web URL: olivetti.it, Focus: Microcomputers, minicomputers and telecom products, Ownrshp: FO, Empl: 57,000, Sales ($M): 6,035, Fiscal End: 12/95; Roberto Colaninno, CEO

Olympus Image Systems Inc. 2 Corporate Center Dr, Melville NY 11747-3157 USA; 516/844-5000, 800/347-4027 Fax: 516/844-5339, Focus: Page printers, Ownrshp: Sub. Olympus Optical, Japan, Founded: 1990, Tomohiro Kubo, Pres, William H. Boles, VP Sales & Mktng, Dave Veilleux, Mktng Mgr, Andy Schaeffer, Prod Mgr

Omega Research Inc. 9200 Sunset Dr, Miami FL 33173-3266 USA; 305/270-1095, 800/292-3461 Fax: 305/270-8919, Focus: Investment software, Prdts: Wall St Analyst, Ownrshp: PVT, Founded: 1982, Ralph Cruz, VP, Dawn Kozlowski, Mktng Coord, Darla D. Tuttle, PR Dir

Omicron-Center for Information Technology Management (Omicron), 115 Rt 46, Bldg. D-31, Mountain Lakes NJ 07046 USA; 201/335-0240, Fax: 201/335-0289, Web URL: omicronet.com, Focus: MIS management issues, Ownrshp: Nonprofit, Founded: 1980, Empl: 65, Jim Webber, Pres, Email: jwebber@omicronet.com; Don Bussell, Exec Dir, Omicron/Chicago, Teresa Carbone, Participation Coordinator, Jim Webber, Pres

Omni MultiMedia Group 50 Howe Ave, Millbury MA 01527 USA; 508/865-4451, 800/343-7620 Fax: 508/865-1853, Focus: Software publisher, Ownrshp: AMEX, Stk Sym: OMG, Paul F. Johnson, Pres, Robert E. Lee, EVP, CFO

Omnicomp Graphics Corp. 1734 W Sam Houston Pkwy N, Houston TX 77043 USA; 713/464-2990, Fax: 713/827-7540, Focus: Graphics controllers and multimedia products, Ownrshp: PVT, Founded: 1983, Empl: 40, Sales ($M): 7.5, Anthony G. Masraff, CEO, Huling H. Parker, Pres & COO

Omnidata International Inc. 124 S 600 W, PO Box 448, Logan UT 84323-0448 USA; 801/753-7760, Fax: 801/753-6756, Focus: Handheld computers, Prdts: Rugged DOS Terminal, Ownrshp: PVT, Gilbert Larson, Pres, Aaron Cartwright, Mktng Mgr

Omron Advanced Systems Inc. 3945 Freedom Cr, #700, Santa Clara CA 95054 USA; 408/727-6644, Focus: Utility software, Ownrshp: Sub Omron, Japan

ON Technology Corp. 1 Cambridge Ctr, Cambridge MA 02142-1604 USA; 617/374-1400, 800/767-6683 Fax: 617/374-1433, Co Email: info@on.com, Web URL: on.com, Focus: Workgroup software, Prdts: Notework, SofTrack, AuditTrack, Ownrshp: OTC, Stk Sym: ONTC, Founded: 1985, Empl: 350, Sales ($M): 44.1, Fiscal End: 12/95; Christopher Risley, Pres & CEO, Email: crisley@on.com; John Bogdan, VP & CFO, Email: jbogdan@on.com; John Rizzi, VP Sales, Email: jrizzi@on.com; Ivan O'Sullivan, VP Mktng, Email: iosulliv@on.com; Steven Guthrie, Dir PR, Email: sguthrie@on.com

On The Go Software 4350 La Jolla Village Dr, #300, San Diego CA 92122-1244 USA; 619/546-4340, Fax: 619/546-0430, Co Email: 74754.1767@compuserve.com, Focus: Laptop PC software, Prdts: Expense It, Ownrshp: PVT, Founded: 1989, Empl: 10, Robert Crumpler, Pres

OnBase Technology Inc. 14 Hughes St, #B105, Irvine CA 92718 USA; 800/782-5682 Fax: 714/830-5691, Co Email: onbase@deltanet.com, Web URL: onbasetech.com, Focus: Internet directory software, Prdts: DragNet, Ownrshp: PVT, Bruce Sargeant, Pres

OneOnOne Computer Training 2055 Army Trail Rd, Dept. CIA1, Addison IL 60101 USA; 708/628-0500, 800/424-8668 Fax: 708/628-0550, Focus: Audio-based training for PC applications, Ownrshp: Sub. Mosaic Media, Founded: 1976, F. Lee McFadden, Pres

Online Computer Library Center Inc. (OCLC), 6565 Frantz Rd, Dublin OH 43017-3395 USA; 614/764-6000, Fax: 614/764-6096, Web URL: oclc.org, Focus: Nonprofit computer library service, Prdts: FirstSearch, Rick Noble, VP Reference Svc, Nita Dean, Email: nita_dean@oclc.org

Online Environs Inc. 38 Sidney St, #350, Cambridge MA 02139 USA; 617/225-0449, Fax: 617/225-0677, Co Email: info@ole.environs.com, Web URL: environs.com, Focus: 3D software products and World Wide Web services, Richard P. Lawless Jr., Pres, Andrew Yu, VP Mktng, John Ahn, VP Tech, Fritz Francis, VP Ops

Online Interactive Inc. (OLI), 2815 Second Ave, #500, Seattle WA 98121 USA; 206/443-1933, Fax: 206/443-1885, Co Email: @online-interactive.com, Focus: Online stores, Prdts: atOnce Software, FreeShop Online, Founded: 1994, Tim Choate, Pres & CEO, John Ballantine, EVP, Bill Benjamin, Email: wabenjamin@aol.com

ONSALE 1971 Landings Dr, Mountain View CA 94043 USA; 415/428-0600, Fax: 415/428-0163, Co Email: info@onsale.com, Web URL: onsale.com, Focus: Online retail service, Founded: 1994, Jerry Kaplan, Founder, Alan Fisher, SW Partner, Razi Mohiuddin, SW Partner

OnStream Networks Inc. 3393 Octavius Dr, Santa Clara CA 95054-3004 USA; 408/727-4545, Fax: 408/727-5151, Co Email: @onstream.com, Focus: Broadband networking products, Prdts: CLstream ATM Access Family, BMXstream, LXstream, Ownrshp: PVT, Founded: 1989, Empl: 95, James Mongiello, Pres & CEO, Peter Liebowitz, VP Sales, Robert Stiehler, VP Finance, Laura Stiff, PR Mgr, Email: laura@onstream.com

Ontrack Computer Systems Inc. 6321 Bury Dr, Eden Prairie MN 55346 USA; 612/937-1107, 800/752-1333 Fax: 612/937-5815, Co Email: @ontrack.com, Web URL: ontrack.com, Focus: Data recovery service & hard disk utility software, Prdts: Disk Manager, Data Recovery, Ownrshp: PVT, Founded: 1985, Empl: 140, Michael Rogers, CEO, John Pence, Pres, Gary Stevens, SVP Eng, Dave Dehne, Sales Mgr, Pam Bednar, Mktng Mgr, Email: pamb@ontrack.com; Janet M. Hance, PR Coord, Email: janeth@ontrack.com

Ontrack Media Corp. 150-B Shoreline Hwy, #22, Mill Valley CA 94941 USA; 415/331-1692, 800/520-5627 Fax: 415/331-1695, Co Email: 72262.2763@compuserve.com, Focus: Career selection software, Prdts: CareerPath, Ownrshp: PVT, Founded: 1993, Roy Kuklinsky, Pres & CEO, Steve Kimmelman, VP, Donal MacCoon, Dir Marcom, Email: dmaccoon@aol.com

Onyx Graphics Corp. 6915 S High Tech Dr, Midvale UT 84047 USA; 801/568-9900, Fax: 801/568-9911, Focus: Digital color printing systems, Prdts: Imagez, Ownrshp: PVT, Founded: 1989, Empl: 20, Chuck Edwards, Pres, Jim Harre, EVP, Neil Baker, VP Sales & Mktng, Todd Hess, VP Ops & CFO

Opcode Systems 3950 Fabian Way, #100, Palo Alto CA 94303 USA; 415/856-3333, Fax: 415/856-3332, Co Email: @opcode.com, Web URL: opcode.co, Focus: MIDI and music software, Prdts: Studio Vision, EZ Vision, Galaxy, Studio 3, Music shop, Chris Halaby, Pres, Dave Oppenheim, Dir R&D, Sean Casey, CIO, Paul De Benedictis, Email: paul_de_beedictis@opcode.com

Open Horizon Inc. 1301 Shoreway Rd #126, Belmont CA 94002 USA; 415/598-1200, Fax: 415/593-1669, Co Email: info@open-horizon.com, Focus: Products for client/server environments, Prdts: Connection, Nicholas Zaldastani, Pres & CEO

Open Market Inc. 245 First St, Cambridge MA 02142 USA; 617/621-9500, Fax: 617/621-1703, Co Email: info@openmarket.com, Web URL: openmarket.com, Focus: Electronic commerce software, Ownrshp: OTC, Stk Sym: OMKT, Founded: 1994, Empl: 257, Sales ($M): 1.8, Fiscal End: 12/95; Gary Eichhorn, CEO, David Gifford, Chief Scientist, Lawrence Stewart, CTO

Open Software Foundation (OSF), PO Box 2002, Andover MA 01810 USA; 508/474-9258, 800/767-2336 Fax: 508/470-0526, Focus: Develops open standards for software applications, Ownrshp: Nonprofit, Founded: 1988, Empl: 300, David Tory, Pres, Martin Ford, CFO, Peter B. Shaw, VP Sales & Mktng

Open Systems Holdings Corp. 7626 Golden Triangle Dr, Eden Prairie MN 55344-3732 USA; 612/829-0011, 800/528-2276 Fax: 612/829-1493, Co Email: info@osas.com, Web URL: osas.com, Focus: Accounting software, Prdts: Open Systems Accounting Software, Ownrshp: PVT, Founded: 1976, Empl: 120, Sales ($M): 12.0, Michael Bertini, CEO, William Wolff, Pres, John Schmeisser, Controller, Kent Hollrah, Dir Sales, Dianne Kearns, Dir Mktng, Dawn Westerberg, PR Mgr

Open Text Corp. 180 Columbia St W, Waterloo Ontario N2L 3L3 Canada; 519/888-7111, Fax: 519/888-0677, Co Email: @opentext.com, Web URL: opentext.com, Focus: Document mangement products, Prdts: Web Search Server, Ownrshp: PVT, Founded: 1991, Empl: 75, Tom Jenkins, Pres & CEO, Tim Bray, SVP Tech, Mike Farrell, EVP, David Weinberger, VP Mktng & Comm, David Paolini, Dir PR, Email: davep@opentext.com

Open Users Recommended Solutions (OURS), 401 N Michigan Ave, Chicago IL 60611-4267 USA; 312/644-6610, Fax: 312/321-6869, Focus: Organization to improve multivendor computer networks, Ownrshp: Nonprofit, Founded: 1991, Empl: 50

OpenConnect Systems 2711 LBJ Freeway, Dallas TX 75234 USA; 214/484-5200, 800/551-5881 Fax: 214/484-6100, Co Email: info@oc.com, Web URL: oc.com, Focus: Connectivity and internetworking software, Ownrshp: PVT

Operations Control Systems (OCS), 560 San Antonio Rd, #106, Palo Alto CA 94306 USA; 415/493-4122, Fax: 415/493-3393, Focus: Unix system software, Prdts: Express, Ownrshp: PVT, Founded: 1979, Gary Leight, Pres, James Lofink, Dir Mktng, Daniel Cobb, Tech Svcs Mgr

Opis Corp. 1101 Walnut St, Des Moines IA 50309-3425 USA; 515/284-0209, 800/395-0209 Fax: 515/248-5147, Web URL: opis.com, Focus: Customer support system, Prdts: SupportExpress, Founded: 1990, Doug Nicholas, CEO

OPTi Inc. 888 Tasman Dr, Milpitas CA 95035 USA; 408/486-8000, Fax: 408/486-8001, Web URL: opti.com, Focus: Chip sets for PCs, Ownrshp: OTC, Stk Sym: OPTI, Founded: 1989, Empl: 205, Sales ($M): 163.7, Fiscal End: 12/95; Jerry Chang, Chmn & CEO, Raj Jaswa, Pres, Dave Zacaries, COO, Vik Vakil, Marcom Mgr

Optibase Inc. 5000 Quorum Dr, #700, Dallas TX 75240-7024 USA; 214/774-3800, Fax: 214/239-1273, Co Email: @optibase.com, Web URL: optibase.com, Focus: Multimedia and image processing products, Prdts: MPEG LabSuite, MPEG Video Pro, PC Motion, Ownrshp: Sub. Optibase, Israel, Founded: 1988, Empl: 200, Ron Eisenburg, Pres & CTO, Email: rone@optibase.com; Raymond G. Harris, Pres N America, Email: rayh@optibase.com; Mark Fears, Marcom Mgr, Email: markf@optibase.com

Optical Access Int'l. 500 W Cummings Park, Woburn MA 01801 USA; 617/937-3910, Fax: 617/937-3950, Co Email: oai@oai.com, Focus: Optical storage systems, Ownrshp: PVT, Founded: 1989, Willard K. Rice Jr., CEO, Email: rice@oai.com

Optical Coating Laboratory Inc. (OCLI), 2789 Northpoint Pkwy, Santa Rosa CA 95407-7397 USA; 707/545-6440, Fax: 707/525-7410, Focus: Anti-glare filters for CRTs, Prdts: Glare/Guard, Ownrshp: OTC, Stk Sym: OCLI, Founded: 1948, Empl: 1,107, Sales ($M): 169.4, Fiscal End: 10/95; Herbert M. Dwight Jr., Chmn, Pres, CEO, James W. Seeser, VP & CTO, John McCullough, VP, Kenneth D. Pietrelli, VP Corp Svcs, John M. Markovich, VP & CFO

Optical Data Systems Inc. (ODS), 1101 E Arapaho Rd, Richardson TX 75081 USA; 214/234-6400, Fax: 214/234-1467, Focus: LAN and communications products, Ownrshp: OTC, Stk Sym: ODSI, Founded: 1983, Empl: 230, Sales ($M): 111.5, Fiscal End: 12/95; G. Ward Paxton, Chmn, Pres & CEO, Roger Hughes, VP & COO, T. Joe Head, SVP, Terry L. Gaston, VP Mktng, Garry L. Hemphill, VP Ops, Robert Hoskins, Prod Mktng Mgr

Optical Media Int'l. (OMI), 51 E Campbell Ave, #170, Campbell CA 95008-2047 USA; 408/376-3511, Fax: 408/376-3519, Co Email: omi@netcom.com, Focus: CD-ROM production products,

Ownrshp: PVT, Founded: 1985, Empl: 30, Sales ($M): 7, Allen Adkins, Pres & CEO, Ralph Coan, VP & CFO

Optical Storage Technology Assoc. (OSTA), 311 E Carrillo St, Santa Barbara CA 93101 USA; 805/963-3853, Fax: 805/962-1541, Web URL: osta.org, Focus: Promote market acceptance of optical technology for computer storage, Ownrshp: Nonprofit, Founded: 1992, Raymond C. Freeman Jr., Facilitator, Email: ray@osta.org

Opticomm Corp. 5505 Morehouse Dr, #150, San Diego CA 92121 USA; 619/450-0143, Fax: 619/450-0155, Focus: Fiber optic video, audio and data products, Ownrshp: PVT, Founded: 1986, Empl: 12, Sales ($M): 1.5, David Caidar, Pres, Shaya Fainman, Chmn, Ethan Maxon, Sales Mgr, Chris Arnold, Allan Castro

Optima Technology Corp. 17062 Murphy Ave, Irvine CA 92714-5914 USA; 714/476-0515, Fax: 714/476-0613, Co Email: @optimatech.com, Web URL: optimatech.com, Focus: Mass storage products, Prdts: MiniPak, Diskovery, Concorde, Desktape, Ownrshp: PVT, Founded: 1990, Empl: 100, Tarek Ayob, VP Sales & Mktng, Marilyn K. Kruger, Mktng Dir, Email: mkruger@optimatech.com

Optimal Networks 500 Logue Av.e, Mountain View CA 94043 USA; 415/254-5950, Fax: 415/254-5954, Co Email: info@optimal.com, Web URL: optimal.com, Focus: Network modeling, analysis & simulation software, Ownrshp: PVT, Founded: 1993, Empl: 15, J. Edward Snyder, Pres & CEO, Moshe Liran, Chmn & CTO, Email: moshel@optimal.com; Jay Weil, VP Mktng, Email: jayw@optimal.com; Steve Holtzman, VP Fin, Scott Braddock, Account Exec, Email: scott_braddock@arpartners.com

Optimum Resource Inc. 5 Hiltech Ln, Hilton Head Island SC 29926 USA; 803/689-8000, 800/327-1473 Fax: 803/689-8008, Co Email: stickyb@stickybear.com, Web URL: stickybear.com, Focus: Children's educational software, Prdts: Stickybear series, Ownrshp: PVT, Founded: 1981, Empl: 75, Richard Hefter, Pres, Olivia Hefter, EVP, Christopher Guntz, COO, David Kennaugh, VP Sales & Mktng

Optivision Inc. 3450 Hillview Ave, Palo Alto CA 94304 USA; 415/855-0200, Fax: 415/855-0222, Web URL: optivision.com, Focus: Video compression products, Ownrshp: PVT, Founded: 1983, Empl: 94, Joseph W. Goodman, Chmn & CTO, James S. Tyler, Pres & CEO, Ralph Mele, EVP Sales & Mktng, Janek Kaliczak, Dir Bus Dev, Bronwyn Johnston, Marcom Mgr, Email: bronwyn@optivision.com

Opus Systems Inc. 3000 Coronado Dr, Santa Clara CA 95054-3203 USA; 408/562-9340, Fax: 408/562-9341, Co Email: info@opus.com, Web URL: opus.com, Focus: SPARC-compatible add-in boards for PC, Prdts: SPARCard, Ownrshp: PVT, Founded: 1983, Empl: 20, Craig Forney, Pres & CEO, Email: craig@opus.com; Lawrence L. Siebert, VP Mfg, Email: larry@opus.com; Solomon Pelc, VP Sales, Email: spelc@opus.com; Barbara Watanabe, Dir Mktng, Email: barbara@opus.com

Oracle Corp. 500 Oracle Pkwy, Redwood Shores CA 94065 USA; 415/506-7000, Fax: 415/506-7200, Web URL: oracle.com, Focus: Database software, Prdts: Oracle, Ownrshp: OTC, Stk Sym: ORCL, Founded: 1977, Empl: 16,882, Sales ($M): 4,233.3, Fiscal End: 5/96; Lawrence J. Ellison, Chmn, Pres & CEO, Dirk A. Kabcenell, EVP Prod Div, Raymond J. Ln, EVP WW Ops, Raymond L. Ocampo Jr., SVP, Jeffrey O. Henley, EVP & CFO, Catherine Buan

Orchestra MultiSystems Inc. 12300 Edison Way, Garden Grove CA 92641 USA; 714/891-3861, 800/237-9988 Fax: 714/891-2661, Focus: Color monitors, Prdts: Brass Series, Ownrshp: PVT, Founded: 1993, John Hui, CEO

Orchid Technology 45365 Northport Loop W, Fremont CA 94538 USA; 510/683-0300, Fax: 510/490-9312, Focus: Add-in boards, Ownrshp: Sub Micronics, Founded: 1982, Empl: 160, Sales ($M): 27, Fiscal End: 6/91; Greg Reznick, Pres, John Murphy, VP Sales & Mktng, Luong Nguyen, VP Mfg, Tony Rodrigues, Dir Prod Mktng

Osicom Technologies Inc. 1223 Wilshire Blvd, #597, Santa Monica CA 90403-5400 USA; Focus: PCs, peripherals and LAN products, Ownrshp: OTC, Stk Sym: OSIC, Founded: 1981, Empl: 150, Parvinder Chadha, Pres & CEO, Sharon Chadha, CFO

Ositech Communications Inc. 679 Southgate Dr, Guelph Ontario N1G 4S2 Canada; 519/836-8063, 800/563-2386 Fax: 519/836-6156, Focus: PCMCIA cards, Ownrshp: PVT, Mike Dodgson

OST Inc. 14225 Sullyfield Cr, Chantilly VA 22021 USA; 703/817/0400, 800/678-9678 Fax: 703/817/0402, Co Email: info@ost-us.com, Web URL: ost-us.com, Focus: Internetworking products, Prdts: Xcellys, Magellys, Ecom, Ownrshp: Sub. OST, France, Founded: 1980, Empl: 350, Sales ($M): 60, Fiscal End: 12/95; Ed Bursk, Pres, Email: ebk@ost-us.com

Our Business Machines 12901 Ramona Blvd, #J, Irwindale CA 91706 USA; 818/337-9614, Fax: 818/960-1766, Focus: Scanners and peripheral boards, Ownrshp: PVT, Founded: 1986

Output Technology Corp. 2310 N Fancher Rd, Spokane WA 99212-1381 USA; 509/536-0468, Fax: 509/533-1280, Focus: Printers, Ownrshp: PVT, Founded: 1984, Billy R. Anders, Pres & CEO, Linda Hemingway, Dir Mktng, Tom Bloom, Mktng Mgr

P&L Associates 4642 E Chapman Ave, #349, Orange CA 92669 USA; 714/633-5308, 800/843-3997 Fax: 714/532-8204, Focus: Accounting software, Prdts: Ledgers, Ownrshp: PVT, Dave Cantral, Owner, Esther Pederson, VP Mktng

P.I. Engineering Inc. 2296 Williamston Rd, Williamston MI 48895 USA; 517/655-5523, 800/628-3185 Fax: 517/655-4926, Focus: Productive interface products, Prdts: Dual Mouse Adapter, Marjorie Hetherington, VP Sales & Mktng

Pacific Communications Sciences (PCI), 9645 Scranton Rd, San Diego CA 92121-1761 USA; 619/535-9500, Fax: 619/535-9235, Co Email: @pcsi.cirrus.com, Web URL: pcsi.com, Focus: Cellular chips and products, Prdts: PHS Digital Cordless Chip Set, Ownrshp: Sub Cirrus Logic, Founded: 1987, Empl: 500, David Lyon, Pres & CEO, Michael L. Lubin, EVP, Gwen Carlson, Dir Corp Com, Email: glc@pcsi.cirrus.com

Pacific Crest Technologies Inc. PO Box 6319, Anaheim CA 92816-0319 USA; 714/261-6444, Fax: 714/261-6468, Focus: Business card scanner, Prdts: CardGrabber, Ownrshp: PVT

Pacific Data Products 9855 Scranton Rd #B, San Diego CA 92121-1765 USA; 619/552-0880, Fax: 619/552-0889, Focus: Printers, plotters and accessories, Ownrshp: Sub. DCA, Founded: 1986, Tom Bogan, Pres

Pacific HiTech Inc. 3855 S 500 W, #B, Salt Lake City UT 84115 USA; 801/261-1024, Fax: 801/261-0310, Co Email: info@pht.com, Web URL: pht.com, Focus: CD-ROM software, Prdts: Best of Internet, Ownrshp: PVT, Founded: 1992, Empl: 50, Cliff Miller, Pres, Email: cliff@pht.com; Brad Midgley, Email: brad@pht.com; Phil Hatch, Email: phil@pht.com

Pacific Image Communications Inc. 919 S Fremont Ave, #238, Alhambra CA 91803 USA; 818/457-8880, Fax: 818/457-8881, Co Email: pacimage@aol.com, Focus: Image processing and fax communication products, Prdts: SuperVoice Series, SuperFax, Ownrshp: PVT, Founded: 1987, Empl: 10, Patrick Leung, Pres, Abe Chang, Co-founder, Glen U. Sugimoto, Mktng Mgr

Pacific Image Electronics Inc. 3895 Del Amo Blvd, #704, Torrance CA 90503 USA; 310/214-5281, 800/909-9966 Fax: 310/214-5282, Focus: Optical scanning devices, Prdts: ScanAce II, ScanMedia, Founded: 1995, Roger A. Bennett, VP

Pacific Internet 600 Corporate Pointe, #100, Culver City CA 90230-7607 USA; 310/410-9700, 800/572-2638 Fax: 310/410-9727, Co Email: @pacnet.com, Web URL: pacnet.com, Focus: Supplier of Internet products and services, Prdts: WebCube-Internet Server Systems, Ownrshp: PVT, Founded: 1994, Empl: 17, Sales ($M): 2.5, Garry S. Hipsher, Founder, Email: garry@pacnet.com; K. Kamath, Mktng Exec, Email: keshav@pacnet.com; Tania Hayek, Int'l Sales Mgr, Email: tania@pacnet.com; Joseph Riser, Comm

Exec, Email: josephr@pacnet.com

Pacific Micro Data Inc. (PMD), 16751 Millikan Ave, Irvine CA 92714-5009 USA; 714/955-9090, Fax: 714/955-9490, Co Email: @p_micro.com, Focus: Mass storage subsystems, RAID, tape backup and CD-ROM servers, Prdts: MAST 9500, Ownrshp: PVT, Founded: 1989, Sales ($M): 15, Ame Gur, Pres, Email: a_gur@pmicro.com; Maury Loomis, Dir Sales & Mktng, Email: m_loomis@pmicro.com

Pacific Microelectronics Inc. 201 San Antonio Cr, #C250, Mountain View CA 94040 USA; 415/948-6200, Fax: 415/948-6296, Co Email: @netusa.com, Web URL: netusa.com, Focus: Unix to PC connectivity software, Prdts: Mac-In-DOS, Common-Link, Bookshelves on OS/2, Ownrshp: PVT, Founded: 1987, Wun C. Chiou, Chmn & CEO, Email: wchiou@netusa.com; Larry Liang, VP Bus Dev, Bob Adams, Pres & COO, Peter Cataneo, VP Mktng

Pacific Software Publishing Inc. 14405 SE 36th St, #300, Bellevue WA 98006 USA; 206/562-1224, Fax: 206/562-0811, Co Email: 70740.1273@compuserve.com, Focus: Japanese word processor software, Prdts: KanjiWord, Ownrshp: PVT, Founded: 1987, Ken Uchikura, Pres, Bethany Bennett, Mktng Coord, Email: 70740.1273@compuserve.com

Pacific Telecom Inc. 805 Broadway, PO Box 9901, Vancouver WA 98668-8701 USA; 360/905-5800, Focus: Telecom services, Ownrshp: OTC, Stk Sym: PTCM, Founded: 1900, Empl: 2,762, Sales ($M): 648.6, Fiscal End: 12/95; Charles E. Robinson, Chmn, Pres & CEO, James H. Huesgen, EVP & CFO, Diana E. Snowdon, SVP, Wesley E. Carson, VP

Pacific Telesis Group 130 Kearny St, #2926, San Francisco CA 94108 USA; 415/394-3000, Fax: 415/989-7606, Web URL: pactel.com, Focus: A regional Bell operating company (RBOC), Ownrshp: NYSE, Stk Sym: PAC, Founded: 1983, Empl: 48,889, Sales ($M): 9,042.0, Fiscal End: 12/95; Philip J. Quigley, Chmn, Pres & CEO, Jim R. Moberg, EVP, Robert L. Barada, VP Corp Strategy & Dev, Michael J. Fitzpatrick, Pres Pactel Enterprises, William E. Downing, EVP & CFO, Thomas O. Moulton Jr., VP Corp Com

Packard Bell 31717 La Tienda Dr, Westlake Village CA 91362 USA; 818/865-1555, Web URL: packardbell.com, Focus: PCs and peripherals, Ownrshp: OTC, Stk Sym: PBEL, Founded: 1985, Sales ($M): 4,300, Fiscal End: 12/95; Beny Alagem, Chmn & CEO, Pres, Brent Cohen, COO, Mal Ranson, VP Mktng, Doug McCormick, Dir Info Syst

Packard Bell Interactive (PBI), 1201 Third Ave, #2301, Seattle WA 98101 USA; 206/654-4100, 800/632-6437 Fax: 206/654-4188, Focus: Educational children's software, Prdts: There's a Dinosaur in the Garden, Ownrshp: Sub. Packard Bell, Glen Uslan, VP Mktng

Pacom Inc. 1257-B Tasman Dr, #B, Sunnyvale CA 94089-2229 USA; 408/752-1590, Fax: 408/982-9378, Focus: PC peripherals, Ownrshp: PVT, H.S. Han, Pres, Y.C. Song, VP Sales, Young Yoo, Dir Sales & Mktng

PageAhead Software Corp 2125 Western Ave, #301, Seattle WA 98121-9814 USA; 206/441-0340, 800/967-9671 Fax: 206/441-9876, Co Email: info@pageahead.com, Focus: Data access and connectivity software, Prdts: SimbaEngine, SimbaLib, Ownrshp: PVT, Founded: 1990, Empl: 20, Michael Satterfield, Pres, Kirk Herrington, VP Eng, Russ Aldrich, VP Mktng, D. Scott Johnson, Marcom Mgr, Email: scottj@pagehead.com

Paging Network Inc. (PageNet), 4965 Preston Park Blvd, #600, Plano TX 75093 USA; 214/985-4100, Fax: 214/985-6711, Co Email: @pagenet.com, Web URL: pagenet.com, Focus: Digital messaging software, Ownrshp: OTC, Stk Sym: PAGE, Founded: 1981, Empl: 4,676, Sales ($M): 552.6, Fiscal End: 12/95; Glenn W. Marschel, Pres & CEO, George M. Perrin, Chmn, Kenneth W. Sanders, SVP & CFO, Michael A. DiMarco, SVP, Barry Fromberg, SVP, Scott L. Baradell, Mgr Corp Com, Email: scott_baradell@pagenet.com

PairGain Technologies Inc. 14402 Franklin Ave, Tustin CA 92680-7013 USA; 714/832-9924, Fax: 714/832-9922, Web URL: pairgain.com, Focus: Telecom products, Prdts: CooperOptics, HiGain, Campus, Megabit Modem, Ownrshp: OTC, Stk Sym: PAIR, Founded: 1988, Empl: 400, Sales ($M): 107.2, Fiscal End: 12/95; Charles S. Strauch, Chmn & CEO, Howard Flagg, Pres, Charles McBrayer, CFO, Kim Gower, Dir Corp Comm

Palm Computing 4410 El Camino Real, #108, Los Altos CA 94022 USA; 415/949-9560, Fax: 415/949-0147, Co Email: info@palm.com, Web URL: palm.com, Focus: Handheld computing products, Prdts: Graffiti, Ownrshp: PVT, Founded: 1992, Empl: 28, Jeff Hawkins, Chief Tech, Email: jeff@palm.com; Donna Dubinsky, Pres & CEO, Email: donna@palm.com; Ed Colligan, VP Mktng, Email: ed@palm.com

Palo Alto Software 144 E 14th Ave, Eugene OR 97401-3564 USA; 541/683-6162, Fax: 541/683-6250, Web URL: pasware.com, Focus: Business planning software, Prdts: Business Plan Toolkit, Business Plan Pro, Marketing Plan Pro, Ownrshp: PVT, Founded: 1983, Empl: 5, Sales ($M): 0.8, Tim Berry, Pres, Email: timberry@aol.com

Panacea Inc. 600 Suffolk St, Lowell MA 01854-3629 USA; 508/937-1760, 800/7297420 Fax: 508/970-0199, Co Email: sales@panacea.com, Focus: Graphics software, Ownrshp: Sub Spacetec, Founded: 1988, Empl: 10, Dennis T. Gain, Pres, Brad Ek, Dir Eng

Panasonic Communications & Systems Co. 2 Panasonic Way, Secaucus NJ 07094 USA; 201/348-7000, Focus: PCs, printers, scanners, monitors and optical mass storage, Ownrshp: Sub. Matsushita, Japan, Steve Yuhas, Pres, Tim Curran, GM Sales

Panther Software 2629 Manhattan Ave,#278, Hermosa Beach CA 90254 USA; 310/372-6806, Fax: 310/372-2347, Co Email: 71223.2636@compuserve.com, Web URL: panthersoft.com, Focus: File organization software, Prdts: Office Central, Steve Robinson, Pres, Lisa Marie McCroskey, Dir Mktng

Pantone Inc. 590 Commerce Blvd, Carlstadt NJ 07072-3098 USA; 201/935-5500, Fax: 201/896-0242, Co Email: @pantone.com, Focus: Color matching systems, Prdts: Pantone Matching System, Ownrshp: PVT, Founded: 1962, Empl: 125, Lawrence Herbert, Pres & CEO, Richard Herbert, SVP, Lisa Herbert, VP Corp Com

PaperClip Software Inc. 3 University Plaza Dr, #600, Hackensack NJ 07601-6208 USA; 201/487-3503, 800/929-3503 Fax: 201/487-0613, Focus: Document imaging software, Ownrshp: PVT, Founded: 1991

PAR Technology Corp. 8383 Seneca Turnpike, New Hartford NY 13413-4991 USA; 315/738-0600, Fax: 315/738-0411, Web URL: partech.com, Focus: Transaction processing POS systems, Ownrshp: NYSE, Stk Sym: PTC, Founded: 1968, Empl: 903, Sales ($M): 107.4, Fiscal End: 12/95; John W. Sammon Jr., Chmn & Pres, Charles A. Constantino, EVP, Ben F. Williams, VP Bus Dev, Kenneth Giffune, VP Human Resources, Ronald J. Casciano, VP & CFO, Karen L. Sammon, Dir Investor Relations, Email: ksammon@partech.com

Paradigm Software Development Inc. 2510 Western Ave, #500, Seattle WA 98121 USA; 206/728-2281, 800/967-5947 Fax: 206/728-8401, Focus: Employee management software, Prdts: Workwise, Ownrshp: PVT, Founded: 1992, Cliff Monlux, Pres, Stanton Monlux, VP Mktng, Email: stantond@aol.com; Tom Wynne, Head Prod Dev, Kirby Watson, Dir Sales

Paradigm Technology Inc. 71 Vista Montana, San Jose CA 95134 USA; 408/954-0500, Fax: 408/954-8913, Focus: SRAM semiconductors for telecommunications and high-end desk-top computer applications, Stk Sym: PRDM, Founded: 1987, Empl: 150, Sales ($M): 32.5, Fiscal End: 12/94; Michael Gulett, Pres & CEO, Richard Veldhouse, VP Mktng & Sales, Robert McClelland, CFO, Doug Schirle, Controller

ParaGraph Int'l. 1688 Dell Ave, Campbell CA 95008 USA; 408/364-7700, Fax: 408/374-5466, Web URL: paragraph.com, Focus:

Handwriting recognition software, 3D multimedia, Internet, Prdts: CalliGrapher, ParaScript, FreeStyle, Ownrshp: PVT, Founded: 1989, Stephan Pachikov, Pres

Parallax Graphics Inc. 2500 Condensa St, Santa Clara CA 95051 USA; 408/727-2220, Fax: 408/980-5139, Web URL: parallax.com, Focus: Video imaging products, Prdts: XVideo, PowerVideo, Multivideo, MovieStream, Ownrshp: Sub. Dynatech Corp., Founded: 1982, Empl: 50, Frank Florence, Pres, Dennis Drowty, VP Ops, Robert Goodwin, VP Eng, Lee Caswell, VP Sales & Mktng, Email: lee@parallax.com; Barbara Kay, Prod Mktng Mgr, Email: bkay@parallax.com

Parallel PCs Inc. 1404 Durwood Dr, Reading PA 19609 USA; 610/670-1710, Focus: Parallel processing software, Prdts: Synectics, Ownrshp: PVT, Founded: 1988, Steve Rosenberry, Pres, Mario Leone, Dir Eng

Parallel Storage Solutions 116 S Central Ave, Elmsford NY 10523 USA; 914/347-7044, 800/998-7839 Fax: 914/347-4646, Focus: Portable backup products, Prdts: Tape Station Series, PSS-PD Series, Ownrshp: PVT, Founded: 1992, Marvin Hilf, Pres, Jess Hurwitz, Dir Prod Dev

Parallel Technologies Inc. 10603 170th Court NE, Redmond WA 98052 USA; 206/883-6900, Fax: 206/869-9767, Focus: Parallel ports, Ownrshp: PVT, Don Schuman, Pres, Maurice Fuller, Dir Mktng

Parallel Technologies Sales 4240 B St, Auburn WA 98001 USA; 206/813-8728, Fax: 206/813-8730, Focus: Computer accessories, Prdts: Direct Cable Connection, Frank Vlacil, VP

Parametric Technology Corp. 128 Technology Dr, Waltham MA 02154 USA; 617/398-5000, Fax: 617/398-6000, Web URL: ptc.com, Focus: Engineering design software, Ownrshp: OTC, Founded: 1987, Empl: 899, Sales ($M): 441, Fiscal End: 9/95; Steven C. Walske, Pres & CEO, Samuel P. Geisberg, EVP & Chmn, Louis J. Volpe, SVP Mktng & Ops, C. Richard Harrison, SVP Sales, Nancy Herzog

Paramount Interactive 2019 Landings Dr, Mountain View CA 94043-0815 USA; 415/812-8200, Fax: 415/813-8055, Focus: Multimedia entertainment software, Ownrshp: Sub. Paramount Communications

Parana Supplies Corp. 3625 Del Amo Blvd #260, Torrance CA 90503 USA; 310/793-1325, 800/472-7262 Fax: 800/822-1343, Focus: Printer supplies, Ownrshp: PVT, Founded: 1990, Empl: 110, Haruyasu Murasawa, Pres, Masahiro Ueda, EVP, Deena Gribben, Sales Mgr, Bob Anderson, Mktng Mgr

ParaSoft Corp. 2031 S Myrtle Ave, Monrovia CA 91016 USA; 818/305-0041, Fax: 818/305-9048, Co Email: info@parasoft.com, Web URL: parasoft.com, Focus: Software tools for parallel computers, Prdts: Insure++, Ownrshp: PVT, Founded: 1987, Adam Kolawa, Chmn & CEO, Arthur Hicken, Mktng Mgr, Email: ahicken@parasoft.com

ParcPlace-Digitalk Inc. 999 E Arques Ave, Sunnyvale CA 94086-4593 USA; 408/481-9090, 800/759-7272 Fax: 408/481-9095, Co Email: @parcplace.com, Web URL: parcplace.com, Focus: System software, Prdts: Smalltalk 80, Object Builder, Ownrshp: OTC, Stk Sym: PARQ, Founded: 1986, Empl: 322, Sales ($M): 49.6, Fiscal End: 3/96; William P. Lyons, Pres & CEO, Adele Goldberg, Chmn, Peter Deutsch, CTO, Martin Yam, SVP Sales & Mktng, Carolyn V. Aver, VP & CFO, Ellie Victor, Email: ellie@parcplace.com

Paris Business Products 122 Kissel Rd, Burlington NJ 08016 USA; 800/523-6454 Focus: Continuous forms and computer paper, Prdts: PageSaver Plus, Founded: 1964

Parity Software One Harbor Dr, #110, Sausalito CA 94965 USA; 415/332-5656, Fax: 415/332-5657, Co Email: @paritysw.com, Focus: Call processing software, Prdts: VoiceBocx, Kelly Ransom, Email: kellyr@paritysw.com

Parity Systems Inc. 110 Knowles Dr, Los Gatos CA 95030-1828 USA; 408/378-1000, 800/514/4080 Fax: 408/378-1022, Co

Email: inquire@parity.com, Web URL: parity.com, Focus: Unix workstations, peripherals and software, Ownrshp: PVT, Founded: 1986, Empl: 60, Sales ($M): 35, Norbert Witt, Pres & CEO, Nick Ward, VP Fin & CFO, Robbi Robinson, Mktng Mgr, Email: rob@parity.com

ParSoft Corp. 2031 S Myrtle Ave, Monrovia CA 91016-4836 USA; 818/305-0041, Fax: 818/305-9048, Co Email: @parsoft.com, Focus: Software development tools, Prdts: Insight, Ownrshp: PVT, Founded: 1987, Adam Kowala, Chmn & CEO, Jon Flower, Pres, Arthur Hicken, Mktng Dir, Email: ahicken@parasoft.com

Parsons Technology Inc. One Parsons Dr, PO Box 100, Hiawatha IA 52233-0100 USA; 319/395-9626, Fax: 319/395-0217, Focus: PC productivity software, Prdts: Money Counts, Personal Tax Edge, It's Legal, Ownrshp: Sub Intuit, Founded: 1984, Empl: 600, Sales ($M): 41, Fiscal End: 12/93; Bob Parsons, Pres, Joan Dyal, Dir Corp Comm, Scott Porter, CFO

Partners-in-Health Inc. 9619 Chesapeake Dr, San Diego CA 92123 USA; 619/514-4315, Fax: 619/565-1508, Focus: Health care software, Prdts: MLTS-Medicare Log Tracking System, Ownrshp: PVT, Empl: 3, Ian Wisenberg, Pres, Rocky Smolin, VP Mktng

Passport Corp. Mark Centre III, 140 E Ridgewood Ave, Paramus NJ 07652 USA; 201/634-1100, 800/926-6736 Fax: 201/634-0406, Focus: Cross-platform application development environment, Prdts: Passport, Richard Ramsdell, Pres, Alan Tonnesen, EVP, Cynthia Roeth

Pathlight Technology Inc. 767 Warren Rd, Ithaca NY 14850-1255 USA; 607/226-4000, Fax: 607/266-4020, Co Email: @pathlight.com, Focus: SSA adapters and associated software products, Prdts: StreamLine-PCI, Alex Lieb, VP Mktng & Sales, Rahmani Khezri, VP R&D, R. Chris Martens, Dir Mktng, Email: rcm@pathlight.com

Patricia Seybold Group 148 State St, 7th Floor, Boston MA 02109 USA; 617/742-5200, 800/826-2424 Fax: 617/742-1028, Web URL: psgroup.com, Focus: Information on distributed computing for networked organizations, Ownrshp: PVT, Founded: 1985, Empl: 17, Patricia Seybold, Pres & Publisher, Ronni Marshak, VP & Editor-in-Chief

Patton & Patton Software Corp. 16890 Church St, Bldg 16, Morgan Hill CA 95037-5144 USA; 408/778-6557, Fax: 408/778-9972, Focus: Flow charting software, Ownrshp: PVT, Founded: 1982, Empl: 19, Sales ($M): 4.3, Fiscal End: 9/92; William L. Patton Sr., Pres, Bill Patton Jr., GM

Paul Mace Software 400 Williamson Way, Ashland OR 97520 USA; 541/488-2322, 800/944-0191 Fax: 541/488-1549, Web URL: pmace.com, Focus: Windows multimedia authoring tools for the Internet, Prdts: EXPO, Ownrshp: PVT, Founded: 1986, Empl: 12, Paul Mace, CEO, Kathleen Kahle, CFO, Doug Zeffer, Dir Dev

Paychex Inc. 911 Panorama Trail S, Rochester NY 14625-0397 USA; 716/385-6666, Fax: 716/383-3423, Web URL: paychex.com, Focus: Payroll data processing services, Prdts: TAXPAY, PAYCHEX, PAYLINK, Ownrshp: OTC, Stk Sym: PAYX, Founded: 1971, Empl: 3,950, Sales ($M): 325.3, Fiscal End: 5/96; B. Thomas Golisano, Chmn, Pres & CEO, John T. Carlen, EVP, Eugene R. Polisseni, VP Mktng, Walter Turek, VP Sales, G. Thomas Clark, VP & CFO

PC Connection Inc. 6 Mill St, Marlow NH 03456 USA; 603/446-3383, 800/800-1111 Fax: 603/446-7791, Focus: Mail order sales of PC and Mac computers, software and peripherals, Ownrshp: PVT, Founded: 1982, Sales ($M): 250, Fiscal End: 12/95; Patricia Gallup, Chmn & CEO, David Hall, EVP, Wayne Wilson, CFO, Deirdre Nation, Corp Comm

PC Data 11260 Roger Bacon Dr #204, Reston VA 20190 USA; 703/435-1025, Fax: 703/478-0484, Co Email: pcdata@aol.com, Focus: PC software and hardware sales tracking and market shares, Ownrshp: PVT, Founded: 1991, Empl: 10, Ann Stephens, Pres

PC DOCS Inc. 25 Burlington Mall Rd, Burlington MA 01803 USA;

617/273-3800, Fax: 617/272-3693, Co Email: @pcdocs.com, Web URL: pcdocs.com, Focus: Document management software, Prdts: DOCS Open, DOCS Mobile, DOCS Interchange, Ownrshp: Sub PC DOCS Group, Canada, Stk Sym: DOCSF, Founded: 1989, Empl: 160, Sales ($M): 81.2, Fiscal End: 6/96; Scott Kadlec, Pres, Email: scottk@pcdocs.com; Larry Bohn, EVP & GM, Email: larryb@pcdocs.com; Jeff Hoey, VP Sales, Email: jeffh@pcdocs.com; Ann Palermo, VP Mktng, Email: annp@pcdocs.com; Beth Parker, Marcom Mgr, Email: bethp@pcdocs.com

PC Memory Card Int'l. Assoc. (PCMCIA), 2635 N First St, #209, San Jose CA 95134 USA; 408/433-2273, Fax: 408/433-9558, Co Email: office@pcmcia.com, Web URL: pc-card.com, Focus: Advancement of PC memory cards, Ownrshp: Nonprofit, Founded: 1989, Empl: 525, Bill Lempesis, Exec Dir, Stephen Harper, Pres & Chmn, Greg Barr, Sr Comm Specialist, Email: gbarr@pcmcia.org

PC Service Source Inc. 2350 Valley View Ln, Dallas TX 75234 USA; 214/406-8583, 800/727-2787 Fax: 214/406-9081, Focus: Service parts distributor, Ownrshp: OTC, Stk Sym: PCSS, Founded: 1989, Empl: 350, Sales ($M): 68.7, Fiscal End: 12/95; Avery More, Chmn, Mark T. Hilz, Pres & CEO, Danny Hendrix, VP Ops

PC Wholesale 444 Scott Dr, Bloomingdale IL 60108 USA; 708/307-1700, 800/525-4727 Fax: 708/307-2450, Web URL: pcwholesale.com, Focus: PC product distributor, Founded: 1990, Empl: 65, Daniel J. O'Brien, COO

PC-Kwik Corp. 3800 SW Cedar Hills Blvd, #260, Beaverton OR 97005-2035 USA; 503/644-5644, 800/274-5945 Fax: 503/646-8267, Co Email: @pckwik.mhs.compuserve.com, Focus: Utility software, Prdts: PC-Kwik, Ownrshp: Sub. Micro Design, Founded: 1982, Empl: 35, Sales ($M): 3.0, Bruce Schafer, Pres, Email: bruce@pckwik.mhs.compuserve.com; Bob Hughes, Dir Sales & Mktng, Email: bob@pckwik.mhs.compuserve.com; Jana Geary, Marcom Spec

PCI Special Interest Group (PCI), 5200 NE Elam Young Pkwy, Hillsboro OR 97124 USA; 800/433-5177 Fax: 503/693-0920, Co Email: pcisig@teleport.com, Focus: Open use of PCI local bus, Ownrshp: Nonprofit, Founded: 1992

PCs Compleat 34 St Martin Dr, Marlboro MA 01752-3021 USA; 508/480-8500, 800/234-6882 Fax: 508/480-8583, Co Email: sales@pcscompleat.com, Web URL: pcscompleat.com, Focus: Mail order PC sales, Ownrshp: Sub CompUSA, Founded: 1991, Empl: 30, Gordon Hoffstein, Chmn & CEO, Jack Littman-Quinn, Pres & COO, Bill Brown, EVP

PDC 1002 W Ninth Ave, King of Prussia PA 19406 USA; 610/265-3300, Fax: 610/265-2165, Co Email: @pa.pdc.com, Focus: Unix system administration software, Prdts: BudTool, Ownrshp: PVT, Founded: 1986, Empl: 107, Sales ($M): 35, George Wilson, Pres & CEO, Email: gwilson@pa.pdc.com; Don Trimmer, VP Strategic Dev, Email: dtrimmer@eng.pdc.com; Roger Stager, VP Eng, Email: rstager@eng.pdc.com; Karen Kelty, Dir Mktng, Email: kkelty@pa.pdc.com

PDQ Peripherals 3350 Scott Blvd, Bldg. 7, Santa Clara CA 95054 USA; 408/727-2600, 800/737-7462 Fax: 408/727-2435, Co Email: pdq.periph@aol.com, Focus: Designs, manufactures & markets removable mass storage peripheral subsystems, Founded: 1990, Melanie Tunick, Mktng Mgr

Peachtree Software Inc. 1505-C Pavilion Place, Norcross GA 30093 USA; 770/564-5800, 800/228-0068 Fax: 404/564-5888, Focus: Accounting and productivity software, Ownrshp: Sub. ADP, Founded: 1975, Empl: 160, Sales ($M): 40, Ron Verni, Pres, John Vasil, VP Sales

Peak Technologies Group Inc. 600 Madison Ave, 26th Floor, New York NY 10022 USA; 212/832-2833, Fax: 212/832-3151, Focus: Bar code products, Ownrshp: OTC, Stk Sym: PEAK, Founded: 1989, Empl: 813, Sales ($M): 184.6, Fiscal End: 12/95; Nicholas R. Toms, Chmn, Pres & CEO, John R. Coutts, COO, Edward A. Stevens, EVP & CFO, Robert J. Theodore, SVP, Jack A.

Bowser, SVP, Steve Fowler

Pecan Software Corp. 920 Holcomb Bridge Rd, #201, Roswell GA 30078 USA; 770/594-9707, Fax: 770/594-9707, Focus: MVS operations productivity software, Prdts: Smart/Suite, Ownrshp: PVT, Founded: 1987, Empl: 21, John Andrews, Pres, Tari Schreider, Dir Sales & Mktng

Peer-to-Peer Communications Inc. PO Box 640218, San Jose CA 95164 USA; 408/435-2677, 800/420-2677 Fax: 408/435-0895, Web URL: peer-to-peer.com, Focus: Publisher and distributor of computer and technical books, Ownrshp: PVT, Founded: 1994, Rachel Unkefer, CEO, Chris MacIntosh, Ops Mgr

PeerLogic 555 DeHaro St, San Francisco CA 94107-2348 USA; 415/626-4545, 800/733-7601 Fax: 415/626-4710, Co Email: info@peerlogic.com, Web URL: peerlogic.com, Focus: Network communications software, message-oriented middleware, Ownrshp: PVT, Founded: 1986, Empl: 50, Daniel Gregerson, Pres & CEO, Quincy Yu, CFO, Peter Tait, VP Mktng, John Roberts, VP Dev, Jennifer Hart, Dir Prod Mktng, Email: jhart@peerlogic.com

Pencom Systems Inc. 9050 Capitol of Texas Hwy N, Austin TX 78759 USA; 512/343-1111, Fax: 512/346-6444, Co Email: @pencom.com, Web URL: pencom.com, Focus: Open system products and services, Ownrshp: PVT, Founded: 1991, Empl: 550, Sales ($M): 50+, Wade E. Saadi, Chmn, W. Frank King, Pres Pencom SW, Edgar Saadi, SVP, Patrick D. Motola, VP & GM Pencom SW, Edward A. Taylor, EVP

Pennant Systems Co. 150 Kettletown Rd, #4001, Southbury CT 06488-2685 USA; 203/849-6844, Fax: 203/849-6825, Focus: Mainframe and midrange printers and peripherals, Ownrshp: Sub. IBM Corp., Founded: 1991, Empl: 1,883, James T. Vanderslice, Pres

Pennsylvania Technology Council 4516 Henry St, #500, Pittsburgh PA 15213 USA; 412/687-2700, Fax: 412/687-2791, Web URL: techcenter-pgh.com, Focus: Association for technology companies in Pennsylvania, Ownrshp: Nonprofit, Founded: 1983, Empl: 2,000, Raymond R. Christman, Exec Dir

Pentax Technologies Corp. 100 Technology Dr, Broomfield CO 80021 USA; 303/460-1600, 800/543-6144 Fax: 303/460-1628, Co Email: @tech.pentax.com, Focus: Scanners and portable printers, Prdts: PocketJet, DS Series, Ownrshp: Sub. Asahi Optical, Japan, Founded: 1985, Empl: 40, Robert A. Bender, Pres, Robert Ariniello, Dir Sales, Steve Juhasz, Dir Mktng, William Bunker, Dir Eng, Bob Owens, Marcom Mgr, Email: bob.owens@tech.pentax.com

Peoplesoft Inc. 4440 Rosewood Dr, Pleasanton CA 94588 USA; 510/225-3000, 800/947-7754 Fax: 510/225-3100, Co Email: info@peoplesoft.com, Web URL: peoplesoft.com, Focus: C/S business software, Prdts: Peoplesoft Financials, Peoplesoft Manufacturing, Ownrshp: OTC, Stk Sym: PSFT, Founded: 1987, Empl: 1,500, Sales ($M): 227.6, Fiscal End: 12/95; David A. Duffield, Chmn, Pres & CEO, Ken Morris, VP R&D, Albert W. Duffield, SVP WW Ops, Ronald E.F. Codd, CFO, John Cate, Dir PR, Email: john_cate@peoplesoft.com

Percon Inc. 1720 Willow Creek Cr, #530, Eugene OR 97402-9171 USA; 541/344-1189, 800/929-7899 Fax: 541/344-1399, Focus: Bar code products, Prdts: Bar Code EasyWand, Ownrshp: OTC, Stk Sym: PRCN, Founded: 1983, Sales ($M): 12.7, Fiscal End: 12/95; Michael Coughlin, Pres, Fabian Borensztein, Prod Mktng Mgr

Percussion Software Inc. 92 Montvale Ave, #2100, Stoneham MA 02180 USA; 617/438-9900, 800/283-0800 Fax: 617/438-9955, Co Email: questions@percussion.com, Focus: Lotus Notes data integration, Prdts: Notrix Composer, Notrix Composer Live!, Ownrshp: PVT, Founded: 1994, Empl: 30, Sales ($M): 5, Fiscal End: 12/95; Barry Reynolds, Pres, Email: barry_reynolds@percussion.com; Audrey Augun, VP Mktng, Email: audrey_augun@percussion.com; Alan Matthews, CTO, Email: alan_matthews@percussion.com; Bill Langlais, VP Dev, Email:

bill_langlais@percussion.com; Jay Seletz, Dir MIS, Email: jay_seletz@percussion.com; Joyce Radnor, Email: 102052.3240@compuserve.com

Peregrine Systems 12670 High Bluff Dr, San Diego CA 92130 USA; 619/481-5000, 800/638-5231 Fax: 619/481-1751, Web URL: peregrine.com, Focus: Help desk and network management applications, Prdts: Remote Network Monitoring Tools, Founded: 1980, John Moores, Chmn, John Woodall, VP Sales & Mktng

PerfecTouch Inc. 200 S Desplaines, Chicago IL 60661 USA; 800/859-2225 Focus: Keyboards, Prdts: PerfecTouch 101, Neal Taslitz, Pres

Performance Awareness Corp. 8521 Six Forks Rd, #200, Raleigh NC 27615 USA; 919/870-8800, Fax: 919/870-7416, Co Email: info@pacorp.com, Web URL: pacorp.com, Focus: Multi-user benchmarking and software testing, Prdts: preVue, Ownrshp: PVT, Founded: 1986, Paul Chou, Pres, Jeff Schuster, Dir Mktng & Sales, Email: jeff@pacorp.com; Kent Siefkes, Tech Dir, Email: kds@pacorp.com; Keira Stroupe, Marcom Mgr, Email: keira@pacorp.com

Performance Computer 315 Science Pkwy, Rochester NY 14620 USA; 716/256-0200, Fax: 716/256-0791, Focus: SCSI adapters and communications adapters, Ownrshp: PVT, Don Turrell, Pres

Performance Software Inc. 26 Parker St, Newburyport MA 01950 USA; 508/462-0737, Fax: 508/462-4755, Co Email: psiusa@delphi.com, Focus: Automated software testing, Prdts: V-Test, Ownrshp: PVT, John J. Kiley, Pres, Amy S. Krane, Dir Mktng, Email: 75363.1102@compuserve.com

Performance Technologies Inc. 315 Science Pkwy, Rochester NY 14620 USA; 716/256-0200, Fax: 716/256-0791, Co Email: @pt.com, Focus: Workstation peripherals, Ownrshp: OTC, Founded: 1981, Empl: 150, Sales ($M): 17.9, Fiscal End: 12/95; Charles E. Maginness, Chmn & CEO, Donald L. Turrell, Pres & COO, Dorrance W. Lamb, VP & CFO, William E. Mahuson, VP Tech, Leah Wilson, Marcom Coord, Email: ljw@pt.com

Performance Technology Inc. 800 Lincoln Ctr, 7800 IH 10 W, San Antonio TX 78230 USA; 210/979-2000, Fax: 210/979-2002, Web URL: perftech.com, Focus: LAN software and Internet connectivity, Prdts: POWERLan, POWERsave, POWERfusion, Instant Internet, Ownrshp: PVT, Founded: 1985, Empl: 50, Paul Finke, Pres & CEO, Email: paulf@perftech.com; Jonathan C. Schmidt, CTO, Email: jon@perftech.com; Rod Frey, CFO, Email: rod@perftech.com; Kathy Donzis, PR Mgr, Email: kathy@perftech.com

Peripheral Land Inc. (PLI), 47421 Bayside Pkwy, Fremont CA 94538 USA; 510/657-2211, Fax: 510/683-9713, Co Email: D0495@applelink.com, Focus: Removable hard disks, Ownrshp: PVT, Founded: 1985, Empl: 105, Sales ($M): 26, Leo Berenguel, Pres, Daniel Losky, VP Mktng, Frank Jaramillo, EVP Sales

Perkin-Elmer Corp. 761 Main Ave, Norwalk CT 06859-0310 USA; 203/762-1000, Fax: 203/762-6000, Web URL: perkin-elmer.com, Focus: Computer-based instruments, Ownrshp: NYSE, Stk Sym: PKN, Founded: 1937, Empl: 5,600, Sales ($M): 1,113.6, Fiscal End: 6/95; Tony L. White Kelley, Chmn, Pres & CEO, Peter Barrett, VP WW Sales & Svc, Stephen O. Jaeger, VP & CFO, Joseph E. Malandrakis, VP WW Ops, Julianne A. Grace, VP Corp Rel

Perot Systems 1801 Robert Fulton Dr, #200, Reston VA 22091 USA; 703/716-1400, Fax: 703/648-2472, Web URL: perotsystems.com, Focus: Computer services, Ownrshp: PVT, Founded: 1988, Empl: 1,500, Mort Meyerson, Chmn, James Cannavino, Pres & CEO

Persoft Inc. 465 Science Dr, PO Box 44953, Madison WI 53744-4953 USA; 608/273-6000, Fax: 608/273-8227, Co Email: @persoft.com, Web URL: persoft.com, Focus: Network products, Ownrshp: PVT, Founded: 1982, Empl: 135, Sales ($M): 19.5, Fiscal End: 12/96; Thomas Wolfe, Pres & CEO, Susan Hughes, EVP Bus Dev, Steven Entine, VP SW Dev & CTO, Gary Larkins, VP Sales & Mktng, Martin Chiaro, CFO, Marti Westlake, PR Spec, Email: westlake@persoft.com

Personal Computer Rental (PCR), 2557 Rt 130, Cranbury NJ 08512 USA; 609/395-6828, 800/922-8646 Fax: 609/395-7049, Web URL: pcrrent.com, Focus: PC rentals nationwide, Founded: 1983

Personal Library Software Inc. (PLS), 2400 Research Blvd, #350, Rockville MD 20850 USA; 301/990-1155, Fax: 301/963-9738, Co Email: info@pls.com, Focus: Search software for online systems, Ownrshp: PVT, Matthew B. Koll, Pres, Dave Van Daele, VP Sales & Mktng, Adrienne Griffith, Email: adrienne@pls.com

Personal Technology Research 63 Fountain St, #400, Framingham MA 01701 USA; 508/875-5858, Fax: 508/875-2975, Co Email: ptrcorp@aol.com, Focus: Data on retail distribution of information technology products, Ownrshp: PVT, Founded: 1986, Empl: 35, Sales ($M): 3, Casey Dworkin, GM

Personal Training Systems 173 Jefferson Dr, Menlo Park CA 94025-1114 USA; 415/462-2100, 800/832-2499 Fax: 415/462-2101, Co Email: ptssales@ptst.com, Web URL: ptst.com, Focus: PC software tutorials, Ownrshp: PVT, Founded: 1986, Empl: 17, Sales ($M): 3, Ronald Conway, Pres & CEO, Devin Lynch, Dir Sales, Laura Meers, Controller/MIS, Annette Colcord, Marcom Mgr

Personics Corp. 234 Ballardvale St, Wilmington MA 01887-9822 USA; 508/658-0040, 800/445-3311 Fax: 508/988-0105, Focus: PC utility software, Prdts: Monarch, Ownrshp: Sub. Datawatch, Founded: 1984, Empl: 20, Marc Peterson, Pres

Pervasive Software Inc. (BTI), 8834 Capitol of TX Hwy, #300, Austin TX 78759 USA; 512/794-1719, Fax: 512/794-1778, Focus: C/S database software, Prdts: Btrieve, Ownrshp: PVT, Ron Harris, Pres & CEO, Rob Adams

Petrotechnical Open Software Corp. (POSC), 10777 Westheimer Rd, #275, Houston TX 77042 USA; 713/784-1880, Fax: 713/784-9219, Focus: Open system software platform for petroleum industry, Ownrshp: Nonprofit, Founded: 1990, Bill Bartz, Pres & CEO

Pettit & Co. P.C. 12750 Merit Dr, #1440, Dallas TX 75251-1247 USA; 214/458-2221, 800/739-9933 Fax: 214/458-2977, Focus: Accounting software, Prdts: Carillon Financials, Ownrshp: PVT, Founded: 1990, Larry R. Pettit, CEO, Amanda L. Potts

PFM Communications 611 Broadway, #428, New York NY 10012 USA; 212/254-5300, Fax: 212/979-2999, Co Email: talk@pfmc.net, Web URL: pfmc.com, Focus: Internet access provider, Ownrshp: PVT, Founded: 1995, Empl: 6, Marc H. Bell, Pres, Email: mhb@pfm.net; Marc Jaffe, SVP, Email: marc@pfmc.net; Brad Verabay, Dir MIS, Email: biver@pfmc

Phar Lap Software Inc. 60 Aberdeen Ave, Cambridge MA 02138 USA; 617/661-1510, Fax: 617/876-2972, Co Email: info@pharlap.com, Web URL: pharlap.com, Focus: Software development tools for X86 embedded systems, Prdts: TNT Realtime DOS-Extender, Realtime ETS Kernel, TNT Embedded ToolSuite, Ownrshp: PVT, Founded: 1986, Empl: 40, Richard M. Smith, Pres, Robert Moote, VP, John Benfatto, VP, Edward Steinfeld, Dir Mktng, Email: efs@pharlap.com

Phase Systems 19545 NW Von Neumann Dr #210, Beaverton OR 97006 USA; 503/531-2400, 800/845-4064 Fax: 503/531-2401, Co Email: info@phasex.com, Web URL: phasex.com:8000

Philips Electronics Groenewoudseweg 1, BA Eindhoven NL-5621 Netherlands; 31-40-786022, Fax: 31-40-785486, Focus: Consumer electronics and other products, Ownrshp: FO, Empl: 252,000, Sales ($M): 33,689, Fiscal End: 12/94; Cor Boonstra, Chmn & Pres, L.G. Nyberg, Pres Comm Syst, D.G. Eustace, EVP & CFO, F.P. Carrubba, EVP

Philips Home Services Inc. 8 New England Exec. Park, Burlington MA 01803 USA; 617/238-3400, Fax: 617/238-3440, Co Email: phsnews@aol.com, Focus: Screen phones and services, Prdts: Philips P100 Screen Phone, Ownrshp: Sub. Philips, Netherlands, Founded: 1993, Empl: 65, Susan Vladeck, VP Mktng, Paul Chapple, Mgr Media Relations, Keith Decie

Philips Key Modules 2001 Gateway Place, #100, San Jose CA 95110 USA; 408/453-7373, Fax: 408/453-6444, Focus: Computer components and subsystems, Ownrshp: Sub. Philips, Netherlands, Arend Verweij, GM, Hoss Bozorgzad, VP Mktng, Mira Van Roon, Mktng Coord

Philips LMS 4425 ArrowsWest Dr, Colorado Springs CO 80907-3489 USA; 719/593-7900, Fax: 719/599-8713, Focus: Tape and optical drives, Prdts: Infinity 6000 Family, Ownrshp: Sub. Philips Elec. N America, Founded: 1986, Empl: 274, Charles Johnston, Pres & CEO, Todd Gresham, VP Sales & Mktng, Susan Wright, Mgr Marcom, Email: susan_wright@lmsmail.lms.com

Philips Media Home and Family Entertainment 10960 Wilshire Blvd, Los Angeles CA 90024 USA; Focus: CD-ROM-based interactive software, Prdts: GeoSafari, Sarina Simon, Pres

Philips Media OptImage 7185 Vista Dr, W Des Moines IA 50266-9313 USA; 515/225-7000, 800/234-5484 Fax: 515/225-0252, Co Email: info@optimage.com, Focus: Multimedia authoring software, Prdts: Media Mogul, Delta V, ShowMaster, Ownrshp: PVT, Founded: 1989, Empl: 50, Sales ($M): 4, Fiscal End: 12/95; John Gray, Pres, Email: gray@pmpro.com; Bernie Mitchell, VP Edu Publishing, Email: bernmitch@aol.com; Gail Wellington, VP Mktng, Email: gailw@pmpro.com; Dan Godwin, VP Sales, Email: godwin@pmpro.com; Jean Brandenburg, Mktng Coord, Email: jeanb@optimage.com

Philips Semiconductor 811 E Arques Ave, Sunnyvale CA 94088-3409 USA; 408/991-3626, 800/447-1500 Fax: 408/991-2311, Co Email: @scs.philips.com, Web URL: semiconductors.philips.com/ps, Focus: ICs, Ownrshp: Sub. N American Philips, Empl: 19,000, Aurthur van der Poel, Chmn & CEO, Peter Brown, PR Mgr, Email: brownpr@scs.philips.com

Phoenix Technologies Ltd. 2770 De La Cruz Blvd, Santa Clara CA 95050-2624 USA; 408/654-9000, Fax: 408/452-2985, Co Email: @ptltd.com, Web URL: ptltd.com, Focus: BIOS software for Wintel PCs, Ownrshp: OTC, Stk Sym: PTEC, Founded: 1979, Empl: 300, Sales ($M): 53.1, Fiscal End: 9/95; Ronald D. Fisher, Chmn & CEO, Jack Kay, Pres & COO, David A. Cane, VP & CTO, George F. Adams, VP Bus Dev, Robert J. Riopel, CFO, Thomas Benoit

PhotoDisc Inc. 2013 Fourth Ave, 4th Floor, Seattle WA 98121 USA; 206/441-9355, Fax: 206/441-9379, Web URL: photodisc.com, Focus: Digital photography on CD-ROM, Ownrshp: PVT, Founded: 1991, Tom Hughes, Pres, Mark Torrance, Chmn & CEO, Bill Heston, VP Bus Dev, Colleen Maloney, VP, Chris Birkeland, VP Ops & Fin, Julie Huffaker

Photonics Corp. 1515 Centre Pointe Dr, Milpitas CA 95035-8010 USA; 408/955-7930, Fax: 408/955-7950, Focus: Wireless data and communications products, Prdts: Collaborative, Ownrshp: OTC, Stk Sym: PHTX, Founded: 1985, Empl: 14, Sales ($M): 1.6, Fiscal End: 12/93; Gary N. Hughes, Pres & CEO

Physician Micro Systems Inc. (PMSI), 2033 6th Ave, #707, Seattle WA 98121 USA; 206/441-8490, 800/770-7674 Fax: 206/441-8915, Co Email: @pmsi.com, Focus: Medical software, Prdts: Practice Partner, Ownrshp: PVT, Founded: 1983, Empl: 19, Andrew Ury, Pres, Email: andyu@pmsi.com

Pick Systems 1691 Browning, Irvine CA 92714 USA; 714/261-7425, 800/367-7425 Fax: 714/250-8187, Co Email: @pick-sys.com, Web URL: picksys.com, Focus: Multidimensional DBMS software, Prdts: D3, Advanced Pick, Ownrshp: PVT, Founded: 1973, Empl: 100, Sales ($M): 20.0, Fiscal End: 2/95; George Olenik, Pres & CEO, M. Denis Hill, VP Marcom, Email: denis@pick-sys.com; Steve Cobb, VP Sales, Email: steve_cobb@picksys.com; William Rice, VP Sales

Picker Graphic Workstations (PGW), 1301-A Westinghouse Blvd, Charlotte NC 28273-6308 USA; 704/588-4330, 800/862-1746 Fax: 704/588-4595, Co Email: mkt@pgw.picker.com, Web URL: picker.com/pgw, Focus: Graphic accelerators, Ownrshp: Sub. Picker Int'l

PicoPower Technology Inc. 3100 W Warren Ave, Fremont CA 94538-6423 USA; 510/623-8300, Focus: PC power management chips, Ownrshp: Sub Cirrus Logic, Founded: 1991, Empl: 30, Robert Lee, Pres & CEO, John Kenny, VP Eng

PictureTel Corp. 222 Rosewood Dr, Danvers MA 01923-1393 USA; 508/762-5000, 800/716-6000 Fax: 508/762-5245, Web URL: picturetel.com, Focus: Videoconferencing products, Ownrshp: OTC, Stk Sym: PCTL, Founded: 1984, Empl: 1,182, Sales ($M): 346.8, Fiscal End: 12/95; Norman E. Gaut, Chmn, Pres & CEO, Robert F. Mitro, SVP, Joan M. Nevins, VP Mktng, Khoa D. Nguyen, SVP & CTO, Les B. Strauss, SVP & CFO, Ron Taylor, Mgr Media Rel

PictureWorks 125 Towne & Country Dr, Danville CA 94526 USA; 510/855-2001, Fax: 510/8552019, Focus: Color imaging software, Prdts: PhotoEnhancer, Ownrshp: PVT, Lisa Woods, VP Mktng

Pilot Network Services Inc. 1000 Marina Village Pkwy, Alameda CA 94501 USA; 510/748-1850, Fax: 510/748-1849, Co Email: @pilot.net, Web URL: pilot.net, Focus: Internet access services, Ownrshp: PVT, Founded: 1993, Empl: 50, Marketta Silvera, Pres & CEO, Thomas Wadlow, Dir Eng & Dev, Jeff Gall, Dir Sales, Email: gall@pilot.net; Stephanie Fohn, Dir Bus Dev, Robert Carrade, Dir Fin

Pindar Systems 1661 N Swan Rd, #132, Tucson AZ 85712 USA; 520/323-9500, Fax: 520/323-9700, Co Email: pindar@pindarusa.com, Focus: Database publishing systems, Prdts: Pindar's Catalog Management System, Founded: 1995, Empl: 600, Steven Auslander, Email: stevena@pindarusa.com

Pinnacle Business Systems Inc. 46 Pilgrim Rd, Holliston MA 01746 USA; 508/429-5936, Fax: 508/429-5636, Focus: Program management software, Prdts: Program Portfolio Manager, Ownrshp: PVT, Founded: 1980, Ron Pipe, Pres

Pinnacle Micro Inc. 19 Technology, Irvine CA 92718 USA; 714/789-3000, 800/553-7070 Fax: 714/789-3150, Co Email: @pinnacle.com, Focus: Optical storage products and document imaging, Prdts: RCD 5020, Ownrshp: OTC, Stk Sym: PNCL, Founded: 1987, Sales ($M): 81.8, Fiscal End: 12/95; William F. Blum, Pres & CEO, Scott A. Blum, EVP, James G. Hanley, SVP Corp Dev, James Robbins, VP R&D, Kevin L. Lehnert, CFO, Jennifer Blanchfield, Dir Mgr, Email: jenpnclpr@aol.com

Pinnacle Technology Inc. PO Box 128, Kirklin IN 46050 USA; 317/279-5157, 800/525-1650 Co Email: info@pinnacletech.com, Web URL: pinnacletech.com, Focus: Software for OS/2, Prdts: KidProof/2, Desktop Commander, Desktop Observatory, Founded: 1992, Eric A. Henning, VP Sales & Mktng, Email: ehenning@pinnacletech.com

PinPoint Software Corp. 6531 Crown Blvd, #3A, San Jose CA 95120 USA; 408/997-6900, 800/599-3200 Fax: 800/308-3777, Focus: Network analysis software, Prdts: ClickNet, Ownrshp: PVT, Terry Munday, VP Prod Dev

Pioneer New Media Technologies Inc. 2265 E 220th St, Long Beach CA 90810 USA; 800/444-6784 Fax: 310/952-2100, Focus: Optical disks, Ownrshp: Sub. Pioneer, Japan, Founded: 1993, Tom Harga, Pres, Hank Evers, VP Sales & Mktng, Tim Takahashi, VP Eng, Paul Streit, Dir Mktng

Pioneer-Standard Electronics Inc. 4800 E 131st St, Cleveland OH 44105 USA; 216/587-3600, Fax: 216/587-3563, Web URL: pios.com, Focus: Distributes electronic products, Ownrshp: OTC, Stk Sym: PIOS, Founded: 1963, Sales ($M): 1,105.3, Fiscal End: 3/96; James L. Bayman, Chmn, Pres & CEO, Janice M. Margheret, SVP, Arthur Rhein, SVP

Pipeline Digital 46-005 Kawa St, #206, Kaneohe HI 96744 USA; 808/233-1120, Web URL: thepipe.com, Focus: Graphics software, Ownrshp: PVT, Jeff DePonte, Email: jd@thepipe.com

Pitney Bowes Inc. 1 Elmcroft Rd, Stamford CT 06926-0700 USA; 203/356-5000, Fax: 203/351-6709, Web URL: pitneybowes.com, Focus: Office automation systems, Ownrshp: NYSE,

Stk Sym: PBI, Founded: 1920, Empl: 28,000, Sales ($M): 3,554.8, Fiscal End: 12/95; Michael J. Critelli, CEO

Pittsburgh High Tech Council 4516 Henry St, Pittsburgh PA 15213 USA; 412/687-2700, Fax: 412/687-2791, Focus: Organization for Pittsburgh high-tech companies, Ownrshp: Nonprofit

Pivotal Software Inc. 310-260 W Esplanade, N Vancouver BC V7M 3G7 Canada; 604/988-9982, Fax: 604/988-0035, Web URL: pivotal.com, Focus: C/S interaction software, Prdts: Pivotal Relationship, Ownrshp: PVT, Founded: 1991, Empl: 30, Norm Francis, Pres, Email: nfrancis@pivotalsoft.com; Keith Wales, Email: kwales@pivotalsoft.com; Cathy Brown, Email: cbrown@pivotalsoft.com; Sharka Stuyt, Dir Mktng, Email: sharka@pivotal.com; Payman Armin, Email: parmin@pivotalsoft.com

Pixar Animation Studios 1001 W Cutting Blvd, Richmond CA 94804 USA; 510/236-4000, Fax: 510/236-0388, Focus: Image and graphics software, Prdts: RenderMan, Showplace, Ownrshp: OTC, Founded: 1986, Empl: 167, Sales ($M): 12.1, Fiscal End: 12/95; Steven P. Jobs, Chmn & CEO, Edwin E. Catmull, EVP & CTO, Lawrence B. Levy, EVP & CFO

PixelCraft Inc. 130 Doolittle Dr, #19, San Leandro CA 94577 USA; 510/562-2480, 800/933-0330 Fax: 510/562-6451, Focus: Scanning systems and software, Prdts: Pro Imager, ColorAccess, Ownrshp: PVT, Founded: 1992, Jeffrey Tung, Pres, Bruce Mills, VP Mktng & Support

PKWare Inc. 9025 N Deerwood Dr, Brown Deer WI 53223 USA; 414/354-8699, Fax: 414/354-8559, Co Email: info@pkware.com, Web URL: pkware.com, Focus: Data compression software, Prdts: PKZIP, PKLITE, PKWARE Data Compression Libraries, Ownrshp: PVT, Founded: 1986, Empl: 35, Phil Katz, Pres, Bob Gorman, Mktng Mgr, Email: bobg@pkware.com

Planar Systems Inc. 1400 NW Compton Dr, Beaverton OR 97006 USA; 503/690-1100, Fax: 503/690-1541, Focus: EL flat panel displays, Ownrshp: OTC, Stk Sym: PLNR, Founded: 1983, Empl: 450, Sales ($M): 60.4, Fiscal End: 9/94; James M. Hurd, Pres & CEO, Curtis M. Stevens, EVP & CFO, Christopher N. King, EVP & CTO, Malcolm J. Russ, VP

Plantronics 345 Encinal St, Santa Cruz CA 95060 USA; 408/426-5858, Fax: 408/425-8053, Focus: Telephone headsets, Ownrshp: OTC, Founded: 1961, Sales ($M): 183.0, Fiscal End: 3/96; Robert S. Cecil, Chmn & CEO

Plasmon Data Inc. 2045 Junction Ave, San Jose CA 95131-2105 USA; 408/474-0100, 800/445-9400 Fax: 408/474-0111, Co Email: @plasmonca.com, Focus: Optical disk manufacturer, Prdts: CDRecorder, Founded: 1982, Empl: 100, Sales ($M): 30, Fiscal End: 3/95; Peter Helfet, CEO, Phil Storey, Pres, David Kalstrom, SVP

Plastic Thought Inc. 10260-112 St, Edmonton Alberta T5K 1M4 USA; 403/429-5051, 800/635-5715 Fax: 403/426-0632, Co Email: @plasticthought.com, Web URL: 3d-active.com, Focus: 3D software, Prdts: 3d-Active, Ownrshp: PVT, John Davis, VP Mktng & Sales, Email: john@plasticthought.com

Platinum Software Corp. 195 Technology Dr, Irvine CA 92718-2402 USA; 714/453-4000, 800/999-1809 Fax: 714/453-4091, Co Email: @platsoft.com, Web URL: platsoft.com, Focus: Accounting and financial software, Prdts: Platinum for Windows, Ownrshp: OTC, Stk Sym: PSQL, Founded: 1984, Empl: 450, Sales ($M): 40.6, Fiscal End: 6/96; Carmelo J. Santoro, Chmn, L. George Klaus, Pres & CEO, Kevin P. Riegelsberger, VP Sales, Jim Mcmullen, CTO, Michael J. Simmons, CFO, Geri L. Schanz, Dir Corp Comm, Email: gschanz@platsoft.com

Platinum Technology Inc. (PTI), 1815 S Meyers Rd, Oakbrook Terrace IL 60181-5235 USA; 708/620-5000, Fax: 708/691-0710, Web URL: platinum.com, Focus: Mainframe system software, Ownrshp: OTC, Stk Sym: PLAT, Empl: 743, Sales ($M): 275.9, Fiscal End: 12/95; Andrew J. Filipowski, Chmn, Pres & CEO, Paul L. Humenansky, EVP & COO, Thomas A. Slowey, EVP Sales, Paul A. Tatro, EVP Ops, Michael P. Cullinane, SVP & CFO, Michelle

Edelman

Pleiades Research 5904 Monrey Rd, Los Angeles CA 90042 USA; 213/259-1727, Fax: 213/259-1728, Focus: Macintosh voice/fax response products, Prdts: Digital Storefront, Ownrshp: PVT, Steve Nasypany

Plextor 4255 Burton Dr, Santa Clara CA 95054 USA; 408/980-1838, 800/886-3935 Fax: 408/986-1010, Focus: CD-ROMs, Ownrshp: Sub Shinano Kenshi, Japan, Founded: 1990, Robert Tatar, VP, Felix Nemirovsky, Eng Mgr, Email: felixn@netcom.com; Susan Sherman, Marcom Coord

Plexus Software Inc. 1310 Chesapeake Terrace, Sunnyvale CA 94089 USA; 408/747-1210, Fax: 408/727-1245, Focus: Document imaging and workflow software, Ownrshp: Sub BancTec, Founded: 1989, Empl: 180, John A. Torkelson, VP & GM

Plotter Supplies Inc. 10475 Irma Dr, PO Box 330010, Denver CO 80233 USA; 303/450-2900, Fax: 303/450-0926, Focus: Plotter and graphics supplies and accessories, Ownrshp: PVT, Founded: 1983, Empl: 14, Don Stewart, Pres & CEO, Janice Stewart, VP, Brandi Falagrady, Sec & Tres

Plustek USA Inc. 1362 Boreaux Dr, Sunnyvale CA 94089-1005 USA; 408/745-7111, 800/685-8088 Fax: 408/745-7562, Focus: Color scanners, Ownrshp: PVT, David Chen, VP

PNY Electronics Inc. (PNY), 200 Anderson Ave, Moonachie NJ 07074 USA; 201/438-6300, Fax: 201/438-9097, Focus: Computer memory boards, Ownrshp: PVT, Founded: 1985, Empl: 200, Sales ($M): 300, Fiscal End: 12/94; Gadi Cohen, Pres, Ray LeBlanc, VP Sales & Mktng, Michael Ventriello, PR Mgr

PointCast Inc. 10101 N De Anza Blvd, #400, Cupertino CA 95014 408/253-0894, Fax: 408/253-1062, Co Email: @pointcast.cim, Web URL: pointcast.com, Focus: Internet content delivery software, Ownrshp: PVT, Founded: 1992, Empl: 140, Christopher R. Hassett, Pres & CEO

Polaroid Corp. 575 Technology Square, Cambridge MA 02139 USA; 617/577-2000, Fax: 617/577-2800, Focus: Magnetic media, peripherals and photographic products, Ownrshp: NYSE, Stk Sym: PRD, Founded: 1939, Empl: 12,000, Sales ($M): 2,236.9, Fiscal End: 12/95

Polhemus Inc. 1 Hercules Dr, PO Box 560, Colchester VT 05446 USA; 802/655-3159, 800/357-4777 Fax: 802/655-1439, Co Email: @polhemus.com, Web URL: polhemus.com/trackers, Focus: 3-D digitizers, 6 degree-of-freedom position input device, Prdts: 3Space, FasTrak, 3Draw, InsideTrak, IsoTrak II, UltraTrak, Ownrshp: Sub. Kaiser Aero & Elec Co., Founded: 1970, Empl: 43, Philip Cooper, Pres, Email: pgc@polhemus.com; Edward Costello, Dir Mktng, Email: ewc@polhemus.com

Policy Management Systems Corp. (PMSC), One PMS Ctr, Blythewood SC 29016 USA; 803/735-4000, Focus: Software for insurance industry, Ownrshp: OTC, Stk Sym: PMSC, Founded: 1972, Empl: 4,655, Sales ($M): 537.3, Fiscal End: 12/95; G. Larry Wilson, Chmn, Pres & CEO, David T. Bailey, EVP, Charles E. Callahan, EVP, Donald A. Coggiola, EVP, Timothy V. Williams, EVP & CFO

Polytel Computer Products Corp. 1287 Hammerwood Ave, Sunnyvale CA 94089 USA; 408/745-1540, 800/245-6655 Fax: 408/745-6340, Co Email: polytel@ix.netcom.com, Web URL: danish.com/polytel, Focus: Programmable touch pad input devices, Prdts: Keyport, Keyport/KBD, Ownrshp: PVT, Founded: 1982, Empl: 6, Sales ($M): 1, Fiscal End: 12/92; John Doering, Pres

Pop Rocket Inc. 181 Downey St, San Francisco CA 94117 USA; 415/731-9112, Fax: 415/731-1710, Web URL: poprocket.com, Focus: Interactive media, Prdts: Total Distortion, Founded: 1991, Empl: 10, Joe Sparks, CEO & Co-founder

Popkin Software & Systems Inc. 11 Park Place, 15th Fl., New York NY 10007-2801 USA; 212/571-3434, 800/732-5227 Fax: 212/571-3436, Co Email: 73362.735@compuserve.com, Focus: CASE tools, Prdts: System Architect, SA Process, SA BPR, Ownrshp: PVT, Founded: 1986, Sales ($M): 10, Ron Scherma, Pres, Jan

Popkin, Chief Scientist, Robert Eddins, VP R&D, Steve Schroer, Dir Sales

PORT Inc. 66 Fort Point St, Norwalk CT 06855 USA; 203/852-1102, Focus: Notebook PC carrying cases, Ownrshp: PVT, W.D. Hollingsworth, Pres, Sean O'Connor, CEO, Dana Hollingsworth, COO, Vince Kelly, VP Sales

Portable Graphics Inc. 3006 Longhorn Blvd, #105, Austin TX 78758-7631 USA; 512/719-8000, 800/580-1166 Fax: 512/832-0752, Co Email: info@portable.com, Web URL: portable.com, Focus: Workstation graphics software, Prdts: NPGL, Open Inventor, OpenGL, EDISON, V-Realm, Ownrshp: Sub. Evans & Sutherland, Founded: 1986, Empl: 21, Bhupi Bhasin, Pres, Tom Johnson, VP Sales & Mktng, Debbie Murphy, VP Mktng, Jacque Hernandez, Marcom Mgr, Email: jacque@portable.com

Portfolio Software Inc. 244 Westchester Ave, #310, White Plains NY 10604-2900 USA; 800/729-3966 Co Email: portfolio@aol.com, Focus: Personal information utilities, Prdts: Day-to-Day, Dynodex, Ownrshp: PVT, Founded: 1988, Empl: 33, Jeffrey Elghanayan, Pres & CEO, Donald Mayer, COO & GM, Email: donmayer@eworld.com; Steve Hofflander, Dir Sales & Mktng, Fritz Martin, Dir Prod Dev, Happy Mayer, Dir Info Syst, Deborah Marchand, Prod Mktng Mgr

Portland Macintosh Users Group (PMUG), PO Box 8949, Portland OR 97207 USA; Co Email: jcdvore@eworld.com, Focus: Macintosh users group, Empl: 1,300

Postalsoft Inc. 4439 Mormron Coulee Rd, La Crosse WI 54601-8231 USA; 608/788-8700, Fax: 608/788-1188, Focus: Mailing software, Ownrshp: PVT, Founded: 1984, Empl: 140, Douglas P. Schmidt, Pres, Lori A. Bush-Ziebell, PR Spec

Power Computing Corp. 1225 Barber Ln, Milpitas CA 95035 USA; 408/526-0500, 800/999-7279 Fax: 408/526-0545, Co Email: info@powercc.com, Web URL: powercc.com, Focus: Macintosh-compatible computers, Ownrshp: PVT, Founded: 1993, Stephen Kahng, Pres, Geoff Burr, VP Sales & Mktng, Henry Hirvela, SVP & CFO, Jon Fitch, Sr Dir Eng, Mike Rosenfelt, Email: miker@powercc.com

Powerhouse Entertainment 14850 Quorum Dr, #200, Dallas TX 75240 USA; 214/933-5400, Fax: 214/933-6322, Co Email: pwrhouse95@aol.com, Focus: Interactive entertainment, Prdts: FastLANE, Ownrshp: PVT, Founded: 1995, Frank Mazza, Pres & CEO, Peter Tarca, VP R&D, Dominick Vitris, VP Sales & Mktng, Patty Saitow, Dir Prod Mktng, Richard Fields, VP & CFO

PowerHouse Software PO Box 621, Chester NY 10918 USA; 800/815-4622 Focus: Desktop publishing tools, Prdts: QuarkXPress XTensions, Mike Gorman, Pres

PowerPro Software 158 Rockharbor Ln, PO Box 4611, Foster City CA 94404 USA; 415/345-9278, Fax: 415/345-5128, Focus: Windows utility software, Ownrshp: PVT, Varsha Narayan, VP Sales & Mktng, Tony Nair, Dir Mktng, Kathy Misra

PowerQuest Corp. 1083 N State St, Orem UT 84057 USA; 801/226-8977, 800/379-2566 Fax: 801/226-8941, Co Email: @powerquest.com, Web URL: powerquest.com, Focus: PC software utilities, Prdts: PartitionMagic, Ownrshp: PVT, Founded: 1993, Eric Ruff, Pres, John Christensen, VP Mktng, Michael Robertson, VP Sales, Candice Steelman, PR Mktng Mgr, Email: candice@powerquest.com

Powersoft Corp 561 Virginia Rd, Concord MA 01742 USA; 508/287-1500, Fax: 508/369-3997, Co Email: @powersoft.com, Focus: Software development tools, Prdts: PowerBuilder, Enterprise Series, Ownrshp: Sub Sybase, Stk Sym: PWRS, Founded: 1974, Sales ($M): 132.6, Fiscal End: 12/94; Mitchell E. Kertzman, Chmn & CEO, David Litwack, Pres, Paul MacKay, SVP Sales, David Dewan, VP Tech, Craig Dynes, CFO

PR Newswire (PRN), 810 7th Ave 35th Fl., New York NY 10019-5818 USA; 212/596-1500, 800/832-5522 Fax: 800/793-9313, Co Email: prnews@attmail.com, Web URL: prnewswire.com, Focus: Distributes press releases to high-tech publications, Ownrshp: PVT,

Founded: 1954, Empl: 300, Ira Krawitz, VP Mktng, Email: ikrawitz@prnews.attmail.com; Susan G. McPherson, Mktng Mgr, Email: smcphers@prnews.attmail.com; Tom Beyer, Hi-tech/Fax-on-demand, Email: tbeyer@prnews.attmail.com; Ian Capps, Pres

PR-Consult 4660 La Jolla Village Dr, #500, San Diego CA 92122 USA; 619/625-4622, Fax: 619/458-0708, Focus: Travel information software, Prdts: Biztrav International, Ownrshp: Sub PR-Consult, Germany, Werner Grohmann, Pres

Practical Peripherals Inc. 5854 Peachtree Corners E, PO Box 921789, Norcross GA 30348-5203 USA; 770/840-6832, Fax: 770/441-1213, Focus: Modems and printer buffers, Prdts: MacClass 288 PCMCIA with EZ-Port, Ownrshp: Sub. Hayes Microcomputer, Founded: 1981, Empl: 89, John W. Murphy, Pres, Barbara Smith, PR Spec, Email: prbarbi@aol.com

Pragmatech Inc. 101 Nicholson Ln, San Jose CA 95134 USA; 408/943-1151, Fax: 408/943-1461, Focus: Electronic manufacturing services, Ownrshp: PVT, Founded: 1982, Joe Drummond, Pres & CEO, Mark Lyell, VP Sales & Mktng

Prairie Group PO Box 65820, 1650 Fuller Rd, W Des Moines IA 50265 USA; 515/225-9620, 800/346-5392 Fax: 515/225-2422, Co Email: prairiesft@aol.com, Web URL: users.aol.com/prairiesft, Focus: Contact management and file management software, Prdts: DiskTop, In/Out, DataView, InTouch, Ownrshp: PVT, Founded: 1994, Empl: 10, John S. Kirk, Manager, Email: johnskirk@aol.com; Richard Kirsner, Manager, Email: richmk@aol.com; Paul Miller, Manager, Email: prairiepem@aol.com; Gil Beecher, Manager, Email: psgilb@aol.com; Katherine Anne Kirk, PR Mgr

Praxisoft Inc. 44071 Tippecanoe Terrace, Ashburn VA 22011 USA; 703/729-3391, 800/557-7294 Fax: 703/729-6875, Co Email: info@praxisoft.com, Focus: Color management software, Prdts: Color Compas, Spot Separator, Ownrshp: PVT, Stephen Mace, VP Sales

PRC Inc. 1500 PRC Dr, McLean VA 22102 USA; 703/556-1000, Web URL: prc.com, Focus: Systems integration and computer services, Ownrshp: Sub. Black & Decker, Empl: 7,500, Sales ($M): 720, Fiscal End: 12/95; Jim Leto, Pres

Precept Software Inc. 1072 Arastradero Rd, Palo Alto CA 94304 USA; 415/845-5200, Fax: 415/845-5235, Web URL: precept.com, Focus: Multimedia networking software, Ownrshp: PVT, Founded: 1995, Empl: 19, Judy Estrin, Pres & CEO

Precision Guides 200 SW Market, #1590, Portland OR 97201 USA; 503/227-6219, Fax: 503/227-4888, Focus: Recreation software, Ownrshp: PVT, Founded: 1977, Jim Wolfston, Pres, John Stedman, Chief Eng

Precision Risc Organization (PRO), 1911 Pruneridge Ave, Cupertino CA 94025 USA; 408/447-4249, Fax: 408/447-7568, Focus: Advancement of the PA-RISC technology, Ownrshp: Nonprofit, Founded: 1992, Empl: 14, Jim Bell, Pres

Premenos Corp. 1000 Burnett Ave, 2nd Floor, Concord CA 94520 USA; 510/602-2000, Fax: 510/602-2024, Co Email: @premenos.com, Web URL: premenos.com, Focus: Electronic commerce software, Prdts: EDI/400, Templar, Ownrshp: PVT, Founded: 1989, Empl: 150, Sales ($M): 20, Fiscal End: 12/94; Lew Jenkins, Chmn, Daniel Federman, Pres & CEO, Rebecca Young, VP Mktng, Robert Davis, VP Sales, Ward Wolff, VP Fin

Premier Industrial Corp. 4500 Euclid Ave, PO Bo 94884, Cleveland OH 44101-8323 USA; 216/391-8300, Fax: 216/391-8323, Focus: Distributor of electronic components and equipment, Ownrshp: NYSE, Stk Sym: PRE, Founded: 1940, Empl: 4,500, Sales ($M): 866, Fiscal End: 5/96; Morton L. Mandel, Chmn, Philip S. Sims, Vice Chmn

Premisys Communications Inc. 48664 Milmont Dr, Fremont CA 94538 USA; 510/353-7600, Fax: 510/353-7601, Co Email: @premisys.com, Focus: Digital networking products, Prdts: IMACS, Ownrshp: OTC, Stk Sym: PRMS, Founded: 1990, Empl: 160, Sales ($M): 30.8, Fiscal End: 6/95; Raymond C. Lin, Pres & CEO, Boris J. Auerbuch, SVP & CTO, William J. Smith, SVP Sales

& Mktng, Barton Y. Shiemura, VP Mktng, Riley R. Willcox, SVP & CFO, Linda DeLuca, Dir Corp Com, Email: linda.deluca@premisys.com

Presence Corp. 5 Hillandale Ave, Stamford CT 06902 USA; 203/358-3950, 800/863-3950 Fax: 203/358-3944, Co Email: @prsnce.com, Web URL: prsnce.com, Focus: Internet software, Prdts: QM Web, Joan Phaup, Email: joan@questionmark.com

Presentation Works 618 Fourth St, #205, Santa Rosa CA 95404 USA; 707/545-1400, 800/303-1400 Fax: 707/542-1468, Co Email: pworks@aol.com, Focus: Computer graphics design services, Ownrshp: PVT, Carol Greenburg, Pres

Price Waterhouse 6500 Rock Spring Dr, Bethesda MD 20817 USA; 301/897-5900, Web URL: pw.com, Focus: Management consulting and systems integration, Ownrshp: PVT, Founded: 1850, Empl: 49,000, Sales ($M): 4,400, Fiscal End: 12/95; Shaun F. O'Malley, CEO

Prima International Inc. 3350 Scott Blvd, Bldg. 7, Santa Clara CA 95054 USA; 408/727-2600, Fax: 408/727-2435, Focus: Hard disks, backup tapes, removable storage and PCMCIA products for the industrial market, Founded: 1978, Empl: 18, Sales ($M): 20, Fiscal End: 7/91; Gene Hellar, Pres, Richard Wacker, Dir, Melanie Tunick, Mktng Mgr

Primary Access Corp. 12230 World Trade Dr, San Diego CA 92128-3765 USA; 619/675-4100, Fax: 619/674-8800, Co Email: @priacc.com, Focus: Network access and cellular modem software, Ownrshp: PVT, Founded: 1988, Andy May, VP Mktng, Mark Forster, Email: mark_forster@priacc.com

Primavera Systems Inc. 2 Bala Plaza, Bala Cynwyd PA 19004 USA; 610/667-8600, Fax: 610/667-7894, Web URL: primavera.com, Focus: Project management software, Prdts: SureTrak Project Manager, Ownrshp: PVT, Founded: 1983, Empl: 205, Sales ($M): 30.0, Fiscal End: 12/95; Joel M. Koppelman, Pres, Richard K. Faris, EVP, John H. Capobianco, VP Mktng, Susan Torzolini, Email: storzoli@primavera.com

Primax Electronics 521 Almanor Ave, Sunnyvale CA 94086-3512 USA; 408/522-1200, 800/338-3693 Fax: 408/522-1299, Web URL: primaxelec.com, Focus: Electronics, network printer products and scanners, Prdts: DataPen, Color Mobile Office, DeskScan Color, Ownrshp: Sub Primax, Taiwan, Founded: 1984, Empl: 2,000, Sales ($M): 110, Ray Sun, Pres, Brian Flaherty, Dir Dist Sales, Victor Chu, Dir OEM Sales, Timothy Chong, Dir Finance & Admin, Tim Daughters, Sr Mktng Mgr

Prime Time Freeware 370 Altair Way, #150, Sunnyvale CA 94086 USA; 408/433-9662, Fax: 408/433-0727, Co Email: ptf@cfcl.com, Focus: Unix software, Ownrshp: PVT, Founded: 1991, David Fickes, Dir Mktng, Email: david@advice.com

Primeline Communications Corp. 621 Elbert Burnett Rd, Canton NC 28716 USA; 704/648-1298, 800/665-4635 Fax: 704/648-8337, Co Email: obwinfo@entrepid.com, Focus: Online shopping software, Ownrshp: PVT, Carl Farrington, Pres

Primus Communications Corp. 1601 5th Ave, #1900, Seattle WA 98101-1672 USA; 206/292-1000, Fax: 206/292-1825, Focus: Customer support software, Prdts: SolutionBuilder, Ownrshp: PVT, Founded: 1986, Steven Sperry, Pres, Dave Hadley, VP Eng, Dave Keel, VP Sales & Svcs, Jene Leiner, Marcom Mgr, Email: jleiner@symbologic.com

Princeton Graphic Systems 2801 S Yale St, #110, Santa Ana CA 92704 USA; 714/751-8405, Fax: 714/751-5736, Focus: Monitors, Prdts: Ultra line, Ownrshp: Sub MAG Invovision Inc., William Wang, Pres, Douglas Woo, EVP, Ron Shiroke, Dir Sales, Jason Sparks, Dir Mktng, Kelli Baker, PR Mgr

Principia Products Inc. 1506 McDaniel Dr, Westchester PA 19380-6682 USA; 610/429-1359, 800/858-0860 Fax: 610/430-3316, Focus: Optical mark reading software, Prdts: Remark Office OMR, Ownrshp: Sub. Compucon Services, Founded: 1991, Bruce D. Holenstein, Pres, Paul J. Holenstein, VP, Victor F. Berutti, VP, Email: 70461.1470@compuserve.com

PrintPaks Inc. 834 SW St Clair Ave, #205, Portland OR 97205 USA; 503/295-6564, Fax: 503/295-6578, Focus: Multimedia software, Prdts: PrintPaks, Ownrshp: PVT, Founded: 1995, Judy Thorpe, Pres, Irit Hillel, Rosie Welch

Printronix Inc. 17500 Cartwright Rd, PO Box 19559, Irvine CA 92713-9559 USA; 714/863-1900, Fax: 714/660-8682, Co Email: @printronix.com, Focus: Printers, Ownrshp: OTC, Stk Sym: PTNX, Founded: 1974, Empl: 840, Sales ($M): 159.3, Fiscal End: 3/96; Robert A. Kleist, Pres & CEO, J. Edward Belt, SVP Eng & CTO, Richard Steele, SVP Sales & Mktng, George L. Harwood, SVP Fin & CFO, C. Victor Fitzsimmons, SVP WW Mfg

Prismark Partners LLC 130 Main St, Cold Spring Harbor NY 11724 USA; 516/367-9187, Fax: 516/367-9223, Co Email: prismark@delphi.com, Focus: Technical and marketing consulting in electronic packaging, Ownrshp: PVT, Founded: 1971, Empl: 35, Charles Lassen, Managing Partner, Brian Swiggett, Managing Partner, Mark Christensen, Consultant

Pritsker Corp. 8910 Purdue Rd, #600, Indianapolis IN 46268 USA; 317/879-1011, Fax: 317/471-6525, Co Email: pccorp@pritsker.wintek.com, Focus: Simulation and modeling software, Prdts: Factor Production Manager, Factor/AIM, ARIS, Ownrshp: PVT, Founded: 1973, Empl: 50, Fiscal End: 12/92; John E. Layden, Pres, Steven D. Duket, VP, William R. Lilegdon, VP, Alice H. Dial, Mgr Marcom

Pro CD Inc. 222 Rosewood Dr, Danvers MA 01923-4520 USA; 508/750-0000, Fax: 508/750-0070, Co Email: sales@procd.com, Web URL: procd.com, Focus: CD-ROM phone directories, Prdts: ProPhone, Ownrshp: Sub. Axciom Corp., Founded: 1992, Empl: 100, Sales ($M): 21.7, Fiscal End: 12/95; James E. Bryant, Pres & CEO, Email: jbryant@procd.com; Scott Beatty, Publisher, Cal Brown, VP Mktng, Greg Andrews, EVP & CFO, Jane Van Saaun

ProAmerica Systems Inc. 959 E Collins Blvd, Richardson TX 75081 USA; 214/680-6257, 800/888-9600 Fax: 214/680-6145, Co Email: @proam.com, Focus: Relational database software incorporating distributed databases & remote database access, Prdts: Service Call Management, Ownrshp: PVT, Founded: 1990, Joe Longoria, Pres, Jeff Longoria, VP Sales & Mktng, Email: jeffl@proam.com

Probe Research Inc. 3 Wing Dr, #240, Cedar Knolls NJ 07927 USA; 201/285-1500, Fax: 201/285-1519, Web URL: proberesearch.com, Focus: Voice processing, image processing and telecom information, Ownrshp: PVT, Founded: 1976, Empl: 25, Victor Schnee, Pres

Process Software Corp. 959 Concord St, Framingham MA 01701 USA; 508/879-6994, 800/722-7770 Fax: 508/879-0042, Co Email: info@process.com, Web URL: process.com, Focus: Network and communication software, Ownrshp: PVT, Founded: 1984, Philip C. Denzer, Pres, Bernard Volz, CTO

Procom Technology Inc. 2181 Dupont Dr, Irvine CA 92715 USA; 714/852-1000, 800/800-8600 Fax: 714/852-1221, Co Email: info@procom.com, Web URL: procom.com, Focus: PC mass storage and multimedia products, Prdts: CD Server-56 Rax, Ownrshp: PVT, Founded: 1987, Empl: 100, Sales ($M): 43.0, Fiscal End: 7/92; Alex Razmjoo, Pres, Nick Shahrestany, EVP, Lewis S. Lustman, Marcom Mgr

Prodigy Inc. 445 Hamilton Ave, White Plains NY 10601 USA; 914/993-8000, 800/776-3449 Co Email: @prodigy.com, Focus: Online services, Ownrshp: PVT, Founded: 1988, Empl: 750, Greg Carr, Chmn, Paul DeLacey, Pres & CEO, Mike Darcy, Email: darcy@prodigy.com

Product Management Group 2251 Green St, San Francisco CA 94123 USA; 415/346-7307, Co Email: 71332.1520@compuserve.com, Focus: Management & marketing consulting to high technology companies, Ownrshp: PVT, Founded: 1992, Chris Kocher, Principal, Steve Weiss, Principal, Paul Davoust, Principal

Product Safety Engineering Inc. 8052 N 56th St, Tampa FL 33617 USA; 813/989-2360, Fax: 813/989-2373, Focus: EMI, UL,

CSA, TUV, FCC and FTZ testing, Ownrshp: PVT, Founded: 1986, Empl: 24

Professional Help Desk (PHD), 800 Summer St, Stamford CT 06901 USA; 203/356-7700, 8004743-7253 Fax: 203/356-7900, Co Email: info@prohelpdesk.com, Web URL: prohelpdesk.com, Focus: Call tracking & natural Intelligence for problem resolution, Prdts: Professional Help Desk, Ownrshp: Sub. Data Systems & Software, Stk Sym: DSSI, Founded: 1993, Empl: 1000, Sales ($M): 80, Fiscal End: 12/94; Isidore Sobkowski, Pres, Email: info@prohelpdesk.com; Frances Tischler, VP Mktng, Email: info@prohelpdesk.com; Jacob Lamm, VP Prod Dev, Email: info@prohelpdesk.com; Fred Harwood, Sales Mgr, Email: info@prohelpdesk.com

ProfitKey International Inc. 382 Main St, Salem NH 03079 USA; 603/898-9800, 800/331-2754 Fax: 603/898-7554, Focus: Manufacturing control software, Ownrshp: PVT, Founded: 1979, Empl: 50, Sales ($M): 12, Robert MacDonald, Pres & CEO, H. Jeffrey Fencer, COO, Joseph D. Zazzo, CFO

Programart Corp. 124 Auburn St, Cambridge MA 02138 USA; 617/661-3020, Web URL: programart.com, Focus: Performance measurement software, Ownrshp: PVT, Founded: 1969, Empl: 176, Sales ($M): 34.3, Fiscal End: 12/95; John E. Thron, Pres

Programmed Logic Corp. (PLC), 200 Cottontail Ln, Somerset NJ 08873 USA; 908/302-0090, Fax: 908/322-1903, Co Email: @plc.com, Focus: Develops middleware for the UNIX operating system and related open-systems technologies, Prdts: SnapShot, Founded: 1986, Jeff Helthall, VP Mktng

Programmer's Paradise Inc. 1163 Shrewsbury Ave, Shrewsbury NJ 07702-4321 USA; 908/389-8950, 800/445-7899 Fax: 908/389-9227, Web URL: programmers.com, Focus: Communications software, Stk Sym: PROG, Founded: 1982, Empl: 64, Sales ($M): 93.3, Fiscal End: 12/95; Roger Paradis, Pres & CEO, Email: rparadis@programmers.com; Joseph V. Popolo, EVP, Email: jpopolo@programmers.com; John P. Broderick, VP Fin & CFO, Email: jbroderi@programmers.com; John DiPilla, MIS Mgr, Email: jdipilla@programmers.com; Jeff Largiader, VP, Email: jlargiad@programmers.com

Programmer's Shop, The 90 Industrial Park Rd, Hingham MA 02043-9845 USA; 617/740-2510, Fax: 617/740-1892, Web URL: computing.supershops.com, Focus: Reseller of technically software and business productivity software, Ownrshp: Sub. Software Developer's Co., Founded: 1983, Barry N. Byoff, Pres, James O'Connor, VP & CFO, Rick Haigis, VP Mktng, Paul Meallo, Dir MIS

Progress Software Corp. 14 Oak Park, Bedford MA 01730 USA; 617/280-4000, Fax: 617/280-4095, Co Email: info@progress.com, Web URL: progress.com, Focus: Language and database software, Prdts: Progress, Ownrshp: OTC, Stk Sym: PRGS, Founded: 1981, Empl: 1,105, Sales ($M): 180.1, Fiscal End: 11/95; Joseph W. Alsop, Pres, Chadwick H. Carpenter, SVP Corp Dev, Cary L. Johnson, SVP Sales & Mktng, Charles A. Ziering, VP Dev & CTO, Joni M. Mace, VP Fin

Progressive Networks 616 First Ave, #701, Seattle WA 98104 USA; 206/447-0567, Fax: 206/223-8221, Co Email: serverinfo@prognet.com, Web URL: prognet.com, Focus: Audio-on-demand for the Internet, Ownrshp: PVT, Founded: 1994, Empl: 75, Rob Glaser, Pres & CEO, Andrew Sharpless, SVP, Phil Barrett, VP SW Dev, Maria Cantwell, VP Mktng, James Wells, VP Sales

Project Software & Development Inc. (PSDI), 20 University Rd, Cambridge MA 02138 USA; 617/661-1444, Web URL: psdi.com, Focus: Asset maintenance and project management software, Prdts: Maximo, Ownrshp: OTC, Stk Sym: PSDI, Founded: 1968, Empl: 205, Sales ($M): 46.3, Fiscal End: 9/95; Robert L. Daniels, Chmn & CEO, Dean F. Goodermote, Pres & COO, William J. Sawyer, EVP, Norman E. Drapeau, VP Sales & Mktng, Paul D. Birch, VP & CFO

PROLIN Software 2420 Sand Hill Rd, #101, Menlo Park CA 94025 USA; 415/854-7489, Fax: 415/854-7537, Web URL: prolin.com, Focus: IT service management systems, Prdts: PROLIN IT Service Manager, Jerome H. Mol, Pres & CEO

Prolink Computer Inc. 15336 E Valley Blvd, City of Industry CA 91746 USA; 818/369-3833, Fax: 818/369-4883, Focus: VGA and multimedia card manufacturing, Ownrshp: Sub. Prolink Microsystems, Frank Tseng, Pres

Promark Software Inc. 2609 Westview Dr, #301, N Vancouver BC V7N 3W9 Canada; 604/988-2051, Fax: 604/988-3040, Co Email: promark@wimsey.com, Web URL: wimsey.com/~promark, Focus: Educational and entertainment software, Prdts: Microclas, Puzzle PC, Ownrshp: Public, Stk Sym: PRMK.F, Founded: 1973, Empl: 10, Sales ($M): 1.0, Fiscal End: 9/93; Robert A. Simington, Pres, John J. Henry, CEO, Cary Chan, Mktng Mgr, Email: carychan@wimsey.com

Promodel Corp. 1875 S State, Orem UT 84058 USA; 801/223-4600, Fax: 801/226-6046, Web URL: promodel.com, Focus: Simulation tools that improve business processes, Prdts: ProcessModel, Scott Baird, Pres

Prophet 21 Inc. 19 W College Ave, Yardley PA 19067 USA; 215/493-8900, 800/776-7438 Fax: 215/321-8001, Web URL: p21.com, Focus: Software for distribution/reseller industry, Prdts: The Prophet 21 System, Ownrshp: OTC, Stk Sym: PXXI, Founded: 1967, Empl: 263, Sales ($M): 30.3, Fiscal End: 6/93; John E. Meggitt, Chmn & CEO, Charles L. Jaffe, VP SW Dev, Charles L. Boyle, EVP & CFO

Prosoft Labs 4725 First St, #270, Pleasanton CA 94566 USA; 510/426-6100, Fax: 510/426-6101, Co Email: prosoft@prosoftlabs.com, Web URL: prosoftlabs.com, Focus: Software testing, Ownrshp: PVT, Founded: 1985, Greg Brewer, Pres, Robert J. Danielson, Mktng Dir

Protec Microsystems Inc. 297 Labrosse, Pointe-Claire Quebec H9R 1A3 Canada; 514/630-5832, Fax: 514/694-6973, Co Email: protec@cam.org, Focus: Networking and peripheral sharing devices, Prdts: PSC, PSM, Hub-8E & Hub-16E, Founded: 1982, Mohammed Boutaleb, Pres, Rene Mallandain, VP Ops, Denis Morneau, VP Sales & Mktng, Blanca Novoa, Int'l Sales & Mktng

Proteon Inc. 9 Technology Dr, Westboro MA 01581-1799 USA; 508/898-2800, Fax: 508/898--214, Co Email: ppacket@proteon.com, Focus: LAN products, Ownrshp: OTC, Stk Sym: PTON, Founded: 1972, Empl: 286, Sales ($M): 75.3, Fiscal End: 12/95; Daniel J. Capone Jr., Pres & CEO, Jeffrey B. Low, VP Mktng, Craig S. Richards, SVP WW Sales, Joseph A. DiGiantommaso, VP & CFO

ProtoView Development Co. 2540 Rt 130, Cranbury NJ 08512 USA; 609/655-5000, Fax: 609/655-5353, Focus: Windows development tools, Prdts: PICS, Ownrshp: PVT, Founded: 1988, Dean Guida, Pres, Don Preuninger, VP New Tech, Karen Miller, Sales Mgr, Randy Miller, Purch Mgr

Provident Ventures Inc. 9525 NE 5th St, Bellevue WA 98004-5422 USA; 206/453-6600, Fax: 206/453-0890, Co Email: info@provident.com, Web URL: provident.com, Focus: Interactive media products, Prdts: Unlocking Our Potential, Founded: 1994, Dave Jaworski, Founder, Email: davidjaw@provident.com

ProVUE Development 18411 Gotchard St, #A, Huntington Beach CA 92648-1208 USA; 800/966-7878 Focus: Macintosh database software, Prdts: Panorama, Ownrshp: PVT, Jim Rea, Pres

Proxim Inc. 295 N Bernardo Ave, Mountain View CA 94043 USA; 415/960-1630, Fax: 415/964-5181, Co Email: @proxim.com, Web URL: proxim.com, Focus: Wireless LAN, Prdts: Range Link Wireless LANs, Ownrshp: OTC, Stk Sym: PROX, Founded: 1984, Empl: 103, Sales ($M): 22.1, Fiscal End: 12/95; David C. King, Chmn, Pres & CEO, Warren Hackbarth, VP Sales, Keith E. Glover, VP & CFO, Juan Grau, VP Eng, Brian Button, VP Mktng, Email: brianb@proxim.com; Dan Toporek, PR Mgr, Email: dant@proxim.com

Proxima Corp. 9440 Carroll Park Dr, San Diego CA 92121-2298 USA; 619/457-5500, Fax: 619/457-9647, Focus: LCD projection panels and power protection products, Ownrshp: OTC, Stk Sym:

PRXM, Founded: 1982, Empl: 689, Sales ($M): 159.8, Fiscal End: 3/96; Kenneth E. Olson, Chmn, John E. Rehfeld, Pres & CEO, Donald S. Houston, VP Sales, Mary M. Zoeller, VP Mktng, Dennis A. Whittler, VP & CFO, George L. Wilson, PR Mgr

PSINET Inc. 510 Huntmar Park Dr, Herndon VA 22070-5100 USA; 703/904-4100, 800/827-7482 Fax: 703/904-4200, Co Email: info@psi.com, Web URL: psi.net, Focus: Internet access provider, Prdts: InterRamp, Pipeline, PSIWeb, Stk Sym: PSIX, Founded: 1989, Empl: 565, Sales ($M): 32.9, Fiscal End: 12/95; William L. Schrader, Chmn, Pres & CEO, Steven A. Schoffstall, VP Sales, Martin L. Schoffstall, SVP & CTO, Daniel P. Cunningham, CFO, Bruce M. Ley, VP, Brian Muys, Mgr Corp Com, Email: muysb@psi.net

Psion Inc. 150 Baker Ave, Concord MA 01742-2121 USA; 508/371-0310, Fax: 508/371-9611, Focus: Notebook and handheld PCs, Ownrshp: Sub. Psion, England, Founded: 1980, Sales ($M): 97.5, Fiscal End: 12/94; David Elder, Pres, David Potter, Chmn & CEO, Sarah Fisher, Dir Mktng, Kristina Girard, Corp Com

Publications & Communications Inc. 12416 Hymeadow Dr, Austin TX 78750 USA; 512/250-9023, Fax: 512/331-3900, Web URL: pcinews.com, Focus: 15+ computer magazines, Prdts: AutoCAD World, RISC World, Unisys World, SG World, Oracle World, Ownrshp: PVT, Gary Pittman, Pres & CEO, Tom Clark, VP Dev

Pulse Metric Inc. 6190 Cornerstone Ct E, #E103, San Diego CA 92121-4701 USA; 619/546-9461, Fax: 619/546-9470, Web URL: pulsemetric.com, Focus: Computer-based healthcare products, Prdts: Dyna Pulse, Ownrshp: PVT, Founded: 1990, Empl: 20, Shiu-Shin Chio, Pres, Wenhu Wang, VP, Richard Franke, Dir Sales & Mktng

Pulver Laboratories Inc. 320 N Santa Cruz Ave, Los Gatos CA 95030-7243 USA; 408/399-7000, Fax: 408/399-7001, Co Email: pulverl@ix.netcom.com, Focus: RF and EMI interference, Ownrshp: PVT, Founded: 1979, Empl: 50, Lee J. Pulver, Pres

Pure Software Inc. 1309 S Mary Ave, Sunnyvale CA 94087 USA; 408/720-1600, Fax: 408/720-9200, Co Email: @pure.com, Web URL: pure.com, Focus: Software development tool, Ownrshp: OTC, Founded: 1990, Sales ($M): 44.0, Fiscal End: 12/95; Reed Hastings, Chmn, Pres & CEO, Aki Fujimura, VP Eng, Rob Dickerson, VP Mktng, Russ Lampert, Dir Fin, Toni Giusti, PR Mgr, Email: tgiusti@pure.com

PureData Ltd. 180 W Beaver Creek Rd, Richmond Hill Ontario L4B 1B4 Canada; 416/731-6444, Fax: 416/731-7017, Focus: LAN products, Prdts: PureLAN, PureFax, Ownrshp: PVT, Founded: 1979, Empl: 110, Nicholas Cosentino, CEO, Brian Stringer, VP Fin, Tim P. Gouldson

Pygmy Computer Systems Inc. 13501 SW 128th St, #204, Miami FL 33186-5863 USA; 305/253-1212, 800/447-9469 Fax: 305/255-1876, Focus: Software for hand-held computers, Prdts: Advantage, Founded: 1984, Mark Geigel

Pyramid Technology Corp. 3860 N First St, San Jose CA 95134-1702 USA; 408/428-9000, Focus: Supermini and minimainframe computers, Ownrshp: OTC, Stk Sym: PYRD, Founded: 1981, Empl: 849, Sales ($M): 218.5, Fiscal End: 9/94; Richard H. Lussier, Chmn & CEO, John S. Chen, Pres & COO, Edward W. Scott, EVP, Kent L. Robertson, SVP & CFO

QLogic Corp. 3545 Harbor Blvd PO Box 5001, Costa Mesa CA 92628-5001 USA; 714/438-2200, 800/662-4471 Fax: 714/668-5090, Focus: SCSI products, Ownrshp: OTC, Stk Sym: QLGC, Sales ($M): 44.9, Fiscal End: 3/94; Mel Gable, Pres & CEO, Thomas R. Anderson, VP & CFO, David Tovey, VP Mktng, Joseph F. Pleso, VP WW Sales, William C. Caldwell, VP Eng, Irene Santoyo

QMS Inc. 1 Magnum Pass, PO Box 81250, Mobile AL 36689-1250 USA; 334/633-4300, 800/523-2696 Fax: 334/633-0013, Web URL: qms.com, Focus: Printers and printer controllers, Prdts: QMS magicolor CX, Ownrshp: NYSE, Stk Sym: AQM, Founded: 1977, Empl: 1,000, Sales ($M): 259.7, Fiscal End: 9/95; James L. Busby,

Chmn, Pres & CEO, Gerald G. Roenker, COO, Email: roenker@qms.com; Gregory R. Jones, VP Gen. Counsel, Email: jonesg@isccclink.qms.com; Donald L. Parker, CTO, Email: dparker@rd.qms.com; James K. Doan, EVP & CFO, Email: johnsont@isccclink.is.qms.com; Robson Grieve, Acct Assoc, Email: robson_grieve@arpartners.com

QSoft Solutions Corp. PO Box 556, 445 W Commercial St, E Rochester NY 14445-0556 USA; 716/264-9700, Fax: 716/264-9702, Focus: Software for process improvements and total quality, Ownrshp: PVT, Founded: 1993, Empl: 4, Paul Wetenhall, Pres, Charlene Desens, Ops Mgr

QSound Labs Inc. 2748 37th Ave NE, Calgary Alberta T1Y 5L3 Canada; 403/291-2492, Fax: 403/250-1521, Web URL: qsound.ca, Focus: Multimedia audio products, Ownrshp: OTC, Stk Sym: QSNDF, Founded: 1988, Empl: 35, Sales ($M): 3, Fiscal End: 12/95; Danny Lowe, Chmn, David Gallagher, Pres, Dirk Smits, VP Mktng, Christine Anderson, Exec Assist

QStar Technologies Inc. 632 Anchors St NW, Ft. Walton Beach FL 32548-3861 USA; 904/243-0900, 800/568-2578 Fax: 904/243-4234, Co Email: info@qstar.com, Web URL: qstar.com, Focus: Open systems data management software, Prdts: QStar Data Director, QStar Jukebox Manager, QStar Secure, Ownrshp: PVT, Founded: 1987, Empl: 75, Sales ($M): 10, Fiscal End: 1995; Brian Swafford, Pres & Pres, Email: brian@qstar.com; Nelson Gomez, VP Sales & Mktng, Email: nelson@qstar.com; Pam Deveney, Dir Finances, Todd Deveney, Mgr Release Eng & Support, Email: todd@qstar.com; Mariam Williams

Quadralay Corp. 3925 W Braker Ln, #337, Austin TX 78759-5321 USA; 512/346-9199, Fax: 512/346-8990, Co Email: @quadralay.com, Focus: Unix software development tools, Prdts: UDT, Ownrshp: PVT, Founded: 1989, Anthony McDow, Pres, Email: combs@quadralay.com

Quadrangle Software Corp. 5200 Venture Dr, #200, Ann Arbor MI 48108 USA; 313/769-1675, Fax: 313/769-1695, Focus: Entertainment/sport software, Prdts: Lights Out Sports Fans, Ownrshp: PVT, Founded: 1991, Mark Brown, Pres, Greg Giltrow, VP Sales & Mktng

Quadrant Components 4378 Enterprise St, Fremont CA 94538 USA; 510/656-9988, Fax: 510/656-2208, Focus: PCs and peripherals, Ownrshp: PVT, Founded: 1990, Jackson Cole, CEO, Jerry Kaner, Pres, Robbie Abreu, VP Mktng & Sales

Qualcomm Inc. 6455 Lusk Blvd, San Diego CA 92121-2779 USA; 619/587-1121, Fax: 619/452-9096, Web URL: qualcomm.com, Focus: Wireless communications products, Ownrshp: OTC, Stk Sym: QCOM, Founded: 1985, Empl: 2,000, Sales ($M): 457, Fiscal End: 9/95; Irwin M. Jacobs, Chmn & CEO, Harvey P. White, Pres, Andrew J. Viterbi, Vice Chmn & CTO, Allen B. Salmasi, Pres Wireless Div, Anthony S. Thornley, VP & CFO, Marilyn Jordan

Qualitas Inc. 7101 Wisconsin Ave, #1386, Bethesda MD 20814 USA; 301/907-6700, Fax: 301/907-0905, Co Email: 75300.1107@compuserve.com, Focus: Memory management software, Prdts: BlueMax, Ownrshp: PVT, Founded: 1983, Empl: 45, Philip S. Abrahams, Pres, Bob Smith, Chmn, Mary Stanley, CEO

Qualitas Trading Co. 2055 Durant Ave, Berkeley CA 94704-1512 USA; 510/848-8080, Fax: 510/848-8009, Web URL: qtc.com, Focus: Distributes Japanese software in the US, Prdts: Japan Ease, Word Hunter, Ownrshp: PVT, Founded: 1986, Kazue Osugi, Email: kazue@qtc.com

Quality Semiconductor Inc. 851 Martin Ave, Santa Clara CA 95050-2903 USA; 408/450-8000, Fax: 408/496-0773, Web URL: qualitysemi.com, Focus: Memory chips, logic chips, clock management chips, Prdts: QuickSwitch, Ownrshp: OTC, Stk Sym: QUAL, Founded: 1988, Empl: 149, Sales ($M): 46.2, Fiscal End: 9/95; Chun-Pang Chiu, Chmn & CEO, R. Paul Gupta, Pres & COO, George Anderl, VP Sales, Stephen H. Vonderach, VP & CFO, Dan E. Andersen, Dir Corp Comm, Email: dan_andersen@qsica.com

Quality Systems Inc. (QSI), 17822 E 17th St, #210, Tustin CA

92780 USA; 714/731-7171, Fax: 714/731-9494, Focus: Computer systems for health care industry, Ownrshp: OTC, Stk Sym: QSII, Founded: 1974, Empl: 128, Sales ($M): 16.7, Fiscal End: 3/96; Sheldon Razin, Chmn & Pres, Robert J. Beck, EVP, Donn Neufeld, VP Ops, Janet Razin, VP, Robert G. McGraw, VP & CFO

Qualix Group Inc. 1900 S Norfolk St, #224, San Mateo CA 94403 USA; 415/572-0200, Fax: 415/572-1300, Co Email: info@qualix.com, Web URL: qualix.com, Focus: C/S middleware software, Prdts: Firstwatch, Netscope, Ownrshp: PVT, Founded: 1990, Empl: 30, Richard Than, Pres, Email: rthan@qualix.com; Jean Kovacs, EVP, Email: jkovacs@qualix.com; Arlington Glaze, VP Sales, Email: aglaze@qualix.com; Bruce Felt, VP Fin, Email: bfelt@qualix.com; Barbara Coll, Email: bcoll@qualix.com

QualSoft Corp. 1860 Embarcadero Rd #175, Palo Alto CA 94303 USA; 415/494-6100, 800/814-6350 Fax: 415/494-6099, Co Email: info@qsoft.com, Web URL: qsoft.com, Focus: Distributes software development & testing tools, Prdts: XFaceMaker, XRT Widgets, Nutcracker, Code Integrity, Ownrshp: PVT, Laurent Gharda, Pres

Qualstar Corp. 6709 Independence Ave, Canoga Park CA 91303-2973 USA; 818/592-0061, Fax: 818/592-0116, Co Email: @qualstar.attmail.com, Web URL: qualstar.com, Focus: Tape drives and tape subsystems, Founded: 1984, Empl: 60, Sales ($M): 10, William Gervais, Pres, Bob Covey, VP Mktng, Email: covey@qualstar.com; Daniel Thorlakson, VP Ops, Richard Nelson, VP Eng

Qualtrak 3160 De La Cruz, #206, Santa Clara CA 95054-2415 USA; 408/748-9500, Fax: 408/748-8468, Co Email: info@qualtrak.com, Focus: Software testing tools, Prdts: Xtester, Ownrshp: PVT, Founded: 1986, Mike Manley, CEO, Lucinda Matlack, VP Ops, Marti Colwell, VP Mktng & Sales, Email: marti@qualtrak.com

Quantum Corp. 500 McCarthy Blvd, Milpitas CA 95035 USA; 408/894-4000, Fax: 408/894-3218, Web URL: quantum.com, Focus: Winchester disk drives, Prdts: Hardcard, Passport, ProDrive, Ownrshp: OTC, Stk Sym: QNTM, Founded: 1980, Empl: 7,000, Sales ($M): 4,422.7, Fiscal End: 3/96; Stephen M. Berkley, Chmn, Michael A. Brown, CEO, William R. Roach, EVP WW Sales, Kenneth R. Pelowski, VP Bus Dev, Joseph T. Rogers, EVP & CFO, Catherine Hartsog, VP Corp Com

Quark Inc. 1800 Grant St, Denver CO 80203 USA; 303/894-8888, Fax: 303/894-3399, Focus: Electronic publishing software, Prdts: QuarkXPress, Ownrshp: PVT, Founded: 1981, Empl: 350, Sales ($M): 110, Fred Ebrahimi, Pres & CEO, Tim Gill, Chmn & SVP R&D

Quarter-Inch Cartridge Dr Standards Inc. (QIC), 311 E Carrillo St, Santa Barbara CA 93101 USA; 805/963-3853, Fax: 805/962-1541, Web URL: qic.org, Focus: Develops standards for quarter inch data cartridge tape drives and media, Ownrshp: Nonprofit, Founded: 1982, Empl: 44, Tim Russell, Chmn, Raymond C. Freeman, Jr., Facilitator, Email: ray@qic.org; Tony Miller, Email: qicpr@aol.com

Quarterdeck Corp. 13160 Mindanao Way, Marina del Rey CA 90292-9705 USA; 310/309-3700, Fax: 310/309-4218, Co Email: info@quarterdeck.com, Web URL: quarterdeck.com, Focus: Utilities, remote computing and Internet software, Prdts: QEMM, CleanSweep, Ownrshp: OTC, Stk Sym: QDEK, Founded: 1981, Empl: 200, Sales ($M): 70.7, Fiscal End: 9/95; Stephen W. Tropp, SVP, James Moise, SVP Sales, Email: investor@quarterdeck.com; Bill Ethier, VP Ops, Frank Greico, CFO, Ellen Spooren, Sr Dir Corp Com, Email: ellen@quarterdeck.com

Quatech Inc. 662 Wolf Ledges Pkwy, Akron OH 44311 USA; 216/434-3154, Fax: 216/434-1409, Co Email: @quatech.com, Focus: PC boards, Ownrshp: PVT, Founded: 1983, Empl: 30, Francis Chen, Pres, Email: chen@quatech.com; Michael Cenker, Sales Mgr, Email: cenker@quatech.com; Michele Holler, Mktng Mgr, Email: holler@quatech.com; Bruce Trier, Tech Sup Mgr, Email: trier@quatech.com

Queue 383 Commerce Dr, Fairfield CT 06432 USA; 203/335-

0906, 800/232-2224 Fax: 203/336-2481, Co Email: queueinc@aol.com, Focus: Education software, Ownrshp: PVT, Founded: 1980, Empl: 50, Sales ($M): 6.0, Jonathan Kantrowitz, CEO, Peter Uhrynowski, CFO

Quibus Enterprises Inc. 3340 Marble Terrace, Colorado Springs CO 80906 USA; 719/527-1384, Focus: Fortran programming tools, Prdts: Forwarn, Fortran Development Tools, Ownrshp: PVT, Founded: 1988, Carol Beckman, Pres, James Davies, VP

QuickMedia Labs Inc. 100 Saratoga Ave, #320, Santa Clara CA 95051 USA; 408/749-9200, Fax: 408/257-9554, Focus: Photo management software, Prdts: Living Album, Ownrshp: PVT, Greg Bethards

QuickShot Technology Inc. 950 Yosemite Dr, Milpitas CA 95035 USA; 408/263-4163, Fax: 408/263-4005, Focus: Game controllers, PC peripherals and multimedia products, Prdts: Command-Pad Pro, Lauren Gee, Mktng Coord

Quill Corp. PO Box 94080, Palatine IL 60094-4080 USA; 800/789-1331 Fax: 800/789-8955, Focus: Office & computer products, Prdts: Quill, Q-Tech, Ownrshp: PVT, Founded: 1956, Empl: 1,000, Sales ($M): 450, Jack Miller, Pres, Harvey L. Miller, Secretary, Arnold Miller, Treas, Nick Montesano, VP Merch, Lowell Meyers, Dir Advertising, Londa S. Della, PR Coord

Quintar Co. 370 Amapola Ave, #106, Torrance CA 90501-1475 USA; 310/320-5700, 800/223-5231 Fax: 310/618-1282, Focus: Printer controllers, Prdts: Q-Script, Ownrshp: Sub Bell & Howell, Founded: 1983, John Farina, Pres, Gary Moskovitz, EVP, Craig Douglas, VP Mktng

Quintus Corp. 47212 Mission Falls Ct, Fremont CA 94539-7820 USA; 510/624-2818, 800/542-1283 Fax: 510/770-1377, Co Email: @quintus.com, Focus: C/S and Prolog-based software, Ownrshp: PVT, Founded: 1984, Empl: 50, Alan Anderson, Pres & CEO, Michael Bedard, VP Fin, David Parker, VP Bus Dev, Email: dave.parker@quintus.com; Beverly Powell, VP Sales, Lisa Green, Mktng Spec, Email: lisa.green@quintus.com

Quixote Corp. 1 E Wacker Dr, Chicago IL 60601 USA; 312/467-6755, Fax: 312/467-1356, Focus: CD manufacturing, software and court reporting machines for legal industry, Ownrshp: OTC, Stk Sym: QUIX, Founded: 1969, Sales ($M): 185.4, Fiscal End: 6/95; Philip E. Rollhaus Jr., Chmn & Pres, Myron R. Shain, Pres Disc Mfg, Michael LaForte, Pres Stenograph Corp, Joan R. Riley, Dir Investor Relations

Qume Inc. 3475-A N First St, San Jose CA 95134-1803 USA; 408/473-1500, Fax: 408/473-1510, Focus: Terminals and monitors, Ownrshp: PVT, Founded: 1973, Tom Offut, GM

Quyen Systems Inc. 9210 Corporate Blvd, #150, Rockville MD 20850-4608 USA; 301/258-5087, Fax: 301/258-5088, Co Email: 70761.1445@compuserve.com, Web URL: quyen.com, Focus: Network diagramming software, Prdts: Netviz, Ownrshp: PVT, Founded: 1986, Empl: 10, Vo Tran, Pres, Email: quyen.systems@his.com; Jacques Jarman, Dir Sales & Mktng, Faith Perry, Prod Coord, Email: 70761.1445@compuserve.com

Racal Electronics Plc Western Rd, Bracknell, Berkshire RG12 1RG UK; 344-481-222, Web URL: racall.com, Focus: Data communications and LAN products, Ownrshp: FO, Empl: 33,700, Sales ($M): 1,510, Fiscal End: 12/95

Racal InterLan Inc. 60 Codman Hill Rd, Boxborough MA 01719-1737 USA; 508/263-9929, Fax: 508/263-8655, Co Email: rimail@interlan.com, Focus: LAN products, Ownrshp: Sub. Racal, UK, Founded: 1989, Empl: 250, Robert A. Steinkrauss, Pres, Brian Fitzgerald, VP Sales, Peter Hall, VP Prod Mktng & Dev, Robin Agarwal

Racal-Datacom 1601 N Harrison Pkwy, PO Box 407044, Sunrise FL 33340-7044 USA; 305/846-1601, 800/722-2555 Fax: 305/846-3935, Co Email: rdl@racal.com, Web URL: racal.com, Focus: Network products, Prdts: PremNet, CMS, Excalibur and ALM Modems, Ownrshp: Sub. Racal, UK, Founded: 1955, Empl: 2,200, Sales ($M): 626, Fiscal End: 3/95; Paul Kozlowski, Chmn, Jack

Hillhouse, PR

Racotek Inc. 7301 Ohms Ln, Minneapolis MN 55439 USA; 612/832-9800, Focus: Telecom software, Ownrshp: PVT, Richard A. Cortese, Pres & CEO, Larry Sanders, VP Mktng

RadioLAN Inc. De Guigne Dr, #D, Sunnyvale CA 94086 USA; 408/524-2600, Fax: 408/524-0600, Focus: Wireless LANs, Ownrshp: PVT, Founded: 1993, Greg Carse, Pres

RadioMail Corp. 2600 Campus Dr, San Mateo CA 94403 USA; 415/286-7800, Fax: 415/286-7801, Co Email: info@radiomail.net, Web URL: radiomail.com, Focus: Wireless Public message service, Ownrshp: PVT, Founded: 1988, Empl: 33, Geoffrey S. Goodfellow, Chmn, D. Bruce Walters, Pres & CEO, Steve Rand, VP Sales & Mktng, Rose N. Williams, VP, Alan Beringsmith, CFO, Mark Elderkind, Prod Mktng Mgr

Radiometrics Midwest Corp. 55 W 22nd St, #106, Lombard IL 60148 USA; 630/932-7262, Focus: FCC testing and compliance, Ownrshp: PVT, Founded: 1983, Dennis Rollinger, CEO

Radish Communications System Inc. 5744 Central Ave, Boulder CO 80301 USA; 303/443-2237, 800/723-4748 Fax: 303/443-1659, Co Email: support@radish.com, Focus: Voice and data communication products, Prdts: VoiceView, Ownrshp: PVT, Founded: 1990, Empl: 50, Richard A. Davis, Chmn & CTO, Email: rdavis@radish.com; David Klein, Pres & CEO, Email: dklein@radish.com; Deanna Watson, Dir Mktng, Email: dwatson@radish.com; Tom Cullen, VP Sales, Email: tcullen@radish.com

Radius Inc. 215 Moffett Park Dr, Sunnyvale CA 94084 USA; 408/541-6100, 800/227-2795 Fax: 408/541-6150, Co Email: support@radius.com, Web URL: radius.com, Focus: Mac OS-based systems and peripherals, Ownrshp: OTC, Stk Sym: RDUS, Founded: 1986, Empl: 250, Sales ($M): 159.6, Fiscal End: 9/92; Chuck Berger, Chmn & CEO, Dennis Dunnigan, CFO, Patrick Burns, D.J. Anderson, Email: dj_anderson@arpartners.com

RAID Advisory Board 3331 Brittain Ave, #4, San Carlos CA 94070 USA; 415/631-7142, Fax: 415/631-7154, Co Email: tforumltd@aol.com, Web URL: raid-advisory.com, Focus: Develop standards for RAID products, Ownrshp: Nonprofit, Founded: 1992, Empl: 50, Joe Molina

Raidtec Corp 105-C Hembree Park Dr, Roswell GA 30076 USA; 770/664-6066, Fax: 770/664-6166, Co Email: raidtec@interramp.com, Focus: Disk arrays, Prdts: Universal Array Controller, Ownrshp: PVT, Founded: 1990, Sales ($M): 5, Fred Stansberry, Pres & CEO, Sheila Thurmond, VP Sales & Mktng, William Bedford, VP Tech Mktng, William Oppermann, Dir Tech

Raima Corp. 1605 NW Sammamish Rd, #200, Issaquah WA 98027 USA; 206/557-0200, Fax: 206/557-5200, Web URL: raima.com, Focus: Database software, Prdts: Raima Database Manager, Raima Object Manager, Velocis Database Server, Ownrshp: PVT, Founded: 1982, Empl: 63, Sales ($M): 8, Stephen P. Smith, Pres & CEO, Email: ssmith@raima.com; Wayne Warren, Mgr Prod Dev, Email: wwarren@raima.com; David C. Morse, Dir Mktng, Email: dmorse@raima.com

Rainbow Technologies Inc. 50 Technology Dr, Irvine CA 92718 USA; 714/450-7300, 800/852-8569 Fax: 714/450-7450, Co Email: info@rnbo.com, Web URL: rnbo.com, Focus: Software protection products, Ownrshp: OTC, Stk Sym: RNBO, Founded: 1984, Empl: 270, Sales ($M): 66.3, Fiscal End: 12/95; Walter W. Straub, Chmn, Pres & CEO, Peter M. Craig, EVP, Paul Bock, VP Bus Dev, Patrick Fevery, VP & CFO, Ann Jones, Email: ajones@rnbo.com

RAM Mobile Data 10 Woodbridge Ctr Dr, #950, Woodbridge NJ 07095 USA; 908/602-5500, Fax: 908/602-5462, Co Email: info@ram.com, Focus: Wireless messaging services, Ownrshp: RAM Broadcasting & BellSouth, Founded: 1989, Empl: 300, Carl R. Aron, Chmn & CEO, William Lenahan, Pres & CEO, Janet Boudris, SVP

Rambus Inc. 2465 Latham St, Mountain View CA 94040 USA; 415/903-3800, Fax: 415/965-1528, Web URL: rambus.com, Focus: High bandwidth memory interface products, Ownrshp: PVT, Founded: 1990, Empl: 70, Bill Davidow, Chmn, Geoff Tate, Pres & CEO, Gary Harmon, VP & CFO, Subodh Toprani, VP Mktng

Rancho Technology Inc. 10783 Bell Ct, Rancho Cucamonga CA 91730-4834 USA; 909/987-3966, Fax: 909/989-2365, Focus: SCSI products, Ownrshp: PVT, Founded: 1983, Empl: 20, Hari Gupta, Pres, John Fobel, VP

Rand McNally New Media 8255 N Central Park Ave, Skokie IL 60076 USA; 847/329-6335, Fax: 847/674-4496, Focus: Travel and mapping software, Prdts: TripMaker, StFinder, Quick Reference Atlas, Ownrshp: Sub Rand McNally, Founded: 1856, Henry J. Feinberg, Pres, Neil Vill, VP & GM, Email: 72254.2555@compuserve.com

Random Access Inc. 1140 Hammond Dr, #I-9250, Atlanta GA 30328 USA; 404/804-1190, Focus: Internet access, Ownrshp: PVT, Gary Random, CEO, Email: gary@random.com

Raosoft Inc. 6645 NE Windermere Rd, Seattle WA 98115 USA; 206/525-4025, Fax: 206/525-4947, Co Email: raosoft@raosoft.com, Web URL: raosoft.com/raosoft, Focus: Statistical, survey on-line data collection and analysis software, Prdts: SURVEY, SURVEYWin, EZ Report, UFill, Ownrshp: PVT, Founded: 1991, Empl: 10, Potluri M. Rao, Chmn, Catherine McDole Rao, Pres, Shanti R. Rao, Treas, Catherine McDole Rao

Rapid City Communications 555 Clyde Ave, #B, Mountain View CA 94043 USA; 415/937-1370, Fax: 415/937-1399, Focus: High-speed Ethernet switches, Ownrshp: PVT, Founded: 1996, Empl: 16, Joseph S. Kennedy, Pres & CEO, Thomas R. McPherson, VP Eng, Milan Momirov, CTO

Raptor Systems Inc. 69 Hickory Dr, Waltham MA 02154 USA; 617/487-7700, Fax: 617/487-6755, Web URL: raptor.com, Focus: Internet security software, Ownrshp: PVT, Robert Steinkrauss, Pres & CEO, David Pensak, CTO, Shaun McConnon, EVP Sales & Mktng, Alan Kirby, VP Eng

Raritan Computer Inc. (RCI), 10-1 Ilene Ct, Belle Mead NJ 08502 USA; 908/874-4072, Fax: 908/874-5274, Co Email: @raritan.com, Web URL: raritan.com, Focus: PC resource sharing products, Prdts: MasterConsole, Ownrshp: PVT, Founded: 1985, Empl: 36, Sales ($M): 12, Ching Hsu, CEO, Robert S. Pollack, VP Mktng

Raster Graphics Inc. 3025 Orchard Pkwy, San Jose CA 95134-9868 USA; 408/232-4000, 800/441-4788 Fax: 408/232-4100, Focus: Large format digital printing systems, Prdts: Digital ColorStation, ProSystem, Onyx Series, Ownrshp: PVT, Founded: 1987, Empl: 120, Rak Kumar, Pres & CEO, Jim Harre, VP Sales & Mktng, Kelli Ramirez, Dir Corp Com

Rational Data Systems Inc. 11 Pimental Ct, Novato CA 94949-5608 USA; 415/382-8400, 800/743-3054 Fax: 415/382-8441, Web URL: rds.com, Focus: E-mail ISP, Web housing-web pages, Ownrshp: PVT, Founded: 1978, Empl: 15, Sales ($M): 2.5, Fiscal End: 12/95; Doug Kaye, Pres, Email: dkaye@rds.com; Marlene Iadavaia, CFO, Email: miadavia@rds.com; Mike Megill, VP, Email: mmegill@rds.com

Rational Software Corp. 2800 San Thomas Expwy., Santa Clara CA 95051-0951 USA; 408/496-3600, 800/728-1212 Fax: 408/496-3636, Co Email: info@rational.com, Web URL: rational.com, Focus: CASE software, Prdts: Rational Apex, Rational Rose, Ownrshp: OTC, Stk Sym: RATL, Founded: 1980, Empl: 520, Sales ($M): 91.1, Fiscal End: 3/96; Michael T. Devlin, Chmn, Email: mtd@rational.com; Paul D. Levy, Pres & CEO, Email: pdl@rational.com; Gerald J. Rudisin, VP Mktng, Email: gjr@rational.com; Timothy Brennan, VP & Acting CFO, Email: tbrennan@rational.com; Kara Myers, PR Specialist, Email: karam@rational.com

Rave Computer Association Inc. 36960 Metro Ct, Sterling Heights MI 48312 USA; 800/966-7283 Fax: 810/939-7431

Raxco Inc. 2440 Research Blvd, #200, Rockville MD 20850 USA; 301/258-2620, Fax: 301/670-3585, Focus: C/S helpdesk software, Ownrshp: PVT, Robin M. Greidoff, Dir Mktng

Ray Dream Inc. 1804 N Shoreline Blvd, Mountain View CA

94043-9894 USA; 415/960-0768, 800/846-0111 Fax: 415/960-1198, Co Email: ray.dream@applelink.com, Web URL: ray-dream.com, Focus: Image utility software, Prdts: Ray Dream Studio, Add Depth, JAG, Ownrshp: PVT, Founded: 1989, Empl: 40, Sales ($M): 7.7, Fiscal End: 12/95; Eric Hautemont, Pres & CEO, Email: eric_hautemont@raydream.com; Joseph Consul, VP & CFO, Email: consul@raydream.com; Mike Vanneman, VP Sales, Email: vanneman@raydream.com; Yann Corno, VP Dev, Email: corno@raydream.com; Pierre Berkaloff, CTO, Email: berkaloff@raydream.com; Teri Chadbourne, PR Dir, Email: teri@raydream.com

Raymond Engineering Inc. 217 Smith St, Middletown CT 06457 USA; 203/632-4643, Focus: Digital mass storage, Ownrshp: Sub. Kaman, Floyd Baranello, Mktng Mgr, Mary Ann Dostaler

Raytheon Co. 141 Spring St, Lexington MA 02173 USA; 617/862-6600, Fax: 617/860-2172, Web URL: raytheon.com, Focus: Electronic systems, Ownrshp: NYSE, Stk Sym: RTN, Founded: 1922, Empl: 71,600, Sales ($M): 11,715.9, Fiscal End: 12/95; Dennis J. Picard, Chmn & CEO

RCS Computer Experience 260 Madison Ave, New York NY 10016 USA; 212/370-9288, Fax: 212/949-1252, Web URL: rcs-net.com, Focus: Computer sales and service--Internet superstore, Founded: 1990, Charles Tebele, Pres, Jeff Kirshblum, VP Internet Svcs

RDI Computer Corp. 2300 Faraday Ave, Carlsbad CA 92008 USA; 619/929-0992, 800/734-5483 Fax: 619/929-9702, Co Email: sales@rdi.com, Focus: SPARC laptop workstation, Prdts: BriteLite, Ownrshp: PVT, Founded: 1989, Roy A. Wright, Pres & CEO, Carl Baldini, VP Eng, Bob Shields, Dir Mktng, Lisa A. Heller, Mgr Marcom

re:Search Int'l. 1 Broadway, Cambridge MA 02142 USA; 617/577-1574, Fax: 617/577-9517, Co Email: rintl@world.std.com, Focus: CD-ROM authoring and retrieval software, Prdts: re:Search, re:Text, cd:Search, API Toolkits, Ownrshp: PVT, Susan T. Kelly, Pres, Charles Kelly, GM, Josephine Sacco, Account Mgr

Read Technologies Inc. 5405 Alton Pkwy, Bldg 5-A, #502, Irvine CA 92714 USA; 714/551-2049, 800/726-2049 Fax: 714/786-5395, Focus: Document retrieval software, Prdts: AutoINDEX, Ownrshp: PVT, Founded: 1987, J.D. Seal, Dir Ops

Read-Rite Corp. 345 Los Coches St, Milpitas CA 95035 USA; 408/262-6700, Fax: 408/956-3205, Focus: Thin film heads, Ownrshp: OTC, Stk Sym: RDRT, Founded: 1983, Empl: 24,000, Sales ($M): 1,003.0, Fiscal End: 9/95; Cyril J. Yansouni, Chmn & CEO, Fred Schwettmann, Pres & COO, Peter G. Bischoff, EVP R&D, Michael A. Klyszeiko, EVP Ops, John T. Kurtzweil, VP & CFO, Steve Polcyn, Dir PR & Investor Relations

Real World Solutions Inc. 700 Gale Dr, #100, Campbell CA 95008-0901 USA; 408/364-7330, Fax: 408/364-7337, Focus: Wireless applications tools, Prdts: Intelligent Mobile Server, Ownrshp: PVT, John Stossel

Reality Online Inc. 2200 Renaissance Blvd, King of Prussia PA 19406-2755 USA; 610/277-7600, Fax: 610/278-6115, Co Email: info@reality-tech.com, Web URL: moneynet.com, Focus: Personal finance software and services, Prdts: Reuters Money Network, WealthBuilder, Ownrshp: Sub. Reuters, Founded: 1987, Empl: 140, Sales ($M): 12, Douglas Alexander, Pres & CEO, Bill Gray, CFO, David Kreda, EVP, Jeff Jones, VP Dev, Rob Lux, Dir MIS, Deb Goldring, Dir Marcom

RealWorld Corp. 670 Commercial St, 3rd Fl, PO Box 9516, Manchester NH 03108-9516 USA; 603/641-0200, 800/678-6336 Fax: 603/641-0230, Focus: Microcomputer accounting software, Ownrshp: PVT, Founded: 1980, Empl: 110, Sales ($M): 8.8, Fiscal End: 12/95; Murray P. Fish, Pres & CEO, Mark Moreau, PR Mgr

Recital Corp. 85 Constitution Ln, Danvers MA 01923 USA; 508/750-1066, Fax: 508/750-8097, Web URL: recital.com, Focus: Software for client/server Unix, Prdts: Recital, Ownrshp: PVT, Founded: 1988, Empl: 50, Barry Mavin, Principle & CEO, Email:

bmavin@recital.com; Donald Sullivan, VP WW Ops, Email: dons@recital.com; Lee Francis, Dir WW Dist, Email: lfrancis@recital.com; Peter Kelly, Dir R&D, Email: pkelly@recital.com; Phillip Rose, Dir Marcom, Email: prose@recital.com

Recognita Corp. of America 3693 Enochs St, Santa Clara CA 95051-0601 USA; 408/736-5446, Fax: 408/736-6112, Co Email: 70313.1266@compuserve.com, Focus: OCR software, Prdts: GO-CR, Recognita Plus, SELECT, Ownrshp: Sub. Recognita, Hungary, Founded: 1989, Empl: 5, Otto Toth, Pres & CEO, Frank Fenyvesl, Dir Sales & Mktng

Recognition International Inc. 2701 E Grauwyler Rd, PO Box 660204, Irving TX 75061 USA; 214/579-6000, Fax: 214/579-6175, Focus: OCR peripherals and document imaging systems, Ownrshp: NYSE, Stk Sym: REC, Founded: 1962, Empl: 1,525, Sales ($M): 219.4, Fiscal End: 10/94; Robert Vanourek, Pres & CEO, Thomas Hoefert, VP & CFO, Dennis Constantine, Pres Systems Div, Thomas Frederick, Pres SW Div, Fredric Zucker, SVP & CTO

Red Wing Business Systems 491 Hwy 19, PO Box 19, Red Wing MN 55066 USA; 612/388-1106, Fax: 612/388-7950, Focus: Accounting and agriculture software, Ownrshp: PVT, Founded: 1979, Empl: 21, Lyle Warrington, Pres

Reed Technology & Information Services Inc. 20251 Century Blvd, Germantown MD 20874-1196 USA; 301/428-3700, 800/922-9204 Fax: 301/428-0224, Co Email: helpdesk@ocs.com, Focus: CD-ROM products, Prdts: Opti-Net, Ownrshp: Sub. Reed Elsevier, Founded: 1979, Empl: 100, Sales ($M): 20, Donna Lynn, CEO, Phung Truong, COO, Mike Romanies, SVP, Sue Rowland, Mktng Coord

Reflex Inc. 2100 196th St SW, #124, Lynnwood WA 98036-7081 USA; 206/487-2798, Fax: 206/486-5136, Focus: PC security software, Founded: 1985, Frank Horwitz, Pres

Regal Electronics Inc. 4251 Burton Dr, Santa Clara CA 95054 USA; 408/988-2288, Fax: 408/988-2797, Focus: Voice, data, video, connectors, switchmode power supplies and speaker products, Founded: 1976, Tony Lee, Pres, Madeleine Lee, CEO, Dave Heath, Prod Mgr

Relationship Software LLC 1393 W 9000 S, #348, W Jordan UT 84088 USA; 801/253-2252, Fax: 801/235-7099, Co Email: gazsys@ix.netcom.com, Prdts: More LovePlay, Heather Wilson

Relay Technology Inc. 1604 Spring Hill Rd, Vienna VA 22182-7509 USA; 703/506-0500, Fax: 703/506-0510, Co Email: info@relay.com, Focus: PC communication software, Prdts: Relay, Ownrshp: PVT, Founded: 1981, Bruce R. Mancinelli, Pres & CEO, Gordon Perrins, SVP R&D, Robert C. Fitzsimmons, SVP Sales & Mktng, Mark Weitner, VP Mktng, Linda S. Silberg, PR Mgr

Reliability Ratings 175 Highland Ave, 4th Floor, PO Box 626, Needham Heights MA 02194-9872 USA; 617/444-5755, Fax: 617/444-8958, Focus: Computer reliability, serviceability and customer satisfaction information, Ownrshp: PVT, Founded: 1989, Kevin Beam, Dir Research, Greg Strakosch, VP

Reliable Source Inc. PO Box 9991, Mobile AL 36691-0991 USA; 205/660-1960, Focus: Forms processing software, Prdts: FormFiller, Ownrshp: PVT, Founded: 1987, Empl: 14, Dennis Vogel, Pres, T.H. Robinson, Treas, Deanna Flynn

Remedy Corp. 1505 Salado Dr, Mountain View CA 94043 USA; 415/903-5200, Fax: 415/903-9001, Web URL: remedy.com, Focus: C/S helpdesk software, Prdts: Action Request System, Flashboards, ARWeb, Ownrshp: OTC, Stk Sym: RMDY, Founded: 1990, Empl: 129, Sales ($M): 40.1, Fiscal End: 12/95; Lawrence L. Garlick, Chmn, Pres, CEO, David A. Mahler, VP Bus Dev, Vasu S. Devan, VP Sales, Mark Freund, VP Mktng, George A. de Urioste, VP Finance & CFO, Mike Lough, Com Mgr

Rendition Inc. 1675 N Shoreline Blvd, Mountain View CA 94043 USA; 415/335-5900, Web URL: rendition.com, Focus: 3D graphics processors, Prdts: Verite, Founded: 1993, Jay Eisenlohr, Co-

Founder & VP Bus Dev, Richard Buchanan, VP Mktng

Repeat-O-Type Manufacturing Corp. 665 State Hwy 23, Wayne NJ 07470-6892 USA; 201/696-3330, 800/288-3330 Fax: 201/694-7287, Co Email: info@repeatotype.com, Web URL: repeatotype.com, Focus: Laser and inkjet printer cartridges, Prdts: Repeat-O-Type Refill Ink Systems, Ownrshp: PVT, Founded: 1931, Empl: 35, Sales ($M): 2, Fiscal End: 12/94; Fred Keen, Pres, Michael Keen, VP, Robert Keen, Secretary, Corinne Rosen, Sales Mgr

Repository Technologies Inc. (RTI), 6825 Hobson Valley Dr, Woodridge IL 60517 USA; 708/515-0780, 800/776-2176 Fax: 708/515-0788, Focus: Software for customer-support systems, Prdts: ControlFirst, Founded: 1990, E. James Emerson, Pres, Kathleen Emerson, VP

ReproCAD Inc. 3650 Mt. Diablo Blvd, #200, Lafayette CA 94549 USA; 510/284-0400, 800/873-7762 Fax: 510/283-7864, Focus: Reprographics and CAD plotting products, N American service bureau network, Prdts: Open Express, Ownrshp: PVT, Founded: 1984, Empl: 9, Ed Severs, Pres & CEO, Margie Wiggins, Dir Admin

Reptron Electronics Inc. 14401 McCormick Dr, Tampa FL 33626-3046 USA; 813/854-2351, Focus: Electronic distributor and contract manufacturing, Ownrshp: OTC, Stk Sym: REPT, Founded: 1973, Empl: 603, Sales ($M): 223.3, Fiscal End: 12/95; Michael L. Musto, Pres & CEO, Patrick J. Flynn, Pres K-Byte Mfg, Robert Moore, VP Corp Ops, Gary Bolohan, EVP Distr, Paul J. Plante, VP & CFO

RESCOM Ventures Inc. 100-383 Dovercourt Dr, Winnipeg Manitoba R3Y 1G4 Canada; 204/488-6242, Fax: 204/488-1861, Focus: Investment management software, Prdts: The Private Investor

ResNova Software 5011 Argosy Dr, #13, Huntington Beach CA 92649 USA; 714/379-9000, Fax: 714/379-9014, Co Email: sales@resnova.com, Focus: Telecom and online service software, Prdts: NovaLink, Ownrshp: PVT, Founded: 1987, Jonathan Kantor, CEO, Email: jon.kantor@resnova.com; Alexander Hopmann, Chmn & Pres, Gregory Herlihy, SVP, Daniel Link, VP Sales, Robert Tudor, VP Dev

Resumix 2953 Bunker Hill Ln, Santa Clara CA 95054 USA; 408/988-0444, 800/988-0003 Fax: 408/727-9893, Co Email: info@resumix.com, Web URL: resumix.com, Focus: Software for recruiting and hiring, Prdts: Resumix, Founded: 1988, Empl: 180, Sales ($M): 25, Fiscal End: 12/95; Stephen J. Ciesinski, Pres & CEO, Jan Wesemann, VP Sales, Joe Hnilo, VP Mktng, Dick Heddleson, CFO, Vicki Araujo, Mktng Spec

Retix 4640 Admiralty Way, N Tower, 6th Fl., Marina del Rey CA 90292-6695 USA; 310/828-3400, Fax: 310/828-2255, Co Email: @retix.com, Web URL: retix.com, Focus: Network products, Prdts: SwitchStak 5000, Metro LAN 5000, Ownrshp: OTC, Stk Sym: RETX, Founded: 1985, Empl: 250, Sales ($M): 38.8, Fiscal End: 12/95; Joe Stephan, Pres & CEO, Philip Mantle, SVP Sales & Mktng, Dave Keaney, VP Ops, Randy Fardal, VP Mktng, Steve Waszak, VP Finance & CFO, Steve Waszak

Reveal Computer Products Inc. 6045 Variel Ave, Woodland Hills CA 91367 USA; 818/704-6300, 800/326-2222 Fax: 818/340-9957, Focus: Multimedia and accessories, Ownrshp: PVT, Bob Anderson, VP Mktng

Revelation Software 181 Harbor Dr, Stamford CT 06902 USA; 203/973-1000, 800/262-4747 Fax: 203/975-8755, Focus: Database software, Prdts: Revelation Reporter, Revelation ViP, Revelation OpenInsight, Ownrshp: PVT, Founded: 1987, Empl: 100, James Acquaviva, Pres, Steve Sneddon, EVP & CTO, Kurt Baker, VP Sales & Svcs, Mark Martin, MIS Mgr, Shelly Racenstein

Revered Technology Inc. 4750 Calle Quetzal, Camarillo CA 93012 USA; 805/445-6655, 800/220-8919 Fax: 805/445-9962, Focus: Presentation notebook PCs, Ownrshp: PVT

Revnet Systems Inc. 4835 University Square, #2, Huntsville AL

35816 USA; 205/721-1420, Fax: 205/721-1041, Co Email: @revnet.com, Web URL: revnet.com, Focus: Group management and list building software for the World Wide Web, Prdts: GroupMaster, Ownrshp: PVT, Walter Thomas, VP Mktng, Email: wthomas@revnet.com

Revolution Software Inc. 19722 E Country Club Dr, Aventura FL 33180-2527 USA; 305/682-8154, Fax: 305/682-1897, Co Email: 71031.2572@compuserve.com, Focus: Mailing lists for computer industry, Ownrshp: PVT, Founded: 1985, Empl: 6, George T. Thibault, Pres

Rexon Inc. 6225 Cochran Rd, Solon OH 44139 USA; 216/349-0600, Fax: 216/349-0851, Focus: PC peripherals, Ownrshp: OTC, Stk Sym: REXN, Founded: 1978, Empl: 1,100, Sales ($M): 204.8, Fiscal End: 9/94; Robert C. Genesi, Chmn & CEO, Hank E. Oberle, Pres & COO, Martin A. Alpert, EVP Bus Dev, Richard A. Peters, EVP Sales & Mktng, Irvin R. Reuling, VP & CFO

Reynolds and Reynolds 115 S Ludlow St, Dayton OH 45401 USA; 513/443-2000, Fax: 513/449-4213, Co Email: @reyrey.com, Web URL: reyrey.com, Focus: Integrated information management systems for automobile retail and healthcare market, Prdts: ERA, Kredo, Ownrshp: NYSE, Stk Sym: REY, Founded: 1886, Empl: 6,036, Sales ($M): 911.0, Fiscal End: 9/95; David R. Holmes, Chmn, Pres & CEO, Joeph N. Bausman, Pres Auto Sys Div, Dale L. Medford, VP & CFO, Robert C. Nevin, Pres Bus Forms Div, Paul Guthrie, VP Corp Com

RFI Controls Co. 320 N Santa Cruz Ave, Los Gatos CA 95030-7243 USA; 408/399-7007, Fax: 408/399-7011, Focus: EMI/RF design engineering service, Ownrshp: PVT, Founded: 1979, Empl: 20, Lee Pulver, Pres, Erec Ferguson, VP Ops

RG Software Systems Inc. 6900 E Camelback Rd, #630, Scottsdale AZ 85251 USA; 602/423-8000, Fax: 602/423-8389, Focus: Security software and solutions, Ownrshp: PVT, Founded: 1984, Ray Glath, Pres, Beverly Ann Glath, VP

RGB Spectrum 950 Marina Village Pkwy, Alameda CA 94501-1047 USA; 510/814-7000, Fax: 510/814-7026, Co Email: sales@rgb.com, Focus: Scan converters and multimedia products, Prdts: RGD/View, RGB/Videolink, Computer Wall, SynchroMaster, Ownrshp: PVT, Founded: 1987, Empl: 40, Robert P. Marcus, Pres, Tony Spica, VP Sales, Carl Lyle, VP Ops

Rhetorex Inc. 151 Albright Way, Los Gatos CA 95030 USA; 408/370-0881, Fax: 408/370-1171, Focus: Voice processing products, Ownrshp: PVT, Alan Wokas, Pres, Evelyn Elkins

Rhintek Inc. PO Box 220, 8835 Columbia 100 Pkwy, Columbia MD 21045 USA; 410/730-2575, Fax: 410/730-5960, Web URL: rhintek.com/rhinek, Focus: PC communication software, Prdts: EMU/470 for DOS & Windows, RhinoCom, Ownrshp: PVT, Founded: 1977, Empl: 15, Rainer McCown, Pres, Heeth Clark, GM

Rhode Island Soft Systems Inc. (RISS), PO Box 748, Woonsocket RI 02895-0784 USA; 401/767-3106, Fax: 401/767-3108, Web URL: risoftsystems.com, Focus: Computer software development and publishing, Prdts: Win Pak, Web Whiz, Icon Pak, Ownrshp: PVT, Founded: 1988, Empl: 9, Eric G. Robichaud, Pres & CEO, Email: 72662.463@compuserve.com; William J. Zitomer, VP Software Eng, Email: 73770.1633@compuserve.com; Rebecca L. Robichaud, CFO, Email: 71231.2614@compuserve.com

Ricoh Co. Ltd. 15-5 Minami-Aoyama 1-chome, Minato-ku, Tokyo 107 JP-107 Japan; 3-3479-3111, Fax: 3-3403-1578, Web URL: ricoh.co.jp, Focus: Photographic, office products, peripherals and laser printers, Ownrshp: FO, Stk Sym: RICOHC, Founded: 1936, Empl: 34,000, Sales ($M): 6,552, Fiscal End: 3/96

Ricoh Corp. 5 Dedrick Place, W Caldwell NJ 07006 USA; 201/882-2000, Fax: 201/882-2506, Focus: Printers, scanners, fax, storage devices & copiers, Ownrshp: Sub Ricoh, Japan, Founded: 1962, Empl: 3,000, Sales ($M): 1,000, Hisashi Kubo, Chmn, Hisao Yuasa, Vice Chmn & CEO, Eric L. Steensburg, Pres & COO, Jim Ivy, EVP, Masaaki Izushima, SVP, Claudia Jones

RightFAX 4400 E Broadway Blvd #312, Tucson AZ 85711 USA;

520/327-1357, Fax: 520/321-7456, Co Email: @rightfax.com, Focus: Fax server products, Prdts: RightFAX, RightFAX OCR Module, RightFAX E-Mail Gateway, Ownrshp: PVT, Founded: 1987, Bradley H. Feder, Pres, Email: bhf@rightfax.com; Joseph J. Cracchiolo, VP, Email: jjc@rightfax.com; Cheri Hilderbrand, Dir Mktng, Email: crh@rightfax.com; Juli Howard, Dir Sales, Email: jah@rightfax.com; Bill St, Dir Tech Support, Email: bds@rightfax.com

Rimage Corp. 7725 Washington Ave S, Minneapolis MN 55439 USA; 612/944-8144, 800/445-8288 Fax: 612/944-7808, Focus: Computer accessory products, Ownrshp: OTC, Stk Sym: RIMG, Founded: 1987, Empl: 154, Sales ($M): 51.5, Fiscal End: 12/95; David J. Suden, Pres, Jon D. Wylie, CFO

Ring King Visibles Inc. 2210 Second Ave, PO Box 599, Muscatine IA 52761-0599 USA; 319/263-8144, Fax: 319/262-6623, Focus: Ergonomic accessories, Prdts: Adjustable Mouse Cradle, Ownrshp: Sub. HON Industries, Keith Metzger, Mktng Svcs Admin

Ring Zero Systems Inc. 1650 S Amphlett Blvd, #300, San Mateo CA 94402 USA; 415/349-6000, Fax: 415/349-9664, Co Email: 70303.3720@compuserve.com, Focus: Telecom and multimedia software, Ownrshp: PVT, Founded: 1992, Empl: 15, Vlad Shmunis, Pres

RISO Inc. PO Box 4020, Woburn MA 0188-4020 USA; 508/777-7377, 800/876-7476 Fax: 508/777-2517, Focus: Printers and publishing systems, Prdts: Risograph, RISO Publisher, Ownrshp: Sub. RISO Kagaku, Japan, Founded: 1986, Empl: 178, Sales ($M): 121, John C. Carillon, Pres & CEO, Hideo Nakamura, VP & CFO, Robert C. Fallows, VP Sales, Alfred N. Frecker, VP Sales, Alex Oshan, Controller

River Run Software Group 8 Greenwich Office Park, Greenwich CT 06831-5149 USA; 203/861-0090, Fax: 203/861-0096, Co Email: 72662.3247@compuserve.com, Focus: Mobile computing and networking products, Prdts: Magic Connection, Mail on the Run!, Magic Genie, Magic Writer, Ownrshp: PVT, Founded: 1988, Empl: 80, Trilok Manocha, Pres, Taffy Holliday, EVP, Robert N. Perry, SVP

Road Warrior Outpost 16580 Harbor Blvd, Fountain Valley CA 92708 USA; 714/418-1400, 800/274-4277 Fax: 714/839-6282, Co Email: warrior@warrior.com, Web URL: warrior.com, Focus: Information, products and services for portable computer users, Ownrshp: Sub. AR Industries, Debra Zimmerman, Mktng Dir, Email: debra@warrior.com

Robocom Systems Inc. 511 Ocean Ave, Massapequa NY 11758 USA; 516/795-5100, 800/795-5100 Fax: 516/795-6933, Focus: Warehouse management software, Ownrshp: PVT, Founded: 1982, Empl: 65, Fiscal End: 6/95, Irwin Balaban, Pres, Larry Klein, EVP, Richard Wilkins

Robotic Industries Assoc. (RIA), 900 Victors Way, PO Box 3724, Ann Arbor MI 48106 USA; 313/994-6088, Fax: 313/994-3338, Focus: Association for companies involved in industrial & service robotics, Ownrshp: Nonprofit, Founded: 1974, Empl: 325, Donald A. Vincent, EVP

Rochelle Communications Inc. 8906 Wall St, #205, Austin TX 78754 USA; 512/339-8188, Focus: Communications products, Prdts: Caller ID, Ownrshp: PVT, Founded: 1989, Empl: 8, Sales ($M): 2, Gilbert A. Amine, Pres & CEO

Rocket Science Games Inc. 139 Townsend St, #100, San Francisco CA 94107-1922 USA; 415/442-5000, Web URL: rocketsci.com, Focus: Entertainment software, Ownrshp: PVT, Founded: 1993, Empl: 120, Steven G. Blank, Pres, Peter Barrett, EVP, Mike Backes, Co-founder, Ron Cobb, Co-founder, Anna Caldwell, PR Coord

Rockwell International Corp. 2201 Seal Beach Blvd, Seal Beach CA 90740-8250 USA; 310/797-3311, Fax: 310/797-5049, Web URL: rockwell.com, Focus: Semiconductor and electronics products, Ownrshp: NYSE, Stk Sym: RQK, Founded: 1928, Empl: 82,671, Sales ($M): 12,981, Fiscal End: 9/95; Donald R. Beall,

Chmn & CEO, Don H. Davis, Pres & COO, Kent. M Black, EVP & COO, Robert R. Lind, VP Corp Dev, W. Michael Barnes, SVP & CFO, William A. Blanning, Dir Media Rel

Rockwell Network Systems 7402 Hollister Ave, Santa Barbara CA 93117-2590 USA; 805/968-4262, 800/262-8023 Fax: 805/968-6478, Web URL: rns.rockwell.com, Focus: LAN hardware and software, Ownrshp: Sub. Rockwell Int'l., Founded: 1981, Empl: 110, Nick Whelan, Bus Dir, Email: nwhelan@rns.com; Bill Smith, Jr., CFO, Email: bsmith@rns.com; Steve Recker, Dir WW Sales, Email: srecker@rns.com; Steve Ricca, Dir Eng, Email: sncca@rns.com; Jason Hendrix, IS Mgr, Email: jhendrix@rns.com; Marianne McCarthy, PR Mgr, Email: marianne@rns.com

Rockwell Semiconductor Systems (DCD), 4311 Jamboree Rd, Newport Beach CA 92658-8902 USA; 714/883-4600, Fax: 714/883-4078, Co Email: @nb.rockwell.com, Focus: Modems, LAN, ISDN and telecom products, Ownrshp: Sub. Rockwell Int'l, Founded: 1975, Empl: 3,000, Dwight W. Decker, Pres, Armando Geday, VP & Multimedia Com Div, Vijay Parikn, Bus Dir Wireless Com Div, Nick Whalen, Network Sys, Eileen Algaze, Marcom Mgr, Email: eileen.algaze@nb.rockwell.com

Rogue Wave Software Inc. 260 SW Madison Ave, PO Box 2328, Corvallis OR 97339 USA; 541/754-3010, 800/487-3217 Fax: 541/757-6650, Co Email: info@roguewave.com, Web URL: roguewave.com, Focus: C++ class libraries, Prdts: Tools.h++, DBtools.h++, Ownrshp: PVT, Founded: 1989, Empl: 178, Thomas Keffer, Pres, Dan Whitaker, EVP, Thomas A. Nora, VP Sales, Mary Rabe, Dir Dev, Joanne Larson, Email: larson@roguewave.com

Roland Corp. US 7200 Dominion Cr, Los Angeles CA 90040-3696 USA; 213/685-5141, Fax: 213/772-0911, Focus: PC sound products, Ownrshp: Sub. Roland, Japan, Empl: 350, Sales ($M): 100+, Dennis M. Houlihan, Pres, Mark S. Malbon, VP & CFO, Melanie L. Chun, Marcom Assist

Roland Digital Group 15271 Barranca Pkwy, Irvine CA 92718-2201 USA; 714/975-0560, Fax: 714/975-0569, Focus: Plotters & plotting devices for sign making & engraving 3D modeling equipment, Prdts: Roland, Ownrshp: Sub. Roland Digital, Japan, Founded: 1983, Empl: 48, Sales ($M): 8.7, Robert Curtis, VP & GM

Romeo Inc. PO Box 17600, Beverly Hills CA 90209-3600 USA; 310/273-1866, Fax: 310/273-2497, Focus: CD-ROM edutainment software, Ownrshp: PVT, Roger M. Reese, Pres, Harold Neiman, Chmn

Romsoft Inc. 5100 Copans Rd, #100, Margate FL 33063 USA; 305/752-5073, 800/859-4441 Fax: 305/752-6430, Focus: CD-ROM software, Ownrshp: PVT, Founded: 1992, Empl: 10, William Proudst, Email: gradient@gosoft.com; Ronald Teblum, Jack Bracewell, Dir Mktng

Rose Electronics 10707 Stancliff, Houston TX 77099 USA; 713/933-7673, 800/333-9343 Fax: 713/933-0044, Focus: Computer networking, Prdts: ServeView, Station Master, ClassView, Ownrshp: PVT, Founded: 1984, Empl: 50, David Rahvar, General Partner, Peter Macourek, Gen Partner, Dick Baker, Mktng Mgr

Ross Systems Inc. 555 Twin Dolphin Dr, Redwood City CA 94065 USA; 415/593-2500, Fax: 415/592-9364, Web URL: ross-inc.com, Focus: Accounting and vertical market software, Ownrshp: OTC, Stk Sym: ROSS, Founded: 1972, Empl: 500, Sales ($M): 76.0, Fiscal End: 6/94; Dennis V. Vohs, Chmn & CEO, J. Patrick Tinley, Pres & COO, Joseph L. Southworth, VP WW Mktng, Selby F. Little, VP & CFO, Cecilia Roach

Ross Technology 5316 Hwy 290 W, Austin TX 78735 USA; 512/436-2000, 800/774-7677 Fax: 512/892-3036, Focus: Supplier of SPARC microprocessors and related products, Ownrshp: OTC, Stk Sym: RTEC, Founded: 1988, Sales ($M): 100.8, Fiscal End: 4/96; Roger D. Ross, Chmn & Pres, David A. Zeleniak, CFO, Email: davez@ross.com; Matthew R. Gutierrez, VP Mktng, Joe D. Jones, VP Ops, John C. Rasco, Marcom Dir, Email: jrasco@ross.com

RSA Data Security Inc. 100 Marine Pkwy, #500, Redwood City

CA 94065 USA; 415/595-8782, Fax: 415/595-1873, Co Email: info@rsa.com, Web URL: rsa.com, Focus: Security software, Prdts: Bsafe, Tipem, CIS, MailSafe, Ownrshp: PVT, Founded: 1982, Empl: 30, James Bidzos, Pres, Kurt Stammberger, Dir Tech Mktng, Email: kurt@rsa.com

RSI Systems Inc. 7400 Metro Blvd #475, One Corporate Park, Edina MN 55439 USA; 612/896-3020, Fax: 612/896-3030, Focus: Telecom products for videoconferencing, collaborative computing & file transfer, Prdts: Eris Visual Communications System, Ownrshp: OTC, Stk Sym: RSIS, Founded: 1993, Doug Clapp, Founder, Marti Miller, VP Eng, Leigh Wilson, Managing Dir

Rubbermaid Office Products Inc. (ROPI), 1427 William Blount Dr, Maryville TN 37801-8249 USA; 615/977-5477, Fax: 615/977-6849, Focus: Computer accessories and furniture, Ownrshp: Sub. Rubbermaid, Founded: 1987, Empl: 70, Carol S. Troyer, Pres & GM, David Nuti, VP Finance & Ops, Terrence Henzey, VP Mktng, Ken Foran, VP R&D, Donna Marino

Rumarson Technologies Inc. (RTI), 363 Market St, Kenilworth NJ 07033 USA; 908/298-9300, 800/929-0029 Fax: 908/298-8229, Focus: Trade-in programs for computer equipment, Prdts: RealTrade, Ownrshp: PVT, Founded: 1992, Empl: 25, Paul Baum, Pres & CEO, Michael Doron, CIO, Gail Bialos, Controller

Run Inc. 900 Corporate Dr, Mahwah NJ 07430-2013 USA; 201/529-4600, 800/478-6929 Fax: 201/529-2090, Co Email: runusa@aol.com, Focus: LAN and file transfer software, Ownrshp: Sub Run, Israel, Steven Holder, Pres

Ryan-McFarland 8911 N Capital of Texas Hwy, Austin TX 78759 USA; 512/343-1010, 800/762-6265 Fax: 512/343-9487, Co Email: info@rmc.liant.com, Focus: Cobol compilers, Ownrshp: Sub Liant Software, Founded: 1970, Empl: 70, John Hatcher, GM, Bob Richardson, Mgr R&D, Donna Jones Cox, Mgr Tech Svcs, Dwight Flinkerbusch, Prod Mktng Mgr, Lana Tangum, Tech Prod Mgr, Ruth Davidson, Email: ruth@rmc.liant.com

S&H Computer Systems Inc. 1027 17th Ave S, Nashville TN 37212 USA; 615/327-3670, Fax: 615/321-5929, Web URL: sandh.com, Focus: PC multiuser operating system, Prdts: TSX series, Ownrshp: PVT, Founded: 1975, Empl: 10, Sales ($M): 1, Fiscal End: 12/94; Harry R. Sanders, Pres, Email: hsanders@sandh.com; Phillip H. Sherrod, VP Dev, Email: psherrod@sandh.com; Richard M. Dohrmann, VP Mktng & Sales, Email: rdohrmann@sandh.com

S&S Software Int'l. Inc. 1 New England Exec Park, Burlington MA 01803 USA; 617/273-7400, 888/377-6766 Fax: 617/273-7474, Co Email: godrsolomons@compuserve.com, Web URL: drsolomon.com, Focus: Anti-virus and security software, Prdts: Dr. Solomon's Anti-Virus Toolkit, Ownrshp: Sub S&S Int'l, UK, Founded: 1984, Empl: 8, Alan Soloman, Chmn, David Banes, VP Ops, Pat Bitton, VP Mktng

S-MOS Systems 2460 N First St, #180, San Jose CA 95131-1002 USA; 408/922-0200, Fax: 408/922-0238, Focus: ICs, boards and contract manufacturing, Ownrshp: Aff. Seiko Epson, Founded: 1983, Sales ($M): 125, Dan Hauer, Pres, Dan Beck

S.H. Pierce & Co. 1 Kendall Square, Bldg. 600, #323, Cambridge MA 02139 USA; 617/338-2222, Fax: 617/338-2223, Focus: Animation flipbook and poster software, Prdts: FlipBook, PosterWorks, Ownrshp: PVT, Founded: 1989, Steve Hollinger, Pres

S3 Inc. 2770 San Tomas Expwy., Santa Clara CA 95051-0968 USA; 408/980-5400, Fax: 408/980-5444, Co Email: @s3.com, Focus: PC graphics products, Prdts: Scenic/Mx2 MPEG Decoder, Virge 3D Accelerator, Ownrshp: OTC, Stk Sym: SIII, Founded: 1989, Empl: 401, Sales ($M): 316.3, Fiscal End: 12/95; Diosdado P. Banatao, Chmn, Terry N. Holdt, Pres & CEO, Ronald T. Yara, VP Strategic Mktng, George A. Hervey, VP & CFO, Paul Crossley, PR Specialist, Email: pcross@s3.com

Safety Software Inc. 114 2nd St NE, Charlottesville VA 22902 USA; 804/296-8789, 800/932-9457 Fax: 804/296-1660, Co Email: safesoft@interserv.com, Focus: Safety and compliance man-

agement software, Prdts: Safety Office Suite, OSHALOG for Windows, Ownrshp: PVT, Founded: 1991, Harry Smith, Pres

Sage Solutions 353 Sacramento St, #1360, San Francisco CA 94111-3620 USA; 415/392-7243, Fax: 415/392-4030, Web URL: sagesolu.com, Focus: C/S software tools, Ownrshp: PVT, Founded: 1993, Empl: 15, Sales ($M): 0.5, Eugene Rooney, Pres, Email: gene.rooney@sagesolu.com; David Stanton, VP, Email: dave.stanton@sagesolu.com

Sales Technologies Inc. 3399 Peachtree Rd, #700, Atlanta GA 30326 USA; 404/841-4000, Focus: Sales automation software, Ownrshp: PVT, Empl: 600, Jeremy M. Davis, Pres, Alan J. Factor, VP Mktng

Sampo Corp. of America 5550 Peachtree Industrial Blvd, Norcross GA 30071 USA; 770/449-6220, Fax: 770/447-1109, Focus: PC monitors, Ownrshp: Sub. Sampo, Taiwan, Founded: 1976, George Korzeniewski, Pres, Victor Chen, CFO, Norman J. Dybowski, Dir Sales & Mktng, Nancy Smith, Email: nmdavis@aol.com

Samsung Electronics America Inc. (SEA), 105 Challenger Rd, Ridgefield Park NJ 07660-0511 USA; 201/229-4000, 800/933-4110 Fax: 201/229-4110, Focus: PCs and peripherals, Ownrshp: Sub. Samsung, Korea, Ki Ryong Song, Pres, Scott Bower, VP Sales & Mktng

Samsung Electronics Co. 250 2-Ka Taepyung-Ro, Chung-ku, Seoul KR S Korea; 822-726-3816, Web URL: samsung.com, Focus: Semiconductor, telecom, computer and electronics products, Ownrshp: FO, Founded: 1938, Sales ($M): 14,000, Fiscal End: 12/95

Samtron Displays Inc. 18600 S Broadwick St, Rancho Dominguez CA 90220-6434 USA; 310/537-7000, Fax: 310/537-1055, Focus: PC monitors, Ownrshp: Sub. Samsung, Korea, Founded: 1987, K.W. Park, Pres, Charles Root, VP Sales & Mktng

Sanar Systems Inc. 3350 Scott Blvd, Bldg 6501, Santa Clara CA 95054 USA; 408/982-0288, Fax: 408/982-9369, Co Email: sales@sanar.com, Focus: SPARC workstations, Ownrshp: PVT, Founded: 1988, Tom Biggs, EVP

Sanctuary Woods Multimedia Corp. 1825 S Grant St, #260, San Mateo CA 94402 USA; 415/286-6000, 800/943-3664 Fax: 415/286-6010, Web URL: sanctuary.com, Focus: Entertainment software, Ownrshp: OTC, Stk Sym: SWMCF, Founded: 1988, Empl: 65, Sales ($M): 6.3, Fiscal End: 12/94; Scott Walchek, Pres & CEO, Paul Salzinger, Dir Strat Sales

SanDisk Corp. 140 Caspain Ct, Sunnyvale CA 94089 USA; 408/542-0500, Fax: 408/542-0403, Co Email: @sandisk.com, Web URL: sandisk.com, Focus: PCMCIA products, Ownrshp: OTC, Stk Sym: SNDK, Founded: 1988, Empl: 225, Sales ($M): 62.8, Fiscal End: 12/95; Eli Harari, Pres & CEO, Irwin Federman, Chmn, Leon Malmed, SVP Mktng & Sales, Cindy Burgdorf, CFO, Jeff Ellerbruch, Prod Mktng Mgr, Bob Goligoski, Mgr PR

Santa Cruz Operation Inc., The (SCO), 400 Encinal St, PO Box 1900, Santa Cruz CA 95061-1900 USA; 408/425-7222, 800/726-8649 Fax: 408/458-4227, Co Email: info@sco.com, Web URL: sco.com, Focus: Unix system software, cross-platform solutions, Prdts: SCO OpenServer, SCO UnixWare, Vision Family, Ownrshp: OTC, Stk Sym: SCOC, Founded: 1979, Empl: 1,175, Sales ($M): 199.3, Fiscal End: 9/95; Lars H. Turndal, Chmn, Email: larst@sco.com; Alok Mohan, Pres & CEO, Email: alokm@sco.com; Douglas L. Michels, EVP & CTO, Email: doug@sco.com; Scott McGregor, SVP Prod, Email: scott@sco.com; Mike Tilson, CIO, Email: mike@sco.com; Monika Laud, Mgr PR, Email: monikal@sco.com

Sanyo-Verbatim CD Company 1767 Sheridan St, Richmond IN 47374-1811 USA; 317/935-7574, Fax: 317/935-7570, Focus: CD-ROM turnkey production services, Founded: 1994, Thomas Ryan, VP Bus Dev, Hideo Nakai, Chief Admin Officer, Mary Campbell

SAP AG Neurorrstrasse 16, Walldorf D-69190 Germany; 6227-34-0, Fax: 6227-34-1282, Web URL: sap-ag.de, Focus: C/S software,

Prdts: R/3, Ownrshp: FO, Founded: 1972, Empl: 7,100, Sales ($M): 1,887, Fiscal End: 12/95; Dietmar Hopp, Chmn, Hasso Plattner, Deputy Chmn, Dieter Matheis, CFO

SAP America Inc. 300 Stevens Dr, Philadelphia PA 19133 USA; 215/521-4500, Fax: 215/521-6290, Web URL: sap.com, Focus: Business management software, Ownrshp: Sub. SAP, Germany, Founded: 1987, Empl: 1,400, Sales ($M): 710, Fiscal End: 12/95; Jeremy Coote, Pres, Paul Wahl, CEO

SAP Users Group 401 N Michigan Ave, Chicago IL 60611-4267 USA; 312/644-6610, Fax: 312/644-0297, Focus: Association for SAP software users, Ownrshp: Nonprofit

Saratoga Group, The 12980 Saratoga Ave, #E, Saratoga CA 95070 USA; 408/446-9115, 800/893-8008 Fax: 408/446-9134, Co Email: saratoga@ix.netcom.com, Focus: Interactive learning software, Ownrshp: PVT, Founded: 1989, Vincent Vaccarello, Pres

Saros Corp. 10900 NE 8th St, 700 Plaza Ctr, Bellevue WA 98004 USA; 206/646-1066, Fax: 206/462-0879, Co Email: @saros.com, Focus: Document management software, Ownrshp: PVT, Founded: 1986, Empl: 90, Wayne Carpenter, Pres & CEO, Mike Kennewick, VP Sales & Mktng, Pin Foo, VP Prod Dev, Brian Cassidy, VP Bus Dev, Wayne Burns, VP & CFO, Christine L. McCaffrey, Dir Corp Com, Email: christinem@saros.com

SAS Institute Inc. 100 SAS Campus Dr, Cary NC 27513 USA; 919/677-8000, Fax: 919/677-8123, Web URL: sas.com, Focus: Integrated applications software, Prdts: SAS System, Ownrshp: PVT, Founded: 1976, Empl: 3,260, Sales ($M): 562.4, Fiscal End: 12/95; James H. Goodnight, Pres, John Sall, SVP, Barrett Joyner, VP NA Sales & Mktng, Michael W. Truell, Sr Media Com Spec, Email: sasmwt@unx.sas.com

SAT-Sagem 20370 Town Ctr Ln, #255, Cupertino CA 95014 USA; 408/446-8690, Fax: 408/446-9766, Co Email: satinfo@sat-usa.com, Focus: ISDN and video conferencing products, Ownrshp: Sub Sagem, France, Dominique Schraen

Sayers Computer Source 1150 Feehanville Dr, Mt. Prospect IL 60056 USA; 708/391-4000, 800/323-5357 Fax: 708/294-0750, Focus: Catalog sales of computer products, Ownrshp: PVT, Founded: 1983, Gale Sayers, Pres & CEO

Sayett Group Inc. 7 Norton St, Honeoye Falls NY 14472-1023 USA; 716/264-9250, Fax: 716/264-9265, Focus: LCD projection and presentation products, Prdts: DataShow, Ownrshp: OTC, Stk Sym: SAYT, Founded: 1986, Empl: 40, Sales ($M): 6.7, Fiscal End: 12/94; Edward J. Kelly, Pres & CEO

SBC Communications Inc. 175 E Houston, San Antonio TX 78299-2933 USA; 210/821-4105, Fax: 210/351-3553, Focus: A regional Bell operating company (RBOC), Ownrshp: NYSE, Stk Sym: SBC, Founded: 1983, Empl: 58,400, Sales ($M): 12,669.7, Fiscal End: 12/95; Edward E. Whitacre Jr., Chmn & CEO, James R. Adams, Group Pres, Charles E. Foster, Group VP, James S. Kahan, SVP Strat Plng, Donald E. Kiernan, SVP & CFO

SBE Inc. 4550 Norris Canyon Rd, San Ramon CA 94583-1369 USA; 510/355-2000, 800/9252666 Fax: 510/355-2020, Web URL: sbei.com, Focus: Communications controllers, Ownrshp: OTC, Stk Sym: SBEI, Founded: 1962, Empl: 165, Sales ($M): 19.4, Fiscal End: 10/95; William R. Gage, Chmn, William B. Heye, Pres & CEO, Eugene K. Buechele, VP Eng, Anthony J. Spielman, VP Sales & Mktng, Timothy J. Repp, VP & CFO

SBT Accounting Systems 1401 Los Gamos Dr, San Rafael CA 94903 USA; 415/444-9900, 800/944-1000 Fax: 415/444-9901, Co Email: sbt@sbtcorp.com, Web URL: sbt.com, Focus: PC accounting software, Prdts: Pro Series, WebTrader, Ownrshp: PVT, Founded: 1980, Empl: 140, Sales ($M): 16.7, Fiscal End: 12/95; Robert H. Davies, Pres & CEO, David R. Harris, VP Sales & Mktng, Email: harr@sbtcorp.com; Cynthia A. Harris, Dir Mktng, Email: char@sbtcorp.com; William E. Meyer, CFO, Thomas K. Spitzer, VP Eng, Kristen Flynn, Email: kfly@sbtcorp.com

Scala Inc. 2323 Horse Pen Rd, #202, Herndon VA 22071 USA; 703/713-0900, Fax: 703/713-1960, Focus: Multimedia authoring

software, Ownrshp: PVT, Founded: 1992, Edward Larese, Pres & CEO, Jon Bohmer, VP Bus Dev, Einar Haugstad, EVP, John Hillman, VP Mktng, Jeffrey Porter, VP Eng

Scan-Optics Inc. (SO), 22 Prestige Park Cr, E Hartford CT 06108 USA; 203/289-6001, Fax: 203/289-9034, Focus: OCR and document management systems, Ownrshp: OTC, Stk Sym: SOCR, Founded: 1968, Empl: 269, Sales ($M): 42.1, Fiscal End: 12/95; Richard I. Tanaka, Chmn & CEO, James C. Mavel, Pres & COO, Richard C. Goyette, VP Sales & Mktng, Jerry Putzer, VP NA Sales, Michael J. Villano, VP & CFO

Scantron Quality Computers 20200 Nine Mile Rd, St Clair Shores MI 48080 USA; 800/777-3642 Fax: 810/774-2698, Co Email: qualitycom@eworld.com, Focus: Internet service for schools and educational software, Ownrshp: PVT, Founded: 1984, Joseph Gleason, Pres, Email: jpgleason@qualitycomp.com; Matt Spatafora, VP, Email: msspata@qualitycomp.com; Thomas Morse, Sr Treas, Carl Sperber, Dir Mktng, Email: cfsperber@qualitycomp.com

Sceptre Technologies Inc. 16800 E Gale Ave, City of Industry CA 91745-1804 USA; 714/369-3698, Fax: 714/369-3488, Focus: Notebook PCs, Wilson Chiu, Pres, Kathy Chou, VP Sales, Keith Hunt, Mktng Mgr

Scholastic Corp. 411 Lafayette St, 4th Floor, New York NY 10003 USA; 212/505-4900, Fax: 212/505-8587, Focus: Educational software, magazines and books, Prdts: Home-Office Computing, Electronic Learning, Ownrshp: OTC, Stk Sym: SCHL, Founded: 1983, Empl: 35, Sales ($M): 749.9, Fiscal End: 5/95

SCI Systems Inc. (SCI), 2101 W Clinton Ave, PO Box 1000, Huntsville AL 35805 USA; 205/998-0592, Fax: 205/882-4466, Web URL: sci.com, Focus: PCs and contract manufacturing, Ownrshp: OTC, Stk Sym: SCIS, Founded: 1961, Empl: 13,185, Sales ($M): 4,545.0, Fiscal End: 6/96; Olin B. King, Chmn & CEO, A. Eugene Sapp Jr., Pres & COO, David F. Jenkins, SVP, Richard A. Holloway, SVP

Science Applications Int'l. Corp. (SAIC), 10260 Campus Point Dr, San Diego CA 92121 USA; 619/546-6000, Fax: 619/535-7191, Web URL: saic.com, Focus: System integration and software development, Ownrshp: PVT, Founded: 1969, Empl: 15,300, Sales ($M): 2,156, Fiscal End: 2/96

Scientific and Engineering Software (SES), 4301 Westbank Dr, Bldg. A, Austin TX 78746-6564 USA; 512/328-5544, Fax: 512/327-6646, Co Email: @ses.com, Focus: Software development tools, Ownrshp: PVT, Michael Turner, VP Mktng, Cliff Moss

Scientific Software-Intercomp Inc. 1801 California St, #295, Denver CO 80202-2699 USA; 303/292-1111, Fax: 303/295-2235, Focus: Software for oil and gas industries, Ownrshp: OTC, Stk Sym: SSFT, Founded: 1968, Empl: 190, Sales ($M): 27.9, Fiscal End: 12/94; E. Allen Breitenbach, Chmn & CEO, George Steel, Pres & COO, Ronald J. Hottovy, VP & CFO, Jim L. Duckworth, SVP Sales

Scientific-Atlanta Inc. 1 Technology Pkwy, Norcross GA 30092 USA; 770/903-5000, Fax: 770/903-4716, Co Email: sciatl.com, Web URL: sciatl.com, Focus: Communication equipment, Prdts: PowerVu, CoAxiom, Ownrshp: NYSE, Stk Sym: SFA, Founded: 1951, Empl: 4,000, Sales ($M): 1,047.9, Fiscal End: 6/96; James V. Napier, Chmn, James F. McDonald, Pres & CEO, Email: james.mcdonald@sciatl.com; H. Allen Ecker, SVP & CTO, Email: allen.ecker@sciatl.com; Raymond D. Lucas, SVP Strategic Officer, Email: ray.lucas@sciatl.com; Harvey A. Wagner, SVP & CFO, Email: harvey.wagner@sciatl.com; Robert S. Meyers, VP Corp Com, Email: robert.meyers@sciatl.com

Scion Corp. 152 W Patrick St, Frederick MD 21701 USA; 301/695-7870, Fax: 301/695-0035, Co Email: d1887@applelink.apple.com, Focus: Medical imaging & machine vision, Prdts: LG-3 Scientific Frame Grabber, TV-3 RS-170 Display Board, Ownrshp: PVT, Founded: 1978, Empl: 5, Tod Weinberg, Pres

Scitex America Corp. 8 Oak Park Dr, Bedford MA 01730-1473 USA; 617/275-5150, 800/685-9462 Fax: 617/275-3430, Web

URL: scitex.com, Focus: Computer imaging systems for prepress applications, Prdts: Scitex Spontane, Scitex Smart Scanners, Ownrshp: Sub. Scitex Corp. Ltd., Israel, Stk Sym: SCIXF, Founded: 1968, Empl: 3,000, Sales ($M): 728.9, Fiscal End: 12/95; Shimon Alon, Pres & CEO, Ray Wilson, VP Bus Ops, William T. Davison, VP Customer Svcs, Charlie Noonan, VP Sales, Brian Nichols, Dir Marcom

Scitor Corp. 333 Middlefield Rd 2nd Fl, Menlo Park CA 94025-3552 USA; 415/462-4200, 800/549-9876 Fax: 415/462-4201, Co Email: info@scitor.com, Web URL: scitor.com, Focus: Project and process management software, Prdts: Project Scheduler, Process Charter, Ownrshp: PVT, Founded: 1979, Empl: 360, Roger E. Meade, Pres & CEO, Julie Clarke, Mktng Dir, Lenore Dowling

SCM Microsystems Inc. 131 Albright Way, #B, Los Gatos CA 95030-1801 USA; 408/395-9292, Fax: 408/395-8782, Focus: PCMCIA products, Ownrshp: PVT, Founded: 1990, John Reimer, Pres

Scopus Technology Inc. 1900 Powell St, #900, Emeryville CA 94608 USA; 510/597-5800, Fax: 510/428-1027, Co Email: info@scopus.com, Web URL: scopus.com, Focus: Workgroup software, Prdts: ProTEAM, WebTEAM, Ownrshp: OTC, Stk Sym: SCOP, Founded: 1991, Empl: 43, Sales ($M): 7, Ori Sasson, CEO, Aaron Omid, VP Sales, Jeff Bork, VP Mktng

Screen Team 303 Broadway #204, Laguna Beach CA 92651 USA; 714/376-2882, Fax: 714/376-2885, Web URL: screenteam.com, Focus: Screen saver software, Ownrshp: PVT, Michael Bivens

Screen USA 5110 Tollview Dr, Rolling Meadows IL 60008 USA; 847/870-7400, Fax: 847/870-0149, Focus: Marketing and service for screen products, Ownrshp: Sub. Dainippon Screen Mfg. Co., Kenneth D. Newton, Pres & CEO, Richard A. Way

Scriptel Holdings Inc. 4145 Arlingate Plaza, Columbus OH 43228 USA; 614/276-8402, Fax: 614/276-7615, Focus: Digitizers, flat panels and cord less pens, Ownrshp: OTC, Stk Sym: SCRH, Founded: 1983, Empl: 26, Sales ($M): 5.2, Fiscal End: 12/93; James W. France Jr., Chmn, Pres & CEO, Edward Palmer, VP & CIO, Thomas P. Martini, CFO, James V. Holloway, Pres Scriptel Corp

Seagate Enterprise Management Software 19925 Stevens Creek Blvd, Cupertino CA 95014-2305 USA; 408/342-4500, 800/525-5645 Fax: 408/342-4600, Co Email: @sems.com, Web URL: sems.com, Focus: Network management software, Prdts: DualManager, Ownrshp: Sub Seagate, Founded: 1995, Empl: 95, Andre Schwager, Pres & CEO, Roselie Buonauro, VP Mktng, Mark Sutter, VP Prod Dev, John Metzger, VP Prod Dev

Seagate Technology 920 Disc Dr, Scotts Valley CA 95066-4544 USA; 408/438-6550, Fax: 408/438-4127, Co Email: @seagate.com, Web URL: seagate.com, Focus: Winchester disk drives, Ownrshp: OTC, Stk Sym: SGAT, Founded: 1978, Empl: 53,900, Sales ($M): 8,588.4, Fiscal End: 6/96; Alan F. Shugart, Chmn, Pres & CEO, Bernard A. Carballo, SVP Sales & Mktng, Stephen J. Luczo, SVP Corp Dev, Ronald D. Verdoorn, SVP Mfg, Donald L. Waite, SVP & CFO, Julie Still, Media Relations

Seattle Silicon Corp. 4122 - 128th Ave SE, #200, Bellevue WA 98006 USA; 206/957-4422, Fax: 206/957-4550, Focus: ASIC and ASSP chips, Ownrshp: PVT, Founded: 1983, Empl: 15, Sales ($M): 5+, John V. Celms, Pres, Thomas E. Krueger, VP Mktng, Douglas Shorb, Sales Mgr

Seattle Support Group 20420 84th Ave S, Kent WA 98032 USA; 206/395-1484, 800/995-9777 Fax: 206/395-1487, Co Email: ssg@seamac.wa.com, Focus: CD-ROM photographic data, Prdts: Color Digital Photos, Color Digital Library, Vintage Quality Photos, Ownrshp: PVT, Empl: 10, Sales ($M): 3, Lee Simpson, CEO, Steve Daniel, Pres

Second Glance Software 7248 Sunset Ave NE, Bremerton WA 98311 USA; 360/692-3694, Fax: 360/692-9241, Co Email: info@secondglance.com, Focus: Document management software, Prdts: ePaper, LaserSeps, Ownrshp: PVT, Founded: 1991, Lance

Gilbert, Pres, Keith Mowry, Email: keith@secondglance.com

Second Wave Inc. 2525 Wallingwood Dr, Bldg. 13, Austin TX 78746-6932 USA; 512/329-9283, Fax: 512/329-9299, Co Email: d0864@applelink.com, Focus: Macintosh peripherals, Ownrshp: PVT, Founded: 1987, Empl: 18, Roger Storer, VP Eng, Lark Doley, VP Mktng

Secure Document Systems Inc. 9485 Regency Square Blvd #520, Jacksonville FL 32225-9100 USA; 904/725-2505, Fax: 904/725-8836, Focus: MICR printing systems and PC/printer/scanning system, Ownrshp: PVT, Founded: 1984, Empl: 50, Neal G. Anderson, Pres, Mark Alexander, EVP, Chuck Gillum, VP Sales & Mktng, Andy Stenson, Dir Ops, Charles Hoeppner, Dir R&D, Martha Parham, Mktng Proj Mgr

Securenet Technologies Inc. 2100 196th St SW, #124, Lynnwood WA 98036 USA; 206/776-2524, 800/673-3539 Fax: 206/776-2891, Co Email: info@securenet.org, Web URL: securenet.org, Focus: Security and anti-virus software, Prdts: AV-Gold, V-Net, ACS Plus, Ownrshp: PVT, Founded: 1993, Frank Horwitz, Pres, Email: flh@securenet.org; James C. Shaeffer, Email: jcs@securenet.org; Krista A. Golden, Email: kag@securenet.com

Security Dynamics Technologies Inc. (SDI), One Alewife Ctr, Cambridge MA 02140-2312 USA; 617/547-7820, Fax: 617/354-8836, Focus: Computer security and access control products, Ownrshp: OTC, Stk Sym: SDTI, Founded: 1984, Empl: 93, Sales ($M): 33.8, Fiscal End: 12/95; Kenneth P. Weiss, Chmn & CTO, Charles R. Stuckey, Pres & CEO, James M. Geary, VP Mktng, Robert W. Fine, VP Sales, Linda E. Saris, VP & CFO, David Hammond

Security Microsystems Inc. 19135 N 94th St, Scottsdale AZ 85255-5531 USA; 800/345-7390 Focus: PC security hardware and software, Prdts: Lockit, DesMaster, Ownrshp: PVT, Founded: 1982, Empl: 6, Ralph Ferrara, Pres, Email: 71171.104@compuserve.com; John Ferrara, VP, Carol Ferrara, Treas, Linda Mullin, VP Mktng

SeeColor Corp. 357 S El Monte Ave, Los Altos CA 94022 USA; 415/949-8610, Fax: 415/949-0840, Co Email: email@seecolorweb.com, Focus: Assembles complete software products for OEM and VAR customers, Prdts: Radiance, Founded: 1988, Karen Barr, VP Sales & Mktng

Seek Systems Inc. 11014 120th Ave NE, Kirkland WA 98003 USA; 206/822-7400, 800/790-7335 Fax: 206/822-3898, Co Email: x@seek.com, Focus: Disk array products, Prdts: Xcelerator, Seek Array, Adaptive RAID, Ownrshp: PVT, Founded: 1983, Empl: 25, Fred Felker, Pres, Linda Scobey, Dir Mktng, John Ford, Sales Mgr

Seer Technologies Inc. 8000 Regency Pkwy, Cary NC 27511 USA; 919/380-5000, Fax: 919/469-1910, Web URL: seer.com, Focus: CASE products, Ownrshp: OTC, Founded: 1990, Empl: 840, Sales ($M): 112.5, Fiscal End: 12/95; Robert A. Minicucci, Chmn, Gene Bedell, Pres & CEO

SEI Corp. 680 E Swedesford Rd, Wayne PA 19087-1658 USA; 610/254-1000, Focus: Computer services to financial institutions, Ownrshp: OTC, Stk Sym: SEIC, Founded: 1968, Empl: 1,300, Sales ($M): 226.0, Fiscal End: 12/95; Alfred P. West, Jr., Chmn & CEO, Henry H. Greer, Pres & COO, Gilbert L. Beebower, EVP, Richard B. Lieb, EVP, Carmen V. Romeo, EVP & CFO, Cris Brookmyer

SEI Information Technology 1030 Higgins Rd, #215, Park Ridge IL 60068-5763 USA; 708/696-4847, Focus: Intelligent Vehicle Highway System software, Ownrshp: PVT, Founded: 1985

Seiko Epson Corp. 3-3-5 Owa 3-chome, Suwa-shi, Nagano-Ken 392 JP-392 Japan; 266-56-1705, Web URL: epson.co.jp, Focus: Printers and PCs, Ownrshp: PVT, Sales ($M): 4,310, Fiscal End: 12/95

Seiko Instruments USA Inc. 1130 Ringwood Ct, San Jose CA 95131 USA; 408/922-5900, Fax: 408/922-5835, Focus: PC printers and peripherals, Ownrshp: Sub. Seiko Instruments, Japan, Founded: 1981, Empl: 300, Lem Fugitt, EVP, Craig Lynar, Dir Mktng, Dave Del Dotto, Dir Sales, Cheryl Landman, Sr Marcom

Mgr

Sejin America Inc. 2004 Martin Ave, Santa Clara CA 95050 USA; 408/980-7550, Fax: 408/980-7562, Focus: PC input devices, Ownrshp: PVT, Founded: 1973, NW. Lee, Pres, Mark Tiddens, VP Sales & Mktng, Roger Urrabazo, Act Mgr

Sema Group Plc 16 Rue Barbes, Montrouge F-92126 France; 1-4092-4092, Focus: Software and computer services, Ownrshp: FO, Empl: 7,500, Sales ($M): 1,067, Fiscal End: 12/95

SEMATECH 2706 Montopolis, Austin TX 78741 USA; 512/356-3137, Fax: 512/356-3135, Focus: Technology for manufacturing integrated circuits, Ownrshp: Nonprofit, Founded: 1987, Empl: 11, William Spencer, Pres & CEO, Jim Owens, COO, Ann Marett, Com Dir

Semiconductor Industry Assoc. (SIA), 181 Metro Dr, ##450, San Jose CA 95110 USA; 408/436-6600, Fax: 408/436-6646, Focus: Represents U.S.-based semiconductor manufacturers, Ownrshp: Nonprofit, Founded: 1977, Empl: 67, Andrew Procassini, Pres, Warren Davis, VP

Semiconductor Research Corp. (SRC), 1101 Slater Rd, Brighton Hall, #120, Durham NC 27703 USA; 919/541-9400, Fax: 919/541-9450, Web URL: src.org, Focus: Semiconductor industry consortium that oversees applied research at universities, Ownrshp: Nonprofit, Founded: 1982, Empl: 60, Larry W. Sumney, Pres & CEO, Robert M. Burger, VP & Chief Scientist

Sendero Corp. 7272 E Indian School Rd, 3rd Floor, Scottsdale AZ 85251 USA; 602/941-8112, 800/321-6899 Fax: 602/946-8224, Co Email: corporate.sales@sendero.fiserv, Focus: Financial software, Prdts: Sendero Vision, Ownrshp: Sub. Fiserv Inc., Founded: 1982, Empl: 100, Roland D. Sullivan, Chmn, Elliot Rosen, Pres & COO, Rob Mackintosh, SVP & CFO, Jeff Wildenthaler, SVP Sales & Mktng, Randi Long, Mgr Corp Com

Sense8 Corp. 100 Shoreline Hwy, #282, Mill Valley CA 94941-3645 USA; 415/331-6318, Fax: 415/331-9148, Web URL: sense8.com, Focus: Virtual reality/visual simulation software, Prdts: World Tool Kit, World Up, Ownrshp: PVT, Founded: 1990, Empl: 40, Tom Coull, Pres, Email: tom@sense8.com; Pat Gelband, VP SW, Email: pat@sense8.com; Mark Kettering, VP Sales, Email: mark@sense8.com; Dave Hinkle, VP Tech, Email: dave@sense8.com; Debbie Nelson, Mktng Dir, Email: debbie@sense8.com

Sentry Publishing Co. Inc. One Research Dr, Westboro MA 01581-3907 USA; 508/366-2031, Fax: 508/366-8104, Focus: Software and client/server computer magazines and demand-side IT market research, Prdts: Client/Server Computing, Software Magazine, Ownrshp: PVT, William A. Gannon, Pres, Donald E. Fagan, SVP & Publisher, Kathleen Flynn, VP Fin & Admin, Michael P. Walsh, SVP Custom Pubs, Cynthia Reenl, Marcom Mgr

Sequel Technology LLC 500 108th Ave NE, #1900, Bellevue WA 98004 USA; 206/646-6780, 800/881-2465 Fax: 206/646-6556, Co Email: @sequeltech.com, Focus: Internet management software, Stuart Rosove, Pres & CEO

Sequent Computer Systems Inc. 15450 SW Koll Pkwy, Beaverton OR 97006-6063 USA; 503/626-5700, Co Email: @sequent.com, Focus: Multiprocessor systems, Ownrshp: OTC, Stk Sym: SQNT, Founded: 1983, Empl: 1,810, Sales ($M): 540.3, Fiscal End: 12/95; Karl C. Powell, Chmn, Pres & CEO, John McAdam, Pres & COO, Robert S. Gregg, SVP & CFO, Wayne A. Pittenger, VP Ops, Robert B. Witt, VP & CIO, Michael Green, Mgr PR, Email: mgreen@sequent.com

Sequoia Systems Inc. 400 Nickerson Rd, Marlboro MA 01752 USA; 508/480-0800, 800/562-0011 Fax: 508/480-0184, Focus: Fault-tolerant computers, Ownrshp: OTC, Stk Sym: SEQS, Founded: 1981, Empl: 164, Sales ($M): 102.2, Fiscal End: 6/96; J. Michael Stewart, Pres & CEO, Jack J. Stiffler, EVP & CTO, Ronald J. Gellert, VP & GM Syst, John M. Owens, VP Eng, Richard B. Goldman, EVP & CFO

Sercomp Corp. 21050 Lassen St, PO Box 4119, Chatsworth CA

91313-4119 USA; 818/341-1680, 800/477-7372 Fax: 818/341-9587, Focus: Printer ribbons, laser toner cassettes and ink jet cartridges, Prdts: neat-jet, Founded: 1978, Scott Montgomery

Serial Storage Architecture Industry Assoc. (SSA IA), Dept H65/B-013, 5600 Cottle Rd, San Jose CA 95193 USA; 408/256-5656, Fax: 408/256-0595, Focus: Association to promote SSA technology, Ownrshp: Nonprofit, Founded: 1995

Servantis Systems Inc. 4411 E Jones Bridge Rd, Norcross GA 30092 USA; 770/441-3387, Fax: 770/242-7935, Web URL: servantis.com, Focus: Financial software for IBM and compatible computers, Prdts: Bank St, InfoVue, Recon Plus for Windows, Ownrshp: PVT, Founded: 1971, Empl: 550, Sales ($M): 63, Robert Campbell, Chmn & Pres, Robert Bowers, EVP Admin, Jim Garrett, EVP Mktng, John Stephens, Pres Payment Prod, D.R. Grimes, EVP Tech

Server Technology Inc. 1288 Hammerwood Ave, Sunnyvale CA 94089 USA; 408/745-0300, 800/835-1515 Fax: 408/745-0392, Co Email: @servertech.com, Web URL: servertech.com, Focus: LAN and communications products, Ownrshp: PVT, Founded: 1984, Empl: 18, Sales ($M): 2, Carrel Ewing, Pres, Brandon Ewing, VP Sales, Mark Bigler, Dir Prod Res, Jack Cleveland, Dir Eng & Ops, Liza Johnson

ServiceWare Inc. 333 Allegheny Ave, Oakmont PA 15139 USA; 412/826-1158, Fax: 412/826-0577, Co Email: info@serviceware.com, Web URL: serviceware.com, Focus: Pre-packaged knowledge bases for the help desk, Prdts: Knowledge-Paks, Jeff Pepper, Pres & CEO, Hilary G. DeBroff, Dir Marcom, Email: debroff@serviceware.com

SETPOINT Inc. 14701 St Mary's Ln, Houston TX 77079-2995 USA; 713/584-1000, Fax: 713/584-4329, Co Email: @setpoint.com, Focus: Computer automation systems for process control, Ownrshp: PVT, Founded: 1977, Empl: 425, Sales ($M): 42, Douglas C. White, Chmn, Pres & CEO, Janice Crawford

ShaBlamm! Computer Corp. 21040 Homestead Rd, #201, Cupertino CA 95014-0238 USA; 408/730-9696, 800/742-2526 Fax: 408/730-4940, Web URL: shablamm.com, Focus: Personal workstations, Prdts: Nitro Personal Workstation, Ownrshp: PVT, Founded: 1993, Empl: 5, Tom North, Pres & CEO, Email: tn@shablamm.com; Joel Scheunberg, VP Mktng & Sales, Email: js@shablamm.com; Duane Claunch, CFO, Email: dc@shablamm.com

Shana Corp. 9744 - 45th Ave, Edmonton Alberta T6E 5C5 Canada; 403/433-3690, Fax: 403/437-4381, Co Email: info@shana.com, Focus: Forms software, Ownrshp: PVT, Founded: 1985, Empl: 21, Sales ($M): 2, Don Murphy, Pres, John Murphy, VP Sales & Mktng, Email: jmurphy@shana.com

Shandwick Technologies 4 Copley Pl. #605, Boston MA 02116-6504 USA; 617/536-0470, Fax: 617/536-2772, Web URL: miller.com, Focus: PR, marketing communications and internet relations, Ownrshp: PVT, Empl: 95, John Miller Jr., Chmn, Andrea Der Boghosian, EVP

Shandwick USA 8400 Normandale Lake Blvd, #500, Bloomington MN 55437 USA; 612/832-5000, Fax: 612/831-8241, Web URL: shandwick.com, Focus: PR and marketing communications, Ownrshp: PVT, Empl: 85, Dennis McGrath, CEO, Chris Malecek, SVP, Email: rcmalecek@shandwick.com; Mary Ellen Amodeo, Acct Supervisor, Email: meamodeo@shandwick.com

Shared Medical Systems Corp. (SMS), 51 Valley Stream Pkwy, Malvern PA 19355 USA; 610/219-6300, Focus: Computer services for health care industry, Ownrshp: OTC, Stk Sym: SMED, Founded: 1969, Empl: 4,826, Sales ($M): 650.6, Fiscal End: 12/95; R. James Macaleer, Chmn, Marvin S. Cadwell, Pres & CEO, Michael B. Costello, VP Admin & Corp Comm, Terrence W. Kyle, VP Fin

Sharp Electronics Corp. Sharp Plaza, Mahwah NJ 07430-2135 USA; 201/529-8200, Fax: 201/529-8919, Focus: PCs, peripherals and electronic products, Ownrshp: Sub. Sharp, Japan, Founded: 1962, Empl: 2,300, Sales ($M): 2,800, Fiscal End: 3/94; Toshiaki

Urushisako, Chmn & Pres, O. Perry Clay, SVP Consumer Electronics Grp, Hiroshi Okamoto, SVP Info Sys Grp, Daniel J. Infanti, VP, Nancy Boyle Levene, Assoc Dir

Sharper Image Corp. 650 Davis St, San Francisco CA 94111 USA; 415/445-6000, 800/344-4444 Co Email: tsi@enet.net, Web URL: sharperimage.com, Focus: Reseller of PCs and electronics products, Ownrshp: OTC, Stk Sym: SHRP, Founded: 1978, Empl: 1,100, Sales ($M): 188.0, Fiscal End: 1/95; Richard Thalheimer, Chmn & CEO, Craig Womack, EVP & COO, Sydney Klevatt, SVP Mktng, Tracey Wan, SVP & CFO, Vincent Barriero, SVP MIS, Lou Soucie, PR Coordinator

Sherpa Corp. 611 River Oaks Pkwy, San Jose CA 95134 USA; 408/433-0455, 800/736-9778 Fax: 408/943-9507, Web URL: sherpa.com, Focus: Product data management software, Prdts: SHERPA, Ownrshp: PVT, Founded: 1985, Empl: 200, Sales ($M): 24.5, Fiscal End: 12/93; John C. Moore, Pres & CEO, Rick Jones, VP Fin, John Claiborne, VP Mktng, Dick Bertrand, VP Eng, Michael Northwood, VP/Dir, Robin Ratajczak, Marcom Mgr, Email: robinr@sherpa.com

Shining Technology Inc. 10533 Progress Way, #C, Cypress CA 90630 USA; 714/761-9598, Fax: 714/761-9624, Focus: I/O devices for laptop, portable and desktop computers, Prdts: CitiROM, Founded: 1992, Empl: 70, Chris C. Wang, Pres & CEO, Gary Shumaker, VP Tech Mktng Svcs

Shiva Corp. 28 Crosby Dr, Bedford MA 01730-1437 USA; 617/270-8300, Fax: 617/270-8599, Co Email: sales@shiva.com, Web URL: shiva.com, Focus: Remote networking products, Prdts: LanRover, NetModem, Ownrshp: OTC, Stk Sym: SHVA, Founded: 1985, Empl: 135, Sales ($M): 117.7, Fiscal End: 12/95; Frank Ingari, Chmn, Pres & CEO, Woody Benson, VP Mktng & Sales, Dennis Chateauneuf, VP Ops, Cynthia Deysher, CFO, Email: deysher@us.shiva.com; Paul Gustafson

SHL Systemhouse Inc. 50 O'Conner St, #501, Ottawa Ontario K1P 6L2 Canada; 613/236-1428, Web URL: shl.com, Focus: Canada's largest systems integrator, Ownrshp: OTC, Stk Sym: SHKIF, Empl: 5,189, Sales ($M): 912.9, Fiscal End: 8/94; John R. Oltman, Chmn & CEO, John W. Bunnell, Pres, Richard H. Beatty, EVP, Dennis B. Maloney, Pres Computing & Netw, William W. Linton, EVP & CFO

Shortcut Software Corp. PO Box 986, Pacific Palisades CA 90272 USA; 310/459-3871, Fax: 310/459-5621, Co Email: 71511.3344@compuserve.com, Focus: PC software utilities, Prdts: Shortcut Guides, Ownrshp: PVT, Howard Weisberg, Pres

Shuttle Technology 43116 Christy St, Fremont CA 94538 USA; 510/656-0180, Fax: 510/656-0390, Focus: Parallel ports and storage management software, Ownrshp: Sub Shuttle, UK, Founded: 1990, Empl: 50, Sales ($M): 6, Alan Jones, Pres & CEO, Tony Ruane, Sales Mgr, George Dundon, Dir Tech Ops, Harvey Ulijohn

Siemens Nixdorf Information Systems Inc. 200 Wheeler Rd, Burlington MA 01803 USA; 617/273-0480, Fax: 617/221-0245, Web URL: sni.com, Focus: Computers and services, Ownrshp: Sub. Siemens Nixdorf, Germany, Empl: 1,900, Richard Lussier, Pres & CEO, Harry Hamilton, EVP, Herb Cline, VP, Heinz Kagerer, VP, Rolf Mailahn, EVP & CFO, Ian Robb

Siemens Nixdorf Informationssysteme AG Otto Hahn Ring 6, Munich D-81739 Germany; 89-636-47759, Web URL: shi.de, Focus: Minicomputers and microcomputers, Ownrshp: Sub. Siemens, Germany, Founded: 1952, Empl: 38,000, Sales ($M): 8,952, Fiscal End: 9/95; Gerhard Schulmeyer, Pres & CEO

Siemens Nixdorf Printing Systems LP 5500 Broken Sound Blvd, Boca Raton FL 33487 USA; 407/997-3100, 800/523-5444 Fax: 407/994-3352, Focus: Printers, Ownrshp: Sub. Siemens Nixdorf, Germany, Empl: 400, Sales ($M): 220, Fiscal End: 10/95; H. Werner Krause, Pres & CEO, Tim Moylan, VP Mktng, Berndt Haserueck, CFO, Dom Caputo, VP Sales, Gretchen DeWeese, Corp Com Mgr

Sierra On-Line Inc. 3380 146th Place SE, #300, Bellevue WA

98007 USA; 206/649-9800, Fax: 206/641-7617, Web URL: sierra.com, Focus: Entertainment and educational software, Prdts: Phantamasgoria, NASCAR, Print Artist, Ownrshp: OTC, Stk Sym: SIER, Founded: 1979, Empl: 540, Sales ($M): 158.2, Fiscal End: 3/96; Ken Williams, Chmn, Pres & CEO, James G. Stanley, EVP, Michael Brochu, CFO, Alan J. Higginson, EVP Mktng & Sales

Sierra Semiconductor Corp. 2075 N Capitol Ave, San Jose CA 95132 USA; 408/263-9300, Fax: 408/263-3337, Focus: CMOS chips and chip sets, Ownrshp: OTC, Stk Sym: SERA, Founded: 1984, Empl: 500, Sales ($M): 188.7, Fiscal End: 12/95; James V. Diller, Chmn & CEO, Richard J. Koeltl, Pres & COO, Alden J. Chauvin Jr., VP Sales, Marc Robinson, VP & CTO, Tom Bakewell, Dir CIS, Gary Breeding, Dir Marcom

Sierra Wireless Inc. 13151 Vanier Place, #260, Richmond BC V6V 2J2 Canada; 604/231-1100, Co Email: info@sierrawireless.ca, Web URL: sierrawireless.ca, Focus: Wireless modems, Ownrshp: PVT, David Sutcliffe, Pres & CEO, Andrew Herries, VP Sales & Mktng

Sigma Designs Inc. 4650 Landings Pkwy, Fremont CA 94538 USA; 510/770-0100, Fax: 510/770-2640, Co Email: @sdesigns.com, Focus: Display and multimedia products, Ownrshp: OTC, Stk Sym: SIGM, Founded: 1982, Empl: 151, Sales ($M): 26.4, Fiscal End: 1/96; Thinh Tran, Chmn, Pres & CEO, Julien Nguyen, Co-Chmn & CTO, Q. Binh Trinh, VP Fin & CFO, Silvio Perich, SVP Sales, Letty Dupuy

SIGS Publications Group 71 W 23rd St, 3rd Floor, New York NY 10010 USA; 212/242-7447, Fax: 212/242-7574, Co Email: 73361.1707@compuserve.com, Web URL: sigs.com, Focus: Technical computer magazines, books and conferences, Prdts: Object Magazine, C++ Report, X Journal, Smalltalk Report, Ownrshp: PVT, Richard P. Friedman, Pres, Margherita R. Monck, GM

Silicom Ltd. 15311 NE 90th St, #101, Redmond WA 98052-3562 USA; 206/882-7995, Fax: 206/882-4775, Focus: Pocket LAN adapters, Ownrshp: OTC, Stk Sym: SILCF, Founded: 1987, Sales ($M): 2.7, Fiscal End: 12/95; Avi Eizenman, Pres & CEO, Caroline J. Takeuchi, VP Sales & Mktng, Peter Dean

Silicon Graphics Inc. 2011 N Shoreline Blvd, Mountain View CA 94043-1389 USA; 415/960-1980, Fax: 415/961-0595, Web URL: sgi.com, Focus: Graphics workstations and supercomputers, Ownrshp: NYSE, Stk Sym: SGI, Founded: 1981, Empl: 10,485, Sales ($M): 2,921.3, Fiscal End: 6/96; Edward R. McCracken, Chmn & CEO, William M. Kelly, VP Bus Dev, Stanley J. Meresman, SVP & CFO, Forest Baskett, SVP R&D, Jill Grossman, Mgr PR

Silicon Valley Research Inc. (SVR), 300 Ferguson Dr, #300, Mountain View CA 94043 USA; 415/962-3000, Fax: 415/962-3001, Focus: Software for IC design, Prdts: SC, GARDS and Floorplacer, Ownrshp: OTC, Stk Sym: SVRL, Sales ($M): 10.9, Fiscal End: 3/96; Robert Anderson, Pres, Cherrie Billings, Controller

Silton-Bookman Systems 20230 Stevens Creek Blvd #D, Cupertino CA 95014-2210 USA; 408/446-1170, 800/932-6311 Fax: 408/446-5705, Co Email: @sbsinc.com, Web URL: sbsinc.com, Focus: Vertical market software, Prdts: Registrar for Windows, Ownrshp: PVT, Founded: 1984, Empl: 38, Sales ($M): 4.3, Richard Silton, Pres, Email: rsilton@sbsinc.com; Sara Padfield, CFO, Email: spadfield@sbsinc.com; Philip Bookman, VP R&D, Email: pbookman@sbsinc.com; Ron Bauer, Mktng Mgr, Email: rbauer@sbsinc.com; Teri Green, Mktng Coord, Email: tgreen@sbsinc.com

SilverLock Software Corp. PO Box 441384, Houston TX 77244-1384 USA; 713/722-9399, Fax: 713/722-0747, Focus: Utility and productivity software, Prdts: Crash Proof, Power Utilities, Ownrshp: PVT, Founded: 1994, Henry E. Millson III, Pres

SilverSun Inc. 302 N Washington Ave, #103E, Moorestown NJ 08057-2452 USA; 609/722-0050, 800/874-5837 Fax: 609/722-1511, Co Email: ssilversun@aol.com, Focus: Entertainment software, Prdts: Cross Wire, Word Crazy, Ownrshp: PVT, Founded: 1993, Empl: 3, Rick Stauffer, Pres, Bill Albright, VP

Silvon Software Inc. 900 Oakmont Ln, #400, Westmont IL 60559 USA; 708/655-3313, 800/262-8296 Fax: 708/655-3377, Focus: Help desk systems, Michael J. Hennel, Pres, Robert J. Siegel, GM

Simba Information Inc. 213 Danbury Rd, PO Box 7430, Wilton CT 06897-7430 USA; 203/834-0033, 800/307-2529 Fax: 203/834-1771, Web URL: simbanet.com, Focus: Publishing industry information and publications, Prdts: Computer Marketing & Distribution, Multimedia Business, Ownrshp: PVT, Alan Brigish, Publisher, Chris Elwell, VP, Tom Niehaus, VP

Simon & Schuster Interactive 1230 6th Ave, New York NY 10020 USA; 212/698-7187, Focus: Entertainment and education software, Ownrshp: Sub Viacom, Stk Sym: VIA, Founded: 1994, Jack Ramanos, CEO

Simple Technology Inc. 3001 Daimler St, Santa Ana CA 92705-5812 USA; 714/476-1180, Fax: 714/476-1209, Focus: PC memory upgrades, Ownrshp: PVT, Founded: 1990, Empl: 160, Sales ($M): 225, Mike Moshayedi, Pres, Manouch Moshayedi, CEO, Mark Moshayedi, COO, Alexx Wood, PR Mgr

Simplex Time Recorder Co. Simplex Plaza, Gardner MA 01441-0001 USA; 508/632-2500, Focus: Time and attendance software, Prdts: WinStar, Ownrshp: PVT, Founded: 1894, Len Harmon

Simucad Inc. 32970 Alvarado-Niles Rd, #744, Union City CA 94587 USA; 415/487-9700, Fax: 415/487-9721, Co Email: @simucad.com, Focus: Logic and fault simulation software, Prdts: Silos, Ownrshp: PVT, Founded: 1981, Bill Fuchs, Pres & CEO, Lyle Stevens, Mktng Admin, Email: lyle@simucad.com

Sir-Tech Software Inc. PO Box 245, Ogdensburg NY 13669-0245 USA; 315/393-6451, Fax: 315/393-1525, Co Email: 76711.33@compuserve.com, Focus: Recreational and home productivity software, Prdts: Wizardry series, Realms of Arkania, Jagged Alliance, Ownrshp: PVT, Founded: 1981, Empl: 20, Norman Sirotek, Pres & CEO, Robert Sirotek, VP, Linda Sirotek, Prod Plng & Acq, Shari T. Mitchell, PR Dir

Siren Software 505 Hamilton Ave, Palo Alto CA 94301 USA; 415/322-0600, 800/457-4736 Fax: 415/322-9999, Co Email: info@siren.com, Focus: C/S mail and fax server software, Ownrshp: Sub Vicor, Jeff Morrison, Managing Dir, Byron Jacobs, Dir Sales & Mktng, Beth Weber, Marcom Mgr, Email: bweber@siren.com

Sirius Publishing Inc. 7320 E Butherus Dr, #100, Scottsdale AZ 85260 USA; 602/951-3288, Fax: 602/951-3884, Co Email: @siriuspub.com, Web URL: siriusnet.com, Focus: Music and multimedia software, Prdts: PC Karaoke, Ownrshp: PVT, Founded: 1993, Empl: 50, Sales ($M): 40, Richard Gnant, Pres, Jim Matney, Corp Com, Email: jim_m@siriuspub.com

Sirius Software Inc. 345 W Second St, #201, Dayton OH 45402-1443 USA; 513/228-4849, 800/788-4849 Fax: 513/228-1159, Co Email: info@siriusacct.com, Web URL: siriusacct.com/sirius, Focus: Accounting software, Prdts: Sirius Business Accounting, Ownrshp: PVT, Founded: 1991, Norm Suda, Pres, Email: norm_suda@siriusacct.com; Bruce Richards, VP, Email: bruce_richards@siriusacct.com

Sirsi Corp. 689 Discovery Dr, Huntsville AL 35806 USA; 205/922-9820, 800/242-2233 Fax: 205/922-9818, Co Email: @sirsi.com, Web URL: sirsi.com, Focus: Network information retrieval systems, Ownrshp: PVT, Founded: 1979, Empl: 70, Jim Young, CEO, Jacky Young, COO, Mike Murdoch, CTO, Alan Davis, Email: aland@sirsi.com

Skipstone Inc. 3925 W Breaker Ln, #425, Austin TX 78759 USA; 512/305-0200, Fax: 512/305-0212, Co Email: sales@skipstone.com, Web URL: skipstone.com, Focus: Products and technology for IEEE 1394 serial bus, Ownrshp: PVT, Founded: 1994, Gary A. Hoffman, CEO, Email: gary@skipstone.com

SkiSoft Publishing Corp. 1644 Massachusetts Ave, #79, Lexington MA 02173 USA; 617/863-1876, Fax: 617/861-0086, Co Email: info@skisoft.com, Web URL: skisoft.com, Focus: Word processing software, Prdts: Eye Relief, Ownrshp: PVT, Founded: 1988, Ken Skier, Pres, Email: ken@skisoft.com; Cynthia Skier, VP

SKY Computers Inc. 27 Industrial Ave, Chelmsford MA 01824 USA; 508/454-6200, 800/486-3400 Fax: 508/459-9873, Co Email: info@sky.com, Focus: Attached processors, Prdts: SKYbolt, SKYstation, SKYvec, SKYchannel, Ownrshp: Sub. Analogic Corp., Founded: 1980, Bruce R. Rusch, Pres, Robert Hoenig, GM, Email: hoenig@sky.com; Dianne Capps, Marcom Mgr, Email: capps@sky.com

SkyNotes Inc. 4270 Prominade Way #P124, Marina Del Rey CA 90292 USA; 310/577-9332, Fax: 310/821-9048, Co Email: @skynotes.com, Focus: Wireless communication software, Prdts: SkyDispatch, SkySales, SkyMemo, Founded: 1994, Empl: 6, Sales ($M): 2, Marc Menowitz, Pres, Email: marc@radiomail.net; Eric Rayl, SVP, Clive S. Stevens, VP Mktng & Sales, Email: clive@radiomail.net; Matt Biel, Admin Accountant, Email: matt@skynotes.com

SkyTel Corp. 200 S Lamar St, Jackson MS 39201 USA; 601/944-1300, Fax: 601/944-7094, Co Email: @skytel.com, Web URL: skytel.com, Focus: Nationwide paging and voice messaging, Ownrshp: Sub. Mobile Telecom, Founded: 1988, Empl: 430, Sales ($M): 85, David W. Garrison, Pres, Ray O'Brien, SVP Mktng, Anne Marie Potts

SL Corp. 240 Tamal Vista Blvd, #110, Corte Madera CA 94925 USA; 415/927-1724, Fax: 415/927-0878, Focus: Graphical modeling software, Prdts: SL-GMS, Ownrshp: PVT, Founded: 1983, Empl: 42, Sales ($M): 10, Fiscal End: 12/95; Thomas Lubinski, Pres & CTO, Peter N. Sherrill, CEO, Linda Cannon, Mktng Mgr, Email: uunet!gandhi!linda

SL Waber Inc. 520 Fellowship Rd, #306-C, Mt. Laurel NJ 08054 USA; 609/866-8888, 800/634-1485 Fax: 609/886-1945, Focus: Power protection equipment, Prdts: UPStart, Ownrshp: Sub. SL Industries, Founded: 1959, Arthur Blumenthal, Pres, David Day, VP Eng & Advanced Tech, Michael Forbeck, Dir Sales & Mktng, Laurie Gahan, Dir Sales & Mktng, Pat Mikucki, Mktng Mgr

Sligos 3 Place de la Pyramide, Cedex 49, Paris La Defense F-92067 France; 1-4900-9000, Web URL: sligos.com, Focus: Computer services, Ownrshp: FO, Empl: 4,500, Sales ($M): 778, Fiscal End: 12/95

Slimyfrog Software 979 Golf Course Dr, Rohnert Park CA 94928 USA; Fax: 707/769-8456, Co Email: slimyfrog@eworld.com, Focus: Utility and entertainment software, Ownrshp: PVT

Smart and Friendly 20520 Nordhoff St, Chatsworth CA 91311 USA; 818/772-8001, 800/959-7001 Fax: 818/772-2888, Focus: Peripherals and multimedia products, Ownrshp: PVT, Founded: 1982, Perry Solomon, Pres & CEO, Marie Solomon, EVP & CFO, Robert Resovich, Eng, Jeremy Gerber, Marcom Mgr

SMART Modular Technologies 45531 Northpoint Loop W, Fremont CA 94538 USA; 510/623-1231, 800/536-1231 Fax: 510/623-1434, Focus: PCMCIA products, Ownrshp: PVT, Founded: 1988, Empl: 120, Ajay Shah, Pres, Mukesh Patel, Sr Ops, Lata Krishnan, VP Fin, Alan Marten, VP Sales, Bettina Babich, Dir Mktng

Smart Software 4 Hill Rd, Belmont MA 02178 USA; 617/489-2743, 800/762-7899 Fax: 617/498-2748, Co Email: info@smartcorp.com, Focus: Sales and business forecasting software, Prdts: SmartForecast, Ownrshp: PVT, Founded: 1983, Empl: 10, Charles N. Smart, Pres, Email: csmart@smartcorp.com; Nelson S. Hartmian, VP, Email: nsh@smartcorp.com; Thomas R. Willemsin, VP, Email: trw@smartcorp.com

Smart Technologies Inc. 1177-11 Ave SW, #600, Calgary Alberta T2R 1K9 Canada; 403/245-0333, Fax: 403/245-0366, Co Email: @smarttech.com, Focus: Electronic whiteboard and conferencing software, Prdts: SMART Board, SMART 2000 Conferencing, Ownrshp: PVT, Founded: 1987, Empl: 70, David A. Martin, Pres, Email: davidmar@smarttech.com; Nancy Knowlton, EVP, Lucien Potwin, VP HW, John Deutsch, VP Sales, Roy M. Anderson, Dir SW Eng, Natalie Young

SmartDesk Inc. 26062 Merit Cr, #106, Laguna Hills CA 92653

USA; 714/582-4020, 800/582-4022 Fax: 714/348-0006, Focus: Desktop management software, Ownrshp: PVT, Founded: 1994, Steven M. Repetti, Pres & CTO, Joseph Sennott, COO, Sheryl Moss, VP Sales & Mktng, Scott J. Thomas, CFO

Smartek Software 2223 Avenida De La Playa, #208, La Jolla CA 92037-0366 USA; 619/456-5064, Fax: 619/456-3928, Co Email: smartekinc@aol.com, Focus: Educational software, Prdts: WordSmart, Ownrshp: PVT, Founded: 1988, Empl: 7, Sales ($M): 1, David Kay, Pres, Will Von Reis, CTO

SMDS Interest Group Inc. (SMDS), 303 Vintage Park Dr, Foster City CA 94404-1138 USA; 415/578-6979, Fax: 415/525-0182, Focus: Promotion and education of SMDS service usage, Ownrshp: Nonprofit, Founded: 1990, Vivian Beaulieu, Exec Dir, Mark Fisher, Pres & Chmn

Smile International Inc. 1575 Sunflower Ave, Costa Mesa CA 92626 USA; 714/546-0336, 800/876-4532 Fax: 714/546-0315, Focus: Monitors, Ownrshp: Sub Kuo Feng, Taiwan, Founded: 1990, Empl: 40, Sherry Chen, Pres, Roy Pacheco, Dir Mktng, Keith Huang, Mgr Tech Sup, Chris Ho, Sales Mgr

Smith Bucklin & Assoc. 401 N Michigan Ave, Chicago IL 60611-4267 USA; 312/321-6830, Fax: 312/6876, Web URL: sba.com, Focus: Associations and tradeshow management, Ownrshp: PVT

Smith Micro Software Inc. 51 Columbia, Aliso Viejo CA 92656 USA; 714/362-5800, Fax: 714/362-2300, Co Email: @smithmicro.com, Focus: Fax, OCR and communication software, Ownrshp: OTC, Stk Sym: SMSI, Founded: 1982, Empl: 75, Sales ($M): 18.0, Fiscal End: 12/95; William W. Smith Jr., Pres & CEO, Rhonda Smith, EVP & COO, Bruce T. Quigley, Dir Mktng, Email: bquigley@smithmicro.com; Robert A. Caggiano, VP Sales & Mktng, Chuck Spear, CFO

SNMP Research International Inc. 3001 Kimberlin Heights Rd, Knoxville TN 37920-9716 USA; 615/573-1434, Fax: 615/573-9197, Web URL: /n/snmp.com, Focus: Network management software, Mary Case, Pres, Email: mary@snmp.com; John Southwood, Sales & Mktng Mgr, Email: john@snmp.com

Society for Computer Simulation (SCS), PO Box 17900, 4838 Ronson Ct, #L, San Diego CA 92117-1810 USA; 619/277-3888, Fax: 619/277-3930, Co Email: @scs.org, Web URL: scs.org, Focus: Advancement of computer simulation technology, Ownrshp: Nonprofit, Founded: 1952, Empl: 2,300, William Gallagher, Exec Dir, Hildy Linn, Pub Mgr, Email: linn@sdsc.edu

Society for Industrial and Applied Mathematics (SIAM), 3600 University City Science Ctr, Philadelphia PA 19104-2688 USA; 215/382-9800, Fax: 215/386-7999, Co Email: siam@siam.org, Web URL: siam.org, Focus: Further application of mathematics to science and technology, Ownrshp: Nonprofit, Founded: 1952, Empl: 8,800, John Guckenheimer, Pres, James M. Crowley, Exec Dir, James Goldman

Society for Information Display (SID), 1526 Brookhollow Dr, #82, Santa Ana CA 92705-5421 USA; 714/545-1526, Fax: 714/545-1547, Web URL: display.org/sid, Focus: Association for display industry, Ownrshp: Nonprofit, Founded: 1962, Empl: 3,700, Lauren K. Kinsey, Exec Dir, Web Howard, Pres

Society for Information Management (SIM), 401 N Michigan Ave, Chicago IL 60611 USA; 312/644-6610, Fax: 312/245-1081, Focus: Association for information managers, Ownrshp: Nonprofit, Founded: 1968, Empl: 2,700

Society for the History of Technology (SHOT), Dept. Soc. Sciences, MI Technological Univ., Houghton MI 49931-1295 USA; 906/487-2113, Fax: 906/487-2468, Focus: History of technology and its impact on society, Ownrshp: Nonprofit, Founded: 1958, Empl: 1,750, Ruth Schwartz Cowan, Pres, Bruce E. Seely, Secretary & Ed

Society of Telecommunications Consultants (STC), 13766 Center St, #212, Carmel Valley CA 93924 USA; 408/659-0110, Fax: 408/659-0144, Co Email: stchdq@attmail.com, Focus: Serves independent telecommunications consultants, Ownrshp: Nonprofit,

Founded: 1976, Empl: 235, Susan Kuttner, Exec Dir

Society of Woman Engineers (SWE), 120 Wall St, 11th Floor, New York NY 10005-3902 USA; 212/509-9577, Fax: 212/509-0224, Co Email: 71764.743@compuserve.com, Web URL: swe.org, Focus: Organization for women engineers, Ownrshp: Nonprofit, Empl: 18,000

Socket Communications Inc. 6500 Kaiser Dr, Fremont CA 94555-3613 USA; 510/744-2700, Co Email: info@socketcom.com, Web URL: socketcom.com, Focus: Wireless data communications products, Ownrshp: PVT, Murray L. Dennis, Pres & CEO, Michael Gifford, EVP

Soft-One Corp. 1121 S Orem Blvd, Orem UT 84058 USA; 801/221-9400, 800/763-7902 Fax: 801/221-9942, Co Email: @soft-one.com, Web URL: softone.com, Focus: Multimedia-based training, Ownrshp: PVT, Founded: 1992, John R. Stevens, Pres, Dave Hales, VP, Teresa Crowell, Corp Com Dir, Email: tcrowell@soft-one.com

SoftArc Inc. 100 Allstate Pkwy, Markham Ontario L3R 6H3 Canada; 905/415-7000, 800/763-8272 Fax: 905/415-7151, Co Email: info@softarc.com, Web URL: softarc.com, Focus: C/S software, Prdts: First Class, Ownrshp: PVT, Founded: 1989, Empl: 70, Steve Asbury, Pres, Scott Welsh, VP, Dallas Kachan, Mgr Sales & Mktng, Email: dallas@softarc.com

Softbank Comdex Inc. 300 First Ave, Needham MA 02194-2722 USA; 617/443-1500, Fax: 617/444-4806, Web URL: comdex.com, Focus: Computer trade shows, Prdts: COMDEX, Windows World, LAN Expo, New Media, Ownrshp: Sub Softbank, Japan, Founded: 1971, Empl: 220, Masayoshi Son, Chmn, Jason E. Chudnofsky, Pres & CEO, Peter Schaw, VP Mktng, Milton Herbert, EVP, Richard L. Schwab, VP Proj Mgmt, Peter B. Young

Softbank Expos 303 Vintage Park Dr, Foster City CA 94404 USA; 415/578-6900, Fax: 508/525-0194, Co Email: info@sbexpos.com, Web URL: sbexpos.com, Focus: Computer trade shows, Ownrshp: Sub Softbank, Japan

Softbank Inc. 60 Garden City, #250, Monterey CA 93940-5341 USA; 408/644-7800, Fax: 408/644-7899, Focus: Software distribution, Ownrshp: Sub. Softbank, Japan, Masayoshi Son, Chmn, David Blumstein, Pres & CEO, Lowell Forte

Softbank Japan Rokubancho SK Bldg, 3 Rokubancho, Chiyoda-ku, Tokyo Jp-102 Japan; 3-3288-7201, Fax: 3-3288-7120, Focus: Computer trade shows, Ownrshp: Sub Softbank, Japan

SoftBooks Inc. 23282 Mill Creel Dr, Laguna Hills CA 92653-1678 USA; 714/586-1284, 800/992-6464 Fax: 714/586-1297, Focus: Electronic books, Ownrshp: PVT, David Mann, Pres, Richard Hart, CFO, Cindy Goss, PR Mgr

Softbridge Inc. 125 Cambridge Park Dr, Cambridge MA 02140 USA; 617/576-2257, Fax: 617/864-7747, Focus: Software testing tool, embeddable Basic language, Prdts: Automated Test Facility, Ownrshp: PVT, Founded: 1982, Empl: 50, Drew Hannah, Pres & CEO, Maureen Rogers, VP Mktng, Scott Sutherland, VP Sales

SoftCop Corp. 935 Sheldon Ct, Burlington Ontario L7L 5K6 Canada; 905/681-3269, Fax: 905/681-8089, Co Email: softcop@netaccess.on.ca, Focus: Software protection products, Ownrshp: FO, Stk Sym: SCOP, Founded: 1993, Fiscal End: 4/94; John Totten, Pres & CEO, Brian Clark, VP Bus Dev & CFO, Peter M. Slocombe, Dir Corp Com

Softcraft Technologies 1430 W Lake Samm Pkwy NE, Bellevue WA 98008 USA; 206/643-7929, Fax: 206/746-4655, Focus: Diagram software, Prdts: Diagram-It, Ownrshp: PVT, Al Buckingham

Softdesk Inc. 7 Liberty Hall Rd, Henniker NH 03242 USA; 603/428-3199, Fax: 603/428-7901, Co Email: info@softdesk.com, Web URL: softdesk.com, Focus: Architecture, engineering and construction application software, Prdts: Building Design & Engineering, Civil/Survey, Ownrshp: OTC, Stk Sym: SDSK, Founded: 1985, Empl: 134, Sales ($M): 35.6, Fiscal End: 12/95; David C. Arnold, Chmn, Pres & CEO, Jesse F. Devitte, EVP Sales & Mktng, John A. Rogers, CFO, R. Drew Ogden, VP Bus Dev, David A.

Paine, VP Tech, Barbara Goode, Email: bgoode@softdesk.com

SofTeam USA Inc. 3000 Chestnut Ave, #108, Baltimore MD 21211 USA; 410/243-1130, 800/305-8326 Fax: 410/243-1259, Co Email: chesa@aol.com, Focus: Sign making software, embroidery punching software, Prdts: Powersign, Punto 3.0, Ownrshp: PVT, Founded: 1992, Empl: 4, George Brecht, Pres, Cesare Fidanza, Chmn

SofTech Inc. 3260 Eagle Park Dr, Grand Rapids MI 49505 USA; 616/957-2330, Focus: Software development and systems integration, Ownrshp: OTC, Stk Sym: SOFT, Founded: 1969, Empl: 39, Sales ($M): 13.7, Fiscal End: 5/96; Norman L. Rasmussen, Pres & CEO, Mark R. Sweetland, VP, Joseph P. Mullaney, VP & CFO, Jean J. Croteau, VP Bus Ops

SoftKey International Inc. 201 Broadway, Cambridge MA 02139 USA; 617/494-1200, Fax: 617/494-1219, Co Email: @softkey.com, Web URL: softkey.com, Focus: Education and entertainment software, Ownrshp: OTC, Stk Sym: SKEY, Founded: 1982, Empl: 850, Sales ($M): 254.7, Fiscal End: 12/95; Michael J. Perik, Chmn & CEO, Kevin O'Leary, Pres, Les Schmidt, COO, Robert Gagnon, EVP, R. Scott Murray, CFO, Karen Goulet, Dir Corp Affairs

SoftKlone 327 Office Plaza Dr, #100, Tallahassee FL 32301-2776 USA; 904/878-8564, 800/634-8670 Fax: 904/877-9763, Co Email: @softklone.com, Web URL: softklone.com, Focus: PC communications products, Prdts: Mirror, Takeover, Information HOT-LINE, Ownrshp: PVT, Founded: 1985, Empl: 26, Sales ($M): 1.5, Fiscal End: 3/91; Bruce O. Justham, Pres, Email: bruce@softklone.com; Kari E. Downey, Sales & Mktng Mgr, Email: kari@softklone.com

Softlab Inc. 1000 Abernathy Rd, #1000, Atlanta GA 30328 USA; 770/668-8811, Web URL: softlab.dc, Focus: Application development tools, Ownrshp: Sub Softlab, Germany, Sales ($M): 132, Fiscal End: 12/95; Ulrich Fahr, Chmn & CEO, Mark Bartolomeo, Pres

Softmart Inc. Oaklands Corporate Ctr, 467 Creamery Way, Exton PA 19341-2508 USA; 610/524-7440, Fax: 610/363-1438, Focus: Resale of software, networks and peripherals for PCs and workstations, Ownrshp: PVT, Founded: 1983, Empl: 200+, A. Richard Sloane, Pres & CEO

SoftQuad International Inc. 56 Aberfoyle Crescent, 5th Fl., Toronto Ontario M8X 2W4 Canada; 416/239-4801, Fax: 416/239-7105, Co Email: mail@sq.com, Web URL: sq.com, Focus: Electronic publishing software for the Internet, Prdts: HoTMetaL PRO, Sales ($M): 7.9, Fiscal End: 12/95; Dave Gurney, Chmn & CEO, Jodi Hazzan, Press & Media Rel, Email: jodi@sq.com

SoftSolutions Technology Corp. 1555 N Technology Way, Orem UT 84057-2395 USA; 801/226-6000, Fax: 801/224-0920, Focus: Document management software, Ownrshp: PVT, Founded: 1989, Empl: 100, Kenneth W. Duncan, Pres, Lee Duncan, VP

SoftSys Inc. 339 Westney Rd S, #204, Broadcast Square, Ajax Ontario L1S 7J6 Canada; 905/619-8093, Fax: 905/619-3013, Focus: Accounting programs, Prdts: EstimatorPlus, Ash Mather, Mktng Dir

SoftTalk Inc. 100 Crescent Rd, Needham MA 02194-1457 USA; 617/433-0800, Fax: 617/433-0911, Co Email: @softtalk.com, Web URL: softtalk.com, Focus: Integration of telephony, LAN and applications software, Prdts: PHONETASTIC, Founded: 1994, Alexander Belfer, Pres & CEO, Mark W. Feldman, VP Sales & Mktng NA, Saul Orbach, VP Sales & Mktng Europe

Software 2000 Inc. 25 Communications Way, Drawer 6000, Hyannis MA 02601 USA; 508/778-2000, Fax: 508/771-9753, Web URL: s2k.com, Focus: Financial, human resources & environmental management software for IBM AS/400, Ownrshp: OTC, Founded: 1981, Empl: 470, Sales ($M): 65.3, Fiscal End: 8/95; Robert A. Pemberton, Chmn & CEO, Frederick Lizza, Pres, Gail M. Fulciniti

Software Affiliates 16633 Ventura Blvd, #1210, Encino CA 91436 USA; 818/385-3710, Fax: 818/385-0233, Focus: MPEG software, Ownrshp: PVT, Rob Edenzon, Pres, Robert Guth

Software AG of N America Inc. 11190 Sunrise Valley Dr, Reston VA 22091 USA; 703/860-5050, Fax: 703/391-6731, Web URL: sagus.com, Focus: Database and connectivity software for mainframe and midrange computers, Prdts: ADABAS, Natural, Entire, Esperanti, Ownrshp: Sub. Software AG, Germany, Founded: 1972, Empl: 700, Sales ($M): 552 WW, Fiscal End: 12/95; Daniel F. Gillis, Pres & CEO

Software Architects Inc. 19102 N Creek Pkwy, #101, Bothell WA 98011-8005 USA; 206/487-0122, Fax: 206/487-0467, Co Email: info@softarch.com, Focus: Macintosh utility software, Prdts: Here & Now, Ownrshp: PVT, Robert Zollo, Pres, Marlowe Fenne

Software Artistry Inc. 9449 Priority Way W, Indianapolis IN 46240-1471 USA; 317/843-1663, 800/795-1993 Fax: 317/843-7477, Web URL: softart.com, Focus: AI software and expert systems, Prdts: Expert Advisor, Knowledge Engine, Ownrshp: OTC, Stk Sym: SWRT, Founded: 1988, Empl: 193, Sales ($M): 25.6, Fiscal End: 12/95; W. Scott Webber, Pres & CEO, Gary E. Lemke, VP Mktng, Email: gelemke@softart.com; Michael Robbins, SVP WW Sales, Steven M. Ehrlich, VP Client Svcs, Stephen R. Head, VP & CFO, Joseph M. Adams, VP PR

Software Clearing House Inc. 895 Central Ave, Cincinnati OH 45202-1961 USA; 513/579-0455, Fax: 513/579-1064, Co Email: info@sch.com, Web URL: sch.com, Focus: Distributes software, Ownrshp: PVT, Founded: 1979, Empl: 98, Edward J. Bauer, Pres & CEO, Email: ebauer@sch.com; Kent Allen, SVP Finance, Email: kallen@sch.com; Greg Philippe, VP Int'l Sales, Email: gphilippe@sch.com; Charles Best, Dir NA Sales, Email: cbest@sch.com; Denise Reier, Prod Mgr, Email: dreier@sch.com

Software Corp. of America 100 Prospect St, Stamford CT 06901 USA; 203/359-2773, 800/966-7722 Fax: 203/359-3198, Co Email: info@talkthru.com, Web URL: talkthru.com, Focus: Communications software, Prdts: TalkThru, Premier MDT, Ownrshp: PVT, Founded: 1981, Empl: 48, Shirley Eis, Pres, Email: eis@radiomail.net; David Feldstein, SVP Sales & Mktng, Email: dfeldstein@talkthru.com; Austin Donaghy, VP & GM, Lance Tishkevich, Email: ltishkevich@talkthru.com

Software Council of Southern California 21041 Southwestern Ave, #160, Torrance CA 90501 USA; 310/328-0043, Fax: 310/215-3623, Focus: Organization for S California software companies, Ownrshp: Nonprofit

Software Designs Unlimited Inc. 1829 E Franklin St, #1020, Chapel Hill NC 27514-5861 USA; 919/968-4567, Fax: 919/968-4576, Co Email: sdu@applelink.com, Focus: Multimedia software development tools, Ownrshp: PVT, Founded: 1988, Leonard Buck, Pres, Chris Ogden, Bus Dir, Email: chris.ogden@applelink.com

Software Developer's Co. Inc., The 90 Industrial Park Rd, Hingham MA 02043 USA; 617/740-0101, Fax: 617/740-4208, Web URL: computing.supershops.com, Focus: System software and development tools, Ownrshp: OTC, Stk Sym: SDEV, Founded: 1985, Empl: 100, Sales ($M): 56.1, Fiscal End: 3/96; Stephen L. Watson, Chmn, Barry N. Bycoff, Pres & CEO, James O'Connor, CFO, Rick Haigis, VP Mktng

Software Development Systems 815 Commerce Dr, #250, Oak Brook IL 60521 USA; 708/368-0400, Fax: 708/990-4641, Co Email: corp@sdsi.com, Focus: Software development tools for embedded systems, Ownrshp: PVT, Founded: 1984, Jim Challenger, Pres, Email: chal@sdsi.com

Software Engineering of America 1230 Hempstead Turnpike, Franklin Square NY 11010 USA; 916/328-7000, Web URL: seasoft.com, Focus: System and utility software, Ownrshp: PVT, Founded: 1982, Empl: 325, Sales ($M): 94.6, Fiscal End: 12/95; Salvatore Simeone, Pres & CEO

Software Forum PO Box 61031, Palo Alto CA 94306 USA; 415/854-7219, Fax: 415/854-8298, Focus: Information exchange and professional development for software entrepreneurs, Ownrshp: Nonprofit, Founded: 1983, Empl: 1,000, Barbara Cass, Exec Dir, Ellen Jamieson, Assist Exec Dir, Karen McCutcheon, Events Coord

Software Marketing Corp. 6300 E Naumann Dr, Paradise Valley AZ 85253-4226 USA; 602/893-3337, Fax: 602/893-2042, Focus: Edutainment software, Ownrshp: PVT

Software Moguls 12301 Whitewater Dr, #160, Minnetonka MN 55343-4107 USA; 612/932-6721, Fax: 612/932-6736, Co Email: info@moguls.com, Focus: Network backup software, Prdts: SM-Arch, Ownrshp: PVT, Founded: 1986, Empl: 30, Sales ($M): 5, Vinod Gupta, Pres & CEO, Email: vinod@moguls.com; Sunil Khadilkar, VP Eng

Software Partners Inc. 2013 Landings Dr, Mountain View CA 94043 USA; 415/428-0160, Fax: 415/428-0163, Focus: PC project management software, Prdts: FreeStyle, Ownrshp: PVT, Founded: 1988, Empl: 6, Alan Fisher, Pres, Razi Mohiuddin, VP Eng

Software Partners/32 Inc. 447 Old Boston Rd, Topsfield MA 01983 USA; 508/887-6409, Fax: 508/887-3680, Co Email: info@softwarepartners.com, Focus: Tape backup, hierarchical storage management and related software tools for minicomputers, Prdts: StorageCenter, THRUnet, Founded: 1983, Philip A. Jamieson, Pres & CEO, Constance McMahon, VP Sales & Mktng, Steve F. Snyder, COO, W. Michael Rieker, CTO

Software Patent Institute (SPI), 2901 Hubbard St, Ann Arbor MI 48105-2467 USA; 313/769-4606, Fax: 313/769-4054, Co Email: spi@iti.org, Web URL: iti.org, Focus: Software-related patent information and technical support, Ownrshp: Nonprofit, Founded: 1992, Roland J. Cole, Exec Dir

Software Productivity Consortium (SPC), SPC Bldg., 2214 Rock Hill Rd, Herndon VA 20170 USA; 703/742-8877, Fax: 703/742-7200, Focus: Software engineering innovations, Ownrshp: Nonprofit, Founded: 1985, Judd Neale, CEO

Software Professionals Inc. 999 Baker Way, #390, San Mateo CA 94404 USA; 415/578-0700, Fax: 415/578-0118, Co Email: info@sftw.com, Focus: Software for automatic systems management, Ownrshp: OTC, Stk Sym: SFTW, Founded: 1986, Empl: 40, Sales ($M): 6.5, Fiscal End: 12/95; Peter J. McDonald, Chmn, Pres & CEO, William Vogel, CTO, Kenneth S. Voss, VP Sales, Michael A. Morgan, VP & CFO

Software Publishers Assoc. (SPA), 1730 M St NW, #700, Washington DC 20036-4510 USA; 202/452-1600, 800/388-7478 Fax: 202/223-8756, Co Email: @spa.org, Web URL: spa.org, Focus: Association for software publishers who produce, release, develop or license microcomputer, Ownrshp: Nonprofit, Founded: 1984, Empl: 1,200, Kenneth Wasch, Pres, John Kernan, Chmn, Dave McClura, Dir Com, Terri Childs, PR Mgr

Software Publishing Corp. (SPC), 111 N Market St, PO Box 11044, San Jose CA 95113 USA; 408/537-3000, 800/336-8360 Fax: 408/450-7915, Co Email: @spco.com, Web URL: spco.com, Focus: Productivity software, Prdts: Harvard Graphics, Superbase, ASAP WebShow, Ownrshp: OTC, Stk Sym: SPCO, Founded: 1980, Empl: 110, Sales ($M): 24.0, Fiscal End: 9/95; Fred M. Gibbons, Chmn, Irfan Salim, Pres & CEO, Brad Peppard, VP Mktng, Miriam K. Frazer, VP & CFO, Viki Page

Software Security Inc. 6 Thorndal Cr, Darien CT 06820-5421 USA; 203/656-3000, 800/841-1316 Fax: 203/656-3932, Focus: Software protection products, Prdts: UniKey, Ownrshp: PVT, Founded: 1982, Empl: 20, Sales ($M): 8, Frederick Engel, Pres & CEO, Wayne Chou, EVP, Richard Erett, EVP, Neil Holzman, VP Sales & Mktng, Debra Cajigas, Mktng Coord

Software Solutions Inc. 3425B Corporate Way, Duluth GA 30136 USA; 770/418-2000, Fax: 770/418-2022, Focus: Vertical software, Ownrshp: PVT, Founded: 1079, Jess Solomon, Pres & CEO, Jerry Buran, VP Sales & Mktng, Rob Russell, VP Dev

Software Sorcery 5405 Morehouse Dr, #200, San Diego CA 92121-4724 USA; 619/452-9901, Fax: 619/452-5079, Focus: CD-ROM entertainment/Prdts: Sea Rogue, Jutland, Aegis, Fast Attack, Ownrshp: PVT, Founded: 1989, Empl: 11, Sales ($M): 2.4, Bernard J. Tyler, Pres & CEO, Susan Jones, VP

Software Spectrum Inc. 2140 Merritt Dr, Garland TX 75041

USA; 214/840-6600, Focus: Software reseller, Ownrshp: OTC, Stk Sym: SSPE, Founded: 1983, Empl: 750, Sales ($M): 352, Fiscal End: 3/95; Judy Sims, Pres & CEO, Deborah Nugent, VP Finance, Rose Hultgren, Mktng Dir, Robert Mercer, CIO

Software Support Inc. 300 International Pkwy, Heathrow FL 32746 USA; 407/333-4433, Fax: 407/333-9080, Co Email: 74107.3470@compuserve.com, Focus: Computer support services, Ownrshp: PVT, Founded: 1991, Empl: 100, Joseph J. Jacoboni, Pres & CEO, Deborah H. O'Connell, VP Finance, Edgar Martinez, Dir Cust Sup, Ingrid B. Arkeilpane, PR Mgr

Software Support Professional Assoc. (SSPA), 11858 Bernardo Olaza Ct, #101C, San Diego CA 92128-2411 USA; 619/674-4864, Fax: 619/674-1192, Co Email: sspa@ix.netcom.com, Focus: Alliance of customer technical support managers, Ownrshp: Nonprofit, Founded: 1989, Empl: 500+, Bill Rose, Exec Dir, John Hamilton, VP Prof Svcs, Email: hamilto2@ix.netcom.com

Software Valley PO Box 658, 1009 University Ave, Morgantown WV 26507-0658 USA; 703/678-8962, Fax: 703/678-8962, Focus: Association for software developers in W Virginia, Ownrshp: Nonprofit, Dick Dowell, Pres & CEO

Software Ventures Corp. 2907 Claremont Ave, #220, Berkeley CA 94705 USA; 510/644-3232, Fax: 510/848-0885, Co Email: sales@svcdudes.com, Web URL: svcdudes.com, Focus: Interactive telecommunication software, Prdts: MicroPhone II, Ownrshp: PVT, Founded: 1985, David Hindawi, Pres, Lawrence Garrigan, Email: press@svcdudes.com

Softwex International Ltd. 325-1130 W Pender St, Vancouver BC V6E 4A4 Canada; 604/689-9720, Fax: 604/688-9961, Co Email: 75117.3573@compuserve.com, Focus: Cost-control business management software, Prdts: LaborCost, Alain D. Barillaud, Sales

Solbourne Computer Inc. 1790 38th St #300, Boulder CO 80301-2604 USA; 303/772-3400, Fax: 303/772-3646, Focus: Oracle financials consulting, Ownrshp: Aff. Matsushita, Japan, Founded: 1986, Empl: 65, Carl Herrman, CEO

Solectek Inc. 6370 Nancy Ridge Dr, #109, San Diego CA 92121-3212 USA; 619/450-1220, 800/437-1518 Fax: 619/457-2681, Focus: Wireless LANs, Ownrshp: PVT, Founded: 1989, James B. DeBello, Chmn & CEO, Jonathon Y.C. Cheah, VP Eng, Philip L. Rugani, VP WW Sales, Dale Sheets, VP Ops, Vanessa Swancott, Email: vswancot@airlan.com

Solectron Corp. 777 Gibraltar Dr, Bldg. 5, Milpitas CA 95035 USA; 408/957-8500, Fax: 408/956-6075, Focus: Printed circuit boards, mass storage and turnkey systems, Ownrshp: NYSE, Stk Sym: SLR, Founded: 1977, Empl: 4,545, Sales ($M): 2,817.2, Fiscal End: 8/96; Charles A. Dickinson, Chmn, Koichi Nishimura, Pres & CEO

Soleil Software 3853 Grove Ct, Palo Alto CA 94303 USA; 415/494-0114, Fax: 415/493-6416, Web URL: soleil.com, Focus: Educational software, Ownrshp: PVT, Founded: 1992, Empl: 10, Ragni Pasturel, Pres & COO, Marc Pasturel, CEO, Barbara Chrisiani, Designer

Solomon Software 200 E Hardin, PO Box 414, Findlay OH 45839 USA; 419/424-0422, 800/476-5666 Fax: 419/424-3400, Co Email: sales@solomon.com, Web URL: solomon.com, Focus: Accounting software for microcomputers, Prdts: Solomon IV for Windows, Ownrshp: PVT, Founded: 1980, Empl: 150, Gary Harpst, Pres, Email: gharpst@solomon.com; Vern Strong, VP Prod Dev, Email: vstrong@solomon.com; Brian Clark, SVP & GM, Email: bclark@solomon.com; Eric Kurjan, VP Sales & Mktng, Email: ekurjan@solomon.com; John Crawford, Info Syst Mgr, Email: jcrawfor@solomon.com; Skip Reardon, Sr Mktng Mgr, Email: Sreardon@solomon.com

Sonera Technologies PO Box 565, Rumson NJ 07760 USA; 908/747-6886, 800/932-6323 Fax: 908/747-4523, Focus: Monitor & video adapter testing and optimization software, Prdts: DisplayMate Series, Ownrshp: Sub. Cactus Computers, Founded: 1984,

Julia Soneira, Pres, Raymond Soneira, VP Dev

Sonic Solutions 101 Rowland Way, #110, Novato CA 94945-5010 USA; 415/893-8000, Fax: 415/893-8008, Focus: Digital audio and network products, Prdts: SSP card, SSP-3 card, Ownrshp: OTC, Stk Sym: SNIC, Founded: 1986, Empl: 80, Sales ($M): 20.3, Fiscal End: 3/95; Robert J. Doris, CEO, James A. Moorer, SVP Audio Dev & Dir, Mary C. Sauer, SVP Mktng & Sales Dir, A. Clay Leighton, VP Fin, Kirk Pausen, VP Sales

Sonic Systems Inc. 575 N Pastoria Ave, Sunnyvale CA 94086-2916 USA; 408/736-1900, Fax: 408/736-7228, Co Email: sales@sonicsys.com, Focus: Macintosh network products, Ownrshp: PVT, Founded: 1991, Frank Leonardi, Pres, Larry Woodard, Dir Mktng

Sonitech International Inc. 14 Mica Ln, Wellesley MA 02181 USA; 617/235-6824, Fax: 617/235-2531, Co Email: info@sonitech.com, Web URL: sonitech.com, Focus: Digital signal processing systems and consulting, Prdts: Spirit DSP Boards, Ownrshp: PVT, Founded: 1989, Empl: 25

Sonnetech Ltd. 350 Townsend St, #409, San Francisco CA 94107-1699 USA; 415/957-9940, 800/847-0725 Fax: 415/957-9942, Co Email: sonnetech@aol.com, Web URL: colorific.com, Focus: Color management and system software for enhancing computer displays, video cards etc., Prdts: Colorific, Ownrshp: Sub. Sonnet Group, William J. Hilliard, Mgng Partner

Sony Corp. 7-35 Kitashinagawa, 6-chome, Shinagawa-ku, Tokyo 141 JP-141 Japan; 3-5448-2111, Fax: 3-5448-2244, Web URL: sony.co.jp, Focus: Peripherals, electronics and consumer electronic products, Ownrshp: NYSE, Stk Sym: SNE, Founded: 1982, Empl: 130,000, Sales ($M): 43,370.0, Fiscal End: 3/96; Norio Ohga, Chmn & CEO, Nobuyuki Idei, Pres

Sony Corp. of America 1 Sony Dr, Park Ridge NJ 07656-8003 USA; 201/930-1000, Web URL: sony.com, Focus: Peripherals, workstations and consumer electronics products, Ownrshp: Sub. Sony, Japan, Founded: 1960, Empl: 13,000, Sales ($M): 5,000

Sony New Technologies Inc. 711 Fifth Ave, New York NY 10022-3109 USA; 212/833-6790, Fax: 212/833-6421, Focus: Entertainment software, Prdts: Reversi, SubShop, John Kelly

Sony Personal Information Co. 3300 Zanker Rd, San Jose CA 95134 USA; Focus: Personal communicators/PDAs, Prdts: Magic Link, Ownrshp: Sub Sony, Kaz Imai, Pres

Sophisticated Circuits Inc. 19017 120th Ave NE, #106, Bothell WA 98011 USA; 206/485-7979, Fax: 206/485-7172, Co Email: marketing@sophcir.com, Focus: Macintosh hardware products, Ownrshp: PVT, Founded: 1985, Empl: 5, Amar Singh, Pres, David Cloutier, VP Sales & Mktng

Soricon Corp. 5621 Arapahoe Rd, Boulder CO 80303-1332 USA; 303/440-2800, Fax: 303/442-2438, Focus: Bar code, MICR and OCR readers, Prdts: MR2000, EFT Products, Ownrshp: OTC, Stk Sym: SRCC, Founded: 1984, Empl: 54, Sales ($M): 10.4, Fiscal End: 12/93; Chris F. Schellhorn, VP Sales & Mktng, GM, David A. Kempf, VP Fin & Admin, Martin Widmann, Dir Mktng, Jamie Bethea, VP Financial Sales, Alan Roberts, VP Ops, Kelly Enders

SourceMate Information Systems Inc. 20 Sunnyside Ave, Mill Valley CA 94941-1928 USA; 415/381-1011, Fax: 415/381-6902, Focus: PC accounting software, Prdts: AccountMate, Ownrshp: PVT, Founded: 1984, Empl: 50, Ben Tse, Pres & CEO, Dennis Lo, Chmn & VP Eng, Shaun Kuhn, Mktng Coord

South Carolina Research Authority (SCRA), 5300 Int'l Blvd, N Charlston SC 29418 USA; 803/760-3575, Co Email: @scra.org, Ownrshp: Nonprofit

Southern Electronics Corp. 4916 N Royal Atlanta Dr, Tucker GA 30085 USA; 770/491-8962, Fax: 404/938-2814, Focus: Distributes computer products, Ownrshp: OTC, Stk Sym: SECX, Founded: 1980, Empl: 225, Sales ($M): 468.3, Fiscal End: 6/96; Gerald Diamond, Chmn & CEO, Ray D. Risner, Pres & COO, Mark Diamond, EVP, Larry G. Ayers, VP & CFO

Southern Maryland Regional Technology Council PO Box 910, La Plata MD 20646-0910 USA; 301/934-5316, Fax: 301/934-8617, Focus: Organization for Maryland high-tech companies, Ownrshp: Nonprofit

Southern Micro Systems Inc. 1145 Rottenwood Dr, #150, Marietta GA 30067 USA; 770/499-9231, Fax: 770/422-1593, Focus: POS and distribution/manufacturing systems integrator, Prdts: Auto ID Data Collection Hardware & Software, Ownrshp: PVT, Founded: 1985, Empl: 15, Sales ($M): 5.3, Fiscal End: 12/95; Michael T. Hill, Pres, Brad Mackett, Sales Mgr

Southern New England Telecom Corp. (SNET), 227 Church St, New Haven CT 06510 USA; 203/771-5200, Fax: 203/865-5198, Web URL: snet.com, Focus: Independent telephone company, Ownrshp: NYSE, Stk Sym: SNG, Founded: 1878, Empl: 9,111, Sales ($M): 1,838.5, Fiscal End: 12/95; Daniel J. Miglio, Chmn & CEO, Donald R. Shassian, SVP & CFO, Jean M. LeVecchia, SVP Org Dev, Madelyn M. DeMatteo, VP Gen Counsel & Sec, Ronald M. Serrano, SVP Corp Dev

Soyo USA Inc. 1209 John Reed Ct, Industry CA 91745-2405 USA; 818/330-1712, Fax: 818/968-4161, Focus: PC motherboards, Founded: 1989, Empl: 12, Sales ($M): 17.0, Alex Yang, VP

Spacetec IMC Corp. 600 Suffolk St, Lowell MA 01854-3629 USA; 508/970-0330, Fax: 508/970-0199, Co Email: @spacetec.com, Ownrshp: PVT, Founded: 1991, Dennis T. Gain, Chmn & CEO

Sparc Int'l. (SI), 535 Middlefield Rd, #210, Menlo Park CA 94025 USA; 415/321-8692, Fax: 415/321-8015, Focus: Evolution of the SPARC microprocessor architecture and establish compliance definition, Ownrshp: Nonprofit, Founded: 1989, Empl: 225, Robert Duncan, Chmn & CEO

SPARC Technology Business 2550 Garcia Ave, Mountain View CA 94043 USA; 415/960-1300, Web URL: sun.com/stb, Focus: SPARC technology products, Ownrshp: Sub. Sun Microsystems, Founded: 1993, Empl: 500, Chester J. Silvestri, Pres, Samuel T. Spadafora, VP Sales, Art Swift, VP Mktng, Sheree Fitzpatrick, Email: sheree.fitzpatrick@eng.sun.com

Spatial Systems Corp. 1757 E Bayshore Rd, #2B, Redwood City CA 94063 USA; 415/365-9242, Fax: 415/365-2751, Focus: Graphical software, Prdts: WizMap, Ownrshp: PVT, Leslie O'Neil

Spatializer Audio Laboratories 20700 Ventura Blvd #134, Woodland Hills CA 91364 USA; 818/227-3370, Fax: 818/227-9750, Co Email: info@spatializer.com, Web URL: spatializer.com, Focus: Audio technologies for entertainment industry, Ownrshp: OTC, Stk Sym: SPAZ, Empl: 27, Steve Gershick, Pres & CEO, Tim Bratton, VP Sales & Mktng, William Craft, CTO, Fred N. Balch, Dir Marcom, Email: fred@spatializer.com

Specialix Inc. 745 Camden Ave, #129, Campbell CA 95008 USA; 408/378-7919, 800/423-5364 Fax: 408/378-0786, Co Email: @specialix.com, Focus: PC I/O boards, Ownrshp: Sub. Specialix, UK, Founded: 1986, Empl: 28, Sales ($M): 6, Hoyt Foucault, Pres, Rick Freedman, Dir Mktng

Specialized Business Solutions PO Box 1904, Dillon CO 80435-1904 USA; 970/262-1720, 800/359-3458 Web URL: some.com/sbs, Focus: POS software, Prdts: Keystroke, Ownrshp: PVT, Founded: 1988, Empl: 8, Michael Gebb, Pres, Dana Bargell, Sales Mgr

Specialty TeleConstructors Inc. 12001 State Hwy 14 N, Cedar Crest NM 87008 USA; 505/281-2197, 800/551-8088 Focus: Communications network services, Ownrshp: CSE, Stk Sym: SCTR, Founded: 1981, Empl: 107, Sales ($M): 8, Fiscal End: 6/95; Michael R. Budagher, Chmn, Pres & CEO, Bruce P. Budagher, VP, Kari A. Young, CFO

Spectragraphics Corp. 9707 Waples St, San Diego CA 92121 USA; 619/450-0611, Fax: 619/450-0218, Web URL: spectra.com, Focus: Software development and graphics terminals, Prdts: Design Conference, TeamSolutions, TeamConference, TeamExchange, Ownrshp: PVT, Founded: 1981, Empl: 260, Sales ($M): 39, Fiscal End: 12/93; Robert L. Blumberg, Chmn, Pres & CEO, Elliot Shev,

VP Sales, Tom Tranchina, SVP & CFO, Paul Wang, SVP, Michael Perry, Dir MIS, Steven Woodward, Corp Com Mgr

SpecTran Corp. 50 Hall Rd, Sturbridge MA 01566 USA; 508/347-2261, Fax: 508/347-2747, Focus: Develops and manufactures glass optical fibers, Ownrshp: OTC, Stk Sym: SPTR, Sales ($M): 38.6, Fiscal End: 12/95; Raymond E. Jaeger, Chmn, Glenn Moore, Pres & CEO, John E. Chapman, EVP & COO, Crawford L. Cutts, VP Bus Dev, Bruce A. Cannon, SVP & CFO

Spectrix Corp. 106 Wilmot Rd #250, Deerfield IL 60015-5150 USA; 847/317-1770, 800/710-1805 Fax: 847/317-1517, Co Email: @spectrixcorp.com, Web URL: spectrixcorp.com, Focus: Wireless network products for portable PCs, Prdts: SpectrixLite, Ownrshp: PVT, Founded: 1987, Empl: 22, Sandy Moore, Pres & CEO, Email: swrm@spectrixcorp.com; Jerry Goudie, VP Sales, C. Thomas Baumgartner, VP Mktng, Email: ctb@spectrixcorp.com

Spectrum Holobyte Inc. 2490 Mariner Square Loop, #100, Alameda CA 94501 USA; 510/522-3584, Fax: 510/522-3587, Web URL: holobyte.com, Focus: Entertainment software, Prdts: Tetris, Falcon, Star Trek: The Next Generation, Ownrshp: OTC, Stk Sym: SBYT, Founded: 1984, Empl: 400, Sales ($M): 57.3, Fiscal End: 3/96; Stephen Race, CEO, Gilman G. Louie, Chmn, Jeff Forester, SVP Sales, Louis Gioia, Chief Mktng Officer, Holly Hartz, VP Corp Comm

Specular International 7 Pomeroy Ln, Amherst MA 01002 USA; 413/253-3100, 800/433-7732 Fax: 413/253-0540, Co Email: info@specular.com, Web URL: specular.com, Focus: Computer graphics software, Prdts: Infini-D, Collage, LogoMotion, TextureScape, BackBurner, Ownrshp: PVT, Founded: 1990, Empl: 45, Adam Lavine, Pres & CEO, Email: adam_lavine@specular.com; Dennis Chen, VP & Chief Scientist, Email: dennis_chen@specular.com; Chris Johnston, Dir Prod Mgmt, Email: chrisj@specular.com; David Trescot, Dir Sales & Mktng, Email: trescot@specular.com; Mark Roblee, Head Inside Sales, Email: sales@specular.com; Dorothy Eckel, Mgr PR, Email: dorothy@specular.com

Speech Systems Inc. (SSI), 2945 Center Green Ct S, Boulder CO 80301-2275 USA; 303/938-1110, Fax: 303/938-1874, Co Email: info@speechsys.com, Focus: Speech recognition software, Ownrshp: PVT, Founded: 1981, Empl: 20, Ivan Perez-Mendez, Pres, Mark T. Anikst, Chief Scientist, Mark S. Hayes, VP Sales, David J. Tradwick, Chief Arch, Deborah E. Parsons, Mktng Mgr, Email: deb@speechsys.com

Spider Island Software 1 Venture, #230, Irvine CA 92718 USA; 714/453-8095, Fax: 714/453-8044, Co Email: info@spiderisland.com, Web URL: spiderisland.com, Focus: Internet server software, Prdts: TeleFinder, Ownrshp: PVT, Founded: 1988, Rusty Tucker

Spirit of St Louis Software Co. 18067 Edison Ave, Chesterfield MO 63005 USA; 314/530-0757, Fax: 314/530-7350, Focus: Interactive training manuals, Prdts: AuthorSoft Multimedia Presentation, Ownrshp: PVT, Ronald A. Peterson, CEO, Frank Friedlein Jr.

Spirit Technologies Inc. 734 Forest St, Malborough MA 01752-3032 USA; 617/630-1250, Focus: PC peripherals, Ownrshp: PVT, David L. Merchant, Pres

Splash Studios Inc. 8573 154th Ave NE, Redmond WA 98052 USA; 206/882-0300, Fax: 206/882-1516, Focus: Children's products, Prdts: Splash Kids, Ownrshp: PVT, Founded: 1994, Patrick Ford, Pres & CEO, Email: fordy@aol.com; Jack Turk, VP & Creative Dir, Howard Phillips, VP Prod Dev, Mark Cutter, Dir Eng

Sprint Corp. PO Box 11315, Kansas City MO 64112 USA; 913/624-3000, Fax: 913/624-2256, Web URL: sprint.com, Focus: Telecom services, Prdts: Sprint Sense, Business Sense, SprintLink, Sprint Mail, Ownrshp: NYSE, Stk Sym: FON, Founded: 1938, Empl: 48,265, Sales ($M): 12,765, Fiscal End: 12/95; William T. Esrey, Chmn & CEO, Gary D. Forsee, Pres & COO Long Dist Div, Wayne D. Peterson, Pres Local Telecom Div, Dennis E. Foster, Pres Cellular Div, Arthur B. Krause, EVP CFO, Richard C. Smith

Jr., VP Quality & PR

SPSS Inc. 444 N Michigan Ave, Chicago IL 60611-3962 USA; 312/329-2400, 800/543-6609 Fax: 312/329-3668, Co Email: @spss.com, Web URL: spss.com, Focus: Statistical analysis and presentation software, Prdts: SPSS, SYSTAT, QI Analyst, Neural Connection, Ownrshp: OTC, Stk Sym: SPSS, Founded: 1975, Empl: 440, Sales ($M): 63.0, Fiscal End: 12/95; Jack Noonan, Pres & CEO, Edward Hamburg, SVP & CFO, Louise Rehling, SVP Prod Dev, Mark Battaglia, VP Corp Mktng, Susan Phelan, VP Sales & Svcs, Larry Mathias, PR Mgr, Email: pr@spss.com

Spur Products Corp. 9288 W Emerald St, Boise ID 83704 USA; 208/377-0001, Fax: 208/377-0090, Focus: Printer controllers, Prdts: USAII, Spurbox, Ownrshp: PVT, Founded: 1972, Empl: 40, Dennis Hicks, Pres & CEO, Email: d.hicks@micron.net; Terry Francis, VP Sales, George McIlvaine, Dir Eng, Rousan Avaregan, Controller, John Baisch, Prod Mkt Mgr, Email: j.baisch@micron.net

Spyglass Inc. 1230 E Diehl Rd, #304, Naperville IL 60563 USA; 708/505-1010, Fax: 708/505-4944, Co Email: mosaic@spyglass.com, Web URL: spyglass.com, Focus: Internet access software, Ownrshp: OTC, Stk Sym: SPYG, Founded: 1990, Empl: 10, Sales ($M): 10.4, Fiscal End: 12/95; Douglas Colbeth, Pres & CEO, Timothy Krauskopf, VP R&D, Sue Sherman

SQA Inc. 10 State St, Woburn MA 01801 USA; 617/392-0110, Fax: 617/932-3280, Focus: Automated software testing software, Prdts: TeamTest, Ownrshp: PVT, Founded: 1990, Empl: 85, Sales ($M): 12.8, Fiscal End: 12/95; Ron Nordin, Pres & CEO, Philip Wallingford, CTO

SQL Financials Int'l. 2 Ravinia Dr, #1000, Atlanta GA 30346 USA; 770/390-3900, 800/437-0734 Fax: 770/390-3999, Focus: C/S applications, Ownrshp: PVT, Founded: 1991, Empl: 135, Don House, Chmn, Joe McCall, CEO, Steve Jeffery, Pres, Gary Rogers, VP Sales, Adriaan Theron, VP Mktng, Noreen Snellman

SRI International (SRI), 333 Ravenswood Ave, Menlo Park CA 94025 USA; 415/326-6200, Fax: 415/326-5512, Focus: High-tech research, development and consulting, Ownrshp: PVT, Founded: 1946, Empl: 2,400, Sales ($M): 300, William Sommers, Pres & CEO, Paul Jorgensen, EVP & COO, Alice Galloway, Marcom

SRS Labs Inc. 2909 Daimler St, Santa Ana CA 92705 USA; 714/442-1070, Fax: 714/852-1099, Web URL: srslabs.com, Focus: 3D audio products, Ownrshp: PVT, Founded: 1993, Thomas C.K. Yuen, Chmn & CEO, Stephen Sedmak, Pres, James Lucas, VP Sales, Janet Biski, CFO, Jennifer A. Drescher, Email: jenniferd@interramp.com

SSI Products Inc. 11836 Clark St, Arcadia CA 91006 USA; 818/305-0508, Fax: 818/305-0201, Focus: Surround sound multimedia notebook PCs, Prdts: All American, James E. Smidt, Pres, John Bernard, SVP Sales & Mktng

Stac Inc. 12636 High Bluff Dr, San Diego CA 92130-2093 USA; 619/794-4300, 800/522-7822 Fax: 619/794-4570, Co Email: @stac.com, Web URL: stac.com, Focus: Systems management software and applications, Prdts: ReachOut, CD-Quick Share, Replica, Stacker, Ownrshp: OTC, Stk Sym: STAC, Founded: 1983, Empl: 150, Sales ($M): 45.8, Fiscal End: 9/95; Gary W. Clow, Pres & CEO, John R. Witzel, VP Finance, John Bromhead, VP Mktng, Email: jbromhead@stac.com; Tom Dilatush, VP Ops, Douglas Whiting, VP Tech

Stage 1 Development Inc. 15375 Barranca Pkwy, #8209, Irvine CA 92718-2213 USA; 714/450-0390, Fax: 714/450-0395, Focus: Financial analysis software, Prdts: CFO Advisor, Ownrshp: PVT, Founded: 1991, Bob Shoemaker, Pres

Stalker Software Inc. 15 Skylark Dr, #21, Larkspur CA 94939 USA; 800/262-4722 Fax: 415/927-1026, Focus: Macintosh network products, Prdts: CommuniGate, Ownrshp: PVT, Founded: 1991, Vladimir Butenko, Pres

Stallion Technologies Inc. 2880 Research Park Dr, #160, Soquel CA 95073 USA; 408/477-0440, 800/347-7979 Fax: 408/

477-0444, Co Email: name@stallion.com, Web URL: stallion.com, Focus: Network connectivity and remote access products, Prdts: EasyConnection, EasyReach, EasyServer, Ownrshp: Sub. Stallion Tech, Australia, Founded: 1987, Empl: 75, W.E. Kiely, Pres & CEO, Email: billk@stallion.com; Mark J. Calkins, EVP Sales & Mktng, Email: mjc@stallion.com; John Havers, GM, Email: johnh@stallion.com; William DeChamps, CFO, Email: billd@stallion.com; Heather Nelson, Mktng Mgr

Standard Microsystems Corp. 80 Arkay Dr, Hauppauge NY 11788 USA; 516/435-6000, Fax: 516/273-5550, Co Email: @smc.com, Focus: PC LAN products, Ownrshp: OTC, Stk Sym: SMSC, Founded: 1971, Empl: 728, Sales ($M): 341.8, Fiscal End: 2/96; Paul Richman, Chmn & CEO, Reginald R. Maton Jr., VP & CIO, Gerald E. Gollub, EVP, Arthur Sidorsky, EVP, Anthony M. D'Agostino, VP Fin

Standard Performance Evaluation Corp. (SPEC), 10754 Ambassador Dr, #201, Manassas VA 22110 USA; 703/331-0180, Fax: 703/331-0181, Co Email: info@specbench.org, Web URL: specbench.org, Focus: Defines performance benchmarks for Unix computers, Prdts: SPEChpc96, Ownrshp: Nonprofit, Founded: 1988, Kaivalya M. Dixit, Pres, Rodney Sanford, Project Admin, Dianne Rice

Staples Inc. 100 Pennsylvania Ave, Framingham MA 01701-9328 USA; 508/370-8500, Fax: 508/370-8956, Web URL: staples.com, Focus: Chain of over 480 office product superstores internationally, Ownrshp: OTC, Stk Sym: SPLS, Founded: 1985, Empl: 19,000, Sales ($M): 3,068.1, Fiscal End: 1/96; Thomas G. Stemberg, Chmn & CEO, Marty Hanaka, Pres & COO, Joseph S. Vassalluzzo, EVP, John B. Wilson, EVP & CFO, Robert Fried, CTO, Susan Grieb, Dir PR

Star Gate Technologies Inc. 29300 Aurora Rd, Solon OH 44139 USA; 216/349-1860, Fax: 216/349-1978, Focus: Network communications products, Ownrshp: Sub. Digi Int'l., Founded: 1983, Empl: 60, Sales ($M): 14.0, Ray D. Wymer, Pres, Keith C. Rericha, EVP, Jan Clark

Star Technologies Inc. 515 Shaw Rd, Sterling VA 20166 USA; 703/689-4400, Fax: 703/478-3600, Co Email: starinfo@star.com, Focus: Image information management, array and image processors, Prdts: Image Management Server, Film Image Scan Interface, Ownrshp: OTC, Stk Sym: STRR, Founded: 1981, Empl: 35, Sales ($M): 4.3, Fiscal End: 3/96; Robert C. Compton, Chmn & CEO, Brenda A. Potosnak, Controller & Treas, Jerry Carter, Customer Svc, Ed Martello, Dir Eng

StarBase Corp. 18872 MacArthur Blvd, #400, Irvine CA 92715 USA; 714/442-4400, Fax: 714/253-6712, Ownrshp: VSE, Stk Sym: SBP, Jack Brantley, VP Mktng

Stardust Technologies 1901 S Bascom Ave, #333, Campbell CA 95008 USA; 408/879-8080, Fax: 408/879-8081, Focus: WinSock interoperability testing, Ownrshp: PVT, Founded: 1994, Karen Milne, Martin Hall, CTO

Starfish Software 1700 Green Hills Rd, Scotts Valley CA 95066 USA; 408/461-5800, 800/765-7839 Fax: 408/461-5900, Co Email: starfish@aol.com, Web URL: starfishsoftware.com, Focus: Utility software, Prdts: Sidekick, Dashboard, Ownrshp: PVT, Founded: 1994, Empl: 60, Sales ($M): 8, Fiscal End: 12/95; Philippe Kahn, Chmn, Ian Robinson, Dir Prod Mgmt, Norman Cheung, CFO, Te Smith, Dir Prod Mktng, Email: tesmith899@aol.com

Starlight Networks 205 Ravendale Dr, Mountain View CA 94043-5216 USA; 415/967-2774, Fax: 415/967-0686, Web URL: starlight.com, Focus: Video network software and servers, Ownrshp: PVT, Founded: 1991, Empl: 40, Jim Long, CEO, Steve Mitchell, VP WW Field Ops

Starlite Software Corp. PO Box 370, Hadlock WA 98339 USA; 360/385-7125, Focus: PC productivity software, Prdts: PC-Write, PC-Browse, Ownrshp: PVT, Founded: 1983, Empl: 20, Sales ($M): 1.5, Gordon Wanner, Pres, Email: gjw@olympus.net

StarNine Technologies Inc. 2550 Ninth St, #112, Berkeley CA

94710 USA; 510/649-4949, Fax: 510/548-0393, Co Email: info@starnine.com, Web URL: starnine.com, Focus: E-mail and Internet software, Ownrshp: Sub Quarterdeck, Founded: 1987, Tom Biddulph, CEO, Rusty Rahm, Pres, Scott Steward, VP Sales & Mktng, David Thompson, Dir Mktng, Email: david@starnine.com; Chuck Shotton, SVP Eng

Starwave Corp. 13810 SE Eastgate Way, #400, Bellevue WA 98005 USA; 206/957-2000, Fax: 206/957-2009, Web URL: starwave.com, Focus: Interactive entertainment software, Ownrshp: PVT, Founded: 1993, Empl: 215, Mike Slade, Pres & CEO, John von der Embse, Dir PR

State Of The Art Inc. 56 Technology Dr, Irvine CA 92718 USA; 714/753-1222, 800/854-3415 Fax: 714/753-1596, Web URL: stateoftheart.com, Focus: Accounting software, Ownrshp: OTC, Stk Sym: SOTA, Founded: 1981, Empl: 264, Sales ($M): 46.1, Fiscal End: 12/95; David W. Hanna, Pres & CEO, George Riviere, VP R&D, Joseph R. Armstrong, VP & CFO, David R. Butler, VP Sales, Geri L. Schanz, VP Corp Com

STB Systems Inc. 1651 N Glenville, #210, PO Box 850957, Richardson TX 75085-0957 USA; 214/234-8750, 800/234-4334 Fax: 214/234-1306, Co Email: @stb.com, Web URL: stb.com, Focus: PC graphics boards, Ownrshp: OTC, Stk Sym: STBI, Founded: 1981, Empl: 105, Sales ($M): 70, Bill Ogle, Pres & CEO, Don Balthaser, VP Eng, John Gunn, Dir Channel Dev, J. Shane Long, VP Sales & Mktng, Randy Eisenbach, COO, Katrina Krebs, PR Mgr, Email: kkrebs@stb.com

Stellar Graphics Corp. 611 Broadway, #428, New York NY 10012 USA; 212/982-0800, Fax: 212/979-2999, Focus: Web page design, Ownrshp: PVT, Founded: 1991, Marc H. Bell, Pres, Email: mhb@pfm.net

StereoGraphics Corp. 2171-H E Francisco Blvd, San Rafael CA 94901 USA; 415/459-4500, Fax: 415/459-3020, Co Email: stereo@well.sf.ca.us, Focus: 3D display systems, Prdts: CrystalEyes, StereoGraphics, Ownrshp: PVT, Founded: 1980, Dick Martin, Pres, Will Cochran, VP Sales & Mktng, Lenny Lipton, VP R&D, Michael Gjerstad, Dir Sales, Craig Rappaport

Sterling Software Inc. 8080 N Central Expwy, #1100, Dallas TX 75206-1895 USA; 214/891-8600, Fax: 214/739-0535, Co Email: @sterling.com, Web URL: sterling.com, Focus: System and productivity software, Ownrshp: NYSE, Stk Sym: SSW, Founded: 1983, Empl: 3,700, Sales ($M): 588.2, Fiscal End: 9/95; Sam Wyly, Chmn, Sterling L. Williams, Pres & CEO, Werner L. Frank, EVP Bus Dev, Warner C. Blow, EVP, George H. Ellis, EVP & CFO, Anne Vahala, VP Corp Com

STF Technologies Inc. (STF), Jct. I-70 & Hwy 23, PO Box 81, Concordia MO 64020 USA; 816/463-7972, 800/771-6208 Fax: 816/463-2179, Co Email: 74740.1244@compuserve.com, Focus: Macintosh fax software, Prdts: FAXstf, Ownrshp: PVT, Founded: 1988, Rick Wyand, Pres & CEO, Steven D. Myers, VP Prod Mgmt

Stiller Research 2625 Ridgeway St, Tallahassee FL 32310-5169 USA; 904/575-0920, 800/788-0787 Fax: 904/575-7884, Co Email: 74777.3004@compuserve.com, Focus: Security and integrity software, Prdts: Integrity Master, Ownrshp: PVT, Founded: 1985, Empl: 5, Wolfgang Stiller, Pres, Dianne Littrell, VP, Email: 72571.3352@compuserve.com; Jerry Olsen

StillWater Media PO Box 789, Northport NY 11768 USA; 516/261-4599, Fax: 516/261-3958, Co Email: 102073.3171@compuserve.com, Focus: Training and educational software, Prdts: GameMill, Sean O'Malley, Dir Mktng

STMS 44880 Falcon Place, #100, Sterling VA 20166 USA; 703/318-7867, 800/875-7867 Fax: 703/318-9734, Co Email: solutions@stms.com, Web URL: stms.com, Focus: Systems integration, Ownrshp: PVT, Founded: 1990, Empl: 40, Sales ($M): 11.5, Fiscal End: 12/94; John Signorello, CEO, Steve Salmon, CTO, Email: ssalmon@stms.com; Peter J. Jacobs, Dir Mktng, Email: pjacobs@stms.com

Stonehouse & Co. 4100 Spring Valley Rd, #400, Dallas TX

75244 USA; 214/960-1566, Fax: 214/770-6909, Web URL: nnc.com/stonehouse/index, Focus: Communication network management services, Prdts: MONIES, Ownrshp: PVT, Founded: 1978, Empl: 60, Sales ($M): 6.5, Fiscal End: 1995; Marshall Roberts, Pres, Donald Ramp, VP Sales & Mktng, Charles Shelton, SVP Prod Research, John Haller, VP Customer Relations, William Amos, VP Tech Svcs, Cheryl End, Sales Support

Storage Computer Corp. 11 Riverside St, Nashua NH 03062-1373 USA; 603/880-3005, Fax: 603/889-7232, Co Email: info@storage.com, Web URL: storage.com, Focus: Storage servers and solid state disk drives, Prdts: RAID 7, Ownrshp: AMEX, Stk Sym: SOS, Founded: 1984, Empl: 38, Sales ($M): 12, Fiscal End: 12/95; Ted Goodlander, Pres & CEO, John O'Brien, VP R&D, Andras Sarkozv, VP Corp Tech, D. Michael Brazao, VP SI, Anne Murphy, VP Mktng, Jennifer Forsyth, Marcom

Storage Solutions Inc. (SSI), 550 West Ave, Stamford CT 06902 USA; 203/325-0035, Fax: 203/327-4675, Co Email: info@ssi.mhs.compuserve.com, Focus: Storage products, Ownrshp: PVT, Founded: 1989, Robert S. Andrew, Pres, Kim H. Hampson

Storage Technology Corp. (StorageTek), 2700 S 88th St, Louisville CO 80028-4310 USA; 303/673-5020, Fax: 303/673-8876, Web URL: stortek.com, Focus: Mainframe and mid-range peripherals, Ownrshp: NYSE, Stk Sym: STK, Founded: 1969, Empl: 9,100, Sales ($M): 1,929.5, Fiscal End: 12/95; Ryal R. Poppa, Chmn, Pres & CEO, Derek A. Thompson, EVP, Lowell Thomas Gooch, EVP Ops, David E. Weiss, EVP, Gregory A. Tymn, SVP & CFO, Lori Roush, Marcom Spec

Storm Software 1861 Landings Dr, Mountain View CA 94043 USA; 415/691-6600, Fax: 415/691-6689, Co Email: sales@storm.com, Focus: Digital photography software, Ownrshp: PVT, Founded: 1990, Empl: 40, Bill Krause, Pres & CEO, Adriaan Ligtenberg, VP & CTO, Barbara Windham, VP Mktng, Rick Cavin, VP Sales, Rick McConnell, VP Fin, Claire Treseler Dean

Strandware Inc. 306 S Barstow St, #205, PO Box 634, Eau Claire WI 54702-0634 USA; 715/833-2331, Fax: 715/833-1995, Web URL: strandware.com, Focus: Bar code and label design software, Prdts: Label Matrix-BackTrack, Ownrshp: PVT, Founded: 1985, Empl: 12, Michael Strand, Pres, Email: ahansen@strandware.com

Strata Inc. 2 W St George Blvd, #2100, St George UT 84770 USA; 801/628-5218, Fax: 801/628-9756, Co Email: @strata3d.com, Web URL: strata3d.com, Focus: Macintosh and Windows 95/NT software, Prdts: StrataVision 3d, StudioPro 3d, MediaPaint-Digital Video Effects, Ownrshp: PVT, Founded: 1988, Empl: 115, Ken Bringhurst, CEO, Scott Lovell, Pres, Gary Bringhurst, VP Eng, Ted Twiggs, CFO, Kevin Clark, Corp Comm Mgr, Email: kevincl@strata3d.com

StrataCom Inc. 1400 Parkmoor Ave, San Jose CA 95126 USA; 408/294-7600, 800/877-0519 Fax: 408/999-0115, Co Email: @stratacom.com, Web URL: stratacom.com, Focus: Telecom products, Ownrshp: OTC, Stk Sym: STRM, Founded: 1986, Empl: 210, Sales ($M): 331.7, Fiscal End: 12/95; Richard M. Moley, Chmn, Pres & CEO, Sanjay Subhedar, VP & CFO, Richard Lowenthal, VP R&D, Geof Kirsch, VP Sales, M. Alex Mendez, VP Mktng, David Callisch, PR Mgr

Strategic Alliance Partners Inc. 7002 Moody St, #112, La Palma CA 90623 USA; 310/860-4029, 800/946-4277 Fax: 310/468-7007, Focus: Educational software, Prdts: Paper Animal Workshop, Ownrshp: PVT, Frank Westall, Pres, Chip Hilts, COO, Brenda Jaeck, Dir Publishing

Stratus Computer Inc. 55 Fairbanks Blvd, Marlboro MA 01752-1298 USA; 508/460-2000, Fax: 508/481-8945, Focus: Fault-tolerant superminicomputers, Ownrshp: NYSE, Stk Sym: SRA, Founded: 1980, Empl: 2,300, Sales ($M): 587.9, Fiscal End: 12/95; William E. Foster, Chmn & CEO, Gary E. Haroian, Pres & COO, Joseph A. D'Angelo, VP Mkt Dev, Richard L. Tarulli, SVP WW Sales & Serv, Robert E. Donahue, VP & CFO, Paul D. LaBelle, PR Mgr, Email:

paul_labelle@vos.stratus.com

Stream Int'l. 105 Rosemont Rd, Westwood MA 02090 USA; 617/751-1000, Web URL: stream.com, Focus: Computer services, Sales ($M): 1,600, Fiscal End: 12/95

Streetlight Software Inc. 324 Ritch St, San Francisco CA 94107 USA; 415/227-4350, Fax: 415/227-4351, Focus: Time and location based software, Prdts: StLink, Founded: 1992, Timothy Catlin, Pres & CEO

Streetwise Software Inc. 2116 Wilshire Blvd, #230, Santa Monica CA 90403 USA; 310/829-7827, 800/743-6765 Fax: 310/828-8258, Focus: Desktop publishing software for WordPerfect, Prdts: By Design, Ownrshp: PVT, Founded: 1989, Empl: 15, Sam Glicksman, Pres, Email: 73323.2305@compuserve.com; Deborah Azar, Co-founder

Structural Dynamics Research Corp. (SDRC), 2000 Eastman Dr, Milford OH 45150-2740 USA; 513/576-2400, Fax: 513/576-2135, Focus: Mechanical design software, Ownrshp: OTC, Stk Sym: SDRC, Founded: 1987, Empl: 1,122, Sales ($M): 204.1, Fiscal End: 12/95; Albert F. Peter, Pres & CEO, Martin Neads, SVP, Albert L. Klosterman, SVP & CTO, Jack W. Martz, SVP, Jeffrey J. Vorholt, VP & CFO

Suburban Maryland Technology Council 2092 Gaither Rd, Rockville MD 20850 USA; 301/258-5005, Fax: 301/208-8227, Focus: Organization for Maryland high-tech companies, Ownrshp: Nonprofit

Sun Microsystems Inc. 2550 Garcia Ave, Mountain View CA 94043-1100 USA; 415/960-1300, Fax: 415/856-2114, Web URL: sun.com, Focus: Workstations, Ownrshp: OTC, Stk Sym: SUNW, Founded: 1982, Empl: 14,500, Sales ($M): 7,094.8, Fiscal End: 6/96; Scott G. McNealy, Chmn, Pres & CEO, Kenneth M. Alvarez, VP, Michael E. Lehman, VP & CFO, Eric E. Schmidt, VP & CTO, William J. Raduchel, VP & CIO, Marty Coleman

Sunburst Communications 101 Castleton St, Pleasantville NY 10570-3498 USA; 914/747-3310, 800/321-7511 Fax: 914/747-4109, Co Email: sunburst@aol.com, Web URL: nysunburst.com, Focus: Educational software, Ownrshp: PVT, Founded: 1972, Empl: 150, Bill Kernahan, CEO, Claire Kubasik

SunExpress Inc. 5 Omni Way, Chelmsford MA 01824-4141 USA; 508/442-000, Fax: 508/250-5536, Focus: Distribute Sun workstation products, Ownrshp: Sub. Sun Microsystems, Founded: 1991, Empl: 185, Dorothy A. Terrell, Pres, Art Carty, VP & GM, Patty Long

SunGard Data Systems Inc. 1285 Drummers Ln, Wayne PA 19087 USA; 610/341-8700, Fax: 215-341-8739, Web URL: sungard.com, Focus: Disaster recovery and investment management services, Ownrshp: OTC, Stk Sym: SNDT, Founded: 1982, Empl: 2,900, Sales ($M): 532.6, Fiscal End: 12/95; James L. Mann, Chmn, Pres & CEO, David A. Wismer, EVP, Richard C. Tarbox, VP Corp Dev, Donna J. Pedrick, VP Human Res, Michael J. Ruane, VP & CFO

SunService 2550 Garcia Ave, Mountain View CA 94043-1100 USA; 415/960-1300, Fax: 415/969-9131, Web URL: sun.com, Focus: Support, education and services to Sun users, Ownrshp: Sub. Sun Microsystems, Lawrence W. Hambley, Pres

SunSoft Inc. 2550 Garcia Ave, Mountain View CA 94043 USA; 415/960-1300, Fax: 415/336-0362, Focus: Unix operating system and application software, Prdts: Solaris, SPARCworks, Interactive Unix, ProWorks, SunNet Manager, Ownrshp: Sub. Sun Microsystems, Founded: 1990, Empl: 1,200, Edward J. Zander, Pres, Jan Pieter Scheerden, VP, Jim Billmaien, VP, Jon Kannagaard, VP, Patrick J. Deagman, VP Fin, Carol A. Sacks, Mgr PR

Supercom Inc. 1225 Greenbriar Dr, #C, Addison IL 60101 USA; 800/888-1888 Focus: PC distributor, Ownrshp: PVT, Founded: 1983

Supra Corp. 312 SE Stonemill Dr, #150, Vancouver WA 98684 USA; 360/604-1400, 800/774-4965 Fax: 360/604-1401, Co Email: supracorp2@aol.com, Web URL: supra.com, Focus: PC modems and peripherals, Prdts: SupraFAXModem, Ownrshp: Sub Diamond Multimedia, Founded: 1985, Empl: 150, John Wiley, Pres, Alan Ackerman, VP, James Cutburth, VP Mktng, Tamara J. Hanna, Marcom Mgr

Surface Mount Technology Assoc. (SMTA), 5200 Wilson Rd, #215, Edina MN 55424 USA; 612/920-7682, Fax: 612/926-1819, Co Email: smta@smta.org, Web URL: smta.org, Focus: Further the interest of surface mount technology through information dissemination, Ownrshp: Nonprofit, Founded: 1984, Empl: 3,100, JoAnn Stromberg, Exec Admin

SVEC Computer Corp. 2691 Richter Ave, #130, Irvine CA 92714 USA; 714/756-2233, 800/756-7832 Fax: 714/756-1340, Co Email: info@svec.com, Web URL: svec.com, Focus: LAN products, Prdts: FD0455 Etherboard-PCI, FD1110 Fast Hub, Ownrshp: PVT, Founded: 1987, Empl: 135, Sales ($M): 31, Fiscal End: 12/95; Frank Lin, Pres, Email: frank.lin@svec.com; Dario Dellamaggiure, Dir Sales & Mktng, Email: dariod@svec.com; Matt Eakin, IS Mgr, Email: matt.eakin@svec.com

SVI Training Products 9364 Cabot Dr, #B, San Diego CA 92126 USA; 619/693-4344, 800/995-2798 Fax: 619/693-3518, Focus: Training software, Prdts: Courseware Customizer

Swan Technologies 3075 Research Dr, State College PA 16801 USA; 814/238-1820, Fax: 814/237-4450, Focus: PC products, Ownrshp: PVT

SWeDE Corp. PO Box 9281, Newport Beach CA 92658-9281 USA; 714/442-6180, Fax: 714/476-0277, Focus: Educational multimedia software development, Prdts: Scavenger Hunt Adventure Series, Ownrshp: PVT, Founded: 1992, Empl: 12, Greg Gentling, Pres, Clay Matsumoto, Bus Ops

Swenson/Falkner Associates Inc. 1111 TCF Tower, 121 S 8th St, Minneapolis MN 55402 USA; 612/371-0000, Focus: PR and marketing communications, Ownrshp: PVT

SWFTE Int'l. 722 Yorklyn Rd, Hockessin DE 19707 USA; 302/234-1740, 800/759-2562 Fax: 302/234-1904, Web URL: swfte.com, Focus: Personal productivity and entertainment and educational software, Prdts: Bicycle Card Software Series, Multimedia Bug Book, Brain Quest, Ownrshp: PVT, Founded: 1983, Empl: 25, Sales ($M): 7.0, Melissa D'Argenzio, PR Dir, Email: 201.8463@mcimail.com

Sybase Inc. 6475 Christie Ave, Emeryville CA 94608 USA; 510/922-3500, Fax: 510/922-3210, Web URL: sybase.com, Focus: Relational database software, Prdts: Sybase SQL Server, Ownrshp: OTC, Stk Sym: SYBS, Founded: 1984, Empl: 1,117, Sales ($M): 956.6, Fiscal End: 12/95; Mark B. Hoffman, Chmn, Mitchell Kertzman, Pres & CEO, David C. Peterschmidt, EVP & COO, Stewart A. Schuster, EVP Mktng, Kathryn C. Nyrop, VP & Treas

Sycom Technologies Inc. 401 City Ave, #200, Bala Cynwyd PA 19004 USA; 610/660-5770, Fax: 610/668-5404, Focus: Personal organizer software, Prdts: Total Recall, Ownrshp: PVT, Ari Naim, Pres

Sykes Enterprises Inc. (SEI), 100 N Tampa St, #3900, Tampa FL 33602 USA; 813/274-1000, 800/867-9537 Fax: 813/273-0148, Focus: Information systems support, services and solutions, Founded: 1977, Empl: 2,000, John H. Sykes, Marcia R. Quinn, Dir Corp Com

Symantec Corp. 10201 Torre Ave, Cupertino CA 95014-2132 USA; 408/253-9600, Fax: 408/253-4694, Co Email: @symantec.com, Web URL: symantec.com, Focus: PC productivity software, Prdts: Norton Utilities, pcAnywhere, ACT, WinFax, Ownrshp: OTC, Stk Sym: SYMC, Founded: 1982, Empl: 1,442, Sales ($M): 445.4, Fiscal End: 3/96; Gordon E. Eubanks Jr., Pres & CEO, Robert R.B. Dykes, EVP Ops & CFO, John C. Laing, EVP Sales, Eugene Wang, EVP, Mark Bailey, SVP Bus Dev, Michael Sweeny

Symark Software 5655 Lindero Canyon Rd, #502, Westlake Village CA 91362 USA; 818/865-6100, 800/234-9072 Fax: 818/889-1894, Co Email: info@symark.com, Focus: Network storage man-

agement software, Prdts: Pakmanager, Diskmizer, Ownrshp: PVT, Founded: 1985, Empl: 25, Robert Sommers, Chmn, Douglas Yarren, Pres

Symbol Technologies Inc. 116 Wilbur Place, Bohemia NY 11716 USA; 516/563-2400, Fax: 516/563-2831, Focus: Portable bar code scanning equipment, Ownrshp: NYSE, Stk Sym: SBL, Founded: 1973, Empl: 2,200, Sales ($M): 555.2, Fiscal End: 12/95; Jerome Swartz, Chmn & CEO, Jan H. Lindelow, Pres & COO, Frederic P. Heiman, EVP & CTO, Richard Bravman, SVP Mktng, Thomas G. Amato, SVP & CFO

Symix Systems Inc. 2800 Corp Exchange Dr, Columbus OH 43231 USA; 614/523-7000, Focus: Business management software, Ownrshp: OTC, Founded: 1979, Empl: 300, Sales ($M): 43.2, Fiscal End: 12/95; Larry J. Fox, Chmn & CEO, Stephen Sasser, Pres

Symmetry Group, The PO Box 26195, Columbus OH 43226 USA; 614/431-2667, 800/346-3938 Fax: 614/431-5734, Focus: Programmer's tools, Prdts: SLATE with Graphics, SCRIPT, Ownrshp: PVT, Founded: 1987, Empl: 4, C. Vincent Phillips, Pres

Symphony Laboratories 2730 Orchard Pkwy, San Jose CA 95134-2012 USA; 408/986-1701, Fax: 408/986-1771, Co Email: @symlab.com, Focus: PC logic and peripheral chips, Ownrshp: PVT, Founded: 1989, Empl: 20, Phil Mak, Pres, Stuart Friedman, VP Sales

Synaptics Inc. 2698 Orchard Pkwy, San Jose CA 95134 USA; 408/434-0110, Focus: Input devices, Prdts: TouchPad, Ownrshp: PVT, Federico Faggin, Pres, Robert Sumbs, VP Mktng & Sales

Sync Research 7 Studebaker, Irvine CA 92718 USA; 714/588-2070, Fax: 714/588-2080, Web URL: sync.com, Focus: Network products, Ownrshp: OTC, Stk Sym: SYNX, Sales ($M): 23, Fiscal End: 12/95; John Rademaker, Pres & CEO, Gregorio Reyes, Chmn, Todd J. Krautkremer, VP Mktng, William O'Connell, VP Sales, Ronald J. Scioscia, VP & CFO

Synchronics 6584 Poplar Ave, #200, Memphis TN 38138 USA; 901/761-1166, 800/852-5852 Fax: 901/683-8303, Focus: POS and vertical market software, Ownrshp: PVT, Founded: 1980, Empl: 36, Jeff Goldstein, Pres, Jody Franklin, Sales Mgr, Phyllis Gay

Syncronys Softcorp 3960 Ince Blvd, Culver City CA 90232 USA; 310/842-9203, Fax: 310/842-9014, Web URL: syncronys.com, Focus: Memory-enhancement and other PC performance software, Prdts: SoftRAM, Ownrshp: OTC, Stk Sym: SYCR, Founded: 1995, Sales ($M): 16.4, Fiscal End: 12/95; Rainer Poertner, Pres & CEO, Daniel Taylor, EVP Mktng, Wendell Brown, VP Tech, Barbara Velline, VP Fin

Syncware Corp. 3025 S Parker Rd, #109, Aurora CO 80014 USA; 303/369-6900, Fax: 303/369-6540, Focus: Forms software, Ownrshp: PVT, Founded: 1993, Alfred Moresi, Pres & CEO, Albert R. Boulerice, Treas, Katherine E. Hines, Office Mgr

Synergy Interactive Corp. (SIC), 444 De Haro St, #123, San Francisco CA 94107 USA; 415/437-2000, Fax: 415/431-3684, Co Email: syncorp@netcom.com, Focus: Multimedia developer, distributor and publisher, Prdts: GADGET, Founded: 1994, Dan McManus, SVP Publishing, Lesli Arbuthnot, Advert & Comm

Synergy Software 2457 Perkiomen Ave, Reading PA 19606 USA; 610/779-0522, Fax: 610/370-0548, Focus: Macintosh terminal emulation and graphing software, Prdts: VersaTerm, KaleidaGraph, VersaTilities, Ownrshp: PVT, Founded: 1984, Empl: 17, Howard R. Maxwell, Pres, Barbara S. Maxwell, VP Mktng

Synnex Information Technologies Inc. 3797 Spinnaker Ct, Fremont CA 94538 USA; 510/656-3333, Fax: 510/440-3777, Focus: Computers and peripherals, Ownrshp: Sub Mitac, Taiwan, C.K. Cheng

Synon Corp. 1100 Larkspur Landing Cr, Larkspur CA 94939 USA; 415/461-5000, Web URL: synon.com, Focus: C/S development software, Ownrshp: PVT, Founded: 1986, Empl: 430, Sales ($M): 72, Fiscal End: 12/95; William O. Grabbe, Chmn, Richard H. Goldberg, Pres & CEO

Synopsys Inc. 700 E Middlefield Rd, Mountain View CA 94043

USA; 415/962-5000, 800/388-9125 Fax: 415/965-8637, Co Email: designinfo@synopsys.com, Web URL: synopsys.com, Focus: Chip design software, Prdts: Design Compiler, Behaviroal Compiler, VHDL System Simulator, Ownrshp: OTC, Stk Sym: SNPS, Founded: 1986, Empl: 1,300, Sales ($M): 265.5, Fiscal End: 9/95; Aart de Geus, Pres & CEO, Harvey C. Jones, Chmn, Bill Lattin, EVP, Larry Woodson, VP Corp Mktng, A. Brooke Seawell, VP & CFO, Lisa Washington, Email: lisaw@synopsys.com

Synthesis Inc. 2120 Ellis St, Bellingham WA 98225 USA; 360/671-0458, Fax: 360/671-0417, Focus: CAD software for mechanical engineering, Prdts: Synthesis Release, Ownrshp: PVT, Founded: 1982, Empl: 5, Cathy Paxton, Owner, Tim Paxton, Pres, Michelle Greening, Mktng Mgr

Syntrex Technologies Inc. 2621 Van Buren Ave, Norristown PA 19403 USA; Focus: Network systems integrator, Ownrshp: PVT, Founded: 1992

SyQuest Technology Inc. 47071 Bayside Pkwy, Fremont CA 94538 USA; 510/226-4000, Fax: 510/226-4100, Focus: Removable Winchester disks, Ownrshp: OTC, Stk Sym: SYQT, Founded: 1982, Empl: 2,409, Sales ($M): 300, Fiscal End: 9/95; Syed H. Iftikar, Chmn, Pres & CEO, Lou Passaro, EVP Ops, Robert Lyon, VP, James Graber, VP Fin, Michelle J. Mihalick

Sys Technology Inc. 6481 Global Dr, Cypress CA 90630-5227 USA; 714/821-3900, 800/613-9963 Fax: 714/821-9592, Co Email: sysmail@systechnology.com, Web URL: systechnology.com, Focus: PC systems and motherboards, Prdts: Sys Performance Series, Ownrshp: PVT, Founded: 1988, Empl: 30, Bill Yen, Pres, Louis Sun, VP Sales, Henry Huang, VP Production, Ed Leckliter, Dir Mktng

Syscom Inc. 400 E Pratt St, #200, Baltimore MD 21202 USA; 410/539-3737, Fax: 410/539-7774, Web URL: syscom-inc.com, Focus: Training software, Prdts: TrainingServer, Frank Parisi

SysKonnect Inc. 1922 Zanker Rd, San Jose CA 95112-4216 USA; 408/437-3800, Fax: 408/437-3866, Focus: C/S high-performance networking solutions, Prdts: SK-NET, SK-FDDI, Ownrshp: PVT, Founded: 1991, Empl: 20, Mike Coker, Pres, Donna Elmore, MVP, Ronald Wacek, EVP, Mike Paluzzi, SVP

Syspro Impact Software Inc. 5 Hutton Centre Dr, #200, Santa Ana CA 92707-5754 USA; 714/437-1000, 800/369-8649 Fax: 714/437-1407, Web URL: ni.net/sysprousa.com, Focus: Accounting and manufacturing software, Prdts: Impact Encore, Impact Award, Ownrshp: PVT, Founded: 1978, Empl: 150, Sales ($M): 10+, Brian Stein, Pres, Joey Benadretti, VP Mktng

Systech Corp. 10505 Sorrento Valley Dr, San Diego CA 92121 USA; 619/453-8970, 800/205-0610 Fax: 619/546-9402, Focus: Communication products, Prdts: Unplug, Etherplex, Ownrshp: PVT, Founded: 1981, Empl: 80, Sales ($M): 20, D. Mark Fowler, Pres & CEO, Lynn King, VP Ops, Bruce Cassell, VP Sales & Mktng, John Stafford, Dir Mktng, Jack Hetzel, VP Fin, Drew Wilkins, Mgr Marcom

System Software Associates Inc. (SSA), 500 W Madison St, Chicago IL 60661 USA; 312/258-6000, Fax: 312/474-7500, Co Email: @ssax.com, Web URL: ssax.com, Focus: Business enterprise information systems, Ownrshp: OTC, Stk Sym: SSAX, Founded: 1981, Empl: 1,500, Sales ($M): 394.4, Fiscal End: 10/95; Roger E. Covey, CEO, Email: rec@ssax.com; Edward R. Koepfler, VP, Adam S. Bartkowski, VP Prod, James V. Franch, VP Tech, Joseph Skadra, VP & CFO

Systemation 2101 S Clermont St, Denver CO 80222-5006 USA; 303/756-1600, Fax: 303/756-2211, Focus: Training software, Michael Kuehn

Systems & Computer Technology Corp. (SCT), 4 Country View Rd, Malvern PA 19355 USA; 610/647-5930, 800/223-7036 Web URL: sctcorp.com, Focus: Software and services for educational institutions, Prdts: BANNER, Ownrshp: OTC, Stk Sym: SCTC, Founded: 1968, Empl: 2,100, Sales ($M): 176.1, Fiscal End: 9/95; Michael J. Emmi, Chmn, Pres & CEO, Michael D. Chamber-

lain, Pres SCT SW, Eric Haskell, SVP & CFO, Paul Engel, VP, Gerald R. Porter, Pres Info Mgmt

Systems & Software Inc. (SSI), 18012 Cowan, #100, Irvine CA 92714-6809 USA; 714/833-1700, Fax: 714/833-1900, Co Email: @syssoft.com, Focus: Software development tools, Ownrshp: PVT, Founded: 1979, Paul Chen, Pres, N.A. Richards, Dir Mktng, Email: nat@syssoft.com

Systems Engineering Solutions Inc. (SESI), 2301 Gallows Rd, #200, Dunn Loring VA 22027 USA; 703/573-4366, 800/462-9470 Fax: 703/207-9146, Focus: Document management systems, Prdts: IMAXIS, Ownrshp: PVT, Founded: 1987, Empl: 400, William Doyle, Dir Mktng, Heather Oles, Prod Mktng Mgr

Systems Integration Associates 11475 Commercial St, #2, Richmond IL 60071 USA; 312/440-1275, Fax: 312/440-9874, Focus: PCs, Ownrshp: PVT, Founded: 1983, Bruce Bohuslav, Pres

Systems Management American Corp. 5 Koger Ctr, #217, Norfolk VA 23502-4107 USA; 804/461-0559, Fax: 804/461-0569, Focus: Systems integration, telecom, imaging and retrieval, communications audits, Ownrshp: PVT, Founded: 1970, Empl: 33, Sales ($M): 18.5, Fiscal End: 9/94; Herman Valentine Sr., Chmn & Pres, Dorothy J. Valentine, COO, Donald R. Davis, SVP, Ronald R. Richards, Dir Comm, Email: ronrich@infi.net

Systems Plus Inc. 500 Clyde Ave, Mountain View CA 94043-2212 USA; 415/969-7047, Fax: 415/969-0118, Web URL: systemsplus.com, Focus: Medical practice management software, Prdts: Medical Manager, Ownrshp: PVT, Founded: 1980, Empl: 80, Sales ($M): 19.8, Fiscal End: 12/95; Rick Mehrlich, Pres, Sam Omron, VP Ops, Email: sam@systemsplus.com; Reba Gibbons, Dir Mktng, Email: reba@systemsplus.com

Systems Science Inc. 1860 Embarcadero Rd, #260, Palo Alto CA 94303 USA; 415/812-1800, Fax: 415/812-1820, Co Email: info@systems.com, Web URL: systems.com, Focus: EDA and testing software, Ownrshp: PVT, Founded: 1986, Daniel Chapiro, CEO

Systems Union Group 10 Bank St, White Plains NY 10606 USA; 914/948-7770, Web URL: systemsunion.com, Focus: Accounting software, Ownrshp: Sub Systems Union, UK, Founded: 1981, Empl: 425, Sales ($M): 59.3, Fiscal End: 12/95; Lawrence B. Helft, CEO

SystemSoft Corp. 2 Vision Dr, 3rd Fl., Natick MA 01760-2059 USA; 508/651-0088, Fax: 508/651-8188, Co Email: @systemsoft.con, Web URL: systemsoft.com, Focus: Power management, BIOS and PCMCIA software, Prdts: CardSoft, PnPView, Ownrshp: OTC, Stk Sym: SYSF, Founded: 1989, Empl: 140, Sales ($M): 24.6, Fiscal End: 1/95; Robert Angelo, Pres & CEO, Russell M. Blair, VP WW Sales, David Sommers, VP & CFO, Jonathan L. Joseph, SVP Prod Mktng, Paul Sereiko

Sytron Corp. 134 Flanders Rd, Westboro MA 01581-5025 USA; 508/898-0100, Fax: 508/898-2677, Focus: LAN back-up software, Ownrshp: Sub. Rexon, Founded: 1983, Empl: 80, Tom Makmann, VP & GM, Kane Pilsbury, VP Fin, Jerry Nine, VP Prod Plng, Mark Townsend, VP Eng, Dan Ross, Superv Info Syst, Lynn Murray, Marcom Mgr

T-HQ 5016 N Pkwy Calabasas, #100, Calabasas CA 91302 USA; 818/591-1310, Fax: 818/591-1615, Focus: Entertainment software, Ownrshp: OTC, Stk Sym: TOYH, Founded: 1990, Empl: 54, Sales ($M): 33.3, Fiscal End: 12/95; Jack Friedman, Pres & CEO

T/Maker Co. 1390 Villa St, Mountain View CA 94041 USA; 415/962-0195, 800/986-2537 Fax: 415/962-0201, Co Email: @tmaker.com, Focus: Image content and desktop publishing software, Prdts: ClickArt, Vroom Books, World's Easiest Software, Ownrshp: Sub. Deluxe Corp., Founded: 1983, Empl: 90, J. Heidi Roizen, Pres & CEO, John Tompane, VP WW Mktng, Diane Kveyenhagen, VP WW Sales, Mark Kailer, VP Fin & Ops, Jim Schnyler, VP CTC Electronic Direct Tech, Michelle Mecham, PR Mgr, Email: michelle_mecham@tmaker.com

Tab Products Co. 1400 Page Mill Rd, Palo Alto CA 94304 USA; 415/852-2400, Fax: 415/852-2679, Focus: Optical document storage, filing and furniture systems, Ownrshp: AMEX, Stk Sym: TBP, Founded: 1950, Empl: 950, Sales ($M): 152.7, Fiscal End: 5/96; Michael A. Dering, Pres & CEO, John W. Peth, EVP & COO, Patricia J. Robitaille, VP Info & Bus Syst, David B. Haskin, VP Mktng, John M. Palmer, VP & CFO

Tactica Corp. 10300 SW Greenburg Rd, #500, Portland OR 97223 USA; 503/293-9585, Fax: 503/293-9590, Co Email: @tactica.com, Web URL: tactica.com, Focus: C/S business software, Prdts: Geneia, Ownrshp: PVT, Founded: 1990, Jin H. Kim, Pres, Eng-Kee Kwang, EVP & CTO, Sunil Pande, VP Mktng, Rolf Kraus, Dir Mktng Dev, Email: rolf@tactica.com; Suresh Kumar, VP Eng, Meredith Smith, Marcom, Email: meredith@tactica.com

Tactics International Ltd. 16 Haverhill St, 3rd Floor, Andover MA 01810 USA; 508/475-4475, Fax: 508/475-2136, Focus: Mapping and information management software, Ownrshp: PVT, Empl: 75, Tony Buxton, Chmn & CEO, David Donelan, Dir Sales, Robert Reading, EVP, Brian Spargo, Mgr Production, Hans Riemer, Dir Mktng

Tadpole Technology Inc. 12012 Technology Blvd, Austin TX 78727-6208 USA; 512/219-2200, 800/232-6656 Fax: 512/219-2222, Co Email: sales@tadpole.com, Focus: Notebook workstations/OEM board level products, Prdts: SPARCbook, Ownrshp: Sub. Tadpole, UK, Founded: 1983, Empl: 160, Sales ($M): 34, George Grey, CEO, Tadpole, UK, Geoff S. Burr, Pres, Deane Curran, VP Sales & Mktng, Stacy Saxon

Tagram Systems Corp. 145-B Edinger Ave, Tustin CA 92680 USA; 714/258-3222, Fax: 714/258-3220, Web URL: tagram.com, Focus: Multimedia PCs, Prdts: Thunderbolt PC, Ownrshp: PVT, Founded: 1991, Empl: 38, Matt H. Hsia, Pres & CEO, Loretta Keng, VP Ops, Jason Moh, GM

Tahoe Peripherals 999 Tahoe Blvd, #301, Incline Village NV 89451 USA; 702/832-3600, 800/288-6040 Fax: 702/832-3611, Focus: PC peripherals, Ownrshp: Sub. Datrontech P.L.C., Scott K. Benson

Take One Concepts (T.O.C.), PO Box 3526, Incline Village NV 89450 USA; 702/832-8499, Fax: 702/832-8499, Focus: Custom screen savers, Prdts: Multimedia Custom Screen Savers, Ownrshp: PVT, Founded: 1995, Thomas O'Connor, Pres

Talaris Systems Inc. PO Box 261580, San Diego CA 92196-1580 USA; 619/587-0787, 800/934-3345 Fax: 619/587-6788, Focus: Intelligent page printers, Ownrshp: PVT, Founded: 1983, Empl: 20, Sales ($M): 5, Fiscal End: 10/95; Calvin E. Burgart, Pres, Email: cal@talaris.com; Gail McBeth, VP Admin, Email: gail@talaris.com; Arlene Davidson, Dir Ops, Email: arlene@talaris.com

Tally Systems Corp. PO Box 70, Hanover NH 03755-0070 USA; 603/643-1300, 800/262-3877 Fax: 603/643-9366, Web URL: tallysys.com, Focus: Asset management, PC inventory and software metering, Prdts: PC Census, NetCensus, CentaMeter, Ownrshp: PVT, Founded: 1990, Empl: 90+, Ted Jastrzembski, Pres, Tom Cecere, VP Strategic Alliances, Ann Gunn, VP, Richard Cohen, VP R&D, Karen Knapp, Dir Prod Mktng, Jennifer deJong, PR Mgr, Email: jennifer_delong@tallysys.com

Tamarack Technologies 1521 Orangewood Ave, Orange CA 92668 USA; 714/744-3979, Fax: 714/744-4582, Focus: Optical and electronic peripherals, Prdts: ArtiScan Pro 24-bit, Ownrshp: PVT, Founded: 1989, David Hsieh, Dir Sales & Mktng

Tandberg Data Inc. 2865-A Park Ctr Dr, Simi Valley CA 93065-6211 USA; 805/579-1000, 800/826-3237 Fax: 805/579-2555, Focus: QIC tape drives, Prdts: TDC Series, Ownrshp: Sub. Tandberg Data, Norway, Founded: 1991, Empl: 50, Sales ($M): 75, David Griffith, Pres & CEO, Richard Severa, VP Channel Sales & Mktng, Kathryn Lodato, Marcom Mgr

Tandem Computers Inc. 10435 N Tantau Ave, Cupertino CA 95014 USA; 408/725-6000, Fax: 408/285-6938, Co Email: @tandem.com, Web URL: tandem.com, Focus: Fault-tolerant computer systems, Ownrshp: NYSE, Stk Sym: TNDM, Founded: 1974, Empl: 8,000, Sales ($M): 2,285, Fiscal End: 9/95; James G. Treybig, Pres

& CEO, Junne Moy, PR Program Mgr, Email: moy_junne@tandem.com

Tandy Corp. 1800 One Tandy Ctr, Ft. Worth TX 76102 USA; 817/390-3700, Fax: 817/390-2647, Web URL: tandy.com, Focus: PC and consumer electronics products reseller, Ownrshp: NYSE, Stk Sym: TAN, Founded: 1921, Empl: 49,300, Sales ($M): 5,839.1, Fiscal End: 12/95; John V. Roach, Chmn, Pres & CEO, Robert M. McClure, SVP, Ronald L. Parrish, VP Corp Dev, Herschel C. Winn, SVP, Richard A. Silvers, VP & CIO, Lou Ann Blaylock, VP Corp Rel

Tangent Color Systems 14 Inverness Dr E, #A-100, Englewood CO 80112 USA; 303/799-6766, 800/875-8264 Fax: 303/799-1606, Focus: Color scanners and systems, Ownrshp: PVT, Founded: 1987, Empl: 22, Sales ($M): 4, Fiscal End: 12/95; Robert Bornhofen, Pres, Ronald Nowak, VP

Tangible Vision Inc. 1933 Loomis Ave, Downers Grove IL 60516 USA; 630/969-7517, 800/763-8634 Fax: 630/969-7523, Focus: Manufacturing software, Prdts: Imprimis, Ownrshp: PVT, Founded: 1993, Empl: 10, Ram Todatry, Pres, Hussein Armouti, VP R&D, John Jaruis, VP Client Svcs, Kathy Harmon, VP Mktng

Tangram Enterprise Solutions Inc. 5511 Capitol Ctr Dr, #400, Raleigh NC 27606 USA; 919/851-6000, 800/482-6472 Fax: 919/851-6004, Co Email: info@tesi.com, Web URL: tesi.com, Focus: Enterprise-wide distributed resource management and asset management, Prdts: AM:PM Distributed Resource Management Solution, Stk Sym: TESI, Founded: 1982, Empl: 100, Sales ($M): 12.7, Fiscal End: 12/95; W. Christopher Jesse, Pres & CEO, Email: chrisj@tesi.com; Stephen H. Groetzinger, VP NA Sales, Email: steveg@tesi.com; Steven F. Kuckes, VP Tech, Email: stevek_unix@tesi.com; Stan Ragsdale, VP Ops, Email: stanr@tesi.com; Diantha Pinner, Dir Marcom, Email: dianthap@tesi.com

TAP Computer Services Inc. 190 Main St, Ogdensburg NJ 07439 USA; 201/827-4911, Fax: 201/827-5335, Focus: LANs and PCs for financial services industry

Tapedisk Corp. 200 Main St, #210, Menominee WI 54751 USA; 715/235-3388, Focus: Backup software, Ownrshp: PVT, Founded: 1992, Roy S. Ostenso, CEO, Email: 73174.2464@compuserve.com; Ralph Shnelvar, Pres, James G. Dempsey, VP R&D

Tapette Corp. 5 Whatney, Irvine CA 92718-2806 USA; 714/588-7000, Focus: Magnetic media duplication and pkg. services, Prdts: Micro-Case, Ownrshp: PVT, Founded: 1971, Empl: 40, James Neiger II, Pres, Philip Cook, VP, Steve Neiger, Sales Mgr

Taras Linguistic Systems Inc. PO Box 1039, Provo UT 84603-1039 USA; 801/375-3456, 800/840-3926 Fax: 801/375-3434, Co Email: taras@itsnet.com, Focus: Language training software, Ownrshp: PVT, Founded: 1991, Empl: 10, Giovanni Tata, Pres & CEO, Rob Walton

Target Software Group Inc. 2901 58th Ave N, St Petersburg FL 33714 USA; 813/528-2477, 800/872-4381 Fax: 813/528-2671, Focus: Financial management software, Ownrshp: PVT, Founded: 1992, Empl: 75, Richard J. Pearce, Pres & CEO, Antonio Santini, Chmn, Joseph Ward, COO, Richard Story, EVP, Jesse Forrest, Dir Mktng

Target Technologies Inc. 6714 Netherlands Dr, Wilmington NC 28405 USA; 910/395-6100, Fax: 910/395-6108, Focus: Desktop video conferencing products, Prdts: C-Phone, Ownrshp: OTC, Stk Sym: CFON, Founded: 1986, Empl: 24, Fiscal End: 2/94; Daniel Flohr, Chmn, Pres & CEO, Tina L. Jacobs, EVP & COO, Paul H. Albritton, VP & CFO, Stuart E. Ross, VP Eng, Barry Rumac, VP Mktng

Tatung Co. 22 Chungshan N Rd, Taipei TW-10451 Taiwan ROC; 2-592-5252, Web URL: tatung.com, Focus: PCs, peripherals and electronic products, Ownrshp: FO, Sales ($M): 3,000, Fiscal End: 12/95; W.S. Lee, Pres

Tatung Co. of America Inc. 2850 El Presidio St, Long Beach CA 90810 USA; 310/637-2105, Fax: 310/637-8484, Focus: PCs and peripherals, Prdts: UNIQ, Ownrshp: Sub. Tatung, Taiwan,

Founded: 1972, Empl: 200, Chieh Sun, Pres, John Morgan, GM Computer Div, Mike Lee, VP Mktng, Larry Chen, VP Mktng

Tatung Science & Technology Inc. (TSTI), 1840 McCarthy Blvd, Milpitas CA 95035-7425 USA; 408/383-0988, 800/659-5902 Fax: 408/383-0886, Co Email: mkt@tsti.com, Web URL: tatung.com/tsti, Focus: SPARC-compatible workstations, Prdts: Ultra SPARC-Driven Compstation U Series, Ownrshp: Sub. Tatung, Taiwan, Founded: 1989, Empl: 70, Kam H. Chan, Pres, Email: kamchan@tsti.com; Forest Lai, VP Eng, James Hwang, Dir. Svcs & Sup

TCA-Information, Technology & Telecommunications (TCA), 74 New Montgomery, #230, San Francisco CA 94105 USA; 415/777-4647, Fax: 415/777-4647, Web URL: tca.org, Focus: Association for telecom professionals, Ownrshp: Nonprofit, Founded: 1961, Empl: 2,500

TDC Interactive (TDC), 2716 Ocean Park Blvd #3085, Santa Monica CA 90405 USA; 310/452-6720, Fax: 310/452-6722, Focus: Interactive software marketing, publication, distribution and production financing, Prdts: ImageKit, Sam Pirnazar, Founder, Gordon Stulberg, Chmn, Lauren A. Berzins, VP Dist, Jeffrey S. Ferguson, Dir Tech

TDK Corp. 1-13-1 Nihonbashi, Chuo-ku Tokyo JP-103 Japan; 3-3278-5111, Focus: Mass storage products and electronic components, Ownrshp: NYSE, Stk Sym: TDK, Founded: 1935, Empl: 29,070, Sales ($M): 5,107.7, Fiscal End: 3/96; Hiroshi Sato, Pres, Makoto Komoda, EVP, Sadao Iwaya, EVP, Michinoti Katayama

TDK USA Corp. 12 Harbor Park Dr, Port Washington NY 11050 USA; 516/625-0100, Focus: Mass storage media, Ownrshp: Sub. TDK, Japan, Francis J. Sweeney

TEAC America Inc. 7733 Telegraph Rd, Montebello CA 90640 USA; 213/726-0303, Fax: 213/727-7652, Focus: Data storage products, Ownrshp: Sub. Teac, Japan, Founded: 1953, Sales ($M): 380, Les Luzar, Div Mgr, Michael Cobery, Sales Mgr, Scott Elrich, Prod Dev & Mktng Mgr, Mike Nguyen

Teacher Support Software Inc. 1035 NW 57 St, Gainesville FL 32605-4486 USA; 904/332-6404, 800/228-2871 Fax: 904/332-6779, Focus: Educational software, Ownrshp: PVT, Founded: 1981, Empl: 10, Tony Domenech, Pres, Lynn Domenech, VP, Shirley Edelstein, Dir PR

Tech Data Corp. 5350 Tech Data Dr, Clearwater FL 34620 USA; 813/539-7429, Fax: 813/538-7050, Co Email: @techdata.com, Web URL: techdata.com, Focus: Distribution of microcomputer products, Ownrshp: OTC, Stk Sym: TECD, Founded: 1974, Empl: 2,265, Sales ($M): 3,086.6, Fiscal End: 1/96; Steven A. Raymond, Chmn & CEO, A. Timothy Godwin, Pres & COO, Peggy K. Caldwell, SVP Mktng, Jeffrey P. Howells, SVP & CFO, Bruce D. Eden, VP MIS, Chuck Miller, Marcom Mgr, Email: cmiller@techdata.com

Tech Electronics Inc. 6420 Atlantic Boulevard, Norcross GA 30071 USA; 770/446-1416, 800/572-4935 Fax: 770/448-5724, Web URL: usa.net/icia/techelec, Focus: Audio visual & video control, routing & retrieval products, Prdts: InSight, Lee Anne Wimberly, Mktng Coord

Tech-Source Inc. 442 S N Lake Blvd, #1008, Altamonte Springs FL 32701 USA; 407/262-7100, 800/338-8301 Fax: 407/339-2554, Co Email: @techsource.com, Focus: Graphics controllers, Prdts: GXTRA, Ownrshp: PVT, Founded: 1987, Empl: 18, Sales ($M): 3.5, Michael J. Tobias, Pres, Email: mike@techsource.com; Joseph D. Lamm, VP & CTO, Email: joe@techsource.com; Raj Gupta, VP & CFO, Email: raj@techsource.com; Richard E. Bendfelt, Dir Sales, Email: dick@techsource.com; Sue Wilcox, MIS Mgr, Email: sue@techsource.com; Tina M. DeVan, Mktng Assist, Email: tina@techsource.com

TechBridge Technology Corp. 5001 Yonge St, #1301, N York Ontario M2N 6P6 Canada; 416/222-8998, 800/463-8998 Fax: 416/222-0168, Co Email: 73532.456@compuserve.com, Focus: OS/2 software development tools, Prdts: Visual Trio, Ownrshp: PVT, Founded: 1991, Alan Ho, EVP, Email: aho@contrad.com;

Darwon Ne, Dir, Douglas Fraser, Bus Dev Mgr

Techbyte International Inc. 908 Niagara Falls Blvd, N Tonawanda NY 14120-2551 USA; 716/743-8052, Fax: 716/694-9092, Co Email: techbyte@buffnet.net, Focus: Educational software, Ownrshp: FO, Founded: 1984, Empl: 25, Serge Boudream, Pres

Techcessories Corp 681 E Brokaw Rd, San Jose CA 95112 USA; 408/436-5510, 800/480-8324 Fax: 408/436-5509, Focus: Accessories, Ownrshp: Sub Sicon, Jack Wang, Pres

Techmedia Computer Systems Corp. 7345 Orangewood Ave, Garden Grove CA 92641 USA; 714/379-6677, Fax: 714/379-9069, Focus: MPEG technologies and multimedia PC systems, Prdts: MotionMEDIA MPEG Playback Card, Andrew Park, Pres & CEO, Mike Forman

Technalysis Corp. 6700 France Ave S, Minneapolis MN 55435 USA; 612/925-5900, Focus: Computer system design & programming services, Ownrshp: OTC, Stk Sym: TECN, Founded: 1967, Empl: 244, Sales ($M): 16.8, Fiscal End: 12/94; Victor A. Rocchio, Chmn & CEO, Jerry J. Snyder, Pres & COO, James M. Clark, VP, Milan L. Elton, VP

Technically Elite Inc. 1686 Dell Ave, Campbell CA 95008-6901 USA; 408/370-4300, Fax: 408/370-4222, Co Email: @tecelite.com, Web URL: tecelite.com, Focus: Network products, Prdts: Network Professor, MeterWare, EtherMeter, TokenMeter, Ownrshp: PVT, David Norman, Chmn & CEO, Russell Dietz, VP Eng, Sandy Traylor, VP Hardware, Richard J. Wixted, VP Mktng

Technologic Software University Tower, 4199 Campus Dr, Irvine CA 92715-9856 USA; 714/509-5000, 800/626-4567 Fax: 714/509-5015, Co Email: ras@technologic.com, Web URL: technologic.com, Focus: Software to improve productivity, performance, availability and efficiency of users, Prdts: RAS, Founded: 1984, Robert Ralston, Dir Prod Mktng, Email: bralston@technologic.com

Technology Association Leaders' Council (TALC), c/o Pro-Line Communications, 13 Crescent Rd, Livingston NJ 07039 USA; 201/716-9457, Fax: 201/533-0463, Focus: Organization for user groups and associations, Ownrshp: Nonprofit, Founded: 1996, Bruce Freeman, Pres

Technology Council of Central Pennsylvania PO Box 60543, Harrisburg PA 17106-0543 USA; 717/238-5333, Fax: 717/238-6006, Focus: Organization for Pennsylvania high-tech companies, Ownrshp: Nonprofit

Technology Council of Greater Philadelphia 435 Devon Park Dr, Wayne PA 19087 USA; 610/975-9430, Fax: 610/975-9432, Focus: Organization for Philadelphia high-tech companies, Ownrshp: Nonprofit

Technology Council of the Center for Economic Growth 1 Keycorp Plaza, #600, Albany NY 12207 USA; 518/465-8975, Fax: 518/465-6681, Focus: Organization for New York high-tech companies, Ownrshp: Nonprofit

Technology Council-Greater Baltimore Committee 111 S Calvert St, #1500, Baltimore MD 21201-6180 USA; 410/385-1545, Fax: 410/385-1545, Focus: Organization for Baltimore high-tech companies, Ownrshp: Nonprofit

Technology Group Inc., The 36 S Charles St, #2200, Baltimore MD 21201 USA; 410/576-2040, Fax: 410/576-1968, Focus: Document & word processing software, Prdts: XyWrite, General Counsel, Weath Transfer Planning, Ownrshp: PVT, Founded: 1988, Empl: 25, Kenneth Frank, Pres

Technology Insight Inc. 33 Washington St, Marblehead MA 01945 USA; 617/639-2570, Fax: 617/639-2570, Focus: C/S tools, data warehousing, rapid prototyping methodologies, Ownrshp: PVT, Founded: 1984, Empl: 2, Pieter Mimno, Pres

Technology Resource Assistance Center Inc. (TRAC), 530 Oak Grove Ave, #101, Menlo Park CA 94025 USA; 415/853-1100, Fax: 415/853-1677, Web URL: tracworld.com, Focus: Fund raising software, Prdts: DonorTrac, TracStar, Ownrshp: PVT, Founded: 1985, Empl: 11, Susan Orr, Pres, Ann Troussieux, VP

Technology Service Solutions 580 E Swedesford Rd, Valley Forge PA 19087 USA; 610/293-2765, Fax: 610/293-5506, Co Email: udib5564@ibmmail.com, Focus: LAN and C/S support and services, Ownrshp: IBM & Kodak, Founded: 1993, Empl: 6,000, Sales ($M): 800, Fiscal End: 12/94; Richard J. Hernandez, CEO, Daniel S. Conors Jr., Pres & COO, Al Andrus, SVP Bus Dev, Burke R. Veley, SVP & CFO, Marcie Berg-Katcher

TechPool Software 1463 Warrensville Ctr Rd, Cleveland OH 44121 USA; 216/382-1234, 800/925-6998 Fax: 216/382-1915, Co Email: info@techpool.com, Web URL: techpool.com, Focus: Graphics software, Prdts: LifeART, Transverter Pro, Ownrshp: PVT, Founded: 1987, Paul Veregge, Pres, Email: paulv@techpool.com; Dian Bolling, Prod Mgr Transverter Pro, Email: dianb@techpool.com; Diana Cox, Prod Mgr LifeART, Email: dianac@techpool.com

TECO Information Systems Co. Inc. 24 E Harbor Dr, Lake Zurich IL 60047 USA; 708/438-3998, Fax: 708/438-8061, Focus: Monitors, desktop scanners and plain paper fax, Prdts: Relisys, Ownrshp: Sub. TECO, Taiwan, Empl: 650, Sales ($M): 250, Fiscal End: 12/94; Ted Huang, Chmn, John Yang, Pres, David Ciembronowicz, VP Sales & Mktng, Email: dtciembro@aol.com

Ted Gruber Software PO Box 13408, Las Vegas NV 89112 USA; 702/735-1980, 800/410-0192 Co Email: fastgraph@aol.com, Focus: Graphics library software, Prdts: Fastgraph, Ownrshp: PVT, Founded: 1987, Empl: 2, Ted Gruber, Pres, Diana Gruber

Tekelec 26580 W Agoura Rd, Calabasas CA 91302 USA; 818/880-5656, Fax: 818/880-6993, Focus: Network diagnostic products, Ownrshp: OTC, Stk Sym: TKLC, Empl: 310, Sales ($M): 75.3, Fiscal End: 12/95; Philip J. Alford, Pres, William C. Shaw, SVP, Allen J. Toomer, SVP, William J. Minchin, VP Ops, Gilles C. Godin, VP & CFO

Teknowledge Inc. 1810 Embarcadero Rd, Palo Alto CA 94303 USA; 415/424-0500, Fax: 415/493-2645, Web URL: teknowledge.com, Focus: Expert system software and intelligent systems engineering, Prdts: M.4, Ownrshp: OTC, Stk Sym: CMTK, Founded: 1981, Empl: 35, Sales ($M): 3.4, Fiscal End: 12/94; Rick Hayes-Roth, Chmn & CEO, Neil Jacobstein, Pres & COO, Dennis Bugbee, Dir Finance

TeKnowlgy Corp 10000 N Central Expwy, #1460, Dallas TX 75231 USA; 214/373-9998, Fax: 214/373-9994, Focus: Computer training and support, Ownrshp: PVT, Founded: 1994, Morti Tenenhaus, Pres & CEO, Avery More, Chmn

Tektronix Color Printing & Imaging Div. 2600 SW Pkwy, PO Box 1000, Wilsonville OR 97070-1000 USA; 503/685-3150, Fax: 503/685-3063, Focus: Color printers, Ownrshp: Sub. Tektronix, Gerry Perkel, Pres, Robert Stewart, VP Mktng, Gary Gillam, VP US Sales, A.J. Rogers, VP Strategic Mktng, Jennifer Jones, PR Mgr, Email: jennifer.l.jones@tek.com

Tektronix Inc. 26600 SW Pkwy Ave, Wilsonville OR 97070-1000 USA; 503/627-7111, Fax: 503/627-5502, Web URL: tek.com, Focus: Display systems, X terminals and measurement products, Ownrshp: NYSE, Stk Sym: TEK, Founded: 1946, Empl: 7,900, Sales ($M): 1,768.9, Fiscal End: 5/96; Jerome J. Meyer, Chmn & CEO, Lucie Fjeldstad, VP, Carl W. Neun, VP & CFO, Richard I. Knight, VP Tech, Michele M. Potter, VP Corp Com

Telamon Corp. 492 Ninth St, #310, Oakland CA 94607-4098 USA; 510/987-7700, Fax: 510/987-7009, Co Email: @telamon.com, Focus: Telecom services, Ownrshp: PVT, Ross Scroggs, Pres

Telco Systems Inc. 63 Nahatan St, Norwood MA 02062-5702 USA; 617/551-0300, Fax: 617/551-0534, Co Email: @telco.com, Web URL: telco.com, Focus: Telecom products, Ownrshp: OTC, Stk Sym: TELC, Founded: 1972, Empl: 400, Sales ($M): 89.1, Fiscal End: 8/95; John A. Ruggiero, Pres & CEO, William B. Smith, Pres & COO, Robert J. Bauer, SVP Int'l Bus Dev, Bill Waters, SVP Sales, Kenneth J. Hamer Rodges, SVP & CTO

Teleadapt Inc. 51 E Campbell Ave, Campbell CA 95008 USA;

408/370-5105, Fax: 408/370-5110, Co Email: 72623.706@compuserve.com, Web URL: teleadapt.com, Focus: Telecom products for portable computers, Prdts: TeleDaptors, Ownrshp: PVT, Gordon Brown, Pres, Heather Hawes, VP

Telebit Corp. 1 Executive Dr, Chelmsford MA 01824 USA; 508/441-2181, Fax: 508/441-9060, Focus: Connectivity products for dial-up communications, Ownrshp: OTC, Stk Sym: TBIT, Founded: 1982, Empl: 250, Sales ($M): 55.9, Fiscal End: 12/95; James D. Norrod, Pres & CEO, Mark R. Wilson, VP Sales & Ops, Stephen L. Dick, VP Corp Mktng, Denis W. Aull, VP Eng & CTO, Brian D. Cohen, VP & CFO

Telebit Software 1315 Chesapeake Terrace, Sunnyvale CA 94089 USA; 408/734-4333, 800/835-3248 Fax: 408/745-3873, Co Email: info@telebit.com, Focus: Information access software, Ownrshp: PVT, Founded: 1990, Empl: 10, Stephen Dick, VP Mktng, Jerry Steach, PR Mgr, Email: jsteach@telebit.com

Telebyte Technology Inc. 270 Pulaski Rd, Greenlawn NY 11740 USA; 516/423-3232, 800/835-3298 Fax: 516/385-8184, Web URL: telebyteusa.com, Focus: Data communication products, Ownrshp: OTC, Stk Sym: TBTI, Founded: 1978, Empl: 40, Sales ($M): 3.8, Fiscal End: 12/94; Joel A. Kramer, Chmn & Pres, Kenneth S. Schneider, VP Sales

Telecommunications Industry Assoc. (TIA), 2500 Wilson Blvd, Arlington VA 22201-3834 USA; 703/907-7700, Focus: Association of manufacturers and suppliers of materials, products, systems and services to, Ownrshp: Nonprofit, Founded: 1979, Empl: 590, Matt Flanigan, Pres, John Major, Chmn, Kathy M. Hammond, Mgr Com

Telecomputer Inc. 17481 Mt. Cliffwood Cr, Fountain Valley CA 92708 USA; 714/438-3993, Fax: 714/438-3994, Focus: Memory modules, Ownrshp: PVT, Founded: 1983, Empl: 75, Sales ($M): 76, Fiscal End: 12/94; Joseph Nguyen, Pres, Lonnie Kay, GM, Thomas Bayens, Dir Mktng

Teledyne Inc. 2049 Century Park E, Los Angeles CA 90067-3101 USA; 310/551-4306, Fax: 310/551-4366, Web URL: tbe.co./teledyne, Focus: Electronic products, Ownrshp: NYSE, Stk Sym: TDY, Founded: 1960, Empl: 40,000, Sales ($M): 2,567.8, Fiscal End: 12/95; William P. Rutledge, Chmn & CEO, Donald B. Rice, Pres & COO, Hudson B. Drake, SVP

TeleMagic Inc. 17950 Preston Rd, #800, Dallas TX 75252 USA; 214/733-4292, 800/835-6244 Fax: 214/733-4251, Focus: Contact management software, Prdts: TeleMagic Enterprise and TeleMagic Professional, Ownrshp: Sub Sage Group, UK, Founded: 1985, Conrad Masterson, Div VP, Email: conradm@onramp.net; Charlie Kirkpatrick, VP Sales, Rita Riddle, Mktng Coord

TELEMATE Software Inc. 4250 Perimeter Park S, #200, Atlanta GA 30341-1201 USA; 770/936-3700, Fax: 770/936-3710, Co Email: info@telemate.com, Web URL: telemate.com, Focus: Telemanagement software, Prdts: TELEMATE Telemanagement Series for Windows, AutoMate/Anytime, Ownrshp: PVT, Founded: 1985, Empl: 72, David Couchman, CEO, Richard L. Mauro, Pres, Heather Whitt, Mktng Mgr

TelePad Corp. 380 Herndon Pkwy, #1900, Herndon VA 22070 USA; 703/834-9000, Fax: 703/834-1235, Focus: Pen computers and total solutions for field force computing, Prdts: TelePad, Systems Integrator, Stk Sym: TPADA, Founded: 1990, Ron Oklewicz, Pres, Joseph Elkins, COO

Telephone and Data Systems Inc. 30 N LaSalle St, #4000, Chicago IL 60602-2507 USA; 312/630-1900, Fax: 312/630-1908, Web URL: teldta.com, Focus: Telecom services, Ownrshp: AMEX, Stk Sym: TDS, Empl: 5,322, Sales ($M): 954.4, Fiscal End: 12/95; LeRoy T. Carlson Jr., Pres & CEO, LeRoy T. Carlson, Chmn, Rudolph E. Hornacek, VP Eng, Michael K. Chesney, VP Corp Dev, Murray L. Swanson, EVP & CFO

Teleport Communications 1 Teleport Dr, Staten Island NY 10311 USA; 718/983-2000, Fax: 718/983-2147, Focus: Telecom services, Ownrshp: PVT, Founded: 1984, Empl: 850, Sales ($M):

100, Robert Annunziata, CEO

Telescape Communications Inc. 555 W Hastings St, Vancouver BC V6B 4N5 Canada; 604/893-7088, Fax: 604/893-7087, Co Email: info@telescape.com, Web URL: telescape.com, Focus: Multimedia conferencing, Prdts: ts intercom, Founded: 1995, Geoffrey C. Hansen, Pres

TeleTypesetting Co. 311 Harvard St, Brookline MA 02146 USA; 617/734-9700, Fax: 617/737-3974, Co Email: @teletype.com, Focus: Electronic graphic and publishing systems, Prdts: T-Script, Books-on-Disk, Digital Gourmet, Ownrshp: PVT, Founded: 1981, Empl: 12, Edward Friedman, Chmn, Marleen Winer, CEO

TeleVideo Systems Inc. 2345 Harris Way, San Jose CA 95131 USA; 408/954-8333, Fax: 408/954-0622, Focus: Video display terminals, Ownrshp: OTC, Stk Sym: TELV, Founded: 1975, Empl: 64, Sales ($M): 16.9, Fiscal End: 10/95; K. Philip Hwang, Chmn & CEO, Richard A. DuBridge, Pres & COO, Kristine E.J. Kim, Dir Mktng, Isaac Levanon, EVP, K. David Kim, VP & CFO

Tellabs 4951 Indiana Ave, Lisle IL 60532 USA; 708/969-8800, Fax: 708/852-7346, Web URL: tellabs.com, Focus: Telecom products, Ownrshp: OTC, Stk Sym: TLAB, Founded: 1975, Empl: 2,300, Sales ($M): 635.2, Fiscal End: 12/95; Michael J. Birck, Pres & CEO, Peter A. Guglielmi, EVP & CFO, Brian J. Jackman, EVP

TELS Corp. (TEL), 406 W S Jordan Pkwy #250, S Jordan UT 84095 USA; 801/571-1182, Fax: 801/571-1942, Focus: Call-accounting and telephone management systems, Ownrshp: OTC, Stk Sym: TELS, Founded: 1981, Empl: 42, Sales ($M): 7.8, Fiscal End: 12/95; John L. Gunter, Chmn & Pres, Stephen M. Nelson, SVP & CFO, Michael J. Allison, VP Sales & Mktng

Telus 10020 100th St, Edmonton Alberta T5J 0N5 Canada; 403/498-7311, 800/667-4871 Fax: 403/498-7399, Focus: Telecom services, Ownrshp: FO, Stk Sym: AGT, Sales ($M): 1,360.1, Fiscal End: 12/94; George K. Petty, Pres & CEO, Jim McDonald, EVP, Frank Parrotta, EVP Corp Dev, Gary Goertz, EVP & CFO

Telxon Corp. 3330 W Market St, Akron OH 44334-0582 USA; 216/867-3700, 800/800-8001 Fax: 216/869-2240, Co Email: sales@telxon.com, Web URL: telxon.com, Focus: Handheld data collection microcomputers, Ownrshp: OTC, Stk Sym: TLXN, Founded: 1969, Empl: 1,850, Sales ($M): 486.5, Fiscal End: 3/96; William J. Murphy, Pres & COO, Robert F. Meyerson, Chmn & CEO, John H. Cribb, Pres Intl Div, Richard Gurda, VP Corp Com

Template Software Inc. 13100 Worldgate Dr, #340, Herndon VA 22070-4382 USA; 703/318-1000, Fax: 703/318-7378, Co Email: info@template.com, Web URL: template.com, Focus: Software templates, Prdts: SNAP, Workflow Template, System Management Template, Founded: 1978, Empl: 75, Joeseph Fox, Chmn, Email: fox@template.com; Linwood Pearce, CEO, Email: lin.pearce@template.com; Andrew B. Ferrentino, Pres, Email: andy@template.com; David Kiker, VP Prod Dev, Email: dave.kiker@template.com; Mary Ann Stoops, Mktng Mgr, Email: maryann.stoops@template.com

Ten X Technology Inc. 13091 Pond Springs Rd, #B200, Austin TX 78729 USA; 512/918-9182, 800/922-9050 Fax: 512/918-9495, Focus: Optical disks subsystems and application accelerators, Prdts: OptiWin, OptiXchange, Capacity PLUS Jukeboxes, Ownrshp: PVT, Founded: 1983, Empl: 28, Sales ($M): 5, Fiscal End: 3/91; Greg Wise, Mktng Mgr

Tenera L.P. 2001 Center St, Berkeley CA 94704-1204 USA; 510/845-5200, Fax: 510/845-8453, Focus: Software and services for utility and other industries, Ownrshp: AMEX, Stk Sym: TLP, Founded: 1974, Empl: 202, Sales ($M): 23.6, Fiscal End: 12/94; Michael D. Thomas, Chmn & CEO, Bradley C. Geddes, Pres & COO, Donald R. Ferguson, SVP, Jeffrey R. Hazarian, VP & CFO

Teradyne Inc. 321 Harrison Ave, Boston MA 02118 USA; 617/482-2700, Fax: 617/422-2910, Web URL: teradyne.com, Focus: Automatic test and EDA systems, Ownrshp: NYSE, Stk Sym: TER, Founded: 1960, Empl: 5,200, Sales ($M): 1,191.0, Fiscal End: 12/95; Alexander V. d'Arbeloff, Chmn & Pres, James A. Prestige, EVP,

Owen W. Robbins, EVP & CFO, George W. Chamillard, Pres & COO, John P. McCabe, VP Info Sys, Frederick T. Van Veen, VP Corp Rel

Terisa Systems 4984 El Camino Real, Los Altos CA 94022-1433 USA; 415/919/1750, Fax: 415/919-1760, Co Email: @terisa.com, Web URL: terisa.com, Focus: Technology for secure Internet transactions, Prdts: SecureWeb Client Toolkit, SecureWeb Server Toolkit, Ownrshp: PVT, Founded: 1995, Empl: 12, David Kaiser, CEO, Allan Schiffman, CTO

TerraGlyph Interactive Studios 1375 Remington Rd, Schaumburg IL 60173 USA; 847/413-4100, Fax: 847/884-0262, Focus: Entertainment software, Founded: 1994, Ken Hansen, VP Publishing

Terran Interactive Inc. 21471 Lee Dr, #B, Los Gatos CA 95030 USA; 408/353-6231, Fax: 408/353-3871, Web URL: terran-int.com, Focus: Multimedia production, Ownrshp: PVT, Founded: 1995, Darren Giles, Tech Dir, Dana Giles, Art Dir, John Geyer, Mktng Dir, Email: jgeyer@netcom.com

Teubner & Associates Inc. Seventh & Main, PO Box 1994, Stillwater OK 74076 USA; 405/624-2254, Fax: 405/624-3010, Co Email: sales@teubner.com, Web URL: teubner.com, Focus: Internet utility software, Prdts: Corridor, Ownrshp: PVT

Texas Caviar Inc. 3933 Steck Ave, #B-115, Austin TX 78759 USA; 512/346-7887, 800/648-1719 Fax: 512/346-1393, Co Email: support@texascaviar.com, Focus: Multimedia educational software, Prdts: Annabel's Drem of Medieval England, Whale of a Tale, Vital Signs, Ownrshp: PVT, Carolyn J. Kuhn, Pres & CEO, Email: cjkuhn@texascaviar.com

Texas Instruments Inc. (TI), 13500 N Central Expwy, PO Box 655474, Dallas TX 75265 USA; 214/995-2551, Fax: 214/995-4360, Web URL: ti.com, Focus: Semiconductors, PCs, peripherals & electronic systems, Ownrshp: NYSE, Stk Sym: TXN, Founded: 1938, Empl: 59,048, Sales ($M): 13,128, Fiscal End: 12/95; Thomas J. Engibous, Pres & CEO, William P. Weber, Vice Chmn, William B. Mitchell, Vice Chmn, William F. Hayes, EVP, William A. Aylesworth, SVP & CFO

Texas Memory Systems 11200 Westheimer Rd, #1000, Houston TX 77042 USA; 713/266-3200, Fax: 713/266-0332, Web URL: texmemsys.com, Focus: DSP and vector processors, Prdts: Viper-5, John Marsh

Texas Microsystems Inc. 5959 Corporate Dr, Houston TX 77036 USA; 713/541-8200, 800/627-8700 Fax: 713/541-8226, Focus: Industrial microcomputer, Founded: 1975, Empl: 150, Sales ($M): 35.7, Fiscal End: 6/92; Wayne Patterson, Chmn & CEO, Michael Stewart, Pres & COO, Sandy Travis

Tharo Systems Inc. PO Box 798, 2866 Nationwide Pkwy, Brunswick OH 44212-0798 USA; 216/273-4408, Fax: 216/225-0099, Co Email: tharo@tharo.com, Web URL: tharo.com/tharo, Focus: Software and label/barcode printers, thermal transfer ribbons and accessories, Prdts: Easylabel Software, Tharo Thermal Transfer Bar Code Label Printer, Ownrshp: PVT, Founded: 1982, Empl: 20, Thomas M. Thatcher, Pres, Christina Benko, VP Mktng & Sales, Anina Auvil, GM

THEOS Software Corp. 1777 Botelho Dr, #360, Walnut Creek CA 94596-5022 USA; 510/935-1118, Fax: 510/938-4367, Focus: PC multiuser operating systems, Ownrshp: PVT, Founded: 1983, Empl: 30, Sales ($M): 10, Timothy Williams, CEO, Jack Dyer, Pres, Kurt Waag, VP Fin & Admin, Shelley Clark, Dir Mktng, Amy Friedman, Mktng Coord

ThinKware 345 Fourth St, San Francisco CA 94107 USA; 415/777-9876, Focus: Distributor of computer music products, Ownrshp: PVT

Thomson Software 101 Merritt 7, Norwalk CT 06856 USA; 203/845-5000, 800/441-6878 Fax: 203/845-5252, Web URL: thomsoft.com, Focus: C/S software, Ownrshp: Sub Thomson-CSF, Founded: 1995, Empl: 470, Sales ($M): 61.3, Fiscal End: 12/95; Jean-Luc Badault, Pres & CEO, Ben Goodwin, NA Pres

Thomson Software Products 10251 Vista Sorrento Pkwy, #300, San Diego CA 92121 USA; 619/457-2700, Fax: 619/452-2117, Focus: GUI development software, Ownrshp: PVT, Ben Goodwin, Pres & CEO

Thoroughbred Software Int'l. Inc. 19 Schoolhouse Rd, PO Box 6712, Somerset NJ 08875-6712 USA; 201/560-1377, Fax: 201/560-1594, Focus: Language and development tools, Prdts: Idol-IV, Ownrshp: PVT, Founded: 1982, Empl: 75, Sales ($M): 8, Carmen T. Randazzo, Pres & COO, Lynn Alexander, VP Sales & Mktng, Roger D. Sparks, VP Prod & Syst

Thot Technologies 271 E Hacienda Ave, Campbell CA 95008-6616 USA; 408/370-4600, Fax: 408/370-4609, Focus: Disk diagnostics products, Ownrshp: PVT, Founded: 1991, Empl: 8, Sales ($M): 2.2, Jim Eckerman, Pres & CEO, Ian Freeman, CTO

Thought I Could 107 University Place, #4D, New York NY 10003 USA; 212/673-9724, Fax: 212/260-1194, Focus: Macintosh utility software, Prdts: Wallpaper, More Wallpaper, CAL, Ownrshp: PVT, Founded: 1988, Linda Kaplan, Pres

Three D Graphics Inc. 1801 Ave of the Stars, Los Angeles CA 90067-5908 USA; 310/553-3313, Fax: 310/788-8975, Co Email: info@threedgraphics.com, Web URL: threedgraphics.com, Focus: Graphics software, Prdts: Perspective, Pixelloom, Compadre, Ownrshp: PVT, Founded: 1985, Empl: 18, Sales ($M): 2, Elmer R. Easton, Pres, Email: elmere@threedgraphics.com

Thru-Put Technologies 2 N First St, 4th Fl., San Jose CA 95113 USA; 408/920-9711, Fax: 408/920-9715, Focus: Scheduling software

ThrustMaster Inc. 7175 NW Evergreen Pkwy, #400, Hillsboro OR 97124 USA; 503/615-3200, Fax: 503/615-3300, Web URL: thrustmaster.com, Focus: PC input and control devices, Ownrshp: OTC, Stk Sym: TMSR, Founded: 1990, Empl: 96, Sales ($M): 19.4, Fiscal End: 12/95; C. Norman Winningstad, Chmn, Stephen A. Aanderud, Pres & CEO, Kevin J. Darby, VP Sales & Mktng, G. Edward Brightman, VP Ops, Kent Koski, VP & CFO, Email: kent@thrustmaster.com; Kent E. Koski, CFO

Tiara Computer Systems 2302 Walsh Ave, Santa Clara CA 95051-1301 USA; 408/496-5460, Focus: LAN hardware and software, Ownrshp: PVT, Empl: 20, Andrei Glasberg, Pres

Tibco Inc. 530 Lytton Ave, 3rd Fl, Palo Alto CA 94301 USA; 415/325-1025, Web URL: tibco.com, Focus: Financial software, Prdts: Information Bus, Ownrshp: Sub Reuters, UK, Founded: 1994, Empl: 325, Sales ($M): 130, Fiscal End: 12/95; Vivek Ranadive, Chmn, Pres & CEO

TIE/Communications Inc. 8500 W 110th St, Overland Park KS 66210 USA; 913/344-0400, Focus: Telecom products, Ownrshp: AMEX, Stk Sym: TIE, Founded: 1971, Empl: 1,100, Sales ($M): 124.9, Fiscal End: 12/94; George N. Benjamin, Pres & CEO, Eric V. Carter, EVP, Robert H. Kalina, VP Eng & Ops, Edward F. Muehlberger, VP

Tiger Direct Inc. 9100 S Dadeland Blvd 15th Floor, Miami FL 33156 USA; 305/443-8212, Fax: 305/444-5010, Focus: Productivity and utility software, Ownrshp: OTC, Stk Sym: TIGR, Founded: 1985, Empl: 200, Sales ($M): 88.1, Fiscal End: 12/94; Gilbert J. Fiorntino, Chmn, Pres & CEO, Ivan Inerfeld, COO, Samuel M. Waksman, VP & CFO

Timberline Software Corp. 9600 SW Nimbus Ave, Beaverton OR 97005-7163 USA; 503/626-6775, Fax: 503/526-8299, Focus: Construction and property management software, Ownrshp: OTC, Stk Sym: TMBS, Founded: 1971, Empl: 214, Sales ($M): 24.8, Fiscal End: 12/95; John Gorman, Chmn & Pres, Leslie F. Clarke II, EVP, John M. Meek, VP R&D, Thomas P. Cox, SVP & CFO, Nicolette D. Johnston, VP Ops

Timeline Inc. 3055 112th Ave NE, #106, Bellevue WA 98004 USA; 206/822-3140, 800/588-7632 Fax: 206/822-1120, Web URL: tmln.com, Focus: Accounting software, Prdts: Metaview, Ownrshp: OTC, Founded: 1977, Empl: 70, Sales ($M): 5.0, Fiscal End: 3/96; John W. Calahan, Pres & CEO, Charles R. Osenbaugh,

CFO, Owen A. Canton, VP Mktng

TimeMaster Corp. 7165 Shady Oak Rd, Eden Prairie MN 55344 USA; 612/941-9080, Fax: 612/947-0841, Focus: Real-time wireless productivity tools, Prdts: LANTracker

Timeslips Corp. 17950 Preston Rd, #800, Dallas TX 75252 USA; 214/248-9232, 800/285-0999 Fax: 214/248-9245, Co Email: 102102.477@compuserve.com, Focus: Time and expense tracking software, Prdts: Timeslips, TimeSheet Professional, Ownrshp: PVT, Founded: 1985, Empl: 50, Mitchell A. Russo, Pres, Neil R. Ayer, VP, Michelle Franklin

Tippecanoe Systems Inc. 5674 Stoneridge Dr, #119, Pleasanton CA 94588 USA; 510/416-8510, Fax: 510/416-8516, Co Email: info@tippecanoe.com, Web URL: tippecanoe.com, Focus: Barcode and indexing software, Prdts: Bars & Stripes, Tecumseh, Ownrshp: PVT, W. Mike Tyler, Pres, Email: mike@tippecanoe.com

Titan Corp. 3033 Science Park Rd, San Diego CA 92121 USA; 619/552-9500, Fax: 619/552-9645, Co Email: corpcomm@titan.com, Web URL: titan.com, Focus: Information systems and support, Prdts: Video PassPort, Mini DAMA, DAMA Link, Express Connection, Ownrshp: NYSE, Stk Sym: TTN, Founded: 1981, Empl: 1,000, Sales ($M): 134.0, Fiscal End: 12/95; Gene W. Ray, Pres & CEO, Ronald B. Gorda, SVP, Frederick L. Judge, SVP, Stephen P. Meyer, SVP, Roger Hay, SVP & CFO, Michelle Mueller, VP Corp Com, Email: mmueller@titan.com

Tivoli Systems Inc. 9442 N Capital of TX Hwy, #500, Austin TX 78759-6311 USA; 512/794-9070, Fax: 512/794-0623, Web URL: tivoli.com, Focus: Distributed systems management software, Prdts: Tivoli Management Environment, Ownrshp: OTC, Stk Sym: TIVS, Founded: 1989, Empl: 217, Sales ($M): 49.6, Fiscal End: 12/95; Franklin Moss, Pres & CEO, Eric L. Moss, Chmn, William Bock, SVP Ops, James Offerdahl, VP & CFO, Chris Grafft, VP Dev, Claire Campbell, Mgr PR

TJT International 14090 E Firestone Blvd, Santa Fe Springs CA 90670 USA; 310/926-5118, 800/888-8992 Fax: 310/404-9482, Focus: Wholesale distributor of hard disk drives and computer peripherals, Ownrshp: PVT

TMS Inc. PO Box 1358, Stillwater OK 74076-1358 USA; 800/944-7654 Fax: 405/377-0452, Co Email: @tms-ok.mhs.compuserve.com, Focus: Software development tools, Prdts: ViewDirector, MasterView, Ownrshp: OTC, Stk Sym: TMSS, Founded: 1981, Empl: 40, Fiscal End: 8/93; J. Richard Phillips, CEO, Maxwell Steinhardt, Pres & COO, Email: maxwell@tm-ok.mhs; Gail Bower, Mktng Dir, Email: gail@tms-ok.mhs

TNT Software Inc. 22170 Mitchell Ln, Antioch IL 60002-8834 USA; 847/838-4323, Focus: Word processing, Prdts: My Word!, The Creator, Ownrshp: PVT, Founded: 1981, Empl: 3, Bruce W. Tonkin, Pres, P.J. Tonkin, VP

Tolly Group, The 2302 Hwy 34, Manasquan NJ 08736-1427 USA; 908/528-3300, 800/933-1699 Fax: 908/528-1888, Co Email: info@tolly.com, Web URL: tolly.com, Focus: Network and telecom product testing, Ownrshp: PVT, Founded: 1982, Empl: 23, Kevin Tolly, Pres & CEO, Email: ktolly@tolly.com; Neil Anderson, COO, Email: nanderson@tolly.com; Caryn Hill, Mktng & PR Specialist, Email: chill@tolly.com

Tom Sawyer Software 1824 Fourth St, Berkeley CA 94710 USA; 510/848-0853, Fax: 510/848-0854, Co Email: info@tomsawyer.com, Web URL: tomsawyer.com, Focus: Graphics layout and editing software, Prdts: Graph Layout Toolkit, Network Layout Assistant, Ownrshp: PVT, Founded: 1992, Empl: 12, Brendan P. Madden, Pres, Email: bmadden@tomsawyer.com; Stephen Powers, VP Eng, Email: spowers@tomsawyer.com; Wendy M. Jones, Dir Sales & Mktng, Email: wjones@tomsawyer.com

Tools & Techniques Inc. 2201 Northland Dr, Austin TX 78756 USA; 512/459-1308, 800/580-4411 Fax: 512/459-1309, Focus: File conversion software, Prdts: Data Junction, Ownrshp: PVT, Darrell Blanford, VP Mktng

Toray Optical Storage Solutions 1875 S Grant St, #720, San

Mateo CA 94402 USA; 415/341-7152, Fax: 415/341-0845, Co Email: info@totay.com, Web URL: toray.com, Focus: Optical storage products, Ownrshp: Sub Toray, Japan, James Rowley, GM, Charles Kobayashi, VP Mktng, Marc Hoover, Sales Mgr

Toshiba America Electronic Components Inc. (TAEC), 9775 Toledo Way, Irvine CA 92718 USA; 714/455-2000, 800/879-4963 Fax: 714/859-3963, Web URL: toshiba.com/taec, Focus: Semiconductors and display devices, Ownrshp: Sub. Toshiba, Japan, Founded: 1984, Empl: 1,600, Sales ($M): 1,100, Annette Birkett, Mgr Marcom

Toshiba America Information Systems Inc. (TAIS), 9740 Irvine Blvd, PO Box 19724, Irvine CA 92718-9724 USA; 714/583-3111, Fax: 714/583-3133, Web URL: toshiba.com, Focus: Laptop and notebook PCs and peripherals, Ownrshp: Sub. Toshiba, Japan, Founded: 1988, Sales ($M): 2,000, Fiscal End: 12/94; Tom Scott, VP & GM, Van Andrews, VP Sales, Tim Kuhlman, VP Svc, Gary Mueller, VP Ops, Tony Sekino, Assist GM, David Ujita, Dir Marcom

Toshiba Corp. 1-1-1 Shibaura 1-chome, Minato-ku, Tokyo 105-01 JP-105-01 Japan; 3-3457-4511, Fax: 3-3456-4776, Web URL: toshiba.co.jp, Focus: Computers, peripherals, semiconductors and electronic products, Ownrshp: FO, Stk Sym: TOSHBA, Founded: 1875, Empl: 162,000, Sales ($M): 54,192, Fiscal End: 3/96; Joichi Aoi, Chmn, Fumino Sato, Pres & CEO

Total Systems Services Inc. 1200 Sixth Ave, PO Box 1755, Columbus GA 31902-1755 USA; 706/649-2204, Fax: 706/649-4266, Focus: Computer services for banks, Prdts: Total System, Total Access, Cardholder System, Merchant System, Ownrshp: OTC, Stk Sym: TSS, Founded: 1982, Empl: 2,269, Sales ($M): 249.7, Fiscal End: 12/95; Richard W. Ussery, Chmn & CEO, Philip W. Tomlinson, Pres, James B. Lipham, CFO & EVP, M. Troy Woods, EVP, William Pruett, EVP, Danita Gibson-Lloyd, Assist VP, Email: danitag@aol.com

Touchstone Software Int'l. 23691 Birtcher Dr, Lake Forest CA 92630-1770 USA; 714/470-1122, 800/786-8663 Fax: 714/470-1121, Focus: Contact management software, Prdts: CheckIt, Ownrshp: OTC, Stk Sym: TSSW, Founded: 1991, Empl: 57, Sales ($M): 12.1, Fiscal End: 12/95; Larry Dingus, Chmn, C. Shannon Jenkins, Pres & CEO, Ronald Maas, EVP & CFO, Donald C. Watters, VP Sales, Bob Foyle, Dir Mktng

TouchVision Systems Inc. 8755 W Higgins Rd, #200, Chicago IL 60631 USA; 312/714-1400, Fax: 312/714-1405, Focus: Video editing software, Prdts: D/Vision, Ownrshp: PVT, Founded: 1990, Bruce A. Rady, Pres & CEO, Rickey Gold, Dir Marcom

Tower Technology Corp. 1501 W Koenig Ln, Austin TX 78756 USA; 512/452-9455, 800/285-5124 Fax: 512/452-1721, Co Email: tower@twr.com, Web URL: twr.com, Focus: Tools for object software development based on Eiffel OOPL, Prdts: TowerEiffel, Ownrshp: PVT, Founded: 1992, Empl: 9, Sales ($M): 0.5, Robert Howard, Pres & CEO, Email: rock@twr.com; Madison Cloutier, VP Mktng & COO, Email: madison@twr.com; Stephen Tynor, VP Dev, Email: tynor@twr.com; Fred Hart, VP Res, Email: hart@twr.com

TPS Electronics 2495 Old Middlefield Way, Mountain View CA 94043 USA; 415/988-0141, 800/526-5920 Fax: 415/988-0289, Focus: Bar code readers, Ownrshp: PVT, Founded: 1978, Joel Postman, Pres, Mark Marshall, VP Mktng

Tracer Technologies Inc. 702 Russell Ave, #450, Gaithersburg MD 20877 USA; 800/872-2370 Fax: 301/977-5222, Focus: Optical storage device drives, jukebox management and file system software, Prdts: Magna, Magna Vault

Tracker Software Inc. 7575 Golden Valley Rd, #375, Minneapolis MN 55427 USA; 612/525-9802, Fax: 612/525-9825, Focus: Contact management software, Prdts: Tracker, Ownrshp: Sub Tracker, Australia, Roger Bushell, Pres, Andrew Donald, US Pres

Traffic USA Inc. 2300 Corporate Blvd, #241, Boca Raton FL 33431-7308 USA; 407/995-5282, Focus: Network fax software,

Prdts: Object-Fax, Ownrshp: Public, FO, Founded: 1987, Empl: 20, Magnus Bergsson, US Sales & Mktng Mgr, Arni Jensen, Leif Jensen, Xenia Moore

Trainwreck Software 352 State St, Albany NY 12210 USA; 518/342-6352, Ownrshp: PVT

Trans-Micro Inc. PO Box 898, Fairfield FL 32634-0898 USA; 407/878-5858, Fax: 407/878-5917, Focus: Forms software, Prdts: Laser Form Energizer, Ownrshp: PVT

Transaction Network Services Inc. (TNS), 1939 Roland Clarke Place, Reston VA 22091 USA; 703/742-0500, Focus: Transaction transport services, Prdts: TransXpress, Card*Tel Fraud Control, Ownrshp: OTC, Stk Sym: TNSI, Founded: 1990, Empl: 95, Sales ($M): 41.4, Fiscal End: 12/95; John J. McDonnell Jr., Pres & CEO, Brian Bates, VP & GM, Richard Sternitzke, CTO, Robert E. Jones, VP & GM Telecom Svcs Div, Karen Kazmark, PR Dir, Email: kkazmark@aol.com

Transaction Processing Performance Council (TPC), c/o Shanley PR, 777 N 1st St, #600, San Jose CA 95112-6311 USA; 408/295-8894, Fax: 408/295-9768, Web URL: tpc.org, Focus: Develops performance benchmark standards for transaction processing applications, Ownrshp: Nonprofit, Founded: 1988, Empl: 45, Kim Shanley, Administrator

Transarc Corp. 707 Grant St, Gulf Tower, Pittsburgh PA 15219 USA; 412/338-4400, Fax: 412/338-4404, Focus: Unix software development tools, Prdts: Encina, Ownrshp: Sub IBM, Founded: 1989, Empl: 200, Sales ($M): 8, Alfred Spector, Pres & CEO, Mark Power

Transend Corp. 225 Emerson St, Palo Alto CA 94301-1026 USA; 415/324-5370, Co Email: transend@vendor.infonet.com, Web URL: transendcorp.com, Focus: E-mail software, Prdts: PC COMplete, MAPI Connectorware for cc:Mail, Ownrshp: PVT, Founded: 1974, Empl: 50, Fred Krefetz, Pres, Email: krefetz@vendor.infonet.com

Transitional Technology Inc. 5401 E La Palma Ave, Anaheim CA 92807 USA; 714/693-1133, Fax: 714/693-0225, Co Email: info@ttech.com, Focus: Backup tape systems and libraries, Ownrshp: PVT, Founded: 1987, Empl: 65, Sales ($M): 20, Fiscal End: 12/95; Matthew T. Goldbach, Pres, Email: matt@ttech.com; Richard B. Martin, SVP Eng, Email: richard@ttech.com; Kathy Drachman, VP Sales & Mktng, Email: kathy@ttech.com; Tony Tombrello, VP Ops, Karen Seelow, Dir Mktng, Email: karen@ttech.com

Transparent Technology Inc. 600 Corporate Pointe, #100, Culver City CA 90230 USA; 310/215-8040, Fax: 310/215-8070, Co Email: @trantech.com, Focus: Software distributor, Founded: 1989, Empl: 22, Sales ($M): 10, Garry S. Hipsher, Pres, Email: garry@trantech.com; Russell Welchel, Controller, Email: russell@trantech.com; M. Cecilia Williams, Ops Mgr, Joseph Riser, Comm Exec, Email: josephr@trantech.com

Traveling Software Inc. 18702 N Creek Pkwy, Bothell WA 98011 USA; 206/483-8088, Fax: 206/487-1284, Co Email: @travsoft.com, Web URL: travsoft.com, Focus: Software for laptop PCs, Prdts: Laplink, CommWorks, Ownrshp: PVT, Founded: 1982, Empl: 120, Sales ($M): 23.2, Fiscal End: 12/95; Mark Eppley, Chmn & CEO, Jonathan Scott, Pres & COO, Andrew Czernek, VP Mktng, Rob Schram, VP Strat Dev, David Payne, VP Fin & Ops

Trax Softworks Inc. 5840 Uplander Way, Culver City CA 90230-6620 USA; 310/649-5800, Fax: 310/649-6200, Co Email: info@traxsoft.com, Focus: Groupware, Prdts: TeamTalk, Anne M. Moriarty, Mgr Marcom

Trend Micro Devices Inc. 10415 Los Alamitos Blvd, Los Alamitos CA 90720-2111 USA; 310/782-8190, Fax: 310/328-5892, Focus: Anti-virus and security software, Prdts: PC-cillin, PC Rx Antivirus, StationLock, ChipAway Virus, Ownrshp: PVT, Founded: 1988, Empl: 70, Steve Chang, Pres

Triad Systems Corp. 3055 Triad Dr, Livermore CA 94550 USA; 510/449-0606, Focus: Computer systems to automotive parts and dealers and dentists, Ownrshp: OTC, Stk Sym: TRSC, Founded: 1972, Empl: 1,450, Sales ($M): 175.1, Fiscal End: 9/95; James R. Porter, Pres & CEO, Shane Gorman, EVP, Jerome W. Carlson, VP & CFO, Thomas J. O'Malley, VP Admin, Donald C. Wood, VP Info Serv

Tribe Computer Works 960 Atlantic Ave, #101, Alameda CA 94501 USA; 510/814-3900, 800/778-7423 Fax: 510/814-3980, Co Email: sales@tribe.com, Web URL: tribe.com, Focus: Internetworking communications products, Prdts: TribeStar. TribeLink Series, Ownrshp: PVT, Founded: 1990, Empl: 35, Jim Li, CEO, Diana Helander, Dir Mktng, Email: dianah@tribe.com

Tricord Systems Inc. 2800 NW Blvd, Plymouth MN 55441-2625 USA; 612/557-9005, Fax: 612/557-8403, Focus: LAN servers, Prdts: PowerFrame, Ownrshp: OTC, Stk Sym: TRCD, Founded: 1987, Empl: 205, Sales ($M): 60.2, Fiscal End: 12/95; John Mitcham, Pres & CEO, Greg Barnum, SVP & CFO

Trident Microsystems Inc. 189 N Bernardo Ave, Mountain View CA 94043-5203 USA; 415/691-9211, Fax: 415/691-9260, Focus: Graphics and imaging boards and chip sets, Ownrshp: OTC, Stk Sym: TRID, Founded: 1987, Empl: 210, Sales ($M): 168.1, Fiscal End: 6/96; Frank C. Lin, Chmn, Pres & CEO, James T. Lindstrom, VP & CFO, Michael T. Morrione, SVP & GM, Jung-Herng Chang, VP Eng

Trilogy Development Group 6034 W Courtyard Dr, #130, Austin TX 78730 USA; 512/794-5900, Fax: 512/794-8900, Co Email: @trilogy.com, Focus: Sales automation software, Prdts: SalesBuilder, Conquer, Ownrshp: PVT, Founded: 1989, Empl: 120, Joe Liemandt, Pres & CEO, Wade Monroe, EVP & CFO, John Price, VP Mktng, Donald Steele, VP Sales, Harry Vonk, VP Consulting

Trio Information Systems 8601 Six Forks Rd, #105, Raleigh NC 27615 USA; 919/846-4990, Fax: 919/846-4997, Focus: Communications software, Ownrshp: PVT, Founded: 1991, Empl: 25, Leif Petterson, Pres, Sean Schultz, VP Prod Dev

Trio Systems 936 E Green St, #105, Pasadena CA 91106 USA; 818/584-9706, Fax: 818/584-0364, Co Email: mail@triosystems.com, Web URL: triosystems.com, Focus: Database software, Prdts: C-Index, Ownrshp: PVT, Founded: 1978, Alan Bartholomew, Owner

TriQuint Semiconductor 3625 SW Murray Blvd, #A, Beaverton OR 97005-2359 USA; 503/644-3535, Fax: 503/644-3198, Focus: Gallium Arsenic semiconductors, Ownrshp: OTC, Stk Sym: TQNT, Founded: 1986, Sales ($M): 45.9, Fiscal End: 12/95; Steven J. Sharp, Chmn, Pres & CEO, Edward C. Winn, VP & CFO, Joseph Martin, VP Corp Dev, Bruce R. Fournier, VP Sales

TriTeal Corp. 2011 Palomar Airport Rd, #200, Carlsbad CA 92009-1431 USA; 619/930-2077, Fax: 619/930-2081, Co Email: info@triteal.com, Focus: C/S software and systems integration, Prdts: TED, Ownrshp: PVT, Founded: 1993, Gregory J. White, Pres & CEO, Oran Thomas, CTO, Jeff Witous, EVP Bus Dev, Rand Schulman, VP Mktng, Shelley Draminski, Mktng Mgr, Email: draminski@triteal.com

Triticom Box 444180, Eden Prairie MN 55344 USA; 612/937-0772, Fax: 612/937-1998, Web URL: triticom.com, Focus: LAN products, Prdts: EtherVision, ArcVision, TokenVision, LANdecoder, Bridge IT!, Ownrshp: PVT, Founded: 1989, Empl: 20, Barry A. Trent, Pres, Email: btrent@triticom.com; Todd Farley, VP SW Dev, Email: tfarley@triticom.com; Scott DesBles, Sales & Mktng Mgr, Email: sdesbles@triticom.com

Triton Technologies Inc. 200 Middlesex Turnpike, Iselin NJ 08830 USA; 908/855-9440, 800/322-9440 Fax: 908/855-9608, Focus: Communication software, Prdts: Co/Session, Ownrshp: Sub Artisoft, Founded: 1985, Empl: 15, Sales ($M): 2.2, David J. Saphier, Pres, Floyd F. Roberts, VP, Peter Byer, VP Sales & Mktng, Kathy Krais, Dir Mktng, Email: 73672.2303@compuserve.com

Triumph Logistic Computers 10772 Noel St, Los Alamitos CA 90720 USA; 714/952-8999, Fax: 714/952-3804, Focus: Graphics

and video boards, Prdts: Triumphony Visual Forge Video Series, Ownrshp: PVT, Founded: 1989, Empl: 7, Sales ($M): 3.0, Fiscal End: 12/94; Simon H. Hwang, Pres, Nina Chou, Marketing/Sales

TRIUS Inc. 231 Sutton St, #2D-3, PO Box 249, N Andover MA 01845-0249 USA; 508/794-9377, 800/468-7487 Fax: 508/688-6312, Co Email: 71333.103@compuserve.com, Focus: Spreadsheet/2D/3D CAD/rendering software, communications software, Prdts: ProtoCAD 3D, As-Easy-As, Odyssey, DraftChoice, Ownrshp: PVT, Founded: 1986, Paris Karahalios, Pres, Email: 72727.616@compuserve.com

True Basic Inc. 12 Commerce Ave, W Lebanon NH 03784 USA; 603/298-8517, 800/436-2111 Fax: 603/298-7015, Co Email: @truebasic.com, Focus: Educational software, information, Prdts: True BASIC, Kemeny-Kurtz Math, QwikINFO, Ownrshp: PVT, Founded: 1983, Empl: 8, Sales ($M): 1, John A. Lutz, Pres & CEO, Email: john@truebasic.com; Thomas E. Kurtz, Secretary, Treas, Email: tom@truebasic.com

True Software Inc. 200 Baker Ave, Concord MA 01742 USA; 508/369-7398, 800/232-2244 Fax: 508/369-8272, Co Email: info@truesoft.com, Web URL: truesoft.com, Focus: Software configuration management, Prdts: Aide~de~Camp/Pro, Ownrshp: PVT, Founded: 1981, Empl: 35, Robert S. Torino, Pres & CEO, Stuart A. Bernstein, VP Sales & Mktng, Email: stu@truesoft.com; Terence P. Halloran, CFO, Michael Hui, VP Prod Ops, Email: mhui@truesoft.com; Dom Macadino, Dir Support Ops, Email: domm@truesoft.com; Jo Ellen Collins, Dir Mktng, Email: jcollins@truesoft.com

Truevision Inc. 2500 Walsh Ave, Santa Clara CA 95051 USA; 408/562-4200, Fax: 408/562-4065, Focus: Graphics hardware and software, Prdts: TARGA, Ownrshp: OTC, Stk Sym: TRUV, Founded: 1984, Empl: 95, Sales ($M): 71.5, Fiscal End: 6/96; Louis J. Doctor, Pres & CEO, Matt Carter, VP Ops, Robert O'Brien, SVP Sales, Didier Bredy, VP Mktng, John Curson, VP & CFO

TRW Inc. (TRW), 1900 Richmond Rd, Cleveland OH 44124-3760 USA; 216/291-7000, 800/650-0879 Web URL: trw.com, Focus: Electronics components and information services, Ownrshp: NYSE, Stk Sym: TRW, Founded: 1901, Empl: 66,500, Sales ($M): 10,172.4, Fiscal End: 12/95; Joseph T. Gorman, Chmn & CEO, Peter S. Hellman, Pres & COO, D. Van Skilling, EVP Info Syst, John P. Stenbit, VP & GM SI, Howard V. Knicely, EVP, Tom Myers

TSANet 7101 College Blvd, #380, Overland Park KS 66210 USA; 913/345-9311, Fax: 913/345-9317, Web URL: tsanet.org, Focus: Technical support network, Ownrshp: Nonprofit, Dennis Smeltzer, Exec Dir

Tseng Labs Inc. (TLI), 6 Terry Dr, Newtown PA 18940 USA; 215/968-0502, Fax: 215/860-7713, Focus: PC graphics boards, Ownrshp: OTC, Stk Sym: TSNG, Founded: 1983, Empl: 55, Sales ($M): 39.3, Fiscal End: 12/95; Jack Tseng, Pres & CEO, John A. Vigna, EVP & COO, David K.P. Hui, EVP, Mark H. Karsch, SVP & CFO, Mitch Paris, Prod Mgr

TT Systems Corp. 9 Odell Plaza, Yonkers NY 10701 USA; 914/968-2100, Fax: 914/968-2155, Focus: Telephone equipment and accessories for small office and home office, Ownrshp: PVT, Founded: 1975, Empl: 25, Daniel S. Leitman, Pres, Valerie Leitman, VP Treasurer, Walter S. Lange, VP Res & Dev

Turner Home Entertainment 1050 Techwood Dr NE, Atlanta GA 30318 USA; 404/885-0505, Focus: Movies, books and education software, Ownrshp: Sub. Turner Broadcasting, Philip Kent, Pres, Stuart Snyder, SVP, Michael Reagan, EVP & Publisher, Marshall D. Orson, VP Bus Affairs, Ronnie Gunnerson, VP PR

Turtle Beach Systems Inc. 52 Grumbacher Rd, York PA 17402 USA; 717/767-0200, Fax: 717/767-6033, Focus: Multimedia sound products, Ownrshp: Sub. Integrated Circuit Syst., Founded: 1985, Roy C. Smith II, Pres, Jeff Klinedinst, VP Mktng, Robert W. Hoke, VP Eng, Curtis Crowe, VP Sales, Daniel J. McGuire, VP Ops, Stacy Pierson, Dir PR

Tusk Inc. 160 SW 12th Ave, #101A, Deerfield Beach FL 33442-

3114 USA; 407/625-1101, Fax: 407/625-1120, Focus: Pen computers hardware and software, Prdts: All Terrain SuperTablet, All Terrain Supertablet II, Ownrshp: PVT, Founded: 1991, Chuck Krallman, CEO & Co-founder, Donald E. Beazley, Chmn & CFO, Kenneth Shaw, CTO, Marlyn Kilpatrick, VP Admin

Tut Systems Inc. 2495 Estand Way, Pleasant Hill CA 94523 USA; 510/682-6510, 800/998-4888 Fax: 510/682-4125, Web URL: tut-sys.com, Focus: LAN products, Prdts: XL Long Distance Ethernet Repeaters, Ownrshp: PVT, Founded: 1989, Matthew Taylor, Chmn, Sal D'Auria, Pres, Michael Sullivan, CFO, Sanne Higgins, Marcom Dir

TUV Product Service Inc. 5 Cherry Hill Dr, Danvers MA 01923 USA; 508/777-7999, Fax: 508/777-8441, Web URL: tuvps.com, Focus: EMI and safety testing, Ownrshp: PVT, Founded: 1990, Empl: 80, Kurt Eise, Pres, John L. Durant, VP, Axel Breidenbach, Lab Equip Mgr

TV/COM International Inc. 16516 Via Esprillo, San Diego CA 92127 USA; 619/451-1500, Fax: 619/451-1505, Focus: Digital video compression, Prdts: Compression NetWORKS, Ownrshp: Sub. Hyundai Electronics Amer, Henk A. Hanselaar, Pres & CEO, Wallace Dieckmann, CFO, Steve White, VP Eng, Mark Brady, VP Sales, Andrea LaVorgna, Marcom Mgr

TView Inc. 7853 SW Cirrus Dr, Beaverton OR 97008 USA; 503/643-1662, 800/356-3983 Fax: 503/671-9066, Co Email: @tview.com, Web URL: tview.com, Focus: PC-to-TV adapters, Ownrshp: PVT, Founded: 1991, Empl: 10, Thomas M. Hamilton, Pres, Mark D. Lieberman, VP Sales & Mktng, Email: markl@tview.com; Steven R. Morton, VP

Twelve Tone Systems Inc. 44 Pleasant St, PO Box 760, Watertown MA 02272 USA; 617/926-2480, Fax: 617/924-6657, Focus: Music software, Prdts: Cakewalk Home Studio, Ownrshp: PVT, Founded: 1987, Empl: 25, Greg Hendershott, Pres, Christopher Rice, Mktng Dir

Twinbridge Software Corp. 1055 Corporate Ctr. Dr, #400, Monterey Park CA 91754 USA; 213/263-3926, 800/894-6114 Fax: 213/263-8126, Co Email: @twinbridge.com, Web URL: twin-bridge.com, Focus: Asian localizing software development, Prdts: TwinBridge Chinese/Japanese Partner for Windows, Ownrshp: PVT, Founded: 1989, Empl: 21, Sales ($M): 1.7, Fu-Kun Lin, Chmn, Edward L. Chang, Pres & CEO, Roy Pacheco, VP Sales & Mktng, Steve Peng, VP Info, Johnny Li, IS Staff, Email: tech-sup@twinbridge.com; Kevin Wu, Mkt Staff

Twinhead Corp. 1537 Centre Pointe Dr, Milpitas CA 95035 USA; 408/945-0808, Fax: 408/945-1080, Focus: Notebook and desktop PCs, Founded: 1984, Empl: 650, Sales ($M): 83, Stanley Chiang, CEO, Charles Chen, Pres, Doug Moglin, Dir Mktng

Tyan Computer Corp. 1645 S Main St, Milpitas CA 95035 USA; 408/956-8000, Fax: 408/956-8044, Focus: PCs and peripherals, Ownrshp: PVT, Founded: 1989, Sales ($M): 10, Fiscal End: 12/94; James Chen, Sales Mgr

U.S. Microcomputer Statistics Committee (USMCSC), c/o ITI, 1250 Eye St NW, #200, Washington DC 20005 USA; 202/626-5730, Fax: 202/638-4922, Focus: PC vendor consortium that tracks PC sales, Ownrshp: Nonprofit, Founded: 1991, Empl: 40, Helga Sayadian, Coordinator

U.S. Product Data Assoc. (US PRO), 5300 Int'l Blvd, Trident Research Ctr, #204, N Charlston SC 29418 USA; 803/760-3327, Fax: 803/760-3349, Co Email: uspro@scra.org, Focus: Development, implementation and testing of product data standards, Ownrshp: Nonprofit, Founded: 1992, Chuck Stark, Progr Dir, Melanie Varn, Progr Admin

U.S. Robotics Inc. 8100 N McCormick Blvd, Skokie IL 60076-5244 USA; 847/882-5010, Fax: 847/982-5203, Co Email: sales-info@usr.com, Web URL: usr.com, Focus: Wide area network access equipment, Prdts: Courier, Shared Access, Blast, Worldport, Sportster, Ownrshp: OTC, Stk Sym: USRX, Founded: 1976, Sales ($M): 1,092, Fiscal End: 9/95; Casey G. Cowell, Chmn, Pres &

CEO, Jonathan N. Zakin, EVP Sales & Mktng, Ross W. Manire, SVP & CFO, Dale M. Walsh, VP Adv Dev, Semir Sirazi, VP R&D, Karen J. Novak

UB Networks 3990 Freedom Cr, PO Box 58030, Santa Clara CA 95052-8030 USA; 408/496-0111, 800/777-4526 Fax: 408/970-7385, Focus: Network systems, Prdts: Access/One, Ownrshp: Sub. Tandem, Founded: 1979, Empl: 1,000, Sales ($M): 365.1, Roel Pieper, Pres & CEO, Doug Wheeler, VP Mktng, Mike Gardner, SVP Cust Ops, John Chenette, SVP Corp Resources, Chris Brennan, CFO, Mari M. Clapp, VP Corp Re

Ubi Soft Entertainment 80 E Sir Francis Drake Blvd, #3E, Larkspur CA 94939 USA; 415/464-4440, Fax: 415/464-4450, Web URL: ubisoft.com, Focus: Entertainment software, Prdts: Rayman, Carrie Tice

Ubique Inc. 657 Mission St, #601, San Francisco CA 94105 USA; 415/896-2434, Fax: 415/541-7775, Co Email: info@ubique.com, Web URL: ubique.com, Focus: Communication software for WWW, Prdts: Virtual Places, Ownrshp: PVT

Ulead Systems Inc. 970 W 190th St, #520, Torrance CA 90502 USA; 310/523-9393, 800/858-5303 Fax: 310/523-9399, Co Email: mkt@ulead.com, Web URL: seednet.tw//~ulead, Focus: Image processing software, video editing software, Prdts: ImagePals2, Media Studio Pro, Ownrshp: PVT, Founded: 1989, Empl: 90, Liming Chen, Pres, Robert C. Hsieh, Co-Chmn, Lotus Chen, VP Prog Office, Steve Stautzenbach, Dir Sales, Email: stevesta@ulead.com

Ultera Systems Inc. 26052 Merit Cr, #106, Laguna Hills CA 92653 USA; 714/367-8800, Fax: 714/367-0758, Co Email: inform@ultera.com, Focus: Storage systems, Prdts: Striper 101 Series, Mo Nourmohamadian, Founder, Cynthia Karch

UltraStat Inc. 4491 Bent Bros Blvd, Colorado City CO 81019 USA; 719/676-4010, 800/460-7828 Focus: Static discharge products, Ownrshp: PVT, Kevin Cooter, Pres

Ultre Division 145 Pinelawn Rd, Melville NY 11747 USA; 516/753-4800, Fax: 516/753-4801, Focus: Imagesetters, Prdts: Ultre*Setter, Ownrshp: Div. Linotype-Hell, Empl: 60+, Edward J. Boyce, Dir Eng, David G. Green, VP & GM, James D. Martin, Dir WW Sales & Mktng, Darryl L. Tjaden, Dir Bus Planning

UMAX Technologies Inc. 3353 Gateway Blvd, Fremont CA 94538-6526 USA; 510/651-4000, Fax: 510/651-8834, Co Email: @umax.com, Focus: Scanners, Prdts: PowerLook, Mirage, PageOffice, Vista S-12, Maxmedia, Ownrshp: Sub. UMAX, Taiwan, Founded: 1989, Empl: 105, Frank Huang, Chmn & CEO, Vincent Tai, Pres, Email: vincent_tai@umax.com; Mike Owen, Prod Mktng Mgr, Email: mike_owen@umax.com; Imelda Valenzuela, Marcom Mgr, Email: imelda_valenzuela@umax.com

Underwriters Laboratories Inc. (UL), 333 Pfingsten Rd, Northbrook IL 60062-2096 USA; 847/272-8800, Fax: 847/272-8129, Focus: Safety standards, testing and ISO 9000 qualification certification, Ownrshp: PVT, Founded: 1894, Tom Castino, Pres, Robert Haugh, Chmn, Joe Bhatia, VP Ext Affairs

Unex Corp. 77 Northeastern Blvd, Nashua NH 03062-3128 USA; 603/598-1100, 800/345-8639 Fax: 603/598-1122, Focus: Telecom peripherals, Ownrshp: Sub. Dynatech, Michael Fairweather, Pres

UniKix Technologies 700 Technology Park, Billerica MA 01821-4134 USA; 800/765-2662 Fax: 508/765-2826, Co Email: @uni-kix.com, Focus: Transaction processing software, Ownrshp: Sub. Bull HN, Founded: 1994, John G. Noonan, Pres, David Matthews, VP Bus Dev, Kent Bradford, VP Sales, Michael Kott, Dir Mktng, Aiden Harney, VP Tech Ops, Michael C. Kott, Mktng Dir, Email: m.kott@unikix.com

Uniplex Inc. 1333 Corporate Dr, #240, Irving TX 75038-2532 USA; 214/556-0106, Fax: 214/831-7100, Co Email: @uni-plex.com, Focus: Enterprise office automation software, Prdts: onGo Office, Ownrshp: Sub. Uniplex, UK, Founded: 1981, Empl: 300, Sales ($M): 56, Fiscal End: 3/94; David McAuley, Pres, Email:

chuckd@uniplex.com; Email: meaghane@uniplex.com

UniPress Software Inc. 2025 Lincoln Hwy, Edison NJ 08817 USA; 908/287-2100, 800/222-0550 Fax: 908/287-4929, Co Email: info@unipress.com, Web URL: unipress.com, Focus: Software for UNIX computers, Ownrshp: PVT, Founded: 1983, Empl: 35, Sales ($M): 5, Fiscal End: 12/91; Mark Krieger, Pres, Email: msk@unipress.com; Fred Pack, VP, Email: fhp@unipress.com; Stephanie Adler, PR Coord, Email: sja@unipress.com

Unison Software Inc. 5101 Patrick Henry Dr, Santa Clara CA 95054-1111 USA; 408/988-2800, Focus: Systems management software, Founded: 1979, Empl: 120, Sales ($M): 30.0, Fiscal End: 5/96; Don H. Lee, Pres & CEO, Mihael A. Casteel, EVP & CTO

UniSQL Inc. 8911 N Capital of TX Hwy, #2300, Austin TX 78759-7200 USA; 512/343-7299, Fax: 512/343-7383, Focus: Database query software, Ownrshp: PVT, Founded: 1990, Empl: 50, Sales ($M): 5, Won Kim, Pres & CEO

Unisync Inc. 735 N Tulare Way, Upland CA 91786-4639 USA; 714/985-5088, Fax: 714/625-7022, Focus: Network products, Prdts: Host Access, Ownrshp: PVT, Founded: 1986, Empl: 15, Sales ($M): 2, Sandra Fallon, Pres

Unisys Corp. PO Box 500, Blue Bell PA 19424-0001 USA; 215/986-4011, Fax: 215/986-6850, Web URL: unisys.com, Focus: Mainframes, minis and microcomputers, software and services, Ownrshp: NYSE, Stk Sym: UIS, Founded: 1886, Empl: 46,300, Sales ($M): 6,202.3, Fiscal End: 12/95; James A. Unruh, Chmn & CEO, Alan G. Lutz, EVP, Lawrence C. Russell, EVP, George T. Robson, SVP & CFO, Dewaine L. Osman, SVP & CIO, Jack F. McHale, VP Inv & Corp Com

United Innovations 120 Whiting Farms Rd, Holyoke MA 01040-2832 USA; 413/533-7500, 800/323-3283 Fax: 413/533-7755, Focus: Plotters, graphics products and computerized engraving machines, Prdts: Signature Engravers Series, MURAL Plotters Series, Ownrshp: PVT, Founded: 1982, Empl: 25, Fiscal End: 12/95; Christopher Parent, Pres, James Richmond, VP, Kacey Kline, Mktng Dir

United States International Trade Commission (USITC), 500 E St SW, Washington DC 20436 USA; 202/205-2000, Fax: 202/205-2798, Focus: Independent, quasi-judicial agency which investigates the effect of foreign trade on the U, Ownrshp: Nonprofit, Founded: 1916, Don Newquist, Chmn

United Technologies Corp. United Technologies Bldg., Hartford CT 06101 USA; 203/728-7000, Web URL: utc.com, Focus: Electronic products and systems, Ownrshp: NYSE, Stk Sym: UTX, Founded: 1934, Empl: 168,600, Sales ($M): 22,802.0, Fiscal End: 12/95; Robert F. Daniell, Chmn, George David, Pres & CEO, Stephen F. Page, EVP & CFO

Unitrac Software Corp. 141 E Michigan Ave, Kalamazoo MI 49007-3911 USA; 616/344-0220, 800/864-8722 Fax: 616/344-2027, Co Email: @unitrac.com, Focus: Contact management software, Prdts: Unitrac, Ownrshp: PVT, Founded: 1981, Empl: 25, Gregory U. Ozuzu, Pres, Email: gozuzu@unitrac.com; Todd A. Mathison, Mgr Tech Sup Svcs, Email: tmathison@unitrac.com; Rori Gammons, Mgr Sales & Mktng, Email: rgammons@unitrac.com; Mark Eiler, Dir Training Svcs, Email: meiler@unitrac.com

Universal Algorithms Inc. (UAI), One SW Columbia #100, Portland OR 97258 USA; 503/973-5200, Fax: 503/973-5252, Web URL: xweb.com, Focus: Space utilization software and on-line application service for colleges, Prdts: Schedule 25, CollegeNET, Model 25, Ownrshp: PVT, Founded: 1977, James A. Wolfston, Founder & Pres

Univision Technologies Inc. 3 Burlington Woods, Burlington MA 01803 USA; 617/221-6700, Fax: 617/221-6777, Web URL: tiac.net.users/univis, Prdts: Chameleon, Falcon, Aurora, Ownrshp: PVT, Founded: 1986, Empl: 25, Sales ($M): 4, Eli Warsawski, Pres, James Rowell, VP Mktng, Julius Perc, VP Eng, Nissim Shani, VP Ops, Bonnie Pietragallo, Corp Comm Mgr

UniWorx Inc. PO Box 910154, San Diego CA 92191 USA; 619/

740-5111, 800/628-8649 Fax: 619/740-0740, Co Email: 73764.2114@compuserve.com, Focus: Unix training software, Ownrshp: PVT, Founded: 1991, Ron Alpert, Pres, Email: ralpert@nunic.nu.edu; Lee Ray, Tech Dir

UnixWare Technology Group (UTG), 190 River Rd, Rm A-226, Summit NJ 07901 USA; 908/522-6027, Fax: 908/522-5015, Co Email: @utg.org, Focus: Advancement of UnixWare and related technologies, Ownrshp: Nonprofit, Founded: 1993, Empl: 23, Lawrence D. Lyle, Pres & CEO, Michael Dortch, VP Mktng, Email: dortch@utg.org; Diane Taggart, Mktng Mgr, Email: diane@utg.org

Upstill Software 1442A Walnut St, Berkeley CA 94709 USA; 510/526-0178, Fax: 510/526-0179, Co Email: upstill@netcom.com, Focus: Cooking software, Prdts: Mangia, Ownrshp: PVT, Steve Upstill, CEO

US West Communication Group 7800 E Orchard Rd, Englewood CO 80111 USA; 303/793-6500, Focus: Regional Bell operating company (RBOC), Ownrshp: NYSE, Stk Sym: USW, Founded: 1983, Empl: 60,778, Sales ($M): 9,484, Fiscal End: 12/95; Solomon D. Trujillo, CEO

US West Media Group 7800 E Orchard Rd, Englewood CO 80111 USA; 303/793-6500, Web URL: uswest.com, Focus: Broadcasting and media, Ownrshp: NYSE, Sales ($M): 2,374, Fiscal End: 12/95; Charles M. Lillis, CEO

USA Technologies Inc. 1265 Drummers Ln #306, 3 Glenhardie Corp Ctr, Wayne PA 19087 USA; 610/989-0340, 800/633-0340 Fax: 610/989-0344, Web URL: usatech.com, Focus: Unattended credit card technology, Prdts: Credit Card Computer Express C3X, Ownrshp: OTC, Stk Sym: USTXP, George Jensen Jr., Chmn, Pres & CEO, Keith Sterling

Usability Professional Assoc. (UPA), 4020 McEwen, #105, Dallas TX 75244-5019 USA; 214/233-9107, Fax: 214/490-4219, Co Email: upadallas@aol.com, Focus: Information exchange on usability methods, tools and technology, Ownrshp: Nonprofit, Founded: 1991, Empl: 450, Janice James, Pres, Dave Rinehart, Co-Chair

Usability Sciences Corp. 5525 McArthur Blvd, #575, Irving TX 75038 USA; 214/550-1599, Fax: 214/550-9148, Web URL: usabilitysciences.com, Focus: Software usability testing, Ownrshp: PVT, Jeff Schueler, Pres

Usability Systems 1150 Alpha Dr, Alpharetta GA 30201 USA; 770/475-3505, Fax: 770/475-4210, Co Email: info@usabilitysystems.com, Web URL: usabilitysystems.com, Focus: Software usability testing, Ownrshp: PVT, Reed Johnson, Pres

User Group Alliance PO Box 29709, Philadelphia PA 19117-0909 USA; Focus: Organization of over 250 user groups, Ownrshp: Nonprofit, Bill Achuff, Co-Dir

User Group Connection Inc. (UGC), 231 Technology Cr, Scotts Valley CA 95066 USA; 408/461-5700, Fax: 408/461-5701, Co Email: ugc@aol.com, Web URL: ugconnection.org, Focus: User group marketing services for software and hardware vendors, Ownrshp: Nonprofit, Ray Kaupp, Pres, Carmela Zamora, Events & Tradeshows, Sam Decker, Mktng Mgr, Email: ugc-sam@eworld.com; Raines Cohen, Com Mgr, Joantha Muse

USoft 1000 Marina Blvd, Brisbane CA 94005 USA; 415/875-3300, 800/367-8763 Fax: 415/875-3333, Co Email: info@usoft.com, Web URL: usoft.com, Focus: C/S software, Prdts: USoft Developer Series, USoft OnLine Series, USoft Report Series, Founded: 1995, Empl: 200, Sales ($M): 20, Fiscal End: 12/95; Karen Mills, Dir Channels Mktng

Utah Information Technologies Assoc. (UITA), 6995 Union Park Ctr, #490, Midvale UT 84047 USA; 801/568-3500, Fax: 801/568-1072, Web URL: uita.org, Focus: Organization of information technology companies in Utah, Ownrshp: Nonprofit, Founded: 1991, Peter G. Genereaux, Pres

UUNET Technologies Inc. 3060 Williams Dr #601, Fairfax VA 22031-4648 USA; 703/206-5600, 800/488-6383 Fax: 703/206-5601, Co Email: uunet@uunet.uu.net, Web URL: uu.net, Focus:

Internet access provider, Prdts: AlterNet TCP/IP Network, Ownrshp: OTC, Stk Sym: UUNT, Founded: 1987, Sales ($M): 94.5, Fiscal End: 12/95; John W. Sidgmore, Pres & CEO, Richard L. Adams, Chmn & CTO, Michael K. Ballard, VP Mktng & Sls, Jeffrey G. Hilber, CFO

UUPlus Development PO Box 6991, 2131 10th St, #C, Los Osos CA 93412 USA; 805/534-9502, Fax: 805/534-1425, Co Email: info@uuplus.com, Focus: MS-DOS to Unix e-mail software, Prdts: UUPlus Light, UUPlus Utilities, Ownrshp: PVT, Founded: 1991, Empl: 3, Steven J. Gunderson, Owner, John H. Bonnett, GM, Email: jhb@uuplus.com

V Communications Inc. 4320 Stevens Creek Blvd #120, San Jose CA 95129-1266 USA; 408/296-4224, 800/648-8266 Fax: 408/296-4441, Web URL: v-com.com, Focus: PC system software, Prdts: System Commander, Sourcer, Windows Source, Ownrshp: PVT, Founded: 1986, Frank van Gilluwe, Pres, John Fink, EVP, Michael Mazzei, VP Sales & Mktng, Email: 75031.3042@compuserve.com

V-Systems Inc. 32232 Paseo Adelanto, #100, San Juan Capistrano CA 92675 USA; 714/489-8778, 800/556-4874 Fax: 714/489-2486, Focus: Unix fax software, Prdts: VSI-Fax, Ownrshp: PVT, Steve Crossley, Bus Dev Mgr, Greg Ballou

Valis Group PO Box 831, Tiburon CA 94920-0831 USA; 415/435-5404, 800/825-4704 Fax: 415/435-9862, Co Email: valisgroup@aol.com, Focus: Special effect software and multimedia, Prdts: MovieFlo', Flo', Metaflo',, Ownrshp: PVT, Founded: 1991, RoseAnn Alspektor, Pres & CEO, Erwin Schalker, COO, Hellene Biedny, Email: helleneb@aol.com

Vamp Inc. 6753 Selma Ave, Los Angeles CA 90028 USA; 213/466-5533, Fax: 213/466-8564, Focus: Engineering software, Prdts: McCad, Ownrshp: PVT, Founded: 1977, Empl: 10, John Soluk, VP Mktng

Vanstar Inc. 5964 W Las Positas Blvd, PO Box 9012, Pleasanton CA 94588 USA; 510/734-4000, Fax: 510/734-4802, Web URL: vanstar.com, Focus: PC systems integration, Ownrshp: PVT, Founded: 1976, Sales ($M): 1,390, Fiscal End: 4/95; William Tauscher, Chmn, Jay Amato, Pres & CEO

Vantive Corp. 2455 Augustine Dr, #101, Santa Clara CA 95054-3002 USA; 408/982-5700, 800/582-6848 Fax: 408/982-5710, Web URL: vantive.com, Focus: C/S customer support software, Ownrshp: OTC, Stk Sym: VNTV, Founded: 1990, Empl: 143, Sales ($M): 25.0, Fiscal End: 12/95; John R. Luongo, Pres & CEO, Steven M. Goldsworthy, Chmn & CTO, Kathy Murphy, CFO, Chris Howard, Mktng Mgr

Varitronic Systems Inc. 300 Interchange N, 300 Hwy 169 S, Minneapolis MN 55426 USA; 612/542-1500, Fax: 612/541-1503, Focus: Thermal transfer printers for presentation and industrial labeling and signage, Ownrshp: OTC, Stk Sym: VRSY, Founded: 1983, Empl: 275, Sales ($M): 44.8, Fiscal End: 7/94; Cynthia J. Trojanowski, Dir Corp Com

VCON Inc. 5000 Quorum, #700, Dallas TX 75240 USA; 214/774-3890, Fax: 214/774-3893, Focus: Desktop videoconferencing products, Prdts: Armada Cruiser 50 System, Empl: 65, Moti Gura, Chmn & CEO, Doron Herzlich, Pres & COO, Yossi Shachar, Dir Ops, Mike Clifford, VP Sales & Mktng

Vdonet Corp. 4009 Miranda Ave, #250, Palo Alto CA 94304 USA; 415/846-7700, Fax: 415/846-7900, Web URL: vdonet.com, Focus: Real-time video over local and wide area networks, Prdts: VDOLive, Ownrshp: PVT, Founded: 1995, Empl: 40, Asaf Mohr

Velan Inc. 4153 24th St, #1, San Francisco CA 94114-3614 USA; 415/647-0798, Fax: 415/647-1069, Co Email: velan@netcom.com, Focus: Educational network systems, Prdts: VNet, VSetup, VComm, VClass, Ownrshp: PVT, Founded: 1986, Empl: 3, Kevin D. Harlbut, Pres

Ventana Communications Group Inc. PO Box 13964, Research Triangle Pk NC 27709-3964 USA; 919/544-9404, 800/743-5369 Fax: 919/544-9472, Co Email: @vmedia.com, Web

URL: vmedia.com, Focus: Computer books and online software, Prdts: WebWalker, Online Companion, Ownrshp: Sub Int'l. Thomson Publishing, Founded: 1986, Empl: 110, Josef Woodman, Pres, Elizabeth Woodman, VP, Katy Dunn, Corp Com Mgr, Email: kdunn@vmedia.com

Venture Economics Inc. 40 W 57th St, New York NY 10019 USA; 212/765-5311, Fax: 212/765-6123, Focus: Tracks venture capital industry and start-up companies, Ownrshp: PVT, Founded: 1961, Empl: 120, Sales ($M): 5, David Devlin, VP & Publisher, Email: devlin@tfn.com; Lisa Vincent, Editor, Renee Deger

Venture Stores Inc. 2001 E Terra Ln, O'Fallon MO 63366-0110 USA; 314/281-6801, Focus: General merchandise discount stores, Ownrshp: NYSE, Stk Sym: VEN, Sales ($M): 2,017.3, Fiscal End: 1/95; Julian Seeherman, Chmn & CEO, Philip G. Otto, Pres, Cliff J. Campeau, SVP Mktng, Eugene Caldwell, CFO

VentureCom Inc. 215 First St, Cambridge MA 02142 USA; 617/661-1230, Fax: 617/577-1607, Co Email: info@vci.com, Focus: Embedded UNIX software tools, Prdts: Component Integrator 2.3, Ownrshp: PVT, Founded: 1980, Empl: 30, Myron Zimmermann, CTO, Email: myron@vci.com; Michael Dexter-Smith, CEO, Email: mds@vci.com; Eric Pickett, Mktng Coord, Email: eric@vci.com

Verbatim Corp. 1200 W.T. Harris Blvd, Charlotte NC 28262 USA; 704/547-6500, Focus: Magnetic media, Ownrshp: Sub. Mitsubishi Kasei, Japan, Founded: 1969, Empl: 1,500, Nicholas Hartery, Pres & CEO, Tatsuo Kunori, SVP, Michael Korizno, VP NA Sales & Mktng, William Kopatich, VP Bus Dev, William Larson, SVP & CFO, Linda Healy

Verbex Voice Systems Inc. 1090 King Georges Post Rd, Bldg. 107, Edison NJ 08837-3701 USA; 908/225-5225, 800/275-8729 Fax: 908/225-7764, Web URL: txtdirect.net/verbex, Focus: Speech recognition software and hardware, Prdts: Listen for Windows, Speech Commander, Ownrshp: PVT, Founded: 1986, Larry Dooling, Pres & CEO, Jurgen C.H. Lemmermann, VP Ops, David Vetter, VP R&D, Eric R. Nahm, VP Mktng & Sales, David Friel

VeriFone Inc. 3 Lagoon Dr, Redwood City CA 94065-1561 USA; 415/591-6500, Fax: 415/598-5504, Web URL: verifone.com, Focus: Transaction automation systems, Ownrshp: NYSE, Stk Sym: VFI, Founded: 1981, Empl: 1,750, Sales ($M): 387.0, Fiscal End: 12/95; Hatim A. Tyabji, Chmn, Pres & CEO, Joseph M. Zaelit, VP & CFO, John A. Hinds, EVP, James A. Palmer, EVP Dev & Mfg, William R. Pape, SVP & CIO, Roger B. Bertman, VP & GM

Verilink Corp. 145 Baytech Dr, San Jose CA 95134 USA; 408/945-1199, 800/837-4546 Fax: 408/262-6260, Co Email: @verilink.com, Web URL: verilink.com, Focus: Integrated access devices, WAN access products for data/telecommunications, Prdts: Access System, Ownrshp: PVT, Founded: 1982, Empl: 150, Leigh Belden, Pres, Steve C. Taylor, Chmn, Edward Ip, CTO, James Regel, VP Sales & Mktng, Henry Tinker, VP Ops, Wendy Holder, Mktng Spec, Email: wendyh@verilink.com

Verisign Inc. PO Box 7030, Mountain View CA 94039-7030 USA; 415/961-7500, Fax: 415/961-7300, Web URL: verisign.com, Focus: Digtal IDs embedded in software, Web servers and clients, Ownrshp: PVT, Founded: 1995, Empl: 30, Stratton Sclavos, CEO

Veritas Software Corp. (VRTS), 1600 Plymouth St, Mountain View CA 94043-1232 USA; 415/335-8000, Fax: 415/335-8050, Co Email: @veritas.com, Web URL: veritas.com, Focus: Unix utility and storage management software, Prdts: Vista, Ownrshp: OTC, Stk Sym: VRTS, Founded: 1989, Empl: 87, Sales ($M): 24.1, Fiscal End: 12/95; Mark Leslie, Pres & CEO, Chuck House, SVP, Chris L. Dier, VP & CFO, Roger Klorese

VeriTest Inc. 3420 Ocean Park Blvd #2030, Santa Monica CA 90405 USA; 310/450-0062, Fax: 310/399-1760, Co Email: @veritest.com, Focus: System compatibility and performance testing, Ownrshp: PVT, Founded: 1987, Empl: 30, Steve Nemzer, Pres, Email: 70353.1763@compuserve.com; Martine Porter-Zasada, VP

Sales & Mktng

Verity Inc. 1550 Plymouth St, Mountain View CA 94043-1230 USA; 415/960-7600, Fax: 415/960-7698, Co Email: info@verity.com, Web URL: verity.com, Focus: Document retrieval products, Prdts: Top Developer's Toolkit, Topic Agents, Topic WebSearcher, Ownrshp: OTC, Stk Sym: VRTY, Founded: 1988, Empl: 200, Sales ($M): 10, Philippe F. Courtot, Chmn, Pres & CEO, Email: pcourtot@verity.com; Don McCauley, CFO, Email: don@verity.com; Marguerite Padovani, Email: mpadovani@verity.com

Vermont Creative Software Pinnacle Meadows, Richford VT 05476 USA; 802/848-7731, 800/848-1248 Fax: 802/848-3502, Co Email: @vtsoft.com, Focus: Programming tools, Prdts: Vermont HighTest, Vermont Views, Ownrshp: PVT, Founded: 1984, Empl: 40, Vince Taylor, Pres, Rich Douglass, CEO

Versit 50 Commerce Dr, Allendale NJ 07401 USA; 201/327-2308, 800/803-6240 Fax: 800/803-6241, Co Email: versit@cup.portal.com, Focus: Interoperability between computer and communications products, Ownrshp: Nonprofit, Founded: 1994

Vertex Communications Corp. PO Box 1277, 2600 N Longview St, Kilgore TX 75663 USA; 903/984-0555, Focus: Communications products, Ownrshp: OTC, Stk Sym: VTEX, Sales ($M): 65.0, Fiscal End: 9/95; J. Rex Vardeman, Chmn, Pres & CEO, A. Don Branum, SVP, William L. Anton, VP Mktng, James D. Carter, VP Fin

Vertex Industries Inc. 23 Carol St, PO Box 996, Clifton NJ 07014-0996 USA; 201/777-3500, Fax: 201/472-0814, Focus: Data collection systems, Prdts: Bridgenet, Ownrshp: OTC, Stk Sym: VETX, Founded: 1974, Empl: 37, Sales ($M): 4.0, Fiscal End: 7/94; James Q. Maloy, Chmn, Ronald C. Byer, Pres, Email: 73051.370@compuserve.com; Kevin Halloran, VP, Joseph Chirco, Dir Sales & Mktng

Vertisoft Systems Inc. 4 Embarcadero Ctr, #3470, San Francisco CA 94111-5980 USA; 415/956-5999, Fax: 415/956-5355, Focus: Utility software, Ownrshp: PVT, Founded: 1982, Anatoly Tikhman, Pres

Viacom New Media 1515 Broadway, New York NY 10036 USA; 212/258-6000, Fax: 212/258-6597, Web URL: viacomnewmedia.com, Focus: Multimedia software, Prdts: ZOOP, Nick Jr. Play Math!, Congo:The Movie-Descent into Zinj, Ownrshp: Sub Viacom, Founded: 1992, Empl: 200, Michele DiLorenzo, Pres, Roberta Jacobs, SVP Sales & Mktng, Stephen Gass, SVP Prod Dev, Betsy Vorce, SVP Comm

ViaGrafix Corp. 5 S Vann St, Pryor OK 74361 USA; 918/825-6700, 800/842-4723 Fax: 918/825-6744, Focus: PC training products, Ownrshp: PVT, Founded: 1990, Empl: 130, Sales ($M): 16.5, Fiscal End: 12/95; Mike Webster, CEO, Bob Webster, CFO, Doug McCabe, Com Dir, Email: 76774.3504@compuserve.com

VictorMaxx Technologies 510 Lake Cook Rd, #100, Deerfield IL 60016 USA; 708/267-0007, Fax: 708/267-0037, Focus: VR products and services, Prdts: CyberMaxx, Ownrshp: OTC, Stk Sym: VMAX, Founded: 1994, Empl: 30, Rick Currie, Pres, Kate Fagan, VP Sales, Max Minkoff, VP Tech, Email: max@mcs.com; Vanessa Dennen, Creative Mktng Spec, Email: cybrmaxx@aol.com

Video Electronics Standards Assoc. (VESA), 2150 N First St, #440, San Jose CA 95131-2029 USA; 408/435-0333, Fax: 408/435-8225, Co Email: @vesa.org, Focus: Promote PC graphics through improved standards, Ownrshp: Nonprofit, Founded: 1989, Empl: 180, Roger L. McKee, Managing Dir, Scott Vouri, Chmn, Janet L. Courtenay, Dir Mktng, Email: courtenay@vesa.com

VideoLabs Inc. 10925 Bren Rd E, Minneapolis MN 55343 USA; 612/988-0055, Fax: 612/988-0066, Co Email: videolabs@flexcam.com, Web URL: flexcam.com, Focus: Desktop video products, Prdts: FlexCam, Ownrshp: OTC, Stk Sym: VLABS, Founded: 1992, Empl: 25, Sales ($M): 8.1, Fiscal End: 12/95; Ward C. Johnson, Pres, Frank Broghammer, COO & CFO, Gary Campbell, VP Sales, Chris Smith, Mktng Mgr

VideoLan Technologies Inc. 100 Mallard Creek Rd, #250, Louisville KY 40207 USA; 502/895-4858, Fax: 502/895-1680, Focus: Multimedia solutions, Prdts: VL 2000, Ownrshp: OTC, Stk Sym: VLNT, Founded: 1994, Empl: 25, Vernon Jackson, Pres, John Haines, CEO, Peter Beck, COO, Bob Werner, VP, Jim Turner

VideoLogic Inc. 1001 Bayhill Dr #310, San Bruno CA 94066-3013 USA; 415/875-0606, Fax: 415/875-4167, Web URL: videologic.com, Focus: Video digitizers, compression and playback products, Prdts: Captivater Pro, Ownrshp: PVT, Founded: 1985, Empl: 200, Tony Maclaren, Pres, Paul McCabe, VP Sales, Brad Allen, Int'l Systems Coord, Lili McGirr, Mktng & PR Mgr

Videomedia Inc. 175 Lewis Rd #23, San Jose CA 95111 USA; 408/227-9977, 800/937-8526 Fax: 408/227-6707, Co Email: go videomedia@compuserve.com, Web URL: videomedia.com, Focus: Video editing products, Prdts: Animax, V-LAN, Oz, VLXi, Ownrshp: PVT, Founded: 1975, Empl: 55, Don Bennett, Pres, Email: dbennett@videomedia.com; Bill Stickney, VP Eng, Marc Harris, Email: mharris@videomedia.com

Videx Inc. 1105 NE Circle Blvd, Corvallis OR 97330-4285 USA; 541/758-0521, Fax: 541/752-5285, Co Email: @videx.com, Web URL: videx.com, Focus: Portable bar code readers, Prdts: Omni-Wand, DuraWand, TimeWand, Touch Probe, Bar Code Labeler, Ownrshp: PVT, Founded: 1979, Empl: 50, Andy Hilverda, Dir Mktng, Teresa Bodwell, Marcom Contact

VidTech Microsystems Inc. 1700 93rd Ln NE, Minneapolis MN 55449-4326 USA; 612/633-6000, Fax: 612/633-9164, Focus: Graphics accelerators, Prdts: FastMax, GraphMax, Ownrshp: PVT, Sean S. Nguyen, CEO, William C. Foster, COO

ViewCom Technology Int'l. 120 Lakeside Ave, #330, Seattle WA 98122-6552 USA; 206/4547374, Fax: 206/454-7273, Co Email: viewcom@aol.com, Focus: Closed-caption TV decoders, closed caption software for PCs, Prdts: Scriber, Telescriber, TV Reader, Ownrshp: PVT, Founded: 1991, Empl: 7, Rick Dortch, CEO

Viewlogic Systems Inc. 293 Boston Post Rd W, Marlboro MA 01752-4615 USA; 508/480-0881, Fax: 508/480-0882, Web URL: viewlogic.com, Focus: Computer-aided engineering software, Ownrshp: OTC, Stk Sym: VIEW, Founded: 1984, Empl: 561, Sales ($M): 121.0, Fiscal End: 12/95; Alain J. Hanover, Chmn & CEO, Gene Robinson, SVP Mktng & Sales, Lorne J. Cooper, SVP Eng & CTO, Ronald R. Benanto, SVP & CFO, David R. Coelho, SVP & Bus Dev, Ron Benanto

Viewpoint Datalabs Int'l. 625 S State St, Orem UT 84058 USA; 801/229-3000, 800/328-2738 Fax: 801/229-3300, Web URL: viewpoint.com, Focus: 3-D models for desktop design, Prdts: Z-Art, Founded: 1988, John Wright, Pres & CEO, Eliot Jacobsen, VP Fin, John Thomas, VP Ops, John Mellor, VP Bus Dev

ViewSonic Corp. 20480 Business Pkwy, Walnut CA 91789 USA; 909/869-7976, 800/888-8583 Fax: 909/468-3756, Focus: Monitors, Prdts: ViewSonic, Ownrshp: Sub. Keypoint Technology, Founded: 1987, Empl: 95, Sales ($M): 110, Fiscal End: 12/93; James Chu, Pres, Jerry Kanaly, VP Ops & CFO, Mark D. Gersh, Prod Mgr, Jeff Gilmore

Viking Components 11 Columbia, Laguna Hills CA 92656 USA; 714/643-7255, 800/338-2361 Fax: 714/643-7250, Focus: System enhancements for notebook and desktop computers, Glenn McCusker, Pres & CEO, David Tremblay, VP Sales, Shannon Biggs, VP Eng, Tom McKinley, VP Ops, Joe Stafford, CFO, Carl Golod, Mktng & Advert Mgr

VIM Inc. (VIM), 4201 N Lexington Ave, MS ARH251, Arden Hills MN 55126 USA; 612/482-4907, Focus: Forum for Control Data Systems computer customers, Ownrshp: Nonprofit, Founded: 1970, Empl: 188, Sandy Rowe, Coordinator

Virgin Interactive Entertainment 108061 Fitch Ave, Irvine CA 92614 USA; 714/833-8710, Fax: 714/833-8717, Web URL: vie.com, Focus: Computer and video games, Ownrshp: Sub Spelling Entertainment, Stk Sym: SP, Founded: 1987, Empl: 230, Martin

Alper, CEO

Virginia Systems Inc. 5509 W Bay Ct, Midlothian VA 23112 USA; 804/739-3200, Fax: 804/739-8376, Co Email: vasys@cris.com, Web URL: cris.com/~vasys, Prdts: Sonar, Ownrshp: PVT, Founded: 1984, Empl: 5, Sales ($M): 0.5, Philip Van Cleave, Pres, Margaret Ross, VP Mktng

Virtek Vision Corp. 450 Phillip St, Waterloo Ontario N2L 5J2 Canada; 519/746-7190, Fax: 519/746-3383, Co Email: @virtek.ca, Focus: Machine vision and pattern analysis, Prdts: LaserEdge, LeatherCam, TrussLine, Stk Sym: VRTK, Founded: 1986, Empl: 50, Sales ($M): 6.2, Fiscal End: 1/95; Norman B. Wright, Pres & CEO, Richard F. Delogu, VP Fin & CFO, Frank Tremblay, VP Eng, Susan Spencer McLean

Virtual I/O Inc. 1000 Lenora St, #600, Seattle WA 98121 USA; 206/382-7410, Fax: 206/382-8810, Co Email: info@vio.com, Web URL: vio.com, Focus: Headset displays, Ownrshp: PVT, Founded: 1993, Empl: 150, C. Gregory Amadon, Chmn & CEO, Linden Rhoads, Pres, Thomas D. Bowen, VP Mktng, Alex Peder, VP Sales

Virtual Media Works PO Box 70030, Sunnyvale CA 94086-0030 USA; 408/739-0301, Fax: 408/739-5551, Co Email: @vmworks.com, Web URL: vmworks.com, Focus: Multimedia CD-ROM software, Prdts: Virtual Tarot, Ownrshp: PVT, Founded: 1992, Jeff Manning, Pres, Email: jeff@vmworks.com; Catherine Cooper, VP Mktng, Email: cath@vmworks.com

Virtual Open Network Environment Corp. (V-ONE), 1803 Research Blvd, #305, Rockville MD 20850-3155 USA; 301/881-2297, Fax: 301/881-5377, Focus: Internet security and smart card products, Ownrshp: PVT, Founded: 1993, James F. Chen, Pres, Jieh-Shan Wang, CTO

Virtual Vineyards 170 State St #250, Los Altos CA 94022 USA; 415/917-5750, Web URL: virtualvin.com, Focus: Direct marketing of food and wine on the Internet, Prdts: Virtual Vineyards, Ownrshp: PVT, Founded: 1994, Empl: 12, Peter Granoff, Co-Founder, Email: corkdork@virtualvin.com; Robert Olson, Co-Founder, Email: rolson@virtualvin.com; Anne K. Delehunt, VP Mktng, Email: delehunt@virtualvin.com; Ruth Colombo, VP Eng, Email: rcolombo@virtualvin.com

Virtus Corp. 118 MacKenan Dr, #250, Cary NC 27511 USA; 919/467-9700, 800/847-8821 Fax: 919/460-4530, Co Email: info@virtus.com, Web URL: virtus.com, Focus: Desktop 3D tools for the Internet, Prdts: WalkThrough, Virtus VR, Alien Skin Textureshop, Ownrshp: PVT, Founded: 1990, Empl: 48, David A. Smith, Chmn & CEO, Email: david.smith@virtus.com; Ted Finch, VP Mktng, Email: ted.finch@virtus.com; Linda Watson, VP Prod Mgmt, Email: linda.watson@virtus.com; Richard Boyd, VP & GM Virtus Works, Email: richard.boyd@virtus.com; Frank boosman, VP & GM Virtus Studios, Email: frank.boosman@virtus.com; Ashley W. Sharp, Media Relations Mgr, Email: ashley.sharp@virtus.com

Visage Inc. 300 Griffin Brook Park Dr, Methuen MA 01844-1873 USA; 508/620-7100, Fax: 508/620-0273, Focus: Multimedia products, Ownrshp: PVT, Founded: 1984, Empl: 10, Sales ($M): 1.5, William Kantor, Pres & CEO

Vishay Intertechnology 63 Lincoln Hwy, Malvern PA 19355-2120 USA; 610/644-1300, Fax: 610/296-0657, Focus: Electronic components, Ownrshp: NYSE, Stk Sym: VSH, Founded: 1962, Empl: 14,200, Sales ($M): 1,224.4, Fiscal End: 12/95; Felix Zandman, Chmn, Donald G. Alfson, VP, Robert A. Freece, SVP, Henry V. Landau, VP

Visigenic Software 951 Mariner's Island Blvd #460, San Mateo CA 94404 USA; 415/286-1900, 800/632-2864 Fax: 415/286-2464, Focus: Components for database application developers, Roger Sippl, Pres & CEO

Visio Corp. 520 Pike St, #1800, Seattle WA 98101 USA; 206/521-4500, Fax: 206/521-4501, Focus: Graphics software, Prdts: Visio, Ownrshp: OTC, Stk Sym: VSIO, Founded: 1990, Empl: 150,

Sales ($M): 39.4, Fiscal End: 12/95; Jeremy Jaech, Pres, Ted Johnson, VP, Dave Walter, VP, Gary Gigot, VP Mktng, Marty Childberg, CFO

Vision Interactive Publishing 17865 Sky Park Cr, #J, Irvine CA 92714 USA; 714/833-1822, Fax: 714/833-3620, Focus: Publishes interactive multimedia entertainment products, Ownrshp: Sub. Vision Interactive UK, Stuart Kaye, Pres, Debbie Brajevich, VP Mktng

Vision Software Tools Inc. 505 Fourteenth St, #940, Oakland CA 94612 USA; 510/238-4100, Fax: 510/238-4101, Co Email: @visionsoft.com, Web URL: vision-soft.com, Focus: Tools for the development of client/server applications, Prdts: Vision Story-Board, VisionBuilder, Founded: 1991, Naren Bakshi, Chmn, Pres & CEO, Kevin Fletcher Tweedy, SVP, Steve Kruse, VP Sales & Mktng, Email: steve@visionsoft.com; David Harrington, VP Eng, Val Huber, VP & CTO

Vision's Edge Inc. 3491-11 Thomasville Rd #177, Tallahassee FL 32308 USA; 904/386-4573, 800/983-6337 Fax: 904/386-2594, Co Email: veiproduct@aol.com, Focus: XTensions developer, Founded: 1991, Empl: 18, Sales ($M): 1.5, Fiscal End: 12/95; Dacques Viker, Founder, Julie W. Roberts, Prod Mgr, Richard Peterson, VP, Sandra Coman, Dir Mktng

Visioneer 2860 W Bayshore Rd, Palo Alto CA 94303 USA; 415/812-6400, 800/787-7007 Fax: 415/855-9750, Co Email: @visioneer.com, Focus: Document management products, Prdts: PaperPort, PaperPort VX, Ownrshp: OTC, Stk Sym: VSNR, Founded: 1992, Sales ($M): 37.3, Fiscal End: 12/95; Mike McConnell, Pres & CEO, Dave Craft, VP Ops, Todd Basche, VP Eng, Marc Randolph, VP Mktng, Email: marc_randolph@visioneer.com; Geoff Darby, VP & CFO

Visionetics Int'l. 21311 Hawthorne Blvd #300, Torrance CA 90503 USA; 310/316-7940, Fax: 310/316-7457, Focus: Video and graphics products, Prdts: VIGA Window, PortaShow, MPEG Master, Ownrshp: PVT, Founded: 1982, Empl: 50, C.H. Lin, Pres

VisionTek Inc. 1175 Lakeside Dr, Gurnee IL 60031 USA; 708/360-7500, 800/726-9695 Fax: 708/360-7401, Co Email: @visiontek.com, Focus: PC and printer memory, Ownrshp: PVT, Founded: 1988, Empl: 300+, Sales ($M): 300+, Fiscal End: 12/95; Mark Polinsky, CEO, Allen Sutker, Chmn & Pres, Craig Gutmann, CFO, Scott Dauer, VP, Dan Rich, Dir MIS, Brian Abrahams, Dir Mktng, Email: brian_abrahams@visiontek.

Visionware 4500 Bohannon Dr, #280, Menlo Park CA 94025-1029 USA; 415/325-2113, 800/949-8474 Fax: 415/325-8710, Co Email: info@visionware.com, Focus: Unix-Windows integration software, Prdts: X Vision, PC-Connect, Ownrshp: Sub. VisionWare, UK, Founded: 1989, Empl: 130, Sales ($M): 12, Fiscal End: 12/94; Tony Denson, Pres, Chris Holmes, Pres US Div, Olin Reams, VP Sales, Caroline Logothesis, Email: caroline@visionware.com

VisiSoft Inc. 10800 Alpharetta Hwy, #537, Roswell GA 30076-1463 USA; 770/320-0077, Fax: 770/320-0450, Co Email: 73752.1223@compuserve.com, Focus: Network management software, Prdts: VisiNet, Ownrshp: PVT, Founded: 1984, Greg Goodall, Pres & CEO

Vista Controls 27825 Fremont Ct, Valencia CA 91355 USA; 805/257-4430, Fax: 805/257-4782, Focus: Control systems & telecom products for defense & aerospace, Ownrshp: PVT, Founded: 1984, Empl: 35, Sales ($M): 7, Fiscal End: 6/95; Ron Rambin, Pres, Richard Copra, Dir Mktng

Visual Edge Software Ltd. 3950 Cote Vertu, St-Laurent Quebec H4R 1V4 Canada; 514/332-6430, Fax: 514/332-5914, Web URL: vedge.com, Focus: Software development tools, Prdts: Object Bridge, Cross-Platform Toolset, Visual Action Toolset, Ownrshp: PVT, Founded: 1985, Empl: 70, Sales ($M): 65, Fiscal End: 12/95; Michael Foody, Pres, Email: mike@vedge.com; John Spencer, VP Bus Dev, Email: vecalif@attmail.com; Eric Rubin, Dir Prod Mktng, Email: erubin@holonet.com; Russell Ure, Dir Eng, Email: russell@vedge.com; Sharon Hunter, Marcom, Email: sharon@vedge.com

Visual Engineering Inc. 2025 Gateway Place, #318, San Jose CA 95110 USA; 408/452-0600, Fax: 408/452-0632, Co Email: info@ve.com, Focus: Presentation graphics, Ownrshp: PVT, Founded: 1983, Bob Glazebrook, Pres, Dave McMurdie, Email: dave@ve.com

Visual Information Development Inc. (VIDI), 136 W Olive Ave, Monrovia CA 91016 USA; 818/358-3936, Fax: 818/358-4766, Co Email: vidisales@aol.com, Focus: RenderMan enhancement software, Ownrshp: PVT, Nick Pavlovic, CEO

Visual Software Inc. 21731 Ventura Blvd, #310, Woodland Hills CA 91364-1845 USA; 818/593-3500, 800/881-4108 Fax: 213/593-3750, Co Email: @vissoft.com, Web URL: 3dplanet.com, Focus: Imaging and 3D graphics software, Prdts: Visual Reality, Ownrshp: Sub Micrografx, Founded: 1991, Empl: 30, Sales ($M): 6.4, Fiscal End: 12/95; Douglas Richard, CEO, Email: dougr@vissoft.com; John Halloran, Pres, Kevin A. Bromber, VP Sales, Serge Jonnaert, Prod Mktng Mgr, Sid Olkes, CFO

Visual World Inc. 511 Sir Francis Drake Blvd, #201, Greenbrae CA 94904 USA; 415/461-6696, Fax: 415/461-6690, Web URL: visualworld.com, Focus: Development software, Dan Kelly, Pres

VISystems Inc. 135 N Plano Rd #206, Richardson TX 75081-3827 USA; 214/960-8649, Fax: 214/458-1116, Focus: Transaction software for mainframes and workstations, Ownrshp: PVT, Founded: 1987, Empl: 45, Elhamy Kamel, Pres & CEO, Jim Henry, EVP

Vitesse Semiconductor Corp. 741 Calle Plano, Camarillo CA 93012 USA; 805/388-3700, Fax: 805/987-5896, Focus: Gallium arsenic (GaAs) digital ICs, Ownrshp: OTC, Stk Sym: VTSS, Founded: 1987, Empl: 215, Sales ($M): 42.9, Fiscal End: 9/95; Louis Tomasetta, Pres & CEO, Bob Phillips, VP Ops, Neil Rappaport, VP Sales, Ira Deyhimy, VP Prod Dev, Gene Hovanec, VP & CFO

Vivid Image Co. 2311 W 205th St, #103, Torrance CA 90501 USA; 310/618-0274, Fax: 310/618-1982, Co Email: net.vividimage@vividimage.com, Focus: Developer and manufacturer of high-speed controllers for digital image production, Prdts: ImageBox & ImageMaster, Ownrshp: PVT, Founded: 1990, Nicholas Vassilakis, Pres & Chmn, George J. Feiss, CFO, Andy Schnoebelen, EVP, Alfredo Donovan, Dir Sales

Vividata Inc. 1250 Addison St, #213A, Berkeley CA 94702-1700 USA; 510/841-6400, Fax: 510/841-9661, Co Email: info@vividata.com, Web URL: vividata.com, Focus: Unix imaging software, Prdts: ScanShop, PostShop, FaxShop, OCR Shop, Ownrshp: PVT, Empl: 10, Sales ($M): 1.5, Mark Liebman, Pres, Email: mark@vividata.com; Alex Cheng, EVP, Email: alex@vividata.com

Vivo Media 115 Northwest First Ave, #201, Portland OR 97209 USA; 503/223-9644, Fax: 503/223-9714, Web URL: vivomedia.com, Focus: Online marketing and service, Shannon Voigt, Pres, Email: shannon@govivo.com; Chris Sallquist, Creative Dir, Email: chris@govivo.com; Brad Lyons, Email: brad@vivomedia.com

VLSI Research Inc. 1754 Technology Dr, #117, San Jose CA 95110 USA; 408/453-8844, Fax: 408/437-0608, Focus: Semiconductors, semiconductor manufacturing and VLSI systems information, Ownrshp: PVT, Founded: 1976, Empl: 18, Sales ($M): 1.3, Jerry D. Hutcheson, CEO, G. Dan Hutcheson, Pres, Richard J. Dexter, VP

VLSI Technology Inc. 1109 McKay Dr, San Jose CA 95131 USA; 408/434-3000, Fax: 408/263-2511, Focus: High-performance computer chips, Ownrshp: OTC, Stk Sym: VLSI, Founded: 1979, Empl: 2,400, Sales ($M): 719.9, Fiscal End: 12/95; Alfred J. Stein, Chmn & CEO, Donald L. Ciffone, VP, L. Don Maulsby, VP WW Sales, Gregory K. Hinckley, VP & CFO, Barbara S. Kalkis, Dir Corp Com

VMark Software Inc. 50 Washington St, Westboro MA 01581-1021 USA; 508/366-3888, Fax: 508/366-3669, Web URL: vmark.com, Focus: Database software, Ownrshp: OTC, Stk Sym: VMRK, Founded: 1984, Empl: 456, Sales ($M): 68.4, Fiscal End: 12/95; Robert M. Morrill, Pres & CEO, James K. Walsh, VP & COO, Thomas M. Palka, VP WW Mktng, Andrew Ridgers, VP Eng & Dev, Charles F. Kane, VP & CFO, Peter L. Fiore, VP Corp Mktng, Email: pfiore@vmark.com

VME Microsystems Int'l. Corp. 12090 S Memorial Pkwy, Huntsville AL 35803 USA; 205/880-0444, 800/322-3616 Fax: 205/882-0859, Focus: VMEbus board products, Ownrshp: PVT, Founded: 1986, Empl: 210, Sales ($M): 24, Fiscal End: 9/95; Carroll Williams, Pres

VocalTec Inc. 157 Veterans Dr, Northvale NJ 07647 USA; 201/768-9400, Fax: 201/768-8893, Web URL: vocaltec.com, Focus: Internet voice communication software and hardware, Prdts: Internet Phone, Internet Wave, VocalChat, Ownrshp: PVT, Founded: 1989, Elon A. Ganor, Chmn & CEO, Ami Tal, COO, Lior Haramaty, VP Tech Mktng, Daniel Nissan, VP Sales & Mktng, Yahal Zilka, CFO, Nancy Scott, Email: nancy@vocaltec.com

Voice Pilot Technologies Inc. 9200 S Dadeland Blvd #304, Miami FL 33156 USA; 305/670-0807, Fax: 305/670-8009, Focus: Voice dictation software, Prdts: VoiceType, Ownrshp: PVT, Richard Grant, Pres

Voice Processing Corp. One Main St, Cambridge MA 02142 USA; 617/494-0100, Fax: 617/494-4970, Web URL: vpro.com, Focus: Automated speech recognition systems for over the telephone use, Founded: 1983, Kelli V. Smith

Voice-it Software Inc. #210-10524 King George Hwy, Surrey BC V3T 2X2 Canada; Focus: Interactive voice response software, Prdts: Tele-Order, Ownrshp: Sub. Voice-it Technologies, Stk Sym: VT

Voicetek Corp. 19 Alpha Rd, Chelmsford MA 01824-4175 USA; 508/250-9393, Fax: 508/250-9378, Focus: Voice processing products, Prdts: Generations, Ownrshp: PVT, Founded: 1981, Empl: 115, Sheldon Dinkes, Pres & CEO, Scott Ganson, VP Sales, Catherine Jaspersohn, Dir Marcom

Voyager Company 578 Broadway, #406, New York NY 10012 USA; 212/431-5199, Fax: 212/431-5799, Focus: CD-ROM software, Ownrshp: PVT, Founded: 1984, Empl: 70, Bob Stein, Publisher

Voysys Corp. 48634 Milmont Dr, Fremont CA 94538 USA; 510/252-1100, 800/786-9797 Fax: 510/252-1101, Co Email: @voysys.com, Focus: Voice transaction applications for small & medium companies, Prdts: Voysystem, VoysAccess, Ownrshp: PVT, Founded: 1986, Empl: 76, Donald Heitt, Chmn & CEO, Barry Obrand, Pres, Michael Seto, VP Mktng, Paul Twombly, VP Tech, Ashlie Bryant, Marcom Mgr, Email: abryant@voysys.com

VRex Inc. 8 Skyline Dr, Hawthorne NY 10532 USA; 914/345-8877, Fax: 914/345-9552, Focus: Notebook PCs and 3D displays, Prdts: CyberBook, Ownrshp: PVT, Sadeg M. Faris, Pres, Suzanne K. McBride, VP

VST Power Systems 1620 Sudbury Rd, #3, Concord MA 01742 USA; 508/287-4600, Fax: 508/287-4068, Focus: Macintosh power products, Ownrshp: PVT, Vincent Fedele, Pres, Susan McNeff

VTEL 108 Wild Basin Rd, Austin TX 78746 USA; 512/314-2700, 800/856-8835 Fax: 512/314-2792, Focus: Videoconferencing products, Prdts: Enterprise Product Series, Ownrshp: OTC, Stk Sym: VTEL, Founded: 1985, Empl: 300, Sales ($M): 54.2, Fiscal End: 1994; Glenn A. Pierce, Pres & COO, Dick Moeller, CEO, Rod Bond, CFO, Tom Stevenson, VP Mktng, Sheri Goodwin, PR Mgr

Vycor Corp. 5411 Berwyn Rd, College Park MD 20740 USA; 301/220-4450, 800/888-9267 Fax: 301/220-0727, Co Email: info@vycor.com/vycor, Web URL: vycor.com/vycor, Focus: C/S tools, Prdts: DP Umbrella SQL, David Mitchell, Pres & CEO, Alyce J. Menton, Dir Mktng

Wacom Technology Corp. 501 SE Columbia Shores Blvd #300,

Vancouver WA 98661 USA; 360/750-8882, Focus: Digitizers and pen input devices, Ownrshp: Sub. Wacom Co. Ltd., Japan, Founded: 1983, Empl: 446, Sales ($M): 123 WW, Fiscal End: 3/95; Masahiko Yamada, Pres, Joe Deal, VP Sales & Mktng, Jeff Nichols, Sr Mktng Mgr

Waggener Edstrom 6915 SW Macadam Ave, #300, Portland OR 97219 USA; 503/245-0905, Fax: 503/244-7261, Co Email: @wagged.com, Focus: PR and marketing communications, Ownrshp: PVT, Empl: 67, Melissa Waggener, Pres, Pam Edstrom, SVP

WAIS Inc. 690 5th St, San Francisco CA 94107 USA; 415/356-5400, Fax: 415/356-5444, Co Email: @wais.com, Web URL: wais.com, Focus: Information publishing software for networks, Prdts: WAISserver, Ownrshp: PVT, Empl: 30, Brewster Kahle, Pres, Bruce Gilliat, VP Sales & Mktng, John Duhring, VP Bus Dev, Dia Cheney, Email: dia@wais.com

Walker Interactive Systems Inc. 303 Second St, San Francisco CA 94107 USA; 415/495-8811, Fax: 415/957-1711, Web URL: walker.com, Focus: Financial management software, Prdts: Tamaris C/S, Walker Client-GUI, Ownrshp: OTC, Stk Sym: WALK, Founded: 1973, Empl: 400, Sales ($M): 58.9, Fiscal End: 12/95; Leonard Y. Liu, Chmn, Pres & CEO, Darrell P. Trimble, VP Mktng, Bruce Pollock, CFO, Dave Parrish, SVP Amer Ops, Linda L. Vetter, SVP R&D, Courtney Zoog, PR Mgr, Email: cxz@walker.com

Walker Richer & Quinn Inc. (WRQ), 1500 Dexter Ave N, Seattle WA 98109-3051 USA; 206/217-7100, Fax: 206/217-0293, Co Email: @wrq.com, Web URL: wrq.com, Focus: Communication software, Prdts: Reflection, Ownrshp: PVT, Founded: 1981, Empl: 425, Sales ($M): 111.6, Fiscal End: 12/95; Doug Walker, Pres, Craig McKibben, VP Eng, Kevin Klustner, VP Sales & Mktng, Gerry Smith, CFO, Andrea Ostlund, Email: andreao@wrq.com

Wall Data Inc. 11332 NE 122nd Way, Kirkland WA 98034-6931 USA; 206/814-9255, 800/755-9255 Fax: 206/814-4300, Web URL: walldata.com, Focus: Connectivity products, Prdts: Rumba, Ownrshp: OTC, Stk Sym: WALL, Founded: 1982, Empl: 654, Sales ($M): 110.7, Fiscal End: 12/95; James Simpson, Chmn, Pres & CEO, John R. Wall, EVP, Gary A. Land, VP Sales & Mktng, Michael Rogers, VP Channel Sales, Kerry Palmer, VP & CFO, Angelo Grestoni

Wallace Computer Services Inc. 4600 W Roosevelt Rd, Hillside IL 60162-2079 USA; 708/449-8600, 800/323-8447 Fax: 708/449-1161, Focus: Computer services and supplies, Ownrshp: NYSE, Stk Sym: WCS, Founded: 1961, Empl: 3,765, Sales ($M): 862.3, Fiscal End: 7/96; Theodore Dimitriou, Chmn, Robert J. Cronin, Pres & CEO, Michael O. Duffield, SVP Ops, Michael J. Halloran, VP & CFO, Michael T. Leatherman, SVP CIO

Walnut Creek CDROM 4041 Pike Ln, #D-891, Concord CA 94520 USA; 510/674-0783, 800/786-9907 Fax: 510/674-0821, Co Email: orders@cdrom.com, Web URL: cdromcom, Focus: CD-ROM software, Prdts: CICA Windows, Simtel for DOS, QR2! Ham Radio, Ownrshp: PVT, Founded: 1991, Empl: 30, Robert A. Bruce, Pres, Email: rab@cdrom.com; Jack Velte, VP, Email: velte@cdrom.com; Carsie McCarty, Email: carsie@cdrom.com

Wang Laboratories Inc. 600 Technology Park Dr, Billerica MA 01821-4130 USA; 508/459-5000, Fax: 508/967-6045, Web URL: wang.com, Focus: Image software and systems integration, Ownrshp: AMEX, Stk Sym: WAN, Founded: 1951, Empl: 5,900, Sales ($M): 1,099.8, Fiscal End: 6/96; Joseph M. Tucci, Chmn & CEO, Donald P. Casey, Pres, David I. Goulden, SVP, David J. Hennessey, VP, Franklyn A. Caine, EVP & CFO

Washington Laboratories Ltd. 7560 Lindbergh Dr, Gaithersburg MD 20879-5414 USA; 301/417-0220, Fax: 301/417-9069, Focus: Compliance testing, product approvals and EMC services, Ownrshp: PVT, Ray Hammonds, Lab Mgr

Washington Software & Digital Media Alliance 3101 Northup Way, Bellevue WA 98024 USA; 206/889-8880, Fax: 206/889-8014, Web URL: wsdma.org, Focus: Promotes Washington

software industry, Ownrshp: Nonprofit, Founded: 1984, Empl: 750, Kathy Wilcox, Exec Dir

Watcom 1450 E American Ln, #1850, Schaumburg IL 60173 USA; 847/706-9600, Fax: 847/706-9696, Focus: Database software, Ownrshp: PVT

Watergate Software Inc. 2000 Powell St, #1200, Emeryville CA 94608 USA; 510/654-5182, Fax: 510/653-4784, Co Email: @ws.com, Web URL: ws.com, Focus: PC diagnostic software, Prdts: PC-Doctor, PC-Doctor Remote Control, Ownrshp: PVT, Founded: 1993, Empl: 10, Sales ($M): 2.0, Fiscal End: 12/95; Steve Siltanen, Pres, Email: steve_s@ws.com; Marie Travers, Mktng Assist

Watermark Software Inc. 15 3rd Ave, Burlington MA 01803-4416 USA; 617/229-2600, Fax: 617/229-2989, Focus: Document imaging software, Ownrshp: Sub Filenet, Founded: 1993, David Skok, Pres & CEO, Kevin Lach, Dir Mktng

Wave Research Inc. 2261 Fifth St, Berkeley CA 94710 USA; 510/704-3900, Fax: 510/704-3950, Co Email: wavw.usa@applelink.com, Web URL: waveresearch.com/wave, Focus: Network management software, Prdts: FileWave, Ownrshp: PVT, Founded: 1991, Empl: 20, Sales ($M): 2.5, Francois Lagae, Pres & CEO, Email: flagae@waveresearch.com; Bill McConnell, Tech Svcs Mgr, Email: bmcconnell@waveresearch.com; Jack Martin, Sales Mgr, Email: jmartin@waveresearch.com

Wavefront Technologies Inc. 530 E Montecito St, Santa Barbara CA 93103 USA; 805/962-8117, Fax: 805/963-0410, Co Email: @wti.com, Focus: 3D graphic software, Prdts: The Visualizer, Ownrshp: OTC, Stk Sym: WAVE, Founded: 1984, Empl: 151, Sales ($M): 27.7, Fiscal End: 12/94; Michael S. Noling, Pres & CEO, Martin Pleahn, EVP, David P. Swan, VP Sales & Mktng

Wayzata Technology Inc. 21 N 4th St, Grand Rapids MN 55744-2719 USA; 218/326-0597, 800/735-7321 Fax: 218/326-0598, Co Email: wayzatatec@aol.com, Web URL: wayzata-tech.com, Focus: CD-ROM software and information, Ownrshp: PVT, Founded: 1989, Empl: 14, Mark Engelhardt, CEO, Email: markengelhardt@wayzata.com; Denny Gibbons, Dir Sales, Email: dennygibbons@wayzata.com

Weber Group Inc. 101 Main St, Cambridge MA 02142 USA; 617/661-7900, Fax: 617/661-0024, Co Email: lweber@weber-grp.com, Web URL: webergroup.com, Focus: PR and marketing communications, Ownrshp: PVT, Founded: 1987, Empl: 89, Cathy Lugbauer, EVP, Email: clugbauer@webergroup.com; William R. Davies, SVP, Email: bdavies@webergroup.com; Lois Kelly, SVP, Email: lkelly@webergroup.com; Larry Weber, Pres, Email: lweber@webergroup.com; Laura Antonucci, VP, Email: lantonucci@webergroup.com

Webnet Technologies Inc. 2551 Tigertail Ave, Miami FL 33133 USA; 305/858-7155, Fax: 305/285-9654, Focus: Internet email systems, Prdts: ewan, Ownrshp: PVT

WebVision Inc. 21550 Oxnard St, Woodland Hills CA 91367 USA; 818/596-2142, Fax: 818/716-2617, Co Email: info@webvision.com, Web URL: webvision.com, Focus: Internet services and products, Ownrshp: PVT

Weitek Corp. 1060 E Arques Ave, Sunnyvale CA 94086 USA; 408/738-8400, Fax: 408/738-1185, Focus: Performance acceleration chips and systems, Ownrshp: OTC, Stk Sym: WWTK, Founded: 1981, Empl: 83, Sales ($M): 17.6, Fiscal End: 12/95; Arthur J. Collmeyer, Chmn, David L. Gellatly, Pres & CEO, Howard J. Gopen, VP Ops, Alan Samuels, VP & CTO

Welch Allyn Inc. 4619 Jordan Rd, Skaneateles Falls NY 13153-0187 USA; 315/685-8945, Fax: 315/685-3172, Focus: Bar code and magnetic strip readers, Ownrshp: PVT, Founded: 1915, Empl: 1,400, William F. Allyn, Pres, Kevin Jost, VP & GM Data Col Div, Richard Thomas, Info Svsc Mgr, Elizabeth Michalec, Marcom Mgr

Welty-Leger Corp. 333 Elm St, Dedham MA 02026-4530 USA; 617/461-8700, Fax: 617/461-0061, Focus: Warehouse/distribution center software and consulting, Prdts: M2 DCMS, Ownrshp:

PVT, Founded: 1987, Empl: 32, Bruce Welty, Pres, Jean-Pierre Leger, EVP, Jack Kennedy, VP Sales & Mktng

Wesson International Inc. 3001 Bee Caves Rd #200, Austin TX 78746-5561 USA; 512/328-0100, Fax: 512/328-7838, Web URL: wesson.com, Focus: Air traffic control simulations, Prdts: Air Traffic Controll, Tracon, Tower, Ownrshp: PVT, Founded: 1988, Empl: 16, Sales ($M): 2.1, Fiscal End: 12/95; Robert B. Wesson, Chmn & CEO, David E. Warner, Pres

Western Digital Corp. 8105 Irvine Ctr Dr, Irvine CA 92718 USA; 714/932-5000, Fax: 714/932-6293, Web URL: wdc.com, Focus: Semiconductors, subsystems and intelligent disk drives, Prdts: Caviar, Ownrshp: NYSE, Stk Sym: WDC, Founded: 1970, Empl: 7,647, Sales ($M): 2,865.2, Fiscal End: 6/96; Charles A. Haggerty, Chmn, Pres & CEO, Kathryn A. Braun, EVP Pers Stor, Kenneth E. Hendrickson, EVP Micro, David W. Schafer, EVP WW Sales, D. Scott Mercer, EVP & CFO, Brenda Bennett, Dir PR

Western Micro Technology 254 E Hacienda Ave, Campbell CA 95008-6617 USA; 408/379-0177, 800/338-1600 Fax: 408/341-4764, Co Email: @westernmicro.com, Web URL: westernmicro.com, Focus: Distributes computers and peripherals, Ownrshp: OTC, Stk Sym: WSTM, Founded: 1977, Empl: 103, Sales ($M): 106.5, Fiscal End: 12/95; P. Scott Munro, Pres & CEO, Email: smunro@westernmicro.com; Donald A. Cochran, VP Sales & Mktng, Email: dcochran@westernmicro.com; James Dorst, CFO, Cynthia S. Fujiwara, Marcom Mgr, Email: cfujiwar@westernmicro.com

Western Microwave Inc. 495 Mercury Dr, Sunnyvale CA 94086 USA; 408/738-2300, Focus: Microwave devices & components, Ownrshp: OTC, Stk Sym: WMIC, Founded: 1962, Empl: 40, Sales ($M): 2.5, Fiscal End: 9/94; Ibrahim Hefni, Pres & CEO

Western Pacific Data Systems 7590 Fay Ave, La Jolla CA 92037-4849 USA; 619/454-0028, 800/367-9737 Focus: Software for fasteners and logistics, Ownrshp: PVT, Founded: 1979, Empl: 100, Margaret Jackson, Pres, Neil Hadfield, CFO & Tech Dir

Western Telematic Inc. 5 Sterling, Irvine CA 92718-2517 USA; 714/586-9950, Fax: 714/583-9514, Co Email: westtel@netcom.com, Focus: Connectivity products, Ownrshp: PVT, Founded: 1964, Empl: 60, David Morrison, Pres, Nancy Dodd, Sales Mgr, Kimberly Copple, Marcom Mgr

Westing Software 134 Redwood Ave, Corte Madera CA 94925 USA; 415/945-3870, Fax: 415/945-3877, Co Email: westing@aol.com, Focus: Software for research problems, Prdts: CARD, John J. Osborn, Pres, Nan Wieser, VP Mktng, Renee Hart, Mktng Mgr

Westinghouse Electric Corp. Westinghouse Bldg., Gateway Ctr, Pittsburgh PA 15222 USA; 412/244-2000, Fax: 412/642-2466, Focus: Electronic products, Ownrshp: NYSE, Stk Sym: WX, Founded: 1886, Sales ($M): 6,296.0, Fiscal End: 12/95; Michael Jordan, CEO

Westrex Int'l. 25 Denby Rd, Boston MA 02134-1694 USA; 617/254-1200, Fax: 617/254-6848, Focus: POS terminals, printers and peripherals, Ownrshp: PVT, Founded: 1978, Don Emello, Pres, Joe Grimaldi, Dir Sales & Mktng

WexTech Systems Inc. 310 Madison Ave, #905, New York NY 10017 USA; 212/949-9595, 800/939-8324 Fax: 212/949-4007, Co Email: 71333.1400@compuserve.com, Focus: Utilities for Microsoft Word, Prdts: Doc-To-Help, Smooth Scaling, Quicture, Ownrshp: PVT, Steven S. Wexler, Pres, Email: 72467.47@compuserve.com; Paul Neshamkin, Dir Tech Support, Email: 70740.3356@compuserve.com; Julianne Sharer, Dir App Dev, Email: 72460.1761@compuserve.com; Jennifer Hitchner, Dir Sales, J.D. King, Dir Marcom, Email: 102124.1525@compuserve.com

White Pine Software Inc. 40 Simon St, #201, Nashua NH 03060-3043 USA; 603/886-9050, Fax: 603/886-9051, Co Email: info@wpine.com, Web URL: wpine.com, Focus: Software, terminal emulation, desktop video conferencing and internet products,

Prdts: eXodus, Enhanced CU-See Me, 5PM, Ownrshp: PVT, Founded: 1984, Empl: 90, Fiscal End: 12/95; Howard Berke, Pres & CEO, Carl Koppel, VP Sales, Kilko Caballero, CTO, Email: sroche@wpine.com; Dave Bundy, VP Eng, Forrest Milkowski, Dir Prod Mktng, Tracy Specht, PR Mgr, Email: tracy@wpine.com

Wildfire Communications Inc. 20 Maguire Rd, Lexington MA 02173 USA; 617/674-1500, 800/94533473 Fax: 617/674-1501, Co Email: info@wildfire.com, Web URL: wildfire.com, Focus: Computer-assisted telephony, Prdts: Electronic Assistant, Founded: 1991, Bill Warner, Founder & CEO, Joseph B. Lassiter III, Pres, Nicholas C. d'Arbeloff, VP Mktng, Leslie Anderson

Williams & Macias Inc. 1863 1st St, Cheney WA 99004-1967 USA; 509/458-6312, Fax: 509/623-4276, Focus: Utility software, Ownrshp: PVT, Founded: 1985, Empl: 4, Sales ($M): 0.3, William Williams, Pres, Mark Macias, CTO

Willowbrook Technologies Inc. 400 N Rivermede, #100, Concord Ontario L4K 3R5 Canada; 905/660-8795, Fax: 905/660-8768, Focus: Products for small offices and home offices, Prdts: E-Z Office, Adam Griff, Pres, Michael Garbe, CEO

Wilson WindowWare Inc. 2701 California Ave SW, #212, Seattle WA 98116 USA; 206/938-1740, 800/762-8383 Fax: 206/935-7129, Co Email: support@windowware.com, Web URL: windowware.com, Focus: Software for Windows automation, Prdts: WinBatch, WinEdit, Address Manager, Ownrshp: PVT, Founded: 1987, Empl: 10, Sales ($M): 3, Morrie Wilson, Pres & CEO, Email: morriew@windowware.com; Nancy Wilson, VP, James Stiles, Prod Mgr, Email: jwstiles@halcyon.com; Jim Stiles, Prod Mgr

Wind River Systems Inc. 1010 Atlantic Ave, Alameda CA 94501 USA; 510/748-4100, 800/545-9463 Fax: 510/814-2010, Web URL: wrs.com, Focus: Real-time OS, Prdts: VxWorks, Ownrshp: OTC, Stk Sym: WIND, Founded: 1981, Empl: 208, Sales ($M): 44.0, Fiscal End: 1/96; Jerry L. Fiddler, Chmn, Ronald A. Abelmann, Pres & CEO, Robert L. Wheaton, VP Sales, David Wilner, CTO, Richard W. Kraber, VP & CFO, De Anna Mekwunye, Corp Com

Windows User Group Network (WUGNET), PO Box 1967, Media PA 19063 USA; 215/565-1861, Fax: 215/565-7106, Focus: Users of Windows and Presentation Manager, Ownrshp: Nonprofit, Founded: 1988, Empl: 4,000, Howard Sobel, Exec Dir

WinSales Inc. 3605 132nd Ave SE, #312, Bellevue WA 98006 USA; 206/747-2464, Fax: 206/747-2955, Focus: Contact management software, Ownrshp: PVT, Torrey Russell

Winsted Corp. 10901 Hampshire Ave S, Minneapolis MN 55438-2385 USA; 612/944-9050, Fax: 612/944-1546, Focus: Computer furniture, Ownrshp: PVT, Founded: 1963, Empl: 52, Sales ($M): 10, Charles Johnson, Pres, Gerald Hoska, VP, Wayne Cook, Sales Dir, Randy Smith

WinWay Corp. 5431 Auburn Blvd #398, Sacramento CA 95841-2801 USA; 916/965-7878, Fax: 916/965-7879, Focus: Job interview software, Prdts: WinWay Resume, Ownrshp: PVT, Founded: 1991, Erez Carmel, Pres

Wireless Access Inc. 2101 Tasman Dr, Santa Clara CA 95054 USA; 408/653-1555, Co Email: @waccess.com, Focus: Wireless products, Ownrshp: PVT, Greg Reyes, Pres & CEO, Gary Hermansen, VP Sales & Mktng, Email: garyh@waccess.com

Wireless Logic Inc. 2021 N Capitol Ave, San Jose CA 95132 USA; 408/262-1876, Fax: 408/262-2903, Ownrshp: PVT, Founded: 1992, John Lee, Pres & CEO, Andrew Varadi, EVP, Daniel Babitch, VP Eng

WizardWorks 3850 Annapolis Ln N #100, Minneapolis MN 55447-5443 USA; 612/559-5140, Fax: 612/559-5126, Web URL: wizardworks.com, Focus: PC productivity and entertainment software, Ownrshp: PVT, Founded: 1990, Empl: 32, Sales ($M): 17, Fiscal End: 12/95; Robert Armstrong, Pres, Paige Carlson, Dir Mktng, Dave Blum, CFO

Wohl Associates 915 Montgomery Ave, #309, Narberth PA 19072-1501 USA; 610/667-4842, Fax: 610/667-3081, Web URL:

wohl.com, Focus: Office automation, desktop computing and end user computing consulting, Ownrshp: PVT, Founded: 1984, Empl: 3, Amy Wohl, Pres, Email: amy@wohl.com

Wolfram Research Inc. 100 Trade Ctr Dr, Champaign IL 61820-7237 USA; 217/398-0700, Fax: 217/398-0747, Co Email: @wri.com, Focus: Mathematical software for microcomputers, Prdts: Mathematica, Ownrshp: PVT, Founded: 1987, Empl: 130, Stephen Wolfram, Pres, Prem Chawla, COO, Jane O. Rich, PR Mgr, Email: rich@wri.com

WordMark International Corp. 101 Park Ctr Plaza, #1111, San Jose CA 95113-2238 USA; 408/975-1100, 800/835-2400 Fax: 408/975-1111, Co Email: wordmark@netcom.com, Focus: Unix word processing and database software, Prdts: WordMark Classic, uniVerse, LinkMark, Ownrshp: PVT, Founded: 1980, Empl: 25+, Jeffrey Weidler, Pres & CEO, Jeff Jakus, VP Sales & COO

WordTech Systems Inc. 1590 Solano Way, Unit C, Concord CA 94520-5300 USA; 510/689-1200, 800/228-3295 Fax: 510/689-1263, Focus: Artificial intelligence, Prdts: VP Expert, Ownrshp: PVT, Founded: 1982, Empl: 25, Sales ($M): 1.0, Fiscal End: 12/94; David B. Miller, Pres & CEO, Lori Mankin, VP Mktng & Sales, Bill Hess, Prod Mgr

Workflow Technologies Inc. 15802 N 50th St, Scottsdale AZ 85254-1684 USA; 602/867-8078, Fax: 602/867-2679, Focus: Lotus Notes software, Prdts: Innovation Customer Management, Innovation Workflow Processing, Ownrshp: PVT, Founded: 1992, Dale Reynolds, Pres, Elen Reynolds, Dir Sale

Workgroup Solutions 76 Blanchard Rd, Burlington MA 01803 USA; 617/229-9000, Fax: 617/229-9991, Focus: Develops ECAD and MCAD data management tool integrations, Terri Delfino-Benado, Mktng Mgr

Working Software Inc. PO Box 1844, Santa Cruz CA 95061-1844 USA; 408/423-5696, 800/229-9675 Fax: 408/423-5699, Co Email: 76004.2072@compuserve.com, Focus: Word processing utilities, Prdts: QuickLetter, Ownrshp: PVT, Founded: 1985, Empl: 8, Dave Johnson, Pres

World Computer Graphics Assoc. (WCGA), 6121 Lincoln Rd, #302, Alexandria VA 22312 USA; 703/642-3050, Fax: 703/642-1663, Co Email: 71064.1116@compuserve.com, Focus: Association for computer graphics industry, Ownrshp: Nonprofit, Founded: 1981, Empl: 13, Caby Smith, Pres & Exec Dir, Joyce Annecillo, Secretary & Treas

World Future Society (WFS), 7910 Woodmont Ave, #450, Bethesda MD 20814 USA; 301/656-8274, Fax: 301/951-0394, Web URL: wfs.org, Focus: Clearinghouse for ideas about the future, Ownrshp: Nonprofit, Founded: 1966, Empl: 30,000, Edward Cornish, Pres

World Library Inc. 2809 Main St, Irvine CA 92714-5901 USA; 714/756-9500, 800/443-0238 Fax: 714/756-9511, Focus: CD-ROM text software, Ownrshp: PVT, Founded: 1989, Empl: 30, Robert Hustwit, Co-founder, William Hustwit, Co-founder

World Ready Software 123 Townsend St, #636, San Francisco CA 93232 USA; 415/957-1300, Fax: 415/957-1314, Co Email: 73232.1100@compuserve.com, Focus: Multi-lingual language software, Ownrshp: PVT, Founded: 1993, Empl: 10, David Greco, Pres

World Software Corp. 124 Prospect St, Ridgewood NJ 07450 USA; 201/444-3228, 800/962-6360 Fax: 201/444-9065, Focus: Document management software, Prdts: WORLDOX, Extend-A-File Plus, Ownrshp: PVT, Founded: 1988, Empl: 15, Thomas W. Burke, Pres, Kristina Burke, VP

Worldata 5200 Town Ctr Cr, Boca Raton FL 33486 USA; 407/393-8200, Fax: 407/368-8345, Focus: List broker for the microcomputer industry, Ownrshp: PVT, Founded: 1975, Empl: 75, Sales ($M): 30, Fiscal End: 12/92; Roy Schwedelson, CEO, Email: rschwedelson@worldata.com; Helene Schwedelson, COO, Email: hschwedelson@worldata.com

Worlds Inc. 510 Third St, San Francisco CA 94107 USA; 415/281-4878, Fax: 415/285-9483, Web URL: worlds.net, Focus: Simulation/VR software for 3D worlds, Prdts: WorldsWare, LifeForm, AlphaWorld, Worlds Chat, Ownrshp: PVT, Founded: 1994, Empl: 100, Dave Gobel, Pres, Donald Fowler, CEO, Greg Vandendries, VP Sales & Mktng, Cole Larson, CTO, Marco DeMiroz, CFO

WorldSoft 14234 Saratoga-Sunnyvale Rd, #1, Saratoga CA 95070 USA; 408/867-6757, 800/225-9299 Fax: 408/867-4875, Co Email: @worldsoft.com, Focus: Word processing and DTP software, Prdts: WorldWrite, Ownrshp: PVT, Founded: 1984, Empl: 20, Bennett Kaplan, CEO, Paul Kewene-Hite, Pres, Gabi Miro, Dir SW Dev, Dan Cook, Prod Mgr, Email: dan_cook@worldsoft.com

Worthington Data Solutions 3004 Mission St, #220, Santa Cruz CA 95060 USA; 408/458-9938, 800/345-4220 Focus: Bar code products, Ownrshp: PVT, Hall Worthington, Pres

Wright Line Inc. 160 Gold Star Blvd, Worcester MA 01606 USA; 508/852-4300, Fax: 508/853-8904, Focus: Computer furniture systems, Ownrshp: PVT, Founded: 1934, Empl: 400, Philip Burkhart, Pres, George Schwarz, VP Sales, Brigitte A. LaMarche, Marcom Spec

Wright Strategies 816 Sea Turf Cr, Solana Beach CA 92075-2311 USA; 619/274-1047, Fax: 619/274-1728, Focus: Mobile data collection software, Prdts: OmniForm, Ownrshp: PVT, Jay Wright Jr., Pres

WritePro Corp. 43 S Highland Ave, Ossining NY 10562 USA; 914/762-1255, 800/755-1124 Fax: 914/762-5871, Co Email: writepro@pipeline.com, Focus: Creative writing tutorial software, Prdts: WritePro, FictionMaster, FirstAid for Writers, Ownrshp: PVT, Founded: 1989, Empl: 7, Sol Stein, Pres, Patricia Stein, VP

Wyle Laboratories 15370 Barranca Pkwy, PO Box 57008, Irvine CA 92619-7008 USA; 714/753-9953, Focus: Distributes electronic components and systems, Ownrshp: NYSE, Stk Sym: WYL, Founded: 1949, Empl: 1,000, Joseph A. Adamczyk, EVP

Wynd Communications Corp. 4251 S Higuera, Bldg 800, San Luis Obispo CA 93401 USA; 800/549-6000 Fax: 800/549-6001, Co Email: info@wynd.net, Focus: Mobile communications services, Prdts: WyndMail, Ownrshp: Sub Call America, Empl: 130, Jeff Buckingham, Pres, Dan Luis, VP, Email: dluis@wynd.net; King R. Lee, CEO

Wyse Technology Inc. 3471 N First St, San Jose CA 95134-1803 USA; 408/473-1200, 800/438-9973 Fax: 408/473-2080, Focus: Terminals, PCs, monitors and UNIX systems, Ownrshp: PVT, Founded: 1981, Empl: 2,000, Sales ($M): 478, Doug Chance, Pres & CEO, Morris Chang, Chmn, Chuck Comiso, SVP Mktng & Ops, Bruce McGeoch, SVP Eng & Tech

X-Rite Inc. 3100 44th St SW, Grandville MI 49418 USA; 616/534-7663, Fax: 616/534-8960, Focus: Color matching systems, Prdts: Digital Swatchbook, Ownrshp: OTC, Stk Sym: XRIT, Founded: 1958, Empl: 517, Sales ($M): 72.6, Fiscal End: 12/95; Ted Thompson, Chmn & CEO, Duane F. Kluting, VP & CFO, Jeffrey L. Smolinski, VP Ops, Joan Andrew, VP Sales & Mktng

X/Open Company Ltd. (X/Open), 1010 El Camino Real, #380, Menlo Park CA 94025 USA; 415/323-7992, Fax: 415/323-8204, Co Email: @xopen.org, Web URL: xopen.org, Focus: Consortium of computer users and vendors developing open, multi-vendor standards, Ownrshp: Nonprofit, Founded: 1984, Empl: 86, Geoffrey Morris, Pres & CEO, Allen Brown, COO, Mike Lambert, VP & CTO, Paul Daffern, CFO, Jeff Hansen, VP Mktng, Email: j.hansen@xopen.org

XANTE Corp. 2559 Emogene St, Mobile AL 36606 USA; 205/476-8189, Fax: 205/476-9421, Focus: Laser printer controllers, Ownrshp: PVT, Founded: 1989, Robert C. Ross, Jr., Pres, J. Mark SWanzy, COO, Martin E. Kennedy, VP Mktng

Xaos Tools 600 Townsend, #270E, San Francisco CA 94103-9692 USA; 415/487-7000, Fax: 415/558-9886, Co Email: macinfo@xaostools.com, Focus: Graphics and animation software, Ownrshp: PVT, Founded: 1991, Empl: 46, Arthur Schwartzberg, Chmn, Robert L. Batty, Pres, Michael Tolson, Chief Scientist, Martyn Crew, Bus Mgr, Kevin McDonald, Mac Bus Mgr, Therese Bruno, PR Mgr

XcelleNet Inc. 5 Concourse Pkwy, #850, Atlanta GA 30328 USA; 770/804-8100, 800/322-3366 Fax: 770/804-8102, Web URL: xcellenet.com, Focus: Network management software, Prdts: RemoteWare, Ownrshp: OTC, Stk Sym: XNET, Founded: 1986, Empl: 138, Sales ($M): 34.1, Fiscal End: 12/95; Dennis M. Crumpler, Chmn & CEO, John C. Bacon, Pres, Sidney V. Sack, CFO, W. Michael Parham, VP Sales, Shereef Navoar, CTO, Mindy Aronin, Mgr PR, Email: mindy.aronin@xcellenet.com

XChange 530 Hampshire St, #401, San Francisco CA 94110 USA; 415/864-7592, Fax: 415/864-7594, Co Email: xchange@slip.net, Focus: Services for QuarkXTensions, William Buckingham, Pres, Elizabeth Davenport, Email: xchangeed@eworld.com

XDB Systems Inc. 9861 Broken Land Pkwy, #156, Columbia MD 21046 USA; 410/312-9300, Fax: 410/312-9500, Co Email: @xdb.com, Focus: Database software, Ownrshp: PVT, Founded: 1986, Empl: 150, S. Bing Yao, Pres & CEO, Rusty Fiste, VP R&D, Kim Ball, VP Prod Dev, John Marrah, COO, Lien Yao, VP Finance, Connie Handen, Email: connieh@xdb.com

XDB User Group 9861 Broken Lance Pkwy, Colombia MD 21046 USA; 410/312-9300, Focus: User group for XDB database software, Ownrshp: Nonprofit, Founded: 1981

Xecom Inc. 374 Turquoise St, Milpitas CA 95035 USA; 408/945-6640, Fax: 408/942-1346, Focus: Embedded modems and telephone line interface modules, Ownrshp: PVT, Founded: 1984, Empl: 100, Sales ($M): 18, Fiscal End: 12/95; Alan Gregory, Pres, Mel Snyder, VP Mktng & Sales, Colin Barry, VP Eng

Xecute Inc. 1163 Inman Ave, #203, Edison NJ 08820 USA; 908/668-5151, 800/468-1115 Fax: 908/756-6869, Co Email: sales@xecute.com, Web URL: xecute.com, Focus: Remote access, interoperability, data and telecommunications, Internet, Prdts: Hummingbird, Shiva, FTP Software, Century Software, Ownrshp: Sub. GBC Tech., Founded: 1990, Empl: 20, Eric R. Korb, Pres, Email: ekorb@xecute.com; Marcy Catelli, Mktng Dir, Email: marcyc@xecute.com; Rajeev Khanolkar, Dir Tech Svcs, Email: rajeev@xecute.com

Xerox ColorgrafX Systems (CGS), 5853 Rue Ferrari, M/S 3-13, San Jose CA 95138 USA; 408/225-2800, 800/538-6477 Fax: 408/727-2399, Focus: Large format digital color printing, Ownrshp: Sub. Xerox, Founded: 1995, Empl: 250, Barry Lathan, Pres & CEO, Frank Shah, VP Eng, Claude Ezran, VP Mktng, Loren Winckler, VP WW Sales, Andreas Godde, CFO & VP Fin

Xerox Corp. PO Box 1600, 800 Long Ridge Rd, Stamford CT 06904 USA; 203/968-3000, Fax: 203/968-4566, Co Email: @xerox.com, Web URL: xerox.com, Focus: Document automation and computer peripherals, Ownrshp: NYSE, Stk Sym: XRX, Founded: 1906, Empl: 101,000, Sales ($M): 16,611.0, Fiscal End: 12/95; Paul A. Allaire, Chmn & CEO, A. Barry Rand, EVP Ops, Peter van Cuylenburg, EVP Ops, Mark B. Myers, SVP Res & Tech, Patricia M. Wallington, VP Info Mgmt, Judd B. Everhart, Mgr Corp PR

Xerox Desktop Document Systems 3400 Hillview Ave, Palo Alto CA 94303 USA; 415/815-6800, Fax: 415/815-6967, Co Email: @adoc.xerox.com, Focus: Document management systems, Ownrshp: Sub Xerox, Paul A. Ricci, Pres, Laura Cory, VP Mktng, Jerry Murch, VP Bus Dev, Stan Swiniarski, VP SW Prod, Fred Kiremidjian, VP Eng, Peter Warren, Marcom Mgr, Email: pwarren@adoc.xerox.com

Xerox Imaging Systems (XIS), 9 Centennial, Peabody MA 01960 USA; 508/977-2000, Fax: 508/977-5307, Focus: Imaging and OCR scanning products, Prdts: Text Bridge Professional Edition, Text Bridge Pro, Ownrshp: Sub. Xerox, Founded: 1988, Empl: 240, Michael Tivnan, GM, Wayne Crandall, VP Sales, Stan Swiniarski, VP SW Prod, Bob Edwards, VP MIS, Melanie Fleming, Dir SW Mktng, Email: mfleming@xis.xerox.com

Xicor Inc. 1511 Buckeye Dr, Milpitas CA 95035 USA; 408/432-

8888, Fax: 408/432-0640, Focus: EEPROM memory chips, Ownrshp: OTC, Stk Sym: XICO, Founded: 1978, Empl: 1,000, Sales ($M): 113.6, Fiscal End: 12/95; Raphael Klein, Chmn & Pres, Bruce W. Mattern, VP Sales & Mktng, Richard V. Orlando, VP Strategic Mktng, William H. Owen, VP Tech, Klaus G. Hendig, VP Fin & Admin

Xilinx Inc. 2100 Logic Dr, San Jose CA 95124-3400 USA; 408/559-7778, Fax: 408/559-7114, Web URL: xilinx.com, Focus: Gate array chips and related software, Ownrshp: OTC, Stk Sym: XLNX, Founded: 1984, Empl: 868, Sales ($M): 560.8, Fiscal End: 3/96; Bernard Vonderschmitt, Chmn, William P. Roelandts, CEO, C. Frank Myers, VP Ops, Gordon M. Steel, VP & CFO, R. Scott Brown, VP Sales

Xinet 2560 Ninth St, #312, Berkeley CA 94710 USA; 510/845-0555, Fax: 510/644-2680, Co Email: sales@xinet.com, Web URL: xinet.com, Focus: Advanced UNIX systems software and networking, Prdts: FullPress, K-AShare, K-FS, K-Spool, Ownrshp: PVT, Founded: 1991, Robert Kridle, Pres, Email: bob@xinet.com; Dick Wrenn, VP Mktng, Email: dick@xinet.com; Scott Seebass, VP Eng, Email: scott@xinet.com; Tony Rotundo, Comm Mgr, Email: tony@xinet.com

Xionics Inc. 70 Blanchard Rd, Burlington MA 01803-5100 USA; 617/229-7000, Prdts: Lightning, ImageSoft, Ownrshp: PVT, Founded: 1978, Empl: 50, David Skok, Chmn, Peter Santeusanio, Pres

Xionix Simulation Inc. 8150 W Royal Ln, #100, Irving TX 75063-2437 USA; 214/929-9999, Fax: 214/929-0444, Focus: Flight management system trainers and devices, Ownrshp: Sub. Evans & Sutherland, David Welham, Pres

Xiox Corp. 577 Airport Blvd, #700, Burlingame CA 94010 USA; 415/375-8188, Fax: 415/342-1139, Focus: Telecom management software, Ownrshp: OTC, Stk Sym: XIOX, Founded: 1982, Empl: 94, Sales ($M): 6.7, Fiscal End: 12/95; William Welling, Chmn & CEO, Richard J. Filak, VP & CFO, Anthony Dilulio, VP Ops, Michael O. O'Connell, VP Mktng, David Y. Schlossman, VP Eng

Xircom Inc. 2300 Corporate Ctr Dr, Thousand Oaks CA 91320 USA; 805/376-9300, Fax: 805/376-9311, Co Email: sales@xircom.com, Web URL: xircom.com, Focus: LAN adapters, Prdts: Pocket LAN Adapter, Ownrshp: OTC, Stk Sym: XIRC, Founded: 1988, Empl: 300, Sales ($M): 131.6, Fiscal End: 9/94; J. Kirk Mathews, Chmn, Dirk I. Gates, Pres & CEO, Jerry N. Ulrich, VP & CFO, Kenneth J. Biba, EVP, Robert W. Bass, VP Ops, Thomas V. Brown, VP Corp Com

XLNT Designs Inc. 15050 Ave of Science, #200, San Diego CA 92128-3419 USA; 619/487-9320, 800/956-8638 Fax: 619/487-9768, Co Email: marcom@xlnt.com, Web URL: xlnt.com, Focus: Network products, Prdts: Quik Stack, Quik Ether, Quik FDDI+, Ownrshp: PVT, Founded: 1989, Empl: 34, Ronald S. Perloff, Pres, Fazil Osman, VP, Roger Moyers, VP Sales & Mktng, Email: roger@xlnt.com; Barbara Hurst, Marcom Mgr, Email: barbara@xlnt.com

Xscribe Corp. 6285 Nancy Ridge Dr, San Diego CA 92121 USA; 619/457-5091, Fax: 619/457-3928, Focus: Computer-aided transcription equipment, Ownrshp: OTC, Stk Sym: XSCR, Founded: 1978, Sales ($M): 18.4, Fiscal End: 3/96; Suren G. Dutia, Pres & CEO, Bruce C. Myers, VP & CFO, Dennis D. Elkins, Pres Legal Syst Div

Xsoft 3400 Hillview Ave, Palo Alto CA 94303 USA; 415/813-6920, 800/428-2995 Fax: 415/813-7162, Co Email: info@xsoft.xerox.com, Web URL: xsoft.com, Focus: Document and office productivity software, Prdts: GlobalView, DocuBuild, Ownrshp: Sub Xerox, Founded: 1991, Empl: 320, Dennis W. Andrews, Pres, Barry Obrand, VP Mktng, George Rossman, VP Dev

XXCAL Testing Laboratories 11500 W Olympic Blvd #325, Los Angeles CA 90064 USA; 310/477-2902, Fax: 310/477-7127, Co Email: @xxcal.com, Focus: Microcomputer hardware, software and connectivity; software test tools and benchmarks, Ownrshp: PVT, Founded: 1976, Empl: 60, Marvin Hoffman, Chmn & CEO, Bill Schoneman, VP Testing Div, Brett Schoneman, WW Mktng Mgr, Email: brett@xxcal.com

Xylogics Inc. 53 Third Ave, Burlington MA 01803 USA; 617/272-8140, Fax: 617/273-5392, Focus: Mass storage and network products, Ownrshp: OTC, Stk Sym: XLXG, Founded: 1977, Empl: 203, Sales ($M): 50.4, Fiscal End: 10/94; Bruce I. Sachs, Pres & CEO, Frank J. Pipp, Chmn, Theodore A. Aronis, VP Ops, Grace M. Carr, VP Sales & Mktng, Maurice L. Castonguay, VP Fin

Xyplex Inc. 295 Foster St, Littleton MA 01460-2016 USA; 508/952-4700, 800/338-5316 Fax: 508/952-4702, Co Email: info@xyplex.com, Web URL: xyplex.com, Focus: LAN and communications products, Prdts: Network 9000 Routing Hub, Ownrshp: Sub. Raytheon, Stk Sym: XPLX, Founded: 1981, Empl: 550, Sales ($M): 76.8, Fiscal End: 12/93; Peter J. Nesbeda, Chmn, Pres & CEO, Gregor N. Ferguson, EVP, George E. Conant, VP Tech, Gilbert M. Kaufman, VP Prod Dev, Raymond DeZenso, VP & CFO, Rachel Winett, PR Mgr

Xyvision Inc. 101 Edgewater Dr, Wakefield MA 01880 USA; 617/245-4100, Fax: 617/246-5308, Co Email: info@xyvision.com, Web URL: xyvision.com, Focus: Computer publishing and color electronic pre-press systems, Ownrshp: OTC, Stk Sym: XYVI, Founded: 1982, Empl: 150, Sales ($M): 22.4, Fiscal End: 3/96; Thomas H. Conway, Chmn, Pres & CEO, Eugene P. Seneta, VP & CFO, James G. Hickey, VP Cust Support, Kevin J. Duffy, VP NA Sales

Yahoo Corp. 110 Pioneer Way, #F, Mountain View CA 94041 USA; 415/934-3230, Fax: 415/934-3248, Co Email: pr@yahoo.com, Web URL: yahoo.com, Focus: Online Internet guide, Ownrshp: PVT, Founded: 1994, Empl: 30, Jerry Yang, Co-founder, David Filo, Co-founder, Tim Brady, Dir Mktng, Email: tim@yahoo.com; Tim Koogle, CEO

Yamaha Corp. of America PO Box 6600, Buena Park CA 90622-6600 USA; 714/522-9011, 800/823-6414 Focus: PC peripherals, Ownrshp: Sub. Yamaha, Japan

Yamaha Systems Technology 100 Century Ctr Ct, #800, San Jose CA 95112 USA; 408/467-2300, Fax: 408/437-8791, Focus: Graphics controllers and CD Storage, Ownrshp: PVT, Founded: 1987, Empl: 15, Ed Kishimune, Pres, Robert Starr, GM Sales & Mktng, David Grenier, GM Admin, Iraj Zarrinnaal, Prod Mgr Com

Yankee Group, The 31 James Ave, Boston MA 02116 USA; 617/956-5000, Fax: 617/367-5760, Web URL: yankeegroup.com, Focus: Telecom, computers, CIM and consumer electronics data and consulting, Ownrshp: PVT, Founded: 1970, Empl: 75, Howard Anderson, Managing Dir

YARC Systems Corp. 975 Business Ctr Cr, Newbury Park CA 91320 USA; 805/499-9444, Fax: 805/499-4048, Focus: Application accelerators, Prdts: MacRageous, Zuma, Hydra, Screamer, Ownrshp: PVT, Founded: 1988, Empl: 23, Sales ($M): 4, Thierry Doyen, Pres, Trevor Marshall, COO, Karsten Jeppesen, VP Eng

Young Minds Inc. 1910 Orange Tree Ln, #300, PO Box 6910, Redlands CA 92374 USA; 909/335-1350, 800/964-4964 Fax: 909/798-0488, Co Email: @ymi.com, Web URL: ymi.com, Focus: CD-ROM management software and mass storage systems, Prdts: CD Studio, SimpliCD, UltraCapacity, MPS, AutoCDR, Ownrshp: PVT, Founded: 1989, Empl: 50, Andrew Young, Chmn, Email: young@ymi.com; Dave Cote, Pres & CEO, Email: cote@ymi.com; Matthew Hornbeck, VP Ops, Genene Miller, GM, Heather Barger, Email: barger@ymi.com

Young Systems Ltd. 6185 Buford Hwy #C-100, Norcross GA 30071 USA; 770/449-0338, Fax: 770/840-9723, Focus: Retail management system for music and video stores, Ownrshp: PVT, Founded: 1984, Empl: 15, Dennis Young, Chmn, Andrea Young, Pres

Z Microsystems Inc. 5945 Pacific Ctr Blvd, #509, San Diego CA 92121-4309 USA; 619/657-1000, Fax: 619/657-1001, Focus:

Secure storage peripherals, Prdts: SMARTpak, TRANZpak, Ownrshp: PVT, Founded: 1986, Empl: 18, Sales ($M): 10, Fiscal End: 12/92; Jack Wade, Pres, Cynthia Riley, Controller, Craig Jack, VP Sales

Z-Code Software Corp. 101 Rowland Way, #300, Novato CA 94945-5010 USA; 415/898-8649, Co Email: info@z-code.com, Focus: Information exchange software, Prdts: Z-Mail, Ownrshp: Sub. NCD, Founded: 1990, Empl: 50, Email: scott@z-code.com

Zadian Technologies Inc. 2305 Bering Dr, San Jose CA 95131 USA; 408/894-0800, Fax: 408/894-0880, Focus: PCMCIA products, Ownrshp: PVT, Zaydoon Jawadi, Pres, Marissa Panlilio

Zadian Technologies Inc. 2305 Bering Dr, San Jose CA 95131 USA; 408/894-0800, Fax: 408/894-0880, Focus: I/O test systems and software, Ownrshp: PVT, Larry Kubo, VP Mktng, Marissa Rivers

Zebra Express PO Box 6129, Palm Harbor FL 34684-0729 USA; 800/401-0060 Focus: PC accounting software, Ownrshp: PVT, Brian McDonald, Pres

Zebra Technologies VTI Inc. 11170 S State St, Sandy UT 84070 USA; 801/576-9700, Fax: 801/576-5538, Focus: PC bar code reader, Prdts: Track-One, Bar-One, Scan-One, Ownrshp: Sub Zebra Technologies, Founded: 1988, David L. Carter, Pres & CEO, William H. Flury, VP Sales, Gordon Sorensen, Dir Sales, Wayne Wilkinson, Dir Mktng, Jeff Boonmee, Dir New Prod, Greg D. Erickson, PR Spec

Zebu Systems L.L.C. PO Box 65057, Seattle WA 98155 USA; 206/781-9566, Fax: 206/782-7191, Co Email: info@zebu.com, Web URL: zebu.com, Prdts: Orion Internet Firewall System, Kevin Pierce

Zenith Electronics Corp. 1000 Milwaukee Ave, Glenview IL 60025-2493 USA; 708/391-7000, Fax: 708/391-7253, Focus: Consumer electronics products and monitors, Ownrshp: NYSE, Stk Sym: ZE, Founded: 1918, Empl: 18,100, Sales ($M): 1,273.9, Fiscal End: 12/95; Albin F. Moscher, Pres & CEO, Philip S. Thompson, SVP Ops, Gerald M. McCarthy, EVP Sales & Mktng, John W. Bowler, VP R&D, Willard C. McNitt, VP & CFO, John I. Taylor, VP Pub Affairs

Zenographics Inc. 34 Executive Park, #150, Irvine CA 92714-6743 USA; 714/851-6352, Fax: 714/851-1314, Focus: Business graphics and imaging software, Prdts: SuperPrint, Mirage, Ownrshp: PVT, Founded: 1979, Empl: 25, Sales ($M): 3.6, Robert E. Romney, Pres & CEO, Ln Freestone, VP Bus Dev, William B. Warshaw, VP Dev, Charles D'Angelo, VP Sales

Ziff-Davis Publishing Co. One Park Ave, New York NY 10016-5255 USA; 212/503-3500, Fax: 212/503-5519, Co Email: firstname_lastname@zd.com, Web URL: zd.com, Focus: Nearly 50 computer magazines and tradeshows, Prdts: PC Mag., PC/Computing, PC Week, MacWeek, MacUser, Window Sources, Ownrshp: Sub Softbank, Japan, Sales ($M): 850, Fiscal End: 12/95; Eric Hippeau, Chmn & CEO, Ronni Sonnenberg, Pres US Pubs, Jeffrey Ballowee, Pres Interactive Media, J.B. Holston II, Pres Int'l Media, William Rosenthal, VP & CFO, Gregory Jarboe, Dir PR

Zilog Inc. 210 E Hacienda Ave, Campbell CA 95008-6600 USA; 408/370-8000, Fax: 408/370-8056, Web URL: zilog.com, Focus: Applications specific integrated circuits, Ownrshp: Public, Stk Sym: ZLOG, Founded: 1975, Empl: 1,450, Sales ($M): 265.1, Fiscal End: 12/95; Edgar A. Sack, Chmn, Pres & CEO, Michael J. Bradshaw, SVP WW Ops, Thomas C. Carson, SVP WW Sales, Dick Moore, SVP Tech, William R. Walker, SVP & CFO, Chris Bradley, Dir Marcom, Email: cbra@zilog.com

Zinc Software 405 S 100 E, 2nd Floor, Pleasant Grove UT 84062 USA; 801/785-8900, 800/638-8665 Fax: 801/785-8996, Co Email: info@zinc.com, Web URL: zinc.com, Focus: Software development tools, Prdts: Zinc Application Framework, Zinc DataConnect, Ownrshp: PVT, Founded: 1990, Empl: 30, Robert Bishop, Pres & CEO, Email: rbishop@zinc.com; Larry Macfarlane, VP Sales, Email: lmacfarlane@zinc.com; Stan McQueen, VP Dev,

Email: smcqueen@zinc.com

Zitel Corp. 47211 Bayside Pkwy, Fremont CA 94538 USA; 510/440-9600, 800/622-5020 Fax: 510/440-9696, Web URL: zitel.com, Focus: Memory systems, microcomputer boards and systems, Ownrshp: OTC, Stk Sym: ZITL, Founded: 1979, Empl: 92, Sales ($M): 23.7, Fiscal End: 9/95; Jack H. King, Pres & CEO, Richard F. Harapat, VP Sales, Frank J. Vukmanic, VP Mktng, Donald F. Olker, VP Mfg, Henry C. Harris, VP & CFO

Zondervan Publishing House 5300 Patterson Ave SE, Grand Rapids MI 49530 USA; 616/698-6900, 800/226-1122 Fax: 616/698-3439, Web URL: zondervan.com, Focus: Audio/video/software interactive CD-ROMs, Prdts: macBible, BibleSource, Read With Me Bible, Ownrshp: Sub. HarperCollins, Founded: 1931, Empl: 300, Bruce Ruskamp, Pres & CEO, Email: bruce.ruskamp@zph.com; Mark Hunt, Pub/Exec Producer, Email: mark.hunt@zph.com; Sue-Anne Boylan, Dir Info Sys, Email: sue-anne.boylan@zph.com; Jonathan Petersen, Dir Media Rel, Email: jonathan.petersen@zph.com

Zoom Telephonics Inc. 207 South St, Boston MA 02111 USA; 617/423-1072, 800/631-3116 Fax: 617/423-9231, Web URL: zoomtel.com, Focus: PC modems, fax modems and digital voice board, Prdts: Zoom/modem, Zoom/fax modems, Stk Sym: ZOOMF, Founded: 1977, Empl: 300, Sales ($M): 96.9, Fiscal End: 12/95; Frank Manning, Pres, Peter Kramer, VP, Lawrence Panaro, CFO, Terry Manning, Dir Mktng, Dean Paragopolous, Leonard Phillips, Marcom Mgr

ZyXEL 4920 E La Palma Ave, Anaheim CA 92807 USA; 714/693-0808, Fax: 714/693-0705, Co Email: techie@zyxel.com, Focus: Data, fax and cellular modems, Ownrshp: PVT, Founded: 1988, Empl: 150, Sales ($M): 15, Fiscal End: 12/93; Gordon Yang, Pres, Susan Yang, Sales Mgr, Munira Brooks, Mktng Mgr, Email: mbrooks@zyxel.com; Nick Doshi, Tech Sup Mgr

Chapter 3

People

People Award Winners

Computer Reseller News: Top 25 Executives

Each year since 1983 Computer Reseller News has ranked the 25 most influential executives in the personal computer industry. The selections made by CRN's editors focus on individuals that have made an impact on the personal computer distribution and reseller community in the last year.

'95 Rank	Name, Company	Title	'94 Salary & Bonus ($K)
1	Bill Gates, Microsoft	Chairman & CEO	458
2	Andrew Grove, Intel	President & CEO	2,100
3	Lewis Platt, Hewlett-Packard	Chairman, President & CEO	1,179
4	Eckhard Pfeiffer, Compaq	President & CEO	3,550
5	Chip Lacy, Ingram Micro	Co-chairman & CEO	600 to 900
6	Louis Gerstner, IBM	Chairman & CEO	4,600
7	Eric Benhamou, 3Com	Chairman & CEO	522
8	Marc Andreessen, Netscape	VP Technology	80
9	Craig Goldman, Chase Manhattan Bank	CIO & Sr. VP	NA
10	Larry Ellison, Oracle	Chairman & CEO	2,410
11	Steve Ballmer, Microsoft	Exec. VP	412
12	John McKenna, Entex Information Services	President	330 to 350
13	Jeff Vinik, Fidelity Investments	Mgr Fidelity Magellan Fund	6,000 to 8,000
14	Jeff McKeever, MicroAge	Chairman & CEO	628
15	Dick Sanford, Intelligent Electronics	Chairman & CEO	850
16	Steve Raymund, Tech Data	Chairman & CEO	622
17	Robert Frankenberg, Novell	Chairman, President & CEO	600
18	Mike Pickett, Merisel	Chairman & CEO	579
19	Beny Alagem, Packard Bell	President & CEO	NA
20	Scott McNealy, Sun Microsystems	Chairman, President & CEO	1,250
21	Ed Anderson, CompuCom Systems	President & CEO	610
22	John Roach, Tandy	Chairman & CEO	1,050
23	Robert Palmer, Digital Equipment	Chairman, President & CEO	1,275
24	Robert Allen, AT&T	Chairman & CEO	3,499
25	Mike Spindler, Apple Computer	President & CEO	934

The Top 25 executives for the last twelve years are shown in the next four tables.

Rank	1994	1993
1	Jim Manzi, Lotus Dev.	Ben Rosen, Compaq Computer
2	Bill Gates, Microsoft	John Sculley, Apple Computer
3	James Burke, IBM	Bill Gates, Microsoft
4	Eckhard Pfeiffer, Compaq	Jim Cannavino, IBM
5	Chip Lacy, Ingram Micro	David Dukes, Ingram Micro
6	Vinod Dham, Intel	Ray Noorda, Novell
7	Lewis Platt, Hewlett-Packard	Andrew Grove, Intel
8	John Connors, Merisel	Finis Conner, Conner Peripherals
9	Ray Noorda, Novell	Mike Pickett, Merisel
10	Dick Sanford, Intelligent Electronics	Nathan Morton, CompUSA
11	Robert Kavner, AT&T	Jim Manzi, Lotus Development
12	Jeff McKeever, MicroAge	Dick Sanford, Intelligent Electronics

Rank	1994	1993
13	Steve Raymund, Tech Data	Bill Tauscher, ComputerLand
14	Safi Qureshey, AST Research	Steve Raymund, Tech Data
15	Nathan Morton, CompUSA	Jerry Sanders, Advanced Micro Devices
16	Elaine Bond, Chase Manhattan Bank	Jeff McKeever, MicroAge
17	Robert Palmer, Digital Equipment	Bob Neighbors, EDS
18	Chip Morris, T. Rowe Price Assoc.	Michael Dell, Dell Computer
19	Bill Tauscher, ComputerLand	B.P. Thacker, Software Negotiation Purchasing Program
20	Bill Fairfield, Inacom	Safi Qureshey, AST Research
21	Phil Ellett, Gates/FA	John Dobson, ITT Commercial Finance
22	Les Alberthal, EDS	Jack Schoof, Artisoft
23	Mike Spindler, Apple Computer	Phil Ellett, Gates/FA Distributing
24	Sheldon Adelson, Interface Group	Ming Chien, First International Computer
25	Kirk Dove, Ross-Dove	Jack Martin, The Asset Group

Rank	1992	1991
1	Ben Rosen, Compaq Computer	Ray Noorda, Novell
2	John Sculley, Apple Computer	Bill Gates, Microsoft
3	Bill Gates, Microsoft	Bill Tauscher, ComputerLand
4	Jim Cannavino, IBM	Jim Cannavino, IBM
5	David Dukes, Ingram Micro	John Sculley, Apple Computer
6	Ray Noorda, Novell	Philippe Kahn, Borland
7	Andrew Grove, Intel	David House, Intel
8	Finis Conner, Conner Peripherals	Andrew T. Dwyer, JWP
9	Mike Pickett, Merisel	David Dukes, Ingram Micro
10	Nathan Morton, CompUSA	Kevin Arquit, Dir. FTC Bureau of Comp.
11	Jim Manzi, Lotus Development	Scott McNealy, Sun Microsystems
12	Dick Sanford, Intelligent Electronics	Rick Inatome, InaCom
13	Bill Tauscher, ComputerLand	Rod Canion, Compaq Computer
14	Steve Raymund, Tech Data	Tom Yuen, AST Research
15	Jerry Sanders, Advanced Micro Devices	Dick Sanford, Intelligent Electronics
16	Jeff McKeever, MicroAge	Jeff McKeever, MicroAge
17	Bob Neighbors, EDS	Finis Conner, Conner Peripherals
18	Michael Dell, Dell Computer	Luther Nussbaum, Evernet Systems
19	B.P. Thacker, Software Negotiation Purchasing Program	Jerry Kaplan, Go Corp.
20	Safi Qureshey, AST Research	Judge Vaughn Walker
21	John Dobson, ITT Commercial Finance	Mike Pickett, Merisel
22	Jack Schoof, Artisoft	Steve Raymund, Tech Data
23	Phil Ellett, Gates/FA Distributing	Nathan Morton, CompUSA
24	Ming Chien, First International Computer	Jerry Sanders, Advanced Micro Devices
25	Jack Martin, The Asset Group	Bob McNamara, Salomon Brothers

	1990	1989	1988	1987
1	Bill Gates, Microsoft	John Akers, IBM	Rod Canion, Compaq Computer	Ned Lautenbach, IBM
2	Ray Noorda, Novell	Rod Canion, Compaq Computer	John Sculley, Apple Computer	Bill Gates, Microsoft
3	David House, Intel	John Sculley, Apple Computer	Victor Alhadeff, Egghead	John Sculley, Apple Computer
4	Rod Canion, Compaq Computer	Bill Gates, Microsoft	Bill Gates, Microsoft	Rod Canion, Compaq Computer
5	Jeff McKeever, MicroAge	Scott McNealy, Sun Micro	Dave Norman, Businessland	Rick Inatome, Inacomp
6	Arthur Block, Manufacturers Hanover	David House, Intel	Andy Grove, Intel	Ken Waters, ComputerLand
7	Ed Anderson, ComputerLand	Dick Sanford, Intelligent Electr.	John Roach, Tandy	Bob Crowell, Neeco

	1990	1989	1988	1987
8	Richard Hackborn, HP	Steve Jobs, NeXT	Curt Crawford, IBM	Jay Gottlieb, Computer Factory
9	John Sculley, Apple Computer	Rick Inatome, Inacomp	Craig Burton, Novell	Victor Alhadeff, Egghead
10	Bill McCracken, IBM	Bill McCracken, IBM	Rick Inatome, Inacomp	Dave Norman, Businessland
11	Andrew T. Dwyer, JWP	Chip Lacy, Ingram Micro	Ken Waters, ComputerLand	Jeff McKeever, MicroAge
12	David Dukes, Ingram Micro	Drew Major, Novell	The DRAM Broker	Chip Lacy, Micro D
13	Dick Sanford, Intelligent Electr.	Frank King, Lotus Development	Chip Lacy, Ingram Micro	John Roach, Tandy
14	Frank King, Lotus Development	Dave Norman, Businessland	Scott McNealy, Sun Micro	Ben Rosen, Sevin Rosen
15	Scott McNealy, Sun Micro	Alan Kay, Apple Computer	Jeff McKeever, MicroAge	Ray Noorda, Novell
16	Mike Pickett, Merisel	Thomas Sherrard, Toshiba	Tom Yuen, AST Research	Peter Siris, Buckingham Research
17	Nathan Morton, CompUSA	John Doerr, Caufield & Byers	Pete Peterson, WordPerfect	Philippe Kahn, Borland
18	Philippe Kahn, Borland	Jeff McKeever, MicroAge	Bob Leff, Softsel	Bert Helfinstein, Entre
19	Rick Inatome, Inacomp	Katherine Hudson, Eastman Kodak	Jay Gottlieb, Computer Factory	William Krause, 3Com
20	David Norman, Businessland	Doug Michels, Santa Cruz Oper	John Rehfeld, Toshiba	Gordon Hoffstein, Microamerica
21	Safi Qureshey, AST Research	John Young, Hewlett-Packard	Wylie Crawford, LANDA	John Warnock, Adobe Systems
22	Enzo Torresi, NetFrame Systems	Steve Raymund, Tech Data	Larry Ellison, Oracle	Pete Peterson, WordPerfect
23	Jonathan Rottenberg, Boston Computer Soc.	John Warnock, Adobe Systems	Gordon Hoffstein, Microamerica	Mark Shumate, Connecting Point
24	Luther Nussbaum, Evernet Syst.	Col. Arlyn Schumacher, Gunther AFB	Michael Dell, Dell Computer	Alex Kask, Microcomputer Managers
25	Steve Raymund, Tech Data	Alan Hald, ABCD	Alan Weinberger, ASCII	Sheldon Adelson, Interface Grp.

	1986	1985	1984	1983
1	Bill Gates, Microsoft	Dave Norman, Businessland	John Sculley, Apple Computer	Don Estridge, IBM
2	Ed Faber, ComputerLand	Bill Millard, ComputerLand	Bill Millard, ComputerLand	Portia Isaacson, Future Comput.
3	Dave Norman, Businessland	Victor Golberg, IBM	William Ladin, ComputerCraft	Rick Inatome, Computer Mart
4	Bill Lowe, IBM	Avner Parnes, MBI	Rick Inatome, Inacomp	Dave Norman, Businessland
5	Rick Inatome, Inacomp	John Sculley, Apple	Jim Edgette, Entre	Warren Winger, CompuShop
6	Jeff McKeever, MicroAge	J. Martin-Musumeci, Micro/Vest	Richard Koon, IBM	Mike Shabazian, ComputerLand
7	Bill Campbell, Apple	Rod Canion, Compaq	Bruce Burdick, ComputerLand	William Ladin, ComputerCraft
8	Michael Shane, Leading Edge	Ken Carpenter, First Software	Bill Gates, Microsoft	Jim Edgette, Entre
9	Harvey Flam, FHP	Alan Hald, MicroAge	John Levy, General Micro	John Sculley, Apple
10	John Martin-Musumeci, Solitaire	Ben Rosen, Sevin Rosen	Portia Isaacson, Future Comput.	Glenn Johnson, Softwaire Centr.
11	Ray Noorda, Novell	Mitch Kapor, Lotus	Ed Ramos, FIS	Jack Tomlinson, ComputerLand
12	Jay Gottlieb, Computer Factory	Ed Esber, Ashton-Tate	Dave Norman, Businessland	Bill Gates, Microsoft
13	Rod Canion, Compaq	Rick Inatome, Inacomp	Alan Hald, MicroAge	Dave Wagman, Softsel
14	Ed Esber, Ashton-Tate	John Dobson, ITT	Warren Winger, CompuShop	Mitch Kapor, Lotus
15	Victor Alhadeff, Egghead	Ed Ramos, Computone/FIS	Steve Jobs, Apple	John Roach, Tandy
16	John Roach, Tandy	Will Luden, Pacific Telesis	John Rollins, Sears	Dan Fylstra, VisiCorp
17	Avner Parnes, MBI	Jay Gottlieb, Computer Factory	Tony Morris, Morris Decision	John Purtell, OnLine Micro Ctr.
18	Alan Hald, MicroAge	Gordon Hoffstein, Microamerica	Mitch Kapor, Lotus	Lorraine Mecca, Micro D
19	Bert Helfinstein, Entre'	Bruce Burdick, ComputerLand	David Cole, Ashton-Tate	Rod Canion, Compaq
20	Frank Barry, Ingram Software	Egil Juliussen, Future Computing	Dave Wagman, Softsel	David Kay, Kaypro
21	Norm Dinnsen, ComputerLand	Ron Siegel, Gateway Computer	Bill Fairfield, ValCom	Joel Shusterman, Franklin
22	Will Luden, Pacific Telesis	Dave Wagman, Softsel	Sheldon Adelson, Interface Grp.	Sheldon Adelson, Interface Grp.
23	Paul Brainerd, Aldus	Michele Preston, L.F. Rothschild	John Boyd, AT&T	Alan Hald, MicroAge
24	Mike Jackson, Qualitech	Safi Qureshey, AST Research	John Roach, Tandy	Ken Olsen, Digital Equipment
25	Mickey Dude, MicroVision	Sheldon Adelson, Interface Grp.	Michele Preston, L.F. Rothschild	Jack Tramiel, Commodore

Infomart: Hall of Fame

"Infomart's information processing Hall of Fame, formed in 1985, recognizes individuals who have made significant scientific, technological and business contributions to the information processing industry"--Infomart

1995 Inductee:
Vinton Cerf, Co-developer of the Internet's TCP/ip protocol
William R. Hewlett, Co-founder of Hewlett-Packard Co.
David Packard, Co-founder of Hewlett-Packard Co.
1994 Inductee:
Dan Bricklin, Co-creator of VisiCalc, the first electronic spreadsheet
1993 Inductee:
Ray Noorda, Chairman, Novell
Andrew Grove, President & CEO, Intel Corp.
1992 Inductee:
Steve Wozniak, Co-Founder of Apple Computer, Inc.
1991 Inductees:
Dr. Robert N. Noyce, Co-Founder of Fairchild Semiconductor and Intel Corporation; Co-Inventor of the integrated circuit
Dr. Marvin Minsky, Professor and Computer Scientist, MIT; pioneer in artificial intelligence, neural networks and robotics
1990 Inductees:
Steven Jobs, Co-Founder of Apple Computer, Inc.
Kenneth H. Olsen, Founder, Digital Equipment Corporation
1989 Inductees:
Bill Gates, Founder and Chief Executive Officer of Microsoft Corporation
Martin A. Goetz, first U.S. software patent, 1968
1988 Inductees:
John Bardeen, Walter Brattain and William Shockley, 1956 co-recipients of the Nobel Prize in Physics for discovery of the transistor
Chester F. Carlson, Inventor of Xerography
Blaise Pascal, French Mathematician, Philosopher and Scientist, whose work on the pressure of liquids resulted in Pascal's Law
1987 Inductees:
John J. Cullinane, Founder and Chairman of the Board of Cullinet Software
Dr. An Wang, Founder and Chief Executive Officer of Wang Laboratories, Inc.
1986 Inductees:
Philip D. Estridge, IBM Vice President whose division fostered the IBM-PC
H. Ross Perot, Founder of EDS Corporation
1985 Inductees:
Dr. Gene Amdahl, considered the father of high-end, plug-compatible computers
Commodore Grace Hopper, developer of the computer language COBOL
Jack St. Clair Kilby, Co-Inventor of the integrated circuit
Senator Frank Lautenberg, Founder of the first major worldwide computer service company
Drs. John Mauchly and J. Presper Eckert, co-developers of the ENIAC which incorporated many of its components into modern computers
Dr. John von Neumann, innovative mathematician who promoted the advantages of binary numbers in computer construction

Excerpted from with permission from Infomart. Copyright © 1995, Infomart, 1950 Stemmons Freeway, Dallas TX 75207 USA.

Upside: All-Star Team

"It has been a banner year for most technology companies: Share prices are soaring, IPOs are oversubscribed and startups are proliferating. So it took an almost flawless performance by an executive or management team to be named to this year's All-Star team. Oracle CEO Larry Ellison, for example, earned 'CEO of the Year' honors by growing his company's leadership position in its existing market against strong competition while pushing boldly into new areas. Judges for the contest, including journalists, executive search consultants and analysts, gave high marks to executives who bounced back from difficult situations, like Michael Dell, as well as those who managed their companies with nary a misstep, like Doug Carlston."--Upside

CEO of the Year: Lawrence J. Ellison, Chairman, President & CEO, Oracle, Redwood City, CA
Runner Up: Stephen M. Case, President & CEO, America Online, Vienna, VA
CEO, Large Company: Rupert Murdoch, Chairman & CEO, News Corp., Sydney, Australia
Runner Up: Lewis Platt, CEO, Hewlett-Packard, Palo Alto, CA
CEO, Small Company: Douglas G. Carlston, Chairman & CEO, Brøderbund Software, Novato, CA
Runner Up: David A. Duffield, Chairman, President, & CEO, PeopleSoft, Pleasanton, CA
CEO, Turnaround: Michael S. Dell, Chairman & CEO, Dell Computer, Austin, TX

Runner Up: Jerome J. Meyer, Chairman & CEO, Tektronix, Wilsonville, OR
CEO, Private Company: Beny Alagem, Chairman, President & CEO, Packard Bell Electronics, Sacramento, CA
Runner Up: Howard Charney, Chairman & CEO, Grand Junction Networks, Fremont CA
CEO, Startup: Deborah A. Coleman, Chairman & CEO, Merix Corp., Forest Grove, OR
Runner Up: Jen-Hsun Huang, President & CEO, NVidia Corp., Sunnyvale, CA
Chairman: James H. Clark, Chairman, Netscape Communications, Mountain View, CA
Runner Up: Sumner Redstone, Chairman, President & CEO, Viacom, New York, NY
Second-in-Command: Sanjay Kumar, President & COO, Computer Associates International, Islandia, NY
Runner Up: Thomas J. Jermoluk, President & COO, Silicon Graphics, Mountain View, CA
R&D Executive: Eric Schmidt, Chief Technology Officer, Sun Microsystems, Mountain View, CA
Runner Up: Marc Andreessen, President of Technology, Netscape Communications, Mountain View, CA
Sales & Marketing Executive: Thomas Herring, VP Marketing & Business Development, Powersoft, Concord, MA
Runner Up: Steve Chadima, VP Marketing, Knowledge Adventure, La Crescenta, CA
Runner Up: Patrick McVeigh, VP Sales, Knowledge Adventure, La Crescenta, CA
Finance Executive: Joseph A. Graziano, Exec. VP & CFO, Apple Computer, Cupertino, CA
Runner Up: Jeffrey O. Henley, Exec. VP & CFO, Oracle, Redwood City, CA
Management Team: Motorola, Schaumburg, IL
Runner Up: Microsoft, Redmond, WA
Board of Directors: Paul G. Allen: Chairman, Asymetrix; Starwave; Interval Research; Ticketmaster Holdings Grp.; Vulcan Northwest and The Paul Allen Group, Bellevue, WA
Carol Bartz: Chairman, President & CEO, Autodesk, Sausalito, CA
Wilfred J. Corrigan: Chairman & CEO, LSI Logic, Milpitas, CA
L. John Doerr: Partner, Kleiner Perkins Caufield & Byers, Menlo Park, CA
Larry W. Sonsini: Partner, Wilson Sonsini Goodrich & Rosati, Palo Alto, CA

People Directory

Aanderud, Stephen A.; Pres & CEO, ThrustMaster Inc.; US; 503/615-3200

Aarons, Chris; Mktng Dir, Mega Drive Systems Inc.; US; 310/247-0006

Abbey, Stephen L.; VP NA Sales & Mktng, Computer Identics Corp.; US; 617/821-0830

Abbott, Jan; Exec Dir, Association of Shareware Professionals; US; 616/788-5131

Abbott, Robert C.; VP Eng, FastComm Communications Corp; US; 703/318-7750

Abbott, Sandy; CFO, Integrated Information Technology; US; 408/727-1885

Abe, Tadashi; VP & GM, Mitsui Comtek Corp.; US; 408/725-8525

Abelmann, Ronald A.; Pres & CEO, Wind River Systems.; US; 510/748-4100

Aberle, Craig L.; Pres, MicroBiz Corp; US; 201/512-0900

Abod, Charles; CFO, Micro Dynamics; US; 301/589-6300, charles_abod@mdl.com

Abraham, Robert C.; VP, Freeman Associates Inc.; US; 805/963-3853

Abrahams, Philip S.; Pres, Qualitas Inc.; US; 301/907-6700

Abrahamsen, Victor; VP, Lansafe Network Services Inc.; US; 212/889-8100

Abram, John; Pres, In-Stat Inc.; US; 602/483-4440

Abrams, Albert N.; Pres, Abrams Creative Services; US; 818/343-6365

Abrams, Charles; Ed-in-Chief, Online Design; US; 415/334-3800

Abrams, Michael; Ed, Workstation Buyer's Guide; US; 619/488-0533

Abrams, Sharlene; VP & CFO, Mercury Interactive Corp.; US; 408/523-9900

Abramson, Morrie K.; Chmn, Pres & CEO, Kent Electronics Corp.; US; 713/780-7770

Abreu, Robbie; VP Mktng & Sales, Quadrant Components; US; 510/656-9988

Abrials, Mark; Mktng Dir, TechNews Inc.; US; 703/848-2800, mabrials@technews.com

Achuff, Bill; Co-Dir, User Group Alliance; US

Acker, Peter C.; EVP, Numera Software; US; 206/622-2233, petera@numera.com

Ackerman, Alan; VP, Supra Corp.; US; 360/604-1400

Ackerman, Don E.; Chmn, Genicom Corp.; US; 703/802-9200

Ackerman, F. Duane; Pres & CEO, Bell-South Corp.; US; 404/249-2000

Acord, Gary; VP & CFO, Artisoft Inc.; US; 520/670-7100

Acquaviva, James; Pres, Revelation

Software; US; 203/973-1000

Adamczyk, Joseph A.; EVP, Wyle Laboratories; US; 714/753-9953

Adamek, Jan; SVP Sales & Mktng, Hummingbird Communications Ltd.; Canada; 905/470-1203

Adams, Allen R.; Group VP, DSC Communications Corp.; US; 214/519-3000

Adams, Bob; Pres & COO, Pacific Microelectronics Inc.; US; 415/948-6200

Adams, Elizabeth; Mgng Dir, Network Management Forum; US; 201/425-1900

Adams, George F.; VP Bus Dev, Phoenix Technologies Ltd.; US; 408/654-9000

Adams, James R.; Group Pres, SBC Communications Inc.; US; 210/821-4105

Adams, Paul; Pres Prod & Bus Dev, Micro Focus Inc.; US; 415/856-4161, pa@mfltd.co.uk

Adams, Randy; Pres, Internet Shopping Network; US; 415/842-7400, randy@internet.net

Adams, Richard J.; Ed, Eljen Publishing Inc.; US; 813/654-1168

Adams, Richard L.; Chmn & CTO, Uunet Technologies; US; 703/206-5600

Adams, Robert B.; Pres & CEO, Dux Software Corp.; US; 415/948-6200

Adams, Tom; Pres, Adam Media Research; US; 408/659-3070, tomadams@ix.netcom.com

Adcock, Sharon; Principal, Adcock Group, The; US; 310/545-9731, skiadcock@aol.com

Addiego, Joseph; VP Sales, Integrated Systems Inc.; US; 408/542-1500

Addison, Craig; Ed-in-Chief, Electronic Business Asia; Hong Kong; 852-965-1555

Addison, Edwin; EVP, Excalibur Technologies Corp.; US; 619/438-7900

Aden, F. Thomas; Pres, ICVerify Inc.; US; 510/553-7500, taden@icverify.com

Adinolfi, John N.; VP Mktng, Hyperion Software; US; 203/703-3000

Adkins, Allen; Pres & CEO, Optical Media Int'l.; US; 408/376-3511

Adkinson, Mike; Pblr, Jaye Communications; US; 404/984-9444

Adler, John G.; Chmn, Adaptec Inc.; US; 408/945-8600

Adorjan, J.J.; Pres, Emerson Electric Co.; US; 314/553-2000

Adrean, Lee; EVP & CFO, First Data Corp.; US; 201/525-4700

Adrian, Peter; Principal, Vital Information Publications; US; 415/345-7018

Adrion, W. Richard; Ed-in-Chief, ACM Transactions on Software Eng. & Methodology; US; 212/869-7440

Afshar, Art; GM, Micro Express Inc.; US; 714/852-1400

Agbay, Albert J.; Chmn & CEO, Nexar Technologies Inc.; US; 508/836-8700

Agger, Dale; Ed Dir, Duke Communications Int'l.; US; 970/663-4700

Aghion, Daniel; VP Mktng, Hayes Microcomputer Prdcts; US; 770/840-9200

Agnello, Anthony; Pres, Ariel Corp.; US; 908/249-2900

Agostini, Giuliu; SVP Fin, Minnesota Minning & Mfng.; US; 612/733-1110

Agrawal, Sid; VP Mktng, Alliance Semiconductor; US; 408/383-4900

Aguilar, Gale R.; Pres & COO, Mitem Corp.; US; 415/323-6164

Aguirre, J.L.; VP, MAG Innovision Inc.; US; 714/751-2008

Ahearn, Kevin; VP Eng, Hand Held Products; US; 704/541-1380

Ahmed, Rizal; Ed, Insider Weekly for AS/400 Managers; US; 617/444-5755

Ahn, John; VP Tech, Online Environs Inc.; US; 617/225-0449

Aiello, David E.; Pres, Chatham Township Data Corp.; US; 201/586-0700

Ajer, Laurin; Controller, Control Concepts; US; 703/876-6444, ajerl@presearch.com

Akay, Vahe; VP Mktng & Sales, Hyundai Digital Media; US; 408/232-8000

Akerson, Daniel; CEO, Nextel Communications; US; 201/438-1400

Akunda, Ellen; Mktng Mgr, Big Software; US; 415/919-0200, ellen@bigbusiness.com

Ala-Pietila, Pekka; Pres Mobil Phones, Nokia Group; Finland; 3580-18071

Alagem, Beny; Chmn, Pres & CEO, Packard Bell; US; 818/865-1555

Alahuhta, Matti; Pres Nokia Telecom, Nokia Group; Finland; 3580-18071

Alampi, Mary; Ed, Information Industry Directory; US; 313/961-2242

Alba, Gregg; Controller, Computone Corp.; US; 770/475-2725

Albers, Raymond J.; VP & CIO, Circuit City Stores Inc.; US; 804/527-4000

Albert, Alan; Chmn & VP Mktng, Attain Corp.; US; 617/776-1110, aalbert@qm.attain.com

Albert, Joice; Treas, Sam Albert Associates; US; 914/723-8296

Albert, Martyn; Pres, Dolphin Inc.; US; 805/371-9493

Albert, Sam; Pres, Sam Albert Assoc; US; 914/723-8296, samalbert@samalbert.com

Alberthal Jr., Lester M.; Chmn, Pres & CEO, EDS; US; 214/604-6000

Albertini, William O.; EVP & CFO, Bell Atlantic Corp.; US; 215/963-6000

Albright, Bill; VP, SilverSun Inc.; US; 609/722-0050

Albritton, Paul H.; VP & CFO, Target Technologies Inc.; US; 910/395-6100

Alcala, Al; VP Mktng & Sales, Linkpro Inc.; US; 714/854-3322

Alden, Christopher J.; Assoc Pblr, Herring Communications; US; 415/865-2277

Aldrich, Russ; VP Mktng, PageAhead Software Corp; US; 206/441-0340

Aldrich-Ruenzel, Nancy; Ed Dir, Step-By-Step Graphics; US; 309/688-8800

Aldridge, David L.; Pres, Aldridge Company, The; US; 713/953-1940

Alex, Bill; Dir Sales, Inforite Corp.; US; 415/571-8766

Alexander, Douglas; Pres & CEO, Reality Online Inc.; US; 610/277-7600

Alexander, Lynn; VP Sales & Mktng, Thoroughbred Software Int'l. Inc.; US; 201/560-1377

Alexander, Mark; EVP, Secure Document Systems Inc.; US; 904/725-2505

Alexander, Pam; Pres, Alexander Communications Inc.; US; 404/897-2300

Alexy, George N.; SVP Mktng, Cirrus Logic Inc.; US; 510/623-8300

Alfiero, Sal S.; Chmn & CEO, Mark IV Industries; US; 716/689-4972

Alford, Philip J.; Pres, Tekelec; US; 818/880-5656

Alford, Robert S.; VP, AGE Logic Inc.; US; 619/755-1000

Alfred, John; VP, Xplor International; US; 310/373-3633

Alfson, Donald G.; VP, Vishay Intertechnology; US; 610/644-1300

Alias, Patrick; EVP Sales & Mktng, Cognex Corp.; US; 508/650-3000

Alker, Pauline L.; Pres & CEO, Network Peripherals; US; 408/321-7300

Allaire, Paul A.; Chmn & CEO, Xerox Corp.; US; 203/968-3000

Allal, Allan; Chmn, Integrated Business Computers; US; 805/527-8792

Alland, James M.; EVP & COO, Medicus Systems Corp.; US; 847/570-7500

Allen, Arthur; Pres & CEO, Allen Systems Group; US; 941/435-2200

Allen, Bill; Dir Mktng, Minuteman; US; 214/446-7363

Allen, Brad; Int Systems Coord, VideoLogic Inc.; US; 415/875-0606

Allen, Curt D.; EVP, Folio Corp.; US; 801/344-3700, callen@folio.com

Allen, David P.; Pres, Boston Media Consultants; US; 617/545-2696, dpallen@tiac.net

Allen, J. Norman; SVP New Prod, Duracell Int'l.; US; 203/791-3010

Allen, Kent; SVP Finance, Software Clearing House Inc.; US; 513/579-0455, kallen@sch.com

Allen, Paul; Chmn, Asymetrix Corp.; US; 206/637-5859

Allen, Peter; Mngg Ed, Computer Security Institute; US; 415/905-2626

Allen, Rex; Pres, Allen Communication; US; 801/537-7800, rallen@allencomm.com

Allen, Robert B.; Ed-in-Chief, ACM Transactions on Information Systems; US; 212/869-7440

Allen, Robert E.; Chmn & CEO, AT&T Corp.; US; 212/387-5400

Allen, Steven W.; CEO, Allen Communication; US; 801/537-7800, sallen@allencomm.com

Allen, Thomas G.; VP Sales & Mktng, Effective Mgmt Sys; US; 414/359-9800

Allewaert, Jack; CFO, Davidson & Associates Inc.; US; 310/793-0600

Alley, Allen H.; VP Prod Dev, In Focus Systems Inc.; US; 503/685-8888

Allinger, Doug; VP Sales, Burton Group, The; US; 801/566-2880

Allison, Andrew; Ed, Inside the New Computer Industry; US; 408/626-4361

Allison, Michael J.; VP Sales & Mktng, Tels Corp.; US; 801/571-1182

Allison, Nicholas H.; Ed-in-Chief, Adobe Magazine; US; 206/628-2321

Allweiss, Jack A.; Pres & CEO, Future Domain Corp.; US; 714/253-0400

Allweiss, Patricia A.; VP & CFO, Future Domain Corp.; US; 714/253-0400

Allyn, William F.; Pres, Welch Allyn Inc.; US; 315/685-8945

Almand, Russ; VP WW Sales, IMP Inc.; US; 408/432-9100

Almon Jr., William J.; VP Sales & Mktng, Integral Periph; US; 303/449-8009

Almquist, Gordon L.; VP & CFO, 3D Systems Corp.; US; 805/295-5600

Alnes, Knut; VP Mktng, Dolphin Inc.; US; 805/371-9493

Alon, Shimon; Pres & CEO, Scitex America Corp.; US; 617/275-5150

Alon, Zvi; Chmn, Pres & CEO, NetManage Inc.; US; 408/973-7171

Alper, Alan; Ed, Computerworld Client/Server Journal; US; 508/879-0700, aalper@cw.com

Alper, Bruce; VP Bus Dev, Cambridge Parallel Processing; US; 714/261-8901, bruce@cppus.com

Alper, Martin; CEO, Virgin Interactive Entertainment; US; 714/833-8710

Alpern, Alan; CFO, Infosafe Systems Inc.; US; 212/867-7200

Alpert, Bruce; Pblr, Dealerscope Consumer Electronics Marketplace; US; 215/238-5300

Alpert, Martin A.; EVP Bus Dev, Rexon Inc.; US; 216/349-0600

Alpert, Ron; Pres, UniWorx Inc.; US; 619/740-5111, ralpert@nunic.nu.edu

Alpert, Seth; Pblr, Data Sources; US; 212/503-5861

Alsop, Joseph W.; Pres, Progress Software Corp.; US; 617/280-4000

Alspektor, RoseAnn; Pres & CEO, Valis Group, The; US; 415/435-5404

Altavilla, Peter T.; Controller, Applied Magnetics Corp.; US; 805/683-5353

Altenhof-Long, Cameron; VP & CTO, Colorbus Inc.; US; 714/852-1850

Altieri, Louis J.; VP Fin & Admin, ECCS Inc.; US; 908/747-6995

Altmeyer, David; VP Prod, Fisher Business Communications Inc.; US; 714/556-1313

Altschuler, Stan; Pres, Strategic Growth Int'l. Inc.; US; 516/829-7111

Alumbaugh, Wendell; Pres, Micro Computer Systems; US; 214/659-1624

Alvarez, Antonio; VP R&D, Cypress Semiconductor Corp.; US; 408/943-2600

Alvarez, Kenneth M.; VP, Sun Microsystems Inc.; US; 415/960-1300

Alvis, Jeff; Dir, Lante Corp.; US; 312/236-5100, jalvis@lante.com

Amadon, C. Gregory; Chmn & CEO, Virtual I/O Inc.; US; 206/382-7410

Amaral, Walter; SVP & CFO, NetManage Inc.; US; 408/973-7171

Amaru, Chris; Lab Dir, Client/Server Today Labs; US; 617/964-3030, chrisa@cstoday.com

Amato, Albert; EVP & CTO, Delrina Corp.; Canada; 416/441-3676

Amato, Jay; Pres & CEO, Vanstar Inc.; US; 510/734-4000

Amato, Thomas G.; SVP & CFO, Symbol Technologies Inc.; US; 516/563-2400

Ambegaonkar, Prakash; Pres, Frontier Technologies Corp.; US; 414/241-4555

Ambrose, John A.; CEO, DeltaPoint Inc.; US; 408/648-4000

Ambrozy, Joseph T.; VP Strat Plng, Bell Atlantic Corp.; US; 215/963-6000

Ambwani, Kailash; Pres & CEO, Gold Disk Inc.; US; 408/982-0200

Amdahl, Carl; Chmn & CTO, NetFrame Systems Inc.; US; 408/474-1000

Amdur, Eli; Corp Sales Mgr, MicroVideo Learning Systems; US; 212/777-9595, eli_amdur@microvideo.com

Ameen, Harry; VP Sales & Mktng, Laptop Solutions Inc.; US; 713/556-5051, hameen@lsi-tx.com

Amelio, Gilbert F.; Pres & CEO, Apple Computer Inc.; US; 408/996-1010

Ames, Julie; Dir PR, Capener Matthews & Walcher; US; 619/238-8500

Amine, Gilbert A.; Pres & CEO, Rochelle Comm.; US; 512/339-8188

Amman, Robert J.; Vice Chmn & COO, First Financial Management Corp.; US; 770/857-0001

Amodeo, Mary Ellen; Acct Supv, Shandwick US; US; 612/832-5000, meamodeo@shandwick.com

Amos, C. Allen; Pres & CEO, Disk Technologies Corp.; US; 407/671-5500

Amos, William; VP Tech Svcs, Stonehouse & Co.; US; 214/960-1566

Amran, Yosi; Chmn & Pres, Individual Inc.; US; 617/273-6000

Amsden, Neal; Pres, Endpoint Marketing Information Systems; US; 408/725-4200

Amthor, Geoffrey R.; Ed & Pblr, Multimedia Today; US; 404/531-0096, amthor@aol.com

Amthor, Lori Wild; Assoc Ed, Multimedia Today; US; 404/531-0096

Amundson, Anthony; Pres, Avalan Technology Inc.; US; 508/429-6482

Amundson, Maria; Sr Partner, A&R Partners Inc.; US; 415/363-0982, maria_amundson@arpartners.com

Andeini, Alan J.; EVP, Comdisco Inc.; US; 847/698-3000

Anderl, George; VP Sales, Quality Semiconductor Inc.; US; 408/450-8000

Anders, Billy R.; Pres & CEO, Output Technology Corp.; US; 509/536-0468

Andersen, Joseph G.; CFO, Comptronix Corp.; US; 615/377-3330

Anderson, Alan; Pres & CEO, Quintus Corp.; US; 510/624-2818

Anderson, Arthur G.; Chmn, Compression Labs Inc.; US; 408/435-3000

Anderson, Bob; Natl Mktng Mgr, Parana Supplies Corp.; US; 310/793-1325

Anderson, Bradbury H.; Pres & COO, Best Buy Co. Inc.; US; 612/947-2000

Anderson, Brett; Ed-in-Chief, Portable Computing; 818/593-6100

Anderson, Carl; Pres, Doremus Public Relations; US; 212/366-3000

Anderson, Carl B.; VP Sales, Dataram Corp.; US; 609/799-0071

Anderson, Charles R.; Pres, Cogent Data Technologies Inc.; US; 360/378-2929, chuck@cogentdata.com

Anderson, Chris; Pres, CD-ROM Today; US

Anderson, Chris; VP Sales & Mktng, JASC Inc.; US; 612/930-9800

Anderson, Christine; Exec Assist, QSound Labs Inc.; Canada; 403/291-2492

Anderson, David L.; EVP, Amdahl Corp.; US; 408/746-6000

Anderson, Deanna; EVP, Cogent Data Technologies Inc.; US; 360/378-2929, deanna@cogentdata.com

Anderson, Donald W.; SVP & CFO, Minnesota Educational Computing Corp.; US; 612/569-1500

Anderson, Douglas T.; VP & CTO, Micro House Int'l.; US; 303/443-3389

Anderson, Edward R.; Pres & CEO, CompuCom Systems; US; 214/265-3600

Anderson, Fred; Ed & Pblr, International Info; US; 603/394-7900

Anderson, Howard; Mgng Dir, Yankee Group, The; US; 617/956-5000

Anderson, James; Ed, Information Systems Security; US; 617/423-2020

Anderson, Jill; CFO, Accolade Inc.; US; 408/985-1700

Anderson, Julie; Dir, InformationWEEK Open Labs; US; 516/562-5000

Anderson, Keith; Exec Dir, Business Technology Assoc.; US; 816/941-3100

Anderson, Larry; EVP, McQuerter Group; US; 619/450-0030

Anderson, Michael H.; Chmn, Pres & CEO, Hogan Systems; US; 214/386-0020

Anderson, Mike; Ed, GIS World; US; 970/223-4848, mike@gisworld.com

Anderson, Mimi; Ed, Culpepper Letter, The; US; 770/668-0616, mimi@culpepper.com

Anderson, Neal G.; Pres, Secure Document Systems Inc.; US; 904/725-2505

Anderson, Neil; COO, Tolly Group, The; US; 908/528-3300, nanderson@tolly.com

Anderson, R. Lynn; CFO, GameTek Inc.; US; 305/935-3995

Anderson, Randy; VP Mktng, Numera Software Corp.; US; 206/622-2233, randya@numera.com

Anderson, Raymond; Chmn, IXI Corp.; US; 408/427-7700

Anderson, Robert; Pres, Silicon Valley Research Inc.; US; 415/962-3000

Anderson, Roy M.; Dir SW Eng, Smart Technologies Inc.; Canada; 403/245-0333

Anderson, Sandra L.; Ed-in-Chief, MacHome Journal; US; 415/957-1911

Anderson, Stephen S.; Pres & CEO, Micro House Int'l.; US; 303/443-3389

Anderson, Steven R.; SVP MIS, Best Buy Co. Inc.; US; 612/947-2000

Anderson, Thomas J.; Pres & COO, Computone Corp.; US; 770/475-2725

Anderson, Thomas R.; VP & CFO, QLogic Corp.; US; 714/438-2200

Anderson, Warren; Pres, Anderson Soft-Teach; US; 408/399-0100

Anderson, Will; Karakas, VanSickle, Ouellette Inc.; US; 503/221-1551

Anderson Jr., Fred D.; VP & CFO, Automatic Data Processing Inc.; US; 201/994-5000

Andre, Michael G.; Sr EVP, Methode Electronics Inc.; US; 708/867-9600

Andrea, Douglas; Co-Pres, Andrea Electronics Corp.; US

Andrea, Frank; CEO & Chmn, Andrea Electronics Corp.; US

Andrea, John; Co-Pres, Andrea Electronics Corp.; US

Andreessen, Marc; SVP Tech, Netscape Communications; US; 415/254-1900

Andres, Marc; Pres, Mouse Products Inc.; US; 214/363-8326

Andrew, Joan; VP Sales & Mktng, X-Rite Inc.; US; 616/534-7663

Andrew, Robert S.; Pres, Storage Solutions Inc.; US; 203/325-0035

Andrews, Christopher B.; VP & CFO, Advanced Visual Systems Inc.; US; 617/890-4300

Andrews, David; Pres, D.H. Andrews Group; US; 203/271-1300

Andrews, Dennis W.; Pres, Xsoft; US; 415/813-6920

Andrews, Greg; EVP & CFO, Pro CD Inc.; US; 508/750-0000

Andrews, John; Pres, Pecan Software Corp.; US; 770/594-9707

Andrews, Robert B.; CEO & Dir, Leverage Software Inc.; US; 703/494-0818

Andrews, Steven R.; VP, AM International Inc.; US; 847/818-1294

Andrews, Van; VP Sales, Toshiba America Information Systems Inc.; US; 714/583-3111

Andrews, William; VP Sales & Mktng, Microcom Inc.; US; 617/551-1000

Andriani, Ronald C.; Pblr, Graphic Arts Monthly; US; 303/470-4445

Andrus, Al; SVP Bus Dev, Technology Service Solutions; US; 610/293-2765

Angel, David L.; Pres & CEO, Informa-

tion Storage Devices; US; 408/369-2400

Angelo, Keith; VP Mktng, Chips & Technologies Inc.; US; 408/434-0600

Angelo, Robert; Pres & CEO, SystemSoft Corp.; US; 508/651-0088

Angelone, Alfred C.; Chmn & CEO, ASA International Ltd.; US; 508/626-2727

Angus, Robert; Pres, A&R Partners Inc.; US; 415/363-0982, bob_angus@arpartners.com

Anikst, Mark T.; Chief Scientist, Speech Systems Inc.; US; 303/938-1110

Annecillo, Joyce; Sec & Trea, World Computer Graphics Assoc.; US; 703/642-3050

Annino, Joseph S.; Pres CACI Prod Co, CACI International; US; 703/841-7800

Annunziata, Robert; CEO, Teleport Communications; US; 718/983-2000

Ano, Harold P.; SVP Mktng, EMC Corp.; US; 508/435-1000

Ansley, Charles H.; SVP, DSC Communications Corp.; US; 214/519-3000

Anthony, Perry; Exec Dir, Institute for Certification of Computing Professionals; US; 847/299-4227, 74040.3722@compuserve.com

Anton, William L.; VP Mktng, Vertex Communications; US; 903/984-0555

Antrim, James; Pres, Antex Electronics Corp.; US; 310/532-3092

Antrobus, Fred; MIS Mgr, Microrim Inc.; US; 206/649-9500, freda@microrim.com

Anundson, Robert; VP Mktng, Adaptive Solutions Inc.; US; 503/690-1236

Aoi, Joichi; Chmn, Toshiba Corp.; Japan; 3-3457-4511

Appel, Andrew W.; Ed-in-Chief, ACM Transactions on Programming Languages & Systems; US; 212/869-7440

Applegate, Larry; VP, Ares Software Corp.; US; 415/578-9090

Applegate, W.M.; Pres & CEO, AG Communication Systems Corp.; US; 602/582-7000

Appleton, Bill; Pres, Cyberflix Inc.; US; 615/546-1157, cyberflix@aol.com

Appleton, Steve; Chmn & CEO, Micron Technology Inc.; US; 208/368-4400

Araiza, Michael; VP Mktng, AbTech Corp.; US; 804/977-0686

Arazi, Efi; Chmn, Electronics for Imaging Inc.; US; 415/286-8600

Arcari, John J.; CFO, LTX Corp.; US; 617/461-1000

Archuleta, George; Pres & CEO, Alantec Corp.; US; 408/955-9000, arch@alantec.com

Aretakis, Nicholas; VP Sales, ESS Technology Inc.; US; 510/226-1088

Arett, Kent; VP Sys & Ops, Damark International Inc.; US; 612/531-0066

Arganbright, David; Pres, Grolier Electronic Publishing Inc.; US; 203/797-3500

Ariniello, Robert; Dir Sales, Pentax Technologies Corp.; US; 303/460-1600

Arlen, Gary; Pres, Arlen Communications Inc.; US; 301/656-7940, gaha@prodigy.com

Arme, Jennifer; VP NA Sales, Continuus Software Corp.; US; 714/453-2200

Armin, Payman; Pivotal Software Inc.; Canada; 604/988-9982, parmin@pivotal-soft.com

Armstrong, Anne A.; Ed-in-Chief, Federal Computer Week; US; 847-291-5214, annea@fcw.com

Armstrong, B.F.; Pres, InfoEdge; US; 203/363-7150

Armstrong, Donald B.; Dir Bus Dev, Elo TouchSystems Inc.; US; 615/482-4100

Armstrong, Joseph R.; VP & CFO, State Of The Art Inc.; US; 714/753-1222

Armstrong, Lou; Pblr, Inside Netware; US; 502/493-3300

Armstrong, Robert; Pres, Wizard-Works; US; 612/559-5140

Armstrong, T. Paul; VP, Micros Systems Inc.; US; 301/210-6000

Arn, Robert; Chmn & Pres, InContext Systems Corp.; Canada; 416/922-0087

Arnaudoff, V. Steven; VP Mktng & Sales, JMR Electronics; US; 818/993-4801

Arndt, Phillip; Pblr, GPS World; US; 503/343-1200

Arnett, Nick; Pres, Multimedia Computing Corp.; US; 408/369-1233

Arnfield, Robin; Ed, Multimedia Business Analyst; UK; 171-896-2222

Arnold, Chris; Opticomm Corp.; US; 619/450-0143

Arnold, David C.; Chmn, Pres & CEO, Softdesk Inc.; US; 603/428-3199

Arnold, John B.; Chmn, Network Equipment Technologies; US; 415/366-4400

Arnold, Richard; Ed & Pblr, Disaster Recovery Journal; US; 314/894-0276

Arnold, Stuart; Pblr, PC Week; US; 617/393-3700, stuart_arnold@zd.com

Arnos, John; VP Sales, Canon Computer Systems Inc.; US; 714/438-3000

Aron, Carl R.; Chmn & CEO, RAM Mobile Data; US; 908/602-5500

Aronis, Theodore A.; VP Ops, Xylogics Inc.; US; 617/272-8140

Arrington, Edward; Chairperson, Desktop Management Task Force; US; 503/264-9300

Arrison, Clement R.; Pres, Mark IV Industries; US; 716/689-4972

Arthur, David; SVP Mfg, Interlink Electronics; US; 805/484-8855

Artuso, Giovanna; Dir Mktng, KL Group Inc.; Canada; 416/594-1026, gba@klg.com

Artzt, Russell M.; EVP R&D, Computer Associates Int'l. Inc.; US; 516/342-5224

Asay, Roger; Pblr, Asay Publishing Co.; US; 417/781-9317

Asbury, Steve; Pres, SoftArc Inc.; Canada; 905/415-7000

Ascolese, Mark A.; VP & GM Svcs, Exide Electronics Grp; US; 919/872-3020

Ash, Donald G.; Pres & CEO, Clary Corp.; US; 818/359-4486

Ash, Isaac; Pblr, Edutainment News; US; 415/883-6351

Ashall, John; VP Sales & Mktng, Carroll Touch Inc.; US; 512/244-3500

Ashay, Roger; Pblr, Computer Locator; US; 417/781-9317

Ashby, H. Lee; Pres, Circle Inc., The; US

Asher, Oren; Pres & CEO, Ditek Int'l.; Canada; 416/479-1990

Ashford, Todd J.; CFO, Logic Devices Inc.; US; 408/737-3300

Ashida, Mark; CEO, Internet Profiles Corp.; US; 415/322-9600

Ashton, Robin; Pblr, R&D Magazine; US; 708/635-8800, rdchi@mcimail.com

Asprey, Robert R.; SVP Eng, Cybex Corp.; US; 205/430-4000

Asprey, William; Exec Dir, Computing Research Assoc. Inc.; US; 202/234-2111

Assia, David; Chmn, Pres & CEO, Magic Software Enterprises; US; 714/250-1718

Asten, Lawrence D.; VP Sales, ADC Telecommunications; US; 612/938-8080

Astley, Robert E.; VP Sales, AGE Logic Inc.; US; 619/755-1000

Aston, Murray; Pres & CTO, Business-Vision Management Systems Inc.; Canada; 905/629-3233

Aston, Robert; Pres, Aplet Warehouse; US; 408/426-4400

Aston, Robert; Pres, Market Vision; US; 408/426-4400

Ater, William C.; VP & CAO, Anacomp Inc.; US; 317/844-9666

Atherly, John; VP Fin, Asymetrix Corp.; US; 206/637-5859

Atkins, Gary; Chmn, Extended Sys; US

Atkinson, Chuck; Pres, CAP Automation; US; 817/560-7007

Atkinson, Jan; VP, CAP Automation; US; 817/560-7007

Attard, Paul G.; Pres & COO, Multicom Publishing Inc.; US; 415/777-5300

Attard, Tamara L.; Chmn & CEO, Multicom Publishing Inc.; US; 415/777-5300

Atwood, E. Terrell; VP, Mitel Corp.; Canada; 613/592-2122

Au, Spenser; Pblr, Asian Sources Computer Products; Hong Kong; 852-25554777

Auckerman, William; Ed-in-Chief, Computing Japan; Japan; 3-3445-2616

Auditore, Stephen; Pres, Zona Research; US; 415/568-5700

Auerbach, Alexander; Pres, Alexander Auerbach & Co. Inc.; US; 818/501-4221

Auerbuch, Boris J.; SVP & CTO, Premisys Communications; US; 510/353-7600

Aufdemberge, James; VP Sales & Mktng, Information Management Associates Inc.; US; 203/925-6800

Augun, Audrey; VP Mktng, Percussion Software Inc.; US; 617/438-9900, audrey_augun@percussion.com

August, Ray; CTO, Great Plains Software; US; 701/281-0550

Augustine, Norman R.; CEO, Lockheed Martin; US; 301/897-6000

Augustyniak, Lisa K.; Pres, Autumn Technologies; US; 813/530-0626

Augustyniak, Peter G.; VP, Autumn Technologies; US; 813/530-0626

Aull, Denis W.; VP Eng & CTO, Telebit Corp.; US; 508/441-2181

Auray, Robert; VP & CFO, Entex Information Services; US; 914/935-3600

Ausman, Richard; Pblr, Lakewood Publications; US; 612/333-0471

Auvil, Anina; GM, Tharo Systems Inc.; US; 216/273-4408

Avaregan, Rousan; Controller, Spur Products Corp.; US; 208/377-0001

Aver, Carolyn V.; VP & CFO, ParcPlace-Digitalk Inc.; US; 408/481-9090

Avery, Hal; Pblr, Object Magazine; US; 212/229-0320

Avery, Marti; Admin Mgr, International Technology Group; US; 415/964-2565

Avida, Dan; Pres & CEO, Electronics for Imaging Inc.; US; 415/286-8600

Axelrod, Stephen D.; Mgng Dir, Wolfe Axelrod Assoc.; US; 212/370-4500

Axt, Bryon D.; COO, Jones Futurex Inc.; US; 916/632-3456

Ayati, Mehrdad; Pres, Industrial CPU Systems Inc.; US; 714/957-2815

Ayer, Neil R.; VP, Timeslips Corp.; US; 214/248-9232

Ayers, Larry G.; VP & CFO, Southern Electronics Corp.; US; 770/491-8962

Ayers, Robert; Chief Eng, Applied Resources Inc.; US; 913/492-8888

Aylesworth, William A.; SVP & CFO, Texas Instruments Inc.; US; 214/995-2551

Ayob, Tarek; VP Sales & Mktng, Optima Technology Corp.; US; 714/476-0515

Azar, Deborah; Co-Founder, Streetwise Software Inc.; US; 310/829-7827

Azcuy, Gregg M.; Pres & COO, ECCS Inc.; US; 908/747-6995

Azzara, Mike; Pblr, CommunicationsWeek; US; 516/562-5530

Azzouz, Kevin; Pres & COO, Arcada Software Inc.; US; 407/333-7500

Baan, Jan; Chmn & CEO, Baan Co.; US; 415/462-4949

Babb, Gerry; Pres, GRB Consulting; US; 408/741-1917

Babitch, Daniel; VP Eng, Wireless Logic Inc.; US; 408/262-1876

Babitsky, Timlynn; Ed, Object Technology, Directory of; US; 212/242-7447

Baceski, Dave; Ed Dir, Omray Inc.; US; 512/250-1700

Bach, Toni; Ed, Enterprise Internetworking Journal; US; 214/669-9000

Bachinsky, Frank W.; VP, Alydaar Software Corp.; US; 704/544-0092

Bachman, Charles W.; Chmn, Cayenne Software; US; 617/273-9003

Bachman, Tom; Pres & CEO, Inteco Corp.; US; 203/866-4400

Bachrach, Bob; Tech Dir, Martin Communications; US; 415/668-2678

Backes, Mike; Co-Founder, Rocket Science Games Inc.; US; 415/442-5000

Bacon, John C.; Pres, XcelleNet Inc.; US; 770/804-8100

Badault, Jean-Luc; Pres & CEO, Thomson Software; US; 203/845-5000

Baer, Nancy; Mktng Mgr, Computer Security Institute; US; 415/905-2626

Baerson, Kevin; Ed, High Performance Computing & Communications Week; US; 202/638-4260

Baessler, Ernest J.; EVP Fin, CalComp Inc.; US; 714/821-2000

Bahash, Robert J.; EVP & CFO, McGraw-Hill Inc.; US; 212/512-2000

Bahr, Ted; Pblr, OS/2 Magazine; US; 415/905-2382

Baiada, Mel; Pres, Bluestone Inc.; US; 609/727-4600

Bailey, Cassanora; Sales Mgr, Apsylog Inc.; US; 415/812-7700

Bailey, Christine E.; Assoc Ed, Retail Systems Reseller; US; 201/895-3300

Bailey, David T.; EVP, Policy Management Systems Corp.; US; 803/735-4000

Bailey, Joe; VP Sales, Abra Cadabra Software; US; 813/527-1111

Bailey, Mark; SVP Bus Dev, Symantec Corp.; US; 408/253-9600

Baird, Robert E.; VP Mktng, Good Guys Inc., The; US; 415/615-5000

Baird, Scott; Pres, Promodel Corp.; US; 801/223-4600

Baisden, Harry L.; Pblr, Multimedia Daily; US; 703/816-8640

Bajarin, Tim; Pres, Creative Strategies; US; 408/985-1110

Bajkowski, John; Ed, Computerized Investing; US; 312/280-0170, jbajowski@aol.com

Baker, Don; Pres, BSG Corp.; US; 713/965-9000

Baker, Edward D.; SVP, Barra Inc.; US; 510/548-5442

Baker, James K.; Chmn & CEO, Dragon Systems Inc.; US; 617/965-5200

Baker, Janet M.; Pres, Dragon Systems Inc.; US; 617/965-5200

Baker, Joanna L.; Dir Membership, Association for Services Management Int'l.; US; 941/275-7887

Baker, Kurt; VP Sales & Svcs, Revelation Software; US; 203/973-1000

Baker, Neil; VP Sales & Mktng, Onyx Graphics Corp.; US; 801/568-9900

Bakewell, Tom; Dir CIS, Sierra Semiconductor Corp.; US; 408/263-9300

Bakshi, Naren; Chmn, Pres & CEO, Vision Software Tools; US; 510/238-4100

Balaban, Irwin; Pres, Robocom Systems Inc.; US; 516/795-5100

Balanson, Richard; EVP & CTO, Maxtor Corp.; US; 408/432-1700

Baldauf, Sari; Pres Cellular Syst, Nokia Group; Finland; 3580-18071

Baldini, Carl; VP Eng, RDI Computer Corp.; US; 619/929-0992

Baldwin, Rand; Exec Dir, Common - A Users Group; US; 312/644-6610

Bales, Robert C.; Exec Dir, National Computer Security Assoc.; US; 717/258-1816

Balkanski, Alexandre A.; EVP & COO, C-Cube Microsystems; US; 408/944-6300

Ball, Charles L.; VP Sales, nView Corp.; US; 804/873-1354

Ball, Ken; Tech Ed Dir, Industry.Net; US; 412/967-3500

Ball, Kim; VP Prod Dev, XDB Systems Inc.; US; 410/312-9300

Ballantine, John; EVP, Online Interactive Inc.; US; 206/443-1933

Ballard, Clint; CEO, Ballard Synergy; US; 360/697-9260

Ballard, Greg; Pres Capcom Ent, Capcom; US; 408/727-0500

Ballard, Michael K.; VP Mktng & Sls, Uunet Technologies; US; 703/206-5600

Ballard, Richard; Dir Sales, Crystal-Graphics Inc.; US; 408/496-6175

Ballmer, Steven A.; EVP, Microsoft Corp.; US; 206/936-4400

Ballowee, Jeffrey; Pres Interactive Media, Ziff-Davis Publishing Co.; US; 212/503-3500

Balthaser, Don; VP Eng, STB Systems Inc.; US; 214/234-8750

Balthazar, James A.; VP Mktng, Convex Computer Corp.; US; 214/497-4000

Banatao, Diosdado P.; Chmn, S3 Inc.; US; 408/980-5400

Banes, David; VP Ops, S&S Software Int'l. Inc.; US; 617/273-7400

Banfield, Jeanne; VP, Advisor Communications Int'l. Inc.; US; 619/483-6400

Bankhead, David R.; SVP & CFO, Hogan Systems Inc.; US; 214/386-0020

Bantleman, John T.; Pres & CEO, LBMS; US; 713/625-9300

Barada, Robert L.; VP Corp Strategy & Dev, Pacific Telesis Grp; US; 415/394-3000

Baranello, Floyd; Mktng Mgr, Raymond Engineering Inc.; US; 203/632-4643

Baranowski, Joe; VP Mktng, Oki Semiconductor; US; 408/720-1900

Barbee, Jean; Exec Dir, Acute Inc.; US; 913/233-1919, barbee@smartnet.net

Barber, Kathryn; VP, LCS Industries Inc.; US; 201/778-5588

Barber, Larry; COO, Integrated Information Technology; US; 408/727-1885

Barber, Paul; VP Sales, DayStar Digital Inc.; US; 770/967-2077

Barbie Kapaun, Marilyn; Ed, Digital Output; US; 404/524-6954

Bardagy, Robert A.; EVP, Comdisco Inc.; US; 847/698-3000

Bargell, Dana; Sales Mgr, Specialized Business Solutions; US; 970/262-1720

Barger, Sean B.; Chmn, Equilibrium; US; 415/332-4343

Barillaud, Alain D.; Sales, Softwex International Ltd.; Canada; 604/689-9720

Barkelew, Bruce; Pres, Datastorm Technologies Inc.; US; 573/443-3282

Barker, Dwight G.; Sales Dir, Neon Software Inc.; US; 510/283-9771, dwight@neon.com

Barker, Floyd; EVP, Coast Manufacturing Co.; US; 914/376-1500

Barker, Lee J.; VP Ops, Chips & Technologies Inc.; US; 408/434-0600

Barker, Richard D.; VP, Adaptiv Software Inc.; US; 714/789-7300, barker@adaptiv.com

Barksdale, James; Pres & CEO, Netscape Communications Corp.; US; 415/254-1900

Barnea, Dan; CEO, New Dimension Software; US; 714/757-4300

Barnes, Greg; Pres, Extensis Corp.; US; 503/274-2020

Barnes, K. Ray; Sec, Learning Services Inc.; US; 541/683-3827, ray@ls.learnserv.com

Barnes, W. Michael; SVP & CFO, Rockwell International; US; 310/797-3311

Barnett, Bruce; Pres & CEO, Cahners Publishing Co.; US; 617/558-4565

Barnett, Chris; Sr Ed, High-Tech Hot Wire/High-Tech Hot Sheet; US; 415/421-6220

Barnett, Holly; VP & GM, Benjamin Group Inc., The; US; 714/753-0755, hbarnett@oc.tbji.com

Barnett, James; Chmn & CEO, Accolade Inc.; US; 408/985-1700

Barnett, Robyn; PR Coord, Fraser/Young Inc.; US; 310/451-0300

Barnsley, Michael F.; CTO, Iterated Systems Inc.; US; 770/840-0310

Barnum, Greg; SVP & CFO, Tricord Systems Inc.; US; 612/557-9005

Baron, Peter; Pres, Baron, McDonald & Wells; US; 770/492-0373, pbaron@bmwpr.com

Baroni III, Roland A.; EVP, NuIQ Software Inc.; US; 914/833-3479, roland@nuiq.com

Barquin, Ramon C.; Pres, Washington Consulting Group; US; 301/951-3021

Barr, Anthony J.; Pres, Barr Systems Inc.; US; 904/371-3050

Barr, Dina; Dir Mktng, Advantage kbs Inc.; US; 908/287-2236, dbarr@akbs.com

Barr, Karen; VP Sales & Mktng, SeeColor Corp.; US; 415/949-8610

Barr, Kay; VP, Barr Systems Inc.; US; 904/371-3050

Barresi, Joseph A.; VP Sales, Elo Touch-Systems Inc.; US; 615/482-4100

Barrett, Craig R.; EVP & COO, Intel Corp.; US; 408/765-8080

Barrett, Jack; CEO, Appoint; US; 510/803-8850

Barrett, Peter; EVP, Rocket Science Games Inc.; US; 415/442-5000

Barrett, Peter; VP WW Sales & Svc, Perkin-Elmer Corp.; US; 203/762-1000

Barrett, Phil; VP SW Dev, Progressive Networks; US; 206/447-0567

Barrett, Tom; Pres, Embedded Systems Products Inc.; US; 713/561-9990, atb@esphou.com

Barriero, Vincent; SVP MIS, Sharper Image Corp.; US; 415/445-6000

Barron, Bryan; Pres, InfoBusiness Inc.; US; 801/221-1100

Barron, Patrick; VP Sales, MicroSolutions Inc.; US; 815/756-3411

Barrow, Michael; VP & CTO, Mesa Group; US; 617/964-7400

Barrow, Rob; CEO, JSB Corp.; US; 408/438-8300

Barry, Colin; VP Eng, Xecom Inc.; US; 408/945-6640

Barry, Doug; Pres, Object Database Management Group; US; 612/953-7250, dbarry@odmg.org

Barry, George; CFO, Microware Systems Corp.; US; 515/224-1929

Barry, George J.; VP & CFO, Comptek Research Inc.; US; 716/677-4070

Barry, John A.; Ed, Sybase Magazine; US; 510/596-3500

Barry, Tim; Pres, Design Technology; US; 619/448-2888

Barry, Timothy C.; Pres & CEO, MicroSpeed Inc.; US

Bartenbach, Bill; Pres, Association of Information & Dissemination Centers; US; 706/542-6820

Barth, Nick; Pres & CEO, Armor Systems Inc.; US; 407/323-9787

Bartholet, Tom; VP Corp Dev, Odetics Inc.; US; 714/774-5000

Bartholomew, Alan; Owner, Trio Systems; US; 818/584-9706

Bartkowski, Adam S.; VP Prod, System Software Associates; US; 312/258-6000

Bartlett, Barry; VP Research, Frost & Sullivan Inc.; US; 415/961-9000

Bartlett, Jeffrey; Exec Ed, UniForum's UniNews; US; 408/986-8840, jeffb@uniforum.org

Bartlett, P.G.; VP Mktng, ArborText Inc.; US; 313/996-3566

Bartolomeo, Mark; Pres, Softlab Inc.; US; 770/668-8811

Barton, Michael; VP Mktng, Component Integration Laboratories; US; 408/864-0300

Bartsch, Arlen; Dir SAles & Mktng, Corel Corp.; Canada; 613/728-8200

Bartz, Bill; Pres & CEO, Petrotechnical Open Software Corp.; US; 713/784-1880

Bartz, Carol; Chmn, Pres & CEO, Autodesk Inc.; US; 415/507-5000

Basche, Todd; VP Eng, Visioneer; US; 415/812-6400

Basilicato, Al; Pres & CEO, Numonics Corp.; US; 215/362-2766

Baskett, Forest; SVP R&D, Silicon Graphics Inc.; US; 415/960-1980

Baskin, Cathryn; Ed, PC World; US;

415/243-0500

Bass, Charlie; Chmn, Meridian Data Inc.; US; 408/438-3100

Bass, Joan; Ed, Computing Research News; US; 202/234-2111, jbass@cra.org

Bass, Juernene; Prod Mgr, Creative Solutions Inc.; US; 410/766-4080

Bass, Robert W.; VP Ops, Xircom Inc.; US; 805/376-9300

Bassari, David; GM, Cougar Mountain Software; US; 208/375-4455

Bassett, William E.; EVP, BancTec Inc.; US; 214/450-7700

Bassi, Bruno; Pres, Computer Economics Inc.; US; 619/438-8100

Bassin, Ron; Pres, Four Season Software; US; 908/248-6667

Baszucki, David; Pres, Knowledge Revolution; US; 415/574-7777

Baszucki, Greg; VP Sales, Knowledge Revolution; US; 415/574-7777

Baszucki, Paul; Chmn, Knowledge Revolution; US; 415/574-7777

Bates, Amy; Ed, Technology Exchange, The; US

Bates, Brian; VP & GM, Transaction Network Services Inc.; US; 703/742-0500

Bates, Diane; Dir Mktng, Melita International; US; 770/446-7800

Bates, Phil; Pres, Artbeats Software Inc.; US; 503/863-4429

Bates, Robert; Pres, Legend Entertainment Co.; US; 703/222-8500

Batesman, Giles H.; Chmn, CompUSA Inc.; US; 214/982-4000

Battaglia, Mark; VP Corp Mktng, SPSS Inc.; US; 312/329-2400

Battaglia, Michael S.; Pres & CEO, Fischer International Systems Corp.; US; 941/643-1500

Battelle, John; Mgng Ed, Wired Magazine; US; 415/904-0660

Battersby, Gregory J.; Author, Multimedia & Technology Licensing Agreements; US

Battista, Richard; CEO, LDB; US; 215/957-0300

Batty, Robert L.; Pres, Xaos Tools; US; 415/487-7000

Bauer, Edward J.; Pres & CEO, Software Clearing House Inc.; US; 513/579-0455, ebauer@sch.com

Bauer, Michael; Pres, Internet Group Inc., The; US; 412/688-9696, bauer@tig.com

Bauer, Robb; GM, Hard Drive Associates Inc.; US; 503/233-2821

Bauer, Robert J.; SVP Int'l Bus Dev, Telco Systems Inc.; US; 617/551-0300

Bauer, Ron; Mktng Mgr, Silton-Bookman Systems; US; 408/446-1170, rbauer@sbsinc.com

Bauer, Roxy; MIS Mgr, Information Hotline; US; 908/536-7673

Bauer, Stan; VP & GM Magnetic Div, Fuji Photo Film US Inc.; US; 914/789-8100

Bauer, Tammy; Mgr End User Scvs,

UNIX System Price Performance Guide; US; 408/748-8649, tammy@aim.com

Bauer, Tammy L.; Dir, Aim Technology; US; 408/748-8649, tammy@aim.com

Baughman, Douglas M.; Contr Ed, Edutainment News; US; 415/883-6351

Baulch, Howard; EVP & CTO, Checkfree Corp.; US; 614/825-3000

Baum, Paul; Pres & CEO, Rumarson Technologies Inc.; US; 908/298-9300

Baumbach, Karl; Dir Bus Dev, 1st Tech Corp.; US; 512/258-3570

Bausman, Joeph N.; Pres Auto Sys Div, Reynolds & Reynolds; US; 513/443-2000

Baute, Joseph A.; Chmn, Nashua Corp.; US; 603/880-2323

Bay, Gretchen J.; Mgng Ed, 3D Design; US; 415/905-2200, gbay@mfi.com

Bayens, Thomas; Dir Mktng, Telecomputer Inc.; US; 714/438-3993

Bayer, Barry D.; Ed, Law Office Technology Review; US; 610/359-9900, bbaygrnn@counsel.com

Bayman, James L.; Chmn, Pres & CEO, Pioneer-Standard Electronics Inc.; US; 216/587-3600

Bayne, Art; Pres, GetC Software Inc.; Canada; 604/254-5521

Bayne, Kim M.; Pres, wolfBayne Communications; US; 719/593-8032

Bayz, George G.; Pres & COO, MAI Systems Corp.; US; 714/580-0700

Beach, Gary; Pblr, Computerworld Client/Server Journal; US; 508/879-0700

Beale, Stephen; Exec Ed, Micro Publishing Press; US; 310/371-5787

Beale, Susan; Ed, ID Systems, European Edition; France; 33-88-606257

Beall, Donald R.; Chmn & CEO, Rockwell International; US; 310/797-3311

Beam, Kevin; Dir Res, Reliability Ratings; US; 617/444-5755

Beame, Carl; Chmn & CTO, Beame & Whitside Software; US; 919/831-8989

Beamsley, Jeff; VP Sales, Hilgraeve Inc.; US; 313/243-0576

Bean, Michael; Arizona Macintosh Users Group; US; 602/553-8966, bean@amug.org

Bearnson, Lisa; Ed-in-Chief, WordPerfect Magazine; US; 801/226-5555, lisabe@wpmag.com

Beasley, William G.; Ed, CALS/CE Report; US; 713/690-7644

Beasley Jr., E.T.; Dir Tech, Data Entry Systems Inc.; US; 205/430-3023

Beatenbough, D.J.; Dir Fin, Cegelec ESCA; US; 206/822-6800

Beatty, Richard H.; EVP, SHL Systemhouse Inc.; Canada; 613/236-1428

Beatty, Scott; Pblr, Pro CD Inc.; US; 508/750-0000

Beaulieu, Vivian; Exec Dir, Frame Relay Forum; US; 415/578-6980

Beaumont, Jeffrey; CFO, CyberMedia Inc.; US; 310/843-0800

Beavers, Kelly; EVP Eng, Datasonix

Corp.; US; 303/545-9500

Beazley, Donald E.; Chmn & CFO, Tusk Inc.; US; 407/625-1101

Beban, Shelley; VP Fin & Admin, Jian Tools for Sales Inc.; US; 415/254-5600, sbeban@jianusa.com

Bechanan, Jim; CFO, Excalibur Technologies Corp.; US; 619/438-7900

Beck, Daniel; VP, Barra Inc.; US; 510/548-5442

Beck, Peter; COO, VideoLan Technologies Inc.; US; 502/895-4858

Beck, Robert J.; EVP, Quality Systems Inc.; US; 714/731-7171

Becker, Hal; CEO, Integrated Circuit Engineering Corp.; US; 602/998-9780

Becker, John C.; EVP, Axent Technologies; US; 301/258-2620

Becker, Larry; CFO, Big Island Communications Inc.; US; 408/342-8300

Beckers, C.E.; SVP, Barra Inc.; US; 510/548-5442

Beckert, Beverly; Mgng Ed, Computer-Aided Engineering; US; 216/696-7000

Beckman, Carol; Pres, Quibus Enterprises Inc.; US; 719/527-1384

Bedard, Michael; VP Fin, Quintus Corp.; US; 510/624-2818

Bedell, Gene; Pres & CEO, Seer Technologies Inc.; US; 919/380-5000

Bedford, William; VP Tech Mktng, Raidtec Corp; US; 770/664-6066

Bedini, John; Pres, Bedini Electronics Inc.; US; 208/667-8300

Bednar, Pam; Mktng Mgr, Ontrack Computer Systems Inc.; US; 612/937-1107, pamb@ontrack.com

Bedrick, Jerry; Pres, Mystic River Software Inc.; US; 617/497-1585

Beebower, Gilbert L.; EVP, SEI Corp.; US; 610/254-1000

Beecher, Gil; Mgr, Prairie Group; US; 515/225-9620, psgilb@aol.com

Beedle, Jack; Chmn, In-Stat Inc.; US; 602/483-4440

Beeman, Gary; Pres, FieldWorks Inc.; US; 612/947-0856

Beer, Bennett J.; Pres, Computer Expressions Inc.; US; 215/487-7700

Beeson, Daryl; Mgr MIS, Andataco; US; 619/453-9191, daryl@andataco.com

Befeler, Mike; Partner, Storage Systems Marketing; US; 303/499-0281, mikebef@aol.com

Begelman, Mark D.; Pres & COO, Office Depot Inc.; US; 407/278-4800

Beggs, John; Pres WW Sales, Micro Focus Inc.; US; 415/856-4161, jnb@mfltd.co.uk

Behrendt, Ken; CFO, Lawson Software; US; 612/379-2633, ken.behrendt@lawson.com

Behrendt, Peter D.; Chmn, Pres & CEO, Exabyte Corp.; US; 303/442-4333

Behrens, Mark; VP Ops, Dallas Digital Corp.; US; 214/424-2800

Beirne, Patrick R.; Chief Eng, Corel

Corp.; Canada; 613/728-8200

Belanger, Donna; Sr Analyst, Software Industry Financial Review; US; 508/366-2031

Belden, John C.; Chmn, Pres & CEO, OCTuS Inc.; US; 619/268-5140

Belden, Leigh; Pres, Verilink Corp.; US; 408/945-1199

Belfer, Alec; EVP Mktng, CallWare Technologies; US; 801/486-9922

Belfer, Alexander; Pres & CEO, Soft-Talk Inc.; US; 617/433-0800

Bell, Anthony G.; VP Tech, Logic Devices Inc.; US; 408/737-3300

Bell, George; CEO, Exite Inc.; US; 415/934-3611

Bell, Jim; Pres, Precision Risc Organization; US; 408/447-4249

Bell, Linda L.; Chief Ed, NASA Tech Briefs; US; 212/490-3999

Bell, Marc H.; Pres, Stellar Graphics Corp.; US; 212/982-0800, mhb@pfm.net

Bell, P. Jackson; EVP & CFO, Conner Peripherals Inc.; US; 408/456-4500

Bell, Warren; Dir Sales, Crystal Inc.; Canada; 604/681-3435

Bellack, Bob; VP Ops, Compton's NewMedia Inc.; US; 619/929-2500

Bellow, Stephen; VP Sales & Mktng, Belkin Components; US; 310/898-1100

Bellows, Bill; Partner, Copithorne & Bellows; US; 415/284-5200

Belluzzo, Richard E.; EVP Computer Org, Hewlett-Packard; US; 408/553-4300

Belson, Ross A.; Pres & COO, General DataComm Industries; US; 203/574-1118

Belt, J. Edward; SVP Eng & CTO, Printronix Inc.; US; 714/863-1900

Ben-Artzi, Amatzia; VP Bus Dev, NetManage Inc.; US; 408/973-7171

Ben-Zvi, Gideon; Pres & CEO, Ligature Software Inc.; US; 617/238-6734

Benadretti, Joey; VP Mktng, Syspro Impact Software Inc.; US; 714/437-1000

Benanto, Ronald R.; SVP & CFO, Viewlogic Systems Inc.; US; 508/480-0881

Benavides, Robert; VP Sales & Mktng, Indiana Cash Drawer; US; 317/398-6643

Bench, Bob; CFO, Cerprobe Corp.; US; 602/497-4200

Benco, David; EVP, Numerical Algorithms Group Inc.; US; 630/971-2337, benco@nag.com

Benda, Victor C.; Pres & COO, Analysts International Corp.; US; 612/835-5900

Bender, Brian W.; VP & CFO, Egghead Inc.; US; 509/922-7031

Bender, Dean; Partner, Bender, Goldman Helper; US; 310/473-4147, d_bender@bgh.com

Bender, Robert A.; Pres, Pentax Technologies Corp.; US; 303/460-1600

Bendfelt, Richard E.; Dir Sales, TechSource Inc.; US; 407/262-7100, dick@techsource.com

Benedict, Kevin; Pres, Life Change Productions; US

Benedict, Stephen H.; Pres, Micro Star Software; US

Benerofe, Stanley; SVP, Avnet Inc.; US; 516/466-7000

Benfatto, John; VP, Phar Lap Software Inc.; US; 617/661-1510

Benfield, Steve; Chmn, PowerBuilder Developer's Journal; US; 201/332-1515

Benford, Elizabeth; EVP Mktng, Computer Product Testing Services Inc.; US; 908/223-5700

Benford, Tom; Pres & CEO, Computer Product Testing Services Inc.; US; 908/223-5700, benfordtom@aol.com

Benhamou, Eric A.; Pres & CEO, 3Com Corp.; US; 408/764-5000

Beninatii, Joseph P.; Chmn, C3 Inc.; US; 703/471-6000

Benjamin, George N.; Pres & CEO, TIE/Communications; US; 913/344-0400

Benjamin, Sheri; Principal, Benjamin Group Inc., The; US; 714/753-0755

Benko, Christina; VP Mktng & Sales, Tharo Systems Inc.; US; 216/273-4408

Benner, Brenda; Mgng Ed, MacWeek; US; 415/243-3500

Bennett, Bill; Pres, Folio Corp.; US; 801/344-3700, bbennett@folio.com

Bennett, Bruce A.; Ed-in-Chief, EDN Products Edition; US; 201/292-5100

Bennett, Don; Pres, Videomedia Inc.; US; 408/227-9977, dbennett@videomedia.com

Bennett, Gary K.; VP Fin & CFO, Gerber Scientific Inc.; US; 860/644-1551

Bennett, George; VP Sales, Memorex Telex Corp.; US; 214/444-3500

Bennett, Mike; Mgng Ed, Multilingual Computing Magazine; US; 208/263-8178

Bennett, Roger A.; VP, Pacific Image Electronics Inc.; US; 310/214-5281

Bennie, Dennis; Chmn & CEO, Delrina Corp.; Canada; 416/441-3676

Bennington, Richard M.; EVP Ops, Office Depot Inc.; US; 407/278-4800

Benson, Craig R.; Chmn & COO, Cabletron Systems; US; 603/332-9400

Benson, Jerry; Pres, NEC Technologies Inc.; US; 508/264-8000

Benson, Paul A.; Pres, Knowledge Media; US; 916/872-7487

Benson, Scott K.; Tahoe Peripherals; US; 702/832-3600

Benson, Woody; VP Mktng & Sales, Shiva Corp.; US; 617/270-8300

Benthall, Timothy; VP Int Com, Information Builders Inc.; US; 212/736-4433

Bentley, Greg; Pres, Bentley Systems Inc.; US; 610/458-5000

Bentley, Richard D.; EVP, Marshall Industries; US; 818/307-6000

Benz, Randy; VP Fin, Energizer Power Systems; US; 904/462-3911

Berenguel, Leo; Pres, Peripheral Land Inc.; US; 510/657-2211

Berey, Don; VP, Blenheim Group US Inc.; US; 201/346-1400, dberey@blenheim.com

Bereziuk, Mike; SVP, National Semiconductor Corp.; US; 408/721-5000

Berger, Chuck; Chmn & CEO, Radius Inc.; US; 408/541-6100

Berger, Robert; Founder & CTO, InterNex Information Services; US; 408/327-2355, rberger@internex.com

Berger, Stacie; Publicist, North Light Books–Div. F&W Publications; US; 513/531-2222

Berghof, Pattie; Ed Assist, Support Solutions; US; 206/619-4357

Bergins, Lewis A.; EVP, Microcom Inc.; US; 617/551-1000

Bergman, Evan; VP, Development Technologies Inc.; US; 803/790-9230

Bergman, Noel J.; Pres, Development Technologies Inc.; US; 803/790-9230

Bergman, Peter; VP Mktng, Canon Computer Systems; US; 714/438-3000

Bergreen, Zack; Pres & CEO, Astea Int'l.; US; 215/822-8888

Bergroth, Ismo; Dir Tech, Data Fellows Inc.; US; 415/354-0233

Bergsson, Magnus; US Sales & Mktng Mgr, Traffic US Inc.; US; 407/995-5282

Beringsmith, Alan; CFO, RadioMail Corp.; US; 415/286-7800

Berkaloff, Pierre; CTO, Ray Dream Inc.; US; 415/960-0768, berkaloff@raydream.com

Berke, Howard; Pres & CEO, White Pine Software Inc.; US; 603/886-9050

Berkley, Stephen M.; Chmn, Quantum Corp.; US; 408/894-4000

Berkman, Robert I.; Ed, Information Advisor; US

Berko, Frank; Chmn & CEO, Moses Computers; US; 408/358-1550

Berkowitz, Barak; VP Sales & Mktng, Logitech Inc.; US; 510/795-8500

Berliant, Jennie; Sales Dir, North Light Books–Div. F&W Publications; US; 513/531-2222

Berman, Donald; Pres, Modgraph Inc.; US; 617/938-4488

Berman, Ferry; Exec Dir, Center for Democracy & Tech; US; 202/637-9800

Berman, J.M.; Pres & CEO, Metrica Inc.; US; 617/756-0022

Berman, Jeffrey S.; Pblr, Digital Systems Journal; US; 215/643-8000

Berman, Michael; VP Mktng, Modgraph Inc.; US; 617/938-4488

Bernard, John; SVP Sales & Mktng, SSI Products Inc.; US; 818/305-0508

Bernier, Brian; EVP, Infographix Technologies Inc.; US; 404/523-4944

Bernstein, Louis; Developer, Bernstein & Associates; US; 770/392-1488

Bernstein, Stuart A.; VP Sales & Mktng, True Software Inc.; US; 508/369-7398, stu@truesoft.com

Berry, Frank; Dir Mktng, Andataco; US; 619/453-9191, frankb@andataco.com

Berry, Fred; Dir Mktng, Arnet Corp.;

Berry, Steve; Pres, Electronic Trend Publications; US; 408/369-7000, saberry@electronictrendpubs.com

Berry, Tim; Pres, Palo Alto Software; US; 541/683-6162, timberry@aol.com

Berry, William A.; SVP & CFO, Compression Labs Inc.; US; 408/435-3000

Berst, Jesse; Founding Ed, Windows Watcher; US; 206/881-7354, jessee@jesseeberst.com

Bertelli, Jay; Pres, Mercury Computer Systems Inc.; US; 508/256-1300

Bertini, Michael; CEO, Open Systems Holdings Corp.; US; 612/829-0011

Bertolami, Mark S.; Group Prod Mgr, Duracell Int'l.; US; 203/791-3010

Bertrand, Dick; VP Eng, Sherpa Corp.; US; 408/433-0455

Bertucci, Nora; Acct Supv, Greenstone Roberts; US; 516/249-3366

Berutti, Victor F.; VP, Principia Products Inc.; US; 610/429-1359, 70461.1470@compuserve.com

Berzins, Lauren A.; VP Dist, TDC Interactive; US; 310/452-6720

Bessette, Robert M.; Pres & CEO, Core Technology Corp.; US; 517/627-1521

Best, Anita; Ed, International Society for Technology in Education; US; 541/346-4414

Best, Charles; Dir NA Sales, Software Clearing House Inc.; US; 513/579-0455, cbest@sch.com

Bethea, Jamie; VP Financial Sales, Soricon Corp.; US; 303/440-2800

Betterly, Laurence L.; CFO, Cray Research Inc.; US; 612/452-6650

Betty, Charles G.; Pres & COO, EarthLink Network Inc.; US; 818/296-2400

Beyer, Tom; Hi-tech/Fax-on-demand, PR Newswire; US; 212/596-1500, tbeyer@prnews.attmail.com

Beylouny, George; SVP Ops, Murata Electronics North America Inc.; US; 404/436-1300

Bhargava, Rajat; Pres & CEO, net.Genesis; US; 617/577-9800

Bhasin, Bhupi; Pres, Portable Graphics Inc.; US; 512/719-8000

Bhat, Jayaram; VP Mktng, Mercury Interactive Corp.; US; 408/523-9900

Bhatia, Joe; VP Ext Affairs, Underwriters Laboratories Inc.; US; 847/272-8800

Biagi, Susan; Sr Ed, Network VAR; US; 415/905-2200

Bialek, Paul; CFO, Edmark Corp.; US; 206/556-8400

Bialek, Stanley; Co-Founder, Number Nine Visual Technology Corp.; US; 617/674-0009

Bialo, Ellen; Pres, Interactive Educational Systems Design Inc.; US; 212/769-1715

Bialos, Gail; Controller, Rumarson Technologies Inc.; US; 908/298-9300

Biba, Kenneth J.; EVP, Xircom Inc.; US; 805/376-9300

Bibby, Malcolm M.; Pres & CEO, Mobile Security Communications; US; 770/594-0424

Biber, Brian; VP, Information Systems Spending; US; 619/438-8100, bbiber@compecon.com

Bickel, Robert W.; Dir Prod, Bluestone Inc.; US; 609/727-4600, bluestone!bickel@uunet.uu

Biddulph, Tom; CEO, StarNine Technologies Inc.; US; 510/649-4949

Bidzos, James; Pres, RSA Data Security Inc.; US; 415/595-8782

Biel, Matt; Admin Accnt, SkyNotes Inc.; US; 310/577-9332, matt@skynotes.com

Bieniek, Daren J.; Pres & CEO, Automated Computer Business Systems; US; 304/296-0290

Bierman, Robert; VP Eng, Magic Quest Inc.; US; 415/321-5838

Bigelow, Stephen J.; Pblr, Dynamic Learning Systems; US; 508/366-9487, sbigelow@cerfnet.com

Biggs, Shannon; VP Eng, Viking Components; US; 714/643-7255

Biggs, Tom; EVP, Sanar Systems Inc.; US; 408/982-0288

Bigler, Mark; Dir Prod Res, Server Technology Inc.; US; 408/745-0300

Bihr, Mary; LucasArts Entertainment Co.; US; 415/472-3400

Bilinski, Andrew E.; Group VP, BDM Int'l.; US; 703/848-5000

Billheimer, Robert A.; Pblr, SCO World; US; 415/941-1550

Billings, Cherrie; Controller, Silicon Valley Research Inc.; US; 415/962-3000

Billmaier, Jim; Pres, Asymetrix Corp.; US; 206/637-5859

Bilodeau, Normand; CFO, BGS Systems Inc.; US; 617/891-0000

Bilous, Michael T.; EVP Sales & Mktng, Chinon America Inc.; US; 310/533-0274

Bilowus, Dennis; Pres, AEC Software Inc.; US; 703/450-1980

Binch, William B.; VP Sales, Business Objects Inc.; US; 408/973-9300

Biner, John; VP, Eagle Point Software; US; 319/556-8392

Bingenheimer, John J.; VP & CFO, CenterLine Software Inc.; US; 617/498-3000

Bingham, H. Raymond; EVP & CFO, Cadence Design Systems Inc.; US; 408/943-1234

Bingham, Kathleen; EVP, FIND/SVP Inc.; US; 212/645-4500

Bingham, Sanford; Pres, Magnetic Press Inc.; US; 212/219-2831

Binns, John; VP Prod Dev, Inference Corp.; US; 415/899-0100

Binstock, Andrew; Ed-in-Chief, UNIX Review; US; 415/358-9500, abinstock@mfi.com

Biran, Chanoch; EVP, Leaf Systems Inc.; US; 508/460-8300

Birch, Eric N.; Pres, Inchcape Inc.; US;

508/689-9355

Birch, Kenneth C.; VP PC Eng, Micron Electronics; US; 208/893-3434

Birch, Paul D.; VP & CFO, Project Software & Development Inc.; US; 617/661-1444

Birck, Michael J.; Pres & CEO, Tellabs; US; 708/969-8800

Bird, Anthony; VP Sales, Evergreen International Technology Inc.; Canada; 604/986-6121

Bird, Robert; VP, Antex Electronics Corp.; US; 310/532-3092

Birkeland, Chris; VP Ops & Fin, Photo-Disc Inc.; US; 206/441-9355

Birkhead, Evan; Ed-in-Chief, Internetwork; US; 215/643-8000, birk-headec@cardinal.com

Birks, Ian T.; Int'l Sales Dir, IDEAS International Pty. Ltd.; Australia; 612-498-7399, ianb@ideas.com.au

Birmar, Kenneth P.; Ed-in-Chief, ACM Transactions on Computer Systems; US; 212/869-7440

Birnbaum, Joel S.; SVP R&D, Hewlett-Packard Co.; US; 408/553-4300

Birnbaum, Richard S.; EVP Ops, Circuit City Stores Inc.; US; 804/527-4000

Birta, Louis; Ed-in-Chief, Simulation; US; 619/277-3888

Birtles, Nicolas; EVP, Centura Software Corp.; US; 415/321-9500

Birtzer, Larry; Pres & COO, Integral Peripherals Inc.; US; 303/449-8009

Bisa, Brian; VP Mktng, Allen Systems Group; US; 941/435-2200

Bischoff, Peter G.; EVP R&D, Read-Rite Corp.; US; 408/262-6700

Biscos, Gilles; Pres, Interquest; US; 804/979-9945, 102063.1421@compuserve.com

Bishop, Robert; Pres & CEO, Zinc Software; US; 801/785-8900, rbishop@zinc.com

Biski, Janet; CFO, SRS Labs Inc.; US; 714/442-1070

Bisnaire, Marc; Pres, LANSource Technologies Inc.; Canada; 416/535-3555

Bitton, Pat; VP Mktng, S&S Software Int'l. Inc.; US; 617/273-7400

Bitz, Francois J.; VP Eng, Fore Systems Inc.; US; 412/772-6600

Bivens, Michael; Screen Team; US; 714/376-2882

Bivolcic, David J.; SVP, ICOT Corp.; US; 408/433-3300

Bixby, Carl L.; Pres & CEO, Interface Systems Inc.; US; 313/769-5900

Bixby, James A.; Chmn, Pres & CEO, Brooktree Corp.; US; 619/452-7580

Black, Edward; Pres, Computer & Communications Industry Assoc.; US; 202/783-0070

Black, Gordon; Chmn & CEO, Gordon S. Black Corp.; US; 716/272-8400

Black, James E.C.; SVP Eng, Boole & Babbage Inc.; US; 408/526-3000

Black, Kent. M; EVP & COO, Rockwell International Corp.; US; 310/797-3311

Black, Lauren L.; Lab Dir, Macworld Labs; US; 415/243-0505, lauren_black@macworld.com

Blackburn, Steven; COO, Apogee Software Ltd.; US; 214/271-1765

Blackford, John; Ed-in-Chief, Computer Shopper; US; 212/503-3900

Blackstock, Mike; VP Dev, GDT Softworks; Canada; 604/291-9121

Blackwell, Larry G.; Chmn, Pres & CEO, Datastream Systems Inc.; US; 803/297-6775

Blackwell, Walter G.; EVP, International Communications Industries Assoc.; US; 703/273-7200

Blaeser, Jack; Pres, Concord Communications Inc.; US; 508/460-4646

Blair, John; Prod Mgr, Mustek Inc.; US; 714/247-1300

Blair, Larry; VP Mktng, Ipsilon Networks Inc.; US; 415/846-4600

Blair, Michael D.; Chmn & CEO, Cyborg Systems Inc.; US; 312/454-1865

Blair, Pamela; Bus Mgr, Machover Associates Corp.; US; 914/949-3777

Blair, Russell M.; VP WW Sales, SystemSoft Corp.; US; 508/651-0088

Blair, William T.; EVP, Diebold Inc.; US; 216/489-4000

Blake, John; Grp Pblr, MacWeek; US; 415/243-3500

Blakeley, Jerry; Pres, Extech Instruments Corp.; US; 617/890-7440

Blakely, Ken; VP Mktng, MacNeal-Schwendler Corp., The; US; 213/258-9111

Blakeman, Kevin; GM, JSB Corp.; US; 408/438-8300

Blanc, Maureen; Partner, Blanc & Otus; US; 415/512-0500

Blanford, Darrell; VP Mktng, Tools & Techniques Inc.; US; 512/459-1308

Blank, Steven G.; Pres, Rocket Science Games Inc.; US; 415/442-5000

Blankman, Howard; Pres, Howard Blankman Inc.; US; 516/338-8300

Blankstein, Stuart; Pres, ACL Inc.; US; 708/981-9212

Blaschke, Charles; Pres, Education Turnkey Systems Inc.; US; 703/536-2310

Blaschke, James; VP Mktng, Adra Systems Inc.; US; 508/937-3700

Blatnik, Greg; VP, Zona Research; US; 415/568-5700

Blazensky, Jason; VP Mktng, Digicom Systems Inc.; US; 408/262-1277

Bleakney, Ronald J.; VP Sales & Mktng, Natural MicroSystems Corp.; US; 508/650-1300

Bledsoe, Gene; Mgng Partner, Casal Group; US; 214/488-7000

Blelock, Julia; VP, IDC/LINK; US; 212/726-0900, jblelock@idcresearch.com

Blenner, Joel; VP Sales, MicroTouch Systems Inc.; US; 508/659-9000

Blessing, Rose; Ed, Publishing & Production Executive; US; 215/238-5300

Blethen, Roger W.; Pres, LTX Corp.; US; 617/461-1000

Blickenstorfer, Conrad H.; Ed-in-Chief, Pen Computing Magazine; US; 916/984-9947, 73602.2535@compuserve.com

Blitz, Dennis; Pres, Dearborn Publishing Group; US; 312/836-4400

Bloch, Paul S.; Co-Chmn & CEO, Mega Drive Systems Inc.; US; 310/247-0006

Block, Greg; VP Logistics, IPC Technologies Inc.; US; 512/339-3500

Bloom, Betty; Dir Client Svcs, Natural Language Inc.; US; 510/814-0500

Bloom, Curt; VP Field Ops, Cayenne Software; US; 617/273-9003

Bloom, Jonathan; VP, McGrath/Power PR; US; 408/727-0351

Bloom, Robert; Pres & CEO, Publicin Bloom; US; 212/370-1313

Bloom, Robert S.; CFO, Acxiom Corp.; US; 501/336-1000

BloomBecker, Jay; Exec Dir, National Center for Computer Crime Data; US; 408/475-4457

Blount, Jack; Pres & CEO, MobileWare Corp.; US; 214/952-1200

Blow, Warner C.; EVP, Sterling Software Inc.; US; 214/891-8600

Blue, Karsten; Pres, CERFnet; US; 619/455-3900

Blum, Brian; Pres, International Interactive Communications Society; US; 503/579-4427

Blum, Dave; CFO, WizardWorks; US; 612/559-5140

Blum, Rod; CEO, Eagle Point Software; US; 319/556-8392

Blum, Scott A.; EVP, Pinnacle Micro Inc.; US; 714/789-3000

Blum, William T.; Pres & CEO, Pinnacle Micro Inc.; US; 714/789-3000

Blumberg, Robert L.; Chmn, Pres & CEO, Spectragraphics Corp.; US; 619/450-0611

Blumenthal, Arthur; Pres, SL Waber Inc.; US; 609/866-8888

Blumstein, David; Pres & CEO, Softbank Inc.; US; 408/644-7800

Blyth, Trevor; VP Dev, Information Storage Devices Inc.; US; 408/369-2400

Bobrow, Elizabeth; Assoc Ed, Midrange Systems; US; 215/643-8000, bobrowef@box101.cardinal.com

Bock, Paul; VP Bus Dev, Rainbow Technologies Inc.; US; 714/450-7300

Bock, William; SVP Ops, Tivoli Systems Inc.; US; 512/794-9070

Boden, Andrew W.; Pblr, EDI, Handbook of; US

Boehlke, Christine; Creative Dir, Phase Two Strategies; US; 415/772-8400, chris_boehlke@p2pr.com

Boehlke, William; Mgng Off, Phase Two Strategies; US; 415/772-8400, william_boehlke@p2pr.com

Boehm, Ron; Pres, Intellimation; US;

805/968-2291

Boetticker, Jeff; CEO, Black Box Corp.; US; 412/746-5500

Bogan, Tom; Pres, Pacific Data Products; US; 619/552-0880

Bogardus, Tim; Ed-in-Chief, Digital Creativity; US; 212/683-3540

Bogdan, John; VP & CFO, ON Technology Corp.; US; 617/374-1400, jbogdan@on.com

Bohannon, Ralph; VP Mfg, Atmel Corp.; US; 408/441-0311

Bohle, Sue; Pres, Bohle Company, The; US; 310/785-0515

Bohmer, Jon; VP Bus Dev, Scala Inc.; US; 703/713-0900

Bohn, Larry; EVP & GM, PC DOCS Inc.; US; 617/273-3800, larryb@pcdocs.com

Bohuslav, Bruce; Pres, Systems Integration Associates; US; 312/440-1275

Boisvert, Ronald F.; Ed-in-Chief, ACM Transactions on Mathematical Software; US; 212/869-7440

Bolan, Michael L.; VP Mktng, Dallas Semiconductor Corp.; US; 214/450-0400

Bolas, Mark; Pres, Fakespace Inc.; US; 415/688-1940, bolas@well.comm

Boles, William H.; VP Sales & Mktng, Olympus Image Systems Inc.; US; 516/844-5000

Bolesky, Edward M.; VP Ops, New England Business Service Inc.; US; 508/448-6111

Bolger, Brenna; Pres, PRx Tech; US; 408/287-1700

Bolin, Diane; Ops Mgr, Currid & Co.; US; 713/789-5995

Bolkan, Jeff; Mgng Ed, PC Graphics & Video; US; 714/513-8400, jvbolkan@pcgv.com

Bolling, Dian; Prod Mgr Transverter Pro, TechPool Software; US; 216/382-1234, dianb@techpool.com

Bolohan, Gary; EVP Distr, Reptron Electronics Inc.; US; 813/854-2351

Bolsvert, William E.; CFO, Attachmate Corp.; US; 206/644-4010

Bolter, Sher; Ed, Corporate Journal, The; US; 502/456-0808, 73774.3240@compuserve.com

Bond, Rod; CFO, Vtel; US; 512/314-2700

Bondi, Kurt; Ed, Inside the Internet; US; 502/491-1900

Boni, Peter J.; Pres & CEO, Cayenne Software; US; 617/273-9003

Bonington, Paul L.; Pblr, Web Week; US; 203/226-6967, bonington@iw.com

Bonnett, John H.; GM, Uuplus Development; US; 805/534-9502, jhb@uuplus.com

Bonnie, Richard J.; Pres AM Graphics, AM International Inc.; US; 847/818-1294

Bonomi, Mauro; CEO, Minerva; US; 408/970-1780

Bonsignore, Michael R.; Chmn & CEO, Honeywell Inc.; US; 612/951-1000

Bookman, Philip; VP R&D, Silton-Bookman Systems; US; 408/446-1170, pbookman@sbsinc.com

Boone, Gregory; Pres, Systems Research Inc.; US; 360/647-7600

Boone, Randy; VP Fin, Indiana Cash Drawer Co.; US; 317/398-6643

Boonmee, Jeff; Dir New Prod, Zebra Technologies VTI Inc.; US; 801/576-9700

Boonstra, Cor; Chmn & Pres, Philips Electronics; Netherlands; 31-40-786022

Boosman, Frank; VP & GM Virtus Studios, Virtus Corp.; US; 919/467-9700, frank.boosman@virtus.com

Booth, Barbara; VP R&D, Interlink Computer Sciences Inc.; US; 510/657-9800

Booth, Willard; Pres, Insight-Onsite; US; 408/252-2260

Boozer, Trent R.; Pres, Vulcan Publications Inc.; US; 205/988-9708

Bopp, David; Dir IS, Concurrent Computer Corp.; US; 908/870-4500

Borden, Barry; Pres, LMA Group Inc.; US; 610/667-3635

Borel, Daniel; Chmn & CEO, Logitech Inc.; US; 510/795-8500

Boren, C. Sidney; SVP Strag Plng, BellSouth Corp.; US; 404/249-2000

Borensztein, Fabian; Prod Mktng Mgr, Percon Inc.; US; 541/344-1189

Borgen, Howard; Pblr, Pen Computing Magazine; US; 916/984-9947, 75162.524@compuserve.com

Bork, Jeff; VP Mktng, Scopus Technology Inc.; US; 510/597-5800

Borkovich, George S.; Pblr, A/E/C Systems Computer Solution; US; 860/666-1326

Borman, Lisa; Pres, Borman Associates; US; 908/233-8800

Bornhofen, Robert; Pres, Tangent Color Systems; US; 303/799-6766

Borowsky, Irvin J.; Chmn, North American Publishing Co.; US; 215/238-5300

Borowsky, Ned S.; Pres & COO, North American Publishing Co.; US; 215/238-5300

Borozan, Dan Duke; VP Ops, Caere Corp.; US; 408/395-7000

Bosanko, Thomas A.; EVP, DataFocus Inc.; US; 703/631-6770, tab@datafocus.com

Bose, Andy; Group VP, IDC/LINK; US; 212/726-0900, bose@idcresearch.com

Bosko, Mark; VP Dev, Helix Technologies; US; 847/465-0242

Bossen, David A.; Chmn & CEO, Measurex Corp.; US; 408/255-1500

Boswell, Gary T.; GM Computer & Monitors, Aydin Corp.; US; 215/657-7510

Bothwell, David; CEO, Howtek Inc.; US; 603/882-5200

Botten, David S.; Pres & CEO, CSPI; US; 508/663-7598

Botti, John T.; Chmn, Pres & CEO, BitWise Designs Inc.; US; 518/356-9741,

jbotti@docstar.com

Bouchard, J. Thomas; SVP HR, International Business Machines Corp.; US; 914/765-1900

Bouchard, Judith W.; Ed, Microcomputer Abstracts; US; 609/654-6266

Boucher, David; Chmn, Interleaf Inc.; US; 617/290-0710

Boucher, Karen; Mkt Analyst, Standish Group, The; US; 508/385-7500, karen@standishgroup.com

Boucher, Laurence B.; CEO, Auspex Systems Inc.; US; 408/986-2000

Boucher, Robert N.; Pres & CEO, Cardinal Business Media Inc.; US; 215/643-8000

Boudream, Serge; Pres, Techbyte International Inc.; US; 716/743-8052

Boudreau, Donald F.; SVP Ops, MathSoft Inc.; US; 617/577-1017

Boudris, Janet; SVP, RAM Mobile Data; US; 908/602-5500

Boulden, Larry; Pblr, Computer-Aided Engineering; US; 216/696-7000

Boulerice, Albert R.; Treas, Syncware Corp.; US; 303/369-6900

Boutaleb, Mohammed; Pres, Protec Microsystems Inc.; Canada; 514/630-5832

Boutin, Robert J.; SVP & CFO, CompuCom Systems; US; 214/265-3600

Bouvard, Jacques; VP Eng, Individual Inc.; US; 617/273-6000

Bouzari, Alex K.; Co-Chmn & Pres, Mega Drive Systems Inc.; US; 310/247-0006

Bowdwn, Eric; Dir, LAN Times Testing Center; US; 801/342-6800

Bowen, Robert C.; SVP, National Computer Systems Inc.; US; 612/829-3000

Bowen, Robert S.; Chmn & CEO, Group 1 Software; US; 301/731-2300

Bowen, Steven A.; COO, American Computer Resources; US; 203/380-4600

Bowen, Thomas D.; VP Mktng, Virtual I/O Inc.; US; 206/382-7410

Bowen Jr., Hubert A.; Pres, American Computer Resources; US; 203/380-4600, bbowen@the-acr.com

Bower, Scott; VP Sales & Mktng, Samsung Electronics America Inc.; US; 201/229-4000

Bowers, Jon; Pres, Atlantic Cable Technology; US

Bowers, Richard A.; Optical Publishing Assoc.; US; 614/442-8805

Bowers, Robert; EVP Admin, Servantis Systems Inc.; US; 770/441-3387

Bowler, John W.; VP R&D, Zenith Electronics Corp.; US; 708/391-7000

Bowler, Kevin; Assist VP, Nissei Sangyo America Ltd.; US; 617/461-8300

Bowman, Charles; Ed, Unix Developer; US; 212/242-7447, cfb@panix.com

Bowman, Kevin; Dir Sales & Mktng, Azerty Inc.; US; 716/662-0200

Bowman, Lynda B.; VP, Merex Corp.; US; 602/921-7077

Bowman Alden, Sally; Exec Dir, Computer Learning Foundation; US; 415/327-3347

Bowser, Jack A.; SVP, Peak Technologies Group Inc.; US; 212/832-2833

Boyce, Edward J.; Dir Eng, Ultre Division; US; 516/753-4800

Boyce, Pat; Pres & COO, Horizons Technology Inc.; US; 619/292-8331

Boyd, Lynne; SVP Gov Ops, JetForm Corp.; US; 703/448-9544

Boyd, Patrick; VP, Center for Multimedia; US; 206/643-9039

Boyd, Richard; VP & GM Virtus Works, Virtus Corp.; US; 919/467-9700, richard.boyd@virtus.com

Boyd, Stowe; Ed, Business Process Strategies; US; 617/648-8702

Boyd, Wesley; Chmn & CEO, Berkeley Systems Inc.; US; 510/540-5535

Boyd-Merritt, Rick; Ed, OEM Magazine; US; 516/562-5624

Boyers, Pat; Exec Dir, Executive Software Int'l.; US; 818/547-2050, pboyers@executive.com

Boylan, Sue-Anne; Dir Info Sys, Zondervan Publishing House; US; 616/698-6900, sue-anne.boylan@zph.com

Boyle, Charles L.; EVP & CFO, Prophet 21 Inc.; US; 215/493-8900

Bozorgzad, Hoss; VP Mktng, Philips Key Modules; US; 408/453-7373

Bracken, Peter A.; CEO, Computer Data Systems Inc.; US; 301/921-7000

Brackhaus, Karl H.; Pres & CEO, Dynapro Systems Inc.; Canada; 604/521-3962

Bradbury, James S.; Ed, MacUser; US; 415/378-5600

Bradford, Kent; VP Sales, UniKix Technologies; US

Bradford, Russ; Pres, Inclination Software Inc.; US; 702/831-5595, russ@isi-inc.com

Bradford, Sandra K.; VP Sales & Mktng, Inclination Software Inc.; US; 702/831-5595, sales@isiinc.com

Bradley, Jack A.; VP & CFO, Network Computing Devices Inc.; US; 415/694-0650

Bradley, John M.; SVP Bus Dev, Liant Software Corp.; US; 508/872-8700

Bradley, Mike; Pres, Cimtek Thomas; US; 615/929-9383

Bradley, Randy; Chmn & CTO, NetPro Computing Inc.; US; 602/941-3600

Bradshaw, Mary I.; Dir Ind Rel, Multimedia Telecommunications Assoc.; US; 202/296-9800

Bradshaw, Michael J.; SVP WW Ops, Zilog Inc.; US; 408/370-8000

Brady, Greg; Pres Field Ops, i2 Technologies Inc.; US; 214/860-6000, greg_brady@i2.com

Brady, J. Michael; Ed, Robotics Research, Int'l Journal of; US; 617/253-2889, jmb@robots.ox.ac.uk

Brady, Jerome D.; Chmn, Pres & CEO, AM International Inc.; US; 847/818-1294

Brady, Mark; VP Sales, TV/COM International Inc.; US; 619/451-1500

Brady, Tim; Dir Mktng, Yahoo Corp.; US; 415/934-3230, tim@yahoo.com

Brainerd, Walter; Co-Ed, Fortran Users Group; US; 714/441-2022, walt@fortran.com

Brajevich, Debbie; VP Mktng, Vision Interactive Publishing; US; 714/833-1822

Brambert, Dave; Ed-in-Chief, Network VAR; US; 415/905-2200

Brand, Robert L.; VP Controller, McDonnell Douglas Corp.; US; 314/232-0232

Brands, Paul A.; CEO, American Management Systems; US; 703/267-8000

Brandt, George F.; Pres & CEO, Advanced Visual Systems Inc.; US; 617/890-4300

Brandt, John R.; Ed-in-Chief, Industry Week; US; 216/696-7000

Brandt, Richard; Exec Ed, Upside; US; 415/377-0950, rbrandt@upside.com

Brandtner, Marty; CEO, Baker & Taylor Software; US; 805/522-9800

Brantley, Jack; VP Mktng, StarBase Corp.; US; 714/442-4400

Branum, A. Don; SVP, Vertex Communications Corp.; US; 903/984-0555

Bratton, Tim; VP Sales & Mktng, Spatializer Audio Laboratories; US; 818/227-3370

Brauchler, Rolf; VP Mktng, Cygnus Support; US; 415/903-1400

Braue, Joseph; Ed-in-Chief, Data Communications; US; 212/512-2699, jbraue@mcgraw-hill.com

Braun, Cedric R.; Mng Ed, UniForum's IT Solutions; US; 408/986-8840, cedric@uniforum.com

Braun, Jeff; Chmn & CEO, Maxis; US; 510/933-5630

Braun, Kathryn A.; EVP Pers Stor, Western Digital Corp.; US; 714/932-5000

Braun, Klaus; Chief Scientist, Systems Research Inc.; US; 360/647-7600

Bravman, Richard; SVP Mktng, Symbol Technologies Inc.; US; 516/563-2400

Bravos, William; Pres, Elgin Interactive Software Inc.; US; 847/697-9654

Braxton, Jerry W.; EVP & CFO, National Data Corp.; US; 404/728-2000

Bray, Tim; SVP Tech, Open Text Corp.; Canada; 519/888-7111

Brazao, D. Michael; VP SI, Storage Computer Corp.; US; 603/880-3005

Brchett, Rainer; Chmn, LBMS; US; 713/625-9300

Breakfield, Hedy; CFO, DocuMagix Inc.; US; 408/434-1138

Brecht, George; Pres, SofTeam US Inc.; US; 410/243-1130

Breck, Joseph J.; Pblr, ECN, Electronic Component News; US; 610/964-4343, jbreck@chilton.com

Bredy, Didier; VP Mktng, Truevision Inc.; US; 408/562-4200

Breeding, Marshall; Ed, Library Software Review; US; 805/499-0721

Breeman, Dan; Mng Ed, Scientific Computing & Automation; US; 201/292-5100, 74677.1126@compuserve.com

Breen, George; Pres, Digital Video Arts Ltd.; US; 215/576-7920, george@dval.com

Breidenbach, Axel; Lab Equip Mgr, TUV Product Service Inc.; US; 508/777-7999

Breitenbach, E. Allen; Chmn & CEO, Scientific Software-Intercomp Inc.; US; 303/292-1111

Bremer, Alicia; Pres & PR Counsel, Bremer Public Relations; US; 801/364-2030

Bremser Jr., George; Chmn, Etak Inc.; US; 415/328-3825

Brennan, Chris; CFO, UB Networks; US; 408/496-0111

Brennan, Katie A.; Pblr, UNIX Review; US; 415/358-9500, kbrennan@mfi.com

Brennan, Timothy; VP, Rational Software Corp.; US; 408/496-3600, tbrennan@rational.com

Breslin, Thomas C.; CFO, Cardinal Business Media Inc.; US; 215/643-8000

Bresman, Tom; CEO, New Horizons Computer Learning Centers Inc.; US; 714/556-1220

Brewer, Brian A.; VP, MCI Business Markets; US; 404/698-8000

Brewer, Ginger; Pres, Ginger Brewer Associates; US; 206/455-3351

Brewer, Greg; Pres, Prosoft Labs; US; 510/426-6100

Brewer, R. Michael; VP Fin, Boca Research Inc.; US; 407/997-6227

Bridges, S. Rutt; VP & CTO, Landmark Graphics Corp.; US

Briggs, Mark R.; SVP, Intelligent Electronics Inc.; US; 610/458-5500

Brigham, Leslie; Brigham Scully; US; 818/716-9021

Brigham, Tom; Principal, Brigham Scully; US; 818/716-9021

Brightman, G. Edward; VP Ops, ThrustMaster Inc.; US; 503/615-3200

Brightman, Tom; VP Bus & Tech, Cyrix Corp.; US; 214/968-8388

Brigish, Alan; Pblr, Simba Information Inc.; US; 203/834-0033

Bringhurst, Gary; VP Eng, Strata Inc.; US; 801/628-5218

Bringhurst, Ken; CEO, Strata Inc.; US; 801/628-5218

Brink, Derek; Dir Bus Dev, Gradient Technologies; US; 508/624-9600

Brinkley, David; Dir, Fujitsu Computer Products; US; 408/432-6333

Brinkman, Jen; Assoc Ed, EDN Products Edition; US; 201/292-5100

Brintnall, John R.; VP & CFO, Computer Network Technology Corp.; US;

612/797-6000

Briscoe, Edward D.; VP Sales, Iomega Corp.; US; 801/778-1000

Briskin, Roman; Dir Int'l Sales, Advanced Electronic Support Products Inc.; US; 305/944-7710

Britts, Bill; VP Mktng & Sales, Advanced Digital Information Corp.; US; 206/881-8004

Brittsan, Robert; Dir Appl Tech, NeoSoft Corp.; US; 541/389-5489

Brix, Kenneth G.; VP Sales, Cognitronics Corp.; US; 203/830-3400

Broad, David; Pres, Digital Wisdom Inc.; US; 804/443-9000

Broady, Vince; Exec Ed, Multimedia World; US; 415/281-8650

Brochu, Michael; CFO, Sierra On-Line Inc.; US; 206/649-9800

Brock, Ernie; VP, Ares Software Corp.; US; 415/578-9090

Brock, Joel; Pres, Data Pro Accounting Software Inc.; US; 813/885-9459

Brock, Ken; Bus Dev Mgr, Compass Design Automation; US; 408/433-4880

Brockett, Patrick J.; EVP Sales & Mktng, National Semiconductor Corp.; US; 408/721-5000

Broderick, John P.; VP Fin & CFO, Programmer's Paradise Inc.; US; 908/389-8950, jbroderi@programmers.com

Brodeur, John; Pres, Brodeur & Partners Inc.; US; 617/622-2869

Brodie, Melvyn; SVP, DiagSoft Inc.; US; 408/438-8247

Brodnick, William J.; CFO, Aironet Wireless Communications Inc.; US; 330/665-7900

Brodsky, Gerard; Pres, American Facsimile Assoc.; US; 215/981-0292

Brody, Dena; VP Admin, Hurwitz Consulting Group; US; 617/965-6900

Broghammer, Frank; COO & CFO, VideoLabs Inc.; US; 612/988-0055

Brogno, Karen; Ed, Information Systems Management; US; 617/423-2020

Brojde, Peter; Pres, Eicon Technology Corp.; 214/239-3270

Bromber, Kevin A.; VP Sales, Visual Software Inc.; US; 818/593-3500

Bromhead, John; VP Mktng, Stac Inc.; US; 619/794-4300, jbromhead@stac.com

Bromley, David; Ed, Do It With Lotus Smart Suite for Windows; US; 617/482-8634

Brookes, Tom; Dep Ed, European Computer Sources; Belgium; 322-766-0045

Brooks, David; Dir Eng, Link Technologies Inc.; US; 408/473-1200

Brooks, Joseph G.; Pres, Brooks Power Systems; US; 215/244-0264

Brooks, Munira; Mktng Mgr, ZyXEL; US; 714/693-0808, mbrooks@zyxel.com

Brooks, Wade; VP, Janus Interactive; US; 503/629-0587

Brosseau, Denise; Mgr US Bus Dev, Lexicus Corp.; US; 415/462-6800,

deniseb@lexicus.mot.com

Broumand, Clifton; Pres, Man & Machine; US; 301/277-3760

Broussard, Bartel H.; VP Mktng, FTP Software Inc.; US; 508/685-4000

Broussard, George; Partner, Apogee Software Ltd.; US; 214/271-1765

Brown, Alex; VP Sales, Humongous Entertainment; US; 206/487-9258

Brown, Allen; COO, X/Open Company Ltd.; US; 415/323-7992

Brown, Bill; EVP, PCs Compleat; US; 508/480-8500

Brown, Bruce E.; VP Dev, Folio Corp.; US; 801/344-3700, bbrown@folio.com

Brown, Cal; VP Mktng, Pro CD Inc.; US; 508/750-0000

Brown, Cathy; Pivotal Software Inc.; Canada; 604/988-9982, cbrown@pivotalsoft.com

Brown, Daniel F.; EVP Sales, CompuCom Systems; US; 214/265-3600

Brown, Donald; Pres, D.H. Brown Associates Inc.; US; 914/937-4302

Brown, Edward; Pres, Healthcare Communications Inc.; US; 402/466-8100

Brown, Edward D.; Pblr, Bedford Communications; US; 212/807-8220

Brown, Gary; VP Fin, Numetrix Ltd.; US; 203/847-3452

Brown, Gordon; Pres, Teleadapt Inc.; US; 408/370-5105

Brown, Janet; VP Ops & COO, NuIQ Software Inc.; US; 914/833-3479, janet@nuiq.com

Brown, Janice L.; Pres, Janice Brown & Assoc. Inc.; US; 603/764-5800

Brown, Jeff; Pres, Data Critical Corp.; US; 206/885-3500

Brown, Joe; VP Mktng, Auspex Systems Inc.; US; 408/986-2000

Brown, M. Ross; VP, Analogic Corp.; US; 508/977-3000

Brown, Mark; Pres, Quadrangle Software Corp.; US; 313/769-1675

Brown, Matthew; VP R&D, Numera Software Corp.; US; 206/622-2233, mattb@numera.com

Brown, Michael A.; CEO, Quantum Corp.; US; 408/894-4000

Brown, Paulette; Dir PR, Penna Powers Cutting & Haynes Inc.; US; 801/531-0973, ppch@xmission.com

Brown, R. Scott; VP Sales, Xilinx Inc.; US; 408/559-7778

Brown, Richard H.; CEO, H&R Block Inc.; US; 816/753-6900

Brown, Robert; Pres, Coda Inc.; US; 603/647-9600

Brown, Robert G.; Pres, Computer Intelligence/InfoCorp; US; 619/450-1667

Brown, Ron; VP Eng, Gemstone Systems Inc.; US

Brown, Ronald D.; VP & CFO, Cincinnati Milacron Inc.; US; 513/841-8100

Brown, Sarah; Ed & Pblr, Card Technology Today; US; 212/221-5000

Brown, Scott W.; Pres & CEO, NuIQ Software Inc.; US; 914/833-3479, scott@nuiq.com

Brown, Walt; VP Field Ops, Make Systems; US; 415/941-9800

Brown, Wendell; VP Tech, Syncronys Softcorp; US; 310/842-9203

Brown Jr., Thomas R.; Chmn, Burr-Brown Corp.; US; 602/746-1111

Brownyard, George; Chmn, International Society of Certified Electronics Technicians; US; 817/921-9101

Brozen, Yale; Pblr, Strategy Plus; US; 802/767-4622

Bruce, Robert A.; Pres, Walnut Creek CDROM; US; 510/674-0783, rab@cdrom.com

Bruer, Rich; VP, McClenahan Bruer Burrows Communications Inc.; US; 503/643-9035, rich@mcbb.com

Bruggeling, Johannes S.; EVP Int'l Ops, Boole & Babbage Inc.; US; 408/526-3000

Bruggere, Thomas H.; Chmn, Mentor Graphics Corp.; US; 503/626-7000

Bruno, Richard; Chmn, Digital Frontiers; US; 847/328-0880, rjbrunoc@aol.com

Bruno, Tetsujii; EVP, Oki America Inc.; US; 201/646-0011

Brush, Chuck; VP Sales & Mktng, Advanced Integration Research Inc.; US; 408/428-0800

Brush, Kathleen E.; VP Mktng, Computer Network Technology Corp.; US; 612/797-6000

Bryant, James E.; Pres & CEO, Pro CD Inc.; US; 508/750-0000, jbryant@procd.com

Bryant, Roy; VP, Interactive Image Technologies Ltd.; Canada; 416/977-5550, rbryant@interactiv.com

Bryden, Melinda A.; CFO, Midisoft Corp.; US; 206/391-3610

Bryndle, Dan; Dir Mktng, ISTR Inc.; US; 716/855-0295

Bryson, Robert; SVP & GM, Canon US Inc.; US; 516/488-6700

Bubb, Howard G.; Pres & CEO, Dialogic Corp.; US; 201/993-3000

Buchan, George; SVP Eng, Insignia Solutions Inc.; US; 408/327-6000

Buchanan, David; EVP, Aurum Software Inc.; US; 408/562-6370

Buchanan, John; EVP & CFO, Delphax Systems; US; 617/828-9917

Buchanan, Leigh; Exec Ed, WebMaster; US; 508/872-0080

Buchanan, Martin; GM, Cray Research Super Servers Inc.; US; 503/641-3151

Buchanan, Susan; EVP, Aurum Software Inc.; US; 408/562-6370

Buchenberger, Franz; CEO, Black Sun Interactive Inc.; US; 415/273-7000

Buck, Leonard; Pres, Software Designs Unlimited Inc.; US; 919/968-4567

Buck, Ron; CEO, IVI Publishing Inc.;

US; 612/996-6000

Buckingham, Jeff; Pres, Wynd Communications Corp.; US

Buckingham, William; Pres, XChange; US; 415/864-7592

Buckley, Philip; Pres, Cambridge Parallel Processing; US; 714/261-8901

Buckley, Tim; VP Sales, Shapeware Corp.; US; 206/521-4500

Budagher, Bruce P.; VP, Specialty Tele-Constructors Inc.; US; 505/281-2197

Budagher, Michael R.; Chmn, Pres & CEO, Specialty TeleConstructors Inc.; US; 505/281-2197

Budelli, Joe G.; VP Sales, Maxsoft-OCRON Inc.; US; 510/252-0200

Budnick, Alfred S.; VP, Cherry Corp.; US; 847/662-9200

Budwey, James N.; Pblr, Horizon House Publications Inc.; US; 617/769-9750

Buechele, Eugene K.; VP Eng, SBE Inc.; US; 510/355-2000

Buehl, Patrick; Pres, Electronic Technology Group Inc.; US; 612/948-3100

Buerger, David J.; EVP, Buerger Media & Marketing Inc.; US; 770/495-7494, dbuerger@pipeline.com

Buerger, Maggie M.; Pres, Buerger Media & Marketing Inc.; US; 770/495-7494, 73441,1262@compuserve.com

Bueschel, Richard T.; Chmn, Infodata Systems Inc.; US; 703/934-5205

Bugbee, Dennis; Dir Fin, Teknowledge Inc.; US; 415/424-0500

Buhay, Rene; Dir Sales & Mktng, Antec Inc.; US; 510/770-1200

Buhler, Mac; PR Contact, Market Data Retrieval; US; 203/926-4800

Bui, John; VP Fin, Centon Electronics Inc.; US; 714/855-9111

Bullas, Roslyn; Mngg Ed, Peachpit Press Inc.; US; 510/548-4393

Buller, Manfred; EVP, BASF Corp.; US; 201/397-2700

Bundy, Dave; VP Eng, White Pine Software Inc.; US; 603/886-9050

Bunker, William; Dir Eng, Pentax Technologies Corp.; US; 303/460-1600

Bunnell, David; Chmn, Upside Publishing Co., The; US; 415/377-0950

Bunnell, John W.; Pres, SHL Systemhouse Inc.; Canada; 613/236-1428

Bunt, Dennis H.; CFO, BitWise Designs Inc.; US; 518/356-9741

Bunte, Alan G.; VP Strat Plng, Norand Corp.; US; 319/369-3100

Bunyan, Chris; Dir, Xephon; US; 817/455-7050, 100325.3711@compuserve.com

Bunzel, David L.; Pres, Santa Clara Consulting; US; 408/450-1365

Buonauro, Roselie; VP Mktng, Seagate Enterprise Management Software; US; 408/342-4500

Buran, Jerry; VP Sales & Mktng, Software Solutions Inc.; US; 770/418-2000

Burdette, Tom; VP Ops, Barco Chromat-

ics; US; 770/493-7000

Burenga, Kenneth L.; Pres & COO, Dow Jones & Company Inc.; US; 212/416-2000

Burgard, Michael J.; Ed-in-Chief, SCO World; US; 415/941-1550, mikeb@sco-world.com

Burgart, Calvin E.; Pres, Talaris Systems Inc.; US; 619/587-0787, cal@talaris.com

Burgdorf, Cindy; CFO, SanDisk Corp.; US; 408/542-0500

Burger, Robert M.; VP & Chief Scientist, Semiconductor Research Corp.; US; 919/541-9400

Burgert, Werner; EVP, BASF Corp.; US; 201/397-2700

Burgess, Angela; Mngg Ed, Computer Magazine; US; 908/981-0060, aburgess@computer.org

Burgess, Chris J.; VP Fin, Micro-Integration Corp.; US; 301/689-0800

Burgess, Daniel B.; EVP Sales & Mktng, General Parametrics Corp.; US; 510/524-3950

Burgess, Julie; Controller, Around Technology Inc.; US; 216/234-6402

Burgess, Wendy; VP Comm, Gandalf Technologies Inc.; Canada; 613/274-6500

Burgher, Mike; EVP Core Tech, Microware Systems Corp.; US; 515/224-1929

Burgum, Douglas; Pres & CEO, Great Plains Software; US; 701/281-0550

Burk, Ron; Ed, Windows Developer's Journal; US; 913/841-1631

Burka, Karen; Ed Dir, Telcos in Interactive Services; US; 203/834-0033

Burke, Brian; Mktng Mgr, Duracom Computer Systems; US; 214/518-1200

Burke, James G.; VP & CFO, C-Cube Microsystems Inc.; US; 408/944-6300

Burke, Ken; SVP & GM, CMS Enhancements Inc.; US; 714/517-0915

Burke, Kristina; VP, World Software Corp.; US; 201/444-3228

Burke, Raymond F.; EVP, NYNEX Corp.; US; 212/395-2121

Burke, Thomas W.; Pres, World Software Corp.; US; 201/444-3228

Burke, Tom; EVP, Mirror Technologies Inc.; US; 612/270-2718

Burke, Tom; VP, Discovery Channel, The; US; 301/986-1999

Burkett, Sonny; GM, Corporate Sources; US; 714/582-1946

Burkhardt, Jeff; VP Sales, Iconovex Corp.; US; 612/896-5100

Burkhardt Jr., Kenneth J.; EVP Bus Dev, Dialogic Corp.; US; 201/993-3000

Burkhart, Philip; Pres, Wright Line Inc.; US; 508/852-4300

Burkland, Arthel; Dir Ops, Express Systems Inc.; US; 206/728-8300

Burkland, Mike; Pres, Eventus Software; US; 415/477-3700

Burnett, Chris; CFO, Micro Star Software; US

Burney, Derek H.; EVP Int'l, BCE Inc.;

Canada; 514/397-7267

Burns, Kevin J.; Chmn & CEO, Intersolv Inc.; US; 301/838-5000

Burns, Patrick; Radius Inc.; US; 408/541-6100

Burns, Wayne; VP & CFO, Saros Corp.; US; 206/646-1066

Burnstein, Jeff; Mngg Dir, Automated Imaging Assoc.; US; 313/994-6088

Burow, David; Group VP, Chronologic Simulation; US; 415/965-3312

Burr, Geoff; VP Sales & Mktng, Power Computing Corp.; US; 408/526-0500

Burr, Geoff S.; Pres, Tadpole Technology Inc.; US; 512/219-2200

Burrowes, Paul; High Technology Careers Magazine; US; 408/970-8800

Burrows, Charlie; VP, McClenahan Bruer Burrows Communications Inc.; US; 503/643-9035, charlie@mcbb.com

Bursk, Ed; Pres, OST Inc.; US; 703/817/0400, ebk@ost-us.com

Burson, Valerie; VP, Aldridge Company, The; US; 713/953-1940

Burt, Peggy; VP Mktng, MobileWare Corp.; US; 214/952-1200, pburt@mobileware.com

Burton, Art; VP Sales & Mktng, Fischer International Systems Corp.; US; 941/643-1500

Burton, Craig; Principal, Burton Group, The; US; 801/566-2880

Burton, Don E.; VP, Arrow Electronics Inc.; US; 516/391-1300

Burwell, Helen P.; Pres, Information Brokers, Burwell World Directory of; US; 713/537-9051, hburwell@ix.nctcom.com

Burwell, Pat; VP, D/M Communications Inc.; US; 617/329-7799

Burwen, Michael; Pres, Palo Alto Management Group Inc.; US; 415/968-4374

Busby, James L.; Chmn, Pres & CEO, QMS Inc.; US; 334/633-4300

Busby, James W.; Pres, Datasouth Computer Corp.; US; 704/523-8500

Buscaino, Dale E.; VP Eng, Futuretouch Corp.; US; 714/558-6824

Busch, Theo; Pres & CEO, Elsa Inc.; US; 408/565-9669

Bushell, Roger; Pres, Tracker Software Inc.; US; 612/525-9802

Bushnell, Art; SVP Sales, Intell.X; US; 703/524-7400

Bushover, Linda; Pres, 1-800 Service Partners; US; 512/719-9335

Bussell, Don; Exec Dir, Omicron-Center for Information Technology Management; US; 201/335-0240

Bussler, Michael L.; Pres, Algor Inc.; US; 412/967-2700

Buswell, Peter S.; Pres, Cobotyx Corp.; US; 203/282-0010

Butchko, Bob; Pres, miro Computer Products Inc.; US; 415/855-0940

Butenhoff, Susan; Principal, Access Public Relations; US; 415/904-7070

Butenko, Vladimir; Pres, Stalker Software Inc.; US

Butlein, Marc; Chmn, Meta Group; US; 203/973-6700

Butler, David R.; VP Sales, State Of The Art Inc.; US; 714/753-1222

Butler, Gary C.; Group Pres, Automatic Data Processing Inc.; US; 201/994-5000

Butler, Matilda; Pres, Knowledge Access Int'l.; US; 415/969-0606

Butler, Robert; Dir Ops, Business Communications Co. Inc.; US; 203/853-4266

Butler, Stephen G.; Chmn & CEO, KPMG Peat Marwick; US; 201/307-7000

Butterfield, Steve; SVP, Fujitsu Computer Products; US; 408/432-6333

Butterworth, Jim; SVP Bus Dev, Okidata; US; 609/235-2600

Button, Brian; VP Mktng, Proxim Inc.; US; 415/960-1630, brianb@proxim.com

Button, Jim; CEO, ButtonWare Inc.; US; 214/713-6370

Butts, Tim; VP Reseller Mktng, ASCII Group Inc., The; US; 301/718/2600

Buxton, Tony; Chmn & CEO, Tactics International Ltd.; US; 508/475-4475

Buzbee, Bruce; Pres, FormalSoft; US; 801/489-3102

Buzen, Jeffrey P.; SVP, BGS Systems Inc.; US; 617/891-0000

Bycoff, Barry N.; Pres & CEO, Software Developer's Co. Inc., The; US; 617/740-0101

Byer, Peter; VP Sales & Mktng, Triton Technologies Inc.; US; 908/855-9440

Byer, Ronald C.; Pres, Vertex Industries Inc.; US; 201/777-3500, 73051.370@compuserve.com

Bynum, Donald P.; Pres & CEO, Itac Systems Inc.; US; 214/494-3073, bynum@moustrak.com

Byoff, Barry N.; Pres, Programmer's Shop, The; US; 617/740-2510

Byram, James; Dir Res, Gistics Inc.; US; 415/461-4305, byram@gistics.com

Byrn, Gordon S.; Chmn, Mitel Corp.; Canada; 613/592-2122

Byrne, John J.; VP Fin, Mark IV Industries; US; 716/689-4972

Byrne, Richard; Pres & CEO, MediaShare Corp.; US; 619/931-7171

Byrne, Wendy; Pblr, CommunicationsWeek Int'l.; US; 516/562-5530

Byxbee, Crawford; VP Prod Eng, Advanced Input Devices; US; 208/765-8000

Cabalka, Pamela; VP Sales, Drake Training & Technologies; US; 612/896-7000

Caballero, Kilko; CTO, White Pine Software Inc.; US; 603/886-9050, sroche@wpine.com

Cable, Kevin M.; Pres & CEO, Numera Software Corp.; US; 206/622-2233, kevinc@numera.com

Cabral, Joseph; Chmn & Pres, Chatsworth Products Inc.; US; 818/735-6100

Cademenos, Stauros; VP Int'l Sales, Focus Enhancements Inc.; US; 617/938-

8088

Cadogen, William J.; Chmn, Pres & CEO, ADC Telecommunications; US; 612/938-8080

Cadwell, Marvin S.; Pres & CEO, Shared Medical Systems Corp.; US; 610/219-6300

Cady, Roger C.; VP Bus Dev, Dynatech Corp.; US; 617/272-6100

Cafiero, Ralph; VP Sales, Aurora Technologies Inc.; US; 617/290-4800

Cagan, Martin; VP R&D, Continuus Software Corp.; US; 714/453-2200

Caggiano, Robert A.; VP Sales & Mktng, Smith Micro Software Inc.; US; 714/362-5800

Caggiula, Chris; VP Mktng, Logicraft Information Systems; US; 603/880-0300, ccaggiula@logicraft.com

Caglayan, Alper; Pres, Charles River Analytics Inc.; US; 617/491-3474

Cahan, Ben; Pres, B.C. Software Inc.; US; 310/636-4711, cahan@bcsoftware.com

Cahill, Conor P.; VP Eng, AIB Software Corp.; US; 703/430-9247, conor.cahill@aib.com

Cahill, John J.; VP Mktng, MicroSpeed Inc.; US

Cahill, John J.; Chmn, Dataram Corp.; US; 609/799-0071

Caidar, David; Pres, Opticomm Corp.; US; 619/450-0143

Cain, Curtis A.; CEO, Adam Software; US; 404/980-0888

Caine, Franklyn A.; EVP & CFO, Wang Laboratories Inc.; US; 508/459-5000

Cairns, David C.; CFO, Baan Co.; US; 415/462-4949

Calahan, John W.; Pres & CEO, Timeline Inc.; US; 206/822-3140

Calcagni, Rob; Dir Sales, Business Research Group; US; 617/630-3900, calcagni@brg.cahners.com

Caldeira, David; VP Prod, Information Management Associates Inc.; US; 203/925-6800

Calderon, Jack; VP Intl Ops, Group Technologies Corp.; US; 813/972-6477, j.calderon@grtk.com

Caldes, Douglas; EVP, Disk Technologies Corp.; US; 407/671-5500

Caldwell, Brian; Pres, Imagina Inc.; US; 503/224-8522, bcaldwell@imagina.com

Caldwell, Eugene; CFO, Venture Stores Inc.; US; 314/281-6801

Caldwell, Jim; Pres & COO, Fourth Shift Corp.; US; 612/851-1900

Caldwell, Kaye; Pres, Computer Software Industry Assoc.; US; 415/948-9192

Caldwell, Peggy K.; SVP Mktng, Tech Data Corp.; US; 813/539-7429

Caldwell, Susan M.; Exec Dir, Information Systems Audit & Control Assoc.; US; 847/253-1545

Caldwell, William C.; VP Eng, QLogic Corp.; US; 714/438-2200

Caldwell-Stair, Lucy; Pblr, Electronic Marketplace Sourcebook; US

Calhoun, Charlton H.; EVP Mktng, Infosafe Systems Inc.; US; 212/867-7200

Calhoun, Sallie; VP Fin, Globetrotter Software; US; 408/370-2800

Calica, Ben; Dir Production, Cyberflix Inc.; US; 615/546-1157, cyberflix@aol.com

Calkins, Ed; VP Mktng, Maximum Strategy Inc.; US; 408/383-1600

Calkins, Mark J.; EVP Sales & Mktng, Stallion Technologies Inc.; US; 408/477-0440, mjc@stallion.com

Callahan, Charles E.; EVP, Policy Management Systems Corp.; US; 803/735-4000

Callahan, John; Ed, Forms Automation Technology Report; US; 206/283-5111

Callahan, Michael E.; VP Sales, Intermec Corp.; US; 206/348-2600

Callan, Earlene; Pres, C Systems Ltd.; US; 903/342-5284

Callan, James; VP, C Systems Ltd.; US; 903/342-5284

Calvfleisch, Robin; News Ed, Canadian Computer Reseller; Canada; 416/596-5000

Camarata, S.J.; Sales & Mktng, ESRI User Group; US; 909/793-2853

Camarro, Kenneth; Pres, Camarro Research; US; 203/336-4566, kcamarro@snet.net

Cameron, Dave; VP, Iiyama North America; US; 215/957-6543

Cameron, Pat; Pblr, InterActivity; US; 415/358-9500

Camp, Susanna; Ed, Internet Gazette; US; 415/776-1888

Campbell, Alastair; Co-Founder, Digital Wisdom Inc.; US; 804/443-9000

Campbell, David M.; SVP, Bolt Beranek & Newman Inc.; US; 617/873-4000

Campbell, Gail; VP Ops, Computer Support Corp.; US; 214/661-8960

Campbell, Gary; VP Sales, VideoLabs Inc.; US; 612/988-0055

Campbell, George; Chmn, Association of Shareware Professionals; US; 616/788-5131

Campbell, Greg; Design Coord, Three Marketeers Advertising Inc.; US; 408/293-3233, greg@3marketeers.com

Campbell, Jennifer; Features Ed, Corel Magazine; US; 512/250-1700, jenc@jumpnet.com

Campbell, Jim; VP Mktng, Distributed Processing Technology; US; 407/830-5522

Campbell, Keith; VP Mktng, American Small Business Computers Inc.; US; 918/825-4844

Campbell, Kirk; Pres & CEO, International Data Corp.; US; 508/872-8200, kcampbell@idcresearch.com

Campbell, Michael H.; Pres, Campbell Software; US; 847/328-3200

Campbell, Robert; Chmn & Pres, Servantis Systems Inc.; US; 770/441-3387

Campbell, Robert; VP & CFO, Micronics Computers Inc.; US; 510/651-2300

Campbell, Scott; Ed, Omray Inc.; US; 512/250-1700, 71164.15@compuserve.com

Campbell, Scott; Ed, Corel Magazine; US; 512/250-1700, scottc@jumpnet.com

Campbell, W. Patrick; EVP Bus Dev, Ameritech Corp.; US; 312/750-5000

Campbell, William; VP Mktng, Alpha Technologies; US; 360/647-2360

Campbell, William V.; Pres & CEO, Intuit Inc.; US; 415/944-6000

Campeau, Cliff J.; SVP Mktng, Venture Stores Inc.; US; 314/281-6801

Campeau, Francois; VP & CFO, Eicon Technology Corp.; 214/239-3270

Camps, Chuck; CFO, Interplay Productions Inc.; US; 714/553-6655

Camus, Luis; Mgng Ed, PC World; US; 415/243-0500

Cancelosi, Anthony J.; VP & GM, ICL Inc.; US; 703/648-3300

Cane, David A.; VP & CTO, Phoenix Technologies Ltd.; US; 408/654-9000

Canfield, Robert C.; SVP, DST Systems Inc.; US; 816/435-1000

Cannada, Charles T.; SVP, LDDS WorldCom; US; 601/360-8600

Cannavino, James; Pres & CEO, Perot Systems; US; 703/716-1400

Cannon, Bruce A.; SVP & CFO, SpecTran Corp.; US; 508/347-2261

Canon, Maggie; Ed-in-Chief, MacUser; US; 415/378-5600

Canright, Mark W.; VP Sales & Mktng, Exabyte Corp.; US; 303/442-4333

Canton, Owen A.; VP Mktng, Timeline Inc.; US; 206/822-3140

Cantral, Dave; Owner, P&L Associates; US; 714/633-5308

Cantwell, Maria; VP Mktng, Progressive Networks; US; 206/447-0567

Canup, Terry; VP Mktng, Aldridge Company, The; 713/953-1940

Capers, Rushton; VP, Disc Manufacturing Inc.; US; 302/479-2500

Caplan, David; CEO, Objectivity; US; 415/254-7100

Caplin, David J.; VP & GM, A/E/C Systems International Inc.; US; 610/458-7070

Capobianco, John H.; VP Mktng, Primavera Systems Inc.; US; 610/667-8600

Capone Jr., Daniel J.; Pres & CEO, Proteon Inc.; US; 508/898-2800

Caponigro, Ralph A.; SVP & CFO, Compuware Corp.; US; 810/737-7300

Capparell, James; Pblr, MacHome Journal; US; 415/957-1911

Capps, Ian; Pres, PR Newswire; US; 212/596-1500

Capstick, John A.; Chmn & CEO, InterTan Inc.; US; 817/348-9701

Caputo, Dom; VP Sales, Siemens Nixdorf Printing Systems LP; US; 407/997-3100

Caracio, Vince; Pres, Harvard Group, The; US; 713/292-3999

Carballo, Bernard A.; SVP Sales & Mktng, Seagate Technology; US; 408/438-6550

Carbone, Teresa; Participation Coord, Omicron-Center for Information Technology Management; US; 201/335-0240

Cardais, Scott; Pres & CEO, Hand Held Products; US; 704/541-1380

Cardell, Christopher S.; SVP & CFO, Mecklermedia Corp.; US; 203/226-6967, scardell@mecklermedia.com

Cardinal, David J.; Pres & CEO, First Floor Inc.; US; 415/968-1101

Cardinale, Rex; VP & GM Internet Div, Global Village Communication; US; 408/523-1000

Cardosi, Johnny; VP, Distributed Processing Technology; US; 407/830-5522

Carey, D. John; Chmn, Integrated Device Technology Inc.; US; 408/727-6116

Cargile, John; Mgng Ed, Software Developer & Pblr; US; 303/745-5711

Carillon, John C.; Pres & CEO, Riso Inc.; US; 508/777-7377

Carinalli, Charles P.; SVP & CTO, National Semiconductor Corp.; US; 408/721-5000

Carioti, Michael; Mktng Mgr, Provantage Corp.; US; 216/494-8715, carioti@provantage.com

Caris, Ted; Pblr, Cambridge Information Group; US; 301/961-6700

Carl, Ed; VP, International TechneGroup Inc.; US; 513/576-3900, ejc@iti-oh.com

Carlen, John T.; EVP, Paychex Inc.; US; 716/385-6666

Carlson, Bart; CEO, Napersoft Inc.; US; 708/420-1515

Carlson, Jerome W.; VP & CFO, Triad Systems Corp.; US; 510/449-0606

Carlson, John; VP Mktng, Elo TouchSystems Inc.; US; 615/482-4100

Carlson, John; Pres, daVinci Public Relations; US; 812/376-0660

Carlson, Laurie; VP Mkt Dev, Access Graphics Inc.; US; 303/938-9333, lcarlson@access.com

Carlson, LeRoy T.; Chmn, Telephone & Data Systems Inc.; US; 312/630-1900

Carlson, Paige; Dir Mktng, WizardWorks; US; 612/559-5140

Carlson, Steve; VP Design Methodology, Escalade; US; 408/654-1600

Carlson Jr., LeRoy T.; Pres & CEO, Telephone & Data Systems Inc.; US; 312/630-1900

Carlston, Douglas G.; Chmn, Broderbund Software Inc.; US; 415/382-4400

Carmakk, John; Pres, Id Software; US; 214/613-3589, john@idsoftware.com

Carmel, Erez; Pres, WinWay Corp.; US; 916/965-7878

Carmeris, Dean; VP Cust Svcs, FTP Software Inc.; US; 508/685-4000

Carnese, Dan; Dir Eng, Independence

Technologies Inc.; US; 510/438-2000

Caron, Paul; Prdts Dir, UNIX Companion; US

Carpenter, Chadwick H.; SVP Corp Dev, Progress Software Corp.; US; 617/280-4000

Carpenter, John; VP Sales, CW Database; US; 508/879-0700

Carpenter, Wayne; Pres & CEO, Saros Corp.; US; 206/646-1066

Carper, Kyle; VP Mktng, AutoTester Inc.; US; 214/363-6181

Carr, Grace M.; VP Sales & Mktng, Xylogics Inc.; US; 617/272-8140

Carr, Greg; Chmn, Prodigy Inc.; US; 914/993-8000

Carrade, Robert; Dir Fin, Pilot Network Services Inc.; US; 510/748-1818

Carrell, Stewart; Chmn, Evans & Sutherland Computer Corp.; US; 801/588-1000

Carrico, William; Chmn, Percept Software Inc.; US; 408/446-7600

Carrier, Jean-Jacques; VP & CFO, Mitel Corp.; Canada; 613/592-2122

Carroll, Ronald C.; Chmn, Continuum Company Inc., The; US; 512/345-5700

Carrubba, F.P.; EVP, Philips Electronics; Netherlands; 31-40-786022

Carse, Greg; Pres, RadioLAN Inc.; US; 408/524-2600

Carson, Thomas; VP & CFO, Access Graphics Inc.; US; 303/938-9333, tomc@access.com

Carson, Thomas C.; SVP WW Sales, Zilog Inc.; US; 408/370-8000

Carson, Wesley E.; VP, Pacific Telecom Inc.; US; 360/905-5800

Carter, David L.; Pres & CEO, Zebra Technologies VTI Inc.; US; 801/576-9700

Carter, E. Follett; EVP Sales & Mktng, Gartner Group; US; 203/964-0096

Carter, Eric V.; EVP, TIE/Communications Inc.; US; 913/344-0400

Carter, James D.; VP Fin, Vertex Communications Corp.; US; 903/984-0555

Carter, Jerry; Customer Svc, Star Technologies Inc.; US; 703/689-4400

Carter, John L.; EVP & CFO, BurrBrown Corp.; US; 602/746-1111

Carter, Larry; VP & CFO, Cisco Systems Inc.; US; 408/526-4000

Carter, Matt; VP Ops, Truevision Inc.; US; 408/562-4200

Carter-Lome, Maxine; Ed Dir, Wireless; US; 201/285-1500

Carthey, Joanne; Pres & CEO, NetPro Computing Inc.; US; 602/941-3600

Cartwright, Donald W.; Pres, International Software Services Inc.; US; 612/935-9339

Carty, Art; VP & GM, SunExpress Inc.; US; 508/442-000

Caruso, Denise; Ed Dir & Pblr, Technology & Media; US

Caruso, Jeff; Ed, DataTrends Publications Inc.; US; 703/779-0574, jpcaruso@aol.com

Caruso, Joseph A.; Principal, Jordan Tamraz Caruso Advertising Inc.; US; 312/951-2000

Carver, Bruce; Pres, Access Software Inc.; US; 801/359-2900

Carveth, John C.; VP Fin, Adaptive Solutions Inc.; US; 503/690-1236

Casale, Robert J.; Group Pres, Automatic Data Processing Inc.; US; 201/994-5000

Casanave, Cory; Co-Pres, Data Access Corp.; US; 305/238-0012

Casanave III, Charles; Co-Pres, Data Access Corp.; US; 305/238-0012

Casas, Linda; CEO, Strategies, A Marketing Communications Corp.; US; 714/957-8880

Casas, Roger; VP Mktng, Morris Media; US; 310/533-4800

Casatelli, Christine; Exec Ed, RS/Magazine; US; 617/739-7001, cmc@cpg.com

Casciano, Ronald J.; VP & CFO, Par Technology Corp.; US; 315/738-0600

Case, Mary; Pres, SNMP Research International Inc.; US; 615/573-1434, mary@snmp.com

Case, Randall B.; Pres & CEO, Cybermedix Inc.; US; 703/917-6600

Case, Stephen M.; Chmn & CEO, America Online Inc.; US; 703/448-8700

Casella, Jim; COO, IDG Communications; US; 617/534-1200

Casey, Dennis; VP, Strategic Research Corp.; US; 805/569-5610

Casey, Donald P.; Pres, Wang Laboratories Inc.; US; 508/459-5000

Casey, Joan Kelleher; Pres, Joan Kelleher Casey PR; US; 617/325-7209

Casey, Michael J.; VP Fin, IQ Software Corp.; US; 770/446-8880

Casey, Patricia; Ed, Tape/Disc Business; US; 914/328-9157

Casey, Sean; CIO, Opcode Systems; US; 415/856-3333

Casilli, Gerald S.; Chmn, Ikos Systems Inc.; US; 408/255-4567

Cason, Don; Dir Sales, NewGen Systems Corp.; US; 714/641-8600

Caspe, Robert A.; Pres, Leaf Systems Inc.; US; 508/460-8300

Cass, Barbara; Exec Dir, Software Forum; US; 415/854-7219

Cassell, Bruce; VP Sales & Mktng, Systech Corp.; US; 619/453-8970

Cassese, John J.; Chmn & Pres, Computer Horizons Corp.; US; 201/402-7400

Cassidy, Brian; VP Bus Dev, Saros Corp.; US; 206/646-1066

Cassidy, Robert; Ed-in-Chief, R&D Magazine; US; 708/635-8800, rdchi@mci-mail.com

Casteel, Mihael A.; EVP & CTO, Unison Software Inc.; US; 408/988-2800

Castellano, Robert N.; Pres, Information Network, The; US; 804/258-3738

Castillo, Joann; Pres, Association of Database Developers; US; 415/281-5638

Castino, Tom; Pres, Underwriters Laboratories Inc.; US; 847/272-8800

Casto, Randall; Pres, Bendata Management Systems; US; 719/531-5007

Castonguay, Maurice L.; VP Fin, Xylogics Inc.; US; 617/272-8140

Castro, Allan; Opticomm Corp.; US; 619/450-0143

Caswell, Lee; VP Sales & Mktng, Parallax Graphics Inc.; US; 408/727-2220, lee@parallax.com

Caswell, Stephen; VP Mktng & Sales, Incomnet Inc.; US; 818/887-3400

Cataldo, Wallace A.; VP Fin, Keane Inc.; US; 617/241-9200

Cataneo, Peter; VP Mktng, Pacific Microelectronics Inc.; US; 415/948-6200

Catelain, Clark W.; SVP Eng, Centura Software Corp.; US; 415/321-9500

Catelli, Marcy; Mktng Dir, Xecute Inc.; US; 908/668-5151, marcyc@xecute.com

Catlin, Timothy; Pres & CEO, Streetlight Software Inc.; US; 415/227-4350

Catmull, Edwin E.; EVP & CTO, Pixar Animation Studios; US; 510/236-4000

Caudill, Craig; Pres, Falcon Systems Inc.; US; 916/928-9255, craig@falcons.com

Causey, Michael; Exec Ed, Mobile Data Report; US; mcausey@cappubs.com

Cavalier, John; Pres & CEO, Antares Alliance Group; US; 972/447-5500

Cavaliere, Judith; Pblr, Business Documents; US; 215/238-5300

Cavanah, Cassandra; Exec Ed, PC Lap-Top Computers Magazine; US; 310/858-7155

Cavataio, Helene; Admin Mgr, Calyx Corp.; US; 414/782-0300

Cave, Bill; Dir Mktng, Mentalix Inc.; US; 214/423-9377

Cavin, Rick; VP Sales, Storm Software; US; 415/691-6600

Cavuoto, James; Ed & Pblr, Micro Publishing Press; US; 310/371-5787

Cecere, Tom; VP Strategic Alliances, Tally Systems Corp.; US; 603/643-1300

Cecil, Robert S.; Chmn & CEO, Plantronics; US; 408/426-5858

Cecrle, Donella; Dir Mktng, Linksys; US; 714/261-1288

Celi, Louis; Mgng Dir Elec Pubs, Economist Intelligence Unit, The; US; 212/554-0600

Celms, John V.; Pres, Seattle Silicon Corp.; US; 206/957-4422

Cenker, Michael; Sales Mgr, Quatech Inc.; US; 216/434-3154, cenker@quatech.com

Centner, Ron; Pres, Centron Software Technologies Inc.; US; 910/215-5708

Ceragioli, Guy C.; VP Mktng, Lahey Computer Systems Inc.; US; 702/831-2500

Cerf, Vinton; Pres, Internet Society; US; 703/648-9888

Cerullo, John; Chmn, Lawson Software; US; 612/379-2633, john.cerullo@law-

son.com

Cervo, Craig; VP R&D, Applix Inc.; US; 508/870-0300

Chadha, Parvinder; Pres & CEO, Osicom Technologies Inc.; US

Chadha, Sharon; CFO, Osicom Technologies Inc.; US

Chadwick, Dan; Pres, Attain Corp.; US; 617/776-1110, dan_chadwick@qm.attain.com

Chaffee, David C.; Sr Ed, Fiber Optics News; US; 301/340-1520, dchaffee@phillips.com

Chaffee, John; Dir Mktng, Extensis Corp.; US; 503/274-2020

Chaimowitz, Ron; Pres, GT Interactive Software; US; 212/726-6500

Chalifoux, Michael T.; SVP & CFO, Circuit City Stores Inc.; US; 804/527-4000

Challenger, Jim; Pres, Software Development Systems; US; 708/368-0400, chal@sdsi.com

Challis, Dave; Dir Bus Dev, Mountain-Gate Data Systems Inc.; US; 702/851-9393

Chalstrom, Brownell; VP Mktng, Jet-Form Corp.; US; 703/448-9544

Chamberlain, Bryan; Ed, Inside Microsoft PowerPoint; US; 502/491-1900

Chamberlain, George A.; CFO, Marcam Corp.; US; 617/965-0220

Chamberlain, Michael D.; Pres SCT SW, Systems & Computer Technology Corp.; US; 610/647-5930

Chamberlain, Robert; SVP Sales, Continuus Software Corp.; US; 714/453-2200

Chamillard, George W.; Pres & COO, Teradyne Inc.; US; 617/482-2700

Chan, Anthony S.; VP & CFO, NexGen Microsystem; US; 408/435-0202

Chan, Demonder; Dir Eng, NovaLink Technologies Inc.; US; 510/249-9777

Chan, Frank; VP Ops, InterNex Information Services; US; 408/327-2355, ftchan@internex.com

Chan, Fred S.L.; Pres & CEO, ESS Technology Inc.; US; 510/226-1088

Chan, John P.; VP Ops, Network Peripherals; US; 408/321-7300

Chan, Kam H.; Pres, Tatung Science & Technology Inc.; US; 408/383-0988, kamchan@tsti.com

Chan, Steven; Pres & CEO, Auravision Corp.; US; 510/252-6800, steve@auravision.com

Chan, Y.M.; Ed, International designers Network; Hong Kong; 852-25285744

Chance, Doug; Pres & CEO, Wyse Technology Inc.; US; 408/473-1200

Chandlee McCabe, Kim; Assoc Pblr, BUS Publishing Group; US; 908/363-0708

Chaney, Elizabeth; Mgng Partner, McKenna Group Inc.; US; 415/494-2030

Chang, Abe; Co-Founder, Pacific Image Communications Inc.; US; 818/457-8880

Chang, Allen; VP, Comtrade; US; 818/961-6688

Chang, Arrina; Admin Secretary, Computer Association of N. America; US; 718/460-9770

Chang, Carl; Ed-in-Chief, IEEE Software; US; 908/981-0060

Chang, Dean; Pres, ActionTec Electronics Inc.; US; 408/739-7000

Chang, Edward L.; Pres & CEO, Twinbridge Software Corp.; US; 213/263-3926

Chang, Jerry; Chmn & CEO, OPTi Inc.; US; 408/486-8000

Chang, John H.; VP Prod Mktng, Insignia Solutions Inc.; US; 408/327-6000

Chang, Jung-Herng; VP Eng, Trident Microsystems Inc.; US; 415/691-9211

Chang, Ming H.; Pres, Chroma ATE Inc.; US; 408/437-0798

Chang, Morris; Chmn, Wyse Technology Inc.; US; 408/473-1200

Chang, Raymond; VP, International Parallel Machines Inc.; US; 508/990-2977, raychang@ici.net

Chang, Robin; Pres, International Parallel Machines Inc.; US; 508/990-2977

Chang, Steve; Pres, Trend Micro Devices Inc.; US; 310/782-8190

Chanoki, Fred; Chmn, Murata Electronics North America Inc.; US; 404/436-1300

Chapiro, Daniel; CEO, Systems Science Inc.; US; 415/812-1800

Chapman, James N.; SVP Sales, Cyrix Corp.; US; 214/968-8388

Chapman, Jim; Dir Sales, Key Tronic Corp.; US; 509/928-8000

Chapman, John E.; EVP & COO, SpecTran Corp.; US; 508/347-2261

Chapman, Lynn C.; VP Prod Dev, Netrix Corp.; US; 703/742-6000

Chapman, Peter; Tech Svs Mgr, 4-Sight LC; US; 515/221-3000

Chappelear, Bob; VP Eng, McAfee Assoc.; US; 408/988-3832

Chapple, Paul; Mgr Media Relations, Philips Home Services Inc.; US; 617/238-3400

Chari, Sri; VP Mktng, CyberMedia Inc.; US; 310/843-0800, 75460.32@compuserve.com

Charlet, Kimberly; Dir Mktng, EAS Technologies Inc.; US; 812/941-9360

Charlton, Thomas E.; Group VP, Andrew Corp.; US; 708/349-3300

Charp, Sylvia; Ed-in-Chief, Technological Horizons in Education Journal; US; 714/730-4011

Chassen, Arthur; Pblr, Beyond Computing; US; 212/745-6347

Chastain, M. Lance; EVP, Interex; US; 316/524-4747

Chateauneuf, Dennis; VP Ops, Shiva Corp.; US; 617/270-8300

Chaudhary, Tariq; Pres, Gigatron Software Corp.; US; 714/261-1777

Chauvin Jr., Alden J.; VP Sales, Sierra Semiconductor Corp.; US; 408/263-9300

Chawla, Prem; COO, Wolfram Research Inc.; US; 217/398-0700

Chay, K.S.; Pres & COO, Creative Labs Inc.; US; 408/428-6600

Cheah, Jonathon Y.C.; VP Eng, Solectek Inc.; US; 619/450-1220

Cheifet, Stewart; Ed, Cheifet Letter, The; US; 603/863-9322, 70555.276@compuserve.com

Chelin, Jeffrey D.; VP, ARC International Corp.; Canada; 416/630-0200

Chellam, Kris; VP & CFO, Atmel Corp.; US; 408/441-0311

Chen, Charles; Pres, Twinhead Corp.; US; 408/945-0808

Chen, Charles W.; Pblr, Dallas Ft. Worth Technology; US; 214/907-9977

Chen, Daphne; VP Ops, Commax Technologies Inc.; US; 408/435-5000

Chen, David; VP, Plustek US Inc.; US; 408/745-7111

Chen, Dennis; VP & Chief Scientist, Specular International; US; 413/253-3100, dennis_chen@specular.com

Chen, Ernest; VP PC Div, First International Computer US; US; 510/252-8888

Chen, Francis; Pres, Quatech Inc.; US; 216/434-3154, chen@quatech.com

Chen, Henry; Pres, Commax Technologies Inc.; US; 408/435-5000

Chen, Henry; Pres, Halskar Systems; US; 510/656-5157

Chen, Hong; CEO, Aimnet Corp.; US; 408/257-0900

Chen, James F.; Pres, Virtual Open Network Environment Corp.; US; 301/881-2297

Chen, Jesse; Pres, BusLogic Inc.; US; 408/492-9090

Chen, Jimmy; Pres, Media Depot; US; 909/629-2597

Chen, John S.; Pres & COO, Pyramid Technology Corp.; US; 408/428-9000

Chen, Liming; Pres, Ulead Systems Inc.; US; 310/523-9393

Chen, Lotus; VP Prog Office, Ulead Systems Inc.; US; 310/523-9393

Chen, Michael; Chmn & Pres, AITech International Corp.; US; 510/226-8960

Chen, Mina; VP, Media Synergy; Canada; 416/369-1100

Chen, Nai-Ling; MIS Mgr, Halskar Systems; US; 510/656-5157

Chen, Paul; Pres, Systems & Software Inc.; US; 714/833-1700

Chen, Paul; Pres, Media Synergy; Canada; 416/369-1100

Chen, Pehong; CEO, Broadvision Inc.; US; 415/943-3600

Chen, Peter; Pres, Mustek Inc.; US; 714/247-1300

Chen, Rita; CFO, Media Depot; US; 909/629-2597

Chen, S. Chris; Pres & CEO, Initio Corp.; US; 408/988-1919

Chen, Sherry; Pres, Smile International Inc.; US; 714/546-0336

Chen, Thomas; VP Ops, CMD Technology Inc.; US; 714/454-0800

Chen, Thomas; VP Mktng, American Advantech Corp.; US; 408/245-6678

Chen, Vicki; Pres, Chem US; US; 510/785-8080

Chen, Victor; CFO, Sampo Corp. of America; US; 770/449-6220

Chen, Wen-hsiung; SVP Res, Compression Labs Inc.; US; 408/435-3000

Chen, William; Dir MIS, InterNex Information Services; US; 408/327-2355, wchen@internex.com

Chenault, Gennifer; Circ Mgr, DataTrends Publications Inc.; US; 703/779-0574

Chenette, John; SVP Corp Resources, UB Networks; US; 408/496-0111

Cheng, Alex; EVP, Vividata Inc.; US; 510/841-6400, alex@vividata.com

Cheng, Gary; Pres & CEO, Destiny Technology Corp.; US; 408/562-1000

Cheng, Sean; VP Fin, Digicom Systems Inc.; US; 408/262-1277

Chernick, Aubrey; Chmn & CEO, Candle Corp.; US; 310/829-5800

Cherry, Peter B.; Chmn, Pres & CEO, Cherry Corp.; US; 847/662-9200

Cherry, Steven; VP Sales & Mktng, Janna Systems Inc.; US; 408/356-6647, stevec@janna.com

Cherubini, Julian; Pres, AliMed Inc.; US; 617/329-2900

Chesney, Michael K.; VP Corp Dev, Telephone & Data Systems Inc.; US; 312/630-1900

Chess, John; GM, Apex Data Inc.; US; 510/416-5656

Chester, Jimmy; Co-Founder, Automated Computer Business Systems; US; 304/296-0290

Cheung, Andrew; Pres, 01 Communique Laboratory Inc.; Canada; 905/795-2888

Cheung, Norman; CFO, Starfish Software; US; 408/461-5800

Cheung, S.C.; Chmn, 01 Communique Laboratory Inc.; Canada; 905/795-2888

Chiang, Stanley; CEO, Twinhead Corp.; US; 408/945-0808

Chiapparone, Paul J.; SVP, EDS; US; 214/604-6000

Chiaro, Martin; CFO, Persoft Inc.; US; 608/273-6000

Chiazza, John J.; CIO, Eastman Kodak Co.; US; 716/724-4000

Chien, Ming; Chmn, First International Computer Inc.; Taiwan ROC; 2-717-4500

Childberg, Marty; CFO, Visio Corp.; US; 206/521-4500

Childers, Adam; Controller, Ansel Communications; US; 206/869-4928

Childs, Bill W.; Pblr & Ed-in-Chief, Healthcare Informatics; US; 303/674-2774

Childs, Warren; Dir Primary Res, Technology Implementation Index; US; 617/630-3900, childs@brg.cahners.com

Chimiklis, Theodore; VP Sales, International Software Group Inc.; US; 617/221-

1450
Chin, Henry W.; VP & CFO, Marshall Industries; US; 818/307-6000

Ching, Wei; Pres, Maxpeed Corp.; US; 415/345-5447

Chio, Shiu-Shin; Pres, Pulse Metric Inc.; US; 619/546-9461

Chiou, Wun C.; Chmn & CEO, Pacific Microelectronics Inc.; US; 415/948-6200, wchiou@netusa.com

Chirco, Joseph; Dir Sales & Mktng, Vertex Industries Inc.; US; 201/777-3500

Chisholm, John; Pres, Decisive Technology Corp.; US; 415/528-4300, jchisholm@decisive.com

Chisholm, Thomas J.; VP R&D, Computer Identics Corp.; US; 617/821-0830

Chism, Robert E.; Dir Prod Ops, Harris Computer Systems Corp.; US; 305/973-5100

Chitty, Charles R.; Pres & CEO, IQ Software Corp.; US; 770/446-8880

Chiu, Chun-Pang; Chmn & CEO, Quality Semiconductor Inc.; US; 408/450-8000

Chiu, Wilson; Pres, Sceptre Technologies Inc.; US; 714/369-3698

Chiumiento, Patrick; VP Sales & Mktng, Databook Inc.; US; 508/762-9779, patc@databook.com

Cho, Eric; VP Sales, Avanti Corp.; US; 408/738-8881

Choate, Tim; Pres & CEO, Online Interactive Inc.; US; 206/443-1933

Chong, Timothy; Dir Fin & Admin, Primax Electronics; US; 408/522-1200

Chou, Kathy; VP Sales, Sceptre Technologies Inc.; US; 714/369-3698

Chou, Paul; Pres, Performance Awareness Corp.; US; 919/870-8800

Chou, Wayne; EVP, Software Security Inc.; US; 203/656-3000

Chowaniec, Adam; Pres, Newbridge Microsystems; Canada; 613/599-3600

Chrisiani, Barbara; Designer, Soleil Software; US; 415/494-0114

Christ, Charles F.; VP, Digital Equipment Corp.; US; 508/493-5111

Christ, John F.; VP Dev, Datastream Systems Inc.; US; 803/297-6775

Christensen, Douglas; VP, Helmers Publishing Inc.; US; 603/924-9631

Christensen, John; VP Mktng, PowerQuest Corp.; US; 801/226-8977

Christensen, Mark; Consultant, Prismark Partners LLC; US; 516/367-9187

Christensen, Steve; Treas, Learning Services Inc.; US; 541/683-3827, steve@ls.learnserv.com

Christiano, Matt; Pres, Globetrotter Software; US; 408/370-2800

Christiansen, Ron; Principal, CF2GS; US; 206/223-6464

Christie, Daniel H.; CFO, Datastream Systems Inc.; US; 803/297-6775

Christiensen, Brenda; Chair, Fibre Channel Assoc.; US; 512/328-8422

Christman, Raymond R.; Exec Dir,

Pennsylvania Technology Council; US; 412/687-2700

Chu, Christopher; SVP Mktng & Sales, Battery Technology Inc.; US; 213/728-7874

Chu, Don; VP, Fidelity International Technologies; US; 908/417-2230

Chu, James; Pres, ViewSonic Corp.; US; 909/869-7976

Chu, Victor; Dir OEM Sales, Primax Electronics; US; 408/522-1200

Chua, John H.C.; Pres & CEO, Future Labs Inc.; US; 408/254-9000, jchua@futurelabs.com

Chuang, Alfred; EVP & CTO, BEA Systems Inc.; US; 408/743-4000

Chubb, W. Morris; CFO, DTC Data Technology Corp.; US; 408/942-4000

Chudnofsky, Jason E.; Pres & CEO, Softbank Comdex Inc.; US; 617/443-1500

Chung, Hoon; VP Consulting, Numetrix Ltd.; US; 203/847-3452

Chung, M.H.; Chmn, Maxtor Corp.; US; 408/432-1700

Church, Kay; CFO, Continuus Software Corp.; US; 714/453-2200

Churchill, Ross; VP Sales & Mktng, Access Graphics Inc.; US; 303/938-9333, ross@access.com

Churcilla, Kenneth R.; Pres, Mentor Market Research; US; 408/268-6333

Chwang, Ronald; Pres & CEO, Acer America Corp.; US; 408/432-6200

Ciarloni, Angie; Com Mgr, 3D/Eye Inc.; US; 770/937-9000, angiec@eye.com

Cibbarelli, Pamela; Ed, Library Automation Software, Systems & Services, Directory of; US; 609/654-6266

Ciembronowicz, David; VP Sales & Mktng, Teco Information Systems Co. Inc.; US; 708/438-3998, dtciembro@aol.com

Ciesinski, Stephen J.; Pres & CEO, Resumix; US; 408/988-0444

Ciffone, Donald L.; VP, VLSI Technology Inc.; US; 408/434-3000

Cimino, R.; GM, Cadec Systems Inc.; US; 603/668-1010

Cingari, John F.; VP Mktng, Datalogix Int'l.; US; 914/747-2900

Cipriano, Mitchell; VP Mktng, Mountain Network Solutions Inc.; US; 408/438-6650

Clabburn, Robin J.T.; VP & CTO, Nashua Corp.; US; 603/880-2323

Cladis, Chris P.; CEO & GM, Fiber & Wireless Inc.; US; 310/787-7097

Claessens, Dominique; Pres, Image Smith Inc.; US; 310/325-1429

Claiborne, John; VP Mktng, Sherpa Corp.; US; 408/433-0455

Clapp, Doug; Founder, RSI Systems Inc.; US; 612/896-3020

Clark, Bill; Dir Sales & Mktng, Oberon Software Inc.; US; 617/494-0990

Clark, Bob; Ed Dir, Smart Electronics; US; 714/572-2255

Clark, Brian; VP Bus Dev & CFO, Soft-

Cop Corp.; Canada; 905/681-3269

Clark, Brian; SVP & GM, Solomon Software; US; 419/424-0422, bclark@solomon.com

Clark, G. Thomas; VP & CFO, Paychex Inc.; US; 716/385-6666

Clark, Gary; VP Purchasing, Centon Electronics Inc.; US; 714/855-9111

Clark, Heeth; GM, Rhintek Inc.; US; 410/730-2575

Clark, James; VP & GM, Alpha Technologies; US; 360/647-2360

Clark, James H.; Chmn, Netscape Communications Corp.; US; 415/254-1900

Clark, James M.; VP, Technalysis Corp.; US; 612/925-5900

Clark, Jay; SVP, White & Co.; US; 415/274-8100

Clark, Jim; Principal, Lloyd & Clark; US; 818/757-0070

Clark, Jim; CFO, Farallon Computing Inc.; US; 510/814-5100

Clark, Katherine K.; Pres & CEO, Landmark Systems Corp.; US; 703/902-8000

Clark, Michael; Dir Eng, Maxum Development Corp.; US; 708/830-1113

Clark, Nancy; Mktng Dir, Exsys Inc.; US; 505/256-8356

Clark, Patrick L.; VP Sales & Mktng, Computervision Corp.; US; 617/275-1800

Clark, Peter; Evaluation Mgr, Computer Product Testing Services Inc.; US; 908/223-5700

Clark, Shelley; Dir Mktng, Theos Software Corp.; US; 510/935-1118

Clark, Tom; VP Dev, Publications & Communications Inc.; US; 512/250-9023

Clark, Jr., Grahame N.; Chmn, Pres & CEO, BancTec Inc.; US; 214/450-7700

Clarke, Julie; Mktng Dir, Scitor Corp.; US; 415/462-4200

Clarke II, Leslie F.; EVP, Timberline Software Corp.; US; 503/626-6775

Clary, John G.; Chmn, Clary Corp.; US; 818/359-4486

Claunch, Duane; CFO, ShaBlamm! Computer Corp.; US; 408/730-9696, dc@shablamm.com

Clavena, Scott; Ed, ISDN User Newsletter; US; 617/232-3111, igiboston@aol.com

Clay, O. Perry; SVP Consumer Electronics Grp, Sharp Electronics Corp.; US; 201/529-8200

Cleage, Erik; VP Mktng, Altera Corp.; US; 408/894-7000

Clear, Geoffrey P.; VP Fin & Admin, MicroTouch Systems Inc.; US; 508/659-9000

Cleary, Larry; VP Sales & Mktng, Allen Communication; US; 801/537-7800

Cleary, Robert T.; CEO, Kinetic Systems Corp.; US; 815/838-0005

Clemm, David; Pres & COO, Gordon S. Black Corp.; US; 716/272-8400

Clendenin, John L.; Chmn, BellSouth Corp.; US; 404/249-2000

Clephan, Simon; VP Sales, ClariNet Communications Corp.; US; 408/296-0366

Clerke, Dennis E.; VP Mktng & Sales, Cardiff Software Inc.; US; 619/761-4515

Cleveland, Jack; Dir Eng & Ops, Server Technology Inc.; US; 408/745-0300

Clifford, Mike; VP Sales & Mktng, Vcon Inc.; US; 214/774-3890

Clifford, William T.; EVP & COO, Gartner Group; US; 203/964-0096

Cline, Herb; VP, Siemens Nixdorf Information Systems Inc.; US; 617/273-0480

Close, Richard C.; Pres & CEO, Computer Identics Corp.; US; 617/821-0830

Close, Zane; Pres & CEO, Cerprobe Corp.; US; 602/497-4200

Cloud, Kevin; Sec, Id Software; US; 214/613-3589, kevin@idsoftware

Clough, William A.; Pres, MicroSlate Inc.; Canada; 514/444-3680

Cloutier, David; VP Sales & Mktng, Sophisticated Circuits Inc.; US; 206/485-7979

Cloutier, Madison; VP Mktng & COO, Tower Technology Corp.; US; 512/452-9455, madison@twr.com

Clow, Gary W.; Pres & CEO, Stac Inc.; US; 619/794-4300

Cluss, Edward M.; Pres & COO, Cypress Research Corp.; US; 408/752-2700

Clyne, Melissa; VP PR Counsel, Bremer Public Relations; US; 801/364-2030

Coan, Ralph; VP & CFO, Optical Media Int'l.; US; 408/376-3511

Cobb, Daniel; Tech Svcs Mgr, Operations Control Systems; US; 415/493-4122

Cobb, Matt; Chmn, Endpoint Marketing Information Systems; US; 408/725-4200

Cobb, Ron; Co-Founder, Rocket Science Games Inc.; US; 415/442-5000

Cobb, Steve; VP Sales, Pick Systems; US; 714/261-7425, steve_cobb@picksys.com

Cobb, Steve; Ed, Inside Microsoft Excel; US; 502/491-1900

Cobery, Michael; Sales Mgr, Teac America Inc.; US; 213/726-0303

Coburn, Karen; Pres, Cutter Information Corp.; US; 617/648-8700, 73352.1625@compuserve.com

Coccoli Palsho, Dorothea; Pres Info Serv, Dow Jones & Company Inc.; US; 212/416-2000

Cochran, Donald A.; VP Sales & Mktng, Western Micro Technology; US; 408/379-0177, dcochran@westernmicro.com

Cochran, John; VP Bus Dev, Miltope Corp.; US; 334/284-8665

Cochran, Will; VP Sales & Mktng, StereoGraphics Corp.; US; 415/459-4500

Codd, Ronald E.F.; CFO, Peoplesoft Inc.; US; 510/225-3000

Coelho, David R.; SVP & Bus Dev, Viewlogic Systems Inc.; US; 508/480-0881

Coffou, Ann; Co-Author, Target Selling

to IT Professionals; US; 617/982-1724

Cogan, James C.; SVP Ops, General Parametrics Corp.; US; 510/524-3950

Cogdale, Paul; Dir Sales, CE Software Inc.; US; 515/221-1801

Coggins, Mark; VP Prod Dev, Interactive Development Environments Inc.; US; 415/543-0900

Coggiola, Donald A.; EVP, Policy Management Systems Corp.; US; 803/735-4000

Coggshall, William L.; Pres, Pacific Media Associates; US; 415/948-3080

Coghlan, Paul; VP & CFO, Linear Technology Corp.; US; 408/432-1900

Cohen, Alexander; Dir Prod Dev, McKinley Group Inc., The; US; 415/331-1884, xcohen@mckinley.com

Cohen, Benjamin; Pres & CEO, Logic Works Inc.; US; 609/514-1177

Cohen, Brent; COO, Packard Bell; US; 818/865-1555

Cohen, Brian; Pres & CEO, Technology Solutions; US; 212/696-2000

Cohen, Brian D.; VP & CFO, Telebit Corp.; US; 508/441-2181

Cohen, David; Sr Ed, CADalyst; US; 714/513-8400

Cohen, Eric; VP Ops, B.C. Software Inc.; US; 310/636-4711, cohen@bcsoftware.com

Cohen, Gadi; Pres, PNY Electronics Inc.; US; 201/438-6300

Cohen, Gerald D.; Pres, Information Builders Inc.; US; 212/736-4433

Cohen, Jacques; Ed-in-Chief, Communications of the ACM; US; 212/869-7440

Cohen, Jerry; Pres, adRem Technologies; US; 201/740-0337

Cohen, Joan; VP Mktng & Bus Dev, Cayenne Software; US; 617/273-9003

Cohen, Martin M.; Pblr, Dealerscope Merchandising; US; 215/238-5300

Cohen, Marvin; SVP, LCS Industries Inc.; US; 201/778-5588

Cohen, Raines; Com Mgr, User Group Connection Inc.; US; 408/461-5700

Cohen, Richard; VP R&D, Tally Systems Corp.; US; 603/643-1300

Cohen, William; Pblr, Haworth Press Inc.; US

Cohl, Claudia; Pblr, Electronic Learning; US; 212/505-4900

Cohn, Mark A.; Chmn & CEO, Damark International Inc.; US; 612/531-0066

Cohn, Robert; Chmn, Pres & CEO, Octel Communications Corp.; US; 408/321-2000

Coker, Drake; Chief Scientist, Acucobol Inc.; US; 619/689-7220, drake@acucobol.com

Coker, Mike; Pres, SysKonnect Inc.; US; 408/437-3800

Coker, Pamela; Pres, Acucobol Inc.; US; 619/689-7220, pamela@acucobol.com

Colaninno, Roberto; CEO, Olivetti & Co.; Italy; 39-125-5200

Colarik, Michael; Pres, Provantage Corp.; US; 216/494-8715, colarik@provantage.com

Colbeth, Douglas; Pres & CEO, Spyglass Inc.; US; 708/505-1010

Coldick, William; Vice Chmn, Focus Enhancements Inc.; US; 617/938-8088

Cole, Calisa; Pres, Cole Communications; US; 415/324-3152

Cole, David; SVP & Pres AOL Enterprise Sol, America Online Inc.; US; 703/448-8700

Cole, David C.; Pres, NaviSoft Inc.; US; 703/448-8700

Cole, David M.; EVP Prod Dev, Chinon America Inc.; US; 310/533-0274

Cole, Gary M.; Pres, Marin Research; US; 415/389-5444

Cole, Jackson; CEO, Quadrant Components; US; 510/656-9988

Cole, Louis C.; Pres & CEO, Legato Systems Inc.; US; 415/812-6000

Cole, Mark L.; VP, Equinox Systems Inc.; US; 305/746-9000

Cole, Rick; Mktng Mgr, Datasym Inc.; Canada; 519/758-5800

Cole, Roland J.; Exec Dir, Software Patent Institute; US; 313/769-4606

Cole, Truman; CFO, Network Peripherals; US; 408/321-7300

Cole Jr., Jeremiah; VP Fin, Focus Enhancements Inc.; US; 617/938-8088

Coleman, Bruce; Pres & CEO, Computer Network Technology Corp.; US; 612/797-6000

Coleman, David; Ed, Virtual Work Groups; US; 630/986-1432

Coleman, Mary; Pres, Aurum Software Inc.; US; 408/562-6370

Coleman, William; Chmn & CEO, BEA Systems Inc.; US; 408/743-4000

Coleman, William R.; SVP Fin, Cincinnati Bell Information Systems; US; 513/784-5900

Coletta, Paul; VP Sales, Delphax Systems; US; 617/828-9917

Colgate, Kevin; VP Sales, CrossWind Technologies Inc.; US; 408/469-1780, kevin@crosswind.com

Collet, Robert D.; Chmn & Pres, Commercial Internet eXchange Assoc.; US; 703/318-7218, rcollet@cix.org

Colligan, Ed; VP Mktng, Palm Computing; US; 415/949-9560, ed@palm.com

Colligan, John C.; Pres & CEO, Macromedia Inc.; US; 415/252-2000

Collins, J. Robert; VP Strat Plng & Dev, E-Systems Inc.; US; 214/661-1000

Collins, Nancy; UG Spec, Borland User Group; US; 408/431-1065, ncollins@wpo.borland.com

Colliton, D. Robert; VP & CFO, Pinnacle Publishing Inc.; US; 206/251-1900

Collmeyer, Arthur J.; Chmn, Weitek Corp.; US; 408/738-8400

Colmenares, Cynthia; VP Sales & Mktng, Comfy Inc.; US; 408/865-1777

Colombo, Ruth; VP Eng, Virtual Vineyards; US; 415/917-5750, rcolombo@virtualvin.com

Colony, George F.; Pres, Forrester Research Inc.; US; 617/497-7090

Colquhoun, Charlie; VP Prod Dev, Durand Communications Network Inc.; US; 805/961-8700

Colwell, Garrick C.; VP Sales & Mktng, Data Race; US; 210/558-1900

Colwell, Marti; VP Mktng & Sales, Qualtrak; US; 408/748-9500, marti@qualtrak.com

Colwell, Sue; Tech Ed, Byte Lab; US; 603/924-9281

Comiso, Charlet T.; Pres, Link Technologies Inc.; US; 408/473-1200

Comiso, Chuck; SVP Mktng & Ops, Wyse Technology Inc.; US; 408/473-1200

Compton, Harold F.; EVP COO, CompUSA Inc.; US; 214/982-4000

Compton, Robert C.; Chmn & CEO, Star Technologies Inc.; US; 703/689-4400

Conant, George E.; VP Tech, Xyplex Inc.; US; 508/952-4700

Condo, Pat; Pres & CEO, Excalibur Technologies Corp.; US; 619/438-7900

Cone, Todd; Dir Info Syst, Big Island Communications Inc.; US; 408/342-8300

Conklin, Kevin; VP Mktng, Concord Communications Inc.; US; 508/460-4646

Conley, Dennis; CIO, Computer Data Systems Inc.; US; 301/921-7000

Conlin, Chris; VP Mktng, Murata Electronics North America Inc.; US; 404/436-1300

Conlin, Kelly; Pres, IDG Communications; US; 617/534-1200

Connell, Byron; Prod Line Mgr, HP Home Products Div.; US; 408/246-4300

Connell, Susan; VP Mktng, Deltec Corp.; US; 619/291-4211, sconnell@deltecpower.com

Conner, Finis F.; Chmn & CEO, Conner Peripherals Inc.; US; 408/456-4500

Conner, Gene; SVP Ops, Advanced Micro Devices Inc.; US; 408/732-2400

Conners Jr., William J.; VP Strategic Bus Dev, Insoft Inc.; US; 717/730-9501

Connery, Brenda; VP Sales, miro Computer Products Inc.; US; 415/855-0940

Connolly, Daniel W.; Ed, Web Apps Magazine; US; 212/242-7447

Connolly, John; VP & CFO, Davox Corp.; US; 508/952-0200

Connolly, Roger; Dir, Fujitsu Active Information; US; connolly@activeinfo.com

Connor, Deni; Ed, NetWare Solutions; US; 512/873-7761, 75730.2465@compuserve.com

Connors, Brian T.; VP Sales, C-Cube Microsystems Inc.; US; 408/944-6300

Connors, Connie; Pres, Connors Communications; US; 415/217-7500, connie@connors.com

Connors, John; Pres US Ops, Merisel Inc.; US; 310/615-3080

Connors, Michael M.; SVP & Pres AOL Tech, America Online Inc.; US; 703/448-8700

Conors Jr., Daniel S.; Pres & COO, Technology Service Solutions; US; 610/293-2765

Conrades, George H.; Pres & CEO, Bolt Beranek & Newman Inc.; US; 617/873-4000

Conroy, John B.; Pres & CEO, Microfield Graphics Inc.; US; 503/626-9393

Conroy, Vince; VP Prod Dev, Evergreen Systems Inc.; US; 415/897-8888

Constant, Anita A.; SVP, Dearborn Publishing Group; US; 312/836-4400

Constantine, Dennis; Pres Systems Div, Recognition International Inc.; US; 214/579-6000

Constantino, Charles A.; EVP, Par Technology Corp.; US; 315/738-0600

Consul, Joseph; VP & CFO, Ray Dream Inc.; US; 415/960-0768, consul@raydream.com

Conte, Brian; CEO, Express Systems Inc.; US; 206/728-8300, brian@express-systems.com

Contreras, Mercy; Pblr, Mobile Computing Technology; US; 770/955-2500

Conurn Perry, Cecillia; Mgng Ed, Enterprise Internetworking Journal; US; 214/669-9000

Converse-Wilson, Lizabeth; GM Enterprise Syst, Apertus Technologies Inc.; US; 612/828-0300

Conway, James; VP & GM, Mass Optical Storage Technologies; US; 714/898-9400

Conway, Kelly D.; VP Sales & Mktng, Multicom Publishing Inc.; US; 415/777-5300

Conway, Ronald; Pres & CEO, Personal Training Systems; US; 415/462-2100

Conway, Thomas H.; Chmn, Pres & CEO, Xyvision Inc.; US; 617/245-4100

Conyers Jr., James B.; VP Bus Dev, ECC International Corp.; US; 610/687-2600

Cook, Frank; VP Ops, DayStar Digital Inc.; US; 770/967-2077

Cook, J. Michael; CEO, Deloitte & Touche; US; 203/761-3000

Cook, Jonathan H.; VP & CFO, Avid Technology Inc.; US; 508/640-6789

Cook, Philip; VP, Tapette Corp.; US; 714/588-7000

Cook, Robert; Pres, Light Source Inc.; US; 415/461-8000

Cook, Scott D.; Chmn, Intuit Inc.; US; 415/944-6000

Cook, Timothy D.; SVP, Intelligent Electronics Inc.; US; 610/458-5500

Cook, Wayne; Sales Dir, Winsted Corp.; US; 612/944-9050

Cook, William; Dir Info Svcs, Institute of Electrical & Electronics Engineers Inc.; US; 212/705-7900

Cooke, Greg; VP Sales, Data Systems Network Corp.; US; 810/489-7117

Cooke, John; VP & GM, Jones Computer Network; US; 303/792-3111

Cooley, Ross; SVP NA, Compaq Computer Corp.; US; 713/370-0670

Cooper, Alan; Pres, Lansafe Network Services Inc.; US; 212/889-8100

Cooper, Catherine; VP Mktng, Virtual Media Works; US; 408/739-0301, cath@vmworks.com

Cooper, Cheryl; Ed-in-Chief, Computer Journal, The; US

Cooper, Doug; Pres, Cooper/Iverson Marketing; US; 619/292-7400, doug@coopiver.com

Cooper, Edward; VP Mktng, Legato Systems Inc.; US; 415/812-6000

Cooper, Eric C.; Chmn & CEO, Fore Systems Inc.; US; 412/772-6600

Cooper, Geoff; VP Info Tech, Access Graphics Inc.; US; 303/938-9333, geoffc@access.com

Cooper, K. Michael; Pres & CEO, Advanced Gravis Computer Technology Ltd.; Canada; 604/431-5020

Cooper, Linda; Exec Dir, Association for Work Process Improvement; US; 617/426-1167

Cooper, Lorne J.; SVP Eng & CTO, Viewlogic Systems Inc.; US; 508/480-0881

Cooper, Milton E.; Pres Systems Group, Computer Sciences Corp.; US; 310/615-0311

Cooper, Philip; Pres, Polhemus Inc.; US; 802/655-3159, pgc@polhemus.com

Cooper, Richard; Chmn, Strategic Growth Int'l. Inc.; US; 516/829-7111

Cooperman, Michael; CFO, Delrina Corp.; Canada; 416/441-3676

Coote, Jeremy; Pres, SAP America Inc.; US; 215/521-4500

Cooter, Kevin; Pres, UltraStat Inc.; US; 719/676-4010

Copithorne, David; Partner, Copithorne & Bellows; US; 415/284-5200

Coppel, Mark; Exec Pblr, Sunworld Online; US; 415/243-4188, mark.coppel@sunworld.com

Copper, Jack; Pres, ArcanaTech; US; 412/441-6611

Copra, Richard; Dir Mktng, Vista Controls; US; 805/257-4430

Corbett, Gerard F.; Dir Corp Comm, Hitachi America Inc.; US; 914/332-5800

Corder, Rodney J.; VP Eng, New Media Corp.; US; 714/453-0100

Corey, Bob L.; EVP & CFO, MTI Technology Corp.; US; 714/970-0300

Cornell, Edward L.; EVP & CFO, OfficeMax Inc.; US; 216/921-6900

Cornish, Edward; Pres, World Future Society; US; 301/656-8274

Corno, Yann; VP Dev, Ray Dream Inc.; US; 415/960-0768, corno@raydream.com

Corporron, Randy J.; EVP, Kent Electronics Corp.; US; 713/780-7770

Corrigan, Wilfred J.; Chmn & CEO, LSI Logic Corp.; US; 408/433-8000

Corsini Jr., Russell V.; VP & CFO, New England Business Service Inc.; US; 508/448-6111

Cortese, Richard A.; Pres & CEO, Racotek Inc.; US; 612/832-9800

Cory, Laura; VP Mktng, Xerox Desktop Document Systems; US; 415/815-6800

Cosentino, Nicholas; CEO, PureData Ltd.; Canada; 416/731-6444

Cosmez, Mark; VP & CFO, International Microcomputer Software Inc.; US; 415/257-3000

Costanza, Veronica; Pblr, Software Development; US; 415/905-2200

Costello, Edward; Dir Mktng, Polhemus Inc.; US; 802/655-3159, ewc@polhemus.com

Costello, Joseph B.; Pres & CEO, Cadence Design Systems Inc.; US; 408/943-1234

Costello, Michael B.; VP Admin & Corp Comm, Shared Medical Systems Corp.; US; 610/219-6300

Costello, Thomas P.; SVP Res & Dev, Intersolv Inc.; US; 301/838-5000

Cote, Dave; Pres & CEO, Young Minds Inc.; US; 909/335-1350, cote@ymi.com

Cote, Debbie; Mktng PR, a/Soft Development Inc.; US; 603/666-6699

Cote, Kathleen A.; Pres & COO, Computervision Corp.; US; 617/275-1800

Cotichini, Christian; Pres, Absolute Software Corp.; Canada; 604/730-9851

Cotignola, Michael; Pres-Elect, International DB2 Users Group; US; 312/644-6610

Cottman, Bruce H.; Pres, I-Kinetics Inc.; US; 617/661-8181

Couch, Bruce; VP, MacAcademy; US; 904/677-1918

Couchman, David; CEO, Telemate Software Inc.; US; 770/936-3700

Coughlin, Catherine; Mgng Ed, Portable Computing; US; 818/593-6100

Coughlin, Michael; Pres, Percon Inc.; US; 541/344-1189

Coull, Tom; Pres, Sense8 Corp.; US; 415/331-6318, tom@sense8.com

Coulling, Robert; Pres, Microspot US Inc.; US; 408/253-2000

Coulter, Cynthia; SVP, Fleishman-Hillard Inc.; US; 213/629-4974

Courtney, Eugene W.; Pres & CEO, HEI Inc.; US; 612/443-2500

Courtot, Philippe F.; Chmn, Pres & CEO, Verity Inc.; US; 415/960-7600, pcourtot@verity.com

Couse, Jonathin; Dir Dev, Microrim Inc.; US; 206/649-9500, jonathinc@microrim.com

Cousins, Bob; VP Tech, UNIX System Price Performance Guide; US; 408/748-8649, rec@aim.com

Coutts, John R.; COO, Peak Technolo-

gies Group Inc.; US; 212/832-2833

Coverston, Harriet; VP SW Dev, Large Storage Configurations; US; 612/482-4535, hgc@lsci.com

Covey, Bob; VP Mktng, Qualstar Corp.; US; 818/592-0061, covey@qualstar.com

Covey, Roger E.; CEO, System Software Associates Inc.; US; 312/258-6000, rec@ssax.com

Covin, John; Chmn, M Technology Assoc.; US; 301/431-4070

Covington, Samuel B.; CEO, Looking Glass Software Inc.; US; 310/348-8240

Cowan, Les; Sr Ed, Micro Publishing News; US; 310/371-5787

Cowan, William W.; VP & CFO, Medicus Systems Corp.; US; 847/570-7500

Cowell, Casey G.; Chmn, Pres & CEO, U.S. Robotics Inc.; US; 847/882-5010

Cowie, Bruce; Pres & COO Broadcast Group, Electrohome Ltd.; Canada; 519/744-7111

Cowley, Jane; Mktng Mgr, ASCII Entertainment Software Inc.; US; 415/780-0800, jane.cowley@asciient.com

Cowpland, Michael C.J.; Chmn, Pres & CEO, Corel Corp.; Canada; 613/728-8200

Cox, C. Lee; Pres & COO, AirTouch Communications; US; 415/658-2000

Cox, David L.; VP Sales & Mktng, Axonix Corp.; US; 801/521-9797

Cox, Diana; Prod Mgr LifeART, TechPool Software; US; 216/382-1234, dianac@techpool.com

Cox, Thomas P.; SVP & CFO, Timberline Software Corp.; US; 503/626-6775

Coyne, John C.; Pres, Data Entry Systems Inc.; US; 205/430-3023

Cracchiolo, Joseph J.; VP, RightFAX; US; 520/327-1357, jjc@rightfax.com

Craft, Betty M.; Ed, Technical Employment News; US; 512/250-9023

Craft, Dave; VP Ops, Visioneer; US; 415/812-6400

Craft, William; CTO, Spatializer Audio Laboratories; US; 818/227-3370

Craft Jr., Lester; Ed, Smart Computer & Software Retailing; US; 910/605-0121

Craig, Brad; VP Mkt & Bus Dev, Forte Technologies Inc.; US; 716/427-8595, bcraig@fortevr.com

Craig, David; VP Sales, Advanced Visual Systems Inc.; US; 617/890-4300

Craig, David; CFO, 7th Level Inc.; US; 818/547-1955

Craig, David W.; VP & CFO, Convex Computer Corp.; US; 214/497-4000

Craig, Peter M.; EVP, Rainbow Technologies Inc.; US; 714/450-7300

Crain, Desmond; VP Imaging Sales, Bluebird Systems; US; 619/438-2220

Cramblitt, Bob; Pres, Cramblitt & Company; US; 919/481-4599

Crandall, Gary; VP R&D, DataPak Software Inc.; US; 360/891-0542, d0142@applelink.com

Crandall, Richard; Chmn, Comshare Inc.; US; 313/994-4800

Crandall, Wayne; VP Sales, Xerox Imaging Systems; US; 508/977-2000

Crane, Christopher J.; Pres, ASA International Ltd.; US; 508/626-2727

Crane, Mark; Pblr, Inside SCO Unix Systems; US; 502/491-1900

Crane, Steve; VP Tech, Activision Inc.; US; 310/473-9200

Cranford, Richard; Ed, 1-2-3 For Windows Report, The; US; 617/482-8634

Craven, Sheila; Pres, Adscope Inc.; US; 541/687-1519, sheilacrav@aol.com

Crawford, Bobby; MIS Mgr, DacEasy Inc.; US; 214/732-7500

Crawford, Diane; Exec Ed, Communications of the ACM; US; 212/869-7440, crawford@acmvm.bitnet

Crawford, J. Douglas; Pres & CEO, Magellan Geographix; US; 805/685-3100

Crawford, John; Info Syst Mgr, Solomon Software; US; 419/424-0422, jcrawfor@solomon.com

Crawford, Liz; Show Manager, Advanstar Expositions; US; 714/513-8400

Crawford, Michael; Pres, MCCommunications Inc.; US; 214/480-8383, mike_crawford@mccom.com

Cray, Richard; VP Creative Dev, Virtual Reality Sourcebook; US; 310/434-4436

Creasy, Robert; Dir Sales, Barco Chromatics; US; 770/493-7000

Credle, John; Pres, Creative Solutions Inc.; US; 410/766-4080

Creede, James; VP Ops, Montage Graphics; US; 408/654-0700

Creel, John; Reg Sales Mgr, ASCII Entertainment Software Inc.; US; 415/780-0800, john.creel@asciient.com

Cregan, J. Gerard; VP Ops, Netrix Corp.; US; 703/742-6000

Crew, Charles A.; VP & CFO, Group 1 Software; US; 301/731-2300

Crew, Martyn; Bus Mgr, Xaos Tools; US; 415/487-7000

Crews, Wes; VP Corp Dev, DataTimes Corp.; US; 405/751-6400

Cribb, John H.; Pres Intl Div, Telxon Corp.; US; 216/867-3700

Crisman, Craig D.; Chmn, Pres, CEO & CFO, Applied Magnetics Corp.; US; 805/683-5353

Critelli, Michael J.; CEO, Pitney Bowes Inc.; US; 203/356-5000

Croall, Ian F.; Ed, Expert Systems Journal; US; 609/654-6266

Crocker, David; Chmn, Intelligent Micro Software Ltd.; US; 407/726-0024, 71333.3555@compuserve.com

Crockett, Diane; VP Mktng, Digital Impact; US; 918/742-2022

Croft, Daniel; SVP Mktng Ops, Ardis; US; 708/913-1215

Crofts, Steven; Pblr & Ed-in-Chief, Database Journal; US; 214/669-9000

Cromer, Deborah; SVP, Golan/Harris

Technologies; US; 415/904-7000

Cron, Kenneth D.; Pres Publishing, CMP Publications Inc.; US; 516/562-5000

Cronin, Daniel J.; VP Mktng, Epoch Inc.; US; 508/435-1000

Cronin, Geoffrey D.; Pres & CEO, F3 Software Corp.; US; 617/270-0001

Cronin, Robert J.; Pres & CEO, Wallace Computer Services Inc.; US; 708/449-8600

Crookston, Clair; EVP, MacAcademy; US; 904/677-1918

Crosby, Terry; Exec Prod, Computer Television Network; US; 916/582-5083

Croson, Jeff; VP Sales, 7th Level Inc.; US; 818/547-1955

Crossley, Steve; Bus Dev Mgr, V-Systems Inc.; US; 714/489-8778

Croteau, Jean J.; VP Bus Ops, SofTech Inc.; US; 616/957-2330

Crouch, Arlen B.; Pres, Franklin Quest Co.; US; 801/975-9992

Crouse, Don; SVP, Large Storage Configurations; US; 612/482-4535, don@lsci.com

Crowder, John; Pres, Learning Services Inc.; US; 541/683-3827, john@ls.learn-serv.com

Crowder, Kevin; VP Prod Integration, Macromedia Digital Arts Group; US; 214/680-2060

Crowe, Brian; VP Sales, Best Power Technology Inc.; US; 608/565-7200

Crowe, Curtis; VP Sales, Turtle Beach Systems Inc.; US; 717/767-0200

Crowe, James Q.; CEO, MFS Communications; US; 402/977-5300

Crowe, Jeffrey; Pres, Edify Corp.; US; 408/982-2000, jcrowe@edify.com

Crowley, Bob; Sales Mgr, Kenan Systems Corp.; US; 617/225-2224

Crowley, David; Dir Mktng Prog, Delphax Systems; US; 617/828-9917, dcrowley@ccmail.delphax.com

Crowley, James M.; Exec Dir, Society for Industrial & Applied Mathematics; US; 215/382-9800

Crowley, Pamela; Pres, Crowley Communications; US; 408/377-8384

Crowley, Powell; VP Bus Dev, Micro Warehouse; US; 203/899-4000

Crozier, Keith; CEO, IntelliLink Corp.; US; 603/888-0666

Cruikshank, Kirk A.; VP Mktng, Arbor Software Corp.; US; 408/727-5800

Cruise, John; Mgng Ed, X-Ray Magazine; US; 415/861-9258, xrayedit@eworld.com

Crumpler, Dennis M.; Chmn & CEO, XcelleNet Inc.; US; 770/804-8100

Crumpler, Robert; Pres, On The Go Software; US; 619/546-4340

Cruz, Ralph; VP, Omega Research Inc.; US; 305/270-1095

Crystal, Richard; Pres & CTO, Graphic Utilities Inc.; US; 408/577-0334

Culbertson, W. James; Pres, InfoAccess

Inc.; US; 206/747-3203

Cullen, Brian D.; SVP, E-Systems Inc.; US; 214/661-1000

Cullen, James G.; Pres, Bell Atlantic Corp.; US; 215/963-6000

Cullen, Scott; Ed, Office Systems; US; 215/628-7716, sculos@aol.com

Cullen, Tom; VP Sales, Radish Communications System Inc.; US; 303/443-2237, tcullen@radish.com

Cullimore, Neil R.; EVP, Continuum Company Inc., The; US; 512/345-5700

Cullinane, Michael P.; SVP & CFO, Platinum Technology Inc.; US; 708/620-5000

Culpepper, Warren; Chmn & Pres, Culpepper & Associates Inc.; US; 770/668-0616, warren@culpepper.com

Cummings, Elaine M.; Mgng Ed, Client/Server Today; US; 617/964-3030, elainec@cstoday.com

Cummings, Frank T.; VP, Logicon Inc.; US; 310/373-0220

Cummings, Joanne; Ed, I/S Analyzer Case Studies; US; 617/444-5755

Cummings, John R.; Chmn, Pres & CEO, Comptek Research Inc.; US; 716/677-4070

Cuneo, Richard; VP US Sales, Autodesk Inc.; US; 415/507-5000

Cunningham, Andrea; Pres, Cunningham Communication Inc.; US; 408/982-0400

Cunningham, Ann Marie; Exec Dir, National Federation of Abstracting & Information Services; US; 215/893-1561

Cunningham, Daniel P.; CFO, PSINET Inc.; US; 703/904-4100

Cunningham, Joan; Dir Sales & Mktng, IntelliTools; US; 415/382-5959

Cunningham, Lori; Sales Manager, Hum-The Government Computer Magazine; Canada; 613/237-4862, loric@hum.com

Cunningham, Peter; Pres & CEO, Input; US; 415/961-3300, pac@input.com

Cunningham, Philip T.; Chmn, Pres & CEO, Microdyne Corp.; US; 703/739-0500

Cunningham, Terry; CEO, Crystal Inc.; Canada; 604/681-3435

Cuppett, Sharon; VP & Mgng Dir, Baron, MacDonald & Wells; US; 770/492-0373, scuppett@bmwpr.com

Curlander, Paul; VP & GM Printing Syst, Lexmark International Inc.; US; 606/232-2000

Curley, Joe; Dir Sales, Deneba Software; US; 305/596-5644

Curley, William C.; VP MIS & Ops, Good Guys Inc., The; US; 415/615-5000

Curns, Ross; VP WW Sales, Mergent Int'l.; US; 860/257-4223, rcurns@mer-gent.com

Curran, Deane; VP Sales & Mktng, Tadpole Technology Inc.; US; 512/219-2200

Curran, Gordon; SVP, Business Research Int'l.; France; 33-5093-0762

Curran, Kevin; Pres & CEO, GCC Technologies Inc.; US; 617/275-5800

Curran, Tim; GM Sales, Panasonic Communications & Systems Co.; US; 201/348-7000

Currid, Cheryl; Pres, Currid & Co.; US; 713/789-5995, cheryl@currid.com

Currie, Edward; Pblr, C++ Journal; US; 516/767-2233

Currie, Peter L.S.; EVP, AT&T Wireless Services; US; 206/827-4500

Currie, Rick; Pres, VictorMaxx Technologies; US; 708/267-0007

Currier, Kenneth; CEO, Expert Software Inc.; US; 305/567-9990

Currier, Sue; Pres, Expert Software Inc.; US; 305/567-9990

Curry, Blair; Treas, Education Turnkey Systems Inc.; US; 703/536-2310

Curry, Janet; JC Promotions; US; 213/782-0266

Curry, Thomas C.; Pres & CEO, Mac-Neal-Schwendler Corp., The; US; 213/258-9111

Curson, John; VP & CFO, Truevision Inc.; US; 408/562-4200

Curtis, Pamela; Controller, Command Technology Corp.; US; 510/521-5900

Curtis, Robert; VP & GM, Roland Digital Group; US; 714/975-0560

Curtis, Ronald; VP Sales, Kubota Pacific Computer Inc.; US; 408/727-8100, rcurtis@kpc.com

Curtis, Susan J.; Pblr, Portable Computing; US; 818/593-6100

Curtner, Craig; Dir Mktng, 4i Solutions Inc.; US

Cusack, Sally; Mkt Analyst, Standish Group, The; US; 508/385-7500, sally@standishgroup.com

Cutburth, James; VP Mktng, Supra Corp.; US; 360/604-1400

Cutler, Matthew J.; Dir Bus Dev, net.Genesis; US; 617/577-9800

Cutler, Scott E.; VP SW, Chips & Technologies Inc.; US; 408/434-0600

Cutter, Mark; Dir Eng, Splash Studios Inc.; US; 206/882-0300

Cutting, Bill; VP, Penna Powers Cutting & Haynes Inc.; US; 801/531-0973, ppch@utu.com

Cutts, Crawford L.; VP Bus Dev, SpecTran Corp.; US; 508/347-2261

Czarnecki, Edward G.; Mgng Dir, China Telecom Report; US; 301/907-0060

Czarnik, Paul; VP Dev, LanQuest Group; US; 510/354-0940

Czekiel, Patricia; Pblr, Corporate Profiles; US; 810/978-3000

Czernek, Andrew; VP Mktng, Traveling Software Inc.; US; 206/483-8088

Czubek, Donald; Pres, Gen 2 Ventures; US; 408/446-2277

Czuchna, Jerry; VP Adv, Jones Computer Network; US; 303/792-3111

d'Abrev, Manuel; Ed-in-Chief, IEEE Design & Test of Computers; US; 908/981-0060

D'Agostino, Anthony M.; VP Fin, Standard Microsystems Corp.; US; 516/435-6000

D'Agostino, Monica; Grp Mgr, Giles Communications; US; 914/241-9112, monica@giles.com

D'Alessandro, Jennifer; Sr Ed, Outsource!; US; 516/562-5000

D'Alessandro, Joseph; Pres & CEO, Falco Data Products; US; 408/745-7123

D'Alessandro, Laura; Mgng Ed, Business Documents; US; 215/238-5300

D'Alessandro, Richard; Pblr, EDI WORLD; US; 305/925-5900

D'Alessio, R. Dale; SVP Sales, Microdyne Corp.; US; 703/739-0500

D'Angelo, Charles; VP Sales, Zenographics Inc.; US; 714/851-6352

D'Angelo, Diane; Mgng Ed, Windows Sources; US; 212/503-4147, diane_d'angelo@zd.com

D'Angelo, Joseph A.; VP Mkt Dev, Stratus Computer Inc.; US; 508/460-2000

d'Arbeloff, Alexander V.; Chmn & Pres, Teradyne Inc.; US; 617/482-2700

d'Arbeloff, Nicholas C.; VP Mktng, Wildfire Communications Inc.; US; 617/674-1500

D'Arezzo, James; VP Mktng, Autodesk Inc.; US; 415/507-5000

D'Auria, Sal; Pres, Tut Systems Inc.; US; 510/682-6510

DaCosta, Bruce J.; Pres & CEO, NetStream Inc.; US; 412/276-9600

Daffern, Paul; CFO, X/Open Company Ltd.; US; 415/323-7992

Dager, Nick; Ed, AV Video & Multimedia Producer; US; 914/328-9157

Daher, Moe; VP Eng, Lead Technologies Inc.; US; 704/332-5532

Dahl, Robert K.; VP & CFO, Ascend Communications Inc.; US; 510/769-6001

Dahl, Yvonne; VP Sales, Electronic Book Technologies Inc.; US; 401/421-9550, ymd@ebt.com

Dahlgren, Dean; Dir Sales & Mktng, Maxum Development Corp.; US; 708/830-1113, dean@maxum.com

Dahlquist, John; VP Mktng, Harmonic Lightwaves; US; 408/970-9880

Dahod, Shabbir; VP, Asymetrix Corp.; US; 206/637-5859

Dailey, Ed; CEO, Informer Computer Systems Inc.; US; 714/891-1112

Daines, Nolan; Pres & CEO, DiviCom Inc.; US; 408/944-6700

Dale, Robert; Chief Architect, Creative Interaction Technologies Inc.; US; 919/419-1694

Daley, Peter; Pres, Daley Marketing Corp.; US; 714/662-0755

Dalrymple, Ted L.; VP Global Mktng, AMP Inc.; US; 717/564-0100

Dalton, George D.; Chmn & CEO, Fiserv Inc.; US; 414/879-5000

Dalton, James E.; VP, Logicon Inc.; US; 310/373-0220

Daltoso, Joseph M.; Chmn, Pres & CEO, Micron Electronics; US; 208/893-3434

Dambrackas, William A.; Pres & CEO, Equinox Systems Inc.; US; 305/746-9000

Dana, Stevan B.; Pblr, Computer Video; US; 703/998-7600

Dang, Gurcharn; Pres, Best Power Technology Inc.; US; 608/565-7200

Dangermond, Jack; Pres, Environmental Systems Research Institute Inc.; US; 909/793-2853

Dangermond, Laura; VP, Environmental Systems Research Institute Inc.; US; 909/793-2853

Daniclewicz, Joe; VP Com, Data Administration Management Assoc.; US; 314/878-3372

Daniel, James R.; SVP & CFO, MicroAge Inc.; US; 602/804-2000

Daniel, Kent; VP & COO, Hands-On Technology; US; 415/579-7755

Daniel, Kevin N.; Dir Mktng, NeoSoft Corp.; US; 541/389-5489, knd@neosoftware.com

Daniel, Scott C.; VP Bus Dev, Futuretouch Corp.; US; 714/558-6824

Daniel, Steve; Pres, Seattle Support Group; US; 206/395-1484

Daniell, Robert F.; Chmn, United Technologies Corp.; US; 203/728-7000

Daniels, Amy C.; Exec Ed, Semiconductor Industry Almanac, The; US; 408/266-4549

Daniels, Robert L.; Chmn & CEO, Project Software & Development Inc.; US; 617/661-1444

Danielson, Robert E.; SVP Info Sys, OfficeMax Inc.; US; 216/921-6900

Dantzler, Jeffrey; Pres, Comtronic Systems Inc.; US; 509/674-7000

Danuloff, Craig; Pres & CEO, Interactive Catalog Corp.; US; 206/623-0977

Darby, Geoff; VP & CFO, Visioneer; US; 415/812-6400

Darby, Kevin J.; VP Sales & Mktng, ThrustMaster Inc.; US; 503/615-3200

Darien III, Frank; Pres, Darien & Kilburn Inc.; US; 415/362-6400

Darien Sr., Frank; EVP, Darien & Kilburn Inc.; US; 415/362-6400

Dash, Glen R.; VP R&D, Inchcape Inc.; US; 508/689-9355

Daub, Kenneth E.; SVP, LTX Corp.; US; 617/461-1000

Dauchy, Eric; Mgng Ed, European Computer Sources; Belgium; 322-766-0045, 73543.3506@compuserve.com

Daudelin, Dennis; Pres, Aurora Technologies Inc.; US; 617/290-4800

Dauer, Scott; VP, VisionTek Inc.; US; 708/360-7500

Dautel, John; VP Programs, Miltope Corp.; US; 334/284-8665

Dauterman, Steve; Dir Dev, LucasArts Entertainment Co.; US; 415/472-3400

Daverio, Rossella; Pblr, Alcatel Telecommunications Review; France; 1-4076-1010

David, Farr; SVP & GM, Canon US Inc.; US; 516/488-6700

David, George; Pres & CEO, United Technologies Corp.; US; 203/728-7000

David, Mark; Ed-in-Chief, Automatic I.D. News; US; 216/243-8100, autoid@en.com

David, Morton E.; Chmn, Pres & CEO, Franklin Electronic Pblrs Inc.; US; 609/386-2500

Davidow, Bill; Chmn, Rambus Inc.; US; 415/903-3800

Davidowicz, Marion; VP, Buyers Laboratory Inc.; US; 201/488-0404

Davidson, Arlene; Dir Ops, Talaris Systems Inc.; US; 619/587-0787, arlene@talaris.com

Davidson, Bob; Chmn & CEO, Davidson & Associates Inc.; US; 310/793-0600

Davidson, Ian Hay; Chmn, McDonnell Information Systems Group; US; 310/306-4000

Davidson, Jan; Pres, Davidson & Associates Inc.; US; 310/793-0600

Davidson, John; Pres, Network TeleSystems; US; 408/523-8100

Davidson, Keith; Exec Dir, Xplor International; US; 310/373-3633

Davidson, Ken; Ed-in-Chief, Circuit Cellar INK: The Computer Applications Journal; US; 860/875-2751, ken.davidson@circellar.com

Davidson, Scott; Exec Ed, PowerProgrammer Magazine; US; 201/332-1515

Davies, Clive B.; VP & COO, Linear Technology Corp.; US; 408/432-1900

Davies, Howard; Sr Partner, Context; England; 071-937-3595

Davies, James; VP, Quibus Enterprises Inc.; US; 719/527-1384

Davies, Jeremy; Sr Partner, Context; England; 071-937-3595

Davies, John L.; SVP & Pres AOL Int'l, America Online Inc.; US; 703/448-8700

Davies, Robert H.; Pres & CEO, SBT Accounting Systems; US; 415/444-9900

Davies, William R.; SVP, Weber Group Inc., The; US; 617/661-7900, bdavies@webergroup.com

Davis, Bart; Prod Mktng Mgr, Iconovex Corp.; US; 612/896-5100

Davis, Daniel; Assoc Ed, Pen Computing Magazine; US; 916/984-9947

Davis, Diane L.; Pres, Black Data Processing Associates; US; 202/775-4301

Davis, Don H.; Pres & COO, Rockwell International Corp.; US; 310/797-3311

Davis, Donald R.; SVP, Systems Management American Corp.; US; 804/461-0559

Davis, Duane; VP MIS, Kent Electronics Corp.; US; 713/780-7770

Davis, Dwight B.; Ed Dir, Windows

Watcher; US; 206/881-7354, ddavis@sbexpos.com

Davis, Jeff; Ed, Inside Paradox for DOS; US; 502/491-1900

Davis, Jeremy M.; Pres, Sales Technologies Inc.; US; 404/841-4000

Davis, Jerry; GM, Analog & Digital Peripherals Inc.; US; 513/339-2241

Davis, John; VP Mktng & Sales, Plastic Thought Inc.; US; 403/429-5051, john@plasticthought.com

Davis, John J.; EVP, CACI International Inc.; US; 703/841-7800

Davis, John P.; Pres, JP Davis & Co.; US; 503/226-0624, 73302.3552@compuserve.com

Davis, L. Miller; Pres, Davis Inc.; US; 202/667-6400

Davis, Leanne; Ed, SoftPub Yellow Pages, The; US; 206/852-7440

Davis, Lee A.; VP, Marin Research; US; 415/389-5444

Davis, Lynn J.; SVP, ADC Telecommunications; US; 612/938-8080

Davis, Paul; Dir Sales & Mktng, Express Systems Inc.; US; 206/728-8300, paul@express-systems.com

Davis, Randall; Pres, American Association for Artificial Intelligence; US; 415/328-3123

Davis, Ray; CEO, CyNet Inc.; US; 713/897-8317

Davis, Richard; EVP, Applix Inc.; US; 508/870-0300

Davis, Richard A.; Chmn & CTO, Radish Communications System Inc.; US; 303/443-2237, rdavis@radish.com

Davis, Richard C.; Pres Intl Ops, Cerplex Group Inc.; US; 714/258-5151, rdavis@cerplex.com

Davis, Rick; VP Mktng & Sales, Hands-On Technology; US; 415/579-7755

Davis, Robert; VP Sales, Premenos Corp.; US; 510/602-2000

Davis, Robert; CEO, Lycos Inc.; US; 508/229-0717

Davis, Warren; VP, Semiconductor Industry Assoc.; US; 408/436-6600

Davis, Wes; Pres & CEO, MicroTouch Systems Inc.; US; 508/659-9000

Davis, Ylonda; UG Mgr, Borland User Group; US; 408/431-1065, ydavis@wpo.borland.com

Davison, William T.; VP Customer Svcs, Scitex America Corp.; US; 617/275-5150

Davoust, Paul; Principal, Product Management Group; US; 415/346-7307

Dawes, Eric; Pres, Center for Multimedia; US; 206/643-9039

Dawson, Keith; Ed, Call Center Magazine; US; 212/691-8215, keith_dawson@mcimail.com

Dawson, Mark; Pres, Knowledge Quest; US; 714/376-8150

Dawson, Rhett; Pres, Information Technology Industry Data Book; US; 202/626-5729

Dawson, Tom; Dir Sales & Mktng, Abacus Accounting Systems Inc.; Canada; 403/488-8100, tomd@abacus-group.com

Dawson, Vic; VP Sales, Manufacturing & Consulting Services Inc.; US; 602/991-8700

Day, David; VP Eng & Advanced Tech, SL Waber Inc.; US; 609/866-8888

Day, Shelley; Pres & CEO, Humongous Entertainment; US; 206/487-9258

Daya, Jackie; EVP & CFO, Cahners Publishing Co.; US; 617/558-4565

Dayton, Doug; Pres, Dayton Associate; US; 206/451-1140

Dayton, Sky; Chmn & CEO, EarthLink Network Inc.; US; 818/296-2400

de Beuckelaer, Gerard; SVP Info Syst, BASF Corp.; US; 201/397-2700

de Fusco, Andre; VP Bus Dev, ACT Networks Inc.; US; 805/388-2474

de Geus, Aart; Pres & CEO, Synopsys Inc.; US; 415/962-5000

de Graaf, Maria; EVP, Silicon Valley Int'l.; US; 408/376-2626

De Jong, Kenneth; Ed-in-Chief, Evolutionary Computation; US; 617/253-2889, ecj@cs.gmu.edu

De Luca, Guerrino; Pres & CEO, Claris Corp.; US; 408/987-7000

de Marcillac, Philippe; SVP WW Research, International Data Corp.; US; 508/872-8200, pdemarcillac@idcresearch.com

de Remer, James; Pres, E-Net Corp.; US; 415/433-3800

de Soto, Joaquin; VP, Deneba Software; US; 305/596-5644

De Taranto, Anthony C.; Pres, Computer Systems Advisers Inc.; US; 201/391-6500

de Urioste, George A.; VP Fin & CFO, Remedy Corp.; US; 415/903-5200

De Wyze, Jeanette; Ed, Computer Aided Design Report; US; 619/488-0533

Dea, Don; VP, Alaris Inc.; US; 510/770-5700

Deagman, Patrick J.; VP Fin, SunSoft Inc.; US; 415/960-1300

Deak, Alex; VP CIO, Metatec Corp.; US; 614/761-2000

Deal, Joe; VP Sales & Mktng, Wacom Technology Corp.; US; 360/750-8882

Deane, Hunter; VP Sales & Mktng, Iconix Software Engineering Inc.; US; 310/458-0092

DeAngelo, Dena; Acct Exec, Three Marketeers Advertising Inc.; US; 408/293-3233, dena@3marketeers.com

Dear, Brian; Pres, Coconut Computing Inc.; US; 619/456-2002

Dearborn, John; VP Sales, Micrografx Inc.; US; 214/234-1769

DeBello, James B.; Chmn & CEO, Solectek Inc.; US; 619/450-1220

DeBlasi, Joseph S.; Exec Dir, Association for Computing Machinery; US; 212/869-7440

DeBoever, Larry; Pres, DeBoever Architectures Inc.; US; 508/371-1557

DeBow, Yvette; Mgng Ed, Interactive Content; US; 212/780-6060

DeBruyn, Dawn J.; Pres, Concurrent Controls Inc.; US; 415/873-6240, ddebruyn@conctrls.com

DeChamps, William; CFO, Stallion Technologies Inc.; US; 408/477-0440, billd@stallion.com

Decker, Dwight W.; Pres, Rockwell Semiconductor Systems; US; 714/883-4600

Decker, Sam; Mktng Mgr, User Group Connection Inc.; US; 408/461-5700, ugc-sam@eworld.com

Decklever, Larry; Pres, Benchmark Laboratories Inc.; US; 612/897-3505

Dees, Jennifer; Ed & Pblr, Digital Chicago; US; 847/439-6575, jdees@digital-chi.com

Dees, Suzanna; Mgng Ed, Digital Chicago; US; 847/439-6575

Deger, Renee; Venture Economics Inc.; US; 212/765-5311

Dehne, Dave; Sales Mgr, Ontrack Computer Systems Inc.; US; 612/937-1107

Dehne, Timothy R.; VP Mktng, National Instruments Corp.; US; 512/794-0100

Deitrick, Mickey; Eng Mgr, Analog & Digital Peripherals Inc.; US; 513/339-2241

Del Corso, Dante; Ed-in-Chief, IEEE Micro; US; 908/981-0060

Del Dotto, Dave; Dir Sales, Seiko Instruments US Inc.; US; 408/922-5900

Del Riesgo, Charles J.; SVP Tech, Cincinnati Bell Information Systems; US; 513/784-5900

DeLacey, Paul; Pres & CEO, Prodigy Inc.; US; 914/993-8000

Delaney, Ben; Ed & Pblr, CyberEdge Journal; US; 415/331-3343, ben@cyber-edge.com

DeLateur, Stephen A.; VP Tech, Elo TouchSystems Inc.; US; 615/482-4100

DeLatte, Herman; COO, Micrografx Inc.; US; 214/234-1769

Delehunt, Anne K.; VP Mktng, Virtual Vineyards; US; 415/917-5750, delehunt@virtualvin.com

Delfino-Benado, Terri; Mktng Mgr, Workgroup Solutions; US; 617/229-9000

DelGatto, Joseph; Ed, EE Product News; US; 914/949-8500, 73414.1271@compuserve.com

DelGiorno, Daniel; Pres, Computer Concepts Corp.; US; 516/244-1500

Delia, Frank S.; VP & CAO, Mentor Graphics Corp.; US; 503/626-7000

Dell, Michael S.; Chmn & CEO, Dell Computer Corp.; US; 512/338-4400

Dell'Oca, Conrad J.; Pres & CEO, Aspec Technology Inc.; US; 408/774-2199

Dellamaggiure, Dario; Dir Sales & Mktng, SVEC Computer Corp.; US; 714/756-2233, dariod@svec.com

Dellomo, Jim; CFO, Byron Preiss Multimedia Co. Inc.; US; 212/989-6252

Delmontagne, Regis J.; Pres, NPES The Association for Suppliers of Printing & Publishing Tech.; US; 703/264-7200

Delogu, Richard F.; VP Fin & CFO, Virtek Vision Corp.; Canada; 519/746-7190

DeLorme, David; Pres, DeLorme Mapping; US; 207/865-1234

DeLuca, Anthony; SVP & CIO, Avnet Inc.; US; 516/466-7000

Delzell, Bob; VP R&D, Gessler Publishing Co.; US; 540/345-1429

DeMarchi, Thomas; VP Sales & Mktng, Corollary Inc.; US; 714/250-4040

deMartin, Michael; Dir, DMCD Interactive Design Services; US; 203/531-4007

DeMarzo, Robert C.; Ed, Computer Reseller News; US; 516/562-5000, rdemarzo@cmp.com

DeMatteo, Daniel A.; Pres & COO, Neostar Retail Group Inc.; US; 214/401-9000

DeMatteo, Madelyn M.; VP Gen Counsel & Sec, Southern New England Telecom Corp.; US; 203/771-5200

DeMelle, Arthur W.; VP & CFO, Data General Corp.; US; 508/898-5000

DeMiroz, Marco; CFO, Worlds Inc.; US; 415/281-4878

Dempsey, James G.; VP R&D, Tapedisk Corp.; US; 715/235-3388

DenAdel, Phillip; VP Ops, Brooktree Corp.; US; 619/452-7580

Denend, Leslie G.; Pres & CEO, Network General Corp.; US; 415/473-2000

Denney, Michael; VP Mktng, BASIS Inc.; US; 510/547-5900

Dennis, Murray L.; Pres & CEO, Socket Communications Inc.; US; 510/744-2700

Dennis, Robert N.; Chmn, FastComm Communications Corp.; US; 703/318-7750

Dennison, Ed; Exec Dir, Chicago Software Assoc.; US; 708/358-0567

Denson, Tony; Pres, Visionware; US; 415/325-2113

Denzer, Philip C.; Pres, Process Software Corp.; US; 508/879-6994

Depalma, Angelo; Ed, Sensor Technology; US; 201/568-4744, stinfo@insights.com

Der Boghosian, Andrea; EVP, Shandwick Technologies; US; 617/536-0470

Dering, Michael A.; Pres & CEO, Tab Products Co.; US; 415/852-2400

DeRose, Gene; Ed Dir, Jupiter Communications Co.; US; 212/780-6060

Desens, Charlene; Ops Mgr, QSoft Solutions Corp.; US; 716/264-9700

Deshpande, Vinay; VP Eng, Digital Tools Inc.; US; 408/366-6920

DeSimone, L.D.; Chmn & CEO, Minnesota Minning & Manufacturing; US; 612/733-1110

Desmond, John; VP & Ed, Software Productivity Group Inc.; US; 508/366-3344

Desmond, Michael; VP, Computer Press Assoc.; US; 201/398-7300

Detwiler, Karen; Ed-in-Chief, Digital Systems Journal; US; 215/643-8000

Deubert, John; Pres, Acquired Knowledge Inc.; US; 619/587-4668

Deutsch, John; VP Sales, Smart Technologies Inc.; Canada; 403/245-0333

Deutsch, Peter; CTO, ParcPlace-Digitalk Inc.; US; 408/481-9090

Devan, Vasu S.; VP Sales, Remedy Corp.; US; 415/903-5200

Deveney, Pam; Dir Fin, QStar Technologies Inc.; US; 904/243-0900

Deveney, Todd; Mgr Rel Eng & Sup, QStar Technologies Inc.; US; 904/243-0900, todd@qstar.com

Devitte, Jesse F.; EVP Sales & Mktng, Softdesk Inc.; US; 603/428-3199

Devlin, David; VP & Pblr, Venture Economics Inc.; US; 212/765-5311, devlin@tfn.com

Devlin, Gerald T.; SVP, AST Research Inc.; US; 714/727-4141

Devlin, Michael T.; Chmn, Rational Software Corp.; US; 408/496-3600, mtd@rational.com

Devlin, Patrick; Dir Prod Mktng, Compusearch Software Systems Inc.; US; 703/893-7200

DeWall, Scott; VP Sales, MediaLogic ADL Inc.; US; 303/939-9780

Dewan, David; VP Tech, Powersoft Corp; US; 508/287-1500

Dexter, Richard J.; VP, VLSI Research Inc.; US; 408/453-8844

Dexter-Smith, Michael; CEO, VentureCom Inc.; US; 617/661-1230, mds@vci.com

Deyhimy, Ira; VP Prod Dev, Vitesse Semiconductor Corp.; US; 805/388-3700

Deyo, Steve; Ed, ComputerUser; US; 612/339-7571

Deysher, Cynthia; CFO, Shiva Corp.; US; 617/270-8300, deysher@us.shiva.com

DeZenso, Raymond; VP & CFO, Xyplex Inc.; US; 508/952-4700

Dham, Vinod; EVP & COO, NexGen Microsystem; US; 408/435-0202

Diamond, Bob; Pres, Imagine That Inc.; US; 408/365-0305

Diamond, Daniel; Exec Ed, Women in Computing; US; 415/513-6800

Diamond, David; Exec Ed, Open Computing; US; 415/513-6800, davidd@uworld.com

Diamond, Gerald; Chmn & CEO, Southern Electronics Corp.; US; 770/491-8962

Diamond, Jim; Dir Dev, Alliance Manufacturing Software Inc.; US; 805/965-3000, development@alliancemfg.com

Diamond, Mark; EVP, Southern Electronics Corp.; US; 770/491-8962

Diamond, Pat; CFO, Imagine That Inc.; US; 408/365-0305

Dias, Keith; VP Sales & Mktng, Atlantic

Cable Technology; US

Diaz, Judy; Sr Assoc, Breakthru Communications; US; 408/252-1734, jdiaz@breakthrucom.com

Dibachi, Farid; Chmn & CTO, Diba; US; 415/482-3300

Dibachi, Farzad; Pres, Diba; US; 415/482-3300

DiBattista, Scott; VP, Provantage Corp.; US; 216/494-8715, dibattista@provantage.com

Diccicco, Mike; Pres, LDB; US; 215/957-0300

Dick, Stephen L.; VP Corp Mktng, Telebit Corp.; US; 508/441-2181

Dicker, Zachary J.; Pblr, Electronic News; US; 212/736-3900

Dickerson, Rob; VP Mktng, Pure Software Inc.; US; 408/720-1600

Dickinson, Charles A.; Chmn, Solectron Corp.; US; 408/957-8500

Dickinson, John; Ed-in-Chief, Computer Life; US; 415/357-5355

Dickinson, Robert D.; VP Sales & Mktng, ConnectSoft; US; 206/827-6467

Dickson, Charles T.; VP & CFO, General Instrument Corp.; US; 312/695-1000

Dickson, Robin; CFO, Harmonic Lightwaves; US; 408/970-9880

Didion, Catherine; Exec Dir, Association for Women in Science; US; 202/326-8940

Dieckmann, Wallace; CFO, TV/COM International Inc.; US; 619/451-1500

Diehl, Richard; Pres & CEO, Graphsoft Inc.; US; 410/290-5114

Diehl, Stanford; Dir, Byte Lab; US; 603/924-9281, sdiehl@bix.com

Diehlman, Ulrike; Mgr Perf Test, PC World Test Center; US; 415/243-0500

Diener, Ronald G.; Pres, Devcom Mid-America Inc.; US; 708/574-3600, uunet!devcom.com!rgd

Dier, Chris L.; VP & CFO, Veritas Software Corp.; US; 415/335-8000

Dietcher, David; VP Eng, Eurom Flashware Inc.; US

Dietz, C. Alex; VP & CIO, Acxiom Corp.; US; 501/336-1000

Dietz, David; SVP Sales, Labtec Enterprises Inc.; US; 360/896-2000

Dietz, Russell; VP Eng, Technically Elite Inc.; US; 408/370-4300

Dietzler, Diane; VP Mktng & Sales, Individual Software Inc.; US; 510/734-6767

Digate, Charles J.; Pres & CEO, MathSoft Inc.; US; 617/577-1017

Diggin, Paul; Acct Exec, D/M Communications Inc.; US; 617/329-7799, dmpaul@aol.com

Diggins, Vance; Pres & CEO, Applicon; US; 313/995-6000

DiGiacomo, Cele; Pres, Fuse Inc.; US; 908/308-9275

DiGiammarino, Peter F.; Pres, Hyperion Software; US; 203/703-3000

DiGiantommaso, Joseph A.; VP &

CFO, Proteon Inc.; US; 508/898-2800

DiGuido, Al; Pblr, Computer Shopper; US; 212/503-3900

Dilatush, Tom; VP Ops, Stac Inc.; US; 619/794-4300

Dilbeck, Ron; Pres & CEO, nCUBE Corp.; US; 415/593-9000

Diller, James V.; Chmn & CEO, Sierra Semiconductor Corp.; US; 408/263-9300

Dillhoff, Richard; CEO, InfoAccess Inc.; US; 206/747-3203

Dillon, John; VP PR, Fraser/Young Inc.; US; 310/451-0300

Dillon, John M.; VP Sales, Arbor Software Corp.; US; 408/727-5800

DiLorenzo, Michele; Pres, Viacom New Media; US; 212/258-6000

Dilulio, Anthony; VP Ops, Xiox Corp.; US; 415/375-8188

Dilworth, Robert P.; Pres & CEO, Metricom Inc.; US; 408/399-8200

DiMarco, Michael A.; SVP, Paging Network Inc.; US; 214/985-4100

DiMaria, Matthew; VP Mktng, Business Objects Inc.; US; 408/973-9300

Dimitriou, Theodore; Chmn, Wallace Computer Services Inc.; US; 708/449-8600

Dineen, Mark; VP, Blenheim Group US Inc.; US; 201/346-1400, mdineen@blenheim.com

Dineley, Doug; Assoc Ed, Computer Currents; US; 510/547-6800

Dinen, Mark; Dir PC Expo, Bruno Blenheim Inc.; US; 201/346-1400

Dingus, Larry; Chmn, Touchstone Software Int'l.; US; 714/470-1122

Dinkes, Sheldon; Pres & CEO, Voicetek Corp.; US; 508/250-9393

Dinsmore III, William A.; Pres & CEO, Learning Company, The; US; 510/792-2101

DiNucci, David E.; Assoc Ed, IRIS Universe; US; 415/390-2079, ded@sgi.com

Diodati, Joseph A.; VP Mktng, Digi Int'l.; US; 612/943-9020

Dionne, Joseph L.; Chmn & CEO, McGraw-Hill Inc.; US; 212/512-2000

DiPaola, John; Pblr, Managing Office Technology; US; 216/696-7000, motstaff@aol.com

Dipietro, Bill; Pres, Cway Software; US; 215/368-9494

DiPietro, Marty C.; VP Ops, NetFrame Systems Inc.; US; 408/474-1000

DiPilla, John; MIS Mgr, Programmer's Paradise Inc.; US; 908/389-8950, jdipilla@programmers.com

Dishman, George; Ed-in-Chief & Pblr, Enterprise Systems Journal; US; 214/669-9000, 76130.221@compuserve.com

Disman, Murray; Pres, Information Associates; US; 415/322-0247

Distefano, Bryan; Dir Sales, Interex; US; 316/524-4747

Dittmann, Bill; Eng, Embedded Systems Products Inc.; US; 713/561-9990, sup-

port@esphou.com

Dittrich, Alan B.; Dir Mktng, Inchcape Inc.; US; 508/689-9355

Dix, John; Ed, Network World; US; 508/875-6400

Dixit, Kaivalya M.; Pres, Standard Performance Evaluation Corp.; US; 703/331-0180

Dixon, Beth; Ulevich & Orrange Inc.; US; 415/329-1590

Dixon, Henry D.; Pres, Datatrac Corp.; US; 770/552-3866

Dixon, John; Prod Mgr, Maxvision; US; 510/252-0267

Djurdjevic, Robert; Pres, Annex Research; US; 602/956-8586

Dmetruk, Steve; VP Sales & Mktng, Melita International; US; 770/446-7800

Doan, James K.; EVP & CFO, QMS Inc.; US; 334/633-4300, johnsont@isc-clink.is.qms.com

Dobyns, Lydia; VP & GM, NaviSoft Inc.; US; 703/448-8700

Dobyns, Samantha G.; Sales Mgr, Mailer's Software; US; 714/492-7000

Doctor, Louis J.; Pres & CEO, Truevision Inc.; US; 408/562-4200

Dodd, Nancy; Sales Mgr, Western Telematic Inc.; US; 714/586-9950

Dodd, Tom E.; VP Mktng, Dynapro Systems Inc.; Canada; 604/521-3962

Dodds, Philip; Pres, Interactive Multimedia Assoc.; US; 410/626-1380

Dodson, Tom; Pres, Duracom Computer Systems; US; 214/518-1200

Doering, John; Pres, Polytel Computer Products Corp.; US; 408/745-1540

Doering, Ruth; EVP, Crescent Communication; US; 404/698-8650, rdoering@crescomm.com

Doherty, Bryan; Sr Mgr, Japan Digital Laboratory Co. Ltd.; US; 805/588-8709, jdldoherty@aol.com

Doherty, Richard E.; Ed-in-Chief, Envisioneering; US; 516/783-6244

Dohrmann, Richard M.; VP Mktng & Sales, S&H Computer Systems Inc.; US; 615/327-3670, rdohrmann@sandh.com

Dolan, Michael G.; VP R&D, Celeritas Technologies Ltd.; US; 714/367-8650

Dolce, Michael; Prod Mgr, K-12 Micro-Media Publishing Inc.; US; 201/529-4500

Dolch, Volker; Pres, Dolch Computer Systems; US; 510/661-2220

Doley, Lark; VP Mktng, Second Wave Inc.; US; 512/329-9283

Dolgicer, Max; Dir, International Systems Group Inc.; US; 212/489-0400

Domenech, Lynn; VP, Teacher Support Software Inc.; US; 904/332-6404

Domenech, Tony; Pres, Teacher Support Software Inc.; US; 904/332-6404

Donaghy, Austin; VP & GM, Software Corp. of America; US; 203/359-2773

Donahue, Julie M.; VP, Bolt Beranek & Newman Inc.; US; 617/873-4000

Donahue, Robert E.; VP & CFO, Stratus

Computer Inc.; US; 508/460-2000

Donahue, Todd; VP, Acquired Knowledge Inc.; US; 619/587-4668

Donald, Andrew; US Pres, Tracker Software Inc.; US; 612/525-9802

Donald, James L.; Chmn, Pres & CEO, DSC Communications Corp.; US; 214/519-3000

Donald, Norman; VP, Bayware Inc.; US; 415/286-4480

Donaldson, Tim; VP Sales & Mktng, Andor Communications Inc.; US; 612/932-4000

Donelan, David; Dir Sales, Tactics International Ltd.; US; 508/475-4475

Dongarra, Jack; Ed-in-Chief, Supercomputing Apps. & High Perf. Computing, Int'l. Journ. of; US; 617/253-2889, dongarra@cs.utk.edu

Donley, M. Beth; VP & CFO, AER Energy Resources Inc.; US; 404/433-2127

Donnelly, Paulette; Ed, Electronic Information Report; US; 203/834-0033

Donofrio, Nicholas; SVP Server Grp, International Business Machines Corp.; US; 914/765-1900

Donoghue, John G.; VP Mktng, MCI Business Markets; US; 404/698-8000

Donoghue, Kenneth L.; Dir PR Group, Keiler & Co.; US; 203/677-8821

Donohue, Patrick M.; VP Mktng, ECC International Corp.; US; 610/687-2600

Donovan, Alfredo; Dir Sales, Vivid Image Co.; US; 310/618-0274

Dooley, Barbara; Mng Ed, Commercial Internet eXchange Assoc.; US; 703/318-7218, imasters@pipeline.com

Dooley, Patrick; Center for Multimedia; US; 206/643-9039

Dooling, Larry; Pres & CEO, Verbex Voice Systems Inc.; US; 908/225-5225

Doran, John J.; EVP, Computer Television Network; US; 916/582-5083

Dorfman, Julius; Chmn, CIMdata Inc.; US; 617/235-4124

Dorfman, Peter; Dir Mktng, Molloy Group Inc., The; US; 201/540-1212, pdorfman@molloy.com

Dorheim, David W.; Pres & CEO, AER Energy Resources Inc.; US; 404/433-2127

Doris, Robert J.; CEO, Sonic Solutions; US; 415/893-8000

Dorman, William H.; Pres & CEO, Drake Training & Technologies; US; 612/896-7000

Doron, Michael; CIO, Rumarson Technologies Inc.; US; 908/298-9300

Dorrian, Jim; Pres & CEO, Arbor Software Corp.; US; 408/727-5800

Dorsch, Jeff; Ed, Electronic News; US; 212/736-3900

Dorst, James; CFO, Western Micro Technology; US; 408/379-0177

Dortch, Michael; VP Mktng, UnixWare Technology Group; US; 908/522-6027, dortch@utg.org

Dortch, Rick; CEO, ViewCom Technology Int'l.; US; 206/4547374

Doshi, Nick; Tech Sup Mgr, ZyXEL; US; 714/693-0808

Dosland, Brad; Mgng Ed, Morph's Outpost on the Digital Frontier; US; 510/704-7171

Dott, Jackson; Pres, Monarch Avalon; US; 410/254-9200

Doucette, Paul F.; SVP, Bell Industries Inc.; US; 310/826-2355

Dougherty, Brian P.; Chmn, Geoworks; US; 510/814-1660

Dougherty, Dale; Chmn, Davenport Group; US; 707/829-0515

Douglas, Craig; VP Mktng, Quintar Co.; US; 310/320-5700

Douglas, David; Tech Dir, Digital Media Int'l.; US; 805/563-9490

Douglass, Rich; CEO, Vermont Creative Software; US; 802/848-7731

Dove, Kelly; Exec Ed, 3D Design; US; 415/905-2200, kdove@mfi.com

Dowdell Jr., Roger B.; Chmn, Pres & CEO, American Power Conversion; US; 401/789-5735

Dowell, Dick; Pres & CEO, Software Valley; US; 703/678-8962

Dowell, Susan P.; EVP & COO, Medicus Systems Corp.; US; 847/570-7500

Dowie, Doug; SVP, Fleishman-Hillard Inc.; US; 213/629-4974

Dowling, Jack D.; VP & CIO, CompuCom Systems; US; 214/265-3600

Downing, William E.; EVP & CFO, Pacific Telesis Group; US; 415/394-3000

Doyen, Thierry; Pres, YARC Systems Corp.; US; 805/499-9444

Doyle, Audrey V.; Mgng Ed, Computer Graphics World; US; 603/891-0123, audreyd@pennwell.com

Doyle, William; Dir Mktng, Systems Engineering Solutions Inc.; US; 703/573-4366

Dozier, Linda; VP & CTO, NaviSoft Inc.; US; 703/448-8700

Drachman, Kathy; VP Sales & Mktng, Transitional Technology Inc.; US; 714/693-1133, kathy@ttech.com

Dragan, Carol A.; Pres & CEO, General Computer Corp.; US; 216/425-3241

Drake, Hudson B.; SVP, Teledyne Inc.; US; 310/551-4306

Drake, Jeff; Sales Dir, Enterprise Solutions Ltd.; US; 805/449-4181

Drake, Keith; Dir R&D, AbTech Corp.; US; 804/977-0686

Drapeau, Norman E.; VP Sales & Mktng, Project Software & Development Inc.; US; 617/661-1444

Drawas, Randy; Pub Dir, MapWorld Magazine; US; 518/285-7340

Dreibelbis, John; Dir Mktng, Hand Held Products; US; 704/541-1380

Dresselhaus, Daniel; Pres, Dresselhaus Computer Products; US; 909/945-5600

Drew, David P.; VP Info Tech, Minnesota Minning & Manufacturing; US; 612/

733-1110

Dreyer, George; Pres, Norman Data Defense Systems Inc.; US; 703/573-8802

Dreyfuss, Joel; Ed-in-Chief, InformationWEEK; US; 516/562-5000

Driber, R. Byron; SVP & COO, Cybex Corp.; US; 205/430-4000

Driscoll, Catherine; Dir Mktng, Hercules Computer Technology Inc.; US; 510/623-6030

Driscoll, Linda; Ed, Telemarketing & Call Center Solutions; US; 203/852-6800

Drobatschewsky, Serge; VP Ops, Encad Inc.; US; 619/452-0882

Droege, Paula; CFO, Droege Computing Services Inc.; US; 919/403-9459

Droege, Tom; Pres, Droege Computing Services Inc.; US; 919/403-9459

Drolet, Michelle; Pres, Compu-Design Group Inc.; US; 508/655-1177

Drowty, Dennis; VP Ops, Parallax Graphics Inc.; US; 408/727-2220

Drozda, Thomas J.; Pblr, Manufacturing Systems; US; 708/665-1000

Drucker, David; Exec Ed, Printers Buyer's Guide & Handbook; US; 212/807-8220

Drucker, Samuel; GM, Cygnus Support; US; 415/903-1400

Drummond, Joe; Pres & CEO, Pragmatech Inc.; US; 408/943-1151

Drury, Robert L.; VP & CFO, Interphase Corp.; US; 214/919-9000

Dube, Al; CFO & Co-Founder, Mergent Int'l.; US; 860/257-4223, adube@mergent.com

Dube, Louise; CFO, Learningways Inc.; US; 617/234-5800

Dubinsky, Donna; Pres & CEO, Palm Computing; US; 415/949-9560, donna@palm.com

Dubner, Ron; VP Sales, Fuji Photo Film US Inc.; US; 914/789-8100

Dubnoff, Steven; Pres, Circle Systems Inc.; US; 206/682-3783

Dubois, Francine; GM, ASD Software Inc.; US; 909/624-2594

DuBridge, Richard A.; Pres & COO, TeleVideo Systems Inc.; US; 408/954-8333

Dubyak, Michael W.; VP NA Syst, Control Data Systems Inc.; US; 612/482-2401

Duce, Stacie; Assist Acc Mgr, Penna Powers Cutting & Haynes Inc.; US; 801/531-0973, ppch@xmission.com

Duckman, Ken; Pres, Laptop Solutions Inc.; US; 713/556-5051

Duckworth, Jim L.; SVP Sales, Scientific Software-Intercomp Inc.; US; 303/292-1111

Duda, Daryl R.; VP Sales, BCB Holdings Inc.; Canada; 905/850-8266

Dudhia, Ismael; Chmn, Mylex Corp.; US; 510/796-6100

Dueger, William; GM, Azerty Inc.; US; 716/662-0200

Duehren, David W.; VP R&D, Brook-

trout Technology Inc.; US; 617/499-4100, dwd@brooktrout.com

Duff, Bruce; VP Mktng, Information Dimensions Inc.; US; 614/761-8083

Duff, Chuck; Pres, Digital Frontiers; US; 847/328-0880, cduff@digfrontiers.com

Duffield, Albert W.; SVP WW Ops, Peoplesoft Inc.; US; 510/225-3000

Duffield, David A.; Chmn, Pres & CEO, Peoplesoft Inc.; US; 510/225-3000

Duffield, Michael O.; SVP Ops, Wallace Computer Services Inc.; US; 708/449-8600

Duffy, Karl; EVP Sales & Mktng, Killen & Associates Inc.; US; 415/617-6130

Duffy, Kevin J.; VP NA Sales, Xyvision Inc.; US; 617/245-4100

Duffy, Michael J.; VP Ops, Intersolv Inc.; US; 301/838-5000

Dugan, Joe; Dir Mktng, NEBS Software & Computer Forms; US; 603/880-5100

Duggan, Donald; Mgng Partner, Network Associates Inc.; US; 801/373-7888, donaldd@netassoc.com

Duhring, John; VP Bus Dev, Wais Inc.; US; 415/356-5400

Duket, Steven D.; VP, Pritsker Corp.; US; 317/879-1011

Dulley, Ben; Pres, New Era Systems Services Ltd.; Canada; 403/231-9800

Dultz, Mark; Ed, Strategy Plus; US; 802/767-4622

Dumit, Thomas A.; VP & CAO, General Instrument Corp.; US; 312/695-1000

Duncan, E. Townes; Chmn & CEO, Comptronix Corp.; US; 615/377-3330

Duncan, Kenneth W.; Pres, SoftSolutions Technology Corp.; US; 801/226-6000

Duncan, Lee; VP, SoftSolutions Technology Corp.; US; 801/226-6000

Duncan, Phil; VP Int'l Sales, Berkeley Systems Inc.; US; 510/540-5535

Duncan, Robert; Chmn & CEO, Sparc Int'l.; US; 415/321-8692

Dundon, George; Dir Tech Ops, Shuttle Technology; US; 510/656-0180

Dungworth, Carl W.; SVP Sales & Mktng, Cray Research Inc.; US; 612/452-6650, mickd@cray.com

Dunham, Michael D.; Pres & CEO, Effective Management Systems; US; 414/359-9800

Dunkle, John; Pres, WorkGroup Technologies Inc.; US; 603/929-1166

Dunn, Fred; VP, Jon Peddie Associates; US; 415/435-1775, 71250.2146@compuserve.com

Dunn, Joseph D.; VP Prod Dev, Macromedia Inc.; US; 415/252-2000

Dunn, Ronald; Exec Dir, Information Industry Assoc.; US; 202/986-0280

Dunne, Kenis; Ed Prod, Smith & Shows Letter; US; 415/329-8880

Dunnigan, Dennis; CFO, Radius Inc.; US; 408/541-6100

Dunstan, Ericson M.; SVP Corp Eng,

Micropolis Corp.; US; 818/709-3300

Duntemann, Jeff; VP & Ed Dir, Coriolis Group Inc.; US; 602/483-0192

Duques, Henry C.; Chmn & CEO, First Data Corp.; US; 201/525-4700

Durand, Andre; Pres & CEO, Durand Communications Network Inc.; US; 805/961-8700

Durando, Paul; VP Fin, Nu Horizons Electronics Corp.; US; 516/226-6000

Durant, John L.; VP, TUV Product Service Inc.; US; 508/777-7999

Durham, David G.; VP Fin, Ciber Inc.; US; 303/220-0100

Durham, David L.; VP & CFO, Future Now; US; 513/792-4500

Durlach, Nathaniel I.; Mgng Ed, Presence: Teleoperators & Virtual Environments; US; 617/253-2889, presence@cbgrle.mit.edu

Durrick, Mark; Pblr, Midrange Systems; US; 215/643-8000

Durrrett, Joe; CEO, Broderbund Software Inc.; US; 415/382-4400

Durwood, Brian; Dir Bus Dev, Maxtek Components Corp.; US; 503/627-4133

Dury, David S.; VP & CFO, NetFrame Systems Inc.; US; 408/474-1000

DuShane, Carolyn; Com Dir, Institute for Certification of Computing Professionals; US; 847/299-4227

Dusseault, Robert; VP Sales & Mktng, Howtek Inc.; US; 603/882-5200

Dust, Robert; Pres, Gyrus Systems Inc.; US; 804/320-1414, bobdust@ix.net-com.com

Dustin, Lori; Dir Bus Dev, Data Translation Inc.; US; 508/481-3700

Dutia, Suren G.; Pres & CEO, Xscribe Corp.; US; 619/457-5091

Dwight Jr., Herbert M.; Chmn, Pres & CEO, Optical Coating Laboratory Inc.; US; 707/545-6440

Dworkin, Casey; GM, Personal Technology Research; US; 508/875-5858

Dworkin, Sidney; Chmn, General Computer Corp.; US; 216/425-3241

Dyal, Joan; Dir Corp Comm, Parsons Technology Inc.; US; 319/395-9626

Dybowski, Norman J.; Dir Sales & Mktng, Sampo Corp. of America; US; 770/449-6220

Dyer, Dyan; Pres, Command Software Systems Inc.; US; 407/575-3200

Dyer, Jack; Pres, Theos Software Corp.; US; 510/935-1118

Dykes, Robert R.B.; EVP Ops & CFO, Symantec Corp.; US; 408/253-9600

Dykes, Ronald M.; EVP & CFO, Bell-South Corp.; US; 404/249-2000

Dykstra, Thomas M.; VP R&D, Effective Management Systems; US; 414/359-9800

Dynes, Craig; CFO, Powersoft Corp; US; 508/287-1500

Dyson, Esther; Pres & Ed., EDventure Holdings Inc.; US; 212/924-8800, edyson@edventure.com

Dyson, Peter E.; Ed, Seybold Report on Publishing Systems; US; 610/565-2480, pdyson@sbexpos.com

Dzubeck, Frank; Pres, Communications Network Architects Inc.; US; 202/775-8000

Eagle, Ron; Pres, Acute Inc.; US; 913/233-1919

Eaken, Kenneth; VP & GM, MapLinx Corp.; US; 214/231-1400

Eakin, Matt; IS Mgr, SVEC Computer Corp.; US; 714/756-2233, matt.eakin@svec.com

Earl, LeRoy D.; VP Sales & Mktng, H.A. Technical Solutions Inc.; US; 612/221-1661

Earl, Paul; CEO, Interactive Training Inc.; US; 508/879-0006

Earl, Paul H.; Pres, CD Solutions Inc.; US; 508/879-0006, phearl@cdsolutions.com

Earle, Richard; VP Mktng, Border Network Technologies Inc.; Canada; 416/368-7157

Earls, Alan; Ed-in-Chief, Chicago Software Newspaper; US

Easton, Elmer R.; Pres, Three D Graphics Inc.; US; 310/553-3313, elmere@threedgraphics.com

Eaton, Lawrence E.; EVP, Minnesota Minning & Manufacturing; US; 612/733-1110

Ebbers, Bernard J.; Pres & CEO, WorldCom; US; 601/360-8600

Ebenezer, Duke; CEO, M4 Solutions Inc.; US; 407/639-6487

Ebling, Thomas D.; SVP Prod Dev, Marcam Corp.; US; 617/965-0220

Ebrahimi, Fred; Pres & CEO, Quark Inc.; US; 303/894-8888

Ecker, H. Allen; SVP & CTO, Scientific-Atlanta Inc.; US; 770/903-5000, allen.ecker@sciatl.com

Eckerman, Jim; Pres & CEO, Thot Technologies; US; 408/370-4600

Eckler, Todd; Dir R&D, Marcus Technology Inc.; US; 212/678-0406

Eddins, Robert; VP R&D, Popkin Software & Systems Inc.; US; 212/571-3434

Eddison, E. Peter; VP Mktng, Fulcrum Technologies Inc.; Canada; 613/238-1761

Eddy, John; VP Fin, New Era Systems Services Ltd.; Canada; 403/231-9800

Edeleanu, John; Pres & CEO, Hercules Computer Technology Inc.; US; 510/623-6030

Edelen, Charity; Ed, Inside Microsoft Windows; US; 502/491-1900

Edelheit, Lewis S.; SVP R&D, General Electric Co.; US; 203/373-2211

Edelman, Joseph M.; VP, Network Long Distance Inc.; US; 504/343-3125

Edelman, Richard; Pres, Edelman Public Relations; US; 212/768-0550

Eden, Bruce D.; VP MIS, Tech Data Corp.; US; 813/539-7429

Edenfield, J. Michael; EVP & COO, American Software Inc.; US; 404/264-5296

Edenfield, James C.; Pres & CEO, American Software Inc.; US; 404/264-5296

Edenholm, Patrik; Pres, Ansel Communications; US; 206/869-4928

Edenzon, Rob; Pres, Software Affiliates; US; 818/385-3710

Edgell, Douglas C.; Pblr, Retail Systems Reseller; US; 201/895-3300

Edling, John; Chmn & Pres, Dycam Inc.; US; 818/998-8008

Edmonston, Jack; Ed & Pblr, Computer Advisers' Media Advisor; US; 508/358-0293, jackedmons@aol.com

Edstrom, Pam; SVP, Waggener Edstrom; US; 503/245-0905

Edwards, Andrew; Pres, Extron Electronics; US; 714/491-1500

Edwards, Bob; VP MIS, Xerox Imaging Systems; US; 508/977-2000

Edwards, Bruce C.; EVP & CFO, AST Research Inc.; US; 714/727-4141

Edwards, Chuck; Pres, Onyx Graphics Corp.; US; 801/568-9900

Edwards, Kim B.; Pres & CEO, Iomega Corp.; US; 801/778-1000

Edwards, Michael; Chmn, Healthcare Communications Inc.; US; 402/466-8100

Edwards, Paul; News Ed, Canadian Computer Reseller; Canada; 416/596-5000

Edwards, Stephen E.; Ed, Seybold Report on Desktop Publishing; US; 610/565-2480, sedwards@sbexpos.com

Edwards, Thomas J.; VP & CTO, Digital Systems Int'l.; US; 206/881-7544

Edwards, Tracy A.; VP & CFO, Bell Industries Inc.; US; 310/826-2355

Efstathiou, Chris; VP Materials, 1st Tech Corp.; US; 512/258-3570

Egan, David; Pres & COO Mag Grp, Mecklermedia Corp.; US; 203/226-6967, degan@mecklermedia.com

Egan, Frank; Ed & Pblr, Electronic Products; US; 516/227-1300

Egan, John R.; EVP Sales & Mktng, EMC Corp.; US; 508/435-1000

Egan, Richard J.; Chmn, EMC Corp.; US; 508/435-1000

Egger, Dale; Acq Mgr, NEWS/400; US; 970/663-4700

Eggert, George; Exec Dir, Data Processing Management Assoc.; US; 708/825-8124

Eggleston, David M.; VP, Fakespace Inc.; US; 415/688-1940

Eggleton, Eric; VP, Discovery Channel, The; US; 301/986-1999

Egolf, Karen; Ed, Business Marketing; US; 312/649-5260

Ehling, Theresa; Acq Ed, MIT Press, The; US; 617/625-8569

Ehrlich, Steven M.; VP Client Svcs, Software Artistry Inc.; US; 317/843-1663

Eichberger, Joseph; Pres, Advanced Matrix Technology Inc.; US; 805/388-5799

Eicher, Lawrence; Sec General, International Organization for Standardization; Switzerland; 22-749-0111

Eichhorn, Gary; CEO, Open Market Inc.; US; 617/621-9500

Eichorn, John E.; Ed, Microcomputer Abstracts; US; 609/654-6266

Eid, Eid; Dir Graphics SW, Corel Corp.; Canada; 613/728-8200

Eige, Bob; VP Ops, Equilibrium; US; 415/332-4343

Eiler, Mark; Dir Training Svcs, Unitrac Software Corp.; US; 616/344-0220, meiler@unitrac.com

Eilers, Robert; Exec Dir, International Communications Assoc.; US; 214/233-3889

Einav, Roni; Chmn, New Dimension Software; US; 714/757-4300

Eiron, Hanoch; VP & GM, Franz Inc.; US; 510/548-3600

Eis, Shirley; Pres, Software Corp. of America; US; 203/359-2773, eis@radiomail.net

Eise, Kurt; Pres, TUV Product Service Inc.; US; 508/777-7999

Eisenbach, Randy; COO, STB Systems Inc.; US; 214/234-8750

Eisenberg, Wayne; Dir Sales, Apex Data Inc.; US; 510/416-5656

Eisenburg, Ron; Pres & CTO, Optibase Inc.; US; 214/774-3800, rone@optibase.com

Eisenhart, Doug; Dir Dev & Lic, Houghton Mifflin Interactive; US; 617/351-5000

Eisenhart, Mary; Ed, MicroTimes; US; 510/934-3700

Eisenlohr, Jay; Co-Founder & VP Bus Dev, Rendition Inc.; US; 415/335-5900

Eizenman, Avi; Pres & CEO, Silicom Ltd.; US; 206/882-7995

Ejabat, Mory; Pres & CEO, Ascend Communications Inc.; US; 510/769-6001

Ek, Brad; Dir Eng, Panacea Inc.; US; 508/937-1760

Eklund, Mel; Sr Tech Consultant, Forward Concepts; US; 602/968-3759

Elam, Theresa; Distr Sales Mgr, Apex Data Inc.; US; 510/416-5656

Elassy, Fay; VP Eng, Cambex Corp.; US; 617/890-6000

Elder, David; Pres, Psion Inc.; US; 508/371-0310

Eldred, Eric; Tech Analyst, Client/Server Today Labs; US; 617/964-3030, erice@cstoday.com

Eldred, Kenneth A.; Chmn, Inmac Corp.; US; 408/727-1970

Elefant, Steve; Pres, IC Systems; US; 510/339-3480

Eleftheriou, Michael G.; VP Ops & Plng, Control Data Systems Inc.; US; 612/482-2401

Elgan, Mike; Ed, Windows Magazine; US; 516/733-8300

Elgar, Eric; Sr Tech Ed, Computer Reseller News Test Center; US; 516/733-6700, eelgar@cmp.com

Elghanayan, Jeffrey; Pres & CEO, Portfolio Software Inc.; US

Elizer, Lee H.; Pres & CEO, MediaLogic ADL Inc.; US; 303/939-9780

Elkins, Dennis D.; Pres Legal Syst Div, Xscribe Corp.; US; 619/457-5091

Elkins, Joseph; COO, TelePad Corp.; US; 703/834-9000

Elko, Lance; Ed Dir, Computer Entertainment News; US; 510/601-9275

Elledge, Marian; VP, Graphic Communications Assoc.; US; 703/519-8160

Ellenberger, Richard G.; SVP, MCI Business Markets; US; 404/698-8000

Ellerbruch, Jeff; Prod Mktng Mgr, SanDisk Corp.; US; 408/542-0500

Elliot, Bryan; CTO, Durand Communications Network Inc.; US; 805/961-8700

Elliott, Jock; VP, Consultech Communications Inc.; US; 518/283-8444

Elliott, Lyle; Pres, Analog & Digital Peripherals Inc.; US; 513/339-2241

Elliott, Stacey; Subs Mgr, Multimedia Wire; US; 301/493-9290, proact@aol.com

Elliott, T. Micahel; Exec Dir, IEEE Computer Society; US; 202/371-0101

Ellis, George H.; EVP & CFO, Sterling Software Inc.; US; 214/891-8600

Ellis, J. Richard; Pres & CEO, Document Imaging Systems Corp.; US; 408/734-5287

Ellison, Chuck; SVP Sales & Mktng, Asymetrix Corp.; US; 206/637-5859

Ellison, Lawrence J.; Chmn, Pres & CEO, Oracle Corp.; US; 415/506-7000

Ellmore, Douglas; National Academy Press; US; 202/334-2612, dellmore@nas.edu

Ells, Barbara; Sr Consultant, MWA Consulting Inc.; US; 415/323-4780

Elmore, Donna; MVP, SysKonnect Inc.; US; 408/437-3800

Elmore, Jerry; Dir Sales, Electronic Form Systems; US; 214/243-4343

Elmore, Valerie E.M.; Mgng Ed, Client/Server Computing; US; 508/366-2031

Elms, Teresa; Ed, IS Budget; US; 619/438-8100, telms@compecon.com

Elpern, Jeff; Pres & CEO, Mainsoft Corp.; US; 408/794-3400

Elrich, Scott; Prod Dev & Mktng Mgr, Teac America Inc.; US; 213/726-0303

Elsner, Edgar; Pres, Elsner Technologies Co.; US; 817/626-4110

Elton, Milan L.; VP, Technalysis Corp.; US; 612/925-5900

Elwell, Chris; VP, Simba Information Inc.; US; 203/834-0033

Emello, Don; Pres, Westrex Int'l.; US; 617/254-1200

Emerson, E. James; Pres, Repository Technologies Inc.; US; 708/515-0780

Emerson, Kathleen; VP, Repository Technologies Inc.; US; 708/515-0780

Emmerson, Troy; Network Admin, Cogent Data Technologies Inc.; US; 360/378-2929, troy@cogentdata.com

Emmi, Michael J.; Chmn, Pres & CEO, Systems & Computer Technology Corp.; US; 610/647-5930

Endo, Yasuo; EVP, Mitsubishi Electric Corp.; Japan; 3-3218-2111

Endress, Paul; Pres, DataTech Software; US; 717/652-4344

Engel, Fred; VP Eng, Concord Communications Inc.; US; 508/460-4646

Engel, Frederick; Pres & CEO, Software Security Inc.; US; 203/656-3000

Engel, Joel S.; VP Tech, Ameritech Corp.; US; 312/750-5000

Engel, Paul; VP, Systems & Computer Technology Corp.; US; 610/647-5930

Engelhardt, Mark; CEO, Wayzata Technology Inc.; US; 218/326-0597, markengelhardt@wayzata.com

Engibous, Thomas J.; Pres & CEO, Texas Instruments Inc.; US; 214/995-2551

English, David; Ed, Computer Entertainment News; US; 510/601-9275

English, Debby; Mgng Ed, Enterprise Systems Journal; US; 214/669-9000

English, Floyd L.; Chmn, Pres & CEO, Andrew Corp.; US; 708/349-3300

Enrado, Patty; Mgng Ed, AI Expert; US; 415/905-2200

Ensler, Howard; Sales Mgr, CopyPro Inc.; US; 510/689-1200

Enstice, Keith J.; SVP Field Ops, Manugistics Inc.; US; 301/984-5000

Entine, Steven; VP SW Dev & CTO, Persoft Inc.; US; 608/273-6000

Entis, Glenn; CEO, DreamWorks Interactive; US; 310/234-7070

Epley, Sherry; Exec Ed, CyberEdge Journal; US; 415/331-3343

Epple, Gary; VP Dev, Dazel Corp.; US; 512/328-6977

Eppley, Mark; Chmn & CEO, Traveling Software Inc.; US; 206/483-8088

Epstein, David I.; VP Eng, NexGen Microsystem; US; 408/435-0202

Epstein, Jerry; EVP & GM, Fleishman-Hillard Inc.; US; 213/629-4974

Epstein, Jonathan; Pblr, PC World Interactive; US; 415/243-0500, jonathan_epstein@pcworld.com

Erett, Richard; EVP, Software Security Inc.; US; 203/656-3000

Erf, Keith; Pres, KyTek Inc.; US; 603/529-2512

Erickson, Jonathan; Ed-in-Chief, Dr. Dobb's Journal; US; 415/358-9500

Erling, Dale R.; Dir Mktng, Angia Communications; US; 801/371-0488

Ermis, J.C.; Dir Conf, Telecommunications Reports/BRP; US; 202/842-3022, jce@brpnyc.mhs.compuserve.com

Ernest, Sebastian; Pres, Computer Dynamics; US; 817/566-5515

Ernsberger, John; Chmn, Itac Systems Inc.; US; 214/494-3073, johne@moustrak.com

Ernst, Lisa; Dir Conf, Association for Computing Machinery; US; 212/869-7440

Erokan, Dennis; Ed-in-Chief, BAM Media; US; 510/934-3700

Erwin, Brian; Dir Sales & Mktng, O'Reilly & Associates Inc.; US; 707/829-0515

Erwin, Douglas J.; EVP & COO, BMC Software Inc.; US; 713/918-8800

Erwin, Val E.; International Compliance Corp.; US; 817/491-3696

Erxleben, William C.; Pres & CEO, Data I/O Corp.; US; 206/881-6444

Escalante, Dana; VP Dev, Pacific Creations; US; 510/658-2703

Esenther, Dan; VP, Elastic Reality Inc.; US; 608/273-6585

Eskew, Michael; Sales Mgr, Exsys Inc.; US; 505/256-8356

Esposito, Donna; Pblr, Communication Systems Design; US; 415/905-2200, desposito@mfi.com

Esposito, Joe; Pres, Computron Software Inc.; US; 201/935-3400

Esrey, William T.; Chmn & CEO, Sprint Corp.; US; 913/624-3000

Essex, Bessie; VP, Aristo-Soft Inc.; US; 510/426-5355

Essex, Dave; Tech Ed, Byte Lab; US; 603/924-9281

Esteverena, Rolando C.; Pres & CEO, ADFlex Solutions Inc.; US; 602/963-4584

Estrada, Sal; VP Ops, ASCII Entertainment Software Inc.; US; 415/780-0800, sal.estrada@asciient.com

Estrin, Judy; Pres & CEO, Precept Software Inc.; US; 415/845-5200

Estroff, Elizabeth; Ed, Online Tactics; US; 203/834-0033, elizabeth_estroff@simbanet.com

Etchison, Jim; Ed, Support Solutions; US; 206/619-4357, jimwriter9@aol.com

Ethier, Bill; VP Ops, Quarterdeck Corp.; US; 310/309-3700

Ettwein, Jim; VP & GM Advisory Svcs, DeBoever Architectures Inc.; US; 508/371-1557

Eubanks Jr., Gordon E.; Pres & CEO, Symantec Corp.; US; 408/253-9600

Euler, Laura; Mgng Ed, Microsoft Interactive Developer; US; 415/833-7100

Eunice, Jonathan; Pres, Illuminata; US; 603/598-0099, jonathan@illuminata.com

Eustace, D.G.; EVP & CFO, Philips Electronics; Netherlands; 31-40-786022

Evangelist, Stacey C.; Mgng Ed., Computer Technology Research Corp.; US; 803/853-6460

Evangelista-Frace, Anna-Maria; Dir Tech Sup, Odyssey Development Inc.; US; 303/689-9998

Evanier, Joel; VP Sales & Mktng, NET-SYS Technologies Inc.; US; 415/833-7500

Evans, Bill; VP Mktng, Objectivity; US;

415/254-7100

Evans, Bob; Dir Electr Pblr, Brooks/Cole Publishing Co.; US; 408/373-0728, bobevans@brookscole.com

Evans, David; Ed, Marketing Computers; US; 212/536-6587, david@marketing-computers.com

Evans, David B.; Pres, EA Research Inc.; US; 510/867-0967

Evans, Duane E.; Pres & CEO, Computer Television Network; US; 916/582-5083

Evans, Gail; Mgng Ed, Repair, Service & Remarketing News; US; 417/781-9317

Evans, Greg; Pres, Wellspring Communications; US; 619/279-1611

Evans, Karen E.; CFO, EA Research Inc.; US; 510/867-0967

Evans, Kathleen; CFO, Wellspring Communications; US; 619/279-1611

Evans, Larry; Chmn & CEO, Aspen Technology Inc.; US; 617/577-0100

Evans, Richard; SVP, NCR Corp.; US; 513/445-5000

Evanson, Robert E.; EVP Corp Dev, McGraw-Hill Inc.; US; 212/512-2000

Everett, George; Prod Mgr, Connectivity Systems; US; 602/813-3288, georgee@datacal.com

Everett, Keith; VP Mktng, Intermec Corp.; US; 206/348-2600

Everett, Robert; EVP, Hilgraeve Inc.; US; 313/243-0576

Everhart, Rodney L.; SVP & CFO, Bellcore; US; 201/829-2000

Evers, Hank; VP Sales & Mktng, Pioneer New Media Technologies Inc.; US

Ewald, Robert H.; Pres & COO, Cray Research Inc.; US; 612/452-6650

Ewing, Brandon; VP Sales, Server Technology Inc.; US; 408/745-0300

Ewing, Carrel; Pres, Server Technology Inc.; US; 408/745-0300

Eyre, Kathy L.; Controller, Mailer's Software; US; 714/492-7000

Ezran, Claude; VP Mktng, Xerox ColorgrafX Systems; US; 408/225-2800

Ezrim, Robert; EVP & Co-Chmn, 7th Level Inc.; US; 818/547-1955

Fabbio, Robert; Pres, Dazel Corp.; US; 512/328-6977

Fabian, Bill; VP, Okidata; US; 609/235-2600

Factor, Alan J.; VP Mktng, Sales Technologies Inc.; US; 404/841-4000

Fadda, Julie; Mgng Ed, Software Development; US; 415/905-2200, jfadda@mfi.com

Fadden, B.J.; Pres & CEO, GTCO Corp.; US; 410/381-6688

Fagan, Donald E.; SVP & Pblr, Sentry Publishing Co. Inc.; US; 508/366-2031

Fagan, Kate; VP Sales, VictorMaxx Technologies; US; 708/267-0007

Faggin, Federico; Pres, Synaptics Inc.; US; 408/434-0110

Faherty, Michael E.; Chmn & CEO,

ECCS Inc.; US; 908/747-6995

Fahr, Ulrich; Chmn & CEO, Softlab Inc.; US; 770/668-8811

Fainman, Shaya; Chmn, Opticomm Corp.; US; 619/450-0143

Fairfield, Bill L.; Pres & CEO, InaCom Corp.; US; 402/392-3900

Fairlie, Rik; Mngg Ed, Mobile Office; US; 310/589-3100

Fairweather, Michael; Pres, Unex Corp.; US; 603/598-1100

Faith, Suzanne; VP Sales, ButtonWare Inc.; US; 214/713-6370

Falagrady, Brandi; Sec & Treas, Plotter Supplies Inc.; US; 303/450-2900

Falanga, Jim; Pres, DataEase International Inc.; US; 203/374-8000

Faletra, Robert; Ed-in-Chief, Computer Reseller News; US; 516/562-5000, rfaletra@cmp.com

Falk, Lawrence; Pblr, Falsoft Inc.; US; 502/228-4492

Fallet, Duncan; Dir Res, Techtel Corp.; US; 510/655-9414

Fallon, Kevin; Pblr, Redgate Communications Corp.; US; 407/231-6904

Fallon, Sandra; Pres, Unisync Corp.; US; 714/985-5088

Fallows, Robert C.; VP Sales, Riso Inc.; US; 508/777-7377

Faltersack, Fred; High Technology Careers Magazine; US; 408/970-8800

Familiant, David G.; EVP Int'l Ops, Gartner Group; US; 203/964-0096

Fantuzzi, Joe; Pres, MultiGen; US; 408/261-4100

Fanwell, Richard; Applix Inc.; US; 508/870-0300

Faran, Mary Ann; Assoc Ed, Law Office Technology Review; US; 610/359-9900

Fardal, Randy; VP Mktng, Retix; US; 310/828-3400

Fargo, Brian; Pres & CEO, Interplay Productions Inc.; US; 714/553-6655

Faries, David; Mngg Partner, Faries & Associates; US; 408/354-7308

Farina, John; Pres, Quintar Co.; US; 310/320-5700

Farina, Robert; Pres & CEO, Global Turnkey Systems Inc.; US; 201/445-5050

Farinelli, Gene; Chmn, Creamer Dickson Basford; US; 212/887-8010

Faris, Richard K.; EVP, Primavera Systems Inc.; US; 610/667-8600

Faris, Sadeg M.; Pres, VRex Inc.; US; 914/345-8877

Farley, David A.; VP & CFO, BMC Software Inc.; US; 713/918-8800

Farley, Todd; VP SW Dev, Triticom; US; 612/937-0772, tfarley@triticom.com

Farmer, Phillip W.; Pres & COO, Harris Corp.; US; 407/727-9100

Farmer, Vic; Ed Dir, Comdex Show Daily; US; 617/449-6600

Farnham, George; Dir Sales, Archetype Inc.; US; 617/890-7544

Farr, Paul V.; VP & GM, Aim Technology; US; 408/748-8649, paul@aim.com

Farre, Tom; Exec Ed, VARBUSINESS; US; 516/562-5000

Farrell, Jack; Pres, LXE; US; 770/447-4224

Farrell, Mike; EVP, Open Text Corp.; Canada; 519/888-7111

Farrell, Stephen C.; Exec Dir, East-West Foundation; US; 617/261-6699

Farrell, Tim; Chmn & CEO, FutureSoft; US; 713/496-9400

Farrill, F. Craig; VP Tech Plng & Dev, AirTouch Communications; US; 415/658-2000

Farrington, Carl; Pres, Primeline Communications Corp.; US; 704/648-1298

Farris, David B.; VP R&D, Boca Research Inc.; US; 407/997-6227

Farris, Tim; Chmn, Pres & CEO, Boca Research Inc.; US; 407/997-6227

Faul, J. Joel; VP Eng, Cardiff Software Inc.; US; 619/761-4515

Faulkner, David J.; Vice Chmn & CFO, Memorex Telex Corp.; US; 214/444-3500

Faunce, Michael; Pres, Autotime Corp.; US; 503/452-8577

Favela, Olivia; VP Sales & Mktng, Information Presentation Technologies Inc.; US; 805/541-3000

Fawcette, James E.; Ed & Pblr, Visual Basic Programmer's Journal; US; 415/833-7100

Fawcette, James E.; Ed & Pblr, Fawcette Technical Publications Inc.; US; 415/833-7100

Fay, Todor; CTO, Blue Ribbon SoundWorks Ltd.; US; 404/315-0212

Fazakerly, William B.; CTO, Ikos Systems Inc.; US; 408/255-4567

Fazen, Bob; VP, EasySpooler; US; 214/522-2324

Fazzini, Larry; VP Corp Resources, InaCom Corp.; US; 402/392-3900

Fedchenko, Richard P.; VP Mkt Dev, 3D Systems Corp.; US; 805/295-5600

Fedele, Vincent; Pres, VST Power Systems; US; 508/287-4600

Feder, Bradley H.; Pres, RightFAX; US; 520/327-1357, bhf@rightfax.com

Federman, Daniel; Pres & CEO, Premenos Corp.; US; 510/602-2000

Federman, Irwin; Chmn, SanDisk Corp.; US; 408/542-0500

Feeley, Bill; VP Sales, Dux Software Corp.; US; 415/948-6200

Feeney, Edward; Pres NA, Liebert Corp.; US; 614/888-0246

Feeney, Hal; Principal, Pathfinder Research Inc.; US; 408/437-1905

Fegreus, Jack; Ed-in-Chief, Client/Server Today; US; 617/964-3030, jackf@cstoday.com

Fegreus, Jack; Ed Dir, Digital News & Review Labs; US; 617/964-3030, jackf@dnr.com

Fei, Peter T.; CEO, GigaTrend Inc.; US; 619/931-9122

Feibus, Mike; Principal, Mercury Research; US; 602/998-9225

Feidelman, Lawrence; Assoc Pblr, Phillips Decision Point Resources; US; 609/424-1100

Feidler, Mark L.; VP Corp Dev, BellSouth Corp.; US; 404/249-2000

Feigenson, Walter; Dir Mktng, Jandel Scientific Inc.; US; 415/453-6700, walterf@jandel.com

Feinberg, Henry J.; Pres, Rand McNally New Media; US; 847/329-6335

Feintuch, Henry; Mgng Partner, KCS&A Public Relations; US; 212/682-6300

Feiss, George J.; CFO, Vivid Image Co.; US; 310/618-0274

Feit, Alexandra; Mgng Ed, Insight Into Emerging Systems Management Solutions; US; 415/323-4780

Feith, Donald; Pres & CEO, Feith Systems & Software Inc.; US; 215/646-8000, don@feith.com

Felcyn, Jim; CFO, Citrix Systems Inc.; US; 305/340-2246

Feld, Bradley A.; Chmn, net.Genesis; US; 617/577-9800

Feldman, Israel; Pblr, Enterprise Reengineering; US; 703/761-0646

Feldman, Jeff; Partner, FS Communications; US; 415/691-1488

Feldman, Mark W.; VP Sales & Mktng NA, SoftTalk Inc.; US; 617/433-0800

Feldman Jr., Daniel S.; Pres, Abacus Concepts Inc.; US; 510/540-1949

Feldstein, David; SVP Sales & Mktng, Software Corp. of America; US; 203/359-2773, dfeldstein@talkthru.com

Felice, Don; Ed, Conference Analysis Newsletter; US; 617/577-9595, dfelice@gigasd.com

Felker, Fred; Pres, Seek Systems Inc.; US; 206/822-7400

Fellowes, Jim; Pres & COO, Fellowes Manufacturing Co.; US; 708/893-1600

Fellowes, John E.; Chmn & CEO, Fellowes Manufacturing Co.; US; 708/893-1600

Fellowes, Peter; EVP, Fellowes Manufacturing Co.; US; 708/893-1600

Fellows, William; Ed, Unigram.X; US; 516/759-7025, wif@panix.com

Felt, Bruce; VP Fin, Qualix Group Inc.; US; 415/572-0200, bfelt@qualix.com

Felt, Richard K.; Pblr, 3X/400 Systems Management; US; 708/427-9512, 71333.730@compuserve.com

Felt, Richard K.; Pblr, Adams/Hunter Publishing; US; 708/427-9512, 71333.730@compuserve.com

Felton, Carol; VP & GM, Simon/McGarry PR; US; 408/746-0911

Felton, Raymond; Dir Sales & Mktng, Fiber & Wireless Inc.; US; 310/787-7097

Femia, Vincent; VP Dev, Concentric Data Systems Inc.; US; 508/366-1122

Fencer, H. Jeffrey; COO, ProfitKey International Inc.; US; 603/898-9800

Feng, Mike; VP, Mustek Inc.; US; 714/247-1300

Fenimore, Scott; VP Mktng & Sales, Data Pro Accounting Software Inc.; US; 813/885-9459

Fenn, Wade R.; SVP Sales, Best Buy Co. Inc.; US; 612/947-2000

Fenner, William I.; VP & COO, Lasergate Systems Inc.; US; 813/725-0882

Ferelli, Mark C.; Sr Ed, Computer Technology Review; US; 310/208-1335, mark_ferelli@wwpi.com

Feretic, Eileen; Ed-in-Chief, Beyond Computing; US; 212/745-6347, eferetic@vnet.ibm.com

Ferguson, Donald R.; SVP, Tenera L.P.; US; 510/845-5200

Ferguson, Erec; VP Ops, RFI Controls Co.; US; 408/399-7007

Ferguson, George E.; Prod Mktng Mgr, Ambit International; US; 415/957-9433

Ferguson, Gregor N.; EVP, Xyplex Inc.; US; 508/952-4700

Ferguson, Jane; Ed, Curriculum Administrator; US; 203/322-1300

Ferguson, Jeffrey S.; Dir Tech, TDC Interactive; US; 310/452-6720

Ferguson, Kevin; Ed, Computer Retail Week; US; 516/733-6800, kferguso@cmp.com

Ferguson, William C.; Chmn, NYNEX Corp.; US; 212/395-2121

Fernandes, Gary J.; SVP, EDS; US; 214/604-6000

Fernandez, Manny; Pres & CEO, Gartner Group; US; 203/964-0096

Ferra, Dennis J.; SVP, Alltel Corp.; US; 501/661-8000

Ferrara, Carol; Treas, Security Microsystems Inc.; US

Ferrara, John; VP, Security Microsystems Inc.; US

Ferrara, Jon V.; EVP, GoldMine Software Corp.; US; 310/454-6800

Ferrara, Ralph; Pres, Security Microsystems Inc.; US; 71171.104@compuserve.com

Ferrara-Kurth, Kierith; Mktng Mgr, Numerical Algorithms Group Inc.; US; 630/971-2337, ferrara@nag.com

Ferraro, Anthony J.; Pblr, IEEE Spectrum; US; 908/981-0060

Ferraro, Opal P.; CFO, Neostar Retail Group Inc.; US; 214/401-9000

Ferrell, Tom; Tech Mktng Mgr, Compatible Systems Corp.; US; 303/444-9532, tom@compatible.com

Ferrentino, Andrew B.; Pres, Template Software Inc.; US; 703/318-1000, andy@template.com

Ferris, Anne M.; Exec Dir, ATM Forum; US; 415/949-6700

Ferris, Nancy; Mgng Ed, Government Computer News; US; 301/650-2000

Festa, John R.; Pres & CEO, Iterated Systems Inc.; US; 770/840-0310

Feuer, Michael; Chmn & CEO, Office-

Max Inc.; US; 216/921-6900

Feuerstein, Jim; SVP & CTO, Docucon Inc.; US; 210/525-9221

Fevery, Patrick; VP & CFO, Rainbow Technologies Inc.; US; 714/450-7300

Fickes, David; Dir Mktng, Prime Time Freeware; US; 408/433-9662, david@advice.com

Fidanza, Cesare; Chmn, SofTeam US Inc.; US; 410/243-1130

Fiddler, Jerry L.; Chmn, Wind River Systems Inc.; US; 510/748-4100

Fidler, William; EVP SW Dev, Motion Pixels; US; 602/951-3288

Fieder, David; Tech Ed, Information-WEEK Open Labs; US; 516/562-5000

Fiedler, David; Ed-in-Chief, Web Developer; US; 203/226-6967, david@webdeveloper.com

Fiehler, Mel; MIS/DP Mgr, Metrologic Instruments Inc.; US; 609/228-8100

Fields, Craig; Pres & CEO, Microelectronics & Computer Technology Corp.; US; 512/343-0978

Fields, Michael; COO, Genasys II Inc.; US; 970/493-0035, mikef@genasys.com

Fields, Richard; VP & CFO, Powerhouse Entertainment; US; 214/933-5400

Fields, Scott; Ed, Do It With Macintosh System 7.5; US; 617/482-8785

Fieser, Barbara; Exec Dir, Computer Law Assoc.; US; 703/560-7747

Filak, Richard J.; VP & CFO, Xiox Corp.; US; 415/375-8188

Filipowski, Andrew J.; Chmn, Pres & CEO, Platinum Technology Inc.; US; 708/620-5000

Fillinich, Paul; Mktng Mgr, AT&T Software Solutions Group; US; 908/580-6444

Filo, David; Co-Founder, Yahoo Corp.; US; 415/934-3230

Finch, Ted; VP Mktng, Virtus Corp.; US; 919/467-9700, ted.finch@virtus.com

Fine, Robert W.; VP Sales, Security Dynamics Technologies Inc.; US; 617/547-7820

Fine Coburn, Karen; Pblr, Corporate Internet Strategies; US; 617/648-8702

Finegold, Aryeh; Chmn & CEO, Mercury Interactive Corp.; US; 408/523-9900

Finerman, Aaron; Ed, Computing Reviews; US; 212/869-7440

Fink, John; EVP, V Communications Inc.; US; 408/296-4224

Finke, James; Pres, Interconsult; US; 603/964-6464

Finke, Paul; Pres & CEO, Performance Technology Inc.; US; 210/979-2000, paulf@perftech.com

Finkel, Mark; CFO, Logic Works Inc.; US; 609/514-1177

Finkelman, Lauren; VP, S&S Public Relations Inc.; US; 847/291-1616, 76225.2253@compuserve.com

Finkelstein, Richard; Pres, Performance Computing; US; 312/549-8325

Finlay, Matthew; Mgng Dir, CD-ROMs

in Print; US; 203/226-6967

Finley, T. Glyn; VP Mkt Res, Electronic Industries Assoc.; US; 703/907-7500

Finn, Peter; Principal, Ruder-Finn; US; 212/593-6393

Finn, Roger A.; VP & COO, MPSI Systems Inc.; US; 918/250-9611

Finnie, Graham; Ed, CommunicationsWeek Int'l.; US; 516/562-5530, @gfinnie.demon.co.uk

Finocchio Jr., Robert J.; EVP, 3Com Corp.; US; 408/764-5000

Fiore Jr., Anthony N.; VP Bus Dev, Computervision Corp.; US; 617/275-1800

Fiorentino, Gilbert; Pres & CEO, Bloc Development Corp.; US; 305/445-0903

Firth, Paul; Pres, LearnIT Corp.; US; 904/375-6655

Fisch, Steven M.; Pres & CEO, International Software Group Inc.; US; 617/221-1450

Fischbach, Gregory; Chmn & CEO, Acclaim Entertainment Inc.; US; 516/624-8888

Fischer, Addison M.; Chmn, Fischer International Systems Corp.; US; 941/643-1500

Fischer, Charles N.; Ed-in-Chief, ACM Letters on Programming Languages & Systems; US; 212/869-7440

Fischer, Dale; VP Intl Sales, Metrologic Instruments Inc.; US; 609/228-8100

Fischer, Kurt; VP, International Compliance Corp.; US; 817/491-3696

Fisco, David; Ed, Java Report; US; 212/242-7447

Fish, Murray P.; Pres & CEO, Real-World Corp.; US; 603/641-0200

Fisher, Alan; SW Partner, Onsale; US; 415/428-0600

Fisher, Alan; Pres, Software Partners Inc.; US; 415/428-0160

Fisher, Bruce; Dir Mktng & Bus Dev, Electronic Form Systems; US; 214/243-4343

Fisher, George; Ed, Data Sources; US; 212/503-5861

Fisher, George M.C.; Chmn, Pres & CEO, Eastman Kodak Co.; US; 716/724-4000

Fisher, Jeffrey; EVP, Foresight Software; US; 770/206-1000

Fisher, Mark; Pres & Chmn, SMDS Interest Group Inc.; US; 415/578-6979

Fisher, Marshall; Chmn & CEO, IdeaFisher Systems Inc.; US; 714/474-8111

Fisher, P. Edward; VP Prod Dev, Micro-Integration Corp.; US; 301/689-0800

Fisher, Robert J.; Pres, Fisher Business Communications Inc.; US; 714/556-1313

Fisher, Ronald D.; Chmn & CEO, Phoenix Technologies Ltd.; US; 408/654-9000

Fisher, Sarah; Dir Mktng, Psion Inc.; US; 508/371-0310

Fishman, Jerald G.; Pres & COO, Analog Devices Inc.; US; 617/329-4700

Fiste, Rusty; VP R&D, XDB Systems

Inc.; US; 410/312-9300

Fitch, Jon; Sr Dir Eng, Power Computing Corp.; US; 408/526-0500

Fitzgerald, Albert; Pres, Answers Research; US; 619/792-4660

Fitzgerald, Brian; VP Sales, Racal Inter-Lan Inc.; US; 508/263-9929

Fitzgerald, Gale S.; Chmn & CEO, Computer Task Group Inc.; US; 716/887-7424, gale.fitzgerald@ctg.com

Fitzgerald, Susan; Exec Dir, Commercial Internet eXchange Assoc.; US; 703/318-7218, sfitzger@cix.org

Fitzgerald, W. Paul; SVP & CFO, EMC Corp.; US; 508/435-1000

FitzGerald, Maura; Pres, FitzGerald Communications Inc.; US; 617/494-9500

Fitzgibbons, Debra J.; Dir Client Svcs, Delphi Consulting Group Inc.; US; 617/247-1025

Fitzpatrick, Michael J.; Pres Pactel Enterprises, Pacific Telesis Group; US; 415/394-3000

Fitzsimmons, C. Victor; SVP WW Mfg, Printronix Inc.; US; 714/863-1900

Fitzsimmons, Robert C.; SVP Sales & Mktng, Relay Technology Inc.; US; 703/506-0500

Fixmer, Timothy J.; Pblr, NEWS/400; US; 970/663-4700

Fjeldstad, Lucie; VP, Tektronix Inc.; US; 503/627-7111

Flack, David; Ed-in-Chief, Open Computing; US; 415/513-6800, davef@uworld.com

Flagg, Howard; Pres, PairGain Technologies Inc.; US; 714/832-9924

Flahertly, Sean; VP Eng, Graphsoft Inc.; US; 410/290-5114

Flaherty, Brian; Dir Dist Sales, Primax Electronics; US; 408/522-1200

Flaherty, Ross A.; Pres, Association for Systems Management; US; 216/243-6900

Flanagan, Bernard T.; VP Mktng, Dow Jones & Company Inc.; US; 212/416-2000

Flanagan, Don; VP Sales, Arcada Software Inc.; US; 407/333-7500

Flanagan, Mark D.; EVP, Kurzweil Applied Intelligence; US; 617/893-5151

Flanagan, Terry; VP, Copia International Ltd.; US; 708/682-8898

Flanayan, Dennis P.; Pres & CEO, Okidata; US; 609/235-2600

Flanders, Scott; Pres, Macmillan Computer Publishing; US; 317/581-3500

Flanigan, Matt; Pres, Telecommunications Industry Assoc.; US; 703/907-7700

Flanigan, William; VP Mktng, Fast-Comm Communications Corp.; US; 703/318-7750

Flannery, Ed; VP & GM, Fibronics International Inc.; US; 508/671-9440, edflannery@fibusa.com

Flannery, Heidi A.; Pres, Fi.Comm; US; 503/221-7407

Flashenberg, Richard; VP, Coast Manufacturing Co.; US; 914/376-1500

Flavio, John J.; SVP & CFO, Digital Systems Int'l.; US; 206/881-7544

Fleiss, Edward; Tech Sales Mgr, Marcus Technology Inc.; US; 212/678-0406

Flemig, Steve; Prod Mktng Mgr, LXE; US; 770/447-4224

Fleming, Maureen; Pres, Digital Information Group; US; 203/348-2751

Fleming, Samuel; CEO, Decision Resources Inc.; US; 617/487-3700

Fleming, Steve; Mgr Ops, AirWorks Media; Canada; 403/424-9922

Flesher, Tom; EVP, E-Net Corp.; US; 415/433-3800

Fletcher Tweedy, Kevin; SVP, Vision Software Tools Inc.; US; 510/238-4100

Fleury, Gerard; CFO, Media Cybernetics L.P.; US; 301/495-3305, gerard@mediacy.com

Flinkerbusch, Dwight; Prod Mktng Mgr, Ryan-McFarland; US; 512/343-1010

Floathe, Maury; Pres, Floathe Johnson Associates Inc.; US; 206/285-6056

Flohr, Daniel; Chmn, Pres & CEO, Target Technologies Inc.; US; 910/395-6100

Flood, Gary; Ed, Software Futures; US; 212/677-0409

Florence, Frank; Pres, Parallax Graphics Inc.; US; 408/727-2220

Flory, Bruce; Dir Mktng, Liant Software Corp.; US; 508/872-8700

Floryan, Lawrence R.; VP & CTO, Banyan Systems Inc.; US; 508/898-1000

Flower, Jon; Pres, ParSoft Corp.; US; 818/305-0041

Flowers, Melvin L.; VP & CFO, ACT Networks Inc.; US; 805/388-2474

Floyd, Chuck; CFO, Inland Assoc.; US; 913/746-7977

Flury, William H.; VP Sales, Zebra Technologies VTI Inc.; US; 801/576-9700

Flynn, Kathleen; VP Fin & Admin, Sentry Publishing Co. Inc.; US; 508/366-2031

Flynn, Michael T.; Pres Com Group, Alltel Corp.; US; 501/661-8000

Flynn, Mike; Pblr, Embedded Systems Programming; US; 415/905-2200, mflynn@mfi.com

Flynn, Patrick J.; Pres K-Byte Mfg, Reptron Electronics Inc.; US; 813/854-2351

Flynt, Larry; Pblr, LFP Inc.; US; 310/858-7155

Fobel, John; VP, Rancho Technology Inc.; US; 909/987-3966

Foden, Athol M.; Mktng Dir, Maxpeed Corp.; US; 415/345-5447, afoden@maxpeed.com

Fogel, Schmuel; VP, Data Systems & Software Inc.; US; 201/529-2026

Fohn, Stephanie; Dir Bus Dev, Pilot Network Services Inc.; US; 510/748-1850

Foley, Barbara; Acct Mgr, D/M Communications Inc.; US; 617/329-7799

Foley, Paul; Co-Founder, Image Axis Inc.; US; 212/989-5000

Foley, Thomas R.; Pres & CEO, Datawatch Corp.; US; 508/988-9700

Folino, Paul F.; Pres & CEO, Emulex Corp.; US; 714/662-5600

Folk, Roy E.; Pres & COO, ClariNet Communications Corp.; US; 408/296-0366, rfolk@clarinet.com

Fong, Peggy; CFO, Hercules Computer Technology Inc.; US; 510/623-6030

Fontana, Richard; Pres, DataViz Inc.; US; 203/268-0030

Foo, Pin; VP Prod Dev, Saros Corp.; US; 206/646-1066

Foody, Michael; Pres, Visual Edge Software Ltd.; Canada; 514/332-6430, mike@vedge.com

Foos, Terri; Pres, McGrath/Power PR; US; 408/727-0351

Foran, Ken; VP R&D, Rubbermaid Office Products Inc.; US; 615/977-5477

Forbeck, Michael; Dir Sales & Mktng, SL Waber Inc.; US; 609/866-8888

Forbes, Ron; CFO, Micro Focus Inc.; US; 415/856-4161, rhf@mfltd.co.uk

Forbes III, Kenneth S.; Pres, Adaptiv Software Inc.; US; 714/789-7300, kforbes@adaptiv.com

Force, Chris; CFO, Datastorm Technologies Inc.; US; 573/443-3282

Force, Peter T.; VP Sales & Mktng, Dynamic Graphics Inc.; US; 309/688-8800

Forcillo, Michael L.; Pblr, PC Graphics & Video; US; 714/513-8400, mforcillo@pcgv.com

Ford, Brian; Pres, Numerical Algorithms Group Inc.; US; 630/971-2337

Ford, Jeff; Tech Ed, WordPerfect for Windows Magazine; US; 801/226-5555

Ford, Joe T.; Chmn, Pres & CEO, Alltel Corp.; US; 501/661-8000

Ford, John; Sales Mgr, Seek Systems Inc.; US; 206/822-7400

Ford, John M.; EVP, ArborText Inc.; US; 313/996-3566

Ford, Ken; Ed-in-Chief, AAAI Press; US; 415/328-3123

Ford, Martin; CFO, Open Software Foundation; US; 508/474-9258

Ford, Patrick; Pres & CEO, Splash Studios Inc.; US; 206/882-0300, fordy@aol.com

Ford Jr., William; VP & GM, Business Research Group; US; 617/630-3900, ford@brg.cahners.com

Forecki, Paul; VP, Sterling Communications Inc.; US; 408/441-4100, pforecki@sterlingpr.com

Forester, Jeff; SVP Sales, Spectrum Holobyte Inc.; US; 510/522-3584

Forkel, Barbara; VP Sales & Mktng, Faulkner Information Services; US; 609/662-2070

Forman, Edward A.; VP Mktng, Connect Inc.; US; 415/254-4000, edforman@connectinc.com

Forney, Craig; Pres & CEO, Opus Systems Inc.; US; 408/562-9340, craig@opus.com

Forquer, Bill; Pres & CEO, Information

Dimensions Inc.; US; 614/761-8083

Forsee, Gary D.; Pres & COO Long Dist Div, Sprint Corp.; US; 913/624-3000

Forst, Elizabeth; Ed-in-Chief, Pix; US; 212/536-5222

Forster, Karl; VP SW Dev, Mastersoft Inc.; US; 602/948-4888, karl@mastersoft.com

Forsyth, R. Hamish; Pres, mFactory Inc.; US; 415/548-0600

Forsythe, Stephanie J.; CFO, DTC Data Technology Corp.; US; 408/942-4000

Fort, Clancy; Pblr, Carronad's Interactive Media Directory; US; 310/493-2330

Fortner, Brand; Chmn, Fortner Research LLC; US; 703/478-0181, brand@fortner.com

Fortun, Wayne M.; CEO, Hutchinson Technology Inc.; US; 612/587-3797

Foss, Gary D.; EVP Mktng, Office Depot Inc.; US; 407/278-4800

Fossum, Jeffrey J.; CFO, Effective Management Systems; US; 414/359-9800

Foster, Charles E.; Group VP, SBC Communications Inc.; US; 210/821-4105

Foster, Dennis E.; CEO, 360 Communications; US; 312/399-2500

Foster, Eagan; VP, Association of Personal Computer Users Group; US

Foster, Jeffrey C.; Dir Mktng, Glare/Guard; US

Foster, Jim; Pres, Abra Cadabra Software; US; 813/527-1111

Foster, Kent B.; Pres, GTE Corp.; US; 203/965-2000

Foster, Larry; Chmn, Pres & CEO, Midisoft Corp.; US; 206/391-3610

Foster, Lynn; Sales Mgr, Fortner Research LLC; US; 703/478-0181, lynn@fortner.com

Foster, Maile; Dir Mktng, Basis Int'l.; US; 505/345-5232, mfoster@basis.com

Foster, Ronald C.; VP Ops, Egghead Inc.; US; 509/922-7031

Foster, Toni L.; Sales Mgr, FTG Data Systems; US; 714/995-3900

Foster, William C.; COO, VidTech Microsystems Inc.; US; 612/633-6000

Foster, William E.; Chmn & CEO, Stratus Computer Inc.; US; 508/460-2000

Foucault, Hoyt; Pres, Specialix Inc.; US; 408/378-7919

Fought, Bonnie E.; VP & CFO, Connectix Corp.; US; 415/571-5100

Foundyller, Charles; Chmn & Pres, Daratech Inc.; US; 617/354-2339

Fournier, Bruce R.; VP Sales, TriQuint Semiconductor; US; 503/644-3535

Fourt, Jean-Francois; Pres, European Economic Development Agency; US; 415/282-6330

Fowler, D. Mark; Pres & CEO, Systech Corp.; US; 619/453-8970

Fowler, Dave; VP Sales & Mktng, Gradient Technologies; US; 508/624-9600

Fowler, David B.; VP Sales & MKtng, FTP Software Inc.; US; 508/685-4000

Fowler, Donald; CEO, Worlds Inc.; US; 415/281-4878

Fowler, Pete R.; VP Sales & Mktng, Brooktree Corp.; US; 619/452-7580

Fowler Ross, Tara; Mgng Ed, AutoCAD World; US; 512/250-9023

Fox, David; Computer Events Directory; US; 415/485-5508, david@kweb.com

Fox, Edward L.; Pres, Fox Electronics; US; 941/693-0099

Fox, Joeseph; Chmn, Template Software Inc.; US; 703/318-1000, fox@template.com

Fox, Kelli; Computer Events Directory; US; 415/485-5508, kelli@kweb.com

Fox, Kimberly; Sec, Upstart Communications; US; 510/420-7979, kfox@upstart.com

Fox, Larry J.; Chmn & CEO, Symix Systems Inc.; US; 614/523-7000

Fox, Leonard; Pres & CEO, LaserScan Systems Inc.; US; 305/777-1300

Fox, Trent; VP Bus Dev, Cyco Int'l.; US; 404/634-3302

Fox Jr., Edward L.; VP Sales & Mktng, Fox Electronics; US; 941/693-0099

Frain, Henry; Pres, Compusearch Software Systems Inc.; US; 703/893-7200

Franca, Franco; VP Mktng, FutureTel Inc.; US; 408/522-1400

France, G. Scott; CEO, InVision Interactive; US; 415/812-7380

France Jr., James W.; Chmn, Pres & CEO, Scriptel Holdings Inc.; US; 614/276-8402

Francesconi, Joseph J.; Pres & CEO, Network Equipment Technologies Inc.; US; 415/366-4400

Franch, James V.; VP Tech, System Software Associates Inc.; US; 312/258-6000

Francis, Fritz; VP Ops, Online Environs Inc.; US; 617/225-0449

Francis, Kenneth A.; EVP, McDonnell Douglas Corp.; US; 314/232-0232

Francis, Lee; Dir WW Dist, Recital Corp.; US; 508/750-1066, lfrancis@recital.com

Francis, Martin S.; Pres, LTX Corp.; US; 617/461-1000

Francis, Norm; Pres, Pivotal Software Inc.; Canada; 604/988-9982, nfrancis@pivotalsoft.com

Francis, Terry; VP Sales, Spur Products Corp.; US; 208/377-0001

Frank, Armin; GM, NSM Jukebox America Inc.; US; 708/860-5100

Frank, Bill; Pres, Augur Visions Inc.; US; 415/493-5011, theaugur@aol.com

Frank, Jeff; SVP Sales, Deltec Corp.; US; 619/291-4211

Frank, Kenneth; Pres, Technology Group Inc., The; US; 410/576-2040

Frank, Maurice; Ed, DBMS; US; 415/358-9500

Frank, Werner L.; EVP Bus Dev, Sterling Software Inc.; US; 214/891-8600

Franke, Richard; Dir Sales & Mktng,

Pulse Metric Inc.; US; 619/546-9461

Franklin, Burke; Pres, Jian Tools for Sales Inc.; US; 415/254-5600, burke@jianusa.com

Franklin, Jody; Sales Mgr, Synchronics; US; 901/761-1166

Franklin Jr., Curtis; Dir, Client/Server Labs; US; 404/552-3645

Frantz, Mark; Ed, Retail Info Systems News; US; 201/895-3397

Frappaolo, Carl; EVP, Delphi Consulting Group Inc.; US; 617/247-1025

Fraser, Rusty; EVP, Champion Business Systems Inc.; US; 303/792-3606

Frauenfelder, Lew; Pres, Datasonix Corp.; US; 303/545-9500

Frazer, Miriam K.; VP & CFO, Software Publishing Corp.; US; 408/537-3000

Frazier, Allen; Chmn & CEO, DP-Tek Inc.; US; 316/687-3000

Frazier, Belinda; VP, Specialized Systems Consultants Inc.; US; 206/782-7733, bbf@ssc.com

Frecker, Alfred N.; VP Sales, Riso Inc.; US; 508/777-7377

Frederick, Thomas; Pres SW Div, Recognition International Inc.; US; 214/579-6000

Fredrickson, Bruce; Pres, Channel Tactics; US; 303/581-0952

Freece, Robert A.; SVP, Vishay Intertechnology; US; 610/644-1300

Freedman, Eugene M.; Chmn, Coopers & Lybrand; US; 212/536-2000

Freedman, Glenn; Pres, L.I.S.T. Inc.; US; 516/482-2345

Freedman, Rick; Dir Mktng, Specialix Inc.; US; 408/378-7919

Freeman, Andrew; Sales & Mktng Dir, Intelligent Micro Software Ltd.; US; 407/726-0024, 100012.1270@compuserve.com

Freeman, Bruce; Pres, ProLine Communications Inc.; US; 201/716-9457

Freeman, Douglas; Partner, Freeman-McCue; US; 714/557-3663

Freeman, Ian; CTO, Thot Technologies; US; 408/370-4600

Freeman, Marshall W.; Pres & CEO, Miller Freeman Inc.; US; 415/905-2200

Freeman, Jr., Raymond C.; Pres, Freeman Associates Inc.; US; 805/963-3853, ray@freemaninc.com

Freer, Carol; Mgng Ed, Online Access; US; 312/573-1700

Freestone, Lane; VP Bus Dev, Zenographics Inc.; US; 714/851-6352

Freid, Wendy; Mktng Mgr, Hertz Computer Corp.; US; 212/684-4141

Freitag, John D.; Chmn, Computone Corp.; US; 770/475-2725

French, Christine; Mgng Ed, Reseller Management; US; 617/558-4772, cfrench@rm.cahners.com

French, Donald D.; VP & GM Computer Prod, Analog Devices Inc.; US; 617/329-4700

French, John G.; Pblr, Electronic Design; US; 201/393-6060

French, Michael; Dir Mkt Res, Mobile Insights Inc.; US; 415/390-9800, mfrench@mobileinsights.com

Frendberg, Robyn E.; Mgng Ed, UNIX Review; US; 415/358-9500

Frenkel, Karen A.; Producer Spec Proj, ACM Press; US; 212/626-0500

Frentz, William; EVP, Number Nine Visual Technology Corp.; US; 617/674-0009

Fresco, Paolo; Vice Chmn, General Electric Co.; US; 203/373-2211

Frese, Vincent; Pres, Maximum Computer Technologies Inc.; US; 770/428-5000, vince@maxtech.com

Freund, Mark; VP Mktng, Remedy Corp.; US; 415/903-5200

Frey, Rod; CFO, Performance Technology Inc.; US; 210/979-2000, rod@perftech.com

Frey Jr., Philip; Chmn, Pres & CEO, Microsemi Corp.; US; 714/979-8220

Fried, Robert; CTO, Staples Inc.; US; 508/370-8500

Friedberger, Roger D.; SVP & CFO, Insignia Solutions Inc.; US; 408/327-6000

Friedland, Richard S.; Chmn & CEO, General Instrument Corp.; US; 312/695-1000

Friedman, Corey; Pblr, Internet World; US; 203/226-6967, cfriedman@mecklermedia.com

Friedman, Edward; Chmn, TeleTypesetting Co.; US; 617/734-9700

Friedman, Jack; Pres & CEO, T-HQ; US; 818/591-1310

Friedman, Joel S.; SVP Ops, General Signal Corp.; US; 203/329-4100

Friedman, Justin; VP, International Technology Consultants; US; 202/234-2138

Friedman, Marc; Dir, Grassroots Research; US; 415/954-5376

Friedman, Mark; Ed & Pblr, Capacity Management Review; US; 813/261-8945

Friedman, Michael J.; Pres & CEO, Pinnacle Publishing Inc.; US; 206/251-1900

Friedman, Richard P.; Pres, SIGS Publications Group; US; 212/242-7447

Friedman, Ronald F.; Pres & COO, Group 1 Software; US; 301/731-2300

Friedman, Ronald F.; Dir, Comnet Corp.; US; 301/918-0400

Friedman, Stuart; VP Sales, Symphony Laboratories; US; 408/986-1701

Friesen, Gerry; Pblr, Telecom Library Inc.; US; 212/691-8215

Frigstad, David; Pres & CEO, Frost & Sullivan Inc.; US; 415/961-9000

Friscia, Tony; Pres, Advanced Manufacturing Research; US; 617/542-6600

Frison, Steve; VP Dev, Now Software Inc.; US; 503/274-2800

Fritsch, Bill; Pres, CF2GS; US; 206/223-6464

Fritz, Ray M.; CFO, Clarify Inc.; US; 408/428-2000

Frohen, Tod W.; SVP Ops, Megahertz Corp.; US; 801/320-7000

Frohman, Doug; VP Bus Dev, Digital Frontiers; US; 847/328-0880, douglasf@digfrontiers.com

Froman, Stuart; Dir Mktng, Aimnet Corp.; US; 408/257-0900

Fromberg, Barry; SVP, Paging Network Inc.; US; 214/985-4100

Frost, Mark; Ed-in-Chief, Net, The; US; 415/696-1661

Frost, Pam; Ed, Advanced Manufacturing Technology; US; 201/568-4744, amtinfo@insights.com

Frudden, Connie; VP Tech Svcs, Gyrus Systems Inc.; US; 804/320-1414, frudden@ix.netcom.com

Frueh, George T.; Mng Ed, ECN, Electronic Component News; US; 610/964-4343, gfrueh@chilton.com

Frustaci, Pat R.; VP Fin, LCS Industries Inc.; US; 201/778-5588

Frye, Russell H.; Pres, Frye Computer Systems Inc.; US; 617/451-5400

Fryer, Jeff; CFO, Cosmi Corp.; US; 310/833-2000

Fu, Jerry; VP Mfg, Lion Optics Corp.; US; 408/954-8089

Fu, Sai-Wai; VP Eng, C-Cube Microsystems Inc.; US; 408/944-6300

Fuchs, Bill; Pres & CEO, Simucad Inc.; US; 415/487-9700

Fuchs, Eli; VP Eng, GCC Technologies Inc.; US; 617/275-5800

Fuente, David I.; Chmn & CEO, Office Depot Inc.; US; 407/278-4800

Fugitt, Lem; EVP, Seiko Instruments US Inc.; US; 408/922-5900

Fujii, Hiro; Pres, Minolta Corp.; US; 201/825-4000

Fujimura, Aki; VP Eng, Pure Software Inc.; US; 408/720-1600

Fulcher, Jim; Sr Ed, Manufacturing Systems; US; 708/665-1000

Fulcher Linkins, Kim; Ed, Sun Observer, The; US; 512/250-9023

Fulgoni, Gian M.; CEO, Information Resources Inc.; US; 312/726-1221

Fullam, Murial; Bus Mgr, Telecom Library Inc.; US; 212/691-8215

Fuller, Dale L.; VP, NEC Technologies Inc.; US; 508/264-8000

Fuller, Heidi; Dir Acct Svcs, Smith & Shows; US; 415/329-8880, fullerh@aol.com

Fuller, Maurice; Dir Mktng, Parallel Technologies Inc.; US; 206/883-6900

Fuller, Sarah; Pres, Decision Resources Inc.; US; 617/487-3700

Fullmer, Paul; Pres & CEO, Selz, Seabolt & Associates Inc.; US; 312/372-7090

Fultz, Robert B.; Dir Sales & Mktng, NovaLink Technologies Inc.; US; 510/249-9777

Fulweiler, Charles R.; CEO, Casady &

Greene Inc.; US; 408/484-9228

Funess, Richar; Pres, Ruder Finn Inc.; US; 312/645-4835

Funk, Paul; Pres, Funk Software Inc.; US; 617/497-6339

Furlong, Bill; Pblr, Business Marketing; US; 312/649-5260

Furness, Thomas A.; Sr Ed, Presence: Teleoperators & Virtual Environments; US; 617/253-2889, presence@cbgrle.mit.edu

Furry, Carl; Exec Ed, IRIS Universe; US; 415/390-2079

Furst, Allen; Pres, Asian Projects; US; 617/576-1389

Furukawa, Hironori; VP & GM, Mitsui Comtek Corp.; US; 408/725-8525

Fylstra, Daniel; Pres & CEO, Frontline Systems Inc.; US; 702/831-0300, dfylstra@frontsys.com

Gabay, Sonya; VP, Young & Associates Inc.; US; 301/309-9404

Gabelhouse, Gary; CEO, Fairfield Research Inc.; US; 402/441-3370

Gable, Gene; Pblr, Publish; US; 415/978-3280, ggable@publish.com

Gable, Mel; Pres & CEO, QLogic Corp.; US; 714/438-2200

Gabral, Gil; Pres & COO, Micom Communications Corp.; US; 805/583-8600

Gaddis, Gayle; Ed, Telecom Strategy Letter, The; US; 212/732-0775

Gaden, Dorothy K.; VP Mktng, Copia International Ltd.; US; 708/682-8898

Gage, Thomas; VP, Gemini Consulting; US; 201/285-9000

Gage, William R.; Chmn, SBE Inc.; US; 510/355-2000

Gagliano, Sam; Pblr, BASIC TWO Report; US; 508/682-8100

Gagliardi, Gary; Pres, FourGen Software Inc.; US; 206/522-0055

Gagnier, Hugh K.; Pres & COO, Eltron International Inc.; US; 805/579-1800

Gagnon, Eric; Author, What's on the Internet; US; 510/548-4393

Gagnon, Jim; CTO, Abacus Concepts Inc.; US; 510/540-1949

Gagnon, Robert; EVP, SoftKey International Inc.; US; 617/494-1200

Gagon, Roger; Tech Ed, WordPerfect Magazine; US; 801/226-5555, rogerg@wpmag.com

Gahan, Laurie; Dir Sales & Mktng, SL Waber Inc.; US; 609/866-8888

Gahman, Gary; Sales Mgr, Boston Computer Exchange; US; 617/542-4414

Gaidano, Scott; Pres, Drive Savers Inc.; US; 415/382-2000

Gain, Dennis T.; Chmn & CEO, Spacetec IMC Corp.; US; 508/970-0330

Gale, James C.; SVP & CFO, Genicom Corp.; US; 703/802-9200

Gale, John; Pres, Information Workstation Group; US; 703/548-4320

Galken, Sergei; Ed, Russian Telecom; US; 617/232-3111, igiboston@aol.com

Gall, Jeff; Dir Sales, Pilot Network Ser-

vices Inc.; US; 510/748-1850, gall@pilot.net

Gallagher, Brian; Assist Ed, Software Developer & Pblr; US; 303/745-5711

Gallagher, David; Pres, QSound Labs Inc.; Canada; 403/291-2492

Gallagher, Philip; Ed Dir, CeBIT News; Belgium; 322-766-0031

Gallagher, Thomas; EVP Chief Legal Counsel, Bull HN Information Systems Inc.; US; 508/294-6000

Gallagher, William; Exec Dir, Society for Computer Simulation; US; 619/277-3888

Gallant, John; Ed-in-Chief, Network World; US; 508/875-6400

Galley, C. James; Dir, PC Labs; US; 212/503-5255

Galliford, Gregory S.; VP Fin, Abacus Concepts Inc.; US; 510/540-1949

Galloway, Benny; CFO, IPC Technologies Inc.; US; 512/339-3500

Gallup, Patricia; Chmn & CEO, PC Connections Inc.; US; 603/446-3383

Galusha, Gary; SVP Mktng, Maxtor Corp.; US; 408/432-1700

Galvin, Christopher B.; Pres & COO, Motorola Inc.; US; 847/576-5000

Galvin, Michael; Chmn & Pres, Media Cybernetics L.P.; US; 301/495-3305

Galvin, Robert W.; Chmn, Motorola Inc.; US; 847/576-5000

Galvin, W.J.; SVP & CFO, Emerson Electric Co.; US; 314/553-2000

Gamba, John F.; SVP, Bell Atlantic Corp.; US; 215/963-6000

Gammons, Rori; Mgr Sales & Mktng, Unitrac Software Corp.; US; 616/344-0220, rgammons@unitrac.com

Gamradt, John; Chmn, Dallas Digital Corp.; US; 214/424-2800

Gang, David; VP Sales & Mktng, First Floor Inc.; US; 415/968-1101

Ganguly, Anik; Pres, Campbell Services Inc.; US; 810/559-5955

Gannes, Stuart; CEO, Books That Work; US; 415/326-4280

Gannon, Edward F.; Dir Mktng & Sales, NetPro Computing Inc.; US; 602/941-3600

Gannon, William A.; Pres, Sentry Publishing Co. Inc.; US; 508/366-2031

Gannon Jr., William; Dir, Sentry Market Research; US; 508/366-2031

Ganor, Elon A.; Chmn & CEO, VocalTec Inc.; US; 201/768-9400

Ganson, Scott; VP Sales, Voicetek Corp.; US; 508/250-9393

Gantz, John; SVP, International Data Corp.; US; 508/872-8200, jgantz@idcresearch.com

Garb, Stuart; Nat'l Sales Mgr, Jazz Speakers; US; 818/336-2689

Garbacz, Gerald G.; Pres & CEO, Nashua Corp.; US; 603/880-2323

Garbe, Michael; CEO, Willowbrook Technologies Inc.; Canada; 905/660-8795

Garber, Jonathan F.; VP Tech, Connectix Corp.; US; 415/571-5100

Garcia, Anne M.; Dir IS, Datamark Inc.; US; 915/778-1944

Garcia, Art; Ed & Pblr, High-Tech Hot Wire/High-Tech Hot Sheet; US; 415/421-6220, agarcia@aol.com

Garcia, John A.; Pres & CEO, NovaLogic Inc.; US; 818/880-1997, jgarcia@nova-logic.com

Gard, Clifford; Dir Sales, Digicom Systems Inc.; US; 408/262-1277

Gardner, Bruce R.; EVP & CFO, Datawatch Corp.; US; 508/988-9700

Gardner, Michael; Pres, IQ Engineering; US; 408/733-1161

Gardner, Mike; SVP Cust Ops, UB Networks; US; 408/496-0111

Gardner, Richard; SVP NA Sales, BMC Software Inc.; US; 713/918-8800

Garlick, Lawrence L.; Chmn, Pres & CEO, Remedy Corp.; US; 415/903-5200

Garman, Nancy; Ed, Online User; US; 203/761-1466, ngarman@well.com

Garofolo, Ross; CFO, Jandel Scientific Inc.; US; 415/453-6700

Garretson, T.H.; Tech Ed, Computer Sources; US; 408/295-5900

Garrett, Bradley; VP Ops, Advanced Input Devices; US; 208/765-8000

Garrett, Jim; EVP Mktng, Servantis Systems Inc.; US; 770/441-3387

Garrick, George; Pres NA Group, Information Resources Inc.; US; 312/726-1221

Garrison, David W.; Pres & COO, NetCom On-Line Communications Services Inc.; US; 408/345-2600

Garrison, Sue; Mgng Ed, 3X/400 Systems Management; US; 708/427-9512, 71333.3316@compuserve.com

Gartner, Gideon; Chmn & CEO, Giga Information Group; US; 617/577-9595

Garvin, Andrew; Pres, FIND/SVP Inc.; US; 212/645-4500

Gasper, David; Pres, Gasper Corp.; US; 513/427-5200

Gass, Stephen; SVP Prod Dev, Viacom New Media; US; 212/258-6000

Gaston, Aaron; Infogrip Inc.; US; 805/652-0770

Gaston, Terry L.; VP Mktng, Optical Data Systems Inc.; US; 214/234-6400

Gates, Dirk I.; Pres & CEO, Xircom Inc.; US; 805/376-9300

Gates, William E.; Ed & Pblr, Midnight Engineering Magazine; US; 719/254-4558

Gates, William H.; Chmn & CEO, Microsoft Corp.; US; 206/936-4400

Gatti, Alessandro; Pres, Cresta Systems Inc.; US; 408/342-9000, alessandro_gatti@cresta.com

Gault, Nick; VP Eng, Common Grounds Software Inc.; US; 415/802-5800

Gaut, Norman E.; Chmn, Pres & CEO, PictureTel Corp.; US; 508/762-5000

Gavenda, Joyce; VP, Summit Strategies Inc.; US; 617/266-9050

Gay, Jonathan; VP Dev, FutureWave Software Inc.; US; 619/637-6190, 71562.2726@compuserve.com

Geary, James M.; VP Mktng, Security Dynamics Technologies Inc.; US; 617/547-7820

Geather Yoshida, Phyllis; Dir Japan Tech, Japanese Technical Literature; US; 202/482-1288

Gebb, Michael; Pres, Specialized Business Solutions; US; 970/262-1720

Geday, Armando; VP & Multimedia Com Div, Rockwell Semiconductor Systems; US; 714/884-4600

Geddes, Berkeley; Pres, Network Professional Assoc.; US; 801/379-0330

Geddes, Bradley C.; Pres & COO, Tenera L.P.; US; 510/845-5200

Geddes Jr., James J.; Pres & CEO, InVision Systems Corp.; US

Geers, Jim; Pres, Aim Technology; US; 408/748-8649, jim@aim.com

Geibel, Jeffrey P.; Mgng Partner, Geibel Marketing Consulting; US; 617/484-8285

Geiger, Barbara; Pres, Boston Computer Exchange; US; 617/542-4414

Geiger, Richard G.; VP Prod Dev, Itron Inc.; US; 509/924-9900

Geis, Greg; Ed, WordPerfectionist, The; US; 502/491-1900

Geis, Jeff; Mktng Mgr, MaxTech Corp.; US; 201/586-3008, jeff_geis@max-corp.com

Geisberg, Samuel P.; EVP & Chmn, Parametric Technology Corp.; US; 617/398-5000

Gelband, Pat; VP SW, Sense8 Corp.; US; 415/331-6318, pat@sense8.com

Gelinas, Tim; VP Eng, CompuServe Internet Div.; US; 206/447-0300

Gellatly, David L.; Pres & CEO, Weitek Corp.; US; 408/738-8400

Gellerman, Ken; VP Govt Sales, MicroVideo Learning Systems; US; 212/777-9595, ken_gellerman@microvideo.com

Gellert, Ronald J.; VP & GM Syst, Sequoia Systems Inc.; US; 508/480-0800

Genereaux, Peter G.; Pres, Utah Information Technologies Assoc.; US; 801/568-3500

Genesi, Robert C.; Chmn & CEO, Rexon Inc.; US; 216/349-0600

Genest, Leonard; Pres, Genovation Inc.; US; 714/833-3355

Gensler, Steve; Founder, IntelliTools; US; 415/382-5959

Gentile, George M.; Chmn & CEO, Gerber Scientific Inc.; US; 860/644-1551

Gentling, Greg; Pres, SWeDE Corp.; US; 714/442-6180

Gentner, Craig M.; SVP & CFO, Network Equipment Technologies Inc.; US; 415/366-4400

Geoffrey, Mary Ellen; Exec Dir, Industry Advisory Council; US; 703/506-9340

George, Dennis; CFO, Eagle Point Software; US; 319/556-8392

Gergacz, David S.; EVP, Cincinnati Bell Inc.; US; 513/397-9900

Gerhardt, David; Exec Dir, Capital Network Inc.; US; 512/305-0826

Gerken, Barry; VP, Concentric Data Systems Inc.; US; 508/366-1122

Gerolstein, Philip J.; VP Sales & Mktng, Courtland Group Inc.; US; 410/730-7668

Gerow, Mike; PR Dir, Wellspring Communications; US; 619/279-1611

Gerpheide, George; Pres, Cirque Corp.; US; 801/467-1100

Gersh, Mark D.; Prod Mgr, ViewSonic Corp.; US; 909/869-7976

Gershick, Steve; Pres & CEO, Spatializer Audio Laboratories; US; 818/227-3370

Gerson, Alex; Sr Mgr Info, LucasArts Entertainment Co.; US; 415/472-3400

Gerson, Fred M.; VP & CFO, Maxis; US; 510/933-5630

Gerson, Robert E.; Ed-in-Chief, TWICE-This Week In Consumer Electronics; US; 303/470-4445, gerson@cahners.com

Gerstner, Louis V.; Chmn & CEO, International Business Machines Corp.; US; 914/765-1900

Gersuk, D. Joseph; VP & CFO, MapInfo Corp.; US; 518/285-6000

Gertsen, Rick; GM, AllMicro Inc.; US; 813/539-7283

Gervais, William; Pres, Qualstar Corp.; US; 818/592-0061

Gescheider, Bruce; Pres, ACCO US Inc.; US; 847/541-9500

Geschickter, Chet; VP Res, Hurwitz Consulting Group; US; 617/965-6900

Geschke, Charles M.; Pres & COO, Adobe Systems Inc.; US; 415/961-4400

Gessini, Lawrence; Pres, International Communications Assoc.; US; 214/233-3889

Getsey, Andy; Pres, Shafer; US; 714/553-1177

Gewirtz, David; Ed, Workspace for Lotus Notes; US; 502/491-1900

Geyer, John; Mktng Dir, Terran Interactive Inc.; US; 408/353-6231, jgeyer@netcom.com

Gharapetian, Allen; Mktng Mgr, Logicode Technology Inc.; US; 805/388-9000

Gharda, Laurent; Pres, QualSoft Corp.; US; 415/494-6100

Giacalone, Louis; Ed & Pblr, TechScan Newsletter; US; 212/741-0045

Giaimo, Gail; Pres, 3G Graphics Inc.; US; 206/774-3518

Giaimo, Glenn; VP, 3G Graphics Inc.; US; 206/774-3518

Giannopoulos, A.L.; Pres & CEO, Micros Systems Inc.; US; 301/210-6000

Gibb, Forbes; Ed, Online & CD-ROM Review; US; 609/654-6266

Gibbons, Denny; Dir Sales, Wayzata Technology Inc.; US; 218/326-0597, dennygibbons@wayzata.com

Gibbons, Fred M.; Chmn, Software Publishing Corp.; US; 408/537-3000

Gibbons, Glen; Ed, GPS World; US; 503/343-1200

Gibbons, John H.; Dir, Office of Science & Technology Policy; US; 202/456-7116

Gibbons, Reba; Dir Mktng, Systems Plus Inc.; US; 415/969-7047, reba@systemsplus.com

Gibbs, David; VP Mac Sales, Insignia Solutions Inc.; US; 408/327-6000

Gibbs, Jon; Dir Sales & Mktng, Century Software; US; 801/268-3088

Gibbs, Julie B.; Ed, Oracle Magazine; US; 415/506-4763, jgibbs@us.oracle.com

Gibbs, William H.; Chmn, Pres & CEO, DH Technology Inc.; US; 619/451-3485

Gibson, Chris; VP Ops, Arcada Software Inc.; US; 407/333-7500

Gibson, Donald J.; SVP, National Computer Systems Inc.; US; 612/829-3000

Gibson, Mary Margaret; Partner, Channel Strategies Inc.; US; 415/614-3740, mmgibson@chanstrat.com

Gibson, Peter; CFO, Formgen; US; 602/443-4109

Gibson, Tom; Exec Dir, International Teleconferencing Assoc.; US

Gibson, William M.; Chmn, Pres & CEO, Manugistics Inc.; US; 301/984-5000

Gien, Michael; VP Mktng & Tech, Chorus Systems Inc.; US; 408/879-1350

Giese, Douglas A.; Pres, Advanced Processing Labs Inc.; US; 619/546-8626

Giesecke, Carol; VP & CFO, Encad Inc.; US; 619/452-0882

Gifford, David; Chief Scientist, Open Market Inc.; US; 617/621-9500

Gifford, Michael; EVP, Socket Communications Inc.; US; 510/744-2700

Giffune, Kenneth; VP Human Res, Par Technology Corp.; US; 315/738-0600

Gigot, Gary; VP Mktng, Visio Corp.; US; 206/521-4500

Gil, Joseph; Chmn, Four Season Software; US; 908/248-6667

Gilbert, Jody; Ed, Inside Microsoft Word 6; US; 502/491-1900

Gilbert, Lance; Pres, Second Glance Software; 360/692-3694

Gilbert, Ron; Co-Founder, Humongous Entertainment; US; 206/487-9258

Gilbert, Steven; VP, Educom; US; 202/872-4200

Gilbertson, Jay P.; VP & CFO, HBO & Co.; US; 770/393-6000

Gilder, George; Ed, Gilder Technology Report; US; 413/274-0211

Giler, Eric; Pres, Brooktrout Technology Inc.; US; 617/499-4100, erg@brooktrout.com

Giles, Dana; Art Dir, Terran Interactive Inc.; US; 408/353-6231

Giles, Darren; Tech Dir, Terran Interactive Inc.; US; 408/353-6231

Giles Jr., Alexander W.; EVP & CFO, Allerion Inc.; US; 201/877-1000

Gilhooly, Kym; Mgng Ed, Software Magazine; US; 508/366-2031

Gill, Thomas J.; VP & CFO, Fore Systems Inc.; US; 412/772-6600

Gill, Tim; Chmn & SVP R&D, Quark Inc.; US; 303/894-8888

Gillach, Joe; COO, Diba; US; 415/482-3300

Gillam, Gary; VP US Sales, Tektronix Color Printing & Imaging Div.; US; 503/685-3150

Gillen, Al; Ed-in-Chief, Midrange Systems; US; 215/643-8000, gillenam@box101.cardinal.com

Gilley, Thomas; SVP, FutureTel Inc.; US; 408/522-1400

Gilliat, Bruce; VP Sales & Mktng, Wais Inc.; US; 415/356-5400

Gilliatt, Eric; VP Mktng, Applied Magic Inc.; US; 619/599-2626

Gilliland, Carol J.; VP Sales & Mktng, Contour Design Inc.; US; 508/937-2422, 102747.1244@compuserve.com

Gillin, Paul; Ed, Computerworld; US; 508/879-0700

Gilliom, Gregor; Sr Ed, CompuServe Magazine; US; 614/457-8600

Gillis, Daniel F.; Pres & CEO, Software AG of North America Inc.; US; 703/860-5050

Gilluly, C.W.; Chmn & CEO, Hadron Inc.; US; 703/359-6404

Gillum, Chuck; VP Sales & Mktng, Secure Document Systems Inc.; US; 904/725-2505

Gilmore, Ronald J.; SVP Mktng & Adv, CompUSA Inc.; US; 214/982-4000

Giltrow, Greg; VP Sales & Mktng, Quadrangle Software Corp.; US; 313/769-1675

Gimpel, James F.; Pres, Gimpel Software; US; 610/584-4261

Gingerich, James G.; SVP & CFO, InterTan Inc.; US; 817/348-9701

Gingerich, John C.; Pres & COO, Measurex Corp.; US; 408/255-1500

Ginn, Sam; Chmn & CEO, AirTouch Communications; US; 415/658-2000

Gintz, Robert F.; VP Dev, Equinox Systems Inc.; US; 305/746-9000

Giodanella, Richard; Chmn, Pres & CEO, Datalogix Int'l.; US; 914/747-2900

Gioia, Louis; CMO, Spectrum Holobyte Inc.; US; 510/522-3584

Giordano, Stephen; Pres & CEO, Commix SP Inc.; US; 703/356-9858

Giovaniello, Anthony; COO, Boundless Technologies; US; 512/346-2447

Girma, Bernard; Pres & CEO, NewGen Systems Corp.; US; 714/641-8600

Gislason, Drew; VP R&D, Datalight Inc.; US; 206/435-8086

Gisonni, Deborah; Pblr, Network Computing; US; 516/562-5071, dgisonni@nwc.com

Gissel, Hans; Pres, International Electrotechnical Commission; Switzerland; 22-919-0211

Gistaro, Edward P.; Chmn & CEO, Docucon Inc.; US; 210/525-9221

Giuffre, Ralph; EVP Mktng, Humongous Entertainment; US; 206/487-9258

Giugliano, Oreste B.; Ed-in-Chief, US Export Computer Directory; US; 305/253-1440

Giuntini, Philip; Pres, American Management Systems; US; 703/267-8000

Gjerstad, Michael; Dir Sales, StereoGraphics Corp.; US; 415/459-4500

Glabe, Bruce; VP & CFO, Individual Inc.; US; 617/273-6000

Glade, John F.; VP Eng & Mfg, Alpha Microsystems; US; 714/957-8500, jfglade@alphamicro.com

Glasberg, Andrei; Pres, Tiara Computer Systems; US; 408/496-5460

Glaser, Michael L.; Pres, Cyma Systems Inc.; US; 602/831-2607

Glaser, Norm; VP Fin, Paul Kagan Assoc.; US; 408/624-1536

Glaser, Rob; Pres & CEO, Progressive Networks; US; 206/447-0567

Glass, Graham W.; Co-Founder, ObjectSpace Inc.; US; 214/934-2496

Glass, Kira; Mktng & PR Mgr, AP Professional; US; 619/699-6735, kglass@acad.com

Glassanos, Thomas; VP Mktng, Edify Corp.; US; 408/982-2000, tglassanos@edify.com

Glassman, David; VP Mktng & Sales, Aladdin Knowledge Systems; US; 212/564-5678

Glath, Beverly Ann; VP, RG Software Systems Inc.; US; 602/423-8000

Glath, Ray; Pres, RG Software Systems Inc.; US; 602/423-8000

Glatzer, Hal; Ed, CPA Computer Journalism Review; US; 212/246-8631, hglatzer@echonyc.com

Glazar, Christian; Assist Ed, Retail Info Systems News; US; 201/895-3397

Glaze, Arlington; VP Sales, Qualix Group Inc.; US; 415/572-0200, aglaze@qualix.com

Glazebrook, Bob; Pres, Visual Engineering Inc.; US; 408/452-0600

Gleason, James C.; VP Ops, Interphase Corp.; US; 214/919-9000

Gleason, Joseph; Pres, Scantron Quality Computers; US; jpgleason@qualitycomp.com

Gleed, John; EVP & CTO, JetForm Corp.; US; 703/448-9544

Gleicher, Alan A.; VP Sales, Intuit Inc.; US; 415/944-6000

Glick, Lisa; Ops Mgr, IT Solutions Inc.; US; 312/474-7700

Glicksman, Sam; Pres, Streetwise Software Inc.; US; 310/829-7827, 73323.2305@compuserve.com

Glidden, Jeffrey D.; VP & CFO, Banyan Systems Inc.; US; 508/898-1000

Glover, Keith E.; VP & CFO, Proxim Inc.; US; 415/960-1630

Glynn, William; CFO, Blyth Software Inc.; US; 415/571-0222

Gnant, Richard; Pres, Sirius Publishing Inc.; US; 602/951-3288

Gobel, Dave; Pres, Worlds Inc.; US; 415/281-4878

Goddard, Larry; VP Sales, Allen Systems Group; US; 941/435-2200

Godde, Andreas; CFO & VP Fin, Xerox ColorgrafX Systems; US; 408/225-2800

Godfrey, Peter; Chmn, Pres & CEO, Micro Warehouse; US; 203/899-4000

Godin, Gilles C.; VP & CFO, Tekelec; US; 818/880-5656

Godsey, Ernest E.; VP Bus Dev, Interphase Corp.; US; 214/919-9000

Godwin, A. Timothy; Pres & COO, Tech Data Corp.; US; 813/539-7429

Godwin, Dan; VP Sales, Philips Media OptImage; US; 515/225-7000, godwin@pmpro.com

Godwin, R. Wayne; EVP, BASF Corp.; US; 201/397-2700

Goebel, Virginia A.; CFO, Algor Inc.; US; 412/967-2700

Goede, Darryl; Chmn, Pres & CEO, AirWorks Media; Canada; 403/424-9922

Goede, Nancy; VP Corp Affairs, AirWorks Media; Canada; 403/424-9922

Goemans, Johan J.; VP MIS, Avery Dennison; US; 818/304-2000

Goertz, Gary; EVP & CFO, Telus; Canada; 403/498-7311

Goetz, Bob P.; SVP Sales, MTI Technology Corp.; US; 714/970-0300

Goff, Sam; Mgng Partner, Essex Interactive Media; US; 201/894-8700

Going, Rolland S.; EVP, Terpin Group, The; US; 310/821-6100, rgoing@la.terpin.com

Golacinski, Michael; EVP Sales & Mktng, Maxell Corp. of America; US; 201/794-5900

Gold, Rickey; Pres, Rickey Gold & Assoc.; US; 708/486-0920

Gold, Steve; European Bureau Chief, Newsbytes; US; 612/430-1100

Goldbach, Matthew T.; Pres, Transitional Technology Inc.; US; 714/693-1133, matt@ttech.com

Goldberg, Adele; Chmn, ParcPlace-Digitalk Inc.; US; 408/481-9090

Goldberg, Bennet R.; EVP Mktng, Inmac Corp.; US; 408/727-1970

Goldberg, David; CEO, 2-Lane Media; US; 310/473-3706

Goldberg, Howard; VP Ops, DynaTek Automation Systems Inc.; Canada; 902/832-3000

Goldberg, Les; Principal, Les Goldberg PR; US; 714/545-3117, 74551.1335@compuserve.com

Goldberg, M. Robert; EVP & GM, Mindscape Inc.; US; 415/883-3000

Goldberg, Michael C.; Pres & CEO, FDP Corp.; US; 305/858-8200

Goldberg, Richard H.; Pres & CEO,

Synon Corp.; US; 415/461-5000

Golding, D. Rex; VP & CFO, 3DO Co.; US; 415/261-3000

Goldklank, Mitchell; SVP Sales & Mktng, LCS Industries Inc.; US; 201/778-5588

Goldman, James; Society for Industrial & Applied Mathematics; US; 215/382-9800

Goldman, Larry; Partner, Bender, Goldman Helper; US; 310/473-4147, larry_goldman@bgh.com

Goldman, Richard; SVP & CFO, Giga Information Group; US; 617/577-9595

Goldman, Richard B.; EVP & CFO, Sequoia Systems Inc.; US; 508/480-0800

Goldman, Robert; Chmn, Pres & CEO, Object Design Inc.; US; 617/674-5000

Goldman, Steve; Pres, Distributed Processing Technology; US; 407/830-5522

Goldner, Doug; Dir Tech Sup, Data Access Corp.; US; 305/238-0012, doug-g@daccess.com

Goldsammler, Barry; VP Ops, Hertz Computer Corp.; US; 212/684-4141

Goldsmith, David; VP Tech Svcs, JourneyWare Media; US; 510/254-4520, david.goldsmith@pobox.com

Goldstein, Barry J.; EVP & CFO, Office Depot Inc.; US; 407/278-4800

Goldstein, David M.; Pres, Channel Marketing Corp.; US; 214/931-2420, david@cmcus.com

Goldstein, Irwin O.; VP & CFO, Adtran Inc.; US; 205/971-8000

Goldstein, Jeff; Pres, Synchronics; US; 901/761-1166

Goldstein, Jerry; VP Mktng, Foresight Software; US; 770/206-1000

Goldstein, Larry; Pblr, PC Digest; US; 215/941-9600

Goldstein, Michael; Ed-in-Chief, LFP Inc.; US; 310/858-7155, 75300.3144@compuserve.com

Goldstein, Morris; Pres, Information Access Co.; US; 415/378-5200

Goldstein, Robert; Pres, Equity Group Inc.,The; US; 212/371-8660

Goldstone, Jerry A.; Pblr, BCR Enterprises Inc.; US; 630/986-1432

Goldsworthy, Steven M.; Chmn & CTO, Vantive Corp.; US; 408/982-5700

Goldwasser, Ralph A.; SVP & CFO, Bolt Beranek & Newman Inc.; US; 617/873-4000

Golisano, B. Thomas; Chmn, Pres & CEO, Paychex Inc.; US; 716/385-6666

Gollobin, Michael L.; Pres, Control Concepts Inc.; US; 703/876-6444, gollobim@presearch.com

Gollub, Gerald E.; EVP, Standard Microsystems Corp.; US; 516/435-6000

Golovin, Jonathan J.; Chmn, Consilium Inc.; US; 415/691-6100

Golson, Barry; Ed-in-Chief, Yahoo! Internet Life; US; 212/503-3835, bgolson@zd.com

Golub, Judith M.; VP & CFO, Software

Maintenance News Inc.; US; 415/969-5522

Gomez, Nelson; VP Sales & Mktng, QStar Technologies Inc.; US; 904/243-0900, nelson@qstar.com

Gonzalez, Marco A.; Pres, Aladdin System Inc.; US; 408/761-6200, marco@aladdinsys.com

Gooch, Tim; Ed, Delphi Developer's Journal; US; 502/491-1900

Good, Fran; VP CFO, Micom Communications Corp.; US; 805/583-8600

Good, Gary; Pres, G.R. Good Communications; US; 206/486-4446

Good, James; VP Sales, Liebert Corp.; US; 614/888-0246

Goodall, Greg; Pres & CEO, VisiSoft Inc.; US; 770/320-0077

Goodall, Steve; Pres, J.D. Power & Associates; US; 818/889-6330

Goodermote, Dean F.; Pres & COO, Project Software & Development Inc.; US; 617/661-1444

Goodfellow, Geoffrey S.; Chmn, Radio-Mail Corp.; US; 415/286-7800

Goodfriend, John; VP, Lanop Corp.; US

Goodhue, Claire; Assoc Pblr, CADENCE Magazine; US; 415/905-2276

Gooding, Richard W.; Pres MAI NA, MAI Systems Corp.; US; 714/580-0700

Goodlander, Ted; Pres & CEO, Storage Computer Corp.; US; 603/880-3005

Goodman, Ford H.; Pres & CEO, CE Software Inc.; US; 515/221-1801

Goodman, John; VP Ops, Davidson & Associates Inc.; US; 310/793-0600

Goodman, Joseph W.; Chmn & CTO, Optivision Inc.; US; 415/855-0200

Goodman, Ken; Ed, Strategic Solutions; US; 206/868-6532

Goodnight, James H.; Pres, SAS Institute Inc.; US; 919/677-8000

Goodrich, Philip A.; VP Corp Dev, General Signal Corp.; US; 203/329-4100

Goodspeed, Mike; GM, Calyx Corp.; US; 414/782-0300

Goodwill, Craig; CEO, EZ Image Inc.; US; 206/840-2004

Goodwin, Ben; NA Pres, Thomson Software; US; 203/845-5000

Goodwin, Bob; VP Sales & Mktng, Input; US; 415/961-3300, bob_goodwin@input.com

Goodwin, Dan; Controller, DacEasy Inc.; US; 214/732-7500

Goodwin, Eric R.; Pres & CEO, Fulcrum Technologies Inc.; Canada; 613/238-1761

Goodwin, Robert; VP Eng, Parallax Graphics Inc.; US; 408/727-2220

Goodwin, Terrence J.; CIO, LaserScan Systems Inc.; US; 305/777-1300

Goossens, Philippe; Ed-in-Chief, Alcatel Telecommunications Review; France; 1-4076-1010

Gopen, Howard J.; VP Ops, Weitek Corp.; US; 408/738-8400

Gopinath, Rajendar; Ed-in-Chief, Asian

Sources Computer Products; Hong Kong; 852-25554777

Goplen, Bruce; VP Adv Tech, Mission Research Corp.; US; 505/768-7727, goplen@mrcwdc.com

Gorda, Ronald B.; SVP, Titan Corp.; US; 619/552-9500

Gordon, Bernard M.; Chmn & CEO, Analogic Corp.; US; 508/977-3000

Gordon, Bill; Dir WW Sales, Allegiant Technologies Inc.; US; 619/587-0500, bill_gordon@allegiant.com

Gordon, Bing; EVP Mktng, Electronic Arts; US; 415/571-7171

Gordon, Gregory J.; EVP & CFO, Microlytics Inc.; US; 716/248-9150, ggordon@microlytics.com

Gordon, Jon; Pres, DiagSoft Inc.; US; 408/438-8247

Gordon, Robert D.; Chmn, Pres & CEO, Apertus Technologies Inc.; US; 612/828-0300

Gordon, Shannon; Dir Fin, Association for Educational Communications & Technology; US; 202/347-7834

Gordon, Steve M.; VP & CFO, Data I/O Corp.; US; 206/881-6444

Gorlicki, Ronny; VP Mktng, CommTouch Software Inc.; US; 408/245-8682

Gorman, Brian; VP Sales, Cascade Systems Inc.; US; 508/794-8000

Gorman, Chuck J.; Pres & CEO, J3 Learning; US; 612/930-0330

Gorman, John; Chmn & Pres, Timberline Software Corp.; US; 503/626-6775

Gorman, Joseph T.; Chmn & CEO, TRW Inc.; US; 216/291-7000

Gorman, Mike; Pres, PowerHouse Software; US

Gorman, Shane; EVP, Triad Systems Corp.; US; 510/449-0606

Goroch, Antonette; Analyst, AIM Report, The; US; 408/659-3070, gorochak@aol.com

Gosizk, Brian K.; VP, Jordan Tamraz Caruso Advertising Inc.; US; 312/951-2000

Gossett, Robert; Pres, Cougar Mountain Software; US; 208/375-4455

Gotcher, Alan J.; SVP Mfg & Tech, Avery Dennison; US; 818/304-2000

Goto, Kirk; SVP & GM BED, Minolta Corp.; US; 201/825-4000

Gott, Bill; Ed, Printer Channel Monitor; US; 408/865-0221

Gott, William E.; Pres, Venture Marketing Strategies; US; 408/865-0221

Gottlieb, Brett; CFO, Upstart Communications; US; 510/420-7979, bgottlieb@upstart.com

Gottlieb, Joe; EVP Sales & Mktng, Meta Group; US; 203/973-6700

Gottsman, John; CEO, Academic Systems; US; 415/694-6850

Goudie, Jerry; VP Sales, Spectrix Corp.; US; 847/317-1770

Gould, Ellen; Assoc Pblr, Visual Basic

Programmer's Journal; US; 415/833-7100

Goulden, David I.; SVP, Wang Laboratories Inc.; US; 508/459-5000

Gowin, John; Ed, Inside Solaris; US; 502/491-1900

Goyette, Richard C.; VP Sales & Mktng, Scan-Optics Inc.; US; 203/289-6001

Grabbe, William O.; Chmn, Synon Corp.; US; 415/461-5000

Grabe, Lennart; SVP Bus Dev, Ericsson; Sweden; 468-719-0000

Grabel, David; VP Prod Dev, F3 Software Corp.; US; 617/270-0001

Graber, James; VP Fin, SyQuest Technology Inc.; US; 510/226-4000

Gradbois, Jerry; Dir Ops, Envisions Solutions Technology Inc.; US

Graettinger, Tim; VP Prod Dev, NeuralWare Inc.; US; 412/787-8222

Graf, James; VP Sales, a/Soft Development Inc.; US; 603/666-6699, sales@asoft-dev.com

Graf, Ken; VP Dev, a/Soft Development Inc.; US; 603/666-6699, support@asoft-dev.com

Grafft, Chris; VP Dev, Tivoli Systems Inc.; US; 512/794-9070

Graham, Donald B.; SVP Ops, National Data Corp.; US; 404/728-2000

Graham, Ed; VP, Eagle Point Software; US; 319/556-8392

Graham, Eric; Chief Scientist, Byte by Byte Corp.; US; 512/795-0150

Graham, Gary; Sales Mgr, Gyrus Systems Inc.; US; 804/320-1414, graham@ahay-net.com

Graham, Howard H.; SVP & CFO, Informix Software Inc.; US; 415/926-6300

Graham, Kenneth R.; COO, Technologic Partners; US; 212/343-1900

Graham, William; Dir Ops, Factura Kiosks Inc.; US; 716/264-9600

Grammer, Jeffrey; Pres & CEO, Databook Inc.; US; 508/762-9779, jhg@databook.com

Grand, Marcia; Pblr, TWICE-This Week In Consumer Electronics; US; 303/470-4445

Granger, Edward; Principal Scientist, Light Source Inc.; US; 415/461-8000

Granmo, Marti; Pres, Hard Drive Associates Inc.; US; 503/233-2821

Granmo, Steve; VP, Hard Drive Associates Inc.; US; 503/233-2821

Granoff, Peter; Co-Founder, Virtual Vineyards; US; 415/917-5750, corkdork@virtualvin.com

Granovetter, Randy; Pres & CEO, Jabra Corp.; US; 619/622-0764

Grant, August E.; Ed, Communication Technology Update; US; 512/258-8898

Grant, Gerry; Founder, DataGrant Internet Services; US; 714/645-7716

Grant, Joseph M.; SVP & CFO, EDS; US; 214/604-6000

Grant, Ney; Pres & CEO, Ibex Technologies Inc.; US; 916/939-8888

Grant, Richard; Pres, Voice Pilot Technologies Inc.; US; 305/670-0807

Grass, Jonathan D.; Ed, WEBsmith; US; 206/782-7733, jong@ssc.com

Grau, Juan; VP Eng, Proxim Inc.; US; 415/960-1630

Graves, David; Tech Ed, Dimensions; US; 303/469-0557

Gray, Barry; VP Fin, Quality Education Data Inc.; US

Gray, Bill; CFO, Reality Online Inc.; US; 610/277-7600

Gray, Bruce W.; Pblr, Infotainment World Inc.; US; 415/349-4300

Gray, Colleen; VP & CFO, Mylex Corp.; US; 510/796-6100

Gray, Jeff; VP Ind Mktng, Globalink Inc.; US; 703/273-5600, jgray@globalink.com

Gray, John; Pres, Philips Media OptImage; US; 515/225-7000, gray@pmpro.com

Gray, Kerry; Pres, Associated Advertising Agency Inc.; US; 316/683-4691

Gray, Matthew H.; Pres, Hilgraeve Inc.; US; 313/243-0576, mgray@hilgraeve.com

Gray, Matthew K.; CTO, net.Genesis; US; 617/577-9800

Gray, Tom; Pres, Arbor Image Corp.; US; 313/741-8700

Grayson, Edward D.; VP Gen Counsel, Honeywell Inc.; US; 612/951-1000

Grayson, Eric; VP Intl Sales, FutureSoft; US; 713/496-9400

Grayson, George; Chmn, Pres & CEO, 7th Level Inc.; US; 818/547-1955

Grayson, J. Paul; Chmn & CEO, Micrografx Inc.; US; 214/234-1769

Grayson Brower, Cathy; Exec Ed, Home-Office Computing; US; 212/505-4220

Grecky, Charles; Pblr, Advanced Imaging; US; 516/845-2700

Greco, David; Pres, World Ready Software; US; 415/957-1300

Greco, Louis A.; CFO, MacNeal-Schwendler Corp., The; US; 213/258-9111

Greelish, David A.; Ed & Pblr, Historically Brewed; US

Green, David G.; VP & GM, Ultre Division; US; 516/753-4800

Green, Douglas; Pblr, Chicago Software Newspaper; US

Green, Gary M.; EVP & COO, Metricom Inc.; US; 408/399-8200

Green, Hugh R.; Pres, Image Consulting Group Inc.; US; 516/351-8942

Green, Michael I.; VP Mktng & Sales, Fore Systems Inc.; US; 412/772-6600

Green, Randall; VP Bus Dev, Durand Communications Network Inc.; US; 805/961-8700

Green, Randy; Pres, GreenTree Associates Inc.; US; 508/263-6900, rangreen@aol.com

Green, Thomas A.; EVP, Computer Data Systems Inc.; US; 301/921-7000

Greenbaum, Richard; VP Sales & Mktng, ABCO Distributors; US; 914/368-1930

Greenberg, Adam; Mgng Ed, Beyond Computing; US; 212/745-6347

Greenberg, Miles R.; VP & CFO, F3 Software Corp.; US; 617/270-0001

Greenburg, Carol; Pres, Presentation Works; US; 707/545-1400

Greene, Tony; VP, Sterling Hager Inc.; US; 617/259-1400

Greener, Richard; Mgng Partner, Essex Interactive Media; US; 201/894-8700

Greenfield, Andrew; Chmn & Pres, Frame Relay Forum; US; 415/578-6980

Greenfield, Carol; Prog Dir, Massachusetts Software Council Inc.; US; 617/437-0600

Greenfield, Gary G.; Pres & COO, Intersolv Inc.; US; 301/838-5000

Greening, Deborah S.; VP Ops, CompuTrac Inc.; US; 214/234-4241

Greening, Michelle; Mktng Mgr, Synthesis Inc.; US; 360/671-0458

Greenwald, Mark; VP Mktng, D&H Distributing Co.; US; ejcv47a@prodigy.com

Greenwald, Ted; Sr Ed, InterActivity; US; 415/358-9500

Greer, Henry H.; Pres & COO, SEI Corp.; US; 610/254-1000

Greer, Ken; Pres, Elan Computer Group Inc.; US; 415/964-2200

Gregerson, Daniel; Pres & CEO, PeerLogic; US; 415/626-4545

Gregg, Harold; Pres, Expert Choice Software; US; 512/422-1622, 70034.227@compuserve.com

Gregg, Robert S.; SVP & CFO, Sequent Computer Systems Inc.; US; 503/626-5700

Gregor, Andy; CFO, GT Interactive Software; US; 212/726-6500

Gregory, Alan; Pres, Xecom Inc.; US; 408/945-6640

Grehan, Rick; Tech Dir, Byte Lab; US; 603/924-9281

Greico, Frank; CFO, Quarterdeck Corp.; US; 310/309-3700

Greidoff, Robin M.; Dir Mktng, Raxco Inc.; US; 301/258-2620

Grenewetzki, David; EVP Prod Dev, Accolade Inc.; US; 408/985-1700

Grenier, David; GM Admin, Yamaha Systems Technology; US; 408/467-2300

Gresham, Todd; VP Sales & Mktng, Philips LMS; US; 719/593-7900

Grevstad, Eric; Ed, Computer Shopper; US; 212/503-3900

Grey, Bernadette; Ed-in-Chief, HomeOffice Computing; US; 212/505-4220

Grey, George; CEO Tadpole UK, Tadpole Technology Inc.; US; 512/219-2200

Gribben, Deena; Natl Sales Mgr, Parana Supplies Corp.; US; 310/793-1325

Grice, Robert; VP & CFO, Newport Systems Solutions Inc.; US; 714/752-1511

Grieves, Michael; Pres, Data Systems Network Corp.; US; 810/489-7117

Griff, Adam; Pres, Willowbrook Technologies Inc.; Canada; 905/660-8795

Griffin, Ed; Pres, Geneva Group of Cos. Inc.; US; 612/546-5620

Griffin, Glenford F.; VP Sales & Mktng, Key Tronic Corp.; US; 509/928-8000

Griffin, Mark A.; VP Sales & Mktng, Maxi Switch Inc.; US; 520/294-5450

Griffin, Wally; Grp Pres, Jones Computer Network; US; 303/792-3111

Griffin, William D.; SVP & CFO, Inference Corp.; US; 415/899-0100

Griffith, David; Pres & CEO, Tandberg Data Inc.; US; 805/579-1000

Griffith, David; Exec Ed, Digital Imaging; US; 310/212-5802

Griffith, Michael; Ed-in-Chief, PowerBuilder Developer's Journal; US; 201/332-1515

Griffiths, David J.; Pres, LaserVend Inc.; US; 801/553-9080

Grimaldi, Joe; Dir Sales & Mktng, Westrex Int'l.; US; 617/254-1200

Grimes, Charles W.; Author, Multimedia & Technology Licensing Agrmnts; US

Grimes, D.R.; EVP Tech, Servantis Systems Inc.; US; 770/441-3387

Grimm, Susan; VP Pub Sys, Penton Publishing Inc.; US; 216/696-7000

Grimsdale, Charles; CEO, Division Inc.; US; 415/364-6067

Grinder, Mike; Ops Mgr, Microport Inc.; US; 408/438-8649, mike@mport.com

Grinnell, J.D.; EVP, TriHouse Group, The; US; 617/544-3088, 72650.1356@compuserve.com

Grinstead, Mary Jane; SVP Dist & Ops, Ardis; US; 708/913-1215

Grinstein, Keith; Pres Cellular Div, AT&T Wireless Services; US; 206/827-4500

Grkavaz, Olga; SVP, Information Technology Assoc. America; US; 703/522-5055

Groetzinger, Stephen H.; VP NA Sales, Tangram Enterprise Solutions Inc.; US; 919/851-6000, steveg@tesi.com

Grohmann, Werner; Pres, PR-Consult; US; 619/625-4622

Gronski, Robert; VP Sales, Common Grounds Software Inc.; US; 415/802-5800

Gross, Brian; VP Eng, Mentalix Inc.; US; 214/423-9377

Gross, Douglas H.; VP, Computer Language Research Inc.; US; 214/250-7000

Gross, Loren D.; VP, Ceridian Corp.; US; 612/853-8100

Gross, Patrick W.; Vice Chmn, American Management Systems; US; 703/267-8000

Gross, Paul; Pres, Grear Group; US; 415/323-8368

Gross, Richard; VP, Antex Electronics Corp.; US; 310/532-3092

Grosse, John; VP Ops, Applied Micro

Circuits Corp.; US; 619/450-9333

Grossman, Franklin; Pres, Nu-Mega Technologies Inc.; US; 603/889-2386

Grosso, Paul B.; VP Res, ArborText Inc.; US; 313/996-3566

Groth, Nancy; Mgng Ed, MacUser; US; 415/378-5600

Grotzinger, Timothy; VP Eng, Laser Communications Inc.; US; 717/394-8634

Grove, Andrew S.; Pres & CEO, Intel Corp.; US; 408/765-8080

Grove, N. Michael; VP Gen Counsel, Bellcore; US; 201/829-2000

Grover, Pragati; Oak Ridge Public Relations Inc.; US; 408/253-5042, pragati@oakridge.com

Groves, Ray J.; CEO, Ernst & Young; US; 212/773-3000

Gruber, Diana; Ted Gruber Software; US; 702/735-1980

Gruber, Glenn; Dir Mktng, Kyocera Electronics Inc.; US; 908/560-3400

Gruber, Ken; VP & CFO, Enteractive Inc.; US; 212/221-6559

Gruber, Ted; Pres, Ted Gruber Software; US; 702/735-1980

Gruder, Robert F.; Pres, Alydaar Software Corp.; US; 704/544-0092

Gruman, Galen; Exec Ed, Macworld; US; 415/243-0505

Grumman, Bryan; Pres & CEO, Gemstone Systems Inc.; US

Grynberg, Ami; Pres, CabiNet Systems Inc.; US; 201/512-1040, ami@cabinet-sys.com

Guan, Loh Ngiang; VP Tech Div, Aztech Labs Inc.; US; 510/623-8988

Guarascio, Anthony R.; VP & CFO, Executone Information Systems Inc.; US; 203/876-7600

Guastaferro, Angelo; Chmn, nView Corp.; US; 804/873-1354

Guckenheimer, John; Pres, Society for Industrial & Applied Mathematics; US; 215/382-9800

Gudmundson, Crandall; Pres, Odetics Inc.; US; 714/774-5000

Gudmundson, Norm; VP Eng, mFactory Inc.; US; 415/548-0600

Gudonis, Paul R.; CEO, BBN Planet Corp.; US; 617/873-8730

Guenthner, David C.; EVP & CFO, InaCom Corp.; US; 402/392-3900

Guerin, Paul F.; VP Sales, MathSoft Inc.; US; 617/577-1017

Guerra, Kenneth J.; VP Fin, Liant Software Corp.; US; 508/872-8700

Guerrieri, Marilyn; CFO, ACI US Inc.; US; 408/252-4444

Guest, Peter; Pres & CEO, Maxtek Components Corp.; US; 503/627-4133

Guglielmi, Peter A.; EVP & CFO, Tellabs; US; 708/969-8800

Guhman, Gary; Ed & Pblr, Soundbyte News; US; 617/542-4414

Guida, Dean; Pres, ProtoView Development Co.; US; 609/655-5000

Guide, Ron; Dir Prof Svcs, Bluestone Inc.; US; 609/727-4600

Guisbond, Lisa; Mgng Ed, WebServer Magazine; US; 617/739-7001, lisa@cpg.com

Gula, James; VP Eng, Corollary Inc.; US; 714/250-4040

Gulett, Michael; Pres & CEO, Paradigm Technology Inc.; US; 408/954-0500

Gullans, Mark; VP Fin, miro Computer Products Inc.; US; 415/855-0940

Gullett, Jan L.; SVP Mktng & Sales, Broderbund Software Inc.; US; 415/382-4400

Gullickson, Betsy; SVP & GM, Ketchum Public Relations; US; 415/984-6100

Gullotti, Russell A.; Pres & CEO, National Computer Systems Inc.; US; 612/829-3000

Gumbs, David; Sales Mgr, Chase Research Inc.; US; 615/872-0770

Gumucio, Marcelo; Pres & CEO, Memorex Telex Corp.; US; 214/444-3500

Gunderson, Steven J.; Owner, Uuplus Development; US; 805/534-9502

Gunerame, Priyan; VP Ops, ECCS Inc.; US; 908/747-6995

Gunji, Hiromi; Pres & CEO, Brother International Corp.; US; 908/356-8880

Gunn, Ann; VP, Tally Systems Corp.; US; 603/643-1300

Gunn, John; Dir Channel Dev, STB Systems Inc.; US; 214/234-8750

Gunst, Robert A.; Pres & CEO, Good Guys Inc., The; US; 415/615-5000

Gunter, John L.; Chmn & Pres, Tels Corp.; US; 801/571-1182

Gunther, Rick; VP Sales, ASAP Software Express Inc.; US; 847/465-3710

Guntz, Christopher; COO, Optimum Resource Inc.; US; 803/689-8000

Gupta, Arun; Chmn & CEO, DataEase International Inc.; US; 203/374-8000

Gupta, Hari; Pres, Rancho Technology Inc.; US; 909/987-3966

Gupta, Narendra K.; Chmn, Integrated Systems Inc.; US; 408/542-1500

Gupta, R. Paul; Pres & COO, Quality Semiconductor Inc.; US; 408/450-8000

Gupta, Raj; VP & CFO, Tech-Source Inc.; US; 407/262-7100, raj@tech-source.com

Gupta, Saroj; Pres, Blackship Computer Systems Inc.; US; 408/432-7500

Gupta, Umang P.; Chmn, Pres & CEO, Centura Software Corp.; US; 415/321-9500

Gupta, Vinod; Pres & CEO, Software Moguls; US; 612/932-6721, vinod@moguls.com

Gur, Ame; Pres, Pacific Micro Data Inc.; US; 714/955-9090, a_gur@pmicro.com

Gur, Sam; Pres, DynaTek Automation Systems Inc.; Canada; 902/832-3000

Gura, Moti; Chmn & CEO, Vcon Inc.; US; 214/774-3890

Gurdon, Stephen; Pres, Axis Communi-

cations Inc.; US; 617/938-1188

Gurney, Christian; VP, CE Software Inc.; US; 515/221-1801

Gurney, Dave; Chmn & CEO, SoftQuad International Inc.; Canada; 416/239-4801

Guthrie, John G.; SVP, BancTec Inc.; US; 214/450-7700

Gutierrez, Matthew R.; VP Mktng, Ross Technology; US; 512/436-2000

Gutierrez, S.; Asst Ed, Computerized Investing; US; 312/280-0170, aai-imike@aol.com

Gutmann, Craig; CFO, VisionTek Inc.; US; 708/360-7500

Gutschow, Todd W.; VP Tech, HNC Software Inc.; US; 619/546-8877

Guttendorf, Richard; Pres & CEO, Laser Communications Inc.; US; 717/394-8634

Gutter, Ellen; VP Sales & Mktng, Hurwitz Consulting Group; US; 617/965-6900

Guttieres-Lasry, Philippe; Pres, E.M.M.E. Interactive; US; 203/406-4041

Guttinger, Martin; Prog Mgr, Localization & Consulting Services; US; 206/443-5627

Guttman, Bill; CEO, n th degree software; US; 702/588-4900

Guttman, Steve; VP Mktng, Fractal Design Corp.; US; 408/688-5300

Guty, Stephen; Ed Dir, Random House Electronic Publishing; US; 212/751-2600

Gutzmer, Howard; Pres & CEO, Konexx; US; 619/622-1400

Guy, Ken; VP Mktng, Micom Communications Corp.; US; 805/583-8600, keng@micom.com

Gwennap, Linley; Ed-in-Chief, Microprocessor Report; US; 707/824-4001, lgwennap@mdr.zd.com

Gyani, Mohan; EVP & CFO, AirTouch Communications; US; 415/658-2000

Gyenes, Andrew; Chmn & CEO, Enteractive Inc.; US; 212/221-6559

Haag, Thomas; VP, TeleSoft Inc.; US; 619/457-2700

Haas, Kenneth H.; Pres & CFO, IntelliCorp Inc.; US; 415/965-5500

Haavind, Bob; Ed-in-Chief, Computer Design; US; 603/891-0123, bobh@pennwell.com

Haber, Shari; SVP, Connors Communications; US; 415/217-7500, shari@connors.com

Haber, Steve; Chmn, Pres & CEO, Insight Development Corp.; US; 510/244-2000

Hackbarth, Warren; VP Sales, Proxim Inc.; US; 415/960-1630

Hackman Jr., George; Lab Mgr, PC/Computing Usability Lab; US; 415/578-7000

Hackwood, Tom; Sls Mgng, Computer Business Review; US; 212/677-0409, tom@apt.usa.globalnews.com.

Hackworth, Michael L.; Pres & CEO, Cirrus Logic Inc.; US; 510/623-8300

Hadaegh, Elliot; VP Mktng & Sales, Logicode Technology Inc.; US; 805/388-9000

Hadaegh, Moe; Pres & CEO, Logicode Technology Inc.; US; 805/388-9000

Haddod, Dale; VP Fin & Ops, Macola Inc.; US; 614/382-5999

Hader, Frank; VP Sales, Datasym Inc.; Canada; 519/758-5800

Hadfield, Jeff; Ed Dir, WordPerfect for Windows Magazine; US; 801/226-5555, hadfield@wpmag.com

Hadfield, Neil; CFO & Tech Dir, Western Pacific Data Systems; US; 619/454-0028

Hadley, Dave; VP Eng, Primus Communications Corp.; US; 206/292-1000

Haerr, Greg; CEO, Century Software; US; 801/268-3088

Hafkemeyer, Peg S.; VP, CyCare Systems Inc.; US; 602/596-4300

Hagan, Jay; VP, Drive Savers Inc.; US; 415/382-2000

Hagan, Mike; VP Sales & Mktng, Associated Research Services Inc.; US; 214/570-7100

Hagen, Todd; VP Fin & Admin, HyperMedia Communications Inc.; US; 415/573-5170, thagen@newmedia.com

Hager, Charles; Pres, Champion Business Systems Inc.; US; 303/792-3606

Hager, Kenneth V.; VP & CFO, DST Systems Inc.; US; 816/435-1000

Hager, Sterling; Pres, Sterling Hager Inc.; US; 617/259-1400

Hagerty, Philip D.; Dir Sales, Intelligance At Large Inc.; US; 215/387-6002, phil.hagerty@beingthere.com

Haggerty, Beth; Pblr, NetGuide; US; 516/562-5000, bhaggert@cmp.com

Haggerty, Charles A.; Chmn, Pres & CEO, Western Digital Corp.; US; 714/932-5000

Hagin, Chris; Assoc Ed, Red Glasses Official Comdex Press Party List; US; 502/456-0808, chagin@atlanta.com

Hagman, Steve; VP Ops, Altima Systems Inc.; US

Hahn, Martin; GM Internet Grp, Apertus Technologies Inc.; US; 612/828-0300

Hahn, Sam; VP Eng, DocuMagix Inc.; US; 408/434-1138

Haigh, Leslie J.; Dir Fin, Fiber & Wireless Inc.; US; 310/787-7097

Haigis, Rick; VP Mktng, Programmer's Shop, The; US; 617/740-2510

Haigis, Rick; VP Mktng, Software Developer's Co. Inc., The; US; 617/740-0101

Haines, John; CEO, VideoLan Technologies Inc.; US; 502/895-4858

Hakain, David; VP IS, Advanstar Communications Inc.; US; 216/826-2859

Hakimoglu, Ayhan; Chmn & CEO, Aydin Corp.; US; 215/657-7510

Halaby, Chris; Pres, Opcode Systems; US; 415/856-3333

Hald, Alan; Vice Chmn, MicroAge Inc.; US; 602/804-2000

Hale, Alan P.; VP Fin, Dallas Semiconductor Corp.; US; 214/450-0400
Hales, Dave; VP, Soft-One Corp.; US; 801/221-9400
Halevi, Shmuel; EVP, Technology Research Group; US; 617/482-4200
Haley, Thomas; Chmn, Iconovex Corp.; US; 612/896-5100
Hall, Curt; Ed, Intelligent Software Strategies; US; 617/648-8702
Hall, David; EVP, PC Connections Inc.; US; 603/446-3383
Hall, Jack; VP Mktng, IPC Technologies Inc.; US; 512/339-3500
Hall, John; VP, EZ Image Inc.; US; 206/840-2004
Hall, Martin; CTO, Stardust Technologies; US; 408/879-8080
Hall, Peter; VP Prod Mktng & Dev, Racal InterLan Inc.; US; 508/263-9929
Hall, Ray; EVP & CEO, Electronics Representatives Assoc.; US; 312/649-1333
Hall, Terry; SVP WW Sales, Cognos Corp.; US; 617/229-6600
Halla, Brian L.; Pres & CEO, National Semiconductor Corp.; US; 408/721-5000
Haller, John; VP Customer Relations, Stonehouse & Co.; US; 214/960-1566
Haller, John F.; VP Tech, MapInfo Corp.; US; 518/285-6000
Halligan, John F.; EVP & CFO, Gartner Group; US; 203/964-0096
Halligan, Rob; Dir Mktng, International Microcomputer Software Inc.; US; 415/257-3000
Hallmen, David; VP Mktng, Arcada Software Inc.; US; 407/333-7500
Halloran, John; Pres, Visual Software Inc.; US; 818/593-3500
Halloran, Kevin; VP, Vertex Industries Inc.; US; 201/777-3500
Halloran, Michael; VP Sales & Mktng, ActionTec Electronics Inc.; US; 408/739-7000
Halloran, Michael J.; VP & CFO, Wallace Computer Services Inc.; US; 708/449-8600
Halloran, Terence P.; CFO, True Software Inc.; US; 508/369-7398
Halperin, Rich; Pres & CEO, JBA Int'l.; US; 847/590-0299
Halpern, Leo; VP Systems, BCB Holdings Inc.; Canada; 905/850-8266
Halpin, James F.; Pres & CEO, CompUSA Inc.; US; 214/982-4000
Hambley, Lawrence W.; Pres, SunService; US; 415/960-1300
Hamburg, Edward; SVP & CFO, SPSS Inc.; US; 312/329-2400
Hamel, David R.; Pres, Boxer Software; US; 603/924-6602, 74777.170@compuserve.com
Hamer, William C.; VP & CTO, ADC Telecommunications; US; 612/938-8080
Hamer Rodges, Kenneth J.; SVP & CTO, Telco Systems Inc.; US; 617/551-0300

Hamerslag, Steve; Vice Chmn, MTI Technology Corp.; US; 714/970-0300
Hamid, Basit; Chmn, Elixir Technologies Corp.; US; 805/641-5900, basit_hamid@notes.elixir.com
Hamilton, A. Peter; COO, Banyan Systems Inc.; US; 508/898-1000
Hamilton, Alison; Dir Channel Mktng, Niles & Associates Inc.; US; 510/559-8592, alison@niles.com
Hamilton, Barry; IS Mgr, Fox Electronics; US; 941/693-0099
Hamilton, Carol; Exec Dir, American Association for Artificial Intelligence; US; 415/328-3123, ncai@aaai.org
Hamilton, Harry; EVP, Siemens Nixdorf Information Systems Inc.; US; 617/273-0480
Hamilton, James O.; Pres, American Business Systems Inc.; US; 508/250-9600
Hamilton, John; VP Prof Svcs, Software Support Professional Assoc.; US; 619/674-4864, hamilto2@ix.netcom.com
Hamilton, Judy; Pres & CEO, Dataquest; US; 408/437-8000
Hamilton, Rex; Elec Eng, Avatar Systems Corp.; US; 408/321-0110
Hamilton, Thomas M.; Pres, TView Inc.; US; 503/643-1662
Hamirani, Bob; Pres, Nexar Technologies Inc.; US; 508/836-8700
Hammer, David; GM, McKinney Public Relations; US; 215/922-3945
Hammer, N. Robert; Chmn, Pres & CEO, Norand Corp.; US; 319/369-3100
Hammergren, Thomas C.; Pres, Objx Inc.; US; 513/398-0300
Hammerly, J.D.; Dir Sales & Mktng, Cegelec ESCA; US; 206/822-6800
Hammerstrom, Dan; CTO, Adaptive Solutions Inc.; US; 503/690-1236
Hammill, Tom; Pres, Digital Animation Corp.; US; 810/354-0890
Hammitt, John; Co-Author, Target Selling to IT Professionals; US; 617/982-1724
Hammond, Jim; Sr Assoc, Breakthru Communications; US; 408/252-1734
Hammond, Michael; VP, Gateway 2000; US; 605/232-2000
Hammonds, Don; Chmn & CEO, Addison-Wesley Publishing Co.; US; 617/944-3700
Hammonds, Ray; Lab Mgr, Washington Laboratories Ltd.; US; 301/417-0220
Hamrick III, Calvin F.; Pblr, CompuServe Magazine; US; 614/457-8600
Hamza, Nadia; Conf Planner, International Association of Science & Tech.; Canada
Han, H.S.; Pres, Pacom Inc.; US; 408/752-1590
Hanada, Akio; Pres, Fujitsu Personal Systems Inc.; US; 408/982-9500
Hanaka, Marty; Pres & COO, Staples Inc.; US; 508/370-8500
Hanawa, Steve; Pres Capcom Digi Studio, Capcom; US; 408/727-0500

Hancock, Bill; EVP, Network-1 Software & Technology; US; 718/932-7599
Handler, Wendy; VP, Connors Communications; US; 415/217-7500, wendy@connors.com
Hanks, Kevin M.; CFO, Number Nine Visual Technology Corp.; US; 617/674-0009
Hanley, James G.; SVP Corp Dev, Pinnacle Micro Inc.; US; 714/789-3000
Hanley, William T.; Pres & CEO, Galileo Electro-Optics Corp.; US; 508/347-9191
Hanlon, Jim; Mktng Mgr, American Business Systems Inc.; US; 508/250-9600
Hanna, David W.; Pres & CEO, State Of The Art Inc.; US; 714/753-1222
Hanna, Samir L.; Pres & CEO, 3D/Eye Inc.; US; 770/937-9000
Hannah, Adam; VP Eng, DataBeam Corp.; US; 606/245-3500, ahannah@databeam.com
Hannah, Drew; Pres & CEO, Softbridge Inc.; US; 617/576-2257
Hannah, Thomas A.; SVP Ops, Good Guys Inc., The; US; 415/615-5000
Hannon, Cyril F.; EVP Ops, LSI Logic Corp.; US; 408/433-8000
Hanover, Alain J.; Chmn & CEO, Viewlogic Systems Inc.; US; 508/480-0881
Hanratty, Brian J.; EVP, Manufacturing & Consulting Services Inc.; US; 602/991-8700
Hanratty, Patrick J.; Pres & CEO, Manufacturing & Consulting Services Inc.; US; 602/991-8700
Hanratty, Scott M.; SVP Mktng & Sales, Manufacturing & Consulting Services Inc.; US; 602/991-8700, scotth@anvil5k.com
Hanschke, Peter; Dir Mktng, Gallium Software Inc.; Canada; 613/721-0902, phanschke@gallium.com
Hanscome, Barbara; Ed-in-Chief, Software Development; US; 415/905-2200, bhanscome@mfi.com
Hanselaar, Henk A.; Pres & CEO, TV/COM International Inc.; US; 619/451-1500
Hansen, Bill; Mktng Mgr, Management Graphics Inc.; US; 612/854-1220
Hansen, Freddy; Pres, International DB2 Users Group; US; 312/644-6610, dkkmdt8x@ibmmail.com
Hansen, Geoffrey C.; Pres, Telescape Communications Inc.; Canada; 604/893-7088
Hansen, John J.; Pres & CEO, Networks Northwest Inc.; US; 206/391-0618, jhansen@networksnw.com
Hansen, Ken; VP Publishing, TerraGlyph Interactive Studios; US; 847/413-4100
Hansen, Paul; Pblr, Hansen Report on Automotive Electronics, The; US; 603/431-5859
Hansen, Paul G.; VP & CFO, Adaptec Inc.; US; 408/945-8600
Hansen, R. Craig; Chmn & CEO, Call-

Ware Technologies; US; 801/486-9922

Hanson, Bill; Pres, Torrey Pines Research; US; 619/929-4800

Hanson, C. Rowland; Vice Chmn, Interactive Catalog Corp.; US; 206/623-0977

Hanson, Joseph J.; Ed-in-Chief, Curriculum Administrator; US; 203/322-1300

Hanswirth, Barbara; Mktng Mgr, Data Systems Network Corp.; US; 810/489-7117

Hantzsche, Lisa; Assistant, Smith & Shows; US; 415/329-8880, lhantzsche@aol.com

Haramaty, Lior; VP Tech Mktng, VocalTec Inc.; US; 201/768-9400

Harapat, Richard F.; VP Sales, Zitel Corp.; US; 510/440-9600

Harari, Eli; Pres & CEO, SanDisk Corp.; US; 408/542-0500

Harari, Steven L.; Pres, Enterprise Integration Technologies; US; 415/617-8000

Harari, Yasha; Dir Membership, Interactive Television Assoc.; US; 202/408-0008

Harawitz, Howard; Pres, Brooklyn North Software Works Inc.; Canada; 902/493-6080

Harbaugh, Stan; VP Ops, Evergreen Technologies Inc.; US; 541/757-0934

Harberg, Al; Pres, DP Directory Inc.; US; 203/659-1065

Harbison, Robert; Pres, DP-Tek Inc.; US; 316/687-3000

Harczak Jr., Harry J.; CFO, Computer Discount Warehouse; US; 847/465-6000

Harders, Bruce; VP Sales, Etak Inc.; US; 415/328-3825

Hardy, Marina; Dir Mktng, Notable Technologies Inc.; US; 206/455-4040, mhardy@notable.com

Hardy, Robbie; Pres, Creative Interaction Technologies Inc.; US; 919/419-1694

Harga, Tom; Pres, Pioneer New Media Technologies Inc.; US

Hargadon, Tom; Ed & Pblr, Inside Report on New Media; US; 415/861-1317, thargadon@aol.com

Hariton, Lorraine; VP Bus Dev, Network Computing Devices Inc.; US; 415/694-0650

Harker, John V.; Chmn, Pres & CEO, In Focus Systems Inc.; US; 503/685-8888

Harkey, Paul; Mktng Mgr, Special Events Management; US; 803/737-9352, harkey@sbt.tec.sc.us

Harkins, Susan; Ed, Inside Microsoft Access; US; 502/491-1900

Harlbut, Kevin D.; Pres, Velan Inc.; US; 415/647-0798

Harlin, Scott; PR Dir, Green Light Communications; US; 714/719-6400, sharlin@grnlt.com

Harmon, Gary; VP & CFO, Rambus Inc.; US; 415/903-3800

Harmon, Kathy; VP Mktng, Tangible Vision Inc.; US; 630/969-7517, kharmon@tangiblevision.com

Harmon, Paul; Ed, Object-Oriented

Strategies; US; 617/648-8702

Harmonay, Maureen; VP, GreenTree Associates Inc.; US; 508/263-6900

Harney, Aiden; VP Tech Ops, UniKix Technologies; US

Harney, John; Inform; US; 301/587-8202, jharney@aiim.mo.md.us

Haroian, Gary E.; Pres & COO, Stratus Computer Inc.; US; 508/460-2000

Harpell, Pat; Pres, Harpell/Martins & Co.; US; 508/371-1510

Harper, David M.; Dir Mktng, National Computer Security Assoc.; US; 717/258-1816

Harper, Richard; Pres, Association of Shareware Professionals; US; 616/788-5131

Harper, Robin; VP Mktng, Maxis; US; 510/933-5630

Harper, Ronald G.; Chmn, Pres & CEO, MPSI Systems Inc.; US; 918/250-9611

Harper, Stephen; Pres & Chmn, PC Memory Card Int'l. Assoc.; US; 408/433-2273

Harple Jr., Daniel L.; Chmn & CEO, Insoft Inc.; US; 717/730-9501

Harpst, Gary; Pres, Solomon Software; US; 419/424-0422, gharpst@solomon.com

Harre, Jim; EVP, Onyx Graphics Corp.; US; 801/568-9900

Harre, Jim; VP Sales & Mktng, Raster Graphics Inc.; US; 408/232-4000

Harrer, Jim; Pres & CEO, Mustang Software Inc.; US; 805/873-2500, jim.harrer@mustang.com

Harrigan, Barry; Pres, National Association of Desktop Pblrs; US

Harrigan, Michael D.; VP, Network Computing Devices Inc.; US; 415/694-0650

Harrington, David; VP Eng, Vision Software Tools Inc.; US; 510/238-4100

Harrington, David L.; Dir Strategy, IBM Personal Software Products; US; 512/823-3176

Harrington, Mark; Mgng Ed, Computer Retail Week; US; 516/733-6800

Harris, Alison; Ed, United Publications Inc.; US; 207/846-0600, aharris@service-news.com

Harris, Amy N.; Ed, Midrange Computing's Showcase; US; 619/931-8615

Harris, Cynthia A.; Dir Mktng, SBT Accounting Systems; US; 415/444-9900, char@sbtcorp.com

Harris, David R.; VP Sales & Mktng, SBT Accounting Systems; US; 415/444-9900, harr@sbtcorp.com

Harris, Frank M.; VP Mktng & Sales, AER Energy Resources Inc.; US; 404/433-2127, 74164.2372@compuserve.com

Harris, Graig; Exec Ed, Leonardo Electronic Almanac; US; 617/253-2889, harri067@maroon.tc.umn.edu

Harris, Greg; Ed, Full Throttle; US; 502/491-1900

Harris, Hardie; Domestic Ops, Group Technologies Corp.; US; 813/972-6477, h.harris@grtk.com

Harris, Henry C.; VP & CFO, Zitel Corp.; US; 510/440-9600

Harris, James D.; Chmn, GameTek Inc.; US; 305/935-3995

Harris, Jed; Pres, Component Integration Laboratories; US; 408/864-0300, jed@cil.org

Harris, Jerome N.; VP Strategic Plng, Lion Optics Corp.; US; 408/954-8089

Harris, Joshua; Pres, Jupiter Communications Co.; US; 212/780-6060

Harris, Michael E.; VP & CFO, Alternative Resources Corp.; US; 708/317-1000

Harris, Raymond G.; Pres N America, Optibase Inc.; US; 214/774-3800, rayh@optibase.com

Harris, Robert; CEO, Harris InfoSource Int'l.; US; 216/425-9000

Harris, Ron; Pres & CEO, Pervasive Software Inc.; US; 512/794-1719

Harris, Thomas; VP, MicroQuest; US; 913/438-2155.

Harris Jr., William H.; EVP, Intuit Inc.; US; 415/944-6000

Harrison, Ben F.; CEO, InterActive PR Inc.; US; 415/703-0400

Harrison, C. Richard; SVP Sales, Parametric Technology Corp.; US; 617/398-5000

Harrison, Darcy; Mktng Dir, Interactive Software Engineering Inc.; US; 805/685-1006, darcy@eiffel.com

Harrison, John V.; VP Dev, IBM Personal Software Products; US; 512/823-3176

Harrison, Wallace S.; Ed-in-Chief, Professional Electronics Directory/Yearbook; US; 817/921-9061

Harslem, Eric F.; SVP, Dell Computer Corp.; US; 512/338-4400

Hart, Fred; VP Res, Tower Technology Corp.; US; 512/452-9455, hart@twr.com

Hart, John; Assist Ed, Boardwatch Magazine; US; 303/973-6038

Hart, Margo M.; VP Human Res, Inmac Corp.; US; 408/727-1970

Hart, Rebecca; Ed, Profiles; US; 617/280-4000

Hart, Richard; CFO, SoftBooks Inc.; US; 714/586-1284

Harte, John; Pres & CEO, MasPar Computer Corp.; US; 408/736-3300

Harter, Jeneane; VP Sales & Mktng, Maris Multimedia; US; 415/492-2819, 100443.3121@compuserve.com

Hartery, Nicholas; Pres & CEO, Verbatim Corp.; US; 704/547-6500

Hartford, Jeff; Circ Dir, Knowledge Industry Publications Inc.; US; 914/328-9157

Hartlet, Robert; Co-Pres, Corporate Communications; US; 206/728-1778

Hartley, John T.; Chmn & CEO, Harris Corp.; US; 407/727-9100

Hartman, Sigmund; CEO, Knowledge Media; US; 916/872-7487

Hartmian, Nelson S.; VP, Smart Software; US; 617/489-2743, nsh@smartcorp.com

Hartsook, Pieter; Ed, Hartsook Letter; US; 510/521-4988, pieter@hartsook.com

Hartzell, Michelle C.; Pres & CEO, NoRad Corp.; US; 310/605-0808

Hartzog, Adrian; VP Eng, ATI Technologies Inc.; Canada; 905/882-2600

Harvey, Anthony M.; Dir Strat Plng, Fiber & Wireless Inc.; US; 310/787-7097

Harvey, Peter; Chmn, BusLogic Inc.; US; 408/492-9090

Harwood, Fred; Sales Mgr, Professional Help Desk; US; 203/356-7700, info@pro-helpdesk.com

Harwood, George L.; SVP Fin & CFO, Printronix Inc.; US; 714/863-1900

Hasan, Syed; Pres, Maxi Switch Inc.; US; 520/294-5450

Haserueck, Berndt; CFO, Siemens Nixdorf Printing Systems LP; US; 407/997-3100

Hashbarger, J. Robert; VP Sales, Intelli-Power Inc.; US; 714/587-0155

Hashimoto, Kaz; Pres, Cygnus Support; US; 415/903-1400

Haskell, Eric; SVP & CFO, Systems & Computer Technology Corp.; US; 610/647-5930

Haskin, David B.; VP Mktng, Tab Products Co.; US; 415/852-2400

Haslam, Peter; GM, Olicom US; US; 214/423-7560, peterh@smtpgwy.olicom-us

Hassett, Christopher R.; Pres & CEO, PointCast Inc.; US; 408/253-0894

Hastings, Reed; Chmn, Pres & CEO, Pure Software Inc.; US; 408/720-1600

Hata, Masato; Pres, FutureTel Inc.; US; 408/522-1400

Hatch, David; Ed, Printout; US; 617/982-9500, dhatch@gigasd.com

Hatch, Mark; VP Mktng, Integrated Computer Solutions Inc.; US; 617/621-0060, mhatch@ics.com

Hatcher, John; GM, Ryan-McFarland; US; 512/343-1010

Hauck, Ervin A.; VP Eng, Future Domain Corp.; US; 714/253-0400

Hauer, Dan; Pres, S-MOS Systems; US; 408/922-0200

Haugh, Robert; Chmn, Underwriters Laboratories Inc.; US; 847/272-8800

Haugstad, Einar; EVP, Scala Inc.; US; 703/713-0900

Haupert, Carolyn S.; SVP & GM, CyData Inc.; US

Hausen, Wolfgang; Pres & CEO, Cardinal Technologies Inc.; US; 717/293-3000, whausen@cardtech.com

Hautemont, Eric; Pres & CEO, Ray Dream Inc.; US; 415/960-0768, eric_hautemont@raydream.com

Havers, John; GM, Stallion Technologies

Inc.; US; 408/477-0440, johnh@stallion.com

Hawes, Heather; VP, Teleadapt Inc.; US; 408/370-5105

Hawkins, Jeff; Chief Tech, Palm Computing; US; 415/949-9560, jeff@palm.com

Hawkins, John L.; EVP, Advisor Communications Int'l. Inc.; US; 619/483-6400

Hawkins, Trip; Pres & CEO, 3DO Co.; US; 415/261-3000

Hawks, Randy; VP & GM Multimedia, AT&T Paradyne; US; 813/530-2000

Hawley, Brian; Pres, Luminex Software Inc.; US; 909/781-4100

Hay, Roger; SVP & CFO, Titan Corp.; US; 619/552-9500

Hayashi, Ken; GM, Dynaware US Inc.; US; 415/349-5700

Haydamack, William J.; VP & GM Des SW, Data I/O Corp.; US; 206/881-6444

Hayden, David; Pres & CEO, McKinley Group Inc., The; US; 415/331-1884, hayden@mckinley.com

Hayek, Tania; Intl Sales Mgr, Pacific Internet; US; 310/410-9700, tania@pac-net.com

Hayes, Chuck; Pres, CH Products; US; 619/598-2518

Hayes, Dennis C.; Chmn & CEO, Hayes Microcomputer Products Inc.; US; 770/840-9200

Hayes, Eric; Mgng Ed, Mac Monthly; US; 510/428-0110

Hayes, Jeanne; Pres & CEO, Quality Education Data Inc.; US; jhayes@qed-data.com

Hayes, John E.; Pblr, Desktop Engineering; US; 603/924-9631

Hayes, Kevin J.; CFO, Methode Electronics Inc.; US; 708/867-9600

Hayes, Larry; Pres, Hayes Marketing Communications; US; 408/453-5357

Hayes, Mark S.; VP Sales, Speech Systems Inc.; US; 303/938-1110

Hayes, Michael P.; Ed, Electronic Education Report; US; 203/834-0033

Hayes, William F.; EVP, Texas Instruments Inc.; US; 214/995-2551

Hayes-Curtis, Brenda; VP Sales & Mktng, CH Products; US; 619/598-2518

Hayes-Roth, Rick; Chmn & CEO, Teknowledge Inc.; US; 415/424-0500

Haynes, Robert L.; Owner, Haynes Group; US; 714/250-8630

Hays, Carol; Pres, Hays Communications; US

Hays, Nancy; Mgng Ed, IEEE Computer Graphics & Applications; US; 908/981-0060

Hays, Walt; VP Prod, Dantz Development Corp.; US; 510/253-3000

Haythorn, Roy W.; Pres & CEO, Microlytics Inc.; US; 716/248-9150

Hazarian, Jeffrey R.; VP & CFO, Tenera L.P.; US; 510/845-5200

Hazel, W. Charles; Chmn, Castelle

Corp.; US; 408/496-0474

Hazen, C. Edward; VP Fin, Avid Technology Inc.; US; 508/640-6789

Head, Christopher A.; EVP, Comptek Research Inc.; US; 716/677-4070

Head, Robert V.; Ed, Government Imaging; US; 301/445-4405

Head, Stephen R.; VP & CFO, Software Artistry Inc.; US; 317/843-1663

Head, T. Joe; SVP, Optical Data Systems Inc.; US; 214/234-6400

Healy, M. Brian; Group VP & CFO, Computer Language Research Inc.; US; 214/250-7000

Healy, Ray M.; VP Sales, Microtest Inc.; US; 602/952-6400

Heaps, Richard J.; VP Bus Dev, Centura Software Corp.; US; 415/321-9500

Hearst III, William R.; Chmn, @Home Network; US; 415/944-7367

Hecht, Howard; Principal, Decisys Inc.; US; 703/742-5400, hhecht@decisys.com

Hecht, Linda; Mktng Mgr, ESRI User Group; US; 909/793-2853

Heddleson, Dick; CFO, Resumix; US; 408/988-0444

Hedges, Tom; Chmn & VP R&D, Fractal Design Corp.; US; 408/688-5300

Hedrick, Lucy; Mgng Ed, InfoEdge; US; 203/363-7150

Heeger, Jim; VP & CFO, Intuit Inc.; US; 415/944-6000

Heer, Brian; Pres & CEO, Van Nostrand Reinhold; US; 212/254-3232

Heffernan, Tom; Pres, Association of Personal Computer Users Group; US

Hefni, Ibrahim; Pres & CEO, Western Microwave Inc.; US; 408/738-2300

Hefter, Olivia; EVP, Optimum Resource Inc.; US; 803/689-8000

Hefter, Richard; Pres, Optimum Resource Inc.; US; 803/689-8000

Heilmeier, George H.; Pres & CEO, Bellcore; US; 201/829-2000

Heiman, Frederic P.; EVP & CTO, Symbol Technologies Inc.; US; 516/563-2400

Heiman, James R.; Pres, First Market Research; US; 617/482-9080

Heimbuck, Jeffrey A.; Pres & CEO, Inmac Corp.; US; 408/727-1970

Heiser, Paul; Pres, Comtech Publishing Ltd.; US; 702/825-9000

Heitt, Donald; Chmn & CEO, Voysys Corp.; US; 510/252-1100

Heizer, Ray; Pres, Heizer Software; US; 510/943-7667

Helfet, Peter; CEO, Plasmon Data Inc.; US; 408/474-0100

Helfgott, Donald J.; VP R&D, Inspiration Software Inc.; US; 503/245-9011

Helft, Lawrence B.; CEO, Systems Union Group; US; 914/948-7770

Helgeson, Richard; VP Sales, Computer Network Technology Corp.; US; 612/797-6000

Hellar, Gene; Pres, Prima International

Inc.; US; 408/727-2600

Heller, Lisa A.; Dir Mktng, Jabra Corp.; US; 619/622-0764, lheller@jabra.com

Heller, Richard A.; Pres & CEO, Lysis Corp.; US; 404/892-3301

Hellman, Peter S.; Pres & COO, TRW Inc.; US; 216/291-7000

Helm, James; VP Ops, Connectware Inc.; US; 214/907-1093

Helmer, John S.; VP, Audio Digital Imaging; US; 708/439-1335

Helmers Jr., Carl T.; Pres, Helmers Publishing Inc.; US; 603/924-9631

Helper, Lee; Partner, Bender, Goldman Helper; US; 310/473-4147, lee_helper@bgh.com

Helsel, Sandra Kay; Ed-in-Chief, Virtual Reality World; US; 203/226-6967

Helsing, Robert; VP, Management Graphics Inc.; US; 612/854-1220

Helthall, Jeff; VP Mktng, Programmed Logic Corp.; US; 908/302-0090

Helvey, Ted; Pres, Big Software Inc.; US; 415/919-0200

Hembery, Ian; VP Mktng & Sales, InContext Systems Corp.; Canada; 416/922-0087

Heming, Rick; VP Ops, Mustang Software Inc.; US; 805/873-2500, rick.heming@mustang.com

Hemingway, Linda; Dir Mktng, Output Technology Corp.; US; 509/536-0468

Hemmelgarn, Don; VP Prod Data Integration, International TechneGroup Inc.; US; 513/576-3900, dmh@iti-oh.com

Hemphill, Garry L.; VP Ops, Optical Data Systems Inc.; US; 214/234-6400

Henchey, Larry; Ed, Video Systems; US; 913/341-1300, 102556.1703@compuserve.com

Hencin, Ron; VP Sales & Mktng, Level Five Research; US; 407/729-6004

Hendershott, Greg; Pres, Twelve Tone Systems Inc.; US; 617/926-2480

Henderson, Edward; Ed & Pblr, Henderson Electronic Market Forecast; US; 415/961-2900

Henderson, Neil; Pres, Accelerated Technology Inc.; US; 334/661-5770

Henderson, Paul; VP Mktng, Center-Line Software Inc.; US; 617/498-3000

Henderson, Phillip L.; VP Eng, Numonics Corp.; US; 215/362-2766

Hendig, Klaus G.; VP Fin & Admin, Xicor Inc.; US; 408/432-8888

Hendren, Jack; Pres & CEO, Ashlar Inc.; US; 408/746-1800

Hendricks, John S.; Chmn & CEO, Discovery Channel, The; US; 301/986-1999

Hendrickson, Craig; VP, American Small Business Computers Inc.; US; 918/825-4844

Hendrickson, Jo-L; Pres & CEO, Individual Software Inc.; US; 510/734-6767

Hendrickson, Kenneth E.; EVP Micro, Western Digital Corp.; US; 714/932-5000

Hendrix, Danny; VP Ops, PC Service

Source Inc.; US; 214/406-8583

Hendrix, Jason; IS Mgr, Rockwell Network Systems; US; 805/968-4262, jhendrix@rns.com

Hengl, Terry; Pblr, PC AI Magazine; US; 602/971-1869

Henigson, Stuart; VP Mktng, Allegiant Technologies Inc.; US; 619/587-0500, stuart_henigson@allegiant.com

Henley, Jeffrey O.; EVP & CFO, Oracle Corp.; US; 415/506-7000

Hennel, Michael J.; Pres, Silvon Software Inc.; US; 708/655-3313

Hennessey, David J.; VP, Wang Laboratories Inc.; US; 508/459-5000

Henning, Eric A.; VP Sales & Mktng, Pinnacle Technology Inc.; US; 317/279-5157, ehenning@pinnacletech.com

Henning, Mike; Founder, Henning Associates; US; 804/295-0554

Henry, Brian C.; EVP & CFO, Cincinnati Bell Inc.; US; 513/397-9900

Henry, Jim; EVP, VISystems Inc.; US; 214/960-8649

Henry, John J.; CEO, Promark Software Inc.; Canada; 604/988-2051

Henry, Maralyn; Treas, Association of Personal Computer Users Group; US

Henry, Wendell; VP Eng, Adaptive Solutions Inc.; US; 503/690-1236

Hensley, Herbert T.; Pres & CEO, Data Race; US; 210/558-1900

Henson, Joe M.; Chmn, Legent Corp.; US; 703/708-3000

Henson, Robin; VP, Ares Software Corp.; US; 415/578-9090

Henzey, Terrence; VP Mktng, Rubbermaid Office Products Inc.; US; 615/977-5477

Hepburn, Peter; Pres, KnowledgeSet Corp.; US; 415/254-5400, phepburn@kset.com

Herald, Kim; Assoc Ed, CD-ROMs in Print; US; 203/226-6967

Herbert, Lawrence; Pres & CEO, Pantone Inc.; US; 201/935-5500

Herbert, Milton; EVP, Softbank Comdex Inc.; US; 617/443-1500

Herbert, Richard; SVP, Pantone Inc.; US; 201/935-5500

Herbert, William; Pres, Coordinated Service Inc.; US; 508/448-3800

Herbold, Robert J.; COO, Microsoft Corp.; US; 206/936-4400

Herlihy, Gregory; SVP, ResNova Software; US; 714/379-9000

Herman, James; VP, Northeast Consulting Resources Inc.; US; 617/654-0600, herman@ncri.com

Herman, Len; VP West Reg, Feith Systems & Software Inc.; US; 215/646-8000, len@feith.com

Hermansen, Gary; VP Sales & Mktng, Wireless Access Inc.; US; 408/653-1555, garyh@waccess.com

Hermsdorff, Dominique; VP Eng, ACI US Inc.; US; 408/252-4444

Hernandez, Emmanuel; CFO, Cypress Semiconductor Corp.; US; 408/943-2600

Hernandez, Richard J.; CEO, Technology Service Solutions; US; 610/293-2765

Herr, Eric; VP & CFO, Autodesk Inc.; US; 415/507-5000

Herrera, Kelly; Sr Act Exec, Daley Marketing Corp.; US; 714/662-0755

Herries, Andrew; VP Sales & Mktng, Sierra Wireless Inc.; Canada; 604/231-1100

Herring, C. Gregg; Pblr, Defense @ Security Electronics; US; 303/220-0600

Herrington, Debbie; VP Mktng, Portable Graphics Inc.; US; 512/719-8000

Herrington, Kirk; VP Eng, PageAhead Software Corp; US; 206/441-0340

Herrman, Carl; CEO, Solbourne Computer Inc.; US; 303/772-3400

Hersee, Steve; Pres, Copia International Ltd.; US; 708/682-8898

Hershenson, Paul; CFO, Art & Logic; US; 818/501-6990

Hershfield, Rob; Mgr Prod Mktng, Concentric Data Systems Inc.; US; 508/366-1122, 70474.3674@compuserve.com

Hershtal, Zev; EVP & COO, BCB Holdings Inc.; Canada; 905/850-8266

Hertz, Eli; Pres, Hertz Computer Corp.; US; 212/684-4141

Hertz, Marilyn; VP, Hertz Computer Corp.; US; 212/684-4141

Hertzberg, Robert; Ed-in-Chief, Web Week; US; 203/226-6967, rob@webweek.com

Hertzfeld, Andrew; VP & SW Wizard, General Magic Inc.; US; 408/774-4000

Hertzog, Mark; Pblr, Publishing & Production Executive; US; 215/238-5300

Hervey, George A.; VP & CFO, S3 Inc.; US; 408/980-5400

Herzing, John; VP Sales & Mktng, Fujitsu Microelectronics Inc.; US; 408/922-9000

Herzka, Dani; VP Mktng, Linotype-Hell Co.; US; 516/434-2000

Herzlich, Doron; Pres & COO, Vcon Inc.; US; 214/774-3890

Herzog, Cade R.; Assoc Pblr, Dallas/Fort Worth Computer Currents; US; 214/690-6222

Herzog, Eric; VP Mktng, Big Software Inc.; US; 415/919-0200, herzog@bigbusiness.com

Hess, Bill; Prod Mgr, WordTech Systems Inc.; US; 510/689-1200

Hess, Bob; CEO, Macro 4 Plc; US; 201/402-8000

Hess, Claudia; Dir Client Svcs, Integrated Strategic Information Services Inc.; US; 415/802-8555

Hess, Steven A.; VP & CFO, Asante Technologies Inc.; US; 408/435-8388

Hess, Todd; VP Ops & CFO, Onyx Graphics Corp.; US; 801/568-9900

Hess, William; Prod Mgr, CopyPro Inc.; US; 510/689-1200

Heston, Bill; VP Bus Dev, PhotoDisc Inc.; US; 206/441-9355

Hetherington, Marjorie; VP Sales & Mktng, P.I. Engineering Inc.; US; 517/655-5523

Hetzel, Jack; VP Fin, Systech Corp.; US; 619/453-8970

Hevenor, Keith V.; Ed, Electronic Publishing & TypeWorld; US; 918/831-9537, keithh@pennwell.com

Hewett, Julian; Mgng Dir, Ovum Ltd.; England; 071-255-2670, jjh@ovum.mhs.compuserve.com

Heye, William B.; Pres & CEO, SBE Inc.; US; 510/355-2000

Heyman, Alfred J.; Dir Dev, MicroMedium Inc.; US; 919/558-9225

Heyman, I. Michael; Sec, Smithsonian Institution; US; 202/357-2700

Heymann, Leonard; Ed-in-Chief, LAN Times; US; 415/513-6800, lenny-heymann@wcmh.com

Heys, Bill; COO, DayStar Digital Inc.; US; 770/967-2077

Heywood, Robert; Mgr IS, Inso Corp.; US; 617/753-6500

Hibbard, Dwight H.; Chmn, Cincinnati Bell Inc.; US; 513/397-9900

Hibner, Geoffrey; CFO, Frontier Technologies Corp.; US; 414/241-4555

Hicken, Arthur; Mktng Dir, ParSoft Corp.; US; 818/305-0041, ahicken@parasoft.com

Hickey, James G.; VP Cust Support, Xyvision Inc.; US; 617/245-4100

Hickey, Michael K.; Pres, Axonix Corp.; US; 801/521-9797

Hicks, Dennis; Pres & CEO, Spur Products Corp.; US; 208/377-0001, d.hicks@micron.net

Hicks, Don; Ed, Amazing Computing for the Commodore Amiga; US; 508/678-4200, donhicks@aol.com

Hicks, Joyce; Pblr, PiM Publications Inc.; US; 508/678-4200

Hicks-Williams, Lucia; VP Strat Plng, General Magic Inc.; US; 408/774-4000

Hicksted, Richard T.; CTO, MTI Technology Corp.; US; 714/970-8583

Hiechel, David J.; Pres & CEO, Eagle Software Inc.; US; 913/823-7257, dave@eaglesoft.com

Higashi, Tadao; EVP, Oki Electric Industry Co. Ltd.; Japan; 3-3501-3111

Higbie, Patrick B.; Chmn & CEO, DataFocus Inc.; US; 703/631-6770, pat@datafocus.com

Higginson, Alan J.; EVP Mktng & Sales, Sierra On-Line Inc.; US; 206/649-9800

Hight, George; Pres, Basis Int'l.; US; 505/345-5232

Hikdreth, Susan; Ed, Software Success; US; 617/444-5755

Hilber, Jeffrey G.; CFO, Uunet Technologies Inc.; US; 703/206-5600

Hildebrand, J.D.; Ed, Windows Tech Journal; US; 541/747-0800

Hildebrandt, Gene; VP Sales & Mktng, Newer Technology; US; 316/685-4904

Hildebrandt, Peter A.; Pres, Computing Information Directory; US; 509/684-7619

Hilderbrand, Cheri; Dir Mktng, RightFAX; US; 520/327-1357, crh@right-fax.com

Hile, John; VP R&D, Hilgraeve Inc.; US; 313/243-0576

Hilf, Marvin; Pres, Parallel Storage Solutions; US; 914/347-7044

Hill, Chad; Pres, Hill Communications; US; 510/945-7910

Hill, Jeannine; EVP, Marken Communications; US; 408/986-0100

Hill, John; Pres, Matrix Communications; US; 419/882-6800, usgal2hdcp@aol.com

Hill, M. Denis; VP Marcom, Pick Systems; US; 714/261-7425, denis@pick-sys.com

Hill, Michael T.; Pres, Southern Micro Systems Inc.; US; 770/499-9231

Hill, Neal; VP Mktng, Cognos Inc.; Canada; 613/738-1440

Hill, Rick; Dir Eng, Arnet Corp.; US; 615/834-8000

Hill, Stephen E.; SVP Corp Dev, Informix Software Inc.; US; 415/926-6300

Hill, Timothy L.; VP Mktng, Iomega Corp.; US; 801/778-1000

Hillel, Irit; PrintPaks Inc.; US; 503/295-6564

Hiller Jr., Stanley; Chmn, Key Tronic Corp.; US; 509/928-8000

Hilliard, William J.; Mgng Partner, Sonnetech Ltd.; US; 415/957-9940

Hillman, John; VP Mktng, Scala Inc.; US; 703/713-0900

Hills, Len; Pres, Competitive Strategies Inc.; US; 408/266-4549, lhills@competitive-strat.com

Hilton, Peter; VP Sales, MicroSlate Inc.; Canada; 514/444-3680

Hilts, Chip; COO, Strategic Alliance Partners Inc.; US; 310/860-4029

Hilverda, Andy; Dir Mktng, Videx Inc.; US; 541/758-0521

Hilz, Mark T.; Pres & CEO, PC Service Source Inc.; US; 214/406-8583

Hinckley, Gregory K.; VP & CFO, VLSI Technology Inc.; US; 408/434-3000

Hindawi, David; Pres, Software Ventures Corp.; US; 510/644-3232

Hindin, Harvey; VP, Emerging Technologies Group Inc.; US; 516/586-8810, hhindin@etg.com

Hinds, John A.; EVP, VeriFone Inc.; US; 415/591-6500

Hinely, Bill; SVP Sales & Mktng, Coda Music Technology; US; 612/937-9611

Hines, Katherine E.; Office Mgr, Syncware Corp.; US; 303/369-6900

Hinkle, Dave; VP Tech, Sense8 Corp.; US; 415/331-6318, dave@sense8.com

Hippeau, Eric; Chmn & CEO, Ziff-Davis

Publishing Co.; US; 212/503-3500

Hipsher, Garry S.; Pres, Transparent Technology Inc.; US; 310/215-8040, garry@trantech.com

Hiquet, Stacy; Pblr, Ziff-Davis Press; US; 510/601-2000

Hirani, Ajit W.; VP & GM, ECC International Corp.; US; 610/687-2600

Hirata, Ryuichi; Pres Capcom US, Capcom; US; 408/727-0500

Hirayama, Tetsuo; Pres, Dempa Publications Inc.; US; 212/682-4755

Hirsch, Abe; VP Mktng, Applix Inc.; US; 508/870-0300, ahirsch@applix.com

Hirschberg, Julia; Ed, Computational Linguistics; US; 617/253-2889, acl@research.att.com

Hirschel, Jo-Ann; Mgng Ed, Family PC; US; 212/503-5255

Hirschfield, Peter; Pblr, Electronic Musician; US; 510/653-3307

Hirvela, Henry; SVP & CFO, Power Computing Corp.; US; 408/526-0500

Hitchcock, Nancy A.; Assoc Ed, Computer Artist; US; 603/891-0123

Hitchner, Jennifer; Dir Sales, WexTech Systems Inc.; US; 212/949-9595

Hitz, Jay; Apps Eng, Extron Electronics; US; 714/491-1500

Hjerpe, William M.; VP & CFO, Honeywell Inc.; US; 612/951-1000

Hnilo, Joe; VP Mktng, Resumix; US; 408/988-0444

Ho, Alan; EVP, TechBridge Technology Corp.; Canada; 416/222-8998, aho@contrad.com

Ho, C.S.; Pres, Mitac International Corp.; Taiwan ROC; 2-501-8231

Ho, Chris; Sales Mgr, Smile International Inc.; US; 714/546-0336

Ho, Eric; Mgng Dir, Accurate Research Inc.; US; 408/523-4788, eric.ho@drcdrom.com

Ho, K.Y.; Pres & CEO, ATI Technologies Inc.; Canada; 905/882-2600

Ho, S.K.; Pres & CEO, Biscom Inc.; US; 508/250-1800

Hoard, Bruce; Exec Ed, Imaging World Magazine; US; 207/236-8524, bruceh@mcimail.com

Hobgood, Allan H.; Pres & COO, Docucon Inc.; US; 210/525-9221

Hobuss, Jim; Pres, HCS Inc.; US; 503/661-3421

Hobuss, Robin; Treas, HCS Inc.; US; 503/661-3421

Hochman, Seth; Sales Mgr, Coast Manufacturing Co.; US; 914/376-1500

Hocutt, Ron; VP Support Svcs, Folio Corp.; US; 801/344-3700, rhocutt@folio.com

Hodel, Alan E.; Ed-in-Chief, Software Quarterly; US; 817/961-6551, hodel@vnet.ibm.com

Hodge, Ron; Sales, Embedded Systems Products Inc.; US; 713/561-9990

Hodges, Ray L.; Ed, Computer Technology Trends: Analyses & Forecasts; US; 512/258-8898

Hodskins, David; Pres, Hodskins Simone & Searls Inc.; US; 415/327-3434

Hoefert, Thomas; VP & CFO, Recognition International Inc.; US; 214/579-6000

Hoenig, Robert; GM, SKY Computers Inc.; US; 508/454-6200, hoenig@sky.com

Hoeppner, Charles; Dir R&D, Secure Document Systems Inc.; US; 904/725-2505

Hoey, Jeff; VP Sales, PC DOCS Inc.; US; 617/273-3800, jeffh@pcdocs.com

Hofflander, Steve; Dir Sales & Mktng, Portfolio Software Inc.; US

Hoffman, Bob; Pres, Commercial Software Inc.; US; 908/985-8966

Hoffman, Dan; Pres, DISC Distributing Corp.; US; 310/787-6800

Hoffman, David; Ed, Information Today; US; 609/654-6266

Hoffman, Gary A.; CEO, Skipstone Inc.; US; 512/305-0200, gary@skipstone.com

Hoffman, Lance; Dir, Institute for Computer & Telecommunications System Policy; US; 202/994-4955

Hoffman, Lou; Pres, Hoffman Agency, The; US; 408/286-2611, lhoffman@hoffman.com

Hoffman, Mark B.; Chmn, Sybase Inc.; US; 510/922-3500

Hoffman, Marvin; Chmn & CEO, XXCAL Testing Laboratories; US; 310/477-2902

Hoffman, Michael; Pres, Alaras Corp.; US; 919/544-1228

Hoffman, Paul S.; Author, Software Legal Book; US

Hoffman, Sharon L.; Ed, Midrange Computing; US; 619/931-8615

Hoffman, Steve; VP Ops, Computer Task Group Inc.; US; 716/887-7424, steve.hoffman@ctg.com

Hoffstein, Gordon; Chmn & CEO, PCs Compleat; US; 508/480-8500

Hogan, Jerry; Nat'l Sales Mgr, Fox Electronics; US; 941/693-0099

Hogan, Kathleen; Ed, CD-ROM Finder; US; 609/654-6266

Hogan, Thomas H.; Pres, Information Today Inc.; US; 609/654-6266

Hogan, Tom; VP Mktng & Sales, Dayna Communications Inc.; US; 801/269-7200, thogan@dayna.com

Hogue, Sue; CFO, Apertus Technologies Inc.; US; 612/828-0300

Hoke, Robert D.; Pres & CEO, nView Corp.; US; 804/873-1354

Hoke, Robert W.; VP Eng, Turtle Beach Systems Inc.; US; 717/767-0200

Holberger, Kenneth; Chmn, Epoch Inc.; US; 508/435-1000

Holder, Steven; Pres, Run Inc.; US; 201/529-4600

Holdreith, Mark J.; Pblr, Windows Magazine; US; 516/733-8300, mholdrei@cmp.com

Holdt, Terry N.; Pres & CEO, S3 Inc.; US; 408/980-5400

Holenstein, Bruce D.; Pres, Principia Products Inc.; US; 610/429-1359

Holenstein, Paul J.; VP, Principia Products Inc.; US; 610/429-1359

Holgberg, Henrik; VP & GM, Ericsson Inc.; US; 201/890-3600

Holiber, William D.; Group Pblr, CurtCo Freedom Group; US; 310/589-3100

Holiday, Joel; CFO, Applied Micro Circuits Corp.; US; 619/450-9333

Holler, Michele; Mktng Mgr, Quatech Inc.; US; 216/434-3154, holler@quatech.com

Holleyman, Robert; Pres, Business Software Alliance; US; 202/872-5500

Holliday, Michael; Pres, Computer-PREP; US; 602/275-7700

Holliday, Taffy; EVP, River Run Software Group; US; 203/861-0090

Hollinger, Bruce A.; Pres & CEO, Macola Inc.; US; 614/382-5999

Hollinger, Steve; Pres, S.H. Pierce & Co.; US; 617/338-2222

Hollingsworth, Dana; COO, Port Inc.; US; 203/852-1102

Hollingsworth, Steve; Dir Mktng, Cadix International Inc.; US; 404/804-9951

Hollingsworth, W.D.; Pres, Port Inc.; US; 203/852-1102

Hollis, Kevin; Dir Sales, BusinessVision Management Systems Inc.; Canada; 905/629-3233

Holloway, James V.; Pres Scriptel Corp, Scriptel Holdings Inc.; US; 614/276-8402

Holloway, Richard A.; SVP, SCI Systems Inc.; US; 205/998-0592

Hollrah, Kent; Dir Sales, Open Systems Holdings Corp.; US; 612/829-0011

Holm, Torben E.; VP Intl Sales, Management Graphics Inc.; US; 612/854-1220

Holmes, Becky; EVP, K.I.O. Corp.; US; 915/774-5355

Holmes, Bill; VP Mktng, California Software Products Inc.; US; 714/973-0440

Holmes, Bill; Pres & CEO, K.I.O. Corp.; US; 915/774-5355

Holmes, Burton; Pres, Burton Holmes Assoc.; US; 212/989-0207

Holmes, Chris; Pres US Div, Visionware; US; 415/325-2113

Holmes, David R.; Chmn, Pres & CEO, Reynolds & Reynolds; US; 513/443-2000

Holmes, Edith; Pblr, Federal Computer Week; US; 847-291-5214

Holmes, Jeff; CEO/Creat Dir, Three Marketeers Advertising Inc.; US; 408/293-3233, jeff@3marketeers.com

Holmes, Kyle; Dir Bus Dev, MCCommunications Inc.; US; 214/480-8383, kyle_holmes@mccom.com

Holmes, Rebecca L.; EVP, Datamark Inc.; US; 915/778-1944

Holmes, Robert; Pres & COO, Acclaim

Entertainment Inc.; US; 516/624-8888

Holmes, William J.; Pres & CEO, Datamark Inc.; US; 915/778-1944

Holston II, J.B.; Pres Int'l Media, Ziff-Davis Publishing Co.; US; 212/503-3500

Holstrom, Pete; VP & GM, Microport Inc.; US; 408/438-8649

Holt, C. Scott; VP Sales, Diamond Multimedia Systems Inc.; US; 408/325-7000

Holt, Connie; Pblr, Online Design; US; 415/334-3800, connie@online-design.com

Holt, David; Mgr SW Dev, O'Neil Electronics; US; 714/727-1234

Holtzman, Steve; VP Fin, Optimal Networks; US; 415/254-5950

Holzaepfel, Cheryl; Ed-in-Chief, Ziff-Davis Press; US; 510/601-2000

Holzer, Elisabeth; Assoc Ed, Yahoo! Internet Life; US; 212/503-3835, eholzer@zd.com

Holzman, Neil; VP Sales & Mktng, Software Security Inc.; US; 203/656-3000

Homer, Mike; VP Mktng, Network TeleSystems; US; 408/523-8100

Homer, Steve; Assist Ed, CeBIT News; Belgium; 322-766-0031

Honaker, Timothy; SVP, Dearborn Publishing Group; US; 312/836-4400

Honeycutt, Robert L.; COO, Barra Inc.; US; 510/548-5442

Honeycutt, Van B.; Pres & CEO, Computer Sciences Corp.; US; 310/615-0311

Honeywell, Nadja; Prog Mgr, Localization & Consulting Services; US; 206/443-5627

Hong, Mike; SVP Sls & Mktng, Liuski International Inc.; US; 770/447-9454

Hood, Jacky; Pres, Crescent Project Management; US; 415/938-4636

Hood, Phil; Ed-in-Chief, HyperMedia Communications Inc.; US; 415/573-5170, phood@newmedia.com

Hooper, Dean; VP US Sales & Mktng, AMP Inc.; US; 717/564-0100

Hooper, Jack; CFO, Business Printing Center; US; 206/869-6319

Hooper, Steve M.; Pres & CEO, AT&T Wireless Services; US; 206/827-4500

Hootnick, Larry; COO, NetManage Inc.; US; 408/973-7171

Hoover, Marc; Sales Mgr, Toray Optical Storage Solutions; US; 415/341-7152

Hoover, William R.; Chmn, Computer Sciences Corp.; US; 310/615-0311

Hopkins, Michael; VP Sales & Mktng, Dotronix Inc.; US; 612/633-1742

Hopkins, Tim; Ed, Collected Algorithms from the ACM; US; 212/869-7440

Hopmann, Alexander; Chmn & Pres, ResNova Software; US; 714/379-9000

Hopp, Dietmar; Chmn, SAP AG; Germany; 6227-34-0

Hopper, Mark E.; Dir Sales, Auravision Corp.; US; 510/252-6800

Hoppmann, David; Pres & CEO, Intell.X; US; 703/524-7400

Horan, James P.; CIO, DST Systems Inc.; US; 816/435-1000

Horgen, Chris H.; Chmn & CEO, Nichols Research Corp.; US; 205/883-1140

Horn, Barry; EVP Sales & Mktng, Attachmate Corp.; US; 206/644-4010

Horn, Cathy; Exec Dir, Intelligent Network Forum; US; chorn@ballistic.com

Hornacek, Rudolph E.; VP Eng, Telephone & Data Systems Inc.; US; 312/630-1900

Hornaday, Bill W.; Mgng Ed, RiSc World; US; 512/250-9023

Hornbeck, Matthew; VP Ops, Young Minds Inc.; US; 909/335-1350

Horowitz, Danny; Mktng Mgr, Best Data Products Inc.; US; 818/773-9600, danny@bdp.mhs.compuserve.com

Horrell, Robert E.; VP Ops, 3D Systems Corp.; US; 805/295-5600

Horton, William J.; EVP Ops, Computer Television Network; US; 916/582-5083

Horwich, Julian; Exec Dir, Corporate Association for Microcomputer Professionals; US; 847/291-1360

Horwitz, Frank; Pres, Securenet Technologies Inc.; US; 206/776-2524, flh@securenet.org

Horwitz, Gerald A.; SVP, Datametrics Corp.; US; 818/598-6200

Horwitz, Robert; Ed-in-Chief, Directions on Microsoft; US; 206/882-3396

Hoshino, Kenji P.; Pres, CMR Publishing Inc.; US; 707/575-4652

Hoska, Gerald; VP, Winsted Corp.; US; 612/944-9050

Hoskins, Brent; Ed, Business Equipment HOTLINE; US; 816/941-3100

Hosono, Akio; Pres, I-O Data Devices Inc.; US; 408/377-7062

Hottovy, Ronald J.; VP & CFO, Scientific Software-Intercomp Inc.; US; 303/292-1111

Hou, Raymond; Pres, ADI Systems Inc.; US; 408/944-0100, rhou@adiusa.com

Hough, D.J.; VP & CIO, Bell Industries Inc.; US; 310/826-2355

Hough, John; Co-Pres, Corporate Communications; US; 206/728-1778

Hough, Michael R.; Pblr, A/E/C Systems Computer Solution; US; 860/666-1326

Houlihan, Dennis M.; Pres, Roland Corp. US; US; 213/685-5141

House, Chuck; SVP, Veritas Software Corp.; US; 415/335-8000

House, David L.; SVP, Intel Corp.; US; 408/765-8080

House, Don; Chmn, SQL Financials Int'l.; US; 770/390-3900

Housten, John; Pres, Azeena Technologies Inc.; US; 310/981-2771

Houston, Donald S.; VP Sales, Proxima Corp.; US; 619/457-5500

Houtz, Jim H.; Chmn, Pres & CEO,

CyCare Systems Inc.; US; 602/596-4300

Hovanec, Gene; VP & CFO, Vitesse Semiconductor Corp.; US; 805/388-3700

Howard, Alan; Ed, Computer Literature Index; US; 602/995-5929

Howard, Alice; VP, Applied Computer Research Inc.; US; 602/995-5929

Howard, Juli; Dir Sales, RightFAX; US; 520/327-1357, jah@rightfax.com

Howard, Larry; Analyst, Infonetics Research Inc.; US; 408/298-7999

Howard, Martha; Mgng Ed, Information Hotline; US; 908/536-7673

Howard, Michael; Pres, Infonetics Research Inc.; US; 408/298-7999, mvhoward@aol.com

Howard, Pat; Pres & CEO, Digital Systems Int'l.; US; 206/881-7544

Howard, Phillip; Pres, Applied Computer Research Inc.; US; 602/995-5929

Howard, Randall; Chmn, Mortice Kern Systems Inc.; Canada; 519/884-2251

Howard, Robert; VP Sales & Mktng, Dynaware US Inc.; US; 415/349-5700

Howard, Robert; Pres & CEO, Tower Technology Corp.; US; 512/452-9455, rock@twr.com

Howard, Robert; Chmn, Howtek Inc.; US; 603/882-5200

Howard, Roger; VP Sales & Mktng, DataViews Corp.; US; 413/586-4144

Howard, Stephen M.; CEO, Make Systems; US; 415/941-9800

Howard, Web; Pres, Society for Information Display; US; 714/545-1526

Howe, Dale; VP Sales, Dazel Corp.; US; 512/328-6977

Howe, Douglas E.; GM, Nikon Electronic Imaging; US; 516/547-4355

Howe, Kevin; Pres & CEO, DacEasy Inc.; US; 214/732-7500

Howe, Richard T.; Sales, Cybermedix Inc.; US; 703/917-6600

Howell, Dave; Ed-in-Chief, IC Master; US; 516/227-1300

Howell, Robert; EVP & GM, Information Access Co.; US; 415/378-5200

Howells, Jeffrey P.; SVP & CFO, Tech Data Corp.; US; 813/539-7429

Howk, Carleton R.; Ed-in-Chief, A-E-C Automation Newsletter; US; 770/565-3282, aecnews@aol.com

Hripko, Mark; VP Prod Dev, InterApps Inc.; US; 310/374-4125, mhripko@aol.com

Hsia, Matt H.; Pres & CEO, Tagram Systems Corp.; US; 714/258-3222

Hsieh, Robert C.; Co-Chmn, Ulead Systems Inc.; US; 310/523-9393

Hsieh, Steve; Pres, Nimax Inc.; US; 619/566-4800

Hsiung, Hugo X.; Ed, Asia IT Journal; US; 415/286-2766, h.hsiung@idg.geis.com

Hsu, Ching; CEO, Raritan Computer Inc.; US; 908/874-4072

Hsu, Gerald C.; Pres & CEO, ArcSys;

US; 408/738-8881

Hsu, Jazz; Pres & CEO, Jazz Speakers; US; 818/336-2689

Hsu, Tony; VP, Jazz Speakers; US; 818/336-2689

Hsueh, Min-Yu; Chmn, Escalade; US; 408/654-1600

Huai, ReiJane; Pres & CEO, Cheyenne Software Inc.; US; 516/484-5110

Huang, April; Fin Mgr, ETC Computer Inc.; US; 510/226-6250

Huang, Elizabeth; CFO, Jazz Speakers; US; 818/336-2689

Huang, Frank; Chmn & CEO, Umax Technologies Inc.; US; 510/651-4000

Huang, George C.; Chmn & CEO, Award Software Int'l. Inc.; US; 415/968-4433

Huang, Henry; VP Production, Sys Technology Inc.; US; 714/821-3900

Huang, Jerry; Prod Mktng Mgr, AITech International Corp.; US; 510/226-8960

Huang, Keith; Mgr Tech Sup, Smile International Inc.; US; 714/546-0336

Huang, Kent; Pres, ETC Computer Inc.; US; 510/226-6250

Huang, Minsiu; VP Ops, ActionTec Electronics Inc.; US; 408/739-7000

Huang, Oliver; Pres, Arc Media Inc.; Canada; 416/410-4429

Huang, Simon; Pres & CEO, CMD Technology Inc.; US; 714/454-0800

Huang, Ted; Chmn, Teco Information Systems Co. Inc.; US; 708/438-3998

Huang, William; Pres, Area Electronics Systems Inc.; US; 714/993-0300

Hubbard, Barbara; Dir Publishing, Mobile Letter; US; 415/390-9800, bhubbard@mobileinsights.com

Hubbard, Jan; Intl Sales Mgr, Multi-Tech Systems Inc.; US; 612/785-3500

Huber, Val; VP & CTO, Vision Software Tools Inc.; US; 510/238-4100

Huber, Walter J.; VP Mktng, Interstar Technologies Inc.; Canada; 514/875-6710, w.huber@ranmar.qc.ca

Huddleston, Randy; Pres, Integrated Business Computers; US; 805/527-8792

Hudelson, Travis; EVP, MicroVideo Learning Systems; US; 212/777-9595, travis_hudelson@microvideo.com

Hudley, David; VP Creative Dir, KSK Communications; US; 703/734-1880

Hudson, Katherine K.; Dir Mktng, Harris Computer Systems Corp.; US; 305/973-5100

Hudson, William J.; Pres & CEO, AMP Inc.; US; 717/564-0100

Huebner, Elizabeth J.; VP & CFO, Fluke Corp.; US; 206/347-6100

Huesgen, James H.; EVP & CFO, Pacific Telecom Inc.; US; 360/905-5800

Huff, Agnes; SVP, Fraser/Young Inc.; US; 310/451-0300

Huff, Gerald B.; VP Dev, Avantos Performance Systems Inc.; US; 510/654-4600

Huffman, Andrew J.; Pres & CEO,

AimTech Corp.; US; 603/883-0220

Hufnagel, Leon C.; Pres, Chilton Co.; US; 610/964-4000

Hughes, Bob; Dir Sales & Mktng, PC-Kwik Corp.; US; 503/644-5644, bob@pckwik.mhs.compuserve.com

Hughes, Claire M.; Asst Ed, Bits & Bytes Review; US; 406/862-7280

Hughes, Gary N.; Pres & CEO, Photonics Corp.; US; 408/955-7930

Hughes, John; Ed & Pblr, Bits & Bytes Review; US; 406/862-7280

Hughes, Phil; Ed, Internet On-Line Guide; US; 206/782-7733

Hughes, Robert C.; VP WW Sales, Data General Corp.; US; 508/898-5000

Hughes, Roger; VP & COO, Optical Data Systems Inc.; US; 214/234-6400

Hughes, Susan; EVP Bus Dev, Persoft Inc.; US; 608/273-6000

Hughes, Susan K.; Pres, Wordright Associates; US; 210/532-2332

Hughes, Tom; Pres, PhotoDisc Inc.; US; 206/441-9355

Huhn, William D.; EVP & COO, Aironet Wireless Communications Inc.; US; 330/665-7900

Hui, David K.P.; EVP, Tseng Labs Inc.; US; 215/968-0502

Hui, John; CEO, Orchestra MultiSystems Inc.; US; 714/891-3861

Hui, Michael; VP Prod Ops, True Software Inc.; US; 508/369-7398, mhui@truesoft.com

Hui, Steve; Pres & CEO, ExperVision Inc.; US; 408/523-0900

Hull, Charles W.; Pres & COO, 3D Systems Corp.; US; 805/295-5600

Hullot, Jean-Marie; CTO, NeXT Inc.; US; 415/366-0900

Hultgren, Rose; Mktng Dir, Software Spectrum Inc.; US; 214/840-6600

Hulton, Jeff; VP Sales, Attain Corp.; US; 617/776-1110, jeff_hulton@qm.attain.com

Humble, Charles F.; Partner, Insync Partners; US; 503/221-1063

Humenansky, Paul L.; EVP & COO, Platinum Technology Inc.; US; 708/620-5000

Hummel, Matt; Creative Dir, Digital Media Int'l.; US; 805/563-9490

Humphrey, Robert; VP Dev, Chronologic Corp.; US; 602/293-3100

Humphreys, Johnny M.; Pres & CEO, Itron Inc.; US; 509/924-9900

Humphreys, Steven C.; Pres, Caere Corp.; US; 408/395-7000

Hundley Jr., George Lee; Pblr, Smart Computer & Software Retailing; US; 910/605-0121

Hundt, Reed; Chmn of Commission, Federal Communications Commission; US; 202/418-0200

Hung, Nelson; GM, Halskar Systems; US; 510/656-5157

Hung, Winston; VP SW Dev, Initio

Corp.; US; 408/988-1919

Hunt, Mark; Pub/Exec Producer, Zondervan Publishing House; US; 616/698-6900, mark.hunt@zph.com

Hunt, Thomas J.; VP Sales & Mktng, Disk Technologies Corp.; US; 407/671-5500, tom-hunt@radiomail.net

Hunteman, Rick; Dir Sales, Minuteman; US; 214/446-7363

Hunter, Bradfield; SVP Sales, CTX International Inc.; US; 909/598-8094

Hunter, Lee; Mgng Ed & Pblr, Hum-The Government Computer Magazine; Canada; 613/237-4862, lee.hunter@hum.com

Hunter, Scott; VP Eng, Mustang Software Inc.; US; 805/873-2500

Huntington, Dustin; Pres, Exsys Inc.; US; 505/256-8356

Hupp, Alan W.; VP Mktng, Drake Training & Technologies; US; 612/896-7000

Hurd, James M.; Pres & CEO, Planar Systems Inc.; US; 503/690-1100

Hurdelbrink, Emit; VP, National Systems Programmers Assoc.; US; 414/423-2420

Hurley, Colleen; Bus Mgr, CD Solutions Inc.; US; 508/879-0006, cvhurley@cdsolutions.com

Hurley, John C.; VP, Cypress Research Corp.; US; 408/752-2700

Hurley, Sean T.; VP Ops, Linear Technology Corp.; US; 408/432-1900

Hurlow, Mark; Sr Lab Analyst, Macworld Labs; US; 415/243-0505, mark_hurlow@macworld.com

Hurst, Kenneth R.; Chmn, 100VG-Any-LAN Forum; US; 916/348-0212

Hurtado, Jose; Pres & CEO, M-USA Business Systems Inc.; US; 214/386-6100

Hurwitz, Jess; Dir Prod Dev, Parallel Storage Solutions; US; 914/347-7044

Hurwitz, Judith; Pres, Hurwitz Consulting Group; US; 617/965-6900, jhurwitz@world.std.com

Husted, Todd; VP Support Prod, Logical Operations; US; 716/240-7500

Huston, Preston; Chmn, Associated Advertising Agency Inc.; US; 316/683-4691

Hustwit, Robert; Co-Founder, World Library Inc.; US; 714/756-9500

Hustwit, William; Co-Founder, World Library Inc.; US; 714/756-9500

Hutcheson, G. Dan; Pres, VLSI Research Inc.; US; 408/453-8844

Hutcheson, Jerry D.; CEO, VLSI Research Inc.; US; 408/453-8844

Hutchinson, Anne L.; Dir Mktng, Gryphon Software Corp.; US; 619/536-8815

Hutchinson, Peter; Pblr, Dr. Dobb's Journal; US; 415/358-9500

Hutchison, Donald; VP Sales & Mktng, NetCom On-Line Communications Services Inc.; US; 408/345-2600

Hutchison, Roger; Pres & CEO, CD ROM-USA Inc.; US; 303/384-3922

Huxsaw, Charles F.; Pblr, Law Office

Technology Review; US; 610/359-9900

Huyett, John P.; VP & CFO, Avanti Corp.; US; 408/738-8881

Hwang, James; Dir Svcs & Sup, Tatung Science & Technology Inc.; US; 408/383-0988

Hwang, K. Philip; Chmn & CEO, TeleVideo Systems Inc.; US; 408/954-8333

Hwang, Rose; Pres & CEO, Alpha Systems Lab Inc.; US; 714/252-0117

Hwang, Simon H.; Pres, Triumph Logistic Computers; US; 714/952-8999

Hwang, Y.M.; Pres, American Advantech Corp.; US; 408/245-6678

Hwe Huh, Hyung; CTO, Diamond Multimedia Systems Inc.; US; 408/325-7000

Hyams, Peter; Ed, Expert Systems Journal; US; 609/654-6266

Hyatt, Tom; VP & CFO, Connectware Inc.; US; 214/907-1093

Hypponen, Ari; Dir Dev, Data Fellows Inc.; US; 415/354-0233

I'Anson, Stephen Mark; Pres & CEO, Integrated Micro Products Inc.; US; 214/980-2771

Iacobucci, Edward E.; Chmn, Citrix Systems Inc.; US; 305/340-2246

Iadavaia, Marlene; CFO, Rational Data Systems Inc.; US; 415/382-8400, miadavia@rds.com

Iannucci, John; CEO, E Corp.; US

Ianuzzi, Steve; CEO, Blenheim Group US Inc.; US; 201/346-1400

Ianuzzi, Jr., Ralph R.; Pres, Bruno Blenheim Inc.; US; 201/346-1400

Ianuzzi, Sr., Ralph J.; Chmn, Bruno Blenheim Inc.; US; 201/346-1400

Idei, Nobuyuki; Pres, Sony Corp.; Japan; 3-5448-2111

Iftikar, Syed H.; Chmn, Pres & CEO, SyQuest Technology Inc.; US; 510/226-4000

Illig, Clifford W.; Pres & COO, Cerner Corp.; US; 816/221-1024

Illson, James E.; SVP & CFO, Merisel Inc.; US; 310/615-3080

Imai, Kaz; Pres, Sony Personal Information Co.; US

Imai, Minoru; EVP, Oki Electric Industry Co. Ltd.; Japan; 3-3501-3111

Iman, Rocky; Sales Mgr, Maxi Switch Inc.; US; 520/294-5450

Imbler, Stephen V.; SVP & CFO, Centura Software Corp.; US; 415/321-9500

Inatome, Rick; Chmn, InaCom Corp.; US; 402/392-3900

Indvik, Kurt; Pblr & Ed-in-Chief, InfoText; US; 310/724-6783, kindvik@aol.com

Inerfeld, Ivan; COO, Tiger Direct Inc.; US; 305/443-8212

Infanti, Daniel J.; VP, Sharp Electronics Corp.; US; 201/529-8200

Infinger, James L.; VP & CIO, CompUSA Inc.; US; 214/982-4000

Inga, Kandra; VP Sales, Morris Media;

US; 310/533-4800

Ingari, Frank; Chmn, Pres & CEO, Shiva Corp.; US; 617/270-8300

Ingham, Gary; VP Mktng, Positive Support Review Inc.; US; 310/453-6100, ingham@psrinc.com

Ingleman, John A.; VP & CFO, Hutchinson Technology Inc.; US; 612/587-3797

Ingram, Pat; Dir Computing, Ovum Ltd.; England; 071-255-2670, pmi@ovum.mhs.compuserve.com

Inoue, Osamu; Pres, Fuji Photo Film US Inc.; US; 914/789-8100

Interlandi, Daniel G.; SVP Sales & Mktng, Micros Systems Inc.; US; 301/210-6000

Ioele, Tony; VP, Digital Equipment Computer Users Society; US; 508/841-3346

Iorillo, Richard; Pres, Eurom Flashware Inc.; US

Ip, Edward; CTO, Verilink Corp.; US; 408/945-1199

Irie, Hide; Pres, ASCII Entertainment Software Inc.; US; 415/780-0800, hide.irie@asciient.com

Irsfeld, Mitch; Ed-in-Chief, CommunicationsWeek; US; 516/562-5530

Irwin, David; CEO, Irwin Ink; US; 619/483-4333

Isaac, J.R.; Ed, IT-Digest; India; 642-6030, isaac@iris.ernet.in

Isaacs, Craig; VP Sales & Mktng, Dantz Development Corp.; US; 510/253-3000, craig_isaacs@dantz.com

Isaacson, Portia; Pres, Dream IT Inc.; US; 303/417-9313, portia@dreamit.com

Isherwood, Charles S.; SVP & CFO, IMP Inc.; US; 408/432-9100

Ishii, Ione; VP Ops, KnowledgeSet Corp.; US; 415/254-5400, iishii@kset.com

Isley, Larry; Dir, AT&T Software Solutions Group; US; 908/580-6444

Ismach, Robert; Pres, JYACC Inc.; US; 212/267-7722

Israel, David; VP Publishing, Macmillan Computer Publishing; US; 317/581-3500

Israel, Lillian; Dir Memb, Association for Computing Machinery; US; 212/869-7440

Israel, Sharon; Act Mgr, FitzGerald Communications Inc.; US; 617/494-9500

Itsu, Gerald C.; Chmn, Pres & CEO, Avanti Corp.; US; 408/738-8881

Ivers, Jim; Assoc Ed, Virtual Reality World; US; 203/226-6967

Iverson, Gregory R.; VP Mktng, Interphase Corp.; US; 214/919-9000

Iverson, Lorraine; CEO, Cooper/Iverson Marketing; US; 619/292-7400, lorraine@coopiver.com

Ivie, Judith K.; Mgng Ed, A/E/C Systems Computer Solution; US; 860/666-1326

Ivy, Jim; EVP, Ricoh Corp.; US; 201/882-2000

Iwaya, Sadao; EVP, TDK Corp.; Japan;

3-3278-5111

Izushima, Masaaki; SVP, Ricoh Corp.; US; 201/882-2000

Jablo, Michael; VP SW Sales & Mktng, Engineering Animation Inc.; US; 515/296-9908

Jack, Craig; VP Sales, Z Microsystems Inc.; US; 619/657-1000

Jackman, Brian J.; EVP, Tellabs; US; 708/969-8800

Jackson, Brett; SVP Sales & Mktng, Axent Technologies; US; 301/258-2620

Jackson, Charlie; Chmn, FutureWave Software Inc.; US; 619/637-6190

Jackson, Kent M.; Pres, TriHouse Group, The; US; 617/544-3088, 71232.1307@compuserve.com

Jackson, Larry; Pblr, Repair, Service & Remarketing News; US; 417/781-9317

Jackson, Margaret; Pres, Western Pacific Data Systems; US; 619/454-0028

Jackson, Richard D.; Vice Chmn & COO, First Financial Management Corp.; US; 770/857-0001

Jackson, Vernon; Pres, VideoLan Technologies Inc.; US; 502/895-4858

Jackson, William L.; VP Mfg, Logic Devices Inc.; US; 408/737-3300

Jacob, George; VAR Mgr, Image-X; US; 805/964-3537, george@imagexx.com

Jacob, Mark; Past Pres, Houston Area Apple Users Group; US; 713/522-2179

Jacobi, William G.; EVP, Dun & Bradstreet Corp., The; US; 203/834-4200

Jacoboni, Joseph J.; Pres & CEO, Software Support Inc.; US; 407/333-4433

Jacobs, Byron; Dir Sales & Mktng, Siren Software; US; 415/322-0600

Jacobs, Elizabeth W.; Pres, Infogrip Inc.; US; 805/652-0770, 76106.430@compuserve.com

Jacobs, Gerard M; Co-Chmn, General Parametrics Corp.; US; 510/524-3950

Jacobs, Irwin; Pres & CEO, DataViews Corp.; US; 413/586-4144

Jacobs, Irwin M.; Chmn & CEO, Qualcomm Inc.; US; 619/587-1121

Jacobs, Roberta; SVP Sales & Mktng, Viacom New Media; US; 212/258-6000

Jacobs, Tina L.; EVP & COO, Target Technologies Inc.; US; 910/395-6100

Jacobsen, Earl; Pres, Central Data Corp.; US; 217/359-8010

Jacobsen, Eliot; VP Fin, Viewpoint Datalabs Int'l.; US; 801/229-3000

Jacobsen, Mike; CFO, FourGen Software Inc.; US; 206/522-0055

Jacobson, Andrew; Pblr, BRP Publications Inc.; US; 202/842-3006

Jacobstein, Neil; Pres & COO, Teknowledge Inc.; US; 415/424-0500

Jaech, Jeremy; Pres, Visio Corp.; US; 206/521-4500

Jaeck, Brenda; Dir Publishing, Strategic Alliance Partners Inc.; US; 310/860-4029

Jaeger, Raymond E.; Chmn, SpecTran Corp.; US; 508/347-2261

Jaeger, Stephen O.; VP & CFO, Perkin-Elmer Corp.; US; 203/762-1000

Jaffe, Bruce M.; Pres & COO, Bell Industries Inc.; US; 310/826-2355

Jaffe, Charles L.; VP SW Dev, Prophet 21 Inc.; US; 215/493-8900

Jaffe, Marc; SVP, PFM Communications; US; 212/254-5300, marc@pfmc.net

Jaffe, Mark; VP Mktng, JYACC Inc.; US; 212/267-7722

Jagadeesh, B.V.; VP Eng, Exodus Communications Inc.; US; 408/522-8450

Jahnke, William; Sales Mgr, NAFT International Ltd.; US; 212/982-0800, william_jahnke@naft.com

Jakus, Jeff; VP Sales & COO, WordMark International Corp.; US; 408/975-1100

James, Gary; Mgng Ed, Smart Computer & Software Retailing; US; 910/605-0121

James, Jamie G.; Pres, James Agency PR; US; 818/766-8404

James, Janice; Pres, Usability Professional Assoc.; US; 214/233-9107

James, Kelly; VP, Louis James & Associates; US; 801/553-8669, kjames@lja.com

James, Laura; Sales & Mktng Mgr, Romtec plc; UK; 1628-770077

James, Lee; Principal, Alliance Consulting Group Inc.; US; 503/452-5920

James, Louis; Pres, Louis James & Associates; US; 801/553-8669, lejames@lja.com

James, Richard; CEO, Labtec Enterprises Inc.; US; 360/896-2000

Jameson Harker, Susan; Pblr, Microsoft SQL Server Professional; US; 206/251-1900

Jamieson, Ellen; Assist Exec Dir, Software Forum; US; 415/854-7219

Jamieson, Philip A.; Pres & CEO, Software Partners/32 Inc.; US; 508/887-6409

Jamperti, Steve; Dir Res, Imagine That Inc.; US; 408/365-0305

Janal, Daniel; Pres, Janal Communications; US; 510/648-1961

Jansen, Scott; Dir Eng, Maxtek Components Corp.; US; 503/627-4133

Jansson, Hakon; SVP Tech, Ericsson; Sweden; 468-719-0000

Janulaitis, M. Victor; Pres & CEO, Positive Support Review Inc.; US; 310/453-6100, vjanulaitis@psrinc.com

Jaramillo, Frank; EVP Sales, Peripheral Land Inc.; US; 510/657-2211

Jarman, Jacques; Dir Sales & Mktng, Quyen Systems Inc.; US; 301/258-5087

Jaros, Tony; Assoc Mgng Ed, Web Developer; US; 203/226-6967, tjaros@webdeveloper.com

Jaross, Richard H.; Exec Dir, UniForum Monthly; US; 408/986-8840, rich@uniforum.org

Jarrett, John P.; VP SW Eng, Maximum Computer Technologies Inc.; US; 770/428-5000

Jarvi, Kent; CFO, Airsoft Inc.; US; 408/777-7500, jarvi@airsoft.com

Jarvie, Paul; VP Mktng, ASAP Software

Express Inc.; US; 847/465-3710

Jarvis, Mike; Sr Ed, CSG Information Services; US; 813/664-6800

Jastrzembski, Ted; Pres, Tally Systems Corp.; US; 603/643-1300

Jaswa, Raj; Pres, OPTi Inc.; US; 408/486-8000

Jawadi, Zaydoon; Pres, Zadian Technologies Inc.; US; 408/894-0800

Jaworski, Dave; Founder, Provident Ventures Inc.; US; 206/453-6600, david-jaw@provident.com

Jeapes, Ben; Ed, Expert Systems Journal; US; 609/654-6266

Jeffery, Brian; Mgng Dir, International Technology Group; US; 415/964-2565

Jeffery, Steve; Pres, SQL Financials Int'l.; US; 770/390-3900

Jeffrey, Glenn W.; EVP, Ceridian Corp.; US; 612/853-8100

Jehle, Kathryn A.; SVP & CFO, Comshare Inc.; US; 313/994-4800

Jelinek, Richard C.; Chmn, Pres & CEO, Medicus Systems Corp.; US; 847/570-7500

Jenkins, Bruce; VP, Daratech Inc.; US; 617/354-2339

Jenkins, C. Shannon; Pres & CEO, Touchstone Software Int'l.; US; 714/470-1122

Jenkins, Cameron; VP Mktng, Acucobol Inc.; US; 619/689-7220, cameron@acu-cobol.com

Jenkins, David F.; SVP, SCI Systems Inc.; US; 205/998-0592

Jenkins, John; Pres, Cobb Group, The; US; 502/491-1900

Jenkins, Kimberly; Exec Dir, Highway 1; US; 202/628-3922

Jenkins, Lew; Chmn, Premenos Corp.; US; 510/602-2000

Jenkins, Pat; VP, Britt Productions; US; 770/988-9957

Jenkins, R. Gregory; SVP & CFO, Avery Dennison; US; 818/304-2000

Jenkins, Robert S.; SVP, TriHouse Group, The; US; 617/544-3088, 72642.3360@compuserve.com

Jenkins, Sam; Sales Mgr, Special Events Management; US; 803/737-9352, jenkins@sbt.tec.sc.us

Jenkins, Terrell; Pres, Britt Productions; US; 770/988-9957

Jenkins, Tom; Pres & CEO, Open Text Corp.; Canada; 519/888-7111

Jenks, Andrew; Ed, TechNews Inc.; US; 703/848-2800, ajenks@technews.com

Jennings, Andrew; SVP WW Sales, Giga Information Group; US; 617/577-9595

Jennings, Joseph; Chmn, GCI Jennings; US; 415/974-6200

Jennings, T. Benjamin; Co-Chmn, General Parametrics Corp.; US; 510/524-3950

Jensen, Arni; Traffic US Inc.; US; 407/995-5282

Jensen, Craig; Pres, Crystal Group Inc.;

US; 319/378-1636

Jensen, Craig; Chmn & CEO, Executive Software Int'l.; US; 818/547-2050, cjensen@executive.com

Jensen, Kenneth R.; Sr EVP & CFO, FIserv Inc.; US; 414/879-5000

Jensen, Leif; Traffic US Inc.; US; 407/995-5282

Jensen, Max; Pres & CEO, Olicom US; US; 214/423-7560, maxj@smtpgwy.oli-com-us

Jensen, William T.; Pres, Methode Electronics Inc.; US; 708/867-9600

Jensen Jr., George; Chmn, Pres & CEO, US Technologies Inc.; US; 610/989-0340

Jeon, I.B.; VP, Hyundai Electronics America; US; 408/232-8000

Jeppesen, Karsten; VP Eng, YARC Systems Corp.; US; 805/499-9444

Jepson, Charles W.; Pres & CEO, Interlink Computer Sciences Inc.; US; 510/657-9800

Jergensen, Harley; VP, Fargo Electronics Inc.; US; 612/941-9470

Jermoluk, Thomas A.; Pres & CEO, @Home Network; US; 415/944-7367

Jerney, John; Ed, Pen-Based Computing; Canada; 604/472-1315, jerney@net-com.com

Jernstedt, Rich; Pres & CEO, Golin/Harris Communications Inc.; US; 312/836-7100

Jerome, John; CMO, Business Printing Center; US; 206/869-6319

Jesberg, Randy; New Bus Dev, AutoTester Inc.; US; 214/363-6181

Jesse, W. Christopher; Pres & CEO, Tangram Enterprise Solutions Inc.; US; 919/851-6000, chrisj@tesi.com

Jieh, Austin; Chmn, Lion Optics Corp.; US; 408/954-8089

Jobs, Steven P.; Chmn & CEO, Pixar Animation Studios; US; 510/236-4000

Joe, Steven; Dir Ops, D-Link Systems Inc.; US; 714/455-1688, sjoe@irv-ine.dlink.com

Joelson, Mitchell; EVP, Accent Software Int'l. Ltd.; US; 714/223-0620

Johansen, Bob; Pres, Institute for the Future; US; 415/854-6322

Johansen, Donald E.; VP Bus Dev, CSPI; US; 508/663-7598

Johnson, Abigail R.; Dir Strat Comm & PR, Roeder-Johnson; US; 415/802-1850, abigail@roederj.com

Johnson, Brian; VP Adv Dev, DiviCom Inc.; US; 408/944-6700

Johnson, Cary L.; SVP Sales & Mktng, Progress Software Corp.; US; 617/280-4000

Johnson, Charles; Pres, Winsted Corp.; US; 612/944-9050

Johnson, Charles P.; Chmn & CEO, General DataComm Industries Inc.; US; 203/574-1118

Johnson, Cindy E.; VP Info Sys, LSI Logic Corp.; US; 408/433-8000

Johnson, D. LaMont; Ed, Computers in the Schools; US

Johnson, Dave; Pres, Working Software Inc.; US; 408/423-5696

Johnson, David M.; Pblr, SoftPub Yellow Pages, The; US; 206/852-7440

Johnson, Eric; VP Mktng, Activision Inc.; US; 310/473-9200

Johnson, Gary; VP Sales & Mktng, Berkeley Software Design Inc.; US; 719/593-9445, garyj@bsdi.com

Johnson, Gary; Pblr, MSP Communications; US; 612/339-7571

Johnson, George; Pres, Cosmi Corp.; US; 310/833-2000

Johnson, J. Scott; Pres, Ntergaid Inc.; US; 203/783-1280

Johnson, Jack L.; Sec, Atomic City Electronics Inc.; US; 505/662-7059

Johnson, James; Chmn, Standish Group, The; US; 508/385-7500, jim@standishgroup.com

Johnson, Jan; VP PR, Roberts, Mealer & Co. Inc.; US; 714/957-1314, 560.2742@mcimail.com

Johnson, Margaret E.; Exec Dir, Black Data Processing Associates; US; 202/775-4301

Johnson, Mark; EVP Bus Dev, Checkfree Corp.; US; 614/825-3000

Johnson, Michael K.; Ed, Linux Journal; US; 206/782-7733, ljeditor@ssc.com

Johnson, Paul F.; Pres, Omni MultiMedia Group; US; 508/865-4451

Johnson, Reed; Pres, Usability Systems; US; 770/475-3505

Johnson, Robin; CEO, Infoseek Corp.; US; 408/567-2700

Johnson, Ron; Prod Dev, Allen Communication; US; 801/537-7800, rjohnson@allencomm.com

Johnson, Rusty; VP Sales, IPC Technologies Inc.; US; 512/339-3500

Johnson, Sam; VP, Mobile Security Communications; US; 770/594-0424

Johnson, Stephen C.; Pres & CEO, Komag Inc.; US; 408/946-2300

Johnson, Stephen C.; Pres, Usenix Assoc.; US; 510/528-8649

Johnson, Stephen C.; Dir Exec Svcs, Roeder-Johnson; US; 415/802-1850, stephen@roederj.com

Johnson, Steve; EVP New Media, Microware Systems Corp.; US; 515/224-1929

Johnson, Steven; VP Mktng, Evergreen Technologies Inc.; US; 541/757-0934, stevenj@evertech.com

Johnson, Ted; VP, Visio Corp.; US; 206/521-4500

Johnson, Tim; SVP, Golan/Harris Technologies; US; 415/904-7000

Johnson, Tom; VP Sales & Mktng, Portable Graphics Inc.; US; 512/719-8000

Johnson, Tony; Conf Coord, Telecommunications Reports/BRP; US; 202/842-3022, alj@brpnyc.mhs.compuserve.com

Johnson, W. Daniel; SVP Corp Dev,

Hogan Systems Inc.; US; 214/386-0020

Johnson, Ward C.; Pres, VideoLabs Inc.; US; 612/988-0055

Johnson, Warren J.; VP Corp Dev, Exide Electronics Group; US; 919/872-3020

Johnston, Charles; Pres & CEO, Philips LMS; US; 719/593-7900

Johnston, Charles B.; VP Tech, Drake Training & Technologies; US; 612/896-7000

Johnston, Chris; Dir Prod Mgmt, Specular International; US; 413/253-3100, chrisj@specular.com

Johnston, Mark W.; VP Prod Mktng, Microtest Inc.; US; 602/952-6400

Johnston, Nicolette D.; VP Ops, Timberline Software Corp.; US; 503/626-6775

Johnston, Ronald; COO, Globalink Inc.; US; 703/273-5600

Johnston, Ronald W.; CFO, Globalink Inc.; US; 703/273-5600

Johnston Turner, Mary; VP, Northeast Consulting Resources Inc.; US; 617/654-0600, turner@ncri.com

Jonas, Peggy; COO, Design Technology; US; 619/448-2888

Jones, Alan; Pres & CEO, Shuttle Technology; US; 510/656-0180

Jones, Alice; Mgr Corp Com, Micro Dynamics Ltd.; US; 301/589-6300, alice_jones@mdl.com

Jones, Arnold; Dir R&D, Micro Design Int'l. Inc.; US; 407/677-8333

Jones, Bob; VP Programming, Jones Computer Network; US

Jones, Callie; Ed, Silicon Graphics World; US; 512/250-9023

Jones, Dale; VP Sales & Svc, Alpha Technologies; US; 360/647-2360

Jones, Donald H.; Chmn, Nets Inc.; US; 412/967-3500, donjones@industry.net

Jones, Glenn R.; Pres & CEO, Jones Computer Network; US; 303/792-3111

Jones, Greg; Mktng Mgr, HP Home Products Div.; US; 408/246-4300

Jones, Gregory R.; VP Gen Counsel, QMS Inc.; US; 334/633-4300, jonesg@iscclink.qms.com

Jones, Harvey C.; Chmn, Synopsys Inc.; US; 415/962-5000

Jones, Jeff; VP Dev, Reality Online Inc.; US; 610/277-7600

Jones, Joe D.; VP Ops, Ross Technology; US; 512/436-2000

Jones, Lisa; Mktng Dir, Fortner Research LLC; US; 703/478-0181, lisa@fortner.com

Jones, Myron D.; Pres, NMB Technologies Inc.; US; 818/341-3355

Jones, Randall; Exec Sec, Association for Computers & the Humanities; US; 801/378-3513

Jones, Reese; Chmn, Farallon Computing Inc.; US; 510/814-5100

Jones, Richard; VP Mktng & Sales, Chat-

sworth Products Inc.; US; 818/735-6100

Jones, Rick; VP Fin, Sherpa Corp.; US; 408/433-0455

Jones, Robert; Dir Radiocom Bureau, International Telecommunications Union; Switzerland; 22-730-5111

Jones, Robert E.; VP & GM Telecom Svcs Div, Transaction Network Services Inc.; US; 703/742-0500

Jones, Robin; Mktng Dir, Charles River Analytics Inc.; US; 617/491-3474

Jones, Ron L.; Pres & CEO, Colossal Graphics Inc.; US; 415/858-2993

Jones, Steve; Chmn, JSB Corp.; US; 408/438-8300

Jones, Susan; VP, Software Sorcery; US; 619/452-9901

Jones, Tom; VP Mktng, Nets Inc.; US; 412/967-3500, tomjones@industry.net

Jones, Tom; Pres & GM, Infomart; US; 214/746-3500

Jones, Wendy M.; Dir Sales & Mktng, Tom Sawyer Software; US; 510/848-0853, wjones@tomsawyer.com

Jones Cox, Donna; Mgr Tech Svcs, Ryan-McFarland; US; 512/343-1010

Jong, S.H.; Pres, Genova; US; 310/538-4102

Jonnaert, Serge; Prod Mktng Mgr, Visual Software Inc.; US; 818/593-3500

Jorasch, Craig; Pres, Metropolis Software Inc.; US; 415/462-2200

Jordan, Charles A.; Principal, Jordan Tamraz Caruso Advertising Inc.; US; 312/951-2000

Jordan, Edward B.; VP & CFO, Dialogic Corp.; US; 201/993-3000

Jordan, Larry; VP Mktng, Integrated Device Technology Inc.; US; 408/727-6116

Jordan, Lyle W.; VP Ops, In Focus Systems Inc.; US; 503/685-8888

Jordan, Michael; CEO, Westinghouse Electric Corp.; US; 412/244-2000

Jordan, Robert; Pblr, Online Access; US; 312/573-1700

Jordan Grey, Melissa; Pres, Blue Ribbon SoundWorks Ltd.; US; 404/315-0212

Jorgensen, Paul; EVP & COO, SRI International; US; 415/326-6200

Jose, Gary; VP New Bus Dev, Individual Software Inc.; US; 510/734-6767

Joseph, Adam C.; Pres, AIB Software Corp.; US; 703/430-9247, adam.joseph@aib.com

Joseph, Jonathan L.; SVP Prod Mktng, SystemSoft Corp.; US; 508/651-0088

Joseph, Michael T.; Pres, LDI Open Software; US; 216/498-5500

Joseph, Moses; VP Mktng, Integrated Systems Inc.; US; 408/542-1500

Joseph, Stan; CEO, AIB Software Corp.; US; 703/430-9247, stan.joseph@aib.com

Joseph, Stephen A.; VP R&D, Learning Company, The; US; 510/792-2101

Joslin, Charles; Ed, Inside R&D; US; 201/568-4744, irdinfo@insights.com

Jossi, Frank; Mgng Ed, Presentations Magazine; US; 612/333-0471, frankj2092@aol.com

Jost, Allen P.; VP Bus Dev, HNC Software Inc.; US; 619/546-8877

Jost, Kevin; VP & GM Data Col Div, Welch Allyn Inc.; US; 315/685-8945

Joukhadar, Kristina; Sr Mgng Ed, Object Magazine; US; 212/229-0320

Jourdenais, Mark; Info Syst Mgr, Honeybee Software Inc.; Canada; 514/989-5030

Joyal, James; EVP, Sterling Hager Inc.; US; 617/259-1400, jim@sterhag.shore.net

Joyner, Barrett; VP NA Sales & Mktng, SAS Institute Inc.; US; 919/677-8000

Judge, Frederick L.; SVP, Titan Corp.; US; 619/552-9500

Juhasz, Steve; Dir Mktng, Pentax Technologies Corp.; US; 303/460-1600

Juliussen, Egil; Pres & Ed, Computer Industry Almanac Inc.; US; 702/749-5053, cialmanac@aol.com

Junell, Sandy; VP Fin, AIQ Systems Inc.; US; 702/831-2999

Junius, Daniel M.; VP & CFO, Nashua Corp.; US; 603/880-2323

Junkemeier, William; VP & CFO, Databook Inc.; US; 508/762-9779

Jurenko, John A.; VP Sales & Mktng, Adtran Inc.; US; 205/971-8000

Jurewicz, Robert E.; Dir, National Power Laboratory; US; 608/565-7200

Jurgensen, David J.; SVP, Magni Systems Inc.; US; 503/626-8400

Justham, Bruce O.; Pres, SoftKlone; US; 904/878-8564, bruce@softklone.com

Justus, Betsy; Exec Dir, North Carolina Electronics & Information Technologies Assoc.; US; 919/787-8818

Jutila, John; VP Intl Sales, Laser Communications Inc.; US; 717/394-8634

Kaan, Gil; Assoc Ed, InfoText; US; 310/724-6783

Kabay, Michel E.; Dir Ed, National Computer Security Assoc.; US; 717/258-1816

Kabayashi, Akira; Sr EVP, NEC Corp.; Japan; 3-3454-1111

Kabcenell, Dirk A.; EVP Prod Div, Oracle Corp.; US; 415/506-7000

Kacer, Mark; VP & CFO, Equinox Systems Inc.; US; 305/746-9000

Kadlec, Scott; Pres, PC DOCS Inc.; US; 617/273-3800, scottk@pcdocs.com

Kadner, Steve; Pres, Aeon Systems Inc.; US; 505/828-9120

Kaecheley, Barbara; Dir Print Prod, Vector Directory: Messaging Systems; US; 617/862-7607

Kagan, David; VP Mktng, Artel Software Inc.; US; 617/566-0870

Kagan, Paul; Pres, Kagan World Media Inc.; US; 408/624-1536

Kagerer, Heinz; VP, Siemens Nixdorf Information Systems Inc.; US; 617/273-

0480

Kahan, James S.; SVP Strat Plng, SBC Communications Inc.; US; 210/821-4105

Kahle, Brewster; Pres, Wais Inc.; US; 415/356-5400

Kahle, Kathleen; CFO, Paul Mace Software; US; 541/488-2322

Kahn, Alan; VP Sales, Aspen Systems Inc.; US; 303/431-4606, alank@asp-sys.com

Kahn, Jonathan; Dir Sales & Mktng, Aladdin System Inc.; US; 408/761-6200, jonkahn@aladdinsys.com

Kahn, Judy; VP PR, Shafer; US; 714/553-1177

Kahn, Philippe; Chmn, Starfish Software; US; 408/461-5800

Kahn, Scott; SR Info Sys Admin, Hyper-Media Communications Inc.; US; 415/573-5170

Kahng, Stephen; Pres, Power Computing Corp.; US; 408/526-0500

Kailer, Mark; VP Fin & Ops, T/Maker Co.; US; 415/962-0195

Kairis, Craig; VP Bus Dev, Data Critical Corp.; US; 206/885-3500

Kaisen, Kenneth R.; VP Info Syst, New England Business Service Inc.; US; 508/448-6111

Kaiser, David; CEO, Terisa Systems; US; 415/919/1750

Kaku, Ryuzaburo; Chmn, Canon Inc.; Japan; 3-33758-2111

Kale, Vadya; Dir Tech, Maxtek Components Corp.; US; 503/627-4133

Kali, Jonathan Eran; Mgr R&D, Ligature Software Inc.; US; 617/238-6734

Kaliczak, Janek; Dir Bus Dev, Optivision Inc.; US; 415/855-0200

Kalina, Robert H.; VP Eng & Ops, TIE/Communications Inc.; US; 913/344-0400

Kallasvuo, Olli-Pekka; EVP & CFO, Nokia Group; Finland; 3580-18071

Kallman, Thomas; VP, Kallman Associates; US; 201/652-7070

Kallman, Jr., Gerald; VP, Kallman Associates; US; 201/652-7070

Kallman, Sr., Gerald G.; Pres, Kallman Associates; US; 201/652-7070

Kalman, David M.; Pblr, DBMS; US; 415/358-9500

Kalstrom, David; SVP, Plasmon Data Inc.; US; 408/474-0100

Kamath, K.; Mktng Exec, Pacific Internet; US; 310/410-9700, keshav@pacnet.com

Kambury, Dennis; VP Dev, Janus Interactive; US; 503/629-0587

Kamel, Elhamy; Pres & CEO, VISystems Inc.; US; 214/960-8649

Kaminer, David A.; Pres, Kaminer Group, The; US; 914/332-4114, dkaminer@aol.com

Kamins, David; VP Eng, Advanced Visual Systems Inc.; US; 617/890-4300

Kamm Jr., Ervin F.; Pres & CEO, Digi Int'l.; US; 612/943-9020

Kammersgard, Dana; VP Mktng, Arte-

con; US; 619/931-5500

Kanai, Tsutomu; Pres, Hitachi Ltd.; Japan; 3-3258-1111

Kanaly, Jerry; VP Ops & CFO, ViewSonic Corp.; US; 909/869-7976

Kane, Charles F.; VP & CFO, VMark Software Inc.; US; 508/366-3888

Kane, Harvey S.; Pres & COO, GBC Technologies; US; 609/767-2500

Kane, John; Pres, Kane & Associates; US; 415/591-2110

Kane, Larry I.; Pres & CEO, Alternative Resources Corp.; US; 708/317-1000

Kane, Robert W.; Dir, ZD Labs; US; 415/513-8000

Kane, Sanford L.; VP, Data Systems & Software Inc.; US; 201/529-2026

Kane, Stephen D.; Vice Chmn & CAO, First Financial Management Corp.; US; 770/857-0001

Kaneko, Hisashi; Pres, NEC Corp.; Japan; 3-3454-1111

Kaner, Jerry; Pres, Quadrant Components; US; 510/656-9988

Kang, Jay; Dir Tech Sup, Genova; US; 310/538-4102

Kangas, Jim; Ops Mgr, Falcon Systems Inc.; US; 916/928-9255, kangas@falcons.com

Kann, Peter R.; Chmn & CEO, Dow Jones & Company Inc.; US; 212/416-2000

Kannagaard, Jon; VP, SunSoft Inc.; US; 415/960-1300

Kanno, Junjiro; VP, Nissei Sangyo America Ltd.; US; 617/461-8300

Kantor, Jonathan; CEO, ResNova Software; US; 714/379-9000, jon.kantor@resnova.com

Kantor, William; Pres & CEO, Visage Inc.; US; 508/620-7100

Kantrowitz, Jonathan; CEO, Queue; US; 203/335-0906

Kao, Roger; Pres, D-Link Systems Inc.; US; 714/455-1688

Kaplan, Bennett; CEO, WorldSoft; US; 408/867-6757

Kaplan, Jerry; Founder, Onsale; US; 415/428-0600

Kaplan, Ken; Pres & CEO, Microware Systems Corp.; US; 515/224-1929

Kaplan, Linda; Pres, Thought I Could; US; 212/673-9724

Kaplan, Michael; Pres, AllMicro Inc.; US; 813/539-7283

Kaplan, Ron; CFO, Fischer International Systems Corp.; US; 941/643-1500

Kaplan, Stephen; VP Fin & Ops, Janna Systems Inc.; US; 408/356-6647

Kaplan, Warren J.; EVP & CFO, Net-Com On-Line Communications Services Inc.; US; 408/345-2600

Kaplowitz, Harry; Pres, Infodata Systems Inc.; US; 703/934-5205

Kappel, Michael L.; VP, HBO & Co.; US; 770/393-6000

Kara, Dan; Dir Res, Software Productivity Group Inc.; US; 508/366-3344,

76102.1465@compuserve.com

Karaffa, Mike; VP Sales & Mktng, FutureSoft; US; 713/496-9400

Karahalios, Paris; Pres, Trius Inc.; US; 508/794-9377, 72727.616@compuserve.com

Karakas, Steve; Partner, Karakas, Van-Sickle, Ouellette Inc.; US; 503/221-1551

Karasek, Walter; VP, Lotus Notes Advisor; US; 619/483-6400

Karels, Mike; Chief Syst Arch, Berkeley Software Design Inc.; US; 719/593-9445, karels@bsdi.com

Karesky, Ray; Pres, Merex Corp.; US; 602/921-7077

Karish, Charles; VP, Mindcraft Inc.; US; 415/323-9000, karish@mindcraft.com

Karjian, Ronald; Mgng Ed, Computer Design; US; 603/891-0123, rkarjian@pennwell.com

Karlsson, Mikael; Chmn, Axis Communications Inc.; US; 617/938-1188

Karmanos Jr., Peter; Chmn & CEO, Compuware Corp.; US; 810/737-7300

Karney, Tim; Pblr, TechNews Inc.; US; 703/848-2800

Karol, Michael; Mgng Ed, Graphic Arts Monthly; US; 303/470-4445

Karon, Gail; Mgr Prof Svs, Bluebird Systems; US; 619/438-2220

Karsch, Mark H.; SVP & CFO, Tseng Labs Inc.; US; 215/968-0502

Karsilovsky, Peter; Author, Online Services: International Markets; US; 203/834-0033

Kasabian, Anna; VP, DRK Inc.; US; 617/542-5848

Kasabian, David; Pres, DRK Inc.; US; 617/542-5848

Kaser, Richard; Ed Dir, NFAIS Newsletter; US; 215/893-1561, nfais@hslc.org

Kaseta, Bob; VP Eng, Miltope Corp.; US; 334/284-8665

Kashani, Farhad; VP Ops, Link Technologies Inc.; US; 408/473-1200

Kask, Alex; Exec Dir, Microcomputer Managers Assoc. Inc.; US; 908/585-9091, 418.5392@mcimail.com

Kass, Daniel B.; VP Ops, Computer Discount Warehouse; US; 847/465-6000

Kasten, Alex S.; Sr Ed, Multimedia Monitor; US; 703/241-1799

Kasten, Roger; VP Tech, Newer Technology; US; 316/685-4904

Katai, Kenneth; VP Dev, Maximum Strategy Inc.; US; 408/383-1600

Katashiba, Ken; Pres & CEO, Fujitsu Microelectronics Inc.; US; 408/922-9000

Kato, Kiroku; Pres & CEO, Inforite Corp.; US; 415/571-8766

Kato, Kotaro; SVP, NEC America; US; 516/753-7000

Katz, B. Jeffrey; VP Mktng, Atmel Corp.; US; 408/441-0311

Katz, Joel; VP & GM Info Enterprise Sys, GTE Government Systems, Information Systems Div.; US; 703/818-4000

Katz, Leland J.; Dir Sales & Mktng, Software Productivity Group Inc.; US; 508/366-3344, 76102.1472@compuserve.com

Katz, Peter; VP Mktng, Micro Focus Inc.; US; 415/856-4161, pek@mfltd.co.uk

Katz, Phil; Pres, PKWare Inc.; US; 414/354-8699

Katzive, Robert H.; VP, Disk/Trend Inc.; 415/961-6209

Katzman, Elliot; CFO, Atria Software; US; 617/676-2400, elliot@atria.com

Kaufer, David; Co-Founder, Kaufer Miller Communications; US; 206/450-9965, dkaufer@aol.com

Kaufer, Stephen; VP R&D, CenterLine Software Inc.; US; 617/498-3000

Kauffman, Maury S.; Mgng Partner, Kauffman Group; US; 609/482-8288, mkauffman@mcimail.com

Kauffman, Will; SVP & COO, Komag Inc.; US; 408/946-2300

Kaufman, Alan W.; VP Sales, Cheyenne Software Inc.; US; 516/484-5110

Kaufman, Gary C.; VP & CFO, Micros Systems Inc.; US; 301/210-6000

Kaufman, Gilbert M.; VP Prod Dev, Xyplex Inc.; US; 508/952-4700

Kaufman, Roger; CFO, Computer Outsourcing Services Inc.; US; 212/564-3730

Kaufman, Stephen P.; Pres & CEO, Arrow Electronics Inc.; US; 516/391-1300

Kaufmann, James; VP Sales & Mktng, Mass Optical Storage Technologies; US; 714/898-9400

Kaufmann, Todd; Internet Group Inc., The; US; 412/688-9696, tad@tig.com

Kaupp, Ray; Pres, User Group Connection Inc.; US; 408/461-5700

Kauser, Nicolas; EVP & CTO, AT&T Wireless Services; US; 206/827-4500

Kavetas, Harry L.; SVP & CFO, Eastman Kodak Co.; US; 716/724-4000

Kawai, Shosuke; EVP, Epson America Inc.; US; 310/782-0770

Kawalek, Nadine A.; Pres & CEO, Kawalek & Assoc.; US; 415/296-7744, nkawalek@well.com

Kawamata, Masaharu; Pres & CEO, Oberon Software Inc.; US; 617/494-0990

Kawaura, Terry; Chmn & Pres, Konica Business Machines US Inc.; US; 203/683-2222

Kay, David; Pres, Smartek Software; US; 619/456-5064

Kay, Jack; Pres & COO, Phoenix Technologies Ltd.; US; 408/654-9000

Kay, Ken; Exec Dir, Computer Systems Policy Project; US; 202/393-1010

Kay, Lonnie; GM, Telecomputer Inc.; US; 714/438-3993

Kay, Roger L.; Co-Author, Target Selling to IT Professionals; US; 617/982-1724

Kaye, Bea; VP, KPR Inc.; US; 818/368-8212, beakpr@aol.com

Kaye, David; Pres, KPR Inc.; US; 818/368-8212, dkayekpr@aol.com

Kaye, Doug; Pres, Rational Data Systems Inc.; US; 415/382-8400, dkaye@rds.com

Kaye, Steve; GM, GTCO Corp.; US; 410/381-6688

Kaye, Stuart; Pres, Vision Interactive Publishing; US; 714/833-1822

Kayye, Gary; VP Sales, Extron Electronics; US; 714/491-1500

Kazares, Linda; Pres, Ambit International; US; 415/957-9433

Kazarian, Sam; VP Ops, Adaptec Inc.; US; 408/945-8600

Kazmi, Mutahir; Controller, Audio Digital Imaging; US; 708/439-1335

Keane, John F.; Pres & CEO, Keane Inc.; US; 617/241-9200

Keaney, Dave; VP Ops, Retix; US; 310/828-3400

Kearl, Lloyd E.; VP Fin, Dynapro Systems Inc.; Canada; 604/521-3962

Kearns, Dianne; Dir Mktng, Open Systems Holdings Corp.; US; 612/829-0011

Kedar, Ofir; Pres, MITI; US; 415/326-5000, ofirk@miti.com

Kee, Richard; Fin Dir, Ovum Ltd.; England; 071-255-2670, rek@ovum.mhs.compuserve.com

Keefe, Michael N.; VP Eng, Cognitronics Corp.; US; 203/830-3400

Keel, Dave; VP Sales & Svcs, Primus Communications Corp.; US; 206/292-1000

Keel, Judith K.; Exec Dir, Computer Measurement Group Inc.; US; 630/655-1812

Keen, Fred; Pres, Repeat-O-Type Manufacturing Corp.; US; 201/696-3330

Keen, Michael; VP, Repeat-O-Type Manufacturing Corp.; US; 201/696-3330

Keen, Robert; Sec, Repeat-O-Type Manufacturing Corp.; US; 201/696-3330

Keenan, Kathy; Pres, Oak Ridge Public Relations Inc.; US; 408/253-5042, kathy@oakridge.com

Keenan, Tom; VP & CFO, Oak Ridge Public Relations Inc.; US; 408/253-5042, tom@oakridge.com

Keene, Alvin G.; Pres, Information Management Institute Inc.; US; 207/892-5269

Keene, Greg; VP Ops, Client/Server Labs; US; 404/552-3645

Keene, Terry; VP Tech, Client/Server Labs; US; 404/552-3645

Keep, Sherri; International Management Graphics User's Group; US; 612/854-1220

Keffer, Thomas; Pres, Rogue Wave Software Inc.; US; 541/754-3010

Kegg, Richard L.; VP Tech, Cincinnati Milacron Inc.; US; 513/841-8100

Kehler, Thomas P.; Pres & CEO, Connect Inc.; US; 415/254-4000

Kehoe, Shawn; CFO, Amtex Software Corp.; Canada; 613/967-7900

Keiler, Richard W.; Pres, Keiler & Co.; US; 203/677-8821

Keiper, William C.; Chmn & CEO, Artisoft Inc.; US; 520/670-7100

Kelby, Scott; Ed-in-Chief & Pblr, Mac Today; US; 813/733-6225

Keller, May; EVP, Analog & Digital Peripherals Inc.; US; 513/339-2241

Keller, Richard J.; VP & CFO, Intercim Corp.; US; 612/894-9010

Kelley, Brian J.; Pres & CEO, Cognitronics Corp.; US; 203/830-3400

Kelley, Tony L. White; Chmn, Pres & CEO, Perkin-Elmer Corp.; US; 203/762-1000

Kelly, Brian; Ed, Multimedia Business Report; US; 203/834-0033

Kelly, Brian G.; CFO & COO, Activision Inc.; US; 310/473-9200

Kelly, Charles; Sec, Association of Personal Computer Users Group; US

Kelly, Charles; GM, re:Search Int'l.; US; 617/577-1574

Kelly, Dan; Pres, Visual World Inc.; US; 415/461-6696

Kelly, David L.; VP HW Eng, Advanced Logic Research; US; 714/581-6770

Kelly, Edward J.; Pres & CEO, Sayett Group Inc.; US; 716/264-9250

Kelly, J. Michael; SVP Fin, GTE Corp.; US; 203/965-2000

Kelly, John; Pres & CEO, JetForm Corp.; US; 703/448-9544

Kelly, John J.; VP & Gen Counsel, Electronic Industries Assoc.; US; 703/907-7500

Kelly, Kevin; Exec Ed, Wired Magazine; US; 415/904-0660

Kelly, Kim Horan; Pblr, Information Systems Security; US; 617/423-2020

Kelly, Lois; SVP, Weber Group Inc., The; US; 617/661-7900, lkelly@webergroup.com

Kelly, Maureen; Dir MIS, Gandalf Technologies Inc.; Canada; 613/274-6500

Kelly, Michael; Dir Sales, ILT Systems Inc.; US; 212/629-5790

Kelly, Michael F.; Pres, Techtel Corp.; US; 510/655-9414

Kelly, Peter; Dir R&D, Recital Corp.; US; 508/750-1066, pkelly@recital.com

Kelly, Robert; Pres & CEO, Bull HN Information Systems Inc.; US; 508/294-6000

Kelly, Susan T.; Pres, re:Search Int'l.; US; 617/577-1574

Kelly, Terence P.; Chmn, Macro 4 Plc; US; 201/402-8000

Kelly, Thomas F.; EVP & CFO, Cirrus Logic Inc.; US; 510/623-8300

Kelly, Vince; VP Sales, Port Inc.; US; 203/852-1102

Kelly, William M.; VP Bus Dev, Silicon Graphics Inc.; US; 415/960-1980

Kelsch, Bob; EVP & COO, General Magic Inc.; US; 408/774-4000

Kemler, David; VP Mktng & Sales, Information Builders Inc.; US; 212/736-4433

Kemp, Graham; Pres, G2 Research Inc.; US; 415/964-2400

Kemp, Jack; CFO, Franz Inc.; US; 510/

548-3600

Kemp, Thomas L.; EVP & COO, Miller Freeman Inc.; US; 415/905-2200

Kempf, David A.; VP Fin & Admin, Soricon Corp.; US; 303/440-2800

Kenber, Chris; Pres & CEO, Interactive Development Environments Inc.; US; 415/543-0900

Kendall, Andra J.S.; News Ed, PickWorld; US; 714/261-7425

Kendall, Clifford M.; Chmn, Computer Data Systems Inc.; US; 301/921-7000

Kendrick, Doug; Pres, COM&DIA; US; 919/848-0001, dkendric@aol.com

Keng, Loretta; VP Ops, Tagram Systems Corp.; US; 714/258-3222

Kennaugh, David; VP Sales & Mktng, Optimum Resource Inc.; US; 803/689-8000

Kennedy, Douglas; EVP, FDP Corp.; US; 305/858-8200

Kennedy, Jack; VP Sales & Mktng, Welty-Leger Corp.; US; 617/461-8700

Kennedy, Joseph S.; Pres & CEO, Rapid City Communications; US; 415/937-1370

Kennedy, Karen; Pres, KSK Communications; US; 703/734-1880

Kennedy, Kevin; VP Mktng, DIC Digital Supply Corp.; US; 201/692-7700

Kennedy, Lee; Dir Sales & Mktng, Envelope Manager Software; US

Kennedy, Mark; Dir Sales, Carbela Tek Inc.; US; 415/873-6484

Kennedy, Martin E.; VP Mktng, Xante Corp.; US; 205/476-8189

Kennedy, Terry; Ed & Pblr, High-Technology Services Management; US; 941/275-7887

Kennewick, Mike; VP Sales & Mktng, Saros Corp.; US; 206/646-1066

Kenny, John; VP Eng, PicoPower Technology Inc.; US; 510/623-8300

Kenny, Richard T.; Tech/Svc Mgr, American Computer Resources; US; 203/380-4600, rkenny@the-acr.com

Kent, Philip; Pres, Turner Home Entertainment; US; 404/885-0505

Keough, Lee; Exec Ed, Data Communications; US; 212/512-2699, lkeogh@mcgraw-hill.com

Keough, Michael D.; SVP Sales, Megahertz Corp.; US; 801/320-7000

Kephatt, Dean; VP, Connors Communications; US; 415/217-7500

Keppler, Kay; Ed, AI Expert; US; 415/905-2200

Kerfoot, Greg; Pres, Crystal Inc.; Canada; 604/681-3435

Kernahan, Bill; CEO, Sunburst Communications; US; 914/747-3310

Kernan, John; Chmn, Software Pblrs Assoc.; US; 202/452-1600

Kerr, Jill L.; VP Sales & Mktng, ASCII Group Inc., The; US; 301/718/2600

Kerr, John; Ed-in-Chief, Client/Server Computing; US; 508/366-2031

Kerscher, Kim; SVP, Spindler Organiza-

tion Inc.; US; 213/930-0811

Kertzman, Mitchell; Pres & CEO, Sybase Inc.; US; 510/922-3500

Kerutis, Jay; VP Mktng & Sales, New Media Corp.; US; 714/453-0100

Keshian, Dan; Pres, Avid Technology Inc.; US; 508/640-6789

Kessman, Alan; Chmn, Pres & CEO, Executone Information Systems Inc.; US; 203/876-7600

Kestler, Eric; Mgng Ed, Enterprise Reengineering; US; 703/761-0646

Ketchum, John W.; Pres, Loeffler Ketchum Mountjoy PR; US; 704/364-8969

Ketner, Jeff; Pres, Ketner Group; US; 512/794-8876, jketner@ketnergroup.com

Kettering, Mark; VP Sales, Sense8 Corp.; US; 415/331-6318, mark@sense8.com

Keudell, Craig; Dir Sales, Extensis Corp.; US; 503/274-2020

Kewene-Hite, Paul; Pres, WorldSoft; US; 408/867-6757

Keys, David; VP Corp Dev, Fulcrum Technologies Inc.; Canada; 613/238-1761

Keyworth, G.A.; Chmn, NovaLink Technologies Inc.; US; 510/249-9777

Khadilkar, Sunil; VP Eng, Software Moguls; US; 612/932-6721

Khalsa, Arjan; Pres, IntelliTools; US; 415/382-5959

Khambaty, Moiz B.; VP Tech, IMP Inc.; US; 408/432-9100

Khanolkar, Rajeev; Dir Tech Svcs, Xecute Inc.; US; 908/668-5151, rajeev@xecute.com

Khezri, Rahmani; VP R&D, Pathlight Technology Inc.; US; 607/226-4000

Kibiloski, Sean; Mgng Ed, Computer Times; US; 502/339-9672

Kibiloski, Terry; Ed, Louisville Computer Times; US; 502/339-9672

Kiel, Keith; VP, MacAcademy; US; 904/677-1918

Kiely, W.E.; Pres & CEO, Stallion Technologies Inc.; US; 408/477-0440, billk@stallion.com

Kieran, Shirley; Pres, Best-Seller Inc.; Canada; 514/337-3000

Kiernan, Donald E.; SVP & CFO, SBC Communications Inc.; US; 210/821-4105

Kiessling, Greg; Pres, KL Group Inc.; Canada; 416/594-1026

Kight, Peter; CEO, Checkfree Corp.; US; 614/825-3000

Kiker, David; VP Prod Dev, Template Software Inc.; US; 703/318-1000, dave.kiker@template.com

Kilarski, Doug; Mkt Analyst, Aspen; US; 404/848-7751

Kilbane, Doris; Mgng Ed, Automatic I.D. News; US; 216/243-8100

Kilcullen, John J.; Pres & CEO, IDG Books Worldwide; US; 415/655-3000

Kiley, John J.; Pres, Performance Software Inc.; US; 508/462-0737

Kilhoffer, Angela; Pres, Irwin Ink; US; 619/483-4333

Kill, Robert H.; Pres & CEO, Ciprico Inc.; US; 612/551-4000

Kille, Steve; CEO, Isode Consortium; US; 512/305-0280

Killen, Michael; Pres, Killen & Associates Inc.; US; 415/617-6130

Killoran, Joseph F.; VP & CFO, Control Data Systems Inc.; US; 612/482-2401

Kilpatrick, Marlyn; VP Admin, Tusk Inc.; US; 407/625-1101

Kilroy, Kevin; Pres, ManTech Solutions Corp.; US; 703/913-2400

Kim, Jin H.; Pres, Tactica Corp.; US; 503/293-9585

Kim, K. David; VP & CFO, TeleVideo Systems Inc.; US; 408/954-8333

Kim, Kristine E.J.; Dir Mktng, TeleVideo Systems Inc.; US; 408/954-8333

Kim, Kug-Ho; Chmn, AST Research Inc.; US; 714/727-4141

Kim, Won; Pres & CEO, UniSQL Inc.; US; 512/343-7297

Kim, Won; Ed-in-Chief, ACM Transactions on Database Systems; US; 212/869-7440

Kim, Y.H.; Pres & CEO, Hyundai Electronics America; US; 408/232-8000

Kim, Young-Soo; Pres, AST Research Inc.; US; 714/727-4141

Kimihira, Ryozo; EVP, EJ Bilingual Inc.; US; 310/320-8139

Kimmel, Charles F.; VP & CFO, AGE Logic Inc.; US; 619/755-1000

Kimmelman, Steve; VP, Ontrack Media Corp.; US; 415/331-1692

Kinard, Karen A.; Ed, Cable-Telco Report, The; US; 202/842-3006

Kinch, Chuck; COO, New Horizons Computer Learning Centers Inc.; US; 714/556-1220

King, Art; Pres, FaxBack Inc.; US; 503/690-6357

King, Christopher N.; EVP & CTO, Planar Systems Inc.; US; 503/690-1100

King, David; Pres & CEO, DK&A Inc.; US; 619/488-8118

King, David C.; Chmn, Pres & CEO, Proxim Inc.; US; 415/960-1630

King, Elliot; Ed, Scientific Computing & Automation; US; 201/292-5100, 71127.1231@compuserve.com

King, Jack H.; Pres & CEO, Zitel Corp.; US; 510/440-9600

King, Joseph S.; Ed, Retail Systems Reseller; US; 201/895-3300

King, Kenneth; Pres, Educom; US; 202/872-4200

King, Llewellyn; Pblr, High Performance Computing & Communications Week; US; 202/638-4260

King, Lynn; VP Ops, Systech Corp.; US; 619/453-8970

King, Olend; VP Cust Scvs, Acer America Corp.; US; 408/432-6200

King, Olin B.; Chmn & CEO, SCI Systems Inc.; US; 205/998-0592

King, Paul; GM, Binar Graphics Inc.; US; 415/491-1565

King, Richard W.; EVP Netware Group, Novell Inc.; US; 801/222-6000

King, Rod; VP Mktng, Fuji Photo Film US Inc.; US; 914/789-8100

King, W. Frank; Pres Pencom SW, Pencom Systems Inc.; US; 512/343-1111

Kingsbury, Brad; VP Tech, CyberMedia Inc.; US; 310/843-0800

Kingsley, Daniel; Exec Dir, National Venture Capital Assoc.; US; 703/351-5267

Kinnear, Kim; VP Eng, Aurora Technologies Inc.; US; 617/290-4800

Kinnear, Timothy W.; VP Fin, Cyrix Corp.; US; 214/968-8388

Kinninger, Terry; CFO, MetaTools Inc.; US; 805/566-6200

Kinsey, Lauren K.; Exec Dir, Society for Information Display; US; 714/545-1526

Kinsinger, Dwain; VP Sales, Hand Held Products; US; 704/541-1380

Kinzelberg, Chad; VP Mktng, Caere Corp.; US; 408/395-7000

Kipp, Gordon F.; VP Info Serv, BancTec Inc.; US; 214/450-7700

Kirby, Alan; VP Eng, Raptor Systems Inc.; US; 617/487-7700

Kirby, Harland; VP Mktng, AirWorks Media; Canada; 403/424-9922

Kirby, Mike; Chmn & CEO, NCL America Computer Products Inc.; US; 408/737-2496

Kirchner, Tom; Pres, Electronic Systems Technology Inc.; US; 509/735-9092

Kiremidjian, Fred; VP Eng, Xerox Desktop Document Systems; US; 415/815-6800

Kirk, John S.; Mgr, Prairie Group; US; 515/225-9620, johnskirk@aol.com

Kirk, Spencer F.; Pres, Megahertz Corp.; US; 801/320-7000

Kirkey, David G.; VP Sales & Mktng, Advanced Logic Research; US; 714/581-6770

Kirkpatrick, Charlie; VP Sales, TeleMagic Inc.; US; 214/733-4292

Kirkpatrick, David; CFO, Cabletron Systems; US; 603/332-9400

Kirsch, Geof; VP Sales, StrataCom Inc.; US; 408/294-7600

Kirshblum, Jeff; VP Internet Svcs, RCS Computer Experience; US; 212/370-9288

Kirsner, Richard; Mgr, Prairie Group; US; 515/225-9620, richmk@aol.com

Kirsten, John; VP WW Sales, Interactive Development Environments Inc.; US; 415/543-0900

Kirwan, John; Tech Svcs Mgr, Mailer's Software; US; 714/492-7000

Kirzner, Rikki; Tech Ed, Women in Computing; US; 415/513-6800

Kis, Daphne; Pblr & VP, EDventure Holdings Inc.; US; 212/924-8800, daphne@edventure.com

Kishimune, Ed; Pres, Yamaha Systems

Technology; US; 408/467-2300

Kisor, Gregory; Pres & CEO, Information Technologies Research Inc.; US; 407/852-9919

Kissell, Lenny; Mktng Mgr, Artbeats Software Inc.; US; 503/863-4429

Kister, Jack; VP Eng, Diamond Multimedia Systems Inc.; US; 408/325-7000

Kittrell, Marty R.; VP & CFO, Exide Electronics Group; US; 919/872-3020

Kivolowitz, Perry; Pres, Elastic Reality Inc.; US; 608/273-6585

Klapow, Steven; Mgng Ed, Multimedia Producer; US; 914/328-9157

Klatell, Robert E.; SVP & CFO, Arrow Electronics Inc.; US; 516/391-1300

Klatt, Cory; CTO, Business Printing Center; US; 206/869-6319

Klatt, Jennifer; Dir Fin, Avantos Performance Systems Inc.; US; 510/654-4600

Klaus, Christopher; CEO, Internet Security Systems Inc.; US; 770/395-0150

Klaus, L. George; Pres & CEO, Platinum Software Corp.; US; 714/453-4000

Klawitter, Ronald F.; VP Fin, Key Tronic Corp.; US; 509/928-8000

Klein, Barry; Pblr & Ed, Computer Catalogs: Shop by Mail, Phone or Fax; US

Klein, Bruce A.; Chmn, Cerplex Group Inc.; US; 714/258-5151, wklein@cerplex.com

Klein, Christoph; Pres & CEO, AdLib MultiMedia Inc.; Canada; 418/522-6100

Klein, David; Pres & CEO, Radish Communications System Inc.; US; 303/443-2237, dklein@radish.com

Klein, Jeff; Pres, Honeybee Software Inc.; Canada; 514/989-5030

Klein, John; Pres, McDonnell Information Systems Group; US; 310/306-4000

Klein, Ken; VP Sales, Mercury Interactive Corp.; US; 408/523-9900

Klein, Larry; EVP, Robocom Systems Inc.; US; 516/795-5100

Klein, Patrick; VP Sales, Alantec Corp.; US; 408/955-9000, aklein@alantec.com

Klein, Raphael; Chmn & Pres, Xicor Inc.; US; 408/432-8888

Klein, Sarah; Ed, Compu-Mart; US; 214/238-1133

Klein, Timothy; Pres & CEO, ATTO Technology Inc.; US; 716/691-1999

Kleinerman, Aurel; CEO, Mitem Corp.; US; 415/323-6164

Kleinman, Neil; Pres, Pacific Technology Assoc.; US; 818/342-1101

Kleinrock, Dr. Leonard; CEO, Technology Transfer Institute; US; 310/394-8305

Kleist, Robert A.; Pres & CEO, Printronix Inc.; US; 714/863-1900

Kleppe, Johanna; Pblr, 3D Design; US; 415/905-2200, jkleppe@mfi.com

Klessig, Karl; Pres & CEO, Enterprise Solutions Ltd.; US; 805/449-4181

Klevatt, Sydney; SVP Mktng, Sharper Image Corp.; US; 415/445-6000

Klimasauskas, Jane; Pres & CEO, NeuralWare Inc.; US; 412/787-8222

Kline, Allan M.; CFO, Dynatech Corp.; US; 617/272-6100

Kline, Barbara; Pres, Breakthru Communications; US; 408/252-1734, bkline@breakthrucom.com

Kline, Paul; VP Sales, Nu Horizons Electronics Corp.; US; 516/226-6000

Kline, Robert; COO, DK&A Inc.; US; 619/488-8118

Kline, Rodger S.; EVP & COO, Acxiom Corp.; US; 501/336-1000

Kline Pope, Barbara; Mktng Dir, National Academy Press; US; 202/334-2612, bkline@nas.edu

Klinedinst, Jeff; VP Mktng, Turtle Beach Systems Inc.; US; 717/767-0200

Klingman, Ed; Pres, ISDN*tek; US; 415/712-3000

Klosterman, Albert L.; SVP & CTO, Structural Dynamics Research Corp.; US; 513/576-2400

Kluge, John W.; Chmn, WorldCom; US; 601/360-8600

Klusner, Diane; Adv Sales Dir, Electronic Servicing & Technology; US; 913/492-4857

Klustner, Kevin; VP Sales & Mktng, Walker Richer & Quinn Inc.; US; 206/217-7100

Kluting, Duane F.; VP & CFO, X-Rite Inc.; US; 616/534-7663

Klynas, Scott; Pres, Klynas Engineering; US; 805/583-1133

Klyszeiko, Michael A.; EVP Ops, Read-Rite Corp.; US; 408/262-6700

Knapp, Karen; Dir Prod Mktng, Tally Systems Corp.; US; 603/643-1300

Knapp, Richard; CEO, GTM Software; US; 801/235-7000

Knapp Jr., Arthur F.; SVP & CFO, Boole & Babbage Inc.; US; 408/526-3000, aknapp@boole.com

Knapper, Tim; VP, Lawrence Productions; US; 616/665-7075, tknapper@aol.com

Knicely, Howard V.; EVP, TRW Inc.; US; 216/291-7000

Knight, Charles F.; Chmn & CEO, Emerson Electric Co.; US; 314/553-2000

Knight, Darrell; Pres, Expert Graphics Inc.; US; 404/320-0800, darrell@expertg.com

Knight, Fred S.; Ed, Business Communications Review; US; 630/986-1432

Knight, Gordon; CTO, Maxoptix Corp.; US; 510/353-9700

Knight, Peter; VP Bus Dev, Conner Peripherals Inc.; US; 408/456-4500

Knight, Richard I.; VP Tech, Tektronix Inc.; US; 503/627-7111

Knott, Sandie; Pres, Communication Collective, The; US; 408/261-0797

Knowles, C. Harry; Pres & CEO, Metrologic Instruments Inc.; US; 609/228-8100

Knowles, Janet; VP Admin, Metrologic

Instruments Inc.; US; 609/228-8100

Knowlton, Nancy; EVP, Smart Technologies Inc.; Canada; 403/245-0333

Knox, Steve; Pres, Driftwood Systems Inc.; US; 206/775-6495, fortknox@driftwood.com

Knudsen, Chris L.; VP Mktng, Cross-Wind Technologies Inc.; US; 408/469-1780, chris@crosswind.com

Ko, Larry; VP HW Dev, Initio Corp.; US; 408/988-1919

Kobayashi, Charles; VP Mktng, Toray Optical Storage Solutions; US; 415/341-7152

Koblick, Geoffrey; Chmn, International Microcomputer Software Inc.; US; 415/257-3000

Koch, Howard; VP Mktng, Etak Inc.; US; 415/328-3825

Kocher, Chris; Principal, Product Management Group; US; 415/346-7307

Kocher, Joel J.; Pres & COO, Artisoft Inc.; US; 520/670-7100

Kockwood, Anthony J.; Ed-in-Chief, Desktop Engineering; US; 603/924-9631, lockwood@bix.com

Kodinsky, Ed; Pres, Conextions Inc.; US; 508/689-3570

Kodis, Robert D.; Pres, Di-An Controls Inc.; US; 508/559-8000

Koeller, David H.; Pres Group Practice, CyCare Systems Inc.; US; 602/596-4300

Koeltl, Richard J.; Pres & COO, Sierra Semiconductor Corp.; US; 408/263-9300

Koeneman, Carl F.; EVP & CFO, Motorola Inc.; US; 847/576-5000

Koenen, Glenn; Exec Dir, Independent Computer Consultants Assoc.; US; 314/997-4633

Koenig, Joseph; Pres, Interactive Image Technologies Ltd.; Canada; 416/977-5550, jkoenig@omteractiv.com

Koepfler, Ed; Pres & CEO, Interleaf Inc.; US; 617/290-0710, ekoepfler@ileaf.com

Koepfler, Edward R.; VP, System Software Associates Inc.; US; 312/258-6000

Koepsell, Roxanne M.; VP Mktng, Neostar Retail Group Inc.; US; 214/401-9000

Koestner, George; CFO, BusLogic Inc.; US; 408/492-9090

Kohaui, Igal; Chmn, DSP Group Inc.; US; 408/986-4300

Kohavi, Ezra; VP Ops, Intelligent Computer Solutions; US; 818/998-5805

Kohn, Robert H.; SVP, Borland Int'l.; US; 408/431-1000

Kohras, Nicholas; EVP, MicroSlate Inc.; Canada; 514/444-3680

Kokos, Jerry; GM, NEBS Software & Computer Forms; US; 603/880-5100

Kokubo, Koshi; VP Bus Dev, Maxoptix Corp.; US; 510/353-9700

Kolawa, Adam; Chmn & CEO, ParaSoft Corp.; US; 818/305-0041

Kolgraf, Ron; Pblr, Marketing Computers; US; 212/536-6587, ron@marketing-

computers.com

Kolifrath, Chuck; GM, Inchcape Testing Services; US; 508/263-2662

Koll, Matthew B.; Pres, Personal Library Software Inc.; US; 301/990-1155

Koloski, Milissa; SVP, IDG Books Worldwide; US; 415/655-3000

Kolson, Ronald J.; EVP & COO, Micros Systems Inc.; US; 301/210-6000

Kolstad, Rob; Pres, Berkeley Software Design Inc.; US; 719/593-9445, kolstad@bsdi.com

Komoda, Makoto; EVP, TDK Corp.; Japan; 3-3278-5111

Kompan, Jack; Pblr, EDN Asia; Hong Kong; 852-965-1555

Kondo, Hideyo; CEO, FirePower Systems Inc.; US; 415/462-3000

Kong, Jonathan; VP Eng, Integrix Inc.; US; 805/375-1055

Kong, Victor L.; Chmn & CEO, Magni Systems Inc.; US; 503/626-8400

Konitsney, Jennifer; CFO, Campbell Services Inc.; US; 810/559-5955

Kontomerkos, Andrew; SVP, Execu-tone Information Systems Inc.; US; 203/876-7600

Kontopidis, George D.; VP Eng, Natural MicroSystems Corp.; US; 508/650-1300

Koo, James T.; Pres, DTC Data Technology Corp.; US; 408/942-4000

Koogle, Tim; CEO, Yahoo Corp.; US; 415/934-3230

Koontz, Mary Jean; Pres, Pacific Creations; US; 510/658-2703, 76373.3050@compuserve.com

Koop, Linda; Ed, Computer Publishing & Advertising Report; US; 203/834-0033

Kopatich, William; VP Bus Dev, Verbatim Corp.; US; 704/547-6500

Kopeck, Ron; Pres & CEO, LanQuest Group; US; 510/354-0940

Kopp, Urs B.; Pres, ALOS Micrographics Corp.; US; 914/457-4400

Koppel, Carl; VP Sales, White Pine Software Inc.; US; 603/886-9050

Koppelman, Joel M.; Pres, Primavera Systems Inc.; US; 610/667-8600

Korb, Eric R.; Pres, Xecute Inc.; US; 908/668-5151, ekorb@xecute.com

Korizno, Michael; VP NA Sales & Mktng, Verbatim Corp.; US; 704/547-6500

Kornatowski, John; Pres, Empress Software Inc.; US; 301/220-1919, jkornatowski@empress.com

Korstoff, Kathryn; Pres, Sage Research Inc.; US; 508/655-5400, kathryn@sageresearch.com

Korzeniewski, George; Pres, Sampo Corp. of America; US; 770/449-6220

Kosarow, Alex; Dir Exp Sales, DynaTek Automation Systems Inc.; Canada; 902/832-3000

Koski, Kent; VP & CFO, ThrustMaster Inc.; US; 503/615-3200, kent@thrustmas-

ter.com

Koss, John C.; Chmn, Koss Corp.; US; 414/964-5000

Koss, Michael J.; Pres & CEO, Koss Corp.; US; 414/964-5000

Kostic, Mark; Tech Dir, Phillips Decision Point Resources; US; 609/424-1100

Kostiuk, George; Pres, Lanworks Technologies Inc.; Canada; 905/238-5528, george@lanworks.com

Kosugi, Haruo; VP, I-O Data Devices Inc.; US; 408/377-7062

Kotick, Robert A.; Chmn & CEO, Activision Inc.; US; 310/473-9200

Kott, Michael; Dir Mktng, UniKix Technologies; US

Koulopoulos, Thomas M.; Pres, Delphi Consulting Group Inc.; US; 617/247-1025

Koulouris, Mitchell; Pblr, Oracle Informant; US; 916/686-6610

Kovacs, Jean; EVP, Qualix Group Inc.; US; 415/572-0200, jkovacs@qualix.com

Kovaly, Kenneth; Pres, Technical Insights; US; 201/568-4744

Kowala, Adam; Chmn & CEO, ParSoft Corp.; US; 818/305-0041

Kowalczyk, Mercy; Exec Dir, IEEE Transactions on Image Processing; US; 908/981-0060

Koz, Mark; CTO, FutureTel Inc.; US; 408/522-1400

Kozel, Ed; CTO, Cisco Systems Inc.; US; 408/526-4000

Kozlowski, Dawn; Mktng Coord, Omega Research Inc.; US; 305/270-1095

Kozlowski, Paul; Chmn, Racal-Datacom; US; 305/846-1601

Kraber, Richard W.; VP & CFO, Wind River Systems Inc.; US; 510/748-4100

Kraft, Gordon H.; Chmn & CEO, DiagSoft Inc.; US; 408/438-8247

Kraiman, Stephen; VP Prod Dev, Digital Video Arts Ltd.; US; 215/576-7920

Krall, Gary; VP Mktng, Airsoft Inc.; US; 408/777-7500, gary@airsoft.com

Krallman, Chuck; CEO & Co-founder, Tusk Inc.; US; 407/625-1101

Kramarz, Rob; Pres, 1776 Inc.; US; 310/215-1776

Kramer, Joel A.; Chmn & Pres, Telebyte Technology Inc.; US; 516/423-3232

Kramer, Peter; VP, Zoom Telephonics Inc.; US; 617/423-1072

Kramer, Robert S.; Chmn, Adam Software; US; 404/980-0888

Krane, Amy S.; Dir Mktng, Performance Software Inc.; US; 508/462-0737, 75363.1102@compuserve.com

Krapf, Chuck; VP Dev, Arbor Image Corp.; US; 313/741-8700

Kraska, Paul; Prod Mktng Mgr, Multi-Tech Systems Inc.; US; 612/785-3500

Krasny, Michael; Chmn & CEO, Computer Discount Warehouse; US; 847/465-6000

Kratzer, Andy; Sr SW Eng, Eagle Software Inc.; US; 913/823-7257, andy@eaglesoft.com

Kraus, Rolf; Dir Mktng Dev, Tactica Corp.; US; 503/293-9585, rolf@tactica.com

Krause, Arthur B.; EVP CFO, Sprint Corp.; US; 913/624-3000

Krause, Bill; Pres & CEO, Storm Software; US; 415/691-6600

Krause, H. Werner; Pres & CEO, Siemens Nixdorf Printing Systems LP; US; 407/997-3100

Krause, Kai; Co-Founder, MetaTools Inc.; US; 805/566-6200

Krause, Rick; Pres, CompuAdd Corp.; US; 512/250-1489

Krause III, Edward J.; Pres & CEO, E.J. Krause & Associates Inc.; US; 301/986-7800

Krauskopf, Timothy; VP R&D, Spyglass Inc.; US; 708/505-1010

Krautkremer, Todd J.; VP Mktng, Sync Research; US; 714/588-2070

Krawitz, Ira; VP Mktng, PR Newswire; US; 212/596-1500, ikrawitz@prnews.att-mail.com

Kreaden, Mike; VP Eng, Honeybee Software Inc.; Canada; 514/989-5030

Kreda, David; EVP, Reality Online Inc.; US; 610/277-7600

Krefetz, Fred; Pres, Transend Corp.; US; 415/324-5370, krefetz@vendor.info-net.com

Kreidler, William J.; VP Ops, FileNet Corp.; US; 714/966-3400

Kreisberg, Robert S.; Pres, Opus Marketing; US; 714/581-0962, bob@opus-marketing.com

Krelle, Dana B.; VP Sales & Mktng, Nex-Gen Microsystem; US; 408/435-0202

Kretschman, Brian; Dir Sales, Computone Corp.; US; 770/475-2725, brian@computone.com

Kretzmer, W. Brian; VP & CFO, MAI Systems Corp.; US; 714/580-0700

Kreysar, Rick; VP Mktng, McAfee Assoc.; US; 408/988-3832

Kridle, Robert; Pres, Xinet; US; 510/845-0555, bob@xinet.com

Krieger, Mark; Pres, UniPress Software Inc.; US; 908/287-2100, msk@uni-press.com

Krischik, Harry; Chmn, AmeriQuest Technologies Inc.; US; 714/222-6000

Krishan, Baldev; Pres & CEO, NovaLink Technologies Inc.; US; 510/249-9777

Krishnan, Kaylan V.; VP SW Prod, NovaLink Technologies Inc.; US; 510/249-9777

Krishnan, Lata; VP Fin, SMART Modular Technologies; US; 510/623-1231

Krol, John; Ed, Telecommunications Directory; US; 313/961-2242

Krook, Chris; VP Fin, mFactory Inc.; US; 415/548-0600

Krouse, John; Author, 101 CAD/CAM Traps; US; 619/488-0533

Krueger, Richard; VP Mktng, Meridian

Data Inc.; US; 408/438-3100

Krueger, Thomas E.; VP Mktng, Seattle Silicon Corp.; US; 206/957-4422

Kruse, Steve; VP Sales & Mktng, Vision Software Tools Inc.; US; 510/238-4100, steve@visionsoft.com

Kruy, Joseph F.; Chmn, Pres & CEO, Cambex Corp.; US; 617/890-6000

Krysick, Bill; CFO, Green Light Communications; US; 714/719-6400, bkrysick@grnlt.com

Kuang, Sigun; Purchaser, CAF Technology Inc.; US; 818/369-3690

Kubo, Hisashi; Chmn, Ricoh Corp.; US; 201/882-2000

Kubo, Larry; VP Mktng, Zadian Technologies Inc.; US; 408/894-0800

Kubo, Tomohiro; Pres, Olympus Image Systems Inc.; US; 516/844-5000

Kucera, Ken; Pres, First Byte; US; 310/793-0610

Kucharvy, Thomas; Pres, Summit Strategies Inc.; US; 617/266-9050, tomk@summitstrat.com

Kuckes, Steven F.; VP Tech, Tangram Enterprise Solutions Inc.; US; 919/851-6000, stevek_unix@tesi.com

Kuckro, Rod W.; Ed, Report on Electronic Commerce; US; 202/842-0520

Kuehn, Michael; CEO, miro Computer Products Inc.; US; 415/855-0940

Kuhlman, Steve; VP Sales & Mktng, Monotype Typography Inc.; US; 847/718-0400, stevek@monotypeusa.com

Kuhlman, Tim; VP Svc, Toshiba America Information Systems Inc.; US; 714/583-3111

Kuhn, Carolyn J.; Pres & CEO, Texas Caviar Inc.; US; 512/346-7887, cjkuhn@texascaviar.com

Kuklinsky, Roy; Pres & CEO, Ontrack Media Corp.; US; 415/331-1692

Kull, David; Ed, Data Management, Handbook of; US; 617/423-2020

Kumano, Aki; Mech Eng, Avatar Systems Corp.; US; 408/321-0110

Kumar, Rajeev; GM, Blackship Computer Systems Inc.; US; 408/432-7500

Kumar, Rak; Pres & CEO, Raster Graphics Inc.; US; 408/232-4000

Kumar, Sanjay; Pres & COO, Computer Associates Int'l. Inc.; US; 516/342-5224

Kumar, Suresh; VP Eng, Tactica Corp.; US; 503/293-9585

Kunori, Tatsuo; SVP, Verbatim Corp.; US; 704/547-6500

Kunysz, Laura; EVP, Casady & Greene Inc.; US; 408/484-9228

Kunysz, Terry; Pres, Casady & Greene Inc.; US; 408/484-9228

Kunz, William E.; Pres & CEO, Mountain Network Solutions Inc.; US; 408/438-6650

Kunze, Fritz; Chmn & Pres, Franz Inc.; US; 510/548-3600

Kuperstein, Michael; Pres, Miros Inc.; US; 617/235-0330

Kurjan, Eric; VP Sales & Mktng, Solomon Software; US; 419/424-0422, ekurjan@solomon.com

Kursham, Bobbi; VP, Gessler Publishing Co.; US; 540/345-1429

Kursham, Richard; CEO, Gessler Publishing Co.; US; 540/345-1429

Kurtz, Thomas E.; Sec & Treas, True Basic Inc.; US; 603/298-8517, tom@true-basic.com

Kurtzweil, John T.; VP & CFO, Read-Rite Corp.; US; 408/262-6700

Kusch, Bruce; VP Sales, KnowledgeSet Corp.; US; 415/254-5400, bkusch@kset.com

Kushniruk, Dwayne; Pres & CEO, Abacus Accounting Systems Inc.; Canada; 403/488-8100

Kusma, Taissa; Past Pres, Association of Information & Dissemination Centers; US; 706/542-6820

Kusumoto, Sam; Chmn, Minolta Corp.; US; 201/825-4000

Kutnick, Dale; Pres, Meta Group; US; 203/973-6700

Kutten, L.J.; Pblr, Kutish Publications Inc.; US

Kuttner, Susan; Exec Dir, Society of Telecommunications Consultants; US; 408/659-0110

Kuwae, Manabu; VP & GM, Hitachi America Ltd.; US; 914/332-5800

Kveyenhagen, Diane; VP WW Sales, T/Maker Co.; US; 415/962-0195

Kwang, Eng-Kee; EVP & CTO, Tactica Corp.; US; 503/293-9585

Kyle, Bruce; MIS Dir, DataPak Software Inc.; US; 360/891-0542

Kyle, Robert C.; CEO, Dearborn Publishing Group; US; 312/836-4400

Kyle, Terrence W.; VP Fin, Shared Medical Systems Corp.; US; 610/219-6300

Kyo, Michael; Pres, AVerMedia Inc.; US; 510/770-9899

L'Allier, Jim; VP Prod Dev, National Education Training Group; US; 708/369-3000

L'Heureux, David; Dir Mktng, Big Island Communications Inc.; US; 408/342-8300, david@big-island.com

La Prad, Robert C.; Exec Dir, Association for Systems Management; US; 216/243-6900

La Rue, Kevin; Dir Mkt Dev, Allegiant Technologies Inc.; US; 619/587-0500, kevin_larue@allegiant.com

Labarge, Charles A.; VP Corp Svcs, BCE Inc.; Canada; 514/397-7267

Labban, Harvey; Dir Mktng, Alps America; US; 408/432-6000

Labreche, Sylvie; Electronic Commerce World; Canada; 514/288-3555

Lace, Karrie Jo; Pres, Comfy Inc.; US; 408/865-1777

Lach, Henry J.; VP Mktng, EveryWare Development Corp.; Canada; 905/819-1173, hlach@everyware.com

Lach, Kevin; Dir Mktng, Watermark Software Inc.; US; 617/229-2600

Lachman, Ron; Pres & CEO, Lachman Technology Inc.; US; 708/505-9100

LaCilento, Susan; Single Source Marketing Inc.; US; 714/545-1338

Lack, Curtis W.; CFO, CE Software Inc.; US; 515/221-1801

Lacoe, Rudy; VP, KnowledgePoint; US; 707/762-0333

LaCommare, Bill; Pres, Interactive Solutions Inc.; US; 510/734-0730

LaCommare, Steve; VP Sales, Interactive Solutions Inc.; US; 510/734-0730

Lacy, John A.; Pres & CEO, International Information Management Congress; US; 303/440-7085

Ladd, David; EVP, Octel Communications Corp.; US; 408/321-2000

Ladd, Ivor; VP Tech, Empress Software Inc.; US; 301/220-1919, iladd@empress.com

LaForte, Michael; Pres Stenograph Corp, Quixote Corp.; US; 312/467-6755

LaFrenz, Dale E.; Pres & CEO, Minnesota Educational Computing Corp.; US; 612/569-1500

Lagae, Francois; Pres & CEO, Wave Research Inc.; US; 510/704-3900, flagae@waveresearch.com

Lages, Beverly; Pres, Lages & Associates Inc.; US; 714/453-8080

Laginski, Michael; COO, Fulcrum Technologies Inc.; Canada; 613/238-1761

LaGrow, Craig; Pblr, Morph's Outpost on the Digital Frontier; US; 510/704-7171

Lahey, Thomas M.; Pres & CEO, Lahey Computer Systems Inc.; US; 702/831-2500

Lai, Forest; VP Eng, Tatung Science & Technology Inc.; US; 408/383-0988

Lai, K. Larry; Pres, Escalade; US; 408/654-1600

Laing, John C.; EVP Sales, Symantec Corp.; US; 408/253-9600

Laing, Scott; Dir Dev, Brand X Software; US; 804/355-0374

Lake, Rod; High Technology Careers Magazine; US; 408/970-8800

Lakritz, David; Pres & CEO, Language Automation Inc.; US; 415/571-7877, dave@lai.com

Lam, Anne; VP Bus Dev, CyberMedia Inc.; US; 310/843-0800, 74044.3466@compuserve.com

Lam, Clarence; Prod Mgr, ExperVision Inc.; US; 408/523-0900

Lam, Kai; VP R&D, Microtek Lab Inc.; US; 310/297-5000

Lam, Lit; Sr Mktng Mgr, Hyundai Digital Media; US; 408/232-8000

Lam, Steve; CEO, Minuteman; US; 214/446-7363

Lam, Tsui Sung; Pres & COO, Flextronics Int'l.; US; 408/428-1300

LaMacchia, John T.; Pres & CEO, Cincinnati Bell Inc.; US; 513/397-9900

Lamb, Dorrance W.; VP & CFO, Performance Technologies Inc.; US; 716/256-0200

Lamb, John A.; VP R&D, MicroHelp Inc.; US; 770/516-0899

Lamb, Steven; Pres & CEO, Border Network Technologies Inc.; Canada; 416/368-7157

Lambert, Garvin; Dir Sales & Mktng, Ovum Ltd.; England; 071-255-2670, grl@ovum.mhs.compuserve.com

Lambert, James L.; Pres & CEO, Artecon; US; 619/931-5500

Lambert, Leanne; Promotions Mgr, Advanstar Expositions; US; 714/513-8400

Lambert, Mike; VP & CTO, X/Open Company Ltd.; US; 415/323-7992

Lambourne, Mark; CEO, Attack Systems Int'l.; US; 415/421-8191

Lamdoun, Craig; VP Fin & Admin, Kentek Information Systems Inc.; US; 303/440-5500

Lamkin, Bill; Ed, Inside Visual Basic for Windows; US; 502/491-1900

Lamm, Jacob; VP Prod Dev, Professional Help Desk; US; 203/356-7700, info@prohelpdesk.com

Lamm, Joseph D.; VP & CTO, TechSource Inc.; US; 407/262-7100, joe@techsource.com

Lamond, Pierre; Chmn, Cypress Semiconductor Corp.; US; 408/943-2600

Lamont, David X.; Dir Mktng, FWB Inc.; US; 415/325-4392

Lamorticelli, James T.; VP Mktng, NovaLogic Inc.; US; 818/880-1997, jlamorticelli@novalogic.com

Lamparski, Paul; CFO, Bentley Systems Inc.; US; 610/458-5000

Lampert, Russ; Dir Fin, Pure Software Inc.; US; 408/720-1600

Lampman, Dean; Ed-in-Chief, Unisphere; US; 214/669-9000

Lancaster, Sharon; Mgr, Darnell Group, The; US; 909/279-6684

Land, Gary A.; VP Sales & Mktng, Wall Data Inc.; US; 206/814-9255

Landan, Amnon; COO, Mercury Interactive Corp.; US; 408/523-9900

Landau, Henry V.; VP, Vishay Intertechnology; US; 610/644-1300

Landau, John; VP Mktng, Dialogic Corp.; US; 201/993-3000

Landes, Robert N.; Sr EVP, McGraw-Hill Inc.; US; 212/512-2000

Landgraf, William; Pres, Commcrypt Inc.; US; 301/470-2500

Landies, Gordon A.; SVP Comp Prod, Mindscape Inc.; US; 415/883-3000

Landin, Bo; SVP Mktng, Ericsson; Sweden; 468-719-0000

Landry, Richard; Pblr & CEO, HyperMedia Communications Inc.; US; 415/573-5170, rlandry@newmedia.com

Landton, Christopher G.; Chief Ed, Artificial Life; US; 617/253-2889, cgl@santafe.edu

Lane, Dick; VP Sales & Mktng, Connectware Inc.; US; 214/907-1093

Lane, Marlene; Ed Dir, Computer Video; US; 703/998-7600

Lane, Raymond J.; EVP WW Ops, Oracle Corp.; US; 415/506-7000

Lanese, Herbert J.; EVP & CFO, McDonnell Douglas Corp.; US; 314/232-0232

Lang, Frederick W.; Chmn & CEO, Analysts International Corp.; US; 612/835-5900

Lang, John; COO, Epson America Inc.; US; 310/782-0770

Lang, Kathryn; Partner, Windham/Lang Group; US; 415/563-4545, klang@netcom.com

Langa, Fred; Ed Dir, Windows Magazine; US; 516/733-8300

Lange, Walter S.; VP Res & Dev, TT Systems Corp.; US; 914/968-2100

Langen, Mary; Ed-in-Chief, ID Systems; US; 603/924-9631

Langer, Joseph; Pres, Nelco Inc.; US; 414/337-1000

Langer, Steven; Pblr, Compensation in the MIS/dp Field; US; 708/672-4200

Langlais, Bill; VP Dev, Percussion Software Inc.; US; 617/438-9900, bill_langlais@percussion.com

Langley, Juliet; Assoc Pblr, Ziff-Davis Press; US; 510/601-2000

Langmack, Pete; Pres, Henry Russell Bruce PR; US; 319/298-0242

Lannan, Ted; Pres, Fairfield Research Inc.; US; 402/441-3370

Laor, Raviv; CFO, Infographix Technologies Inc.; US; 404/523-4944

Lapides, Robert M.; VP LPI, Liant Software Corp.; US; 508/872-8700

Lapointe, Michel; Pres, DAP Technologies; US; 813/969-3271

LaPolla, Greg; Dir R&D, Linksys; US; 714/261-1288

Laposky, John; Mngg Ed, TWICE-This Week In Consumer Electronics; US; 303/470-4445

Laracey, Kevin; VP Mktng, Elixir Technologies Corp.; US; 805/641-5900, kevin_laracey@notes.elixi.com

Larese, Edward; Pres & CEO, Scala Inc.; US; 703/713-0900

Large, Gordon M.; SVP & CFO, Interleaf Inc.; US; 617/290-0710, glarge@ileaf.com

Largent, William H.; EVP & CFO, Metatec Corp.; US; 614/761-2000

Lari, Humayun; Pres, Lari Software Inc.; US; 919/968-0701

Larkins, Gary; VP Sales & Mktng, Persoft Inc.; US; 608/273-6000

Laroche, Joel; Pblr, Pixel Vision; US; 212/581-3000

LaRoche, John; Exec Dir, Infrared Data Assoc.; US; 510/934-6546, jlaroche@netcom.com

Larocque, Yves; VP Fin & GM, DAP

Technologies; US; 813/969-3271

LaRoque, Kent; Pres, Foresight Software; US; 770/206-1000

Larrimore, David; VP Mktng, Destiny Technology Corp.; US; 408/562-1000

Larsen, Dick; Mgng Ed, Communications Industries Report; US; 703/273-7200, dlarsen@atwood.com

Larsen, Larry; VP, Bit 3 Computer Corp.; US; 612/881-6955

Larsen, Scott; Ed-in-Chief, WordPerfect for Windows Magazine; US; 801/226-5555, scottla@wpmag.com

Larson, Bill; Pres & CEO, McAfee Assoc.; US; 408/988-3832, larson@mcafee.com

Larson, Cole; CTO, Worlds Inc.; US; 415/281-4878

Larson, Gilbert; Pres, Omnidata International Inc.; US; 801/753-7760

Larson, Gordon L.; Mgr & Ed, PC Pocketbook; US

Larson, Joseph C.; Pres, Cardiff Software Inc.; US; 619/761-4515

Larson, Keith; VP Mktng, Astea Int'l.; US; 215/822-8888

Larson, William; SVP & CFO, Verbatim Corp.; US; 704/547-6500

Lasker, Valerie; VP Eng, Percept Software Inc.; US; 408/446-7600

Lassen, Charles; Mgng Partner, Prismark Partners LLC; US; 516/367-9187

Lassiter III, Joseph B.; Pres, Wildfire Communications Inc.; US; 617/674-1500

Lathan, Barry; Pres & CEO, Xerox ColorgrafX Systems; US; 408/225-2800

Latif, Aamer; Pres & CEO, ICOT Corp.; US; 408/433-3300

Latman, Linda; SVP, Equity Group Inc.,The; US; 212/371-8660

Lattin, Bill; EVP, Synopsys Inc.; US; 415/962-5000

Latzke, David; VP & CFO, Fourth Shift Corp.; US; 612/851-1900

Lau, James; VP Eng, Network Appliance Corp.; US; 415/428-5100, jlau@netapp.com

Lau, Lee; VP Strat Plng, ATI Technologies Inc.; Canada; 905/882-2600

Lau, Philip; VP, Alaris Inc.; US; 510/770-5700

Laub, Steven A.; VP & GM, Lattice Semiconductor Corp.; US; 503/681-0118

Laude, Denise; Mktng Mgr, Auerbach Publications; US; 617/423-2020

Laughlin, Chuck; Pres, Corporate Visions Inc.; US; 918/488-0301

Laurencelle, Matthew; Dir Member Svcs, Interactive Television Assoc.; US; 202/408-0008

Lauterback, Klaus D.; VP, Cherry Corp.; US; 847/662-9200

LaValle, Russ; VP Ops, Brand X Software; US; 804/355-0374

Lavine, Adam; Pres & CEO, Specular International; US; 413/253-3100, adam_lavine@specular.com

Lavine, Eileen M.; Pres, Information Services Inc.; US; 301/656-2942

Lavine, Lisa L.; Mktng Mgr, Attack Systems Int'l.; US; 415/421-8191

Law, Bruce; Dir Mktng, Network Professional Assoc.; US; 801/379-0330

Law, Marilyn; Ed, Software Information Database on CD-ROM; US; 317/251-7727

Lawless Jr., Richard P.; Pres, Online Environs Inc.; US; 617/225-0449

Lawlor, Patrick; Sales Mgr, Commax Technologies Inc.; US; 408/435-5000

Lawrence, John; Chmn, Lawrence Productions; US; 616/665-7075

Lawrence, William S.; VP & CFO, General DataComm Industries Inc.; US; 203/574-1118

Laws, David A.; Pres & CEO, IMP Inc.; US; 408/432-9100

Lawson, A. Lowell; Chmn & CEO, E-Systems Inc.; US; 214/661-1000

Lawson, James H.; VP WW Sales, Auspex Systems Inc.; US; 408/986-2000

Lawson, Richard; Pres & CEO, Lawson Software; US; 612/379-2633, richard.lawson@lawson.com

Lawson, William; Dir MIS & COO, Lawson Software; US; 612/379-2633, william.b.lawson@lawson.com

Lawton, Stephen; Ed-in-Chief, Digital News & Review; US; 303/470-4445

Layden, John E.; Pres, Pritsker Corp.; US; 317/879-1011

Lazareck, Leslie; Pres, Blue Sky Software Corp.; US; 619/459-6365

Le Count, Chuck; Project Mgr, Benchmark Laboratories Inc.; US; 612/897-3505

Le Vay, Hal; Principal, Porter, Le Vay & Rose Inc.; US; 212/564-4700

Lea, Wayne A.; Pres, Speech Science Institute-Speech Science Publications; US; 612/890-4343

Leach, M. Robert; SVP Consulting, Cadence Design Systems Inc.; US; 408/943-1234

Leadbetter, Dan; Ed, Smart Electronics; US; 714/572-2255

Leahy, Robert C.; VP Fin & Ops, Brooktrout Technology Inc.; US; 617/499-4100, bcl@brooktrout.com

Leard, Juanita; Partner & GM, Insync Partners; US; 503/221-1063

Leary, Tim; VP Sales, Expert Software Inc.; US; 305/567-9990

Leatherman, Michael T.; SVP CIO, Wallace Computer Services Inc.; US; 708/449-8600

LeBeau, Dan; SVP WW Sales, Cisco Systems Inc.; US; 408/526-4000

LeBlanc, Elaine; SVP, AimTech Corp.; US; 603/883-0220

LeBlanc, Ray; VP Sales & Mktng, PNY Electronics Inc.; US; 201/438-6300

Leblang, David; CTO, Atria Software; US; 617/676-2400

LeBoss, Bruce; Pres, ChipShots Inc.; US; 408/541-8744

Lebu, Barry J.; Pres & CEO, Jazz Multimedia Inc.; US; 408/727-8900

Ledvig, Pat; VP Fin, Minuteman; US; 214/446-7363

Ledwell, David T.; VP & GM DHTech, DH Technology Inc.; US; 619/451-3485

Lee, Adeline; Pub Dir, International designers Network; Hong Kong; 852-25285744

Lee, Andrew; Pres, Antec Inc.; US; 510/770-1200

Lee, Ben; Pres, Cadix International Inc.; US; 404/804-9951

Lee, Charles R.; Chmn & CEO, GTE Corp.; US; 203/965-2000

Lee, Chong-Moon; Chmn, Diamond Computer Systems Inc.; US; 408/736-2000

Lee, Christopher P.; Pres, Best!Ware; US; 201/586-8986

Lee, Dave; MIPS ABI Group; US; 415/933-2082

Lee, Don H.; Pres & CEO, Unison Software Inc.; US; 408/988-2800

Lee, Esther W.; VP & CFO, Auspex Systems Inc.; US; 408/986-2000

Lee, Gwong-Yih; Pres & CEO, Digicom Systems Inc.; US; 408/262-1277

Lee, J.A.N.; Ed-in-Chief, Annals of the History of Computing; US; 908/981-0060

Lee, Jimmy; Pres, Advanced Integration Research Inc.; US; 408/428-0800

Lee, Joe; Pres, CAF Technology Inc.; US; 818/369-3690

Lee, John; Pres & CEO, Wireless Logic Inc.; US; 408/262-1876

Lee, Johnny; VP, Alaris Inc.; US; 510/770-5700

Lee, K. Patrick; VP Sales, AutoTester Inc.; US; 214/363-6181

Lee, King R.; CEO, Wynd Communications Corp.; US

Lee, Linda; Mgng Ed, NADTP Journal; US; 508/887-7900

Lee, Madeleine; CEO, Regal Electronics Inc.; US; 408/988-2288

Lee, Mary T.; Mgng Ed, Computer Sources; US; 408/295-5900

Lee, N.W.; Pres, Sejin America Inc.; US; 408/980-7550

Lee, Paulette; Mgng Ed., Redgate Communications Corp.; US; 407/231-6904

Lee, Robert; Pres & CEO, PicoPower Technology Inc.; US; 510/623-8300

Lee, Robert E.; EVP & CFO, Omni MultiMedia Group; US; 508/865-4451

Lee, Robert P.; Chmn, Pres & CEO, Insignia Solutions Inc.; US; 408/327-6000

Lee, Shih-Chi; Pres, Microtek Lab Inc.; US; 310/297-5000

Lee, Shirley; EVP, Liuski International Inc.; US; 770/447-9454

Lee, Tiffeny; Mktng Mgr, NeuralWare Inc.; US; 412/787-8222

Lee, Tony; Pres, Regal Electronics Inc.; US; 408/988-2288

Lee, W.S.; Pres, Tatung Co.; Taiwan

ROC; 2-592-5252

Leeds, Michael S.; Pres & CEO, CMP Publications Inc.; US; 516/562-5000

Leehey, Jonathan R.; VP Eng, nuLogic; US; 617/444-7680

Lefebvre, Richard A.; Pres & CEO, Axent Technologies; US; 301/258-2620

Lefkof, Alan B.; Pres & CEO, Farallon Computing Inc.; US; 510/814-5100

Lefton Jr., Al Paul; Pres & CEO, Al Paul Lefton Co. Inc.; US; 215/923-9600

Legarza, Mitch R.; CEO, AIQ Systems Inc.; US; 702/831-2999

Legat, M. Geoffrey; Pres, Micro Design Int'l. Inc.; US; 407/677-8333

Leger, Jean-Pierre; EVP, Welty-Leger Corp.; US; 617/461-8700

Lehman, Michael E.; VP & CFO, Sun Microsystems Inc.; US; 415/960-1300

Lehmann, Leonard A.; Chmn, Global Village Communication; US; 408/523-1000

Lehnert, Kevin L.; CFO, Pinnacle Micro Inc.; US; 714/789-3000

Leight, Gary; Pres, Operations Control Systems; US; 415/493-4122

Leighton, A. Clay; VP Fin, Sonic Solutions; US; 415/893-8000

Leighton, Carolyn; Exec Dir, International Network of Women in Technology; US

Leighton, F. Thomson; Ed-in-Chief, Journal of the ACM; US; 212/869-7440

Leitman, Daniel S.; Pres, TT Systems Corp.; US; 914/968-2100

Leitman, Valerie; VP Treas, TT Systems Corp.; US; 914/968-2100

Lekas, Joyce; Pres, Lekas Group, The; US; 415/948-8907

Lemerise, Paul M.; SVP MIS, Merisel Inc.; US; 310/615-3080

Lemke, Gary E.; VP Mktng, Software Artistry Inc.; US; 317/843-1663, gelemke@softart.com

Lemley, John T.; VP & CFO, Evans & Sutherland Computer Corp.; US; 801/588-1000, jlemley@es.com

Lemmermann, Jurgen C.H.; VP Ops, Verbex Voice Systems Inc.; US; 908/225-5225

Lemmons, Philip; Ed-in-Chief, PC World; US; 415/243-0500

Lemon, Jason; CEO, International TechneGroup Inc.; US; 513/576-3900

Lemount, David; VP & COO, Concentra Corp.; US; 617/229-4600

Lempesis, Bill; Exec Dir, PC Memory Card Int'l. Assoc.; US; 408/433-2273

Lenahan, William; Pres & CEO, RAM Mobile Data; US; 908/602-5500

Lenches, Jeffrey J.; EVP, Electronics for Imaging Inc.; US; 415/286-8600

Lennon, Elizabeth B.; Ed, CSL Newsletter; US; 301/975-2832, elizabeth.lennon@nist.gov

Lennox, David; Pres, Media Logic; US; 508/695-2006

Lent, Jo-Anne; Mgng Partner, Interconsult; US; 603/964-6464

Lentz, Hillman; VP Sales, Cyco Int'l.; US; 404/634-3302

Lenzi, Marie A.; Ed, Object Magazine; US; 212/229-0320

Leon, Steven J.; Pres, Technopolis Communication; US; 310/670-5606

Leonard, Andy; Pres, Cinemar Corp.; US; 503/646-2800

Leonard, Donald; VP & CFO, Mustang Software Inc.; US; 805/873-2500

Leonard, Gregory M.; Principal, Information Architects, The; US; 415/948-3927, gmleonard@aol.com

Leonard, M. Russell; EVP & COO, Howtek Inc.; US; 603/882-5200

Leonardi, Frank; Pres, Sonic Systems Inc.; US; 408/736-1900

Leone, Mario; Dir Eng, Parallel PCs Inc.; US; 610/670-1710

Leonsis, Ted; SVP & Pres AOL Svcs Co, America Online Inc.; US; 703/448-8700

LePage, Rick; Ed-in-Chief, MacWeek; US; 415/243-3500

Leppek, Sherry; Assist Ed, Mac Monthly; US; 510/428-0110

Lerner, Harry; VP Fin, Information Builders Inc.; US; 212/736-4433

Lerner, Mark; CFO, Van Nostrand Reinhold; US; 212/254-3232

Lerner, Ned; Principal, Looking Glass Technologies Inc.; US; 617/441-6333

Lernout, Jo; Mgng Dir, Lernout & Hauspie Speech Products; US; 617/238-0960

Leslie, Mark; Pres & CEO, Veritas Software Corp.; US; 415/335-8000

Leto, Jim; Pres, PRC Inc.; US; 703/556-1000

Leung, Patrick; Pres, Pacific Image Communications Inc.; US; 818/457-8880

Leung, Steve; Chmn, DocuMagix Inc.; US; 408/434-1138

Leung, William C.; VP Ops, Asante Technologies Inc.; US; 408/435-8388

Lev, Amir; VP R&D, CommTouch Software Inc.; US; 408/245-8682

Levanon, Isaac; EVP, TeleVideo Systems Inc.; US; 408/954-8333

LeVecchia, Jean M.; SVP Org Dev, Southern New England Telecom Corp.; US; 203/771-5200

LeVeille, Greg; Pres, Silicon Valley Int'l.; US; 408/376-2626

Level, Leon J.; VP & CFO, Computer Sciences Corp.; US; 310/615-0311

Levenberg, Andy; Mgng Ed, NetGuide; US; 516/562-5000

Levenson, Bruce; CEO, United Communications Group; US; 301/816-8950

Levenson, Robert J.; EVP, First Data Corp.; US; 201/525-4700

Leverett, Alan; Mgr Bus Dev, Connectware Inc.; US; 214/907-1093

Levi, David; Chmn & CEO, Natural MicroSystems Corp.; US; 508/650-1300

Levi, Giorgio; Ed-in-Chief, Journal of

Functional & Logic Programming; US; 617/253-2889, jflp.op@ls5.informatik.uni-dortmund

Levin, Amy; VP, Levin PR & Marketing Inc.; US; 914/993-0900

Levin, Dan; Pres & CFO, Books That Work; US; 415/326-4280

Levin, Donald; Pres, Levin PR & Marketing Inc.; US; 914/993-0900

Levin, Seth; Pres, Gessler Publishing Co.; US; 540/345-1429

Levine, David; Dir Mktng, Micro Central; US; 908/360-0300

Levine, Elliot; CFO, Cheyenne Software Inc.; US; 516/484-5110

Levine, Gary W.; VP & CFO, CSPI; US; 508/663-7598

Levine, Jerry; Pres & CEO, AutoTester Inc.; US; 214/363-6181

Levine, Joel M.; Tech Mktng Mgr, Cadix International Inc.; US; 404/804-9951

Levine, Martin; VP Tech, Datapro Information Services Group; US; 609/764-0100

Levine, Paul H.; Pres & CEO, Atria Software; US; 617/676-2400

Levine, S. Robert; Pres & CEO, Cabletron Systems; US; 603/332-9400

LeVine, Larry; Consultant, Schwartz Associates, The; US; 415/965-4561

Levitt, Jason; Sr Tech Ed, InformationWEEK Open Labs; US; 516/562-5000

Levy, Doug; VP Corp Com, Deneba Software; US; 305/596-5644

Levy, Jacob; EVP Ops, Graphic Utilities Inc.; US; 408/577-0334

Levy, Joseph L.; Pblr, CIO; US; 508/872-0080

Levy, Lawrence B.; EVP & CFO, Pixar Animation Studios; US; 510/236-4000

Levy, Michael; Pres, Forminco; Canada; 514/444-9488

Levy, Paul D.; Pres & CEO, Rational Software Corp.; US; 408/496-3600, pdl@rational.com

Levy, Stephen R.; Chmn, Bolt Beranek & Newman Inc.; US; 617/873-4000

Levy, Yacov; CEO, Lernout & Hauspie Speech Products; US; 617/238-0960

Lewak, Jerzy; Pres, Nisus Software Inc.; US; 619/481-1477, jerzy@nisus-soft.com

Lewandowski, Bob; VP Sys, ASAP Software Express Inc.; US; 847/465-3710

Lewchuk, Gordon N.; Pres & CEO, APS America Ltd.; US; 704/364-3346

Lewis, Andrew; Pres & CEO, DayStar Digital Inc.; US; 770/967-2077

Lewis, David; Ed Dir, North Light Books-Div. F&W Publications; US; 513/531-2222

Lewis, Jamie; Pres, Burton Group, The; US; 801/566-2880

Lewis, Jan; Pres, Lewis Research Corp.; US; 408/730-5829

Lewis, Jim; Pres, Globalink Inc.; US; 703/273-5600, jlewis@globalink.com

Lewis, John C.; Chmn, Amdahl Corp.; US; 408/746-6000

Lewis, Lee B.; VP & CFO, Andor Communications Inc.; US; 612/932-4000

Lewis, Mark C.; Prod Mgr, CalComp Inc.; US; 714/821-2000

Lewis, Mark S.; SVP, Electronic Arts; US; 415/571-7171

Lewis, Richard H.; VP WW Sales, Network General Corp.; US; 415/473-2000

Lewis, Ted E.; VP & COO, Moses Computers; US; 408/358-1550

Ley, Bruce M.; VP, PSINET Inc.; US; 703/904-4100

Ley, Tony; Pres & CEO, Harmonic Lightwaves; US; 408/970-9880

Leyton, Spencer; EVP Mktng & Sales, DeltaPoint Inc.; US; 408/648-4000

Li, Chuang; VP Eng, Micronics Computers Inc.; US; 510/651-2300

Li, Jim; CEO, Tribe Computer Works; US; 510/814-3900

Li, Johnny; IS Staff, Twinbridge Software Corp.; US; 213/263-3926, techsup@twin-bridge.com

Li, Peter; Pres, Peter Li Inc.; US; 415/439-5600

Liang, Larry; VP Bus Dev, Pacific Microelectronics Inc.; US; 415/948-6200

Liao, Duke; Pres, DTK Computer Inc.; US; 818/810-0098

Liao, Wun-Yann; Pres, Metra Information Systems Inc.; US; 510/226-9188

Liao, Yuh-Zen; VP Tech, ArcSys; US; 408/738-8881

Liautaud, Bernard; Pres & CEO, Business Objects Inc.; US; 408/973-9300

Liberman, Allen; VP, Trade Quotes Inc.; US; 617/492-0600

Libit, Jordan M.; VP Mktng, FileNet Corp.; US; 714/966-3400

Lichtman, Igal; Pres & CEO, Magic Solutions Inc.; US; 201/587-1515

Lidner, James A.; Chmn, Pres & CEO, Digital Communications Associates Inc.; US; 770/442-4000

Lidner, James D.; Pres & CEO, Attachmate Corp.; US; 206/644-4010

Lieb, Alex; VP Mktng & Sales, Pathlight Technology Inc.; US; 607/226-4000

Lieb, Richard B.; EVP, SEI Corp.; US; 610/254-1000

Lieberman, Mark D.; VP Sales & Mktng, TView Inc.; US; 503/643-1662, markl@tview.com

Liebhaber, Richard T.; EVP & CTO, MCI Communications Corp.; US; 202/872-1600

Liebman, Bill; SVP, Audits & Surveys; US; 212/627-9700

Liebman, Mark; Pres, Vividata Inc.; US; 510/841-6400, mark@vividata.com

Liebman, Seymour; SVP & GM, Canon US Inc.; US; 516/488-6700

Liebowitz, Peter; VP Sales, OnStream Networks Inc.; US; 408/727-4545

Liemandt, Joe; Pres & CEO, Trilogy Development Group; US; 512/794-5900

Lien, Jorgen; Founder, Blue Sky Software

Corp.; US; 619/459-6365

Lievense, Robert J.; EVP, Dun & Bradstreet Corp., The; US; 203/834-4200

Ligget, Woody; VP Sales, n th degree software; US; 702/588-4900

Liggio, Art; Dir Training, Bluestone Inc.; US; 609/727-4600

Lightfoot, Beverley; Mktng Dir, Cobalt Blue; US; 770/518/1116

Lightfoot, Clyde; Software Dev Mgr, Cobalt Blue; US; 770/518/1116

Ligon, W. Augustine; SVP Corp Plng, Circuit City Stores Inc.; US; 804/527-4000

Ligtenberg, Adriaan; VP & CTO, Storm Software; US; 415/691-6600

Lilegdon, William R.; VP, Pritsker Corp.; US; 317/879-1011

Lillis, Charles M.; CEO, US West Media Group; US; 303/793-6500

Lilly, E. Brooks; Pres, Applied Resources Inc.; US; 913/492-8888

Lilly, Maureen; Admin Dir, M Technology Assoc.; US; 301/431-4070

Lilly, Meredith; Dir Corp Comm, Applied Resources Inc.; US; 913/492-8888

Lim, Jenna; Nat'l Sales Mgr, Falcon Systems Inc.; US; 916/928-9255, jenna@falcons.com

Limacher, Marc; Mgng Dir, Integrated Strategic Information Services Inc.; US; 415/802-8555, 73244.2556@compuserve.com

Lin, C.H.; Pres, Visionetics Int'l.; US; 310/316-7940

Lin, Frank; Pres, SVEC Computer Corp.; US; 714/756-2233, frank.lin@svec.com

Lin, Frank C.; Chmn, Pres & CEO, Trident Microsystems Inc.; US; 415/691-9211

Lin, Fu-Kun; Chmn, Twinbridge Software Corp.; US; 213/263-3926

Lin, Jeff; Pres & CEO, Asante Technologies Inc.; US; 408/435-8388

Lin, Nan-Sheng; EVP Eng, Digicom Systems Inc.; US; 408/262-1277

Lin, Patrick; Pres, Fairstone Technologies Corp.; US; 516/261-0023

Lin, Raymond C.; Pres & CEO, Premisys Communications Inc.; US; 510/353-7600

Lin, Vincent; Dir Mktng, ADI Systems Inc.; US; 408/944-0100, vlin@adiusa.com

Lincoln, Howard; Chmn, Nintendo of America Inc.; US; 206/882-2040

Lind, Jeffrey; GM, Compliance West; US; 619/755-5525

Lind, Kenneth H.; VP Fin, Franklin Electronic Pblrs Inc.; US; 609/386-2500

Lind, Robert R.; VP Corp Dev, Rockwell International Corp.; US; 310/797-3311

Lindan, Anthony; Mktng Dir, Arc Media Inc.; Canada; 416/410-4429

Lindelow, Jan H.; Pres & COO, Symbol Technologies Inc.; US; 516/563-2400

Lindenfelder, Mitch; Dir Fin & Admin,

DataFocus Inc.; US; 703/631-6770, mitch@datafocus.com

Linderholm, Owen; Ed-in-Chief, PC World Interactive; US; 415/243-0500

Lindgren, Brian; Ed & Pblr, Triad Services Inc.; US; 803/763-9997

Lindgren, Brian; Ed, Computer Technology Research Corp.; US; 803/853-6460

Lindholm, Elizabeth; Exec Ed, Datamation; US; 617/558-4281, elindholm@datamation.cahners.com

Lindsay, Andrew; Sr Ed, Publishing & Multimedia; US

Lindsay, Mary; Pres, Lindsay PR; US; 408/984-7242

Lindseth, Jon A.; Chmn, AER Energy Resources Inc.; US; 404/433-2127

Lindstrom, James T.; VP & CFO, Trident Microsystems Inc.; US; 415/691-9211

Lindstrom, Robert L.; Ed, Multimedia Producer; US; 914/328-9157

Lineback, J. Robert; Ed-in-Chief, Electronic Business Today; US; 617/964-3030

Ling, Lorraine; Pres & CEO, Extend Inc.; US; 510/484-0395

Ling, Paul; Pres & CEO, Creative Digital Research; US; 408/255-0999

Ling, Paul; Dir Bus Dev, Extend Inc.; US; 510/484-0395

Lingren, Brian J.; Ed, Mantek Services Inc.; US; 803/552-6671

Linhardt, Carl; VP Mktng, Cypress Research Corp.; US; 408/752-2700

Link, Daniel; VP Sales, ResNova Software; US; 714/379-9000

Linker, Sheldon; VP, Linker Systems Inc.; US; 714/552-1904, sol@linker.com

Linn, Hildy; Pub Mgr, Society for Computer Simulation; US; 619/277-3888, linn@sdsc.edu

Linton, William W.; EVP & CFO, SHL Systemhouse Inc.; Canada; 613/236-1428

Lipham, James B.; CFO & EVP, Total Systems Services Inc.; US; 706/649-2204

Lipka, Kristie; Ed, Reliability Rating's AS/400 Client/Server Report; US; 617/444-5755

Lippincott, Douglas E.; Pres & CEO, FTG Data Systems; US; 714/995-3900, 70444.66@compuserve.com

Lipscomb, Ken O.; Pres, Infographix Technologies Inc.; US; 404/523-4944

Lipscomb, Thomas H.; Pres, Infosafe Systems Inc.; US; 212/867-7200, tom@infosafe.com

Lipton, Amy; Exec Ed, HomePC; US; 516/562-7673

Lipton, Lenny; VP R&D, StereoGraphics Corp.; US; 415/459-4500

Liran, Moshe; Chmn & CTO, Optimal Networks; US; 415/254-5950, moshel@optimal.com

Lissauer, Annette; VP Sales, Individual Inc.; US; 617/273-6000

Lissauer, Michael; VP Mktng, Business-Wire; US

Litle, Thomas J.; Chmn & Pres, LitleNet; US; 603/894-9000

Little, Meredith; Ed, Inside Word; US; 502/493-3300

Little, Rich; Pres, Lead Technologies Inc.; US; 704/332-5532

Little, Selby F.; VP & CFO, Ross Systems Inc.; US; 415/593-2500

Little, Will; SVP, Informer Computer Systems Inc.; US; 714/891-1112

Littman-Quinn, Jack; Pres & COO, PCs Compleat; US; 508/480-8500

Littrell, Dianne; VP, Stiller Research; US; 904/575-0920, 72571.3352@compuserve.com

Litwack, David; Pres, Powersoft Corp; US; 508/287-1500

Litwin, Barry; VP R&D, Hummingbird Communications Ltd.; Canada; 905/470-1203

Liu, Leonard Y.; Chmn, Pres & CEO, Walker Interactive Systems Inc.; US; 415/495-8811

Liu, Leonard Y.W.; COO, Cadence Design Systems Inc.; US; 408/943-1234

Liu, Morries; Chmn & CEO, Liuski International Inc.; US; 770/447-9454

Liu, Richard; VP Sales & Mktng, Chem US; 510/785-8080

Liu, William W.; Pres, MediAlive; US; 408/752-8500

Liu, Y.C.; Pres, CTX International Inc.; US; 909/598-8094

Livingstone, John; CEO, Absolute Software Corp.; Canada; 604/730-9851

Lizza, Frederick; Pres, Software 2000 Inc.; US; 508/778-2000

Lloyd, Michael; Principal, Lloyd & Clark; US; 818/757-0070

Lloyd, Robert E.; Chmn & CEO, Mindscape Inc.; US; 415/883-3000

Lloyd, Terrie; Pblr, Computing Japan; Japan; 3-3445-2616

Lo, Dennis; Chmn & VP Eng, SourceMate Information Systems Inc.; US; 415/381-1011

Lo, Jason; Pres, Integrix Inc.; US; 805/375-1055

Lockhart, Michael D.; Chmn, Pres, CEO & COO, General Signal Corp.; US; 203/329-4100

Loeffler, W.G.; Chmn, Loeffler Ketchum Mountjoy PR; US; 704/364-8969

Lofink, James; Dir Mktng, Operations Control Systems; US; 415/493-4122

Logan, James D.; Chmn, MicroTouch Systems Inc.; US; 508/659-9000

Logan, John; Pres, Aberdeen Group Inc.; US; 617/723-7890

Lokey, Larry I.; Pres & GM, Business-Wire; US

Lombardi, John A.; VP Sales & Mktng, Best Power Technology Inc.; US; 608/565-7200

Lomen, Arlyn; VP & CFO, Damark International Inc.; US; 612/531-0066

London, Jack P.; Chmn, Pres & CEO, CACI International Inc.; US; 703/841-7800

London, Mitchell B.; Pres & CEO, ConnectSoft; US; 206/827-6467, 75540.3170@compuserve.com

Long, Gary R.; Pres, CalComp Inc.; US; 714/821-2000

Long, J. Shane; VP Sales & Mktng, STB Systems Inc.; US; 214/234-8750

Long, Jim; COO, Champion Business Systems Inc.; US; 303/792-3606

Long, Jim; CEO, Starlight Networks; US; 415/967-2774

Long, W. Michael; Pres & CEO, Continuum Company Inc., The; US; 512/345-5700

Long, William; EVP, Boundless Technologies; US; 512/346-2447

Longo Jr., Edward H.; SVP Info Svcs, Keane Inc.; US; 617/241-9200

Longobardi, Gene; VP Ops, New Horizons Computer Learning Centers Inc.; US; 714/556-1220

Longoria, Jeff; VP Sales & Mktng, ProAmerica Systems Inc.; US; 214/680-6257, jeffl@proam.com

Longoria, Joe; Pres, ProAmerica Systems Inc.; US; 214/680-6257

Longson, Jim; Pres & CEO, Compton's NewMedia Inc.; US; 619/929-2500

Lonsdale, David; VP WW Sales, Integrated Micro Products Inc.; US; 214/980-2771

Lonstein, Zach; Chmn, Pres & CEO, Computer Outsourcing Services Inc.; US; 212/564-3730

Lookabaugh, Tom; VP R&D, DiviCom Inc.; US; 408/944-6700

Loomis, Maury; Dir Sales & Mktng, Pacific Micro Data Inc.; US; 714/955-9090, m_loomis@pmicro.com

Lopas, Rene; Nat'l Sales Mgr, Altima Systems Inc.; US

Lopatin, Jay; Pres & GM, Micro Central; US; 908/360-0300

Lopatin, Matt; Vendor Acq, Micro Central; US; 908/360-0300

Lopez, Zeke; VP Sales & Mktng, O'Neil Electronics; US; 714/727-1234

Lopinto, John; Pres, Communications Specialties Inc.; US; 516/273-0404, john@commspecial.com

LoPinto, Richard; VP, Nikon Electronic Imaging; US; 516/547-4355

Lorence, Kurt; Project Mgr, Internet Group Inc., The; US; 412/688-9696, kurt@tig.com

Lorentzen, Stephen R.; Pres & COO, Blyth Software Inc.; US; 415/571-0222

Lorimer, Eric R.; VP & CFO, Fakespace Inc.; US; 415/688-1940

LoSasso, Angela; Sr Ed, Computer Sources; US; 408/295-5900

Losky, Daniel; VP Mktng, Peripheral Land Inc.; US; 510/657-2211

Louderback, Jim; Ed-in-Chief, Windows Sources; US; 212/503-4147, jim_louderback@zd.com

Loufek, Gretchen; VP Fin, Ripley-Woodbury Marketing Communications; US; 310/860-7336

Louie, Gilman G.; Chmn, Spectrum Holobyte Inc.; US; 510/522-3584

Louis, Tristan; Exec Dir, iWORLD; US; 203/226-6967

Lovato, Darryl; Dir Dev Tech, Aladdin System Inc.; US; 408/761-6200, dlovato@aladdinsys.com

Love, Ransom; VP Mktng, Caldera; US; 801/229-1675

Love, Richard; VP, Torrey Pines Research; US; 619/929-4800

Lovell, Scott; Pres, Strata Inc.; US; 801/628-5218

Low, Jeffrey B.; VP Mktng, Proteon Inc.; US; 508/898-2800

Lowafer, David; Pres & COO Visual Comm Group, Electrohome Ltd.; Canada; 519/744-7111

Lowe, Danny; Chmn, QSound Labs Inc.; Canada; 403/291-2492

Lowe, David B.; VP Sales, Brooktrout Technology Inc.; US; 617/499-4100, dbl@brooktrout.com

Lowe, Janet; VP, Cplex Optimization Inc.; US; 702/831-7744, janet@cplex.com

Lowe, Ken; Eng Mgr, MAG Innovision Inc.; US; 714/751-2008

Lowe, Todd; Pres, Cplex Optimization Inc.; US; 702/831-7744, tlowe@cplex.com

Lowell, Michael J.; VP & CFO, Alpha Microsystems; US; 714/957-8500

Lowenstein, Douglas; Pres, Interactive Digital Software Assoc.; US; 202/833-4372

Lowenthal, Richard; VP R&D, StrataCom Inc.; US; 408/294-7600

Lowery Jr., W. Wilson; Chmn, IBM Credit Corp.; US; 203/973-7000

Lowrey, Lang; Pres & CEO, Anacomp Inc.; US; 317/844-9666

Lowrey, Tyler; Vice Chmn & COO, Micron Technology Inc.; US; 208/368-4400

Lowry, James; CEO, Gold Standard Multimedia Inc.; US; 904/373-1100

Lowry, Phillip; VP Bus Dev, Motion Pixels; US; 602/951-3288

Lu, David; Pres DFI-USA, Diamond Flower Electric Instrument Co. Inc.; US; 916/568-1234

Lu, Gene; Chmn, Pres & CEO, Advanced Logic Research; US; 714/581-6770

Lu, Y.C.; Pres & CEO, Diamond Flower Electric Instrument Co. Inc.; US; 916/568-1234

Lubeck, Scott; Dir, National Academy Press; US; 202/334-2612

Lubin, Michael L.; EVP, Pacific Communications Sciences; US; 619/535-9500

Lubinski, Thomas; Pres & CTO, SL Corp.; US; 415/927-1724

Lubman, Irving; Chmn, Nu Horizons Electronics Corp.; US; 516/226-6000

Lucanegro, Cheryl A.; Assoc Pblr, Upside Publishing Co., The; US; 415/377-0950, clucanegro@upside.com

Lucarini, Dan; Dir Mktng, Information Management Research Inc.; US; 303/689-0022

Lucas, James; VP Sales, SRS Labs Inc.; US; 714/442-1070

Lucas, John C.; EVP, Knozall Systems Inc.; US; 602/545-0006, johnl@tesi.com

Lucas, Leo; CTO, AimTech Corp.; US; 603/883-0220

Lucas, Raymond D.; SVP Strat Officer, Scientific-Atlanta Inc.; US; 770/903-5000, ray.lucas@sciatl.com

Lucas, William A.; Pres, Vector Directory: Messaging Systems; US; 617/862-7607, 4401232@mcimail.com

Lucchese, Alphonse M.; Chmn, Davox Corp.; US; 508/952-0200

Lucente, Darrell; VP Sales, American Power Conversion; US; 401/789-5735

Lucente, Ed; Pres & CEO, Liant Software Corp.; US; 508/872-8700

Lucivero, James P.; VP Sales, Nexar Technologies Inc.; US; 508/836-8700

Luck, Dale; Pres, GfxBase Inc.; US; 408/262-1469, d.luck@ieee.org

Luckey, George H.; EVP, OfficeMax Inc.; US; 216/921-6900

Lucky, Robert W.; Corp VP Applied Res, Bellcore; US; 201/829-2000

Luczo, Stephen J.; SVP Corp Dev, Seagate Technology; US; 408/438-6550

Ludwick, Andrew K.; Pres & CEO, Bay Networks Inc.; US; 408/988-2400

Lueck, Laurence; Ed & Pblr, Magnetic Media International Newsletter; US; 808/373-5330

Lugbauer, Cathy; EVP, Weber Group Inc., The; US; 617/661-7900, clugbauer@webergroup.com

Luhmann, Rick; Ed, Computer Telephony; US; 212/691-8215, rluhman@mcimail.com

Luhn, Robert; Ed-in-Chief, Computer Currents; US; 510/547-6800

Luis, Dan; VP, Wynd Communications Corp.; US; dluis@wynd.net

Lukas, Vincent; Mktng Mgr, Jazz Speakers; US; 818/336-2689

Luke, Christopher; Pres, Comtrade; US; 818/961-6688

Luke, Rachel; Acct Mgr, Comtrade; US; 818/961-6688

Luke, Robert S.; EVP, CTX International Inc.; US; 909/598-8094

Lukis, Larry J.; EVP & CTO, LaserMaster Corp.; US; 612/941-8687

Lum, Sunny; VP Ops, ACC Technology Group; US; 714/454-2441

Lummis, Larry; VP WW Sales, Micronics Computers Inc.; US; 510/651-2300

Lund, Bill; Sys Admin, Advantage kbs Inc.; US; 908/287-2236, blund@akbs.com

Lund, Patricia; CEO, Upstart Communications; US; 510/420-7979, plund@upstart.com

Lundberg, Abbie; Ed, CIO; US; 508/872-0080

Lundeen, David; CFO, BSG Corp.; US; 713/965-9000

Lundeen, Tim; Pres, Lundeen & Associates; US; 510/521-5855

Lundell, Donald R.; Pres, Knozall Systems Inc.; US; 602/545-0006, donl@tesi.com

Lundell, Gail A.; Dir Marcom, Knozall Systems Inc.; US; 602/545-0006, gaill@tesi.com

Lundin, Kent; VP Mktng, Capsoft Dev. Corp.; US; 801/763-3915

Lundquist, Eric; Ed-in-Chief, PC Week; US; 617/393-3700, eric_lundquist@zd.com

Lung, James; VP Eng, Destiny Technology Corp.; US; 408/562-1000

Lungo, Robert J.; VP & CFO, Howtek Inc.; US; 603/882-5200

Lunt, E. James; Chmn & CEO, DataCal Corp.; US; 602/831-3100

Luo, Zong; VP R&D, Mannesmann Tally Corp.; US; 206/251-5500

Luongo, John R.; Pres & CEO, Vantive Corp.; US; 408/982-5700

Luschemat, Rob; Natl Sales Mgr, nuLogic; US; 617/444-7680

Lusk, Alice; SVP & CIO, NCR Corp.; US; 513/445-5000

Luskin, Bernard J.; Pres, Jones Digital Century Inc.; US; 303/792-3100

Lussier, Richard; Pres & CEO, Siemens Nixdorf Information Systems Inc.; US; 617/273-0480

Lutkowitz, Mark; Pres, Trans-Formation Inc.; US; 205/970-2250

Luttrell, Ken; VP & GM, Arnet Corp.; US; 615/834-8000

Lutz, Alan G.; EVP, Unisys Corp.; US; 215/986-4011

Lutz, John A.; Pres & CEO, True Basic Inc.; US; 603/298-8517, john@truebasic.com

Luu, Jose; VP Eng, Mainsoft Corp.; US; 408/774-3400

Lux, Rob; Dir MIS, Reality Online Inc.; US; 610/277-7600

Lux, Robert; Pres & CEO, BayStone Software; US; 408/370-9301, bob@baystone.com

Luzar, Les; Div Mgr, Teac America Inc.; US; 213/726-0303

Ly, Linus; Mgng Ed, Multimedia Source Book; US; 212/293-3900

Lycklama, Edward; Co-Founder, KL Group Inc.; Canada; 416/594-1026

Lyell, Mark; VP Sales & Mktng, Pragmatech Inc.; US; 408/943-1151

Lyle, Carl; VP Ops, RGB Spectrum; US; 510/814-7000

Lyle, Lawrence D.; Pres & CEO, UnixWare Technology Group; US; 908/522-6027

Lynar, Craig; Dir Mktng, Seiko Instruments US Inc.; US; 408/922-5900

Lynch, Clifford; Pres, American Society for Information Science; US; 301/495-0900

Lynch, Devin; Dir Sales, Personal Training Systems; US; 415/462-2100

Lynch, Rick; Nat'l Sales Mgr, Data Entry Systems Inc.; US; 205/430-3023

Lynch, Shawna; VP Home Ent, Bender, Goldman Helper; US; 310/473-4147, shawna_lynch@bgh.com

Lynch, Tom; VP Sales & Mktng, MicroHelp Inc.; US; 770/516-0899

Lynch Weinstein, Eileen; VP Eng, Advantage kbs Inc.; US; 908/287-2236, eweinstein@akbs.com

Lynn, Donna; CEO, Reed Technology & Information Services Inc.; US; 301/428-3700

Lynn, Kurt; VP Sales & Mktng, Kolvox Communications Inc.; Canada; 416/221-2400

Lynn, Whitney; Pres & CEO, Borland Int'l.; US; 408/431-1000

Lynton, Linda; Ed-in-Chief, International Business; US

Lyon, David; Pres & CEO, Pacific Communications Sciences; US; 619/535-9500

Lyon, Robert; VP, SyQuest Technology Inc.; US; 510/226-4000

Lyons, J. David; EVP Mktng & Sales, National Data Corp.; US; 404/728-2000

Lyons, John; VP Mktng Prog, Entex Information Services; US; 914/935-3600

Lyons, Michael; CEO, Dynasty Technology; US; 708/355-8300

Lyons, Tom; CTO, Ipsilon Networks Inc.; US; 415/846-4600

Lyons, William J.; Pres, Intentia Int'l.; US; 847/768-1300

Lyons, William P.; Pres & CEO, ParcPlace-Digitalk Inc.; US; 408/481-9090

Lysaugh, Thomas F.; VP Mktng, GTE Corp.; US; 203/965-2000

Lytton, Nina; Ed, Crossroads A-list; US; 617/859-0859

Lytton, Robert; Dir Info Tech, Micrografx Inc.; US; 214/234-1769

Ma, Joy; Ed, PC Games; US; 415/349-4300

Maas, Ronald; EVP & CFO, Touchstone Software Int'l.; US; 714/470-1122

Macadino, Dom; Dir Support Ops, True Software Inc.; US; 508/369-7398, domm@truesoft.com

Macaleer, R. James; Chmn, Shared Medical Systems Corp.; US; 610/219-6300

Macaw, Chris; Sales Mgr, Cougar Mountain Software; US; 208/375-4455

MacDonald, Donna; Mktng Mgr, Hi Resolution Inc.; US; 508/463-6953

MacDonald, Michael; Ed-in-Chief, PowerProgrammer Magazine; US; 201/332-1515

MacDonald, Robert; Pres & CEO, ProfitKey International Inc.; US; 603/898-9800

MacDonald, Stephen A.; SVP, Adobe Systems Inc.; US; 415/961-4400

MacDonald, Walter R.; CFO, Gandalf Technologies Inc.; Canada; 613/274-6500

MacDougal, Gary; Pres & COO, Eclipse Systems Inc.; US

Mace, Joni M.; VP Fin, Progress Software Corp.; US; 617/280-4000

Mace, Paul; CEO, Paul Mace Software; US; 541/488-2322

Mace, Stephen; VP Sales, Praxisoft Inc.; US; 703/729-3391

Mace, Tom; Exec Dir, UniForum Association; US; 408/986-8840, tom@uniforum.org

Macfarlane, Larry; VP Sales, Zinc Software; US; 801/785-8900, lmacfarlane@zinc.com

Machala, Edward W.; VP Ops, American Power Conversion; US; 401/789-5735

Machiz, Leon; Chmn & CEO, Avnet Inc.; US; 516/466-7000

Machover, Carl; Pres, Machover Associates Corp.; US; 914/949-3777

Macias, Mark; CTO, Williams & Macias Inc.; US; 509/458-6312

MacIntosh, Chris; Ops Mgr, Peer-to-Peer Communications Inc.; US; 408/435-2677

MacIntyre, Doug; Pres & CEO, Dun & Bradstreet Software Services Inc.; US; 404/239-2000

MacIver, Kenny; Ed, Computer Business Review; US; 212/677-0409, cbred@power.globalnews.com

Mack, David; VP, WorkGroup Technologies Inc.; US; 603/929-1166

Mackay, Duncan; Chief Eng, Mirus Industries Corp.; US; 408/980-6600

MacKay, Bruce A.; Pres & CEO, Mirus Industries Corp.; US; 408/980-6600

MacKay, Paul; SVP Sales, Powersoft Corp; US; 508/287-1500

MacKenzie, Heather; Dir Mktng, Crystal Inc.; Canada; 604/681-3435

Mackett, Brad; Sales Mgr, Southern Micro Systems Inc.; US; 770/499-9231

Mackintosh, Rob; SVP & CFO, Sendero Corp.; US; 602/941-8112

Maclaren, Tony; Pres, VideoLogic Inc.; US; 415/875-0606

MacLean, Randy; CEO, Formgen; US; 602/443-4109

Macleod, Donald; EVP & CFO, National Semiconductor Corp.; US; 408/721-5000

MacMillan, Scott D.; Marcom; nuLogic; US; 617/444-7680

MacNeal, Richard H.; Chmn, MacNeal-Schwendler Corp., The; US; 213/258-9111

Macourek, Peter; Gen Partner, Rose Electronics; US; 713/933-7673

Macrae, Douglas; Chmn, GCC Technol-

ogies Inc.; US; 617/275-5800

Madan, Herbert; Pres & CEO, NETSYS Technologies Inc.; US; 415/833-7500

Madavi, Syrus P.; Pres & CEO, Burr-Brown Corp.; US; 602/746-1111

Madden, Brendan P.; Pres, Tom Sawyer Software; US; 510/848-0853, bmadden@tomsawyer.com

Madden, Wayne; Pblr, Duke Communications Int'l.; US; 970/663-4700

Madesre, Christopher; Sales Mgr, Cyberian Outpost Inc.; US; 203/927-2050, cdm@cybout.com

Madland, Glen; Chmn, Integrated Circuit Engineering Corp.; US; 602/998-9780

Madlin, Nancy; Ed, Pix; US; 212/536-5222

Madnick, Marc; EVP, B.C. Software Inc.; US; 310/636-4711, madnick@bcsoftware.com

Madsen, Peter C.; Pres & CEO, Fast-Comm Communications Corp.; US; 703/318-7750

Maffei, Eric J.; Ed-in-Chief, Microsoft Interactive Developer; US; 415/833-7100

Mafrica, Leonard; Dir Ed Svcs, Association for Services Management Int'l.; US; 941/275-7887

Magadieu, Cheryl; Ed, 1-2-3 For Windows Report, The; US; 617/482-8634

Magee, Keith; VP Sales & Mktg, Computer Support Corp.; US; 214/661-8960

Magee, Kenneth; Pres, Evergreen Technologies Inc.; US; 541/757-0934

Magee, Marshall; Pres & CEO, Magee Enterprises Inc.; US; 770/446-6611

Magee, Stan; Ed, Software Engineering Standards & Specifications; US; 303/792-2181, 73211.2144@compuserve.com

Maggi, Al Dei; VP Field Ops, Integrated Micro Products Inc.; US; 214/980-2771

Maginness, Charles E.; Chmn & CEO, Performance Technologies Inc.; US; 716/256-0200

Maginniss, Chris; EVP & CFO, Microdyne Corp.; US; 703/739-0500

Maglione, Fred R.; VP Sales & Mktng, Lasergate Systems Inc.; US; 813/725-0882

Magney, Phil; Pres, Associated Research Services Inc.; US; 214/570-7100

Maher, Bob; VP Eng, Interleaf Inc.; US; 617/290-0710, bmaher@ileaf.com

Maher, Kathleen; Ed-in-Chief, CADENCE Magazine; US; 415/905-2276

Maher, Tom; EVP WW Ops, Avatar Systems Corp.; US; 408/321-0110

Mahler, David A.; VP Bus Dev, Remedy Corp.; US; 415/903-5200

Mahoney, David C.; Chmn, Pres & CEO, Banyan Systems Inc.; US; 508/898-1000

Mahoney, Matthew; Research Dir, IDC Government; US; 703/876-5055

Mahoney, Robert W.; Chmn, Pres & CEO, Diebold Inc.; US; 216/489-4000

Mahuson, William E.; VP Tech, Performance Technologies Inc.; US; 716/256-

0200

Mai, Chao C.; SVP, Dallas Semiconductor Corp.; US; 214/450-0400

Mailahn, Rolf; EVP & CFO, Siemens Nixdorf Information Systems Inc.; US; 617/273-0480

Maine, Douglas L.; CFO, MCI Communications Corp.; US; 202/872-1600

Maitano, Philip; Mgr SW Dev, Mailer's Software; US; 714/492-7000

Major, John; Chmn, Telecommunications Industry Assoc.; US; 703/907-7700

Major, Kathleen M.; Mgng Ed, C++ Report; US; 212/242-7447

Mak, Albert; VP Mktng, ESS Technology Inc.; US; 510/226-1088

Mak, Phil; Pres, Symphony Laboratories; US; 408/986-1701

Makarenko, Alexander; EVP & GM, Mecom Software; US; 404/564-0473

Makino, Dan; EVP, Nanao US Corp.; US; 310/325-5202

Makmann, Tom; VP & GM, Sytron Corp.; US; 508/898-0100

Makowski, Joe; VP Support Svcs, Computer Task Group Inc.; US; 716/887-7424, joseph.makowski@ctg.com

Malandrakis, Joseph E.; VP WW Ops, Perkin-Elmer Corp.; US; 203/762-1000

Malbon, Mark S.; VP & CFO, Roland Corp. US; US; 213/685-5141

Malcolm, Daniel J.; SVP & COO, American Healthware Systems Inc.; US; 718/435-6300

Malcolm, Michael; SVP Strat Dev, Network Appliance Corp.; US; 415/428-5100

Malecek, Chris; SVP, Shandwick US; US; 612/832-5000, rcmalecek@shandwick.com

Maleval, Jean-Jacques; Ed & Pblr, Computer Data Storage Newsletter; France; 331-42463056

Malin, John; VP Ops, Modgraph Inc.; US; 617/938-4488

Malina, Roger F.; Exec Ed, Leonardo & Leonardo Music Journal; US; 617/253-2889, isast@sfsu.edu

Mallandain, Rene; VP Ops, Protec Microsystems Inc.; Canada; 514/630-5832

Mallicoat, Samuel W.; Chmn & VP R&D, Microfield Graphics Inc.; US; 503/626-9393

Malloy, Rich; Ed-in-Chief, Mobile Office; US; 310/589-3100, malloy@mobileoffice.com

Malmed, Leon; SVP Mktng & Sales, SanDisk Corp.; US; 408/542-0500

Malone, Michael; Pres, Gryphon Software Corp.; US; 619/536-8815

Malone, Tim; Analyst & Ed, PC Pocketbook; US

Maloney, Basil W.; Dir Mktng, Magic Software Enterprises Inc.; US; 714/250-1718

Maloney, Colleen; VP, PhotoDisc Inc.; US; 206/441-9355

Maloney, Dennis B.; Pres Computing &

Netw, SHL Systemhouse Inc.; Canada; 613/236-1428

Maloney, Derek; Prod Mktng Mgr, Apex Data Inc.; US; 510/416-5656

Maloy, James Q.; Chmn, Vertex Industries Inc.; US; 201/777-3500

Maltempo, Robert S.; EVP, Continuum Company Inc., The; US; 512/345-5700

Maltin, Andrew; Co-Founder, Insights Software; US; 310/577-1185

Mamchur Schwartz, Vira; Mgng Ed, Internet World; US; 203/226-6967, vira@iw.com

Manahan, Myra J.; Pres, Single Source Marketing Inc.; US; 714/545-1338

Mancinelli, Bruce R.; Pres & CEO, Relay Technology Inc.; US; 703/506-0500

Mancini, John; Exec Dir, Association for Information & Image Management; US; 301/587-8202

Mancino, Chuck; Pblr, Corry Publishing; US; 814/664-8624

Mandel, Morton L.; Chmn, Premier Industrial Corp.; US; 216/391-8300

Mandel, Paul; Pres, APS Technologies; US; 816/483-1600

Mandelbaum, Mark; Dir Pubs, ACM Press; US; 212/626-0500

Mandich, Mitchell; VP NA Sales, NeXT Inc.; US; 415/366-0900

Manferdelli, John; Pres, Natural Language Inc.; US; 510/814-0500

Mangold, Greg; VP Mktng, Avail Systems Corp; US; 303/444-4018

Manire, Ross W.; SVP & CFO, U.S. Robotics Inc.; US; 847/882-5010

Mankin, Lori; VP Mktng & Sales, WordTech Systems Inc.; US; 510/689-1200

Manley, Mike; CEO, Qualtrak; US; 408/748-9500

Mann, Darlene K.; VP Mktng, Avantos Performance Systems Inc.; US; 510/654-4600

Mann, David; Pres, SoftBooks Inc.; US; 714/586-1284

Mann, James L.; Chmn, Pres & CEO, SunGard Data Systems Inc.; US; 610/341-8700

Mann, Marvin L.; Chmn, Lexmark International Inc.; US; 606/232-2000

Mann, Shel; Dir Consumer Prod, J3 Learning; US; 612/930-0330

Mannheimer, Lee R.; Dir Sales, JMR Electronics Inc.; US; 818/993-4801

Manning, Frank; Pres, Zoom Telephonics Inc.; US; 617/423-1072

Manning, Jeff; Pres, Virtual Media Works; US; 408/739-0301, jeff@vmworks.com

Manning, Terry; Dir Mktng, Zoom Telephonics Inc.; US; 617/423-1072

Manno, Eugene; Chmn, Pres & CEO, Arix Corp.; US; 408/541-8700

Manocha, Trilok; Pres, River Run Software Group; US; 203/861-0090

Manousos, Stephen; VP Sales, Fractal

Design Corp.; US; 408/688-5300

Mans, David P.; Pres & CEO, My Software Co.; US; 415/473-3600

Mansfield, J. Patrick; Pres US Sales, Bull HN Information Systems Inc.; US; 508/294-6000

Mansfield, Kirby A.; VP Mktng, Inso Corp.; US; 617/753-6500

Mantelman, Lee; Ed-in-Chief, Imaging Magazine; US; 212/691-8215, lee@nyoffice.mhs.compuserve.com

Mantle, Philip; SVP Sales & Mktng, Retix; US; 310/828-3400

Manzi, Jim; Pres & CEO, Nets Inc.; US; 412/967-3500, jimmanzi@industry.net

Maples, Michael J.; EVP, Microsoft Corp.; US; 206/936-4400

March, Richard; Ed, VARBUSINESS; US; 516/562-5000

March, Rod G.; VP, First Floor Inc.; US; 415/968-1101

Marchionni, Carmen J.; VP Mktng, Dataram Corp.; US; 609/799-0071

Marcotte, Timothy A.; VP Ops & CFO, Now Software Inc.; US; 503/274-2800

Marcus, Irwin; Pres, Marcus Technology Inc.; US; 212/678-0406

Marcus, Lynne; Pres, Marcus + Co.; US; 617/232-1370, lsmarcus@netcom.com

Marcus, Robert P.; Pres, RGB Spectrum; US; 510/814-7000

Marengi, Joseph; Pres, Novell Inc.; US; 801/222-6000

Margalit, Yanki; Pres, Aladdin Knowledge Systems; US; 212/564-5678

Margheret, Janice M.; SVP, Pioneer-Standard Electronics Inc.; US; 216/587-3600

Margolis, Harry W.; Chmn & CEO, CompuTrac Inc.; US; 214/234-4241

Margolis, Paul A.; Chmn, Marcam Corp.; US; 617/965-0220

Marguiles, David M.; EVP, Cerner Corp.; US; 816/221-1024

Marin, Cynthia; Mktng Mgr, Chinon America Inc.; US; 310/533-0274

Marinaro, Edward; Pres & CEO, Network Computing Devices Inc.; US; 415/694-0650

Marino, Carl T.; Pblr, Industry Week; US; 216/696-7000

Marino, Robert J.; SVP Fed Ops, C3 Inc.; US; 703/471-6000

Marino, Sal F.; Chmn & CEO, Penton Publishing Inc.; US; 216/696-7000

Marinstein, Jeff; Pres, Contingency Planning Research Inc.; US; 914/696-4500

Maris, Nick; Chmn, Maris Multimedia; US; 415/492-2819

Marken, Andy; Pres, Marken Communications; US; 408/986-0100

Markkula Jr., A.C.; Vice Chmn, Apple Computer Inc.; US; 408/996-1010

Markman, Steve; Chmn, Pres & CEO, General Magic Inc.; US; 408/774-4000

Markman, Steven; EVP Info Access, Novell Inc.; US; 801/222-6000

Markovich, John M.; VP & CFO, Optical Coating Laboratory Inc.; US; 707/545-6440

Markowicz, Victor; Co-Chmn, Gtech Corp.; US; 401/392-1000

Markowitz, Michael C.; Chief Ed, EDN Asia; Hong Kong; 852-965-1555, ednmarkowitz@mcimail.com

Markowsky, George; Pres, Maine Software Developers Assoc.; US; 207/866-0496

Marks, Howard E.; EVP Studios, Activision Inc.; US; 310/473-9200

Marks, Jack; EVP, Graphic Utilities Inc.; US; 408/577-0334

Marks, Jo; Chmn, Harlequin Inc.; US; 617/374-2400

Marks, Michael E.; Chmn & CEO, Flextronics Int'l.; US; 408/428-1300

Marks, Robert; VP Mfg, Acer America Corp.; US; 408/432-6200

Marley, James E.; Chmn, AMP Inc.; US; 717/564-0100

Marrah, John; COO, XDB Systems Inc.; US; 410/312-9300

Marrin, Dr. Yvette; Pres, National Cristina Foundation; US; 203/622-6000

Marriner, William L.; EVP & CFO, Exabyte Corp.; US; 303/442-4333

Marschel, Glenn W.; Pres & CEO, Paging Network Inc.; US; 214/985-4100

Marsh, Donald H.; Pres & CEO, Marsh Software Systems; US; 704/788-9335

Marsh, Julia A.; Ed, New Telecom Quarterly; US; 512/258-8898, march@tfi.com

Marsh, Sarah T.; VP, Marsh Software Systems; US; 704/788-9335

Marsh-Wetherell, Barbara; Principal, Marsh-Wetherell Market Relations; US; 510/933-1907

Marshak, David; Author, Understanding & Leveraging Lotus Notes Release 4; US; 617/742-5200

Marshak, Ronni; VP & Ed-in-Chief, Patricia Seybold Group; US; 617/742-5200

Marshall, Charlotte; Pres, Charlotte Marshall & Associates; US; 310/379-6104

Marshall, David; Pres & CEO, JourneyWare Media; US; 510/254-4520, dpmars@ix.netcom.com

Marshall, Frank J.; VP & GM, Cisco Systems Inc.; US; 408/526-4000

Marshall, Gordon S.; Chmn, Marshall Industries; US; 818/307-6000

Marshall, Mark; VP Mktng, TPS Electronics; US; 415/988-0141

Marshall, Morry; Dir Analysts, In-Stat Inc.; US; 602/483-4440

Marshall, Trevor; COO, YARC Systems Corp.; US; 805/499-9444

Marte, Janine; Assoc Ed, Computing Channels; US

Martell, Robert E.; Pres & CEO, Avatar Systems Corp.; US; 408/321-0110

Martello, Ed; Dir Eng, Star Technologies

Inc.; US; 703/689-4400

Marten, Alan; VP Sales, SMART Modular Technologies; US; 510/623-1231

Martin, Andrea; Pres, Martin Communications; US; 415/668-2678

Martin, Bryan; CTO, Integrated Information Technology Inc.; US; 408/727-1885

Martin, David; VP & GM, Carroll Touch Inc.; US; 512/244-3500

Martin, David A.; Pres, Smart Technologies Inc.; Canada; 403/245-0333, davidmar@smarttech.com

Martin, Dick; Pres, StereoGraphics Corp.; US; 415/459-4500

Martin, Fritz; Dir Prod Dev, Portfolio Software Inc.; US

Martin, James D.; Dir WW Sales & Mktng, Ultre Division; US; 516/753-4800

Martin, Jean-Paul; VP Eng, Media Cybernetics L.P.; US; 301/495-3305

Martin, Jeremy; VP R&D, BusinessVision Management Systems Inc.; Canada; 905/629-3233

Martin, Joanne; Ed, Supercomputing Apps. & High Perf. Computing, Int'l. Journ. of; US; 617/253-2889, dongarra@cs.utk.edu

Martin, Joelle M.; Pblr, Internet Week; US; 301/340-1520, emullally@phillips.com

Martin, John C.; Pres Retail Stores, OfficeMax Inc.; US; 216/921-6900

Martin, John F.; Pblr, Scientific Computing & Automation; US; 201/292-5100

Martin, Joseph; VP Corp Dev, TriQuint Semiconductor; US; 503/644-3535

Martin, Mark; MIS Mgr, Revelation Software; US; 203/973-1000

Martin, Richard; Nat'l Sales Mgr, American Business Systems Inc.; US; 508/250-9600

Martin, Richard B.; SVP Eng, Transitional Technology Inc.; US; 714/693-1133, richard@ttech.com

Martin, Robert; Ed, Cisco World; US; 512/250-9023

Martin, Ron; Pres, Ron Martin & Assoc. Inc.; US; 201/579-3369

Martin, T.W.; Dir Sales, NeoSoft Corp.; US; 541/389-5489, twm@neosoftware.com

Martin, Terence D.; EVP & CFO, General Signal Corp.; US; 203/329-4100

Martinez, Edgar; Dir Cust Sup, Software Support Inc.; US; 407/333-4433

Martinez, Joseph; Pres, DIC Digital Supply Corp.; US; 201/692-7700

Martinez, Ken; Pres, Houston Area Apple Users Group; US; 713/522-2179

Martinez Jr, Miguel A.; VP & CFO, Elek-Tek; US; 847/677-7660

Martini, Thomas P.; CFO, Scriptel Holdings Inc.; US; 614/276-8402

Martino, Gary; VP & CFO, Information Management Associates Inc.; US; 203/925-6800

Martz, Jack W.; SVP, Structural Dynamics Research Corp.; US; 513/576-2400

Marushima, Giichi; Chief R&D, Canon Inc.; Japan; 3-33758-2111

Marvin, Michael D.; Chmn, MapInfo Corp.; US; 518/285-6000

Marwick, Roma; Mktng Mgr, Crystal-Graphics Inc.; US; 408/496-6175

Marymee, Carla B.; Pblr, Sybase Magazine; US; 510/596-3500

Masich, Jeffrey; Pres, Computing Technology Industry Assoc.; US; 630/268-1818

Maslana, Richard; VP Ops, Farallon Computing Inc.; US; 510/814-5100

Maslyn, James P.; SVP & CFO, Mindscape Inc.; US; 415/883-3000

Mason, David H.; Pres, Northeast Consulting Resources Inc.; US; 617/654-0600, mason@ncri.com

Mason, Greg; Pblr, Multimedia World; US; 415/281-8650

Mason, Roger; VP & CFO, Concurrent Computer Corp.; US; 908/870-4500

Mason, Susan A.; Principal, Information Architects, The; US; 415/948-3927, susanmason@aol.com

Mason, Victoria; Ed-in-Chief, BRP Publications Inc.; US; 202/842-3006

Mason, William; Pres & CEO, Adra Systems Inc.; US; 508/937-3700

Masraff, Anthony G.; CEO, Omnicomp Graphics Corp.; US; 713/464-2990

Massa, Jeff; SVP Bus Dev, Intell.X; US; 703/524-7400

Massero, Bob; Exec Dir, North American Ingres User Assoc.; US; 408/649-0644

Massey, Bob; Pres & CEO, CompuServe Inc.; US; 614/457-8600

Massie, Thomas; Chmn & CEO, Focus Enhancements Inc.; US; 617/938-8088

Masson, Bernard; VP & GM DHPrint, DH Technology Inc.; US; 619/451-3485

Masters, Del W.; Pres & CEO, Maximum Strategy Inc.; US; 408/383-1600

Masters, Melvin L.; Chmn, Pres & CEO, LaserMaster Corp.; US; 612/941-8687

Masterson, Conrad; Div VP, TeleMagic Inc.; US; 214/733-4292, conradm@onramp.net

Matera, John; VP WW Sales, Keyfile Corp.; US; 603/883-3000, johnmatera@keyfile.com

Matheis, Dieter; CFO, SAP AG; Germany; 6227-34-0

Mathews, Andrew W.; VP Sales, Datawatch Corp.; US; 508/988-9700

Mathews, Greg; Dir Sales, Arcland; US; 610/993-9904

Mathews, J. Kirk; Chmn, Xircom Inc.; US; 805/376-9300

Mathias, Don; COO, Mesa Communications Inc.; US; 714/260-3905, dwmathias@aol.com

Mathieson, Neil G.; VP Sales, Data I/O Corp.; US; 206/881-6444

Mathis, Thomas; Pres, Carina Software; US; 510/355-1266

Mathison, Todd A.; Mgr Tech Sup Svcs, Unitrac Software Corp.; US; 616/344-0220, tmathison@unitrac.com

Matic, Branko; Chmn, Matrox Graphics Inc.; Canada; 514/685-2630

Matlack, Lucinda; VP Ops, Qualtrak; US; 408/748-9500

Maton Jr., Reginald R.; VP & CIO, Standard Microsystems Corp.; US; 516/435-6000

Matson, Bill; Sales Mgr, Autotime Corp.; US; 503/452-8577

Matsui, Ken; Pres, Chinon America Inc.; US; 310/533-0274

Matsumoto, Clay; Bus Ops, SWeDE Corp.; US; 714/442-6180

Matsutani, Takashi; Pres, Fujitsu Systems Business of America Inc.; US; 408/988-8012

Mattern, Bruce W.; VP Sales & Mktng, Xicor Inc.; US; 408/432-8888

Matteucci, Paul; CEO, Mpath Interactive Inc.; US; 408/342-8800

Matthes, Lynne; Pblr, Microsoft Interactive Developer; US; 415/833-7100

Matthews, Alan; CTO, Percussion Software Inc.; US; 617/438-9900, alan_matthews@percussion.com

Matthews, David; VP Bus Dev, UniKix Technologies; US

Matthews, Jim; Pres & CEO, Capener Matthews & Walcher; US; 619/238-8500

Matthews, Nancy; Dir Sales, Arnet Corp.; US; 615/834-8000

Matthews, Pete; VP Mktng, Forte Technologies Inc.; US; 716/427-8595, pmatthews@fortevr.com

Matthews, Terry; Chmn, Newbridge Networks Corp.; Canada; 604/430-3600

Matthies, William; Pres, Verity Group Inc.; US; 714/680-9611, verbill@aol.com

Matthys, Mark; Partner, Casal Group; US; 214/488-7000, mmattys.casal@onramp.net

Mattia, Thomas; Pres, GCI Jennings; US; 415/974-6200

Mattingly, Kimberly; Dir Mktng Dev, Niles & Associates Inc.; US; 510/559-8592, kimberly@niles.com

Mattos, Tom; Mgng Ed, Dallas Ft. Worth Technology; US; 214/907-9977

Maule, Rick; VP Mktng, Concurrent Computer Corp.; US; 908/870-4500

Maulsby, L. Don; VP WW Sales, VLSI Technology Inc.; US; 408/434-3000

Mauro, Richard L.; Pres, Telemate Software Inc.; US; 770/936-3700

Mauro, Rosemary; Dir, Fuse Inc.; US; 908/308-9275

Mautner, Stephen; Exec Ed, National Academy Press; US; 202/334-2612, smautner@nas.edu

Mavel, James C.; Pres & COO, Scan-Optics Inc.; US; 203/289-6001

Maville, Nancy; VP Fin & Admin, High Performance Systems Inc.; US; 603/643-9636

Mavin, Barry; Principle & CEO, Recital Corp.; US; 508/750-1066, bmavin@recital.com

Mawhinney, David; VP Adv Apps, Nets Inc.; US; 412/967-3500, davemawhinney@industry.net

Maxon, Ethan; Sales Mgr, Opticomm Corp.; US; 619/450-0143

Maxwell, Barbara S.; VP Mktng, Synergy Software; US; 610/779-0522

Maxwell, Christine; Pblr, McKinley Group Inc., The; US; 415/331-1884, maxwell@mckinley.com

Maxwell, Howard R.; Pres, Synergy Software; US; 610/779-0522

Maxwell, Isabel; VP Strat Plng, McKinley Group Inc., The; US; 415/331-1884, max@mckinley.com

Maxwell, Kim; Chmn & Pres, ADSL Forum; US; 415/378-6680, adslforum@aol.com

May, Andy; VP Mktng, Primary Access Corp.; US; 619/675-4100

May, Christy; Pres, D/M Communications Inc.; US; 617/329-7799, dmchristy@aol.com

May, Doug; VP Mktng, Fujitsu Computer Products; US; 408/432-6333

May, Joel A.; Pres, Harmonic Vision; US; 847/467-2395

Mayer, Denny; VP Sales, InVision Interactive; US; 415/812-7380

Mayer, Donald; COO & GM, Portfolio Software Inc.; US; donmayer@eworld.com

Mayer, Gordon E.; Pres & CEO, Geoworks; US; 510/814-1660

Mayer, Happy; Dir Info Syst, Portfolio Software Inc.; US

Mayer, Harold F.; VP Admin, Cognitronics Corp.; US; 203/830-3400

Mayer, Robert; VP Sales, International Microcomputer Software Inc.; US; 415/257-3000

Mayer, Susan; SVP Corp Dev, MCI Communications Corp.; US; 202/872-1600

Mayes, John; Pres, Network Translation Inc.; US; 415/494-6387

Mayhew, Mary Ann; EVP Bus Dev, Computer Data Systems Inc.; US; 301/921-7000

Mazner, Martin; Pres, BookMaker Corp.; US; 415/345-8160, 228.2035@mcimail.com

Mazor, Barry; Ed-in-Chief, Advanced Imaging; US; 516/845-2700

Mazza, Frank; Pres & CEO, Powerhouse Entertainment; US; 214/933-5400

Mazzei, Michael; VP Sales & Mktng, V Communications Inc.; US; 408/296-4224, 75031.3042@compuserve.com

McAdam, John; Pres & COO, Sequent Computer Systems Inc.; US; 503/626-5700

McAdams Jr., Robert; EVP & CFO, Measurex Corp.; US; 408/255-1500

McAfee, Eric A.; CFO, New Media Corp.; US; 714/453-0100

McAfee, John; Chmn & CTO, McAfee Assoc.; US; 408/988-3832

McAlister, Deborah; Holland McAlister PR; US; 214/669-3456

McAllister, Pam; Pblr, Computer Technology Review; US; 310/208-1335, pam_johnson@wwpi.com

McAloon, Brian; VP Sales, Analog Devices Inc.; US; 617/329-4700

McArthur, Larry; Pres & CEO, Aries Technology Inc.; US; 508/453-5310

McAuley, David; Pres, Uniplex Inc.; US; 214/556-0106

McBeth, Gail; VP Admin, Talaris Systems Inc.; US; 619/587-0787, gail@talaris.com

McBrayer, Charles; CFO, PairGain Technologies Inc.; US; 714/832-9924

McBride, Suzanne K.; VP, VRex Inc.; US; 914/345-8877

McBride, Walter J.; SVP & CFO, Emulex Corp.; US; 714/662-5600

McCabe, John P.; VP Info Sys, Teradyne Inc.; US; 617/482-2700

McCabe, Kathryn; Ed-in-Chief, Online Access; US; 312/573-1700

McCabe, Paul; VP Sales, VideoLogic Inc.; US; 415/875-0606

McCall, Bob; VP Sales, Abacus Concepts Inc.; US; 510/540-1949, sales@abacus.com

McCall, Charles W.; Pres & CEO, HBO & Co.; US; 770/393-6000

McCall, Joe; CEO, SQL Financials Int'l.; US; 770/390-3900

McCann Jr., Russell F.; Pres & CEO, Ares Software Corp.; US; 415/578-9090

McCarron, Dean; Principal, Mercury Research; US; 602/998-9225

McCarron, Dean A.; Founder, PC Processors & Chip Sets; US; 602/998-9225

McCarthy, Gerald M.; EVP Sales & Mktng, Zenith Electronics Corp.; US; 708/391-7000

McCarthy, Guy; Pres & CEO, Fortner Research LLC; US; 703/478-0181, guy@fortner.com

McCarthy, Ken; Pblr, Internet Gazette; US; 415/776-1888

McCarthy, Michael E.; Ed-in-Chief & Pblr, Sunworld Online; US; 415/243-4188, michael.mccarthy@sunworld.com

McCarty, Bill; Dir, Center for Software Development; US; 408/494-8378, mccarty@center.org

McCarty, Michael W.; EVP Sales, HBO & Co.; US; 770/393-6000

McCaughey, Lori; VP, K-12 MicroMedia Publishing Inc.; US; 201/529-4500

McCauley, Don; CFO, Verity Inc.; US; 415/960-7600, don@verity.com

McCauley, Herbert N.; VP Info Mgmt, Harris Corp.; US; 407/727-9100

McChristy, Neal; Assoc Ed, Repair, Service & Remarketing News; US; 417/781-9317

McClanathan, Joe; VP & GM, Energizer Power Systems; US; 904/462-3911

McClean, William; Ed, ICECAP Report; US; 602/998-9780, 73512.304@compuserve.com

McClelland, Robert; CFO, Paradigm Technology Inc.; US; 408/954-0500

McClenahan, Kerry; Pres, McClenahan Bruer Burrows Communications Inc.; US; 503/643-9035, kerry@mcbb.com

McClimans, Fred; Principal, Decisys Inc.; US; 703/742-5400, fmcclimans@decisys.com

McCloskey, Peter F.; Pres, Electronic Industries Assoc.; US; 703/907-7500

McCloskey Jr., Richard D.; Pres & CEO, Angia Communications; US; 801/371-0488

McClura, Dave; Dir Com, Software Pblrs Assoc.; US; 202/452-1600

McClure, David; Exec Dir, Association of Online Professionals; US; 703/924-9594

McClure, Robert M.; SVP, Tandy Corp.; US; 817/390-3700

McConaughey, Steve; Dir Mktng, Common Grounds Software Inc.; US; 415/802-5800

McConnel, John; Pres, Medic Computer Systems; US; 919/847-8102

McConnell, Bill; Tech Svcs Mgr, Wave Research Inc.; US; 510/704-3900, bmcconnell@waveresearch.com

McConnell, Matt; Pres & CEO, Compatible Systems Corp.; US; 303/444-9532, matt@compatible.com

McConnell, Mike; Pres & CEO, Visioneer; US; 415/812-6400

McConnell, Rick; VP Fin, Storm Software; US; 415/691-6600

McConnon, Shaun; EVP Sales & Mktng, Raptor Systems Inc.; US; 617/487-7700

McCormack, Marianne; Service Mgr, NAFT Computer Service Corp.; US; 212/982-9800

McCormick, Carl; Pres & CEO, Group Technologies Corp.; US; 813/972-6477, c.mccormick@grtk.com

McCormick, Doug; Dir Info Syst, Packard Bell; US; 818/865-1555

McCormick, John J.; Ed, InformationWEEK; US; 516/562-5000

McCourt, Mark; EVP & Pblr, Software Productivity Group Inc.; US; 508/366-3344, 76102.1473@compuserve.com

McCown, Rainer; Pres, Rhintek Inc.; US; 410/730-2575

McCoy, Mike; Pres, Advanced Digital Systems; US; 310/926-1928

McCracken, Edward R.; Chmn & CEO, Silicon Graphics Inc.; US; 415/960-1980

McCracken, William; GM Fullfillment, IBM Personal Computer Co.; US; 914/766-3700

McCraken, John P.; Int'l Acct Mgr, Award Software Int'l. Inc.; US; 415/968-

4433
McCranie, J. Daniel; VP Mktng & Sales, Cypress Semiconductor Corp.; US; 408/943-2600

McCreary, Lew; Ed Dir, CIO; US; 508/872-0080, mccreary@cio.com

McCrocklin, John; Sr Advisor, Attack Systems Int'l.; US; 415/421-8191

McCrorey, Catherine; Mgng Ed, Computerworld Client/Server Journal; US; 508/879-0700

McCue, Dan; Partner, Freeman-McCue; US; 714/557-3663

McCulloch, Christine; Mktng Dir, Grassroots Research; US; 415/954-5376

McCullough, John; VP, Optical Coating Laboratory Inc.; US; 707/545-6440

McCullough, Patrick D.; VP Info Syst, Neostar Retail Group Inc.; US; 214/401-9000

McCullough, Thomas A.; EVP, DST Systems Inc.; US; 816/435-1000

McCurry, James B.; Chmn & CEO, Neostar Retail Group Inc.; US; 214/401-9000

McCusker, Glenn; Pres & CEO, Viking Components; US; 714/643-7255

McCutcheon, Doug; CFO, Asyst; US; 510/661-5023

McDermaid, Anne; Sales & Mktng Mgr, Creative Solutions Inc.; US; 410/766-4080

McDermott, Joseph; VP & CTO, Datalogix Int'l.; US; 914/747-2900

McDermott, LeeAnne; Ed-in-Chief, GamePro; US; 415/349-4300

McDole Rao, Catherine; Pres, Raosoft Inc.; US; 206/525-4025

McDonald, Beverly; Principal, Baron, McDonald & Wells; US; 770/492-0373, bmcdonald@bmwpr.com

McDonald, Brian; Pres, Zebra Express; US

McDonald, Carol L.; Pres, McDonald & Associates; US; 402/691-8248

McDonald, James F.; Pres & CEO, Scientific-Atlanta Inc.; US; 770/903-5000, james.mcdonald@sciatl.com

McDonald, Jim; EVP, Telus; Canada; 403/498-7311

McDonald, Jim; Eng Mgr, Creative Solutions Inc.; US; 410/766-4080

McDonald, Kevin; Mac Bus Mgr, Xaos Tools; US; 415/487-7000

McDonald, Peter J.; Chmn, Pres & CEO, Software Professionals Inc.; US; 415/578-0700

McDonald, Roy K.; Pres & CEO, Connectix Corp.; US; 415/571-5100

McDonald, Tom; VP & CFO, National Education Training Group; US; 708/369-3000

McDonnell, John F.; Chmn, McDonnell Douglas Corp.; US; 314/232-0232

McDonnell, Neil; VP Sales & Mktng, Dynapro Systems Inc.; Canada; 604/521-3962

McDonnell, Thomas A.; Pres & CEO,

DST Systems Inc.; US; 816/435-1000

McDonnell Jr., John J.; Pres & CEO, Transaction Network Services Inc.; US; 703/742-0500

McDonough, Joseph E.; VP & CFO, Analog Devices Inc.; US; 617/329-4700

McDonough, Kevin C.; SVP Eng, Cyrix Corp.; US; 214/968-8388

McDougall, Paul; Ed-in-Chief, Pre; US; 212/683-3540

McDow, Anthony; Pres, Quadralay Corp.; US; 512/346-9199

McDowall, Ian E.; VP, Fakespace Inc.; US; 415/688-1940

McElwain, Brian J.; VP Sales & Mktng, 01 Communique Laboratory Inc.; Canada; 905/795-2888

McEnany, Lee; VP, Bohle Company, The; US; 310/785-0515

McEwen, Neal W.; VP & CFO, Iterated Systems Inc.; US; 770/840-0310

McFadden, Dave; Pres, MorseMcFadden Communications Inc.; US; 206/889-0528

McFadden, F. Lee; Pres, OneOnOne Computer Training; US; 708/628-0500

McFarland, Mike; SVP Sales & Mktng, Inforite Corp.; US; 415/571-8766

McFarland, Tom; Pres, Century Software; US; 801/268-3088

McFarlane, Robert; CEO, Micro 2000 Inc.; US; 818/547-0125

McGahan, J. Perry; VP Prod Dev, Courtland Group Inc.; US; 410/730-7668

McGannon, Thomas; VP, Metropolis Software Inc.; US; 415/462-2200

McGarr, Michael S.; Ed, EDI WORLD; US; 305/925-5900

McGee, Darren; Ed, Fox Pro Developers Journal; US; 502/491-1900

McGee, Frank; VP Dev, Elixir Technologies Corp.; US; 805/641-5900, frank_mcgee@notes.elixir.com

McGeever, Christine; Mgng Ed, Visual Basic Programmer's Journal; US; 415/833-7100

McGeoch, Bruce; SVP Eng & Tech, Wyse Technology Inc.; US; 408/473-1200

McGettigan, Patrick H.; Chmn, Landmark Systems Corp.; US; 703/902-8000

McGill, Brian; Dev Mgr, Kenan Systems Corp.; US; 617/225-2224

McGinley, William J.; Chmn, Methode Electronics Inc.; US; 708/867-9600

McGinty, Jim; Pres, Cambridge Information Group; US; 301/961-6700

McGovern, Patrick J.; Chmn, IDG Communications; US; 617/534-1200

McGowan, Steve; VP Eng, Forte Technologies Inc.; US; 716/427-8595, sbm@servtech.com

McGowan, Terry; Pres & CEO, Action Technologies Inc.; US; 510/521-6190

McGrath, Dennis; CEO, Shandwick US; US; 612/832-5000

McGrath, Gerald M.; VP & CFO, Analysts International Corp.; US; 612/835-5900

McGrath, T.E.; SVP Imaging Grp, Fuji Photo Film US Inc.; US; 914/789-8100

McGrath Brooks, Roseanne; Mgng Ed, Ent; US; 215/643-8000, brooksrm@cardinal.com

McGraw, George P.; Pres & GM, CompuTrac Inc.; US; 214/234-4241, georgem@ctinc.com

McGraw, Paul; EVP, APS Technologies; US; 816/483-1600

McGraw, Robert G.; VP & CFO, Quality Systems Inc.; US; 714/731-7171

McGraw III, Harold; Pres & COO, McGraw-Hill Inc.; US; 212/512-2000

McGrawth, Paul K.; VP & CFO, Cayenne Software; US; 617/273-9003

McGreggor, Keith; Pres, BeInfinite Inc.; US

McGregor, Scott; SVP Prod, Santa Cruz Operation Inc., The; US; 408/425-7222, scott@sco.com

McGrory, Malcolm; Pres, Cascade Systems Inc.; US; 508/794-8000

McGuire, Daniel J.; VP Ops, Turtle Beach Systems Inc.; US; 717/767-0200

McGuire, James S.; COO, BGS Systems Inc.; US; 617/891-0000

McHale, Greg; VP Mktng, Number Nine Visual Technology Corp.; US; 617/674-0009

McHale, Steve; Ed, Canadian Computer Reseller; Canada; 416/596-5000

McHale, William P.; VP Sales & Mktng, F3 Software Corp.; US; 617/270-0001

McHenry, Julie; CEO, Wilson McHenry Co.; US; 415/638-3400, jmchenry@wmc.com

McIlvaine, George; Dir Eng, Spur Products Corp.; US; 208/377-0001

McIlwain, Don C.; VP Ops, Apertus Technologies Inc.; US; 612/828-0300

McIndoe, Darrell B.; VP IS, Nichols Research Corp.; US; 205/883-1140

McInerney, Robert J.; Pres Commercial Syst, Arrow Electronics Inc.; US; 516/391-1300

McInroy, Bill; Pres, Elixir Technologies Corp.; US; 805/641-5900, bill_mcinroy@notes.elixir.com

McIntosh, Jim; Pres, GDT Softworks; Canada; 604/291-9121

McIntosh, John; Partner, Storage Systems Marketing; US; 303/499-0281, jwmci@aol.com

McIntosh, Lance; VP Fin, ATI Technologies Inc.; Canada; 905/882-2600

McIntosh, Mac; Mac McIntosh Co., The; US; 310/376-1221

McIntyre, Pam; Mgng Ed, M Computing; US; 301/431-4070, mta1994@aol.com

McIntyre, Thomas; VP Chapters, Digital Equipment Computer Users Society; US; 508/841-3346

McKee, Alan; VP Dev, Aspen Technology Inc.; US; 617/577-0100

McKee, Roger L.; Mgng Dir, Video Electronics Standards Assoc.; US; 408/435-0333

McKee Jr, E. Stanton; SVP & CFO, Electronic Arts; US; 415/571-7171

McKeever, Jeffrey D.; Chmn & CEO, MicroAge Inc.; US; 602/804-2000

McKelvie, Charles; Dir Fin, Carbela Tek Inc.; US; 415/873-6484

McKenna, Dennis; SVP Sales & Mktng, Hyundai Electronics America; US; 408/232-8000

McKenna, John; Pres & CEO, Entex Information Services; US; 914/935-3600

McKenna, Regis; Chmn, McKenna Group Inc.; US; 415/494-2030

McKenna, Tom; Pres, InterGroup Technologies Inc.; US; 206/643-8089, tomm@connected.com

McKenzie, Dan; Pres & CEO, Every-Ware Development Corp.; Canada; 905/819-1173

McKeon, Paul; Pres, Crescent Communication; US; 404/698-8650, pmckeon@crescomm.com

McKibben, Craig; VP Eng, Walker Richer & Quinn Inc.; US; 206/217-7100

McKiernan, William; CEO, Cybersource Corp.; US; 408/556-9306

McKinley, Tom; VP Ops, Viking Components; US; 714/643-7255

McKinney, Bea; VP, askSam Systems; US; 904/584-6590

McKinney, Harry W.; GM, HP Home Products Div.; US; 408/246-4300

McKinney, Michael H.; Chmn, askSam Systems; US; 904/584-6590

McKinney, Michael J.; EVP & CFO, askSam Systems; US; 904/584-6590

McLachlan, John; Pblr, Telecommunication Markets; UK; 171-896-2222

McLagam, Donald; Pres & CEO, Desktop Data Inc.; US; 617/229-3000

McLaughlin, Jack; Ed & Pblr, Rumors & Raw Data; US; 619/328-3700

McLawhorn, Carl; Pres, Forvus Research Inc.; US; 919/954-0063

McLean, Laurie; Pres & CEO, McLean Public Relations; US; 415/513-8800, laurie_mclean@mcleanpr.co

Mclenda, Mike; Ed, Electronic Musician; US; 510/653-3307

McLeod, Douglas B.; Ed, Computer Industry Report; US; 617/872-8200

McLeod, Jonah; Ed-in-Chief, Integrated System Design; US; 415/903-0140, jonah@asic.com

McLeod, Kate; Pres, McLeod Group, The; US; 212/255-2507

McMahon, Constance; VP Sales & Mktng, Software Partners/32 Inc.; US; 508/887-6409

McMahon, Mike; EVP, Oberon Software Inc.; US; 617/494-0990

Mcmanns, Neil; Exec Ed, Digital Media; US; 415/575-3775, neilm@digmedia.com

McManus, Dan; SVP Pbls, Synergy Interactive Corp.; US; 415/437-2000

McManus, Mark; Ed-in-Chief, Computer Economics Inc.; US; 619/438-8100, mmcmanus@compecon.com

McMaster, Carolyn; Mgng Ed, NewMedia; US; 415/573-5170

McMillan, Bob; CFO, New Horizons Computer Learning Centers Inc.; US; 714/556-1220

McMillan, Tom; Ed, Color Publishing; US; 603/891-9166, tomm@pennwell.com

McMillian, Lonnie S.; VP Eng, Adtran Inc.; US; 205/971-8000

Mcmullen, Jim; CTO, Platinum Software Corp.; US; 714/453-4000

McMullen, Melanie; Ed-in-Chief, LAN Magazine; US; 415/905-2200, mmcmullen@mfi.com

McNab, Ron; VP Sales & Mktng, Lanworks Technologies Inc.; Canada; 905/238-5528, ran@lanworks.com

McNabb, Paul A.; VP, Argus Systems Group Inc.; US; 217/384-6300, mcnabb@argus.cu-online.com

McNamara, George; Ed Dir, Computer Technology Review; US; 310/208-1335, george_mcnamara@wwpi.com

McNannay, Dennis; Prod Mgr, DataPak Software Inc.; US; 360/891-0542

McNealy, Scott G.; Chmn, Pres & CEO, Sun Microsystems Inc.; US; 415/960-1300

McNiel, James P.; VP Bus Dev, Cheyenne Software Inc.; US; 516/484-5110

McNitt, Willard C.; VP & CFO, Zenith Electronics Corp.; US; 708/391-7000

McPherson, Paul; Pblr, Color Publishing; US; 603/891-9166, paulm@pennwell.com

McPherson, Susan G.; Mktng Mgr, PR Newswire; US; 212/596-1500, smcphers@prnews.attmail.com

McPherson, Thomas R.; VP & GM, Hughes Network Systems-DirecPC; US; 301/428-5500

McQueen, Stan; VP Dev, Zinc Software; US; 801/785-8900, smcqueen@zinc.com

McQuerter, Gregory; Pres, McQuerter Group; US; 619/450-0030

McQuigg, Clancy; Pres, Leverage Software Inc.; US; 703/494-0818

McRea, Roger; VP, Musicware; US; 206/881-9797

McSweeney, Michael; Exec Dir, Standards Council of Canada; Canada; 613/238-3222

McVaney, C. Edward; Pres & CEO, J.D. Edwards & Co.; US

McWatters, C. Dennis; VP Sales, Concurrent Computer Corp.; US; 908/870-4500

Mead, Peter; VP Mktng, Executive Software Int'l.; US; 818/547-2050, pmead@executive.com

Meade, Roger E.; Pres & CEO, Scitor Corp.; US; 415/462-4200

Meader, Peggy; Pres, Inland Assoc.; US; 913/746-7977

Meadlock, James; Chmn & CEO, Intergraph Corp.; US; 205/730-8302

Meador, Wes E.; EVP, Maximum Strategy Inc.; US; 408/383-1600

Meallo, Paul; Dir MIS, Programmer's Shop, The; US; 617/740-2510

Means, Peter; Pres, NovaStor Corp.; US; 805/579-6700, peter@novastor.com

Mecham, Nick; Mgr, Improve Technologies; US; 801/224-6550, nickm@transera.com

Meckler, Alan M.; Chmn & CEO, Mecklermedia Corp.; US; 203/226-6967, ameck@mecklermedia.com

Medford, Dale L.; VP & CFO, Reynolds & Reynolds; US; 513/443-2000

Medich, Cathy; Exec Dir, CommerceNet; US; 415/617-8790

Medley, Jerry; Dir Sales, Bit 3 Computer Corp.; US; 612/881-6955

Medrano, Roberto; VP WW Mktng, Milkyway Networks Corp.; US; 408/467-3868

Meehan, James; Chmn, Pres & CEO, CenterLine Software Inc.; US; 617/498-3000

Meehan, Peter; Pres & CEO, Loox Software Inc.; US; 415/903-0942, peter@loox.com

Meek, John M.; VP R&D, Timberline Software Corp.; US; 503/626-6775

Meeley, Stephen; Prod Mgmt, Data Access Corp.; US; 305/238-0012, stephen-m@daccess.com

Meeran, Saleem; Pres, Image-X; US; 805/964-3537, saleem@imagexx.com

Meerow, Burt; Pblr, Printer Impressions; US; 201/488-0404

Meers, Laura; Controller/MIS, Personal Training Systems; US; 415/462-2100

Meers, Trevor; Asst Ed, PC Novice; US; 402/479-2141

Meffert, George; EVP, Energizer Power Systems; US; 904/462-3911

Meggitt, John E.; Chmn & CEO, Prophet 21 Inc.; US; 215/493-8900

Megill, Mike; VP, Rational Data Systems Inc.; US; 415/382-8400, mmegill@rds.com

Mehrlich, Rick; Pres, Systems Plus Inc.; US; 415/969-7047

Mehta, Jay; VP Fin, Oki America Inc.; US; 201/646-0011

Meier, George B.; Pres, G. Meier Inc.; US; 201/376-8181, gmeier@aol.com

Meier, Pat; Pres, Pat Meier Associates Inc.; US; 415/957-5999, patmeier@pat-meier.com

Meise, Richard G.; Pres & CEO, Microtest Inc.; US; 602/952-6400

Melancon Jr., DeJean; Pres, Advantage kbs Inc.; US; 908/287-2236, dmelancon@akbs.com

Mele, Ralph; EVP Sales & Mktng, Optivision Inc.; US; 415/855-0200

Meling, Lawrence A.; VP Mktng, Ikos Systems Inc.; US; 408/255-4567

Melissa, Raymond F.; Pres, Mailer's Software; US; 714/492-7000
Melkerson, Al; Pres, Microvitec Inc.; US; 404/964-9288
Mellin, Michael; Pres & CEO, Hands-On Technology; US; 415/579-7755
Mello, Adrian; Ed-in-Chief, Macworld; US; 415/243-0505
Mellor, John; VP Bus Dev, Viewpoint Datalabs Int'l.; US; 801/229-3000
Melnicki, Steve; VP Ops, Inforite Corp.; US; 415/571-8766
Melson, James; Chmn, Melson Technologies; US; 847/291-4000
Melvin, Jeffrey J.; VP Sales, Inso Corp.; US; 617/753-6500
Melzer, Edward A.; VP & CFO, Intelligent Electronics Inc.; US; 610/458-5500
Menas, Gregory W.; Pres, Interex; US; 316/524-4747
Mendelsohn, Alex; Ed-in-Chief, Portable Design; US; 918/835-3161, alexm@pennwell.com
Mendez, M. Alex; VP Mktng, Strata-Com Inc.; US; 408/294-7600
Mendoza, Jim; Dir Training, Comprehend Franchise Corp.; US; 954/921-6040
Mendoza, Tom; VP NA Sales, Network Appliance Corp.; US; 415/428-5100, tmendoza@netapp.com
Meneau, Christophe; Pres, Graphic Development Int'l.; US; 415/382-6600
Menendez, Manny; Pres, Deneba Software; US; 305/596-5644
Meng, William; Pres, Marasys Inc.; US; 208/772-0248
Menn, Don; Ed-in-Chief, Multimedia World; US; 415/281-8650
Menowitz, Marc; Pres, SkyNotes Inc.; US; 310/577-9332, marc@radiomail.net
Menzel, David B.; CFO, Campbell Software; US; 847/328-3200
Menzel, Robert T.; CP & GM, Harris Computer Systems Corp.; US; 305/973-5100
Menzilcioglu, Onat; Pres, Fore Systems Inc.; US; 412/772-6600
Mercer, D. Scott; EVP & CFO, Western Digital Corp.; US; 714/932-5000
Mercer, Robert; CIO, Software Spectrum Inc.; US; 214/840-6600
Merchant, David L.; Pres, Spirit Technologies Inc.; US; 617/630-1250
Meredith, Gary E.; SVP, Evans & Sutherland Computer Corp.; US; 801/588-1000, gmeredith@es.com
Meredith, Thomas J.; CFO, Dell Computer Corp.; US; 512/338-4400
Meresman, Stanley J.; SVP & CFO, Silicon Graphics Inc.; US; 415/960-1980
Merker, Lance; Sales & Mktng Mgr, Mainstay; US; 805/484-9400
Merlo, Saverio; SVP Mktng, Boole & Babbage Inc.; US; 408/526-3000
Merrick, George A.; VP Display Bus, Dynatech Corp.; US; 617/272-6100
Merrifield, Ed; CFO, DiagSoft Inc.; US;

408/438-8247
Merrin, Seymour; Pres, Merrin Information Services Inc.; US; 415/493-5050
Mertens, Daniel J.; VP Ops, MicroSpeed Inc.; US
Meshi, Joseph; EVP & CFO, Genovation Inc.; US; 714/833-3355
Metcalfe, Jane; Pres, Wired Ventures Inc.; US; 415/276-5000
Metzger, Daniel; VP Mktng, Lawson Software; US; 612/379-2633, daniel@metzger@lawson.com
Metzger, Irwin J.; CFO, Forte Technologies Inc.; US; 716/427-8595
Metzger, John; VP Prod Dev, Seagate Enterprise Management Software; US; 408/342-4500
Meub, Dan; VP Mktng & Sales, Now Software Inc.; US; 503/274-2800
Meuller, Ray; Chmn, Colorado Software Assoc.; US; 303/220-2000
Mewhorter, Mark; VP Progression Sys Dev, Macola Inc.; US; 614/382-5999
Meyer, Bertrand; Pres, Interactive Software Engineering Inc.; US; 805/685-1006, bertrand@eiffel.com
Meyer, Carol; Pblr, Computing Reviews; US; 212/869-7440
Meyer, Daniel J.; Chmn & CEO, Cincinnati Milacron Inc.; US; 513/841-8100
Meyer, Jean-Arcady; Ed, Adaptive Behavior; US; 617/253-2889, meyer@biologie.ens.fr
Meyer, Jerome J.; Chmn & CEO, Tektronix Inc.; US; 503/627-7111
Meyer, John; Dir Tech, Lante Corp.; US; 312/236-5100, jmeyer@lante.com
Meyer, Ray; Pres, Deltec Corp.; US; 619/291-4211
Meyer, Stephen P.; SVP, Titan Corp.; US; 619/552-9500
Meyer, Thomas C.; SVP Ops, Blyth Software Inc.; US; 415/571-0222
Meyer, William E.; CFO, SBT Accounting Systems; US; 415/444-9900
Meyers, Lowell; Dir Adv, Quill Corp.; US
Meyerson, Adam; Dir, PC/Computing Usability Lab; US; 415/578-7000
Meyerson, Mort; Chmn, Perot Systems; US; 703/716-1400
Meyerson, Robert F.; Chmn & CEO, Telxon Corp.; US; 216/867-3700
Mezger, Dieter; Pres, Compass Design Automation; US; 408/433-4880
Miau, Matthew; CEO, Mitac International Corp.; Taiwan ROC; 2-501-8231
Michael, Derrek J.; Dir Ops, Mega Drive Systems Inc.; US; 310/247-0006
Michalski, Jerry; Mgng Ed, EDventure Holdings Inc.; US; 212/924-8800, jerry@edventure.com
Michela, Catherine; VP Mktng, Intell.X; US; 703/524-7400
Michels, Douglas L.; EVP & CTO, Santa Cruz Operation Inc., The; US; 408/425-7222, doug@sco.com

Mickelson, Mark; VP, Hitachi Data Systems; US; 408/970-1000
Middleton, Don; Dir Strat Sales, Black & White Software; US; 408/369-7400
Midgley, Brad; Pacific HiTech Inc.; US; 801/261-1024, brad@pht.com
Mielcarski, Robert J.; VP R&D, Dynapro Systems Inc.; Canada; 604/521-3962
Miglio, Daniel J.; Chmn & CEO, Southern New England Telecom Corp.; US; 203/771-5200
Migliore, John J.; Pres & CEO, Adaptive Solutions Inc.; US; 503/690-1236
Mihalic, Steve; Tech Mgr, Around Technology Inc.; US; 216/234-6402
Mikelk, Terry; VP, Parks Associates; US; 214/490-1113
Mikita, Rich; GM, CW Database; US; 508/879-0700
Milano, Dominic; Ed, InterActivity; US; 415/358-9500
Milenbach, Julian; Dir, PC World Test Center; US; 415/243-0500
Miley, Derrick; CEO, Big Island Communications Inc.; US; 408/342-8300
Milkowski, Forrest; Dir Prod Mktng, White Pine Software Inc.; US; 603/886-9050
Millard, John B.; Pres & CEO, Mitel Corp.; Canada; 613/592-2122
Millard, Ralph A.; Dir Bus Dev, Energizer Power Systems; US; 904/462-3911
Millard III, Harrison K.; Chmn & Pres, Atomic City Electronics Inc.; US; 505/662-7059
Miller, Arnold; Treas, Quill Corp.; US
Miller, Art; Pres & CEO, Microrim Inc.; US; 206/649-9500, artm@microrim.com
Miller, B. Scott; VP Prod Dev, Group 1 Software; US; 301/731-2300
Miller, Beth; CFO, Casady & Greene Inc.; US; 408/484-9228
Miller, Charles D.; Chmn & CEO, Avery Dennison; US; 818/304-2000
Miller, Cliff; Pres, Pacific HiTech Inc.; US; 801/261-1024, cliff@pht.com
Miller, Cory J.; VP & CFO, Ciprico Inc.; US; 612/551-4000
Miller, Curt; Dir Eng, Notable Technologies Inc.; US; 206/455-4040, cmiller@notable.com
Miller, David; Dir Mktng, Frost & Sullivan Inc.; US; 415/961-9000, dmiller@frost.com
Miller, David B.; Pres & CEO, WordTech Systems Inc.; US; 510/689-1200
Miller, Doug; VP Mktng, Dazel Corp.; US; 512/328-6977
Miller, Douglas; VP Ops, Itac Systems Inc.; US; 214/494-3073, miller@moustrak.com
Miller, Eddie; Pres, CIMdata Inc.; US; 617/235-4124
Miller, Erik; VP & CFO, Meridian Data Inc.; US; 408/438-3100

Miller, Genene; GM, Young Minds Inc.; US; 909/335-1350

Miller, Graham C.C.; Chmn, LTX Corp.; US; 617/461-1000

Miller, Hank; Pres, H.F. Miller Associates; US; 408/354-4222

Miller, Harris; Pres, Information Technology Assoc. America; US; 703/522-5055, hmiller@itaa.org

Miller, Harvey L.; Sec, Quill Corp.; US

Miller, Jack; Pres, Quill Corp.; US

Miller, James D.; VP Strategy, Ceridian Corp.; US; 612/853-8100

Miller, Jamie; CFO & Dir Ops, Interactive Catalog Corp.; US; 206/623-0977

Miller, Janice; Exec Dir, Women in Information Processing; US; 202/328-6161

Miller, Jeff; Dir Prod Mgmt, NMB Technologies Inc.; US; 818/341-3355

Miller, Jeffrey A.; Pres & CEO, Documentum Inc.; US; 510/463-6800

Miller, John E.; Chmn, Intermetrics Inc.; US; 617/661-1840

Miller, Judith; Principal, Tech Trade Assoc.; US; 803/785-5497

Miller, Julia; CEO & Dir Bus Dev, Black & White Software; US; 408/369-7400

Miller, Karen; Sales Mgr, ProtoView Development Co.; US; 609/655-5000

Miller, Katherine; Assoc Ed, Gale Directory of Databases; US; 313/961-2242

Miller, Kathleen; PR Consultant, Nickelsen Communications; US; 510/845-8804, janedeaux@aol.com

Miller, Lewis E.; Pres & COO, Future Now; US; 513/792-4500

Miller, Mark; VP Sales & Mktng, Escalade; US; 408/654-1600

Miller, Mark; VP, Comprehend Franchise Corp.; US; 954/921-6040

Miller, Marti; VP Eng, RSI Systems Inc.; US; 612/896-3020

Miller, Michael J.; Ed-in-Chief, PC Magazine; US; 212/503-5255

Miller, Pam; Co-Founder, Kaufer Miller Communications; US; 206/450-9965, pammilpr@aol.com

Miller, Paul; Mgr, Prairie Group; US; 515/225-9620, prairiepem@aol.com

Miller, Paul G.; Chmn, Large Storage Configurations; US; 612/482-4535, pgm@lsci.com

Miller, Randy; Purch Mgr, ProtoView Development Co.; US; 609/655-5000

Miller, Richard K.; Pres, Richard K. Miller & Assoc. Inc.; US; 770/416-0006

Miller, Robert L.; Chmn & CEO, Language Publications Interactive; US; 212/620-3193

Miller, Rockey L.; Ed & Pblr, Multimedia Alert; US; 703/241-1799

Miller, Scott; Partner, Apogee Software Ltd.; US; 214/271-1765

Miller, Sharon B.; Superv, Access Public Relations; US; 415/904-7070

Miller, Stephanie; Acct Exec, Penna

Powers Cutting & Haynes Inc.; US; 801/531-0973, ppch@xmission.com

Miller, Steven; VP Mktng, Light Source Inc.; US; 415/461-8000

Miller, Thomas O.; VP Mobile Syst, Norand Corp.; US; 319/369-3100

Miller, Tom; VP Corp Plng, Fujitsu Microelectronics Inc.; US; 408/922-9000

Miller, William; Chmn, Borland Int'l.; US; 408/431-1000

Miller, William J.; Chmn & CEO, Avid Technology Inc.; US; 508/640-6789

Miller Jr., John; Chmn, Shandwick Technologies; US; 617/536-0470

Milletti, Umberto; Dir Prod Dev, Knowledge Revolution; US; 415/574-7777

Milligan, Lee; CFO, NovaLogic Inc.; US; 818/880-1997, lmilligan@novalogic.com

Millison, Doug; Ed-in-Chief, Morph's Outpost on the Digital Frontier; US; 510/704-7171

Millman, Jeffrey; EVP, Computer Outsourcing Services Inc.; US; 212/564-3730

Mills, Bruce; VP Mktng & Support, PixelCraft Inc.; US; 510/562-2480

Mills, Karen; Dir Channel Mktng, USoft; US; 415/875-3300

Mills, Kathy J.; Mgng Ed, International Business; US

Mills, Robert; Ed, Computer-Aided Engineering; US; 216/696-7000

Millson III, Henry E.; Pres, SilverLock Software Corp.; US; 713/722-9399

Millstein, Julian; Ed, Computer Law Strategist; US; 212/779-9200, mmstrat@ljextra.com

Milne, Bob; Mgng Ed, Electronic Design; US; 201/393-6060

Milne, Karen; Stardust Technologies; US; 408/879-8080

Mimica, Ivan; Pres & CEO, Articulate Systems Inc.; US; 617/935-5656

Mimno, Pieter; Pres, Technology Insight Inc.; US; 617/639-2570

Minchin, William J.; VP Ops, Tekelec; US; 818/880-5656

Minear, Candee; Ad Dir, Scout Business Software Directory; US; 303/772-0321

Minicucci, Robert A.; Chmn, Seer Technologies Inc.; US; 919/380-5000

Minihane, Peter J.; EVP & CFO, Microcom Inc.; US; 617/551-1000

Minkoff, Max; VP Tech, VictorMaxx Technologies; US; 708/267-0007, max@mcs.com

Minor, Michael J.; CEO, Blyth Software Inc.; US; 415/571-0222

Minteer, Robert; VP, Gyrus Systems Inc.; US; 804/320-1414, rminteer@ix.netcom.com

Mintz, Andrew; Pblr, Multimedia Producer; US; 914/328-9157

Mintz, Elyse; VP Mktng, Colorgraphic Communications Corp.; US; 770/455-3921

Mintz, Ezra; Pres, Colorgraphic Commu-

nications Corp.; US; 770/455-3921

Mintz, Gilbert; Founding Partner, Broadview Associates; US; 201/461-7929

Mirabella, Richard; VP Sales & Mktng, Globetrotter Software; US; 408/370-2800

Miranker, Glen; VP HW Eng, FirePower Systems Inc.; US; 415/462-3000

Mirarooni, Eddie; Chmn & CEO, MagicRAM; US; 213/413-9999

Miro, Gabi; Dir SW Dev, WorldSoft; US; 408/867-6757

Miscione, Gene; Pres & CEO, Centon Electronics Inc.; US; 714/855-9111

Miskin, Donna; Mgng Ed, CommunicationsWeek; US; 516/562-5530, 5983683@mcimail.com

Misumi, Tac; Mktng Mgr, Fujitsu Systems Business of America Inc.; US; 408/988-8012

Mita, Katsushige; Chmn, Hitachi Ltd.; Japan; 3-3258-1111

Mitarai, Hajime; Pres, Canon Inc.; Japan; 3-33758-2111

Mitcham, John; Pres & CEO, Tricord Systems Inc.; US; 612/557-9005

Mitchell, Bernie; VP Edu Publishing, Philips Media OptImage; US; 515/225-7000, bernmitch@aol.com

Mitchell, Bruce; VP Mktng, MITI; US; 415/326-5000, brucem@miti.com

Mitchell, Chad L.; CTO, Great Wave Software; US; 408/438-1990

Mitchell, Charles; Pblr, Springhouse Corp.; US; 215/628-7716

Mitchell, David; Pres & CEO, Vycor Corp.; US; 301/220-4450

Mitchell, David T.; Pres & COO, Conner Peripherals Inc.; US; 408/456-4500

Mitchell, James F.; SVP & CTO, Davox Corp.; US; 508/952-0200

Mitchell, John; Ed, Dell Insider; US; 512/250-9023

Mitchell, John F.; Vice Chmn, Motorola Inc.; US; 847/576-5000

Mitchell, Richard; Dir Res, Jandel Scientific Inc.; US; 415/453-6700

Mitchell, Stacy McKee; CEO, Great Wave Software; US; 408/438-1990

Mitchell, Steve; VP WW Field Ops, Starlight Networks; US; 415/967-2774

Mitchell, William B.; Vice Chmn, Texas Instruments Inc.; US; 214/995-2551

Mitro, Robert F.; SVP, PictureTel Corp.; US; 508/762-5000

Mitsch, Ronald A.; EVP, Minnesota Minning & Manufacturing; US; 612/733-1110

Miura, Masaaki; VP & GM, Mitsui Comtek Corp.; US; 408/725-8525

Miyakawa, Mark; Pres & COO, NCL America Computer Products Inc.; US; 408/737-2496

Miyasaka, Kiyoshi; VP Spec Proj, Fujitsu Microelectronics Inc.; US; 408/922-9000

Mize, Scott; Ed, DV Finance Report; US; 415/357-9400

Mizner, Steve; VP Media Dir, KSK Communications; US; 703/734-1880, 710.0099@mcimail.com

Mladen, Caryn; Ed-in-Chief, Multimedia Online; US; 407/231-6904

Moberg, Jim R.; EVP, Pacific Telesis Group; US; 415/394-3000

Modena Barasch, Rachel; Oak Ridge Public Relations Inc.; US; 408/253-5042, rachel@oakridge.com

Modry, Jiri; VP Mktng & Sales, Encad Inc.; US; 619/452-0882

Moeller, Dick; CEO, Vtel; US; 512/314-2700

Moffitt, Phillip; Chmn & CEO, Light Source Inc.; US; 415/461-8000

Moh, Jason; GM, Tagram Systems Corp.; US; 714/258-3222

Mohan, Alok; Pres & CEO, Santa Cruz Operation Inc., The; US; 408/425-7222, alokm@sco.com

Mohiuddin, Razi; SW Partner, Onsale; US; 415/428-0600

Mohr, Asaf; Vdonet Corp.; US; 415/846-7700

Mohr, August; Ed-in-Chief, Inside SCO Unix Systems; US; 502/491-1900

Mohr, Rick; Dir Dev, Archetype Inc.; US; 617/890-7544

Mohta, Pushpendra; Exec Dir, CERFnet; US; 619/455-3900, pushp@cerf.net

Moise, James; SVP Sales, Quarterdeck Corp.; US; 310/309-3700, investor@quarterdeck.com

Mokhoff, Nicolas; Exec Ed, Electronic Engineering Times; US; 516/562-5000, nmokhoff@eet.cmp.com

Mol, Jerome H.; Pres & CEO, Prolin Software; US; 415/854-7489

Molden, Richard W.; Pblr, Internetwork; US; 215/643-8000, moldenrw@cardinal.com

Moldstad, Frank; Ed-in-Chief, PC Graphics & Video; US; 714/513-8400, fmoldstad@pcgv.com

Moley, Richard M.; Chmn, Pres & CEO, StrataCom Inc.; US; 408/294-7600

Molina, Joe; RAID Advisory Board; US; 415/631-7142

Molinari, Alfred; Chmn & CEO, Data Translation Inc.; US; 508/481-3700

Molinari, John A.; VP & GM Multimedia, Data Translation Inc.; US; 508/481-3700

Molino, Joe; CFO, Digital Directory Assistance Inc.; US; 301/657-8548, joem@dda-inc.com

Mollema, Esther; Pres, American Institute; US; 212/661-3500

Molloy, Bruce G.; Chmn & CEO, Molloy Group Inc., The; US; 201/540-1212

Moloney, Jack; EVP & GM, MicroSolutions Inc.; US; 815/756-3411

Momirov, Milan; CTO, Rapid City Communications; US; 415/937-1370

Monaco, Stephen; VP Mktng, Datastorm Technologies Inc.; US; 573/443-3282

Monaghan, Dan; VP Mktng, Graphsoft Inc.; US; 410/290-5114, dan@graphsoft.com

Monahan, Grace; EVP, CMP Publications Inc.; US; 516/562-5000

Monash, Curt A.; Ed & Pblr, Monash Software Letter; US; 212/315-3120, monashinfo@mcimail.com

Monck, Margherita R.; GM, SIGS Publications Group; US; 212/242-7447

Mongiello, James; Pres & CEO, OnStream Networks Inc.; US; 408/727-4545

Monlux, Cliff; Pres, Paradigm Software Development Inc.; US; 206/728-2281

Monlux, Stanton; VP Mktng, Paradigm Software Development Inc.; US; 206/728-2281, stantond@aol.com

Monroe, Eric; Chmn & Pres, Image Society Inc.; US; 602/839-8709

Monroe, Jean; Chmn & CEO, Audio Digital Imaging; US; 708/439-1335

Monroe, Kevin; GM Corp Sec, Audio Digital Imaging; US; 708/439-1335

Monroe, Wade; EVP & CFO, Trilogy Development Group; US; 512/794-5900

Montague, William P.; EVP & CFO, Mark IV Industries; US; 716/689-4972

Montesano, Nick; VP Merch, Quill Corp.; US

Montevecchio, Albert J.; Chmn, Pres & CEO, Moscom Corp.; US; 716/381-6000

Montgomery, David W.; VP & CFO, Advanstar Communications Inc.; US; 216/826-2859

Montgomery, Gerard; Pres & CEO, AbTech Corp.; US; 804/977-0686

Montgomery, Henry; CFO, Mobius Computer Corp.; US; 510/460-5252

Montgomery, Jeff; Chmn, ElectroniCast Corp.; US; 415/343-1398

Montgomery, Scott; VP Prod Dev, Envelope Manager Software; US

Montgomery, Stephen; VP, ElectroniCast Corp.; US; 415/343-1398

Montross, Al; Pres & CEO, Mylex Corp.; US; 510/796-6100

Montry, Gerald F.; SVP & CFO, DSC Communications Corp.; US; 214/519-3000

Monty, Jean C.; Pres & CEO, Northern Telecom Ltd.; Canada; 905/566-3178

Mooar, William; Pres & CEO, Coast Manufacturing Co.; US; 914/376-1500

Mooers, John; VP, Green Light Communications; US; 714/719-6400, jmooers@grnlt.com

Mooers, Robert; Ad Dir, Green Light Communications; US; 714/719-6400, rmooers@grnlt.com

Mooers, Tom; Pres & GM, Green Light Communications; US; 714/719-6400, tmooers@grnlt.com

Moon, Michael; Dir Exec Programs, Gistics Inc.; US; 415/461-4305, moon@gistics.com

Moore, Andy; Ed-in-Chief, Imaging World Magazine; US; 207/236-8524

Moore, Autumn; Dir Sales & Mktng, Microspot US Inc.; US; 408/253-2000

Moore, Bob; Pres, Moore Information Systems; US; 818/704-7722, b.moore@ix.netcom.com

Moore, Bob; CEO, MorseMcFadden Communications Inc.; US; 206/889-0528

Moore, Bruce; Pres & COO, Auspex Systems Inc.; US; 408/986-2000

Moore, Christopher J.; Controller, Gemstone Systems Inc.; US

Moore, Cutch; VP Sales, Nets Inc.; US; 412/967-3500, cutchmoore@industry.net

Moore, D. Larry; Pres & COO, Honeywell Inc.; US; 612/951-1000

Moore, Dick; SVP Tech, Zilog Inc.; US; 408/370-8000

Moore, Donnie M.; SVP & CFO, Cognos Inc.; Canada; 613/738-1440

Moore, Ernest; Co-Owner, Balt Inc.; US; 817/697-4953

Moore, George; VP Plng, Logitech Inc.; US; 510/795-8500

Moore, Glenn; Pres & CEO, SpecTran Corp.; US; 508/347-2261

Moore, Gordon E.; Chmn, Intel Corp.; US; 408/765-8080

Moore, John C.; Pres & CEO, Sherpa Corp.; US; 408/433-0455

Moore, John R.; VP Ops, Edmark Corp.; US; 206/556-8400

Moore, Lorraine; Co-Owner, Balt Inc.; US; 817/697-4953

Moore, Mark; VP Eng, Diba; US; 415/482-3300

Moore, Myra; Ed, Pathfinder; US; 214/490-1113

Moore, Rich; VP R&D, Capcom Digital Studios, Capcom; US; 408/727-0500

Moore, Robert; VP Corp Ops, Reptron Electronics Inc.; US; 813/854-2351

Moore, Roberta; Pres, Qualitative Marketing; US; 408/295-5524

Moore, Sandy; Pres & CEO, Spectrix Corp.; US; 847/317-1770, swrm@spectrixcorp.com

Moore, Tom; Pblr, Electronics Strategies; US; 617/345-2704

Moorer, James A.; SVP Audio Dev & Dir, Sonic Solutions; US; 415/893-8000

Moores, John; Chmn, Peregrine Systems; US; 619/481-5000

Moote, Robert; VP, Phar Lap Software Inc.; US; 617/661-1510

Moran, Chuck; Pres, National Education Training Group; US; 708/369-3000

Moran, Tim; Exec Ed, OEM Magazine; US; 516/562-5624

Morawski, Ted; MIS Mgr, Associated Business Publications Co.; US; 212/490-3999

Mordaunt, Cynthia; VP Mktng, Horizons Technology Inc.; US; 619/292-8331

More, Avery; Chmn, TeKnowlgy Corp;

US; 214/373-9998

More, Avery; Chmn, PC Service Source Inc.; US; 214/406-8583

Morel, Brigitte; GM, Business Research Int'l.; France; 33-5093-0762

Moreland, Mike; VP Sales & Ops, 1st Tech Corp.; US; 512/258-3570

Moresi, Alfred; Pres & CEO, Syncware Corp.; US; 303/369-6900

Morgan, Henry; EVP & CFO, Connect Inc.; US; 415/254-4000

Morgan, James D.; VP & Chief Scientist, Comptek Research Inc.; US; 716/677-4070

Morgan, John; GM Computer Div, Tatung Co. of America Inc.; US; 310/637-2105

Morgan, Michael A.; VP & CFO, Software Professionals Inc.; US; 415/578-0700

Morgan Caesar, Minda; Ed, Internet Week; US; 301/340-1520

Morgan, Jr., Charles D.; Chmn, Pres & CEO, Acxiom Corp.; US; 501/336-1000

Morgenstern, George; Chmn, Pres & CEO, Data Systems & Software Inc.; US; 201/529-2026

Morgenstern, Joseph; Ed, Israel High-Tech & Investment Report; Israel; 3-523-5279

Morgridge, John P.; Chmn, Cisco Systems Inc.; US; 408/526-4000

Mori, Michael; Ed, PCMCIA Developer's Guide; US; 408/749-0130

Morley Foster, Cathy; VP, White & Co.; US; 415/274-8100

Morneau, Denis; VP Sales & Mktng, Protec Microsystems Inc.; Canada; 514/630-5832

Moro, Wendy; Partner, Windham/Lang Group; US; 415/563-4545, wmoro@net-com.com

Moroney, William; Pres, Multimedia Telecommunications Assoc.; US; 202/296-9800

Moroz, Mike; VP Retail Mktng, Damark International Inc.; US; 612/531-0066

Morrill, Jane; Mgng Ed, Windows NT; US; 303/663-4700

Morrill, Robert M.; Pres & CEO, VMark Software Inc.; US; 508/366-3888

Morrione, Michael T.; SVP & GM, Trident Microsystems Inc.; US; 415/691-9211

Morris, Bill; Pres, CoMark Technologies Inc.; US; 214/233-7091

Morris, Dawn; Pres, Morris Media; US; 310/533-4800

Morris, Geoffrey; Pres & CEO, X/Open Company Ltd.; US; 415/323-7992

Morris, George; Chmn & CEO, Morris Media; US; 310/533-4800

Morris, Gerald F.; EVP & CFO, Diebold Inc.; US; 216/489-4000

Morris, Hal; Tech Ed, Microcomputer Trainer, The; US; 201/330-8923

Morris, Judy; VP, Crescent Communication; US; 404/698-8650, jmorris@cres-

comm.com

Morris, Ken; VP R&D, Peoplesoft Inc.; US; 510/225-3000

Morris, Larry G.; Actg CFO, Micrografx Inc.; US; 214/234-1769

Morris, Leila; Mgng Ed, InfoText; US; 310/724-6783

Morris, Lewis C.; Pres, Cylink Corp.; US; 408/735-5800

Morris, Tony; Principal, Morris & Associates; US; 617/556-8960

Morrise, Marshall; Pres, Capsoft Dev. Corp.; US; 801/763-3915

Morrison, David; Pres, Western Telematic Inc.; US; 714/586-9950

Morrison, Jeff; Mgng Dir, Siren Software; US; 415/322-0600

Morse, Alan C.; VP R&D & CTO, DataViews Corp.; US; 413/586-4144

Morse, Clint; Pres, Apex Computer; US; 206/867-1900

Morse, David C.; Dir Mktng, Raima Corp.; US; 206/557-0200, dmorse@raima.com

Morse, Thomas; Sr Treas, Scantron Quality Computers; US

Morsillo, Leon; VP Prod Eng & Tech, Datacap Systems Inc.; US; 215/699-7051

Mortenson, Jerald H.; VP & CFO, HEI Inc.; US; 612/443-2500

Morton, Steven R.; VP, TView Inc.; US; 503/643-1662

Moscher, Albin F.; Pres & CEO, Zenith Electronics Corp.; US; 708/391-7000

Moses, Debra; Assoc, Martin Communications; US; 415/668-2678, d143j@aol.com

Moshayedi, Manouch; CEO, Simple Technology Inc.; US; 714/476-1180

Moshayedi, Mark; COO, Simple Technology Inc.; US; 714/476-1180

Moshayedi, Mike; Pres, Simple Technology Inc.; US; 714/476-1180

Moshir, Sean; Pres, High Technology Software Corp.; US; 602/970-1025

Moskovitz, Gary; EVP, Quintar Co.; US; 310/320-5700

Moskun, James; Chmn, Nu-Mega Technologies Inc.; US; 603/889-2386

Moss, Eric L.; Chmn, Tivoli Systems Inc.; US; 512/794-9070

Moss, Franklin; Pres & CEO, Tivoli Systems Inc.; US; 512/794-9070

Moss, Sheryl; VP Sales & Mktng, Smart-Desk Inc.; US; 714/582-4020

Moss, Sylvia; Writer, Levin PR & Marketing Inc.; US; 914/993-0900

Moss, Yvette; Sales Admin, MicroClean Inc.; US; 408/995-5062

Mostrom, Michael A.; Div Mgr Plasma Sciences, Mission Research Corp.; US; 505/768-7727, mmostrom@rt66.com

Motola, Patrick D.; VP & GM Pencom SW, Pencom Systems Inc.; US; 512/343-1111

Mott, Stephen Craig; Pres & CEO, Cognitive Systems Inc.; US; 203/356-7756

Motte, Keith; Network Admin Mgr, Compton's NewMedia Inc.; US; 619/929-2500

Mount, Bob; Pres & CEO, International Power Technologies; US; 801/224-4828

Mountanos, William P.; Pres & CEO, Fast Electronic U.S. Inc.; US; 415/295-3500

Moursund, David; CEO, International Society for Technology in Education; US; 541/346-4414

Moutrie, Chester L.; VP Eng, Intercim Corp.; US; 612/894-9010

Moyers, Roger; VP Sales & Mktng, XLNT Designs Inc.; US; 619/487-9320, roger@xlnt.com

Moylan, Tim; VP Mktng, Siemens Nixdorf Printing Systems LP; US; 407/997-3100

Mruz, Michael J.; Pres & COO, Nichols Research Corp.; US; 205/883-1140

Muehlberger, Edward F.; VP, TIE/Communications Inc.; US; 913/344-0400

Mueller, Gary; VP Ops, Toshiba America Information Systems Inc.; US; 714/583-3111

Mueller, Harald; VP Ops, Eicon Technology Corp.; 214/239-3270

Mueller, Jayne; Pres, Dynamic Graphics Inc.; US; 309/688-8800

Mueller, Kent C.; Pres & CEO, Mastersoft Inc.; US; 602/948-4888, kent@mastersoft.com

Mueller, Kurt; Chmn & CEO, Dataware Technologies Inc.; US; 617/621-0820

Mueller, Lawrence A.; SVP WW Ops, American Software Inc.; US; 404/264-5296

Mugas, Carol; Pres, Data Administration Management Assoc.; US; 314/878-3372

Muirhead, E. Rust; Sec, Alydaar Software Corp.; US; 704/544-0092

Mulholland, James J.; VP Sales & Mktng, Evergreen Systems Inc.; US; 415/897-8888

Mullally, Ellen; Mgng Ed, Fiber Optics News; US; 301/340-1520

Mullaney, John K.; VP Sales & Mktng, Netrix Corp.; US; 703/742-6000

Mullaney, Joseph P.; VP & CFO, SofTech Inc.; US; 616/957-2330

Mullarkey, Vincent J.; VP & CFO, Digital Equipment Corp.; US; 508/493-5111

Mullen, David; VP & CFO, Borland Int'l.; US; 408/431-1000

Mullen, James X.; Pres, Mullen; US; 508/468-1155

Mullenger, Dirk; Mgr Event Mktng, Information Technology Services Marketing Assoc.; US; 617/862-8500

Muller, Anthony R.; SVP Ops, Centigram Communications Corp.; US; 408/944-0250

Muller, Michael; Chmn, Connect Inc.; US; 415/254-4000

Mulligan, Margaret; PR Dir, CoMark Technologies Inc.; US; 214/233-7091

Mullin, Linda; VP Mktng, Security Microsystems Inc.; US

Muma, Leslie M.; Pres & COO, Flserv Inc.; US; 414/879-5000

Muma, Stephen; Pres, Sierra/Alliance Inc.; US; 602/991-5836

Mun, Michael; Pres, Aztech Labs Inc.; US; 510/623-8988

Munday, Terry; VP Prod Dev, PinPoint Software Corp.; US; 408/997-6900

Mundell, Jacqueline; Exec Dir, Library & Information Technology Assoc.; US; 312/280-4270

Munn, David; Dir Membership, Information Technology Services Marketing Assoc.; US; 617/862-8500

Munn, Richard; Pres, Information Technology Services Marketing Assoc.; US; 617/862-8500

Munns, Ian; SVP Mktng & Tech, Mitel Corp.; Canada; 613/592-2122

Munro, P. Scott; Pres & CEO, Western Micro Technology; US; 408/379-0177, smunro@westernmicro.com

Munro, William; Pres, Mannesmann Tally Corp.; US; 206/251-5500

Muns, Ron; Chmn & CEO, Bendata Management Systems; US; 719/531-5007

Munshani, Shanker; Pres, Micronics Computers Inc.; US; 510/651-2300

Munson, Jr., David C.; Ed-in-Chief, IEEE Transactions on Image Processing; US; 908/981-0060

Muntz, Richard R.; Ed-in-Chief, ACM Computing Surveys; US; 212/869-7440

Murach, Mike; Pres, Mike Murach & Associates Inc.; US; 209/440-9071

Murasawa, Haruyasu; Pres, Parana Supplies Corp.; US; 310/793-1325

Murase, Haruso; Pres & CEO, Canon US Inc.; US; 516/488-6700

Murch, Jerry; VP Bus Dev, Xerox Desktop Document Systems; US; 415/815-6800

Murdakes, James; Pres & CEO, Large Storage Configurations; US; 612/482-4535, jmurdaks@lsci.com

Murdoch, Mike; CTO, Sirsi Corp.; US; 205/922-9820

Muro, Kathy; VP, FDP Corp.; US; 305/858-8200

Murphy, Anne; VP Mktng, Storage Computer Corp.; US; 603/880-3005

Murphy, Don; Pres, Shana Corp.; Canada; 403/433-3690

Murphy, George W.; Pres & CEO, ECC International Corp.; US; 610/687-2600

Murphy, Jeff; VP Mfg, Cardinal Technologies Inc.; US; 717/293-3000, jeffm@cardtech.com

Murphy, John; VP Sales & Mktng, Shana Corp.; Canada; 403/433-3690, jmurphy@shana.com

Murphy, John; VP Sales & Mktng, Orchid Technology; US; 510/683-0300

Murphy, John W.; Pres, Practical Peripherals Inc.; US; 770/840-6832

Murphy, Kathy; CFO, Vantive Corp.; US; 408/982-5700

Murphy, Kathy; Pblr, New Media Publications; US; 512/873-7761, 75730.2465@compuserve.com

Murphy, Keith; VP Dist Sales, NovaStor Corp.; US; 805/579-6700, keith@novastor.com

Murphy, Martin; Pres, Faulkner Information Services; US; 609/662-2070

Murphy, Michael; Ed & Pblr, California Technology Stock Letter; US; 415/726-8495

Murphy, Roger J.; Pres & CEO, Aironet Wireless Communications Inc.; US; 330/665-7900

Murphy, Shaun; Mktng Mgr, 3D/Eye Inc.; US; 770/937-9000

Murphy, William J.; Pres & COO, Telxon Corp.; US; 216/867-3700

Murray, Dave; SVP, Neale-May & Partners Inc.; US; 415/328-5555

Murray, Edward; VP Eng, Inforite Corp.; US; 415/571-8766

Murray, Mark; Dir SW Dev, Direct Technology; US; 212/475-2747

Murray, R. Scott; CFO, SoftKey International Inc.; US; 617/494-1200

Murray, Robert J.; Chmn, Pres & CEO, New England Business Service Inc.; US; 508/448-6111

Murray, Valerie; Ed, IDG's Windows 95 Journal; US; 617/482-8785

Murton, Kenneth G.; Pres & CEO, BCB Holdings Inc.; Canada; 905/850-8266

Muse, Dan; Exec Ed, Family PC; US; 212/503-5255

Musick, Darrell; VP Mktng & Sales, Energizer Power Systems; US; 904/462-3911

Musto, Michael L.; Pres & CEO, Reptron Electronics Inc.; US; 813/854-2351

Muth, Mike; Ed, Delph Report, The; US; 617/247-1025

Muzzy, Peter; Pres, Lattice Inc.; US

Myers, Bruce C.; VP & CFO, Xscribe Corp.; US; 619/457-5091

Myers, C. Frank; VP Ops, Xilinx Inc.; US; 408/559-7778

Myers, Mark B.; SVP Res & Tech, Xerox Corp.; US; 203/968-3000

Myers, Neil; Founding Partner, Network Associates Inc.; US; 801/373-7888, neilm@netassoc.com

Myers, Ray G.; VP Quality, Network Appliance Corp.; US; 415/428-5100, rgm@netapp.com

Myers, Richard C.; VP Admin, Hutchinson Technology Inc.; US; 612/587-3797

Myers, Steven D.; VP Prod Mgmt, STF Technologies Inc.; US; 816/463-7972

Myrick, Jake; Co-Founder, Big Top Productions Inc.; US; 415/978-5363

Myrick, Jim; Co-Founder, Big Top Productions Inc.; US; 415/978-5363

Myrmo, Erik R.; VP Eng, Computone Corp.; US; 770/475-2725, erik@compu-

tone.com

Nabors, Clyde W.; Exec Dir, National Electronics Service Dealers Assoc.; US; 817/921-9061

Nace, Ted; Pblr, Peachpit Press Inc.; US; 510/548-4393

Nadata, Arthur; Pres & Treas, Nu Horizons Electronics Corp.; US; 516/226-6000

Nadeau, Michael; Ed, I+Way; US; 603/924-7271, mnadeau@ix.netcom.com

Nadon, Donald J.; VP Sales, National Instruments Corp.; US; 512/794-0100

Nafus, Edward C.; EVP, First Data Corp.; US; 201/525-4700

Nag, Ronjon; GM, Lexicus Corp.; US; 415/462-6800

Nagano, Nario; VP Sales & Mktng, AIWA America; US; 201/512-3600

Nagel, David C.; SVP R&D, Apple Computer Inc.; US; 408/996-1010

Nagel, Paul; SVP Eng, Megahertz Corp.; US; 801/320-7000

Nagel, Robert H.; EVP Tech, Infosafe Systems Inc.; US; 212/867-7200

Nagy, Dennis A.; SVP Sales, MacNeal-Schwendler Corp., The; US; 213/258-9111

Nagy, Terry; Ops Mgr, Apogee Software Ltd.; US; 214/271-1765

Nahm, Eric R.; VP Mktng & Sales, Verbex Voice Systems Inc.; US; 908/225-5225

Naim, Ari; Pres, Sycom Technologies Inc.; US; 610/660-5770

Nair, Tony; Dir Mktng, PowerPro Software; US; 415/345-9278

Najda, Andrew; Pres & CEO, Number Nine Visual Technology Corp.; US; 617/674-0009

Nakai, Hideo; Chief Admin Off, Sanyo-Verbatim CD Company; US; 317/935-7574

Nakamura, Hideo; VP & CFO, Riso Inc.; US; 508/777-7377

Nakao, M. Bruce; SVP & CFO, Adobe Systems Inc.; US; 415/961-4400

Nakatsu, Peg; Bus Mgr, SoftPub Yellow Pages, The; US; 206/852-7440

Nakell, Chuck; Dir Mktng, Inspiration Software Inc.; US; 503/245-9011, cnakell@mcimail.com

Nalevanko, Tom; Pres, Mainstay; US; 805/484-9400

Naman, Mard; Mgng Ed, Publish; US; 415/978-3280, mnaman@publish.com

Nance, Richard E.; Ed-in-Chief, ACM Transactions on Modeling & Computer Simulations; US; 212/869-7440

Napier, James V.; Chmn, Scientific-Atlanta Inc.; US; 770/903-5000

Napolitan, J'Amy; VP & Sr Analyst, Infonetics Research Inc.; US; 408/298-7999, jamynap@aol.com

Narang, Charles K.; Pres, NCI Information Systems Inc.; US; 703/893-8623

Narayan, Varsha; VP Sales & Mktng, PowerPro Software; US; 415/345-9278

Narisawa, Goro; GM, Japan Digital Laboratory Co. Ltd.; US; 805/588-8709

Narodick, Sally G.; Chmn & CEO, Edmark Corp.; US; 206/556-8400

Nashleanas, Patricia; Pres, Eden Systems Corp.; US; 317/848-9600, patnash@edensys.com

Nashleanas, Richard P.; CEO, Eden Systems Corp.; US; 317/848-9600, ricknash@edensys.com

Nason, Duane; Ed-in-Chief, Mac Monthly; US; 510/428-0110

Nassr Jr., John; Bus Mgr, JobShop Software Solutions; Canada; 514/697-8621

Naterman, Lois; Pblr, dot.COM; US; 203/853-4266

Nathan, Joseph A.; Pres & COO, Compuware Corp.; US; 810/737-7300

Nathan, Russ V.; Mgng Dir, Romtec plc; UK; 1628-770077

Natkin, Hy; Ed-in-Chief, ECN, Electronic Component News; US; 610/964-4343, hnatkin@chilton.com

Naturman, Louis; Pres, Business Communications Co. Inc.; US; 203/853-4266

Natwick, Bob; VP Sales, DiviCom Inc.; US; 408/944-6700

Navid, Mike; CFO, MagicRAM; US; 213/413-9999

Navoar, Shereef; CTO, XcelleNet Inc.; US; 770/804-8100

Ne, Darwon; Dir, TechBridge Technology Corp.; Canada; 416/222-8998

Neads, Martin; SVP, Structural Dynamics Research Corp.; US; 513/576-2400

Neal, David; CFO, Creative Interaction Technologies Inc.; US; 919/419-1694

Neal, Philip M.; Pres & COO, Avery Dennison; US; 818/304-2000

Neal, Scotty R.; Pres, AT&T CommVault Systems; US; 908/935-8000

Neale, Jennifer; Pblr, LAN Times; US; 415/513-6800

Neale, Judd; CEO, Software Productivity Consortium; US; 703/742-8877

Neale-May, Donovan; Pres, Neale-May & Partners Inc.; US; 415/328-5555

Nealon, David J.; VP WW Ops, Micronics Computers Inc.; US; 510/651-2300

Neason, Rob; Pres, New Machine Publishing; US; 310/581-3600, neason@newmachine.com

Nee, Eric; Ed-in-Chief, Upside; US; 415/377-0950, enee@upside.com

Needleman, Raphael; Ed-in-Chief, BYTE Magazine; US; 603/924-9281

Needleman, Theodore; Ed-in-Chief, Accounting Technology; US; 212/967-7000, tedneedleman@mcimail.com

Neff, Jerome; Grp Pres, Penton Publishing Inc.; US; 216/696-7000

Nei, Chu; VP Eng, Maxpeed Corp.; US; 415/345-5447

Neiger, Steve; Sales Mgr, Tapette Corp.; US; 714/588-7000

Neiger II, James; Pres, Tapette Corp.; US; 714/588-7000

Neill, Gary; CFO, Dazel Inc.; US; 512/328-6977

Neilson, Robert D.; VP Mktng, Itron Inc.; US; 509/924-9900

Neiman, Harold; Chmn, Romeo Inc.; US; 310/273-1866

Nelson, Andrew; Creative Dir, Cyberflix Inc.; US; 615/546-1157, cyberflix@aol.com

Nelson, Curtis; VP Sales & Mktng, Crystal Group Inc.; US; 319/378-1636

Nelson, Dana R.; VP Sales & Mktng, Digi Int'l.; US; 612/943-9020

Nelson, Diane; Principal, Nelson Henning Group; US; 415/967-2387

Nelson, Fritz; Ed, Network Computing; US; 516/562-5071, fnelson@nwc.com

Nelson, Greg; Pres, Nelson's Computer Services; US; 708/965-7325

Nelson, Greg H.; VP App & Sales, ADFlex Solutions Inc.; US; 602/963-4584

Nelson, Jay J.; Ed, Design Tools Monthly; US; 303/444-6876

Nelson, Kathy; Mgng Ed., Duke Communications Int'l.; US; 970/663-4700

Nelson, Neal; Pres, Neal Nelson & Associates; US; 312/755-1000

Nelson, Richard; VP Eng, Qualstar Corp.; US; 818/592-0061

Nelson, Stephen M.; SVP & CFO, Tels Corp.; US; 801/571-1182

Nemirovsky, Felix; Eng Mgr, Plextor; US; 408/980-1838, felixn@netcom.com

Nemnom, Elias; CFO, MEDE America Corp.; US; 216/425-3241

Nemzer, Steve; Pres, VeriTest Inc.; US; 310/450-0062, 70353.1763@compuserve.com

Nesbeda, Peter J.; Chmn, Pres & CEO, Xyplex Inc.; US; 508/952-4700

Nesbitt, Vance; Chmn & CEO, Kent Marsh Ltd.; US; 713/522-5625

Nesdore, Paul; Pblr, Digital News & Review; US; 303/470-4445, pauln@dnr.cahners.com

Neshamkin, Paul; Dir Tech Sup, Wex-Tech Systems Inc.; US; 212/949-9595, 70740.3356@compuserve.com

Nesmith, Brian; Pres & CEO, Ipsilon Networks Inc.; US; 415/846-4600

Neubart, Michael; Ed-in-Chief, Internet World; US; 203/226-6967, neubarth@iw.com

Neubert, Thomas; VP & GM, Elsa Inc.; US; 408/565-9669, thomasn@elsa-usa.mhs

Neufeld, Donn; VP Ops, Quality Systems Inc.; US; 714/731-7171

Neun, Carl W.; VP & CFO, Tektronix Inc.; US; 503/627-7111

Neurath, Paul; Principal, Looking Glass Technologies Inc.; US; 617/441-6333

Nevin, George; Sales & Mktng Mgr, Cimtek Thomas; US; 615/929-9383

Nevin, Robert C.; Pres Bus Forms Div, Reynolds & Reynolds; US; 513/443-2000

Nevins, Joan M.; VP Mktng, PictureTel Corp.; US; 508/762-5000

New, Michael; Dir Mktng, InfoAccess Inc.; US; 206/747-3203

Newberry, Thomas L.; Chmn, American Software Inc.; US; 404/264-5296

Newell, Bill; Pres & CEO, Micro Dynamics Ltd.; US; 301/589-6300, bill_newell@mdl.com

Newell, Christopher; Pres, Musitek; US; 805/646-8051

Newell, Martin; CTO, Ashlar Inc.; US; 408/746-1800

Newman, Alexander; Exec Dir, Sun User Group Inc.; US; 617/232-0514

Newman, Blair T.; Ed, Edge, The; US; 5748015@mcimail.com

Newman, Dale; VP Sales & Mktng, Formgen; US; 602/443-4109

Newman, David; Mktng Dir, Island Software Corp.; US; 415/491-1000

Newman, Keith; Pblr, Computer Retail Week; US; 516/733-6800, knewman@cmp.com

Newquist, Harvey; Pres, Relayer Group; US; 212/369-6340

Newton, Charles; Pres, Newton-Evans Research Co. Inc.; US; 410/465-7316

Newton, Harry; Pblr, Telecom Library Inc.; US; 212/691-8215, harrynewton@mcimail.com

Newton, Kenneth D.; Pres & CEO, Screen US; US; 847/870-7400

Newton, Paul E.; Pres & CEO, Boole & Babbage Inc.; US; 408/526-3000

Ng, Kanhom; Pres, Kanesmen Corp.; US; 408/263-9881

Ng, Laurence; Pblr, International designers Network; Hong Kong; 852-25285744

Ng, Patricia; VP Sales & Mktng, Aztech Labs Inc.; US; 510/623-8988

Ng, Susan; Mktng Dir, Kanesmen Corp.; US; 408/263-9881, susan_ng@kansmen.com

Ngai, Henry; VP Eng, D-Link Systems Inc.; US; 714/455-1688

Nguyen, Joseph; Pres, Telecomputer Inc.; US; 714/438-3993

Nguyen, Julien; Co-Chmn & CTO, Sigma Designs Inc.; US; 510/770-0100

Nguyen, Khoa D.; SVP & CTO, Picture-Tel Corp.; US; 508/762-5000

Nguyen, Luong; VP Mfg, Orchid Technology; US; 510/683-0300

Nguyen, Sean S.; CEO, VidTech Microsystems Inc.; US; 612/633-6000

Nguyen, Thomas; VP Eng, Advanced Integration Research Inc.; US; 408/428-0800

Nicas, Peter; Pblr, Client/Server Today; US; 617/964-3030, nicas@cstoday.com

Nicholas, Carolann; AT&T Global Product Compliance Laboratory; US; 908/834-1800

Nicholas, Charles R.; EVP & CFO, Andrew Corp.; US; 708/349-3300

Nicholas, Donald L.; Pblr, Internet Voyager; US; nicholas@bdc.iii.net

Nicholas, Doug; CEO, Opis Corp.; US;

515/284-0209

Nicholl, Ray; Co-Founder, DataViz Inc.; US; 203/268-0030

Nichols, Brenda; VP, Parker, Nichols & Co. Inc.; US; 508/369-2100, 481.8432@mcimail.com

Nichols, Corwin L.; Pres, MicroTech Conversion Systems Inc.; US; 415/424-1174

Nichols, Eirwen; Dir Telecom, Ovum Ltd.; England; 071-255-2670

Nichols, Jeff; Sr Mktng Mgr, Wacom Technology Corp.; US; 360/750-8882

Nichols, Roy J.; SVP & CTO, Nichols Research Corp.; US; 205/883-1140

Nickelsen, Myrna; Principal, Nickelsen Communications; US; 510/845-8804, mnickelsen@aol.com

Nickless, James P.; VP Ops, Mobile Security Communications; US; 770/594-0424

Nicol, Helen; Pblr, Multimedia Business Analyst; UK; 171-896-2222

Nicolai, Frank A.; EVP & CFO, American Management Systems; US; 703/267-8000

Nicoletti, Thomas J.; VP & CFO, Altera Corp.; US; 408/894-7000

Nicols, Maureen; NA Agent, Xephon; US; 817/455-7050

Niehaus, Ed; Sr Partner, Niehaus/Ryan/Haller; US; 415/615-7900, ed@nrh.com

Niehaus, Tom; VP, Simba Information Inc.; US; 203/834-0033

Nielsen, Cyndee; VP Mktng, Expert Graphics Inc.; US; 404/320-0800, cyndee@expertg.com

Nielson Jr., Lars P.; Nat'l Sales Mgr, DataCal Corp.; US; 602/831-3100, 74111.3420@compuserve.com

Nierenberg, Roy A.; Pres, Experience In Software Inc.; US; 510/644-0694

Nies, Thomas M.; Pres & CEO, Cincom Systems Inc.; US; 513/662-2300

Nikaido, Taeko; VP Mktng, Comtech Publishing Ltd.; US; 702/825-9000

Niles, Richard; Pres, Niles & Associates Inc.; US; 510/559-8592

Nilles, Tony; Sales Mgr, Numerical Algorithms Group Inc.; US; 630/971-2337, nilles@nag.com

Nine, Jerry; VP Sales & Mktng, National Education Training Group; US; 708/369-3000

Nishimoto, Hiroaki; VP Bus Dev, Oberon Software Inc.; US; 617/494-0990

Nishimura, Koichi; Pres & CEO, Solectron Corp.; US; 408/957-8500

Nishizawa, Yasunori; Sr Mngg Dir, Oki Electric Industry Co. Ltd.; Japan; 3-3501-3111

Nissan, Daniel; VP Sales & Mktng, VocalTec Inc.; US; 201/768-9400

Niwa, Norio; Pres & CEO, Epson America Inc.; US; 310/782-0770

Noack, Jerry C.; VP & Group Pblr, Lakewood Publications; US; 612/333-0471

Noble, Carla; Pblr, Adobe Magazine; US; 206/628-2321

Noble, Richard W.; Controller US Ops., ARC International Corp.; Canada; 416/630-0200

Noble, Rick; VP Reference Svc, Online Computer Library Center Inc.; US; 614/764-6000

Nolan, Kathleen Lopez; Ed, Gale Directory of Databases; US; 313/961-2242

Nolan, Robert J.; Pblr, PC/Computing; US; 415/578-7000

Noling, Michael S.; Pres & CEO, Wavefront Technologies Inc.; US; 805/962-8117

Nolley, Robert; Dir, International Parallel Machines Inc.; US; 508/990-2977

Noon, John P.; Pblr, Syllabus Press; US; 408/773-0670

Noonan, Charlie; VP Sales, Scitex America Corp.; US; 617/275-5150

Noonan, Jack; Pres & CEO, SPSS Inc.; US; 312/329-2400

Noonan, John G.; Pres, UniKix Technologies; US

Noorda, Ray; Chmn, CrystalGraphics Inc.; US; 408/496-6175

Noorderhaven, Henk J.; Pres, Elektroson US; US; 610/617-0850

Nora, Thomas A.; VP Sales, Rogue Wave Software Inc.; US; 541/754-3010

Norby, R. Douglas; SVP & CFO, Mentor Graphics Corp.; US; 503/626-7000

Nordin, Ron; Pres & CEO, SQA Inc.; US; 617/392-0110

Nordling, Tamis; Mngg Ed, Adobe Magazine; US; 206/628-2321

Norman, David; Chmn & CEO, Technically Elite Inc.; US; 408/370-4300

Norman, Lane H.; Pres, National Electronics Service Dealers Assoc.; US; 817/921-9061

Norman, Robert A.; Pres, Amquest Corp.; US; 717/569-8030

Norris, Charles A.; CFO, Corel Corp.; Canada; 613/728-8200

Norris, David L.; VP & Co-Founder, ObjectSpace Inc.; US; 214/934-2496

Norrod, James D.; Pres & CEO, Telebit Corp.; US; 508/441-2181

North, Robert L.; Pres & CEO, HNC Software Inc.; US; 619/546-8877

North, Tom; Pres & CEO, ShaBlamm! Computer Corp.; US; 408/730-9696, tn@shablamm.com

Northwood, Michael; VP/Dir, Sherpa Corp.; US; 408/433-0455

Norton, Margaret; VP, Octel Communications Corp.; US; 408/321-2000

Norton, Robert; EVP, Cambex Corp.; US; 617/890-6000

Norton, Sarah E.; Dir Mktng, Business Research Group; US; 617/630-3900, norton@brg.cahners.com

Norton, Thomas; Andrea Electronics Corp.; US

Norwood, Diva; Pblr, Automatic I.D.

News; US; 216/243-8100, advansta@village.ios.com

Nosbaum, LeRoy D.; EVP UtiliNet Div, Metricom Inc.; US; 408/399-8200

Notebaert, Richard C.; Chmn & CEO, Ameritech Corp.; US; 312/750-5000

Nouray, Allen; VP Ops, MagicRAM; US; 213/413-9999

Nourmohamadian, Mo; Founder, Ultera Systems Inc.; US; 714/367-8800

Novarina, Raymond C.; VP Eng, Concurrent Controls Inc.; US; 415/873-6240, rnovarina@conctrls.com

Novitsky, Donna J.H.; VP Mktng, Clarify Inc.; US; 408/428-2000

Novoa, Blanca; Intl Sales & Mktng, Protec Microsystems Inc.; Canada; 514/630-5832

Novotny, Neal; VP Prod R&D, Jian Tools for Sales Inc.; US; 415/254-5600, nnovotny@jianusa.com

Nowak, Ronald; VP, Tangent Color Systems; US; 303/799-6766

Noxon, Woody; Pres, Consortium for Advanced Manufacturing-International Inc.; US; 817/860-1654

Nozaki, Akihiko; Pres, Nissei Sangyo America Ltd.; US; 617/461-8300

Nugent, Deborah; VP Fin, Software Spectrum Inc.; US; 214/840-6600

Nugent, Robert M.; SVP Sales, Centigram Communications Corp.; US; 408/944-0250

Nulph, Christopher D.; Pres, DataPak Software Inc.; US; 360/891-0542, d0142@applelink.com

Nulph, Mark A.; VP Sales & Mktng, DataPak Software Inc.; US; 360/891-0542

Nunez, Ramon A.; Pres & CEO, Ikos Systems Inc.; US; 408/255-4567

Nurie, Ghulam; Dir Mktng, Chronologic Simulation; US; 415/965-3312

Nuti, David; VP Fin & Ops, Rubbermaid Office Products Inc.; US; 615/977-5477

Nyberg, L.G.; Pres Comm Syst, Philips Electronics; Netherlands; 31-40-786022

Nyberg, Lars; Chmn & CEO, NCR Corp.; US; 513/445-5000

Nye, Bruce D.; VP CFO, Cerplex Group Inc.; US; 714/258-5151, bnye@cerplex.com

Nyer, Barry; Mktng Dir, AliMed Inc.; US; 617/329-2900

Nyrop, Kathryn C.; VP & Treas, Sybase Inc.; US; 510/922-3500

Nystrom, Raymond E.; VP & CFO, Inmac Corp.; US; 408/727-1970

Nyweide, Jeff; Pres & COO, Dataware Technologies Inc.; US; 617/621-0820

O'Brien, Daniel J.; COO, PC Wholesale; US; 708/307-1700

O'Brien, Jeffrey M.; Sr Ed, Marketing Computers; US; 212/536-6587, jeff@marketingcomputers.com

O'Brien, John; VP R&D, Storage Computer Corp.; US; 603/880-3005

O'Brien, Matt; Pres, Communications

O'Brien, R. Andrew; VP Mktng & Bus Dev, Brooktrout Technology Inc.; US; 617/499-4100, aob@brooktrout.com

O'Brien, Ray; SVP Mktng, SkyTel Corp.; US; 601/944-1300

O'Brien, Robert; SVP Sales, Truevision Inc.; US; 408/562-4200

O'Brien, Sara; Assist Ed, Cheifet Letter, The; US; 603/863-9322, 74774.75@compuserve.com

O'Brien, Susan; VP Bus Dev, DeBoever Architectures Inc.; US; 508/371-1557

O'Callaghan, James; EVP, Cirque Corp.; US; 801/467-1100

O'Connell, Cynthia; VP R&D, Compusearch Software Systems Inc.; US; 703/893-7200

O'Connell, Deborah H.; VP Sales, Software Support Inc.; US; 407/333-4433

O'Connell, Michael O.; VP Mktng, Xiox Corp.; US; 415/375-8188

O'Connell, Rick; Dir Sales, Focus Enhancements Inc.; US; 617/938-8088

O'Connell, William; VP Sales, Sync Research; US; 714/588-2070

O'Conner, William Y.; Pres & COO, Gtech Corp.; US; 401/392-1000

O'Connor, Edward K.; Pblr, Government Imaging; US; 301/445-4405

O'Connor, James; CFO, Software Developer's Co. Inc., The; US; 617/740-0101

O'Connor, Marianne; Pres, Sterling Communications Inc.; US; 408/441-4100, moc@sterlingpr.com

O'Connor, Sean; CEO, Port Inc.; US; 203/852-1102

O'Connor, Thomas; Pres, Take One Concepts; US; 702/832-8499

O'Connor Abrams, Michela; Pblr, Open Computing; US; 415/513-6800, michela-abrams@wcmh.com

O'Conor, Rodney; Pres, Cameron Assoc.; US; 212/644-9560

O'Deady, Mark; Ed, Strategic Solutions; US; 206/868-6532

O'Dell, Wally; Pres WW, Liebert Corp.; US; 614/888-0246

O'Donald, Jay R.; VP Eng, Emulex Corp.; US; 714/662-5600

O'Donnell, Irene; VP Admin, Keyfile Corp.; US; 603/883-3800, ireneodonnell@keyfile.com

O'Donnell, Jack R.; EVP & CFO, Anacomp Inc.; US; 317/844-9666

O'Donnell, Jim; Ed, Notes Report, The; US; 617/482-8634

O'Donnell, Michael J.; Chmn, Pres & CEO, Allerion Inc.; US; 201/877-1000

O'Donnell, Tim; Pres, Advanced RISC Machines; US; 408/399-5199

O'Fallon, John; Pres, Maxum Development Corp.; US; 708/830-1113

O'Gara, Maureen; Pblr, Unigram.X; US; 516/759-7025

O'Grady, Paul; Chmn & CEO, Micro

Focus Inc.; US; 415/856-4161, pog@mfltd.co.uk

O'Hara, Stephen C.; Pres & CEO, Andor Communications Inc.; US; 612/932-4000

O'Kane, John T.; VP MIS, Executone Information Systems Inc.; US; 203/876-7600

O'Leary, Kevin; Pres, SoftKey International Inc.; US; 617/494-1200

O'Leary, Patrick; VP Mktng, Cognos Corp.; US; 617/229-6600

O'Leary, Terry; Pres, Greenberg Seronick & Partners; US; 617/267-4949

O'Malley, Joseph; SVP Sales, Okidata; US; 609/235-2600

O'Malley, Sean; Dir Mktng, StillWater Media; US; 516/261-4599

O'Malley, Shaun F.; CEO, Price Waterhouse; US; 301/897-5900

O'Malley, Thomas J.; VP Admin, Triad Systems Corp.; US; 510/449-0606

O'Mary, Gary; Co-Founder, Computer Fun; US; 619/271-9090, garyo@computerfun.com

O'Meara, William J.; Pres & CEO, C-Cube Microsystems Inc.; US; 408/944-6300

O'Neil, Tim; Pres, O'Neil Electronics; US; 714/727-1234

O'Neill, Beth; Client Svcs Mgr, Cutter Information Corp.; US; 617/648-8700

O'Neill, Brian; Adv Mgr, Simulation Software, Directory of; US; 619/277-3888, oneill@sdsc.edu

O'Neill, Kevin; Co-Founder, Image Axis Inc.; US; 212/989-5000

O'Neill, Kevin; VP Research, Business Research Group; US; 617/630-3900, oneill@brg.cahners.com

O'Pry, Tim; Pres & CEO, MicroHelp Inc.; US; 770/516-0899

O'Reilly, Charles; EVP, JMR Electronics Inc.; US; 818/993-4801

O'Reilly, Tim; Pres, O'Reilly & Associates Inc.; US; 707/829-0515

O'Reilly, Tom; Ed, DVD Report; US; 914/328-9157

O'Rourke, John; CMO, Kenan Systems Corp.; US; 617/225-2224, johno@kenan.com

O'Rourke Jr., James F.X.; CEO, Bruno Blenheim Inc.; US; 201/346-1400

O'Sullivan, Cara; Ed-in-Chief, Infobase Technology Magazine; US; 801/299-6700, cosulliv@folio.com

O'Sullivan, Ivan; VP Mktng, ON Technology Corp.; US; 617/374-1400, iosulliv@on.com

O'Toole, Annrai; VP Dev, Iona Technologies; US; 508/460-6888

Oaas, T. Erik; VP & CFO, Micron Electronics; US; 208/893-3434

Oakley, Elizabeth; Pres, Oakley Publishing; US; 541/747-0800

Oberle, Hank E.; Pres & COO, Rexon Inc.; US; 216/349-0600

Oberteuffer, John A.; Pres, Voice Information Associates Inc.; US; 617/861-6680, jober24@aol.com

Obrand, Barry; Pres, Voysys Corp.; US; 510/252-1100

Ocampo Jr., Raymond L.; SVP, Oracle Corp.; US; 415/506-7000

Ochel, Kent; Pres, Business Resource Software; US; 512/251-7541

Ochlis, Samuel; Chmn, CSPI; US; 508/663-7598

Ochs, Paul G.; Pblr, DataTrends Publications Inc.; US; 703/779-0574

Odeen, Philip A.; Pres & CEO, BDM Int'l.; US; 703/848-5000

Odeyard, Gary; VP & GM, Shafer; US; 714/553-1177

Odom, Bruce; Pblr, Out of the Blue; US

Oestreicher, Don; VP Eng, Airsoft Inc.; US; 408/777-7500, dono@airsoft.com

Offerdahl, James; VP & CFO, Tivoli Systems Inc.; US; 512/794-9070

Offut, Tom; GM, Qume Inc.; US; 408/473-1500

Ogden, Chris; Bus Dir, Software Designs Unlimited Inc.; US; 919/968-4567, chris.ogden@applelink.com

Ogden, R. Drew; VP Bus Dev, Softdesk Inc.; US; 603/428-3199

Ogle, Bill; Pres & CEO, STB Systems Inc.; US; 214/234-8750

Ohanian, Michael; Pres, Intermec Corp.; US; 206/348-2600

Ohga, Norio; Chmn & CEO, Sony Corp.; Japan; 3-5448-2111

Okamoto, Hiroshi; SVP Info Sys Grp, Sharp Electronics Corp.; US; 201/529-8200

Oklewicz, Ron; Pres, TelePad Corp.; US; 703/834-9000

Okuno, Mike; Pres, Kyocera Electronics Inc.; US; 908/560-3400

Olenik, George; Pres & CEO, Pick Systems; US; 714/261-7425

Oleson, Ray J.; Pres CACI Inc., CACI International Inc.; US; 703/841-7800

Oliver, Christopher J.; Dir Eng, Cabletron Systems; US; 603/332-9400

Oliver, Jan; Mngg Ed, Multimedia Today; US; 404/531-0096

Olker, Donald F.; VP Mfg, Zitel Corp.; US; 510/440-9600

Olkes, Sid; CFO, Visual Software Inc.; US; 818/593-3500

Ollila, Jorma; Chmn, Pres & CEO, Nokia Group; Finland; 3580-18071

Olsen, Glenn; Pblr, X-Ray Magazine; US; 415/861-9258, xraypub@eworld.com

Olsen, Gordon; VP, High Technology Marketing; US; 508/478-2392, olsen@htm.com

Olsen Jr., Dan R.; Ed-in-Chief, ACM Transactions on Computer-Human Interaction; US; 212/869-7440

Olson, Chuck; Pres, Learningways Inc.; US; 617/234-5800

Olson, Craig; VP Mktng, BayStone Software; US; 408/370-9301, craig@bay-stone.com

Olson, Dwight; VP Ops, Micom Communications Corp.; US; 805/583-8600

Olson, Kenneth E.; Chmn, Proxima Corp.; US; 619/457-5500

Olson, Larry D.; EVP Sales, Kent Electronics Corp.; US; 713/780-7770

Olson, Robert; Co-Founder, Virtual Vineyards; US; 415/917-5750, rolson@virtualvin.com

Olson, Terry; Pres, Information Resource Group; US; 810/978-3000

Oltman, John R.; Chmn & CEO, SHL Systemhouse Inc.; Canada; 613/236-1428

Olver, Tama H.; VP Info Svcs, Amdahl Corp.; US; 408/746-6000

Omaru, Mike; Pres, Iiyama North America; US; 215/957-6543

Omid, Aaron; VP Sales, Scopus Technology Inc.; US; 510/597-5800

Omron, Sam; VP Ops, Systems Plus Inc.; US; 415/969-7047, sam@systemsplus.com

Ongarato, Mike; VP Sales & Mktng, LANcast; US; 603/880-1833, mike-ong@aol.com

Opfer, James E.; Group VP R&D, Komag Inc.; US; 408/946-2300

Opie, John; Vice Chmn, General Electric Co.; US; 203/373-2211

Opitz, Scott; Sales & Mktng Dir, Conextions Inc.; US; 508/689-3570

Opolko, Phyllis; VP Mktng, Monarch Avalon; US; 410/254-9200

Oppenheim, Dave; Dir R&D, Opcode Systems; US; 415/856-3333

Oppenheimer, Charlie; VP & GM Mac Div, Global Village Communication; US; 408/523-1000

Opper, Susanna; Pres, Susanna Opper & Assoc.; US; 413/528-6513

Oppermann, William; Dir Tech, Raidtec Corp; US; 770/664-6066

Orasin, Frank; CFO, Berkeley Software Design Inc.; US; 719/593-9445, orasin@bsdi.com

Orbach, Bob; Pres, Orbach Inc.; US; 212/667-5083

Orbach, Saul; VP Sales & Mktng Europe, SoftTalk Inc.; US; 617/433-0800

Orban, George P.; Chmn, Egghead Inc.; US; 509/922-7031

Orchard, Frank; VP Dev, Foresight Software; US; 770/206-1000

Ordish, Jonathan; Ed, Inside WordPerfect; US; 502/491-1900

Oriani, Peggy; Dir Mktng, Legend Entertainment Co.; US; 703/222-8500

Orlando, Richard V.; VP Strategic Mktng, Xicor Inc.; US; 408/432-8888

Orlando, Robert P.; VP & CFO, MathSoft Inc.; US; 617/577-1017

Orletsky, Terry; VP, Abacus Accounting Systems Inc.; Canada; 403/488-8100

Ormandy, Roman; Pres, Caligari Corp.; US; 415/390-9600

Orr, James F.; Pres & CEO, Cincinnati Bell Information Systems; US; 513/784-5900

Orr, Joel; Pres, Orr Associates Int'l.; US; 804/467-2677, joel_oor@mcimail.com

Orr, Susan; Pres, Technology Resource Assistance Center Inc.; US; 415/853-1100

Orrange, William; Pres, Ulevich & Orrange Inc.; US; 415/329-1590

Orsini, Tom T.; SVP Fin & Dev, Alltel Corp.; US; 501/661-8000

Orson, Marshall D.; VP Bus Affairs, Turner Home Entertainment; US; 404/885-0505

Osborn, John J.; Chmn, Jandel Scientific Inc.; US; 415/453-6700

Osborn, Joseph; Pres, Jandel Scientific Inc.; US; 415/453-6700, joe@jandel.com

Osborn, Todd S.; VP Sales, Gateway 2000; US; 605/232-2000

Osborne, Lynn; Ed, Storage Source; US; 303/415-0858, losborne@aol.com

Osborne, Ronald W.; EVP & CFO, BCE Inc.; Canada; 514/397-7267

Oseka, Juliet; Asst Ed, PC Novice; US; 402/479-2141

Osenbaugh, Charles R.; CFO, Timeline Inc.; US; 206/822-3140

Oshan, Alex; Controller, Riso Inc.; US; 508/777-7377

Osman, Dewaine L.; SVP & CIO, Unisys Corp.; US; 215/986-4011

Osman, Fazil; VP, XLNT Designs Inc.; US; 619/487-9320

Ostenso, Roy S.; CEO, Tapedisk Corp.; US; 715/235-3388, 73174.2464@compuserve.com

Osugi, Kazue; Qualitas Trading Co.; US; 510/848-8080, kazue@qtc.com

Oswald, Charles W.; Chmn, National Computer Systems Inc.; US; 612/829-3000

Oswald, Daniel; Pres, MultiLing International Inc.; US; 801/377-2000

Ota, Chris; Mktng Mgr, Nanao US Corp.; US; 310/325-5202

Ota, William T.; Pblr/Pres/CEO, Advisor Communications Int'l. Inc.; US; 619/483-6400, 71154.3123@compuserve.com

Ott, Ed; VP, Four Season Software; US; 908/248-6667

Ott, Robert W.; VP Sales, IQ Software Corp.; US; 770/446-8880

Otto, Philip G.; Pres, Venture Stores Inc.; US; 314/281-6801

Otus, Simone; Partner, Blanc & Otus; US; 415/512-0500

Ousley, James E.; Pres & CEO, Control Data Systems Inc.; US; 612/482-2401

Ouye, Mike; VP Eng, First Floor Inc.; US; 415/968-1101

Ovelleyye, Daniel; VP Eng, MicroSlate Inc.; Canada; 514/444-3680

Overby, John; Pres & CEO, Advanced Hardware Architecture; US; 509/334-1000

Overton, Russell G.; SVP Bus Dev, HBO & Co.; US; 770/393-6000

Ow, Peter; EVP, Everex Systems Inc.; US; 510/498-1111

Owen, Barry; Mgng Ed, PC World Interactive; US; 415/243-0500

Owen, Brian D.; Pres & CEO, MapInfo Corp.; US; 518/285-6000

Owen, David P.; VP Corp Dev & Strat, Network Equipment Technologies Inc.; US; 415/366-4400

Owen, Maria; CEO, Montage Graphics; US; 408/654-0700

Owen, Mike; Prod Mktng Mgr, Umax Technologies Inc.; US; 510/651-4000, mike_owen@umax.com

Owen, Scott; VP & COO, Information Storage Devices Inc.; US; 408/369-2400

Owen, William H.; VP Tech, Xicor Inc.; US; 408/432-8888

Owens, Jim; COO, Sematech; US; 512/356-3137

Owens, John M.; VP Eng, Sequoia Systems Inc.; US; 508/480-0800

Owens, Park; VP Mktng, Fellowes Manufacturing Co.; US; 708/893-1600

Owens, Ross; Mgng Ed, InfoWorld; US; 415/572-7341

Owens, Stanley; Chmn, ASAP Software Express Inc.; US; 847/465-3710

Ownby, Starr; Sales Mgr, Design Technology; US; 619/448-2888

Oxenhorn, Eli; Chmn, Cheyenne Software Inc.; US; 516/484-5110

Oyler, James R.; Pres & CEO, Evans & Sutherland Computer Corp.; US; 801/588-1000, joyler@es.com

Ozuzu, Gregory U.; Pres, Unitrac Software Corp.; US; 616/344-0220, gozuzu@unitrac.com

Pacey, Gordon; VP Ops, Cambridge Parallel Processing; US; 714/261-8901, gordon@cppus.com

Pacheco, Roy; VP Sales & Mktng, Twinbridge Software Corp.; US; 213/263-3926

Pachikov, Stephan; Pres, ParaGraph Int'l.; US; 408/364-7700

Paciello, Michael; SVP, Nexar Technologies Inc.; US; 508/836-8700

Pack, Fred; VP, UniPress Software Inc.; US; 908/287-2100, fhp@unipress.com

Pack, Jeff; Pres, Chase Research Inc.; US; 615/872-0770

Packert, Bonnie; EVP, HyperLogic Corp.; US; 619/746-2765, bpackert@hyperlogic.com

Paddock, Norman; Exec Dir, Association of Desk-Top Pblrs; US; 619/563-9714

Padfield, Sara; CFO, Silton-Bookman Systems; US; 408/446-1170, spadfield@sbsinc.com

Padilla, Therese G.; Prod Mgr, Command Software Systems Inc.; US; 407/575-3200, padilla@commandcom.com

Padveen, Stewart; Pres, LinkStar Communications Corp.; US; 954/426-5465

Padwick, Armanda; Dir Fin, Crystal Inc.; Canada; 604/681-3435

Page, Loraine; Ed, Link-Up; US; 609/654-6266

Page, Scott; EVP, 7th Level Inc.; US; 818/547-1955

Page, Stephen F.; EVP & CFO, United Technologies Corp.; US; 203/728-7000

Pageler, John; VP Sales, Cogent Data Technologies Inc.; US; 360/378-2929, john@cogentdata.com

Paglierani, John; VP Prod Dev, Mesa Group; US; 617/964-7400

Pagnozzi, Dominick; VP, ABCO Distributors; US; 914/368-1930

Pahwa, Ash; Pres, CD-ROM Strategies Inc.; US; 714/453-1702

Paine, David A.; VP Tech, Softdesk Inc.; US; 603/428-3199

Paine, Jeff; VP Mktng, Eicon Technology Corp.; 214/239-3270

Paisley, Christopher B.; VP & CFO, 3Com Corp.; US; 408/764-5000

Paisley, William; EVP, Knowledge Access Int'l.; US; 415/969-0606

Pajari, George; Pres, Faximum Software Inc.; Canada; 604/925-3600

Pakacs, Katherine; Mgng Dir, Communications Managers Assoc.; US; 201/425-1700

Palermo, Ann; VP Mktng, PC DOCS Inc.; US; 617/273-3800, annp@pcdocs.com

Palermo, Mary Dean; SVP & CFO, Aspen Technology Inc.; US; 617/577-0100

Paley, M. Greg; GM & SVP, Award Software Int'l. Inc.; US; 415/968-4433

Palka, Thomas M.; VP WW Mktng, VMark Software Inc.; US; 508/366-3888

Palkovich, Jeff G.; VP Ops, Damark International Inc.; US; 612/531-0066

Pallace, Bob; Pres, Pallace Inc.; US; 301/622-5100

Pallatta, Mike; VP Sales, Magic Solutions Inc.; US; 201/587-1515

Palm, Debra; Mgng Dir, International Interactive Communications Society; US; 503/579-4427

Palmer, Charles L.; Chmn, Minnesota Educational Computing Corp.; US; 612/569-1500

Palmer, Edward; VP & CIO, Scriptel Holdings Inc.; US; 614/276-8402

Palmer, James A.; EVP Dev & Mfg, VeriFone Inc.; US; 415/591-6500

Palmer, James T.; Chmn & CEO, Horizons Technology Inc.; US; 619/292-8331

Palmer, Jeffrey H.; VP, BBN Software Products Corp.; US; 617/873-5000

Palmer, John M.; VP & CFO, Tab Products Co.; US; 415/852-2400

Palmer, Kerry; VP & CFO, Wall Data Inc.; US; 206/814-9255

Palmer, Mike; Pres, Direct Technology; US; 212/475-2747

Palmer, Robert B.; Pres & CEO, Digital Equipment Corp.; US; 508/493-5111

Palmisano, Sam J.; Pres & CEO, Integrated Systems Solutions Corp.; US

Paluck, Robert J.; Chmn & CEO, Convex Computer Corp.; US; 214/497-4000

Paluzzi, Mike; SVP, SysKonnect Inc.; US; 408/437-3800

Pampel, Roland D.; Pres & CEO, Microcom Inc.; US; 617/551-1000

Panagakos, Pauline; Mgng Ed, Portable Design; US; 918/835-3161, paulinep@pennwell.com

Panaro, Lawrence; CFO, Zoom Telephonics Inc.; US; 617/423-1072

Pancoast, Judy; VP Sales & Mktng, Magee Enterprises Inc.; US; 770/446-6611

Pande, Sunil; VP Mktng, Tactica Corp.; US; 503/293-9585

Panetta, Louis; EVP, Fujitsu Personal Systems Inc.; US; 408/982-9500

Pankonien, Gary; Chmn, 1st Tech Corp.; US; 512/258-3570

Panos, Dave; VP Mktng, DataBeam Corp.; US; 606/245-3500, dpanos@databeam.com

Panos, Gregory P.; Ed & Pblr, SophisTech Research; US; 310/434-4436

Paone, Joe; Tech Ed, Internetwork; US; 215/643-8000, paoneja@cardinal.com

Papciak, Wally; EVP & COO, Quality Education Data Inc.; US; wpapciak@qed-data.com

Pape, Robert G.; CFO, ADFlex Solutions Inc.; US; 602/963-4584

Pape, William R.; SVP & CIO, VeriFone Inc.; US; 415/591-6500

Papermaster, Steven G.; Chmn & CEO, BSG Corp.; US; 713/965-9000

Paquette, Richard; Pblr, BBS Magazine; US; 609/953-9110, publisher@bbsmag.com

Paradis, Roger; Pres & CEO, Programmer's Paradise Inc.; US; 908/389-8950, rparadis@programmers.com

Paragopolous, Dean; Zoom Telephonics Inc.; US; 617/423-1072

Parazin, Diane; Acct Dir, Lages & Associates Inc.; US; 714/453-8080

Pardoe, Terry; EVP, International Management Services Inc.; US; 508/520-1555

Pardue, Andrew S.; VP Ops, Datatrac Corp.; US; 770/552-3866

Pare, Don; Pres & CEO, Caravelle Networks Corp.; Canada; 613/225-1172, dpare@caravelle.com

Parent, Christopher; Pres, United Innovations; US; 413/533-7500

Parham, W. Michael; VP Sales, XcelleNet Inc.; US; 770/804-8100

Parikh, Jiren; GM, Elektroson US; US; 610/617-0850, jparikh@elektroson.com

Parikh, Mihir; CEO, Asyst; US; 510/661-5023

Parikn, Vijay; Bus Dir Wireless Com Div, Rockwell Semiconductor Systems; US; 714/883-4600

Parini, Joe; Pres, Fibronics International Inc.; US; 508/671-9440, joe-parine@fibusa.com

Paris, Raymond W.; VP, Keane Inc.;

US; 617/241-9200

Park, Andrew; Pres & CEO, Techmedia Computer Systems Corp.; US; 714/379-6677

Park, C.S.; Pres & CEO, Maxtor Corp.; US; 408/432-1700

Park, K.W.; Pres, Samtron Displays Inc.; US; 310/537-7000

Park, William; EVP Mktng, Genova; US; 310/538-4102

Parker, Cary; VP Mktng, Nelco Inc.; US; 414/337-1000

Parker, David; VP Bus Dev, Quintus Corp.; US; 510/624-2818, dave.parker@quintus.com

Parker, Donald L.; CTO, QMS Inc.; US; 334/633-4300, dparker@rd.qms.com

Parker, Fred; Dir Mktng, CERFnet; US; 619/455-3900, fparker@cerf.net

Parker, H. Dennison; Pres & Pblr, GIS World Inc.; US; 970/223-4848

Parker, Huling H.; Pres & COO, Omnicomp Graphics Corp.; US; 713/464-2990

Parker, Jeff; Pblr, Directions on Microsoft; US; 206/882-3396

Parker, Keith R.; Ed, Data Analysis Group; US; 707/539-3009

Parker, Kevin; Ed, Manufacturing Systems; US; 708/665-1000

Parker, Reny; VP, Data Analysis Group; US; 707/539-3009

Parker, Robert G.; VP Mktng, Atria Software; US; 617/676-2400

Parker, Steve; Pres, Parker, Nichols & Co. Inc.; US; 508/369-2100

Parker, Tim; Tech Ed, SCO World; US; 415/941-1550, timp@scoworld.com

Parket, Brad; Founder, American Internet Corp.; US; 617/276-4500

Parkinson, Joseph L.; Chmn, Pres & CEO, Integrated Information Technology Inc.; US; 408/727-1885

Parks, Bob; VP Mktng, Kentek Information Systems Inc.; US; 303/440-5500

Parks, Tricia; Pres, Parks Associates; US; 214/490-1113

Parkus, Lawrence; VP Corp Dev, Computer Sciences Corp.; US; 310/615-0311

Parman, Joan; VP, G.R. Good Communications; US; 206/486-4446

Parra, Victor; Pres, Electronic Messaging Assoc.; US; 703/524-5550

Parrish, Charles M.; GM Mobile Data, GTE Personal Communications Services; US; 404/391-8000

Parrish, Dave; SVP Amer Ops, Walker Interactive Systems Inc.; US; 415/495-8811

Parrish, Edward A.; Ed-in-Chief, Computer Magazine; US; 908/981-0060, computer@wpi.edu

Parrish, Ronald L.; VP Corp Dev, Tandy Corp.; US; 817/390-3700

Parrish, Tom; Ed, Mobile Computing Technology; US; 770/955-2500

Parrotta, Frank; EVP Corp Dev, Telus; Canada; 403/498-7311

Parson, Laurence D.; VP & GM, Glare/Guard; US

Parsons, Bob; Pres, Parsons Technology Inc.; US; 319/395-9626

Parsons, John A.; Chmn & Pres, Micro-Integration Corp.; US; 301/689-0800

Parsons, Keith; Tech Mgr, Network Professional Assoc.; US; 801/379-0330

Parsons, Roger B.; Pres & CEO, Delphax Systems; US; 617/828-9917

Parzybok, William G.; Chmn & CEO, Fluke Corp.; US; 206/347-6100

Paschal, Allen; Pres & CEO, DataTimes Corp.; US; 405/751-6400

Paschal, John M.; Pres DataTimes Info Partner, DataTimes Corp.; US; 405/751-6400

Passaro, Lou; EVP Ops, SyQuest Technology Inc.; US; 510/226-4000

Passmore, David; Pres, Decisys Inc.; US; 703/742-5400, dpassmore@decisys.com

Pasturel, Marc; CEO, Soleil Software; US; 415/494-0114

Pasturel, Ragni; Pres & COO, Soleil Software; US; 415/494-0114

Patalano, Salvatore F.; COO, LaserScan Systems Inc.; US; 305/777-1300

Pate, Donald; VP Sales, BusLogic Inc.; US; 408/492-9090

Patel, Mukesh; Sr Ops, SMART Modular Technologies; US; 510/623-1231

Patel, Shirish; Pres, CoSystems Inc.; US; 408/522-0500, shirish@cosystems.com

Paterson, Colin; Sec, Franklin Datacom Inc.; US; 805/373-8688

Patil, Suhas S.; Chmn & EVP, Cirrus Logic Inc.; US; 510/623-8300

Patono, Patti; Dir Spec Projects, J.D. Power & Associates; US; 818/889-6330

Patrick, Chuck; Dir Dev, Bluestone Inc.; US; 609/727-4600

Patrick, John; VP Mktng, Davidson & Associates Inc.; US; 310/793-0600

Patterson, Dave; Chmn, Computing Research Assoc. Inc.; US; 202/234-2111

Patterson, David F.; VP Sales & Mktng, Datatrac Corp.; US; 770/552-3866

Patterson, James L.; Chmn, Clarify Inc.; US; 408/428-2000

Patterson, Neal L.; Chmn & CEO, Cerner Corp.; US; 816/221-1024

Patterson, Wayne; Chmn & CEO, Texas Microsystems Inc.; US; 713/541-8200

Patton, Carole; Pblr, Mendham Technology Group; US; 201/543-2273

Patton Jr., Bill; GM, Patton & Patton Software Corp.; US; 408/778-6557

Patton Sr., William L.; Pres, Patton & Patton Software Corp.; US; 408/778-6557

Patty, Alan P.; SVP Sales, Inference Corp.; US; 415/899-0100

Paty, Diana; Dir Sales, Odyssey Development Inc.; US; 303/689-9998

Paul, Larry; Bus Mgr, Thomas Public Relations Inc.; US; 516/549-7575

Paul, Lois; Pres, Lois Paul & Partners; US; 617/238-5700

Paulet, Bruno; Pres, Apsylog Inc.; US; 415/812-7700

Paulsen, Paul; VP, J2 Marketing Services; US; 714/529-2527

Paustian, Chuck; Mng Ed, Crain Communications Inc.; US; 312/649-5260

Pavia, Jim; Ed-in-Chief, Dealerscope Consumer Electronics Marketplace; US; 215/238-5300, jpavia@napco.com

Pavicic, Brian; Dir Sales, InfoAccess Inc.; US; 206/747-3203

Pavlovic, Nick; CEO, Visual Information Development Inc.; US; 818/358-3936

Pavoney, Howard; Pres, Micros-To-Mainframes Inc.; US; 914/268-5000

Pawlik, Michael M.; VP Mktng, Burr-Brown Corp.; US; 602/746-1111

Paxton, Cathy; Owner, Synthesis Inc.; US; 360/671-0458

Paxton, G. Ward; Chmn, Pres & CEO, Optical Data Systems Inc.; US; 214/234-6400

Paxton, Tim; Pres, Synthesis Inc.; US; 360/671-0458

Payne, A. Brent; Pres, DataCal Corp.; US; 602/831-3100

Payne, Anna; Partner, EDI, spread the word!; US; 214/243-3456

Payne, David; VP Fin & Ops, Traveling Software Inc.; US; 206/483-8088

Payne, John; Pres, Ex Machina Inc.; US; 212/843-0000

Payne, Robert; Partner, EDI, spread the word!; US; 214/243-3456

Payne, T. Hunt; SVP Sales & Mktng, Komag Inc.; US; 408/946-2300

Payne-Taylor, Christopher; Dir Mktng, Japan Entry; US; 508/352-7788

Payre, Denis; COO, Business Objects Inc.; US; 408/973-9300

Pazian, Steve; Pres & CEO, Mobile-Comm; US; 601/966-0888

Peager, Jeff; Adv Mgr, Azerty Inc.; US; 716/662-0200

Peak, Michael; Principal, Peak Public Relations; US; 408/446-0407

Pearce, John; CEO, MediaMap; US; 617/374-9300

Pearce, Linwood; CEO, Template Software Inc.; US; 703/318-1000, lin.pearce@template.com

Pearce, Richard; Pres, Ca$hGraf; US; 813/528-2477

Pearkins, Jon; Pres, Adiant Corp.; Canada; 403/998-0607

Pearlman, Earl; Pres & CEO, MTI Technology Corp.; US; 714/970-0300

Pearlman, Ellen; Ed-in-Chief, HomePC; US; 516/562-7673

Pearlman, Lawrence; Chmn, Pres & CEO, Ceridian Corp.; US; 612/853-8100

Pearlstine, Norman; Pres, Technology & Media; US

Pearson, Resa Quinn; Principal, Pearson Communications; US; 408/496-5885

Peck, Darryl; Pres, Cyberian Outpost Inc.; US; 203/927-2050,

dpeck@cybout.com

Peck, Richard; VP Bus Dev, O'Reilly & Associates Inc.; US; 707/829-0515

Peddie, Jon; Ed-in-Chief, Jon Peddie Associates; US; 415/435-1775, 71250.2146@compuserve.com

Peder, Alex; VP Sales, Virtual I/O Inc.; US; 206/382-7410

Pedersen, Severen; Dir Sales, Aspen Systems Inc.; US; 303/431-4606, severenp@aspsys.com

Pederson, Esther; VP Mktng, P&L Associates; US; 714/633-5308

Pederson, Robin; SVP WW Sales & Mktng, Great Plains Software; US; 701/281-0550

Pedrick, Donna J.; VP Human Res, SunGard Data Systems Inc.; US; 610/341-8700

Peebler, Robert P.; Pres, CEO & COO, Landmark Graphics Corp.; US

Peed, Tom; Pblr, Peed Corp.; US; 402/479-2141

Peeler, John R.; VP, Dynatech Corp.; US; 617/272-6100

Peffer, Paul; Pres & CEO, Colorbus Inc.; US; 714/852-1850

Pegan, Mike; EVP Sales & Mktng, IDG Books Worldwide; US; 415/655-3000

Peisel, William; VP Eng, Digital Products Inc.; US; 617/647-1234

Peitler, Michael A.; VP WW Sales, Emulex Corp.; US; 714/662-5600

Pelc, Solomon; VP Sales, Opus Systems Inc.; US; 408/562-9340, spelc@opus.com

Pell Jr., Richard; Mgng Ed, Electronic Products; US; 516/227-1300

Pellatt, Peter; CFO, Abacus Accounting Systems Inc.; Canada; 403/488-8100

Pelletier, Jerry; Pres, Imateq Systems Corp.; Canada; 403/285-9551

Pelowski, Kenneth R.; VP Bus Dev, Quantum Corp.; US; 408/894-4000

Peltz, David; Pres, CADventures; US; 818/998-6157

Pemberton, Adam C.; Pblr, CD-ROM Professional; US; 203/761-1466

Pemberton, Jefferey K.; Pblr, Online User; US; 203/761-1466

Pemberton, Robert A.; Chmn & CEO, Software 2000 Inc.; US; 508/778-2000

Pence, John; Pres, Ontrack Computer Systems Inc.; US; 612/937-1107

Pence, Roger; Ed, Roger Pence's Microsoft & the AS/400 Letter; US; 617/444-5755

Pencsak, Nancy; Partner, Channel Strategies Inc.; US; 415/614-3740, npencsak@chanstrat.com

Pendell, Chuck; VP Sales, Action Technologies Inc.; US; 510/521-6190

Peng, Steve; VP Info, Twinbridge Software Corp.; US; 213/263-3926

Penn, Richard J.; VP Sales & Mktng, Hutchinson Technology Inc.; US; 612/587-3797

Pensak, David; CTO, Raptor Systems

Inc.; US; 617/487-7700

Peppard, Brad; VP Mktng, Software Publishing Corp.; US; 408/537-3000

Pepper, Jeff; Pres & CEO, ServiceWare Inc.; US; 412/826-1158

Pepper, Jeffrey M.; VP & Ed Dir, AP Professional; US; 619/699-6735, publisher@igc.org

Pepper, John; Pres, Pepper & Associates Inc.; US; 913/345-8008

Perakis, James A.; Pres & CEO, Hyperion Software; US; 203/703-3000

Peranich, David; Dir Sales, Decisive Technology Corp.; US; 415/528-4300

Perc, Julius; VP Eng, Univision Technologies Inc.; US; 617/221-6700

Perenon, Adrian; Dir Mktng, Brooks/Cole Publishing Co.; US; 408/373-0728, adrianperenon@brookscole.com

Perez-Mendez, Ivan; Pres, Speech Systems Inc.; US; 303/938-1110

Perham, Leonard; Pres & CEO, Integrated Device Technology Inc.; US; 408/727-6116

Perich, Silvio; SVP Sales, Sigma Designs Inc.; US; 510/770-0100

Perik, Michael J.; Chmn & CEO, SoftKey International Inc.; US; 617/494-1200

Perkel, Gerry; Pres, Tektronix Color Printing & Imaging Div.; US; 503/685-3150

Perkins, Anthony B.; Pblr, Herring Communications Inc.; US; 415/865-2277, tony@herring.com

Perkins, Carl C.; Pres & CEO, New Media Corp.; US; 714/453-0100

Perkins, Jeffrey; Pres, Circuit Research Corp.; US; 603/880-4000

Perkins, Jim; Pres, Formgen; US; 602/443-4109

Perkins, Kathy; Dir Mktng, Odyssey Development Inc.; US; 303/689-9998

Perkins, Michael C.; Sr Ed, Red Herring, The; US; 415/865-2277

Perkins, Russell; Pres, Multimedia Business & Marketing Sourcebook; US; 215/238-5300

Perlegos, George; Chmn, Pres & CEO, Atmel Corp.; US; 408/441-0311

Perloff, Ronald S.; Pres, XLNT Designs Inc.; US; 619/487-9320

Perrault, Bill; VP Mktng & Sales, Compton's NewMedia Inc.; US; 619/929-2500

Perrett, George W.; VP, Interface Systems Inc.; US; 313/769-5900

Perrier, Carolyn; Dir Peripheral Mktng, Canon Computer Systems Inc.; US; 714/438-3000

Perrin, Charles R.; CEO, Duracell Int'l.; US; 203/791-3010

Perrin, George M.; Chmn, Paging Network Inc.; US; 214/985-4100

Perrin, Mark C.; SVP Bus Dev, Digital Systems Int'l.; US; 206/881-7544

Perrins, Gordon; SVP R&D, Relay Technology Inc.; US; 703/506-0500

Perry, Chris; Dir Mktng, Falco Data

Products; US; 408/745-7123

Perry, Harriett; VP, Jostens Home Learning; US; 619/587-0087

Perry, Michael; Dir MIS, Spectragraphics Corp.; US; 619/450-0611

Perry, Randy; Sales Mgr, Aspen Systems Inc.; US; 303/431-4606, randyp@asp-sys.com

Perry, Robert N.; SVP, River Run Software Group; US; 203/861-0090

Perry, Shelley; Dir Mktng, Logic Works Inc.; US; 609/514-1177

Person, Carol; Exec Ed, Macworld; US; 415/243-0505

Persson, Conrad; Ed, Electronic Servicing & Technology; US; 913/492-4857, cpersedit@aol.com

Perusse, Dawn; Pres, Corporate Solutions; US

Pesko, Rebecca M.; Assoc Pblr, Print on Demand Business; US; 617/834-0001

Pesko, Jr., Charles A.; Pblr, Print on Demand Business; US; 617/834-0001

Pesochinsky, Nina; Partner, Erich Stein Communications; US; 303/722-4343

Peter, Albert F.; Pres & CEO, Structural Dynamics Research Corp.; US; 513/576-2400

Peters, Eric C.; VP Tech, Avid Technology Inc.; US; 508/640-6789

Peters, Frank; Pres, Franklin Datacom Inc.; US; 805/373-8688

Peters, Gale; VP Sales & Mktng, Datacap Systems Inc.; US; 215/699-7051

Peters, Richard A.; EVP Sales & Mktng, Rexon Inc.; US; 216/349-0600

Peterschmidt, David C.; EVP & COO, Sybase Inc.; US; 510/922-3500

Petersen, James F.; Chmn, Best Programs Inc.; US; 703/709-5200

Petersen, Kent; VP, Iiyama North America; US; 215/957-6543

Peterson, Allen; EVP, Fourth Shift Corp.; US; 612/851-1900

Peterson, Bob; Dir Merge Prod, Locus Computing Corp.; US; 310/670-6500, bobp@locus.com

Peterson, Cornelius; Pres & CEO, Digital Products Inc.; US; 617/647-1234

Peterson, Daniel S.; Pres, Musicware; US; 206/881-9797

Peterson, Eric; Pres, Cambridge Software Group Inc.; US; 617/577-0600, eric-peterson@csgnotes@notes.net

Peterson, Gwen; VP Mktng, Clarity Software Inc.; US; 415/691-0320, info@.clarity.com

Peterson, Jack H.; Dir Strat Plng, ActionTec Electronics Inc.; US; 408/739-7000

Peterson, John E.; Admin of Ops, Business Applications Performance Corp.; US; 408/988-7654

Peterson, Marc; Pres, Personics Corp.; US; 508/658-0040

Peterson, Marco D.; VP Mktng, Datawatch Corp.; US; 508/988-9700

Peterson, Mary Margaret; Mgng Ed, UniForum Monthly; US; 408/986-8840, meg@uniforum.org

Peterson, Michael; Pres, Strategic Research Corp.; US; 805/569-5610

Peterson, Pete; Fitnesoft Inc.; US; 801/221-7777

Peterson, Richard; VP, Vision's Edge Inc.; US; 904/386-4573

Peterson, Ronald A.; CEO, Spirit of St. Louis Software Co.; US; 314/530-0757

Peterson, Scott A.; Pres, Byte by Byte Corp.; US; 512/795-0150

Peterson, Terry; Ed, Business System Magazine; US; 814/664-8624

Peterson, Thomas L.; VP, Musicware; US; 206/881-9797

Peterson, Tom; Nat'l Sales Mgr, Management Graphics Inc.; US; 612/854-1220

Peterson, Vernon C.; CFO, Byte by Byte Corp.; US; 512/795-0150

Peterson, Wayne D.; Pres Local Telecom Div, Sprint Corp.; US; 913/624-3000

Peterson, William T.; VP Mktng, Artisoft Inc.; US; 520/670-7100

Peth, John W.; EVP & COO, Tab Products Co.; US; 415/852-2400

Petracca, Steve; Chmn, Micro Channel Developers Assoc.; US; 916/222-2262

Petralia, Ronald P.; VP Sales, MicroSpeed Inc.; US

Petrocelli, Pat; CFO, Chinon America Inc.; US; 310/533-0274

Petronis, Scott; Assist Ed, MapWorld Magazine; US; 518/285-7340

Petsch, Gregory E.; SVP Corp Ops, Compaq Computer Corp.; US; 713/370-0670

Petska-Juliussen, Karen; Chmn & Ed-in-Chief, Computer Industry Almanac Inc.; US; 702/749-5053, cialmanac@aol.com

Petterson, Leif; Pres, Trio Information Systems; US; 919/846-4990

Pettinella, Nicholas A.; VP & CFO, Intermetrics Inc.; US; 617/661-1840

Pettis, Chuck; SVP, Floathe Johnson Associates Inc.; US; 206/285-6056

Pettit, Larry R.; CEO, Pettit & Co. P.C.; US; 214/458-2221

Petty, George K.; Pres & CEO, Telus; Canada; 403/498-7311

Pettyjohn, Bruce; Pres, Artistic Visions; US; 408/378-1435

Peverell, Raymond E.; SVP Sales & Mktng, Network Equipment Technologies Inc.; US; 415/366-4400

Pfeiffer, Eckhard; Pres & CEO, Compaq Computer Corp.; US; 713/370-0670

Pfeiffer, Jay; Pres, Pfeiffer Public Relations Inc.; US; 303/393-7044

Phan, Mitchell; VP, Alpha Systems Lab Inc.; US; 714/252-0117

Phee, Howard; CFO, DynaTek Automation Systems Inc.; Canada; 902/832-3000

Phelan, Ken; CEO, MicroBiz Corp; US; 201/512-0900

Phelan, Mark; EVP Sales & Mktng,

Checkfree Corp.; US; 614/825-3000

Phelan, Susan; VP Sales & Svcs, SPSS Inc.; US; 312/329-2400

Phelps, Barry; Chmn, Micom Communications Corp.; US; 805/583-8600

Philippe, Greg; VP Intl Sales, Software Clearing House Inc.; US; 513/579-0455, gphilippe@sch.com

Phillips, Bob; VP Ops, Vitesse Semiconductor Corp.; US; 805/388-3700

Phillips, C. Vincent; Pres, Symmetry Group, The; US; 614/431-2667

Phillips, Dan; VP Sales, Concord Communications Inc.; US; 508/460-4646

Phillips, Gary; Mktng Dir, Micro Computer Systems Inc.; US; 214/659-1624

Phillips, Howard; VP Prod Dev, Splash Studios Inc.; US; 206/882-0300

Phillips, J. Richard; CEO, TMS Inc.; US

Phillips, John; Pres, Technology Transfer Institute; US; 310/394-8305

Phillips, Jon; Ed, Blaster; US

Phillips, Leonard; Pres, Trade Quotes Inc.; US; 617/492-0600

Piazza, Maryanne; Dir Mktng, Grolier Electronic Publishing Inc.; US; 203/797-3500

Picard, Dennis J.; Chmn & CEO, Raytheon Co.; US; 617/862-6600

Pick, Ed; VP, FDP Corp.; US; 305/858-8200

Pickering, Mark; Tech Dir, AdLib MultiMedia Inc.; Canada; 418/522-6100

Pieper, Roel; Pres & CEO, UB Networks; US; 408/496-0111

Pieplow, Daniel; VP Fin & Ops, Micro Design Int'l. Inc.; US; 407/677-8333

Pierce, Craig C.; Pblr, Lotus Publishing Corp.; US; 617/482-8634

Pierce, Craig S.; Pblr, IDG Newsletters Corp.; US; 617/482-8785

Pierce, Glenn A.; Pres & COO, Vtel; US; 512/314-2700

Pierce, Mark; VP Sales, JourneyWare Media; US; 510/254-4520, 73052.73@compuserve.com

Pierce, Michael L.; EVP Ops, ADFlex Solutions Inc.; US; 602/963-4584

Piercey, Chuck; Exec Dir, International Association of HP Computing Professionals; US; 408/747-0227

Pierrat, Michel; Pres & CEO, EncyNova Int'l.; US; 303/404-3583, pierrat@csn.net

Pietrelli, Kenneth D.; VP Corp Svcs, Optical Coating Laboratory Inc.; US; 707/545-6440

Pietropaolo, Joseph J.; VP & CFO, Gtech Corp.; US; 401/392-1000

Pikcilingis, David; Pres, Boston Business Computing Ltd.; US; 508/725-3222, dcpik@bbc.com

Pilch, Patrick D.; CFO, Andrea Electronics Corp.; US

Pile, Jim; Ed, Do It With Microsoft Office For Windows; US; 617/482-8785

Pilsbury, Kane; VP Fin, Sytron Corp.; US; 508/898-0100

Pimentel, Albert A.; SVP & CFO, LSI Logic Corp.; US; 408/433-8000

Pinalto, Larry; CFO, MITI; US; 415/326-5000, larryp@miti.com

Pine, Ted; Principal, InfoTech; US; 802/763-2097

Pinkerton, Janet; Mgng Ed, Dealerscope Consumer Electronics Marketplace; US; 215/238-5300, jpinkerton@napco.com

Pinkus, Claudio; Pres, IDOC Inc.; US; 310/446-4666, claudio@idocinc.com

Pinsonneault, Alan; VP Ops, Mannesmann Tally Corp.; US; 206/251-5500

Pinter, Marco; Pres, Digital Media Int'l.; US; 805/563-9490

Pipe, Ron; Pres, Pinnacle Business Systems Inc.; US; 508/429-5936

Pipkin, Chester; Pres, Belkin Components; US; 310/898-1100

Pipp, Frank J.; Chmn, Xylogics Inc.; US; 617/272-8140

Pippin, John E.; Chmn & CEO, LXE; US; 770/447-4224

Pirnazar, Sam; Founder, TDC Interactive; US; 310/452-6720

Pisacreta, Edward; Ed, Computer Law Strategist; US; 212/779-9200

Pittard, M. Tarlton; Vice Chmn & CFO, First Financial Management Corp.; US; 770/857-0001

Pittenger, Wayne A.; VP Ops, Sequent Computer Systems Inc.; US; 503/626-5700

Pittman, Gary; Pres & CEO, Publications & Communications Inc.; US; 512/250-9023

Pittsman, Santo J.; VP & CFO, MobileComm; US; 601/966-0888

Pizzarro, Richard; Chief Eng, Insoft Inc.; US; 717/730-9501

Planitzer, Russell E.; Chmn & CEO, Computervision Corp.; US; 617/275-1800

Plansky, Paul L.; Ed, HTE Research Inc.; US; 415/871-4377

Plant, Donald; Controller, Factura Kiosks Inc.; US; 716/264-9600

Plante, Paul J.; VP & CFO, Reptron Electronics Inc.; US; 813/854-2351

Plante, Richard A.; Pres & COO, Encad Inc.; US; 619/452-0882

Platt, Lewis E.; Chmn, Pres & CEO, Hewlett-Packard Co.; US; 408/553-4300

Plattner, Hasso; Dep Chmn, SAP AG; Germany; 6227-34-0

Plauger, P.J.; Ed, C/C++ Users Journal; US; 913/841-1631

Plaut, David; VP Sales, Chatham Township Data Corp.; US; 201/586-0700

Plavin, Gary; VP & GM, ASL LCD Inc.; US; 201/896-8888

Pleahn, Martin; EVP, Wavefront Technologies Inc.; US; 805/962-8117

Pleso, Joseph F.; VP WW Sales, QLogic Corp.; US; 714/438-2200

Plimpton, Jack; Pres, Japan Entry; US; 508/352-7788

Plotkin, Joyce; Exec Dir, Massachusetts

Software Council Inc.; US; 617/437-0600

Plumer, Chris; EVP, KSK Communications; US; 703/734-1880

Podradchik, Steven; Pres, Medio Multimedia Inc.; US; 206/867-5500

Poduska, John W.; Chmn, Advanced Visual Systems Inc.; US; 617/890-4300

Poei, Robin; Dir Ops, NewGen Systems Corp.; US; 714/641-8600

Poertner, Rainer; Pres & CEO, Syncronys Softcorp; US; 310/842-9203

Pogue, David; CEO, Stackig; US; 703/734-3300

Poindexter, Valerie; VP AD Sales, Asay Publishing Co.; US; 417/781-9317

Poitras, Adrian J.; Ed, Computer Technology Trends: Analyses & Forecasts; US; 512/258-8898

Polasky, Carol; CFO, Dallas Digital Corp.; US; 214/424-2800

Poler, Ariel; Pres, Internet Profiles Corp.; US; 415/322-9600

Polifrone, Anthony; Pres, Buyers Laboratory Inc.; US; 201/488-0404

Polinsky, Mark; CEO, VisionTek Inc.; US; 708/360-7500

Polishuk, Paul; Pres, Information Gatekeepers Inc.; US; 617/738-8088, igiboston@aol.com

Polishuk, Peter; Mktng Mgr, Information Gatekeepers Inc.; US; 617/738-8088

Polisseni, Eugene R.; VP Mktng, Paychex Inc.; US; 716/385-6666

Politi, Stan; Pblr, Computer Currents Publishing Inc.; US; 510/547-6800

Politis, David L.; Pres, Politis & Associates; US; 801/569-2592, dpolitis@altatech.com

Pollack, Robert S.; VP Mktng, Raritan Computer Inc.; US; 908/874-4072

Pollak, David; Pres, Athena Design Inc.; US; 617/617-6372

Pollare, Carrie; EVP, DISC Distributing Corp.; US; 310/787-6800

Polley, R. Stephen; Chmn & CEO, Interphase Corp.; US; 214/919-9000

Pollizzi III, Joseph A.; Pres, Digital Equipment Computer Users Society; US; 508/841-3346

Pollock, Bruce; CFO, Walker Interactive Systems Inc.; US; 415/495-8811

Pollock, John; Chmn & CEO, Electrohome Ltd.; Canada; 519/744-7111

Pollock, Steve; VP Prod Mktng, Claris Corp.; US; 408/987-7000

Poludnewycz, Andrei; EVP Prod, Information Management Associates Inc.; US; 203/925-6800

Pomerantz, Anita; Contr Ed, Process Insight Review; US; 716/264-9700

Pontcher, Lynn; Admin Dir, International Information Management Congress; US; 303/440-7085

Pontikes, William N.; EVP, Comdisco Inc.; US; 847/698-3000

Pool, David; Pres, CompuServe Internet Div.; US; 206/447-0300

Poole, Sam; Pres, Maxis; US; 510/933-5630

Pope, David; Ed Dir, Digital Imaging; US; 310/212-5802

Pope, James W.; VP & CFO, E-Systems Inc.; US; 214/661-1000

Pope, Stephen T.; Ed, Computer Music Journal; US; 617/253-2889, cmj@cnmat.cnmat.berkeley.edu

Popek, Gerald J.; Chmn, Locus Computing Corp.; US; 310/670-6500

Poper, Toni; Pres, Linker Systems Inc.; US; 714/552-1904, tmp@linker.com

Popkin, Jan; Chief Scientist, Popkin Software & Systems Inc.; US; 212/571-3434

Popolo, Joseph V.; EVP, Programmer's Paradise Inc.; US; 908/389-8950, jpopolo@programmers.com

Poppa, Ryal R.; Chmn, Pres & CEO, Storage Technology Corp.; US; 303/673-5020

Poppel, Harvey; Partner, Broadview Associates; US; 201/461-7929

Porat, Eli; Pres & CEO, DSP Group Inc.; US; 408/986-4300

Porter, Gerald R.; Pres Info Mgmt, Systems & Computer Technology Corp.; US; 610/647-5930

Porter, James N.; Pres, Disk/Trend Inc.; US; 415/961-6209

Porter, James R.; Pres & CEO, Triad Systems Corp.; US; 510/449-0606

Porter, Jeffrey; VP Eng, Scala Inc.; US; 703/713-0900

Porter, John A.; Vice Chmn, LDDS WorldCom; US; 601/360-8600

Porter, Julie; VP & Consultant, Kawalek & Assoc.; US; 415/296-7744

Porter, Michael J.; Pres, Porter, Le Vay & Rose Inc.; US; 212/564-4700

Porter, Patrick L.; Ed-in-Chief, Software Magazine; US; 508/366-2031

Porter, Robyn M.; Sr Acct Exec, FSA Corp.; Canada; 403/264-4822

Porter, Scott; CFO, Parsons Technology Inc.; US; 319/395-9626

Porter, Stephen; Ed, Computer Graphics World; US; 603/891-0123, stevep@pennwell.com

Porter, Thomas A.; Pblr & GM, Discovery Channel, The; US; 301/986-1999

Porter-Zasada, Martine; VP Sales & Mktng, VeriTest Inc.; US; 310/450-0062

Portesy, Tom; VP, Blenheim Group US Inc.; US; 201/346-1400, tportesy@blenheim.com

Porto, Bryan D.; VP, MPSI Systems Inc.; US; 918/250-9611

Post, Grace; VP Mktng, Verity Group Inc.; US; 714/680-9611

Posth, Mark L.; Ed, MacHome Journal; US; 415/957-1911

Postman, Joel; Pres, TPS Electronics; US; 415/988-0141

Potosnak, Brenda A.; Controller & Treas, Star Technologies Inc.; US; 703/689-4400

Potsus, Whitney; Asst Ed, PC Novice; US; 402/479-2141

Potter, David; Chmn & CEO, Psion Inc.; US; 508/371-0310

Potter, Michael U.; Chmn & CEO, Cognos Inc.; Canada; 613/738-1440

Potter, Robert J.; Pres, R.J. Potter Co.; US; 214/869-8270

Potts, Gary; Pres & CEO, Maxoptix Corp.; US; 510/353-9700

Potts, Rodney; Chmn, Coda Inc.; US; 603/647-9600

Potwin, Lucien; VP HW, Smart Technologies Inc.; Canada; 403/245-0333

Poupart, Andrew; VP Ops, Component Integration Laboratories; US; 408/864-0300

Powell, Beverly; VP Sales, Quintus Corp.; US; 510/624-2818

Powell, Bill; VP Bus Strat, Aspen; US; 404/848-7751

Powell, Karl C.; Chmn, Pres & CEO, Sequent Computer Systems Inc.; US; 503/626-5700

Powell, Ronald J.; Pblr & Exec Ed, Data Management Review; US; 414/792-9696, rpowell@dmreview.com

Powell, Ronald J.; Pblr, Powell Publishing Inc.; US; 414/792-9696, rpowell@dmreview.com

Power, Dave; Chmn, J.D. Power & Associates; US; 818/889-6330

Power, Richard; Ed, Computer Security Journal; US; 415/905-2626

Powers, John H.; Exec Dir, Institute of Electrical & Electronics Engineers Inc.; US; 212/705-7900

Powers, Michael; Treas, Connect Tech Inc.; Canada; 519/836-1291, mike@connecttech.com

Powers, Roger W.; Pblr, Dallas/Fort Worth Computer Currents; US; 214/690-6222

Powers, Stephen; VP Eng, Tom Sawyer Software; US; 510/848-0853, spowers@tomsawyer.com

Poynder, Richard; Ed, Information World Review; US; 609/654-6266

Pozzi, Marti; VP Sales, Avantos Performance Systems Inc.; US; 510/654-4600

Prahsker, Dalia; Pres, New Dimension Software; US; 714/757-4300

Prakash, Jay; Pres, Strategic Focus; US; 408/942-1500

Pramberger, Joseph T.; Ed & Pblr, NASA Tech Briefs; US; 212/490-3999

Prather, Ron; VP Sales & Mktng, Epson America Inc.; US; 310/782-0770

Pratt, David; Pres, Digital Vision Inc.; US; 617/329-5400

Pratt, David B.; SVP, Adobe Systems Inc.; US; 415/961-4400

Pratt, Diane; Dir Prod Dev, KnowledgePoint; US; 707/762-0333

Pratt, Gregory A.; Pres & COO, Intelligent Electronics Inc.; US; 610/458-5500

Pratt, John R.; VP Mktng, Digital Vision

Inc.; US; 617/329-5400

Preiss, Byron; Chmn, Pres & CEO, Byron Preiss Multimedia Co. Inc.; US; 212/989-6252

Preller, David; MIS Mgr, Acecad Inc.; US; 408/655-1900

Premo, David; VP Grp Pbls, Argus Integrated Media; US; 303/220-0600

Presley, Jerry; VP, Micro Computer Systems Inc.; US; 214/659-1624

Presotto, David L.; Ed, Computing Systems; US; 617/253-2889, journal@usenix.org

Prestige, James A.; EVP, Teradyne Inc.; US; 617/482-2700

Preston, Richard T.; Pres & CEO, Common Grounds Software Inc.; US; 415/802-5800, rpreston@commonground.com

Preuninger, Don; VP New Tech, ProtoView Development Co.; US; 609/655-5000

Previte, Richard; Pres & COO, Advanced Micro Devices Inc.; US; 408/732-2400

Price, Beverly; VP, FDP Corp.; US; 305/858-8200

Price, John; VP Mktng, Trilogy Development Group; US; 512/794-5900

Price, Timothy F.; Pres, MCI Business Markets; US; 404/698-8000

Priestly, Ernest; Pres & CEO, Aristo-Soft Inc.; US; 510/426-5355

Prior, Jack; Pres & CEO, Gallium Software Inc.; Canada; 613/721-0902, jprior@gallium.com

Pritchard, William L.; VP PR, Fisher Business Communications Inc.; US; 714/556-1313

Privateer, Pete; SVP Ops, Axent Technologies; US; 301/258-2620

Privitera, Dennis; Exec Dir, Help Desk Institute; US; 719/531-5138

Probst, Lawrence F.; Chmn, Pres & CEO, Electronic Arts; US; 415/571-7171

Probst, Worth; Chmn, Colorbus Inc.; US; 714/852-1850

Procassini, Andrew; Pres, Semiconductor Industry Assoc.; US; 408/436-6600

Proctor, Joseph; VP Info Syst, Advanced Micro Devices Inc.; US; 408/732-2400

Proesel, Ronald; Pres, MicroSolutions Inc.; US; 815/756-3411

Prokosch, Wilson; VP NA Sales, Olicom US; US; 214/423-7560, wilsonp@smtpgwy@olicom-us.com

Prophet, Andy; Pres, AP Research; US; 408/253-6567

Prothro, C.V.; Chmn, Pres & CEO, Dallas Semiconductor Corp.; US; 214/450-0400

Proudfoot, Mark A.; VP Mktng, Micro-Integration Corp.; US; 301/689-0800

Proudst, William; Romsoft Inc.; US; 305/752-5073, gradient@gosoft.com

Provance, Michael; Bus Mgr, Internet Group Inc., The; US; 412/688-9696, pra@tig.com

Provencher, Karen; Pblr, Unix Business Software Directory; US; 215/643-8000

Prowse, W. James; SVP Mktng, Compuware Corp.; US; 810/737-7300

Pruett, William; EVP, Total Systems Services Inc.; US; 706/649-2204

Pryor, Bill; VP R&D, DeltaPoint Inc.; US; 408/648-4000

Pryor, Douglas; Ed Dir, Computer Publishing Group Inc.; US; 617/739-7001, dpryor@cpg.com

Puckett, Bernard; CEO, Mobile Telecommunications Technologies Corp.; US; 601/944-1300

Puette, Robert L.; Pres & CEO, NetFrame Systems Inc.; US; 408/474-1000

Puffer, C.J.; Pres, Avalon Marcom; US; 707/837-8950, bycjpuffer@aol.com

Pugh, Carl S.; Pres & COO Tradeshow Grp, Mecklermedia Corp.; US; 203/226-6967, cpugh@mecklermedia.com

Pugh, John; Ed, Smalltalk Report, The; US; 212/242-7447

Pugh, Michael; VP Bus Dev, Digital Media Int'l.; US; 805/563-9490, mikeadmi&aol.com

Pulaski, Eric; Pres, LAN Support Group Inc.; US; 713/789-0881

Pulver, Lee J.; Pres, Pulver Laboratories Inc.; US; 408/399-7000

Purcell, David A.; Chmn & CEO, Encad Inc.; US; 619/452-0882

Purcell, Steven; VP & CFO, Micro Warehouse; US; 203/899-4000

Purdom, Ned; VP, Purdom Public Relations; US; 415/588-5700

Purdom, Paul; Pres, Purdom Public Relations; US; 415/588-5700

Purdy, Gloria M.; CFO, Interlink Computer Sciences Inc.; US; 510/657-9800

Purdy, J. Gerry; Pres & CEO, Mobile Insights Inc.; US; 415/390-9800, gpurdy@mobileinsights.com

Purkis, Leonard C.; SVP & CFO, Iomega Corp.; US; 801/778-1000

Purnell, Walt; Pres & CFO, Ardis; US; 708/913-1215

Putterman, Leland D.; VP WW Mktng, BMC Software Inc.; US; 713/918-8800

Putzer, Jerry; VP NA Sales, Scan-Optics Inc.; US; 203/289-6001

Pyles, Jon; Pblr, Stuff You Gotta Know About Windows; US; 502/491-1900

Pytka, Stephen M.; EVP, Biscom Inc.; US; 508/250-1800

Quan, Henry; VP Mktng, ATI Technologies Inc.; Canada; 905/882-2600

Quarles, J.R.; VP Prod Plng, Cadec Systems Inc.; US; 603/668-1010

Queller, Abe; Prod Mgr, ExcellNet Communications; US; 818/340-6430

Quickmire, Carl; Conf Mgr, Special Events Management; US; 803/737-9352, quickmire@sbt.tec.sc.us

Quigley, Bruce T.; Dir Mktng, Smith Micro Software Inc.; US; 714/362-5800, bquigley@smithmicro.com

Quigley, Philip J.; Chmn, Pres & CEO, Pacific Telesis Group; US; 415/394-3000

Quiner, Quent; Sales Mgr, K.I.O. Corp.; US; 915/774-5355

Quinlan, Michael; Pres & CEO, Marcam Corp.; US; 617/965-0220

Quint, Barbara; Ed, Searcher; US; 609/654-6266

Quirk, Kevin; Prod Mgr, Applied Resources Inc.; US; 913/492-8888

Quist, Erik S.; GM, Cyberflix Inc.; US; 615/546-1157, cyberflix@aol.com

Rabe, Mary; Dir Dev, Rogue Wave Software Inc.; US; 541/754-3010

Rabette, Michael S.; COO, Carbela Tek Inc.; US; 415/873-6484

Rabie, Charlie; VP Prod Mgmt, Dataware Technologies Inc.; US; 617/621-0820

Rabin, Neal; Pres, Miramar Systems Inc.; US; 805/966-2432

Rabinowitz, Joseph; CEO, JMR Electronics Inc.; US; 818/993-4801

Rabins, Selwyn; Co-Chmn, AlphaBlox Corp.; US; 617/229-2924

Race, David; VP Strat Plng, Distributed Processing Technology; US; 407/830-5522

Race, Stephen; CEO, Spectrum Holobyte Inc.; US; 510/522-3584

Raddi, William J.; SVP & CTO, Exide Electronics Group; US; 919/872-3020

Rademaker, John; Pres & CEO, Sync Research; US; 714/588-2070

Raduchel, William J.; VP & CIO, Sun Microsystems Inc.; US; 415/960-1300

Rady, Bruce A.; Pres & CEO, TouchVision Systems Inc.; US; 312/714-1400

Raeburn, Anthony; Gen Sec, International Electrotechnical Commission; Switzerland; 22-919-0211

Rafer, Scott; Dir Sales & Mktng, EA Research Inc.; US; 510/867-0967

Rafferty, Mark H.; VP & CFO, FastComm Communications Corp.; US; 703/318-7750

Rafferty, Robin; VP Mktng, Abacus Concepts Inc.; US; 510/540-1949, marketing@abacus.com

Rafuse, Mark; VP & CFO, Liuski International Inc.; US; 770/447-9454

Ragon, Phillip T.; Pres, InterSystems Corp.; US; 617/621-0600

Ragsdale, Stan; VP Ops, Tangram Enterprise Solutions Inc.; US; 919/851-6000, stanr@tesi.com

Rahm, Rusty; Pres, StarNine Technologies Inc.; US; 510/649-4949

Rahvar, David; Gen Partner, Rose Electronics; US; 713/933-7673

Raichyk, Isaac; Pres, Kolvox Communications Inc.; Canada; 416/221-2400

Raikes, Jeffrey S.; SVP, Microsoft Corp.; US; 206/936-4400

Rains, Kevin; CFO, MultiGen; US; 408/261-4100

Raitt, David I.; Ed, Electronic Library, The; US; 609/654-6266

Rajaji, Raghavan; SVP & CFO, BancTec Inc.; US; 214/450-7700

Raleigh, Lisa; Mng Ed, Technology & Media; US

Ramanos, Jack; CEO, Simon & Schuster Interactive; US; 212/698-7187

Rambin, Ron; Pres, Vista Controls; US; 805/257-4430

Ramella, Daniel J.; Pres & COO, Penton Publishing Inc.; US; 216/696-7000

Ramo, John; Pres & COO, Enteractive Inc.; US; 212/221-6559

Ramp, Donald; VP Sales & Mktng, Stonehouse & Co.; US; 214/960-1566

Ramquist, Lars; Pres & CEO, Ericsson; Sweden; 468-719-0000

Ramsdell, Richard; Pres, Passport Corp.; US; 201/634-1100

Ramsey, Donald A.; Pres & CEO, Arcland; US; 610/993-9904

Ramsey, John; Pres & CEO, Access Graphics Inc.; US; 303/938-9333, jramsey@access.com

Ranadive, Vivek; Chmn, Pres & CEO, Tibco Inc.; US; 415/325-1025

Rand, A. Barry; EVP Ops, Xerox Corp.; US; 203/968-3000

Rand, Steve; VP Sales & Mktng, RadioMail Corp.; US; 415/286-7800

Randag, Bill; VP Sales & Mktng, K.I.O. Corp.; US; 915/774-5355

Randag Jr, William F.; VP Sales & Mktng, Datamark Inc.; US; 915/778-1944

Randazzo, Carmen T.; Pres & COO, Thoroughbred Software Int'l. Inc.; US; 201/560-1377

Randesi, Stephen J.; Chmn, Gen 2 Ventures; US; 408/446-2277

Randolph, Marc; VP Mktng, Visioneer; US; 415/812-6400, marc_randolph@visioneer.com

Random, Gary; CEO, Random Access Inc.; US; 404/804-1190, gary@random.com

Ranelli, Melody; CFO, Best Programs Inc.; US; 703/709-5200

Rankin, Ernest; Pres, Rankin Group Ltd., The; US; 714/937-9100

Ransdell, Carl; VP New Tech, Numera Software Corp.; US; 206/622-2233, carlr@numera.com

Ranson, Mal; VP Mktng, Packard Bell; US; 818/865-1555

Ranucci, Rick; Pblr, BradyGames; US; 317/581-3500

Rao, Connie; Asst Ed, Venture Marketing Strategies; US; 408/865-0221

Rao, Potluri M.; Chmn, Raosoft Inc.; US; 206/525-4025

Rao, Shanti R.; Treas, Raosoft Inc.; US; 206/525-4025

Rapalus, Patrice; Dir, Computer Security Institute; US; 415/905-2626, prapalus@mfi.com

Rappaport, Andrew; Pres, Technology Research Group; US; 617/482-4200

Rappaport, Neil; VP Sales, Vitesse Semiconductor Corp.; US; 805/388-3700

Raskin, Robin; Ed, PC Magazine; US; 212/503-5255

Rasmussen, Michael; VP SW Eng, Analogic Corp.; US; 508/977-3000

Rasmussen, Neil M.; VP, American Power Conversion; US; 401/789-5735

Rasmussen, Norman L.; Pres & CEO, SofTech Inc.; US; 616/957-2330

Rasmussen, Paul; Pres & CEO, Beame & Whitside Software Ltd.; US; 919/831-8989

Ratcliffe, Mitch; Ed-in-Chief, Digital Media; US; 415/575-3775, godsdog@dig-media.com

Rathbun, Bob; VP Mktng, Cyberian Outpost Inc.; US; 203/927-2050, rdr@cybout.com

Rattazzi, Gianluca; Pres & CEO, Meridian Data Inc.; US; 408/438-3100

Rauch, Wendy; Pres, Emerging Technologies Group Inc.; US; 516/586-8810, wrauch@etg.com

Raup, Ron; Pres, Coda Music Technology; US; 612/937-9611

Rauth, Ray; Pres, Independent Computer Consultants Assoc.; US; 314/997-4633, 70007.4251@compuserve.com

Ravid, Gonen; Pres, Intelligent Computer Solutions; US; 818/998-5805

Ravitch, Carl; EVP, Audits & Surveys; US; 212/627-9700

Rawson, Andrew; VP Mktng, Magic Solutions Inc.; US; 201/587-1515

Ray, Gene W.; Pres & CEO, Titan Corp.; US; 619/552-9500

Ray, Glenn R.; Pres & CEO, Celeritas Technologies Ltd.; US; 714/367-8650

Ray, Lee; Tech Dir, UniWorx Inc.; US; 619/740-5111

Rayl, Eric; SVP, SkyNotes Inc.; US; 310/577-9332

Raymond, Liz; Actg Mgr, Three Marketeers Advertising Inc.; US; 408/293-3233, liz@3marketeers.com

Raymund, Steven A.; Chmn & CEO, Tech Data Corp.; US; 813/539-7429

Raza, S. Atiq; Chmn, Pres & CEO, Nex-Gen Microsystem; US; 408/435-0202

Razin, Janet; VP, Quality Systems Inc.; US; 714/731-7171

Razin, Sheldon; Chmn & Pres, Quality Systems Inc.; US; 714/731-7171

Razmjoo, Alex; Pres, Procom Technology Inc.; US; 714/852-1000

Rea, Jim; Pres, ProVUE Development; US

Reading, Robert; EVP, Tactics International Ltd.; US; 508/475-4475

Reagan, Michael; EVP & Pblr, Turner Home Entertainment; US; 404/885-0505

Reams, Olin; VP Sales, Visionware; US; 415/325-2113

Reardon, John; GM, RTC Group, The; US; 714/489-7575

Recht, Steve; CFO, Auravision Corp.; US; 510/252-6800, srecht@auravision.com

Recine, Thomas D.; VP Mktng, Linear Technology Corp.; US; 408/432-1900

Recker, Steve; Dir WW Sales, Rockwell Network Systems; US; 805/968-4262, srecker@rns.com

Reda, Ralph; VP Sales, Objectivity; US; 415/254-7100

Redmond, Paul A.; Chmn, Itron Inc.; US; 509/924-9900

Rednick, Melvyn; Pres & CEO, Incomnet Inc.; US; 818/887-3400

Redon, Olivier; Bus Mgr, Localization & Consulting Services; US; 206/443-5627

Reed, Carl; CTO, Genasys II Inc.; US; 970/493-0035, carlr@genasys.com

Reed, Cartwright; Pres, Intelligence At Large Inc.; US; 215/387-6002

Reed, Howard A.; Pblr, Curriculum Administrator; US; 203/322-1300

Reed, Mark E.; VP Sales & Mktng, In Focus Systems Inc.; US; 503/685-8888

Reed, Randall R.; CFO, Microfield Graphics Inc.; US; 503/626-9393

Reed, Robert; Pres, Reed, Revell-Pechar; US; 206/462-4777, breed@rrp.com

Reed, Sandy; Ed-in-Chief, InfoWorld; US; 415/572-7341

Reedy, Matthew C.; Chmn & VP Dev, IQ Software Corp.; US; 770/446-8880

Reeks, Kevin; VP Govt Sys, Argus Systems Group Inc.; US; 217/384-6300

Reese, Roger M.; Pres, Romeo Inc.; US; 310/273-1866

Reeve, Vicki L.; Mgng Ed, Multimedia Monitor; US; 703/241-1799

Rega, Regina; Ed, CD-ROMs in Print; US; 203/226-6967

Regan, Marian; Ed, SRC Newsletter; US; 919/541-9400, marian@src.org

Regberg, Marc; VP, Venture Development Corp.; US; 508/653-9000

Regel, James; VP Sales & Mktng, Verilink Corp.; US; 408/945-1199

Regenbauma, Allan; VP Sales, Network Connection Inc., The; US; 770/751-0889, regenbauma@tnc.www.com

Register, Ron H.; Dep Dir Mgmt, Defense Advanced Research Projects Agency; US; 703/696-2444

Regnier, Scott; Reg Sales Mgr, 4-Sight LC; US; 515/221-3000

Rehfeld, John E.; Pres & CEO, Proxima Corp.; US; 619/457-5500

Rehling, Louise; SVP Prod Dev, SPSS Inc.; US; 312/329-2400

Reichert, Carl; EVP, Cranel Inc.; US; 614/431-8000

Reichle, Bill; Purchasing Mgr, Cyberian Outpost Inc.; US; 203/927-2050

Reid, David T.; VP Sales, Advanced Gravis Computer Technology Ltd.; Canada; 604/431-5020

Reid, Edward J.; Ed, Findex, Worldwide Directory of Market Research Reports; US; 301/961-6700

Reid, Peter C.; VP & CFO, Fulcrum Technologies Inc.; Canada; 613/238-1761

Reid, Sherry; VP Ops, Drake Training & Technologies; US; 612/896-7000

Reimer, John; Pres, SCM Microsystems Inc.; US; 408/395-9292

Reinhart, Frank; Pres & CEO, Linkpro Inc.; US; 714/854-3322

Reisch, Dave; Mgr MIS, Macola Inc.; US; 614/382-5999

Remer, Daniel; Pres, Island Software Corp.; US; 415/491-1000

Remer, Paul; GM, Island Software Corp.; US; 415/491-1000

Reno, John F.; Pres & CEO, Dynatech Corp.; US; 617/272-6100

Repetti, Peter Q.; VP & CFO, Manugistics Inc.; US; 301/984-5000

Repetti, Steven M.; Pres & CTO, Smart-Desk Inc.; US; 714/582-4020

Repp, Timothy J.; VP & CFO, SBE Inc.; US; 510/355-2000

Rericha, Keith C.; EVP, Star Gate Technologies Inc.; US; 216/349-1860

Reseska, Matthew; Pblr, EE Product News; US; 914/949-8500, 73414.1271@compuserve.com

Resovich, Robert; Eng, Smart & Friendly; US; 818/772-8001

Ressier, Richard S.; Chmn & CEO, MAI Systems Corp.; US; 714/580-0700

Rethmeier, Ken; Pblr, CPA PC Network Advisor; US

Reuling, Irvin R.; VP & CFO, Rexon Inc.; US; 216/349-0600

Reusing, Guadalupe; Pres, Memory Experts Int'l.; Canada; 514/333-5010

Reuterdahl, Thomas; VP Prod Dev, GameTek Inc.; US; 305/935-3995

Revell-Pechar, Ann; VP PR, Reed, Revell-Pechar; US; 206/462-4777, annrp@rrp.com

Revis, Jennifer; VP, Technology Solutions; US; 212/696-2000

Reyes, Greg; Pres & CEO, Wireless Access Inc.; US; 408/653-1555

Reyes, Greg L.; VP RF Syst, Norand Corp.; US; 319/369-3100

Reyes, Gregorio; Chmn, Sync Research; US; 714/588-2070

Reynolds, Barry; Pres, Percussion Software Inc.; US; 617/438-9900, barry_reynolds@percussion

Reynolds, Carolanne; VP, Faximum Software Inc.; Canada; 604/925-3600

Reynolds, Clark E.; Chmn, Alpha Microsystems; US; 714/957-8500

Reynolds, Dale; Pres, Workflow Technologies Inc.; US; 602/867-8078

Reynolds, Elen; Dir Sales, Workflow Technologies Inc.; US; 602/867-8078

Reynolds, Jack; Chmn, First Market Research; US; 617/482-9080

Reynolds, Louis R.; Pres & CEO, Electronic Book Technologies Inc.; US; 401/421-9550

Reynolds, Michael; VP Sales, Digital

Impact; US; 918/742-2022

Reynolds, Robert E.; VP Ops, Burr-Brown Corp.; US; 602/746-1111

Reznick, Greg; Pres, Orchid Technology; US; 510/683-0300

Rhein, Arthur; SVP, Pioneer-Standard Electronics Inc.; US; 216/587-3600

Rhines, Walden C.; Pres & CEO, Mentor Graphics Corp.; US; 503/626-7000

Rhoads, Linden; Pres, Virtual I/O Inc.; US; 206/382-7410

Rhodes, Wayne; Ed-in-Chief, 3X/400 Systems Management; US; 708/427-9512, 71333.730@compuserve.com

Rhyins, Will; Pblr, Multimedia Source Book; US; 212/293-3900

Ricca, Steve; Dir Eng, Rockwell Network Systems; US; 805/968-4262, sncca@rns.com

Ricci, Paul A.; Pres, Xerox Desktop Document Systems; US; 415/815-6800

Ricci, Ron; Principal New Bus, Cunningham Communication Inc.; US; 408/982-0400

Ricciardi, L.R.; SVP, International Business Machines Corp.; US; 914/765-1900

Ricciardi, Lucy Rae; VP & CFO, Hyperion Software; US; 203/703-3000

Ricciardi, Wayne; VP Sales & Mktng, Auravision Corp.; US; 510/252-6800, wricciardi@auravision.com

Riccomi, Alfred; Pres, Multimedia Systems; US; 214/644-8875

Rice, Charles B.; VP & Tech Dir, AGE Logic Inc.; US; 619/755-1000

Rice, Donald B.; Pres & COO, Teledyne Inc.; US; 310/551-4306

Rice, Jerry; Dir IS, Chatsworth Products Inc.; US; 818/735-6100

Rice, Marnie; Office Mgr, Center for Software Development; US; 408/494-8378

Rice, Peter J.; CFO, Data Translation Inc.; US; 508/481-3700

Rice, Tom; CEO, FutureTel Inc.; US; 408/522-1400

Rice, William; VP Sales, Pick Systems; US; 714/261-7425

Rice Jr., Willard K.; CEO, Optical Access Int'l.; US; 617/937-3910, rice@oai.com

Rich, Dan; Dir MIS, VisionTek Inc.; US; 708/360-7500

Richard, Douglas; CEO, Visual Software Inc.; US; 818/593-3500, dougr@vis-soft.com

Richard, Eric R.; VP Eng, net.Genesis; US; 617/577-9800

Richards, Bruce; VP, Sirius Software Inc.; US; 513/228-4849, bruce_richards@siriusacct.com

Richards, Claudia; Ed, Marketing Surveys Index; UK; 494-676186

Richards, Craig; VP Mktng, Dun & Bradstreet Software Services Inc.; US; 404/239-2000

Richards, Craig S.; SVP WW Sales, Pro-

teon Inc.; US; 508/898-2800

Richards, N.A.; Dir Mktng, Systems & Software Inc.; US; 714/833-1700, nat@syssoft.com

Richards, Ronald R.; Dir Comm, Systems Management American Corp.; US; 804/461-0559, ronrich@infi.net

Richards, Stu; Mktng Dir, DeLorme Mapping; US; 207/865-1234, richards@delorme.com

Richards, Waldo R.; SVP, Mentor Graphics Corp.; US; 503/626-7000

Richardsen, Bruce; Ed, AMR Report; US; 617/542-6600

Richardson, Belinda; Admin, Blackship Computer Systems Inc.; US; 408/432-7500

Richardson, Bob; Mgr R&D, Ryan-McFarland; US; 512/343-1010

Richardson, Frank M.; Pres & CEO, Firefox Inc.; US; 408/321-8344

Richardson, Jim; VP & CFO, Network General Corp.; US; 415/473-2000

Richardson, Kevin G.; VP Gov Rel, Electronic Industries Assoc.; US; 703/907-7500

Richburg, Joseph; Chmn & CEO, Kaseworks Inc.; US; 770/448-4240

Richell, Elizabeth; VP Mktng, California Software Products Inc.; US; 714/973-0440

Richman, Mitch; COO, InVision Interactive; US; 415/812-7380

Richman, Paul; Chmn & CEO, Standard Microsystems Corp.; US; 516/435-6000

Richmond, Barry; Pres, High Performance Systems Inc.; US; 603/643-9636

Richmond, James; VP, United Innovations; US; 413/533-7500

Rickard, Jack; Ed & Pblr, Boardwatch Magazine; US; 303/973-6038

Rickey, David M.; Pres & CEO, Applied Micro Circuits Corp.; US; 619/450-9333

Ricks, Dennis; Pres & CEO, Crystal-Graphics Inc.; US; 408/496-6175

Riden, Eugene; Dir Bus Rel, Lante Corp.; US; 312/236-5100, eriden@lante.com

Ridenhour, Mike; Pres, Keyspan; US; 510/222-0131

Ridgers, Andrew; VP Eng & Dev, VMark Software Inc.; US; 508/366-3888

Riebel, Steven W.; VP & CFO, Data Race; US; 210/558-1900

Riedler, Alfred; CFO, Bluebird Systems; US; 619/438-2220

Riedman, Laurie; Pres, Riedman Communications Inc.; US; 716/396-3100

Riegel, Dave L.; EVP & COO, Exabyte Corp.; US; 303/442-4333

Riegelsberger, Kevin P.; VP Sales, Platinum Software Corp.; US; 714/453-4000

Rieger, Robert J.; Chmn & CEO, NetCom On-Line Communications Services Inc.; US; 408/345-2600

Rieker, W. Michael; CTO, Software Partners/32 Inc.; US; 508/887-6409

Riera, Joseph D.; VP Info Syst, Apple

Computer Inc.; US; 408/996-1010

Rieves, S.L.; VP Info Syst, Emerson Electric Co.; US; 314/553-2000

Rigas, John; Pres, Microsystems Engineering Co.; US; 630/261-0111

Riley, Bernard L.; VP & CFO, Dataram Corp.; US; 609/799-0071

Riley, Bill; VP Sales, Individual Software Inc.; US; 510/734-6767

Riley, Cynthia; Controller, Z Microsystems Inc.; US; 619/657-1000

Riley, David; Pres & CEO, NeoSoft Corp.; US; 541/389-5489

Riley, Dennis; VP Mktng, InfoBusiness Inc.; US; 801/221-1100

Riley, Michael H.; VP Mktng, Anacomp Inc.; US; 317/844-9666

Rinas, Kay; Dir Bus Dev, MAG Innovision Inc.; US; 714/751-2008

Rinat, Zack; CEO, NetDynamics; US; 415/969-6665

Rinehart, Dave; Co-Chmn, Usability Professional Assoc.; US; 214/233-9107

Riner, Wil; Chmn & CEO, Network Connection Inc., The; US; 770/751-0889

Ring, Ed; CFO, Upside Publishing Co., The; US; 415/377-0950, edring@upside.com

Ringe, Leslie; Pblr, Digital Age; US; 215/643-8000

Rinzel, Michael; Co-author & Ed, America Online Report; US; 212/780-6060

Riopel, Robert J.; CFO, Phoenix Technologies Ltd.; US; 408/654-9000

Ripp, Robert; VP & CFO, AMP Inc.; US; 717/564-0100

Risher, James A.; Pres & CEO, Exide Electronics Group; US; 919/872-3020

Risley, Christopher; Pres & CEO, ON Technology Corp.; US; 617/374-1400, crisley@on.com

Risner, Ray D.; Pres & COO, Southern Electronics Corp.; US; 770/491-8962

Ristow, Beverly; Pres, Beverly Ristow PR; US; 408/247-1564

Rittenbery, Gerry; VP, Kyocera Electronics Inc.; US; 908/560-3400

Rittenmeyer, Ronald; Pres & COO, Merisel Inc.; US; 310/615-3080

Ritz, Charles; Co-Ed, Fortran Users Group; US; 714/441-2022

Rivero, Manuel; Pres, Intelecsis Inc.; US; 210/682-0649

Riviere, George; VP R&D, State Of The Art Inc.; US; 714/753-1222

Rizai, Matthew M.; Pres & CEO, Engineering Animation Inc.; US; 515/296-9908

Rizzi, John; VP Sales, ON Technology Corp.; US; 617/374-1400, jrizzi@on.com

Rizzo, Tony; Ed-in-Chief, NetGuide; US; 516/562-5000, trizzo@cmp.com

Roach, John V.; Chmn, Pres & CEO, Tandy Corp.; US; 817/390-3700

Roach, Stan; EVP Sales & Mktng, Accolade Inc.; US; 408/985-1700

Roach, William R.; EVP WW Sales,

Quantum Corp.; US; 408/894-4000

Robb, Heather; Act Mgr, FitzGerald Communications Inc.; US; 617/494-9500

Robb, Jim; VP WW Sales, FourGen Software Inc.; US; 206/522-0055

Robbins, James; VP R&D, Pinnacle Micro Inc.; US; 714/789-3000

Robbins, Michael; SVP WW Sales, Software Artistry Inc.; US; 317/843-1663

Robbins, Owen W.; EVP & CFO, Teradyne Inc.; US; 617/482-2700

Robert, Chris; Pres & CEO, Epoch Inc.; US; 508/435-1000

Robert, Christopher D.; Pres & CEO, Keyfile Corp.; US; 603/883-3800, chrisrobert@keyfile.com

Roberts, Alan; VP Ops, Soricon Corp.; US; 303/440-2800

Roberts, Buz; Dir Eng, Big Island Communications Inc.; US; 408/342-8300

Roberts, Carol; Dir Fin, Carroll Touch Inc.; US; 512/244-3500

Roberts, Floyd F.; VP, Triton Technologies Inc.; US; 908/855-9440

Roberts, Fred; VP & CFO, Allen Systems Group; US; 941/435-2200

Roberts, Gregg; VP Fin, Ioline Corp.; US; 206/821-2140

Roberts, Janice M.; VP Mktng, 3Com Corp.; US; 408/764-5000

Roberts, John; VP Dev, PeerLogic; US; 415/626-4545

Roberts, Julie W.; Prod Mgr, Vision's Edge Inc.; US; 904/386-4573

Roberts, Linda; Acct Exec, Alexander Auerbach & Co. Inc.; US; 818/501-4221

Roberts, Marshall; Pres, Stonehouse & Co.; US; 214/960-1566

Roberts, Roger; Pres & CEO, Citrix Systems Inc.; US; 305/340-2246

Roberts, William M.; Pres, Brooks/Cole Publishing Co.; US; 408/373-0728

Roberts Jr., Bert C.; Chmn & CEO, MCI Communications Corp.; US; 202/872-1600

Robertson, Kent L.; SVP & CFO, Pyramid Technology Corp.; US; 408/428-9000

Robertson, Les; VP Sales & Mktng, Minuteman; US; 214/446-7363

Robertson, Mark A.; VP Ops, Future Domain Corp.; US; 714/253-0400

Robertson, Michael; VP Sales, PowerQuest Corp.; US; 801/226-8977

Robertson, Sue; EVP, Archetype Inc.; US; 617/890-7544

Robertson, William; Pblr, Corporate Intranet Solutions; US

Robichaud, Eric G.; Pres & CEO, Rhode Island Soft Systems Inc.; US; 401/767-3106, 72662.463@compuserve.com

Robichaud, Rebecca L.; CFO, Rhode Island Soft Systems Inc.; US; 401/767-3106, 71231.2614@compuserve.com

Robinson, Brian; Mgng Ed, Envisioneering; US; 516/783-6244

Robinson, Charles E.; Chmn, Pres & CEO, Pacific Telecom Inc.; US; 360/905-

5800

Robinson, David; EVP Sales, Chorus Systems Inc.; US; 408/879-1350

Robinson, Gene; SVP Mktng & Sales, Viewlogic Systems Inc.; US; 508/480-0881

Robinson, Ian; Dir Prod Mgmt, Starfish Software; US; 408/461-5800

Robinson, Lisa; SVP, Fleishman-Hillard Inc.; US; 213/629-4974

Robinson, Marc; VP & CTO, Sierra Semiconductor Corp.; US; 408/263-9300

Robinson, Marla; Pres, Breakthrough Productions; US; 916/265-0911

Robinson, Richard; Dir SW Dev, Infographix Technologies Inc.; US; 404/523-4944

Robinson, Richard W.; Ed-in-Chief, BBS Magazine; US; 609/953-9110, editor@bbsmag.com

Robinson, Robert A.; Dir Sales, Initio Corp.; US; 408/988-1919

Robinson, Steve; Pres, Panther Software; US; 310/372-6806

Robinson, T.H.; Treas, Reliable Source Inc.; US; 205/660-1960

Robitaille, Patricia J.; VP Info & Bus Syst, Tab Products Co.; US; 415/852-2400

Roblee, Mark; Head Inside Sales, Specular International; US; 413/253-3100, sales@specular.com

Robson, George T.; SVP & CFO, Unisys Corp.; US; 215/986-4011

Roby, Jerry; Pres & CEO, IMC Networks Corp.; US; 714/724-1070, jroby@imcnetworks.com

Rocchio, Victor A.; Chmn & CEO, Technalysis Corp.; US; 612/925-5900

Roche, Bill; Ed-in-Chief, Smart Electronics; US; 714/572-2255

Roche, Jim; VP & GM, Newbridge Microsystems; Canada; 613/599-3600

Roche, Kevin J.; VP & CFO, Dow Jones & Company Inc.; US; 212/416-2000

Rock, Terrence L.; Pres, Convex Computer Corp.; US; 214/497-4000

Rockenbach, Philip C.; CEO, Harmonic Vision; US; 847/467-2395

Rockom, Joseph W.; VP & CFO, Ikos Systems Inc.; US; 408/255-4567

Rodgers, Derryl; Dir Tech Ops, Acucobol Inc.; US; 619/689-7220, derryl@acucobol.com

Rodgers, T.J.; Pres & CEO, Cypress Semiconductor Corp.; US; 408/943-2600

Rodin, Robert; Pres & CEO, Marshall Industries; US; 818/307-6000

Roditti, Esther C.; Ed & Pblr, Computer Law & Tax Report; US; 212/879-3325

Rodrigues, Daniel; Pblr, Circuit Cellar INK: The Computer Applications Journal; US; 860/875-2751

Rodrigues, Tony; Dir Prod Mktng, Orchid Technology; US; 510/683-0300

Rodriguez, Juan; Chmn, Datasonix Corp.; US; 303/545-9500

Rodriguez, P. Steven; VP Mktng &

Sales, Celeritas Technologies Ltd.; US; 714/367-8650

Rodriguez, Richard L.; Pres & COO, Elek-Tek; US; 847/677-7660

Rodts, Gerald; VP & GM, DAP Technologies; US; 813/969-3271

Rodwick, Paul; EVP, Attachmate Corp.; US; 206/644-4010

Roehm, Fred; Mktng Mgr, Extended Systems; US

Roelandts, Willem P.; SVP & GM Comp Syst, Hewlett-Packard Co.; US; 408/553-4300

Roelandts, William P.; CEO, Xilinx Inc.; US; 408/559-7778

Roenker, Gerald G.; COO, QMS Inc.; US; 334/633-4300, roenker@qms.com

Roeser, Robert R.; Pres & CEO, Elo TouchSystems Inc.; US; 615/482-4100

Rogers, A.J.; VP Strategic Mktng, Tektronix Color Printing & Imaging Div.; US; 503/685-3150

Rogers, Bruce; Pres, Rogers Communications; US; 617/224-1100

Rogers, Gary; VP Sales, SQL Financials Int'l.; US; 770/390-3900

Rogers, Gerald D.; Pres & CEO, Cyrix Corp.; US; 214/968-8388

Rogers, John; EVP & CFO, Cognex Corp.; US; 508/650-3000

Rogers, John A.; CFO, Softdesk Inc.; US; 603/428-3199

Rogers, Joseph T.; EVP & CFO, Quantum Corp.; US; 408/894-4000

Rogers, Mark; VP, Folio Corp.; US; 801/344-3700, mrogers@folio.com

Rogers, Maureen; VP Mktng, Softbridge Inc.; US; 617/576-2257

Rogers, Michael; CEO, Ontrack Computer Systems Inc.; US; 612/937-1107

Rogers, Michael; VP Channel Sales, Wall Data Inc.; US; 206/814-9255

Rogers, Mike; Pblr, Computerworld; US; 508/879-0700

Rogers, Scott; Exec Ed, Osborne McGraw-Hill; US; 510/549-6600

Rohrs, Roger; Pblr, Orion Blue Book, Computers; US; 602/951-1114, orion@netzone.com

Roizen, J. Heidi; Pres & CEO, T/Maker Co.; US; 415/962-0195

Rokus, Josef W.; VP & CFO, Galileo Electro-Optics Corp.; US; 508/347-9191

Roland, Paul G.; Chmn, Anacomp Inc.; US; 317/844-9666

Rolland, Kurt E.; CTO & VP Res, Multicom Publishing Inc.; US; 415/777-5300

Rollhaus Jr., Philip E.; Chmn & Pres, Quixote Corp.; US; 312/467-6755

Rollinger, Dennis; CEO, Radiometrics Midwest Corp.; US; 630/932-7262

Rollins, Joel B.; VP & CFO, National Instruments Corp.; US; 512/794-0100

Rollinson, Bill; VP Mktng, Internet Shopping Network; US; 415/842-7400, bill@internet.net

Rollwagen, John; Chmn, Computer

Network Technology Corp.; US; 612/797-6000

Roloff, Jeffrey; Chmn, Central Data Corp.; US; 217/359-8010

Roman, John; Dir Mktng, miro Computer Products Inc.; US; 415/855-0940

Romanies, Mike; SVP, Reed Technology & Information Services Inc.; US; 301/428-3700

Romano, John; R&D Mgr, HP Home Products Div.; US; 408/246-4300

Romei, Lura; Ed, Managing Office Technology; US; 216/696-7000, luraomei@ad.com

Romeo, Carmen V.; EVP & CFO, SEI Corp.; US; 610/254-1000

Romero, Liliana C.; Mgng Ed, US Export Computer Directory; US; 305/253-1440

Romney, Brad; Pres & CEO, Dayna Communications Inc.; US; 801/269-7200, bromney@dayna.com

Romney, Robert E.; Pres & CEO, Zenographics Inc.; US; 714/851-6352

Roncarelli, Robi; Pblr & Ed, Pixel-The Computer Animation News People Inc.; Canada; 416/424-4657

Roome, Hugh; Pblr, Home-Office Computing; US; 212/505-4220

Rooney, Eugene; Pres, Sage Solutions; US; 415/392-7243, gene.rooney@sagesolu.com

Rooney, Thomas D.; VP & CFO, AM International Inc.; US; 847/818-1294

Root, Charles; VP Sales & Mktng, Samtron Displays Inc.; US; 310/537-7000

Ros, Carl W.; EVP & CFO, Ericsson; Sweden; 468-719-0000

Rosati Jr., Joseph A.; VP, ISTR Inc.; US; 716/855-0295

Rose, Bill; Exec Dir, Software Support Professional Assoc.; US; 619/674-4864

Rose, Carl R.; Pres, Cyber-Safe; US; 713/784-2374, carl@da.com

Rose, Daniel; Pres, Rose Associates; US; 415/941-1215

Rose, David S.; Chmn & CEO, Ex Machina Inc.; US; 212/843-0000

Rose, Jasper; Mgr Bus Dev, Fujitsu Active Information; US; jrose@activeinfo.com

Rose, Joe; VP Fin, Basis Int'l.; US; 505/345-5232

Rose, Joe A.; EVP Info Serv, National Data Corp.; US; 404/728-2000

Rose, John; CFO, Cardinal Technologies Inc.; US; 717/293-3000, johnr@cardtech.com

Rose, Kassie; Ed, CompuServe Magazine; US; 614/457-8600

Rosebush, Judson; Ed, Pixel Vision; US; 212/581-3000

Rosen, David; Ed-in-Chief, Multimedia Online; US; 407/231-6904

Rosen, Elliot; Pres & COO, Sendero Corp.; US; 602/941-8112

Rosen, Emanuel; VP Mktng, Niles & Associates Inc.; US; 510/559-8592, manu@niles.com

Rosen, Fredric K.; SVP, Gerber Scientific Inc.; US; 860/644-1551

Rosen, Jane; Mgng Ed, PowerProgrammer Magazine; US; 201/332-1515

Rosenberg, Doug; Pres, Iconix Software Engineering Inc.; US; 310/458-0092

Rosenberg, John S.; Ed, Business Documents; US; 215/238-5300

Rosenberry, Steve; Pres, Parallel PCs Inc.; US; 610/670-1710

Rosenblatt, Alfred; Mgng Ed, IEEE Spectrum; US; 908/981-0060, a.rosenblatt@ieee.org

Rosenfeld, Larry; Pres, Stackig; US; 703/734-3300

Rosenfeld, Larry; Pres & CEO, Concentra Corp.; US; 617/229-4600

Rosengarten, Felix; VP & CFO, Information Storage Devices Inc.; US; 408/369-2400

Rosenker, Mark V.; VP Public Affairs, EIA Trade Directory & Membership List; US; 703/907-7500

Rosenschein, Jeffrey; VP R&D, Accent Software Int'l. Ltd.; US; 714/223-0620

Rosenschein, Robert; Pres, Accent Software Int'l. Ltd.; US; 714/223-0620

Rosensweig, Daniel; Pblr, PC Magazine; US; 212/503-5255

Rosenthal, Paul; Mktng Dir, Computer Software Agreements; US

Rosenthal, Paula; VP, Firefly Software Corp.; US; 516/935-7060

Rosenthal, William; VP & CFO, Ziff-Davis Publishing Co.; US; 212/503-3500

Rosenthal, William A.; Pres, Logical Operations; US; 716/240-7500

Rosenzweig, Fred; VP Mfg, Electronics for Imaging Inc.; US; 415/286-8600

Rosetto, Louis; Pblr, Wired Ventures Inc.; US; 415/276-5000

Rosol, Michael; VP Sales & Mktng, Datasonix Corp.; US; 303/545-9500

Rosove, Stuart; Pres & CEO, Sequel Technology LLC; US; 206/646-6780

Ross, Dan; Superv Info Syst, Sytron Corp.; US; 508/898-0100

Ross, JoAnne; Controller, Itac Systems Inc.; US; 214/494-3073, joanne@moustrak.com

Ross, John; GM, Applied Magnetics Corp.; US; 805/683-5353

Ross, Kenneth M.; EVP Dev, Connect Inc.; US; 415/254-4000

Ross, Margaret; VP Mktng, Virginia Systems Inc.; US; 804/739-3200

Ross, Michael; Dir Sales, Equilibrium; US; 415/332-4343

Ross, Michael M.; Pres & CEO, Network Long Distance Inc.; US; 504/343-3125

Ross, Michael R.; VP Sales & Mktng, Interex; US; 316/524-4747

Ross, Raymond E.; Pres & COO, Cincinnati Milacron Inc.; US; 513/841-8100

Ross, Richard; Pblr, Electronic Servicing & Technology; US; 913/492-4857

Ross, Roger D.; Chmn & Pres, Ross Technology; US; 512/436-2000

Ross, Stuart E.; VP Eng, Target Technologies Inc.; US; 910/395-6100

Ross, Jr., Robert C.; Pres, Xante Corp.; US; 205/476-8189

Rossi, Alan J.; Group VP, Andrew Corp.; US; 708/349-3300

Rossi, Joe; Ed, Unisys World; US; 512/250-9023

Rossman, George; VP Dev, Xsoft; US; 415/813-6920

Rossotti, Charles O.; Chmn, American Management Systems; US; 703/267-8000

Rotenberg, Marc; Dir, Electronic Privacy Information Center; US; 202/544-9240

Roth, Andrew; VP Mktng, ACCO US Inc.; US; 847/541-9500

Rothman, Barry; EVP, Greenstone Roberts; US; 516/249-3366

Rothman, Dan; Dir Sales & Mktng, Fairstone Technologies Corp.; US; 516/261-0023

Rothman, Stephen H.; Co-CEO, Micros-To-Mainframes Inc.; US; 914/268-5000

Rothrock, Edwin; Dir Sales & Mktng, C/C++ Users Journal; US; 913/841-1631, edwin@rdpub.com.

Rothschild, Leigh M.; Pres & Pblr, IntraCorp Inc.; US; 305/591-5900

Rottenberg, Alan; SVP, Cognos Inc.; Canada; 613/738-1440

Roub, Bryan R.; SVP & CFO, Harris Corp.; US; 407/727-9100

Roucher, Thierry; Ed-in-Chief, Alcatel Telecommunications Review; France; 1-4076-1010

Rousseau, John; Pblr, GamePro; US; 415/349-4300

Rovinson, Mike; Mgng Ed, Electronic Business Today; US; 617/964-3030

Rowe, Sandy; Coord, Vim Inc.; US; 612/482-4907

Rowell, Dave; Tech Ed, Byte Lab; US; 603/924-9281

Rowell, James; VP Mktng, Univision Technologies Inc.; US; 617/221-6700

Rowen, Chris; VP Eng, Logicraft Information Systems; US; 603/880-0300

Rowinski, Jan; VP Ops, MicroSlate Inc.; Canada; 514/444-3680

Rowland, Dennis H.; VP & CFO, Geoworks; US; 510/814-1660

Rowley, James; GM, Toray Optical Storage Solutions; US; 415/341-7152

Roy, Philippe; Dir Mktng, Kinetic Systems Corp.; US; 815/838-0005

Royan, Patrick; VP & CFO, Alantec Corp.; US; 408/955-9000, royan@alantec.com

Rozhin, Dona; Mkt Dev Mgr, HP Home Products Div.; US; 408/246-4300

Ruane, Michael J.; VP & CFO, SunGard

Data Systems Inc.; US; 610/341-8700

Ruane, Tony; Sales Mgr, Shuttle Technology; US; 510/656-0180

Rubattino, Gina; Pres, Pixel Relations; US; 415/474-0407

Rubell, Victor; Assoc Ed, Electronic Education Report; US; 203/834-0033

Rubin, Barbara; Bus Mgr, National Electronics Service Dealers Assoc.; US; 817/921-9061

Rubin, Eric; Dir Prod Mktng, Visual Edge Software Ltd.; Canada; 514/332-6430, erubin@holonet.com

Rubin, Fred; VP, Entex Information Services; US; 914/935-3600

Rubin, Howard; Ed, IT Metrics Strategies; US; 617/648-8702

Rubin, Kim; VP Eng, GreenSpring Computers Inc.; US; 415/327-1200, kim@gspring.com

Rubinsky, Yuri; Pres, SoftQuad Inc.; US; 416/239-4801

Rubinstein, Dick; Ed, Internet Voyager; US; dickr@id.wing.net

Rubinstein, Jon; COO, FirePower Systems Inc.; US; 415/462-3000

Ruby, Dan; Ed-in-Chief, NetSmart; US; 415/522-2411, druby@smarter.com

Rudd, Andrew; Chmn & CEO, Barra Inc.; US; 510/548-5442

Rudin, Zelda; VP, A&R Partners Inc.; US; 415/363-0982

Rudisin, Gerald J.; VP Mktng, Rational Software Corp.; US; 408/496-3600, gjr@rational.com

Ruditsky, Barry; VP OEM Sales, DataBeam Corp.; US; 606/245-3500, bruditsky@databeam.com

Rudy, Bob; VP Sales & Mktng, CMD Technology Inc.; US; 714/454-0800

Ruegg, Randall L.; CFO, LaserMaster Corp.; US; 612/941-8687

Ruehle, William J.; EVP & CFO, Bay Networks Inc.; US; 408/988-2400

Ruettgers, Michael C.; Pres & CEO, EMC Corp.; US; 508/435-1000

Ruff, Eric; Pres, PowerQuest Corp.; US; 801/226-8977

Rugani, Philip L.; VP WW Sales, Solectek Inc.; US; 619/450-1220

Ruggiero, John A.; Pres & CEO, Telco Systems Inc.; US; 617/551-0300

Rulfs, Jim; VP Bus Dev, Notable Technologies Inc.; US; 206/455-4040, jrulfs@notable.com

Runck, Robert; Ed-in-Chief, NADTP Journal; US; 508/887-7900

Rundall, Rick; GM, Scout Business Software Directory; US; 303/772-0321

Runnion III, Charles S.; EVP Sales & Mktng, Cerner Corp.; US; 816/221-1024

Runtagh, Hellene S.; Pres & CEO, GE Information Services; US; 301/340-4000

Runyan, Bob; EVP, Lahey Computer Systems Inc.; US; 702/831-2500

Rusch, Bruce R.; Pres & COO, Analogic Corp.; US; 508/977-3000

Rusert, Mike; VP Ops, Canon Computer Systems Inc.; US; 714/438-3000

Rush, Nicholas; VP Prod, Berkeley Systems Inc.; US; 510/540-5535

Rushalko, Kevin B.; Pblr, ID Systems; US; 603/924-9631

Rushen, Frank J.; Pres, Instruments Specialties Co. Inc.; US; 717/424-8510

Ruskamp, Bruce; Pres & CEO, Zondervan Publishing House; US; 616/698-6900, bruce.ruskamp@zph.com

Russ, Malcolm J.; VP, Planar Systems Inc.; US; 503/690-1100

Russell, Anne M.; Ed Dir, Pre; US; 212/683-3540, anne_russell@cowlesbiz.com

Russell, Christine; CFO, Cygnus Support; US; 415/903-1400

Russell, Grant N.; CTO, Advanced Gravis Computer Technology Ltd.; Canada; 604/431-5020

Russell, John; Ed-in-Chief, Reseller Management; US; 617/558-4772, jruss@rm.cahners.com

Russell, Lawrence C.; EVP, Unisys Corp.; US; 215/986-4011

Russell, Marianne; VP & Ed Dir, Van Nostrand Reinhold; US; 212/254-3232

Russell, Rob; VP Dev, Software Solutions Inc.; US; 770/418-2000

Russell, Tim; Chmn, Quarter-Inch Cartridge Drive Standards Inc.; US; 805/963-3853

Russian, David H.; VP & CFO, Brooktree Corp.; US; 619/452-7580

Russo, Douglas J.; EVP & COO, 4i Solutions Inc.; US

Russo, Mitchell A.; Pres, Timeslips Corp.; US; 214/248-9232

Rutgers, Arnold; VP Mktng, Control Data Systems Inc.; US; 612/482-2401

Ruth, Josy; VP Eng, Cambridge Parallel Processing; US; 714/261-8901, josy@cppus.com

Rutkowski, Anthony M.; Exec Dir, Internet Society; US; 703/648-9888

Rutledge, William P.; Chmn & CEO, Teledyne Inc.; US; 310/551-4306

Ryan, Bill; Sr Partner, Niehaus/Ryan/Haller; US; 415/615-7900, bill@nrh.com

Ryan, Bruce J.; EVP & CFO, Amdahl Corp.; US; 408/746-6000

Ryan, James J.; VP Info Mgmt, Data General Corp.; US; 508/898-5000

Ryan, Joseph D.; VP, Funk Software Inc.; US; 617/497-6339

Ryan, Lisa R.; Mngg Ed, Data Management Review; US; 414/792-9696

Ryan, Lou; EVP Sales, Delrina Corp.; Canada; 416/441-3676

Ryan, Mark; Eng Mgr, Microport Inc.; US; 408/438-8649, mark@mport.com

Ryan, Thomas; VP Bus Dev, Sanyo-Verbatim CD Company; US; 317/935-7574

Ryan, Tom; Nat'l Acct Mgr, AP Professional; US; 619/699-6735, tryan@acad.com

Ryan, Vincent; Assoc Ed, Software Mar-

keting Journal; US; 415/296-7744

Ryan, Will; Partner, Susanna Opper & Assoc.; US; 413/528-6513

Ryono, Byron; Dir Bus Dev, First Floor Inc.; US; 415/968-1101

Saadi, Edgar; SVP, Pencom Systems Inc.; US; 512/343-1111

Saadi, Wade E.; Chmn, Pencom Systems Inc.; US; 512/343-1111

Saal, Harry; Chmn, Network General Corp.; US; 415/473-2000

Sabatt, Chuck; Exec Sec, Imaging Technologies Assoc.; US; 508/775-3433

Sachs, Bruce I.; Pres & CEO, Xylogics Inc.; US; 617/272-8140

Sacilotto, Jeff; Sr Lab Analyst, Macworld Labs; US; 415/243-0505, jeff_sacilotto@macworld.com

Sacino, Carole; Pblr, Datamation; US; 617/558-4281

Sack, Edgar A.; Chmn, Pres & CEO, Zilog Inc.; US; 408/370-8000

Sack, Sidney V.; CFO, XcelleNet Inc.; US; 770/804-8100

Sacks, Andrew; Dir Sales, Black & White Software; US; 408/369-7400

Sacks, Holly; VP MKtng, Micropolis Corp.; US; 818/709-3300

Sacks, Martin; Pres & CEO, International Microcomputer Software Inc.; US; 415/257-3000

Sacks, S. Henry; Pblr & CEO, Computer Publishing Group Inc.; US; 617/739-7001, shs@cpg.com

Sadler, Allen; VP Ops, Alantec Corp.; US; 408/955-9000, sadler@alantec.com

Sadler, William S.; CEO & Pres, Dotronix Inc.; US; 612/633-1742

Sadowski, Raymond; SVP & CFO, Avnet Inc.; US; 516/466-7000

Sage, Karen; EVP, Corporate Visions Inc.; US; 918/488-0301

Sahin, Kenan; Pres, Kenan Systems Corp.; US; 617/225-2224

Saito, Kunisho; Pres & CEO, NEC Electronics Inc.; US; 415/960-6000

Saitow, Patty; Dir Prod Mktng, Powerhouse Entertainment; US; 214/933-5400

Sakai, Akihiko; VP, Epson America Inc.; US; 310/782-0770

Sakata, Kay; VP Int'l Sales, Bluebird Systems; US; 619/438-2220

Salamon, Simon; VP, IDC/LINK; US; 212/726-0900, ssalamon@idcresearch.com

Salerno, Frederic V.; Vice Chmn, NYNEX Corp.; US; 212/395-2121

Sales, Don; VP Sales, Blackship Computer Systems Inc.; US; 408/432-7500

Saliba, Bonnie; VP, MacAcademy; US; 904/677-1918

Salim, Irfan; Pres & CEO, Software Publishing Corp.; US; 408/537-3000

Salisbury, Alan; COO, Microelectronics & Computer Technology Corp.; US; 512/343-0978

Salisbury, Alan B.; Pres, Learning Tree

Int'l.; US; 703/709-9019

Sall, John; SVP, SAS Institute Inc.; US; 919/677-8000

Sallquist, Chris; Creative Dir, Vivo Media; US; 503/223-9644, chris@govivo.com

Salmasi, Allen B.; Pres Wireless Div, Qualcomm Inc.; US; 619/587-1121

Salmon, Steve; CTO, STMS; US; 703/318-7867, ssalmon@stms.com

Salmons, Jim; Ed, Object Technology, Directory of; US; 212/242-7447

Salvatroi, Jai; Mgr Ops, Microworks Corp.; US; 201/492-1691

Salzinger, Paul; Dir Strat Sales, Sanctuary Woods Multimedia Corp.; US; 415/286-6000

Sameh, Ahmed; Ed-in-Chief, IEEE Computational Science & Engineering; US; 908/981-0060

Sammon Jr., John W.; Chmn & Pres, Par Technology Corp.; US; 315/738-0600

Sammons, John; Pres, Business Applications Performance Corp.; US; 408/988-7654

Samper, J. Phillip; Chmn & CEO, Cray Research Inc.; US; 612/452-6650

Sample, David M.; SVP, Hyperion Software; US; 203/703-3000

Sampson, Deborah; Chmn, Independent Computer Consultants Assoc.; US; 314/997-4633, 70007.4250@compuserve.com

Sampson, Marcia; Exec Ed, Publishing & Multimedia; US

Samsel, Jon; Pblr, Carronad's Interactive Media Directory; US; 310/493-2330

Samuels, Alan; VP & CTO, Weitek Corp.; US; 408/738-8400

Sanchez, Steve; SVP, BBDO; US; 415/274-6200

Sandapen, Sheila; Ed, IDG's Windows 95 Journal; US; 617/482-8785

Sander, Joe; VP WW Sales, Insoft Inc.; US; 717/730-9501

Sandera, Jiri; VP Eng, Microsemi Corp.; US; 714/979-8220

Sanders, Dawn; Dir Sup, Alliance Manufacturing Software Inc.; US; 805/965-3000, support@alliancemfg.com

Sanders, Harry R.; Pres, S&H Computer Systems Inc.; US; 615/327-3670, hsanders@sandh.com

Sanders, Kenneth W.; SVP & CFO, Paging Network Inc.; US; 214/985-4100

Sanders, Larry; VP Mktng, Racotek Inc.; US; 612/832-9800

Sanders, Larry; Pres & CEO, Fujitsu Computer Products; US; 408/432-6333

Sanders, William L.; VP Info Syst, Honeywell Inc.; US; 612/951-1000

Sanders III, Jerry; Chmn & CEO, Advanced Micro Devices Inc.; US; 408/732-2400

Sandler, Minda; Mgng Ed, Net, The; US; 415/696-1661

Sandone, Randall J.; Pres & CEO, Argus Systems Group Inc.; US; 217/384-

6300, sandone@argus.cu-online.com

Sanfillippo, John; Dir Ops, Carbela Tek Inc.; US; 415/873-6484

Sanford, Curtis N.; VP Sales, Ascend Communications Inc.; US; 510/769-6001

Sanford, Richard D.; Chmn & CEO, Intelligent Electronics Inc.; US; 610/458-5500

Sanford, Rodney; Project Admin, Standard Performance Evaluation Corp.; US; 703/331-0180

Sanford, S. Ted; VP Sales & Mktng, Canary Communications Inc.; US; 408/453-9201

Sangster, Denise; Pres, Global Touch Inc.; US; 510/649-1100

Sangveraphunsiri, Vic; VP Syst Eng, Advanced Logic Research; US; 714/581-6770

Sansbury, James; VP Tech, Altera Corp.; US; 408/894-7000

Santarini II, Michael; Assoc Ed, Integrated System Design; US; 415/903-0140, michael@asic.com

Santeusanio, Peter; Pres, Xionics Inc.; US; 617/229-7000

Santini, Antonio; Chmn, Target Software Group Inc.; US; 813/528-2477

Santoro, Carmelo J.; Chmn, Platinum Software Corp.; US; 714/453-4000

Santos, Dan; Dir Mktng, Musicware; US; 206/881-9797

Santos, Enrico; CFO, Fortner Research LLC; US; 703/478-0181, rico@fortner.com

Santullo, Michael; CEO, Four11 Corp.; US; 415/617-2000

Saphier, David J.; Pres, Triton Technologies Inc.; US; 908/855-9440

Sapienza, Michael; VP Mktng, Checkfree Corp.; US; 614/825-3000

Saponaro, Joseph A.; Pres & CEO, Intermetrics Inc.; US; 617/661-1840

Sapp Jr., A. Eugene; Pres & COO, SCI Systems Inc.; US; 205/998-0592

Sapunov, Stanislaw; Pres, Mecom Software; US; 404/564-0473

Sarath, Patrice; Ed, Access to Wang; US; 512/873-7761

Sarbin, Hershel B.; Pres & CEO, Cowles Business Media; US; 212/683-3540

Sargeant, Bruce; Pres, OnBase Technology Inc.; US

Sarin, Arun; SVP Corp Dev, AirTouch Communications; US; 415/658-2000

Saris, Linda E.; VP & CFO, Security Dynamics Technologies Inc.; US; 617/547-7820

Sarkozv, Andras; VP Corp Tech, Storage Computer Corp.; US; 603/880-3005

Sarma, Pat; EVP, American Megatrends Inc.; US; 770/263-8181

Sasaki, Richard; Dir Fin, Maxtek Components Corp.; US; 503/627-4133

Sasek, Joseph; VP WW Sales, Livingston Enterprises Inc.; US; 510/426-0770

Sasser, Stephen; Pres, Symix Systems

Inc.; US; 614/523-7000

Sasson, Ori; CEO, Scopus Technology Inc.; US; 510/597-5800

Satchell, Mark; Pblr, APT Data Services Inc.; US; 212/677-0409, mark@apt.usa.globalnews.com

Sato, Fumino; Pres & CEO, Toshiba Corp.; Japan; 3-3457-4511

Sato, Hiroshi; Pres, TDK Corp.; Japan; 3-3278-5111

Sato, Takeshi; Chief Rep, Oki America Inc.; US; 201/646-0011

Satterfield, Michael; Pres, PageAhead Software Corp; US; 206/441-0340

Satwalekar, Mukund; Data International Inc.; US; 908/232-3485

Sauer, Mary C.; SVP Mktng & Sales Dir, Sonic Solutions; US; 415/893-8000

Sauerland, John F.; CFO, ICVerify Inc.; US; 510/553-7500, jsauerland@icverify.com

Saul, Shai; VP Bus Dev, Aladdin Knowledge Systems; US; 212/564-5678

Saunders, Ann; CFO & Bus Mgr, Boston Computer Exchange; US; 617/542-4414

Saunders, Michael; VP, Luminex Software Inc.; US; 909/781-4100

Saurette, Al; VP Bus Dev, New Era Systems Services Ltd.; Canada; 403/231-9800

Savadove, Gary; SVP Mktng, Labtec Enterprises Inc.; US; 360/896-2000

Savage, Betty J.; VP & CFO, Inso Corp.; US; 617/753-6500

Saviers, F. Grant; Pres & CEO, Adaptec Inc.; US; 408/945-8600

Sawamura, Shiko; Pres & CEO, Oki Electric Industry Co. Ltd.; Japan; 3-3501-3111

Sawe, Anvil; VP & GM, Hyundai Digital Media; US; 408/232-8000

Sawyer, Judith; VP, Coordinated Service Inc.; US; 508/448-3800

Sawyer, Susan; Dir Mktng, Gigatron Software Corp.; US; 714/261-1777, s_sawyer@gsclion.com

Sawyer, William J.; EVP, Project Software & Development Inc.; US; 617/661-1444

Saxena, Jit; Pres & CEO, Applix Inc.; US; 508/870-0300

Sayadian, Helga; Coord, U.S. Microcomputer Statistics Committee; US; 202/626-5730

Sayed, Anita; Pres, IEM Inc.; US; 970/221-3005

Sayed, Hushi; CEO, IEM Inc.; US; 970/221-3005

Sayers, Gale; Pres & CEO, Sayers Computer Source; US; 708/391-4040

Scallan, Todd; Dir Corp Partnership, Black & White Software; US; 408/369-7400

Scanlin, David L.; VP Sales, Learning Company, The; US; 510/792-2101

Scanlon, F. Taylor; VP WW Mktng, Compass Design Automation; US; 408/433-4880

Scapicchio, Mark; Ed, Ami Pro Report, The; US; 617/482-8634

Scarff, Dennis; VP Intl Dist, Apogee Software Ltd.; US; 214/271-1765

Scartz, Don T.; VP Fin, LXE; US; 770/447-4224

Schacht, Henry; Chmn & CEO, Lucent Technologies; US; 908/582-8500

Schaeberle, Gregg; Sales Dir, Compulink Management Center Inc.; US; 310/212-5465

Schaeffer, Andy; Prod Mgr, Olympus Image Systems Inc.; US; 516/844-5000

Schaeffer, Gordon; VP Mktng, Four-Gen Software Inc.; US; 206/522-0055

Schafer, Bruce; Pres, PC-Kwik Corp.; US; 503/644-5644, bruce@pck-wik.mhs.compuserve.com

Schafer, David W.; EVP WW Sales, Western Digital Corp.; US; 714/932-5000

Schaffer, Adam; VP Mktng, Micro Warehouse; US; 203/899-4000

Schaffer, Donna; Dir Ops, Microprocessor Report; US; 707/824-4001, dschaffer@mdr.zd.com

Schaffhauser, Dian; Ed-in-Chief, Smart Access; US; 206/251-1900

Schaffner, Brian; Ed, Paradox for Windows Developer's Journal; US; 502/491-1900

Schalker, Erwin; COO, Valis Group, The; US; 415/435-5404

Schantz, Herbert F.; Pres, HLS Associates Int'l.; US; 703/444-7037

Schantz, Letty L.M.; Chmn, HLS Associates Int'l.; US; 703/444-7037

Schaper, C. James; SVP WW Sales & Mktng, Banyan Systems Inc.; US; 508/898-1000

Schaper, Jim; EVP & COO, Dun & Bradstreet Software Services Inc.; US; 404/239-2000

Schar, Daniel R.; VP, Hergo Ergonomic Support Systems Inc.; US; 212/684-4666

Schaw, Peter; VP Mktng, Softbank Comdex Inc.; US; 617/443-1500

Scheaffer, Michael; Dir Fin, Notable Technologies Inc.; US; 206/455-4040, mscheaffer@notable.com

Schechter, Robert; Pres, Natural Micro-Systems Corp.; US; 508/650-1300

Scheen, Sue; VP Channel Sales, Mastersoft Inc.; US; 602/948-4888, sue@mastersoft.com

Scheerden, Jan Pieter; VP, SunSoft Inc.; US; 415/960-1300

Scheffer, Richard; VP Mktng, Forte Software Inc.; US; 510/869-3400

Scheider, Sam; Dir IS, Cognex Corp.; US; 508/650-3000

Scheine, Arnold J.; Pres & CEO, LCS Industries Inc.; US; 201/778-5588

Scheland, Carla; Dir Client Svcs, n th degree software; US; 702/588-4900

Schellhase, James; CFO, IntelliQuest; US; 512/329-2424

Schellhorn, Chris F.; VP Sales & Mktng,

GM, Soricon Corp.; US; 303/440-2800

Schember, Jack; Ed-in-Chief & Pblr, Response TV; US; 714/513-8400

Schengili, Joseph; Pres, Numetrix Ltd.; US; 203/847-3452

Schengili, Veerle; VP Ops, Numetrix Ltd.; US; 203/847-3452

Schenker, Jennifer L.; Sr Exec Ed, CommunicationsWeek Int'l.; US; 516/562-5530, jschenke@cmp.com

Schenkler, Sheldon M.; VP & CFO, Cambex Corp.; US; 617/890-6000

Scherb, Jeff; SVP & CTO, Dun & Bradstreet Software Services Inc.; US; 404/239-2000

Scherer, Barbara V.; VP & CFO, Micropolis Corp.; US; 818/709-3300

Scherle, Rick; Pres, Kelly Micro Systems Inc.; US

Scherma, Ron; Pres, Popkin Software & Systems Inc.; US; 212/571-3434

Scherpenberg, F.A.; VP Computer Prod, Dallas Semiconductor Corp.; US; 214/450-0400

Scherrer, Jon L.; VP, Midisoft Corp.; US; 206/391-3610

Scheunberg, Joel; VP Mktng & Sales, ShaBlamm! Computer Corp.; US; 408/730-9696, js@shablamm.com

Schewe, Steve; Pres & CEO, Mirror Technologies Inc.; US; 612/270-2718

Schickler, Peter; Ed-in-Chief, Inside dBase for Windows; US; 502/491-1900

Schiffman, Allan; CTO, Terisa Systems; US; 415/919/1750

Schild, Ken; MIS Admin, Abra Cadabra Software; US; 813/527-1111

Schiller, Victor H.; Chmn & CEO, Eclipse Systems Inc.; US

Schilling, Susan L.; SVP Dev, Minnesota Educational Computing Corp.; US; 612/569-1500

Schimicci, Frank; Pres & CEO, Ioline Corp.; US; 206/821-2140

Schimmoeller, Gerald; VP & CFO, Concentra Corp.; US; 617/229-4600

Schinas, John P.; Chmn, Digi Int'l.; US; 612/943-9020

Schirle, Doug; Controller, Paradigm Technology Inc.; US; 408/954-0500

Schlanger, Florenic; VP Client Svcs, Magic Solutions Inc.; US; 201/587-1515

Schleider, Michael; VP Sales & Mktng, IMC Networks Corp.; US; 714/724-1070, mschleider@imcnetworks.com

Schloemer, Gregory J.; VP, ALOS Micrographics Corp.; US; 914/457-4400

Schlosky, Dan; Principal, Marcom Strategies; US; 310/820-6629, dschlosky@aol.com

Schlossman, David Y.; VP Eng, Xiox Corp.; US; 415/375-8188

Schlueter, Jeffrey L.; VP, CyData Inc.; US

Schmeisser, John; Controller, Open Systems Holdings Corp.; US; 612/829-0011

Schmelzer, Dean C.; EVP Mktng &

Sales, Flserv Inc.; US; 414/879-5000

Schmidt, Doug; Ed, C++ Report; US; 212/242-7447, schmidt@cs.wustl.edu

Schmidt, Douglas P.; Pres, Postalsoft Inc.; US; 608/788-8700

Schmidt, Eric E.; VP & CTO, Sun Microsystems Inc.; US; 415/960-1300

Schmidt, Jill; SVP, Fellowes Manufacturing Co.; US; 708/893-1600

Schmidt, Jonathan C.; CTO, Performance Technology Inc.; US; 210/979-2000, jon@perftech.com

Schmidt, Les; COO, Learning Company, The; US; 510/792-2101

Schmidt, Les; COO, SoftKey International Inc.; US; 617/494-1200

Schmidt, Matthew; Partner, FS Communications; US; 415/691-1488

Schmidt, Noel; VP Ops, Architecture Technology Corp.; US; 612/935-2035

Schmidt, Ronald V.; EVP & CTO, Bay Networks Inc.; US; 408/988-2400

Schmitt, Dave; Dir Prod Dev, IntelliTools; US; 415/382-5959

Schmuller, Joseph; Ed-in-Chief, PC AI Magazine; US; 602/971-1869

Schnaidt, Patricia; Ed-in-Chief, Network Computing; US; 516/562-5071, pschnaidt@nwc.com

Schnee, Victor; Pres, Probe Research Inc.; US; 201/285-1500

Schneider, Bernie; VP Mktng, Ascend Communications Inc.; US; 510/769-6001

Schneider, Edward; Sr Ed, Computer Buyer's Guide & Handbook; US; 212/807-8220

Schneider, Kenneth S.; VP Sales, Telebyte Technology Inc.; US; 516/423-3232

Schneider, Seth T.; Ed-in-Chief, Multilingual Computing Magazine; US; 208/263-8178

Schneiderman, Steve; Pblr, Network VAR; US; 415/905-2200, ayoung@mfi.com

Schneur, Avner; CTO, Astea Int'l.; US; 215/822-8888

Schnoebelen, Andy; EVP, Vivid Image Co.; US; 310/618-0274

Schnyder, Phil; Pres & CEO, askSam Systems; US; 904/584-6590

Schnyler, Jim; VP CTC Electronic Direct Tech, T/Maker Co.; US; 415/962-0195

Schoch, Claude; CEO, Digital Directory Assistance Inc.; US; 301/657-8548, claudes@dda-inc.com

Schoch, Eric; VP Mktng, Digital Directory Assistance Inc.; US; 301/657-8548, erics@dda-inc.com

Schoech, Dick; Ed, Computers in Human Services; US

Schoeller, Fred; Pres, Computer Support Corp.; US; 214/661-8960

Schoen, Claire; Ed Dir, Electronic Media for School Market: Review Trends & Forecasts; US; 203/834-0033

Schoenfeld, Adam; Ed, Online Marketplace; US; 212/780-6060

Schoenfeld, Lee H.; SVP Mktng, Best Buy Co. Inc.; US; 612/947-2000

Schoeniger, Eric; Ed-in-Chief, Ent; US; 215/643-8000, schoeniger@cardinal.com

Schoffstall, Martin L.; SVP & CTO, PSI-NET Inc.; US; 703/904-4100

Schoffstall, Steven A.; VP Sales, PSINET Inc.; US; 703/904-4100

Schon, Jeffrey; CEO, Living Books; US; 415/352-5200

Schonau, Mark R.; CFO, CyCare Systems Inc.; US; 602/596-4300

Schoneman, Bill; VP Testing Div, XXCAL Testing Laboratories; US; 310/477-2902

Schrader, Lisa; Sales & Mktng Mgr, Pearson Communications; US; 408/496-5885, schrader@pearson.com

Schrader, William L.; Chmn, Pres & CEO, PSINET Inc.; US; 703/904-4100

Schraff, Bryan; Pres, Schraff Group; US; 714/556-6800, bschraff@schraff-group.com

Schrago, Dianee; Pres, S&S Public Relations Inc.; US; 847/291-1616

Schraith, James T.; Pres & CEO, Cerplex Group Inc.; US; 714/258-5151, jschraith@cerplex.com

Schram, Rob; VP Strat Dev, Traveling Software Inc.; US; 206/483-8088

Schreiber, Rich; Pres, ATB Associates; US; 617/239-1793

Schreider, Tari; Dir Sales & Mktng, Pecan Software Corp.; US; 770/594-9707

Schreier, Paul; Ed, Personal Engineering & Instrumentation News; US; 603/427-1377

Schroeder, John; Mgr Eng, Basis Int'l.; US; 505/345-5232, jfs@basis.com

Schroeder, Leslie; Pres, Leslie Schroeder PR & Marketing; US; 408/446-9158

Schroeder, William J.; Pres & CEO, Diamond Multimedia Systems Inc.; US; 408/325-7000

Schroer, Steve; Dir Sales, Popkin Software & Systems Inc.; US; 212/571-3434

Schueler, Jeff; Pres, Usability Sciences Corp.; US; 214/550-1599

Schulman, Rand; VP Mktng, TriTeal Corp.; US; 619/930-2077

Schulmeyer, Gerhard; Pres & CEO, Siemens Nixdorf Informationssysteme AG; Germany; 89-636-47759

Schultz, Eric V.; Chmn & CEO, Mesa Group; US; 617/964-7400

Schultz, Gary; Mktng Dir, MaxTech Corp.; US; 201/586-3008, gary_schultz@maxcorp.com

Schultz, Gary G.; Principal Analyst, Multimedia Research Group; US; 408/524-9767

Schultz, James L.; Pres & CEO, Computer Research Inc.; US; 412/262-4430

Schultz, Ronnie; SysOp, GameNet Corp.; US; 212/254-5300, ronnie_schultz@gamenet.com

Schultz, Sabrina; Mgr Mktng & Sales,

Command Technology Corp.; US; 510/521-5900

Schultz, Sean; VP Prod Dev, Trio Information Systems; US; 919/846-4990

Schultz, Tim; VP Eng, Compatible Systems Corp.; US; 303/444-9532, tim@compatible.com

Schulz, Duane; Pres & CEO, Now Software Inc.; US; 503/274-2800

Schulze, Richard M.; Chmn & CEO, Best Buy Co. Inc.; US; 612/947-2000

Schumacker, Robert A.; Pres Simulation Div, Evans & Sutherland Computer Corp.; US; 801/588-1000

Schuman, Don; Pres, Parallel Technologies Inc.; US; 206/883-6900

Schupp, David O.; VP, Interface Systems Inc.; US; 313/769-5900

Schussel, George; CEO, Digital Consulting Inc.; US; 508/470-3880

Schussler, Terry R.; Principle, Gray Matter Design; US; 415/243-0394, schussler@aol.com

Schuster, Jeff; Dir Mktng & Sales, Performance Awareness Corp.; US; 919/870-8800, jeff@pacorp.com

Schuster, Larry; VP Sales & Mktng, Link Technologies Inc.; US; 408/473-1200

Schuster, Stewart A.; EVP Mktng, Sybase Inc.; US; 510/922-3500

Schwab, Izzy; Pres, D&H Distributing Co.; US

Schwab, Richard L.; VP Proj Mgmt, Softbank Comdex Inc.; US; 617/443-1500

Schwager, Andre; Pres & CEO, Seagate Enterprise Management Software; US; 408/342-4500

Schwartz, Ben; VP Mktng, Nu Horizons Electronics Corp.; US; 516/226-6000

Schwartz, Dan; Pblr, HomePC; US; 516/562-7673

Schwartz, Deborah; Assoc Ed, Digital Age; US; 215/643-8000, schwartzdr@cardinal.com

Schwartz, Ephraim; Ed-in-Chief, Computer Buyer's Guide & Handbook; US; 212/807-8220

Schwartz, Gary M.; EVP & GM Cons Div, Franklin Electronic Pblrs Inc.; US; 609/386-2500

Schwartz, Jonathan; Pres & CEO, Lighthouse Design Ltd.; US; 415/570-7736

Schwartz, Nancy; Mgr, Infomart Corporate Evaluation Center; US; 214/746-3500

Schwartz, Peter A.; SVP & CFO, Computer Associates Int'l. Inc.; US; 516/342-5224

Schwartz, Richard L.; SVP & CTO, Borland Int'l.; US; 408/431-1000

Schwartz, Tom; Pres, Schwartz Associates, The; US; 415/965-4561, tjs@cup.portal.com

Schwartz Cowan, Ruth; Pres, Society for the History of Technology; US; 906/487-2113

Schwartzberg, Arthur; Chmn, Xaos

Tools; US; 415/487-7000

Schwarz, George; VP Sales, Wright Line Inc.; US; 508/852-4300

Schwarz, John G.; VP Mktng, IBM Personal Software Products; US; 512/823-3176

Schwedelson, Helene; COO, Worldata; US; 407/393-8200, hschwedelson@worldata.com

Schwedelson, Roy; CEO, Worldata; US; 407/393-8200, rschwedelson@worldata.com

Schweibold, S. Brad; Dir Sales, Eden Systems Corp.; US; 317/848-9600, essales@edensys.com

Schweiker, Anthony; Pres, K-12 Micro-Media Publishing Inc.; US; 201/529-4500

Schwenk Jr., Harold S.; Chmn, Pres & CEO, BGS Systems Inc.; US; 617/891-0000

Schwerin, Julie B.; Pres, InfoTech; US; 802/763-2097

Schwerin, Tamy; Dir Sales & Ops, Blast Software Inc.; US; 919/542-3007

Schwettmann, Fred; Pres & COO, Read-Rite Corp.; US; 408/262-6700

Scioscia, Ronald J.; VP & CFO, Sync Research; US; 714/588-2070

Scirica, Joe; VP Prod Dev, Maxis; US; 510/933-5630

Sciuto, John J.; Pres & CEO Fed Syst, Comptek Research Inc.; US; 716/677-4070

Sclavos, Stratton; CEO, Verisign Inc.; US; 415/961-7500

Scobey, Linda; Dir Mktng, Seek Systems Inc.; US; 206/822-7400

Scoll, Joan; Dir MIS, Intermec Corp.; US; 206/348-2600

Scoroposki, James; EVP, Acclaim Entertainment Inc.; US; 516/624-8888

Scott, Craig; VP Sales & Mktng, GDT Softworks; Canada; 604/291-9121

Scott, Daniel; Pres, Business Products Industry Assoc.; US; 703/549-9040

Scott, Edward W.; EVP, Pyramid Technology Corp.; US; 408/428-9000

Scott, Gerald R.; VP, Jones Futurex Inc.; US; 916/632-3456

Scott, Gord; Dir Fin, GDT Softworks; Canada; 604/291-9121

Scott, Gordon; CFO, Advanced Hardware Architecture; US; 509/334-1000

Scott, H. David; EVP & GM, Barco Chromatics; US; 770/493-7000, scott@barco.com

Scott, John B.; VP R&D & Mktng, Andrew Corp.; US; 708/349-3300

Scott, Jonathan; Pres & COO, Traveling Software Inc.; US; 206/483-8088

Scott, Karyn; GM, Gray Matter Design; US; 415/243-0394

Scott, Roger; Pres, Dallas Digital Corp.; US; 214/424-2800

Scott, Stephen; Dir Sales & Mktng, Droege Computing Services Inc.; US; 919/403-9459

Scott, Susan; Pblr & CEO, Upside Publishing Co., The; US; 415/377-0950, sscott@upside.com

Scott, Thomas; EVP, Data Entry Systems Inc.; US; 205/430-3023

Scott, Tom; VP & GM, Toshiba America Information Systems Inc.; US; 714/583-3111

Scott Jr., Edward; EVP Ops, BEA Systems Inc.; US; 408/743-4000

Scott-Jackson, Dennis; VP Dev, Advanced Gravis Computer Technology Ltd.; Canada; 604/431-5020

Scroggs, Ross; Pres, Telamon Corp.; US; 510/987-7700

Scull, David J.; Pres & CEO, IPC Technologies Inc.; US; 512/339-3500

Seaborn, True; Pblr, IEEE Computer Society Press; US; 714/821-8380, t.seaborn@computer.org

Seago, Sandy; VP Sales & Mktng, Computer Group Inc., The; US; 614/876-8600

Seal, J.D.; Dir Ops, Read Technologies Inc.; US; 714/551-2049

Seaman, David R.; CTO, Blyth Software Inc.; US; 415/571-0222

Seaman, Mark; VP, Cardiff Software Inc.; US; 619/761-4515

Searle, Gregg A.; EVP, Diebold Inc.; US; 216/489-4000

Searls, Doc; Principal, Searls Group, The; US; 415/593-5590

Seawell, A. Brooke; VP & CFO, Synopsys Inc.; US; 415/962-5000

Sebeck, Mike; Sales Dir, Micro Dynamics Ltd.; US; 301/589-6300, mike_sebeck@mdl.com

Sedmak, Stephen; Pres, SRS Labs Inc.; US; 714/442-1070

Seebach, Joseph W.; VP Bus Dev, Arcada Software Inc.; US; 407/333-7500

Seebass, Scott; VP Eng, Xinet; US; 510/845-0555, scott@xinet.com

Seeherman, Julian; Chmn & CEO, Venture Stores Inc.; US; 314/281-6801

Seeley, Jeanne; VP Fin, Apple Computer Inc.; US; 408/996-1010

Seely, Bruce E.; Sec & Ed, Society for the History of Technology; US; 906/487-2113

Seely, Mark; VP Dev, Calyx Corp.; US; 414/782-0300

Seeser, James W.; VP & CTO, Optical Coating Laboratory Inc.; US; 707/545-6440

Seethaler, Mark; CFO, Dayna Communications Inc.; US; 801/269-7200, mseethaler@dayna.com

Seidel, Robert W.; Dir, Charles Babbage Institute; US; 612/624-5050, rws@maroon.tc.umn.edu

Seiden, Jeffrey S.; Pres, nuLogic; US; 617/444-7680

Seiden, Paul; Sales Mgr, Communications Specialties Inc.; US; 516/273-0404, pseiden@commspecial.com

Seidenberg, Ivan G.; Pres & CEO, NYNEX Corp.; US; 212/395-2121

Seigel, J.W.; VP Mktng, AG Communication Systems Corp.; US; 602/582-7000

Seiler, Melvin; EVP & COO, Micro Warehouse; US; 203/899-4000

Seippel, William H.; VP & CFO, Landmark Graphics Corp.; US

Sejnowski, Terrence; Ed-in-Chief, Neural Computation; US; 617/253-2889, terry@salk.edu

Sekhar, Chandra; Pres & CEO, Exodus Communications Inc.; US; 408/522-8450

Sekimoto, Dr. Tadahiro; Chmn, NEC Corp.; Japan; 3-3454-1111

Sekino, Tony; Assist GM, Toshiba America Information Systems Inc.; US; 714/583-3111

Selbe, Ann; VP Sales, Colorbus Inc.; US; 714/852-1850

Selby, Fred H.; SVP Sales, FileNet Corp.; US; 714/966-3400

Selby, Laurence; Pblr, Computer Software Agreements; US

Seletz, Jay; Dir MIS, Percussion Software Inc.; US; 617/438-9900, jay_seletz@percussion.com

Self, Nancy M.; VP Admin, Micron Technology Inc.; US; 208/368-4400

Selinsky, Ted; Mgng Ed, NASA Tech Briefs; US; 212/490-3999

Selven, Karen; VP Mktng, Electronic Trend Publications; US; 408/369-7000, kselven@electronictrendpubs.com

Selvin, Neil; Pres & CEO, Global Village Communication; US; 408/523-1000

Sembler, Floyd; Pblr, International Business; US

Semich, J. William; Ed-in-Chief, Datamation; US; 617/558-4281, bsemich@cahners.com

Sene, Jamie; VP Mktng, AllMicro Inc.; US; 813/539-7283

Seneta, Eugene P.; VP & CFO, Xyvision Inc.; US; 617/245-4100

Sennott, Joseph; COO, SmartDesk Inc.; US; 714/582-4020

Senter, Alan Z.; SVP & CFO, NYNEX Corp.; US; 212/395-2121

Serlin, Omri; Pres, Itom International Co.; US; 415/948-4516, omris@cup.portal.com

Sernovitz, Andy; Pres, Interactive Television Assoc.; US; 202/408-0008

Serpa, Bruce; US Sales Mgr, Calluna Technology Inc.; US; 408/453-4753

Serrano, Ronald M.; SVP Corp Dev, Southern New England Telecom Corp.; US; 203/771-5200

Servi, Ruben; Mktng Dir, IDOC Inc.; US; 310/446-4666, ruben@idocinc.com

Servoss, Marcus E.; Pres, Servoss PR; US; 303/777-6200

Seto, Michael; VP Mktng, Voysys Corp.; US; 510/252-1100

Severa, Richard; VP Channel Sales & Mktng, Tandberg Data Inc.; US; 805/579-1000

Severino, Paul J.; Chmn, Bay Networks

Inc.; US; 408/988-2400

Severs, Ed; Pres & CEO, ReproCAD Inc.; US; 510/284-0400

Sexton, Kenneth A.; VP & CFO, Intersolv Inc.; US; 301/838-5000

Seybold, Andrew M.; Ed-in-Chief, Andrew Seybold's Outlook on Communications & Computing; US; 408/338-7701, aseybold@mcimail.com

Seybold, Jonathan W.; Pblr, Seybold Report on Desktop Publishing; US; 610/565-2480, jseybold@sbexpos.com

Seybold, Linda M.; Mgng Ed, Andrew Seybold's Outlook on Communications & Computing; US; 408/338-7701, 74431.1647@compuserve.com

Seybold, Patricia; Pres & Pblr, Patricia Seybold Group; US; 617/742-5200

Seymour, Jonathan; Pres, Gold Standard Multimedia Inc.; US; 904/373-1100

Shachar, Yossi; Dir Ops, Vcon Inc.; US; 214/774-3890

Shackil, Al; Pblr, Personal Engineering & Instrumentation News; US; 603/427-1377

Shaeffer, James C.; Securenet Technologies Inc.; US; 206/776-2524, jcs@securenet.org

Shafer, Chip; Chmn, Shafer; US; 714/553-1177

Shaffer, Oren G.; EVP & CFO, Ameritech Corp.; US; 312/750-5000

Shaffer, Richard; Principal, Technologic Partners; US; 212/343-1900

Shah, Ajay; Pres, SMART Modular Technologies; US; 510/623-1231

Shah, Frank; VP Eng, Xerox ColorgrafX Systems; US; 408/225-2800

Shah, Kim; VP Mktng, Arcland; US; 610/993-9904

Shahrestany, Nick; EVP, Procom Technology Inc.; US; 714/852-1000

Shaikh, Mohammed; Chmn, Image-X; US; 805/964-3537, mohammed@imagexx.com

Shain, Ken; Pres, Cyco Int'l.; US; 404/634-3302

Shain, Myron R.; Pres, Disc Manufacturing Inc.; US; 302/479-2500

Shaker, James; Pblr, PRG Guide; US; 413/664-6185

Shandle, Jack; Ed-in-Chief, Electronic Design; US; 201/393-6060

Shani, Nissim; VP Ops, Univision Technologies Inc.; US; 617/221-6700

Shanker, Subramonian; Pres, American Megatrends Inc.; US; 770/263-8181

Shanks, Janet W.; CFO, DH Technology Inc.; US; 619/451-3485

Shanks, Patricia; Pres, BASIS Inc.; US; 510/547-5900

Shanley, Kim; Admin, Transaction Processing Performance Council; US; 408/295-8894

Shannon, Terry C.; Ed, Shannon Knows DEC; US; 603/465-3821

Shanny, Noam; EVP Eng, Ligature Software Inc.; US; 617/238-6734

Shanon, Greg; Pres, InfoStructure Services & Technologies Inc.; US; 515/296-6903

Shapiro, Sally; Mng Ed, MapWorld Magazine; US; 518/285-7340

Sharer, Julianne; Dir App Dev, WexTech Systems Inc.; US; 212/949-9595, 72460.1761@compuserve.com

Sharfman, Nahum; Pres, CommTouch Software Inc.; US; 408/245-8682

Sharma, Ken; Sr Partner, i2 Technologies Inc.; US; 214/860-6000, ken_sharma@i2.com

Sharma, Raghu; Pres, Multi-Tech Systems Inc.; US; 612/785-3500

Sharony, Meir; VP Sales & Mktng, Intelligent Computer Solutions; US; 818/998-5805

Sharp, James M.; Pres, Itsunami Inc.; US; 510/841-7271

Sharp, Richard L.; Chmn, Pres & CEO, Circuit City Stores Inc.; US; 804/527-4000

Sharp, Steven J.; Chmn, Pres & CEO, TriQuint Semiconductor; US; 503/644-3535

Sharpf, Norman W.; Pres, Graphic Communications Assoc.; US; 703/519-8160

Sharples, Brian; Pres, IntelliQuest; US; 512/329-2424

Sharpless, Andrew; SVP, Progressive Networks; US; 206/447-0567

Shassian, Donald R.; SVP & CFO, Southern New England Telecom Corp.; US; 203/771-5200

Shatas, Remigius G.; SVP & CTO, Cybex Corp.; US; 205/430-4000

Shaw, Claudia; VP Sales, Colorgraphic Communications Corp.; US; 770/455-3921

Shaw, Debbie; Pblr, E-mail, Buyers Guide to Electronic Commerce; US; 770/578-4980

Shaw, Jack; Pres, Electronic Commerce Strategies Inc.; US; 770/951-2648

Shaw, Kenneth; CTO, Tusk Inc.; US; 407/625-1101

Shaw, Peter B.; VP Sales & Mktng, Open Software Foundation; US; 508/474-9258

Shaw, Peter J.; Pres & CEO, AGE Logic Inc.; US; 619/755-1000

Shaw, William C.; SVP, Tekelec; US; 818/880-5656

Shawhan, Jerry; VP, Cincom Systems Inc.; US; 513/662-2300

Shaya, Jacob; EVP & Chief Scientist, Ligature Software Inc.; US; 617/238-6734

Sheer, William; CabiNet Systems Inc.; US; 201/512-1040, william@cabinet-sys.com

Sheerin, Matthew; Exec Ed, Electronic Buyers' News; US; 516/562-5000, msheerin@cmp.com

Sheeth, Jay; Dir Mktng, GTE Personal Communications Services; US; 404/391-8000

Sheets, Dale; VP Ops, Solectek Inc.; US; 619/450-1220

Shelton, Charles; SVP Prod Researc, Stonehouse & Co.; US; 214/960-1566

Shelton, James H.; Ed, CD-ROM Finder; US; 609/654-6266

Shelton, Monty; Pres, Future Trends Software Inc.; US; 214/224-3288

Shelton, Ted; Pres & CEO, IT Solutions Inc.; US; 312/474-7700

Shemas, George; VP Prod Dev, Information Dimensions Inc.; US; 614/761-8083

Shen, Ann; VP Sales & Mktng, Award Software Int'l. Inc.; US; 415/968-4433

Shepard, Bob; Research, Darnell Group, The; US; 909/279-6684

Shepard, Jeff; Pblr, Darnell Group, The; US; 909/279-6684, jshepard@darnell.com

Sherer, Scott; Pres, National Systems Programmers Assoc.; US; 414/423-2420

Sherick, Mike; Nat'l Sales Mgr, Japan Digital Laboratory Co. Ltd.; US; 805/588-8709

Sheridan, Thomas B.; Sr Ed, Presence: Teleoperators & Virtual Environments; US; 617/253-2889, presence@cbgrle.mit.edu

Sherman, Christopher V.; Pblr & Ed, Multimedia Wire; US; 301/493-9290, mmwire@aol.com

Sherman, J. Richard; Pres, RCI Ltd.; US; 612/858-8830, rcisherm@epx.cis.umn.edu

Sherman, Randall; Pres, New Venture Forecasting; US; 415/337-9171

Sherrill, Peter N.; CEO, SL Corp.; US; 415/927-1724

Sherrill, Roy L.; Pres, Datalight Inc.; US; 206/435-8086

Sherrod, Maggie; Mktng Mgr, Jostens Home Learning; US; 619/587-0087

Sherrod, Phillip H.; VP Dev, S&H Computer Systems Inc.; US; 615/327-3670, psherrod@sandh.com

Sherwin, Elton; VP Mktng, Lexicus Corp.; US; 415/462-6800, eltons@lexicus.mot.com

Sherwin, Richard M.; Ed-in-Chief, Dealerscope Merchandising; US; 215/238-5300

Sherwood, Scott W.; SVP Human Resources, Cadence Design Systems Inc.; US; 408/943-1234

Sheth, Arun P.; VP Sales, Kinetic Systems Corp.; US; 815/838-0005

Shev, Elliot; VP Sales, Spectragraphics Corp.; US; 619/450-0611

Shieh, Sam; VP Eng, Metra Information Systems Inc.; US; 510/226-9188

Shields, Bob; Dir Mktng, RDI Computer Corp.; US; 619/929-0992

Shiemura, Barton Y.; VP Mktng, Premisys Communications Inc.; US; 510/353-7600

Shih, Stan; Chmn & CEO, Acer Inc.; Taiwan ROC; 2-545-5288

Shillman, Robert J.; Chmn, Pres &

CEO, Cognex Corp.; US; 508/650-3000

Shimomura, Tokihiko; GM, Oki America Inc.; US; 201/646-0011

Shin, Chen-Hwa; Pres & CEO, Lion Optics Corp.; US; 408/954-8089

Shiohama, Larry; Natl Sales Mgr, Mitek Systems Inc.; US; 619/587-9157

Shipley, Chris; Ed, DemoLetter; US; 415/312-0691

Shipley, Dan; Dir Prod Mktng, Caravelle Networks Corp.; Canada; 613/225-1172

Shipman, G. William; Pres, IntelliPower Inc.; US; 714/587-0155

Shipp, Michael; Pres, Chromatic Communications Enterprises Inc.; US; 510/945-1602

Shippee, Richard R.; Dir Pubs, UniForum Monthly; US; 408/986-8840, dick@uniforum.org

Shirer, Michael; Pres, Management Software Assoc.; US; 617/232-4111

Shires, Philip; Pres & CEO, Kentek Information Systems Inc.; US; 303/440-5500

Shirk, Dave; VP Sales & Mktng, Macola Inc.; US; 614/382-5999

Shirley, Richard; SVP, Enterprise Solutions Ltd.; US; 805/449-4181

Shiroke, Ron; Dir Sales, MAG Innovision Inc.; US; 714/751-2008

Shmunis, Vlad; Pres, Ring Zero Systems Inc.; US; 415/349-0600

Shnelvar, Ralph; Pres, Tapedisk Corp.; US; 715/235-3388

Shockley, Rich; EVP, Apex Computer; US; 206/867-1900

Shoemaker, Bob; Pres, Stage 1 Development Inc.; US; 714/450-0390

Shohara, Sumi; VP Mktng, Action Technologies Inc.; US; 510/521-6190

Shohfi, David; VP Sales & Mktng, Jian Tools for Sales Inc.; US; 415/254-5600, shohfi@jianusa.com

Shomo, William L.; VP Prod Research, Micro-Integration Corp.; US; 301/689-0800

Shorb, Douglas; Sales Mgr, Seattle Silicon Corp.; US; 206/957-4422

Short, Jerry; VP Bus Dev, Digital Impact; US; 918/742-2022

Short, Louise; Pres & CEO, Digital Impact; US; 918/742-2022

Shotton, Chuck; SVP Eng, StarNine Technologies Inc.; US; 510/649-4949

Shotwell, Jay; Pres, Shotwell Public Relations Inc.; US; 408/727-4356

Shough, Terry; VP Sales, Edify Corp.; US; 408/982-2000, terrys@edify.com

Showers, Dale C.; Chmn, Andor Communications Inc.; US; 612/932-4000

Shows, Winnie; Pres, Smith & Shows; US; 415/329-8880, wshows@aol.com

Shray, Steven L.; VP & COO, Micro-Tech Conversion Systems Inc.; US; 415/424-1174

Shriver, Bruce; Pres, Genesis 2 Inc.; US; 914/762-3251

Shugart, Alan F.; Chmn, Pres & CEO, Seagate Technology; US; 408/438-6550

Shukla, Anu; COO, mFactory Inc.; US; 415/548-0600

Shulman, Dean F.; SVP Mktng, Brother International Corp.; US; 908/356-8880

Shulte, Richard; Ed, NT Developer; US; 541/747-0800

Shum, Martin; Chmn, Pres & CEO, ACT Networks Inc.; US; 805/388-2474

Shumaker, Gary; VP Tech Mktng Svcs, Shining Technology Inc.; US; 714/761-9598

Shumate, Robert L.; Pres, Helix Technologies; US; 847/465-0242

Shur, Vadim; VP NA Sales, CabiNet Systems Inc.; US; 201/512-1040, vadim@cabinet-sys.com

Shwed, Gil; Chmn, Check Point Software Technologies Inc.; US; 617/859-9051

Sibayan, Fred; VP Sales & Mktng, Exodus Communications Inc.; US; 408/522-8450

Siboni, Roger S.; Dep Chmn, KPMG Peat Marwick; US; 201/307-7000

Sichler, Joseph E.; CFO, CMP Publications Inc.; US; 516/562-5000

Siclari-Lee, Paulette; Ed, Macintosh Multimedia Product Registry; US; 407/231-6904

Sidgmore, John W.; Pres & CEO, Uunet Technologies Inc.; US; 703/206-5600

Sidhu, Sanjiv; Pres, i2 Technologies Inc.; US; 214/860-6000, sanjiv_sidhu@i2.com

Sidorsky, Arthur; EVP, Standard Microsystems Corp.; US; 516/435-6000

Siebenaler, Rick A.; Dir SW Dev, Harris Computer Systems Corp.; US; 305/973-5100

Siebert, Lawrence L.; VP Mfg, Opus Systems Inc.; US; 408/562-9340, larry@opus.com

Siefkes, Kent; Tech Dir, Performance Awareness Corp.; US; 919/870-8800, kds@pacorp.com

Siegel, Robert J.; GM, Silvon Software Inc.; US; 708/655-3313

Siegert, Paul; Pres, Mentalix Inc.; US; 214/423-9377

Siemon, Marta; Partner, Insync Partners; US; 503/221-1063, martas@insyncp.com

Sigel, E. Courtney; Chmn, Pres & CEO, Harris Computer Systems Corp.; US; 305/973-5100

Sigel, Susan; VP, National Association of Desktop Pblrs; US

Signorello, John; CEO, STMS; US; 703/318-7867

Siilasmaa, Risto; Pres & CEO, Data Fellows Inc.; US; 415/354-0233

Silber, Tony; Mgng Ed, Web Week; US; 203/226-6967, tsilber@webweek.com

Sileo, Lorraine; Author, Online Services: Review Trends & Forecasts; US; 203/834-0033

Sills, Stanley S.; Chmn & CEO, PTN Publishing Co.; US; 516/845-2700

Siltanen, Steve; Pres, Watergate Software Inc.; US; 510/654-5182, steve_s@ws.com

Silton, Richard; Pres, Silton-Bookman Systems; US; 408/446-1170, rsilton@sbsinc.com

Silver, Catherine; VP Sales, Herring Communications Inc.; US; 415/865-2277

Silvera, Marketta; Pres & CEO, Pilot Network Services Inc.; US; 510/748-1850

Silverman, Arnold N.; Chmn, ICOT Corp.; US; 408/433-3300

Silverman, Barry; Dir, Institute for Artificial Intelligence; US; 202/994-5079

Silverman, Nat; Pres, Nathan J. Silverman Co. PR; US; 847/328-4292, natsilv@aol.com

Silverman, William; Pres, William Silverman & Co.; US; 216/696-7750

Silvers, Richard A.; VP & CIO, Tandy Corp.; US; 817/390-3700

Silverstein, Jeff; Ed & Pblr, Digital Information Group; US; 203/840-0045

Silvestri, Chester J.; Pres, Sparc Technology Business; US; 415/960-1300

Silvius, Susan; Mgr Usability Test, PC World Test Center; US; 415/243-0500

Sim, W.H.; Chmn & CEO, Creative Labs Inc.; US; 408/428-6600

Simeon, Yvette; Mgng Ed, Digital Kids Report; US; 212/780-6060

Simeone, Salvatore; Pres & CEO, Software Engineering of America; US; 916/328-7000

Simeone-Ambert, Doreen; Partner, D.H. Andrews Group; US; 203/271-1300

Simerath, Hal; VP Prod Dev, CalComp Inc.; US; 714/821-2000

Simington, Robert A.; Pres, Promark Software Inc.; Canada; 604/988-2051

Simko, Robert; Exec Dir, International Technology Group; US; 415/964-2565

Simmons, George; CFO, Digital Products Inc.; US; 617/647-1234

Simmons, Michael J.; CFO, Platinum Software Corp.; US; 714/453-4000

Simmons, Wayne; VP Sales, Fujitsu Computer Products; US; 408/432-6333

Simon, Diana; Ed, Digital Kids Report; US; 212/780-6060

Simon, Janson; Ed-in-Chief, Chicago Journal of Theoretical Computer Science; US; 617/253-2889, chicago-journal@cs.uchicago.edu

Simon, Michael S.; VP Sales, AIB Software Corp.; US; 703/430-9247, mike.simon@aib.com

Simon, Sarina; Pres, Philips Media Home & Family Entertainment; US

Simon, Steve; CEO, S&S Public Relations Inc.; US; 847/291-1616

Simonds, Jonathan; Pres, Information Presentation Technologies Inc.; US; 805/541-3000

Simonds, Kenneth W.; Chmn, MasPar Computer Corp.; US; 408/736-3300

Simons, Todd; Mktng Dir, Franklin Quest Co.; US; 801/975-9992

Simonsen, Jill; Mgng Ed, Selling Networks; US; 415/513-6800

Simonson, Ray; Pres, Xplor International; US; 310/373-3633

Simpson, Charlie; Ed-in-Chief, Digital Age; US; 215/643-8000, simpsoncm@cardinal.com

Simpson, James; Chmn, Pres & CEO, Wall Data Inc.; US; 206/814-9255

Simpson, Lee; CEO, Seattle Support Group; US; 206/395-1484

Simpson, Scott; Dir PR, Schraff Group; US; 714/556-6800

Sims, Arthur B.; Chmn & CEO, 3D Systems Corp.; US; 805/295-5600

Sims, Judy; Pres & CEO, Software Spectrum Inc.; US; 214/840-6600

Sims, Philip S.; Vice Chmn, Premier Industrial Corp.; US; 216/391-8300

Sing, Y.W.; Vice Chmn, Integrated Information Technology Inc.; US; 408/727-1885

Singer, Steve; Pres, Micro Format Inc.; US; 847/520-4699

Singh, Amar; Pres, Sophisticated Circuits Inc.; US; 206/485-7979

Singh, Inder; Pres & CEO, Lynx Real-Time Systems Inc.; US; 408/879-3900

Singh, Jagdeep; Pres & CEO, Airsoft Inc.; US; 408/777-7500, jagdeep@airsoft.com

Sinisgalli, Peter F.; EVP & CFO, Dun & Bradstreet Software Services Inc.; US; 404/239-2000

Sinkewiz, Giles; VP & GM Integrated Cust Sol, GTE Government Systems, Information Systems Div.; US; 703/818-4000

Sinyard, Bobbi; Pblr, Windows Tech Journal; US; 541/747-0800

Sipe, Russell; Pblr, Computer Gaming World; US

Sipkovich, Ronald J.; VP & CFO, Advanced Logic Research; US; 714/581-6770

Sipowicz, Steven; CFO, Integrated Systems Inc.; US; 408/542-1500, ssipowicz@isi.com

Sippl, Roger; Pres & CEO, Visigenic Software; US; 415/286-1900

Sirazi, Semir; VP R&D, U.S. Robotics Inc.; US; 847/882-5010

Sirotek, Linda; Prod Plng & Acq, Sir-Tech Software Inc.; US; 315/393-6451

Sirotek, Norman; Pres & CEO, Sir-Tech Software Inc.; US; 315/393-6451

Sirotek, Robert; VP, Sir-Tech Software Inc.; US; 315/393-6451

Sisto, Al; Pres & CEO, DocuMagix Inc.; US; 408/434-1138

Sisto, Leslie; Grp Pblr, Cutter Information Corp.; US; 617/648-8700, 73352.1625@compuserve.com

Sit, Hon P.; VP Eng, Hercules Computer Technology Inc.; US; 510/623-6030

Sitarski, Ed; VP R&D, Numetrix Ltd.; US; 203/847-3452

Sivin-Kachala, Jay; VP, Interactive Educational Systems Design Inc.; US; 212/769-1715

Skadra, Joseph; VP & CFO, System Software Associates Inc.; US; 312/258-6000

Skaff, George; VP Mktng, DocuMagix Inc.; US; 408/434-1138

Skapinker, Mark; Pres, Delrina Corp.; Canada; 416/441-3676

Skaradowski, Susan K.; Mng Ed, Internet Voyager; US; sueskara@aol.com

Skates, Ronald L.; Pres & CEO, Data General Corp.; US; 508/898-5000

Skelton, Thomas A.; EVP & COO, Manugistics Inc.; US; 301/984-5000

Skemp, Randy L.; SVP, CyCare Systems Inc.; US; 602/596-4300

Skiba, Tom; CFO, IVI Publishing Inc.; US; 612/996-6000

Skier, Cynthia; VP, SkiSoft Publishing Corp.; US; 617/863-1876

Skier, Ken; Pres, SkiSoft Publishing Corp.; US; 617/863-1876, ken@skisoft.com

Skiles, David W.; VP Sales & Mktng, Galileo Electro-Optics Corp.; US; 508/347-9191

Skilling, D. Van; EVP Info Syst, TRW Inc.; US; 216/291-7000

Skinner, Donald K.; Chmn & CEO, Eltron International Inc.; US; 805/579-1800

Skok, David; Pres & CEO, Watermark Software Inc.; US; 617/229-2600

Skok, Michael; Chmn, AlphaBlox Corp.; US; 617/229-2924

Skoog, Norma; VP, Future Now; US; 513/792-4500

Skov, Andrea R.; VP Mktng, ICVerify Inc.; US; 510/553-7500, askov@icverify.com

Slade, John; Pres, Knowledge Garden Inc.; US; 516/862-0600, jslade@kgarden.com

Slade, Mike; Pres & CEO, Starwave Corp.; US; 206/957-2000

Slagowitz, Martin; VP Prof Svcs, Information Builders Inc.; US; 212/736-4433

Slater, Alan P.; EVP, Group 1 Software; US; 301/731-2300

Slater, Michael; Pres, MicroDesign Resources Inc.; US; 707/824-4004, mslater@mdr.zd.com

Slavin, Jack; VP Sales, AimTech Corp.; US; 603/883-0220

Slawetsky, Louis E.; Pblr, Office Product Analyst, The; US; 716/232-5320

Slette, Mike; VP Bus Dev, Great Plains Software; US; 701/281-0550

Slevin, Jack; Pres & CEO, Comdisco Inc.; US; 847/698-3000

Slingerlend, Mac J.; EVP & CFO, Ciber Inc.; US; 303/220-0100

Slipson, Alan; VP, Corollary Inc.; US; 714/250-4040

Sloan, Alan D.; EVP, Iterated Systems Inc.; US; 770/840-0310

Sloane, A. Richard; Pres & CEO, Soft-

mart Inc.; US; 610/524-7440

Slome, B.P.; Pres, ABCO Distributors; US; 914/368-1930

Slome, Roz; VP, ABCO Distributors; US; 914/368-1930

Sloss, Craig; Prod Mktng Mgr, Nanao US Corp.; US; 310/325-5202

Sloss, Rodney F.; VP Fin, Lattice Semiconductor Corp.; US; 503/681-0118

Slovick, Murray; Ed & Assoc Pblr, IEEE Spectrum; US; 908/981-0060, m.slovick@ieee.org

Slowey, Thomas A.; EVP Sales, Platinum Technology Inc.; US; 708/620-5000

Slutzky, Joel; Chmn & CEO, Odetics Inc.; US; 714/774-5000

Smaby, Gary; Pres, Smaby Group; US; 612/333-0002

Smaldrone, Thomas E.; Pres Mktng Group, Cincinnati Bell Information Systems; US; 513/784-5900

Smart, Charles N.; Pres, Smart Software; US; 617/489-2743, csmart@smartcorp.com

Smart, J. Larry; Pres & CEO, Micropolis Corp.; US; 818/709-3300

Smart, John R.; VP Mktng, Innovative Tech Systems Inc.; US; 215/441-5600

Smarte, Gene; Ed-in-Chief, CADalyst; US; 714/513-8400

Smelek, Raymond A.; Pres & CEO, Extended Systems; US

Smeltzer, Dennis; Exec Dir, TSANet; US; 913/345-9311

Smidt, James E.; Pres, SSI Products Inc.; US; 818/305-0508

Smith, Art; Compulink Management Center Inc.; US; 310/212-5465, 75162.2305@compuserve.com

Smith, Bob; Chmn, Qualitas Inc.; US; 301/907-6700

Smith, Brent; Pblr, FoxTalk; US; 206/251-1900

Smith, Caby; Pres & Exec Dir, World Computer Graphics Assoc.; US; 703/642-3050

Smith, Cathy; Pres, Rourke & Co.; US; 617/267-0042

Smith, Clive G.; VP Bus Dev, Geoworks; US; 510/814-1660

Smith, Daniel; CEO, Cascade Communications; US; 508/692-2600

Smith, Darrell; VP Prod Dev, Motion Pixels; US; 602/951-3288

Smith, Dave; Acc Mgr, Penna Powers Cutting & Haynes Inc.; US; 801/531-0973, ppch@xmission.com

Smith, David; Chmn, Magic Quest Inc.; US; 415/321-5838

Smith, David A.; Chmn & CEO, Virtus Corp.; US; 919/467-9700, david.smith@virtus.com

Smith, Douglas; VP Sales & Mktng, Davox Corp.; US; 508/952-0200

Smith, Douglas P.; VP & CFO, Computervision Corp.; US; 617/275-1800

Smith, Esther T.; CEO & Pres, Tech-

News Inc.; US; 703/848-2800, esmith@technews.com

Smith, Gerry; EVP & COO, Core Int'l.; US; 407/997-6055

Smith, Gerry; CFO, Walker Richer & Quinn Inc.; US; 206/217-7100

Smith, Gordon; Application Partners Inc.; US; 908/549-5464

Smith, Guy; VP, Intellimation; US; 805/968-2291

Smith, Harry; Pres, Safety Software Inc.; US; 804/296-8789

Smith, Howard J.; Pres & CEO, Clarity Software Inc.; US; 415/691-0320

Smith, Hyrum W.; CEO, Franklin Quest Co.; US; 801/975-9992

Smith, J. Neil; Pres, Melita International; US; 770/446-7800

Smith, Jay A.; Pres, Jasmine Multimedia; US; 818/780-3344

Smith, Kent D.; EVP Cust Ops, Legato Systems Inc.; US; 415/812-6000

Smith, Kevin; VP Mktng, BateTech Software Inc.; US; 303/763-8333, kevins@batetech.com

Smith, Lowell R.; Corp VP, BDM Int'l.; US; 703/848-5000

Smith, Marc C.; Chmn, Pres & CEO, Adtran Inc.; US; 205/971-8000

Smith, Mark; Ed Dir, Windows NT; US; 303/663-4700, mark@winntmag.com

Smith, Mark S.; VP Sales, Network Peripherals; US; 408/321-7300

Smith, Melany; Mktng Dir, Micro Dynamics Ltd.; US; 301/589-6300, melany_smith@mdl.com

Smith, Mike; GM Connectivity Group, Locus Computing Corp.; US; 310/670-6500

Smith, Paul; VP Mktng, Asante Technologies Inc.; US; 408/435-8388

Smith, Peter J.; Pres & CEO, Ansys Inc.; US

Smith, Randall; Pres & CEO, MacAcademy; US; 904/677-1918

Smith, Randall S.; Pres Info Svcs, Information Resources Inc.; US; 312/726-1221

Smith, Raymond W.; Chmn & CEO, Bell Atlantic Corp.; US; 215/963-6000

Smith, Rhonda; EVP & COO, Smith Micro Software Inc.; US; 714/362-5800

Smith, Richard M.; Pres, Phar Lap Software Inc.; US; 617/661-1510

Smith, Rick L.; VP & CFO, Datalogix Int'l.; US; 914/747-2900

Smith, Robert C.; Pres, CBIS Inc.; US; 770/446-1332

Smith, Robert L.; VP Eng, KnowledgeSet Corp.; US; 415/254-5400, rlsmith@kset.com

Smith, Robert S.; VP Bus Dev, General DataComm Industries Inc.; US; 203/574-1118

Smith, Rodney; Chmn, Pres & CEO, Altera Corp.; US; 408/894-7000

Smith, Roger; DB/Pub MIS Mgr, Educom; US; 202/872-4200

Smith, Roger; VP Sales & Mktng, Crescent Project Management; US; 415/938-4636

Smith, Roscoe; Pblr, AV Video & Multimedia Producer; US; 914/328-9157

Smith, Ryan; IS Mgr, Angia Communications; US; 801/371-0488

Smith, Sally; Pres, S.S. Smith & Associates Inc.; US; 513/897-0654

Smith, Sam K.; Chmn, Landmark Graphics Corp.; US

Smith, Stephen; VP Sales & Mktng, E.M.M.E. Interactive; US; 203/406-4041

Smith, Stephen D.; Dir Mktng, Digital Animation Corp.; US; 810/354-0890

Smith, Stephen P.; Pres & CEO, Raima Corp.; US; 206/557-0200, ssmith@raima.com

Smith, Steven; Mgng Ed, Service & Support World; US; 512/250-9023

Smith, Steven B.; SVP Mktng, Megahertz Corp.; US; 801/320-7000

Smith, Theodore J.; Chmn, Pres & CEO, FileNet Corp.; US; 714/966-3400

Smith, Tom; EVP, Datastorm Technologies Inc.; US; 573/443-3282

Smith, Tomec; Pres, InfoCenter; US; 303/751-8880

Smith, Tony; Dir, Special Events Management; US; 803/737-9352, smitht@sbt.tec.sc.us

Smith, William B.; Pres & COO, Telco Systems Inc.; US; 617/551-0300

Smith, William J.; SVP Sales & Mktng, Premisys Communications Inc.; US; 510/353-7600

Smith II, Roy C.; Pres, Turtle Beach Systems Inc.; US; 717/767-0200

Smith III, Roscoe C.; SVP Group Pblr, Knowledge Industry Publications Inc.; US; 914/328-9157, kipi1@applelink.com

Smith Jr., Robert L.; Exec Dir, Interactive Services Assoc.; US; 301/495-4955

Smith Jr., William W.; Pres & CEO, Smith Micro Software Inc.; US; 714/362-5800

Smith, Jr., Bill; CFO, Rockwell Network Systems; US; 805/968-4262, bsmith@rns.com

Smith-Dzubeck, Kathryn; EVP, Communications Network Architects Inc.; US; 202/775-8000

Smith-Moritz, Geoff; Ed, Rapid Prototyping Report; US; 619/488-0533

Smithson, Franchon M.; SVP & CFO, Legent Corp.; US; 703/708-3000

Smits, Dirk; VP Mktng, QSound Labs Inc.; Canada; 403/291-2492

Smolenski, Loretta R.; Ed, Newton-Evans Research Co. Inc.; US; 410/465-7316

Smolin, Rocky; VP Mktng, Partners-in-Health Inc.; US; 619/514-4315

Smolinski, Jeffrey L.; VP Ops, X-Rite Inc.; US; 616/534-7663

Smoot, Oliver; EVP, Information Technology Industry Council; US; 202/737-8888

Smyth, Peter; VP Sales, Altera Corp.; US; 408/894-7000

Snapp, Cheryl; Founding Partner, Network Associates Inc.; US; 801/373-7888, cheryls@netassoc.com

Snedacker, Dianne; Pres, Ketchum Public Relations; US; 415/984-6100

Snedaker, Carl; VP Eng, DiagSoft Inc.; US; 408/438-8247

Sneddon, Steve; EVP & CTO, Revelation Software; US; 203/973-1000

Snell, David; VP Eng, ATTO Technology Inc.; US; 716/691-1999

Snider, James; Vice Chair, 1394 Trade Assoc.; US; 512/305-0202

Snow, Dean; Pres, Comprehend Franchise Corp.; US; 954/921-6040

Snowden, Guy B.; Co-Chmn & CEO, Gtech Corp.; US; 401/392-1000

Snowdon, Diana E.; SVP, Pacific Telecom Inc.; US; 360/905-5800

Snyder, Becky; Pblr, Intellimation; US; 805/968-2291

Snyder, Bill; CFO, Integrated Device Technology Inc.; US; 408/727-6116

Snyder, Bob; GM, European Computer Sources; Belgium; 322-766-0045

Snyder, J. Edward; Pres & CEO, Optimal Networks; US; 415/254-5950

Snyder, Jackie; Mktng Dir, Byron Preiss Multimedia Co. Inc.; US; 212/989-6252

Snyder, Jerry J.; Pres & COO, Technalysis Corp.; US; 612/925-5900

Snyder, John; VP Inv Rel, Kaufer Miller Communications; US; 206/450-9965, jsnyderir@aol.com

Snyder, Kevin; Controller, Axonix Corp.; US; 801/521-9797

Snyder, Mel; VP Mktng & Sales, Xecom Inc.; US; 408/945-6640

Snyder, Peter; Pres, Miller/Shandwick Technologies; US; 617/536-0470

Snyder, Richard; EVP Ops, Cognex Corp.; US; 508/650-3000

Snyder, Richard D.; Pres & COO, Gateway 2000; US; 605/232-2000

Snyder, Steve F.; COO, Software Partners/32 Inc.; US; 508/887-6409

Snyder, Stuart; SVP, Turner Home Entertainment; US; 404/885-0505

So, Yin; Pres, Allodyne Inc.; US; 510/770-1101

Sobel, Howard; Exec Dir, Windows User Group Network; US; 215/565-1861

Sobiloff, Peter B.; VP Ops, Datalogix Int'l.; US; 914/747-2900

Sobkowski, Isidore; Pres, Professional Help Desk; US; 203/356-7700, info@prohelpdesk.com

Sobol, Michael I.; Pblr, Infosecurity News; US; 508/879-9792

Soderbergh, Christine; Pres, Christine Soderbergh PR; US; 310/394-7763

Soechtig, Jacqueline E.; Chmn, Pres & CEO, Lasergate Systems Inc.; US; 813/725-0882

Soejima, Toshihiro; Pres & CEO, Mitsui Comtek Corp.; US; 408/725-8525

Solberg, Ronald D.; Pres, EasyCom Inc.; US; 630/969-1441

Soley, Richard; VP, Object Management Group; US; 508/820-4300

Solley, Michael W.; VP SI, Nichols Research Corp.; US; 205/883-1140

Sollitto, Vincent; VP & GM, Fujitsu Microelectronics Inc.; US; 408/922-9000

Sollman, George H.; Pres & CEO, Centigram Communications Corp.; US; 408/944-0250

Soloman, Alan; Chmn, S&S Software Int'l. Inc.; US; 617/273-7400

Solomon, Jess; Pres & CEO, Software Solutions Inc.; US; 770/418-2000

Solomon, Joy; GM, IVI Publishing Inc.; US; 612/996-6000

Solomon, Lewis; Pres, Venture Development Corp.; US; 508/653-9000

Solomon, Marie; EVP & CFO, Smart & Friendly; US; 818/772-8001

Solomon, Mark; Ed, Exploring Windows NT; US; 502/491-1900

Solomon, Perry; Pres & CEO, Smart & Friendly; US; 818/772-8001

Solomon, Robert M.; Dir Mktng, Brand X Software; US; 804/355-0374

Solomon, Steve; VP SW Prod, Farallon Computing Inc.; US; 510/814-5100

Soluk, John; VP Mktng, Vamp Inc.; US; 213/466-5533

Some, Norman M.; Chmn & CEO, GBC Technologies; US; 609/767-2500

Sommer, Steven R.; VP Mktng, Informix Software Inc.; US; 415/926-6300

Sommerhauser, Charles; Principal, Walt & Sommerhauser Communications; US; 408/496-0900

Sommers, David; VP & CFO, SystemSoft Corp.; US; 508/651-0088

Sommers, Robert; Chmn, Symark Software; US; 818/865-6100

Sommers, William; Pres & CEO, SRI International; US; 415/326-6200

Somogyi, Lel F.; Pres, Around Technology Inc.; US; 216/234-6402, lsomogyi@aroundtech.com

Son, Masayoshi; Chmn, Softbank Comdex Inc.; US; 617/443-1500

Soneira, Julia; Pres, Sonera Technologies; US; 908/747-6886

Soneira, Raymond; VP Dev, Sonera Technologies; US; 908/747-6886

Sones, Aaron H.; Pres, Hunter Digital; US; 310/471-5852

Song, Ki Ryong; Pres, Samsung Electronics America Inc.; US; 201/229-4000

Song, Y.C.; VP Sales, Pacom Inc.; US; 408/752-1590

Songhurst, Ruth; Pres, Mortice Kern Systems Inc.; Canada; 519/884-2251

Sonksen, David R.; VP & CFO, Microsemi Corp.; US; 714/979-8220

Sonnenberg, Ronni; Pres US Pubs, Ziff-Davis Publishing Co.; US; 212/503-3500

Sonntag, Albert; VP Ops, Broderbund Software Inc.; US; 415/382-4400

Sopp, William; VP Sales & Mktng, Konexx; US; 619/622-1400, bsopp@konexx.com

Soreide, Phil; VP & Creative Dir, Ripley-Woodbury Marketing Communications; US; 310/860-7336

Sorensen, Gordon; Dir Sales, Zebra Technologies VTI Inc.; US; 801/576-9700

Sorensen, Jack; Pres, LucasArts Entertainment Co.; US; 415/472-3400

Sorensen, Robert A.; CFO, Angia Communications; US; 801/371-0488

Sorg, Patricia; Client Svcs Mgr, Market Trends Digest; US; 410/465-7316

Sorhaug, Asbjorn; EVP & COO, LANcast; US; 603/880-1833, asbjorns@aol.com

Sorkin, Fred; Pres, Hummingbird Communications Ltd.; Canada; 905/470-1203

Sosbee, Roberta; Sales Dir, Great Wave Software; US; 408/438-1990

Sotomayor, Bernardo; VP & GM, Iconovex Corp.; US; 612/896-5100

Soule, Nathan; Acct Supv, Robert Wick Public Relations Inc.; US; 212/682-0600

Souter, Justin; CEO, Art & Logic; US; 818/501-6990

Southwood, John; Sales & Mktng Mgr, SNMP Research International Inc.; US; 615/573-1434, john@snmp.com

Southworth, Joseph L.; VP WW Mktng, Ross Systems Inc.; US; 415/593-2500

Southworth, Robert; Treas, Electronic Systems Technology Inc.; US; 509/735-9092

Sowers, Brad; VP WW Mktng, Memorex Telex Corp.; US; 214/444-3500

Spadafora, Samuel T.; VP Sales, Sparc Technology Business; US; 415/960-1300

Spain, Jennifer; Dir Ops, NAFT International Ltd.; US; 212/982-0800, jen_spain@naft.com

Spampinato, Janice; VP Sales & Mktng, Ag Group Inc., The; US; 510/937-7900

Spargo, Brian; Mgr Prdtn, Tactics International Ltd.; US; 508/475-4475

Sparkman, George; Pblr, Computer Hot Line; US

Sparks, Bryan; Pres, Caldera; US; 801/229-1675

Sparks, Jason; Dir Mktng, Princeton Graphic Systems; US; 714/751-8405

Sparks, Joe; CEO & Co-founder, Pop Rocket Inc.; US; 415/731-9112

Sparks, Roger D.; VP Prod & Syst, Thoroughbred Software Int'l. Inc.; US; 201/560-1377

Spatafora, Matt; VP, Scantron Quality Computers; US; msspata@quality-comp.com

Spatz, Bruce; VP & Ed-in-Chief, Sybex; US; 510/523-8233

Spazante, William A.; CFO, General Parametrics Corp.; US; 510/524-3950

Spear, Chuck; CFO, Smith Micro Software Inc.; US; 714/362-5800

Spears, Robert M.; VP, Gateway 2000; US; 605/232-2000

Spector, Alfred; Pres & CEO, Transarc Corp.; US; 412/338-4400

Spector, Gregory; SVP, GCI Jennings; US; 415/974-6200

Spence, Stephen P.; VP Sales, Choreo Systems Inc.; Canada; 613/238-1050, steves@choreo.ca

Spencer, John; VP Bus Dev, Visual Edge Software Ltd.; Canada; 514/332-6430, vecalif@attmail.com

Spencer, Michael E.; VP Mktng & Sales, Minden Group Inc.; US; 408/399-6645

Spencer, William; Pres & CEO, Sematech; US; 512/356-3137

Sperry, Steven; Pres, Primus Communications Corp.; US; 206/292-1000

Spica, Tony; VP Sales, RGB Spectrum; US; 510/814-7000

Spielman, Anthony J.; VP Sales & Mktng, SBE Inc.; US; 510/355-2000

Spilke, Howard; VP R&D, Atria Software; US; 617/676-2400

Spilo, Michael L.; Pres, Helix Software Co. Inc.; US

Spindler, Paul; Pres, Spindler Organization Inc.; US; 213/930-0811

Spink, Leslie; Exec Ed, Insight Into Emerging Systems Management Solutions; US; 415/323-4780

Spinner, Bob A.; VP Sales, Clarify Inc.; US; 408/428-2000

Spitz, Robert; VP Ops, Feith Systems & Software Inc.; US; 215/646-8000

Spitzer, David; VP & CFO, NeuralWare Inc.; US; 412/787-8222

Spitzer, Thomas K.; VP Eng, SBT Accounting Systems; US; 415/444-9900

Spizziri, Martha; Exec Ed, Digital News & Review; US; 303/470-4445, ms@dnr.cahners.com

Spofford, John; Ed, Computer Video; US; 703/998-7600

Sprague, Tony; Tech Mgr, Intelligent Micro Software Ltd.; US; 407/726-0024, 100066.517@compuserve.com

Spring, Steve; Pres, Aspen Systems Inc.; US; 303/431-4606

Springer, Bill; Pblr, United Publications Inc.; US; 207/846-0600, bspring@servicenews.com

Sprinzen, Marty; Chmn, Pres & CEO, Forte Software Inc.; US; 510/869-3400

Spurlock, Duane; Ed, Inside WordPerfect for Windows; US; 502/491-1900

Squeri, Denis J.; VP Sales, My Software Co.; US; 415/473-3600

Squires, Gary R.; Pblr, Government Computer News; US; 301/650-2000

St. Charles, David P.; Pres & CEO, Integrated Systems Inc.; US; 408/542-1500

St. Clare, Mark S.; SVP & CFO, FileNet Corp.; US; 714/966-3400, mstclare@filenet.com

Staab, H. Peter; VP Eng, ACT Networks Inc.; US; 805/388-2474

Staadecker, Joel; Pres & CEO, Allegiant Technologies Inc.; US; 619/587-0500, staad@allegiant.com

Stacey, Doug; Ed Dir, International DB2 Users Group; US; 312/644-6610

Stacey, Mark; VP Sales & Mktng, Omray Inc.; US; 512/250-1700

Staciokas, Leon J.; SVP & COO, Iomega Corp.; US; 801/778-1000

Stackpole, Kerry; Pres, Association for Work Process Improvement; US; 617/426-1167

Stacy, John M.; VP Mktng & Sales, Learning Company, The; US; 510/792-2101

Staedke, John; Pres & CEO, Hitachi Data Systems; US; 408/970-1000

Stafford, James F.; Pres & CEO, Chips & Technologies Inc.; US; 408/434-0600

Stafford, Jan; Exec Ed, Office World News; US; 908/785-1616

Stafford, Jim; Pblr, Computer Life; US; 415/357-5355

Stafford, Joe; CFO, Viking Components; US; 714/643-7255

Stafford, John; Dir Mktng, Systech Corp.; US; 619/453-8970

Stager, Roger; VP Eng, PDC; US; 610/265-3300, rstager@eng.pdc.com

Stagno, Anthony; VP Ops, Ascend Communications Inc.; US; 510/769-6001

Stahlman, Mark; Pres, New Media Assoc.; US; 212/349-2700

Stahnke, Lizanna; SVP, Microdyne Corp.; US; 703/739-0500

Staiano, Edward; Chmn, Network Computing Devices Inc.; US; 415/694-0650

Staiano, Edward F.; Pres & GM, Motorola Computer Group; US; 602/438-3000

Stambler, Sarah; Pres, Sarah Stambler's Marketing with Technology News; US; 212/222-1765, sarah@mwt.com

Stamen, Jeffrey P.; Pres SW Group, Information Resources Inc.; US; 312/726-1221

Stamm, David; Pres & CEO, Clarify Inc.; US; 408/428-2000

Stanfield, Jim; Ed, Inside DOS; US; 502/491-1900

Stanford, Donald L.; SVP Tech, Gtech Corp.; US; 401/392-1000

Stange, Karen; MIS Mgr, Drive Savers Inc.; US; 415/382-2000

Stanger, Donna G.; VP Prod Dev, Edmark Corp.; US; 206/556-8400

Stanley, Brad; Pres, KnowledgeBroker Inc.; US; 702/852-5711

Stanley, Chuck; Pblr, BAM Media; US; 510/934-3700

Stanley, James G.; EVP, Sierra On-Line Inc.; US; 206/649-9800

Stanley, Mary; CEO, Qualitas Inc.; US; 301/907-6700

Stanley, Susan; VP, Engineered Software; US; 910/299-4843

Stanley, Thomas E.; SVP & Pblr, Merriam-Webster Inc.; US; 413/734-3134

Stanley Jr., W. L.; Pres & CEO, Engineered Software; US; 910/299-4843

Stansberry, Fred; Pres & CEO, Raidtec Corp; US; 770/664-6066

Stansell, Michael W.; VP Ops, Microfield Graphics Inc.; US; 503/626-9393

Stanton, David; VP, Sage Solutions; US; 415/392-7243, dave.stanton@sagesolu.com

Stanton, Paul A.; VP Mktng, Mecklermedia Corp.; US; 203/226-6967, stanton@mecklermedia.com

Staple, Gregory C.; Pres, TeleGeography Inc.; US; 202/467-0017

Stapleton, Deborah A.; Pres, Stapleton Communications Inc.; US; 415/988-9207

Stapleton, Raymond D.; SVP, Genicom Corp.; US; 703/802-9200

Stark, Chuck; Prog Dir, U.S. Product Data Assoc.; US; 803/760-3327

Starkey, Neil; EVP & CTO, DataBeam Corp.; US; 606/245-3500, nstarkey@databeam.com

Starks, Michael; Pres, 3DTV Corp.; US; 415/479-3516, starks@stereospace.com

Starr, Robert; GM Sales & Mktng, Yamaha Systems Technology; US; 408/467-2300

Stasior, Matthew; Insights Software; US; 310/577-1185

Stata, Ray; Chmn & CEO, Analog Devices Inc.; US; 617/329-4700

Staudt, Thomas P.; Pres & CEO, MEDE America Corp.; US; 216/425-3241

Stauffer, Gordon R.; VP Dev, Cybermedix Inc.; US; 703/917-6600

Stauffer, Rick; Pres, SilverSun Inc.; US; 609/722-0050

Stautzenbach, Steve; Dir Sales, Ulead Systems Inc.; US; 310/523-9393, stevesta@ulead.com

Stavisky, Robin D.; Mgng Partner, New Venture Marketing; US; 415/473-9990, rdsnvm@aol.com

Stavropulos, Peter; Dir Comm, Bull HN Information Systems Inc.; US; 508/294-6000

Stawarz, Jean; Oak Ridge Public Relations Inc.; US; 408/253-5042, jean@oakridge.com

Stead, Jerre; CEO, Ingram Micro Inc.; US; 714/566-1000

Stearns, Greg; CEO, CH Products; 619/598-2518

Stecher, Greg; CFO, Genasys II Inc.; US; 970/493-0035, gregs@genasys.com

Stedman, John; Chief Eng, Precision Guides; US; 503/227-6219

Steel, George; Pres & COO, Scientific Software-Intercomp Inc.; US; 303/292-1111

Steel, Gordon M.; VP & CFO, Xilinx Inc.; US; 408/559-7778

Steele, Bob; Mgng Dir, International

Association for Management Automation; US; 941/275-7887

Steele, Donald; VP Sales, Trilogy Development Group; US; 512/794-5900

Steele, Jane; Assoc/Res Assist, Windham/Lang Group; US; 415/563-4545, jdsteele@netcom.com

Steele, Richard; SVP Sales & Mktng, Printronix Inc.; US; 714/863-1900

Steele, Robert M.; Exec Dir, Association for Services Management Int'l.; US; 941/275-7887

Steensburg, Eric L.; Pres & COO, Ricoh Corp.; US; 201/882-2000

Steere, Leslie; Mgng Ed, Oracle Magazine; US; 415/506-4763, lsteere@us.oracle.com

Steffan, Mike; Pres Distribution, InaCom Corp.; US; 402/392-3900

Steffann, Lawrence F.; VP Ops, Boca Research Inc.; US; 407/997-6227

Steffensen, Dwight A.; Chmn & CEO, Merisel Inc.; US; 310/615-3080

Steger, Hal; VP, mFactory Inc.; US; 415/548-0600

Stein, Alfred J.; Chmn & CEO, VLSI Technology Inc.; US; 408/434-3000

Stein, Bob; Pblr, Voyager Company, The; US; 212/431-5199

Stein, Brian; Pres, Syspro Impact Software Inc.; US; 714/437-1000

Stein, Charles W.; Pres & CEO, Netrix Corp.; US; 703/742-6000

Stein, Erich; Principal, Erich Stein Communications; US; 303/722-4343, erich.stein@ossinc.net

Stein, J. Ditter; Pres & CEO, BASF Corp.; US; 201/397-2700

Stein, Larry A.; Pres, FarPoint Communications; US; 805/726-4420

Stein, Patricia; VP, WritePro Corp.; US; 914/762-1255

Stein, Sol; Pres, WritePro Corp.; US; 914/762-1255

Steinbach, Leonard; Pres, Microcomputer Managers Assoc. Inc.; US; 908/585-9091, lstein@nln.org

Steinberg, Martin; Pres, Odyssey Development Inc.; US; 303/689-9998

Steinerd, Robert J.; VP, Dataquest; US; 408/437-8000

Steinert, Tom; Ed-in-Chief, Interactive Week; US; 516/229-3700, tomhyphen@onramp.net

Steinfeld, Edward; Dir Mktng, Phar Lap Software Inc.; US; 617/661-1510, efs@pharlap.com

Steinhardt, Maxwell; Pres & COO, TMS Inc.; US; maxwell@tm-ok.mhs

Steinke, Steve; Sr Ed, LAN Magazine; US; 415/905-2200, ssteinke@mfi.com

Steinkrauss, Robert; Pres & CEO, Raptor Systems Inc.; US; 617/487-7700

Steinkrauss, Robert A.; Pres, Racal InterLan Inc.; US; 508/263-9929

Stella, Carl C.; SVP, Datametrics Corp.; US; 818/598-6200

Stelzer, David F.; Pres Com Solutions, Cincinnati Bell Information Systems; US; 513/784-5900

Stemberg, Thomas G.; Chmn & CEO, Staples Inc.; US; 508/370-8500

Stenbit, John P.; VP & GM SI, TRW Inc.; US; 216/291-7000

Stenson, Andy; Dir Ops, Secure Document Systems Inc.; US; 904/725-2505

Stephan, Joe; Pres & CEO, Retix; US; 310/828-3400

Stephansen, Stephan; VP Mktng & Sales, Information Storage Devices Inc.; US; 408/369-2400

Stephens, Ann; Pres, PC Data; US; 703/435-1025

Stephens, Bob; COO, Adaptec Inc.; US; 408/945-8600

Stephens, Bryn; Sales Mgr, Acecad Inc.; US; 408/655-1900

Stephens, John; Pres Payment Prod, Servantis Systems Inc.; US; 770/441-3387

Stephens, Phil; VP Ops, Indiana Cash Drawer Co.; US; 317/398-6643

Stephenson, Larry J.; Pres & CEO, Newport Systems Solutions Inc.; US; 714/752-1511

Stephenson Jr., James M.; Chmn & Pres, Kinetic Systems Corp.; US; 815/838-0005

Sterken, James J.; Pres & CEO, ArborText Inc.; US; 313/996-3566

Sterling, John M.; VP Sales, Datastream Systems Inc.; US; 803/297-6775

Stern, Michael M.; VP Ops, CSPI; US; 508/663-7598

Stern, Paul G.; Chmn, Northern Telecom Ltd.; Canada; 905/566-3178

Sternbach, Eric; Pres, MicroVideo Learning Systems; US; 212/777-9595, eric_sternbach@microvideo.com

Sterne, Rick; Pres, Datasym Inc.; Canada; 519/758-5800

Sternick, Wendy; Pres, Kaetron Software Corp.; US; 713/298-1500

Sternitzke, Richard; CTO, Transaction Network Services Inc.; US; 703/742-0500

Steuri, John E.; CEO Alltel Info Svcs, Alltel Corp.; US; 501/661-8000

Steven, Alain; Pres, Cegelec ESCA; US; 206/822-6800

Stevens, Bob; Pres, Magic Quest Inc.; US; 415/321-5838

Stevens, Bridget; Dir Acct Svcs, MCCommunications Inc.; US; 214/480-8383, bridget_stevens@mccom.com

Stevens, Clive S.; VP Mktng & Sales, SkyNotes Inc.; US; 310/577-9332, clive@radiomail.net

Stevens, Curtis M.; EVP & CFO, Planar Systems Inc.; US; 503/690-1100

Stevens, Edward A.; EVP & CFO, Peak Technologies Group Inc.; US; 212/832-2833

Stevens, Edward P.; Pres, Emis Software Inc.; US; 210/822-8499

Stevens, Gary; SVP Eng, Ontrack Computer Systems Inc.; US; 612/937-1107

Stevens, John R.; Pres, Soft-One Corp.; US; 801/221-9400

Stevens, Lyle; Mktng Admin, Simucad Inc.; US; 415/487-9700, lyle@simucad.com

Stevenson, Bobby G.; Chmn, Pres & CEO, Ciber Inc.; US; 303/220-0100

Stevenson, Gregory D.; EVP Ops, Micron Electronics; US; 208/893-3434

Stevenson, Mirek; Chmn & Pres, Quantum Group Int'l.; US; 914/694-3260

Stevenson, Tom; VP Mktng, Vtel; US; 512/314-2700

Steward, Scott; VP Sales & Mktng, Star-Nine Technologies Inc.; US; 510/649-4949

Stewart, Don; Pres & CEO, Plotter Supplies Inc.; US; 303/450-2900

Stewart, J. Michael; Pres & CEO, Sequoia Systems Inc.; US; 508/480-0800

Stewart, Janice; VP, Plotter Supplies Inc.; US; 303/450-2900

Stewart, Kirk; CEO, Manning Selvage & Lee; 212/213-0909

Stewart, Lawrence; CTO, Open Market Inc.; US; 617/621-9500

Stewart, Linda; Ed, NCSA News; US; 717/258-1816

Stewart, Michael; Pres & COO, Texas Microsystems Inc.; US; 713/541-8200

Stewart, Robert; VP Mktng, Tektronix Color Printing & Imaging Div.; US; 503/685-3150

Stich, Fred; CTO, Best Power Technology Inc.; US; 608/565-7200

Stick, Karman; Ingram Laboratories; US; 714/566-1000

Stickley, Lyndon; Pres, 4-Sight LC; US; 515/221-3000

Stickney, Bill; VP Eng, Videomedia Inc.; US; 408/227-9977

Stickrod, Randall L.; Exec Dir, micro Computer Inc.; US; 415/855-0940

Sticksez, Kelly A.; VP, Channel Marketing Corp.; US; 214/931-2420, kelly@cmcus.com

Stiehler, Robert; VP Fin, OnStream Networks Inc.; US; 408/727-4545

Stiffler, Jack J.; EVP & CTO, Sequoia Systems Inc.; US; 508/480-0800

Stihl, John T.; Chmn, Pres & CEO, Concurrent Computer Corp.; US; 908/870-4500

Stikeleather, Gregory; Pres & CEO, aha!software corp.; US; 415/988-2080, 426.2752@mcimail.com

Stiles, James; Prod Mgr, Wilson WindowWare Inc.; US; 206/938-1740, jwstiles@halcyon.com

Stiller, Wolfgang; Pres, Stiller Research; US; 904/575-0920

Stinton, Jim; CIO, MEDE America Corp.; US; 216/425-3241

Stitt, Gordon L.; VP & GM Spec Prod, Network Peripherals; US; 408/321-7300

Stock, Frank; VP Dev, n th degree soft-

ware; US; 702/588-4900

Stockdill, Shay; Principal, Strategies, A Marketing Communications Corp.; US; 714/957-8880

Stockner, Rene; GM, Navision Software US Inc.; US; 770/564-8000

Stockwell, Barbara; VP & Assoc Pblr, Knowledge Industry Publications Inc.; US; 914/328-9157

Stolinsky, Peter; VP Mktng, Castelle Corp.; US; 408/496-0474

Stoll, Peter; VP Fin, JYACC Inc.; US; 212/267-7722

Stone, Chris; Dir Bus Dev, MountainGate Data Systems Inc.; US; 702/851-9393

Stone, Christopher; Pres, Object Management Group; US; 508/820-4300

Stone, Jordan; Sr Analyst, Infonetics Research Inc.; US; 408/298-7999

Stone, Warren; Pres & COO, Addison-Wesley Publishing Co.; US; 617/944-3700

Stonecipher, Chuck; COO, Advanced Digital Information Corp.; US; 206/881-8004

Stonecipher, Harry C.; Pres & CEO, McDonnell Douglas Corp.; US; 314/232-0232

Stoner, David M.; EVP Ops, Marcam Corp.; US; 617/965-0220

Stopa, Lawrence; Dir Tech Mktng, Jordan Tamraz Caruso Advertising Inc.; US; 312/951-2000

Storer, Larry; Ed Dir, Cisco World; US; 512/250-9023, storer@pcinews.com

Storer, Roger; VP Eng, Second Wave Inc.; US; 512/329-9283

Storey, Phil; Pres, Plasmon Data Inc.; US; 408/474-0100

Storrison, William E.; SVP Ops, Ciber Inc.; US; 303/220-0100

Story, James Michael; Pblr, James Publishing & Assoc.; US; 214/238-1133

Story, Mike; Pblr, THE*MART; US; 214/238-1133

Story, Richard; EVP, Target Software Group Inc.; US; 813/528-2477

Stouffer, Richard K.; Pres, North Shore Systems Inc.; US; 702/831-1108

Stoughton, Thom; VP Cust Support Svcs, InterApps Inc.; US; 310/374-4125, tstoughton@aol.com

Stout, Alan; Pres, ISTR Inc.; US; 716/855-0295

Stoutenborough, Ross; Pres, CAD Research; US; 714/662-4970

Stoutenborough, Tara; Pres, Strategies, A Marketing Communications Corp.; US; 714/957-8880

Stover, Joyce; VP, Pinnacle Peak Publishing Ltd.; US; 602/585-5580

Stover, Richard N.; Pblr, Pinnacle Peak Publishing Ltd.; US; 602/585-5580

Stover, Wilbur; VP & CFO, Micron Technology Inc.; US; 208/368-4400

Strachan, James; Pblr, Asian Sources MediaGroup; US; 408/295-4500

Stradford, Daniel P.; SVP Sales &

Mktng, Flextronics Int'l.; US; 408/428-1300

Strain, Carl E.; VP Ops & CFO, Microtest Inc.; US; 602/952-6400

Strakosch, Greg; Pblr, United Communications Group; US; 301/816-8950, gstrakos@ucg.com

Strand, Michael; Pres, Strandware Inc.; US; 715/833-2331, ahansen@strand-ware.com

Strang, Dale; Pub & Pres, Digital Video Magazine; US; 415/522-2400

Strange, Jack; VP Sales & Mktng, Caligari Corp.; US; 415/390-9600

Strange, Michael R.; EVP, Franklin Electronic Pblrs Inc.; US; 609/386-2500

Strapko, Peter; Mgng Dir, Weka Publishing; US

Strashun Whitcher, Joann; Ed-in-Chief, Print on Demand Business; US; 617/834-0001

Stratton, Paul B.; VP Mktng, Duracell Int'l.; US; 203/791-3010

Straub, Walter W.; Chmn, Pres & CEO, Rainbow Technologies Inc.; US; 714/450-7300

Strauch, Charles S.; Chmn & CEO, Pair-Gain Technologies Inc.; US; 714/832-9924

Strauss, Les B.; SVP & CFO, PictureTel Corp.; US; 508/762-5000

Strauss, Will; Pres, Forward Concepts; US; 602/968-3759

Strautman, Richard L.; VP, DH Technology Inc.; US; 619/451-3485

Strecker, William; VP & CTO, Digital Equipment Corp.; US; 508/493-5111

Street, Bill; Dir Tech Sup, RightFAX; US; 520/327-1357, bds@rightfax.com

Street, Jules; VP, Killen & Associates Inc.; US; 415/617-6130

Streit, Paul; Dir Mktng, Pioneer New Media Technologies Inc.; US

Strickland, Samuel R.; EVP & CFO, CACI International Inc.; US; 703/841-7800

Strief, Jeffrey L.; SVP, CMP Publications Inc.; US; 516/562-5000

Stringer, Brian; VP Fin, PureData Ltd.; Canada; 416/731-6444

Stringer, Mike; Pres, Stringer Furtado + Shaw; US; 617/272-0444

Strobel, Mark D.; VP Sales & Mktng, Fargo Electronics Inc.; US; 612/941-9470

Strohl, Philip; Dir Res & Pubs, Interactive Television Assoc.; US; 202/408-0008

Strohmeyer, Ken; Orion Blue Book, Computers; US; 602/951-1114, kenstr@aol.com

Strom, Terence M.; Pres & CEO, Egghead Inc.; US; 509/922-7031

Stromberg, JoAnn; Exec Admin, Surface Mount Technology Assoc.; US; 612/920-7682

Strong, Vern; VP Prod Dev, Solomon Software; US; 419/424-0422, vstrong@solomon.com

Stuart, Bruce R.; Pres, ChannelCorp

Management Consultants Inc.; Canada; 604/263-6811

Stuart, Marg A.; Pblr, ChannelCorp Management Consultants Inc.; Canada; 604/263-6811

Stubblefield, Jerry W.; VP & CFO, nView Corp.; US; 804/873-1354

Stuckey, Charles R.; Pres & CEO, Security Dynamics Technologies Inc.; US; 617/547-7820

Stuckey, M.M.; Chmn & CEO, Fourth Shift Corp.; US; 612/851-1900

Stuhlmann, Ellen H.; Pblr, Philips Business Information Inc.; US; 301/340-1520

Stulberg, Gordon; Chmn, TDC Interactive; US; 310/452-6720

Stumpf, Kevin; Assoc Ed, Historically Brewed; US

Stuppy, John; Ed, Journal of Office Technology; US; 703/924-9688

Sturgeon Jr., James D.; VP Ops, Datametrics Corp.; US; 818/598-6200

Sturgill, Rhonda; Ops Mgr, Acecad Inc.; US; 408/655-1900

Stussi, Doug; CFO, DataTimes Corp.; US; 405/751-6400

Stuyt, Sharka; Dir Mktng, Pivotal Software Inc.; Canada; 604/988-9982, sharka@pivotal.com

Su, Kevin; COO, Nimax Inc.; US; 619/566-4800

Subbloie, Albert; Pres & CEO, Information Management Associates Inc.; US; 203/925-6800

Subhedar, Sanjay; VP & CFO, StrataCom Inc.; US; 408/294-7600

Suchman, Carol; EVP, Technology Solutions; US; 212/696-2000

Suda, Norm; Pres, Sirius Software Inc.; US; 513/228-4849, norm_suda@sirius-acct.com

Suden, David J.; Pres, Rimage Corp.; US; 612/944-8144

Suer, Myles; Dir Mktng, 1394 Trade Assoc.; US; 512/305-0202

Sugiura, Go; Chmn, Altima Systems Inc.; US

Sugiyama, Mineo; Pres & CEO, NEC America; US; 516/753-7000

Sullivan, Barry; Dir SW Components Div, Gallium Software Inc.; Canada; 613/721-0902, bsullivan@gallium.com

Sullivan, Donald; VP WW Ops, Recital Corp.; US; 508/750-1066, dons@recital.com

Sullivan, Eamon; Mgng Tech Dir, PC Week Labs; US; 415/513-8000, eamon_sullivan@zd.com

Sullivan, Garrett; CFO, Cognitronics Corp.; US; 203/830-3400

Sullivan, Godfrey; VP Americas, Autodesk Inc.; US; 415/507-5000

Sullivan, Jon Fox; Pblr, Federal Internet Source, The; US

Sullivan, Michael; CFO, Tut Systems Inc.; US; 510/682-6510

Sullivan, Robert E.; SVP Admin, Harris

Corp.; US; 407/727-9100

Sullivan, Roger; VP Mktng, Keyfile Corp.; US; 603/883-3800, rogersullivan@keyfile.com

Sullivan, Roland D.; Chmn, Sendero Corp.; US; 602/941-8112

Sullivan, Scott D.; CFO, WorldCom; US; 601/360-8600

Sullivan, Steve; VP Sales, Elektroson US; US; 610/617-0850

Sullivan, Tim; Pres & CEO, Connectware Inc.; US; 214/907-1093

Sully, Sandra L.; VP MIS, 3Com Corp.; US; 408/764-5000

Sumbs, Robert; VP Mktng & Sales, Synaptics Inc.; US; 408/434-0110

Summers, Dave; CFO, ExperVision Inc.; US; 408/523-0900

Summers, Doug; Sales Dir, Microtek Lab Inc.; US; 310/297-5000

Summers, Kent; Dir Mktng, Electronic Book Technologies Inc.; US; 401/421-9550, kjs@ebt.com

Sumner, Kelly; COO, GameTek Inc.; US; 305/935-3995

Sumney, Larry W.; Pres & CEO, Semiconductor Research Corp.; US; 919/541-9400

Sun, Bosco; Pres & CEO, Camintonn Z-RAM Corp.; US; 714/454-1500

Sun, Chieh; Pres, Tatung Co. of America Inc.; US; 310/637-2105

Sun, David; VP Eng, Kingston Technology Corp.; US; 714/435-2600

Sun, Louis; VP Sales, Sys Technology Inc.; US; 714/821-3900

Sun, Ray; Pres, Primax Electronics; US; 408/522-1200

Sundheim, Jeff; Pblr, VARBUSINESS; US; 516/562-5000

Surber, W. Allen; SVP, Genicom Corp.; US; 703/802-9200

Susser, Elan; Pres, GoldMine Software Corp.; US; 310/454-6800

Sutcliffe, David; Pres & CEO, Sierra Wireless Inc.; Canada; 604/231-1100

Suter, Albert E.; Sr Vice Chmn & COO, Emerson Electric Co.; US; 314/553-2000

Sutherland, Scott; VP Sales, Softbridge Inc.; US; 617/576-2257

Sutker, Allen; Chmn & Pres, VisionTek Inc.; US; 708/360-7500

Sutter, Blanche M.; VP & CFO, Caere Corp.; US; 408/395-7000

Sutter, Larry; Chmn, Cadre Technologies Inc.; US; 401/351-5950, lsutter@cadre.com

Sutter, Mark; VP Prod Dev, Seagate Enterprise Management Software; US; 408/342-4500

Sutton, Paul; VP WW Sales, IntelliCorp Inc.; US; 415/965-5500

Sutton, Richard; Dir Eng, EA Research Inc.; US; 510/867-0967

Sutton II, James O.; Chmn & CEO, National Computers Plus; US; 918/664-0690

Suwannukul, Van; Chmn, Hercules Computer Technology Inc.; US; 510/623-6030

Suzuki, Makoto; Pres, Hitachi Telecom US Inc.; US; 770/446-8820

Suzuki, Tadashi; Sr EVP, NEC Corp.; Japan; 3-3454-1111

Swadley, Richard; Pres & Pblr, Sams Publishing; US; 317/581-3500

Swafford, Brian; Pres, QStar Technologies Inc.; US; 904/243-0900, brian@qstar.com

Swain, William D.; CFO, Metricom Inc.; US; 408/399-8200

Swan, David P.; VP Sales & Mktng, Wavefront Technologies Inc.; US; 805/962-8117

Swan, Michael J.; Pres, Neon Software Inc.; US; 510/283-9771

Swank, Richard B.; CEO, Advanstar Communications Inc.; US; 216/826-2859

Swanson, Murray L.; EVP & CFO, Telephone & Data Systems Inc.; US; 312/630-1900

Swanson, Robert H.; CEO, Litton Industries Inc.; US; 818/598-5000

Swanson Jr., Robert H.; Pres & CEO, Linear Technology Corp.; US; 408/432-1900

Swanzy, J. Mark; COO, Xante Corp.; US; 205/476-8189

Swartz, Jeff; SVP Mktng, Giga Information Group; US; 617/577-9595

Swartz, Jeffrey; Principal, Daly-Swartz Public Relations; US; 714/361-6888

Swartz, Jerome; Chmn & CEO, Symbol Technologies Inc.; US; 516/563-2400

Swayne, Gregory M.; Pres, Adam Software; US; 404/980-0888

Sweas, Gerald J.; VP & CFO, Norand Corp.; US; 319/369-3100

Swedburg, Richard; Eng Mgr, Electronic Technology Group Inc.; US; 612/948-3100

Swedlow, Erica; Pres, EBS Public Relations Inc.; US; 847/714-8600

Sweeney, Jack; Ed, Washington Technology; US; 703/848-2800, jsweeney@technews.com

Sweeney, Jim; Mktng Mgr, Empress Software Inc.; US; 301/220-1919, jsweeney@empress.com

Sweeney, Patrick; VP & CFO, Inchcape Inc.; US; 508/689-9355

Sweetland, Mark R.; VP, SofTech Inc.; US; 616/957-2330

Swensrud II, S. Blake; Pres, International Technology Consultants; US; 202/234-2138

Swift, Art; VP Mktng, Sparc Technology Business; US; 415/960-1300

Swift, Myles; Pres, Computer Assistance Inc.; US; 503/895-3347

Swift, Patricia; VP, Computer Assistance Inc.; US; 503/895-3347

Swiggett, Brian; Mgng Partner, Prismark Partners LLC; US; 516/367-9187

Swindler, Dale; VP Sales, Eagle Software Inc.; US; 913/823-7257, dale@eagle-soft.com

Swiniarski, Stan; VP SW Prod, Xerox Desktop Document Systems; US; 415/815-6800

Swistak, Gregory; Pres, Factura Kiosks Inc.; US; 716/264-9600

Swistak, Paul; Dir Sales & Mktng, Factura Kiosks Inc.; US; 716/264-9600

Switz, Robert E.; VP & CFO, ADC Telecommunications; US; 612/938-8080

Sykes, Ed; VP R&D, Make Systems; US; 415/941-9800

Sykes, John H.; Sykes Enterprises Inc.; US; 813/274-1000

Sykes, W. David; Pres, Andataco; US; 619/453-9191, dave@andataco.com

Sylvester, Tim; Digital News & Review Labs; US; 617/964-3030, tims@dnr.com

Szambelan, Lawrence J.; VP Info Syst, MicroAge Inc.; US; 602/804-2000

Szczepaniak, Joseph; VP Sales, Grolier Electronic Publishing Inc.; US; 203/797-3500

Szirom, Steve Z.; Exec Ed, HTE Research Inc.; US; 415/871-4377, szirom@hte-sibs.com

Szklanka, Eli; VP, ASA International Ltd.; US; 508/626-2727

Szlam, Aleksander; Chmn & CEO, Melita International; US; 770/446-7800

Szretter, Hank; Pres, E.E.S. Companies Inc.; US; 508/653-6911

Szretter, June; VP Mktng, E.E.S. Companies Inc.; US; 508/653-6911

Szulik, Matthew J.; SVP Sales & Mktng, MapInfo Corp.; US; 518/285-6000

Taglia, Joseph; SVP, Mountain Network Solutions Inc.; US; 408/438-6650

Tahmassebi, David; Sr Mktng Mgr, Hyundai Digital Media; US; 408/232-8000, dtahmassebi@hea.com

Tai, Ken; CEO, InterNex Information Services; US; 408/327-2355, ktai@internex.net

Tai, Vincent; Pres, Umax Technologies Inc.; US; 510/651-4000, vincent_tai@umax.com

Tait, Peter; VP Mktng, PeerLogic; US; 415/626-4545

Takahashi, Tim; VP Eng, Pioneer New Media Technologies Inc.; US

Takashiro, Tsuyoshi; Pres, Future Pirates Inc.; US; 310/396-6788

Takazawa, Makomoto; Pres & CEO, Core Int'l.; US; 407/997-6055

Takeda, Becky; Dir Mktng, Apex Data Inc.; US; 510/416-5656

Takeuchi, Caroline J.; VP Sales & Mktng, Silicom Ltd.; US; 206/882-7995

Takeuchi, Masakazu; Pres & CEO, Gradco US Inc.; US; 714/206-6100

Tal, Ami; COO, VocalTec Inc.; US; 201/768-9400

Talbott, James; Ed, Personal Property Taxation of Computer Software; US; 610/

975-9619

Talsky, Gene R.; Pres, Promark Consulting Services; US; 603/632-7951, gtalsky@mcimail.com

Tan, Eugene; Dir Mktng, Cogent Electronics Inc.; US; 415/591-6617

Tan, James; Pres, Multiwave Innovation Inc.; US; 408/379-2900

Tan, K.H.; Pres, Cogent Electronics Inc.; US; 415/591-6617

Tan, Kit; CFO, Acculogic Inc.; US; 714/454-2441

Tan, Manuel C.; Pres & COO, Liuski International Inc.; US; 770/447-9454

Tanaka, Hiroshi; EVP, Canon Inc.; Japan; 3-33758-2111

Tanaka, Richard I.; Chmn & CEO, Scan-Optics Inc.; US; 203/289-6001

Tang, Ding-Yuan; Pres, Maxsoft-OCRON Inc.; US; 510/252-0200, ding@maxsoft-ocron.com

Tangum, Lana; Tech Prod Mgr, Ryan-McFarland; US; 512/343-1010

Tanner, Michael; VP Ops, Aurora Technologies Inc.; US; 617/290-4800

Tannheimer, Gregory L.; EVP, Intermec Corp.; US; 206/348-2600

Taradalsky, Morris; Pres & CEO, MicroNet Technology Inc.; US; 714/453-6000

Tarantino, Robert V.; Pres & CEO, Dataram Corp.; US; 609/799-0071

Tarbini, Judith A.; Pres, Complete Communications; US; 510/855-9522, jtarbini@aol.com

Tarbox, Richard C.; VP Corp Dev, SunGard Data Systems Inc.; US; 610/341-8700

Tarca, Peter; VP R&D, Powerhouse Entertainment; US; 214/933-5400

Tarello, John A.; SVP & Treas, Analogic Corp.; US; 508/977-3000

Tarolla, Ken; VP Dev, Expert Software Inc.; US; 305/567-9990

Tarr, Gary M.; Pres, Cyborg Systems Inc.; US; 312/454-1865

Tarter, Jeffrey; Ed & Pblr, Soft-letter; US; 617/924-3944

Tarulli, Richard L.; SVP WW Sales & Serv, Stratus Computer Inc.; US; 508/460-2000

Taschek, John; Mgng Tech Dir, PC Week Labs; US; 415/513-8000, john_taschek@zd.com

Tash, Martin; Pres, Plenum Publishing Corp.; US; 212/620-8000

Taslitz, Neal; Pres, PerfecTouch Inc.; US

Tata, Giovanni; Pres & CEO, Taras Linguistic Systems Inc.; US; 801/375-3456

Tatar, Robert; VP, Plextor; US; 408/980-1838

Tate, Dana; VP, Microcomputer Managers Assoc. Inc.; US; 908/585-9091, 70272.154@compuserve.com

Tate, Geoff; Pres & CEO, Rambus Inc.; US; 415/903-3800

Tate, Mary Ann; Dir Mktng, Quality

Education Data Inc.; US

Tatham, Bill; Pres & CEO, Janna Systems Inc.; US; 408/356-6647

Tatro, Paul A.; EVP Ops, Platinum Technology Inc.; US; 708/620-5000

Tatsuno, Sheridan; Pblr, Dreamscape Productions; US; 408/685-8818

Taube, Glenn; VP, Control Concepts Inc.; US; 703/876-6444, taubeg@presearch.com

Tauscher, William; Chmn, Vanstar Inc.; US; 510/734-4000

Tax, Joel P.; Santa Clara Consulting; US; 408/450-1365

Taylor, Bart; Assoc Pblr, Windows NT; US; 303/663-4700

Taylor, Bruce; Grp Pblr, Imaging World Magazine; US; 207/236-8524

Taylor, Bruce M.; Pres, American Small Business Computers Inc.; US; 918/825-4844

Taylor, Craig S.; VP Eng, Geoworks; US; 510/814-1660

Taylor, Daniel; EVP Mktng, Syncronys Softcorp; US; 310/842-9203

Taylor, Donald S.; Pres, Aydin Corp.; US; 215/657-7510

Taylor, Doug; Mktng Mgr, Level Five Research; US; 407/729-6004, doug@l5r.com

Taylor, Edward A.; EVP, Pencom Systems Inc.; US; 512/343-1111

Taylor, Gerald H.; Pres & COO, MCI Communications Corp.; US; 202/872-1600

Taylor, Graham; VP, Inteco Corp.; US; 203/866-4400

Taylor, Harry; VP, Duracell Int'l.; US; 203/791-3010

Taylor, Jason; Prod Mktng Mgr, 4-Sight LC; US; 515/221-3000

Taylor, Jeffrey W.; VP & CFO, National Computer Systems Inc.; US; 612/829-3000

Taylor, Jim; VP Mktng Sales, MicroClean Inc.; US; 408/995-5062

Taylor, Matthew; Chmn, Tut Systems Inc.; US; 510/682-6510

Taylor, Sandy; Mkt Analyst, Standish Group, The; US; 508/385-7500, sandy@standishgroup.com

Taylor, Steve C.; Chmn, Verilink Corp.; US; 408/945-1199

Taylor, Tiffany; Ed, Inside Paradox for Windows; US; 502/491-1900

Taylor, Tom; Partner, Storage Systems Marketing; US; 303/499-0281, tomroger@aol.com

Taylor, Trey; Pres, Interactive Marketing Institute; US; 202/624-7372

Taylor, Vince; Pres, Vermont Creative Software; US; 802/848-7731

Taylor, Volney; EVP, Dun & Bradstreet Corp., The; US; 203/834-4200

Taylor, Wendy; Exec Ed, PC/Computing; US; 415/578-7000

Taylor Jr., George J.; Chmn & CEO,

Cobotyx Corp.; US; 203/282-0010

Tchong, Michael; VP Mktng, MetaTools Inc.; US; 805/566-6200

Tebbe, Mark A.; Pres, Lante Corp.; US; 312/236-5100, mtebbe@lante.com

Tebele, Charles; Pres, RCS Computer Experience; US; 212/370-9288

Teblum, Ronald; Romsoft Inc.; US; 305/752-5073

Tebo, Mitch; Pblr, Adweek's Directory of Interactive Marketing; US

Teglovic, Stephen M.; VP Eng, ConnectSoft; US; 206/827-6467

Tehrani, Jadji; Pblr & Ed-in-Chief, Telemarketing & Call Center Solutions; US; 203/852-6800

Teich, Tim; VP Sales & Mktng, Advanced Input Devices; US; 208/765-8000

Teige, Peter; Sr Ed, Mobile Letter; US; 415/390-9800, pteige@mobilein-sights.com

Teitelman, Warren; VP Eng, BayStone Software; US; 408/370-9301

Tellez, Lorenzo; VP & CFO, C3 Inc.; US; 703/471-6000

Temin, Thomas R.; Ed, Government Computer News; US; 301/650-2000, editor@gcn.com

Tenenhaus, Morti; Pres & CEO, TeKnowlogy Corp; US; 214/373-9998

Tennant, Rich; 5th Wave by Rich Tennant, The; US; 508/546-2448

Tennant, Richard G.; VP & CFO, Netrix Corp.; US; 703/742-6000

Tenney, Arnold S.; Pres & CEO, ARC International Corp.; Canada; 416/630-0200

Tensillo, Kevin; Ed, Communications News; US; 972/644-0830

Teo, Peter; Dir Ops, Aztech Labs Inc.; US; 510/623-8988

Teresi, Robert; Chmn & CEO, Caere Corp.; US; 408/395-7000

Terpin, Michael J.; Pres, Terpin Group, The; US; 310/821-6100

Terrell, Dorothy A.; Pres, SunExpress Inc.; US; 508/442-000

Terry, Colleen; VP Sales & Mktng, Clear Software Inc.; US; 617/965-6755

Terry, Kathy; VP Corp, Balt Inc.; US; 817/697-4953

Teter, James; Pres, Management Graphics Inc.; US; 612/854-1220

Tetiva, Tim; Pres & CEO, Command Technology Corp.; US; 510/521-5900

Teza, Jeffrey R.; VP Tech & Bus Dev, Brooktree Corp.; US; 619/452-7580

Thalheimer, Richard; Chmn & CEO, Sharper Image Corp.; US; 415/445-6000

Than, Richard; Pres, Qualix Group Inc.; US; 415/572-0200, rthan@qualix.com

Thatcher, David; CFO, Diba; US; 415/482-3300

Thatcher, Thomas M.; Pres, Tharo Systems Inc.; US; 216/273-4408

Thayer, Michael; Dir Eng, Factura Kiosks Inc.; US; 716/264-9600

Theodore, Robert J.; SVP, Peak Technologies Group Inc.; US; 212/832-2833

Theriault, Richard; Sr Ed, Mac Today; US; 813/733-6225

Theron, Adriaan; VP Mktng, SQL Financials Int'l.; US; 770/390-3900

Thewes, Thomas; Vice Chmn, Compuware Corp.; US; 810/737-7300

Theye, Terry L.; Chmn & CEO, Future Now; US; 513/792-4500

Thibault, Aline; VP, FitzGerald Communications Inc.; US; 617/494-9500

Thibault, George T.; Pres, Revolution Software Inc.; US; 305/682-8154

Thibault, Roger C.; Ed & Pblr, Yellowstone Information Services; US; 614/944-1657

Thiel, Fred; VP Mktng & Sales, Alta Research Corp.; US; 305/428-8538

Thieman, Michael A.; EVP Sales & Mktng, HNC Software Inc.; US; 619/546-8877

Thoben, E. Michael; Chmn, Pres & CEO, Interlink Electronics; US; 805/484-8855

Thoma, Michael; SVP Mktng, Inference Corp.; US; 415/899-0100

Thoma, Mike; VP Prod Dev, My Software Co.; US; 415/473-3600

Thoman, G. Richard; SVP & CFO, International Business Machines Corp.; US; 914/765-1900

Thomas, Allison; Principal, Allison Thomas Assoc.; US; 213/937-2300

Thomas, Gary; Co-Founder, Insights Software; US; 310/577-1185

Thomas, Gary M.; Dir Sales, Magni Systems Inc.; US; 503/626-8400

Thomas, James M.; VP, Microsemi Corp.; US; 714/979-8220

Thomas, John; VP Ops, Viewpoint Datalabs Int'l.; US; 801/229-3000

Thomas, Karen; Pres & CEO, Thomas Public Relations Inc.; US; 516/549-7575, 310.3946@mcimail.com

Thomas, Leo J.; Group VP, Eastman Kodak Co.; US; 716/724-4000

Thomas, Lynda K.; VP Admin, CompuTrac Inc.; US; 214/234-4241

Thomas, Michael D.; Chmn & CEO, Tenera L.P.; US; 510/845-5200

Thomas, Oran; CTO, TriTeal Corp.; US; 619/930-2077

Thomas, Patrick H.; Chmn, Pres & CEO, First Financial Management Corp.; US; 770/857-0001

Thomas, Patti; CFO, Falcon Systems Inc.; US; 916/928-9255, patti@falcons.com

Thomas, Raymond V.; VP & CFO, HNC Software Inc.; US; 619/546-8877

Thomas, Richard; Info Svsc Mgr, Welch Allyn Inc.; US; 315/685-8945

Thomas, Roberta; Pblr, Pre; US; 212/683-3540, roberta_thomas@cowles-biz.com

Thomas, Ronald B.; Chmn, Ciprico Inc.;

US; 612/551-4000

Thomas, Scott J.; CFO, SmartDesk Inc.; US; 714/582-4020

Thomas, Stephen; Pres, Datapro Information Services Group; US; 609/764-0100

Thomas, Walter; VP Mktng, Revnet Systems Inc.; US; 205/721-1420, wthomas@revnet.com

Thomas Gooch, Lowell; EVP Ops, Storage Technology Corp.; US; 303/673-5020

Thomasmeyer, William; Pres & CEO, Logicraft Information Systems; US; 603/880-0300

Thompson, Bentham; Mgng Ed, Online Design; US; 415/334-3800, ben@online-design.com

Thompson, David; Dir Mktng, StarNine Technologies Inc.; US; 510/649-4949, david@starnine.com

Thompson, Derek A.; EVP, Storage Technology Corp.; US; 303/673-5020

Thompson, Gary; CFO, Legato Systems Inc.; US; 415/812-6000

Thompson, Gary; Pres, Golan/Harris Technologies; US; 415/904-7000

Thompson, George A.; Sr Ed, HP Professional; US; 215/643-8000, thompsonga@box101.cardinal.com

Thompson, James F.; VP & CFO, Itron Inc.; US; 509/924-9900

Thompson, John M.; COO, Innovative Tech Systems Inc.; US; 215/441-5600

Thompson, John W.; GM PSP Div, IBM Personal Software Products; US; 512/823-3176

Thompson, Michael C.; VP Ops, Comptronix Corp.; US; 615/377-3330

Thompson, Philip S.; SVP Ops, Zenith Electronics Corp.; US; 708/391-7000

Thompson, Stephen A.; SVP, Cahners Publishing Co.; US; 617/558-4565

Thompson, Ted; Chmn & CEO, X-Rite Inc.; US; 616/534-7663

Thompson, William M.; Pres & CEO, Innovative Tech Systems Inc.; US; 215/441-5600

Thomsen, Carsten; VP Eng, National Instruments Corp.; US; 512/794-0100

Thomsen, Mel; Principal, Pathfinder Research Inc.; US; 408/437-1905

Thorell, Lisa; VP Mktng, CompuServe Internet Div.; US; 206/447-0300

Thorlakson, Daniel; VP Ops, Qualstar Corp.; US; 818/592-0061

Thornley, Anthony S.; VP & CFO, Qualcomm Inc.; US; 619/587-1121

Thornton, Stephen F.; Chmn, Pres & CEO, Cybex Corp.; US; 205/430-4000

Thornton, Tim; Pblr, Digital Output; US; 404/524-6954

Thorpe, Judy; Pres, PrintPaks Inc.; US; 503/295-6564

Thrailkill, Howard A.; EVP & COO, Adtran Inc.; US; 205/971-8000

Thron, John E.; Pres, Programart Corp.; US; 617/661-3020

Thuma, David; Dir Mktng, Abra Cadabra

Software; US; 813/527-1111

Thurber, Kenneth; Pres, Architecture Technology Corp.; US; 612/935-2035

Thurk, Michael C.; SVP Mktng, General DataComm Industries Inc.; US; 203/574-1118

Thurman, Harry L.; VP Bus Dev, E-Systems Inc.; US; 214/661-1000

Thurmond, Sheila; VP Sales & Mktng, Raidtec Corp; US; 770/664-6066

Thyggersen, Steve; Pres, Janus Interactive; US; 503/629-0587

Ticktin, Neil; Pblr, Xplain Corp.; US; 805/494-9797

Tiddens, Mark; VP Sales & Mktng, Sejin America Inc.; US; 408/980-7550

Tierney, Gretta; Assoc Coord, ADSL Forum; US; 415/378-6680

Tierney, Peter R.; Chmn, Pres & CEO, Inference Corp.; US; 415/899-0100

Tikhman, Anatoly; Pres, Vertisoft Systems Inc.; US; 415/956-5999

Tilbury, Hal; Pres & CEO, Bluebird Systems; US; 619/438-2220

Till, Jim; VP Sales, Compton's NewMedia Inc.; US; 619/929-2500

Tillar, Gregory T.; Pres & COO, Metatec Corp.; US; 614/761-2000

Tilson, Mike; CIO, Santa Cruz Operation Inc., The; US; 408/425-7222, mike@sco.com

Tinkel, Kathleen; Ed & Pblr, MacPrePres; US; 203/227-2357

Tinker, Henry; VP Ops, Verilink Corp.; US; 408/945-1199

Tinley, J. Patrick; Pres & COO, Ross Systems Inc.; US; 415/593-2500

Tinsley, Tom; Pres, Baan Co.; US; 415/462-4949

Tippett, Peter S.; Pres, National Computer Security Assoc.; US; 717/258-1816

Tippett, Richard; VP Mfg, CalComp Inc.; US; 714/821-2000

Tippetts, Matthew; VP Prod Dev, Info-Business Inc.; US; 801/221-1100

Tischler, Frances; VP Mktng, Professional Help Desk; US; 203/356-7700, info@prohelpdesk.com

Tishkevich, Lance; Software Corp. of America; US; 203/359-2773, ltishkevich@talkthru.com

Tissier, Suzanne M.; Assist Ed, High-Technology Services Management; US; 941/275-7887

Titch, Steve; Ed Dir, Telephony; US; 312/595-1080

Titterton, Lewis H.; EVP Sales, MEDE America Corp.; US; 216/425-3241

Tivnan, Michael; GM, Xerox Imaging Systems; US; 508/977-2000

Tjaden, Darryl L.; Dir Bus Plng, Ultre Division; US; 516/753-4800

Tnanian, Avadis; VP Eng, NeXT Inc.; US; 415/366-0900

Tobaccowala, Toby; CEO, Commerce Direct International Inc.; Canada; 604/861-3217

Tobeck, Tim L.; Pblr, Electronic Business Today; US; 617/964-3030

Tobias, Michael J.; Pres, Tech-Source Inc.; US; 407/262-7100, mike@tech-source.com

Tobin, Jacquelin; Mng Ed, Pix; US; 212/536-5222

Todatry, Ram; Pres, Tangible Vision Inc.; US; 630/969-7517

Todd, Lee T.; Pres & CEO, DataBeam Corp.; US; 606/245-3500, ltodd@databeam.com

Tognini, Eileen; VP Sales & Mktng, Development Technologies Inc.; US; 803/790-9230

Tognoli, Greg; VP Sales & Mktng, KnowledgePoint; US; 707/762-0333

Toksu Gould, Kismet; Pblr, Interactive Marketing News; US; 301/340-1520

Tolhurst, William A.; VP Eng, Mobile Security Communications; US; 770/594-0424

Tolladay, Laura; Mktng Dir, Art & Logic; US; 818/501-6990

Tolle Jr., Kenneth E.; Ed-in-Chief, Inside Netware; US; 502/493-3300

Tolly, Kevin; Pres & CEO, Tolly Group, The; US; 908/528-3300, ktolly@tolly.com

Tolonen, James R.; SVP & CFO, Novell Inc.; US; 801/222-6000

Tolson, Michael; Chief Scientist, Xaos Tools; US; 415/487-7000

Tom, Sherman W.; VP Ops, Mylex Corp.; US; 510/796-6100

Tomasetta, Louis; Pres & CEO, Vitesse Semiconductor Corp.; US; 805/388-3700

Tomasetti, Thomas; Pres & CEO, Consilium Inc.; US; 415/691-6100

Tomasi, Robert; VP Ops, NetCom On-Line Communications Services Inc.; US; 408/345-2600

Tomb, Jay; Ed-in-Chief, Xplorer, The Journal of Electronic Document Systems; US; 310/373-3633

Tombrello, Tony; VP Ops, Transitional Technology Inc.; US; 714/693-1133

Tomescu, Radu; EVP, Ansel Communications; US; 206/869-4928, tomescu@ansel.com

Tomlinson, Philip W.; Pres, Total Systems Services Inc.; US; 706/649-2204

Tompane, John; VP WW Mktng, T/Maker Co.; US; 415/962-0195

Toms, Nicholas R.; Chmn, Pres & CEO, Peak Technologies Group Inc.; US; 212/832-2833

Tondi, Genevieve; Dir Sales & Mktng, Infographix Technologies Inc.; US; 404/523-4944

Tonkin, Bruce W.; Pres, TNT Software Inc.; US; 847/838-4323

Tonkin, P.J.; VP, TNT Software Inc.; US; 847/838-4323

Tonnesen, Alan; EVP, Passport Corp.; US; 201/634-1100

Tooker, Gary L.; Vice Chmn & CEO,

Motorola Inc.; US; 847/576-5000

Toomer, Allen J.; SVP, Tekelec; US; 818/880-5656

Toomey Jr., Daniel C.; VP & CFO, Eltron International Inc.; US; 805/579-1800

Topfer, Morton L.; Vice Chmn, Dell Computer Corp.; US; 512/338-4400

Topper, Andrew; Pres, Foresite Systems; US; 517/337-7050

Topping, Paul R.; Pres, Design Science Inc.; US; 310/433-0685, pault@mathtype.com

Toprani, Subodh; VP Mktng, Rambus Inc.; US; 415/903-3800

Torino, Robert S.; Pres & CEO, True Software Inc.; US; 508/369-7398

Torkelson, John A.; VP & GM, Plexus Software Inc.; US; 408/747-1210

Torrance, Mark; Chmn & CEO, PhotoDisc Inc.; US; 206/441-9355

Tory, David; Pres, Open Software Foundation; US; 508/474-9258

Toso, Victor; Pres, Nada Chair; US; 612/623-4436

Toth, Otto; Pres & CEO, Recognita Corp. of America; US; 408/736-5446

Totten, John; Pres & CEO, SoftCop Corp.; Canada; 905/681-3269

Tovey, David; VP Mktng, QLogic Corp.; US; 714/438-2200

Townsend, Mark; VP Eng, Sytron Corp.; US; 508/898-0100

Townsend, Mark; VP Adv Tech, National Education Training Group; US; 708/369-3000

Trachtman, Les; Chmn, Northeast Software Assoc.; US; 203/321-3711

Tradwick, David J.; Chief Arch, Speech Systems Inc.; US; 303/938-1110

Trainer, Susan; Assoc, Martin Communications; US; 415/668-2678, susanpr1@aol.com

Tran, Thinh; Chmn, Pres & CEO, Sigma Designs Inc.; US; 510/770-0100

Tran, Vinh; Pres, Canary Communications Inc.; US; 408/453-9201

Tran, Vo; Pres, Quyen Systems Inc.; US; 301/258-5087, quyen.systems@his.com

Tranchina, Tom; SVP & CFO, Spectragraphics Corp.; US; 619/450-0611

Travers, Paul; Pres, Forte Technologies Inc.; US; 716/427-8595, ptravers@fortevr.com

Traylor, Sandy; VP Hardware, Technically Elite Inc.; US; 408/370-4300

Treadwell, Joann; Ed, Business Geographics; US; 970/223-4848, joann@gis-world.com

Tredennick, Nick; Pres, Tredennick Inc.; US; 408/395-6552, bozo@tredennick.com

Trefethen, Eugene; GM, Fox Electronics; US; 941/693-0099

Treiber, Jason; Fin Mgr, Konexx; US; 619/622-1400

Tremblay, Daniel-Victor; Sales Dir,

AdLib MultiMedia Inc.; Canada; 418/522-6100

Tremblay, David; VP Sales, Viking Components; US; 714/643-7255

Tremblay, Frank; VP Eng, Virtek Vision Corp.; Canada; 519/746-7190

Trempont, Dominique; CFO, NeXT Inc.; US; 415/366-0900

Trent, Barry A.; Pres, Triticom; US; 612/937-0772, btrent@triticom.com

Trescot, David; Dir Sales & Mktng, Specular International; US; 413/253-3100, trescot@specular.com

Tresman, Ian; Pblr, Multilingual PC Directory; UK; 181-953-7722, iantresman@easy.netco.uk

Trevithick, Paul; Pres & CEO, Archetype Inc.; US; 617/890-7544

Trevor, Fred; VP Ops, GreenSpring Computers Inc.; US; 415/327-1200, fred@gspring.com

Treybig, James G.; Pres & CEO, Tandem Computers Inc.; US; 408/725-6000

Triant, Deborah; Pres & CEO, Check Point Software Technologies Ltd.; US; 617/859-9051

Trier, Bruce; Tech Sup Mgr, Quatech Inc.; US; 216/434-3154, trier@quatech.com

Trifari, John; Pres, John Trifari Public Relations; US; 408/541-9192

Trifari, Karen; VP & CFO, NCL America Computer Products Inc.; US; 408/737-2496

Trigilio, Bonnie; VP Admin, Courtland Group Inc.; US; 410/730-7668

Trigilio, Jr., George J.; Pres & CEO, Courtland Group Inc.; US; 410/730-7668

Trikha, Satish; VP Sales, ACC Technology Group; US; 714/454-2441

Trimble, Darrell P.; VP Mktng, Walker Interactive Systems Inc.; US; 415/495-8811

Trimderger, John R.; COO & CFO, Dauphin Technology Inc.; US; 847/971-3400

Trimm, Gary; Pres & CEO, Compression Labs Inc.; US; 408/435-3000

Trimmer, Don; VP Strategic Dev, PDC; US; 610/265-3300, dtrimmer@eng.pdc.com

Trinh, Q. Binh; VP Fin & CFO, Sigma Designs Inc.; US; 510/770-0100

Trino, Joseph; Pres & COO, Kaseworks Inc.; US; 770/448-4240

Triola, Dennis; Pblr, Video Systems; US; 913/341-1300

Tripp, Leonard L.; Ed, Software Engineering Standards & Specifications; US; 303/792-2181

Trivisonno, Nicholas L.; EVP Strat Plng, GTE Corp.; US; 203/965-2000

Trojan, Dean; VP Fin, Colorbus Inc.; US; 714/852-1850

Trom, Jeff D.; VP, Engineering Animation Inc.; US; 515/296-9908

Tropp, Stephen W.; SVP, Quarterdeck

Corp.; US; 310/309-3700

Trottier, Lorne; Pres, Matrox Graphics Inc.; Canada; 514/685-2630

Troussieux, Ann; VP, Technology Resource Assistance Center Inc.; US; 415/853-1100

Troy, Michael; Pres & CEO, KnowledgePoint; US; 707/762-0333

Troyer, Carol S.; Pres & GM, Rubbermaid Office Products Inc.; US; 615/977-5477

Trpik, Joseph R.; EVP, Association for Services Management Int'l.; US; 941/275-7887

Truchard, James; Chmn, Pres & CEO, National Instruments Corp.; US; 512/794-0100

Trudeau, Molly M.; Mngg Ed, GPS World; US; 503/343-1200

Truesdell, Joanne; VP Dev, Cway Software; US; 215/368-9494

Truet, Bick; Pres, Technologies Research Group; US; 908/730-9050

Trujillo, Solomon D.; CEO, US West Communication Group; US; 303/793-6500

Truong, Phung; COO, Reed Technology & Information Services Inc.; US; 301/428-3700

Tryfon, George; Sales Mgr, Cadix International Inc.; US; 404/804-9951

Tsakiris, Alex T.; Pres, Mind Path Technologies; US; 214/233-9296

Tsantes, John; Pres, Tsantes & Associates; US; 408/452-8700

Tsao, Janie C.; Pres, Linksys; US; 714/261-1288

Tsao, Victor; Dir Ops, Linksys; US; 714/261-1288

Tschunke, Jochen; Chmn, Computer 2000; Germany; 89-724-90276

Tse, Ben; Pres & CEO, SourceMate Information Systems Inc.; US; 415/381-1011

Tseng, Frank; Pres, Prolink Computer Inc.; US; 818/369-3833

Tseng, Jack; Pres & CEO, Tseng Labs Inc.; US; 215/968-0502

Tseng, Tim; Tech Mgr, ETC Computer Inc.; US; 510/226-6250

Tsubota, Yasuhiro; Pres & CEO, Canon Computer Systems Inc.; US; 714/438-3000

Tsuei, Dan; CFO, DTK Computer Inc.; US; 818/810-0098

Tsui, Cyrus Y.; Chmn, Pres & CEO, Lattice Semiconductor Corp.; US; 503/681-0118

Tsui, Steve; VP Sales, Acer America Corp.; US; 408/432-6200

Tu, John; Pres, Kingston Technology Corp.; US; 714/435-2600

Tucci, Joseph M.; Chmn & CEO, Wang Laboratories Inc.; US; 508/459-5000

Tuck, Larry; Ed, Lakewood Publications; US; 612/333-0471, ltuck@aol.com

Tucker, Bruce; VP Bus, Network Music Inc.; US; 619/451-6400

Tucker, Dean; VP Sales, Cardinal Technologies Inc.; US; 717/293-3000, deant@cardtech.com

Tucker, John W.; VP Sales & Mktng, ACT Networks Inc.; US; 805/388-2474

Tucker, Kerry; Pres, Nuffer, Smith, Tucker Inc.; US; 619/296-0605

Tucker, Louhon; VP Fin, Best Power Technology Inc.; US; 608/565-7200

Tucker, Michael J.; Exec Ed, SunExpert; US; 617/739-7001, mjt@cpg.com

Tudor, Robert; VP Dev, ResNova Software; US; 714/379-9000

Tullio, Douglas J.; Pres & CEO, Alpha Microsystems; US; 714/957-8500, dtullio@alphamicro.com

Tullo, Patrick J.; EVP Sales, Cray Research Inc.; US; 612/452-6650

Tulloch, John N.; Mngg Dir, IDEAS International Pty. Ltd.; Australia; 612-498-7399, johnt@ideas.com.au

Tung, Jeffrey; Pres, PixelCraft Inc.; US; 510/562-2480

Tung, Michael; VP Fin, Acer America Corp.; US; 408/432-6200

Tuori, Martin; VP Tech, Kolvox Communications Inc.; Canada; 416/221-2400, mtuori@kolvox.com

Turek, Walter; VP Sales, Paychex Inc.; US; 716/385-6666

Turk, Jack; VP & Creative Dir, Splash Studios Inc.; US; 206/882-0300

Turk, Mary; Acct Exec, Levin PR & Marketing Inc.; US; 914/993-0900

Turley, Jim; Author, Selecting a High-Performance Embedded Microprocessor; US; 707/824-4001

Turndal, Lars H.; Chmn, Santa Cruz Operation Inc., The; US; 408/425-7222, larst@sco.com

Turner, Don; CFO, 1st Tech Corp.; US; 512/258-3570

Turner, Douglas M.; Dir Sales & Mktng, Direct Technology; US; 212/475-2747

Turner, Joseph; VP, Adscope Inc.; US; 541/687-1519

Turner, Khoi; VP Prod Dev, 4i Solutions Inc.; US

Turner, Michael; VP Mktng, Scientific & Engineering Software; US; 512/328-5544

Turner, R. Brough; SVP Ops, Natural MicroSystems Corp.; US; 508/650-1300

Turner, Richard; Dir Sales & Mktng, Direct Technology; US; 212/475-2747

Turrell, Don; Pres, Performance Computer; US; 716/256-0200

Turrell, Donald L.; Pres & COO, Performance Technologies Inc.; US; 716/256-0200

Turull, Ron; Ed, Inside ILE; US; 617/444-5755

Tuttle, Margaret; VP Mktng & Dist, Enteractive Inc.; US; 212/221-6559

Twiggs, Ted; CFO, Strata Inc.; US; 801/628-5218

Twombly, Paul; VP Tech, Voysys Corp.; US; 510/252-1100

Twombly, Steve; Pblr, Reseller Management; US; 617/558-4772, stevet@rm.cahners.com

Tworek, Richard M.; SVP, Infodata Systems Inc.; US; 703/934-5205

Tyabji, Hatim A.; Chmn, Pres & CEO, VeriFone Inc.; US; 415/591-6500

Tye, Cary; VP, Feith Systems & Software Inc.; US; 215/646-8000

Tyler, Bernard J.; Pres & CEO, Software Sorcery; US; 619/452-9901

Tyler, James S.; Pres & CEO, Optivision Inc.; US; 415/855-0200

Tyler, W. Mike; Pres, Tippecanoe Systems Inc.; US; 510/416-8510, mike@tippecanoe.com

Tyler, William; Pres & CEO, Brand X Software; US; 804/355-0374

Tymn, Gregory A.; SVP & CFO, Storage Technology Corp.; US; 303/673-5020

Tynor, Stephen; VP Dev, Tower Technology Corp.; US; 512/452-9455, tynor@twr.com

Typaldos, Andreas; Chmn & CEO, Computron Software Inc.; US; 201/935-3400

Tyre, Terian; Mgng Ed, Technological Horizons in Education Journal; US; 714/730-4011

Uchikura, Ken; Pres, Pacific Software Publishing Inc.; US; 206/562-1224

Uecker-Rust, Jodi; VP Employee Svcs, Great Plains Software; US; 701/281-0550

Ueda, Masahiro; EVP, Parana Supplies Corp.; US; 310/793-1325

Uemo, Korchi; Pres, Hitachi America Ltd.; US; 914/332-5800

Uhl, James C.; Pblr, Integrated System Design; US; 415/903-0140, jimu@asic.com

Uhrynowski, Peter; CFO, Queue; US; 203/335-0906

Ulevich, Janis; VP, Ulevich & Orrange Inc.; US; 415/329-1590

Ulrich, Jerry N.; VP & CFO, Xircom Inc.; US; 805/376-9300

Underwood, George B.; VP Sales, ArborText Inc.; US; 313/996-3566

Ungaro, Colin; Pblr, Network World; US; 508/875-6400

Unger, Sarah; Com Mgr, Hanover Fairs US Inc.; US; 609/987-1202

Unkefer, Rachel; CEO, Peer-to-Peer Communications Inc.; US; 408/435-2677

Unkefer, Ronald A.; Chmn, Good Guys Inc., The; US; 415/615-5000

Uno, Keiichi; VP Bus Dev, FirePower Systems Inc.; US; 415/462-3000

Unruh, James A.; Chmn & CEO, Unisys Corp.; US; 215/986-4011

Uphoff, Tony L.; Pblr, InformationWEEK; US; 516/562-5000

Upp, Elizabeth A.; Mgng Ed, X Journal, The; US; 212/242-7447

Uppal, Sanjay; VP Mktng, ATM Forum; US; 415/949-6700

Upstill, Steve; CEO, Upstill Software;

US; 510/526-0178

Urban, Randell L.; CFO, ArcanaTech; US; 412/441-6611

Urban, William P.; Pblr & Pres, BUS Publishing Group; US; 908/363-0708

Ure, Russell; Dir Eng, Visual Edge Software Ltd.; Canada; 514/332-6430, russell@vedge.com

Urschel, Locke; Dir Sls, Alliance Manufacturing Software Inc.; US; 805/965-3000, sales@alliancemfg.com

Urschel, William; Pres, Alliance Manufacturing Software Inc.; US; 805/965-3000, urschelw@alliancemfg.com

Urushisako, Toshiaki; Chmn & Pres, Sharp Electronics Corp.; US; 201/529-8200

Ury, Andrew; Pres, Physician Micro Systems Inc.; US; 206/441-8490, andyu@pmsi.com

Usher, John; Pres, Greystone Peripherals Inc.; US; 408/866-4739

Uslan, Glen; VP Mktng, Packard Bell Interactive; US; 206/654-4100

Ussery, Richard W.; Chmn & CEO, Total Systems Services Inc.; US; 706/649-2204

Uttarwar, Mohan; Pres, Digital Tools Inc.; US; 408/366-6920

Uttarwar, Vijay; VP Fin, Digital Tools Inc.; US; 408/366-6920

Vaccarello, Vincent; Pres, Saratoga Group, The; US; 408/446-9115

Vadasz, Leslie L.; SVP Bus Dev, Intel Corp.; US; 408/765-8080

Vafier, Frank; EVP, JYACC Inc.; US; 212/267-7722

Vagnoni, David J.; EVP, Computer Research Inc.; US; 412/262-4430

Vail, Michael; SVP Sales, Astea Int'l.; US; 215/822-8888

Valentine, Dorothy J.; COO, Systems Management American Corp.; US; 804/461-0559

Valentine Sr., Herman; Chmn & Pres, Systems Management American Corp.; US; 804/461-0559

Vallee, Roy; Pres & COO, Avnet Inc.; US; 516/466-7000

Vallerand, Andre; Pres, Electronic Commerce World; Canada; 514/288-3555

Valovic, Thomas S.; Ed-in-Chief, Telecommunications Magazine; US; 617/769-9750

Van, Tien; Pres, Informer Computer Systems Inc.; US; 714/891-1112

Van Buren, John J.; SVP & CFO, Datametrics Corp.; US; 818/598-6200

Van Cleave, Philip; Pres, Virginia Systems Inc.; US; 804/739-3200

Van Cleef, Lisa; VP, Big Top Productions Inc.; US; 415/978-5363

van Cuylenburg, Peter; EVP Ops, Xerox Corp.; US; 203/968-3000

Van Daele, Dave; VP Sales & Mktng, Personal Library Software Inc.; US; 301/990-1155

Van Daele, David; SVP, Infodata Systems Inc.; US; 703/934-5205

Van den Broucke, Luc; Pres, Barco Chromatics; US; 770/493-7000

van der Poel, Aurthur; Chmn & CEO, Philips Semiconductor; US; 408/991-3626

van Gilluwe, Frank; Pres, V Communications Inc.; US; 408/296-4224

Van Guilder, Phil; VP Sales & Mktng, Dallas Digital Corp.; US; 214/424-2800

van Hamersveld, Chris; Pres, Looking Glass Software Inc.; US; 310/348-8240

Van Horn, Charles; Exec Dir, ITA; US; 609/279-1700

Van Pelt, Janet; CFO, MicroHelp Inc.; US; 770/516-0899

Van Siclen, John W.; VP Mktng & Sales, NetFrame Systems Inc.; US; 408/474-1000

Vana-Paxhia, Steven; Chmn & CTO, MathSoft Inc.; US; 617/577-1017

Vana-Paxhia, Steven R.; Pres & CEO, Inso Corp.; US; 617/753-6500

Vance, Kenneth; Co-Founder, Automated Computer Business Systems; US; 304/296-0290

Vance, Vicki; Dir Mktng, Falcon Systems Inc.; US; 916/928-9255, vicki@falcons.com

Vancil, Richard; VP Mktng, Individual Inc.; US; 617/273-6000

Vandendries, Greg; VP Sales & Mktng, Worlds Inc.; US; 415/281-4878

Vanderploeg, Martin J.; EVP, Engineering Animation Inc.; US; 515/296-9908

Vanderpool, Rufe; COO & VP, Microrim Inc.; US; 206/649-9500, rufev@microrim.com

Vanderslice, James T.; Pres, Pennant Systems Co.; US; 203/849-6844

Vanderslice, John; EVP, Aydin Corp.; US; 215/657-7510

Vanjoff, Barbara; VP Sales, Chancery Software Ltd.; Canada; 604/294-1233

VanMondfrans, Kevin; Mktng Mgr, Century Software; US; 801/268-3088

Vanneman, Mike; VP Sales, Ray Dream Inc.; US; 415/960-0768, vanneman@raydream.com

Vanourek, Robert; Pres & CEO, Recognition International Inc.; US; 214/579-6000

VanSickle, Sharon; Partner, Karakas, VanSickle, Ouellette Inc.; US; 503/221-1551

Vanston, John; Chmn, Technology Futures Inc.; US; 512/258-8898

Vanston, Lawrence K.; Pblr, Technology Futures Inc.; US; 512/258-8898

Varadi, Andrew; EVP, Wireless Logic Inc.; US; 408/262-1876

Vardeman, J. Rex; Chmn, Pres & CEO, Vertex Communications Corp.; US; 903/984-0555

Varn, Melanie; Progr Admin, U.S. Product Data Assoc.; US; 803/760-3327

Varnum, Duane; Dir Prod Mktng, CE Software Inc.; US; 515/221-1801

Vasil, John; Dir Sales, NEBS Software & Computer Forms; US; 603/880-5100

Vasil, John; VP Sales, Peachtree Software Inc.; US; 770/564-5800

Vassalluzzo, Joseph S.; EVP, Staples Inc.; US; 508/370-8500

Vassilakis, Nicholas; Pres & Chmn, Vivid Image Co.; US; 310/618-0274

Vassiliades, Thomas A.; Chmn, Pres & CEO, Gandalf Technologies Inc.; Canada; 613/274-6500

Vaughn, John E.; Pres Info Ind Svcs, Ameritech Corp.; US; 312/750-5000

Vaughn, Pam; Dir Fin & Mfg, Express Systems Inc.; US; 206/728-8300, pam@express-systems.com

Veaner, Daniel; Pres, EmmaSoft Software Co. Inc.; US; 607/533-4685

Veaner, Karen M.; VP, EmmaSoft Software Co. Inc.; US; 607/533-4685

Veilleux, Dave; Mktng Mgr, Olympus Image Systems Inc.; US; 516/844-5000

Veitch, Jim; VP Tech, Franz Inc.; US; 510/548-3600

Veldhouse, Richard; VP Mktng & Sales, Paradigm Technology Inc.; US; 408/954-0500

Veley, Burke R.; SVP & CFO, Technology Service Solutions; US; 610/293-2765

Vellante, David; SVP, International Data Corp.; US; 508/872-8200, dvellante@idcresearch.com

Velline, Barbara; VP Fin, Syncronys Softcorp; US; 310/842-9203

Velte, Jack; VP, Walnut Creek CDROM; US; 510/674-0783, velte@cdrom.com

Venator, John A.; EVP & CEO, Computing Technology Industry Assoc.; US; 630/268-1818

Venman, Joshua C.; R&D Dir, IDEAS International Pty. Ltd.; Australia; 612-498-7399, joshv@ideas.com.au

Venter, Robert; Exec Dir, Portable Computer & Communication Assoc.; US; 408/338-0924

Verabay, Brad; Dir MIS, PFM Communications; US; 212/254-5300, biver@pfmc

Verderico, Patrick; CFO, Creative Labs Inc.; US; 408/428-6600

Verdoorn, Ronald D.; SVP Mfg, Seagate Technology; US; 408/438-6550

Verdu, Mike; Chmn, Legend Entertainment Co.; US; 703/222-8500

Vereen, Linsey; Ed, Embedded Systems Programming; US; 415/905-2200, lvereen@mfi.com

Veregge, Paul; Pres, TechPool Software; US; 216/382-1234, paulv@techpool.com

Verheecke, Robert P.; CFO, Business Objects Inc.; US; 408/973-9300

Verma, Umesh K.; Pres & CEO, Blue Lance; US; 713/680-1187

Vermes, Douglas B.; VP Software Dev, NuIQ Software Inc.; US; 914/833-3479, doug@nuiq.com

Vernadakis, George; Ed, Interactive Week; US; 516/229-3700, gvernada@zd.com

Verni, Ron; Pres, Peachtree Software Inc.; US; 770/564-5800

Vernon, Mark; Pres, ACI US Inc.; US; 408/252-4444

Verrilli, Ronald J.; CFO, American Computer Resources; US; 203/380-4600

Verschueren, Joe; CEO, Business Printing Center; US; 206/869-6319, joev@parallel-comm.com

Verson, Marissa; Pres, InterActive PR Inc.; US; 415/703-0400

Verweij, Arend; GM, Philips Key Modules; US; 408/453-7373

Vessels, Stuart; Ed, 123 Users Journal; US; 502/491-1900

Vestal, Chris; Pblr, Telecom Publishing Group; US

Vetras, Daniel P.; VP Cons Sales, Edmark Corp.; US; 206/556-8400

Vetter, David; VP R&D, Verbex Voice Systems Inc.; US; 908/225-5225

Vetter, Linda L.; SVP R&D, Walker Interactive Systems Inc.; US; 415/495-8811

Via, George C.; EVP Cust Solutions, Bellcore; US; 201/829-2000

Vick, Gailen; VP Mktng & Sales, Avatar Systems Corp.; US; 408/321-0110, gailenvic@aol.com

Vieau, David P.; VP WW Mkt Dev, American Power Conversion; US; 401/789-5735

Vieth, M. Kathy; Pres & COO, Coloray; US; 510/623-3300

Vieth, Richard; VP Sales & Mktng, Future Labs Inc.; US; 408/254-9000, rvieth@futurelabs.com

Vigna, John A.; EVP & COO, Tseng Labs Inc.; US; 215/968-0502

Viker, Dacques; Founder, Vision's Edge Inc.; US; 904/386-4573

Vill, Neil; VP & GM, Rand McNally New Media; US; 847/329-6335, 72254.2555@compuserve.com

Villano, Michael J.; VP & CFO, Scan-Optics Inc.; US; 203/289-6001

Villinger, Armand; VP Electronics Group, Hearst Business Publishing; US; 516/227-1300

Vincent, Donald A.; EVP, Robotic Industries Assoc.; US; 313/994-6088

Vincent, Lisa; Ed, Venture Economics Inc.; US; 212/765-5311

Vincenzo, Ray; Dir PR, Imagio; US; 206/625-0252

Vines, Kenneth R.; VP Fin, DSC Communications Corp.; US; 214/519-3000

Viola, Michael R.; Pres & CEO, Intercim Corp.; US; 612/894-9010

Virden, P. Shelton; VP Sales, Now Software Inc.; US; 503/274-2800

Virga, Bruce A.; VP Sales & Mktng, Design Science Inc.; US; 310/433-0685, brucev@mathtype.com

Visaggi, John; Pres, DDC Publishing Inc.; US; 212/986-7300

Vitak, Dave; Dir Prod Mktng, Navision Software US Inc.; US; 770/564-8000

Viterbi, Andrew J.; Vice Chmn & CTO, Qualcomm Inc.; US; 619/587-1121

Vitorelo, Terry; VP Ops, BusinessWire; US

Vitris, Dominick; VP Sales & Mktng, Powerhouse Entertainment; US; 214/933-5400

Vizard, Michael; Exec Ed, InfoWorld; US; 415/572-7341

Vla-Koch, Vanessa; VP Ops, Mobile Insights Inc.; US; 415/390-9800, vvlay@mobileinsight.com

Vlacil, Frank; VP, Parallel Technologies Sales; US; 206/813-8728

Vladeck, Susan; VP Mktng, Philips Home Services Inc.; US; 617/238-3400

Vobach, Arnold R.; Chmn, Cyber-Safe; US; 713/784-2374

Voci, Valerie; Sponsorship Mktng, Telecommunications Reports/BRP; US; 202/842-3022, vmv@brpnyc.mhs.compuserve.com

Vogel, Dennis; Pres, Reliable Source Inc.; US; 205/660-1960

Vogel, Jeff; Dir Eng, Electronic Book Technologies Inc.; US; 401/421-9550, jlv@ebt.com

Vogel, Robert; Pres, Consultech Communications Inc.; US; 518/283-8444

Vogel, William; CTO, Software Professionals Inc.; US; 415/578-0700

Vohs, Dennis V.; Chmn & CEO, Ross Systems Inc.; US; 415/593-2500

Voigt, Shannon; Pres, Vivo Media; US; 503/223-9644, shannon@govivo.com

Vokoun, Greg; VP Prod Dev, Cyma Systems Inc.; US; 602/831-2607

Volk, Steven B.; Chmn & CEO, Integral Peripherals Inc.; US; 303/449-8009

Volker, Michael; CEO, Mindflight Technology Inc.; US; 604/294-6465

Volpe, Louis J.; SVP Mktng & Ops, Parametric Technology Corp.; US; 617/398-5000

Volz, Bernard; CTO, Process Software Corp.; US; 508/879-6994

Volz, William J.; Pres, Logic Devices Inc.; US; 408/737-3300

Von Ehr, James; VP & GM, Macromedia Digital Arts Group; US; 214/680-2060

von Halle, Barbara; Ed, Data Management, Handbook of; US; 617/423-2020

Von Lintig, John; VP & CFO, Magic Solutions Inc.; US; 201/587-1515

von Mayrhauser, Anneliese; VP Conf & Tutorials, IEEE Computer Society; US; 202/371-0101

Von Reis, Will; CTO, Smartek Software; US; 619/456-5064

von Vital, Leonard W.; CFO, Astea Int'l.; US; 215/822-8888

Vonderach, Stephen H.; VP & CFO, Quality Semiconductor Inc.; US; 408/450-

8000

Vonderschmitt, Bernard; Chmn, Xilinx Inc.; US; 408/559-7778

Vonk, Harry; VP Consulting, Trilogy Development Group; US; 512/794-5900

Vorholt, Jeffrey J.; VP & CFO, Structural Dynamics Research Corp.; US; 513/576-2400

Vosicky, John J.; EVP & CFO, Comdisco Inc.; US; 847/698-3000

Voss, Kenneth S.; VP Sales, Software Professionals Inc.; US; 415/578-0700

Vouri, Scott; Pres, Binar Graphics Inc.; US; 415/491-1565

Vu, Hung; Pres & CEO, Milkyway Networks Corp.; US; 408/467-3868

Vukmanic, Frank J.; VP Mktng, Zitel Corp.; US; 510/440-9600

Vukovic, Phil; Pres, Bit 3 Computer Corp.; US; 612/881-6955

Waag, Kurt; VP Fin & Admin, Theos Software Corp.; US; 510/935-1118

Wacek, Ronald; EVP, SysKonnect Inc.; US; 408/437-3800

Wacker, Christopher; VP Mktng & Sales, Compulink Management Center Inc.; US; 310/212-5465

Wacker, Nien-Ling; Pres & CEO, Compulink Management Center Inc.; US; 310/212-5465

Wacker, Richard; Dir, Prima International Inc.; US; 408/727-2600

Waclo, John; Pres, Elite Software; US; johnw@eliteinc.com

Wada, Yoichi; Pres, Computer Applications America Co. Ltd.; US; 212/332-2580

Waddell, John C.; Chmn, Arrow Electronics Inc.; US; 516/391-1300

Waddell, Richard; Dir Mktng, Mannesmann Tally Corp.; US; 206/251-5500

Wade, Brian J.; VP Sales & Mktng, Network-1 Software & Technology; US; 718/932-7599

Wade, Jack; Pres, Z Microsystems Inc.; US; 619/657-1000

Wadlow, Thomas; Dir Eng & Dev, Pilot Network Services Inc.; US; 510/748-1850

Waggener, Melissa; Pres, Waggener Edstrom; US; 503/245-0905

Wagner, Edward; Pres, Computer Technology Research Corp.; US; 803/853-6460

Wagner, Edward R.; Pblr, Multimedia Intelligence; US; 803/853-6460

Wagner, Harvey A.; SVP & CFO, Scientific-Atlanta Inc.; US; 770/903-5000, harvey.wagner@sciatl.com

Wagner, Heidi; Admin, Computer Press Assoc.; US; 201/398-7300

Wagner, Russell A.; VP, Datastream Systems Inc.; US; 803/297-6775

Wahl, Gloria; Pres, InterNex Information Services; US; 408/327-2355, gwahl@internex.com

Wahl, Paul; CEO, SAP America Inc.; US; 215/521-4500

Wai, Gilbert; SVP Prod Dev, Legato Systems Inc.; US; 415/812-6000

Wainwright, Julie; Pres & COO, Berkeley Systems Inc.; US; 510/540-5535

Waite, Donald L.; SVP & CFO, Seagate Technology; US; 408/438-6550

Waitt, Theodore W.; Chmn & CEO, Gateway 2000; US; 605/232-2000

Wakerly, John; EVP & CTO, Alantec Corp.; US; 408/955-9000, jfw@alantec.com

Waksman, Samuel M.; VP & CFO, Tiger Direct Inc.; US; 305/443-8212

Walchek, Scott; Pres & CEO, Sanctuary Woods Multimedia Corp.; US; 415/286-6000

Wald, Scott; Pres & CEO, ASAP Software Express Inc.; US; 847/465-3710

Waldheim, Peter; EVP, Interactive Television Assoc.; US; 202/408-0008

Waldman, Todd; Pres, Acecad Inc.; US; 408/655-1900

Waldron, James J.; VP Bus Dev, MicroTouch Systems Inc.; US; 508/659-9000

Waldron, Steve; Pres, Iconovex Corp.; US; 612/896-5100

Wales, Keith; Pivotal Software Inc.; Canada; 604/988-9982, kwales@pivotalsoft.com

Walker, Allen; VP R&D, DacEasy Inc.; US; 214/732-7500

Walker, David N.; VP & Controller, BDM Int'l.; US; 703/848-5000

Walker, Doug; Pres, Walker Richer & Quinn Inc.; US; 206/217-7100

Walker, James M.; VP & CFO, Global Village Communication; US; 408/523-1000

Walker, Lloyd; VP Dev, Human Code Inc.; US; 512/477-5455

Walker, William R.; SVP & CFO, Zilog Inc.; US; 408/370-8000

Wall, Gerald A.; VP & CFO, Digi Int'l.; US; 612/943-9020

Wall, John R.; EVP, Wall Data Inc.; US; 206/814-9255

Wall, Patrick; Pres, A-R Editions Inc.; US; 608/836-9000

Wallace, Dan B.; VP, Logicon Inc.; US; 310/373-0220

Wallace, James; Pres, Cranel Inc.; US; 614/431-8000

Wallace, Louis R.; Ed-in-Chief, Digital Video Magazine; US; 415/522-2400, lou@dv.com

Wallace, Mike; VP Tech Support, Calyx Corp.; US; 414/782-0300

Wallace, Richard; Ed-in-Chief, Electronic Engineering Times; US; 516/562-5000, rwallace@eet.cmp.com

Wallace, Rick W.; Exec Dir, Association of Color Thermal Transfer Technology Inc.; US; 716/691-5817

Wallach, June; VP, IDC/LINK; US; 212/726-0900, jwallach@idcresearch.com

Wallach, Steven J.; SVP Tech, Convex Computer Corp.; US; 214/497-4000

Wallack, Iris; Pblr, Information Hotline; US; 908/536-7673

Waller, Keith; Mgng Ed, CeBIT News; Belgium; 322-766-0031

Wallet, Bill; VP Sales & Mktng, Client/Server Labs; US; 404/552-3645

Wallin, Robert; Pres, Applied Magic Inc.; US; 619/599-2626

Wallingford, Philip; CTO, SQA Inc.; US; 617/392-0110

Wallington, Patricia M.; VP Info Mgmt, Xerox Corp.; US; 203/968-3000

Walsh, Dale M.; VP Adv Dev, U.S. Robotics Inc.; US; 847/882-5010

Walsh, James K.; VP & COO, VMark Software Inc.; US; 508/366-3888

Walsh, Jesse; Pres, Jesse Walsh Communications; US; 616/695-5948

Walsh, John J.; SVP Plng & Strat, Compression Labs Inc.; US; 408/435-3000

Walsh, Michael J.; Pres, Internet Info; US; 703/578-4800

Walsh, Michael P.; SVP Custom Pubs, Sentry Publishing Co. Inc.; US; 508/366-2031

Walsh, Miles; VP Mktng, Macromedia Inc.; US; 415/252-2000

Walsh, Shaun; VP OEM Sales, NovaStor Corp.; US; 805/579-6700, shaun@novastor.com

Walske, Steven C.; Pres & CEO, Parametric Technology Corp.; US; 617/398-5000

Walt, Robert; Principal, Walt & Sommerhauser Communications; US; 408/496-0900

Walter, Dave; VP, Visio Corp.; US; 206/521-4500

Walter, Janice; Ed, Inside Microsoft Office; US; 502/491-1900

Walters, Chipp; Pres & CEO, Human Code Inc.; US; 512/477-5455

Walters, D. Bruce; Pres & CEO, RadioMail Corp.; US; 415/286-7800

Walters, Liz; COO, Human Code Inc.; US; 512/477-5455

Walters, Richard F.; Exec Ed, M Computing; US; 301/431-4070, walters@cs.ucdavis.edu

Walters, Steve; Chmn & Pres, ATM Forum; US; 415/949-6700

Walton, Mark; VP Mktng & Sales, 3D/Eye Inc.; US; 770/937-9000, mawa@eye.com

Walton, Tiffany A.; Mgng Ed, Multimedia Business & Marketing Sourcebook; US; 215/238-5300

Wambolt, Ronald R.; SVP WW Sales, Fluke Corp.; US; 206/347-6100

Wan, Tracey; SVP & CFO, Sharper Image Corp.; US; 415/445-6000

Wandell, Bo; VP Sales, CompuServe Internet Div.; US; 206/447-0300

Wandishin, John; Dir Mktng, Brother International Corp.; US; 908/356-8880

Wang, Andrew; Pres, Bayware Inc.; US; 415/286-4480

Wang, Cathy; Mktng Mgr, Accurate

Research Inc.; US; 408/523-4788, cathy.wang@drcdrom.com

Wang, Charlene; Pres, First International Computer Inc.; Taiwan ROC; 2-717-4500

Wang, Charles B.; Chmn & CEO, Computer Associates Int'l. Inc.; US; 516/342-5224

Wang, Chris C.; Pres & CEO, Shining Technology Inc.; US; 714/761-9598

Wang, Eugene; EVP, Symantec Corp.; US; 408/253-9600

Wang, Gigi; SVP, International Data Corp.; US; 508/872-8200, gwang@idcresearch.com

Wang, Jack; Pres, Techcessories Corp; US; 408/436-5510

Wang, Jieh-Shan; CTO, Virtual Open Network Environment Corp.; US; 301/881-2297

Wang, Joe; Pres, 20/20 Software Inc.; US; 503/520-0504

Wang, Paul; SVP, Spectragraphics Corp.; US; 619/450-0611

Wang, Qing Ren; CTO, ExperVision Inc.; US; 408/523-0900

Wang, Robert; VP R&D, CMD Technology Inc.; US; 714/454-0800

Wang, Steve; Pres, Contour Design Inc.; US; 508/937-2422

Wang, Wenhu; VP, Pulse Metric Inc.; US; 619/546-9461

Wang, William; Pres, MAG Innovision Inc.; US; 714/751-2008

Wangman, Carl A.; Exec Dir, Information Systems Security Assoc. Inc.; US; 847/657-6746

Wanner, Gordon; Pres, Starlite Software Corp.; US; 360/385-7125, gjw@olympus.net

Warburton, Jim; Pres, Baker & Taylor Software; US; 805/522-9800

Ward, Joseph; COO, Target Software Group Inc.; US; 813/528-2477

Ward, Nick; VP Fin & CFO, Parity Systems Inc.; US; 408/378-1000

Ward, Robert; Pblr, R&D Publications Inc.; US; 913/841-1631

Warf, Albert W.; Group VP, Diebold Inc.; US; 216/489-4000

Wark, John R.; Pres & CEO, Continuus Software Corp.; US; 714/453-2200

Warkenton, Peter; Pres, California Software Products Inc.; US; 714/973-0440

Warmenhoven, Daniel J.; Pres & CEO, Network Appliance Corp.; US; 415/428-5100

Warner, Bill; Founder & CEO, Wildfire Communications Inc.; US; 617/674-1500

Warner, David E.; Pres, Wesson International Inc.; US; 512/328-0100

Warner, Jim; Dir Dev, International Software Group Inc.; US; 617/221-1450

Warner, John D.; Pres, Boeing Computer Services Co.; US; 206/655-2121

Warnick, John; CFO, Lasergate Systems Inc.; US; 813/725-0882

Warnock, John E.; Chmn & CEO, Adobe Systems Inc.; US; 415/961-4400

Warnock, John J.; SVP & CFO, FTP Software Inc.; US; 508/685-4000

Warnshuis, Edward W.; Pblr, Technological Horizons in Education Journal; US; 714/730-4011

Warren, Walter D.; SVP Ops, Data Race; US; 210/558-1900

Warren, Wayne; Mgr Prod Dev, Raima Corp.; US; 206/557-0200, wwarren@raima.com

Warrier, Unni; Pres, CyberMedia Inc.; US; 310/843-0800

Warrington, Lyle; Pres, Red Wing Business Systems; US; 612/388-1106

Warsawski, Eli; Pres, Univision Technologies Inc.; US; 617/221-6700

Warshaw, William B.; VP Dev, Zenographics Inc.; US; 714/851-6352

Wasch, Kenneth; Pres, Software Pblrs Assoc.; US; 202/452-1600

Waserman, Anthony I.; Chmn, Interactive Development Environments Inc.; US; 415/543-0900

Washburn, David; Dir Sales & Mktng, Improve Technologies; US; 801/224-6550, davidw@transera.com

Wason, Wes; Sales & Mktng Mgr, ASD Software Inc.; US; 909/624-2594

Waszak, Steve; VP Fin & CFO, Retix; US; 310/828-3400

Watanabe, Laurie; Mgng Ed, Enterprise Communications; US; 714/513-8400

Waters, Bill; SVP Sales, Telco Systems Inc.; US; 617/551-0300

Waters, Crystal; Reviews Ed, Net, The; US; 415/696-1661

Waters, Kenneth R.; Pres, MicroAge Inc.; US; 602/804-2000

Waters, Martin C.; Pres & CEO, Locus Computing Corp.; US; 310/670-6500

Wathor, Doug; VP Sales & Mktng, InfoImaging Technologies Inc.; US; 415/960-0100

Watkins, Fred; Pres, HyperLogic Corp.; US; 619/746-2765, fwatkins@hyperlogic.com

Watkins, Pam; Pub Dir, Computer Reseller News; US; 516/562-5000, pwatkins@cmp.com

Watson, Deanna; Dir Mktng, Radish Communications System Inc.; US; 303/443-2237, dwatson@radish.com

Watson, Kirby; Dir Sales, Paradigm Software Development Inc.; US; 206/728-2281

Watson, Linda; VP Prod Mgmt, Virtus Corp.; US; 919/467-9700, linda.watson@virtus.com

Watson, Max P.; Chmn, Pres & CEO, BMC Software Inc.; US; 713/918-8800

Watson, Stephen L.; Chmn, Software Developer's Co. Inc., The; US; 617/740-0101

Watson, Todd L.; Assist Ed, Software Quarterly; US; 817/961-6551,

radar@vnet.ibm.com

Watt, Karen; Pblr, Midrange Computer Directories; US; 810/978-4300

Watters, Donald C.; VP Sales, Touchstone Software Int'l.; US; 714/470-1122

Watterson, Karen; Ed, Microsoft SQL Server Professional; US; 206/251-1900

Watts, Karen; Pblr, DP Blue Book Co., The; US; 810/978-4300

Waxman, Barry; VP Sales, Mylex Corp.; US; 510/796-6100

Waylan, C.J.; EVP, GTE Personal Communications Services; US; 404/391-8000

Wayman, Lance; VP Ops, Compulink Management Center Inc.; US; 310/212-5465

Wayman, Robert P.; EVP & CFO, Hewlett-Packard Co.; US; 408/553-4300

Weatherford, Thom; VP & CFO, Logitech Inc.; US; 510/795-8500

Weaver, Alan L.; SVP, Cerplex Group Inc.; US; 714/258-5151, aweaver@cerplex.com

Weaver, Gary D.; SVP Mfg, AST Research Inc.; US; 714/727-4141

Weaver, Phil; SVP Sales & Mktng, Jet-Form Corp.; US; 703/448-9544

Webb, Dorothy; SVP, Best Programs Inc.; US; 703/709-5200

Webb, Joe; VP Sales, AllMicro Inc.; US; 813/539-7283

Webb, Kaaren; Dir Prod Dev, Jostens Home Learning; US; 619/587-0087

Webb, Rick; Dir Sales, Centon Electronics Inc.; US; 714/855-9111

Webber, Jeff; Pres, Mobius Computer Corp.; US; 510/460-5252

Webber, Jim; Pres, Omicron-Center for Information Technology Management; US; 201/335-0240, jwebber@omicronet.com

Webber, W. Scott; Pres & CEO, Software Artistry Inc.; US; 317/843-1663

Weber, Jeffrey A.; VP Ops & Fin, Computer Identics Corp.; US; 617/821-0830

Weber, Larry; Pres, Weber Group Inc., The; US; 617/661-7900, lweber@webergroup.com

Weber, Lisa; VP Mktng, CD ROM-USA Inc.; US; 303/384-3922

Weber, William P.; Vice Chmn, Texas Instruments Inc.; US; 214/995-2551

Webster, Bob; CFO, ViaGrafix Corp.; US; 918/825-6700

Webster, David; Ed & Pblr, Software Developer & Pblr; US; 303/745-5711

Webster, Don; VP Ops, Graphsoft Inc.; US; 410/290-5114

Webster, George K.; Pres & CEO, Miltope Corp.; US; 334/284-8665

Webster, Mike; CEO, ViaGrafix Corp.; US; 918/825-6700

Webster, Ralph L.; VP & CFO, Logicon Inc.; US; 310/373-0220

Webster, Robert E.; VP, American Small Business Computers Inc.; US; 918/825-4844

Weed, Robert; Pres, Chronologic Corp.;

US; 602/293-3100

Weedfald, Peter C.; Pblr, Windows Sources; US; 212/503-4147

Weedmark, Richard; VP Bus Dev, Gilmore Corp.; Canada; 613/237-7770

Weeks, Doyle C.; SVP & CFO, Cybex Corp.; US; 205/430-4000

Wegbreit, Ben; Chmn & CEO, Kubota Pacific Computer Inc.; US; 408/727-8100

Weger, Jeff; MIS Mgr, Evergreen Technologies Inc.; US; 541/757-0934

Wegman, David; COO, Magic Software Enterprises Inc.; US; 714/250-1718

Wehle, John; VP Eng, Feith Systems & Software Inc.; US; 215/646-8000

Wehrer, Wayne; Dir Eng, Carroll Touch Inc.; US; 512/244-3500

Weidler, Jeffrey; Pres & CEO, Word-Mark International Corp.; US; 408/975-1100

Weil, Jay; VP Mktng, Optimal Networks; US; 415/254-5950, jayw@optimal.com

Weinbach, Arthur F.; Pres & COO, Automatic Data Processing Inc.; US; 201/994-5000

Weinberg, Tod; Pres, Scion Corp.; US; 301/695-7870

Weinberger, Alan; Chmn, Pres & CEO, ASCII Group Inc., The; US; 301/718/2600

Weinberger, David; VP Mktng & Comm, Open Text Corp.; Canada; 519/888-7111

Weinberger, George; Pres, American Healthware Systems Inc.; US; 718/435-6300

Weiner, Bruce; Pres, Mindcraft Inc.; US; 415/323-9000, bruce@mindcraft.com

Weiner, Rick; Ed, Out of the Blue; US

Weinfurter, Daniel J.; EVP, Alternative Resources Corp.; US; 708/317-1000

Weingart, Norman; VP, Communications Specialties Inc.; US; 516/273-0404, normanw@commspecial.com

Weingarten, Fred W.; Ed Dir, Computing Research News; US; 202/234-2111, weingarten@cra.org

Weingarten, Ira; Pres, Equity Communications; US; 805/897-1880

Weinkrantz, Alan; Pres, Alan Weinkrantz And Co.; US; 210/820-3070, aweinkrantz@mcimail.com

Weinkrantz, Barbara; VP, Alan Weinkrantz And Co.; US; 210/820-3070

Weinman, Elliot D.; Pres, Software Productivity Group Inc.; US; 508/366-3344, 76102.1473@compuserve.com

Weinstein, David M.; VP Mktng, Centigram Communications Corp.; US; 408/944-0250

Weinstein, Joel; Pres, High Technology Marketing; US; 508/478-2392, joel@htm.com

Weir, Bernard J.; VP Prod Dev, FTG Data Systems; US; 714/995-3900

Weir, James; Exec Dir, Information User Assoc.; US; 312/644-6610

Weisberg, David S.; Pblr & Ed, Engineering Automation Report; US; 303/770-1728, dweisbrg@eareport.com

Weisberg, Howard; Pres, Shortcut Software Corp.; US; 310/459-3871

Weisenberg, Robert E.; VP Ops & GM, Effective Management Systems; US; 414/359-9800

Weiskamp, Keith; Pblr, PC Techniques; US; 602/483-0192

Weiskamp, Keith; Pres & Pblr, Coriolis Group Inc.; US; 602/483-0192

Weismann, Rodger; VP & CFO, Forte Software Inc.; US; 510/869-3400

Weiss, David E.; EVP, Storage Technology Corp.; US; 303/673-5020

Weiss, Kenneth P.; Chmn & CTO, Security Dynamics Technologies Inc.; US; 617/547-7820

Weiss, Michael; Pres, MWA Consulting Inc.; US; 415/323-4780

Weiss, Steve; Principal, Product Management Group; US; 415/346-7307

Weiss-Morris, Loretta; Ed & Pblr, Microcomputer Trainer, The; US; 201/330-8923

Weissman, Robert E.; Chmn & CEO, Dun & Bradstreet Corp., The; US; 203/834-4200

Weitner, Mark; VP Mktng, Relay Technology Inc.; US; 703/506-0500

Weitzner, Steve; Pblr, OEM Magazine; US; 516/562-5624

Welch, Marianne; Pres, Welch Communications; US; 408/395-7363

Welch, Rosie; PrintPaks Inc.; US; 503/295-6564

Welch Jr., John F.; Chmn & CEO, General Electric Co.; US; 203/373-2211

Welchel, Russell; Controller, Transparent Technology Inc.; US; 310/215-8040, russell@trantech.com

Weldler, David; VP, Data Systems & Software Inc.; US; 201/529-2026

Weldor, Jinty; DB Solutions Dir, Romtec plc; UK; 1628-770077

Welham, David; Pres, Xionix Simulation Inc.; US; 214/929-9999

Welke, Elton; Pblr & GM, Microsoft Press; US; 206/882-8080

Welke, Larry; Pres, ICP; US; 317/251-7727

Weller, Edward; GM, Sterling Hager Inc.; US; 617/259-1400

Welling, William; Chmn & CEO, Xiox Corp.; US; 415/375-8188

Wellington, David; Pres, CrossWind Technologies Inc.; US; 408/469-1780, david@crosswind.com

Wellington, Gail; VP Mktng, Philips Media OptImage; US; 515/225-7000, gailw@pmpro.com

Wells, James; VP Sales, Progressive Networks; US; 206/447-0567

Wells, John; Tech Ed, PickWorld; US; 714/261-7425

Wells, Terry L.; Principal, Baron,

McDonald & Wells; US; 770/492-0373, twells@bmwpr.com

Welsh, Dennie; Chmn, Integrated Systems Solutions Corp.; US

Welsh, Michelle; VP Mktng, FutureWave Software Inc.; US; 619/637-6190, 73124.3426@compuserve.com

Welsh, Scott; VP, SoftArc Inc.; Canada; 905/415-7000

Welter, Brian; VP Eng, Interactive Catalog Corp.; US; 206/623-0977

Welty, Bill; Chmn, Action Technologies Inc.; US; 510/521-6190

Welty, Bruce; Pres, Welty-Leger Corp.; US; 617/461-8700

Wen, Yeh-Tsong; VP Eng, LANcast; US; 603/880-1833

Wenig, Raymond; Pres, International Management Services Inc.; US; 508/520-1555, rwening@delphi.com

Wenig, Sandra; VP, International Management Services Inc.; US; 508/520-1555

Wenning, Rob; Pblr, CSG Information Services; US; 813/664-6800

Wenninger, Fred; Pres & COO, Key Tronic Corp.; US; 509/928-8000

Wenzel, Robert J.; COO, LaserMaster Corp.; US; 612/941-8687

Werner, Bob; VP, VideoLan Technologies Inc.; US; 502/895-4858

Werthman, Scott; Pblr, Software Quarterly; US; 817/961-6551

Wesemann, Jan; VP Sales, Resumix; US; 408/988-0444

Wesolek, Robert; COO, Kent Marsh Ltd.; US; 713/522-5625

Wesson, Robert B.; Chmn & CEO, Wesson International Inc.; US; 512/328-0100

West, Donald; Ed, Telemedia Week; US; 617/964-3030

West, J. Thomas; SVP, Data General Corp.; US; 508/898-5000

West, John; Pres & CEO, Cimlinc Inc.; US; 708/250-0090

West, W. Michael; EVP, Octel Communications Corp.; US; 408/321-2000

West, Jr., Alfred P.; Chmn & CEO, SEI Corp.; US; 610/254-1000

Westall, Frank; Pres, Strategic Alliance Partners Inc.; US; 310/860-4029

Westerman, Peter; Pblr, Windows Developer's Journal; US; 913/841-1631

Westerman III, John L.; VP & CFO, Continuum Company Inc., The; US; 512/345-5700

Western, James; VP & GM, Angia Communications; US; 801/371-0488

Westhaver, Mona; Pres, Inspiration Software Inc.; US; 503/245-9011

Westmoreland, Nicole; Sr Ed, Communication Systems Design; US; 415/905-2200, nwestmoreland@mfi.com

Weston, Josh S.; Chmn & CEO, Automatic Data Processing Inc.; US; 201/994-5000

Westover, Matt; Nat'l Sales Mgr,

Andataco; US; 619/453-9191, matt.westover@andataco.com

Westwood, Paula; Ed Assist, Online User; US; 203/761-1466

Wetenhall, Paul; Pres, QSoft Solutions Corp.; US; 716/264-9700

Wetherbee, Ann; Prod Mgr, D/M Communications Inc.; US; 617/329-7799

Wetmore, David F.; EVP & COO, Legent Corp.; US; 703/708-3000

Wetsel, Gary A.; EVP & CFO, Octel Communications Corp.; US; 408/321-2000

Wettreich, Daniel; Chmn & CEO, Camelot Corp.; US; 214/733-3005

Wexler, Steven S.; Pres, WexTech Systems Inc.; US; 212/949-9595, 72467.47@compuserve.com

Weyand, William J.; EVP Sales, Measurex Corp.; US; 408/255-1500

Whalen, Nick; Network Sys, Rockwell Semiconductor Systems; US; 714/883-4600

Whaley, Amy K.; Accountant, HTE Research Inc.; US; 415/871-4377

Wheaton, Robert L.; VP Sales, Wind River Systems Inc.; US; 510/748-4100

Wheeler, Doug; VP Mktng, UB Networks; US; 408/496-0111

Wheeler, Wendell; Pres, Electronic Form Systems; US; 214/243-4343

Whelan, Greg; VP, ADSL Forum; US; 415/378-6680, greg.whelan@analog.com

Whelan, Nick; Bus Dir, Rockwell Network Systems; US; 805/968-4262, nwhelan@rns.com

Whitacker, Jim; CIO, Network General Corp.; US; 415/473-2000

Whitacre Jr., Edward E.; Chmn & CEO, SBC Communications Inc.; US; 210/821-4105

Whitaker, Dan; EVP, Rogue Wave Software Inc.; US; 541/754-3010

Whitaker, Jerry; Ed-in-Chief, Video Systems; US; 913/341-1300, jwhitaker@msn.com

Whitchurch, Woody; CFO, Distributed Processing Technology; US; 407/830-5522

White, Charles; Pres, Black & White Software; US; 408/369-7400

White, Cheri L.; VP & CFO, CompuTrac Inc.; US; 214/234-4241

White, Daryl J.; SVP & CFO, Compaq Computer Corp.; US; 713/370-0670

White, Donald; CEO, Interference Control Technologies; US; 540/347-0030

White, Douglas C.; Chmn, Pres & CEO, Setpoint Inc.; US; 713/584-1000

White, George P.; Pres, Corollary Inc.; US; 714/250-4040

White, Gregory J.; Pres & CEO, TriTeal Corp.; US; 619/930-2077

White, Harvey P.; Pres, Qualcomm Inc.; US; 619/587-1121

White, John W.; VP & CIO, Compaq Computer Corp.; US; 713/370-0670

White, Paul; Ed, Smalltalk Report, The;

US; 212/242-7447

White, Peter; US Ed., Computergram; US; 212/677-0409

White, Phillip E.; Chmn, Pres & CEO, Informix Software Inc.; US; 415/926-6300

White, Rene; Principal, White & Co.; US; 415/274-8100

White, Steve; VP Eng, TV/COM International Inc.; US; 619/451-1500

White, Stuart; VP Svcs & Sup, CompuServe Internet Div.; US; 206/447-0300

White, Warren; Pres, FutureSoft; US; 713/496-9400

Whitehouse, Harry T.; Pres, Envelope Manager Software; US

Whiteside, Fred; Mgr R&D, Beame & Whitside Software Ltd.; US; 919/831-8989

Whiteside, Stephen; Mgr Enterprise Solutions, EveryWare Development Corp.; Canada; 905/819-1173

Whiting, Douglas; VP Tech, Stac Inc.; US; 619/794-4300

Whiting, Jerry; Pres, Azalea Software Inc.; US; 206/932-4030

Whitlock, Mary Ann; Mktng Dir, Microtek Lab Inc.; US; 310/297-5000

Whitman, Ira C.; SVP R&D, BitWise Designs Inc.; US; 518/356-9741

Whitmore, Sam; Ed Dir, PC Week; US; 617/393-3700, sam_whitmore@zd.com

Whitney, Peter; VP & GM, Mind Path Technologies; US; 214/233-9296, pwhitney@aol.com

Whitney, Walter; Sales Mgr RTC Group, RTC Group, The; US; 714/489-7575

Whitney-Smedt, Suzanne; Mktng Mgr, ACI US Inc.; US; 408/252-4444

Whittler, Dennis A.; VP & CFO, Proxima Corp.; US; 619/457-5500

Wible, Scott R.; Mgng Ed, Healthcare Informatics; US; 303/674-2774

Wichmann, Scott; VP Fin, Linksys; US; 714/261-1288

Wick, Robert; Pres, Robert Wick Public Relations Inc.; US; 212/682-0600

Widman, Jake; Ed, Publish; US; 415/978-3280, jwidman@publish.com

Widmann, Martin; Dir Mktng, Soricon Corp.; US; 303/440-2800

Wiebe, James; Pres, Newer Technology; US; 316/685-4904

Wielage, Edward A.; Cogent Technologies Inc.; US; 717/283-2257

Wiener, Hesh; Ed & Pblr, Technology News of America Co. Inc.; US; 212/334-9750

Wiener, Richard; Ed, Journal of Object-Oriented Programming; US; 212/242-7447

Wienkoop, Glenn R.; EVP, Measurex Corp.; US; 408/255-1500

Wieser, Nan; VP Mktng, Westing Software; US; 415/945-3870

Wiggins, Margie; Dir Admin, Repro-CAD Inc.; US; 510/284-0400

Wight, Robert; Pres, Avail Systems Corp; US; 303/444-4018

Wilbur, Jay; CEO, Id Software; US; 214/613-3589, jay@idsoftware.com

Wilcox, David; SVP, Dataware Technologies Inc.; US; 617/621-0820

Wilcox, Kathy; Exec Dir, Washington Software & Digital Media Alliance; US; 206/889-8880

Wilcox, Sue; MIS Mgr, Tech-Source Inc.; US; 407/262-7100, sue@techsource.com

Wilczak, John; Chmn, Pres & CEO, MetaTools Inc.; US; 805/566-6200

Wilde, Timothy; Pres & CEO, Connexperts; US; 214/233-8800

Wilde, William P.; VP Sales & Mktng, Minnesota Educational Computing Corp.; US; 612/569-1500

Wildenthaler, Jeff; SVP Sales & Mktng, Sendero Corp.; US; 602/941-8112

Wilder, Ron; Ed, Inside Filemaker Pro; US; 502/491-1900

Wilder, Throop; Founder & CEO, American Internet Corp.; US; 617/276-4500

Wiley, John; Pres, Supra Corp.; US; 360/604-1400

Wiley, Joseph L.; VP & CFO, American Software Inc.; US; 404/264-5296

Wiley Priestley, Nadine; CFO, Maximum Strategy Inc.; US; 408/383-1600

Wilhelm, Richard M.; VP Mktng, Helix Technologies; US; 847/465-0242

Wilk, Robert; Pres, International Association for Computer Systems Security; US; 516/499-1616

Wilker, Harry R.; SVP, Broderbund Software Inc.; US; 415/382-4400

Wilkes, Ed; Dir Sales & Mktng, MountainGate Data Systems Inc.; US; 702/851-9393

Wilkins, Jeffrey M.; Chmn & CEO, Metatec Corp.; US; 614/761-2000

Wilkins, Katie; Dep Mgng Dir, Romtec plc; UK; 1628-770077

Wilkins, R.D.; VP Sales, Cadec Systems Inc.; US; 603/668-1010

Wilkinson, Mark; Acct Mgr, Image-X; US; 805/964-3537, mark@imagexx.com

Wilkinson, Peter; Assoc Ed, Business Equipment HOTLINE; US; 816/941-3100

Wilkinson, Wayne; Dir Mktng, Zebra Technologies VTI Inc.; US; 801/576-9700

Willcox, Riley R.; SVP & CFO, Premisys Communications Inc.; US; 510/353-7600

Willemsin, Thomas R.; VP, Smart Software; US; 617/489-2743, trw@smartcorp.com

Willenborg, Jim; Chmn & VP Mktng, My Software Co.; US; 415/473-3600

Willens, Ronald; EVP, Livingston Enterprises Inc.; US; 510/426-0770

Willens, Steven; Pres & CEO, Livingston Enterprises Inc.; US; 510/426-0770

Willets, Larry; Ed, Enterprise Reengineering; US; 703/761-0646

Williams, Anthony; EVP & CFO,

Acclaim Entertainment Inc.; US; 516/624-8888

Williams, Ben F.; VP Bus Dev, Par Technology Corp.; US; 315/738-0600

Williams, Byron; Ed, Inside AutoCAD; US; 502/491-1900

Williams, Carroll; Pres, VME Microsystems Int'l. Corp.; US; 205/880-0444

Williams, Elizabeth; Marcom Mgr, Lanworks Technologies Inc.; Canada; 905/238-5528, liz@lanworks.com

Williams, Gregg; Ed, Apple Directions; US; 408/974-3264, greggw@apple.com

Williams, James B.; Pres & COO, Inter-Tan Inc.; US; 817/348-9701

Williams, Ken; Chmn, Pres & CEO, Sierra On-Line Inc.; US; 206/649-9800

Williams, Lora; VP Mktng, Sybex; US; 510/523-8233

Williams, M. Cecilia; Ops Mgr, Transparent Technology Inc.; US; 310/215-8040

Williams, Martha E.; Ed, Online & CD-ROM Review; US; 609/654-6266

Williams, Michael; Acct Exec, Ripley-Woodbury Marketing Communications; US; 310/860-7336

Williams, Richard; CFO, Alpha Technologies; US; 360/647-2360

Williams, Robert; VP Mktng, NetManage Inc.; US; 408/973-7171

Williams, Rose N.; VP, RadioMail Corp.; US; 415/286-7800

Williams, Sean; Dir Mktng, Carbela Tek Inc.; US; 415/873-6484

Williams, Stephen; European Sales Dir, IDEAS International Pty. Ltd.; Australia; 612-498-7399, stevew@ideasinternational.com

Williams, Sterling L.; Pres & CEO, Sterling Software Inc.; US; 214/891-8600

Williams, Theodore; Chmn & CEO, Bell Industries Inc.; US; 310/826-2355

Williams, Timothy; CEO, Theos Software Corp.; US; 510/935-1118

Williams, Timothy V.; EVP & CFO, Policy Management Systems Corp.; US; 803/735-4000

Williams, Tom; Pres, Combinet Inc.; US; 408/522-9020

Williams, Tom; CTO, Cobotyx Corp.; US; 203/282-0010

Williams, William; Pres, Williams & Macias Inc.; US; 509/458-6312

Williamson, Glen T.; Pres, Mountain-Gate Data Systems Inc.; US; 702/851-9393

Willisobert, R.; Project Mgr, Graphics Performance Characterization Committee; US; 703/331-0180

Willmott, Tom; Ed & VP, New Technology Impact; US; 617/723-7890

Wilmott, Tina; VP, Terpin Group, The; US; 310/821-6100, twilmott@sf.terpin.com

Wilnai, Dan; Pres, Computer Access Technology Corp.; US; 408/727-6600

Wilner, David; CTO, Wind River Sys-

tems Inc.; US; 510/748-4100

Wilson, Carol; Exec Ed, Interactive Week; US; 516/229-3700, cwilson@zd.com

Wilson, Debra; VP DP, Research Results Inc.; US; 508/345-5510

Wilson, Elise; Pblr, Application Development Trends; US; 508/652-1100

Wilson, G. Larry; Chmn, Pres & CEO, Policy Management Systems Corp.; US; 803/735-4000

Wilson, George; Pres & CEO, PDC; US; 610/265-3300, gwilson@pa.pdc.com

Wilson, Graham J.S.; Chmn, Miller Freeman Inc.; US; 415/905-2200

Wilson, John B.; EVP & CFO, Staples Inc.; US; 508/370-8500

Wilson, John W.; Ed, ComputerLetter; US; 212/343-1900

Wilson, Johnny; Ed, Computer Gaming World; US

Wilson, L.R.; Chmn, Pres & CEO, BCE Inc.; Canada; 514/397-7267

Wilson, Lee; VP Mktng, Chancery Software Ltd.; Canada; 604/294-1233

Wilson, Lerry; Pres, Wilson McHenry Co.; US; 415/638-3400, lwilson@wmc.com

Wilson, Mark R.; VP Sales & Ops, Telebit Corp.; US; 508/441-2181

Wilson, Michael; VP Fin & CFO, Advanced Input Devices; US; 208/765-8000

Wilson, Morrie; Pres & CEO, Wilson WindowWare Inc.; US; 206/938-1740, morriew@windowware.com

Wilson, Nancy; VP, Wilson Window-Ware Inc.; US; 206/938-1740

Wilson, Ralph; EVP, Improve Technologies; US; 801/224-6550

Wilson, Ray; VP Bus Ops, Scitex America Corp.; US; 617/275-5150

Wilson, Richard; Pres, Application Partners Inc.; US; 908/549-5464

Wilson, Richard D.; VP Sales, Micro-Tech Conversion Systems Inc.; US; 415/424-1174

Wilson, Ron; CEO, Improve Technologies; US; 801/224-6550

Wilson, Ryan; Karakas, VanSickle, Ouellette Inc.; US; 503/221-1551

Wilson, Steve; Pres, ButtonWare Inc.; US; 214/713-6370

Wilson, Wayne; CFO, PC Connections Inc.; US; 603/446-3383

Wilson Jr., Thomas W.; Chmn, Information Resources Inc.; US; 312/726-1221

Wimberley, Keith; Dir Mktng, Insoft Inc.; US; 717/730-9501

Winckler, Loren; VP WW Sales, Xerox ColorgrafX Systems; US; 408/225-2800

Winder, Edwin C.; SVP Sales, Informix Software Inc.; US; 415/926-6300

Windham, Barbara; VP Mktng, Storm Software; US; 415/691-6600

Windham, Laurie; Partner, Windham/Lang Group; US; 415/563-4545,

lwindham@netcom.com

Winebaum, Jake; Ed & Pblr, Family PC; US; 212/503-5255

Winer, Marleen; CEO, TeleTypesetting Co.; US; 617/734-9700

Wing, Howard; VP Sales & Mktng, Maxoptix Corp.; US; 510/353-9700

Wing, Sidney E.; Pres & CEO, Datametrics Corp.; US; 818/598-6200

Wingren, W. Martin; Chmn, Cypress Research Corp.; US; 408/752-2700

Winkler, Lisa; Exec Dir, Enterprise Computer Telephony; US; 415/578-6852

Winn, D. Clive; Pres, Fitnesoft Inc.; US; 801/221-7777

Winn, Edward C.; VP & CFO, TriQuint Semiconductor; US; 503/644-3535

Winn, Francis W.; Chmn, Computer Language Research Inc.; US; 214/250-7000

Winn, George M.; Pres & COO, Fluke Corp.; US; 206/347-6100

Winn, Herschel C.; SVP, Tandy Corp.; US; 817/390-3700

Winn, Paul T.; Pres & CEO, Genicom Corp.; US; 703/802-9200

Winn, Stephen T.; Pres & CEO, Computer Language Research Inc.; US; 214/250-7000

Winningstad, C. Norman; Chmn, ThrustMaster Inc.; US; 503/615-3200

Winsky, Gregory J.; SVP, Franklin Electronic Pblrs Inc.; US; 609/386-2500

Winston, Judie; Pblr, Newstips Electronic Ed.ial Bulletin; US; 216/338-8400

Winston, Marty; Ed, Newstips Electronic Ed.ial Bulletin; US; 216/338-8400, 75250.3467@compuserve.com

Winston, Morton M.; Chmn, NoRad Corp.; US; 310/605-0808

Winston, Peter; Pres & CEO, Integrated Computer Solutions Inc.; US; 617/621-0060, winston@ics.com

Winters, Mary-Frances; Pres, Winters Group Inc., The; US; 716/546-7480

Winther, Mark; VP, IDC/LINK; US; 212/726-0900, mwinther@idcresearch.com

Wirth, Ken; VP MKtng, Diamond Multimedia Systems Inc.; US; 408/325-7000

Wirth, Steven P.; Pblr, EDN Products Edition; US; 201/292-5100

Wirths, Craig; COO, Durand Communications Network Inc.; US; 805/961-8700

Wise, Greg; Mktng Mgr, Ten X Technology Inc.; US; 512/918-9182

Wise, Mark; CEO, Rowland Co., The; US; 212/527-8800

Wise, Michael V.; VP Ops, CompuCom Systems; US; 214/265-3600

Wise, Stuart; Pblr, Computer Law Strategist; US; 212/779-9200

Wisenberg, Ian; Pres, Partners-in-Health Inc.; US; 619/514-4315

Wismer, David A.; EVP, SunGard Data Systems Inc.; US; 610/341-8700

Withrow, Lawrence; VP Sales, Computer Product Testing Services Inc.; US; 908/223-5700

Witkowicz, Tad; Pres & CEO, Cross-Comm Corp.; US; 508/481-4060

Witmer, Donald; COO & CFO, DeltaPoint Inc.; US; 408/648-4000, don_witmer@deltapoint.com

Witous, Jeff; EVP Bus Dev, TriTeal Corp.; US; 619/930-2077

Witsaman, Mark; SVP Tech, Mobile-Comm; US; 601/966-0888

Witt, Norbert; Pres & CEO, Parity Systems Inc.; US; 408/378-1000

Witt, Robert B.; VP & CIO, Sequent Computer Systems Inc.; US; 503/626-5700

Witt, Scott; Ed, How to Conquer the Software Market; US; 914/268-5925

Wittkopp, Dan; VP Fin & Admin, Cogent Data Technologies Inc.; US; 360/378-2929

Wittlen, Michael; Pres, E Corp.; US

Witzel, John R.; VP Fin, Stac Inc.; US; 619/794-4300

Wixted, Richard J.; VP Mktng, Technically Elite Inc.; US; 408/370-4300

Wodyka, Mark; VP Sales & Mktng, AITech International Corp.; US; 510/226-8960

Woelbruck, David; Ed, HP Chronicle; US; 512/250-9023

Wohl, Amy D.; Pres, Wohl Associates; US; 610/667-4842, awohl@mcimail.com

Wohlfahrt, Jeffrey; Pres, Advanced Concepts Inc.; US; 414/963-0999

Wokas, Alan; Pres, Rhetorex Inc.; US; 408/370-0881

Wolf, Jeff; VP Fin, Link Technologies Inc.; US; 408/473-1200

Wolf, Tom; VP Sales & Mktng, Eiger Labs Inc.; US; 408/774-3456

Wolf, Vickie; CFO, Nimax Inc.; US; 619/566-4800

Wolfe, Gordon H.; Mgng Dir, Wolfe Axelrod Assoc.; US; 212/370-4500

Wolfe, L. Stephen; Pres, CAD/CAM Publishing Inc.; US; 619/488-0533

Wolfe, Thomas; Pres & CEO, Persoft Inc.; US; 608/273-6000

Wolff, Ward; VP Fin, Premenos Corp.; US; 510/602-2000

Wolff, William; Pres, Open Systems Holdings Corp.; US; 612/829-0011

Wolfram, Stephen; Pres, Wolfram Research Inc.; US; 217/398-0700

Wolfston, James A.; Founder & Pres, Universal Algorithms Inc.; US; 503/973-5200

Wolfston, Jim; Pres, Precision Guides; US; 503/227-6219

Womack, Craig; EVP & COO, Sharper Image Corp.; US; 415/445-6000

Womble, James T.; EVP, Acxiom Corp.; US; 501/336-1000

Wong, Amy S.; CFO, AVerMedia Inc.; US; 510/770-9899, amyw@aver.com

Wong, Frank T.; VP Fin, Micros-To-

Mainframes Inc.; US; 914/268-5000

Wong, John; VP, Aydin Corp.; US; 215/657-7510

Wong, Njai; VP Prod Dev, Empress Software Inc.; US; 301/220-1919, nwong@empress.com

Wong, Shuh Hai; Network Mgr, ExperVision Inc.; US; 408/523-0900, shuh-hai@pebble.expervision.com

Wong, Wilson; VP & Co-Chmn, Asante Technologies Inc.; US; 408/435-8388

Woo, Douglas; EVP, Princeton Graphic Systems; US; 714/751-8405

Wood, Charles C.; Ed & Pblr, Information Security Policies Made Easy; US; 415/332-7763

Wood, Donald C.; VP Info Serv, Triad Systems Corp.; US; 510/449-0606

Wood, Donald F.; EVP Ricochet Div, Metricom Inc.; US; 408/399-8200

Wood, Graham; CFO, Foresight Software; US; 770/206-1000

Wood, John B.; Pres & CEO, C3 Inc.; US; 703/471-6000

Wood, Karen; VP Sales, Gemstone Systems Inc.; US

Wood, Richard; CFO & VP Fin, Make Systems; US; 415/941-9800

Wood, Richard B.; VP & CFO, Macromedia Inc.; US; 415/252-2000

Wood, Steve; Pres & CEO, Notable Technologies Inc.; US; 206/455-4040, swood@notable.com

Woodall, John; VP Sales & Mktng, Peregrine Systems; US; 619/481-5000

Woodard, Larry; Dir Mktng, Sonic Systems Inc.; US; 408/736-1900

Woodbury, Mick; Pres, Ripley-Woodbury Marketing Communications; US; 310/860-7336

Woodhull, John R.; Pres & CEO, Logicon Inc.; US; 310/373-0220

Woodland, Charlotte; Sales Mgr, Micro Central; US; 908/360-0300

Woodman, Elizabeth; VP, Ventana Communications Group Inc.; US; 919/544-9404

Woodman, Josef; Pres, Ventana Communications Group Inc.; US; 919/544-9404

Woodruff, Michael; Dir Ops, Ardis; US; 708/913-1215

Woods, Lisa; VP Mktng, PictureWorks; US; 510/855-2001

Woods, M. Troy; EVP, Total Systems Services Inc.; US; 706/649-2204

Woods, Wendy; Ed-in-Chief, Newsbytes; US; 612/430-1100

Woodsmall, Dana; Pblr, CADalyst; US; 714/513-8400

Woodson, Larry; VP Corp Mktng, Synopsys Inc.; US; 415/962-5000

Woodward, Victor; VP Ops, Firefox Inc.; US; 408/321-8344

Woog, Kenneth M.; Pres, Futuretouch Corp.; US; 714/558-6824

Worcester, Chad; Dir Multimedia, J3

Learning; US; 612/930-0330

Workman, Jim; Ed-in-Chief & Pblr, Mac Today; US; 813/733-6225

Workman, Mike; SVP & CTO, Conner Peripherals Inc.; US; 408/456-4500

Worthen, David; Pres, Connect Tech Inc.; Canada; 519/836-1291, djw@connecttech.com

Worthen, Jim; Pres, J2 Marketing Services; US; 714/529-2527

Worthen, John D.; Pres & CEO, Mergent Int'l.; US; 860/257-4223

Worthington, Hall; Pres, Worthington Data Solutions; US; 408/458-9938

Worthington, Shari; Pres, Cirrus Technology; US; 508/755-5242

Worthman, Susan; Exec Dir, Multimedia Development Group; US; 415/553-2300

Wortman, Victor; Pres, Victor Wortman Co., The; US; 310/393-6281

Wozniak, Steve; Ed Dir, Envisioneering; US; 516/783-6244

Wrathall, T. Wallace; Pres & CEO, Comshare Inc.; US; 313/994-4800

Wreden, Nick; Pres, Aspen; US; 404/848-7751

Wrenn, Dick; VP Mktng, Xinet; US; 510/845-0555, dick@xinet.com

Wright, Anne; Dir Computer Group, Rourke & Co.; US; 617/267-0042

Wright, Bruce T.; VP, Nashua Corp.; US; 603/880-2323

Wright, Dan; VP & CFO, Electrohome Ltd.; Canada; 519/744-7111

Wright, Graham; VP Tech, Beame & Whitside Software Ltd.; US; 919/831-8989

Wright, Guy; Exec Ed, OS/2 Magazine; US; 415/905-2382, gwright@mfi.com

Wright, John; Pres & CEO, Viewpoint Datalabs Int'l.; US; 801/229-3000

Wright, Leslie; VP & CFO, Fractal Design Corp.; US; 408/688-5300

Wright, Norman B.; Pres & CEO, Virtek Vision Corp.; Canada; 519/746-7190

Wright, Roy A.; Pres & CEO, RDI Computer Corp.; US; 619/929-0992

Wright Jr., Jay; Pres, Wright Strategies; US; 619/274-1047

Wrixon, Ann; Exec Dir, BMUG Inc.; US; 510/549-2684

Wu, Joe; VP, Chroma ATE Inc.; US; 408/437-0798

Wu, Peter; Dir Eng, Nimax Inc.; US; 619/566-4800

Wu, Sheng-Chuan; VP Bus Dev, Franz Inc.; US; 510/548-3600

Wu, Tsung-Ching; EVP Tech, Atmel Corp.; US; 408/441-0311

Wu, W. Norman; Pres & CEO, Avantos Performance Systems Inc.; US; 510/654-4600, 615.6237@mcimail.com

Wujcik, Anne; Pres, Wujcik & Associates; US; 703/519-3557, annewujcik@aol.com

Wulkan, Maks; EVP, Eicon Technology

Corp.; 214/239-3270

Wyand, Rick; Pres & CEO, STF Technologies Inc.; US; 816/463-7972

Wyckoff, Kurt D.; Dir Sales & Mktng, AEC Software Inc.; US; 703/450-1980

Wylie, Jon D.; CFO, Rimage Corp.; US; 612/944-8144

Wylie, Margie; Ed, Digital Media; US; 415/575-3775, zeke@digmedia.com

Wyly, Sam; Chmn, Sterling Software Inc.; US; 214/891-8600

Wyman, Mead; CFO, Dataware Technologies Inc.; US; 617/621-0820

Wymer, Ray D.; Pres, Star Gate Technologies Inc.; US; 216/349-1860

Wynne, Tom; Head Prod Dev, Paradigm Software Development Inc.; US; 206/728-2281

Wynnyckyj, Mike; VP Sales & Mktng, Lava Computer Mfg. Inc.; Canada; 416/674-5942, 75662.110@compuserve.com

Wynnyckyj, Roman; Pres, Lava Computer Mfg. Inc.; Canada; 416/674-5942

Wyrick, Kenneth L.; VP Sales & Mktng, Boca Research Inc.; US; 407/997-6227

Xenakis, Suzanne; Acct Mgr, Smith & Shows; US; 415/329-8880, suzannex@aol.com

Yablon, Jeff; Pres, Computer Press Assoc.; US; 201/398-7300

Yacenda, Michael W.; EVP, Executone Information Systems Inc.; US; 203/876-7600

Yaker, Israel M.; Pres, MultiWriter Software; US; 201/837-0420

Yam, Martin; SVP Sales & Mktng, ParcPlace-Digitalk Inc.; US; 408/481-9090

Yamada, Masahiko; Pres, Wacom Technology Corp.; US; 360/750-8882

Yamaguchi, Roland; VP Ops, Canary Communications Inc.; US; 408/453-9201

Yamamoto, Tom; Pres, Murata Electronics North America Inc.; US; 404/436-1300

Yamazaki, Yas; Chmn, Mass Optical Storage Technologies; US; 714/898-9400

Yamnitsky, Boris; Pres, Artel Software Inc.; US; 617/566-0870

Yanakakis, Paul; VP Fin, International Software Group Inc.; US; 617/221-1450

Yanamoto, Arthur; Ops Mgr, Axxon Computer Corp.; Canada; 519/974-0163

Yang, Alex; VP, Soyo US Inc.; US; 818/330-1712

Yang, Frank; Dir Sales, ETC Computer Inc.; US; 510/226-6250

Yang, Gordon; Pres, ZyXEL; US; 714/693-0808

Yang, Jerry; Co-Founder, Yahoo Corp.; US; 415/934-3230

Yang, John; Pres, Teco Information Systems Co. Inc.; US; 708/438-3998

Yang, Lou; VP Eng, Destiny Technology Corp.; US; 408/562-1000

Yang, Susan; Sales Mgr, ZyXEL; US; 714/693-0808

Yaniger, Stuart I.; VP R&D, Interlink Electronics; US; 805/484-8855

Yansouni, Cyril J.; Chmn & CEO, Read-Rite Corp.; US; 408/262-6700

Yao, Lien; VP Fin, XDB Systems Inc.; US; 410/312-9300

Yao, S. Bing; Pres & CEO, XDB Systems Inc.; US; 410/312-9300

Yap, Harvey; CFO, Decisive Technology Corp.; US; 415/528-4300

Yara, Ronald T.; VP Strategic Mktng, S3 Inc.; US; 408/980-5400

Yariagadda, Rambabu; CFO, Living Books; US; 415/352-5200

Yarren, Douglas; Pres, Symark Software; US; 818/865-6100

Yarrington, Jeff; VP Sales, InterApps Inc.; US; 310/374-4125, jeff-yarr@aol.com

Yasinovsky, Vadim; Pres, Clear Software Inc.; US; 617/965-6755

Yasno, Igor; Pres, Diamond Optimum Systems; US; 818/224-2010

Yates, William A.; SVP Sales & Mktng, Interlink Electronics; US; 805/484-8855

Yau, Alfred; Pres, J-Mark Computer Corp.; US; 818/856-5800

Yazbek, Michel A.; SVP Sales & Mktng, Mesa Group; US; 617/964-7400

Yedwab, Gadi; VP Eng, MITI; US; 415/326-5000, gadiy@miti.com

Yelich, Mark; Ed & Pblr, Dimensions; US; 303/469-0557

Yellin, Robert; SVP & CTO, Legent Corp.; US; 703/708-3000

Yellowlees, Robert A.; Chmn & CEO, National Data Corp.; US; 404/728-2000

Yen, Bill; Pres, Sys Technology Inc.; US; 714/821-3900

Yen, Hsin; CEO, InteliSys Inc.; US

Yeung, Gilbert; SW Dev Mgr, Lanworks Technologies Inc.; Canada; 905/238-5528, gilbert@lanworks.com

Ynostroza, Roger; Ed, Graphic Arts Monthly; US; 303/470-4445

Yokoyama, Douglas J.; VP Sales & Mktng, Integrated Micro Solutions Inc.; US; 408/3698282

Yong, Alan; Chmn, Pres & CEO, Dauphin Technology Inc.; US; 847/971-3400

Yonker, Michael D.; VP IS & CFO, In Focus Systems Inc.; US; 503/685-8888

Yoo, Young; Dir Sales & Mktng, Pacom Inc.; US; 408/752-1590

Yost, Denny; Ed-in-Chief & Pblr, Enterprise Internetworking Journal; US; 214/669-9000

Young, Andrea; Pres, Young Systems Ltd.; US; 770/449-0338

Young, Andrew; Chmn, Young Minds Inc.; US; 909/335-1350, young@ymi.com

Young, Angela; Pblr, LAN Magazine; US; 415/905-2200, ayoung@mfi.com

Young, Cynthia; Pres, Classroom Connect; US

Young, Dennis; Chmn, Young Systems Ltd.; US; 770/449-0338

Young, Ellie; Exec Dir, Usenix Assoc.; US; 510/528-8649

Young, Fred C.; CFO, Black Box Corp.; US; 412/746-5500

Young, J. Thomas; VP Ops, Connect-Soft; US; 206/827-6467

Young, Jacky; COO, Sirsi Corp.; US; 205/922-9820

Young, Jean; Pres, Young & Associates Inc.; US; 301/309-9404

Young, Jeremy; Ed, Electronic Buyers' News; US; 516/562-5000, jyoung@cmp.com

Young, Jim; CEO, Sirsi Corp.; US; 205/922-9820

Young, John; Chmn, Novell Inc.; US; 801/222-6000

Young, Kari A.; CFO, Specialty Tele-Constructors Inc.; US; 505/281-2197

Young, Katherine C.; SVP Ops, Maxtor Corp.; US; 408/432-1700

Young, Lucy; Exec Dir, Dauphin Technology Inc.; US; 847/971-3400

Young, Peter R.; Exec Dir, National Commission on Library & Information Sciences; US; 202/606-9200

Young, Rebecca; VP Mktng, Premenos Corp.; US; 510/602-2000

Young, Richard; Pres, JVC Information Products Co.; US; 714/261-1292

Young, Robbin; Mgng Dir, Windows Watcher; US; 206/881-7354, ryoung@sbexpos.com

Young, Robert; VP Mktng, Cardinal Technologies Inc.; US; 717/293-3000, byoung@cardtech.com

Young, Roger A.; VP & CFO, BDM Int'l.; US; 703/848-5000

Young, Willis; VP & CFO, Hayes Microcomputer Products Inc.; US; 770/840-9200

Youngblood, Gerald; Pres, Boundless Technologies; US; 512/346-2447

Yourdon, Ed; Ed, American Programmer; US; 617/648-8702

Yu, Allen; Pres, Empac International Corp.; US; 510/683-8800

Yu, Andrew; VP Mktng, Online Environs Inc.; US; 617/225-0449

Yu, Hong; Pres & CEO, LANcast; US; 603/880-1833

Yu, Jonathan K.; VP Ops, Lattice Semiconductor Corp.; US; 503/681-0118

Yu, Quincy; CFO, PeerLogic; US; 415/626-4545

Yu, Raymond; Pres, Alaris Inc.; US; 510/770-5700

Yuasa, Hisao; Vice Chmn & CEO, Ricoh Corp.; US; 201/882-2000

Yuen, Andy T.S.; VP Int'l Ops, Microsemi Corp.; US; 714/979-8220

Yuen, Thomas C.K.; Chmn & CEO, SRS Labs Inc.; US; 714/442-1070

Yuhas, Steve; Pres, Panasonic Communications & Systems Co.; US; 201/348-7000

Yurtin, Wayne; Co-Founder, AllPen Software; US; 408/399-8800

Yuval, Cohen; VP Mktng, DSP Group Inc.; US; 408/986-4300

Zabetian, Mahboud; Pres & CEO, Ag Group Inc., The; US; 510/937-7900

Zabkar, Joe; Pres, GreenSpring Computers Inc.; US; 415/327-1200, joe@gspring.com

Zacaries, Dave; COO, OPTi Inc.; US; 408/486-8000

Zachan, Michael P.; Pres, Acculogic Inc.; US; 714/454-2441

Zachan, Mike; Pres, Computer Peripherals Inc.; US; 714/454-2441

Zacharias, Greg; VP, Charles River Analytics Inc.; US; 617/491-3474

Zachmann, Will; Pres, Canopus Research; US; 617/934-9800, wfz@canopusresearch.com

Zack, Darryl; VP Sales, JYACC Inc.; US; 212/267-7722

Zadeh, Ali H.; VP Sales & Mktng, Initio Corp.; US; 408/988-1919, aliz@initio.com

Zadeh, Mark; SVP Intl Sales, Labtec Enterprises Inc.; US; 360/896-2000

Zaelit, Joseph M.; VP & CFO, VeriFone Inc.; US; 415/591-6500

Zagaris, Michael P.; CEO, Mobile Products Inc.; US; 209/526-7119

Zahner, John; Ed, HeadsUp; US

Zaidi, Feroz; Co-Chmn, Elixir Technologies Corp.; US; 805/641-5900, ferozzaidi@notes.elixir.com

Zajas, Jeff; MIS Dir, International Association of HP Computing Professionals; US; 408/747-0227

Zak, George R.; VP Mktng, Analysts International Corp.; US; 612/835-5900

Zakhariya, Ramiz H.; Pres, Micro Channel Developers Assoc.; US; 916/222-2262, rzakhari@interserv.com

Zakin, Jonathan N.; EVP Sales & Mktng, U.S. Robotics Inc.; US; 847/882-5010

Zaks, Irving; VP & GM Govt Sys, GTE Government Systems, Information Systems Div.; US; 703/818-4000

Zaks, Rory K.; VP Retail, Elek-Tek; US; 847/677-7660

Zakzeski, Jim; VP Sales & Mktng, Cubix Corp.; US; 702/888-1000

Zaldastani, Nicholas; Pres & CEO, Open Horizon Inc.; US; 415/598-1200

Zaman, Bruce; Pres, Best Data Products Inc.; US; 818/773-9600

Zambonini, Renato; Pres & COO, Cognos Inc.; Canada; 613/738-1440

Zamora, Carmela; Events & Tradeshows, User Group Connection Inc.; US; 408/461-5700

Zandan, Peter; CEO, IntelliQuest; US; 512/329-2424

Zander, Edward J.; Pres, SunSoft Inc.; US; 415/960-1300

Zandman, Felix; Chmn, Vishay Intertechnology; US; 610/644-1300

Zappacosta, Pierluigi; Pres, Logitech Inc.; US; 510/795-8500

Zaremba, James; Grp Pres, Penton Publishing Inc.; US; 216/696-7000

Zarrella, John; Pres, Research Results Inc.; US; 508/345-5510

Zayas, Ron; Dir Mktng, FTG Data Systems; US; 714/995-3900, ronzayas@aol.com

Zazzo, Joseph D.; CFO, ProfitKey International Inc.; US; 603/898-9800

Zeffer, Doug; Dir Dev, Paul Mace Software; US; 541/488-2322

Zeichick, Alan; Ed-in-Chief, OS/2 Magazine; US; 415/905-2382, zeichick@acm.org

Zeigler, Terry; Pres, Datacap Systems Inc.; US; 215/699-7051

Zeis, Michael; Pres, Blackstone Research Associates; US; 508/278-3449

Zelencik, Stephen; SVP & CMO, Advanced Micro Devices Inc.; US; 408/732-2400

Zeleniak, David A.; CFO, Ross Technology; US; 512/436-2000, davez@ross.com

Zelnick, Nate; Ed, Internet Business Report; US; 212/780-6060

Zeman, Greg; Pres, Computer Discount Warehouse; US; 847/465-6000

Zemel, Tami; Mgng Ed, Dr. Dobb's Journal; US; 415/358-9500

Zemke, E. Joseph; Pres & CEO, Amdahl Corp.; US; 408/746-6000

Zenisek, Tom; Pres & Chmn, Enterprise Computer Telephony; US; 415/578-6852

Zenor, Stanley; Exec Dir, Association for Educational Communications & Technology; US; 202/347-7834

Zerbe, Mark A.; EVP Ops, Kent Electronics Corp.; US; 713/780-7770

Zhivago, Kristin; Partner, Zhivago Marketing Partners; US; 415/328-6000, kristin@zhivago.com

Zhivago, Philip; Partner, Zhivago Marketing Partners; US; 415/328-6000

Zhu, George; Dir Prod Dev, MaxTech Corp.; US; 201/586-3008, george_zhu@maxcorp.com

Zhu, Min; VP & CTO, Future Labs Inc.; US; 408/254-9000

Zieber, Fred; Pres, Pathfinder Research Inc.; US; 408/437-1905

Ziedenberg, Erica; Partner, Windham/Lang Group; US; 415/563-4545, eziedenberg@netcom.com

Ziegel, Robert; Grp Pblr, Computer Design; US; 603/891-0123, bobz@pennwell.com

Ziems, Charlotte; Exec Ed & Test Ctr Dir, Infoworld Test Center; US; 415/572-7341, charlotte_ziems@infoworld.com

Ziering, Charles A.; VP Dev & CTO, Progress Software Corp.; US; 617/280-4000

Zilber, Jon; Ed-in-Chief, PC/Computing; US; 415/578-7000

Zilka, Yahal; CFO, VocalTec Inc.; US; 201/768-9400

Zimmer, Mark; Pres & CEO, Fractal Design Corp.; US; 408/688-5300

Zimmerman, Marc; Sales Mgr, Comtronic Systems Inc.; US; 509/674-7000

Zimmermann, Hubert; Chmn & CEO, Chorus Systems Inc.; US; 408/879-1350

Zimmermann, Myron; CTO, VentureCom Inc.; US; 617/661-1230, myron@vci.com

Zinsli, Peter F.; VP Mktng, Microfield Graphics Inc.; US; 503/626-9393

Zipper, Stuart; Ed, ClieNT Server News; US; 516/759-7025

Zirkle, David H.; Pres & CEO, FTP Software Inc.; US; 508/685-4000

Zirngibl, Arno; Chmn, Provantage Corp.; US; 216/494-8715, zirngibl@provantage.com

Zisman, Michael; EVP & CEO, Lotus Development Corp.; US; 617/577-8500

Zito, Larry; EVP, Attachmate Corp.; US; 206/644-4010

Zitomer, William J.; VP Software Eng, Rhode Island Soft Systems Inc.; US; 401/767-3106, 73770.1633@compuserve.com

Zlotogorski, Herbert; COO, Accent Software Int'l. Ltd.; US; 714/223-0620

Zoeller, Mary M.; VP Mktng, Proxima Corp.; US; 619/457-5500

Zoellner, Jack; VP Ops, Champion Business Systems Inc.; US; 303/792-3606

Zollo, Robert; Pres, Software Architects Inc.; US; 206/487-0122

Zoukis, Paul J.; SVP Sales & Mktng, Hogan Systems Inc.; US; 214/386-0020

Zucker, Frederic; Pres & CEO, Advanced Input Devices; US; 208/765-8000

Zulch, Larry; Pres & Co-Founder, Dantz Development Corp.; US; 510/253-3000

Zulch, Richard; VP Eng & Co-Founder, Dantz Development Corp.; US; 510/253-3000

Zung, David; Sales Dir, CAF Technology Inc.; US; 818/369-3690

Zuuring, Peter; Pres & CEO, Amtex Software Corp.; Canada; 613/967-7900

Zvegintzov, Nicholas; Pres, Software Maintenance News Inc.; US; 415/969-5522

Zwica, Tom; Pres, Interactive Design Consultants; US; 309/944-8108, tomz@idc.geneseo.com

Zwick, Nicholas; Chmn, Dialogic Corp.; US; 201/993-3000

Zwicker, Dave; VP Sales, Gradient Technologies; US; 508/624-9600

Chapter 4

Products and
Technologies

Product Awards

Computer Industry Almanac: Product Awards

Each year the Computer Industry Almanac will be listing the most interesting, innovative and useful new products. These awards grew from the most common question we are asked at trade shows: "Have you seen anything interesting?" So we decided to list what we think are the most interesting or innovative or fun or surprising products we have seen or used in the last year. In other words, any product that evokes excitement. These awards are highly opinionated and may be unusual, but we think they deserve recognition. There is no limit to the type of products on the list other than they be personal computer related. It can be service, software, hardware, peripheral, publications, information, etc. We tend to pick products that are not well known. This list is not ranked and is in alphabetical order by product name.

Product Name	Company	City, State	Product Type
1995-1996 CIA Product Awards			
CleanSweep 95	Quarterdeck	Marina del Rey, CA	Utility software
First Aid 95	CyberMedia	Santa Monica, CA	Utility software
FrontPage	Microsoft	Redmond, WA	Web page development software
Internet Explorer	Microsoft	Redmond, WA	Web browser
Monte Python's Complete Waste of Time	7th Level	Los Angeles, CA	Entertainment
Note It	Gigatron Software	Los Angeles, CA	Document utility software
PageMaker 6.0	Adobe	Mountain View, CA	Desktop publishing software
PkZip	PKWare	Brown Deer, WI	Data compression software
Windows 95	Microsoft	Redmond, WA	Operating system and user interface
1994-1995 CIA Product Awards			
Arts & Letters Express 5	Computer Support	Dallas, TX	Illustration software
Designer 3	Ray Dream	Mountain View, CA	3D illustration software
FrameMaker 5	Frame Technology	San Jose, CA	Desktop publisher
Gone fishing	Amtex	Belleville, Ontario, Canada	Fishing simulation game
Navigator	Netscape	Mountain View, CA	Web browser
Paradox for Windows 5.0	Borland	Scotts Valley, CA	Database software
Quicken 4.0	Intuit	Mountain View, CA	Financial management software
1993-1994 CIA Product Awards			
Access 2.0	Microsoft	Redmond, WA	Database software
Art Gallery	Microsoft	Redmond, WA	Art pictures
Charisma 4.0	Micrografx	Richardson, TX	Presentation software
eWorld	Apple Computer	Cupertino, CA	Online service
Kids Zoo	Knowledge Adventure	La Crescenta, CA	Educational software
LANtastic Version 6	Artisoft	Tucson, AZ	LAN software
Mouse-Trak	ITAC Systems	Garland, TX	Trackball
Office	Microsoft	Redmond, WA	Software suite
Piano	Musicware	Redmond, WA	Piano teaching software
Studio 8	Electronic Arts	San Mateo, CA	Drawing software

Computer Industry Almanac: Very Influential Products

There are thousands of products introduced each year, but only a handful leave a lasting impression on the computer industry. Computer Industry Almanac will select a few products each year that we consider the most influential products introduced in the last year. To be included in this list, the products can be a best seller, use new technology, have step function performance or price/performance improvements, be innovative or be the start of something big. The products are listed alphabetically.

Product Name	Company	Product Type	Reason
1995-1996 VIPs			
Aspire	Acer America	Personal Computer	Innovative
Destination	Gateway 2000	PC with large screen TV	Trendsetter
Internet Phone	Intel	Phone emulation software	Potential Internet standard
Java	Sun Microsystems	Interpretive language	Future impact
LaserJet 5L	Hewlett-Packard	Laser printer	Best seller
Macintosh clones	Power Computing	Personal computer	Future impact
OfficeJet	Hewlett-Packard	Multifunction printer	Trendsetter, best seller
Pentium Pro	Intel	Microprocessor	Future impact
Pentium Pro SMP systems	Numerous	Multiprocessor servers	Future impact
Portege 610CT	Toshiba	Subnotebook PC	Trendsetter
ThinkPad 501C	IBM	Subnotebook PC	Innovative
ThinkPad 760CD	IBM	Ultrathin notebook PC	Trendsetter
UltraSPARC	Sun Microsystems	64-bit microprocessor	Trend setter
Universal Serial Bus	Intel-led consortium	High-speed serial bus	Future impact
Windows 95	Microsoft	Client operating system	Best seller
Windows NT 4.0	Microsoft	Server and client operating system	Future impact
WorldNet	AT&T	Internet access service	Price trend setter, best seller
Zip	Iomega	100MB floppy disk drive	Best seller
1994-1995 VIPs			
Access 2.0	Microsoft	Database software	Best seller
America Online	America Online	Online service	Best seller
Internet phone	VocalTec	Phone emulation software	Future impact
Magic Cap	General Magic	Software agent	Innovative
Navigator 1.0	Netscape	Internet browser	Best seller
Notes 4.0	Lotus	Groupware software	Best seller
Office 4	Microsoft	Suite software	Best seller
Pentium	Intel	Microprocessor	Best seller
PowerMac	Apple	Desktop PC	Best seller, Future impact
World Wide Web	Numerous	Information distribution standard	Future impact
1993-1994 VIPs			
i486DX4	Intel Corp.	Microprocessor	Best seller
Microsoft Office	Microsoft Corp	Application suit	Best seller
MS-DOS 6.2	Microsoft Corp.	Operating system	Best seller
Newton	Apple Computer	Personal Digital Assistant	Future impact
Notes 3.0	Lotus Development	Groupware	Trendsetter
OS/2 for Windows	IBM Corp.	Operating system	Best seller
PowerPC 603	IBM & Motorola	Microprocessor	Future impact
Power Macintosh	Apple Computer	Personal computer	Future impact
PCI bus	Intel-led consortium	High-speed bus	Best Seller
Plug & Play	Microsoft-led consortium	Interface convention	Future impact
Presario	Compaq Computer	Home PC	Best seller
Toshiba Portege 3400	Toshiba	Subnotebook PC	Trendsetter
Windows NT	Microsoft Corp.	Operating System	Future impact

Macworld: World Class Awards

"Once a year, Macworld takes time out to recognize the vibrancy and dedication to excellence that have always characterized the Macintosh market. We sift through thousands of offerings to find the few products that deserve to be viewed as superior--not just in comparison to their competition, but on an absolute standard of quality, value and performance.

'To make our selection, we deployed the most rigorous and multifaceted evaluation process ever used in the computer press. Over several months we polled our editors and expert authors about their views on hundreds of contenders. To be considered products had to be shipping as of December 1, 1995; we did not restrict our candidates to products that shipped in 1995--no matter when a product first became available, if we thought it was great, we considered it for an award."--Macworld

Award	Company	Product
Most Innovative Company	Apple Computer	QuickDraw 3D, QuickTime VR & more
Most Promising New Product	Netscape Communications	Navigator
Best New Technology	Apple Computer	QuickDraw 3D
Product of the Year	Netscape Communications	Navigator
Computer System	Apple Computer	Power Macintosh 7500/100
Storage	Iomega	Zip
Input Device	Wacom Technologies	ArtPad
System Enhancement/Software	Connectix	Speed Doubler
System Enhancement/Hardware	Visioneer	PaperPort Vx
Graphics Utility	Equilibrium Technology	DeBabelizer
Illustration Software	Macromedia	FreeHand
Image-Editing Software	Adobe Systems	Photoshop
Page-Layout/Design-Tool Software	Quark	QuarkXPress
Page-Layout/Design-Tool Software	Adobe Systems	PageMaker
Paint Software	Fractal Design	Painter
Professional Display	Radius	PressView series
Scanner	Agfa	Arcus II
Video Display Card	Radius	Thunder IV & ThunderColor series
Graphic Design Printer	3M Printing & Publishing Systems	Rainbow 2720
Accounting Software	BestWare	M.Y.O.B.
Core Business Software	Claris	FileMaker Pro
Data Presentation Software	DeltaPoint Software	DeltaGraph Pro
Presentation Software	Adobe Systems	Persuasion
Business Printer	Apple Computer	LaserWriter 16/600 PS
Multimedia Authoring	Macromedia	Director
Video-Production Tool	Adobe Systems	After Effects
Audio-Production Tool	OSC	Deck II
CAD Software	Graphsoft	MiniCad
Modeling/Rendering Software	MetaTools	KPT Bryce
Modeling/Rendering Software	Specular International	Infini-D
Digital Camera	Eastman Kodak	DC40
Developer Tool/Programming Environment	Metrowerks	CodeWarrior
Mathematics Software	Wolfram Research	Mathematica
Technical/Statistics Software	National Instruments	LabView
Personal Productivity Software	Now Software	Now Contact & Now Up-to-Date
Personal Productivity Software	Claris	ClarisWorks
Personal Printer	Hewlett-Packard	LaserJet 5MP
Game	Bungie Software	Marathon

Award	Company	Product
Game	Brøderbund Software	Myst
Web-Site Manager	Quarterdeck/StarNine Technologies	WebStar
Networking Hardware	Farallon Computing	AirDock

Excerpted with permission from Macworld, March 1996, p 96. Copyright © 1996, Macworld published at 501 Second Street, San Francisco CA 94107 U.S.

NewMedia: Invision Awards

"Can a mere idea burst into flame? Yes, and tonight we honor the best and brightest! An acknowledged hallmark of creative combustion and technical trailblazing, The NewMedia Invision Awards were established in 1993 to identify and highlight the most innovative new media applications. This year, the program expanded to include 30 online opportunities for World Wide Web developers."--NewMedia

Product	Company	Audience/Category	Award
Beyond the Wall: Stories Behind the Vietnam Wall	Magnet Interactive Studios	Adult Reference	Best of Show
TerraQuest	Brad Johnson Presents	Overall Design Online	Best of Online
Training and Support			
SGSS 2000: The Power of Service	ITT Sheraton, Powerhouse Interactive, CF Video	Employee Orientation	Gold/Excellence
Actions & Attitudes: The Customer Service Simulation	Micromentor Inc.	Sales Training/Support	Gold
Hunter Engineering Web for Sales Representatives	Hunter Engineering Co.	Sales Training/Support Online	Gold
AT&T Branch Management Simulation	Micromentor Inc.	Technical Training/Support	Gold
Hunter Engineering Web for Technical and Training Representatives	Hunter Engineering Co.	Technical Training/Support Online	Gold
Windows NT System Administration	Global Knowledge Network Inc.	Product Training/Customer Support	Gold
C/NET online audio tour	C/NET: the computer network	Product Training/Customer Support Online	Gold
Personal and Nonprofit Projects			
Public Shelter	EJL Productions LLC	Personal	Gold/Excellence
Crime Scouts	Opportune Press Inc.	Nonprofit	Gold
Rock the Vote Website	AND Interactive Communications Corp.	Nonprofit Online	Gold
Education			
Emerging Communications Technologies	International University College	Higher Education Online	Gold/Excellence
Oval Office: Challenge of the Presidency	Meridian Creative Group-Larson Texts	Middle/High School	Gold
VizAbility	PWS Publishing Co.	Higher Education	Gold
Sales and Marketing			
Surf This Disc	Enlighten	Product Catalog	Gold/Excellence
Miller Highway Interactive	Marcato Multimedia, Neoscape, MAFF/X	Corporate Presentation	Gold
Bad Mojo	Pulse Entertainment	Corporate Image	Gold
Genie Val-Pak Laptop Sales	Galileo	Sales Presentation	Gold
Tales from Lantropolis	Elvis & Bonaparte Inc.	Interactive Advertisement	Gold
Toy Story Website	2-Lane Media, Bonifer/Bogner, Canto-5	Online Advertising/Promotion	Gold
Photodisc web site	PhotoDisc Inc.	Online Catalog/Direct Sales	Gold
Health Navigator Kiosk	Multimedia Resources Inc.	Marketing/Sales Kiosk	Gold
Entertainment and Edutainment			
Critical Mass: America's Race to Build the Atomic Bomb	Corbis Corp.	Adult Entertainment	Gold/Excellence

Product	Company	Audience/Category	Award
Operation: Weather Disaster	Human Code Inc.	Children	Gold
Inventor Labs	Red Hill Studio	Young Adult	Gold/Excellence
24 Hours in Cyberspace	Against All Odds Productions	Adult Entertainment Online	Gold
The East Village	Marinex Multimedia Corp.	Adult Entertainment Online	Gold
Star Trek Klingon	Simon & Schuster Interactive	Interactive Movie	Gold
Toy Story Website	2-Lane Media, Bonifer/Bogner, Canto-5	Movie/TV-Related Online	Gold
Primus "Tales from the Punchbowl"	Ion/Interscope	Enhanced Music	Gold
Jazz Central Station	N2K Entertainment	Music-Related Online	Gold
Arcade America	7th Level Inc.	Arcade Game	Gold
Gearheads	R/GA Interactive	Arcade Game	Gold
The Residents Bad Day on the Midway	Inscape	Adventure/Role Playing Game	Gold
Bad Mojo	Pulse Entertainment	Strategy/Puzzle Game	Gold
Treasure Chest	Sirius Publishing Inc.	Strategy/Puzzle Game	Gold
MultiPlayer BattleTech Solaris	Kesmai Corp.	Online/Multiuser Game	Gold
Technical and Creative Excellence			
Bad Mojo	Pulse Entertainment	Best Story/Script	Gold/Excellence
Bad Mojo	Pulse Entertainment	Best Graphics	Gold
MapQuest	MapQuest, GeoSystems	Graphics Online	Gold
Rock the Vote Website	AND Interactive Communications Corp.	Graphics Online	Gold
Candidate 96	AND Interactive Communications Corp.	Best Interface/Online	Gold
Arcade America	7th Level Inc.	Best Animation	Gold
TerraQuest	Brad Johnson Presents	Overall Design Online	Gold
Living Home Premier Issue	Novo Media Group	Best Pacage Design	Gold
Information/Reference			
Beyond the Wall: Stories Behind the Vietnam Wall	Magnet Interactive Studios	Adult Reference	Gold/Excellence
Microsoft Encarta 96 Encyclopedia	Microsoft	Adult Reference	Gold
www.harappa.com	Harappa	Adult Online Reference	Gold
A Jack Kerouac ROMnibus	Penguin Books USA, Mind & Motion	Electronic Book	Gold
Men Are From Mars, Women Are From Venus	AOL Productions Inc.	Book/CD-ROM	Gold
AirMedia Live!	Ex Machina Inc.	Online News Information	Gold
search.com	C/NET:the computer network	Online Index	Gold
Palace Infotainment Center	Technology Applications Group Inc.	Information/Education Kiosk	Gold

The 1995 gold winners are shown in the next table.

Product	Company	Audience/Category	Award
Passage to Vietnam	Ad-Hoc Interactive, Against All Odds Productions, Interval Research	Book/CD-ROM	Best of Show
Education			
Dime! Interactive	D.C. Heath & Co.	Young Adult	Gold/Excellence
Thinkin' Things	Edmark Corp.	Children	Gold
Video Producer	Co/Op Media	Higher Education	Gold
Information & Reference			
The Cartoon History of the Universe	Human Code, Putnam New Media	Electronic Books	Gold/Excellence
Tibet: Exploring Life on the Plateau	Grid Media Ltd.	Encyclopedia/Reference	Gold
Passage to Vietnam	Ad-Hoc Interactive, Against All Odds Productions, Interval Research	Book/CD-ROM	Gold
Just Think (an interactive) Issue 2	Ad-Hoc Interactive	Interactive Periodicals	Gold
Games			

Product	Company	Audience/Category	Award
Road Rash	Electronic Arts	Arcade	Gold/Excellence
Who Killed Taylor French?	Creative Multimedia	Adventure/Role Playing	Gold
The 11th Hour: The Sequel to The 7th Guest	Trilobyte	Strategy/Puzzle	Gold
Training			
Lexus Labs	Lexus-Toyota, Internal & External Communication	Sales/Management Training	Gold/Excellence
WinAlign Multimedia	Hunter Engineering Co.	Manufacturing/Technical Training & Support	Gold
Personal Protective Equipment	Coastal Video Communications Corp.	Manufacturing/Technical Training & Support	Gold
Interactive Regional Anesthesia	Churchill Livingstone Interactive Publications	Health Care & Medical Training	Gold
Consumer			
Passage to Vietnam	Ad-Hoc Interactive, Against All Odds Productions, Interval Research	Adult Edutainment	Gold/Excellence
The Cartoon History of the Universe	Human Code, Putnam New Media	Adult Edutainment	Gold
A Passion for Art: Renoir, Cezanne, Matisse and Dr. Barnes	Corbis	Adult Edutainment	Gold
Dazzeloids	Center for Advanced Whimsy, Voyager Co.	Children	Gold
A.D.A.M.: The Inside Story	A.D.A.M. Software	Young Adult	Gold
The Vortex: Quantum Gate II	Hyperbole Studios	Interactive Movies	Gold
The Residents' Gingerbread Man	Ion	Interactive Music	Gold
Rain: A Multimedia Adventure	Learning Edge	Information/Education Kiosk	Gold
Sales & Marketing			
Bose Multimedia Speaker Demonstration	Bose Corp.	Product Demonstration	Gold/Excellence
Herman Miller Concept Book/Sales Presentation	Clement Mok Designs	Corporate/Sales Presentation	Gold
Toyota Auto Show CDi	McGill Multimedia	Interactive Advertising & Promotion	Gold
CompuServeCD	CompuServe	Online Promotion	Gold
1995 Acura Interactive	Digital Facades Corp.	Marketing/Sales Kiosk	Gold
Labatt Customer Loyalty Program	O'Hara Systems, Hughes Rapp Collin	Marketing/Sales Kiosk	Gold
Personal & Group Projects			
Lebuse's Letters	Robert Linehan	General Information	Gold/Excellence
Convergence Career Paths CD-ROM Series: Career Paths in Finance/Career Paths in Accounting	Convergence Multimedia	Education	Gold
Technical and Creative Excellence			
Seeing Time	Red Hill Studio	Video	Gold/Excellence
Under A Killing Moon	Access Software	Story/Script	Gold
Blown Away	IVI Publishing, Imagination Pilots	Graphic Design	Gold
Monty Python's Complete Waste of Time	7th Level	Programming	Gold
Buried in Time: The Journeyman Project 2	Presto Studios, Sanctuary Woods	Animation	Gold
Cyberwar PC CD-ROM	Sales Curve Interactive	Audio/Soundtrack	Gold
A Passion for Art: Renoir, Cezanne, Matisse and Dr. Barnes	Corbis	Interface Design	Gold
Megadeth, Arizona	Capitol Records	Online Interface	Gold
Cyberwar PC CD-ROM	Sales Curve Interactive	CD-ROM Packaging	Gold

The 1994 gold winners are shown in the next table.

Product	Company	Category/Audience	Award
Consumer Games			

Product	Company	Category/Audience	Award
Travelrama USA	Apple/Zenda Studio	Edutainment: Children (3-12)	Gold/Excellence
Myst	Brøderbund Software	Adventure	Gold/Excellence
The 7th Guest	Trilobyte	Adventure	Gold/Excellence
The Tortoise and the Hare	Living Books	Edutainment: Children (3-12)	Gold/Excellence
The Magic Death	Creative Multimedia	Other	Gold/Excellence
Comanche CD	NovaLogic	Simulations	Gold
Consumer: General			
Berlitz for Business Japanese	Sierra On-Line	Adult Enrichment	Gold/Excellence
Lenny's Musictoons	Paramount Interactive	Interactive Music	Gold/Excellence
Red Shift Multimedia Astronomy	Maris Multimedia	Adult Enrichment	Gold
Birdsong	Mackerel Interactive Media	Adult Enrichment	Gold
Microsoft Art Gallery	Microsoft	Adult Enrichment	Gold
Voyeur	Philips Interactive Media	Interactive Movies	Gold
Make My Video: INXS	Digital Pictures	Interactive Music	Gold
Corporate			
This Old Pump	Nolan Multimedia	Technical Training	Gold/Excellence
McDonald's Service Enhancement Training	Andersen Consulting	Sales/Management Training	Gold/Excellence
UPS Uniting the World	Floyd Design	Other	Gold
Skyvision	Artemis Alliance	Manufacturing/Tech Support	Gold
Education			
Discovering French Interactive	D.C. Heath & Co.	K-12 Application	Gold/Excellence
Addition and Its Processes	American Instit. of Learning	Other	Gold/Excellence
Life Moves: The Process of Recovery	American Instit. of Learning	Other	Gold/Excellence
Cytovision	John Moores Univ. Open Lrng.	Other	Gold/Excellence
HIV & AIDS: An Interactive Curriculum	Interactive Media Lab Dartm.	Other	Gold
Sales/Marketing			
Singapore Post	North Communications	Point of Sale Kiosk	Gold/Excellence
The iStation	Intouch Group	Advertisement	Gold/Excellence
Mackerel Stack 2.0	Mackerel Interactive Media	Advertisement	Gold/Excellence
The Affluent Investor	Wall Street Journal	Sales Presentation	Gold
DMI Interactive Gallery	Disc Manufacturing	Product Demo Disk	Gold
World Tour Golf	Media Design	Advertisement	Gold
Home Survival Toolkit	Books That Work	Advertisement	Gold
West End Post Interactive Electronic Bus. Card	West End Post Interactive	Other	Gold
Technical/Creative Excellence			
Total Distortion	Pop Rocket	Audio/Soundtrack	Gold/Excellence
World Tour Golf	Media Design	Interface Design	Gold/Excellence
The 7th Guest	Trilobyte	Programming	Gold/Excellence
The 7th Guest	Trilobyte	Animation/Graphics	Gold/Excellence
Virtual Adventures: Loch Ness Adventure	Iwerks Entertainment	Other	Gold/Excellence
En Passant: Experiences in Interactive Shopping	Medior	Best Programming	Gold
En Passant: Experiences in Interactive Shopping	Medior	Interface Design	Gold
Szabo International	BVR Group	Other	Gold
Information/Reference			
Cytovision Laser	John Moores Univ. Open Lrng.	Catalog Reference Guide	Gold/Excellence
Journey to The Source	Grid Media	Book Adaptation	Gold/Excellence
AARX: Kronolog II	Human Code	Other	Gold/Excellence
Sitting on the Farm	Sanctuary Woods	Book Adaptation	Gold

Product	Company	Category/Audience	Award
End-User			
Brothers	Brother's Network	Other	Gold/Excellence
Bell High School Video Portfolios	Brian Reilly	K-12 Education	Gold/Excellence
Arris Imaging System	Chiropractic Consultants	Other	Gold/Excellence
The Dynamic Spine	Phila. Clg. of Osteopathic Med	Higher Education	Gold

Excerpted with permission from NewMedia. Copyright © 1996, NewMedia, 901 Mariner's Island Blvd., Ste. 365, San Mateo CA 94404 USA.

PC Magazine: Awards for Technical Excellence

Since 1984, PC Magazine has presented the Awards for Technical Excellence. The 1995 competition is the 12th annual awards presented. The awards acknowledge and honor the work of the engineers, programmers and business leaders whose creativity and energy have driven--and continue to drive--this industry. To be eligible for this year's awards, products had to ship during the period from October 1, 1994, to September 30, 1995.

1995 Winner	Company	Category
Microsoft Windows 95	Microsoft Corp.	Operating Systems
Borland Delphi Client/Server	Borland International	Development Tools
Microsoft Access for Windows 95	Microsoft Corp.	Application Software
IBM ThinkPad 760CD	IBM PC Co.	Systems
IBM TrackWrite Keyboard	IBM PC Co.	Design
ForeRunner ATM Product Family	Fore Systems	Networking
Java	Sun Microsystems	Internet Tools
Snappy Video Snapshot	Play Inc.	Peripherals
Phaser 340	Tektronix	Printers
Descent	Interplay Productions Inc.	After Hours
Bill Gates and Paul Allen	Microsoft Corp.	Lifetime Achievement
Brad Silverberg and the Windows 95 team	Microsoft Corp.	Person of the Year

Previous Winners:

1994 Winner	Company	Category
Microsoft Windows NT Workstation Version 3.5	Microsoft Corp.	System Software
dBase 5.0 for Windows	Borland International	Development Tools
Microsoft Office Version 4.2	Microsoft Corp.	Application Software
trueSpace	Caligari Corp	Graphics Software
AirAccess Version 2.0	AirSoft Inc.	Networking Software
NCSA Mosaic	National Center for Supercomputing Applications, University of Illinois	Communications Software
V.34 Communications Protocol	International Telecommunications Union	Communications Standard
Stacker Version 4.0	Stac Electronics	Utility Software
Toshiba Portege Series	Toshiba America Information Systems Inc.	Hardware
Xircom CreditCard Ethernet+Modem	Xircom Inc.	Networking Hardware
IBM's magnetoresistive & PRML hard disk technology	IBM Storage Systems Division	Components
Doom	id Software	After Hours
Vinton Cerf and Robert Kahn	-	Lifetime Achievement
Jim Manzi and Ray Ozzie	Lotus Development Corp.	Person of the Year

1993 Winner	Company	Category
Microsoft OLE 2.0	Microsoft Corp.	Operating Systems & Software Standards

1993 Winner	Company	Category
WinScope, Version 1.1	Periscope Co., The	Development Tools
Lotus Improv for Windows, Release 2.1	Lotus Development	Application Software
Adobe Acrobat	Adobe Systems	Graphics Software
Microsoft Windows NT, Advanced Server	Microsoft Corp.	Networking Software
IBM ThinkPad 700C Family	IBM	Systems
Apple Newton MessagePad	Apple Computer	Design
Intel Pentium	Intel	Components/Subsystems
Wellfleet Backbone Concentrator Node	Wellfleet Communications	Networking Hardware
HP DeskJet 1200C	Hewlett-Packard	Peripherals
Brøderbund's Living Books	Brøderbund Software	After Hours
Jack S. Kilby and Robert N. Noyce	-	Lifetime Achievement
Andrew S. Grove	Intel Corp.	Person of the Year

1992 Winner	Company	Category
PCMCIA, Release 2.0	PC Memory Card International Assoc.	Hardware Standards
OS/2, Version 2.0	IBM Corp.	Operating Systems & Software Standards
Borland C++ 3.1	Borland International Inc.	Development Tools
Quattro Pro for Windows	Borland International Inc.	Applications
Fractal Design Painter Version 1.2	Fractal Design Corp.	Graphics Applications
Compaq Deskpro 66/M	Compaq Computer	Systems
Toshiba T4400SXC	Toshiba America Information Systems	Portable Computers
Ecosys a-Si Printer FS-1500A	Kyocera Electronics Inc.	Printers
NEC InterSect CDR-74	NEC	Peripherals
AMD 3.3-volt CPU	Advanced Micro Devices	Components/Subsystems
Windows for Workgroups	Microsoft Corp.	Networking/Communications
Interactive Books	Knowledge Adventure	After Hours
Raymond J. Noorda	Novell	Lifetime Achievement
Michael S. Dell	Dell Computer Corp.	Person of the Year

1991 Winner	Company	Category
PenPoint	Go Corp.	Standards and Operating Systems
Microsoft Visual Basic	Microsoft Corp.	Development Tools
Stacker, Version 1.1	Stac Electronics	Utilities
FOXPRO, VERSION 2.0	Fox Software Inc.	Applications Software
Toshiba T2200SX	Toshiba America Information Systems	Portable Computers
IBM LaserPrinter 10	Lexmark International Inc.	Printers
Altair Wireless Ethernet	Motorola Inc.	Connectivity
SIMEARTH	Maxis* Dist. by Brøderbund Software Inc.	After Hours
Philip D. (Don) Estridge	IBM Corp.	Person of the PC Decade
Daniel Bricklin and Robert Frankston	-	Lifetime Achievement
Philippe Kahn	Borland International Inc.	Person of the Year

1990 Winner	Company	Category
LANtastic Voice Adapter	Artisoft Inc.	Connectivity
Xircom Pocket LAN Adapter	Xircom Inc.	Design
Turbo C++ Professional	Borland International	Development Tools
Edsun Continuous Edge Graphics	Edsun Laboratories Inc.	Emerging Technology
Compton's MultiMedia Encyclopedia	Britannica Software Inc.	Entertainment/After Hours
HP LaserJet III	Hewlett-Packard Co.	Hardware

1990 Winner	Company	Category
HP NewWave, Version 3.0	Hewlett-Packard Co.	Operating Environments
Compaq Systempro	Compaq Computer Corp.	PCs
Sharp PC-6220	Sharp Electronics Corp.	Portables
TravelMate 2000	Texas Instruments	Portables
Developer's RenderMan	Pixar	Software
Adele Goldberg	ParcPlace Systems	Lifetime Achievement
Finis Conner	Conner Peripherals	Person of the Year
Terry Johnson	PrairieTek	Person of the Year

1989 Winner	Company	Category
Audio Visual Connection	IBM	Hardware
Autodesk Animator	Autodesk	Graphics
IBM LaserPrinter	IBM	Printers
Magellan	Lotus Development	Utilities
Multiscope OS/2 Debugger	Logitech	Development Tools
NetWare 386, Version 3.0	Novell	Connectivity
OS/2, Version 1.2	IBM and Microsoft	Operating Environments
The Poqet PC	Poqet Computer	Portables
Quattro Pro	Borland International	Applications
Roland LAPC-I	Roland U.S.	Entertainment/After Hours
John Warnock	Adobe Systems	Lifetime Achievement
Joseph R. Canion	Compaq Computer	Person of the Year

1988 Winner	Company	Category
All Chargecard	All Computers	Add-in Boards
ALR FlexCache 25386	Advanced Logic Research	Desktop Machines
Intel 80386 Design Team	Intel	Persons of the Year
Kurta IS/1 Cordless Stylus/Puck	Kurta	Hardware
Lahey FORTRAN 286 & 386	Lahey Computer Systems	Compilers/Languages
Micrografx Designer	Micrografx	Graphics Software
Microsoft Mouse	Microsoft	Design
NEC UltraLite	NEC Home Electronics (U.S.A)	Portables
Q&A 3.0	Symantec	Application
Dennis Ritchie	AT&T Bell Laboratories	Lifetime Achievement
SunRiver Workstation	SunRiver	Connectivity
Turbo Debugger	Borland International	Development Tools
VM/386	Intelligent Graphics	386 Software

1987 Winner	Company	Category
AutoShade	Autodesk	Graphics Software
Compaq Portable 386	Compaq Computer	Portable Computers
Compaq Deskpro 386/20	Compaq Computer	Desktop Computers
Douglas Englebart	McDonnell Douglas Info. System Group	Lifetime Achievement
LIM expansion memory specification 4.0	Lotus Development, Intel, Microsoft	Utilities
Lucid 3D	Personal Computer Support Group	Application Software
Micro Channel architecture	IBM	Special Award
Microsoft Excel for Windows	Microsoft	Application Software
Microsoft Windows/386	Microsoft	Operating Environments
Publisher's Type Foundry	ZSoft	Desktop Publishing

1987 Winner	Company	Category
QuickBASIC 4.0	Microsoft	Development Tools
3Com 10Mb Twisted Pair	3Com	Connectivity
Turbo Pascal 4.0	Borland International	Development Tools
Zenith Perfect Monitor Model ZCM-1490	Zenith Data Systems	Hardware

1986 Winner	Company	Category
Advanced Netware/286	Novell	Networking
Compaq Deskpro 386	Compaq Computer	Desktop Computers
Bill Gates	Microsoft	Special Award
HAL	Lotus Development	Software Add-ons
Microsoft Windows 1.03	Microsoft	Environments
NEC MultiSync	NEC Home Electronics	Graphics Hardware
NewViews	Q.W. Page Associates	Application Software
Perspective	Three D Graphics	Graphics Software
QuickBASIC 2	Microsoft	Programming Languages
TIPS	Island Graphics	Graphics Software
Toshiba T3100	Toshiba America	Portable Computers
What's Best	General Optimization	Software Add-ons
Zenith Z-181 Portable PC	Zenith Data Systems	Portable Computers

1985 Winner	Company	Category
Apple LaserWriter	Apple Computer	N/A
Mike Brown	Central Point Software	Special Award
EGA CHIPSet	Chips & Technologies	N/A
Freelance	Lotus Development	N/A
IBM Proprinter	IBM	N/A
Javelin	Javelin Software	N/A
LANLink	The Software Link	N/A
Plus Hardcard	Plus Development	N/A
Trailblazer modem	Telebit	N/A

1984 Winner	Company	Category
Enable	The Software Group	N/A
Framework	Ashton-Tate	N/A
Infoscope	Microsoft	N/A
Intel 80286	Intel	N/A
PC Blue Series	Public domain	N/A
Turbo Pascal	Borland International	N/A

N/A: Not Applicable: Winners were not designated by category in 1984 and 1985.

PC World: Best Products of 1996

"We mailed ballots to 1900 subscribers, consultants, computer professionals and user group presidents and asked them to vote on the products that PC World editors nominated for World Class Awards. When there was a difference of 1% or less in the number of votes a product received, we called a tie. In write-in categories with fewer than 100 total votes, the winning product was required to have a lead of only one vote."--PC World.

1996 Winners			
	Category	Company	Product
Product of the Year		Netscape	Navigator 2.0
On The Desktop	Business Desktop Computer	Gateway 2000	Gateway 200 Professional line
	Home Desktop Computer	Gateway 2000	Gateway 200 Family PC line
	Operating System/Environment	Microsoft	Windows 95
	Input/Pointing Device	Microsoft	Microsoft Natural Keyboard
		Logitech	MouseMan '96
	Monitor 15"	NEC	MultiSync XV 15+
	Monitor 17"	NEC	MultiSync XV 17+
On The Road	Laptop/Notebook Computer	IBM	ThinkPad 755CD
	Subnotebook Computer	IBM	ThinkPad 701C
	PC Card Modem	Hayes Microcomputer	Optima 288 V.34+Fax With EZJack
	Personal Digital Assistant	Apple	Newton
		Hewlett-Packard	OmniGo 100 Organizer Plus
	Wireless Communications Device	SkyTel	SkyCard PCMCIA Card
The Printed Page	High-End Color Printer	Epson	Stylus Pro/Pro XI
		Tektronix	Phaser 340
	Personal Color Printer	Hewlett-Packard	DeskJet 850C/855C
	Personal Monochrome Printer	Hewlett-Packard	LaserJet 5/5M
	Multifunction Device	Hewlett-Packard	OfficeJet LX
	Scanner	Hewlett-Packard	ScanJet 4C
Most Promising Newcomers	Hardware	Intel	Pentium Processor 166MHz
	Hardware	Intel	Pentium Pro Processor
	Hardware	Iomega	Zip Drive
	Software	Netscape	Navigator
In A Wired World	Online Service	America Online	America Online
	Web Site	Yahoo	Yahoo
	Internet Service Provider	Netcom	
	Fax-Modem	U.S. Robotics	Sportster 28.8 Faxmodem
	Fax Software	Symantec	WinFax Pro 7.0
	Communications	Datastorm	Procomm Plus 3.0 for Windows
	LAN E-Mail Package	Lotus	cc:Mail for Windows
	Remote Access/Remote Control	Symantec	Norton pcAnywhere-32
	Internet Interface/Utility	Netscape	Navigator 2.0
	Web Authoring Tool	Microsoft	Internet Assistant
Motion and Sound	Graphics Accelerator Board	Diamond Multimedia	Stealth64 Video 3200
	Sound Card	Creative Labs	Sound Blaster 16
	Multimedia Upgrade Kit	Creative Labs	Discovery Multimedia Upgrade Kit
	Business Tool	Microsoft	Office for Windows 95
	Children's Education CD-ROM	Microsoft	Encarta
	Adult Education CD-ROM	Microsoft	Encarta
	Reference CD-ROM	Microsoft	Encarta
	Entertainment CD-ROM	Microsoft	Cinemania
	CD-ROM Game--Adults	Brøderbund	Myst
	CD-ROM Game--Children	Brøderbund	Where in the World Is Carmen Sandiego?

	Category	Company	Product
	1996 Winners		
Storage	Hard Drive	Western Digital	Caviar AC31600
	Removable Portable Drive	Iomega	Zip drive
	Tape Backup Drive	Hewlett-Packard	Colorado T1000-E
	CD-ROM Drive	NEC	MultiSpin 6X
	Writable CD-ROM Drive	Hewlett-Packard	SureStore CD-Writer 4020
	Optical Drive	Pinnacle Micro	Apex
Service and Support	Hardware	Hewlett-Packard	
	Software	Microsoft	
Loser Of The Year		Microsoft	Windows 95
Applications	Word Processor	Microsoft	Word 6.0
	Spreadsheet	Microsoft	Excel 5.0
	Database--Personal	Microsoft	Access 2.0
	Database--Professional	Microsoft	Access 2.0
	Applications Suite	Microsoft	Office 95
	Desktop Publishing	Adobe	PageMaker 6.01
	Presentation Graphics	Microsoft	PowerPoint 4.0
	Draw Software	Corel	CorelDraw 6.0
	Computer-Aided Design	Autodesk	AutoCAD R13
	3D Graphics	Autodesk	3D Studio 4.0
	Image Editing/Paint	Adobe	Photoshop 3.05
Working Together	Groupware Application Environment	Lotus	Notes Release 4
	Group Discussion	Netscape	Collabra Share 2.2
	Document/Video Conferencing	Intel	ProShare Video Conferencing System 200
	Electronic Document Distribution	Adobe	Acrobat 2.1
	Network Server	Hewlett-Packard	NetServer line
		IBM	PC Server line
	LAN Operating System (Peer-to-Peer)	Microsoft	Windows NT
	LAN Operating System (Server-Based)	Novell	NetWare 4.1
	Workgroup Color Printer	Hewlett-Packard	Color LaserJet 5
	Workgroup Monochrome Printer	Hewlett-Packard	LaserJet 5M Plus
The Basic Tools	Utility Collection	Symantec	Norton Utilities for Windows 95
	Windows Shell	Symantec	Norton Navigator for Windows 95
	OCR Software	Caere	OmniPage Pro 6.0
	Shareware/Freeware	PKWare	PKZip version 2
	Backup Software	Hewlett-Packard	Colorado Backup for Windows 95
	Program Language/Development Tool	Microsoft	Visual Basic 4.0
	Forms Software	Symantec	FormFlow 2.0
Getting Organized	Personal Information Manager	Lotus	Organizer 2.1
	Contact Manager	Symantec	Act 2.0 for Windows
	Project Manager	Microsoft	Project for Windows 95
	Accounting	Intuit	QuickBooks 4.0
	Personal Finance	Intuit	Quicken 5 for Windows 95
	Tax Planning/Preparation	Intuit	TurboTax
Mail-Order Company		PC Connection	

The 1995 winners are shown in the next table.

		1995 Winners	
	Category	Company	Product
Product of the Year		IBM	OS/2 Warp 3.0
Desktop Dynamos	Business Desktop Computer	Dell	Dimension XPS P90
	Home Desktop Computer	Micron	P90 Home MPC
	Operating System/Environment	IBM	OS/2 Warp 3.0
	Input/Pointing Device	Microsoft	Microsoft Mouse 2.0
	Monitor	ViewSonic	ViewSonic 17
	Graphics Accelerator Board	Diamond	Diamond Stealth 64 DRAM
Power Apps	Word Processor	Microsoft	Word 6.0 for Windows
	Spreadsheet	Microsoft	Excel 5.0
	Database	Microsoft	Access 2.0
	Applications Suite	Microsoft	Office Professional 4.3
Sound, Fury and Fun	Sound Card	Creative Labs	Sound Blaster 16
	CD-ROM Drive	Plextor	Plextor 4Plex
	Multimedia Upgrade Kit	Creative Labs	Edutainment CD 16
	Business Application (CD-ROM)	Intuit	Quicken 4.0 for Windows
	Children's Education (CD-ROM)	Microsoft	Encarta '95
	Reference: (CD-ROM)	Microsoft	Encarta '95
	Game--Adult (CD-ROM)	Brøderbund	Myst
	Game--Children (CD-ROM)	Brøderbund	Just Grandma and Me
	Non--CD-ROM Game	id Software	Doom II
On the Road	Notebook Computer	Toshiba	Toshiba T4900CT
	Subnotebook Computer	Toshiba	Toshiba Portégé T3600CT
	PC Card (PCMCIA)	Xircom	Xircom Credit Card Ethernet
	Personal Digital Assistant	Sony	Magic Link
Cold, Hard Storage	Hard Drive	Western Digital	Caviar AC31000
	Removable/Portable Drive	Iomega	Bernoulli 150 Insider
	Tape Backup Drive	Hewlett-Packard	Colorado Jumbo 250
	Optical Drive	Pinnacle Micro	Tahoe 230
LAN Links	Network Server	Compaq	ProLiant 2000
	LAN Operating System (Peer-to-Peer)	Microsoft	Windows for Workgroups 3.11
	LAN Operating System (Server-Based)	Novell	NetWare 3.12
	Groupware Application	Lotus	Notes
	LAN E-Mail Package	Lotus	cc:Mail Desktop Release 2.0 for Windows
Making Connections	Fax-Modem	U.S. Robotics	Sportster 14.4 Data/Fax Modem
	Fax Software	Delrina	WinFax Pro 4.0
	Communications Software	Datastorm	ProComm Plus 2.0 for Windows
	Internet Interface/Utility	Netscape	Navigator 1.0
	Online Service:	CompuServe	CompuServe
	BBS	The WELL	The WELL
	Internet Access Provider	Netcom	
Off the Page	Scanner	Hewlett-Packard	ScanJet Iicx
	OCR Software	Caere	OmniPage Professional 5.0
Page Pumpers	Laser/Dye-Sublimation Printer (Color)	Fargo & Hewlett-Packard	PrimeraPro & Color LaserJet
	Laser Printer (Monochrome)	Hewlett-Packard	LaserJet 4
	Inkjet Printer (Color)	Hewlett-Packard	DeskJet 560C
	Inkjet Printer (Monochrome)	Hewlett-Packard	DeskJet 540

	Category	Company	Product
		1995 Winners	
Swiss Army Knives	Utility Collection	Symantec	Norton Utilities 8.0
	Windows Shell	Symantec	Norton Desktop 3.0 for Windows
	Backup Software	Symantec	Norton Backup 8.0
	Shareware	PKWare	PKZip 2.04g
Presentation Is Everything	Desktop Publishing	Adobe	PageMaker 5.0
	Font Software	Adobe	Type Manager 3.0
	Presentation Graphics	Microsoft	PowerPoint 4.0
	Draw Software	Corel	CorelDraw 5.0
	Image Editing/Paint	Adobe	Photoshop 3.0
Power Tools	Computer-Aided Design	Autodesk	AutoCAD
	Programming Language	Microsoft	Visual Basic 3.0
Keep Your Ducks in a Row	Project Manager	Microsoft	Project 4.0
	Personal Information Manager	Lotus	Organizer 2.0
	Contact Manager	Symantec	Act 2.0 for Windows
	Forms Software	Delrina	PerForm for Windows
Money, Money, Money	Accounting	Intuit	QuickBooks 3.0 for Windows
	Personal Finance	Intuit	Quicken 4.0 for Windows
	Tax Planning/Preparation	Intuit	TurboTax for Windows
Who Can You Trust?	Service and Support (Hardware)	Dell & Compaq	
	Service and Support (Software)	Microsoft	
	Mail-Order Company	PC Connection	

Product and Technology Trends

Multimedia PC Systems: Network Delivery of Multimedia

The need for delivery of information to more people, more effectively, over distance, in less time--be that information used for business, education, entertainment or process control--is a driving force which continuously grows without any bounds. It again appears we are very fortunate indeed that the technologies required to satisfy that need have emerged in the nick of time. Interactive multimedia systems connected over the Internet, *the Information Chisolm Trail* which offers the promise to evolve into the storied Information Superhighway, have become widely available just as the need for delivery of information is growing to unprecedented proportions.

Multimedia plus the Internet, combined with the first *killer ap* of hypertext linkages to data on inter networked servers, have led to the creation of the World Wide Web. Text, static graphics, animation, sound, photo realistic images and motion video are routinely used to deliver information interactively over the Internet.

The New Capabilities

Reach out and touch the information that is needed and wanted: Users no longer are limited to the information delivered by a relatively small number of local newspapers, local radio and TV broadcast stations and neighborhood cable channels; all chosen to appeal to the broadest (and lowest) common denominator of tastes and interests among all potential receivers of that information. Over the Internet, users can access the multimedia information they need and want, from wherever and whenever it may be available, be it about a sporting event involving their favorite contestants as it occurs, be it breaking news or archived information, be it educational, entertainment, personal or business related.

Tell me a story:

Electronic media like all the media that preceded it delivers information through the presentation of stories. Multimedia technologies make it possible to tell stories more effectively than technologies which precede it, technologies which will continue to be used where they offer the best choices serving specific needs and wants. Those information delivery technologies include text and static graphic computer communications, color displays, text-only output, motion video, audio, print on paper, handwritten script, text and graphic symbols chiseled on masonry, plus the earliest information delivery system of all--wandering story tellers delivering business, educational, entertainment and political information to all of us whether we want it or not.

Receive and send, see and be seen:

Users no longer are limited to receiving information alone, but also can send information to anywhere in the world. They too can employ multimedia technologies to deliver information to more people, more effectively, in less time. As is so often the case, the timely availability of required technology once again proves that necessity is the mother of invention.

From wherever one needs to be or wants to be:

Multimedia technologies make the *Interactive Dramatization of Information* possible.

Networked systems make it possible to access and deliver information from and to anywhere in the world. Together, they make it possible for their users to participate in *virtual* meetings with peers, superiors and customers from wherever they need or want to be: virtual meetings to work with peer groups, department meetings, training classes, meetings to learn about solutions to new and old problems, about resolutions to new and old issues, new regulations, new products, new services and competitors' offerings; meetings delivering information about the organization's differentiated and superior offerings to customers which serve to make it unique.

Standard features

The need for delivery of information is not new. It has existed since the human race started to develop civilization. Today, the new media for the delivery of information is based upon digital electronics. Graphics and color became standard features in personal computing systems during the last decade. During this decade we are beginning to witness audio and motion-video also becoming standard features.

Already, Sun Microsystems' UltraSPARC™ processor includes multiple data stream instructions that facilitate the implementation of audio and video codecs using software alone. Intel has disclosed their MMX™ (MultiMedia eXtensions) to the Pentium™ processor and it is expected that before the end of 1997 all Pentium and PentiumPro™ processors. As graphics and color have become standard features, soon the mainstream personal computing systems will include multimedia functions as standard features as well. Competitors will have to respond with similar if not identical features, or limit themselves to niche market segments.

The Needs and Wants Being Served

The need being served by multimedia systems is to provide viable substitutes for traditional ways of exchanging organizational information and knowledge among the members of organizations which emphasize: frequent and direct contact with customers, allocation of decision making authority and responsibility among all members of work groups and/or employ nationally distributed and even globally distributed *virtual* work groups.

Today, computers add the capability of interacting with the *delivery of information,* making it possible to evaluate alternative what-if scenarios. They make it possible to navigate through enormous volumes of information that otherwise would not be fathomable due to the magnitude of the task.

During the last 150 years: photography, telegraphy, the phonograph, telephony, movies, radio, television and computers have achieved enormous strides in the *delivery of information.* Yes, *computers* also belong to that list. Computers deliver information about the data they manipulate, about the data they manage and store, about the alphanumeric and graphical data they sort and search. They deliver information by presenting it in visual and audible forms, be it alphanumerical or graphical employing print or CRT displays, that can more easily understood by more people, more effectively, in less time.

Definitions of "Multimedia"

A precise definition of "Multimedia" is:
an adjective! "Multimedia" much too often is misused in the most fundamental way. "Multimedia" is *not* a noun. Using it as if it were a noun leads to unclear definitions and a lot of confusion. Using it for what it is, an adjective modifying the meanings of nouns without completely changing those meanings, makes for a clearer definition.

There are "multimedia" databases, "multimedia" displays, "multimedia" presentations, "multimedia" terminals, etc. There are many "multimedia" things, but no noun named multimedia. But defining the word as being an adjective is not sufficient.

A more common definition of "Multimedia" is:
    "Multimedia is any combination of available media which stimulates the senses
    to best deliver information. Today, interactive multimedia computer systems
    employ: text, static 2-D & 3-D graphics, color, sound, photo realistic images,
    animated graphics and motion video."

Virtual Reality?

In the future where will the never-ending quest for improved *delivery of information* lead? It appears to be leading to the vision called Virtual Reality. *Perhaps* it might even make it possible for us to *virtually immerse ourselves* in 3-D *tactile simulations* of the very information we seek. *More likely,* or at least in the near term, it will enable us to *browse through* 3-D visible and audible *representations* of the information we seek and/or deliver.

Delivery of Information *is* what it's all about. --Alfred Riccomi

Computer Industry Almanac: Future Technology Trends

The underlying technologies of computers continue to advance at a very rapid pace. In this section a review of advances and trends in the main technologies for building computers is presented. Expected technology changes over the next few years and their implications on computer products are projected. A few hot product trends such as the Internet, multimedia, computer platform portability, microprocessor and OS/GUI trends are also discussed. The projected capabilities of typical personal computers in year 2002 round out this section.

Semiconductor Technology Trends

Semiconductors and magnetic disks are the two most important technologies for improving computers. Semiconductor memory chips quadruple in size every three or three and a half years. A few years ago 1-Mbit random access memory (RAM) chips were prevalent, but have peaked in importance. Four-Mbit RAM chips are the leading device. Sixteen-Mbit chips are in volume production and these chips will become the leader this year. Sixty-four-Mbit chips will be prevalent in the 1998 timeframe. By the turn of the century 256-Mbit RAM will be in full production. The prices of RAM chips have declined an average of 20% per year in the last 25 years. The prices of RAM chips did not decline much in the 1992 to 1995 time period due to under-production in the semiconductor industry. In late 1995 the price picture was reversed as production caught up with demand. In the last nine months memory prices dropped over 50% and the price per bit is back on its 20% per year price decline. The long term price trend for RAM chips is to continue to decline 20% per year.

The use of removable memory cards using RAM, ROM and programmable ROM chips will grow substantially in the late 1990s. There are now two interface standards--the PC Card (i.e. PCMCIA) and the smaller which will make a competitive market and increase usage. In a few years removable memory cards with 32-, 64-, 128- and even 256MByte capacity will be common. These cards will be used in PDAs, pocket, sub-notebook and notebook computers. They will also be used in desktop PCs, peripherals (i.e., laser printers), fax machines, copiers and many other electronic products.

Semiconductors also improve the speed of computers through faster microprocessors, faster memory chips, faster graphics, faster peripheral interfaces or faster buses. Microprocessor performance improves more than 50% per year and will continue at this pace for the foreseeable future. RISC techniques and other performance enhancements will be used by both future RISC processors and by the Intel's Pentium-family of microprocessors. The resulting advances in microprocessor speed are one reason microprocessor performance will continue improving and will surpass mainframe computers in power and may even rival supercomputers in the late-1990s. In 1989 Intel introduced the 80486 microprocessor which is three to four times the performance of the 80386. In March 1993, Intel introduced the Pentium microprocessor which is three to four times the performance of the 80486. In 1995 Pentium became the workhorse of PCs and it is time to introduce the Pentium successor: Pentium Pro, which is 2.5 times faster than the Pentium. Since the IBM PC was introduced in 1981, the raw microprocessor speed for personal computers has increased over 500 times. Another 10-fold increase is expected by the turn of the century.

The processor of the large computer is not improving as fast and uses multiple processors to improve performance. The RISC microprocessors are already being used in midrange computers and this trend will accelerate as RISC processors are now moving to 64-bit architecture. Microprocessor versions of mainframe computers are now available and will dominate the mainframe computer systems. A technology called Very Long Instruction Word (VLIW) is a likely candidate for next generation microprocessors. In a few years the microprocessor will be prevalent as the processor in just about all computers--from the PC to the massively-parallel computer.

Semiconductors have improved from a single transistor per chip to many million transistors per chip in the last 35 years. The question is how long can these improvements continue? There is general agreement that the current technology trends will at least last another 10 years and probably another 15 years. ICs will probably be using 3D transistor structures by the end of this period to maintain the technology advances. By year 2010 or so, semiconductor technology will be bumping up against the laws of quantum physics. It is likely that chips after that time will use quantum physics to gain further improvements.

Mass Storage Technology Trends

Magnetic disks are about 35 years old, but the technology continues to advance rapidly. Currently, disks quadruple their storage capacity every four years at the same price point. Additionally, new product segments are regularly introduced at lower price points and smaller physical sizes. Examples are the 3.5-inch hard disk and 3.5-inch floppy disk drive. In 1989 the first 2.5-inch hard disk appeared and there are now 1.8-inch hard disks. These products are aimed at notebook and subnotebook computers and will increase their capabilities and/or shrink their size. Optical disks are now emerging as a viable competitor to magnetic disks.

Optical disks have larger storage capacities, but have slower performance than magnetic disks. The competition from optical disks will speed up the magnetic disk advances. The two disk technologies will co-exist for many years. Currently the CD-ROM is seeing strong growth as it is now a built-in device for nearly all desktop and mini-tower PCs. The specifications for the next generation CD-ROM has been finalized and agreed on by the consumer electronics, computer and movie industries. It is currently called the Digital Video Disk (DVD) and will store music, movies and computer data. The single sided DVD will store 4.7 or 7.5 GBytes. A double sided DVD will store up to 17 GBytes. The first DVD drives are expected in late 1996 and will be priced in the $500 range soon after introduction. It will be 1998-99 until the DVD will start replacing the CD-ROM in a major way.

In the 1970s the dominant disk technology was the removable hard disk. The removable disk media was used for backup, off-line storage and to interchange data between computers. In the 1980s the removable media disk was largely replaced by the fixed disk. The 1990s have seen the return of the removable hard disk. The popularity of the removable hard disk is increasing and large development efforts are taking place to bring out small, removable hard disks that are usable with personal computers. In the last year Iomega's Zip drive, a 3.5 inch floppy disk drive with a 100 MByte capacity, has been very successful.

Another important trend in the disk industry is the use of arrays of small disks to supplement or replace the large mainframe computer disk. These disk arrays have higher performance, better reliability and lower prices than large disks. They have also become important for computer networks as mass storage for network servers.

Today all mass storage technologies store bits in 2D, whether it is magnetic disks, optical disks or magnetic tape systems. Holographic storage technologies have shown promise for a long time, but it is probably the 21st century before holographic mass storage products will be available. In a decade or so, new mass storage technologies may appear that store bits in 3D to gain higher storage densities.

Printer Technology Trends

All aspects of printers are improving rapidly--print quality, speed, quietness and price. Printer speed is doubling every four years. Page printers and inkjet printers are changing the most. The laser printer is the most popular page printer, due to its print quality, versatility and price-performance. The low-end laser printer is now priced below $400. Currently 30% of printers sold are laser printers--up from one in 10 in 1987. The price decline of the laser printer will continue and this will further increase its sales volume. Most laser printers sold to date have 300 dots per inch resolution, but the 600 dpi laser printer is now taking over. The color laser printer is also emerging as a mainstream product. Color laser printer prices are still too high ($5,000 plus) for widespread use, but we will see dramatic price declines in the next few years.

The inkjet printing technology has seen phenomenal growth in the last four years. This is due to its quietness, color capability and low power consumption. Inkjet print quality is nearly as good as the laser printer, but the price is considerably less than laser printers. The inkjet printer is the choice for notebook computers and for the home market. The inkjet printer has also become the leading technology for color printing. The inkjet color printer is now available for less than $350. Currently over 55% of printers sold are inkjet printers and over 95% of those have color capabilities.

Until 1992 the workhorse printer for the microcomputer industry was the impact matrix printer. It is still advancing in print quality, speed and price-performance. Nevertheless, non-impact printer technologies will continue to take market share away from the impact printer. The impact matrix printer now accounts for less than 10% of printer unit sales, which is down from 80% in 1987 and 45% in 1992.

Two new printer segments are emerging that are likely to become popular. Multifunction printers do three functions: printing, copying and faxing. Multifunction printers are growing rapidly--especially in the home-office and small business segments. The other printer segment is the photography printer which is used to make copies of digital images stored in computers or from digital cameras.

Display Technology Trends

Graphics and display quality have already improved substantially due to the graphical user interface. Multimedia, 3D graphics, visualization software and virtual reality applications will need even better graphics and display technology in the future. In the PC market, color monitors have overtaken the use of monochrome monitors and now over 95% of monitors sold are color. The display resolution is also improving. For workstations a display resolution of 1,024 x 1,280 pixels is standard. The PC resolution is lower, but it is also getting better. The VGA display specifications used by IBM's PS/2 in 1987 became the standard with 640 x 400 pixels. Now the standard display resolution for the PC is moving to 1,024 x 768 pixels.

The size of the display is also increasing. The need for better ergonomics will increase the average display size in the next few years. Not everybody needs a full-page display, a 2 to 4 inch larger monitor can substantially lower the eye strain and fatigue of heavy computer users. In the PC industry large and full-page monitors account for 10% to 15% of color monitors and 20% to 25% of monochrome monitor unit sales, but are likely to triple their market share in the next 3-5 years.

Display technology improvements are also crucial for laptop computers. LCD technology has come a long way since laptop computers first appeared. The first laptop PCs were truly personal as only the user could read the display. Liquid crystal displays will remain the dominant technology in the 1990s. But the biggest improvement is the availability of the color LCD at affordable prices. In 1992 notebook and laptop PCs with an active matrix color LCD had a price premium of $2,000 to $3,000, and declined to $1,000 or less in 1994. Now notebook PCs with color have only a few hundred dollars price premium and over 85% of notebook PCs sold have color displays. Other flat display technologies are also used with portable computers, but primarily with high-end products due to their high price and high-power consumption.

The development of high-definition TV will have a significant impact on computer technology and will be especially important for flat display technologies. A U.S. standard will probably be finalized in 1996 and HDTV sets will appear by 1997. Flat displays are a major goal for HDTV sets and the huge technology investments will directly benefit the computer industry. As these flat displays become available in the late-1990s, they will be used in computers.

Networking Technology Trends

Computer networking has become a crucial technology. Computers are connected to each other via local networks, modems, fax, fax modems or any other technology. Networks are connected to other networks via high speed communication links. And the number of computers connected to CompuServe, Prodigy, America Online and other online services have surpassed 10 million. The Internet has seen incredible growth in the last two years and has over 30 million computers connected.

The local area network is the most important connectivity product. It takes stand-alone PCs and makes them into multiuser systems with all the advantages. It also allows networks of PCs and/or workstations to replace large and expensive mainframes and minicomputer systems at much better price/performance. LANs will become increasingly important and the percentage of microcomputers hooked to a LAN will continue increasing. Today over 50% of office PCs are connected to a LAN and just about all workstations are networked. The Ethernet is the most popular LAN technology. Currently the most popular Ethernet LANs transfer data at 10 Mbps. The emerging Fast Ethernet with 100 Mbps looks like the winner in high-performance LANs. By the late 1990s nearly all office PCs in use will be hooked to LANs. The recent introduction of wireless LANs will make local networks even more versatile.

A new connectivity segment has grown up almost overnight--internetworking. As the number of LANs grew, the need for connecting them increased and internetworking took off. The main products of internetworking are bridges which connect similar networks; routers which connect dissimilar networks and gateways which connect and translate between vastly different networks. The internetworking products will grow in performance and features, but will drop in price as is normal in the computer industry. An emerging technology called ATM (Asynchronous Transfer Mode) is likely to become the main internetworking standard due to its transmission efficiency and multimedia capability. ATM is a cell switching technology that combines the best of packet and circuit switching. ATM will have a high transfer rate to handle voice, data, image and video information. ATM also has the potential to be a major LAN technology in 5-10 years.

Connectivity via modems is also important. Most modems sold today have 14,400 baud transmission speed, but 28,800 baud modems are making a strong showing. Currently over one in four PCs have a modem, but the percentage is much higher for portable PCs. In a few years nearly half of the PCs will have modems, but a large majority will have communications capabilities via LANs. Fax modems are also growing in importance--especially for notebook computers. Many of the PDAs will have advanced communications capabilities including fax modems that can be used with cellular phone networks. The speed of these phone modems will not increase very much in the future and the race is on to find higher speed technologies that can meet the future needs of the Internet and other communications applications.

A new wireless technology, the Personal Communications Services (PCS), is expected to compete favorably with current cellular technology in a few years. Since PCS is expected to cost less than cellular phone service, it will make wireless connectivity cost effective for most portable PC users.

The TV cable network can also be used for data transmission via a so-called cable modem. Such devices are now emerging. They are currently expensive, but prices will decline as production increases. Cable modems allow high transfer rates to the consumer, but much slower transfer rates the other way. The cable TV companies have a great opportunity to deliver Internet/web data to the consumers at rates that are 100 times higher than phone modems.

ISDN (Integrated Service Digital Network) is now available in most communities and may become a popular technology. ISDN allows computer communications without modems at 64 Kbps or 128 Kbps. The phone companies charge 50% to 100% more for an ISDN line than a regular phone line. The main problem with ISDN is that it is difficult to install and the phone companies have limited experience in implementing ISDN. ISDN has a short term opportunity, but is likely to be eclipsed in a few years by other technologies such as cable modems and ADSL.

The most promising high-speed data transmission technologies are the ADSL, HDSL and VDSL. These three technologies use the existing telephone lines to deliver a quantum leap in transmission speed. High Data Rate Digital Subscriber Line (HDSL) uses two pairs of wires to transmit 1.5 Mbps. This technology is likely to replace existing T1 lines due to its lower cost than T1. HDSL is furthest along of the DSL technologies.

Asymmetric Digital Subscriber Line (ADSL) has tremendous potential as connection to consumers and businesses. ADSL can transfer 1.5 to 8 Mbps upstream to the customer and 16K to 640 Kbps downstream from the customer. Numerous ADSL trials are under way and ADSL is likely to be in volume production in the 1988 timeframe.

Very High Data Rate Digital Subscriber Line (VDSL) has tremendous speed: 12.9 Mbps for up to 4,500 feet and 52.9 Mbps for up to 1,000 feet. VDSL is a technology further in the future.

Two communications technologies that are 5 to 10 years down the road may eventually have a major impact--optical fibers to homes and businesses and low-orbit satellites. Both technologies will take a long time to implement due to tremendous implementation costs--tens of billions of dollars. Fiber optics lines to homes and business will happen sooner or later and will solve all foreseeable bandwidth problems. Low-orbit satellites are a risky business and may never happen due to the large up front investment before any revenues are realized. Low-orbit satellites would become the ultimate wireless technology.

Input/Output Technology Trends

The keyboard is by far the most common input device and it will continue to hold this distinction for a long time. Keyboard technology is very stable and few changes are taking place. Cordless keyboards are available and are likely to see much more usage in the future. Improved keyboard ergonomics are now important due to growing problems with repetitive stress injuries. Ergonomic keyboards are now available and accessories to improve the ergonomics of standard keyboards are readily available and should be used by all computer users.

A pointing device is used with over 70% of PCs in use, but over 90% of PCs sold today come with a pointing device. The popularity of Windows and other graphical user interfaces will assure that a pointing device will be used with the vast majority of PCs in the late 1990s. What type of pointing device is less clear. The mouse is the overwhelming choice today, but it may not be tomorrow. The drawback of the mouse is extra desk space. A variety of technologies are likely to share the pointing function. The mouse will remain the most popular device, but its market share will decline. The stylus used with pen-based computers will become a mouse competitor and trackballs will see continued usage--especially on notebook computers. A special keyboard key that emulates mouse movement is also a strong alternative for portable and desktop computers.

Scanners and software that recognize ordinary printed text have a good future and are likely to be in common use in the 1990s. Currently the desktop scanner is too expensive for widespread use--especially the color scanner. The handheld scanner is less expensive, but is less accurate in use. Several companies have included a scanner as part of the keyboard. To improve the capability of these peripherals requires lots of memory, processing power and knowledge-based software that will recognize the desired patterns. Sooner or later the required power and memory will be available at a cost-effective price. As scanner prices decline and accuracy improves their popularity will steadily increase.

Speech-recognition technology reached the niche-product stage a few years ago. Speech-recognition products are quite useful provided the application requires a vocabulary of less than a thousand words. Speech systems with thousands of words in their vocabulary are now available at attractive prices. Each year the size of the speech-recognition vocabulary grows at any given price point. In a few years PC-based speech-recognition capability will reach thousands of words with some training. Then the usage of speech recognition will increase rapidly. If speech recognition takes off soon, it is likely to impact handwriting recognition in a negative way and could prevent widespread usage of handwriting recognition.

The first handwriting recognition pad was introduced in the early 1980s, but the technology was too expensive and too limited to catch on. The technology reappeared in 1989 with the GRiDPad notebook computer. Numerous pen-based computers were introduced in the early 1990s. The acceptance of pen-computers has been slower than anticipated--primarily due to unrealistic expectations. The writing that can be recognized is still limited, but as the technology improves most of the restrictions will go away. The pen-based computer is primarily used to replace data-entry applications which use clipboards. As so-called pen-centric software is introduced, pen computers will become general purpose computers and the market for pen computers may take off in a few years. The handwriting recognition and input pad technology may also supplement the keyboard in desktop computers.

Speech synthesizers are already affordable and used successfully in specialized applications such as voice mail and sound for recreational software. But it will take multimedia computers to put the technology in common usage. In this decade speech synthesis will be built into most PCs as the technology becomes inexpensive and useful for multimedia computers and voice-mail communications.

Video conferencing has been around for a long time, but has been too expensive for widespread use. Video compression hardware and software is changing the economics of video conferencing. Desktop video conferencing systems based on PCs are likely to see widespread use in the next few years.

Software Technology Trends

Object technology is destined to dramatically change the computer industry. It is not a new software technology because it has been around since the mid-1970s. The basic idea is to treat information as objects that have certain characteristics. This simple idea has far reaching implications that makes it faster and easier to develop and maintain software. In a nutshell--object technology makes it possible to reuse software instead of starting from scratch each time. Hence object-oriented programming is here to stay and it will have a very positive impact on future software products. But object-oriented technology still needs well designed products, good programmers and thorough testing. There is currently an intense battle to set object technology standards between Microsoft's OLE and the Apple/IBM/Novel-led consortium's OpenDoc. It is unlikely that either contender will dominate and the software developers will have to live with two de facto standards.

The software agent or intelligent agent may be the next hot technology. It shows tremendous potential, but runs the risk of near-term disappointment due to overpromises and overhype. Software agents span a wide spectrum, but are essentially smart programs that can engage and help all types of computer users with their tasks. Software agent technology is in its infancy and will be a hot research topic for years to come. Software agents are already becoming useful as information filters and information finders. AT&T has launched an online service called PersonaLink that is designed for software agents based on General Magic's Telescript and Magic Cap software. Programs that manage messaging functions such as e-mail and to search for information on the Internet will start the software agent revolution.

Visualization software provides representation of complex scientific problems, advanced 3D design problems and similar applications. It is only a few years old, but promises to have a significant impact. Visualization software takes a large amount of three dimensional data and generates many types of visual images. Visualization software originated on high-end workstations due to the computing power needed--especially graphics performance. Over the next couple of years visualization software will appear for high-end PCs.

Multimedia software is one of the most frequently used buzz words in the computer industry. Multimedia is the use of multiple types of information. A good example is a CD-ROM based encyclopedia. It has the text and figures like a normal encyclopedia in book form. The multimedia encyclopedia also has recorded speeches or video clips from famous people and may have video showing how an engine or other device works. In a nutshell, multimedia software stimulates the senses by using text, graphics, still and moving images, sound, speech and music. Down the road multimedia may also stimulate smell, taste and motion.

Multimedia software has the biggest potential to change entertainment and education. However, multimedia software is difficult to develop and will require some patience. There is little doubt that multimedia is extremely important, but will take longer to develop than most of us would like. Business software will also go multimedia. Documents will have text, drawings, video clips and speech. E-mail will become e-mail/voice mail. Databases will store text, graphics, images, speech and so on.

The software to access the Internet's World Wide Web has exploded in the last three years and is vastly improving the information storage and retrieval capabilities of the Internet. The web has become a de facto standard for storing, finding and transferring information on the Internet. It is the largest client/server system available. The web uses hypertext to store its information, it handles multimedia documents and has a common user interface (Internet browser). It is impacting information distribution via CD-ROM and will continue dramatic growth.

There is a tremendous battle between Netscape and Microsoft to set the standard for the Internet browser. Netscape has the lead with its Navigator software, but Microsoft's Internet Explorer has narrowed the technology and feature lead that Netscape had a year ago. We will most likely have two de facto standards in the browser market for the foreseeable future.

Today Java is one of the biggest buzz words in the computer industry. Java was announced by Sun Microsystems in June 1995. Java is an interpretive language based on C++, an object oriented language. Java's future importance is because it is platform independent and can run on any computer and because it can be distributed easily via the Internet to any computer. This opens the possibility of creating a software platform that can eventually rival the Microsoft Windows platform. Software applications written in the Java language can de downloaded via the Internet (or any other communication link) to any computer and executed with a Java interpreter. The Java interpreter software would also be downloaded. Initially these applications are likely to be small and are therefore called applets. However, Java programs can be large if the computer that downloads the program has enough memory and the communication link has enough bandwidth. There is a lot of excitement in the computer industry about Java--partly because of the market opportunity and partly because Java is perceived as a strong competitor to the Wintel standard if it becomes a new computer platform.

It is generally acknowledged that the software technology has not kept up with the hardware advances. Two articles by Ted Lewis ("The Next 10,000 Years", Computer Magazine, March & April 1996) have some interesting perspectives on where software and hardware technologies are going in the next 16 years (10,000 is base 2 and hence means 16 years). These two articles suggest that software should be built from new-era languages using frameworks, component technologies and applets. The new-era languages are much improved versions of today's object technologies. The articles also suggest that the key software building blocks are created by software artists. As the technology improves the user will adapt the software building blocks to their specific applications.

Technology Trend Summary

There are a variety of other technologies that have the potential to improve computers over the next 10 years. A few are listed in Figure 4.1 along with key potential technologies discussed in the previous sections. Note that this chart shows the estimated time when major impact occurs. The technologies are usually emerging earlier than listed and major impact occurs a few years later.

Figure 4.1: Computer Technology Impact				
Years Until Impact	1-2 Years	3-5 Years	6-10 Years	Over 10 Years
Revolutionary Technologies	o Internet/Web o Intranets o Java computer platform	o Virtual Reality (VR) o 3D Web information o E-cash/cyber cash		o Optical computers o Superconducting computers
Computer Architecture	o PC SMP servers o Network computer (NC)	o Information appliances o Neural networks	o Self-diagnosing PCs o Self-repairing PCs	
Software Technologies	o Object technology o Software agents	o Security software o E-commerce software	o Software based on applets, frameworks & components	o User adapted software
Network/Telecom Technologies	o ISDN o Fast Ethernet o Cable TV modem	o ADSL modem o ATM internetworking o PCS/wireless	o Desktop ATM o Optical fibers to homes o Low orbit satellites	
Mass Storage	o Read-only DVD o 100 MByte floppy disks	o Erasable DVD	o Holographic storage	o New 3D mass storage technologies
Printing/Input Technologies	o Multifunction printers o Color page printers o Photo-realistic printers	o Speech recognition o 3D pointing devices o Handwriting recognition	o Natural language o Gesture recognition	o Brainwave recognition
Display/Graphics/ Output Technologies	o Video compression o Desktop video conferencing	o High definition TV o New flat displays	o 3D display technologies o Virtual retinal display	
Semiconductor Components	o 64-Mbit RAM chip o 64-bit microprocessors	o 256-Mbit RAM chip o VLIW microprocessors	o 1024-Mbit RAM chip o 3D chips	o 4096-Mbit RAM chip o Quantum-based chips

The Internet and the World-Wide Web have already had tremendous impact on the computer industry and more will follow. The corporate version of the Internet, the intranet, is further increasing the impact of this technology. The addition of Java to the Internet has the potential of making another major computing platform that can be targeted by software developers. These subjects are discussed further in the next section.

Electronic cash (e-cash) or cyber cash is a payment concept that is rapidly becoming a payment method for the Internet and electronic commerce in general. E-cash is likely to advance electronic commerce and may also have an impact on the world's financial system.

Symmetrical Multi-Processor (SMP) systems have been available for large computers and the workstation market for a long time. SMP systems expand the performance range of single processor systems. SMP versions of the Pentium Pro are starting to appear, and are likely to make an even larger impact due to their low prices compared to larger systems.

Two new computer product segments are emerging that have the potential to have a large impact on the computer industry in the next five years. The Network Computer (NC) is a low cost device that functions as an Internet access device. Oracle, IBM, Sun Microsystems, Apple, Netscape and many others are supporting a common

NC specification. NCs are expected to be generally available in 1997. The NC is an example of an application specific computer.

Several companies are working on another application specific, simple-to-use computer category called information appliances. Most of these products are aimed at the home market and the consumer electronics companies are interested in entering this market. Information appliances are also expected to be available in 1997. Time will tell which application specific computers will be most successful. Both NCs and information appliances will be discussed in the next section.

Multimedia PC is no longer on the top 5 buzz word list, but continues to advance and increase in importance. Video compression and decompression will soon be a standard feature on most PCs--especially home PCs. The Intel Pentium with multimedia capabilities will be available in 1997 and will provide step function improvements for multimedia applications ranging from video conferencing to simulation games.

It is easy to see why Hollywood is interested in the multimedia PC. In a couple of years a multimedia hit title will sell a few million copies in the U.S. at a price of $30 to $50. Hence the revenue potential is $60M to $100M. By the end of the decade a multimedia hit title could sell 10M units at the same price point and could bring in retail revenues of $0.5B. By comparison a movie is considered a hit when it generates $100M in U.S. movie theaters. I predict that the multimedia PC will evolve into the personal movie theater in five years or so.

Artificial or virtual reality (VR) is a promising, but mostly a futuristic concept. VR means a computer-simulated environment that changes based on your action. In some ways virtual reality is the next generation of multimedia. The environment that can be simulated today is crude, but will improve in proportion to computer technology gains. VR technology is in its infancy, but experiments range from architecture, entertainment and physics to medical rehabilitation and psychotherapy. The interest in VR is extremely wide and far-flung--from computer scientists to a new subculture (cyberpunks). There are already movies based on VR-themes and numerous consumer magazines have covered virtual reality (i.e. Time Magazine). Initially we will see special purpose computers to do VR applications (Entertainment VR machines are already available). But it will take a few years until virtual reality simulations appear realistic. At the end of the decade VR could have a major impact on computer applications.

Neural-network computers have far reaching implications. Neural nets are modeled after the way the brain works. The result is a computer that is much better at learning new tasks than traditional computers. The technology is in its infancy and will be greatly improved. Neural-net computers are already used in specialized applications. As the capability of specialized neural-network chips increase, their use will spread. We also need to learn more about how the brain works to expand neural-network capabilities. In the late 1990s neural-network computers have the potential to make a major impact on computer technology. In the 21st century a combination of bio and electrical engineering may bring us bio-chips for neural networks.

Superconducting technology can be used to design extremely fast chips. The drawback has been the great expense of cooling the equipment to extremely low temperatures. The advances in warmer superconducting materials is promising and could finally make superconductive chips viable. However, it will be 10 years until superconductive computers are commercially available. Special purpose usage could be possible at an earlier date.

The dream of optical computers is at least 30 years old. Progress has been made, but optical computers remain elusive. It is possible we may see special purpose optical computers in this decade, but general-purpose optical computers will have to wait until the 21st century.

Significant computer improvements are coming from telecom and networking technologies. Telecom/networking advances are improving computing in four different areas:
1. Faster internetworking technologies such as ATM and/or Gigabit Ethernet.
2. Faster LAN and networking such as Fast Ethernet and later desktop ATM.
3. Faster computer communications from 28.8 Kbps modems and ISDN, later from cable modems and ADSL and eventually fiber optics lines to homes and offices.
4. Wireless communication via the cellular network, later via PCS and eventually from low orbit satellites.

In many ways the personal computer is becoming a major communication tool as much as data processing tools and personal productivity tools.

Hot Computer Industry Issues

This section discusses a few topics that are hot. The topics may be hot due to rapid market growth, future market potential and impact or because a topic's uncertainty or confusion is important to understand. The subjects discussed are the Internet, multimedia computers, RISC-based computers, graphics user interface/operating systems and potential impact of portable OSs and application programming interface (API) standards.

Internet and Intranets

The Internet is without doubt the hottest topic in the computer industry today--and deservedly so! The Internet or its successor has the potential to rival the combined impact of the phone, TV and PC in 10 to 15 years. The Internet is not one network, but is a network of over 30,000 networks, over 3M computer hosts and over 35M users (i.e. e-mail addresses) in the U.S. and worldwide.

The Internet has been around for a long time and traces its roots back to 1969 when the Department of Defense started the ARPANET. In the 1970s and 1980s the Internet grew as a network for government-sponsored and university-based research. In the mid-1980s the National Science Foundation (NSF) actively promoted the Internet as part of the regional supercomputer centers. At this time the Internet was not intended for commercial usage. In the late 1980s as commercial users started connecting to the Internet in large numbers, the NSF developed an "acceptable use policy" to prevent for-profit use on the NSF portion of the Internet. In 1985 there were only about 1,000 computers connected to the Internet, which grew 100-fold by 1990. The number of Internet host computers surpassed one million in 1993.

A major milestone occurred in 1991 when for-profit, commercial Internet connections became available, as the first Internet service providers emerged. Commercial use of the Internet grew quickly in the early 1990s as the number of national and regional Internet service providers increased rapidly. The second major milestone came in mid-1993 when the Mosaic software browser appeared. Mosaic quickly became the standard interface to the Internet's World Wide Web and greatly simplified Internet access. Mosaic and the many Mosaic-compatible programs such as Netscape Navigator and Spry's Internet in a Box made it possible for "mere mortals" to use the Internet. The Mosaic graphical user interface, which is now called the Internet or web browser, quickly became the standard software interface for Internet access.

Today there are two main web browser vying for dominance--Netscape's Navigator and Microsoft's Internet Explorer. Netscape has the clear market share lead, but Microsoft is making progress and will remain a formidable competitor to Netscape.

The Internet is successful because it is an open system and it is not controlled by any vendor or group of vendors. It also has a robust structure because it does not have an achilles heel that may bring down the whole system. But better software security and data protection is required for future electronic commerce growth.

A key element in continued Internet success is that it has reached a critical mass that attracts the best and the brightest in the computer industry and beyond. This means the information will become better and more comprehensive, electronic commerce will blossom and more people and companies will be attracted to the Internet. The people interaction will fill all tastes and interests and the software interface will become easier to use, which starts another growth cycle. But this rapid growth will strain the Internet infrastructure and create temporary bottlenecks and usage problems.

In the last year corporate networks using the Internet technology standards have sprung up in a major way. These networks are called intranets. Corporations have realized that an intranet solution is the answer to many information distribution applications--for internal company applications, for suppliers and even for customers of a company. Intranet applications in many cases are used instead of client/server systems at much lower costs and lower complexity. Today intranets are even hotter than the Internet. Intranet servers, server software and web content creation tools are growing dramatically.

A unique characteristic of the Internet is very rapid technology advances. No segment of the computer industry is changing as fast as the Internet. In two years Netscape has developed three versions of the Navigator browser. Both Netscape and Microsoft shipped version 3.0 of their browsers in August 1996 and the next versions are due in 9 months or less.

Java

Two years ago Java only meant coffee. Today it is one of the biggest buzz words in the computer industry. Java was announced by Sun Microsystems in June 1995. Java is an interpretive language based on C++, an object oriented language (Java has been called C++ minus minus). Hence, Java is based on two software technologies that have been around for a long time--language interpreters and object technology. So why is Java so hot? Because two other events have made the combination of the two technologies very viable--the Internet and today's microprocessor performance. In a nutshell, the right infrastructure is available to support Java or a similar product.

A big problem for interpreters is that they are usually 5 to 10 times slower than assembly language or compiled code. In the early 1980s, the UCSD p-code interpreter was available for the IBM PC, but it failed because it was too slow and because the users did not buy the relatively expensive interpreter software. Some p-code programs were successful because they included the interpreter with the program (i.e. PFS:File), but eventually they were rewritten in other languages. The speed of today's microprocessors lowers this problem and in the future additional speed will minimize this drawback. A Java interpreter chip will eliminate the interpreter speed problem.

The Internet makes distribution of the interpreter and large amounts of application software very cost effective. The Internet eliminates expensive and cumbersome software manufacturing, warehousing, distribution and retailing. It also solves most of the shelf space problem, where most software retailers can display and sell a limited number of software titles. The Internet adds one more advantage: a viable method for renting the application for use one or more times.

The third element that makes Java hot is that the major computer vendors are looking for a product or strategy that can compete with the Wintel standard. Java is believed to be this product. This fact is a main reason for the rapid support by nearly all major hardware and software vendors within 9 months of Java's introduction.

Microsoft is not sitting still and has made great progress in embracing the Internet in the last year. Microsoft has also licensed Java, but Java is only part of Microsoft's strategy. Microsoft's ActiveX, OCX and Visual Basic are well established and have a large base of software developers that have over 1,500 software components available. The software development tools are also much further along than Java tools. The main drawback of the ActiveX portfolio is that it only runs on the Wintel standard. If Microsoft moves to a cross-platform strategy for ActiveX (i.e. Macintosh and Unix) it will be an even more formidable competitor to Java.

The outlook for Java is quite promising, but I do not believe it will replace the Wintel standard in the next decade. Instead Java will become a complementary product used on PCs and on emerging product categories such as the NC and on some information appliances. However, Java will receive strong competition from Microsoft's ActiveX products and maybe from future similar products.

Network Computers

The Network Computer (NC) has gotten a lot of attention in 1996. The concept was originally promoted by Larry Ellison of Oracle starting in late 1995. The reason for a network computer is the rise of the Internet--a computer dedicated to accessing the Internet or intranets as they grow in importance. It is believed that the NC will cost less than a PC, because it will not have mass storage devices and will have a web browser instead of Windows or Macintosh operating software. It is also believed that the NC will have much lower support costs than a PC.

Oracle, IBM, Sun Microsystems, Netscape, Apple and many other companies agreed on a standard for NCs in June 1996. By early 1997 numerous NCs are expected to be available. By late 1997 we will know whether NCs will become an instant success or a potential success story that needs further work and more infrastructure (i.e. more bandwidth to the Internet). It will probably be too early to know if the NC is a bust, like some people believe.

It is reasonable to believe that the NC will have some success, but it will certainly not be a PC-killer. To be successful, the NC needs Internet bandwidth and today only large corporations have that bandwidth. Hence, its initial success has to come in the corporate marketplace. At the end of the decade the NC may have an opportunity in the home market, but by that time there may already be information appliances established in the home that access the Internet.

The size of the NC market is debated heatedly among the market researchers and analysts. It will probably grow to 5% to 10% of the PC unit market in 5 to 6 years or 5M to 10M units sold per year worldwide by 2002.

Information Appliances

Information appliance is a broad term and is not as well defined as the network computer. It has different meaning to different people. An information appliance is an inexpensive, easy-to-use computer that is dedicated to do one or a few similar functions. A TV that has built-in Internet access is an information appliance. A telephone that can compose, send and receive email and faxes is an information appliance. A device that can manage a check book register, print checks, access bank and financial information and buy and sell stocks is an information appliance. A product that can run educational programs from a variety of sources is an information appliance. A machine that simplifies kitchen tasks such as cooking, menu planning, ordering and shopping is an information appliance. In many ways PDAs are information appliances with a handheld form factor. There are many other variations of functions that can be done efficiently by such application specific computers.

The big question is which functions will succeed as information appliances. Some will do very well and others will fail miserably. Information appliances will have to cost a few hundred dollars or add a few hundred dollars to an existing product to be successful. The products have to save the owner time, money and/or add significant capabilities to functions the users are performing. Over time the information appliances have to become more powerful without adding complexity or increasing in price. Much future functionality will depend on receiving real-time information from the Internet (i.e. product reviews, comparative shopping and availability for large purchases). This means that the information appliances need Internet access capabilities either built-in or via another device. It is not far-fetched to postulate a family of information appliances that have stand-alone operation most of the time, but can also be hooked together to provide additional functions.

All of the functions that will be done with information appliances can also be accomplished with a PC. And if many information appliances were used, the price may be as high or higher than buying a PC. Even so there is a potentially large market for information appliances. The main reasons are a low entry price and easier to use product. These two features mean that many customers would buy an information appliance, but would not purchase a PC because they could not afford one or they would not take the time to learn to use a PC.

It is difficult to project the market potential for information appliances--especially because many will be included with other products or will be an upgrade of other devices. Here are a few speculations that may illuminate the information appliance potential. If 10% of TVs sold in the U.S. in year 2000 have Internet access, this is a market of 2.5M information appliances. If 10% of all cellular phones sold in the U.S. in year 2000 had e-mail and fax functions, this is a market potential of 1M to 1.5M units. If 2% of households with two wage earners bought a kitchen specific information appliance in year 2000, the market potential is about 0.5M units. If 3% of the car buyers (new or used) in year 2000 bought an information appliance that finds the best deal and availability, the number of such devices sold would be in the 1M range.

Microprocessor Wars

Reduced Instruction Set Computers or RISC have received much attention in the last few years. RISC processors are primarily used in workstations and include Sun's SPARC, MIPS Computer Rx000, HP's Precision Architecture, Digital Equipment Alpha, IBM's RS/6000 and IBM/Motorola's PowerPC. The claim is that RISC is much faster than Complex Instruction Set Computers (CISC) such as Intel 80486, Pentium and Pentium Pro. The performance advantage that RISC has over CISC is not likely to grow and may be smaller in the future. The RISC performance is rarely large enough to swing the purchase decision.

The reason is that many of the techniques used by RISC processors are not an inherent advantage and can and will be used by the CISC processor designers.   Intel's Pentium and Pentium Pro are using many of the performance techniques used by RISC processors. The result is that the performance gap between the best CISC-based and RISC-based microprocessors is narrowing and in three to five years may be small enough that it is not a significant factor in product selections. However, the performance of typical workstations will remain well above the typical PC. The reason is that workstations will be designed with higher performance and more expensive components.

This microprocessor war has raged for five years and will probably continue for another five years. The only sure winner is the Intel Pentium family and there is little doubt that it will continue the 386/486 dominance. It is reasonable to expect that the Pentium, Pentium Pro and its successor will account for 80% to 85% of the microprocessor sales for PCs and other computers. Currently worldwide computer sales are over 65M units per year and growing at about 15% to 20% per year. Among the RISC contenders it looks like the PowerPC has won the battle for first place and it is a four-way battle for second place between SPARC, Rx000, HP PA and DEC Alpha. In the workstation market SPARC is ahead due to its usage by the leading workstation vendor--Sun Microsystems, but Apple's Macintosh volume makes the PowerPC the clear RISC leader.

Figure 4.2 shows the leading microprocessor families, including four Intel families and all the main RISC processors. The ARM microprocessor is also listed as it likely to be a candidate for network computers and information appliances. Sun is designing a Java interpreter chip and such products may also be used in NCs and some information appliances. The installed base of the microprocessors as of 3Q 1996 have been estimated along with the yearly shipment rate for 1996-97 and 1998-99. When a new microprocessor is just taking off, the yearly shipment rate changes dramatically. An estimate of the installed base for each microprocessor at year-end 2000 has also been projected. Note that these projections are based on current trends and unexpected events could change the numbers considerably.

Figure 4.2: Microprocessors: Status and Projections						
Microprocessors	Volume Shipments	Major Vendors Using	Installed Base 3Q'96	Yearly Shipments '96-97	Yearly Shipments '98-99	Installed Base Year 2000
Intel 486 & Compatibles	1990	All PC vendors	90-95M	2-4M	negl.	40-45M
Intel Pentium & Compatibles	1993	All PC vendors	65-70M	55-60M	10-30M	160-170M
Intel Pentium Pro & Compatibles	1996	All PC vendors	0.5-1M	1-10M	40-70M	190-200M
Intel P7 & Compatibles	1998	All PC vendors	na	na	1-10M	65-75M
PowerPC Family	1994	Apple, Motorola, IBM	8-9M	4-6M	7-9M	50-60M
SPARC Family	1987	Sun Microsystems	2-2.1M	0.5-0.65M	0.7-1M	5-7M
MIPS Rx000 Family	1987	Silicon Graphics	0.8-0.9M	0.2-0.3M	0.3-0.5M	2.5-4M
Precision Architecture	1991	Hewlett-Packard	0.6-0.7M	0.25-0.35M	0.4-0.6M	2.5-4M
Alpha Family	1993	Digital	0.2-0.3M	0.12-0.2M	0.3-0.4M	1-2M
ARM Family	1993	Apple, Acorn	0.2-0.3M	0.2-0.3M	0.4-0.6M	1-3M
Java Interpreter Chip	1997-98	Network Computer vendors	na	na	0.1-1M	2-10M

Figure 4.2 shows that it will be very difficult to unseat Intel as the dominant microprocessor vendor. Based on current product trends, only the PowerPC has significant volume potential. The emergence of the NC, information appliances and possible PDA success provide new opportunities for the RISC processors, but it is unclear which RISC architectures will benefit. It is also uncertain how large these opportunities are. Therefore, the year 2000 range of the installed base of the RISC processors is quite large. A reasonable projection is that each of the three application specific computer categories have a volume opportunity of a few million units per year by the end of the decade. If any of the product categories are really successful, the real volume potential is 6 to 10 years down the road (i.e. tens of millions of units sold per year).

SPARC has been quite successful, but primarily due to Sun's clout in the workstation market. SPARC-based products from other vendors are minor players, but this could change as the SPARC architecture is now more open than before. To hedge its bets, Sun is now promoting its Solaris operating system across multiple processor platforms.

The third place is a battle between SPARC, HP PA, Alpha and MIPS Rx000. Currently SPARC is ahead due to Sun's strength. The ACE Rx000 consortium has faded away and the Rx000's chance to overtake SPARC's lead rests on the success of Windows NT and high volume applications in the consumer market. The Rx000 will be used in Nintendo's new video game machine and in Sony and other Japanese consumer electronics products. These high volume applications will be good for Rx000 pricing and technology investments, but will only be marginally helpful in the software war. The consumer applications are not included in the installed base figures in Figure 4.2.

HP's PA is a potent product and is currently a workstation performance leader. However, HP has been slow to sign up allies and most of the leading companies have already chosen sides. Thus it may already be too late for HP's PA to become a standard. However, the joint development with Intel will probably make the PA architecture a survivor due to the next generation compatibility with Intel.

Alpha has a position similar to the PA, but its late market entry makes it very difficult to become a market leader. Alpha is also a performance leader, but it lacks support from major computer companies. The Alpha will do well in replacing DEC's proprietary VAX minicomputers, but its overall success depends on Windows NT success and on DEC's ability to sign up additional computer vendors to use Alpha.

The Intel P7 is an interesting microprocessor because Intel and Hewlett-Packard are working together on this product. This future microprocessor will be compatible with both the x86 and HP PA, but it will not be available until 1998 or later. The P7 is expected to be a 64-bit processor and there will probably be Intel and HP versions.

Software Platforms

In the last five years a fierce battle took place over who would dominate the graphical user interface and accompanying operating system. Microsoft has won this battle convincingly and currently has 170M plus users worldwide. The Macintosh is a distant second about 25M users, followed by OS/2 with 12M users and all Unix versions at nearly 6M users. The Sun Solaris base is the largest Unix segment with about 1.6M users.

Microsoft won this battle as much by its own actions as the inaction and plain incompetence by the competing vendors. Apple and IBM made the most blunders and have had three chances to give Windows serious competition. Apple could have licensed the Macintosh operating system to other PC vendors in the late 1980s or early 1990s. The earlier this had happened, the higher the Macintosh market share would have become. This opportunity closed in 1992-93 timeframe as Windows 3.1 grew dramatically. IBM had its chance with OS/2 in the 1991-93 timeframe to become a strong second to Windows, but failed to capitalize on its opportunity. The final opportunity for IBM and Apple was with the PowerPC alliance. If they had settled on using only the Macintosh OS on the PowerPC in 1992, it could have challenged the Wintel standard. Even if Apple and IBM settle on the Macintosh today, it will become a strong second standard. Current trends will mire Apple and IBM as weak second and third players after Windows.

The Unix community has not done much better. Unix never had a chance to become the dominant desktop PC operating system, but it should have been its birthright to be the dominant server operating system. All it needed was to make one Unix version the dominant one instead of having four, five or six competing versions. Several times the major vendors have said they would work on making one or two standards. But a few years went by and it became clear they were only paying lip service to these agreements. The result is that Novell NetWare became the leading server operating system. In the next few years Windows NT will probably surpass NetWare as the leading server OS and Unix will be a distant third.

As in the past, much of the actions are directed to diffuse Intel and Microsoft's power to evolve their current standards (sometimes called Wintel). For a while Lotus Notes looked like it could challenge Wintel in the office market, but the Internet growth wiped out that opportunity. Notes will still be a significant software platform and is likely to have more users than Unix in a few years.

In 1995 many companies realized the Internet phenomenon created new opportunities. There is even a chance to challenge the Wintel standard by making the Internet into a software platform. This is the reason for the tremendous support that Sun Microsystems' Java has received. The Internet is a software platform because the Java interpreter can be downloaded to any computer with Internet access. The software vendors write their software in the Java language and these programs can also be downloaded to any computer with Internet access. However, this can also take place for any other interpretive language. Microsoft also has such a language, Visual

Basic and its ActiveX strategy. Since intranets use Internet technologies, the intranet users may also become part of the Internet software platform.

To get an idea of what the software platform choices are, the next figure shows key parameters of the leading software platforms. An estimate of the installed base as of 3Q 1996 is shown for each software platform. The yearly shipments or increase for the remainder of the decade has also been estimated. Note that yearly shipments do not add directly to the installed base due to replacement sales. A projection for the installed base at year-end 2000 is included for each software platform. Note that these projections are based on current trends and there may be unexpected events that could change the numbers considerably

Figure 4.3: Software Platforms: Status and Projections					
Software Platforms	Microproces-sor Focus	Other Microprocessors	Installed Base 3Q'96	Yearly Ship-ments/Increase	Installed Base 2000
Macintosh	PowerPC	680x0	25M	4-6M	35-40M
MS-DOS/PC-DOS	Pentium	x86	180M	3-4M	5-10M
Windows 3.x	Pentium	x86	130M	3-4M	5-10M
Windows 95	Pentium	x86	50M	50-70M	300-400M
Windows NT	Pentium	PowerPC, Alpha, MIPS	3M	3-10M	30-50M
IBM OS/2	Pentium	x86	12M	2-4M	20-30M
Sun Solaris (Unix)	SPARC	Pentium, PowerPC	1.6M	0.7-1.5M	5-10M
SCO Xenix/Unix	Pentium	x86	1M	0.2-0.5M	3-5M
Other Unix	Many	Many	3M	0.2-0.4M	4-6M
All Unix	Many	Many	5.6M	1.1-2.4M	12-20M
Novell NetWare	Pentium	Many	4M	0.9-1.5M	9-12M
Lotus Notes Installed Base	Pentium	Many	5M	4-8M	20-30M
Internet Host Computers	Many	Many	8-10M	8-15M	60-75M
Computers that Access the Internet	Many	Many	35-40M	25-50M	250-300M
Computers with Internet Email Access	Many	Many	50-60M	45-60M	350-450M
Intranets	Many	Many	na	na	na

There are some interesting observations and projections that can be drawn from this chart. All software platforms are planned for the Intel Pentium family. Hence, there is no question that Intel will remain the volume leader. Intel's microprocessor shipments will surpass 60M units in 1996.

MS-DOS remains the largest OS installed base with about 180M users including Windows 3.x users. Microsoft Windows 3.0/3.1 remains the largest GUI software platform. Windows 95 is both a 32-bit operating system and graphical user interface and is replacing both MS-DOS and Windows 3.x. Windows 95 shipped in August 1995 with phenomenal publicity and its installed base has already exceeded 50M units worldwide and may surpass 70M units at year-end 1996. By year-end 1997, Windows 95 will have surpassed the Windows 3.x user base.

Windows NT includes both the server and client versions. The client version is about 80% to 85% of the total units. Windows NT is on its way to becoming the leading server operating system in a couple of years.

The Apple Macintosh has an installed base of over 25M units, which will help establish the PowerPC and will maintain the Macintosh OS as a leading product. Apple started to licence the Mac OS in late 1994 but moved slowly at first. Apple is now more aggressive and the Macintosh clones are starting to do well. Power Computing has been most successful so far. The Macintosh will be leading OS for the PowerPC, but will get strong competition as a server OS from Windows NT.

IBM's OS/2 now has an installed base over 12M, which is 2X higher than all Unix versions combined. Current monthly sales rates are equal to or better than the Macintosh OS/GUI. IBM has scaled down its expectations for OS/2 and is focusing on the server market and on its traditional customers in large corporations. The future of IBM's OS/2 is clouded due to IBM's acquisition of Lotus Notes. Will Notes become IBM's main strategy to battle

Microsoft instead of OS/2? From the projections of Figure 4.3, Notes will have a larger installed base than OS/2 by the end of the decade.

The Unix software platforms will battle in the workstation market and as servers in the client/server market and will not have much of an impact in the PC market. In the client/server market Unix will compete with Novell's NetWare and the server version of Windows NT and OS/2. Solaris should do well due to Sun's strong position in the workstation market. SCO and HP have taken over Novell's UnixWare and will jointly develop a 64-bit Unix that so far has received strong support from other Unix vendors. This will make SCO/HP UnixWare a strong competitor to Solaris.

It is difficult to estimate and project the Internet, because it changes so fast. In the past the Internet has doubled in size every year since 1988. From a software platform potential there are three parts of the Internet: Internet host computers, Internet users via Internet access providers and users with Internet email access. There are currently nearly 10M Internet host computers. It is difficult to grow 100% per year for an extended time and to be conservative, lower Internet growth rates (65% per year) are used for the rest of the decade. This means that there will be 60M to 75M internet host computers by year-end 2000.

The number of Internet users via Internet access providers is currently 35M to 40M worldwide. A 65% growth rate per year would bring the number of Internet users to 250M to 300M by year 2000. The number of computer users with Internet email capabilities is currently in the 50-60M range, which could grow to 350-450M by year 2000. Even Internet email users can receive a Java interpreter and Java-based software and be part of this Internet software platform. The hard part is to estimate what portion of theoretical Internet software platform will buy and use the available software.

The intranet size is even harder to estimate and project, because it is so new and many corporations are not giving out much information about their intranet plans.

Platform Portability Potential

A goal in the computer industry, at least from the users' point of view, is to have application portability between different computing platforms. This goal is no longer as elusive as it once seemed. There are six distinct trends in the computer industry that are improving or will improve platform portability in the future:

1. Portable operating systems
2. Standard application programmer interfaces (APIs)
3. Object technology and reusable software components
4. Emulation of other microprocessors
5. Future microprocessors with multiple instruction sets
6. Internet as a software platform

The more application software portability there is, the happier the computer users will be.

Portable Operating Systems

Unix was the first portable operating system and it has been available on multiple hardware platforms for over 25 years. Unix's importance accelerated in the 1980s with the growth of the workstation industry. Microsoft's decision to make Windows NT a portable operating system was a watershed event and it is now available on all major microprocessors. The Macintosh OS is also becoming a portable operating system. In the future, all important operating systems will become portable. Even Microsoft's Windows 95 is likely to become portable in its next generation implementation.

API Standards

The importance of API standards is primarily due to the growth of the Windows software base. It is the strategy of several vendors to tap into the Windows software base through the use and emulation of the Windows API. Compatibility in the Unix market is shifting to compliance with the COSE Spec 1170 list of Unix application programmer interfaces. It is likely that this trend will grow in importance and numerous APIs from multimedia and object technology to networking, telecom, 3D visualization and client/server will become standards.

Object Technology

The increasing usage of object technology will have a positive impact on software portability. Object technology is and will be used to build portable operating systems. This technology also makes it easier to develop portable application software. The greatest potential of object technology is the promise of reusable software components. Reusable software components promise increased software productivity and more reliable software. Eventually software artists may construct superior software components that are licensed for use by software publishers.

Microprocessor Emulation

Emulation of other processors' instruction sets have been around almost as long as the computer industry. The main disadvantage with emulation is that it is usually five to ten times slower than native operation, but in some cases this is still a viable option. When a new processor came along, backwards compatibility was usually accomplished by emulation of older processors. In this case, the new processor is considerably faster than the older processor and this makes emulation acceptable. Currently workstations use their RISC processors to emulate the Intel x86 microprocessors to tap into the Windows software base. Today such emulation by RISC processors yields x86 performance that is 30% to 50% slower than the real thing. In the next generation of microprocessors this gap is likely to narrow as the designers add features that speed up the emulation process.

Microprocessors with Multiple Instruction Sets

Presently there is no microprocessor that executes multiple instruction sets because the technology is not far enough along to do so cost-effectively. But as the microprocessor technology advances, this will become feasible--probably in a year or two. When this happens there are likely to be lawsuits flying, but this will only be a temporary slow down. It is likely that in five years, the RISC microprocessor will include emulation of the x86 instruction set. In fact, without this feature many of the RISC microprocessors will not survive. There has already been trade press rumors that IBM is considering to do so with the PowerPC.

Internet as a Software Platform

We have already talked about looking at the Internet as a platform. This may be the biggest factor in making application portability between different computing platforms. If this trend is successful, a significant portion of tomorrow's software base will work on multiple computing platforms. It is likely that there will be multiple successful software platforms using the Internet as a base. Java is the software platform receiving the most attention, but Microsoft's ActiveX is also likely to succeed. And there is no reason why smaller, niche oriented software bases cannot be quite as successful as Internet software platforms.

New Technologies to Watch For

There are a few additional products, technologies or trends that are important and are likely to have a market impact in the next few years as shown in the next table. Some will be successful and others will fade away.

Figure 4.4: Products/Technologies To Watch		
Vendor(s)	Product or Technology	Importance
Intel	P55C microprocessor	A Pentium microprocessor with accelerated multimedia capabilities
Netscape & Microsoft	Navigator vs. Internet Explorer	Battle to lead in web browser software
Many	Universal Serial Bus (USB)	High-speed serial bus that is a likely dominant I/O standard
Adobe	Acrobat	Potential standard for electronic document distribution
Apple, IBM & Motorola	PowerPC Reference Platform	A standard for PowerPC computers including the Macintosh
Many	NC Reference Profile	Likely standard for network computers that access the Internet
Microsoft vs OpenDoc	Object technology standards	Who will set the object technology API standards?
Many	Moving Worlds	Potential standard for 3D web pages--based on VRML

Vendor(s)	Product or Technology	Importance
	Figure 4.4: Products/Technologies To Watch	
Microsoft, Intel & others	Simply Interactive PC (SIPC)	Future standard for low-cost, entertainment-focused PC
@Home	Cable TV information delivery	Innovative content delivery to PCs via cable TV modems
PointCast	PointCast	Screen saver that delivers news from web servers to PCs
Microsoft	ActiveX, OCX, Visual Basic	Microsoft's roadmap to give Java competition as an Internet platform
Many	Web content development tools	What company will lead this new, important software segment?
Many	Processor for application specific PCs	Which MPU will lead the NC, PDA & information appliance markets?
TV Interactive	Touch-sensitive smart paper	Can be used as an inexpensive remote control device
Apple	Meta Content Format (MCF)	Open file format standard for finding web information
Many	Off-line browsers	Retrieves specified web content during off-peak hours
Microsoft	Graphics technology (Talisman)	Workstation graphics performance on PCs

A new Intel Pentium microprocessor will have a major impact on the PC market in 1997. The code name is P55C and it will be available in 1Q 1997 in volume production. This microprocessor is a Pentium with added multimedia capabilities and it will quickly be a major product.

Netscape's Navigator is currently the clear market leader in Internet browsing software with over 70% market share. There were numerous competitors to Netscape in 1994 and 1995, but Microsoft has become the main competitor. Both Netscape and Microsoft introduced version 3.0 of their product in August 1996. Microsoft's Internet Explorer has now caught up with Navigator's features and functionality. Microsoft still lags in market share, but I believe Microsoft will narrow the gap in the next year.

The Universal Serial Bus is a new high-speed serial I/O bus that is endorsed by all major PC vendors. USB will make major strides in 1997 and is likely to replace the serial, parallel, keyboard and mouse ports in a few years.

Adobe's Acrobat is currently the leading software technology/standard for distributing electronic documents. Adobe is hoping that Acrobat will be as successful as Postscript is. Acrobat will have to contend will other products, but the main competition may come from the World Wide Web's HTML. HTML is currently much simpler than Acrobat, but HTML is so successful and there will surely be a more capable HTML2 and HTML3.

The PowerPC Reference Platform has been defined and finally includes the Macintosh. It will be a much stronger standard with the Macintosh included. But several years have been wasted that translate to lower market share than looked feasible a few years ago.

The Network Computer Reference Profile is a specification for network computers that has the support of Apple, IBM, Netscape, Oracle, Sun Microsystems and many other companies. It will likely be the dominant standard in the NC market.

There is currently a battle to set object technology standards between Microsoft's OLE and OpenDoc, which is supported by Apple, IBM, Novell and others. Hopefully, a compromise is possible to settle on just one standard, but it is more likely that we will have to live with both.

The web needs to store three dimensional information and Moving World is a proposed standard for 3D information storage on the Web. The standard is based on the Virtual Reality Modeling Language (VRML) and is supported by 56 vendors including Netscape and Silicon Graphics.

Microsoft, Intel and other companies are defining the specification for a low-cost, home PC that will also be a good game computer. This effort is called Simply Interactive PC or SIPC. It will compete with video game machines and probably some of the information appliances. It is too early to project how successful it will be.

@Home is a start-up company that has received lots of attention because it plans to deliver information to PC users over cable TV networks. It is funded by TCI, the largest U.S. cable company.

Another start-up company receiving attention is PointCast. It has developed a screen saver program that delivers information to PC users from Internet web sites. CNN is one of the providers of information. The users can select what types of information to be downloaded.

Microsoft's ActiveX, OCX (formerly called OLE) and Visual Basic will give Java strong competition and will probably take a significant share of the Internet interpreter/applet software market. It will also become an Internet software platform. Will there also be a Visual Basic interpreter chip?

A new software segment has risen overnight: web page software development and management tools. Several start-up software companies were the pioneers and some have already been successful. Microsoft bought Vermeer Technologies for $130M in stocks.

The microprocessor battle for a new multi-million unit market opportunity is heating up: application specific PCs such as the PDA, NC and information appliance. It will most likely be a battle between the ARM, x86, PowerPC, Rx000 microprocessors and Java chips.

Future Computer Product Categories

The computer product segments shown in Figure 1.4 are likely to change in the next five years. The main differences are a wealth of server computers and probably a proliferation of application specific PCs. Minicomputers, mainframes and supercomputers will become server computers. Server computers are all the network servers used in local area networks, intranets and other networks. Another change is that the distinction between PCs and workstations will be much smaller than today. Hence they are not listed separately, but notebooks and desktop computers deserve separate segment designations. The projected rise of application specific PCs will add a variety of dedicated function computers for the office and home markets.

The resulting product segments are shown in Figure 4.5. By year 2002 the computer industry will evolve to three main computer platforms. These three categories have very different hardware, operating software and application software requirements:

1. Server computers: Servers include LAN and network servers, web, intranet and Internet servers and several types of specialized servers. The specialized servers range from transaction and database servers to simulation and video and virtual reality servers. Video servers will deliver streams of video such as movies on demand to hundreds of customers. Virtual reality servers will create realistic 3-dimensional words for customers to explore and experience by using client computers. Supercomputers and massively-parallel computers will be the ultimate compute servers for very large problems. Minicomputer and mainframe computers can remain as legacy servers for a while, but must evolve to open system servers or face extinction.

2. Desktop and notebook client computers: This category includes PCs, workstations and single-user supercomputers. These computers are quite powerful in stand-alone operation and gain additional capabilities from server computers.

3. Application specific PCs: This segment consists of all PDAs, network computers and information appliances. Most of these devices have limited stand-alone power and get much of their capabilities from interaction with server computers--either by downloading programs or data or both. Some application specific PCs will have stand-alone operation as the primary mode and will only occasionally rely on servers.

2002 Computer Product Segments

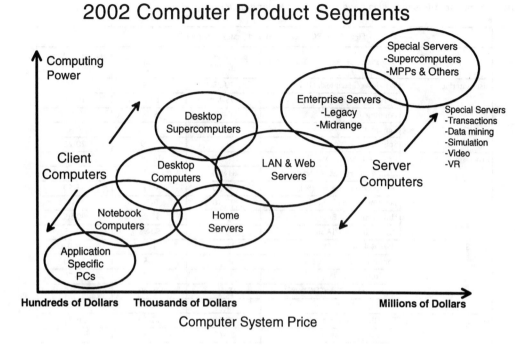

Figure 4.5

The market characteristics are also very different for the three platforms. The server segment is in its growth phase and is attracting many new and existing competitors. The desktop segment is in its mature phase with moderate growth and intense competition. The notebook segment is growing strongly, but will enter its mature phase by the end of the decade. The distinction between PCs and workstations will have disappeared by year 2002. The application specific PC segment, including PDAs, NCs and information appliances, is in the emerging phase and is wide open. The application specific PC segments will be characterized by standards battles--from microprocessors to operating systems, GUIs and languages.

The enterprise server segment includes the mainframe or legacy systems and midrange computers. The special server segment includes supercomputers and massively parallel processors (MPP) and numerous new or emerging servers. Data mining servers are products that sift through large databases to find specific patterns. Video servers store movies and other video information and deliver the video on demand to client computers. Virtual reality servers will generate 3D virtual worlds for different types of applications. LAN and web servers will be the largest segments in unit shipment with millions of products sold per year. By the turn of the century we will also see the emergence of server computers used in homes. Such home servers will be used in households with multiple consumer PCs and in home offices. Home servers may also play a role in home automation systems that will control household equipment in the future.

The next figure shows projected technology trends for the three main categories of personal computers by the year 2000. The percentage of application specific PCs, notebook PCs and desktop or minitower PCs sold with various new technologies and features are estimated. Docking station features are included for notebook PCs.

The user interface will consist of two types of products--the evolution of the traditional Macintosh and Windows interface and a simpler user interface that will probably be based on the Internet browser interface. It is possible the simple user interface may be based on other products such as Microsoft's SIPC or possibly future products.

The PC processor power in year 2000 will be equal to the Pentium Pro for application specific PCs, twice that power for notebook PCs and at least 3x the power of the Pentium Pro for desktop PCs. Many PCs will also have a multimedia processor to handle speech recognition, handwriting recognition and video compression/decompression. Some products may also have Java or other language interpreters.

Features	Capability or % of PCs Sold With:	Application Specific PCs	Notebook PCs	Desktop/Mini-tower PCs
	Figure 4.6: PC Technology and Features in Year 2000			
User Interface	Windows/Macintosh GUI (%)	20-25	90-95	90-95
	Browser/simple GUI (%)	75-80	10-15	10-15
	Pointing device (%)	90-100	95-100	95-100
	Pen input (%)	25-30	20-25	7-10
	Speech input (%)	3-5	8-10	20-25
Processor & Memory	Processor power (MIPS)	200-400	700-900	1,000-1,200
	Main memory size (MByte)	64-128	128-256	256-512
	Multimedia processor (%)	35-30	35-40	45-50
	Java/interpreter chip (%)	30-40	0-10	0-10
	Universal Serial Bus (%)	30-40	85-90	90-95
	PC Card/PCMCIA slots (%)	90-95	90-95	30-35
Mass Storage	Hard disk drive (%)	15-20	100	100
	Removable disk drive (%)	negl.	3-5	15-20
	CD-ROM drive (%)	5-10	30-35	45-50
	Digital Video Disk (DVD) (%)	5-10	25-30	35-40
	Erasable DVD (%)	1-2	3-5	20-25
Display	TV/HDTV as display (%)	40-50	15-20	20-25
	Color display (%)	55-60	95-98	97-100
	Full page display (%)	negl.	1-2	15-20
Printer	Monochrome page printer (%)	3-5	10-12	25-35
	Color page printer (%)	negl.	negl.	7-10
	Color inkjet printer (%)	35-40	40-45	50-55
	Multifunction printer (%)	2-3	3-5	10-15
	Photo-realistic printer (%)	1-2	2-3	5-8
Input Devices	Color scanner (%)	3-5	1-2	8-10
	Digital video camera (%)	2-3	5-7	15-20
	Natural/ergonomic keyboard (%)	negl.	2-3	5-10
Connectivity	Internet/intranet access (%)	50-60	85-90	90-95
	Phone modem (%)	10-15	25-30	30-35
	Wireless modem (%)	5-10	25-30	negl.
	Cable modem (%)	15-20	5-10	10-15
	ISDN/ADSL interface (%)	15-20	10-15	20-25
	LAN/network interface (%)	15-20	35-40	50-55

All notebook and desktop PCs will have multi-gigabyte hard disk drives and will also have either a CD-ROM or a digital video disk (DVD). Some application specific PCs will have mass storage devices, but many will rely on networks for their storage functions.

A large portion of these PCs will have Internet/intranet access and other communications capabilities. The connection media will have much higher bandwidth than today. The LAN interface standard will be 100 Mbps and even gigabit transfer rates will be on the horizon either through desktop ATM or gigabit Ethernet. Cable modems and ADSL will be delivering multi-megabits per second to homes and offices. Wireless modems via digital cellular phones and their emerging competitor--personal communications systems (PCS)--will keep notebook PCs in contact with the rest of the world.

Year 2002 PC Capabilities

To summarize the technology trends, the next figures project what the typical PCs sold in year 2002 are likely to look like. Remember that projections like these usually turn out to be conservative. Five figures show products that are based on evolution of current technologies--subnotebook and notebook PCs, typical home desktop PCs and office desktop PCs and personal workstations. Four more figures add the capabilities of emerging technologies: application specific PCs in general and PDAs in particular, the multimedia PC/TV and the virtual reality PC.

The notebook PC is growing rapidly--both in capabilities and sales volume. The notebook PC, five years down the road, will be very powerful as shown in Figure 4.7. A flat, color display with 1,024 x 1,280 resolution will provide excellent graphics. The processor will consist of a Pentium Pro +2 microprocessor with 512 MBytes of RAM. Digital wireless fax/modem with encryption capabilities will provide secure communications back to the office, the Internet, intranets or to online services. Connectivity via the public ISDN or ADSL system will also be possible. When used in the office, the notebook PC will communicate via LANs. The notebook PC will have a five gigabyte hard disk and a digital video disk that can read CD-ROMs and other optical disks. PC cards with capacities of 256 MBytes to 2,048 MBytes will provide extra program or data storage. The PC card slots may also be used for peripheral functions.

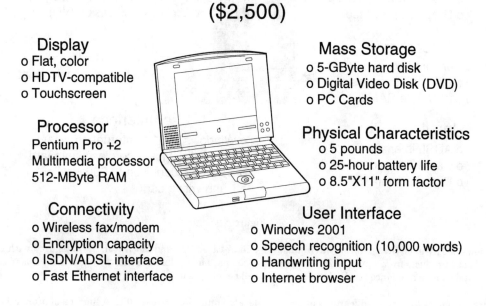

2002 Notebook PC
($2,500)

Display
o Flat, color
o HDTV-compatible
o Touchscreen

Processor
Pentium Pro +2
Multimedia processor
512-MByte RAM

Connectivity
o Wireless fax/modem
o Encryption capacity
o ISDN/ADSL interface
o Fast Ethernet interface

Mass Storage
o 5-GByte hard disk
o Digital Video Disk (DVD)
o PC Cards

Physical Characteristics
o 5 pounds
o 25-hour battery life
o 8.5"X11" form factor

User Interface
o Windows 2001
o Speech recognition (10,000 words)
o Handwriting input
o Internet browser

Figure 4.7

The typical notebook PC in year 2002 may have a cordless keyboard. The user interface will be Windows 2001 or Windows NT 6.0. Handwriting recognition will have matured, and some users will choose to have pen input included with their notebook PCs. Speech recognition will be included with a vocabulary of 10,000 words. The weight will be about 5 pounds and the price will be in the $2,500 range.

The typical 2002 desktop home PC is shown in Figure 4.8. It will cost about $2,000. This desktop computer has tremendous capability compared to current PCs. A Pentium Pro +2 microprocessor with 15 to 20 times the performance of today's Pentium or PowerPC will be standard. Memory size will be at least 512 MBytes.

The home PC will have advanced multimedia features including a special purpose processor that will compress and decompress images, recognize handwriting and speech input and generate speech, music and sounds. It will also have a digital video disk that will be able to read music CDs, CD-ROMs and other optical disks. If erasable DVDs are available at this time, it will go a long way toward solving the backup problems most PC users currently have. Otherwise a 100 MB floppy disk will be used for backup. The hard disk will have at least 5,000-MByte storage. The color display will have 1,024 x 1,280 resolution and will be HDTV-compatible. Hard-copy output will be provided by a color multifunction printer that will print, scan and fax. This printer will also print photographs, but some photographers will choose a photo-realistic printer to improve the picture quality.

Internet access will be common either via a cable modem or ADSL or ISDN interfaces. Many home computers will also have digital video cameras for use with video conferencing or the long-awaited video phone. The home PC will be able to send data, voice and images and even video conferencing over the public telecom network-- whether it is supplied by the local phone company, long distance phone company, cable company or other communications service suppliers.

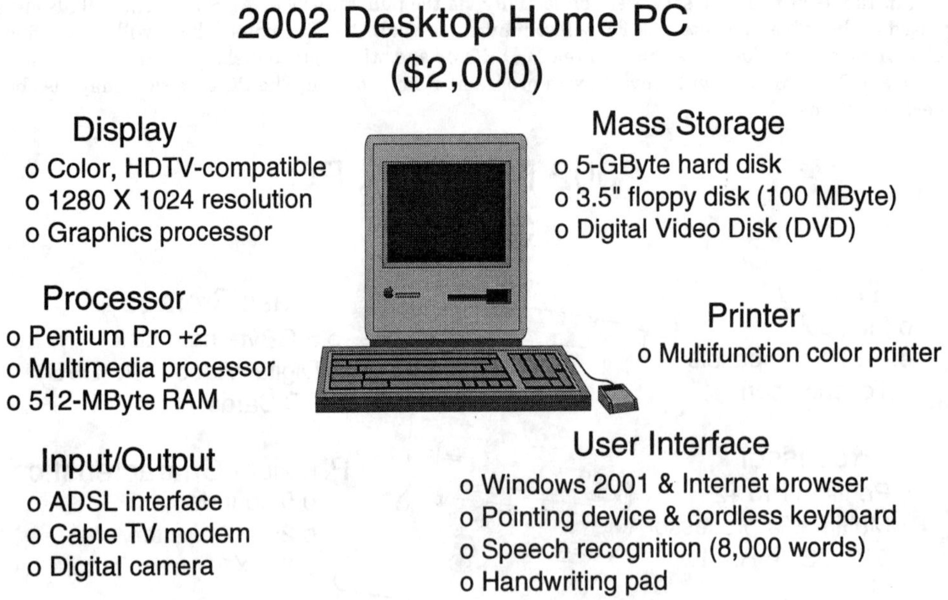

2002 Desktop Home PC
($2,000)

Display
o Color, HDTV-compatible
o 1280 X 1024 resolution
o Graphics processor

Processor
o Pentium Pro +2
o Multimedia processor
o 512-MByte RAM

Input/Output
o ADSL interface
o Cable TV modem
o Digital camera

Mass Storage
o 5-GByte hard disk
o 3.5" floppy disk (100 MByte)
o Digital Video Disk (DVD)

Printer
o Multifunction color printer

User Interface
o Windows 2001 & Internet browser
o Pointing device & cordless keyboard
o Speech recognition (8,000 words)
o Handwriting pad

Figure 4.8

Windows 2001 will be the operating environment for Intel-based PCs and Macintosh 8 will be used with PowerPC-based products from Apple, IBM and other Mac-compatible vendors. An interface to a home bus to communicate and control appliances and other equipment will be an option.

Figure 4.9 shows the expected features of a typical desktop office PC in year 2002. A high-resolution, full-page color display which is HDTV-compatible is standard. The processor will be a Pentium Pro +2 with 20 times the performance of the 1996 Pentium. In Intel's code name convention this will be the P8 processor. It will have a phenomenal 100 million transistors and a clock rate of 500 MHz or higher. There will be one or more co-processors handling speech and handwriting recognition and multimedia tasks such as video compression/decompression and 3D graphics.

Standard memory size will be at least 512 MBytes RAM and maybe 1,024 MBytes. Connectivity will be via LAN for workgroup interaction and via ADSL for remote communication. The LAN connection will most likely be Fast Ethernet at 100 Mbps. The LAN interface may be using ATM technology with its high speed and high bandwidth. Mass storage includes a 10 gigabyte hard disk, a 100 MByte floppy disk drive (primarily for backwards compatibility) and a QIC tape backup system. A multifunction erasable digital video disk is likely to be a standard device. The DVD will read CDs, CD-ROMs and any other optical media. CD-ROMs and/or DVDs will be used as software distribution media, but the Internet will also be a major software distribution media. Video conferencing will be based on 30 frames per second and full TV resolution.

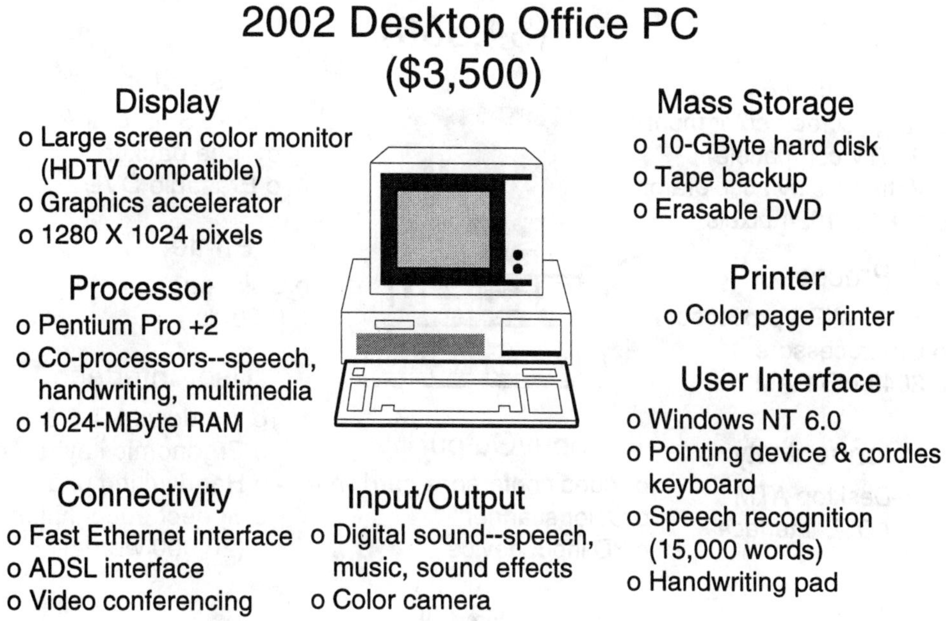

2002 Desktop Office PC
($3,500)

Display

o Large screen color monitor
  (HDTV compatible)
o Graphics accelerator
o 1280 X 1024 pixels

Processor

o Pentium Pro +2
o Co-processors--speech,
  handwriting, multimedia
o 1024-MByte RAM

Connectivity

o Fast Ethernet interface
o ADSL interface
o Video conferencing

Input/Output

o Digital sound--speech,
  music, sound effects
o Color camera

Mass Storage

o 10-GByte hard disk
o Tape backup
o Erasable DVD

Printer

o Color page printer

User Interface

o Windows NT 6.0
o Pointing device & cordles
  keyboard
o Speech recognition
  (15,000 words)
o Handwriting pad

Figure 4.9

A color page printer will be the printer of choice with a 10 page-per-minute speed and at least 600 dots-per-inch resolution and may have built-in scanning capability. A color video camera may also be common. The user interface will be Windows NT's successor--probably version 6.0. A pointing device and cordless keyboard will be standard. Handwriting recognition using a pad may be popular depending on speech input capabilities. Speech recognition with a vocabulary of 15,000 words can be expected. The price will be about $3,500.

The year 2002 personal workstation is shown in Figure 4.10. It uses a 5,000 plus MIPS processor that may be using RISC technology and other computer architecture advances. The processor will use 64-bit architecture. The personal workstation will cost around $4,500 in year 2002 and will have one or more co-processors for performance enhancements. The memory size is 2 GBytes or higher.

This desktop computer will have a full-page color display and color page printer. The main difference between the personal workstation and the typical office desktop PC will be the graphics performance which is higher on the personal workstation. 3D graphics capabilities will be standard in this timeframe and will require a 3D input device.

The personal workstation will have tremendous mass storage devices. A 20 GByte hard disk will be standard and a QIC tape backup device will be need to protect all this data. An erasable digital video disk will also be used with most products. Connectivity will be provided by desktop ATM or gigabit Ethernet interfaces. Some products will also use ADSL via public network connections.

The operating environment will primarily be Windows NT, but Solaris and other Unix-based software will be used. This will be the power-users' machine and due to heavy usage a variety of man-machine interface technologies will be available. No input and control device is ideal and a multiplicity of devices will limit repetitive stress injuries. This means that ergonomic/natural keyboards, handwriting and speech recognition will be common.

2002 Personal Workstation
($4,500)

Display
o Large screen color monitor
  (HDTV compatible)
o Virtual reality accelerator
o 1280 X 1024 pixels

Processor
o 5,000 MIPS processor
o Co-processors
o 2048-MB RAM

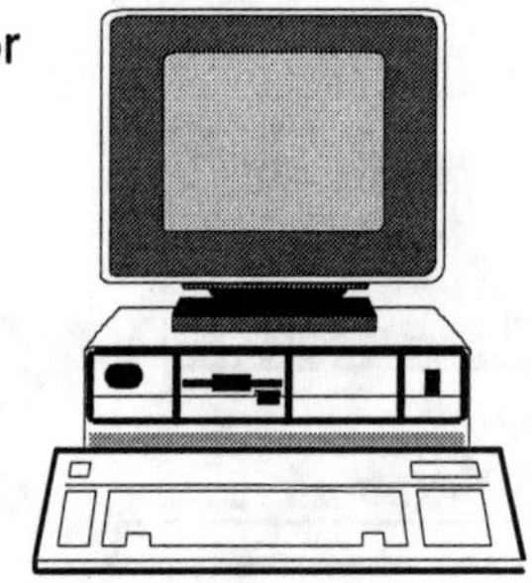

Connectivity
o Desktop ATM
o ADSL interface

Input/Output
o Video conference hardware
o Color scanner
o 3D input device

Mass Storage
o 20-GB hard disk
o Tape backup
o Erasable DVD

Printer
o Color page printer
  (600 dpi)

User Interface
o Windows NT 6.0
o Ergonomic keyboard
o Handwriting pad
o Speech recognition
  (20,000 words)

Figure 4.10

The 2002 application specific PCs are shown in Figure 4.11. There will be a wide range of devices and it is diffi-cult to project what these emerging products will look like. The PDA will range in price from a few hundred dol-lars to nearly $2,000. PDAs will remain small, handheld devices that range from simple organizer/schedulers to multifunction devices with wireless communications, Internet access, smart software agents and productivity enhancing applications. The PDA processor in year 2002 will have more power than today's Pentium Pro and may be based on Intel or emerging RISC microprocessors. The user interface will be much simpler than today's Macintosh or Windows 95, but it is unclear what it will be. Microsoft's Windows CE for consumer electronics products and Microsoft's SIPC are two candidates. A browser-based operating system is another candidate.

The Network Computer will have price range of $400-$800 and will be focused on Internet, intranet and other network access applications. The processor will range from a third generation Pentium or PowerPC to any other RISC chip. The software user interface will be based on an evolution of today's Internet browser.

The features of the information appliances are the hardest to predict. Today it is unclear what functions will be successful in information appliances, but there are probably a few products that will be established by the turn of the century. It is likely that some of the PDA and NC functions will be implemented as information appliances for the home market--especially Internet and smart communications functions. Other information appliance functions will be in association with existing home devices ranging from TVs and photography equipment to kitchen appliances. Home automation functions such as control and management of heating, air conditioning, pools/spas, security and lighting may also be the target of information appliances.

Figure 4.11: Application Specific PCs in Year 2002			
Capability/Features	PDAs	Network Computers	Information Appliances
Typical Price ($)	200-1,500	400-800	200-600
Form Factor	Phone-Handheld	Notebook-Desktop	Numerous
Styling/Color	Office	Office	Consumer electronics
User Interface	Simple GUI	Browser	Browser-simple GUI
Pointing Device	Yes	Yes	Yes

Figure 4.11: Application Specific PCs in Year 2002			
Capability/Features	PDAs	Network Computers	Information Appliances
Pen Input	Some	No	Some
Speech Input	Some	No	Some
Processor Power (MIPS)	400-800	700-900	400-800
Main Memory Size (MByte)	128-256	256-512	128-256
Multimedia Processor	Some	Some	Some
Java/Interpreter Chip	Some	Yes	Some
Universal Serial Bus	Yes	Yes	Yes
PC Card/PCMCIA Slots	Yes	Some	Some
Hard Disk Drive	Some	Some	Some
CD-ROM Drive	No	Some	Some
Digital Video Disk (DVD)	No	Some	Some
TV/HDTV as Display	No	No	Some
Color Display	Yes	Yes	Yes
Color Inkjet Printer	Some	Some	Some
Multifunction Printer	Some	No	Some
Photo-Realistic Printer	No	No	Some
Scanner	No	No	Some
Internet/Intranet Access	Most	Yes	Some
Phone Modem	Some	Some	Some
Wireless Modem	Some	No	No
Cable Modem	No	Some	Some
ISDN/ADSL Interface	Some	Some	Some
LAN/Network Interface	Some	Some	No

Due to large variations in application specific computers, the characteristics are listed in general terms and few specifics are available. These devices will all have a lot of memory since few will have mass storage devices. If Java or other interpretive languages become popular, some devices--especially NCs--will use interpreter chips to speed up the processing. These devices will also have some peripheral functions and the Universal Serial Bus is the most likely standard for such connections. Some of the application specific PCs will have a built-in color display, but many will use TVs and later high-definition TVs (HDTV) as the display. Most of the application specific PCs will have good communications features to download software and information. Others may have CD-ROMs and later DVDs as software distribution media. Many of the application specific PCs will be focused on vertical markets--both for business and consumer segments.

An example of a vertical information appliance is the photography assistant. Such a product will manage, access, scan, edit and store digital images. It will take images from digital cameras or other digital sources as well as convert analog frames from VCRs or other analog video sources into digital images. A built-in scanner will convert existing pictures to digital form. It will download images from the Internet or receive family photos via email. It will edit, enhance and add special effects to the digital images. The product will also categorize and store the images on different mass storage devices. Compression and decompression hardware will be included to save on storage capacity. This information appliance will be able to retrieve individual images or presentations of images and use displays such as TVs, monitors or projection displays. Initially, a product such as this will probably cost less than $1,000, but with reasonable volume production should reach the $500 price point or less--excluding the mass storage devices.

By 2002 PDAs will either be established or will have disappeared. There will be a spectrum of PDAs. At the low end, dedicated-function PDAs will cost a few hundred dollars and will have functions similar to pocket organizers. At the midrange, PDAs will cost $500-600 and will be primarily communication devices. A typical high-end PDA is shown in Figure 4.12. This product has both communications and computing functions and will cost about $1,000.

2002 Personal Digital Assistant
($1,000)

Display
o Flat, color
o SuperVGA resolution
o Touchscreen

Processor
o Pentium +2
o 256-MByte RAM

Connectivity
o Wireless fax/modem
o ISDN, ADSL or LAN interface
o Infrared local communications

Mass Storage
o 500-MByte hard disk
o 512-MByte Flash memory
o PC cards

Physical Characteristics
o Pocket size
o >1 pound
o 50-hour battery life

User Interface
o Simple GUI/Internet browser
o Writing stylus
o Mini-keyboard

Figure 4.12

There is currently much speculation about TV set-top boxes that would add intelligence to the TV so it can connect to the information superhighway. By year 2002, this vision will have become a reality, but the question is whether this product will be TV or PC based. Both approaches will probably be successful in the marketplace. TVs will add Internet functionality and TV receiver functions will be added to PCs. The TV with Internet features are included in the information appliance segment. The resulting multimedia PC/TV is shown in Figure 4.13.

Its features will be similar to the typical home desktop PC, but with less mass storage capabilities. Hardware and software to handle images, video, speech and music will be included. The key to managing images and video is compression hardware and software. A multimedia processor and MIDI interface will take care of speech and music. A multifunction DVD will be crucial for storing these multimedia objects. The optical disk will play audio CDs, read CD-ROMs and erasable optical disks and will be the main mass storage device. A multifunction color printer for printing images, data and text will be a useful addition.

The TV receiving function will take a few ICs and is easily included at less than $100. After TV programming and Internet access, the applications for this machine are hard to project. Multimedia entertainment will undoubtedly be plentiful. But multimedia education and adult training software will be more important. Software that's the equivalent of an expert in nearly every field such as lawyer, doctor, accountant or financial planner will be common. As is prevalent today, office software will also be heavily used on this home PC. We will also see Hollywood-based entertainment software and this platform will be a movie and TV delivery system.

2002 Multimedia PC/TV
($1,000)

Display
o Color, HDTV-compatible
o Optional projection display
o Video accelerator

Processor
o Pentium Pro +2
o Multimedia processor
o 512-MByte RAM

Connectivity
o Cable TV modem
o TV signal receiver
o ADSL interface
o Internet access

Mass Storage
o Multifunction DVD
o 1-GB hard disk
o PC cards

Printer
o Multifunction color printer

Multimedia I/O
o Text-to-speech
o MIDI interface
o Video I/O
o Digital audio

User Interface
o Windows SIPC and
  Internet browser
o Pointing device
o Cordless keyboard
o Remote controller

Figure 4.13

2002 Virtual Reality PC
($3,000)

Display
o 3D color display system
  (HDTV compatible)
o 3D graphics accelerator

Processor
o Pentium Pro +3
o Virtual reality
  processor
o 1024-MB RAM

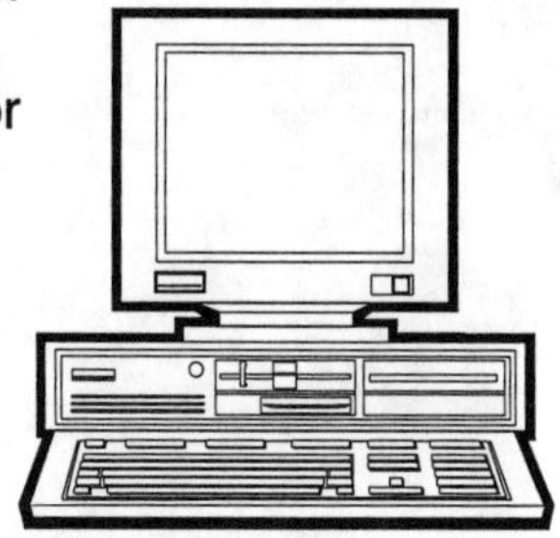

Connectivity
o Fast Ethernet interface
  or cable TV modem
o ADSL interface

Mass Storage
o 5-GB hard disk
o Multifunction DVD

Printer
o Color multifunction
  printer

Input/Output
o 3D input device
o Video camera

User Interface
o Windows 2001
  & Internet browser
o Handwriting pad
o Speech recognition
  (8,000 words)

Figure 4.14

Virtual reality is receiving tremendous attention, but today the technology is primitive--even using high-end workstations. By 2002, technology will advance enough to allow a capable VR-based PC. Figure 4.14 shows the projected features of a PC configured for virtual reality applications. It is a high-end desktop home PC with added 3D graphics and display capabilities. The key is a high-performance co-processor dedicated to virtual reality and related software. The system price is about $3,000. However, a stripped system without printer, LAN interface and hard disk would be priced in the $2,000 range. The most difficult feature to predict is the 3D color display system. Most likely there will also be a helmet or goggle-like device for intense virtual-reality experience. Virtual reality will require a 3D-input device. A 3D trackball may be used (a six degree of freedom device), but gloves and other new devices are likely to emerge.

The applications for this machine are even harder to project. Virtual reality-based multimedia entertainment software will undoubtedly be plentiful. A business version of this product with higher capabilities is also likely to appear that will be used to design all types of products--from buildings and landscaping to cars and planes. But it will also be used to buy a new house in a distant location or to visit an art museum.

Computer Industry Almanac: Further Information

There are many sources of information to follow technology, market and strategy trends. Most of the sources are publications that follows specific technology areas. Here are a few publications that are recommended. A few publications that are very market oriented are included because they add perspectives on where new technologies are going. For additional details, these publications are listed in Chapter 12 of the Computer Industry Almanac.

Publication, Format, Technology Focus
• Andrew Seybold's Outlook, Newsletter, Product and technology trends in the PC industry
• Communications of the ACM, Magazine, Software technology and computer science
• ComputerLetter, Newsletter, Analysis; business and technology trends
• Computer Magazine (IEEE), Magazine, Hardware and software technology; computer architecture
• Dempa Digest, Newsletter, Summary information on Japan's electronics and computer industries
• Envisioneering, Newsletter, PC, multimedia, graphics and electronics technology trends
• Gilder Technology Report, Newsletter, Technology trends, especially the impact of future telecom bandwidth
• Hartsook Letter, Newsletter, Analysis and trends in the Macintosh market
• Microprocessor Report, Newsletter, Microprocessor technology and computer architecture trends
• Mobile Letter, Newsletter, Mobile computing and data communications
• Newsbytes, E-mail/fax, Information and analysis of important new product announcements
• OEM Magazine, Magazine, Technology trends for software and systems integrators
• P.C. Letter, Newsletter, Analysis and opinions on PC industry trends and events
• PC Graphics Report, Newsletter, Graphics technology trends
• Red Herring, Magazine, Financial and investment news on high-tech companies
• Release 1.0, Newsletter, Software technology analysis and trends
• Soft•letter, Newsletter, PC software trends and strategies
• Windows Watcher, Newsletter, Microsoft technology and market trends

Chapter 5

Advertising and Marketing

Advertising and Marketing Rankings and Awards

Adscope: Top 150 Computer Advertisers

Adscope tracks computer print advertising in computer and business magazines. The top 150 advertisers for 1995 are ranked in the next table. These 150 companies spent an estimated $1.26B on print ads in 1995.

Rank	Advertiser	Ads	Pages	Est Exp-$K
1	IBM Corporation	2,984	4,177.8	93,297.0
2	Microsoft Corporation	1,769	3,321.0	69,503.9
3	Compaq Computer Corporation	938	1,770.6	36,668.1
4	Digital Equipment Corporation	1,191	1,838.6	35,920.5
5	Hewlett-Packard	1,210	2,005.0	33,857.0
6	Dell Computer Corporation	867	1,571.7	33,534.9
7	Gateway 2000	520	1,762.4	32,846.1
8	Lotus Development Corporation	591	1,091.1	27,009.5
9	Apple Computer, Inc.	833	1,380.4	26,684.4
10	Novell, Inc.	792	1,416.4	23,342.0
11	Acer America Corp.	519	1,025.4	21,119.4
12	Toshiba America Information Systems	641	760.6	20,194.4
13	NCR Corporation	391	798.5	18,292.8
14	AT&T End User Organization	701	759.3	17,817.4
15	Computer Associates Int'l.,Inc.	941	1,158.8	17,543.6
16	Corel Systems Corp.	952	989.9	15,900.7
17	Sprint Communications Company	456	465.6	15,155.8
18	Hewlett-Packard [Printer/plotter]	667	717.1	14,974.5
19	Dow Jones & Co.	601	194.4	14,801.1
20	Midwest Micro Peripherals	342	906.5	14,018.6
21	Zeos International, Ltd.	319	625.0	13,593.1
22	Micron Electronics, Inc.	401	776.1	13,546.2
23	NEC Technologies, Inc.	423	722.5	13,122.9
24	CDW Computer Centers, Inc.	267	582.5	12,798.7
25	Texas Instruments Personal Productivity	334	416.6	12,765.3
26	Intel Corporation	374	619.6	12,725.2
27	Un Microsystems, Inc.	477	650.2	12,080.2
28	3Com Corporation	475	728.2	11,752.1
29	Ingram Micro, Inc.	804	1,189.6	11,618.7
30	American Power Conversion Corp.	667	722.9	11,442.3
31	Epson America, Inc.	392	598.2	10,982.0
32	Unisys Corporation	358	491.7	10,359.8
33	SAS Institute, Inc.	405	459.9	10,065.2
34	Advanced Micro Devices/AMD	325	605.4	9,845.7
35	Xerox Corporation	327	355.4	9,630.6
36	USA Flex	208	547.0	9,494.9
37	NEC Technologies, Inc.	303	573.4	9,457.4
38	Zenith Data Systems	292	428.9	9,289.6
39	Canon U.S.A., Inc.	406	372.3	9,084.1
40	AST Research, Inc.	269	299.3	8,262.9
41	ALR/Advanced Logic Research, Inc.	434	442.7	7,772.4

Rank	Advertiser	Ads	Pages	Est Exp-$K
42	America Online, Inc.	374	536.4	7,294.3
43	Oracle Corporation [Hq]	466	495.0	7,257.7
44	Tektronix, Inc.	481	532.1	7,249.2
45	Symantec Corporation	368	389.1	7,183.6
46	Sony Corporation Of America	327	641.9	7,110.4
47	NetManage, Inc.	602	467.5	7,020.0
48	Insight Direct, Inc.	191	378.9	6,950.7
49	U.S. Robotics, Inc.	321	469.9	6,742.4
50	Merisel	502	663.1	6,730.5
51	PCs Compleat, Inc.	120	297.0	6,649.4
52	Quantex Microsystems, Inc.	109	435.0	6,516.8
53	Kingston Technology Corp.	309	322.8	6,354.5
54	Adobe Systems, Inc.	453	433.1	6,230.0
55	Motorola Semiconductor Products	360	478.6	6,157.0
56	Motorola	303	357.8	5,802.9
57	NEC Electronics, Inc.	238	393.7	5,729.6
58	Cabletron Systems, Inc.	302	407.2	5,691.1
59	CompuServe Information	520	398.4	5,650.8
60	Sharp Electronics Corporation	257	298.0	5,619.7
61	Texas Instruments-Semiconductor Group	552	626.3	5,619.5
62	IPC Technologies, Inc.	154	226.2	5,605.9
63	SunSoft	289	345.1	5,526.0
64	Intel Corporation/PCED Division	292	321.6	5,517.1
65	Skytel, Inc.	234	179.1	5,417.6
66	AT&T Paradyne Corporation	276	354.5	5,210.1
67	Creative Labs, Inc.	355	435.0	5,169.8
68	Canon Computer Systems, Inc.	130	255.1	5,005.9
69	Bay Networks, Inc.	333	351.5	4,838.1
70	Tech Data Corporation	400	499.8	4,728.5
71	Quarterdeck Corp.	306	295.3	4,714.7
72	ViewSonic Corp.	240	310.5	4,692.5
73	Pinnacle Micro, Inc.	310	314.8	4,676.5
74	Fujitsu America/Computer Prod. Div	144	254.0	4,610.8
75	Silicon Graphics, Inc.	213	279.7	4,595.8
76	EMC Corporation	202	196.1	4,575.3
77	Northern Telecom, Inc.	405	402.9	4,513.7
78	Adaptec, Inc.	281	301.9	4,477.6
79	Prodigy Services Co.	196	363.0	4,472.8
80	Bellsouth Corporation	112	100.4	4,451.7
81	LG Group/LG Semicon	227	301.0	4,431.5
82	Ricoh Corporation	203	185.7	4,395.0
83	3M Company [Hq's]	227	298.1	4,366.9
84	Canon U.S.A., Inc./Printer Div.	152	159.4	4,365.6
85	Conner Peripherals, Inc.	281	294.8	4,271.3
86	Powersoft Corporation	281	307.6	4,270.8
87	GTE Corp.	92	133.2	4,248.4
88	AT&T Network Systems	285	622.2	4,181.1
89	Lexmark International, Inc.	230	221.8	4,128.6
90	APS Technologies	155	292.2	4,085.9
91	Analog Devices, Inc.	318	546.3	3,971.3

Rank	Advertiser	Ads	Pages	Est Exp-$K
92	AMP, Inc.	362	414.2	3,863.9
93	Attachmate Corporation	249	303.0	3,823.3
94	Delrina Technology, Inc.	234	245.7	3,803.3
95	CompUSA	124	146.3	3,802.3
96	Micro Focus, Inc.	211	209.7	3,796.1
97	MCI Communications Corp.	225	169.7	3,778.0
98	First Source International, Inc.	100	165.0	3,776.6
99	Xircom, Inc.	145	205.2	3,746.5
100	Toshiba America/Electronic Component	534	456.5	3,704.7
101	Sybase, Inc.	166	199.8	3,686.6
102	Samsung Electronics America, Inc.	142	233.0	3,674.8
103	Information Builders, Inc.	324	259.5	3,569.4
104	Lambda Electronics, Inc.	265	505.3	3,532.0
105	Informix Software, Inc.	256	254.3	3,439.9
106	Softbank Exposition & Conf. Co.	309	307.3	3,438.9
107	PC Connection, Inc.	63	124.0	3,266.6
108	Megahertz Corporation	203	211.0	3,236.7
109	Okidata Corporation	148	160.1	3,173.7
110	CompuServe/Spry/Internet Division	221	237.6	3,065.4
111	La Cie, Ltd.	131	222.5	3,064.3
112	Walker Richer & Quinn, Inc.	245	272.4	3,038.0
113	Mita Copystar America, Inc.	79	72.9	3,014.2
114	National Semiconductor Corp. [Hq]	333	373.0	3,008.6
115	Hewlett-Packard [Test Equipment]	505	485.4	2,988.8
116	MEI/Micro Center	160	193.0	2,975.1
117	Platinum Technology	221	252.3	2,961.0
118	Creative Computers/PC Mall/Macmal	63	142.0	2,948.4
119	Samsung Information Systems	170	175.5	2,948.3
120	Cybex Corporation	477	220.1	2,939.4
121	Intuit, Inc.	182	174.7	2,924.1
122	Intergraph Corporation	339	352.1	2,917.6
123	Princeton Graphic Systems	130	198.2	2,911.1
124	Associates Mega Sub-System, Inc.	77	122.2	2,883.2
125	Microcom, Inc.	126	143.0	2,873.2
126	EDS/Electronic Data Systems Corp.	234	268.3	2,870.9
127	Western Digital Corporation	188	170.4	2,844.9
128	Centura Software Corporation	138	201.0	2,844.8
129	Caere Corporation	155	137.8	2,811.8
130	Multiple Zones International, Inc.	84	139.0	2,804.8
131	Mag Innovision, Inc.	125	185.2	2,786.0
132	EPS Technologies, Inc.	79	167.3	2,783.7
133	Texas Instruments-Information Tech. Group	122	127.7	2,780.3
134	Hewlett-Packard/Scanner Products	114	122.6	2,778.7
135	Seagate Technology, Inc.	146	166.0	2,762.3
136	Autodesk, Inc.	238	357.9	2,745.3
137	Standard Microsystems Corporation	210	221.6	2,698.7
138	Samsung Semiconductor, Inc.	181	337.2	2,653.1
139	Progress Software Corporation	161	173.4	2,644.8
140	IBM Microelectronics	114	231.0	2,644.5
141	Boxlight Corporation	423	187.5	2,637.4

Rank	Advertiser	Ads	Pages	Est Exp-$K
142	PSInet	245	203.1	2,605.6
143	Panasonic Office Automation	250	230.5	2,594.2
144	Keystone Learning Systems	226	199.8	2,593.8
145	FTP Software, Inc.	258	202.3	2,586.0
146	Diamond Multimedia Systems, Inc.	192	201.0	2,581.2
147	Bell Microproducts, Inc.	146	93.7	2,578.8
148	Cisco Systems, Inc.	146	175.3	2,559.8
149	SGS-Thomson Microelectronics	113	219.6	2,553.1
150	Rockwell International	36	48.9	2,502.0
	Totals	52,487	71,463.5	1,261,068.8

Excerpted with permission from Adscope, April 1996. Copyright © 1996, Adscope, Inc., 1601 Oak Street, Ste. B, Eugene OR 97401 USA.

CreaTECH: Marcom Awards

"The 5th Annual Awards marked the beginning of the Marcom Hall of fame. The first inductee is Steve Hayden of Ogilvy & Mather (formerly Creative Director at Chiat/Day) who created the Macintosh '1984' commercial. 'This is clearly the best high tech commercial ever made--even after 11 years this ad, which showed that technology could liberate, still defines the spirit of the Mac and may also be the defining ad of the New Media society,' said Alan Brody Marcom Awards Program Director.

'The Grand Marquee Award: goes to a category-winning ad that sums up the state of the industry for this Marcom Year. This year it goes to a very daring ad that came from the consumer electronics area that challenged and won the heart of the Marcoms--the 'Techie' category.

'Judges on both coasts resisted this award because it came out of consumer electronics. But they all agreed this was the best ad they saw at the show and they HAD to give them this award.

'The Bright Idea Award: The Bright idea award is an opportunity for us to reward a contestant that has produced an ad or campaign that puts an entirely refreshing spin on the subject. This year, the Bright Idea Award went to Brueckner Interactive for a self promotion floppy disk that proved that interactive is not just about links and jumps, it is about being engaging."--CreaTECH

Corporate Image
Winner: TFA Communications for SPS Payment
Runner-Up: MCCommunications for SPS Payment
Finalist: Novar International
Saatchi & Saatchi for Hewlett-Packard

New Product (Hardware/Software)
Winner: Mobium for Decisionmark
Runner-Up: Miller/Kadanoff for Navisoft
Finalist: Merisel for NEC

New Company Ad, Special Mention
Mobium for TSS

Computers (all platforms)
Winner: FCB/Technology Group for Tandem Computers Inc.
Runner-Up: FCB/Technology Group for Tandem Computers Inc.
Finalist: Ammirati & Puris/Lintas for Compaq Computer Corporation

Software (languages & utilities)
Winner: FCB/Technology Group for Adobe Systems
Runner-Up: FCB/Technology for Cheyenne Software Inc.
Finalist: CF2GS for WRQ

Peripherals
Winner: FCB/Technology Group for Epson America
Runner-Up: FCB/Technology for Epson America

Networking
Winner: MCCommunications for Fujitsu Network Transmission Systems
Runner-Up: Merisel for 3Com
Finalist: Clark & Co. for Microtest Inc.

Òtechie Ad
Winner: RDA International Inc. for Denon Electronics
Runner-Up: Resource for Creative Labs
Finalist: TRW Systems for TRW Integration Group

Business-to-Business
Winner: McCann-Erickson for AT&T
Runner-Up: Saatchi & Saatchi for Hewlett-Packard
Finalist: Mobium for Decisionmark

TV Commercial
Winner: Saatchi & Saatchi for Hewlett-Packard
Runner-Up: Griffin Bacal for Sharp Electronics Corp.
Finalist: Poppe Tyson for Toshiba

Public Relations

Introduction of a New Product
Winner: Schwartz Communications for Wildfire Communications
Runner-Up: Alexander Communications for Rand McNally
Finalist: Gibson Communications for Zenith Data Systems

Press Kit
Winner: Delrina Corporation
Runner-Up: Network Associates for Lexmark International Inc.
Finalist: Chicken Boy Productions for Origin Systems

Press Conference/Event
Winners (Tie): Connors Communications
The Hoffman Agency for Hewlett-Packard Information Storage Group
Runner-Up: The Horn Group for Edify Corporation

Corporate Image
Winner: The Horn Group for PeopleSoft
Runner-Up: Connors Communications for Sega of America
Finalists: MCCommunications for Incite
The Townsend Agency for TriTeal Corporation

Marketing Communications

Integrated Marketing
Winner: Activision
Runner-Up: TV Guide On Screen
Finalists: Miller/Kadanoff for Navisoft
Resource for Apple Computer

Packaging
Winner: SWFTE International Ltd.
Runner-Up: Chicken Boy Productions for Origin Systems
Finalists: Pro CD Inc

Direct Mail
Winner: TFA Communications for R.R. Donnelley & Sons Company
Runner-Up: Miller/Kadanoff for 3Com
Finalists: Mobium for Powers Process Controls
Mobium for TSS
Barry Blau & Partners for IBM
Directech Inc. for Digital Equipment Corp.

Video
Winner: N.W. Ayer & Partners for AT&T
Runner-Up: IBM
Finalist: Hewlett-Packard

International Marketing
Winner: International Data Group
Runner-Up: Miller/Kadanoff for 3Com

Print Collateral
Winner: Greco Etheridge Group for Interactive Week
Runner-Up: Serino Associates for LANart Corporation
Finalists: Greenstone Roberts Advertising, IBM

Low-Budget Categories

Low-Budget Print Ad
Winner: Miller/Kadanoff
Runner-Up: RDA International Inc. for NAD Electronics
Finalist: Greco Etheridge for Interactive Week

Low-Budget Marketing or PR Program
Winner: Miller/Kadanoff
Runner-Up: Mobium for TSS
Finalist: Varitel for ITS Northern California Chapter

Interactive Categories

CD ROM-Based Ad
Winner: Novo Media Group for Toyota Motor Sales
Runner-Up: Macromedia Inc.
Finalist: Mobium for R.R. Donnelley & Sons Company

World Wide Web or Online Ad
Winner: Cuniff Interactive and Fry Multimedia for Van den Bergh Foods
Runner-Up: Doremus Advertising
Finalist: Resource for Burton Snowboards

Floppy-Based Ad
Winner: Brueckner Interactive for Duval Woglom Brueckner
Runner-Up: 2-Lane Media for WarnerActive
Finalist: Media Logic for A&M Records
Enlighten

Interactive Kiosk
Winner: intouch group inc
Runner-Up: Big Hand Productions for Interactive People System
Finalist: Multimedia Resources for Blue Cross Blue Shield of Massachusetts

Demo Disk
Winner: Resource for Eaton IDT
Runner-Up: Spiralock Corporation
Finalist: The HyperMedia Group for Microsoft Corp.

Consumer Electronics Categories

Interactive PR, Special Mentions
Block Interactive
Red Dot Interactive for NBC

Consumer Electronics Print Ad
Winner: RDA International for Denon Electronics
Runner-Up: Thiel Audio
Finalist: RDA International

Consumer Electronics TV Commercial, Special Mention

RDA International for Denon Electronics

Consumer Electronics Integrated Marketing Business-to-Business Campaign
Winner: RDA International for Acclaim Entertainment
Runner-Up: Scott Anderson Group for Microware Systems, Corp.

PR & Marketing Communications Service Firms Directory

A&R Partners Inc. 509 Seaport Court, Port of Redwood City CA 94063 USA; 415/363-0982, Fax: 415/363-1299, Co Email: info@arpartners.com, Focus: PR and marketing communications, Ownership: PVT, Yr Founded: 1989, Empl: 21, Robert Angus, President, Email: bob_angus@arpartners.com; Zelda Rudin, VP, Maria Amundson, Sr Partner, Email: maria_amundson@arpartners.com; Julie Costantino, Media & Res Mgr, Email: julie_constantino@arpartners.com

Abrams Creative Services 4647 Caritina Drive, Tarzana CA 91356 USA; 818/343-6365, Fax: 818/343-6366, Focus: PR and marketing communications, Ownership: PVT, Albert N. Abrams, President

Access Public Relations 101 Howard Street 2nd Floor, San Francisco CA 94105 USA; 415/904-7070, Fax: 415/904-7055, Co Email: @accesspr.com, Focus: PR and marketing communications, Ownership: PVT, Empl: 15, Susan Butenhoff, Principal, Sharon B. Miller, Supervisor

Adcock Group, The 4108 Highland Ave #AA, Manhattan Beach CA 90266 USA; 310/545-9731, Fax: 310/545-5939, Co Email: skiadcock@aol.com, Focus: PR and marketing communications, Ownership: PVT, Sharon Adcock, Principal, Email: ski-adcock@aol.com

Adiant Corp. 54015 Range Road 212, Ardrossan Alberta T8G 2C2 Canada; 403/998-0607, Fax: 403/998-4872, Co Email: 71231.3005@compuserve.com, Focus: IBM mainframe software and related product testing and PR, Ownership: PVT, Yr Founded: 1987, Jon Pearkins, President

* Co. Inc. 100 Independence Mall W, Philadelphia PA 19106 USA; 215/923-9600, Fax: 215/351-4299, Focus: PR and marketing communications, Ownership: PVT, Empl: 70, Al Paul Lefton Jr., President & CEO, Betsy Amoroso, Acct. Exec./PR

Alan Weinkrantz And Co. 3737 Broadway #340, San Antonio TX 78209 USA; 210/820-3070, Fax: 210/820-3080, Co Email: 70610.632@compuserve.com, Focus: PR and marketing communications, Ownership: PVT, Empl: 5, Alan Weinkrantz, President, Email: aweinkrantz@mcimail.com; Barbara Weinkrantz, VP

Alexander Auerbach & Co. Inc. 3887 Dixie Canyon Ave, Sherman Oaks CA 91423-4839 USA; 818/501-4221, 800/871-5263 Fax: 818/501-4211, Co Email: alexauer@ix.netcom.com, Focus: PR and marketing communications, Ownership: PVT, Yr Founded: 1986, Empl: 4, Alexander Auerbach, President, Linda Roberts, Acct Exec

Alexander Communications Inc. 400 Colony Square #980, Atlanta GA 30361 USA; 404/897-2300, Fax: 404/897-2311, Web URL: alexander-pr.com, Focus: PR and marketing communications, Ownership: PVT, Empl: 40, Pam Alexander, President

Alliance Consulting Group Inc. 10250 SW Greenburg Road #213, Portland OR 97223-5461 USA; 503/452-5920, Fax: 503/452-5930, Focus: PR and marketing communications, Ownership: PVT, Lee James, Principal

Allison Thomas Assoc. 5670 Wilshire Blvd #2500, Los Angeles CA 90036 USA; 213/937-2300, Fax: 213/939-7211, Focus: PR and marketing communications, Ownership: PVT, Allison Thomas, Principal

Aspen 3340 Peachtree Road #1800, Atlanta GA 30326 USA; 404/848-7751, 800/731-4940 Fax: 404/848-7752, Co Email: aspennow@aol.com, Focus: Business development for high-tech firms, Ownership: PVT, Empl: 5, Nick Wreden, President, Doug Kilarski, Mkt Analyst, Bill Powell, VP, Bus Strategies

Associated Advertising Agency Inc. 4601 E Douglas, Wichita KS 67218 USA; 316/683-4691, Fax: 316/683-1990, Focus: PR and marketing communications, Ownership: PVT, Empl: 30, Preston Huston, Chairman, Kerry Gray, President

Avalon Marcom 1070 Elsbree Lane, Windsor CA 95492 USA; 707/837-8950, Fax: 707/837-8950, Focus: PR and marketing communications, Ownership: PVT, C.J. Puffer, President, Email: bycjpuffer@aol.com

Barker Campbell & Farley 240 Business Park Drive, Virginia Beach VA 23462 USA; 804/497-4811, Fax: 804/497-4660, Focus: PR and marketing communications, Ownership: PVT, Empl: 45

Baron, McDonald & Wells 6292 Lawrenceville Hwy NW #C, Tucker GA 30084 USA; 770/492-0373, Fax: 770/492-0374, Co Email: bmwpr@bmwpr.com, Web URL: mindspring.com/~bm&w/bmwhome, Focus: PR and marketing strategies, Ownership: PVT, Yr Founded: 1992, Peter Baron, President, Email: pbaron@bmwpr.com; Beverly McDonald, Principal, Email: bmcdonald@bmwpr.com; Terry L. Wells, Principal, Email: twells@bmwpr.com; Sharon Cuppett, VP & Mgng Dir, Email: scuppett@bmwpr.com

Barton-Gilanelli & Assoc. Inc. 51 N Mascher Street, Philadelphia PA 19106 USA; 215/592-8601, Fax: 215/592-0086, Focus: PR and marketing communications, Ownership: PVT

BBDO 170 Maiden Lane, San Francisco CA 94108 USA; 415/274-6200, Fax: 415/291-0715, Focus: PR and marketing communications, Ownership: PVT, Empl: 50, Steve Sanchez, SVP

Bender, Goldman Helper (BG&H), 11500 W. Olympic Blvd #655, Los Angeles CA 90064 USA; 310/473-4147, Fax: 310/478-4727, Focus: PR and marketing communications, Ownership: PVT, Yr Founded: 1986, Empl: 55+, Dean Bender, Partner, Email: d_bender@bgh.com; Larry Goldman, Partner, Email: larry_goldman@bgh.com; Lee Helper, Partner, Email: lee_helper@bgh.com; Shawna Lynch, VP, Home Ent., Email: shawna_lynch@bgh.com; Shawn Blake, VP, TV Div., Email: shawn_blake@bgh.com

Benjamin Group Inc., The (TBGI), 100 Pacifica Ave #480, Irvine CA 92718 USA; 714/753-0755, Fax: 714/753-0844, Co Email: @oc.tbgi.com, Focus: PR and marketing communications, Ownership: PVT, Empl: 6, Sheri Benjamin, Principal, Holly Barnett, VP & GM, Email: hbarnett@oc.tbji.com

Beverly Ristow PR 1031 Daisy Ct, Sunnyvale CA 94086 USA; 408/247-1564, Fax: 408/984-8857, Focus: PR and marketing communications, Ownership: PVT, Beverly Ristow, President

Blanc & Otus 135 Main Street 12th Floor, San Francisco CA 94105 USA; 415/512-0500, Fax: 415/512-0600, Focus: PR and marketing communications, Ownership: PVT, Empl: 13, Maureen Blanc, Partner, Simone Otus, Partner

Bohle Company, The 1999 Avenue of the Stars #550, Los Angeles CA 90067 USA; 310/785-0515, Fax: 310/286-9551, Co Email: @bohle.com, Focus: PR and marketing communications, Ownership: PVT, Empl: 14, Sue Bohle, President, Lee McEnany, VP

Borman Associates 932 South Ave, Westfield NJ 07090 USA; 908/233-8800, Fax: 908/233-5161, Focus: PR and marketing communications, Ownership: PVT, Lisa Borman, President

Boston Communications 376 Boylston Street, Boston MA 02116 USA; 617/247-1112, Fax: 617/247-2272, Focus: PR and marketing communications, Ownership: PVT

Boston Media Consultants 19 Damon Road Sandhills, Scituate MA 02066 USA;

617/545-2696, Fax: 617/545-3464, Co Email: dpallen@tiac.net, Focus: PR and marketing communications, Ownership: PVT, David P. Allen, President, Email: dpallen@tiac.net

Bozell PR 75 Rockefeller Plaza, New York NY 10019-6908 USA; 212/484-7400, Focus: PR and marketing communications, Ownership: PVT

Breakthru Communications 1340 S DeAnza Blvd #205, San Jose CA 95129 USA; 408/252-1734, Co Email: break-thru@breakthrucom.com, Focus: PR and marketing communications, Ownership: PVT, Yr Founded: 1989, Empl: 3, Barbara Kline, President, Email: bkline@break-thrucom.com; Judy Diaz, Sr Assoc, Email: jdiaz@breakthrucom.com; Jim Hammond, Sr Assoc

Bremer Public Relations 307 W 200 South #3005, Salt Lake City UT 84101 USA; 801/364-2030, Fax: 801/364-2037, Focus: Marketing communication services, Ownership: PVT, Yr Founded: 1987, Empl: 10, Alicia Bremer, President, PR Counsel, Melissa Clyne, VP, PR Counsel

Brigham Scully 6351 Owensmouth Ave #101B, Woodland Hills CA 91367 USA; 818/716-9021, Fax: 818/716-9579, Co Email: 74503.2442@compuserve.com, Focus: PR and marketing communications, Yr Founded: 1974, Empl: 4, Tom Brigham, Principal, Leslie Brigham

Britt Productions 1100 Circle 75 Pkwy #650, Atlanta GA 30339 USA; 770/988-9957, Fax: 770/859-9424, Focus: PR and marketing communications, Ownership: PVT, Empl: 4, Terrell Jenkins, President, Pat Jenkins, VP

Brodeur & Partners Inc. 9 Hillside Ave, Waltham MA 02154 USA; 617/622-2869, Fax: 617/622-2828, Co Email: @bro-deur.com, Focus: PR and marketing communications, Ownership: PVT, Empl: 60, John Brodeur, President

Buerger Media & Marketing Inc. 3455 Peachtree Industrial Blvd Bldg 271, Duluth GA 30136-2657 USA; 770/495-7494, Fax: 770/495-7595, Co Email: 73441.1262@compuserve.com, Focus: Strategic PR and marketing consulting and interactive market services, Ownership: PVT, Yr Founded: 1992, Empl: 2, Maggie M. Buerger, President, Email: 73441,1262@compuserve.com; David J. Buerger, EVP, Email: dbuerger@pipe-line.com

Burson-Marstellar 230 Park Ave S, New York NY 10003 USA; 212/614-4000, Fax: 212/598-6944, Focus: PR and marketing communications, Ownership: PVT, Empl: 2,000

Burton Holmes Assoc. 2 Grove Street, New York NY 10014 USA; 212/989-0207, Fax: 212/255-9289, Focus: PR and marketing communications, Ownership: PVT, Burton Holmes, President

Business Communications Co. Inc. 25 Van Zant Street, Norwalk CT 06855-1781 USA; 203/853-4266, Fax: 203/853-0348, Co Email: buscom2@aol.com, Web URL: vyne.com/bcc, Focus: Information and PR on telecom & electronics, Ownership: PVT, Yr Founded: 1971, Empl: 20, Louis Naturman, President, Robert Butler, Dir Ops

Business-to-Business Marketing Communications 900 Ridgefield Drive #330, Raleigh NC 27609 USA; 919/872-8172, Fax: 919/872-8875, Focus: PR and marketing communications, Ownership: PVT

BusinessWire 44 Montgomery Street 39th Floor, San Francisco CA 94104 USA; 800/227-0845 Fax: 415/788-5335, Focus: Distributes press releases to publications, Ownership: PVT, Larry I. Lokey, President & GM, Terry Vitorelo, VP Ops, Michael Lissauer, VP Mktng

Cameron Assoc. 424 Madison Ave 5th Floor, New York NY 10017 USA; 212/644-9560, Fax: 212/644-9817, Focus: PR and marketing communications, Ownership: PVT, Rodney O'Conor, President

Capener Matthews & Walcher 620 C Street 6th Floor, San Diego CA 92101 USA; 619/238-8500, Fax: 619/238-8505, Focus: PR and marketing communications, Ownership: PVT, Empl: 35, Jim Matthews, President & CEO, Julie Ames, Dir PR

Casal Group 14465 Webb Chapel #212, Dallas TX 75234 USA; 214/488-7000, Fax: 214/488-7020, Co Email: casal@onramp.net, Focus: VARs and system integrator information and PR, Ownership: PVT, Yr Founded: 1985, Empl: 35, Gene Bledsoe, Managing Partner, Mark Matthys, Partner, Email: mmat-tys.casal@onramp.net

CF2GS 1008 Western Ave, Seattle WA 98104 USA; 206/223-6464, Fax: 206/223-2765, Focus: PR and marketing communications, Ownership: PVT, Empl: 40, Bill Fritsch, President, Ron Christiansen, Principal

Charlotte Marshall & Associates 1638 Third Street #2, Manhattan Beach CA 90266 USA; 310/379-6104, Fax: 310/376-4776, Co Email: charmarpr@aol.com, Focus: PR and marketing communications, Ownership: PVT, Charlotte Marshall, President

ChipShots Inc. 586 Weddell Drive #4, Sunnyvale CA 94089 USA; 408/541-8744, Fax: 408/541-2185, Focus: Strategic communications and marketing services, Ownership: PVT, Bruce LeBoss, President

Christine Soderbergh PR 15257 Earlham Street, Pacific Palisades CA 90272 USA; 310/394-7763, Fax: 310/459-8835, Focus: PR and marketing communications, Ownership: PVT, Christine Soderbergh, President

Cirrus Technology 49 Migley Lane, Worcester MA 01604 USA; 508/755-5242, Fax: 508/795-1636, Focus: PR and marketing communications, Ownership: PVT, Empl: 5, Shari Worthington, President

Cole Communications 125 University Ave, Palo Alto CA 94301 USA; 415/324-3152, Fax: 415/324-3290, Co Email: cal-isa@aol.com, Focus: PR and marketing communications, Ownership: PVT, Empl: 5, Calisa Cole, President

CoMark Technologies Inc. 12700 Park Central Drive #1605, Dallas TX 75251 USA; 214/233-7091, Fax: 214/233-3672, Co Email: 71344.1761@compuserve.com, Focus: PR and marketing communications, Ownership: PVT, Bill Morris, President, Margaret Mulligan, PR Dir

Communication Collective, The 1420 Lexington Street, Santa Clara CA 95050-5313 USA; 408/261-0797, Fax: 408/261-9972, Focus: PR and marketing communications, Ownership: PVT, Sandie Knott, President

Complete Communications 81 Milano Ct #143, Danville CA 94526-1963 USA; 510/855-9522, Fax: 510/855-9521, Co Email: jtarbini@aol.com, Focus: PR and marketing communications, Ownership: PVT, Yr Founded: 1993, Empl: 6, Judith A. Tarbini, President, Email: jtar-bini@aol.com; Patrice Reed, Exec Assist

Connors Communications 45 Belden Place, San Francisco CA 94104-2808 USA; 415/217-7500, Fax: 415/217-7503, Co Email: webmaster@connors.com, Web URL: connors.com, Focus: PR and marketing communications, Ownership: PVT, Empl: 30, Connie Connors, President, Email: connie@connors.com; Shari Haber, SVP, Email: shari@connors.com; Wendy Handler, VP, Email: wendy@con-nors.com; Dean Kephatt, VP

Consultech Communications Inc. 120 Defreest Drive, Troy NY 12180 USA; 518/283-8444, Fax: 518/283-0830, Focus: PR, marketing communications and direct marketing software, Ownership: PVT, Yr Founded: 1981, Empl: 15, Robert Vogel, President, Jock Elliott, VP

Cooper/Iverson Marketing 8334 Claremont Mesa Blvd #214, San Diego CA 92111 USA; 619/292-7400, Fax: 619/571-2769, Co Email: coopiver@cerf.net, Focus: PR and marketing communications, Ownership: PVT, Yr Founded: 1990, Empl: 10, Doug Cooper, President, Email: doug@coopiver.com; Lorraine Iverson, CEO, Email: lorraine@coopiver.com

Copithorne & Bellows 100 First Street #2600, San Francisco CA 94105-2634 USA; 415/284-5200, Fax: 415/495-3992, Co Email: @sf.cbpr.com, Focus: PR and marketing communications, Ownership: PVT, David Copithorne, Partner, Bill Bellows, Partner

Corporate Communications 2121 Fifth Ave, Seattle WA 98121 USA; 206/728-1778, Fax: 206/728-1106, Focus: PR and marketing communications, Ownership: PVT, Robert Hartlet, Co-president, John Hough, Co-president

Cramblitt & Company 1135 Kildaire Farm Road, Cary NC 27511 USA; 919/481-4599, Fax: 919/481-4639, Co Email: cramco@interpath.com, Focus: PR and marketing communications, Ownership: PVT, Empl: 4, Bob Cramblitt, Chairman

Creamer Dickson Basford 1633 Broadway, New York NY 10019 USA; 212/887-8010, Fax: 212/887-8081, Focus: PR and marketing communications, Ownership: PVT, Empl: 75, Gene Farinelli, Chairman

Crescent Communication 1200 Ashwood Pkwy #400, Atlanta GA 30338 USA; 404/698-8650, Fax: 404/698-8651, Co Email: pmckeon@crescomm.com, Focus: PR and marketing communications, Ownership: PVT, Yr Founded: 1985, Empl: 30, Paul McKeon, President, Email: pmckeon@crescomm.com; Ruth Doering, EVP, Email: rdoering@crescomm.com; Judy Morris, VP, Email: jmorris@crescomm.com

Crowley Communications 880 E Campbell Ave #202, Campbell CA 95008-2341 USA; 408/377-8384, Focus: PR and marketing communications, Ownership: PVT, Pamela Crowley, President

Cunningham Communication Inc. 3945 Freedom Circle 9th Fl, Santa Clara CA 95054 USA; 408/982-0400, Fax: 408/982-0403, Web URL: ccipr.com, Focus: PR and marketing communications, Ownership: PVT, Empl: 90, Andrea Cunningham, President, Ron Ricci, Principal New Bus

D/M Communications Inc. 651 Clapboardtree St, Westwood MA 02090 USA; 617/329-7799, Fax: 617/461-8266, Focus: PR and marketing communications, Ownership: PVT, Empl: 9, Christy May, President, Email: dmchristy@aol.com; Pat Burwell, VP, Ann Wetherbee, Prod Mgr, Barbara Foley, Acct Mgr, Paul Diggin, Acct Exec, Email: dmpaul@aol.com

Daly-Swartz Public Relations 940 Calle Amanecer #H, San Clemente CA 92673 USA; 714/361-6888, Fax: 714/361-6891, Co Email: kzwk88a@prodigy.com, Focus: PR and marketing communications, Ownership: PVT, Empl: 1, Jeffrey Swartz, Principal

Darien & Kilburn Inc. 639 Front Street 4th Floor, San Francisco CA 94111 USA; 415/362-6400, Fax: 415/362-3223, Focus: PR and marketing communications, Ownership: PVT, Empl: 15, Frank Darien III, President, Frank Darien Sr., EVP

daVinci Public Relations 1537 Washington Street, Columbus IN 47201 USA; 812/376-0660, Fax: 812/376-8137, Focus: PR and marketing communications,

Ownership: PVT, John Carlson, President

DDB Needham 200 Crescent Court, Dallas TX 75201 USA; 214/969-9000, Fax: 214/855-2317, Focus: PR and marketing communications, Ownership: PVT

Desmond Towey & Assoc. 515 Madison Ave #1909, New York NY 10022 USA; 212/888-7600, Focus: Investor relations and marketing communications, Ownership: PVT

Doremus Public Relations 200 Varick Street, New York NY 10014 USA; 212/366-3000, Fax: 212/366-3632, Web URL: netresource.com/wsn, Focus: PR and marketing communications, Ownership: PVT, Carl Anderson, President

DRK Inc. 101 Summer Street Church Green, Boston MA 02110 USA; 617/542-5848, Fax: 617/542-5545, Co Email: info@drk.com, Web URL: drk.com, Focus: PR and marketing communications, Ownership: PVT, Empl: 20, David Kasabian, President, Anna Kasabian, VP

Duval Woglom Brueckner Partners Inc. 585 Commercial Street, Boston MA 02109 USA; 617/248-1881, Fax: 617/248-1874, Focus: Advertising, marketing and PR, Ownership: PVT

EasyCom Inc. 1032-61st Street, Downers Grove IL 60516 USA; 630/969-1441, Fax: 630/515-8092, Focus: PR and marketing communications, Ownership: PVT, Ronald D. Solberg, President

EBS Public Relations Inc. 3100 Dundee Road #308, Northbrook IL 60062 USA; 847/714-8600, Fax: 847/714-9001, Co Email: @ebspr.com, Focus: PR and marketing communications, Ownership: PVT, Erica Swedlow, President

Edelman Public Relations 1500 Broadway, New York NY 10036 USA; 212/768-0550, Fax: 212/704-0128, Web URL: edelman.com, Focus: PR and marketing communications, Ownership: PVT, Empl: 170, Richard Edelman, President

Elgin Syferd DDB Needham 1008 Western Ave, Seattle WA 98104 USA; Focus: PR, advertising and marketing communications, Ownership: PVT

Equity Communications 1512 Grand Ave #200, Santa Barbara CA 93103 USA; 805/897-1880, Fax: 805/897-1883, Focus: PR and marketing communications, Ownership: PVT, Ira Weingarten, President

Equity Group Inc.,The 919 Third Ave 18th Fl, New York NY 10022 USA; 212/371-8660, Fax: 212/421-1278, Focus: PR and marketing communications, Ownership: PVT, Robert Goldstein, President, Linda Latman, SVP

Erich Stein Communications 700 E Speer Blvd, Denver CO 80203 USA; 303/722-4343, Fax: 303/722-5353, Co Email: erich.stein@ossinc.net, Focus: PR and marketing communications, Ownership: PVT, Yr Founded: 1988, Empl: 2, Erich

Stein, Principal, Email: erich.stein@oss-inc.net; Nina Pesochinsky, Partner

Farago Advertising 101 Fifth Ave, New York NY 10003 USA; 212/243-0864, Fax: 212/243-1682, Focus: PR and marketing communications, Ownership: PVT, Empl: 25

Faries & Associates 67 Central Ave, Los Gatos CA 95032 USA; 408/354-7308, Fax: 408/395-6670, Focus: PR and marketing communications, Ownership: PVT, Empl: 2, David Faries, Managing Partner

Fi.Comm 200 SW Market Street #1895, Portland OR 97201 USA; 503/221-7407, Fax: 503/221-7402, Focus: PR and financial communications, Ownership: PVT, Heidi A. Flannery, President

Fisher Business Communications Inc. 5 Hutton Centre Drive #120, Santa Ana CA 92707-5754 USA; 714/556-1313, Fax: 714/556-1216, Co Email: info@fbiz.com, Focus: PR and marketing communications, Ownership: PVT, Empl: 15, Robert J. Fisher, President, David Altmeyer, VP Prod, William L. Pritchard, VP PR

FitzGerald Communications Inc. (FGCI), 245 First Street 12th Floor, Cambridge MA 02142 USA; 617/494-9500, Fax: 617/494-1818, Co Email: fitzcomm.com, Web URL: fitzgerald.com, Focus: PR and marketing communications, high technology focused and investor relations, Ownership: PVT, Yr Founded: 1993, Empl: 50, Maura FitzGerald, President, Aline Thibault, VP, Sharon Israel, Act Mgr, Heather Robb, Act Mgr, Candace Fitzgerald, Mktng Dir, Email: cfitzgerald@fitzcomm.com

Fleishman-Hillard Inc. 515 S Flower Street, 7th Floor, Los Angeles CA 90071 USA; 213/629-4974, Fax: 213/623-6495, Focus: PR and marketing communications, Ownership: PVT, Empl: 50, Jerry Epstein, EVP & GM, Lisa Robinson, SVP, Cynthia Coulter, SVP, Doug Dowie, SVP

Floathe Johnson Associates Inc. 190 Queen Anne Ave N #350, Seattle WA 98109 USA; 206/285-6056, Fax: 206/301-4338, Web URL: floathe.com, Focus: PR and marketing communications, Ownership: PVT, Empl: 50, Maury Floathe, President, Chuck Pettis, SVP

Freeman-McCue 3 Hutton Center Drive #960, Santa Ana CA 92707 USA; 714/557-3663, Fax: 714/557-6690, Focus: PR and marketing communications, Ownership: PVT, Douglas Freeman, Partner, Dan McCue, Partner

FS Communications 888 Villa St #410, Mountain View CA 94041 USA; 415/691-1488, Fax: 415/960-0541, Focus: PR and marketing communications, Ownership: PVT, Jeff Feldman, Partner, Matthew Schmidt, Partner

G.R. Good Communications 24014 57th Ave SE, Woodinville WA 98072 USA; 206/486-4446, Fax: 206/485-7001,

Co Email: ggood@halcyon.com, Focus: PR and marketing communications for computer and electronics companies, Ownership: PVT, Empl: 3, Gary Good, President, Joan Parman, VP

GCI Jennings 131 Steuart Street #400, San Francisco CA 94105 USA; 415/974-6200, Fax: 415/974-6226, Co Email: 6304272@mcimail.com, Focus: PR and marketing consulting, Ownership: PVT, Empl: 22, Joseph Jennings, Chairman, Thomas Mattia, President, Gregory Spector, SVP

Geibel Marketing Consulting PO Box 611, Belmont MA 02178-0005 USA; 617/484-8285, Fax: 617/489-3567, Co Email: 74752.3072@compuserve.com, Focus: Software marketing programs, sales support programs and PR services, Ownership: PVT, Jeffrey P. Geibel, Managing Partner

Gilbert Whitney & Johns 110 S Jefferson Road, Whippany NJ 07981 USA; 201/386-1776, Fax: 201/386-0589, Focus: Advertising, PR and marketing, Ownership: PVT

Giles Communications 19 N Moger Ave, Mt. Kisco NY 10549 USA; 914/241-9112, Fax: 914/241-9293, Co Email: @giles.com, Focus: PR and marketing communications, Ownership: PVT, Monica D'Agostino, Grp Mgr, Email: monica@giles.com

Ginger Brewer Associates PO Box 53288, Bellevue WA 98015-3288 USA; 206/455-3351, Fax: 206/454-3481, Focus: Press receptions at trade shows, Ownership: PVT, Empl: 2, Ginger Brewer, President

Golan/Harris Technologies 101 Howard Street 2nd Floor, San Francisco CA 94105-1616 USA; 415/904-7000, Fax: 415/904-7025, Web URL: golanharris.com, Focus: PR and marketing communications, Ownership: PVT, Empl: 60, Gary Thompson, President, Tim Johnson, SVP, Deborah Cromer, SVP

Golin/Harris Communications Inc. 500 N Michigan Ave #200, Chicago IL 60611 USA; 312/836-7100, Fax: 312/836-7170, Focus: PR and marketing communications, Ownership: PVT, Empl: 300, Rich Jernstedt, President & CEO

Grear Group 231 Washington Ave, Palo Alto CA 94301 USA; 415/323-8368, Fax: 415/323-8369, Focus: PR and marketing communications, Ownership: PVT, Paul Gross, President

Green Light Communications (GLC), 366 San Miguel Drive, Newport Beach CA 92660 USA; 714/719-6400, Fax: 714/719-6414, Web URL: grnlt.com, Focus: PR and marketing communications, advertising & online services, Ownership: PVT, Yr Founded: 1993, Empl: 15, Tom Mooers, Pres & GM, Email: tmooers@grnlt.com; Robert Mooers, Ad Dir,

Email: rmooers@grnlt.com; Scott Harlin, PR Dir, Email: sharlin@grnlt.com; John Mooers, VP, Email: jmooers@grnlt.com; Bill Krysick, CFO, Email: bkrysick@grnlt.com

Greenberg Seronick & Partners 855 Boylston Street, Boston MA 02116 USA; 617/267-4949, Fax: 617/267-7322, Web URL: tiac.net/users/gsandp, Focus: PR, new media and marketing communications, Ownership: PVT, Terry O'Leary, President

Greenstone Roberts 1 Huntington Quadrangle, Melville NY 11747 USA; 516/249-3366, Fax: 516/249-7048, Focus: PR and marketing communications, Stock Symbol: GRRI, Barry Rothman, EVP, Nora Bertucci, Acct Supervisor

H.F. Miller Associates 688 Bicknell Road, Los Gatos CA 95030-1644 USA; 408/354-4222, Fax: 408/354-4333, Focus: PR and marketing communications, Ownership: PVT, Empl: 4, Hank Miller, President

Harpell/Martins & Co. 66 Commonwealth Ave, Concord MA 01742 USA; 508/371-1510, Fax: 508/369-7561, Focus: PR and marketing communications, Ownership: PVT, Pat Harpell, President

Hayes Marketing Communications 2055 Gateway Place #260, San Jose CA 95110 USA; 408/453-5357, Fax: 408/453-5342, Co Email: hayesadv@mcimail.com, Focus: PR and marketing communications, Ownership: PVT, Empl: 4, Larry Hayes, President

Hays Communications 1286 Highway 237, Mount Vernon WA 98273 USA; 800/597-3094 Fax: 360/428-3707, Focus: PR and marketing communications, Ownership: PVT, Empl: 3, Carol Hays, President

Henry Russell Bruce PR 401 First Street SE #200, Cedar Rapids IA 52402 USA; 319/298-0242, Fax: 319/298-0243, Focus: PR and marketing communications, Ownership: PVT, Empl: 40, Pete Langmack, President

High Technology Marketing 12 Rosenfeld Ave, Milford MA 01757 USA; 508/478-2392, 800/739-8898 Fax: 508/473-9035, Co Email: joel@htm.com, Focus: PR and marketing communications, Ownership: PVT, Empl: 18, Joel Weinstein, President, Email: joel@htm.com; Gordon Olsen, VP, Email: olsen@htm.com; Email: marcom@htm.com

Hill Communications 123 Ipswich Way, Pleasant Hill CA 94523 USA; 510/945-7910, Fax: 510/934-3126, Focus: PR and marketing communications, Ownership: PVT, Chad Hill, President

Hodskins Simone & Searls Inc. 255 Lytton Ave, Palo Alto CA 94301-1035 USA; 415/327-3434, Fax: 415/327-3438, Web URL: hodskins.com, Focus: PR and marketing communications, Ownership:

PVT, David Hodskins, President

Hoffman Agency, The 10 S 3rd Street 5th Floor, San Jose CA 95113-2503 USA; 408/286-2611, Fax: 408/286-0133, Focus: PR and marketing communications, Ownership: PVT, Yr Founded: 1987, Empl: 26, Lou Hoffman, President, Email: lhoffman@hoffman.com

Holland McAlister PR 9441 LBJ Fwy #513, Dallas TX 75243 USA; 214/669-3456, Fax: 214/669-3223, Co Email: 74240.321@compuserve.com, Focus: PR and marketing communications, Ownership: PVT, Deborah McAlister

Horn Group, The 500 Airport Blvd #345, Burlingame CA 94010 USA; 415/579-6400, Fax: 415/579-3688, Co Email: @horngroup.com, Focus: PR and marketing communications, Ownership: PVT

Howard Blankman Inc. 125 Jericho Tpk #200, Jericho NY 11753-1016 USA; 516/338-8300, Fax: 516/338-5043, Web URL: hblank.com, Focus: PR and marketing communications, Ownership: PVT, Empl: 15, Howard Blankman, President

HWH Public Relations 1414 Avenue of the Americas, New York NY 10019 USA; 212/355-5049, Fax: 212/593-0065, Focus: PR and marketing communications, Ownership: PVT

Imagio 3116 Occidental Ave S #400, Seattle WA 98104 USA; 206/625-0252, Fax: 206/625-0271, Co Email: imagio1@aol.com, Focus: Advertising and PR, Ownership: PVT, Ray Vincenzo, Dir PR

InfoTech PO Box 150, Skyline Drive, Woodstock VT 05091-0150 USA; 802/763-2097, Fax: 802/763-2098, Co Email: infotech@valley.net, Focus: CD-ROM and multimedia software information and PR services, Ownership: PVT, Yr Founded: 1984, Empl: 3, Ted Pine, Principal, Julie B. Schwerin, President

Ingalls, Quinn & Johnson 1 Design Center Place, Boston MA 02110 USA; 617/295-7000, Fax: 617/295-7514, Focus: PR and marketing communications, Ownership: PVT, Empl: 210

Insync Partners 115 NW 1st Ave #300, Portland OR 97209-4023 USA; 503/221-1063, Fax: 503/221-6953, Co Email: @insyncp.com, Focus: PR and marketing communications, Ownership: PVT, Yr Founded: 1985, Empl: 15, Charles F. Humble, Partner, Marta Siemon, Partner, Email: martas@insyncp.com; Juanita Leard, Partner & GM, Shannon Voigt, Partner

InterActive PR Inc. 600 Townsend Street #349E, San Francisco CA 94103 USA; 415/703-0400, Fax: 415/703-0469, Co Email: info@ipri.com, Focus: PR and marketing communications, Ownership: PVT, Marissa Verson, President, Ben F. Harrison, CEO

Irwin Ink 8686 Villa La Jolla Dr #4, La

Jolla CA 92037 USA; 619/483-4333, Fax: 619/483-3444, Focus: PR and marketing communications, Ownership: PVT, David Irwin, CEO, Angela Kilhoffer, President

J2 Marketing Services 505 Mercury Lane, Brea CA 92621 USA; 714/529-2527, Fax: 714/671-1645, Focus: PR and marketing communications, Ownership: PVT, Yr Founded: 1971, Empl: 20, Jim Worthen, President, Paul Paulsen, VP, Lana Perry, Dir PR, Email: 73410,2672@compuserve.com

James Agency PR 3630 Coldwater Canyon Ave, Studio City CA 91604 USA; 818/766-8404, Fax: 818/508-0562, Focus: PR and marketing communications, Ownership: PVT, Empl: 10, Jamie G. James, President

Janal Communications 11 Lakefield Court, Danville CA 94506 USA; 510/648-1961, Fax: 510/648-1779, Co Email: dan@janal.com, Web URL: janal.com, Focus: PR and marketing communications, Ownership: PVT, Empl: 3, Daniel Janal, President

Janice Brown and Assoc. Inc. PO Box 219, Wentworth NH 03282-0219 USA; 603/764-5800, Focus: PR and marketing communications, Ownership: PVT, Empl: 1, Janice L. Brown, President

JC Promotions PO Box 481296, Los Angeles CA 90048 USA; 213/782-0266, Fax: 213/782-0268, Co Email: jcpromo@aol.com, Focus: Marketing communications, Ownership: PVT, Janet Curry

Jesse Walsh Communications 115 E Front Street, Buchanan MI 49107 USA; 616/695-5948, Fax: 616/695-7623, Focus: PR and marketing communications, Ownership: PVT, Jesse Walsh, President

Joan Kelleher Casey PR 174 Bonad Rd, Chestnut Hill MA 02167 USA; 617/325-7209, Focus: PR and marketing communications, Ownership: PVT, Joan Kelleher Casey, President

John Trifari Public Relations 1160 B La Rochelle Terrace, Sunnyvale CA 94089 USA; 408/541-9192, Co Email: trifari@aol.com, Focus: PR and marketing communications, Ownership: PVT, Empl: 3, John Trifari, President

Jordan Tamraz Caruso Advertising Inc. (JTC), 1419 N Wells Street, Chicago IL 60610-1395 USA; 312/951-2000, Fax: 312/951-9827, Focus: Marketing communications, PR and advertisibg services, Ownership: PVT, Yr Founded: 1968, Empl: 100, Charles A. Jordan, Principal, Joseph A. Caruso, Principal, Brian K. Gosizk, VP, Lawrence Stopa, Dir Tech Mktng

JP Davis & Co. 522 SW 5th Ave #1010, Portland OR 97204 USA; 503/226-0624, Fax: 503/226-0653, Co Email: john@jpdavis.com, Web URL: teleport.com/~jpdavis, Focus: PR and marketing communications, Ownership: PVT,

Yr Founded: 1994, Empl: 3, John P. Davis, President, Email: 73302.3552@compuserve.com; Jennifer Turnbell, Assoc., Email: 102030.2027@compuserve.com

Kaminer Group, The 183 Martling Ave, Tarrytown NY 10591-4703 USA; 914/332-4114, Email: dkaminer@aol.com, Focus: PR and marketing communications, Ownership: PVT, David A. Kaminer, President, Email: dkaminer@aol.com

Kane & Associates 2622 Lincoln Ave, Belmont CA 94002 USA; 415/591-2110, Fax: 415/591-9467, Focus: PR and marketing communications, Ownership: PVT, Empl: 3, John Kane, President

Karakas, VanSickle, Ouellette Inc. (KVO), 200 SW Market Street #1400, Portland OR 97201-5741 USA; 503/221-1551, Fax: 503/221-0564, Co Email: @kvo.com, Web URL: kvo.com, Focus: PR and marketing communications, Ownership: PVT, Yr Founded: 1983, Empl: 75, Steve Karakas, Partner, Sharon VanSickle, Partner, Will Anderson, Ryan Wilson

Kaufer Miller Communications 1750 112th Ave NE #D-154, Bellevue WA 98004 USA; 206/450-9965, Fax: 206/450-9963, Co Email: @kmcomm.com, Focus: PR and marketing communications, Ownership: PVT, Empl: 8, Pam Miller, Co-founder, Email: pammilpr@aol.com; David Kaufer, Co-founder, Email: dkaufer@aol.com; John Snyder, VP Investor Relations, Email: jsnyderir@aol.com

Kawalek & Assoc. 525 Market Street 36th Fl, San Francisco CA 94105 USA; 415/296-7744, Fax: 415/296-7766, Web URL: kawalek@aol.com, Focus: Software magazine, PR and marketing communications, Prdts: Software Marketing Journal, Ownership: PVT, Yr Founded: 1987, Empl: 20, Nadine A. Kawalek, President & CEO, Email: nkawalek@well.com; Julie Porter, VP & Consultant, April Davis, Mktng Coord

KCS&A Public Relations 820 Second Ave, New York NY 10017-4504 USA; 212/682-6300, Fax: 212/697-0910, Co Email: kcsa@aol.com, Web URL: kcsa.com, Focus: PR and marketing communications, Ownership: PVT, Empl: 40, Henry Feintuch, Managing Partner

Keiler & Co. 304 Main Street, Farmington CT 06032-2957 USA; 203/677-8821, Fax: 203/676-8164, Focus: PR and marketing communications, Ownership: PVT, Empl: 75, Richard W. Keiler, President, Kenneth L. Donoghue, Dir PR Group

Ketchum Public Relations 55 Union Street, San Francisco CA 94111-1266 USA; 415/984-6100, Fax: 415/982-0505, Focus: PR and marketing communications, Ownership: PVT, Empl: 45, Dianne Snedacker, President, Betsy Gullickson, SVP & GM

Ketner Group 4131 Spicewood Springs

Road #I-2, Austin TX 78759 USA; 512/794-8876, Fax: 512/794-9923, Web URL: ketnergroup.com, Focus: PR and marketing communications, Ownership: PVT, Jeff Ketner, President, Email: jketner@ketnergroup.com

Kleier Communications Inc. 1833 Windsor Place, Louisville KY 40204 USA; 502/456-5191, Fax: 502/458-6169, Focus: PR and marketing communications, Ownership: PVT

KPR Inc. 17057 Chatsworth Street, Granada Hills CA 91344-5845 USA; 818/368-8212, Fax: 818/368-8857, Co Email: dkayekpr@aol.com, Focus: PR and marketing communications, Ownership: PVT, Yr Founded: 1976, Empl: 8, David Kaye, President, Email: dkayekpr@aol.com; Bea Kaye, VP, Email: beakpr@aol.com

KSK Communications 8618 Westwood Center Drive, Vienna VA 22182-2222 USA; 703/734-1880, Fax: 703/821-2756, Focus: PR and marketing communications, Ownership: PVT, Yr Founded: 1983, Empl: 35, Karen Kennedy, President, Chris Plumer, EVP, Steve Mizner, VP Media Dir, Email: 710.0099@mcimail.com; David Hudley, VP Creative Dir, Jenny Morgan, VP PR, Email: 715.0094@mcimail.com

Lages & Associates Inc. 15635 Alton Pkwy #125, Irvine CA 92718 USA; 714/453-8080, Fax: 714/453-8242, Co Email: 76400.2765@compuserve.com, Focus: PR and marketing communications for high technology and interactive entertainment, Ownership: PVT, Yr Founded: 1988, Empl: 7, Beverly Lages, President, Diane Parazin, Acct Dir

LDB 455 Business Center Drive, Horsham PA 19044 USA; 215/957-0300, Fax: 215/672-9373, Focus: PR and marketing communications, Ownership: PVT, Empl: 30, Richard Battista, CEO, Mike Diccicco, President

Lekas Group, The 245 Del Monte Ave #100, Los Altos CA 94022-1206 USA; 415/948-8907, Fax: 415/948-7928, Co Email: lekas@aol.com, Focus: PR and marketing communications, Ownership: PVT, Empl: 8, Joyce Lekas, President

Les Goldberg PR 1570 Brookhollow Drive #200, Santa Ana CA 92705-5428 USA; 714/545-3117, Fax: 714/545-1197, Co Email: rtnh60a@prodigy.com, Focus: PR and marketing communications, Ownership: PVT, Yr Founded: 1985, Empl: 6, Les Goldberg, Principal, Email: 74551.1335@compuserve.com

Leslie Schroeder PR & Marketing 10151 Western Drive, Cupertino CA 95014 USA; 408/446-9158, Fax: 408/257-1478, Co Email: 73510.3271@compuserve.com, Focus: PR and marketing communications, Ownership: PVT, Leslie Schroeder, President

Levin PR & Marketing Inc. 30 Glenn

Street, White Plains NY 10603-3213 USA; 914/993-0900, Fax: 914/993-9589, Co Email: levinpr@aol.com, Focus: PR and marketing communications, Ownership: PVT, Yr Founded: 1984, Empl: 5, Donald Levin, President, Amy Levin, VP, Mary Turk, Acct Exec, Sylvia Moss, Writer

Lindsay PR 151 Buckingham #296, Santa Clara CA 95051 USA; 408/984-7242, Fax: 408/985-9976, Focus: PR and marketing communications, Ownership: PVT, Mary Lindsay, President

Lloyd & Clark 5530 Corbin Ave #323, Tarzana CA 91356 USA; 818/757-0070, Fax: 818/757-0083, Focus: PR and marketing communications, Ownership: PVT, Empl: 9, Michael Lloyd, Principal, Jim Clark, Principal

Loeffler Ketchum Mountjoy PR 2101 Rexford Road #200E, Charlotte NC 28211-3477 USA; 704/364-8969, Fax: 704/364-8470, Focus: PR and marketing communications, Ownership: PVT, Empl: 40, W.G. Loeffler, Chairman, John W. Ketchum, President

Lois Paul & Partners 25 Corporate Drive, PO Box 3182, Burlington MA 01803 USA; 617/238-5700, Fax: 617/238-5999, Co Email: info_east@lpp.com, Focus: PR and marketing communications, Ownership: PVT, Empl: 30, Lois Paul, President

Louis James & Associates 11275 S Rick Circle, S. Jordan UT 84095 USA; 801/553-8669, Fax: 801/553-8579, Web URL: lja@lja.com, Focus: PR and marketing communications, Ownership: PVT, Empl: 7, Louis James, President, Email: lejames@lja.com; Kelly James, VP, Email: kjames@lja.com

Manning Selvage & Lee 79 Madison Ave, New York NY 10016-7880 USA; 212/213-0909, Fax: 212/213-7199, Focus: PR and marketing communications, Ownership: PVT, Empl: 85, Kirk Stewart, CEO

Marcom Strategies 1516 S Bundy Drive #202, Los Angeles CA 90025 USA; 310/820-6629, Fax: 310/820-3158, Focus: PR and marketing communications, Ownership: PVT, Empl: 4, Dan Schlosky, Principal, Email: dschlosky@aol.com

Marcus + Co. 54 Stearns Road, Brookline MA 02146 USA; 617/232-1370, Fax: 617/232-0535, Co Email: lsmarcus@ix.netcom.com, Focus: PR and marketing communications, Ownership: PVT, Yr Founded: 1992, Lynne Marcus, President, Email: lsmarcus@netcom.com

Marken Communications 3375 Scott Blvd #108, Santa Clara CA 95054-3111 USA; 408/986-0100, Fax: 408/986-0162, Co Email: marken@cerfnet.com, Focus: PR and marketing communications, Ownership: PVT, Yr Founded: 1977, Empl: 6, Andy Marken, President, Jeannine Hill, EVP

Marsh-Wetherell Market Relations 121 Arlene Drive, Walnut Creek CA 94595-1730 USA; 510/933-1907, Fax: 510/933-2474, Focus: PR and marketing communications, Ownership: PVT, Barbara Marsh-Wetherell, Principal

Martin Communications 59 Kittredge Terrace, San Francisco CA 94118 USA; 415/668-2678, Fax: 415/668-3041, Co Email: martcom@aol.com, Focus: PR and marketing communications, Ownership: PVT, Yr Founded: 1992, Andrea Martin, President, Susan Trainer, Associate, Email: susanpr1@aol.com; Debra Moses, Associate, Email: d143j@aol.com; Bob Bachrach, Tech Dir

Matrix Communications 5693 N Main Street, Sylvania OH 43560 USA; 419/882-6800, 800/572-0945 Fax: 419/885-2311, Focus: PR and marketing communications, Ownership: PVT, Yr Founded: 1988, Empl: 8, John Hill, President, Email: usgal2hdcp@aol.com

McClenahan Bruer Burrows Communications Inc. 12655 SW Center Street #180, Beaverton OR 97005-1600 USA; 503/643-9035, Fax: 503/643-8072, Focus: PR and marketing communications, Ownership: PVT, Yr Founded: 1993, Empl: 14, Rich Bruer, VP, Email: rich@mcbb.com; Kerry McClenahan, President, Email: kerry@mcbb.com; Charlie Burrows, VP, Email: charlie@mcbb.com

MCCommunications Inc. 8131 LBJ Fwy #275, Dallas TX 75251-1322 USA; 214/480-8383, Fax: 214/669-8447, Web URL: mccom.com, Focus: PR, advertising and marketing communications, Ownership: PVT, Yr Founded: 1986, Empl: 38, Michael Crawford, President, Email: mike_crawford@mccom.com; Kyle Holmes, Dir Bus Dev, Email: kyle_holmes@mccom.com; Bridget Stevens, Dir Acct Svcs, Email: bridget_stevens@mccom.com; Sheridan Stancliff, Pr Rep, Email: sheridan_stancliff@mccom.com

McGrath/Power PR 3945 Freedom Circle #690, Santa Clara CA 95054-1225 USA; 408/727-0351, Fax: 408/727-2695, Focus: PR and marketing communications, Ownership: PVT, Empl: 9, Terri Foos, President, Jonathan Bloom, VP

McKenna Group Inc. 1755 Embarcadero Road, Palo Alto CA 94303 USA; 415/494-2030, Fax: 415/494-8660, Focus: PR and marketing communications, Ownership: PVT, Empl: 100, Regis McKenna, Chairman, Elizabeth Chaney, Managing Partner

McKinney Public Relations 870 Curtis Center, One Independence Square W, Philadelphia PA 19106 USA; 215/922-3945, Fax: 215/922-7353, Focus: PR and marketing communications, Ownership: PVT, David Hammer, GM

McLean Public Relations 901 Mariner's Island Blvd #375, San Mateo CA 94404 USA; 415/513-8800, Fax: 415/513-8810, Co Email: @mcleanpr.com, Focus: PR and marketing communications, Ownership: PVT, Empl: 12, Laurie McLean, President & CEO, Email: laurie_mclean@mcleanpr.co

McLeod Group, The 43 W 24th Street, New York NY 10010 USA; 212/255-2507, Fax: 212/255-4434, Co Email: 73704.2002@compuserve.com, Focus: PR and marketing communications, Ownership: PVT, Empl: 2, Kate McLeod, President

McQuerter Group 5752 Oberlin Drive #106, San Diego CA 92121-1748 USA; 619/450-0030, Fax: 619/450-0967, Focus: PR and marketing communications, Ownership: PVT, Empl: 16, Gregory McQuerter, President, Larry Anderson, EVP

Mesa Communications Inc. 17320 Red Hill Ave #108, Irvine CA 92714-5644 USA; 714/260-3905, Fax: 714/261-5425, Focus: PR and marketing communications, Ownership: PVT, Don Mathias, COO, Email: dwmathias@aol.com

Miller/Shandwick Technologies 4 Copley Pl #605, Boston MA 02116 USA; 617/536-0470, Fax: 617/536-2772, Web URL: millercom.com, Focus: High-tech PR, Ownership: PVT, Peter Snyder, President

MJC Communications PO Box 205, Hales Corners WI 53130-0205 USA; 414/425-6164, Fax: 414/425-6865, Focus: PR and marketing communications, Ownership: PVT

MorseMcFadden Communications Inc. 610 Market Street #100, Kirkland WA 98033 USA; 206/889-0528, Fax: 206/889-0917, Web URL: morsepr.com, Focus: PR and marketing communications, Ownership: PVT, Bob Moore, CEO, Dave McFadden, President

Mullen 36 Essex Street, Wenham MA 01984 USA; 508/468-1155, Fax: 508/468-1133, Web URL: mullen.com, Focus: PR and marketing communications, Ownership: PVT, James X. Mullen, President

MWW/Savitt Inc. 1191 Second Ave #840, Seattle WA 98101 USA; 206/685-8505, Fax: 206/689-8508, Focus: PR and marketing communications, Ownership: PVT

Nathan J. Silverman Co. PR 1830 Sherman Ave #401, Evanston IL 60201 USA; 847/328-4292, Fax: 847/328-4317, Focus: PR and marketing communications, Ownership: PVT, Nat Silverman, President, Email: natsilv@aol.com

Neale-May & Partners Inc. 409 Sherman Ave, Palo Alto CA 94306-1827 USA; 415/328-5555, Fax: 415/328-5016, Focus: PR and marketing communications, Ownership: PVT, Empl: 20, Donovan

Neale-May, President, Dave Murray, SVP
Nelson Henning Group 217 Ada Ave
#55, Mountain View CA 94043 USA;
415/967-2387, Fax: 415/967-2591, Co
Email: 76470.1530@compuserve.com,
Focus: PR and marketing communications,
Ownership: PVT, Diane Nelson, Principal
Network Associates Inc. 80 E 100
North, Provo UT 84606 USA; 801/373-
7888, Fax: 801/373-8680, Co Email:
403.6034@mcimail.com, Web URL:
netassoc.com, Focus: PR and marketing
communications, Ownership: PVT, Yr
Founded: 1991, Empl: 25, Cheryl Snapp,
Founding Partner, Email: cheryls@netas-
soc.com; Neil Myers, Founding Partner,
Email: neilm@netassoc.com; Donald Dug-
gan, Managing Partner, Email:
donaldd@netassoc.com
New Venture Marketing 1100 Alma St,
Menlo Park CA 94025 USA; 415/473-
9990, Fax: 415/473-9999, Focus: PR and
marketing communications, Ownership:
PVT, Empl: 8, Robin D. Stavisky, Manag-
ing Partner, Email: rdsnvm@aol.com
Nickelsen Communications 2560
Ninth Street #315B, Berkeley CA 94710
USA; 510/845-8804, Fax: 510/845-8909,
Co Email: 634.5628@mcimail.com,
Focus: PR and marketing communications,
Ownership: PVT, Myrna Nickelsen, Princi-
pal, Email: mnickelsen@aol.com; Kathleen
Miller, PR Consultant, Email: jan-
edeaux@aol.com
Niehaus/Ryan/Haller 601 Gateway
Blvd #930, S. San Francisco CA 94080-
7009 USA; 415/615-7900, Fax: 415/615-
7901, Co Email: firstname@nrh.com,
Focus: PR and marketing communications,
Ownership: PVT, Empl: 8, Ed Niehaus, Sr
Partner, Email: ed@nrh.com; Bill Ryan, Sr
Partner, Email: bill@nrh.com
Nuffer, Smith, Tucker Inc. 3170 Fourth
Ave 3rd Floor, San Diego CA 92103 USA;
619/296-0605, Fax: 619/296-8530, Co
Email: nst@cts.com, Focus: PR and mar-
keting communications, Ownership: PVT,
Kerry Tucker, President
Oak Ridge Public Relations Inc.
21771 Stevens Creek Blvd, Cupertino CA
95014-1175 USA; 408/253-5042, Fax:
408/253-0936, Web URL: oakridge.com,
Focus: PR and marketing communications,
Ownership: PVT, Empl: 6, Kathy Keenan,
President, Email: kathy@oakridge.com;
Tom Keenan, VP & CFO, Email:
tom@oakridge.com; Jean Stawarz, Email:
jean@oakridge.com; Rachel Modena Bara-
sch, Email: rachel@oakridge.com; Pragati
Grover, Email: pragati@oakridge.com
Opus Marketing 23151 Moulton Pkwy,
Laguna Hills CA 92653 USA; 714/581-
0962, Fax: 714/581-1497, Web URL:
opusmarketing.com, Focus: Staffing, team
building and management consulting,
Ownership: PVT, Robert S. Kreisberg,
President, Email: bob@opusmarket-

ing.com
Pallace Inc. 11931 Tech Road, Silver
Spring MD 20904 USA; 301/622-5100,
Fax: 301/220-3730, Focus: PR and mar-
keting communications, Ownership: PVT,
Empl: 45, Bob Pallace, President
Parker, Nichols & Co. Inc. 72 Junction
Square, Concord MA 01742 USA; 508/
369-2100, Fax: 508/369-2106, Co Email:
327.0114@mcimail.com, Focus: PR and
marketing communications, Ownership:
PVT, Steve Parker, President, Brenda
Nichols, VP, Email: 481.8432@mci-
mail.com
Pat Meier Associates Inc. 123
Townsend #102, San Francisco CA 94107
USA; 415/957-5999, Fax: 415/957-1733,
Co Email: @patmeier.com, Focus: PR and
marketing communications, Ownership:
PVT, Empl: 8, Pat Meier, President,
Email: patmeier@patmeier.com
Peak Public Relations 21710 Stevens
Creek Blvd #220, Cupertino CA 95014
USA; 408/446-0407, Fax: 408/446-0450,
Co Email: peakpr@aol.com, Focus: PR
and marketing communications, Owner-
ship: PVT, Yr Founded: 1983, Empl: 5,
Michael Peak, Principal
Pearson Communications 2700 Augus-
tine Drive #298, Santa Clara CA 95054
USA; 408/496-5885, Fax: 408/496-5881,
Focus: Strategic marketing communica-
tions, Ownership: PVT, Yr Founded:
1988, Resa Quinn Pearson, Principal, Lisa
Schrader, Sales & Mktng Mgr, Email:
schrader@pearson.com
Penna Powers Cutting & Haynes Inc.
(PPCH), 136 S Main Street #600, Salt Lake
City UT 84101-1601 USA; 801/531-0973,
Fax: 801/363-2315, Focus: PR and mar-
keting communications, Ownership: PVT,
Yr Founded: 1989, Empl: 5, Bill Cutting,
VP, Email: ppch@utu.com; Paulette
Brown, Dir PR, Email: ppch@xmis-
sion.com; Dave Smith, Acc Mgr, Email:
ppch@xmission.com; Stephanie Miller,
Account, Email: ppch@xmission.com; Sta-
cie Duce, Assist Acc Mgr, Email:
ppch@xmission.com; Paulette Brown, Dir
PR, Email: ppch@xmission.com
Pepper & Associates Inc. 6900 College
Blvd #650, Overland Park KS 66211 USA;
913/345-8008, Fax: 913/345-1735,
Focus: PR and marketing communications,
Ownership: PVT, John Pepper, President
Pfeiffer Public Relations Inc. (PPR),
600 S Cherry Street #515, Denver CO
80222 USA; 303/393-7044, Fax: 303/
393-7122, Focus: Investor relations and
corporate communications, Ownership:
PVT, Yr Founded: 1982, Empl: 6, Jay Pfe-
iffer, President
Phase Two Strategies 170 Colombus
Ave #300, San Francisco CA 94133 USA;
415/772-8400, Fax: 415/989-8186, Co
Email: @p2pr.com, Focus: PR and marketing communications, Ownership: PVT,

Empl: 20, William Boehlke, Managing
Officer, Email:
william_boehlke@p2pr.com; Christine
Boehlke, Creative Dir, Email:
chris_boehlke@p2pr.com
Pixel Relations 1106 Taylor Street, San
Francisco CA 94108 USA; 415/474-0407,
Fax: 415/474-0477, Co Email: pix-
elpr@aol.com, Focus: PR and marketing
communications, Ownership: PVT, Gina
Rubattino, President
Politis & Associates 9500 S 500 W
#105, Sandy UT 84070-6655 USA; 801/
569-2592, Fax: 801/569-1133, Co Email:
dpolitis@altatech.com, Focus: PR and
marketing communications and advertising,
Ownership: PVT, Yr Founded: 1990,
Empl: 6, David L. Politis, President, Email:
dpolitis@altatech.com
Porter, Le Vay & Rose Inc. 7 Penn
Plaza, New York NY 10001 USA; 212/
564-4700, Fax: 212/244-3075, Focus: PR
and marketing communications, Ownership: PVT, Hal Le Vay, Principal, Michael
J. Porter, President
PR Newswire (PRN), 810 7th Ave 35th
Fl, New York NY 10019-5818 USA; 212/
596-1500, 800/832-5522 Fax: 800/793-
9313, Co Email: prnews@attmail.com,
Web URL: prnewswire.com, Focus: Dis-
tributes press releases to high-tech publica-
tions, Ownership: PVT, Yr Founded:
1954, Empl: 300, Ira Krawitz, VP Mktng,
Email: ikrawitz@prnews.attmail.com;
Susan G. McPherson, Mktng Mgr, Email:
smcphers@prnews.attmail.com; Tom
Beyer, Hi-tech/Fax-on-demand, Email:
tbeyer@prnews.attmail.com; Ian Capps,
President
ProLine Communications Inc. 13
Crescent Road, Livingston NJ 07039 USA;
201/716-9457, Fax: 201/533-0463, Co
Email: 323.9739@mcimail.com, Focus:
PR and marketing communications, Own-
ership: PVT, Bruce Freeman, President
PRx Tech 97 S Second Street #300, San
Jose CA 95113 USA; 408/287-1700, Fax:
408/993-2251, Co Email: prx@aol.com,
Focus: PR and marketing communications,
Ownership: PVT, Empl: 40, Brenna
Bolger, President
Publicin Bloom 304 E 45th Street, New
York NY 10017 USA; 212/370-1313, Fax:
212/984-1695, Focus: PR and marketing
communications, Ownership: PVT, Empl:
110, Robert Bloom, President & CEO
Publicity Plus 8026 E State Road 46,
Nashville IN 47448 USA; 812/988-8600,
Fax: 812/988-9550, Focus: PR and mar-
keting communications, Ownership: PVT
Purdom Public Relations 395 Oyster
Point Blvd #319, S. San Francisco CA
94080 USA; 415/588-5700, Fax: 415/
588-1643, Focus: PR and marketing com-
munications, Ownership: PVT, Empl: 17,
Paul Purdom, President, Ned Purdom, VP
Rainier Co. 206 Worcester Road, PO

Box 134, Princeton MA 01541-0134 USA; 508/464-5302, Fax: 598/464-2968, Co Email: rainier@world.std.com, Focus: Marketing communications, Ownership: PVT

Rankin Group Ltd., The 2119 W Orangewood Ave, Orange CA 92668-1941 USA; 714/937-9100, Fax: 714/937-9111, Co Email: rankin@pacbell.net, Focus: PR and marketing communications, Ownership: PVT, Ernest Rankin, President

Reed, Revell-Pechar 1239 120th NE #G, Bellevue WA 98005 USA; 206/462-4777, Fax: 206/462-4779, Co Email: annrp@rrp.com, Web URL: rrp.com, Focus: PR and marketing communications, Ownership: PVT, Yr Founded: 1991, Empl: 6, Robert Reed, President, Email: breed@rrp.com; Ann Revell-Pechar, VP PR, Email: annrp@rrp.com

Rickey Gold & Assoc. 419 W Briar Pl #B, Chicago IL 60657-4710 USA; 708/486-0920, Fax: 708/486-1413, Focus: PR and marketing communications, Ownership: PVT, Rickey Gold, President

Riedman Communications Inc. 131 East Street, Canandaigua NY 14424 USA; 716/396-3100, Fax: 716/396-5941, Focus: PR and marketing communications, Ownership: PVT, Laurie Riedman, President

Ripley-Woodbury Marketing Communications 11100 Artesia Blvd #B, Cerritos CA 90703 USA; 310/860-7336, Fax: 310/860-6128, Focus: PR and marketing communications, Ownership: PVT, Empl: 15, Mick Woodbury, President, Phil Soreide, VP & Creative Dir, Michael Williams, Acct Exec, Gretchen Loufek, VP Finance

RMR & Associates Inc. 1401 Rockville Pike #510, Rockville MD 20852 USA; 301/217-0009, Fax: 301/217-5966, Web URL: rmr.com, Focus: Advertising, marketing & PR, Ownership: PVT

Robert Wick Public Relations Inc. (RWPR), 305 Madison Ave #3219, New York NY 10165 USA; 212/682-0600, Fax: 212/682-3131, Co Email: 73160.1124@compuserve.com, Focus: PR and marketing communications, Ownership: PVT, Yr Founded: 1982, Empl: 4, Robert Wick, President, Nathan Soule, Acct Supervisor

Roberts, Mealer & Co. Inc. 3 Hutton Centre #700, Santa Ana CA 92707 USA; 714/957-1314, Fax: 714/957-0805, Focus: PR and marketing communications, Ownership: PVT, Jan Johnson, VP PR, Email: 560.2742@mcimail.com

Rocket, Burkhead, Lewis & Winslow 8601 Six Forks Road, PO Box 18189, Raleigh NC 27619-8189 USA; 919/848-5531, Fax: 919/848-2614, Focus: Advertising, marketing and PR, Ownership: PVT

Roeder-Johnson 655 Skyway #130, San Carlos CA 94070 USA; 415/802-1850,

Fax: 415/593-5515, Co Email: firstname@roederj.com, Web URL: roederj.com, Focus: PR and marketing communications, Ownership: PVT, Empl: 2, Abigail R. Johnson, Dir Strat Comm & PR, Email: abigail@roederj.com; Stephen C. Johnson, Dir Exec Svcs, Email: stephen@roederj.com

Rogers Communications 301 Edgewater Place #302, Wakefield MA 01880-6209 USA; 617/224-1100, Fax: 617/224-1239, Focus: PR and marketing communications, Ownership: PVT, Empl: 8, Bruce Rogers, President

Ron Martin & Assoc. Inc. 9 Union Place, Newton NJ 07860 USA; 201/579-3369, Fax: 201/579-0195, Focus: PR and marketing communications, Ownership: PVT, Ron Martin, President

Rourke & Co. 1 Exeter Place, Boston MA 02116-2836 USA; 617/267-0042, Fax: 617/267-1862, Co Email: rourke@applelink.com, Focus: PR and marketing communications, Ownership: PVT, Cathy Smith, President, Anne Wright, Dir Computer Group

Rowland Co., The 1675 Broadway, New York NY 10019 USA; 212/527-8800, Fax: 212/527-8989, Focus: PR and marketing communications, Ownership: PVT, Empl: 100, Mark Wise, CEO

Ruder Finn Inc. 444 N Michigan Ave #1600, Chicago IL 60611-3901 USA; 312/645-4835, Fax: 312/645-4843, Focus: Integrated marketing communication consulting, Ownership: PVT, Empl: 12, Richar Funess, President

Ruder-Finn 301 E 57th St, New York NY 10022 USA; 212/593-6393, Fax: 212/715-1661, Focus: PR and marketing communications, Ownership: PVT, Peter Finn, Principal

S&S Public Relations Inc. 40 Skokie Blvd #200, Northbrook IL 60062 USA; 847/291-1616, Fax: 847/291-1758, Focus: PR and marketing communications, Ownership: PVT, Dianee Schrago, President, Steve Simon, CEO, Lauren Finkelman, VP, Email: 76225.2253@compuserve.com

S.S. Smith & Associates Inc. 8572 Old Stage Road, Waynesville OH 45068-9745 USA; 513/897-0654, Fax: 513/897-0655, Co Email: sssmith@dnaco.com, Focus: PR and marketing communications, Ownership: PVT, Empl: 4, Sally Smith, President

Schraff Group 3158 Redhill Ave #200, Costa Mesa CA 92626 USA; 714/556-6800, Fax: 714/556-1739, Web URL: schraffgroup.com, Focus: PR and marketing communications, Ownership: PVT, Yr Founded: 1976, Bryan Schraff, President, Email: bschraff@schraffgroup.com; Scott Simpson, Dir PR

Searls Group, The 3240 Melody Drive, San Carlos CA 94070 USA; 415/593-5590, Fax: 415/593-6190, Focus: PR and mar-

keting communications, Ownership: PVT, Empl: 4, Doc Searls, Principal

Selz, Seabolt & Associates Inc. 221 N LaSalle, Chicago IL 60601 USA; 312/372-7090, Fax: 312/372-6160, Co Email: info@selz.com, Web URL: selz.com, Focus: PR and marketing communications, Ownership: PVT, Empl: 35, Paul Fullmer, President & CEO

Servoss PR 455 Sherman Street #455, Denver CO 80203 USA; 303/777-6200, Fax: 303/744-7541, Focus: PR and marketing communications, Ownership: PVT, Empl: 9, Marcus E. Servoss, President

Shafer 18200 Von Karman Ave 8th Floor, Irvine CA 92715-1087 USA; 714/553-1177, Fax: 714/553-9446, Focus: PR advertising and marketing communications, Ownership: PVT, Yr Founded: 1982, Empl: 52, Chip Shafer, Chairman, Judy Kahn, VP PR, Andy Getsey, President, Gary Odeyard, VP & GM

Shandwick Technologies 4 Copley Pl #605, Boston MA 02116-6504 USA; 617/536-0470, Fax: 617/536-2772, Web URL: miller.com, Focus: PR, marketing communications and internet relations, Ownership: PVT, Empl: 95, John Miller Jr., Chairman, Andrea Der Boghosian, EVP

Shandwick USA 8400 Normandale Lake Blvd #500, Bloomington MN 55437 USA; 612/832-5000, Fax: 612/831-8241, Web URL: shandwick.com, Focus: PR and marketing communications, Ownership: PVT, Empl: 85, Dennis McGrath, CEO, Chris Malecek, SVP, Email: rcmalecek@shandwick.com; Mary Ellen Amodeo, Acct Supervisor, Email: meamodeo@shandwick.com

Shotwell Public Relations Inc. 2700 Augustine Drive #239, Santa Clara CA 95054 USA; 408/727-4356, Fax: 408/727-4699, Co Email: louieyan@pacbell.net, Focus: PR and marketing communications, Ownership: PVT, Jay Shotwell, President

Simon/McGarry PR 1230 Oakmead Pkwy #318, Sunnyvale CA 94086 USA; 408/746-0911, Fax: 408/746-0915, Co Email: smcgarrypr@aol.com, Focus: PR and marketing communications, Ownership: PVT, Empl: 6, Carol Felton, VP & GM

Single Source Marketing Inc. 2850 Mesa Verde Drive E #G, Costa Mesa CA 92626 USA; 714/545-1338, Fax: 714/545-5371, Focus: PR and marketing communications, Ownership: PVT, Myra J. Manahan, President, Susan LaCilento

Smith & Shows 28 Holbrook Ln, Atherton CA 94027-2037 USA; 415/329-8880, Fax: 415/329-1408, Focus: PR for networking, software development and UNIX vendors, Ownership: PVT, Yr Founded: 1984, Empl: 5, Winnie Shows, President, Email: wshows@aol.com; Heidi Fuller, Dir Acct Svcs, Email: fullerh@aol.com;

Suzanne Xenakis, Acct Mgr, Email: suzan-nex@aol.com; Lisa Hantzsche, Assistant, Email: lhantzsche@aol.com

Smith Masar Johnston 3530 Camino del Rio N #309, San Diego CA 92108 USA; 619/281-8991, Fax: 619/283-1696, Focus: PR and marketing communications, Ownership: PVT

Spindler Organization Inc. 6100 Wilshire Blvd #840, Los Angeles CA 90048 USA; 213/930-0811, Fax: 213/930-1241, Focus: PR and marketing communications, Ownership: PVT, Empl: 20, Paul Spindler, President, Kim Kerscher, SVP

Stackig 7680 Old Springhouse Road, McLean VA 22102-4350 USA; 703/734-3300, Fax: 703/556-0319, Co Email: stackig@digex.com, Focus: PR and marketing communications, Ownership: PVT, Larry Rosenfeld, President, David Pogue, CEO

Stapleton Communications Inc. 1101 San Antonio Road, Mountain View CA 94043 USA; 415/988-9207, Fax: 415/988-9209, Focus: PR and marketing communications, Ownership: PVT, Deborah A. Stapleton, President

Sterling Communications Inc. 100 Century Center Court #420, San Jose CA 95112 USA; 408/441-4100, Fax: 408/441-4101, Co Email: info@sterlingpr.com, Focus: PR and marketing communications, Ownership: PVT, Empl: 12, Marianne O'Connor, President, Email: moc@sterlingpr.com; Paul Forecki, VP, Email: pforecki@sterlingpr.com

Sterling Hager Inc. 2 Lewis Street, Lincoln MA 01773 USA; 617/259-1400, Fax: 617/259-1512, Web URL: sterlinghager.com, Focus: PR and marketing communications, Ownership: PVT, Yr Founded: 1984, Empl: 22, Sterling Hager, President, James Joyal, EVP, Email: jim@sterhag.shore.net; Edward Weller, GM, Tony Greene, VP

Strategic Growth Int'l. Inc. 111 Great Neck Road #606, Great Neck NY 10021 USA; 516/829-7111, Fax: 516/829-8319, Focus: PR and marketing communications, Ownership: PVT, Empl: 10, Richard Cooper, Chairman, Stan Altschuler, President

Strategies, A Marketing Communications Corp. 150 Paularino Ave #140, Costa Mesa CA 92626-3318 USA; 714/957-8880, Fax: 714/957-1373, Co Email: 75443.2120@compuserve.com, Focus: PR and marketing communications, Ownership: PVT, Yr Founded: 1991, Empl: 11, Linda Casas, CEO, Tara Stoutenborough, President, Shay Stockdill, Principal

Stringer Furtado + Shaw 3 Burlington Woods Drive, Burlington MA 01803 USA; 617/272-0444, Fax: 617/245-8498, Co Email: mikestringer@stringerco.com, Focus: PR and marketing communications, Ownership: PVT, Mike Stringer, President

Sutton Communications 13614 Boquita Dr, Del Mar CA 92014 USA; 619/456-1701, Focus: PR and marketing communications, Ownership: PVT, Marsha Sutton, President

Switzer Communications 21 Tamal Vista Blvd #135, Corte Madera CA 94925 USA; 415/945-7070, Fax: 415/945-3235, Co Email: @switz.com, Focus: PR and marketing communications, Ownership: PVT

Technology Solutions 475 Park Ave S 5th Floor, New York NY 10016-6901 USA; 212/696-2000, Fax: 212/696-3733, Co Email: @tsipr.com, Focus: PR and marketing communications, Ownership: PVT, Empl: 20, Brian Cohen, President & CEO, Carol Suchman, EVP, Jennifer Revis, VP

Technopolis Communication 4841 Shenandoah Ave, Los Angeles CA 90056-1062 USA; 310/670-5606, Fax: 310/670-2064, Co Email: teknopolis@aol.com, Focus: PR, marketing communications & marketing services for hardware, software & svcs companies, Ownership: PVT, Steven J. Leon, President

Terpin Group, The 4676 Admiralty Way #520, Marina del Rey CA 90292 USA; 310/821-6100, Fax: 310/577-9646, Co Email: ttg@la.terpin.com, Focus: PR and marketing communications, Ownership: PVT, Empl: 10, Michael J. Terpin, President, Rolland S. Going, EVP, Email: rgoing@la.terpin.com; Tina Wilmott, VP, Email: twilmott@sf.terpin.com

Thomas Public Relations Inc. 775 Park Ave Huntington Atrium, Huntington NY 11743 USA; 516/549-7575, Fax: 516/549-1129, Co Email: 73740.2661@compuserve.com, Focus: PR and marketing communications, Ownership: PVT, Yr Founded: 1992, Empl: 6, Karen Thomas, President & CEO, Email: 310.3946@mci-mail.com; Larry Paul, Bus Mgr

Three Marketeers Advertising Inc. 40 S Market Street 3rd Floor, San Jose CA 95113 USA; 408/293-3233, Fax: 408/293-2433, Co Email: info@3marketeers.com, Web URL: 3marketeers.com, Focus: PR and marketing communications, Ownership: PVT, Empl: 9, Jeff Holmes, CEO/Creative Dir, Email: jeff@3marketeers.com; Liz Raymond, Actg Mgr, Email: liz@3marketeers.com; Greg Campbell, Design Coord, Email: greg@3marketeers.com; Dena DeAngelo, Acct Exec, Email: dena@3marketeers.com

Toms & Assoc. 1565 Emory St, San Jose CA 95126-2018 USA; 408/993-1617, Fax: 408/971-3931, Focus: PR and marketing communications, Ownership: PVT, Beverly Toms, President

TriHouse Group, The 51 Williamsburg Lane, Scituate MA 02066 USA; 617/544-3088, Fax: 617/545-8349, Co Email:

71232.1307@compuserve.com, Focus: Marketing communications, Ownership: PVT, Empl: 5, Kent M. Jackson, President, Email: 71232.1307@compuserve.com; Robert S. Jenkins, SVP, Email: 72642.3360@compuserve.com; J.D. Grinnell, EVP, Email: 72650.1356@compuserve.com

Tsantes & Associates 2480 N First Street #280, San Jose CA 95113-2019 USA; 408/452-8700, Fax: 408/452-8703, Web URL: tsantes.com, Focus: PR and marketing communications, Ownership: PVT, Empl: 7, John Tsantes, President

Ulevich & Orrange Inc. 459 Hamilton Ave #304, Palo Alto CA 94301 USA; 415/329-1590, Fax: 415/329-1542, Focus: PR and marketing communications, Ownership: PVT, Empl: 3, William Orrange, President, Janis Ulevich, VP, Beth Dixon

Upstart Communications 4053 Harland Street #118, Emeryville CA 94608 USA; 510/420-7979, Fax: 510/426-7980, Focus: PR and marketing communications, Ownership: PVT, Empl: 12, Patricia Lund, CEO, Email: plund@upstart.com; Brett Gottlieb, CFO, Email: bgottlieb@upstart.com; Kimberly Fox, Secretary, Email: kfox@upstart.com

Victor Wortman Co., The 305 San Vicente Blvd #110, Santa Monica CA 90402 USA; 310/393-6281, Fax: 310/394-6988, Focus: PR and marketing communications, Ownership: PVT, Victor Wortman, President

Waggener Edstrom 6915 SW Macadam Ave #300, Portland OR 97219 USA; 503/245-0905, Fax: 503/244-7261, Co Email: @wagged.com, Focus: PR and marketing communications, Ownership: PVT, Empl: 67, Melissa Waggener, President, Pam Edstrom, SVP

Walt & Sommerhauser Communications 2700 Augustine Drive #200, Santa Clara CA 95054 USA; 408/496-0900, Fax: 408/496-2978, Focus: PR and marketing communications, Ownership: PVT, Empl: 7, Robert Walt, Principal, Charles Sommerhauser, Principal

Weber Group Inc., The 101 Main Street, Cambridge MA 02142 USA; 617/661-7900, Fax: 617/661-0024, Co Email: lweber@webergrp.com, Web URL: webergroup.com, Focus: PR and marketing communications, Ownership: PVT, Yr Founded: 1987, Empl: 89, Cathy Lugbauer, EVP, Email: clugbauer@webergroup.com; William R. Davies, SVP, Email: bdavies@webergroup.com; Lois Kelly, SVP, Email: lkelly@webergroup.com; Larry Weber, President, Email: lweber@webergroup.com; Laura Antonucci, VP, Email: lantonucci@webergroup.com

Welch Communications 1 University Ave, Los Gatos CA 95030 USA; 408/395-7363, Co Email: welchcom@aol.com,

Focus: PR and marketing communications, Ownership: PVT, Marianne Welch, President

Wellspring Communications 7975 Raytheon Road #340, San Diego CA 92111 USA; 619/279-1611, Fax: 619/279-1613, Focus: High-technology, business-to-business PR and marketing communications, Ownership: PVT, Yr Founded: 1985, Empl: 6, Greg Evans, President, Mike Gerow, PR Dir, Kathleen Evans, CFO

White & Co. 170 Maiden Lane, San Francisco CA 94108 USA; 415/274-8100, Fax: 415/274-8113, Co Email: whiteco@bbdowest.com, Web URL: whiteco.com, Focus: PR, marketing communications and technology consulting, Ownership: PVT, Yr Founded: 1988, Empl: 15, Rene White, Principal, Jay Clark, SVP, Cathy Morley Foster, VP

William Silverman & Co. 1111 Superior Ave E #1700, Cleveland OH 44114-2507 USA; 216/696-7750, Fax: 216/696-8751, Focus: PR and marketing communications, Ownership: PVT, Empl: 25, William Silverman, President

Wilson McHenry Co. 2929 Campus Drive, San Mateo CA 94403 USA; 415/638-3400, Fax: 415/638-3434, Web URL: wmc.com, Focus: PR and marketing communications, Ownership: PVT, Empl: 10, Lerry Wilson, President, Email: lwilson@wmc.com; Julie McHenry, CEO, Email: jmchenry@wmc.com

Windham/Lang Group 240 Cervantes Blvd, San Francisco CA 94123 USA; 415/563-4545, Focus: PR and marketing communications, Ownership: PVT, Laurie Windham, Partner, Email: lwindham@netcom.com; Kathryn Lang, Partner, Email: klang@netcom.com; Wendy Moro, Partner, Email: wmoro@netcom.com; Erica Ziedenberg, Partner, Email: eziedenberg@netcom.com; Jane Steele, Assoc./Res Assist., Email: jdsteele@netcom.com

wolfBayne Communications PO Box 50287, Colorado Springs CO 80949-0287 USA; 719/593-8032, Co Email: kimmik@wolfbayne.com, Web URL: bayne.com/wolfbayne, Focus: PR, marketing communications & Internet marketing, Ownership: PVT, Kim M. Bayne, Pres

Wolfe Axelrod Assoc. 420 Lexington Ave #2635, New York NY 10170 USA; 212/370-4500, Fax: 212/370-4505, Co Email: 76015.440@compuserve.com, Focus: PR and financial communications, Ownership: PVT, Stephen D. Axelrod, Mng Dir, Gordon H. Wolfe, Mng Dir

Wordright Associates 825 E Guenther Street, San Antonio TX 78210-1237 USA; 210/532-2332, Fax: 210/532-2023, Co Email: 71634.34@compuserve.com, Focus: PR and marketing communications, Ownership: PVT, Empl: 2, Susan K. Hughes, President

Young & Associates Inc. 1688 E Gude Drive #301, Rockville MD 20850-5306 USA; 301/309-9404, Fax: 301/309-1804, Focus: PR and marketing communications, Ownership: PVT, Empl: 7, Jean Young, President, Sonya Gabay, VP

Zhivago Marketing Partners 70 Princeton Road, Menlo Park CA 94025 USA; 415/328-6000, Fax: 415/322-9149, Co Email: @zhivago.com, Focus: PR and marketing communications, Ownership: PVT, Empl: 2, Kristin Zhivago, Partner, Email: kristin@zhivago.com; Philip Zhivago, Partner

Chapter 6

Conferences and Trade Shows

Conference Directory

A/E/C SYSTEMS '97
6/17/97 to 6/19/97, Focus: Computer buyers from design and construction industries, Pennsylvania Convention Center, Philadelphia, PA U.S., Sponsor: A/E/C Systems International Inc., 415 Eagleview Blvd, #106, Exton PA 19341 U.S.; 610/458-7070, Fax: 610/458-7171, 800/451-1196, Email: aecsys@ix.netcom .com, Web URL: aecsystems.com, Contact: David Caplin, Atten.: 25,000+, Exhibitors: 450+

A/E/C SYSTEMS Fall '97
11/03/97 to 11/06/97, Focus: Computer buyers from design and construction industries, San Diego, CA U.S., Sponsor: A/E/C Systems International Inc., 415 Eagleview Blvd, #106, Exton PA 19341 U.S.; 610/458-7689, Fax: 610/458-7171, 800/451-1196, Email: aecsys@ix.netcom.com, Web URL: aecsystems.com, Contact: Sharon Price, Exhibitors: 400+

ACM Conference on Communications & Computer Security
4/02/97 to 4/04/97, Focus: Computer and communication security, Zurich, Switzerland, Sponsor: ACM, 1515 Broadway, 17th Floor, New York NY 10036 U.S.; 212/869-7440

ACM Conference on Human Factors & Computing Systems, CHI 97
3/22/97 to 3/27/97, Convention Center, Atlanta, GA U.S., Sponsor: ACM, 1515 Broadway, 17th Floor, New York NY 10036 U.S.; 212/869-7440, Web URL: acm.org/sighci/chi97

ACM Conference on Programming Language Design
6/16/97 to 6/20/97, Focus: Programming language design, Las Vegas, NV U.S., Sponsor: ACM, 1515 Broadway, 17th Floor, New York NY 10036 U.S.; 212/869-7440

AIIM Show and Conference
4/14/97 to 4/17/97, Focus: Document management, Jacob K. Javits Convention Center, New York, NY U.S., Sponsor: Association for Information and Image Management Int'l, 1100 Wayne Ave, #1100, Silver Spring MD 20910 U.S.; 301/587-8202, Fax: 301/588-4838, 800/477-2446, Email: aiim@aiim .org, Web URL: aiim.org, Exhibitors: 350+

ATM Year 1997
6/23/97 to 6/27/97, Focus: ATM technologies, business opportunities and new applications, San Jose, CA U.S., Sponsor: Technology Transfer Institute, 741 10th Street, Santa Monica CA 90402-2899 U.S.; 310/394-8305, Fax: 310/451-2104, 800/200-4884, Email: custserv@tticom.com, Web URL: tticom.com/atm, 2nd Sponsor: Business Communications Review, Atten.: 1,000+

Advanced Speech Applications & Technologies, ASAT
4/14/97 to 4/16/97, Focus: Speech technologies, San Francisco, CA U.S., Sponsor: Advanstar Expositions, 7500 Old Oak Blvd, Cleveland OH 44130 U.S.; 216/826-2806, 800/777-4442, Email: expos@advanstar-expos.com, Web URL: advanstar-expos.com, 2nd Sponsor: AT&T

Agenda 98
10/19/97 to 10/21/97, Focus: PC industry direction, Scottsdale, AZ U.S., Sponsor: InfoWorld Conference & Media Group, 155 Bovet Road, #800, San Mateo CA 94402 U.S.; 415/572-7341, Fax: 415/286-2750, 800/633-4312, Web URL: conferences.infoworld.com

Asia and South Pacific Design Automation Conference, ASP-DAC
1/28/97 to 1/31/97, Focus: Design automation, International Conference Hall, Makuhari, Japan, Sponsor: ACM, 1515 Broadway, 17th Floor, New York NY 10036 U.S.; 212/869-7440, 2nd Sponsor: IPSJ

Association of Color Thermal Transfer Tech. Technical Conf.
1/12/97 to 1/15/97, Focus: Color thermal transfer technology, Loews Ventana Canyon Resort, Tucson, AZ U.S., Sponsor: Association of Color Thermal Transfer Technology, 310 Commerce Drive, #228, Amherst NY 14228-2396 U.S.; 716/691-5817, Fax: 716/691-3395, Contact: Rick W. Wallace

Business OnLine '97
4/22/97 to 4/24/97, Focus: Electronic commerce, Paris, France, Sponsor: Giga Information Group, 1 Longwater Circle, Norwell MA 02061-1620 U.S.; 617/982-9500, Fax: 617/982-1724, 800/874-9980, Email: conferences@gigaweb .com, Web URL: gigaweb .com, 2nd Sponsor: Arthur D. Little

Business OnLine '97
6/24/97 to 6/26/97, Focus: Electronic commerce, Sheraton Palace Hotel, San Francisco, CA U.S., Sponsor: Giga Information Group, 1 Longwater Circle, Norwell MA 02061-1620 U.S.; 617/982-9500, Fax: 617/982-1724, 800/874-9980, Email: conferences@gigaweb .com, Web URL: gigaweb.com/businessonline, 2nd Sponsor: Oracle

Business Online Conference
12/03/96 to 12/04/96, Focus: Executive guide to Internet and Intranet strategy, San Diego, CA U.S., Sponsor: Digital Consulting Inc., 204 Andover Street, Andover MA 01810 U.S.; 508/470-3880, Fax: 508/470-0526, 800/324-3976, Email: dciconf1@aol.com, Web URL: dciexpo.com

Business Online Conference

4/01/97 to 4/03/97, Focus: Executive guide to Internet and Intranet strategy, Orlando, FL U.S., Sponsor: Digital Consulting Inc., 204 Andover Street, Andover MA 01810 U.S.; 508/470-3880, Fax: 508/470-0526, 800/324-3976, Email: dciconf1@aol.com, Web URL: dciexpo.com

Business Process & Workflow '97
3/02/97 to 3/05/97, Focus: Technology and management, Walt Disney World Dolphin, Orland, FL U.S., Sponsor: Giga Information Group, 1 Longwater Circle, Norwell MA 02061-1620 U.S.; 617/982-9500, Fax: 617/982-1724, 800/874-9980, Email: conferences@gigaweb.com, Web URL: gigaweb.com, Contact: Martha Popoloski, 2nd Sponsor: XSoft

CES Habitech '97
6/24/97 to 6/26/97, Focus: Consumer electronics and home automation, Dallas, TX U.S., Sponsor: Consumer Electronics Shows, 2500 Wilson Blvd, Arlington VA 22201-3834 U.S.; 703/907-7600, Fax: 703/907-7601, Email: zoogang@ix.net-com.com, Web URL: eia.org/ceg, Contact: Cynthia Upson, 2nd Sponsor: Electronics Industries Assoc.

CES Mobile Electronics '97
4/04/97 to 4/06/97, Focus: Mobile electronics products, Atlanta, GA U.S., Sponsor: Electronic Industries Assoc., 2500 Wilson Blvd, Arlington VA 22201-3834 U.S.; 703/907-7600, Fax: 703/907-7601, Email: zoogang@ix.netcom.com, Web URL: eia.org/ceg, Contact: Cynthia Upson, Atten.: 5,000+

CES Spring, CES
6/02/97 to 6/05/97, Focus: Consumer products, Atlanta, GA U.S., Sponsor: Consumer Electronics Manufacturers Association, 2500 Wilson Blvd, Arlington VA 22201-3834 U.S.; 703/907-7674, Fax: 703/907-7690, Contact: Cynthia Upson

Comdex/Argentina '97
5/20/97 to 5/23/97, Focus: PC and LAN products, Predio Ferial de Palermo, Buenos Aires, Argentina, Sponsor: Softbank Expos, 300 First Ave, Needham MA 02194-2722 U.S.; 617/449-6600, Fax: 617/449-6953, Email: info@sbexpos.com, Web URL: sbexpos.com

Comdex/Asia at Singapore Informatics
10/07/97 to 10/09/97, Focus: PC and LAN products, Singapore International Convention & Expo, Singapore, Sponsor: Softbank Expos, 300 First Ave, Needham MA 02194-2722 U.S.; 617/449-6600, Fax: 617/449-6953, Email: info@sbex-pos.com, Web URL: sbexpos.com

Comdex/Canada '97
7/09/97 to 7/11/97, Focus: PC and LAN products, Metro Toronto Convention Ctr

& SkyDome, Toronto, Canada, Sponsor: Softbank Expos, 300 First Ave, Needham MA 02194-2722 U.S.; 617/449-6600, Fax: 617/449-6953, Email: info@sbex-pos.com, Web URL: sbexpos.com, Contact: Cheryl Delgreco

Comdex/China
2/25/97 to 3/01/97, Focus: PC and LAN products, China International Exhibition Centre, Beijing, China, Sponsor: Softbank Expos, 300 First Ave, Needham MA 02194-2722 U.S.; 617/449-6600, Fax: 617/449-6953, Email: info@sbex-pos.com, Web URL: sbexpos.com

Comdex/ComExpo Mexico '97
2/25/97 to 2/28/97, Focus: PC and LAN products, Sports Palace, Mexico City, Mexico, Sponsor: Softbank Expos, 300 First Ave, Needham MA 02194-2722 U.S.; 617/449-6600, Fax: 617/449-6953, Email: info@sbexpos.com, Web URL: sbexpos.com, Contact: Kim Pappas, Atten.: 60,000+, Exhibitors: 325+

Comdex/Consumer Expo
12/06/96 to 12/15/96, Focus: PC and LAN products, Parque Anhembi, Sao Paulo, Brazil, Sponsor: Softbank Expos, 300 First Ave, Needham MA 02194-2722 U.S.; 617/449-6600, Fax: 617/449-6953, Email: info@sbexpos.com, Web URL: sbexpos.com

Comdex/Espanol '96
12/04/96 to 12/07/96, Focus: PC and LAN products, Miami Beach Convention Center, Miami Beach, FL U.S., Sponsor: Softbank Expos, 300 First Ave, Needham MA 02194-2722 U.S.; 617/449-6600, Fax: 617/449-6953, Email: info@sbex-pos.com, Web URL: sbexpos.com

Comdex/Espanol '97
12/09/97 to 12/11/97, Focus: PC and LAN products, Miami Beach Convention Center, Miami Beach, FL U.S., Sponsor: Softbank Expos, 300 First Ave, Needham MA 02194-2722 U.S.; 617/449-6600, Fax: 617/449-6953, Email: info@sbex-pos.com, Web URL: sbexpos.com

Comdex/Fall '96
11/18/96 to 11/22/96, Focus: PC and LAN products, Las Vegas Convention Center, Las Vegas, NV U.S., Sponsor: Softbank Expos, 300 First Ave, Needham MA 02194-2722 U.S.; 617/449-6600, Fax: 617/449-6953, Email: info@sbex-pos.com, Web URL: sbexpos.com, Contact: Kim Pappas, Atten.: 210,000+, Exhibitors: 2,100+

Comdex/Fall '97
11/17/97 to 11/21/97, Focus: PC and LAN products, Las Vegas Convention Center, Las Vegas, NV U.S., Sponsor: Softbank Expos, 300 First Ave, Needham MA 02194-2722 U.S.; 617/449-6600, Fax: 617/449-6953, Email: info@sbex-pos.com, Web URL: sbexpos.com

Comdex/IT Forum France
2/03/97 to 2/07/97, Focus: PC and LAN

products, Parc des Expositions, Paris, France, Sponsor: Softbank Expos, 300 First Ave, Needham MA 02194-2722 U.S.; 617/449-6600, Fax: 617/449-6953, Email: info@sbexpos.com, Web URL: sbexpos.com

Comdex/IT India
12/04/96 to 12/07/96, Focus: PC and LAN products, Pragati Maidan, New Delhi, India, Sponsor: Softbank Expos, 300 First Ave, Needham MA 02194-2722 U.S.; 617/449-6600, Fax: 617/449-6953, Email: info@sbexpos.com, Web URL: sbexpos.com

Comdex/Japan
4/08/97 to 4/11/97, Focus: PC and LAN products, Nippon Convention Center, Tokyo, Japan, Sponsor: Softbank Expos, 300 First Ave, Needham MA 02194-2722 U.S.; 617/449-6600, Fax: 617/449-6953, Email: info@sbexpos.com, Web URL: sbexpos.com

Comdex/Korea
8/26/97 to 8/30/97, Focus: PC and LAN products, Korea Exhibition Center, Seoul, Korea, Sponsor: Softbank Expos, 300 First Ave, Needham MA 02194-2722 U.S.; 617/449-6600, Fax: 617/449-6953, Email: info@sbexpos.com, Web URL: sbexpos.com

Comdex/PacRim '97
1/21/97 to 1/23/97, Focus: PC and LAN products, Trade & Convention Center, Vancouver, BC, Canada, Sponsor: Softbank Expos, 300 First Ave, Needham MA 02194-2722 U.S.; 617/449-6600, Fax: 617/449-6953, Email: info@sbex-pos.com, Web URL: sbexpos.com, Atten.: 35,000+, Exhibitors: 300+

Comdex/Quebec SCIB '97
10/07/97 to 10/09/97, Focus: PC and LAN products, Palais des Congres, Montreal, Quebec, Sponsor: Softbank Expos, 300 First Ave, Needham MA 02194-2722 U.S.; 617/449-6600, Fax: 617/449-6953, Email: info@sbexpos.com, Web URL: sbexpos.com, Contact: Kim Pappas, Atten.: 20,000+, Exhibitors: 150+

Comdex/Spring '97
6/02/97 to 6/05/97, Focus: PC and LAN products, Georgia World Congress Center, Atlanta, GA U.S., Sponsor: Softbank Expos, 300 First Ave, Needham MA 02194-2722 U.S.; 617/449-6600, Fax: 617/449-6953, Email: info@sbex-pos.com, Web URL: sbexpos.com, Contact: Amy McNamara, Atten.: 100,000+, Exhibitors: 1,100+

Comdex/Sucesu Rio '97
4/08/97 to 4/13/97, Focus: PC and LAN products, Rio Centro, Rio de Janeiro, Brazil, Sponsor: Softbank Expos, 300 First Ave, Needham MA 02194-2722 U.S.; 617/449-6600, Fax: 617/449-6953, Email: info@sbexpos.com, Web URL: sbexpos.com, Contact: Kim Pappas, Atten.: 75,000+, Exhibitors: 275+

Comdex/Sucesu-SP Brazil '97
8/18/97 to 8/22/97, Focus: PC and LAN products, Parque Anhembi, Sao Paulo, Brazil, Sponsor: Softbank Expos, 300 First Ave, Needham MA 02194-2722 U.S.; 617/449-6600, Fax: 617/449-6953, Email: info@sbexpos.com, Web URL: sbexpos.com

Comdex/UK '97
4/22/97 to 4/25/97, Focus: PC and LAN products, Earls Court 2 Exhibition Centre, London, England, Sponsor: Softbank Expos, 300 First Ave, Needham MA 02194-2722 U.S.; 617/449-6600, Fax: 617/449-6953, Email: info@sbex-pos.com, Web URL: sbexpos.com, Contact: Kim Pappas, Atten.: 50,000+, Exhibitors: 250+

CeBIT '97
3/13/97 to 3/19/97, Focus: Computer technology trends and products, Hannover Fairgrounds, Hannover, Germany, Sponsor: Hannover Fairs U.S. Inc., 103 Carnegie Center, Princeton NJ 08540 U.S.; 609/987-1202, Fax: 609/987-0092, Contact: Mette Fisker Petersen, Atten.: 600,000, Exhibitors: 6,507

Christmas Computer Show & Christmas Computer Entertainment
11/28/96 to 12/01/96, Focus: PCs, accessories etc., London, England, Sponsor: IDG World Expos, 111 Speen St., Box 9107, Framingham MA 01701-9107 U.S.; 508/879-6700, Fax: 508/872-8237, 800/225-4698, Web URL: idg.com

Client/Server Application Packages
12/10/96 to 12/12/96, Focus: Client/server applications, Navy Pier, Chicago, IL U.S., Sponsor: Digital Consulting Inc., 204 Andover Street, Andover MA 01810 U.S.; 508/470-3880, Fax: 508/470-0526, 800/324-3976, Email: dciconf@aol.com, Web URL: dciexpo.com

Client/Server Application Packages
3/25/97 to 3/27/97, Focus: Client/server applications, Phoenix, AZ U.S., Sponsor: Digital Consulting Inc., 204 Andover Street, Andover MA 01810 U.S.; 508/470-3880, Fax: 508/470-0526, 800/324-3976, Email: dciconf@aol.com, Web URL: dciexpo.com

Client/Server Application Packages
4/15/97 to 4/17/97, Focus: Client/server applications, Toronto, Canada, Sponsor: Digital Consulting Inc., 204 Andover Street, Andover MA 01810 U.S.; 508/470-3880, Fax: 508/470-0526, 800/324-3976, Email: dciconf@aol.com, Web URL: dciexpo.com

ComNet '97
2/03/97 to 2/06/97, Focus: Voice, data and telecom technologies and trends, Convention Center, Washington, DC U.S., Sponsor: MHA Event Management, 1400 Providence Hwy, PO Box 9103, Norwood MA 02062 U.S.; 617/440-0366, Fax: 617/440-0359, 800/315-1133, Email:

webmaster@mha.com, Web URL: mha
.com/comnet, Atten.: 35,000, Exhibitors:
450

Commerce on the Internet

1/27/97 to 1/29/97, Focus: Security,
Web sites, customizing software for the
Internet, San Diego, CA U.S., Sponsor:
National Computer Security Association,
10 S Courthouse Ave, Carlisle PA 17013
U.S.; 717/258-1816, Fax: 717/243-8642,
Email: conferences@ncsa.com, Web URL:
ncsa.com

Communication Design Engineering Conference

3/24/97 to 3/26/97, Focus: Designing the
latest telecommunications & data commu-
nications systems, Washington Convention
Center, Washington, DC U.S., Sponsor:
Miller Freeman Inc., 600 Harrison Street,
San Francisco CA 94107 U.S.; 415/905-
2354, Fax: 415/905-2220, 800/441-8826,
Web URL: mfi.com, Contact: Natasha
Claro, 2nd Sponsor: Communication Sys-
tem Design

Compuexpo

10/15/97 to 10/20/97, Bogota, Colombia, Sponsor: IDG World Expos, 111 Speen
St., Box 9107, Framingham MA 01701-
9107 U.S.; 508/879-6700, Fax: 508/872-
8237, 800/225-4698, Web URL: idg.com

Computer Games Developers' Conference, CGDC

4/26/97 to 4/29/97, Focus: Game devel-
opment, Santa Clara Convention Center,
Santa Clara, CA U.S., Sponsor: Miller
Freeman Inc., 600 Harrison Street, San
Francisco CA 94107 U.S.; 415/905-2354,
Fax: 415/905-2220, 800/441-8826, Web
URL: mfi.com

Computer Personnel Research Conference

4/03/97 to 4/05/97, San Francisco, CA
U.S., Sponsor: ACM, 1515 Broadway,
17th Floor, New York NY 10036 U.S.;
212/869-7440, Web URL: acm.org/
sigcpr/cigcpr97

Computer Security Applications Conference

12/09/96 to 12/13/96, Focus: Computer
security, San Diego Hyatt Islandia, San
Diego, CA U.S., Sponsor: National Computer Security Association, 10 S Courthouse Ave, Carlisle PA 17013 U.S.; 717/
258-1816, Fax: 717/243-8642, Email:
conferences@ncsa.com, Web URL:
ncsa.com, 2nd Sponsor: Applied Computer
Security Associates

Computer Training & Support Conference

9/14/97 to 9/16/97, Focus: Tools and
technologies for computer training and support, Opryland, Nashville, TN U.S., Sponsor: Softbank Expos, 10 Presidents
Landing, Medford MA 02155 U.S.; 617/
393-3344, Fax: 616/393-3322, 800/348-
7246, Email: info@sbexpos.com, Web
URL: sbexpos.com, Atten.: 4,500+,

Exhibitors: 160

ComputerMania-Denver, CO

12/06/96 to 12/08/96, Focus: Entertainment, educational and home office products, Denver Convention Center, Denver,
CO U.S., Sponsor: Softbank Expos, 303
Vintage Park Drive, Foster City CA 94404
U.S.; 415/578-6900, Fax: 415/525-0194,
800/472-3976, Email: info@sbex-
pos.com, Web URL: sbexpos.com

Computers, Freedom & Privacy '97

3/11/97 to 3/14/97, SF Airport Hyatt
Regency, San Franicsco, CA U.S., Sponsor:
ACM, 1515 Broadway, 17th Floor, New
York NY 10036 U.S.; 212/869-7440

Computerworld Expo China

9/08/97 to 9/12/97, Focus: Client/
server computing, Beijing, China, Sponsor: IDG World Expos, 111 Speen St., Box
9107, Framingham MA 01701-9107 U.S.;
508/879-6700, Fax: 508/872-8237, 800/
225-4698, Web URL: idg.com

Computerworld Expo New Zealand

3/18/97 to 3/20/97, Focus: Client/
server computing, Auckland, New
Zealand, Sponsor: IDG World Expos, 111
Speen St., Box 9107, Framingham MA
01701-9107 U.S.; 508/879-6700, Fax:
508/872-8237, 800/225-4698, Web
URL: idg.com

Computerworld Expo South China

6/16/97 to 6/19/97, Focus: Client/
server computing, Guangdong, China,
Sponsor: IDG World Expos, 111 Speen St.,
Box 9107, Framingham MA 01701-9107
U.S.; 508/879-6700, Fax: 508/872-8237,
800/225-4698, Web URL: idg.com

Computerworld Expo Vietnam

3/06/97 to 3/10/97, Focus: Client/
server computing, Ho Chi Minh City, Vietnam, Sponsor: IDG World Expos, 111
Speen St., Box 9107, Framingham MA
01701-9107 U.S.; 508/879-6700, Fax:
508/872-8237, 800/225-4698, Web
URL: idg.com

Conference on Information, Communications & Signal Processing, ICICS'97

9/09/97 to 9/12/97, Singapore, Sponsor:
IEEE, 1730 Massachusetts Ave NW, Wash-
ington DC 20036 U.S.; 202/371-0101,
Web URL: computer.org,

Coninfo

5/13/97 to 5/16/97, Focus: Computer &
IT, Santa Catarina, Brazil, Sponsor: Fenasoft, 3250 Mary St., #205, Miami FL
33133 U.S.; 305/446-3041, Fax: 305/
446-3815, Web URL: fenasoft.com.br

Consumer Online Services Conference

3/03/97 to 3/05/97, Focus: Online products, technologies and trends, New York,
NY U.S., Sponsor: Jupiter Communications, 627 Broadway, New York NY 10012
U.S.; 212/780-6060, Fax: 212/780-6075,
800/488-4345, Email: jupiter@jup.com,
Web URL: jup.com, Contact: Harry Lar-

son

DB/Expo East

12/02/96 to 12/06/96, Focus: Database,
client/server and data warehousing technologies, Jacob K. Javits Convention Center, New York, NY U.S., Sponsor:
Blenheim Group, Ft. Lee Executive Park, 1
Executive Drive, Ft. Lee NJ 07024 U.S.;
201/346-1400, Fax: 201/346-1532, 800/
829-3976, Email: ascully@blenheim.com,
Web URL: shownet.com, Contact: Annie
Scully, Exhibitors: 400+

DB/Expo West

5/13/97 to 5/15/96, Focus: Database, cli-
ent/server and data warehousing technologies, Moscone Center, San Francisco, CA
U.S., Sponsor: Blenheim Group, Ft. Lee
Executive Park, 1 Executive Drive, Ft. Lee
NJ 07024 U.S.; 201/346-1400, Fax: 201/
346-1532, 800/829-3976, Email:
mhavilan@blenheim.com, Web URL:
shownet.com, Contact: Mark Haviland,
Exhibitors: 200+

DRTV Expo & Conference

4/29/97 to 5/01/97, Focus: Direct
response television, Long Beach Convention Center, Long Beach, CA U.S., Sponsor: Advanstar Expositions, 7500 Old Oak
Blvd, Cleveland OH 44130 U.S.; 216/826-
2806, Fax: 216/826-2801, 800/854-3112,
Email: advanstar@advanstar-expos.com,
Web URL: advanstar-expos.com/drtv,
Exhibitors: 100+

Data Warehouse World

4/08/97 to 4/10/97, Focus: Database
technology, San Jose, CA U.S., Sponsor:
Digital Consulting Inc., 204 Andover
Street, Andover MA 01810 U.S.; 508/
470-3880, Fax: 508/470-0526, 800/324-
3976, Email: dciconf1@aol.com, Web
URL: dciexpo.com

Data Warehouse World

4/15/97 to 4/17/97, Focus: Database
technology, Toronto, Canada, Sponsor:
Digital Consulting Inc., 204 Andover
Street, Andover MA 01810 U.S.; 508/
470-3880, Fax: 508/470-0526, 800/324-
3976, Email: dciconf1@aol.com, Web
URL: dciexpo.com

Data Warehousing & DSS/EIS Conference

3/10/97 to 3/11/97, Focus: Data warehousing, Sheraton Grande Torrey Pines, La
Jolla, CA U.S., Sponsor: Giga Information
Group, 1 Longwater Circle, Norwell MA
02061-1620 U.S.; 617/982-9500, Fax:
617/982-1724, 800/874-9980, Email:
conferences@gigaweb.com, Web URL:
gigaweb.com, 2nd Sponsor: Decision Support Technology

Data Warehousing Conference

11/03/97 to 11/04/97, Focus: Data warehousing, Westin, Copley Square, Boston,
MA U.S., Sponsor: Giga Information
Group, 1 Longwater Circle, Norwell MA
02061-1620 U.S.; 617/982-9500, Fax:
617/982-1724, 800/874-9980, Email:

conferences@gigaweb.com, Web URL: gigaweb.com, 2nd Sponsor: Decision Support Technology

Data Warehousing Conference & OLAP Forum

2/25/97 to 2/27/97, Focus: Database technology trends, Orlando, FL U.S., Sponsor: Digital Consulting Inc., 204 Andover Street, Andover MA 01810 U.S.; 508/470-3880, Fax: 508/470-0526, 800/324-3976, Email: dciconf@aol.com, Web URL: dciexpo.com, 2nd Sponsor: Meta Group

DataStorage 2000

9/25/00 to 9/27/00, Focus: Data storage industry, San Jose, CA U.S., Sponsor: Forum Management, Conferences Etc, 2680 Bayshore Pkwy, #214, Mt. View CA 94043 U.S.; 415/968-2836, Fax: 415/968-5392, Contact: Darlene Plamondon, 2nd Sponsor: DISK/TREND Inc. and Freeman Associates Inc.

DataStorage 97

9/15/97 to 9/17/97, Focus: Data storage industry, Fairmont, San Jose, CA U.S., Sponsor: Forum Management, Conferences Etc, 2680 Bayshore Pkwy, #214, Mt. View CA 94043 U.S.; 415/968-2836, Fax: 415/968-5392, Email: dsforum.com/dsconf, Contact: Darlene Plamondon, 2nd Sponsor: DISK/TREND Inc. and Freeman Associates Inc.

DataStorage 98

9/08/98 to 9/10/98, Focus: Data storage industry, San Jose, CA U.S., Sponsor: Forum Management, Conferences Etc, 2680 Bayshore Pkwy, #214, Mt. View CA 94043 U.S.; 415/968-2836, Fax: 415/968-5392, Contact: Darlene Plamondon, 2nd Sponsor: DISK/TREND Inc. and Freeman Associates Inc.

DataStorage 99

9/27/99 to 9/29/99, Focus: Data storage industry, San Jose, CA U.S., Sponsor: Forum Management, Conferences Etc, 2680 Bayshore Pkwy, #214, Mt. View CA 94043 U.S.; 415/968-2836, Fax: 415/968-5392, Contact: Darlene Plamondon, 2nd Sponsor: DISK/TREND Inc. and Freeman Associates Inc.

Database & Client/Server World

12/10/96 to 12/12/96, Focus: Data warehousing, Internet, client/server, Navy Pier, Chicago, IL U.S., Sponsor: Digital Consulting Inc., 204 Andover Street, Andover MA 01810 U.S.; 508/470-3880, Fax: 508/470-0526, 800/324-3976, Email: dciconf@aol.com, Web URL: dciexpo.com, 2nd Sponsor: Computer Associates

Database & Client/Server World

4/15/97 to 4/17/97, Focus: Data warehousing, Internet, client/server, Toronto, Canada, Sponsor: Digital Consulting Inc., 204 Andover Street, Andover MA 01810 U.S.; 508/470-3880, Fax: 508/470-0526, 800/324-3976, Email: dciconf@aol.com, Web URL: dciexpo.com

Database/Client-Server Conference and Expo

7/15/97 to 7/17/97, Beijing, China, Sponsor: IDG World Expos, 111 Speen St., Box 9107, Framingham MA 01701-9107 U.S.; 508/879-6700, Fax: 508/872-8237, 800/225-4698, Web URL: idg.com

Demo 97

2/09/97 to 2/12/97, Focus: New products and technologies, Indian Wells, CA U.S., Sponsor: InfoWorld Conference & Media Group, 155 Bovet Road, #800, San Mateo CA 94402 U.S.; 415/572-7341, Fax: 415/286-2750, 800/633-4312, Email: demo@pcletter.com, Web URL: demo.com, 2nd Sponsor: PC Letter

Design Automation Conference '97, DAC

6/09/97 to 6/13/97, Focus: Computer design technology, Anaheim Convention Center, Anaheim, CA U.S., Sponsor: IEEE-CS, 1730 Massachusetts Ave NW, Washington DC 20036 U.S.; 202/371-0101, Web URL: computer.org, 2nd Sponsor: ACM SIGODA, Atten.: 18,000, Exhibitors: 150

Electronic Components and Technology Conference

5/18/97 to 5/21/97, Fairmont, San Jose, CA U.S., Sponsor: Electronic Industries Assoc., 2500 Wilson Blvd, Arlington VA 22201-3834 U.S.; 703/907-7600, Fax: 703/907-7601, Email: zoogang@ix.netcom.com, Web URL: eia.org/ceg, Contact: Mark V. Rosenker

Electronic Entertainment Expo, E3

6/19/97 to 6/21/97, Focus: Interactive electronic entertainment, Georgia World Congress Center, Atlanta, GA U.S., Sponsor: MHA Event Management, 1400 Providence Hwy, PO Box 9103, Norwood MA 02062 U.S.; 617/440-0366, Fax: 617/440-0359, 800/315-1133, Email: webmaster@mha.com, Web URL: mha.com/e3/, 2nd Sponsor: Interactive Digital Software Association, Atten.: 40,000, Exhibitors: 450+

Entertainment, Education Electronic Expo, E4

7/24/97 to 7/27/97, Mexico City, Mexico, Sponsor: IDG World Expos, 111 Speen St., Box 9107, Framingham MA 01701-9107 U.S.; 508/879-6700, Fax: 508/872-8237, 800/225-4698, Web URL: idg.com

Expo Comm Argentina

10/07/97 to 10/10/97, Focus: Telecom industry, Buenos Aires, Argentina, Sponsor: E.J. Krause & Assoc. Inc., 7315 Wisconsin Ave, #450N, Bethesda MD 20814 U.S.; 301/986-7800, Fax: 301/986-4538

Expo Comm China 97

11/11/97 to 11/15/97, Focus: Telecom industry, Guangzhou, China, Sponsor: E.J. Krause & Assoc. Inc., 7315 Wisconsin Ave, #450N, Bethesda MD 20814 U.S.; 301/986-7800, Fax: 301/986-4538, Contact:

Ron Akins

Expo Comm Mexico 97

2/11/97 to 2/14/97, Focus: Telecom industry, Mexico City, Mexico, Sponsor: E.J. Krause & Assoc. Inc., 7315 Wisconsin Ave, #450N, Bethesda MD 20814 U.S.; 301/986-7800, Fax: 301/986-4538, Contact: Ron Akins, Atten.: 25,000, Exhibitors: 190

Expo Comm USA

6/02/97 to 6/05/97, Focus: Telecom, computer and office automation, Georgia World Congress Center, Atlanta, GA U.S., Sponsor: E.J. Krause & Assoc. Inc., 7315 Wisconsin Ave, #450N, Bethesda MD 20814 U.S.; 301/986-7800, Fax: 301/986-4538

Expo Comm Wireless Hong Kong

3/04/97 to 3/06/97, Focus: Telecom industry, Hong Kong, Sponsor: E.J. Krause & Assoc. Inc., 7315 Wisconsin Ave, #450N, Bethesda MD 20814 U.S.; 301/986-7800, Fax: 301/986-4538

ExpoCorp

4/28/97 to 4/30/97, Focus: Computer hardware and software, Sao Paulo, Brazil, Sponsor: Fenasoft, 3250 Mary St., #205, Miami FL 33133 U.S.; 305/446-3041, Fax: 305/446-3815, Web URL: fenasoft.com.br

FAXWORLD '96

12/09/96 to 12/11/96, Focus: Utilizing or implementing fax-integrated messaging technologies, Hyatt Regency, Burlingame, CA U.S., Sponsor: Giga Information Group, 1 Longwater Circle, Norwell MA 02061-1620 U.S.; 617/982-9500, Fax: 617/878-6650, 800/874-9980, Email: conferences@gigaweb.com, Web URL: gigaweb.com

FOSE '97, FOSE

3/18/97 to 3/20/97, Focus: Federal and military computer buyers and resellers, Washington, DC U.S., Sponsor: Reed Exhibition Cos., 383 Main Ave, Norwalk CT 06851 U.S.; 203/840-5634, Fax: 203/840-9646, 800/354-4003, Web URL: fose.reedexpo.com, Atten.: 80,000, Exhibitors: 450

FedNet

12/04/97 to 12/05/97, Focus: Network use in government organizations, Washington, DC U.S., Sponsor: Reed Exhibition Cos., 383 Main Ave, Norwalk CT 06851 U.S.; 203/840-5634, Fax: 203/840-9646, 800/354-4003, Web URL: fednet.reedexpo.com

Federal Imaging '97

12/04/97 to 12/05/97, Focus: Imaging use in government organizations, Washington, DC U.S., Sponsor: Reed Exhibition Cos., 383 Main Ave, Norwalk CT 06851 U.S.; 203/840-5634, Fax: 203/840-9646, 800/354-4003, Web URL: federalimaging.reedexpo.com, Atten.: 7,000, Exhibitors: 150

Fenasoft
7/21/97 to 7/26/97, Focus: International software & hardware, Anhembi Exposition Center, Sao Paulo, Brazil, Sponsor: Fenasoft, 3250 Mary St., #205, Miami FL 33133 U.S.; 305/446-3041, Fax: 305/446-3815, Web URL: fenasoft.com.br, Atten.: 625,000, Exhibitors: 1,600

GigaWorld '97
6/08/97 to 6/12/97, Hyatt Regency at Gainey Ranch, Scottsdale, AZ U.S., Sponsor: Giga Information Group, 1 Longwater Circle, Norwell MA 02061-1620 U.S.; 617/982-9500, Fax: 617/982-1724, 800/874-9980, Email: conferences@gigaweb.com, Web URL: gigaweb.com

Giganet: The Gigabit Networks and Systems Conference
11/18/96 to 11/20/96, Santa Clara, CA U.S., Sponsor: Technology Transfer Institute, 741 10th Street, Santa Monica CA 90402-2899 U.S.; 310/394-8305, Fax: 310/451-2104, 800/200-4884, Email: custserv@tticom.com, Web URL: tticom.com/atm

Government, Business & Education Tech Expo
5/28/97 to 5/30/97, Honolulu, HI U.S., 3450 Palmer Drive, #7280, Cameron Park CA 95682 U.S.; 916/672-1860, Fax: 916/672-0946, 800/474-3976, Contact: Karyn Epp

Graphic Communications 3
5/15/97 to 5/17/97, Focus: Graphic communications, Pennsylvania Convention Center, Philadelphia, PA U.S., Sponsor: Advanstar Expositions, 7500 Old Oak Blvd, Cleveland OH 44130 U.S.; 216/826-2806, Fax: 216/826-2801, Email: advanstar@advanstar-expos.com, Web URL: advanstar-expos.com

ID Expo and MDCC
5/13/97 to 5/16/97, Focus: Bar code and mobile communication product and technology, Pennsylvania Convention Center, Philadelphia, PA U.S., Sponsor: Advanstar Expositions, 7500 Old Oak Blvd, Cleveland OH 44130 U.S.; 216/826-2806, Fax: 216/826-2801, 800/331-5706, Email: advanstar@advanstar-expos.com, Web URL: advanstar-expos.com, 2nd Sponsor: Automatic I.D. News, Exhibitors: 275+

ID Info Los Angeles '96
12/04/96 to 12/05/96, Focus: Automatic Data Capture, Los Angeles Airport Hilton, Los Angeles, CA U.S., Sponsor: Advanstar Expositions, 131 W. 1st Street, Duluth MN 55802-2065 U.S.; 218/723-9130, Fax: 218/723-9122, 800/331-5706, Email: advanstar@advanstar-expos.com, Web URL: advanstar-expos.com/idexpo, 2nd Sponsor: Automatic I.D. News

ID Info Los Angeles '97
12/02/97 to 12/03/97, Focus: Automatic Data Capture, Los Angeles Airport Hilton, Los Angeles, CA U.S., Sponsor: Advanstar

Expositions, 7500 Old Oak Blvd, Cleveland OH 44130 U.S.; 216/826-2806, Fax: 216/826-2801, Email: advanstar@advanstar-expos.com, Web URL: advanstar-expos.com, 2nd Sponsor: Automatic I.D. News

ID Info Minneapolis
9/09/97 to 9/10/97, Hyatt Regency, Minneapolis, MN U.S., Sponsor: Advanstar Expositions, 7500 Old Oak Blvd, Cleveland OH 44130 U.S.; 216/826-2806, Fax: 216/826-2801, Email: advanstar@advanstar-expos.com, Web URL: advanstar-expos.com

IEEE International Conference on Robotics & Automation
4/20/97 to 4/25/97, Focus: Robotics and computer automation, Albuquerque, NM U.S., Sponsor: IEEE, 1730 Massachusetts Ave NW, Washington DC 20036 U.S.; 202/371-0101, Web URL: computer.org

IEEE International Symposium on Information Theory
6/29/97 to 7/04/97, Focus: Information science, Ulm, Germany, Sponsor: IEEE, 1730 Massachusetts Ave NW, Washington DC 20036 U.S.; 202/371-0101, Web URL: computer.org

IEEE Virtual Reality International Symposium, VRAIS '97
3/01/97 to 3/05/97, Focus: Virtual reality technology, Albuquerque, NM U.S., Sponsor: IEEE, 1730 Massachusetts Ave NW, Washington DC 20036 U.S.; 202/371-0101, Web URL: computer.org

IEEE-ISSCC International Solid State Circuits Conference, IEEE-ISSCC
2/06/97 to 2/08/97, Focus: Semiconductor technology, San Francisco, CA U.S., Sponsor: IEEE, 1730 Massachusetts Ave NW, Washington DC 20036 U.S.; 202/371-0101, Web URL: computer.org

IT Forum
9/16/97 to 9/18/97, Focus: Enterprise technology, Jacob K. Javits Convention Center, New York, NY U.S., Sponsor: Blenheim Group, Ft. Lee Executive Park, 1 Executive Drive, Ft. Lee NJ 07024 U.S.; 201/346-1400, Fax: 201/346-1532, 800/829-3976, Email: mhaviland@blenheim.com, Web URL: shownet.com, Contact: Mark Haviland, Exhibitors: 400+

Impact! '96
11/27/96 to 11/29/96, Focus: New screening applications and high-fidelity printing, Ramada O'Hare, Chicago, IL U.S., Sponsor: Graphic Communications Association, 100 Daingerfield Road, Alexandria VA 22314-2888 U.S.; 703/519-8160, Fax: 703/548-2867, Web URL: gca.org

Information Superhighway Summit Asia
9/02/97 to 9/05/97, Focus: Coming developments & what is available today, Singapore, Sponsor: IDG World Expos, 111 Speen St., Box 9107, Framingham MA

01701-9107 U.S.; 508/879-6700, Fax: 508/872-8237, 800/225-4698, Web URL: idg.com, 2nd Sponsor: ComNet

Ink Jet and Thermal Printing-Europe
3/19/97 to 3/21/97, Focus: Ink jet and thermal printing marketplace, Steigenberger Hotel, Berlin, Germany, Sponsor: Giga Information Group, 1 Longwater Circle, Norwell MA 02061-1620 U.S.; 617/982-9500, Fax: 617/982-1724, 800/874-9980, Email: conferences@gigaweb.com, Web URL: gigaweb.com, Contact: Martha Popoloski

International Computer & Networks Expo
5/14/97 to 5/18/97, Focus: PCs and networking, Shanghai, China, Sponsor: IDG World Expos, 111 Speen St., Box 9107, Framingham MA 01701-9107 U.S.; 508/879-6700, Fax: 508/872-8237, 800/225-4698, Web URL: idg.com

International Conference on Computer Architecture
5/31/97 to 6/04/97, Westin Hotel, Denver, CO U.S., Sponsor: ACM, 1515 Broadway, 17th Floor, New York NY 10036 U.S.; 212/869-7440

International Conference on Functional Programming '97
6/09/97 to 6/11/97, Amsterdam, Netherlands, Sponsor: ACM, 1515 Broadway, 17th Floor, New York NY 10036 U.S.; 212/869-7440

International Conference on Intelligent User Interfaces
1/06/97 to 1/09/97, Focus: Intelligent user interfaces, Hilton at Walt Disney World, Orlando, FL U.S., Sponsor: ACM, 1515 Broadway, 17th Floor, New York NY 10036 U.S.; 212/869-7440, 2nd Sponsor: American Association of Artificial Intelligence

International Conference on Parallel & Distributed Computing
3/19/97 to 3/21/97, Focus: Parallel and distributed computer system technology, Shanghai, China, Sponsor: IEEE, 1730 Massachusetts Ave NW, Washington DC 20036 U.S.; 202/371-0101, Web URL: computer.org

International Conference on Parallel & Distributed Info. Sys.
12/18/96 to 12/20/96, Eden Roc Spa & Resort, Miami, FL U.S., Sponsor: ACM, 1515 Broadway, 17th Floor, New York NY 10036 U.S.; 212/869-7440, 2nd Sponsor: IEEE-CS

International Conference on Software Engineering, ICSE 97
5/19/97 to 5/23/97, Focus: Software engineering technology, Sheraton Boston Hotel & Towers, Boston, MA U.S., Sponsor: ACM, 1515 Broadway, 17th Floor, New York NY 10036 U.S.; 212/869-7440, Web URL: ics.uci.edu/icse97, 2nd Sponsor: IEEE-CS TCSE

International Conference on Super-

computing, ICS
7/07/97 to 7/11/97, Focus: Supercomputing, Vienna, Austria, Sponsor: ACM, 1515 Broadway, 17th Floor, New York NY 10036 U.S.; 212/869-7440

International DB2 Users Group North American Conference, IDUG
5/11/97 to 5/15/97, Focus: DB2 products and applications, Chicago Hilton & Towers, Chicago, IL U.S., Sponsor: International DB2 Users Group, 401 N Michigan Ave, Chicago IL 60611 U.S.; 312/644-6610, Fax: 312/321-6869, Email: idug@mcs.com, Web URL: idug.org, Atten.: 1,700+

International Symposium on High Perf. Computer Architecture
2/01/97 to 2/05/97, Focus: Computer architecture, San Antonio, TX U.S., Sponsor: IEEE-CS, 1730 Massachusetts Ave NW, Washington DC 20036 U.S.; 202/371-0101, Web URL: computer.org

Internet Commerce Expo Hong Kong
8/05/97 to 8/08/97, Focus: Applications and products for Internet, Hong Kong, Sponsor: IDG World Expos, 111 Speen St., Box 9107, Framingham MA 01701-9107 U.S.; 508/879-6700, Fax: 508/872-8237, 800/225-4698, Web URL: idg.com

Internet Commerce Expo Taiwan,
5/26/97 to 5/28/97, Focus: Applications and products for Internet, Taipei, Taiwan, Sponsor: IDG World Expos, 111 Speen St., Box 9107, Framingham MA 01701-9107 U.S.; 508/879-6700, Fax: 508/872-8237, 800/225-4698, Web URL: idg.com

Internet Developers' Competition
2/17/97 to 2/19/97, Focus: Internet information, San Jose, CA U.S., Sponsor: Digital Consulting Inc., 204 Andover Street, Andover MA 01810 U.S.; 508/470-3880, Fax: 508/470-0526, 800/324-3976, Email: dciconf@aol.com, Web URL: dciexpo.com

Internet Expo, Web World & EMail World
2/17/97 to 2/19/97, Focus: Internet information, San Jose, CA U.S., Sponsor: Digital Consulting Inc., 204 Andover Street, Andover MA 01810 U.S.; 508/470-3880, Fax: 508/470-0526, 800/324-3976, Email: dciconf@aol.com, Web URL: dciexpo.com

Internet Expo, Web World & EMail World
3/25/97 to 3/27/97, Focus: Internet information, London, England, Sponsor: Digital Consulting Inc., 204 Andover Street, Andover MA 01810 U.S.; 508/470-3880, Fax: 508/470-0526, 800/324-3976, Email: dciconf@aol.com, Web URL: dciexpo.com

Internet Expo, Web World & EMail World
4/22/97 to 4/24/97, Focus: Internet information, Chicago, IL U.S., Sponsor: Digital Consulting Inc., 204 Andover

Street, Andover MA 01810 U.S.; 508/470-3880, Fax: 508/470-0526, 800/324-3976, Email: dciconf@aol.com, Web URL: dciexpo.com

Internet World Argentina
4/08/97 to 4/11/97, Focus: Internet information and technology, Buenos Aires, Argentina, Sponsor: Mecklermedia, 20 Ketchum Street, Westport CT 06880 U.S.; 203/226-6967, Fax: 203/226-6976, 800/632-5537, Email: info@mecklermedia.com, Web URL: iworld.com/shows, Contact: Francie Coulter

Internet World Asia '97
3/19/97 to 3/21/97, Focus: Internet & worldwide web, Kuala Lumpur, Malaysia, Sponsor: Mecklermedia, 20 Ketchum Street, Westport CT 06880 U.S.; 203/226-6967, Fax: 203/226-6976, 800/632-5537, Email: iwconf@mecklermedia.com, Web URL: iworld.com/shows

Internet World Australia Pacific '97
8/12/97 to 8/14/97, Focus: Internet & worldwide web, Sydney, Australia, Sponsor: Mecklermedia, 20 Ketchum Street, Westport CT 06880 U.S.; 203/226-6967, Fax: 203/226-6976, 800/632-5537, Email: iwconf@mecklermedia.com, Web URL: iworld.com/shows

Internet World Canada
1/07/97 to 1/10/97, Focus: Internet & worldwide web, Toronto Convention Center, Toronto, Canada, Sponsor: Mecklermedia, 20 Ketchum Street, Westport CT 06880 U.S.; 203/226-6967, Fax: 203/226-6976, 800/632-5537, Email: iwconf@mecklermedia.com, Web URL: iworld.com/shows, Atten.: 15,000

Internet World Chile
10/07/97 to 10/10/97, Focus: Internet information and technology, Fisa Cordillera, Chile, Sponsor: Mecklermedia, 20 Ketchum Street, Westport CT 06880 U.S.; 203/226-6967, Fax: 203/226-6976, 800/632-5537, Email: info@mecklermedia.com, Web URL: iworld.com/shows, Contact: Francie Coulter

Internet World Colombia
3/27/97 to 3/29/97, Focus: Internet information and technology, Bogota, Colombia, Sponsor: Mecklermedia, 20 Ketchum Street, Westport CT 06880 U.S.; 203/226-6967, Fax: 203/226-6976, 800/632-5537, Email: info@mecklermedia.com, Web URL: iworld.com/shows, Contact: Francie Coulter

Internet World Fall '96
12/09/96 to 12/13/96, Focus: Internet & worldwide web, Jacob K. Javits Convention Ctr, New York, NY U.S, Sponsor: Mecklermedia, 20 Ketchum St, Westport CT 06880 U.S.; 203/226-6967, Fax: 203/226-6976, 800/632-5537, Email: iwconf@mecklermedia.com, Web URL: iworld.com/shows, Contact: Francie Coulter, Atten.: 50,000, Exhibitors: 400+

Internet World Fall '97

12/08/97 to 12/12/97, Focus: Internet & worldwide web, Jacob K. Javits Convention Center, New York, NY U.S., Sponsor: Mecklermedia, 20 Ketchum Street, Westport CT 06880 U.S.; 203/226-6967, Fax: 203/226-6976, Email: iwconf@mecklermedia.com, Web URL: iworld.com/shows

Internet World International@Singapore
1/23/97 to 1/25/97, Focus: Internet & worldwide web, Singapore, Sponsor: Mecklermedia, 20 Ketchum Street, Westport CT 06880 U.S.; 203/226-6967, Fax: 203/226-6976, 800/632-5537, Email: iwconf@mecklermedia.com, Web URL: iworld.com/shows

Internet World Israel
6/18/97 to 6/20/97, Focus: Internet information and technology, Jerusalem Convention Center, Israel, Sponsor: Mecklermedia, 20 Ketchum Street, Westport CT 06880 U.S.; 203/226-6976, 800/632-5537, Email: info@mecklermedia.com, Web URL: iworld.com/shows, Contact: Francie Coulter, 2nd Sponsor: People & Computers Group

Internet World Japan
7/23/97 to 7/25/97, Focus: Internet & worldwide web, Tokyo, Japan, Sponsor: Mecklermedia, 20 Ketchum Street, Westport CT 06880 U.S.; 203/226-6967, Fax: 203/226-6976, 800/632-5537, Email: iwconf@mecklermedia.com, Web URL: iworld.com/shows

Internet World Mexico
6/04/97 to 6/06/97, Focus: Internet & worldwide web, Mexico City, Mexico, Sponsor: Mecklermedia, 20 Ketchum Street, Westport CT 06880 U.S.; 203/226-6967, Fax: 203/226-6976, 800/632-5537, Email: iwconf@mecklermedia.com, Web URL: iworld.com/shows

Internet World Shanghai-China
6/11/97 to 6/13/97, Focus: Internet & worldwide web, Shanghai, China, Sponsor: Mecklermedia, 20 Ketchum Street, Westport CT 06880 U.S.; 203/226-6967, Fax: 203/226-6976, 800/632-5537, Email: iwconf@mecklermedia.com, Web URL: iworld.com/shows

Internet World Spring '97
3/10/97 to 3/14/97, Focus: Internet & worldwide web, Los Angeles Convention Center, Los Angeles, CA U.S., Sponsor: Mecklermedia, 20 Ketchum Street, Westport CT 06880 U.S.; 203/226-6967, Fax: 203/226-6976, 800/632-5537, Email: iwconf@mecklermedia.com, Web URL: iworld.com/shows, Contact: Francie Coulter, 2nd Sponsor: Internet World Magazine, Atten.: 40,000+

Internet World UK Spring '97
5/20/97 to 5/22/97, Focus: Internet & worldwide web, London, England, Sponsor: Mecklermedia, 20 Ketchum Street, Westport CT 06880 U.S.; 203/226-6967,

Fax: 203/226-6976, 800/632-5537, Email: iwconf@mecklermedia.com, Web URL: iworld.com/shows

Internet+Intranet, I2

2/18/97 to 2/20/97, Focus: Internet and intranet information, Hynes Convention Center, Boston, MA U.S., Sponsor: Blenheim Group, Ft. Lee Executive Park, 1 Executive Drive, Ft. Lee NJ 07024 U.S.; 201/346-1400, Fax: 201/346-1532, 800/829-3976, Email: mhavilan@blenheim.com, Web URL: shownet.com, Contact: Mark Haviland

Internet+Intranet, I2

5/13/97 to 5/15/96, Focus: Internet and intranet information, Moscone Center, San Francisco, CA U.S., Sponsor: Blenheim Group, Ft. Lee Executive Park, 1 Executive Drive, Ft. Lee NJ 07024 U.S.; 201/346-1400, Fax: 201/346-1532, 800/829-3976, Email: mhavilan@blenheim.com, Web URL: shownet.com, Contact: Mark Haviland

Internet+Intranet, I2

9/16/97 to 9/18/97, Focus: Internet and intranet information, Jacob K. Javits Convention Center, New York, NY U.S., Sponsor: Blenheim Group, Ft. Lee Executive Park, 1 Executive Drive, Ft. Lee NJ 07024 U.S.; 201/346-1400, Fax: 201/346-1532, 800/829-3976, Email: mhaviland@blenheim.com, Web URL: shownet.com, Contact: Mark Haviland

Jakarta Computer Expo

5/20/97 to 5/27/97, Focus: PCs, Jakarta, Indonesia, Sponsor: IDG World Expos, 111 Speen St., Box 9107, Framingham MA 01701-9107 U.S.; 508/879-6700, Fax: 508/872-8237, 800/225-4698, Web URL: idg.com

JavaOne

4/02/97 to 4/04/97, Focus: Java software development, Moscone Center, San Francisco CA U.S., Sponsor: Softbank Expos, PO Box 5855, San Mateo CA 94402 U.S.; 415/578-6900, Fax: 415/525-0199, 800/488-2883, Web URL: java.sun.com/javaone

M/cad Expo 97

6/16/97 to 6/19/97, Focus: CAD, Pennsylvania Convention Center, Philadelphia, PA U.S., Sponsor: A/E/C Systems International Inc., 415 Eagleview Blvd, #106, Exton PA 19341 U.S.; 610/458-7070, Fax: 610/458-7171, 800/451-1196, Email: aecsys@ix.netcom.com, Web URL: aecsystems.com, Contact: Carmella Colacchio, 2nd Sponsor: Computer-Aided Engineering, Atten.: 25,000, Exhibitors: 450+

Macworld

1/07/97 to 1/10/97, Focus: Macintosh computers, peripherals & software, Moscone Center, San Francisco, CA U.S., Sponsor: MHA Event Management, 1400 Providence Hwy, PO Box 9103, Norwood MA 02026 U.S.; 617/440-0366, Fax: 617/440-0359, 800/315-1133, Email:

webmaster@mha.com, Web URL: mha.com/macworldexpo, Atten.: 72,000, Exhibitors: 400+

Macworld Expo Australia '97

11/13/97 to 11/15/97, Focus: Macintosh computers, peripherals & software, Sydney, Australia, Sponsor: IDG World Expos, 111 Speen St., Box 9107, Framingham MA 01701-9107 U.S.; 508/879-6700, Fax: 508/872-8237, 800/225-4698, Web URL: idg.com

Macworld Expo Mexico

9/30/97 to 10/02/97, Focus: Macintosh computers, peripherals & software, Mexico City, Mexico, Sponsor: IDG World Expos, 111 Speen St., Box 9107, Framingham MA 01701-9107 U.S.; 508/879-6700, Fax: 508/872-8237, 800/225-4698, Web URL: idg.com

Macworld Expo Tokyo

2/19/97 to 2/22/96, Focus: Macintosh computers, peripherals & software, Tokyo, Japan, Sponsor: IDG World Expos, 111 Speen St., Box 9107, Framingham MA 01701-9107 U.S.; 508/879-6700, Fax: 508/872-8237, 800/225-4698, Web URL: idg.com

Macworld Expo/Boston

8/06/97 to 8/08/97, Focus: Macintosh products and trends, World Trade Center & Bayside Expo Ctr., Boston, MA U.S., Sponsor: MHA Event Management, 1400 Providence Hwy, PO Box 9103, Norwood MA 02062 U.S.; 617/440-0466, Fax: 617/440-0357, 800/315-1133, Email: webmaster@mha.com, Web URL: mha.com, 2nd Sponsor: International Data Group, Atten.: 58,600+

Meta Data Conference

3/17/97 to 3/20/97, Dallas, TX U.S., Sponsor: Technology Transfer Institute, 741 10th Street, Santa Monica CA 90402-2899 U.S.; 310/394-8305, Fax: 310/451-2104, 800/200-4884, Email: custserv@tticom.com, Web URL: tticom.com/atm

Microprocessor Forum 97

10/13/97 to 10/16/97, Focus: Microprocessors, Fairmont, San Jose, CA U.S., Sponsor: MicroDesign Resources, 874 Gravenstein Hwy S., Sebastopol CA 95472 U.S.; 707/824-4001, Fax: 707/823-0504, 800/527-0288, Email: mpf@mdr.zd.com, Web URL: chipanalyst.com

Mobile Insights '97

2/23/97 to 2/25/97, Focus: Mobile computing and data communications, Laguna Nigel, CA U.S., Sponsor: Mobile Insights Inc., 2001 Landings Drive, Mt. View CA 94043 U.S.; 415/390-9800, Fax: 415/919-0930, Web URL: mobileinsights.com

Mobile World

11/12/96 to 11/13/96, Focus: Improving business productivity through mobile computing, Atlanta, GA U.S., Sponsor: Digital Consulting Inc., 204 Andover St, Andover MA 01810 U.S.; 508/470-3880, Fax:

508/470-0526, 800/324-3976, Email: dciconf1@aol.com, Web URL: dciexpo.com

Motion Expo with Powersystems World

9/09/97 to 9/11/97, Baltimore Convention Center, Baltimore, MD U.S., Sponsor: Advanstar Expositions, 7500 Old Oak Blvd, Cleveland OH 44130 U.S.; 216/826-2806, Fax: 216/826-2801, Email: advanstar@advanstar-expos.com, Web URL: advanstar-expos.com

Multimedia China 97

4/24/97 to 4/27/97, Focus: Multimedia, Beijing, China, Sponsor: Seventh Wave, 10211 Sunland Blvd, Shadow Hills CA 91040-1739 U.S.; 818/353-8652, Fax: 818/353-8215, Email: info@wave7.com, Web URL: wave7.com, Atten.: 60,000+, Exhibitors: 210+

NetWorld+Interop-East

10/06/97 to 10/10/97, Focus: Local and wide are networks, computer hardware and software, Georgia World Congress Center, Atlanta, GA U.S., Sponsor: Softbank Expos, 303 Vintage Park Drive, Foster City CA 94404 U.S.; 415/578-6900, Fax: 415/525-0194, 800/472-3976, Email: info@sbexpos.com, Web URL: sbexpos.com, Atten.: 50,000, Exhibitors: 500

NetWorld+Interop-Frankfurt

6/23/97 to 6/27/97, Focus: Local and wide area networks, computer hardware and software, Frankfurt, Germany, Sponsor: Softbank Messe & Konferenz, Riesstrasse 25, Munich D-80992 Germany; 49 89 1431 2481, Fax: 49 89 1431 2486, Email: info@sbexpos.com, Web URL: sbexpos.com, Atten.: 21,000, Exhibitors: 332

NetWorld+Interop-Paris

9/22/97 to 9/26/97, Focus: Local and wide area networks, computer hardware and software, Porte de Versailles, Paris, France, Sponsor: Softbank Expos, 300 First Ave, Needham MA 02194-2722 U.S.; 617/449-6600, Fax: 617/449-6953, Email: info@sbexpos.com, Web URL: sbexpos.com, Atten.: 30,235, Exhibitors: 320

NetWorld+Interop-Sydney

11/25/96 to 11/29/96, Focus: Local and wide are networks, computer hardware and software, Sydney Exhibition & Conference Centre, Sydney Australia, Sponsor: Softbank Expos, 303 Vintage Park Drive, Foster City CA 94404 U.S.; 415/578-6900, Fax: 415/525-0194, 800/472-3976, Email: info@sbexpos.com, Web URL: sbexpos.com

NetWorld+Interop-Tokyo

7/21/97 to 7/25/97, Focus: Local and wide area networks, computer hardware and software, Makuhari Messe, Tokyo, Japan, Sponsor: Softbank Japan, Rokubancho SK Bldg, 3 Rokubancho, Chiyoda-ku, Tokyo JP-102 Japan; 81 3 3288 7201, Fax:

81 3 3288 7120, Email: info@sbex-
pos.com, Web URL: sbexpos.com, Atten.:
40,000, Exhibitors: 170

NetWorld+Interop-West
5/05/97 to 5/09/97, Focus: Local and
wide are networks, computer hardware &
software, Las Vegas Convention Cntr, Las
Vegas, NV U.S., Sponsor: Softbank Expos,
303 Vintage Park Dr, Foster City CA
94404 US; 415/578-6900, Fax: 415/525-
0194, 800/472-3976, Email: info@sbex-
pos.com, Web URL: sbexpos.com, Atten.:
50,000, Exhibitors: 600

Network World Unplugged
4/09/97 to 4/10/97, Focus: Mobile,
remote access and wireless solutions, San
Jose, CA U.S., Sponsor: IDG World
Expos, 111 Speen St., Box 9107, Framingham MA 01701-9107 U.S.; 508/879-
6700, Fax: 508/872-8237, 800/225-4698,
Web URL: idg.com

Network World Unplugged '97
12/03/97 to 12/04/97, Focus: Mobile,
remote access and wireless solutions, Boston, MA U.S., Sponsor: IDG World Expos,
111 Speen St., Box 9107, Framingham MA
01701-9107 U.S.; 508/879-6700, Fax:
508/872-8237, 800/225-4698, Web
URL: idg.com

Networking China
9/08/97 to 9/12/97, Focus: Networking
products and applications, Beijing, China,
Sponsor: IDG World Expos, 111 Speen St,
Box 9107, Framingham MA 01701-9107
U.S; 508/879-6700, Fax: 508/872-8237,
800/225-4698, Web URL: idg.com

Networks Expo & Mactivity '97
2/18/97 to 2/20/97, Focus: LAN and network products and technology, Hynes Convention Center, Boston, MA U.S.,
Sponsor: Blenheim Group, Ft. Lee Executive Park, 1 Executive Drive, Ft. Lee NJ
07024 U.S.; 201/346-1400, Fax: 201/
346-1532, 800/829-3976, Email:
mhavilan@blenheim.com, Web URL:
shownet.com, Contact: Mark Haviland,
Atten.: 35,000+, Exhibitors: 250+

Networks Expo & Windows World
10/28/97 to 10/30/97, Focus: Networking, communication and interoperability
products, Infomart, Dallas, TX U.S., Sponsor: Blenheim Group, Ft. Lee Executive
Park, 1 Executive Drive, Ft. Lee NJ 07024
U.S.; 201/346-1400, Fax: 201/346-1532,
800/829-3976, Email: mhaviland@blen-
heim.com, Web URL: shownet.com, Contact: Mark Haviland, Atten.: 31,638+,
Exhibitors: 250+

**Nomadic Computing & Communica-
tions Conference**, NOMADIC
3/18/97 to 3/20/97, Washington, DC
U.S., Sponsor: Technology Transfer Institute, 741 10th Street, Santa Monica CA
90402-2899 U.S.; 310/394-8305, Fax:
310/451-2104, 800/200-4884, Email:
custserv@tticom.com, Web URL: tti-
com.com/atm

Object World East
3/02/97 to 3/07/97, Focus: Object-oriented programming, Hynes Convention
Center, Boston, MA U.S., Sponsor: Object
World Corp., 492 Old Connecticut Path,
Framingham MA 01701 U.S.; Fax: 508/
872-6500, 800/969-4664

Object World Frankfurt
10/10/97 to 10/12/97, Focus: Object-
oriented programming, Frankfurt, Germany, Sponsor: IDG World Expos; 111
Speen St., Box 9107, Framingham MA
01701-9107 U.S.; 508/879-6700, Fax:
508/872-8237, 800/225-4698, Web
URL: idg.com, Contact: Matt Mandino

Object World Sydney
8/26/97 to 8/29/97, Focus: Object-oriented programming, Sydney, Australia,
Sponsor: IDG World Expos, 111 Speen St.,
Box 9107, Framingham MA 01701-9107
U.S.; 508/879-6700, Fax: 508/872-8237,
800/225-4698, Web URL: idg.com, Contact: Matt Mandino

Object World Tokyo
10/03/97 to 10/05/97, Focus: Object-
oriented programming, Tokyo, Japan,
Sponsor: IDG World Expos, 111 Speen St.,
Box 9107, Framingham MA 01701-9107
U.S.; 508/879-6700, Fax: 508/872-8237,
800/225-4698, Web URL: idg.com, Contact: Matt Mandino

Object World West
7/22/97 to 7/27/97, Focus: Object-oriented programming, Moscone Center, San
Francisco, CA U.S., Sponsor: Object
World Corp., 492 Old Connecticut Path,
Framingham MA 01701 U.S.; Fax: 508/
872-6500, 800/969-4664

**Office Equipment & Supplies, Com-
puters & Communications Int'l**
10/12/97 to 10/14/97, Panama, Sponsor:
IDG World Expos, 111 Speen St., Box
9107, Framingham MA 01701-9107 U.S.;
508/879-6700, Fax: 508/872-8237, 800/
225-4698, Web URL: idg.com

**On Demand Digital Printing & Pub-
lishing**
5/06/97 to 5/08/97, Focus: Digital printing and publishing, Jacob K. Javits Convention Center, New York, NY U.S., Sponsor:
Expocon Management Assoc., 363 Reef
Road, PO Box 915, Fairfield CT 06430-
0915 U.S.; 203/256-4700, Fax: 203/256-
4730, Email: ondemand@expocon.com,
Web URL: expocon.com, 2nd Sponsor:
Xerox, Exhibitors: 200+

PC Card '97
4/08/97 to 4/10/97, Focus: PCMCIA
technology and trends, San Jose, CA U.S.,
Sponsor: Digital Consulting Inc., 204
Andover Street, Andover MA 01810 U.S.;
508/470-3880, Fax: 508/470-0526, 800/
324-3976, Email: dciconf1@aol.com,
Web URL: dciexpo.com, 2nd Sponsor:
Epson, Intel, Motorola & SunDisk

PC Expo, WEB.X & Networks Expo
6/17/97 to 6/19/97, Focus: PC and LAN

products, Jacob K. Javits Convention Center, New York, NY U.S., Sponsor: Blenheim Group, Ft. Lee Executive Park, 1
Executive Drive, Ft. Lee NJ 07024 U.S.;
201/346-1400, Fax: 201/346-1532, 800/
829-3976, Email: mhaviland@blen-
heim.com, Web URL: shownet.com, Contact: Mark Haviland, Atten.: 130,000+

PC Tech Forum
5/19/97 to 5/22/97, Focus: Technologies and markets of the next generation of
PCs, Hyatt Regency, Burlingame, CA U.S.,
Sponsor: MicroDesign Resources, 874
Gravenstein Hwy S., Sebastopol CA 95472
U.S.; 707/824-4001, Fax: 707/823-0504,
800/527-0288, Web URL: chipana-
lyst.com

PC World Expo/Chongqing
12/04/96 to 12/07/96, Focus: PCs and
LANs, Chongqing, China, Sponsor: IDG
World Expos, 111 Speen St., Box 9107,
Framingham MA 01701-9107 U.S.; 508/
879-6700, Fax: 508/872-8237, 800/225-
4698, Web URL: idg.com

PC World Expo/Stockholm
1/27/97 to 1/29/97, Focus: PC and LAN
products, Stockholm, Sweden, Sponsor:
IDG World Expos, 111 Speen St., Box
9107, Framingham MA 01701-9107 U.S.;
508/879-6700, Fax: 508/872-8237, 800/
225-4698, Web URL: idg.com

**PC World, Internet China, Interac-
tive Multimedia China**
4/03/97 to 4/08/97, Focus: PCs and
LANs, Internet and multimedia, Beijing,
China, Sponsor: IDG World Expos, 111
Speen St., Box 9107, Framingham MA
01701-9107 U.S.; 508/879-6700, Fax:
508/872-8237, 800/225-4698, Web
URL: idg.com

Plug.In '97
7/16/97 to 7/18/96, Focus: Technology
in music, New York, NY U.S., Sponsor:
Jupiter Communications, 627 Broadway,
New York NY 10012 U.S.; 212/780-6060,
Fax: 212/780-6075, 800/488-4345,
Email: jupiter@jup.com, Web URL:
jup.com

Power '97
10/12/97 to 10/15/97, Focus: Power
requirements for mobile computing &
wireless communications, Santa Clara Convention Center, Santa Clara, CA U.S.,
Sponsor: Giga Information Group, 1 Longwater Circle, Norwell MA 02061-1620
U.S.; 617/982-9500, Fax: 617/982-1724,
800/874-9980, Email: confer-
ences@gigaweb.com, Web URL:
gigaweb.com, 2nd Sponsor: Arthur D. Little, Atten.: 500+

**Principles & Practices of Parallel
Programming**, PPoPP
6/18/97 to 6/21/97, Focus: Parallel programming, Alexis Park Resort, Las Vegas,
NV U.S., Sponsor: ACM, 1515 Broadway,
17th Floor, New York NY 10036 U.S.;
212/869-7440

Print 97
9/03/97 to 9/10/97, Focus: Printing and publishing technologies, McCormick Place, Chicago, IL U.S., Sponsor: Graphic Arts Show Co., 1899 Preston White Drive, Reston VA 22091-4326 U.S.; 703/264-7200, Fax: 703/620-9187, Email: 70732.2023@compuserve.com, Contact: John Grossi, Atten.: 90,000, Exhibitors: 900

Romanian Computer Show, ROCS 10/16/97 to 10/19/97, Bucharest, Romania, Sponsor: IDG World Expos, 111 Speen St., Box 9107, Framingham MA 01701-9107 U.S.; 508/879-6700, Fax: 508/872-8237, 800/225-4698, Web URL: idg.com

SIGGRAPH 97
8/03/97 to 8/08/97, Focus: Computer graphics & interactive techniques, Los Angeles Convention Center, Los Angeles, CA U.S., Sponsor: Smith, Bucklin & Assoc., 401 N Michigan Ave, PO Box 95316, Chicago IL 60611 U.S.; 312/321-6830, Fax: 312/321-6876, Email: siggraph97@siggraph.org, 2nd Sponsor: ACM, Atten.: 30,000+

SPA 1997 Annual Conference
9/06/97 to 9/10/97, Focus: PC software industry, Washington, DC U.S., Sponsor: Software Publishers Assoc., 1730 M Street NW, #700, Washington DC 20036-4510 U.S.; 202/452-1600, Fax: 202/223-8756, Web URL: spa.org, Atten.: 1,200

SPA 1997 Spring Symposium
3/01/97 to 3/05/97, Focus: PC software industry, San Diego, CA U.S., Sponsor: Software Publishers Assoc., 1730 M Street NW, #700, Washington DC 20036-4510 U.S.; 202/452-1600, Fax: 202/223-8756, Web URL: spa.org, Atten.: 1,200

SPA 1998 Annual Conference
9/12/98 to 9/16/98, Focus: PC software industry, Chicago, IL U.S., Sponsor: Software Publishers Assoc., 1730 M Street NW, #700, Washington DC 20036-4510 U.S.; 202/452-1600, Fax: 202/223-8756, Web URL: spa.org, Atten.: 1,200

SPA 1998 Spring Symposium
3/21/98 to 3/26/98, Focus: PC software industry, San Jose, CA U.S., Sponsor: Software Publishers Assoc., 1730 M Street NW, #700, Washington DC 20036-4510 U.S.; 202/452-1600, Fax: 202/223-8756, Web URL: spa.org, Atten.: 1,200

Scantech Expo Europe
11/18/97 to 11/20/97, Koln Messe, Koln, Germany, Sponsor: Advanstar Expositions, 7500 Old Oak Blvd, Cleveland OH 44130 U.S.; 216/826-2806, Fax: 216/826-2801, Email: advanstar@advanstar-expos.com, Web URL: advanstar-expos.com

Seybold Seminars-Germany
11/19/96 to 11/21/96, Focus: Printing, publishing and new media equipment, Frankfurt, Germany, Sponsor: Softbank

Messe & Konferenz, Riesstrasse 25, Munich D-80992 Germany; 49 89 1431 2481, Fax: 49 89 1431 2486, Email: info@sbex-pos.com, Web URL: sbexpos.com

Seybold Seminars-New York
4/22/97 to 4/25/97, Focus: Printing, publishing and new media equipment, Jacob K. Javits Convention Center, New York, NY U.S., Sponsor: Softbank Expos, 303 Vintage Park Drive, Foster City CA 94404 U.S.; 415/578-6900, Fax: 415/525-0194, 800/472-3976, Email: info@sbexpos.com, Web URL: sbex-pos.com, Atten.: 20,000, Exhibitors: 200

Seybold Seminars-San Francisco
9/30/97 to 10/03/97, Focus: Printing, publishing and new media equipment, Moscone Center, San Francisco, CA U.S., Sponsor: Softbank Expos, 303 Vintage Park Drive, Foster City CA 94404 U.S.; 415/578-6900, Fax: 415/525-0194, 800/472-3976, Email: info@sbexpos.com, Web URL: sbexpos.com, Atten.: 40,000, Exhibitors: 350

Seybold Seminars-Tokyo
12/02/96 to 12/05/96, Focus: Printing, publishing and new media equipment, Tokyo International Exhibition Center, Tokyo, Japan, Sponsor: Softbank Japan, Rokubancho SK Bldg, 3 Rokubancho, Chiyoda-ku, Tokyo JP-102 Japan; 81 3 3288 7201, Fax: 81 3 3288 7120, Email: info@sbexpos.com, Web URL: sbex-pos.com

Seybold Seminars-Tokyo
12/11/97 to 12/14/97, Focus: Printing, publishing and new media equipment, Tokyo International Exhibition Center, Tokyo, Japan, Sponsor: Softbank Japan, Rokubancho SK Bldg, 3 Rokubancho, Chiyoda-ku, Tokyo JP-102 Japan; 81 3 3288 7201, Fax: 81 3 3288 7120, Email: info@sbexpos.com, Web URL: sbex-pos.com

Simulation Conference '96
12/08/96 to 12/11/96, Hotel del Coronado, San Diego, CA U.S., Sponsor: ACM, 1515 Broadway, 17th Floor, New York NY 10036 U.S.; 212/869-7440, Email: brunner@systemflow.com, 2nd Sponsor: IEEE-ICS

Simulation Conference '97
12/07/97 to 12/10/97, Atlanta, GA U.S., Sponsor: ACM, 1515 Broadway, 17th Floor, New York NY 10036 U.S.; 212/869-7440

Software Marketing Executive Forum '96
12/08/96 to 12/11/96, Focus: Business, legislative, technological & regulatory issues, Ritz-Carlton, Aspen, CO U.S., Sponsor: Software Marketing Journal, 525 Market Street, #1600, San Francisco CA 94105 U.S.; 415/546-5585, Fax: 415/546-5599, Email: smj@well.com, Contact: Stuart Rauch, 2nd Sponsor: Kawalek & Associates, Atten.: 175

Spotlight 97
7/20/97 to 7/22/97, Focus: Interactive media, Laguna Nigel, CA U.S., Sponsor: InfoWorld Publishing Company, 155 Bovet Road, #800, San Mateo CA 94402 U.S.; 415/572-7341, Fax: 415/286-2750, 800/633-4312, Web URL: conferences.info-world.com, 2nd Sponsor: Infotainment World, Atten.: 250

Supercomputing Conference '97
11/16/97 to 11/21/97, San Jose Convention Center, San Jose, CA U.S., Sponsor: ACM, 1515 Broadway, 17th Floor, New York NY 10036 U.S.; 212/869-7440

Support Services--Nashville
3/09/97 to 3/12/97, Focus: Support products & services for help desk, network, software etc., Opryland, Nashville, TN U.S., Sponsor: Softbank Technology Group, 1755 Telstar Drive, #101, Colorado Springs CO 80920-1017 U.S.; 719/531-5138, Fax: 719/528-4250, 800/248-5667, Web URL: sbexpos.com, 2nd Sponsor: Help Desk Institute, Atten.: 6,000, Exhibitors: 125

Support Services--San Francisco
10/07/97 to 10/10/97, Focus: Support products & services for help desk, network, software etc., Moscone Center, San Francisco CA U.S., Sponsor: Softbank Technology Group, 1755 Telstar Drive, #101, Colorado Springs CO 80920-1017 U.S.; 719/531-5138, Fax: 719/528-4250, 800/248-5667, Web URL: sbexpos.com, 2nd Sponsor: Help Desk Institute, Atten.: 6,000, Exhibitors: 125

Surface Mount International: Advanced Electronics Mfg. Tech.
9/07/97 to 9/11/97, Focus: Electronic products manufactured using surface mount and related tech., San Jose Convention Center, San Jose, CA U.S., Sponsor: ARI, 1420 MacArthur Drive, Carrollton TX 75007 U.S.; 214/323-0575, Fax: 214/466-4611, Web URL: surfacemount.com, 2nd Sponsor: Electronic Industries Association, Atten.: 1,000+, Exhibitors: 360

TRI-Ada '96
12/03/96 to 12/07/96, Philadelphia Marriott, Philadelphia, PA U.S., Sponsor: Ada Information Clearinghouse, PO Box 1866, Falls Church VA 22041 U.S.; 703/681-2869, Fax: 703/681-2869, 800/232-4211, Email: adainfo@sw-eng.falls-church.va.us, Web URL: sw-eng.falls-church.va.us, 2nd Sponsor: ACM

UNIX World
6/24/97 to 6/26/97, Focus: UNIX & open systems, Mexico City, Mexico, Sponsor: IDG World Expos, 111 Speen St., Box 9107, Framingham MA 01701-9107 U.S.; 508/879-6700, Fax: 508/872-8237, 800/225-4698, Web URL: idg.com

UniForum '97
3/10/97 to 3/14/97, Focus: UNIX & open systems, Moscone Center, San Francisco, CA U.S., Sponsor: Softbank Expos,

300 First Ave, Needham MA 02194-2722
U.S.; 617/449-6600, Fax: 617/449-6953,
Email: info@sbexpos.com, Web URL:
sbexpos.com, Contact: Suzanne Lonergan,
2nd Sponsor: Uniforum, Atten.: 25,000+,
Exhibitors: 350+

Web Developer '97
5/28/97 to 5/30/97, Focus: Internet &
worldwide web, Chicago, IL U.S., Spon-
sor: Mecklermedia, 20 Ketchum Street,
Westport CT 06880 U.S.; 203/226-6967,
Fax: 203/226-6976, 800/632-5537,
Email: iwconf@mecklermedia.com, Web
URL: iworld.com/shows

Web Interactive '97
7/23/97 to 7/25/97, Focus: Internet
product innovations, Santa Clara Convention Cntr, Santa Clara, CA U.S., Sponsor:
Mecklermedia, 20 Ketchum Street, Westport
CT 06880 U.S.; 203/226-6967, Fax: 203/
226-6976, 800/632-5537, Email:
info@mecklermedia.com, Web URL:
iworld.com/shows, Contact: Francie
Coulter, Atten.: 3,300+, Exhibitors: 55+

Web Interactive Australia '97
5/27/97 to 5/29/97, Focus: Internet &
worldwide web, Melbourne, Australia,
Sponsor: Mecklermedia, 20 Ketchum
Street, Westport CT 06880 U.S.; 203/
226-6967, Fax: 203/226-6976, 800/632-
5537, Email: iwconf@mecklermedia.com,
Web URL: iworld.com/shows

Web Market West
12/02/96 to 12/03/96, Focus: Building
businesses on the Internet, The Palace
Hotel, San Francisco, CA U.S., Sponsor:
Red Herring, 1550 Bryant Street, #950,
San Francisco CA 94103 U.S.; 415/865-
2277, Fax: 415/865-0453, Email:

events@herring.com, Web URL: her-
ring.com, Contact: Laura Bartholomew,
2nd Sponsor: Microsoft

Windows Solutions--Japan
12/10/96 to 12/13/96, Focus: Tools and
technologies for building Windows enterprise solutions, Makuhari Messe, Tokyo,
Japan, Sponsor: Softbank Japan, Rokubancho SK Bldg, 3 Rokubancho, Chiyoda-ku,
Tokyo JP-102 Japan; 81 3 3288 7201, Fax:
81 3 3288 7210, Email: info@sbex-
pos.com, Web URL: sbexpos.com, Atten.:
23,000, Exhibitors: 81

Windows Solutions--Japan
12/08/97 to 12/12/97, Focus: Tools and
technologies for building Windows enterprise solutions, Makuhari Messe, Tokyo,
Japan, Sponsor: Softbank Japan, Rokubancho SK Bldg, 3 Rokubancho, Chiyoda-ku,
Tokyo JP-102 Japan; 81 3 3288 7201, Fax:
81 3 3288 7210, Email: info@sbex-
pos.com, Web URL: sbexpos.com, Atten.:
23,000, Exhibitors: 81

Windows World--Dallas 97
9/09/97 to 9/11/97, Focus: PC Windows
applications, Dallas Convention Center,
Dallas, TX U.S., Sponsor: Softbank Expos,
300 First Ave, Needham MA 02194-2722
U.S.; 617/449-6600, Fax: 617/449-6953,
Email: info@sbexpos.com, Web URL:
sbexpos.com, Contact: Peter B. Young,
Atten.: 10,000, Exhibitors: 100+

Winter CES'97, WCES
1/09/97 to 1/12/97, Focus: Consumer
electronics and computer products for
resellers, Sands Expo & Convention Center, Las Vegas, NV U.S., Sponsor: Consumer Electronics Shows, 2500 Wilson
Blvd, Arlington VA 22201-3834 U.S.;

703/907-7600, Fax: 703/907-7601,
Email: zoogang@ix.netcom.com, Web
URL: eia.org/cema, Contact: Cynthia
Upson, 2nd Sponsor: Electronics Industries
Assoc., Atten.: 100,000, Exhibitors: 1,750

Winter CES'98, WCES
1/08/98 to 1/11/98, Focus: Consumer
electronics and computer products for
resellers, Las Vegas, NV U.S., Sponsor:
Consumer Electronics Shows, 2500 Wilson
Blvd, Arlington VA 22201-3834 U.S.;
703/907-7600, Fax: 703/907-7601,
Email: zoogang@ix.netcom.com, Web
URL: eia.org/ceg, Contact: Cynthia
Upson, 2nd Sponsor: Electronics Industries
Assoc., Atten.: 80,000, Exhibitors: 1,750

Year 2000
12/10/96 to 12/12/96, Focus: Year 2000
questions and answers, Navy Pier, Chicago,
IL U.S., Sponsor: Digital Consulting Inc.,
204 Andover Street, Andover MA 01810
U.S.; 508/470-3880, Fax: 508/470-0526,
800/324-3976, Email: dciconf@aol.com,
Web URL: dciexpo.com

Year 2000
3/25/97 to 3/27/97, Focus: Year 2000
questions and answers, Phoenix, AZ U.S.,
Sponsor: Digital Consulting Inc., 204
Andover Street, Andover MA 01810 U.S.;
508/470-3880, Fax: 508/470-0526, 800/
324-3976, Email: dciconf@aol.com, Web
URL: dciexpo.com

Conference Directory-- by Date

11/18/96 to 11/22/96
Comdex/Fall '96, Las Vegas Convention Center, Las Vegas, NV U.S., Focus: PC and LAN products, Sponsor: Softbank Expos, 300 First Ave, Needham MA 02194-2722 U.S.; 617/449-6600, Fax: 617/449-6953, Email: info@sbex-pos.com, Web URL: sbexpos.com, Contact: Kim Pappas, Atten.: 210,000+, Exhibitors: 2,100+

12/02/96 to 12/06/96
DB/Expo East, Jacob K. Javits Convention Center, New York, NY U.S., Focus: Database, client/server and data warehousing technologies, Sponsor: Blenheim Group, Ft. Lee Executive Park, 1 Executive Drive, Ft. Lee NJ 07024 U.S.; 201/346-1400, Fax: 201/346-1532, 800/829-3976, Email: ascully@blenheim.com, Web URL: shownet.com, Exhibitors: 400+

12/02/96 to 12/05/96
Seybold Seminars-Tokyo, Tokyo International Exhibition Center, Tokyo, Japan, Focus: Printing, publishing and new media equipment, Sponsor: Softbank Japan, Rokubancho SK Bldg, 3 Rokubancho, Chiyoda-ku, Tokyo JP-102 Japan; 81 3 3288 7201, Fax: 81 3 3288 7120, Email: info@sbexpos.com, Web URL: sbex-pos.com

12/02/96 to 12/03/96
Web Market West, The Palace Hotel, San Francisco, CA U.S., Focus: Building businesses on the Internet, Sponsor: Red Herring, 1550 Bryant Street, #950, San Francisco CA 94103 U.S.; 415/865-2277, Fax: 415/865-0453, Email: events@herring.com, Web URL: herring.com, Contact: Laura Bartholomew, 2nd Sponsor: Microsoft

12/03/96 to 12/04/96
Business Online Conference, San Diego, CA U.S., Focus: Executive guide to Internet and Intranet strategy, Sponsor: Digital Consulting Inc., 204 Andover Street, Andover MA 01810 U.S.; 508/470-3880, Fax: 508/470-0526, 800/324-3976, Email: dciconf1@aol.com, Web URL: dciexpo.com

12/03/96 to 12/07/96
TRI-Ada '96, Philadelphia Marriott, Philadelphia, PA U.S., Sponsor: Ada Information Clearinghouse, PO Box 1866, Falls Church VA 22041 U.S.; 703/681-2869, Fax: 703/681-2869, 800/232-4211, Email: adainfo@sw-eng.falls-church.va.us, Web URL: sw-eng.falls-church.va.us, 2nd Sponsor: ACM

12/04/96 to 12/07/96

Comdex/Espanol '96, Miami Beach Convention Center, Miami Beach, FL U.S., Focus: PC and LAN products, Sponsor: Softbank Expos, 300 First Ave, Needham MA 02194-2722 U.S.; 617/449-6600, Fax: 617/449-6953, Email: info@sbex-pos.com, Web URL: sbexpos.com

12/04/96 to 12/07/96
Comdex/IT India, Pragati Maidan, New Delhi, India, Focus: PC and LAN products, Sponsor: Softbank Expos, 300 First Ave, Needham MA 02194-2722 U.S.; 617/449-6600, Fax: 617/449-6953, Email: info@sbexpos.com, Web URL: sbex-pos.com

12/04/96 to 12/05/96
ID Info Los Angeles '96, Los Angeles Airport Hilton, Los Angeles, CA U.S., Focus: Automatic Data Capture, Sponsor: Advanstar Expositions, 131 W. 1st Street, Duluth MN 55802-2065 U.S.; 218/723-9130, Fax: 218/723-9122, 800/331-5706, Email: advanstar@advanstar-expos.com, Web URL: advanstar-expos.com/idexpo, 2nd Sponsor: Automatic I.D. News

12/04/96 to 12/07/96
PC World Chongqing, Chongqing, China, Focus: PCs and LANs, Sponsor: IDG World Expos, 111 Speen St., Box 9107, Framingham MA 01701-9107 U.S.; 508/879-6700, Fax: 508/872-8237, 800/225-4698, Web URL: idg.com

12/06/96 to 12/15/96
Comdex/Consumer Expo, Parque Anhembi, Sao Paulo, Brazil, Focus: PC and LAN products, Sponsor: Softbank Expos, 300 First Ave, Needham MA 02194-2722 U.S.; 617/449-6600, Fax: 617/449-6953, Email: info@sbexpos.com, Web URL: sbexpos.com

12/06/96 to 12/08/96
ComputerMania-Denver, CO, Denver Convention Center, Denver, CO U.S., Focus: Entertainment, educational and home office products, Sponsor: Softbank Expos, 303 Vintage Park Drive, Foster City CA 94404 U.S.; 415/578-6900, Fax: 415/525-0194, 800/472-3976, Email: info@sbexpos.com, Web URL: sbex-pos.com

12/08/96 to 12/11/96
Simulation Conference '96, Hotel del Coronado, San Diego, CA U.S., Sponsor: ACM, 1515 Broadway, 17th Floor, New York NY 10036 U.S.; 212/869-7440, Email: brunner@systemflow.com, 2nd Sponsor: IEEE-ICS

12/08/96 to 12/11/96
Software Marketing Executive Forum '96, Ritz-Carlton, Aspen, CO U.S., Focus: Business, legislative, technological & regulatory issues, Sponsor: Software Marketing Journal, 525 Market Street, #1600, San Francisco CA 94105 U.S.; 415/546-5585, Fax: 415/546-5599, Email: smj@well.com, Contact: Stuart Rauch, 2nd Sponsor: Kawalek & Associates,

Atten.: 175

12/09/96 to 12/13/96
Computer Security Applications Conference, San Diego Hyatt Islandia, San Diego, CA U.S., Focus: Computer security, Sponsor: National Computer Security Association, 10 S Courthouse Ave, Carlisle PA 17013 U.S.; 717/258-1816, Fax: 717/243-8642, Email: conferences@ncsa.com, Web URL: ncsa.com, 2nd Sponsor: Applied Computer Security Associates

12/09/96 to 12/11/96
FAXWORLD '96, Hyatt Regency, Burlingame, CA U.S., Focus: Utilizing or implementing fax-integrated messaging technologies, Sponsor: Giga Information Group, 1 Longwater Circle, Norwell MA 02061-1620 U.S.; 617/982-9500, Fax: 617/878-6650, 800/874-9980, Email: conferences@gigaweb.com, Web URL: gigaweb.com

12/09/96 to 12/13/96
Internet World Fall '96, Jacob K. Javits Convention Center, New York, NY U.S., Focus: Internet & worldwide web, Sponsor: Mecklermedia, 20 Ketchum Street, Westport CT 06880 U.S.; 203/226-6967, Fax: 203/226-6976, 800/632-5537, Email: iwconf@mecklermedia.com, Web URL: iworld.com/shows, Contact: Francie Coulter, Atten.: 50,000, Exhibitors: 400+

12/10/96 to 12/12/96
Client/Server Application Packages, Navy Pier, Chicago, IL U.S., Focus: Client/server applications, Sponsor: Digital Consulting Inc., 204 Andover Street, Andover MA 01810 U.S.; 508/470-3880, Fax: 508/470-0526, 800/324-3976, Email: dciconf@aol.com, Web URL: dciexpo.com

12/10/96 to 12/12/96
Database & Client/Server World, Navy Pier, Chicago, IL U.S., Focus: Data warehousing, Internet, client/server, Sponsor: Digital Consulting Inc., 204 Andover Street, Andover MA 01810 U.S.; 508/470-3880, Fax: 508/470-0526, 800/324-3976, Email: dciconf@aol.com, Web URL: dciexpo.com, 2nd Sponsor: Computer Associates

12/10/96 to 12/13/96
Windows Solutions-Japan, Makuhari Messe, Tokyo, Japan, Focus: Tools and technologies for building Windows enterprise solutions, Sponsor: Softbank Japan, Rokubancho SK Bldg, 3 Rokubancho, Chiyoda-ku, Tokyo JP-102 Japan; 81 3 3288 7201, Fax: 81 3 3288 7210, Email: info@sbexpos.com, Web URL: sbex-pos.com, Atten.: 23,000, Exhibitors: 81

12/10/96 to 12/12/96
Year 2000, Navy Pier, Chicago, IL U.S., Focus: Year 2000 questions and answers, Sponsor: Digital Consulting Inc., 204 Andover Street, Andover MA 01810 U.S.; 508/470-3880, Fax: 508/470-0526, 800/324-3976, Email: dciconf@aol.com, Web URL: dciexpo.com

12/18/96 to 12/20/96
International Conference on Parallel & Distributed Info. Sys., Eden Roc Spa & Resort, Miami, FL U.S., Sponsor: ACM, 1515 Broadway, 17th Floor, New York NY 10036 U.S.; 212/869-7440, 2nd Sponsor: IEEE-CS

1/06/97 to 1/09/97
International Conference on Intelligent User Interfaces, Hilton at Walt Disney World, Orlando, FL U.S., Focus: Intelligent user interfaces, Sponsor: ACM, 1515 Broadway, 17th Floor, New York NY 10036 U.S.; 212/869-7440, 2nd Sponsor: American Association of Artificial Intelligence

1/07/97 to 1/10/97
Internet World Canada, Toronto Convention Center, Toronto, Canada, Focus: Internet & worldwide web, Sponsor: Mecklermedia, 20 Ketchum Street, Westport CT 06880 U.S.; 203/226-6967, Fax: 203/226-6976, 800/632-5537, Email: iwconf@mecklermedia.com, Web URL: iworld.com/shows, Atten.: 15,000

1/07/97 to 1/10/97
Macworld, Moscone Center, San Francisco, CA U.S., Focus: Macintosh computers, peripherals & software, Sponsor: MHA Event Management, 1400 Providence Hwy, PO Box 9103, Norwood MA 02026 U.S.; 617/440-0366, Fax: 617/440-0359, 800/315-1133, Email: webmaster@mha.com, Web URL: mha.com/macworldexpo, Atten.: 72,000, Exhibitors: 400+

1/09/97 to 1/12/97
Winter CES'97, WCES, Sands Expo & Convention Center, Las Vegas, NV U.S., Focus: Consumer electronics and computer products for resellers, Sponsor: Consumer Electronics Shows, 2500 Wilson Blvd, Arlington VA 22201-3834 U.S.; 703/907-7600, Fax: 703/907-7601, Email: zoogang@ix.netcom.com, Web URL: eia.org/cema, Contact: Cynthia Upson, 2nd Sponsor: Electronics Industries Assoc., Atten.: 100,000, Exhibitors: 1,750

1/12/97 to 1/15/97
Association of Color Thermal Transfer Tech. Technical Conf., Loews Ventana Canyon Resort, Tucson, AZ U.S., Focus: Color thermal transfer technology, Sponsor: Association of Color Thermal Transfer Technology, 310 Commerce Drive, #228, Amherst NY 14228-2396 U.S.; 716/691-5817, Fax: 716/691-3395, Contact: Rick W. Wallace

1/21/97 to 1/23/97
Comdex/PacRim '97, Trade & Convention Center, Vancouver, BC, Canada, Focus: PC and LAN products, Sponsor: Softbank Expos, 300 First Ave, Needham MA 02194-2722 U.S.; 617/449-6600, Fax: 617/449-6953, Email: info@sbexpos.com, Web URL: sbexpos.com, Atten.: 35,000+, Exhibitors: 300+

1/23/97 to 1/25/97
Internet World International@Singapore, Singapore, Focus: Internet & worldwide web, Sponsor: Mecklermedia, 20 Ketchum Street, Westport CT 06880 U.S.; 203/226-6967, Fax: 203/226-6976, 800/632-5537, Email: iwconf@mecklermedia.com, Web URL: iworld.com/shows

1/27/97 to 1/29/97
Commerce on the Internet, San Diego, CA U.S., Focus: Security, Web sites, customizing software for the Internet, Sponsor: National Computer Security Association, 10 S Courthouse Ave, Carlisle PA 17013 U.S.; 717/258-1816, Fax: 717/243-8642, Email: conferences@ncsa.com, Web URL: ncsa.com

1/27/97 to 1/29/97
PC World Expo/Stockholm, Stockholm, Sweden, Focus: PC and LAN products, Sponsor: IDG World Expos, 111 Speen St., Box 9107, Framingham MA 01701-9107 U.S.; 508/879-6700, Fax: 508/872-8237, 800/225-4698, Web URL: idg.com

1/28/97 to 1/31/97
Asia and South Pacific Design Automation Conference, ASP-DAC, International Conference Hall, Makuhari, Japan, Focus: Design automation, Sponsor: ACM, 1515 Broadway, 17th Floor, New York NY 10036 U.S.; 212/869-7440, 2nd Sponsor: IPSJ

2/01/97 to 2/05/97
International Symposium on High Perf. Computer Architecture, San Antonio, TX U.S., Focus: Computer architecture, Sponsor: IEEE-CS, 1730 Massachusetts Ave NW, Washington DC 20036 U.S.; 202/371-0101, Web URL: computer.org

2/03/97 to 2/07/97
Comdex/IT Forum France, Parc des Expositions, Paris, France, Focus: PC and LAN products, Sponsor: Softbank Expos, 300 First Ave, Needham MA 02194-2722 U.S.; 617/449-6600, Fax: 617/449-6953, Email: info@sbexpos.com, Web URL: sbexpos.com

2/03/97 to 2/06/97
ComNet '97, Convention Center, Washington, DC U.S., Focus: Voice, data and telecom technologies and trends, Sponsor: MHA Event Management, 1400 Providence Hwy, PO Box 9103, Norwood MA 02062 U.S.; 617/440-0366, Fax: 617/440-0359, 800/315-1133, Email: webmaster@mha.com, Web URL: mha.com/comnet, Atten.: 35,000, Exhibitors: 450

2/06/97 to 2/08/97
IEEE-ISSCC International Solid State Circuits Conference, IEEE-ISSCC, San Francisco, CA U.S., Focus: Semiconductor technology, Sponsor: IEEE, 1730 Massachusetts Ave NW, Washington DC 20036 U.S.; 202/371-0101, Web URL: computer.org

2/09/97 to 2/12/97
Demo 97, Indian Wells, CA U.S., Focus:

New products and technologies, Sponsor: InfoWorld Conference & Media Group, 155 Bovet Road, #800, San Mateo CA 94402 U.S.; 415/572-7341, Fax: 415/286-2750, 800/633-4312, Email: demo@pcletter.com, Web URL: demo.com, 2nd Sponsor: PC Letter

2/11/97 to 2/14/97
Expo Comm Mexico 97, Mexico City, Mexico, Focus: Telecom industry, Sponsor: E.J. Krause & Assoc. Inc., 7315 Wisconsin Ave, #450N, Bethesda MD 20814 U.S.; 301/986-7800, Fax: 301/986-4538, Contact: Ron Akins, Atten.: 25,000, Exhibitors: 190

2/17/97 to 2/19/97
Internet Developers' Competition, San Jose, CA U.S., Focus: Internet information, Sponsor: Digital Consulting Inc., 204 Andover Street, Andover MA 01810 U.S.; 508/470-3880, Fax: 508/470-0526, 800/324-3976, Email: dciconf@aol.com, Web URL: dciexpo.com

2/17/97 to 2/19/97
Internet Expo, Web World & EMail World, San Jose, CA U.S., Focus: Internet information, Sponsor: Digital Consulting Inc., 204 Andover Street, Andover MA 01810 U.S.; 508/470-3880, Fax: 508/470-0526, 800/324-3976, Email: dciconf@aol.com, Web URL: dciexpo.com

2/18/97 to 2/20/97
Internet+Intranet, I2, Hynes Convention Center, Boston, MA U.S., Focus: Internet and intranet information, Sponsor: Blenheim Group, Ft. Lee Executive Park, 1 Executive Drive, Ft. Lee NJ 07024 U.S.; 201/346-1400, Fax: 201/346-1532, 800/829-3976, Email: mhavilan@blenheim.com, Web URL: shownet.com, Contact: Mark Haviland

2/18/97 to 2/20/97
Networks Expo & Mactivity '97, Hynes Convention Center, Boston, MA U.S., Focus: LAN and network products and technology, Sponsor: Blenheim Group, Ft. Lee Executive Park, 1 Executive Drive, Ft. Lee NJ 07024 U.S.; 201/346-1400, Fax: 201/346-1532, 800/829-3976, Email: mhavilan@blenheim.com, Web URL: shownet.com, Contact: Mark Haviland, Atten.: 35,000+, Exhibitors: 250+

2/19/97 to 2/22/96
Macworld Expo Tokyo, Tokyo, Japan, Focus: Macintosh computers, peripherals & software, Sponsor: IDG World Expos, 111 Speen St., Box 9107, Framingham MA 01701-9107 U.S.; 508/879-6700, Fax: 508/872-8237, 800/225-4698, Web URL: idg.com

2/23/97 to 2/25/97
Mobile Insights '97, Laguna Nigel, CA U.S., Focus: Mobile computing and data communications, Sponsor: Mobile Insights Inc., 2001 Landings Drive, Mt. View CA 94043 U.S.; 415/390-9800, Fax: 415/919-0930, Web URL: mobileinsights.com

2/25/97 to 3/01/97
Comdex/China, China International Exhibition Centre, Beijing, China, Focus: PC and LAN products, Sponsor: Softbank Expos, 300 First Ave, Needham MA 02194-2722 U.S.; 617/449-6600, Fax: 617/449-6953, Email: info@sbexpos.com, Web URL: sbexpos.com

2/25/97 to 2/28/97
Comdex/ComExpo Mexico '97, Sports Palace, Mexico City, Mexico, Focus: PC and LAN products, Sponsor: Softbank Expos, 300 First Ave, Needham MA 02194-2722 U.S.; 617/449-6600, Fax: 617/449-6953, Email: info@sbexpos.com, Web URL: sbexpos.com, Contact: Kim Pappas, Atten.: 60,000+, Exhibitors: 325+

2/25/97 to 2/27/97
Data Warehousing Conference & OLAP Forum, Orlando, FL U.S., Focus: Database technology trends, Sponsor: Digital Consulting Inc., 204 Andover Street, Andover MA 01810 U.S.; 508/470-3880, Fax: 508/470-0526, 800/324-3976, Email: dci-conf@aol.com, Web URL: dciexpo.com, 2nd Sponsor: Meta Group

3/01/97 to 3/05/97
IEEE Virtual Reality International Symposium, VRAIS '97, Albuquerque, NM U.S., Focus: Virtual reality technology, Sponsor: IEEE, 1730 Massachusetts Ave NW, Washington DC 20036 U.S.; 202/371-0101, Web URL: computer.org

3/01/97 to 3/05/97
SPA 1997 Spring Symposium, San Diego, CA U.S., Focus: PC software industry, Sponsor: Software Publishers Assoc., 1730 M Street NW, #700, Washington DC 20036-4510 U.S.; 202/452-1600, Fax: 202/223-8756, Web URL: spa.org, Atten.: 1,200

3/02/97 to 3/05/97
Business Process & Workflow '97, Walt Disney World Dolphin, Orland, FL U.S., Focus: Technology and management, Sponsor: Giga Information Group, 1 Longwater Circle, Norwell MA 02061-1620 U.S.; 617/982-9500, Fax: 617/982-1724, 800/874-9980, Email: conferences@gigaweb.com, Web URL: gigaweb.com, Contact: Martha Popoloski, 2nd Sponsor: XSoft

3/02/97 to 3/07/97
Object World East, Hynes Convention Center, Boston, MA U.S., Focus: Object-oriented programming, Sponsor: Object World Corp., 492 Old Connecticut Path, Framingham MA 01701 U.S.; Fax: 508/872-6500, 800/969-4664

3/03/97 to 3/05/97
Consumer Online Services Conference, New York, NY U.S., Focus: Online products, technologies and trends, Sponsor: Jupiter Communications, 627 Broadway, New York NY 10012 U.S.; 212/780-6060, Fax: 212/780-6075, 800/488-4345,

Email: jupiter@jup.com, Web URL: jup.com, Contact: Harry Larson

3/04/97 to 3/06/97
Expo Comm Wireless Hong Kong, Hong Kong, Focus: Telecom industry, Sponsor: E.J. Krause & Assoc. Inc., 7315 Wisconsin Ave, #450N, Bethesda MD 20814 U.S.; 301/986-7800, Fax: 301/986-4538

3/06/97 to 3/10/97
Computerworld Expo Vietnam, Ho Chi Minh City, Vietnam, Focus: Client/server computing, Sponsor: IDG World Expos, 111 Speen St., Box 9107, Framingham MA 01701-9107 U.S.; 508/879-6700, Fax: 508/872-8237, 800/225-4698, Web URL: idg.com

3/09/97 to 3/12/97
Support Services-Nashville, Opryland, Nashville, TN U.S., Focus: Support products & services for help desk, network, software etc., Sponsor: Softbank Technology Group, 1755 Telstar Drive, #101, Colorado Springs CO 80920-1017 U.S.; 719/531-5138, Fax: 719/528-4250, 800/248-5667, Web URL: sbexpos.com, 2nd Sponsor: Help Desk Institute, Atten.: 6,000, Exhibitors: 125

3/10/97 to 3/11/97
Data Warehousing & DSS/EIS Conference, Sheraton Grande Torrey Pines, La Jolla, CA U.S., Focus: Data warehousing, Sponsor: Giga Information Group, 1 Longwater Circle, Norwell MA 02061-1620 U.S.; 617/982-9500, Fax: 617/982-1724, 800/874-9980, Email: conferences@gigaweb.com, Web URL: gigaweb.com, 2nd Sponsor: Decision Support Technology

3/10/97 to 3/14/97
Internet World Spring '97, Los Angeles Convention Center, Los Angeles, CA U.S., Focus: Internet & worldwide web, Sponsor: Mecklermedia, 20 Ketchum Street, Westport CT 06880 U.S.; 203/226-6967, Fax: 203/226-6976, 800/632-5537, Email: iwconf@mecklermedia.com, Web URL: iworld.com/shows, Contact: Francie Coulter, 2nd Sponsor: Internet World Magazine, Atten.: 40,000+

3/10/97 to 3/14/97
UniForum '97, Moscone Center, San Francisco, CA U.S., Focus: UNIX & open systems, Sponsor: Softbank Expos, 300 First Ave, Needham MA 02194-2722 U.S.; 617/449-6600, Fax: 617/449-6953, Email: info@sbexpos.com, Web URL: sbexpos.com, Contact: Suzanne Lonergan, 2nd Sponsor: Uniforum, Atten.: 25,000+, Exhibitors: 350+

3/11/97 to 3/14/97
Computers, Freedom & Privacy '97, SF Airport Hyatt Regency, San Franicsco, CA U.S., Sponsor: ACM, 1515 Broadway, 17th Floor, New York NY 10036 U.S.; 212/869-7440

3/13/97 to 3/19/97
CeBIT '97, Hannover Fairgrounds, Han-

nover, Germany, Focus: Computer technology trends and products, Sponsor: Hannover Fairs U.S. Inc., 103 Carnegie Center, Princeton NJ 08540 U.S.; 609/987-1202, Fax: 609/987-0092, Contact: Mette Fisker Petersen, Atten.: 600,000, Exhibitors: 6,507

3/17/97 to 3/20/97
Meta Data Conference, Dallas, TX U.S., Sponsor: Technology Transfer Institute, 741 10th Street, Santa Monica CA 90402-2899 U.S.; 310/394-8305, Fax: 310/451-2104, 800/200-4884, Email: custserv@tti-com.com, Web URL: tticom.com/atm

3/18/97 to 3/20/97
Computerworld Expo New Zealand, Auckland, New Zealand, Focus: Client/server computing, Sponsor: IDG World Expos, 111 Speen St., Box 9107, Framingham MA 01701-9107 U.S.; 508/879-6700, Fax: 508/872-8237, 800/225-4698, Web URL: idg.com

3/18/97 to 3/20/97
FOSE '97, FOSE, Washington, DC U.S., Focus: Federal and military computer buyers and resellers, Sponsor: Reed Exhibition Cos., 383 Main Ave, Norwalk CT 06851 U.S.; 203/840-5634, Fax: 203/840-9646, 800/354-4003, Web URL: fose.reedexpo.com, Atten.: 80,000, Exhibitors: 450

3/18/97 to 3/20/97
Nomadic Computing & Communications Conference, NOMADIC, Washington, DC U.S., Sponsor: Technology Transfer Institute, 741 10th Street, Santa Monica CA 90402-2899 U.S.; 310/394-8305, Fax: 310/451-2104, 800/200-4884, Email: custserv@tticom.com, Web URL: tticom.com/atm

3/19/97 to 3/21/97
Ink Jet and Thermal Printing-Europe, Steigenberger Hotel, Berlin, Germany, Focus: Ink jet and thermal printing marketplace, Sponsor: Giga Information Group, 1 Longwater Circle, Norwell MA 02061-1620 U.S.; 617/982-9500, Fax: 617/982-1724, 800/874-9980, Email: conferences@gigaweb.com, Web URL: gigaweb.com, Contact: Martha Popoloski

3/19/97 to 3/21/97
International Conference on Parallel & Distributed Computing, Shanghai, China, Focus: Parallel and distributed computer system technology, Sponsor: IEEE, 1730 Massachusetts Ave NW, Washington DC 20036 U.S.; 202/371-0101, Web URL: computer.org

3/19/97 to 3/21/97
Internet World Asia '97, Kuala Lumpur, Malaysia, Focus: Internet & worldwide web, Sponsor: Mecklermedia, 20 Ketchum Street, Westport CT 06880 U.S.; 203/226-6967, Fax: 203/226-6976, 800/632-5537, Email: iwconf@mecklermedia.com, Web URL: iworld.com/shows

3/22/97 to 3/27/97

ACM Conference on Human Factors & Computing Systems, CHI 97, Convention Center, Atlanta, GA U.S., Sponsor: ACM, 1515 Broadway, 17th Floor, New York NY 10036 U.S.; 212/869-7440, Web URL: acm.org/sigchi/chi97

3/24/97 to 3/26/97
Communication Design Engineering Conference, Washington Convention Center, Washington, DC U.S., Focus: Designing the latest telecommunications & data communications systems, Sponsor: Miller Freeman Inc., 600 Harrison Street, San Francisco CA 94107 U.S.; 415/905-2354, Fax: 415/905-2220, 800/441-8826, Web URL: mfi.com, Contact: Natasha Claro, 2nd Sponsor: Communication System Design

3/25/97 to 3/27/97
Client/Server Application Packages, Phoenix, AZ U.S., Focus: Client/server applications, Sponsor: Digital Consulting Inc., 204 Andover Street, Andover MA 01810 U.S.; 508/470-3880, Fax: 508/470-0526, 800/324-3976, Email: dciconf@aol.com, Web URL: dciexpo.com

3/25/97 to 3/27/97
Internet Expo, Web World & EMail World, London, England, Focus: Internet information, Sponsor: Digital Consulting Inc., 204 Andover Street, Andover MA 01810 U.S.; 508/470-3880, Fax: 508/470-0526, 800/324-3976, Email: dciconf@aol.com, Web URL: dciexpo.com

3/25/97 to 3/27/97
Year 2000, Phoenix, AZ U.S., Focus: Year 2000 questions and answers, Sponsor: Digital Consulting Inc., 204 Andover Street, Andover MA 01810 U.S.; 508/470-3880, Fax: 508/470-0526, 800/324-3976, Email: dciconf@aol.com, Web URL: dciexpo.com

3/27/97 to 3/29/97
Internet World Colombia, Bogota, Colombia, Focus: Internet information and technology, Sponsor: Mecklermedia, 20 Ketchum Street, Westport CT 06880 U.S.; 203/226-6967, Fax: 203/226-6976, 800/632-5537, Email: info@mecklermedia.com, Web URL: iworld.com/shows, Contact: Francie Coulter

4/01/97 to 4/03/97
Business Online Conference, Orlando, FL U.S., Focus: Executive guide to Internet and Intranet strategy, Sponsor: Digital Consulting Inc., 204 Andover Street, Andover MA 01810 U.S.; 508/470-3880, Fax: 508/470-0526, 800/324-3976, Email: dciconf1@aol.com, Web URL: dciexpo.com

4/02/97 to 4/04/97
ACM Conference on Communications & Computer Security, Zurich, Switzerland, Focus: Computer and communication security, Sponsor: ACM, 1515 Broadway, 17th Floor, New York NY 10036 U.S.; 212/869-7440

4/02/97 to 4/04/97
JavaOne, Moscone Center, San Francisco CA U.S., Focus: Java software development, Sponsor: Softbank Expos, PO Box 5855, San Mateo CA 94402 U.S.; 415/578-6900, Fax: 415/525-0199, 800/488-2883, Web URL: java.sun.com/javaone

4/03/97 to 4/05/97
Computer Personnel Research Conference, San Francisco, CA U.S., Sponsor: ACM, 1515 Broadway, 17th Floor, New York NY 10036 U.S.; 212/869-7440, Web URL: acm.org/sigcpr/cigcpr97

4/03/97 to 4/08/97
PC World, Internet China, Interactive Multimedia China, Beijing, China, Focus: PCs and LANs, Internet and multimedia, Sponsor: IDG World Expos, 111 Speen St., Box 9107, Framingham MA 01701-9107 U.S.; 508/879-6700, Fax: 508/872-8237, 800/225-4698, Web URL: idg.com

4/04/97 to 4/06/97
CES Mobile Electronics '97, Atlanta, GA U.S., Focus: Mobile electronics products, Sponsor: Electronic Industries Assoc., 2500 Wilson Blvd, Arlington VA 22201-3834 U.S.; 703/907-7600, Fax: 703/907-7601, Email: zoogang@ix.netcom.com, Web URL: eia.org/ceg, Contact: Cynthia Upson, Atten.: 5,000+

4/08/97 to 4/11/97
Comdex/Japan, Nippon Convention Center, Tokyo, Japan, Focus: PC and LAN products, Sponsor: Softbank Expos, 300 First Ave, Needham MA 02194-2722 U.S.; 617/449-6600, Fax: 617/449-6953, Email: info@sbexpos.com, Web URL: sbexpos.com

4/08/97 to 4/13/97
Comdex/Sucesu Rio '97, Rio Centro, Rio de Janeiro, Brazil, Focus: PC and LAN products, Sponsor: Softbank Expos, 300 First Ave, Needham MA 02194-2722 U.S.; 617/449-6600, Fax: 617/449-6953, Email: info@sbexpos.com, Web URL: sbexpos.com, Contact: Kim Pappas, Atten.: 75,000+, Exhibitors: 275+

4/08/97 to 4/10/97
Data Warehouse World, San Jose, CA U.S., Focus: Database technology, Sponsor: Digital Consulting Inc., 204 Andover Street, Andover MA 01810 U.S.; 508/470-3880, Fax: 508/470-0526, 800/324-3976, Email: dciconf1@aol.com, Web URL: dciexpo.com

4/08/97 to 4/11/97
Internet World Argentina, Buenos Aires, Argentina, Focus: Internet information and technology, Sponsor: Mecklermedia, 20 Ketchum Street, Westport CT 06880 U.S.; 203/226-6967, Fax: 203/226-6976, 800/632-5537, Email: info@mecklermedia.com, Web URL: iworld.com/shows, Contact: Francie Coulter

4/08/97 to 4/10/97
PC Card '97, San Jose, CA U.S., Focus: PCMCIA technology and trends, Sponsor:

Digital Consulting Inc., 204 Andover Street, Andover MA 01810 U.S.; 508/470-3880, Fax: 508/470-0526, 800/324-3976, Email: dciconf1@aol.com, Web URL: dciexpo.com, 2nd Sponsor: Epson, Intel, Motorola & SunDisk

4/09/97 to 4/10/97
Network World Unplugged, San Jose, CA U.S., Focus: Mobile, remote access and wireless solutions, Sponsor: IDG World Expos, 111 Speen St., Box 9107, Framingham MA 01701-9107 U.S.; 508/879-6700, Fax: 508/872-8237, 800/225-4698, Web URL: idg.com

4/14/97 to 4/17/97
AIIM Show and Conference, Jacob K. Javits Convention Center, New York, NY U.S., Focus: Document management, Sponsor: Association for Information and Image Management Int'l, 1100 Wayne Ave, #1100, Silver Spring MD 20910 U.S.; 301/587-8202, Fax: 301/588-4838, 800/477-2446, Email: aiim@aiim.org, Web URL: aiim.org, Exhibitors: 350+

4/14/97 to 4/16/97
Advanced Speech Applications & Technologies, ASAT, San Francisco, CA U.S., Focus: Speech technologies, Sponsor: Advanstar Expositions, 7500 Old Oak Blvd, Cleveland OH 44130 U.S.; 216/826-2806, 800/777-4442, Email: expos@advanstar-expos.com, Web URL: advanstar-expos.com, 2nd Sponsor: AT&T

4/15/97 to 4/17/97
Client/Server Application Packages, Toronto, Canada, Focus: Client/server applications, Sponsor: Digital Consulting Inc., 204 Andover Street, Andover MA 01810 U.S.; 508/470-3880, Fax: 508/470-0526, 800/324-3976, Email: dciconf@aol.com, Web URL: dciexpo.com

4/15/97 to 4/17/97
Data Warehouse World, Toronto, Canada, Focus: Database technology, Sponsor: Digital Consulting Inc., 204 Andover Street, Andover MA 01810 U.S.; 508/470-3880, Fax: 508/470-0526, 800/324-3976, Email: dciconf1@aol.com, Web URL: dciexpo.com

4/15/97 to 4/17/97
Database & Client/Server World, Toronto, Canada, Focus: Data warehousing, Internet, client/server, Sponsor: Digital Consulting Inc., 204 Andover Street, Andover MA 01810 U.S.; 508/470-3880, Fax: 508/470-0526, 800/324-3976, Email: dciconf@aol.com, Web URL: dciexpo.com

4/20/97 to 4/25/97
IEEE International Conference on Robotics & Automation, Albuquerque, NM U.S., Focus: Robotics and computer automation, Sponsor: IEEE, 1730 Massachusetts Ave NW, Washington DC 20036 U.S.; 202/371-0101, Web URL: computer.org

4/22/97 to 4/24/97
Business OnLine '97, Paris, France, Focus: Electronic commerce, Sponsor: Giga Infor-

mation Group, 1 Longwater Circle, Norwell MA 02061-1620 U.S.; 617/982-9500, Fax: 617/982-1724, 800/874-9980, Email: conferences@gigaweb.com, Web URL: gigaweb.com, 2nd Sponsor: Arthur D. Little

4/22/97 to 4/25/97
Comdex/UK '97, Earls Court 2 Exhibition Centre, London, England, Focus: PC and LAN products, Sponsor: Softbank Expos, 300 First Ave, Needham MA 02194-2722 U.S.; 617/449-6600, Fax: 617/449-6953, Email: info@sbexpos.com, Web URL: sbexpos.com, Contact: Kim Pappas, Atten.: 50,000+, Exhibitors: 250+

4/22/97 to 4/24/97
Internet Expo, Web World & EMail World, Chicago, IL U.S., Focus: Internet information, Sponsor: Digital Consulting Inc., 204 Andover Street, Andover MA 01810 U.S.; 508/470-3880, Fax: 508/470-0526, 800/324-3976, Email: dci-conf@aol.com, Web URL: dciexpo.com

4/22/97 to 4/25/97
Seybold Seminars-New York, Jacob K. Javits Convention Center, New York, NY U.S., Focus: Printing, publishing and new media equipment, Sponsor: Softbank Expos, 303 Vintage Park Drive, Foster City CA 94404 U.S.; 415/578-6900, Fax: 415/525-0194, 800/472-3976, Email: info@sbexpos.com, Web URL: sbexpos.com, Atten.: 20,000, Exhibitors: 200

4/24/97 to 4/27/97
Multimedia China 97, Beijing, China, Focus: Multimedia, Sponsor: Seventh Wave, 10211 Sunland Blvd, Shadow Hills CA 91040-1739 U.S.; 818/353-8652, Fax: 818/353-8215, Email: info@wave7.com, Web URL: wave7.com, Atten.: 60,000+, Exhibitors: 210+

4/26/97 to 4/29/97
Computer Games Developers' Conference, CGDC, Santa Clara Convention Center, Santa Clara, CA U.S., Focus: Game development, Sponsor: Miller Freeman Inc., 600 Harrison Street, San Francisco CA 94107 U.S.; 415/905-2354, Fax: 415/905-2220, 800/441-8826, Web URL: mfi.com

4/28/97 to 4/30/97
ExpoCorp, Sao Paulo, Brazil, Focus: Computer hardware and software, Sponsor: Fenasoft, 3250 Mary St., #205, Miami FL 33133 U.S.; 305/446-3041, Fax: 305/446-3815, Web URL: fenasoft.com.br

4/29/97 to 5/01/97
DRTV Expo & Conference, Long Beach Convention Center, Long Beach, CA U.S., Focus: Direct response television, Sponsor: Advanstar Expositions, 7500 Old Oak Blvd, Cleveland OH 44130 U.S.; 216/826-2806, Fax: 216/826-2801, 800/854-3112, Email: advanstar@advanstar-expos.com, Web URL: advanstar-expos.com/drtv, Exhibitors: 100+

5/05/97 to 5/09/97
NetWorld+Interop-West, Las Vegas Convention Center, Las Vegas, NV U.S., Focus: Local and wide are networks, computer hardware and software, Sponsor: Softbank Expos, 303 Vintage Park Drive, Foster City CA 94404 U.S.; 415/578-6900, Fax: 415/525-0194, 800/472-3976, Email: info@sbexpos.com, Web URL: sbexpos.com, Atten.: 50,000, Exhibitors: 600

5/06/97 to 5/08/97
On Demand Digital Printing & Publishing, Jacob K. Javits Convention Center, New York, NY U.S., Focus: Digital printing and publishing, Sponsor: Expocon Management Assoc., 363 Reef Road, PO Box 915, Fairfield CT 06430-0915 U.S.; 203/256-4700, Fax: 203/256-4730, Email: ondemand@expocon.com, Web URL: expocon.com, 2nd Sponsor: Xerox, Exhibitors: 200+

5/11/97 to 5/15/97
International DB2 Users Group North American Conference, IDUG, Chicago Hilton & Towers, Chicago, IL U.S., Focus: DB2 products and applications, Sponsor: International DB2 Users Group, 401 N Michigan Ave, Chicago IL 60611 U.S.; 312/644-6610, Fax: 312/321-6869, Email: idug@mcs.com, Web URL: idug.org, Atten.: 1,700+

5/13/97 to 5/16/97
Coninfo, Santa Catarina, Brazil, Focus: Computer & IT, Sponsor: Fenasoft, 3250 Mary St., #205, Miami FL 33133 U.S.; 305/446-3041, Fax: 305/446-3815, Web URL: fenasoft.com.br

5/13/97 to 5/15/96
DB/Expo West, Moscone Center, San Francisco, CA U.S., Focus: Database, client/server and data warehousing technologies, Sponsor: Blenheim Group, Ft. Lee Executive Park, 1 Executive Drive, Ft. Lee NJ 07024 U.S.; 201/346-1400, Fax: 201/346-1532, 800/829-3976, Email: mhavilan@blenheim.com, Web URL: shownet.com, Contact: Mark Haviland, Exhibitors: 200+

5/13/97 to 5/16/97
ID Expo and MDCC, Pennsylvania Convention Center, Philadelphia, PA U.S., Focus: Bar code and mobile communication product and technology, Sponsor: Advanstar Expositions, 7500 Old Oak Blvd, Cleveland OH 44130 U.S.; 216/826-2806, Fax: 216/826-2801, 800/331-5706, Email: advanstar@advanstar-expos.com, Web URL: advanstar-expos.com, 2nd Sponsor: Automatic I.D. News, Exhibitors: 275+

5/13/97 to 5/15/96
Internet+Intranet, I2, Moscone Center, San Francisco, CA U.S., Focus: Internet and intranet information, Sponsor: Blenheim Group, Ft. Lee Executive Park, 1 Executive Drive, Ft. Lee NJ 07024 U.S.; 201/346-1400, Fax: 201/346-1532, 800/829-3976, Email: mhavilan@blen-

heim.com, Web URL: shownet.com, Contact: Mark Haviland

5/14/97 to 5/18/97
International Computer & Networks Expo, Shanghai, China, Focus: PCs and networking, Sponsor: IDG World Expos, 111 Speen St., Box 9107, Framingham MA 01701-9107 U.S.; 508/879-6700, Fax: 508/872-8237, 800/225-4698, Web URL: idg.com

5/15/97 to 5/17/97
Graphic Communications 3, Pennsylvania Convention Center, Philadelphia, PA U.S., Focus: Graphic communications, Sponsor: Advanstar Expositions, 7500 Old Oak Blvd, Cleveland OH 44130 U.S.; 216/826-2806, Fax: 216/826-2801, Email: advanstar@advanstar-expos.com, Web URL: advanstar-expos.com

5/18/97 to 5/21/97
Electronic Components and Technology Conference, Fairmont, San Jose, CA U.S., Sponsor: Electronic Industries Assoc., 2500 Wilson Blvd, Arlington VA 22201-3834 U.S.; 703/907-7600, Fax: 703/907-7601, Email: zoogang@ix.netcom.com, Web URL: eia.org/ceg, Contact: Mark V. Rosenker

5/19/97 to 5/23/97
International Conference on Software Engineering, ICSE 97, Sheraton Boston Hotel & Towers, Boston, MA U.S., Focus: Software engineering technology, Sponsor: ACM, 1515 Broadway, 17th Floor, New York NY 10036 U.S.; 212/869-7440, Web URL: ics.uci.edu/icse97, 2nd Sponsor: IEEE-CS TCSE

5/19/97 to 5/22/97
PC Tech Forum, Hyatt Regency, Burlingame, CA U.S., Focus: Technologies and markets of the next generation of PCs, Sponsor: MicroDesign Resources, 874 Gravenstein Hwy S., Sebastopol CA 95472 U.S.; 707/824-4001, Fax: 707/823-0504, 800/527-0288, Web URL: chipanalyst.com

5/20/97 to 5/23/97
Comdex/Argentina '97, Predio Ferial de Palermo, Buenos Aires, Argentina, Focus: PC and LAN products, Sponsor: Softbank Expos, 300 First Ave, Needham MA 02194-2722 U.S.; 617/449-6600, Fax: 617/449-6953, Email: info@sbexpos.com, Web URL: sbexpos.com

5/20/97 to 5/22/97
Internet World UK Spring '97, London, England, Focus: Internet & worldwide web, Sponsor: Mecklermedia, 20 Ketchum Street, Westport CT 06880 U.S.; 203/226-6967, Fax: 203/226-6976, 800/632-5537, Email: iwconf@mecklermedia.com, Web URL: iworld.com/shows

5/20/97 to 5/27/97
Jakarta Computer Expo, Jakarta, Indonesia, Focus: PCs, Sponsor: IDG World Expos, 111 Speen St., Box 9107, Framingham MA 01701-9107 U.S.; 508/879-6700, Fax:

508/872-8237, 800/225-4698, Web URL: idg.com

5/26/97 to 5/28/97
Internet Commerce Expo Taiwan, ICE, Taipei, Taiwan, Focus: Applications and products for Internet, Sponsor: IDG World Expos, 111 Speen St., Box 9107, Framingham MA 01701-9107 U.S.; 508/879-6700, Fax: 508/872-8237, 800/225-4698, Web URL: idg.com

5/27/97 to 5/29/97
Web Interactive Australia '97, Melbourne, Australia, Focus: Internet & worldwide web, Sponsor: Mecklermedia, 20 Ketchum Street, Westport CT 06880 U.S.; 203/226-6967, Fax: 203/226-6976, 800/632-5537, Email: iwconf@mecklermedia.com, Web URL: iworld.com/shows

5/28/97 to 5/30/97
Government, Business & Education Tech Expo, Honolulu, HI U.S., 3450 Palmer Drive, #7280, Cameron Park CA 95682 U.S.; 916/672-1860, Fax: 916/672-0946, 800/474-3976, Contact: Karyn Epp

5/28/97 to 5/30/97
Web Developer '97, Chicago, IL U.S., Focus: Internet & worldwide web, Sponsor: Mecklermedia, 20 Ketchum Street, Westport CT 06880 U.S.; 203/226-6967, Fax: 203/226-6976, 800/632-5537, Email: iwconf@mecklermedia.com, Web URL: iworld.com/shows

5/31/97 to 6/04/97
International Conference on Computer Architecture, Westin Hotel, Denver, CO U.S., Sponsor: ACM, 1515 Broadway, 17th Floor, New York NY 10036 U.S.; 212/869-7440

6/02/97 to 6/05/97
CES Spring, CES, Atlanta, GA U.S., Focus: Consumer products, Sponsor: Consumer Electronics Manufacturers Association, 2500 Wilson Blvd, Arlington VA 22201-3834 U.S.; 703/907-7674, Fax: 703/907-7690, Contact: Cynthia Upson

6/02/97 to 6/05/97
Comdex/Spring '97, Georgia World Congress Center, Atlanta, GA U.S., Focus: PC and LAN products, Sponsor: Softbank Expos, 300 First Ave, Needham MA 02194-2722 U.S.; 617/449-6600, Fax: 617/449-6953, Email: info@sbexpos.com, Web URL: sbexpos.com, Contact: Amy McNamara, Atten.: 100,000+, Exhibitors: 1,100+

6/02/97 to 6/05/97
Expo Comm U.S., Georgia World Congress Center, Atlanta, GA U.S., Focus: Telecom, computer and office automation, Sponsor: E.J. Krause & Assoc. Inc., 7315 Wisconsin Ave, #450N, Bethesda MD 20814 U.S.; 301/986-7800, Fax: 301/986-4538

6/04/97 to 6/06/97
Internet World Mexico, Mexico City, Mexico, Focus: Internet & worldwide web, Sponsor: Mecklermedia, 20 Ketchum

Street, Westport CT 06880 U.S.; 203/226-6967, Fax: 203/226-6976, 800/632-5537, Email: iwconf@mecklermedia.com, Web URL: iworld.com/shows

6/08/97 to 6/12/97
GigaWorld '97, Hyatt Regency at Gainey Ranch, Scottsdale, AZ U.S., Sponsor: Giga Information Group, 1 Longwater Circle, Norwell MA 02061-1620 U.S.; 617/982-9500, Fax: 617/982-1724, 800/874-9980, Email: conferences@gigaweb.com, Web URL: gigaweb.com

6/09/97 to 6/13/97
Design Automation Conference '97, DAC, Anaheim Convention Center, Anaheim, CA U.S., Focus: Computer design technology, Sponsor: IEEE-CS, 1730 Massachusetts Ave NW, Washington DC 20036 U.S.; 202/371-0101, Web URL: computer.org, 2nd Sponsor: ACM SIGODA, Atten.: 18,000, Exhibitors: 150

6/09/97 to 6/11/97
International Conference on Functional Programming '97, Amsterdam, Netherlands, Sponsor: ACM, 1515 Broadway, 17th Floor, New York NY 10036 U.S.; 212/869-7440

6/11/97 to 6/13/97
Internet World Shanghai-China, Shanghai, China, Focus: Internet & worldwide web, Sponsor: Mecklermedia, 20 Ketchum Street, Westport CT 06880 U.S.; 203/226-6967, Fax: 203/226-6976, 800/632-5537, Email: iwconf@mecklermedia.com, Web URL: iworld.com/shows

6/16/97 to 6/20/97
ACM Conference on Programming Language Design, Las Vegas, NV U.S., Focus: Programming language design, Sponsor: ACM, 1515 Broadway, 17th Floor, New York NY 10036 U.S.; 212/869-7440

6/16/97 to 6/19/97
Computerworld Expo South China, Guangdong, China, Focus: Client/server computing, Sponsor: IDG World Expos, 111 Speen St., Box 9107, Framingham MA 01701-9107 U.S.; 508/879-6700, Fax: 508/872-8237, 800/225-4698, Web URL: idg.com

6/16/97 to 6/19/97
M/cad Expo 97, Pennsylvania Convention Center, Philadelphia, PA U.S., Focus: CAD, Sponsor: A/E/C Systems International Inc., 415 Eagleview Blvd, #106, Exton PA 19341 U.S.; 610/458-7070, Fax: 610/458-7171, 800/451-1196, Email: aecsys@ix.netcom.com, Web URL: aecsystems.com, Contact: Carmella Colacchio, 2nd Sponsor: Computer-Aided Engineering, Atten.: 25,000, Exhibitors: 450+

6/17/97 to 6/19/97
A/E/C SYSTEMS '97, Pennsylvania Convention Center, Philadelphia, PA U.S., Focus: Computer buyers from design and construction industries, Sponsor: A/E/C Systems International Inc., 415 Eagleview Blvd, #106, Exton PA 19341 U.S.; 610/

458-7070, Fax: 610/458-7171, 800/451-1196, Email: aecsys@ix.netcom.com, Web URL: aecsystems.com, Contact: David Caplin, Atten.: 25,000+, Exhibitors: 450+

6/17/97 to 6/19/97
PC Expo, WEB.X & Networks Expo, Jacob K. Javits Convention Center, New York, NY U.S., Focus: PC and LAN products, Sponsor: Blenheim Group, Ft. Lee Executive Park, 1 Executive Drive, Ft. Lee NJ 07024 U.S.; 201/346-1400, Fax: 201/346-1532, 800/829-3976, Email: mhaviland@blenheim.com, Web URL: shownet.com, Contact: Mark Haviland, Atten.: 130,000+

6/18/97 to 6/20/97
Internet World Israel, Jerusalem Convention Center, Israel, Focus: Internet information and technology, Sponsor: Mecklermedia, 20 Ketchum Street, Westport CT 06880 U.S.; 203/226-6967, Fax: 203/226-6976, 800/632-5537, Email: info@mecklermedia.com, Web URL: iworld.com/shows, Contact: Francie Coulter, 2nd Sponsor: People & Computers Group

6/18/97 to 6/21/97
Principles & Practices of Parallel Programming, PPoPP, Alexis Park Resort, Las Vegas, NV U.S., Focus: Parallel programming, Sponsor: ACM, 1515 Broadway, 17th Floor, New York NY 10036 U.S.; 212/869-7440

6/19/97 to 6/21/97
Electronic Entertainment Expo, E3, Georgia World Congress Center, Atlanta, GA U.S., Focus: Interactive electronic entertainment, Sponsor: MHA Event Management, 1400 Providence Hwy, PO Box 9103, Norwood MA 02062 U.S.; 617/440-0366, Fax: 617/440-0359, 800/315-1133, Email: webmaster@mha.com, Web URL: mha.com/e3/, 2nd Sponsor: Interactive Digital Software Association, Atten.: 40,000, Exhibitors: 450+

6/23/97 to 6/27/97
ATM Year 1997, San Jose, CA U.S., Focus: ATM technologies, business opportunities and new applications, Sponsor: Technology Transfer Institute, 741 10th Street, Santa Monica CA 90402-2899 U.S.; 310/394-8305, Fax: 310/451-2104, 800/200-4884, Email: custserv@tticom.com, Web URL: tticom.com/atm, 2nd Sponsor: Business Communications Review, Atten.: 1,000+

6/23/97 to 6/27/97
NetWorld+Interop-Frankfurt, Frankfurt, Germany, Focus: Local and wide area networks, computer hardware and software, Sponsor: Softbank Messe & Konferenz, Riesstrasse 25, Munich D-80992 Germany; 49 89 1431 2481, Fax: 49 89 1431 2486, Email: info@sbexpos.com, Web URL: sbexpos.com, Atten.: 21,000, Exhibitors: 332

6/24/97 to 6/26/97

Business OnLine '97, Sheraton Palace Hotel, San Francisco, CA U.S., Focus: Electronic commerce, Sponsor: Giga Information Group, 1 Longwater Circle, Norwell MA 02061-1620 U.S.; 617/982-9500, Fax: 617/982-1724, 800/874-9980, Email: conferences@ gigaweb.com, Web URL: gigaweb.com/ businessonline, 2nd Sponsor: Oracle
6/24/97 to 6/26/97
CES Habitech '97, Dallas, TX U.S., Focus: Consumer electronics and home automation, Sponsor: Consumer Electronics Shows, 2500 Wilson Blvd, Arlington VA 22201-3834 U.S.; 703/907-7600, Fax: 703/907-7601, Email: zoogang@ix.net-com.com, Web URL: eia.org/ceg, Contact: Cynthia Upson, 2nd Sponsor: Electronics Industries Assoc.
6/24/97 to 6/26/97
UNIX World, Mexico City, Mexico, Focus: UNIX & open systems, Sponsor: IDG World Expos, 111 Speen St., Box 9107, Framingham MA 01701-9107 U.S.; 508/879-6700, Fax: 508/872-8237, 800/ 225-4698, Web URL: idg.com
6/29/97 to 7/04/97
IEEE International Symposium on Information Theory, Ulm, Germany, Focus: Information science, Sponsor: IEEE, 1730 Massachusetts Ave NW, Washington DC 20036 U.S.; 202/371-0101, Web URL: computer.org
7/07/97 to 7/11/97
International Conference on Supercomputing, ICS, Vienna, Austria, Focus: Supercomputing, Sponsor: ACM, 1515 Broadway, 17th Floor, New York NY 10036 U.S.; 212/869-7440
7/09/97 to 7/11/97
Comdex/Canada '97, Metro Toronto Convention Ctr & SkyDome, Toronto, Canada, Focus: PC and LAN products, Sponsor: Softbank Expos, 300 First Ave, Needham MA 02194-2722 U.S.; 617/449-6600, Fax: 617/449-6953, Email: info@sbex-pos.com, Web URL: sbexpos.com, Contact: Cheryl Delgreco
7/15/97 to 7/17/97
Database/Client-Server Conference and Expo, Beijing, China, Sponsor: IDG World Expos, 111 Speen St., Box 9107, Framingham MA 01701-9107 U.S.; 508/879-6700, Fax: 508/872-8237, 800/225-4698, Web URL: idg.com
7/16/97 to 7/18/96
Plug.In '97, New York, NY U.S., Focus: Technology in music, Sponsor: Jupiter Communications, 627 Broadway, New York NY 10012 U.S.; 212/780-6060, Fax: 212/780-6075, 800/488-4345, Email: jupiter@jup.com, Web URL: jup.com
7/20/97 to 7/22/97
Spotlight 97, Laguna Nigel, CA U.S., Focus: Interactive media, Sponsor: Info-World Publishing Company, 155 Bovet Road, #800, San Mateo CA 94402 U.S.;

415/572-7341, Fax: 415/286-2750, 800/ 633-4312, Web URL: conferences.info-world.com, 2nd Sponsor: Infotainment World, Atten.: 250
7/21/97 to 7/26/97
Fenasoft, Anhembi Exposition Center, Sao Paulo, Brazil, Focus: International software & hardware, Sponsor: Fenasoft, 3250 Mary St., #205, Miami FL 33133 U.S.; 305/446-3041, Fax: 305/446-3815, Web URL: fenasoft.com.br, Atten.: 625,000, Exhibitors: 1,600
7/21/97 to 7/25/97
NetWorld+Interop-Tokyo, Makuhari Messe, Tokyo, Japan, Focus: Local and wide area networks, computer hardware and software, Sponsor: Softbank Japan, Rokubancho SK Bldg, 3 Rokubancho, Chiyoda-ku, Tokyo JP-102 Japan; 81 3 3288 7201, Fax: 81 3 3288 7120, Email: info@sbexpos.com, Web URL: sbex-pos.com, Atten.: 40,000, Exhibitors: 170
7/22/97 to 7/27/97
Object World West, Moscone Center, San Francisco, CA U.S., Focus: Object-oriented programming, Sponsor: Object World Corp., 492 Old Connecticut Path, Framingham MA 01701 U.S.; Fax: 508/ 872-6500, 800/969-4664
7/23/97 to 7/25/97
Internet World Japan, Tokyo, Japan, Focus: Internet & worldwide web, Sponsor: Mecklermedia, 20 Ketchum Street, Westport CT 06880 U.S.; 203/226-6967, Fax: 203/226-6976, 800/632-5537, Email: iwconf@mecklermedia.com, Web URL: iworld.com/shows
7/23/97 to 7/25/97
Web Interactive '97, Santa Clara Convention Center, Santa Clara, CA U.S., Focus: Internet product innovations, Sponsor: Mecklermedia, 20 Ketchum Street, Westport CT 06880 U.S.; 203/226-6967, Fax: 203/226-6976, 800/632-5537, Email: info@mecklermedia.com, Web URL: iworld.com/shows, Contact: Francie Coulter, Atten.: 3,300+, Exhibitors: 55+
7/24/97 to 7/27/97
Entertainment, Education Electronic Expo, E4, Mexico City, Mexico, Sponsor: IDG World Expos, 111 Speen St., Box 9107, Framingham MA 01701-9107 U.S.; 508/ 879-6700, Fax: 508/872-8237, 800/225-4698, Web URL: idg.com
8/03/97 to 8/08/97
SIGGRAPH 97, Los Angeles Convention Center, Los Angeles, CA U.S., Focus: Computer graphics & interactive techniques, Sponsor: Smith, Bucklin & Assoc., 401 N Michigan Ave, PO Box 95316, Chicago IL 60611 U.S.; 312/321-6830, Fax: 312/321-6876, Email: siggraph97@sig-graph.org, 2nd Sponsor: ACM, Atten.: 30,000+
8/05/97 to 8/08/97
Internet Commerce Expo Hong Kong, ICE, Hong Kong, Focus: Applications and

products for Internet, Sponsor: IDG World Expos, 111 Speen St., Box 9107, Framingham MA 01701-9107 U.S.; 508/879-6700, Fax: 508/872-8237, 800/225-4698, Web URL: idg.com
8/06/97 to 8/08/97
Macworld Expo/Boston, World Trade Center & Bayside Expo Ctr., Boston, MA U.S., Focus: Macintosh products and trends, Sponsor: MHA Event Management, 1400 Providence Hwy, PO Box 9103, Norwood MA 02062 U.S.; 617/440-0466, Fax: 617/440-0357, 800/315-1133, Email: webmaster@mha.com, Web URL: mha.com, 2nd Sponsor: International Data Group, Atten.: 58,600+
8/12/97 to 8/14/97
Internet World Australia Pacific '97, Sydney, Australia, Focus: Internet & worldwide web, Sponsor: Mecklermedia, 20 Ketchum Street, Westport CT 06880 U.S.; 203/226-6967, Fax: 203/226-6976, 800/ 632-5537, Email: iwconf@mecklerme-dia.com, Web URL: iworld.com/shows
8/18/97 to 8/22/97
Comdex/Sucesu-SP Brazil '97, Parque Anhembi, Sao Paulo, Brazil, Focus: PC and LAN products, Sponsor: Softbank Expos, 300 First Ave, Needham MA 02194-2722 U.S.; 617/449-6600, Fax: 617/449-6953, Email: info@sbexpos.com, Web URL: sbexpos.com
8/26/97 to 8/30/97
Comdex/Korea, Korea Exhibition Center, Seoul, Korea, Focus: PC and LAN products, Sponsor: Softbank Expos, 300 First Ave, Needham MA 02194-2722 U.S.; 617/449-6600, Fax: 617/449-6953, Email: info@sbexpos.com, Web URL: sbexpos.com
8/26/97 to 8/29/97
Object World Sydney, Sydney, Australia, Focus: Object-oriented programming, Sponsor: IDG World Expos, 111 Speen St., Box 9107, Framingham MA 01701-9107 U.S.; 508/879-6700, Fax: 508/872-8237, 800/225-4698, Web URL: idg.com, Contact: Matt Mandino
9/02/97 to 9/05/97
Information Superhighway Summit Asia, Singapore, Focus: Coming developments & what is available today, Sponsor: IDG World Expos, 111 Speen St., Box 9107, Framingham MA 01701-9107 U.S.; 508/ 879-6700, Fax: 508/872-8237, 800/225-4698, Web URL: idg.com, 2nd Sponsor: ComNet
9/03/97 to 9/10/97
Print 97, McCormick Place, Chicago, IL U.S., Focus: Printing and publishing technologies, Sponsor: Graphic Arts Show Co., 1899 Preston White Drive, Reston VA 22091-4326 U.S.; 703/264-7200, Fax: 703/620-9187, Email: 70732.2023@ compuserve.com, Contact: John Grossi, Atten.: 90,000, Exhibitors: 900
9/06/97 to 9/10/97

SPA 1997 Annual Conference, Washington, DC U.S., Focus: PC software industry, Sponsor: Software Publishers Assoc., 1730 M Street NW, #700, Washington DC 20036-4510 U.S.; 202/452-1600, Fax: 202/223-8756, Web URL: spa.org, Atten.: 1,200
9/07/97 to 9/11/97
Surface Mount International: Advanced Electronics Mfg. Tech., San Jose Convention Center, San Jose, CA U.S., Focus: Electronic products manufactured using surface mount and related tech., Sponsor: ARI, 1420 MacArthur Drive, Carrollton TX 75007 U.S.; 214/323-0575, Fax: 214/466-4611, Web URL: surfacemount.com, 2nd Sponsor: Electronic Industries Association, Atten.: 1,000+, Exhibitors: 360
9/08/97 to 9/12/97
Computerworld Expo China, Beijing, China, Focus: Client/server computing, Sponsor: IDG World Expos, 111 Speen St., Box 9107, Framingham MA 01701-9107 U.S.; 508/879-6700, Fax: 508/872-8237, 800/225-4698, Web URL: idg.com
9/08/97 to 9/12/97
Networking China, Beijing, China, Focus: Networking products and applications, Sponsor: IDG World Expos, 111 Speen St., Box 9107, Framingham MA 01701-9107 U.S.; 508/879-6700, Fax: 508/872-8237, 800/225-4698, Web URL: idg.com
9/09/97 to 9/12/97
Conference on Information, Communications & Signal Processing, ICICS'97, Singapore, Sponsor: IEEE, 1730 Massachusetts Ave NW, Washington DC 20036 U.S.; 202/371-0101, Web URL: computer.org
9/09/97 to 9/10/97
ID Info Minneapolis, Hyatt Regency, Minneapolis, MN U.S., Sponsor: Advanstar Expositions, 7500 Old Oak Blvd, Cleveland OH 44130 U.S.; 216/826-2806, Fax: 216/826-2801, Email: advanstar@advanstar-expos.com, Web URL: advanstar-expos.com
9/09/97 to 9/11/97
Motion Expo with Powersystems World, Baltimore Convention Center, Baltimore, MD U.S., Sponsor: Advanstar Expositions, 7500 Old Oak Blvd, Cleveland OH 44130 U.S.; 216/826-2806, Fax: 216/826-2801, Email: advanstar@advanstar-expos.com, Web URL: advanstar-expos.com
9/09/97 to 9/11/97
Windows World-Dallas 97, Dallas Convention Center, Dallas, TX U.S., Focus: PC Windows applications, Sponsor: Softbank Expos, 300 First Ave, Needham MA 02194-2722 U.S.; 617/449-6600, Fax: 617/449-6953, Email: info@sbexpos.com, Web URL: sbexpos.com, Contact: Peter B. Young, Atten.: 10,000, Exhibitors: 100+
9/14/97 to 9/16/97
Computer Training & Support Conference, Opryland, Nashville, TN U.S., Focus:

Tools and technologies for computer training and support, Sponsor: Softbank Expos, 10 Presidents Landing, Medford MA 02155 U.S.; 617/393-3344, Fax: 616/393-3322, 800/348-7246, Email: info@sbexpos.com, Web URL: sbexpos.com, Atten.: 4,500+, Exhibitors: 160
9/15/97 to 9/17/97
DataStorage 97, Fairmont, San Jose, CA U.S., Focus: Data storage industry, Sponsor: Forum Management, Conferences Etc, 2680 Bayshore Pkwy, #214, Mt. View CA 94043 U.S.; 415/968-2836, Fax: 415/968-5392, Email: dsforum.com/dsconf, Contact: Darlene Plamondon, 2nd Sponsor: DISK/TREND Inc. and Freeman Associates Inc.
9/16/97 to 9/18/97
IT Forum, Jacob K. Javits Convention Center, New York, NY U.S., Focus: Enterprise technology, Sponsor: Blenheim Group, Ft. Lee Executive Park, 1 Executive Drive, Ft. Lee NJ 07024 U.S.; 201/346-1400, Fax: 201/346-1532, 800/829-3976, Email: mhaviland@blenheim.com, Web URL: shownet.com, Contact: Mark Haviland, Exhibitors: 400+
9/16/97 to 9/18/97
Internet+Intranet, I2, Jacob K. Javits Convention Center, New York, NY U.S., Focus: Internet and intranet information, Sponsor: Blenheim Group, Ft. Lee Executive Park, 1 Executive Drive, Ft. Lee NJ 07024 U.S.; 201/346-1400, Fax: 201/346-1532, 800/829-3976, Email: mhaviland@blenheim.com, Web URL: shownet.com, Contact: Mark Haviland
9/22/97 to 9/26/97
NetWorld+Interop-Paris, Porte de Versailles, Paris, France, Focus: Local and wide area networks, computer hardware and software, Sponsor: Softbank Expos, 300 First Ave, Needham MA 02194-2722 U.S.; 617/449-6600, Fax: 617/449-6953, Email: info@sbexpos.com, Web URL: sbexpos.com, Atten.: 30,235, Exhibitors: 320
9/30/97 to 10/02/97
Macworld Expo Mexico, Mexico City, Mexico, Focus: Macintosh computers, peripherals & software, Sponsor: IDG World Expos, 111 Speen St., Box 9107, Framingham MA 01701-9107 U.S.; 508/879-6700, Fax: 508/872-8237, 800/225-4698, Web URL: idg.com
9/30/97 to 10/03/97
Seybold Seminars-San Francisco, Moscone Center, San Francisco, CA U.S., Focus: Printing, publishing and new media equipment, Sponsor: Softbank Expos, 303 Vintage Park Drive, Foster City CA 94404 U.S.; 415/578-6900, Fax: 415/525-0194, 800/472-3976, Email: info@sbexpos.com, Web URL: sbexpos.com, Atten.: 40,000, Exhibitors: 350
10/03/97 to 10/05/97
Object World Tokyo, Tokyo, Japan,

Focus: Object-oriented programming, Sponsor: IDG World Expos, 111 Speen St., Box 9107, Framingham MA 01701-9107 U.S.; 508/879-6700, Fax: 508/872-8237, 800/225-4698, Web URL: idg.com, Contact: Matt Mandino
10/06/97 to 10/10/97
NetWorld+Interop-East, Georgia World Congress Center, Atlanta, GA U.S., Focus: Local and wide are networks, computer hardware and software, Sponsor: Softbank Expos, 303 Vintage Park Drive, Foster City CA 94404 U.S.; 415/578-6900, Fax: 415/525-0194, 800/472-3976, Email: info@sbexpos.com, Web URL: sbexpos.com, Atten.: 50,000, Exhibitors: 500
10/07/97 to 10/09/97
Comdex/Asia at Singapore Informatics, Singapore International Convention & Expo, Singapore, Focus: PC and LAN products, Sponsor: Softbank Expos, 300 First Ave, Needham MA 02194-2722 U.S.; 617/449-6600, Fax: 617/449-6953, Email: info@sbexpos.com, Web URL: sbexpos.com
10/07/97 to 10/09/97
Comdex/Quebec SCIB '97, Palais des Congres, Montreal, Quebec, Focus: PC and LAN products, Sponsor: Softbank Expos, 300 First Ave, Needham MA 02194-2722 U.S.; 617/449-6600, Fax: 617/449-6953, Email: info@sbexpos.com, Web URL: sbexpos.com, Contact: Kim Pappas, Atten.: 20,000+, Exhibitors: 150+
10/07/97 to 10/10/97
Expo Comm Argentina, Buenos Aires, Argentina, Focus: Telecom industry, Sponsor: E.J. Krause & Assoc. Inc., 7315 Wisconsin Ave, #450N, Bethesda MD 20814 U.S.; 301/986-7800, Fax: 301/986-4538
10/07/97 to 10/10/97
Internet World Chile, Fisa Cordillera, Chile, Focus: Internet information and technology, Sponsor: Mecklermedia, 20 Ketchum Street, Westport CT 06880 U.S.; 203/226-6967, Fax: 203/226-6976, 800/632-5537, Email: info@mecklermedia.com, Web URL: iworld.com/shows, Contact: Francie Coulter
10/07/97 to 10/10/97
Support Services-San Francisco, Moscone Center, San Francisco CA U.S., Focus: Support products & services for help desk, network, software etc., Sponsor: Softbank Technology Group, 1755 Telstar Drive, #101, Colorado Springs CO 80920-1017 U.S.; 719/531-5138, Fax: 719/528-4250, 800/248-5667, Web URL: sbexpos.com, 2nd Sponsor: Help Desk Institute, Atten.: 6,000, Exhibitors: 125
10/10/97 to 10/12/97
Object World Frankfurt, Frankfurt, Germany, Focus: Object-oriented programming, Sponsor: IDG World Expos, 111 Speen St., Box 9107, Framingham MA 01701-9107 U.S.; 508/879-6700, Fax:

508/872-8237, 800/225-4698, Web URL: idg.com, Contact: Matt Mandino
10/12/97 to 10/14/97
Office Equipment & Supplies, Computer & Communication Int'l, Panama, Sponsor: IDG World Expos, 111 Speen St., Box 9107, Framingham MA 01701-9107 U.S.; 508/879-6700, Fax: 508/872-8237, 800/225-4698, Web URL: idg.com
10/12/97 to 10/15/97
Power '97, Santa Clara Convention Center, Santa Clara, CA U.S., Focus: Power requirements for mobile computing & wireless communications, Sponsor: Giga Information Group, 1 Longwater Circle, Norwell MA 02061-1620 U.S.; 617/982-9500, Fax: 617/982-1724, 800/874-9980, Email: conferences@gigaweb.com, Web URL: gigaweb.com, 2nd Sponsor: Arthur D. Little, Atten.: 500+
10/13/97 to 10/16/97
Microprocessor Forum 97, Fairmont, San Jose, CA U.S., Focus: Microprocessors, Sponsor: MicroDesign Resources, 874 Gravenstein Hwy S., Sebastopol CA 95472 U.S.; 707/824-4001, Fax: 707/823-0504, 800/527-0288, Email: mpf@mdr.zd.com, Web URL: chipanalyst.com
10/15/97 to 10/20/97
Compuexpo, Bogota, Colombia, Sponsor: IDG World Expos, 111 Speen St., Box 9107, Framingham MA 01701-9107 U.S.; 508/879-6700, Fax: 508/872-8237, 800/225-4698, Web URL: idg.com
10/16/97 to 10/19/97
Romanian Computer Show, ROCS, Bucharest, Romania, Sponsor: IDG World Expos, 111 Speen St., Box 9107, Framingham MA 01701-9107 U.S.; 508/879-6700, Fax: 508/872-8237, 800/225-4698, Web URL: idg.com
10/19/97 to 10/21/97
Agenda 98, Scottsdale, AZ U.S., Focus: PC industry direction, Sponsor: InfoWorld Conference & Media Group, 155 Bovet Road, #800, San Mateo CA 94402 U.S.; 415/572-7341, Fax: 415/286-2750, 800/633-4312, Web URL: conferences.infoworld.com
10/28/97 to 10/30/97
Networks Expo & Windows World, Infomart, Dallas, TX U.S., Focus: Networking, communication and interoperability products, Sponsor: Blenheim Group, Ft. Lee Executive Park, 1 Executive Drive, Ft. Lee NJ 07024 U.S.; 201/346-1400, Fax: 201/346-1532, 800/829-3976, Email: mhaviland@blenheim.com, Web URL: shownet.com, Contact: Mark Haviland, Atten.: 31,638+, Exhibitors: 250+
11/03/97 to 11/06/97
A/E/C SYSTEMS Fall '97, San Diego, CA U.S., Focus: Computer buyers from design and construction industries, Sponsor: A/E/C Systems International Inc., 415 Eagleview Blvd, #106, Exton PA 19341 U.S.; 610/458-7689, Fax: 610/458-7171, 800/

451-1196, Email: aecsys@ix.netcom.com, Web URL: aecsystems.com, Contact: Sharon Price, Exhibitors: 400+
11/03/97 to 11/04/97
Data Warehousing Conference, Westin, Copley Square, Boston, MA U.S., Focus: Data warehousing, Sponsor: Giga Information Group, 1 Longwater Circle, Norwell MA 02061-1620 U.S.; 617/982-9500, Fax: 617/982-1724, 800/874-9980, Email: conferences@gigaweb.com, Web URL: gigaweb.com, 2nd Sponsor: Decision Support Technology
11/11/97 to 11/15/97
Expo Comm China 97, Guangzhou, China, Focus: Telecom industry, Sponsor: E.J. Krause & Assoc. Inc., 7315 Wisconsin Ave, #450N, Bethesda MD 20814 U.S.; 301/986-7800, Fax: 301/986-4538, Contact: Ron Akins
11/13/97 to 11/15/97
Macworld Expo Australia '97, Sydney, Australia, Focus: Macintosh computers, peripherals & software, Sponsor: IDG World Expos, 111 Speen St., Box 9107, Framingham MA 01701-9107 U.S.; 508/879-6700, Fax: 508/872-8237, 800/225-4698, Web URL: idg.com
11/16/97 to 11/21/97
Supercomputing Conference '97, San Jose Convention Center, San Jose, CA U.S., Sponsor: ACM, 1515 Broadway, 17th Floor, New York NY 10036 U.S.; 212/869-7440
11/17/97 to 11/21/97
Comdex/Fall '97, Las Vegas Convention Center, Las Vegas, NV U.S., Focus: PC and LAN products, Sponsor: Softbank Expos, 300 First Ave, Needham MA 02194-2722 U.S.; 617/449-6600, Fax: 617/449-6953, Email: info@sbexpos.com, Web URL: sbexpos.com
11/18/97 to 11/20/97
Scantech Expo Europe, Koln Messe, Koln, Germany, Sponsor: Advanstar Expositions, 7500 Old Oak Blvd, Cleveland OH 44130 U.S.; 216/826-2806, Fax: 216/826-2801, Email: advanstar@advanstar-expos.com, Web URL: advanstar-expos.com
12/02/97 to 12/03/97
ID Info Los Angeles '97, Los Angeles Airport Hilton, Los Angeles, CA U.S., Focus: Automatic Data Capture, Sponsor: Advanstar Expositions, 7500 Old Oak Blvd, Cleveland OH 44130 U.S.; 216/826-2806, Fax: 216/826-2801, Email: advanstar@advanstar-expos.com, Web URL: advanstar-expos.com, 2nd Sponsor: Automatic I.D. News
12/03/97 to 12/04/97
Network World Unplugged '97, Boston, MA U.S., Focus: Mobile, remote access and wireless solutions, Sponsor: IDG World Expos, 111 Speen St., Box 9107, Framingham MA 01701-9107 U.S.; 508/879-6700, Fax: 508/872-8237, 800/225-4698, Web URL: idg.com

12/04/97 to 12/05/97
FedNet, Washington, DC U.S., Focus: Network use in government organizations, Sponsor: Reed Exhibition Cos., 383 Main Ave, Norwalk CT 06851 U.S.; 203/840-5634, Fax: 203/840-9646, 800/354-4003, Web URL: fednet.reedexpo.com
12/04/97 to 12/05/97
Federal Imaging '97, Washington, DC U.S., Focus: Imaging use in government organizations, Sponsor: Reed Exhibition Cos., 383 Main Ave, Norwalk CT 06851 U.S.; 203/840-5634, Fax: 203/840-9646, 800/354-4003, Web URL: federalimaging.reedexpo.com, Atten.: 7,000, Exhibitors: 150
12/07/97 to 12/10/97
Simulation Conference '97, Atlanta, GA U.S., Sponsor: ACM, 1515 Broadway, 17th Floor, New York NY 10036 U.S.; 212/869-7440
12/08/97 to 12/12/97
Internet World Fall '97, Jacob K. Javits Convention Center, New York, NY U.S., Focus: Internet & worldwide web, Sponsor: Mecklermedia, 20 Ketchum Street, Westport CT 06880 U.S.; 203/226-6967, Fax: 203/226-6976, Email: iwconf@mecklermedia.com, Web URL: iworld.com/shows
12/08/97 to 12/12/97
Windows Solutions-Japan, Makuhari Messe, Tokyo, Japan, Focus: Tools and technologies for building Windows enterprise solutions, Sponsor: Softbank Japan, Rokubancho SK Bldg, 3 Rokubancho, Chiyoda-ku, Tokyo JP-102 Japan; 81 3 3288 7201, Fax: 81 3 3288 7210, Email: info@sbexpos.com, Web URL: sbexpos.com, Atten.: 23,000, Exhibitors: 81
12/09/97 to 12/11/97
Comdex/Espanol '97, Miami Beach Convention Center, Miami Beach, FL U.S., Focus: PC and LAN products, Sponsor: Softbank Expos, 300 First Ave, Needham MA 02194-2722 U.S.; 617/449-6600, Fax: 617/449-6953, Email: info@sbexpos.com, Web URL: sbexpos.com
12/11/97 to 12/14/97
Seybold Seminars-Tokyo, Tokyo International Exhibition Center, Tokyo, Japan, Focus: Printing, publishing and new media equipment, Sponsor: Softbank Japan, Rokubancho SK Bldg, 3 Rokubancho, Chiyoda-ku, Tokyo JP-102 Japan; 81 3 3288 7201, Fax: 81 3 3288 7120, Email: info@sbexpos.com
1/08/98 to 1/11/98
Winter CES'98, WCES, Las Vegas, NV U.S., Focus: Consumer electronics and computer products for resellers, Sponsor: Consumer Electronics Shows, 2500 Wilson Blvd, Arlington VA 22201-3834 U.S.; 703/907-7600, Fax: 703/907-7601, Email: zoogang@ix.netcom.com, Web URL: eia.org/ceg, Contact: Cynthia

Upson, 2nd Sponsor: Electronics Industries Assoc., Atten.: 80,000, Exhibitors: 1,750

3/21/98 to 3/26/98
SPA 1998 Spring Symposium, San Jose, CA U.S., Focus: PC software industry, Sponsor: Software Publishers Assoc., 1730 M Street NW, #700, Washington DC 20036-4510 U.S.; 202/452-1600, Fax: 202/223-8756, Web URL: spa.org, Atten.: 1,200

9/08/98 to 9/10/98
DataStorage 98, San Jose, CA U.S., Focus: Data storage industry, Sponsor: Forum Management, Conferences Etc, 2680 Bayshore Pkwy, #214, Mt. View CA 94043 U.S.; 415/968-2836, Fax: 415/968-5392, Contact: Darlene Plamondon, 2nd Spon-

sor: DISK/TREND Inc. and Freeman Associates Inc.

9/12/98 to 9/16/98
SPA 1998 Annual Conference, Chicago, IL U.S., Focus: PC software industry, Sponsor: Software Publishers Assoc., 1730 M Street NW, #700, Washington DC 20036-4510 U.S.; 202/452-1600, Fax: 202/223-8756, Web URL: spa.org, Atten.: 1,200

9/27/99 to 9/29/99
DataStorage 99, San Jose, CA U.S., Focus: Data storage industry, Sponsor: Forum Management, Conferences Etc, 2680 Bayshore Pkwy, #214, Mt. View CA 94043 U.S.; 415/968-2836, Fax: 415/968-5392, Contact: Darlene Plamondon, 2nd Spon-

sor: DISK/TREND Inc. and Freeman Associates Inc.

9/25/2000 to 9/27/2000
DataStorage 2000, San Jose, CA U.S., Focus: Data storage industry, Sponsor: Forum Management, Conferences Etc, 2680 Bayshore Pkwy, #214, Mt. View CA 94043 U.S.; 415/968-2836, Fax: 415/968-5392, Contact: Darlene Plamondon, 2nd Sponsor: DISK/TREND Inc. and Freeman Associates Inc.

Conference Company Directory

A/E/C Systems International Inc. 415 Eagleview Blvd #106, Exton PA 19341 U.S.; 610/458-7070, 800/451-1196 Fax: 610/458-7171, Web URL: aecsystems.com, Focus: Computer tradeshows and publications, Prdts: A/E/C Systems, Ownership: PVT, Founded: 1979, Empl: 100, David J. Caplin, VP & GM, Kimber McEntee, Mktng Coord

Advanstar Expositions 201 E Sandpointe Ave #600, Santa Ana CA 92707-5761 U.S.; 714/513-8400, Fax: 714/513-8481, Focus: Thermal entertainment, film, TV & video theater, Ownership: PVT, Founded: 1984, Liz Crawford, Show Manager, Leanne Lambert, Promotions Mgr

AIC Conferences Inc. 50 Broad Street 19th Floor, New York NY 10004 U.S.; 212/952-1899, 800/409-4242 Fax: 212/248-7374, Focus: Online publishing conferences, Trina Johnston, GM Media & Com

American Association for Artificial Intelligence (AAAI), 445 Burgess Drive, Menlo Park CA 94025-3442 U.S.; 415/328-3123, Fax: 415/321-4457, Co Email: info@aaai.org, Web URL: aaai.org, Focus: Study and application of artificial intelligence science and technology, Ownership: Nonprofit, Founded: 1980, Empl: 10,000, Carol Hamilton, Exec Dir, Email: ncai@aaai.org; Randall Davis, President

American Electronics Assoc. (AEA), 5201 Great America Pkwy #520, Santa Clara CA 95054 U.S.; 408/987-4200, Fax: 408/970-8565, Co Email: @aeanet.org, Web URL: aeanet.org, Focus: Serves and represents the nation's electronics industry, Ownership: Nonprofit, Founded: 1943, Empl: 3,500

American Institute 708 Third Ave 3rd Floor, New York NY 10017-4103 U.S.; 212/661-3500, 800/345-8016 Fax: 212/661-0204, Co Email: hands-on@amer-inst.com, Web URL: amer-inst.com, Focus: Computer training courses and seminars, Ownership: Sub Institute for Int'l. Res., Esther Mollema, President, Kim Rascoll, Mktng Asst

Applied Computer Research Inc. PO Box 82266, Phoenix AZ 85068-9280 U.S.; 602/995-5929, 800/234-2227 Fax: 602/995-0905, Focus: Information, publications & conferences on applications development & product marketing, Ownership: PVT, Founded: 1971, Phillip Howard, President, Alice Howard, VP, Karen Hedden, Mktng Mgr

Association Exposition & Services

383 Main Ave, Norwalk CT 06851 U.S.; 203/840-4820, Fax: 203/840-4821, Focus: Telecom conferences, Ownership: Sub Reed Exhibition

Association for Computing Machinery (ACM), 1515 Broadway 17th Floor, New York NY 10036-5701 U.S.; 212/869-7440, Fax: 212/944-1318, Co Email: @acm.org, Web URL: acm.org, Focus: Educational and scientific society for computer professionals, Ownership: Nonprofit, Founded: 1947, Empl: 80,000, Joseph S. DeBlasi, Exec Dir, Lillian Israel, Dir Memb, Lisa Ernst, Dir Conf, John A. Osmundsen, Assoc Dir Pub Affairs

Association for Information and Image Management (AIIM), 1100 Wayne Ave #1100, Silver Spring MD 20910 U.S.; 301/587-8202, Fax: 301/587-2711, Web URL: aiim.org, Focus: Advancing technology for capture, storage and retrieval of image documents, Prdts: AIIM Show, Ownership: Nonprofit, Founded: 1945, Empl: 9,000, John Mancini, Exec Dir

Association of Color Thermal Transfer Technology Inc. (ACT), 310 Commerce Drive #228, Amherst NY 14228-2396 U.S.; 716/691-5817, Fax: 716/691-3395, Focus: Promote color thermal transfer printer technology, Ownership: Nonprofit, Founded: 1993, Rick W. Wallace, Exec Dir

Automatic ID Manufacturers Inc. 1326 Freeport Road, Pittsburgh PA 15238 U.S.; 412/963-8588, Prdts: Scantech, Ownership: PVT

Blenheim Group USA Inc. Ft Lee Exec Park, One Exec Drive, Ft. Lee NJ 07024 U.S.; 201/346-1400, 800/829-3976 Fax: 201/346-1532, Web URL: shownet.com, Focus: Computer tradeshows, Prdts: PC Expo, Networks Expo, UNIX Expo, DB/Expo, Ownership: Public, Steve Ianuzzi, CEO, Mark Dineen, VP, Email: mdineen@blenheim.com; Tom Portesy, VP, Email: tportesy@blenheim.com; Don Berey, VP, Email: dberey@blenheim.com; Annie Scully, PR Director, Email: ascully@blenheim.com

Business Technology Assoc. (BTA), 12411 Wornall Road, Kansas City MO 64145 U.S.; 816/941-3100, Fax: 816/941-4838, Web URL: btanet.org, Focus: Association for resellers of office automation equipment and LANs, Ownership: Nonprofit, Founded: 1926, Empl: 6,000, Keith Anderson, Exec Dir, Jan Kitta, Marcom Mgr

CMP Trade Show & Conference Services (CMP), 1 Jericho Plz 2nd Fl Wing A, Jericho NY 11753 U.S.; 516/733-6770, 800/972-5244 Fax: 516/733-6730, Co Email: confreg@cmp.com, Focus: Enterprise-wide client/server solutions, Ownership: PVT, Founded: 1988

Computer Security Institute (CSI),

600 Harrison Street, San Francisco CA 94107 U.S.; 415/905-2626, Fax: 415/905-2218, Co Email: csi@mfi.com, Web URL: gosci.com/csi, Focus: Information for protecting an organization's information assets, Prdts: Network Security, CSI Annual Conference, Ownership: Nonprofit, Founded: 1974, Empl: 3,100, Patrice Rapalus, Dir, Email: prapalus@mfi.com; Nancy Baer, Mktng Mgr, Peter Allen, Managing Ed

Computing Technology Industry Assoc. (CTIA), 450 E 22nd Street #230, Lombard IL 60148-6156 U.S.; 630/268-1818, Fax: 630/268-1384, Co Email: comptiahq@aol.com, Web URL: comptia.org, Focus: Association for computer resellers and vendors, Ownership: Nonprofit, Founded: 1982, Empl: 500, John A. Venator, EVP & CEO, Jeffrey Masich, President

Consumer Electronics Shows (CES), 2500 Wilson Blvd, Arlington VA 22201-3834 U.S.; 703/907-7674, Fax: 703/907-7690, Focus: Consumer electronics tradeshows for resellers, Prdts: SCES, WCES, Ownership: PVT

Convention Data Services Inc. PO Box 1328, Hyannis MA 02601 U.S.; Fax: 508/778-7718, Focus: Computer tradeshows, Ownership: PVT

Data Processing Management Assoc. (DPMA), 505 Busse Hwy, Park Ridge IL 60068-3191 U.S.; 708/825-8124, Fax: 708/825-1693, Focus: Broader understanding of the methods and principles of data processing systems, Ownership: Nonprofit, Founded: 1951, Empl: 30,000, George Eggert, Exec Dir

Dataquest 1290 Ridder Park Drive, San Jose CA 95131-2398 U.S.; 408/437-8000, Fax: 408/437-0292, Co Email: @dataquest.com, Focus: PC, workstation, supercomputer, mass storage, printer & semiconductor information, Ownership: Sub Gartner Group, Founded: 1971, Judy Hamilton, President & CEO, Robert J. Steinerd, VP, Paul Wheaton, Media Rel Mgr

Delphi Consulting Group Inc. 100 City Hall Plaza, Boston MA 02108-2106 U.S.; 617/247-1025, Fax: 617/247-4957, Focus: Seminars and consulting on electronic document management, Ownership: PVT, Founded: 1988, Empl: 20, Thomas M. Koulopoulos, President, Carl Frappaolo, EVP, Debra J. Fitzgibbons, Dir Client Svcs, Mary Ann Kozlowski, Mgr PR

Digital Consulting Inc. (DCI), 204 Andover Street, Andover MA 01810 U.S.; 508/470-3880, 800/324-3976 Fax: 508/470-0526, Focus: Seminars, conferences on CASE, database, PCs and other topics, Ownership: PVT, Founded: 1981, Empl: 70, Sales($M): 10, George Schussel, CEO

Digital Equipment Computer Users Society (DECUS), 334 S Street SHR 3-1/

T25, Shrewsbury MA 01545-4195 U.S.; 508/841-3346, 800/333-8755 Fax: 508/841-3357, Co Email: information@decus.org, Focus: Users group for Digital Equipment products, Prdts: DECUS Symposia & Trade Shows, DECUS University, Ownership: Nonprofit, Founded: 1961, Empl: 53,000, Joseph A. Pollizzi III, President, Tony Ioele, VP, Thomas McIntyre, VP Chapters, Paul Murphy, Email: murphy@decus.org

Disk/Trend Inc. 1925 Landings Drive, Mountain View CA 94043 U.S.; 415/961-6209, Fax: 415/969-2560, Co Email: dtinfo@disktrend.com, Focus: Publishes annual Disk/Trend reports on rigid, disk drive arrays and optical disk drives, Ownership: PVT, Founded: 1977, Empl: 4, James N. Porter, President, Robert H. Katzive, VP

E.J. Krause & Associates Inc. 7315 Wisconsin Ave #450N, Bethesda MD 20814 U.S.; 301/986-7800, Fax: 301/986-4538, Focus: International telecom tradeshows, Ownership: PVT, Founded: 1985, Edward J. Krause III, President & CEO, Ron Akins, VP Tech Group

Electronic Industries Assoc. (EIA), 2500 Wilson Blvd, Arlington VA 22201-3834 U.S.; 703/907-7500, Fax: 703/907-7501, Co Email: @eia.org, Web URL: eia.org, Focus: Trade organization of computer, communications and electronics manufacturers, Ownership: Nonprofit, Founded: 1924, Empl: 1,000, Peter F. McCloskey, President, John J. Kelly, VP & Gen Counsel, T. Glyn Finley, VP Mkt Res, Kevin G. Richardson, VP Gov Rel, Mark V. Rosenker, VP Pub Aff

Expocon Management Associates Inc. 363 Reef Road, PO Box 915, Fairfield CT 06430 U.S.; 203/256-4700, Fax: 203/256-4730, Co Email: @expocon.com, Web URL: expocon.com, Focus: Electronics, data collection and printing tradeshows, Prdts: Abilities Expo, ADA, East Coast Video Show, Sensors Expo, IDENTIMEX, Ownership: PVT, Drew Jenkins, Show Manager

Fenasoft Feiras Comercials Ltda. 3250 Mary Street #205, Miami FL 33133 U.S.; 305/446-3041, Fax: 305/446-3815, Focus: Fenasoft computer tradeshow in Sao Paulo, Brazil, Prdts: Fenasoft, Ownership: PVT

Forum Management, Conferences Etc 2500 Bayshore Pkwy #214, Mountain View CA 94043 U.S.; 415/968-2836, Fax: 415/968-5392, Focus: Computer conference management, Ownership: PVT

Freeman Associates Inc. 311 E Carrillo Street, Santa Barbara CA 93101 U.S.; 805/963-3853, Fax: 805/962-1541, Co Email: freemaninc@aol.com, Web URL: freemaninc.com, Focus: Market analysis and consulting on tape and optical storage; Co-sponsors DataStorage conf., Ownership:

PVT, Founded: 1977, Empl: 8, Raymond C. Freeman, Jr., President, Email: ray@freemaninc.com; Robert C. Abraham, VP

Gartner Group 56 Top Gallant Road, PO Box 10212, Stamford CT 06904-2212 U.S.; 203/964-0096, Fax: 203/967-6143, Web URL: gartner.com, Focus: Information on mainframe, mini and PCs, LANs, software, office automation & telecom, Ownership: NASDAQ, Stock Symbol: GART, Founded: 1979, Empl: 1,175, Sales($M): 229.2, Fiscal End: 9/95; Manny Fernandez, President & CEO, William T. Clifford, EVP & COO, E. Follett Carter, EVP Sales & Mktng, David G. Familiant, EVP Int'l Ops, John F. Halligan, EVP & CFO, Kate Berg, Mgr Media Rel

Giga Information Group 1 Kendall Square Bldg 1400W, Cambridge MA 02139 U.S.; 617/577-9595, 800/874-9980 Fax: 617/577-1649, Co Email: @gigasd.com, Web URL: gigaweb.com, Focus: Electronic imaging, information processing and telecom data, Ownership: Sub Giga Information, Founded: 1979, Empl: 300, Sales($M): 28, Gideon Gartner, Chairman & CEO, Jeff Swartz, SVP Mktng, Richard Goldman, SVP & CFO, Andrew Jennings, SVP WW Sales, Martha Popoloski

Global Touch Inc. 2980 Adeline, Berkeley CA 94703 U.S.; 510/649-1100, Fax: 510/649-1155, Focus: International distribution channel data and conferences, Ownership: PVT, Founded: 1989, Denise Sangster, President

Graphic Arts Show Co. 1899 Preston White Drive, Reston VA 22091-4367 U.S.; 703/264-7200, Fax: 703/620-9187, Co Email: 70732.2023@compuserve.com, Focus: Printing and graphic communications industry tradeshows, Prdts: CONCEPPTS, Midwest Graphics, Graph Expo, Graphic Arts, PRINT, Ownership: PVT, Founded: 1982, Regis J. Delmontagne, President

Graphic Communications Assoc. (GCA), 100 Daingerfield Road, Alexandria VA 22314-2804 U.S.; 703/519-8160, Fax: 703/548-2867, Web URL: printing.org, Focus: Association for printing and publishing industries, Ownership: Nonprofit, Founded: 1966, Empl: 350, Norman W. Sharpf, President, Marian Elledge, VP

Hannover Fairs USA Inc. 103 Carnegie Center, Princeton NJ 08540 U.S.; 609/987-1202, Fax: 609/987-0092, Focus: Electronics tradeshows in Hannover, Germany, Prdts: CeBit, Hannover Fair, Ownership: PVT, Sarah Unger, Com Mgr, Mette Fisker Petersen, Project Manager

Herring Communications Inc. 1550 Bryant Street #950, San Francisco CA 94103-4832 U.S.; 415/865-2277, Fax: 415/865-2280, Co Email: info@herring.com, Web URL: herring.com, Focus:

High-tech financial magazine and conferences, Prdts: Red Herring, Ownership: PVT, Anthony B. Perkins, Publisher, Christopher J. Alden, Assoc Pub, Catherine Silver, VP Sales

IDG Communications (IDG), 1 Exeter Plaza 15th Fl, Boston MA 02116 U.S.; 617/534-1200, Fax: 617/859-8642, Focus: Over 200 computer magazines in 60+ countries, Prdts: CIO, Computerworld, InfoWorld, Macworld, Network World, PC World, Ownership: PVT, Empl: 5,000, Sales($M): 1,400, Fiscal End: 12/95; Patrick J. McGovern, Chairman, Kelly Conlin, President, Jim Casella, COO

IDG World Expos 111 Speen Street, PO Box 9107, Framingham MA 01701-9107 U.S.; 508/879-6700, 800/225-4698 Fax: 508/872-8237, Web URL: idg.com, Focus: PC, workstations, software and communications tradeshows, Prdts: MacWorld, SunWorld, Windows World, ComNet, Object World, Ownership: PVT

IEEE Computer Society (IEEE-CS), 1730 Massachusetts Ave NW, Washington DC 20036-1992 U.S.; 202/371-0101, Fax: 202/728-9614, Web URL: computer.org, Focus: Association for computer professionals, Ownership: Nonprofit, Founded: 1951, Empl: 100,000, T. Micahel Elliott, Exec Dir, Anneliese von Mayrhauser, VP Conf & Tutorials

Information Industry Assoc. (IIA), 1625 Massachusetts Ave NW #700, Washington DC 20036 U.S.; 202/986-0280, Fax: 202/638-4403, Web URL: infoindustry.org, Focus: Association for companies that create, use or distribute information electronically, Ownership: Nonprofit, Founded: 1968, Empl: 550, Ronald Dunn, Exec Dir, VP

Information Management Institute Inc. PO Box 1449, Windham ME 04062 U.S.; 207/892-5269, Fax: 207/892-7356, Focus: Printing technology conferences, Prdts: Ink Jet Printing, Laser Printing, Thermal Printing, Ownership: PVT, Alvin G. Keene, President

Information Services Inc. (IS), 4733 Bethesda Ave #700, Bethesda MD 20814 U.S.; 301/656-2942, Fax: 301/656-3179, Focus: Promote Australian computer exhibitions in US, Prdts: PC-The Personal Computer Show, Ownership: PVT, Founded: 1968, Eileen M. Lavine, President

Information Technology Assoc. America (ITAA), 1616 N Ft Myer Drive #1300, Arlington VA 22209-9998 U.S.; 703/522-5055, Fax: 703/525-2279, Web URL: itaa.com, Focus: Trade association for software & services firms, Ownership: Nonprofit, Founded: 1960, Empl: 650, Harris Miller, President, Olga Grkavaz, SVP

Information Technology Industry Council (ITI), 1250 Eye Street NW

#200, Washington DC 20005 U.S.; 202/737-8888, Fax: 202/638-4922, Web URL: itic.com, Focus: Association for information technology industry, Ownership: Nonprofit, Founded: 1916, Empl: 28, Oliver Smoot, EVP

Information Technology Services Marketing Assoc. (ITSMA), 175 Bedford Street #7, Lexington MA 02173 U.S.; 617/862-8500, Fax: 617/674-1355, Co Email: itsma@aol.com, Focus: Association of high-tech service marketers and managers, Prdts: MarketingServices conf., Ownership: Nonprofit, Founded: 1994, Empl: 55, Richard Munn, President, David Munn, Dir Membership, Dirk Mullenger, Mgr Event Mktng

InfoWorld Publishing Co. 155 Bovet Road #800, San Mateo CA 94402 U.S.; 415/572-7341, 800/432-2478 Fax: 415/312-0547, Web URL: infoworld.com, Focus: Computer publications and conferences, Ownership: PVT

Institute of Electrical and Electronics Engineers Inc. (IEEE), 345 E 47th Street, New York NY 10017-2394 U.S.; 212/705-7900, Fax: 212/752-4929, Web URL: ieee.org, Focus: Association for electrical and computer engineers, Ownership: Nonprofit, Founded: 1884, Empl: 320,000, John H. Powers, Exec Dir, William Cook, Dir Info Svcs

International Communications Assoc. (ICA), 12750 Merit Drive #710 LB-89, Dallas TX 75251-1240 U.S.; 214/233-3889, 800/422-4636 Fax: 214/233-2813, Web URL: icanet.com, Focus: Major user organization for voice, data and image telecom, Prdts: ICA Expo, Ownership: Nonprofit, Founded: 1948, Empl: 700, Robert Eilers, Exec Dir, Lawrence Gessini, President, Michael Case

International Database Management Assoc. Inc. 10675 Treena St #103, San Diego CA 92131 U.S.; 800/767-7469 Fax: 619/271-1032, Focus: PC tradeshows, Prdts: International Spectrum, Ownership: PVT

International DB2 Users Group (IDUG), 401 N Michigan Ave, Chicago IL 60611-4267 U.S.; 312/644-6610, Fax: 312/321-6869, Co Email: idug@mcs.com, Focus: Users of IBM's DB2 software, Ownership: Nonprofit, Founded: 1988, Empl: 2,130, Freddy Hansen, President, Email: dkkmdt8x@ibmmail.com; Michael Cotignola, President-Elect, Doug Stacey, Editorial Dir

Jupiter Communications Co. 627 Broadway 2nd Fl, New York NY 10012-2612 U.S.; 212/780-6060, 800/488-4345 Fax: 212/780-6075, Co Email: jup5@aol.com, Web URL: jup.com/jupiter, Focus: Telecom, information services and videotex information, publications & conferences, Ownership: PVT, Founded:

1986, Empl: 6, Joshua Harris, President, Gene DeRose, Ed Dir

Kallman Associates 20 Harrison Ave, Waldwick NJ 07463 U.S.; 201/652-7070, Fax: 201/652-3898, Focus: Trade show representation, Ownership: PVT, Founded: 1961, Gerald G. Kallman, Sr., President, Thomas Kallman, VP, Gerald Kallman, Jr., VP

Knowledge Industry Publications Inc. (KIPI), 701 Westchester Ave, White Plains NY 10604 U.S.; 914/328-9157, 800/800-5474 Fax: 914/328-9093, Web URL: kipinet.com, Focus: Computer, video and multimedia magazines and conferences, Prdts: AV Video, Computer Pictures, Tape/Disc Business, Ownership: PVT, Roscoe C. Smith III, SVP, Group Pub, Email: kipi1@applelink.com; Barbara Stockwell, VP & Assoc Pub, Jeff Hartford, Circ Dir

Mecklermedia Corp. 20 Ketchum Street, Westport CT 06880 U.S.; 203/226-6967, Fax: 203/454-5840, Co Email: info@mecklermedia.com, Web URL: iworld.com, Focus: Internet publications, tradeshows and consulting, Prdts: Internet World, Web Week, Web Developer, Ownership: NASDAQ, Stock Symbol: MECK, Founded: 1971, Empl: 87, Sales($M): 14.5, Fiscal End: 9/95; Alan M. Meckler, Chairman & CEO, Email: ameck@mecklermedia.com; David Egan, Pres & COO Mag Grp, Email: degan@mecklermedia.com; Carl S. Pugh, Pres & COO Tradeshow Grp, Email: cpugh@mecklermedia.com; Paul A. Stanton, VP Mktng, Email: stanton@mecklermedia.com; Christopher S. Cardell, SVP & CFO, Email: scardell@mecklermedia.com; Francie Coulter, Dir PR, Email: fcoulter@mecklermedia.com

MHA Event Management 1400 Province Hwy, PO Box 9103, Norwood MA 02062-9103 U.S.; 617/440-0366, 800/315-1133 Fax: 617/440-0359, Focus: Tradeshow management, Prdts: Macworld, Ownership: PVT

MicroDesign Resources Inc. 874 Gravenstein Hwy S #14, Sebastopol CA 95472 U.S.; 707/824-4004, 800/527-0288 Fax: 707/823-0504, Web URL: chipanalyst.com, Focus: Consulting & conferences on microprocessors, semiconductor, workstation and PC technology, Ownership: PVT, Founded: 1987, Empl: 12, Michael Slater, President

Miller Freeman Inc. 600 Harrison Street, San Francisco CA 94107 U.S.; 415/905-2200, 800/829-2505 Fax: 415/905-2389, Web URL: mfi.com, Focus: Computer and high-tech magazines and tradeshows, Prdts: DBMS, OS/2, CADENCE, AI Expert, LAN, STACKS, UNIX Review, Ownership: PVT, Graham J.S. Wilson, Chairman, Marshall W. Freeman, President & CEO, Thomas L. Kemp, EVP &

COO

Mobile Insights Inc. 2001 Landings Drive, Mountain View CA 94043 U.S.; 415/390-9800, Fax: 415/919-0930, Web URL: mobileinsights.com, Focus: Market research and conferences for the mobile computing and communications industry, Ownership: PVT, J. Gerry Purdy, President & CEO, Email: gpurdy@mobileinsights.com; Michael French, Dir Mkt Res, Email: mfrench@mobileinsights.com; Vanessa Vla-Koch, VP Ops, Email: vvlay@mobileinsight.com

MPC Trade Shows Inc. PO Box 42007, Houston TX 77242 U.S.; 713/974-5252, 800/717-7469 Fax: 713/974-5459, Web URL: mpcshows.com, Focus: Computer tradeshows, Ownership: PVT

National Computer Security Assoc. (NCSA), 10 S Courthouse Ave, Carlisle PA 17013 U.S.; 717/258-1816, Fax: 717/243-8642, Co Email: @ncsa.com, Web URL: ncsa.com, Focus: Microcomputer security and computer viruses, Ownership: Nonprofit, Founded: 1989, Empl: 1,600, Robert C. Bales, Exec Dir, Michel E. Kabay, Dir Ed, David M. Harper, Dir Mktng, Peter S. Tippett, President, Larry Teien, PR Mgr

Object World Corp. 492 Old Connecticut Path, Framingham MA 01701 U.S.; 800/969-4664 Fax: 508/872-6500, Focus: Object programming conferences, Ownership: PVT

Reed Exhibition Cos 383 Main Ave, Norwalk CT 06851 U.S.; 800/791-3673 Fax: 203/840-9800, Focus: Computer tradeshows, Prdts: FOSE, FedNet, Federal Imaging, Ownership: Sub Reed Elsevier

RTC Group, The 27312 Calle Arroyo, Rancho Viejo CA 92675 U.S.; 714/489-7575, Fax: 714/489-8502, Focus: Computer trade shows, Prdts: Real-Time Computer Show, PC Advanced Technologies Show, Ownership: Sub Concept Development, Founded: 1987, John Reardon, GM, Walter Whitney, Sales Mgr RTC Group

SIGS Publications Group 71 W. 23rd Street 3rd Floor, New York NY 10010 U.S.; 212/242-7447, Fax: 212/242-7574, Co Email: 73361.1707@compuserve.com, Web URL: sigs.com, Focus: Technical computer magazines, books and conferences, Prdts: Object Magazine, C++ Report, X Journal, Smalltalk Report, Ownership: PVT, Richard P. Friedman, President, Margherita R. Monck, GM

Smith Bucklin & Assoc. 401 N Michigan Ave, Chicago IL 60611-4267 U.S.; 312/321-6830, Fax: 312/6876, Web URL: sba.com, Focus: Associations and tradeshow management, Ownership: PVT

Society for Computer Simulation (SCS), PO Box 17900, 4838 Ronson Ct #L, San Diego CA 92117-1810 U.S.; 619/277-3888, Fax: 619/277-3930, Co Email: @scs.org, Web URL: scs.org, Focus:

Advancement of computer simulation technology, Ownership: Nonprofit, Founded: 1952, Empl: 2,300, William Gallagher, Exec Dir, Hildy Linn, Pub Mgr, Email: linn@sdsc.edu

Society of Manufacturing Engineers (SME), 1 SME Drive, Dearborn MI 48121 U.S.; 313/271-1500, Focus: CAD/CAM/CAE/CIM tradeshows, Prdts: AutoFact, Ownership: PVT

Softbank Comdex Inc. 300 First Ave, Needham MA 02194-2722 U.S.; 617/443-1500, Fax: 617/444-4806, Web URL: comdex.com, Focus: Computer trade shows, Prdts: Comdex, Windows World, LAN Expo, New Media, Ownership: Sub Softbank, Japan, Founded: 1971, Empl: 220, Masayoshi Son, Chairman, Jason E. Chudnofsky, President & CEO, Peter Schaw, VP Mktng, Milton Herbert, EVP, Richard L. Schwab, VP Proj Mgmt, Peter B. Young

Softbank Expos 303 Vintage Park Drive, Foster City CA 94404 U.S.; 415/578-6900, Fax: 508/525-0194, Co Email: info@sbexpos.com, Web URL: sbexpos.com, Focus: Computer trade shows, Ownership: Sub Softbank, Japan

Softbank Japan Rokubancho SK Bldg, 3 Rokubancho, Chiyoda-ku, Tokyo Jp-102 Japan; 3-3288-7201, Fax: 3-3288-7120, Focus: Computer trade shows, Ownership: Sub Softbank, Japan

Softbank Technology Group 1755 Telstar Drive #101, Colorado Springs CO 80920-1017 U.S.; 719/531-5138, 800/248-5667 Fax: 719/528-4250, Focus: Computer support conferences, Ownership: Sub Softbank, Japan

Software Productivity Group Inc. 180 Turnpike Road, Westboro MA 01581 U.S.; 508/366-3344, 800/808-3976 Fax: 508/366-8030, Co Email: general@spgnet.com, Web URL: spgnet.com, Focus: Software technology research and consulting, software magazine & conferences, Prdts: Application Development Trends, Ownership: PVT, Founded: 1989, Empl:

20+, Elliot D. Weinman, President, Email: 76102.1473@compuserve.com; Mark McCourt, EVP & Pub, Email: 76102.1473@compuserve.com; Leland J. Katz, Dir Sales & Mktng, Email: 76102.1472@compuserve.com; Dan Kara, Dir Res, Email: 76102.1465@compuserve.com; John Desmond, VP & Editor

Software Publishers Assoc. (SPA), 1730 M Street NW #700, Washington DC 20036-4510 U.S.; 202/452-1600, 800/388-7478 Fax: 202/223-8756, Co Email: @spa.org, Web URL: spa.org, Focus: Association for software publishers who produce, release, develop or license microcomputer, Ownership: Nonprofit, Founded: 1984, Empl: 1,200, Kenneth Wasch, President, John Kernan, Chairman, Dave McClura, Dir Com, Terri Childs, PR Mgr

Special Events Management 111 Executive Center Drive, Columbia SC 29210 U.S.; 803/737-9352, 800/553-7702 Fax: 803/737-7440, Co Email: smitht@sbt.tec.sc.us, Focus: International trade shows and professional conferences, Ownership: PVT, Founded: 1982, Empl: 10, Tony Smith, Dir, Email: smitht@sbt.tec.sc.us; Paul Harkey, Mktng Mgr, Email: harkey@sbt.tec.sc.us; Sam Jenkins, Sales Mgr, Email: jenkins@sbt.tec.sc.us; Carl Quickmire, Conference Mgr, Email: quickmire@sbt.tec.sc.us

Technology Exchange Co. 1 Jacob Way, Reading MA 01867 U.S.; 617/944-3700, 800/662-4282 Fax: 617/942-3002, Focus: Technical training for computer professionals, Ownership: Sub Addison-Wesley

Technology Standards Group Inc. 1083 Waterville Lake Road, Chula Vista CA 91915 U.S.; 619/656-9660, Fax: 619/656-9661, Focus: Seminars on LANs and computer technology, Ownership: PVT, Founded: 1986

Technology Transfer Institute 741 10th Street, Santa Monica CA 90402 U.S.;

310/394-8305, 800/4884 Fax: 310/451-2104, Co Email: custserv@tti.com, Web URL: tti.com, Focus: Seminars & conferences on computer management, software development, networks & databases, Ownership: PVT, Founded: 1972, Empl: 12, John Phillips, President, Dr. Leonard Kleinrock, CEO

Telecommunications Reports/BRP 1333 H St NW 2nd Fl W Tower, Washington DC 20005 U.S.; 202/842-3022, 800/822-6338 Fax: 202/842-3023, Web URL: brp.com, Focus: Telecom policy & technology trends & issues, Ownership: PVT, Founded: 1934, J.C. Ermis, Dir Conf, Email: jce@brpnyc.mhs.compuserve.com; Tony Johnson, Conf Coord, Email: alj@brpnyc.mhs.compuserve.com; Valerie Voci, Sponsorship Mktng, Email: vmv@brpnyc.mhs.compuserve.com

Usenix Assoc. (USENIX), 2560 Ninth Street #215, Berkeley CA 94710 U.S.; 510/528-8649, Fax: 510/548-5738, Focus: Services and technical information for users of UNIX, Ownership: Nonprofit, Founded: 1975, Empl: 4,900, Ellie Young, Exec Dir, Stephen C. Johnson, President

Wave Technologies Int'l. 10845 Olive Blvd #250, St. Louis MO 63141 U.S.; 314/995-5767, 800/828-2050 Co Email: info@wavetech.com, Web URL: wavetech.com, Focus: Computer training seminars and courses, Ownership: PVT

Xplor International , 24238 Hawthorne Blvd, Torrance CA 90505-6505 U.S.; 310/373-3633, 800/669-7567 Fax: 310/375-4240, Co Email: info@explor.org, Web URL: xplor.org, Focus: Association for electronic document printing users, Ownership: Nonprofit, Founded: 1980, Empl: 1,550, Keith Davidson, Exec Dir, Ray Simonson, President, John Alfred, VP, James Porter, Mgr Com, Email: jporter@xplor.com

Chapter 7

Headlines and History

Headlines

These headlines are compiled by Computer Industry Almanac from many sources. Events are shown by month.

January 1993

- Aldus debuts PageMaker 5.0 for the Macintosh.
- Sears sells its Business Systems Centers to InaCom.
- Cisco Systems rolled out its next-generation platform, Cisco 7000.
- IBM ships the 200,000th AS/400 computer.
- Silicon Graphics introduces its most powerful graphics supercomputer, which will be 10 times faster than current systems.
- Intergraph announces a new family of CAD/CAM workstations.
- Supercomputer Systems runs out of money and ceases operation after IBM declines to add to its $100M investment.
- Borland introduces Paradox for Windows.
- IBM announces its worst loss ever, $4.97B, and the first ever operating quarterly loss in 4Q 1992.
- Intel is readying a line of 486 microprocessors, the S series, with built-in power management features.
- IBM's chairman John Akers resigns, which starts an extremely visible search for his replacement.

February 1993

- Unofficial reports say the FTC failed to reach a decision after 30 months investigation of Microsoft's business practices.
- General Magic, an Apple spin-off, debuts Telescripts, a communications-intensive operating system for PDAs.
- IBM introduces 9 new RS/6000 models priced from $3,995 for an entry level M20 to $312,000 to an eight processor SP1 9076.
- Zenith Data Systems and Government Technology Systems win the U.S. Department of Defense's Desktop IV contract for the second time. The contract is for up to 300,000 PCs and office automation software worth $740M.
- Novell announces NetWare Lite 1.1 for DOS and Windows.
- IBM introduces mid-life kickers for its ES/900 mainframe computers--ten water-cooled models and eight air-cooled models.
- Sun Microsystems and Novell disclose plans to bring out a NetWare 4.0 version for SPARC computers.
- NeXT sells its hardware business to Canon and will concentrate its efforts on the Nextstep software business.
- Lotus introduces Improv for Windows--a 3D spreadsheet program at a low introductory price of $99.
- IBM announces 14 new AS/400 models, the F series, ranging in price from $10K to $1.1M with availability in December 1993.

March 1993

- After the World Trade Center bombing several disaster recovery service vendors were in demand.
- Novell formally announces NetWare 4.0.
- Compaq starts selling PCs by direct marketing/direct response channels.
- Borland introduces dBase IV Version 2.0.
- The East Coast Blizzard of the Century collapsed a roof of an EDS data center and cut off service to 5,000 ATMs for several days.
- NuTek USA, a small start-up company, announced a workalike Macintosh PC.
- CompuAdd abandons computer retailing and will close its 110 stores by year-end 1993.
- Microsoft rolls out the second version of Windows NT beta-test software.
- Control Data Systems signs a letter of intent to buy Evernet, a $40M network integrator.
- Digital licenses Mitsubishi as second source for the Alpha chip.
- Intel formally announces the Pentium microprocessor.
- SunSoft introduces PC-NFS 5.0 which connects DOS and Windows PCs to NFS computers.
- Lotus introduces Notes 3.0 with first shipment in late April.
- JWP puts its information Services division on the selling block.
- IBM, HP, Sun Microsystems and Unix Systems Laboratory announces the Common Open Systems Environment (COSE) for workstations.
- PC demand outstrips supply due to component shortages. IBM has two month delay on PS/Value Points and a $1B backlog on its ThinkPad 700 notebook PC. Apple, Compaq and AST Research also report shortages.
- Microsoft ships MS-DOS 6.0.
- After tremendous publicity on the search for IBM's new CEO, the choice is finally made public: Louis Gerstner.

April 1993

- Cray Computer introduces the long awaited Cray 3 supercomputer priced from $2.95M to $30M for 16 processors.
- IBM PC Co. introduces 40 new models in the PS/Value Point family.
- Canon introduces the NoteJet 486 notebook PC with built-in bubble jet printer.
- Motorola starts shipping the first PowerPC RISC processor chips.
- Sun Microsystems announces SPARCstation 10 Model 30LC and Model 51 workstations.
- Digital adds three workstations to its AXP line ranging in price from $5K to $70K.
- AMD wins a legal battle to use Intel's 486 microcode and will start shipping AMD 486 chips.
- IBM makes its $6.1B Adstar storage business an independent subsidiary with former California congressman Ed Zschau as chairman.
- Amdahl announces lay-offs of 1,100 people (13% of its workforce) due to declining profits for its mainframe computers.

• Borland offers its Office software suite which include WordPerfect's word processing software.
• Microsoft is considering moving Windows NT to other RISC platforms including PowerPC, SPARC and HP PA.

May 1993

• Several PC vendors announce efforts to make environmentally friendly PCs. Efforts will be made to design PCs that have recyclable parts.
• Oracle talks about its plans for Oracle Version 8.0 which will be available in December 1994.
• HP will build-in infrared links as a way of transferring data between portable and desktop PCs or between desktop PCs.
• Sun announces Windows Application Binary Interface (WABI), which Sun says will allow Unix workstations with X Windows to run many Windows applications.
• Microsoft announces plans to make the Windows application programming interface available on Unix and Macintosh computers.
• Microsoft also announced that Object Linking and Embedding, OLE 2.0, will be a major bridge to its second generation Windows NT version (code-named Cairo), which is expected to be available in late 1994.
• IBM adds the ThinkPad 720 and 720C notebook PCs.
• IBM adds two RS/6000 workstations--Model 230 and 550L.
• Microsoft says it shipped 3M MS-DOS 6.0 in the first two months after introduction.
• Apple details software migration paths between the Macintosh and PowerPC.
• IBM says it will sell its version of MS-DOS to the whole PC market.
• Pentium-based PCs finally ship.
• Microsoft officially unveils Windows NT at COMDEX/Spring.
• IBM introduces OS/2 Version 2.1.
• IBM and Microsoft confirm they are working on porting Windows NT to the PowerPC.

June 1993

• MCI announces it will form a global network partnership with British Telecom
• Microsoft upgrades its Access database with version 1.1.
• Lotus acquires Approach Software, a database software company, for about $20M.
• Microsoft unveils a software framework for connecting PCs to copiers, faxes and telecom devices--called Microsoft at Work (MAW).
• Lotus ships 1-2-3 Release 4 for Windows and Improv 2.1.
• EPA's Energy Star Initiative is officially unveiled and most PC vendors support the program with announcements of energy efficient PCs.
• IBM announces PC-DOS 6.1, Pen for OS/2 and several multimedia products.
• HP introduces several low-cost PCs in its Vectra VL line. HP also releases the OmniBook 300 subnotebook PC.
• COSE delivers its spec for a common Unix desktop to X/Open.
• Apple, Borland, IBM, Novell and WordPerfect released their plan for OpenDoc, a set of object technologies for multiple platforms.
• Novell unwraps its blueprint for AppWare architecture, a common high-level API that can link to a range of networks, GUIs and clients.

July 1993

• Sun Microsystems teams with Intergraph to port Windows NT to the SPARC platform.
• IBM PC Co. upgrades and expands its ValuePoint line.
• Toshiba debuts the T6600 multimedia laptop PC with built-in CD-ROM.
• IBM also introduces its Ambra PC line, a low-cost PC mail order brand which does not use the IBM name.
• Sun enters the X terminal market. Sun also releases its fiscal year revenue figures of $4.31B.
• IBM discloses that 85,000 people will leave IBM in 1993 and takes a $8.9B in write-offs to cover plant closings and work force reductions.

August 1993

• Apple ships the Newton MessagePad--its first Personal Digital Assistant.
• Dell announces three desktop PC lines: the new NetPlex, OptiPlex and upgrades to the Dimension line.
• Stratus introduces low-end fault-tolerant Unix servers with a starting price of $60K.
• Sharp jumps on the Newton bandwagon and unveils the PI-7000 Expert Pad, which is based on the Newton Intelligence software.
• Gateway 2000 releases a color subnotebook PC called ColorBook.
• MFS Datanet reveals an ATM network between 14 cities is up and running.
• Motorola discloses it has licensed Windows NT for the PowerPC.
• AT&T announces it will acquire McCaw Cellular for $12.6B.
• Compaq introduces a PC family targeted for the home market, which is called Presario.
• Two pen-computer pioneers--Go and EO--merge and retain the EO name.
• FTC ends its probe of Microsoft without any actions, but the Antitrust Division of the Department of Justice will launch its investigation.
• Digital says it will license IBM's NetView.
• Toshiba expands its Satellite notebook line with the T1950 series.
• Over 75 Unix vendors agree to develop a set of standard APIs for all major Unix versions, The APIs will be ready in mid-1994.
• Microsoft ships its long awaited Windows NT.

September 1993

• Microsoft outlines the Plug and Play plan which will minimize add-in card incompatibilities when implemented by late 1994.

- IBM introduces three AS/400 models targeted for the server market; hardware prices start at $17K.
- Sun Microsystems introduces clustered network file servers.
- Wang emerges from its Chapter 11 bankruptcy protection.
- Oracle discloses its blueprint for Oracle Office, which will compete with Lotus Notes.
- David Packard retires as Chairman of Hewlett-Packard.
- IBM debuts its first workstations based on the PowerPC chip, the Powerstation 25T and Powerserver 250.
- Digital ships Windows NT with its Alpha-based PCs.
- Frame Technology introduces FrameMaker 4 desktop publishing program.
- Microsoft lowers the price of Windows NT Advanced Server to only $1,495 for a 1,000 user network from $36,500 previously.
- ComputerLand agrees to sell its franchising and distribution business to Merisel for $110M.

October 1993

- Microsoft introduces Windows for Workgroups 3.11.
- Digital announces two Alpha-based workstations and three servers.
- Novell transfers the Unix trademark to X/Open. X/Open will certify that an operating system is Unix compliant.
- John Sculley resigns from Apple and becomes Chairman & CEO of Spectrum Information Technologies.
- WordPerfect ships WordPerfect 6.0 for Windows
- Novell releases Personal NetWare peer-to-peer networking software.
- Microsoft announces MS-DOS 6.2 and Word 6.0 for Windows.
- Apple unveils the Quadra 610 which has a 68040 and a 486 microprocessor and can run both Mac and Windows software.
- Bell Atlantic and Tele-Communications announce they will merge at a deal valued at $12B. A frenzy of headlines on the Information Super-highway follows from the computer press to the popular press. The deal is later cancelled.

November 1993

- Digital announces high-end PCs using the PCI bus and either 486, Pentium or Alpha microprocessors.
- Amdahl says it will reduce its workforce by 24%, will drop several Unix projects and will sell Sun Unix products instead.
- Toshiba introduces its Portege T3400 subnotebook PCs, shipments will start in January 1994.
- Everex emerges from Chapter 11 bankruptcy protection.
- Ray Noorda sets his retirement date from Novell for June 1994
- IBM announces OS/2 for Windows, which upgrades the Windows environment to OS/2.
- Compton's NewMedia claims it has received a core patent for multimedia applications, which is later overturned.
- Lotus extends its joint marketing and OS/2 development agreement.
- Sun Microsystems licenses NextStep and makes a $10M investment in NeXT.
- IBM's Ambra subsidiary introduces a subnotebook PC starting at $1,900 and a high-end color notebook PC.

December 1993

- Microsoft shows an early version of Chicago or Windows 4.0 to 5,000+ software developers.
- Apple hosts a Newton software developers conference with over 1,000 attendees.
- WordPerfect names Adrian Rietveld as new CEO.
- Compaq exits the network printer market.
- IBM says it will sell its Federal Systems division ($2.2B in yearly revenue) to Loral for $1.6B.
- Oracle ships Oracle Office 2.0.

January 1994

- Apple enters the online service market by announcing eWorld.
- HP becomes a Taligent partner and buys 15% from Apple and IBM.
- Silicon Graphics upgrades its Indy workstations with the 150MHz R4400 microprocessor.
- Apple announces it will provide PowerPC upgrade boards for current Macintoshes.
- Numerous native PowerPC applications for the Macintosh are previewed at MacWorld.
- IBM unveils its plan to migrate the AS/400 to the PowerPC hardware platform by 1995.
- NCR changes name to AT&T Global Information Solutions.
- Apple officially announced it will licence its Macintosh operating system to companies using the PowerPC.
- HP introduces a PA-RISC workstation, the HP 9000 Model 712 starting at $4K.
- Borland ships BorlandOffice 2.0.
- General Magic demonstrates Magic Cap and Telescript.
- Novell ships NetWare 4.01, an upgrade of NetWare 4.0.
- Apple is working on a 3D Quickdraw for both Macintosh and Windows.

February 1994

- Compaq ships its Contura Aero subnotebook PC, which starts at $1,400.
- IBM drops its right to build the Pentium.

• Lotus ships cc:Mail Mobile for Windows and Notes for Solaris--its first Unix version.
• Microsoft ships Excel 5.0 and also adopts TCP/IP as its networking protocol of choice.
• John Sculley leaves Spectrum Information Technologies, while lawsuits fly (which are later dropped).
• Stac Electronics wins its lawsuit (and $120M) against Microsoft's use of data compression in MS-DOS 6.x.
• Dell reenters the notebook PC market buy reselling units made by AST Research.
• Bell Atlantic and Tele-Communications abandon their merger.
• Apple upgrades its Newton with the MessagePad 110.
• Intel unveils its Graphics Library (IGL), a 3D API for PCs.

March 1994

• Macintoshes using the PowerPC start shipping--three models are available: the 6100, 7100 and 8100
• Court awards AMD right to use Intel microprocessor microcode.
• Intel introduces the 486DX4, a clock-tripling chip and over 30 vendors introduce PCs using the DX4.
• NexGen ships its NX586 microprocessor--a Pentium class processor.
• Convex Computer introduces a massively parallel computer using up to 128 PA-7100 RISC microprocessors.
• IBM announces a RS/6000 laptop workstation.
• Sun Microsystems makes a buyout royalty deal with Novell for Unix System V Release 4 for $82.5M.
• Aldus and Adobe agree to merge in a transaction worth $525M and will form a $0.5B software company.
• ComputerLand changes name to Vanstar after selling its franchising and distribution business to Merisel.
• Sun Microsystems announces its SPARCstation 20.
• Apple announces software that will emulate the Macintosh on Sun and HP workstations.
• Novell says it will acquire WordPerfect for $1.14B and will buy Borland's Quattro Pro for $145M.
• EDS wins an outsourcing contract from Xerox that could be worth over $4B in 10 years.
• Taligent gives its first public demonstration of a major part of its object-oriented OS, Frameworks.
• Novell outlines its strategy for adding platform independent Symmetrical Multiprocessing capabilities to NetWare by year-end 1997.
• Informix ships its first multiprocessing database, OnLine 7.0.
• IBM introduces its first ATM product, an ATM adapter card for the RS/6000.
• AT&T and Lotus unveil plans for electronic information services using Lotus' Notes servers.

April 1994

• Microsoft ships Access 2.0 and FoxPro 2.6 database programs.
• Compaq says it is experimenting with a PowerPC-based server using Windows NT.
• Robert J. Frankenberg, a former HP executive, becomes Novell's President & CEO.
• Sun Microsystems introduces Solaris 2.4 for Unix workstations and for X86-based computers.
• Wang ships Open/Profound, a document management program for Windows.
• Symantec says it will purchase Central Point Software at an estimated value of $60M.
• Digital introduces Alpha-based SMP AXP 21000 servers starting at $19K.
• IBM agrees to build Cyrix 486-compatible chips.
• Lotus will back-off the Macintosh application market and will primarily focus on Windows and OS/2 platforms.
• Apple unveils a family of PowerPC-based servers, the WorkGroup Server WS 6150, WS 8150 and WS 9150.
• HP announces OpenView for Windows, a network management program.
• Compaq replaces its DeskPro/M series with the DeskPro XL range.
• Intel proposed the MPS 1.1 MultiProcessor Specification and gains support from PC and operating system vendors.
• Novell and Apple plan to develop a NetWare version for Power Macs.
• IBM PC Co. President Robert J. Corrigan resigns and is replaced by G. Richard Thoman.

May 1994

• Digital confirms it will lay off 20,000 people and sell off some of its business.
• IBM realigns its sales force from a geographic organization to an industry focused orientation.
• Microsoft and Texas Instruments agree to jointly develop a database repository specification.
• IBM introduces OS/400 version 3, several RISC-ready AS/400 models and per-user software pricing.
• AT&T and Novell announce they will construct a public network service based on NetWare.
• Computer Associates and EDS settle their two year old lawsuit and clears CA to make a $305M bid for The ASK Group.
• IBM unveils several RS/6000 workstations (Models 41T and 3BT) and servers (Models C10 and 59H).
• IBM announces a low-end family of PC servers using the EISA and PCI buses instead of the MCA bus.
• Sprint and EDS talk about merger, which is later abandoned.
• Microsoft says it will no longer use suggested retail pricing.
• HP announces four new workstation models in the HP 9000 family--HP 715 and 725--with entry prices from $10K to $20K.
• Sun Microsystems announces its SPARCstation 5.
• The first PCs using the PowerPC Reference Platform specs are unveiled.
• IBM says it shipped its 5 millionth copy of OS/2. Microsoft says it shipped its 50 millionth copy of Windows.
• Lotus says it will purchase the developer of Notes, Iris Associates, for $84M in stocks.
• Radius and SuperMac agree to merge in a deal worth $81M.
• Intergraph bets the company on Windows NT and Pentium and will migrate its product line from Unix/Clipper and Unix/SPARC.

• On Technology acquires Da Vinci Systems, an e-mail vendor with a 2 million user base.

June 1994

• Taligent releases the beta version of its long awaited object-oriented building blocks for operating systems.
• HP forms a systems integration subsidiary called the Solutions Integration Group.
• Intel and HP announce an alliance to produce a microprocessor compatible with both the X86 and HP-PA in the 1998 timeframe.
• Compaq lowers prices on its PCs.
• Oracle unveils Version 7.1 of its database program.
• NexGen formalizes an agreement with IBM Microelectronics to manufacture its Nx586, a Pentium-compatible microprocessor.
• MIPS rolls out its 64-bit RISC microprocessor--the R8000.
• WordPerfect upgrades its Office Suite with Version 4.1.
• IBM unveils its ATM product map and strategy and introduces five ATM switches.
• Borland announces dBase for Windows.
• Lotus says it will buy SoftSwitch, a message integration provider, for about 3 million shares.
• AT&T and Silicon Graphics launch Interactive Digital Solutions, a joint venture to deliver multimedia services.
• IBM introduces its Ramac RAID storage systems.
• Microsoft makes its first public showing of Windows 4.0 (code named Chicago) and starts its beta testing.
• Microsoft settles its lawsuit with Stac Electronics as Microsoft buys 15% of Stac for $40M and licences its technology for $43M.
• Open Software Foundation releases OSF/1 1.3 microkernel-based OS and OSF/Motif 2.0 GUI.
• IBM and Sun Microsystems agree to put Solaris on the PowerPC.
• IBM shows a pre-beta version of its Workspace OS for handheld computers at a tradeshow in Taiwan (Code-name EOS).

July 1994

• Wellfleet and SynOptics agree to merge in a transaction worth $1B.
• PowerPC 603 microprocessors are now available. 1M PowerPC 601 chips have been sold to date.
• Digital takes a $1.2B restructuring charge to layoff 20,000 employees in the next 12 months.
• Sun Microsystems and Thomson Consumer Electronics announce a joint venture to provide digital interactive video servers.
• Cisco Systems says it will acquire Newport Systems Solutions for 4.2M shares.
• Dell withdraws from the PC retail business and will concentrate on direct marketing and VARs.
• Digital unveils the DEC 3000 Model 700 and Model 900 workstations and AdvantageCluster server with up to 16 Alpha chips.
• Microsoft settles a four year old federal antitrust investigation. Microsoft agrees to modify its OS licensing terms with PC manufacturers.
• Digital agrees to sell its disk business to Quantum for $400M (DEC's annual disk revenue is about $700M).
• IBM says it will close its Ambra PC subsidiary and will cut the head-count of the PC Co. by 20%.
• Compaq holds the No. 1 spot in worldwide PC shipments for 2Q94 with 1.5M units, followed by IBM with 0.9M and Apple with 0.85M.
• Seagate will buy Palidrome, a publisher of storage management software, for $69M.

August 1994

• Sterling Software will acquire KnowledgeWare for $113M.
• Dell reenters the notebook PC market with the Latitude line ranging from 486DX2 to Pentium-based models.
• IBM ships a new version of its Unix operating system--AIX 4.1.
• Storage Technology plans to acquire Network Systems for 8.5M shares worth about $315M.
• TCI and other cable TV companies will buy $2B in phone equipment to compete in the local phone business.
• Bell Atlantic and Nynex sue to block AT&T's acquisition of McCaw Cellular.
• Microsoft says it shipped 0.8M Access database programs in the last three months and 2M units since introduction in November 1992.
• IBM plans to offer an electronic software shopping, ordering and delivery services for companies through its Global Network next year.
• Compaq and Microsoft say they will put warning labels on computer keyboards to avoid hand and wrist injuries.
• AT&T Global Information Solutions (formerly NCR) introduces several notebook and multimedia PCs.
• Lotus says it is working on a desktop version of its Notes software.
• Thousands of people worldwide have been infected from the kaos4 virus by downloading erotic software from an Internet bulletin board.
• Novell and Microsoft call a truce to their feud as Bill Gates and Robert Frankenberg meet to discuss future cooperation.
• AT&T and Intel announce they will develop software to bridge their competing desktop video conferencing standards.
• Software Publishers Association reports CD-ROM software sales revenue increased 366% in 1Q'94 versus last year.
• Thinking Machines, the pioneer in massively parallel computers, files for Chapter 11 bankruptcy protection.
• Novell says it will lay off 1,750 workers in the next 6 months.

September 1994

• Microsoft introduces a Window specific ergonomic keyboard.
• Microsoft says Chicago will be called Windows 95 and will be released in 1H'95.
• Compaq unveils 12 Presario models that will use AMD's 486 microprocessors.
• Apple will finally let other companies make Macintosh-compatible computers and expects the first clones to be available in mid-95.
• IBM announces its Aptiva line of multimedia PCs which replace the PS/1 family.
• Spry rolls out Internet In A Box, the first commercial software package for Internet access.

• Bill Gates is swamped with 5,000 e-mail messages after The New Yorker publishes his Internet address.
• Cray Research introduces the J916, first in a series of low-cost supercomputers.
• HP offers two workgroup laser printers--the LaserJet 4V and 4MV.
• Microsoft, Lockheed and Southwestern Bell plan to offer advanced TV services.
• Sony's PDA, the Magic Link, hits the market and marks the debut of software agents that can perform a variety of tasks by connecting to AT&T's PersonaLink service.
• Microsoft completes its acquisition of Altamira Software--a company focusing on color imaging.
• Sun Microsystems announces its Netra servers for PC LANs.
• Digital introduces the Alpha AXP 21164 microprocessor with a 300 MHz clock rate and over 1-billion-instructions-per-second.
• Microsoft unveils Windows NT 3.5 (code name Daytona).
• Oracle brings out its Document groupware software to compete with Lotus Notes.
• Prodigy and CompuServe announces the addition of Internet service to their members.

October 1994

• Bill Gates tops the Forbes 400 list of America's richest people and is worth $9.3B.
• HP offers two mobile inkjet printers that weigh 4 pounds and are half the size of notebook PCs.
• Motorola's computer division introduces PowerPC-based computers and plans to use Windows NT.
• Mead says it has agreed to sell its Lexis/Nexis online service to Reed Elsevier for $1.5B.
• Rumors circulate that Motorola, IBM or AT&T will acquire all or part of Apple.
• Intel introduces the fifth member of the Pentium, a 50/75MHz version targeted for notebook PCs.
• IBM launches its OS/2 Warp with built-in Internet access.
• Microsoft says it will buy Intuit for $1.5B, the largest PC software acquisition ever.
• HP debuts the OfficeJet personal printer/fax/copier combination priced at $959.
• AMD announced its Pentium-class microprocessor, called the K5. Production is expected in 1H'95.
• Investment firm Forstmann Little buys Ziff-Davis Publishing for $1.4B.
• Macromedia says it will acquire Altsys for $69M. Altsys is the creator of FreeHand.
• Artisoft makes LANtastic available for OS/2.
• Toshiba licenses the PowerPC and plans to use it in a variety of systems.
• Sun Microsystems beefs up its SPARCserver 1000 and SPARCcenter 2000 products with 60 MHz SuperSPARC microprocessors.
• IBM introduces PowerPC-based symmetrical multiprocessor (SMP) servers.
• IBM revamps it PC product line. ValuePoint and PS/2 merge into the IBM PC Desktop Series. IBM also announces the PC Server 500 family.
• SunSoft launches its SolarNet PC LAN administration software, which can manage hundreds of PCs from centralized consoles.
• MIPS Technologies unveils its 64-bit RISC processor, the R10000, with a 200 MHz clock rate.
• SynOptics and Wellfleet complete their merger and changes name to Bay Networks.
• Cisco outbids IBM and buys Kalpana for $204M. Kalpana has an installed base of 20K Ethernet switches totaling 150K ports.

November 1994

• Apple was the top seller of PCs in the U.S. in 3Q'94, but Compaq retains the lead worldwide. Apple shipped 160K Power Macs in the USA in 3Q or 25% of its total.
• Softbank Corp. says it will purchase Ziff's tradeshow business including Interop for $202M.
• HP, Quantum and Seagate said they will support the Ultra SCSI (40 MBytes per second) and Fibre Channel Arbitrated Loop (FC-AL) which has 100 MBytes per second transfer rate.
• Microsoft will buy NextBase, a mapping and route-planning software company.
• Novell's stock surged on rumors that IBM might be planning a takeover.
• Microsoft says it has contracted with five companies to provide additional telephone support during the Windows 95 launch.
• Apple and IBM agree to support a common PowerPC hardware architecture. The first machines will be ready in 1996.
• Sun Microsystems hires many of Thinking Machines top engineers to develop massively parallel computers.
• WordPerfect unveils WordPerfect 6.1 for Windows.
• America Online buys two software companies. BookLink Technologies produces InternetWorks. NaviSoft makes software to put text and other content into electronic form.
• Hyundai Electronics America says it will buy AT&T's NCR Microelectronic Products Division for $300M.
• HP introduces its first Omnibook color notebook PC, the Omnibook 600.
• Microsoft starts a $100M TV and print advertising campaign to build overall brand awareness.
• Adobe Photoshop 3.0 for Windows is now available at a suggested price of $895.
• IBM announces its VoiceType Dictation software for Windows. Users can dictate 70 to 100 words per minute using a 20,000 word vocabulary.
• Sybase will buy Powersoft for $944M in stocks.
• Microsoft previews its online service at COMDEX/Fall (Microsoft Network) which will be part of Windows 95.
• AT&T will buy the remaining portion of Sierra On-Line's ImagiNation Network for $40M.
• IBM says it has signed agreements with three leading German PC vendors, Vobis, Escom and Comtech, to preload OS/2 Warp on their PCs.
• Hayes Microcomputer files for Chapter 11 reorganization.
• MCI introduces an Internet connection service.
• A subtle flaw in Intel's Pentium can generate errors in complex math calculations.
• Microsoft is shipping the second major beta version of Windows 95.
• Rumors fly that Oracle will buy Lotus Development.

December 1994

• Apple's notebook PCs are ranked first in customer satisfaction by a J.D. Power study, closely followed by IBM and Compaq.
• Apple, AT&T, IBM and Siemens form an alliance, called Versit, to set software standards for computer data transfers.
• FCC opens the bidding on 99 licenses for PCS phones in 51 markets.
• Intel says there is an 1 in 9 billion chance the average user will get an error because of the Pentium math flaw.
• IBM says the Pentium flaw could produce an error as often as once every 24 days in certain spreadsheet applications. IBM stops shipping PCs with Pentium microprocessors until the flaw has been fixed.
• Intel receives much criticism for its handling of the Pentium flaw. Intel is only replacing Pentium chips to users with heavy math applications.
• Despite the Pentium flaw furor, sales continue strongly.
• Cisco signs an agreement to buy LightStream's ATM business for $120M.
• Apple says it has granted a license to Bandai to make a multi-purpose video game machine based on the Macintosh architecture.
• TCI buys a 20% share in Microsoft's Network for $125M.
• Intel issues an apology and announces it will offer free Pentium replacements to all users. The new chips will be sent within 60 days.
• Microsoft's Windows 95 is now projected to ship in August 1995.
• AT&T buys the Interchange Online Network from Ziff-Davis.
• Prodigy says it will offer its Internet World Wide Web browser to its users free of charge.
• Apple's System 8 (code name Copeland) operating system is expected to ship in mid-1996 instead of mid-1995.
• Intel's next generation microprocessor, code name P6, is expected at COMDEX/Fall 1995.
• Beta version of NetWare 4.1 is getting good reviews.
• Powersoft ships its Enterprise Series 4.0 client server development software.
• Apple licenses its first Macintosh-compatible system vendor--Power Computing Corp.
• IBM says it has sold over 0.8M copies of OS/2 Warp worldwide in less than two months.

January 1995

• Microsoft shows BOB, a new user interface that runs on top of Windows.
• Apple denies the rumors that Oracle, Philips and Matsushita are interested in buying Apple.
• General Magic announces it has filed for an IPO.
• Uunet Technologies and Microsoft will build the largest dial-up TCP/IP network in the world. The network will be operated by Uunet and will provide Internet access to Microsoft Network users.
• Microsoft signs an agreement to license Spyglass' Mosaic World Wide Web browser software.
• CompuServe unveils numerous services for Lotus Notes users.
• Intel takes a charge of $475M against its 4Q'94 earnings for replacing the flawed Pentiums.
• Borland says it will lay off 40% of its workforce (650 people). Its president also resigns.
• IBM reports its first full-year profit since 1990--a profit of $3B. IBM shipped 4.1M PCs in 1994--a 3% decline from 1993.
• Unisys says it will lay of 4,000 employees in the next 60 days.
• Novell announces UnixWare 2.0 with volume shipments in March.
• Intel announces its Pentium Overdrive 66MHz processor which can upgrade most 50 MHz 486SX2, DX2 and 25MHz 486 PCs.
• Internet provides critical information on the devastating Kobe earthquake--including news and photographs.
• Microsoft is set to beta test its Windows NT Enhanced Server on the PowerPC platform.
• Lotus drops prices on Notes and offers a low-cost run-time client version with a street price in the $120 range.
• Judge Stanley Sporkin, who is handling the Microsoft/Department of Justice antitrust settlement, is asking for more information.
• Siemens Nixdorf agrees to purchase Pyramid Technology for $207M.

February 1995

• Judge Stanley Sporkin rejects the antitrust settlement between Microsoft and Department of Justice. Both say they will appeal the ruling as the judge overstepped his jurisdiction.
• A new form of CDs, CD Plus, which adds interactive visuals to CD audio is ready for release.
• Microsoft and Intuit postpone to May 30 the date for completing Microsoft's $1.5B acquisition of Intuit.
• Sun Microsystems introduces additional models in its Voyager portable workstations.
• Cray Research launches the Cray T90 with up to 32 processors and peak performance of 60 Gigaflops. Prices range from $2.5M to $30M.
• A standard battle for the digital video disk (DVD) is heating up between Sony-Philips and a consortium led by Toshiba and Time-Warner. The DVD is expected to replace the VCR and will also be used in multimedia PCs.
• Softbank, a Japanese software distributor and tradeshow firm, buys Interface Group's tradeshows--including COMDEX--for $800M plus.
• USA and China avert a trade war with an accord that cracks down on Chinese copyright pirates and protects intellectual property--including computer software.
• Radius says it will start making Power Mac clones in mid-1995.
• Samsung buys a 40% stake in AST for $378M.
• Microsoft says it will support the Desktop Management Interface (DMI) in Windows 95.
• Apple sues Intel and Microsoft over the use of Apple's QuickTime video software in Microsoft's Video for Windows and Intel's Display Control Interface.
• Silicon Graphics buys Alias Research and Wavefront Technologies in a stock swap worth $500M.
• Intel releases information on the P6: 2X performance of Pentium, available in 2H'95 and volume production in mid-1996.
• NeXT plans to port its products to Windows 95 and NT.

• VocalTec releases its Internet Phone, which can use the Internet to make calls anywhere in the world. Motorola will also use the software in some of its modems.

March 1995

• Microsoft's third beta version of Windows 95 is released to 50,000 testers.
• Digital announces LinkWorks 3, a groupware product.
• Bertelsman says it will start its own European online service to compete with Europe Online, which will start operation in 1995.
• CompuServe will acquire Spry and its Internet browser software for $100M.
• Eastman Kodak and Sun Microsystems will co-develop digital technology for image distribution over the Internet.
• Hewlett-Packard starts a new round of PC price cuts, which are followed by all major PC vendors.
• Zenith Electronics backs Toshiba/Time-Warner's CVD technology.
• Microsoft co-founder Paul Allen invests $500M in DreamWorks SKG, the new entertainment company created by Steven Spielberg, Jeffrey Katzenberg and David Geffen.
• Netscape says it has signed up Apple, IBM, Microsoft, Sun Microsystems and others to use its new Internet security technology.
• SunSoft starts distributing its new object-based operating system code named Spring.
• Microsoft and DreamWorks SKG are forming a joint venture to develop interactive games and adventure software.
• MCI unveils its marketplaceMCI, a service that will provide millions of users with Internet access and electronic shopping.
• Eastman Kodak unveils a wealth of digital photography products and services.
• Cray Computer files for Chapter 11 bankruptcy protection.
• Microhelp says it sold over 0.5M copies of Uninstaller in 1994.
• Intel introduces a 120MHz Pentium and lowers prices of other Pentium MPUs. Leading PC vendors announce products using the new chip.
• Pacific Bell says it will offer Internet access to businesses in May.
• Compaq says it will use NexGen's 586 microprocessor in addition to Intel's Pentium.
• Compaq introduces numerous business PCs and lowers the price of older models up to 23%. Many models include desktop management tools.
• The auction for PCS ends after 3 months of bidding with 18 players offering $7B for the wireless licenses.
• Microsoft says Cairo, the next major release of Windows NT will be available in late 1996.
• The U.S. Court of Appeals reverses a ruling that said Quattro Pro infringed on Lotus 1-2-3. A possible $100M in damages payment from Borland to Lotus had been expected. Lotus will appeal to a higher court.
• IBM announces the ThinkPad 701C (code named Butterfly) subnotebook PC. Its innovative design allows a full size keyboard that hangs over the edges when opened.
• A furor is created by Dan Farmer because he is planning to release a program called SATAN (Security Analysis Tool for Auditing Networks) via the Internet. The program searches for security flaws, but there is fear it may also become a hacker tool.
• Adobe disclosed an alliance with IBM to jointly develop publishing systems that use Adobe's Acrobat and Postscript and IBM's Advanced Function Presentation architecture. IBM will preload the Acrobat Reader on the majority of its PCs.

April 1995

• Tandem unveils a fault-tolerant Web server called CyberWeb.
• Hewlett-Packard enters the consumer PC market with an aggressively priced family of products. HP also cuts prices on its OmniBook notebook PCs up to 15%.
• China says it will open the Internet to the public this month.
• Craig McCaw says he will invest up to $1.1B in Nextel.
• Microsoft releases a preview version of Windows 95 to the first 400,000 users that ask. The price is $32.
• Digital introduces its top-of-the-line Alpha server called TurboLaser with a starting price of $200K.
• Microsoft announces Plus!, a new utility program to enhance its upcoming Windows 95.
• MCI Communications and the National Science Foundation unveil a national communications network, called the very high-speed Backbone Network (vBNS) which will connect five U.S. supercomputing sites.
• The U.S. Department of Justice files an antitrust suit to block Microsoft's acquisition of Intuit.

May 1995

• Leading computer and media companies agree on an erasable compact disk format.
• Intel reduces the Pentium microprocessor prices up to 31%.
• Lotus ships the InterNotes Web Publisher which translates Notes databases into the web's HTML format.
• Compaq, 3M and Matsushita announce the joint development of a 120Mbyte floppy disk that is compatible with current 3.5" diskettes.
• IBM introduces two ThinkPad PCs. One model has a snap-out panel that can be used with overhead projectors.
• Prodigy offers its customers the opportunity to publish their own web pages.
• MCI Communications will invest up to $2B in News Corp. They will distribute News Corp.'s electronic information over MCI's network.
• Intel plans to enlist power users to test its P6 chip to avoid flaws similar to what happened to the Pentium.
• Intuit signs agreements with 12 banks to offer bank-at-home services for Quicken.
• Seagate says it is buying Frye Computer Systems which makes LAN software utilities.
• NBC announced it will provide a wide range of programming for Microsoft's online network.
• IBM introduces OS/2 Warp Connect with additional network features. IBM's cumulative sales of OS/2 is 9M units including 2M OS/2 Warp.
• Power Computing introduces three PowerPC Macintosh clones.
• Sun Microsystems introduces Hot Java, an interpretive language that can spice up web pages via small Java based applications called applets.
• Microsoft ends its plan to acquire Intuit, due to the long delays battling the government's antitrust suit.

- Compaq announces the ProLiant 4500 SMP-based server which is designed to use Windows NT.
- America Online plans to buy Medior ($30M) and WAIS ($15M), two software companies that specialize in online products.
- Computer Associates plans to offer $1.78B to buy Legent Corp.
- Hewlett-Packard has developed a medical notebook PDA which allows doctors to monitor a patient remotely.
- Intel's 90MHz Pentium for notebook PCs invades the market.
- Digital announces OpenVMS 6.2 operating system for its 10M VAX computer user base.
- Microsoft reorganizes its top management after Mike Maples announces he will retire in July.
- Santa Cruz Operation announces its SCO OpenServer 5, a Unix operating systems.
- Two Smalltalk software companies agree to merge. ParcPlace issues 3.8M shares worth $48M for all of Digitalk's stocks.
- McAfee plans to buy Saber Software for $40.6M.
- Netscape says it will use Java in its upcoming Navigator 2.0 browser.
- Internet service providers PSI and Uunet go public.

June 1995

- The U.S. Patent and Trade Office proposes new guidelines to clear up confusion surrounding software patents.
- DreamWorks SKG and Silicon Graphics will build a complete digital studio for $50M.
- Compaq asks for $585M in damages from Packard Bell in a copyright infringement lawsuit.
- America Online acquires Global Network Navigator for $11M.
- A New York court rules a $200M libel suit can proceed against Prodigy because Prodigy edits its content and hence is a publisher.
- IBM announces a PS/2 server with a System/390 processor board and MVS, VM or VSE operating system.
- IBM offers to purchase Lotus Development for $60 per share or $3.3B in cash in a hostile takeover bid.
- Taligent releases its first object-oriented product called CommonPoint.
- Cyrix launches a low-end Pentium competitor it is calling 5x86.
- Hewlett-Packard announces new high-end graphics workstations--the J Series. HP also says it will offer optimized Windows NT servers.
- Intel unveils the 133MHz Pentium microprocessors.
- The U.S. Court of Appeals overturns Judge Stanley Sporkin's rejection of the Microsoft antitrust decree. The antitrust decree will stand.
- Iomega announces an internal version of its Zip disk drive. It stores up to 100Mbytes and is used instead of a floppy disk.
- Windows NT for the PowerPC starts shipping.
- IBM announces its second generation microprocessor-based System 3090 mainframe system.
- Minitel, which has provided videotex services in France since 1980, will add Internet access.
- The antitrust division of the Justice Department is scrutinizing the planned Microsoft Network.
- EDS buys A.T. Kearney for $628M--half in cash and half in stocks. A.T. Kearney is a leading consulting firm with 1994 revenue of $346M.
- Lotus agrees to IBM's takeover after the price is raised to $64 per share or $3.52B--the largest software acquisition ever.
- Apple introduces the high-end Power Mac 9500 based on the PowerPC 604 microprocessor.
- Canon announces several computers based on the PowerPC 603 and 604 microprocessors.
- IBM introduces five RS/6000 workstations and three servers. IBM also announces its first PCs using the PowerPC--the Power Series 850 and ThinkPad Power Series 850.
- Adobe Systems says it will acquire Frame Technology for $500M in stocks.
- Apple announces a new version of QuickTime for Windows.
- Web software developer Spyglass goes public.

July 1995

- IBM will build Mac-compatible PCs for Radius.
- Packard Bell sells a 20% stake to NEC Corp. for $170M.
- Forbes Magazine says Bill Gates is the richest man in the world with assets valued at $12.9B.
- BankAmerica and NationsBank say they have completed their acquisition of Meca Software from H&R Block for $35M.
- The U.S. Postal Service and Premenos will test software that will authenticate messages sent over the Internet--i.e. an electronic postmark.
- Symantec will acquire Canadian software company Delrina for $415M.
- Hewlett-Packard introduces two high-end color inkjet printers, DeskJet 1600 starting at $1,400.
- AT&T buys an $8M equity stake in BBN Planet, a leading Internet service provider.
- LG Group of Korea will acquire a controlling interest in Zenith Electronics for $351M. After the transaction LG will own 58% of Zenith.
- Microsoft will distribute Money, its personal finance software, for free for two months after its introduction in August.
- Intel is developing a Pentium microprocessor for multimedia applications called the P55C. It is expected to be available in 1996.
- Intuit says it will offer home banking services for 19 banks through Quicken.
- Apple introduces the Performa 5200CD and 6200CD PowerPC-based products for the home and multimedia markets.
- 15 companies, including Apple, Compaq, IBM and Oracle, have teamed up to support an open cross-platform standard for multimedia objects.
- 3Com will acquire Chipcom for $775M in stocks.

August 1995

- Digital post its first annual profit since 1990.
- IBM's CEO, Louis Gerstner, concedes OS/2 has lost the battle versus Windows. IBM will now focus OS/2 on large corporations and as a server operating system.
- Cray Computer shuts its doors after spending more than $200M without completing its first supercomputer.
- AT&T, Sony and NTT will start an online service in Japan in 1996.

- Microsoft licenses Digital's clustering software technology for use in Windows NT.
- The Justice Department says it will not take antitrust action against Microsoft Network before it is launched on August 24.
- MCI is merging its online business with News Corp.'s Delphi service. The new service will operate on the web.
- Quix says it has moved the Mac OS to the PowerPCs, but Apple declines to license this product.
- Sun Microsystems co-founder Andreas Bechtolsheim resigns as VP of Technology to start a computer networking company.
- Hewlett-Packard upgrades its SureStore optical disk jukebox system with a maximum storage of 2,381GBytes.
- GM says it will spin off EDS as an independent company by early 1996.
- Netscape goes public at $28, peaks at $75 and closes the first day at $58.25--giving a stock valuation of $2.2B.
- Intel announces a beta-test program for the P6 for several hundred power users.
- Radius and Daystar Digital unveil their Power Macintosh clones.
- Apple updates its Macintosh notebooks with the first PowerPC-based products.
- The Microsoft/Department of Justice antitrust agreement is finally signed.
- Microsoft paid the Rolling Stones $4M to use their song "Start Me Up" in the Windows 95 launch.
- VeriFone buys Enterprise Integration Technologies, an Internet software and consulting company, for $28M.
- Microsoft launches Windows 95 with unparalleled press coverage, hoopla and sales. TV programs, newspapers and magazines are full of Windows 95 stories. Many stores opened at midnight to sell Windows 95. The most visible product launch ever in any industry.
- Major computer vendors including IBM, HP, Digital and Intel agree to develop an API standard for 64-bit Unix specifications.
- Windows 95 support lines are jammed and have long waiting times in the days after its launch.

September 1995

- Intel announces the Pentium Overdrive, a Pentium upgrade for high-end 486 systems, for $299.
- Bay Networks will purchase Xylogics for $300M in stock.
- Sun Microsystems sets up a division, called JavaSoft, to focus on Java application development technology.
- Novell turns future development of Unix to Santa Cruz Operation and Hewlett-Packard. SCO takes over the System V source code and UnixWare 2.x in exchange for 6.1M SCO shares valued at $60M. HP will handle the development of next generation 64-bit Unix.
- Two competing camps agree on a single format for the digital video disk. It will store a 133 minute movie at the highest video and audio quality or 4.7 gigabytes. The DVD will also play CD-ROMs and audio CDs. The first products are expected in 2H'96.
- Hewlett-Packard introduces the HP 5L laser printer with a $479 price.
- AT&T says it will split into three independent companies: telephone services, computer systems and telecom products.
- MCI plans to buy SHL Systemhouse for $1B.
- Intel gives the P6 a name: Pentium Pro.
- Seagate reaches an agreement to buy Conner Peripherals for $1.1B.
- Netscape will acquire Collabra Software for $108M in stocks. Collabra develops groupware software.
- Hewlett-Packard will acquire Convex for $150M in stocks.
- AT&T launches business Internet services.
- Novell presents its vision and roadmap for its networking future--Novell Embedded Systems Technology. NEST is projected to connect up to 1B intelligent devices by 2000 including computers, appliances and other products using microprocessors.
- Lexmark says it will go public later this year. Lexmark's 1994 revenue was $1.85B.
- Chen Systems announces its first product--the CS-1000 midrange server. The company was founded by Steve Chen, the designer of Cray Research's most popular supercomputer.
- First Windows 95 specific viruses appear.
- Netscape introduces Navigator 2.0.

October 1995

- Hewlett-Packard unveils the CopyJet, a combination color copier and color printer, with a price range of $2,495 to $3,199.
- Lotus signs licensing agreement with 11 telecom companies to make Notes available on their public networks--including Deutche Telekom, BT, Telecom Italia, Malaysian Telecom, NTT, U.S. West and SNET.
- Philips introduces an Internet access product based on its CD-I player and a TV. It will be sold by its CD-Online subsidiary for $163 excluding the CD-I player and the TV.
- IBM announces the ThinkPad 760 notebook PCs with multimedia capabilities. IBM also upgrades its PC servers, workstation and midrange servers and related software.
- Oracle chairman Larry Ellison says it may sell low-cost Network Computers in 1Q'96 for Internet access.
- Storage Technology introduces the Kodiak RAID mainframe storage system.
- Netscape began its Bug Bounty program and offers cash prices to anyone discovering serious flaws in its web browser software.
- Through Corbis, a company he owns, Bill Gates bought the electronic rights to the Bettman Archieve containing 11.5 million photographs--a visual history of the 20th century.
- AT&T puts Paradyne, a datacom equipment supplier up for sale.
- Sun Microsystems upgrades its SPARCserver 1000E and SPARCcenter 2000E.
- Lotus president Jim Manzi resigns and is replaced by Michael Zisman.
- Data General shows its first Pentium-based servers that will replace the 88000-based products.
- Advanced Micro Devices agrees to acquire NexGen for $860M in stock. NexGen makes Pentium-compatible microprocessors.
- Caere buys ViewStar for $40M in stock.
- Vermeer Technologies start shipping FrontPage, a Web development program.
- Be, a start-up company founded by Jean-Louis Gassee, introduces a PowerPC-based computer with proprietary OS for the digital audio and video markets.
- Oracle says it will embed Sun Microsystems' Java in Powerbrowser.

• Macromedia will release Java-based development tools.
• Microsoft says it shipped 7M Windows 95 in less than two months--3M upgrades and 4M on new PCs.
• SoftKey unveils an unsolicited stock and cash bid of $606M for Learning Co., which challenges Brøderbund's agreement to acquire Learning Co. Softkey also offers to buy Minnesota Educational Computing for $370M.

November 1995

• Sun Microsystems announces its first workstations and servers based on the 64-bit UltraSPARC chip.
• Apple, IBM and Motorola release the Common Hardware Reference Platform (CHRP) specifications for PowerPC-based computers. CHRP is renamed PowerPC Platform.
• Intel officially rolls out the Pentium Pro microprocessor.
• Microsoft outsources its PC and network support to Entex Information for three years for $40M.
• Borland and Spyglass throw their support behind Sun Microsystems' Java.
• Softbank reaches an agreement to buy Ziff-Davis for $2.1B.
• Numerous PC vendors show Pentium Pro products at COMDEX/Fall.
• Apple and IBM disband Kaleida Labs. Apple will continue development of the cross-platform multimedia ScriptX technology. IBM retains rights to use the technology.
• Apple announces the Newton 2.0 operating system.
• Lotus introduces SmartSuite 96 for Windows 95.
• Lexmark goes public at a price of $21 per share for a market value of $1.5B.
• Novell ships the Macintosh client (MacIPX) for NetWare 4.
• Cray Research unveils its second generation massively-parallel processor T3E with 16 to 128 Alpha microprocessors starting at $1M.
• Sun Microsystems releases Solaris 2.5 for SP'RC, PowerPC and X86.
• Cabletron plans to buy Standard Microsystems' Enterprise Networking Business for $77.5M.
• Microsoft rolls out Internet Explorer 2.0.

December 1995

• Sun Microsystems and Netscape introduce JavaScript, a simplified version of Java, for building web software.
• Microsoft outlines a broad strategy to enter the Internet market including licensing Sun's Java.
• Softkey wins the battle with Brøderbund and will acquire the Learning Co. for $606M.
• IBM and Adobe Systems will license Java.
• Exponential Technology announces it will make PowerPC chips starting in 1997.
• Lotus drops the price of client desktop Notes from $155 to $69. Lotus also license Java for use in Notes 4.0.
• Microsoft buys 50% of NBC's America's Talking cable channel for $200M. NBC and Microsoft will later launch a 24-hour news station delivered on cable, Internet and Microsoft Network.
• Fore Systems and Alantec will merge in a deal worth $684M.
• Apple, IBM and HP say they will shut down Taligent. IBM will take over Taligent's products.
• AT&T will eliminate 40,000 jobs and take a $6B pretax charge to cover the cost of splitting into three companies.

January 1996

• Apple announces Media Tool 2.0, an object-based, cross-platform multimedia authoring tool.
• Power Computing unveils its entry level PowerCurve Macintosh clones.
• AT&T's computer group goes back to the future: the new name is NCR Corp. again.
• U.S. Supreme Court upholds a court ruling that leaves Borland the winner in a 5.5 year "look-and-feel" battle with Lotus' 1-2-3 spreadsheet.
• Apple announces a loss of $69M for the 4Q'95 quarter, which starts the most tumultuous and negative month in Apple's history.
• Microsoft introduces animation software for Windows NT from its Softimage division to compete with Silicon Graphics workstations.
• Sun Microsystems says it is in merger talks with Apple. Apple rejects Sun's bid as too low.
• DRAM prices are dropping again after three years of firm prices.
• Compaq and Intel end their feud and sign a 10-year cross-licensing patent agreement.
• Lotus announces Notes 4.0.
• IBM kills the OS/2 version for the PowerPC.
• Silicon Graphics upgrades its product line using the MIPS R5000 and R10000 microprocessors.
• After 7 months of brewing, Sun's Java finally ships.
• Microsoft buys Vermeer Technologies, a web software developer, for $130M in stocks.
• Apple ousts Michael Spindler and appoints Gilbert Amelio as Chairman & CEO.
• Digital will exit the home PC market to concentrate on the business PC market.

February 1996

• Corel says it will acquire WordPerfect for $113M in stock, $11M in cash and a minimum of $70M in royalties for Novell's Groupwise and Envoy over 5 years.
• IBM will buy client/server software developer Tivoli for $743M.
• Sun Microsystems plans to develop a Java interpreter chip by 1997.
• A unique events takes place: "24 Hours in Cyberspace". On February 8th 1,000 photographers fan out around the globe to document how the online digital revolution is changing people's lives. The result is broadcast over the Internet in real time.

• Apple's new CEO, Gilbert Amelio, says the company is not for sale.
• Numerous PC vendors start shipping Pentium Pro systems.
• Packard Bell acquires Zenith Data Systems in a complex deal worth $650M. Packard Bell gets $650M from NEC and Groupe Bull in return for preferred stock.
• AT&T rolls out its WorldNet Internet access service including free access for a limited time. AT&T is swamped and cannot meet initial demand.
• Toshiba says it will enter the desktop PC business later this year.
• The semiconductor industry's key indicator, the book-to-bill ratio, turned its worst performance in five years.
• IBM announces software that can turn its mainframe and midrange computers into web servers.
• H&R Block plans to spin off its CompuServe business as a separate company.
• Microsoft ships the first of two beta test versions of Windows NT 4.0 to 120,000 users.
• The telecom deregulation bill is finally passed, which allows cable TV, long distance and local phone companies to compete against each other.
• Motorola and Sun Microsystems announce an alliance to build high-speed Internet access systems for home users.
• Microsoft bundles its Internet Information Server for free with Windows NT.
• Compaq and Packard Bell settle their suits accusing each other of selling computers that had some old or used parts as new PCs.
• Novell ships its Client 32 for Windows 95.
• IBM will support Windows NT and Sun Solaris on the RS/6000.
• Microsoft reorganizes and makes an Internet division headed by Brad Silverberg.
• Apple licenses the Mac OS to Motorola including the right to sublicense the Mac OS to other companies.
• NEC and other MIPS architecture vendors say they will support the 64-bit Unix that HP and SCO will deliver in 1998.
• A group of 56 vendors, including Silicon Graphics and Netscape, support an extension to Virtual Reality Modeling Language (VRML) called Moving World for 3D web pages.
• Silicon Graphics agrees to buy Cray Research for $739M in stock.
• U.S. West plans to buy Continental Cablevision, the third largest cable TV operator, for $10.8B.
• MasterCard and Visa release joint specs for secured credit card transactions over the Internet.

March 1996

• Compaq aggressively lowered its high-end PC and server prices.
• Apple says it will cease operation of its online service, eWorld.
• Singapore announces it will filter what the average user can see and say on the Internet.
• Fujitsu says it will enter the U.S. notebook PC market in 2Q'96.
• Digital releases entry-level (AlphaStation 255) and mid-range workstations (AlphaStation 500).
• Apple unveils its latest Newton, the MessagePad 130, starting at $800.
• Lucent Technologies, AT&T's telecom equipment business, file the largest IPO ever--111M shares for over $3B.
• Microsoft ships Exchange messaging and groupware software.
• David Packard, a co-founder of Hewlett-Packard, dies at age 83.
• Cyrix says it will enter the PC motherboard and system business
• Novell licenses Java.
• Microsoft outlines its ActiveX software component platform strategy that includes OLE.
• Gateway 2000 introduces Destination, a PC with a large screen TV.
• Motorola introduces a smart phone that can access the Internet and send and receive faxes.

April 1996

• Pactel agrees to a $16.7B acquisition by SBC Communications, a first-ever union of Baby Bells.
• Bill Gates outlines Microsoft's strategy for an easy to use home PC called Simply Interactive PC or SIPC.
• Netscape and GE Information Service form Actra Business Systems to develop electronic commerce software.
• Yahoo! goes public and soars from $13 to $33 per share in its first day of trading.
• McAfee Associates propose to buy Cheyenne Software for nearly $1B. Due to Cheyenne's opposition the offer is later dropped.
• AT&T Labs hires Apple's chief technologist, David C. Nagel, to be its first president.
• Apple posts a record $740M loss in its fiscal second quarter ending in March.
• Bell Atlantic and Nynex announce a merger in a deal worth $23B.
• Paul Allen signs an exclusive 14-month option to buy the Seattle Seahawks football team for nearly $200M.
• CompuServe's IPO is priced at $30 per share and raises $454M for its parent H&R Block.
• Cisco Systems agrees to buy StrataCom for stocks worth about $4B.
• Compaq, Data General, ICL, NCR, Olivetti, Siemens-Nixdorf and Unisys agree to use Santa Cruz Operation's Unix for Pentium computers.
• Microsoft and Casio agree to work together on hand-held computers and appliance-like devices.
• Sun Microsystems strikes deals with Microsoft and other companies to bundle Java with their operating systems.
• Computer Sciences agrees to acquire Continuum for stocks valued at $1.44B.
• General Motors approves a spin-off for EDS. EDS will pay GM $500M and give GM discounted services for 10 years.
• Lucent Technologies goes public and raises over $3B.
• Microsoft says it plans to dismantle its Microsoft Network and recreate it on the Internet.
• Intel upgrades its ProShare video conferencing system.
• Apple says Copeland, the next generation Mac OS, will be delayed until mid 1997.
• IBM unveils its next OS/2 Warp upgrade, code named Merlin which will ship in 2H'96.
• Security Dynamics Technologies and RSA Data Security will merge in a deal worth $300M.

• Lycos, Exite and Yahoo!, three Internet content search companies, go public.

May 1996

• MFS Communications agrees to buy Uunet Technologies for about $2B.
• Lucent Technologies introduces Inferno, a network operating system and Limbo, a programming language.
• IBM and Sears sell Prodigy for close to $250M in cash and stock to a group of investors.
• IBM and 10 big banks form a company called Inet that will offer complete home banking services.
• Gilbert Amelio outlines Apple's strategy including product streamlining, Internet focus and alternative platforms such as low-cost information appliances.
• IBM announces home automation software for its PCs.
• IBM becomes a licensee of the Mac OS including permission to sublicense to other companies.
• Microsoft reaches agreements with four cable companies including Time-Warner and Comcast to use Windows NT as the software foundation for their Internet telecom networks.
• Intel lowers Pentium prices 15% to 30%.
• Tandem says it will make its fault-tolerant software available for Windows NT.
• IBM unveils NetCommerce, the first end-to-end electronic commerce solution based on the Secure Electronic Transmission protocol.
• A General Accounting Office report estimates that hackers attack Pentagon computers 250,000 times per year.
• Amdahl introduces Windows NT and Pentium Pro-based servers.
• Oracle, IBM, Sun Microsystems, Apple and Netscape support the Network Computer specifications (NC Reference Profile), a low-cost disk-less Internet access device.
• IBM and Apple will co-develop a notebook PC that runs the Mac OS.
• IBM introduces the ThinkPad 560, an ultraslim notebook PC.
• Silicon Graphics says it will migrate the Cray supercomputer product line to the MIPS microprocessors by year 2000.
• A National Research Council report recommends promoting and relaxing export control of encryption software.

June 1996

• Microsoft says it will license its VBA technology for customizing its own applications programs.
• Packard Bell and NEC will combine their PC businesses (except in Japan and China), which forms a $8B company called Packard Bell NEC.
• CompuServe licenses Microsoft Windows NT Normandy server software in return for including CompuServe's online software in Windows 95.
• The Clinton administration is planning an anti-terror cyberteam to battle electronic terrorist attacks.
• Pure Software and Atria Software agree to merge in a stock deal worth $973M.
• John Sculley, former Apple CEO, forms investment firm with his two brothers.
• IBM says it will support Windows and Windows NT for all of its product line.
• Apple ships Cyberdog, its integrated software suite for Internet access.
• JavaSoft, a Sun Microsystems division, releases JavaOS, a compact operating system for Internet computers and PDAs.
• IBM says it will resell Storage Technology's mainframe disk drive systems.
• EDS is spun off from GM.
• A panel of federal judges blocks Congress' legislative curbs on "indecent" material on the Internet contained in the telecom deregulation bill passed in February.
• Compaq wins its largest server order--8,500 ProSignia 300 running Windows NT from GM for its dealer network.
• IBM upgrades its OS/400 with Internet support features including browser access and security.
• Hewlett-Packard introduces its first 64-bit HP 9000 workstations starting at $24K.
• IBM plans to port Windows NT applications to OS/390 via Bristol Technology's Wind/U application development software.
• Sony enters the U.S. home PC market with a 200MHz Pentium-based product.
• Motorola introduces digital 2-way radio to compete with cellular phones. Nextel is the main customer.
• VeriFone offers a secure Internet payment system for banks to sell to merchants.
• IBM introduces Aptiva PCs with game enhancing 3D technology.
• Compaq rolls out three new notebook PCs including the Armada ultrathin models.
• Andersen Consulting and BBN form a venture to design and sell Internet-based business services.
• IBM reaches a pact with the Justice Department to end the restrictions from its 1956 consent decree.
• Most major PC vendors introduce 200MHz Pentium computers.
• Ross Technology shows a PC add-in board that allows SPARC/Solaris software to run on Windows computers.
• Fujitsu enters the U.S. portable PC business with three lines of Pentium-based notebook PCs.
• IBM says Notes is now available in 850 cities in 100 countries via the IBM Global Network.
• The first PCs with the Universal Serial Bus, a new standard for peripheral connection, are announced.
• Toshiba, Compaq, Texas Instruments and Acer release new notebook PCs.
• Microsoft unwraps its Windows NT server clustering roadmap (code name Wolfpack).
• Samsung says it will second source Digital's Alpha chip and will use Alpha chips in future computer systems.
• Power Computing wins an order for 3,000 Macintoshes from Lockheed Martin.

July 1996

• Microsoft says it will add Internet functions to its operating systems and applications.

• Philips and Sony unveil plans to market set-top boxes that will offer Internet access on a TV.
• Bill Gates tops Forbes' billionaire list as the world's richest man with a net worth of $18B.
• Compaq revamps and expands its Presario PC line for the home computer market.
• IBM shows off its system for the Olympics which includes four System/390 mainframes, two RS/6000 SP massively parallel processors, 80 AS/400, 7,000 PCs and 300 networks.
• Microsoft's CityScape development project, a nationwide network of online community guides crammed with local listings, maps, reviews and retail ads, is creating anxiety in the newspaper industry.
• Digital says it will lay off 7,000 people and take a $475M charge against earnings due to slow PC and European revenue.
• NeXT Software ships OpenStep for Windows NT.
• Compaq unveils three desktop PC lines including a low-priced PC family starting at $1,100.
• Intel introduces free Internet phone software that can be down-loaded from Intel's web server.
• Rockwell says it will acquire chip maker Brooktree for $275M.
• AT&T and Microsoft agree to market each others Internet products.
• Department of Energy announces a $193M, four-year deal with IBM to build the world's fastest computer--3 trillion operations per second and 2.5 trillion bytes of memory.
• IBM receives bad publicity due to problems with its computer system at the Olympics in Atlanta.
• Analysts says Apple may emulate the Wintel standard as part of the Copeland OS due in mid-97.
• Microsoft releases Windows NT 4.0 to manufacturing a month earlier than expected.
• Canon sells its PowerPC systems developer, FirePower, to Motorola.

August 1996

• Intel says it will delay its Pentium multimedia chip, code name P55C, from 4Q'96 to 1Q'97.
• Compaq forms a division to make workstations.
• Microsoft asks Netscape to "cease and desist" using price comparisons of its server software, which potentially violates Microsoft's Windows NT workstation license.
• America Online is disconnected from its 6 million customers for 19 hours while upgrading its internal software.
• Intel lowers Pentium and Pentium Pro prices, but says it will skip its normal November price decrease.
• Microsoft ships a new version of its web browser, Internet Explorer 3.0.
• Netscape ships a new version of its web browser, Navigator 3.0.
• Softbank plans to buy 80% of Kingston Technology, a vendor of memory cards and systems, for $1.5B.
• IBM, Compaq, Sun Microsystems and other high-tech companies invest $100M in the Java Fund, a venture capital fund that will invest in 20-25 Java-based software start-up companies.
• Power Computing and Umax Computer introduce entry-level Macintosh clones.
• Robert Frankenberg resigns as CEO at Novell.
• Sprint offers Internet service for the consumer market.
• Zenith Electronics wins $1B order for digital TV set-top boxes from Americast for a minimum order of 3M units starting in 1997.
• Netscape forms Navio Communications to build Internet software for TVs, phones, cars and other consumer devices.
• AT&T's Alex Mandl resigns as president to take the top job at Associated Communications, a small wireless, start-up company.
• WorldCom, the 4th largest long distance phone company, offers $12.4 to buy MFS Communications.
• @Home announces partnerships with 60 media companies including USA Today, NY Times and Wall Street Journal. @Home will launch its cable information delivery system in Fremont, CA this fall with TCI.
• Time-Warner Cable says it will offer Internet Access service to its cable subscribers in Akron and Canton, OH beginning in September.
• IBM says it is building a series of object frameworks in Java for use in developing industry-specific business applications.
• Amdahl unveils four Pentium Pro, Windows NT-based EnVista servers for Internet, database, groupware and branch office applications.
• SunRiver Data releases its first Network Computer and changes its name to Boundless Technologies.
• Novell announces IntranetWare, which includes NetWare 4.11, a web server and browser and Novell's Internet Access Server.

September 1996

• Cisco to buy Granite Systems, a manufacturer of high-speed network switching gear, for $220M.
• H&R Block says it will keep its 80% ownership of CompuServe for now.
• IBM introduces it first Network Computer, called the Network Station. It is a business oriented, PowerPC-based machine with a $700 price excluding monitor.
• America Online creates barricades against cyberspace junk mailings and starts blocking email from 5 major Internet bulk-mail operators.
• Ford unveils the first car totally designed by computer, the Puma, which will be sold in Europe.
• IBM introduces its third generation microprocessor-based mainframes.
• Toshiba ships its first desktop PCs.
• An Internet access provider is nearly shutdown by a hacker using hundreds of bogus information requests per second.
• Compaq introduces a network router, Fast Ethernet devices and network management software in its Netelligent product line.
• Netscape opens AppFoundry, a web site that features free Java-based applications for Netscape's browser.
• Motorola introduces Macintosh-compatible PC and Windows NT PowerPC servers.
• Microsoft unveils its Windows CE operating system for handheld PCs.
• The Justice Department launches an antitrust investigation of Microsoft's Internet business.
• Web TV boxes that connect TVs to the Internet ships from Philips and Sony.

History

Computer Industry Almanac has derived these historical milestones from a wide variety of sources.

3000 BC: Dust abacus is invented, probably in Babylonia.
1800 BC: Babylonian mathematician develops algorithms to resolve numerical problems.
500 BC: Bead and wire abacus originates in Egypt.
200 AD: Saun-pan computing tray is used in China; soroban computing tray used in Japan.
1000: Gerbert of Aurillac or Pope Sylvester II devises a more efficient abacus.
1617: Scottish inventor John Napier uses bones to demonstrate division by subtraction and multiplication by addition.
1622: William Oughtred develops the slide rule in England.
1624: Wilhelm Schickard builds first four-function calculator-clock at the University of Heidelberg.
1642: Blaise Pascal builds the first numerical calculating machine in Paris.
1673: Gottfried Leibniz builds a mechanical calculating machine that multiplies, divides, adds and subtracts.
1780: American Benjamin Franklin discovers electricity.
1805: Joseph-Marie Jacquard invents perforated card for use on his loom.
1822: In England Charles Babbage designs a Difference Engine to calculate logarithms, but the machine is never built.
1833: Charles Babbage designs the Analytical Machine that follows instructions from punched-cards. It is the first general purpose computer.
1842: Lady Ada Byron, Countess of Lovelace and daughter of Lord Byron, documents Babbage's work and writes programs for Babbage.
1854: Irishman George Boole publishes The Mathematical Analysis of Logic using the binary system now known as Boolean algebra.
1855: George and Edvard Scheutz of Stockholm build the first practical mechanical computer based on Babbages work.
1876: Telephone is invented by Alexander Graham Bell.
1884: Herman Hollerith applies for patents for automatic punch-card tabulating machine.
1884: Institute of Electrical Engineers (IEE) is founded.
1886: William Burroughs develops the first commercially successful mechanical adding machine.
1889: Patent is issued for Hollerith tabulating machine.
1890: Dr. Herman Hollerith constructs an electromechanical machine using perforated cards for use in the U.S. census.
1896: Hollerith founds the Tabulating Machine Co. and constructs a sorting machine.
1903: Nikola Tesla, a Yugoslavian who worked for Thomas Edison, patents electrical logic circuits called gates or switches.
1911: Computing-Tabulating-Recording Company is formed through a merger of the Tabulating Company (founded by Hollerith), the Computing Scale Company, and the International Time Recording Company.
1912: Institute of Radio Engineers (IRE) is formed.
1914: Thomas J. Watson becomes President of Computing-Tabulating-Recording Company.
1921: Czech word robot is used to describe mechanical workers in the play R.U.R. by Karel Capek.
1924: Computing-Tabulating-Recording Company changes its name to International Business Machines.
1925: Vannevar Bush, builds a large scale analog calculator, the differential analyzer, at MIT.
1927: First public demonstration of television. Radio-telephone becomes operational between London and New York.
1927: Powers Accounting Machine Company becomes the Tabulating Machines Division of Remington-Rand Corp.
1928: A Russian immigrant, Vladimir Zworykin, invents the cathode ray tube (CRT).
1931: First calculator, the Z1, is built in Germany by Konrad Zuse.
1933: First electronic talking machine, the Voder, is built by Dudley, who follows in 1939 with the Vocoder (Voice coder).
1936: Englishman Alan M. Turing while at Princeton University formalizes the notion of calculableness and adapts the notion of algorithm to the computation of functions. Turing's machine is defined to be capable of computing any calculable function.
1937: George Stibitz builds the first binary calculator at Bell Telephone Laboratories.
1938: Hewlett-Packard Co. is founded to make electronic equipment.
1939: First Radio Shack catalog is published.
1939: John V. Atanasoff designs a prototype for the ABC (Atanasoff-Berry Computer) with the help of graduate student Clifford Berry at Iowa State College. In 1973 a judge ruled it the first automatic digital computer.
1940: At Bell Labs, George Stibitz demonstrates the Complex Number Calculator, which may be the first digital computer.
1940: First color TV broadcast.
1940: Remote processing experiments, conducted by Bell Laboratories, create the first terminal.
1941: Colossus computer is designed by Alan M. Turing and built by M.H.A. Neuman at the University of Manchester, England.
1941: Konrad Zuse builds the Z3 computer in Germany, the first calculating machine with automatic control of its operations.
1944: Colossus Mark II is built in England.
1944: Mark I (IBM ASCC) is completed, based on the work of Professor Howard H. Aiken at Harvard and IBM. It is a relay-based computer.
1944: Grace Murray Hopper starts a distinguished career in the computer industry by being the first programmer for the Mark I.
1945: John von Neumann paper describes stored-program concept for EDVAC.
1946: Binac (Binary Automatic Computer), the first computer to operate in real time, is started by Eckert and Mauchly; it is completed in 1949.
1946: ENIAC (Electronic Numerical Integrator and Computer), with 18,000 vacuum tubes, is dedicated at the University of Pennsylvania. It was 8 by 100 feet and weighed 80 tons. It could do 5,000 additions and 360 multiplications per second.
1946: Eckert-Mauchly Computer Corporation is formed as the Electronic Control Co. to design a Universal Automatic Computer (Univac).
1946: Term bit for binary digit is used for first time by John Tukey.
1947: Alan M. Turing publishes an article on Intelligent Machinery which launches artificial intelligence.
1947: Association for Computing Machinery (ACM) is formed.
1948: EDSAC (Electronic Delay Storage Automatic Calculator) is developed at the University of Cambridge by Maurice V. Wilkes.

1948: IBM introduces the 604 electronic calculator.

1948: IBM builds the Selective Sequence Electronic Calculator (SSEC), a computer with 12,000 tubes.

1948: Transistor is invented by William Bradford Shockley with John Bardeen and Walter H. Brattain.

1949: EDVAC (Electronic Discrete Variable Automatic Computer) supports the first tests of magnetic disks.

1949: Jay Forrester uses iron cores as main memory in Whirlwind. Forrester patent is issued in 1956.

1949: Claude Shannon of MIT builds the first chess playing machine.

1950: Maurice V. Wilkes at Cambridge University uses assembler (symbolic assembly language) on EDSAC.

1950: Remington-Rand acquires Eckert-Mauchly Computer Corp.

1950: SEAC (Standards Eastern Automatic Computer) is delivered to the National Bureau of Standards.

1951: First Joint Computer Conference is held.

1951: Maurice V. Wilkes introduces the concept of microprogramming.

1951: IEEE Computer Society is formed.

1951: UNIVAC I is installed at the Bureau of Census using a magnetic tape unit as a buffer memory.

1951: Grace Hopper writes the first compiler for UNIVAC 1.

1951: Wang Laboratories, Inc. is founded by An Wang in Boston.

1951: Whirlwind computer becomes operational at MIT. It was the first real-time computer and was designed by Jay Forrester and Ken Olsen.

1952: First computer manual is written by Fred Gruenberger.

1952: IBM introduces the 701, its first electronic stored-program computer.

1952: Nixdorf Computer is founded in Germany.

1952: Remington-Rand acquires Engineering Research Associates (ERA).

1952: RCA develops Bizmac with iron-core memory and a magnetic drum supporting the first database.

1952: UNIVAC I predicts an Eisenhower landslide with 7% of the votes, just one hour after the polls close.

1952: U.S. Department of Justice sues IBM for monopolizing the punched-card accounting machine industry.

1953: Burroughs Corp. installs the Universal Digital Electronic Computer (UDEC) at Wayne State University.

1953: First high-speed printer is developed by Remington-Rand for use on the Univac.

1953: First magnetic tape device, the IBM 726, is introduced with 100 character-per-inch density and 75 inches-per-second speed.

1953: IBM ships its first stored-program computer, the 701. It is a vacuum tube, or first generation, computer.

1954: FORTRAN is created by John Backus at IBM. Harlan Herrick runs the first successful FORTRAN program.

1954: Gene Amdahl develops the first operating system, used on IBM 704.

1955: First SHARE users group meeting is held.

1955: Remington-Rand merges with Sperry Gyroscope to form Sperry-Rand.

1956: APT (Automatic Programmed Tool) is developed by D.T. Ross.

1956: Burroughs acquires Electrodata and the Datatron computer, which becomes the Burroughs 205.

1956: Government antitrust suit against IBM is settled; consent decree requires IBM to sell as well as lease machines.

1956: A. Newell, D. Shaw and F. Simon invent IPL (Information Processing Language.)

1956: RCA ships the Bizmac.

1956: T.J. Watson, Jr. assumes presidency of IBM.

1956: The acronym artificial intelligence is coined by John McCarthy.

1957: Control Data Corporation is formed by William C. Norris and a group of engineers from Sperry-Rand.

1957: Digital Equipment Corporation is founded by Ken Olsen.

1957: First issue of Datamation is released.

1957: Honeywell joins with Raytheon to ship the Datamatic 1000.

1958: ALGOL, first called IAL (International Algebraic Language), is presented in Zurich.

1958: First virtual memory machine, Atlas, is installed in England by Feranti. It was developed at University of Manchester by R.M. Kilburn.

1958: First electronic computers are built in Japan by NEC: the NEC-1101 and -1102.

1958: Frank Rosenblatt builds the Perceptron Mark I using a CRT as an output device.

1958: LISP is developed on the IBM 704 at MIT under John McCarthy.

1958: Seymour Cray builds the first fully transistorized supercomputer for Control Data Corp., the CDC 1604.

1958: Jack Kilby of Texas Instruments makes the first integrated circuit.

1959: COBOL is defined by the Conference on Data System Languages (Codasyl), based on Grace Hoppers Flow-Matic.

1959: First packaged program is sold by Computer Science Corporation.

1959: IBM introduces the 1401. Over 10,000 units will be delivered during its lifetime.

1959: IBM ships its first transistorized, or second generation, computers, the 1620 and 1790.

1959: Jack S. Kilby at Texas Instruments files a patent for the first integrated circuit.

1959: Robert Noyce of Fairchild Semiconductor develops the monolithic idea for integrated circuits.

1960: Benjamin Curley develops the first minicomputer, the PDP-1, at Digital Equipment Corporation.

1960: COBOL runs on UNIVAC II and RCA 501.

1960: Control Data Corporation delivers its first product, a large scientific computer named the CDC 1604.

1960: Digital ships the first small computer, the PDP-1.

1960: First electronic switching central office becomes operational in Chicago.

1960: Removable disks first appear.

1961: AFIPS (American Federation of Information Processing Societies) forms.

1961: Multiprogramming runs on Stretch computer. Time-sharing runs at MIT on IBM 709 and 7090 computers by F. Corbato.

1961: IBM delivers the Stretch computer to Los Alamos. This transistorized computer with 64-bit data paths is the first to use eight-bit bytes.

1962: APL (A Programming Language) is developed by Ken Iverson, Harvard University and IBM.

1962: First general-purpose simulation languages are proposed: (1) SIMSCRIPT by the Rand Corporation, and (2) GPSS by IBM.

1962: IBM markets 1311 using removable disks.

1962: IBM's U.S.-based annual revenues from computer products reaches $1 billion and for the first time surpasses its other revenue.

1962: H. Ross Perot founds EDS (Electronic Data Systems) in Dallas, TX.

1963: Control Data acquires Bendix Corp. computer division.

1963: Conversational graphics consoles are developed by General Motors (DAC-1) and MIT Lincoln Laboratories (Sketchpad), resulting in computer-aided design (CAD). Sketchpad uses the first light-pen, developed by Ivan Sutherland.

1963: DEC ships the first PDP-5 minicomputer.

1963: Tandy acquires Radio Shack (9 stores).

1964: IBM announces the System 360, the first family of compatible computers.

1964: Control Data Corporation introduces the CDC 6000, which uses 60-bit words and parallel processing. CDC ships the 6600, the most powerful computer for several years. It was designed by Seymour Cray.

1964: BASIC (Beginners All-purpose Symbolic Instruction Language) created by Tom Kurtz and John Kemeny of Dartmouth.

1964: Graphic tablet is developed by M.R. Davis and T.D. Ellis at Rand Corporation.

1964: Honeywell introduces the H-200 attacking IBM's installed base of 1400 systems.

1964: NCR introduces the 315/100.

1965: CDC founds the Control Data Institute to provide computer-related education.

1965: Digital ships the first PDP-8 minicomputer.

1965: First computer science Ph.D. is granted to Richard L. Wexelblat at the University of Pennsylvania.

1965: IBM ships the first System 360, its first integrated circuit-based, or third generation, computer.

1966: Honeywell acquires Computer Control Company, a minicomputer manufacturer.

1966: Scientific Data Systems (SDS) introduces Sigma 7.

1966: Texas Instruments offers the first solid-state hand-held calculator.

1967: Digital introduces the PDP-10 computer.

1967: A.H. Bobeck at Bell Laboratories develops bubble memory.

1967: Burroughs ships the B3200.

1967: First issue of Computerworld is published.

1968: Dendral, the first medical diagnostic medical program, is created by Joshua Lederberg at Stanford University.

1968: Univac introduces the 9400 computer.

1968: Integrated Electronics (Intel) Corp. is founded by Gordon Moore and Robert Noyce.

1969: Edson deCastro leaves DEC to start Data General Corp. and introduces the Nova, the first 16-bit minicomputer.

1969: First International Joint Conference on Artificial Intelligence is held.

1969: IBM unbundles hardware and software; introduces a minicomputer line, System/3.

1969: Lockheed Electronics ships the MAC-16.

1969: PASCAL compiler is written by Nicklaus Wirth and installed on the CDC 6400.

1969: Object technology is first used by a Norwegian--Kristian Nygaard.

1970: Computer Logic Systems ships SLS-18.

1970: Digital ships its first 16-bit minicomputer, the PDP-11/20.

1970: Data General ships SuperNova.

1970: First ACM Computer Chess tournament is held.

1970: Honeywell acquires General Electric's computer operations. 1970: IBM ships its first System 370, a fourth generation, computer.

1970: Xerox Data Systems introduces the CF-16A.

1971: Computer Automation introduces the Alpha-16.

1971: IBM introduces the 370/135 and 370/195 mainframe computers.

1971: Floppy disks are introduced to load the IBM 370 microcode.

1971: Intel Corporation announces the first microprocessor, the Intel 4004, developed by a team headed by Marcian E. Hoff.

1971: John Blankenbaker builds the first personal computer, the Kenbak I.

1971: NCR introduces the Century 50.

1971: Sperry-Rand takes over the RCA computer product line.

1972: Cray Research is founded.

1972: First electronic pocket calculator is developed by Jack Kilby, Jerry Merryman, and Jim VanTassel of Texas Instruments.

1972: Gary Kildall at Naval Postgraduate School writes PL/1, the first programming language for the Intel 4004 microprocessor.

1972: Intel introduces the 8008, an 8 bit microprocessor.

1972: Prime Computer is founded.

1973: First National Computer Conference (NCC) is held in New York City.

1973: IBM settles a lawsuit by Control Data, selling Service Bureau Corporation (SBC) to Control Data.

1973: PROLOG language is developed by Alain Comerauer at the University of Marseilles-Luminy, France.

1973: R2E markets the MICRAL, the first microcomputer in France.

1973: Winchester disk drives are first introduced by IBM, who uses the term as a code name for its Model 3340 direct-access storage device.

1974: Digital enters the Fortune 500 ranking of the largest industrial companies.

1974: Intel introduces the 8080, an 8 bit microprocessor that will be used in numerous personal computers.

1974: Zilog is formed.

1974: Motorola introduces the 6800 microprocessor.

1974: The first Creative Computer magazine is published

1975: Cray Research introduces the Cray-1 supercomputer.

1975: Homebrew Computer Club, considered the first personal computer users group, is formed.

1975: MITS introduces the Altair personal computer, named after a Star Trek episode, A Voyage to Altair. The kit cost $397 for a 256 byte computer. The I/O consisted of switches and lights. It was designed by Ed Roberts and Bill Yates.

1975: Microsoft is founded after Bill Gates and Paul Allen adapt and sell BASIC to MITS for the Altair PC.

1975: The first computer store opens in Santa Monica, CA.

1975: Xerox withdraws from the mainframe computer industry.

1975: Sphere introduces the first complete desktop computer.

1975: IMSAI builds the first clone computer, which helps establish the Altair's S-100 bus as a de facto standard.

1975: Processor Technology and Cromemco announce S-100 compatible computers.

1976: First fault-tolerant computer, the T/16, is introduced by Tandem.

1976: MYCIN, an expert system to diagnose and treat infectious blood diseases, is developed at Stanford University by E. Shortliffe.

1976: NEC System 800 and 900 general-purpose mainframes are introduced.

1976: Seymour Cray engineers and delivers Cray 1 with 200,000 freon-cooled ICs and 100 million floating point operations per second.

1976: Superminicomputers are introduced by Perkin-Elmer and Gould SEL.

1976: Zilog Z-80 chip is introduced.

1976: MOS Technology introduces 6502 microprocessor.

1976: Gary Kildall writes the CP/M operating system and founds Digital Research.

1976: Electric Pencil, the first PC word processing program is announced.

1976: Apple Computer is founded and introduces the Apple I.

1977: Apple Computer announces the Apple II personal computer.

1977: Commodore and Tandy begin selling personal computers.

1977: Digital introduces its first 32-bit superminicomputer, the VAX-11/780.

1977: Datapoint introduces ARC system, the first local area network.

1977: First ComputerLand franchise store opens in Morristown, NJ under the name Computer Shack.

1977: North Star and Pertec introduce PCs with 5.25" floppy disks.

1977: Heathkit brings out computer kits for hobbyists.

1978: Sprint business service is inaugurated.

1978: Texas Instruments introduces the Speak-and-Spell educational toy featuring digital speech synthesis.

1978: Total computers in use in the U.S. exceed a half million units.

1978: Digital ships its first VAX-11/780.

1978: The first COMDEX trade show is held.

1979: Ada language is developed by a team at CII-Honeywell Bull (France) directed by Jean Ichbiah.

1979: The Source and CompuServe Information Services go online.

1979: VisiCalc, the first electronic spreadsheet software, is shown at the West Coast Computer Faire.

1979: Texas Instruments introduces the TI-99/4 home computer.

1979: Hayes introduces the first PC modem.

1979: Wordstar, one of the best-selling word processing programs for PCs, is released by Micropro (later called Wordstar International).

1980: Control Data Corporation introduces the Cyber 205 supercomputer.

1980: First issue of InfoWorld is published.

1980: Microsoft licenses UNIX operating system from Bell Laboratories and introduces its Xenix adaptation.

1980: Sinclair introduces the ZX80 PC with an entry price under $200.

1980: Total computers in use in the U.S. exceed one million units.

1981: Commodore introduces the VIC-20 home computer, which sells over one million units.

1981: IBM enters the personal computer market, creating a de facto standard.

1981: Osborne Computer introduces the Osborne 1, the first portable computer.

1981: Digital introduces the first dual processor minicomputer, the VAX-11/782.

1982: AT&T agrees to give up 22 Bell System companies in settling a 13-year-old lawsuit brought by the Justice Department.

1982: Compaq Computer incorporates.

1982: Sun Microsystems is founded.

1982: Microsoft licenses MS-DOS to 50 microcomputer manufacturers in the first 16 months of availability.

1982: Time Magazine names the computer its Man of the Year.

1982: U.S. drops IBM antitrust suit begun in 1969.

1983: Compaq ships its first computer in January and sells $111M, the greatest first-year sales in the history of American business.

1983: Cray 2 computer introduced with one billion FLOPs (floating point operations per second) performance rating.

1983: Lotus 1-2-3 replaces VisiCalc as the spreadsheet software of choice for microcomputers.

1983: NEC announces the SX-1 and SX-2 supercomputers.

1983: Total computers in use in the U.S. exceed ten million units.

1984: Apple introduces the Macintosh computer.

1984: IBM introduces the PC AT (Advanced Technology). IBM merges with Rolm Corp., which becomes a telecommunications subsidiary.

1984: The Tandy 1000 personal computer becomes the #1 selling IBM PC-compatible in its first year.

1985: IBM delivers the new 3090 Sierra systems.

1985: Aldus introduces PageMaker for the Macintosh and starts the desktop publishing era.

1986: Burroughs merges with Sperry to form Unisys Corporation, second only to IBM in computer revenues.

1986: Compaq makes the Fortune 500 list. Introduces its first Intel 80386-based PC.

1986: Computerworld publishes its 1,000th issue on November 3.

1986: HP introduces its Spectrum line of reduced instruction set computers (RISC).

1986: The number of computers in the U.S. exceeds 30 million.

1987: IBM introduces its PS/2 family and ships over 1 million units by year end.

1987: Cray Research introduces the Cray 2S which is 40% faster than the Cray 2.

1987: ETA Systems introduces its ETA-10 family of supercomputers.

1987: Sun Microsystems introduces its first workstation based on the SPARC RISC microprocessor.

1987: Apple introduces the Macintosh II and Macintosh SE and HyperCard.
1987: IBM introduces its Systems Applications Architecture (SAA).
1987: Digital introduces Vaxstation 2000 workstation computer, and the MicroVAX 3500 and 3600.
1987: Aldus introduces PageMaker for the IBM PC and compatible computers.
1987: Compaq reaches a billion dollar in sales in its fifth year of operation.
1987: Conner Peripherals beats Compaq's first year sales record: $113M vs $111M.
1987: Computer Associates acquires UCCEL in the largest ever software acquisition ($780M).
1987: IBM invests in Steve Chens Supercomputer Systems, Inc.
1987: Digital ships its 100,000th VAX.
1987: Apple spins off its application software business as a separate company and names it Claris.
1987: Texas Instruments introduces the first AI microprocessor chip.
1988: Digital introduces VAXstation 8000.
1988: Cray Research introduces the Cray Y-MP, a $20M supercomputer.
1988: IBM introduces a new mainframe computer operating system called MVS/ESA.
1988: IBM announces its long awaited Silverlake mid-range computers called AS/400.
1988: Motorola announces the 88000, a RISC microprocessor.
1988: The first 3D graphics supercomputers are announced by Apollo, Ardent and Stellar.
1988: The first PS/2-compatible computers are announced by Tandy, Dell Computer and others.
1988: Unisys introduces the 2200/400 family to replace its mid-range 1100 series.
1988: AT&T announces plan to acquire 20% of Sun Microsystems, and that Sun will help AT&T develop the next version of UNIX.
1988: BM, DEC, HP, Apollo and several other major computer companies form the Open Software Foundation to set a UNIX counterstandard.
1988: Sun Microsystems surpasses the $1 billion sales mark, and introduces 80386-based workstations.
1988: IBM and Sears joint videotex venture starts operation under the Prodigy name.
1988: Sematech picks Austin, TX as its headquarters and the consortium will be headed by Robert Noyce.
1988: A consortium of PC companies led by Compaq introduces the EISA counter standard to IBM's PS/2 MicroChannel bus.
1988: IBM introduces the ES/3090 S series mainframe computer.
1988: IBM wins a $3.6B contract to build the next generation air traffic control system.
1988: Unisys acquires Convergent Technologies for $350M.
1988: Computer Associates acquires Applied Data Research for $170M from Ameritech.
1988: A nondestructive worm spreads via the Internet network and brings several thousand computers to their knees.
1989: Solbourne Computer introduces the first Sun 4-compatible computer.
1989: Digital announces a workstation using Mips Computer's RISC microprocessor.
1989: Microsoft buys a 20% stake in Santa Cruz Operation, a major Unix software developer.
1989: Intel announces the 80486 microprocessor and the I860 RISC/coprocessor chip. Both chips have over one million transistors.
1989: Hewlett-Packard acquires Apollo for $476M.
1989: Sun Microsystems introduces its SPARCstation, a low-end RISC workstation with an entry price of only $9,000.
1989: Control Data discontinues its ETA supercomputer subsidiary.
1989: IBM announces the Officevision software using the SAA protocol, which runs on PS/2s, PS/2 LANs, AS/400 and mainframe computers.
1989: Cray restructures itself into two companies: Cray Research which continues with its current business and Cray Computer Corp. headed by Seymour Cray, which will develop a gallium arsenide-based supercomputer.
1989: NeXT sells a 16.6% share to Canon for $100M.
1989: Seagate buys Control Data's Imprimis disk drive subsidiary for $450M.
1989: Computer Associates acquires Cullinet for $333M.
1989: Prime Computer agrees to be bought by a J.H. Whitney-formed company, ending a long and acrimonious takeover battle by MAI Basic.
1989: Apple introduces its long awaited portable Macintosh.
1989: The worldwide number of computers in use surpasses 100M units.
1989: Poqet announces the first pocket sized MS-DOS compatible computer.
1989: Grid introduces a laptop computer with a touch sensitive pad that recognizes handwriting--the GridPad.
1989: The number of computers in the U.S. exceeds 50M units.
1989: The notebook computer becomes a full function computer including hard and floppy disk with the arrival of Compaq's LTE family.
1989: Digital Equipment extends the VAX-family into the mainframe arena with the VAX 9000.
1989: The first EISA-based personal computers arrive.
1989: The first 80486-based computers are introduced.
1989: Dun & Bradstreet acquires MSA in a major software acquisition worth $333M.
1990: Motorola introduces the 68040 microprocessor.
1990: IBM announces its RISC Station 6000 family of high performance workstations.
1990: Intel introduces the 80386SL microprocessor for notebook PCs.
1990: Digital introduces a fault-tolerant VAX computer.
1990: Cray Research unveils an entry-level supercomputer, the Y-MP2E, with a starting price of $2.2M.
1990: Microsoft introduces Windows 3.0.
1990: Lotus wins its look and feel suit against Paperback Software's spreadsheet program.
1990: IBM ships the PS/1, a computer for consumers and home offices.
1990: IBM announces the System 390 (code name Summit), its mainframe computer for the 1990s.
1990: Microsoft's fiscal year revenue ending 6/30/90 exceeds $1B.
1990: NCR abandons its proprietary mainframes in favor of systems based on single or multiple Intel 486 and successor microprocessors.
1990: Apple introduces its low-end Macintoshes: The Classic, LC and IISI.
1990: Intel launches a parallel supercomputer using over 500 860 RISC microprocessors.

1990: Sun Microsystems brings out the SPARCstation 2.

1990: Microsoft along with IBM, Tandy, AT&T and others announced hardware and software specifications for multimedia platforms.

1990: The first SPARC compatible workstations are introduced.

1990: The number of Internet host computers surpass 100,000.

1990: Kalpana introduces the first Ethernet switch.

1991: Go Corp. releases PenPoint, an operating system for pen-based computers.

1991: Advanced Micro Devices announces its AMD 386 microprocessor to compete with Intel's 386 chips.

1991: Notebook PCs are introduced by most PC vendors.

1991: HP unveils its RISC-based 9000 Series 700 workstations with exceptional price-performance.

1991: Compaq leads a group of companies to launch the Advanced Computing Environment (ACE) to set a standard for PCs and workstations.

1991: The Federal Trade Commission launches an investigation into Microsoft's business practices.

1991: Intel introduces the 486SX, a lower priced 486 chip.

1991: NCR agrees to be acquired by AT&T in a deal valued at $7.4B.

1991: Apple releases the System 7.0 operating system for Macintosh.

1991: Wang will resell IBM's PS/2, RS/6000 and minicomputers. IBM will invest $100M in Wang.

1991: Microsoft rolls out DOS 5.0 with great success.

1991: Major changes among PC dealers as ComputerLand acquires Nynex's computer stores, CompuCom acquires Computer Factory, ValCom and Inacomp merge, JWP buys Businessland and Intelligent Electronics acquires BizMart.

1991: Borland buys Ashton-Tate for $440M.

1991: SunSoft, a Sun Microsystems subsidiary, announces Solaris which is a Unix operating system for SPARC workstations and 386/486 PCs.

1991: The Bell companies receive permission to enter the online information services market.

1991: Apple &IBM sign historic deal--including 2 joint ventures: Kaleida to develop multimedia products, Taligent to develop object software.

1991: Apple rolls out its PowerBook notebook and Quadra Macintosh PCs.

1991: Wavetracer introduces its Zephyr massively parallel computer system with up to 8,192 processors.

1991: IBM reorganizes itself into more autonomous business units and several divisions become wholly-owned subsidiaries.

1991: AT&T/NCR agrees to acquire Teradata for $520M.

1991: Many computer companies have loses including Compaq, DEC, IBM, Lotus and Unisys, primarily due to work force reduction costs.

1991: The first general purpose pen-based notebook computers are introduced.

1991: IBM has its first revenue decline in 45 years.

1992: IBM invests $100M in Groupe Bull.

1992: Silicon Graphics buys Mips Computer in a $400M stock swap.

1992: IBM releases OS/2 Version 2.0 and ships over 1M units.

1992: Microsoft introduces Windows 3.1 and ships nearly 10M units.

1992: The core of Apple's lawsuit versus Microsoft Windows is dismissed.

1992: Sun Microsystems launches a new generation of SPARC computers--the SPARCstation 10 family.

1992: Compaq announces several new lines of PCs and becomes a price trend setter. Its low-price strategy is very successful.

1992: Ken Olsen resigns from Digital after 25 years at the helm.

1992: Sears and IBM form a new venture, named Advantis, to compete in the value added network service market.

1992: Wang Laboratories files for Chapter 11 bankruptcy protection.

1992: IBM makes the IBM PC Co. a subsidiary.

1992: IBM follows Compaq's strategy and introduces aggressively priced PCs--also with good success.

1992: Compaq enters the Japanese market with aggressively priced PCs--as much as 50% lower than Japanese PC prices.

1992: Digital announces its next generation computer architecture--the RISC-based Alpha.

1992: Microsoft introduces Windows for Workgroups.

1992: Intel says its next microprocessor will be called Pentium instead of 586.

1992: Hewlett-Packard ships the LaserJet 4, a 600 by 600 dots per inch resolution laser printer.

1992: Novell to acquire Unix Systems Laboratory, including Univel, from AT&T for $350M.

1993: IBM reports its worst year in history with a loss of $4.97B on revenues of $64.5B.

1993: IBM chairman John Akers resigns. After the most publicity ever for an executive search, Louis Gerstner becomes the new CEO.

1993: General Magic debuts Telescripts, a communications-intensive operating system for PDAs.

1993: NeXT sells its hardware business to Canon and will concentrate its efforts on the NeXTStep software business.

1993: Novell unveils NetWare 4.0.

1993: IBM introduces the F series of the AS/400.

1993: Lotus announces Notes 3.0.

1993: Motorola starts shipping the first PowerPC microprocessor.

1993: IBM's storage division, Adstar, becomes a subsidiary.

1993: Microsoft unveils Windows NT.

1993: Pentium-based systems start shipping.

1993: EPA's Energy Star Initiative is unveiled and most PC vendors support the program with announcements of energy efficient PCs.

1993: Apple ships the Newton MessagePad--its first Personal Digital Assistant.

1993: AT&T announces it will acquire McCaw Cellular for $12.6B.

1993: Compaq introduces the Presario, a PC family targeted for the home market.

1993: The number of Internet host computers pass 1M units.

1993: FTC ends its probe of Microsoft without any action, but the Antitrust Division of the Department of Justice will launch its investigation.

1993: Microsoft outlines the Plug and Play and Microsoft at Work (MAW) initiatives.

1993: IBM debuts its first workstations based on the PowerPC chip.

1993: Novell transfers the Unix trademark to X/Open and it will certify that an operating system is Unix compliant.

1993: IBM announces OS/2 for Windows, which upgrades the Windows environment to OS/2.

1993: Sun Microsystems licenses NeXTStep and makes a $10M investment in NeXT.

1993: IBM says it will sell its Federal Systems division ($2.2B in yearly revenue) to Loral for $1.6B.

1994: Macintoshes using the PowerPC start shipping.

1994: Intel introduces the 486DX4 clock-tripling microprocessor.

1994: Aldus and Adobe agree to merge in a transaction worth $525M and will form a $0.5B+ software company.

1994: Novell says it will acquire WordPerfect for $1.14B and will buy Borland's Quattro Pro for $145M.

1994: Digital says it will lay off 20,000 people and will sell off some of its business.

1994: Wellfleet and SynOptics agree to merge in a transaction worth $1B.

1994: Compaq takes the No. 1 spot in worldwide PC shipments for the first time.

1994: Microsoft settles a four year old federal antitrust investigation.

1994: Apple licenses the Macintosh operating system for the first time.

1994: John Sculley leaves Apple after 10 years at the helm.

1994: The number of email users in the U.S. surpass 20M people.

1994: Netscape is founded by Jim Clark and Marc Andreessen.

1994: Bill Gates tops the Forbes 400 list of America's richest people and is worth $9.3B.

1994: A subtle flaw in Intel's Pentium microprocessor creates tremendous amount of bad publicity.

1994: Sybase buys Powersoft for $944M.

1994: FCC opens the bidding on 99 licenses for PCS phone systems in 51 markets.

1994: The Internet bursts on the front page of computer publications.

1995: Softbank buys the Interface Group's tradeshow division for $800M.

1995: The first Macintosh clones ship from Power Computing, Radius and Daystar Digital.

1995: Numerous Internet software companies are acquired at very high prices.

1995: The Department of Justice files an antitrust suit to block Microsoft's acquisition of Intuit. Microsoft later ends the acquisition attempt.

1995: Sun Microsystems introduces Java, an interpretive language that can spice up web pages.

1995: IBM acquires Lotus Development for $3.52B.

1995: Forbes says Bill Gates is the richest man in the world with assets valued at $12.9B.

1995: 3Com acquires Chipcom for $775M in stock.

1995: Netscape goes public with a first day closing price that gives the company a $2.2B valuation.

1995: Windows 95 is launched with the largest press coverage of any product in any industry.

1995: Seagate buys Conner Peripherals for $1.1B.

1995: Apple, IBM and Motorola release the Common Hardware Reference Platform (CHRP) specs for PowerPC computers.

1995: Intel introduces the Pentium Pro microprocessor.

1995: Lotus Notes users exceed 1M units.

1995: Sun Microsystems ships workstations based on the 64-bit UltraSPARC.

1995: Softbank buys Ziff-Davis for $2.1B.

1995: Apple, IBM and HP say they will shut down Taligent.

1996: Internet fever reaches a peak: Internet software companies are bought at very high prices, companies with Internet products go public with extreme valuations, Internet start-up companies proliferates and the press and media is saturated with Internet stories and publicity.

1996: IBM buys client/server software developer Tivoli for $743M.

1996: A telecom deregulation bill passes that allows cable TV, long distance and local telephone companies to compete against each other.

1996: Silicon Graphics buys Cray Research, the leading supercomputer vendor, for $739M.

1996: AT&T enters the Internet service provider market with aggressive pricing.

1996: Motorola and IBM license Apple's Mac OS including sublicensing to other vendors.

1996: AT&T spins off Lucent Technologies, its telecom equipment manufacturing business, in the largest U.S. IPO ever.

1996: After 4 years of stable prices, DRAMs drop dramatically and catches up with historical trends.

1996: SBC Communications says it will acquire Pacific Telesis in a $16.7B.

1996: Bell Atlantic and Nynex announce a merger valued at $23B.

1996: IBM and Sears sell their Prodigy online service to a group of investors for $250M.

1996: H&R Block spins off CompuServe online service in an IPO.

1996: MFS Communications agrees to buy Uunet Technologies, an Internet service provider, for $2B.

1996: DRAM memory prices drop dramatically after four years of stable pricing.

1996: EDS is spun off from GM.

1996: Microsoft moves its Microsoft Network online service to the Internet.

1996: The first macro virus, World Concept, which is attached to Microsoft Word 6 files, becomes the number 1 virus in record time.

1996: Intranets, corporate networks that use Internet technology, becomes a hot topic and grows dramatically.

1996: The Universal Serial Bus, a new peripheral interface bus, emerges as a standard personal computer I/O bus.

1996: The computers in use in the U.S. surpass 100M units.

1996: Microsoft ships Windows NT 4.0.

1996: Forbes says Bill Gates is the richest man in the world with assets valued at $18B.

1996: Packard Bell and NEC will combine their PC businesses, except in Japan and China.

1996: IBM reaches a pact with the Justice Department to end the restrictions from the 1956 consent decree.

1996: The first Network Computers ship from IBM and others.

1996: Year 2000 software date problems hit the front page and receives deserved attention.

1996: Microsoft and Netscape ship version 3.0 of their Internet browsers--Internet Explorer and Navigator.

Copyright © November 1996, Computer Industry Almanac, 702/749-5053, 800/377-6810 (U.S. only).

Chapter 8

Employment, Salaries and Wealth

Employment

Computerworld: 100 Best Places to Work

"Computerworld's third annual Best Places to Work ranking captures the essence of what it takes to be an out-standing IS organization. Various criteria were used in our weighted-average formula; all of them play an important role in creating an environment where IS professionals can thrive.

'Who: Computerworld considered a diversity of organizations for inclusion on the Best Places list. We started with last year's 100 ranking and added the 1995 Fortune 500 list, which includes both manufacturing and service companies. In addition, we included large government agencies, both state and federal, colleges and universities and about 40 of the largest management consulting and systems integration firms. In all, Computerworld surveyed more than 1,100 organizations. The primary contact within these organizations was the most senior information systems manager.

'What: We asked these IS managers 31 questions covering a wide range of employee-related topics: benefits, salary levels, salary increases, staff growth, staff promotions, employee turnover rates, training budgets and number of training days, use of technology and diversity in the workplace. In most questions, we asked respondents to identify a range, rather than a specific number.

'These nine topics were each given a numerical value, which were then summed, using a weighted-average formula, to determine the total score for the organization. These scores then became the basis for ranking the organizations and selecting the final 100 Best Places to Work."--Computerworld

Rank	Company	Industry	IS Staff Changes (%)		Avg. Salary Incr.(%)		IS Staff Diversity (%)	
			Actual '95	Proj. '96	Actual '95	Proj. '96	Women	Minorities
1	Cisco Systems	Computer products	20+	20+	7-9	10+	20-39	20-38
2	Informix Software	Computer products	10-20	20+	7-9	10+	40-49	1-19
3	Computer Associates Int'l.	Computer products	10-20	20+	10+	10+	40-49	20-39
4	Sears, Roebuck & Co.	Wholesale & retail	10-20	1-4	10+	7-9	40-49	20-39
5	Xerox	Computer products	10-20	10-20	10+	10+	40-49	20-39
6	Massachusetts Mutual	Insurance	1-4	10-20	7-9	10+	50-74	1-19
7	Price Waterhouse LLP	Prof. svcs. & consulting	20+	20+	10+	10+	20-39	1-19
8	Southwest Airlines Co.	Transportation services	20+	20+	7-9	7-9	40-49	1-19
9	American Management Sys.	Prof. svcs. & consulting	20+	10-20	10+	10+	20-39	1-19
10	Enserch Corp.	Mining, forest prod, oil & gas	10-20	5-9	7-9	7-9	40-49	20-39
11	Home Depot	Wholesale & retail	10-20	5-9	7-9	7-9	40-49	1-19
12	University of Miami	Education	1-4	1-4	4-6	4-6	40-49	50-74
13	First NBD Chicago	Financial svcs. & banking	10-20	10-20	10+	7-9	20-39	20-39
14	University of WI, Stevens Pt.	Education	10-20	20+	4-6	4-6	20-39	0
15	Caterpillar	Industrial equipment	1-4	5-9	7-9	7-9	40-49	20-39
16	Key Services	Financial svcs. & banking	10-20	10-20	7-9	7-9	20-39	1-19
17	U.S. Arms Control & Disarmament Agency	Government	10-20	0	1-3	1-3	50-74	50-74
18	Crown Central Petroleum	Mining, forest prod, oil & gas	10-20	10-20	4-6	4-6	40-49	1-19
19	Fifth Third Bancorp	Financial svcs. & banking	20+	10-20	7-9	7-9	20-39	1-19
20	E-Systems	Appliances & electrical equip.	5-9	5-9	7-9	7-9	20-39	1-19
21	Entergy	Telecom & utilities	0	10-20	10+	10+	20-39	1-19
22	Tech Data	Wholesale & retail	20+	10-20	4-6	4-6	20-39	20-39
23	Sherwin-Williams	Chemicals & pharmaceuticals	5-9	1-4	4-6	4-6	20-39	1-19
24	Campbell Soup	Food & beverage	-20+	1-4	7-9	4-6	40-49	1-19
25	PacifiCare Health Sys.	Health care	20+	10-20	4-6	4-6	40-49	40-49

Rank	Company	Industry	IS Staff Changes (%)		Avg. Salary Incr.(%)		IS Staff Diversity (%)	
			Actual '95	Proj. '96	Actual '95	Proj. '96	Women	Minorities
26	Amgen	Chemicals & pharmaceuticals	10-20	5-9	4-6	4-6	NA	NA
27	AT&T	Telecom & utilities	1-4	1-4	10+	10+	50-74	1-19
28	Maytag	Appliances & electrical equip.	20+	10-20	4-6	4-6	20-39	1-19
29	Duff & Phelps Credit Rating	Financial svcs. & banking	20+	20+	7-9	7-9	1-19	20-39
30	AMOCO	Mining, forest prod, oil & gas	1-4	1-4	7-9	4-6	20-39	20-39
31	Mellon Bank	Financial svcs. & banking	5-9	0	4-6	4-6	20-39	1-19
32	State Street Bank & Trust	Financial svcs. & banking	-1--4	10-20	10+	10+	40-49	1-19
33	U.S. Dept Housing & Urban Dev	Government	5-9	1-4	4-6	4-6	50-74	50-74
34	Owens Corning	Metals, bldg materials & glass	-1--4	-5--9	10+	10+	20-39	1-19
35	Outboard Marine	Industrial equipment	10-20	20+	4-6	4-6	20-39	1-19
36	First Bank System	Financial svcs. & banking	20+	5-9	4-6	4-6	20-39	1-19
37	Anheuser-Busch	Food & beverage	5-9	20+	4-6	4-6	20-39	20-39
38	Avon Products	Cosmetics	5-9	5-9	10+	7-9	20-39	20-39
39	Pepsico	Food & beverage	0	1-4	4-6	4-6	40-49	1-19
40	University of CA, Davis	Education	20+	20+	4-6	4-6	40-49	50-74
41	Tyco International	Appliances & electrical equip.	0	1-4	7-9	7-9	50-74	1-19
42	Caliber Technology	Transportation services	10-20	5-9	4-6	4-6	20-39	1-19
43	UNUM	Financial svcs. & banking	0	0	10+	10+	NA	1-19
44	Fleet Services	Financial svcs. & banking	20+	10-20	4-6	4-6	40-49	1-19
45	SunTrust Services	Financial svcs. & banking	20+	5-9	10+	10+	20-39	1-19
46	Wal-Mart Stores	Wholesale & retail	5-9	1-4	7-9	10+	NA	NA
47	U.S. Healthcare	Insurance	20+	20+	4-6	4-6	20-39	1-19
48	Farmland Industries	Wholesale & retail	1-4	0	4-6	4-6	40-49	1-19
49	Minnesota Mutual Life Insur.	Insurance	1-4	5-9	4-6	4-6	40-49	1-19
50	United HealthCare	Health care	10-20	20+	4-6	4-6	20-39	20-39
51	Equitable Cos., The	Financial svcs. & banking	0	5-9	7-9	7-9	40-49	20-39
52	Barnett Technologies	Financial svcs. & banking	10-20	5-9	4-6	4-6	20-39	20-39
53	Deloitte & Touche	Prof. svcs. & consulting	10-20	5-9	4-6	4-6	20-39	1-19
54	Microsoft	Computer products	20+	20+	7-9	7-9	20-39	1-19
55	Interpublic Group of Cos.	Prof. svcs. & consulting	5-9	1-4	4-6	4-6	40-49	1-19
56	Willamette Industries	Wholesales & retail	20+	5-9	10+	7-9	40-49	1-19
57	N. Dakota State Univ.-Fargo	Education	10-20	10-20	1-3	1-3	50-74	0
58	Consolidated Freightways	Transportation services	5-9	5-9	4-6	1-3	20-39	1-19
59	Parker Hannifin Corp.	Metals, bldg materials & glass	10-20	5-9	NA	NA	20-39	1-19
60	Tosco	Mining, forest prod, oil & gas	20+	10-20	4-6	4-6	20-39	1-19
61	Kansas State Univ.-Manhattan	Education	5-9	1-4	4-6	4-6	50-74	20-39
62	University of Notre Dame	Education	5-9	5-9	1-3	1-3	20-39	20-39
63	Cone Mills	Apparel & textile	5-9	1-4	4-6	4-6	20-39	1-19
64	Bowling Green State Univ.	Education	0	1-4	4-6	4-6	50-74	0
65	Diamond Shamrock	Mining, forest prod, oil & gas	-1--4	0	4-6	4-6	20-39	20-39
66	Chrysler	Automotive	1-4	1-4	10+	10+	1-19	1-19
67	Honeywell	Appliances & electrical equip.	0	0	4-6	4-6	40-49	1-19
68	AMP	Appliances & electrical equip.	5-9	5-9	4-6	4-6	20-39	1-19
69	Board of Gov., Fed. Reserve Sys.	Government	1-4	1-4	4-6	1-3	40-49	20-39
70	Booz Allen & Hamilton	Prof. svcs. & consulting	10-20	5-9	7-9	7-9	20-39	50-74
71	Phelps Dodge	Mining, forest prod, oil & gas	10-20	20+	4-6	4-6	20-39	1-19
72	Bear Stearns & Co.	Financial svcs. & banking	10-20	10-20	4-6	10+	20-39	20-39
73	Teachers Ins Annuity Assoc	Insurance	5-9	1-4	4-6	4-6	20-39	40-49
74	Northwestern Mutual Life Ins	Insurance	0	1-4	4-6	4-6	40-49	1-19

Rank	Company	Industry	IS Staff Changes (%)		Avg. Salary Incr.(%)		IS Staff Diversity (%)	
			Actual '95	Proj. '96	Actual '95	Proj. '96	Women	Minorities
75	Comerica	Financial svcs. & banking	0	5-9	4-6	4-6	40-49	1-19
76	Bausch & Lomb	Health care	5-9	-1--4	4-6	4-6	40-49	1-19
77	Champion International	Mining, forest prod, oil & gas	5-9	1-4	4-6	4-6	20-39	1-19
78	Rohm & Haas Co.	Chemical & pharmaceuticals	0	1-4	1-3	1-3	20-39	1-19
79	First Commerce	Financial svcs. & banking	5-9	5-9	7-9	7-9	50-74	NA
80	Florida Atlantic University	Education	1-4	1-4	4-6	1-3	20-39	20-39
81	Detroit Edison	Telecom & utilities	1-4	1-4	4-6	4-6	20-39	20-39
82	Reynolds Metals	Metals, bldg materials & glass	1-4	5-9	4-6	4-6	20-39	1-19
83	State of WV, Dept. of Admin.	Government	-1--4	1-4	4-6	4-6	20-39	1-19
84	U.S. Dept. of Justice	Government	0	0	4-6	4-6	40-49	50-74
85	Standard Commercial	Tobacco	10-20	0	10+	NA	20-39	1-19
86	Lithonia Lighting	Appliances & electrical equip.	5-9	5-9	4-6	4-6	50-74	1-19
87	Pacific Telesis Group	Telecom & utilities	5-9	5-9	4-6	4-6	50-74	20-39
88	EMC	Computer products	20+	5-9	4-6	4-6	20-39	20-39
89	Turner Corp., The	Construction	20+	5-9	7-9	4-6	20-39	1-19
90	University of Delaware-Newark	Education	0	0	4-6	4-6	50-70	1-19
91	Fluor	Construction	0	NA	4-6	4-6	20-39	1-19
92	State of Alabama	Government	5-9	1-4	7-9	7-9	20-39	1-19
93	Phillips-Van Heusen	Apparel & textile	1-4	1-4	4-6	4-6	40-49	1-19
94	General Mills	Food & beverage	0	0	4-6	4-6	40-49	1-19
95	Computer Task Group	Prof. svcs. & consulting	10-20	10-20	4-6	4-6	20-39	1-19
96	Hewlett-Packard	Computer products	10-20	5-9	7-9	7-9	20-39	20-39
97	Sallie Mae Servicing	Financial svcs. & banking	0	0	4-6	4-6	40-49	20-39
98	People's Bank	Financial svcs. & banking	10-20	5-9	4-6	4-6	20-39	20-39
99	AMR, The Sabre Group	Transportation services	10-20	5-9	10+	7-9	20-39	20-39
100	National Semiconductor	Appliances & electrical equip.	-10--20	-10--20	7-9	7-9	40-49	20-39

Excerpted with permission from Computerworld, June, 1996, p. 72. Copyright © 1996, CW Publishing Inc., Framingham MA 01701 USA.

Forbes: U.S. Jobs & Productivity

"Surprise: Despite all the talk about downsizing, America's largest corporations added to their payrolls last year.

'For most of the past decade and a half, employment at Forbes 500s companies has been shrinking, even while their sales have been rising. Big corporations have simply learned to make better use of their workers.

'The past year has seen an interruption in that long-running trend. The 787 companies listed in one or more of our rankings employed 20.4M people at year-end, a bit more than a 1% gain from 1994. The payroll growth didn't hurt productivity: Combined sales for these companies gained 10% from the previous year, a good 7% after inflation. Combined profits were up 12%."--Forbes

Rank	Company	Per Employee ($K)					Empl (#K)
		Profits	Sales	Sales Rank	Assets	Assets Rank	
Computers & Communications--Major Systems							
1	Compaq Computer	50.2	939.0	1	497.5	1	15.7
2	Silicon Graphics	36.7	395.9	6	359.1	4	6.3
3	Dell Computer	33.6	653.8	3	265.2	5	8.1
4	Teradyne	32.9	245.8	12	211.3	9	4.8
5	Sun Microsystems	30.8	440.7	5	225.4	7	14.5

Rank	Company	Per Employee ($K)					Empl (#K)
		Profits	Sales	Sales Rank	Assets	Assets Rank	
6	Hewlett-Packard	25.7	328.6	8	252.6	6	102.0
7	Gateway 2000	25.2	535.4	4	163.7	11	6.9
8	IBM	18.8	323.2	9	360.7	3	222.6
9	Apple Computer	10.5	714.5	2	411.5	2	15.9
10	Tandem Computers	8.8	268.6	10	213.8	8	8.4
11	Digital Equipment	7.0	234.0	13	162.3	12	61.7
12	Raychem	6.8	168.7	14	152.9	14	9.5
13	Harris	6.2	131.9	16	113.1	15	26.6
14	SCI Systems	4.7	266.5	11	96.2	16	13.2
15	Unisys	-14.9	148.2	15	170.0	10	41.9
16	AST Research	-39.7	356.1	7	160.1	13	6.6
	Industry Medians	14.7	325.9		212.6		
Computers & Communications--Peripherals							
1	Cisco Systems	194.1	817.1	4	724.6	1	3.3
2	Micron Technology	150.5	587.1	5	538.3	2	6.8
3	EMC	94.7	556.9	8	506.0	3	3.5
4	Intel	88.1	400.3	13	432.5	7	40.5
5	Linear Technology	83.3	242.9	18	331.7	14	1.4
6	Applied Materials	65.7	422.3	11	380.7	11	8.5
7	LSI Logic	61.5	327.1	14	477.3	4	3.9
8	3Com	54.4	583.4	6	408.3	9	3.1
9	Bay Networks	52.7	416.9	12	344.7	13	4.1
10	Atmel	46.5	259.6	17	376.4	12	2.4
11	Tellabs	42.8	235.3	20	204.5	20	2.7
12	U.S. Robotics	39.9	455.1	10	311.1	15	2.4
13	Cabletron Systems	31.0	201.8	23	177.7	21	5.3
14	Arrow Electronics	29.8	870.5	3	397.2	10	6.8
15	Fore Systems	27.8	229.5	21	461.6	6	0.9
16	Advanced Micro (AMD)	24.5	198.1	24	247.1	18	12.3
17	Analog Devices	23.8	177.9	25	229.7	19	5.7
18	Varian Associates	21.8	239.5	19	144.5	23	6.6
19	Avnet	19.1	533.1	9	273.6	16	9.0
20	Texas Instruments	18.8	226.5	22	159.0	22	58.0
21	Molex	14.1	135.8	27	141.2	24	9.8
22	National Semiconductor	12.4	129.0	28	125.2	26	20.8
23	Western Digital	11.9	317.8	15	118.4	28	7.6
24	AMP	11.4	139.8	26	120.4	27	37.4
25	Solectron	11.2	276.5	16	139.5	25	8.8
26	Tech Data	8.8	1,262.4	2	426.9	8	2.4
27	Quantum	7.6	574.5	7	260.7	17	7.3
28	Read-Rite	7.1	52.1	30	45.4	30	20.8
29	Seagate Technology	6.1	85.5	29	59.6	29	64.3
30	Merisel	-2.9	1,835.4	1	464.6	5	3.2
	Industry Medians	26.2	297.2		292.4		
Computers & Communications--Software							
1	Altera	112.2	518.9	2	924.5	1	0.8
2	Microsoft	102.1	411.9	4	505.6	5	18.0
3	Xilinx	89.6	533.1	1	687.5	2	1.0
4	Parametric Tech	54.0	262.9	9	296.6	10	1.7

Rank	Company	Per Employee ($K)					Empl (#K)
		Profits	Sales	Sales Rank	Assets	Assets Rank	
5	BMC Software	52.8	298.2	6	407.4	7	1.3
6	Adobe Systems	48.1	392.6	5	455.6	6	1.9
7	Novell	42.9	265.7	8	315.2	9	7.5
8	Informix	38.8	261.0	10	248.3	12	2.7
9	PeopleSoft	29.5	228.5	11	315.4	8	1.0
10	Oracle	27.0	197.0	12	144.1	14	19.2
11	America Online	1.8	287.3	7	279.6	11	2.5
12	Intuit	-1.6	179.4	14	186.6	13	2.7
13	Netscape Communications	-7.8	181.7	13	512.9	4	0.4
14	Computer Associates	-14.4	423.3	3	646.6	3	7.6
	Industry Medians	40.9	276.5		361.4		
	Computers & Communications--Telecommunications						
1	Ascend Communications	145.6	712.3	2	1,597.4	3	0.2
2	PanAmSat	115.4	764.2	1	9,465.9	1	0.2
3	Cascade Communications	78.2	414.9	4	344.2	17	0.3
4	StrataCom	64.6	408.6	5	363.8	14	0.8
5	WorldCom	35.7	485.3	3	873.6	4	7.5
6	Citizens Utilities	35.2	236.1	13	865.5	6	4.5
7	DSC Communications	34.2	252.3	11	330.9	20	5.6
8	SBC Communications	32.0	214.6	14	372.6	13	59.1
9	Ameritech	31.1	208.3	15	340.4	19	64.5
10	Bell Atlantic	27.8	200.3	16	360.3	15	67.1
11	GTE	23.4	183.8	24	340.9	18	108.6
12	u.S. West	23.2	185.5	23	324.5	21	51.1
13	Alltel	22.0	193.2	22	315.1	23	16.1
14	Pacific Telesis	20.9	180.0	27	315.3	22	50.2
15	Frontier	20.7	306.0	7	301.0	25	7.0
16	AirTouch Communications	20.3	249.0	12	868.9	5	6.5
17	Sprint	19.5	262.9	10	310.8	24	48.5
18	S. New England Telecom	17.9	194.9	21	288.8	27	9.4
19	Telephone & Data Systems	17.8	163.3	28	593.7	8	5.8
20	BellSouth	17.4	199.1	17	354.8	16	89.8
21	Nynex	15.7	196.7	20	384.6	11	68.2
22	Qualcomm	13.6	180.5	26	379.4	12	2.5
23	Motorola	13.0	197.4	19	166.4	30	137.0
24	MCI Communications	12.7	354.2	6	447.9	10	43.1
25	General Instrument	10.1	197.7	18	187.1	29	12.3
26	AT&T	0.5	263.7	9	294.4	26	301.9
27	360° Communications	-0.5	265.1	8	626.8	7	3.1
28	Paging Network	-10.2	149.0	29	283.2	28	4.3
29	MFS Communications	-82.9	180.6	25	578.1	9	3.2
30	Nextel Communications	-128.2	86.7	30	2,663.0	2	2.1
	Industry Medians	20.5	204.3		357.6		

Excerpted with permission from Forbes Magazine, April 22, 1996, p. 278. Copyright © 1996, Forbes Inc., USA.

Source Edp: Computer Job Trends

"Rapidly changing technologies are completely redefining the way companies manage their information resources and, in essence, altering the information technology job market. Today only half of the jobs in information technology industry are in the MIS departments. Now a third of the information technology jobs are filled through outsourcing or consulting profession versus in-house MIS departments. A limited number of jobs that design, develop, manufacture and sell hardware and software products are still in-house at companies. Systems development has been moved to the user departments in many organizations, leaving the MIS department to maintain the tools and the databases.

'Here are some highlight of trends we see developing in the industry, along with specific skills that hiring managers are requiring in information technology professionals."--Source Edp

Client/Server Systems Explosion

The area currently in greatest demand in the information technology industry is client/server architecture. Most companies in today's marketplace are either in a client/server environment or are migrating to client/server systems. A key trend in the industry is the reengineering of legacy systems to fit into a client/server architecture with a GUI front-end and other database servers. The goal is to transition data and applications off the mainframe into a more cost-efficient, flexible, user-friendly environment.

Client/server systems combine local area networks (LANs) and relational databases to run distributed applications. These distributed applications run on both central-site file servers under multi-tasking operating systems such as Unix, OS/2 or Windows NT and single-user workstations running graphical-user interfaces such as X-Windows or OSF/Motif under Unix, Microsoft Windows and Mac OS. They are written in high-level languages and GUI development tools such as Visual Basic, Visual C++ and Powerbuilder. The applications are connected via LAN technology such as TCP/IP, Novell NetWare, DECnet and NT Server.

Demand for client/server application, design and development professionals is really strong in the current marketplace. Many development positions will emerge for professionals with object-oriented design and programming skills using C++. This is a completely new method of developing computer software that can be very complex, usually performed by a software engineer. In addition, positions will emerge for systems analysts and application developers who will be building systems using objects created by the software engineers.

On the client side of the equation, a demand exists for professionals that have the ability to develop front-end applications and are familiar with key development tools such as Informix 4GL, Progress, Uniface, Delphi, SAP and BPCS. They should also possess Windows-based graphical user interface skills and be familiar with Visual Basic, Visual C++ and Powerbuilder.

On the server side, a demand exists for professionals who have strong working knowledge of one or more of the following operating systems such as Unix, Windows NT or OS/2. They should also be proficient in one or more of the following database management systems such as Oracle, Sybase, Informix or DB-2.

Consulting on the Rise

The recession and corporate downsizing forced individuals into consulting, but it has evolved into a popular and marketable career choice. Today, the information technology industry is comprised of 70% permanent employees and 30% consultants. By 2000 this percentage break is projected to be the reverse--70% consultants and 30% permanent employees.

Increasing numbers of information technology professionals are becoming full-time consultants, moving from project to project and client to client. Companies in today's marketplace generally have a core group of employees that work on specific product offerings and a mix of consultants that specializes in particular technologies. The hiring of consultants has filled specific needs. Plus consultants have enabled the companies to remain competitive since the development of new applications now only takes a few months from start to finish.

Companies are looking for consultants who have a "specific" skill set primarily in one of the latest technologies as it applies to their business needs. In addition to proficiency in one or more of the latest technologies, consultants should have good interpersonal skills and the ability to work well under pressure.

The demand for consultants is strong in the following areas: client/server; EDI (Electronic Data Interchange); WAN (Wide Area Networking); and LAN (Local Area Networking).

The Internet Tidal Wave

The Internet is not the wave of the future--it is here now. The Internet was originally designed by and for researchers at universities nationwide and within the government. Today, in the United States, almost half of all Fortune 500 companies use and have presence on the Internet. It currently connects to over 150 countries and is utilized by more than 37 million people worldwide!

Companies are scrambling to take advantage of this powerful new business tool. They are looking for ways to effectively market and sell their respective products and service online by utilizing the Internet.

Companies are looking for professionals that are well versed in the dominant Internet applications such as email, World Wide Web (WWW), Wide Area Information Server (WAIS), Gopher and Mosaic. They must also know how to effectively create and manage a hypertext home page while linking it to strategic points within the World Wide Web. These professionals should also have keen interpersonal skills and an understanding of basic marketing and business principles. Multimedia experience is a plus.

Mainframe's Role Diminishes

Although the mainframe will continue to be the workhorse of information processing for a few years, its role is diminishing. Many companies are migrating to the cost-effective, flexible client/server systems. The focus on mainframe systems has changed in 2 ways. Organizations today are utilizing large, standard packaged applications in place of custom software packages capable of running on the mainframe. Now the mainframe acts as a central receptacle for corporate data and a server hub in enterprise-wide cooperative processing environments.

Companies are looking for professionals who have mainframe experience but are also well versed in client/server technology. There is still some demand for mainframe maintenance programmers. However with the increased migration of companies to client/server architecture this demand is dwindling. In order to be more marketable, mainframe professionals need to become experienced in client/server technology.

Software Development Exhibits Growth

Software development will continue to be a lucrative and competitive market. The software labor market is much more about a "profession" than an industry because it cuts across nearly all other industries. Companies are hiring talented professionals to help manage their information, conduct initial product analysis and work in the quality assurance and end-user support areas.

The continued growth of the software industry has created a strong demand for detail-oriented software engineers specializing in software quality control and technical professionals who have good customer service skills and business savy.

Excerpted with permission from Source Edp. Copyright © 1996, Source Edp, P.O. Box 809030, Dallas TX 75380 USA.

Source Edp: Computer Position Responsibilities

"Source Edp is a leading recruiting firm devoted exclusively to the computer profession. With over 50 offices across North America, Source Edp is well informed about computer careers. We have defined responsibilities for key computer positions and their positions as follows."--Source Edp

Systems Development

Windows Systems Developer: Develops and supports graphical user interface applications. Programs in Power-builder, Visual Basic or Visual C++. Knows how to access relational databases like Sybase, Oracle or Access. Skilled in OLE, SDK, MFL, DLL and DDE. Applications are generally written for networked and client/server environments.

Unix Systems Developer: Develops software for distributed or centralized systems. Analyzes, designs and codes with definitive understanding of the application. Expertise with Unix and C. Familiar with C++, X-Windows, Motif and InterProcess Communications. Capable of integrating systems to a two- or three-tier architecture.

Client/Server Programmer/Analyst: Analyzes and designs programming applications for a client/server architecture. Knowledgeable of ODBC, Windows NT, Macintosh, Novell, OS/2, Windows 95, Unix, APIs and RPCs.

Mainframe Programmer/Analyst: Codes and maintains business applications. Develops and supports large-scale batch or high-volume transaction environments that require IBM/MVS mainframe processing power. Programs in business-oriented languages such as Cobol and CICS or fourth generation languages.

Midrange Programmer/Analyst: Develops and supports enterprise-oriented applications or general business applications. Programs in business-oriented languages such as Cobol and RPG/400 or fourth generation languages on AS/400 computers.

Software Engineer: Designs and develops systems-level software such as OSs, network and database management, languages and graphical user interfaces. Programs in languages such as C, C++, assembly or Smalltalk.

Voice/Telecommunications Engineer
Designs and implements voice networks and integrates telephony hardware and network services. Experienced in traffic engineering and carrier management. Works with call processing applications such as IVR and call centers. Strong network hardware knowledge and communications experience.

Business Systems

Business Systems Analyst: Works directly with management and users to analyze, specify and design business applications. Develops detailed functional, system and program specifications using structured design methodologies and computer- aided software engineering (CASE) tools. Must have strong business sense and keen communications skills. Works with both the information system team and the strategic planning business group.

Consultant: Facilitates organizational change while providing subject matter expertise on technical, functional and business topics during the development or implementation of enterprise-wide automated systems. Performs business requirements analysis, recommends selection of package software, develops proposals for consulting services and manages implementation projects at client sites. Provides expert knowledge of products like SAP R/3, Peoplesoft HRMS/Financials and SmartStream.

EDI Analyst: Introduces EDI standards and technology. Makes decisions for information construction and selects resources for EDI processing and application expansion. Coordinates processing and transmission schedules plus mapping of standard data formats. Generally serves as a key contact for trading partners and value-added network consultants.

Specialists

Database Analyst: Uses data modeling techniques to analyze and specify data usages within an application area. Defines both logical views and physical data structures. In the client/server environments, defines the back end.

Database Administrator: Administers and controls an organization's data resources. Uses data dictionary software packages to ensure data integrity and security, recover corrupted data and eliminate data redundancy; and uses tuning tools to improve database performance.

Internet Specialist: Well versed in the dominant Internet applications such as email, World Wide Web (WWW), Wide Area Information Server (WAIS), Gopher and Mosaic. Must know how to effectively create and manage hypertext home page and link it to the appropriate strategic points within the World Wide Web. Should possess keen interpersonal skills and understand basic marketing and business principles. Multimedia experience is a plus.

System Administrator/Manager: Installs operating systems software, database management systems software, compilers and utilities. Monitors and tunes systems software, peripherals and networks. Installs new users, creates batch administration scripts and runs systems backups. Resolves systems problems.

PC Software Specialist: Works with microcomputer applications including word processors, spreadsheets, presentation graphics, database management systems, electronic mail and communications. Also evaluates, installs and supports PCs and various printer, graphics and storage peripherals. Adds new users to the system and trains them. Performs system backups and data recovery. Often works in a help desk environment fielding calls from end users.

LAN Administrator: Installs and maintains local area network's hardware and software. Troubleshoots network usage and computer peripherals. Installs new users. Performs system backups and data recovery. Resolves LAN communications problems.

Wide Area Network (WAN) Administrator: Evaluates, selects, installs and maintains wide area networks. Provides WAN transport services. Performs analysis and diagnostics. Works with network hardware like routers, hubs and multiplexers. Familiar with WAN routing protocols such as SLIP and X.25.

Voice Analyst: Designs voice networks integrating telephony hardware and network services. Supports systems development in telephony intensive applications such as Interactive Voice Response (IVR) and call centers. Experienced in traffic engineering and carrier management. Understands network hardware and is familiar with PBX and ACD systems planning.

Data Communications Analyst: Installs, maintains and troubleshoots data networks. Utilizes one or more of the following: T-1s, TCP/IP, Fiber Optics, SNA or Frame Relay for communications. Assists users with problems related to connectivity. Analyzes data flow. Configures modems, DSUs, multiplexers and routers. Utilizes network tools such as Netview or Netspy.

Network Engineer: High-level LAN/WAN technician. Plans, implements and supports network solutions between multiple platforms. Installs and maintains local area network hardware and software. Troubleshoots network usage and computer peripherals. CNE certification is a plus.

Mainframe Systems Programmer: Installs and maintains mainframe operating systems, communications software, database management software, compilers and utility programs. Provides technical support to applications programmers, hardware/software evaluation and planning. Creates and modifies special purpose utility programs. Ensures system's efficiency and integrity.

Unix Systems Administrator: Installs and maintains Unix operating systems. Configures Unix boxes, establishes standards and evaluates hardware and software products. Must be familiar with shell-and kernel-level programming. Troubleshoots networking and operating system problems.

Edp Auditor: Analyzes the system function and operations to determine adequate security and control. Evaluates systems and operational procedures and reports findings to senior management. Writes ad hoc report programs using fourth generation languages and specialized audit software.

Technical Writer/Editor: Works directly with systems analysts and programmers to write and edit program and system documentation, user manuals, training courses and procedures. Also prepares proposals and technical reports.

Management

MIS Director/Chief Information Officer: Determines the overall strategic direction and business contribution of the information systems function.

Manager of Business Application: Plans and oversees multiple projects and project managers. Works with CIO and senior management to determine systems development strategy and standards. Administers department budget and reviews project managers.

VP/Manager of Customer Support: In software vendor environment, manages pre-sales and post-sales support, help-line and documentation. For large packages, manages development of customization of the core product for specific customers.

Project Leader: Coordinates resources, schedules and communications for application development projects. Develops project schedules and assigns tasks. Performs both systems analysis and programming. Serves as contact with user groups and systems management.

Technical Services Director: Plans and overseas the research, evaluation and integration of new technology, systems development, methodologies, data administration, capacity planning, training and technical support.

Project Manager: Plans and oversees the development and support of a specific application or functional area. Administers performance appraisals, salaries, hiring and budgets.

Sales

Account Representative: Identifies and contacts sales prospects, analyzes customer's needs, proposes business solutions and negotiates and oversees the implementation of new products.

Pre/Post Sales Support Representatives: Supports the sales effort by analyzing customer requirements, proposing and demonstrating technical solutions, ensuring acceptable product installation, training users and providing technical support and problem resolution.

Data Center/Computer Operations

Data Center Manager: Plans and directs all computer and peripheral machine operations, data entry, data control scheduling and quality control.

Operations Support Technician: Analyzes and supports computer operations by controlling production applications, monitoring system resources and response time and providing first-line support for operational problems.

Communications/Network Operator: Monitors and maintains communications network operations. Troubleshoots communications hardware and software and transmission problems.

Source Engineering: Opportunities in the 1990s

"Engineering professionals can look forward to another year of hiring and stable employment. The hiring opportunities will continue to increase during 1996 for all levels of engineering professionals. During 1994 the three-year hiring freeze ended, creating opportunities throughout 1995 for employment at all levels of experience. Small to mid-size companies expanded rapidly in 1995 by hiring mid- to senior-level engineers while larger firms returned to the practise of hiring new graduates."--Source Engineering

Consulting: The recession forces companies and individuals into consulting, but it has evolved into a popular and marketable career option. Increasing numbers of engineers are becoming full-time consultants, moving from project to project and client to client. Consulting provides a diversity of work for the mid-career engineers and reduced work time for those nearing retirement.

Engineers who choose consulting as a career path must maintain up-to-date technical skills and become more flexible in their approach to work. Engineering consultants who are the most in demand have technological skills within a specific industry.

Software Development: The greatest growth area within the engineering industry is in the software market. Today, the software labor market has developed into a profession because it crosses nearly all industry lines. Companies are hiring engineering talent to help manage the information flow as well as to design, develop and test new products. In this environment, the skills in demand are database design and development plus administration experience. Additionally, proficiency in either MS-Windows or Windows 95 and C++ is required. It would also be desirable to have user-interface development experience.

New operating systems and the expanded use of older ones continue to create demands for software engineers who understand OS terminals, database design and API programming. The ratio of software engineers to other engineers will climb rapidly over the next few years. Software engineering will continue to dominate the hiring focus in engineering. The language highest in demand is C++/OOD with one of the Windows option such as Windows 95, MS-Windows, NT or Motif. Knowledge of both MS-Windows and Unix is a highly marketable combination and will soon be a necessity. The greatest software growth will be in Windows internals, GUI, data communications, telephony and database programming and client/server architecture.

Technical Support: The growth of software has generated a market for technical support personnel. Programmers who seek a change in direction will find an opportunity to combine engineering knowledge, people skills and business savvy in these support positions. One to two years of software development experience provides a good base for a technical support position, but senior positions are also available.

Software QA Test: The increasing size and complexity of software projects has created a strong demand for test and software quality assurance engineers. Software engineers who are able to visualize the complete system and have test experience, along with formalized training in quality assurance techniques, are in high demand.

System Administration: The technology and economics of networking computer systems within a company have developed a career path in systems and network administration, including upper management. Opportunities are increasing for individuals with knowledge of at least three types of platforms. The best combination of experience is MS-Windows, Windows NT, Unix and Novell. Also preferred are engineers with CNE credentials.

Digital Hardware Design: Because of the increased complexity of products, system design concepts for both IC and board level design are needed, creating a demand for ASIC engineers. ASIC engineers are needed to bridge IC and board level design, offering maximum flexibility to system design engineers.

Analog Hardware Design: This discipline requires a high degree of expertise and specialization. This creates superior opportunities at the IC and board design level. Analog design opportunities are predominantly in the RF/modem and cellular applications.

IC Design: CAD systems have simplified IC design. As a result, some of the creativity has been removed from standard products. But new challenges remain. These are in chip sets, mixed mode and full custom design, especially DSP for multimedia and image processing.

Source Engineering: Position Responsibilities

"It is important to have a broad perspective of the engineering profession before planning a career. The position descriptions listed here will show you the many opportunities available within the field."--Source Engineering

Engineering:

Director of Engineering/VP: Only a select few can expect to reach this level. This is a highly visible management position which often completely supplants direct technical work. Individuals in this position generally oversees major short- and long-term projects, manage groups of people and have overall bottom-line responsibility.

Engineering Manager: Interfaces with top engineering and all levels of management within the company. Demonstrates tactical and strategic decision making abilities that influence the success of the organization.

Group Leader/Section Head: Responsible for the design and development of one or more prominent systems or product lines as well as overseeing the people working on the project. Provides technical guidance and motivates subordinates.

Principal Engineer/Project Leader: Typically leads one to five engineers in the design and development of a product or one or more of its components. Coordinates the talents of people in groups to complete breadboard designs and production prototypes. Provides final release of designs to production and presents reports to management on the team's progress.

Engineer/Senior Engineer: Completes the development and documentation of design from initial breadboard concept to final debugging. Assists in overall product specification and participates in the final approval and release of designs to the production stage.

R&D Technician: Assigned as part of a team usually with engineers or senior engineers to support the development of new products or the enhancement of existing ones. Helps with breadboard concepts, develops prototypes and completes designs as assigned. Troubleshoots and debugs designs.

Software QA Engineer: Develops QA test procedures, automates test tools and conducts testing. Highly involved in the overall development of the product. Writes and utilizes shell scripts in support of test efforts.

Draftperson/Designer/CAD: Meets organization's documentation standards in converting verbal sketch concepts into drawings for release to manufacturing vendors and user manuals.

Marketing

Director of Sales or Marketing/VP: Identifies new opportunities for profit and presents strategic plans that help attain goals. Supevises and plans the implementation of programs and monitors their success or failure. Develops promotional and sales opportunities and directs the efforts of others in the organization.

Sales/Marketing Manager: Formulates business goals. Develops new business and sells new products and product enhancements to existing client base. Creates effective tools utilized by the sales staff to market and sell the product. Provides training for the sales staff to keep them up-to-date on the product and any product enhancements. Compensation is usually a base salary plus an incentive program which is tied directly to the goals attained by the sales and marketing team.

Product Manager: Responsible for the success of an assigned product or product line. Develops product descriptions and marketing literature. Also helps create promotional campaigns to the target market. Individuals in this position often have direct profit and loss responsibility.

Sales Engineer: Qualifies prospective clients, identifies their needs and presents products in configurations that will achieve the client's goals. Compensation is frequently based on performance.

Applications Engineer: Supports the sales effort and participates at product demonstrations and trade shows. Writes product application data sheets and discusses technical application details with potential customers and users. Interfaces daily with customers and sales engineers.

Salaries

Computerworld: Salary Survey

"Unequal opportunity. Salaries on the rise, but women still underrepresented in top FIS ranks.

'The good news: On average, information systems salaries increased faster than the national average for most other professions last year. The bad news: When it comes to IS jobs, women are still badly underrepresented...

'Overall, this year's survey found that women account for just over 37% of IS professionals, which is 7% below the national average of women in the total work-force, according to the Department of Commerce.

'Despite the persistent gender gap, both sexes made above-average salary gains last year. In fact, 1994 was a year in which the pie got bigger in virtually every IS job category. While the Department of Commerce figures show wages and salaries for other professions rose by just 3% in the 12 months ended in June 1995, Computerworld Salary Survey data shows that IS salary increases averaged 4.5%. Overall IS salary growth even outpaced other fields including engineering, sales and human resources.

'Computerworld, in cooperation with the Society for Information Management, conducted a nationwide survey of IS employees to determine total compensation, salary increases, fringe benefits and turnover in the IS field. The mail survey was conducted in May and June 1995. A total of 987 responses were received."--Computerworld

Job Titles:	Top IS Management				Networks				Systems Dev	
	CIO/VP	Dir, Sys Dev	Dir, Net-works	Dir, IS Ops	Mgr Voice/ Data omm	Comm Specialist	Network Admin	LAN Mgr	Prjt Mgr, Sys & Prog	Sr Sys Analyst
Average	82,129	67,276	65,110	60,196	57,139	44,588	41,240	44,175	55,331	50,388
Bonus	9,439	5,706	4,940	5,179	3,139	2,386	1,640	2,627	3,055	1,522
Total	91,568	72,982	70,050	65,375	60,278	46,974	42,880	46,802	58,386	51,910
Industry, Nonmanufacturing										
Bus Svc IS	140,500	87,400	79,500	70,500	72,000	53,250	48,250	48,500	71,250	60,250
Banking	118,973	96,500	94,953	81,380	78,375	53,914	46,035	54,376	72,706	59,913
Media	98,292	72,750	65,500	68,463	62,500	82,667	39,155	43,000	62,125	56,143
Insurance	96,056	74,742	74,325	67,606	71,638	44,957	44,076	50,858	59,117	52,665
Retail	95,778	71,235	65,400	68,236	52,325	44,450	40,184	39,218	57,105	47,864
Bus Svc Non-IS	90,881	75,194	60,857	64,205	58,857	40,083	42,656	45,545	53,620	51,120
Health	88,853	69,311	64,750	57,617	51,864	43,000	41,018	46,094	55,459	51,936
Utilities	88,334	69,000	76,833	62,600	73,500	58,000	49,000	44,875	57,214	52,633
Transportation	85,591	69,633	53,650	61,167	80,000	44,000	39,333	41,500	53,448	53,358
Distribution	78,955	60,818	55,000	59,293	70,000	51,000	38,500	41,375	60,900	48,833
Education	73,764	57,957	54,267	52,239	47,167	39,154	41,200	39,739	50,176	46,132
Nonprofit	72,329	58,950	54,375	60,271	60,700	46,250	45,938	45,714	53,833	50,550
Government	69,440	59,528	54,941	60,371	54,100	40,946	41,552	NA	51,990	48,372
Industry, Manufacturing										
Consumer Products	130,700	95,278	112,133	81,375	66,000	39,333	44,200	59,300	69,929	57,500
Food & Beverage	122,455	96,778	108,250	96,967	72,800	55,350	51,583	56,000	63,667	59,250
Consumer Electronics	108,173	79,906	NA	62,069	72,750	45,350	48,000	46,542	71,750	61,000
Forest Products	100,938	69,125	65,000	55,343	51,250	44,500	40,167	44,667	52,667	46,000
Apparel/Textile	94,889	63,600	79,000	53,500	54,667	40,000	33,667	44,182	52,583	45,000
Chemical	91,800	68,879	118,500	82,250	61,667	51,250	41,667	52,500	68,929	54,000
Industry Equipment	79,958	63,233	62,000	NA	NA	NA	37,816	43,729	62,009	56,820
Metal/Plast./Rubber	77,642	83,111	55,125	58,221	70,500	40,857	40,556	47,786	52,714	47,167

Job Titles:	Top IS Management				Networks				Systems Dev	
	CIO/VP	Dir, Sys Dev	Dir, Net-works	Dir, IS Ops	Mgr Voice/Data omm	Comm Specialist	Network Admin	LAN Mgr	Prjt Mgr, Sys & Prog	Sr Sys Analyst
Company Size										
Under $100M	74,112	61,460	56,398	55,658	53,851	42,663	39,580	42,920	53,900	48,069
$100M-$500M	97,518	71,814	63,345	66,869	56,599	46,342	43,977	45,298	60,347	52,163
Over $500M	131,639	93,526	90,721	84,682	69,157	51,635	47,401	50,715	62,896	56,765

Job Titles	Systems Development								Tech Srvics/Oper	
	Systems Analyst	Sr Sys Prgrmmr	Systems Prgrmmr	Sr Prgrmmr /Analyst	Prgrmmr /Analyst	Database Manager	Database Analyst	Data Security Admin Anal	Computer Ops Mgr	Comp Ops Super
Average	43,710	48,635	41,117	44,263	36,274	53,610	46,766	46,170	47,624	38,167
Bonus	1,706	3,096	770	1,718	929	2,059	1,008	1,314	1,921	1,358
Total	45,416	51,731	41,887	45,981	37,203	55,669	47,774	47,484	49,545	39,525
Industry, Nonmanufacturing										
Business Service IS	49,000	67,000	53,625	49,800	39,000	51,500	40,500	51,500	62,500	43,000
Utilities	48,250	49,500	45,900	46,577	43,271	62,000	48,250	NA	57,267	50,250
Transportation	46,655	49,000	45,000	47,200	37,544	43,000	41,500	NA	51,667	44,500
Banking	46,500	57,900	49,150	57,465	46,147	60,000	55,000	46,357	51,317	38,417
Media	44,667	54,000	42,500	45,214	34,667	79,500	43,500	NA	46,667	39,050
Insurance	44,518	49,804	40,900	43,117	37,072	59,763	51,125	46,138	58,256	39,693
Government	43,557	NA	39,324	43,796	36,019	52,438	43,765	45,273	43,988	37,655
Health	43,314	51,334	41,925	47,769	36,705	52,425	47,071	46,600	46,406	38,660
Distribution	43,071	50,667	40,800	42,429	37,500	70,500	42,800	NA	46,864	34,250
Retail	42,417	48,527	44,875	42,006	34,209	56,800	53,625	48,200	45,600	37,055
Bus. Service Non-IS	38,214	45,600	30,000	44,776	35,792	46,845	38,333	35,500	44,300	38,250
Nonprofit	38,000	49,750	45,333	40,650	32,409	58,000	42,750	50,000	46,429	37,900
Education	37,833	42,964	34,364	NA	32,796	47,944	50,500	47,750	39,536	37,636
Industry, Manufacturing										
Consumer Product	62,667	58,667	57,500	54,417	42,750	68,375	52,000	41,000	72,000	37,500
Metal/Plast./Rubber	56,000	41,429	37,767	42,700	36,726	45,708	41,000	45,000	51,429	39,625
Food & Beverage	55,250	49,800	43,000	45,667	39,180	71,750	54,333	56,500	57,460	44,850
Chemical	53,000	60,500	44,000	49,000	38,834	52,000	45,000	50,000	53,750	49,667
Consumer Electronics	51,667	55,660	40,000	55,234	43,274	64,000	55,000	NA	51,500	38,500
Forest Products	43,333	45,250	42,333	44,188	40,083	43,625	40,000	46,500	46,417	31,000
Apparel/Textile	36,333	42,333	41,667	44,000	37,893	50,000	42,000	NA	47,321	39,937
Industry Equipment	NA	56,500	39,867	53,600	34,001	NA	55,000	NA	54,738	NA
Company Size										
Under $100M	40,806	48,514	39,898	43,589	35,304	48,365	41,490	43,625	44,662	37,396
$100M-$500M	46,174	50,358	42,031	48,278	38,060	56,069	50,520	50,750	47,267	36,509
Over $500M	50,144	54,977	45,500	48,160	39,932	61,062	49,628	48,034	59,517	44,180

Job Titles	Technical Services/Operations Cont.			PC End-User Support				
	Lead Computer Oper	Computer Operator	Technical Specialist	Microcomp/End-User comp Mgr	Tech Spprt Mgr/Help Desk Mgr	Help Desk Operator	PC Tech Spprt Specialist	Business Services Analyst
Average	29,361	24,681	35,927	47,543	40,440	28,940	32,239	36,569
Bonus	943	702	874	2,282	1,316	546	806	636
Total	30,304	25,383	36,801	49,825	41,756	29,486	33,045	37,205

Job Titles	Technical Services/Operations Cont.			PC End-User Support				
	Lead Computer Oper	Computer Operator	Technical Specialist	Microcomp/ End-User comp Mgr	Tech Spprt Mgr/Help Desk Mgr	Help Desk Operator	PC Tech Spprt Specialist	Business Services Analyst
Industry, Nonmanufacturing								
Bus. Service Non-IS	33,209	24,885	35,571	43,667	42,668	34,500	32,155	38,200
Insurance	32,979	25,609	40,313	60,550	53,250	29,138	33,182	32,667
Media	32,042	25,278	36,667	61,800	38,500	23,667	27,571	40,600
Business Service IS	32,000	23,750	NA	69,000	NA	28,750	32,567	49,000
Government	31,341	26,686	31,206	49,199	40,447	27,393	33,804	29,636
Utilities	30,806	27,900	45,025	58,500	24,500	39,167	40,825	43,000
Health	30,306	23,453	35,520	48,736	40,833	30,088	31,911	37,625
Banking	29,367	24,155	32,571	48,031	39,250	31,591	36,765	41,800
Education	28,787	25,208	33,958	46,233	34,806	24,364	30,541	35,643
Transportation	28,717	30,875	33,500	54,000	44,500	34,400	30,833	NA
Retail	28,529	22,788	33,950	36,682	37,100	22,857	30,778	39,333
Nonprofit	28,357	24,643	35,500	35,100	36,714	28,071	34,350	35,500
Distribution	26,255	24,559	44,400	49,333	32,167	31,250	33,400	29,500
Industry, Manufacturing								
Consumer Products	36,000	28,056	45,000	73,500	56,250	29,667	38,700	50,000
Food & Beverage	35,333	27,056	41,275	71,650	NA	28,375	36,357	51,667
Consumer Electronics	33,344	28,813	41,641	43,625	52,000	29,000	39,750	44,000
Chemical	31,333	NA	NA	71,000	NA	33,667	41,000	35,000
Forest Products	30,500	25,800	37,167	45,750	40,000	30,750	40,000	37,500
Metal/Plast./Rubber	27,164	23,669	38,740	45,000	NA	31,125	31,857	NA
Industrial Equipment	26,510	24,233	24,733	44,000	NA	NA	28,925	39,000
Apparel/Textile	26,043	22,436	NA	49,333	NA	23,000	33,083	NA
Company Size								
Under $100M	29,215	24,108	32,729	45,228	35,937	29,934	31,683	35,053
$100M-$500M	30,376	26,147	38,583	47,228	41,342	28,073	32,853	39,500
Over $500M	32,448	27,161	40,665	59,309	49,877	30,561	36,499	39,510

Excerpted with permission from Computerworld, September 4, 1995, p. 69. Copyright © 1995, CW Publishing Inc., Framingham MA 01701 USA.

Positive Support Review: Data Processing Compensation

"PSR Review Methodology: The Compensation Review utilized data from Positive Support Review's Compensation Database for Management Information System professionals. This database contains compensation information on many Southern California firms. The database is classified by normalized job position, taking into account similarities in job function and responsibilities, rather than merely job title.

'From this database, compensation benchmark ranges are established for each normalized job position. In analyzing the survey data, the upper and lower quartiles are eliminated to determine PSR's Benchmark Ranges. The benchmark ranges are then used to assess the alignment of a company's actual compensation to the marketplace for each job function. The results can be assessed using the following guidelines:

• Below Benchmark Range: Highly impacted by forces of the marketplace.
• Within Benchmark Range: Subject to the normal forces of the marketplace for similar job function(s) and responsibilities.
• Above Benchmark Range: Not subject to the forces of the marketplace.

'Reviews were conducted from the standpoint of a comparison of base salary and, when appropriate, from the additional standpoint of total compensation. Total compensation is determined by adding the budgetary bonus amounts and an equivalent cash value for 'above-standard' compensation to an individual's base salary.

'The Compensation Review data was divided into two categories. Large companies represent companies whose gross revenues are equal to or greater than $500M. Mid-sized companies are companies whose gross revenues are less than $500M."--Positive Support Review

Company Size	Title	Base Salary ($)		Including Perks ($)		PSR Bench-mark ($)
		Minimum	Maximum	Minimum	Maximum	
Large	VP - Chief Information Officer (CIO)	93,600	194,500	110,000	292,575	246,900
Large	VP - Administration	61,830	87,878	61,830	114,445	101,300
Large	VP - Consulting Services	82,000	102,300	86,000	105,900	100,900
Large	VP - Information Services	79,510	126,900	104,539	158,625	145,100
Large	VP - Technical Services	80,000	100,990	80,000	127,869	115,900
Large	Director - I.S. Planning	79,464	126,100	89,000	157,625	140,500
Large	Director - Production/Data Center	74,000	147,700	74,000	177,240	151,400
Large	Director - Systems & Programming	82,160	130,300	84,000	162,875	143,200
Large	Manager - Computer Operations	57,517	87,900	59,438	96,690	87,400
Large	Manager - Microcomputer Technology	52,889	78,225	61,591	81,725	76,700
Large	Manager - Network Services	50,000	72,100	50,000	75,449	69,100
Large	Manager - Operating Systems Production	52,416	78,738	57,658	85,203	78,300
Large	Manager - Production Services	51,635	72,808	54,021	74,281	69,200
Large	Manager - Production Support	47,268	58,039	53,212	64,036	61,300
Large	Manager - Systems & Programming	62,000	75,186	62,000	78,584	74,400
Large	Manager - Technical Services	49,877	76,700	50,000	85,324	76,500
Large	Manager - Training & Documentation	64,890	76,100	64,941	77,542	74,400
Large	Manager Transaction Processing	60,887	76,208	65,710	81,031	77,200
Large	Manager - Voice & Data Communications	46,800	105,976	50,000	109,976	95,000
Large	Capacity Planning Supervisor	44,783	60,426	44,783	60,426	56,500
Large	Change Control Supervisor	38,000	62,700	38,000	63,954	57,500
Large	Computer Operations - Shift Manager	46,548	62,700	46,548	63,954	59,600
Large	Computer Operations - Shift Supervisor	30,000	48,426	30,000	48,426	43,800
Large	Database Manager	56,995	72,100	56,995	73,542	69,400
Large	Data Communications Manager	43,000	69,157	43,000	69,157	62,600
Large	Data Entry Supervisor	27,612	46,398	27,612	46,398	41,700
Large	Information Center Manager	73,400	86,000	73,400	86,000	82,900
Large	Lead Customer Service Manager	65,130	85,700	65,130	85,700	80,600
Large	Office Automation Applications Manager	73,760	86,400	73,760	86,400	83,200
Large	Production Control Specialist	35,779	39,779	35,779	39,779	38,800
Large	Production Services Supervisor	54,270	62,300	54,270	62,300	60,300
Large	Project Manager - Applications	47,700	62,956	47,700	69,279	63,900
Large	Project Manager - Distributed Systems	62,740	78,600	62,740	78,600	74,600
Large	Project Manager - Network Technical Services	61,900	73,000	61,900	73,000	70,200
Large	Project Manager - Systems	53,368	66,896	56,345	69,951	66,500
Large	Supervisor - Hardware Installations	32,994	41,828	32,994	41,828	39,600
Large	Supervisor - Microcomputer Support	48,438	58,025	48,438	63,694	59,900
Large	Supervisor - Network Services	40,482	48,980	40,482	48,980	46,900
Large	Voice Communications Manager	52,430	72,000	52,430	72,000	67,100
Large	Change Control Analyst	35,946	39,940	35,946	39,940	38,900
Large	Computer Operator	25,642	45,851	25,642	45,851	40,800
Large	Data Center Facility Administration	29,718	43,845	29,718	43,845	40,300

Company Size	Title	Base Salary ($)		Including Perks ($)		PSR Bench- mark ($)
		Minimum	Maximum	Minimum	Maximum	
Large	Data Entry Clerk	21,699	30,832	21,699	30,832	28,500
Large	Data Security Administration	32,220	55,808	32,864	55,808	50,100
Large	Database Specialist	44,980	55,210	48,701	60,210	57,300
Large	Disaster Recovery Coordinator	51,140	64,600	51,140	64,600	61,200
Large	Forms & Graphics Designer	32,972	49,080	32,972	49,080	45,100
Large	4th GL Specialist	49,150	63,500	49,150	63,500	59,900
Large	Hardware Installations Coordinator	56,770	71,300	56,770	71,300	67,700
Large	IS Planning Analyst	50,810	60,900	50,810	60,900	58,400
Large	LAN Applications Support Analyst	39,090	54,500	39,090	55,590	51,500
Large	Network Control Analyst	38,912	55,803	38,912	55,803	51,600
Large	Network Services Administrator	38,031	52,829	38,031	52,829	49,100
Large	Network Technician	41,730	55,300	45,313	55,590	53,000
Large	Operations Analyst	37,529	50,588	37,529	50,588	47,300
Large	Personal Computer Specialist	34,499	44,133	35,305	44,133	41,900
Large	Production Control Analyst	47,860	57,400	47,860	57,400	55,000
Large	Programmer/Analyst	47,125	59,321	48,330	59,321	56,600
Large	Senior Network Specialist	54,430	64,700	55,559	64,700	62,400
Large	Software Engineer	70,434	82,900	70,434	82,900	79,800
Large	Systems Analyst	46,865	65,378	46,865	65,378	60,700
Large	Systems Programmer	40,799	70,280	40,799	70,280	62,900
Large	Systems Support Specialist	42,050	56,500	43,067	57,630	54,000
Large	Tape Librarian	24,137	39,263	24,137	39,263	35,500
Large	Technical Services Specialist	31,900	49,228	31,900	49,228	44,900
Large	Technical Specialist	35,100	39,000	35,100	42,386	40,600
Large	Voice Communications Coordinator	30,000	50,180	30,000	50,180	45,100
Medium	VP - Chief Information Officer (CIO)	70,500	190,000	76,140	205,200	172,900
Medium	VP - Administration	55,513	81,500	60,087	86,500	79,900
Medium	VP - Consulting Services	82,620	91,800	87,577	97,308	94,900
Medium	VP - Information Services	57,786	89,762	67,981	101,090	92,800
Medium	VP - Technical Services	65,917	95,000	89,264	109,875	104,700
Medium	Director - I.S. Planning	64,869	86,000	64,869	93,000	86,000
Medium	Director - Production/Data Center	52,000	99,000	55,120	99,000	88,000
Medium	Director - Systems & Programming	57,838	81,516	57,838	87,268	79,900
Medium	Manager - Computer Operations	47,267	62,771	49,188	64,951	61,000
Medium	Manager - Microcomputer Technology	47,228	55,236	49,500	60,525	57,800
Medium	Manager - Network Services	45,298	89,000	47,925	89,000	78,700
Medium	Manager - Operating Systems Production	48,852	86,000	51,024	86,000	77,300
Medium	Manager - Production Services	46,342	61,814	47,000	65,233	60,700
Medium	Manager - Production Support	45,998	55,000	45,998	56,109	53,600
Medium	Manager - Systems & Programming	55,000	71,800	55,000	73,000	68,500
Medium	Manager - Technical Services	41,342	78,000	42,658	78,000	69,200
Medium	Manager - Training & Documentation	55,890	66,100	55,890	66,100	63,500
Medium	Manager Transaction Processing	45,015	63,100	46,598	63,100	59,000
Medium	Manager - Voice & Data Communications	45,475	79,000	45,475	83,000	73,600
Medium	Capacity Planning Supervisor	41,000	61,000	41,000	61,000	56,000
Medium	Change Control Supervisor	24,500	40,000	24,500	40,000	36,100
Medium	Computer Operations - Shift Manager	35,537	49,267	35,537	49,267	45,800
Medium	Computer Operations - Shift Supervisor	27,000	55,000	27,000	55,000	48,000
Medium	Database Manager	49,000	60,069	49,000	62,128	58,800

Company Size	Title	Base Salary ($)		Including Perks ($)		PSR Bench-mark ($)
		Minimum	Maximum	Minimum	Maximum	
Medium	Data Communications Manager	46,475	60,600	46,475	60,600	57,100
Medium	Data Entry Supervisor	31,678	40,600	31,678	40,600	38,400
Medium	Information Center Manager	57,330	67,700	57,330	67,700	65,100
Medium	Lead Customer Service Manager	31,678	65,000	31,678	65,000	56,700
Medium	Office Automation Applications Manager	56,370	69,300	56,370	69,300	66,100
Medium	Production Control Specialist	24,128	47,000	24,128	47,000	41,300
Medium	Production Services Supervisor	49,500	59,000	49,500	59,000	56,600
Medium	Project Manager - Applications	45,000	63,000	45,000	65,169	60,100
Medium	Project Manager - Distributed Systems	49,955	65,000	52,473	65,000	61,900
Medium	Project Manager - Network Technical Services	54,340	64,600	54,340	64,600	62,000
Medium	Project Manager - Systems	51,312	64,347	53,098	67,454	63,900
Medium	Supervisor - Hardware Installations	39,470	48,300	39,470	48,300	46,100
Medium	Supervisor - Microcomputer Support	41,325	56,600	41,325	56,600	52,800
Medium	Supervisor - Network Services	38,930	47,700	38,930	47,700	45,500
Medium	Voice Communications Manager	42,300	57,917	42,300	61,713	56,900
Medium	Change Control Analyst	32,580	42,200	32,580	42,200	39,800
Medium	Computer Operator	21,000	40,000	22,000	40,000	35,500
Medium	Data Center Facility Administration	26,607	39,900	26,607	39,900	36,600
Medium	Data Entry Clerk	15,624	26,249	15,624	26,249	23,600
Medium	Data Security Administration	42,700	46,750	42,700	46,750	45,700
Medium	Database Specialist	41,369	56,057	41,369	56,057	52,400
Medium	Disaster Recovery Coordinator	42,570	55,300	42,570	55,300	52,100
Medium	Forms & Graphics Designer	30,880	47,200	30,880	47,200	43,100
Medium	4th GL Specialist	39,740	53,600	39,740	53,600	50,100
Medium	Hardware Installations Coordinator	52,600	69,000	52,600	69,000	64,900
Medium	IS Planning Analyst	33,300	59,500	33,300	59,500	53,000
Medium	LAN Applications Support Analyst	32,000	44,000	32,000	44,000	41,000
Medium	Network Control Analyst	35,280	48,000	35,280	48,000	44,800
Medium	Network Services Administrator	34,166	45,977	34,166	45,977	43,000
Medium	Network Technician	32,000	43,500	32,000	43,500	40,600
Medium	Operations Analyst	29,955	42,172	29,955	42,172	39,100
Medium	Personal Computer Specialist	27,780	42,000	27,780	42,000	38,400
Medium	Production Control Analyst	38,680	51,200	38,680	51,200	48,100
Medium	Programmer/Analyst	40,000	56,911	40,000	56,911	52,700
Medium	Senior Network Specialist	42,800	52,000	42,800	52,000	49,700
Medium	Software Engineer	60,600	72,600	60,600	72,600	69,600
Medium	Systems Analyst	28,000	51,835	29,680	51,835	46,300
Medium	Systems Programmer	42,031	55,000	42,031	55,000	51,800
Medium	Systems Support Specialist	32,400	53,000	32,400	53,000	47,900
Medium	Tape Librarian	23,000	38,000	23,000	38,000	34,300
Medium	Technical Services Specialist	23,000	38,583	23,000	38,583	34,700
Medium	Technical Specialist	29,700	33,000	29,700	33,000	32,200
Medium	Voice Communications Coordinator	27,900	31,000	27,900	31,000	30,200

Source Edp: National and Local Salaries

"The 1996 salary survey numbers are based on analysis of the current salaries of more than 95,000 information technology professionals culled from our nationwide database and supplemental resources. National and local metropolitan salaries are tabulated by position titles and levels of responsibility.

'Salary ranges include the twentieth upper and lower percentiles in each category. The twentieth percentile represents the figure at which 20% of the respondents earn that salary or less. The median represents the figure at which half earn more and half earn less. The eightieth percentile represents the figure at which 20% earn that salary or more."--Source Edp

National Salaries ($K)	Median Salaries ($K)	20%	Median	80%
	Systems Development			
Mainframe	Junior Programmer	32	34	39
	Programmer/Analyst	34	41	46
	Senior Programmer/Analyst	41	49	59
Midrange	Junior Programmer	28	33	39
	Programmer/Analyst	33	40	46
	Senior Programmer/Analyst	41	50	63
Client/Server	Junior Programmer	30	35	41
	Programmer/Analyst	36	43	50
	Senior Programmer/Analyst	43	52	65
GUI	Junior Programmer	28	34	40
	Programmer/Analyst	35	42	49
	Senior Programmer/Analyst	41	50	62
Software Engineer	Junior Engineer	32	37	47
	Software Engineer	35	45	50
	Senior Software Engineer	32	55	69
	Business Systems			
	Business Analyst	41	50	61
	Consultant	47	59	83
	EDI Analyst	41	47	58
	Specialist			
Database Management	Database Analyst	44	54	62
	Database Administrator	52	59	69
LAN Administrator		36	43	54
Network Engineer		40	48	60
PC Specialist	PC Software Specialist	30	36	47
	PC Analyst	34	45	55
Systems Administrator/Manager		40	48	59
WAN Administration	Voice Analyst	38	48	60
	Data Communication Analyst	46	55	69
	WAN Administrator	39	47	58
Systems Programmer		44	54	64
Edp Auditing	Edp Auditor	29	42	38
	Senior Edp Auditor	42	53	63
Technical Writing	Writer	27	34	41
	Editor	33	44	53
Systems Architect		41	49	61
	Management			
MIS Director/CIO	Small/Medium Shop	53	66	83
	Large Shop	78	97	125

National Salaries ($K)	Median Salaries ($K)	20%	Median	80%
Manager of Business Applications		60	72	89
Applications Development		62	74	91
Technical Services		58	70	87
VP/Manager of Systems Engineering		63	76	94
VP/Manager of Customer Support		55	67	82
Project Manager		52	63	78
Project Leader		44	54	66
Sales				
Account Representative		50	69	94
Pre/Post Sales Support Representative		43	52	64
Management		58	86	115
Data Centers				
Data Center Manager		44	58	75
Operations Support	Technician	23	29	36
	Senior Technician	30	38	48
Communications/Network	Operator	24	33	39
	Senior Operator	33	44	57

"Our annual salary survey shows the median salaries for computer information technology professionals from coast to coast. Median salaries are used in order to keep our salary survey representative and unaffected by extremes."--Source Edp

Local Salaries ($K)	New England				Mid-Atlantic			
	NH	Boston	Hartford	Upper Fairfield/ N Haven	Westch. Lower Fairfield	New York City	NJ Central & Northern	Long Island
Systems Development								
Mainframe Junior Programmer	33.1	37.3	33.5	36.9	38.9	37.0	36.7	33.4
Mainframe Programmer/Analyst	41.5	46.7	45.2	46.7	45.2	47.3	44.7	43.8
Mainframe Senior Programmer/Analyst	50.6	58.6	51.5	55.4	57.0	59.4	57.0	55.4
Midrange Junior Programmer	34.3	32.1	32.7	35.0	36.2	36.5	34.5	34.2
Midrange Programmer/Analyst	39.4	45.2	38.2	39.1	48.2	48.1	45.1	44.9
Midrange Senior Programmer/Analyst	47.7	58.0	48.2	48.4	61.4	62.6	57.5	56.6
Client/Server Junior Programmer	36.7	37.4	35.5	37.2	40.3	42.5	37.0	35.9
Client/Server Programmer/Analyst	44.2	48.7	42.4	44.1	51.0	55.0	52.0	47.4
Client/Server Senior Programmer/Analyst	52.4	56.3	49.0	52.0	62.2	67.0	55.0	52.0
GUI Junior Programmer	33.2	40.8	35.3	36.9	38.9	39.9	36.7	34.8
GUI Programmer/Analyst	44.2	46.5	44.8	47.3	48.9	47.6	47.2	46.0
GUI Senior Programmer/Analyst	46.6	57.0	54.0	57.3	59.3	59.8	55.8	55.7
Junior Software Engineer	42.4	44.9	39.5	38.0	45.5	45.8	43.5	42.1
Software Engineer	50.2	53.5	46.0	47.5	55.4	55.5	52.9	51.6
Senior Software Engineer	58.5	67.0	60.2	61.0	64.9	62.1	66.0	63.3
Business Systems								
Business Analyst	46.6	47.6	47.1	52.0	54.8	53.3	51.7	49.5
Consultant	63.8	65.1	56.2	63.9	73.4	70.2	68.9	72.4
EDI Analyst	42.4	45.9	47.0	47.2	49.8	57.5	55.3	44.3
Specialists								
Database Analyst	52.5	53.6	55.8	58.5	61.7	60.8	58.2	54.2
Database Administrator	63.4	64.7	52.7	58.3	73.0	80.2	72.5	56.0
LAN Administrator	44.3	47.9	43.5	47.0	48.0	51.7	47.0	45.5

Local Salaries ($K)	New England				Mid-Atlantic			
	NH	Boston	Hartford	Upper Fairfield/ N Haven	Westch. Lower Fairfield	New York City	NJ Central & Northern	Long Island
Network Engineer	56.7	57.9	44.1	46.1	50.4	55.0	52.0	47.5
PC Software Specialist	39.4	42.1	37.6	38.1	41.9	44.5	37.7	38.9
PC Analyst	47.1	49.3	46.3	48.2	55.4	55.0	51.2	51.2
Systems Administrator/Manager	48.6	54.3	47.6	50.6	53.4	59.9	56.6	51.1
Voice Analyst	47.6	48.6	50.6	53.0	55.9	54.3	52.7	50.2
Data Communications Analyst	58.4	59.6	55.5	58.2	61.3	65.4	57.8	63.0
WAN Administrator	45.9	46.8	46.5	49.2	50.7	52.3	48.9	46.1
Systems Programmer	60.0	61.2	54.7	57.3	60.4	59.6	57.0	56.7
Edp Auditor	40.4	45.4	40.2	40.6	40.3	50.4	50.8	42.4
Senior Edp Auditor	53.0	54.1	53.4	52.6	65.4	61.8	60.3	62.4
Technical Writer	38.2	38.1	33.8	33.2	39.0	38.4	38.8	37.8
Technical Editor	46.4	47.3	43.3	48.2	50.8	48.4	47.9	50.5
Systems Architect	49.1	50.1	44.9	47.0	52.9	59.2	60.7	51.5
Management								
MIS Director/CIO: Small/Medium Shop	66.7	68.1	64.1	67.2	70.8	75.6	75.0	56.7
MIS Director/CIO: Large Shop	90.6	102.3	99.6	97.8	105.2	130.5	105.0	77.4
Manager of Business Applications	79.6	81.2	76.3	80.2	90.1	80.0	75.0	72.0
Applications Development	69.6	71.0	73.9	77.4	81.6	85.8	77.0	76.5
Technical Services	60.1	78.0	76.9	78.5	86.2	85.3	82.2	85.4
VP/Manager of Systems Engineering	87.3	89.1	78.5	78.0	86.7	90.0	83.0	81.3
VP/Manager of Customer Support	70.0	71.4	66.9	69.7	84.0	85.0	62.0	67.4
Project Manager	60.4	72.0	61.3	67.3	70.9	75.6	66.9	62.4
Project Leader	50.4	58.9	53.6	56.1	63.2	66.4	55.8	54.4
Sales								
Account Representative	70.0	71.4	59.4	62.2	80.0	75.9	61.9	56.7
Pre/Post Sales Support Rep.	50.2	55.3	52.6	51.6	54.4	58.9	51.3	54.4
Management	84.3	86.0	84.4	88.4	93.2	88.8	87.9	85.1
Data Center								
Data Center Manager	63.0	64.3	58.2	57.5	67.3	77.8	62.5	72.7
Operations Support: Technician	25.5	26.0	30.2	32.2	32.3	34.3	30.1	34.7
Operations Support: Senior Technician	41.3	42.7	35.9	37.6	43.7	50.1	39.9	41.8
Communications/Network: Operator	32.8	33.5	34.8	36.5	38.5	36.6	36.3	29.6
Communications/Network: Sr. Operator	48.9	47.9	46.6	48.8	51.1	49.1	48.6	43.0

Local Salaries ($K)	Mid-Atlantic				East North Central			
	Phil S NJ	Baltimore	Washington DC	Upstate NY	Western MI	Detroit	Cleveland/ Akron	Pittsburgh
Systems Development								
Mainframe Junior Programmer	35.4	30.0	37.1	29.2	33.0	34.8	33.5	31.8
Mainframe Programmer/Analyst	42.2	39.9	49.5	37.0	37.5	40.0	37.0	38.2
Mainframe Senior Programmer/Analyst	51.0	48.0	55.0	38.7	47.3	48.0	42.9	42.1
Midrange Junior Programmer	31.2	30.5	35.8	27.2	33.3	31.4	31.1	29.6
Midrange Programmer/Analyst	41.0	37.4	39.7	37.0	37.8	38.9	39.0	37.8
Midrange Senior Programmer/Analyst	55.4	48.0	50.6	50.8	48.8	50.0	44.3	45.8
Client/Server Junior Programmer	35.0	32.0	39.4	36.6	36.0	37.0	38.1	32.7
Client/Server Programmer/Analyst	42.0	44.1	48.3	41.5	45.0	45.0	45.7	37.0

Local Salaries ($K)	Mid-Atlantic				East North Central			
	Phil S NJ	Baltimore	Washing-ton DC	Upstate NY	Western MI	Detroit	Cleve-land/ Akron	Pittsburgh
Client/Server Senior Programmer/Analyst	55.0	51.6	58.7	49.2	54.0	55.0	50.5	46.0
GUI Junior Programmer	32.0	32.9	38.6	33.3	35.8	36.2	30.9	31.9
GUI Programmer/Analyst	38.8	39.4	42.0	38.3	39.2	41.3	36.3	34.9
GUI Senior Programmer/Analyst	51.0	51.5	52.7	49.2	46.0	52.1	43.3	44.7
Junior Software Engineer	36.4	33.8	39.7	35.7	36.8	38.7	33.2	32.8
Software Engineer	47.9	47.1	47.6	40.9	40.7	45.8	40.3	40.2
Senior Software Engineer	55.1	57.5	58.2	56.4	51.1	59.3	47.0	50.1
Business Systems								
Business Analyst	52.0	46.2	52.6	41.2	50.4	51.0	46.5	44.8
Consultant	61.3	59.3	64.0	50.6	62.0	62.8	53.5	55.1
EDI Analyst	51.2	42.0	50.1	40.7	45.8	46.1	41.0	40.8
Specialists								
Database Analyst	64.2	50.2	61.1	46.4	56.8	57.1	44.7	50.5
Database Administrator	55.0	58.8	64.8	56.3	52.0	63.5	52.2	51.8
LAN Administrator	44.0	40.5	47.6	38.4	37.0	44.3	41.6	39.3
Network Engineer	50.0	47.1	54.2	45.4	41.0	52.0	41.2	42.0
PC Software Specialist	40.0	37.5	40.0	34.1	32.8	31.0	33.3	34.7
PC Analyst	49.3	39.9	46.9	37.8	43.5	45.2	40.1	42.6
Systems Administrator/Manager	53.4	44.6	55.1	40.1	49.1	49.2	42.4	43.7
Voice Analyst	50.8	43.4	55.4	42.0	51.4	51.8	35.1	45.7
Data Communications Analyst	55.8	51.8	60.8	56.0	56.4	53.7	44.2	50.2
WAN Administrator	51.0	40.1	47.2	41.5	44.0	48.1	44.2	42.0
Systems Programmer	55.0	51.0	59.9	45.4	55.6	54.0	48.0	49.5
Edp Auditor	48.5	39.4	47.9	33.5	37.1	45.9	39.2	33.0
Senior Edp Auditor	56.7	55.9	55.0	53.0	51.0	55.7	47.2	45.4
Technical Writer	36.6	35.8	37.1	31.5	32.2	30.5	27.8	31.5
Technical Editor	46.2	42.9	45.2	38.2	46.7	40.0	40.3	41.6
Systems Architect	51.0	41.9	49.1	37.3	45.6	45.0	48.7	40.6
Management								
MIS Director/CIO: Small/Medium Shop	72.0	71.6	89.4	53.2	65.2	68.2	56.3	58.0
MIS Director/CIO: Large Shop	95.0	88.2	120.5	67.4	82.6	96.0	74.5	73.5
Manager of Business Applications	76.0	67.8	78.0	72.3	65.0	72.3	59.8	68.2
Applications Development	74.3	68.9	80.9	61.4	66.0	78.3	64.9	66.9
Technical Services	77.0	67.6	69.8	62.8	62.0	66.1	62.1	57.7
VP/Manager of Systems Engineering	82.0	67.8	85.1	65.2	65.0	72.0	63.2	71.0
VP/Manager of Customer Support	79.0	66.1	78.2	64.9	60.0	65.0	60.2	72.0
Project Manager	64.6	59.9	70.3	53.3	65.3	67.0	56.3	58.1
Project Leader	53.9	50.0	58.7	44.5	54.5	55.1	51.1	48.5
Sales								
Account Representative	59.7	65.3	70.8	56.2	70.0	64.2	55.4	64.0
Pre/Post Sales Support Rep.	49.5	66.1	53.9	40.9	50.1	51.8	43.2	47.7
Management	84.8	88.9	92.3	82.7	85.8	90.0	74.0	76.3
Data Center								
Data Center Manager	55.2	51.2	64.0	45.6	55.8	63.5	48.2	49.7
Operations Support: Technician	29.2	26.9	29.6	22.5	27.5	26.0	27.1	24.5
Operations Support: Senior Technician	36.0	37.2	39.2	38.3	36.4	34.4	31.5	32.4
Communications/Network: Operator	30.0	32.5	38.1	28.9	35.4	33.4	30.5	31.5

Local Salaries ($K)	Mid-Atlantic				East North Central			
	Phil S NJ	Baltimore	Washington DC	Upstate NY	Western MI	Detroit	Cleveland/ Akron	Pittsburgh
Communications/Network: Sr. Operator	37.6	43.5	44.1	38.7	42.0	43.0	35.2	42.2

Local Salaries ($K)	East North Central				West North Central			
	Indianapolis/Ft. Wayne	Cincinnati/Dayton	Columbus	Louisville	Minneapolis/St. Paul	Green Bay/Fox Valley	Milwaukee	Chicago
Systems Development								
Mainframe Junior Programmer	31.2	36.0	29.9	30.2	34.2	29.3	33.1	36.4
Mainframe Programmer/Analyst	34.7	38.1	38.8	34.5	41.8	38.8	39.9	46.4
Mainframe Senior Programmer/Analyst	44.0	46.2	45.3	45.5	48.0	43.5	45.3	48.1
Midrange Junior Programmer	30.9	32.1	30.1	28.1	33.6	27.3	29.5	36.0
Midrange Programmer/Analyst	34.4	37.3	38.9	34.5	37.9	36.2	39.2	44.6
Midrange Senior Programmer/Analyst	40.9	47.1	46.0	40.0	44.2	38.5	40.8	47.7
Client/Server Junior Programmer	30.4	31.2	31.2	30.0	34.1	29.1	31.2	38.5
Client/Server Programmer/Analyst	33.6	38.5	41.1	35.0	43.0	36.7	38.7	46.2
Client/Server Senior Programmer/Analyst	43.6	47.6	50.3	44.0	52.0	44.8	49.5	53.5
GUI Junior Programmer	31.2	31.4	29.2	30.2	34.3	29.4	30.7	36.4
GUI Programmer/Analyst	36.8	40.6	35.5	37.1	42.4	37.1	41.9	45.9
GUI Senior Programmer/Analyst	42.3	46.3	42.8	47.2	49.0	41.2	48.7	53.7
Junior Software Engineer	32.1	36.6	33.5	31.1	34.1	30.2	34.9	37.4
Software Engineer	42.3	43.0	41.5	34.4	48.2	36.0	39.9	51.0
Senior Software Engineer	49.0	51.2	49.9	46.4	58.0	41.9	47.9	61.6
Business Systems								
Business Analyst	43.9	46.5	46.5	42.5	50.0	45.4	48.5	51.2
Consultant	54.0	57.2	50.2	52.3	57.7	50.8	53.2	63.0
EDI Analyst	39.9	42.3	40.3	48.2	47.3	49.1	51.2	51.9
Specialists								
Database Analyst	49.4	52.3	45.0	47.9	55.0	46.5	52.4	57.7
Database Administrator	51.9	53.4	53.1	53.2	60.6	47.2	52.4	62.0
LAN Administrator	42.8	52.5	40.7	38.3	41.7	36.2	37.9	44.9
Network Engineer	41.2	48.0	44.8	45.0	52.0	39.1	41.0	51.5
PC Software Specialist	35.7	36.9	34.5	31.8	37.7	36.1	33.7	41.2
PC Analyst	37.9	40.1	41.5	43.2	45.0	41.0	44.7	49.2
Systems Administrator/Manager	42.8	45.3	42.3	38.1	46.2	40.3	45.1	49.9
Voice Analyst	44.8	47.4	39.2	52.0	46.2	42.2	44.1	52.2
Data Communications Analyst	49.1	52.0	47.6	54.1	52.7	46.3	52.0	57.3
WAN Administrator	37.8	51.1	46.9	45.0	47.7	43.7	46.9	54.0
Systems Programmer	48.4	54.4	50.8	46.9	55.2	50.4	51.9	56.5
Edp Auditor	45.6	34.2	36.0	37.1	45.2	39.1	45.3	47.1
Senior Edp Auditor	53.3	47.1	46.5	43.1	55.9	47.9	52.6	57.6
Technical Writer	31.5	33.5	27.4	33.0	33.8	30.7	29.4	32.7
Technical Editor	40.7	43.1	39.9	39.4	46.7	38.3	40.1	47.5
Systems Architect	39.7	46.7	44.5	45.4	51.0	41.7	45.3	55.5
Management								
MIS Director/CIO: Small/Medium Shop	56.8	60.1	55.9	55.0	70.0	55.2	63.1	77.3
MIS Director/CIO: Large Shop	85.4	92.2	98.5	92.4	119.0	78.9	85.0	123.1
Manager of Business Applications	67.1	65.8	63.5	64.0	70.1	70.3	79.9	74.9

Local Salaries ($K)	East North Central				West North Central			
	Indianapo-lis/Ft. Wayne	Cincin-nati/Day-ton	Columbus	Louisville	Minnea-polis/St. Paul	Green Bay/Fox Valley	Milwau-kee	Chicago
Applications Development	65.4	69.3	63.3	69.9	72.9	68.0	70.1	81.4
Technical Services	63.3	59.8	63.0	68.9	70.0	60.3	63.8	78.7
VP/Manager of Systems Engineering	77.7	74.5	68.3	68.0	72.1	65.5	68.5	81.3
VP/Manager of Customer Support	58.9	69.8	55.1	62.1	68.0	NA	65.3	71.5
Project Manager	64.9	60.2	58.9	58.3	65.7	53.5	56.5	66.3
Project Leader	50.2	52.3	50.5	50.0	53.0	44.7	46.7	55.3
Sales								
Account Representative	57.0	71.4	68.7	59.9	66.6	60.2	68.9	67.5
Pre/Post Sales Support Rep.	50.9	50.8	45.4	42.3	52.2	41.1	45.7	50.9
Management	74.7	79.1	70.5	72.4	91.6	70.3	73.6	95.0
Data Center								
Data Center Manager	59.0	59.0	56.2	58.0	68.7	45.8	47.9	70.3
Operations Support: Technician	23.9	28.2	23.9	26.0	37.0	31.5	37.0	31.4
Operations Support: Senior Technician	31.7	33.6	32.8	30.8	45.3	33.5	45.3	40.0
Communications/Network: Operator	30.8	32.6	27.2	32.0	36.3	34.3	30.4	36.0
Communications/Network: Sr. Operator	41.3	43.7	39.2	42.8	46.3	45.7	40.7	43.5

Local Salaries ($K)	West North Central				South Atlantic			
	Omaha/Des Moines	St. Louis	Kansas City	Wichita/Topeka	Atlanta	Char-lotte, NC	Raleigh/Durham/Greens-boro	Tampa/Orlando
Systems Development								
Mainframe Junior Programmer	30.5	30.3	31.8	29.3	36.8	37.3	37.6	31.9
Mainframe Programmer/Analyst	35.0	39.4	40.5	36.8	39.5	39.1	39.4	38.0
Mainframe Senior Programmer/Analyst	44.1	46.2	47.3	47.3	51.1	49.3	49.8	48.1
Midrange Junior Programmer	28.4	30.5	29.8	27.2	38.4	34.7	35.0	33.3
Midrange Programmer/Analyst	36.4	37.3	39.6	37.2	44.2	38.4	42.4	38.8
Midrange Senior Programmer/Analyst	43.0	46.8	44.3	38.4	53.8	49.0	49.4	50.5
Client/Server Junior Programmer	29.9	31.6	30.1	29.8	38.4	37.0	37.0	35.2
Client/Server Programmer/Analyst	34.2	45.3	34.2	34.1	46.7	42.0	42.2	43.6
Client/Server Senior Programmer/Analyst	44.1	53.2	45.7	45.5	55.3	53.0	53.7	53.2
GUI Junior Programmer	30.6	30.4	29.8	29.3	37.3	37.3	37.7	30.5
GUI Programmer/Analyst	33.5	38.6	38.3	32.1	46.3	40.9	43.8	39.3
GUI Senior Programmer/Analyst	42.9	48.0	47.3	41.1	55.2	52.3	52.8	46.8
Junior Software Engineer	31.4	31.2	30.6	30.1	40.8	38.4	38.7	30.9
Software Engineer	40.2	43.7	43.6	37.6	47.8	42.4	42.8	43.1
Senior Software Engineer	47.4	49.2	49.6	45.6	57.2	53.3	53.8	56.8
Business Systems								
Business Analyst	48.1	47.1	48.8	47.7	56.8	52.5	53.0	40.8
Consultant	52.9	52.5	51.5	50.7	75.7	64.6	65.2	48.5
EDI Analyst	42.9	42.3	44.3	42.9	49.2	47.8	48.2	44.5
Specialists								
Database Analyst	48.4	48.1	49.5	46.4	61.2	59.1	59.7	45.8
Database Administrator	52.7	54.9	55.1	55.1	68.5	61.4	59.7	56.2
LAN Administrator	37.7	39.2	36.7	36.1	52.4	46.0	46.4	45.9
Network Engineer	31.7	44.1	32.4	32.2	55.3	53.0	54.2	48.7

Local Salaries ($K)	West North Central				South Atlantic			
	Omaha/ Des Moines	St. Louis	Kansas City	Wichita/ Topeka	Atlanta	Char- lotte, NC	Raleigh/ Durham/ Greens- boro	Tampa/ Orlando
PC Software Specialist	31.3	33.4	33.1	31.3	39.4	37.9	37.3	33.8
PC Analyst	37.1	42.7	36.1	41.4	47.4	45.3	45.7	39.9
Systems Administrator/Manager	41.9	45.2	40.8	40.2	53.8	51.2	51.7	44.4
Voice Analyst	43.9	43.6	42.7	42.0	46.8	53.6	54.0	39.1
Data Communications Analyst	52.5	51.2	51.1	50.5	55.4	58.8	59.3	49.3
WAN Administrator	36.7	47.3	37.5	37.3	46.7	50.0	52.2	46.1
Systems Programmer	53.1	51.6	53.3	52.5	57.9	58.0	58.5	49.8
Edp Auditor	37.4	43.0	39.3	39.9	40.6	42.2	44.0	39.6
Senior Edp Auditor	49.8	50.7	50.4	47.7	50.8	53.2	53.7	49.7
Technical Writer	27.5	35.1	29.8	28.2	33.3	33.6	33.9	28.2
Technical Editor	39.9	42.6	41.4	40.7	42.5	48.7	49.1	34.0
Systems Architect	38.9	41.4	37.9	37.3	65.0	47.5	51.4	47.9
Management								
MIS Director/CIO: Small/Medium Shop	61.3	68.3	66.9	66.8	78.4	67.9	68.5	58.3
MIS Director/CIO: Large Shop	81.2	100.0	102.1	87.8	122.7	86.0	86.8	83.4
Manager of Business Applications	62.9	60.2	64.2	63.8	91.4	65.0	67.2	66.8
Applications Development	64.1	63.7	66.1	68.6	78.8	78.3	79.0	71.3
Technical Services	66.1	67.1	63.9	63.9	81.2	67.6	72.5	59.3
VP/Manager of Systems Engineering	68.4	69.7	69.1	68.4	88.1	70.0	83.9	75.8
VP/Manager of Customer Support	46.8	62.6	47.2	47.7	56.0	60.0	63.1	61.7
Project Manager	55.7	57.9	54.2	53.4	68.2	68.0	68.6	54.2
Project Leader	46.5	52.3	53.3	44.5	56.4	56.8	57.3	45.8
Sales								
Account Representative	69.7	74.5	71.6	66.9	74.7	71.6	69.1	68.2
Pre/Post Sales Support Rep.	46.5	55.2	48.7	46.7	65.2	52.2	52.7	47.5
Management	73.2	80.5	71.2	70.1	98.4	89.4	90.2	89.0
Data Center								
Data Center Manager	51.0	48.8	52.0	51.3	61.1	58.2	58.7	53.0
Operations Support: Technician	26.5	23.3	27.0	21.0	35.7	28.7	28.9	26.1
Operations Support: Senior Technician	33.3	30.9	33.8	31.8	39.4	38.0	38.3	34.6
Communications/Network: Operator	30.2	27.0	29.4	26.8	32.2	36.9	37.2	33.6
Communications/Network: Sr. Operator	40.5	37.0	39.4	36.0	43.1	49.4	49.8	45.0

Local Salaries ($K)	S Atlantic	South Central					Mountain	
	Miami	Tulsa/ Okla- homa City	Memphis/ Nashville	Dallas/ Ft. Worth	San Anto- nio/Aus- tin	Houston	Denver	Phoenix
Systems Development								
Mainframe Junior Programmer	33.0	32.1	28.6	34.7	32.1	33.2	35.0	33.7
Mainframe Programmer/Analyst	39.0	37.6	36.6	42.3	38.5	38.8	42.0	39.4
Mainframe Senior Programmer/Analyst	49.2	45.3	42.9	49.0	47.7	49.5	48.2	44.6
Midrange Junior Programmer	30.3	29.9	26.6	32.3	30.6	35.1	35.0	31.4
Midrange Programmer/Analyst	36.1	37.4	35.2	39.8	33.9	41.6	41.0	38.7
Midrange Senior Programmer/Analyst	45.9	42.2	42.1	45.6	43.2	49.7	47.6	46.5
Client/Server Junior Programmer	36.0	31.1	30.0	33.6	33.1	36.7	34.5	30.9
Client/Server Programmer/Analyst	46.1	35.1	35.0	40.2	40.1	44.5	43.3	45.3

Local Salaries ($K)	S Atlantic	South Central					Mountain	
	Miami	Tulsa/ Okla- homa City	Memphis/ Nashville	Dallas/ Ft. Worth	San Anto- nio/Aus- tin	Houston	Denver	Phoenix
Client/Server Senior Programmer/Analyst	54.2	45.9	44.0	52.1	46.6	50.9	52.5	51.2
GUI Junior Programmer	32.6	32.2	28.7	33.4	32.9	33.3	34.4	33.8
GUI Programmer/Analyst	38.6	35.2	38.7	42.5	36.1	42.6	43.6	39.9
GUI Senior Programmer/Analyst	45.7	45.1	45.7	51.0	46.2	49.7	55.8	47.4
Junior Software Engineer	35.6	33.1	29.5	36.0	33.9	39.1	38.5	38.7
Software Engineer	44.6	36.6	32.6	45.8	39.9	47.8	43.0	38.4
Senior Software Engineer	55.3	45.9	46.7	56.8	47.0	53.9	56.6	53.7
Business Systems								
Business Analyst	49.1	48.5	46.4	56.1	49.1	52.1	47.0	50.4
Consultant	56.3	55.6	49.6	66.0	55.4	57.6	57.8	58.4
EDI Analyst	49.4	41.1	46.4	44.4	40.8	46.9	42.8	43.2
Specialists								
Database Analyst	51.6	50.9	45.4	59.6	49.9	52.7	53.0	53.5
Database Administrator	60.6	55.9	52.9	61.9	50.9	65.6	58.7	57.7
LAN Administrator	47.9	39.6	39.3	42.8	40.6	43.6	44.7	41.7
Network Engineer	46.0	33.2	45.0	42.6	41.3	58.5	65.3	48.0
PC Software Specialist	33.4	31.6	30.5	36.4	30.1	38.5	35.3	30.9
PC Analyst	39.6	39.1	41.8	42.2	42.8	42.9	40.6	41.0
Systems Administrator/Manager	48.1	44.1	39.3	47.6	45.2	45.7	45.9	46.3
Voice Analyst	46.7	46.1	41.1	46.5	42.4	47.8	48.0	48.5
Data Communications Analyst	51.3	50.6	52.6	54.7	48.9	52.4	52.7	53.2
WAN Administrator	43.0	38.1	44.1	46.4	40.3	46.9	42.0	42.8
Systems Programmer	50.6	53.4	44.5	53.9	51.1	51.7	51.9	52.4
Edp Auditor	41.5	40.0	35.7	41.6	38.1	39.5	40.2	39.0
Senior Edp Auditor	52.1	45.8	40.9	49.5	46.1	47.4	49.6	48.1
Technical Writer	30.0	28.9	30.1	31.2	29.6	32.6	30.1	30.4
Technical Editor	42.5	41.9	37.4	45.3	43.0	43.4	43.6	44.1
Systems Architect	53.0	40.9	44.7	49.5	44.6	49.3	45.2	43.0
Management								
MIS Director/CIO: Small/Medium Shop	59.3	68.3	55.7	68.9	60.3	60.6	66.6	61.5
MIS Director/CIO: Large Shop	90.6	99.0	91.2	126.0	101.4	99.9	85.5	77.9
Manager of Business Applications	65.0	65.1	65.0	70.4	61.7	81.6	67.0	57.4
Applications Development	75.7	67.4	68.8	79.1	69.1	76.4	75.7	76.1
Technical Services	64.1	68.4	70.8	74.3	71.6	69.1	60.5	61.1
VP/Manager of Systems Engineering	65.0	69.7	64.0	92.4	84.3	93.1	74.5	75.3
VP/Manager of Customer Support	56.2	47.6	63.0	64.3	69.9	77.7	73.5	62.0
Project Manager	59.3	58.6	59.0	67.4	65.3	66.5	60.9	61.6
Project Leader	49.5	48.9	49.8	58.1	52.4	55.4	54.7	51.4
Sales								
Account Representative	67.1	67.9	59.1	85.9	75.8	72.3	56.3	56.9
Pre/Post Sales Support Rep.	46.9	52.4	40.1	56.1	46.4	56.9	46.7	47.2
Management	89.0	91.5	68.6	94.1	91.4	84.3	80.0	80.9
Data Center								
Data Center Manager	50.7	56.7	57.2	60.7	57.9	55.5	56.5	52.6
Operations Support: Technician	28.1	24.7	26.0	26.7	24.4	29.5	25.7	25.9
Operations Support: Senior Technician	33.1	37.3	29.2	35.3	32.6	38.6	34.0	34.4
Communications/Network: Operator	32.2	31.8	28.3	32.4	28.6	35.6	33.0	33.4

Local Salaries ($K)	S Atlantic	South Central					Mountain	
	Miami	Tulsa/ Oklahoma City	Memphis/ Nashville	Dallas/ Ft. Worth	San Antonio/Austin	Houston	Denver	Phoenix
Communications/Network: Sr. Operator	43.1	42.5	44.4	44.3	41.6	44.0	44.2	44.7

Local Salaries ($K)	Mountain	Pacific						Canada
	Albuquerque	Seattle	Portland	San Fran/ San Jose	Los Angeles	Orange County	San Diego	Toronto
Systems Development								
Mainframe Junior Programmer	31.9	33.8	34.7	38.6	38.1	37.9	35.1	40.0
Mainframe Programmer/Analyst	37.9	41.3	42.0	48.2	47.7	47.2	42.0	47.7
Mainframe Senior Programmer/Analyst	46.4	51.5	50.5	55.0	58.0	55.0	51.0	53.2
Midrange Junior Programmer	31.9	34.0	35.5	36.2	36.4	35.5	33.2	33.6
Midrange Programmer/Analyst	36.8	37.9	39.3	47.0	47.3	46.9	43.0	41.4
Midrange Senior Programmer/Analyst	43.2	54.1	50.1	57.2	57.1	56.0	52.3	49.8
Client/Server Junior Programmer	28.9	39.5	40.0	40.7	39.2	38.4	35.5	38.4
Client/Server Programmer/Analyst	37.9	49.1	55.0	58.2	47.8	46.2	43.2	47.9
Client/Server Senior Programmer/Analyst	44.2	61.3	65.0	71.3	60.1	58.0	54.0	56.7
GUI Junior Programmer	28.8	40.5	38.2	38.7	37.0	36.3	35.7	34.6
GUI Programmer/Analyst	37.2	49.2	47.3	48.7	46.9	46.3	44.4	42.4
GUI Senior Programmer/Analyst	42.4	58.4	53.5	61.0	58.6	58.1	54.0	52.8
Junior Software Engineer	37.1	40.5	44.0	46.1	42.0	41.1	39.8	39.5
Software Engineer	42.2	51.0	53.0	58.2	48.5	47.0	43.6	48.6
Senior Software Engineer	51.8	63.1	65.0	72.2	62.1	61.0	52.4	59.4
Business Systems								
Business Analyst	49.1	47.7	52.0	61.5	56.5	55.8	54.0	53.8
Consultant	50.4	58.6	53.7	66.9	66.1	65.0	61.1	64.2
EDI Analyst	43.7	41.1	48.9	55.5	58.2	55.3	51.0	51.3
Specialists								
Database Analyst	44.5	54.2	53.0	61.2	61.0	60.0	55.0	52.9
Database Administrator	53.8	57.5	60.0	68.2	69.2	66.0	60.1	62.8
LAN Administrator	43.1	41.8	43.4	47.7	48.1	46.0	42.3	46.7
Network Engineer	45.0	54.1	49.0	59.6	60.3	58.1	53.0	55.6
PC Software Specialist	28.2	38.0	38.2	42.5	45.4	44.1	37.7	42.5
PC Analyst	35.3	47.5	46.4	52.0	53.1	52.2	48.8	46.2
Systems Administrator/Manager	38.8	46.5	52.4	61.6	61.8	60.4	49.0	58.2
Voice Analyst	38.5	45.0	54.8	55.5	52.1	51.9	48.3	45.4
Data Communications Analyst	47.8	53.3	60.2	67.0	60.0	59.8	55.0	55.6
WAN Administrator	41.4	47.5	53.7	72.0	55.2	61.2	41.7	50.1
Systems Programmer	44.3	52.6	59.3	60.1	62.0	61.2	57.0	61.5
Edp Auditor	39.1	40.9	39.6	48.4	52.6	50.8	43.2	54.3
Senior Edp Auditor	46.9	48.3	54.4	62.8	63.8	63.6	55.8	63.6
Technical Writer	27.5	35.5	44.7	47.7	42.0	41.2	37.7	41.3
Technical Editor	38.8	44.2	54.5	59.5	50.8	50.0	47.3	50.6
Systems Architect	42.5	48.8	49.9	77.4	61.2	78.6	73.0	51.0
Management								
MIS Director/CIO: Small/Medium Shop	57.8	61.6	72.0	78.0	76.1	75.0	73.1	66.8
MIS Director/CIO: Large Shop	73.4	98.1	91.5	120.4	128.8	125.6	115.4	91.2
Manager of Business Applications	72.8	71.0	75.0	96.0	83.1	82.1	81.2	77.7
Applications Development	68.3	71.0	80.1	96.4	86.9	85.0	77.4	74.8

| Local Salaries ($K) | Mountain | Pacific | | | | | | Canada |
	Albuquer-que	Seattle	Portland	San Fran/San Jose	Los Ange-les	Orange County	San Diego	Toronto
Technical Services	59.7	71.5	69.1	85.3	86.0	84.0	80.0	66.1
VP/Manager of Systems Engineering	72.5	81.5	85.1	98.0	85.4	83.1	75.6	78.2
VP/Manager of Customer Support	55.7	75.0	65.0	87.0	86.1	85.1	81.9	68.4
Project Manager	57.9	61.7	68.2	76.0	74.3	73.1	69.0	66.5
Project Leader	49.1	51.5	58.1	67.0	65.3	64.1	60.3	58.3
Sales								
Account Representative	55.5	73.6	64.4	112.0	78.6	77.8	74.0	71.8
Pre/Post Sales Support Rep.	42.9	47.4	53.4	80.0	64.2	63.4	60.1	55.4
Management	66.3	87.3	91.4	120.0	97.6	96.1	94.2	111.2
Data Center								
Data Center Manager	48.5	52.8	NA	70.0	72.7	69.0	63.0	60.2
Operations Support								
Operations Support: Technician	23.9	31.8	NA	44.3	35.0	34.6	33.4	38.5
Operations Support: Senior Technician	32.0	42.0	NA	49.4	49.1	47.3	44.1	42.8
Communications/Network								
Communications/Network: Operator	26.3	33.5	NA	35.3	36.1	34.8	30.1	38.8
Communications/Network: Sr. Operator	36.6	48.1	NA	42.1	48.2	46.2	39.1	49.2

Excerpted with permission from Source Edp. Copyright © 1996, Source Edp, P.O. Box 809030, Dallas TX 75380 USA.

Source Engineering: Engineering Salaries

"The 1996 salary survey numbers are based on analysis of the current salaries of more than 20,000 engineering professionals culled from our nationwide database and supplemental resources. National and local metropolitan salaries are tabulated by position titles and levels of responsibility. Our annual salary survey shows the median salaries for engineering and manufacturing professionals from coast to coast."--Source Engineering

Salary ($K)	Boston/NH	Dallas	LA/Orange Cty	San Diego	San Fran/San Jose	Portland	Median
Design Development							
Software							
Junior Engineer	45.0	36.4	40.1	39.8	47.7	44.5	42
Engineer	50.0	49.4	48.0	43.6	53.7	52.5	50
Senior Engineer	55.0	52.5	62.0	52.4	58.6	61.0	57
Principal Engineer	65.0	59.3	68.3	63.7	69.9	65.0	65
Staff/Project Leader	75.0	69.9	80.0	74.5	83.7	75.2	75
Manager	90.0	81.4	86.1	84.4	91.3	85.0	86
Director	110.0	98.2	96.5	92.3	110.4	101.0	100
Technical Support	45.0	48.4	47.1	45.2	53.4	52.0	48
Digital Analog Design							
Junior Engineer	43.0	34.9	38.1	37.7	48.3	43.4	41
Engineer	47.0	48.5	45.8	44.4	52.4	47.1	47
Senior Engineer	52.0	53.1	56.0	55.2	64.0	53.8	54
Principle Engineer	62.0	58.9	64.7	63.8	67.1	55.0	63
Staff/Project Leader	75.0	70.1	80.0	73.9	82.2	73.8	74
Semiconductor Design							
Junior Engineer	48.1	39.1	40.5	39.9	54.1	48.6	44

Salary ($K)	Boston/ NH	Dallas	LA/ Orange Cty	San Diego	San Fran/ San Jose	Portland	Median
Engineer	52.2	42.4	45.4	43.3	58.6	52.7	49
Senior Engineer	60.0	51.3	58.5	57.2	69.3	54.2	58
Principle Engineer	75.0	62.3	65.6	64.5	79.0	64.8	65
Staff/Project Leader	80.0	68.9	76.1	74.2	84.1	75.6	76
Mechanical/Robotics							
Junior Engineer	41.5	33.7	42.9	39.1	46.7	41.9	42
Engineer	45.1	37.2	47.5	44.6	50.6	45.5	45
Senior Engineer	46.4	43.0	59.8	58.5	54.4	46.8	51
Principle Engineer	58.0	53.1	69.1	53.7	63.5	58.2	58
Staff/Project Leader	70.9	63.9	69.7	69.1	79.7	71.6	70
Small Group Manager	83.4	76.4	78.4	74.2	93.8	84.2	81
Large Group Manager/Director	98.3	92.4	92.5	86.7	110.4	99.2	95
Vice President	115.5	102.8	103.1	95.8	129.8	124.8	109
Manufacturing							
Equipment/Test/QA/IE							
Junior Engineer	38.4	31.2	35.2	32.2	43.2	38.8	37
Engineer	41.7	33.9	41.8	42.1	53.7	42.1	42
Senior Engineer	46.6	45.8	44.2	46.9	62.4	45.0	46
Principle Engineer	56.0	46.6	56.0	56.3	70.3	60.1	56
Staff/Project Leader	69.2	56.2	66.5	68.2	77.7	69.8	69
Small Group Manager	73.8	65.4	68.2	72.9	83.0	74.5	73
Large Group Manager/Director	86.9	78.5	82.0	89.1	97.7	87.8	87
Vice President	97.5	94.3	97.3	95.1	109.5	98.4	97
Marketing							
Direct Sales/Product Management							
<2 years	49.5	40.2	38.4	41.0	55.6	49.9	45
2-3 years	53.6	43.6	46.0	44.5	60.3	54.1	50
4-6 years	55.2	50.2	57.0	57.0	72.8	55.7	56
>6 years	61.1	63.5	64.5	65.2	78.9	61.7	64
Area Sales Manager	73.2	70.0	74.0	72.4	88.9	73.9	74
Small Group Manager	83.1	74.3	78.7	79.0	99.0	83.9	81
Large Group Manager	94.0	80.1	87.2	84.9	111.9	94.9	91
Vice President	110.3	98.6	100.2	96.1	131.4	111.4	105
Miscellaneous							
Technical Writer							
<2 years	39.5	32.0	30.1	32.7	44.3	39.8	36
2-3 years	42.8	34.8	34.2	35.5	48.1	43.2	39
4-6 years	44.1	37.8	40.1	36.5	49.5	44.5	42
>6 years	48.8	45.7	46.6	40.5	58.9	49.3	48
Staff/Project Leader	55.9	49.7	54.0	46.3	62.8	56.4	55
Field Eng/Customer Support							
<2 years	41.3	33.6	34.4	35.6	46.5	41.7	38
2-3 years	44.8	36.4	39.1	40.1	50.4	45.3	42
4-6 years	46.2	42.7	44.5	46.2	58.5	46.6	46
>6 years	51.1	50.2	49.0	58.0	65.3	51.6	51
Staff/Project Leader	62.6	58.5	56.6	65.4	70.3	63.2	63

Wealth

Computer Reseller News: Top Executives—Salaries & Compensation

"Of the more than 300 executive pay packages reviewed--ranging from chief executives to vice presidents at companies from AT&T Corp. to Wang Laboratories--businesses paid 50 of these leaders $1M or more in straight cash compensation during 1995. The top 150 paid executives received an average salary of slightly more than $1M, an impressive increase over last year's average of $765,666. This year's median salary was $780,211.

'In its first-ever look at stock options, CRN's survey uncovered more than 100 executives who received options to buy stock in their companies that could reap them another $1M in value by the time they are exercised--assuming a modest stock growth rate of 7.5%. Overall, about three-fourths of the executive pay packages examined contained options to buy company stock at a discounted or fixed rate."--Computer Reseller News

Rank	Executive	Company	1995 Pay ($)	% Chg Over '94	Stk Op Realizable
1	Charles Wang	Computer Associates	5,585,000	-17	12,022,557
2	Louis Gerstner	IBM	4,775,000	4	8,293,500
3	Eckhard Pfeiffer	Compaq	3,625,000	2	12,492,853
4	Lawrence Ellison	Oracle	3,343,090	39	17,128,197
5	Sanjay Kumar	Computer Associates	3,317,000	59	8,619,144
6	Jerry Sanders	Advanced Micro	3,005,848	-34	0
7	Scott McNealy	Sun Microsystems	3,000,000	147	5,563,539
8	Casey Cowell	U.S. Robotics	2,799,000	92	2,833,862
9	Andrew Grove	Intel	2,756,700	31	4,871,000
10	Robert Allen	AT&T	2,677,500	-20	10,843,320
11	Jerry Junkins	Texas Instruments	2,542,050	32	5,146,144
12	Bert Roberts	MCI	2,190,000	25	3,063,105
13	Raymond Lane	Oracle	2,127,434	74	8,564,099
14	Craig Barrett	Intel	2,067,500	33	3,247,350
15	Gary Tooker	Motorola	2,020,000	2	5,184,000
16	Richard Previte	Advanced Micro (AMD)	2,019,252	-16	3,931,845
17	John McCartney	U.S. Robotics	1,739,400	59	1,889,242
18	Jonathan Zakin	U.S. Robotics	1,739,400	59	1,889,242
19	Tyler Lowrey	Micron Technology	1,695,274	61	1,212,600
20	Steven Appleton	Micron Technology	1,689,540	57	1,212,600
21	Stephen Kaufman	Arrow	1,688,295	28	1,222,750
22	Leon Machiz	Avnet	1,660,000	33	4,946,200
23	Christopher Galvin	Motorola	1,570,000	5	3,888,000
24	Lewis Platt	Hewlett-Packard	1,530,755	30	1,281,600
25	Jeffrey Henley	Oracle	1,519,582	75	8,564,099
26	Russell Artzt	Computer Associates	1,504,000	-6	6,236,754
27	Ross Manire	U.S. Robotics	1,449,500	202	1,889,242
28	Michael Hackworth	Cirrus Logic	1,448,980	64	6,209,493
29	Edward McCracken	Silicon Graphics	1,445,671	15	6,753,927
30	William Miller	Quantum	1,431,023	177	1,789,063
31	Michael Spindler	Apple	1,424,912	53	4,792,561
32	William Hoover	Computer Sciences	1,362,404	10	0
33	Gerald H. Taylor	MCI	1,325,000	38	2,042,070
34	Sam Wyly	Sterling Software	1,300,000	11	59,770,382
35	David House	Intel	1,293,400	15	913,300
36	Robert Palmer	Digital Equipment	1,275,016	42	16,653,641

Rank	Executive	Company	1995 Pay ($)	% Chg Over '94	Stk Op Realizable
37	Gerhard Parker	Intel	1,264,500	34	1,623,650
38	Frank Gill	Intel	1,255,000	21	1,623,650
39	Thomas Jermoluk	Silicon Graphics	1,250,997	37	14,685,807
40	Ned Lautenbach	IBM	1,240,000	16	3,317,300
41	Jerome Meyer	Tektronix	1,224,094	42	0
42	John M. Thompson	IBM	1,218,334	21	3,317,300
43	Sterling Williams	Sterling Software	1,200,000	14	20,948,355
44	Gary Stimac	Compaq	1,170,000	17	4,195,533
45	Richard Thoman	IBM	1,125,000	41	2,902,725
46	Bill Fairfield	Inacom	1,102,815	134	132,803
47	Andreas Barth	Compaq	1,092,932	20	3,269,801
48	Jeffrey McKeever	MicroAge	1,068,815	70	0
49	Dirk Kabcenell	Oracle	1,055,378	165	6,834,604
50	Michael Krasny	CDW Computer	1,044,370	122	0
51	James Halpin	CompUSA	990,000	124	1,405,125
52	Walden Rhines	Mentor Graphics	983,050	45	1,561,465
53	Suhas Patil	Cirrus Logic	968,386	60	1,166,885
54	John Roach	Tandy	918,339	-13	5,242,645
55	Ross Cooley	Compaq	910,000	2	2,271,859
56	Edward Zander	Sun Microsystems	900,000	51	2,225,415
57	Gregory Petsch	Compaq	875,000	9	3,589,876
58	Enrico Pesatori	Digital Equipment	870,000	53	7,105,493
59	Joseph Tucci	Wang	870,000	34	2,560,200
60	Alan Hald	MicroAge	869,331	185	0
61	Ray Vallee	Avnet	864,000	23	4,949,600
62	Robert Bishop	Silicon Graphics	855,772	39	2,667
63	Stephen Zelencik	Advanced Micro (AMD)	848,410	-12	1,965,922
64	Phillip White	Informix	821,667	20	5,070,391
65	Michael Brown	Quantum	819,124	149	1,073,438
66	Michael Dell	Dell Computer	818,032	128	0
67	Gregory Zeman	CDW Computer	817,177	-24	0
68	David Holmes	Reynolds & Reynolds	815,355	3	740,138
69	Robert Frankenberg	Novell	813,166	58	0
70	Edward Heitzeberg	Micron Technology	813,047	92	808,400
71	Wilbur Stover	Micron Technology	810,230	134	727,560
72	Gerald Diamond	Southern Electronics	800,667	83	0
73	Kenneth Smith	Micron Technology	797,172	98	808,400
74	Ian Diery	Apple	790,636	31	2,817,193
75	Joseph Roebuck	Sun Microsystems	781,648	55	445,083
76	Teruyasu Sekimoto	Silicon Graphics	778,773	70	1,822,451
77	William Roach	Quantum	760,953	168	715,625
78	Kenneth Lee	Quantum	751,501	172	715,625
79	Douglas Bartek	Cirrus Logic	744,171	24	833,489
80	Robert Herbold	Microsoft	740,133	NA	19,785,387
81	Michael Canning	Cirrus Logic	730,501	96	833,489
82	James Dixon	CompuCom	726,020	17	1,166,884
83	Edward Anderson	CompuCom	726,020	17	0
84	Joseph Rodgers	Quantum	723,452	143	715,625
85	Donald Baldwin	Micron Technology	721,027	79	646,720
86	Michael Seedman	U.S. Robotics	719,800	122	1,889,242

Rank	Executive	Company	1995 Pay ($)	% Chg Over '94	Stk Op Realizable
87	Gordon Marshall	Marshall Industries	708,262	0	0
88	Lawrence Hambley	Sun Microsystems	702,618	49	1,854,513
89	William Raduchel	Sun Microsystems	699,769	38	2,225,415
90	Carlo Giersch	Arrow	698,178	13	489,100
91	Marvin Burkett	Advanced Micro (AMD)	692,897	-20	1,965,922
92	Sam Srinivasan	Cirrus Logic	684,096	43	1,800,336
93	Robert Rodin	Marshall Industries	683,616	35	0
94	Eugene Conner	Advanced Micro (AMD)	681,001	-19	1,965,922
95	Gary Lauer	Silicon Graphics	676,807	26	3,642,236
96	Steven Menefee	Arrow	670,712	20	1,930,950
97	Charles Geschke	Adobe	668,322	14	2,323,242
98	John Warnock	Adobe	668,322	14	2,323,242
99	Joseph Graziano	Apple	664,213	30	0
100	John Cassese	Computer Horizons	660,000	39	583,443
101	Safi Qureshey	AST Research	656,172	-24	770,977
102	Charles Wyly	Sterling Software	650,000	11	29,885,242
103	James Abrahamson	Oracle	650,000	-23	0
104	Carl Neun	Tektronix	639,614	34	0
105	Robert Throop	Arrow	627,765	-24	489,100
106	Frederick Forsyth	Apple	622,353	36	2,822,055
107	Steven Raymund	Tech Data	622,000	-22	NA
108	Warner Blow	Sterling Software	621,610	11	964,386
109	Daniel Eilers	Apple	618,983	32	10,037,985
110	Daniel Kass	CDW Computer	616,352	19	0
111	Rudi Lamprecht	Tektronix	605,529	137	213,120
112	Charles Christ	Digital Equipment	600,006	90	6,220,768
113	Terence Strom	Egghead	600,000	-45	569,551
114	George Ellis	Sterling Software	600,000	14	6,445,648
115	James Busby	QMS	595,832	0	38,128
116	James Buckley	Apple	586,448	19	9,623,325
117	Richard Rose	Dataflex	583,816	42	0
118	William Tauscher	Vanstar	580,008	NA	2,167,072
119	Frank Ingari	Shiva	577,230	75	0
120	Richard Belluzzo	Hewlett-Packard	576,112	23	400,500
121	Joseph Parkinson	Micron Technology	572,745	-57	0
122	Michael Bealmear	Sybase	568,306	147	2,774,675
123	Robert Klatell	Arrow	561,600	-1	733,650
124	William Strecker	Digital Equipment	560,008	31	2,842,197
125	Joseph Marengi	Novell	552,618	11	0
126	Harold Compton	CompUSA	550,000	NA	1,106,301
127	Daniel Brown	CompuCom	543,900	17	583,442
128	Gordon Eubanks	Symantec	537,842	21	0
129	Bernard Vergnes	Microsoft	526,445	6	7,959,819
130	John Rando	Digital Equipment	523,089	102	5,921,244
131	Douglas Norby	Mentor Graphics	523,015	32	360,287
132	Eric Benhamou	3Com	521,518	9	3,665,254
133	Donald Casey	Wang	510,000	-19	1,684,342
134	Robert Schultz	Inacom	506,280	134	84,994
135	P.T. Winn	Genicom	504,382	16	61,816
136	Robert Nevin	Reynolds & Reynolds	499,877	8	343,397

Rank	Executive	Company	1995 Pay ($)	% Chg Over '94	Stk Op Realizable
137	Daniel Terpack	Tektronix	499,873	43	140,040
138	James Tolonen	Novell	498,529	13	0
139	Mary Burnside	Novell	489,489	10	0
140	Richard Bentley	Marshall Industries	471,354	10	0
141	Franklyn Caine	Wang	470,625	NA	3,087,243
142	Gordon McLenithan	Dataflex	462,812	24	0
143	George DeSola	Inacom	460,771	118	84,994
144	William Larson	McAfee Associates	449,684	13	11,150,831
145	Dennis McEvoy	Sybase	449,038	63	3,934,600
146	Michael Maples	Microsoft	446,846	-9	0
147	Michael Steffan	Inacom	445,799	142	84,994
148	Jeremiah van Vuuren	Wang	445,105	30	875,858
149	Gene Lu	Advanced Logic Research (ALR)	444,479	7	506,240
150	Howard Graham	Informix	444,333	25	2,433,788

Excerpted with permission from Computer Reseller News, June 3, 1996, p. 142. Copyright © 1996, CMP Publications Inc. All rights reserved. CMP Publications Inc., 600 Community Drive, Manhasset NY 11030 USA.

Computer Reseller News: Top Executives—Stock Holdings

"As for stock holdings, the surge in technology stocks over the past year resulted in the barrier to entry on the Top 150 list more than doubling. While it only took a stock value of $3.3M to make the list a year ago, that number is now up to $7.3M."--Computer Reseller News

'95 Rank	Executive	Company	Current Val ($)	% Chg Over '94
1	Bill Gates	Microsoft	16,509,530,700	63
2	Paul Allen	Microsoft	6,405,518,340	61
3	William Hewlett	Hewlett-Packard	3,621,268,000	73
4	Steven Ballmer	Microsoft	3,504,473,388	65
5	Lawrence Ellison	Oracle	3,461,171,521	72
6	Gordon Moore	Intel	3,250,176,792	65
7	Theodore Waitt	Gateway 2000	1,376,091,531	105
8	James Clark	Netscape	1,327,977,500	NA
9	Robert Levine	Cabletron	966,036,671	98
10	Charles Wang	Computer Associates	867,260,635	173
11	Craig Benson	Cabletron	834,296,739	85
12	Michael Dell	Dell	702,118,244	62
13	Robert Galvin	Motorola	628,001,477	-20
14	John Doerr	Netscape	626,845,000	NA
15	David Dunn	Iomega	576,950,420	NA
16	James Barksdale	Netscape	547,605,000	NA
17	Michael Krasney	CDW Computer	496,471,759	50
18	Raymond Noorda	Novell	385,019,205	-31
19	Casey Cowell	U.S. Robotics	310,264,980	630
20	Richard Adams	Uunet	300,508,600	NA
21	John Morgridge	Cisco	288,683,304	38
22	Alan Ashton	Novell	232,836,917	-46
23	Andrew Grove	Intel	155,622,496	99
24	Martin Sprinzen	Forte Software	148,581,817	NA
25	Marc Andreessen	Netscape	141,500,000	NA

'95 Rank	Executive	Company	Current Val ($)	% Chg Over '94
26	Scott McNealy	Sun Microsystems	131,543,587	63
27	Peter Godfrey	Micro Warehouse	130,651,316	4
28	Christopher Galvin	Motorola	117,187,470	-40
29	John McCartney	U.S. Robotics	113,439,040	NA
30	Robert Bishop	Silicon Graphics	112,660,836	-14
31	Rodger Dowdell	American Power Conversion (APC)	112,569,205	-30
32	A.C. Markkula	Apple	99,461,879	-42
33	Jonathan Zakin	U.S. Robotics	96,309,890	NA
34	Leslie Vadasz	Intel	92,494,506	95
35	Stephen Kaufman	Arrow	90,182,549	NA
36	Christopher Oliver	Cabletron	89,459,338	NA
37	James Sha	Netscape	84,900,000	NA
38	John Cassese	Computer Horizons	76,109,590	NA
39	Craig Barrett	Intel	75,262,626	163
40	John Sidgmore	Uunet	72,959,332	NA
41	Edward McCracken	Silicon Graphics	68,514,787	-3
42	Benjamin Rosen	Compaq	68,318,019	23
43	Eckhard Pfeiffer	Compaq	62,607,673	46
44	Neil Rasmussen	American Power Conversion (APC)	62,166,623	-32
45	Robert Klatell	Arrow	57,407,973	NA
46	Conway Rulon-Miller	Netscape	56,600,000	NA
47	Richard Schell	Netscape	56,600,000	NA
48	Bernard Vergnes	Microsoft	54,434,250	58
49	John Warnock	Adobe	53.966,204	-13
50	Louis Gerstner	IBM	52,525,146	233
51	Kim Edwards	Iomega	50,727,356	NA
52	Robert Epstein	Sybase	49,727,459	NA
53	John Waddell	Arrow	49,307,477	NA
54	Robert Allen	AT&T	47,822,959	33
55	Mark Hoffman	Sybase	47,709,311	NA
56	Bert Roberts	MCI	45,545,238	NA
57	Anton Radman	Iomega	45,289,292	NA
58	Jerry Junkins	Texas Instruments	44,411,240	8
59	William Hoover	Computer Sciences	44,219,499	NA
60	Leon Staciokas	Iomega	42,906,400	NA
61	Ross Manire	U.S. Robotics	40,607,685	NA
62	Lewis Platt	Hewlett-Packard	40,237,750	122
63	Charles Geschke	Adobe	38,511,230	-16
64	Steven Raymund	Tech Data	35,303,355	-20
65	Richard Sanford	Intelligent Electronics	35,040,430	0
66	Eric Benhamou	3Com	34,527,197	85
67	Marc Butlein	Meta Group	33,787,648	NA
68	Dale Kutnick	Meta Group	33,787,616	NA
69	Gary Tooker	Motorola	33,561,350	2
70	William Tauscher	Vanstar	31,259,158	NA
71	David House	Intel	30,608,857	NA
72	Russell Artzt	Computer Associates	30,275,082	NA
73	Thomas Perkins	Tandem	28,389,015	NA
74	Gerhard Parker	Intel	28,165,785	NA
75	Philippe Kahn	Borland	27,580,093	269

'95 Rank	Executive	Company	Current Val ($)	% Chg Over '94
76	John Chambers	Cisco	27,369,944	72
77	Frank Gill	Intel	27,052,180	122
78	Phillip White	Informix	26,189,111	NA
79	Dirk Kabcenell	Oracle	26,153,759	NA
80	Jeffrey Henley	Oracle	25,465,625	NA
81	Jerry Sanders	Advanced Micro (AMD)	24,614,213	108
82	Robert Palmer	Digital Equipment	24,590,664	51
83	William Weisz	Motorola	24,423,183	NA
84	Gordon Marshall	Marshall Industries	24,194,081	-28
85	Carol Bartz	Autodesk	23,705,039	31
86	Norman Gaut	PictureTel	23,076,714	NA
87	Emanuel Landsman	American Power Conversion (APC)	22,693,125	NA
88	Ned Lautenbach	IBM	21,989,839	NA
89	John M. Thompson	IBM	21,588,804	NA
90	Safi Qureshey	AST Research	21,402,769	-63
91	Frank Marshall	Cisco	20,440,000	48
92	Tim Krauskopf	Spyglass	20,311,813	NA
93	Edward Staiano	Motorola	19,689,722	NA
94	Stephen MacDonald	Adobe	18,670,815	-8
95	J. Paul Grayson	Micrografx	17,806,890	215
96	Joseph Squarzini	Uunet	17,742,795	NA
97	Jeffrey Hilber	Uunet	16,975,539	NA
98	Bernhard Hubert	Computer Horizons	16,939,228	NA
99	Srini Nageshwar	Iomega	15,817,254	NA
100	Douglas Colbeth	Spyglass	15,799,928	NA
101	Mitchell Kertzman	Sybase	15,773,609	NA
102	Douglas Becker	Sylvan Learning Systems	15,744,683	NA
103	Christopher Hoehn-Saric	Sylvan Learning Systems	15,744,683	NA
104	Andreas Barth	Compaq	15,369,019	46
105	Raymond Lane	Oracle	15,186,048	NA
106	Michael Hackworth	Cirrus Logic	14,758,940	NA
107	John Adler	Adaptec	14,616,268	NA
108	Grant Saviers	Adaptec	14,087,939	NA
109	Edward Briscoe	Iomega	14,023,125	NA
110	Suhas Patil	Cirrus Logic	13,828,904	NA
111	Leon Machiz	Avnet	13,780,751	42
112	Jerome Meyer	Tektronix	13,671,735	-20
113	Stuart Smith	Handex	13,331,505	NA
114	David Wagman	Merisel	13,276,250	3
115	Thomas Jermoluk	Silicon Graphics	13,195,190	108
116	Michael Spindler	Apple	13,084,195	24
117	Atiq Raza	Advanced Micro (AMD)	12,962,863	NA
118	Stephen Levy	Bolt Beranek & Newman	12,425,744	NA
119	Marc Porat	General Magic	12,363,311	-53
120	Rick Inatome	Inacom	12,294,623	127
121	James Treybig	Tandem	11,679,479	NA
122	Robert North	HNC Software	11,493,791	NA
123	William Hayes	Texas Instruments	11,308,553	NA
124	Gary Stimac	Compaq	10,912,879	87
125	George Conrades	Bolt Beranek & Newman	10,750,257	NA

'95 Rank	Executive	Company	Current Val ($)	% Chg Over '94
126	ReiJane Huai	Cheyenne Software	10,582,043	NA
127	Robert Leff	Merisel	10,219,426	-7
128	Curtis Smith	Handex	10,155,544	NA
129	Sanjay Kumar	Computer Associates	10,152,781	NA
130	Gerald Poch	AmeriData	10,041,382	NA
131	Eric Herr	Autodesk	9,977,039	117
132	Ronald Fisher	Phoenix Technologies	9,820,125	NA
133	Leonard Fassler	AmeriData	9,817,506	NA
134	William Miller	Quantum	9,797,776	NA
135	Andrew Hertzfeld	General Magic	9,397,513	NA
136	James Halpin	CompUSA	9,148,569	NA
137	Bruce Nakao	Adobe	9,143,993	7
138	David Litwack	Sybase	9,063,150	NA
139	Richard Thoman	IBM	8,987,638	NA
140	Michael Emmi	Systems and Computer	8,794,705	-7
141	James Abrahamson	Oracle	8,713,564	NA
142	Edward Anderson	CompuCom	8,332,500	NA
143	James McCleary	AmeriData	8,196,966	NA
144	Daniel Brown	CompuCom	8,104,278	NA
145	Edward Machala	American Power Conversion (APC)	7,804,250	-51
146	Khoa Nguyen	PictureTel	7,796,547	NA
147	Edward Heitzeberg	Micron Technology	7,741,313	NA
148	Richard Previte	Advanced Micro (AMD)	7,618,483	NA
149	Samuel Stroum	Egghead	7,327,152	NA
150	Gerald Diamond	Southern Electronics	7,267,657	-88

Forbes: World's Billionaires

"Great fortunes are made in times of rapid social, technological and economic change by those who grasp the meaning of the changes early on. That's why the big fortunes matter. They spring up like plants after a spring rain wherever economics come to life and there is solid economic progress.

'Primarily as a reflection of Wall Street's continuing boom, together with the changes wrought by the computer revolution, the number of billion-dollar fortunes in the U.S. climbed by 20, to 149, in the past year. The U.S. is thus still home to a third of the world's great fortunes, though Asia is gaining. The value of Bill Gate's Microsoft holdings increased by $5.1B to reach $18B. Gates is typical in a way: Many of the new U.S. fortunes are built on computer and communication technologies."--Forbes

Computer Industry Almanac has selected only the billionaires that derive their wealth from or are investing heavily in the computer, electronics or telecommunications industries.

1995 Name	Country	Wealth Source	Net Worth ($B)
William H. Gates	United States	Microsoft	18.0
Paul G. Allen	United States	Microsoft	7.5
Kenneth R. Thomson	Canada	Thomson Corp., media, online services	7.4
Carlos Slim Helu & family	Mexico	Telefonos de Mexico, International Wireless, Prodigy	6.1
Walter Haefner	Switzerland	Computer Associates, software, automobiles	5.5
Lawrence J. Ellison	United States	Oracle, software	4.9

1995 Name	Country	Wealth Source	Net Worth ($B)
Lee Kun-hee & family	Korea	Samsung, electronics, memory chips	4.9
Masayoshi Son	Japan	Softbank, COMDEX, Ziff-Davis	4.6
Dhanin Chearavanont	Thailand	Diversified, TelecomAsia	4.2
Steven Anthony Ballmer	United States	Microsoft	3.7
William Redington Hewlett	United States	Hewlett-Packard	3.6
McCaw family	United States	McCaw Cellular	3.6
Yue-Che Wang & family	Taiwan	Plastics, electronics, First International Computer	3.5
Gordon Earle Moore	United States	Intel, semiconductors	3.4
Koo Cha-kyung & family	Korea	Appliances, electronics, LG Group, Zenith	2.9
Dietmar Hopp & family	Germany	SAP, software	2.7
H. Ross Perot	United States	Computer services	2.6
von Siemens family	Germany	Siemens, electronics, semiconductors, computers	2.6
Jamie Zobel de Ayala & family	Philippines	Diversified, Globe Telecom	2.6
Alejo Peralta & family	Mexico	Manufacturing, telecom	2.5
Banyong Lamsam & family	Thailand	Banking, telecom	2.5
Akio Morita & family	Japan	Sony, real estate, food	2.3
Thaksin Shinawatra & family	Thailand	Shinawatra Computer & Communications	2.1
Roberto Marinho	Brazil	Media, cellular phones	2.1
Ziff family	United States	Publishing	2.0
John Gokongwei Jr.	Philippines	Diversified, Digitel Telecom	2.0
Hasso Plattner	Germany	SAP, software	1.8
Boonchai Bencharongkul	Thailand	United Communication Industry	1.7
Klaus Tschira & family	Germany	SAP, software	1.6
Theodore W. Waitt	United States	Gateway 2000, personal computers	1.6
Robert William Galvin	United States	Motorola	1.5
Karl Diehl & family	Germany	Defense, electronics	1.5
Bernardo Garza Sada & family	Mexico	Diversified, telecom	1.5
Serge Dassault & family	France	Aerospace, electronics	1.4
Tajudin Ramli	Malaysia	Celcom, cellular phone service	1.4
Hiroshi Yamauchi	Japan	Nintendo, video games	1.4
Takemitsu Takizaki	Japan	Factory automation sensors	1.4
Hans-Werner Hector	Germany	SAP, software	1.3
David Geffen	United States	Music	1.3
Masafumi Miyamoto & family	Japan	Square Co., video game software	1.3
Hixon family	United States	Connectors	1.2
Luiz Alberto Garcia & family	Brazil	Grupo ABC Algar, telecom	1.2
Kazuo Inamori	Japan	Kyocera, electronics	1.1
Eugenio Garza Laguera & family	Mexico	Banking, beverage, telecom	1.1
March family	Spain	Diversified, cellular phones	1.1
Craig O. McCaw	United States	McCaw Cellular	1.0

The billionaires in the computer, electronics and telecommunications industries for 1994 are listed below.

1994 Name	Country	Wealth Source	Net Worth ($B)
William H. Gates III	United States	Microsoft	12.9
Dhanin Chearavanont	Thailand	Agribusiness, telecom, TelecomAsia	5.5
Paul G. Allen	United States	Microsoft	5.3
Gordon Earle Moore	United States	Intel	5.3
Walter Haefner	Switzerland	Software, Computer Associates	4.4
Lawrence J. Ellison	United States	Oracle	3.8

1994 Name	Country	Wealth Source	Net Worth ($B)
David Packard	United States	Hewlett-Packard	3.4
Koo Cha-kyung & family	Korea	Appliances, electronics, LG Group	2.9
William Redington Hewlett	United States	Hewlett-Packard	2.6
Steven Anthony Ballmer	United States	Microsoft	2.5
McCaw family	United States	McCaw Cellular	2.5
Henry Ross Perot	United States	Computer services	2.5
Alejo Peralta & family	Mexico	Industry, telecom, Grupo Iusacell	2.3
Dietmar Hopp & family	Germany	Software, SAP AG	2.1
Thaksin Shinawatra & family	Thailand	Shinawatra Computer & Telecom	2.1
von Siemens family	Germany	Electronics, heavy industry, Siemens	2.0
Yue-Che Wang & family	Taiwan	Plastics, electronics	2.0
Hasso Plattner	Germany	Software, SAP	1.9
Masayoshi Son	Japan	Software, tradeshows, Softbank Corp.	1.9
Klaus Tschira	Germany	Software, SAP	1.8
Robert Edward Turner	United States	Turner Broadcasting Systems	1.7
Boonchai Bencharongkul & family	Thailand	Telecom, United Communications Industry	1.6
Adisai Bodharamik	Thailand	Jasmine International	1.6
Chantal Grundig	Germany	Electronics, Grundig	1.6
Ziff family	United States	Publishing	1.5
Serge Dassault & family	France	Aerospace, electronics, Dassault Aviation	1.4
Hans-Werner Hector	Germany	Software, SAP	1.4
T. Ananda Krishnan	Malaysia	Telecom, diversified, Binariang	1.4
Robert William Galvin	United States	Motorola	1.4
Hixon family	United States	Connectors	1.3
Waitt family	United States	Gateway 2000	1.2
Kazuo Inamori	Japan	Electronics, Kyocera	1.2
Tajudin Ramli	Malaysia	Telecom, Technology Resources Industries	1.1
David Geffen	United States	Recording	1.0
Javier Garza Calderón & family	Mexico	Telecom	1.0
Morita family	Japan	Sony	1.0
Hiroshi Yamauchi	Japan	Nintendo	1.0

Chapter 9

International Marketplace

International Marketplace

Computer Industry Almanac: Computers in Use by Country

The countries with the most computers are shown in Figure 9.1. It is primarily the largest industrialized countries that make this list. This figure shows the number of total computers and the number of personal computers in use at year-end from 1985 to 1995 with projections for year 2000.

The U.S. is the clear leader and has over five times as many computers as Japan and nearly seven times as many computers as Germany. Even when compared to all of Europe the U.S. has nearly twice as many computers in use. At year-end 1995, 26 countries had over one million computers in use, up from 11 countries in 1991. Six more countries may surpass the million mark in 1996. The number of computers in the former Soviet Union has grown rapidly as the cold war came to an end. Currently there is 2.7 million computers in Russia compared to less than 0.3 million in 1989.

In the U.S. PCs account for over 95% of total computers. Worldwide PCs also account for over 95% of the total number of computers. Workstations is the second largest category, but only contributes about 3% of all computers.

Figure 9.1: Countries With The Most Computers (#M)										
Country	Computers In Use	1985	1988	1989	1991	1992	1993	1994	1995	2000
U.S.	Total Computers	21.5	40.8	47.6	62.0	68.2	76.5	85.8	96.2	160.5
	Total PCs	19.1	37.9	44.5	58.6	64.6	72.6	81.5	91.5	154.0
Japan	Total Computers	2.1	5.1	6.4	9.2	10.8	12.6	14.9	18.3	46.8
	Total PCs	1.8	4.7	5.9	8.7	10.2	12.0	14.2	17.4	45.0
Germany	Total Computers	1.9	4.2	5.2	7.3	8.7	10.4	12.3	14.2	29.8
	Total PCs	1.6	3.9	4.9	6.9	8.3	9.9	11.7	13.5	28.6
U.K.	Total Computers	2.1	4.3	5.2	7.2	8.4	9.6	10.9	12.6	26.0
	Total PCs	1.8	3.9	4.8	6.8	7.9	9.1	10.4	12.0	25.0
France	Total Computers	1.3	3.1	4.0	5.7	6.5	7.5	8.6	10.0	21.8
	Total PCs	1.1	2.9	3.7	5.4	6.2	7.1	8.2	9.5	21.0
Canada	Total Computers	0.9	2.0	2.5	3.7	4.3	5.2	6.2	7.2	15.3
	Total PCs	0.8	1.9	2.4	3.5	4.1	5.0	5.9	6.9	14.7
Italy	Total Computers	0.9	2.1	2.6	3.7	4.3	5.0	5.9	6.7	17.5
	Total PCs	0.8	1.9	2.4	3.5	4.1	4.8	5.6	6.4	16.8
Australia	Total Computers	0.34	0.95	1.24	2.1	2.7	3.4	4.0	4.8	10.2
	Total PCs	0.28	0.87	1.15	1.96	2.6	3.2	3.8	4.6	9.8
South Korea	Total Computers	0.13	0.28	0.43	1.0	1.4	1.9	2.6	3.5	10.6
	Total PCs	0.10	0.26	0.40	0.9	1.3	1.8	2.5	3.4	10.2
Spain	Total Computers	0.20	0.50	0.79	1.44	1.8	2.3	2.9	3.5	8.1
	Total PCs	0.17	0.46	0.73	1.35	1.7	2.2	2.7	3.3	7.8
Netherlands	Total Computers	0.32	0.76	1.02	1.65	2.0	2.4	2.8	3.3	7.1
	Total PCs	0.27	0.70	0.95	1.55	1.9	2.3	2.7	3.2	6.8
China	Total Computers	0.12	0.28	0.40	0.67	0.92	1.34	2.0	2.9	13.3
	Total PCs	0.09	0.25	0.36	0.63	0.87	1.26	1.9	2.8	12.7
Russia	Total Computers	0.10	0.23	0.34	0.65	0.93	1.37	1.9	2.7	9.2
	Total PCs	0.08	0.20	0.31	0.61	0.88	1.29	1.8	2.6	8.8
Mexico	Total Computers	0.15	0.37	0.49	0.87	1.21	1.61	2.05	2.6	6.3
	Total PCs	0.12	0.34	0.46	0.82	1.14	1.52	1.94	2.4	6.0
Brazil	Total Computers	0.10	0.24	0.31	0.62	0.91	1.27	1.76	2.4	7.8
	Total PCs	0.08	0.22	0.29	0.59	0.86	1.20	1.67	2.3	7.5

Figure 9.1: Countries With The Most Computers (#M)										
Country	Computers In Use	1985	1988	1989	1991	1992	1993	1994	1995	2000
Worldwide Total	Total Computers	38.1	79.4	97.0	136.9	159.2	186.9	218.8	257.2	556.9
	Total PCs	33.2	73.4	90.6	129.4	150.8	177.4	208.0	245.0	535.6

In Figure 9.2 the market shares of computers in use are displayed for the U.S., Japan and Europe. At year-end 1995 the U.S. accounted for 37.4% of all computers in use in the world--down from 45.3% in 1991 and 56.5% in 1985. The European countries account for another 21% and Japan uses about 7% of the installed computers. All other countries have the remaining 34.4% or 88+ million computers. In Europe, Germany accounts for 5.5%, U.K. 4.9%, France 3.9% and Italy 2.6%. Outside the U.S., Europe and Japan, Canada and Australia are the largest computer markets with 2.8% and 1.9% of the installed base of computers. The U.S. share will continue to slip by about 1.6% each year because other countries' computer acquisitions are growing faster than the U.S. and due to higher replacement rates in the U.S.

The market shares of the world's computing power are also shown in Figure 9.2. Computer Industry Almanac has estimated the computing power for each country by assigning a MIPS value for each type of computer. Even though we can argue about the MIPS rating of computers, the values assigned are consistent and provide a reasonable framework for country comparisons. The U.S. dominance is even higher in computing power (41.7%) than in computers in use since the U.S. has more of the latest and most powerful computers. Europe has 26% and Japan has 7% of the world's computing power. All remaining countries have only 25% of the world's computing power. Russia is growing fast, but has only 0.8% of the total computing power in the world (The former Soviet Union or CIS has a 1.4% share). China is also growing rapidly and has 1% share of the world's computing power.

Figure 9.2: U.S. versus Europe versus Japan										
Country	% Market Share	1985	1988	1989	1991	1992	1993	1994	1995	2000
U.S.	Total Computers	56.45	51.45	49.03	45.25	42.84	40.95	39.22	37.41	28.81
	Computing Power	59.71	56.53	53.97	50.18	47.65	45.62	43.70	41.68	33.52
	Total PCs	57.57	51.64	49.11	45.30	42.85	40.93	39.17	37.34	28.76
Japan	Total Computers	5.57	6.46	6.55	6.73	6.81	6.76	6.81	7.11	8.41
	Computing Power	5.77	6.55	6.60	6.81	6.87	6.79	6.84	7.12	8.79
	Total PCs	5.32	6.40	6.51	6.70	6.79	6.75	6.81	7.10	8.40
Europe	Total Computers	16.96	18.33	19.36	20.49	20.95	21.09	21.11	21.04	21.88
	Computing Power	22.31	23.81	24.74	25.78	26.23	26.31	26.29	26.08	27.83
	Total PCs	21.09	23.39	24.55	25.56	26.18	26.40	26.47	26.33	27.01

Figure 9.3 shows the top 15 countries in computer density. The industrialized countries in Europe and North America account for 12 of the top 15 countries. The U.S. has 365 computers in use per 1,000 people which is over 8 times higher than the worldwide average. The U.S. computers per capita increases by about 30-35 units per year for each 1,000 people. Australia and Norway are next with 264 and 259 computers per 1,000 people. The Scandinavian countries rank high due to a high percentage of service industries (including a large government sector) and advanced manufacturing industries. The U.K. also ranks high due to a larger home computer market than most other countries. Worldwide the number of computers increases by about 6-7 units per 1,000 people per year.

Figure 9.3: Computers Per Capita										
Rank	Computers/1000 People	1985	1988	1989	1991	1992	1993	1994	1995	2000
1	U.S.	90.1	166.0	191.7	245.4	266.9	296.6	329.2	364.7	580.0
2	Australia	21.5	58.4	75.3	120.5	155.0	191.9	222.7	264.3	525.7
3	Norway	28.4	61.2	77.7	120.7	148.2	180.5	218.5	259.5	515.4
4	Canada	36.4	77.4	96.2	136.6	157.5	189.0	219.2	254.8	511.9

Rank	Computers/1000 People	1985	1988	1989	1991	1992	1993	1994	1995	2000
	Figure 9.3: Computers Per Capita									
5	Denmark	25.9	58.6	76.7	127.3	153.8	184.6	217.2	252.5	510.2
6	Finland	25.4	56.2	76.0	119.3	146.2	178.8	211.0	245.5	505.0
7	Sweden	24.5	58.5	77.0	114.2	139.6	169.9	204.0	244.1	508.9
8	New Zealand	25.7	57.2	73.5	115.6	136.4	159.8	191.2	224.8	499.2
9	U.K.	36.4	74.8	90.7	125.7	144.8	164.8	187.4	216.5	441.1
10	Netherlands	22.4	51.9	69.2	109.7	131.1	156.9	184.3	214.8	450.3
11	Switzerland	24.2	53.0	70.2	109.0	126.6	149.5	174.3	201.6	443.7
12	Singapore	17.8	46.5	59.7	84.7	104.8	126.9	153.8	188.8	412.0
13	Belgium	20.1	47.0	63.2	100.2	117.3	138.3	161.2	188.6	405.2
14	Ireland	23.8	54.1	68.3	102.0	117.4	136.1	159.1	186.4	404.1
15	Germany	24.0	54.2	67.6	91.5	108.6	129.2	151.3	174.6	361.8
	Europe	14.3	31.7	40.8	60.2	71.0	83.5	97.3	113.4	248.9
	Worldwide	7.8	15.4	18.5	25.2	29.1	33.6	38.8	44.9	90.3

At year-end 1995 there were over 61,000 mainframe computers in the world--including a thousand supercomputers. The installed base of midrange computers exceeds 12 million including workstations and minicomputers. The installed base of mainframe and minicomputers may soon decrease as lower priced workstation servers and PC servers are taking over many of their functions. The number of PCs in use surpassed 245 million units worldwide during 1995. This includes all office PCs (desktop, laptop and notebook) and all home computers. The total number of computers in use worldwide surpassed 100 million units in 1989, 200M in 1994 and will exceed 300 million in 1997 and should pass 500 million by year 2000. Currently the installed base of computers is increasing by 35 million to 40 million units per year. The sales per year is higher because 40% to 45% of the unit sales are replacing older models and hence do not increase the number in use.

Computer Industry Almanac: International Statistics

How many computers are in use in the world? And how many computers are installed in various countries? Those are the questions Computer Industry Almanac answers in this table. There is only sketchy country by country data available that we are aware of, and hence we had to estimate some of the information shown below. We have used published data from all the major market research companies such as IDC, Dataquest, Computer Intelligence, Giga Information Group and the foreign market research companies such as Context, Romtec and ResearchAsia. We have also used U.N., U.S. and other countries government data. Data for Japan is based on JEIDA shipment statistics. Numerous bits and pieces of information from other sources, such as SPA's International Resource Directory and Guide, have been used in the estimates.

This year we are showing the historical data from 1980 to 1995 and projections for year 2000. The computers in use include mainframe computers, midrange computers, workstations and personal computers. A market share of the total computers have been calculated for each country. The PCs account for over 90% of all computers in all countries. The data includes estimated computing power in MIPS (millions of instructions per second) and each country's share of total worldwide MIPS. We also calculated computers per capita and computing power per capita. The MIPS per capita is indexed versus the U.S.'s 100 for each country.

Designation		2000	1995	1994	1993	1992	1991	1989	1988	1985	1980
Argentina											
Population--Est.	#M	36.2	34.3	33.9	33.5	33.1	32.7	31.9	31.5	30.7	28.2
Computer in Use	#M	2.3	0.90	0.71	0.55	0.41	0.29	0.18	0.14	0.06	0.007
Computer in Use--Share	%	0.409	0.349	0.327	0.293	0.255	0.211	0.187	0.170	0.149	0.145
Computers/1000 People	#	62.9	26.2	21.1	16.3	12.2	8.9	5.7	4.3	1.8	0.27

Designation		2000	1995	1994	1993	1992	1991	1989	1988	1985	1980
Computing Power--MIPS	#K	938,000	25,774	9,179	2,964	1,040	485	204	127	34.7	2.16
Computing Power--Share	%	0.381	0.312	0.293	0.264	0.232	0.194	0.175	0.162	0.148	0.118
MIPS/1000 People	#	25,914	752	271	88	31.4	14.9	6.4	4.0	1.13	0.08
Index versus U.S.'s 100	#	8.68	5.76	5.16	4.45	3.75	3.00	2.53	2.24	1.93	1.44
Australia											
Population--Est.	#M	19.4	18.3	18.1	17.8	17.6	17.3	16.5	16.3	15.6	14.6
Computer in Use	#M	10.2	4.8	4.0	3.4	2.7	2.1	1.2	0.95	0.34	0.039
Computer in Use--Share	%	1.83	1.88	1.84	1.83	1.71	1.52	1.28	1.20	0.88	0.76
Computers/1000 People	#	525.7	264.3	222.7	191.9	155.0	120.5	75.3	58.4	21.5	2.7
Computing Power--MIPS	#K	4,721,000	155,950	57,782	20,658	7,749	3,843	1,497	947	215	12.9
Computing Power--Share	%	1.92	1.89	1.84	1.84	1.73	1.54	1.29	1.21	0.91	0.70
MIPS/1000 People	#	243,471	8,513	3,199	1,159	440	222	91.0	58.3	13.7	0.88
Index versus U.S.'s 100	#	81.5	65.2	60.9	58.4	52.6	44.8	36.0	32.5	23.4	16.6
Austria											
Population--Est.	#M	8.11	7.99	7.96	7.92	7.88	7.67	7.59	7.58	7.55	7.55
Computer in Use	#M	2.81	1.27	1.09	0.92	0.77	0.64	0.40	0.29	0.12	0.016
Computer in Use--Share	%	0.504	0.494	0.498	0.494	0.486	0.466	0.411	0.365	0.315	0.306
Computers/1000 People	#	346.3	159.1	136.9	116.7	98.1	83.1	52.5	38.2	15.9	2.1
Computing Power--MIPS	#K	1,301,000	40,933	15,656	5,579	2,197	1,176	482	289	76.6	5.2
Computing Power--Share	%	0.528	0.495	0.500	0.497	0.489	0.471	0.414	0.370	0.327	0.280
MIPS/1000 People	#	160,377	5,123	1,967	704	279	153	63.5	38.1	10.2	0.69
Index versus U.S.'s 100	#	53.7	39.2	37.4	35.5	33.3	30.9	25.1	21.2	17.3	13.0
Belgium											
Population--Est.	#M	10.14	10.08	10.06	10.04	10.02	9.92	9.89	9.88	9.86	9.85
Computer in Use	#M	4.1	1.9	1.6	1.4	1.2	0.99	0.62	0.46	0.20	0.027
Computer in Use--Share	%	0.738	0.739	0.741	0.743	0.738	0.726	0.644	0.585	0.520	0.513
Computers/1000 People	#	405.2	188.6	161.2	138.3	117.3	100.2	63.2	47.0	20.1	2.7
Computing Power--MIPS	#K	1,903,000	61,230	23,294	8,384	3,340	1,833	755.1	462.8	126.4	8.76
Computing Power--Share	%	0.772	0.741	0.743	0.746	0.744	0.734	0.649	0.593	0.539	0.478
MIPS/1000 People	#	187,654	6,074	2,316	835	333	185	76.4	46.8	12.8	0.89
Index versus U.S.'s 100	#	62.83	46.51	44.08	42.07	39.83	37.25	30.18	26.10	21.86	16.76
Brazil											
Population--Est.	#M	169.5	160.7	158.5	156.7	154.8	151.9	150.8	150.7	139.8	122.8
Computer in Use	#M	7.8	2.4	1.8	1.3	0.91	0.62	0.31	0.24	0.10	0.014
Computer in Use--Share	%	1.40	0.942	0.806	0.680	0.571	0.456	0.322	0.303	0.269	0.262
Computers/1000 People	#	46.1	15.1	11.1	8.1	5.9	4.1	2.1	1.6	0.73	0.11
Computing Power--MIPS	#K	2,817,000	60,755	19,752	5,993	2,022	904	294	187	53.3	3.4
Computing Power--Share	%	1.14	0.735	0.630	0.534	0.450	0.362	0.253	0.239	0.227	0.187
MIPS/1000 People	#	16,617	378	125	38.3	13.1	6.0	2.0	1.2	0.38	0.028
Index versus U.S.'s 100	#	5.56	2.89	2.37	1.93	1.56	1.20	0.77	0.69	0.65	0.53
Bulgaria											
Population--Est.	#M	8.74	8.78	8.78	8.83	8.93	8.91	8.97	8.97	8.97	8.84
Computer in Use	#M	0.68	0.25	0.20	0.16	0.12	0.09	0.054	0.042	0.019	0.002
Computer in Use--Share	%	0.122	0.099	0.092	0.085	0.075	0.065	0.055	0.053	0.049	0.047
Computers/1000 People	#	77.8	29.0	23.0	17.9	13.5	9.9	6.0	4.7	2.1	0.28
Computing Power--MIPS	#K	245,000	6,399	2,276	752	272	131	51.8	34.0	9.8	0.62
Computing Power--Share	%	0.100	0.077	0.073	0.067	0.061	0.053	0.045	0.044	0.042	0.034
MIPS/1000 People	#	28,081	729	259	85.2	30.5	14.7	5.78	3.79	1.09	0.070
Index versus U.S.'s 100	#	9.40	5.58	4.94	4.29	3.64	2.97	2.28	2.11	1.86	1.32
Canada											

Designation		2000	1995	1994	1993	1992	1991	1989	1988	1985	1980
Population--Est.	#M	29.9	28.4	28.1	27.8	27.4	26.8	26.3	26.1	25.4	24.1
Computer in Use	#M	15.3	7.2	6.2	5.2	4.3	3.7	2.5	2.0	0.92	0.13
Computer in Use--Share	%	2.75	2.82	2.82	2.81	2.71	2.68	2.61	2.54	2.43	2.55
Computers/1000 People	#	511.9	254.8	219.2	189.0	157.5	136.6	96.2	77.4	36.4	5.46
Computing Power--MIPS	#K	7,081,000	233,417	88,488	31,688	12,278	6,764	3,060	2,015	590	43.4
Computing Power--Share	%	2.87	2.82	2.82	2.82	2.74	2.71	2.63	2.58	2.52	2.38
MIPS/1000 People	#	237,073	8,207	3,149	1,141	447	252	116	77.2	23.2	1.80
Index versus U.S.'s 100	#	79.4	62.8	59.9	57.5	53.5	50.8	46.0	43.0	39.6	34.0
Chile											
Population--Est.	#M	15.21	14.16	13.91	13.74	13.50	13.29	12.83	12.64	12.04	11.09
Computer in Use	#M	0.89	0.37	0.30	0.24	0.18	0.15	0.085	0.055	0.024	0.003
Computer in Use--Share	%	0.159	0.143	0.138	0.128	0.114	0.107	0.087	0.070	0.063	0.059
Computers/1000 People	#	58.3	25.9	21.8	17.4	13.4	11.1	6.6	4.4	1.98	0.27
Computing Power--MIPS	#K	320,000	9,233	3,403	1,133	407	215	83.3	45.2	12.8	0.77
Computing Power--Share	%	0.130	0.112	0.109	0.101	0.091	0.086	0.072	0.058	0.054	0.042
MIPS/1000 People	#	21,041	652	245	82.5	30.2	16.2	6.50	3.58	1.06	0.069
Index versus U.S.'s 100	#	7.04	4.99	4.66	4.15	3.60	3.27	2.57	1.99	1.81	1.30
China											
Population--Est.	#M	1,260	1,203	1,190	1,178	1,164	1,151	1,112	1,088	1,038	985
Computer in Use	#M	13.3	2.9	2.0	1.3	0.92	0.67	0.40	0.28	0.12	0.012
Computer in Use--Share	%	2.38	1.13	0.908	0.717	0.580	0.489	0.408	0.355	0.308	0.239
Computers/1000 People	#	10.5	2.41	1.67	1.14	0.79	0.58	0.36	0.26	0.11	0.013
Computing Power--MIPS	#K	5,465,000	83,385	25,498	7,251	2,367	1,123	445	264	71.8	3.58
Computing Power--Share	%	2.22	1.01	0.814	0.646	0.527	0.450	0.383	0.338	0.306	0.195
MIPS/1000 People	#	4,337	69.3	21.4	6.16	2.03	0.98	0.40	0.24	0.07	0.004
Index versus U.S.'s 100	#	1.45	0.53	0.41	0.31	0.24	0.20	0.16	0.14	0.12	0.068
Colombia											
Population--Est.	#M	39.2	36.2	35.5	34.9	34.3	33.8	32.0	31.3	29.4	26.6
Computer in Use	#M	2.0	0.69	0.52	0.39	0.29	0.21	0.12	0.084	0.033	0.004
Computer in Use--Share	%	0.356	0.267	0.237	0.206	0.183	0.157	0.119	0.106	0.088	0.072
Computers/1000 People	#	50.6	19.0	14.6	11.0	8.5	6.3	3.6	2.7	1.1	0.14
Computing Power--MIPS	#K	818,000	19,709	6,663	2,089	747	360	130	79.1	20.5	1.1
Computing Power--Share	%	0.332	0.238	0.213	0.186	0.166	0.144	0.112	0.101	0.088	0.059
MIPS/1000 People	#	20,873	544	188	59.8	21.8	10.6	4.1	2.5	0.70	0.041
Index versus U.S.'s 100	#	6.99	4.17	3.57	3.01	2.60	2.15	1.61	1.41	1.19	0.77
Czech Republic											
Population--Est.	#M	10.61	10.43	10.41	10.39	10.37	10.36	10.35	10.34	10.34	10.29
Computer in Use	#M	1.4	0.50	0.38	0.30	0.23	0.16	0.084	0.055	0.025	0.003
Computer in Use--Share	%	0.250	0.194	0.171	0.159	0.141	0.117	0.087	0.069	0.066	0.063
Computers/1000 People	#	131.1	47.7	36.0	28.6	21.7	15.5	8.1	5.3	2.4	0.32
Computing Power--MIPS	#K	502,000	12,532	4,229	1,413	510	239	81.5	43.8	13.1	0.83
Computing Power--Share	%	0.204	0.152	0.135	0.126	0.114	0.096	0.070	0.056	0.056	0.045
MIPS/1000 People	#	47,331	1,202	406	136	49.2	23.0	7.87	4.24	1.26	0.080
Index versus U.S.'s 100	#	15.8	9.2	7.7	6.9	5.9	4.6	3.1	2.4	2.2	1.5
Denmark											
Population--Est.	#M	5.26	5.20	5.19	5.18	5.17	5.13	5.13	5.13	5.10	5.12
Computer in Use	#M	2.7	1.3	1.1	0.96	0.79	0.65	0.39	0.30	0.13	0.017
Computer in Use--Share	%	0.482	0.510	0.515	0.511	0.499	0.477	0.405	0.378	0.347	0.330
Computers/1000 People	#	510.2	252.5	217.2	184.6	153.8	127.3	76.7	58.6	25.9	3.3
Computing Power--MIPS	#K	1,243,000	42,286	16,185	5,770	2,257	1,206	475	299	84.3	5.6

Designation		2000	1995	1994	1993	1992	1991	1989	1988	1985	1980
Computing Power--Share	%	0.504	0.512	0.517	0.514	0.503	0.483	0.408	0.383	0.359	0.307
MIPS/1000 People	#	236,283	8,132	3,121	1,115	437	235	92.6	58.4	16.5	1.10
Index versus U.S.'s 100	#	79.1	62.3	59.4	56.2	52.2	47.4	36.6	32.6	28.1	20.7
Finland											
Population--Est.	#M	5.15	5.09	5.07	5.05	5.03	4.99	4.96	4.95	4.91	4.78
Computer in Use	#M	2.6	1.2	1.1	0.90	0.74	0.60	0.38	0.28	0.12	0.016
Computer in Use--Share	%	0.467	0.486	0.488	0.483	0.462	0.435	0.389	0.351	0.328	0.302
Computers/1000 People	#	505.0	245.5	211.0	178.8	146.2	119.3	76.0	56.2	25.4	3.3
Computing Power--MIPS	#K	1,204,000	40,256	15,353	5,451	2,091	1,098	456	278	79.7	5.14
Computing Power--Share	%	0.489	0.487	0.490	0.485	0.466	0.440	0.392	0.356	0.340	0.281
MIPS/1000 People	#	233,847	7,909	3,031	1,079	415	220	91.9	56.1	16.2	1.08
Index versus U.S.'s 100	#	78.3	60.6	57.7	54.4	49.6	44.4	36.3	31.3	27.7	20.3
France											
Population--Est.	#M	59.4	58.1	57.9	57.6	57.3	56.6	56.0	55.8	55.0	53.9
Computer in Use	#M	21.8	10.0	8.6	7.5	6.5	5.7	4.0	3.1	1.3	0.16
Computer in Use--Share	%	3.92	3.88	3.92	4.01	4.10	4.15	4.15	3.92	3.45	3.02
Computers/1000 People	#	368.1	171.7	148.3	130.2	114.1	100.5	71.9	55.7	23.9	2.9
Computing Power--MIPS	#K	10,116,000	321,372	123,279	45,269	18,568	10,489	4,863	3,104	839	51.4
Computing Power--Share	%	4.10	3.89	3.93	4.03	4.14	4.20	4.18	3.97	3.58	2.82
MIPS/1000 People	#	170,450	5,530	2,131	786	324	185	86.9	55.6	15.2	0.95
Index versus U.S.'s 100	#	57.1	42.3	40.6	39.6	38.7	37.4	34.3	31.0	26.0	18.0
Germany											
Population--Est.	#M	82.2	81.3	81.1	80.8	80.4	79.6	77.6	77.6	77.6	78.3
Computer in Use	#M	29.8	14.2	12.3	10.4	8.7	7.3	5.2	4.2	1.9	0.22
Computer in Use--Share	%	5.34	5.52	5.61	5.58	5.49	5.32	5.41	5.30	4.89	4.30
Computers/1000 People	#	361.8	174.6	151.3	129.2	108.6	91.5	67.6	54.2	24.0	2.8
Computing Power--MIPS	#K	13,777,000	457,363	176,220	62,994	24,827	13,429	6,341	4,193	1,187	73.1
Computing Power--Share	%	5.59	5.53	5.62	5.61	5.53	5.38	5.45	5.37	5.06	4.00
MIPS/1000 People	#	167,526	5,623	2,173	780	309	169	81.7	54.0	15.3	0.93
Index versus U.S.'s 100	#	56.1	43.1	41.4	39.3	36.9	34.0	32.3	30.1	26.1	17.6
Greece											
Population--Est.	#M	10.88	10.65	10.54	10.47	10.39	10.04	10.04	10.02	9.92	9.64
Computer in Use	#M	1.36	0.51	0.44	0.37	0.30	0.25	0.16	0.12	0.049	0.003
Computer in Use--Share	%	0.244	0.200	0.201	0.196	0.189	0.184	0.169	0.156	0.128	0.063
Computers/1000 People	#	124.7	48.3	41.7	35.0	29.0	25.1	16.3	12.4	4.9	0.34
Computing Power--MIPS	#K	559,000	14,767	5,644	1,985	772	422	184	116	30.0	0.94
Computing Power--Share	%	0.227	0.179	0.180	0.177	0.172	0.169	0.158	0.149	0.128	0.051
MIPS/1000 People	#	51,415	1,387	535	190	74.3	42.1	18.4	11.6	3.02	0.098
Index versus U.S.'s 100	#	17.2	10.6	10.2	9.6	8.9	8.5	7.3	6.5	5.2	1.8
Hong Kong											
Population--Est.	#M	5.59	5.54	5.61	5.65	5.75	5.86	5.71	5.65	5.42	5.06
Computer in Use	#M	2.0	0.95	0.75	0.59	0.44	0.33	0.18	0.14	0.060	0.008
Computer in Use--Share	%	0.364	0.370	0.344	0.316	0.279	0.241	0.189	0.172	0.158	0.150
Computers/1000 People	#	363.1	171.5	134.3	104.4	77.4	56.3	32.1	24.1	11.1	1.5
Computing Power--MIPS	#K	939,000	30,615	10,815	3,564	1,264	608	221	136	38.3	2.57
Computing Power--Share	%	0.381	0.370	0.345	0.317	0.282	0.243	0.190	0.174	0.163	0.140
MIPS/1000 People	#	168,134	5,523	1,929	630	220	104	38.8	24.1	7.1	0.51
Index versus U.S.'s 100	#	56.3	42.3	36.7	31.8	26.3	20.9	15.3	13.4	12.1	9.6
Hungary											
Population--Est.	#M	10.37	10.32	10.33	10.32	10.45	10.56	10.57	10.59	10.64	10.71

Designation		2000	1995	1994	1993	1992	1991	1989	1988	1985	1980
Computer in Use	#M	1.6	0.56	0.44	0.34	0.25	0.18	0.093	0.069	0.030	0.004
Computer in Use--Share	%	0.285	0.218	0.202	0.180	0.156	0.134	0.096	0.087	0.079	0.072
Computers/1000 People	#	153.3	54.4	42.7	32.6	23.8	17.3	8.8	6.5	2.8	0.35
Computing Power--MIPS	#K	574,000	14,132	4,972	1601	563	272	89.9	55.5	15.7	0.94
Computing Power--Share	%	0.233	0.171	0.159	0.143	0.125	0.109	0.077	0.071	0.067	0.051
MIPS/1000 People	#	55,345	1,369	481	155	53.9	25.8	8.5	5.2	1.47	0.088
Index versus U.S.'s 100	#	18.5	10.5	9.2	7.8	6.4	5.2	3.4	2.9	2.5	1.7
India											
Population--Est.	#M	1,018	937	919	903	887	870	833	817	768	692
Computer in Use	#M	6.3	1.6	1.2	0.83	0.61	0.43	0.27	0.19	0.08	0.008
Computer in Use--Share	%	1.124	0.616	0.528	0.444	0.385	0.313	0.280	0.241	0.210	0.157
Computers/1000 People	#	6.15	1.69	1.26	0.92	0.69	0.49	0.33	0.23	0.104	0.012
Computing Power--MIPS	#K	2,259,000	39,797	12,970	3,928	1,377	629	267	157	42.8	2.12
Computing Power--Share	%	0.916	0.481	0.414	0.350	0.307	0.252	0.230	0.201	0.183	0.115
MIPS/1000 People	#	2,219	42.5	14.1	4.3	1.6	0.72	0.32	0.19	0.056	0.003
Index versus U.S.'s 100	#	0.743	0.325	0.269	0.219	0.185	0.146	0.127	0.107	0.095	0.058
Indonesia											
Population--Est.	#M	219.5	203.6	200.4	197.2	194.1	193.6	187.7	184.0	175.0	154.9
Computer in Use	#M	3.4	0.98	0.71	0.52	0.37	0.26	0.15	0.10	0.042	0.005
Computer in Use--Share	%	0.609	0.380	0.327	0.277	0.231	0.192	0.153	0.128	0.110	0.095
Computers/1000 People	#	15.5	4.8	3.6	2.6	1.9	1.4	0.79	0.55	0.24	0.032
Computing Power--MIPS	#K	1,224,000	24,542	8,032	2,452	826	385	146	83.1	22.4	1.24
Computing Power--Share	%	0.496	0.297	0.256	0.218	0.184	0.154	0.126	0.106	0.096	0.068
MIPS/1000 People	#	5,575	121	40.1	12.4	4.3	2.0	0.78	0.45	0.13	0.008
Index versus U.S.'s 100	#	1.87	0.92	0.76	0.63	0.51	0.40	0.31	0.25	0.22	0.15
Ireland											
Population--Est.	#M	3.63	3.55	3.54	3.53	3.52	3.49	3.55	3.53	3.59	3.40
Computer in Use	#M	1.5	0.66	0.56	0.48	0.41	0.36	0.24	0.19	0.085	0.010
Computer in Use--Share	%	0.263	0.257	0.257	0.257	0.259	0.260	0.250	0.241	0.224	0.202
Computers/1000 People	#	404.1	186.4	159.1	136.1	117.4	102.0	68.3	54.1	23.8	3.1
Computing Power--MIPS	#K	679,000	21,312	8,093	2,901	1,174	657	293	191	54.4	3.46
Computing Power--Share	%	0.276	0.258	0.258	0.258	0.261	0.263	0.252	0.244	0.232	0.188
MIPS/1000 People	#	187,116	6,003	2,286	822	333	188	82.5	54.0	15.2	1.02
Index versus U.S.'s 100	#	62.6	46.0	43.5	41.4	39.8	37.9	32.6	30.1	25.8	19.2
Israel											
Population--Est.	#M	5.51	5.14	5.04	4.92	4.80	4.56	4.37	4.30	4.13	3.74
Computer in Use	#M	1.8	0.74	0.56	0.46	0.39	0.33	0.23	0.19	0.079	0.009
Computer in Use--Share	%	0.318	0.286	0.255	0.249	0.246	0.241	0.236	0.234	0.208	0.174
Computers/1000 People	#	320.9	143.0	110.7	94.4	81.6	72.3	52.5	43.2	19.2	2.4
Computing Power--MIPS	#K	819,000	23,680	8,017	2,805	1,113	608	277	185	50.6	2.97
Computing Power--Share	%	0.332	0.286	0.256	0.250	0.248	0.243	0.238	0.237	0.216	0.162
MIPS/1000 People	#	148,627	4,607	1,590	570	232	133	63.5	43.1	12.2	0.79
Index versus U.S.'s 100	#	49.8	35.3	30.3	28.7	27.7	26.9	25.1	24.0	20.9	15.0
Italy											
Population--Est.	#M	58.9	58.3	58.1	58.0	57.9	57.8	57.6	57.5	57.1	56.5
Computer in Use	#M	17.5	6.7	5.9	5.0	4.3	3.7	2.6	2.1	0.92	0.12
Computer in Use--Share	%	3.14	2.61	2.70	2.70	2.70	2.71	2.66	2.60	2.41	2.27
Computers/1000 People	#	296.9	115.0	101.8	87.0	74.3	64.1	44.9	35.9	16.1	2.1
Computing Power--MIPS	#K	8,093,000	215,826	85,009	30,477	12,218	6,832	3,125	2,058	586	38.6
Computing Power--Share	%	3.28	2.61	2.71	2.71	2.72	2.74	2.69	2.64	2.50	2.11

Designation		2000	1995	1994	1993	1992	1991	1989	1988	1985	1980
MIPS/1000 People	#	137,472	3,705	1,462	525	211	118	54.2	35.8	10.3	0.68
Index versus U.S.'s 100	#	46.0	28.4	27.8	26.5	25.2	23.8	21.4	20.0	17.5	12.9
Japan											
Population--Est.	#M	127.6	125.5	125.1	124.7	124.3	124.0	123.2	122.6	120.7	116.8
Computer in Use	#M	46.8	18.3	14.9	12.6	10.8	9.2	6.4	5.1	2.1	0.24
Computer in Use--Share	%	8.41	7.11	6.81	6.76	6.81	6.73	6.55	6.46	5.57	4.69
Computers/1000 People	#	367.0	145.6	119.2	101.3	87.2	74.3	51.6	41.8	17.6	2.1
Computing Power--MIPS	#K	21,678,000	588,618	214,187	76,319	30,816	16,997	7,682	5,118	1,352	88.7
Computing Power--Share	%	8.79	7.12	6.84	6.79	6.87	6.81	6.60	6.55	5.77	4.86
MIPS/1000 People	#	169,954	4,690	1,712	612	248	137	62.3	41.7	11.2	0.76
Index versus U.S.'s 100	#	56.9	35.9	32.6	30.8	29.6	27.6	24.6	23.3	19.1	14.3
Malaysia											
Population--Est.	#M	22.0	19.7	19.3	18.9	18.4	18.0	16.7	16.4	15.5	13.8
Computer in Use	#M	2.5	0.81	0.62	0.46	0.33	0.23	0.10	0.07	0.027	0.003
Computer in Use--Share	%	0.449	0.315	0.282	0.247	0.207	0.171	0.101	0.092	0.071	0.054
Computers/1000 People	#	113.9	41.1	32.1	24.4	17.9	13.1	5.9	4.5	1.7	0.20
Computing Power--MIPS	#K	1,030,000	23,245	7,907	2,483	838	389	106	65.1	16.0	0.81
Computing Power--Share	%	0.418	0.281	0.252	0.221	0.187	0.156	0.091	0.083	0.068	0.044
MIPS/1000 People	#	46,929	1,179	411	132	45.4	21.6	6.3	4.0	1.03	0.06
Index versus U.S.'s 100	#	15.7	9.03	7.82	6.64	5.43	4.36	2.49	2.21	1.76	1.11
Mexico											
Population--Est.	#M	102.9	94.0	92.1	90.4	90.2	90.0	86.4	83.5	79.7	68.7
Computer in Use	#M	6.3	2.6	2.0	1.6	1.2	0.87	0.49	0.37	0.15	0.020
Computer in Use--Share	%	1.12	1.00	0.936	0.859	0.758	0.635	0.505	0.461	0.394	0.388
Computers/1000 People	#	60.7	27.4	22.2	17.7	13.4	9.7	5.7	4.4	1.9	0.29
Computing Power--MIPS	#K	2,575,000	73,811	26,223	8,647	3,067	1,440	528	325	89.1	5.8
Computing Power--Share	%	1.04	0.893	0.837	0.770	0.683	0.577	0.454	0.416	0.380	0.317
MIPS/1000 People	#	25,024	785	285	95.6	34.0	16.0	6.1	3.9	1.1	0.08
Index versus U.S.'s 100	#	8.38	6.01	5.42	4.82	4.06	3.22	2.42	2.17	1.91	1.59
Netherlands											
Population--Est.	#M	15.80	15.45	15.37	15.28	15.19	15.02	14.79	14.72	14.48	14.14
Computer in Use	#M	7.1	3.3	2.8	2.4	2.0	1.6	1.0	0.76	0.32	0.037
Computer in Use--Share	%	1.28	1.29	1.29	1.28	1.25	1.20	1.05	0.96	0.85	0.73
Computers/1000 People	#	450.3	214.8	184.3	156.9	131.1	109.7	69.2	51.9	22.4	2.6
Computing Power--MIPS	#K	3,295,000	106,898	40,689	14,473	5,658	3,039	1,237	762	207	12.8
Computing Power--Share	%	1.34	1.29	1.30	1.29	1.26	1.22	1.06	0.98	0.88	0.70
MIPS/1000 People	#	208,544	6,919	2,647	947	372	202	83.6	51.8	14.3	0.91
Index versus U.S.'s 100	#	69.8	53.0	50.4	47.7	44.5	40.8	33.1	28.9	24.4	17.1
New Zealand											
Population--Est.	#M	3.48	3.41	3.39	3.37	3.34	3.31	3.37	3.34	3.27	3.11
Computer in Use	#M	1.7	0.77	0.65	0.54	0.46	0.38	0.25	0.19	0.084	0.010
Computer in Use--Share	%	0.312	0.298	0.296	0.288	0.286	0.279	0.255	0.241	0.221	0.202
Computers/1000 People	#	499.2	224.8	191.2	159.8	136.4	115.6	73.5	57.2	25.7	3.4
Computing Power--MIPS	#K	804,000	24,695	9,303	3,252	1,294	706	299	191	53.6	3.46
Computing Power--Share	%	0.326	0.299	0.297	0.290	0.288	0.283	0.257	0.244	0.229	0.188
MIPS/1000 People	#	231,173	7,242	2,747	965	387	213	88.9	57.1	16.4	1.11
Index versus U.S.'s 100	#	77.4	55.5	52.3	48.6	46.3	43.0	35.1	31.8	28.0	20.9
Norway											
Population--Est.	#M	4.39	4.33	4.31	4.30	4.29	4.27	4.20	4.19	4.15	4.09
Computer in Use	#M	2.3	1.1	0.94	0.78	0.64	0.52	0.33	0.26	0.12	0.016

Designation		2000	1995	1994	1993	1992	1991	1989	1988	1985	1980
Computer in Use--Share	%	0.406	0.437	0.431	0.415	0.399	0.376	0.336	0.323	0.309	0.302
Computers/1000 People	#	515.4	259.5	218.5	180.5	148.2	120.7	77.7	61.2	28.4	3.8
Computing Power--MIPS	#K	1,048,000	36,197	13,538	4,686	1,806	951	394	256	75.1	5.14
Computing Power--Share	%	0.425	0.438	0.432	0.417	0.402	0.381	0.339	0.328	0.320	0.281
MIPS/1000 People	#	238,668	8,359	3,139	1,090	421	223	93.9	61.1	18.1	1.26
Index versus U.S.'s 100	#	79.9	64.0	59.8	54.9	50.3	44.9	37.1	34.0	30.8	23.7

Peru

Designation		2000	1995	1994	1993	1992	1991	1989	1988	1985	1980
Population--Est.	#M	26.26	24.09	23.63	23.21	22.80	22.36	21.45	21.27	19.70	17.30
Computer in Use	#M	1.16	0.43	0.35	0.27	0.20	0.16	0.10	0.076	0.031	0.004
Computer in Use--Share	%	0.208	0.169	0.158	0.144	0.128	0.118	0.104	0.095	0.081	0.072
Computers/1000 People	#	44.2	18.0	14.6	11.6	8.9	7.2	4.7	3.6	1.6	0.22
Computing Power--MIPS	#K	479,000	12,494	4,450	1,464	527	275	111	69.5	18.3	1.08
Computing Power--Share	%	0.194	0.151	0.142	0.130	0.117	0.110	0.096	0.089	0.078	0.059
MIPS/1000 People	#	18,240	519	188	63.1	23.1	12.3	5.19	3.27	0.928	0.062
Index versus U.S.'s 100	#	6.11	3.97	3.59	3.18	2.76	2.48	2.05	1.82	1.58	1.17

Philippines

Designation		2000	1995	1994	1993	1992	1991	1989	1988	1985	1980
Population--Est.	#M	81.6	73.3	69.8	68.5	67.2	65.8	64.9	63.2	56.8	51.1
Computer in Use	#M	1.7	0.66	0.53	0.41	0.33	0.26	0.16	0.12	0.042	0.005
Computer in Use--Share	%	0.309	0.257	0.242	0.222	0.206	0.188	0.165	0.149	0.112	0.095
Computers/1000 People	#	21.11	9.01	7.59	6.06	4.88	3.91	2.46	1.87	0.75	0.10
Computing Power--MIPS	#K	621,000	16,582	5,950	1,964	735	377	157	96.9	22.8	1.24
Computing Power--Share	%	0.252	0.201	0.190	0.175	0.164	0.151	0.135	0.124	0.097	0.068
MIPS/1000 People	#	7,614	226	85.3	28.7	10.9	5.74	2.42	1.53	0.40	0.024
Index versus U.S.'s 100	#	2.55	1.73	1.62	1.45	1.31	1.16	0.96	0.85	0.68	0.46

Poland

Designation		2000	1995	1994	1993	1992	1991	1989	1988	1985	1980
Population--Est.	#M	39.5	38.8	38.7	38.5	38.4	37.8	38.2	38.0	37.3	35.6
Computer in Use	#M	3.8	1.2	0.97	0.76	0.59	0.44	0.24	0.16	0.055	0.006
Computer in Use--Share	%	0.676	0.478	0.445	0.408	0.370	0.323	0.250	0.203	0.145	0.122
Computers/1000 People	#	95.2	31.7	25.1	19.8	15.4	11.7	6.4	4.2	1.48	0.18
Computing Power--MIPS	#K	1,359,000	30,930	10,963	3,635	1,335	657	235	130	28.7	1.6
Computing Power--Share	%	0.551	0.374	0.350	0.324	0.297	0.263	0.202	0.166	0.123	0.087
MIPS/1000 People	#	34,387	797	283	94.4	34.8	17.4	6.15	3.42	0.77	0.045
Index versus U.S.'s 100	#	11.51	6.11	5.40	4.75	4.16	3.50	2.43	1.90	1.31	0.84

Portugal

Designation		2000	1995	1994	1993	1992	1991	1989	1988	1985	1980
Population--Est.	#M	10.74	10.56	10.53	10.49	10.45	10.39	10.46	10.39	10.05	9.78
Computer in Use	#M	1.7	0.74	0.62	0.51	0.41	0.33	0.20	0.14	0.06	0.007
Computer in Use--Share	%	0.309	0.289	0.282	0.272	0.260	0.243	0.205	0.179	0.154	0.144
Computers/1000 People	#	160.1	70.3	58.6	48.5	39.7	32.0	19.1	13.7	5.9	0.8
Computing Power--MIPS	#K	708,000	21,283	7,907	2,740	1,054	551	215	126	34.9	2.2
Computing Power--Share	%	0.287	0.257	0.252	0.244	0.235	0.221	0.184	0.162	0.149	0.118
MIPS/1000 People	#	65,939	2,015	751	261	101	53.1	20.5	12.1	3.5	0.22
Index versus U.S.'s 100	#	22.1	15.4	14.3	13.2	12.1	10.7	8.1	6.8	5.9	4.2

Romania

Designation		2000	1995	1994	1993	1992	1991	1989	1988	1985	1980
Population--Est.	#M	23.4	23.2	23.2	23.2	23.3	23.4	23.2	23.0	22.7	22.2
Computer in Use	#M	1.05	0.39	0.31	0.24	0.19	0.15	0.090	0.067	0.033	0.004
Computer in Use--Share	%	0.188	0.150	0.141	0.131	0.121	0.112	0.092	0.084	0.081	0.073
Computers/1000 People	#	44.7	16.7	13.3	10.5	8.3	6.5	3.9	2.9	1.4	0.17
Computing Power--MIPS	#K	378,000	9,732	3,475	1,164	437	228	86.8	53.7	16.0	0.94
Computing Power--Share	%	0.153	0.118	0.111	0.104	0.097	0.091	0.075	0.069	0.068	0.052
MIPS/1000 People	#	16,148	420	150	50.2	18.8	9.7	3.7	2.3	0.70	0.04

Designation		2000	1995	1994	1993	1992	1991	1989	1988	1985	1980
Index versus U.S.'s 100	#	5.41	3.21	2.85	2.53	2.25	1.96	1.48	1.30	1.20	0.80
Russia											
Population--Est.	#M	151.5	149.9	149.6	149.3	149.0	148.7	146.7	145.9	143.3	139.1
Computer in Use	#M	9.2	2.7	1.9	1.4	0.93	0.65	0.34	0.23	0.10	0.014
Computer in Use--Share	%	1.65	1.05	0.883	0.731	0.586	0.478	0.346	0.284	0.270	0.265
Computers/1000 People	#	60.6	18.0	12.9	9.1	6.3	4.4	2.3	1.5	0.72	0.099
Computing Power--MIPS	#K	3,313,000	67,655	21,716	6,471	2,095	959	330	185	55.2	3.58
Computing Power--Share	%	1.34	0.819	0.693	0.576	0.467	0.384	0.284	0.236	0.236	0.195
MIPS/1000 People	#	21,876	451	145	43.3	14.1	6.45	2.25	1.27	0.386	0.026
Index versus U.S.'s 100	#	7.32	3.46	2.76	2.18	1.68	1.30	0.89	0.71	0.66	0.48
Saudi Arabia											
Population--Est.	#M	22.3	18.7	18.1	17.6	17.1	17.9	16.1	15.5	11.2	10.0
Computer in Use	#M	1.5	0.65	0.54	0.44	0.36	0.29	0.17	0.12	0.04	0.004
Computer in Use--Share	%	0.271	0.252	0.246	0.235	0.223	0.210	0.172	0.151	0.092	0.072
Computers/1000 People	#	67.9	34.6	29.7	24.9	20.8	16.1	10.4	7.8	3.1	0.38
Computing Power--MIPS	#K	622,000	18,566	6,894	2,369	903	477	180	107	20.8	1.08
Computing Power--Share	%	0.252	0.225	0.220	0.211	0.201	0.191	0.155	0.137	0.089	0.059
MIPS/1000 People	#	27,971	991	380	134	52.8	26.7	11.2	6.91	1.86	0.109
Index versus U.S.'s 100	#	9.36	7.59	7.24	6.77	6.31	5.38	4.41	3.85	3.18	2.05
Singapore											
Population--Est.	#M	3.03	2.89	2.86	2.83	2.80	2.76	2.67	2.65	2.56	2.41
Computer in Use	#M	1.25	0.55	0.44	0.36	0.29	0.23	0.16	0.12	0.046	0.004
Computer in Use--Share	%	0.224	0.212	0.201	0.192	0.184	0.171	0.164	0.155	0.120	0.075
Computers/1000 People	#	412.0	188.8	153.8	126.9	104.8	84.7	59.7	46.5	17.8	1.6
Computing Power--MIPS	#K	578,000	17,591	6,323	2,168	834	431	193	123	29.1	1.29
Computing Power--Share	%	0.235	0.213	0.202	0.193	0.186	0.173	0.166	0.158	0.124	0.070
MIPS/1000 People	#	190,782	6,081	2,210	766	298	156	72.2	46.4	11.4	0.53
Index versus U.S.'s 100	#	63.9	46.6	42.1	38.6	35.6	31.5	28.5	25.9	19.4	10.1
Slovakia											
Population--Est.	#M	5.59	5.43	5.40	5.38	5.35	5.32	5.24	5.21	5.12	4.97
Computer in Use	#M	0.63	0.24	0.19	0.15	0.11	0.081	0.038	0.025	0.011	0.001
Computer in Use--Share	%	0.113	0.093	0.086	0.078	0.069	0.059	0.039	0.032	0.029	0.025
Computers/1000 People	#	112.2	43.9	34.8	27.2	20.6	15.2	7.3	4.8	2.2	0.26
Computing Power--MIPS	#K	227,000	5,999	2,121	696	250	120	37.0	20.1	5.8	0.32
Computing Power--Share	%	0.092	0.073	0.068	0.062	0.056	0.048	0.032	0.026	0.025	0.018
MIPS/1000 People	#	40,528	1,104	393	130	46.7	22.6	7.1	3.9	1.14	0.07
Index versus U.S.'s 100	#	13.6	8.46	7.47	6.53	5.59	4.55	2.79	2.15	1.94	1.23
South Africa											
Population--Est.	#M	51.3	45.1	43.9	42.8	41.7	40.6	38.5	35.1	32.5	30.3
Computer in Use	#M	2.35	0.90	0.72	0.56	0.44	0.33	0.19	0.14	0.035	0.004
Computer in Use--Share	%	0.422	0.351	0.330	0.301	0.275	0.239	0.199	0.170	0.091	0.072
Computers/1000 People	#	45.8	20.0	16.5	13.2	10.5	8.1	5.0	3.9	1.07	0.12
Computing Power--MIPS	#K	968,000	25,925	9,274	3,050	1,122	548	216	127	21.3	1.08
Computing Power--Share	%	0.393	0.314	0.296	0.272	0.250	0.220	0.186	0.162	0.091	0.059
MIPS/1000 People	#	18,862	575	211	71	27	14	5.6	3.6	0.66	0.04
Index versus U.S.'s 100	#	6.32	4.40	4.02	3.59	3.21	2.72	2.22	2.01	1.12	0.67
South Korea											
Population--Est.	#M	47.9	45.6	45.1	44.6	44.1	43.1	43.4	42.8	42.6	38.1
Computer in Use	#M	10.6	3.5	2.6	1.9	1.4	1.0	0.43	0.28	0.13	0.01
Computer in Use--Share	%	1.91	1.38	1.20	1.01	0.87	0.73	0.44	0.35	0.33	0.19

Designation		2000	1995	1994	1993	1992	1991	1989	1988	1985	1980
Computers/1000 People	#	222.1	77.9	58.1	42.3	31.6	23.3	9.9	6.5	2.9	0.26
Computing Power--MIPS	#K	4,925,000	114,453	37,713	11,430	3,983	1,868	522	279	83.5	3.27
Computing Power--Share	%	2.00	1.38	1.20	1.02	0.89	0.75	0.45	0.36	0.36	0.18
MIPS/1000 People	#	102,907	2,513	837	256	90.3	43.3	12.0	6.51	1.96	0.086
Index versus U.S.'s 100	#	34.5	19.2	15.9	12.9	10.8	8.7	4.8	3.6	3.3	1.6
Spain											
Population--Est.	#M	40.0	39.4	39.3	39.2	39.2	39.4	39.4	39.2	38.8	37.5
Computer in Use	#M	8.1	3.5	2.9	2.3	1.8	1.4	0.79	0.50	0.20	0.019
Computer in Use--Share	%	1.45	1.35	1.30	1.24	1.16	1.05	0.81	0.63	0.52	0.36
Computers/1000 People	#	201.7	88.0	72.6	59.1	47.2	36.4	20.0	12.8	5.1	0.50
Computing Power--MIPS	#K	3,733,000	111,634	40,992	13,995	5,251	2,647	950	501	126	6.4
Computing Power--Share	%	1.51	1.35	1.31	1.25	1.17	1.06	0.82	0.64	0.54	0.35
MIPS/1000 People	#	93,400	2,833	1,042	357	134	67.2	24.1	12.8	3.26	0.17
Index versus U.S.'s 100	#	31.3	21.7	19.8	18.0	16.0	13.5	9.5	7.1	5.5	3.2
Sweden											
Population--Est.	#M	8.99	8.82	8.77	8.73	8.69	8.56	8.40	8.39	8.35	8.31
Computer in Use	#M	4.6	2.2	1.8	1.5	1.2	0.98	0.65	0.49	0.20	0.021
Computer in Use--Share	%	0.822	0.837	0.818	0.794	0.762	0.714	0.666	0.619	0.536	0.406
Computers/1000 People	#	508.9	244.1	204.0	169.9	139.6	114.2	77.0	58.5	24.5	2.5
Computing Power--MIPS	#K	2,120,000	69,349	25,715	8,958	3,446	1,804	781	490	130	6.9
Computing Power--Share	%	0.860	0.839	0.821	0.798	0.768	0.723	0.671	0.627	0.555	0.378
MIPS/1000 People	#	235,667	7,861	2,931	1,026	397	211	93.0	58.4	15.6	0.83
Index versus U.S.'s 100	#	78.90	60.19	55.79	51.69	47.40	42.46	36.76	32.53	26.59	15.67
Switzerland											
Population--Est.	#M	7.27	7.09	7.04	6.99	6.94	6.78	6.60	6.59	6.46	6.39
Computer in Use	#M	3.2	1.4	1.2	1.0	0.88	0.74	0.46	0.35	0.16	0.016
Computer in Use--Share	%	0.579	0.555	0.561	0.559	0.552	0.539	0.477	0.440	0.410	0.301
Computers/1000 People	#	443.7	201.6	174.3	149.5	126.6	109.0	70.2	53.0	24.2	2.4
Computing Power--MIPS	#K	1,493,000	46,007	17,622	6,312	2,498	1,363	560	348	99.6	5.14
Computing Power--Share	%	0.606	0.557	0.562	0.562	0.556	0.546	0.481	0.446	0.425	0.280
MIPS/1000 People	#	205,469	6,494	2,504	903	360	201	84.8	52.9	15.4	0.80
Index versus U.S.'s 100	#	68.8	49.7	47.7	45.5	43.0	40.5	33.5	29.5	26.3	15.2
Taiwan											
Population--Est.	#M	22.4	21.5	21.3	21.1	20.9	20.7	20.2	20.0	19.3	17.9
Computer in Use	#M	5.2	2.1	1.7	1.4	1.1	0.89	0.51	0.35	0.14	0.015
Computer in Use--Share	%	0.935	0.819	0.777	0.737	0.694	0.647	0.522	0.440	0.378	0.289
Computers/1000 People	#	232.1	97.9	79.9	65.3	52.9	42.9	25.0	17.5	7.4	0.8
Computing Power--MIPS	#K	2,414,000	67,925	24,483	8,348	3,162	1,650	613	350	96.0	4.86
Computing Power--Share	%	0.979	0.822	0.781	0.743	0.704	0.661	0.527	0.448	0.410	0.265
MIPS/1000 People	#	107,550	3,159	1,151	396	151	79.8	30.3	17.5	5.0	0.27
Index versus U.S.'s 100	#	36.0	24.2	21.9	19.9	18.1	16.1	12.0	9.7	8.5	5.1
Thailand											
Population--Est.	#M	63.6	60.3	59.4	58.7	58.0	56.8	54.2	54.6	51.6	47.0
Computer in Use	#M	3.3	1.1	0.79	0.58	0.43	0.30	0.15	0.10	0.04	0.004
Computer in Use--Share	%	0.590	0.413	0.361	0.313	0.268	0.219	0.159	0.128	0.112	0.072
Computers/1000 People	#	51.7	17.6	13.3	10.0	7.4	5.3	2.8	1.9	0.82	0.08
Computing Power--MIPS	#K	1,355,000	30,473	10,131	3,165	1,094	503	173	94.9	26.0	1.08
Computing Power--Share	%	0.550	0.369	0.323	0.282	0.244	0.202	0.149	0.122	0.111	0.059
MIPS/1000 People	#	21,306	506	170	53.9	18.9	8.9	3.2	1.7	0.51	0.023
Index versus U.S.'s 100	#	7.13	3.87	3.25	2.72	2.25	1.79	1.26	0.97	0.86	0.43

Designation		2000	1995	1994	1993	1992	1991	1989	1988	1985	1980
Turkey											
Population--Est.	#M	69.6	63.4	62.1	60.9	59.7	58.6	55.4	54.2	50.7	45.1
Computer in Use	#M	1.9	0.92	0.79	0.68	0.52	0.38	0.21	0.12	0.04	0.004
Computer in Use--Share	%	0.343	0.357	0.363	0.364	0.325	0.278	0.216	0.156	0.112	0.072
Computers/1000 People	#	27.4	14.5	12.8	11.2	8.7	6.5	3.8	2.3	0.84	0.08
Computing Power--MIPS	#K	787,000	26,380	10,199	3,683	1,327	638	235	116	26.0	1.08
Computing Power--Share	%	0.319	0.319	0.325	0.328	0.296	0.256	0.202	0.149	0.111	0.059
MIPS/1000 People	#	11311	416	164	60.5	22.2	10.9	4.2	2.1	0.51	0.02
Index versus U.S.'s 100	#	3.79	3.19	3.13	3.05	2.66	2.20	1.68	1.19	0.88	0.45
U.K.											
Population--Est.	#M	59.0	58.3	58.1	58.0	57.8	57.5	57.0	56.9	56.4	56.3
Computer in Use	#M	26.0	12.6	10.9	9.6	8.4	7.2	5.2	4.3	2.1	0.29
Computer in Use--Share	%	4.67	4.91	4.98	5.11	5.26	5.28	5.33	5.36	5.40	5.67
Computers/1000 People	#	441.1	216.5	187.4	164.8	144.8	125.7	90.7	74.8	36.4	5.2
Computing Power--MIPS	#K	12,043,000	406,620	156,556	57,702	23,774	13,331	6,249	4,247	1,253	96.4
Computing Power--Share	%	4.89	4.92	5.00	5.14	5.30	5.34	5.37	5.44	5.34	5.28
MIPS/1000 People	#	204,294	6,975	2,693	995	411	232	110	74.6	22.2	1.7
Index versus U.S.'s 100	#	68.40	53.40	51.26	50.14	49.15	46.72	43.32	41.56	37.85	32.27
Ukraine											
Population--Est.	#M	51.9	51.9	51.9	51.8	51.8	51.7	51.4	51.3	50.8	50.0
Computer in Use	#M	2.4	0.55	0.41	0.30	0.20	0.14	0.08	0.07	0.03	0.004
Computer in Use--Share	%	0.422	0.212	0.187	0.160	0.128	0.102	0.084	0.084	0.085	0.072
Computers/1000 People	#	45.3	10.5	7.9	5.8	3.9	2.7	1.6	1.3	0.64	0.075
Computing Power--MIPS	#K	850,000	13,732	4,613	1,423	461	207	79.4	53.7	17.0	0.94
Computing Power--Share	%	0.345	0.166	0.147	0.127	0.103	0.083	0.068	0.069	0.072	0.051
MIPS/1000 People	#	16,359	265	89.0	27.5	8.9	4.0	1.5	1.05	0.33	0.019
Index versus U.S.'s 100	#	5.48	2.03	1.69	1.38	1.06	0.81	0.61	0.58	0.57	0.36
U.S.											
Population--Est.	#M	276.6	263.8	260.7	258.1	255.5	252.5	248.2	246.0	238.6	227.7
Computer in Use	#M	160.5	96.2	85.8	76.5	68.2	62.0	47.6	40.8	21.5	3.3
Computer in Use--Share	%	28.8	37.4	39.2	41.0	42.8	45.3	49.0	51.5	56.4	63.8
Computers/1000 People	#	580.0	364.7	329.2	296.6	266.9	245.4	191.7	166.0	90.1	14.4
Computing Power--MIPS	#K	82,619,000	3,445,401	1,369,420	512,373	213,869	125,251	62,797	44,150	13,999	1,208
Computing Power--Share	%	33.5	41.7	43.7	45.6	47.6	50.2	54.0	56.5	59.7	66.2
MIPS/1000 People	#	298,673	13,060	5,253	1,985	837	496	253	179	58.7	5.31
Index versus U.S.'s 100	#	100	100	100	100	100	100	100	100	100	100
Venezuela											
Population--Est.	#M	23.2	21.0	20.5	20.1	20.1	20.2	19.3	18.8	17.3	14.5
Computer in Use	#M	1.43	0.61	0.49	0.40	0.32	0.25	0.15	0.11	0.042	0.004
Computer in Use--Share	%	0.257	0.236	0.225	0.214	0.201	0.184	0.152	0.135	0.110	0.072
Computers/1000 People	#	61.6	28.9	24.0	19.9	16.0	12.5	7.7	5.7	2.4	0.26
Computing Power--MIPS	#K	590,000	17,435	6,323	2,164	821	422	166	100	25.7	1.08
Computing Power--Share	%	0.239	0.211	0.202	0.193	0.183	0.169	0.142	0.128	0.109	0.059
MIPS/1000 People	#	25,415	830	308	108	40.9	20.9	8.6	5.3	1.5	0.07
Index versus U.S.'s 100	#	8.51	6.36	5.86	5.42	4.89	4.22	3.40	2.97	2.52	1.41
Europe											
Population--Est.	#M	489.6	477.1	474.6	472.0	469.8	466.0	460.9	458.4	450.7	437.6
Computer in Use	#M	121.9	54.1	46.2	39.4	33.4	28.1	18.8	14.5	6.5	0.82
Computer in Use--Share	%	21.88	21.04	21.11	21.09	20.95	20.49	19.36	18.33	16.96	15.87
Computers/1000 People	#	248.9	113.4	97.3	83.5	71.0	60.2	40.8	31.7	14.3	1.87

Designation		2000	1995	1994	1993	1992	1991	1989	1988	1985	1980
Computing Power--MIPS	#K	68,599,000	2,155,848	823,782	295,547	117,724	64,348	28,780	18,599	5,231	343
Computing Power--Share	%	27.83	26.08	26.29	26.31	26.23	25.78	24.74	23.81	22.31	18.75
MIPS/1000 People	#	140,111	4,518	1,736	626	251	138	62.4	40.6	11.6	0.78
Index versus U.S.'s 100	#	46.9	34.6	33.0	31.5	29.9	27.8	24.7	22.6	19.8	14.8
Other Countries											
Population--Est.	#M	1,717	1,523	1,481	1,446	1,412	1,412	1,344	1,310	1,202	1,038
Computer in Use	#M	85.9	34.4	28.5	23.6	19.5	16.2	10.6	8.4	3.5	0.26
Computer in Use--Share	%	15.42	13.39	13.02	12.63	12.23	11.82	10.97	10.53	9.29	5.13
Computers/1000 People	#	50.0	22.6	19.2	16.3	13.8	11.5	7.9	6.4	2.9	0.26
Computing Power--MIPS	#K	26,297,000	880,524	308,036	100,969	36,445	18,052	7,394	4,267	1,262	89.2
Computing Power--Share	%	10.67	10.65	9.83	8.99	8.12	7.23	6.35	5.46	5.38	4.881
MIPS/1000 People	#	15,320	578	208	69.8	25.8	12.8	5.5	3.3	1.05	0.086
Index versus U.S.'s 100	#	5.13	4.43	3.96	3.52	3.08	2.58	2.17	1.82	1.79	1.62
Worldwide											
Population--Est.	#M	6,170	5,734	5,638	5,555	5,472	5,423	5,239	5,143	4,865	4,457
Computer in Use	#M	556.9	257.2	218.8	186.9	159.2	136.9	97.0	79.4	38.1	5.16
Computer in Use--Share	%	100	100	100	100	100	100	100	100	100	100
Computers/1000 People	#	90.3	44.9	38.8	33.6	29.1	25.2	18.5	15.4	7.8	1.16
Computing Power--MIPS	#K	246,509,000	8,265,419	3,133,533	1,123,206	448,875	249,590	116,349	78,099	23,446	1,835
Computing Power--Share	%	100	100	100	100	100	100	100	100	100	100
MIPS/1000 People	#	39,954	1,441	556	202	82.0	46.0	22.2	15.2	4.8	0.41
Index versus U.S.'s 100	#	13.38	11.04	10.58	10.19	9.80	9.28	8.78	8.46	8.21	7.72

By year-end 1995 there were 257M computers in use worldwide. In the next five years this figure will double.

Computer Industry Almanac: Further Information

Information on the international computer markets is hard to find and is often expensive. We have found one excellent source, which is published by the Software Publishers Association and is called "International Resource Directory and Guide". It is prepared by GreenTree Associates and contains a wealth of information on just about every significant country in the world.

Another useful publication is "Marketscan International", which provides market statistics and research data about computer markets around the world. Both publications are listed in the publications directory in Chapter 12 of the Computer Industry Almanac.

Computerworld: Global 100

"In the premier issue of The Global 100, Computerworld's objective was to present a list--not a ranking--of 100 outstanding users of information technology from around the world. Besides naming outstanding companies, Computerworld wanted the list to reflect leading information technology users in diverse industries and countries from all regions of the globe. The result is an eclectic combination of organizations from 31 countries: Some are globally integrated corporations, some are international or national leaders and some are government agencies. All have passed muster based on a combination of qualitative and quantitative analysis.

From the 500-plus nominations they received from 40 countries in January, Computerworld researchers gathered financial and IS data about each company from public sources, from the nominated companies and from IDG publications around the world.

The final Global 100 listing was selected by Computerworld's Special Projects Team based on research and analysis of available data on organization size, industry position, geographic location, country leadership in IS and the use of information technology."--Computerworld

Company	Industry	Country	Revenue ($M)	Profit ($M)	# IS Employees	IS Spending ($M)
ABB Asea Brown Boveri Ltd.	Industrial Equipment	Switzerland	28,000	2,200	5,000	700
AGFA Gevaert NV	Appliances & Electronics	Belgium	7,000	5	200	30
AMR Corp.	Transportation	U.S.	15,800	-110	> 5000	250-499
Aerospatiale	Transportation	France	9,500	-25	500-999	250-499
Amadeus	Transportation	France	130	4	500-999	50-99
Arab National Bank	Banking	Saudi Arabia	507	108	138	26
Arcelik AS	Appliances & Electronics	Turkey	1,270	112	245	90
Australia & New Zealand Banking Grp	Banking	Australia	5,179	185	100-249	100-249*
BMW	Automotive	Germany	16,710	297	1,000	323
Banco Ambrosiano Veneto S.p.A.	Banking	Italy	NA	103	470	90
Banco Bradesco SA	Banking	Brazil	12,160	374	2,500	150
Banco Exterior de Espana	Banking	Spain	3,787	228	NA	NA
BankExim	Banking	Indonesia	550	75	130	10
Barclays Bank PLC	Banking	UK	11,000	3,900	2,500-4,999	> 1,000
Bass PLC	Food & Beverage	UK	7,034	551	500-999	100-249
British Petroleum Co. PLC	Oil & Gas	UK	52,425	1,345	1,000-2,499	500-1,000
The Broken Hill Proprietary Co.	Metals	Australia	12,218	948	1,000-2,499	100-249
CNP Assurances SA	Insurance	France	14,600	236	227	113
Codelco Chile--Div Chuquicamata	Metals	Chile	1,592	456	< 100	5-9
CSX Corp.	Transportation	U.S.	9,500	993	1,200	160
Cemex SA	Mining & Process Mfg.	Mexico	2,976	537	100-249	25-49
The Charles Schwab Corp.	Financial Services	U.S.	1,060	135	500-999	100-249
The Chase Manhattan Corp.	Banking	U.S.	11,187	1,205	3,500	600
Chicago Mercantile Exchange	Financial Services	U.S.	145	20	175	34
The Coca-Cola Co.	Food & Beverage	U.S.	13,957	2,176	100-249	100-249
Coles Myer Ltd.	Retail	Australia	11,300	353	1,000	188
The Dai-Ichi Kangyo Bank Ltd.	Banking	Japan	27,778	117	500-999	NA
Deutsche Bank AG	Banking	Germany	NA	3	2,000	975
Deutsche Bundespost Telekom	Communications	Germany	33,971	-1,655	2,500-4,999	500-1,000
Deutsche Lufthansa AG	Transportation	Germany	10,193	6,680	1,000-2,499	NA
ENEL S.p.A.	Utilities	Italy	21,304	NA	1,300	297
Eli Lilly & Co.	Pharmaceuticals	U.S.	6,452	480	2,500-4,999	250-499
Emirates Airlines	Transportation	United Arab Emirates	645	55	270	28
Fiat S.p.A.	Automotive	Italy	31,850	-1	1,000-2,499	60
Fidelity Investments	Financial Services	U.S.	2,800	NA	1,000-2499	250-499
First National Bank Holdings Ltd.	Banking	South Africa	NA	216	1,000-2,499	63
Fisher & Paykel Ltd.	Appliances & Electronics	New Zealand	420	NA	70	NA
Ford Motor Co.	Automotive	U.S.	108,521	2,529	2,500-4,999	250-499
Glaxo Holdings PLC	Pharmaceuticals	UK	8,852	2,039	NA	NA
Groupe Paribas	Banking	France	5,760	580	1,000-2,499	250-499
Hindustan Lever Ltd.	Consumer Products & Apparel	India	800	74	< 100	5-9
Hyundai Corp.	Automotive	South Korea	11,300	181	100-249	50-99
ITT Hartford	Insurance	U.S.	10,066	493	1,000-2,499	100-249
Information & Decision Support Ctr	Government	Egypt	14	0	312	11
Japan Finance Corp for Small Business	Government	Japan	27	0	< 100	1-4
Jusco Co. Ltd.	Retail	Japan	14,419	74	NA	NA

Company	Industry	Country	Revenue ($M)	Profit ($M)	# IS Employees	IS Spending ($M)
Kao Corp.	Consumer Products & Apparel	Japan	7,503	215	NA	135
Kvaerner Engineering AS	Industrial Equipment	Norway	3,263	130	250-499	50-99
The Kwangju Bank Ltd.	Banking	South Korea	NA	NA	81	9
MCI Communications Corp.	Communications	U.S.	13,300	795	2,500-4,999	500-1,000
Merrill Lynch & Co., Inc.	Financial Services	U.S.	16,588	1,359	2,500-4,999	500-1,000
Metropolitan Toronto Police	Government	Canada	517	0	165	17
Michigan Dept. of Social Services	Government	U.S.	7,500	0	250-499	50-99
Misumi Corp.	Industrial Equipment	Japan	190	NA	11	NA
NSK Ltd.	Industrial Equipment	Japan	3,157	35	100-249	25-49
National Computer Board	Government	Singapore	50	0	1,000-2,499	25-49
National Informatics Centre	Government	India	25	0	2,500-4,999	25-49
New Zealand Inland Revenue Dept.	Government	New Zealand	375	0	343	61
Nike, Inc.	Consumer Products & Apparel	U.S.	3,790	299	250-499	10-24
Nippon Telegraph & Telephone Corp.	Communications	Japan	64,586	484	> 5,000	> 1,000*
The Nomura Securities Co. Ltd.	Financial Services	Japan	6,585	480	< 100	NA
PECO Energy Co.	Utilities	U.S.	4,000	1,000	215	110
Petroleo Brasileiro SA-Petrobras	Oil & Gas	Brazil	18,029	673	1,000-2,499	100-249
Phillips Petroleum Co.	Oil & Gas	U.S.	12,400	484	500-999	100-249
Pohang Iron & Steel Co. Ltd.	Metals	South Korea	8,650	950	1,000-2,499	50-99
Privatbank, Commercial Bank	Banking	Ukraine	194	10	49	1
Qantas Airways Ltd.	Transportation	Australia	4,853	115	500-999	100-249
Rolls Royce PLC	Transportation	UK	5,205	114	500-999	100-249
Royal Dutch PTT Telecom B.V.	Communications	Netherlands	6,000	1,000	2,500-4,999	250-499
The Royal Hong Kong Jockey Club	Recreational Services	Hong Kong	8,700	237	250-499	50-99
Ryder Systems, Inc.	Transportation	U.S.	4,217	-61	500-999	100-249
Saab-Scania AB	Automotive	Sweden	13,319	199	250-499	NA
Samsung Electronics Co. Ltd.	Appliances & Electronics	South Korea	10,000	467	> 5,000	> 1,000
Scandinavian Airlines System	Transportation	Sweden	4,560	202	1,000	53
Seiyu Ltd.	Retail	Japan	10,195	50	< 100	50-99
Sevel Argentina SA	Automotive	Argentina	1,890	84	NA	100-249
Seven Eleven Japan Co. Ltd.	Retail	Japan	1,881	448	< 100	50-99
Singapore Network Services	Communications	Singapore	16	2	100-249	5-9
Skoda automobilova AS	Automotive	Czech Republic	1,191	1	169	11
Sumitomo Group	Banking	Japan	165,051	71	NA	NA
Swissair	Transportation	Switzerland	4,300	40	500-999	100-249
Tata Engineering & Locomotive Co.	Automotive	India	1,200	NA	475	25
The Tata Iron & Steel Co. Ltd.	Metals	India	1,219	58	250-499	5-9
Telecom Australia	Communications	Australia	9,500	1,500	2,500-4,999	500-1,000
Telecom Italia S.p.A.	Communications	Italy	18,680	2,087	1,000-2,499	500-1,000
Tokyo Electric Power Co., Inc.	Utilities	Japan	47,339	622	NA	NA
Toronto Stock Exchange	Financial Services	Canada	55	NA	200	21
Toyota Motor Corp.	Automotive	Japan	94,600	1,270	1,000-2,499	35
TransCanada Pipelines Ltd.	Oil & Gas	Canada	3,205	269	100-249	25-49
United Health Care Corp.	Insurance	U.S.	3,769	288	500-999	100-249
United Parcel Service, Inc.	Transportation	U.S.	19,600	900	4,000	200
Varig Brasilian Airlines SA	Transportation	Brazil	2,035	0	420	45
Vale Do Rio Doce, Companhia	Mining & Process Mfr.	Brazil	2,269	645	325	45
Volvo AB	Automotive	Sweden	14,252	198	1,000-2,499	250-499
Wal-Mart Stores, Inc.	Retail	U.S.	67,345	2,333	1,000-2,499	250-499

Company	Industry	Country	Revenue ($M)	Profit ($M)	# IS Employees	IS Spending ($M)
Washington State Dept. of Info. Svcs.	Government	U.S.	90	0	420	90
Wells Fargo & Co.	Banking	U.S.	4,854	612	1,000-2,499	100-249
Weyerhaeuser Co.	Mining & Process Mfg.	U.S.	10,398	1,197	500-999	100-249
Winterthur Swiss Versicherungs	Insurance	Switzerland	12,019	219	1,000-2,499	250-499
Xerox Corp.	Appliances & Electronics	U.S.	17,410	-126	1,000-2,499	500-1,000

*Computerworld estimate

Excerpted with permission from Computerworld, May 1, 1995, p. 54. Copyright © 1995, CW Publishing Inc., Framingham MA 01701 USA

Datamation: Global 100

"On this, the 20th anniversary of the Datamation 100, a dozen companies joined the billionaire's club, bringing the roster to 75, up from 63 in 1994, 52 five years ago and 31 a decade ago. Based on that rate of entry, the entire Datamation 100 will be members within five years."--Datamation

'95 Rank	'94 Rank	Company	Country	'95 IT Rev ($M)	'94 IT Rev ($M)	Net Inc ($M)	Tot '95 Rev ($M)	IT Rev/Total Rev (%)
1	1	IBM	U.S.	71,940	64,052	4,178	71,940	100.0
2	2	Fujitsu	Japan	26,798	21,331	671	39,974	67.0
3	3	Hewlett-Packard	U.S.	26,073	19,200	2,433	32,510	80.2
4	4	NEC	Japan	19,350	18,726	700	43,000	45.0
5	5	Hitachi	Japan	16,208	13,699	NA	85,306	19.0
6	8	Compaq Computer	U.S.	14,800	10,866	789	14,800	100.0
7	6	Digital Equipment	U.S.	14,400	13,500	431	14,400	100.0
8	9	EDS	U.S.	12,422	10,052	939	12,422	100.0
9	7	AT&T (incl. NCR & Lucent)	U.S.	11,384	11,459	139	79,609	14.3
10	10	Toshiba	Japan	11,380	9,936	850	54,192	18.9
11	11	Apple Computer	U.S.	11,378	9,549	167	11,378	100.0
12	12	Siemens Nixdorf	Germany	8,951	7,209	16	8,951	100.0
13	24	Seagate Technology	U.S.	8,200	3,500	NA	8,200	100.0
14	19	Microsoft	U.S.	7,418	4,650	1,838	7,418	100.0
15	14	Matsushita	Japan	7,026	6,059	1,017	78,069	9.0
16	17	Sun Microsystems	U.S.	6,500	5,348	447	6,500	100.0
17	13	Unisys	U.S.	6,202	6,216	-625	6,202	100.0
18	18	Olivetti	Italy	6,035	5,303	NA	6,035	100.0
19	26	Acer	Taiwan	5,700	3,200	NA	5,700	100.0
20	15	Canon	Japan	5,616	5,708	429	11,948	47.0
21	16	Groupe Bull	France	5,300	5,388	61	5,300	100.0
22	23	Dell Computer	U.S.	5,296	3,500	272	5,300	100.0
23	22	NTT Data	Japan	5,287	3,800	81	5,287	100.0
24	20	Xerox	U.S.	4,668	3,983	-472	16,611	28.1
25	32	Packard Bell	U.S.	4,300	2,600	NA	4,300	100.0
26	34	Andersen Consulting	U.S.	4,220	2,452	NA	4,220	100.0
27	25	Quantum	U.S.	4,174	3,286	56	4,174	100.0
28	21	Mitsubishi	Japan	4,145	3,848	NA	34,543	12.0
29	27	Computer Sciences	U.S.	4,100	3,085	133	4,100	100.0
30	28	Cap Gemini Sogeti	France	3,785	2,955	NA	4,205	90.0
31	31	Gateway 2000	U.S.	3,676	2,700	173	3,676	100.0
32	39	Intel	U.S.	3,240	2,304	3,556	16,202	20.0

'95 Rank	'94 Rank	Company	Country	'95 IT Rev ($M)	'94 IT Rev ($M)	Net Inc ($M)	Tot '95 Rev ($M)	IT Rev/Total Rev (%)
33	33	Computer Associates	U.S.	3,196	2,455	700	3,196	100.0
34	-	ADP	U.S.	3,157	NA	422	3,157	100.0
35	30	Oki	Japan	3,071	2,805	343	6,980	44.0
36	37	Motorola	U.S.	2,974	2,372	1,781	27,037	11.0
37	36	Oracle	U.S.	2,707	2,377	423	2,707	100.0
38	49	Cisco Systems	U.S.	2,668	1,500	634	2,668	100.0
39	47	Silicon Graphics	U.S.	2,541	1,631	237	2,732	93.0
40	38	AST Research	U.S.	2,349	2,311	-263	2,349	100.0
41	45	Western Digital	U.S.	2,340	1,900	91	2,340	100.0
42	40	KPMG Peat Marwick	U.S.	2,300	2,300	NA	7,500	30.7
43	41	Tandem	U.S.	2,285	2,108	108	2,285	100.0
44	42	Lockheed Martin	U.S.	2,057	2,070	683	22,853	9.0
45	44	Novell	U.S.	2,040	1,998	338	2,040	100.0
46	43	Seiko Epson	Japan	2,026	2,026	NA	4,310	47.0
47	29	Ricoh	Japan	1,966	2,867	NA	6,552	30.0
48	63	3Com	U.S.	1,963	1,014	176	1,963	100.0
49	48	Storage Technology	U.S.	1,929	1,625	-142	1,929	100.0
50	51	EMC	U.S.	1,921	1,377	365	1,921	100.0
51	58	SAP	Germany	1,887	1,130	283	1,887	100.0
52	53	Entex Information Services	U.S.	1,785	1,300	NA	1,785	100.0
53	55	Bay Networks	U.S.	1,700	1,200	221	1,700	100.0
54	46	Amdahl	U.S.	1,516	1,639	29	1,516	100.0
55	52	Lexmark	U.S.	1,478	1,350	32	2,158	68.5
56	-	SAIC	U.S.	1,401	NA	57	2,156	65.0
57	50	Samsung	Korea	1,400	1,400	NA	14,000	10.0
58	54	Texas Instruments	U.S.	1,313	1,238	1,088	13,128	10.0
59	77	Kingston Technology	U.S.	1,300	802	NA	1,300	100.0
60	86	Coopers & Lybrand	U.S.	1,260	591	NA	6,300	20.0
61	69	Maxtor	U.S.	1,230	891	-82	1,230	100.0
62	57	Data General	U.S.	1,205	1,142	-66	1,205	100.0
63	-	Stream International	U.S.	1,200	NA	NA	1,600	75.0
64	56	Alcatel Business Systems	France	1,156	1,189	-5,000	28,890	4.0
65	72	LM Ericsson	Sweden	1,107	840	762	13,836	8.0
66	65	Finsiel	Italy	1,103	937	40	1,103	100.0
67	76	Cabletron Systems	U.S.	1,100	811	202	1,100	100.0
68	59	Intergraph	U.S.	1,098	1,041	-45	1,098	100.0
69	75	Wang Laboratories	U.S.	1,095	821	-81	1,095	100.0
70	-	U.S. Robotics	U.S.	1,092	379	89	1,092	100.0
71	68	Sema Group	France	1,067	913	43	1,067	100.0
72	82	Mitac	Taiwan	1,062	600	6	1,062	100.0
73	70	General Electric	U.S.	1,050	889	7	70,000	1.5
74	-	Nomura	Japan	1,042	NA	18	1,240	84.0
75	61	Tatung	Taiwan	1,032	1,030	NA	3,000	34.4
76	71	MCI	U.S.	992	860	548	15,265	6.5
77	66	Memorex Telex	U.S.	981	934	NA	981	100.0
78	74	Sybase	U.S.	957	826	-20	957	100.0
79	-	Alltel	U.S.	927	862	355	3,110	29.8
80	62	Price Waterhouse	U.S.	880	1,020	NA	4,400	20.0
81	80	Sony	Japan	847	684	NA	43,328	2.0

'95 Rank	'94 Rank	Company	Country	'95 IT Rev ($M)	'94 IT Rev ($M)	Net Inc ($M)	Tot '95 Rev ($M)	IT Rev/Total Rev (%)
82	78	British Telecom	UK	838	775	NA	20,942	4.0
83	-	Micron Electronics	U.S.	833	NA	43	1,300	64.1
84	-	Sligos	France	778	739	16	778	100.0
85	85	Adobe Systems	U.S.	762	598	94	762	100.0
86	83	First International Computer	Taiwan	725	600	NA	725	100.0
87	100	Informix Software	U.S.	714	469	98	714	100.0
88	-	Fiserv	U.S.	703	580	-60	703	100.0
89	67	Cray Research	U.S.	676	922	-226	676	100.0
90	81	Comparex	Germany	670	678	42	670	100.0
91	-	Ceridian	U.S.	667	458	59	1,333	50.0
92	89	Ernst & Young	U.S.	653	557	NA	6,870	9.5
93	-	Shared Medical Systems	U.S.	651	551	40	651	100.0
94	-	PRC	U.S.	648	795	NA	720	90.0
95	79	Newbridge Networks	Canada	641	737	138	641	100.0
96	-	Intec	Japan	637	621	4	637	100.0
97	-	American Management Systems	U.S.	632	460	29	632	100.0
98	96	Sterling Software	U.S.	610	490	92	610	100.0
99	84	Racal Electronics	UK	604	600	66	1,510	40.0
100	-	Deloitte & Touche	U.S.	600	600	NA	1,200	50.0
		Total		**443,804**	**NA**	**NA**	**1,056,990**	**42.0**

Excerpted with permission from Datamation, June 15, 1996, p. 32. Copyright © 1996, The Cahners Publishing Company, Newton MA 02158 USA.

Chapter 10

Forecasts and Sales Estimates

Information and Electronics

Information Technology Industry Council: Computer and Business Equipment Industry

"Worldwide revenue of the U.S. computer and business equipment sector of the industry, which consists of four major parts, is projected to have reached $316.7B in 1991, an increase of 9.5% from 1990. During the forecast period to the year 2002, the CAGR is expected to be 10.0%. This would increase revenue to $901.2B. The largest part of this sector consists of computers and related equipment which accounted for approximately 52.8% of the total, or $167.2B, in 1991. By 2002, with a CAGR of 8.7%, computers and related equipment are forecast to generate revenue of $418.0B and represent 46.4% of this industry's total."--Information Technology Industry Council

Worldwide Revenue of U.S. Computer and Business Equipment Industry							
Year	Total Rev. ($B)	Domestic Rev. ($B)	Foreign Rev. ($B)	Computer Equipment ($B)	Software & Services ($B)	Business Equipment ($B)	Manifold Business Forms ($B)
1960	4.50	NA	NA	1.50	NA	2.50	0.50
1965	8.20	NA	NA	3.00	0.20	4.21	0.79
1970	20.52	14.16	6.36	10.50	2.50	6.20	1.32
1975	45.95	33.54	12.41	27.85	6.50	9.28	2.32
1976	50.15	37.11	13.04	30.70	7.00	10.00	2.45
1977	56.47	42.92	13.55	34.90	8.00	10.60	2.97
1978	67.40	49.20	18.20	41.52	10.00	12.50	3.38
1979	77.82	56.81	21.01	47.10	13.50	13.10	4.12
1980	91.17	66.55	24.62	55.10	18.00	13.50	4.57
1981	102.52	75.86	26.66	61.80	21.00	14.70	5.02
1982	114.16	81.05	33.11	69.00	23.50	16.50	5.16
1983	131.55	86.82	44.73	79.15	28.20	18.72	5.48
1984	154.32	101.85	52.47	91.80	35.25	21.35	5.92
1985	171.12	111.23	59.89	101.00	40.70	23.10	6.32
1986	183.65	117.54	66.11	107.60	45.00	24.40	6.65
1987	205.48	129.45	76.03	118.40	53.95	26.10	7.03
1988	235.33	145.83	89.50	131.80	68.05	27.90	7.58
1989	259.95	158.55	101.40	142.00	79.85	30.05	8.05
1990	289.29	174.95	114.34	154.80	94.10	31.95	8.44
1991	316.72	191.30	125.42	167.20	107.15	33.55	8.82
1992	347.48	209.10	138.38	180.70	121.96	35.56	9.26
1993	382.55	228.50	154.05	196.10	138.81	37.87	9.77
1994	420.69	249.50	171.19	212.90	157.15	40.33	10.31
1995	462.90	272.50	190.40	231.60	177.53	42.95	10.82
1996	509.67	297.60	212.07	252.00	200.56	45.75	11.36
2002	901.19	499.10	402.09	418.00	401.21	66.75	15.23
CAGR '81-'91 (%)	11.9	9.7	16.7	10.5	17.7	8.6	5.8
CAGR '91-'02 (%)	10.0	9.1	11.2	8.7	12.8	6.5	5.1

Excerpted with permission from Information Technology Industry Council, The Information Technology Industry Data Book 1960-2002. Copyright © 1992, ITI,1250 Eye Street NW, Washington DC 20005 USA.

Information Technology Industry Council: Information Industry

The following information has been extracted from CBEMA's The Information Technology Industry Data Book 1960-2002. All revenues are in current billion dollars.

	Worldwide Revenue of U.S. Information Technology Industry				
Year	Total ($B)	Domestic ($B)	Foreign ($B)	Computer & Business Equip. Industry ($B)	Telecommunications Industry ($B)
1960	15.30	NA	NA	4.50	10.80
1965	25.50	NA	NA	8.20	17.30
1970	54.54	NA	NA	20.52	34.02
1975	111.05	NA	NA	45.95	65.10
1976	122.28	NA	NA	50.15	72.13
1977	137.88	NA	NA	56.47	81.41
1978	159.52	NA	NA	67.40	92.12
1979	181.23	NA	NA	77.82	103.41
1980	203.91	174.09	29.82	91.17	112.74
1981	229.10	196.60	32.50	102.52	126.58
1982	252.79	213.32	39.47	114.16	138.63
1983	277.68	228.89	48.79	131.55	146.13
1984	313.92	255.21	58.71	154.32	159.60
1985	337.75	271.88	65.87	171.12	166.63
1986	358.57	286.18	72.39	183.65	174.92
1987	391.48	308.80	82.68	205.48	186.00
1988	431.96	334.84	97.12	235.33	196.63
1989	466.40	356.47	109.93	259.95	206.45
1990	505.04	382.75	122.29	289.29	215.75
1991	542.23	408.75	133.48	316.72	225.51
1992	582.82	434.34	148.48	347.48	235.34
1993	629.20	464.19	165.01	382.55	246.65
1994	679.11	496.09	183.02	420.69	258.42
1995	733.68	530.47	203.21	462.90	270.78
1996	793.42	565.55	227.87	509.67	283.75
2002	1,273.18	834.45	438.73	901.19	371.99
CAGR '81-'91 (%)	9.0	7.6	15.2	11.9	5.9
CAGR '91-'02 (%)	8.1	6.7	11.4	10.0	4.7

Excerpted with permission from Information Technology Industry Council, The Information Technology Industry Data Book 1960-2002. Copyright © 1992, ITI,1250 Eye Street NW, Washington DC 20005 USA.

Information Technology Industry Council: Information Industry versus GNP

"Each year since 1970, with the single exception of 1976, the information technology industry has grown at a more rapid rate than the overall economy (GNP). Revenue in the information technology industry, in current dollars, increased by an average annual compound growth rate (CAGR) of 13.7% in the 1971-1981 period and 9.0% for the years 1981-1991. GNP increased 10.7% and 6.5% during the comparable periods. During this twenty-year time frame, computer equipment revenue has outpaced the growth of the other components of the information technology industry, rising from $14.0B in 1970 to an estimated $167.2B in 1991. Its CAGR for

1971-1981 was 16.0% and for 1981-1991 is estimated to have been 10.5%."--Information Technology Industry Council

Year	Gross Natl Prdct (GNP) ($B)	Growth Rate (%)	Total IT Ind Rev ($B)	Growth Rate (%)	Comp & Bus Equip Ind Rev ($B)	Growth Rate (%)	Telecom Ind Rev ($B)	Growth Rate (%)
1970	1,015.5	5.4	54.5	19.3	20.5	14.5	34.0	22.3
1971	1,102.7	8.6	63.4	16.3	24.9	21.5	38.5	13.2
1972	1,212.8	10.0	73.1	15.3	29.5	18.5	43.6	13.2
1973	1,359.3	12.1	85.1	16.4	35.0	18.6	50.1	14.9
1974	1,472.8	8.3	99.2	16.6	41.4	18.3	57.8	15.4
1975	1,598.4	8.5	111.1	12.0	46.0	11.1	65.1	12.6
1976	1,782.8	11.5	122.3	10.1	50.2	9.1	72.1	10.8
1977	1,990.5	11.7	137.9	12.8	56.5	12.5	81.4	12.9
1978	2,249.7	13.0	159.5	15.7	67.4	19.3	92.1	13.1
1979	2,508.2	11.5	181.2	13.6	77.8	15.4	103.4	12.3
1980	2,732.0	8.9	203.9	12.5	91.2	17.2	112.7	9.0
1981	3,052.6	11.7	229.1	12.4	102.5	12.4	126.6	12.3
1982	3,166.0	3.7	252.9	10.4	114.2	11.4	138.7	9.5
1983	3,405.7	7.6	277.7	9.8	131.6	15.2	146.1	5.4
1984	3,772.2	10.8	313.9	13.0	154.3	17.2	159.6	9.2
1985	4,014.9	6.4	337.8	7.6	171.1	10.9	166.6	4.4
1986	4,231.6	5.4	358.6	6.2	183.7	7.4	174.9	5.0
1987	4,515.6	6.7	391.5	9.2	205.5	11.9	186.0	6.3
1988	4,873.7	7.9	432.0	10.3	235.3	14.5	196.6	5.7
1989	5,200.8	6.7	466.4	8.0	260.0	10.5	206.5	5.0
1990	5,465.1	5.1	505.0	8.3	289.2	11.2	215.8	4.5
1991	5,639.3	3.2	542.1	7.3	316.6	9.5	225.5	4.5
1992	5,823.5	3.3	581.3	7.2	345.4	9.1	235.9	4.6
1993	6,142.0	5.5	625.0	7.5	378.0	9.4	247.0	4.7
1994	6,502.0	5.9	672.8	7.6	413.9	9.5	258.8	4.8
1995	6,931.0	6.6	725.2	7.8	453.9	9.7	271.2	4.8
1996	7,402.0	6.8	782.2	7.9	498.0	9.7	284.3	4.8
2002	11,056.2		1,250.1		873.5		376.6	
CAGR '71-'81 (%)		10.7		13.7		15.2		12.6
CAGR '81-'91 (%)		6.3		9.0		11.9		5.9
CAGR '91-'02 (%)		6.3		7.9		9.7		4.8

Computers

Computer Industry Almanac: U.S. PC Market

The PC market has had exceptional growth in the last two years--primarily caused by strong home/consumer sales. In 1995 the PC unit sales exceeded the total number of cars and trucks sold in the U.S. for the first time. There are potential problems with the consumer market becoming such a large portion of the total PC market. The consumer market is more volatile than the business market. Hence the PC market forecast for the late 1990s has more uncertainty. The PC unit sales for 12 different distribution channels are summarized in the table below:

U.S. PC Unit Sales (#K)	1992	1993	1994	1995	1996	1997	1998	1999	2000
Traditional Computer Dealers	3,952	4,231	4,486	5,234	5,672	5,907	6,092	6,229	6,367
Computer Superstores	564	835	1,269	1,796	2,284	2,760	3,213	3,650	4,102
VARs/Systems Integrators	1,023	1,067	1,153	1,275	1,359	1,441	1,522	1,600	1,679
Local Assemblers	1,215	1,382	1,606	1,667	1,680	1,693	1,705	1,705	1,699
Office Product Superstores	253	372	534	750	954	1,149	1,346	1,551	1,760
Consumer Electronics Stores	809	898	1,048	1,112	1,179	1,245	1,310	1,373	1,435
Consumer Electronics Superstores	378	600	1,104	1,625	2,130	2,587	3,029	3,465	3,864
Warehouse Clubs	233	316	470	584	696	801	898	995	1,096
Other Mass Merchants	511	632	915	1,197	1,380	1,562	1,742	1,932	2,131
Direct Marketing/Mail Order	1,650	2,050	2,630	3,180	3,650	4,090	4,490	4,855	5,225
Direct Sales Force	655	580	545	510	480	450	425	400	380
Other Distribution Channels	535	590	655	722	781	837	883	931	979
Total US PC Unit Sales	11,778	13,553	16,415	19,652	22,245	24,524	26,656	28,686	30,719
Yearly Growth Rate (%)	16.4	15.1	21.1	19.7	13.2	10.2	8.7	7.6	7.1

The traditional computer dealers will remain the largest distribution channel--especially for office PCs. Computer superstores will grow dramatically and unit sales will increase over seven-fold from 1992 to 2000. PC sales in office product superstores will grow by nearly 7X in the same time frame. Consumer electronics superstore PC sales will grow more than 10X from 1992 to 2000. The market share of traditional computer dealers will decline to less than 21% of the U.S. total by 2000. Computer superstores will sell over 13% of the total in 2000. The direct marketing channel--including mail order companies--already accounts for over 16% of annual PC sales, but will not increase its market share very much because most of the price advantage of direct marketing has disappeared. As a group the mass merchant channels will grow from 14% plus in 1990 to about 36% in 1995 and nearly 47% in 2000. PC revenue by distribution channel is summarized in the next table.

U.S. PC Revenue ($M)	1992	1993	1994	1995	1996	1997	1988	1999	2000
Traditional Computer Dealers	10,764	11,638	12,490	14,869	16,235	16,898	17,515	18,188	18,742
Computer Superstores	1,222	2,001	3,147	4,869	6,267	7,531	8,819	10,001	11,128
VARs/Systems Integrators	4,195	4,477	4,973	5,535	6,042	6,440	6,802	7,118	7,438
Local Assemblers	2,544	3,054	3,702	3,875	3,946	4,012	4,066	4,099	4,093
Office Product Superstores	500	850	1,270	1,919	2,438	2,925	3,468	4,006	4,520
Consumer Electronics Stores	1,429	1,814	2,261	2,476	2,640	2,776	2,949	3,083	3,209
Consumer Electronics Superstores	694	1,258	2,469	3,732	4,902	5,935	7,039	8,151	9,017
Warehouse Clubs	415	645	1,018	1,309	1,561	1,769	2,006	2,236	2,451
Other Mass Merchants	899	1,267	1,956	2,662	3,103	3,486	3,881	4,265	4,687
Direct Marketing/Mail Order	4,129	5,300	7,330	9,500	11,237	12,733	14,254	15,560	16,845
Direct Sales Force	1,838	1,654	1,574	1,546	1,480	1,407	1,343	1,280	1,219
Other Distribution Channels	1,273	1,402	1,498	1,891	2,028	2,147	2,272	2,390	2,515
Total US PC Revenue	29,903	35,361	43,668	54,183	61,878	68,061	74,414	80,377	85,864

U.S. PC Revenue ($M)	1992	1993	1994	1995	1996	1997	1988	1999	2000
Yearly Growth Rate (%)	19.5	18.3	23.5	24.0	14.2	10.0	9.3	8.0	6.8

Traditional computer dealers will remain the largest PC distribution channel by revenue. Direct marketing has grown strongly and became the second largest channel in 1993. The revenue is only for PCs and peripherals sold with the initial purchase (except printers), but excludes other PC-related sales such as software and aftermarket peripherals. The market share of traditional computer dealers will decline less than in unit market share due to higher average prices than consumer oriented channels. As a group the retail channels will grow from 9.6% in 1990 to over 31% in 1995 and nearly 41% in 2000.

PC Microprocessor Trends

For each distribution channel the microprocessor trends were projected. In the 386- and 486-eras direct marketing, traditional computer dealers, VARs and direct sales force adopt the latest microprocessors first, while the consumer-oriented channels adopt new technology at a later date. But the adoption of the Pentium reversed that trend. The consumer-oriented channels were much quicker to adopt the Pentium PCs than the business-oriented channels. This is due to the explosion of multimedia applications for the home/consumer market. The growing use of MPEG video in multimedia applications is likely to repeat the Pentium trend for the transition to the Pentium Pro/686 microprocessor and to the P7 microprocessor later in the decade. A summary of the microprocessor market shares for all distribution channels is shown below:

MPU Market Shares (%)	1990	1991	1992	1993	1994	1995	1996	1997	1998	1999	2000
8088/86	10.6	5.3	1.5	-	-	-	-	-	-	-	-
286	36.4	20.5	4.3	0.1	-	-	-	-	-	-	-
386SX	23.4	36.7	39.6	8.7	0.6	-	-	-	-	-	-
386DX	19.5	22.2	19.4	7.4	0.8	0.03	-	-	-	-	-
486SX/SL	-	0.8	8.1	33.7	28.7	3.6	0.1	-	-	-	-
486DX	0.4	2.6	15.2	36.7	46.3	37.6	4.3	0.1	-	-	-
Pentium/586	-	-	-	0.5	10.9	45.6	80.8	74.7	40.9	5.4	0.1
Pentium Pro/686/P6	-	-	-	-	-	-	1.0	10.5	43.4	76.7	71.7
P7	-	-	-	-	-	-	-	-	-	1.0	10.4
Total 80x86	90.6	88.1	88.0	87.2	87.3	86.8	86.1	85.3	84.2	83.1	82.2
PowerPCs	-	-	-	-	3.4	7.0	10.9	13.2	15.1	16.3	17.1
Other Microprocessors	9.4	11.9	12.0	12.8	9.3	6.2	3.0	1.2	0.6	0.6	0.6

Computer Industry Almanac: Worldwide Workstation Market

This forecast includes technical and commercial workstations as well as workstation servers. The workstation market continues to grow. Much of the current and future workstation growth is coming from LAN, Internet and intranet servers. In 1995 the workstation unit sales exceeded a million units for the first time and will surpass 2.5M units in 1999 for a compound annual growth rate of 24%. Sun Microsystems and its SPARC architecture will remain the volume leader. The unit sales for the major workstation architectures are summarized in the table below:

Worldwide Workstation Unit Sales (#K)	1991	1992	1993	1994	1995	1996	1997	1998	1999
SPARC-based Workstations	201	229	295	343	421	518	629	755	899
PowerPC & RS/6000 Workstations	50	66	81	106	152	207	293	385	494
Precision Architecture Workstations	20	55	71	113	164	232	306	374	451
MIPS Architecture Workstations	89	102	116	134	155	183	229	293	373
Alpha-based Workstations	-	2	24	58	90	127	180	235	292

Worldwide Workstation Unit Sales (#K)	1991	1992	1993	1994	1995	1996	1997	1998	1999
Other Workstations	176	150	126	103	73	33	7	-	-
Total Worldwide Workstation Unit Sales	**537**	**604**	**715**	**856**	**1,056**	**1,302**	**1,644**	**2,042**	**2,509**
Yearly Growth Rate (%)	27.7	12.6	33.3	19.6	23.4	23.3	26.3	24.2	22.9

The PowerPC and RS/6000 category includes IBM's workstations. Hewlett-Packard is the major supplier of PA-based workstations. Silicon Graphics is the largest vendor using the MIPS Rx000 architecture. Digital Equipment is the dominant vendor providing Alpha workstations. The "Other" category includes workstations based on the 68000, 88000 and Clipper microprocessors.

Worldwide revenue for each of the major workstation architectures is summarized in the next table.

Worldwide Workstation Revenue ($B)	1991	1992	1993	1994	1995	1996	1997	1998	1999
SPARC-based Workstations	3.58	3.99	4.82	5.29	6.51	7.78	9.24	10.90	12.80
PowerPC & RS/6000 Workstations	1.08	1.25	1.48	1.79	2.40	3.07	4.00	4.93	5.96
Precision Architecture Workstations	0.39	0.96	1.24	1.84	2.62	3.61	4.68	5.65	6.72
MIPS Architecture Workstations	2.12	2.26	2.59	3.11	3.65	4.46	5.09	6.06	7.39
Alpha-based Workstations	-	0.04	0.41	0.96	1.44	1.98	2.71	3.44	4.15
Other Workstations	3.07	2.47	1.95	1.50	0.99	0.41	0.08	-	-
Total Worldwide Workstation Revenue	**10.2**	**11.0**	**12.5**	**14.5**	**17.6**	**21.3**	**25.8**	**31.0**	**37.0**
Yearly Growth Rate (%)	22.9	7.2	13.7	16.1	21.5	21.0	21.1	20.1	19.5

The worldwide workstation market exceeded $17B in 1995 and will grow to $37B in 1999 for a compound annual growth rate of 20.4%. The SPARC compatible workstation segment will remain the clear leader with over a third of the market.

Copyright © 1996. Computer Industry Almanac Inc., 702/749-5053, 800/377-6810 (U.S. only). USA.

Consumer Electronics Manufacturers Association: U.S. Home Computer Market

"The personal computer has finally come into its own as an accepted and desired member of the American household. 1995 was the first year in which dollar sales of PCs were higher than that of all television sets, as dollar sales of PCs grew a little more than 35%. Sales of PCs to consumers represented about 45% of all PC sales in the United States in 1995."--Consumer Electronics Manufacturers Association

U.S. Consumer PC Market	1990	1991	1992	1993	1994	1995
Unit Sales to Dealers (#K)	4,000	3,900	4,875	5,850	6,725	8,400
Unit Growth (%)	-	-2.5	25.0	20.0	15.0	24.9
Factory Sales ($M)	4,187	4,287	5,573	6,921	8,070	10,920
Revenue Growth (%)	-	2.4	30.0	24.2	16.6	35.3
Average Unit Price ($)	1,047	1,099	1,143	1,183	1,200	1,300

The U.S. consumer PC factory sales, including imports, are shown below. Total PC, peripherals and software sales are also compared to all consumer electronics sales. The consumer PC share of total consumer electronics sales is growing rapidly.

U.S. Factory Sales ($M)	1985	1986	1987	1988	1989	1990	1991	1992	1993	1994	1995
Personal Computers	2,175	3,060	3,100	3,340	3,711	4,187	4,287	5,573	6,921	8.070	10,920
Computer Peripherals	-	-	-	-	-	1,980	2,060	2,220	2,450	3,100	3,850
Computer Software	-	-	-	-	-	971	1,045	1,250	1,600	2,050	2,500

U.S. Factory Sales ($M)	1985	1986	1987	1988	1989	1990	1991	1992	1993	1994	1995
Computer Total	-	-	-	-	-	7,138	7,392	9,043	10,971	13,220	17,270
Consumer Electronics Total	22,940	26,740	29,164	32,236	33,373	43,033	42,668	46,165	51,215	56,292	61,693
Computer Portion (%)	-	-	-	-	-	16.6	17.3	19.6	21.4	23.5	28.0

Excepted with permission from The Year in Consumer Electronics 95. Copyright © 1996, Consumer Electronics Manufacturers Association, 2500 Wilson Blvd., Arlington VA 22201-3834 USA.

Data Analysis Group: Computer Market

"These forecasts of the total U.S. market (final sales) are based on data reported in Computer Industry Forecasts since 1984. All forecasts are computed with a statistical model which weighs information inversely to time from reporting. Forecasts are updated in January and July. There is approximately 90% confidence that forecasts lie within the Low and High limits. Product categories are presented in order appearing in Computer Industry Forecasts. Definitions are presented in alphabetical order."--Data Analysis Group

Product Categories	Year	Low	Mid	High
Mainframe Computers ($B)	1993	10.3	11.6	13.1
	1994	9.9	11.6	13.2
	1995	9.8	11.5	13.5
	1996	9.3	11.3	13.4
	1997	8.8	11.0	13.2
	1998	8.4	10.7	13.2
	1999	7.9	10.4	12.9
Mainframe CAGR (%)	1996-99	-5.4	-2.7	-1.4
Minicomputers ($B)	1993	7.6	8.6	9.7
	1994	7.4	8.6	9.8
	1995	7.2	8.5	9.9
	1996	6.8	8.3	9.9
	1997	6.4	8.1	9.6
	1998	6.1	7.8	9.6
	1999	5.6	7.4	9.1
Minicomputers CAGR (%)	1996-99	-6.5	-4.0	-2.5
Total Mainframes & Minicomputers ($B)	1993	15.6	20.2	23.2
	1994	15.0	20.2	23.4
	1995	14.8	20.0	23.9
	1996	14.1	19.6	23.7
	1997	13.2	19.1	23.3
	1998	12.6	18.5	23.2
	1999	11.7	17.8	22.4
Total Mainframes & Minicomputers CAGR (%)	1996-99	-5.9	-3.2	-1.8
Supercomputers ($B)	1993	1.7	1.9	2.4
	1994	1.9	2.2	2.8
	1995	1.9	2.6	2.9
	1996	2.5	3.0	3.8
	1997	2.7	3.4	4.2
	1998	3.1	4.0	5.1
	1999	3.6	4.6	6.1
Supercomputers CAGR (%)	1996-99	13.0	16.0	16.7

Product Categories	Year	Low	Mid	High
Workstations ($B)	1993	7.8	10.1	11.8
	1994	8.7	11.4	13.5
	1995	10.5	12.9	16.8
	1996	10.5	14.7	17.3
	1997	13.0	16.7	22.1
	1998	13.6	18.9	23.9
	1999	16.2	21.6	29.5
Workstations CAGR (%)	1996-99	15.7	13.7	19.5
Personal Computers ($B)	1993	29.5	36.3	39.9
	1994	31.7	38.5	44.8
	1995	32.6	41.2	47.9
	1996	34.1	44.5	52.2
	1997	36.0	48.0	57.6
	1998	39.7	52.3	66.3
	1999	39.4	56.0	68.5
Personal Computers CAGR (%)	1996-99	5.0	8.0	9.5
Portable, Notebook, Subnotebook & Laptop Computers ($B)	1993	6.2	6.7	8.4
	1994	6.7	8.1	9.5
	1995	7.4	9.8	10.9
	1996	8.8	11.9	13.5
	1997	10.7	14.2	17.1
	1998	11.9	16.5	19.9
	1999	14.3	19.2	25.0
Portable, Notebook, Subnotebook & Laptop Computers CAGR (%)	1996-99	17.5	17.3	22.6
Portable, Handheld Computers ($B)	1994	-	-	-
	1995	0.6	0.8	0.9
	1996	0.8	1.1	1.2
	1997	1.2	1.4	1.8
	1998	1.3	1.8	2.2
	1999	1.7	2.3	3.0
Portable, Handheld Computers CAGR (%)	1996-99	30.0	29.0	35.7
Portable, Pen-based Computers ($B)	1994	-	-	-
	1995	1.4	1.6	2.0
	1996	1.5	2.0	2.3
	1997	2.1	2.5	3.4
	1998	2.5	3.2	4.2
	1999	3.1	3.9	5.4
Portable, Pen-based Computers CAGR (%)	1996-99	28.3	24.5	33.9
Total, Portable Computers ($B)	1993	5.8	6.7	7.9
	1994	6.5	8.1	9.2
	1995	10.1	12.2	14.9
	1996	12.5	14.9	19.1
	1997	14.2	18.2	22.7
	1998	14.6	21.5	24.3
	1999	19.5	25.3	34.0
Total, Portable Computers CAGR (%)	1996-99	16.1	19.2	21.1

Product Categories	Year	Low	Mid	High
LAN Server Market ($B)	1993	6.5	7.1	9.0
	1994	6.6	8.2	9.5
	1995	7.8	9.5	11.7
	1996	7.9	10.9	12.5
	1997	9.9	12.5	16.3
	1998	9.6	14.3	16.5
	1999	12.7	16.3	23.0
LAN Server Market CAGR (%)	1996-99	17.1	14.2	22.4

Frost & Sullivan: U.S. Low-End Workstation Market

"U.S. sales of low-end workstations to the commercial marketplace will more than triple from $3.6B in 1994 to $11.2B by the year 1999, growing at a 21% compound annual rate.

'Enterprise-level workstations will pace the market, increasing their share from 15% of overall market revenues in 1993 to 44% by 1999 while personal computer-level workstations, hammered by downward price pressures, dip in share from 69 to 39% in the same period.

'While enterprise-level workstations will see the most rapid growth, with a 45% CAGR projected for the 1993-1999 period, and become the largest workstation segment, PC-level workstations will grow at a still-healthy 11% CAGR--the slowest among product segments--in the face of severe price competition.

'Introduction of next-generation processors suitable for PC platforms will broaden system capabilities and allow many more small businesses to enter the distributed computing arena. By removing barriers that have historically separated PCs from workstations, these new processor families have extended the commercial market for these workstations.

'Competitive pressures have brought steadily declining prices and profit margins with low-end workstation companies relying on high-volume economies of scale to support their aggressive pricing. Competition is particularly intense in entry-level and PC-level segments as platforms based on next-generation processors span barriers historically dividing these sectors. Although the main focus of competition has thus far been between market leaders, clone/compatible vendors will become more involved as the commercial market develops."--Frost & Sullivan

Year	Units (K)	Unit Growth (%)	Rev. ($B)	Rev. Growth (%)
1992	345.0	-	2.89	-
1993	457.3	32.6	3.61	25.1
1994	536.4	17.3	4.17	15.5
1995	656.4	22.4	5.00	19.9
1996	839.2	27.8	6.22	24.3
1997	1,105.0	31.7	7.83	25.9
1998	1,399.1	26.6	9.50	21.3
1999	1,742.8	24.6	11.24	18.4
1992-99 CAGR		26.0	-	21.4

Computer Segments

Data Analysis Group: Computer Segments Products Market

"These forecasts of the total U.S. market (final sales) are based on data reported in Computer Industry Forecasts since 1984. All forecasts are computed with a statistical model which weighs information inversely to time from reporting. Forecasts are updated in January and July. There is approximately 90% confidence that forecasts lie within the Low and High limits. Product categories are presented in order appearing in Computer Industry Forecasts. Definitions are presented in alphabetical order."--Data Analysis Group

Product Categories	Year	Low	Mid	High
Multimedia, Hardware & Software ($B)	1993	3.1	4.0	4.2
	1994	4.7	5.4	6.6
	1995	5.9	7.2	8.6
	1996	7.6	9.5	11.7
	1997	10.2	12.5	16.3
	1998	11.1	16.3	18.4
	1999	16.7	21.1	29.1
Multimedia, Hardware & Software CAGR (%)	1996-99	30.0	30.5	35.7
Videoconferencing, Equipment and Services ($B)	1993	1.0	1.3	1.4
	1994	1.4	1.8	2.1
	1995	2.0	2.5	3.2
	1996	2.5	3.3	4.1
	1997	3.6	4.5	6.2
	1998	4.8	6.0	8.4
	1999	6.2	8.0	11.2
Videoconferencing, Equipment and Services CAGR (%)	1996-99	34.9	34.0	39.4

Frost & Sullivan: U.S. Desktop Publishing Equipment Market

"The U.S. desktop publishing equipment market will more than triple, growing from $7.5B in 1994 to $27B by the year 2001, at a 20% compound annual rate.

'Output devices will increase their share of total market revenues from 33% in 1994 to 36% in 2001 as storage systems likewise increase their share from 15 to 17% while software's dips from 15 to 10% in the same period.

'The share of computer systems, at 32% of revenues in 1994, will remain relatively stable during the forecast period.

'Desktop publishing has progressed rapidly in the past decade from industry buzzword to multibillion-dollar market, representing at once a major computer industry application sector and the publishing industry's fastest-growing segment. Recent technological advances have eroded most of the processing barriers that prevented imaging technology implementation in desktop publishing applications."--Frost & Sullivan

Unit Shipment & Revenue Forecasts (U.S.)											
Year	1991	1992	1993	1994	1995	1996	1997	1998	1999	2000	2001
Units (M)	3.2	3.9	4.6	5.3	6.0	6.9	8.1	9.6	11.4	13.8	16.8
Revenues ($B)	5.50	5.99	6.65	7.54	8.69	10.25	12.21	14.72	17.93	21.95	26.99

Unit Shipment & Revenue Forecasts (U.S.)										
Year	1991	1992	1993	1994	1995	1996	1997	1998	1999	2000	2001
% Revenue Growth Rate	-	8.9	11.1	13.4	15.3	18.0	19.2	20.6	21.8	22.5	23.0

Compound Annual Growth Rate (1994-2001): 20.0%

Note: All figures are rounded.

Frost & Sullivan: U.S. Hospital Information System Market

"U.S. sales of hospital information systems (HIS) will more than double from $1.5B in 1994 to $4.2B by the year 2001, growing at a 16% compound annual rate...

'Integrated HIS packages, along with computer-based patient records (CPRs) and electronic medical records (EMRs), will lead industry growth while growth of other standalone products is sapped by the strong market-place impact of integrated products...

'Open-architecture solutions are increasingly preferred to design systems responding to the needs of multiple departments and facilities as the industry re-engineers its processes in response to intensifying competitive pressures and regulatory strictures. Industry consolidation, including acquisitions of clinics, nursing homes, out-patient services and home healthcare agencies by hospitals, is additionally forcing them into more integrated HIS programs."--Frost & Sullivan

Year	1991	1992	1993	1994	1995	1996	1997	1998	1999	2000	2001
Revenue ($M)	1,308.8	1,324.7	1,383.9	1,507.7	1,731.6	2,096.7	2,582.4	3,152.1	3,614.2	3,924.8	4,147.9
% Revenue Growth	-	1.2	4.5	8.9	14.8	21.1	23.2	22.1	14.7	8.6	5.7

CAGR: 15.6%

HLS Associates: U.S. Automated Forms Processing Market

The U.S. automated forms processing market is projected to be a $4.2B market in 1996 and is projected to grow 16.4% in 1997 to $4.9B.

U.S. Automated Forms Processing Markets ($M)		
Market Segment	1996	1997
Total Item Processing	1,150	1,300
Total Document Processing	3,060	3,610
Total Transaction Processing	4,210	4,900
Document Processing Systems	872	1,002
Vertical Market		
Government	210	240
Financial Services	90	100
Wholesale and Retail	20	30
Health Care	200	220
Manufacturing	10	15

U.S. Automated Forms Processing Markets ($M)		
Market Segment	1996	1997
Utilities/Transportation	70	80
Insurance	45	55
Other	12	12
Total Vertical Markets	657	752

The U.S. OCR systems market is estimated to be worth $124M in 1996 and $159M in 1997 for a 28.5% growth.

U.S. Automatic Data Capture OCR Markets		
OCR Market	1996	1997
Item Processing ($M)	25.0	34.5
Document Processing ($M)	39.0	54.8
Transaction Processing ($M)	64.0	89.3
High-End Automatic Text Recognition ($M)	60.0	70.0
Total Automatic Data Capture ($M)	124.0	159.3
OCR Systems (# Units)		
Large	90	96
Medium	380	440
Client/Server	240	307
Total Document Processing	710	843
Item Processing	200	230
High Volume	340	402
Total OCR Systems	1,250	1,475

Excerpted with permission from HLS Associates, August, 1996. Copyright © 1996, HLS Associates, 19 Halifax Court, Sterling VA 22170 USA.

Machover Associates: Worldwide Computer Graphics Market

The commercial and industrial computer graphics applications markets will grow from $43.3B in 1995 to $81.9B in the year 2000 for a compound annual growth rate of 14%. The multimedia market, which includes desktop video, will remain the largest segment.

Graphics Segments	1995 ($B)	2000 ($B)	CAGR %
CAD/CAM	11.9	15.2	5
Art/Animation	3.4	7.4	17
Multimedia (including desktop video)	14.7	29.5	15
Realtime Simulation	0.7	1.3	13
Scientific Visualization	2.9	6.5	18
Graphic Arts	4.0	11.2	23
Virtual Reality	0.4	2.1	39
Other	5.5	8.7	10
Total	43.3	81.9	14

Excerpted with permission from Machover Assoc., Nov. 1995. Copyright © 1995, Machover Assoc., 152A Longview Ave., White Plains NY 10605 U.S.

Voice Information Associates: Automatic Speech Recognition Market

"The end user value of the automatic speech recognition market (ASR) is projected to grow to $944M by 1998 up from a value of $347.2M in 1994 and $19.3M in 1986...

'Revenues to vendors of ASR equipment/technology are projected to reach $810.7M by 1998, up from $298.2M in 1994 and $17M in 1986. This rapid market growth is the result of a combination of improving speech technology (software) and the availability of powerful processing capability in relatively low-cost personal computers."-- Voice Information Associates

Market ($M)	Pre-1986 (Cumul.)	1986	1987	1988	1989	1990	1991	1992	1993	1994	1995	1996	1997	1998
ASR End-User	38.2	19.3	29.9	48.3	69.2	92.2	133.8	189.3	259.7	347.2	456.6	589.1	750.8	944.0
ASR Vendor	35.5	17.0	25.9	40.7	56.4	73.5	107.6	159.2	222.5	298.2	393.2	508.5	647.0	810.7

The ASR market has been segment into six areas.

Market Segment	1994 Revenue ($M)	1998 Revenue ($M)	CAGR % ('94-98)
Computer Control	32.2	102.1	33.3
Speech-to-Text	70.7	218.9	32.6
Telephone	85.9	260.2	32.0
Voice Verification	20.3	47.0	23.5
Data Entry	55.2	116.7	20.6
Consumer	34.0	65.7	18.0
Total	**298.2**	**810.7**	**28.4**

Peripherals

Business Communications: U.S. Internetworking Market

"The forecast for internetworking products and services annual revenue in 2005 will be over $156B, up from $82B in 1995, reflecting an average annual growth rate of 6.7%. BCC notes that the convergence factors that have brought computers and communications together are more crisply definable than ever before. Computers are moving into the home and adding multimedia and/or video capability. The microelectronics evolution meanwhile made it possible for the cable television to be a computer in itself. Communications via fiber optics can now offer tremendous capacity scenarios.

'The two larger markets are video and information services. Video services at $27.2B in 1995, will reach a $62B level by 2005, according to BCC analysis. Information services in that same period are expected to grow from a $29.2B level in 1995 to $42.1B in 2005."--Business Communications Company

	1995 ($B)	2005 ($B)	AAGR (%) 1995-2005
Video Services	27.2	62.0	8.6
Information Services	29.2	42.1	3.8
Video Sales & Rentals	16.4	28.3	5.6
Transmission Services	6.5	11.7	6.1
Equipment & Software	2.8	12.3	16
Total	**82.1**	**156.4**	**6.7**

Excerpted with permission from Business Comm., July 12 1995. Copyright © 1995, Business Communications, 25 Van Zant St., Norwalk CT 06855 U.S.

Business Communications: Worldwide Flat-Panel Display Market

"In 1994, worldwide shipments of CRT displays were valued at $14B. By the end of the decade, shipments of CRT displays will reach a market value of $21.8B as a result of 7.7% average annual growth. Approximately 104M CRT displays will be shipped in 2000. Shipments of the flat-panel display were valued at $5.4B in 1994. Of the flat-panel displays, liquid crystal display technology will experience the most rapid rise with annual shipments growing at 21% annually over the next six years. Both active matrix and passive matrix technology will benefit from the dramatic growth of portable computing, improved technology and lower fabrication costs. Liquid crystal displays for instrumentation also will experience rapid growth.

'Both plasma and electroluminescent (EL) flat-panel technologies will experience rising demand. Plasma shipments, driven by television, computer and large area display applications, will grow at an average annual rate of 12.3% through 2000. Shipments of EL displays, used for computers and monitoring applications, will exceed 10% annually over the course of the decade. Meanwhile, the more traditional vacuum fluorescent and light emitting diode displays will grow at a more moderate pace in the coming years. Both types of displays will find continued use in instrumentation and monitoring applications."--Business Communications Company

Display Shipments ($B)	1994	2000	% AAGR 1994-2000
CRT	14.0	21.8	7.7
Flat Panel	5.4	11.9	14.1
Total	**19.4**	**33.7**	**9.6**

Excerpted with permission from Business Comm., Dec. 1994. Copyright © 1994, Business Communications, 25 Van Zant St., Norwalk CT 06855 U.S.

Business Communications: Worldwide PCMCIA/PC Card Market

"By 2000, the PC card market revenues will approach $7B, growing at an impressive annual rate of over 50%. Current trends indicate that the PCMCIA/PC card interface will take its place as the peripheral and upgrade solution of choice across all computer lines well into the 21st century. There are also strong indications that the form factor will spread to virtually every corner of the electronics market, from automobiles to television.

'Communications cards currently hold the largest market share, representing some 50% of current revenues. Price drops will bring these cards into line with standard factors, now some 40 to 50% less costly than the PCM-CIA/PC card equivalents. Revenue from this segment will still represent 20% of the market in the year 2000, with an annual growth rate of just under 30%. Memory and mass storage will ultimately represent over 50% of all revenues, returning PCMCIA technology to its roots in memory expansion. The ever increasing demands for memory storage bodes well for miniature hard disk drives, while we feel that flash technology still is up to two years away from solid acceptance. This is due primarily to continued high prices.

'Other applications making use of the PCMCIA technology, such as multi-function cards, pager cards, personal security cards and some that have yet to be developed, are a largely untapped source of revenues for card vendors. This portion of the market is projected to represent almost 30% of total revenues."--Business Communications Company

Market Segments	Communications Cards		Memory/Mass Storage		Other Applications		Totals	
Year	Units (#M)	($B)	Units (#M)	($B)	Units (#M)	($B)	Units (#M)	($B)
1994	1.3	0.3	1.3	0.3	0.1	0.0	2.7	0.6
1996	4.0	0.8	5.3	0.9	1.5	0.5	10.8	2.2
1998	8.3	1.2	13.2	2.5	4.7	1.1	26.2	4.8
2000	12.6	1.3	22.3	3.7	8.7	2.0	43.6	7.0
AAGR (%) 1994-2000	46.0	27.7	60.6	52.0	114.2	101.4	59.0	50.6

Excerpted with permission from Business Comm., March 1995. Copyright ©1995, Business Communications, 25 Van Zant St., Norwalk CT 06855 U.S.

Computer Industry Almanac: U.S. PC Printer Market

The PC market has had exceptional growth in the last two years--primarily caused by strong home/consumer sales. Since printer sales are proportional to PC sales, printers also had exceptional growth in the last few years. In 1995 the PC unit sales exceeded the total number of cars and trucks sold in the U.S. for the first time. In 1996 the printer unit sales will exceed the number of cars and trucks sold in the U.S.. There are potential problems with the consumer market becoming such a large portion of the total PC market. The consumer market is more volatile than the business market. Hence the PC and printer market forecasts for the late 1990s have more uncertainty. The printer unit sales by 12 different distribution channels are summarized in the table below:

Printer Unit Sales (#K)	1992	1993	1994	1995	1996	1997	1988	1999	2000
Traditional Computer Dealers	3,458	3,681	2,916	2,539	2,552	2,599	2,619	2,710	2,802
Computer Superstores	733	1,169	1,980	2,873	3,768	4,678	5,575	6,461	7,384
VARs/Systems Integrators	890	923	986	1,071	1,148	1,225	1,301	1,368	1,436
Local Assemblers	286	329	392	392	395	389	384	375	365
Office Product Superstores	408	728	1,205	1,755	2,347	2,988	3,649	4,342	5,052
Consumer-Electronics Stores	534	601	702	795	879	953	1,035	1,106	1,170
Consumer-Electronics Superstores	271	450	845	1,390	1,853	2,316	2,802	3,274	3,709
Warehouse Clubs	155	215	327	435	539	649	754	860	965
Other Mass Merchants	309	395	590	856	1,042	1,226	1,429	1,633	1,833
Direct Marketing/Mail Order	1,257	1,609	2,051	2,496	2,865	3,211	3,570	3,884	4,206
Direct Sales Force	491	441	411	377	350	324	306	288	274

Printer Unit Sales (#K)	1992	1993	1994	1995	1996	1997	1988	1999	2000
Other Distribution Channels	368	416	465	509	559	607	645	684	725
Total U.S. Printer Unit Sales	9,161	10,958	12,870	15,488	18,298	21,165	24,068	26,985	29,919
Yearly Growth Rate (%)	22.4	19.6	17.4	20.3	18.1	15.7	13.7	12.1	10.9
All Retail Channels	2,411	3,559	5,648	8,103	10,428	12,810	15,243	17,676	20,112

Traditional computer dealers are rapidly losing market share and are now being surpassed as the largest printer distribution channel by the computer superstores. Printer sales in traditional computer dealers started declining in 1994 as many buyers are shifting to lower priced channels. Both the direct marketing/mail order channel and the office-product superstores will surpass the printer sales of traditional computer dealers in the next years. Computer superstores will grow strongly and unit sales will increase 20 fold from 1991 to 2000 and became the largest channel for printers in 1995. Printer sales in office product superstores will grow more than 32X in the same time frame as these stores increasingly specialize in printer sales. Consumer-electronics superstore printer sales will grow 25 times from 1991 to 2000. Printer revenue by distribution channel is summarized below:

Printer Revenue ($M)	1992	1993	1994	1995	1996	1997	1998	1999	2000
Traditional Computer Dealers	2,817	2,900	2,333	2,218	2,350	2,454	2,467	2,518	2,541
Computer Superstores	447	637	968	1,382	1,796	2,180	2,561	2,936	3,314
VARs/Systems Integrators	1,026	1,089	1,198	1,351	1,420	1,487	1,541	1,583	1,616
Local Assemblers	191	208	233	263	276	274	264	250	233
Office Product Superstores	197	324	502	733	1,002	1,261	1,515	1,782	2,056
Consumer-Electronics Stores	234	271	326	357	393	421	445	461	473
Consumer-Electronics Superstores	126	208	378	624	841	1,043	1,239	1,426	1,596
Warehouse Clubs	63	89	144	197	247	292	333	368	402
Other Mass Merchants	140	178	278	394	483	563	642	718	793
Direct Marketing/Mail Order	853	1,016	1,298	1,687	2,014	2,290	2,531	2,723	2,908
Direct Sales Force	434	398	391	368	345	324	305	288	275
Other Distribution Channels	244	253	275	300	329	353	368	381	393
Total Printer Revenue	6,772	7,572	8,325	9,875	11,496	12,942	14,211	15,433	16,601
Yearly Growth Rate (%)	16.5	11.8	10.0	18.6	16.4	12.6	9.8	8.6	7.6
All Retail Channels	1,206	1,708	2,597	3,687	4,763	5,761	6,735	7,691	8,634

The traditional computer dealers sell higher priced printers than the superstores and retain its revenue lead through 1997. Computer superstores will grow strongly and become the largest channel in 1998 followed by the direct marketing/mail order channel.The revenue market share of traditional computer dealers will decline less than in unit market share due to higher average prices than consumer oriented channels--$874 in 1995 for traditional computer dealers versus $455 for all retail-oriented channels.

Printer Technology Trends

For each distribution channel the sales of different printer technologies were projected. Four technology categories were used: Impact matrix, laser, inkjet and other printers and plotters. The laser printer category is actually the page printers and it includes LED and other page printer technologies. The "other printer & plotter" category includes thermal printers, thermal-transfer printers, all plotters technologies, line printers and the emerging multifunction-printer products.

The multifunction printer category took off in 1995 and about 200,000 multifunction printers were sold last year--more than a 20 fold increase over 1994. Multifunction printers will continue to increase the "other" category substantially in the next few years. Color-thermal transfer printers are also growing well--especially with the traditional computer dealers. Sales of thermal-transfer printers were in the 30,000 to 40,000 range in 1995. A summary of printer sales by technology for all channels is shown below:

Printer Unit Sales	1991	1992	1993	1994	1995	1996	1997	1998	1999	2000
Impact Matrix (#K)	4,035	4,206	4,064	2,680	1,688	1,240	984	775	650	519

Printer Unit Sales	1991	1992	1993	1994	1995	1996	1997	1998	1999	2000
Laser/Page (#K)	2,292	2,968	3,592	4,256	4,942	5,725	6,452	7,159	7,833	8,527
Inkjet (#K)	1,045	1,869	3,181	5,783	8,457	10,610	12,684	14,726	16,734	18,711
Other Printer/Plotters (#K)	113	118	120	151	401	723	1,046	1,407	1,768	2,161
Impact Matrix (#%)	53.9	45.9	37.1	20.8	10.9	6.8	4.6	3.2	2.4	1.7
Laser/Page Share (#%)	30.7	32.4	32.8	33.1	31.9	31.3	30.5	29.7	29.0	28.5
Inkjet Share (#%)	14.0	20.4	29.0	44.9	54.6	58.0	59.9	61.2	62.0	62.5
Other Printer/Plotters (#%)	1.5	1.3	1.1	1.2	2.6	3.9	4.9	5.8	6.6	7.2

The serial impact-matrix printer category was the volume leader in 1993, but its market share is declining rapidly due to the advances of inkjet and to a lesser degree--laser technologies. In 1994 both inkjet and laser printer categories surpassed the sales of impact matrix printers. Inkjet printers grew dramatically in 1994 and became the unit leader. Inkjet yearly sales will increase by a factor of nearly 18 from 1991 to 2000. Revenue growth and revenue market shares are shown below:

Printer Revenue	1991	1992	1993	1994	1995	1996	1997	1998	1999	2000
Impact Matrix ($M)	1,530	1,466	1,317	827	530	405	336	278	240	197
Laser/Page ($M)	3,619	4,267	4,720	5,071	5,512	6,044	6,505	6,901	7,323	7,767
Inkjet ($M)	605	971	1,450	2,327	3,284	4,108	4,847	5,524	6,155	6,755
Other Printers/Plotters ($M)	101	99	92	120	555	942	1,254	1,507	1,713	1,880
Impact Matrix ($%)	26.3	21.7	17.4	9.9	5.4	3.5	2.6	2.0	1.6	1.2
Laser/Page Share ($%)	62.3	63.0	62.3	60.9	55.8	52.6	50.3	48.6	47.5	46.8
Inkjet Share ($%)	10.4	14.3	19.2	27.9	33.3	35.7	37.5	38.9	39.9	40.7
Other Printers/Plotters ($%)	1.7	1.5	1.2	1.4	5.6	8.2	9.7	10.6	11.1	11.3

Laser printers continue to be the leader in revenue with about 56% of the market which will decline about 9% by year 2000. Due to an average price that is currently 3X the average price of inkjet products, laser printers will retain the lead in revenue. Inkjet printer revenues are growing over 11X between 1991 and 2000 and surpassed the impact matrix printer market share in 1993. The "Other" category consists of older technologies such as thermal, fully-formed-character printers and PC plotters which have declined in importance and thermal-transfer color printers and multifunction printers that are increasing in importance. Average multifunction printers are selling in the $700-$800 range. Multifunction printer revenues were $150M to $200M in the U.S. in 1995. The typical price for thermal transfer printers is $4,000 and up. The estimated revenue for thermal-transfer printers was also in the $150M to $200M range in 1995.

Data Analysis Group: Peripherals Market

"These forecasts of the total U.S. market (final sales) are based on data reported in Computer Industry Forecasts since 1984. All forecasts are computed with a statistical model which weighs information inversely to time from reporting. Forecasts are updated in January and July. There is approximately 90% confidence that forecasts lie within the Low and High limits. Product categories are presented in order appearing in Computer Industry Forecasts. Definitions are presented in alphabetical order."--Data Analysis Group

Product Categories	Year	Low	Mid	High
Printers, Impact ($B)	1993	3.8	4.2	4.8
	1994	3.4	4.2	4.5
	1995	3.7	4.1	5.1
	1996	3.2	3.8	4.6
	1997	2.8	3.5	4.2
	1998	2.5	3.1	3.9
	1999	1.8	2.6	2.9
Printers, Impact CAGR (%)	1996-99	-17.7	-12.0	-14.2
Printers, Non-impact ($B)	1993	5.7	7.3	7.6
	1994	6.3	8.2	8.6
	1995	8.0	9.1	11.6
	1996	7.9	10.1	11.8
	1997	8.4	11.2	13.2
	1998	9.0	12.3	14.6
	1999	10.0	13.8	17.1
Printers, Non-impact CAGR (%)	1996-99	8.5	10.8	13.2
Total Printers ($B)	1993	9.9	11.5	12.9
	1994	10.7	12.4	14.4
	1995	11.1	13.2	15.7
	1996	11.2	13.9	16.5
	1997	11.4	14.7	17.5
	1998	11.9	15.4	19.0
	1999	12.4	16.4	20.7
Total Printers CAGR (%)	1996-99	3.4	5.5	7.8
Hard Disk Drives ($B)	1993	13.0	15.0	16.6
	1994	13.8	15.7	17.6
	1995	14.7	16.4	18.7
	1996	14.3	17.2	19.4
	1997	14.9	18.0	21.4
	1998	14.9	18.9	22.8
	1999	14.9	19.8	24.3
Hard Disk Drives CAGR (%)	1996-99	1.3	4.8	7.9
Floppy Disk Drives ($B)	1993	1.7	2.0	2.3
	1994	1.7	2.0	2.3
	1995	1.7	2.0	2.3
	1996	1.6	1.9	2.2
	1997	1.6	1.9	2.2
	1998	1.5	1.9	2.1
	1999	1.5	1.8	2.1
Floppy Disk Drives CAGR (%)	1996-99	-1.7	-2.3	-1.7
Optical Disk Drives ($B)	1993	1.5	2.0	2.1
	1994	2.0	2.3	2.9
	1995	2.1	2.7	3.3
	1996	2.4	3.0	3.9
	1997	2.6	3.4	4.4
	1998	3.1	4.3	5.6
	1999	3.5	5.4	6.4
Optical Disk Drives CAGR (%)	1996-99	12.8	21.1	17.8

Product Categories	Year	Low	Mid	High
Total Disk Drives ($B)	1993	15.6	19.0	21.1
	1994	16.4	20.0	22.5
	1995	17.6	21.0	24.5
	1996	18.0	22.1	25.9
	1997	18.5	23.3	27.6
	1998	20.2	25.0	31.2
	1999	20.8	27.0	33.3
Total Disk Drives CAGR (%)	1996-99	5.0	6.8	8.7
Terminals, General Purpose ($B)	1993	4.8	5.3	5.8
	1994	4.9	5.6	6.3
	1995	5.0	5.8	6.7
	1996	5.1	6.1	7.1
	1997	5.2	6.4	7.5
	1998	5.3	6.7	8.0
	1999	5.5	7.1	8.6
Terminals, General Purpose CAGR (%)	1996-99	2.4	5.2	6.8
X-Terminals ($B)	1994	0.5	0.7	0.8
	1995	0.7	0.9	1.2
	1996	0.7	1.1	1.3
	1997	0.9	1.3	1.7
	1998	1.0	1.5	2.2
	1999	1.2	1.8	2.7
X-Terminals CAGR (%)	1996-99	17.9	19.1	26.1
Scanners ($B)	1993	0.6	0.7	0.9
	1994	0.7	0.9	1.2
	1995	0.7	1.1	1.2
	1996	0.9	1.3	1.6
	1997	1.0	1.5	1.9
	1998	1.2	1.7	2.4
	1999	1.4	1.9	2.8
Scanners CAGR (%)	1996-99	16.2	14.8	21.4
Power Protection ($B)	1993	0.8	1.1	1.2
	1994	1.0	1.3	1.5
	1995	1.0	1.4	1.7
	1996	1.2	1.6	2.2
	1997	1.3	1.8	2.7
	1998	1.2	2.0	2.8
	1999	1.2	2.2	3.2
Power Protection CAGR (%)	1996-99	0.2	12.0	12.7

Disk/Trend: Worldwide Disk Drive Arrays Market

"Disk drive arrays have become a major part of the data storage industry... worldwide sales revenues will exceed $7.7B in 1995 as the result of shipments of more than 565,000 arrays. Disk drive array sales for network, mini-computer and multiuser markets are expected to remain the largest product group with more than $10B in 1998 revenues. However, disk drive array sales revenues for mainframe computers are expected to peak in 1996--not because less storage capacity will be shipped, but due to continuous price reductions for the large quantity of disk drives shipped with mainframe disk arrays."--Disk/Trend

Worldwide Sales Revenues ($M)	Shipments				
Systems	1994	1995	1996	1997	1998
Single-User	16.0	20.6	29.8	35.1	42.6
Networks, Minicomputers, Multiuser	3,821.0	4,667.9	6,054.4	8,139.6	10,269.9
Mainframe	1,853.0	3,014.3	3,412.8	3,191.3	2,752.8
Very High Performance	54.6	73.2	84.2	94.4	97.2
Total, All Arrays	**5,744.6**	**7,776.0**	**9,581.2**	**11,460.4**	**13,162.5**
+%	67.2	35.4	23.2	19.6	14.9

Excerpted with permission from Disk/Trend, May 15, 1995. Copyright © 1995, Disk/Trend, Inc., 1925 Landings Drive, Mountain View CA 94043 U.S.

Disk/Trend: Worldwide Magnetic Rigid-Disk Drive Market

"The growth outlook for the rigid disk drive industry is better than ever, as demand for on-line data storage continues to be enhanced by new applications and new software. 1996 worldwide shipments of rigid disk drives are estimated at 109.2M units, an increase of 21.9% over last year. During the disk drive industry's 40 year history, There has been a continuous trend toward drives with smaller disks. That trend continues for the industry's mainstream disk drives, and after 1996, no drives with disks larger than 5.25 inches are expected to remain in production. 3.5 inch drives continue to dominate shipments for desktop personal computers, network file servers and mainframe storage systems. Shipments of 2.5 inch drives, mostly installed in notebook computers, and 1.8 inch drives used with a variety of specialized systems, are also expected to continue growing.

Drive Shipments (#K)	1995 Ship-ments	Forecast			
		1996	1997	1998	1999
10-14 Inch	5.9	0.3	-	-	-
6.5-9.5 Inch	11.8	1.0	-	-	-
5.25 Inch	706.8	4,389.8	5,075.0	5,425.0	5,445.0
3.5 Inch	77,775.8	91,895.1	108,075.0	125,870.0	144,265.0
2.5-3 Inch	10,637.8	12,536.0	14,445.0	17,030.0	19,415.0
1.8 Inch or Less	418.8	370.0	630.0	865.0	1,120.0
Total, All Groups	**89,556.9**	**109,192.2**	**128,225.0**	**149,190.0**	**170,245.0**
Growth (%)	27.9	21.9	17.4	16.4	14.1

'Dramatic annual increases in disk recording densities, combined with mushrooming demand for data storage, are pushing up typical disk drive capacities faster than ever. In 1995, drives in the 500 megabyte to 1 gigabyte range dominated worldwide shipments, but 1-2 gigabyte drives have jumped into the lead in 1996 with forecasted shipments of 47.2M units. By 1999, drives in the 5-10 gigabyte range are projected to outsell all others, with a total of 65M drives."--Disk/Trend

Capacity of Shipments (TeraByte)s	1995 Shipments	Forecast			
		1996	1997	1998	1999
Disk Cartridge Drives	105	1,002	2,304	5,135	9,035
Fixed Disk Drives:					
<300 Megabytes	1,527	233	60	29	18
300-500 Megabytes	5,170	654	291	200	185
500 Megabytes to 1 Gigabyte	28,860	27,757	10,202	3,718	1,188
1-2 Gigabytes	24,121	63,260	31,373	12,578	3,359
2-3 Gigabytes	10,775	41,620	119,623	65,560	57,061

Capacity of Shipments (TeraByte)s	1995 Shipments	Forecast			
		1996	1997	1998	1999
3-5 Gigabytes	7,120	16,128	95,904	278,258	185,187
5-10 Gigabytes	2,974	12,469	35,712	256,613	454,793
>10 Gigabytes	25	920	10,420	77,377	643,766
Total Capacity in Terabytes	**80,677**	**164,033**	**305,889**	**699,468**	**1,354,592**

Disk/Trend: Worldwide Optical Disk Drive Market

"Booming sales of CD-ROM drives during the last two years have provided a major boost to overall sales of optical disk drives, with the industry's 1994 revenues climbing to $3.7B, a one-year jump of 68%. 1994's shipments of 24M CD-ROM drives provided 77% of all optical disk drive sales revenues, with continuing growth for CD-ROM drives expected to top 34M in 1995 increasing to almost 61M drives in 1998.

'The emergence of CD-ROM drives as a major computer industry product area has prompted numerous new programs in related product lines. In addition to the impact on software publishing and distribution, increasing CD-ROM demand has stimulated development of CD-ROM format disk libraries for applications of all sizes."--Disk/Trend

Optical Disk Drives					
Worldwide Shipments (#K)	1994	1995	1996	1997	1998
CD-ROM	24,048.2	34,218.4	44,619.0	55,725.0	60,923.0
Read/Write <1 Gigabyte	724.2	1,081.4	1,554.3	2,580.2	5,583.2
Read/Write >1 Gigabyte	8.6	20.8	98.1	279.1	1,339.5
Total, All Drives	**24,781.0**	**35,320.6**	**46,271.4**	**58,584.3**	**67,845.7**
+%	114.8	42.5	31.0	26.6	15.8

Note: Read/write drives include write-once, rewritable and multifunction types.

Optical Disk Libraries					
Worldwide Shipments (#K)	1994	1995	1996	1997	1998
CD-ROM	52,753	139,055	316,597	662,233	1,260,293
Read/Write, 1-39 Disks	12,740	18,636	21,700	24,890	27,896
Read/Write, 40-69 Disks	1,832	2,701	3,194	3,627	4,010
Read/Write, >70 Disks	2,749	3,329	3,931	4,527	5,130
Total, All Libraries	**70,074**	**163,722**	**345,422**	**695,277**	**1,297,329**
+%	104.7	133.6	111.0	101.3	86.6

Disk/Trend: Worldwide Removable Data Storage Market

"Overall sales revenue growth for the removable data storage products included in the report is expected to increase only from $2.9B to $3.1B in the five year period ending in 1998, the increase in unit shipments during the same period is projected to increase manyfold for most of the product groups. The fastest growing product group is expected to be high capacity floppy drives, forecasted to jump from 203,500 drives in 1994 to 3.4M in 1998.

'Low-capacity floppy drives are included in the Disk/Trend Report on removable data storage for the first time this year, providing extremely high shipment levels, but very low pricing. The 1994 total for 8, 5.25 and 3.5 inch floppy drives was 75.5M drives, with the 1998 total projected at 92.9M. Total 1994 sales revenues of $2.3B for all types of low-capacity floppy drives are destined to slump to $1.7B in 1998, as average prices decline faster than shipments increase and as older drive models sold at higher prices disappear from the market."--Disk/Trend

Worldwide Shipments (#K)	1994 Shipments	Forecast			
		1995	1996	1997	1998
PCMCIA Flash Cards	491.9	835.4	1,347.5	1,965.3	2,780.5
PCMCIA Rigid Disk Drives	156.1	319.0	570.0	785.0	990.0
Rigid-Disk Cartridge Drives	468.4	742.0	1,300.0	1,680.0	1,985.0
Small-Optical Disk Drives	482.8	596.8	728.5	882.0	1,007.5
High-Capacity Flexible Disk Drives	203.5	475.0	1,205.0	2,235.0	3,430.0
Low-Capacity Flexible Disk Drives	75,514.0	78,204.0	82,178.0	87,138.0	92,930.0
Total Shipments	**77,316.7**	**81,172.2**	**87,329.0**	**94,685.3**	**103,123.0**
Growth (%)	15.3	5.0	7.6	8.4	8.9

Excerpted with permission from Disk/Trend, September 12, 1995. Copyright © 1995, Disk/Trend, Inc., 1925 Landings Dr., Mt. View CA 94043 USA.

Freeman Associates: Worldwide Automated Optical Library Products Market

"The worldwide market for automated optical library products will grow from $380M in 1994 to $943M in 2000, a rate of 16%... Libraries based on three optical disk technologies are analyzed through the year 2000... The authors predict combined shipments of all classes of automated optical libraries to grow from 76,000 units in 1994 to more than 2M units in 2000, a 73% compound annual growth rate. The difference in growth rates between revenues and shipments reflects anticipated price erosion and the growth popularity of smaller, lower cost libraries.

'CD-ROM/CD-R devices will increasingly dominate the market for optical disk libraries throughout the forecast period, growing from 72% of all units shipped in 1994 to 96% of all units in 2000. In terms of revenue, however, the CD-ROM/CD-R class of products commanded a mere 11% of total revenue in 1994, behind the 3.5-inch to 5.25-inch and the 12-inch and 14-inch product classes. Only by 1996 will CD-ROM/CD-R libraries move into second position to eventually earn 41% of the 2000 revenue total.

'The 3.5-inch to 5.25-inch library groups accounted for 24% of industry units and 56% of revenue in 1994 and are forecast to shrink to 3% and 42% respectively in 2000. As in the CD-ROM/CD-R field, a very active market for low-end libraries will spur demand, accounting for 77% of shipments in the 2000 market. Annual growth of 31% will pace the largest segment of this product class--libraries utilizing fewer than 30 disks--to more than 53,800 units delivered in 2000. Libraries with 30 to 99 disks will lead the revenue race until 1997, when more compact devices move into the lead. Products with 100 or more disks represent the smallest of these product segments, despite annual shipment growth of 15%.

'The 12-inch and 14-inch optical library groups will continue modest growth in shipments from 2,600 units in 1994 to 5,000 units in 2000. Such products will maintain a capacity and performance edge over 5.25-inch libraries, providing an upgrade path to a dedicated cadre of write-once users."--Freeman Associates

	1994	1995	1996	1998	2000
Unit Shipments (K)					
3.5-Inch to 5.25-Inch	18	26	35	54	70
12-Inch and 14-Inch	3	3	4	4	5
CD-ROM/CD-R	55	301	603	1,330	1,966

	1994	1995	1996	1998	2000
Total Shipments	76	330	642	1,388	2,041
Installed Base	162	485	1,111	3,388	6,590
Revenue ($M)					
3.5-Inch to 5.25-Inch	215	255	286	349	396
12-Inch and 14-Inch	124	137	144	154	161
CD-ROM/CD-R	41	92	152	276	386
Total Revenue	380	484	582	779	943

Freeman Associates: Worldwide Automated Tape Libraries Market

"The worldwide market for automated tape libraries will grow from $1.5B in 1995 to $2.1B in 2001. The appeal of these libraries will be enhanced by forthcoming advances in the underlying storage technologies, enabling automated libraries to meet the needs of ever-more demanding applications. In spite of lower-than-expected shipments in 1995, demand for libraries using DAT technology is expected to grow rapidly. Shipments of 2,599 units in 1995 will increase to more than 34,000 units in 2001 and revenue will expand from $19M to $152M. With initial shipments in 1989, 8-millimeter was the first small-form factor tape technology to be used in an automated setting. Unit shipments of these libraries will lead the market throughout the forecast period, growing from 11,412 in 1995 to nearly 38,600 in 2001."--Freeman Associates

Year	1995	1996	1997	2001
Unit Shipments				
DAT	2,599	6,690	13,100	34,271
8-Millimeter	11,412	16,052	20,738	38,577
DLT	1,260	6,649	11,915	26,000
Half-Inch Cartridge	2,288	2,507	2,737	3,117
Half-Inch Helical	58	74	92	163
19-Millimeter	97	111	110	6
Total Shipments	17,714	32,083	48,692	102,134
Growth From Previous Year (%)	174	81	52	9
Installed Base at Year End	33,763	65,087	112,329	414,035
Revenue ($M)				
DAT	19	48	81	152
8-Millimeter	84	111	132	214
DLT	67	215	338	548
Half-Inch Cartridge	1,241	1,198	1,239	1,162
Half-Inch Helical	7	7	9	10
19-Millimeter	44	48	45	2
Total Revenue	1,462	1,627	1,844	2,088
Growth From Previous Year (%)	6	11	13	-1

Freeman Associates: Worldwide High Performance Tape Market

"High performance tape drives are playing an increasingly important role on networked environments for secondary storage and the rapid backing up of record large numbers of files...

'New product developments in high-performance tape, such as the introduction of 128-track half-inch cartridge models, are responsible for this overall market trend. A shift away from reel drives to higher-priced 128-track and StorageTek's RedWood helical-scan products is reflected in revenue growth, rising from $961M in 1994 to $1.4B in 2000, a 7% annualized rate... Shipments totaled 74,100 units in 1994, a decline of 7% from the previous year, and will decline again in 1995, but will climb to 78,200 in 2000, an effective growth rate of 1% for the six-year period. Half-inch cartridge drives will lead the growth with a projected 96% of the high performance market by 2000, while reel drives will dwindle from 40% of the 1994 total to 0% by 2000. Shipments of helical scan drives will grow to 4% of the high-performance market during this period...

'Sales of half-inch reel-to-reel magnetic-tape drives have dropped each year since peaking at 189,000 units in 1985. This decline is projected to continue unabated--shipments of reel drives will drop from 29,900 in 1994 to 1,200 in 1999, their final year of shipment.

'...helical scan products are on an upswing, principally because of the introductions of half-inch RedWood technology by StorageTek and Akebono by Sony. Shipments in the half-inch helical scan product category, which also includes VHS data drives, will rise from 294 units in 1994 to 1,525 in 2000, a 32% compounded rate of growth....revenue to surge in the same six-year period from $4.6M to $114M, an annual growth rate of 71%."--Freeman Associates

	1994	1995	1996	1998	2000
Unit Shipments (K)					
Half-Inch Cartridge	43.6	47.5	56.9	71.1	74.9
Half-Inch Reel	29.9	22.8	15.2	4.3	0
Helical Scan	0.6	0.9	1.4	2.4	3.3
Total Shipments	**74.1**	**71.2**	**73.5**	**77.8**	**78.2**
Installed Base	**643**	**574**	**522**	**463**	**450**
Revenue ($M)					
Half-Inch Cartridge	785	883	1,051	1,325	1,240
Half-Inch Reel	146	111	72	20	0
Helical Scan	30	63	97	159	184
Total Revenue	**961**	**1,057**	**1,220**	**1,504**	**1,424**

Freeman Associates: Worldwide Mid-Range Tape Market

"Worldwide market demand for computer tape drives utilizing DAT, 8mm and compact half-inch serpentine technology will approach $1.5B at OEM price levels in 2000, an 8% annual growth rate from $955M in 1994. In 1995 the market for these mid-range tape drives is projected to grow at a 34% rate in units and a 22% rate in revenue, driven largely by the rapid growth of DAT deliveries... High volume shipments of workstations, networked systems and small business computers have generated a growing requirement for high-capacity disk-backup solutions... A wide variety of new small-form-factor tape drives is responding to this market opportunity, offering ever lower prices, larger capacities and higher performance...

'A well-defined migration path offering faster and higher capacity drives--and rapidly declining prices--have solidified DAT's position in the highly-competitive small-tape market. DAT drives currently provide 2 GB (DDS) to 12 GB (DDS-3) of uncompressed storage capacity. These devices have wide appeal due to their compact, low-cost media and their ability to fit within a 3.5-inch package.

'Shipments of DAT drives reached 820,000 units in 1994--up 60% from the prior year. Unit shipments are projected to exceed 1.8M in 2000, a 14% annual growth rate during the forecast period. Declining prices will limit compound revenue growth to 9% over this period, however, from $571M in 1994 to $974 in 2000, expressed at OEM levels. Revenue from 2 GB models peaked in 1994 at $418M and will cease in 1998. Revenue from 4 GB models will surpass that of 2 GB models in 1995 and will combine with future models to reach $974M in 2000.

'The late 1995 introduction of the Mammoth product expanded the capacity range of eight-millimeter drives from 2.5 GB to 20 GB, all in 5.25-inch half-high packages. Eight-millimeter products continue to grow in popularity, due in part to aggressive marketing and an ambitious migration path to higher capacity and performance... Use of automated media libraries and changers will maintain this appeal: Eight-millimeter products will encounter keen competition from both above and below, however, as DAT, quarter-inch and DLT tape products target similar opportunities."--Freeman Associates

	1994	1995	1996	2000
Unit Shipments (K)				
DAT	820	1,149	1,370	1,803
8-Millimeter	203	216	228	284
Half-Inch Serpentine	49	72	96	158
Total Shipments	1,072	1,437	1,694	2,245
Growth (%)	48	34	18	6
Installed Base	2,736	3,875	5,124	9,275
Revenue ($M)				
DAT	571	739	835	974
8-Millimeter	282	282	298	333
Half-Inch Serpentine	102	143	169	198
Total Revenue	955	1,164	1,302	1,505
Growth (%)	35	22	12	1

Excerpted with permission from Freeman Assoc., Dec. 27 1995. Copyright © 1995, Freeman Assoc., 311 E. Carrillo St., Santa Barbara CA 93101 U.S.

Freeman Associates: Worldwide Minicartridge Market

"Ever-expanding shipments of hard-disk drives of ever-increasing capacities are fueling a strong pull-through of companion-tape drives. This demand greatly benefits quarter-inch cartridge drives and is reflected in forecasts of increasing future demand. Industry revenue for all classes of quarter-inch cartridge drives, both minicartridge and data-cartridge units, will expand to $844M at OEM levels in 2000, a 7% compounded annual growth rate from the $568M value of the 1994 market. The authors predict combined shipments of these products to grow from 3.6M units in 1994 to 7.5M in 2000, a 13% annual rate.

'Drives using compact minicartridges will be the fastest-growing category of quarter-inch devices... The introduction of higher-capacity media choices is a prime reason for the expected growth of minicartridge drives. Shipment growth from nearly 2.9M minicartridge drives in 1994 to 7.2M in 2000--a 17% annual rate. A strong shift to higher capacity models is predicted within these projections. Demand for 5.25-inch data-cartridge drives eased off to 735K units in 1994 from a peak of 868K units in 1992. This decline is expected to continue, with total data-cartridge drive shipments subsiding to 220K units in 2000. OEM-level revenues will recede from $263M in 1994 to $100M in 2000."--Freeman Associates

	1994	1995	1996	2000
Unit Shipments (K)				
Minicartridge	2,880	3,585	4,387	7,238
Data Cartridge	735	562	427	220
Total Drives	3,615	4,147	4,814	7,458
Growth From Previous Year (%)	20	15	16	8
Installed Base at Year End	11,231	13,399	15,759	26,920
Revenue ($M at OEM Level)				
Minicartridge	305	393	493	744

	1994	1995	1996	2000
Data Cartridge	263	198	162	100
Total Revenue	**568**	**591**	**655**	**844**
Growth From Previous Year (%)	2	4	11	0

Freeman Associates: Worldwide Optical Data Storage Market

"The optical disk drive industry shipped 21.3M units into data storage markets in 1994 and is projected to deliver more than 34.5M units in 1995--a 62% rate of growth. This demand is forecast to expand at an average yearly rate of 21% to 67.2M units in 2000...

'...the worldwide market for optical disk drives will exceed $8.2B at OEM price levels in 2000, an 18% compounded growth rate from the $3.1B value of the 1994 market. While total drive shipments in 1994 were up 145% over 1993 levels, revenue was up by only 74%... This difference in rates is due to a shift in mix toward lower-cost CD-ROM drives and to falling prices for all categories of optical products. CD-ROM devices accounted for 96.9% of all optical drives shipped for computer use and 76% of total revenue in 1994. Rewritable products followed with 2.9% of shipments and 17.6% of revenue. Write-once products comprised the remainder."--Freeman Associates

Shipments (#K)	1994	1995	1996	2000
Rewritable	608	1,144	1,941	6,188
Write-Once	56	185	348	580
CD-ROM	20,672	33,204	40,800	60,400
Total Shipments	**21,336**	**34,533**	**43,089**	**67,168**
% Growth	145	62	25	7
Installed Base	32,935	60,493	89,818	180,336

Revenue ($M)	1994	1995	1996	2000
Rewritable	543	659	933	2,154
Write-Once	194	274	332	250
CD-ROM	2,351	3,477	4,027	5,798
Total Revenue	**3,088**	**4,410**	**5,292**	**8,202**
% Growth	74	43	20	4

Frost & Sullivan: Multimedia Hardware & Software Markets

"Driven by maturing and proliferating development tools, multimedia's ability to bring together motion video, sound, animation, still images and text on a personal computer or workstation is expected to make it the most common form of computing. By the end of the decade, most computer platforms should include multimedia elements. These will likely be integrated on the motherboard, or be included as add-on components. Training, presentation, point-of-sale and referencing databases all benefit from the speed and interactivity of computers. These functions also benefit from the power and effective communication inherent in sound, moving video and animation."--Frost & Sullivan

Total U.S. Revenue, 1990 - 2000		
Year	Revenues ($B)	% Rev. Growth Rate
1990	3.14	-

Total U.S. Revenue, 1990 - 2000		
Year	Revenues ($B)	% Rev. Growth Rate
1991	3.39	7.9
1992	3.91	15.4
1993	4.92	25.8
1994	6.87	39.7
1995	9.78	42.4
1996	14.09	44.0
1997	18.34	30.1
1998	21.42	16.8
1999	22.44	4.7
2000	22.19	(1.1)
Compound Annual Growth Rate (1993-2000): 24.0%		

Note: All figures are rounded.

Total Worldwide % of Revenues by Product Type, 1990 - 2000					
Year	Computing Platforms	Authoring Software	Video Products	Audio Products	Animation Software
1990	84.7	6.4	0.8	6.3	1.7
1991	81.5	7.2	1.7	7.5	2.1
1992	76.7	7.9	4.0	9.0	2.5
1993	69.4	8.4	9.0	10.3	2.9
1994	62.0	8.5	14.9	11.4	3.1
1995	58.5	9.1	17.8	11.1	3.6
1996	57.7	9.8	18.9	9.7	3.9
1997	58.3	11.0	18.6	8.2	3.9
1998	58.3	12.3	18.9	6.9	3.6
1999	58.2	12.4	19.9	6.2	3.3
2000	57.0	13.3	21.1	5.6	3.0

Frost & Sullivan: Worldwide Optical Disk Market

"Worldwide sales of optical disk drives and media will more than quadruple from $2.6B in 1993 to $11.5B by the year 2000, growing at a 24% compound annual rate, while unit growth reaches an even greater 44% CAGR.

'As of 1994, CD-ROM accounted for 96% of market revenues and rewritable drives and media 4%.

'In 1994, 40% of PCs were shipped with CD-ROM drives already installed, with major firms like Apple, IBM and Compaq including them as standard equipment on most models. By the end of the decade, a projected 90% of PCs will ship with CD-ROM drives.

'Optical storage will increasingly be adopted for mainstream applications as it is seen to provide removable, high-capacity, random access media offering long-term data integrity and resistance to magnetic corruption.

'Rewritable drive shipments, which is so far representing a relatively small market, grew at an estimated 31% rate in 1994. Rewritable firms are hoping next-generation capacity drives such as 230 and 640 megabyte 3.5-inch drives will allow their products to compete for multimedia development and playback, and for desktop publishing. At the same time, these capacity increases are putting rewritable drives further from the sub-$500 price point important to mass market buyers.

'CD-recordable drive firms have had better success pushing prices down to mass market levels. The jukebox market, which includes 5.25-inch, 12- and 14-inch and CD-ROM jukeboxes, is also emerging as storage demands rise and the number of available CD-ROM titles passes 8,000.

'Optical and magnetic superresolution will play major roles in increasing capacity by 1996, reducing laser beam size and so facilitating higher bit-density. After a long slow development curve, optical storage technology will see frequent capacity and performance increases in the near future, helping it penetrate applications until now inaccessible.''--Frost & Sullivan

Year	Units (M)	Unit Growth (%)	Rev. ($B)	Rev. Growth (%)
1990	17.0	-	0.78	-
1991	33.0	88.3	1.06	35.9
1992	59.4	85.8	1.61	51.8
1993	103.3	73.9	2.55	58.7
1994	194.7	88.5	3.92	53.5
1995	328.4	68.7	5.19	32.5
1996	497.6	51.5	6.44	24.2
1997	700.4	40.8	7.67	19.0
1998	898.6	28.3	8.92	16.3
1999	1,092.9	21.6	10.19	14.2
2000	1,307.4	19.6	11.55	13.4
CAGR (1990-2000)	-	54.4	-	30.9

Giga Information Group: U.S. Infrared Technology Market

"Infrared (IR) technology, seen as a cordless serial port primarily linking mobile devices to computing platforms, is poised to replace local data transmission links in mobile and desktop computers and to provide additional connections to other devices, such as PDAs...

'A small portion of today's notebooks and subnotebooks offer IrDA (Infrared Data Association) standardized ports and it is likely that the majority will incorporate IrDA, at least as an option, within the next 12 to 18 months.

	1995	1996	1997	1998
U.S. Unit Shipments (#K)	4,233	4,762	5,336	5,957
% IR Implementation	32	85	100	100
% Slow IR (SIR) 115 Kbps/1,000 Kbps	90	60	25	0
% Fast IR (FIR) 4,000 Kbps/10,000 Kbps	10	40	75	100

'The wide use of infrared devices in the home, primarily television and VCR remote controls, has painlessly trained a large population of potential 'beamers' in the usage requirements and limits of IR transmission.

'BIS believes IR technology will quickly find its way into printers, desktop systems, watches and other common devices. However, the keys to high-value, fast adoption IR-enabled products will be the integration of mobile and stationary devices and the flexible distribution of functions between these types of devices. Fortunately, these characteristics are central to the directions of IrDA's future.''--Giga Information Group

Giga Information Group: U.S. Multifunction Products Market

"The U.S. market for multifunction products is forecasted to reach more than $2.8B in 1995, accounting for 1.3M units being sold... Multifunction products are a combination of two or more of the print, fax, copy and/or scan functions in one machine.

'In 1994, the U.S. multifunction products market surpassed $1B, selling over 310,000 units. BIS forecasts that 7.2M units will be sold by 1999, accounting for more than $10B! This represents a compound annual growth rate of 88%. Interestingly, more than two-thirds of the units sold in 1999 will be low-end products and will be targeted to small offices/home offices and individual desktops in corporations."--Giga Information Group

Year	1992	1993	1994	1995	1996	1997	1998	1999
All MFPs (#K)	51	91	311	1,342	2,841	4,450	5,773	7,223

Excerpted with permission, Aug. 1995. Copyright © 1995, Giga Information Grp., 1 Kendall Sq, Bldg 1400W, Cambridge MA 02139 U.S.

Pacific Media Associates: Worldwide LCD Projector Market

"...Pacific Media Associates has estimated that the worldwide market will grow from $434M in 1994 to $2,077M in 1999, a compound annual growth rate of 36%. Contributing to this growth rate will be a continued expansion in the numbers of manufacturers--including some giant companies that have not yet participated in this market--and models--including a broadening variety of configurations--as well as lower prices due to both improved technology and competitive necessity.

'Many users strongly prefer projectors to panels because of their fully-integrated designs, which reduce setup time and clutter in demonstration and presentation situations... Furthermore, the continued miniaturization of these products matches their growing use for portable applications. And, as compared to panels, the ability to design compact and streamlined models, as well as to reduce their manufacturing costs dramatically, results from eliminating the rather severe constraint of the overhead projector."--Pacific Media Associates

Year	1989	1990	1991	1992	1993	1994	1995	1996	1997	1998	1999
LCD Projectors ($M)	23	42	56	83	171	434	763	1,160	1,499	1,806	2,077

Excerpted with permission from Pacific Media Assoc., April 27 1995. Copyright © 1995, Pacific Media Associ., 1121 Clark Ave., Mt. View CA 94040 U.S.

Pacific Media Associates: Worldwide LCD Projection Panel Market

"...Pacific Media Associates has estimated that the worldwide market will grow from $674M in 1994 to $1,361M in 1999, a compound annual growth rate of 14%. According to the firm's analysis, continued improvements in technology and inclusion of advanced features from the earlier high-end models, coupled with declining prices and growing user awareness, will help keep demand growing at double-digit rates.

'...the research firm has concluded that the technologies and features expected to grow faster than their alternatives include 'high color' (over 512 colors), high resolution (over 640 X 480), active matrix materials and built-in video. Most users will continue to pay well for fully-featured units..."--Pacific Media Associates

Year	1989	1990	1991	1992	1993	1994	1995	1996	1997	1998	1999
Worldwide Sales ($M)	132	167	278	376	469	674	940	1,155	1,273	1,335	1,361

Excerpted with permission from Pacific Media Assoc., April 28 1995. Copyright © 1995, Pacific Media Assoc., 1121 Clark Ave., Mt. View CA 94040 U.S.

Software and Service

Data Analysis Group: Software and Services Market

"These forecasts of the total U.S. market (final sales) are based on data reported in Computer Industry Forecasts since 1984. All forecasts are computed with a statistical model which weighs information inversely to time from reporting. Forecasts are updated in January and July. There is approximately 90% confidence that forecasts lie within the Low and High limits. Product categories are presented in order appearing in Computer Industry Forecasts. Definitions are presented in alphabetical order."--Data Analysis Group

Product Categories	Year	Low	Mid	High
Systems Integration ($B)	1993	12.4	17.0	18.6
	1994	15.4	19.2	23.9
	1995	15.7	21.5	25.1
	1996	19.3	24.3	31.9
	1997	19.3	27.5	32.8
	1998	23.1	30.8	40.7
	1999	23.2	34.5	42.2
Systems Integration CAGR (%)	1996-99	6.3	12.3	9.8
EDI Software & Services ($B)	1993	0.3	0.4	0.5
	1994	0.4	0.5	0.6
	1995	0.5	0.8	0.9
	1996	0.6	1.0	1.2
	1997	0.8	1.3	1.7
	1998	1.0	1.6	2.4
	1999	1.0	2.0	2.8
EDI Software & Services CAGR (%)	1996-99	16.5	25.1	31.1
Multiuser Software ($B)	1993	18.5	21.0	23.5
	1994	19.4	22.3	25.8
	1995	19.6	23.5	27.1
	1996	19.9	24.7	28.6
	1997	20.3	25.8	30.5
	1998	21.1	26.8	33.0
	1999	20.9	27.7	34.1
Multiuser Software CAGR (%)	1996-99	1.6	4.0	6.0
PC Software ($B)	1993	6.3	7.0	8.0
	1994	6.6	7.6	8.8
	1995	7.2	8.3	9.9
	1996	7.7	9.0	11.1
	1997	8.1	9.7	12.2
	1998	8.4	10.4	13.2
	1999	8.3	11.2	13.5
PC Software CAGR (%)	1996-99	2.4	7.7	6.8

Forward Concepts: Worldwide Teleconferencing Market

"The overall teleconferencing industry will grow from over $866M in 1995 to over $3.6B in 2000, a 33% growth rate. Some segments, however, such as group videoconferencing, will actually decline in overall market revenues. Such a decline will occur because growth in unit volumes will not be able to keep pace with declines in unit prices. Price declines will be most aggressive at the desktop level, as cameras, codecs and software all experience price decreases. The study concludes that the industry is on the threshold of achieving the price levels needed for wide scale acceptance."--Forward Concepts

Teleconferencing Segments ($M)	1995	2000
Group Videoconferencing	635	405
Desktop Videoconferencing	120	1,632
Gateways/MCUs	44	377
Videophones	37	582
Data Conferencing	30	646
Total	**866**	**3,642**

The telecom delivery media for the desktop videoconferencing market is shown below.

Year ($M)	1995	1996	1997	1998	1999	2000	CAGR (%)
Phone (POTS)	16	106	217	443	665	762	116.6
ISDN	78	80	86	89	92	96	4.2
LAN	26	41	76	119	274	328	66.0
Cable TV	0	8	24	74	155	236	133.1
ATM	1	10	14	28	105	211	191.6
Total	**121**	**245**	**417**	**753**	**1,291**	**1,633**	**68.3**

Excerpted with permission from Forward Concepts, Dec. 11 1995. Copyright © 1995, Forward Concepts, 1575 W University Dr. #111, Tempe AZ 85281 U.S.

Frost & Sullivan: U.S. Banking Automation Software Market

"U.S. banking automation software markets will more than double from $1.6B in 1994 to $3.6B by the year 2001, growing at a 13% compound annual rate...

'The share of overall market revenue generated by banking operations software will rise from 47% in 1994 to 51% in 2001 while the investment analysis software share correspondingly dips from 36 to 32% and that of electronic funds transfer (EFT) holds steady at 17% in the same period...

'Adoption of new technologies will be slower than often anticipated, due to the large costs of investment, implementation and training, and banks' reluctance to invest in client-server systems requires major restructuring of both information technology departments and information systems, favoring gradual migration rather than rapid and wholesale shifts to new systems.

'Besides client/server architecture and object-oriented programming, the increased use of graphical-user interfaces (GUIs) will be a major programming trend."--Frost & Sullivan

Year	Revenues ($M)	% Growth
1991	1,093.0	11.0
1992	1,212.7	13.4
1993	1,375.8	13.6
1994	1,562.5	13.9
1995	1,780.0	14.9
1996	2,045.0	14.4
1997	2,340.4	12.8
1998	2,639.8	11.6

Year	Revenues ($M)	% Growth
1999	2,946.5	10.7
2000	3,260.8	9.6
2001	3,572.7	-
CAGR: 12.5%		

Frost & Sullivan: U.S. CASE/OOPS Software Market

"The U.S. market for CASE/OOPS software will more than double from $1.6B in 1994 to $4.2B by the year 2001, growing at a 15% compound annual rate. Both object-oriented technologies and client-server environments are driving a resurgence of CASE/OOPS software tools frequently used in the business re-engineering process."-- Frost & Sullivan

Year	Revenues ($M)	Revenue Growth (%)
1991	361.2	-
1992	544.3	50.7
1993	1,068.4	96.3
1994	1,589.8	48.8
1995	2,060.4	29.6
1996	2,524.0	22.5
1997	2,826.8	12.0
1998	3,050.2	7.9
1999	3,300.3	8.2
2000	3,676.5	11.4
2001	4,235.3	15.2
1991-2001 Compound Annual Growth Rate is 27.9%		

Frost & Sullivan: U.S. Data Compression Market

"Paced by tremendous growth in motion-video compression, the U.S. data compression market will grow to eight times its present size, from $161M in 1994 to $1.3B by the year 2001, at a 35% compound annual rate.

'Motion-video will increase its share of this total market from 45% of revenues in 1994 to 70% in 2001 while speech compression dips in share from 43 to 28% though growing dramatically in absolute terms and still image and text compression plummets form 12 to 2% in the same period.

'End-user adoption has increased as technology evolved, standards developed and prices declined. The industry is set for a growth explosion with the outlook dramatically improved from five years ago, when this market was beset by costly products, a dearth of standards and low general understanding of the technologies. Digital television is expected to take off in the 1995-96 period with many cable subscribers switching to digital TV and high growth continuing the rest of the decade. Motion-video compression growth will also be driven by videoconferencing and video CD and authoring applications. Videoconferencing will show substantial growth potential as prices decline and desktop conferencing on personal computers becomes a presence."--Frost & Sullivan

Year	Units (K)	Unit Grwth (%)	Rev. ($M)	Rev. Grwth (%)
1991	1,760.8	-	49.9	-
1992	2,395.5	36.0	67.1	34.5

Year	Units (K)	Unit Grwth (%)	Rev. ($M)	Rev. Grwth (%)
1993	3,590.9	49.9	98.8	47.2
1994	5,828.3	62.3	160.6	62.5
1995	9,896.6	69.8	278.9	73.6
1996	16,183.2	63.6	462.5	65.9
1997	23,383.4	44.5	664.5	43.7
1998	30,192.2	29.1	854.3	28.6
1999	36,688.5	21.5	1,024.1	19.9
2000	42,427.0	15.6	1,169.8	14.2
2001	47,505.9	12.0	1,289.0	10.2
1991-2001 CAGR	-	39.0	-	38.4

Excerpted with permission from Frost & Sullivan, March 1995. Copyright © 1995, Frost & Sullivan, 2525 Charleston Rd., Mt. View CA 94043 USA.

Frost & Sullivan: Worldwide EDI Market

"The worldwide electronic data interchange (EDI) market will more than quadruple from $700M in 1994 to $3.2B by the year 2001, growing at a 24% compound annual rate. Value-added network services will rise in revenue percentage of the market from 80% in 1994 to 85% in 2001 while software correspondingly dips from 20 to 15% in the same period while growing strongly in absolute terms."--Frost & Sullivan

Year	Revenue ($M)	Rev. Growth (%)
1991	250.60	-
1992	360.59	43.9
1993	510.27	41.5
1994	699.01	37.0
1995	928.17	32.8
1996	1,199.92	29.3
1997	1,520.54	26.7
1998	1,867.02	22.8
1999	2,269.20	21.5
2000	2,726.74	20.2
2001	3,195.44	17.2
1991-2001 Compound Annual Growth Rate is 28.2%.		

Excerpted with permission from Frost & Sullivan, March 1995. Copyright © 1995, Frost & Sullivan, 2525 Charleston Rd., Mt. View CA 94043 U.S.

Frost & Sullivan: Worldwide Geographical Information Systems Market

"Worldwide markets for geographical information systems (GIS) software and services will more than triple from $1.2B in 1993 to $3.8B in 1999, growing at a 21% compound annual rate. The share spent on software will rise from 46% in 1993 to 52% by 1999."--Frost & Sullivan

Year	1989	1990	1991	1992	1993	1994	1995	1996	1997	1998	1999
Revenue ($B)	0.66	0.76	0.89	1.04	1.24	1.49	1.80	2.18	2.63	3.17	3.82
Revenue Growth (%)	-	15.9	16.8	17.6	18.7	20.1	20.3	21.6	20.6	20.4	20.4

1989-1999 Compound Annual Growth Rate: 19.2%.

Giga Information Group: Worldwide Workflow Tools Software Market

"The worldwide market for workflow tools, which includes development tools, the workflow engine, database and desktop runtime components, is projected to grow from $213M in 1994 to $824M in 1999. Moreover, the total value of workflow-enabled software, which is application software bundled with workflow tools as part of a business solution, and workflow tools software (not counting custom applications) will grow from $580M in 1994 to almost $3B in 1999!

Giga Information Group segments the workflow software market into three categories: •Production Workflow deals with transaction-orientated, high-value, repetitive processes such as insurance claims or accounts payable. It represents the largest segment of the workflow tools market, growing to $482M in 1999.

•Collaborative Workflow deals with high-value, non-repetitive, generally nontransaction-orientated processes such as new product development, sales force automation or technical document assembly. Projected to grow to $104M in 1999, this segment represents the smallest, but in many ways the most visible segment of the workflow tools market.

•Administrative/Ad Hoc Workflow deals with low-value processes generally connected to routine office work, like travel expense reporting or budgeting, rather than processes integral to the line of business. This segment is expected to grow to $237M in 1999.--Giga Information Group

Workflow Tools Software	1993	1994	1995	1996	1997	1998	1999
Revenue ($M)	139.72	212.53	329.81	465.06	573.24	699.82	823.72

Software Publishers Association: North American PC Software Market

"The combined sales of personal computer application software in the United States and Canada reached $7.53B in 1995, a 12% increase from a revised $6.7B in 1994. Fourth quarter 1995 sales were $2.07B, down 8.8% from the record Q4 94, where sales were $2.27B. For the year, unit sales in North America increased 60% and were up 35% for Q4 95 over the same period in 1994. Worldwide unit sales increased 37% for Q4 95 and 71% for the year as a whole."--Software Publishers Association

1995 North American PC Software Sales ($M)				
Software Platforms	PC/MS-DOS	Windows	Macintosh	Other	Total
Entertainment	288.0	274.2	86.9	NA	649.1
Home Education	36.3	423.6	108.9	2.9	571.6
Finance	82.3	294.8	50.7	NA	427.7
Word Processors	25.5	987.3	63.5	9.3	1,085.7
Spreadsheets	12.3	803.4	46.8	2.8	865.2
Databases	9.2	305.3	25.1	NA	340.4
Integrated	2.1	84.7	45.3	NA	132.1
Utilities	76.2	297.9	51.6	26.7	452.4
Presentation Graphics	1.5	315.0	29.9	NA	347.1
Drawing & Painting	NA	150.5	159.0	7.5	317.0

1995 North American PC Software Sales ($M)					
Software Platforms	PC/MS-DOS	Windows	Macintosh	Other	Total
Desktop Publishing	NA	179.4	82.6	NA	262.0
Other Graphics	17.2	278.3	68.2	NA	364.1
Project Management	7.6	164.2	16.8	NA	188.7
Personal Information Managers	1.0	204.0	27.3	NA	232.6
Languages & Tools	8.6	231.6	8.0	1.2	249.3
Other Productivity	149.5	660.1	184.1	46.5	1,040.3
Total	717.4	5,654.3	1,054.7	98.9	7,525.3

Note that the SPA's software market estimates are based on sales reports from their members, which include most of the important U.S. software vendors. Hence this is probably the best market data available for the PC software market. However, the overall PC software market is likely 10-15% bigger than SPA 's sales report due to the large number of small software companies that do not report sales data to SPA.

1994 North American PC Software Sales ($M)					
Software Platforms	PC/MS-DOS	Windows	Macintosh	Other	Total
Entertainment	182.1	190.6	82.0	NA	454.8
Home Education	171.7	324.4	116.3	8.4	566.2
Finance	116.2	233.6	46.5	NA	398.5
Word Processors	95.3	826.9	94.0	13.1	1,029.3
Spreadsheets	62.2	689.3	69.0	8.7	829.2
Databases	29.6	279.5	41.1	1.3	350.1
Integrated	6.8	75.1	48.4	NA	130.2
Utilities	104.1	154.7	50.5	15.3	326.6
Presentation Graphics	9.5	258.7	45.0	1.0	314.2
Drawing & Painting	NA	119.6	209.9	10.6	364.3
Desktop Publishing	NA	123.2	72.2	NA	195.5
Other Graphics	38.0	211.3	67.6	1.3	313.2
Project Management	18.6	139.5	14.0	NA	172.1
Personal Information Managers	4.4	135.9	23.4	NA	163.9
Languages & Tools	17.1	143.4	13.7	2.9	176.9
Other Productivity	160.7	458.1	174.3	36.0	816.9
Total	1,132.5	4,441.2	1,225.1	103.8	6,717.8

The "other" category includes software for the Apple II, Commodore Amiga and other proprietary platforms.

1993 North American PC Software Sales ($M)					
Software Platforms	PC/MS-DOS	Windows	Macintosh	Other	Total
Entertainment	357.7	48.0	51.1	2.5	459.3
Home Education	130.7	105.2	45.3	2.6	277.5
Finance	181.2	135.1	40.0	NA	356.8
Word Processors	222.7	676.0	105.9	22.7	1,027.4
Spreadsheets	159.9	563.8	71.5	20.7	815.9
Databases	133.0	217.9	38.1	1.0	388.7
Integrated	17.2	47.5	47.9	1.7	114.3
Utilities	128.7	126.9	51.0	4.3	314.1
Presentation Graphics	41.2	214.5	40.6	5.0	301.3
Drawing & Painting	1.8	96.8	159.8	1.2	259.6
Desktop Publishing	NA	148.0	92.4	NA	241.5

1993 North American PC Software Sales ($M)					
Software Platforms	PC/MS-DOS	Windows	Macintosh	Other	**Total**
Other Graphics	52.6	106.0	79.9	2.1	**235.2**
Project Management	49.1	151.8	28.2	NA	**229.1**
Languages & Tools	33.1	122.6	21.8	5.2	**182.6**
Other Productivity	318.6	358.5	138.6	31.8	**848.5**
Total	**2,037.2**	**3,292.0**	**1,052.2**	**1,05.6**	**6,329.2**

1992 was the last year MS-DOS software sales exceeded Windows applications.

1992 North American PC Software Sales ($M)					
Software Platforms	PC/MS-DOS	Windows	Macintosh	Other	**Total**
Entertainment	267.2	29.6	31.4	13.6	**341.8**
Home Education	104.3	12.4	22.6	6.7	**146.1**
Finance	220.3	45.0	30.9	NA	**296.3**
Word Processors	249.0	417.9	144.3	18.4	**829.5**
Spreadsheets	332.1	343.6	92.5	27.0	**795.3**
Databases	267.2	31.2	48.2	1.8	**348.5**
Integrated	66.4	28.9	47.6	5.3	**148.1**
Utilities	154.4	98.8	68.3	NA	**322.3**
Presentation Graphics	94.0	142.4	49.0	3.8	**289.3**
Drawing & Painting	2.5	145.0	110.3	4.0	**261.8**
Desktop Publishing	10.1	75.8	53.8	NA	**140.6**
Other Graphics	103.4	87.5	69.9	3.5	**264.2**
Languages & Tools	79.0	87.1	18.3	75.0	**259.5**
Other Productivity	633.9	389.4	202.5	76.4	**1,302.2**
Total	**2,583.8**	**1,934.6**	**989.7**	**237.2**	**5,745.4**

1991 North American PC Software Sales ($M)					
Software Platforms	PC/MS-DOS	Windows	Macintosh	Other	**Total**
Entertainment	210.6	12.2	25.0	16.3	**265.4**
Home Education	76.0	NA	13.8	9.6	**99.3**
Finance	188.5	13.9	23.7	NA	**220.3**
Word Processors	442.6	253.3	92.5	24.2	**812.4**
Spreadsheets	408.4	208.6	97.8	24.4	**739.1**
Databases	267.8	2.9	40.1	NA	**309.7**
Integrated	84.8	11.2	24.7	7.3	**127.9**
Utilities	207.8	21.6	46.7	1.0	**277.8**
Presentation Graphics	151.4	50.3	35.1	4.5	**242.5**
Drawing & Painting	2.0	69.6	108.9	3.0	**185.2**
Desktop Publishing	19.3	73.3	44.8	1.8	**140.4**
Other Graphics	101.8	12.2	66.2	6.9	**193.0**
Languages & Tools	89.2	57.2	20.7	84.5	**250.6**
Other Productivity	577.9	143.0	209.9	88.0	**1,086.6**
Total	**2,962.7**	**989.0**	**823.5**	**270.1**	**5,036.6**

Telecommunications

Data Analysis Group: Telecommunications Market

"These forecasts of the total U.S. market (final sales) are based on data reported in Computer Industry Forecasts since 1984. All forecasts are computed with a statistical model which weighs information inversely to time from reporting. Forecasts are updated in January and July. There is approximately 90% confidence that forecasts lie within the Low and High limits. Product categories are presented in order appearing in Computer Industry Forecasts. Definitions are presented in alphabetical order."--Data Analysis Group

Product Categories	Year	Low	Mid	High
Frame Relays ($B)	1993	-	-	-
	1994	-	-	-
	1995	0.8	1.0	1.3
	1996	1.1	1.5	1.8
	1997	1.7	2.2	2.9
	1998	2.3	3.0	4.1
	1999	3.2	4.1	5.8
Frame Relays CAGR (%)	1996-99	42.5	39.9	47.1
Modems ($B)	1993	1.6	2.0	2.3
	1994	1.7	2.2	2.6
	1995	1.8	2.3	2.9
	1996	1.9	2.5	3.1
	1997	2.0	2.6	3.4
	1998	2.0	2.8	3.5
	1999	2.2	3.0	3.9
Modems CAGR (%)	1996-99	5.0	6.0	8.5
Network Connectors ($B)	1993	0.8	1.0	1.1
	1994	0.9	1.2	1.4
	1995	1.1	1.3	1.7
	1996	1.2	1.5	2.1
	1997	1.3	1.7	2.2
	1998	1.5	1.9	2.7
	1999	1.5	2.1	2.8
Network Connectors CAGR (%)	1996-99	7.1	12.0	10.6

Frost & Sullivan: U.S. Mobile Services Market

"The U.S. mobile communications services market will more than triple from $26.3B in 1994 to $92.5B by the year 2001, growing at a 20% compound annual rate.

'The share of total mobile market revenues going to cellular and emerging PCS (personal communications services) will rise from 68% in 1994 to 71% in 2001 while that going to paging dips from 26 to 22% in the same period.

'The share of revenues paid for by personal non-business end-users will balloon from 6% in 1994 to 17% by the year 2001 and that going to blue-collar applications increase from 11 to 17% while dominant shares going to

sales and general business applications decline, respectively, from 41 to 32% and 40 to 29% in the same period."-
-Frost & Sullivan

Year	1991	1992	1993	1994	1995	1996	1997	1998	1999	2000	2001
Revenues ($M)	12,650	16,516	20,484	26,334	33,567	40,397	48,036	55,269	64,979	78,250	92,537
% Revenue Growth	-	30.6	24.0	26.7	27.5	20.3	18.9	15.1	17.6	20.4	18.3

CAGR: 19.7%

Frost & Sullivan: U.S. Optic Fiber Market

"Spurred by intensifying competition between telephone and cable companies for communications control of the 'local loop,' the U.S. market for optic fiber products in local telecommunications systems will more than triple from $761M in 1994 to nearly $2.5B by the year 2000, growing at a 21% compound annual rate. As of 1994, some 76% of market revenues were derived from sales to dominant local exchange carriers (LECs), 17% cable television companies and 6% emerging alternative local carriers, often called CAPs (competitive access providers).

'Telephone and cable companies are positioning themselves to poach on each others' traditional turf as the legal strictures preserving their respective monopolies erode. For both categories of provider as well as the small alternative CAPs, increased bandwidth provided by optic fiber will be crucial to fulfilling their emerging full-service role. Telcos and cable companies each want to be the primary future suppliers of both voice and video services. The converging goal of multiple providers is to offer a single high-bandwidth access line supporting future digital services by any medium, whether voice, data or video. Some analysts feel the cable companies need to safeguard their position by expanding their one-way video networks into two-way interactive networks. Telephone companies are in the early stages of volume deployment of fiber-in-the-loop (FITL) systems. Larger cable TV operators are at the same time upgrading their aging coaxial networks to fiber. CAPs, meanwhile, who have always used fiber, are expanding their networks into wider geographical areas.

'As all three categories of providers continue their fiber network deployment, led by the telcos with their huge installations, the fiber in the loop market will grow at a high rate--projected at over 70% in 1995 though dropping significantly thereafter."--Frost & Sullivan

U.S. Fiber-in-the-Loop Market		
Year	Revenue ($M)	Rev. Growth (%)
1990	74.17	-
1991	88.90	19.8
1992	248.63	180.0
1993	428.91	72.5
1994	761.17	77.5
1995	1,303.90	71.3
1996	1,631.65	25.1
1997	1,836.96	12.6
1998	2,028.91	10.4
1999	2,228.86	9.8
2000	2,458.92	10.3

1990-2000 Compound Annual Growth Rate is 41.9%. 1993-2000 CAGR is 21.6%.

Frost & Sullivan: U.S. Wireless Hardware Market

"The U.S. market for wireless office equipment will expand by nearly 20 times from $101M in 1993 to $1.9B by the year 2000 at a 52% compound annual rate. The already-dominant wireless local area network (LAN) segment will increase its share of total revenues from 68% in 1993 to 91% of the much-larger market of 2000 while the share of the voice segment--though growing strongly in absolute terms--will plummet from 23 to 8% and that of integrated voice/data equipment from 10 to 2% in the same period."--Frost & Sullivan

Year	Revenue ($M)	Rev. Growth (%)
1990	7.3	-
1991	19.4	165.8
1992	44.2	127.8
1993	100.7	127.8
1994	206.1	104.7
1995	359.7	74.5
1996	565.3	57.2
1997	836.9	48.0
1998	1,155.9	38.1
1999	1,522.1	31.7
2000	1,923.1	26.3

1990-2000 Compound Annual Growth Rate is 74.6%.

Giga Information Group: U.S. Fax Machine Market

"Standalone fax machines are evolving to multifunctional machines with PC and network connectivity. More than one million multifunction, plain paper fax machines will be sold by 1998, making these multifunction devices the leader of all fax machines sold.

'Optional PC fax, printing and scanning functions (in that order of priority) are offered by most fax machine manufacturers today. The devices remain fax-focused. They offer full-capacity fax machine capability but limited printing and scanning support. Most use the serial port for printing which is slow and is best used for casual applications. Many also provide 200 dpi (dots-per-inch) scanning, while the standard for office scanning is 300 dpi or higher. The optional functions are positioned as add-on features rather than as primary attributes of the product. This will change as the category matures."--Giga Information Group

Fax Machines (#K)	1992	1993	1994	1995	1996	1997	1998
Thermal, Standalone	1,458	1,646	1,698	1,564	1,381	1,172	941
Plain Paper, Standalone	442	674	1,052	1,121	1,169	1,203	1,184
Plain Paper, Multifunction	12	19	130	425	765	1,035	1,350
Total	**1,912**	**2,339**	**2,880**	**3,110**	**3,315**	**3,410**	**3,475**

Other Markets

Business Communications: U.S. Automatic ID Systems Market

"Automatic Identification (auto ID) systems have become an integral part of the manufacturing, retail, shipping, healthcare and financial industries. Since the 1970's when the bar code was developed for the grocery store business, to current developments in biometrics and smart cards, auto ID has grown by leaps and bounds as an industry.

'...the total value of domestic sales, including exports, of automatic ID systems will reach over $8B by 2000, up from $4.3B in 1994, reflecting an average annual growth rate (AAGR) of 10.9%. Industry sales are expected to grow at between 20-24% in the first three years of the forecast period and then taper off towards year 2000.

'Bar code systems account for the largest volume and highest growth rate of automatic ID sales.

'Magnetic stripe cards, including smart cards, are the second largest automatic ID technology. Although the smart card is more active in the European and Asian markets, it has very strong potential in the U.S. Sales of magnetic strip systems reached $608M in 1994 and are forecast to have an AAGR of 9.2% to reach over $1B by 2000."--Business Communications Company

% Market Value of U.S. Sales, 2000		
Bar Code	Magnetic Stripe	All Other
74.3	12.7	13.0

Value of Sales, 1994-2000	1994 ($M)	2000 ($M)	AAGR (%) 1994-2000
Bar Code	3,042	6,009	12.0
Magnetic Stripe	608	1,028	9.2
All Other	694	1,051	7.2
Total	**4,344**	**8,088**	**10.9**

Business Communications: U.S. Electronic Banking Services Market

"Revenues generated from the provision of electronic banking services have steadily gained in importance and should continue to do so, increasing 12% annually from $11.0B in 1994 to $21.4B in the year 2000.

'In retail banking, customers want the flexibility and convenience of being able to bank at many different locales and at different times. As a result, banks are having to extend their provision of services with automated teller machines (ATMs), telephone banking, banking by personal computer and in the future, interactive videobanking through cable television. The services provided in these electronic banking outlets will include simple transactions, to a whole host of banking services including: loan applications, stock trading and other financial products. By 2000, the home computer banking market is expected to approach $205M, reflecting an annual average growth rate of 93%

'All of this heightened activity in electronic banking means that banks will continue to invest in ATM and other information technologies as a means of achieving further improvements in service delivery, productivity, competitiveness and for revenue diversification purposes. In addition, the retail sector in particular will boost its purchases of POS terminals and consumers will begin investing in some of the technologies of the next decade, namely screen-based telephones and set-top interactive television devices. As a result, it is likely that sales of

ATMs, POS terminals and other electronic banking devices will increase 17% per year, from $734M in 1994 to $1.9B in the year 2000."--Business Communications Company

Item	1990 ($M)	1994 ($M)	2000 ($M)	1994-2000 AAGR (%)
ATMs	2,554	4,011	6,945	9.6
POS Terminals	44	193	855	28.2
Home Computer Banking	negl.	3	205	102.2
Telephone Banking	45	78	190	16.0
Interactive TV Banking	negl.	1	75	105.4
Smart Cards	-	negl.	85	135.0
Other Electronic Funds Transfer	4,336	6,310	13,025	12.8
Total Electronic Banking Services	**6,979**	**10,957**	**21,380**	**11.8**

Business Communications: U.S. Interactive TV Market

"The results of current interactive television tests, FCC standards and licensing procedures and strategic alliances between leading industry partners are greatly affecting the growth prospects of the interactive industry. Interactive television is an emerging industry and has no peers or predecessors, especially in the home entertainment sectors. Interactivity, or the ability of the viewers to interact with the source of the television programs they watch, is a revolutionary concept. The industry is poised to take advantage of the new options that the viewers will have when the services are implemented and quick acceptance, very rapid market penetration and explosive growth are anticipated.

'...substantial efforts are being made to deliver interactive TV services on satellite, coaxial telephone and terrestrial media. However BCC notes that fiber optic lines are the most favored transmission medium for these services. While the primary or trunk lines are already in place, mostly owned by long distance telephone companies, fiber-to-home will be installed in major markets to provide interactive services.

'...the installation of fiber optic lines to homes will grow from $100M in 1996 to $4.5B in 2000, accounting for an annual average growth rate (AAGR) of 575%. These lines will be used for a variety of interactive services and represent the bulk of the investment that will go into providing the services.

'Furthermore the growth in the number of homes using interactive services will burgeon from a low base of 50,000 in 1996 to 22.5M by 2000, accounting for an AAGR of 575% as well. In addition to basic services, many of these homes will subscribe to additional interactive programs such as home health information, on-line video programs, etc.

'The BCC analysis which goes on to measure the effects of interactive TV on equipment notes that the overall revenues from the five major types of equipment will grow from $283.75M in 1996 to $13,450M by 2000, registering an annual aggregate growth rate of 187%."--Business Communications Company

Equipment ($M, 1994 Constant)	1996	1997	1998	1999	2000	AAGR %
Analog to Digital Systems	5.00	7.22	10.83	14.85	25.50	50.8
Video Servers	48.75	89.00	202.50	495.00	900.00	109.0
Digital Switches	150.00	300.00	600.00	1200.00	2400.00	100.0
Home Basement Boxes	5.00	75.00	150.00	750.00	1,125.00	487.5
Home TV Receivers	75.00	900.00	1,125.00	3,750.00	9,000.00	374.6
Total	**283.75**	**1,371.22**	**2,088.33**	**6,209.85**	**13,450.50**	**187.0**

Frost & Sullivan: U.S. Infrared Sensor Market

"Paced by increasing commercial applications, U.S. infrared sensor markets will double from $648M in 1994 to over $1.3B by the year 2001. Commercial sales will grow from 22% of total revenues in 1994 to 33% in 2001 while dominant military sales correspondingly decline in share from 78 to 67% in the same period.

'Major emerging commercial application areas include industrial process control, environmental monitoring, space-based programs, drug and law enforcement, search and rescue and medical applications. Reduction in system prices to levels affordable for commercial end-users will be crucial to commercial market expansion. Price, by contrast, was distinctly less important to the military market than performance."--Frost & Sullivan

Year	Units	Unit Growth (%)	Revenue ($M)	Rev. Growth (%)
1991	258,017.8	-	641.2	-
1992	283,584.0	9.9	647.9	1.1
1993	316,914.5	11.8	653.3	0.8
1994	357,126.7	12.7	658.7	0.8
1995	959,491.1	168.7	666.6	1.2
1996	2,272,468.4	136.8	688.3	3.3
1997	5,063,020.0	122.8	720.0	4.6
1998	9,107,831.0	79.9	809.6	12.4
1999	16,519,668.9	81.4	991.4	22.5
2000	30,337,869.8	83.6	1,202.0	21.2
2001	56,104,010.9	84.9	1,447.9	20.5
1991-2001CAGR	-	71.3	-	8.5

Frost & Sullivan: U.S. Intelligent Transport System Market

"The U.S. market for intelligent transportation systems (ITS) will grow by more than six times from $99M in 1994 to $656M by the year 2001 at a 31% compound annual rate.

'Advanced vehicle control systems will explode in share from 7% of the total market in 1994 to 33% in 2001 as advanced traveler information systems similarly balloon form 2 to 25% while the currently dominant commercial vehicle operations market, though growing healthily in absolute terms, drops in share from 62 to 27% in the same period.

'Many ITS products are already available with many more ready to be soon brought to market. Prices will decline sharply over the years ahead. As vehicle detection radars, beacon transceivers, weigh-in-motion systems, ATIS and other systems advance from prototype to production, average costs will fall substantially. As these technologies mature and proliferate, the number of vendors will meanwhile increase, along with price competition.

'Real-time updated route guidance and electronic toll collection could significantly boost the carrying capacity of road networks, crucial in areas where urban highways are unable to expand in the face of prohibitive land costs. ITS projects are also designed to improve auto safety and reduce vehicle emissions.

'Growing consumer awareness later in the decade will stimulate further ITS deployment. Taxpayers able to actually see ITS infrastructure functioning properly will be more likely to support government funding. This factor will help growth accelerate from 24% in 1994 to 36% by 1999 on a much larger base."--Frost & Sullivan

Year	1991	1992	1993	1994	1995	1996	1997	1998	1999	2000	2001	CAGR
U.S. Revenues ($M)	53.1	65.2	80.1	99.4	131.8	174.3	232.9	313.6	427.1	545.3	656.1	
Growth (%)		22.8	22.9	24.0	32.6	32.2	33.6	34.7	36.2	27.7	20.3	30.9

Frost & Sullivan: Worldwide Barcode Equipment Market

"Led by software growth, the worldwide barcode equipment market will more than double from $2.2B in 1993 vendor revenues to $5.6B by the year 2000, growing at a 15% compound annual rate. Thirty-four percent of 1994 market revenues will be accounted for by scanners, 27% terminals, 21% printers and 18% software.

'Market growth is being driven by dropping prices for both barcode equipment and computers as well as work-force reductions, technology advances and increasing repetitive strain injury claims, which shift employer preferences away from employee keyboard use toward barcodes.

'Dropping prices, new niche-oriented products and introduction of advanced 2D symbologies have meanwhile opened up entirely new markets for barcode products. Symbology support is becoming a bigger issue as barcode applications proliferate. Since many large stores sell products spanning many application industries, scanners will need to support an increasing variety of symbologies.

'Lines traditionally demarcating competitive technologies have grown increasingly blurred. CCD technology advances allow these scanners to work in short-range scanning applications, fostering competition with laser technology. Advances in barcode label media have promoted greater competition between thermal direct and transfer vendors. There are new higher-performance products and wireless products.

'The printer market has seen migration from impact to dedicated thermal direct and thermal transfer printers for higher resolutions. Introduction of high-speed scanners and verifiers will further promote market growth."--Frost & Sullivan

Year	(#K)	Unit Grwth (%)	Rev. ($M)	Rev. Grwth (%)
1990	2,152.6	-	1,564.2	-
1991	2,597.8	20.7	1,729.5	10.6
1992	2,957.8	13.9	1,921.7	11.1
1993	3,431.4	16.0	2,156.3	12.2
1994	4,036.2	17.6	2,438.3	13.1
1995	4,744.4	17.5	2,775.8	13.8
1996	5,589.3	17.8	3,181.5	14.6
1997	6,560.6	17.4	3,672.5	15.4
1998	7,580.4	15.5	4,242.5	15.5
1999	8,770.4	15.7	4,897.5	15.4
2000	10,156.6	15.8	5,644.9	15.3
1990-2000 CAGR:	-	16.8	-	13.7

Frost & Sullivan: Worldwide Programmable Logic Controller Market

"The worldwide programmable logic controller (PLC) market will more than double from $4.2B in 1993 to $8.6B in the year 2000 at an 11% compound annual rate.

'The revenue share of small PLCs will grow from 30% in 1993 to 35% in 2000 while that of medium PLCs dips from 30 to 26% and that of large units from 16 to 9% in the same period. The share of market revenue accounted for by software will meanwhile increase from 9 to 12% and that of fault-tolerant PLCs from 2 to 5% in the forecast period.

'Demand for PLCs is growing as automation intensifies across end-user industries including automotive, food processing, chemical, pharmaceutical, metal, pulp and paper, waste-water management, medical and electronics. While the U.S. and Europe remain the largest PLC markets, major opportunities are opening in Latin America and Southeast Asia as those regions rapidly industrialize and construct new automated manufacturing facilities.

'The PLC industry is dominated by a few multinationals including Siemens, Mitsubishi and Omron of Japan, Allen-Bradley and GE Fanuc (a collaboration between General Electric and Japan's Fanuc). These firms dominate the micro, small, medium and large segments. A number of smaller firms, meanwhile, focus on specific geographic or end-user markets."--Frost & Sullivan

Year	Units (K)	Unit Growth (%)	Revenue ($M)	Revenue Growth (%)
1990	5,622.5	-	3,309.4	-
1991	6,201.7	10.3	3,574.1	8.0
1992	6,835.2	10.2	3,860.8	8.0
1993	7,634.5	11.7	4,208.6	9.0
1994	8,627.4	13.0	4,648.5	10.5
1995	9,850.7	14.2	5,197.0	11.8
1996	11,323.2	14.9	5,840.4	12.4
1997	12,920.5	13.9	6,540.2	12.0
1998	14,565.0	12.7	7,249.6	10.8
1999	16,201.8	11.2	7,944.0	9.6
2000	17,784.2	9.8	8,605.0	8.3
1990-2000 CAGR	-	12.2	-	10.0

Excerpted with permission from Frost & Sullivan, Jan., 1995. Copyright © 1995, Frost & Sullivan, 2525 Charleston Road, Mountain View CA 94043 USA.

Giga Information Group: Automotive Electronics Market

"The total demand for automotive electronics was valued at $11.3B in 1994, and is forecast to rise to 16.1B in 1999. This includes electronic system control units in passenger vehicle production in North America, Europe and Japan.

'The implementation of automotive electronic systems has significantly increased in recent years. This, combined with a general recovery in key world car markets last year, resulted in a 1994 automotive electronics growth of 24%! The market is forecast to continue expanding as car makers respond to legislative, consumer and competitor pressures."--Giga Information Group

Automotive Electronics Segments ($M)	1994	1999	CAGR (%)
Driver Information (i.e. instrumentation, heads-up display, navigation, collision avoidance)	470	970	15.6

Automotive Electronics Segments ($M)	1994	1999	CAGR (%)
Vehicle Security (i.e. keyless entry, vehicle immobilizer)	588	1,080	12.9
Chassis Systems (i.e. ABS, traction, suspension, variable-assist power steering)	1,800	2,700	8.5
Body Systems (i.e. air-bags, A/C, lighting, multiplexing, comfort, convenience)	2,300	3,800	10.6
Powertrain Control (i.e. engine/emission control, fuel economy, on-board diagnostics)	6,200	7,500	3.9
Total Automotive Electronics	**11,300**	**16,100**	**7.3**

Giga Information Group: Worldwide Color TV Production Market

"Worldwide production of color television receivers reached 115M units in 1994, an increase of 7% over the previous year and is expected to reach 140M units by 1998. The market is worth $35B at trade price levels. More than half of all receivers are now manufactured in the Far East and SE Asia regions.

`Thailand and Malaysia have been major beneficiaries of foreign investment in recent years and together now account of annual production of 13M CTVs. There are growing signs, however, of expansion into new markets, including India, Pakistan and Vietnam. Western Europe and North America, including Mexico, account for 19% and 20% of world CTV production respectively. Manufacturers will maintain a presence in these regions, since it is uneconomical to ship many larger screen television receivers across long distances. In fact, there has been a surge in production in North America in recent years, driven by the recovery in the U.S. domestic market and by growing demand in Mexico.

`The battle for leadership in the world CTV market remains tightly contested; 8 companies each produce more than 5M receivers each year, with the three leading producers, Matsushita, Philips and Sony (including their subsidiaries) each producing between 9 and 11M sets during 1993."--Giga Information Group

Country (#M)	1990 (Est.)	1994 (Est.)	% Change
S. Korea	12.4	16.0	+29
China	10.2	14.0	+37
Japan	13.2	10.6	-20
Thailand	2.5	7.5	+300
Malaysia	3.3	5.5	+67
Others	8.9	7.8	-12
Total Far East & SE Asia:	50.5	61.4	+22
U.K.	4.2	6.0	+43
Germany	3.5	3.5	0
France	2.3	3.3	+43
Italy	2.3	3.1	+35
Others	6.0	6.3	+5
Total Western Europe:	18.3	22.2	+21
North America (USA, Mexico & Canada)	16.5	23.0	+39
E. Europe and CIS	8.4	5.2	-38
Rest of World	4.3	3.8	-12
Total Worldwide Production	**98.0**	**115.2**	**+18**

VLSI Research: Top 10 Worldwide Semiconductor Companies

"The worldwide semiconductor market grew by just under 40% in 1995, according to preliminary data released by VLSI Research Inc. Semiconductor sales by merchant producers reached $142B in 1995, captive sales achieved $9.9B and totaled $152B, a hefty 36.8% increase over 1994's sales.

'Turning our attention to the top ten semiconductor suppliers and capital spenders, the 1995 list looks much like 1994. Intel, the largest chip maker, has also been the largest spender for several years in a row, showing how capital expenditures play a direct role in increasing a corporation's market share. Korean companies, which were small a few years ago, have quickly risen in their ranking by outspending their Japanese and U.S. counterparts. Samsung, the third largest spender in 1995, rose one notch to become the 6th largest chip maker in 1995. They are also the largest DRAM manufacturer in the world."--VLSI Research

	Top-Ten Semiconductor Suppliers			
95 Rank	Company	Country	95 Rev ($M)	1994 Rank
1	Intel	United States	13,997	1
2	NEC	Japan	10,632	2
3	Toshiba	Japan	9,619	3
4	Motorola	United States	9,278	4
5	Hitachi	Japan	8,607	5
6	Samsung	Korea	7,787	7
7	Texas Instruments	United States	7,782	8
8	IBM	United States	6,601	6
9	Fujitsu	Japan	5,367	9
10	Mitsubishi	Japan	5,164	10

	Top-Ten Capital Spenders			
95 Rank	Company	Country	95 Expen ($M)	1994 Rank
1	Intel	United States	3,276	1
2	Motorola	United States	2,113	3
3	Samsung	Korea	1,903	2
4	LG Semicon	Korea	1,726	6
5	NEC	Japan	1,599	10
6	Texas Instruments	United States	1,423	7
7	Hitachi	Japan	1,386	5
7	Fujitsu	Japan	1,386	4
9	Hyundai	Korea	1,325	9
10	Toshiba	Japan	1,172	8

International Markets

Frost & Sullivan: European Computer Peripheral Market

"After slow growth rates during the global recession, the European market for computer peripherals has quickly gathered pace and is estimated to have been worth $23.48B in 1994. This represented an increase of 6.3% on the previous year. The market, including disk drives, keyboards, monitors, mouse devices and modems, could grow to reach a value of $32.63B by 2000.

'Looking forward, the report suggests that the two largest segments, monitors and disk drives, will experience the greatest technological change. In the case of monitors, worth $8.43B in 1994, energy saving monitors are expected to become common place providing prices decrease to compete more effectively with standard versions. Larger screens are also being developed for multi-media applications and anti-glare screens are also becoming more prevalent.

'There is a battle going on in the $7.43B disk drive market between CD-ROMs and 3.5-inch floppy drives. Frost & Sullivan anticipates that most PC's in the future will probably have built in CD-ROM drives thereby cutting out the need for 3.5-inch software applications. This sector has good growth prospects throughout the forecast period and should be worth over $10.92B by the end of the century.

'In the modem and mouse-device sectors, currently worth $3.51B and $998M respectively, technological developments will include a continued trend towards cableless communication using infrared technology.

'New software applications for image stitching will boost the growth of hand-held scanners and ergonomic design considerations will remain important in the keyboard, scanner and mouse-device sectors.

'Pricing has always been a significant issue in the computer peripherals market with the average price for all product categories having declined substantially in the recent past. This trend is not expected to continue however and price stabilization is expected towards the end of the review period. In absolute terms, the average price for computer peripherals add-ons was $331 in 1990. It decreased to $308 in 1993 and should stabilize at around $286 by the year 2000.

'Germany, with 20.4% of the total, was the largest national market for peripherals in 1994 followed by the U.K. with 17.9% and France with 17.2%"--Frost & Sullivan

Year	Units (M)	Unit Growth (%)	Revenue ($B)	Revenue Growth (%)
1990	60.4	-	19.97	-
1991	63.7	5.5	20.54	2.9
1992	65.9	3.5	20.80	1.3
1993	71.7	8.8	22.06	6.1
1994	77.9	8.6	23.49	6.4
1995	83.9	7.7	24.94	6.2
1996	90.3	7.6	26.49	6.2
1997	96.2	6.5	27.96	5.5
1998	102.2	6.2	29.49	5.5
1999	108.3	6.0	31.04	5.3
2000	114.2	5.4	32.64	5.1
1990-2000 CAGR	-	6.6	-	5.0

Frost & Sullivan: European PCN Market

"Personal Communications Networks (PCNs), a service which is defined as offering personal communications at a cost level that is sufficiently low as to attract a mass subscriber audience, are poised for a mass market breakthrough towards the end of the decade. PCNs are likely to challenge the role of the fixed network. This scenario has been much encouraged by the attitude of the European Union Commission towards telecommunications industry liberalization.

'Frost & Sullivan believes that the emergent demand for personal communications could be satisfied to a greater or lesser extent by three alternative technologies--DCS 1800, DECT and conventional GSM networks--with Digital European Cordless Telephony (DECT) as the access mechanism and channel for high density local area traffic and DCS 1800 for the true mobile applications. Although PCNs will most frequently be based upon DCS 1800, in practice there is some technology overlap, and indeed potential technology sharing, which can make alternative approaches feasible.

'Once intelligent networks are developed, which will be towards the end of this decade, their combination with DECT and DCS 1800 will make them strongly competitive with conventional cellular communications, which additionally they will offer an alternative to the fixed network local loop. PCNs market breakthrough will be led by Germany, the United Kingdom and France.

'Fast progress in the other countries is much more doubtful, and if PCNs are not launched until GSM networks have become well-established, their operators could have problems of financial viability. Using a number of key market parameters, an optimistic scenario forecasts 26.5M subscribers by 1999, while the pessimistic outcome is only 13.8M users in the same year."--Frost & Sullivan

Year	1993	1994	1995	1996	1997	1998	1999
Optimistic	3.5	270.0	1,193.5	3,530.0	8,368.8	14,531.3	21,100.0
Pessimistic	3.5	186.3	687.5	1,825.5	4,157.5	8,063.1	12,631.3

Frost & Sullivan: European Printer Market

"Although the European printer market is expected to grow in overall revenue terms in the period up to the year 2000, some product sectors will experience declining market share and negative revenue growth rates. The market, valued at almost $5.83B in 1994, is forecast to grow to a value of nearly $7.78B by the turn of the century. This revenue growth reflects even stronger growth in unit shipments from 9.3M to 15.2M over the same period.

'But some market segments are not expected to benefit from the overall expansion in the market place. Dot matrix printers, which currently account for 13.3% of the market (in revenue terms) are only expected to take a 6% share of the market by 2000. This will represent a negative annual compound growth of 10.2%. Line printer revenues are also forecast to fall over the period from $348.1M to $248.7M representing a negative compound annual growth rate of 4.7%.

'The non-impact segments on the other hand will grow strong in unit shipment term--strong enough over the forecast period to more than offset price erosion and produce substantial revenue growth. This segment should be worth $2.6B by 2000. Laser printer revenues are also forecast to grow from almost $2.3B in 1994 to reach $3.89B in 2000. Thermal transfer printers, the final product segment covered in the report will also grow in value terms but represents a relatively small sector of the overall printer market."--Frost & Sullivan

Year	Units (M)	Unit Growth (%)	Revenue ($B)	Revenue Growth (%)
1990	7.37		6.85	-
1991	7.48	1.5	6.47	-5.5

Year	Units (M)	Unit Growth (%)	Revenue ($B)	Revenue Growth (%)
1992	7.75	3.6	6.20	-4.0
1993	8.50	9.7	6.11	-1.6
1994	9.31	9.5	5.82	-4.6
1995	10.40	11.7	6.00	3.1
1996	11.55	11.1	6.36	5.9
1997	12.64	9.4	6.76	6.3
1998	13.59	7.5	7.14	5.6
1999	14.44	6.3	7.48	4.7
2000	15.20	5.3	7.80	4.1
1990-2000 CAGR	-	7.5	-	1.3

Frost & Sullivan: European Workstation Market

"The European markets for commercial and technical workstations are both strong and growing rapidly. The European market value of commercial and technical workstations was $20B and $3.37B respectively in 1993. Commercial workstations now represent one of the largest hardware product markets in the whole information technology business, and the business is currently at the watershed of a major change. This change is being led by the introduction of much faster Pentium and PowerPC processors in volume. These technologies provide much greater performance which, in turn, has encouraged suppliers to provide greater storage capacities and better management type software. Shipment values for commercial workstations rose by 10.9% in value terms and by 19.4% in volume in 1993--a year which was scarred by economic recession in most of Europe. While this rate of growth can not be expected to be maintained, value shipments are expected to be worth over $30.26B by 1999.

'Technical workstations represent one of the strongest information technology markets in Europe. Another strong performer in the recession years, growth in this market is expected to gather pace in the years to come and technical workstation shipments are expected to be worth nearly $5.9B by 1999. Within the commercial workstations market, the industrial sector, worth $10.42B in 1993, is expected to continue to be the major end-user and should account for sales worth almost $14.37B by 1999. Within the technical workstation market, the personal computer sector will display the strongest growth rates in both volume and value terms. This sector should be worth over $869M by 1999."--Frost & Sullivan

Year	1993	1994	1995	1996	1997	1998	1999
Commercial Workstations ($M)	22,154	23,937	25,674	27,143	28,353	29,350	30,261
Technical Workstations ($M)	3,369	3,793	4,289	4,733	5,145	5,469	5,887
Total Workstations ($M)	25,523	27,730	29,963	31,876	33,498	34,819	36,148

Giga Information Group: Canadian Wireless Market

"The Canadian markets for cellular, paging and wireless data are anticipated to grow to a combined installed base of almost 12 million subscribers by the end of the year 2000! This represents a penetration of the Canadian population of 43%, achieved by a compound annual growth rate of 28% over the next five years. This will grow from just under 3 million wireless subscribers at the end of 1994.

'Most of the growth will be attributed to cellular services as new markets are penetrated with consumer-oriented products and tariffing. Both Rogers Cantel and the Mobility Canada affiliates launched shrink-wrapped cell-phone-in-a-box through retail during 1994. The products target the consumer and SOHO (small office/home office) markets. In the six to nine months since they have been available, Cantel's Amigo and Mobility Canada's Liberti have been far more successful than either operator had anticipated."--Giga Information Group

Installed Base (K)	Wireless Data	Cellular	Paging	Total
1994	33	1,900	800	2,733
2000	651	6,543	4,623	11,817

Excerpted with permission from Giga Information Group, May 9, 1995. Copyright © 1995, Giga Information Group, One Kendall Square, Bldg. 1400W, Cambridge MA 02139 USA.

Giga Information Group: European Consumer Electronics Market

"Demand for consumer electronics products fell by 7% in Western Europe in 1993, from $41.1B to $38.8B (value measured at retail level, including tax). Sales in 1994 are forecast to fall a further 1%, to $38.1B. Price competition remains intense, and demand for 'big ticket' items remains subdued by lack of consumer confidence. In 1995, with an improved economic background and growing consumer confidence, Giga Information Group forecasts 2% growth for the European Consumer Electronics sector."--Giga Information Group

Retail Value ($B)	1992	1993	1994	1998
Car Audio	4.3	4.3	4.5	5.8
Home Audio	8.1	7.7	7.5	7.5
Personal/Portable Audio	3.6	3.5	3.6	4.0
Satellite Receivers	1.0	1.0	1.1	1.3
Camcorders	4.2	3.4	3.0	3.9
VCRs	6.3	5.7	5.6	6.0
Television Receivers	13.6	12.7	12.8	14.0
Total	**41.1**	**38.3**	**38.1**	**42.5**

Excerpted with permission from Giga Information Group, September 21, 1994. Copyright © 1994, Giga Information Group, One Kendall Square, Bldg. 1400W, Cambridge MA 02139 USA.

Giga Information Group: European Mobile Communications Service and Equipment Markets

"Mobile communications services and equipment markets are expected to increase to $30.1B and $8.1B respectively by 1998... Over the forecast period, these represent compound annual growth rates of 25% and 15% respectively. The mobile communications market is one of the fastest-growing sectors of the European telecommunications market. In 1993, total European sales of mobile communications services were valued at $10B and corresponding sales of equipment accounted for $4.0B. In terms of revenue, these sectors represent 7% and 33% of the total European telecommunications services and terminal equipment markets respectively."--Giga Information Group

Sales Revenue ($M) by Industry Sector					% CAGR '93-98
Telecoms Services	1992	1993	1994	1998	
Mobile Communications	7,736	9,993	14,751	28,757	30
Wireline Voice (estimate)	128,620	132,864	136,850	156,127	4
Facsimile	6,507	8,097	9,504	12,972	15
Total Service's Market	**142,863**	**150,954**	**161,105**	**197,856**	**7**
Mobile Communications	3,570	3,975	5,177	8,124	15
Customer Premises Voice	6,350	6,144	6,203	6,210	-

Sales Revenue ($M) by Industry Sector					% CAGR '93-98
Telecoms Services	1992	1993	1994	1998	
Facsimile	2,232	1,955	1,718	1,365	-7
Total Equipment Market	**12,152**	**12,074**	**13,098**	**15,699**	**5**
Total Market	**155,015**	**162,978**	**174,172**	**213,555**	**6**

Excerpted with permission from Giga Information Group, August 22, 1995. Copyright © 1995, Giga Information Group, One Kendall Square, Bldg. 1400W, Cambridge MA USA.

Romtec: European Cellular Market

"By the year 2000, the German market will lead the European cellular customer base, with the U.K. following closely behind. Together they will account for 39% of European customers. The Italian and French markets will also play significant roles with market shares of 15% and 11% respectively. Swedish operators will continue to be the most successful in Europe as their innovative market strategies will push the Swedish penetration rate to the highest in Europe. As a result, the Swedish market will gain 9% of the cellular customer base in the year 2000.

'GSM (Global System Mobile Communications) services will account for the majority of services by the year 2000 with a European market share of 66%, up from 27% by the year 1994. The uptake of GSM services will be reflected in the strong growth of unit shipments which are expected to peak in 1999, reaching nearly 12M units, compared with 8.3M units in 1994. By the end of the decade the vast majority of shipments will be digital, as the demand for analog terminals will collapse dramatically and will only account for 2% European unit shipments."--Romtec

Year	1994	1995	1996	1997	1998	1999	2000
Installed Base (#)	14,148,800	20,039,650	26,224,500	31,865,000	36,826,500	41,034,500	44,514,000

Excerpted with permission from Romtec, June 22, 1995. Copyright © 1995, Romtec Plc, Vanwall Road, Maidenhead, Berks SL6 4UB England.

Romtec: European Data Network Termination Points

"The installed base of data connections to public networks in Europe will grow from approximately 6M in 1995 to 11.1M in year 2000. The current domination of connections to leased circuits and PSTN will be overtaken by ISDN--with it becoming the single biggest category by 2000. Frame Relay and ATM services will experience rapid growth over the next five years but they will remain niche market services."--Romtec

Data Network Technologies	Units 95 (#K)	Units 2000 (#K)	% Share 95	% Share 2000
PSTN	1,995.7	2,115.8	33	19
ISDN	483.8	5,233.9	8	47
ALC	1,572.4	1,002.2	26	9
DLC	1,270.0	1,781.8	21	16
PSDN	604.8	890.9	10	8
CSDN	121.0	-	2	-
Frame Relay & ATM	-	111.4	-	1
Total NTPs	**6,047.6**	**11,136.0**	**100**	**100**

Excerpted with permission from Romtec, September 18, 1995. Copyright © 1995, Romtec Plc, Vanwall Road, Maidenhead, Berks SL6 4UB England.

Internet and Online Markets

General Magic: Fastest Growing Internet Domains

"The latest results from the Internet's most basic and longest continuing measurement of its size were just released by Mark Lottor of Network Wizards at Menlo Park CA U.S. The Domain Survey attempts to discover every host on the Internet by doing a complete search of the Domain Name System. The results were gathered during July 1996.

'Lottor's measurements show that the Internet currently consists of countless autonomous networks, representing 488,000 domains, with 12,881,000 "advertised" connected computers in 156 countries and territories. Because of the unknown and potentially unlimited numbers of multiuser computers and network or application gateways, it is not possible to correlate any of this information with the number of end users. Further processing and analyzing Lottor's data over the past several years reveals the following newsworthy and highlights:
• The figure of 12.8M hosts represents a current annual host growth rate of 72%, and was very close to the predicted number based on the average growth rate over the past four years. In other words, the Internet's exponential growth rate continues unabated.
• Considering the increasing tendency of hiding large numbers of hosts behind firewalls, the actual number of connected hosts is likely far higher.
• Hosts named "WWW" constitute by far the largest and fastest number of hosts--212,000 computers (up from 75,000 in January 1996 and 16,000 in July 1995) and increasing at the annual rate of 1,165%.
• The largest single domain is .com with 3.3M hosts, and now constitutes 26% of all hosts.
• Forty-two country and global top level domains are experiencing annual growth rates in excess of 100%.
• Among country and global top level domains above the 10,000 mark, the most rapidly growing included: China, Brazil, Russian Federation, Hungary, Czech Rep., Portugal, .US, Japan, South Africa, Singapore.
• In absolute numbers, the most rapidly growing domains were .com, .net, .edu, Japan, .US, .mil, UK--all with six month increases in excess of 100,000 hosts.
• Without subsequent processing to attribute the three letter global domains to a country previously done by John Quarterman of MIDS <http://www.mids.org/, its not possible to determine final country figures. However, it appears approximately that the same 60% - 40% balance between U.S. versus non-U.S., proportions remain. Quarterman should be contacted regarding the availability of this information.
• The domains of 23 countries or territories appeared on the host count for the first time--apparently connecting since January 1996. However, these hosts may not necessarily be actually in the country."--General Magic)

Domain (1H 1996)	January 1996	July 1996	Increase
.com	2,430,954	3,323,647	892,693
.net	758,597	1,232,902	474,305
.edu	1,793,491	2,114,851	321,360
Japan-dom	269,327	496,427	227,100
USA-dom	233,912	432,727	198,815
.mil	258,791	431,939	173,148
UK-dom	451,750	579,492	127,742
Germany-dom	452,997	548,168	95,171
Australia-dom	309,562	397,460	87,898
Finland-dom	211,900	277,207	65,307
.org	265,327	327,148	61,821
France-dom	137,217	189,786	52,569
Canada-dom	372,891	424,356	51,465
.gov	312,330	361,065	48,735
Italy-dom	73,364	113,776	40,412
Netherlands-dom	174,888	214,704	39,816
Sweden-dom	149,877	186,312	36,435
South Africa-dom	48,277	83,349	35,072

Domain (1H 1996)	January 1996	July 1996	Increase
Norway-dom	88,356	120,780	32,424
Brazil-dom	20,113	46,854	26,741
Denmark-dom	51,827	76,955	25,128
New Zealand-dom	53,610	77,886	24,276
Korea-dom	29,306	47,973	18,667
Austria-dom	52,728	71,090	18,362
Russian Fed (RU-dom)	32,022	17,702	14,320
Switzerland-dom	85,844	102,691	16,847
Singapore-dom	22,769	38,376	15,607
Czech-dom	16,786	32,219	15,433
Poland-dom	24,945	38,432	13,487
Hungary-dom	11,750	25,109	13,359
Belgium-dom	30,535	43,311	12,776
Israel-dom	29,503	39,611	10,108

-dom indicates country top level domain, exclusive from any .com, .net, .org, or .int global top level domains that may also be located in the country. In the past, about 80% have been in the U.S. Fastest Growing Internet Domains In 2nd Half 1995 (In Relative Annualized %):

Domain	January 1996 #	July 1996 #	Increase %
Swaziland-dom	1	49	4,800
Sri Lanka-dom	6	234	3,800
Pakistan-dom	17	386	2,171
New Caledonia-dom	1	19	1,800
Azerbaijan-dom	1	18	1,700
Saudi Arabia-dom	27	275	919
Andorra-dom	10	81	710
Belize-dom	1	8	700
Kenya-dom	17	133	682
Namibia-dom	11	84	664
Malta-dom	68	476	600
Guatemala-dom	27	159	489
China-dom	2,146	11,282	426
Barbados-dom	2	9	350
Belarus-dom	23	103	348
Jordan-dom	19	79	316
Lebanon-dom	88	359	308
Cuba-dom	1	4	300
Senegal-dom	14	46	229
Nepal-dom	19	60	216
San Marino-dom	90	277	208
Liechtenstein-dom	44	134	205
Tonga-dom	1	3	200
Kazakhstan-dom	187	545	191
Romania-dom	954	2,725	186
Peru-dom	813	2,269	179
India-dom	788	2,176	176
Macedonia-dom	39	94	141
Cyprus-dom	384	919	139
Bolivia-dom	66	154	133
Brazil-dom	20,113	46,854	133

Domain	January 1996 #	July 1996 #	Increase %
Colombia-dom	2,262	5,265	133
Gibraltar-dom	26	60	131
Indonesia-dom	2,351	5,262	124
Russian Fed. (RU-dom)	14,320	32,022	124
Bulgaria-dom	1,013	2,254	123
Albania-dom	36	77	114
Hungary-dom	11,750	25,109	114
Lithuania-dom	630	1,335	112
Uzbekistan-dom	35	74	111
Malaysia-dom	4,194	8,541	104
Nicaragua-dom	141	285	102
Macau-dom	65	129	98
Georgia-dom	60	119	98
Ukraine-dom	2,318	4,499	94
Czech-dom	16,786	32,219	92
Anguilla-dom	23	44	91
Slovakia-dom	2,913	5,498	89
Portugal-dom	9,359	17,573	88
El Salvador-dom	23	43	87
U.S.-dom	233,912	432,727	85
Japan-dom	269,327	496,427	84
Bermuda-dom	608	1,099	81
Latvia-dom	1,631	2,932	80
Argentina-dom	5,312	9,415	77
Monaco-dom	56	99	77
Philippines-dom	1,771	3,117	76
Costa Rica-dom	1,495	2,582	73
South Africa-dom	48,277	83,349	73
Slovenia-dom	5,870	9,949	69
Singapore-dom	22,769	38,376	69
.mil	258,791	431,939	67
Bahrain-dom	142	236	66
Luxembourg-dom	1,756	2,877	64
Korea-dom	29,306	47,973	64
.net	758,597	1,232,902	63
Estonia-dom	4,129	6,605	60
Kuwait-dom	1,233	1,963	59
Greenland-dom	88	140	59
Thailand-dom	4,055	6,362	57
Italy-dom	73,364	113,776	55
Poland-dom	24,945	38,432	54
Morocco-dom	234	351	50
Vatican-dom	2	3	50
Denmark-dom	51,827	76,955	48
Mexico-dom	13,787	20,253	47
Chile-dom	9,027	13,239	47
New Zealand-dom	53,610	77,886	45
Turkey-dom	5,345	7,743	45
Greece-dom	8,787	12,689	44
Venezuela-dom	1,165	1,679	44

Domain	January 1996 #	July 1996 #	Increase %
Ireland-dom	15,036	21,464	43
Belgium-dom	30,535	43,311	42
Uruguay-dom	626	878	40
Panama-dom	148	207	40
France-dom	137,217	189,786	38
Egypt-dom	591	817	38
.com	2,430,954	3,323,647	37
Norway-dom	88,356	120,780	37
Hong Kong-dom	17,693	24,133	36
Armenia-dom	77	105	36
Austria-dom	52,728	71,090	35
Israel-dom	29,503	39,611	34
Cote d'Ivoire-dom	3	4	33
Finland-dom	211,900	277,207	31
United Arab Emir-dom	365	469	28
Australia-dom	309,562	397,460	28
UK-dom	451,750	579,492	28
Sweden-dom	149,877	186,312	24
Iceland-dom	8,719	10,810	24
.int	1,557	1,930	24
.org	265,327	327,148	23
Netherlands-dom	174,888	214,704	23
Taiwan-dom	25,273	30,645	21
Germany-dom	452,997	548,168	21
Ecuador-dom	504	609	21
Trinidad and T.-dom	55	66	20
Switzerland-dom	85,844	102,691	20
Jamaica-dom	164	195	19
Russia-dom	11,481	13,601	18
.edu	1,793,491	2,114,851	18
Guam-dom	55	64	16
Spain-dom	53,707	62,447	16
.gov	312,330	361,065	16
Canada-dom	372,891	424,356	14
Iran-dom	271	307	13
Algeria-dom	16	18	13
Fiji-dom	52	58	12
Croatia-dom	2,230	2,480	11
Brunei Darussalam-dom	156	170	9
Uganda-dom	58	60	3

Country or Territory Hosts First Appearing July 1996			
Angola	Aruba	Benin	Burkina Faso
Central African Republic	Djibouti	Dominica	Guyana
Honduras	Madagascar	Mali	Mauritius
Mongolia	Mozambique	Netherlands Antilles	Niger
Paraguay	Qatar	Saint Lucia	Suriname
Vanuatu	Vietnam	Virgin Islands (U.S.)	

Chapter 11

Associations and Organizations

Associations and Organizations Directory

100VG-AnyLAN Forum (VGF), PO Box 1378, N. Highlands CA 95660 USA; 916/348-0212, Co Email: vgf@any-lan.win.com, Focus: Interoperability testing, certification and implementation of IEEE 802.12, Ownership: Nonprofit, Kenneth R. Hurst, Chmn

1394 Trade Assoc. c/o Skipstone, 3925 W Breaker Lane #425, Austin TX 78759 USA; 512/305-0202, Fax: 512/305-0212, Co Email: ipra@netcom.com, Web URL: firewire.org, Focus: Promote IEEE 1394 high-speed serial bus, Ownership: Nonprofit, Yr Founded: 1994, Empl: 25+, Gary A. Hoffman, Chmn, Email: gary@skipstone.com; James Snider, Vice Chair, Myles Suer, Dir Mktng

ACM SIG on Ada Programming Language (SIGADA), 1515 Broadway 17th Floor, New York NY 10036 USA; 212/626-0611, Fax: 212/302-5826, Focus: Technical and organizational aspects of the Ada language, Ownership: Nonprofit, Empl: 3,629

ACM SIG on APL Programming Language (SIGAPL), 1515 Broadway 17th Floor, New York NY 10036 USA; 212/626-0611, Fax: 212/302-5826, Focus: Development and application of the APL language, Ownership: Nonprofit, Empl: 898

ACM SIG on Applied Computing (SIGAPP), 1515 Broadway 17th Floor, New York NY 10036 USA; 212/626-0611, Fax: 212/302-5826, Focus: Integration of graphics, databases, communications & software engineering, Ownership: Nonprofit, Empl: 422

ACM SIG on Architecture of Computer Systems (SIGARCH), 1515 Broadway 17th Floor, New York NY 10036 USA; 212/626-0611, Fax: 212/302-5826, Focus: Design and organization of computer systems, Ownership: Nonprofit, Empl: 4,920

ACM SIG on Artificial Intelligence (SIGART), 1515 Broadway 17th Floor, New York NY 10036 USA; 212/626-0611, Fax: 212/302-5826, Focus: Special interest group on knowledge-based systems, Ownership: Nonprofit, Empl: 8,205

ACM SIG on Automata and Computability Theory (SIGACT), 1515 Broadway 17th Floor, New York NY 10036 USA; 212/626-0611, Fax: 212/302-5826, Focus: Theoretical computer science including analysis of algorithms, automata & semantics, Ownership: Nonprofit, Empl: 2,175

ACM SIG on Biomedical Computing (SIGBIO), 1515 Broadway 17th Floor, New York NY 10036 USA; 212/626-0611, Fax: 212/302-5826, Focus: Computer use in biomedical applications, Ownership: Nonprofit, Empl: 875

ACM SIG on Business Information Technology (SIGBIT), 1515 Broadway 17th Floor, New York NY 10036 USA; 212/626-0611, Fax: 212/302-5826, Focus: Technologies and methodologies for improving effectiveness in business information systems, Ownership: Nonprofit, Empl: 3,190

ACM SIG on Computer Graphics (SIGGRAPH), 1515 Broadway 17th Floor, New York NY 10036 USA; 212/626-0611, Fax: 212/302-5826, Focus: Computer graphics R&D, technologies and applications, Ownership: Nonprofit, Empl: 12,590

ACM SIG on Computer Personnel Research (SIGCPR), 1515 Broadway 17th Floor, New York NY 10036 USA; 212/626-0611, Fax: 212/302-5826, Focus: Computer personnel management, selection, evaluation and training techniques, Ownership: Nonprofit, Empl: 235

ACM SIG on Computer Science Education (SIGCSE), 1515 Broadway 17th Floor, New York NY 10036 USA; 212/626-0611, Fax: 212/302-5826, Focus: Development, implementation and evaluation of computer science programs and courses, Ownership: Nonprofit, Empl: 2,730

ACM SIG on Computer Uses in Education (SIGCUE), 1515 Broadway 17th Floor, New York NY 10036 USA; 212/626-0611, Fax: 212/302-5826, Focus: Improved concepts, methods and policies for instructional computing, Ownership: Nonprofit, Empl: 1,300

ACM SIG on Computers and Human Interaction (SIGCHI), 1515 Broadway 17th Floor, New York NY 10036 USA; 212/626-0611, Fax: 212/302-5826, Focus: Human-computer interaction and user interfaces, Ownership: Nonprofit, Empl: 5,948

ACM SIG on Computers and Society (SIGCAS), 1515 Broadway 17th Floor, New York NY 10036 USA; 212/626-0611, Fax: 212/302-5826, Focus: Computer impact on society--ethical and philosophical implications, Ownership: Nonprofit, Empl: 1,500

ACM SIG on Computers and the Physically Handicapped (SIGCAPH), 1515 Broadway 17th Floor, New York NY 10036 USA; 212/626-0611, Fax: 212/302-5826, Focus: Computer solution for disabled people, Ownership: Nonprofit, Yr Founded: 1970, Empl: 387

ACM SIG on Data Communication (SIGCOMM), 1515 Broadway 17th Floor, New York NY 10036 USA; 212/626-0611, Fax: 212/302-5826, Focus: Computer networks and communications, Ownership: Nonprofit, Empl: 4,800

ACM SIG on Design Automation (SIGDA), 1515 Broadway 17th Floor, New York NY 10036 USA; 212/302-5826, Focus: Computer applications in electrical and electronics design fields, Ownership: Nonprofit, Empl: 2,185

ACM SIG on Hypertext/Hypermedia (SIGLINK), 1515 Broadway 17th Floor, New York NY 10036 USA; 212/626-0611, Fax: 212/302-5826, Focus: Research on hypertext and hypermedia applications, Ownership: Nonprofit, Empl: 220

ACM SIG on Information Retrieval (SIGIR), 1515 Broadway 17th Floor, New York NY 10036 USA; 212/626-0611, Fax: 212/302-5826, Focus: Computer applications of information retrieval and dissemination, Ownership: Nonprofit, Empl: 1,669

ACM SIG on Management of Data (SIGMOD), 1515 Broadway 17th Floor, New York NY 10036 USA; 212/626-0611, Fax: 212/302-5826, Focus: Development, management and evaluation of database technology, Ownership: Nonprofit, Empl: 4,045

ACM SIG on Measurement and Evaluation (SIGMETRICS), 1515 Broadway 17th Floor, New York NY 10036 USA; 212/626-0611, Fax: 212/302-5826, Focus: Computer system performance measurements and related subjects, Ownership: Nonprofit, Empl: 1,872

ACM SIG on Microprogramming (SIGMICRO), 1515 Broadway 17th Floor, New York NY 10036 USA; 212/626-0611, Fax: 212/302-5826, Focus: Microprogramming, firmware, computer architecture and VLSI implementations, Ownership: Nonprofit, Empl: 1,155

ACM SIG on Numerical Mathematics (SIGNUM), 1515 Broadway 17th Floor, New York NY 10036 USA; 212/626-0611, Fax: 212/302-5826, Focus: Computational mathematics: numerical algorithms, mathematical software, computation theory, Ownership: Nonprofit, Empl: 1,162

ACM SIG on Office Information Systems (SIGOIS), 1515 Broadway 17th Floor, New York NY 10036 USA; 212/626-0611, Fax: 212/302-5826, Focus: Computing techniques in office activities, Ownership: Nonprofit, Empl: 1,649

ACM SIG on Operating Systems

(SIGOPS), 1515 Broadway 17th Floor, New York NY 10036 USA; 212/626-0611, Fax: 212/302-5826, Focus: Operating system technology for multi-programming, multi-processing and timesharing, Ownership: Nonprofit, Empl: 6,620

ACM SIG on Programming Language FORTH (SIGFORTH), 1515 Broadway 17th Floor, New York NY 10036 USA; 212/626-0611, Fax: 212/302-5826, Focus: Development and research on Forth and its applications, Ownership: Nonprofit, Empl: 432

ACM SIG on Programming Languages (SIGPLAN), 1515 Broadway 17th Floor, New York NY 10036 USA; 212/869-7440, Fax: 212/302-5826, Focus: Practical and theoretical aspects on all programming languages, Ownership: Nonprofit, Empl: 10,250

ACM SIG on Security and Audit Control (SIGSAC), 1515 Broadway 17th Floor, New York NY 10036 USA; 212/626-0611, Fax: 212/302-5826, Focus: Technology for computer and data security, Ownership: Nonprofit, Empl: 1,157

ACM SIG on Simulation and Modeling (SIGSIM), 1515 Broadway 17th Floor, New York NY 10036 USA; 212/626-0611, Fax: 212/302-5826, Focus: Development, methodology and applications of computer simulation, Ownership: Nonprofit, Empl: 1,935

ACM SIG on Small and Personal Computing Systems and Applications (SIGSMALL/PC), 1515 Broadway 17th Floor, New York NY 10036 USA; 212/626-0611, Fax: 212/302-5826, Focus: Architecture and applications of personal and small computers, Ownership: Nonprofit, Empl: 4,330

ACM SIG on Software Engineering (SIGSOFT), 1515 Broadway 17th Floor, New York NY 10036 USA; 212/626-0611, Fax: 212/302-5826, Focus: Software engineering techniques, principles and practice, Ownership: Nonprofit, Empl: 9,800

ACM SIG on Symbolic and Algebraic Manipulation (SIGSAM), 1515 Broadway 17th Floor, New York NY 10036 USA; 212/626-0611, Fax: 212/302-5826, Focus: Practical and theoretical aspects of algorithms and data structures, Ownership: Nonprofit, Empl: 902

ACM SIG on Systems Documentation (SIGDOC), 1515 Broadway 17th Floor, New York NY 10036 USA; 212/626-0611, Fax: 212/302-5826, Focus: Techniques for reference material and user documentation, Ownership: Nonprofit, Empl: 1,086

ACM SIG on University and College Computing Services (SIGUCCS), 1515 Broadway 17th Floor, New York NY 10036 USA; 212/626-0611, Fax: 212/302-5826, Focus: Development and guidance on computer usage in universities, Ownership:

Nonprofit, Empl: 1,005
Acute Inc. (ACUTE), 700 SW Jackson Street #702, Topeka KS 66603-3740 USA; 913/233-1919, Fax: 913/357-6629, Co Email: barbee@smartnet.com, Focus: Computer applications information for CPAs, Ownership: Nonprofit, Yr Founded: 1965, Empl: 1,400, Jean Barbee, Exec Dir, Email: barbee@smartnet.net; Ron Eagle, Pres

Ada Information Clearinghouse (AdaIC), PO Box 1866, Falls Church VA 22041 USA; 800/232-4211 Fax: 703/681-2869, Co Email: adainfo@sw-eng.falls-church.va, Web URL: sw-eng.falls-church.va.us, Focus: Information on the Ada community

ADSL Forum 303 Vintage Park Drive, Foster City CA 94404-1138 USA; 415/378-6680, Fax: 415/525-0182, Co Email: adslforum@adsl.com, Focus: Promote use of Asymmetric Digital Subscriber Line technology, Ownership: Nonprofit, Yr Founded: 1994, Gretta Tierney, Assoc Coord, Kim Maxwell, Chmn & Pres, Email: adslforum@aol.com; Greg Whelan, VP, Email: greg.whelan@analog.com

Amdahl Users Group (AUG), 1250 E Arques Ave MS 215, Sunnyvale CA 94088-3470 USA; 408/746-8888, Focus: Users of Amdahl products and services, Ownership: Nonprofit, Yr Founded: 1976, Empl: 700

American Association for Artificial Intelligence (AAAI), 445 Burgess Drive, Menlo Park CA 94025-3442 USA; 415/328-3123, Fax: 415/321-4457, Co Email: info@aaai.org, Web URL: aaai.org, Focus: Study and application of artificial intelligence science and technology, Ownership: Nonprofit, Yr Founded: 1980, Empl: 10,000, Carol Hamilton, Exec Dir, Email: ncai@aaai.org; Randall Davis, Pres

American Association for the Advancement of Science (AAAS), 1200 New York Ave NW, Washington DC 20005 USA; 202/326-6400, Fax: 202/682-0816, Web URL: aaas.org, Focus: Furthers the work of scientists, fosters scientific freedom and responsibility, Ownership: Nonprofit, Yr Founded: 1848, Empl: 141,000

American Electronics Assoc. (AEA), 5201 Great America Pkwy #520, Santa Clara CA 95054 USA; 408/987-4200, Fax: 408/970-8565, Co Email: @aeanet.org, Web URL: aeanet.org, Focus: Serves and represents the nation's electronics industry, Ownership: Nonprofit, Yr Founded: 1943, Empl: 3,500

American Facsimile Assoc. (AFA), 2200 Ben Franklin Pkwy #N-108, Philadelphia PA 19130 USA; 215/981-0292, Fax: 215/981-0295, Focus: Information for fax industry, Ownership: Nonprofit, Yr Founded: 1986, Gerard Brodsky, Pres
American Mobile Telecommunications Assoc. (AMTA), 1150 18th Street

#250, Washington DC 20036 USA; 202/331-7773, Fax: 202/331-9062, Focus: Association for wireless industry, Ownership: Nonprofit

American National Standards Institute (ANSI), 11 W 42nd Street, New York NY 10036 USA; 212/642-4900, Fax: 212/398-0023, Focus: Coordinates and approves American National Standards. Is US member to ISO and IEC, Ownership: Nonprofit, Yr Founded: 1918, Empl: 1,600

American Society for Information Science (ASIS), 8720 Georgia Ave #501, Silver Spring MD 20910 USA; 301/495-0900, Fax: 301/495-0810, Focus: Improve access to information through policy, technology and research, Ownership: Nonprofit, Yr Founded: 1937, Empl: 3,700, Clifford Lynch, Pres

American Software Association-Div. of ITAA (ASA), c/o ITAA, 1616 N Ft Myer Drive #1300, Arlington VA 22209 USA; 703/522-5055, Fax: 703/525-2279, Focus: Association for software companies, Ownership: Nonprofit

American Software Users Group (ASUG), 401 N Michigan Ave, Chicago IL 60611-4267 USA; 312/644-6610, Fax: 312/321-6869, Focus: Users of American Software's products, Ownership: Nonprofit, Yr Founded: 1981, Empl: 2,000

Apple Dealers Assoc. (ADA), 450 E 22nd Street #230, Lombard IL 60148-6158 USA; 630/268-1818, Fax: 630/240-1384, Focus: Association for Apple resellers, Ownership: Nonprofit, Empl: 500, Elizabeth G. Berglund, Dir Marcom

ARCNET Trade Assoc. (ATA), 2460 Wisconsin Ave, Downers Grove IL 60515 USA; 630/960-5130, Fax: 630/963-2122, Web URL: arcnet.org, Focus: Arcnet LAN vendor association, Ownership: Nonprofit, Yr Founded: 1987, Empl: 50

Arizona Macintosh Users Group (AMUG), 4131 N 24th Street #A-120, Phoenix AZ 85016 USA; 602/553-8966, Fax: 602/553-8771, Co Email: info@amug.org, Web URL: amug.org, Focus: Macintosh users in 38 states and 15 countries, Ownership: Nonprofit, Empl: 1,900, Michael Bean, Email: bean@amug.org

Arizona Software Assoc. 3900 E Camelback #200, Phoenix AZ 85018 USA; 602/912-5351, Fax: 602/957-4828, Focus: Organization for software companies in Arizona, Ownership: Nonprofit

Association for Computers and the Humanities (ACH), College of Humanities, Brigham Young Univ, Provo UT 84602 USA; 801/378-3513, Fax: 801/378-4649, Focus: Promotes scholarships and applied studies in using computers in humanities, Ownership: Nonprofit, Yr Founded: 1978, Empl: 400, Randall Jones, Exec Secretary

Association for Computing Machin-

ery (ACM), 1515 Broadway 17th Floor, New York NY 10036-5701 USA; 212/869-7440, Fax: 212/944-1318, Co Email: @acm.org, Web URL: acm.org, Focus: Educational and scientific society for computer professionals, Ownership: Nonprofit, Yr Founded: 1947, Empl: 80,000, Joseph S. DeBlasi, Exec Dir, Lillian Israel, Dir Memb, Lisa Ernst, Dir Conf, John A. Osmundsen, Assoc Dir Pub Affairs

Association for Educational Communications and Technology (AECT), 1025 Vermont Ave NW #820, Washington DC 20005 USA; 202/347-7834, Fax: 202/347-7839, Web URL: aect.org, Focus: Educational technology such as computerized instruction, Ownership: Nonprofit, Stanley Zenor, Exec Dir, Shannon Gordon, Dir Fin, Marry Kavalier, Dir Pubs

Association for Information and Image Management (AIIM), 1100 Wayne Ave #1100, Silver Spring MD 20910 USA; 301/587-8202, Fax: 301/587-2711, Web URL: aiim.org, Focus: Advancing technology for capture, storage and retrieval of image documents, Prdts: AIIM Show, Ownership: Nonprofit, Yr Founded: 1945, Empl: 9,000, John Mancini, Exec Dir

Association for Services Management Int'l. (AFSM), 1342 Colonial Blvd #25, Ft. Myers FL 33907 USA; 941/275-7887, 800/444-9786 Focus: Association for high-tech services and support, Ownership: Nonprofit, Joseph R. Trpik, EVP, Robert M. Steele, Exec Dir, Joanna L. Baker, Dir Membership, Leonard Mafrica, Dir Ed Svcs

Association for Systems Management (ASM), 1433 W Bagley Road, PO Box 38370, Cleveland OH 44138-0370 USA; 216/243-6900, Fax: 216/234-2930, Focus: Continuing education for information systems professional, Ownership: Nonprofit, Yr Founded: 1947, Empl: 6,000, Robert C. La Prad, Exec Dir, Ross A. Flaherty, Pres

Association for Women in Computing 41 Sutter Street #1006, San Francisco CA 94104 USA; 415/905-4663, Co Email: awc@acm.org, Web URL: halcyon.com/monih/awc, Focus: Association for women in the computer industry, Ownership: Nonprofit, Yr Founded: 1978

Association for Women in Science (AWIS), 1200 New York Ave NW #650, Washington DC 20005 USA; 202/326-8940, Fax: 202/326-8960, Co Email: awis@awis.org, Focus: Expanding educational and career opportunities for women in the sciences, Ownership: Nonprofit, Empl: 5,000, Catherine Didion, Exec Dir

Association for Work Process Improvement 185 Devonshire Street, Boston MA 02110 USA; 617/426-1167, Fax: 617/521-8675, Co Email: tawpi@aol.com, Focus: Data capture, document, remittance and electronic process-

ing applications, Ownership: Nonprofit, Yr Founded: 1970, Empl: 1,000, Linda Cooper, Exec Dir, Kerry Stackpole, Pres

Association of Color Thermal Transfer Technology Inc. (ACT), 310 Commerce Drive #228, Amherst NY 14228-2396 USA; 716/691-5817, Fax: 716/691-3395, Focus: Promote color thermal transfer printer technology, Ownership: Nonprofit, Yr Founded: 1993, Rick W. Wallace, Exec Dir

Association of Database Developers (ADD), 3165 16th Street, San Francisco CA 94103 USA; 415/281-5638, Focus: Organization for software developers using Xbase, Ownership: Nonprofit, Yr Founded: 1982, Empl: 160, Joann Castillo, Pres

Association of Desk-Top Publishers (AD-TP), 3401-A 800 Adams Ave, San Diego CA 92116 USA; 619/563-9714, Fax: 619/280-3778, Focus: Trade association for desktop publishers, Ownership: Nonprofit, Yr Founded: 1986, Norman Paddock, Exec Dir

Association of Information and Dissemination Centers (ASIDIC), PO Box 8105, Athens GA 30603 USA; 706/542-6820, Focus: Organization for database producers and users, Ownership: Nonprofit, Yr Founded: 1968, Empl: 80, Bill Bartenbach, Pres, Taissa Kusma, Past Pres, Jeanette Webb, Email: jwebb@uga.cc.uga.edu

Association of Online Professionals 6010 Burdon Court #302, Alexandria VA 22315 USA; 703/924-9594, Fax: 703/924-9594, Focus: Organization for online users, Ownership: Nonprofit, Empl: 200, David McClure, Exec Dir

Association of Personal Computer Users Group (APCUG), 1730 M Street NW #700, Washington DC 20036 USA; Focus: Helping user groups worldwide, Empl: 425, Tom Heffernan, Pres, Eagan Foster, VP, Charles Kelly, Sec, Maralyn Henry, Treas

Association of Shareware Professionals (ASP), 545 Grover Road, Muskegon MI 49442-9427 USA; 616/788-5131, Fax: 616/788-2765, Co Email: @asp-shareware.org, Web URL: asp-shareware.org, Focus: Association for shareware software vendors and authors, Ownership: Nonprofit, Yr Founded: 1987, Empl: 1,500, George Campbell, Chmn, Richard Harper, Pres, Jan Abbott, Exec Dir

Association of the DEC Marketplace (DDA), 107 S Main Street, Chelsea MI 48118 USA; 313/475-8333, 800/DDA-1130 Fax: 313/475-4671, Web URL: dda.org, Focus: Serves vendors and consumers of the open Digital marketplace, Yr Founded: 1982

Association of the Institute of Certification of Computer Prof. (AICCP), 2200 E Devon Ave #247, Des Plaines IL

60018 USA; 847/299-4227, Fax: 847/299-4280, Focus: Certification of computer professionals, Ownership: Nonprofit

ATM Forum (ATM), 2570 W El Camino Real #304, Mountain View CA 94040-1313 USA; 415/949-6700, Fax: 415/949-6705, Co Email: info@atmforum.com, Web URL: atmforum.com, Focus: Speed development of Asynchronous Transfer Mode products, Ownership: Nonprofit, Yr Founded: 1991, Empl: 580, Steve Walters, Chmn & Pres, Anne M. Ferris, Exec Dir, Sanjay Uppal, VP Mktng

Austin Software Council 8920 Business Park Drive, Austin TX 78759 USA; 512/794-9994, Fax: 512/794-9997, Focus: Organization for Austin software companies, Ownership: Nonprofit

Automated Imaging Assoc. (AIA), 900 Victors Way PO Box 3724, Ann Arbor MI 48106 USA; 313/994-6088, Fax: 313/994-3338, Focus: Productive use of image processing and machine vision, Ownership: Nonprofit, Jeff Burnstein, Mngng Dir

Black Data Processing Associates (BDPA), 1250 Connecticut Ave NW #700, Washington DC 20036 USA; 202/775-4301, 800/727-2372 Fax: 202/637-9195, Focus: Educational opportunities and information sharing, Ownership: Nonprofit, Yr Founded: 1975, Empl: 2,000, Margaret E. Johnson, Exec Dir, Diane L. Davis, Pres

BMUG Inc. (BMUG), 1442A Walnut Street #62, Berkeley CA 94709-1496 USA; 510/549-2684, Fax: 510/849-9026, Co Email: bmuginfo@bmug.org, Web URL: bmug.org, Focus: PC users group, Ownership: Nonprofit, Yr Founded: 1984, Empl: 12,000, Ann Wrixon, Exec Dir

Borland User Group 1800 Green Hills Road, Scotts Valley CA 95066 USA; 408/431-1065, Fax: 408/431-4175, Focus: Users of Borland's language and application software, Ownership: Nonprofit, Ylonda Davis, UG Mgr, Email: ydavis@wpo.borland.com; Nancy Collins, UG Spec, Email: ncollins@wpo.borland.com

Business Applications Performance Corp. (BAPC), 2200 Mission College Blvd RNB4-21, Santa Clara CA 95051 USA; 408/988-7654, Fax: 408/765-4920, Co Email: john_peterson@bapco.com, Web URL: bapco.com, Focus: Develop applications-based industry standard benchmarks, Ownership: Nonprofit, Yr Founded: 1991, Empl: 19, John Sammons, Pres, John E. Peterson, Admin of Ops

Business Products Industry Assoc. (BPIA), 301 N Fairfax Street, Alexandria VA 22314 USA; 703/549-9040, Fax: 703/683-7552, Web URL: recyclefurn.org, Focus: Association for resellers of office products, Ownership: Nonprofit, Yr Founded: 1904, Empl: 7,000, Daniel Scott, Pres

Business Software Alliance 2001 L St

NW #400, Washington DC 20036 USA; 202/872-5500, Fax: 202/872-5501, Co Email: software@bsa.org, Web URL: bsa.org/bsa, Focus: Prevention of software piracy, Ownership: Nonprofit, Yr Founded: 1988, Robert Holleyman, Pres, Diane Smiroldo

Business Technology Assoc. (BTA), 12411 Wornall Road, Kansas City MO 64145 USA; 816/941-3100, Fax: 816/941-4838, Web URL: btanet.org, Focus: Association for resellers of office automation equipment and LANs, Ownership: Nonprofit, Yr Founded: 1926, Empl: 6,000, Keith Anderson, Exec Dir, Jan Kitta, Marcom Mgr

Cable Television Laboratories Inc. (CableLabs), 400 Centennial Pkwy, Louisville CO 80027-1208 USA; 303/661-9100, Fax: 303/661-9199, Web URL: cablelabs.com, Focus: R&D consortium for the cable TV industry, Ownership: Nonprofit, Donald Frazier

Cable/Information Technology Convergence Forum c/o CableLabs, 400 Centennial Pkwy, Louisville CO 80027-1208 USA; 303/661-9100, Fax: 303/661-9199, Focus: Communications between computer and cable TV companies, Ownership: Nonprofit, Yr Founded: 1994

Canadian Information Processing Society 430 King Street W #106, Toronto Ontario M5V 1L5 Canada; 416/593-4040, Focus: Association for Canadian computer professionals, Ownership: Nonprofit, Yr Founded: 1958, Empl: 5,000

Capital Network Inc. 3925 W Braker Lane #406, Austin TX 78759-5321 USA; 512/305-0826, Fax: 512/305-0836, Co Email: david@ati.utexas.edu, Focus: Economic development organization for high-tech companies, Ownership: Nonprofit, Yr Founded: 1989, David Gerhardt, Exec Dir

CDPD Forum Inc. (CDPD), 401 N Michigan Ave, Chicago IL 60611 USA; 800/335-2373 Focus: Support development of nationwide CDPD network, Ownership: Nonprofit, Yr Founded: 1994, Empl: 57

CED Research Triangle Software Developers Roundtable PO Box 13353, Research Triangle Pk NC 27709 USA; 919/460-5355, Fax: 919/460-3861, Focus: High-tech organization for North Carolina, Ownership: Nonprofit

Cellular Telecommunications Industry Assoc. 1250 Connecticut Ave NW, Washington DC 20036 USA; 202/785-0081, Fax: 202/776-0540, Focus: Association for cellular phone vendors, Ownership: Nonprofit

Center for Democracy and Technology 1634 Eye St NW #1100, Washington DC 20006 USA; 202/637-9800, Fax: 202/637-0968, Co Email: info@cdt.org, Web URL: cdt.org, Ownership: Nonprofit,

Jerry Berman, Exec Dir

Central & Eastern Europe Business Information Center (EEBIC), ITA Dept of Commerce Rm 7412, Washington DC 20230 USA; 202/482-2645, Fax: 202/482-4473, Focus: Clearinghouse for information on opportunities in Eastern Europe, Ownership: Nonprofit, Yr Founded: 1990

Charles Babbage Institute (CBI), 103 Walter Library Univ of Minnesota, Minneapolis MN 55455 USA; 612/624-5050, Fax: 612/624-8054, Co Email: cbi@vx.cis.umn.edu, Web URL: cbi.itdean.umn.edu/cbi, Focus: Archival collection and researches history of information processing and computing, Ownership: Nonprofit, Yr Founded: 1978, Robert W. Seidel, Dir, Email: rws@maroon.tc.umn.edu

Chicago Software Assoc. 2 N Riverside Plaza #2400, Chicago IL 60606 USA; 708/358-0567, Fax: 708/358-0586, Focus: Association for Chicago area software developers, Ownership: Nonprofit, Ed Dennison, Exec Dir

Cincom International Users Group 2300 Montana Ave, Cincinnati OH 45211-3899 USA; 513/662-2300, Fax: 513/481-8332, Focus: Organization for users of Cincom products, Ownership: Nonprofit

Coleman Computer Assoc. 7380 Pkwy Drive, La Mesa CA 91942-1532 USA; 619/465-4063, Focus: Association for computer professionals, Ownership: Nonprofit, Yr Founded: 1967

Colorado Advanced Software Institute 1898 S Flatirons Court #5A, Boulder CO 80301 USA; 303/440-3695, Fax: 303/440-4083, Focus: Organization for Colorado software companies, Ownership: Nonprofit

Colorado Software Assoc. 190 E 9th Ave #300, Denver CO 80203 USA; 303/220-2000, Fax: 303/220-2120, Focus: Association for Colorado software developers, Ownership: Nonprofit, Ray Meuller, Chmn

CommerceNet 800 El Camino Real, Menlo Park CA 94025 USA; 415/617-8790, Fax: 415/617-1516, Co Email: info@commerce.net, Web URL: commerce.net, Focus: Consortium to create an Internet electronic marketplace, Ownership: Nonprofit, Yr Founded: 1994, Empl: 135, Cathy Medich, Exec Dir

Commercial Internet eXchange Assoc. (CIX), 1035 Sterling Road #201, Herndon VA 22071 USA; 703/318-7218, Fax: 703/904-0646, Co Email: @cix.org, Web URL: cix.org/cixhome, Focus: Association for internet information providers, Ownership: Nonprofit, Empl: 180, Susan Fitzgerald, Exec Dir, Email: sfitzger@cix.org; Robert D. Collet, Chmn & Pres, Email: rcollet@cix.org; Barbara Dooley, Managing Ed, Email: imasters@pipeline.com

Common - A Users Group 401 N Michigan Ave, Chicago IL 60611-4267 USA; 312/644-6610, Fax: 312/644-0297, Focus: Users group for IBM AS/400, RS/6000, System/36, 38, 88, IBM 43xx, 9379 & 370 Architectures, Ownership: Nonprofit, Yr Founded: 1960, Empl: 4,000, Rand Baldwin, Exec Dir

Communications Managers Assoc. (CMA), 1201 Mt Kemble Ave, Morristown NJ 07960 USA; 201/425-1700, Fax: 201/425-0777, Web URL: cma.org, Focus: Information sharing, education and enhancement of the telecommunications profession, Ownership: Nonprofit, Yr Founded: 1948, Empl: 500, Matt O'Brien, Pres, Katherine Pakacs, Managing Dir

Compact Flash Assoc. (CFA), PO Box 51537, Palo Alto CA 94303 USA; 415/843-1220, Fax: 415/493-1871, Co Email: info@compactflash.org, Web URL: compactflash.org, Focus: Association for compact flash card vendors, Prdts: Compact Flash Specification Standard, Ownership: Nonprofit, Yr Founded: 1995, Empl: 30, Bill Frank, Exec Dir, Email: billfrank@compactflash.org

Component Integration Laboratories (CI Labs), PO Box 61747, Sunnyvale CA 94088-1747 USA; 408/864-0300, Fax: 408/0380, Co Email: cilabs@cil.org, Focus: Develop object technology standards-OpenDoc, Ownership: Nonprofit, Jed Harris, Pres, Email: jed@cil.org; Andrew Poupart, VP Ops, Michael Barton, VP Mktng

Computer & Automated Systems Assoc. of the SME (CASA/SME), 1 SME Drive, PO Box 930, Dearborn MI 48121 USA; 313/271-1500, Fax: 313/271-2861, Focus: Association for computer and automated systems professionals, Ownership: Nonprofit, Yr Founded: 1974, Empl: 10,000

Computer and Communications Industry Assoc. (CCIA), 666 Eleventh Street NW 6th Fl, Washington DC 20001 USA; 202/783-0070, Fax: 202/783-0534, Co Email: ccia@aol.com, Focus: Association for computer and communications industry, Ownership: Nonprofit, Yr Founded: 1972, Empl: 65, Edward Black, Pres

Computer Association of N. America (CANA), 136-21 Rosevelt Ave 3rd Floor, Flushing NY 11354 USA; 718/460-9770, Fax: 718/460-9771, Ownership: Nonprofit, Yr Founded: 1991, Arrina Chang, Admin. Secretary

Computer Emergency Response Team Coordination Center (CERT), CMU Software Eng Institute, Pittsburgh PA 15213 USA; 412/268-7090, Co Email: cert@cert.org, Focus: Respond to computer security incidents on the Internet, Ownership: Nonprofit

Computer Law Assoc. (CLA), 3028 Javier Road #500E, Fairfax VA 22031 USA; 703/560-7747, Fax: 703/207-7028, Co Email: clanet@aol.com, Web URL: cla.org, Focus: Information for attorneys in computer law, Ownership: Nonprofit, Yr Founded: 1971, Empl: 1,300, Barbara Fieser, Exec Dir

Computer Learning Foundation (CLF), 2431 Park Blvd, PO Box 60007, Palo Alto CA 94306-0007 USA; 415/327-3347, Fax: 415/327-3349, Co Email: clf@legal.com, Focus: Effective and ethical use of technology among educators, parents and youth, Ownership: Nonprofit, Yr Founded: 1987, Empl: 200+, Sally Bowman Alden, Exec Dir

Computer Leasing & Remarketing Assoc. Inc. (CDLA), 401 N Michigan Ave, Chicago IL 60611-4267 USA; 312/644-6610, Fax: 312/321-6869, Focus: Represents companies that buy, sell, lease and broker computers and high-tech equipment, Ownership: Nonprofit, Yr Founded: 1981, Empl: 260, Douglas B. McAllister, Dir Com

Computer Measurement Group Inc. (CMG), 414 Plaza Drive #209, Westmont IL 60559 USA; 630/655-1812, Fax: 630/655-1813, Web URL: cmg.cs.csi.cuny.edu, Focus: Performance, planning and management of computer systems, Ownership: Nonprofit, Yr Founded: 1975, Judith K. Keel, Exec Dir

Computer Press Assoc. (CPA), 631 Henmar Drive, Landing NJ 07850 USA; 201/398-7300, Fax: 201/398-3888, Co Email: 102751.1445@compuserve.com, Focus: Promotes excellence in computer journalism, Ownership: Nonprofit, Yr Founded: 1983, Empl: 350, Jeff Yablon, Pres, Michael Desmond, VP, Heidi Wagner, Admin

Computer Security Institute (CSI), 600 Harrison Street, San Francisco CA 94107 USA; 415/905-2626, Fax: 415/905-2218, Co Email: csi@mfi.com, Web URL: gosci.com/csi, Focus: Information for protecting an organization's information assets, Prdts: Network Security, CSI Annual Conference, Ownership: Nonprofit, Yr Founded: 1974, Empl: 3,100, Patrice Rapalus, Dir, Email: prapalus@mfi.com; Nancy Baer, Mktng Mgr, Peter Allen, Managing Ed

Computer Software Industry Assoc. (CSIA), 101 First Street #324, Los Altos CA 94022 USA; 415/948-9192, Focus: Educates members on California and federal software legislation, Ownership: Nonprofit, Yr Founded: 1982, Empl: 125, Kaye Caldwell, Pres

Computer Systems Policy Project (CSPP), 1001 G Street NW #900E, Washington DC 20001 USA; 202/393-1010, Web URL: cspp.org, Focus: Promotes creation of national information infrastructure, Ownership: Nonprofit, Yr Founded: 1989,

Ken Kay, Exec Dir

Computing Research Assoc. Inc. (CRA), 1875 Connecticut Ave NW #718, Washington DC 20009 USA; 202/234-2111, Fax: 202/667-1066, Web URL: cra.org, Focus: Promote computing technology research, Ownership: Nonprofit, Yr Founded: 1972, Empl: 150, William Asprey, Exec Dir, Dave Patterson, Chmn

Computing Technology Industry Assoc. (CTIA), 450 E 22nd Street #230, Lombard IL 60148-6156 USA; 630/268-1818, Fax: 630/268-1384, Co Email: comptiahq@aol.com, Web URL: comptia.org, Focus: Association for computer resellers and vendors, Ownership: Nonprofit, Yr Founded: 1982, Empl: 500, John A. Venator, EVP & CEO, Jeffrey Masich, Pres

Comshare Users Group 555 Briarwood Circle, Ann Arbor MI 48108 USA; 313/994-4800, Focus: Users of Comshare software products, Ownership: Nonprofit, Ricia Hughes

Connect, The User Group for Texas Instruments Software 401 N Michigan Ave, Chicago IL 60611-4267 USA; 312/644-6610, Fax: 312/644-0297, Focus: Association for TI software users, Ownership: Nonprofit

Consortium for Advanced Manufacturing-International Inc. (CAM-I), 3301 Airport Fwy #324, Bedford TX 76021 USA; 817/860-1654, Fax: 817/275-6450, Co Email: @cam-i.com, Focus: Cooperative R&D in Computer Integrated Manufacturing (CIM), Ownership: Nonprofit, Yr Founded: 1972, Empl: 80, Woody Noxon, Pres

Copyright Office 101 Independence Ave, Washington DC 20559 USA; 202/707-3000, Fax: 202/707-8366, Focus: Information on copyright law, registration, procedures and requirements, Ownership: Nonprofit

Corporate Association for Microcomputer Professionals (CAMP), 950 Skokie Blvd #310, Northbrook IL 60062 USA; 847/291-1360, Fax: 847/291-1360, Focus: Association of corporate MIS director, Ownership: Nonprofit, Yr Founded: 1984, Empl: 4,000+, Julian Horwich, Exec Dir

Data Administration Management Assoc. (DAMA), PO Box 6096, Chesterfield MO 63006-6096 USA; 314/878-3372, Fax: 314/878-4016, Focus: Information management issues, Ownership: Nonprofit, Yr Founded: 1986, Empl: 3,000, Carol Mugas, Pres, Joe Daniclewicz, VP Com

Data Processing Management Assoc. (DPMA), 505 Busse Hwy, Park Ridge IL 60068-3191 USA; 708/825-8124, Fax: 708/825-1693, Focus: Broader understanding of the methods and principles of data processing systems, Ownership: Non-

profit, Yr Founded: 1951, Empl: 30,000, George Eggert, Exec Dir

Davenport Group c/o O'Reilly, 101 Morris Street #A, Sebastopol CA 95472 USA; 707/829-0515, Fax: 707/829-0104, Focus: Establish common interchange format among UNIX software vendors, Ownership: Nonprofit, Yr Founded: 1992, Dale Dougherty, Chmn

Defense Advanced Research Projects Agency (DARPA), 3701 N Fairfax Drive, Arlington VA 22203-1714 USA; 703/696-2444, Fax: 703/696-2207, Focus: Manages high-risk, high-payoff basic research and applied technology programs, Ownership: Nonprofit, Yr Founded: 1958, Ron H. Register, Deputy Dir Mgmt

Defense Technical Information Center 8275 John Jay Kingman Rd, Ft Belvoir VA 22060-6218 USA; 703/767-9100, Fax: 703/767-9183, Web URL: dtic.mil, Focus: Repository of Defense Department's research and development efforts, Ownership: Nonprofit

Desktop Management Task Force (DMTF), 2111 NE 25th Street, Hillsboro OR 97209-4023 USA; 503/264-9300, Fax: 503/264-9027, Co Email: @dmtf.org, Focus: Open, standard for managing desktop systems, Ownership: Nonprofit, Yr Founded: 1992, Empl: 300, Edward Arrington, Chairperson

Digital Equipment Computer Users Society (DECUS), 334 S Street SHR 3-1/T25, Shrewsbury MA 01545-4195 USA; 508/841-3346, 800/333-8755 Fax: 508/841-3357, Co Email: information@decus.org, Focus: Users group for Digital Equipment products, Prdts: DECUS Symposia & Trade Shows, DECUS University, Ownership: Nonprofit, Yr Founded: 1961, Empl: 53,000, Joseph A. Pollizzi III, Pres, Tony Ioele, VP, Thomas McIntyre, VP Chapters, Paul Murphy, Email: murphy@decus.org

East-West Foundation 23 Drydock Ave 3rd Fl, Boston MA 02210 USA; 617/261-6699, Fax: 617/261-6644, Co Email: ewedf@ix.netcom.com, Focus: Donations of surplus computers for use in Eastern-Europe, Ownership: Nonprofit, Yr Founded: 1990, Stephen C. Farrell, Exec Dir

Educom 1112 16th Street NW #600, Washington DC 20036 USA; 202/872-4200, Fax: 202/872-4318, Focus: Consortium of universities regarding computer and communication in higher education, Ownership: Nonprofit, Yr Founded: 1964, Kenneth King, Pres, Steven Gilbert, VP, Roger Smith, DB/Pub MIS Manager, Windy Rickard Bollentin, PR/Pub

Electro Federation Canada 10 Carleson Court #210, Rexdale Ontario M9W 6L2 Canada; 416/674-7410, Fax: 416/674-7412, Focus: Association for Canadian electronics industry, Ownership: Nonprofit

Electronic Commerce World 380 St Antoine #3280W, Montreal Quebec H2Y 3X7 Canada; 514/288-3555, Fax: 514/288-4199, Co Email: institute@ecworld.org, Web URL: ecworld.org, Focus: Research, education and information on EDI, Ownership: Nonprofit, Yr Founded: 1992, Empl: 15, Andre Vallerand, Pres, Sylvie Labreche

Electronic Document Systems Foundation 24238 Hawthorne Blvd, Torrance CA 90505-6505 USA; 310/373-3633, 800/669-7567 Fax: 310/375-4240, Co Email: info@xplor.org, Web URL: xplor.org, Focus: Electronic document systems industry and society, Ownership: Nonprofit, Ray Simonson, Chmn

Electronic Industries Assoc. (EIA), 2500 Wilson Blvd, Arlington VA 22201-3834 USA; 703/907-7500, Fax: 703/907-7501, Co Email: @eia.org, Web URL: eia.org, Focus: Trade organization of computer, communications and electronics manufacturers, Ownership: Nonprofit, Yr Founded: 1924, Empl: 1,000, Peter F. McCloskey, Pres, John J. Kelly, VP & Gen Counsel, T. Glyn Finley, VP Mkt Res, Kevin G. Richardson, VP Gov Rel, Mark V. Rosenker, VP Pub Aff

Electronic Messaging Assoc. 1655 N Ft Meyer Drive #850, Arlington VA 22209 USA; 703/524-5550, Fax: 703/524-5558, Co Email: info@ema.org, Web URL: ema.org, Focus: Association for electronic messaging users & vendors, Ownership: Nonprofit, Yr Founded: 1983, Empl: 400, Victor Parra, Pres, Mark Rockwell, PR Mgr

Electronic Privacy Information Center 666 Pennsylvania Ave SE, Washington DC 20003 USA; 202/544-9240, Fax: 202/547-5482, Co Email: info@epic.org, Web URL: epic.org, Focus: Research on privacy, information access & computer security, Ownership: Nonprofit

Electronics and Business Equipment Assoc. (EEA), Russell Square House 10-12 Russell Square, London WC1B 5AE England; 071-331-2000, Fax: 071-331-2040, Focus: Represents electronics, telecom and business equipment industries, Ownership: Nonprofit, Yr Founded: 1946

Electronics Representatives Assoc. (ERA), 20 E Huron Street, Chicago IL 60611 USA; 312/649-1333, Fax: 312/649-9509, Co Email: info@era.org, Web URL: era.org, Focus: Networking for manufacturers to find sales representatives to carry their product lines, Ownership: Nonprofit, Yr Founded: 1935, Empl: 2,200, Ray Hall, EVP & CEO

Energy Star Computers US EPA, Global Change Div 6202J, Washington DC 20460 USA; 202/775-6650, Fax: 202/775-6680, Focus: Promotes usage of energy efficient computers, Ownership: Nonprofit, Yr Founded: 1992

Enterprise Computer Telephony (ECTF), 303 Vintage Park Drive, Foster City CA 94404 USA; 415/578-6852, Fax: 415/378-6692, Focus: Open forum on interoperability in computer telephony industry, Ownership: Nonprofit, Yr Founded: 1995, Lisa Winkler, Exec Dir, Tom Zenisek, Pres & Chmn

ESRI User Group 380 New York Street, Redlands CA 92373 USA; 909/793-2853, 800/447-9778 Fax: 909/793-3051, Co Email: info@esri.com, Web URL: esri.com, Focus: Users of ESRI geographical information system products, Ownership: PVT, Yr Founded: 1969, Empl: 800, Sales($M): 155, Fiscal End: 94; Jack Dangermond, Pres, S.J. Camarata, Sales & Mktng, Linda Hecht, Mktng Mgr, Lisa Backman, Email: ibackman@esri.com

European Committee for Electrotechnical Standardization (CENELEC), 35 rue de Stassart, Brussels B-1050 Belgium; 2-519-6871, Fax: 2-519-6919, Focus: European standards organization (one of three), Ownership: Nonprofit, Yr Founded: 1973

European Committee for Standardization (CEN), 36 rue de Stassart, Brussels B-1050 Belgium; 322-519-6811, Fax: 322-519-6819, Focus: Develops technical standards for Europe, Ownership: Nonprofit, Yr Founded: 1961

European Economic Development Agency 3181 Mission Street #119, San Francisco CA 94110 USA; 415/282-6330, Fax: 415/282-7904, Focus: Assistance to find European site locations, Ownership: Nonprofit, Jean-Francois Fourt, Pres

European Strategic Program for R&D in Information Technology (ESPRIT), c/o European Commission, Brussels B-1050 Belgium; 322-235-1603, Fax: 322-235-3821, Focus: European high-tech research consortium, Ownership: Nonprofit

Export/Import Bank of the United States 811 Vermont Ave NW, Washington DC 20571 USA; 202/565-3900, 800/565-3946 Web URL: exim.gov, Focus: Aids in exporting US goods and services, Ownership: Nonprofit, Yr Founded: 1934

Federal Communications Commission (FCC), 1919 M Street NW, Washington DC 20554 USA; 202/418-0200, Web URL: fcc.gov, Focus: Regulates broadcast and communications transmission industries Ownership: Nonprofit, Yr Founded: 1934, Reed Hundt, Chmn of Commission

Federation of International Distributors (FED), 532 Great Road, Acton MA 01720 USA; 508/263-6900, Fax: 508/263-6565, Focus: Association of software distributors and republishers, Ownership: Nonprofit, Yr Founded: 1989, Empl: 50, Randy Green, Exec Dir

Fibre Channel Assoc. (FCA), 950 Westbank Drive #207, Austin TX 78746 USA;

512/328-8422, Fax: 512/328-8423, Co Email: fca@fibrechannel.com, Web URL: fibrechannel.com, Focus: Promotion of Fibre Channel technology, Ownership: Nonprofit, Yr Founded: 1993, Brenda Christiensen, Chair

Fibre Channel Loop Community (FCLC), PO Box 2161, Saratoga CA 95070 USA; 408/867-6630, Web URL: tachyon.rose.hp.com/fclc, Focus: Promote Fibre Channel-Arbitrated Loop as serial interface standard, Ownership: Nonprofit, Yr Founded: 1995, Empl: 40

Fortran Users Group (FUG), PO Box 4201, Fullerton CA 92634 USA; 714/441-2022, Fax: 714/441-2022, Web URL: fortran.com, Focus: Updates Fortran users on standards, programming trends and reviews products, Ownership: Nonprofit, Yr Founded: 1987, Charles Ritz, Co-Editor, Walter Brainerd, Co-Editor

Frame Relay Forum (FRF), 303 Vintage Park Drive, Foster City CA 94404 USA; 415/578-6980, Fax: 415/525-0182, Co Email: frf@sbexpos.com, Web URL: frame-relay.indiana.edu, Focus: Promotion of frame relay technology usage, Ownership: Nonprofit, Yr Founded: 1991, Vivian Beaulieu, Exec Dir, Andrew Greenfield, Chmn & Pres

Fuse Inc. (FUSE), 200 Craig Road #G, Manalapan NJ 07726 USA; 908/308-9275, Fax: 908/308/9277, Focus: Users of Information Builders' products: Focus, Level5, EDA/SQL, Ownership: Nonprofit, Yr Founded: 1979, Empl: 8,000, Cele DiGiacomo, Pres, Rosemary Mauro, Dir

Graphic Communications Assoc. (GCA), 100 Daingerfield Road, Alexandria VA 22314-2804 USA; 703/519-8160, Fax: 703/548-2867, Web URL: printing.org, Focus: Association for printing and publishing industries, Ownership: Nonprofit, Yr Founded: 1966, Empl: 350, Norman W. Sharpf, Pres, Marian Elledge, VP

Graphics Performance Characterization Committee (GPC), 10754 Ambassador Drive #201, Manassas VA 22111 USA; 703/331-0180, Fax: 703/331-0181, Co Email: info@specbench.org, Web URL: specbench.org/gpc, Focus: Defines standard benchmarks for measuring graphics performance, Ownership: Nonprofit, Yr Founded: 1987, R. Willisobert, Project Mgr, Rodney Sanford, Project Admin

Guide International Corp. (GUIDE), 401 N Michigan Ave, Chicago IL 60611 USA; 312/644-6610, Fax: 312/321-6869, Focus: Users of IBM 309X, 308X, 4300, 9370, AS/400 and 390 architecture computers, Ownership: Nonprofit, Yr Founded: 1956, Empl: 1,700

Help Desk Institute (HDI), 1755 Telstar Drive #101, Colorado Springs CO 80920-1017 USA; 719/531-5138, Fax: 719/528-4250, Web URL: helpdeskinst.com, Focus: Training and education for help desk professionals, Ownership: PVT, Yr Founded: 1989, Empl: 25, Dennis Privitera, Exec Dir

Highway 1 601 Pennsylvania Ave NW, Washington DC 20004 USA; 202/628-3900, Fax: 202/628-3922, Web URL: highway1.org, Focus: Information on new computer technologies to members of Congress, Kimberly Jenkins, Exec Dir

Home Recording Rights Coalition (HRRC), PO Box 33576, 1145 19th Street NW, Washington DC 20033 USA; 800/282-8273 Co Email: hrrc@access.digex.com, Web URL: digex.net/hrrc, Focus: Protect consumer's fair use right of electronic/computer products, Ownership: Nonprofit, Yr Founded: 1981, Ruth Rodgers

Houston Area Apple Users Group (HAAUG), PO Box 610150, Houston TX 77208-0150 USA; 713/522-2179, Fax: 713/956-9049, Focus: Apple II, Macintosh and Newton users, Ownership: Nonprofit, Empl: 1,000, Ken Martinez, Pres, Mark Jacob, Past Pres

HP Convex User Group (CUG), 3000 Waterview Pkwy, Richardson TX 75080 USA; 214/497-4000, Fax: 214/497-4141, Focus: Users of Convex minisupercomputers, Ownership: Nonprofit, Yr Founded: 1986

IEEE Computer Society (IEEE-CS), 1730 Massachusetts Ave NW, Washington DC 20036-1992 USA; 202/371-0101, Fax: 202/728-9614, Web URL: computer.org, Focus: Association for computer professionals, Ownership: Nonprofit, Yr Founded: 1951, Empl: 100,000, T. Micahel Elliott, Exec Dir, Anneliese von Mayrhauser, VP Conf & Tutorials

Image Society Inc. PO Box 6221, Chandler AZ 85246 USA; 602/839-8709, Co Email: image@acvax.inre.asu.edu, Focus: Advancing real-time visual simulation technology and applications, Ownership: Nonprofit, Yr Founded: 1987, Empl: 600, Eric Monroe, Chmn & Pres, VP

Imaging Technologies Assoc. (ITA), 25 Mid-Tech Drive #C, W. Yarmouth MA 02673 USA; 508/775-3433, Fax: 508/790-4778, Focus: Association of printer supplies manufacturers, Ownership: Nonprofit, Yr Founded: 1922, Chuck Sabatt, Exec Secretary, Chuck Sabatt, Exec Secretary

Independent Computer Consultants Assoc. (ICCA), 933 Gardenview Office Pkwy, St. Louis MO 63141 USA; 314/997-4633, Fax: 314/567-5133, Co Email: 70007.1407@compuserve.com, Focus: Association for computer consultants, Ownership: Nonprofit, Yr Founded: 1976, Empl: 2,100, Glenn Koenen, Exec Dir, Deborah Sampson, Chmn, Email: 70007.4250@compuserve.com; Ray Rauth, Pres, Email: 70007.4251@compuserve.com

Industry Advisory Council 7777 Lees-

burg Pike #3LS, Falls Church VA 22043 USA; 703/506-9340, Fax: 703/506-9309, Focus: Organization for computer vendors, Mary Ellen Geoffrey, Exec Dir

Information Industry Assoc. (IIA), 1625 Massachusetts Ave NW #700, Washington DC 20036 USA; 202/986-0280, Fax: 202/638-4403, Web URL: infoindustry.org, Focus: Association for companies that create, use or distribute information electronically, Ownership: Nonprofit, Yr Founded: 1968, Empl: 550, Ronald Dunn, Exec Dir, VP

Information Systems Audit & Control Assoc. (ISACA), 3701 Algonquin Road #1010, Rolling Meadows IL 60008 USA; 847/253-1545, Fax: 847/253-1443, Web URL: isaca.org, Focus: Advancement of information system audit and control, Ownership: Nonprofit, Yr Founded: 1969, Empl: 13,500, Susan M. Caldwell, Exec Dir

Information Systems Consultants Assoc. (ISCA), PO Box 467190, Atlanta GA 30346 USA; 770/491-1500, Fax: 770/491-3600, Focus: Computer consultants association, Ownership: Nonprofit, Yr Founded: 1986, Empl: 200

Information Systems Security Assoc. Inc. (ISSA), 1926 Waukegan Road #1, Glenview IL 60025 USA; 847/657-6746, Co Email: issa@mcs.com, Web URL: uhsa.uh.edu/issa, Focus: Association for information security professionals, Ownership: Nonprofit, Yr Founded: 1981, Empl: 2,000, Carl A. Wangman, Exec Dir

Information Technology Assoc. America (ITAA), 1616 N Ft Myer Drive #1300, Arlington VA 22209-9998 USA; 703/522-5055, Fax: 703/525-2279, Web URL: itaa.org, Focus: Trade association for software & services firms, Ownership: Nonprofit, Yr Founded: 1960, Empl: 650, Harris Miller, Pres, Email: hmiller@itaa.org; Olga Grkavaz, SVP

Information Technology Foundation 1616 N Ft Myer Drive #1300, Arlington VA 22209-9998 USA; 703/522-5055, Fax: 703/525-2279, Focus: Information technologies to benefit disabled persons, Ownership: Nonprofit, Yr Founded: 1986

Information Technology Industry Council (ITI), 1250 Eye Street NW #200, Washington DC 20005 USA; 202/737-8888, Fax: 202/638-4922, Web URL: itic.com, Focus: Association for information technology industry, Ownership: Nonprofit, Yr Founded: 1916, Empl: 28, Oliver Smoot, EVP

Information Technology Service (IRMS), 18th & F Street NW Rm G241, Washington DC 20405 USA; 202/501-1000, Focus: Manages the government's information resources including telecom & computers, Ownership: Nonprofit, Yr Founded: 1948

Information Technology Services

Marketing Assoc. (ITSMA), 175 Bedford Street #7, Lexington MA 02173 USA; 617/862-8500, Fax: 617/674-1355, Co Email: itsma@aol.com, Focus: Association of high-tech service marketers and managers, Prdts: MarketingServices conf., Ownership: Nonprofit, Yr Founded: 1994, Empl: 55, Richard Munn, Pres, David Munn, Dir Membership, Dirk Mullenger, Mgr Event Mktng

Information User Assoc. (IUA), 401 N Michigan Ave, Chicago IL 60611-4267 USA; 312/644-6610, Fax: 312/321-6869, Focus: Organization for Computer Associates products, Ownership: Nonprofit, Yr Founded: 1974, Empl: 550, James Weir, Exec Dir

Infrared Data Assoc. (IrDA), PO Box 3883, Walnut Creek CA 94598 USA; 510/934-6546, Fax: 510/943-5600, Co Email: info@irda.org, Web URL: irda.org, Focus: Interoperable IR data interconnection standard, Ownership: Nonprofit, Empl: 130, John LaRoche, Exec Dir, Email: jlaroche@netcom.com

Institute for Artificial Intelligence GWU, 707 22nd St NW, Washington DC 20052 USA; 202/994-5079, Fax: 202/994-0245, Web URL: seas.gwu.edu/seas/institutes/iai, Focus: Research and information on intelligent software technology, Barry G. Silverman, Dir

Institute for Certification of Computing Professionals (ICCP), 2200 E Devon Ave #247, Des Plaines IL 60018 USA; 847/299-4227, Fax: 847/299-4280, Co Email: 74040.3722@compuserve.com, Focus: Certification of computer professionals, Ownership: Nonprofit, Yr Founded: 1973, Perry Anthony, Exec Dir, Email: 74040.3722@compuserve.com; Carolyn DuShane, Com Dir

Institute for Computer & Telecommunications System Policy GWU, 801 22nd St NW, Washington DC 20052 USA; 202/994-4955, Fax: 202/994-0227, Co Email: instctp@seas.gwu.edu, Web URL: seas.gwu.edu/seas/ictsp, Focus: Research and policy issues on computer & telecom technology, Lance J. Hoffman, Dir

Institute for Computer Capacity Management (ICCM), 1020 8th Ave S #6, Naples FL 33940 USA; 941/261-8945, Fax: 941/261-5466, Focus: Computer performance and capacity management, Ownership: Nonprofit, Phillip Howard, Pres, Suzanne Howard, Mktng Mgr

Institute of Electrical and Electronics Engineers Inc. (IEEE), 345 E 47th Street, New York NY 10017-2394 USA; 212/705-7900, Fax: 212/752-4929, Web URL: ieee.org, Focus: Association for electrical and computer engineers, Ownership: Nonprofit, Yr Founded: 1884, Empl: 320,000, John H. Powers, Exec Dir, William Cook, Dir Info Svcs

Intelligent Network Forum (IN Forum), 11312 LBJ Fwy #600-1114, Dallas TX 75238 USA; Web URL: inf.org, Focus: Association for the intelligent network industry, Ownership: Nonprofit, Yr Founded: 1996, Cathy Horn, Exec Dir, Email: chorn@ballistic.com

Interactive Digital Software Assoc. 919 18th St NW, Washington DC 20006 USA; 202/833-4372, Fax: 202/833-4431, Focus: Association for entertainment software publishers, Ownership: Nonprofit, Douglas Lowenstein, Pres

Interactive Marketing Institute 1001 Pennsylvania Ave NW, Washington DC 20004 USA; 202/624-7372, Fax: 202/624-7222, Focus: Advance electronic commerce, Trey Taylor, Pres

Interactive Multimedia Assoc. (IMA), 48 Maryland Ave #202, Annapolis MD 21401 USA; 410/626-1380, Fax: 410/263-0590, Co Email: info@ima.org, Web URL: ima.org, Focus: Association for multimedia industry, Ownership: Nonprofit, Yr Founded: 1987, Empl: 280, Philip Dodds, Pres

Interactive Services Assoc. (ISA), 8403 Colesville Road #865, Silver Spring MD 20910 USA; 301/495-4955, Fax: 301/495-4959, Co Email: isa@isa.net, Web URL: isa.net/isa, Focus: Online services and interactive information, Ownership: Nonprofit, Robert L. Smith Jr., Exec Dir

Interactive Television Assoc. (ITA), 1030 Fifteenth Street NW #1053, Washington DC 20005 USA; 202/408-0008, Fax: 202/408-0111, Co Email: intertv@aol.com, Focus: Association to advance interactive TV, Ownership: Nonprofit, Yr Founded: 1993, Empl: 13, Andy Sernovitz, Pres, Peter Waldheim, EVP, Yasha Harari, Dir Membership, Matthew Laurencelle, Dir Member Svcs, Philip Strohl, Dir Res & Pubs

International Association for Computer Systems Security 6 Swarthmore Lane, Dix Hills NY 11746 USA; 516/499-1616, Focus: Association for computer security, Ownership: Nonprofit, Robert Wilk, Pres

International Association for Management Automation (IAMA), 1342 Colonial Blvd #25, Ft. Myers FL 33907 USA; 941/275-7887, 800/333-9786 Fax: 941/275-0794, Web URL: afsmi@afsmi.org, Focus: Management automation, Empl: 5,000+, Bob Steele, Mgng Dir

International Association of HP Computing Professionals (INTEREX), 1192 Borregas Ave, Sunnyvale CA 94089 USA; 408/747-0227, Fax: 408/747-0947, Focus: Hewlett-Packard computer users, Ownership: Nonprofit, Yr Founded: 1974, Empl: 8,000, Chuck Piercey, Exec Dir, Jeff Zajas, MIS Dir, Denise Garlow, Com Mgr

International Association of Knowl-edge Engineers 973D Russell Ave, Gaithersburg MD 20879 USA; 301/948-5390, Fax: 301/926-4243, Focus: Association for knowledge engineering industry, Ownership: Nonprofit

International Association of Science and Tech. (IAST), 4500 16th Ave NW #80, Calgary Alberta K3B 0M6 Canada; 800/995-2161 Fax: 403/247-6851, Co Email: iasted@orion.oac.uci.edu, Ownership: Nonprofit, Nadia Hamza, Conf Planner

International Communications Assoc. (ICA), 12750 Merit Drive #710 LB-89, Dallas TX 75251-1240 USA; 214/233-3889, 800/422-4636 Fax: 214/233-2813, Web URL: icanet.com, Focus: Major user organization for voice, data and image telecom, Prdts: ICA Expo, Ownership: Nonprofit, Yr Founded: 1948, Empl: 700, Robert Eilers, Exec Dir, Lawrence Gessini, Pres, Michael Case

International Communications Industries Assoc. (ICIA), 11242 Wapless Mill Road, Fairfax VA 22030 USA; 703/273-7200, Fax: 703/278-8082, Co Email: icia@icia.org, Web URL: usa.net/icia, Focus: Association for firms selling video, audio-visual and computer products, Ownership: Nonprofit, Yr Founded: 1949, Empl: 950, Walter G. Blackwell, EVP

International Council for Computer Communication (ICCC), PO Box 9745, Washington DC 20016 USA; 703/836-7787, Co Email: 1713789@mcimail.com, Web URL: ncst@ernet.int/icc, Focus: Advance R&D, applications and education of computer communication, Ownership: Nonprofit, Yr Founded: 1972, Empl: 100

International DB2 Users Group (IDUG), 401 N Michigan Ave, Chicago IL 60611-4267 USA; 312/644-6610, Fax: 312/321-6869, Co Email: idug@mcs.com, Focus: Users of IBM's DB2 software, Ownership: Nonprofit, Yr Founded: 1988, Empl: 2,130, Freddy Hansen, Pres, Email: dkkmdt8x@ibm-mail.com; Michael Cotignola, Pres-Elect, Doug Stacey, Editorial Dir

International Electrotechnical Commission (IEC), 3 rue de Varembe, PO Box 131, Geneva 20 CH-1211 Switzerland; 22-919-0211, Fax: 22-919-0300, Focus: International standards for the electrical and electronic industries, Ownership: Nonprofit, Yr Founded: 1906, Hans Gissel, Pres, Anthony Raeburn, General Secretary

International Engineering Consortium 303 E Wacker Drive #740, Chicago IL 60601-5212 USA; 312/938-3500, Fax: 312/938-8787, Ownership: Nonprofit, Yr Founded: 1944

International Federation for Information Processing (IFIP), 16 Place Longemalle, Geneva CH-1204 Switzerland; 22-282-649, Fax: 22-781-232, Focus: Organization for information science and technology associations, Ownership: Nonprofit, Yr Founded: 1960, Empl: 45

International Information Integrity Institute (I-4), c/o SRI, 333 Ravenswood Ave AH 344, Menlo Park CA 94025-3493 USA; 415/859-4729, Fax: 415/859-2986, Focus: Promotes information security as management responsibility, Ownership: Nonprofit, Yr Founded: 1986, Empl: 65

International Information Management Congress (IMC), 1650 38th Street #205W, Boulder CO 80301-2623 USA; 303/440-7085, Fax: 303/440-7234, Web URL: iimc.org, Focus: Document and electronic imaging, Ownership: Nonprofit, Yr Founded: 1963, Empl: 85, Lynn Pontcher, Admin Dir, John A. Lacy, Pres & CEO, Lase Low

International Interactive Communications Society (IICS), 14657 SW Teal Blvd #119, Beaverton OR 97007 USA; 503/579-4427, Fax: 503/579-6272, Focus: Advancement of multimedia and interactive technologies, Ownership: Nonprofit, Yr Founded: 1983, Empl: 3,000, Debra Palm, Managing Dir, Brian Blum, Pres

International Management Graphics User's Group 1401 E 79th Street, Minneapolis MN 55425 USA; 612/854-1220, Fax: 612/851-6159, Focus: Users of Management Graphics' products, Ownership: Nonprofit, Sherri Keep

International Oracle User Group (IOUG), 401 N Michigan Ave, Chicago IL 60611 USA; 312/245-1579, Focus: Umbrella organization for all Oracle software user groups, Ownership: Nonprofit, Yr Founded: 1981

International Organization for Standardization (ISO), 1 rue de Varembe, Geneva 20 CH-1211 Switzerland; 22-749-0111, Fax: 22-733-3430, Focus: Worldwide federation of 100+ countries' national standards bodies, Ownership: Nonprofit, Yr Founded: 1947, Lawrence Eicher, Secretary General, Anke Varcin, Head Press Svcs

International Society for Mini and Microcomputers (ISMM), 4500 16th Ave NW #80, Calgary Alberta K3B 0M6 Canada; 403/288-1195, Fax: 403/247-6851, Ownership: Nonprofit, Nadia Hamza, Conf Planner

International Society for Technology in Education (ISTE), 1787 Agate Street, Eugene OR 97403-1923 USA; 541/346-4414, Fax: 541/346-5890, Focus: Supports computer use and technology in the classroom, Ownership: Nonprofit, Yr Founded: 1979, Empl: 13,000, David Moursund, CEO, Anita Best, Editor

International Society of Certified Electronics Technicians (ISCET), 2708 W Berry Street #3, Ft. Worth TX 76109 USA; 817/921-9101, Fax: 817/921-3741, Focus: Certifies electronics technicians,

Ownership: Nonprofit, Yr Founded: 1970, Empl: 2,000, Clyde W. Nabors, Exec Dir, Barbara Rubin, Bus Mgr, George Brownyard, Chmn

International Tandem Users' Group (ITUG), 401 N Michigan Ave, Chicago IL 60611-4267 USA; 312/321-6851, Fax: 312/245-1085, Focus: Advance effective utilization of Tandem Computers via member information exchange, Ownership: Nonprofit, Yr Founded: 1978, Empl: 1,000

International Telecommunications Union (ITU), Place des Nations, Geneva 20 CH-1211 Switzerland; 22-730-5111, Fax: 22-733-7256, Focus: Produces telecom standards through 2 committees-- CCITT (Telephone & Telegraph) and CCIR (R, Ownership: Nonprofit, Yr Founded: 1865, Robert Jones, Dir Radiocom Bureau

International Teleconferencing Assoc. (ITCA), 1650 Tysons Blvd #200, McLean VA 22102 USA; 800/360-4822 Fax: 703/506-3266, Focus: Teleconferencing industry, Ownership: Nonprofit, Tom Gibson, Exec Dir

International Television Assoc. (ITVA), 6311 N O'Connor Road #230, Irving TX 75039 USA; 214/869-1112, Fax: 214/869-2980, Co Email: itvahq@ix.netcom.com, Web URL: itva.org, Focus: Visual communications

International Trade Admin., Science & Electronics (S&E), 14th Street & Constitution Ave NW, Washington DC 20230 USA; 202/482-3809, Focus: Seeks to improve export competitiveness of U.S. high-tech firms, Ownership: Nonprofit, Yr Founded: 1984

Internet Society 12020 Sunrise Valley Drive #270, Reston VA 22091 USA; 703/648-9888, 800/468-9507 Fax: 703/648-9887, Web URL: isoc.org, Focus: Association for users of the Internet, Ownership: Nonprofit, Empl: 5,000, Anthony M. Rutkowski, Exec Dir, Vinton Cerf, Pres

Isode Consortium 3925 W Braker Lane, Austin TX 78759 USA; 512/305-0280, Fax: 512/305-0285, Web URL: isode.com, Focus: Promote and develop the ISODE package of OSI applications, Ownership: Nonprofit, Yr Founded: 1992, Steve Kille, CEO

ITA (ITA), 182 Nasau Street #209, Princeton NJ 08542 USA; 609/279-1700, Fax: 609/279-1999, Co Email: ita@bccom.com, Focus: Trends and innovations in magnetic and optical media, Ownership: Nonprofit, Yr Founded: 1970, Empl: 450, Charles Van Horn, Exec Dir

Japan Information Processing Development Center (JIPDEC), Kikai Shinko Bldg 3-5-8, Shibakoen, Minato-ku, Tokyo 105 J-105 Japan; 03-3432-9382, Fax: 03-3432-9389, Focus: Promotion of computer and information processing industry, Ownership: Nonprofit, Yr Founded: 1967, Empl: 239

Laddis Group, The 10754 Ambassador Drive #201, Manassas VA 22110 USA; 703/331-0181, Fax: 703/331-0181, Co Email: info@specbench.com, Web URL: specbench.com, Focus: Develop benchmarks for comparing NFS file server performance, Ownership: Nonprofit, Yr Founded: 1990

Library & Information Technology Assoc. (LITA), 50 E Huron Street, Chicago IL 60611 USA; 312/280-4270, Fax: 312/280-3257, Co Email: lita@ala.org, Focus: Information technologies for libraries, Ownership: Nonprofit, Jacqueline Mundell, Exec Dir

M Technology Assoc. (MTA), 1738 Elton Road #205, Silver Spring MD 20903-1725 USA; 301/431-4070, Fax: 301/431-0017, Co Email: mta1994@aol.com, Web URL: members.aol.com/mta1994, Focus: Association for MUMPS computer language users, Ownership: Nonprofit, Yr Founded: 1971, Empl: 1,800, John Covin, Chmn, Maureen Lilly, Admin Dir

Macscitech Assoc. 49 Midgley Lane, Worcester MA 01604 USA; 508/755-5242, Fax: 508/795-1636, Web URL: macscitech.org, Focus: Enhance scientific and engineering use of Apple Macintosh, Ownership: Nonprofit, Yr Founded: 1991, Empl: 1,500, Shari Worthington, Exec Dir

Maine Software Developers Assoc. 17 Oak Street, PO Box 492, Orono ME 04473-0492 USA; 207/866-0496, Fax: 207/866-0362, Focus: Association for software developers in Maine, Ownership: Nonprofit, George Markowsky, Pres

Management Software Assoc. (TMSA), 35 Gardner Road, Brookline MA 02146 USA; 617/232-4111, Fax: 617/734-3308, Focus: Promote growth of business management software, Ownership: Nonprofit, Yr Founded: 1993, Empl: 10, Michael Shirer, Pres

Massachusetts Software Council Inc. 1 Exeter Plaza #200, Boston MA 02116 USA; 617/437-0600, Fax: 617/437-9686, Web URL: swcouncil.org, Focus: Promotes Massachusetts software industry, Ownership: Nonprofit, Yr Founded: 1985, Empl: 350, Joyce Plotkin, Exec Dir, Carol Greenfield, Program Dir

Michigan Technology Council 2005 Baits Drive, Ann Arbor MI 48109 USA; 313/763-9757, Fax: 313/936-2746, Focus: High-tech organization for Michigan, Ownership: Nonprofit

Micro Channel Developers Assoc. (MCDA), 2280 N Bechelli Lane #B, Redding CA 96002 USA; 916/222-2262, 800/438-6232 Fax: 916/222-2528, Web URL: microchannel.inter.net, Focus: Promote Micro Channel compatible products, Ownership: Nonprofit, Yr Founded: 1990, Empl: 66, Steve Petracca, Chmn, Ramiz H. Zakhariya, Pres, Email: rza-

khari@interserv.com

Microcomputer Managers Assoc. Inc. (MMA), PO Box 4615, Warren NJ 07059 USA; 908/585-9091, Focus: Organization focused on technology management issues, Ownership: Nonprofit, Yr Founded: 1982, Empl: 1,000, Alex Kask, Exec Dir, Email: 418.5392@mcimail.com; Leonard Steinbach, Pres, Email: lstein@nln.org; Dana Tate, VP, Email: 70272.154@compuserve.com

Microelectronics & Computer Technology Corp. (MCC), PO Box 200195, Austin TX 78720 USA; 512/343-0978, Fax: 512/338-3892, Focus: Cooperative R&D organization with focus on application-driven information technology, Ownership: Nonprofit, Yr Founded: 1982, Craig Fields, Pres & CEO, Alan Salisbury, COO

Mindshare User Group Program 1 Microsoft Way, Redmond WA 98052 USA; 206/882-8080, 800/228-6738 Fax: 206/936-2483, Co Email: mindshar@microsoft.com, Web URL: microsoft.com/mindshar, Focus: Umbrella organization for Microsoft local and special interest groups, Ownership: Nonprofit

Minnesota Software Assoc. 1200 Washington Ave S, Minneapolis MN 55415 USA; 612/338-4631, Fax: 612/337-3400, Focus: Organization for Minnesota software companies, Ownership: Nonprofit

MIPS ABI Group (MSIG), c/o SGI, 2011 N Shoreline MS 9L-855, Mountain View CA 94043 USA; 415/933-2082, Focus: Unix SVR4 object code compatibility for MIPS RISC computers, Ownership: Nonprofit, Yr Founded: 1991, Dave Lee

Multimedia Development Group (MDG), 2601 Mariposa Street, San Francisco CA 94110 USA; 415/553-2300, Fax: 415/553-2403, Co Email: mdgoffice@aol.com, Focus: Promote multimedia industry growth, Ownership: Nonprofit, Empl: 300, Susan Worthman, Exec Dir

Multimedia Telecommunications Assoc. (MMTA), 1820 Jefferson Place NW #100, Washington DC 20036 USA; 202/296-9800, Fax: 202/296-9810, Web URL: mmta.org, Focus: Protects and expands competitive markets (domestic/foreign) for telecommunications, Ownership: Nonprofit, Yr Founded: 1970, Empl: 650, William Moroney, Pres, Mary I. Bradshaw, Dir Ind Rel

National Academy of Engineering 2101 Constitution Ave NW, Washington DC 20418 USA; 202/334-1562, Fax: 202/334-1595, Web URL: nas.edu, Focus: Advises federal government and encourages technical and engineering research and education, Ownership: Nonprofit, Yr Founded: 1964, Empl: 1700, Doug Wolford, Dir Ext Affairs

National Academy of Sciences 2101

Constitution Ave NW, Washington DC 20418 USA; 202/334-2138, Fax: 202/334-1597, Web URL: nas.edu, Focus: Advises federal government and furthers the interest of science and its use, Ownership: Nonprofit, Yr Founded: 1863, Empl: 1200, Lee Tune

National Aeronautics and Space Administration (NASA), 400 Maryland Ave SW, Washington DC 20546 USA; 202/358-0000, Web URL: nasa.gov, Ownership: Nonprofit, Yr Founded: 1958

National Association of Computer Consultants Businesses 10255 W Higgins #800, Rosemont IL 60019 USA; 847-297-5607, Focus: Organization for computer consultants

National Association of Desktop Publishers (NADTP), 462 Old Boston Street #62, Topsfield MA 01983 USA; 800/874-4113 Fax: 508/887-6117, Focus: Association for desktop publishing users, Ownership: Nonprofit, Yr Founded: 1986, Empl: 13,000, Barry Harrigan, Pres, Susan Sigel, VP

National Center for Computer Crime Data (NCCCD), 1222 17th Ave #B, Santa Cruz CA 95062 USA; 408/475-4457, Fax: 408/475-5336, Co Email: nudnic@ix.netcom.com, Focus: Statistics and information on computer crimes, Ownership: Nonprofit, Yr Founded: 1980, Empl: 6, Jay BloomBecker, Exec Dir

National Center for Education Statistics 555 New Jersey Ave NW, Washington DC 20208 USA; 202/219-1828, Fax: 202/219-1736, Focus: Analyzes data on the performance of the US educational system, Ownership: Nonprofit

National Center for Supercomputing Applications (NCSA), 605 E Springfield Ave, Champaign IL 61820 USA; 217/244-3049, Fax: 217/244-9195, Focus: High-performance computing research, Prdts: NCSA Mosaic, Ownership: Nonprofit, Yr Founded: 1985, John R. Melchi, Pub Info Officer, Email: jmelchi@ncsa.uiuc.edu

National Commission on Library & Information Sciences 1110 Vermont Ave NW #820, Washington DC 20005-3522 USA; 202/606-9200, Fax: 202/606-9203, Focus: Independent federal agency advising Pres & Congress on library and information policy, Ownership: Nonprofit, Yr Founded: 1970, Peter R. Young, Exec Dir

National Computer Security Assoc. (NCSA), 10 S Courthouse Ave, Carlisle PA 17013 USA; 717/258-1816, Fax: 717/243-8642, Co Email: @ncsa.com, Web URL: ncsa.com, Focus: Microcomputer security and computer viruses, Ownership: Nonprofit, Yr Founded: 1989, Empl: 1,600, Robert C. Bales, Exec Dir, Michel E. Kabay, Dir Ed, David M. Harper, Dir Mktng, Peter S. Tippett, Pres, Larry Teien, PR Mgr

National Computer Security Center (NCSC), 9800 Savage Road, Ft. George G. Mead MD 20755-6000 USA; 410/859-4371, Fax: 410/859-4375, Focus: Advance computer security, Ownership: Nonprofit, Yr Founded: 1981

National Cristina Foundation (NCF), 591 W Putnam Ave, Greenwich CT 06830 USA; 203/622-6000, 800/274-7846 Fax: 203/622-6270, Co Email: ncf-nasd@gteens.com, Focus: Obtains used or surplus microcomputers for free distribution to groups serving disabled an, Ownership: Nonprofit, Yr Founded: 1985, Dr. Yvette Marrin, Pres

National Electronics Service Dealers Assoc. (NESDA), 2708 W Berry Street #3, Ft. Worth TX 76109-2356 USA; 817/921-9061, Fax: 817/921-3741, Focus: Association for computer and electronic service industry, Ownership: Nonprofit, Yr Founded: 1963, Empl: 900, Clyde W. Nabors, Exec Dir, Barbara Rubin, Bus Mgr, Lane H. Norman, Pres

National Federation of Abstracting & Information Services (NFAIS), 1518 Walnut Street #307, Philadelphia PA 19102-3403 USA; 215/893-1561, Fax: 215/893-1564, Co Email: nfais@hslc.org, Focus: Information for producers, distributors and corporate users of information, Ownership: Nonprofit, Yr Founded: 1958, Empl: 70, Ann Marie Cunningham, Exec Dir

National Institute of Standards and Technology (NIST), Route I-270 & Quince Orchard Rd, Gaithersburg MD 20899-0001 USA; 301/975-2762, Fax: 301/926-1630, Co Email: inquires@nist.gov, Web URL: nist.gov, Focus: Promotes US economic growth by application of technology, measurements and standards, Ownership: Nonprofit, Yr Founded: 1901

National Research Council (NRC), 2101 Constitution Ave NW, Washington DC 20418 USA; 202/334-2138, Fax: 202/334-1597, Focus: Operating arm of the National Academy of Sciences and National Academy of Engineering, Ownership: Nonprofit, Yr Founded: 1968

National Science & Technology Council (NSTC), Old Executive Office Bldg, Washington DC 20500 USA; 202/456-6100, Fax: 202/456-6026, Focus: Coordinates among agencies with research and development programs, Ownership: Nonprofit, Yr Founded: 1993

National Science Foundation (NSF), 4201 Wilson Blvd, Arlington VA 22230 USA; 703/306-1234, Fax: 703/306-0202, Web URL: nsf.com, Focus: Promotes the progress of science and engineering through the support of research and education, Ownership: Nonprofit, Yr Founded: 1950

National Security Agency/Central Security Service (NSA/CSS), 9800 Savage Road, Ft. George G. Mead MD 20755-6000 USA; 301/688-6524, Focus: 3 main missions: information system security, operations security & foreign intelligence, Ownership: Nonprofit, Yr Founded: 1952

National Systems Programmers Assoc. (NaSPA), 4811 S 76th Street #210, Milwaukee WI 53220-9933 USA; 414/423-2420, Fax: 414/423-2433, Focus: Association for corporate computing professionals, Ownership: Nonprofit, Yr Founded: 1986, Empl: 29,000, Scott Sherer, Pres, Emit Hurdelbrink, VP

National Technical Information Center (NTIS), 5285 Port Royal Road, Springfield VA 22161 USA; 703/487-4650, Fax: 703/321-8547, Focus: Distributes computer information, software & databases developed by the U.S. government, Ownership: Nonprofit, Yr Founded: 1945

National Technical Information Service (NTIS), 5285 Port Royal Road, Springfield VA 22161 USA; 703/487-4650, Fax: 703/321-8547, Web URL: fedworld.gov, Focus: Central source for sale of government-sponsored scientific & technical reports, Ownership: Nonprofit, Yr Founded: 1945

National Telecommunications & Information Administration (NTIA), HCHB, 14th & Constitution Ave NW Rm 4898, Washington DC 20230 USA; 202/482-1551, Fax: 202/482-1635, Co Email: ntia@doc.gov, Focus: Supports development and growth of telecom, information and related industries, Ownership: Nonprofit, Yr Founded: 1978

National Venture Capital Assoc. 1655 N Ft Myer Drive #700, Arlington VA 22209 USA; 703/351-5267, Fax: 703/351-5268, Focus: Venture capital industry trends, Ownership: Nonprofit, Empl: 300, Daniel Kingsley, Exec Dir

NetWare Users Int'l. (NUI), 122 E 1700 South, Provo UT 84606 USA; 801/222-6000, 800/638-9273 Focus: Umbrella organization of over 220 worldwide Novell NetWare user groups, Ownership: Nonprofit, Yr Founded: 1985, Empl: 90,000

Network Management Forum 1201 Mt Kemble Ave, Morristown NJ 07960-6628 USA; 201/425-1900, Fax: 201/425-1515, Web URL: mnf.org, Focus: Association for network interoperability, Ownership: Nonprofit, Elizabeth Adams, Managing Dir

Network Professional Assoc. (NPA), 151 E 1700 South, Provo UT 84606 USA; 801/379-0330, Fax: 801/379-0331, Focus: Organization for network computing service professionals, Ownership: Nonprofit, Yr Founded: 1991, Empl: 11,000, Berkeley Geddes, Pres, Bruce Law, Dir Mktng, Keith Parsons, Tech Mgr, Gerry Dye, Dir Int'l Rel

New Hampshire High Tech Council PO Box 10308, Bedford NH 03110-0308

USA; 603/647-8324, Fax: 603/668-3906, Focus: High-tech organization for New Hampshire, Ownership: Nonprofit

New Information Industry Cooperative Endeavor (NIICE), c/o X/Open, 1010 El Camino Real #380, Menlo Park CA 94025 USA; 415/323-7992, Fax: 415/323-8204, Co Email: @xopen.co.uk, Focus: Database software interoperability, Ownership: Nonprofit, Yr Founded: 1995

NIST Computer Systems Laboratory (CSL), Route I-270 & Quince Orchard Rd, Gaithersburg MD 20899-0001 USA; 301/975-2832, Fax: 301/948-1784, Co Email: @enh.nist.org, Focus: Supports development of computer technology advances, Ownership: Nonprofit, Yr Founded: 1972

NIST Computing and Applied Mathematics Laboratory Route I-270 & Quince Orchard Rd B118, Gaithersburg MD 20899-0001 USA; 301/975-2732, Fax: 301/963-9137, Ownership: Nonprofit

North American Data General Users Group (NADGUG), c/o Nth Degree, 490 Boston Post, Sudbury MA 01776 USA; 508/443-3330, 800/253-3902 Fax: 508/443-4715, Focus: Interchange of ideas and information among DG computer users, Ownership: Nonprofit, Yr Founded: 1973, Empl: 2,100

North American Ingres User Assoc. (NAIUA), 2107 Del Monte Ave, Monterey CA 93940 USA; 408/649-0644, Fax: 408/649-4124, Co Email: info@naiua.org, Web URL: naiua.org, Focus: Users of Ingres database software, Ownership: Nonprofit, Yr Founded: 1981, Empl: 4,000, Bob Massero, Exec Dir

North American ISDN Users' Forum (NIU), c/o NTIS, Route I-270 & Quince Orchard Rd, Gaithersburg MD 20899-0001 USA; 301/975-4858, Focus: Implementation of ISDN applications, Ownership: Nonprofit, Yr Founded: 1988, Anne Enright Shepherd

North Carolina Electronics & Information Technologies Assoc. (NCEITA), 3203 Woman's Club Drive #220, Raleigh NC 27612 USA; 919/787-8818, Fax: 919/783-9058, Focus: Association for NC's electronics and information companies, Ownership: Nonprofit, Betsy Justus, Exec Dir

Northeast Software Assoc. c/o Hyperion Software, 777 Long Ridge Rd, Stamford CT 06902 USA; 203/321-3711, Fax: 203/968-2932, Focus: Association for software developers in Connecticut and New York, Ownership: Nonprofit, Les Trachtman, Chmn

Northeast Technical Assoc. (NTA), c/o ProLine Communications, 13 Crescent Road, Livingston NJ 07039 USA; 201/716-9457, Fax: 201/533-0463, Focus: Organization for computer companies in the northeast, Ownership: Nonprofit,

Bruce Freeman, Pres

Northern Virginia Technology Council 8391 Old Courthouse Road #300, Vienna VA 22182 USA; 703/734-9500, Fax: 703/734-2836, Focus: Organization for Virginia high-tech companies, Ownership: Nonprofit

NPES The Association for Suppliers of Printing & Publishing Tech. (NPES), 1899 Preston White Drive, Reston VA 20191-4367 USA; 703/264-7200, Fax: 703/620-0994, Co Email: npes@npes.org, Web URL: npes.org, Focus: Association for companies in the printing, publishing and graphic communications, Ownership: Nonprofit, Yr Founded: 1933, Empl: 300, Regis J. Delmontagne, Pres

NTIS Federal Computer Products Center 5285 Port Royal Road Rm 1025S, Springfield VA 22161 USA; 703/487-4763, Ownership: Nonprofit

Object Management Group (OMG), 492 Old Connecticut Path, Framingham MA 01701 USA; 508/820-4300, Fax: 508/820-4303, Web URL: omg.org, Focus: Industry standard object-oriented application integration environment, Ownership: Nonprofit, Yr Founded: 1989, Empl: 250, Christopher Stone, Pres, Richard Soley, VP

Office of Science & Technology Policy (OSTP), Old Executive Office Bldg Rm 424, Washington DC 20500 USA; 202/456-7116, Fax: 202/456-6022, Focus: Examines current state of U.S. science & technology; gives advice & makes recommendations, Ownership: Nonprofit, Yr Founded: 1976, John H. Gibbons, Dir

Omicron-Center for Information Technology Management (Omicron), 115 Route 46 Bldg D-31, Mountain Lakes NJ 07046 USA; 201/335-0240, Fax: 201/335-0289, Web URL: omicronet.com, Focus: MIS management issues, Ownership: Nonprofit, Yr Founded: 1980, Empl: 65, Jim Webber, Pres, Email: jwebber@omicronet.com; Don Bussell, Exec Dir, Omicron/Chicago, Teresa Carbone, Participation Coordinator, Jim Webber, Pres

Open Software Foundation (OSF), PO Box 2002, Andover MA 01810 USA; 508/474-9258, 800/767-2336 Fax: 508/470-0526, Focus: Develops open standards for software applications, Ownership: Nonprofit, Yr Founded: 1988, Empl: 300, David Tory, Pres, Martin Ford, CFO, Peter B. Shaw, VP Sales & Mktng

Open Users Recommended Solutions (OURS), 401 N Michigan Ave, Chicago IL 60611-4267 USA; 312/644-6610, Fax: 312/321-6869, Focus: Organization to improve multivendor computer networks, Ownership: Nonprofit, Yr Founded: 1991, Empl: 50

Optical Publishing Assoc. (OPA), PO

Box 21268, Columbus OH 43221 USA; 614/442-8805, Fax: 614/442-8815, Focus: Development of optical publishing technologies, standards and markets, Ownership: Nonprofit, Yr Founded: 1988, Richard A. Bowers

Optical Storage Technology Assoc. (OSTA), 311 E Carrillo Street, Santa Barbara CA 93101 USA; 805/963-3853, Fax: 805/962-1541, Web URL: osta.org, Focus: Promote market acceptance of optical technology for computer storage, Ownership: Nonprofit, Yr Founded: 1992, Raymond C. Freeman Jr., Facilitator, Email: ray@osta.org

Patent & Trademark Office (PTO), 2121 Crystal Drive, Arlington VA 22202 USA; 703/305-8341, Web URL: uspto.gov, Focus: Examines & issues patents & registers trademarks, Ownership: Nonprofit, Yr Founded: 1790

PC Memory Card Int'l. Assoc. (PCMCIA), 2635 N First Street #209, San Jose CA 95134 USA; 408/433-2273, Fax: 408/433-9558, Co Email: office@pcmcia.com, Web URL: pc-card.com, Focus: Advancement of PC memory cards, Ownership: Nonprofit, Yr Founded: 1989, Empl: 525, Bill Lempesis, Exec Dir, Stephen Harper, Pres & Chmn, Greg Barr, Sr Comm Specialist, Email: gbarr@pcmcia.org

PCI Special Interest Group (PCI), 5200 NE Elam Young Pkwy, Hillsboro OR 97124 USA; 800/433-5177 Fax: 503/693-0920, Co Email: pcisig@teleport.com, Focus: Open use of PCI local bus, Ownership: Nonprofit, Yr Founded: 1992

Pennsylvania Technology Council 4516 Henry Street #500, Pittsburgh PA 15213 USA; 412/687-2700, Fax: 412/687-2791, Web URL: techcenter-pgh.com, Focus: Association for technology companies in Pennsylvania, Ownership: Nonprofit, Yr Founded: 1983, Empl: 2,000, Raymond R. Christman, Exec Dir

Petrotechnical Open Software Corp. (POSC), 10777 Westheimer Road #275, Houston TX 77042 USA; 713/784-1880, Fax: 713/784-9219, Focus: Open system software platform for petroleum industry, Ownership: Nonprofit, Yr Founded: 1990, Bill Bartz, Pres & CEO

Pittsburgh High Tech Council 4516 Henry Street, Pittsburgh PA 15213 USA; 412/687-2700, Fax: 412/687-2791, Focus: Organization for Pittsburgh high-tech companies, Ownership: Nonprofit

Portable Computer & Communication Assoc. (PCCA), PO Box 924, Brookdale CA 95007 USA; 408/338-0924, Fax: 408/338-7806, Web URL: outlook.com/pcca, Focus: Forum for mobile computing and communication, Ownership: Nonprofit, Yr Founded: 1992, Andrew M. Seybold, Pres, Robert Venter, Exec Dir

Precision Risc Organization (PRO),

1911 Pruneridge Ave, Cupertino CA 94025 USA; 408/447-4249, Fax: 408/447-7568, Focus: Advancement of the PA-RISC technology, Ownership: Nonprofit, Yr Founded: 1992, Empl: 14, Jim Bell, Pres

Primavera Users Group (P3NET), 2 Bala Plaza, Bala Cynwyd PA 19004 USA; 610/667-8600, Fax: 610/660-5857, Web URL: primavera.com, Focus: Primavera project management software users, Ownership: Nonprofit, Empl: 15,000

Quarter-Inch Cartridge Drive Standards Inc. (QIC), 311 E Carrillo Street, Santa Barbara CA 93101 USA; 805/963-3853, Fax: 805/962-1541, Web URL: qic.org, Focus: Develops standards for quarter inch data cartridge tape drives and media, Ownership: Nonprofit, Yr Founded: 1982, Empl: 44, Tim Russell, Chmn, Raymond C. Freeman, Jr., Facilitator, Email: ray@qic.org; Tony Miller, Email: qicpr@aol.com

Quest, JD Edwards Users Group 401 N Michigan Ave, Chicago IL 60611-4267 USA; 312/644-6610, Fax: 312/644-0297, Focus: Association for JD Edwards software users

RAID Advisory Board 3331 Brittain Ave #4, San Carlos CA 94070 USA; 415/631-7142, Fax: 415/631-7154, Co Email: tforumltd@aol.com, Web URL: raid-advisory.com, Focus: Develop standards for RAID products, Ownership: Nonprofit, Yr Founded: 1992, Empl: 50, Joe Molina

Robotic Industries Assoc. (RIA), 900 Victors Way PO Box 3724, Ann Arbor MI 48106 USA; 313/994-6088, Fax: 313/994-3338, Focus: Association for companies involved in industrial & service robotics, Ownership: Nonprofit, Yr Founded: 1974, Empl: 325, Donald A. Vincent, EVP

SAP Users Group 401 N Michigan Ave, Chicago IL 60611-4267 USA; 312/644-6610, Fax: 312/644-0297, Focus: Association for SAP software users, Ownership: Nonprofit

Sematech 2706 Montopolis, Austin TX 78741 USA; 512/356-3137, Fax: 512/356-3135, Focus: Technology for manufacturing integrated circuits, Ownership: Nonprofit, Yr Founded: 1987, Empl: 11, William Spencer, Pres & CEO, Jim Owens, COO, Ann Marett, Com Dir

Semiconductor Industry Assoc. (SIA), 181 Metro Drive #450, San Jose CA 95110 USA; 408/436-6600, Fax: 408/436-6646, Focus: Represents U.S.-based semiconductor manufacturers, Ownership: Nonprofit, Yr Founded: 1977, Empl: 67, Andrew Procassini, Pres, Warren Davis, VP

Semiconductor Research Corp. (SRC), 1101 Slater Road Brighton Hall #120, Durham NC 27703 USA; 919/541-9400, Fax: 919/541-9450, Web URL: src.org, Focus: Semiconductor industry consortium that oversees applied research

at universities, Ownership: Nonprofit, Yr Founded: 1982, Empl: 60, Larry W. Sumney, Pres & CEO, Robert M. Burger, VP & Chief Scientist

Serial Storage Architecture Industry Assoc. (SSA IA), c/o IBM, 5600 Cottle Road Dept H65/B-013, San Jose CA 95193 USA; 408/256-5656, Fax: 408/256-0595, Focus: Association to promote SSA technology, Ownership: Nonprofit, Yr Founded: 1995

Share Inc. (SHARE), 401 N Michigan Ave #2400, Chicago IL 60611-4267 USA; 312/822-0932, Fax: 312/321-6869, Focus: User group for large IBM computers, Ownership: Nonprofit, Yr Founded: 1955, Empl: 2,500

Small Business Administration (SBA), 409 3rd Street SW MC 2110, Washington DC 20416 USA; 202/205-6600, 800/827-5722 Fax: 202/205-6028, Web URL: sba.gov, Focus: Provides small firms participation in NSF-sponsored research, Ownership: Nonprofit, Yr Founded: 1953, D.J. Caufield, Public Info Spec

SMDS Interest Group Inc. (SMDS), 303 Vintage Park Drive, Foster City CA 94404-1138 USA; 415/578-6979, Fax: 415/525-0182, Focus: Promotion and education of SMDS service usage, Ownership: Nonprofit, Yr Founded: 1990, Vivian Beaulieu, Exec Dir, Mark Fisher, Pres & Chmn

Smithsonian Institution 1000 Jefferson Drive SW, Washington DC 20560 USA; 202/357-2700, 800/766-2149 Web URL: si.edu, Focus: World's largest museum complex--including many technology exhibits, Ownership: Nonprofit, Yr Founded: 1846, I. Michael Heyman, Secretary

Society for Computer Simulation (SCS), PO Box 17900, 4838 Ronson Ct #L, San Diego CA 92117-1810 USA; 619/277-3888, Fax: 619/277-3930, Co Email: @scs.org, Web URL: scs.org, Focus: Advancement of computer simulation technology, Ownership: Nonprofit, Yr Founded: 1952, Empl: 2,300, William Gallagher, Exec Dir, Hildy Linn, Pub Mgr, Email: linn@sdsc.edu

Society for Industrial and Applied Mathematics (SIAM), 3600 University City Science Center, Philadelphia PA 19104-2688 USA; 215/382-9800, Fax: 215/386-7999, Co Email: siam@siam.org, Web URL: siam.org, Focus: Further application of mathematics to science and technology, Ownership: Nonprofit, Yr Founded: 1952, Empl: 8,800, John Guckenheimer, Pres, James M. Crowley, Exec Dir, James Goldman

Society for Information Display (SID), 1526 Brookhollow Drive #82, Santa Ana CA 92705-5421 USA; 714/545-1526, Fax: 714/545-1547, Web URL: display.org/sid, Focus: Association for display industry, Ownership: Nonprofit, Yr

Founded: 1962, Empl: 3,700, Lauren K. Kinsey, Exec Dir, Web Howard, Pres

Society for Information Management (SIM), 401 N Michigan Ave, Chicago IL 60611 USA; 312/644-6610, Fax: 312/245-1081, Focus: Association for information managers, Ownership: Nonprofit, Yr Founded: 1968, Empl: 2,700

Society for the History of Technology (SHOT), Dept Soc Sciences, MI Technological Univ, Houghton MI 49931-1295 USA; 906/487-2113, Fax: 906/487-2468, Focus: History of technology and its impact on society, Ownership: Nonprofit, Yr Founded: 1958, Empl: 1,750, Ruth Schwartz Cowan, Pres, Bruce E. Seely, Secretary & Ed

Society of Telecommunications Consultants (STC), 13766 Center Street #212, Carmel Valley CA 93924 USA; 408/659-0110, Fax: 408/659-0144, Co Email: stchdq@attmail.com, Focus: Serves independent telecommunications consultants, Ownership: Nonprofit, Yr Founded: 1976, Empl: 235, Susan Kuttner, Exec Dir

Society of Woman Engineers (SWE), 120 Wall Street 11th Floor, New York NY 10005-3902 USA; 212/509-9577, Fax: 212/509-0224, Co Email: 71764.743@compuserve.com, Web URL: swe.org, Focus: Organization for women engineers, Ownership: Nonprofit, Empl: 18,000

Software Council of Southern California 21041 Southwestern Ave #160, Torrance CA 90501 USA; 310/328-0043, Fax: 310/215-3623, Focus: Organization for S. California software companies, Ownership: Nonprofit

Software Forum PO Box 61031, Palo Alto CA 94306 USA; 415/854-7219, Fax: 415/854-8298, Focus: Information exchange and professional development for software entrepreneurs, Ownership: Nonprofit, Yr Founded: 1983, Empl: 1,000, Barbara Cass, Exec Dir, Ellen Jamieson, Assist Exec Dir, Karen McCutcheon, Events Coord

Software Patent Institute (SPI), 2901 Hubbard Street, Ann Arbor MI 48105-2467 USA; 313/769-4606, Fax: 313/769-4054, Co Email: spi@iti.org, Web URL: iti.org, Focus: Software-related patent information and technical support, Ownership: Nonprofit, Yr Founded: 1992, Roland J. Cole, Exec Dir

Software Productivity Consortium (SPC), 2214 Rock Hill Road SPC Bldg, Herndon VA 20170 USA; 703/742-8877, Fax: 703/742-7200, Focus: Software engineering innovations, Ownership: Nonprofit, Yr Founded: 1985, Judd Neale, CEO

Software Publishers Assoc. (SPA), 1730 M Street NW #700, Washington DC 20036-4510 USA; 202/452-1600, 800/388-7478 Fax: 202/223-8756, Co Email:

@spa.org, Web URL: spa.org, Focus: Association for software publishers who produce, release, develop or license microcomputer, Ownership: Nonprofit, Yr Founded: 1984, Empl: 1,200, Kenneth Wasch, Pres, John Kernan, Chmn, Dave McClura, Dir Com, Terri Childs, PR Mgr

Software Support Professional Assoc. (SSPA), 11858 Bernardo Olaza Court #101C, San Diego CA 92128-2411 USA; 619/674-4864, Fax: 619/674-1192, Co Email: sspa@ix.netcom.com, Focus: Alliance of customer technical support managers, Ownership: Nonprofit, Yr Founded: 1989, Empl: 500+, Bill Rose, Exec Dir, John Hamilton, VP Prof Svcs, Email: hamilto2@ix.netcom.com

Software Valley PO Box 658, 1009 University Ave, Morgantown WV 26507-0658 USA; 703/678-8962, Fax: 703/678-8962, Focus: Association for software developers in West Virginia, Ownership: Nonprofit, Dick Dowell, Pres & CEO

Southern Maryland Regional Technology Council PO Box 910, La Plata MD 20646-0910 USA; 301/934-5316, Fax: 301/934-8617, Focus: Organization for Maryland high-tech companies, Ownership: Nonprofit

Sparc Int'l. (SI), 535 Middlefield Road #210, Menlo Park CA 94025 USA; 415/321-8692, Fax: 415/321-8015, Focus: Evolution of the SPARC microprocessor architecture and establish compliance definition, Ownership: Nonprofit, Yr Founded: 1989, Empl: 225, Robert Duncan, Chmn & CEO

Standard Performance Evaluation Corp. (SPEC), 10754 Ambassador Drive #201, Manassas VA 22110 USA; 703/331-0180, Fax: 703/331-0181, Co Email: info@specbench.org, Web URL: specbench.org, Focus: Defines performance benchmarks for Unix computers, Prdts: SPEChpc96, Ownership: Nonprofit, Yr Founded: 1988, Kaivalya M. Dixit, Pres, Rodney Sanford, Project Admin, Dianne Rice

Standards Council of Canada (SCC), 45 O'Conner Street #1200, Ottawa Ontario K1P 6N7 Canada; 613/238-3222, Fax: 613/995-4564, Focus: Works with Canadian standards organizations to ensure availability of appropriate standard, Ownership: Nonprofit, Yr Founded: 1970, Michael McSweeney, Exec Dir

Suburban Maryland Technology Council 2092 Gaither Road, Rockville MD 20850 USA; 301/258-5005, Fax: 301/208-8227, Focus: Organization for Maryland high-tech companies, Ownership: Nonprofit

Sun User Group Inc. (SUG), 1330 Beacon Street #344, Brookline MA 02146-3202 USA; 617/232-0514, Fax: 617/232-1347, Co Email: office@sug.org, Web URL: sug.org, Focus: Sun workstation

computer users, Ownership: Nonprofit, Yr Founded: 1983, Empl: 6,500, Alexander Newman, Exec Dir, Charles Sumner, Dir Mktng, Email: sumner@sug.org

Surface Mount Technology Assoc. (SMTA), 5200 Wilson Road #215, Edina MN 55424 USA; 612/920-7682, Fax: 612/926-1819, Co Email: smta@smta.org, Web URL: smta.org, Focus: Further the interest of surface mount technology through information dissemination, Ownership: Nonprofit, Yr Founded: 1984, Empl: 3,100, JoAnn Stromberg, Exec Admin

TCA-Information, Technology & Telecommunications (TCA), 74 New Montgomery #230, San Francisco CA 94105 USA; 415/777-4647, Fax: 415/777-4647, Web URL: tca.org, Focus: Association for telecom professionals, Ownership: Nonprofit, Yr Founded: 1961, Empl: 2,500

Technology Administration Main Commerce Bldg, Washington DC 20230 USA; 202/482-1575, Fax: 202/501-2492, Focus: Encourages new technologies and its commercialization. Oversees NIST, NTIA and NTIS, Ownership: Nonprofit

Technology Administration, Technology Policy 14th Street & Constitution Ave NW, Washington DC 20230 USA; 202/482-5687, Focus: Promotes productivity and international competitiveness of U.S. industry, Ownership: Nonprofit, Yr Founded: 1962

Technology Association Leaders' Council (TALC), c/o ProLine Communications, 13 Crescent Road, Livingston NJ 07039 USA; 201/716-9457, Fax: 201/533-0463, Focus: Organization for user groups and associations, Ownership: Nonprofit, Yr Founded: 1996, Bruce Freeman, Pres

Technology Council of Central Pennsylvania PO Box 60543, Harrisburg PA 17106-0543 USA; 717/238-5333, Fax: 717/238-6006, Focus: Organization for Pennsylvania high-tech companies, Ownership: Nonprofit

Technology Council of Greater Philadelphia 435 Devon Park Drive, Wayne PA 19087 USA; 610/975-9430, Fax: 610/975-9432, Focus: Organization for Philadelphia high-tech companies, Ownership: Nonprofit

Technology Council of the Center for Economic Growth 1 Keycorp Plaza #600, Albany NY 12207 USA; 518/465-8975, Fax: 518/465-6681, Focus: Organization for New York high-tech companies, Ownership: Nonprofit

Technology Council-Greater Baltimore Committee 111 S Calvert Street #1500, Baltimore MD 21201-6180 USA; 410/385-1545, Fax: 410/385-1545, Focus: Organization for Baltimore high-tech companies, Ownership: Nonprofit

Telecommunications Industry Assoc. (TIA), 2500 Wilson Blvd, Arlington VA 22201-3834 USA; 703/907-7700, Focus: Association of manufacturers and suppliers of materials, products, systems and services to, Ownership: Nonprofit, Yr Founded: 1979, Empl: 590, Matt Flanigan, Pres, John Major, Chmn, Kathy M. Hammond, Mgr Com

Transaction Processing Performance Council (TPC), c/o Shanley PR, 777 N 1st Street #600, San Jose CA 95112-6311 USA; 408/295-8894, Fax: 408/295-9768, Web URL: tpc.org, Focus: Develops performance benchmark standards for transaction processing applications, Ownership: Nonprofit, Yr Founded: 1988, Empl: 45, Kim Shanley, Administrator

TSANet 7101 College Blvd #380, Overland Park KS 66210 USA; 913/345-9311, Fax: 913/345-9317, Web URL: tsanet.org, Focus: Technical support network, Ownership: Nonprofit, Dennis Smeltzer, Exec Dir

U.S. Microcomputer Statistics Committee (USMCSC), c/o ITI, 1250 Eye St NW #200, Washington DC 20005 USA; 202/626-5730, Fax: 202/638-4922, Focus: PC vendor consortium that tracks PC sales, Ownership: Nonprofit, Yr Founded: 1991, Empl: 40, Helga Sayadian, Coordinator

U.S. Product Data Assoc. (US PRO), 5300 Int'l Blvd Trident Research Center #204, N. Charlston SC 29418 USA; 803/760-3327, Fax: 803/760-3349, Co Email: uspro@scra.org, Focus: Development, implementation and testing of product data standards, Ownership: Nonprofit, Yr Founded: 1992, Chuck Stark, Progr Dir, Melanie Varn, Progr Admin

Underwriters Laboratories Inc. (UL), 333 Pfingsten Road, Northbrook IL 60062-2096 USA; 847/272-8800, Fax: 847/272-8129, Focus: Safety standards, testing and ISO 9000 qualification certification, Ownership: PVT, Yr Founded: 1894, Tom Castino, Pres, Robert Haugh, Chmn, Joe Bhatia, VP Ext Affairs

UniForum Association (UniForum), 2901 Tasman Drive #205, Santa Clara CA 95054 USA; 408/986-8840, 800/255-5620 Fax: 408/986-1645, Web URL: uniforum.org, Focus: Vendor-independent association dedicated to promoting UNIX and open systems and services, Ownership: Nonprofit, Yr Founded: 1980, Empl: 6,500, Tom Mace, Exec Dir, Email: tom@uniforum.org

United States Information Agency (USIA), 301 4th Street SW, Washington DC 20547 USA; 202/619-4700, Fax: 202/619-6988, Web URL: usia.gov, Focus: "PR agency for the USA". Operates Voice of America, Worldnet TV, Ownership: Nonprofit

United States International Trade

Commission (USITC), 500 E Street SW, Washington DC 20436 USA; 202/205-2000, Fax: 202/205-2798, Focus: Independent agency which investigates the effect of foreign trade on the U.S., Ownership: Nonprofit, Yr Founded: 1916

UnixWare Technology Group (UTG), 190 River Road Rm A-226, Summit NJ 07901 USA; 908/522-6027, Fax: 908/522-5015, Co Email: @utg.org, Focus: Advancement of UnixWare and related technologies, Ownership: Nonprofit, Yr Founded: 1993, Empl: 23, Lawrence D. Lyle, Pres & CEO, Michael Dortch, VP Mktng, Email: dortch@utg.org; Diane Taggart, Mktng Mgr, Email: diane@utg.org

Usability Professional Assoc. (UPA), 4020 McEwen #105, Dallas TX 75244-5019 USA; 214/233-9107, Fax: 214/490-4219, Co Email: upadallas@aol.com, Focus: Information exchange on usability methods, tools and technology, Ownership: Nonprofit, Yr Founded: 1991, Empl: 450, Janice James, Pres, Dave Rinehart, Co-Chair

Usenix Assoc. (USENIX), 2560 Ninth Street #215, Berkeley CA 94710 USA; 510/528-8649, Fax: 510/548-5738, Focus: Services and technical information for users of UNIX, Ownership: Nonprofit, Yr Founded: 1975, Empl: 4,900, Ellie Young, Exec Dir, Stephen C. Johnson, Pres

User Group Alliance PO Box 29709, Philadelphia PA 19117-0909 USA; Focus: Organization of over 250 user groups, Ownership: Nonprofit, Bill Achuff, Co-Dir

User Group Connection Inc. (UGC), 231 Technology Circle, Scotts Valley CA 95066 USA; 408/461-5700, Fax: 408/461-5701, Co Email: ugc@aol.com, Web URL: ugconnection.org, Focus: User group marketing services for software and hardware vendors, Ownership: Nonprofit, Ray Kaupp, Pres, Carmela Zamora, Events & Tradeshows, Sam Decker, Mktng Mgr, Email: ugcsam@eworld.com; Raines Cohen, Com Mgr, Joantha Muse

Utah Information Technologies Assoc. (UITA), 6995 Union Park Center #490, Midvale UT 84047 USA; 801/568-3500, Fax: 801/568-1072, Web URL: uita.org, Focus: Organization of information technology companies in Utah, Ownership: Nonprofit, Yr Founded: 1991, Peter G. Genereaux, Pres

Versit 50 Commerce Drive, Allendale NJ 07401 USA; 201/327-2308, 800/803-6240 Fax: 800/803-6241, Co Email: versit@cup.portal.com, Focus: Interoperability between computer and communications products, Ownership: Nonprofit, Yr Founded: 1994

Video Electronics Standards Assoc. (VESA), 2150 N First Street #440, San Jose CA 95131-2029 USA; 408/435-0333, Fax: 408/435-8225, Co Email: @vesa.org, Focus: Promote PC graphics through improved standards, Ownership: Nonprofit, Yr Founded: 1989, Empl: 180, Roger L. McKee, Managing Dir, Scott Vouri, Chmn, Janet L. Courtenay, Dir Mktng, Email: courtenay@vesa.com

Vim Inc. (VIM), 4201 N Lexington Ave MS ARH251, Arden Hills MN 55126 USA; 612/482-4907, Focus: Forum for Control Data Systems computer customers, Ownership: Nonprofit, Yr Founded: 1970, Empl: 188, Sandy Rowe, Coordinator

Washington Software & Digital Media Alliance 3101 Northup Way, Bellevue WA 98024 USA; 206/889-8880, Fax: 206/889-8014, Web URL: wsdma.org, Focus: Promotes Washington software industry, Ownership: Nonprofit, Yr Founded: 1984, Empl: 750, Kathy Wilcox, Exec Dir

Windows User Group Network (WUGNET), PO Box 1967, Media PA 19063 USA; 215/565-1861, Fax: 215/565-7106, Focus: Users of Windows and Presentation Manager, Ownership: Nonprofit, Yr Founded: 1988, Empl: 4,000, Howard Sobel, Exec Dir

Women in Information Processing (WIP), PO Box 39173, Washington DC 20016 USA; 202/328-6161, Focus: Information for professionals in information processing industry, Ownership: Nonprofit, Yr Founded: 1979, Empl: 3,000, Janice Miller, Exec Dir

World Computer Graphics Assoc. (WCGA), 6121 Lincoln Road #302, Alexandria VA 22312 USA; 703/642-3050, Fax: 703/642-1663, Co Email: 71064.1116@compuserve.com, Focus: Association for computer graphics industry, Ownership: Nonprofit, Yr Founded: 1981, Empl: 13, Caby Smith, Pres & Exec Dir, Joyce Annecillo, Secretary & Treas

World Future Society (WFS), 7910 Woodmont Ave #450, Bethesda MD 20814 USA; 301/656-8274, Fax: 301/951-0394, Web URL: wfs.org, Focus: Clearinghouse for ideas about the future, Ownership: Nonprofit, Yr Founded: 1966, Empl: 30,000, Edward Cornish, Pres

X/Open Company Ltd. (X/Open), 1010 El Camino Real #380, Menlo Park CA 94025 USA; 415/323-7992, Fax: 415/323-8204, Co Email: @xopen.org, Web URL: xopen.org, Focus: Consortium of computer users and vendors developing open, multi-vendor standards, Ownership: Nonprofit, Yr Founded: 1984, Empl: 86, Geoffrey Morris, Pres & CEO, Allen Brown, COO, Mike Lambert, VP & CTO, Paul Daffern, CFO, Jeff Hansen, VP Mktng, Email: j.hansen@xopen.org

XDB User Group 9861 Broken Lance Pkwy, Colombia MD 21046 USA; 410/312-9300, Focus: User group for XDB database software, Ownership: Nonprofit, Yr Founded: 1981

Xplor International (Xplor), 24238 Hawthorne Blvd, Torrance CA 90505-6505 USA; 310/373-3633, 800/669-7567 Fax: 310/375-4240, Co Email: info@explor.org, Web URL: xplor.org, Focus: Association for electronic document printing users, Ownership: Nonprofit, Yr Founded: 1980, Empl: 1,550, Keith Davidson, Exec Dir, Ray Simonson, Pres, John Alfred, VP, James Porter, Mgr Com, Email: jporter@xplor.com

Chapter 12

Publications

Publication Rankings

Adscope: Leading Computer Magazines

The top magazines ranked by computer advertising revenues are shown below for the last three years. PC Magazine remains the clear leader with 1995 advertising revenues of nearly $214M. Computer Shopper is the leader in ad pages with over 8,100 pages. The top 10 magazines had computer advertising revenues of over $1B in 1995.

Rank	Publication--1995	# Ad Pages	% Change	Ad Rev. ($K)	% Change
1	PC Magazine	7,359	1.20	213,851	6.30
2	Wall Street Journal, The	1,473	10.77	129,360	16.83
3	PC Week	7,049	3.02	118,026	11.41
4	Computer Shopper	8,159	-1.27	103,313	11.95
5	Computerworld	4,668	5.50	87,320	17.18
6	PC World	2,912	13.50	86,102	31.12
7	Computer Reseller News	7,420	-8.17	80,028	8.94
8	InfoWorld	4,550	-0.13	79,623	6.63
9	BusinessWeek	1,612	22.63	74,843	29.02
10	PC Computing	3,056	16.46	70,201	24.67
	Subtotal	**48,258**	**2.08**	**1,042,669**	**14.23**

Several computer magazines experienced strong advertising revenue growth in 1994: Computer Shopper with a 48% increase and Computer Reseller News with 30% growth. InfoWorld had the best growth in ad pages with nearly 25% increase over 1993.

Rank	Publication--1994	# Ad Pages	% Change	Ad Rev. ($K)	% Change
1	PC Magazine	7,272	2.97	201,181	10.22
2	Wall Street Journal, The	1,330	-0.67	110,721	3.05
3	PC Week	6,843	23.41	105,936	16.87
4	Computer Shopper	8,264	3.55	92,289	48.14
5	Computerworld	4,424	9.94	74,515	18.40
6	InfoWorld	4,556	24.86	74,673	27.06
7	Computer Reseller News	8,081	11.82	73,464	30.24
8	PC World	2,566	0.27	65,667	8.01
9	BusinessWeek	1,315	-4.78	58,008	0.37
10	PC Computing	2,624	-14.37	56,308	-2.68
11	InformationWeek	2,617	12.80	41,758	19.32
12	CommunicationsWeek	3,061	13.45	38,712	20.39
	Subtotal	**52,953**	**8.40**	**993,232**	**14.88**

Computer Reseller News and Computerworld grew strongly in 1993 both in ad revenue and ad pages. PC Magazine has been the leader in ad revenue for over 10 years.

Rank	Publication--1993	# Ad Pages	% Change	Ad Rev. ($K)	% Change
1	PC Magazine	7,062	1.90	182,518	9.53
2	Wall Street Journal, The	1,339	2.70	107,449	7.30
3	PC Week	5,545	5.86	90,647	7.20
4	Computerworld	4,024	31.20	62,936	32.91
5	Computer Shopper	7,981	-7.63	62,298	5.00
6	PC World	2,559	1.59	60,796	31.03

Rank	Publication--1993	# Ad Pages	% Change	Ad Rev. ($K)	% Change
7	InfoWorld	3,649	4.68	58,769	11.42
8	PC Computing	3,064	3.93	57,858	14.65
9	BusinessWeek	1,381	-0.81	57,797	3.17
10	Computer Reseller News	7,227	39.76	56,406	39.24
11	MacUser	2,417	-6.05	37,924	2.02
12	Macworld	2,235	-8.82	36,984	-5.87
	Subtotal	**48,483**	**6.04**	**872,382**	**11.75**

Computer Press Association: Computer Press Awards

The 11th Annual Computer Press Awards honored top journalists who excelled in their coverage of the information industries in 1994. Citizen America Corporation and The Computer Press Association have sponsored the Computer Press Awards from 1985 to 1992. In 1993 3M Storage Products took on the sponsorship of the awards. As the oldest and most distinguished writing competition of its kind, it allows journalists to be recognized by their peers. Some of the award categories have changed over time.

Breaking News:
1995 Winner: "Lotus on the block", Michael Fitzgerald, Suruchi Mohan and Patricia Keefe, Computerworld
1995 Runner-Up: "IT bullish on IBM-Lotus pairing", Charles Cooper, Paula Rooney and John Dodge, PC Week
1995 Runner-Up: "I Want Lotus!", Craig Zarley, Edward F. Moltzen and Barbara Darrow, Computer Reseller News
1994 Winner: "Microsoft, Justice Dept. Discussing a Settlement", Elizabeth Corcoran, The Washington Post
1994 Runner-Up: "Intel Pentium Bug", Steve Young, CNN
1994 Runner-Up: "Hackers Storm DoD Nets", Bob Brewin and Elizabeth Sikorovsky, Federal Computer Week
Investigative News Story or Series:
1995 Winner: "The Point-Five Percent Solution and Mr. Toad's Wild Ride", Brock N. Meeks, Cyberwire Dispatch
1995 Runner-Up: "Ticket To Nowhere", Joseph Maglitta, Computerworld
1995 Runner-Up: "Invasions of Privacy", Jeffrey Rothfeder, Christina Wood and Richard Overton, PC World
1994 Winner: "The Humbling of John Sculley", Lawrence Hooper and Jesse Kornbluth, Worth
1994 Runner-Up: "Microsoft Develops More Than Software", Jack Sweeney, Computer Reseller News
1994 Runner-Up: "Dangerous E-Mail", Stephanie Stahl, InformationWeek
Expository Feature or Series:
1995 Winner: "The Software Revolution", Amy Cortese and Team, BusinessWeek
1995 Runner-Up: "Building Binge", Bill Snyder and Larry Aragon, PC Week/Inside
1995 Runner-Up: "The Once and Future Microsoft", G. Pascal Zachary, Upside
1994 Winner: "The Last Harpoon", Wendy Goldman Rohm, Eric Nee and Karen Southwick, Upside Magazine
1994 Runner-Up: "Culture Club", Michael Meyer and Nancy Hass, Newsweek
1994 Runner-Up: "Breaking into the Men's Club", Bronwyn Fryer, Rusty Weston and Roderick Simpson, Open Computing
How-To Feature or Series:
1995 Winner: "Windows 95 Superguide", Ed Bott, Wendy Taylor and Woody Leonhard, PC/Computing
1995 Runner-Up: "The Information Byways", Charles Bowen and Andrea Linne, HomePC
1995 Runner-Up: "Moving Clients to Windows 95", Doug Wilson and Tom Farre, VARBusiness
1994 Winner: "Windows Detective: Solving the Mysteries of Error Messages", Michael Lasky and Steve Fox, PC World
1994 Runner-Up: "Memory Not Included", Jeremy Schlosberg and Andrea Linne, HomePC Magazine
1994 Runner-Up: "Are You Breaking the Law?" James Martin and Kathy Abes, Macworld
Product Analysis Feature or Series:
1995 Winner: "Windows 95 Superguide", Ed Bott, Wendy Taylor and Woody Leonhard, PC/Computing
1995 Runner-Up: Next-Generation Routing: Making Sense of the Marketectures", Stephen Saunders, Lee Keough and Aaron Fischer, Data Comm.
1995 Runner-Up: "Are You Ready for Electronic Partnering", Joshua Macht and David Freedman, Inc. Magazine
1994 Winner: "Notes: Mailboxes, Etc." Ed Bott and Elizabeth Longsworth, PC/Computing
1994 Runner-Up: "The Road to PowerMac", Andrew Gore, Bob O'Donnell and Anita Malnig, MacWeek
1994 Runner-Up: "Killer Color Notebooks", Marty Jerome and Wendy Taylor, PC/Computing
Technical Feature or Series:
1995 Winner: "The Future of SCSI", Jim Heid and Dan Littman, Macworld Communications
1995 Runner-Up: "The CW Guide to High-end Desktop PCs", James M. Connolly, Cathleen Gagne and Rosemary Cafasso, Computerworld
1995 Runner-Up: "M-Bone", Kevin Wendle, Win Baker and Om Dixon, C/NET: The Computer Network
1994 Winner: "Energy Management: Keeping Your Portable Going and Going", Ron Wilson, OEM Magazine

1994 Runner-Up: "Transforming the PC: Plug and Play", Tom Halfhill, Richard Friedman and Warren Williamson, Byte Magazine

1994 Runner-Up: "V.34 Modems: Watch the Fine Print", Kieran Taylor, Lee Keough and Aaron Fischer, Data Communications Magazine

News Story in a General Interest Publication:

1993 Winner: "IBM's New Boss," Catherine Arnst, Business Week

1993 Runner-up: "Novell: End of an Era?," Kathy Rebello, Business Week

1993 Runner-up: "Big Brother's Holding Company," Jolie Solomon, Newsweek

1992 Winner: "On The Spot," John Wilke, The Wall Street Journal

1992 Runner-up: "Compaq: The Making of a Comeback," Catherine Arnst and Stephanie Forest, BusinessWeek

1992 Runner-up: "Operation Desert Sneak," Gina Smith and Katie Rabin, San Francisco Examiner

1991 Winner: G. Pascal Zachary and Stephen Kreider Yoder, Wall Street Journal

1990 Winner: Andrew Tanzer, New, Improved Color Computer, Forbes

1989 Winner: Jonathan Levine, Neil Gross and John Carey, Is the U.S. Selling Its High-Tech Soul to Japan?, BusinessWeek

News Story in a Computer Publication:

1993 Winner: "DOS 6.0," Stuart Johnson, Doug Barney and Kevin Strehlo, Infoworld

1993 Runner-up: "Software Price War Threatens Free Support," T.C. Doyle, Diana Hwang and Heather Clancy, Computer Reseller News

1993 Runner-up: "Stop! Is Your New Software Secondhand?," Roberta Furger, PC World

1992 Winner: "Scam!," Roberta Furger and Mike Hogan, PC World

1992 Runner-up: "CA Business Policies Anger Some Large Shops," Johanna Ambrosio, Computerworld

1992 Runner-up: "DISA to Services: Apocalypse Now," Bob Brewin, Federal Computer Week

1991 Winner: Peter Krass, InformationWeek

1990 Winner: Alice LaPlante and Ed Scannell, IBM/Microsoft Alliance Crumbling, InfoWorld

1989 Winner: Bruce Caldwell, Washington's Revolving Door Crisis, InformationWeek

Feature in a General Interest Publication:

1993 Winner: "Cracking the Code," Mark Uehling, Popular Science

1993 Runner-up: "Gerstner's New Vision for IBM," David Kirkpatrick, Fortune

1993 Runner-up: "Stalking Stealth Viruses," Christopher O'Malley, Popular Science

1992 Winner: "Deconstructing The Computer Industry," John Verity, BusinessWeek

1992 Runner-up: "Bottom Fishing," Michael Allen, The Wall Street Journal

1992 Runner-up: "Interactive Television," Michael Antonoff, Popular Science Magazine

1991 Winner: Elizabeth Corcoran, Scientific American

1990 Winner: Gregg Pascal Zachary, Venture-Capital Star, Kleiner Perkins, Flops as a Maker of Laptops, The Wall Street Journal

1989 Winner: Brenton R. Schlender, How Steve Jobs Linked up with IBM, Fortune

Feature In Computer Publication:

1993 Winner: "Will the FTC Come to Its Senses about Microsoft's Mischief?," Wendy Goldman-Rohm, Upside

1993 Runner-up: "Multimedia Explosion," Ed Bott and John Montgomery, PC/Computing

1993 Runner-up: "Bosses with X-Ray Eyes" and "Privacy in Peril," Charles Piller, Macworld

1992 Winner: "America's Shame: Separate Realities, and Official Word," Charles Piller and Morton Kondrake; Macworld; Liza Weiman and Cheryl England, editors

1992 Runner-up: "E-Mail Snooping," Jeffrey Rothfeder, Rochelle Garner and Lewis D'Vorkin; Corporate Computing

1992 Runner-up: "It's All Right Now," Richard Rapaport, David Bunnel and Eric Nee; Upside

1991 Winner: Preston Gralla, PC/Computing

1990 Winner: Jonathan Littman, The Shockwave Rider, PC/Computing

1989 Winner: Dennis Livingston, Federal Systems Integration, Systems Integration

Opinion or Editorial:

1995 Winner: "The Once and Future Microsoft", G. Pascal Zachary, Upside

1995 Runner-Up: "A Rotten Apple", Eric Nee, Upside

1995 Runner-Up: "Famous Last Words", Stephen Levy and Deborah Branscum, Macworld Communications

1994 Winner: "A Native Need for Narrative" Phil Hood and Mary McFall, NewMedia

1994 Runner-Up: "No Guts", Paul Gillin, Computerworld

1994 Runner-Up: "Significa: Team Players", J.D. Hildebrand and Bobbi Sinyard, Windows Tech Journal

1993 Winner: "Maybe This Sounds Strange, But I'm Starting to Sour on Suites," Cheryl Currid, Windows

1993 Runner-up: "Installer Hell," Michael Crichton, Byte

1993 Runner-up: "The Windows NT Sleight of Hand: Microsoft's Artful Promotion," John Dvorak, PC/Computing

1992 Winner: "Conspicuous Consumer: Smart Company, Foolish Choices," Deborah Branscum and Charles Barrett, Macworld

1992 Runner-up: "PCs are PCs, and TVs are TVs, And Nary the Twain Shall Meet," John C. Dvorak, PC/Computing

1992 Runner-up: "The FBI Wants to Tap Your Network," David Bunnell, NewMedia

1991 Winner: Douglas Adams, MacUser

1990 Winner: John Dvorak, The Decline of Civilization, DEC Professional

1989 Winner: Paul Somerson, untitled column, PC/Computing

Hardware Product Review:

1995 Winner: "Your Portable Persona", Bill Howard and Richard Fisco, PC Magazine

1995 Runner-Up: "Branch-Office Routers: No Match For Frame Relay", David Newman, Donald Marks and Dennis Mendyk, Data Communications

1995 Runner-Up: "Internet Servers: New Internet Support for Information Systems", Lisa Stapleton, Steve Irwin and Greg Johnson, InfoWorld

1994 Winner: "Power Macs: Full Speed Ahead", Cheryl England, Stephan Somogyi and Henry Bortman, MacUser

1994 Runner-Up: "Consumer Lab", Sean Fulton and Melanie Berger, HomePC

1994 Runner-Up: "CD-R: Out of the Oven and Pipin Hot", Ean Houts, Jeff Angus and Bob Gale, InfoWorld

1993 Winner: "The Newton Generation," Henry Bortman, MacWeek
1993 Runner-up: "Working Away," Owen Linzmayer, MacUser
1993 Runner-up: "Unwrapping the Packard Bell Legend," Doug Wilson, Computer Sources
1992 Winner: "What's The Right Size?," Bill Catchings and Mark L. Van Name, Corporate Computing
1992 Runner-up: "386 and 486 Notebooks: Fitting the World Inside Your Briefcase," Bill Howard and Chris Barr; PC Magazine
1992 Runner-up: "50-MHz 486DX PCs," Siobhan Nash and Gregory S. Smith, InfoWorld
1991 Winner: Russell Ito, MacUser
1990 Winner: Cheryl England Spencer, Low Capacity Drives, Macworld
1989 Winner: Bill Howard and Bruce Brown, 286 Laptops: Compute En Route

Software Product Review:
1995 Winner: "Easy Money: Personal Finance Software", Peter Scisco, Daniel Tynan and Anita Hamilton, PC World
1995 Runner-Up: "Desktop Videoconferencing: Not Ready for Prime Time", Kieran Taylor, Lee Keough and Dennis Mendyk, Data Communications
1995 Runner-Up: "ClarisWorks 4.0", David Pogue and Wendy Sharp, Macworld Communications
1994 Winner: "Live Picture", Deke McClelland and Carol Person, Macworld
1994 Runner-Up: "AlisaMail: The Best Yet, But Don't Attach Your Sales Contract", Steve Irwin and Lisa Stapleton, InfoWorld
1993 Winner: "DOS 6.0," Chris DeVoney and Paul Somerson, PC/Computing
1993 Runner-up: "32-Bit Desktop Operating Systems," Les Kend and Siobhan Nash, InfoWorld
1993 Runner-up: "The Windows Spreadsheet Challenge," Richard Scoville and Steve Adams, PC World
1992 Winner: "QuickTime In Action," Russell Ito and James Bradbury, MacUser
1992 Runner-up: "Presentation Software Playoffs," Deke McClelland and Steve Fox, PC World
1992 Runner-up: "The Future is Now: ObjectVision Brings a View of What's to Come," Jack W. Crenshaw, Windows Tech Journal
1991 Winner: Craig Stinson, PC Magazine
1990 Winner: Michael Miley, Mail Call, MacUser
1989 Winner: David Buerger, Mary O'Donnell and Tracey Capen, Move over, Netware?, InfoWorld

Broad-Interest Newspaper:
1995 Winner: Computer Reseller News, Robert Faletra, Robert C. DeMarzo and Ed Sperling
1995 Runner-Up: Runner-Up: PC Week, Dan Farber, John Dodge and Rob O'Regan
1995 Runner-Up: San Francisco Chronicle, Jeff Pelline, David Einstein and Michelle Quinn
1994 Winner: The Arizona Republic, Dan Hontz
1994 Runner-Up: Computer Currents, Robert Luhn
1994 Runner-Up: Computer User, Steve Deyo

Trade Newspaper:
1995 Winner: Federal Computer Week, Anne Armstrong, Joanne Connelly and Carolyn Marsan
1995 Runner-Up: Inter@ctive Week, Tom Steinert-Threlkeld, George Vernadakis and Carol Wilson
1994 Winner: Computer Reseller News, Robert Faletra
1994 Runner-Up: CommunicationsWeek, Becky McAdams
1994 Runner-Up: Micro Publishing News, James Cavuoto, Stephen Ball and David Pope

Computer Newspaper (circulation less than 100,000):
1993 Winner: Electronic Buyers News
1993 Runner-up: Government Computer News
1993 Runner-up: Service News
1992 Winner: Computer Retail Week
1992 Runner-up: Government Computer News
1992 Runner-up: MacWeek

Computer Newspaper (circulation more than 100,000):
1993 Winner: Computerworld
1993 Runner-up: Communications Week
1993 Runner-up: Computer Reseller News
1992 Winner: Computerworld
1992 Runner-up: Electronic Engineering Times
1992 Runner-up: PC Week

Computer Newspaper (circulation over 50,000):
1991 Winner: PC Week
1990 Winner: Computer Reseller News
1989 Winner: Computer Systems News

Computer Newspaper (circulation under 50,000):
1991 Winner: Computer Retail Week
1990 Winner: Computer Retail Week
1989 Winner: Macintosh News

Broad-Interest Magazine:
1995 Winner: HomePC, Ellen Pearlman
1995 Runner-Up: Family PC, Robin Raskin
1995 Runner-Up: PC World, The PC World Staff
1994 Winner: Wired, Louis Rosetto
1994 Runner-Up: Byte, Dennis Allen
1994 Runner-Up: HomePC Magazine, Ellen Pearlman

Technical Trade Magazine:
1995 Winner: Computerworld, Paul Gilian, Maryfran Johnson and Patricia Keefe
1995 Runner-Up: OEM Magazine, Rick Boyd-Merritt, Tim Moran and David Lieberman
1995 Runner-Up: Computer Reseller News, Robert Faletra, Robert C. DeMarzo and Ed Sperling
1994 Winner: Datamation, Kevin Strehlo and Christopher Lewis
1994 Runner-Up: Data Communications, Joseph Brane, Lee Keough and Ken Surabian
1994 Runner-Up: Windows Tech Journal, J.D. Hildebrand, Cecilia Hagen and Wanda Walker
Non-Technical Trade Magazine:
1995 Winner: Inter@ctive Week, Tom Steinert-Threlkeld, George Vernadakis and Carol Wilson
1995 Runner-Up: Upside, Eric Nee
1995 Runner-Up: Computer Graphics World, Stephen Porter
1994 Winner: PC Magazine, Michael Miller, Robin Raskin and Nick Stam
1994 Runner-Up: Computer Artist Magazine, Tom McMillan
1994 Runner-Up: Forbes ASAP, Richard Karlgaard
Computer Magazine (circulation less than 100,000):
1993 Winner: Upside
1993 Runner-up: Computer Artist
1993 Runner-up: VAR Business
1992 Winner: CIO Magazine
1992 Runner-up: NewMedia Magazine
1992 Runner-up: VARBusiness
Computer Magazine (circulation more than 100,000):
1993 Winner: Macworld
1993 Runner-up: NewMedia
1993 Runner-up: PC Magazine
1992 Winner: Macworld
1992 Runner-up: Byte
1992 Runner-up: PC Magazine
Computer Magazine (circ. over 50,000):
1991 Winner: Macworld
1990 Winner: Macworld
1989 Winner: Personal Computing
Computer Magazine (circ. under 50,000):
1991 Winner: Computers in Accounting
1990 Winner: Workstation News
1989 Winner: VARBusiness
Rookie of the Year:
1995 Winner: C/NET Online, Christopher Barr, Kevin Wendle and Fred Sotherland
1995 Runner-Up: Delphi Informant, Jerry Coffey and Mitchell Koulouris
1995 Runner-Up: Inter@ctive Week, Tom Steinert-Threlkeld, George Vernadakis and Carol Wilson
1994 Winner: HomePC Magazine, Ellen Pearlman
1994 Runner-Up: Game Developer Magazine, Larry O'Brien
1994 Runner-Up: Hot Wired, Louis Rossetto, Andrew Anker and Chip Bayers
1993 Winner: OS/2 Professional
1993 Runner-up: Windows Sources
1992 Winner: Windows Tech Journal
1992 Runner-up: Corporate Computing Magazine
Newsletter:
1995 Winner: Windows Watcher, Jesse Berst, Dwight Davis and Robin Young
1995 Runner-Up: The Seybold Report on Publishing Systems, Stephen Edwards, Mark Walter and Andrew Tribute
1995 Runner-Up: DV Full Motion, Linda Laflamme
1994 Winner: Microprocessor Report, Michael Slater and Linley Gwennap
1994 Runner-Up: Release 1.0, Jerry Michalski and Esther Dyson
1994 Runner-Up: Windows Watcher, Jesse Berst, Dwight Dans and Robin Young
1993 Winner: Microprocessor Report
1993 Runner-up: Macromedia User Journal
1993 Runner-up: Windows Watcher
1992 Winner: Rel-EAST
1992 Runner-up: LaserJet Journal
1992 Runner-up: P.C. Letter
1991 Winner: Windows Watcher
1990 Winner: LaserJet Journal
1989 Winner: Sourcefile
On-Line Publication:
1995 Winner: ZD Net/World Wide Web Edition, Tom Schmidt, Jerome Tuccille and Scott Hacker
1995 Runner-Up: C/NET Online, Christopher Barr, Kevin Wendle and Fred Sotherland
1994 Winner: Hot Wired, Louis Rossetto, Andrew Anker and Chip Bayers

1994 Runner-Up: Computer Retail Week, Mike Harris
1994 Runner-Up: WEBster, The Cyberspace Surfer, Dianne Husum and Jim Crawley
1992 Winner: Newsbytes News Network
1992 Runner-up: The Computer Club
1991 Winner: Computer Club, Prodigy Services
1990 Winner: Newsbytes News Network
1989 Winner: The Well

Nonfiction Computer Book:
1995 Winner: "How Computers Work", Ron White, Valerie Haynes Perry and Bruce Lundquist, Ziff-Davis Press
1995 Runner-Up: "Hoover's Guide to Computer Companies", The Reference Press, Inc.
1995 Runner-Up: "Be Your Own Headhunter", Pam Dixon, Sylvia Tiersten and Charles Levine, Random House
1994 Winner: "Mailing List Services On Your Home-Based PC"
1994 Runner-Up "The Brainmakers", David Freedman
1994 Runner-Up: "The Internet", Paul Hoffman
1993 Winner: "Visualization of Natural Phenomena," Robert Wolff and Larry Yaeger
1993 Runner-up: "The Software Developer's and Marketer's Legal Companion," Gene Landy
1993 Runner-up: "Jargon", Robin Williams and Steve Cummings
1992 Winner: "Privacy For Sale: How Computerization Has Made Everyone's Private Life an Open Secret," Jeffrey Rothfeder and Robert Bender
1992 Runner-up: "The Computer Industry Almanac 1992," Egil Juliussen and Karen Petska-Juliussen
1992 Runner-up: "The Hacker Crackdown: Law & Disorder on the Electronic Frontier," Bruce Sterling and Betsy Mitchell
1991 Winner: Computers and Society: Impact!, David O. Arnold
1990 Winner: Guy Kawasaki, The Macintosh Way
1989 Winner: Microsoft Press, Microsoft CD-ROM Yearbook 1989-1990

Introductory How-to-Book: Systems:
1995 Winner: "The Internet for Teachers", Bard Williams, Bill Helling and Pat Seiler, IDG Books Worldwide
1995 Runner-Up: "Yahoo! Unplugged: Your Discovery Guide to The Web", Jerry Yang, David Filo with Charles Seiter, Paul Hoffman, Tom Negrino, Dave Taylor and Karen Heyman, IDG Books Worldwide
1995 Runner-Up: "How To Use The Internet, Second Edition", Marietta Tretter, Margo Hill and Martha Barrera, Ziff-Davis Press
1994 Winner: "The PC Bible", Eric Knorr
1994 Runner-Up: "The Internet for Macs for Dummies", Charles Seiter, Shawn MacLaren and Mary Bednarek
1994 Runner-Up: "The Non-Designers Design Book", Robin Williams
1993 Winner: "How Networks Work," Frank Derfler, Jr. and Les Freed
1993 Runner-up: "The Internet for Dummies," John Levine and Carol Baroudi
1993 Runner-up: "Roger C. Parker's One Minute Designer," Roger Parker
1992 Winner: "Danny Goodman's Macintosh Handbook - Featuring System 7," Danny Goodman and Richard Saul Wurman, Bantam Electronic Publishing
1992 Runner-up: "PCs For Dummies," Dan Gookin and Andy Rathbone
1992 Runner-up: "Van Wolverton's Guide to DOS 5," Van Wolverton, Debra Miller and Steve Lambert
1991 Winner: Getting Started with the Apple Macintosh, Neil Salkind

Introductory How-to-Book: Software:
1995 Winner: "Windows 95 Simplified", Ruth Maran, Kelleigh Wing, Paul Lofthouse, IDG Books Worldwide
1995 Runner-Up: "Macworld Freehand 5 Bible, Second Edition", Deke McClelland, Susan Pines and Andy Cummings, IDG Books Worldwide
1995 Runner-Up: "Real Life Windows 95", Dan Gookin, Corbin Collins and Mary C. Corder, IDG Books Worldwide
1994 Winner: "Windows 3.1 for Dummies", 2nd Edition, Andy Rathbone, Julie King and Mary Bednarek
1994 Runner-Up: "How To Use WordPerfect 6.0 for Windows", Eric Stone
1994 Runner-Up: "Windows 3.1 Simplified, Expanded", Ruth Maran and Judy Maran
1993 Winner: "DOS for Dummies, Second Edition," Dan Gookin
1993 Runner-up: "The Create It! Kit," Kim Baker and Sunny Baker
1993 Runner-up: "How to Use Word," Eric Stone
1992 Winner: ""Windows 3.1 Programming for Mere Mortals," Woody Leonhard, Addison-Wesley Publishing Company
1992 Runner-up: "PageMaker 4: An Easy Desk Reference," Robin Williams
1992 Runner-up: "WordPerfect for Dummies," Dan Gookin, Sandy Blackthorn and John Kilcullen
1991 Winner: Microsoft Excel: Step by Step, Microsoft Corp.

Advanced How-to-Book: Systems:
1995 Winner: "PCI System Architecture, Third Edition", Tom Shanley and Don Anderson, Addison-Wesley Publishing Company
1995 Runner-Up: Animation and 3D Modeling on the Mac", Dan Foley and Melora Foley, Peachpit Press
1995 Runner-Up: "The Indispensable PC Hardware Book, Second Edition", Hans-Peter Messmer, Addison-Wesley Publishing Company
1994 Winner: "Macworld Networking Bible," 2nd Edition, Dave Kosnir, Joel Snyder and Andy Cummings
1994 Runner-Up: "The Icon Book: Visual Symbols for Computer Systems and Documentation", William Horton and Terri Hudson
1994 Runner-Up: "Understanding Desktop Color," 2nd Edition, Michael Kieran
1993 Winner: "Network World Network Security Secrets," David Stang and Sylvia Moon
1993 Runner-up: "The Windows 3.1 Bible," Fred Davis and Sylvia Paul
1993 Runner-up: "Hard Disk Secrets," John Goodman
1992 Winner: "Macworld Music and Sound Bible," Christopher Yavelow and Jeremy Judson, IDG Books Worldwide
1992 Runner-up: "DOS 5," Alfred Glossbrenner and Debra Miller
1992 Runner-up: "Undocumented Windows," Andrew Schulman, David Maxey and Matt Pietrek

1991 Winner: The Art of Computer Systems Analysis, Raj Jain

Advanced How-to-Book: Software:

1995 Winner: "The KPT Bryce Book", Susan Kitchens, Addison-Wesley Publishing Company

1995 Runner-Up: "Windows 95 System Programming Secrets", Matt Pietrek, Clare Mansfield and James Finnegan, IDG Books Worldwide

1994 Winner: "The Photoshop Wow! Book," Windows Edition, Linnea Dayton and Jack Davis

1994 Runner-Up: "PC Game Programming Explorer", Dave Roberts and Keith Weiskamp

1994 Runner-Up: "Real World Freehand 4", Olav Martin Dvern

1993 Winner: "Hacker's Guide to Word for Windows," Woody Leonard and Vincent Chen

1993 Runner-up: "Real-World PageMaker 5.0," Bruce Fraser and Steve Roth

1993 Runner-up: "Access Basic Cookbook," Chris St. Valentine

1992 Winner: "Macintosh Human Interface Guidelines," Apple Computer, Inc.; Addison Wesley Publishing

1992 Runner-up: "Moving from C to C++," Greg Perry

1992 Runner-up: "Windows API Bible: The Definitive Programmer's Reference," Mitchell Waite and James L. Conger; Waite Group Press

1991 Winner: Real World PageMaker 4, Jesse Berst, Stephen Roth, Olav Martin Kvern, and Scott Dunn

CD-ROM Publications:

1995 Winner: CD-ROM, "Spring 1995", Paul Sommerson and Mark C. Li, PC/Computing

1995 Runner-Up: "Multimedia World Live", Russell Glitman and Kate Rowland

Best How-to Book:

1990 Winner: Mitchell Waite and Stephen Prata, The Waite Group's New C Primer Plus

1989 Winner: Ronnie Shushan and Don Wright, Desktop Publishing by Design

Best Software Product-Specific Book:

1990 Winner: Gordon McComb, WordPerfect 5.1 Macros and Templates

1989 Winner: Cary Prague and James Hammit, dBase IV Programming

Best Hardware Product-Specific Book:

1989 Winner: Neil J. Salkind, The Big Mac Book

Radio Program/Series:

1995 Winner: The Personal Computer Show, Joe King

1995 Runner-Up: C/NET, Brian Cooley

1995 Runner-Up: The CompuDudes, Peter Cook, Scott Manning and Justin Roman

1994 Winner: On Computers, Gina Smith, Jerry Kay and Renn Vara

1994 Runner-Up: The Personal Computer Show, Joe King, Hank Lee and Dave Burstein

1992 Winner: Horizons: "Push Button Magic," Harriet Baskas, Marcie Sillman and Donna Limerick, National Public Radio

1992 Runner-up: "The Personal Computer Show," Joe King, Hank Kee and Dave Burstein, WBAI-FM

1992 Runner-up: "Software/Hardtalk with John C. Dvorak;" John C. Dvorak, Maureen McGinley and John Moss

1991 Winner: Computing Success!, Business Radio Network

1990 Winner: Joe King, Producer/Host, The Personal Computer Show, WBAI New York

Columnist:

1995 Winner: "Random Access", Stephen Levy, Newsweek

1995 Runner-Up: "Consumer Watch", Roberta Furger and Christina Wood, PC World

1995 Runner-Up: "Computer Pursuits", Nelson King, Computer User

1994 Winner: "Logout", Gary Andrew Poole and David Diamond, Open Computing

1994 Runner-Up: "Iconoclast", Steven Levy and Deborah Branscum, Macworld

1994 Runner-Up: "Consumer Watch by Roberta Furger", Roberta Furger, PC World

1993 Winner: Deborah Branscum, Macworld

1993 Runner-up: Andy Ihnatko, MacUser

1993 Runner-up: Gary Andrew Poole, UnixWorld

1992 Winner: Bill Machrone, PC Magazine

1992 Runner-up: Steven Levy, Macworld

1992 Runner-up: Andy Ihnatko, MacUser

1991 Winner: Deborah Branscum, Macworld

1990 Winner: Jerry Borrell, Macworld

1989 Winner: John Dvorak, PC Magazine

Television Program/Series:

1995 Winner: C/NET, Kevin Wendle, Frank Voci, Fred Sotherland, Win Baker and Stace Felder

1995 Runner-Up: Minerva's Machine, Karen A. Frenkel and Stephen Schmidt

1994 Winner: User's Group, Stewart Cheifet, Giles Bateman and Robin Ray

1994 Runner-Up: The Computer Chronicles, Sara O'Brien and Stewart Cheifet

1994 Runner-Up: Computer 101, Shelley Angers, Sara O'Brien and Stewart Cheifet

1993 Winner: CNN Science and Technology Week, Cable News Network

1991 Winner: Business World, ABC News

1990 Winner: Computer Chronicles, Stewart Cheifet and Sara O'Brien

1989 Winner: Business World, ABC News

Publication Directory

This directory contains 1,190 publications such as magazines, newspapers, directories, journals and periodicals. A "free" subscription means its free to qualified subscribers. The price for non-qualified subscribers may also be listed. If there are two prices listed, the first price is the member price and the other is the non-member price. All prices are for subscribers in the U.S. Foreign subscribers normally pay more.

All Web URL addresses start with: http://www., which is not listed in the directory.

The Publications Directory is available for sales on diskette from the Computer Industry Almanac. For inclusion in future edition of the Almanac, send the information about your publication directly to us. There is no charge for this listing.

1-2-3 For Windows Report, The
Publishing Co: Lotus Publishing Corp., 77 Franklin Street #310, Boston, MA 02110, USA; 617/482-8634, Fax: 617/422-8189, Focus: Tips and techniques for Lotus 1-2-3 for Windows users; Format: Newsletter; Craig G. Pierce, Pblshr Richard Cranford, Ed. Cheryl Magadieu, Ed. Freq: Monthly, Price/yr-$:69/89/99

101 CAD/CAM Traps
Publishing Co: CAD/CAM Publishing Inc., 1010 Turquoise Street, #320, San Diego, CA 92109-1268, USA; 619/488-0533, Fax: 619/488-6052, Co Email: cad-circ@aol.com; Focus: How to organize, plan and budget for a CAD/CAM system; Format: Factbook; John Krouse, Author Price/yr-$:79.95

123 Users Journal
Publishing Co: Cobb Group, The, 9420 Bunsen Pkwy. #300, Louisville, KY 40220, USA; 502/491-1900, Fax: 502/491-8050, Co Email: cobb@aol.com; Web URL: cobb.com; Focus: News and tips for users of Lotus 1-2-3 spreadsheet; Format: Newsletter; Stuart Vessels, Ed. Freq: Monthly, Price/yr-$:59

2021 AD: Visions of the Future
Publishing Co: International Engineering Consortium, 303 E Wacker Drive, #740, Chicago, IL 60601-5212, USA; 312/938-3500, Fax: 312/938-8787, Focus: Future information and communications age, featuring over 70 futurist experts; Format: Report; Price/yr-$:475

3D Design
Publishing Co: Miller Freeman Inc., 600 Harrison Street, San Francisco, CA 94107-1391, USA; 415/905-2200, Fax: 415/905-2234, Co Email: @mfi.com; Focus: Information on 3D software and hardware; Format: Magazine; Johanna Kleppe, Pblshr Email: jkleppe@mfi.com; Kelly Dove, Exec Ed. Email: kdove@mfi.com; Gretchen J. Bay, Mgng Ed. Email: gbay@mfi.com; Freq: Monthly, Price/yr-$:29.95

3X/400 Systems Management
Publishing Co: Adams/Hunter Publishing, 2101 S. Arlington Heights Rd., #150, Arlington Heights, IL 60005, USA; 708/427-9512, Fax: 708/427-2006, Co Email: 71333.3316@compuserve.com; Focus: Decision support for IBM midrange systems managers; Format: Magazine; Wayne Rhodes, Ed-in-Chief Email: 71333.730@compuserve.com; Richard K. Felt, Pblshr Email: 71333.730@compuserve.com; Sue Garrison, Mgng Ed. Email: 71333.3316@compuserve.com; Circ.: 58,000, Freq: Monthly, Price/yr-$:Free/42

A-E-C Automation Newsletter
Publishing Co: Technology Publications Inc., 5920 Roswell Road #B107336, Atlanta, GA 30328-4922, USA; 770/565-3282, Fax: 770/565-3286, Co Email: aec-news@aol.com; Focus: News, information and analysis on CAE, CAD, GIS applications; Format: Newsletter; Carleton R. Howk, Ed-in-Chief Email: aec-news@aol.com; Circ.: 4,300, Freq: Monthly, Price/yr-$:225

A/E/C Systems Computer Solution
Publishing Co: A/E/C Systems Inc., PO Box 310318, Newington, CT 06131-0318, USA; 860/666-1326, Fax: 203/666-4782, Focus: Computer use in design/construction industries; Format: Magazine; George S. Borkovich, Pblshr Judith K. Ivie, Mgng Ed. Michael R. Hough, Pblshr Freq: 6/Year, Price/yr-$:36

AC's Guide to the Commodore Amiga
Publishing Co: PiM Publications Inc., PO Box 2140, Fall River, MA 02722, USA; 508/678-4200, Fax: 508/675-6002, Focus: Product guide for all Amiga hardware and software; Format: Magazine; Don Hicks, Ed. Email: donhicks@aol.com; Joyce Hicks, Pblshr Circ.: 25,000, Freq: 2/Year, Price/yr-$:12/issue

Accelerating PC Graphics
Publishing Co: Mercury Research, 7950 E. Acoma Drive, #203, Scottsdale, AZ 85260, USA; 602/998-9225, Fax: 602/998-4338, Co Email: service@mercury.org; Focus: Technology trends and forecast on PC graphics; Format: Book; Mike Feibus, Founder Dean A. McCarron, Founder Price/yr-$:1,995

Access to Wang
Publishing Co: New Media Publications, 10711 Burnet Road, #305, Austin, TX 78758-4459, USA; 512/873-7761, Fax: 512/873-7782, Focus: News, reviews and information for Wang system users; Format: Magazine; Patrice Sarath, Ed. Kathy Murphy, Pblshr Circ.: 10,000, Freq: Monthly, Price/yr-$:Free/38

Access/Visual Basic Advisor
Publishing Co: Advisor Publications Inc., 4010 Morena Blvd, San Diego, CA 92117, USA; 619/483-6400, Fax: 619/483-9851, Co Email: 71154.3123@compuserve.com; Focus: News and information for dBase users; Format: Magazine; William T. Ota, Pblr/Pres/CEO John L. Hawkins, Ed-in-Chief & EVP Jeanne Banfield, VP Circ.: 33,000, Freq: Monthly, Price/yr-$:29

Accounting Technology
Publishing Co: Faulkner & Gray Inc., 11 Penn Plaza, 17th Floor, New York, NY 10001, USA; 212/967-7000, Fax: 212/563-3930, Focus: Applying technical solutions to accounting; Format: Magazine; Theodore Needleman, Ed-in-Chief Email: tedneedleman@mcimail.com; Circ.: 30,000, Freq: 11/year, Price/yr-$:58

ACM Computing Surveys
Publishing Co: Association for Computing Machinery, 1515 Broadway, 17th Floor, New York, NY 10036, USA; 212/869-7440, Fax: 212/869-0481, Web URL: acm.org; Focus: Perspectives on hardware, software, systems and other topics; Format: Magazine; Richard R. Muntz, Ed-in-Chief Carol Meyer, Pblshr Circ.: 18,000, Freq: 4/Year, Price/yr-$:21

ACM Guide to Computing Literature
Publishing Co: Association for Computing Machinery, 1515 Broadway, 17th Floor, New York, NY 10036, USA; 212/869-7440, Fax: 212/944-1318, Web URL: acm.org; Focus: Index of computer science literature; Format: Index; Freq: Annual, Price/yr-$:100

ACM Interactions
Publishing Co: Association for Computing Machinery, 1515 Broadway, 17th Floor,

New York, NY 10036, USA; 212/869-7440, Fax: 212/869-0481, Web URL: acm.org; Focus: Human-computer interaction; Format: Magazine; Carol Meyer, Pblshr Freq: 6/Year, Price/yr-$:45

ACM Letters on Programming Languages & Systems
Publishing Co: Association for Computing Machinery, 1515 Broadway, 17th Floor, New York, NY 10036, USA; 212/869-7440, Fax: 212/869-0481, Web URL: acm.org; Focus: Research and algorithms on programing languages and systems; Format: Magazine; Charles N. Fischer, Ed-in-Chief Carol Meyer, Pblshr Circ.: 2,200, Freq: 4/Year, Price/yr-$:26/105

ACM Transactions on Computer Systems
Publishing Co: Association for Computing Machinery, 1515 Broadway, 17th Floor, New York, NY 10036, USA; 212/869-7440, Fax: 212/869-0481, Web URL: acm.org; Focus: Technical information on computer system design and architecture; Format: Magazine; Kenneth P. Birmar, Ed-in-Chief Carol Meyer, Pblshr Circ.: 5,260, Freq: 4/Year, Price/yr-$:32

ACM Transactions on Computer-Human Interaction
Publishing Co: Association for Computing Machinery, 1515 Broadway, 17th Floor, New York, NY 10036, USA; 212/869-7440, Fax: 212/869-0481, Web URL: acm.org; Focus: Software, hardware and human aspects of computer interaction; Format: Magazine; Dan R. Olsen Jr., Ed-in-Chief Carol Meyer, Pblshr Freq: 4/Year, Price/yr-$:30

ACM Transactions on Database Systems
Publishing Co: Association for Computing Machinery, 1515 Broadway, 17th Floor, New York, NY 10036, USA; 212/869-7440, Fax: 212/869-0481, Web URL: acm.org; Focus: Technical information on database theory and applications; Format: Magazine; Won Kim, Ed-in-Chief Carol Meyer, Pblshr Circ.: 6,433, Freq: 4/Year, Price/yr-$:31

ACM Transactions on Information Systems
Publishing Co: Association for Computing Machinery, 1515 Broadway, 17th Floor, New York, NY 10036, USA; 212/869-7440, Fax: 212/869-0481, Web URL: acm.org; Focus: Technical information on hypertext, object-oriented systems, AI and other topics; Format: Magazine; Robert B. Allen, Ed-in-Chief Carol Meyer, Pblshr Circ.: 4,573, Freq: 4/Year, Price/yr-$:32

ACM Transactions on Mathematical Software
Publishing Co: Association for Computing Machinery, 1515 Broadway, 17th Floor, New York, NY 10036, USA; 212/869-7440, Fax: 212/869-0481, Web URL: acm.org; Focus: Research on mathematical algorithms and software development; Format: Magazine; Ronald F. Boisvert, Ed-in-Chief Carol Meyer, Pblshr Circ.: 3,114, Freq: 4/Year, Price/yr-$:32

ACM Transactions on Modeling & Computer Simulations
Publishing Co: Association for Computing Machinery, 1515 Broadway, 17th Floor, New York, NY 10036, USA; 212/869-7440, Fax: 212/869-0481, Web URL: acm.org; Focus: Peer-reviewed papers on discrete-event computer simulation; Format: Magazine; Richard E. Nance, Ed-in-Chief Carol Meyer, Pblshr Circ.: 2,400, Freq: 4/Year, Price/yr-$:36

ACM Transactions on Programming Languages & Systems
Publishing Co: Association for Computing Machinery, 1515 Broadway, 17th Floor, New York, NY 10036, USA; 212/869-7440, Fax: 212/869-0481, Web URL: acm.org; Focus: Research and algorithms on programing languages and systems; Format: Magazine; Andrew W. Appel, Ed-in-Chief Carol Meyer, Pblshr Circ.: 7,077, Freq: 6/Year, Price/yr-$:44

ACM Transactions on Software Eng. & Methodology
Publishing Co: Association for Computing Machinery, 1515 Broadway, 17th Floor, New York, NY 10036, USA; 212/869-7440, Fax: 212/869-0481, Web URL: acm.org; Focus: Peer-reviewed information on theory and application of software engineering; Format: Magazine; W. Richard Adrion, Ed-in-Chief Carol Meyer, Pblshr Circ.: 6,319, Freq: 4/Year, Price/yr-$:28

ACR Library of Programmers & Developers Tools
Publishing Co: Applied Computer Research Inc., PO Box 82266, Phoenix, AZ 85071-2266, USA; 602/995-5929, Fax: 602/995-0905, Focus: Directory of software development tools; Format: Directory; Freq: 1/Year, Price/yr-$:275

Adaptive Behavior
Publishing Co: MIT Press Journals, 55 Hayward Street, Cambridge, MA 02142, USA; 617/253-2889, Fax: 617/258-6779, Co Email: journals-orders@mit.edu; Web URL: mitpress.mit.edu; Focus: Research adaptive behavior in natural/artificial systems; Format: Magazine; Jean-Arcady Meyer, Ed. Email: meyer@biologie.ens.fr; Circ.: 500, Freq: 4/Year, Price/yr-$:50

Adobe Magazine
Publishing Co: Adobe Systems Inc., 411 First Ave S., Seattle, WA 98104-2871, USA; 206/628-2321, Fax: 206/343-3273, Co Email: magazine.editor@adobe.com; Focus: Desktop publishing and Adobe's products; Format: Magazine; Carla Noble, Pblshr Nicholas H. Allison, Ed-in-Chief Tamis Nordling, Mngg Ed. Freq: 8/Year, Price/yr-$:Free/35

Advanced Imaging
Publishing Co: PTN Publishing Co., 445 Broad Hollow Road, Melville, NY 11747, USA; 516/845-2700, Fax: 516/845-2797, Focus: Multimedia technology and trends; Format: Magazine; Barry Mazor, Ed-in-Chief Charles Grecky, Pblshr Circ.: 60,000, Freq: Monthly, Price/yr-$:Free/60

Advanced Intelligent Network News
Publishing Co: Phillips Business Information Inc., 1201 Seven Locks Road, #300, Potomac, MD 20854-1110, USA; 301/340-1520, Fax: 301/424-4297, Co Email: pbi@phillips.com; Web URL: phillips.com; Focus: Analysis of intelligent network services, technology and business; Format: Newsletter; Freq: 25/Year, Price/yr-$:597

Advanced Manufacturing Technology
Publishing Co: Technical Insights Inc., PO Box 1304, Ft. Lee, NJ 07024-9967, USA; 201/568-4744, Fax: 201/568-8247, Co Email: amtinfo@insights.com; Web URL: insights.com; Focus: News, trends and analysis of manufacturing automation and technologies; Format: Newsletter; Pam Frost, Ed. Email: amtinfo@insights.com; Kenneth A. Kovaly, Pblshr Email: amtinfo@insights.com; Freq: Monthly, Price/yr-$:630

Adweek's Directory of Interactive Marketing
Publishing Co: Adweek Directories, 1515 Broadway, New York, NY 10036, USA; Focus: Over 2,000 companies whose focus in digital media in marketing; Format: Factbook; Mitch Tebo, Pblshr Freq: Annual, Price/yr-$:199

AEA Directory
Publishing Co: American Electronics Association, 5201 Great American Pkwy., PO Box 54990, Santa Clara, CA 95056-0990, USA; 408/987-4200, Fax: 408/970-8565, Web URL: aeanet.org; Focus: Listing of over 2,900 high-tech companies; Format: Directory; Freq: Annual, Price/yr-$:95/195

AEC Hardware and Software Buyers Guide
Publishing Co: A/E/C Systems Inc., PO Box 310318, Newington, CT 06131-0318, USA; 860/666-1326, Fax: 203/666-4782, Focus: Listing of AEC products; Format: Directory; Michael Hough, Pblshr Freq: Annual, Price/yr-$:30

Agora Digital Talent Sourcebook
221 Main Street, #700, San Francisco, CA 94105-1919, USA; 415/543-8290, Fax: 415/543-8232, Focus: Listing of products and services for Macintosh; Format: Directory; Circ.: 20,000, Freq: 2/Year, Price/yr-$:60

AI Directory
Publishing Co: American Association for Artificial Intelligence, 445 Burgess Drive,

Menlo Park, CA 94025-3496, USA; 415/328-3123, Fax: 415/321-4457, Co Email: info@aaai.org; Web URL: aaai.org; Focus: Directory of companies, people and services in the AI industry; Format: Directory; Carol Hamilton, Exec Dir Email: info@aaai.org; Circ.: 10,000, Freq: Annual, Price/yr-$:40/60

AI Expert

Publishing Co: Miller Freeman Inc., 600 Harrison Street, San Francisco, CA 94107-1391, USA; 415/905-2200, Fax: 415/905-2234, Focus: News and trends for developers and users of AI applications; Format: Magazine; Kay Keppler, Ed. Patty Enrado, Mgng Ed. Circ.: 35,000, Freq: Monthly, Price/yr-$:42

AI Magazine

Publishing Co: American Association for Artificial Intelligence, 445 Burgess Drive, Menlo Park, CA 94025-3496, USA; 415/328-3123, Fax: 415/321-4457, Co Email: info@aaai.org; Web URL: aaai.org; Focus: Technical articles on AI; Format: Magazine; Carol Hamilton, Exec Dir Email: info@aaai.org; Circ.: 15,000, Freq: 4/Year, Price/yr-$:40

AI Today

Publishing Co: Yellowstone Information Services, 605 Brady Ave, Steubenville, OH 43952-1459, USA; 614/282-2797, Fax: 614/282-2798, Focus: Information on AI, expert systems and neural networks; Format: Newsletter; Roger C. Thibault, Ed. & Pblr Circ.: 5,000, Freq: 6/Year, Price/yr-$:50

AIM Report, The

Publishing Co: Adams Media Research, 15B W Carmel Valley Road, Carmel Valley, CA 93924, USA; 408/659-3070, Fax: 408/659-4330, Focus: Interactive multimedia technology and trends; Format: Newsletter; Tom Adams, Pres Email: tomadams@ix.netcom.com; Antonette Goroch, Analyst Email: gorochak@aol.com; Freq: 22/Year, Price/yr-$:550

AIX Update

Publishing Co: Xephon, 1301 W. Hwy 407, #201-450, Lewisville, TX 75067, USA; 817/455-7050, Fax: 817/455-2492, Focus: News, tips and software to improve AIX; Format: Magazine; Freq: 4/Year, Price/yr-$:245

Alcatel Telecommunications Review

Publishing Co: Alcatel, 54,rue La Boetie, Paris, F-75008, France; 1-4076-1010, Fax: 1-4076-1400, Focus: Telecom advances, applications and services; Format: Magazine; Rossella Daverio, Pblshr Philippe Goossens, Ed-in-Chief Thierry Roucher, Ed-in-Chief Freq: 4/Year, Price/yr-$:Free

Alpha Forum

Publishing Co: Pinnacle Publishing Inc., 18000 72nd Ave S. #217, Kent, WA 98032, USA; 206/251-1900, Fax: 206/251-5057, Web URL: pinpub.com; Focus: Information for Alpha Four database users;

Format: Newsletter; Dian Schaffhauser, Ed-in-Chief Brent Smith, Pblshr Freq: Monthly, Price/yr-$:79

Alpha Visual FX

Publishing Co: Miller Freeman Inc., 411 Borel Ave, #100, San Mateo, CA 94402-3522, USA; 415/358-9500, Fax: 415/358-9855, Format: Magazine

Amazing Computing for the Commodore Amiga

Publishing Co: PiM Publications Inc., PO Box 2140, Fall River, MA 02722, USA; 508/678-4200, Fax: 508/675-6002, Focus: Timely information for serious Amiga PC users; Format: Magazine; Don Hicks, Ed. Email: donhicks@aol.com; Joyce Hicks, Pblshr Circ.: 30,000, Freq: Monthly, Price/yr-$:29

America Online Report

Publishing Co: Jupiter Communications Co., 627 Broadway, 2nd Fl, New York, NY 10012, USA; 212/780-6060, Fax: 212/780-6075, Co Email: jup5@aol.com; Web URL: jup.com/jupiter; Focus: Market research study & analysis of online services; Format: Factbook; Michael Rinzel, Co-author & Ed. Freq: Annual, Price/yr-$:450

American Electronics Companies in Japan, Directory of

Publishing Co: American Electronics Association, 5201 Great American Pkwy., PO Box 54990, Santa Clara, CA 95054, USA; 408/987-4200, Fax: 408/970-8565, Web URL: aeanet.org; Focus: Profiles of US electronics companies' operation in Japan; Format: Directory; Freq: Semiannual, Price/yr-$:95/150

American Programmer

Publishing Co: Cutter Information Corp., 37 Broadway, Arlington, MA 02174-5539, USA; 617/648-8702, Fax: 617/648-1950, Co Email: 74107.653@compuserve.com; Web URL: cutter.com; Focus: Software technology trends and developments; Format: Newsletter; Ed Yourdon, Ed. Karen Coburn, Group Pblshr Email: 73352,1625@compuserve.com; Freq: Monthly, Price/yr-$:435

Ami Pro Report, The

Publishing Co: Lotus Publishing Corp., 77 Franklin Street #310, Boston, MA 02110, USA; 617/482-8634, Fax: 617/422-8189, Focus: Tips and techniques for Lotus Ami Pro users; Format: Newsletter; Craig G. Pierce, Pblshr Mark Scapicchio, Ed. Cheryl Magadieu, Ed. Freq: Monthly, Price/yr-$:69/89/99

AMR Report

Publishing Co: Advanced Manufacturing Research Inc., 2 Oliver Street, 5th Floor, Boston, MA 02109-4901, USA; 617/542-6600, Fax: 617/542-5670, Co Email: info@advmfg.com; Web URL: terra.net/amr; Focus: News and analysis on manufacturing information strategies; Format: Newsletter; Bruce Richardsen, Ed. Tony Friscia, Pblshr & Pres Circ.: 3,500, Freq:

10/Year

Amy D. Wohl's TrendsLetter

Publishing Co: Wohl Associates, 915 Montgomery Ave, #309, Narberth, PA 19072, USA; 610/667-4842, Fax: 610/667-3081, Co Email: awohl@mcimail.com; Focus: Analysis and opinions on emerging technologies; Format: Newsletter; Amy D. Wohl, Ed. Email: awohl@mcimail.com; Freq: Monthly, Price/yr-$:495

Andrew Seybold's Outlook

Publishing Co: Pinecrest Press Inc., PO Box 917, Brookdale, CA 95007, USA; 408/338-7701, Fax: 408/338-7806, Co Email: aseybold@mcimail.com; Focus: Reviews, opinions and trends in mobile computing; Format: Newsletter; Andrew M. Seybold, Ed-in-Chief Email: aseybold@mcimail.com; Linda M. Seybold, Mgng Ed. Email: 74431.1647@compuserve.com; Freq: Monthly, Price/yr-$:395/425

Annals of the History of Computing

Publishing Co: IEEE Computer Society, 445 Hoes Lane, PO Box 1331, Piscataway, NJ 08855-1331, USA; 908/981-0060, Fax: 908/981-9667, Co Email: @ieee.org; Web URL: ieee.org; Focus: Chronicles of vital contributions and their impact on society; Format: Magazine; J.A.N. Lee, Ed-in-Chief True Seaborn, Pblshr Freq: 4/Year, Price/yr-$:26

Annex Computer Report

Publishing Co: Annex Holdings Corp., 5110 N 40th Street, #100, Phoenix, AZ 85018, USA; 602/956-8586, Fax: 602/956-8594, Focus: News, analysis and pricing trend for IBM and other mainframe computers; Format: Newsletter; Robert Djurdjevic, Ed. Freq: Monthly, Price/yr-$:775

ANSI Catalog of American National Standards

Publishing Co: American National Standards Institute, 11 W. 42nd Street, New York, NY 10036, USA; 212/642-4900, Fax: 212/398-0023, Web URL: ansi.org; Focus: Listing of nearly 10,500 national standards; Format: Directory; Freq: Annual, Price/yr-$:20

Apple Directions

Publishing Co: Apple Computer Inc., 1 Infinite Loop, Cupertino, CA 95014, USA; 408/974-3264, Web URL: devworld.apple.com; Focus: Apple's strategy, technology and direction; Format: Newsletter; Gregg Williams, Ed. Email: greggw@apple.com; Freq: Monthly, Price/yr-$:49

Application Development Strategies

Publishing Co: Cutter Information Corp., 37 Broadway, Arlington, MA 02174-5539, USA; 617/648-8702, Fax: 617/648-1950, Co Email: 74107.653@compuserve.com; Web URL: cutter.com; Focus: Information on CASE, Client/Server and software development technologies; Format: Newsletter; Ed Yourdon, Ed. Karen Coburn, Group Pblshr Email: 73352.1625@compuserve.com; Freq: Monthly, Price/yr-$:427

Application Development Trends
Publishing Co: Software Productivity Group Inc., 1 Apple Hill, #301, Natick, MA 01532, USA; 508/652-1100, Fax: 508/393-3388, Web URL: spgnet.com; Focus: Information and trends for software developers; Format: Magazine; John Desmond, Ed. Elise Wilson, Pblshr Freq: 13/Year, Price/yr-$:Free/49

Applications & System Software
Publishing Co: Faulkner Information Services, 7905 Browning Road, Pennsauken, NJ 08109-4319, USA; 609/662-2070, Fax: 609/662-0905, Co Email: faulkner@faulkner.com; Web URL: faulkner.com; Focus: Product information on micro, mid-size and mainframe software; Format: Loose-leaf; Martin Murphy, Pblshr Freq: Monthly, Price/yr-$:1,035

Applications Development Software
Publishing Co: Datapro Information Services Group, 600 Delran Pkwy., Delran, NJ 08705-9904, USA; 609/764-0100, Fax: 609/764-2811, Co Email: datapro@mhh.com; Web URL: datapro.com; Focus: Information on software development tools for mainframe and mid-range computers; Format: CD-ROM; Freq: Monthly

Applications Software, Management of
Publishing Co: Datapro Information Services Group, 600 Delran Pkwy., Delran, NJ 08705-9904, USA; 609/764-0100, Fax: 609/764-2811, Co Email: datapro@mhh.com; Web URL: datapro.com; Focus: Information for software development and DP managers; Format: CD-ROM; Freq: Monthly

Artificial Life
Publishing Co: MIT Press Journals, 55 Hayward Street, Cambridge, MA 02142, USA; 617/253-2889, Fax: 617/258-6779, Co Email: journals-orders@mit.edu; Web URL: mitpress.mit.edu; Focus: Research on natural/artificial life-systems; Format: Magazine; Christopher G. Landton, Chief Ed. Email: cgl@santafe.edu; Circ.: 1,300, Freq: 4/Year, Price/yr-$:50

AS/400 Application Development Today
Publishing Co: IIR Publications Inc., 5650 El Camino Real, #225, Carlsbad, CA 92008-9711, USA; 619/931-8615, Fax: 619/931-9935, Web URL: as400.com; Focus: AS/400 software development trends and technology; Format: Newsletter; Freq: 6/Year, Price/yr-$:89

AS/400 Connectivity Expert
Publishing Co: IIR Publications Inc., 5650 El Camino Real, #225, Carlsbad, CA 92008-9711, USA; 619/931-8615, Fax:

619/931-9935, Web URL: as400.com; Focus: Technical and management aspects of AS/400 connectivity; Format: Newsletter; Freq: 6/Year, Price/yr-$:89

AS/400 Manufacturing & Distribution Today
Publishing Co: IIR Publications Inc., 5650 El Camino Real, #225, Carlsbad, CA 92008-9711, USA; 619/931-8615, Fax: 619/931-9935, Web URL: as400.com; Focus: AS/400 in manufacturing and distribution industries; Format: Newsletter; Freq: 6/Year, Price/yr-$:89

Asia IT Journal
Publishing Co: IDG Asia Business Development, 155 Bovet Road, #650, San Mateo, CA 94402, USA; 415/286-2766, Fax: 415/286-2790, Focus: Information on Asian computer market; Format: Newsletter; Hugo X. Hsiung, Ed. Email: h.hsiung@idg.geis.com; Freq: Monthly, Price/yr-$:395

Asian Sources Computer Products
Publishing Co: Asian Sources Media Group, 22/F Vita Tower, 29 Wong Chuk Hang Rd, Box 8952, Hong Kong, Hong Kong; 852-25554777, Fax: 852-28700940, Focus: Product news and sources for computer products from Asia; Format: Magazine; Spenser Au, Pblshr Rajendar Gopinath, Ed-in-Chief Freq: Monthly, Price/yr-$:75/150

ASR News
Publishing Co: Voice Information Association 14 Glenn Road S, PO Box 625, Lexington, MA 02173, USA; 617/861-6680, Fax: 617/863-8790, Web URL: tia.net/users/asrnews; Focus: News on automatic speech recognition industry; Format: Newsletter; John Oberteuffer, Pblshr Email: jober24@aol.com; Freq: Monthly, Price/yr-$:295

Asynchronous Transfer Mode
Publishing Co: Information Gatekeepers Inc., 214 Harvard Ave, Boston, MA 02134, USA; 617/232-3111, Fax: 617/734-8562, Co Email: igiboston@aol.com; Focus: ATM technology, standards, applications and markets; Format: Newsletter; Paul Polishuk, Ed. & Pblr Email: igiboston@aol.com; Freq: Monthly, Price/yr-$:545/595

Atlanta Computer Currents
Publishing Co: Jaye Communications Inc., 550 Interstate N Pkwy NW, #150, Atlanta, GA 30339, USA; 770/984-9444, Fax: 770/612-0780, Web URL: sid.com; Focus: Information for computer users in the southeast; Format: Newspaper; Mike Adkinson, Ed. & Pblr Circ.: 41,000, Freq: Monthly, Price/yr-$:15

AutoCAD Tech Journal
Publishing Co: Miller Freeman Inc., 600 Harrison Street, San Francisco, CA 94107-1391, USA; 415/905-2200, Fax: 415/905-2234, Focus: Information for AutoCAD users; Format: Magazine

AutoCAD World
Publishing Co: Publications & Communications Inc., 12416 Hymeadow Drive, Austin, TX 78750-1896, USA; 512/250-9023, Fax: 512/331-3900, Co Email: @pcinews.com; Web URL: pcinews.com/pci; Focus: Information for AutoCAD users; Format: Tabloid; Robert Martin, Ed. Larry Storer, Ed-in-Chief Tara Fowler Ross, Mngg Ed. Circ.: 30,000, Freq: Monthly, Price/yr-$:38/75

Automatic I.D. News
Publishing Co: Advanstar Communications Inc., 7500 Old Oak Blvd, Cleveland, OH 44130-3369, USA; 216/243-8100, Fax: 216/891-2733, Co Email: autoid@en.com; Web URL: autoidnews.com; Focus: Automated data capture products, technology and case studies; Format: Tabloid; Mark David, Ed-in-Chief Email: autoid@en.com; Diva Norwood, Pblshr Email: advansta@village.ios.com; Doris Kilbane, Mngg Ed. Circ.: 75,000, Freq: Monthly, Price/yr-$:Free/41

AV Video & Multimedia Producer
Publishing Co: Knowledge Industry Publishing, 701 Westchester Ave, White Plains, NY 10604, USA; 914/328-9157, Fax: 914/328-9093, Co Email: avmmp@kipi.com; Web URL: kipi.com; Focus: Information on computer graphics, video, audio, presentation & multimedia; Format: Magazine; Nick Dager, Ed. Roscoe Smith, Pblshr Circ.: 60,000, Freq: Monthly, Price/yr-$:53

Bank Automation News
Publishing Co: Phillips Business Information Inc., 1201 Seven Locks Road, #300, Potomac, MD 20854-1110, USA; 301/340-1520, Fax: 301/424-4297, Co Email: pbi@phillips.com; Web URL: phillips.com; Focus: News, analysis and trends in banking automation; Format: Newsletter; Freq: 25/Year, Price/yr-$:595

Bank Systems & Technology
Publishing Co: Miller Freeman Inc., 1515 Broadway, 32rd Floor, New York, NY 10036, USA; 212/869-1300, Fax: 212/302-6273, Focus: Technology trends for bank management; Format: Magazine; Circ.: 26,000, Freq: Monthly, Price/yr-$:56

BASIC TWO Report
Publishing Co: Midware Technology, 3 Ballard Way, Lawrence, MA 01843, USA; 508/682-8100, Fax: 508/682-9785, Co Email: email@midware.com; Web URL: midware.com; Focus: News, reviews and information for users of the Basic-2 language; Format: Magazine; Sam Gagliano, Pblshr Circ.: 2,500, Freq: 4/Year, Price/yr-$:Free/30

BASICPro
Publishing Co: Fawcette Technical Publications, 209 Hamilton Ave, Palo Alto, CA 94301-2530, USA; 415/917-7650, Fax: 415/853-0230, Focus: Information for

Basic programmers; Format: Magazine; James E. Fawcette, Ed. & Pblr Freq: 6/Year, Price/yr-$:34

BBS Magazine
Publishing Co: Callers Digest Inc., 701 Stokes Road, Medford, NJ 08055, USA; 609/953-9110, Fax: 609/953-7961, Co Email: @bbsmag.com; Focus: Information on the bulletin boards, online services and Internet; Format: Magazine; Richard Paquette, Pblshr Email: publisher@bbsmag.com; Richard W. Robinson, Ed-in-Chief Email: editor@bbsmag.com; Circ.: 48,000, Freq: Monthly, Price/yr-$:36

Beyond Computing
Publishing Co: IBM & New York Times Custom Publishing, 590 Madison Ave, 8th Floor, New York, NY 10022, USA; 212/745-6347, Fax: 212/745-6058, Web URL: beyondcomputingmag.com; Focus: Integration of business strategy and information technology; Format: Magazine; Arthur Chassen, Pblshr Eileen Feretic, Ed-in-Chief Email: eferetic@vnet.ibm.com; Adam Greenberg, Mgng Ed. Circ.: 150,000, Freq: 9/Year, Price/yr-$:Free/40

Bits & Bytes Review
Publishing Co: Bits & Bytes Computer Resources, 623 N. Iowa Ave, Whitefish, MT 59937, USA; 406/862-7280, Co Email: xb.j24@Forsythe.Stanford.edu; Focus: Reviews and news of computer products and resources for academic users; Format: Newsletter; Claire M. Hughes, Asst Ed. John Hughes, Ed. & Pblshr Freq: 4/Year, Price/yr-$:55/70

Blaster
Publishing Co: Blaster Publishing Inc., PO Box 469037, Escondido, CA 92046-9820, USA; Fax: 510/704-7128, Focus: Information for youths empowered by digital technology; Format: Magazine; Craig LaGrow, Pblshr Doug Millison, Ed-in-Chief Jon Phillips, Ed. Freq: Monthly, Price/yr-$:19.95

Boardwatch Magazine
Publishing Co: Boardwatch Magazine, 8500 W. Bowles Ave #210, Littleton, CO 80123-3275, USA; 303/973-6038, Fax: 303/973-3731, Co Email: @boardwatch.com; Focus: Guide to online services; Format: Magazine; Jack Rickard, Ed. & Pblr John Hart, Assist Ed. Freq: Monthly, Price/yr-$:36

boot Magazine
PO Box 51481, Boulder, CO 80323-1481, USA; Web URL: bootnet.com; Focus: Information on PC and software; Format: Magazine; Price/yr-$:39

Borland C++ Developer's Journal
Publishing Co: Cobb Group, The, 9420 Bunsen Pkwy. #300, Louisville, KY 40220, USA; 502/491-1900, Fax: 502/491-8050, Co Email: cobb@aol.com; Web URL: cobb.com; Focus: Tips and techniques for Borland C++ users; Format: Newsletter; Tim Gooch, Ed. Freq:

Monthly, Price/yr-$:69

Broadband Networking
Publishing Co: Datapro Information Services Group, 600 Delran Pkwy., Delran, NJ 08705-9904, USA; 609/764-0100, Fax: 609/764-2811, Co Email: datapro@mhh.com; Web URL: datapro.com; Focus: Information on high-speed communications products and technologies; Format: CD-ROM; Freq: Monthly

Broadband Networking News
Publishing Co: Phillips Business Information Inc., 1201 Seven Locks Road, #300, Potomac, MD 20854-1110, USA; 301/340-1520, Fax: 301/424-4297, Co Email: pbi@phillips.com; Web URL: phillips.com; Focus: News, standards and trends in the broadband networking industry; Format: Newsletter; Freq: 25/Year, Price/yr-$:597

Burton Group News Analysis, The
Publishing Co: Burton Group, 7040 Union Park Center, Midvale, UT 84047, USA; 801/566-2880, Fax: 801/566-3611, Co Email: info@tbg.com; Web URL: tbg.com; Focus: Summary and analysis of important network computing news events; Format: Newsletter; Jamie Lewis, Ed. Craig Burton, Pblshr Freq: Monthly, Price/yr-$:795

Burton Group Report on Network Computing
Publishing Co: Burton Group, 7040 Union Park Center, Midvale, UT 84047, USA; 801/566-2880, Fax: 801/566-3611, Co Email: info@tbg.com; Web URL: tbg.com; Focus: In-depth analysis and evaluation of strategic issues in network computing; Format: Newsletter; Jamie Lewis, Ed. Craig Burton, Pblshr Freq: Monthly, Price/yr-$:1,895

Business Communications Review
Publishing Co: BCR Enterprises Inc., 950 York Road, #203, Hinsdale, IL 60521, USA; 630/986-1432, Fax: 630/323-5324, Co Email: info@bcr.com; Web URL: bcr.com; Focus: Information on voice and data communications; Format: Magazine; Fred S. Knight, Ed. Jerry A. Goldstone, Pblshr Freq: Monthly, Price/yr-$:45

Business Computing Brief
Publishing Co: FT Telecoms & Media Publishing, Maple House, 149 Tottenham Court Road, London, W1P 9LL, UK; 171-896-2222, Fax: 171-896-2274, Format: Newsletter; Price/yr-$:419

Business Documents
Publishing Co: North American Publishing Co., 401 N. Broad Street, Philadelphia, PA 19108, USA; 215/238-5300, Fax: 215/238-5457, Co Email: editor@bfls.napco.com; Focus: Electronic and printed forms; Format: Magazine; Judith Cavaliere, Pblshr John S. Rosenberg, Ed. Laura D'Alessandro, Mgng Ed. Freq: 10/year, Price/yr-$:198/238

Business Equipment HOTLINE
Publishing Co: Business Technology Assoc., 12411 Wornall Road, Kansas City, MO 64175-1166, USA; 816/941-3100, Fax: 816/941-8034, Focus: News on business equipment; Format: Loose-leaf; Brent Hoskins, Ed. Peter Wilkinson, Assoc Ed. Circ.: 1,000, Freq: Bimonthly, Price/yr-$:30

Business Geographics
Publishing Co: GIS World Inc., 166 E. Boardwalk, #250, Ft. Collins, CO 805252, USA; 970/223-4848, Fax: 970/223-5700, Co Email: firstname@gisworld.com; Web URL: gisworld.com; Focus: Information on geographic technology uses; Format: Magazine; Joann Treadwell, Ed. Email: joann@gisworld.com; Freq: 6/Year, Price/yr-$:92

Business Marketing
Publishing Co: Crain Communications Inc., 740 N. Rush Street, Chicago, IL 60611-2590, USA; 312/649-5260, Fax: 312/649-5462, Web URL: adage.com; Focus: News and information about high-tech marketing; Format: Newspaper; Bill Furlong, Pblshr Karen Egolf, Ed. Freq: Monthly, Price/yr-$:44

Business Process Strategies
Publishing Co: Cutter Information Corp., 37 Broadway, Arlington, MA 02174-5539, USA; 617/648-8702, Fax: 617/648-1950, Co Email: 74107.653@compuserve.com; Web URL: cutter.com; Focus: Business process and reengineering; Format: Newsletter; Stowe Boyd, Ed. Karen Coburn, Group Pblshr Email: 73352.1625@compuserve.com; Freq: Monthly, Price/yr-$:395

Business System Magazine
Publishing Co: Corry Publishing, 2820 W. 21st Street, Erie, PA 16506-2970, USA; 814/664-8624, Fax: 814/664-7781, Focus: News and information for resellers of office automation products; Format: Magazine; Terry Peterson, Ed. Chuck Mancino, Pblshr Circ.: 35,000, Freq: Monthly, Price/yr-$:Free/39

BYTE Magazine
Publishing Co: McGraw-Hill Inc., One Phoenix Mill Lane, Peterborough, NH 03458, USA; 603/924-9281, Fax: 603/924-2550, Co Email: 71367.1054@compuserve.com; Focus: Product information, reviews and news for knowledgeable PC users; Format: Magazine; David Egan, Pblshr Raphael Needleman, Ed-in-Chief Circ.: 505,000, Freq: Monthly, Price/yr-$:29.95

C++ Journal
Publishing Co: Imagesoft Inc., 2 Haven Ave, Port Washington, NY 11050, USA; 516/767-2233, Focus: News, tips and techniques for C++ users; Format: Magazine; Edward Currie, Pblshr Circ.: 15,000, Freq: 4/Year, Price/yr-$:32

C++ Report

Publishing Co: SIGS Publications Group, 71 W. 23rd Street, 3rd Floor, New York, NY 10010, USA; 212/242-7447, Fax: 212/242-7574, Co Email: 73361.1707@compuserve.com; Web URL: sigs.com; Focus: Information for C++ programmers; Format: Magazine; Richard P. Friedman, Pblshr Kathleen M. Major, Mgng Ed. Doug Schmidt, Ed. Email: schmidt@cs.wustl.edu; Freq: 10/Year, Price/yr-$:69

C/C++ Users Journal
Publishing Co: Miller Freeman Inc., 1601 W. 23rd Street, #200, Lawrence, KS 66046, USA; 913/841-1631, Fax: 913/841-2624, Co Email: cujsub@rdpub.com; Focus: Advanced solutions for C/C++ programmers; Format: Magazine; P.J. Plauger, Ed. Peter Hutchinson, Pblshr Edwin Rothrock, Dir Sales & Mktg Email: edwin@rdpub.com.; Circ.: 40,000, Freq: Monthly, Price/yr-$:34.95

Cable Optics
Publishing Co: Information Gatekeepers Inc., 214 Harvard Ave, Boston, MA 02134, USA; 617/232-3111, Fax: 617/734-8562, Co Email: igiboston@aol.com; Focus: Fiber optics technology and applications for CATV industry; Format: Newsletter; Paul Polishuk, Ed. & Pblr Email: igiboston@aol.com; Freq: Monthly, Price/yr-$:545/595

Cable-Telco Report, The
Publishing Co: BRP Publications Inc., 1333 H Street NW #1100. W. Tower, Washington, DC 20005, USA; 202/842-3006, Fax: 202/842-3047, Co Email: brp@access.digex.net; Focus: Follows competition & collaboration with cable TV & telephone cos. to bring services; Format: Newsletter; Andrew Jacobson, Pblshr Victoria A. Mason, Ed.-in-Chief Karen A. Kinard, Ed. Freq: Biweekly, Price/yr-$:547

CAD Rating Guide, The
Publishing Co: ZEM Press, 8220 Stone Trail Drive, Bethesda, MD 20817-4556, USA; 301/365-1159, Fax: 319/365-4586, Co Email: 72377.2060@compuserve.com; Focus: Evaluation of over 140 CAD programs; Format: Factbook; Freq: Annual, Price/yr-$:150

CAD/CAM, CAE: Survey, Review and Buyer's Guide
Publishing Co: Daratech Inc., 140 Sixth Street, Cambridge, MA 02142, USA; 617/354-2339, Fax: 617/354-7822, Co Email: daratech@daratech.com; Web URL: daratech.com; Focus: News, surveys, reviews, profiles and analysis of the CAD/CAM/CAE industries; Format: Newsletter; Bruce Jenkins, Ed. Charles Foundyller, Pblshr Freq: Monthly, Price/yr-$:972

CADalyst
Publishing Co: Advanstar Communications Inc., 201 E Sandpointe Ave, #600, Santa Ana, CA 92707-5761, USA; 714/513-8400, Fax: 714/513-8612, Co Email: 73417.167@compuserve.com; Web URL: advanstar.com/cadalyst; Focus: News and reviews for AutoCad users; Format: Magazine; Dana Woodsmall, Pblshr Gene Smarte, Ed-in-Chief David Cohen, Sr Ed. Circ.: 70,000, Freq: Monthly, Price/yr-$:39

CADENCE Magazine
Publishing Co: Miller Freeman Inc., 600 Harrison Street, San Francisco, CA 94107-1391, USA; 415/905-2276, Fax: 415/905-2499, Co Email: 76703.756@compuserve.com; Web URL: mfi.com/cadence; Focus: Using AutoCAD in professional environment; Format: Magazine; Kathleen Maher, Ed-in-Chief Johanna Kleppe, Pblshr Claire Goodhue, Assoc Pblshr Circ.: 73,000, Freq: Monthly, Price/yr-$:40

Calendars Directory
Publishing Co: Press Access, 120 Boylston Street, 10th Fl., Boston, MA 02166, USA; 617/542-6670, Fax: 617/542-6671, Co Email: faimc@aol.com; Focus: Editorial schedule of leading computer publications; Format: Directory; Freq: Annual

California Technology Stock Letter
Publishing Co: Murenove Inc., PO Box 308, Half Moon Bay, CA 94019-9911, USA; 415/726-8495, Fax: 415/726-8494, Focus: News and analysis of computer and high technology companies (Registered Investment Adviser; Format: Newsletter; Michael Murphy, Ed. & Pblr Freq: 24/year, Price/yr-$:295

Call Center Magazine
Publishing Co: Telecom Library Inc., 12 W. 21st Street, 10th Floor, New York, NY 10010, USA; 212/691-8215, Fax: 212/691-1191, Co Email: 6274700@mcimail.com; Focus: Information for companies using computers and high-tech to build sales and deliver customers; Format: Magazine; Keith Dawson, Ed. Email: keith_dawson@mcimail.com; Harry Newton, Pblshr Email: harrynewton@mcimail.com; Circ.: 47,000, Freq: Monthly, Price/yr-$:14

CALS/CE Report
Publishing Co: Knowledge Base Int'l., 5700 NW Central Drive, #160, Houston, TX 77092, USA; 713/690-7644, Fax: 713/690-7645, Co Email: 75250.3326@compuserve.com; Focus: Information on DoD's CALS and CE initiatives; Format: Newsletter; William G. Beasley, Ed. Freq: Monthly, Price/yr-$:295

Canadian Computer Reseller
Publishing Co: Maclean Hunter Ltd., 777 Bay Street, Toronto, Ontario M5W 1A7, Canada; 416/596-5000, Fax: 416/593-3166, Co Email: ccr@inforamp.net; Focus: Information for Canadian computer resellers; Format: Magazine; Steve McHale, Ed. Paul Edwards, News Ed. Robin Calvfleisch, News Ed. Circ.: 15,000,

Freq: 24/Year

Capacity Management Review
Publishing Co: ICCM, a Demand Technology Company, 1020 8th Ave S. #6, Naples, FL 33940, USA; 813/261-8945, Fax: 813/261-5456, Focus: Information on computer performance and capacity management; Format: Newsletter; Mark Friedman, Ed. & Pblr Phillip Howard, Ed. Freq: Monthly, Price/yr-$:295

Card Technology Today
Publishing Co: SJB Services, 576 5th Ave, #1103, New York, NY 10036, USA; 212/221-5000, Fax: 212/221-5958, Focus: Application and technology news about memory cards, smart cards, IC cards etc.; Format: Newsletter; Sarah Brown, Ed. & Pblr Freq: 10/Year, Price/yr-$:475

Carronad's Interactive Media Directory
Publishing Co: Carronade Group, The, 7140 E Ring Street, Long Beach, CA 90808, USA; 310/493-2330, Fax: 310/493-5119, Co Email: fort@sirius.com; Web URL: carronade.com; Focus: Listing of multimedia products and vendors; Format: Directory; Jon Samsel, Pblshr Clancy Fort, Pblshr Freq: 2/Year, Price/yr-$:150

CD-ROM Computing: State of the Market
Publishing Co: Fairfield Research Inc., 5815 S 58th Street, Lincoln, NE 68516-3688, USA; 402/441-3370, Fax: 402/441-3389, Co Email: fairfield@cybersurvey.com; Web URL: cybersurvey.com; Focus: Survey-based data on CD-ROM ownership and usage; Format: Factbook; Ted Lannan, Pres Freq: Annual, Price/yr-$:795

CD-ROM Finder
Publishing Co: Information Today Inc., 143 Old Marlton Pike, Medford, NJ 08055-8750, USA; 609/654-6266, Fax: 609/654-4309, Co Email: custserv@infotoday.com; Web URL: infotoday.com; Focus: Listing of over 2,000 CD-ROM titles; Format: Directory; James H. Shelton, Ed. Kathleen Hogan, Ed. Freq: Annual, Price/yr-$:70

CD-ROM Professional
Publishing Co: Pemberton Press, 462 Danbury Road, Wilton, CT 06897-2126, USA; 203/761-1466, Fax: 203/761-1444, Focus: Information on CD-ROM industry; Format: Magazine; Adam C. Pemberton, Pblshr Freq: Monthly, Price/yr-$:55

CD-ROM Today
Publishing Co: GP Publications Inc., 1350 Bayshore Hwy, #210, Burlingame, CA 94010-1811, USA; Focus: CD-ROM and personal multimedia applications; Format: Magazine; Lance Elko, Edit Dir Chris Anderson, Pres Circ.: 132,000, Freq: Monthly, Price/yr-$:49.95

CD-ROMs in Print
Publishing Co: Mecklermedia, 20 Ketchum Street, Westport, CT 06880-9760, USA; 203/226-6967, Fax: 203/454-5840, Co

Email: info@mecklermedia.com; Focus: Directory of 8,000 CD-ROM titles & 4,000 companies in worldwide market; Format: Directory/CD-ROM; Matthew Finlay, Mngg Dir Regina Rega, Ed. Kim Herald, Assoc Ed. Freq: Annual, Price/yr-$:130/50

CeBIT News
Publishing Co: Asian Sources Media Group, Hoornzeelstraat 21A, Brussels, B-3080, Belgium; 322-766-0031, Fax: 322-768-0084, Focus: Newspaper at CeBIT trade show; Format: Newspaper; Philip Gallagher, Ed. Dir Keith Waller, Mngg Ed. Steve Homer, Assist Ed

CeBIT: Guide to the USA Pavilion
Publishing Co: Asian Sources Media Group, Hoornzeelstraat 21A, Brussels, B-3080, Belgium; 322-766-0031, Fax: 322-768-0084, Focus: Directory of American technology at CeBIT trade show; Format: Directory; Philip Gallagher, Ed. Dir

Channelmarker Letter, The
Publishing Co: Merrin Information Services Inc., 2275 E. Bayshore Road, #101, Palo Alto, CA 94303, USA; 415/493-5050, Fax: 415/493-5480, Focus: News, opinions and analysis of PC distribution channels and dealer-vendor relations; Format: Newsletter; Seymour Merrin, Ed. & Pblr Freq: Monthly, Price/yr-$:499/599

Charles Babbage Institute Newsletter
Publishing Co: Charles Babbage Institute, Univ. Minnesota, 103 Walter Lib, 117 Pleasent St., Minneapolis, MN 55455, USA; 612/624-5050, Fax: 612/625-8054, Co Email: cbi@vx.cis.umn.edu; Web URL: cbi.umn.edu; Focus: History of information processing; Format: Newsletter

Cheifet Letter, The
Publishing Co: Computer Chronicles, PCTV, 322 N Main Street, Newport, NH 03773, USA; 603/863-9322, Fax: 603/863-7316, Co Email: 74774.13@compuserve.com; Web URL: pctv.com; Focus: PC trends as seen on PBS TV series Computer Chronicles; Format: Newsletter; Stewart Cheifet, Ed. Email: 70555.276@compuserve.com; Sara O'Brien, Assist Ed. Email: 74774.75@compuserve.com; Circ.: 2,875, Freq: 8/Year, Price/yr-$:32.50

Chicago Journal of Theoretical Computer Science
Publishing Co: MIT Press Journals, 55 Hayward Street, Cambridge, MA 02142, USA; 617/253-2889, Fax: 617/258-6779, Co Email: journals-orders@mit.edu; Web URL: mitpress.mit.edu; Focus: Research on mathematical foundations of computing.; Format: Internet; Janson Simon, Ed.-in-Chief Email: chicago-journal@cs.uchica; Circ.: 150, Price/yr-$:30

Chicago Software Newspaper
2 N Riverside Plaza, #2400, Chicago, IL 60606, USA; Co Email: chisoft@aol.com;

Web URL: chisoft.com; Focus: Midwest software information; Format: Newspaper; Douglas Green, Pblshr Alan Earls, Ed-in-Chief

China Telecom Report
Publishing Co: ITC Publications, 4340 East-West Hwy, #1020, Bethesda, MD 20814-4411, USA; 301/907-0060, Fax: 301/907-6555, Co Email: 71011.2475@compuserve.com; Focus: News, analysis and forecast on Chinese telecom market; Format: Newsletter; Edward G. Czarnecki, Mngg Dir Freq: Monthly, Price/yr-$:679

CICS Update
Publishing Co: Xephon, 1301 W. Hwy 407, #201-450, Lewisville, TX 75067, USA; 817/455-7050, Fax: 817/455-2492, Focus: News, tips and software to improve IBM's CICS; Format: Magazine; Freq: Monthly, Price/yr-$:225

CIO
Publishing Co: CIO Communications Inc., 492 Old Connecticut Path, Framingham, MA 01701-9208, USA; 508/872-0080, Fax: 508/879-7784, Web URL: cio.com; Focus: Management perspectives for CIO, MIS and executives interested in information issues; Format: Magazine; Lew McCreary, Ed. Dir Joseph L. Levy, Pblshr Abbie Lundberg, Ed. Circ.: 80,000, Freq: 21/Year, Price/yr-$:Free/98

Circuit Cellar INK: The Computer Applications Journal
Publishing Co: Circuit Cellar Inc., 4 Park Street, Suite 20, Vernon, CT 06066, USA; 860/875-2751, Fax: 860/872-2204, Co Email: editor@circellar.com; Focus: Information on embedded computer applications; Format: Magazine; Ken Davidson, Ed.-in-Chief Email: ken.davidson@circellar.co; Daniel Rodrigues, Pblshr Circ.: 45,000, Freq: Monthly, Price/yr-$:21.95

Cisco World
Publishing Co: Publications & Communications Inc., 12416 Hymeadow Drive, Austin, TX 78750-1896, USA; 512/250-9023, Fax: 512/331-3900, Co Email: @pcinews.com; Web URL: pcinews.com/pci; Focus: Internetworking and technology; Format: Magazine; Larry Storer, Ed. Dir Robert Martin, Ed. Circ.: 20,000, Freq: Monthly, Price/yr-$:92/140

Classroom Connect
Publishing Co: Wentworth Worldwide Media, 1866 Colonial Village Ln., Lancaster, PA 17601, USA; 717/393-1000, Fax: 717/393-5752, Co Email: connect@classroom.net; Web URL: classroom.net; Focus: Road map to help teachers & students travel the information highway.; Format: Newsletter; Circ.: 20,000, Freq: 9/Year, Price/yr-$:39

Client Server Management HandiGuide
Publishing Co: Positive Support Review Inc., 2500 Broadway, #320, Santa Monica,

CA 90404-3061, USA; 310/453-6100, Fax: 310/453-6253, Co Email: info@psrinc.com; Focus: Information for managing and implementing C/S systems; Format: Book/diskette; M. Victor Janulaitis, Pblr & Ed. Price/yr-$:395/795

ClieNT Server News
Publishing Co: G2 Computer Intelligence Inc., 3 Maple Place, PO Box 7, Glen Head, NY 11545-9864, USA; 516/759-7025, Fax: 516/759-7028, Focus: News, trends and analysis of Microsoft Windows NT; Format: Newsletter; Maureen O'Gara, Pblshr Stuart Zipper, Ed. Freq: Weekly, Price/yr-$:595

Client/Server Analyst
Publishing Co: Datapro Information Services Group, 600 Delran Pkwy., Delran, NJ 08705-9904, USA; 609/764-0100, Fax: 609/764-2811, Co Email: datapro@mhh.com; Web URL: datapro.com; Focus: Information on C/S products, technology & trends; Format: CD-ROM; Freq: Monthly

Client/Server Computing
Publishing Co: Sentry Publishing Company Inc., 1 Research Drive, #400B, Westborough, MA 01581-3907, USA; 508/366-2031, Fax: 508/366-8104, Co Email: clientserver@mcimail.com; Focus: News and information on next generation information systems; Format: Magazine; John Kerr, Ed-in-Chief Donald E. Fagan, Pblshr Valerie E.M. Elmore, Mngg Ed. Circ.: 90,000, Freq: Monthly, Price/yr-$:Free/65

Client/Server Computing
Publishing Co: Faulkner Information Services, 7905 Browning Road, Pennsauken, NJ 08109-4319, USA; 609/662-2070, Fax: 609/662-0905, Co Email: faulkner@faulkner.com; Web URL: faulkner.com; Focus: Management and implementation issues on C/S platforms, architecture, software and systems; Format: Loose-leaf; Martin Murphy, Pblshr Freq: Monthly, Price/yr-$:1,545

Client/Server Today
Publishing Co: Cahners Publishing Co., 275 Washington Street, Newton, MA 02158-1630, USA; 617/964-3030, Fax: 617/558-4759, Co Email: @cstoday.com; Focus: Client/server products, technologies and trends; Format: Magazine; Jack Fegreus, Ed.-in-Chief Email: jackf@cstoday.com; Peter Nicas, Pblshr Email: nicas@cstoday.com; Elaine M. Cummings, Mngg Ed. Email: elainec@cstoday.com; Freq: Monthly, Price/yr-$:Free/65

Client/Server Tool Watch
Publishing Co: Hurwitz Consulting Group Inc., 29 Crafts Street, #270, Newton, MA 02158, USA; 617/965-6900, Fax: 617/965-6901, Web URL: bluestone.com/hurwitz; Focus: News and analysis of software development tools; Format: Newsletter; Judith S. Hurwitz, Ed. & Pblr Email: jhur-

witz@world.std.com; Chet Geschickter, Sr Ed. Freq: Monthly, Price/yr-$:347

Cognizer Almanac 1996-1997
Publishing Co: Cognizer Co., 801 W. El Camino Real, #150, Mt. View, CA 94040, USA; 415/965-4561, Fax: 415/968-0834, Focus: Source book on neural net, fuzzy logic, genetic algorithms and virtual reality; Format: Directory; Tom Schwartz, Pres Email: tjs@cup.portal.com; Freq: Annual, Price/yr-$:395

Collected Algorithms from the ACM
Publishing Co: Association for Computing Machinery, 1515 Broadway, 17th Floor, New York, NY 10036, USA; 212/869-7440, Fax: 212/944-1318, Web URL: acm.org; Focus: Machine-readable code listing of algorithms published in ACM journals; Format: Magazine; Tim Hopkins, Ed. Carol Meyer, Pblshr Circ.: 2,000, Freq: 4/Year, Price/yr-$:90

Color Business Report
Publishing Co: Blackstone Research Associates, PO Box 345, Uxbridge, MA 01569-0345, USA; 508/278-3449, Fax: 508/278-7975, Focus: Color printers, color copiers, color scanners and related products; Format: Newsletter; Michael Zeis, Ed. & Pblr Freq: Monthly, Price/yr-$:375/425

Color Publishing
Publishing Co: PennWell Publishing Co., 10 Tera Blvd, 5th Floor, Nashua, NH 03062-2801, USA; 603/891-9166, Fax: 603/891-0539, Co Email: @pennwell.com; Web URL: pennwell.com; Focus: Color electronic publishing and pre-press; Format: Magazine; Tom McMillan, Ed. Email: tomm@pennwell.com; Paul McPherson, Pblshr Email: paulm@pennwell.com; Circ.: 23,000, Freq: 6/Year, Price/yr-$:Free/20

Comdex Show Daily
Publishing Co: Softbank COMDEX, 300 First Ave, Needham, MA 02194, USA; 617/449-6600, Fax: 617/449-5756, Focus: Daily newspaper at COMDEX Fall and Spring trade shows; Format: Newspaper; Vic Farmer, Ed. Dir Circ.: 44,000, Freq: Daily, Price/yr-$:Free

Common Knowledge
Publishing Co: IIR Publications Inc., 5650 El Camino Real, #225, Carlsbad, CA 92008-9711, USA; 619/931-8615, Fax: 619/931-9935, Web URL: as400.com; Format: Magazine

Communication Systems Design
Publishing Co: Miller Freeman Inc., 600 Harrison Street, San Francisco, CA 94107-1391, USA; 415/905-2200, Fax: 415/905-2499, Focus: Information on communications design issues; Format: Magazine; Donna Esposito, Pblshr Email: desposito@mfi.com; Nicole Westmoreland, Sr Ed. Email: nwestmoreland@mfi.com; Price/yr-$:50

Communication Technology Update
Publishing Co: Technology Futures Inc.,

13740 Research Blvd, #C-1, Austin, TX 78726-1859, USA; 512/258-8898, Fax: 512/258-0087, Co Email: info@tfi.com; Web URL: tfi.com; Focus: Communication technologies; Format: Factbook; August E. Grant, Ed. Price/yr-$:45

Communication Today
Publishing Co: Phillips Business Information Inc., 1201 Seven Locks Road, #300, Potomac, MD 20854-1110, USA; 301/340-1520, Fax: 301/424-4297, Co Email: pbi@phillips.com; Web URL: phillips.com; Focus: News and information on telecom industry; Format: Newsletter; Freq: Daily, Price/yr-$:1,495

Communications Business & Finance
Publishing Co: BRP Publications Inc., 1333 H Street NW #1100. W. Tower, Washington, DC 20005, USA; 202/842-3006, Fax: 202/842-3047, Co Email: brp@access.digex.net; Focus: Finance & investment activities in converging telecom, cable TV, wireless & multimedia ind; Format: Newsletter; Victoria Mason, Ed-in-Chief Andrew Jacobson, Pblshr Freq: Biweekly, Price/yr-$:547

Communications Industries Report
Publishing Co: International Communications Industries Assoc., 11242 Waples Mill Road, #200, Fairfax, VA 22030, USA; 703/273-7200, Fax: 703/278-8082, Co Email: icia@icia.org; Web URL: usa.net/icia; Focus: Information and news on video, multimedia, telecom, interactive and computer industries; Format: Newspaper; Dick Larsen, Mgng Ed. Email: dlarsen@atwood.com; Price/yr-$:Free/35

Communications Networking Services
Publishing Co: Datapro Information Services Group, 600 Delran Pkwy., Delran, NJ 08705-9904, USA; 609/764-0100, Fax: 609/764-2811, Co Email: datapro@mhh.com; Web URL: datapro.com; Focus: Information for managing phone and data services; Format: CD-ROM; Freq: Monthly

Communications News
Publishing Co: Nelson Publishing, 305 Spring Creek Village, Dallas, TX 75248, USA; 972/644-0830, Co Email: ktensillo@mcimail.com; Focus: Applications for networking and information management; Format: Magazine; Kevin Tensillo, Ed. Circ.: 71,000, Freq: Monthly, Price/yr-$:Free/35

Communications of the ACM
Publishing Co: Association for Computing Machinery, 1515 Broadway, 17th Floor, New York, NY 10036, USA; 212/869-7440, Fax: 212/869-0481, Web URL: acm.org; Focus: ACM membership magazine containing technical papers on computer science; Format: Magazine; Mark Mandelbaum, Dir Pubs Jacques Cohen, Ed.-in-Chief Diane Crawford, Exec. Ed.

Email: crawford@acmvm.bitnet; Circ.: 85,000, Freq: Monthly, Price/yr-$:31

Communications Standards & Architecture
Publishing Co: Datapro Information Services Group, 600 Delran Pkwy., Delran, NJ 08705-9904, USA; 609/764-0100, Fax: 609/764-2811, Co Email: datapro@mhh.com; Web URL: datapro.com; Focus: Detailed specifications of proprietary and open telecom standards; Format: CD-ROM; Freq: Monthly

CommunicationsWeek
Publishing Co: CMP Publications Inc., 600 Community Drive, Manhasset, NY 11030, USA; 516/562-5530, Fax: 516/562-5055, Co Email: cwk@halldata.com; Web URL: commweek.com; Focus: News about the communications industry; Format: Newspaper; Mike Azzara, Pblshr Mitch Irsfeld, Ed-in-Chief Donna Miskin, Mgng Ed. Email: 5983683@mcimail.com; Circ.: 165,000, Freq: Weekly, Price/yr-$:Free/155

CommunicationsWeek Int'l.
Publishing Co: CMP Publications Inc., 600 Community Drive, Manhasset, NY 11030, USA; 516/562-5530, Fax: 516/365-5474, Focus: International communications industry; Format: Newspaper; Wendy Byrne, Pblshr Graham Finnie, Ed. Email: @gfinnie.demon.co.uk; Jennifer L. Schenker, Sr Exec Ed. Email: jschenke@cmp.com; Freq: Weekly, Price/yr-$:Free/150

Compensation in the MIS/dp Field
Publishing Co: Abbott, Langer & Assoc., 548 First Street, Crete, IL 60417, USA; 708/672-4200, Fax: 708/672-4674, Focus: Salary and bonus information; Format: Factbook; Steven Langer, Pblshr Freq: Annual, Price/yr-$:750

Compu-Mart
Publishing Co: James Publishing & Associates, 899 Presial Drive, #110, Richardson, TX 75081-2953, USA; 214/238-1133, Fax: 214/238-1132, Co Email: themartmag@aol.com; Focus: PC product ads and news; Format: Magazine; James Michael Story, Pblshr Sarah Klein, Ed. Circ.: 35,000, Freq: Weekly, Price/yr-$:80

CompuServe Magazine
Publishing Co: CompuServe Inc., 5000 Arlington Centre Blvd., Columbus, OH 43220, USA; 614/457-8600, Co Email: 70003.3731@compuserve.com; Focus: Information on CompuServe's online services and computer information industry; Format: Magazine; Calvin F. Hamrick III, Pblshr Kassie Rose, Ed. Gregor Gilliom, Sr Ed. Circ.: 550,000, Freq: Monthly, Price/yr-$:Free/30

Computational Linguistics
Publishing Co: MIT Press Journals for ACL, 55 Hayward Street, Cambridge, MA 02142, USA; 617/253-2889, Fax: 617/258-6779, Co Email: journals-

orders@mit.edu; Web URL: mit-press.mit.edu; Focus: Natural/artificial language-system design/analysis; Format: Magazine; Julia Hirschberg, Ed. Email: acl@research.att.com; Circ.: 1,500, Freq: 4/Year, Price/yr-$:98

Computer Advertising & Marketing Strategies
Publishing Co: Simba Information Inc., 11 River Bend Drive S, PO Box 4234, Stamford, CT 06807-0234, USA; 203/834-0033, Fax: 203/358-5825, Co Email: simba@aol.com; Web URL: simba-net.com; Focus: Review, trends & forecasts for computer advertising; Format: Reference book; Chris Elwell, Gr Pblr Freq: Annual, Price/yr-$:1,150

Computer Advisers' Media Advisor
PO Box 67, Wayland, MA 01778-9914, USA; 508/358-0293, Fax: 508/358-2798, Focus: Information for computer media advertisers; Format: Newsletter; Jack Edmonston, Ed. & Pblr Email: jacked-mons@aol.com; Freq: Monthly, Price/yr-$:249

Computer Aided Design Report
Publishing Co: CAD/CAM Publishing Inc., 1010 Turquoise Street, #320, San Diego, CA 92109-1268, USA; 619/488-0533, Fax: 619/488-6052, Focus: News, analysis and survey results about the CAD/CAM market; Format: Newsletter; Jeanette De Wyze, Ed. L. Stephen Wolfe, Pblshr Freq: Monthly, Price/yr-$:189

Computer Animation Producers, Directory of
Publishing Co: Pixel-The Computer Animation News People Inc., 109 Vanderhoof Ave #2, Toronto, Ontario M4G 2H7, Canada; 416/424-4657, Fax: 416/424-1812, Focus: Listing of computer animation companies, schools, products and people; Format: Directory; Robi Roncarelli, Ed. & Pblr Price/yr-$:64

Computer Applications in Power Magazine
Publishing Co: IEEE Power Engineering Society, 445 Hoes Lane, PO Box 1331, Piscataway, NJ 08855-1331, USA; 908/981-0060, Fax: 908/981-9667, Co Email: @ieee.org; Web URL: ieee.org; Focus: Computer applications for design, operation and control of power systems; Format: Magazine; Freq: 4/Year, Price/yr-$:Assn. Dues

Computer Artist
Publishing Co: PennWell Publishing Co., 10 Tara Blvd. 5th Floor, Nashua, NH 03062-2801, USA; 603/891-0123, Fax: 603/891-0539, Co Email: @pennwell.com; Web URL: pennwell.com; Focus: Digital imaging, illustration and design; Format: Magazine; Tom McMillan, Ed. Email: tomm@pennwell.com; Paul McPherson, Pblshr Nancy A. Hitchcock, Assoc Ed. Circ.: 20,000, Freq: 6/Year, Price/yr-$:29.70

Computer Business Review
Publishing Co: APT Data Services Inc., 27 E 21st Street, 3rd Floor, New York, NY 10010, USA; 212/677-0409, Fax: 212/677-0463, Co Email: @apt.usa.globalnews.com; Web URL: power.globalnews.com; Focus: Computer, communications & microelectronics industries; Format: Newsletter; Kenny MacIver, Ed. Email: cbred@power.globalnews.co; Mark Satchell, Pblshr Email: mark@apt.usa.globalnews.com; Tom Hackwood, Sls Mgng Email: tom@apt.usa.globalnews.com.; Freq: Monthly, Price/yr-$:195/295

Computer Buyer's Guide & Handbook
Publishing Co: Bedford Communications, 150 Fifth Ave, New York, NY 10011, USA; 212/807-8220, Fax: 212/807-8737, Focus: PC product reviews, comparisons and special issues on desktop publishing, printers, laser; Format: Magazine; Ephraim Schwartz, Ed.-in-Chief Edward Brown, Pblshr Edward Schneider, Sr. Ed. Circ.: 50,000, Freq: Monthly, Price/yr-$:36

Computer Catalogs: Shop by Mail, Phone or Fax
Publishing Co: Todd Publications, PO Box 301, West Nyack, NY 10994, USA; Fax: 914/358-6213, Focus: Consumer guide of over 350 mail order catalogs; Format: Reference Book; Barry Klein, Pblr & Ed. Freq: Yearly, Price/yr-$:25

Computer Currents
Publishing Co: Computer Currents Publishing Inc., 5720 Hollis, Emeryville, CA 94608, USA; 510/547-6800, Fax: 510/547-4613, Co Email: 73554.3010@compuserve.com; Focus: Regional editions to users in Bay Area, S. California, Boston, Houston, Dallas & Atlanta; Format: Newspaper; Stan Politi, Pblshr Robert Luhn, Ed.-in-Chief Doug Dineley, Assoc Ed. Circ.: 400,000, Freq: 24/Year, Price/yr-$:29.95

Computer Data Storage Newsletter
Publishing Co: Micro-Journal Publishing Co., 11 rue de Provence, Paris, F-75009, France; 331-42463056, Fax: 331-48242276, Co Email: 100565.3667@compuserve.com; Focus: News and information on magnetic and optical disk and tape industry; Format: Newsletter; Jean-Jacques Maleval, Ed. & Pblr Circ.: 500, Freq: Monthly, Price/yr-$:325

Computer Design
Publishing Co: PennWell Publishing Co., 10 Tara Blvd. 5th Floor, Nashua, NH 03062-2801, USA; 603/891-0123, Fax: 603/891-0514, Co Email: @pennwell.com; Web URL: computer-design.com; Focus: Computer system design, development and system integration; Format: Magazine; Ronald Karjian, Mgng Ed. Email: rkarjian@pennwell.com;

Bob Haavind, Ed-in-Chief Email: bobh@pennwell.com; Robert Ziegel, Grp Pblshr Email: bobz@pennwell.com; Freq: 13/Year, Price/yr-$:Free/99

Computer Economics Report
Publishing Co: Computer Economics Inc., 5841 Edison Place, Carlsbad, CA 92008, USA; 619/438-8100, Fax: 619/431-1126, Co Email: cer@compecon.com; Focus: New, views and analysis on medium and large computers (cost comparisons, price/performance; Format: Newsletter; Mark McManus, Ed.-in-Chief Email: mmc-manus@compecon.com; Bruno Bassi, Pblshr Freq: Monthly, Price/yr-$:595

Computer Economics Sourcebook
Publishing Co: Computer Economics Inc., 5841 Edison Place, Carlsbad, CA 92008, USA; 619/438-8100, Fax: 619/431-1126, Co Email: ces@compecon.com; Focus: Prices, residual value and price/performance of computer systems; Format: Newsletter; Mark McManus, Ed.-in-Chief Email: mmcmanus@compecon.com; Bruno Bassi, Pblshr Freq: Annual, Price/yr-$:1,495

Computer Entertainment News
Publishing Co: CEN Publishing Inc., 360 Mountain Avenue, Piedmont, CA 94611, USA; 510/601-9275, Fax: 510/658-3757, Co Email: cennews@aol.com; Focus: Entertainment and education software news for software resellers; Format: Newspaper; Lance Elko, Ed. Dir David English, Ed. Freq: 24/Year, Price/yr-$:Free/147

Computer Events Directory
Publishing Co: KnowledgeWeb, Inc., 9 Laurel Place, #7, San Rafael, CA 94901, USA; 415/485-5508, Fax: 415/485-5508, Co Email: info@kweb.com; Web URL: www.kweb.com; Focus: Listing of computer conferences and events; Format: Email, Online; David Fox, Email: david@kweb.com; Kelli Fox, Email: kelli@kweb.com; Circ.: 50,000+, Freq: Daily, Price/yr-$:Free

Computer Fraud & Security
Publishing Co: Elsevier Science, PO Box 945, Madison Square Station, New York, NY 10160-0757, USA; 212/633-3750, Fax: 212/633-3764, Focus: Computer security information; Format: Factbook; Circ.: 2,000, Price/yr-$:352

Computer Gaming World
Publishing Co: Ziff-Davis Publishing Co., 135 Main Street, San Francisco, CA 94105-1812, USA; Fax: 714/283-3444, Focus: Strategy & adventure game software; Format: Magazine; Johnny Wilson, Ed. Russell Sipe, Pblshr Circ.: 110,000, Freq: Monthly, Price/yr-$:28

Computer Graphics World
Publishing Co: PennWell Publishing Co., 10 Tara Blvd. 5th Floor, Nashua, NH 03062-2801, USA; 603/891-0123, Fax: 603/891-0539, Co Email: @pennwell.com; Web URL: pennwell.com;

Focus: News and information about computer graphics products and technology; Format: Magazine; Stephen Porter, Ed. Email: stevep@pennwell.com; Audrey V. Doyle, Mngng Ed. Email: audreyd@pennwell.com; Circ.: 70,300, Freq: Monthly, Price/yr-$:Free/48

Computer Hot Line
Publishing Co: United Advertising Periodicals, 15400 Knoll Trail, #330, Dallas, TX 75248, USA; Fax: 214/233-5514, Focus: Ads for buying and selling new and used computers, services & supplies; Format: Magazine; George Sparkman, Pblshr Circ.: 20,000, Freq: Weekly, Price/yr-$:119

Computer Industry Almanac
Publishing Co: Computer Industry Almanac Inc., PO Box 600, Glenbrook, NV 89413, USA; 702/749-5053, Fax: 702/749-5864, Co Email: cialmanac@aol.com; Focus: Reference book about the computer industry; Format: Almanac/CD/Onlin; Karen Petska-Juliussen, Ed.-in-Chief Email: cialmanac@aol.com; Egil Juliussen, Pres Email: cialmanac@aol.com; Freq: Annual, Price/yr-$:53/63

Computer Industry Forecasts
Publishing Co: Data Analysis Group, 5100 Cherry Creek Rd, PO Box 128, Cloverdale, CA 95425, USA; 707/539-3009, Fax: 707/486-5618, Co Email: dataag@interserv.com; Focus: Summary of forecast and market shares for computers, peripherals and software from over 60; Format: Factbook; Keith R. Parker, Ed. Reny Parker, Editorial Assist Freq: 4/Year, Price/yr-$:325

Computer Industry Report
Publishing Co: International Data Corp., 5 Speen Street, Framingham, MA 01701-9908, USA; 617/872-8200, Fax: 617/626-4205, Focus: News, trends, analysis and statistics on the computer industry; Format: Newsletter; Freq: 24/year, Price/yr-$:495

Computer Journal, The
Publishing Co: Adventure Publishing, PO Box 700686, Tulsa, OK 74170-0686, USA; Fax: 918/621-2135, Focus: Non-technical computer newspaper; Format: Newspaper; Cheryl Cooper, Ed-in-Chief Circ.: 30,000, Freq: Monthly, Price/yr-$:24

Computer Law & Tax Report
Publishing Co: Roditti Reports Corp., 954 Lexington Ave, #283, New York, NY 10021, USA; 212/879-3325, Fax: 212/879-4496, Focus: News, tax developments and legislation regarding computer law; Format: Newsletter.Book; Esther C. Roditti, Ed. & Pblr Freq: Monthly, Price/yr-$:280/380

Computer Law Forms Handbook
Publishing Co: Clark Boardman Callagan, 155 Pfingsten Road, Deerfield, IL 60015-4998, USA; 847/948-7000, Fax: 847/948-9340, Co Email: cbcservice@cbclegal.com; Web URL: cbclegal.com; Focus:

Over 100 computer law forms; Format: Factbook; Freq: Annual, Price/yr-$:110

Computer Law Strategist
Publishing Co: Leader Publications, 345 Park Ave S., New York, NY 10010, USA; 212/779-9200, Fax: 212/696-1848, Focus: Trends and actions from top law firms regarding computer cases; Format: Newsletter; Julian Millstein, Ed. Email: mmstrat@ljextra.com; Stuart Wise, Pblshr Edward Pisacreta, Ed. Freq: Monthly, Price/yr-$:214

Computer Life
Publishing Co: Ziff-Davis Publishing Co., 135 Main Street, San Francisco, CA 94105, USA; 415/357-5355, Fax: 415/357-5455, Co Email: ceditors.notes@mail.zd.ziff.co; Focus: Information on home PCs and high-tech products; Format: Magazine; John Dickinson, Ed-in-Chief Jim Stafford, Pblshr Chris Shipley, Ed. Circ.: 300,000, Freq: Monthly, Price/yr-$:25

Computer Literature Index
Publishing Co: Applied Computer Research Inc., PO Box 82266, Phoenix, AZ 85071-2266, USA; 602/995-5929, Fax: 602/995-0905, Focus: Indexes over 300 periodicals, books, conference & government reports by subject & author; Format: Index; Alan Howard, Ed. Phillip Howard, Pblshr Freq: 4/Year, Price/yr-$:198.50

Computer Locator
Publishing Co: Asay Publishing, PO Box 670, Joplin, MO 64802-0670, USA; 417/781-9317, Fax: 417/781-0427, Focus: Information for computer resellers; Format: Newspaper; Roger Ashay, Pblshr Freq: Monthly, Price/yr-$:29

Computer Magazine
Publishing Co: IEEE Computer Society, 445 Hoes Lane, PO Box 1331, Piscataway, NJ 08855-1331, USA; 908/981-0060, Fax: 908/981-9667, Web URL: computer.org; Focus: Membership publication of IEEE Computer Society; Format: Magazine; Edward A. Parrish, Ed.-in-Chief Email: computer@wpi.edu; True Seaborn, Pblshr Email: t.seaborn@computer.org; Angela Burgess, Mngng Ed. Email: aburgess@computer.org; Circ.: 90,000, Freq: Monthly, Price/yr-$:Assn. Dues

Computer Magazine Publishing Market Forecast
Publishing Co: Simba Information Inc., 11 River Bend Drive S, PO Box 4234, Stamford, CT 06807-0234, USA; 203/834-0033, Fax: 203/358-5825, Co Email: simba@aol.com; Web URL: simba-net.com; Focus: Analysis of the computer magazine publishing industry; Format: Factbook; Chris Elwell, Gr Pblr Freq: Annual, Price/yr-$:1,995

Computer Monthly
Publishing Co: Vulcan Publications Inc., 1 Chase Corporate Drive, #300, Birmingham, AL 35244, USA; 205/988-9708, Fax: 205/987-3227, Focus: Listing of new and

used computer products; Format: Magazine; Trent R. Boozer, Pblshr Circ.: 90,000, Freq: 24/Year, Price/yr-$:Free

Computer Music Journal
Publishing Co: MIT Press Journals, 55 Hayward Street, Cambridge, MA 02142, USA; 617/253-2889, Fax: 617/258-6779, Co Email: journals-orders@mit.edu; Web URL: mitpress.mit.edu.; Focus: Technical musical information for computer music, digital sound synthesis, multimedia.; Format: Magazine; Stephen T. Pope, Ed. Email: cmj@cnmat.cnmat.berkeley.; Circ.: 3,900, Freq: 4/Year, Price/yr-$:45

Computer Price Watch
Publishing Co: Orion Research Corp., 14555 N. Scottsdale Road, #330, Scottsdale, AZ 85254-3457, USA; 602/951-1114, Fax: 602/951-1117, Co Email: orion@bluebook.com; Web URL: bluebook.com; Focus: Used values on computers and selected software; Format: Reference book; Roger Rohrs, Pblshr Email: orion@bluebook.com; Ken Strohmeyer, Email: kenstr@aol.com; Price/yr-$:40

Computer Publishing & Advertising Report
Publishing Co: Simba Information Inc., 11 River Bend Drive S, PO Box 4234, Stamford, CT 06807-0234, USA; 203/834-0033, Fax: 203/358-5825, Co Email: simba@aol.com; Web URL: simba-net.com; Focus: News and analysis on computer publishing and advertising; Format: Newsletter; Chris Elwell, Gr Pblr Linda Koop, Ed. Freq: 24/Year, Price/yr-$:525

Computer Publishing Market Forecast
Publishing Co: Simba Information Inc., 11 River Bend Drive S, PO Box 4234, Stamford, CT 06807-0234, USA; 203/834-0033, Fax: 203/358-5825, Co Email: simba33@aol.com; Web URL: simba-net.com; Focus: Statistics and forecast of the computer publishing industry; Format: Factbook; Chris Elwell, Pblshr Freq: Annual, Price/yr-$:1,995

Computer Reseller News
Publishing Co: CMP Publications Inc., 600 Community Drive, Manhasset, NY 11030, USA; 516/562-5000, Fax: 516/562-5636, Web URL: crn.com; Focus: News, reviews and trends about the computer reseller community; Format: Newspaper; Robert Faletra, Ed-in-Chief Email: rfaletra@cmp.com; Pam Watkins, Pub Dir Email: pwatkins@cmp.com; Robert C. DeMarzo, Ed. Email: rdemarzo@cmp.com; Circ.: 71,000, Freq: Weekly, Price/yr-$:Free/199

Computer Retail Week
Publishing Co: CMP Publications Inc., 600 Community Drive, Manhasset, NY 11030, USA; 516/733-6800, Web URL: techweb.cmp.com/crw; Focus: Computer retail stores, superstores, warehouse clubs

and department stores; Format: Newspaper; Keith Newman, Pblshr Email: knewman@cmp.com; Kevin Ferguson, Ed. Email: kferguso@cmp.com; Mark Harrington, Mngng Ed. Circ.: 28,000, Freq: Weekly, Price/yr-$:Free/180

Computer Retailers, Dealers & Distributors
Publishing Co: CSG Information Services, 3922 Coconut Palm Drive, Tampa, FL 33619-8321, USA; 813/664-6800, Fax: 813/664-6888, Focus: Directory of over 2,400 computer resellers with over 28,000 locations; Format: Directory; Mike Jarvis, Ed. Freq: Annual, Price/yr-$:275/795

Computer Security Journal
Publishing Co: Computer Security Institute, 600 Harrison Street, San Francisco, CA 94107, USA; 415/905-2626, Fax: 415/905-2218, Co Email: csi@mfi.com; Web URL: gocsi.com/csi; Focus: Technical articles on computer security; Format: Magazine; Richard Power, Ed. Circ.: 3,000, Freq: 2/Year, Price/yr-$:197

Computer Select
Publishing Co: Ziff Desktop Information, One Park Ave, New York, NY 10157, USA; 212/503-4400, Fax: 212/503-4414, Focus: One year of full text or abstract of hundreds of computer magazines; Format: CD-ROM; Freq: Monthly, Price/yr-$:1,395

Computer Shopper
Publishing Co: Ziff-Davis Publishing Co., One Park Ave, New York, NY 10016, USA; 212/503-3900, Fax: 212/503-3999, Web URL: cshopper.com; Focus: Reviews and large ad section for new/used computers, peripherals, software and employment.; Format: Newspaper; John Blackford, Ed-in-Chief Al DiGuido, Pblshr Eric Grevstad, Ed. Circ.: 435,000, Freq: 12/Year, Price/yr-$:39.50

Computer Software Agreements
Publishing Co: Warren Gorham Lamont, 31 St. James Ave, Boston, MA 02116-9372, USA; Fax: 617/451-0908, Co Email: sales@wgl.com; Web URL: wgl.com; Focus: Sample software agreements with explanations; Format: Looseleaf; Laurence Selby, Pblshr Paul Rosenthal, Mktng Dir Freq: 2/year, Price/yr-$:195

Computer Software Protection
Publishing Co: Clark Boardman Callagan, 155 Pfingsten Road, Deerfield, IL 60015-4998, USA; 847/948-7000, Fax: 847/948-9340, Co Email: cbcservice@cbclegal.com; Web URL: cbclegal.com; Focus: Software copyright, patents, trademarks, trade secrets, etc.; Format: Factbook; Freq: Annual, Price/yr-$:325

Computer Sources
Publishing Co: Asian Sources Media Group, 1038 Leigh Ave, #100, San Jose, CA 95126-4155, USA; 408/295-5900, Fax: 408/295-4595, Focus: PC product news

for resellers, OEMs and system integrators; Format: Magazine; Mary T. Lee, Mngng Ed. Angela LoSasso, Sr Ed. T.H. Garretson, Tech Ed. Circ.: 40,000, Freq: Monthly, Price/yr-$:Free

Computer Systems Laboratory
Publishing Co: National Institute of Standards & Technology, Technology Bldg, Rm B151, Gaithersburg, MD 20899-0001, USA; 301/975-2832, Fax: 301/948-1784, Co Email: mailserv@nist.gov; Format: Newsletter; Elizabeth B. Lennon, Ed. Email: lennon@enh.nist.gov; Freq: Monthly, Price/yr-$:Free

Computer Systems Series: Peripherals
Publishing Co: Datapro Information Services Group, 600 Delran Pkwy., Delran, NJ 08705-9904, USA; 609/764-0100, Fax: 609/764-2811, Co Email: datapro@mhh.com; Web URL: datapro.com; Focus: Information on peripherals; Format: CD-ROM; Freq: Monthly

Computer Systems Series: Software
Publishing Co: Datapro Information Services Group, 600 Delran Pkwy., Delran, NJ 08705-9904, USA; 609/764-0100, Fax: 609/764-2811, Co Email: datapro@mhh.com; Web URL: datapro.com; Focus: Analysis and evaluation of midrange to mainframe software packages; Format: CD-ROM; Freq: Monthly

Computer Systems Series: Systems & Overviews
Publishing Co: Datapro Information Services Group, 600 Delran Pkwy., Delran, NJ 08705-9904, USA; 609/764-0100, Fax: 609/764-2811, Co Email: datapro@mhh.com; Web URL: datapro.com; Focus: Information on computer products and technologies; Format: CD-ROM; Freq: Monthly

Computer Technology Review
Publishing Co: West World Productions Inc., 924 Westwood Blvd. #650, Los Angeles, CA 90024-2910, USA; 310/208-1335, Fax: 310/208-1054, Co Email: @wwpi.com; Focus: Computer technology reviews and trends for system integrators/VARs/OEMs; Format: Newspaper; George McNamara, Ed. Dir Email: george_mcnamara@wwpi.com; Pam McAllister, Pblshr Email: pam_johnson@wwpi.com; Mark C. Ferelli, Sr Ed. Email: mark_ferelli@wwpi.com; Circ.: 71,000, Freq: Monthly, Price/yr-$:Free/84

Computer Technology Trends: Analyses and Forecasts
Publishing Co: Technology Futures Inc., 13740 Research Blvd, #C-1, Austin, TX 78726-1859, USA; 512/258-8898, Fax: 512/258-0087, Co Email: info@tfi.com; Web URL: tfi.com; Focus: Technical progress in computers; Format: Factbook;

Adrian J. Poitras, Ed. Ray L. Hodges, Ed. Price/yr-$:995

Computer Telephony
Publishing Co: Computer Telephony Publishing Inc., 12 W. 21st Street, 10th Floor, New York, NY 10010, USA; 212/691-8215, Fax: 212/691-1191, Web URL: computertelephony.com; Focus: Computer and telephone integration; Format: Magazine; Harry Newton, Ed.-in-Chief Email: harrynewton@mcimail.com; Gerry Friesen, Pblshr Rick Luhmann, Ed. Email: rluhman@mcimail.com; Freq: Monthly, Price/yr-$:Free/17

Computer Times
Publishing Co: Louisville Computer Times, 3135 Sunfield Circle, Louisville, KY 40241, USA; 502/339-9672, Fax: 502/426-7585, Co Email: edcomtimes@prodigy.com; Focus: 8 regional newspaper in Ohio, Indiana, Kentucky & Tennessee; Format: Newspaper; Terry Kibiloski, Ed. Sean Kibiloski, Mngng Ed. Circ.: 60,000, Freq: Monthly, Price/yr-$:12

Computer Trade Show World
Publishing Co: Publications & Communications Inc., 12416 Hymeadow Drive, Austin, TX 78750-1896, USA; 512/250-9023, Fax: 512/331-6779, Co Email: @pcinews.com; Web URL: pcinews.com/pci; Focus: Listing of upcoming computer tradeshows; Format: Online; Freq: Bimonthly, Price/yr-$:45/75

Computer Video
Publishing Co: JRS Publishing, 5827 Columbia Pike, 3rd Fl., Falls Church, VA 22041, USA; 703/998-7600, Fax: 703/998-2966, Focus: Information on video and computer graphics equipment; Format: Magazine; Stevan B. Dana, Pblshr John Spofford, Ed. Marlene Lane, Ed. Dir Freq: Bimonthly, Price/yr-$:Free

Computer-Aided Engineering
Publishing Co: Penton Publishing Inc., 1100 Superior Ave, Cleveland, OH 44114-2543, USA; 216/696-7000, Fax: 216/696-1309, Co Email: 72302.247@compuserve.com; Web URL: penton.com; Focus: Computer systems and applications in design, analysis, manufacturing and product management; Format: Magazine; Larry Boulden, Pblshr Robert Mills, Ed. Beverly Beckert, Mngng Ed. Circ.: 60,000, Freq: Monthly, Price/yr-$:50

Computergram
Publishing Co: APT Data Services Inc., 928 Broadway, #800, New York, NY 10010, USA; 212/677-0409, Fax: 212/677-0463, Co Email: @apt.usa.globalnews.com; Web URL: power.globalnews.com; Focus: Summary of computer industry news story; Format: Fax, e-mail; Mark Satchell, Pblshr Email: mark@apt.usa.globalnews.c; Peter White, US Ed. Freq: Daily, Price/yr-$:995

Computerized Investing
Publishing Co: American Association of Individual Investors, 625 N. Michigan Ave,

#1900, Chicago, IL 60611, USA; 312/280-0170, Fax: 312/280-1625, Co Email: aaiigenl@aol.com; Focus: News and analysis about computerized investing; Format: Newsletter; John Bajkowski, Ed. Email: jbajowski@aol.com; S. Gutierrez, Asst Ed. Email: aaiimike@aol.com; Circ.: 40,000, Freq: Bimonthly, Price/yr-$:30/60

ComputerLetter
Publishing Co: Technologic Partners, 120 Wooster Street, New York, NY 10012, USA; 212/343-1900, Fax: 212/343-1915, Focus: News, analysis and business trends in the computer industry; Format: Newsletter; Richard Shaffer, Ed. & Pblr John W. Wilson, Ed. Kenneth R. Graham, COO Freq: 40/year, Price/yr-$:595

Computers in Healthcare
Publishing Co: Argus Integrated Media, 6300 S Syracuse Way, #650, Englewood, CO 80111, USA; 303/220-0600, Fax: 303/267-0234, Focus: Information for computer users in the healthcare fields; Format: Magazine; Circ.: 16,500, Freq: 12/Year, Price/yr-$:29

Computers in Human Services
Publishing Co: Haworth Press Inc., 10 Alice Street, Binghamton, NY 13904-1580, USA; Fax: 800/895-0582, Focus: Computer usage in human services; Format: Journal; Dick Schoech, Ed. Freq: 4/Year, Price/yr-$:45

Computers in Libraries
Publishing Co: Information Today Inc., 143 Old Marlton Pike, Medford, NJ 08055-8750, USA; 609/654-6266, Fax: 609/654-4309, Co Email: custserv@infotoday.com; Web URL: infotoday.com; Focus: News and information about library information technology; Format: Magazine; David Hoffman, Ed. Freq: 10/Year, Price/yr-$:88

Computers in the Schools
Publishing Co: Haworth Press Inc., 10 Alice Street, Binghamton, NY 13904-1580, USA; Fax: 800/895-0582, Focus: School usage of computer; Format: Journal; D. LaMont Johnson, Ed. William Cohen, Pblshr Freq: 4/Year, Price/yr-$:40

ComputerUser
Publishing Co: MSP Communications, 220 S. 6th Street, #500, Minneapolis, MN 55402-4507, USA; 612/339-7571, Fax: 612/339-5806, Focus: Regional newspapers in 14 cities; Format: Newsprint Magazine; Steve Deyo, Ed. Gary Johnson, Pblshr Circ.: 650,000, Freq: Monthly, Price/yr-$:Free/25

Computerworld
Publishing Co: CW Publishing, 500 Old Connecticut Path, Framingham, MA 01701-9171, USA; 508/879-0700, Fax: 508/875-8931, Co Email: @cw.com; Web URL: computerworld.com; Focus: News and information about the computer industry for information systems managers; Format: Newspaper; Paul Gillin, Ed.

Mike Rogers, Pblshr Circ.: 140,000, Freq: Weekly, Price/yr-$:48

Computerworld Client/Server Journal
Publishing Co: CW Publishing, 500 Old Connecticut Path, Framingham, MA 01701-9171, USA; 508/879-0700, Fax: 508/872-2364, Co Email: @cw.com; Focus: Mgng next generation information systems; Format: Magazine; Gary Beach, Pblshr Alan Alper, Ed. Email: aalper@cw.com; Catherine McCrorey, Mgng Ed. Freq: Monthly, Price/yr-$:Free

Computing Channels
Publishing Co: Computing Technology Industry Association, 450 E 22nd Street, #230, Lombard, IL 60148-6158, USA; Format: Magazine; John A. Venator, Pblshr Janine Marte, Assoc Ed. Freq: 13/Year

Computing Information Directory
Publishing Co: Hildebrandt Inc., PO Box 534, Colville, WA 99114, USA; 509/684-7619, Fax: 509/684-7619, Co Email: darlench@wsu.edu; Focus: Computing literature index; Format: Handbook; Peter A. Hildebrandt, Pres Freq: Annual, Price/yr-$:230

Computing Japan
Publishing Co: LINC Japan Ltd., Hiroo AK Bldg 4F, 5-25-2 Hiroo, Shibuya-ku, Tokyo, JP-105, Japan; 3-3445-2616, Fax: 3-3447-4925, Focus: Information on Japanese computer industry; Format: Magazine; Terrie Lloyd, Pblshr William Auckerman, Ed-in-Chief Price/yr-$:70/130

Computing Research News
Publishing Co: Computing Research Association, 1875 Connecticut Ave NW, #718, Washington, DC 20009, USA; 202/234-2111, Fax: 202/667-1066, Co Email: info@cra.org; Web URL: cra.org; Focus: News, trends and analysis of federal and private computing research; Format: Newspaper; Joan Bass, Ed. Email: jbass@cra.org; Fred W. Weingarten, Ed. Dir Email: weingarten@cra.org; Circ.: 5,000, Freq: 5/Year, Price/yr-$:Free/25

Computing Reviews
Publishing Co: Association for Computing Machinery, 1515 Broadway, 17th Floor, New York, NY 10036, USA; 212/869-7440, Fax: 212/944-1318, Web URL: acm.org; Focus: Reviews and critiques selected refereed articles, books, conference and proceeding papers; Format: Magazine; Aaron Finerman, Ed. Carol Meyer, Pblshr Circ.: 7,000, Freq: Monthly, Price/yr-$:40

Computing Systems
Publishing Co: MIT Press Journals for the USENIX Association, 55 Hayward Street, Cambridge, MA 02142, USA; 617/253-2889, Fax: 617/258-6779, Co Email: journals-orders@mit.edu; Web URL: mit-press.mit.edu; Focus: Research on advanced operating systems, languages & networks; Format: Magazine; David L.

Presotto, Ed. Email: journal@usenix.org; Circ.: 6.300, Freq: 4/Year, Price/yr-$:60.00

Computing Teacher, The
Publishing Co: International Society for Technology in Education, 1787 Agate Street, Eugene, OR 97403-1923, USA; 541/346-4414, Fax: 541/346-5890, Focus: Information for teachers using computers for pre-college education; Format: Magazine; Anita Best, Ed. Circ.: 12,000, Freq: 8/Year, Price/yr-$:Free/46

CompuTrade Int'l.
Publishing Co: Arco Publication Inc., 3F-2, Section 1, No 5, Pateh Road, Taipei, Taiwan ROC; 2-396-5128, Fax: 2-396-4511, Focus: Asian PC product trends for OEM and volume buyers; Format: Newspaper; Freq: 24/Year, Price/yr-$:220

Conference Analysis Newsletter
Publishing Co: Giga Information Group, 1 Kendall Square, Bldg 1400W, Cambridge, MA 02139, USA; 617/577-9595, Fax: 617/577-1649, Focus: Detailed reports and critiques on computer conferences; Format: Newsletter; Don Felice, Ed. Email: dfelice@gigasd.com; Freq: 24/Year, Price/yr-$:495

Consumer Online Services Report
Publishing Co: Jupiter Communications Co., 627 Broadway, New York, NY 10012, USA; 212/780-6060, Fax: 212/780-6075, Co Email: jup5@aol.com; Web URL: jup.com/jupiter; Focus: Analysis, forecasts development in the online market; Format: Factbook; Freq: Annual, Price/yr-$:1,895

Converging Communications Technologies
Publishing Co: Faulkner Information Services, 7905 Browning Road, Pennsauken, NJ 08109-4319, USA; 609/662-2070, Fax: 609/662-0905, Co Email: faulkner@faulkner.com; Web URL: faulkner.com; Focus: Profiles of services, providers and emerging communications technologies; Format: Loose-leaf; Martin Murphy, Pblshr Freq: Monthly, Price/yr-$:1,555

Copier Review
Publishing Co: Buyers Laboratory Inc., 20 Railroad Ave, Hackensack, NJ 07601, USA; 201/488-0404, Fax: 201/488-0461, Focus: News, prices and test results on copiers & multifunction devices; Format: Newsletter; Anthony Polifrone, Pres Marion Davidowitz, VP Burt Meerow, Pblr Freq: Monthly, Price/yr-$:385

Copier SpecCheck Guide
Publishing Co: Dataquest Inc., 26254 Golden Valley Road, #401, Santa Clarita, CA 95351, USA; 805/298-3261, Fax: 805/298-4388, Co Email: mmakers@net-com.com; Web URL: net-com.com~mmakers; Focus: Specifications of copiers; Format: Directory; Freq: 4/Year, Price/yr-$:40

Corel Magazine
Publishing Co: Omray Inc., 9801 Anderson Mill Rd, #207, Austin, TX 78750, USA; 512/250-1700, Fax: 512/219-3156, Co Email: 71164.15@compuserve.com; Web URL: corelmag.com; Focus: Information for Corel software users; Format: Magazine; Scott Campbell, Ed. Email: scottc@jumpnet.com; Jennifer Campbell, Features Ed. Email: jenc@jumpnet.com; Dave Baceski, Pblshr Circ.: 40,000, Freq: Monthly, Price/yr-$:39.95

CorelDRAW
Publishing Co: Cobb Group, The, 9420 Bunsen Pkwy. #300, Louisville, KY 40220, USA; 502/491-1900, Fax: 502/491-8050, Co Email: cobb@aol.com; Web URL: cobb.com; Focus: Tips and techniques for CorelDraw; Format: Newsletter; Freq: 10/Year, Price/yr-$:59

Corporate Internet Strategies
Publishing Co: Cutter Information Corp., 37 Broadway, Arlington, MA 02174-5552, USA; 617/648-8702, Fax: 617/648-1950, Co Email: 74107.653@compuserve.com; Web URL: cutter.com; Focus: Internet management and technical challenges; Format: Newsletter; Karen Fine Coburn, Pblshr Ed. Yourdon, Ed. Freq: Monthly, Price/yr-$:417

Corporate Intranet Solutions
Publishing Co: Gartner Group, PO Box 4332, Greenwich, CT 06830-9630, USA; Fax: 203/316-6774, Web URL: gartner.com; Focus: Intranet planning, development and transition; Format: Newsletter; William Robertson, Pblshr Freq: Monthly, Price/yr-$:495

Corporate Journal, The
2100 Douglas Blvd, Louisville, KY 40205, USA; 502/456-0808, Fax: 502/458-5066, Focus: Ed. insert in corporate newsletters; Sher Bolter, Ed.

Corporate Profiles
Publishing Co: IRG, 35200 Dequindre, Sterling Heights, MI 48310-4857, USA; 810/978-3000, Fax: 810/978-3010, Focus: Overview of a company's hardware and software; Format: Newsletter; Patricia Czekiel, Pblshr Freq: Monthly, Price/yr-$:250-500

Corporate Software & Solutions
Publishing Co: Datapro Information Services Group, 600 Delran Pkwy., Delran, NJ 08705-9904, USA; 609/764-0100, Fax: 609/764-2811, Co Email: datapro@mhh.com; Web URL: datapro.com; Focus: Information on corporate and departmental software; Format: CD-ROM; Freq: Monthly

CPA Computer Journalism Review
Publishing Co: Computer Press Association, 2E South Bldg. The Piano Factory,454 W 46th Street, New York, NY 10036, USA; 212/246-8631, Fax: 212/977-5894, Focus: Computer journalism; Format: Newsletter; Hal Glatzer, Ed. Email:

hglatzer@echonyc.com; Freq: Bimonthly
CPA PC Network Advisor
Publishing Co: Harcourt Brace Professional Publishing, 6277 Sea Harbor Drive, Orlando, FL 32821-9816, USA; Fax: 800/336-7377, Focus: Tips and information on PC networks; Format: Newsletter; Ken Rethmeier, Pblshr Freq: Monthly, Price/yr-$:217

Crossroads A-list
Publishing Co: Open Systems Advisors Inc., 268 Newbury Street, Boston, MA 02116-2403, USA; 617/859-0859, Fax: 617/859-0853, Co Email: finnerty@crossroads-osa.com; Web URL: crossroads-osa.com; Focus: Directory of newly proven products; Format: Online; Nina Lytton, Ed. Price/yr-$:free

CSL Newsletter
Publishing Co: National Institute of Standards & Technology, Technology Bldg, Rm B151, Gaithersburg, MD 20899-0001, USA; 301/975-2832, Fax: 301/948-1784, Co Email: @nist.gov; Focus: News about computer activities from the National Institute of Standards & Technology; Format: Newsletter; Elizabeth B. Lennon, Ed. Email: elizabeth.lennon@nist.gov; Freq: Monthly, Price/yr-$:Free

Culpepper Letter, The
Publishing Co: Culpepper & Associates Inc., 7000 Peachtree-Dunwoody Road, Bldg 10, Atlanta, GA 30328, USA; 770/668-0616, Fax: 770/668-1095, Co Email: @culpepper.com; Focus: Software sales productivity, pricing and promotion; Format: Newsletter; Mini Anderson, Ed. Email: mimi@culpepper.com; Warren Culpepper, Pblshr Email: warren@culpepper.com; Freq: Monthly, Price/yr-$:269

Current and Future Danger: Computer Crime and Information Warfare
Publishing Co: Computer Security Institute, 600 Harrison Street, San Francisco, CA 94107, USA; 415/905-2626, Fax: 415/905-2218, Co Email: prapalus@mfi.com; Focus: Areas of computer crime; Format: Newsletter; Richard Power, Ed. Price/yr-$:37

Curriculum Administrator
Publishing Co: Educational Media Inc., 992 High Ridge Road, Stamford, CT 06905, USA; 203/322-1300, Fax: 203/329-9177, Focus: Computer news for school district administrators; Format: Magazine; Joseph J. Hanson, Ed.-in-Chief Howard A. Reed, Pblshr Jane Ferguson, Ed. Circ.: 55,000, Freq: 10/Year, Price/yr-$:Free

CyberEdge Journal
Publishing Co: CyberEdge Information Services, 1 Gate Six Road, #G, Sausalito, CA 94965, USA; 415/331-3343, Fax: 415/331-3643, Co Email: info@cyberedge.com; Web URL: cyberedge.com; Focus: Information on VR and cybernetics; Format: Newsletter; Ben Delaney, Ed. &

Pblr Email: ben@cyberedge.com; Sherry Epley, Exec Ed. Freq: 6/Year, Price/yr-$:249

Dallas Ft. Worth Technology
Publishing Co: City Publishing Inc., 801 E. Campbell Road, #170, Richardson, TX 75081-1856, USA; 214/907-9977, Fax: 214/783-8854, Co Email: 71163.2653@compuserve.com; Focus: High-tech industry in Dallas-Ft. Worth area; Format: Newspaper; Tom Mattos, Mgng Ed. Charles W. Chen, Pblshr Circ.: 30,000, Freq: Monthly, Price/yr-$:Free

Dallas/Fort Worth Computer Currents
Publishing Co: Power Media Group, 1600 Promenade Center, #809, Richardson, TX 75080, USA; 214/690-6222, Fax: 214/690-6333, Co Email: currents@computek.net; Web URL: onramp.net/ccurrent; Focus: Computer users in Dallas/Fort Worth area; Format: Newspaper; Roger W. Powers, Pblshr Cade R. Herzog, Assoc Pblr Freq: Monthly, Price/yr-$:Free

Data Base Management
Publishing Co: Auerbach Publications, 31 St. James Ave, Boston, MA 02116-9372, USA; 617/423-2020, Fax: 617/451-0908, Co Email: 73752.2270@compuserve.com; Web URL: wgl.com; Focus: Information on selecting, implementing and maintaining database systems; Format: Loose-leaf; Kim Horan Kelly, Pblshr Freq: 6/Year, Price/yr-$:405

Data Based Advisor
Publishing Co: Advisor Publications Inc., 4010 Morena Blvd, San Diego, CA 92117, USA; 619/483-6400, Fax: 619/483-9851, Co Email: 71154.3123@compuserve.com; Focus: News and information for Lotus Notes users; Format: Magazine; William T. Ota, Pblr/Pres/CEO John L. Hawkins, Ed-in-Chief & EVP Jeanne Banfield, VP Circ.: 38,000, Freq: Monthly, Price/yr-$:39

Data Center Management, Handbook of
Publishing Co: Auerbach Publications, 31 St. James Ave, Boston, MA 02116-9372, USA; 617/423-2020, Fax: 617/451-0908, Co Email: 73752.2270@compuserve.com; Web URL: wgl.com; Focus: Information on managing data centers; Format: Handbook; Freq: Annual, Price/yr-$:150

Data Center Operations Management
Publishing Co: Auerbach Publications, 31 St. James Ave, Boston, MA 02116-9372, USA; 617/423-2020, Fax: 617/451-0908, Co Email: 73752.2270@compuserve.com; Web URL: wgl.com; Focus: Information on managing data centers; Format: Loose-leaf; Kim Horan Kelly, Pblshr Freq: 6/Year, Price/yr-$:405

Data Communications
Publishing Co: McGraw-Hill Inc., 1221 Avenue of the Americas, New York, NY 10020, USA; 212/512-2699, Fax: 212/

512-6833, Co Email: datacomm@mcgraw-hill.com; Focus: News and information on telecommunications and networking; Format: Magazine; Joseph Braue, Ed.-in-Chief Email: jbraue@mcgraw-hill.com; Lee Keough, Executive Ed. Email: lkeogh@mcgraw-hill.com; Circ.: 90,000, Freq: 16/Year, Price/yr-$:Free/125

Data Communications Management
Publishing Co: Auerbach Publications, 31 St. James Ave, Boston, MA 02116-9372, USA; 617/423-2020, Fax: 617/451-0908, Co Email: 73752.2270@compuserve.com; Web URL: wgl.com; Focus: Service on planning, developing and operating communications systems; Format: Loose-leaf; Kim Horan Kelly, Pblshr Freq: 6/Year, Price/yr-$:405

Data Management Review
Publishing Co: Powell Publishing Inc., 19380 Emerald Drive, Brookfield, WI 53045-3617, USA; 414/792-9696, Fax: 414/792-9777, Co Email: 74164.2427@compuserve.com; Web URL: dmreview.com; Focus: Client/server and object technology solutions; Format: Magazine; Lisa R. Ryan, Mgng Ed. Ronald J. Powell, Pblshr & Exec Ed. Email: rpowell@dmreview.com; Circ.: 53,196, Freq: Monthly, Price/yr-$:Free/35

Data Management, Handbook of
Publishing Co: Auerbach Publications, 31 St. James Ave, Boston, MA 02116-9372, USA; 617/423-2020, Fax: 617/451-0908, Co Email: 73752.2270@compuserve.com; Web URL: wgl.com; Focus: How-to-for data management functions; Format: Factbook; Barbara von Halle, Ed. David Kull, Ed. Freq: Annual, Price/yr-$:150

Data Networking
Publishing Co: Datapro Information Services Group, 600 Delran Pkwy., Delran, NJ 08705-9904, USA; 609/764-0100, Fax: 609/764-2811, Co Email: datapro@mhh.com; Web URL: datapro.com; Focus: Information on networking equipment and services, internetworking and interoperability; Format: CD-ROM; Freq: Monthly

Data Networks
Publishing Co: Faulkner Information Services, 7905 Browning Road, Pennsauken, NJ 08109-4319, USA; 609/662-2070, Fax: 609/662-0905, Co Email: faulkner@faulkner.com; Web URL: faulkner.com; Focus: LANs, internetworking, data communications systems and software; Format: Loose-leaf; Martin Murphy, Pblshr Freq: Monthly, Price/yr-$:2,285

Data Security Management
Publishing Co: Auerbach Publications, 31 St. James Ave, Boston, MA 02116-9372, USA; 617/423-2020, Fax: 617/451-0908, Co Email: 73752.2270@compuserve.com; Web URL: wgl.com; Focus: Information on technology and management for secure computer systems; Format: Loose-leaf;

Kim Horan Kelly, Pblshr Freq: 6/Year, Price/yr-$:405

Data Sources
Publishing Co: Ziff Communications Co., One Park Ave, New York, NY 10016-0317, USA; 212/503-5861, Fax: 212/503-5800, Focus: Listing of 75,000 computer-related products and vendors (Also on CD-ROM); Format: Directory; George Fisher, Ed. Seth Alpert, Pblshr Freq: 2/Year, Price/yr-$:595

Database Journal
Publishing Co: Cardinal Business Media Inc., 12225 Greenville Ave, #700, Dallas, TX 75243, USA; 214/669-9000, Fax: 214/669-9909, Co Email: 73430.2350@compuserve.com; Focus: News and technical information for database users and developers; Format: Magazine; Steven Crofts, Pblr & Ed-in-Chief Denny Yost, Assoc Pblr Circ.: 35,000, Freq: 6/Year, Price/yr-$:Free

Database Programming & Design
Publishing Co: Miller Freeman Inc., 600 Harrison Street, San Francisco, CA 94107-1391, USA; 415/905-2200, Fax: 415/905-2234, Focus: Technical information for database users; Format: Magazine; Circ.: 32,000, Freq: Monthly, Price/yr-$:47

DataLaw Report, The
Publishing Co: Clark Boardman Callagan, 155 Pfingsten Road, Deerfield, IL 60015-4998, USA; 847/948-7000, Fax: 847/948-9340, Co Email: cbcservice@cbclegal.com; Web URL: cbclegal.com; Focus: Analysis and information on global computer law; Format: Newsletter; Freq: 6/Year, Price/yr-$:250

Datamation
Publishing Co: Cahners Publishing Co., 275 Washington Street, Newton, MA 02158-1630, USA; 617/558-4281, Fax: 617/558-4506, Web URL: datamation.com; Focus: News and trends in the computer industry for information technology managers; Format: Magazine; J. William Semich, Ed.-in-Chief Email: bsemich@cahners.com; Carole Sacino, Pblshr Elizabeth Lindholm, Exec Ed. Email: elindholm@datamation.cahners.com; Circ.: 210,000, Freq: 24/Year, Price/yr-$:Free/75

DataTrends Report on DEC
Publishing Co: DataTrends Publications Inc., 30-C Catoctin Circle SE, Leesburg, VA 22075, USA; 703/779-0574, Fax: 703/779-2267, Co Email: dtrends@aol.com; Focus: Analysis and predictions of DEC's products and strategies; Format: Newsletter; Jeff Caruso, Ed. Email: jpcaruso@aol.com; Paul G. Ochs, Pblshr Freq: Monthly, Price/yr-$:625

DB2 Update
Publishing Co: Xephon, 1301 W. Hwy 407, #201-450, Lewisville, TX 75067, USA; 817/455-7050, Fax: 817/455-2492, Focus: News, tips and software to improve

IBM's DB2; Format: Magazine; Freq: Monthly, Price/yr-$:325

dBase Advisor
Publishing Co: Advisor Publications Inc., 4010 Morena Blvd, San Diego, CA 92117, USA; 619/483-6400, Fax: 619/483-9851, Co Email: 71154.3123@compuserve.com; Focus: News and information for dBase users; Format: Magazine; William T. Ota, Pblr/Pres/CEO John L. Hawkins, Ed-in-Chief & EVP Jeanne Banfield, VP Circ.: 25,000, Freq: 6/Year, Price/yr-$:29

DBMS
Publishing Co: Miller Freeman Inc., 411 Borel Ave, #100, San Mateo, CA 94402-3522, USA; 415/358-9500, Fax: 415/358-9855, Co Email: dbms@mfi.com; Web URL: dbmsmag.com; Focus: Database professionals who develop for client/server systems; Format: Magazine; David M. Kalman, Pblshr Maurice Frank, Ed. Circ.: 67,000, Freq: 13/Year, Price/yr-$:25

Dealerscope Consumer Electronics Marketplace
Publishing Co: North American Publishing Co., 401 N. Broad Street, Philadelphia, PA 19108, USA; 215/238-5300, Fax: 215/238-5457, Co Email: @napco.com; Focus: For CE, PC and major appliance retailers; Format: Tabloid; Bruce Alpert, Pblshr Jim Pavia, Ed-in-Chief Email: jpavia@napco.com; Janet Pinkerton, Mgng Ed. Email: jpinkerton@napco.com; Freq: Monthly, Price/yr-$:65

Dealerscope Goldbook
Publishing Co: North American Publishing Co., 401 N. Broad Street, Philadelphia, PA 19108, USA; 215/238-5300, Fax: 215/238-5283, Focus: Listing of consumer electronics vendors; Format: Directory/CD-ROM; Freq: Annual, Price/yr-$:349

Dealerscope Merchandising
Publishing Co: North American Publishing Co., 401 N. Broad Street, Philadelphia, PA 19108, USA; 215/238-5300, Fax: 215/238-5457, Co Email: @dm.napco; Focus: Information for consumer electronics and computer dealers; Format: Magazine; Martin M. Cohen, Pblshr Richard M. Sherwin, Ed.-in-Chief Janet Pinkerton, Mgng Ed. Freq: 6/Year, Price/yr-$:65

Defense @ Security Electronics
Publishing Co: Argus Business Publishing, 6300 S Syracuse Way, #650, Englewood, CO 80111, USA; 303/220-0600, Fax: 303/721-7227, Focus: Information on military electronics and security; Format: Magazine; C. Gregg Herring, Pblshr Circ.: 44,000, Freq: Monthly, Price/yr-$:38

Dell Insider
Publishing Co: Publications & Communications Inc., 12416 Hymeadow Drive, Austin, TX 78750-1896, USA; 512/250-9023, Fax: 512/331-3900, Co Email: @pcinews.com; Web URL: pcinews.com/pci; Focus: News for Dell computer users; Format: Magazine; Larry Storer, Ed-in-Chief

John Mitchell, Ed. Circ.: 20,000, Freq: Monthly, Price/yr-$:45

Delph Report, The
Publishing Co: Delphi Consulting Group, 100 City Hall Plaza, Boston, MA 02108-2106, USA; 617/247-1025, Fax: 617/247-4957, Web URL: delphigroup.com; Focus: News and information on EDMS, tends, technology business issues in text retrieval.; Format: Newsletter; Carl Frappaolo, Mgng Ed. Mike Muth, Ed. Freq: Monthly, Price/yr-$:195

Delphi Developer
Publishing Co: Pinnacle Publishing Inc., 18000 72nd Ave S. #217, Kent, WA 98032, USA; 206/251-1900, Fax: 206/251-5057, Web URL: pinpub.com; Focus: Information for Delphi users; Format: Newsletter; Freq: Monthly, Price/yr-$:79

Delphi Developer's Journal
Publishing Co: Cobb Group, The, 9420 Bunsen Pkwy. #300, Louisville, KY 40220, USA; 502/491-1900, Fax: 502/491-8050, Co Email: cobb@aol.com; Web URL: cobb.com; Focus: Tips and techniques for Borland Delphi users; Format: Newsletter; Tim Gooch, Ed. Freq: Monthly, Price/yr-$:59

Delphi Informant
Publishing Co: Informant Communications Group Inc., 10519 E. Stockton Blvd. #142, Elk Grove, CA 95624-9704, USA; 916/686-6610, Fax: 916/686-8497, Web URL: informant.com; Format: Magazine; Mitchell Koulouris, Pblshr Circ.: 14,000, Freq: Monthly, Price/yr-$:49.95

Delphi Workflow Report, The
Publishing Co: Delphi Consulting Group, 100 City Hall Plaza, Boston, MA 02108-2106, USA; 617/247-1511, Fax: 617/247-4957, Focus: Electronic document management systems; Format: Newsletter; Mike Muth, Ed. Thomas M. Kouloupoulos, Mgng Ed. Freq: Monthly, Price/yr-$:195

DemoLetter
Publishing Co: InfoWorld Publishing Co., 155 Bovet Road, #800, San Mateo, CA 94402-9821, USA; 415/312-0691, Fax: 415/312-0547, Co Email: info@pcletter.com; Web URL: pcletter.com; Focus: Analysis and opinions on events and products in the PC industry; Format: Newsletter; Chris Shipley, Ed. Circ.: 1,000, Freq: 22/Year, Price/yr-$:495

Dempa Digest
Publishing Co: Dempa Publications Inc., 275 Madison Ave, New York, NY 10016-1101, USA; 212/682-3755, Fax: 212/682-2730, Focus: News and information on Japan's electronics industry; Format: Newsletter; Tetsuo Hirayama, Pres Freq: Weekly, Price/yr-$:350

Design Tools Monthly
Publishing Co: The Nelson Group, 2111 30th Street, #H, Boulder, CO 80301-1125, USA; 303/444-6876, Fax: 303/440-3641, Web URL: ares.csd.net/~dtm;

Focus: News and information on electronic pre-press; Format: Newsletter; Jay J. Nelson, Ed. Freq: Monthly, Price/yr-$:99

Desktop Engineering
Publishing Co: Helmers Publishing Inc., 174 Concord Street, Peterborough, NH 03458-0874, USA; 603/924-9631, Fax: 603/924-7408, Co Email: de-editor@gold.mv.net; Focus: Computer information for engineers; Format: Magazine; Anthony J. Kockwood, Ed-in-Chief Email: lockwood@bix.com; John E. Hayes, Pblshr

Desktop Software & Solutions
Publishing Co: Datapro Information Services Group, 600 Delran Pkwy., Delran, NJ 08705-9904, USA; 609/764-0100, Fax: 609/764-2811, Co Email: datapro@mhh.com; Web URL: datapro.com; Focus: INformation on PC software; Format: CD-ROM; Freq: Monthly

Digital Age
Publishing Co: Cardinal Business Media Inc., 1300 Virginia Drive, #400, Ft. Washington, PA 19034-3225, USA; 215/643-8000, Fax: 215/643-3901, Co Email: @cardinal.com; Focus: Information for users of Digital Equipment Corp. technology; Format: Magazine; Charlie Simpson, Ed.-in-Chief Email: simpsoncm@cardinal.com; Leslie Ringe, Pblshr Deborah Schwartz, Assoc Ed. Email: schwartzdr@cardinal.com; Circ.: 50,000, Freq: Monthly, Price/yr-$:Free/30

Digital Chicago
Publishing Co: Peregrine Marketing Assoc. Inc., 515 E Golf Road, #201, Arlington Heights, IL 60005, USA; 847/439-6575, Co Email: digitalchi@aol.com; Web URL: digitalchi.com; Focus: Information for computer and Internet users in the Chicago area; Format: Magazine; Jennifer Dees, Ed. & Pblr Email: jdees@digitalchi.com; Suzanna Dees, Mgng Ed. Freq: 6/Year, Price/yr-$:15

Digital Creativity
Publishing Co: Cowles Business Media, 470 Park Ave S, #7N, New York, NY 10016, USA; 212/683-3540, Fax: 212/683-4364, Co Email: @cowlesbiz.com; Focus: People and processes of digital creativity; Format: Magazine; Roberta Thomas, Pblshr Email: roberta_thomas@cowlesbiz.; Anne M. Russell, Ed. Dir Email: anne_russell@cowlesbiz.com; Tim Bogardus, Ed-in-Chief Freq: 6/Year, Price/yr-$:36

Digital Directions Report
Publishing Co: Computer Economics Inc., 5841 Edison Place, Carlsbad, CA 92008, USA; 619/438-8100, Fax: 619/431-1126, Co Email: ddr@compecon.com; Focus: Financial, analysis, trends and forecasts on DEC computers; Format: Newsletter; Mark McManus, Ed.-in-Chief Email: mmcmanus@compecon.com; Bruno Bassi,

Pblshr Freq: Monthly, Price/yr-$:525

Digital Imaging
Publishing Co: Micro Publishing Press, 2340 Plaza del Amo, #100, Torrance, CA 90501, USA; 310/212-5802, Fax: 310/212-5226, Co Email: mcimpn; Focus: Information for users of graphics services; Format: Magazine; James Cavuoto, Ed. & Pblr David Griffith, Exec Ed. David Pope, Ed. Dir Circ.: 60,000, Freq: 6/Year, Price/yr-$:Free/25

Digital Kids Report
Publishing Co: Jupiter Communications Co., 627 Broadway, New York, NY 10012, USA; 212/780-6060, Fax: 212/780-6075, Co Email: jup5@aol.com; Web URL: jup.com/jupiter; Focus: News on interactive/online information for kids; Format: Newsletter; Gene DeRose, Pblshr Diana Simon, Ed. Yvette Simeon, Mgng Ed. Freq: Monthly, Price/yr-$:425

Digital Media
Publishing Co: Seybold Publications, 444 De Haro Street, #126, San Francisco, CA 94107, USA; 415/575-3775, Fax: 610/575-3780, Co Email: info@digmedia.com; Web URL: digmedia.com; Focus: Multimedia and related subjects; Format: Newsletter; Mitch Ratcliffe, Ed-in-Chief Email: godsdog@digmedia.com; Margie Wylie, Ed. Email: zeke@digmedia.com; Neil Mcmanns, Exec Ed. Email: neilm@digmedia.com; Freq: Monthly, Price/yr-$:395

Digital News & Review
Publishing Co: Cahners Publishing Co., 8773 S Ridgeline Blvd, Highlands Ranch, CO 80126-2329, USA; 303/470-4445, Fax: 303/470-4280, Co Email: @dnr.cahners.com; Focus: Product and technology trends for DEC computers; Format: Newspaper; Paul Nesdore, Pblshr Email: pauln@dnr.cahners.com; Stephen Lawton, Ed.-in-Chief Martha Spizziri, Exec Ed. Email: ms@dnr.cahners.com; Circ.: 89,000, Freq: Monthly, Price/yr-$:Free/96

Digital Output
Publishing Co: Axle Communications Inc., 250 Williams Street, #2212, Atlanta, GA 30303, USA; 404/524-6954, Fax: 404/524-7167, Co Email: digiout1@aol.com; Web URL: mindspring.com/digiout; Focus: Electronic publishing business news; Format: Tabloid; Tim Thornton, Pblshr Marilyn Barbie Kapaun, Ed. Freq: 12/Year, Price/yr-$:41

Digital Publisher
Publishing Co: Information Today Inc., 143 Old Marlton Pike, Medford, NJ 08055-8750, USA; 609/654-6266, Fax: 609/654-4309, Co Email: custserv@infotoday.com; Web URL: infotoday.com; Focus: Digital documents & multimedia information over networks and on disks; Format: Magazine; Peter Hyams, Ed. Freq: Monthly, Price/yr-$:179

Digital Systems Journal

Publishing Co: Cardinal Business Media Inc., 1300 Virginia Drive, #400, Ft. Washington, PA 19034-3225, USA; 215/643-8000, Fax: 215/643-8099, Focus: Software journal for Digital programming professionals; Format: Magazine; Karen Detwiler, Ed.-in-Chief Jeffrey S. Berman, Pblshr Circ.: 7,500, Freq: Bimonthly, Price/yr-$:60

Digital Unix News

Publishing Co: Publications & Communications Inc., 12416 Hymeadow Drive, Austin, TX 78750-1896, USA; 512/250-9023, Fax: 512/331-3900, Co Email: dec-news@pcinews.lonestar.org; Web URL: pcinews.com/pci; Focus: News and information for users of DEC Unix products; Format: Newspaper; Larry Storer, Ed.-in-Chief Kim Fulcher Linkins, Ed. Circ.: 20,000, Freq: 6/Year, Price/yr-$:Free/49

Digital Video

Publishing Co: Miller Freeman Inc., 600 Harrison Street, San Francisco, CA 94107-1391, USA; 415/905-2200, Fax: 415/905-2234, Format: Magazine

Digital Video Magazine

Publishing Co: ActiveMedia, 600 Townsend Street, #170E, San Francisco, CA 94103, USA; 415/522-2400, Fax: 415/522-2409, Focus: Desktop video products; Format: Magazine; Louis R. Wallace, Ed.-in-Chief Email: lou@dv.com; Dale Strang, Pblr & Pres Circ.: 75,000, Freq: Monthly, Price/yr-$:24.95

Dimensions

Publishing Co: Computerized Pricing Systems, 13650 Silverton Drive, Broomfield, CO 80020, USA; 303/469-0557, Fax: 303/460-0228, Co Email: 71175.1133@compuserve.com; Focus: Technical information for 4th Dimension database software users; Format: Magazine; Mark Yelich, Ed. & Pblr David Graves, Tech Ed. Freq: 6/Year, Price/yr-$:69/99

Directions on Microsoft

Publishing Co: Redmond Communications Inc., 15127 NE 24th Street, #293, Redmond, WA 98052, USA; 206/882-3396, Fax: 206/885-0848, Focus: Microsoft's products, services and strategic directions; Format: Newsletter; Robert Horwitz, Ed-in-Chief Jeff Parker, Pblshr Freq: 10/Year, Price/yr-$:595

Directory Publishing

Publishing Co: Simba Information Inc., 11 River Bend Drive S, PO Box 4234, Stamford, CT 06807-0234, USA; 203/834-0033, Fax: 203/358-5825, Co Email: simba33@aol.com; Web URL: simba-net.com; Focus: Directory publishing industry: Books, CD-ROMs, web and online; Format: Factbook; Freq: Annual, Price/yr-$:159

Disaster Recovery Journal

Publishing Co: Systems Support Inc., PO Box 510110, St. Louis, MO 63151, USA;

314/894-0276, Fax: 314/894-7474, Web URL: drj.com; Focus: Information on contingency planning, security and disaster recovery; Format: Magazine; Richard Arnold, Ed. & Pblr Circ.: 29,000, Freq: 4/Year, Price/yr-$:Free

Discontinued Copier Guide

Publishing Co: Dataquest Inc., 26254 Golden Valley Road, Bldg. 401, Santa Clarita, CA 95351, USA; 805/298-3261, Fax: 805/298-4388, Co Email: mmakers@net-com.com; Web URL: net-com.com~mmakers; Focus: Specifications and listing of discontinued copiers; Format: Directory; Freq: Annual, Price/yr-$:95

Display Devices

Publishing Co: Dempa Publications Inc., 275 Madison Ave, New York, NY 10016-1101, USA; 212/682-4755, Fax: 212/682-2730, Focus: Trends and display products--CRTs, ELs, LCDs, LEDs, PDPs and VFDs; Format: Magazine; Tetsuo Hirayama, Pres Freq: 2/Year, Price/yr-$:30

Distributed Computing Monitor

Publishing Co: Patricia Seybold Group, 148 State Street, 7th Floor, Boston, MA 02109-9990, USA; 617/742-5200, Fax: 617/742-1028, Web URL: psgroup.com; Focus: News, research and analysis on LANs, servers and networking; Format: Newsletter; Patricia B. Seybold, Pblshr Freq: Monthly, Price/yr-$:539

Distributed Systems Management Report.

Publishing Co: DataTrends Publications Inc., 30-C Catoctin Circle SE, Leesburg, VA 22075, USA; 703/779-0574, Fax: 703/779-2267, Co Email: dtrends@aol.com; Focus: News and analysis on distributed systems--vendors, products and technologies; Format: Newsletter; Jeff Caruso, Ed. Email: jpcaruso@aol.com; Paul G. Ochs, Pblshr Freq: Monthly, Price/yr-$:550

Do It With Lotus Smart Suite for Windows

Publishing Co: Lotus Publishing Corp., 77 Franklin Street #310, Boston, MA 02110, USA; 617/482-8634, Fax: 617/422-8189, Focus: Tips and techniques for Lotus Smart Suite users; Format: Newsletter; Craig G. Pierce, Pblshr Valerie Murray, Ed. David Bromley, Ed. Freq: Monthly, Price/yr-$:69/89/109

Do It With Macintosh System 7.5

Publishing Co: IDG Newsletters Corp., 77 Franklin Street, Boston, MA 02110-1510, USA; 617/482-8785, Fax: 617/338-0164, Focus: Tips and techniques for Mac System 7.5 users; Format: Newsletter; Craig G. Pierce, Pblshr Scott Fields, Ed. Sheila Sandapen, Ed. Freq: Monthly, Price/yr-$:69/89/109

Do It With Microsoft Office For Windows

Publishing Co: IDG Newsletters Corp., 77 Franklin Street, Boston, MA 02110-1510,

USA; 617/482-8785, Fax: 617/338-0164, Focus: Tips and techniques for Microsoft Office Users; Format: Newsletter; Craig G. Pierce, Pblshr Jim Pile, Ed. Cheryl Magadieu, Ed. Freq: Monthly, Price/yr-$:69/89/109

Do It With Microsoft Publisher for Windows

Publishing Co: IDG Newsletters Corp., 77 Franklin Street, Boston, MA 02110-1510, USA; 617/482-8785, Fax: 617/338-0164, Focus: Tips and techniques for Microsoft Pblshr users; Format: Newsletter; Craig G. Pierce, Pblshr Scott Fields, Ed. David Bromley, Ed. Freq: Monthly, Price/yr-$:69/89/109

Document Imaging Report

Publishing Co: Phillips Business Information Inc., 1201 Seven Locks Road, #300, Potomac, MD 20854-1110, USA; 301/340-1520, Fax: 301/424-4297, Co Email: pbi@phillips.com; Web URL: phillips.com; Focus: Information on imaging industry; Format: Newsletter; Freq: 25/Year, Price/yr-$:597

Document Imaging Systems

Publishing Co: Datapro Information Services Group, 600 Delran Pkwy., Delran, NJ 08705-9904, USA; 609/764-0100, Fax: 609/764-2811, Co Email: datapro@mhh.com; Web URL: datapro.com; Focus: Information on document imaging products and vendors; Format: CD-ROM; Freq: Monthly

Document Management

Publishing Co: Pinnacle Peak Publishing Ltd., 8711 E. Pinnacle Peak Road, #249, Scottsdale, AZ 85255-3555, USA; 602/585-5580, Fax: 602/585-7417, Web URL: docmanage.com; Focus: Document management trends and technologies; Format: Magazine; Richard N. Stover, Pblr & Mgng Ed. Herbert F. Schantz, Assoc Ed. Freq: 6/Year, Price/yr-$:30

Document Management & Imaging Systems

Publishing Co: Faulkner Information Services, 7905 Browning Road, Pennsauken, NJ 08109-4319, USA; 609/662-2070, Fax: 609/662-0905, Co Email: faulkner@faulkner.com; Web URL: faulkner.com; Focus: Reports on document management & imaging system technologies, vendors and products; Format: Looseleaf; Martin Murphy, Pblshr Freq: Monthly, Price/yr-$:1,120

Document Management Newstakes

Publishing Co: Dataquest Inc., 251 River Oaks Pkwy, San Jose, CA 95134, USA; 408/468-8000, Fax: 408/954-1780, Web URL: dataquest.com; Focus: Information on document management; Format: Newsletter; Freq: Monthly, Price/yr-$:595

DOS Authority, The

Publishing Co: Cobb Group, The, 9420 Bunsen Pkwy. #300, Louisville, KY 40220, USA; 502/491-1900, Fax: 502/

491-8050, Co Email: cobb@aol.com; Web
URL: cobb.com; Focus: Tips and techniques for advanced MS-DOS users; Format: Newsletter; Freq: 24/Year, Price/yr-
$:69

DOS Software Connection
Publishing Co: Cobb Group, The, 9420
Bunsen Pkwy. #300, Louisville, KY
40220, USA; 502/491-1900, Fax: 502/
491-8050, Co Email: cobb@aol.com; Web
URL: cobb.com; Format: Newsletter;
Price/yr-$:59

DOS World
Publishing Co: IDG Communications/
Peterborough, 86 Elm Street, Peterbor-
ough, NH 03458, USA; 603/924-0100,
Fax: 603/924-6972, Focus: Review of
DOS and Windows software; Format:
Magazine; Michael Nadeau, Ed. Email:
mnadeau@ix.netcom.com; Freq: 6/Year

dot.COM
Publishing Co: Business Communications
Co. Inc., 25 Van Zant Street, Norwalk, CT
06855, USA; 203/853-4266, Fax: 203/
853-0348, Web URL: buscom.com; Focus:
News, information and products for the
Internet market; Format: Newsletter; Lois
Naterman, Pblshr Freq: Monthly, Price/yr-
$:375

**DP Blue Books, The Computer
Installation Source**
Publishing Co: DP Blue Book Co., The,
35200 Dequindre, #100, Sterling Heights,
MI 48310-4857, USA; 810/978-4300,
Fax: 810/978-4310, Focus: State and pro-
vincial directories of computer users; For-
mat: Directory; Karen Watt, Pblshr Freq:
Annual, Price/yr-$:295-695

Dr. Dobb's Journal
Publishing Co: Miller Freeman Inc., 411
Borel Ave, #100, San Mateo, CA 94402-
3522, USA; 415/358-9500, Fax: 415/358-
9749, Web URL: ddj.com; Focus: Infor-
mation for the professional programmer;
Format: Magazine; Jonathan Erickson, Ed.-
in-Chief Peter Hutchinson, Pblshr Tami
Zemel, Mgng Ed. Circ.: 115,227, Freq:
Monthly, Price/yr-$:34.95

Dr. Dobb's Sourcebook
Publishing Co: Miller Freeman Inc., 411
Borel Ave, #100, San Mateo, CA 94402-
3522, USA; 415/358-9500, Fax: 415/358-
9749, Web URL: ddj.com; Format: Directory

DV Finance Report
Publishing Co: Digital Video Magazine, 330
Townsend Street, #235, San Francisco, CA
94107, USA; 415/357-9400, Fax: 415/
357-9401, Co Email: titles@netcom.com;
Focus: Information on multimedia, digital
and interactive media; Format: Newsletter;
Scott Mize, Ed. Freq: Monthly, Price/yr-
$:395

DVD Report
Publishing Co: Knowledge Industry Pub-
lishing, 701 Westchester Ave, White
Plains, NY 10604, USA; 914/328-9157,

Fax: 914/328-9093, Web URL: kipi.com;
Focus: Information on the DVD market;
Format: Newsletter; Tom O'Reilly, Ed.
Freq: 12/Year, Price/yr-$:697

**E-mail, Buyers Guide to Electronic
Commerce**
Publishing Co: Electronic Commerce Strategies, 1685 Barn Swallow Road, Marietta,
GA 30062, USA; 770/578-4980, Fax:
770/973-9984, Web URL: e-com.com/
strategies; Focus: Products, services and
trends in paperless technologies; Format:
Directory; Debbie Shaw, Pblshr Jack Shaw,
Pres Circ.: 30,000, Freq: 2/Year, Price/
yr-$:25/issue

Eastern Telecom Report
Publishing Co: ITC Publications, 4340
East-West Hwy, #1020, Bethesda, MD
20814-4411, USA; 301/907-0060, Fax:
301/907-6555, Focus: News, analysis and
forecast on Eastern European telecom market; Format: Newsletter; Edward G. Czarnecki, Mngg Dir Circ.: 1,000, Freq:
Monthly, Price/yr-$:749

Easy ACT!
Publishing Co: Pinnacle Publishing Inc.,
18000 72nd Ave S. #217, Kent, WA
98032, USA; 206/251-1900, Fax: 206/
251-5057, Web URL: pinpub.com; Focus:
Information for Clipper database users;
Format: Newsletter; Freq: Monthly

ECN, Electronic Component News
Publishing Co: Chilton Co., 1 Chilton
Way, Radnor, PA 19089, USA; 610/964-
4343, Fax: 610/964-4348, Co Email: ecn-
info@chilton.com; Web URL:
ecnmag.com; Focus: Electronic and com-
puter product news and reviews; Format:
Newspaper; Hy Natkin, Ed.-in-Chief
Email: hnatkin@chilton.com; Joseph J.
Breck, Pblshr Email: jbreck@chilton.com;
George T. Frueh, Mngg Ed. Email:
gfrueh@chilton.com; Freq: Monthly,
Price/yr-$:Free/50

eCommerce Report
Publishing Co: Cobb Group, The, 9420
Bunsen Pkwy. #300, Louisville, KY
40220, USA; 502/491-1900, Fax: 502/
491-8050, Co Email: cobb@aol.com; Web
URL: cobb.com; Format: Newsletter;
Price/yr-$:395

**Economics of Multimedia Title Pub-
lishing**
Publishing Co: Simba Information Inc., 11
River Bend Drive S, PO Box 4234, Stamford, CT 06807-0234, USA; 203/834-
0033, Fax: 203/358-5825, Co Email: sim-
bamkt@aol.com; Web URL: simba-
net.com; Focus: Market analysis, statistics
and choices for multimedia publishing business; Format: Factbook; Chris Elwell,
Pblshr Freq: Annual, Price/yr-$:895

Edge, The
Publishing Co: Arcadia Pacific Corp., 1545
Viewsite Drive, Los Angeles, CA 90069-
1322, USA; Co Email: 71700.1412@com-
puserve.com; Focus: Information on PDAs,

personal information managers and related
topics; Format: Newsletter; Blair T. Newman, Ed. Email: 5748015@mcimail.com;
Freq: Monthly

**EDI Forum: The Journal of Electronic
Commerce**
Publishing Co: EDI Group Ltd., PO Box
710, Oak Park, IL 60303, USA; 708/848-
0135, Fax: 708/848-0270, Co Email:
dmferguson@attmail.com; Focus: Information on EDI and electronic commerce;
Format: Magazine; Freq: 4/Year, Price/yr-
$:250

EDI News
Publishing Co: Phillips Business Information Inc., 1201 Seven Locks Road, #300,
Potomac, MD 20854-1110, USA; 301/
340-1520, Fax: 301/424-4297, Co Email:
pbi@phillips.com; Web URL: phil-
lips.com; Focus: News and trends in the
electronic data interchange industry; Format: Newsletter; Freq: 25/Year, Price/yr-
$:597

EDI Update
Publishing Co: IBC Publishing Ltd., 290
Eliot St., Box 91004, Ashland, MA 01721-
9104, USA; 508/881-2800, Focus: International EDI developments; Format: Newsletter; Freq: 10/Year, Price/yr-$:470

EDI WORLD
Publishing Co: EDI WORLD Inc., 2021
Coolidge Street, Hollywood, FL 33020-
2400, USA; 305/925-5900, Fax: 305/925-
7533, Co Email: ediworld@aol.com; Web
URL: ediworld.com; Focus: Electronic
commerce and EDI; Format: Magazine;
Michael S. McGarr, Ed. Richard D'Alessan-
dro, Pblshr Circ.: 49,000, Freq: Monthly,
Price/yr-$:45

EDI Yellow Pages Int'l.
Publishing Co: EDI, spread the word!,
13805 Wooden Creek Drive, Dallas, TX
75244, USA; 214/243-3456, Fax: 214/
243-7265, Focus: Lists over 21,000 worldwide companies using EDI and lists EDI
products and services; Format: Directory;
Anna Payne, Ed. & Pblr Circ.: 35,000,
Freq: Annual, Price/yr-$:34

EDI, Handbook of
Publishing Co: Warren Gorham Lamont,
31 St. James Ave, Boston, MA 02116-
9372, USA; Fax: 617/451-0908, Co
Email: sales@wgl.com; Web URL:
wgl.com; Focus: Information on using EDI;
Format: Loose-leaf; Andrew W. Boden,
Pblshr Price/yr-$:126

Editors Directory
Publishing Co: Press Access, 120 Boylston
Street, 10th Fl., Boston, MA 02166, USA;
617/542-6670, Fax: 617/542-6671, Co
Email: faimc@aol.com; Focus: Listing of
editors of computer publications; Format:
Directory; Freq: Annual

EDN
Publishing Co: Cahners Publishing Co.,
275 Washington Street, Newton, MA
02158-1630, USA; 617/964-3030, Fax:

617/558-4470, Focus: News, product reviews and product comparisons for electronic engineers; Format: Magazine; Circ.: 161,500, Freq: 48/Year, Price/yr-$:Free/160

EDN Asia
Publishing Co: Cahners Asia Ltd., 19/F 8 Commercial Tower, 8 Sun Yip Street, Choiwan, Hong Kong; 852-965-1555, Fax: 852/976-0706, Co Email: ednasia@mcimail.com; Focus: Technology, products and design information for electronic engineers in Asia; Format: Magazine; Michael C. Markowitz, Chief Ed. Email: edn-markowitz@mcimail.com; Jack Kompan, Pblshr Circ.: 28,000, Freq: Monthly, Price/yr-$:Free/125

EDN Products Edition
Publishing Co: Gordon Publications Inc., 301 Gibraltar Drive, Morris Plains, NJ 07950-0650, USA; 201/292-5100, Fax: 201/292-0783, Focus: New products, technology for electronics designers and systems integrators; Format: Newspaper; Steven P. Wirth, Pblshr Bruce A. Bennett, Ed.-in-Chief Jen Brinkman, Assoc Ed. Circ.: 132,000, Freq: 12/Year, Price/yr-$:Free

EDP Audit, Control and Security Newsletter
Publishing Co: Auerbach Publications, 31 St. James Ave, Boston, MA 02116-9372, USA; 617/423-2020, Fax: 617/451-0908, Co Email: 73752.2270@compuserve.com; Web URL: wgl.com; Focus: News and techniques on auditing, control and systems security; Format: Newsletter; Kim Horan Kelly, Pblshr Freq: Monthly, Price/yr-$:142

EDP Auditing
Publishing Co: Auerbach Publications, 31 St. James Ave, Boston, MA 02116-9372, USA; 617/423-2020, Fax: 617/451-0908, Co Email: 73752.2270@compuserve.com; Web URL: wgl.com; Focus: Information on auditing computer-based systems; Format: Loose-leaf; Kim Horan Kelly, Pblshr Freq: 6/Year, Price/yr-$:405

Education Empowerment
Publishing Co: Empower Tools, 5610 Buckingham Palace Court, Alexandria, VA 22315-4120, USA; 703/924-9688, Fax: 703/924-9683, Focus: Education technology for K-12, higher education and training; Format: Magazine; John Stuppy, Ed.

Edutainment News
8 Digital Drive, #101, Novato, CA 94949, USA; 415/883-6351, Fax: 415/883-0893, Focus: Education and entertainment products; Format: Magazine; Isaac Ash, Pblshr Douglas M. Baughman, Contr Ed. Freq: 6/Year

EE Product News
Publishing Co: Intertec Publishing Corp., 707 Westchester Ave, White Plains, NY 10604, USA; 914/949-8500, Fax: 914/682-0922, Co Email: 73414.1271@com-

puserve.com; Focus: News and reviews of new electronic products; Format: Magazine; Joseph DelGatto, Ed. Email: 73414.1271@compuserve.com; Matthew Reseska, Pblshr Email: 73414.1271@compuserve.com; Circ.: 102,500, Freq: Monthly, Price/yr-$:Free/52

EIA Trade Directory & Membership List
Publishing Co: Electronic Industries Association, 2500 Wilson Blvd, Arlington, VA 22201-3834, USA; 703/907-7500, Fax: 703/907-7501, Co Email: @eia.org; Web URL: eia.org; Focus: List over 1,000 electronics companies; Format: Factbook; Peter F. McCloskey, Pres John J. Kelly, VP Mark V. Rosenker, VP Public Affairs Freq: Annual, Price/yr-$:200

Electronic Business Asia
Publishing Co: Cahners Asia Ltd., 19/F 8 Commercial Tower, 8 Sun Yip Street, Chaiwan, Hong Kong; 852-965-1555, Fax: 852/976-0706, Focus: News and analysis of the Asian electronics industry; Format: Magazine; Craig Addison, Ed.-in-Chief Jack Kompan, Pblshr Circ.: 31,000, Freq: Monthly, Price/yr-$:Free/142

Electronic Business Today
Publishing Co: Cahners Publishing Co., 275 Washington Street, Newton, MA 02158-1630, USA; 617/964-3030, Fax: 617/558-4970, Co Email: ebt@cahners.com; Focus: Vendor selection and partnering strategies; Format: Magazine; Tim L. Tobeck, Pblshr J. Robert Lineback, Ed.-in-Chief Mike Rovinson, Mgng Ed. Freq: Monthly, Price/yr-$:Free/65

Electronic Buyers' News
Publishing Co: CMP Publications Inc., 600 Community Drive, Manhasset, NY 11030, USA; 516/562-5000, Fax: 516/562-5123, Co Email: @cmp.com; Web URL: techweb.cmp.com/ebn; Focus: Newspaper for OEM product sourcing and vendor partnering; Format: Newspaper; Jeremy Young, Ed. Email: jyoung@cmp.com; Mark Holdreith, Pblshr Email: mholdrei@cmp.com; Matthew Sheerin, Exec Ed. Email: msheerin@cmp.com; Circ.: 62,000, Freq: 51/Year, Price/yr-$:Free/149

Electronic Commerce
Publishing Co: Phillips Business Information Inc., 1201 Seven Locks Road, #300, Potomac, MD 20854-1110, USA; 301/340-1520, Fax: 301/424-4297, Co Email: pbi@phillips.com; Web URL: phillips.com; Focus: News, trends and analysis of electronic commerce; Format: Newsletter; Price/yr-$:697

Electronic Design
Publishing Co: Penton Publishing Inc., 611 Route #46 West, Hasbrouck Heights, NJ 07604, USA; 201/393-6060, Fax: 201/393-0204, Web URL: penton.com; Focus: News, applications and product reports for engineers and engineering managers; Format: Magazine; Jack Shandle, Ed.-in-Chief

John G. French, Pblshr Bob Milne, Mgng Ed. Circ.: 165,000, Freq: 28/Year, Price/yr-$:Free/105

Electronic Education Report
Publishing Co: Simba Information Inc., 11 River Bend Drive S, PO Box 4234, Stamford, CT 06807-0234, USA; 203/834-0033, Fax: 203/358-5825, Co Email: simba99@aol.com; Web URL: simbanet.com; Focus: Convergence of technology and learning; Format: Newsletter; Chris Elwell, Gr Pblr Michael P. Hayes, Ed. Victor Rubell, Assoc Ed. Freq: 24/Year, Price/yr-$:349

Electronic Engineering Times
Publishing Co: CMP Publications Inc., 600 Community Drive, Manhasset, NY 11030, USA; 516/562-5000, Fax: 516/562-5325, Co Email: eetimes@eet.cmp.com; Web URL: techweb.cmp.com/eet; Focus: Product, technology, professional and business news for electronic engineers; Format: Newspaper; Steve Weitzner, Pblshr Email: sweitzner@eet.cmp.com; Richard Wallace, Ed-in-Chief Email: rwallace@eet.cmp.com; Nicolas Mokhoff, Exec Ed. Email: nmokhoff@eet.cmp.com; Circ.: 127,500, Freq: Weekly, Price/yr-$:Free/149

Electronic Engineers Master Catalog
Publishing Co: Hearst Business Publishing/UTP Div., 645 Stewart Ave, Garden City, NY 11530, USA; 516/227-1300, Fax: 516/227-1453, Web URL: eemonline.com; Focus: Listing of electronics manufacturers and distributors; Format: Directory; Armand Villinger, Pblshr Freq: Annual, Price/yr-$:115

Electronic Information Report
Publishing Co: Simba Information Inc., 11 River Bend Drive S, PO Box 4234, Stamford, CT 06807-0234, USA; 203/834-0033, Fax: 203/358-5825, Co Email: simba99@aol.com; Web URL: simbanet.com; Focus: News and information on electronic publishing and online information; Format: Newsletter; Chris Elwell, Gr Pblr Lorraine Sileo, Ed. Dir Paulette Donnelly, Ed. Freq: 46/Year, Price/yr-$:479

Electronic Learning
Publishing Co: Scholastic Inc., 411 Lafayette Street, 4th Floor, New York, NY 10003, USA; 212/505-4900, Fax: 212/505-8587, Focus: News, reviews and perspectives for educational computer & technology users; Format: Magazine; Claudia Cohl, Pblshr Circ.: 70,000, Freq: 8/Year, Price/yr-$:Free/24

Electronic Library, The
Publishing Co: Information Today Inc., 143 Old Marlton Pike, Medford, NJ 08055-8750, USA; 609/654-6266, Fax: 609/654-4309, Co Email: custserv@infotoday.com; Web URL: infotoday.com; Focus: Impact of computerized storage systems on libraries and information centers; Format: Magazine; David I. Raitt, Ed. Freq: 6/Year,

Price/yr-$:120

Electronic Mail & Messaging Systems
Publishing Co: BRP Publications Inc., 1333 H Street NW #1100. W. Tower, Washington, DC 20005, USA; 202/842-3022, Fax: 202/842-1875, Co Email: brp@access.digex.net; Focus: News and analysis on technology, applications, and market trends in E-mail, fax, etc.; Format: Newsletter; Freq: biweekly, Price/yr-$:595

Electronic Manufacturers Directory
Publishing Co: Harris InfoSource International, 2057 Aurora Road, Twinsburg, OH 44087, USA; 216/425-9000, Fax: 216/425-4328, Focus: Listing of over 15,000 electronics firms and 46,000 executives; Format: Directory; Robert Harris, CEO Freq: Annual, Price/yr-$:160,00

Electronic Market Data Book
Publishing Co: Electronic Industries Association, 2500 Wilson Blvd, Arlington, VA 22201-3834, USA; 703/907-7500, Fax: 703/907-7501, Co Email: @eia.org; Web URL: eia.org; Focus: Historical data and forecast of electronics industry segments; Format: Directory; Peter F. McCloskey, Pres John J. Kelly, VP Mark V. Rosenker, VP Public Affairs Freq: Annual, Price/yr-$:75/150

Electronic Marketplace Report
Publishing Co: Simba Information Inc., 11 River Bend Drive S, PO Box 4234, Stamford, CT 06807-0234, USA; 203/834-0033, Fax: 203/358-5825, Co Email: simba99@aol.com; Web URL: simbanet.com; Focus: News and information on electronic shopping and commerce; Format: Newsletter; Chris Elwell, Gr Pblr Lorraine Sileo, Ed. Dir Karen Burka, Ed. Freq: 24/Year, Price/yr-$:449

Electronic Marketplace Sourcebook
Publishing Co: Thompson Publishing Group, 1725 K Street NW, Washington, DC 20006, USA; Fax: 800/926-2012, Focus: Listing of companies in electronic marketing; Format: Loose-leaf; Lucy Caldwell-Stair, Pblshr Price/yr-$:349

Electronic Media
Publishing Co: Crain Communications Inc., 740 N. Rush Street, Chicago, IL 60611-2590, USA; 312/649-5260, Web URL: adage.com; Focus: Regional newspaper; Format: Newspaper; Freq: Weekly, Price/yr-$:99

Electronic Media for School Market: Review Trends & Forecasts
Publishing Co: Simba Information Inc., 11 River Bend Drive S, PO Box 4234, Stamford, CT 06807-0234, USA; 203/834-0033, Fax: 203/358-5825, Co Email: simbainfo@simbanet.com; Web URL: simbanet.com; Focus: Scholastics and forecasts on new technology integration in schools; Format: Factbook; Claire Schoen, Ed. Dir Freq: Annual, Price/yr-$:1,095

Electronic Media News Mail

Publishing Co: Microinfo Ltd., PO Box 3, Omega Park, Alton, Hants, GU34 2PG, UK; 01420-86848, Fax: 01420-89889, Co Email: emedia@ukminfo.demon.co.uk; Focus: Worldwide electronic media publishing; Format: E-mail Newsletter; Price/yr-$:100 pounds

Electronic Messaging News
Publishing Co: Phillips Business Information Inc., 1201 Seven Locks Road, #300, Potomac, MD 20854-1110, USA; 301/340-1520, Fax: 301/424-4297, Co Email: pbi@phillips.com; Web URL: phillips.com; Focus: News, standards and trends in the electronic messaging industry; Format: Newsletter; Freq: 25/Year, Price/yr-$:597

Electronic Musician
Publishing Co: Cardinal Music & Entertainment Group, 6400 Hollis Street, #12, Emeryville, CA 94608, USA; 510/653-3307, Fax: 510/653-5142, Focus: Music synthesizer and computer music products; Format: Magazine; Mike Mclenda, Ed. Peter Hirschfield, Pblshr Circ.: 60,300, Freq: Monthly, Price/yr-$:24

Electronic News
Publishing Co: International Publishing Corp., 302 5th Avenue, 4th Fl., New York, NY 10001, USA; 212/736-3900, Fax: 212/736-5125, Co Email: enews@sumnet.com; Web URL: sumnet.com/enews; Focus: News about the electronics industry; Format: Tabloid; Zachary J. Dicker, Pblshr Jeff Dorsch, Ed. Circ.: 85,000, Freq: 51/Year, Price/yr-$:129

Electronic Products
Publishing Co: Hearst Business Publishing/UTP Div., 645 Stewart Ave, Garden City, NY 11530, USA; 516/227-1300, Fax: 516/227-1901, Web URL: electronicproducts.com; Focus: Electronic product and technology news for engineers; Format: Magazine; Frank Egan, Ed. & Pblr Richard Pell Jr., Mngd Ed. Circ.: 124,000, Freq: Monthly, Price/yr-$:Free/50

Electronic Publishing & TypeWorld
Publishing Co: PennWell Publishing Co., 1421 South Sheridan, Tulsa, OK 74112, USA; 918/831-9537, Fax: 918/831-9497, Co Email: @pennwell.com; Web URL: pennwell.com; Focus: News and information about electronic publishing; Format: Newspaper; Keith V. Hevenor, Ed. Email: keithh@pennwell.com; Paul McPherson, Pblshr Freq: 18/Year, Price/yr-$:Free/30

Electronic Servicing & Technology
Publishing Co: CQ Communications Inc., PO Box 12487, Overland Park, KS 66282-2487, USA; 913/492-4857, Fax: 913/492-4857, Focus: News and information for electronic service technicians; Format: Magazine; Conrad Persson, Ed. Email: cpersedit@aol.com; Richard Ross, Pblshr Diane Klusner, Adv Sales Dir Circ.: 30,000, Freq: Monthly, Price/yr-$:24

Electronics Purchasing
Publishing Co: Cahners Publishing Co., 275 Washington Street, Newton, MA 02158-1630, USA; 617/558-4723, Fax: 617/558-4327, Focus: Product news for buyers of electronics and computers; Format: Magazine; Freq: Monthly, Price/yr-$:Free/65

Electronics Strategies
Publishing Co: Investext Group, The, 22 Pittsburgh Street, Boston, MA 02210-9630, USA; 617/345-2704, Fax: 617/330-1986, Focus: Investment research reports on electronics and computer companies; Format: CD-ROM; Tom Moore, Pblshr Freq: 4/Year, Price/yr-$:2,995

Embedded Systems Programming
Publishing Co: Miller Freeman Inc., 600 Harrison Street, San Francisco, CA 94107-1391, USA; 415/905-2200, Fax: 415/905-2234, Web URL: embedded.com; Focus: Technical information for designing embedded computer systems; Format: Magazine; Linsey Vereen, Ed. Email: lvereen@mfi.com; Mike Flynn, Pblshr Email: mflynn@mfi.com; Circ.: 40,000, Freq: Monthly, Price/yr-$:50

End-User Computing Management
Publishing Co: Auerbach Publications, 31 St. James Ave, Boston, MA 02116-9372, USA; 617/423-2020, Fax: 617/451-0908, Co Email: 73752.2270@compuserve.com; Web URL: wgl.com; Focus: Information on planning and control information centers and end-user computing; Format: Loose-leaf; Kim Horan Kelly, Pblshr Freq: 6/Year, Price/yr-$:495

Engineering Automation Report
Publishing Co: Technology Automation Services, PO Box 3593, Englewood, CO 80155-3593, USA; 303/770-1728, Fax: 303/770-3660, Focus: News and analysis of computer, graphics and data communications for engineering managers; Format: Newsletter; David S. Weisberg, Pblr & Ed. Email: dweisbrg@eareport.com; Freq: Monthly, Price/yr-$:225

Ent
Publishing Co: Cardinal Business Media Inc., 1300 Virginia Drive, #400, Ft. Washington, PA 19034-3225, USA; 215/643-8000, Fax: 215/643-3901, Web URL: cardinal.com/ent; Focus: Enterprise solutions for Windows NT users; Format: Magazine; Mark Durrick, Pblshr Eric Schoeniger, Ed-in-Chief Email: schoeniger@cardinal.com; Roseanne McGrath Brooks, Mngg Ed. Email: brooksrm@cardinal.com; Freq: Monthly, Price/yr-$:Free

Enterprise Communications
Publishing Co: Advanstar Communications Inc., 201 E Sandpointe Ave, #600, Santa Ana, CA 92707-5761, USA; 714/513-8400, Fax: 714/513-8482, Focus: Voice, data and video integration; Format: Magazine; Kurt Indvik, Ed-in-Chief & Pblr Email: kindvik@aol.com; Laurie

Watanabe, Mngng Ed. Freq: Monthly, Price/yr-$:39

Enterprise Communications
Publishing Co: Faulkner Information Services, 7905 Browning Road, Pennsauken, NJ 08109-4319, USA; 609/662-2070, Fax: 609/662-0905, Co Email: faulkner@faulkner.com; Web URL: faulkner.com; Focus: Information on LANs, networking and telecom; Format: Loose-leaf; Martin Murphy, Pblshr Freq: Monthly, Price/yr-$:4,995

Enterprise Computing
Publishing Co: Faulkner Information Services, 7905 Browning Road, Pennsauken, NJ 08109-4319, USA; 609/662-2070, Fax: 609/662-0905, Co Email: faulkner@faulkner.com; Web URL: faulkner.com; Focus: Information on all computers, peripherals and software; Format: CD-ROM; Martin Murphy, Pblshr Freq: Monthly, Price/yr-$:4,155

Enterprise Internetworking Journal
Publishing Co: Cardinal Business Media Inc., 12225 Greenville Ave, #700, Dallas, TX 75243, USA; 214/669-9000, Fax: 214/669-9909, Co Email: 73430.2344@compuserve.com; Focus: Information on internetworking for IBM-based systems; Format: Magazine; Denny Yost, Ed-in-Chief & Pblr Cecillia Conurn Perry, Mngng Ed. Toni Bach, Ed. Circ.: 20,000, Freq: Monthly, Price/yr-$:Free

Enterprise Reengineering
Publishing Co: TFG Publishing Co., 7777 Leesburg Pike, #315-N, Falls Church, VA 22043, USA; 703/761-0646, Fax: 703/761-0766, Co Email: tfg.bpr.er@his.com; Focus: Reengineering technology and implementation; Format: Tabloid; Israel Feldman, Pblshr Larry Willets, Ed. Eric Kestler, Mngng Ed. Freq: 6/Year, Price/yr-$:Free

Enterprise Systems Journal
Publishing Co: Cardinal Business Media Inc., 12225 Greenville Ave, #700, Dallas, TX 75243, USA; 214/669-9000, Fax: 214/669-9909, Web URL: btb.com/cardinal; Focus: News and technical information for users of IBM mainframe and compatible systems; Format: Magazine; George Dishman, Ed-in-Chief & Pblr Email: 76130.221@compuserve.com; Debby English, Mngng Ed. Circ.: 100,000, Freq: Monthly, Price/yr-$:Free/60

Envisioneering
Publishing Co: Kyra Communications, 3864 Bayberry Lane, Seaford, NY 11783-1503, USA; 516/783-6244, Fax: 516/679-8167, Web URL: gate.woz.org/envisioneering; Focus: Insight, news and perspectives on PCs, audio, video, graphics and multimedia; Format: Newsletter; Richard E. Doherty, Ed-in-Chief Steve Wozniak, Ed. Dir Brian Robinson, Mngng Ed. Freq: 24/Year, Price/yr-$:395

European Computer Sources

Publishing Co: Asian Sources Media Group, Hoornzeelstraat 21A, Tervuren, B-3080, Belgium; 322-766-0045, Fax: 322-768-0084, Co Email: 100135.1344@compuserve.com; Focus: News and information for European PC resellers; Format: Magazine; Eric Dauchy, Mngng Ed. Email: 73543.3506@compuserve.com; Bob Snyder, GM Tom Brookes, Deputy Ed. Circ.: 32,000, Freq: Monthly, Price/yr-$:75

European Electronics Directory
Publishing Co: Elsevier, PO Box 150, Kidlington, Oxford, OX5 1AS, UK; Focus: Listing of 4,500 European electronics companies; Format: Directory; Freq: Annual, Price/yr-$:390

Event Happenings
Publishing Co: Tech Trade Assoc., 8 Combahee Road, Hilton Head, SC 29928-3316, USA; 803/785-5497, Fax: 803/785-5498, Focus: Happenings at high-tech tradeshows, conferences & symposiums; Format: Newsletter; Judith Miller, Principal Circ.: 3,000, Freq: Quarterly, Price/yr-$:30

Evolutionary Computation
Publishing Co: MIT Press Journals, 55 Hayward Street, Cambridge, MA 02142, USA; 617/253-2889, Fax: 617/258-6779, Co Email: journals-orders@mit.edu; Web URL: mitpress.mit.edu; Focus: Research on evolutionary computer systems that can evolve as natural life-forms do; Format: Magazine; Kenneth De Jong, Ed.-in-Chief Email: ecj@cs.gmu.edu; Circ.: 650, Freq: 4/Year, Price/yr-$:48

Expert Systems Journal
Publishing Co: Information Today Inc., 143 Old Marlton Pike, Medford, NJ 08055-8750, USA; 609/654-6266, Fax: 609/654-4309, Co Email: custserv@infotoday.com; Web URL: infotoday.com; Focus: Technical articles on AI and knowledge systems; Format: Magazine; Ian F. Croall, Ed. Ben Jeapes, Ed. Peter Hyams, Ed. Freq: 4/Year, Price/yr-$:132

Expert, The
Publishing Co: Cobb Group, The, 9420 Bunsen Pkwy. #300, Louisville, KY 40220, USA; 502/491-1900, Fax: 502/491-8050, Co Email: cobb@aol.com; Web URL: cobb.com; Focus: News, tips and techniques for Microsoft Excel Windows users; Format: Newsletter; Steve Cobb, Ed. Freq: Monthly, Price/yr-$:79

Exploring Oracle DBMS
Publishing Co: Cobb Group, The, 9420 Bunsen Pkwy. #300, Louisville, KY 40220, USA; 502/491-1900, Fax: 502/491-8050, Co Email: cobb@aol.com; Web URL: cobb.com; Focus: Tips and techniques for Oracle DBMS; Format: Newsletter; Price/yr-$:129

Exploring Oracle Designer 2000/ Developer 2000
Publishing Co: Cobb Group, The, 9420 Bunsen Pkwy. #300, Louisville, KY

40220, USA; 502/491-1900, Fax: 502/491-8050, Co Email: cobb@aol.com; Web URL: cobb.com; Focus: Tips and techniques for Oracle Designer 2000/Developer 2000; Format: Newsletter; Price/yr-$:129

Exploring Sybase SQL Server
Publishing Co: Cobb Group, The, 9420 Bunsen Pkwy. #300, Louisville, KY 40220, USA; 502/491-1900, Fax: 502/491-8050, Co Email: cobb@aol.com; Web URL: cobb.com; Focus: Tips and techniques for Sybase SQL Server; Format: Newsletter; Price/yr-$:129

Exploring the Net using Internet Explorer/MSN
Publishing Co: Cobb Group, The, 9420 Bunsen Pkwy. #300, Louisville, KY 40220, USA; 502/491-1900, Fax: 502/491-8050, Co Email: cobb@aol.com; Web URL: cobb.com; Focus: Tips and techniques for using Internet Explorer/MSN; Format: Newsletter; Price/yr-$:49

Exploring Windows NT
Publishing Co: Cobb Group, The, 9420 Bunsen Pkwy. #300, Louisville, KY 40220, USA; 502/491-1900, Fax: 502/491-8050, Co Email: cobb@aol.com; Web URL: cobb.com; Focus: Tips and techniques for Microsoft Windows NT users; Format: Newsletter; Mark Solomon, Ed. Freq: Monthly, Price/yr-$:119

Family PC
Publishing Co: Ziff-Davis Publishing Co., One Park Ave, New York, NY 10016-5255, USA; 212/503-5255, Fax: 212/503-5519, Focus: Information for home PC users; Format: Magazine; Jake Winebaum, Ed. & Pblr Dan Muse, Exec Ed. Jo-Ann Hirschel, Mngng Ed. Freq: 10/Year, Price/yr-$:14.95

Fax SpecCheck Guide
Publishing Co: Dataquest Inc., 26254 Golden Valley Road, Bldg. 401, Santa Clarita, CA 95351, USA; 805/298-3261, Fax: 805/298-4388, Co Email: mmakers@netcom.com; Web URL: netcom.com~mmakers; Focus: Specifications of fax machines; Format: Directory; Freq: 4/Year, Price/yr-$:45

Fax-Accessible Database
Publishing Co: Buyers Laboratory Inc., 20 Railroad Ave, Hackensack, NJ 07601, USA; 201/488-0404, Fax: 201/488-0461, Focus: Online database of office product specifications: fax, copiers & printers; Format: Fax-on-demand; Anthony Polifrone, Pres Marion Davidowitz, VP Burt Meerow, Pblr Price/yr-$:150

FAXreporter
Publishing Co: Buyers Laboratory Inc., 20 Railroad Ave, Hackensack, NJ 07601, USA; 201/488-0404, Fax: 201/488-0461, Focus: News, analysis and test results on fax machines & multifunction devices; Format: Newsletter; Anthony Polifrone, Pres Marion Davidowitz, VP Burt Meerow, Pblr

Freq: Monthly, Price/yr-$:365

FDDI News

Publishing Co: Information Gatekeepers Inc., 214 Harvard Ave, Boston, MA 02134, USA; 617/232-3111, Fax: 617/734-8562, Co Email: igiboston@aol.com; Focus: FDDI technology, markets, products and applications; Format: Newspaper; Paul Polishuk, Ed. & Pblr Email: igiboston@aol.com; Freq: Monthly, Price/yr-$:545/595

Federal Computer Week

Publishing Co: IDG Communications Inc., 3110 Fairview Park Drive, #1040, Falls Church, VA 22042-7890, USA; 847-291-5214, Co Email: @fcw.com; Web URL: fcw.com; Focus: News about the federal government's purchase and use of information technology; Format: Newspaper; Anne A. Armstrong, Ed.-in-Chief Email: annea@fcw.com; Edith Holmes, Pblshr Circ.: 75,000, Freq: 36/Year, Price/yr-$:Free/95

Federal Internet Source, The

Publishing Co: National Journal, 1501 M Street NW, #300, Washington, DC 20005, USA; Fax: 202/739-8540, Focus: Listing of government Internet services; Format: Directory; Jon Fox Sullivan, Pblshr Freq: Annual, Price/yr-$:19

Federal Taxation of Computer Software

Publishing Co: Kutish Publications Inc., PO Box 113, 125 Strafford Ave, Wayne, PA 19087-0113, USA; 610/975-9619, Fax: 610/975-9623, Focus: Information on federal taxation of software; Format: Directory; L.J. Kutten, Pblshr Freq: Annual, Price/yr-$:125

Fiber Datacom

Publishing Co: Information Gatekeepers Inc., 214 Harvard Ave, Boston, MA 02134, USA; 617/232-3111, Fax: 617/734-8562, Co Email: igiboston@aol.com; Focus: News and information on applications of fiber optics in data communication; Format: Newsletter; Paul Polishuk, Ed. & Pblr Email: igiboston@aol.com; Freq: Monthly, Price/yr-$:545/595

Fiber in the Loop

Publishing Co: Information Gatekeepers Inc., 214 Harvard Ave, Boston, MA 02134, USA; 617/232-3111, Fax: 617/734-8562, Co Email: igiboston@aol.com; Focus: Fiber technology to homes, products, trials and services; Format: Newsletter; Paul Polishuk, Ed. & Pblr Email: igiboston@aol.com; Freq: 26/Year, Price/yr-$:545/595

Fiber Optics and Communications

Publishing Co: Information Gatekeepers Inc., 214 Harvard Ave, Boston, MA 02134, USA; 617/232-3111, Fax: 617/734-8562, Co Email: igiboston@aol.com; Focus: News, technology and market trends on fiber optics in communications systems; Format: Newsletter; Paul Polishuk, Ed. &

Pblr Email: igiboston@aol.com; Freq: Monthly, Price/yr-$:545/595

Fiber Optics Business

Publishing Co: Information Gatekeepers Inc., 214 Harvard Ave, Boston, MA 02134, USA; 617/232-3111, Fax: 617/734-8562, Co Email: igiboston@aol.com; Focus: Business developments and market trends in the fiber optics industry; Format: Newsletter; Paul Polishuk, Ed. & Pblr Email: igiboston@aol.com; Freq: 26/Year, Price/yr-$:545/595

Fiber Optics News

Publishing Co: Phillips Business Information Inc., 1201 Seven Locks Road, #300, Potomac, MD 20854-1110, USA; 301/340-1520, Fax: 301/309-3847, Co Email: pbi@phillips.com; Web URL: phillips.com; Focus: Update and analysis on today's fiber optic business opportunities; Format: Newsletter; David C. Chaffee, Sr Ed. Email: dchaffee@phillips.com; Joelle M. Martin, Pblshr Email: emullally@phillips.com; Ellen Mullally, Mgng Ed. Freq: 50/Year, Price/yr-$:697

Fiber Optics Sensors and Systems

Publishing Co: Information Gatekeepers Inc., 214 Harvard Ave, Boston, MA 02134, USA; 617/232-3111, Fax: 617/734-8562, Co Email: igiboston@aol.com; Focus: Fiber optic applications to sensors technology, markets, products and applications; Format: Newsletter; Paul Polishuk, Ed. & Pblr Email: igiboston@aol.com; Freq: Monthly, Price/yr-$:545/594

Fiber Optics Weekly Update

Publishing Co: Information Gatekeepers Inc., 214 Harvard Ave, Boston, MA 02134, USA; 617/232-3111, Fax: 617/734-8562, Co Email: igiboston@aol.com; Focus: News, information and market trends on fiber optics; Format: Newsletter; Paul Polishuk, Ed. & Pblr Email: igiboston@aol.com; Freq: 52/Year, Price/yr-$:545/595

Fiber Optics Yellow Pages

Publishing Co: Information Gatekeepers Inc., 214 Harvard Ave, Boston, MA 02134, USA; 617/232-3111, Fax: 617/734-8562, Co Email: igiboston@aol.com; Focus: Directory and information on fiber optics industry worldwide; Format: Directory; Paul Polishuk, Ed. & Pblr Email: igiboston@aol.com; Freq: Annual, Price/yr-$:90/110

Findex, Worldwide Directory of Market Research Reports

Publishing Co: Cambridge Information Group, 7200 Wisconsin Ave, Bethesda, MD 20814-4823, USA; 301/961-6700, Fax: 301/961-6720, Co Email: market@csa.com; Web URL: csa.com; Focus: Directory of market research reports, studies and surveys; Format: Directory; Edward J. Reid, Ed. Ted Caris, Pblshr Freq: Annual, Price/yr-$:385

Forms Automation Technology

Report

Publishing Co: Information Technology Research, 220 W. Mercer Street, #500, Seattle, WA 98119, USA; 206/283-5111, Fax: 206/727-6940, Focus: Forms automation news, trend and technologies; Format: Newsletter; John Callahan, Ed. Freq: 16/Year, Price/yr-$:395-595

Fortran Journal

Publishing Co: Fortran Users Group, PO Box 4201, Fullerton, CA 92634, USA; 714/441-2022, Fax: 714/441-2022, Co Email: @fortran.com; Web URL: fortran.com/fortran; Focus: News and information about the Fortran marketplace; Format: Newsletter; Walt Brainerd, Co-Ed Email: walt@fortran.com; Charles Ritz, Co-Ed Freq: 6/Year, Price/yr-$:28/100

Four Hundred, The

Publishing Co: Technology News of America Co., Inc., 110 Greene Street, New York, NY 10012, USA; 212/334-9750, Fax: 212/334-9491, Co Email: technews@worldnet.com; Focus: Information systems strategies for users of IBM midrange systems; Format: Newsletter; Hesh Wiener, Ed. & Pblr Freq: Monthly, Price/yr-$:199

Fox Pro Developers Journal

Publishing Co: Cobb Group, The, 9420 Bunsen Pkwy. #300, Louisville, KY 40220, USA; 502/491-1900, Fax: 502/491-8050, Co Email: cobb@aol.com; Web URL: cobb.com; Focus: News, tips and tricks for Microsoft Fox Pro developers; Format: Newsletter; Darren McGee, Ed. Freq: Monthly, Price/yr-$:89

FoxPro Advisor

Publishing Co: Advisor Publications Inc., 4010 Morena Blvd, San Diego, CA 92117, USA; 619/483-6400, Fax: 619/483-9851, Co Email: 71154.3123@compuserve.com; Focus: News and information for FoxPro users; Format: Magazine; William T. Ota, Pblr/Pres/CEO Email: 71154.3123@compuserve.com; John L. Hawkins, Ed-in-Chief & EVP Jeanne Banfield, VP Circ.: 22,500, Freq: Monthly, Price/yr-$:49

FoxTalk

Publishing Co: Pinnacle Publishing Inc., 18000 72nd Ave S. #217, Kent, WA 98032, USA; 206/251-1900, Fax: 206/251-5057, Web URL: pinpub.com; Focus: Information and utilities for Microsoft Fox-Pro users; Format: Newsletter; Dian Schaffhauser, Ed.-in-Chief Brent Smith, Pblshr Freq: Monthly, Price/yr-$:179

FT Systems

Publishing Co: ITOM Int'l. Co., PO Box 1450, Los Altos, CA 94023, USA; 415/948-4516, Fax: 415/948-9153, Focus: Analyzes technical and market trends in fault-tolerant and transaction systems; Format: Newsletter; Omri Serlin, Ed. & Pblr Email: omris@cup.portal.com; Freq: Monthly, Price/yr-$:695

Full Throttle
Publishing Co: Cobb Group, The, 9420 Bunsen Pkwy. #300, Louisville, KY 40220, USA; 502/491-1900, Fax: 502/491-8050, Co Email: cobb@aol.com; Web URL: cobb.com; Focus: Tips and tricks for Microsoft Flight Simulator users; Format: Newsletter; Greg Harris, Ed. Freq: Bi-Monthly, Price/yr-$:39

Future Media
PO Box 11632, Berkeley, CA 94701-2632, USA; 510/548-0341, Fax: 510/843-3628, Focus: Multimedia; Format: Newsletter

Gale Directory of Databases: CD-ROM, Diskette, Magnetic Tape, etc
Publishing Co: Gale Research Inc., 835 Penobscot Bldg, Detroit, MI 48226, USA; 313/961-2242, Fax: 313/961-6815, Co Email: galenp@conch.aa.msen.com; Focus: Description & contact information on over 4,400 databases on electronic media; Format: Directory; Kathleen Lopez Nolan, Ed. Katherine Miller, Assoc Ed. Freq: 2/Year, Price/yr-$:130

Gale Directory of Databases: Online Databases
Publishing Co: Gale Research Inc., 835 Penobscot Bldg, Detroit, MI 48226, USA; 313/961-2242, Fax: 313/961-6815, Co Email: galenp@conch.aa.msen.com; Focus: Description & contact information on over 5,400 online databases; Format: Directory; Kathleen Lopez Nolan, Ed. Katherine Miller, Assoc Ed. Freq: 2/Year, Price/yr-$:210

Game Developer
Publishing Co: Miller Freeman Inc., 600 Harrison Street, San Francisco, CA 94107-1391, USA; 415/905-2200, Fax: 415/905-2234, Focus: Information for game developers; Format: Magazine; Veronica Costanza, Pblshr Freq: 6/Year, Price/yr-$:39.95

Game Hits
Publishing Co: Infotainment World Inc., 951 Mariner's Island Blvd, #700, San Mateo, CA 94404-1561, USA; 415/349-4300, Fax: 415/349-8347, Format: Magazine; Freq: Monthly

GamePro
Publishing Co: Infotainment World Inc., 951 Mariner's Island Blvd, #700, San Mateo, CA 94404-1561, USA; 415/349-4300, Fax: 415/349-8347, Focus: Video games for Nintendo, Sega and Atari; Format: Magazine; LeeAnne McDermott, Ed.-in-Chief John Rousseau, Pblshr Circ.: 300,000, Freq: Monthly, Price/yr-$:24.95

GartnerLetter-Microsoft Tracker
Publishing Co: Gartner Group, PO Box 4332, Greenwich, CT 06830-9630, USA; Fax: 203/316-6774, Web URL: gartner.com; Focus: Tracking, assessing and analyzing Microsoft; Format: Newsletter; William P. Robertson, Pblshr Freq: Monthly, Price/yr-$:495

GartnerLetter-Personal Computing

News and Analysis
Publishing Co: Gartner Group, PO Box 4332, Greenwich, CT 06830-9630, USA; Fax: 203/316-6774, Web URL: gartner.com; Focus: Technologies and products of personal computing; Format: Newsletter; William P. Robertson, Pblshr Freq: Monthly, Price/yr-$:495

Geibel Report, The
Publishing Co: Geibel Marketing Consulting, PO Box 611, Belmont, MA 02178-0005, USA; 617/484-8285, Fax: 617/489-3567, Co Email: 74752.3072@compuserve.com; Focus: Software marketing strategies and techniques--especially for vertical markets; Format: Newsletter; Jeff Geibel, Mngng Partner Freq: 6/Year, Price/yr-$:50

Georgia Technology Sourcebook
Publishing Co: Jaye Communications Inc., 550 Interstate N Pkwy NW, #150, Atlanta, GA 30339, USA; 770/984-9444, Fax: 770/612-0780, Web URL: sid.com; Focus: Listing of 1,600 high-tech companies in Georgia; Format: Directory; Freq: Annual, Price/yr-$:30/80

Gilder Technology Report
Publishing Co: Gilder Technology Group Inc., PO Box 660, Housatonic, MA 01236, USA; 413/274-0211, Fax: 413/274-0213, Co Email: gtg@gilder.com; Focus: Telecom technology trends and its impact on the computer business; Format: Newsletter; George Gilder, Ed. Freq: Monthly, Price/yr-$:295

GIS World
Publishing Co: GIS World Inc., 155 E. Boardwalk, #250, Ft. Collins, CO 805252, USA; 970/223-4848, Fax: 970/223-5700, Co Email: firstname@gisworld.com; Web URL: gisworld.com; Focus: Information on Geographic Information Systems; Format: Magazine; Mike Anderson, Ed. Email: mike@gisworld.com; Circ.: 20,000, Freq: 12/Year, Price/yr-$:72

Global Network Management
Publishing Co: Datapro Information Services Group, 600 Delran Pkwy., Delran, NJ 08705-9904, USA; 609/764-0100, Fax: 609/764-2811, Co Email: datapro@mhh.com; Web URL: datapro.com; Focus: Information on managing global networks; Format: CD-ROM; Freq: Monthly

Government Computer News
Publishing Co: Cahners Publishing Co., 8601 Georgia Ave, #300, Silver Spring, MD 20910, USA; 301/650-2000, Fax: 301/650-2111, Co Email: editor@gcn.com; Web URL: gcn.com; Focus: Serves computer users throughout the Federal Government; Format: Newspaper; Thomas R. Temin, Ed. Email: editor@gcn.com; Gary R. Squires, Pblshr Nancy Ferris, Mngng Ed. Circ.: 80,000, Freq: Biweekly, Price/yr-$:Free/95.90

Government Imaging

Publishing Co: GI Communications Corp. Inc., 1738 Elton Road, #304, Silver Spring, MD 20903-1725, USA; 301/445-4405, Fax: 301/445-5722, Web URL: clark.net/pub/govimag; Focus: Imaging application news for government users; Format: Newspaper; Edward K. O'Connor, Pblshr Robert V. Head, Ed. Circ.: 32,000, Freq: Monthly, Price/yr-$:25

GPC Quarterly Report, The
Publishing Co: Standard Performance Evaluation Corp., 10754 Ambassador Drive, #201, Manassas, VA 22110, USA; 703/331-0180, Fax: 703/331-0181, Co Email: info@specbench.org; Web URL: specbench.org/gpc; Focus: Graphics performance standards activities and benchmark results; Format: Online; Bob Cramblitt, Ed. Freq: 4/Year, Price/yr-$:195

GPS World
Publishing Co: Advanstar Communications Inc., 859 Willamette Street, Eugene, OR 97401-6806, USA; 503/343-1200, Fax: 503/344-3514, Co Email: mggpsworld@aol.com; Focus: Technology and products for the Global Positioning System; Format: Tabloid; Phillip Arndt, Pblshr Glen Gibbons, Ed. Molly M. Trudeau, Mngng Ed. Freq: Monthly, Price/yr-$:64

Graphic Arts Monthly
Publishing Co: Cahners Publishing Co., 8773 S Ridgeline Blvd, Highlands Ranch, CO 80126-2329, USA; 303/470-4445, Fax: 303/470-4280, Focus: News and information about the commercial printing industry.; Format: Magazine; Roger Ynostroza, Ed. Ronald C. Andriani, Pblshr Michael Karol, Mngng Ed. Circ.: 89,000, Freq: Monthly, Price/yr-$:Free/90

Guide to Global Messaging
Publishing Co: Vector Directory Services Inc., 34 Clarke Street, Lexington, MA 02173, USA; 617/862-7607, Fax: 617/862-6887, Co Email: 4401232@mcimail.com; Focus: Information on global messaging; Format: Directory; William A. Lucas, Pres Email: 4401232@mcimail.com; Freq: Annual, Price/yr-$:26

Hansen Report on Automotive Electronics, The
Publishing Co: Paul Hansen Associates, 11 Wentworth Rd, Rye, NH 03045-6106, USA; 603/431-5859, Fax: 603/431-5791, Focus: Global news and analysis of electronics in cars; Format: Newsletter; Paul Hansen, Pblshr Freq: 10/Year, Price/yr-$:427

Hard Disk Technical Guide
Publishing Co: MicroHouse, 4900 Pearl East, Circle, #101, Boulder, CO 80301, USA; 303/443-3388, Fax: 303/443-3323, Web URL: microhouse.com; Focus: Directory and specs of PC hard drives, controllers, BIOS drivers and interface type; Format: Book; Steve Anderson, Pres/CEO

Doug Anderson, VP/CTO Price/yr-
$:49.95

Hard Drives, Encyclopedia of
Publishing Co: Micro House International,
4900 Pearl East Circle, #101, Boulder, CO
80301, USA; 303/443-3388, Fax: 303/
443-3323, Web URL: microhouse.com;
Focus: Directory and specs of hard disk
drives; Format: Directory; Steve Anderson,
Pres & CEO Doug Anderson, VP & CTO
Freq: 2/Year, Price/yr-$:169

Hartsook Letter
3131 Marina Drive, Alameda, CA 94501,
USA; 510/521-4988, Fax: 510/521-3572,
Co Email: pieter@hartsook.com; Web
URL: hartsook.com; Focus: Information
and analysis of the Macintosh market; For-
mat: Newsletter/WWW; Pieter Hartsook,
Ed. Email: pieter@hartsook.com; Freq:
Monthly, Price/yr-$:275

HeadsUp
Publishing Co: Individual Inc., 8 New
England Exec Park-West, Burlington, MA
01803-9622, USA; Fax: 800/417-1000,
Focus: Personalized daily news service via
fax; Format: Fax; John Zahner, Ed. Freq:
Daily

Healthcare Informatics
Publishing Co: Health Data Analysis Inc.,
2902 Evergreen Pkwy, #100, PO Box
2830, Evergreen, CO 80439-9904, USA;
303/674-2774, Fax: 303/674-3134,
Focus: Computers in healthcare applications; Format: Magazine; Bill W. Childs,
Pblshr & Ed-in-Chief Scott R. Wible, Mngg
Ed. Freq: Monthly, Price/yr-$:34.95

**Henderson Electronic Market Fore-
cast**
Publishing Co: Henderson Ventures, 101
First Street, #444, Los Altos, CA 94022,
USA; 415/961-2900, Fax: 415/961-3090,
Focus: Worldwide market forecasts of elec-
tronics industries including computers;
Format: Newsletter; Edward Henderson,
Ed. & Pblr Freq: 11/year, Price/yr-$:750

**High Performance Computing &
Communications Week**
Publishing Co: King Publishing Group, 627
National Press Bldg., Washington, DC
20045, USA; 202/638-4260, Fax: 202/
662-9744, Focus: News about high perfor-
mance computing and communication mar-
kets; Format: Newsletter; Kevin Baerson,
Ed. Llewellyn King, Pblshr Freq: Weekly,
Price/yr-$:725

High Technology Careers Magazine
Publishing Co: Westech Expocorp, 4701
Patrick Henry Drive, #1901, Santa Clara,
CA 95054-1847, USA; 408/970-8800,
Fax: 408/980-5103, Focus: Career news
and high-tech job ads; Format: Newspaper;
Paul Burrowes, Fred Faltersack, Rod Lake,
Circ.: 137,000, Freq: 6/Year, Price/yr-
$:Free/29

**High-Tech Hot Wire/High-Tech Hot
Sheet**
Publishing Co: Hot Sheet Publishing, 114

Sansome Street, #1224, San Francisco, CA
94104-3823, USA; 415/421-6220, Fax:
415/421-6225, Co Email: medi-
amark@aol.com; Focus: High-technology
media trends and personalities; Format: Fax
newsletter; Art Garcia, Ed. & Pblr Email:
agarcia@aol.com; Chris Barnett, Sr Ed.
Freq: 24/Year, Price/yr-$:349

High-Tech Marketing News
Publishing Co: wolfBayne Communica-
tions, PO Box 50287, Colorado Springs,
CO 80949, USA; 719/593-8032, Co
Email: htmnews@wolfbayne.com; Web
URL: bayne.com/wolfbayne/htmnews.;
Focus: Marketing communications; For-
mat: Newsletter; Kim M. Bayne, Pblshr
Email: kimmik@wolfbayne.com

**High-Technology Services Manage-
ment**
Publishing Co: AFSM Int'l. Inc., 1342
Colonial Blvd, #25, Ft. Myers, FL 33907,
USA; 941/275-7887, Co Email:
afsmi@afsmi.org; Web URL: afsmi.com;
Focus: Membership publication for AFSM
Int'l.; Format: Magazine; Terry Kennedy,
Ed. & Pblr Suzanne M. Tissier, Assist Ed.
Freq: 12/Year, Price/yr-$:65

**High-Technology Services Manage-
ment-Suppliers' Directory**
Publishing Co: AFSM Int'l. Inc., 1342
Colonial Blvd, #25, Ft. Myers, FL 33907,
USA; 941/275-7887, Co Email:
afsmi@afsmi.org; Web URL: afsmi.com;
Focus: Guide to products and services; For-
mat: Magazine; Terry Kennedy, Ed. & Pblr
Suzanne M. Tissier, Assist Ed. Freq:
Annual, Price/yr-$:25

Historically Brewed
Publishing Co: Historical Computer Society, 2962 Park Street, #3, Jacksonville, FL
32205-8032, USA; Co Email: histori-
cal@aol.com; Focus: Historical and retro-
spective on the computer industry; Format:
Magazine; David A. Greelish, Ed. & Pblr
Kevin Stumpf, Assoc Ed. Freq: 6/Year,
Price/yr-$:18/24

**Hollywood Interactive Entertain-
ment Directory**
Publishing Co: Hollywood Creative Directory, 3000 W Olympic Blvd, #2525, Santa
Monica, CA 90404, USA; 310/315-4815,
Fax: 310/315-4816, Co Email: hcd@hol-
lyvision.com; Web URL: hollyvision.com;
Focus: Listing of interactive entertainment
companies; Format: Directory; Circ.:
2,000, Freq: Annual, Price/yr-$:49.50

Home Banking Report
Publishing Co: Jupiter Communications
Co., 627 Broadway, 2nd Fl, New York, NY
10012, USA; 212/780-6060, Fax: 212/
780-6075, Co Email: jup5@aol.com; Web
URL: jup.com/jupiter; Focus: Home banking trends and info; Format: Factbook;
Gene DeRose, Pblshr Freq: Annual, Price/
yr-$:1,395

Home PC: State of the Market
Publishing Co: Fairfield Research Inc.,

5815 S 58th Street, Lincoln, NE 68516-
3688, USA; 402/441-3370, Fax: 402/441-
3389, Co Email: fairfield@cybersur-
vey.com; Web URL: cybersurvey.com;
Focus: Survey-based data on home PC
ownership and usage; Format: Factbook;
Ted Lannan, Pres Freq: Annual, Price/yr-
$:795

Home Shopping Report
Publishing Co: Jupiter Communications
Co., 627 Broadway, 2nd Fl, New York, NY
10012, USA; 212/780-6060, Fax: 212/
780-6075, Co Email: jup5@aol.com; Web
URL: jup.com/jupiter; Focus: Technology
and market for interactive shopping; Format: Factbook; Gene DeRose, Ed. Freq:
Annual, Price/yr-$:995

Home-Office Computing
Publishing Co: Scholastic Inc., 411 Lafayette Street, 4th Floor, New York, NY
10003, USA; 212/505-4220, Fax: 212/
505-4260, Focus: News, perspectives and
reviews for people with a home-office; Format: Magazine; Hugh Roome, Pblshr Bernadette Grey, Ed.-in-Chief Cathy Grayson
Brower, Exec Ed. Circ.: 360,000, Freq:
Monthly, Price/yr-$:19.97

HomePC
Publishing Co: CMP Publications Inc., 600
Community Drive, Manhasset, NY 11030,
USA; 516/562-7673, Fax: 516/562-7007,
Co Email: homepc@aol.com; Web URL:
techweb.cmp.com/hpc; Focus: Informa-
tion for Home PC users; Format: Maga-
zine; Dan Schwartz, Pblshr Ellen Pearlman,
Ed.-in-Chief Amy Lipton, Exec Freq:
Monthly, Price/yr-$:22

**How to Conquer the Software Mar-
ket**
Publishing Co: Micro Software Marketing,
PO Box 380, Congers, NY 10920, USA;
914/268-5925, Focus: Marketing, publicity and strategies for marketing software;
Format: Book; Scott Witt, Ed. Price/yr-
$:135

How to Maximize Your PC
Publishing Co: WEKA Publishing, 1077
Bridgeport Ave, Shelton, CT 06484, USA;
Fax: 203/944-3663, Focus: Loose-leaf
information on upgrading and expanding
PCs; Format: Loose-leaf; Peter Strapko,
Mngg Dir Circ.: 30,000, Freq: 4/Year,
Price/yr-$:59.95

HP Chronicle
Publishing Co: Publications & Communica-
tions Inc., 12416 Hymeadow Drive, Aus-
tin, TX 78750-1896, USA; 512/250-9023,
Fax: 512/331-3900, Co Email: @pcin-
ews.com; Web URL: pcinews.com/pci;
Focus: Information and product reviews for
HP 3000 users; Format: Magazine; Larry
Storer, Ed. Dir David Woelbruck, Ed.
Circ.: 17,000, Freq: Monthly, Price/yr-
$:45/75

HP Professional
Publishing Co: Cardinal Business Media
Inc., 1300 Virginia Drive, #400, Ft. Wash-

ington, PA 19034-3225, USA; 215/643-8000, Fax: 215/643-8099, Focus: News, reviews and information for HP computer users; Format: Magazine; Charlie Simpson, Ed-in-Chief Email: simpsoncm@box101.cardinal; Leslie Ringe, Pblshr George A. Thompson, Sr Ed. Email: thompsonga@box101.cardinal.com; Circ.: 35,000, Freq: Monthly, Price/yr-$:Free/30

hp-ux/usr
Publishing Co: INTEREX, 1192 Borregas Ave, Sunnyvale, CA 94089, USA; 408/747-0227, Fax: 408/747-0947, Web URL: interex.org; Focus: Information for HP Unix users; Format: Magazine; Circ.: 11,000, Freq: 6/Year, Price/yr-$:Free/49.50

Hum-The Government Computer Magazine
Publishing Co: Hum Communications Ltd., 557 Cambridge Street S., #202, Ottawa, Ontario K1S 4J4, Canada; 613/237-4862, Fax: 613/237-4232, Focus: Information for government computer users in Canada; Format: Magazine; Lee Hunter, Mgng Ed. & Pblr Email: lee.hunter@hum.com; Lori Cunningham, Sales Manager Email: loric@hum.com; Circ.: 13,005, Freq: Monthly, Price/yr-$:19

I+Way
Publishing Co: IDG Communications/Peterborough, 86 Elm Street, Peterborough, NH 03458, USA; 603/924-7271, Fax: 603/924-7013, Focus: Information on the Internet; Format: Magazine; Michael Nadeau, Ed. Email: mnadeau@ix.net-com.com

I/S Analyzer Case Studies
Publishing Co: United Communications Group, 175 Highland Ave, Needham, MA 02194, USA; 617/444-5755, Fax: 617/444-8958, Web URL: ucg.com; Focus: Case studies on reengineering, C/S, object technology, etc.; Format: Newsletter; Greg Strakosch, Pblshr Email: gstrakos@ucg.com; Joanne Cummings, Ed. Freq: Monthly, Price/yr-$:325

IBEX Bulletin, The
Publishing Co: Xephon, 1301 W. Hwy 407, #201-450, Lewisville, TX 75067, USA; 817/455-7050, Fax: 817/455-2492, Focus: Survey data from IBM Mainframe User Information Exchange--a panel of 1,500 mainframe users; Format: Newsletter; Freq: Monthly, Price/yr-$:460

IBM Terminology, The Handbook of
Publishing Co: Xephon, 1301 W. Hwy 407, #201-450, Lewisville, TX 75067, USA; 817/455-7050, Fax: 817/455-2492, Focus: Guide to IBM products, concepts and strategies; Format: Factbook; Freq: 2/Year, Price/yr-$:100

IC Master
Publishing Co: Hearst Business Publishing/UTP Div., 645 Stewart Ave, Garden City, NY 11530, USA; 516/227-1300, Fax:

516/227-1453, Focus: Listing of over 80,000 commercial ICs; Format: Directory; Armand Villinger, Pblshr Dave Howell, Ed.-in-Chief Freq: Annual, Price/yr-$:185

ICECAP Report
Publishing Co: Integrated Circuit Engineering Corp., 15022 N. 75th Street, Scottsdale, AZ 85260-2476, USA; 602/998-9780, Fax: 602/948-1925, Focus: News, reviews, analysis and forecasts on the semiconductor industry; Format: Newsletter; William McClean, Ed. Email: 73512.304@compuserve.com; Circ.: 300, Freq: Monthly, Price/yr-$:495

ID Systems
Publishing Co: Helmers Publishing Inc., 174 Concord Street, Peterborough, NH 03458-0874, USA; 603/924-9631, Fax: 603/924-7408, Focus: Covers automated data collection systems including barcode & other keyless data entry tech; Format: Magazine; Kevin B. Rushalko, Pblshr Carl T. Helmers Jr., Ed.ial Dir Mary Langen, Ed.-in-Chief Circ.: 73,500, Freq: Monthly, Price/yr-$:Free/55

ID Systems, European Edition
Publishing Co: Helmers Publishing Inc., 16 rue Sleidan, Strasbourg, F-67000, France; 33-88-606257, Fax: 33-88-600583, Focus: Covers automated data collection systems in Europe including barcode & keyless; Format: Magazine; Kevin B. Rushalko, Pblshr Mary Langen, Ed.-in-Chief Susan Beale, Ed. Circ.: 23,000, Freq: 9/year

IDG's Windows 95 Journal
Publishing Co: IDG Newsletters Corp., 77 Franklin Street, Boston, MA 02110-1510, USA; 617/482-8785, Fax: 617/338-0164, Focus: Tips and techniques for Windows 95 users; Format: Newsletter; Craig G. Pierce, Pblshr Valerie Murray, Ed. Sheila Sandapen, Ed. Freq: Monthly, Price/yr-$:99/119/129

IEC Annual Review of Communications
Publishing Co: International Engineering Consortium, 303 E Wacker Drive, #740, Chicago, IL 60601-5212, USA; 312/938-3500, Fax: 312/938-8787, Focus: Information for information industry, telecommunications professionals & educators; Format: Report; Price/yr-$:195

IEEE Communications Magazine
Publishing Co: IEEE Communications Society, 445 Hoes Lane, PO Box 1331, Piscataway, NJ 08855-1331, USA; 908/981-0060, Fax: 908/981-9776, Co Email: @ieee.org; Web URL: ieee.org; Focus: Technical information on communications trends; Format: Magazine; Circ.: 37,000, Freq: Monthly, Price/yr-$:39

IEEE Computational Science & Engineering
Publishing Co: IEEE Computer Society, 445 Hoes Lane, PO Box 1331, Piscataway, NJ 08855-1331, USA; 908/981-0060, Fax:

908/981-9667, Co Email: @ieee.org; Web URL: ieee.org; Focus: Science and engineering that use computers as their main tool; Format: Magazine; Ahmed Sameh, Ed.-in-Chief True Seaborn, Pblshr Email: t.seaborn@computer.org; Freq: 4/Year, Price/yr-$:22/27

IEEE Computer Graphics and Applications
Publishing Co: IEEE Computer Society, 445 Hoes Lane, PO Box 1331, Piscataway, NJ 08855-1331, USA; 908/981-0060, Fax: 908/981-9667, Co Email: @ieee.org; Web URL: ieee.org; Focus: Technical information on computer graphics applications, research and technology; Format: Magazine; Nancy Hays, Mgng Ed. True Seaborn, Pblshr Email: t.seaborn@computer.org; Circ.: 8,000, Freq: 6/Year, Price/yr-$:31/36

IEEE Design and Test of Computers
Publishing Co: IEEE Computer Society, 445 Hoes Lane, PO Box 1331, Piscataway, NJ 08855-1331, USA; 908/981-0060, Fax: 908/981-9667, Co Email: @ieee.org; Web URL: ieee.org; Focus: Technical information on computer design and testing; Format: Magazine; Manuel d'Abrev, Ed.-in-Chief True Seaborn, Pblshr Email: t.seaborn@computer.org; Circ.: 8,000, Freq: 4/Year, Price/yr-$:28/33

IEEE Expert
Publishing Co: IEEE Computer Society, 445 Hoes Lane, PO Box 1331, Piscataway, NJ 08855-1331, USA; 908/981-0060, Fax: 908/981-9667, Co Email: @ieee.org; Web URL: ieee.org; Focus: Technical information on expert systems; Format: Magazine; True Seaborn, Pblshr Email: t.seaborn@computer.org; Circ.: 15,000, Freq: 6/year, Price/yr-$:31

IEEE Membership Directory
Publishing Co: IEEE, 445 Hoes Lane, PO Box 1331, Piscataway, NJ 08855-1331, USA; 908/981-0060, Fax: 908/981-9667, Co Email: @ieee.ogr; Web URL: ieee.org; Focus: Listing of 300,000+ IEEE members (CD-ROM $100); Format: Directory; Freq: Annual, Price/yr-$:70

IEEE Micro
Publishing Co: IEEE Computer Society, 445 Hoes Lane, PO Box 1331, Piscataway, NJ 08855-1331, USA; 908/981-0060, Fax: 908/981-9667, Co Email: @ieee.org; Web URL: ieee.org; Focus: Technical information on microcomputer system design, technology and applications; Format: Magazine; Dante Del Corso, Ed.-in-Chief True Seaborn, Pblshr Email: t.seaborn@computer.org; Circ.: 22,000, Freq: 6/Year, Price/yr-$:29/34

IEEE Multimedia
Publishing Co: IEEE Computer Society, 445 Hoes Lane, PO Box 1331, Piscataway, NJ 08855-1331, USA; 908/981-0060, Fax: 908/981-9667, Co Email: @ieee.org; Web URL: ieee.org; Focus: Technical

information on multimedia hardware and software; Format: Magazine; True Seaborn, Pblshr Email: t.seaborn@computer.org; Circ.: 8,000, Freq: 4/Year, Price/yr-$:22/27

IEEE Network Magazine
Publishing Co: IEEE Communications Society, 445 Hoes Lane, PO Box 1331, Piscataway, NJ 08855-1331, USA; 908/981-0060, Fax: 908/981-9776, Co Email: @ieee.org; Web URL: ieee.org; Focus: Technical information on computer communication; Format: Magazine; Freq: 6/Year, Price/yr-$:26

IEEE Parallel & Distributed Technology
Publishing Co: IEEE Computer Society, 445 Hoes Lane, PO Box 1331, Piscataway, NJ 08855-1331, USA; 908/981-0060, Fax: 908/981-9667, Co Email: @ieee.org; Web URL: ieee.org; Focus: Technical information on parallel computer systems; Format: Magazine; True Seaborn, Pblshr Email: t.seaborn@computer.org; Freq: 4/Year, Price/yr-$:26/31

IEEE Personal Communications
Publishing Co: IEEE Communications Society, 445 Hoes Lane, PO Box 1331, Piscataway, NJ 08855-1331, USA; 908/981-0060, Fax: 908/981-9776, Co Email: @ieee.org; Web URL: ieee.org; Focus: Technical information on nomadic communications and computing; Format: Magazine; Freq: 6/Year, Price/yr-$:22

IEEE Potentials
Publishing Co: IEEE, 445 Hoes Lane, Piscataway, NJ 08855-1331, USA; 908/981-0060, Fax: 908/981-9667, Co Email: @ieee.org; Web URL: ieee.ogr; Focus: Career news for computer and electronics students; Format: Magazine; Freq: 6/Year, Price/yr-$:15

IEEE Robotics and Automation Magazine
Publishing Co: IEEE Robotics and Automation Society, 445 Hoes Lane, PO Box 1331, Piscataway, NJ 08855-1331, USA; 908/981-0060, Fax: 908/981-9667, Co Email: @ieee.org; Web URL: ieee.org; Focus: Technical information on robotics and automation Theory; Format: Magazine; Freq: 4/Year, Price/yr-$:Assn. Dues/7

IEEE Software
Publishing Co: IEEE Computer Society, 445 Hoes Lane, PO Box 1331, Piscataway, NJ 08855-1331, USA; 908/981-0060, Fax: 908/981-9667, Co Email: @ieee.org; Web URL: ieee.org; Focus: Technical information on software development; Format: Magazine; Carl Chang, Ed.-in-Chief True Seaborn, Pblshr Email: t.seaborn@computer.org; Circ.: 25,000, Freq: 6/Year, Price/yr-$:31/36

IEEE Spectrum
Publishing Co: IEEE, 445 Hoes Lane, PO Box 1331, Piscataway, NJ 08855-1331, USA; 908/981-0060, Fax: 908/981-9667,

Co Email: @ieee.org; Web URL: spectrum.ieee.org; Focus: Electronics, computer technology and social issues of technology; Format: Magazine; Murray Slovick, Ed. & Assoc Pblr Email: m.slovick@ieee.org; Alfred Rosenblatt, Mgng Ed. Email: a.rosenblatt@ieee.org; Anthony J. Ferraro, Pblshr Circ.: 300,000, Freq: Monthly, Price/yr-$:40

IEEE Technical Activities Guide
Publishing Co: IEEE, 445 Hoes Lane, PO Box 1331, Piscataway, NJ 08855-1331, USA; 908/981-0060, Fax: 908/981-9667, Co Email: @ieee.org; Web URL: ieee.org; Focus: Five years listing of IEEE conferences; Format: Directory; Freq: 4/Year

IEEE Technology and Society Magazine
Publishing Co: IEEE, 445 Hoes Lane, PO Box 1331, Piscataway, NJ 08855-1331, USA; 908/981-0060, Fax: 908/981-9667, Co Email: @ieee.org; Web URL: ieee.org; Focus: Impact of computer and electronics technology; Format: Magazine; Freq: 4/Year, Price/yr-$:24

IEEE Transactions on Communications
Publishing Co: IEEE Communications Society, 445 Hoes Lane, PO Box 1331, Piscataway, NJ 08855-1331, USA; 908/981-0060, Fax: 908/981-9776, Co Email: @ieee.org; Web URL: ieee.org; Focus: Technical papers on communications topics; Format: Magazine; Freq: Monthly, Price/yr-$:27

IEEE Transactions on Computer-Aided Design of ICs & Systems
Publishing Co: IEEE Circuits and Systems Society, 445 Hoes Lane, PO Box 1331, Piscataway, NJ 08855-1331, USA; 908/981-0060, Fax: 908/981-9667, Co Email: @ieee.org; Web URL: ieee.org; Focus: Technical articles on ICs and systems CAD; Format: Magazine; Freq: Monthly, Price/yr-$:21/26

IEEE Transactions on Computers
Publishing Co: IEEE Computer Society, 445 Hoes Lane, PO Box 1331, Piscataway, NJ 08855-1331, USA; 908/981-0060, Fax: 908/981-9667, Co Email: @ieee.org; Web URL: ieee.org; Focus: Technical papers on computation, information processing, applications & computer systems d; Format: Magazine; Circ.: 15,000, Freq: Monthly, Price/yr-$:31/36

IEEE Transactions on Fuzzy Systems
Publishing Co: IEEE Circuits and Systems Society, 445 Hoes Lane, PO Box 1331, Piscataway, NJ 08855-1331, USA; 908/981-0060, Fax: 908/981-9667, Co Email: @ieee.org; Web URL: ieee.org; Focus: Technical articles on fuzzy logic and systems; Format: Magazine; Freq: 4/Year, Price/yr-$:19/27

IEEE Transactions on Image Processing
Publishing Co: IEEE Signal Processing Soci-

ety, 445 Hoes Lane, PO Box 1331, Piscataway, NJ 08855-1331, USA; 908/981-0060, Fax: 908/981-9667, Co Email: sp.info@ieee.org; Web URL: ieee.org; Focus: Technical articles on signal processing and image processing; Format: Magazine; David C. Munson, Jr., Ed.-in-Chief Mercy Kowalczyk, Exec Dir Circ.: 3,200, Freq: Monthly, Price/yr-$:36

IEEE Transactions on Information Theory
Publishing Co: IEEE Information Theory Society, 445 Hoes Lane, PO Box 1331, Piscataway, NJ 08855-1331, USA; 908/981-0060, Fax: 908/981-9667, Co Email: @ieee.org; Web URL: ieee.org; Focus: Technical data on information theory; Format: Magazine; Freq: 7/Year, Price/yr-$:Assn. Dues

IEEE Transactions on Knowledge & Data Engineering
Publishing Co: IEEE Computer Society, 445 Hoes Lane, PO Box 1331, Piscataway, NJ 08855-1331, USA; 908/981-0060, Fax: 908/981-9667, Co Email: @ieee.org; Web URL: ieee.org; Focus: Technical articles on knowledge engineering and AI; Format: Magazine; Freq: 6/Year, Price/yr-$:31/36

IEEE Transactions on Neural Networks
Publishing Co: IEEE Circuits and Systems Society, 445 Hoes Lane, PO Box 1331, Piscataway, NJ 08855-1331, USA; 908/981-0060, Fax: 908/981-9667, Co Email: @ieee.org; Web URL: ieee.org; Focus: Science and technology of neural networks; Format: Magazine; Freq: 6/Year, Price/yr-$:28/40

IEEE Transactions on Parallel & Distributed Systems
Publishing Co: IEEE Computer Society, 445 Hoes Lane, PO Box 1331, Piscataway, NJ 08855-1331, USA; 908/981-0060, Fax: 908/981-9667, Co Email: @ieee.org; Web URL: ieee.org; Focus: Technical information on parallel and distributed systems and applications; Format: Magazine; Freq: Monthly, Price/yr-$:31/36

IEEE Transactions on Pattern Analysis & Machine Intelligence
Publishing Co: IEEE Computer Society, 445 Hoes Lane, PO Box 1331, Piscataway, NJ 08855-1331, USA; 908/981-0060, Fax: 908/981-9667, Co Email: @ieee.org; Web URL: ieee.org; Focus: Technical information on pattern recognition and machine intelligence; Format: Magazine; Freq: Monthly, Price/yr-$:31/36

IEEE Transactions on Software Engineering
Publishing Co: IEEE Computer Society, 445 Hoes Lane, PO Box 1331, Piscataway, NJ 08855-1331, USA; 908/981-0060, Fax: 908/981-9667, Co Email: @ieee.org; Web URL: ieee.org; Focus: Technical papers on software engineering; Format:

Magazine; Freq: Monthly, Price/yr-$:30/35

IEEE Transactions on VLSI Systems
Publishing Co: IEEE Circuits and Systems Society, 445 Hoes Lane, PO Box 1331, Piscataway, NJ 08855-1331, USA; 908/981-0060, Fax: 908/981-9667, Co Email: @ieee.org; Web URL: ieee.org; Focus: Technical articles on very large scale integrated circuits; Format: Magazine; Freq: 4/Year, Price/yr-$:17

IEEE/ACM Transactions on Networking
Publishing Co: IEEE & ACM, 445 Hoes Lane, PO Box 1331, Piscataway, NJ 08855-1331, USA; 908/981-0060, Fax: 908/981-9667, Co Email: @ieee.org; Web URL: ieee.org; Focus: Technical information on communications networks; Format: Magazine; Freq: 6/Year, Price/yr-$:31

Imaging Magazine
Publishing Co: Telecom Library Inc., 12 W. 21st Street, 10th Floor, New York, NY 10010, USA; 212/691-8215, Fax: 212/691-1191, Web URL: imagingmagazine.com; Focus: Information on imaging products and technology; Format: Magazine; Lee Mantelman, Ed.-in-Chief Email: lee@nyoffice.mhs.compuser; Harry Newton, Ed. Email: harrynewton@mcimail.com; Gerry Friesen, Pblshr Circ.: 60,000, Freq: Monthly, Price/yr-$:18

Imaging Supplies Annual
Publishing Co: Giga Information Group, 1 Longwater Circle, Norwell, MA 02061, USA; 617/982-9500, Fax: 617/878-6650, Focus: Directory of imaging supplies products and vendors; Format: Directory; Jeff Swartz, Exec Pblr David Hatch, Ed. Email: dhatch@gigasd.com; Freq: Annual, Price/yr-$:125

Imaging Supplies Monthly
Publishing Co: Giga Information Group, 1 Longwater Circle, Norwell, MA 02061, USA; 617/892-9500, Fax: 617/878-6650, Focus: Ribbons, toner cartridges and supplies for printers and copiers; Format: Newsletter; Jeff Swartz, Pblshr Dave Hatch, Email: dhatch@gigasd.com; Circ.: 650, Freq: Monthly, Price/yr-$:350

Imaging World Magazine
Publishing Co: Cardinal Business Media Inc., Bayview St. at Sharp's Wharf, PO Box 1358, Camden, ME 04843, USA; 207/236-8524, Fax: 207/236-6452, Web URL: iwmag.com; Focus: Imaging technology and trends; Format: Newspaper; Bruce Hoard, Exec Ed. Email: bruceh@mcimail.com; Bruce Taylor, Grp Pblshr Andy Moore, Ed-in-Chief Circ.: 60,000, Freq: Monthly, Price/yr-$:Free/48

IMC Journal
Publishing Co: International Information Management Congress, 1650 38th Street, #205W, Boulder, CO 80301, USA; 303/440-7085, Fax: 303/440-7234, Focus:

Information on international document imaging; Format: Magazine; Bruce Taylor, Ed. & Pblr Bruce Hoard, Exec Ed. Freq: 6/Year, Price/yr-$:38

Impact Printer Guide
Publishing Co: Dataquest Inc., 26254 Golden Valley Road, Bldg. 401, Santa Clarita, CA 95351, USA; 805/298-3261, Fax: 805/298-4388, Co Email: mmakers@netcom.com; Web URL: netcom.com~mmakers; Focus: Specifications of dot matrix and line printers; Format: Directory; Freq: 2/Year, Price/yr-$:99

In-Stat Electronics Report
Publishing Co: In-Stat Inc., PO Box 14667, 7418 E Helm Drive, Scottsdale, AZ 85267-4667, USA; 602/483-4440, Fax: 602/483-0400, Web URL: instat.com; Focus: News, forecasts and analysis of the semiconductor market; Format: Newsletter; Jack Beedle, Chmn John Abram, Pres Morry Marshall, Dir Analysis Freq: Monthly, Price/yr-$:795

In-Stat Information Alert
Publishing Co: In-Stat Inc., PO Box 14667, 7418 E Helm Drive, Scottsdale, AZ 85267-4667, USA; 602/483-4440, Fax: 602/483-0400, Web URL: instat.com; Focus: News of the semiconductor market; Format: Fax bulletin; Jack Beedle, Chmn John Abram, Pres Morry Marshall, Dir Analysis Freq: Weekly, Price/yr-$:795

Industry Pulse, The
Publishing Co: VLSI Research Inc., 1754 Technology Drive, #117, San Jose, CA 95110, USA; 408/453-8844, Fax: 408/437-0608, Focus: Statistics on the semiconductor, semiconductor equipment and electronics industries; Format: Newsletter; Freq: Monthly, Price/yr-$:110/150

Industry Week
Publishing Co: Penton Publishing Inc., 1100 Superior Ave, Cleveland, OH 44114-2543, USA; 216/696-7000, Fax: 216/696-7670, Co Email: 74774.2327@compuserve.com; Web URL: penton.com; Focus: Management in administration, finance, productions, engineering, purchasing, marketing and; Format: Magazine; Carl T. Marino, Pblshr John R. Brandt, Ed.-in-Chief Freq: 25/Year, Price/yr-$:Free/60

Industry.Net
Publishing Co: Automation New Network, PO Box 38357, Pittsburgh, PA 15238-8357, USA; 412/967-3500, Fax: 412/967-3504, Co Email: @industry.net; Web URL: industry.net; Focus: Regional industry information; Format: Magazine; Don Jones, Pblshr Ken Ball, Tech Ed. Dir Freq: 16/Year, Price/yr-$:Free/68

Infobase Technology Magazine
Publishing Co: Folio Corp., 5072 N 300 W, Provo, UT 84604-5652, USA; 801/299-6700, Fax: 801/229-6787, Focus: Information for Folio Infobase users; Format: Online magazine; Cara O'Sullivan,

Ed.-in-Chief Email: cosulliv@folio.com; Freq: 6/Year, Price/yr-$:Free

Infoperspectives
Publishing Co: Technology News of America Co., Inc., 110 Greene Street, New York, NY 10012, USA; 212/334-9750, Fax: 212/334-9491, Co Email: technews@worldnet.com; Focus: Information systems strategies at large companies; Format: Newsletter; Hesh Wiener, Ed. & Pblr Freq: Monthly, Price/yr-$:485

Inform
Publishing Co: Association for Information & Image Management, 1100 Wayne Avenue, #1100, Silver Spring, MD 20910, USA; 301/587-8202, Fax: 301/587-5129, Co Email: @aiim.mo.md.us; Focus: Applications of micrographics, imaging and document management; Format: Magazine; John Harney, Email: jharney@aiim.mo.md.us; Circ.: 40,000, Freq: 10/Year, Price/yr-$:85

Information & Interactive Service Report
Publishing Co: BRP Publications Inc., 1333 H Street NW, 2nd Fl., Washington, DC 20005, USA; 202/842-0520, Fax: 212/475-1790, Co Email: brp@access.digex.net; Focus: News on information delivery, products & markets-video text, home banking, etc; Format: Newsletter; Rod W. Kuckro, Ed. Nate Zelnick, Associate Ed. Andrew Jacobson, Pblshr Freq: biweekly, Price/yr-$:495

Information Advisor
Publishing Co: FIND/SVP, 625 Avenue of the Americas, New York, NY 10011, USA; Fax: 212/645-7681, Co Email: @findsvp.com; Web URL: findsvp.com; Focus: Tips and techniques for finding online business information; Format: Newsletter; Robert I. Berkman, Ed. Freq: Monthly, Price/yr-$:130

Information Brokers, Burwell World Directory of
Publishing Co: Burwell Enterprises, 3724 FM 1960 W. #214, Houston, TX 77068-3528, USA; 713/537-9051, Fax: 713/537-8332, Co Email: 75120.50@compuserve.com; Focus: Listing of 1,700 companies offering online research services or document delivery; Format: Directory/disk; Helen P. Burwell, Pres Email: hburwell@ix.nctcom.com; Freq: Annual, Price/yr-$:99/150

Information Hotline
Publishing Co: Science Associates/Int'l. Inc., 6 Hastings Road, Marlboro, NJ 07746, USA; 908/536-7673, Fax: 908/536-7673, Focus: News and trends in information and library sciences; Format: Newsletter; Martha Howard, Mgng Ed. Iris Wallack, Pblshr Roxy Bauer, MIS Manager Freq: 10/Year, Price/yr-$:150

Information Industry Bulletin
Publishing Co: Digital Information Group, PO Box 110235, Stamford, CT 06911-

0235, USA; 203/840-0045, Fax: 203/977-8310, Co Email: 75120.2616@compuserve.com; Focus: Information about the information industry; Format: Newsletter; Jeff Silverstein, Ed. & Pblr Freq: Weekly, Price/yr-$:395

Information Industry Directory
Publishing Co: Gale Research Inc., 835 Penobscot Bldg, Detroit, MI 48226, USA; 313/961-2242, Fax: 313/961-6083, Co Email: galenp@conch.aa.msen.com; Focus: Descriptive listing of nearly 6,000 producers and vendors of electronic information; Format: Directory; Mary Alampi, Ed. Freq: Annual, Price/yr-$:475

Information Management: Strategy, Systems & Technologies
Publishing Co: Auerbach Publications, 31 St. James Ave, Boston, MA 02116-9372, USA; 617/423-2020, Fax: 617/451-0908, Co Email: 73752.2270@compuserve.com; Web URL: wgl.com; Focus: How-to reference on information systems operation; Format: Loose-leaf; Kim Horan Kelly, Pblshr Freq: 6/Year, Price/yr-$:505

Information Sciences & Technology, Annual Review of
Publishing Co: Information Today Inc., 143 Old Marlton Pike, Medford, NJ 08055-8750, USA; 609/654-6266, Fax: 609/654-4309, Co Email: custserv@infotoday.com; Web URL: infotoday.com; Focus: Reviews and trends in the information systems and services industry; Format: Factbook; Martha E. Williams, Ed. Freq: Annual, Price/yr-$:76/95

Information Security
Publishing Co: Datapro Information Services Group, 600 Delran Pkwy., Delran, NJ 08705-9904, USA; 609/764-0100, Fax: 609/764-2811, Co Email: datapro@mhh.com; Web URL: datapro.com; Focus: Information about security technologies; Format: Newsletter; Freq: Monthly

Information Security Policies Made Easy
Publishing Co: Baseline Software, PO Box 1219, Sausalito, CA 94966, USA; 415/332-7763, Fax: 415/332-8032, Co Email: infosec@baselinesoft.com; Web URL: baselinesoft.com/people/infose; Focus: Pre-written policies for information security, planning and implementation; Format: Book/diskette; Charles C. Wood, Ed. & Pblr Price/yr-$:495

Information Security Services
Publishing Co: Datapro Information Services Group, 600 Delran Pkwy., Delran, NJ 08705-9904, USA; 609/764-0100, Fax: 609/764-2811, Co Email: datapro@mhh.com; Web URL: datapro.com; Focus: Information about security technologies and government regulations; Format: CD-ROM; Freq: Monthly

Information Sources
Publishing Co: Information Industry

Assoc., 1625 Massachusetts Ave NW, #700, Washington, DC 20036, USA; 202/986-0280, Fax: 202/638-4403, Web URL: infoindustry.org; Focus: Directory of over 500 information industry companies; Format: Directory; Freq: Annual, Price/yr-$:30/158

Information Strategy: The Executive's Journal
Publishing Co: Auerbach Publications, 31 St. James Ave, Boston, MA 02116-9372, USA; 617/423-2020, Fax: 617/451-0908, Co Email: 73752.2270@compuserve.com; Web URL: wgl.com; Focus: Information for implementing and managing end-user computing; Format: Newsletter; Kim Horan Kelly, Pblshr Freq: Monthly, Price/yr-$:145

Information Systems Management
Publishing Co: Auerbach Publications, 31 St. James Ave, Boston, MA 02116-9372, USA; 617/423-2020, Fax: 617/451-0908, Co Email: 73752.2270@compuserve.com; Web URL: wgl.com; Focus: Practical advice on managing IS departments; Format: Magazine; Karen Brogno, Ed. Circ.: 5,000, Freq: 4/Year, Price/yr-$:134

Information Systems Security
Publishing Co: Auerbach Publications, 31 St. James Ave, Boston, MA 02116-9372, USA; 617/423-2020, Fax: 617/451-0908, Co Email: 73752.2270@compuserve.com; Web URL: wgl.com; Focus: Information on security planning, implementation and management; Format: Reference book; Kim Horan Kelly, Pblshr James Anderson, Ed. Freq: 4/Year, Price/yr-$:158

Information Systems Security Products & Services Catalogue
Publishing Co: Defense Dept./NSA, US Government Printing Office, Washington, DC 20402, USA; 202/512-1800, Fax: 202/512-2250, Focus: Listing of government approved security products; Format: Directory; Freq: 4/Year, Price/yr-$:55

Information Systems Spending
Publishing Co: Computer Economics Inc., 5841 Edison Place, Carlsbad, CA 92008, USA; 619/438-8100, Fax: 619/431-1126, Co Email: iss@compecon.com; Focus: DP spending, staffing, leasing and applications trends; Format: Factbook; Brian Biber, VP Email: bbiber@compecon.com; Freq: Annual, Price/yr-$:895

Information Technology Industry Data Book
Publishing Co: Information Technology Industry Council (ITI), 1250 Eye Street NW, #200, Washington, DC 20005, USA; 202/626-5729, Fax: 202/638-4922, Web URL: itic.org; Focus: Information industry statistics from 1960 with forecast to 2005; Format: Factbook; Rhett Dawson, Pres Oliver Smoot, EVP Freq: Annual, Price/yr-$:165.90

Information Technology Market Sourcebook

Publishing Co: Frost & Sullivan, 2525 Charleston Road, Mt. View, CA 94043, USA; 415/961-9000, Fax: 415/961-5042, Web URL: frost.com; Focus: Forecasts, trends and market data; Format: Report; Freq: Annual, Price/yr-$:695

Information Technology Strategic Alliances Database
Publishing Co: Itsunami Inc., PO Box 4756, Berkeley, CA 94704, USA; 510/841-7271, Fax: 510/848-6897, Focus: Summaries of strategic relationships in the information industry; Format: Diskette; James M. Sharp, Ed. & Pblr Freq: 4/Year, Price/yr-$:2,500

Information Technology/21st Century
Publishing Co: Computer Technology Research Corp., 6 North Atlantic Wharf, Charleston, SC 29401-2150, USA; 803/853-6460, Fax: 803/853-7210, Co Email: report@ctrcorp.com; Web URL: ctrcorp.com; Focus: News & information about the PC marketplace-hardware, software, etc.; Format: Newsletter; Edward R. Wagner, Pres, Pblr Stacey Evangelist, Ed-in-Chief Freq: Monthly, Price/yr-$:390

Information Today
Publishing Co: Information Today Inc., 143 Old Marlton Pike, Medford, NJ 08055-8750, USA; 609/654-6266, Fax: 609/654-4309, Co Email: custserv@infotoday.com; Web URL: infotoday.com; Focus: News and information about electronic information services; Format: Magazine; David Hoffman, Ed. Freq: 11/Year, Price/yr-$:48

Information World Review
Publishing Co: Information Today Inc., 143 Old Marlton Pike, Medford, NJ 08055-8750, USA; 609/654-6266, Fax: 609/654-4309, Co Email: custserv@infotoday.com; Web URL: infotoday.com; Focus: News and information about European electronic information services; Format: Magazine; Richard Poynder, Ed. Freq: 11/Year, Price/yr-$:63

InformationWEEK
Publishing Co: CMP Publications Inc., 600 Community Drive, Manhasset, NY 11030, USA; 516/562-5000, Fax: 516/562-5036, Web URL: techweb.cmp.com/iwk; Focus: News and trends for information managers; Format: Magazine; Joel Dreyfuss, Ed.-in-Chief Tony L. Uphoff, Pblshr John J. McCormick, Ed. Circ.: 191,000, Freq: Weekly, Price/yr-$:Free/64

Infosecurity News
498 Concord Street, Framingham, MA 01702-2357, USA; 508/879-9792, Fax: 508/879-0348, Co Email: isn@nustu,ccmail.compuserve.co; Focus: Information systems security; Format: Magazine; Michael I. Sobol, Pblshr Price/yr-$:Free

InfoText
Publishing Co: GPG Publishing Inc., 9200

Sunset Blvd., #612, Los Angeles, CA 90069, USA; 310/724-6783, Focus: Interactive voice applications for non-technical users; Format: Magazine; Kurt Indvik, Pblr & Ed-in-Chief Leila Morris, Mngd Ed. Gil Kaan, Assoc Ed. Circ.: 17,000, Freq: 6/Year, Price/yr-$:Free/30

InfoVision ComForum Report
Publishing Co: International Engineering Consortium, 303 E Wacker Drive, #740, Chicago, IL 60601-5212, USA; 312/938-3500, Fax: 312/938-8787, Focus: Expert predictions for the information industry; Format: Report; Price/yr-$:475

InfoWorld
Publishing Co: InfoWorld Publishing Co., 155 Bovet Road, #800, San Mateo, CA 94402, USA; 415/572-7341, Fax: 415/358-1269, Co Email: 73267.1537@compuserve.com; Web URL: infoworld.com; Focus: News, reviews and product comparisons for PC buyers; Format: Newspaper; Sandy Reed, Ed.-in-Chief Michael Vizard, Exec Ed. Ross Owens, Mngd Ed. Circ.: 250,000, Freq: Weekly, Price/yr-$:Free/145

Inside AutoCAD
Publishing Co: Cobb Group, The, 9420 Bunsen Pkwy. #300, Louisville, KY 40220, USA; 502/491-1900, Fax: 502/491-8050, Co Email: cobb@aol.com; Web URL: cobb.com; Focus: News, tips and tricks for AutoCAD users; Format: Newsletter; Byron Williams, Ed. Freq: Bimonthly, Price/yr-$:89

Inside Corel WordPerfect Suite
Publishing Co: Cobb Group, The, 9420 Bunsen Pkwy. #300, Louisville, KY 40220, USA; 502/491-1900, Fax: 502/491-8050, Co Email: cobb@aol.com; Web URL: cobb.com; Focus: News, tips and tricks for Corel WordPerfect Suite; Format: Newsletter; Price/yr-$:69

Inside Corel WordPerfect Suite 7
Publishing Co: Cobb Group, The, 9420 Bunsen Pkwy. #300, Louisville, KY 40220, USA; 502/491-1900, Fax: 502/491-8050, Co Email: cobb@aol.com; Web URL: cobb.com; Focus: News, tips and tricks for Corel WordPerfect Suite 7; Format: Newsletter; Price/yr-$:69

Inside dBase
Publishing Co: Cobb Group, The, 9420 Bunsen Pkwy. #300, Louisville, KY 40220, USA; 502/491-1900, Fax: 502/491-8050, Co Email: cobb@aol.com; Web URL: cobb.com; Focus: Tips and techniques for dBase users; Format: Newsletter; Jeff Davis, Ed. Freq: Monthly, Price/yr-$:69

Inside dBase for Windows
Publishing Co: Cobb Group, The, 9420 Bunsen Pkwy. #300, Louisville, KY 40220, USA; 502/491-1900, Fax: 502/491-8050, Co Email: cobb@aol.com; Web URL: cobb.com; Focus: Tips and techniques for dBase for Windows users; For-

mat: Newsletter; Peter Schickler, Ed. Peter Schickler, Ed.-in-Chief Freq: Monthly, Price/yr-$:69

Inside DOS
Publishing Co: Cobb Group, The, 9420 Bunsen Pkwy. #300, Louisville, KY 40220, USA; 502/491-1900, Fax: 502/491-8050, Co Email: cobb@aol.com; Web URL: cobb.com; Focus: News, tips and techniques for MS-DOS users; Format: Newsletter; Jim Stanfield, Ed. Freq: Monthly, Price/yr-$:49

Inside Filemaker Pro
Publishing Co: Cobb Group, The, 9420 Bunsen Pkwy. #300, Louisville, KY 40220, USA; 502/491-1900, Fax: 502/491-8050, Co Email: cobb@aol.com; Web URL: cobb.com; Focus: News, tips and techniques for Filemaker Pro Macintosh users; Format: Newsletter; Ron Wilder, Ed. Freq: Monthly, Price/yr-$:59

Inside ILE
Publishing Co: United Communications Group, 175 Highland Ave, Needham, MA 02194, USA; 617/444-5755, Fax: 617/444-8958, Web URL: ucg.com; Focus: Information for ILE users; Format: Newsletter; Greg Strakosch, Pblshr Email: gstrakos@ucg.com; Ron Turull, Ed. Freq: Monthly, Price/yr-$:99

Inside LANtastic
Publishing Co: Cobb Group, The, 9420 Bunsen Pkwy. #300, Louisville, KY 40220, USA; 502/491-1900, Fax: 502/491-8050, Co Email: cobb@aol.com; Web URL: cobb.com; Focus: News, tips and techniques for LANtastic users; Format: Newsletter; John Gowin, Ed. Freq: Monthly, Price/yr-$:99

Inside Microsoft Access
Publishing Co: Cobb Group, The, 9420 Bunsen Pkwy. #300, Louisville, KY 40220, USA; 502/491-1900, Fax: 502/491-8050, Co Email: cobb@aol.com; Web URL: cobb.com; Focus: News, tips and tricks for Microsoft Access users; Format: Newsletter; Susan Harkins, Ed. Freq: Monthly, Price/yr-$:59

Inside Microsoft Excel
Publishing Co: Cobb Group, The, 9420 Bunsen Pkwy. #300, Louisville, KY 40220, USA; 502/491-1900, Fax: 502/491-8050, Co Email: cobb@aol.com; Web URL: cobb.com; Focus: News, tips and techniques for Microsoft Excel users on the Macintosh; Format: Newsletter; Steve Cobb, Ed. Freq: Monthly, Price/yr-$:59

Inside Microsoft Office
Publishing Co: Cobb Group, The, 9420 Bunsen Pkwy. #300, Louisville, KY 40220, USA; 502/491-1900, Fax: 502/491-8050, Co Email: cobb@aol.com; Web URL: cobb.com; Focus: News, tips and tricks for Microsoft Office users; Format: Newsletter; Janice Walter, Ed. Freq: Monthly, Price/yr-$:69

Inside Microsoft Office 95

Publishing Co: Cobb Group, The, 9420 Bunsen Pkwy. #300, Louisville, KY 40220, USA; 502/491-1900, Fax: 502/491-8050, Co Email: cobb@aol.com; Web URL: cobb.com; Focus: News, tips and tricks for Microsoft Office 95 users; Format: Newsletter; Price/yr-$:59

Inside Microsoft PowerPoint
Publishing Co: Cobb Group, The, 9420 Bunsen Pkwy. #300, Louisville, KY 40220, USA; 502/491-1900, Fax: 502/491-8050, Co Email: cobb@aol.com; Web URL: cobb.com; Focus: News, tips and tricks for Microsoft PowerPoint users; Format: Newsletter; Bryan Chamberlain, Ed. Freq: Monthly, Price/yr-$:49

Inside Microsoft Project
Publishing Co: Cobb Group, The, 9420 Bunsen Pkwy. #300, Louisville, KY 40220, USA; 502/491-1900, Fax: 502/491-8050, Co Email: cobb@aol.com; Web URL: cobb.com; Focus: Tips and techniques for Microsoft Project users; Format: Newsletter; Freq: 6/Year, Price/yr-$:49

Inside Microsoft Project for Windows 95
Publishing Co: Cobb Group, The, 9420 Bunsen Pkwy. #300, Louisville, KY 40220, USA; 502/491-1900, Fax: 502/491-8050, Co Email: cobb@aol.com; Web URL: cobb.com; Focus: Tips and techniques for Microsoft Project for Windows 95 users; Format: Newsletter; Price/yr-$:59

Inside Microsoft Visual C++
Publishing Co: Cobb Group, The, 9420 Bunsen Pkwy. #300, Louisville, KY 40220, USA; 502/491-1900, Fax: 502/491-8050, Co Email: cobb@aol.com; Web URL: cobb.com; Focus: News and information for Visual C++ users; Format: Newsletter; Freq: Monthly, Price/yr-$:69

Inside Microsoft Windows
Publishing Co: Cobb Group, The, 9420 Bunsen Pkwy. #300, Louisville, KY 40220, USA; 502/491-1900, Fax: 502/491-8050, Co Email: cobb@aol.com; Web URL: cobb.com; Focus: Tips and techniques for Microsoft Windows users; Format: Newsletter; Charity Edelen, Ed. Freq: Monthly, Price/yr-$:49

Inside Microsoft Windows 95
Publishing Co: Cobb Group, The, 9420 Bunsen Pkwy. #300, Louisville, KY 40220, USA; 502/491-1900, Fax: 502/491-8050, Co Email: cobb@aol.com; Web URL: cobb.com; Focus: News and tips for Microsoft Windows 95; Format: Newsletter; Price/yr-$:49

Inside Microsoft Windows: Networking Edition
Publishing Co: Cobb Group, The, 9420 Bunsen Pkwy. #300, Louisville, KY 40220, USA; 502/491-1900, Fax: 502/491-8050, Co Email: cobb@aol.com; Web URL: cobb.com; Focus: News and tips for Microsoft Windows in network applica-

tions; Format: Newsletter; Charity Edelen, Ed. Freq: Monthly, Price/yr-$:59

Inside Microsoft Word 6
Publishing Co: Cobb Group, The, 9420 Bunsen Pkwy. #300, Louisville, KY 40220, USA; 502/491-1900, Fax: 502/491-8050, Co Email: cobb@aol.com; Web URL: cobb.com; Focus: News, tips and tricks for Microsoft Word 6 users; Format: Newsletter; Jody Gilbert, Ed. Freq: Monthly, Price/yr-$:59

Inside Microsoft Word 6/Mac
Publishing Co: Cobb Group, The, 9420 Bunsen Pkwy. #300, Louisville, KY 40220, USA; 502/491-1900, Fax: 502/491-8050, Co Email: cobb@aol.com; Web URL: cobb.com; Focus: News and tips for Macintosh Word 6 users; Format: Newsletter; Jody Gilbert, Ed. Freq: Bimonthly, Price/yr-$:59

Inside Microsoft Works
Publishing Co: Cobb Group, The, 9420 Bunsen Pkwy. #300, Louisville, KY 40220, USA; 502/491-1900, Fax: 502/491-8050, Co Email: cobb@aol.com; Web URL: cobb.com; Focus: News and tips for Microsoft Works users on the Macintosh; Format: Newsletter; Jim Stanfield, Ed. Freq: Monthly, Price/yr-$:49

Inside Microsoft Works for Windows
Publishing Co: Cobb Group, The, 9420 Bunsen Pkwy. #300, Louisville, KY 40220, USA; 502/491-1900, Fax: 502/491-8050, Co Email: cobb@aol.com; Web URL: cobb.com; Focus: News and tips for Microsoft Works for Windows users; Format: Newsletter; Jim Stanfield, Ed. Freq: Monthly, Price/yr-$:49

Inside Microsoft Works for Windows 95
Publishing Co: Cobb Group, The, 9420 Bunsen Pkwy. #300, Louisville, KY 40220, USA; 502/491-1900, Fax: 502/491-8050, Co Email: cobb@aol.com; Web URL: cobb.com; Focus: News and tips for Microsoft Works for Windows 95 users; Format: Newsletter; Price/yr-$:49

Inside Netscape Navigator
Publishing Co: Cobb Group, The, 9420 Bunsen Pkwy. #300, Louisville, KY 40220, USA; 502/491-1900, Fax: 502/491-8050, Co Email: cobb@aol.com; Web URL: cobb.com; Focus: News and tips for Netscape Navigator; Format: Newsletter; Price/yr-$:49

Inside Netware
Publishing Co: Cobb Group, The, 9420 Bunsen Pkwy. #300, Louisville, KY 40220, USA; 502/493-3300, Fax: 502/491-8050, Co Email: cobb@aol.com; Web URL: cobb.com; Focus: Tips and techniques for NetWare users; Format: Newsletter; Kenneth E. Tolle Jr., Ed-in-Chief Lou Armstrong, Pblshr Freq: Monthly, Price/yr-$:99

Inside OS/2
Publishing Co: Cobb Group, The, 9420 Bunsen Pkwy. #300, Louisville, KY 40220, USA; 502/491-1900, Fax: 502/491-8050, Co Email: cobb@aol.com; Web URL: cobb.com; Focus: Tips and techniques for OS/2 users; Format: Newsletter; Mark Solomon, Ed. Freq: Monthly, Price/yr-$:59

Inside PageMaker
Publishing Co: Cobb Group, The, 9420 Bunsen Pkwy. #300, Louisville, KY 40220, USA; 502/491-1900, Fax: 502/491-8050, Co Email: cobb@aol.com; Web URL: cobb.com; Focus: Tips and techniques for PageMaker users; Format: Newsletter; Freq: Monthly, Price/yr-$:59

Inside Paradox for DOS
Publishing Co: Cobb Group, The, 9420 Bunsen Pkwy. #300, Louisville, KY 40220, USA; 502/491-1900, Fax: 502/491-8050, Co Email: cobb@aol.com; Web URL: cobb.com; Focus: News and tips for users of Paradox DOS version; Format: Newsletter; Jeff Davis, Ed. Freq: Monthly, Price/yr-$:119

Inside Paradox for Windows
Publishing Co: Cobb Group, The, 9420 Bunsen Pkwy. #300, Louisville, KY 40220, USA; 502/491-1900, Fax: 502/491-8050, Co Email: cobb@aol.com; Web URL: cobb.com; Focus: Tips and techniques for Paradox for Windows users; Format: Newsletter; Tiffany Taylor, Ed. Freq: Bimonthly, Price/yr-$:79

Inside Performa
Publishing Co: Cobb Group, The, 9420 Bunsen Pkwy. #300, Louisville, KY 40220, USA; 502/491-1900, Fax: 502/491-8050, Co Email: cobb@aol.com; Web URL: cobb.com; Focus: Tips and techniques for Performa; Format: Newsletter; Price/yr-$:49

Inside QuattroPro
Publishing Co: Cobb Group, The, 9420 Bunsen Pkwy. #300, Louisville, KY 40220, USA; 502/491-1900, Fax: 502/491-8050, Co Email: cobb@aol.com; Web URL: cobb.com; Focus: News and tips for using Borland's Quattro spreadsheet; Format: Newsletter; Stuart Vessels, Ed. Freq: Monthly, Price/yr-$:59

Inside QuattroPro For Windows
Publishing Co: Cobb Group, The, 9420 Bunsen Pkwy. #300, Louisville, KY 40220, USA; 502/491-1900, Fax: 502/491-8050, Co Email: cobb@aol.com; Web URL: cobb.com; Focus: News and tips for using Borland's QuattroPro for Windows spreadsheet; Format: Newsletter; Susan Harkins, Ed. Freq: Monthly, Price/yr-$:59

Inside R&D
Publishing Co: Technical Insights Inc., PO Box 1304, Ft. Lee, NJ 07024-9967, USA; 201/568-4744, Fax: 201/568-8247, Co Email: irdinfo@insights.com; Web URL: insights.com; Focus: Trends and analysis of high-tech R&D; Format: Newsletter; Charles Joslin, Ed. Email: ird-info@insights.com; Kenneth A. Kovaly, Pblshr Email: irdinfo@insights.com; Freq: Weekly, Price/yr-$:790

Inside Report on New Media
Publishing Co: Conference Communications Inc., PO Box 77270, San Francisco, CA 94107, USA; 415/861-1317, Fax: 415/431-9368, Format: Newsletter; Tom Hargadon, Ed. & Pblr Email: thargadon@aol.com; Freq: 22/Year, Price/yr-$:495

Inside SCO Unix Systems
Publishing Co: Cobb Group, The, 9420 Bunsen Pkwy. #300, Louisville, KY 40220, USA; 502/491-1900, Fax: 502/491-8050, Co Email: cobb@aol.com; Web URL: cobb.com; Focus: Tips and techniques for SCO ODS and Unix/Xenix; Format: Newsletter; Mark Crane, Pblshr August Mohr, Ed.-in-Chief Freq: 10/Year, Price/yr-$:99

Inside Solaris
Publishing Co: Cobb Group, The, 9420 Bunsen Pkwy. #300, Louisville, KY 40220, USA; 502/491-1900, Fax: 502/491-8050, Co Email: cobb@aol.com; Web URL: cobb.com; Focus: Tips and techniques for Sun Solaris users; Format: Newsletter; John Gowin, Ed. Freq: Monthly, Price/yr-$:99

Inside the Internet
Publishing Co: Cobb Group, The, 9420 Bunsen Pkwy. #300, Louisville, KY 40220, USA; 502/491-1900, Fax: 502/491-8050, Co Email: cobb@aol.com; Web URL: cobb.com; Focus: Tips and techniques for using the Internet; Format: Newsletter; Kurt Bondi, Ed. Freq: Monthly, Price/yr-$:69

Inside the New Computer Industry
25420 Via Cicindela, Carmel, CA 93923-8412, USA; 408/626-4361, Fax: 408/626-4362, Focus: News, analysis and perspectives on open systems and RISC; Format: Newsletter; Andrew Allison, Ed. Freq: 11/Year, Price/yr-$:675

Inside Version 3
Publishing Co: United Communications Group, 175 Highland Ave, Needham, MA 02194, USA; 617/444-5755, Fax: 617/444-8958, Web URL: ucg.com; Focus: Information for users of AS/400 operating systems; Format: Newsletter; Greg Strakosch, Pblshr Email: gstrakos@ucg.com; Ron Turull, Ed. Freq: Monthly, Price/yr-$:99

Inside Visual Basic for Windows
Publishing Co: Cobb Group, The, 9420 Bunsen Pkwy. #300, Louisville, KY 40220, USA; 502/491-1900, Fax: 502/491-8050, Co Email: cobb@aol.com; Web URL: cobb.com; Focus: News and tips for Visual Basic users; Format: Newsletter; Bill Lamkin, Ed. Freq: Monthly, Price/yr-$:59

Inside Visual dBase for Windows
Publishing Co: Cobb Group, The, 9420 Bunsen Pkwy. #300, Louisville, KY 40220, USA; 502/491-1900, Fax: 502/

491-8050, Co Email: cobb@aol.com; Web URL: cobb.com; Focus: News and tips for Visual dBase for Windows; Format: Newsletter; Price/yr-$:69

Inside Visual FoxPro

Publishing Co: Cobb Group, The, 9420 Bunsen Pkwy. #300, Louisville, KY 40220, USA; 502/491-1900, Fax: 502/491-8050, Co Email: cobb@aol.com; Web URL: cobb.com; Focus: News and tips for Visual FoxPro users; Format: Newsletter; Price/yr-$:89

Inside Word

Publishing Co: Cobb Group, The, 9420 Bunsen Pkwy. #300, Louisville, KY 40220, USA; 502/493-3300, Fax: 502/491-8050, Co Email: cobb@aol.com; Web URL: cobb.com; Focus: News and tips for Microsoft Word for Macintosh users; Format: Newsletter; Meredith Little, Ed. Freq: Monthly, Price/yr-$:59

Inside Word for Windows

Publishing Co: Cobb Group, The, 9420 Bunsen Pkwy. #300, Louisville, KY 40220, USA; 502/491-1900, Fax: 502/491-8050, Co Email: cobb@aol.com; Web URL: cobb.com; Focus: Tips and techniques for users of Microsoft Word for Windows; Format: Newsletter; Meredith Little, Ed. Freq: Monthly, Price/yr-$:79

Inside WordPerfect

Publishing Co: Cobb Group, The, 9420 Bunsen Pkwy. #300, Louisville, KY 40220, USA; 502/491-1900, Fax: 502/491-8050, Co Email: cobb@aol.com; Web URL: cobb.com; Focus: News, tips and information for WordPerfect users; Format: Newsletter; Jonathan Ordish, Ed. Freq: Monthly, Price/yr-$:69

Inside WordPerfect for Windows

Publishing Co: Cobb Group, The, 9420 Bunsen Pkwy. #300, Louisville, KY 40220, USA; 502/491-1900, Fax: 502/491-8050, Co Email: cobb@aol.com; Web URL: cobb.com; Focus: News, tips and information for WordPerfect for Windows users; Format: Newsletter; Duane Spurlock, Ed. Freq: Monthly, Price/yr-$:69

Insider for Lotus cc:Mail, The

Publishing Co: Cobb Group, The, 9420 Bunsen Pkwy. #300, Louisville, KY 40220, USA; 502/491-1900, Fax: 502/491-8050, Co Email: cobb@aol.com; Web URL: cobb.com; Focus: News, tips and information for Lotus cc:Mail; Format: Newsletter; Price/yr-$:89

Insider Weekly for AS/400 Managers

Publishing Co: United Communications Group, 175 Highland Ave, Needham, MA 02194, USA; 617/444-5755, Fax: 617/444-8958, Web URL: ucg.com; Focus: News, analysis and information for AS/400 managers; Format: Newsletter; Greg Strakosch, Pblshr Email: gstrakos@ucg.com; Rizal Ahmed, Ed. Freq: 48/Year, Price/yr-$:395

Insight Into Emerging Systems Man-

agement Solutions

Publishing Co: MWA Consulting Inc., 261 Hamilton Ave, #421, Palo Alto, CA 94301, USA; 415/323-4780, Fax: 415/323-4794, Co Email: insight-mwa@aol.com; Focus: Information on the Desktop Management Task Force; Format: Newsletter; Michael Weiss, Ed. & Pblr Alexandra Feit, Mgng Ed. Leslie Spink, Exec Ed. Freq: 4/Year

Insight IS

Publishing Co: Xephon, 1301 W. Hwy 407, #201-450, Lewisville, TX 75067, USA; 817/455-7050, Fax: 817/455-2492, Focus: News, analysis and trends for mainframes and IS; Format: Newsletter; Freq: Monthly, Price/yr-$:290

Insurance & Technology

Publishing Co: Miller Freeman Inc., 1515 Broadway, 32rd Floor, New York, NY 10036, USA; 212/869-1300, Fax: 212/302-6273, Focus: Information on computer automation in the insurance industry; Format: Magazine; Freq: Monthly

Integrated System Design

Publishing Co: Verecom Group, 5150 El Camino Real, #D31, Los Altos, CA 94022-9873, USA; 415/903-0140, Fax: 415/903-0151, Web URL: netline.com/isd; Focus: Technologies for system design; Format: Magazine; Jonah McLeod, Ed.-in-Chief Email: jonah@asic.com; James C. Uhl, Pblshr Email: jimu@asic.com; Michael Santarini II, Assoc Ed. Email: michael@asic.com; Circ.: 51,000, Freq: Monthly, Price/yr-$:Free/48

Intelligent Software Strategies

Publishing Co: Cutter Information Corp., 37 Broadway, Arlington, MA 02174-5539, USA; 617/648-8702, Fax: 617/648-1950, Co Email: 74107.653@compuserve.com; Web URL: cutter.com; Focus: Information on AI, expert systems, CASE, neural nets and natural languages; Format: Newsletter; Curt Hall, Ed. Karen Coburn, Group Pblshr Email: 73352.1625@compuserve.com; Circ.: 700, Freq: Monthly, Price/yr-$:447

Interactive Communications

Publishing Co: Computer Technology Research Corp., 6 North Atlantic Wharf, Charleston, SC 29401-2150, USA; 803/853-6460, Fax: 803/853-7210, Co Email: report@ctrcorp.com; Web URL: ctrcorp.com; Focus: News and information about the communications market; Format: Newsletter; Edward R. Wagner, Pres Stacey Evangelist, Ed-in-Chief Freq: Monthly, Price/yr-$:460

Interactive Content

Publishing Co: Jupiter Communications Co., 627 Broadway, New York, NY 10012, USA; 212/780-6060, Fax: 212/780-6075, Co Email: jup5@aol.com; Web URL: jup.com/jupiter; Focus: Consumer online services information; Format: Newsletter; Gene DeRose, Pblshr Michael Rin-

zel, Ed. Yvette DeBow, Mgng Ed. Freq: Monthly, Price/yr-$:555

Interactive Daily

Publishing Co: Phillips Business Information Inc., 1201 Seven Locks Road, #300, Potomac, MD 20854-1110, USA; 301/340-1520, Fax: 301/309-3847, Co Email: pbi@phillips.com; Web URL: phillips.com; Focus: Daily news briefing on interactive entertainment; Format: Fax; Freq: Daily, Price/yr-$:995

Interactive Home

Publishing Co: Jupiter Communications Co., 627 Broadway, New York, NY 10012, USA; 212/780-6060, Fax: 212/780-6075, Co Email: jup5@aol.com; Web URL: jup.com/jupiter; Focus: News and information on interactive consumer technologies; Format: Newsletter; Gene DeRose, Pblshr Freq: Monthly, Price/yr-$:475

Interactive Informer, The

Publishing Co: CD3 Consulting Inc., PO Box 4406, Stamford, CT 06907-0406, USA; 203/968-6700, Fax: 203/968-8757, Focus: News and information on interactive software development; Format: Newsletter; Freq: 9/Year, Price/yr-$:395

Interactive Marketing News

Publishing Co: Phillips Business Information Inc., 1201 Seven Locks Road, #300, Potomac, MD 20854-1110, USA; 301/340-1520, Fax: 301/309-3847, Co Email: pbi@phillips.com; Web URL: phillips.com; Focus: New media marketing opportunities; Format: Newsletter; Kismet Toksu Gould, Pblshr Freq: 25/Year, Price/yr-$:595

Interactive TV Report

Publishing Co: Simba Information Inc., 11 River Bend Drive S, PO Box 4234, Stamford, CT 06807-0234, USA; 203/834-0033, Fax: 203/358-5825, Co Email: simbamkt@aol.com; Web URL: simba-net.com; Focus: News and information in interactive TV; Format: Newsletter; Chris Elwell, Pblshr Freq: 12/Year, Price/yr-$:595

Interactive TV Sourcebook

Publishing Co: Broadcast Information Bureau, 401 N Broad Street, 5th Floor, Philadelphia, PA 19108, USA; 215/238-5300, Fax: 215/238-5412, Focus: Information on the interactive TV industry; Format: Factbook; Price/yr-$:395

Interactive TV Strategies

Publishing Co: Telecom Publishing Group, 1101 King Street, #444, Alexandria, VA 22314-2968, USA; Fax: 800/645-4104, Web URL: cappubs.com; Focus: News and information on interactive TV trials; Format: Newsletter; Michael Causey, Exec Ed. Email: mcausey@cappubs.com; Chris Vestal, Pblshr Freq: 24/Year, Price/yr-$:425

Interactive TV: Profiles & Analysis

Publishing Co: Simba Information Inc., 11 River Bend Drive S, PO Box 4234, Stamford, CT 06807-0234, USA; 203/834-0033, Fax: 203/358-5825, Co Email: simbamkt@aol.com; Web URL: simbanet.com; Focus: Trends, participants and tests in interactive TV; Format: Report; Chris Elwell, Pblshr Freq: Annual, Price/yr-$:1395

Interactive Video News
Publishing Co: Phillips Business Information Inc., 1201 Seven Locks Road, #300, Potomac, MD 20854-1110, USA; 301/340-1520, Fax: 301/309-3847, Co Email: pbi@phillips.com; Web URL: phillips.com; Focus: News and information on interactive video; Format: Newsletter; Freq: 25/Year, Price/yr-$:597

Interactive Week
Publishing Co: InterActive Enterprises, 100 Quentin Roosevelt Blvd, #508, Garden City, NY 11530, USA; 516/229-3700, Fax: 516/229-3707, Web URL: interactive-week.com/~intweek; Focus: Information on the interactive and online industries; Format: Newspaper; Carol Wilson, Exec Ed. Email: cwilson@zd.com; Tom Steinert, Ed.-in-Chief Email: tomhyphen@onramp.net; George Vernadakis, Ed. Email: gvernada@zd.com; Freq: 18/Year, Price/yr-$:Free/60

InterActivity
Publishing Co: Miller Freeman Inc., 411 Borel Ave, San Mateo, CA 94402-3522, USA; 415/358-9500, Fax: 415/358-9527, Co Email: interactivity@mfi.com; Focus: Multimedia how to magazine; Format: Magazine; Pat Cameron, Pblshr Dominic Milano, Ed. Ted Greenwald, Sr Ed. Circ.: 50,000, Freq: Monthly, Price/yr-$:59.95

InterAd
Publishing Co: Jupiter Communications Co., 627 Broadway, 2nd Fl, New York, NY 10012, USA; 212/780-6060, Fax: 212/780-6075, Co Email: jup5@aol.com; Web URL: jup.com/jupiter; Focus: Internet and online ad information; Format: Newsletter; Gene DeRose, Pblshr Freq: Monthly, Price/yr-$:375

International Business
Publishing Co: IB Communications Inc., 9 East 40 Street, 10th Floor, New York, NY 10016, USA; Format: Magazine; Floyd Sembler, Pblshr Linda Lynton, Ed-in-Chief Kathy J. Mills, Mgng Ed. Freq: Monthly, Price/yr-$:48

International Designers Network
Publishing Co: Systems Design Ltd., Shop C, 5-9 Gresson Street, Wanchai, Hong Kong; 852-25285744, Fax: 852-25291296, Co Email: idn@hkstar.com; Web URL: hkstar.com/idn; Focus: Magazine; Laurence Ng, Pblshr Adeline Lee, Pub Dir Y.M. Chan, Ed. Freq: 6/Year, Price/yr-$:180/200

International Distribution Channels Database
Publishing Co: Ideas + Information Inc., Hilltop Business Center, S Hampton, NH

03827, USA; 603/394-7900, Fax: 603/394-7601, Co Email: info@interinfo.com; Web URL: interinfo.com; Focus: Data on over 9,000 resellers; Format: Database; Fred Anderson, Ed. & Pblshr Freq: 4/Year, Price/yr-$:750-1,500

International Electronics Contacts
Publishing Co: Electronic Industries Association, 2500 Wilson Blvd, Arlington, VA 22201-3834, USA; 703/907-7500, Fax: 703/907-7501, Co Email: @eia.org; Web URL: eia.org; Focus: Lists over 700 information sources in 70 countries; Format: Directory; Freq: Annual, Price/yr-$:40/70

International Info
Publishing Co: Ideas + Information Inc., Hilltop Business Center, S Hampton, NH 03827, USA; 603/394-7900, Fax: 603/394-7601, Co Email: info@interinfo.com; Web URL: interinfo.com; Focus: Information on international markets and channels; Format: Report; Fred Anderson, Ed. & Pblshr Freq: 4/Year, Price/yr-$:250

International Resource Guide, The
Publishing Co: Software Pblshrs Association, 1730 M. Street NW, #700, Washington, DC 20036-4510, USA; 202/452-1600, Fax: 202/223-8756, Focus: Information on international software markets; Format: Directory; Randy Green, Ed. Freq: 4/Year, Price/yr-$:495/1750

International Telecom Regulatory Environments
Publishing Co: Datapro Information Services Group, 600 Delran Pkwy., Delran, NJ 08705-9904, USA; 609/764-0100, Fax: 609/764-2811, Co Email: datapro@mhh.com; Web URL: datapro.com; Focus: Information on global telecom environments and standards; Format: CD-ROM; Freq: Monthly

International Ventures in Interactive Television
Publishing Co: Simba Information Inc., 11 River Bend Drive S, PO Box 4234, Stamford, CT 06807-0234, USA; 203/834-0033, Fax: 203/358-5825, Co Email: simbamkt@aol.com; Web URL: simbanet.com; Focus: International developments and ventures in interactive television; Format: Loose-leaf; Price/yr-$:1,295

Internet Advisor
Publishing Co: Advisor Publications Inc., 4010 Morena Blvd, San Diego, CA 92117, USA; 619/483-6400, Fax: 619/483-9851, Co Email: 71154.3123@compuserve.com; Focus: Internet and online service users; Format: Magazine; William T. Ota, Pblr/Pres/CEO John L. Hawkins, Ed-in-Chief & EVP Jeanne Banfield, VP Circ.: 25,000, Freq: Bimonthly, Price/yr-$:39

Internet as a Business Resource
Publishing Co: Faulkner Information Services, 7905 Browning Road, Pennsauken, NJ 08109-4319, USA; 609/662-2070, Fax:

609/662-0905, Co Email: faulkner@faulkner.com; Web URL: faulkner.com; Focus: Guide to doing business on the Internet, web and online; Format: Loose-leaf; Martin Murphy, Pblshr Freq: Monthly, Price/yr-$:499

Internet Business Advantage
Publishing Co: Cobb Group, The, 9420 Bunsen Pkwy. #300, Louisville, KY 40220, USA; 502/491-1900, Fax: 502/491-8050, Co Email: cobb@aol.com; Web URL: cobb.com; Focus: News, tips and information for business on the Internet; Format: Newsletter; Price/yr-$:59

Internet Business Advantage
Publishing Co: Wentworth Worldwide Media, 1866 Colonial Village Ln., Lancaster, PA 17601, USA; 717/393-1000, Fax: 717/393-5752, Focus: How to successfully conduct business on the Internet; Format: Newsletter; Circ.: 20,000, Freq: Monthly, Price/yr-$:99

Internet Business Report
Publishing Co: Jupiter Communications Co., 627 Broadway, New York, NY 10012-2612, USA; 212/780-6060, Fax: 212/780-6075, Co Email: jup5@aol.com; Web URL: jup.com; Focus: News, analysis and information about the Internet; Format: Newsletter; Gene DeRose, Pblshr Nate Zelnick, Ed. Yvette DeBow, Mgng Ed. Freq: Monthly, Price/yr-$:395

Internet Gazette
Publishing Co: e-media, 2130 Fillmore Street, #288, San Francisco, CA 94115, USA; 415/776-1888, Co Email: gazette@e-media.com; Focus: Internet information; Format: Newspaper; Ken McCarthy, Pblshr Susanna Camp, Ed. Freq: 8/Year, Price/yr-$:10

Internet Marketing & Technology Report
Publishing Co: Computer Economics Inc., 5841 Edison Place, Carlsbad, CA 92008, USA; 619/438-8100, Fax: 619/431-1126, Co Email: subs@cei.mhs.compuserve.com; Focus: Information on online opportunities; Format: Newsletter; Mark McManus, Ed.-in-Chief Freq: Monthly, Price/yr-$:387

Internet On-Line Guide
Publishing Co: Specialized Systems Consultants Inc., PO Box 55549, Seattle, WA 98155, USA; 206/782-7733, Fax: 206/782-7191, Co Email: sales@ssc.com; Web URL: ssc.com; Focus: Information for newcomers to the Internet; Format: Factbook; Phil Hughes, Ed. Price/yr-$:3

Internet Systems
Publishing Co: Miller Freeman Inc., 600 Harrison Street, San Francisco, CA 94107-1391, USA; 415/905-2200, Fax: 415/905-2234, Focus: Information for Internet developers; Format: Magazine

Internet Voyager
Publishing Co: Blue Dolphin Communications Inc., 83 Boston Post Road, Sudbury,

MA 01776, USA; Focus: Internet content information; Format: Newsletter; Donald L. Nicholas, Pblshr Email: nicholas@bdc.iii.net; Dick Rubinstein, Ed. Email: dickr@id.wing.net; Susan K. Skaradowski, Mgng Ed. Email: sueskara@aol.com; Freq: 12/Year, Price/yr-$:78

Internet Week
Publishing Co: Phillips Business Information Inc., 1201 Seven Locks Road, #300, Potomac, MD 20854-1110, USA; 301/340-1520, Fax: 301/424-4297, Co Email: pbi@phillips.com; Web URL: phillips.com; Focus: News and analysis of Internet business opportunities; Format: Newsletter; Joelle M. Martin, Pblshr Minda Morgan Caesar, Ed. Freq: 50/Year, Price/yr-$:697

Internet White Pages
Publishing Co: IDG Books Worldwide, 919 E Hillsdale Blvd, #400, Foster City, CA 94404, USA; 415/655-3000, Fax: 415/655-3299, Web URL: idgbooks.com; Focus: Listing of 100,000 Internet addresses; Format: Directory; Price/yr-$:30

Internet World
Publishing Co: Mecklermedia, 20 Ketchum Street, Westport, CT 06880-9760, USA; 203/226-6967, Fax: 203/454-5840, Co Email: iwedit@mecklermedia.com; Web URL: internetworld.com; Focus: News and information for Internet users; Format: Magazine; Corey Friedman, Pblshr Email: cfriedman@mecklermedia.co; Michael Neubart, Ed.-in-Chief Email: neubarth@iw.com; Vira Mamchur Schwartz, Mgng Ed. Email: vira@iw.com; Circ.: 100,000+, Freq: Monthly, Price/yr-$:29

Internet, Commercial User's Guide to the
Publishing Co: Thompson Publishing Group, 1725 K Street NW, Washington, DC 20006, USA; Fax: 800/926-2012, Focus: Business users' guide to the Internet; Format: Loose-leaf; Lucy Caldwell-Stair, Pblshr Price/yr-$:298

Internet, The
Publishing Co: Software Productivity Group Inc., 1 Apple Hill, #301, Natick, MA 01532, USA; 508/652-1100, Fax: 508/393-3388, Web URL: spgnet.com; Focus: Information about the Internet; Format: Magazine; Freq: 2/Year

Internetwork
Publishing Co: Cardinal Business Media Inc., 1300 Virginia Drive, #400, Ft. Washington, PA 19034-3225, USA; 215/643-8000, Fax: 215/643-8099, Web URL: internetworkweb.com; Focus: News, reviews and information about networks and interoperability; Format: Tabloid; Evan Birkhead, Ed.-in-Chief Email: birkheadec@cardinal.com; Richard W. Molden, Pblshr Email: moldenrw@cardinal.com; Joe Paone, Tech Ed. Email:

paoneja@cardinal.com; Circ.: 100,000, Freq: Monthly, Price/yr-$:Free/75

Interoperability
Publishing Co: Miller Freeman Inc., 600 Harrison Street, San Francisco, CA 94107-1391, USA; 415/905-2200, Fax: 415/905-2587, Format: Magazine

IntraNet Magazine
Publishing Co: Network World Inc./IDG, 161 Worcester Road, PO Box 9172, Framingham, MA 01701-9172, USA; 508/875-6400, Fax: 508/820-3467, Co Email: nwnews@nww.com; Web URL: nwfusion.com; Focus: Information on intranets; Format: Magazine

IRIS Universe
Publishing Co: Silicon Graphics Inc., 2011 N. Shoreline Blvd, MS 415, Mt. View, CA 94039, USA; 415/390-2079, Fax: 415/390-1737, Co Email: universe@corp.sgi.com; Web URL: sgi.com/technology/publication; Focus: Visual computing applications and technology; Format: Magazine; Carl Furry, Exec Ed. David E. DiNucci, Assoc Ed. Email: ded@sgi.com; Circ.: 52,000, Freq: 4/Year, Price/yr-$:Free

IS Budget
Publishing Co: Computer Economics Inc., 5841 Edison Place, Carlsbad, CA 92008, USA; 619/438-8100, Fax: 619/431-1126, Co Email: custserv@compecon.com; Focus: News and analysis of DP expenses and DP productivity; Format: Newsletter; Teresa Elms, Ed. Email: telms@compecon.com; Bruno Bassi, Pblshr Freq: Monthly, Price/yr-$:495

IS Position Descriptions HandiGuide
Publishing Co: Positive Support Review Inc., 2500 Broadway, #320, Santa Monica, CA 90404-3061, USA; 310/453-6100, Fax: 310/453-6253, Co Email: info@psrinc.com; Focus: Computer job descriptions; Format: Book/diskette; M. Victor Janulaitis, Pblr & Ed. Freq: Annual, Price/yr-$:395/795

IS, Communication & DP Metrics HandiGuide
Publishing Co: Positive Support Review Inc., 2500 Broadway, #320, Santa Monica, CA 90404-3061, USA; 310/453-6100, Fax: 310/453-6253, Co Email: info@psrinc.com; Focus: Over 150 metrics for benchmarking information systems performance; Format: Book/diskette; M. Victor Janulaitis, Pblr & Ed. Freq: Annual, Price/yr-$:395/795

ISDN
Publishing Co: Information Gatekeepers Inc., 214 Harvard Ave, Boston, MA 02134, USA; 617/232-3111, Fax: 617/734-8562, Co Email: igiboston@aol.com; Focus: Technology trends, markets and applications of ISDN; Format: Newsletter; Paul Polishuk, Ed. & Pblr Email: igiboston@aol.com; Freq: Monthly, Price/yr-$:545/595

ISDN News
Publishing Co: Phillips Business Information Inc., 1201 Seven Locks Road, #300, Potomac, MD 20854-1110, USA; 301/340-1520, Fax: 301/424-4297, Co Email: pbi@phillips.com; Web URL: phillips.com; Focus: News, analysis and trends in the ISDN market; Format: Newsletter; Freq: 25/Year, Price/yr-$:597

ISDN User Newsletter
Publishing Co: Information Gatekeepers Inc., 214 Harvard Ave, Boston, MA 02134, USA; 617/232-3111, Fax: 617/734-8562, Co Email: igiboston@aol.com; Focus: ISDN applications, products and vendors information; Format: Magazine; Scott Clavena, Ed. Email: igiboston@aol.com; Paul Polishuk, Pblshr Email: igiboston@aol.com; Freq: 6/Year, Price/yr-$:70/85

ISDN Yellow Pages
Publishing Co: Information Gatekeepers Inc., 214 Harvard Ave, Boston, MA 02134, USA; 617/232-3111, Fax: 617/734-8562, Co Email: igiboston@aol.com; Focus: Directory and information on ISDN industry worldwide; Format: Directory; Paul Polishuk, Ed. & Pblr Email: igiboston@aol.com; Freq: Annual, Price/yr-$:69.95

Israel High-Tech & Investment Report
PO Box 33633, Tel Aviv 61336, Israel; 3-523-5279, Fax: 3-522-7799, Focus: News and information on high-tech in Israel; Format: Newsletter; Joseph Morgenstern, Ed. Freq: 11/Year, Price/yr-$:95

IT Metrics Strategies
Publishing Co: Cutter Information Corp., 37 Broadway, Arlington, MA 02174-5539, USA; 617/648-8702, Fax: 617/648-1950, Co Email: 74107.653@compuserve.com; Web URL: cutter.com; Format: Newsletter; Howard Rubin, Ed. Karen Coburn, Group Pblshr Email: 73352.1625@compuserve.com; Freq: Monthly, Price/yr-$:485

IT-Digest
Publishing Co: IRIS-Div of NIIT, 8 Balaji Estate, Kalkaji, New Delhi 110 019, India; 642-6030, Fax: 648-2053, Co Email: @iris.ernet.com; Focus: News and information on the Indian computer market; Format: Newsletter; J.R. Isaac, Ed. Email: isaac@iris.ernet.in; Freq: Monthly, Price/yr-$:100/200

ITAA's Software & Services Tax Report
Publishing Co: Information Technology Association of America, 1616 N. Ft. Myer Drive, #1300, Arlington, VA 22209-9998, USA; 703/522-5055, Fax: 703/525-2279, Web URL: itaa.org; Focus: State by state sales and use tax regulations; Format: Factbook; Freq: Annual, Price/yr-$:150/195

iWORLD
Publishing Co: Mecklermedia, 20 Ketchum

Street, Westport, CT 06880-9760, USA;
203/226-6967, Fax: 203/454-5840, Co
Email: info@mecklermedia.com; Web
URL: iworld.com; Focus: Internet industry; Format: Electronic Newspaper; Tristan
Louis, Exec Dir Freq: Daily

Japan Electronics Almanac
Publishing Co: Dempa Publications Inc.,
275 Madison Ave, New York, NY 10016-
1101, USA; 212/682-4755, Fax: 212/682-
2730, Focus: Profiles of Japanese electronics companies; Format: Directory; Tetsuo
Hirayama, Pres Freq: Annual, Price/yr-
$:68

Japan Electronics Buyer's Guide
Publishing Co: Dempa Publications Inc.,
275 Madison Ave, New York, NY 10016-
1101, USA; 212/752-3003, Fax: 212/752-
3289, Focus: Listing of 1,700+ products
and 1,700+ Japanese companies; Format:
Directory; Tetsuo Hirayama, Pres Freq:
Annual, Price/yr-$:210

Japanese Technical Literature
Publishing Co: Office of International
Technology Policy & Programs, 14th &
Constitution Ave NW, Rm 4230 HCHB,
Washington, DC 20230, USA; 202/482-
1288, Fax: 202/482-0365, Co Email:
pgenther@banyan.doc.gov; Web URL:
doc.gov/aptp; Focus: Review on Japanese
technical information; Format: Newsletter; Phyllis Geather Yoshida, Dir Japan
Tech Circ.: 3,100, Freq: Monthly, Price/
yr-$:Free

Japanese Technical Reports, Directory of
Publishing Co: National Technical Information Service, 5285 Port Royal Road, Rm
1303, Springfield, VA 22161, USA; 703/
487-4650, Fax: 703/321-8547, Focus:
Summaries of Japanese technical reports;
Format: Directory; Freq: Annual, Price/
yr-$:35

Java Report
Publishing Co: SIGS Publications Group,
71 W. 23rd Street, 3rd Floor, New York,
NY 10010, USA; 212/242-7447, Fax:
212/242-7574, Co Email: @sigs.com;
Web URL: sigs.com; Focus: Building applications using Java; Format: Magazine; Richard P. Friedman, Pblshr David Fisco, Ed.
Freq: 10/Year, Price/yr-$:60

JavaWorld
Publishing Co: International Data Group,
501 Second Street, #600, San Francisco,
CA 94107, USA; 415/267-1710, Focus:
Information for Java users; Format: Magazine

Jones Computer Network
Publishing Co: Jones Education Networks
Inc., 9697 E Mineral Ave, PO Box 3309,
Englewood, CO 80155-3309, USA; Fax:
303/784-8049, Focus: Information on
computer products; Format: TV cable
channel; Bob Jones, VP Programming
**Journal of Asia Electronics Union
(AEU)**

Publishing Co: Dempa Publications Inc.,
275 Madison Ave, New York, NY 10016-
1101, USA; 212/682-4755, Fax: 212/682-
2730, Focus: Product, technology and business news about Asian/Pacific Rim countries' electronics indus; Format:
Newspaper; Tetsuo Hirayama, Pres Freq:
Bimonthly, Price/yr-$:65

Journal of Business Strategy
Publishing Co: Faulkner & Gray Inc., 11
Penn Plaza, 17th Floor, New York, NY
10001, USA; 212/967-7000, Fax: 212/
967-7155, Focus: Strategic trends and
applications of information technology for
senior level planners; Format: Magazine;
Circ.: 25,000, Freq: 6/Year, Price/yr-
$:105

**Journal of Electronic Engineering
(JEE)**
Publishing Co: Dempa Publications Inc.,
275 Madison Ave, New York, NY 10016-
1101, USA; 212/682-4755, Fax: 212/682-
2730, Focus: Product and technology news
about the electronics industry; Format:
Newspaper; Tetsuo Hirayama, Pres Freq:
Monthly, Price/yr-$:115

Journal of Functional and Logic Programming
Publishing Co: MIT Press Journals, 55 Hayward Street, Cambridge, MA 02142, USA;
617/253-2889, Fax: 617/258-6779, Co
Email: journals-orders@mit.edu; Web
URL: mitpress.mit.edu; Focus: Research
on functional logic computer-programming.; Format: Internet; Giorgio Levi, Ed-in-Chief Email: jflp.op@ls5.informatik.un; Circ.: 100, Price/yr-$:30

Journal of Object-Oriented Programming
Publishing Co: SIGS Publications Group,
71 W. 23rd Street, 3rd Floor, New York,
NY 10010, USA; 212/242-7447, Fax:
212/242-7574, Co Email:
73361.1707@compuserve.com; Web
URL: sigs.com; Focus: Latest research,
applications and technical data on object-oriented languages; Format: Magazine;
Richard Wiener, Ed. Richard P. Friedman,
Pblshr Circ.: 24,000, Freq: 9/year, Price/
yr-$:69

Journal of Office Technology
Publishing Co: Empower Tools, 5610
Buckingham Palace Court, Alexandria, VA
22315-4120, USA; 703/924-9688, Fax:
703/924-9683, Focus: Office technology
trends; Format: Magazine; John Stuppy,
Ed. Freq: Monthly, Price/yr-$:100

Journal of the ACM
Publishing Co: Association for Computing
Machinery, 1515 Broadway, 17th Floor,
New York, NY 10036, USA; 212/869-
7440, Fax: 212/869-0481, Web URL:
acm.org; Focus: Peer-reviewed articles on
computer science technology and theory;
Format: Magazine; F. Thomson Leighton,
Ed.-in-Chief Mark Mandelbaum, Dir Pubs
Circ.: 9,161, Freq: 6/Year, Price/yr-$:40

**Journal of the Electronics Industry
(JEI)**
Publishing Co: Dempa Publications Inc.,
275 Madison Ave, New York, NY 10016-
1101, USA; 212/682-4755, Fax: 212/682-
2730, Focus: Product and technology news
about the Japanese and worldwide consumer electronics industry; Format: Newspaper; Tetsuo Hirayama, Pres Freq:
Monthly, Price/yr-$:150

LAN
Publishing Co: Information Gatekeepers
Inc., 214 Harvard Ave, Boston, MA 02134,
USA; 617/232-3111, Fax: 617/734-8562,
Co Email: igiboston@aol.com; Focus:
Worldwide technology trends, applications and markets for LANs; Format:
Newsletter; Paul Polishuk, Ed. & Pblr
Email: igiboston@aol.com; Freq: Monthly,
Price/yr-$:545/595

LAN Magazine
Publishing Co: Miller Freeman Inc., 600
Harrison Street, San Francisco, CA 94107-
1391, USA; 415/905-2200, Fax: 415/905-
2587, Co Email: lanmag@mci.com; Web
URL: lanmag.com; Focus: Information,
reviews and news on LAN products, installation, management and maintenance; Format: Magazine; Melanie McMullen, Ed-in-Chief Email: mmcmullen@mfi.com;
Angela Young, Pblshr Email:
ayoung@mfi.com; Steve Steinke, Sr Ed.
Email: ssteinke@mfi.com; Circ.: 81,385,
Freq: 13/Year, Price/yr-$:29.95

LAN Times
Publishing Co: McGraw-Hill Inc., 1900
O'Farrell Street, #200, San Mateo, CA
94403-1311, USA; 415/513-6800, Fax:
415/513-6985, Co Email: @wcmh.com;
Web URL: wcmh.com/lantimes; Focus:
News, reviews and trends about the computer network industry; Format: Newspaper; Leonard Heymann, Ed.-in-Chief
Email: lenny-heymann@wcmh.com; Jennifer Neale, Pblshr Circ.: 175,000, Freq:
26/Year, Price/yr-$:Free/150

LANs and Internetworking
Publishing Co: Datapro Information Services Group, 600 Delran Pkwy., Delran,
NJ 08705-9904, USA; 609/764-0100, Fax:
609/764-2811, Co Email:
datapro@mhh.com; Web URL:
datapro.com; Focus: Information on LANs
and internetworking products, trends and
technologies; Format: CD-ROM; Freq:
Monthly

Large & Midrange Systems & Software
Publishing Co: Faulkner Information Services, 7905 Browning Road, Pennsauken,
NJ 08109-4319, USA; 609/662-2070, Fax:
609/662-0905, Co Email:
faulkner@faulkner.com; Web URL:
faulkner.com; Focus: Product information
on large & midrange computers, peripherals and software; Format: Loose-leaf; Martin Murphy, Pblshr Freq: Monthly, Price/

yr-$:1,450

Latin American Telecom Report
Publishing Co: ITC Publications, 4340 East-West Hwy, #1020, Bethesda, MD 20814-4411, USA; 301/907-0060, Fax: 301/907-6555, Focus: News, analysis and forecast on Latin American telecom market; Format: Newsletter; Edward G. Czarnecki, Mngng Dir Freq: Monthly, Price/yr-$:679

Law & Regulation in European Multimedia
Publishing Co: FT Telecoms & Media Publishing, Maple House, 149 Tottenham Court Road, London, W1P 9LL, UK; 171-896-2222, Fax: 171-896-2274, Focus: Legal information on European multimedia; Format: Newsletter; Price/yr-$:742

Law and Business of Computer Software
Publishing Co: Clark Boardman Callagan, 155 Pfingsten Road, Deerfield, IL 60015-4998, USA; 847/948-7000, Fax: 847/948-9340, Co Email: cbcservice@cbcle-gal.com; Web URL: cbclegal.com; Focus: Overview of computer laws; Format: Factbook; Freq: Annual, Price/yr-$:115

Law of Computer Technology
Publishing Co: Warren Gorham Lamont, 31 St. James Ave, Boston, MA 02116-9372, USA; Fax: 617/451-0908, Co Email: sales@wgl.com; Web URL: wgl.com; Focus: Developments in computer technology law; Format: Loose-leaf; Laurence Selby, Pblshr Paul Rosenthal, Mktng Dir Freq: 3/Year, Price/yr-$:159.50

Law Office Technology Review
Publishing Co: Altman Weil Pensa Publications, PO Box 625, 2 Campus Blvd, Newtown Square, PA 19073, USA; 610/359-9900, Fax: 610/359-0467, Focus: Software and hardware news and reviews for law office computer users; Format: Newsletter; Barry D. Bayer, Ed. Email: bbaygrnn@counsel.com; Mary Ann Faran, Assoc Ed. Charles F. Huxsaw, Pblshr Freq: Monthly, Price/yr-$:195

Leonardo and Leonardo Music Journal
Publishing Co: MIT Press Journals for Leonardo/Int'l. Society, 55 Hayward Street, Cambridge, MA 02142, USA; 617/253-2889, Fax: 617/258-6779, Co Email: journals-orders@mit.edu; Web URL: mit-press.mit.edu; Focus: Visual artists/musicians who use science/technology; Format: Magazine; Roger F. Malina, Exec Ed. Email: isast@sfsu.edu; Circ.: 2,400, Freq: 5/Year, Price/yr-$:55/70

Leonardo Electronic Almanac
Publishing Co: MIT Press Journals for Leonardo/Int'l. Society, 55 Hayward Street, Cambridge, MA 02142, USA; 617/253-2889, Fax: 617/258-6779, Co Email: journals-orders@mit.edu; Web URL: mit-press.mit.edu; Focus: Visual artists/musi-

cians who use science/technology.; Format: Internet; Graig Harris, Exec Ed. Email: harri067@maroon.tc.umn.ed; Circ.: 250, Freq: 12/Year, Price/yr-$:15/25

Library & Information Sciences
Publishing Co: National Technical Information Service, 5285 Port Royal Road, Rm 1303, Springfield, VA 22161, USA; 703/487-4630, Fax: 703/321-8547, Focus: Abstracts US government reports on information systems, electronic technology, marketing a; Format: Newsletter; Freq: Weekly, Price/yr-$:105

Library Automation Software, Systems & Services, Directory of
Publishing Co: Information Today Inc., 143 Old Marlton Pike, Medford, NJ 08055-8750, USA; 609/654-6266, Fax: 609/654-4309, Co Email: custserv@infotoday.com; Web URL: infotoday.com; Focus: Directory of library automation products; Format: Directory; Pamela Cibbarelli, Ed. Freq: Biannual, Price/yr-$:79

Library Software Review
Publishing Co: Sage Publications Inc., 2455 Teller Road, Thousand Oaks, CA 91320, USA; 805/499-0721, Fax: 805/499-0971, Focus: News and reviews on computer products for libraries; Format: Magazine; Marshall Breeding, Ed. Freq: 4/Year, Price/yr-$:152

LightWavePro
Publishing Co: Miller Freeman Inc., 411 Borel Ave, #100, San Mateo, CA 94402-3522, USA; 415/358-9500, Fax: 415/358-9855, Format: Magazine

Link-Up
Publishing Co: Information Today Inc., 143 Old Marlton Pike, Medford, NJ 08055-8750, USA; 609/654-6266, Fax: 609/654-4309, Co Email: custserv@infotoday.com; Web URL: infotoday.com; Focus: On-line computer communications and information gathering for computer users; Format: Magazine; Loraine Page, Ed. Circ.: 10,000, Freq: 6/Year, Price/yr-$:29

Linux Journal
Publishing Co: SSC, PO Box 85867, Seattle, WA 98155-1867, USA; 206/782-7733, Fax: 206/782-7191, Co Email: subs@ssc.com; Web URL: ssc.com; Focus: News and information for Linux users; Format: Magazine; Phil Hughes, Pblshr Email: phil@ssc.com; Michael K. Johnson, Ed. Email: ljeditor@ssc.com; Belinda Frazier, Assoc Producer Email: bbf@ssc.com; Circ.: 30,000, Freq: Monthly, Price/yr-$:22

Local Area Networks
Publishing Co: Faulkner Information Services, 7905 Browning Road, Pennsauken, NJ 08109-4319, USA; 609/662-2070, Fax: 609/662-0905, Co Email: faulkner@faulkner.com; Web URL: faulkner.com; Focus: Guide to LAN administration including solutions and products;

Format: CD-ROM; Martin Murphy, Pblshr Freq: Monthly, Price/yr-$:1,035

Local Area Networks, Handbook of
Publishing Co: Auerbach Publications, 31 St. James Ave, Boston, MA 02116-9372, USA; 617/423-2020, Fax: 617/451-0908, Co Email: 73752.2270@compuserve.com; Web URL: wgl.com; Focus: Practical information for solving LAN problems; Format: Handbook; Freq: Annual, Price/yr-$:150

LOCALNetter Newsletter
Publishing Co: Architecture Technology Corp., PO Box 24344, Minneapolis, MN 55424, USA; 612/935-2035, Fax: 612/829-5871, Focus: News, reviews and analysis of LAN products and technologies; Format: Newsletter; Kenneth Thurber, Ed. & Pblr Freq: Monthly, Price/yr-$:300

Lotus Notes Advisor
Publishing Co: Advisor Publications Inc., 4010 Morena Blvd, San Diego, CA 92117, USA; 619/483-6400, Fax: 619/483-9851, Co Email: 71154.3123@compuserve.com; Focus: News and information for Lotus Notes users; Format: Magazine; William T. Ota, Pblr/Pres/CEO Email: 71154.3123@compuserve.com; John L. Hawkins, Ed-in-Chief & EVP Walter Karasek, VP Circ.: 25,000, Freq: 6/Year, Price/yr-$:39

M Computing
Publishing Co: M Technology Assoc., 1738 Elton Road, #205, Silver Spring, MD 20903, USA; 301/431-4070, Fax: 301/431-0017, Co Email: mta1994@aol.com; Focus: Information for M Technologies user; Format: Magazine; Richard F. Walters, Exec Ed. Email: walters@cs.ucdavis.edu; Pam McIntyre, Mngng Ed. Email: mta1994@aol.com; Circ.: 3,500, Freq: 5/Year, Price/yr-$:75

Mac Monthly
Publishing Co: Solotech Publishing, 1412 62nd Street, Emeryville, CA 94608, USA; 510/428-0110, Fax: 510/428-0550, Co Email: macmonthly@aol.com; Focus: Macintosh computer users; Format: Tabloid; Duane Nason, Ed.-in-Chief Eric Hayes, Mngng Ed. Sherry Leppek, Assist Ed. Circ.: 30,000, Freq: Monthly, Price/yr-$:Free/11

Mac Today
Publishing Co: KW Publishing Inc., 2194 Main Street, #K, Dunedin, FL 34698, USA; 813/733-6225, Fax: 813/733-1370, Co Email: mactoday@aol.com; Focus: Information for Macintosh users in the Southeast USA; Format: Tabloid; Scott Kelby, Ed-in-Chief & Pblr Jim Workman, Ed-in-Chief & Pblr Richard Theriault, Sr Ed. Freq: 12/Year, Price/yr-$:20

MacAddict
PO Box 58253, Boulder, CO 80323-8253, USA; Web URL: macaddict.com; Focus: Information for the Macintosh; Format: Magazine; Price/yr-$:40

MacAuthority Software Connection
Publishing Co: Cobb Group, The, 9420 Bunsen Pkwy. #300, Louisville, KY 40220, USA; 502/493-3300, Fax: 502/491-8050, Co Email: cobb@aol.com; Web URL: cobb.com; Format: Newsletter; Price/yr-$:59

MacAuthority, The
Publishing Co: Cobb Group, The, 9420 Bunsen Pkwy. #300, Louisville, KY 40220, USA; 502/493-3300, Fax: 502/491-8050, Co Email: cobb@aol.com; Web URL: cobb.com; Focus: Tips and techniques for Macintosh users; Format: Newsletter; Ron Wiler, Ed. Freq: Monthly, Price/yr-$:49

MacHome Journal
Publishing Co: MacHome Journal, 612 Howard Street, 6th Floor, San Francisco, CA 94105, USA; 415/957-1911, Fax: 415/882-9502, Co Email: letters@machome.com; Focus: Information for consumer users of the Macintosh; Format: Magazine; James Capparell, Pblshr Sandra L. Anderson, Ed-in-Chief Mark L. Posth, Ed. Circ.: 125,000, Freq: 12/Year, Price/yr-$:23.95

Macintosh Market Review & Forecast
3131 Marina Drive, Alameda, CA 94501, USA; 510/521-4988, Fax: 510/521-3572, Co Email: pieter@hartsook.com; Web URL: hartsook.com; Focus: Forecasts and shipment data for Apple's Macintosh; Format: Factbook; Pieter Hartsook, Ed. Email: pieter@hartsook.com; Freq: 2/Year, Price/yr-$:3,000

Macintosh Market--Executive Summary
3131 Marina Drive, Alameda, CA 94501, USA; 510/521-4988, Fax: 510/521-3572, Co Email: pieter@hartsook.com; Web URL: hartsook.com; Focus: Summary of Macintosh market research reports; Format: Newsletter; Pieter Hartsook, Ed. Email: pieter@hartsook.com; Freq: Monthly, Price/yr-$:275

Macintosh Multimedia Product Registry
Publishing Co: Redgate Communications Corp., 660 Beachland Blvd, Vero Beach, FL 32963, USA; 407/231-6904, Fax: 407/231-7872, Focus: Listing of over 8,000 Macintosh products and product reviews; Format: Directory; Paulette Siclari-Lee, Ed. Kevin Fallon, Pblshr Circ.: 40,000, Freq: 4/Year, Price/yr-$:40

MacPrePres
Publishing Co: PrePress Information, Inc., 12 Burr Road, Westport, CT 06880, USA; 203/227-2357, Fax: 203/454-4962, Focus: Fax delivered information about desktop publishing; Format: Fax; Kathleen Tinkel, Ed. & Pblr Freq: 45/Year, Price/yr-$:195

MacTech Magazine
Publishing Co: Xplain Corp., PO Box

5200, Westlake Village, CA 91359-5200, USA; 805/494-9797, Fax: 805/494-9798, Co Email: info@mactech.com; Web URL: mactech.com; Focus: Technical information for Macintosh programmers & developers; Format: Magazine; Neil Ticktin, Pblshr Freq: Monthly, Price/yr-$:47

MacUser
Publishing Co: Ziff-Davis Publishing Co., 950 Tower Lane, Foster City, CA 94404, USA; 415/378-5600, Fax: 415/378-5675, Co Email: letters@macuser.ziff.com; Web URL: macuser.ziff.com/macuser; Focus: Reviews, product testing and news for Macintosh users; Format: Magazine; Maggie Canon, Ed-in-Chief James S. Bradbury, Ed. Nancy Groth, Mngg Ed. Circ.: 421,000, Freq: Monthly, Price/yr-$:27

MacWeek
Publishing Co: Ziff-Davis Publishing Co., 301 Howard Street, San Francisco, CA 94105, USA; 415/243-3500, Fax: 415/243-3651, Co Email: macweek@macweek.com; Web URL: macweek.com; Focus: Provides news and information for Macintosh business buyers; Format: Newspaper; Rick LePage, Ed.-in-Chief Brenda Benner, Mgng Ed. John Blake, Grp Pblshr Circ.: 95,000, Freq: 47/Year, Price/yr-$:Free/125

Macworld
Publishing Co: Macworld Communications Inc., 501 Second Street, San Francisco, CA 94107, USA; 415/243-0505, Fax: 415/442-0766, Co Email: macworld@macworld.com; Web URL: macworld.com; Focus: Informs Macintosh users of new products and applications; Format: Magazine; Adrian Mello, Ed-in-Chief Galen Gruman, Exec Ed. Carol Person, Exec Ed. Circ.: 566,000, Freq: Monthly, Price/yr-$:30

Magnetic Media International Newsletter
Publishing Co: Magnetic Media Information Services, 841 Ikena Circle, Honolulu, HI 96821, USA; 808/373-5330, Fax: 808/377-5668, Focus: Tape, disk, optical, film, solid state and other media; Format: Newsletter; Laurence Lueck, Ed. & Pblr Circ.: 550, Freq: Bimonthly, Price/yr-$:1,500

Management Center Operations
Publishing Co: International Association for Management Automation, 1342 Colonial Blvd, #25, Ft. Myers, FL 33907, USA; 941-275-7887, Co Email: afsmi@afsmi.org; Focus: Aspects of services management; Format: Magazine; Leonard Mafrica, Ed. Suzanne M. Tissier, Ed. Assist Freq: 6/Year, Price/yr-$:Free/125

Managing Data Networks
Publishing Co: Datapro Information Services Group, 600 Delran Pkwy., Delran, NJ 08705-9904, USA; 609/764-0100, Fax: 609/764-2811, Co Email: datapro@mhh.com; Web URL:

datapro.com; Focus: Information on networking planning, implementation and management; Format: CD-ROM; Freq: Monthly

Managing Distributed Systems
Publishing Co: Faulkner Information Services, 7905 Browning Road, 114 Cooper Center, Pennsauken, NJ 08109-4319, USA; 609/662-2070, Fax: 609/662-0905, Co Email: faulkner@faulkner.com; Web URL: faulkner.com; Focus: Information on distributed systems; Format: Newsletter; Martin Murphy, Pblshr Freq: Monthly, Price/yr-$:515

Managing Information Technology
Publishing Co: Datapro Information Services Group, 600 Delran Pkwy., Delran, NJ 08705-9904, USA; 609/764-0100, Fax: 609/764-2811, Co Email: datapro@mhh.com; Web URL: datapro.com; Focus: Information on issues, trends and concepts about information systems; Format: CD-ROM; Freq: Monthly

Managing LANs
Publishing Co: Datapro Information Services Group, 600 Delran Pkwy., Delran, NJ 08705-9904, USA; 609/764-0100, Fax: 609/764-2811, Co Email: datapro@mhh.com; Web URL: datapro.com; Focus: Information on LAN products, technologies and trends; Format: CD-ROM; Freq: Monthly

Managing Office Technology
Publishing Co: Penton Publishing Inc., 1100 Superior Ave, Cleveland, OH 44114-2543, USA; 216/696-7000, Fax: 216/696-7648, Web URL: penton.com; Focus: News and analysis of computers and office equipment; Format: Magazine; Lura Romei, Ed. Email: luraomei@ad.com; John DiPaola, Pblshr Email: motstaff@aol.com; Circ.: 130,000, Freq: Monthly, Price/yr-$:45

Managing System Development
Publishing Co: Applied Computer Research Inc., PO Box 82266, Phoenix, AZ 85071-2266, USA; 602/995-5929, Fax: 602/995-0905, Focus: News, analysis and information on system and software development; Format: Newsletter; Alan Howard, Ed. Phillip Howard, Pblshr Freq: Monthly, Price/yr-$:198.50

Managing Voice Networks
Publishing Co: Datapro Information Services Group, 600 Delran Pkwy., Delran, NJ 08705-9904, USA; 609/764-0100, Fax: 609/764-2811, Co Email: datapro@mhh.com; Web URL: datapro.com; Focus: Information on voice network technologies and trends; Format: CD-ROM; Freq: Monthly

Manufacturing Automation
Publishing Co: Vital Information Publications, 754 Caravel Lane, Foster City, CA 94941, USA; 415/345-7018, Fax: 415/345-7018, Focus: News, analysis, trends and forecasts about the international factory

automation and CIM ma; Format: Newsletter; Peter Adrian, Ed. & Prncpl Circ.: 300, Freq: Monthly, Price/yr-$:325

Manufacturing Systems
Publishing Co: Hitchcock Publishing Co., 191 S. Gary Ave, Carol Stream, IL 60188-2292, USA; 708/665-1000, Fax: 708/462-2225, Web URL: manufacturingsystems.com; Focus: Management of integrated manufacturing; Format: Magazine; Thomas J. Drozda, Pblshr Kevin Parker, Ed. Jim Fulcher, Sr Ed. Freq: Monthly, Price/yr-$:70

MapWorld Magazine
Publishing Co: MapInfo Corp., One Global View, Troy, NY 12180, USA; 518/285-7340, Co Email: mapworld.mag@mapinfo.com; Focus: Desktop mapping; Format: Magazine; Randy Drawas, Pub Dir Sally Shapiro, Mng Ed. Scott Petronis, Assist Ed

Market Intelligence Report, The
Publishing Co: Fairfield Research Inc., 5620 S. 49th Street, Lincoln, NE 68516, USA; 402/441-3370, Fax: 402/441-3389, Co Email: fairfield@cybersurvey.com; Web URL: cybersurvey.com; Focus: Growth trends and sales projections for electronic game and interactive media, PCs, etc; Format: Newsletter; Ted Lannan, Pres Freq: Monthly, Price/yr-$:487

Market Trends Digest
Publishing Co: Newton-Evans Research Co. Inc., 10176 Baltimore National Pike, #204, Ellicott City, MD 21042, USA; 410/465-7316, Fax: 410/750-7429, Co Email: fkjn43ac@prodigy.com; Focus: Multi-client studies, survey results on computer, communications & control system; Format: Newsletter; Loretta R. Smolenski, Ed. Charles Newton, Pblshr Patricia Sorg, Client Svcs Mgr Freq: Monthly, Price/yr-$:295

Marketing Computers
Publishing Co: ASM Publications Inc., 1515 Broadway, 12th Floor, New York, NY 10036, USA; 212/536-6587, Fax: 212/536-6551, Web URL: marketingcomputers.com; Focus: Information on computer advertising and marketing strategies; Format: Magazine; Ron Kolgraf, Pblshr Email: ron@marketingcomputers.co; David Evans, Ed. Email: david@marketingcomputers.com; Jeffrey M. O'Brien, Sr Ed. Email: jeff@marketingcomputers.com; Circ.: 16,000, Freq: 23/Year, Price/yr-$:495

Marketing Surveys Index
PO Box 480, Beaconsfiels, Buckinghamshire, HP9 2RS, UK; 494-676186, Fax: 494-676186, Focus: Listing of market research reports; Format: Directory; Claudia Richards, Ed. Freq: 10/Year, Price/yr-$:370

Marketing Technology
Publishing Co: Zhivago Marketing Partners, 70 Princeton Rd., Menlo Park, CA

94025-5327, USA; 415/328-8600, Fax: 415/322-9149, Co Email: kristin@zhivago.com; Focus: Effective marketing for high-tech products & marketing using technical tools; Format: Newsletter; Kristin Zhivago, Ed. Email: kristin@zhivago.com; Philip Zhivago, Pblshr Freq: Monthly, Price/yr-$:269

Marketscan International
Publishing Co: CMP Media, 2800 Campus Drive, San Mateo, CA 94403, USA; 415/525-4300, Fax: 415/513-4482, Focus: International news on the PC and LAN market; Format: Newsletter; Freq: Monthly

Mathematica Journal
Publishing Co: Miller Freeman Inc., 600 Harrison Street, San Francisco, CA 94107-1391, USA; 415/905-2200, Fax: 415/905-2234, Focus: News and information for Mathematica users; Format: Magazine; Circ.: 4,500, Freq: 4/Year, Price/yr-$:55

MechanCAD
Publishing Co: Miller Freeman Inc., 600 Harrison Street, San Francisco, CA 94107-1391, USA; 415/905-2200, Fax: 415/905-2234, Format: Magazine

Media Computing
Publishing Co: Dreamscape Productions, 510 Woodhaven, Aptos, CA 95003, USA; 408/685-8818, Fax: 408/685-8819, Co Email: statsuno@aol.com; Focus: Analysis of US multimedia computing and technology trends; Format: Newsletter; Sheridan Tatsuno, Ed. & Pblr Freq: Monthly, Price/yr-$:495/550

MediaMap
Publishing Co: MediaMap, 215 First Street, 3rd Floor, Cambridge, MA 02142-9750, USA; 617/374-9300, Fax: 617/374-9345, Co Email: info@mediamap.com; Web URL: mediamap.com; Focus: Profiles of leading computer press editors and analysts; Format: Directory; John Pearce, CEO Freq: 4/Year, Price/yr-$:1,695

MediaMap Alert
Publishing Co: MediaMap, 215 First Street, 3rd Floor, Cambridge, MA 02142-9750, USA; 617/374-9300, Fax: 617/374-9345, Co Email: info@mediamap.com; Web URL: mediamap.com; Focus: News, analysis and information about national & int'l computer publications and trade shows; Format: Newsletter; Freq: Monthly, Price/yr-$:295

MediaMap Western Europe
Publishing Co: MediaMap, 215 First Street, 3rd Floor, Cambridge, MA 02142-9750, USA; 617/374-9300, Fax: 617/374-9345, Co Email: info@mediamap.com; Web URL: mediamap.com; Focus: Profiles of leading computer press editors and analysts in Europe; Format: Directory; John Pearce, CEO Freq: 2/Year, Price/yr-$:995/1,695

MediaMap/Business & Finance
Publishing Co: MediaMap, 215 First Street,

3rd Floor, Cambridge, MA 02142-9750, USA; 617/374-9300, Fax: 617/374-9345, Co Email: info@mediamap.com; Focus: Media information database; Format: Directory; John Pearce, CEO Freq: Monthly

Metrics for the Internet & Information Technology HandiGuide
Publishing Co: Positive Support Review Inc., 2500 Broadway Street, Santa Monica, CA 90404-3061, USA; 310/453-6100, Fax: 310/453-6253, Focus: Industry specific measure for financial svcs, distribution, manufacturing, education etc.; Format: Book; M. Victor Janulaitis, Pres & CEO

Metropolitan Area Networks (MAN)
Publishing Co: Information Gatekeepers Inc., 214 Harvard Ave, Boston, MA 02134, USA; 617/232-3111, Fax: 617/734-8562, Co Email: igiboston@aol.com; Focus: News, technology, products, applications and services on MAN; Format: Newsletter; Paul Polishuk, Ed. & Pblr Email: igiboston@aol.com; Freq: Monthly, Price/yr-$:545/595

MFP Advocate, The
Publishing Co: Camarro Research, 580 Commerce Drive, Fairfield, CT 06432, USA; 203/336-4566, Fax: 203/331-0470, Focus: Multifunction Product and Market Newsletter; Format: Newsletter; Kenneth Camarro, Pblshr Freq: Monthly, Price/yr-$:395

Micro House Technical Library
Publishing Co: Micro House International, 4900 Pearl East Circle, #101, Boulder, CO 80301, USA; 303/443-3388, Fax: 303/443-3323, Web URL: microhouse.com; Focus: Directory and specs of hard disk drives, network cards, main boards and peripheral cards; Format: CD-Rom; Steve Anderson, Pres/CEO Doug Anderson, VP/CTO Freq: 4/Year, Price/yr-$:249.00

Micro Publishing News
Publishing Co: Micro Publishing Press, 21150 Hawthorne Blvd. #104, Torrance, CA 90503, USA; 310/371-5787, Focus: Electronic publishing news for California users; Format: Newspaper; James Cavuoto, Ed. & Pblr Les Cowan, Sr Ed. Stephen Beale, Exec Ed. Circ.: 40,000, Freq: Monthly, Price/yr-$:Free/25

Micro Software Marketing
Publishing Co: Micro Software Marketing, PO Box 380, Congers, NY 10920, USA; 914/268-5925, Focus: News and information about the microcomputer software industry; Format: Newsletter; Scott Witt, Ed. & Pblr Freq: Monthly, Price/yr-$:87

Microcomputer Abstracts
Publishing Co: Information Today Inc., 143 Old Marlton Pike, Medford, NJ 08055-8750, USA; 609/654-6266, Fax: 609/654-4309, Co Email: custserv@infotoday.com; Web URL: infotoday.com; Focus: Abstracts of leading microcomputer jour-

nals and magazines; Format: Book, CD-ROM; Judith W. Bouchard, Ed. John E. Eichorn, Ed. Freq: 4/Year, Price/yr-$:195

Microcomputer Software, Directory of
Publishing Co: Datapro Information Services Group, 600 Delran Pkwy., Delran, NJ 08705-9904, USA; 609/764-0100, Fax: 609/764-2811, Co Email: datapro@mhh.com; Web URL: datapro.com; Focus: Information on over 18,000 microcomputer programs; Format: CD-ROM; Freq: Monthly

Microcomputer Trainer, The
Publishing Co: Systems Literacy Inc., 696 Ninth Street, PO Box 2487, Secaucus, NJ 07096-2487, USA; 201/330-8923, Fax: 201/330-0163, Focus: Information about microcomputer training; Format: Newsletter; Loretta Weiss-Morris, Ed. & Pblr Hal Morris, Tech Ed. Freq: Monthly, Price/yr-$:195/265

MicroLeads Reseller Directory
Publishing Co: Chromatic Communications Enterprises, Inc., PO Box 30127, Walnut Creek, CA 94598-9878, USA; 510/945-1602, Fax: 707/746-0542, Focus: Listing of over 6,000 computer retailers ($995 on diskette).; Format: Directory; Michael Shipp, Ed. & Pblr Freq: Annual, Price/yr-$:595

MicroLeads Vendor Directory
Publishing Co: Chromatic Communications Enterprises, Inc., PO Box 30127, Walnut Creek, CA 94598-9878, USA; 510/945-1602, Fax: 707/746-0542, Focus: Listing of over 7,000+ microcomputer vendors ($495 on diskette); Format: Directory; Michael Shipp, Ed. & Pblr Freq: Annual, Price/yr-$:495

Microprocessor Report
Publishing Co: MicroDesign Resources, 874 Gravenstein Hwy S. #14, Sebastopol, CA 95472, USA; 707/824-4001, Fax: 707/823-0504, Co Email: lgwennap@mdr.zd.com; Web URL: chipanalyst.com; Focus: In-depth analysis of new microprocessor developments; Format: Newsletter; Michael Slater, Pblr & Ed. Dir Email: mslater@mdr.zd.com; Linley Gwennap, Ed-in-Chief Email: lgwennap@mdr.zd.com; Donna Schaffer, Dir Ops Email: dschaffer@mdr.zd.com; Freq: 17/Year, Price/yr-$:495

Microsfocus COBOL Developers Journal
Publishing Co: Cobb Group, The, 9420 Bunsen Pkwy. #300, Louisville, KY 40220, USA; 502/493-3300, Fax: 502/491-8050, Co Email: cobb@aol.com; Web URL: cobb.com; Focus: Tips and techniques for Microsfocus COBOL developers; Format: Newsletter; Price/yr-$:149

Microsoft Access 95 Developers Journal
Publishing Co: Cobb Group, The, 9420 Bunsen Pkwy. #300, Louisville, KY

40220, USA; 502/493-3300, Fax: 502/491-8050, Co Email: cobb@aol.com; Web URL: cobb.com; Focus: Tips and techniques for Microsoft Access 95 developers; Format: Newsletter; Price/yr-$:89

Microsoft Interactive Developer
Publishing Co: Fawcette Technical Publications, 209 Hamilton Ave, Palo Alto, CA 94301-2500, USA; 415/833-7100, Fax: 415/853-0230, Co Email: 75451.2343@compuserve.com; Web URL: microsoft.com/mind; Focus: Internet development; Format: Magazine; Eric J. Maffei, Ed-in-Chief Laura Euler, Mgng Ed. Lynne Matthes, Pblshr Freq: Monthly, Price/yr-$:33

Microsoft SQL Server Professional
Publishing Co: Pinnacle Publishing Inc., 18000 72nd Ave S. #217, Kent, WA 98032, USA; 206/251-1900, Fax: 206/251-5057, Web URL: pinpub.com; Focus: Tips and solutions for Microsoft SQL Server users; Format: Loose-leaf; Susan Jameson Harker, Pblshr Karen Watterson, Ed. Freq: Monthly, Price/yr-$:199

Microsoft Systems Journal
Publishing Co: Miller Freeman Inc., 600 Harrison Street, San Francisco, CA 94107-1391, USA; 415/905-2200, Fax: 415/905-2234, Focus: News and information for programmers developing in Microsoft environments; Format: Magazine; Eric J. Maffei, Ed-in-Chief Peter Westerman, Pblshr Circ.: 40,000, Freq: Monthly, Price/yr-$:50

Microsystems, Software & LANs
Publishing Co: Faulkner Information Services, 7905 Browning Road, Pennsauken, NJ 08109-4319, USA; 609/662-2070, Fax: 609/662-0905, Co Email: faulkner@faulkner.com; Web URL: faulkner.com; Focus: Product and technology information on PCs, servers, LANs, peripherals and software; Format: Loose-leaf; Martin Murphy, Pblshr Freq: Monthly, Price/yr-$:1,535

MicroTimes
Publishing Co: BAM Media Inc., 3470 Buskirk Ave, Pleasant Hill, CA 94523, USA; 510/934-3700, Fax: 510/934-3958, Co Email: microx@well.sf.ca.us; Focus: News, reviews and perspectives for PC users in California; Format: Newspaper; Dennis Erokan, Ed-in-Chief Chuck Stanley, Pblshr Mary Eisenhart, Ed. Circ.: 235,000, Freq: 14/Year, Price/yr-$:35/65

Midnight Engineering Magazine
1700 Washington Ave, Rocky Ford, CO 81067, USA; 719/254-4558, Fax: 719/254-4517, Focus: Resources and insight for entrepreneurial engineers; Format: Magazine; William E. Gates, Ed. & Pblr Circ.: 10,000, Freq: 6/Year, Price/yr-$:24

Midrange Computer Directories
Publishing Co: DP Blue Book Co., The, 35200 Dequindre, #100, Sterling Heights, MI 48310-4857, USA; 810/978-4300,

Fax: 810/978-4310, Focus: Loose-leaf reports on over 150,000 computer sites in N. America; Format: Loose-leaf; Karen Watt, Pblshr Freq: Monthly

Midrange Computing
Publishing Co: IIR Publications Inc., 5650 El Camino Real, #225, Carlsbad, CA 92008-9711, USA; 619/931-8615, Fax: 619/931-9935, Web URL: as400.com; Focus: Technical information about IBM midrange systems; Format: Newspaper; Sharon L. Hoffman, Ed. Circ.: 20,000, Freq: Monthly, Price/yr-$:99

Midrange Computing's Showcase
Publishing Co: IIR Publications Inc., 5650 El Camino Real, #225, Carlsbad, CA 92008-9711, USA; 619/931-8615, Fax: 619/931-9935, Web URL: as400.com; Focus: Product news for IBM midrange systems; Format: Newspaper; Amy N. Harris, Ed. Circ.: 95,000, Freq: 9/Year, Price/yr-$:Free

Midrange Systems
Publishing Co: Cardinal Business Media Inc., 1300 Virginia Drive, #400, Ft. Washington, PA 19034-3225, USA; 215/643-8000, Fax: 215/643-8099, Web URL: cardinal.com/midrange; Focus: News and trends for IBM midrange computer users; Format: Magazine; Al Gillen, Ed.-in-Chief Email: gillenam@box101.cardinal.; Mark Durrick, Pblshr Elizabeth Bobrow, Assoc Ed. Email: bobrowef@box101.cardinal.com; Circ.: 53,000, Freq: Semi-monthly, Price/yr-$:Free

Mobile Communications
Publishing Co: FT Telecoms & Media Publishing, Maple House, 149 Tottenham Court Road, London, W1P 9LL, UK; 171-896-2222, Fax: 171-896-2274, Focus: Information on mobile communications trends; Format: Newsletter; Price/yr-$:1,005

Mobile Communications Int'l.
Publishing Co: Cheerman Ltd., 301-305 Euston Road, London, NW1 3SS, UK; 71-383-5757, Fax: 71-383-3181, Focus: Information on the global mobile communication market; Format: Magazine; Freq: Monthly, Price/yr-$:90

Mobile Computing Technology
Publishing Co: Intertec Publishing Corp., 6151 Powers Ferry Road NW, Atlanta, GA 30339-2941, USA; 770/955-2500, Web URL: argusinc.com; Focus: News and technical information on mobile computing; Format: Magazine; Tom Parrish, Ed. Mercy Contreras, Pblshr Freq: 6/Year, Price/yr-$:Free/32

Mobile Data Report
Publishing Co: Telecom Publishing Group, 1101 King Street, #444, Alexandria, VA 22314-2968, USA; Fax: 800/645-4104, Co Email: mdr@cappubs.com; Web URL: cappubs.com/tpg; Focus: News, trends and information about mobile communications; Format: Newsletter; Michael Cau-

sey, Exec Ed. Email:
mcausey@cappubs.com; Chris Vestal,
Pblshr Freq: 24/Year, Price/yr-$:597

Mobile Letter
Publishing Co: IDG Newsletters Corp., 77
Franklin Street, Boston, MA 02110-1510,
USA; 617/482-8785, Fax: 617/338-0164,
Focus: Tips and techniques for Mobile
Computing Professionals; Format: News-
letter; Craig G. Pierce, Pblshr Freq:
Monthly, Price/yr-$:595/695

Mobile Letter
Publishing Co: Mobile Computing Insights
Inc., 2001 Landings Drive, Mt. View, CA
94043, USA; 415/390-9800, Fax: 415/
919-0930, Co Email: @mobilein-
sights.com; Web URL: mobilein-
sights.com; Focus: Information and news
on mobile computing and communications;
Format: Newsletter; J. Gerry Purdy, Ed-
in-Chief Email: gpurdy@mobilein-
sights.com; Peter Teige, Sr Ed. Email:
pteige@mobileinsights.com; Barbara Hubbard, Dir Publishing Email: bhub-
bard@mobileinsights.com; Freq:
Monthly, Price/yr-$:595

Mobile Office
Publishing Co: CurtCo Freedom Group,
29160 Heathercliff Road, #200, Malibu,
CA 90265, USA; 310/589-3100, Fax:
310/589-3131, Co Email: @mobileof-
fice.com; Web URL: mobileoffice.com;
Focus: News and information on portable
office products; Format: Magazine; William D. Holiber, Gr Pblr Rich Malloy, Ed-
in-Chief Email: malloy@mobileoffice.com;
Rik Fairlie, Mgng Ed. Circ.: 105,000,
Freq: Monthly, Price/yr-$:Free/24

Mobile Phone News
Publishing Co: Phillips Business Information Inc., 1201 Seven Locks Road, #300,
Potomac, MD 20854-1110, USA; 301/
340-1520, Fax: 301/309-3847, Co Email:
pbi@phillips.com; Web URL: phil-
lips.com; Focus: News mobile phone market; Format: Magazine; Freq: 50/Year,
Price/yr-$:697

Monash Software Letter
Publishing Co: Monash Information Services, 61 W. 62nd Street, New York, NY
10023, USA; 212/315-3120, Fax: 212/
399-3268, Co Email: monashinfo@mci-
mail.com; Focus: Software industry trends,
analysis and technology; Format: Newsletter; Curt A. Monash, Ed. & Pblr Email:
monashinfo@mcimail.com; Freq:
Monthly, Price/yr-$:347

Monitor
Publishing Co: Information Today Inc., 143
Old Marlton Pike, Medford, NJ 08055-
8750, USA; 609/654-6266, Fax: 609/654-
4309, Co Email: custserv@infotoday.com;
Web URL: infotoday.com; Focus: News
and analysis of the online and electronic
publishing industry; Format: Newsletter;
Freq: Monthly, Price/yr-$:290

Morph's Outpost on the Digital

Frontier
Publishing Co: Morph's Outpost Inc., 2223
Shattuck Avenue, Berkeley, CA 94704,
USA; 510/704-7171, Fax: 510/704-7128,
Co Email: info@morph.com; Focus: For
builders on the information superhighway;
Format: Newspaper; Craig LaGrow, Pblshr
Doug Millison, Ed.-in-Chief Brad Dosland,
Mgng Ed. Circ.: 35,000, Freq: Monthly,
Price/yr-$:39.95

**Multifunction Product and Market
Trend Report**
Publishing Co: Camarro Research, 580
Commerce Drive, Fairfield, CT 06432,
USA; 203/336-4566, Fax: 203/331-0470,
Focus: Trends, analysis and outlook on
multifunction products; Format: Factbook;
Kenneth Camarro, Pblshr Price: Annual,
Price/yr-$:1,695

Multilingual Computing Magazine
319 N First Ave, Sandpoint, ID 83864,
USA; 208/263-8178, Fax: 208/263-6310,
Co Email: info@multiligual.com; Focus:
Language technology trends; Format: Mag-
azine; Seth T. Schneider, Ed-in-Chief Mike
Bennett, Mgng Ed. Freq: 6/Year, Price/
yr-$:35

Multilingual PC Directory
Publishing Co: Knowledge Computing, 9
Ashdown Drive, Borehamwood, Herts,
WD6 4LZ, UK; 181-953-7722, Fax: 181-
905-1879, Co Email: 72240.3447@com-
puserve.com; Web URL: knowl-
edge.co.uk; Focus: Directory of
information on multilingual and foreign
language PC software; Format: Directory/
disk/w; Ian Tresman, Pblshr Email:
iantresman@easy.netco.uk; Circ.: 1,000,
Freq: 4/Year, Price/yr-$:20-50

Multimedia Alert
Publishing Co: Future Systems Inc., PO
Box 26, Falls Church, VA 22040-0026,
USA; 703/241-1799, Fax: 703/532-0529,
Co Email: 71333.2753@compuserve.com;
Focus: News on interactive multimedia
industry; Format: Fax, e-mail; Rockley L.
Miller, Ed. & Pblr Freq: Weekly, Price/yr-
$:395

**Multimedia and Technology Licens-
ing Agreements**
Publishing Co: Warren Gorham Lamont,
31 St. James Ave, Boston, MA 02116-
9372, USA; Fax: 617/451-0908, Co
Email: sales@wgl.com; Web URL:
wgl.com; Focus: Forms and commentary to
help draft and negotiate winning deals; Format: Loose-leaf; Gregory J. Battersby,
Author Charles W. Grimes, Author Price/
yr-$:150

**Multimedia Business & Marketing
Sourcebook**
Publishing Co: Broadcast Information
Bureau, 401 N Broad Street, 5th Floor,
Philadelphia, PA 19108, USA; 215/238-
5300, Fax: 215/238-5283, Web URL:
napco.com; Focus: Guide to the multime-
dia industry; Format: Factbook; Tiffany A.

Walton, Mgng Ed. Russell Perkins, Pres
Freq: Annual, Price/yr-$:195

Multimedia Business Analyst
Publishing Co: FT Telecoms & Media Publishing, Maple House, 149 Tottenham
Court Road, London, W1P 9LL, UK; 171-
896-2222, Fax: 171-896-2274, Focus:
Developments in multimedia and interactive media; Format: Newsletter; Helen
Nicol, Pblshr Robin Arnfield, Ed. Freq:
24/Year, Price/yr-$:664

Multimedia Business Report
Publishing Co: Simba Information Inc., 11
River Bend Drive S, PO Box 4234, Stamford, CT 06807-0234, USA; 203/834-
0033, Fax: 203/358-5825, Co Email: sim-
bainfo@simbanet.com; Web URL: simba-
net.com; Focus: Information on the
multimedia industry; Format: Newsletter;
Lorraine Sileo, Ed. Dir Brian Kelly, Ed.
Tom O'Reilly, Ed. Freq: 46/Year, Price/
yr-$:479

Multimedia Daily
Publishing Co: Pasha Publications, 1616 N.
Ft. Myer Drive, #1000, Arlington, VA
22209-3107, USA; 703/816-8640, Fax:
703/528-3742, Focus: News and informa-
tion on the multimedia industry; Format:
Fax; Harry L. Baisden, Pblshr Freq: Daily,
Price/yr-$:595

Multimedia Intelligence
Publishing Co: Computer Technology
Research Corp., 6 North Atlantic Wharf,
Charlston, SC 29401-2150, USA; 803/
853-6460, Fax: 803/853-7210, Co Email:
report@ctrcorp.com; Web URL: ctr-
corp.com; Focus: News & information
about the multimedia marketplace-stan-
dards, hardware, software, etc.; Format:
Newsletter; Edward R. Wagner, Pblshr
Stacey Evangelist, Ed-in-Chief Freq:
Monthly, Price/yr-$:390

Multimedia Monitor
Publishing Co: Future Systems Inc., PO
Box 26, Falls Church, VA 22040-0026,
USA; 703/241-1799, Fax: 703/532-0529,
Co Email: 71333.2753@compuserve.com;
Focus: Information on interactive multime-
dia industry; Format: Newsletter; Rockey
L. Miller, Ed. & Pblr Vicki L. Reeve, Mgng
Ed. Alex S. Kasten, Sr Ed. Freq: Monthly,
Price/yr-$:395

**Multimedia Network Technology
Report**
Publishing Co: DataTrends Publications
Inc., 30-C Catoctin Circle SE, Leesburg,
VA 22075, USA; 703/779-0574, Fax:
703/779-2267, Co Email:
dtrends@aol.com; Focus: News & infor-
mation on networked multimedia commu-
nications products, tech, standard, etc.;
Format: Newsletter; Jeff Caruso, Ed.
Email: jpcaruso@aol.com; Paul G. Ochs,
Pblshr Freq: Biweekly, Price/yr-$:395

Multimedia Online
Publishing Co: Redgate Communications
Corp., 660 Beachland Blvd, Vero Beach, FL

32963, USA; 407/231-6904, Fax: 407/231-7872, Co Email: reviewz@aol.com; Focus: America Online's guide to multimedia; Format: Magazine; Kevin Fallon, Pblshr David Rosen, Ed-in-Chief Caryn Mladen, Ed-in-Chief Freq: 4/Year

Multimedia Producer
Publishing Co: Knowledge Industry Publications Inc., 701 Westchester Ave, #109W, White Plains, NY 10604-3098, USA; 914/328-9157, Fax: 914/328-9093, Co Email: mmediapro@aol.com; Web URL: kipinet.com; Focus: Strategies to help developers and creators of interactive multimedia; Format: Magazine; Robert L. Lindstrom, Ed. Steven Klapow, Mngg Ed. Andrew Mintz, Pblshr Circ.: 45,000, Freq: Monthly, Price/yr-$:40

Multimedia Source Book
Publishing Co: Hi-Tech Media Inc., 445 5th Ave, 27th Floor, New York, NY 10016, USA; 212/293-3900, Fax: 212/293-7909, Co Email: msb@i-2000.com; Web URL: mmsourcebook.com/msb; Focus: Guide to multimedia products & services; Format: Book; Will Rhyins, Pblshr Linus Ly, Mngg Ed. Freq: 2/Year, Price/yr-$:49.95

Multimedia Title Publishing: Review, Trends & Forecast
Publishing Co: Simba Information Inc., 11 River Bend Drive S, PO Box 4234, Stamford, CT 06807-0234, USA; 203/834-0033, Fax: 203/358-5825, Co Email: simbainfo@simbanet.com; Web URL: simbanet.com; Focus: Information for publishers of multimedia CD-ROM titles; Format: Loose-leaf; Michael Hayes, Sr Mngg Ed. Freq: Annual, Price/yr-$:1,300

Multimedia Today
Publishing Co: IBM Corp., 4280 Twin Rivers Drive, Gainesville, GA 30504, USA; 404/531-0096, Fax: 404/531-1002, Co Email: 71572.2720@compuserve.com; Focus: Multimedia products and technology; Format: Magazine; Geoffrey R. Amthor, Ed. & Pblr Email: amthor@aol.com; Jan Oliver, Mngg Ed. Lori Wild Amthor, Assoc Ed. Freq: 4/Year, Price/yr-$:20

Multimedia Week
Publishing Co: Phillips Business Information Inc., 1201 Seven Locks Road, #300, Potomac, MD 20854-1110, USA; 301/340-1520, Fax: 301/424-4297, Co Email: pbi@phillips.com; Web URL: phillips.com; Focus: News, trends and business opportunities in the multimedia industry; Format: Newsletter; Freq: 50/Year, Price/yr-$:697

Multimedia Wire
Publishing Co: ProActive Media Inc., 5601 Grosvenor Lane, Bethesda, MD 20814, USA; 301/493-9290, Fax: 301/493-8996, Co Email: mmwire@aol.com; Web URL: mmwire.com; Focus: Information on multimedia industry; Format: Fax/E-mail;

Christopher V. Sherman, Pblshr & Ed. Email: mmwire@aol.com; Stacey Elliott, Subs Mgr Email: proact@aol.com; Freq: Daily, Price/yr-$:445

Multimedia Wire+
Publishing Co: Phillips Business Information Inc., 1201 Seven Locks Road, #300, Potomac, MD 20854-1110, USA; 301/340-1520, Fax: 301/424-4297, Co Email: pbi@phillips.com; Web URL: phillips.com; Focus: News and information in the multimedia market; Format: Newsletter; Freq: Daily, Price/yr-$:495

Multimedia World
Publishing Co: PCW Communications Inc., 501 Second Street, #600, San Francisco, CA 94107, USA; 415/281-8650, Fax: 415/281-3915, Co Email: 75300.2503@compuserve.com; Focus: News and information on multimedia PCs; Format: Magazine; Greg Mason, Pblshr Don Menn, Ed.-in-Chief Vince Broady, Exec Ed. Freq: Monthly, Price/yr-$:15

Music & Computers
Publishing Co: Miller Freeman Inc., 600 Harrison Street, San Francisco, CA 94107-1391, USA; 415/905-2200, Fax: 415/905-2234, Format: Magazine

MVS Update
Publishing Co: Xephon, 1301 W. Hwy 407, #201-450, Lewisville, TX 75067, USA; 817/455-7050, Fax: 817/455-2492, Focus: Tools and techniques for enhancing IBM's MVS software; Format: Magazine; Freq: Monthly, Price/yr-$:430

NADTP Journal
Publishing Co: National Association of Desktop Pblshrs, 462 Old Boston Street, #62, Topsfield, MA 01983-1232, USA; 508/887-7900, Fax: 508/887-9245, Co Email: nadtp@aol.com; Focus: Membership publication for NADTP; Format: Magazine; Barry Harrigan, Pblshr Robert Runck, Ed.-in-Chief Linda Lee, Mngg Ed. Circ.: 20,000, Freq: Monthly, Price/yr-$:48/95

NASA Tech Briefs
Publishing Co: Associated Business Publications Co., 317 Madison Avenue, #921, New York, NY 10017-5391, USA; 212/490-3999, Fax: 212/986-7864, Co Email: ntb_edit@interramp.com; Web URL: nasatech.com; Focus: Information about NASA technology, patents and programs; Format: Magazine; Joseph T. Pramberger, Ed. & Pblr Ted Selinsky, Mngg Ed. Linda L. Bell, Chief Ed. Circ.: 203,000, Freq: Monthly, Price/yr-$:Free/75

NCSA News
Publishing Co: National Computer Security Assoc., 10 S Courthouse Ave, Carlisle, PA 17013, USA; 717/258-1816, Fax: 717/243-8642, Co Email: newseditor@ncsa.com; Focus: Journal of the NCSA; Format: Magazine; Linda Stewart, Ed. Freq: 4/Year

Net, The

Publishing Co: Imagine Publishing Inc., 1350 Old Bayshore Hwy, #210, Burlingame, CA 94010, USA; 415/696-1661, Fax: 415/696-1678, Co Email: talktous@thenet-usa.com; Web URL: thenet-usa.com; Focus: Information for Internet users; Format: Magazine; Mark Frost, Ed.-in-Chief Minda Sandler, Mngg Ed. Crystal Waters, Reviews Ed. Freq: Monthly, Price/yr-$:49.95

NetGuide
Publishing Co: CMP Publications Inc., 600 Community Drive, Manhasset, NY 11030, USA; 516/562-5000, Fax: 516/562-7406, Co Email: netmail@netguide.cmp.com; Web URL: netguidemag.com; Focus: Guide for online users; Format: Magazine; Beth Haggerty, Pblshr Email: bhaggert@cmp.com; Tony Rizzo, Ed.-in-Chief Email: trizzo@cmp.com; Andy Levenberg, Mngg Ed. Circ.: 200,000+, Freq: Monthly, Price/yr-$:23

Netscape World
Publishing Co: International Data Group, 501 Second Street, #600, San Francisco, CA 94107, USA; 415/267-4527, Focus: Information for Netscape software users; Format: Magazine

NetSmart
600 Townsend Street, #170E, San Francisco, CA 94103, USA; 415/522-2411, Fax: 415/522-2409, Focus: Internet products and trends; Format: Magazine; Dan Ruby, Ed.-in-Chief Email: druby@smarter.com; Freq: Monthly

Netware Software Connection
Publishing Co: Cobb Group, The, 9420 Bunsen Pkwy. #300, Louisville, KY 40220, USA; 502/493-3300, Fax: 502/491-8050, Co Email: cobb@aol.com; Web URL: cobb.com; Format: Newsletter; Price/yr-$:59

NetWare Solutions
Publishing Co: New Media Publications, 10711 Burnet Road, #305, Austin, TX 78758-4459, USA; 512/873-7761, Fax: 512/873-7782, Co Email: 75730.2465@compuserve.com; Focus: News, applications and products for NetWare system managers; Format: Magazine; Deni Connor, Ed. Email: 75730.2465@compuserve.com; Kathy Murphy, Pblshr Email: 75730.2465@compuserve.com; Circ.: 40,000, Freq: Monthly, Price/yr-$:Free/24

Network Analyst
Publishing Co: Datapro Information Services Group, 600 Delran Pkwy., Delran, NJ 08705-9904, USA; 609/764-0100, Fax: 609/764-2811, Co Email: datapro@mhh.com; Web URL: datapro.com; Focus: Network management product announcements and events; Format: Newsletter; Freq: Monthly

Network Computing
Publishing Co: CMP Publications Inc., 600 Community Drive, Manhasset, NY 11030,

USA; 516/562-5071, Fax: 516/562-7293, Co Email: @nwc.com; Web URL: networkcomputing.com; Focus: Reviews and technical information about network products and system development; Format: Magazine; Deborah Gisonni, Pblshr Email: dgisonni@nwc.com; Patricia Schnaidt, Ed.-in-Chief Email: pschnaidt@nwc.com; Fritz Nelson, Ed. Email: fnelson@nwc.com; Circ.: 190,000, Freq: 20/Year, Price/yr-$:Free/65

Network Economics Letter
Publishing Co: Computer Economics Inc., 5841 Edison Place, Carlsbad, CA 92008, USA; 619/438-8100, Fax: 619/431-1126, Co Email: custserv@compecon.com; Focus: Cost of ownership, networking standards and technology trends; Format: Newsletter; Mark McManus, Ed.-in-Chief Email: mmcmanus@compecon.com; Bruno Bassi, Pblshr Email: bbassi@compecon.com; Freq: Monthly, Price/yr-$:395

Network Management Systems & Strategies
Publishing Co: DataTrends Publications Inc., 30-C Catoctin Circle SE, Leesburg, VA 22075, USA; 703/779-0574, Fax: 703/779-2267, Co Email: dtrends@aol.com; Focus: Guide to new network management products, technologies and standards; Format: Newsletter; Jeff Caruso, Ed. Email: jpcaruso@aol.com; Paul G. Ochs, Pblshr Email Gennifer Chenault, Circ Mgr Freq: 24/Year, Price/yr-$:465

Network Services
Publishing Co: Datapro Information Services Group, 600 Delran Pkwy., Delran, NJ 08705-9904, USA; 609/764-0100, Fax: 609/764-2811, Co Email: datapro@mhh.com; Web URL: datapro.com; Focus: Information on international network services market; Format: CD-ROM; Freq: Monthly

Network VAR
Publishing Co: Miller Freeman Inc., 600 Harrison Street, San Francisco, CA 94107-1391, USA; 415/905-2200, Fax: 415/905-2234, Co Email: @mfi.com; Focus: Information for network VARs and integrators; Format: Magazine; Steve Schneiderman, Pblshr Email: ayoung@mfi.com; Dave Brambert, Ed.-in-Chief Susan Biagi, Sr Ed. Circ.: 30,600, Freq: Monthly, Price/yr-$:Free/39

Network World
Publishing Co: Network World Inc./IDG, 161 Worcester Road, PO Box 9172, Framingham, MA 01701-9172, USA; 508/875-6400, Fax: 508/820-3467, Co Email: nwnews@nww.com; Web URL: nwfusion.com; Focus: News and information for network and telecommunications users; Format: Newspaper; John Gallant, Ed.-in-Chief Colin Ungaro, Pblshr John Dix, Ed. Circ.: 150,000, Freq: Weekly, Price/yr-$:Free/129

Neural Computation

Publishing Co: MIT Press Journals, 55 Hayward Street, Cambridge, MA 02142, USA; 617/253-2889, Fax: 617/258-6779, Co Email: journals-orders@mit.edu; Web URL: mitpress.mit.edu; Focus: Research results on neural computation; Format: Magazine; Terrence Sejnowski, Ed-in-Chief Email: terry@salk.edu; Circ.: 2,100, Freq: 8/Year, Price/yr-$:78

New Media Markets
Publishing Co: FT Telecoms & Media Publishing, Maple House, 149 Tottenham Court Road, London, W1P 9LL, UK; 171-896-2222, Fax: 171-896-2274, Format: Newsletter; Price/yr-$:1,110

New Media Week
Publishing Co: Phillips Business Information Inc., 1201 Seven Locks Road, #300, Potomac, MD 20854-1110, USA; 301/340-1520, Fax: 301/424-4297, Co Email: pbi@phillips.com; Web URL: phillips.com; Focus: News and information on emerging media market; Format: Newsletter; Freq: 50/Year, Price/yr-$:595

New Technology Impact
Publishing Co: Aberdeen Group, 1 Boston Place, 29th Floor, Boston, MA 02108, USA; 617/723-7890, Fax: 617/723-7897, Web URL: aberdeen.com; Focus: Downsizing and open systems business and technology issues; Format: Loose-leaf; Tom Willmott, Ed. & VP Freq: Monthly, Price/yr-$:3,995

New Telecom Quarterly
Publishing Co: Technology Futures Inc., 13740 Research Blvd, #C-1, Austin, TX 78726-1859, USA; 512/258-8898, Fax: 512/258-0087, Co Email: ntg@tfi.com; Web URL: ntq.com; Focus: Information on the global telecom market and technology; Format: Factbook; Julia A. Marsh, Ed. Email: march@tfi.com; Lawrence K. Vanston, Pblshr Freq: 4/Year, Price/yr-$:120

NewMedia
Publishing Co: HyperMedia Communications Inc., 901 Mariner Island Blvd., #365, San Mateo, CA 94404, USA; 415/573-5170, Fax: 415/573-5131, Web URL: hyperstand.com; Focus: Multimedia products and technology; Format: Magazine; Phil Hood, Ed.-in-Chief Richard Landry, Pblshr & CEO Carolyn McMaster, Mgng Ed. Circ.: 250,000, Freq: 16/Year, Price/yr-$:Free/52

News IS
Publishing Co: Xephon, 1301 W. Hwy 407, #201-450, Lewisville, TX 75067, USA; 817/455-7050, Fax: 817/455-2492, Focus: News and commentary on IBM's mainframe business and IS issues; Format: Newsletter; Freq: Weekly, Price/yr-$:775

NEWS/400
Publishing Co: Duke Communications Int'l., 221 E. 29th Street, PO Box 3438, Loveland, CO 80538-2725, USA; 970/663-4700, Fax: 970/663-3285, Web URL: duke.com; Focus: Technical information

for IBM AS/400 users; Format: Magazine; Kathy Nelson, Mgng Pblr Timothy J. Fixmer, Pblshr Dale Egger, Acq Mgr Circ.: 31,000, Freq: Monthly, Price/yr-$:119

Newsbytes
Publishing Co: Newsbytes News Network, 406 Olive Street W., Stillwater, MN 55082-4945, USA; 612/430-1100, Fax: 612/430-0441, Co Email: 72241.337@compuserve.com; Focus: Web-site computer & telecom real-time wire service; Format: Online; Wendy Woods, Ed.-in-Chief Steve Gold, European Bureau Chief Freq: Weekly

Newstips Electronic Editorial Bulletin
Publishing Co: Newstips Inc., 13830 Braeburn Lane, Novelty, OH 44072, USA; 216/338-8400, Fax: 216/338-3480, Co Email: newstips@newstips.com; Focus: Publicity for computer industry press members; Format: Fax or e-mail; Marty Winston, Ed. Email: 75250.3467@compuserve.com; Judie Winston, Pblshr Circ.: 1,500, Freq: Weekly, Price/yr-$:Free

NFAIS Newsletter
Publishing Co: National Federation of Abstracting & Info. Serv., 1518 Walnut Street, Philadelphia, PA 19102, USA; 215/893-1561, Fax: 215/893-1564, Co Email: nfais@hslc.org; Focus: Review and analysis of information industry trends; Format: Loose-leaf; Richard Kaser, Ed. Dir Email: nfais@hslc.org; Circ.: 600, Freq: Monthly, Price/yr-$:110/125

Nonimpact Printer Guide
Publishing Co: Dataquest Inc., 26254 Golden Valley Road, Bldg. 401, Santa Clarita, CA 95351, USA; 805/298-3261, Fax: 805/298-4388, Co Email: mmakers@netcom.com; Web URL: netcom.com~mmakers; Focus: Specifications of laser printers and inkjet printers; Format: Directory; Freq: 2/Year, Price/yr-$:48

Notes Report, The
Publishing Co: Lotus Publishing Corp., 77 Franklin Street #310, Boston, MA 02110, USA; 617/482-8634, Fax: 617/422-8189, Focus: Tips and techniques for Lotus Notes users; Format: Newsletter; Craig G. Pierce, Pblshr Jim O'Donnell, Ed. Sheila Sandapen, Ed. Freq: Monthly, Price/yr-$:295/325/335

Novell Companion, The
Publishing Co: WEKA Publishing, 1077 Bridgeport Ave, Shelton, CT 06484, USA; Fax: 203/944-3663, Focus: Information using Novell NetWare; Format: Loose-leaf; Freq: 4/Year, Price/yr-$:89

NT Developer
Publishing Co: Oakley Publishing, PO Box 70167, Eugene, OR 97401, USA; 541/747-0800, Fax: 541/746-0071, Focus: Technical information for programmers using Windows NT; Format: Magazine;

Richard Shulte, Ed. Bobbi Sinyard, Pblshr
Freq: Monthly, Price/yr-$:130/160

NTIS Alert on Communication
Publishing Co: National Technical Information Service, 5285 Port Royal Road, Rm
1303, Springfield, VA 22161, USA; 703/
487-4650, Fax: 703/321-8547, Focus:
Abstract of government communication
research; Format: Newsletter; Freq: 24/
Year, Price/yr-$:150

**NTIS Alert on Computers, Control &
Information Theory**
Publishing Co: National Technical Informa-
tion Service, 5285 Port Royal Road, Rm
1303, Springfield, VA 22161, USA; 703/
487-4650, Fax: 703/321-8547, Focus:
Abstract of government computer research;
Format: Newsletter; Freq: 24/Year,
Price/yr-$:150

NTIS Alert on Foreign Technology
Publishing Co: National Technical Informa-
tion Service, 5285 Port Royal Road, Rm
1303, Springfield, VA 22161, USA; 703/
487-4650, Fax: 703/321-8547, Focus:
Summaries of foreign technology research;
Format: Newsletter; Freq: 24/Year,
Price/yr-$:165

Object Magazine
Publishing Co: SIGS Publications Group,
236 W 26th Street, #7SW, New York, NY
10001, USA; 212/229-0320, Fax: 212/
807-9111, Co Email: 70754.1111@com-
puserve.com; Web URL: sigs.com; Focus:
Advice and news on managing and implementing object oriented technology; Format: Magazine; Marie A. Lenzi, Ed. Hal
Avery, Pblshr Kristina Joukhadar, Sr Mgng
Ed. Circ.: 20,000, Freq: Monthly, Price/
yr-$:45

Object Observer
Publishing Co: G2 Computer Intelligence
Inc., 3 Maple Place, PO Box 7, Glen Head,
NY 11545-9864, USA; 516/759-7025,
Fax: 516/759-7028, Format: Newsletter;
Maureen O'Gara, Pblshr William Fellows,
Ed. Email: wif@panix.com; Freq: Occa-
sional

Object Technology, Directory of
Publishing Co: SIGS Publications Group,
71 W. 23rd Street, 3rd Floor, New York,
NY 10010, USA; 212/242-7447, Fax:
212/242-7574, Co Email:
73361.1707@compuserve.com; Web
URL: sigs.com; Focus: Source book on
companies, products and services for the
object oriented programming industry;
Format: Directory; Jim Salmons, Ed. Timlynn Babitsky, Ed. Freq: Annual, Price/yr-
$:49

Object-Oriented Strategies
Publishing Co: Cutter Information Corp.,
37 Broadway, Arlington, MA 02174-5539,
USA; 617/648-8702, Fax: 617/648-1950,
Co Email: 74107.653@compuserve.com;
Web URL: cutter.com; Focus: Trends and
information on object-oriented technology;
Format: Newsletter; Paul Harmon, Ed.

Karen Coburn, Group Pblshr Email:
73352.1625@compuserve.com; Circ.:
1,300, Freq: Monthly, Price/yr-$:497

OEM Magazine
Publishing Co: CMP Publications Inc., 600
Community Drive, Manhasset, NY 11030,
USA; 516/562-5624, Fax: 516/562-5325,
Web URL: techweb.cmp.com/oem;
Focus: Technology and trends for system
and software builders; Format: Magazine;
Rick Boyd-Merritt, Ed. Steve Weitzner,
Pblshr Tim Moran, Exec Ed. Freq: 11/
Year, Price/yr-$:Free/79

Office Dealer
Publishing Co: Springhouse Corp., 1111
Betlehem Pike, Box 908, Springhouse, PA
19477-0908, USA; 215/628-7716, Fax:
215/540-8041, Focus: News and product
information for office system dealers; Format: Magazine; Scott Cullen, Ed. Email:
sculos@aol.com; Charles Mitchell, Pblshr
Circ.: 19,500, Freq: 6/Year, Price/yr-
$:Free

Office Equipment & Products (OEP)
Publishing Co: Dempa Publications Inc.,
275 Madison Ave, New York, NY 10016-
1101, USA; 212/682-3755, Fax: 212/682-
2730, Focus: Product and technology news
on the Japanese and worldwide computer
and office equipment in; Format: Newspaper; Tetsuo Hirayama, Pres & Ed. Freq:
Monthly, Price/yr-$:130

Office Product Analyst
Publishing Co: Dataquest Inc., 26254
Golden Valley Road, Bldg. 401, Santa Clarita, CA 95351, USA; 805/298-3261, Fax:
805/298-4388, Co Email: mmakers@net-
com.com; Web URL: net-
com.com~mmakers; Format: Newsletter;
Freq: 12/Year, Price/yr-$:199

Office Product Analyst, The
Publishing Co: Industry Analysts Inc., 50
Chestnut Street, #900, Rochester, NY
14604, USA; 716/232-5320, Fax: 716/
454-5760, Focus: Cost/performance analy-
sis of PCs and office products; Format:
Newsletter; Louis E. Slawetsky, Pblshr
Freq: Monthly, Price/yr-$:195

Office Systems
Publishing Co: Springhouse Corp., 1111
Betlehem Pike, Box 908, Springhouse, PA
19477-0908, USA; 215/628-7716, Fax:
215/540-8041, Focus: News and information about office system automation; Format: Magazine; Scott Cullen, Ed. Email:
sculos@aol.com; Charles Mitchell, Pblshr
Circ.: 100,000, Freq: Monthly, Price/yr-
$:Free

Office World News
Publishing Co: BUS Publishing Group, 366
Ramtown Greenville Road, Howell, NJ
07731, USA; 908/785-1616, Focus: News
and information on business equipment and
supplies for dealers/resellers; Format: Tabloid; William P. Urban, Pblshr Kim Chandlee McCabe, Assoc Pblr & E-in-C Jan
Stafford, Exec Ed. Circ.: 31,500, Freq:

Monthly, Price/yr-$:Free/50

**On the Internet: User Demographics
and Trends**
Publishing Co: Simba Information Inc., 11
River Bend Drive S, PO Box 4234, Stamford, CT 06807-0234, USA; 203/834-
0033, Fax: 203/358-5825, Co Email:
simba99@aol.com; Web URL: simba-
net.com; Focus: Marketing on the Internet;
Format: Loose-leaf; Price/yr-$:1,150

Online & CD-ROM Review
Publishing Co: Information Today Inc., 143
Old Marlton Pike, Medford, NJ 08055-
8750, USA; 609/654-6266, Fax: 609/654-
4309, Co Email: custserv@infotoday.com;
Web URL: infotoday.com; Focus: Review
and trends in the online information industry; Format: Magazine; Martha E. Williams, Ed. Forbes Gibb, Ed. Freq: 6/Year,
Price/yr-$:120

Online Access
Publishing Co: Chicago Fine Print Inc., 900
N. Franklin, #310, Chicago, IL 60614,
USA; 312/573-1700, Fax: 312/573-0520,
Focus: News, directories and how to use
online information services & BBS; Format:
Magazine; Robert Jordan, Pblshr Kathryn
McCabe, Ed.-in-Chief Carol Freer, Mgng
Ed. Circ.: 100,000, Freq: 8/Year, Price/
yr-$:24

Online Advertising Report
Publishing Co: Jupiter Communications
Co., 627 Broadway, 2nd Fl, New York, NY
10012, USA; 212/780-6060, Fax: 212/
780-6075, Co Email: jup5@aol.com; Web
URL: jup.com/jupiter; Focus: Online ad
information; Format: Factbook; Gene
DeRose, Pblshr Freq: Annual, Price/yr-
$:1,395

Online Design
Publishing Co: OnLine Design Publications, 2261 Market Street, #331, San Francisco, CA 94114, USA; 415/334-3800,
Fax: 415/621-6760, Co Email: @online-
design.com; Focus: Information on electronic design; Format: Magazine; Connie
Holt, Pblshr Email: connie@online-
design.com; Charles Abrams, Ed-in-Chief
Bentham Thompson, Mgng Ed. Email:
ben@online-design.com; Freq: 12/Year,
Price/yr-$:15

Online Kids Report
Publishing Co: Jupiter Communications
Co., 627 Broadway, 2nd Fl, New York, NY
10012, USA; 212/780-6060, Fax: 212/
780-6075, Co Email: jup5@aol.com; Web
URL: jup.com/jupiter; Focus: Information
on kids online usage; Format: Factbook;
Gene DeRose, Pblshr Price/yr-$:875

Online Marketplace
Publishing Co: Jupiter Communications
Co., 627 Broadway, New York, NY
10012, USA; 212/780-6060, Fax: 212/
780-6075, Co Email: jup5@aol.com; Web
URL: jup.com/jupiter; Focus: News on
electronic commerce in the home; Format:
Newsletter; Gene DeRose, Pblshr Adam

Schoenfeld, Ed. Yvette Simeon, Mgng Ed. Freq: Monthly, Price/yr-$:545

Online Services: International Markets
Publishing Co: Simba Information Inc., 11 River Bend Drive S, PO Box 4234, Stamford, CT 06807-0234, USA; 203/834-0033, Fax: 203/358-5825, Co Email: simbainfo@simbanet.com; Web URL: simbanet.com; Focus: International online services market; Format: Factbook; Chris Elwell, Gr Pblr Peter Karsilovsky, Author Freq: Annual, Price/yr-$:1,995

Online Services: Review Trends & Forecasts
Publishing Co: Simba Information Inc., 11 River Bend Drive S, PO Box 4234, Stamford, CT 06807-0234, USA; 203/834-0033, Fax: 203/358-5825, Co Email: simbainfo@simbanet.com; Web URL: simbanet.com; Focus: Statistics and forecasts about online services and companies; Format: Factbook; Chris Elwell, Pblsr Lorraine Sileo, Author Freq: Annual, Price/yr-$:995

Online Services: State of the Market
Publishing Co: Fairfield Research Inc., 5815 S 58th Street, Lincoln, NE 68516-3688, USA; 402/441-3370, Fax: 402/441-3389, Co Email: fairfield@cybersurvey.com; Web URL: cybersurvey.com; Focus: Survey-based data on online services usage; Format: Factbook; Ted Lannan, Pres Freq: Annual, Price/yr-$:795

Online Tactics
Publishing Co: Simba Information Inc., 11 River Bend Drive S, PO Box 4234, Stamford, CT 06807-0234, USA; 203/834-0033, Fax: 203/358-5825, Co Email: simbainfo@simbanet.com; Web URL: simbanet.com; Focus: Information for Web and online users; Format: Newsletter; Chris Elwell, Gr Pblr Elizabeth Estroff, Ed. Email: elizabeth_estroff@simbanet.com; Freq: 12/Year, Price/yr-$:345

Online User
Publishing Co: Online Inc., 462 Danbury Road, Wilton, CT 06897-2126, USA; 203/761-1466, Fax: 203/761-1444, Co Email: online@well.com; Web URL: onlineinc.com/online; Focus: Online information for knowledge workers; Format: Magazine; Jefferey K. Pemberton, Pblsr Nancy Garman, Ed. Email: ngarman@well.com; Paula Westwood, Ed. Assist Freq: 6/Year, Price/yr-$:24

Only The Best
Publishing Co: Association for Supervision & Curriculum Dev., 1250 N. Pitt Street, Alexandria, VA 22314, USA; 703/549-9110, Fax: 703/549-3891, Web URL: ascd.org; Focus: Annual guide to the highest rated educational software; Format: Directory; Freq: Annual, Price/yr-$:25/30

OPAC Directory
Publishing Co: Information Today Inc., 143

Old Marlton Pike, Medford, NJ 08055-8750, USA; 609/654-6266, Fax: 609/654-4309, Co Email: custserv@infotoday.com; Web URL: infotoday.com; Focus: List of modem phone number & Internet addresses of online public access catalogs; Format: Directory; Freq: Annual, Price/yr-$:70

Open Computing
Publishing Co: McGraw-Hill Inc., 1900 O'Farrell Street, #200, San Mateo, CA 94403-1311, USA; 415/513-6800, Fax: 415/513-6985, Co Email: @uworld.com; Focus: News, reviews and trends in the Unix and open systems market; Format: Magazine; David Flack, Ed.-in-Chief Email: davef@uworld.com; Michela O'Connor Abrams, Pblshr David Diamond, Exec Ed. Email: davidd@uworld.com; Circ.: 94,000, Freq: Monthly, Price/yr-$:18

Open Information Systems
Publishing Co: Patricia Seybold Group, 148 State Street, 7th Floor, Boston, MA 02109-9990, USA; 617/742-5200, Fax: 617/742-1028, Web URL: psgroup.com; Focus: News, opinions, reviews and analysis of the UNIX marketplace; Format: Newsletter; Patricia Seybold, Pblshr Freq: Monthly, Price/yr-$:531

Open Systems Economics Letter
Publishing Co: Computer Economics Inc., 5841 Edison Place, Carlsbad, CA 92008, USA; 619/438-8100, Fax: 619/431-1126, Co Email: ose@compecon.com; Focus: Listing of information and outsourcing service providers; Format: Newsletter; Mark McManus, Ed.-in-Chief Email: mcmanus@compecon.com; Bruno Bassi, Pblshr Freq: Annual, Price/yr-$:395

Open Systems Products Directory
Publishing Co: UniForum Assoc., 2901 Tasman Drive, #205, Santa Clara, CA 95054-1100, USA; 408/986-8840, Fax: 408/986-1645, Co Email: pubs@uniforum.org; Web URL: uniforum.org; Focus: Directory of Unix & open systems products and vendors; Format: Directory; Tom Mace, Exec Dir Dick Shippee, Dir Pubs Email: dick@uniforum.org; Circ.: 15,000, Freq: Annual, Price/yr-$:100

Optical Memory News
Publishing Co: Phillips Business Information Inc., 1201 Seven Locks Road, #300, Potomac, MD 20854-1110, USA; 301/340-1520, Fax: 301/424-4297, Co Email: pbi@phillips.com; Web URL: phillips.com; Focus: News and analysis of the optical memory industry; Format: Newsletter; Freq: 25/Year, Price/yr-$:597

Oracle Developer
Publishing Co: Pinnacle Publishing Inc., 18000 72nd Ave S. #217, Kent, WA 98032, USA; 206/251-1900, Fax: 206/251-5057, Web URL: pinpub.com; Focus: Information and utilities for Oracle developers; Format: Newsletter; Freq: Monthly

Oracle Informant
Publishing Co: Informant Communications

Group Inc., 10519 E. Stockton Blvd. #142, Elk Grove, CA 95624-9704, USA; 916/686-6610, Fax: 916/686-8497, Web URL: informant.com; Focus: Information for Borland dBase Windows users; Format: Magazine; Mitchell Koulouris, Pblshr Circ.: 15,000, Freq: Monthly, Price/yr-$:49.95

Oracle Magazine
Publishing Co: Oracle Corp., 500 Oracle Pkwy. MS 659510, Redwood Shores, CA 94065, USA; 415/506-4763, Fax: 415/506-7122, Co Email: oramag@us.oracle.com; Focus: Oracle software users; Format: Magazine, CD; Julie B. Gibbs, Ed. Email: jgibbs@us.oracle.com; Leslie Steere, Mgng Ed. Email: lsteere@us.oracle.com; Circ.: 70,000, Freq: 6/Year, Price/yr-$:Free

Orion Blue Book, Computers
Publishing Co: Orion Research Corp., 14555 N. Scottsdale Road, #330, Scottsdale, AZ 85254-3457, USA; 602/951-1114, Fax: 602/951-1117, Co Email: orion@bluebook.com; Web URL: netzone.com/orion; Focus: Prices for over 32,000 used computer products; Format: Directory; Roger Rohrs, Pblshr Email: orion@netzone.com; Ken Strohmeyer, Email: kenstr@aol.com; Freq: 4/Year, Price/yr-$:200

OS/2 Magazine
Publishing Co: Miller Freeman Inc., 600 Harrison Street, San Francisco, CA 94107-1391, USA; 415/905-2382, Fax: 415/905-2499, Co Email: 76703.756@compuserve.com; Focus: OS/2 in business environments; Format: Magazine; Alan Zeichick, Ed-in-Chief Email: zeichick@acm.org; Ted Bahr, Pblshr Guy Wright, Exec Ed. Email: gwright@mfi.com; Circ.: 60,000, Freq: Monthly, Price/yr-$:30

OSINetter Newsletter
Publishing Co: Architecture Technology Corp., PO Box 24344, Minneapolis, MN 55424, USA; 612/935-2035, Fax: 612/829-5871, Focus: News, products and standards activities regarding Open Systems Interconnection; Format: Newsletter; Kenneth Thurber, Ed. & Pblr Freq: Monthly, Price/yr-$:372

Out of the Blue
Publishing Co: Blue Moon Communications Inc., 405 Tarrytown Road, Rm 361, White Plains, NY 10607, USA; Fax: 914/761-7305, Focus: News and information for ex-IBM employees; Format: Newsletter; Rick Weiner, Ed. Bruce Odom, Pblshr Freq: Monthly, Price/yr-$:40

Outsource!
Publishing Co: CMP Publications Inc., 600 Community Drive, Manhasset, NY 11030, USA; 516/562-5000, Focus: OEM manufacturing outsourcing; Format: Magazine; Mark Holdreith, Pblshr Matthew Sheerin, Ed. Jennifer D'Alessandro, Sr Ed. Circ.:

24,000, Freq: 6/Year, Price/yr-$:Free

Pacific Rim Media

Publishing Co: Dreamscape Productions, 510 Woodhaven, Aptos, CA 95003, USA; 408/685-8818, Fax: 408/685-8819, Co Email: statsuno@aol.com; Focus: Analysis of Pacific Rim high-tech companies and technology trends; Format: Newsletter; Sheridan Tatsuno, Ed. & Pblr Freq: 4/Year, Price/yr-$:395/450

Paradox for Windows Developer's Journal

Publishing Co: Cobb Group, The, 9420 Bunsen Pkwy. #300, Louisville, KY 40220, USA; 502/491-1900, Fax: 502/491-8050, Co Email: cobb@aol.com; Web URL: cobb.com; Focus: Tips and techniques for Paradox database developers and programmers; Format: Newsletter; Brian Schaffner, Ed. Freq: Monthly, Price/yr-$:119

Paradox Informant

Publishing Co: Informant Communications Group Inc., 10519 E. Stockton Blvd, #142, Elk Grove, CA 95624-9704, USA; 916/686-6610, Fax: 916/686-8497, Web URL: informant.com; Focus: Information for Borland Paradox users; Format: Magazine; Mitchell Koulouris, Pblshr Circ.: 18,000, Freq: Monthly, Price/yr-$:49.95

Pathfinder

Publishing Co: Parks Assoc., 5310 Harvest Hill Road, #235, LB 162, Dallas, TX 75230, USA; 214/490-1113, Fax: 214/490-1133, Co Email: 76002,2162@compuserve.com; Focus: Information and analysis on home automation industry; Format: Newsletter; Tricia Parks, Exec Ed. Myra Moore, Ed. Circ.: 100, Freq: Bi-monthly, Price/yr-$:395

PC AI Magazine

3310 W. Bell Road, #119, Phoenix, AZ 85023-2968, USA; 602/971-1869, Fax: 602/971-2321, Co Email: info@pcai.com; Web URL: pcai.com; Focus: Intelligent solutions for desktop computers; Format: Magazine; Joseph Schmuller, Ed.-in-Chief Terry Hengl, Pblshr Freq: 6/Year, Price/yr-$:28

PC Audio Technology & Chip Sets

Publishing Co: Mercury Research, 7950 E. Acoma Drive, #203, Scottsdale, AZ 85260, USA; 602/998-9225, Fax: 602/998-4338, Co Email: service@mercury.org; Focus: Market strategy and forecast on PC audio technology; Format: Book; Mike Feibus, Founder Dean A. McCarron, Founder Price/yr-$:1,995

PC Digest

Publishing Co: National Software Testing Laboratories Inc., 625 Ridge Pike, Bldg D, Conshohocken, PA 19428, USA; 215/941-9600, Fax: 215/941-9952, Web URL: nstl.com; Focus: Reports on comparative testing of PCs and peripherals; Format: Newsletter; Larry Goldstein, Pblshr Freq: Monthly, Price/yr-$:452

PC Games

Publishing Co: Infotainment World Inc., 951 Mariner's Island Blvd, #700, San Mateo, CA 94404, USA; 415/349-4300, Fax: 415/349-8347, Focus: Computer and CD-ROM entertainment software; Format: Magazine; Bruce W. Gray, Pblshr Joy Ma, Ed. Freq: Monthly, Price/yr-$:25

PC Graphics & Video

Publishing Co: Advanstar Communications Inc., 201 E Sandpointe Ave, #600, Santa Ana, CA 92707-5761, USA; 714/513-8400, Fax: 714/513-8612, Co Email: @pcgv.com; Web URL: pcgv.com; Focus: Graphics, video and multimedia; Format: Magazine; Frank Moldstad, Ed-in-Chief Email: fmoldstad@pcgv.com; Michael L. Forcillo, Pblshr Email: mforcillo@pcgv.com; Jeff Bolkan, Mgng Ed. Email: jvbolkan@pcgv.com; Circ.: 75,000, Freq: Monthly, Price/yr-$:Free/30

PC Graphics Report, The

Publishing Co: Jon Peddie Associates, 4 St. Gabrielle Court, Tiburon, CA 94920, USA; 415/435-1775, Fax: 415/435-1599, Co Email: info@jpa-pcgr.com; Web URL: jpa-pcgr.com; Focus: News, analysis and opinions on PC graphics industry; Format: Newsletter; Fred Dunn, Ed. Email: 71250.2146@compuserve.com; Jon Peddie, Ed.-in-Chief Email: 71250.2146@compuserve.com; Circ.: 130, Freq: Weekly, Price/yr-$:2,100

PC LapTop Computers Magazine

Publishing Co: LFP Inc., 9171 Wilshire Blvd. #300, Beverly Hills, CA 90210, USA; 310/858-7155, Fax: 310/274-7985, Focus: News, features, buyers guide and applications for laptop computers; Format: Magazine; Larry Flynt, Pblshr Michael Goldstein, Ed.-in-Chief Cassandra Cavanah, Exec Ed. Circ.: 70,000, Freq: Monthly, Price/yr-$:24.95

PC Magazine

Publishing Co: Ziff-Davis Publishing Co., One Park Ave, New York, NY 10016-5802, USA; 212/503-5255, Fax: 212/503-5519, Web URL: ziff.com/~pcmag; Focus: Reviews, product tests and news for IBM-standard PC users; Format: Magazine; Daniel Rosensweig, Pblshr Michael J. Miller, Ed.-in-Chief Robin Raskin, Ed. Circ.: 925,000, Freq: 22/Year, Price/yr-$:49.97

PC Novice

Publishing Co: Peed Corp., 120 W. Harvest Drive, Lincoln, NE 68521-9966, USA; 402/479-2141, Fax: 402/479-2104, Co Email: 74644.3017@compuserve.com; Focus: Tutorial and information for PC newcomers; Format: Magazine; Juliet Oseka, Asst Ed. Trevor Meers, Asst Ed. Whitney Potsus, Asst Ed. Circ.: 310,000, Freq: Monthly, Price/yr-$:24

PC Pocketbook

Publishing Co: Price Books and Forms Inc.,

751 N. Coney Ave, PO Box 9512, Azusa, CA 91702-9512, USA; Fax: 818/334-8158, Focus: Prices of PC and peripheral configurations; Format: Directory; Gordon L. Larson, Mgr & Ed. Tim Malone, Analyst & Ed. Freq: 6/Year, Price/yr-$:36.90

PC Policies and Procedures HandiGuide

Publishing Co: Positive Support Review Inc., 2500 Broadway, #320, Santa Monica, CA 90404-3061, USA; 310/453-6100, Fax: 310/453-6253, Co Email: info@psrinc.com; Focus: Information on managing and supporting PCs in corporations; Format: Book/diskette; M. Victor Janulaitis, Pblr & Ed. Freq: Annual, Price/yr-$:395/795

PC Processors and Chip Sets

Publishing Co: Mercury Research, 7950 E. Acoma Drive, #203, Scottsdale, AZ 85260, USA; 602/998-9225, Fax: 602/998-4338, Co Email: service@mercury.org; Focus: Market strategy and forecast report on PC processors and chip sets; Format: Book; Mike Feibus, Founder Dean A. McCarron, Founder Price/yr-$:1,995

PC SoftDIR

Publishing Co: El Jen Inc., PO Box 3065, 2839 Timber Knoll, Brandon, FL 33509-3065, USA; 813/654-1168, Fax: 813/654-8906, Co Email: softdir@aol.com; Web URL: netusa.com/pcsoft/softdir; Focus: Directory of 4,500 DOS/Windows programs and 500+ publishers; Format: Windows-Baseed E; Richard J. Adams, Ed. Freq: 4/Year, Price/yr-$:30/80

PC Support Expert

Publishing Co: IIR Publications Inc., 5650 El Camino Real, #225, Carlsbad, CA 92008-9711, USA; 619/931-8615, Fax: 619/931-9935, Web URL: as400.com; Focus: PC support for AS/400 systems; Format: Newsletter; Freq: 6/Year, Price/yr-$:89

PC Techniques

Publishing Co: Coriolis Group Inc., 7339 E. Acoma Drive, #7, Scottsdale, AZ 85260, USA; 602/483-0192, Fax: 602/483-0193, Co Email: orders@coriolis.com; Web URL: coriolis.com; Focus: Technical information for PC programmers; Format: Magazine; Jeff Duntemann, Ed.-in-Chief Keith Weiskamp, Pblshr Circ.: 30,000, Freq: 6/Year, Price/yr-$:21.95

PC Today

Publishing Co: Peed Corp., 120 W. Harvest Drive, Lincoln, NE 68521-9966, USA; 402/479-2141, Fax: 402/477-9252, Focus: Product specs, prices and information for PC users; Format: Magazine; Tom Peed, Pblshr Circ.: 65,000, Freq: Monthly, Price/yr-$:24

PC Toolbox, The

Publishing Co: Dynamic Learning Systems, PO Box 805, Marlboro, MA 01752, USA;

508/366-9487, Fax: 508/898-9995, Co Email: 73652.3205@compuserve.com; Web URL: dlspubs.com; Focus: PC optimization and repair tips; Format: Newsletter; Stephen J. Bigelow, Pblr & Ed. Email: sbigelow@cerfnet.com; Freq: 6/Year, Price/yr-$:39

PC Upgrade
Publishing Co: Bedford Communications, 150 Fifth Ave, New York, NY 10011, USA; 212/807-8220, Fax: 212/807-8737, Focus: Guide to building and expanding computer systems; Format: Magazine; Edward D. Brown, Pblshr Ephraim Schwartz, Ed.-in-Chief Edward Schneider, Sr Ed. Freq: 6/Year, Price/yr-$:24

PC Week
Publishing Co: Ziff-Davis Publishing Co., 10 Press Landing, Medford, MA 02155, USA; 617/393-3700, Fax: 617/393-3701, Web URL: pcweek.com; Focus: News, reviews and information for MS-DOS PC users and buyers; Format: Newspaper; Stuart Arnold, Pblshr Email: stuart_arnold@zd.com; Eric Lundquist, Ed.-in-Chief Email: eric_lundquist@zd.com; Sam Whitmore, Ed.ial Dir Email: sam_whitmore@zd.com; Circ.: 220,000, Freq: Weekly, Price/yr-$:Free/195

PC World
Publishing Co: PCW Communications Inc., 501 Second Street, #600, San Francisco, CA 94107, USA; 415/243-0500, Fax: 415/442-1891, Co Email: letters@pcworld.com; Web URL: pcworld.com; Focus: News, information and hands-on articles for IBM PC user; Format: Magazine; Philip Lemmons, Ed-in-Chief Cathryn Baskin, Ed. Luis Camus, Mgng Ed. Circ.: 916,000, Freq: Monthly, Price/yr-$:30

PC World Interactive
Publishing Co: PCW Communications Inc., 501 Second Street, #600, San Francisco, CA 94107, USA; 415/243-0500, Fax: 415/546-1673, Focus: 12 months of articles and graphics from PC World & online links to companies, interactive; Format: CD-ROM; Jonathan Epstein, Pblshr Email: jonathan_epstein@pcworld.; Owen Linderholm, Ed-in-Chief Barry Owen, Mgng Ed. Circ.: 50,000, Freq: 4/Year, Price/yr-$:50

PC/Computing
Publishing Co: Ziff-Davis Publishing Co., 950 Tower Lane, Foster City, CA 94404, USA; 415/578-7000, Fax: 415/578-7029, Co Email: 76000.21@compuserve.com; Focus: Reviews, news and perspectives for active home and office PC users; Format: Magazine; Wendy Taylor, Exec Ed. Jon Zilber, Ed.-in-Chief Robert J. Nolan, Pblshr Circ.: 750,000, Freq: Monthly, Price/yr-$:25

PCMCIA Developer's Guide
Publishing Co: Sycard Technology, 1180-F

Miraloma Way, Sunnyvale, CA 94086, USA; 408/749-0130, Fax: 408/749-1323, Focus: Information for engineers designing PCMCIA products; Format: Reference Book; Michael Mori, Ed. Freq: Annual, Price/yr-$:90

PCNetter Newsletter
Publishing Co: Architecture Technology Corp., PO Box 24344, Minneapolis, MN 55424, USA; 612/935-2035, Fax: 612/829-5871, Focus: News, trends & analysis of PCs & workstations, w/emphasis on datacom; Format: Newsletter; Kenneth Thurber, Ed. & Pblr Freq: Monthly, Price/yr-$:275

PCS Week
Publishing Co: Phillips Business Information Inc., 1201 Seven Locks Road, #300, Potomac, MD 20854-1110, USA; 301/340-1520, Fax: 301/309-3847, Co Email: pbi@phillips.com; Web URL: phillips.com; Focus: News and information about PCS and cellular phone industry; Format: Newsletter; Freq: 50/Year, Price/yr-$:697

Pen Computing Magazine
Publishing Co: Pen Computing Inc., 120 Waterboro Square, Folsom, CA 95630, USA; 916/984-9947, Fax: 916/984-9939, Co Email: 73602.2535@compuserve.com; Focus: Pen-based computer technology and products; Format: Magazine; Howard Borgen, Pblshr Email: 75162.524@compuserve.com; Conrad H. Blickenstorfer, Ed-in-Chief Email: 73602.2535@compuserve.com; Daniel Davis, Assoc Ed. Freq: 6/Year, Price/yr-$:24

Pen-Based Computing
Publishing Co: Volksware Inc., 2301-349 W. Georgia Street, Vancouver, BC V6B 3W5, Canada; 604/472-1315, Fax: 604/472-1315, Focus: Pen-based computers; Format: Newsletter; John Jerney, Ed. Email: jerney@netcom.com; Freq: 10/Year, Price/yr-$:200/240

Personal Engineering and Instrumentation News
Publishing Co: PEC Inc., PO Box 430, Rye, NH 03870-0430, USA; 603/427-1377, Fax: 603/427-1388, Web URL: pein.com; Focus: Technical information for engineers who use PCs; Format: Magazine; Paul Schreier, Ed. Al Shackil, Pblshr Circ.: 51,000, Freq: Monthly, Price/yr-$:Free

Personal Property Taxation of Computer Software
Publishing Co: Kutish Publications Inc., PO Box 113, 125 Strafford Ave, Wayne, PA 19087-0113, USA; 610/975-9619, Fax: 610/975-9623, Focus: State-by-state personal property software taxation rules; Format: Factbook; James Talbott, Ed. L.J. Kutten, Pblshr Freq: Annual, Price/yr-$:125

PickWorld
Publishing Co: Pick Systems, 1691 Browning, Irvine, CA 92714, USA; 714/261-

7425, Fax: 714/250-8187, Co Email: @picksys.com; Focus: Information for VARs, developers and users of the Pick operating system; Format: Magazine; M. Denis Hill, Ed. Andra J.S. Kendall, News Ed. John Wells, Tech Ed. Circ.: 25,000, Freq: 6/Year, Price/yr-$:Free/55

Pix
Publishing Co: Photo District News, 1515 Broadway, New York, NY 10036, USA; 212/536-5222, Fax: 212/536-5224, Focus: Convergence of photo, imaging and computer technology; Format: Tabloid; Elizabeth Forst, Ed-in-Chief Nancy Madlin, Ed. Jacquelin Tobin, Mgng Ed. Freq: 6/Year, Price/yr-$:Free

Pixel Vision
154 W. 57th Street, #826, New York, NY 10019, USA; 212/581-3000, Fax: 212/757-8283, Focus: Computer imaging; Format: Magazine; Judson Rosebush, Ed. Joel Laroche, Pblshr Circ.: 10,000, Freq: 5/Year

Pixel-The Computer Animation Newsletter
Publishing Co: Pixel-The Computer Animation News People Inc., 109 Vanderhoof Ave #2, Toronto, Ontario M4G 2H7, Canada; 416/424-4657, Fax: 416/424-1812, Focus: News and information on computer animation market; Format: Newsletter; Robi Roncarelli, Ed. & Pblr Freq: Monthly, Price/yr-$:215

Portable Computing
Publishing Co: Cowles Business Media, 23622 Calabasas Road, #123, Calabasas, CA 91302-1576, USA; 818/593-6100, Fax: 818/593-6153, Focus: Information for portable PC users; Format: Magazine; Susan J. Curtis, Pblshr Brett Anderson, Ed.-in-Chief Catherine Coughlin, Mgng Ed. Freq: Monthly, Price/yr-$:25

Portable Computing Letter, The
Publishing Co: Yellowstone Information Services, 605 Brady Ave, Steubenville, OH 43952-1459, USA; 614/282-2797, Fax: 614/282-2798, Focus: Portable computing hardware and software; Format: Newsletter; Roger C. Thibault, Ed. & Pblr Circ.: 2,000, Freq: 6/Year, Price/yr-$:50

Portable Design
Publishing Co: PennWell Publishing Co., 1421 S Sheridan Road, Tulsa, OK 74112, USA; 918/835-3161, Fax: 918/831-9497, Co Email: @pennwell.com; Web URL: pennwell.com; Focus: Mobile computing and communications; Format: Magazine; Alex Mendelsohn, Ed-in-Chief Email: alexm@pennwell.com; Robert Ziegel, Grp Pblshr Email: bobz@pennwell.com; Pauline Panagakos, Mgng Ed. Email: paulinep@pennwell.com; Freq: Monthly

PowerBuilder Advisor
Publishing Co: Advisor Publications Inc., 4010 Morena Blvd, San Diego, CA 92117, USA; 619/483-6400, Fax: 619/483-9851, Co Email: 71154.3123@compuserve.com;

Focus: News and information for Power-Builder users; Format: Magazine; William T. Ota, Pblr/Pres/CEO Email: 71154.3123@compuserve.com; John L. Hawkins, Ed-in-Chief & EVP Walter Karasek, VP Circ.: 25,000, Freq: Bi-Monthly, Price/yr-$:39

PowerBuilder Developer's Journal

Publishing Co: Sys-Con Publications Inc., 46 Holly Street, Jersey City, NJ 07305-9838, USA; 201/332-1515, Fax: 201/333-7361, Co Email: 73611.756@compuserve.com; Focus: Information for Powerbuilder developers; Format: Magazine; Steve Benfield, Chmn Michael Griffith, Ed.-in-Chief Scott Davidson, Mgng Ed. Freq: Monthly, Price/yr-$:119

PowerProgrammer Magazine

Publishing Co: Sys-Con Publications Inc., 46 Holly Street, Jersey City, NJ 07305-9838, USA; 201/332-1515, Fax: 201/333-7361, Co Email: 73611.756@compuserve.com; Focus: Information for Powerbuilder programmers; Format: Magazine; Michael MacDonald, Ed.-in-Chief Scott Davidson, Exec Ed. Jane Rosen, Mgng Ed. Freq: 6/Year, Price/yr-$:41

Pre

Publishing Co: Cowles Business Media, 470 Park Ave S, #7N, New York, NY 10016, USA; 212/683-3540, Fax: 212/683-4364, Co Email: @cowlesbiz.com; Focus: Technology solutions for prepublishing professionals; Format: Magazine; Roberta Thomas, Pblshr Email: roberta_thomas@cowlesbiz.; Anne M. Russell, Ed. Dir Email: anne_russell@cowlesbiz.com; Paul McDougall, Ed-in-Chief Freq: 8/Year, Price/yr-$:45

Presence: Teleoperators and Virtual Environments

Publishing Co: MIT Press Journals, 55 Hayward Street, Cambridge, MA 02142, USA; 617/253-2889, Fax: 617/258-6779, Co Email: journals-orders@mit.edu; Web URL: mitpress.mit.edu; Focus: Research on teleoperators and virtual reality environments; Format: Magazine; Thomas B. Sheridan, Sr Ed. Email: presence@cbgrle.mit.edu; Thomas A. Furness, Sr Ed. Email: presence@cbgrle.mit.edu; Nathaniel I. Durlach, Mgng Ed. Email: presence@cbgrle.mit.edu; Circ.: 1,650, Freq: 4/Year, Price/yr-$:56

Presentations Magazine

Publishing Co: Lakewood Publications Inc., 50 South 9th Street, Minneapolis, MN 55402, USA; 612/333-0471, Fax: 612/333-6526, Focus: News and information about computer-based and other presentation products; Format: Magazine; Larry Tuck, Ed.-at-Lrg Email: ltuck@aol.com; Frank Jossi, Mgng Ed. Email: frankj2092@aol.com; Richard Ausman, Pblshr Circ.: 70,000, Freq: Monthly, Price/yr-$:Free/50

PRG Guide

Publishing Co: Publications Resource Group, PO Box 765, N. Adams, MA 01247, USA; 413/664-6185, Fax: 413/664-9343, Web URL: prgguide.com; Focus: Communications industry publications; Format: Magazine; James Shaker, Pblshr Price/yr-$:Free

Print on Demand Business

Publishing Co: CAP Ventures, One Snow Rd., Marshfield, MA 02050, USA; 617/834-0001, Fax: 617/834-0002, Focus: Information on printing industry; Format: Magazine; Charles A. Pesko, Jr., Pblshr Joann Strashun Whitcher, Ed.-in-Chief Rebecca M. Pesko, Assoc Pub Freq: Bimonthly, Price/yr-$:36

Printed Circuit Fabrication

Publishing Co: Miller Freeman Inc., 600 Harrison Street, San Francisco, CA 94107-1391, USA; 415/905-2200, Fax: 415/905-2234, Focus: Manufacturing of printed circuit boards; Format: Magazine; Circ.: 22,000, Freq: Monthly, Price/yr-$:Free/40

Printer Channel Monitor

Publishing Co: Venture Marketing Strategies, 5150 Graves Ave, #11H, San Jose, CA 95129, USA; 408/865-0221, Fax: 408/865-1523, Co Email: 73364.3116@compuserve.com; Focus: News & analysis for printer market planning; Format: Newsletter; Bill Gott, Ed. Connie Rao, Res Assist Freq: Monthly, Price/yr-$:295/350

Printer Impressions

Publishing Co: Buyers Laboratory Inc., 20 Railroad Ave, Hackensack, NJ 07601, USA; 201/488-0404, Fax: 201/488-0461, Focus: News, analysis and test reports on printers and multifunction devices; Format: Newsletter; Anthony Polifrone, Pres Marion Davidowitz, VP Burt Meerow, Pblr Freq: Monthly, Price/yr-$:365

Printers Buyer's Guide & Handbook

Publishing Co: Bedford Communications, 150 Fifth Ave, New York, NY 10011, USA; 212/807-8220, Fax: 212/807-8737, Focus: Information on printers; Format: Magazine; Edward D. Brown, Pblshr Ephraim Schwartz, Ed.-in-Chief David Drucker, Exec Ed. Freq: Monthly, Price/yr-$:36

Printout

Publishing Co: Giga Information Group, 1 Longwater Circle, Norwell, MA 02061, USA; 617/982-9500, Fax: 617/878-6650, Focus: Developments in printer and related industries; Format: Newsletter; Jeff Swartz, Pblshr David Hatch, Ed. Email: dhatch@gigasd.com; Circ.: 300, Freq: Monthly, Price/yr-$:392

Proceedings of the IEEE

Publishing Co: IEEE, 445 Hoes Lane, PO Box 1331, Piscataway, NJ 08855-1331, USA; 908/981-0060, Fax: 908/981-9667, Co Email: @ieee.org; Web URL: ieee.org;

Focus: In-depth reviews and tutorials of computer and electronics technology; Format: Magazine; Freq: Monthly, Price/yr-$:23

Process Insight Review

Publishing Co: QSoft Solutions Corp., PO Box 556, 445 W Commercial Street, E. Rochester, NY 14445-0556, USA; 716/264-9700, Fax: 716/264-9702, Focus: Analysis of software for reengineering, TQM, groupware & MBAWare; Format: Newsletter; Paul Wetenhall, Mgng Ed. Anita Pomerantz, Cntrib Ed. Freq: 11/Year, Price/yr-$:395

Processor, The

Publishing Co: Peed Corp., 120 W. Harvest Drive, Lincoln, NE 68501-9966, USA; 402/479-2141, Fax: 402/477-9252, Web URL: processor.com; Focus: PC product specification listings; Format: Newspaper; Tom Peed, Ed. & Pblr Circ.: 250,000, Freq: 52/Year, Price/yr-$:59

Professional Electronics Directory/Yearbook

Publishing Co: National Electronics Service Dealers Assoc., 2708 W. Berry Street, Ft. Worth, TX 76109-2397, USA; 817/921-9061, Fax: 817/921-3741, Focus: Technical and reference information for electronics professionals; Format: Directory; Wallace S. Harrison, Ed.-in-Chief Clyde W. Nabors, Pblshr Circ.: 10,000+, Freq: Annual, Price/yr-$:12

Profiles

Publishing Co: Progress Software Corp., 14 Oak Park, Bedford, MA 01730, USA; 617/280-4000, Focus: Information on C/S and visual development; Format: Magazine; Rebecca Hart, Ed. Freq: 3/Year

PRTECH

Publishing Co: Cardinal Business Media Inc., 12225 Greenville Ave, #700, Dallas, TX 75243, USA; 214/669-9000, Fax: 214/669-9909, Web URL: prtech.com; Focus: Updated high-technology news; Format: Online

PSR Reviews

Publishing Co: Positive Support Review Inc., 2500 Broadway, #320, Santa Monica, CA 90404-3061, USA; 310/453-6100, Fax: 310/453-6253, Co Email: info@psrinc.com; Web URL: psrinc.compsr; Focus: Perspectives on PC, LAN and MIS management issues; Format: Newsletter; M. Victor Janulaitis, Pblshr & Ed. Email: victor@psrinc.com; Freq: 6/Year, Price/yr-$:60

Publish

Publishing Co: International Data Group, 501 Second Street, San Francisco, CA 94107, USA; 415/978-3280, Fax: 415/975-2613, Co Email: 76127.205@compuserve.com; Web URL: publish.com; Focus: Desktop & personal publishing with emphasis on using integrated text & graphics; Format: Magazine; Jake Widman, Ed. Email: jwidman@publish.com; Mard

Naman, Mgng Ed. Email: mnaman@publish.com; Gene Gable, Pblshr Email: gable@publish.com; Circ.: 125,000, Freq: Monthly, Price/yr-$:Free/40

Publishing & Multimedia
Publishing Co: DTPI, 462 Old Boston Street, Topsfield, MA 01983-1232, USA; Focus: Desktop publishing, graphic design and multimedia; Format: Magazine; Barry Harrigan, Ed. & Pblr Marcia Sampson, Exec Ed. Andrew Lindsay, Sr Ed. Price/yr-$:Free

Publishing & Production Executive
Publishing Co: North American Publishing Co., 401 N. Broad Street, Philadelphia, PA 19108, USA; 215/238-5300, Fax: 215/238-5457, Co Email: @ppe.napco.com; Focus: Buyers of printing, prepress and publishing systems; Format: Magazine; Rose Blessing, Ed. Mark Hertzog, Pblshr Circ.: 30,000, Freq: Monthly, Price/yr-$:Free

Quicksense for Windows
Publishing Co: Cobb Group, The, 9420 Bunsen Pkwy. #300, Louisville, KY 40220, USA; 502/491-1900, Fax: 502/491-8050, Co Email: cobb@aol.com; Web URL: cobb.com; Focus: Tips and information for Quicken users; Format: Newsletter; Freq: Monthly, Price/yr-$:39

R&D Magazine
Publishing Co: Cahners Publishing Co., 1350 E. Touhy Ave, Des Plaines, IL 60018, USA; 708/635-8800, Fax: 708/390-2618, Co Email: rdchi@mcimail.com; Web URL: cahners.com/mags/mainmagd; Focus: News and analysis of advances in science & technology; Format: Magazine; Robert Cassidy, Ed.-in-chief Email: rdchi@mcimail.com; Robin Ashton, Pblshr Email: rdchi@mcimail.com; Circ.: 100,000, Freq: Monthly, Price/yr-$:Free/80

RACF Update
Publishing Co: Xephon, 1301 W. Hwy 407, #201-450, Lewisville, TX 75067, USA; 817/455-7050, Fax: 817/455-2492, Focus: News, tips and software to improve RACF security; Format: Magazine; Freq: Monthly, Price/yr-$:175

Rapid Prototyping Report
Publishing Co: CAD/CAM Publishing Inc., 1010 Turquoise Street, #320, San Diego, CA 92109-1268, USA; 619/488-0533, Fax: 619/488-6052, Focus: Desktop manufacturing industry; Format: Newsletter; Geoff Smith-Moritz, Ed. L. Stephen Wolfe, Pblshr Freq: Monthly, Price/yr-$:295

Red Glasses Official Comdex Press Party List
Publishing Co: Corporate Journal, The, 2100 Douglass Blvd, Louisville, KY 40205, USA; 502/456-0808, Fax: 502/458-5066, Co Email: 74774.3240@compuserve.com; Focus: Listing of press events at the Comdex trade shows; Format: Newsletter; Sher Bolter, Ed. Email: 73774.3240@com-

puserve.com; Chris Hagin, Assoc Ed. Email: chagin@atlanta.com; Price/yr-$:Free

Red Herring, The
Publishing Co: Herring Communications Inc., 1550 Bryant Street, #950, San Francisco, CA 94103, USA; 415/865-2277, Fax: 415/865-2280, Co Email: info@herring.com; Web URL: herring.com; Focus: Financial and investment news for high-tech companies; Format: Magazine; Christopher J. Alden, Exec Ed. Email: chris@herring.com; Anthony B. Perkins, Ed-in-Chief & Pblr Email: tony@herring.com; Michael C. Perkins, Sr Ed. Freq: Monthly, Price/yr-$:69

Release 1.0
Publishing Co: EDventure Holdings Inc., 104 Fifth Ave, 20th Fl, New York, NY 10011-6987, USA; 212/924-8800, Fax: 212/924-0240, Co Email: info@edventure.com; Focus: Analysis and opinions on software, AI, CASE, groupware, text management and PC events; Format: Newsletter; Esther Dyson, Ed. Daphne Kis, Pblshr Jerry Michalski, Mgng Ed. Freq: 11/Year, Price/yr-$:595/650

Reliability Rating's AS/400 Client/Server Report
Publishing Co: United Communications Group, 175 Highland Ave, Needham, MA 02194, USA; 617/444-5755, Fax: 617/444-8958, Web URL: ucg.com; Focus: Buyers guide for AS/400 C/S products; Format: Newsletter; Greg Strakosch, Pblshr Email: gstrakos@ucg.com; Kristie Lipka, Ed. Freq: Monthly, Price/yr-$:395

Repair, Service & Remarketing News
Publishing Co: Asay Publishing, PO Box 670, Joplin, MO 64802-0670, USA; 417/781-9317, Fax: 417/781-0427, Focus: Information on repair and service; Format: Newspaper; Larry Jackson, Pblshr Gail Evans, Mgng Ed. Neal McChristy, Assoc Ed. Freq: Monthly, Price/yr-$:89/110

Report on Electronic Commerce
Publishing Co: BRP Publications Inc., 1333 H Street, #200 W., Washington, DC 20005, USA; 202/842-0520, Fax: 212/475-1790, Co Email: brp@access.digex.net; Focus: Information and issues for the superhighway; Format: Newsletter; Andrew Jacobson, Pblshr Rod W. Kuckro, Ed. Freq: Biweekly, Price/yr-$:554

Report on IBM, The
Publishing Co: DataTrends Publications Inc., 30-C Catoctin Circle SE, Leesburg, VA 22075, USA; 703/779-0574, Fax: 703/779-2267, Co Email: dtrends@aol.com; Focus: News and analysis on IBM; Format: Newsletter; Jeff Caruso, Ed. Email: jpcaruso@aol.com; Paul G. Ochs, Pblshr Freq: Weekly, Price/yr-$:775

Report on Microsoft, The
Publishing Co: DataTrends Publications

Inc., 30-C Catoctin Circle SE, Leesburg, VA 22075, USA; 703/779-0574, Fax: 703/779-2267, Co Email: dtrends@aol.com; Focus: News, analysis and information about Microsoft; Format: Newsletter; Jeff Caruso, Ed. Email: jpcaruso@aol.com; Paul G. Ochs, Pblshr Freq: 24/Year, Price/yr-$:395

Report on Object Analysis and Design
Publishing Co: SIGS Publications Group, 71 W. 23rd Street, 3rd Floor, New York, NY 10010, USA; 212/242-7447, Fax: 212/242-7574, Co Email: 73361.1707@compuserve.com; Web URL: sigs.com; Focus: Language-independent analysis, design and modeling; Format: Magazine; Richard P. Friedman, Pblshr Richard Wiener, Ed. Freq: 6/Year, Price/yr-$:99/199

Reseller Management
Publishing Co: Cahners Publishing Co., 275 Washington Street, Newton, MA 02158-1630, USA; 617/558-4772, Fax: 617/558-4757, Co Email: resellermgmt@mcimail.com; Focus: Profitable strategies for value added resellers; Format: Magazine; Steve Twombly, Pblshr Email: stevet@rm.cahners.com; John Russell, Ed.-in-Chief Email: jruss@rm.cahners.com; Christine French, Mgng Ed. Email: cfrench@rm.cahners.com; Circ.: 68,000, Freq: 14/Year, Price/yr-$:Free/60

Reseller Management Handbook
Publishing Co: ChannelCorp Products Inc., 2991 W. 42nd Ave, Vancouver, BC V6N 3G8, Canada; 604/263-6811, Fax: 604/263-4914, Co Email: cph@mala.bc.ca; Focus: Management information for computer resellers and vendors; Format: Factbook; Marg A. Stuart, Pblshr Bruce R. Stuart, Ed. Freq: Annual, Price/yr-$:95

Response TV
Publishing Co: Advanstar Communications Inc., 201 E Sandpointe Ave, #600, Santa Ana, CA 92707-5761, USA; 714/513-8400, Fax: 714/513-8482, Focus: News and information on interactive TV; Format: Newsletter; Jack Schember, Ed-in-Chief & Pblr Freq: Monthly

Retail Automation, Reports on
Publishing Co: Datapro Information Services Group, 600 Delran Pkwy., Delran, NJ 08705-9904, USA; 609/764-0100, Fax: 609/764-2811, Co Email: datapro@mhh.com; Web URL: datapro.com; Focus: Information on automation equipment for retailers; Format: CD-ROM; Freq: Monthly

Retail Info Systems News
Publishing Co: Edgell Communications, 10 W Hannover Ave, #107, Randolph, NJ 07869-4214, USA; 201/895-3397, Fax: 201/895-9363, Co Email: edgell@planet.net; Focus: Technology for retailers; Format: Tabloid; Douglas C.

Edgell, Pblshr Mark Frantz, Ed. Christian Glazar, Assist Ed. Freq: 9/Year, Price/yr-$:50

Retail Systems Reseller
Publishing Co: Edgell Communications, 10 W Hannover Ave, #107, Randolph, NJ 07869-4214, USA; 201/895-3300, Fax: 201/895-7711, Co Email: edgell@planet.net; Focus: Information for retail technology resellers; Format: Magazine; Douglas C. Edgell, Pblshr Joseph S. King, Ed. Christine E. Bailey, Assoc Ed. Circ.: 15,000, Freq: 10/Year, Price/yr-$:Free/36

RiSc World
Publishing Co: Publications & Communications Inc., 12416 Hymeadow Drive, Austin, TX 78750-1896, USA; 512/250-9023, Fax: 512/331-6779, Co Email: @pcinews.com; Web URL: pcinews.com/pci; Focus: News, reviews and technical information for IBM RS 6000 users; Format: Newspaper; Larry Storer, Ed.-in-Chief Bill W. Hornaday, Mgng Ed. Circ.: 15,000, Freq: Monthly, Price/yr-$:45/75

Robotics Research, Int'l Journal of
Publishing Co: MIT Press Journals, 55 Hayward Street, Cambridge, MA 02142, USA; 617/253-2889, Fax: 617/258-6779, Co Email: journals-orders@mit.edu; Web URL: mitpress.mit.edu; Focus: Research and trends in the robotics sensory-control related fields; Format: Magazine; J. Michael Brady, Ed. Email: jmb@robots.ox.ac.uk; Circ.: 1.300, Freq: 6/Year, Price/yr-$:82

Roger Pence's Microsoft and the AS/400 Letter
Publishing Co: United Communications Group, 175 Highland Ave, Needham, MA 02194, USA; 617/444-5755, Fax: 617/444-8958, Web URL: ucg.com; Focus: Information for AS/400 managers using Microsoft AS/400 environment; Format: Newsletter; Greg Strakosch, Pblshr Email: gstrakos@ucg.com; Roger Pence, Ed. Freq: 24/Year, Price/yr-$:195

Roncarelli Report on Computer Animation Industry
Publishing Co: Pixel-The Computer Animation News People Inc., 109 Vanderhoof Ave #2, Toronto, Ontario M4G 2H7, Canada; 416/424-4657, Fax: 416/424-1812, Co Email: pixel@infoamp.net; Web URL: gsfmicro.com/pixel/home; Focus: Review and forecast of computer animation industry; Format: Factbook; Robi Roncarelli, Ed. & Pblr Freq: Annual, Price/yr-$:1,295

RS/Magazine
Publishing Co: Computer Publishing Group Inc., 320 Washington Street, Brookline, MA 02146-3202, USA; 617/739-7001, Fax: 617/739-7003, Co Email: cmc@cpg.com; Web URL: cpg.com; Focus: News and information for IBM RS/6000 users; Format: Magazine; Douglas

Pryor, Ed. Dir Email: dpryor@cpg.com; S. Henry Sacks, Pblshr Email: shs@cpg.com; Christine Casatelli, Exec Ed. Email: cmc@cpg.com; Circ.: 38,000, Freq: Monthly, Price/yr-$:Free/60

Rumors and Raw Data
Publishing Co: Business Research Consultant Inc., PO Box 1646, Rancho Mirage, CA 92270, USA; 619/328-3700, Fax: 619/328-2474, Co Email: jackmcla@aol.com; Focus: Intelligence on disk drive an disk drive component industry; Format: Newsletter; Jack McLaughlin, Ed. & Pblr Freq: Weekly, Price/yr-$:12,000

Russian Telecom
Publishing Co: Information Gatekeepers Inc., 214 Harvard Ave, Boston, MA 02134, USA; 617/232-3111, Fax: 617/734-8562, Co Email: igiboston@aol.com; Focus: Information on Russian/CIS telecom market, applications and vendors; Format: Newsletter; Sergei Galken, Ed. Email: igiboston@aol.com; Paul Polishuk, Pblshr Freq: 12/Yearly, Price/yr-$:545/595

Sales and Use Tax of Computer Software
Publishing Co: Kutish Publications Inc., PO Box 181916, Coronado, CA 92178-1916, USA; Fax: 800/803-9623, Focus: State-by-state software taxation rules; Format: Factbook; L.J. Kutten, Pblshr Freq: Annual, Price/yr-$:450

Sarah Stambler's Marketing with Technology News
Publishing Co: TechProse Inc., 370 Central Park W, #210, New York, NY 10025, USA; 212/222-1765, Fax: 212/678-6357, Co Email: sarah.mwt.com; Focus: Information on fax marketing and online marketing; Format: Fax; Sarah Stambler, Pres Email: sarah@mwt.com; Price/yr-$:149

Scientific Computing & Automation
Publishing Co: Gordon Publications Inc., 301 Gibraltar Drive, PO Box 650, Morris Plains, NJ 07950-0650, USA; 201/292-5100, Fax: 201/898-9281, Focus: Information for scientists & engineers using computing for R & D; Format: Magazine; John F. Martin, Pblshr Dan Breeman, Mgng Ed. Email: 74677.1126@compuserve.com; Elliot King, Ed. Email: 71127.1231@compuserve.com; Circ.: 70,000, Freq: Monthly, Price/yr-$:Free/60

SciTech Journal
Publishing Co: MacSciTech Association, 49 Midgley Lane, Worcester, MA 01604, USA; 508/755-5242, Fax: 508/795-1636, Co Email: scitechmac@aol.com; Web URL: macscitech.org; Focus: Scientific and engineering applications of the Macintosh; Format: Magazine; Shari L.S. Worthington, Ed. Freq: 6/Year

SCO World
Publishing Co: Venture Publishing Inc., 480 San Antonio Road, Mt. View, CA 94040-1218, USA; 415/941-1550, Fax: 415/941-1504, Focus: News and informa-

tion for SCO Xenix/Unix and ODT users; Format: Magazine; Robert A. Billheimer, Pblshr Michael J. Burgard, Ed.-in-Chief Email: mikeb@scoworld.com; Tim Parker, Tech Ed. Email: timp@scoworld.com; Freq: Monthly, Price/yr-$:17.50

Scout Business Software Directory
Publishing Co: Software Press, PO Box 389, Longmont, CO 80501, USA; 303/772-0321, Fax: 303/772-4069, Focus: Listing of software for AS/400, S/36, S/38, R4000, client server and PC/LAN; Format: Directory; Rick Rundall, GM Candee Minear, Ad Dir Freq: 2/Year, Price/yr-$:65

Searcher
Publishing Co: Information Today Inc., 143 Old Marlton Pike, Medford, NJ 08055-8750, USA; 609/654-6266, Fax: 609/654-4309, Co Email: custserv@infotoday.com; Web URL: infotoday.com; Focus: Information for database searchers, brokers and consultants; Format: Magazine; Barbara Quint, Ed. Freq: 10/Year, Price/yr-$:56

Selecting a High-Performance Embedded Microprocessor
Publishing Co: MicroDesign Resources, 874 Gravenstein Hwy S. #14, Sebastopol, CA 95472, USA; 707/824-4001, Fax: 707/823-0504, Web URL: chipanalyst.com; Focus: Aspects of embedded microprocessors; Format: Factbook; Jim Turley, Author Price/yr-$:1,995

Selling Networks
Publishing Co: McGraw-Hill Inc., 1900 O'Farrell Street, #200, San Mateo, CA 94403-1311, USA; 415/513-6800, Fax: 415/513-6819, Focus: News and information for network resellers; Format: Magazine; Michela O'Connor Abrams, Pblshr Leonard Heymann, Ed. Jill Simonsen, Mgng Ed. Freq: 6/Year, Price/yr-$:Free

Semiconductor Industry Almanac, The
Publishing Co: Competitive Strategies Inc., 1750 Clarence Court, San Jose, CA 95124-1201, USA; 408/266-4549, Fax: 408/264-0221, Focus: Information on semiconductor industry and its applications; Format: Fact book; Len Hills, Ed. Amy C. Daniels, Exec Ed. Freq: Annual, Price/yr-$:299

Semiconductor Industry and Business Survey
Publishing Co: HTE Research Inc., 400 Oyster Point Blvd, #220, S. San Francisco, CA 94080, USA; 415/871-4377, Fax: 415/871-0531, Focus: News, analysis, trends and views on semiconductor business; Format: Newsletter; Paul L. Plansky, Ed-in-Chief Steve Z. Szirom, Exec Ed. Freq: 18/Year, Price/yr-$:495

Sensor Business Digest
Publishing Co: Vital Information Publications, 754 Caravel Lane, Foster City, CA 94404, USA; 415/345-7018, Fax: 415/345-7018, Focus: News, trends and analy-

sis on sensors and instrumentation markets; Format: Newsletter; Peter Adrian, Ed. & Prncpl Circ.: 200, Freq: Monthly, Price/yr-$:325

Sensor Technology
Publishing Co: Technical Insights Inc., PO Box 1304, Ft. Lee, NJ 07631-9967, USA; 201/568-4744, Fax: 201/568-8247, Co Email: stinfo@insights.com; Web URL: insights.com; Focus: News and analysis of sensor technology and products; Format: Newsletter; Angelo Depalma, Ed. Email: stinfo@insights.com; Kenneth A. Kovaly, Pblshr Email: stinfo@insights.com; Freq: Monthly, Price/yr-$:610

Sensors Magazine
Publishing Co: Helmers Publishing Inc., 174 Concord Street, Peterborough, NH 03458, USA; 603/924-9631, Fax: 603/924-7408, Focus: News and information on computer-based sensors; Format: Magazine; Circ.: 63,000, Freq: 13/year, Price/yr-$:Free/55

Serlin Report on Parallel Processing
Publishing Co: ITOM Int'l. Co., PO Box 1450, Los Altos, CA 94023, USA; 415/948-4516, Fax: 415/948-9153, Focus: Technical and market developments in supercomputers, minisupers and parallel systems; Format: Newsletter; Omri Serlin, Ed. & Pblr Email: omris@cup.portal.com; Freq: Monthly, Price/yr-$:695

Service & Support World
Publishing Co: Publications & Communications Inc., 12416 Hymeadow Drive, Austin, TX 78750-1896, USA; 512/250-9023, Fax: 512/331-3900, Co Email: @pcinews.com; Web URL: pcinews.com/pci; Focus: Information for maintenance and service managers; Format: Magazine; Larry Storer, Ed.-in-Chief Steven Smith, Mgng Ed. Circ.: 32,000, Freq: Monthly, Price/yr-$:Free/30

Service Industry Newsletter
Publishing Co: Dataquest, 251 River Oaks Pkwy, San Jose, CA 95134, USA; 408/468-8000, Fax: 408/954-1780, Web URL: dataquest.com; Focus: Digest of key events in the high-tech service industry; Format: Newsletter; Freq: Monthly, Price/yr-$:245

Service News
Publishing Co: United Publications Inc., 38 Lafayette Street, PO Box 995, Yarmouth, ME 04096, USA; 207/846-0600, Fax: 207/846-0657, Co Email: @service-news.com; Web URL: servicenews.com; Focus: News about and for computer service and support professionals; Format: Magazine; Alison Harris, Ed. Email: aharris@servicenews.com; Bill Springer, Pblshr Email: bspring@servicenews.com; Circ.: 45,000, Freq: 14/Year, Price/yr-$:Free/45

Seybold Bulletin on Computer Publishing
Publishing Co: Seybold Publications, 428 E. Baltimore Ave, PO Box 500, Media, PA 19063-9938, USA; 610/565-2480, Fax: 610/565-1858, Co Email: ciacona@sbex-pos.com; Focus: News and information on computer publishing; Format: Email/Fax; Freq: 52/Year, Price/yr-$:245/445

Seybold Report on Desktop Publishing
Publishing Co: Seybold Publications, 428 E. Baltimore Ave, PO Box 644, Media, PA 19063-9938, USA; 610/565-2480, Fax: 610/565-4659, Co Email: ciacona@sbex-pos.com; Focus: Information and reviews of desktop publishing products; Format: Newsletter; Jonathan W. Seybold, Pblshr Email: jseybold@sbexpos.com; Stephen E. Edwards, Ed. Email: sedwards@sbex-pos.com; Peter E. Dyson, Ed. Email: pdyson@sbexpos.com; Freq: Monthly, Price/yr-$:245

Seybold Report on Publishing Systems
Publishing Co: Seybold Publications, 428 E. Baltimore Ave, PO Box 644, Media, PA 19063-9938, USA; 610/565-2480, Fax: 610/565-4659, Co Email: ciacona@sbex-pos.com; Focus: News, reviews and trends on electronic prepress products; Format: Newsletter; Jonathan W. Seybold, Pblshr Email: jseybold@sbexpos.com; Stephen E. Edwards, Ed. Email: sedwards@sbex-pos.com; Peter E. Dyson, Ed. Email: pdyson@sbexpos.com; Freq: 22/Year, Price/yr-$:365

Shannon Knows DEC
Publishing Co: Illuminata, 3 Depot Rd, PO Box 1585, Hollis, NH 03049, USA; 603/465-3821, Fax: 603/465-3951, Co Email: newsletter@illuminata.com; Focus: Updates on DEC; Format: Newsletter; Jonathan Eunice, Pblshr Terry C. Shannon, Ed. Freq: 24/Year, Price/yr-$:295

SIAM Journal on Computing
Publishing Co: Society for Industrial & Applied Mathematics, 3600 University City Science Center, Philadelphia, PA 19104-2688, USA; 215/382-9800, Fax: 215/386-7999, Co Email: siam@siam.org; Web URL: siam.org; Focus: Peer-reviewed research articles on mathematics in computer science; Format: Magazine; Freq: Bimonthly, Price/yr-$:48/198

SIAM Journal on Scientific & Statistical Computing
Publishing Co: Society for Industrial & Applied Mathematics, 3600 University City Science Center, Philadelphia, PA 19104-2688, USA; 215/382-9800, Fax: 215/386-7999, Co Email: siam@siam.org; Web URL: siam.org; Focus: Peer-reviewed articles on research in scientific and statistical computations; Format: Magazine; Freq: Bimonthly, Price/yr-$:48/210

SIAM News
Publishing Co: Society for Industrial & Applied Mathematics, 3600 University City Science Center, Philadelphia, PA 19104-

2688, USA; 215/382-9800, Fax: 215/386-7999, Co Email: siam@siam.org; Web URL: siam.org; Focus: Membership publication for SIAM; Format: Magazine; Freq: Monthly, Price/yr-$:15

Silicon Graphics World
Publishing Co: Publications & Communications Inc., 12416 Hymeadow Drive, Austin, TX 78750-1896, USA; 512/250-9023, Fax: 512/331-3900, Co Email: sgi@pcin-ews.lonestar.org; Web URL: pcin-ews.com/pci; Focus: News, features and reviews of Silicon Graphics workstation products; Format: Newspaper; Callie Jones, Ed. Larry Storer, Ed.-in-Chief Circ.: 20,000, Freq: Monthly, Price/yr-$:Free/45

Simply Secure
Publishing Co: Cobb Group, The, 9420 Bunsen Pkwy. #300, Louisville, KY 40220, USA; 502/491-1900, Fax: 502/491-8050, Co Email: cobb@aol.com; Web URL: cobb.com; Focus: Tips and information for Simply Money & Tax users; Format: Newsletter; Freq: Monthly, Price/yr-$:39

Simulation
Publishing Co: Society for Computer Simulation, PO Box 17900, San Diego, CA 92177, USA; 619/277-3888, Fax: 619/277-3930, Co Email: @scs.org; Web URL: scs.org; Focus: Technical information on computer simulation; Format: Magazine; Hildy Linn, Mgng Ed. Email: linn@sdsc.edu; Louis Birta, Ed-in-Chief Freq: Monthly, Price/yr-$:149

Simulation Software, Directory of
Publishing Co: Society for Computer Simulation, PO Box 17900, San Diego, CA 92177, USA; 619/277-3888, Fax: 619/277-3930, Co Email: scs@sdsc.edu; Web URL: scs.org; Focus: Listing of computer simulation software; Format: Directory; Hildy Linn, Mgng Ed. Email: linn@sdsc.edu; Brian O'Neill, Adv Mgr Email: oneill@sdsc.edu; Circ.: 25,000, Freq: Annual, Price/yr-$:40

SLC
Publishing Co: Soft•letter, 17 Main Street, Watertown, MA 02172-9807, USA; 617/924-3944, Fax: 617/924-7288, Focus: Classified marketplace for the software industry; Format: Newsletter; Jeffrey Tarter, Pblshr Freq: 6/Year, Price/yr-$:Free/25

Smalltalk Report, The
Publishing Co: SIGS Publications Group, 71 W. 23rd Street, 3rd Floor, New York, NY 10010, USA; 212/242-7447, Fax: 212/242-7574, Co Email: 73361.1707@compuserve.com; Web URL: sigs.com; Focus: News and trends for smalltalk programmers; Format: Newsletter; John Pugh, Ed. Paul White, Ed. Freq: 9/Year, Price/yr-$:89

Smart Access
Publishing Co: Pinnacle Publishing Inc.,

18000 72nd Ave S. #217, Kent, WA 98032, USA; 206/251-1900, Fax: 206/251-5057, Web URL: pinpub.com; Focus: Information and utilities for Microsoft Access users; Format: Newsletter; Dian Schaffhauser, Ed.-in-Chief Susan Jameson Harker, Pblshr Freq: Monthly, Price/yr-$:139

Smart Computer & Software Retailing

Publishing Co: Cahners Publishing Co., PO Box 2754, High Pointe, NC 27261, USA; 910/605-0121, Fax: 910/605-1143, Co Email: 75300.2101@compuserve.com; Focus: News for computer and software retailers; Format: Tabloid; George Lee Hundley Jr., Pblshr Lester Craft Jr., Ed. Gary James, Mgng Ed. Freq: 21/Year, Price/yr-$:Free/75

Smart Electronics

Publishing Co: McMullen & Yee Publishing Inc., 774 S. Placentia Ave, Placentia, CA 92670, USA; 714/572-2255, Focus: Computer-related products for small office/home office users; Format: Magazine; Bill Roche, Ed.-in-Chief Bob Clark, Ed. Dir Dan Leadbetter, Ed. Freq: 6/Year, Price/yr-$:19.95

SMT Trends

Publishing Co: New Insights, 303 Vallejo Street, Crockett, CA 94525, USA; 510/787-2273, Fax: 510/787-2273, Focus: News, trends and analysis of surface mount technology and electronic packaging markets; Format: Newsletter; Michael New, Ed. & Pblr Circ.: 200, Freq: Monthly, Price/yr-$:325

SNA Perspectives

Publishing Co: SNA Perspectives, 12980 Saratoga Ave, #e, Saratoga, CA 95070, USA; 408/446-9115, Fax: 408/446-9134, Co Email: g2vdon@cerf.net; Focus: News and analysis of IBM's SAA, SNA, DIA & DDM products & strategies; Format: Newsletter; Donald Czubek, Ed. Freq: Monthly, Price/yr-$:395

SNA Update

Publishing Co: Xephon, 1301 W. Hwy 407, #201-450, Lewisville, TX 75067, USA; 817/455-7050, Fax: 817/455-2492, Focus: Tools and techniques for enhancing IBM's SNA; Format: Magazine; Freq: 4/Year, Price/yr-$:165

Snapshots

Publishing Co: Patricia Seybold Group, 148 State Street, 7th Floor, Boston, MA 02109-9990, USA; 617/742-5200, Fax: 617/742-1028, Web URL: psgroup.com; Focus: Parts of editorials, features, news column or case study; Format: Newsletter; Patricia Seybold, Pblshr Freq: Monthly, Price/yr-$:95

Soft•letter

Publishing Co: Soft•letter 17 Main Street, Watertown, MA 02172-9807, USA; 617/924-3944, Fax: 617/924-7288, Focus: Trends and strategies in software publish-

ing; annual ranking of top 100 software companies; Format: Newsletter; Jeffrey Tarter, Ed. & Pblr Freq: 24/year, Price/yr-$:345

SoftPub Yellow Pages, The

Publishing Co: SoftPub Group Inc., 24705 214th Ave SE, Maple Valley, WA 98038, USA; 206/852-7440, Fax: 206/413-0747, Co Email: 75021.605@compuserve.com; Focus: Directory of suppliers to the software industry; Format: Directory; David M. Johnson, Pblshr Leanne Davis, Ed. Peg Nakatsu, Bus Mgr Circ.: 35,000, Freq: Annual, Price/yr-$:49

Software Analyst

Publishing Co: G. Meier Inc., PO Box 104, Millburn, NJ 07041, USA; 201/376-8181, Fax: 201/376-8335, Co Email: gmeier@aol.com; Focus: Market shares of software products; Format: Newsletter; George B. Meier, Pblshr Email: gmeier@aol.com; Freq: Monthly, Price/yr-$:1,500

Software Copyright Handbook

Publishing Co: SSC, PO Box 55549, Seattle, WA 98155-0549, USA; 206/782-7733, Fax: 206/782-7191, Co Email: @ssc.com; Web URL: ssc.com; Focus: Information on how to copyright software; Format: Reference book; Price/yr-$:10

Software Developer & Publisher

Publishing Co: Webcom Communications Corp., 10555 E Dartmouth, #330, Aurora, CO 80014-2633, USA; 303/745-5711, Fax: 303/745-5712, Co Email: 74262.103@compuserve.com; Web URL: infowebcom.com; Focus: Information on the software industry; Format: Magazine; David Webster, Ed. & Pblr John Cargile, Mgng Ed. Brian Gallagher, Assist Ed. Freq: 6/Year, Price/yr-$:36

Software Development

Publishing Co: Miller Freeman Inc., 600 Harrison Street, San Francisco, CA 94107-1391, USA; 415/905-2200, Fax: 415/905-2234, Web URL: sdmagazine.com; Focus: News, reviews and trends about computer language products; Format: Magazine; Barbara Hanscome, Ed-in-Chief Email: bhanscome@mfi.com; Veronica Costanza, Pblshr Julie Fadda, Mgng Ed. Email: jfadda@mfi.com; Circ.: 72,000, Freq: Monthly, Price/yr-$:39

Software Digest

Publishing Co: National Software Testing Laboratories, Inc., 625 Ridge Pike, Bldg D, Conshohocken, PA 19428, USA; 609/426-5526, Web URL: nstl.com; Focus: Reports on comparative testing on PC software; Format: Newsletter; Larry Goldstein, Pblshr Freq: Monthly, Price/yr-$:462

Software Economics Letter

Publishing Co: Computer Economics Inc., 5841 Edison Place, Carlsbad, CA 92008, USA; 619/438-8100, Fax: 619/431-1126, Co Email: swn@compecon.com; Focus: Software prices, discounts, licensing and

cost of ownership; Format: Newsletter; Mark McManus, Ed.-in-Chief Email: mmc-manus@compecon.com; Bruno Bassi, Pblshr Freq: Monthly, Price/yr-$:395

Software Engineering Standards & Specifications

Publishing Co: Global Professional Publications, 15 Inverness Way E, Englewood, CO 80112, USA; 303/792-2181, Fax: 303/397-7935, Focus: 220 software engineering standards, reports from 46 standards development organizations; Format: Directory/Index; Stan Magee, Ed. Email: 73211.2144@compuserve.com; Leonard L. Tripp, Ed. Price/yr-$:79.50

Software Engineering Strategies

Publishing Co: Auerbach Publications, 31 St. James Ave, Boston, MA 02116-9372, USA; 617/423-2020, Fax: 617/451-0908, Co Email: 73752.2270@compuserve.com; Web URL: wgl.com; Focus: Information on CASE, object technology and emerging software trends; Format: Newsletter; Kim Horan Kelly, Pblshr Freq: 6/Year, Price/yr-$:125

Software Futures

Publishing Co: APT Data Services Inc., 27 E 21st Street, 3rd Floor, New York, NY 10010, USA; 212/677-0409, Fax: 212/677-0463, Co Email: @apt.usa.global-news.com; Web URL: power.global-news.com; Focus: Information on software development; Format: Newsletter; Mark Satchell, Pblshr Email: mark@apt.usa.glo-balnews.c; Gary Flood, Ed. Freq: Monthly, Price/yr-$:495

Software Industry Bulletin

Publishing Co: Digital Information Group, PO Box 110235, Stamford, CT 06911-0235, USA; 203/840-0045, Fax: 203/977-8310, Co Email: 75120.2616@compuserve.com; Focus: News and analysis on the software industry; Format: Newsletter; Jeff Silverstein, Pblr Freq: 48/Year, Price/yr-$:395

Software Industry Financial Review

Publishing Co: Sentry Market Research, 1 Research Drive, #400B, Westborough, MA 01581-3907, USA; 508/366-2031, Fax: 508/836-4732, Web URL: sentrytech.com; Focus: Financial comparisons of leading software companies; Format: Factbook; Bill Gannon Jr., Research Dir Donna Belanger, Sr Analyst Freq: Annual, Price/yr-$:795

Software Information Database on CD-ROM

Publishing Co: ICP Inc., 823 E. Westfield Blvd., Indianapolis, IN 46220-1715, USA; 317/251-7727, Fax: 317/251-7813, Co Email: info@icp.com; Web URL: icp.com; Focus: Information on 5,000 vendors and 18,000 micro, mini and mainframe software products; Format: CD-ROM; Marilyn Law, Ed. Larry Welke, Pblshr Freq: 4/Year

Software Law Bulletin

Publishing Co: Kutish Publications Inc., PO Box 113, 125 Strafford Ave, Wayne, PA 19087-0113, USA; 610/975-9619, Fax: 610/975-9623, Focus: News and developments affecting software law; Format: Newsletter; L.J. Kutten, Pblshr Freq: 10/Year, Price/yr-$:280

Software Legal Book
Publishing Co: Shafer Books Inc., PO Box 40, Croton-on-Hudson, NY 10520-0040, USA; Fax: 914/271-5193, Focus: Software rights and contracts; Format: Factbook; Paul S. Hoffman, Author Price/yr-$:235

Software Magazine
Publishing Co: Sentry Publishing Company Inc., 1 Research Drive, #400B, Westborough, MA 01581-3907, USA; 508/366-2031, Fax: 508/366-8104, Co Email: softwaremagazine@mcimail.com; Focus: News and information for professional software developers, managers and users; Format: Magazine; Patrick L. Porter, Ed-in-Chief Donald E. Fagan, Pblshr Kym Gilhooly, Mgng Ed. Circ.: 100,000, Freq: Monthly, Price/yr-$:Free/75

Software Market Survey
Publishing Co: Sentry Market Research, 1 Research Drive, #400B, Westborough, MA 01581-3907, USA; 508/366-2031, Fax: 508/836-4732, Web URL: sentrytech.com; Focus: Survey-based information on the software industry; Format: Factbook; Bill Gannon Jr., Research Dir Freq: Annual, Price/yr-$:997

Software Marketing Journal
Publishing Co: Kawalek & Assoc., 455 The Embarcadero, San Francisco, CA 94111, USA; 415/296-7744, Fax: 415/296-7766, Focus: Business and marketing issues for software executives; Format: Magazine; Nadine A. Kawalek, Ed-in-Chief & Pblr Vincent Ryan, Assoc Ed. Circ.: 3,000, Freq: 6/Year, Price/yr-$:395

Software Quarterly
Publishing Co: IBM Corp., 1 E. Kirkwood Blvd., MS 40-B3-04, Roanoke, TX 76299-0015, USA; 817/961-6551, Focus: IBM software technology; Format: Magazine; Alan E. Hodel, Ed.-in-Chief Email: hodel@vnet.ibm.com; Scott Werthman, Pblshr Todd L. Watson, Assist Ed. Email: radar@vnet.ibm.com; Freq: 4/Year, Price/yr-$:Free/19

Software Success
Publishing Co: United Communications Group, 175 Highland Ave, Needham, MA 02194, USA; 617/444-5755, Fax: 617/444-8958, Web URL: ucg.com; Focus: News, analysis and research result on management and operation of software publishers; Format: Newsletter; Susan Hikdreth, Ed. Circ.: 2,000, Freq: Monthly, Price/yr-$:257

Software Taxation Letter
Publishing Co: Kutish Publications Inc., PO Box 181916, Coronado, CA 92178, USA; Fax: 800/803-9623, Focus: Software taxa-

tion issues; Format: Newsletter; L.J. Kutten, Pblshr Freq: 10/Year, Price/yr-$:275

Software, Directory of
Publishing Co: Datapro Information Services Group, 600 Delran Pkwy., Delran, NJ 08705-9904, USA; 609/764-0100, Fax: 609/764-2811, Co Email: datapro@mhh.com; Web URL: datapro.com; Focus: Information on over 8,000 mainframe and minicomputer programs; Format: CD-ROM; Freq: Monthly

SoftWatch
Publishing Co: Applied Computer Research Inc., PO Box 82266, Phoenix, AZ 85071-2266, USA; 602/995-5929, Fax: 602/995-0905, Focus: Software article highlights for over 300 periodicals; Format: Index; Alan Howard, Ed. Freq: 4/Year, Price/yr-$:95

Soundbyte News
Publishing Co: Boston Computer Exchange, 210 South Street, 6th Floor, Boston, MA 02111-2725, USA; 617/542-4414, Fax: 617/542-8849, Co Email: 4726199@mcimail.com; Focus: Used computer price index and PC news events; Format: Fax; Gary Guhman, Ed. & Pblr Freq: Weekly, Price/yr-$:Free

SRC Newsletter
Publishing Co: Semiconductor Research Corp., PO Box 12053, Research Triangle Park, NC 27709, USA; 919/541-9400, Fax: 919/541-9450, Co Email: @src.org; Focus: Information about SRC's research activities; Format: Newsletter; Marian Regan, Ed. Email: marian@src.org; Freq: Monthly, Price/yr-$:Free

State and Use Taxation of Computer Software
Publishing Co: Software Taxation Institute, PO Box 10170, Reno, NV 89510-0170, USA; Fax: 800/803-9623, Focus: State-by-state guide to software taxation issues; Format: Reference Book; Freq: Annual, Price/yr-$:475

State Computer Laws
Publishing Co: Clark Boardman Callagan, 155 Pfingsten Road, Deerfield, IL 60015-4998, USA; 847/948-7000, Fax: 847/948-9340, Co Email: cbcservice@cbclegal.com; Web URL: cbclegal.com; Focus: Contracts, liability, taxation and other legal aspects by states; Format: Factbook; Freq: Annual, Price/yr-$:105

Step-By-Step Electronic Design
Publishing Co: Step-By-Step Publishing, PO Box 1901, Peoria, IL 61656-9941, USA; 309/688-8800, Fax: 309/688-6579, Focus: Design tips for users of desktop publishing software; Format: Newsletter; Nancy Aldrich-Ruenzel, Edtrl Dir Freq: Monthly, Price/yr-$:48

Step-By-Step Graphics
Publishing Co: Step-By-Step Publishing, PO Box 1901, Peoria, IL 61656-9941, USA; 309/688-8800, Fax: 309/688-6579, Focus: Information for users of desktop publishing software; Format: Magazine;

Nancy Aldrich-Ruenzel, Edit Dir Freq: 6/Year, Price/yr-$:42

Storage Source
Publishing Co: Storage Systems Marketing, 1235 Wildwood Road, Boulder, CO 80303, USA; 303/415-0858, Fax: 303/727-4262, Co Email: storagesys@aol.com; Focus: Storage systems sales & marketing; Format: Newsletter; Lynn Osborne, Ed. Email: losborne@aol.com; Freq: Bimonthly, Price/yr-$:295

Strategic Partnering
Publishing Co: ChannelCorp Products Inc., 2991 W. 42nd Ave, Vancouver, BC V6N 3G8, Canada; 604/263-6811, Fax: 604/263-4914, Focus: Strategic partnering information for computer vendors and resellers; Format: Factbook; Marg Stuart, Pblshr Bruce R. Stuart, Ed. Freq: Annual, Price/yr-$:100

Strategic Solutions
Publishing Co: Good Publishing Group Ltd., 22845 NE 8th, #161, Redmond, WA 98053, USA; 206/868-6532, Fax: 206/868-8921, Focus: Marketing issues for hardware and software companies; Format: Newsletter; Ken Goodman, Ed. Mark O'Deady, Ed. Circ.: 2,500, Freq: Monthly, Price/yr-$:225

Strategy Plus
Publishing Co: Strategy Plus Inc., PO Box 21, Hancock, VT 05748, USA; 802/767-4622, Fax: 802/767-3382, Focus: Review and information for computer game users; Format: Magazine; Mark Dultz, Ed. Yale Brozen, Pblshr Freq: Monthly, Price/yr-$:32

Stuff You Gotta Know About Windows
Publishing Co: Cobb Group, The, 9420 Bunsen Pkwy. #300, Louisville, KY 40220, USA; 502/491-1900, Fax: 502/491-8050, Co Email: cobb@aol.com; Web URL: cobb.com; Focus: Tips and techniques for Microsoft Windows users; Format: Newsletter; Jon Pyles, Pblshr Tiffany Taylor, Ed. Freq: Monthly, Price/yr-$:39

Sun Observer, The
Publishing Co: Publications & Communications Inc., 12416 Hymeadow Drive, Austin, TX 78750-1896, USA; 512/250-9023, Fax: 512/331-3900, Co Email: @pcinews.com; Web URL: pcinews.com/pci; Focus: News and information for the Sun Microsystems community; Format: Magazine; Larry Storer, Ed.-in-Chief Email: storer@pcinews.com; Kim Fulcher Linkins, Ed. Circ.: 30,000, Freq: Monthly, Price/yr-$:45/75

SunExpert
Publishing Co: Computer Publishing Group Inc., 320 Washington Street, Brookline, MA 02146-3202, USA; 617/739-7001, Fax: 617/739-7003, Co Email: @cpg.com; Web URL: cpg.com; Focus: News, reviews and information for SPARC workstation users; Format: Magazine; Dou-

glas Pryor, Ed.-in-Chief Email: dpryor@cpg.com; S. Henry Sacks, Pblshr Email: shs@cpg.com; Michael J. Tucker, Exec Ed. Email: mjt@cpg.com; Circ.: 64,000, Freq: Monthly, Price/yr-$:Free/60

Sunworld Online
Publishing Co: IDG Communications Inc., 501 Second Street, San Francisco, CA 94107, USA; 415/243-4188, Fax: 415/267-1732, Co Email: @sunworld.com; Web URL: sun.com/sunworldonline; Focus: Product reviews and news for Sun users; Format: Online; Michael E. McCarthy, Ed-in-Chief & Pblr Email: michael.mccarthy@sunworld; Mark Coppel, Exec Pblr Email: mark.coppel@sunworld.com; Circ.: 50,000, Freq: Monthly, Price/yr-$:Free

Supercomputing Apps. & High Perf. Computing, Int'l. Journ. of
Publishing Co: MIT Press Journals, 55 Hayward Street, Cambridge, MA 02142, USA; 617/253-2889, Fax: 617/258-6779, Co Email: journals-orders@mit.edu; Web URL: mitpress.mit.edu; Focus: Peer-reviewed research papers on supercomputing applications; Format: Magazine; Joanne Martin, Ed. Email: dongarra@cs.utk.edu; Jack Dongarra, Ed-in-Chief Email: dongarra@cs.utk.edu; Circ.: 650, Freq: 4/Year, Price/yr-$:75

Support Solutions
Publishing Co: High Tech High Touch Solutions Inc., 16625 Redmond Way, #M-475, Redmond, WA 98052-9874, USA; 206/619-4357, Fax: 206/788-1595, Focus: Customer service and support; Format: Magazine; Jim Etchison, Ed. Email: jimwriter9@aol.com; Pattie Berghof, Ed. Assist Freq: Monthly, Price/yr-$:69

Sybase Magazine
Publishing Co: Sybase Inc., 6475 Christie Ave, Emeryville, CA 94608, USA; 510/596-3500, Focus: Enterprise client/server computing; Format: Magazine; John A. Barry, Ed. Carla B. Marymee, Pblshr Freq: 4/Year, Price/yr-$:Free/30

SysAdmin
Publishing Co: Miller Freeman Inc., 1601 W. 23rd Street, #200, Lawrence, KS 66046-2700, USA; 913/841-1631, Fax: 913/841-2624, Co Email: sasub@rdpub.com; Focus: Unix systems administration information; Format: Magazine; Circ.: 14,000, Freq: 6/Year, Price/yr-$:39

Systems Development Management
Publishing Co: Auerbach Publications, 31 St. James Ave, Boston, MA 02116-9372, USA; 617/423-2020, Fax: 617/451-0908, Co Email: 73752.2270@compuserve.com; Web URL: wgl.com; Focus: Information on managing and performing system development; Format: Loose-leaf; Kim Horan Kelly, Pblshr Freq: 6/Year, Price/yr-$:405

TAG's Channel Compass

Publishing Co: Ambit Group, The, 665 Third Street, #508, San Francisco, CA 94107, USA; 415/957-9433, Fax: 415/957-0504, Co Email: ambitsf@aol.com; Focus: Report on channels of distribution and channel development; Format: Newsletter; Linda Kazares, Ed. & Pblr Freq: Monthly, Price/yr-$:395

Tape/Disc Business
Publishing Co: Knowledge Industry Publishing, 701 Westchester Ave, White Plains, NY 10604, USA; 914/328-9157, Fax: 914/328-9093, Co Email: kipa.mktg@kipi.com; Web URL: kipi.com; Focus: Information for manufacturers, dealers and duplicators of magnetic and optical media; Format: Magazine; Patricia Casey, Ed. Barbara Stockwell, Pblshr Circ.: 43,000, Freq: Monthly, Price/yr-$:74

Target Selling to IT Professionals
Publishing Co: Giga Information Group, One Longwater Circle, Norwell, MA 02061-1620, USA; 617/982-1724, Fax: 617/982-9500, Focus: Understanding the range of IT organizational models and job functions; Format: Book; Roger L. Kay, Co-Author John Hammitt, Co-Author Ann Coffou, Co-Author Price/yr-$:995

Technical Employment News
Publishing Co: Publications & Communications Inc., 12416 Hymeadow Drive, Austin, TX 78750-1896, USA; 512/250-9023, Fax: 512/331-3900, Co Email: @pcinews.com; Web URL: pcinews.com/pci; Focus: Contract employment and job shopper industry; Format: Magazine; Betty M. Craft, Ed. Tom Clark, Pblshr Circ.: 10,000, Freq: Weekly, Price/yr-$:55-175

Technical Support
Publishing Co: NaSPA, 7044 S. 13th Street, Oak Creek, WI 53154-9920, USA; Fax: 414/768-8001, Focus: Technical management strategies, interoperability insights, systems strategies etc.; Format: Magazine

Technological Horizons in Education Journal
Publishing Co: T.H.E. Journal, 150 El Camino Real, #112, Tustin, CA 92680-3670, USA; 714/730-4011, Fax: 714/730-3739, Co Email: thejournal@earthlink.net; Web URL: thejournal.com; Focus: Educational news concerning computers, remote learning and high tech products; Format: Magazine; Dr. Sylvia Charp, Ed-in-Chief Edward W. Warnshuis, Pblshr Terian Tyre, Mngg Ed. Circ.: 150,000, Freq: 11/year, Price/yr-$:Free/29

Technology & Learning
Publishing Co: Peter Li, Inc., 22 Front Street, #401, San Francisco, CA 94111, USA; 415/438-5600, Fax: 415/439-5619, Web URL: techlearning.com; Focus: Educational use of computers in the classroom; Format: Magazine; Peter Li, Pblshr Circ.: 80,000, Freq: 8/Year, Price/yr-$:24

Technology & Media
Publishing Co: Technology & Media Group, Inc., 1 Longwater Circle, Norwell, MA 02061, USA; Focus: Communication, information and entertainment; Format: Newsletter; Denise Caruso, Edit Dir & Pblr Norman Pearlstine, Pres Lisa Raleigh, Mngg Ed. Freq: Monthly, Price/yr-$:595/770

Technology Events Calendar & Worldwide Directory
Publishing Co: Tech Trade Assoc., 8 Combahee Road, Hilton Head, SC 29928-3316, USA; 803/785-5497, Fax: 803/785-5498, Focus: Calender & reference guide to high-tech tradeshows, conferences and symposiums; Format: Directory; Judith Miller, Principal Circ.: 3,000, Freq: Annual, Price/yr-$:40

Technology Exchange, The
Publishing Co: Technology Board of Trade, 2665 N 1st Street, #102, San Jose, CA 95134-2033, USA; Co Email: tecboard@aol.com; Focus: Listing of technologies available for licensing; Format: Newsletter; Amy Bates, Ed. Freq: 6/Year, Price/yr-$:149

Technology Implementation Index
Publishing Co: Business Research Group, 275 Washington Street, Newton, MA 02158-1630, USA; 617/630-3900, Fax: 617/558-4585, Co Email: @brg.cahners.com; Focus: Tracks implementation of emerging technologies in leading US companies; Format: Newsletter; Warren Childs, Dir Primary Res Email: childs@brg.cahners.com; Freq: 4/Year, Price/yr-$:3,500

TechNotes
Publishing Co: Jaye Communications Inc., 3200 Professional Pkwy, #245, Atlanta, GA 30339-9828, USA; 770/984-9444, Fax: 770/612-0780, Web URL: sid.com; Focus: Calendar of high-tech events in Georgia; Format: Fax/Online; Freq: Weekly

TechScan Newsletter
Publishing Co: Richmond Research Inc., Box 537 Vlg. Station, New York, NY 10014-0537, USA; 212/741-0045, Fax: 212/243-7356, Co Email: techscan@pipeline.com; Focus: Information on how to use technology to solve business problems; Format: Newsletter; Louis Giacalone, Ed. & Pblr Circ.: 2,500, Freq: Monthly, Price/yr-$:87.50

Telco Competition Report
Publishing Co: BRP Publications Inc., 1333 H Street NW #1100. W. Tower, Washington, DC 20005, USA; 202/842-3006, Fax: 202/842-3047, Co Email: brp@access.digex.net; Focus: Business news, federal/state regulatory & legislative battles to open up telecom svcs.; Format: Newsletter; Freq: Biweekly, Price/yr-$:459

Telcos in Interactive Services

Publishing Co: Simba Information Inc., 11 River Bend Drive S, PO Box 4234, Stamford, CT 06807-0234, USA; 203/834-0033, Fax: 203/358-5825, Co Email: simbainfo@simbanet.com; Web URL: simbanet.com; Focus: Telephone companies current and future in interactive services; Format: Newsletter; Karen Burka, Ed. Dir Price/yr-$:1,995

TELE*MGR
Publishing Co: James Publishing & Associates, 899 Presial, #110, Richardson, TX 75081, USA; 214/238-1133, Fax: 214/238-1132, Co Email: themartmag@aol.com; Focus: Telecom equipment for purchasing managers; Format: Magazine; James Michael Story, Pblshr Sarah Klein, Ed. Circ.: 40,000

tele.com
Publishing Co: McGraw-Hill Cos., PO Box 464, Hightstown, NJ 08520-0464, USA; Fax: 212/512-3351, Focus: Next generation services; Format: Magazine; Joseph Braue, Ed. Dir

Telecom Advertising Report
Publishing Co: Simba Information Inc., 11 River Bend Drive S, PO Box 4234, Stamford, CT 06807-0234, USA; 203/834-0033, Fax: 203/358-5825, Co Email: simbainfo@simbanet.com; Web URL: simbanet.com; Focus: Information on telecom ad spending; Format: Newsletter; Freq: 24/Year, Price/yr-$:498

Telecom Calendar
Publishing Co: Information Gatekeepers Inc., 214 Harvard Ave, Boston, MA 02134, USA; 617/232-3111, Fax: 617/734-8562, Co Email: igiboston@aol.com; Focus: Worldwide 10 year calendar of telecom, computer and electronics conferences and trade show; Format: Newsletter; Paul Polishuk, Ed. & Pblr Email: igiboston@aol.com; Freq: 4/Year, Price/yr-$:250/300

Telecom Industry Advertising & Market Forecast
Publishing Co: Simba Information Inc., 11 River Bend Drive S, PO Box 4234, Stamford, CT 06807-0234, USA; 203/834-0033, Fax: 203/358-5825, Co Email: simbainfo@simbanet.com; Web URL: simbanet.com; Focus: Information on telecom ad spending; Format: Factbook; Freq: Annual, Price/yr-$:1,595

Telecom Outlook Report
Publishing Co: International Engineering Consortium, 303 E Wacker Drive, #740, Chicago, IL 60601-5212, USA; 312/938-3500, Fax: 312/938-8787, Focus: Future of global telecommunications and information services industries; Format: Report; Price/yr-$:1,295

Telecom Sources
Publishing Co: Asian Sources Media Group, 1210 S Bascom Ave, #205, San Jose, CA 95128-3535, USA; 408/295-4500, Fax: 408/295-0889, Focus: Telecom product

news for resellers, OEMs and system integrators; Format: Magazine; Price/yr-$:65/95

Telecom Standards
Publishing Co: Information Gatekeepers Inc., 214 Harvard Ave, Boston, MA 02134, USA; 617/232-3111, Fax: 617/734-8562, Co Email: igiboston@aol.com; Focus: News about standards activities around the world; Format: Newsletter; Paul Polishuk, Ed. & Pblr Email: igiboston@aol.com; Freq: Monthly, Price/yr-$:545/595

Telecom Strategy Letter, The
Publishing Co: Northern Business Information, 1221 Avenue of the Americas, New York, NY 10020-1001, USA; 212/732-0775, Fax: 212/233-6233, Focus: Analyzes competition and strategic developments in telecom; Format: Newsletter; Gayle Gaddis, Ed. Circ.: 400, Freq: Monthly, Price/yr-$:995

Telecommunication Market Sourcebook
Publishing Co: Frost & Sullivan, 2525 Charleston Road, Mt. View, CA 94043, USA; 415/961-9000, Fax: 415/961-5042, Web URL: frost.com; Focus: Telecom market, data and statistics; Format: Directory; Price/yr-$:995

Telecommunication Markets
Publishing Co: FT Telecoms & Media Publishing, Maple House, 149 Tottenham Court Road, London, W1P 9LL, UK; 171-896-2222, Fax: 171-896-2274, Focus: Information on the worldwide telecom market; Format: Newsletter; John McLachlan, Pblshr Freq: 23/Year, Price/yr-$:997

Telecommunications Directory
Publishing Co: Gale Research Inc., 835 Penobscot Bldg, Detroit, MI 48226, USA; 313/961-2242, Fax: 313/961-6083, Co Email: galenp@conch.aa.msen.com; Focus: Listing of over 2,500 national and international communications systems and services; Format: Directory; John Krol, Ed. Freq: Biannual, Price/yr-$:345

Telecommunications Magazine
Publishing Co: Horizon House Publications Inc., 685 Canton Street, Norwood, MA 02062, USA; 617/769-9750, Fax: 617/762-9071, Co Email: telecomm@world.std.com; Web URL: telecoms-mag.com/tcs; Focus: News and technical information on the US telecom industry; Format: Magazine; Thomas S. Valovic, Ed-in-Chief James N. Budwey, Pblshr Circ.: 55,000, Freq: Monthly, Price/yr-$:Free/85

Telecommunications Market Review & Forecast
Publishing Co: Multimedia Telecommunications Assoc., 1820 Jefferson Place NW, #100, Washington, DC 20036, USA; 202/296-9800, Fax: 202/296-4993, Web URL: mmta.org; Focus: Review and forecast of telecommunications products and services;

Format: Factbook; Freq: 2/Year, Price/yr-$:498

Telecommunications Networks, Systems & Services
Publishing Co: Faulkner Information Services, 7905 Browning Road, Pennsauken, NJ 08109-4319, USA; 609/662-2070, Fax: 609/662-0905, Co Email: faulkner@faulkner.com; Web URL: faulkner.com; Focus: Voice services, providers and equipment; Format: Loose-leaf; Martin Murphy, Pblshr Freq: Monthly, Price/yr-$:1,450

Telecommunications Reports
Publishing Co: BRP Publications Inc., 1333 H Street NW #1100. W. Tower, Washington, DC 20005, USA; 202/842-3006, Fax: 202/842-3047, Co Email: brp@access.digex.net; Focus: Technology development and policy issues in the telecommunications industry; Format: Newsletter; Freq: Weekly, Price/yr-$:895

Telecommunications Reports Int'l.
Publishing Co: BRP Publications Inc., 1333 H Street NW #1100. W. Tower, Washington, DC 20005, USA; 202/842-3006, Fax: 202/842-3047, Co Email: brp@access.digex.net; Focus: News and information on global telecom issues; Format: Newsletter; Freq: Biweekly, Price/yr-$:897

Telecommunications Sourcebook
Publishing Co: Multimedia Telecommunications Assoc., 1820 Jefferson Place NW, #100, Washington, DC 20036, USA; 202/296-9800, Fax: 202/296-4993, Web URL: mmta.org; Focus: Listing of telecommunications products and services; Format: Directory; Freq: Annual, Price/yr-$:53

Telecommunications Week
Publishing Co: BRP Publications Inc., 1333 H Street NW #1100. W. Tower, Washington, DC 20005, USA; 202/842-3006, Fax: 202/842-3047, Co Email: brp@access.digex.net; Focus: 8-page report on major domestic telecom news developments; Format: Newsletter; Freq: Weekly, Price/yr-$:395

Telefacts
Publishing Co: Datapro Information Services Group, 600 Delran Pkwy., Delran, NJ 08705-9904, USA; 609/764-0100, Fax: 609/764-2811, Co Email: datapro@mhh.com; Web URL: datapro.com; Focus: Information on new market opportunities; Format: Newsletter; Freq: Monthly

Telemarketing & Call Center Solutions
Publishing Co: Technology Marketing Corp., One Technology Plaza, Norwalk, CT 06854, USA; 203/852-6800, Fax: 203/853-2845, Web URL: tmcnet.com; Focus: Telemarketing; Format: Magazine; Jadji Tehrani, Pblr & Ed-in-Chief Linda Driscoll, Ed. Freq: Monthly, Price/yr-$:49

Telemedia Week

Publishing Co: Cahners Publishing Co., 275 Washington Street, Newton, MA 02158-1630, USA; 617/964-3030, Focus: Information on the new media industry; Format: Magazine; Donald West, Ed. Freq: Weekly

Telephony
Publishing Co: Intertec Publishing Corp., 1 IBM Plaza, 23rd Fl, Chicago, IL 60611, USA; 312/595-1080, Fax: 312/595-0295, Focus: Telecom technology trends and products; Format: Magazine; Steve Titch, Ed. Dir Freq: Weekly

Text Retrieval Systems
Publishing Co: Delphi Consulting Group, 100 City Hall Plaza, Boston, MA 02108-2106, USA; 617/247-1511, Fax: 617/247-4957, Focus: Information on text retrieval industry; Format: Loose-leaf; Thomas M. Kouloupoulos, Pblshr Freq: Monthly, Price/yr-$:1,599

THE*MART
Publishing Co: James Publishing & Associates, 899 Presial, #100, Richardson, TX 75081, USA; 214/238-1133, Fax: 214/238-1132, Co Email: themart-mag@aol.com; Focus: Telecom equipment and service; Format: Magazine; Mike Story, Pblshr Sarah Klein, Ed. Circ.: 32,000, Freq: Monthly, Price/yr-$:40

ThePage
Publishing Co: Cobb Group, The, 9420 Bunsen Pkwy. #300, Louisville, KY 40220, USA; 502/491-1900, Fax: 502/491-8050, Co Email: cobb@aol.com; Web URL: cobb.com; Focus: Desktop publishing and graphics design for Macintosh users; Format: Newsletter; Bryan Chamberlain, Ed. Freq: Monthly, Price/yr-$:69

Token Perspectives Newsletter
Publishing Co: Architecture Technology Corp., PO Box 24344, Minneapolis, MN 55424, USA; 612/935-2035, Fax: 612/829-5871, Focus: News and analysis of IBM Token Ring compatible LAN products & FDDI products; Format: Newsletter; Kenneth Thurber, Ed. & Pblr Freq: Monthly, Price/yr-$:312

Top Computer Executives, Directory of
Publishing Co: Applied Computer Research Inc., PO Box 82266, Phoenix, AZ 85071-2266, USA; 602/995-5929, Fax: 602/995-0905, Focus: Listing of key MIS executives at medium and large US mainframe sites; Format: Directory; Alan Howard, Ed. Freq: 2/Year, Price/yr-$:520

TPC Quarterly Report
Publishing Co: Transaction Processing Performance Council, c/o Shanley PR, 777 N. First Street #600, San Jose, CA 95112-6311, USA; 408/295-8894, Fax: 408/295-9768, Web URL: tpc.org; Focus: Listing of transaction benchmark performance results; Format: Newsletter; Freq: 4/Year, Price/yr-$:375/599

TR Wireless News

Publishing Co: BRP Publications Inc., 1333 H Street NW #1100. W. Tower, Washington, DC 20005, USA; 202/842-3006, Fax: 202/842-3047, Co Email: brp@access.digex.net; Focus: Covers several areas of wireless communications field, including satellites, radio, etc.; Format: Newsletter; Freq: Biweekly, Price/yr-$:497

Tradeshow Report
Publishing Co: MediaMap, 215 First Street, 3rd Floor, Cambridge, MA 02142-9750, USA; 617/374-9300, Fax: 617/374-9345, Co Email: info@mediamap.com; Web URL: mediamap.com; Focus: Directory and analysis of computer tradeshows; Format: Directory; Freq: Annual, Price/yr-$:795

TWICE-This Week In Consumer Electronics
Publishing Co: Cahners Publishing Co., 8773 S Ridgeline Blvd, Highlands Ranch, CO 80126-2329, USA; 303/470-4445, Fax: 303/470-4280, Focus: News on consumer electronics industry; Format: Newspaper; Robert E. Gerson, Ed.-in-Chief Email: gerson@cahners.com; Marcia Grand, Pblshr John Laposky, Mngg Ed. Freq: 28/Year, Price/yr-$:Free/90

U.S. Government Software for Mainframes and Microcomputers
Publishing Co: National Technical Information Service, 5285 Port Royal Road, Rm 1303, Springfield, VA 22161, USA; 703/487-4650, Fax: 703/321-8547, Focus: Directory of software and tools available from NTIS; Format: Directory; Freq: Annual, Price/yr-$:59

Understanding and Leveraging Lotus Notes Release 4
Publishing Co: Patricia Seybold Group, 148 State Street, 7th Floor, Boston, MA 02109-9990, USA; 617/742-5200, Fax: 617/742-1028, Web URL: psgroup.com; Focus: Planning for and deploying Lotus Notes; Format: Loose-leaf; David Marshak, Author Price/yr-$:495

UniForum Monthly
Publishing Co: UniForum Assoc., 2901 Tasman Drive, #205, Santa Clara, CA 95054-1100, USA; 408/986-8840, Fax: 408/986-1645, Co Email: pubs@uniforum.org; Web URL: uniforum.org; Focus: Membership magazine for UniForum; Format: Magazine; Mary Margaret Peterson, Mngg Ed. Email: meg@uniforum.org; Richard R. Shippee, Dir Pubs Email: dick@uniforum.org; Richard H. Jaross, Exec Dir Email: rich@uniforum.org; Circ.: 15,000, Freq: Monthly, Price/yr-$:24

UniForum's IT Solutions
Publishing Co: UniForum Assoc., 2901 Tasman Drive, #205, Santa Clara, CA 95054-1100, USA; 408/986-8840, Fax: 408/986-1645, Co Email: pubs@uniforum.org; Web URL: uniforum.org; Focus:

Unix and open technologies; Format: Magazine; Richard R. Shippee, Dir Pubs Email: dick@uniforum.org; Jeffrey Bartlett, Exec Ed. Email: jeffb@uniforum.org; Cedric R. Braun, Mngg Ed. Email: cedric@uniforum.com; Freq: Monthly, Price/yr-$:24

UniForum's UniNews
Publishing Co: UniForum Assoc., 2901 Tasman Drive, #205, Santa Clara, CA 95054-1100, USA; 408/986-8840, Fax: 408/986-1645, Co Email: pubs@uniforum.org; Web URL: uniforum.org; Focus: Unix and open technologies; Format: Newsletter; Jeffrey Bartlett, Exec Ed. Cedric Braun, Mngg Ed. Price/yr-$:12

Unigram.X
Publishing Co: G2 Computer Intelligence Inc., 3 Maple Place, PO Box 7, Glen Head, NY 11545-9864, USA; 516/759-7025, Fax: 516/759-7028, Focus: Breaking news on the worldwide UNIX market; Format: Newsletter; Maureen O'Gara, Pblshr William Fellows, Ed. Freq: Weekly, Price/yr-$:595

Unisphere
Publishing Co: Cardinal Business Media Inc., 12225 Greenville Ave, #700, Dallas, TX 75243, USA; 214/669-9000, Fax: 214/669-9909, Co Email: 73430.2347@compuserve.com; Web URL: btb.com/cardinal/uni; Focus: News and technical information for users of Unisys computer systems and services; Format: Magazine; Dean Lampman, Ed-in Chief George Dishman, Pub Dir Debby English, Mngg Ed. Circ.: 20,000, Freq: Monthly, Price/yr-$:Free/80

Unisys World
Publishing Co: Publications & Communications Inc., 12416 Hymeadow Drive, Austin, TX 78750-1896, USA; 512/250-9023, Fax: 512/331-3900, Co Email: @pcinews.com; Web URL: pcinews.com/pci; Focus: Information, product news and review, user profiles and user group news for Unisys compute; Format: Newspaper; Larry Storer, Ed.-in-Chief Gary Pittman, Pblshr Joe Rossi, Ed. Circ.: 15,000, Freq: Monthly, Price/yr-$:92/145

UNIX & Open Systems
Publishing Co: Datapro Information Services Group, 600 Delran Pkwy., Delran, NJ 08705-9904, USA; 609/764-0100, Fax: 609/764-2811, Co Email: datapro@mhh.com; Web URL: datapro.com; Focus: Information on open systems and Unix market; Format: CD-ROM; Freq: Monthly

Unix Business Software Directory
Publishing Co: CBM Books, 1300 Virginia Drive, #400, Ft. Washington, PA 19034, USA; 215/643-8000, Fax: 215/643-8099, Focus: Listing of Unix software; Format: Directory; Karen Provencher, Pblshr Freq: Annual, Price/yr-$:150

UNIX Companion
Publishing Co: WEKA Publishing, 1077

Bridgeport Ave, Shelton, CT 06484, USA; Fax: 203/944-3663, Focus: UNIX administrator's reference; Format: Loose-leaf; Paul Caron, Prdts Dir Freq: 4/Year, Price/yr-$:89

Unix Developer
Publishing Co: SIGS Publications Group, 71 W. 23rd Street, 3rd Floor, New York, NY 10010, USA; 212/242-7447, Fax: 212/242-7574, Co Email: 71700.3570@compuserve.com; Web URL: sigs.com; Focus: Information for Unix developers; Format: Magazine; Richard P. Friedman, Pblshr Charles Bowman, Ed. Freq: 10/Year, Price/yr-$:Free

UNIX Review
Publishing Co: Miller Freeman Inc., 411 Borel Ave, #100, San Mateo, CA 94402-3522, USA; 415/358-9500, Fax: 415/358-9739, Web URL: mfi.com/unixrev; Focus: Technical information about UNIX for software developers, VARs, OEMs and SIs; Format: Magazine; Andrew Binstock, Ed.-in-Chief Email: kbrennan@mfi.com; Katie A. Brennan, Pblshr Email: kbrennan@mfi.com; Robyn E. Frendberg, Mgng Ed. Circ.: 75,000, Freq: 13/Year, Price/yr-$:Free/55

UNIX System Price Performance Guide
Publishing Co: AIM Technology, 4699 Old Ironside Drive, #400, Santa Clara, CA 95054, USA; 408/748-8649, Fax: 408/748-0161, Co Email: benchinfo@aim.com; Web URL: aim.com; Focus: Performance ratings of Unix computers; Format: Factbook; Bob Cousins, VP Tech Email: rec@aim.com; Jim Geers, Pblshr Tammy Bauer, Mgr End User Scvs Email: tammy@aim.com; Circ.: 20,000, Freq: 4/Year, Price/yr-$:30

Update: The Executive's Purchasing Advisor
Publishing Co: Buyers Laboratory Inc., 20 Railroad Ave, Hackensack, NJ 07601, USA; 201/488-0404, Fax: 201/488-0461, Focus: Information and purchasing advice for office products; Format: Newsletter; Anthony Polifrone, Pres Marion Davidowitz, VP Burt Meerow, Pblr Freq: Monthly, Price/yr-$:115

Upside
Publishing Co: Upside Publishing Co., The, 2015 Pioneer Court, San Mateo, CA 94403-1736, USA; 415/377-0950, Fax: 415/377-1962, Co Email: editorial@upside.com; Web URL: upside.com; Focus: Analysis and profiles of companies and people in the computer and high-tech industries; Format: Magazine; Eric Nee, Ed-in-Chief Email: enee@upside.com; Susan Scott, Pblshr Email: sscott@upside.com; Richard Brandt, Exec Ed. Email: rbrandt@upside.com; Circ.: 70,000, Freq: Monthly, Price/yr-$:48

USA Export Computer Directory
Publishing Co: USA Export Publications

Inc., PO Box 161137, Miami, FL 33116-1137, USA; 305/253-1440, Fax: 305/256-9525, Focus: Listing of US computer companies exporting to Latin America; Format: Directory; Liliana C. Romero, Mgng Ed. Oreste B. Giugliano, Ed.-in-Chief Circ.: 40,000, Freq: Annual, Price/yr-$:Free

Used Copier Report
Publishing Co: Dataquest Inc., 26254 Golden Valley Road, Bldg. 401, Santa Clarita, CA 95351, USA; 805/298-3261, Fax: 805/298-4388, Co Email: mmakers@netcom.com; Web URL: netcom.com~mmakers; Focus: Information on used copiers; Format: Newsletter; Freq: 12/Year, Price/yr-$:199

Value Added Resellers
Publishing Co: CSG Information Services, 3922 Coconut Palm Drive, Tampa, FL 33619-8321, USA; 813/664-6800, Fax: 813/664-6888, Focus: Directory of over 4,000 VARs; Format: Directory; Mike Jarvis, Ed. Freq: Annual, Price/yr-$:275/795

Valuing Software Businesses
Publishing Co: Digital Information Group, PO Box 110235, Stamford, CT 06911-0235, USA; 203/840-0942, Fax: 203/977-8310, Co Email: 75120.2616@compuserve.com; Focus: Analysis and statistics on valuing software companies; Format: Factbook; Jeff Silverstein, Ed. & Pblr Price/yr-$:395

VARBUSINESS
Publishing Co: CMP Publications Inc., 600 Community Drive, Manhasset, NY 11030, USA; 516/562-5000, Fax: 516/562-7098, Web URL: techweb.cmp.com/var; Focus: News and information for Value-Added Resellers (VARs); Format: Magazine; Richard March, Ed. Jeff Sundheim, Pblshr Tom Farre, Exec Ed. Circ.: 60,000, Freq: Monthly, Price/yr-$:Free/89

Vector Directory: Messaging Systems
Publishing Co: Vector Directory Services Inc., 34 Clarke Street, Lexington, MA 02173, USA; 617/862-7607, Fax: 617/862-6887, Co Email: 4401232@mci-mail.com; Focus: Listing of company e-mail information; Format: Directory; William A. Lucas, Pres Email: 4401232@mci-mail.com; Barbara Kaecheley, Dir Print Prod Freq: 2/Year, Price/yr-$:229

Venture Capital Directory, Vankirk's
Publishing Co: Vankirk Business Information, 2800 Shirlington Road, #904, Arlington, VA 22206, USA; 703/379-9200, Fax: 703/379-8017, Focus: Listing of over 1,800 venture capital firms; Format: Directory; Freq: Annual, Price/yr-$:325/490

Venture Capital Journal
Publishing Co: Venture Economics Inc., 40 W. 57th Street, 11th Floor, New York, NY 10019, USA; 212/765-5311, Fax: 212/765-6123, Focus: News and analysis of the venture capital industry; Format: Newsletter; Freq: Monthly, Price/yr-$:725

Venture Capital Sources, Pratt's Guide to
Publishing Co: Venture Economics Inc., 40 W. 57th Street, 11th Floor, New York, NY 10019, USA; 212/765-5311, Fax: 212/956-0112, Focus: Listing of over 950 venture capital sources; Format: Directory; Freq: Annual, Price/yr-$:249

Verbum
Publishing Co: Verbum Inc., 123 Townsend, #645, San Francisco, CA 94107, USA; 415/777-9901, Fax: 415/777-9929, Co Email: info@verbum.com; Web URL: verbum.com; Focus: PC art and design including multimedia, DTP and digital art; Format: Web site

Video Systems
Publishing Co: Intertec Publishing Corp., 9800 Metcalfe Ave, Overland Park, KS 66212-2215, USA; 913/341-1300, Fax: 913/967-1904, Focus: News and information about desktop video, multi-media and video products; Format: Magazine; Jerry Whitaker, Ed.-in-Chief Email: jwhitaker@msn.com; Dennis Triola, Pblshr Larry Henchey, Ed. Email: 102556.1703@compuserve.com; Circ.: 40,000, Freq: Monthly, Price/yr-$:Free/50

Video Technology News
Publishing Co: Phillips Business Information Inc., 1201 Seven Locks Road, #300, Potomac, MD 20854-1110, USA; 301/340-1520, Fax: 301/424-4297, Co Email: pbi@phillips.com; Web URL: phillips.com; Focus: Video technology news and trends; Format: Newsletter; Freq: 25/Year, Price/yr-$:697

Video Toaster User
Publishing Co: Miller Freeman Inc., 600 Harrison Street, San Francisco, CA 94107-1391, USA; 415/905-2200, Fax: 415/905-2234

Video, Multimedia & Audio-Visual Products, Dir. of
Publishing Co: International Communications Industries Assoc., 11242 Wapless Mill Road, Fairfax, VA 22030, USA; 703/273-7200, Fax: 703/278-8082, Focus: Listing of 2,500 video, computer and AV products; Format: Directory; Freq: Annual, Price/yr-$:80/95

Virtual Reality Sourcebook
Publishing Co: SophisTech Research, 347 Orizaba Ave, Long Beach, CA 90814, USA; 310/434-4436, Fax: 310/434-4730, Co Email: virtual8Qaol.com; Web URL: users.aol.com/virtual8/vrs; Focus: Directory of virtual reality products, companies and services; Format: Book/diskette; Gregory P. Panos, Ed. & Pblr Richard Cray, VP Creative Dev Circ.: 10,000, Freq: Annual, Price/yr-$:60

Virtual Reality World
Publishing Co: Mecklermedia, 20 Ketchum Street, Westport, CT 06880-9760, USA; 203/226-6967, Fax: 203/454-5840, Co

Email: info@mecklermedia.com; Focus: Virtual reality development and use; Format: Magazine; Alan M. Meckler, Pblshr Sandra Kay Helsel, Ed.-in-Chief Jim Ivers, Assoc Ed. Circ.: 15,200, Freq: 6/Year, Price/yr-$:29

Virtual Work Groups
Publishing Co: BCR Enterprises Inc., 950 York Road, #203, Hinsdale, IL 60521, USA; 630/986-1432, Fax: 630/323-5324, Co Email: info@bcr.com; Web URL: bcr.com; Focus: Virtual offices and collaborative computing; Format: Magazine; David Coleman, Ed. Jerry A. Goldstone, Pblshr Freq: 6/Year, Price/yr-$:Free

Visual Basic Developer
Publishing Co: Pinnacle Publishing Inc., 18000 72nd Ave S. #217, Kent, WA 98032, USA; 206/251-1900, Fax: 206/251-5057, Web URL: pinpub.com; Focus: Information and utilities for Visual Basic developers; Format: Newsletter; Freq: Monthly

Visual Basic Programmer's Journal
Publishing Co: Fawcette Technical Publications, 209 Hamilton Ave, Palo Alto, CA 94301-2530, USA; 415/833-7100, Fax: 415/853-0230, Co Email: vbpj@compuserve.com; Web URL: windx.com; Focus: Information for Visual Basic programmers; Format: Magazine; James E. Fawcette, Ed. & Pblr Ellen Gould, Assoc Pblr Christine McGeever, Mngg Ed. Circ.: 100,000, Freq: 12/Year, Price/yr-$:35

Visual C++ Developer
Publishing Co: Pinnacle Publishing Inc., 18000 72nd Ave S. #217, Kent, WA 98032, USA; 206/251-1900, Fax: 206/251-5057, Web URL: pinpub.com; Focus: Information and utilities for Visual C++ developers; Format: Newsletter; Freq: Monthly

Visual Objects Advisor
Publishing Co: Advisor Publications Inc., 4010 Morena Blvd, San Diego, CA 92117, USA; 619/483-6400, Fax: 619/483-9851, Co Email: 71154.3123@compuserve.com; Focus: News and information for CA-Visual Objects users; Format: Magazine; William T. Ota, Pblr/Pres/CEO Email: 71154.3123@compuserve.com; John L. Hawkins, Ed-in-Chief & EVP Jeanne Banfield, VP Circ.: 25,000, Freq: 6/Year, Price/yr-$:39.00

VM Update
Publishing Co: Xephon, 1301 W. Hwy 407, #201-450, Lewisville, TX 75067, USA; 817/455-7050, Fax: 817/455-2492, Focus: Tools and techniques for enhancing IBM's VM software; Format: Magazine; Freq: Monthly, Price/yr-$:235

Voice Technology & Service News
Publishing Co: Phillips Business Information Inc., 1201 Seven Locks Road, #300, Potomac, MD 20854-1110, USA; 301/340-1520, Fax: 301/424-4297, Co Email: pbi@phillips.com; Web URL: phil-

lips.com; Focus: News, analysis and trends in the voice communications market; Format: Newsletter; Freq: 25/Year, Price/yr-$:597

VSAM Update
Publishing Co: Xephon, 1301 W. Hwy 407, #201-450, Lewisville, TX 75067, USA; 817/455-7050, Fax: 817/455-2492, Focus: News, tips and software to improve IBM's VSAM; Format: Magazine; Freq: 4/Year, Price/yr-$:160

VSE Update
Publishing Co: Xephon, 1301 W. Hwy 407, #201-450, Lewisville, TX 75067, USA; 817/455-7050, Fax: 817/455-2492, Focus: Tips and techniques to improve IBM's VSE; Format: Magazine; Freq: 4/Year, Price/yr-$:135

Wall Street & Technology
Publishing Co: Miller Freeman Inc., 1515 Broadway, 32rd Floor, New York, NY 10036, USA; 212/869-1300, Fax: 212/302/6273, Focus: Information on using computer in the financial industry; Format: Magazine; Circ.: 31,000, Freq: 13/Year, Price/yr-$:65

Wang in the News
Publishing Co: Publications & Communications Inc., 12416 Hymeadow Drive, Austin, TX 78750-1896, USA; 512/250-9023, Fax: 512/331-3900, Co Email: @pcinews.com; Web URL: pcinews.com/pci; Focus: Information, product news and reviews for WANG computer users; Format: Magazine; Larry Storer, Ed. Dir Steven Smith, Ed. Circ.: 12,000, Freq: Monthly, Price/yr-$:45/75

Washington Technology
Publishing Co: TechNews Inc., 8500 Leesburg Pike, #7500, Vienna, VA 22182-2412, USA; 703/848-2800, Fax: 703/848-2353, Co Email: technews@access.digex.net; Web URL: wtonline.com/wtonline; Focus: Business news about high technology; Format: Newspaper; Tim Karney, Pblshr Esther T. Smith, Ed.-at-Large Email: esmith@technews.com; Jack Sweeney, Ed. Email: jsweeney@technews.com; Circ.: 30,000, Freq: 26/Year, Price/yr-$:Free/49

Washington Telecom News
Publishing Co: Phillips Business Information Inc., 1201 Seven Locks Road, #300, Potomac, MD 20854-1110, USA; 301/340-1520, Fax: 301/309-3847, Co Email: pbi@phillips.com; Web URL: phillips.com; Focus: News and information on communications technology; Format: Magazine; Freq: Monthly, Price/yr-$:697

Wayzata World Factbook
Publishing Co: Wayzata Technology Inc., 21 NE 4th Street, Grand Rapids, MN 55744-2719, USA; 218/326-0597, Fax: 218/326-0598, Co Email: wayzatatec@aol.com; Web URL: wayzatatech.com; Focus: CD-ROM with information and maps on the countries of the

world; Format: CD-ROM; Dennis Gibbons, Dir Sls & Mktng Email: dennygibbons@wayzatatech.; Freq: Annual, Price/yr-$:25

Web Apps Magazine
Publishing Co: SIGS Publications Group, 71 W. 23rd Street, 3rd Floor, New York, NY 10010, USA; 212/242-7447, Fax: 212/242-7574, Co Email: 71700.3570@compuserve.com; Web URL: sigs.com; Focus: Information for web users; Format: Magazine; Richard P. Friedman, Pblshr Daniel W. Connolly, Ed. Freq: 6/Year, Price/yr-$:60

Web Developer
Publishing Co: Mecklermedia, 20 Ketchum Street, Westport, CT 06880-9760, USA; 203/226-6967, Fax: 203/454-5840, Co Email: info@mecklermedia.com; Web URL: mecklerweb.com; Focus: Information on Web development, software, hardware and networking; Format: Magazine; Paul L. Bonington, Pblshr Email: bonington@iw.com; David Fiedler, Ed-in-Chief Email: david@webdeveloper.com; Tony Jaros, Assoc Mngg Ed. Email: tjaros@webdeveloper.com; Freq: 6/Year, Price/yr-$:29

Web Magazine
Publishing Co: International Data Group, 501 Second Street, #600, San Francisco, CA 94107, USA; 415/267-4586, Focus: Information for web users; Format: Magazine

Web Techniques
Publishing Co: Miller Freeman Inc., 600 Harrison Street, San Francisco, CA 94107-1391, USA; 415/905-2200, Fax: 415/905-2234, Focus: Information for web developers

Web Week
Publishing Co: Mecklermedia, 20 Ketchum Street, Westport, CT 06880-9760, USA; 203/226-6967, Fax: 203/454-5840, Co Email: info@mecklermedia.com; Web URL: webweek.com; Focus: News, analysis and information on Internet's World-Wide Web; Format: Tabloid; Paul Bonington, Pblshr Email: bonington@iw.com; Robert Hertzberg, Ed.-in-Chief Email: rob@webweek.com; Tony Silber, Mngg Ed. Email: tsilber@webweek.com; Circ.: 25,000, Freq: Monthly, Price/yr-$:Free/129

WebMaster
Publishing Co: International Data Group, 492 Old Connecticut Path, PO Box 9208, Framingham, MA 01701-9208, USA; 508/872-0080, Fax: 508/879-7784, Web URL: web.master.com; Focus: Business on the Internet; Format: Magazine; Lew McCreary, Ed-in-Chief, Pblshr Email: mccreary@cio.com; Leigh Buchanan, Exec Ed. Joseph L. Levy, Grp Pblshr Freq: Bimonthly, Price/yr-$:30

WebServer Magazine
Publishing Co: Computer Publishing

Group Inc., 320 Washington Street, Brookline, MA 02146-3202, USA; 617/739-7001, Fax: 617/739-7003, Co Email: @cpg.com; Web URL: cpg.com; Focus: Technical information for Web server management; Format: Magazine; S. Henry Sacks, Pblshr Email: shs@cpg.com; Douglas Pryor, Ed-in-Chief Email: dpryor@cpg.com; Lisa Guisbond, Mgng Ed. Email: lisa@cpg.com; Circ.: 60,000, Freq: 6/Year, Price/yr-$:60

WEBsmith

Publishing Co: SSC, PO Box 55549, Seattle, WA 98155-0549, USA; 206/782-7733, Fax: 206/782-7191, Co Email: websmith@ssc.com; Web URL: ssc.com/websmith; Focus: The how-to magazine of the web; Format: Magazine; Belinda Frazier, Pblshr Email: bbf@ssc.com; Jonathan D. Grass, Ed. Email: jong@ssc.com; Circ.: 20,000, Freq: Monthly, Price/yr-$:24

What's on the Internet

Publishing Co: Peachpit Press, 2414 Sixth Street, Berkeley, CA 94710, USA; 510/548-4393, Fax: 510/548-5991, Co Email: @peachpit.com; Web URL: peachpit.com; Focus: Guide to USENET Newsgroups; Format: Factbook; Eric Gagnon, Author Freq: Semi-Annual, Price/yr-$:40

Wide Area Communications

Publishing Co: Datapro Information Services Group, 600 Delran Pkwy., Delran, NJ 08705-9904, USA; 609/764-0100, Fax: 609/764-2811, Co Email: datapro@mhh.com; Web URL: datapro.com; Focus: Information on emerging telecom and networking products and technologies; Format: CD-ROM; Freq: Monthly

Windows 95 Professional

Publishing Co: Cobb Group, The, 9420 Bunsen Pkwy. #300, Louisville, KY 40220, USA; 502/491-1900, Fax: 502/491-8050, Co Email: cobb@aol.com; Web URL: cobb.com; Focus: Tips and news for Windows 95 Professional users; Format: Newsletter; Price/yr-$:99

Windows Developer's Journal

Publishing Co: Miller Freeman Inc., 1601 W. 23rd Street, #200, Lawrence, KS 66046, USA; 913/841-1631, Fax: 913/841-2624, Co Email: wdsub@rdpub.com; Focus: Information for advanced Windows programmers; Format: Magazine; Ron Burk, Ed. Peter Westerman, Pblshr Circ.: 20,000, Freq: Monthly, Price/yr-$:34.99

Windows Magazine

Publishing Co: CMP Publications Inc., 1 Jericho Plaza, Jericho, NY 11753, USA; 516/733-8300, Fax: 516/733-8390, Co Email: winmag@aol.com; Web URL: winmag.com; Focus: News and reviews about Windows products; Format: Magazine; Fred Langa, Ed. Dir Mark J. Holdreith, Pblshr Mike Elgan, Ed. Circ.: 450,000, Freq: 14/Year, Price/yr-$:25

Windows NT

Publishing Co: Duke Communications Int'l., PO Box 3438, Loveland, CO 80539-9977, USA; 303/663-4700, Fax: 303/667-2321, Co Email: winntmag@duke.com; Web URL: winntmag.com; Focus: Information for users of Windows NT; Format: Magazine; Mark Smith, Ed. Dir Email: mark@winntmag.com; Bart Taylor, Associate Pblshr Jane Morrill, Mgng Ed. Circ.: 50,000, Freq: Monthly, Price/yr-$:40

Windows Report, The

Publishing Co: Cobb Group, The, 9420 Bunsen Pkwy. #300, Louisville, KY 40220, USA; 502/491-1900, Fax: 502/491-8050, Co Email: cobb@aol.com; Web URL: cobb.com; Focus: Information for Microsoft Windows users; Format: Newsletter; Jonathan Ordish, Ed. Freq: 24/Year, Price/yr-$:149

Windows Software Connection

Publishing Co: Cobb Group, The, 9420 Bunsen Pkwy. #300, Louisville, KY 40220, USA; 502/491-1900, Fax: 502/491-8050, Co Email: cobb@aol.com; Web URL: cobb.com; Format: Newsletter; Price/yr-$:59

Windows Sources

Publishing Co: Ziff-Davis Publishing Co., One Park Ave, New York, NY 10016, USA; 212/503-4147, Fax: 212/503-4199, Web URL: wsources.com; Focus: Information on Windows products; Format: Magazine; Peter C. Weedfald, Pblshr Jim Louderback, Ed.-in-Chief Email: jim_louderback@zd.com; Diane D'Angelo, Mgng Ed. Email: diane_d'angelo@zd.com; Circ.: 320,000, Freq: Monthly, Price/yr-$:28

Windows Tech Journal

Publishing Co: Oakley Publishing, PO Box 70167, Eugene, OR 97401, USA; 541/747-0800, Fax: 541/746-0071, Focus: Programming techniques for Windows developers; Format: Magazine; J.D. Hildebrand, Ed. Bobbi Sinyard, Pblshr Circ.: 25,000, Freq: Monthly, Price/yr-$:30

Windows Watcher

Publishing Co: CompuTh!nk, Inc., 15127 NE 24th Street, #344, Redmond, WA 98052-5530, USA; 206/881-7354, Fax: 206/883-1452, Focus: News and information on the Windows market; Format: Newsletter; Jesse Berst, Founding Ed. Email: jessee@jesseeberst.com; Dwight B. Davis, Ed. Dir Email: ddavis@sbexpos.com; Robbin Young, Mgng Dir Email: ryoung@sbexpos.com; Freq: Monthly, Price/yr-$:495

Wired Magazine

Publishing Co: Wired USA Ltd., 544 Second Street, San Francisco, CA 94107-1427, USA; 415/904-0660, Fax: 415/904-0669, Co Email: subscription@wired.com; Web URL: hotwired.com; Focus: Trends and opinions on the digital world of computer, telecom and entertainment; Format: Magazine; Louis Rosetto, Ed. & Pblr Kevin

Kelly, Exec Ed. John Battelle, Mgng Ed. Freq: Monthly, Price/yr-$:40

Wireless

Publishing Co: Wireless Publishing Co., 3 Wing Drive, #240, Cedar Knolls, NJ 07927-1000, USA; 201/285-1500, Fax: 201/285-1519, Web URL: wireless-mag.com; Focus: Wireless technology and products; Format: Magazine; Victor Schnee, Pblshr Maxine Carter-Lome, Ed. Dir Freq: 11/Year, Price/yr-$:Free/55

Wireless Business & Finance

Publishing Co: Phillips Business Information Inc., 1201 Seven Locks Road, #300, Potomac, MD 20854-1110, USA; 301/340-1520, Fax: 301/340-0542, Co Email: pbi@phillips.com; Web URL: phillips.com; Focus: News, analysis and trends in the wireless business; Format: Newsletter; Freq: 25/Year, Price/yr-$:697

Wireless Cellular Telecommunications

Publishing Co: Information Gatekeepers Inc., 214 Harvard Ave, Boston, MA 02134, USA; 617/232-3111, Fax: 617/734-8562, Co Email: igiboston@aol.com; Focus: News and technology on cellular applications; Format: Newsletter; Paul Polishuk, Ed. & Pblr Email: igiboston@aol.com; Freq: Monthly, Price/yr-$:545/595

Wireless Communications

Publishing Co: Faulkner Information Services, 7905 Browning Road, Pennsauken, NJ 08109-4319, USA; 609/662-2070, Fax: 609/662-0905, Co Email: faulkner@faulkner.com; Web URL: faulkner.com; Focus: Mobile computing, paging, PCS and cellular radio; Format: Loose-leaf; Martin Murphy, Pblshr Freq: Monthly, Price/yr-$:799

Wireless Data News

Publishing Co: Phillips Business Information Inc., 1201 Seven Locks Road, #300, Potomac, MD 20854-1110, USA; 301/340-1520, Fax: 301/424-4297, Co Email: pbi@phillips.com; Web URL: phillips.com; Focus: Wireless data news, analysis, applications and trends; Format: Newsletter; Freq: 25/Year, Price/yr-$:597

Wireless Messaging Report

Publishing Co: BRP Publications Inc., 1333 H Street NW #1100. W. Tower, Washington, DC 20005, USA; 202/842-3022, Fax: 202/842-1875, Co Email: brp@access.digex.net; Focus: Messaging, data and information services in wireless market; Format: Newsletter; Freq: biweekly, Price/yr-$:449

Wireless PCS

Publishing Co: Information Gatekeepers Inc., 214 Harvard Ave, Boston, MA 02134, USA; 617/232-3111, Fax: 617/734-8562, Co Email: igiboston@aol.com; Focus: Personal Communications services technology, markets and applications; Format: Newsletter; Paul Polishuk, Ed. & Pblr Email: igi-

boston@aol.com; Freq: Monthly, Price/
yr-$:545/595

**Wireless Satellite & Broadcasting
Telecommunications**
Publishing Co: Information Gatekeepers
Inc., 214 Harvard Ave, Boston, MA 02134,
USA; 617/232-3111, Fax: 617/734-8562,
Co Email: igiboston@aol.com; Focus:
Applications, technology and markets for
broadcasting and satellites; Format: News-
letter; Paul Polishuk, Ed. & Pblr Email: igi-
boston@aol.com; Freq: Monthly, Price/
yr-$:545/595

**Wireless Spectrum Management
Telecommunications**
Publishing Co: Information Gatekeepers
Inc., 214 Harvard Ave, Boston, MA 02134,
USA; 617/232-3111, Fax: 617/734-8562,
Co Email: igiboston@aol.com; Focus:
Telecom news, technology, markets and
applications; Format: Newsletter; Paul Pol-
ishuk, Ed. & Pblr Email: igibos-
ton@aol.com; Freq: Monthly, Price/yr-
$:545/595

Wireless Telecommunications
Publishing Co: Information Gatekeepers
Inc., 214 Harvard Ave, Boston, MA 02134,
USA; 617/232-3111, Fax: 617/734-8562,
Co Email: igiboston@aol.com; Focus:
Wireless applications such as LANs, build-
ings and point-of-sale technology; Format:
Newsletter; Paul Polishuk, Ed. & Pblr
Email: igiboston@aol.com; Freq: Monthly,
Price/yr-$:545/595

Women in Computing
Publishing Co: McGraw-Hill Inc., 1900
O'Farrell Street, #200, San Mateo, CA
94403-1311, USA; 415/513-6800, Fax:
415/513-6985, Co Email: @wcmh.com;
Focus: Information for women in the computer industry; Format: Newsletter; Michela O'Connor Abrams, Pblshr Email:
michela-abrams@wcmh.com; Daniel Diamond, Exec Ed. Rikki Kirzner, Tech Ed.
Freq: Monthly, Price/yr-$:50

WordPerfect for Windows Magazine
Publishing Co: Ivy International Communications Inc., 270 W Center Street, Orem,
UT 84057, USA; 801/226-5555, Fax:
801/226-8804, Co Email:
wpwinmag@wpmag.com; Web URL:
wpmag.com; Focus: News, tips, macros
and reviews for WordPerfect for Windows
users; Format: Magazine; Jeff Hadfield, Ed.
Dir Email: hadfield@wpmag.com; Scott
Larsen, Ed.-in-Chief Email: scot-
tla@wpmag.com; Jeff Ford, Tech Ed.
Circ.: 200,000, Freq: Monthly, Price/yr-
$:24

WordPerfect Magazine
Publishing Co: Ivy International Communi-
cations Inc., 270 W Center Street, Orem,
UT 84057, USA; 801/226-5555, Fax:
801/226-8804, Co Email: @wpmag.com;
Focus: News, tips, macros and reviews for
WordPerfect users; Format: Magazine; Jeff
Hadfield, Ed. Dir Email: had-

field@wpmag.com; Lisa Bearnson, Ed-in-
Chief Email: lisabe@wpmag.com; Roger
Gagon, Tech Ed. Email: rog-
erg@wpmag.com; Circ.: 180,000, Freq:
Monthly, Price/yr-$:24

WordPerfectionist, The
Publishing Co: Cobb Group, The, 9420
Bunsen Pkwy. #300, Louisville, KY
40220, USA; 502/491-1900, Fax: 502/
491-8050, Co Email: cobb@aol.com; Web
URL: cobb.com; Focus: News, tips and
techniques for WordPerfect users; Format:
Newsletter; Greg Geis, Ed. Freq: Monthly,
Price/yr-$:69

Workbench Focus
Publishing Co: HCS Inc., 18004 SE Marie
Street, Portland, OR 97236-1338, USA;
503/661-3421, Fax: 503/661-2477,
Focus: News and information for MicroFo-
cus software users; Format: Newsletter;
Robin Hobuss, Ed. Freq: 4/Year, Price/yr-
$:40

**Workflow: The New Information
Systems Infrastructures**
Publishing Co: Delphi Consulting Group,
100 City Hall Plaza, Boston, MA 02108-
2106, USA; 617/247-1025, Fax: 617/247-
4957, Focus: Development, evaluation &
implementation of workflow solutions;
Format: Loose-leaf; Thomas M. Koulopoulos, Pblshr Freq: Monthly, Price/yr-
$:1,200

Workgroup Computing Report
Publishing Co: Patricia Seybold Group, 148
State Street, 7th Floor, Boston, MA 02109-
9990, USA; 617/742-5200, Fax: 617/742-
1028, Web URL: psgroup.com; Format:
Newsletter; Patricia B. Seybold, Pblshr
Freq: Monthly, Price/yr-$:385

Workgroup Computing Series
Publishing Co: Datapro Information Services Group, 600 Delran Pkwy., Delran,
NJ 08705-9904, USA; 609/764-0100, Fax:
609/764-2811, Co Email:
datapro@mhh.com; Web URL:
datapro.com; Focus: 10-volume loose-leaf
information on workgroup/distributed systems; Format: CD-ROM; Freq: Monthly

Workspace for Lotus Notes
Publishing Co: Cobb Group, The, 9420
Bunsen Pkwy. #300, Louisville, KY
40220, USA; 502/491-1900, Fax: 502/
491-8050, Co Email: cobb@aol.com; Web
URL: cobb.com; Focus: Tips and information for Lotus Notes users; Format: Newsletter; David Gewirtz, Ed. Freq: Monthly,
Price/yr-$:149

Workstation Buyer's Guide
Publishing Co: CAD/CAM Publishing Inc.,
1010 Turquoise Street, #320, San Diego,
CA 92109-1268, USA; 619/488-0533,
Fax: 619/488-6052, Focus: Criteria for
comparison shopping workstations; Format: Book; Michael Abrams, Ed. Price/yr-
$:14.95

Workstations & Servers
Publishing Co: Datapro Information Ser-

vices Group, 600 Delran Pkwy., Delran,
NJ 08705-9904, USA; 609/764-0100, Fax:
609/764-2811, Co Email:
datapro@mhh.com; Web URL:
datapro.com; Focus: Information on workstations and server products; Format: CD-
ROM; Freq: Monthly

World Wide Web Journal
Publishing Co: O'Reilly & Associates Inc.,
103 Morris Street, #A, Sebastopol, CA
95472, USA; 707/829-0515, Fax: 707/
829-0104, Web URL: ora.com; Focus:
Web topics like legal issues and security;
Format: Magazine; Freq: 4/Year

X Journal, The
Publishing Co: SIGS Publications Group,
71 W. 23rd Street, 3rd Floor, New York,
NY 10010, USA; 212/242-7447, Fax:
212/242-7574, Co Email:
71700.3570@compuserve.com; Web
URL: sigs.com; Focus: Latest thinking,
technology and news on X windows systems; Format: Magazine; Charles F. Bowman, Ed-in-Chief Email: cfb@panix.com;
Elizabeth A. Upp, Mngg Ed. Circ.: 15,000,
Freq: 7/Year, Price/yr-$:39

X Resource, The
Publishing Co: O'Reilly & Associates Inc.,
103 Morris Street, #A, Sebastopol, CA
95472, USA; 707/829-0515, Fax: 707/
829-0104, Co Email: info@ora.com; Web
URL: ora.com; Focus: Technical information on X Window systems; Format: Magazine; Freq: 4 or 5/Year, Price/yr-$:65 or
90

X-Ray Magazine
Publishing Co: X.ALT Publishing, 530
Hampshire Street, #401, San Francisco,
CA 94110, USA; 415/861-9258, Fax:
415/864-7594, Focus: Publishing, work-
group & multimedia technology for Quark
users; Format: Magazine; Glenn Olsen,
Pblshr Email: xraypub@eworld.com; John
Cruise, Mngg Ed. Email:
xrayedit@eworld.com; Freq: 6/Year,
Price/yr-$:Free

**Xplorer, The Journal of Electronic
Document Systems**
Publishing Co: Xplor Int'l., 24238 Haw-
thorne Blvd., Torrance, CA 90505-6505,
USA; 310/373-3633, Fax: 310/375-4240,
Co Email: info@xplor.org; Web URL:
xplor.org; Focus: Electronic Document
Systems Association; Format: Magazine;
Jay Tomb, Ed.-in-Chief Keith T. Davidson,
Pblshr Circ.: 5,000, Freq: Semi-annual,
Price/yr-$:25/50

Yahoo! Internet Life
Publishing Co: Ziff-Davis Publishing Co.,
One Park Ave, New York, NY 10016,
USA; 212/503-3835, Web URL: yil.com;
Focus: Online guide to the Internet; For-
mat: Online; Barry Golson, Ed-in-Chief
Email: bgolson@zd.com; Elisabeth Holzer,
Assoc Ed. Email: eholzer@zd.com; Freq:
Daily, Price/yr-$:Free/20

Yearbook of World Electronics Data:

America, Japan, Asia Pacific
Publishing Co: Business Research Group,
275 Washington Street, Newton, MA
02158-1630, USA; 617/630-3900, Fax:
617/558-4585, Focus: Market data, forecasts and production statistics on computers
and electronics; Format: Factbook; Sarah E.
Norton, Dir Mktng Email:
norton@brg.cahners.com; Freq: Annual,
Price/yr-$:1,360

**Yearbook of World Electronics Data:
East Europe**
Publishing Co: Business Research Group,
275 Washington Street, Newton, MA
02158-1630, USA; 617/630-3900, Fax:
617/558-4585, Focus: Market data, forecasts and production statistics on computers
and electronics; Format: Factbook; Sarah E.
Norton, Dir Mktng Email:
norton@brg.cahners.com; Freq: 0.5/
year, Price/yr-$:865

**Yearbook of World Electronics Data:
Emerging Countries**
Publishing Co: Business Research Group,

275 Washington Street, Newton, MA
02158-1630, USA; 617/630-3900, Fax:
617/558-4585, Focus: Market data, forecasts and production statistics on computers
and electronics; Format: Factbook; Sarah E.
Norton, Dir Mktng Email:
norton@brg.cahners.com; Freq: 0.5/
year, Price/yr-$:790

**Yearbook of World Electronics Data:
West Europe**
Publishing Co: Business Research Group,
275 Washington Street, Newton, MA
02158-1630, USA; 617/630-3900, Fax:
617/558-4585, Focus: Market data, forecasts and production statistics on computers
and electronics; Format: Factbook; Sarah E.
Norton, Dir Mktng Email:
norton@brg.cahners.com; Freq: Annual,
Price/yr-$:910

**Yellowstone Desktop Publishing Let-
ter, The**
Publishing Co: Yellowstone Information
Services, 605 Brady Ave, Steubenville, OH
43952-1459, USA; 614/282-2797, Fax:

614/282-2798, Focus: Desktop publishing
information; Format: Newsletter; Roger C.
Thibault, Ed. & Pblr Circ.: 5,000, Freq: 6/
Year, Price/yr-$:50

Yellowstone Multimedia Letter, The
Publishing Co: Yellowstone Information
Services, 605 Brady Ave, Steubenville, OH
43952-1459, USA; 614/282-2797, Fax:
614/282-2798, Focus: Multimedia applica-
tions, products, news and trends; Format:
Newsletter; Roger C. Thibault, Ed. & Pblr
Circ.: 5,000, Freq: 6/Year, Price/yr-$:50

Yellowstone Windows Letter, The
Publishing Co: Yellowstone Information
Services, 605 Brady Ave, Steubenville, OH
43952-1459, USA; 614/282-2797, Fax:
614/282-2798, Focus: Windows applica-
tions, products, news and trends; Format:
Newsletter; Roger C. Thibault, Ed. & Pblr
Circ.: 2,000, Freq: 6/Year, Price/yr-$:50

Publishers Directory

A-R Editions Inc. 801 Deming Way, Madison WI 53717 USA; 608/836-9000, 800/736-0070 Fax: 608/831-8200, Focus: Computer music books, Ownership: PVT, Patrick Wall, Pres

A/E/C Systems International Inc. 415 Eagleview Blvd #106, Exton PA 19341 USA; 610/458-7070, 800/451-1196 Fax: 610/458-7171, Web URL: aecsystems.com, Focus: Computer tradeshows and publications, Prdts: A/E/C Systems, Ownership: PVT, Yr Founded: 1979, Empl: 100, David J. Caplin, VP & GM, Kimber McEntee, Mktng Coord

AAAI Press 445 Burgess Drive, Menlo Park CA 94025 USA; 415/328-3123, Fax: 415/321-4457, Co Email: press@aaai.org, Web URL: aaai.org, Focus: AI books, Ownership: PVT, Carol Hamilton, Exec Dir, Ken Ford, Ed.-in-Chief

Abacus 5370 52nd Street SE, Grand Rapids MI 49512 USA; 616/698-0330, Fax: 616/698-0325, Focus: Books on programming languages, Ownership: PVT, Yr Founded: 1978

ACM Press 1515 Broadway 17th Floor, New York NY 10036 USA; 212/626-0500, Fax: 212/944-1318, Focus: Technical computer magazines and books, Ownership: PVT, Karen A. Frenkel, Producer Spec Proj, Mark Mandelbaum, Dir Pubs

Adams New Media 260 Center Street, Holbrook MA 02343 USA; 617/767-8100, Fax: 617/767-0994, Co Email: @adamsonline, Focus: Publisher of electronic products, Ownership: Sub. Adams Media Corp., David B. Wood, Dir Publicity, Email: dwood@adamsonline.com

Adams/Hunter Publishing 2101 S Arlington Heights Road #150, Arlington Heights IL 60005 USA; 708/427-9512, Fax: 708/427-2006, Focus: Midrange systems magazine, Prdts: 3X/400 Systems Management, Ownership: PVT, Richard K. Felt, Pblr, Email: 71333.730@compuserve.com

Addison-Wesley Publishing Co. 1 Jacob Way, Reading MA 01867 USA; 617/944-3700, Fax: 617/944-7273, Co Email: @aw.com, Focus: Pblr of books and software, Ownership: PVT, Yr Founded: 1942, Empl: 1,000, Don Hammonds, Chmn & CEO, Warren Stone, Pres & COO

Advanstar Communications Inc. 7500 Old Oak Blvd, Cleveland OH 44130-3369 USA; 216/826-2859, Fax: 216/891-2733, Focus: Computer magazines and newsletters, Prdts: Automatic I.D. News, CADalyst, High Color, PC Graphics & Video, Ownership: PVT, Richard B. Swank, CEO, David W. Montgomery, VP & CFO, David Hakain, VP IS

Adventure Publishing PO Box 700686, Tulsa OK 74170-0686 USA; 800/726-7667 Fax: 918/621-2135, Focus: Computer newspapers, Ownership: PVT

Advisor Communications Int'l. Inc. 4010 Morena Blvd #200, San Diego CA 92117 USA; 619/483-6400, 800/336-6060 Fax: 619/483-9851, Focus: Software user magazines, Prdts: Clipper Advisor, Data Based Advisor, Ownership: PVT, William T. Ota, Pres & CEO, John L. Hawkins, EVP, Jeanne Banfield, VP

Andrew Allison 25420 Via Cicindela, Carmel CA 93923-8412 USA; Focus: Computer industry consulting, Prdts: Inside the New Computer Industry, Ownership: PVT, Andrew Allison, Pblr & Ed.

AP Professional 525 B Street #1900, San Diego CA 92101-4495 USA; 619/699-6735, 313-1277 Fax: 619/699-6380, Co Email: app@acad.com, Web URL: apnet.com, Focus: Multimedia, Internet, graphics, scientific computer, programming & networking books, Stock Symbol: HARG, Fiscal End: 10/95; Jeffrey M. Pepper, VP & Ed Dir, Email: publisher@igc.org; Kira Glass, Mktng & PR Mgr, Email: kglass@acad.com; Tom Ryan, Nat'l Acct Mgr, Email: tryan@acad.com; Josh Mills, Publicist, Email: jmills@acad.com

Applied Computer Research Inc. PO Box 82266, Phoenix AZ 85068-9280 USA; 602/995-5929, 800/234-2227 Fax: 602/995-0905, Focus: Information, publications & conferences on applications development & product marketing, Ownership: PVT, Yr Founded: 1971, Phillip Howard, Pres, Alice Howard, VP, Karen Hedden, Mktng Mgr

APT Data Services Inc. 928 Broadway #800, New York NY 10010 USA; 212/677-0409, Fax: 212/677-0463, Web URL: power.globalnews.com, Focus: Publishes computer newsletters, Ownership: PVT, Mark Satchell, Pblr

Argus Integrated Media 6300 S Syracuse Way #650, Englewood CO 80111 USA; 303/220-0600, Fax: 303/267-0234, Focus: Computer and high-tech magazines, Ownership: PVT, David Premo, VP, Grp Pblr

Asay Publishing Co. PO Box 670, Joplin MO 64802-0670 USA; 417/781-9317, 800/825-9633 Fax: 417/781-0427, Focus: Pblr of office and computer magazines, Ownership: PVT, Yr Founded: 1987, Empl: 47, Roger Asay, Pblr, Valerie Poindexter, VP AD Sales

Asian Sources MediaGroup 1210 S Bascom Ave #205, San Jose CA 95128-3535 USA; 408/295-4500, Fax: 408/295-0889, Focus: 30+ high-tech magazines in Asia, Europe and US, Prdts: Asian Sources,

Telecom Sources, Ownership: PVT, James Strachan, Pblr

Associated Business Publications Co. 317 Madison Ave #921, New York NY 10017 USA; 212/490-3999, Fax: 212/986-7864, Focus: High-tech magazines, Prdts: NASA Tech Briefs, Laser Tech Briefs, Technology 200X, Ownership: PVT, Ted Morawski, MIS Mgr

Association for Computing Machinery (ACM), 1515 Broadway 17th Floor, New York NY 10036-5701 USA; 212/869-7440, Fax: 212/944-1318, Co Email: @acm.org, Web URL: acm.org, Focus: Educational and scientific society for computer professionals, Ownership: Nonprofit, Yr Founded: 1947, Empl: 80,000, Joseph S. DeBlasi, Exec Dir, Lillian Israel, Dir Memb, Lisa Ernst, Dir Conf, John A. Osmundsen, Assoc Dir Pub Affairs

Auerbach Publications 31 St James Ave, Boston MA 02111 USA; 617/423-2020, 800/950-1216 Fax: 617/451-0908, Co Email: 73752.2270@compuserve.com, Web URL: wgl.com, Focus: Books, journals and reference services on MIS/DP management, Ownership: Sub Warren Gorman Lamont, Denise Laude, Mktng Mgr

BAM Media 3470 Buskirk Ave, Pleasant Hill CA 94523 USA; 510/934-3700, Fax: 510/934-3958, Web URL: microtimes.com, Focus: Regional computer magazine, Prdts: MicroTimes, BAM, The Rocket, Ownership: PVT, Yr Founded: 1984, Empl: 80, Dennis Erokan, Ed.-in-Chief, Chuck Stanley, Pblr

BCR Enterprises Inc. 950 York Road #203, Hinsdale IL 60521 USA; 630/986-1432, Fax: 630/323-5324, Co Email: info@bcr.com, Web URL: bcr.com, Focus: Voice and data communication magazines, Ownership: PVT, Jerry A. Goldstone, Pblr

Bedford Communications 150 Fifth Ave, New York NY 10011 USA; 212/807-8220, Fax: 212/807-8737, Focus: Computer product review magazines, Ownership: PVT, Edward D. Brown, Pblr

BradyGames 201 W 103rd Street, Indianapolis IN 46290-1097 USA; 317/581-3500, Fax: 317/581-3550, Web URL: mcp.com, Focus: Computer game books, Ownership: Sub Macmillan Computer Pub, Rick Ranucci, Pblr

BRP Publications Inc. 1333 H St NW #1100 W Tower, Washington DC 20005 USA; 202/842-3006, Fax: 202/842-3047, Co Email: brp@access.digex.net, Focus: E-mail, telecom and online information and publications, Ownership: PVT, Yr Founded: 1977, Andrew Jacobson, Pblr, Victoria Mason, Ed-in-Chief

BUS Publishing Group 1905 Swarthmore Ave, Lakewood NJ 08701-4541 USA; 908/363-0708, Fax: 908/367-2426, Focus: Office technology magazine, Prdts: Office World News, Ownership: PVT, Yr Founded: 1972, William P. Urban, Pblr & Pres, Kim Chandlee McCabe, Assoc Pblr

Business Research Group (BRG), 275 Washington Street, Newton MA 02158 USA; 617/630-3900, 800/828-6344 Fax: 617/558-4585, Co Email: info@brg.cahners.com, Focus: Information, publications & consulting in C/S, networking, wireless & telecom, Ownership: PVT, Yr Founded: 1988, Empl: 21, Sales($M): 1.5, William Ford Jr., VP & GM, Email: ford@brg.cahners.com; Kevin O'Neill, VP Research, Email: oneill@brg.cahners.com; Sarah E. Norton, Dir Mktng, Email: norton@brg.cahners.com; Rob Calcagni, Dir Sales, Email: calcagni@brg.cahners.com

CAD/CAM Publishing Inc. 1010 Turquoise St #320, San Diego CA 92109-1268 USA; 619/488-0533, Fax: 619/488-6052, Co Email: cadcirc@aol.com, Focus: CAD/CAM, CAE and rapid prototyping information and publications, Prdts: Computer Aided Design Report, Rapid Prototyping Report, Ownership: PVT, Yr Founded: 1981, Empl: 9, L. Stephen Wolfe, Pres

Cahners Publishing Co. 275 Washington Street, Newton MA 02158 USA; 617/558-4565, Fax: 617/558-4228, Focus: 20+ computer and high-tech magazines, Prdts: Datamation, Design News, Digital News & Review, EDN, TWICE, GCN, Ownership: PVT, Bruce Barnett, Pres & CEO, Stephen A. Thompson, SVP, Jackie Daya, EVP & CFO

Cambridge University Press 40 W 20th Street, New York NY 10011-4211 USA; 212/924-3900, 800/872-7423 Fax: 212/691-3239, Co Email: market@cup.org, Web URL: cup.org, Focus: Computer science books, Ownership: PVT

Cardinal Business Media Inc. 1300 Virginia Drive #400, Ft. Washington PA 19034 USA; 215/643-8000, Fax: 215/643-8099, Web URL: cardinal.com, Focus: 10+ magazines, newsletters and computer books on midrange computers, Prdts: DEC Professional, HP Professional, LAN Computing, Midrange System, Ownership: PVT, Robert N. Boucher, Pres & CEO, Thomas C. Breslin, CFO

CBM Books 1300 Virginia Drive #400, Ft. Washington PA 19034 USA; 800/285-1755 Fax: 215/643-8099, Co Email: 76702.1564@compuserve.com, Focus: Unix and networking books, Ownership: Sub Cardinal Business Media

Chilton Co. 1 Chilton Way, Radnor PA 19089 USA; 610/964-4000, Fax: 610/964-4348, Focus: High-tech magazines, Prdts: ECN, I&CS, Quality, Ownership: PVT, Leon C. Hufnagel, Pres

ClariNet Communications Corp.

4880 Stevens Creek Blvd #206, San Jose CA 95129-1034 USA; 408/296-0366, Fax: 408/296-1668, Co Email: info@clari.net, Web URL: clari.net, Focus: Internet newspaper, Ownership: PVT, Yr Founded: 1989, Empl: 15, Sales($M): 1+, Roy E. Folk, Pres & COO, Email: rfolk@clari-net.com; Simon Clephan, VP Sales

Classroom Connect 1866 Colonial Village Lane, PO Box 10488, Lancaster PA 17605-0488 USA; 800/638-1639 Fax: 717/393-5752, Co Email: info@classroom.net, Web URL: classroom.net, Focus: Publishes multimedia Internet education materials for K-12 teachers and students, Ownership: Div. Wentworth Worldwide Media, Cynthia Young, Pres, Kim E. Conlin, Email: kconlin@classroom.com

CMP Publications Inc. 600 Community Drive, Manhasset NY 11030-3847 USA; 516/562-5000, Fax: 516/562-5055, Co Email: @cmp.com, Web URL: techweb.cmp.com, Focus: 15+ computer magazines, Prdts: CommunicationsWeek, CRN, CRW, EET, InformationWeek, Windows, Ownership: PVT, Sales($M): 380, Fiscal End: 12/95; Michael S. Leeds, Pres & CEO, Grace Monahan, EVP, Jeffrey L. Strief, SVP, Kenneth D. Cron, Pres Publishing, Joseph E. Sichler, CFO, Barbara Kerbel

Cobb Group, The 9420 Bunsen Pkwy #300, Louisville KY 40220 USA; 502/491-1900, Fax: 502/491-4200, Web URL: cobb.com, Focus: 40+ computer software newsletters, books and software, Ownership: Sub. Ziff-Davis, John Jenkins, Pres

Computer Currents Publishing Inc. 5720 Hollis, Emeryville CA 94608 USA; 510/547-6800, Fax: 510/547-4613, Focus: Reginal computer newspapers, Ownership: Sub IDG, Stan Politi, Pblr

Computer Industry Almanac Inc. PO Box 600, 1639 Logan Creek Drive, Glenbrook NV 89413-0600 USA; 702/749-5053, 800/377-6810 Fax: 702/749-5864, Co Email: cialmanac@aol.com, Focus: Pblr of Computer Industry Almanac, market research and PC consulting, Prdts: Computer Industry Almanac, Ownership: PVT, Yr Founded: 1986, Empl: 4, Karen Petska-Juliussen, Chmn & E-in-C, Email: 73543.3506@compuserve.com; Egil Juliussen, Pres & Ed, Email: cialmanac@aol.com

Computer Publishing Group Inc. 320 Washington Street, Brookline MA 02146 USA; 617/739-7001, Fax: 617/739-7003, Co Email: @cpg.com, Web URL: cpg.com, Focus: Workstation magazines, Prdts: RS/Magazine, SunExpert, WebServer Magazine, Ownership: PVT, Yr Founded: 1989, Empl: 25, Fiscal End: 12/95; S. Henry Sacks, Pblr & CEO, Email: shs@cpg.com; Douglas Pryor, Editorial Dir, Email: dpryor@cpg.com

Coriolis Group Inc. 7339 E Acoma Drive #7, Scottsdale AZ 85260 USA; 602/483-0192, 800/410-0192 Fax: 602/483-0193, Co Email: orders@coriolis.com, Web URL: coriolis.com, Focus: Pblr of computer magazines, books and software, Prdts: PC Techniques, Ownership: PVT, Yr Founded: 1989, Empl: 22, Keith Weiskamp, Pres & Pblr, Jeff Duntemann, VP & Ed Dir, Shannon Karl, Publicity Dir, Email: sbounds@coriolis.com

Corry Publishing 2820 W 21st Street, Erie PA 16506-2970 USA; 814/664-8624, Fax: 814/664-7781, Focus: Office automation magazine, Prdts: Business System Magazine, Ownership: PVT, Chuck Mancino, Pblr

Cowles Business Media 470 Park Ave S #7N, New York NY 10016 USA; 212/683-3540, Fax: 212/683-4364, Web URL: cowlesbiz.com, Focus: Mobile computing magazines, Ownership: PVT, Hershel B. Sarbin, Pres & CEO

Crain Communications Inc. 740 N Rush Street, Chicago IL 60611-2590 USA; 312/649-5260, Fax: 312/649-5462, Focus: High-tech marketing magazine, Prdts: Business Marketing, Ownership: PVT, Chuck Paustian, Mgng Ed

Crescent Project Management 1931 Old Middlefield Way #C, Mountain View CA 94043 USA; 415/938-4636, Fax: 415/938-4164, Co Email: crescent86@aol.com, Focus: Support center publications, Prdts: Support Center Masterplan, Jacky Hood, Pres, Roger Smith, VP Sales & Mktng

CSG Information Services 3922 Coconut Palm Drive, Tampa FL 33619 USA; 813/664-6800, 800/927-9292 Fax: 813/664-6882, Focus: Computer reseller directories, Prdts: Computer Retailers, Dealers & Distributors, Value Added Resellers, Ownership: PVT, Rob Wenning, Pblr, Mike Jarvis, Sr Ed.

CurtCo Freedom Group 29160 Heathercliff Road #200, Malibu CA 90265 USA; 310/589-3100, Fax: 310/589-3131, Web URL: mobileoffice.com, Focus: Computer magazine, Prdts: Mobile Office, Ownership: PVT, William D. Holiber, Group Pub

Data Analysis Group 5100 Cherry Creek Road, PO Box 128, Cloverdale CA 95425 USA; 707/539-3009, Fax: 707/486-5618, Co Email: dataag@interserv.com, Focus: Market forecast information on the computer industry, Ownership: PVT, Yr Founded: 1979, Empl: 5, Keith Parker, Pres, Reny Parker, VP

Datapro Information Services Group 600 Delran Pkwy, Delran NJ 08705-9904 USA; 609/764-0100, Fax: 609/764-8953, Co Email: datapro@mgh.com, Web URL: datpro.com, Focus: 40+ loose-leaf publications on technology, products and management, Ownership: Sub McGraw-Hill, Yr Founded: 1971, Empl: 450, Sales($M): 55, Stephen Thomas, Pres, Martin Levine, VP Tech

DataTrends Publications Inc. 30-C Catoctin Circle SE, Leesburg VA 22075 USA; 703/779-0574, 800/766-8130 Fax: 703/779-2267, Co Email: dtrends@aol.com, Focus: Newsletters on companies and product trends, Prdts: Report on IBM, Report on Microsoft, Datatrends Report on DEC, Ownership: PVT, Yr Founded: 1983, Empl: 5, Jeff Caruso, Ed., Email: jpcaruso@aol.com; Paul G. Ochs, Pblr, Gennifer Chenault, Circ Mgr

DDC Publishing Inc. 275 Madison 12th Fl, New York NY 10016 USA; 212/986-7300, 800/528-3897 Fax: 212/689-6857, Focus: Quick reference PC software books, Ownership: PVT, John Visaggi, Pres

Dempa Publications Inc. 275 Madison Ave, New York NY 10016 USA; 212/682-4755, Fax: 212/682-2730, Focus: High-tech newspapers, magazines and newsletters in Japan and, Prdts: Dempa Shimbun, AEU, JEE, JEI, OEP, Dempa Digest, Ownership: PVT, Tetsuo Hirayama, Pres

Digital Consulting Inc. (DCI), 204 Andover Street, Andover MA 01810 USA; 508/470-3880, 800/324-3976 Fax: 508/470-0526, Focus: Seminars, conferences on CASE, database, PCs and other topics, Ownership: PVT, Yr Founded: 1981, Empl: 70, Sales($M): 10, George Schussel, CEO

Digital Information Group PO Box 110235, Stamford CT 06911-0235 USA; 203/348-2751, Fax: 203/977-8310, Focus: Directories and factbooks on information industry, Prdts: Software Industry Factbook, CD-ROM Factbook, Online Factbook, Ownership: PVT, Yr Founded: 1985, Maureen Fleming, Pres, Jeff Silverstein, Ed. & Pblr

Digital Press 313 Washington Street, Newton MA 02158-1626 USA; 617/928-2500, Fax: 617/928-2620, Web URL: bh.com/bh/dp, Focus: Technical computer books, Ownership: Sub Digital Equipment, John Shirley, Prod Mgr, Email: john.shirley@repp.com

DP Blue Book Co., The 35200 Dequindre #100, Sterling Heights MI 48310 USA; 810/978-4300, Fax: 810/978-4310, Focus: Directories of computer users, Ownership: PVT, Karen Watts, Pblr

Dreamscape Productions 510 Woodhaven, Aptos CA 95003 USA; 408/685-8818, Fax: 408/685-8819, Focus: Computer newsletters, Ownership: PVT, Sheridan Tatsuno, Pblr

Duke Communications Int'l. 221 E 29th Street, PO Box 3438, Loveland CO 80538-2725 USA; 970/663-4700, 800/621-1544 Fax: 970/663-3285, Co Email: editors@duke.com, Web URL:

news400.com, Focus: AS/400 computer magazine, Prdts: NEWS/400, Ownership: PVT, Wayne Madden, Pblr, Kathy Nelson, Mng Ed., Dale Agger, Editorial Dir

Dynamic Learning Systems PO Box 805, Marlboro MA 01752 USA; 508/366-9487, Fax: 508/898-9995, Co Email: 73652.3205@compuserve.com, Web URL: dlspubs.com, Focus: PC service publications, Ownership: PVT, Yr Founded: 1989, Stephen J. Bigelow, Pblr, Email: sbigelow@cerfnet.com

EDventure Holdings Inc. 104 Fifth Ave, New York NY 10011-6987 USA; 212/924-8800, Fax: 212/924-0240, Co Email: info@edventure.com, Focus: Release 1.0 newsletter on emerging software, Ownership: PVT, Yr Founded: 1983, Empl: 6, Sales($M): 2, Esther Dyson, Pres & Ed., Email: edyson@edventure.com; Daphne Kis, Pblr & VP, Email: daphne@edventure.com; Jerry Michalski, Mng Ed, Email: jerry@edventure.com

Eljen Publishing Inc. 2839 Timber Knoll, PO Box 3065, Brandon FL 33509-3065 USA; 813/654-1168, Fax: 813/654-8906, Co Email: softdir@aol.com, Web URL: netusa.com/pcsoft/softdir, Focus: PC software directory, Prdts: PC Softdir, Ownership: PVT, Richard J. Adams, Ed.

Elsevier Science 655 Avenue of the Americas, New York NY 10010 USA; 212/989-5800, 888/437-4636 Focus: Technical computer books, Ownership: PVT

Falsoft Inc. 9509 US Hwy 42, PO Box 385, Prospect KY 40059 USA; 502/228-4492, Fax: 502/228-5121, Focus: Computer magazine and newsletter, Prdts: PCM, PC Kids, Ownership: PVT, Lawrence Falk, Pblr

Faulkner Information Services 114 Cooper Center, 7905 Browning Road, Pennsauken NJ 08109-4319 USA; 609/662-2070, 800/843-0460 Fax: 609/662-3380, Web URL: faulkner.com, Focus: Information services on computer and communications products, Ownership: PVT, Yr Founded: 1985, Empl: 90, Martin Murphy, Pres, Barbara Forkel, VP Sales & Mktng

Fawcette Technical Publications Inc. 209 Hamilton Ave, Palo Alto CA 94301 USA; 415/833-7100, 800/848-5523 Fax: 415/853-0230, Focus: Programming magazines, Ownership: PVT, James E. Fawcette, Ed. & Pblr

Gale Research Inc. 835 Penobscott Bldg, 645 Giswold Street, Detroit MI 48226 USA; 313/961-2242, 800/877-4253 Fax: 800/414-5043, Focus: Directories of CD-ROMs, databases and online services, Prdts: Information Industry, Telecom, CD-ROM, Online Databases, Ownership: PVT

GIS World Inc. 155 E Boardwalk Drive #250, Ft. Collins CO 80525 USA; 970/223-4848, Fax: 970/223-5700, Web URL:

gisworld.com, Focus: Geographic information systems magazines and books, Prdts: GIS World, Business Geographics, Ownership: PVT, H. Dennison Parker, Pres & Pblr

Gower Old Post Road, Brookfield VT 05036-9704 USA; 802/276-3162, 800/535-9544 Fax: 802/276-3837, Focus: Information management books, Ownership: PVT

Harris InfoSource Int'l. 2057 Aurora Road, Twinsburg OH 44087 USA; 216/425-9000, 800/888-5900 Fax: 216/425-4328, Focus: Directories of manufacturing companies, Ownership: PVT, Robert Harris, CEO

Haworth Press Inc. 10 Alice Street, Binghamton NY 13904-1580 USA; 800/342-9678 Fax: 800/895-0582, Focus: Computer magazines, computer and human services books, Prdts: Computers in Human Services, Computers in Schools, Ownership: PVT, William Cohen, Pblr

Hearst Business Publishing 645 Stewart Ave, Garden City NY 11530 USA; 516/227-1300, 800/833-7138 Fax: 516/227-1453, Focus: High-tech magazines and directories, Prdts: Electronic Products, IC Master, Ownership: PVT, Armand Villinger, VP Electronics Group

Helmers Publishing Inc. 174 Concord Street, Peterborough NH 03458-0874 USA; 603/924-9631, Fax: 603/924-7408, Focus: High-tech magazines and books on bar coding, data entry and desktop engineering software, Prdts: ID Systems, Sensors Magazine, Desktop Engineering, Ownership: PVT, Douglas Christensen, VP, Carl T. Helmers Jr., Pres

Herring Communications Inc. 1550 Bryant Street #950, San Francisco CA 94103-4832 USA; 415/865-2277, Fax: 415/865-2280, Co Email: info@herring.com, Web URL: herring.com, Focus: High-tech financial magazine and conferences, Prdts: Red Herring, Ownership: PVT, Anthony B. Perkins, Pblr, Christopher J. Alden, Assoc Pub, Catherine Silver, VP Sales

Holister Associates PO Box 575, Lyons CO 80540 USA; 303/682-2634, Fax: 303/682-2654, Focus: Computer reference books, Ownership: PVT

Horizon House Publications Inc. 685 Canton Street, Norwood MA 02062 USA; 617/769-9750, 800/225-9977 Fax: 617/762-9071, Focus: Telecom magazine, Ownership: PVT, James N. Budwey, Pblr

HyperMedia Communications Inc. 901 Mariner's Island Blvd #365, San Mateo CA 94404 USA; 415/573-5170, 800/832-3513 Fax: 415/573-5131, Co Email: mktg@newmedia.com, Web URL: hyperstand.com, Focus: Multimedia magazine, Prdts: NewMedia, Macromedia User Journal, Stock Symbol: HPR, Yr Founded: 1992, Empl: 40, Sales($M): 7.4, Fiscal

End: 1/95; Richard Landry, Pblr & CEO, Email: rlandry@newmedia.com; Phil Hood, Ed.-in-Chief, Email: phood@new-media.com; Todd Hagen, VP Fin & Admin, Email: thagen@newmedia.com; Scott Kahn, SR Info Sys Admin, Susan Lake, Dir Mktng, Email: slake@newmedia.com

IDG Books Worldwide 919 E Hillsdale Blvd #400, Foster City CA 94404 USA; 415/655-3000, Fax: 415/655-3299, Co Email: @idgbooks.com, Focus: PC books, Ownership: PVT, Sales($M): 112, Fiscal End: 12/95; John J. Kilcullen, Pres & CEO, Mike Pegan, EVP Sales & Mktng, Milissa Koloski, SVP, Linda White

IDG Communications (IDG), 1 Exeter Plaza 15th Fl, Boston MA 02116 USA; 617/534-1200, Fax: 617/859-8642, Focus: Over 200 computer magazines in 60+ countries, Prdts: CIO, Computer-world, InfoWorld, Macworld, Network World, PC World, Ownership: PVT, Empl: 5,000, Sales($M): 1,400, Fiscal End: 12/95; Patrick J. McGovern, Chmn, Kelly Conlin, Pres, Jim Casella, COO

IDG Newsletters Corp. 77 Franklin Street #310, Boston MA 02110 USA; 617/482-8785, 800/807-0771 Fax: 617/338-0164, Focus: Computer newsletters, Ownership: Sub IDG, Craig S. Pierce, Pblr

IEEE Computer Society (IEEE-CS), 1730 Massachusetts Ave NW, Washington DC 20036-1992 USA; 202/371-0101, Fax: 202/728-9614, Web URL: computer.org, Focus: Association for computer professionals, Ownership: Nonprofit, Yr Founded: 1951, Empl: 100,000, T. Micahel Elliott, Exec Dir, Anneliese von Mayrhauser, VP Conf & Tutorials

IEEE Computer Society Press 10662 Los Vaqueros Circle, PO Box 3014, Los Alamitos CA 90720-1264 USA; 714/821-8380, Fax: 714/821-4010, Focus: Magazines and books for IEEE Computer Society members, Prdts: Computer Magazine, Expert, Micro, Multimedia, Software, Ownership: PVT, True Seaborn, Pblr

IEEE Press 345 E 47th Street, New York NY 10017 USA; 212/705-7555, 800/678-4333 Fax: 212/705-7453, Web URL: ieee.org, Focus: Technical magazines, journals and books for IEEE members, Ownership: PVT

IIR Publications Inc. 5650 El Camino Real #225, Carlsbad CA 92008 USA; 619/931-8615, 800/477-5665 Fax: 619/931-9935, Web URL: as400.com, Focus: Computer magazines and newsletters, Prdts: Midrange Computing, Ownership: PVT

InfoEdge 2 Stamford Landing, Stamford CT 06903 USA; 203/363-7150, 800/544-7337 Fax: 203/363-7156, Co Email: infoedge@futuris.net, Web URL: info-edge.com, Focus: Information technology reports, Ownership: PVT, Empl: 10, Sales($M): 2.1, B.F. Armstrong, Pres, Lucy Hedrick, Mgng Ed

Information Gatekeepers Inc. 214 Harvard Ave, Boston MA 02134 USA; 617/738-8088, Fax: 617/734-8562, Co Email: igiboston@aol.com, Focus: Information on LANS, fiber optics, ISDN, wireless and telecom, Ownership: PVT, Yr Founded: 1978, Empl: 15, Sales($M): 2, Paul Polishuk, Pres, Email: igiboston@aol.com; Peter Polishuk, Mktng Mgr

Information Resource Group (IRG), 35200 Dequindre, Sterling Heights MI 48310-4857 USA; 810/978-3000, Fax: 810/978-3010, Web URL: irg.ppcix.net-com.com, Focus: Database and research on 150,000 computer sites and 1M corporate and MIS executives, Prdts: IRG Database, Ownership: PVT, Yr Founded: 1982, Empl: 100, Terry Olson, Pres

Information Today Inc. 143 Old Marlton Pike, Medford NJ 08055 USA; 609/654-6266, 800/300-9868 Fax: 609/654-4309, Co Email: custserv@infotoday.com, Web URL: infotoday.com, Focus: Computer newsletters, magazines and directories, Ownership: PVT, Thomas H. Hogan, Pres

Infotainment World Inc. 951 Mariner's Island Blvd #700, San Mateo CA 94404 USA; 415/349-4300, Fax: 415/349-8347, Focus: Computer and CD-ROM entertainment software magazines, Prdts: PC Games, GamePro, Ownership: PVT, Bruce W. Gray, Pblr

InfoWorld Publishing Co. 155 Bovet Road #800, San Mateo CA 94402 USA; 415/572-7341, 800/432-2478 Fax: 415/312-0547, Web URL: infoworld.com, Focus: Computer publications and conferences, Ownership: PVT

International Thomson Computer Press 20 Park Plaza #1001, Boston MA 02116 USA; 617/695-1419, 800/842-3636 Fax: 617/695-1615, Co Email: itcp@itp.thomson.com, Web URL: thomson.com/intlitcp, Focus: Computer books, Ownership: Sub Int'l. Thomson Publishing, Kathleen Raftery, Email: kraftery@thomson.com

IW Publishing Bayview Street at Sharp's Wharf, Camden ME 04843 USA; 207/236-8524, Fax: 207/236-6452, Web URL: imagngwrld@aol.com, Focus: Imaging technology magazine, Prdts: Imaging World Magazine, Ownership: PVT, Bruce Taylor, Pres, Dan Bolita, News Ed

James Publishing & Assoc. 899 Presial Road #110, Richardson TX 75081 USA; 214/238-1133, 800/864-1177 Fax: 214/238-1132, Focus: Computer magazines, Ownership: PVT, James Michael Story, Pblr

Jaye Communications 550 Interstate N Pkwy NW #150, Atlanta GA 30334-5008 USA; 404/984-9444, Fax: 404/612-0780, Focus: Regional computer publications, Prdts: Atlanta Computer Currents, Technology South, Ownership: PVT, Mike

Adkinson, Pblr

Jones Digital Century Inc. 9697 E Mineral Ave, PO Box 3309, Englewood CO 80155-3309 USA; 303/792-3100, Fax: 303/792-5608, Web URL: digitalcentury.com, Focus: Electronic publishing, Prdts: Jones Telecommunications Encyclopedia Update, Ownership: Sub. Jones Interactive, Bernard J. Luskin, Pres

Jupiter Communications Co. 627 Broadway 2nd Fl, New York NY 10012-2612 USA; 212/780-6060, 800/488-4345 Fax: 212/780-6075, Co Email: jup5@aol.com, Web URL: jup.com/jupiter, Focus: Telecom, information services and videotex information, publications & conferences, Ownership: PVT, Yr Founded: 1986, Empl: 6, Joshua Harris, Pres, Gene DeRose, Ed Dir

Kawalek & Assoc. 525 Market Street 36th Fl, San Francisco CA 94105 USA; 415/296-7744, Fax: 415/296-7766, Web URL: kawalek@aol.com, Focus: Software magazine, PR and marketing communications, Prdts: Software Marketing Journal, Ownership: PVT, Yr Founded: 1987, Empl: 20, Nadine A. Kawalek, Pres & CEO, Email: nkawalek@well.com; Julie Porter, VP & Consultant, April Davis, Mktng Coord

Knowledge Industry Publications Inc. (KIPI), 701 Westchester Ave, White Plains NY 10604 USA; 914/328-9157, 800/800-5474 Fax: 914/328-9093, Web URL: kipinet.com, Focus: Computer, video and multimedia magazines and conferences, Prdts: AV Video, Computer Pictures, Tape/Disc Business, Ownership: PVT, Roscoe C. Smith III, VP, Group Pub, Email: kipi1@applelink.com; Barbara Stockwell, VP & Assoc Pub, Jeff Hartford, Circ Dir

Kutish Publications Inc. PO Box 181916, Coronado CA 92178 USA; 800/342-9621 Fax: 800/803-9623, Focus: Newsletters and directories on computer taxation and law, Ownership: PVT, L.J. Kutten, Pblr

Lakewood Publications 50 S 9th Street, Minneapolis MN 55402 USA; 612/333-0471, 800/328-4329 Fax: 612/333-6526, Co Email: presmag@aol.com, Focus: Presentation magazine, Ownership: PVT, Yr Founded: 1988, Jerry C. Noack, VP & Group Pub, Richard Ausman, Pblr, Larry Tuck, Ed.

LFP Inc. 9171 Wilshire Blvd #300, Beverly Hills CA 90210 USA; 310/858-7155, Fax: 310/274-7985, Focus: Computer magazines, Prdts: PC LapTop Computers, Ownership: PVT, Michael Goldstein, Ed.-in-Chief, Email: 75300.3144@compuserve.com; Larry Flynt, Pblr

Lotus Publishing Corp. 77 Franklin Street #310, Boston MA 02110 USA; 617/482-8634, Fax: 617/422-8189, Focus: Newsletters on Lotus products, Craig C.

Pierce, Pblr

Louisville Computer Times 3135 Sunfield Circle, Louisville KY 40241 USA; 502/339-9672, Fax: 502/426-7585, Focus: Regional computer newspapers, Prdts: Computer Times, Ownership: PVT, Terry Kibiloski, Ed.

MacHome Journal 612 Howard Street 6th Fl, San Francisco CA 94105 USA; 415/957-1911, Fax: 415/882-9502, Focus: Computer magazines, Ownership: PVT, James Capparell, Pblr

Macmillan Computer Publishing (MCP), 201 W 103rd Street, Indianapolis IN 46290-1097 USA; 317/581-3500, 800/428-5331 Fax: 317/581-3550, Web URL: mcp.com, Focus: PC productivity software and computer books, Prdts: Adobe Press, Brady, Hayden, New Riders, Que, Sams, Ownership: Sub Macmillan Publishing USA, Yr Founded: 1981, Empl: 250, Scott Flanders, Pres, David Israel, VP Publishing, Cyndy Warren, Email: 75677.720@compuserve.com

Marcel Dekker Inc. 270 Madison Ave, New York NY 10016 USA; 212/696-9000, 800/228-1160 Focus: Technical computer and telecom books, Ownership: PVT

McGraw-Hill Inc. 1221 Avenue of the Americas, New York NY 10020-1095 USA; 212/512-2000, Fax: 212/512-3511, Web URL: mcgraw-hill.com, Focus: Numerous computer and telecom magazines, Prdts: BYTE, Data Communications, LAN Times, Open Computing, Ownership: NYSE, Yr Founded: 1925, Empl: 15,004, Sales($M): 2,935.3, Fiscal End: 12/95; Joseph L. Dionne, Chmn & CEO, Harold McGraw III, Pres & COO, Robert N. Landes, Sr EVP, Robert E. Evanson, EVP Corp Dev, Robert J. Bahash, EVP & CFO

McKinley Group Inc., The 85 Liberty Ship Way #201, Sausalito CA 94965-1768 USA; 415/331-1884, Fax: 415/331-8600, Co Email: @mckinley.com, Web URL: mckinley.com, Focus: Internet information directories, Prdts: Magellan, McKinley Internet Yellow Pages, Ownership: PVT, Yr Founded: 1993, Empl: 50, David Hayden, Pres & CEO, Email: hayden@mckinley.com; Christine Maxwell, Pblr, Email: maxwell@mckinley.com; Isabel Maxwell, VP Strat Plng, Email: max@mckinley.com; Alexander Cohen, Dir Prod Dev, Email: xcohen@mckinley.com; Helene Atkin, Dir Media Rel, Email: hfa@mckinley.com

Mecklermedia Corp. 20 Ketchum Street, Westport CT 06880 USA; 203/226-6967, Fax: 203/454-5840, Co Email: info@mecklermedia.com, Web URL: iworld.com, Focus: Internet publications, tradeshows and consulting, Prdts: Internet World, Web Week, Web Developer, Ownership: NASDAQ, Stock Symbol: MECK, Yr Founded: 1971, Empl: 87,

Sales($M): 14.5, Fiscal End: 9/95; Alan M. Meckler, Chmn & CEO, Email: ameck@mecklermedia.com; David Egan, Pres & COO Mag Grp, Email: degan@mecklermedia.com; Carl S. Pugh, Pres & COO Tradeshow Grp, Email: cpugh@mecklermedia.com; Paul A. Stanton, VP Mktng, Email: stanton@mecklermedia.com; Christopher S. Cardell, SVP & CFO, Email: scardell@mecklermedia.com; Francie Coulter, Dir PR, Email: fcoulter@mecklermedia.com

MediaMap 215 First Street 3rd Floor, Cambridge MA 02142-1293 USA; 617/374-9300, Fax: 617/374-9345, Web URL: mediamap.com, Focus: Computer publications and tradeshows information, Ownership: PVT, Yr Founded: 1985, John Pearce, CEO

Mendham Technology Group 144 Talmadge Road, Mendham NJ 07945 USA; 201/543-2273, Fax: 201/543-6033, Focus: Newsletters on Windows and multimedia, Ownership: PVT, Carole Patton, Pblr

Micro House Int'l. Inc. 2477 N 55th Street #101, Boulder CO 80301 USA; 303/443-3389, 800/926-8299 Fax: 303/443-3323, Web URL: microhouse.com, Focus: PC diagnostic software & PC books, Prdts: DrivePro, EZ-Drive, Micro House Technical Library, Ownership: PVT, Yr Founded: 1989, Stephen S. Anderson, Pres & CEO, Douglas T. Anderson, VP & CTO

Micro Publishing Press 21150 Hawthorne Blvd #104, Torrance CA 90503 USA; 310/371-5787, Fax: 310/542-0849, Focus: Desktop publishing magazines and books, Prdts: Digital Imaging, Micro Publishing News, Ownership: PVT, James Cavuoto, Ed. & Pblr, Stephen Beale, Exec Ed

Microsoft Press 1 Microsoft Way, Redmond WA 98052-6399 USA; 206/882-8080, 800/677-7377 Fax: 206/936-7329, Co Email: msp@compuserve.com, Web URL: microsoft.com/mspress, Focus: PC and Mac software books, Ownership: Sub Microsoft, Stock Symbol: MSFT, Elton Welke, Pblr & GM

Mike Murach & Associates Inc. 2466 Westshaw Lane #101, Fresno CA 93711 USA; 209/440-9071, Fax: 209/275-9035, Focus: Pblr of PC and mainframe computer books, Ownership: PVT, Mike Murach, Pres

Miller Freeman Inc. 600 Harrison Street, San Francisco CA 94107 USA; 415/905-2200, 800/829-2505 Fax: 415/905-2389, Web URL: mfi.com, Focus: Computer and high-tech magazines and tradeshows, Prdts: DBMS, OS/2, CADENCE, AI Expert, LAN, STACKS, UNIX Review, Ownership: PVT, Graham J.S. Wilson, Chmn, Marshall W. Freeman, Pres & CEO, Thomas L. Kemp, EVP & COO

MIT Press, The 55 Hayward Street, Cam-

bridge MA 02142-1399 USA; 617/625-8569, Web URL: mitpress.mit.edu, Focus: Computer science books, Ownership: PVT, Theresa Ehling, Acq Ed

MSP Communications 220 S 6th Street #500, Minneapolis MN 55402-4507 USA; 612/339-7571, Fax: 612/339-5806, Focus: Regional computer newspapers, Prdts: ComputerUser, Ownership: PVT, Gary Johnson, Pblr

National Academy Press 2101 Constitution Ave NW, Washington DC 20418 USA; 202/334-2612, Fax: 202/334-2793, Co Email: slubeck@nas.edu, Web URL: nas.edu, Focus: Technology assessment books, Ownership: PVT, Scott Lubeck, Dir, Stephen Mautner, Exec Ed., Email: smautner@nas.edu; Barbara Kline Pope, Mktng Dir, Email: bkline@nas.edu; Douglas Ellmore, Internet, Email: dellmore@nas.edu; Mary Herbenick, Mktng Specialist, Email: mherbeni@nas.edu

National Technical Information Service (NTIS), 5285 Port Royal Road, Springfield VA 22161 USA; 703/487-4650, Fax: 703/321-8547, Web URL: fedworld.gov, Focus: Central source for sale of government-sponsored scientific & technical reports, Ownership: Nonprofit, Yr Founded: 1945

Nelson Publishing 305 Spring Creek Vlg, Dallas TX 75248 USA; 972/644-0830, Focus: Telecom magazine, Prdts: Communications News, Ownership: PVT

New Media Publications 10711 Burnett Road #305, Austin TX 78759-4459 USA; 512/873-7761, Fax: 512/873-7782, Focus: Computer magazines, Prdts: Access to Wang, NetWare Solutions, Ownership: PVT, Kathy Murphy, Pblr

North American Publishing Co. 401 N Broad Street, Philadelphia PA 19108 USA; 215/238-5300, Fax: 215/238-5457, Focus: Printing and publishing magazines, Prdts: Publishing & Production Executive, Business Documents, Ownership: PVT, Irvin J. Borowsky, Chmn, Ned S. Borowsky, Pres & COO

North Light Books-Div. F&W Publications 1507 Dana Ave, Cincinnati OH 45207 USA; 513/531-2222, 800/289-0963 Fax: 513/531-4744, Focus: Graphics design and computer graphics, Ownership: PVT, David Lewis, Ed.ial Dir, Jennie Berliant, Sales Dir, Stacie Berger, Publicist

O'Reilly & Associates Inc. 103 Morris Street #A, Sebastopol CA 95472 USA; 707/829-0515, 800/998-9938 Fax: 707/829-0104, Co Email: order@ora.com, Web URL: ora.com, Focus: Software, books on Unix, Internet and Worldwide Web Journal, Prdts: Website, The Whole Internet User's Guide & Catalog, WWW Journal, Ownership: PVT, Yr Founded: 1978, Empl: 140, Tim O'Reilly, Pres, Brian Erwin, Dir Sales & Mktng, Richard Peck, VP Bus Dev, Sara Winge, PR Dir,

Email: sara@ora.com

Oakley Publishing PO Box 70167, Eugene OR 97401 USA; 541/747-0800, Fax: 541/746-0071, Focus: Windows and NT magazines, Prdts: NT Developer, Windows Tech Journal, Ownership: PVT, Elizabeth Oakley, Pres

Omray Inc. 9801 Anderson Mill Road #207, Austin TX 78750 USA; 512/250-1700, 800/486-3282 Fax: 512/250-1016, Web URL: corelmag.com, Focus: Computer magazines and multimedia, Prdts: Corel Magazine, Corel Expert User CD-ROM, Corelectronic, Ownership: PVT, Yr Founded: 1992, Sales($M): 12, Scott Campbell, Ed., Email: 71164.15@compuserve.com; Dave Baceski, Editorial Dir, Mark Stacey, VP Sales & Mktng

Osborne McGraw-Hill 2600 10th Street, Berkeley CA 94710 USA; 510/549-6600, Fax: 510/549-6603, Focus: PC software books, Ownership: PVT, Scott Rogers, Exec Ed

Peachpit Press Inc. 2414 Sixth Street, Berkeley CA 94710 USA; 510/548-4393, 800/283-9444 Fax: 510/548-5991, Co Email: @peachpit.com, Web URL: peachpit.com, Focus: Mac and Windows software books, Prdts: Macintosh Bible, Windows Bible, PC Bible, Ownership: PVT, Ted Nace, Pblr, Roslyn Bullas, Mgng Ed, Trish Booth, Email: trish@peachpit.com

Peed Corp. 120 W Harvest Drive, Lincoln NE 68501 USA; 402/479-2141, 800/247-4880 Fax: 402/477-9252, Web URL: processor.com, Focus: PC magazines, Prdts: PC Catalog, Processor, PC Novice, PC Today, Ownership: PVT, Tom Peed, Pblr

PennWell Publishing Co. 10 Tara Blvd, Nashua NH 03026-2801 USA; 603/891-9166, Fax: 603/891-0539, Web URL: pennwell.com, Focus: Numerous computer and high-tech magazines, Prdts: Color Publishing, Computer Design, Computer Graphics World, Ownership: PVT

Penton Publishing Inc. 1100 Superior Ave, Cleveland OH 44114-2543 USA; 216/696-7000, Fax: 216/696-0836, Web URL: penton.com, Focus: Computers and office equipment magazines, Ownership: PVT, Yr Founded: 1903, Empl: 1,250, Sal F. Marino, Chmn & CEO, Daniel J. Ramella, Pres & COO, Jerome Neff, Grp Pres, James Zaremba, Grp Pres, Susan Grimm, VP Pub Sys, Jenny Febbo, Dir Corp Comm, Email: jfebbo@penton.com

Peter Li Inc. 222 Front Street #401, San Francisco CA 94111 USA; 415/439-5600, Fax: 415/439-5619, Web URL: techlearning.com, Focus: Educational computer magazine, Prdts: Technology & Learning, Ownership: PVT, Peter Li, Pres

Phillips Business Information Inc. (PBI), 1201 Seven Locks Road #300, Potomac MD 20854 USA; 301/340-1520, Fax:

301/424-4297, Co Email: @phillips.com, Focus: 20+ telecom and computer newsletters, Prdts: AIN Report, EDI News, ISDN News, Multimedia Week, Data Channels, Ownership: Sub Phillips Publishing, Ellen H. Stuhlmann, Pblr, Barbara Van Gorder

PiM Publications Inc. PO Box 2140, Fall River MA 02722 USA; 508/678-4200, 800/345-3360 Fax: 508/675-6002, Focus: Amiga PC magazines, Ownership: PVT, Joyce Hicks, Pblr

Pinnacle Peak Publishing Ltd. 8711 E Pinnacle Peak Road #249, Scottsdale AZ 85255 USA; 602/585-5580, Fax: 602/585-7417, Web URL: docmanage.com, Focus: Document management products and technology consulting, Prdts: Document Management & Windows Imaging, Ownership: PVT, Yr Founded: 1988, Empl: 5, Richard N. Stover, Pblr, Joyce Stover, VP

Pinnacle Publishing Inc. 18000 72nd Ave S #217, Kent WA 98032-0888 USA; 206/251-1900, Fax: 206/251-5057, Web URL: pinpub.com, Focus: PC utility software and computer newsletters, Ownership: PVT, Yr Founded: 1986, Empl: 32, Sales($M): 6.7, Fiscal End: 12/95; Michael J. Friedman, Pres & CEO, D. Robert Colliton, VP & CFO

Pixel-The Computer Animation News People Inc. 109 Vanderhoof Ave #2, Toronto Ontario M4G 2H7 Canada; 416/424-4657, Fax: 416/424-1812, Co Email: pixel@inforamp.net, Web URL: gsfmicro.com/pixel, Focus: Information, directory and reports on computer animation and graphics markets, Ownership: PVT, Yr Founded: 1983, Empl: 3, Robi Roncarelli, Pblr & Ed.

Plenum Publishing Corp. 233 Spring Street, New York NY 10013-1578 USA; 212/620-8000, 800/221-9369 Fax: 212/463-0742, Focus: Computer science books, Ownership: PVT, Martin Tash, Pres

Positive Support Review Inc. (PSR), 2500 Broadway Street #320, Santa Monica CA 90404-3061 USA; 310/453-6100, Fax: 310/453-6253, Co Email: info@psrinc.com, Web URL: psrinc.com/psr, Focus: Mission-critical information systems consulting and books, Ownership: PVT, Yr Founded: 1982, M. Victor Janulaitis, Pres & CEO, Email: vjanulaitis@psrinc.com; Gary Ingham, VP Mktng, Email: ingham@psrinc.com

Powell Publishing Inc. 19380 Emerald Drive, Brookfield WI 53045 USA; 414/792-9696, Fax: 414/792-9777, Web URL: dmreview.com, Focus: Database magazine, Prdts: Data Management Review, Ownership: PVT, Ronald J. Powell, Pblr, Email: rpowell@dmreview.com

Probe Publishing Corp. 3 Wing Drive #240, Cedar Knolls NJ 07927-1000 USA; 201/285-1500, Fax: 201/285-1519,

Focus: Wireless magazine and 10+ telecom newsletters, Prdts: Wireless, Ownership: PVT

Provantage Corp. 7249 Whipple Ave NW, N. Canton OH 44720-7143 USA; 216/494-8715, 800/336-1166 Fax: 216/494-5260, Co Email: @provantage.com, Web URL: provantage.com, Focus: Reseller of hardware, software and accessories, Prdts: E-Catalog, Ownership: PVT, Michael Colarik, Pres, Email: colarik@provantage.com; Arno Zirngibl, Chmn, Email: zirngibl@provantage.com; Scott DiBattista, VP, Email: dibattista@provantage.com; Michael Carioti, Mktng Mgr, Email: carioti@provantage.com; George Wuerthele, Email: wuerthele@provantage.com

PTN Publishing Co. 445 Broad Hollow Road, Melville NY 11747 USA; 516/845-2700, Fax: 516/845-2787, Focus: AV and imaging magazines, Prdts: AVC Presentation, Advanced Imaging, Ownership: PVT, Stanley S. Sills, Chmn & CEO

Publications & Communications Inc. 12416 Hymeadow Drive, Austin TX 78750 USA; 512/250-9023, Fax: 512/331-3900, Web URL: pcinews, Focus: 15+ computer magazines, Prdts: AutoCAD World, RISC World, Unisys World, SG World, Oracle World, Ownership: PVT, Gary Pittman, Pres & CEO, Tom Clark, VP Dev

R&D Publications Inc. 1601 W 23rd Street #200, Lawrence KS 66046-0127 USA; 913/841-1631, Fax: 913/841-2624, Web URL: rdpub.com, Focus: Technical computer magazines and programming books, Ownership: PVT, Robert Ward, Pblr

Random House Electronic Publishing 201 E 50th Street, New York NY 10022 USA; 212/751-2600, 800/733-3000 Fax: 212/572-4997, Focus: PC/Mac software books, Ownership: PVT, Stephen Guty, Editorial Dir

Redgate Communications Corp. 660 Beachland Blvd, Vero Beach FL 32963 USA; 407/231-6904, 800/333-8760 Fax: 407/231-7872, Focus: Macintosh products directories, multimedia publications, Prdts: Macintosh Multimedia Product Registry, Multimedia Today, Ownership: PVT, Yr Founded: 1983, Kevin Fallon, Pblr, Paulette Lee, Mng Ed.

Sage Publications 2455 Teller Road, Thousand Oaks CA 91320 USA; 805/499-0721, Fax: 805/499-0871, Focus: Books, journals and newsletters, Ownership: PVT

Sams Publishing 201 W 103rd Street, Indianapolis IN 46290-1097 USA; 317/581-3500, Fax: 317/581-3550, Focus: Borland-based books, Ownership: Div. MacMillan Computer Pub., Richard Swadley, Pres & Pblr

Scholastic Corp. 411 Lafayette Street 4th Floor, New York NY 10003 USA; 212/505-4900, Fax: 212/505-8587, Focus:

Educational software, magazines and books, Prdts: Home-Office Computing, Electronic Learning, Ownership: OTC, Stock Symbol: SCHL, Yr Founded: 1983, Empl: 35, Sales($M): 749.9, Fiscal End: 5/95

Sentry Publishing Co. Inc. 1 Research Drive, Westboro MA 01581-3907 USA; 508/366-2031, Fax: 508/366-8104, Focus: Software and client/server computer magazines and demand-side IT market research, Prdts: Client/Server Computing, Software Magazine, Ownership: PVT, William A. Gannon, Pres, Donald E. Fagan, SVP & Pblr, Kathleen Flynn, VP Fin & Admin, Michael P. Walsh, SVP Custom Pubs, Cynthia Reenl, Marcom Mgr

SIGS Publications Group 71 W. 23rd Street 3rd Floor, New York NY 10010 USA; 212/242-7447, Fax: 212/242-7574, Co Email: 73361.1707@compuserve.com, Web URL: sigs.com, Focus: Technical computer magazines, books and conferences, Prdts: Object Magazine, C++ Report, X Journal, Smalltalk Report, Ownership: PVT, Richard P. Friedman, Pres, Margherita R. Monck, GM

Simba Information Inc. 213 Danbury Road, PO Box 7430, Wilton CT 06897-7430 USA; 203/834-0033, 800/307-2529 Fax: 203/834-1771, Web URL: simba-net.com, Focus: Publishing industry information and publications, Prdts: Computer Marketing & Distribution, Multimedia Business, Ownership: PVT, Alan Brigish, Pblr, Chris Elwell, VP, Tom Niehaus, VP

Software Maintenance News Inc. 4546 El Camino Real B10 #237, Los Altos CA 94022 USA; 415/969-5522, Fax: 415/969-5949, Co Email: 73670.2227@compuserve.com, Focus: Software management books and newsletter, Prdts: Software Management Technology Reference Guide, Ownership: PVT, Nicholas Zvegintzov, Pres, Judith M. Golub, VP & CFO

Software Productivity Group Inc. 180 Turnpike Road, Westboro MA 01581 USA; 508/366-3344, 800/808-3976 Fax: 508/366-8030, Co Email: general@spgnet.com, Web URL: spgnet.com, Focus: Software technology research and consulting, software magazine & conferences, Prdts: Application Development Trends, Ownership: PVT, Yr Founded: 1989, Empl: 20+, Elliot D. Weinman, Pres, Email: 76102.1473@compuserve.com; Mark McCourt, EVP & Pub, Email: 76102.1473@compuserve.com; Leland J. Katz, Dir Sales & Mktng, Email: 76102.1472@compuserve.com; Dan Kara, Dir Res, Email: 76102.1465@compuserve.com; John Desmond, VP & Ed.

Specialized Systems Consultants Inc. PO Box 55549, Seattle WA 98155-0549 USA; 206/782-7733, Fax: 206/782-7191, Co Email: sales@ssc.com, Web URL: ssc.com, Focus: Unix reference and tutorial

books, Prdts: Tcl and Tk Pocket References, WEBnut, Ownership: PVT, Yr Founded: 1983, Empl: 19, Belinda Frazier, VP, Email: bbf@ssc.com

Speech Science Institute-Speech Science Publications PO Box 240428, Apple Valley MN 55124 USA; 612/890-4343, Co Email: 76331.1241@compuserve.com, Focus: Speech recognition technology books, Ownership: PVT, Wayne A. Lea, Pres

Springer-Verlag New York Inc. 175 Fifth Ave, New York NY 10010 USA; 212/460-1500, Fax: 212/473-6272, Focus: Computer science books and journals, Ownership: PVT

Springhouse Corp. 1111 Betlehem Pike, PO Box 908, Springhouse PA 19477-0908 USA; 215/628-7716, Fax: 215/540-8041, Focus: Office system magazine, Ownership: PVT, Charles Mitchell, Pblr

SSC PO Box 55549, Seattle WA 98155 USA; 206/782-7733, Fax: 206/782-7191, Web URL: ssc.com, Focus: Computer magazines, Prdts: Websmith, Linux Journal, Ownership: PVT

St. Martin's Press 175 Fifth Ave, New York NY 10010 USA; 212/674-5151, 800/221-7954 Fax: 212/420-9314, Focus: Computer books, Ownership: PVT

Sybex 2021 Challenger Drive, Alameda CA 94501 USA; 510/523-8233, 800/227-2346 Fax: 510/523-2373, Focus: Computer books, Ownership: PVT, Yr Founded: 1976, Bruce Spatz, VP & Ed.-in-Chief, Lora Williams, VP Mktng

Syllabus Press 1307 S Mary Ave #211, Sunnyvale CA 94087 USA; 408/773-0670, Fax: 408/746-2711, Co Email: info@syllabus.com, Web URL: syllabus.com, Focus: High-tech magazines and conferences for educational market, Prdts: Syllabus, Query, HEPC, Ownership: PVT, Yr Founded: 1987, Empl: 30, John P. Noon, Pblr

Tech Trade Assoc. 8 Combahee Road, Hilton Head Island SC 29928-3316 USA; 803/785-5497, Fax: 803/785-5498, Focus: Info. about high-tech editors, analysts, tradeshows and conferences, Prdts: Technology Events Calendar, News@beats PR Software, Event Happenings, Ownership: PVT, Judith Miller, Principal

TechNews Inc. 8500 Leesburg Pike #7500, Vienna VA 22182-2412 USA; 703/848-2800, Fax: 703/848-2353, Co Email: technews@technews.com, Web URL: wtonline.com/wtonline, Focus: High-tech newspaper, Prdts: Washington Technology, Ownership: PVT, Yr Founded: 1986, Empl: 35, Tim Karney, Pblr, Andrew Jenks, Ed., Email: ajenks@technews.com; Mark Abrials, Mktng Dir, Email: mabrials@technews.com; Esther Smith, CEO & Pres, Email: esmith@technews.com

Technology News of America Co. Inc. 110 Greene Street, New York NY 10012 USA; 212/334-9750, Co Email: technews@worldnet.net, Focus: Computer newsletters, Prdts: Infoperspectives, Four Hundred, Ownership: PVT, Hesh Wiener, Ed. & Pblr

Telecom Library Inc. 12 W 21 Street 10th Floor, New York NY 10010 USA; 212/691-8215, 800/542-7279 Fax: 212/691-1191, Web URL: telecomlibrary.com, Focus: Telecom and networking books and magazines, Prdts: Call Center Magazine, Teleconnect Magazine, Imaging Magazine, Ownership: PVT, Yr Founded: 1978, Empl: 85, Harry Newton, Pblr, Gerry Friesen, Pblr, Murial Fullam, Bus Mgr

Telecom Publishing Group 1101 King Street #444, Alexandria VA 22314 USA; 800/327-7205 Fax: 800/645-4104, Web URL: cappubs.com, Focus: Telecom and computer newsletters, Prdts: Mobile Data Report, Information Networks, Ownership: PVT, Chris Vestal, Pblr

UniForum Association (UniForum), 2901 Tasman Drive #205, Santa Clara CA 95054 USA; 408/986-8840, 800/255-5620 Fax: 408/986-1645, Web URL: uniforum.org, Focus: Vendor-independent association dedicated to promoting UNIX and open systems and services, Ownership: Nonprofit, Yr Founded: 1980, Empl: 6,500, Tom Mace, Exec Dir, Email: tom@uniforum.org

United Communications Group 11300 Rockville Pike #1100, Rockville MD 20852-3030 USA; 301/816-8950, Fax: 301/816-8945, Focus: 10+ computer workstation, software and midrange newsletters, Prdts: I/S Analyzer Case Studies, AS/400 Advisor, Software Success, Ownership: PVT, Greg Strakosch, Pblr, Bruce Levenson, CEO

United Publications Inc. 38 Lafayette Street, PO Box 995, Yarmouth ME 04096 USA; 207/846-0600, Fax: 207/846-0657, Web URL: servicenews.com, Focus: Computer service magazine, Prdts: Service News, Ownership: PVT, Bill Springer, Pblr, Email: bspring@servicenews.com; Alison Harris, Ed., Email: aharris@servicenews.com

Upside Publishing Co., The 2015 Pioneer Court, San Mateo CA 94403 USA; 415/377-0950, 888/387-7433 Fax: 415/377-1961, Web URL: upside.com, Focus: High-tech financial magazine, Prdts: Upside, Ownership: PVT, David Bunnell, Chmn, Susan E. Scott, Pblr & CEO, Email: sscott@upside.com; Cheryl A. Lucanegro, Assoc Pub, Email: clucanegro@upside.com; Ed Ring, CFO, Email: edring@upside.com

Van Nostrand Reinhold 115 5th Ave, New York NY 10003 USA; 212/254-3232, 800/842-3636 Fax: 212/505-6219, Co Email: @vnr.com, Focus: Computer science books, Prdts: Doing Business on the Internet, Ownership: PVT, Yr Founded: 1978, Brian Heer, Pres & CEO, Marianne Russell, VP & Ed.ial Dir, Mark Lerner, CFO, Jacqueline Jeng, Email: jjeng@vnr.com

Vital Information Publications 754 Caravel Lane, Foster City CA 94404 USA; 415/345-7018, Fax: 415/345-7018, Focus: High-tech newsletters, Prdts: Manufacturing Automation, Sensor Business Digest, Ownership: PVT, Peter Adrian, Principal

Vulcan Publications Inc. 1 Chase Corporate Drive #300, Birmingham AL 35244 USA; 205/988-9708, Focus: Computer magazines, Prdts: Computer Monthly, Ownership: PVT, Trent R. Boozer, Pres

Weka Publishing 1077 Bridgeport Ave, Shelton CT 06484 USA; 800/222-9352 Fax: 203/944-3663, Focus: Computer publications, Ownership: PVT, Peter Strapko, Mgng Dir

West World Productions Inc. 924 Westwood Blvd #650, Los Angeles CA 90024-2910 USA; 310/208-1335, Fax: 310/208-1054, Web URL: wwpi.com, Focus: Technology trend magazine, Prdts: Computer Technology Review, Ownership: PVT

Wired Ventures Inc. 520 Third St, San Francisco CA 94107 USA; 415/276-5000, Fax: 415/276-5100, Web URL: hot-

wired.com, Focus: Computer magazine, Prdts: Wired, Ownership: PVT, Jane Metcalfe, Pres, Louis Rosetto, Pblr

WorldCom 515 E Amite Street, Jackson MS 39201-2702 USA; 601/360-8600, 800/844-1009 Fax: 704/255-8719, Web URL: wcom.com, Focus: PC software books, Ownership: NASDAQ, Stock Symbol: WCOM, Sales($M): 3,639.9, Fiscal End: 12/95; Bernard J. Ebbers, Pres & CEO, John W. Kluge, Chmn, Scott D. Sullivan, CFO

Xephon 1301 W Hwy 407 #201-450, Lewisville TX 75067 USA; 817/455-7050, Fax: 817/455-2492, Web URL: xephon.co.uk, Focus: Mid-range and mainframe computer information and publications, Ownership: PVT, Maureen Nicols, NA Agent, Chris Bunyan, Dir, Email: 100325.3711@compuserve.com

Xplain Corp. PO Box 5200, Westlake Village CA 91359-5200 USA; 805/494-9797, Fax: 805/494-9798, Co Email: info@mactech.com, Web URL: mactech.com, Focus: Macintosh magazines, Prdts: MacTech Magazine, Ownership: PVT, Neil Ticktin, Pblr

Yellowstone Information Services RR 2, PO Box 42A, Bloomingdale OH 43910-9802 USA; 614/944-1657, Fax: 614/944-1668, Focus: Computer newsletters, high-tech mailing lists, Prdts: Portable Computing Letter, The Internet Trail, Ownership:

PVT, Yr Founded: 1986, Roger C. Thibault, Ed. & Pblr

Ziff-Davis Press 5903 Christie Ave, Emeryville CA 94608-1925 USA; 510/601-2000, Fax: 510/601-2099, Co Email: firstname_lastname@zd.com, Web URL: zd.com, Focus: PC books, Ownership: PVT, Stacy Hiquet, Pblr, Juliet Langley, Assoc Pblr, Cheryl Holzaepfel, Ed.-in-Chief

Ziff-Davis Publishing Co. 1 Park Ave, New York NY 10016-5255 USA; 212/503-3500, Fax: 212/503-5519, Co Email: firstname_lastname@zd.com, Web URL: zd.com, Focus: Nearly 50 computer magazines and tradeshows, Prdts: PC Mag., PC/Computing, PC Week, MacWeek, MacUser, Window Sources, Ownership: Sub Softbank, Japan, Sales($M): 850, Fiscal End: 12/95; Eric Hippeau, Chmn & CEO, Ronni Sonnenberg, Pres US Pubs, Jeffrey Ballowee, Pres Interactive Media, J.B. Holston II, Pres Int'l Media, William Rosenthal, VP & CFO, Gregory Jarboe, Dir PR

Chapter 13

Research

Market Research Company Directory

Aberdeen Group Inc. 1 Boston Place 29th Floor, Boston MA 02108 USA; 617/723-7890, Fax: 617/723-7897, Web URL: aberdeen.com, Focus: Management consulting and custom market research, Ownership: PVT, Empl: 15, John Logan, Pres

Adam Media Research 15B W Carmel Valley Rd, Carmel Valley CA 93924 USA; 408/659-3070, 800/868-8124 Fax: 408/659-4330, Focus: Interactive multimedia research and consulting, Ownership: PVT, Tom Adams, Pres, Email: tomadams@ix.netcom.com

Adscope Inc. 1601 Oak St #B, Eugene OR 97401 USA; 541/687-1519, Focus: Tracks print ads in computer, telecom and electronics publications, Ownership: PVT, Founded: 1981, Empl: 16, Sheila Craven, Pres, Email: sheilacrav@aol.com; Joseph Turner, VP

Advanced Manufacturing Research 2 Oliver St 5th Floor, Boston MA 02103-4901 USA; 617/542-6600, Fax: 617/542-5670, Co Email: info@advmfg.com, Web URL: advmfg.com, Focus: Manufacturing information, CIM, industrial software and controls, Ownership: PVT, Founded: 1986, Empl: 30, Sales($M): 1.5, Tony Friscia, Pres

Ambit International 665 Third St #508, San Francisco CA 94107 USA; 415/957-9433, Fax: 415/957-0504, Co Email: ambitsf@aol.com, Focus: Distribution channel information, Ownership: PVT, Founded: 1988, Empl: 3, Linda Kazares, Pres, George E. Ferguson, Prod. Mktng. Mgr.

Annex Research 5110 N 40th St #100, Phoenix AZ 85018 USA; 602/956-8586, Fax: 602/956-8594, Focus: Information on IBM and plug compatible mainframe and mid-range computers, Ownership: PVT, Founded: 1978, Robert Djurdjevic, Pres

Answers Research 462 Stevens Ave #303, Solana Beach CA 92075-2066 USA; 619/792-4660, Fax: 619/792-1075, Focus: PC industry information, Ownership: PVT, Founded: 1991, Empl: 15, Albert Fitzgerald, Pres

AP Research 19672 Stevens Creek Blvd #175, Cupertino CA 95014-2465 USA; 408/253-6567, Focus: PCMCIA cards and microcomputer IC information, Ownership: PVT, Founded: 1992, Andy Prophet, Pres

Applied Computer Research Inc. PO Box 82266, Phoenix AZ 85068-9280 USA; 602/995-5929, 800/234-2227 Fax: 602/995-0905, Focus: Information, publications & conferences on applications development & product marketing, Ownership: PVT, Founded: 1971, Phillip Howard, Pres, Alice Howard, VP, Karen Hedden, Mktng Mgr

Architecture Technology Corp. PO Box 24344, Minneapolis MN 55424 USA; 612/935-2035, Fax: 612/829-5871, Focus: Information on communication systems, LANs and distributed systems, Ownership: PVT, Founded: 1981, Empl: 25, Sales($M): 2, Kenneth Thurber, Pres, Noel Schmidt, VP Ops

Arlen Communications Inc. 7315 Wisconsin Ave #600E, Bethesda MD 20814 USA; 301/656-7940, Fax: 301/656-3204, Focus: Electronic publishing & retailing, telebanking, videotex and interactive TV information, Ownership: PVT, Founded: 1980, Empl: 6, Gary Arlen, Pres, Email: gaha@prodigy.com

Asian Projects 134 Hamilton St, Cambridge MA 02139 USA; 617/576-1389, Fax: 617/576-1391, Focus: Asian high-tech market information, Ownership: PVT, Founded: 1993, Allen Furst, Pres

Associated Research Services Inc. 4320 N Beltline #A202, Irving TX 75038 USA; 214/570-7100, Fax: 214/570-4201, Web URL: arso.com, Focus: Marketing and promotion data on PCs, printers and workstations, Ownership: PVT, Founded: 1987, Empl: 17, Phil Magney, Pres, Mike Hagan, VP Sales & Mktng

ATB Associates 25 Livermore Rd, Wellesley MA 02181 USA; 617/239-1793, Fax: 617/237-2842, Focus: Computer market information, Ownership: PVT, Rich Schreiber, Pres

Audits & Surveys 650 Avenue of the Americas, New York NY 10011 USA; 212/627-9700, Fax: 212/627-2034, Web URL: surveys.com, Focus: PC sales tracking data, Ownership: PVT, Carl Ravitch, EVP, Bill Liebman, SVP

Augur Visions Inc. 101 First St #505, Los Altos CA 94022 USA; 415/493-5011, Fax: 415/493-1871, Focus: PCs, multimedia, mass storage, networking and distribution channel data, Ownership: PVT, Founded: 1988, Empl: 12, Bill Frank, Pres, Email: theaugur@aol.com

Blackstone Research Associates 10 River Rd, Uxbridge MA 01569-0314 USA; 508/278-3449, Fax: 508/278-7975, Focus: Printers, copiers, desktop publishing and reprographics information, Ownership: PVT, Founded: 1990, Michael Zeis, Pres

Boston Computer Exchange 210 South St 6th Fl, Boston MA 02111-2725 USA; 617/542-4414, 800/262-6399 Fax: 617/542-8849, Focus: Brokers used computers and data on used computer prices, Ownership: PVT, Founded: 1981, Empl: 12, Sales($M): 10, Barbara Geiger, Pres, Ann Saunders, CFO, Bus Mgr, Gary Gahman, Sales Mgr

Broadview Associates 1 Bridge Plaza, Ft. Lee NJ 07024 USA; 201/461-7929,

Fax: 201/346-9191, Web URL: broadview.com, Focus: Statistics on mergers and acquisitions in the information technology industry, Ownership: PVT, Founded: 1973, Empl: 85, Gilbert Mintz, Founding Partner, Harvey Poppel, Partner

BRP Publications Inc. 1333 H St NW #1100 W Tower, Washington DC 20005 USA; 202/842-3006, Fax: 202/842-3047, Co Email: brp@access.digex.net, Focus: E-mail, telecom and online information and publications, Ownership: PVT, Founded: 1977, Andrew Jacobson, Publisher, Victoria Mason, Ed-in-Chief

Burton Group, The 7040 Union Park Center, Midvale UT 84047 USA; 801/566-2880, Fax: 801/566-3611, Co Email: info@tbg.com, Web URL: tbg.com, Focus: Research, market analysis and consulting on network computing, Ownership: PVT, Founded: 1989, Empl: 12, Craig Burton, Principal, Jamie Lewis, Pres, Doug Allinger, VP Sales

Business Communications Co. Inc. 25 Van Zant St, Norwalk CT 06855-1781 USA; 203/853-4266, Fax: 203/853-0348, Co Email: buscom2@aol.com, Web URL: vyne.com/bcc, Focus: Information and PR on telecom & electronics, Ownership: PVT, Founded: 1971, Empl: 20, Louis Naturman, Pres, Robert Butler, Dir Ops

Business Research Group (BRG), 275 Washington St, Newton MA 02158 USA; 617/630-3900, 800/828-6344 Fax: 617/558-4585, Co Email: info@brg.cahners.com, Focus: Information, publications & consulting in C/S, networking, wireless & telecom, Ownership: PVT, Founded: 1988, Empl: 21, Sales($M): 1.5, William Ford Jr., VP & GM, Email: ford@brg.cahners.com; Kevin O'Neill, VP Research, Email: oneill@brg.cahners.com; Sarah E. Norton, Dir Mktng, Email: norton@brg.cahners.com; Rob Calcagni, Dir Sales, Email: calcagni@brg.cahners.com

Business Research Int'l. 233 Chemin des Bridants, Megeve F-74120 France; 33-5093-0762, Fax: 33-5091-9173, Co Email: 100652.3505@compuserve.com, Focus: European distribution channels and end user research, Ownership: PVT, Founded: 1993, Brigitte Morel, GM, Gordon Curran, SVP

C Systems Ltd. 1006 N Plum St, PO Box 708, Winnsboro TX 75494 USA; 903/342-5284, Fax: 903/342-5803, Co Email: csystems@e-tex.com, Focus: Tracks advertising activities of high-tech and consumer companies, Ownership: PVT, Founded: 1975, Empl: 20, Earlene Callan, Pres, James Callan, VP

CAD Research 3184-D Airway Ave, Costa Mesa CA 92626 USA; 714/662-

4970, Fax: 714/662-0304, Web URL: cad-research.com, Focus: Information on software and hardware for CAD/CAM/MCAE, Ownership: PVT, Founded: 1988, Empl: 20, Ross Stoutenborough, Pres

CAD/CAM Publishing Inc. 1010 Turquoise St #320, San Diego CA 92109-1268 USA; 619/488-0533, Fax: 619/488-6052, Co Email: cadcirc@aol.com, Focus: CAD/CAM, CAE and rapid prototyping information and publications, Prdts: Computer Aided Design Report, Rapid Prototyping Report, Ownership: PVT, Founded: 1981, Empl: 9, L. Stephen Wolfe, Pres

CADventures 18105-1 Andrea Circle N, Northridge CA 91325 USA; 818/998-6157, Fax: 818/998-0973, Focus: CAD market and technology information, Ownership: PVT, David Peltz, Pres

Camarro Research 580 Commerce Drive, Fairfield CT 06432-5513 USA; 203/336-4566, Fax: 203/331-0470, Co Email: kcamarro@snet.net, Focus: Computer fax boards and systems, fax machines, fax industry & printer information, Ownership: PVT, Founded: 1983, Empl: 5, Kenneth Camarro, Pres

Cambridge Information Group 7200 Wisconsin Ave #601, Bethesda MD 20814 USA; 301/961-6700, Fax: 301/961-6720, Web URL: csa.com, Focus: Annual directory of market research reports, studies and surveys, Prdts: Findex, Ownership: PVT, Founded: 1971, Empl: 60, Jim McGinty, Pres, Ted Caris, Publisher

Canopus Research PO Box 2805, 160 Standish St, Duxbury MA 02331 USA; 617/934-9800, Fax: 617/934-9888, Web URL: canopusresearch.com, Focus: Information on computer and communications markets, Ownership: PVT, Founded: 1983, Empl: 1, Will Zachmann, Pres, Email: wfz@canopusresearch.com

Casal Group 14465 Webb Chapel #212, Dallas TX 75234 USA; 214/488-7000, Fax: 214/488-7020, Co Email: casal@onramp.net, Focus: VARs and system integrator information and PR, Ownership: PVT, Founded: 1985, Empl: 35, Gene Bledsoe, Managing Partner, Mark Matthys, Partner, Email: mmattys.casal@onramp.net

CCMI 11300 Rockville Pike #1100, Rockville MD 20852-3030 USA; 301/816-8950, Fax: 301/816-8945, Focus: Statistics on telecom rates and tariffs, Ownership: PVT, Empl: 15

Channel Marketing Corp. 17400 N Dallas Pkwy #105, Dallas TX 75287 USA; 214/931-2420, Fax: 214/931-5505, Co Email: info@cmcus.com, Focus: Channel research consulting, trends and analysis, Ownership: PVT, Founded: 1988, Empl: 21, David M. Goldstein, Pres, Email: david@cmcus.com; Kelly A. Sticksez, VP, Email: kelly@cmcus.com

Channel Strategies Inc. (CSI), 299 California Ave #200, Palo Alto CA 94306 USA; 415/614-3740, Fax: 415/614-3745, Co Email: info@chanstrat.com, Web URL: chanstrat.com, Focus: Distribution channel information for hardware & software vendors, Ownership: PVT, Founded: 1985, Empl: 5, Mary Margaret Gibson, Partner, Email: mmgibson@chanstrat.com; Nancy Pencsak, Partner, Email: npencsak@chanstrat.com

Channel Tactics 4876 Idylwild Trail, Boulder CO 80301 USA; 303/581-0952, Fax: 303/581-0953, Co Email: 74431.55@compuserve.com, Focus: Consulting on distribution channels, Ownership: PVT, Founded: 1992, Bruce Fredrickson, Pres

ChannelCorp Management Consultants Inc. 2991 W 42nd Ave, Vancouver BC V6N 3G8 Canada; 604/263-6811, Fax: 604/263-4914, Focus: Distribution channel consulting, executive education & research, Ownership: PVT, Bruce R. Stuart, Pres, Margaret A. Stuart

Chromatic Communications Enterprises Inc. PO Box 30127, Walnut Creek CA 94598 USA; 510/945-1602, 800/782-3475 Fax: 707/746-0542, Focus: Database of microcomputer vendors and dealers, Ownership: PVT, Founded: 1982, Empl: 6, Michael Shipp, Pres

CIMdata Inc. 177 Worcester St #301, Wellesley MA 02181 USA; 617/235-4124, Fax: 617/235-4793, Focus: Information on CAD/CAM and CIM technology and markets, Ownership: PVT, Founded: 1983, Empl: 15, Julius Dorfman, Chmn, Eddie Miller, Pres

Cimtek Thomas 2700 S Roan St #203, Johnson City TN 37601 USA; 615/929-9383, 800/246-7353 Fax: 615/929-9445, Focus: Database of installed base of factory automation equip & database of WW expanding plants, Ownership: PVT, Founded: 1985, Empl: 10, Mike Bradley, Pres, George Nevin, Sales & Mktng Mgr

Communications Network Architects Inc. PO Box 32063, Washington DC 20007 USA; 202/775-8000, Fax: 202/785-1817, Focus: Network technology and trend information, Ownership: PVT, Founded: 1973, Empl: 17, Frank Dzubeck, Pres, Kathryn Smith-Dzubeck, EVP

Competitive Strategies Inc. 1750 Clarence Court, San Jose CA 95124-1201 USA; 408/266-4549, Fax: 408/264-0221, Web URL: competitive-strat.com, Focus: Information on applications of semiconductors, Prdts: Semiconductor Industry Almanac, Ownership: PVT, Founded: 1991, Empl: 3, Len Hills, Pres, Email: lhills@competitive-strat.com

Computer Economics Inc. 5841 Edison Place, Carlsbad CA 92008 USA; 619/438-8100, Fax: 619/431-1126, Co Email: custserv@compecon.com, Focus: Mainframe, workstations and mid-range computers;

forecast of residual value, new products, Ownership: PVT, Founded: 1979, Empl: 25, Bruno Bassi, Pres, Mark McManus, Editor-in-Chief, Email: mmcmanus@compecon.com

Computer Industry Almanac Inc. PO Box 600, 1639 Logan Creek Drive, Glenbrook NV 89413-0600 USA; 702/749-5053, 800/377-6810 Fax: 702/749-5864, Co Email: cialmanac@aol.com, Focus: Publisher of Computer Industry Almanac, market research and PC consulting, Prdts: Computer Industry Almanac, Ownership: PVT, Founded: 1986, Empl: 4, Karen Petska-Juliussen, Chmn & E-in-C, Email: 73543.3506@compuserve.com; Egil Juliussen, Pres & Ed, Email: cialmanac@aol.com

Computer Intelligence/InfoCorp 3344 N Torrey Pines Court, La Jolla CA 92037 USA; 619/450-1667, Fax: 619/452-7491, Focus: Database of computer installations--including mainframe, mini, PC & telecom, Ownership: PVT, Founded: 1969, Robert G. Brown, Pres

Computer Technology Research Corp. (CTR), 6 N Atlantic Wharf, Charleston SC 29401-2115 USA; 803/853-6460, Fax: 803/853-7210, Co Email: ctr-reports@aol.com, Web URL: sims.net/ctr, Focus: Mainframe, midrange, microcomputers & telecom information, Ownership: PVT, Founded: 1979, Empl: 25, Edward Wagner, Pres, Brian Lindgren, Editor, Stacey C. Evangelist, Mngng Editor

Context 435 London House 26-40 Kensington High St, London W8 4PF England; 071-937-3595, Fax: 071-937-1159, Focus: Track European PC product sales and prices, Ownership: PVT, Founded: 1983, Empl: 49, Jeremy Davies, Sr Partner, Howard Davies, Sr Partner

Contingency Planning Research Inc. 4 W Red Oak Lane 1st Fl, White Plains NY 10604 USA; 914/696-4500, 800/277-5511 Fax: 914/696-4580, Focus: Research and consulting in disaster recovery, contingency planning and risk management, Ownership: PVT, Founded: 1987, Empl: 15, Jeff Marinstein, Pres, Ellen Gold, Mktng Dir

Coordinated Service Inc. 20A Court St, Groton MA 01450 USA; 508/448-3800, Fax: 508/448-0060, Focus: On-line database of service companies; mergers and acquisition brokering to third parties, Ownership: PVT, Founded: 1974, Empl: 3, Sales($M): 0.3, William Herbert, Pres, Judith Sawyer, VP

Creative Strategies 4010 Moorpark Ave #212, San Jose CA 95117-1843 USA; 408/985-1110, Fax: 408/985-1114, Focus: Computers, CAD/CAM, AI, office automation and telecom, Ownership: PVT, Founded: 1969, Empl: 12, Tim Bajarin, Pres

Culpepper & Associates Inc. 7000

Peachtree-Dunwoody Rd Bldg 10, Atlanta GA 30328 USA; 770/668-0616, Fax: 770/668-1095, Focus: Information on software industry business practices, Ownership: PVT, Founded: 1979, Empl: 16, Sales($M): 1, Warren Culpepper, Chmn & Pres, Email: warren@culpepper.com

Currid & Co. 11000 Richmond Ave #140, Houston TX 77042 USA; 713/789-5995, Fax: 713/789-5994, Web URL: currid.com, Focus: Technology assessment for Fortune 500 companies and computer industry clients, Ownership: PVT, Founded: 1991, Empl: 16, Cheryl Currid, Pres, Email: cheryl@currid.com; Diane Bolin, Ops Mgr

Cutter Information Corp. (CIC), 37 Broadway, Arlington MA 02174 USA; 617/648-8700, 800/964-8700 Fax: 617/648-8707, Co Email: 74107.653@compuserve.com, Web URL: cutter.com, Focus: Information technology for newsletters, Ownership: PVT, Founded: 1986, Empl: 30, Karen Coburn, Pres, Beth O'Neill, Client Svcs Mgr, Leslie Sisto, Grp Pub, Email: 73352.1625@compuserve.com

CW Database 500 Old Connecticut Path, Framingham MA 01701 USA; 508/879-0700, Fax: 508/879-0184, Focus: Databases of computer sites, 7,000 VARs and 38,000 IS professionals, Ownership: Sub Computerworld, Rich Mikita, GM, John Carpenter, VP Sales

D.H. Andrews Group 700 W Johnson Ave, Cheshire CT 06410 USA; 203/271-1300, Fax: 203/272-8744, Focus: Information, reports, seminars, consulting and strategic planning on the IBM AS/400, Ownership: PVT, Founded: 1984, Empl: 25, Sales($M): 3, David Andrews, Pres, Doreen Simeone-Ambert, Partner

D.H. Brown Associates Inc. 222 Grace Church St, Port Chester NY 10573 USA; 914/937-4302, Fax: 914/937-2485, Web URL: dhbrown.com, Focus: CAD/CAM market, workstations, PCs and object-oriented programming information, Ownership: PVT, Founded: 1985, Donald Brown, Pres

Daley Marketing Corp. 151 Kalmus H4, Costa Mesa CA 92626 USA; 714/662-0755, Fax: 714/662-0717, Co Email: daleydmc@ix.netcom.com, Web URL: dmc.netcom.com, Focus: Computer prices, residual values and used computer pricing, Ownership: PVT, Founded: 1980, Empl: 7, Peter Daley, Pres, Kelly Herrera, Sr Act Exec

Daratech Inc. 140 Sixth St, Cambridge MA 02142 USA; 617/354-2339, Fax: 617/354-7822, Co Email: daratech@daratech.com, Web URL: daratech.com, Focus: CAD/CAM, CAE, GIS, multimedia and workstations data--including user surveys, Ownership: PVT, Founded: 1978, Empl: 15, Charles

Foundyller, Chmn & Pres, Bruce Jenkins, VP

Darnell Group, The 4720 Crestview Drive, Norco CA 91760 USA; 909/279-6684, Fax: 909/273-9505, Co Email: jshepard@darnell.com, Focus: Market research on power conversion, batteries and UPS, Ownership: PVT, Jeff Shepard, Publisher, Email: jshepard@darnell.com; Bob Shepard, Research, Sharon Lancaster, Manager

Data Analysis Group 5100 Cherry Creek Rd, PO Box 128, Cloverdale CA 95425 USA; 707/539-3009, Fax: 707/486-5618, Co Email: dataag@interserv.com, Focus: Market forecast information on the computer industry, Ownership: PVT, Founded: 1979, Empl: 5, Keith Parker, Pres, Reny Parker, VP

Datapro Information Services Group 600 Delran Pkwy, Delran NJ 08705-9904 USA; 609/764-0100, Fax: 609/764-8953, Co Email: datapro@mgh.com, Web URL: datpro.com, Focus: 40+ loose-leaf publications on technology, products and management, Ownership: Sub McGraw-Hill, Founded: 1971, Empl: 450, Sales($M): 55, Stephen Thomas, Pres, Martin Levine, VP Tech

Dataquest 1290 Ridder Park Drive, San Jose CA 95131-2398 USA; 408/437-8000, Fax: 408/437-0292, Co Email: @dataquest.com, Focus: PC, workstation, supercomputer, mass storage, printer & semiconductor information, Ownership: Sub Gartner Group, Founded: 1971, Judy Hamilton, Pres & CEO, Robert J. Steinerd, VP, Paul Wheaton, Media Rel Mgr

Davis Inc. PO Box 21717, Washington DC 20009-9717 USA; 202/667-6400, Fax: 202/667-6512, Focus: Desktop imaging information, Ownership: PVT, L. Miller Davis, Pres

Dayton Associate 477 123rd Place NE, Bellevue WA 98005 USA; 206/451-1140, Fax: 206/451-8505, Co Email: dougdayton@msn.com, Focus: Strategic marketing and technical communication, Ownership: PVT, Founded: 1985, Doug Dayton, Pres

DeBoever Architectures Inc. Damonmill Square #5C, Concord MA 01742 USA; 508/371-1557, 800/313-2037 Fax: 508/371-1558, Web URL: lrdeulharet.com, Focus: Information on computer connectivity, system integration and telecom, Ownership: PVT, Founded: 1987, Empl: 8, Larry DeBoever, Pres, Susan O'Brien, VP Bus Dev, Jim Ettwein, VP & GM Advisory Svcs

Decision Resources Inc. 1100 Winter St, Waltham MA 02154 USA; 617/487-3700, Fax: 617/487-5750, Focus: Information and consulting on computers, telecom, electronics & emerging technologies, Ownership: PVT, Empl: 100, Sales($M): 10, Sarah Fuller, Pres, Samuel Fleming, CEO,

Cindy Corona, Mktng Mgr

Decisys Inc. 45615 Willow Pond Plz, Sterling VA 20164 USA; 703/742-5400, Fax: 703/742-8038, Web URL: decisys.com, Focus: Network integration consulting, Ownership: PVT, Founded: 1994, Empl: 6, David Passmore, Pres, Email: dpassmore@decisys.com; Fred McClimans, Principal, Email: fmcclimans@decisys.com; Howard Hecht, Principal, Email: hhecht@decisys.com

Delphi Consulting Group Inc. 100 City Hall Plaza, Boston MA 02108-2106 USA; 617/247-1025, Fax: 617/247-4957, Focus: Seminars and consulting on electronic document management, Ownership: PVT, Founded: 1988, Empl: 20, Thomas M. Koulopoulos, Pres, Carl Frappaolo, EVP, Debra J. Fitzgibbons, Dir Client Svcs, Mary Ann Kozlowski, Mgr PR

Digital Consulting Inc. (DCI), 204 Andover St, Andover MA 01810 USA; 508/470-3880, 800/324-3976 Fax: 508/470-0526, Focus: Seminars, conferences on CASE, database, PCs and other topics, Ownership: PVT, Founded: 1981, Empl: 70, Sales($M): 10, George Schussel, CEO

Disk/Trend Inc. 1925 Landings Drive, Mountain View CA 94043 USA; 415/961-6209, Fax: 415/969-2560, Co Email: dtinfo@disktrend.com, Focus: Publishes annual Disk/Trend reports on rigid, disk drive arrays and optical disk drives, Ownership: PVT, Founded: 1977, Empl: 4, James N. Porter, Pres, Robert H. Katzive, VP

DP Directory Inc. 525 Goodale Hill Rd, Glastonbury CT 06033 USA; 203/659-1065, Fax: 203/659-4700, Focus: Databases and mailing lists of computer magazines, columnists, editors and user groups, Ownership: PVT, Founded: 1984, Empl: 3, Al Harberg, Pres

Dream IT Inc. 2620 7th St, Boulder CO 80304 USA; 303/417-9313, Fax: 303/473-9670, Co Email: @dreamit.com, Web URL: dreamit.com, Focus: Mobile computing, wireless communications, pens, digitizers and consulting, Ownership: PVT, Founded: 1991, Empl: 3, Sales($M): O.6, Portia Isaacson, Pres, Email: portia@dreamit.com

Economist Intelligence Unit, The 111 W 57th St, New York NY 10019 USA; 212/554-0600, Fax: 212/586-1181, Focus: Information technology usage data, Ownership: PVT, Louis Celi, Mgng Dir Elec Pubs

EDI, spread the word! 13805 Wooded Creek Drive, Dallas TX 75244 USA; 214/243-3456, 800/777-5006 Fax: 214/243-7265, Focus: Market research and consulting on EDI, Ownership: PVT, Founded: 1986, Empl: 9, Robert Payne, Partner, Anna Lee Payne, Partner

Education Turnkey Systems Inc. 256 N Washington St, Falls Church VA 22046 USA; 703/536-2310, Fax: 703/536-3225,

Focus: Education market for computer-based instruction and multimedia, Ownership: PVT, Founded: 1969, Empl: 8, Charles Blaschke, Pres, Blair Curry, Treas

EDventure Holdings Inc. 104 Fifth Ave, New York NY 10011-6987 USA; 212/924-8800, Fax: 212/924-0240, Co Email: info@edventure.com, Focus: Release 1.0 newsletter on emerging software, Ownership: PVT, Founded: 1983, Empl: 6, Sales($M): 2, Esther Dyson, Pres & Editor, Email: edyson@edventure.com; Daphne Kis, Publisher & VP, Email: daphne@edventure.com; Jerry Michalski, Mng Ed, Email: jerry@edventure.com

Electronic Commerce Strategies Inc. 670 Village Trace Bldg 19-310, Marietta GA 30067 USA; 770/951-2648, Fax: 770/951-2649, Co Email: info@e-com.com, Web URL: e-com.com, Focus: Information about the electronic data interchange (EDI) market, Ownership: PVT, Founded: 1985, Empl: 4, Jack Shaw, Pres

Electronic Trend Publications 1975 Hamilton Ave #6, San Jose CA 95125-5630 USA; 408/369-7000, 800/726-6858 Fax: 408/369-8021, Co Email: info@electronictrendpubs.com, Web URL: electronictrendpubs.com, Focus: Information on computer systems and high-tech markets, Ownership: PVT, Founded: 1978, Empl: 10, Sales($M): 1+, Steve Berry, Pres, Email: saberry@electronictrendpubs.com; Karen Selven, VP Mktng, Email: kselven@electronictrendpubs.com

ElectroniCast Corp. 800 S Clarmont #105, San Mateo CA 94402 USA; 415/343-1398, Fax: 415/343-1698, Focus: Fiber optics, networks, interconnection and optoelectronics information, Ownership: PVT, Founded: 1981, Empl: 24, Sales($M): 1.3, Jeff Montgomery, Chmn, Stephen Montgomery, VP

Emerging Technologies Group Inc. 5 Kinsella St, Dix Hills NY 11746 USA; 516/586-8810, Fax: 516/586-3043, Focus: Information, consulting and seminars on C/S computing and cost-of-ownership, Ownership: PVT, Founded: 1987, Empl: 12, Wendy Rauch, Pres, Email: wrauch@etg.com; Harvey Hindin, VP, Email: hhindin@etg.com

Fairfield Research Inc. 5815 S 58th St, Lincoln NE 68516-3688 USA; 402/441-3370, 800/755-0024 Fax: 402/441-3389, Co Email: fairfield@mail.ltec.net, Web URL: cybersurvey.com, Focus: Custom and syndicated surveys of computer users, Ownership: PVT, Founded: 1986, Empl: 75, Gary Gabelhouse, CEO, Ted Lannan, Pres

Faulkner Information Services 114 Cooper Center, 7905 Browning Rd, Pennsauken NJ 08109-4319 USA; 609/662-2070, 800/843-0460 Fax: 609/662-3380, Web URL: faulkner.com, Focus: Information services on computer and communica-

tions products, Ownership: PVT, Founded: 1985, Empl: 90, Martin Murphy, Pres, Barbara Forkel, VP Sales & Mktng

FIND/SVP Inc. 625 Avenue of the Americas, New York NY 10011 USA; 212/645-4500, Fax: 212/645-7681, Focus: Finds information about high tech and other subjects for its subscribers, Ownership: NASDAQ, Founded: 1969, Empl: 170, Sales($M): 28.6, Fiscal End: 12/95; Andrew Garvin, Pres, Kathleen Bingham, EVP

First Market Research 656 Beacon St, Boston MA 02215 USA; 617/482-9080, Fax: 617/482-4017, Web URL: firstmarket.com, Focus: Information on video and telecom, PC software and hardware, fax, phones & copier, Ownership: PVT, Founded: 1967, Empl: 8, James R. Heiman, Pres, Jack Reynolds, Chmn

Foresite Systems PO Box 584, Okemos MI 48805 USA; 517/337-7050, Fax: 517/337-7050, Focus: Software development methodology data, Ownership: PVT, Andrew Topper, Pres

Forrester Research Inc. 1033 Massachusetts Ave, Cambridge MA 02138 USA; 617/497-7090, Fax: 617/868-0577, Web URL: forrester.com, Focus: Analysis of PCs, LANs, software and network management for Fortune 1000 market, Ownership: PVT, Founded: 1983, Empl: 17, George F. Colony, Pres

Forward Concepts 1575 W University Drive #111, Tempe AZ 85281 USA; 602/968-3759, Fax: 602/968-7145, Co Email: fwdconcepts.com, Focus: Electronics systems, semiconductors and digital signal processing information, Ownership: PVT, Founded: 1984, Empl: 5, Will Strauss, Pres, Mel Eklund, Sr Tech Consultant

Freeman Associates Inc. 311 E Carrillo St, Santa Barbara CA 93101 USA; 805/963-3853, Fax: 805/962-1541, Co Email: freemaninc@aol.com, Web URL: freemaninc.com, Focus: Market analysis and consulting on tape and optical storage; Co-sponsors DataStorage conf., Ownership: PVT, Founded: 1977, Empl: 8, Raymond C. Freeman, Jr., Pres, Email: ray@freemaninc.com; Robert C. Abraham, VP

Frost & Sullivan Inc. 2525 Charleston Rd, Mountain View CA 94043 USA; 415/961-9000, Fax: 415/961-5042, Focus: Telecom, computers, office automation, ICs & electronics information, Ownership: PVT, Founded: 1960, Empl: 250, Sales($M): 26, David Frigstad, Pres & CEO, Barry Bartlett, VP Research, David Miller, Dir Mktng, Email: dmiller@frost.com

Fuji-Keizai USA Inc. 141 E 55th St #3F, New York NY 10022 USA; 212/688-2550, Fax: 212/758-9040, Focus: Market research and consulting, Ownership: Sub Fuji-Keizai Zhonglian, Jason Asaeda

Future Technology Surveys Inc. 5880

Live Oak Pkwy #255, Norcross GA 30093-1740 USA; 770/717-0779, Fax: 770/381-9865, Focus: Computers, manufacturing technologies, sensors, energy and environment data, Ownership: PVT, Founded: 1973, Empl: 8, Richard Miller, Pres

G. Meier Inc. PO Box 104, Millburn NJ 07041 USA; 201/376-8181, Fax: 201/376-8335, Co Email: gmeier@aol.com, Focus: PC software sales and market shares tracking, Ownership: PVT, Founded: 1986, George B. Meier, Pres

G2 Research Inc. 883 N Shoreline Blvd #A-210, Mountain View CA 94043 USA; 415/964-2400, Fax: 415/964-2582, Web URL: g2r.com, Focus: Computers, telecom, office automation and system integration information, Ownership: PVT, Founded: 1987, Empl: 50, Graham Kemp, Pres

Gartner Group 56 Top Gallant Rd, PO Box 10212, Stamford CT 06904-2212 USA; 203/964-0096, Fax: 203/967-6143, Web URL: gartner.com, Focus: Information on mainframe, mini and PCs, LANs, software, office automation & telecom, Ownership: NASDAQ, Stock Symbol: GART, Founded: 1979, Empl: 1,175, Sales($M): 229.2, Fiscal End: 9/95; Manny Fernandez, Pres & CEO, William T. Clifford, EVP & COO, E. Follett Carter, EVP Sales & Mktng, David G. Familiant, EVP Int'l Ops, John F. Halligan, EVP & CFO, Kate Berg, Mgr Media Rel

Geibel Marketing Consulting PO Box 611, Belmont MA 02178-0005 USA; 617/484-8285, Fax: 617/489-3567, Co Email: 74752.3072@compuserve.com, Focus: Software marketing programs, sales support programs and PR services, Ownership: PVT, Jeffrey P. Geibel, Managing Partner

Gemini Consulting 25 Airport Rd, Morristown NJ 07960 USA; 201/285-9000, 800/631-8100 Fax: 201/285-9020, Focus: Communications, consumer electronics, computer and content, Prdts: Business Transformation, Ownership: PVT, Founded: 1991, Empl: 1,800, Thomas Gage, VP, Jill Totenberg, VP Comm, Email: jtotenberg@aol.com

Gen 2 Ventures 12980 Saratoga Ave #E, Saratoga CA 95070 USA; 408/446-2277, Fax: 408/446-4755, Focus: Information and consulting on IBM networking and cooperative processing, Ownership: PVT, Founded: 1986, Donald Czubek, Pres, Stephen J. Randesi, Chmn

Genesis 2 Inc. PO Box 642, Millwood NY 10546-0642 USA; 914/762-3251, Fax: 914/941-9181, Co Email: shriver@genesis2.com, Web URL: genesis2.com, Focus: High-performance and parallel computer consulting, Ownership: PVT, Founded: 1991, Bruce Shriver, Pres

Giga Information Group 1 Kendall Square Bldg 1400W, Cambridge MA 02139 USA; 617/577-9595, 800/874-9980 Fax: 617/577-1649, Co Email: @gigasd.com, Web URL: gigaweb.com, Focus: Electronic imaging, information processing and telecom data, Ownership: Sub Giga Information, Founded: 1979, Empl: 300, Sales($M): 28, Gideon Gartner, Chmn & CEO, Jeff Swartz, SVP Mktng, Richard Goldman, SVP & CFO, Andrew Jennings, SVP WW Sales, Martha Popoloski

Gistics Inc. 700 Larkspur Landing Circle #199, Larkspur CA 94939-1754 USA; 415/461-4305, Fax: 415/927-4337, Focus: Multimedia and new media information and consulting, Ownership: PVT, Founded: 1987, Empl: 8, Michael Moon, Dir Exec. Programs, Email: moon@gistics.com; James Byram, Dir Research, Email: byram@gistics.com

Global Touch Inc. 2980 Adeline, Berkeley CA 94703 USA; 510/649-1100, Fax: 510/649-1155, Focus: International distribution channel data and conferences, Ownership: PVT, Founded: 1989, Denise Sangster, Pres

Gordon S. Black Corp. 135 Corporate Woods, Rochester NY 14623-1457 USA; 716/272-8400, Fax: 716/272-8680, Focus: Customer satisfaction surveys for high-tech companies, Ownership: PVT, Founded: 1975, Empl: 30, Gordon Black, Chmn & CEO, David Clemm, Pres & COO

Grassroots Research 4 Embarcadero Center 30th Floor, San Francisco CA 94111 USA; 415/954-5376, Fax: 415/954-8201, Focus: Computer end-user and reseller surveys, Ownership: PVT, Founded: 1984, Marc Friedman, Dir, Christine McCulloch, Mktng Dir

GRB Consulting 19923 Via Escuela Drive, Saratoga CA 95070 USA; 408/741-1917, Fax: 408/867-0427, Focus: Computer product strategy consulting, Ownership: PVT, Founded: 1990, Gerry Babb, Pres

GreenTree Associates Inc. 532 Great Rd, Acton MA 01720 USA; 508/263-6900, Fax: 508/263-6565, Co Email: jan@greentree.com, Web URL: greentree.com, Focus: International computer marketing data and consulting, Ownership: PVT, Founded: 1985, Empl: 7, Randy Green, Pres, Email: rangreen@aol.com; Maureen Harmonay, VP

Griffin Dix Research Associates 1525 Shattuck Ave #E, Berkeley CA 94709-1500 USA; 510/540-6350, Fax: 510/540-6510, Focus: Desktop video and multimedia market research, publishing & prepress industry research, Ownership: PVT

Hartsook Letter, The 3001 Marina Drive, Alameda CA 94501-1637 USA; 510/521-4988, Fax: 510/521-3572,

Focus: Analysis of the Macintosh market, Ownership: PVT, Founded: 1991, Empl: 2, Pieter Hartsook, Editor & Publisher

Harvard Group, The 50 Firefall Court #600, The Woodlands TX 77380 USA; 713/292-3999, Fax: 713/292-2499, Focus: Computer reseller consulting, Ownership: PVT, Founded: 1977, Empl: 6, Sales($M): 1.1, Vince Caracio, Pres

HCS Inc. 18004 SE Marie St, Portland OR 97236-1338 USA; 503/661-3421, Fax: 503/661-2477, Focus: CASE, CAD, software maintenance, PCs, workstations and re-engineering information, Ownership: PVT, Founded: 1988, Empl: 5, Jim Hobuss, Pres, Robin Hobuss, Treas

HLS Associates Int'l. (HLSA), 19 Halifax Court #200, Sterling VA 20165 USA; 703/444-7037, Fax: 703/406-9298, Co Email: hlsassoc@aol.com, Focus: Consulting and info on work process automation using OCR/imaging technologies, Ownership: PVT, Founded: 1987, Empl: 5, Sales($M): 1, Herbert F. Schantz, Pres, Letty L.M. Schantz, Chmn

HTE Research Inc. 400 Oyster Point Blvd #220, S. San Francisco CA 94080 USA; 415/871-4377, Fax: 415/871-0513, Co Email: @hte-sibs.com, Web URL: hte-sibs.com, Focus: Information about the semiconductor industry, Ownership: PVT, Founded: 1979, Empl: 5, Steve Szirom, Pres, Email: szirom@hte-sibs.com; Paul Plansky, Editor, Amy K. Whaley, Accountant

Hurwitz Consulting Group 29 Crafts St #270, Newton MA 02158-1274 USA; 617/965-6900, Fax: 617/965-6901, Focus: Application development software and cross platform infrastructures & systems, Ownership: PVT, Founded: 1992, Empl: 16, Judith Hurwitz, Pres, Email: jhurwitz@world.std.com; Dena Brody, VP Admin, Chet Geschickter, VP Res, Ellen Gutter, VP Sales & Mktng

ICP 823 E Westfield Blvd, Indianapolis IN 46220-1715 USA; 317/251-7727, Fax: 317/251-7813, Co Email: info@icp.com, Web URL: icp.com, Focus: Information on software products and companies, Ownership: PVT, Founded: 1966, Empl: 60, Larry Welke, Pres

IDC Government 3110 Fairview Park Drive #1100, Falls Church VA 22042-4503 USA; 703/876-5055, Fax: 703/876-5077, Web URL: idcg.com, Focus: Information technology data and consulting, Ownership: PVT, Matthew Mahoney, Research Dir

IDC/LINK 2 Park Ave #1420, New York NY 10016 USA; 212/726-0900, Fax: 212/696-8096, Web URL: idcresearch.com, Focus: Electronic information svcs, education market data, mass market computing & telecom, Ownership: IDC, Founded: 1976, Empl: 45, Andy Bose, Group VP, Email: bose@idcresearch.com; Mark Winther,

VP, Email: mwinther@idcresearch.com; Julia Blelock, VP, Email: jblelock@idcresearch.com; Simon Salamon, VP, Email: ssalamon@idcresearch.com; June Wallach, VP, Email: jwallach@idcresearch.com; Elleen Zimber, Grp Op Mgr, Email: ezimbler@idcresearch.com

IDEAS International Pty. Ltd. 802-808 Pacific Hwy, PO Box 315, Gordon NSW 2072 Australia; 612-498-7399, Fax: 612-498-5249, Co Email: ideas.com.au, Web URL: ideas.com.au, Focus: Database of computer systems and performance information, Prdts: Competitive Profiles, Ownership: PVT, Founded: 1981, Empl: 7, Sales($M): 1.0, John N. Tulloch, Managing Dir, Email: johnt@ideas.com.au; Ian T. Birks, Int'l. Sales Dir, Email: ianb@ideas.com.au; Stephen Williams, European Sales Dir, Email: stevew@ideas-international.com; Joshua C. Venman, R&D Dir, Email: joshv@ideas.com.au

Illuminata 187 Main St, Nashua NH 03060 USA; 603/598-0099, Fax: 603/598-0199, Co Email: info@illuminata.com, Web URL: illuminata.com, Focus: Technology assessment and market research, Ownership: PVT, Founded: 1993, Jonathan Eunice, Pres, Email: jonathan@illuminata.com

Image Consulting Group Inc. 315 Walt Whitman Rd #316, Huntington Station NY 11746 USA; 516/351-8942, Fax: 516/351-8944, Focus: Computer imaging market research, Ownership: PVT, Hugh R. Green, Pres

In-Stat Inc. PO Box 14667, Scottsdale AZ 85260-2418 USA; 602/483-4440, Fax: 602/483-0400, Web URL: instat.com, Focus: Information services on semiconductor, computer and communications industries, Prdts: In-Stat Electronics Report, Ownership: PVT, Founded: 1981, Empl: 17, Sales($M): 2.5, Jack Beedle, Founder, John Abram, Pres, Morry Marshall, Dir Analysts

InfoCenter 2280 S Xanadu Way #390, Aurora CO 80014 USA; 303/751-8880, Fax: 303/751-8885, Web URL: websitesurveys.com, Focus: Product development research and customer and web tracking studies, Ownership: PVT, Founded: 1991, Empl: 20, Tomec Smith, Pres

Infonetics Research Inc. 298 S 15th St, San Jose CA 95112-2150 USA; 408/298-7999, Fax: 408/298-2073, Focus: LANs, network management and computer communication information, Ownership: PVT, Founded: 1990, Empl: 10, Sales($M): 1, Michael Howard, Pres, Email: mvhoward@aol.com; J'Amy Napolitan, VP & Sr. Analyst, Email: jamynap@aol.com; Jordan Stone, Sr. Analyst, Larry Howard, Analyst

Information Architects, The 23190 Ravensbury Ave, Los Altos CA 94024 USA; 415/948-3927, Fax: 415/948-3590,

Co Email: gmleonard@aol.com, Focus: SPARC marketplace information, Ownership: PVT, Founded: 1989, Empl: 8, Gregory M. Leonard, Principal, Email: gmleonard@aol.com; Susan A. Mason, Principal, Email: susanmason@aol.com

Information Associates 1259 El Camino Real #231, Menlo Park CA 94025 USA; 415/322-0247, Fax: 415/322-0469, Focus: Workstations, graphics, imaging, visualization and display systems information, Ownership: PVT, Founded: 1989, Empl: 1, Murray Disman, Pres

Information Gatekeepers Inc. 214 Harvard Ave, Boston MA 02134 USA; 617/738-8088, Fax: 617/734-8562, Co Email: igiboston@aol.com, Focus: Information on LANS, fiber optics, ISDN, wireless and telecom, Ownership: PVT, Founded: 1978, Empl: 15, Sales($M): 2, Paul Polishuk, Pres, Email: igiboston@aol.com; Peter Polishuk, Mktng Mgr

Information Network, The 3120 Parkside Lane, Williamsburg VA 23185 USA; 804/258-3738, Fax: 804/258-3820, Focus: IC and computer market research, Ownership: PVT, Robert N. Castellano, Pres

Information Resource Group (IRG), 35200 Dequindre, Sterling Heights MI 48310-4857 USA; 810/978-3000, Fax: 810/978-3010, Web URL: irg.ppcix.net-com.com, Focus: Database and research on 150,000 computer sites and 1M corporate and MIS executives, Prdts: IRG Database, Ownership: PVT, Founded: 1982, Empl: 100, Terry Olson, Pres

Information Workstation Group 1101 King St #601, Alexandria VA 22314 USA; 703/548-4320, Fax: 703/548-4321, Focus: Research and consulting on multimedia, CD-ROM, imaging and advanced information systems, Ownership: PVT, Founded: 1985, John Gale, Pres

InfoTech PO Box 150, Skyline Drive, Woodstock VT 05091-0150 USA; 802/763-2097, Fax: 802/763-2098, Co Email: infotech@valley.net, Focus: CD-ROM and multimedia software information and PR services, Ownership: PVT, Founded: 1984, Empl: 3, Ted Pine, Principal, Julie B. Schwerin, Pres

Input 1881 Landings Drive, Mountain View CA 94043-0848 USA; 415/961-3300, Fax: 415/961-3966, Co Email: @input.com, Focus: Market research on information service, networks, software, SI and electronic commerce, Ownership: PVT, Founded: 1974, Empl: 70, Sales($M): 8, Peter Cunningham, Pres & CEO, Email: pac@input.com; Bob Goodwin, VP Sales & Mktng, Email: bob_goodwin@input.com

Insight-Onsite 1378 Olympus Drive, San Jose CA 95129 USA; 408/252-2260, Fax: 408/252-2299, Co Email: insight-ons@aol.com, Focus: Information on semi-

conductors and PCs, market opportunity reports, Ownership: PVT, Founded: 1978, Empl: 1, Willard Booth, Pres

Institute for the Future 2744 Sand Hill Rd, Menlo Park CA 94025-7020 USA; 415/854-6322, Fax: 415/854-7850, Web URL: iftf.org, Focus: Telecom, teleconferencing, groupware, multimedia workstations & education information, Ownership: PVT, Founded: 1968, Empl: 20, Sales($M): 4, Bob Johansen, Pres

Inteco Corp. 110 Richards Ave, Norwalk CT 06854 USA; 203/866-4400, Fax: 203/852-1599, Focus: Multiclient studies for information and high-tech industries, Ownership: PVT, Founded: 1978, Empl: 40, Tom Bachman, Pres & CEO, Graham Taylor, VP

Integrated Circuit Engineering Corp. 15022 N 75th St, Scottsdale AZ 85260 USA; 602/998-9780, Fax: 602/948-1925, Co Email: icec@primenet.com, Web URL: ice-corp.com, Focus: Information and consulting about the semiconductor industry, Ownership: PVT, Founded: 1964, Empl: 50, Sales($M): 4, Glen Madland, Chmn, Hal Becker, CEO

Integrated Strategic Information Services Inc. (I.S.I.S.), 2516 Hastings Drive #500, Belmont CA 94002 USA; 415/802-8555, Fax: 415/802-9555, Co Email: isis@isisglobal.com, Focus: IT market research, Marc Limacher, Managing Dir, Email: 73244.2556@compuserve.com; Claudia Hess, Dir Client Svcs

IntelliQuest 1250 Capital of Texas Hwy S Bldg 2 Plaza 1, Austin TX 78746 USA; 512/329-2424, Fax: 512/329-0888, Co Email: @intelliquest.com, Web URL: intelliquest.com, Focus: Custom research for technology products and services, Ownership: PVT, Founded: 1985, Empl: 150, Sales($M): 15, Peter Zandan, CEO, Brian Sharples, Pres, James Schellhase, CFO

Interconsult PO Box 880, N. Hampton NH 03862 USA; 603/964-6464, Fax: 603/964-9747, Co Email: 73251.3015@compuserve.com, Focus: International computer market consulting, Ownership: PVT, Founded: 1978, Empl: 5, James Finke, Pres, Jo-Anne Lent, Managing Partner

International Data Corp. (IDC), 5 Speen St, Framingham MA 01701 USA; 508/872-8200, 800/343-4935 Fax: 508/935-4015, Co Email: info@idcresearch.com, Web URL: idcresearch.com, Focus: Market research on computer hardware, software, workgroup applications, PC & services, Ownership: PVT, Founded: 1964, Empl: 500, Sales($M): 130, Fiscal End: 12/95; Kirk Campbell, Pres & CEO, Email: kcampbell@idcresearch.com; Philippe de Marcillac, SVP, WW Research, Email: pdemarcillac@idcresearch.com; David Vellante, SVP, Email: dvellante@idcresearch.com; John Gantz, SVP,

Email: jgantz@idcresearch.com; Gigi Wang, SVP, Email: gwang@idcresearch.com; Chris Whelan, Marcom Mgr, Email: cwhelan@idcresearch.com

International Systems Group Inc. 347 W 57th St #PHB, New York NY 10019 USA; 212/489-0400, Fax: 212/489-1125, Focus: C/S consulting, Ownership: PVT, Founded: 1984, Max Dolgicer, Dir

International Technology Consultants 1724 Kalorama Rd NW #210, Washington DC 20009-2624 USA; 202/234-2138, Fax: 202/483-7922, Focus: Latin American and Eastern Europe telecom market analysis, Ownership: PVT, Founded: 1991, S. Blake Swensrud II, Pres, Justin Friedman, VP

International Technology Group 1503 Grant Rd #180, Mountain View CA 94040-3270 USA; 415/964-2565, Fax: 415/964-2827, Focus: Information services and management consulting in information systems technologies, Ownership: PVT, Founded: 1983, Empl: 8, Sales($M): 0.8, Brian Jeffery, Managing Dir, Robert Simko, Exec Dir, Marti Avery, Admin Mgr

Internet Info 5119A Leesburg Pike #293, Falls Church VA 22041 USA; 703/578-4800, Fax: 703/578-4801, Co Email: info@internetinfo.com, Focus: Market research on Internet, Ownership: PVT, Michael J. Walsh, Pres

Interquest PO Box 6568, Charlottesville VA 22906 USA; 804/979-9945, Fax: 804/979-9959, Focus: Electronic printing and publishing information, Ownership: PVT, Founded: 1988, Empl: 7, Gilles Biscos, Pres, Email: 102063.1421@compuserve.com; Fonda Nyus

Itom International Co. PO Box 1450, Los Altos CA 94023 USA; 415/948-4516, Fax: 415/948-9153, Focus: Fault tolerant computers, transaction processing, parallel processing & RISC information, Ownership: PVT, Founded: 1980, Omri Serlin, Pres

Itsunami Inc. PO Box 4756, Berkeley CA 94704 USA; 510/841-7271, Fax: 510/848-6897, Focus: High-tech partnerships and strategic relations database, Ownership: PVT, Founded: 1983, James M. Sharp, Pres

J.D. Power & Associates 30401 Agoura Rd, Agoura Hills CA 91301 USA; 818/889-6330, Fax: 818/889-3719, Focus: Customer satisfaction research for automobiles, PCs and consumer electronics, Ownership: PVT, Founded: 1968, Empl: 200, Dave Power, Chmn, Steve Goodall, Pres, Patti Patono, Dir Spec Projects

Japan Entry 43 Oak Ridge Rd, PO Box 319, W. Boxford MA 01885 USA; 508/352-7788, Fax: 508/352-7578, Focus: Consulting on strategic partnerships with Japanese companies, Ownership: PVT, Founded: 1988, Empl: 7, Jack Plimpton, Pres, Christopher Payne-Taylor, Dir Mktng

Jon Peddie Associates 4 St Gabrielle Court, Tiburon CA 94920-1619 USA; 415/435-1775, Fax: 415/435-1599, Co Email: info@jpa-pcgr.com, Web URL: jpa-pcgr.com, Focus: Computer graphics information and consulting, Ownership: PVT, Founded: 1984, Empl: 5, Jon Peddie, Pres, Fred Dunn, VP

Jupiter Communications Co. 627 Broadway 2nd Fl, New York NY 10012-2612 USA; 212/780-6060, 800/488-4345 Fax: 212/780-6075, Co Email: jup5@aol.com, Web URL: jup.com/jupiter, Focus: Telecom, information services and videotex information, publications & conferences, Ownership: PVT, Founded: 1986, Empl: 6, Joshua Harris, Pres, Gene DeRose, Ed Dir

Kagan World Media Inc. 126 Clock Tower Place, Carmel CA 93923 USA; 408/624-1536, Fax: 408/625-3225, Focus: Market research on consumer electronics and new media, Ownership: PVT, Paul Kagan, Pres

Kauffman Group 324 Windsor Drive, Cherry Hill NJ 08002-2426 USA; 609/482-8288, Fax: 609/482-8940, Focus: Consulting and information on fax technology, Ownership: PVT, Maury S. Kauffman, Managing Partner, Email: mkauffman@mcimail.com

Killen & Associates Inc. 1212 Parkenson Ave, Palo Alto CA 94301 USA; 415/617-6130, Fax: 415/617-6140, Web URL: killen.com, Focus: Information on telecom, computers, electronic commerce and payment systems, Ownership: PVT, Founded: 1976, Empl: 12, Sales($M): 1.2, Michael Killen, Pres, Jules Street, VP, Karl Duffy, EVP Sales & Mktng

Lewis Research Corp. 137 E Fremont Ave #245, Sunnyvale CA 94087 USA; 408/730-5829, Focus: Information and consulting on the microcomputer industry, Ownership: PVT, Founded: 1985, Jan Lewis, Pres

LMA Group Inc. PO Box 677, Bala Cynwyd PA 19004 USA; 610/667-3635, Fax: 610/667-6226, Co Email: barry@lmagroup.com, Focus: Strategy and management consulting, Ownership: PVT, Founded: 1980, Empl: 2, Barry Borden, Pres

Machover Associates Corp. 152-A Longview Ave, White Plains NY 10605 USA; 914/949-3777, Fax: 914/949-3851, Co Email: machover_associates@mcimail.com, Web URL: cmachover@aol.com, Focus: Computer graphics consulting and information, Ownership: PVT, Founded: 1976, Empl: 5, Carl Machover, Pres, Pamela Blair, Bus Mgr

Magnetic Press Inc. 588 Broadway, #1104, New York NY 10012-5408 USA; 212/219-2831, Fax: 212/334-4729, Web URL: acropolis.com/acropolis, Focus: Telecom, ISDN, videotex, information and

video information services, Ownership: PVT, Founded: 1986, Empl: 6, Sanford Bingham, Pres

Mantek Services Inc. 3216-A Industry Drive, N. Charlston SC 29418 USA; 803/552-6671, 800/2643698 Fax: 803/552-6673, Co Email: mantekpubs@aol.com, Focus: Computer & telecom market research reports, Ownership: PVT, Founded: 1949, Brian J. Lingren, Editor

Market Data Retrieval 16 Progress Drive, Box 2117, Shelton CT 06484-1117 USA; 203/926-4800, Fax: 203/929-5253, Focus: Market research on educational market, Ownership: PVT, Founded: 1969, Mac Buhler, PR contact, John Kelly

Market Vision 326 Pacheco Ave #200, Santa Cruz CA 95062-1233 USA; 408/426-4400, Fax: 408/426-4411, Web URL: apletware.com, Focus: Multimedia market research and consulting, Ownership: PVT, Founded: 1988, Robert Aston, Pres

MediaMap 215 First St 3rd Floor, Cambridge MA 02142-1293 USA; 617/374-9300, Fax: 617/374-9345, Web URL: mediamap.com, Focus: Computer publications and tradeshows information, Ownership: PVT, Founded: 1985, John Pearce, CEO

Mentor Market Research 6214 Meridian Ave, San Jose CA 95120 USA; 408/268-6333, Fax: 408/997-0437, Co Email: mentorms@best.com, Web URL: best.com, Focus: Internet and web consulting, Ownership: PVT, Kenneth R. Churcilla, Pres

Mercury Research 7950 E Acoma Drive #203, Scottsdale AZ 85260 USA; 602/998-9225, Fax: 602/998-4338, Co Email: servic@mercury.org, Focus: PC components market research & consulting; track & forecast PC design & building trends, Ownership: PVT, Mike Feibus, Principal, Dean McCarron, Principal

Merrin Information Services Inc. 2275 E Bayshore Rd #101, Palo Alto CA 94303 USA; 415/493-5050, Fax: 415/493-5480, Focus: PC product marketing and distribution data and consulting, Ownership: PVT, Founded: 1988, Empl: 11, Seymour Merrin, Pres

Meta Group 208 Harbor Drive, Stamford CT 06912 USA; 203/973-6700, Fax: 203/354-8066, Co Email: info@metagroup.com, Web URL: metagroup.com, Focus: Consulting and information on computer technology impact on business, Ownership: NASDAQ, Stock Symbol: METG, Founded: 1989, Empl: 200, Sales($M): 29.6, Fiscal End: 12/95; Dale Kutnick, Pres, Marc Butlein, Chmn, Joe Gottlieb, EVP Sales & Mktng, Heather Whiteman, Mktng Mgr, Email: heatherw@metagroup.com

MicroDesign Resources Inc. 874 Gravenstein Hwy S #14, Sebastopol CA 95472 USA; 707/824-4004, 800/527-

0288 Fax: 707/823-0504, Web URL: chipanalyst.com, Focus: Consulting & conferences on microprocessors, semiconductor, workstation and PC technology, Ownership: PVT, Founded: 1987, Empl: 12, Michael Slater, Pres

Mobile Insights Inc. 2001 Landings Drive, Mountain View CA 94043 USA; 415/390-9800, Fax: 415/919-0930, Web URL: mobileinsights.com, Focus: Market research and conferences for the mobile computing and communications industry, Ownership: PVT, J. Gerry Purdy, Pres & CEO, Email: gpurdy@mobileinsights.com; Michael French, Dir Mkt Res, Email: mfrench@mobileinsights.com; Vanessa Vla-Koch, VP Ops, Email: vvlay@mobileinsight.com

Morris & Associates 211 Congress St 2nd Floor, Boston MA 02110-2410 USA; 617/556-8960, Fax: 617/482-6201, Co Email: 72662.3563@compuserve.com, Focus: Management consulting to PC companies; private venture capital, Ownership: PVT, Founded: 1987, Empl: 2, Tony Morris, Principal

Multimedia Computing Corp. PO Box 60369, Sunnyvale CA 94088-0369 USA; 408/369-1233, Focus: Information on multimedia technology and products, Ownership: PVT, Founded: 1988, Empl: 5, Nick Arnett, Pres

Multimedia Research Group 435 Palo Verde Drive #A, Sunnyvale Ca 94086 USA; 408/524-9767, Fax: 408/524-9770, Focus: Multimedia, interactive and digital video and digital network information, Ownership: PVT, Founded: 1990, Gary G. Schultz, Principal Analyst

Multimedia Systems 3104 Canyon Creek Drive, Richardson TX 75080-1507 USA; 214/644-8875, Fax: 214/644-3364, Co Email: 71207.3244@compuserve.com, Focus: Multimedia market research, Ownership: PVT, Alfred Riccomi, Pres

MWA Consulting Inc. 261 Hamilton Ave #421, Palo Alto CA 94301 USA; 415/323-4780, Fax: 415/323-4794, Focus: Computer printers, image and document processing information, Ownership: PVT, Founded: 1989, Michael Weiss, Pres, Barbara Ells, Sr Consultant

National Center for Computer Crime Data (NCCCD), 1222 17th Ave #B, Santa Cruz CA 95062 USA; 408/475-4457, Fax: 408/475-5336, Co Email: nudnic@ix.netcom.com, Focus: Statistics and information on computer crimes, Ownership: Nonprofit, Founded: 1980, Empl: 6, Jay BloomBecker, Exec Dir

New Media Assoc. 148 Duane St 6th Floor, New York NY 10013-3855 USA; 212/349-2700, Fax: 212/226-8731, Focus: PC and workstation consulting and information, Ownership: PVT, Mark Stahlman, Pres

New Venture Forecasting 99 Cedro

Ave, San Francisco CA 94127 USA; 415/ 337-9171, Fax: 415/333-8453, Focus: Microprocessors consulting and information, Ownership: PVT, Founded: 1982, Randall Sherman, Pres

Newton-Evans Research Co. Inc. 10176 Baltimore National Pike #204, Ellicott City MD 21042 USA; 410/465-7316, Fax: 410/750-7429, Focus: Supercomputers, microcomputers, datacom, control systems & vertical market data, Ownership: PVT, Founded: 1978, Empl: 6, Sales($M): 1, Charles Newton, Pres, Loretta Smolenski, Mgr Ops

Northeast Consulting Resources Inc. (NCRI), 1 Liberty Square 11th Floor, Boston MA 02109 USA; 617/654-0600, Fax: 617/654-0654, Web URL: ncri.com, Focus: Network management, telecom, computer consulting, strategy and management consulting, Ownership: PVT, Founded: 1984, Empl: 22, Sales($M): 3.5, David H. Mason, Pres, Email: mason@ncri.com; James Herman, VP, Email: herman@ncri.com; Mary Johnston Turner, VP, Email: turner@ncri.com

Northern Business Information Inc. 600 Delran Pkwy, Delran NJ 08075 USA; 609/764-0100, Focus: Telecom market information, Ownership: Sub Datapro, Founded: 1976

NPD Group Inc. 900 W Shore Rd, Port Washington NY 11050 USA; 516/625-0700, Fax: 516/625-2444, Focus: Video game market research, Ownership: PVT

Orbach Inc. Oppenheimer Tower/32th Floor, World Financial Ctr, New York NY 10281 USA; 212/667-5083, Fax: 212/ 667-5794, Co Email: 74431.324@compuserve.com, Focus: Consulting on PC distribution, merchandising, software marketing and strategic alliances, Ownership: PVT, Founded: 1989, Bob Orbach, Pres

Orr Associates Int'l. 261 Marsh Island Dr, Chesapeake VA 23320 USA; 804/467-2677, 800/223-3226 Fax: 804/495-8548, Web URL: mysite.com/joeloor, Focus: Computer consulting and research, Ownership: PVT, Joel Orr, Pres, Email: joel_oor@mcimail.com

Ovum Ltd. 1 Mortimer St, London W1N 7RH England; 071-255-2670, Fax: 071-255-1995, Co Email: info@ovum.mhs.compuserve.com, Web URL: ovum.com, Focus: Research and consulting in computing & telecom, Ownership: PVT, Founded: 1985, Empl: 100, Sales($M): 5.5, Julian Hewett, Managing Dir, Email: jjh@ovum.mhs.compuserve.com; Garvin Lambert, Dir Sales & Mktng, Email: grl@ovum.mhs.compuserve.com; Eirwen Nichols, Dir Telecoms, Pat Ingram, Dir Computing, Email: pmi@ovum.mhs.compuserve.com; Richard Kee, Fin Dir, Email: rek@ovum.mhs.compuserve.com; Jennie

Morales, PR Mgr, Email: jhb@ovum.mhs.compuserve.com

Pacific Creations 8 Captain Dr #452, Emeryville CA 94608-1728 USA; 510/ 658-2703, Fax: 510/658-2705, Focus: Multimedia environmental and Japan market research, Ownership: PVT, Mary Jean Koontz, Pres, Email: 76373.3050@compuserve.com; Dana Escalante, VP Dev

Pacific Media Associates 1121 Clark Ave, Mountain View CA 94040-2212 USA; 415/948-3080, Fax: 415/948-3092, Focus: Multimedia and desktop presentations consulting, Ownership: PVT, Founded: 1992, Empl: 2, William L. Coggshall, Pres

Pacific Technology Assoc. 18653 Ventura Blvd #346, Tarzana CA 91356 USA; 818/342-1101, Fax: 818/344-0679, Focus: PCs, workstations and computer graphics consulting, Ownership: PVT, Founded: 1985, Empl: 3, Neil Kleinman, Pres

Palo Alto Management Group Inc. 2672 Bayshore Pkwy #701, Mountain View CA 94043 USA; 415/968-4374, Fax: 415/968-4245, Focus: Technical computing, telecom and smart card information, Ownership: PVT, Founded: 1981, Empl: 10, Michael Burwen, Pres

Parks Associates 5310 Harvest Hill Rd #235 LB 162, Dallas TX 75230-5805 USA; 214/490-1113, 727-5711 Fax: 214/490-1133, Co Email: 76002.2162@compuserve.com, Web URL: homesystems.com/market.data, Focus: Home automation and consumer information services, Ownership: PVT, Founded: 1986, Empl: 12, Sales($M): 0.6, Tricia Parks, Pres, Terry Mikelk, VP, Bronya Coleman, PR Coordinator

Pathfinder Research Inc. 1620 Old Oakland Rd #D-207, San Jose CA 95131 USA; 408/437-1905, Fax: 408/437-8929, Co Email: pfri@netcom.com, Focus: Semiconductor and microelectronics market research, Ownership: PVT, Founded: 1991, Fred Zieber, Pres, Hal Feeney, Principal, Mel Thomsen, Principal

Patricia Seybold Group 148 State St 7th Floor, Boston MA 02109 USA; 617/742-5200, 800/826-2424 Fax: 617/742-1028, Web URL: psgroup.com, Focus: Information on distributed computing for networked organizations, Ownership: PVT, Founded: 1985, Empl: 17, Patricia Seybold, Pres & Publisher, Ronni Marshak, VP & Editor-in-Chief

Paul Kagan Assoc. 126 Clock Tower Place, Carmel CA 93923-8723 USA; 408/ 624-1536, Fax: 408/625-3225, Focus: Market research on entertainment and communications industries, Ownership: PVT, Paul Kagan, Pres, Norm Glaser, VP Fin

PC Data 11260 Roger Bacon Dr #204, Reston VA 20190 USA; 703/435-1025,

Fax: 703/478-0484, Co Email: pcdata@aol.com, Focus: PC software and hardware sales tracking and market shares, Ownership: PVT, Founded: 1991, Empl: 10, Ann Stephens, Pres

Performance Computing 3930 N Pine Grove #1214, Chicago IL 60613 USA; 312/549-8325, Fax: 312/549-4824, Focus: Relational database consulting, Ownership: PVT, Richard Finkelstein, Pres

Personal Technology Research 63 Fountain St #400, Framingham MA 01701 USA; 508/875-5858, Fax: 508/875-2975, Co Email: ptrcorp@aol.com, Focus: Data on retail distribution of information technology products, Ownership: PVT, Founded: 1986, Empl: 35, Sales($M): 3, Casey Dworkin, GM

Phillips Decision Point Resources 1111 Marlkress Rd, Cherry Hill NJ 08003 USA; 609/424-1100, 800/678-4642 Fax: 609/424-1999, Focus: Telecom and data communication products and vendor database, Ownership: PVT, Founded: 1971, Empl: 17, Sales($M): 2.3, Lawrence Feidelman, Assoc. Publisher, Mark Kostic, Tech Dir

Pinnacle Peak Publishing Ltd. 8711 E Pinnacle Peak Rd #249, Scottsdale AZ 85255 USA; 602/585-5580, Fax: 602/ 585-7417, Web URL: docmanage.com, Focus: Document management products and technology consulting, Prdts: Document Management & Windows Imaging, Ownership: PVT, Founded: 1988, Empl: 5, Richard N. Stover, Publisher, Joyce Stover, VP

Pixel-The Computer Animation News People Inc. 109 Vanderhoof Ave #2, Toronto Ontario M4G 2H7 Canada; 416/424-4657, Fax: 416/424-1812, Co Email: pixel@inforamp.net, Web URL: gsfmicro.com/pixel, Focus: Information, directory and reports on computer animation and graphics markets, Ownership: PVT, Founded: 1983, Empl: 3, Robi Roncarelli, Publisher & Editor

Positive Support Review Inc. (PSR), 2500 Broadway St #320, Santa Monica CA 90404-3061 USA; 310/453-6100, Fax: 310/453-6253, Co Email: info@psrinc.com, Web URL: psrinc.com/ psr, Focus: Mission-critical information systems consulting and books, Ownership: PVT, Founded: 1982, M. Victor Janulaitis, Pres & CEO, Email: vjanulaitis@psrinc.com; Gary Ingham, VP Mktng, Email: ingham@psrinc.com

Probe Research Inc. 3 Wing Drive #240, Cedar Knolls NJ 07927 USA; 201/ 285-1500, Fax: 201/285-1519, Web URL: proberesearch.com, Focus: Voice processing, image processing and telecom information, Ownership: PVT, Founded: 1976, Empl: 25, Victor Schnee, Pres

Promark Consulting Services PO Box 1060, Enfield NH 03748-1060 USA; 603/

632-7951, Fax: 603/632-7951, Focus: Channel business development consulting, Ownership: PVT, Founded: 1978, Empl: 3, Gene R. Talsky, Pres, Email: gtalsky@mcimail.com

Qualitative Marketing 12 S First St #900, San Jose CA 95113-2405 USA; 408/295-5524, Fax: 408/998-0285, Co Email: info@qmarketing.com, Web URL: qmarketing.com, Focus: Custom market research and market development, Ownership: PVT, Founded: 1984, Empl: 4, Roberta Moore, Pres

Quality Education Data Inc. 1600 Broadway 12th Floor, Denver CO 80202-4912 USA; 800/525-5811 Fax: 303/860-0238, Co Email: @qeddata.com, Focus: Market research on colleges and schools, Ownership: Sub Peterson's, Empl: 60, Jeanne Hayes, Pres & CEO, Email: jhayes@qeddata.com; Wally Papciak, EVP & COO, Email: wpapciak@qeddata.com; Mary Ann Tate, Dir Mktng, Barry Gray, VP Fin

Quantum Group Int'l. 110 Corporate Park Drive, White Plains NY 10604 USA; 914/694-3260, Fax: 914/694-1797, Focus: Data and consulting on computer and communications hardware and service industries, Ownership: PVT, Founded: 1964, Empl: 25, Mirek Stevenson, Chmn & Pres

R.J. Potter Co. 5215 N O'Connor Blvd #975, Irving TX 75039 USA; 214/869-8270, Fax: 214/869-6593, Co Email: robtpotter@aol.com, Focus: Business and technical consulting, Ownership: PVT, Founded: 1989, Robert J. Potter, Pres

RCI Ltd. 1301 E 79th St #200, Minneapolis MN 55425-1119 USA; 612/858-8830, Fax: 612/858-8834, Web URL: infomall.org/rci, Focus: High performance computing, Ownership: PVT, Empl: 10, J. Richard Sherman, Pres, Email: rcisherm@epx.cis.umn.edu

Relayer Group 1735 York Ave #276, New York NY 10128-6861 USA; 212/369-6340, Focus: Information on AI, multimedia, virtual reality and text management, Ownership: PVT, Founded: 1982, Empl: 6, Harvey Newquist, Pres

Reliability Ratings 175 Highland Ave 4th Floor, PO Box 626, Needham Heights MA 02194-9872 USA; 617/444-5755, Fax: 617/444-8958, Focus: Computer reliability, serviceability and customer satisfaction information, Ownership: PVT, Founded: 1989, Kevin Beam, Dir Research, Greg Strakosch, VP

Research Results Inc. 371 Wanoosnoc Rd, Fitchburg MA 01420 USA; 508/345-5510, Fax: 508/345-5335, Focus: End-user market research, Ownership: PVT, Founded: 1987, John Zarrella, Pres, Debra Wilson, VP DP

Richard K. Miller & Assoc. Inc. 5880 Live Oak Pkwy #270, Norcross GA 30093

USA; 770/416-0006, Fax: 770/416-0052, Focus: Computer graphics data and consulting, Ownership: PVT, Founded: 1972, Richard K. Miller, Pres

Romtec plc Vanwall Rd, Maidenhead Berks SL6 4UB UK; 1628-770077, Fax: 1628-785433, Focus: Directories and information on European computer resellers, Ownership: PVT, Founded: 1982, Empl: 90, Russ V. Nathan, Managing Dir, Katie Wilkins, Deputy Mng Dir, Jinty Weldor, DB Solutions Dir, Laura James, Sales & Mktng Mgr, Claire Esberger, Marcom Mgr

Rose Associates 4 Main St, Los Altos CA 94022 USA; 415/941-1215, Fax: 415/941-2233, Focus: Home automation and electronics material information, Ownership: PVT, Empl: 5, Daniel Rose, Pres

Ruder Finn Inc. 444 N Michigan Ave #1600, Chicago IL 60611-3901 USA; 312/645-4835, Fax: 312/645-4843, Focus: Integrated marketing communication consulting, Ownership: PVT, Empl: 12, Richar Funess, Pres

Sage Research Inc. 220 N Main St #102, Natick MA 01760 USA; 508/655-5400, Fax: 508/655-5516, Focus: Networking and software market research, Ownership: PVT, Founded: 1993, Kathryn Korstoff, Pres, Email: kathryn@sageresearch.com

Sam Albert Associates 27 Kingwood Rd, Scarsdale NY 10583 USA; 914/723-8296, Fax: 914/723-2886, Web URL: samalbert.com, Focus: Information systems consulting, strategic relationships and alliances, Ownership: PVT, Founded: 1989, Sam Albert, Pres, Email: samalbert@samalbert.com; Joice Albert, Treas

Santa Clara Consulting 65 Washington St #170, Santa Clara CA 95050 USA; 408/450-1365, Fax: 408/253-9938, Focus: Mass storage and data recording media consulting, rechargable batteries, printer supplies, Ownership: PVT, Founded: 1980, David L. Bunzel, Pres, Joel P. Tax

Schwartz Associates, The 801 W El Camino Real #150, Mountain View CA 94040 USA; 415/965-4561, 800/965-4561 Fax: 415/968-0834, Focus: AI, neural networks, expert & fuzzy systems, virtual reality and genetic algorithms data, Ownership: PVT, Founded: 1984, Empl: 4, Tom Schwartz, Pres, Email: tjs@cup.portal.com; Larry LeVine, Consultant

Sentry Market Research 1 Research Drive #4008, Westboro MA 01581-3907 USA; 508/366-2031, Fax: 508/366-8104, Focus: Information on software markets, Ownership: Sub Sentry Publishing, Founded: 1981, Empl: 11, Sales($M): 1, William Gannon Jr., Dir

Seybold Publications Inc. 428 E Baltimore Ave, PO Box 644, Media PA 19063-9938 USA; 610/565-2480, Fax: 610/565-4659, Focus: Information on CD-ROM,

desktop and electronic publishing, Ownership: Sub Softbank, Founded: 1970

Sierra/Alliance Inc. 6621 N Scottsdale Rd, Scottsdale AZ 85250-7803 USA; 602/991-5836, Fax: 602/991-0661, Web URL: adc@primenet.com, Focus: Computer buyer research and development, Ownership: PVT, Founded: 1980, Empl: 18, Stephen Muma, Pres

Silicon Valley Int'l. 300 Orchard City Drive, Campbell CA 95008 USA; 408/376-2626, Fax: 408/376-2646, Focus: Computer industry growth and forecasts, Ownership: PVT, Founded: 1987, Empl: 20, Greg LeVeille, Pres, Maria de Graaf, EVP

Simba Information Inc. 213 Danbury Rd, PO Box 7430, Wilton CT 06897-7430 USA; 203/834-0033, 800/307-2529 Fax: 203/834-1771, Web URL: simbanet.com, Focus: Publishing industry information and publications, Prdts: Computer Marketing & Distribution, Multimedia Business, Ownership: PVT, Alan Brigish, Publisher, Chris Elwell, VP, Tom Niehaus, VP

Smaby Group 1315 Foshay Tower, Minneapolis MN 55402 USA; 612/333-0002, Fax: 612/333-0204, Co Email: sgi@smaby.com, Focus: Supercomputers, MPP, server-clusters, digital video and telecom information, Ownership: PVT, Founded: 1989, Empl: 7, Gary Smaby, Pres

Software Productivity Group Inc. 180 Turnpike Rd, Westboro MA 01581 USA; 508/366-3344, 800/808-3976 Fax: 508/366-8030, Co Email: general@spg-net.com, Web URL: spgnet.com, Focus: Software technology research and consulting, software magazine & conferences, Prdts: Application Development Trends, Ownership: PVT, Founded: 1989, Empl: 20+, Elliot D. Weinman, Pres, Email: 76102.1473@compuserve.com; Mark McCourt, EVP & Pub, Email: 76102.1473@compuserve.com; Leland J. Katz, Dir Sales & Mktng, Email: 76102.1472@compuserve.com; Dan Kara, Dir Res, Email: 76102.1465@compuserve.com; John Desmond, VP & Editor

SophisTech Research 347 Orizaba, Long Beach CA 90814 USA; 310/434-4436, Fax: 310/434-2730, Focus: Virtual reality data and consulting, Ownership: PVT, Greg Panos, Pres

SRI International (SRI), 333 Ravenswood Ave, Menlo Park CA 94025 USA; 415/326-6200, Fax: 415/326-5512, Focus: High-tech research, development and consulting, Ownership: PVT, Founded: 1946, Empl: 2,400, Sales($M): 300, William Sommers, Pres & CEO, Paul Jorgensen, EVP & COO, Alice Galloway, Marcom

Standish Group, The 586 Old Kings Hwy, Dennis MA 02638-1906 USA; 508/385-7500, Fax: 508/385-7522, Co Email: @standishgroup.com, Focus: On-line transactions, client/server consulting and electronic commerce, Ownership: PVT, James Johnson, Chmn, Email: jim@standishgroup.com; Sally Cusack, Mkt Analyst, Email: sally@standish-group.com; Sandy Taylor, Mkt Analyst, Email: sandy@standishgroup.com; Karen Boucher, Mkt Analyst, Email: karen@standishgroup.com; Kevin Gallagher, Dir Sales & Mktng, Email: kevin@standishgroup.com

Stanford Resources 3150 Almaden Expwy, San Jose CA 95118 USA; 408/448-4440, Fax: 408/448-4445, Focus: Monitor market research, Ownership: PVT

Storage Systems Marketing 1235 Wildwood Rd, Boulder CO 80303-5641 USA; 303/499-0281, Fax: 303/727-4262, Co Email: storagesys@aol.com, Focus: Storage industry marketing research/sales & marketing process, Prdts: The Storage Source, Ownership: PVT, John McIntosh, Partner, Email: jwmci@aol.com; Tom Taylor, Partner, Email: tom-roger@aol.com; Mike Befeler, Partner, Email: mikebef@aol.com; Lynn Osborne, Partner, Email: losborne@aol.com

Strategic Focus 500 E Calaveras Blvd #321, Milpitas CA 95035 USA; 408/942-1500, Fax: 408/262-1786, Focus: Worldwide CASE market information, Ownership: PVT, Founded: 1986, Jay Prakash, Pres

Strategic Research Corp. 350 S Hope Ave #A-103, Santa Barbara CA 93105 USA; 805/569-5610, Fax: 805/569-2512, Web URL: sresearch.com, Focus: Mass storage, networking and storage management software consulting, publishing & confs., Ownership: PVT, Founded: 1987, Empl: 10, Michael Peterson, Pres, Dennis Casey, VP, Karen Nilsen, PR Coord, Email: knilsen@sresearch.com

Summit Strategies Inc. 360 Newbury St, Boston MA 02115 USA; 617/266-9050, Fax: 617/266-7952, Web URL: summitstrat.com, Focus: C/S, networks and distribution channel consulting, Ownership: PVT, Founded: 1984, Empl: 7, Thomas Kucharvy, Pres, Email: tomk@summitstrat.com; Joyce Gavenda, VP

Susanna Opper & Assoc. 388 West Rd, Alford MA 01266 USA; 413/528-6513, Fax: 413/528-0734, Co Email: sopper@mcimail.com, Focus: Groupware and network group communications consulting, Ownership: PVT, Founded: 1983, Susanna Opper, Pres, Will Ryan, Partner

Systems Research Inc. 211 S Garden St, Bellingham WA 98225-5819 USA; 360/647-7600, Fax: 360/647-0889, Co Email: sysr@pacificrim.net, Web URL: pacificrim.net/~sysr, Focus: Accounting & business information systems for Microsoft Windows, Prdts: Small Business Manager, Ownership: PVT, Founded: 1988, Empl:

2, Gregory Boone, Pres, Klaus Braun, Chief Scientist

Technical Insights PO Box 1304, Ft. Lee NJ 07024-9967 USA; 201/568-4744, Fax: 201/568-8247, Co Email: tiinfo@insights.com, Web URL: insights.com, Focus: AI, neural networks, silicon compilers and biotechnology information, Ownership: PVT, Founded: 1971, Empl: 20, Sales($M): 2.5, Kenneth Kovaly, Pres

Technologic Partners 120 Wooster St, New York NY 10012 USA; 212/343-1900, Fax: 212/343-1915, Focus: Information on PCs and workstations, Ownership: PVT, Founded: 1984, Empl: 15, Richard Shaffer, Principal, Kenneth R. Graham, COO

Technologies Research Group 44 Old Rt 22, PO Box 5277, Clinton NJ 08809-5277 USA; 908/730-9050, Fax: 908/730-9480, Focus: Telecom, computer and info-tainment information, Ownership: PVT, Founded: 1989, Bick Truet, Pres

Technology Futures Inc. 11709 Boulder Lane, Austin TX 78726-1808 USA; 512/258-8898, 800/TEK-FUTR Fax: 512/258-0087, Co Email: info@tfi.com, Web URL: tfi.com, Focus: Technology forecasting and telecom information, Ownership: PVT, Founded: 1978, Empl: 10, John Vanston, Chmn, Lawrence Vanston, Pres, Carrie Vanston, Media Relations

Technology Research Group (TRG), 10 Post Office Sq, Boston MA 02109-4603 USA; 617/482-4200, Fax: 617/482-4585, Focus: Management consulting for computer, software, telecom and semiconductor companies, Ownership: PVT, Founded: 1984, Empl: 11, Sales($M): 17.4, Fiscal End: 3/96; Andrew Rappaport, Pres, Shmuel Halevi, EVP

Technology Transfer Institute 741 10th St, Santa Monica CA 90402 USA; 310/394-8305, 800/4884 Fax: 310/451-2104, Co Email: custserv@tti.com, Web URL: tti.com, Focus: Seminars & conferences on computer management, software development, networks & databases, Ownership: PVT, Founded: 1972, Empl: 12, John Phillips, Pres, Dr. Leonard Kleinrock, CEO

Techtel Corp. 2000 Powell St #1500, Emeryville CA 94608 USA; 510/655-9414, Fax: 510/655-9670, Co Email: techserv@techtel.com, Web URL: techtel.com, Focus: PC end-user surveys and custom research, Ownership: PVT, Founded: 1983, Empl: 12, Michael F. Kelly, Pres, Duncan Fallet, Dir Res

TeleGeography Inc. (TGI), 1150 Connecticut Ave #1000, Washington DC 20036 USA; 202/467-0017, Fax: 202/467-5915, Co Email: info@telegeraphy.com, Web URL: telegeography.com, Focus: Telecom information, Ownership: PVT, Founded: 1992, Gregory C. Staple, Pres

Torrey Pines Research 6359 Paseo del Lago #100, Carlsbad CA 92009 USA; 619/929-4800, Fax: 619/931-1671, Focus: Printer and imaging technology information, Ownership: PVT, Founded: 1987, Bill Hanson, Pres, Richard Love, VP

Trade Quotes Inc. 675 Massachusets Ave, Cambridge MA 02139 USA; 617/492-0600, Fax: 617/354-3355, Focus: Surveys of computer users; Statistical survey processing, Ownership: PVT, Founded: 1970, Empl: 10, Leonard Phillips, Pres, Allen Liberman, VP

Trans-Formation Inc. 3828 Briar Oak Drive, Birmingham AL 35243-4834 USA; 205/970-2250, Fax: 205/970-0363, Focus: Telecom information with focus on transmission equipment markets, Ownership: PVT, Founded: 1986, Mark Lutkowitz, Pres

Tredennick Inc. 1625 Sunset Ridge Rd, Los Gatos CA 95090-9435 USA; 408/395-6552, Fax: 408/395-2025, Focus: Microprocessor technology trend consulting, Ownership: PVT, Founded: 1989, Nick Tredennick, Pres, Email: bozo@tredennick.com

Triad Services Inc. PO Box 80312, Charleston SC 29416-0312 USA; 803/763-9997, Fax: 803/763-0466, Co Email: triadsvcs@gnn.com, Focus: Reports on hardware & software applications, conversion of data from paper to online & CD, Ownership: PVT, Founded: 1996, Brian Lindgren, Editor & Publisher

Venture Development Corp. 1 Apple Hill, Natick MA 01760-9904 USA; 508/653-9000, Fax: 508/653-9836, Co Email: bdc4u@aol.com, Focus: Marketing research and strategic planning for computer, office automation & telecom, Ownership: PVT, Founded: 1971, Empl: 30, Sales($M): 3, Lewis Solomon, Pres, Marc Regberg, VP

Venture Economics Inc. 40 W 57th St, New York NY 10019 USA; 212/765-5311, Fax: 212/765-6123, Focus: Tracks venture capital industry and start-up companies, Ownership: PVT, Founded: 1961, Empl: 120, Sales($M): 5, David Devlin, VP & Publisher, Email: devlin@tfn.com; Lisa Vincent, Editor, Renee Deger

Venture Marketing Strategies 5150 Graves Ave #11H, San Jose CA 95129 USA; 408/865-0221, Fax: 408/865-1523, Co Email: 73364.3116@compuserve.com, Focus: Printer market, technology and distribution consulting, Ownership: PVT, Founded: 1993, William E. Gott, Pres, Connie Rao, Asst Editor

Verity Group Inc. 680 Langsdorf Drive #102, Fullerton CA 92631-3702 USA; 714/680-9611, Fax: 714/680-9676, Focus: Customer satisfaction research, Ownership: PVT, Founded: 1988, William Matthies, Pres, Email: verbill@aol.com; Grace Post, VP Mktng

VLSI Research Inc. 1754 Technology Drive #117, San Jose CA 95110 USA; 408/453-8844, Fax: 408/437-0608, Focus: Semiconductors, semiconductor manufacturing and VLSI systems information, Ownership: PVT, Founded: 1976, Empl: 18, Sales($M): 1.3, Jerry D. Hutcheson, CEO, G. Dan Hutcheson, Pres, Richard J. Dexter, VP

Voice Information Associates Inc. 14 Glen Rd South, PO Box 625, Lexington MA 02173 USA; 617/861-6680, Fax: 617/863-8790, Web URL: tiac.net/users/asrnews, Focus: Speech recognition and synthesis information, Ownership: PVT, Founded: 1990, John A. Oberteuffer, Pres, Email: jober24@aol.com

Washington Consulting Group 4330 E West Hwy 10th Fl, Bethesda MD 20814-4408 USA; 301/951-3021, Focus: Computer consulting, Ownership: PVT, Ramon C. Barquin, Pres

Waterman Associates PO Box 151358, San Rafael CA 94915-1358 USA; 415/721-7377, Focus: Marketing research and strategic planning, Ownership: PVT, Founded: 1984, Terri Eddy

Winters Group Inc., The Temple Bldg 14 Franklin St #920, Rochester NY 14604 USA; 716/546-7480, Fax: 716/546-7427, Focus: Information on computers, telecom and office equipment, Ownership: PVT, Founded: 1984, Empl: 15, Sales($M): 1, Mary-Frances Winters, Pres

Wohl Associates 915 Montgomery Ave #309, Narberth PA 19072-1501 USA; 610/667-4842, Fax: 610/667-3081, Web URL: wohl.com, Focus: Office automation, desktop computing and end user computing consulting, Ownership: PVT, Founded: 1984, Empl: 3, Amy Wohl, Pres, Email: amy@wohl.com

WorkGroup Technologies Inc. 400 Lafayette Rd, Hampton NH 03842-2222 USA; 603/929-1166, Fax: 603/926-9801, Focus: Syndicated & custom market research on mid-range computers, PCs, workstations & groupware, Ownership: NASDAQ, Founded: 1988, Empl: 15, Sales($M): 10.5, Fiscal End: 3/96; John Dunkle, Pres, David Mack, VP

Wujcik & Associates 810 S Alfred St #1, Alexandria VA 22314 USA; 703/519-3557, Fax: 703/548-1037, Focus: K-12 education market research, Ownership: PVT, Founded: 1991, Anne Wujcik, Pres, Email: annewujcik@aol.com

Xephon 1301 W Hwy 407 #201-450, Lewisville TX 75067 USA; 817/455-7050, Fax: 817/455-2492, Web URL: xephon.co.uk, Focus: Mid-range and mainframe computer information and publications, Ownership: PVT, Maureen Nicols, NA Agent, Chris Bunyan, Dir, Email: 100325.3711@compuserve.com

Yankee Group, The 31 James Ave, Boston MA 02116 USA; 617/956-5000, Fax: 617/367-5760, Web URL: yankeegroup.com, Focus: Telecom, computers, CIM and consumer electronics data and consulting, Ownership: PVT, Founded: 1970, Empl: 75, Howard Anderson, Managing Dir

Zona Research 497 Seaport Ct #102-A, Redwood City CA 94063-2730 USA; 415/568-5700, Fax: 415/306-2420, Co Email: info@xbg.com, Web URL: xbg.com, Focus: X window systems data and consulting, Ownership: PVT, Founded: 1990, Empl: 6, Stephen Auditore, Pres, Greg Blatnik, VP

Testing Company Directory

100VG-AnyLAN Forum (VGF), PO Box 1378, N. Highlands CA 95660 USA; 916/348-0212, Co Email: vgf@any-lan.win.com, Focus: Interoperability testing, certification and implementation of IEEE 802.12, Ownership: Nonprofit, Kenneth R. Hurst, Chmn

AT&T Global Product Compliance Laboratory 101 Crawford Corners Rd Rm 11C-196, Holmdel NJ 07733-3030 USA; 908/834-1800, Fax: 908/834-1830, Focus: Testing, certification & education for phone, computer and electronics products, Ownership: PVT, Carolann Nicholas

Adiant Corp. 54015 Range Rd 212, Ardrossan Alberta T8G 2C2 Canada; 403/998-0607, Fax: 403/998-4872, Co Email: 71231.3005@compuserve.com, Focus: IBM mainframe software and related product testing and PR, Ownership: PVT, Founded: 1987, Jon Pearkins, Pres

Aim Technology 4699 Old Ironsides Drive #400, Santa Clara CA 95054-1828 USA; 408/748-8649, Fax: 408/748-0161, Co Email: @aim.com, Focus: Unix performance measurement, system management, network file management, Ownership: PVT, Founded: 1981, Empl: 18, Jim Geers, Pres, Email: jim@aim.com; Paul V. Farr, VP & GM, Email: paul@aim.com; Tammy L. Bauer, Dir, Email: tammy@aim.com; Melanie Deane, Mgr Corp Admin, Email: melanie@aim.com

Benchmark Laboratories Inc. 7600 Parklawn #408, Minneapolis MN 55435 USA; 612/897-3505, Fax: 612/897-3524, Focus: Software testing for MS-DOS, Windows, OS/2, Macintosh, LANs and Unix, Ownership: PVT, Founded: 1987, Empl: 15, Larry Decklever, Pres, Chuck Le Count, Project Mgr

Buyers Laboratory Inc. 20 Railroad Ave, Hackensack NJ 07601 USA; 201/488-0404, Fax: 201/488-0461, Focus: Office product testing and specification guides, Ownership: PVT, Founded: 1961, Empl: 40, Anthony Polifrone, Pres, Marion Davidowicz, VP

Byte Lab 1 Phoenix Mill Lane, Peterborough NH 03458 USA; 603/924-9281, Fax: 603/924-2550, Web URL: byte.com, Focus: Testing and evaluation of PCs, LAN, multimedia and workstations, Ownership: PVT, Founded: 1975, Empl: 11, Stanford Diehl, Dir, Email: sdiehl@bix.com; Rick Grehan, Tech Dir, Dave Rowell, Tech Ed, Dave Essex, Tech Ed, Sue Colwell, Tech Ed

Cardinal Technologies Inc. 1827 Freedom Rd, Lancaster PA 17601 USA; 717/293-3000, Fax: 717/293-3055, Web URL: cardtech.com, Focus: Modems, Prdts: Cardinal 288 Fax Modems, Ownership: PVT, Founded: 1987, Empl: 250, Sales($M): 35,

Wolfgang Hausen, Pres & CEO, Email: whausen@cardtech.com; John Rose, CFO, Email: johnr@cardtech.com; Dean Tucker, VP Sales, Email: deant@cardtech.com; Robert Young, VP Mktng, Email: byoung@cardtech.com; Jeff Murphy, VP Mfg, Email: jeffm@cardtech.com; Tom Ransom, Dir Corp Comm, Email: tomr@cardtech.com

Center for Software Development (CSD), 111 W St John #200, San Jose CA 95113 USA; 408/494-8378, Fax: 408/494-8383, Co Email: info@center.org, Web URL: center.org/csd, Focus: Self-service software testing and porting lab, Ownership: Nonprofit, Marnie Rice, Office Mgr, Bill McCarty, Dir, Email: mccarty@center.org

Client/Server Labs 8601 Dunwoody Place #332, Atlanta GA 30350 USA; 404/552-3645, Fax: 404/993-4667, Focus: C/S product testing, Prdts: RPMark benchmark, Ownership: PVT, Founded: 1995, Terry Keene, VP Tech, Greg Keene, VP Ops, Bill Wallet, VP Sales & Mktng, Curtis Franklin Jr., Dir

Client/Server Today Labs 275 Washington St, Newton MA 02158-1630 USA; 617/964-3030, Fax: 617/558-4759, Co Email: @cstoday.com, Web URL: cstoday.com, Focus: Product testing for Client/Server Today magazine, Ownership: PVT, Founded: 1994, Chris Amaru, Lab Dir, Email: chrisa@cstoday.com; Eric Eldred, Tech Analyst, Email: erice@cstoday.com

Compliance West 11189 Sorrento Valley Rd #103, San Diego CA 92121-1326 USA; 619/755-5525, Fax: 619/452-1810, Focus: Product safety testing for UL, CSA, TUV etc., Ownership: PVT, Founded: 1983, Empl: 7, Jeffrey Lind, GM

Computer Product Testing Services Inc. 2329 Hwy 34 S #201, Manasquan NJ 08736 USA; 908/223-5700, Fax: 908/223-5744, Focus: PC compatibility, performance, functionality and quality assurance testing, Mac testing, Ownership: PVT, Founded: 1983, Empl: 15, Tom Benford, Pres & CEO, Email: benford-tom@aol.com; Elizabeth Benford, EVP Mktng, Lawrence Withrow, VP Sales, Peter Clark, Evaluation Mgr, Nehib Conrad, Admin Assist

Computer Reseller News Test Center 1 Jericho Plaza #A, Jericho NJ 11753 USA; 516/733-6700, Fax: 516/733-8636, Web URL: crn.com, Focus: Product testingfor Computer Reseller News, Ownership: PVT, Eric Elgar, Sr Tech Ed, Email: eelgar@cmp.com

DataFocus Inc. 12450 Fair Lakes Circle #400, Fairfax VA 22033-3831 USA; 703/631-6770, 800/637-8034 Fax: 703/818-

1532, Web URL: datafocus.com, Focus: Systems integration and UNIX to Win 32 migration tools, Prdts: NutCRACKER, Ownership: Sub KTI, Stock Symbol: KTIE, Founded: 1983, Empl: 8090, Sales($M): 12, Fiscal End: 12/95; Patrick B. Higbie, Chmn & CEO, Email: pat@datafocus.com; Thomas A. Bosanko, EVP, Email: tab@datafocus.com; Mitch Lindenfelder, Dir Fin & Admin, Email: mitch@datafocus.com; Wendy Mades, Dir Marcom, Email: wendy@datafocus.com

Digital News & Review Labs 275 Washington St, Newton MA 02158-1611 USA; 617/964-3030, Fax: 617/558-4759, Co Email: @dnr.com, Focus: Tests and evaluates DEC and other workstations, servers and software, Ownership: PVT, Jack Fegreus, Ed Dir, Email: jackf@dnr.com; Tim Sylvester, Email: tims@dnr.com

Inchcape Inc. 1 Tech Drive, Andover MA 01810 USA; 508/689-9355, Fax: 508/689-9353, Web URL: worldlab.com, Focus: Independent testing, inspection and certification, Prdts: ETL Listed, WH Listed, Ownership: PVT, Eric N. Birch, Pres, Glen R. Dash, VP R&D, Alan B. Dittrich, Dir Mktng, Patrick Sweeney, VP & CFO, Cheri Hart, Marcom Mgr

Inchcape Testing Services 593 Massachusetts Ave, Boxborough MA 01719 USA; 508/263-2662, Fax: 508/263-7086, Focus: FCC, product safety and international compliance testing, Ownership: PVT, Founded: 1983, Chuck Kolifrath, GM

Infomart Corporate Evaluation Center 1950 Stemmons Fwy #6038, Dallas TX 75207-3199 USA; 214/746-3500, Fax: 214/746-3501, Web URL: infomart-usa.com, Focus: Multi-vendor testing, Ownership: PVT, Founded: 1994, Nancy Schwartz, Mgr

InformationWEEK Open Labs 600 Community Drive, Manhasset NY 11030 USA; 516/562-5000, Fax: 516/562-5036, Web URL: techweb.com, Focus: Product testing for InformationWEEK, Ownership: PVT, Julie Anderson, Dir, Jason Levitt, Sr Tech Ed, David Fieder, Tech Ed

InfoWorld Test Center Infoworld, 155 Bovet Rd, #800, San Mateo CA 94402 USA; 415/572-7341, Fax: 415/312-0570, Web URL: infoworld.com, Focus: Microcomputer product testing for Infoworld product reviews, Ownership: PVT, Founded: 1987, Empl: 16, Charlotte Ziems, Exec Ed & Test Ctr Dir, Email: charlotte_ziems@infoworld.com

Ingram Laboratories 1395 S Lyon St, Santa Ana CA 92705 USA; 714/566-1000, Focus: Benchmark, acceptance, comparison, compatibility, usability, software and custom testing, Ownership: PVT, Founded: 1982, Empl: 18, Karman Stick

Instruments Specialties Co. Inc. Shielding Way, Delaware Water Gap PA 18327 USA; 717/424-8510, Fax: 717/424-6213, Focus: RFI/EMI shielding, EMC and FCC 15J compliance testing, Ownership: PVT, Founded: 1938, Empl: 330, Frank J. Rushen, Pres

Interference Control Technologies Inc. Route 3, PO Box 2000D, Gainesville VA 22065 USA; 540/347-0030, Fax: 540/347-5813, Focus: Magnetic Interference Control, FCC Parts 15J, MIL-STD-462 and UL compliance testing, Ownership: PVT, Founded: 1970, Empl: 35, Donald White, CEO

International Compliance Corp. 802 N Kealy, Lewisville TX 75057 USA; 817/491-3696, Fax: 817/491-3699, Focus: Compliance testing for FCC, UL, CSA, IEC, TUV, VDE and European CE, Ownership: PVT, Founded: 1986, Empl: 7, Val E. Erwin, Pres, Kurt Fischer, VP

LAN Times Testing Center 441 E Bay Blvd #100, Provo UT 84606 USA; 801/342-6800, Fax: 801/342-6837, Web URL: lantimes.com, Focus: Product testing for LAN Times magazine, Ownership: PVT, Eric Bowdwn, Dir

LanQuest Group 47800 Westinghouse Dr, Fremont CA 94539-7469 USA; 510/354-0940, Fax: 510/354-0950, Co Email: info@lanquest.com, Web URL: lanquest.com, Focus: Network testing and analysis, Prdts: Framethrower, NET/WRx, Ownership: PVT, Founded: 1986, Ron Kopeck, Pres & CEO, Paul Czarnik, VP Dev

MacUser Labs MacUser, 950 Tower Lane 18th Floor, Foster City CA 94404 USA; 415/378-5600, Fax: 415/378-5675, Co Email: letters@macuser.com, Web URL: macuser.ziff.com/macuser, Focus: Product testing for MacUser product reviews, Ownership: PVT, Founded: 1989

Macworld Labs Macworld, 501 Second St, San Francisco CA 94107 USA; 415/243-0505, Fax: 415/442-0766, Co Email: lauren_black@macworld.com, Web URL: macworld.com, Focus: Product testing for Macworld product reviews, Ownership: PVT, Founded: 1983, Empl: 100, Lauren L. Black, Lab Dir, Email: lauren_black@macworld.com; Mark Hurlow, Sr Lab Analyst, Email: mark_hurlow@macworld.com; Jeff Sacilotto, Sr Lab Analyst, Email: jeff_sacilotto@macworld.com

Mindcraft Inc. 410 Cambridge Ave, Palo Alto CA 94306 USA; 415/323-9000, Fax: 415/323-0854, Focus: Testing for POSIX conformance, Ownership: PVT, Founded: 1985, Empl: 15, Bruce Weiner, Pres, Email: bruce@mindcraft.com; Charles Karish, VP, Email: karish@mindcraft.com

NIST Computer Systems Laboratory (CSL), Route I-270 & Quince Orchard Rd, Gaithersburg MD 20899-0001 USA; 301/975-2832, Fax: 301/948-1784, Co Email: @enh.nist.org, Focus: Supports development of computer technology advances, Ownership: Nonprofit, Founded: 1972

National Power Laboratory PO Box 280, Necedah WI 54646 USA; 608/565-7200, Fax: 608/565-2929, Focus: Nationwide power quality testing, Ownership: PVT, Founded: 1988, Robert E. Jurewicz, Dir

National Software Testing Laboratories Inc. 625 Ridge Pike Bldg D, Conshohocken PA 19428-1180 USA; 610/941-9600, 800/257-9402 Fax: 610/941-9952, Focus: Comparison, compatibility and usability testing of PC products, Ownership: PVT, Founded: 1983, Empl: 75

Neal Nelson & Associates 330 N Wabash Ave, Chicago IL 60611-3604 USA; 312/755-1000, Fax: 312/755-1010, Co Email: office@nna.com, Web URL: nna.com, Focus: Performance tests of multiuser systems, networks, web software, databases & other hardware, Ownership: PVT, Founded: 1973, Empl: 11, Neal Nelson, Pres

PC Labs PC Magazine, 1 Park Ave, New York NY 10016 USA; 212/503-5255, Focus: Microcomputer product testing that are the basis for PC Magazine's review, Ownership: PVT, Founded: 1985, C. James Galley, Dir

PC Week Labs 320B Lakeside Drive, Foster City CA 94404 USA; 415/513-8000, Fax: 415/513-8199, Co Email: firstname_lastname@zd.com, Web URL: pcweek.com/reviews, Focus: Product testing for PC Week product reviews, Ownership: PVT, Founded: 1991, Eamon Sullivan, Mgng Tech Dir, Email: eamon_sullivan@zd.com; John Taschek, Mgng Tech Dir, Email: john_taschek@zd.com

PC World Test Center 501 Second St #600, San Francisco CA 94107 USA; 415/243-0500, Fax: 415/442-1891, Co Email: pcworld@aol.com, Web URL: pcworld.com, Focus: Product testing for PC World magazine, Ownership: PVT, Founded: 1992, Julian Milenbach, Dir, Susan Silvius, Mgr Usability testing, Ulrike Diehlman, Mgr Performance testing

PC/Computing Usability Lab 950 Tower Lane 19th Floor, Foster City CA 94404 USA; 415/578-7000, Co Email: 76000.21@compuserve.com, Focus: Usability testing for PC/Computing magazine, Ownership: PVT, Adam Meyerson, Dir, George Hackman Jr., Lab Mgr

Performance Awareness Corp. 8521 Six Forks Rd #200, Raleigh NC 27615 USA; 919/870-8800, Fax: 919/870-7416, Co Email: info@pacorp.com, Web URL: pacorp.com, Focus: Multi-user benchmark-

ing and software testing, Prdts: preVue, Ownership: PVT, Founded: 1986, Paul Chou, Pres, Jeff Schuster, Dir Mktng & Sales, Email: jeff@pacorp.com; Kent Siefkes, Tech Dir, Email: kds@pacorp.com; Keira Stroupe, Marcom Mgr, Email: keira@pacorp.com

Product Safety Engineering Inc. 8052 N 56th St, Tampa FL 33617 USA; 813/989-2360, Fax: 813/989-2373, Focus: EMI, UL, CSA, TUV, FCC and FTZ testing, Ownership: PVT, Founded: 1986, Empl: 24

Prosoft Labs 4725 First St #270, Pleasanton CA 94566 USA; 510/426-6100, Fax: 510/426-6101, Co Email: prosoft@prosoftlabs.com, Web URL: prosoftlabs.com, Focus: Software testing, Ownership: PVT, Founded: 1985, Greg Brewer, Pres, Robert J. Danielson, Mktng Dir

Pulver Laboratories Inc. 320 N Santa Cruz Ave, Los Gatos CA 95030-7243 USA; 408/399-7000, Fax: 408/399-7001, Co Email: pulverl@ix.netcom.com, Focus: RF and EMI interference, Ownership: PVT, Founded: 1979, Empl: 50, Lee J. Pulver, Pres

Radiometrics Midwest Corp. 55 W 22nd St #106, Lombard IL 60148 USA; 630/932-7262, Focus: FCC testing and compliance, Ownership: PVT, Founded: 1983, Dennis Rollinger, CEO

Stardust Technologies 1901 S Bascom Ave #333, Campbell CA 95008 USA; 408/879-8080, Fax: 408/879-8081, Focus: WinSock interoperability testing, Ownership: PVT, Founded: 1994, Karen Milne, Martin Hall, CTO

TUV Product Service Inc. 5 Cherry Hill Drive, Danvers MA 01923 USA; 508/777-7999, Fax: 508/777-8441, Web URL: tuvps.com, Focus: EMI and safety testing, Ownership: PVT, Founded: 1990, Empl: 80, Kurt Eise, Pres, John L. Durant, VP, Axel Breidenbach, Lab Equip Mgr

Tolly Group, The 2302 Hwy 34, Manasquan NJ 08736-1427 USA; 908/528-3300, 800/933-1699 Fax: 908/528-1888, Co Email: info@tolly.com, Web URL: tolly.com, Focus: Network and telecom product testing, Ownership: PVT, Founded: 1982, Empl: 23, Kevin Tolly, Pres & CEO, Email: ktolly@tolly.com; Neil Anderson, COO, Email: nanderson@tolly.com; Caryn Hill, Mktng & PR Specialist, Email: chill@tolly.com

Underwriters Laboratories Inc. (UL), 333 Pfingsten Rd, Northbrook IL 60062-2096 USA; 847/272-8800, Fax: 847/272-8129, Focus: Safety standards, testing and ISO 9000 qualification certification, Ownership: PVT, Founded: 1894, Tom Castino, Pres, Robert Haugh, Chmn, Joe Bhatia, VP Ext Affairs

Usability Sciences Corp. 5525 McArthur Blvd #575, Irving TX 75038

USA; 214/550-1599, Fax: 214/550-9148, Web URL: usabilitysciences.com, Focus: Software usability testing, Ownership: PVT, Jeff Schueler, Pres

Usability Systems 1150 Alpha Drive, Alpharetta GA 30201 USA; 770/475-3505, Fax: 770/475-4210, Co Email: info@usabilitysystems.com, Web URL: usabilitysystems.com, Focus: Software usability testing, Ownership: PVT, Reed Johnson, Pres

VeriTest Inc. 3420 Ocean Park Blvd #2030, Santa Monica CA 90405 USA; 310/450-0062, Fax: 310/399-1760, Co Email: @veritest.com, Focus: System compatibility and performance testing, Owner-ship: PVT, Founded: 1987, Empl: 30, Steve Nemzer, Pres, Email: 70353.1763@compuserve.com; Martine Porter-Zasada, VP Sales & Mktng

Washington Laboratories Ltd. 7560 Lindbergh Drive, Gaithersburg MD 20879-5414 USA; 301/417-0220, Fax: 301/417-9069, Focus: Compliance testing, product approvals and EMC services, Ownership: PVT, Ray Hammonds, Lab Mgr

XXCAL Testing Laboratories 11500 W. Olympic Blvd #325, Los Angeles CA 90064 USA; 310/477-2902, Fax: 310/477-7127, Co Email: @xxcal.com, Focus: Microcomputer hardware, software and connectivity; software test tools and bench-marks, Ownership: PVT, Founded: 1976, Empl: 60, Marvin Hoffman, Chmn & CEO, Bill Schoneman, VP Testing Div, Brett Schoneman, WW Mktng Mgr, Email: brett@xxcal.com

ZD Labs 320B Lakeside Drive, Foster City CA 94404 USA; 415/513-8000, Co Email: firstname_lastname@zd.com, Web URL: zd.com, Focus: Product testing for Ziff-Davis magazines, Ownership: PVT, Founded: 1991, Robert W. Kane, Dir

Chapter 14

Bits, Nibbles and Bytes

Facts and Figures

Computer Ethics Institute: Ten Commandments of Computer Ethics

The Computer Ethics Institute is a coalition of people in the business, computer profession, education, public policy and religious communities that are concerned with the ethical use computers. Dr. Ramon C. Barquin authored the following computer ethics rules in 1992.

1. Thou shalt not use a computer to harm other people.
2. Thou shalt not interfere with other people's computer work.
3. Thou shalt not snoop around in other people's computer files.
4. Thou shalt not use a computer to steal.
5. Thou shalt not use a computer to bear false witness.
6. Thou shalt not copy or use proprietary software for which you have not paid.
7. Thou shalt not use other people's computer resources without authorization or proper compensation.
8. Thou shalt not appropriate other people's intellectual output.
9. Thou shalt think about the social consequences of the program you are writing or the system you are designing.
10. Thou shalt always use a computer in ways that insure consideration and respect for your fellow humans.

Excerpted with permission The Computer Ethics Institute. Copyright © 1992, Computer Ethics Institute, 11 Dupont Circle NW, #900, Washington, DC 20036-1271.

Computer Industry Almanac: Computers per Capita Trends

In 1960 there were only 5,000 computers in use in the U.S. and all were mainframe computers. By 1965 the number of computers in use in the U.S. reached 25,000 and they were still nearly all mainframe computers. By 1970 the U.S. computer installed base reached 80,000 with minicomputers accounting for about 30%. In 1975 the computers in use surpassed 200,000 units and minicomputers accounted for over 50%. The first personal computers, appeared in 1975 and these were assembled from kits.

The increase in computer usage has been phenomenal since the personal computer caught on in the early 1980s. When the PC first appeared in the mid-1970s there was less than one computer per 1,000 people in the U.S. The table below shows the estimated computers per capita trend in the U.S. from 1965 to 1989. The figure clearly shows the explosion in computer usage. In 1965 there was only one computer for each 10,000 people in the United States. In the next ten years computers per capita increased nine-fold. Then came the personal computer. In the following ten years, from 1975 to 1985, the computer density grew 100-fold as the computers per capita zoomed to 90 per 1,000 people.

	1965	1970	1975	1980	1985	1988	1989
Worldwide: Total Computers in Use (#M)	-	-	0.3	5.2	38	79	97
Worldwide: Computers/1000 People	-	-	0.07	1.2	7.8	15.4	18.5
U.S.: Total Computers in Use (#M)	0.025	0.08	0.2	3.3	21.5	41	48
U.S.: Computers/1000 People	0.1	0.3	0.9	14	90	166	192
U.S.: Share of Computers in Use (%)	-	-	67.5	63.5	56.4	51.5	49.0
Worldwide: PCs in Use (#M)	-	-	negl.	2.1	33	73	91
U.S.: PCs in Use (#M)	-	-	negl.	1.4	19	38	45

The PC explosion continued in the 1990s as shown in the next table. In the last ten years, the computers per capita "only" grew 306% to 365 computers per 1,000 people. At year-end 1995 PCs accounted for 347 of the 365 computers per 1,000 people. The computer density will continue to grow strongly in the late 1990s. The yearly sales of computers in the U.S. is over 22M units and will reach over 30M units in the year 2000. The U.S. computer shipment rate is about 82 to 109 per 1,000 people in the 1996 to 2000 timeframe. But since over half of the units sold are replacing older computers, the computer density per 1,000 people increases by about 40 units per year. This indicates that the computers per capita will reach 425 to 440 per 1,000 people by year-end 1997 and 550 to 600 computers per 1,000 people at the end of year 2000.

	1991	1992	1993	1994	1995	1997	2000
Worldwide: Total Computers in Use (#M)	137	159	187	219	257	338	557
Worldwide: Computers/1000 People	25.3	29.1	33.7	38.8	44.9	57.0	90.3
U.S.: Total Computers in Use (#M)	62	68	77	86	96	117	160
U.S.: Computers/1000 People	245	267	297	329	365	433	580
U.S.: Share of Computers in Use (%)	45.3	42.8	41.0	39.2	37.4	35.0	28.8
Worldwide: PCs in Use (#M)	129	151	177	208	245	324	536
U.S.: PCs in Use (#M)	59	65	73	82	92	112	154

The worldwide installed base of computers surpassed 250M in 1995 and will more than double by year 2000 to over 550M. Currently the yearly worldwide shipments of PCs is over 60M worldwide and will be growing 15% to 20% per year the rest of the decade and may surpass 120M units in year 2000. These numbers include mainframes, minicomputers, workstations, office PCs, consumer PCs, emerging low-cost computers such as network computers and information appliances.

Computer Humor

Computer Industry Almanac: Jokes Received Online

The following are jokes that were circulating online and forwarded to us. If you've heard them before, you can laugh again. If you have any good ones, we'd like to have them for the next edition of the Almanac. So send them on to us at cialmanac@aol.com. Enjoy!

More Lightbulb Jokes

Q. How many Help Desk people does it take to change a light bulb?
A. PC Repair has received your mail concerning your hardware problem and has assigned your request Service Order Number 39712. Please use this number for any future reference to this case of trouble. As soon as a technician becomes available, you will be contacted.
Q. How many support staff people does it take to change a light bulb?
A. We have an exact copy of the light bulb here and it seems to be working fine. Can you tell me what kind of system you have? Ok. Just exactly how dark is it? Ok. There could be four or five things wrong. Have you tried the light switch?
Q. How many integration testers does it take to change a light bulb?
A. We just find the problem. We don't fix them.
Q. How many developers does it take to change a light bulb?
A. The light bulb works fine on the systems in all other offices. Why would YOURS not work?
Q. How many software engineers does it take to change a light bulb?
A. That's a hardware problem.
Q. How many hardware engineers does it take to change a light bulb?
A. Tell software to code around it.
Q. How many contract programmers does it take to change a light bulb?
A. Two. One always quits in the middle of the project.
Q. How many help desk techs does it take to change a light bulb?
A. I think that's a device driver problem.
Q. How many Windows programmers does it take to change a light bulb?
A. 472. One to write WinGetLightBulbHandle, one to write WinQueryStatusLightBulb, one to write WinGetLightSwitchHandle...
Q. How many C++ programmers does it take to change a light bulb?
A. You're still thinking procedurally. A properly designed light bulb object would inherit a change method from a generic light bulb class, so all you'd have to do is send it a bulb change message.

One-Liner Grins

Daddy, why doesn't this magnet pick up this floppy disk?
Give me ambiguity or give me something else.
Pentiums melt in your PC, not in your hand.
Error, no keyboard--press F1 to continue.
Artificial Intelligence usually beats real stupidity.
Double your drive space--delete Windows!
Oops. My brain just hit a bad sector.
C program run. C program crash. C programmer quit.
Is reading in the bathroom considered Multi-Tasking?
My computer isn't that nervous... it's just a bit ANSI.
Honey, I Formatted the Kid!
Spelling checkers at maximum! Fire!
Your e-mail has been returned due to insufficient voltage.
Who is General Failure and why is he reading my disk?
Hex dump: Where witches put used curses...
Never violate the Prime Directory! C:\

Multitasking: Screwing up several things at once...
Maniac: An early computer built by nuts...
Stack Error: Lost on a cluttered desk...
Stack Overflow: Too many pancakes...
Capt'n! The spellchecker kinna take this abuse!
C:\BELFRY is where I keep my .BAT files.
ASCII to ASCII, DOS to DOS.
How do I set my laser printer on stun?
"Today's subliminal thought is:""
'Calm down--it's only ones and zeros.'
....now touch these wires to your tongue!'
Computer analyst to programmer: "You start coding. I'll go find out what they want."
According to my calculations the problem doesn't exist.
It said, "Insert disk #3," but only two will fit!
RAM DISK is not an installation procedure!
Computers are only human.
This time it will surely run.
I just found the last bug.
"Real programmers use: COPY CON PROGRAM.EXE"
Logic: The art of being wrong with confidence...
If at first you don't succeed, call it version 1.0
God is REAL, unless explicitly declared INTEGER.
Asking if computers can think is like asking if submarines can swim.
From C:*.* to shining C:*.*
This message transmitted on 100% recycled electrons.
Today's assembler command: EXOP Execute Operator
Justify my text? I'm sorry but it has no excuse.
Programming is an art form that fights back.
Backups? We doan *NEED* no steenking baX%^~,VbKx NO CARRIER
My mail reader can beat up your mail reader.
Nobody has ever, ever, EVER learned all of WordPerfect.
Good programming is 99% sweat and 1% coffee.

How Does a Chicken Cross the Road?

NT Chicken: Will cross the road in June. No, August. September for sure.
OS/2 Chicken: It crossed the road in style years ago, but it was so quiet that nobody noticed.
Win 95 Chicken: You see different colored feathers while it crosses, but cook it and it still tastes like... chicken.
Microsoft Chicken (TM): It's already on both sides of the road. And it just bought the road.
OOP Chicken: It doesn't need to cross the road, it just sends a message.
Assembler Chicken: First it builds the road...
C Chicken: It crosses the road without looking both ways.
C++ Chicken: The chicken wouldn't have to cross the road, you'd simply refer to him on the other side.
VB Chicken: USHighways!TheRoad.cross (aChicken)
Delphi Chicken: The chicken is dragged across the road and dropped on the other side.
Java Chicken: If your road needs to be crossed by a chicken, the server will download one to the other side. (Of course, those are chicklets)
Web Chicken: Jumps out onto the road, turns right, and just keeps on running.
Gopher Chicken: Tried to run, but got flattened by the Web chicken.
Newton Chicken: Can't cluck, can't fly, and can't lay eggs, but you can carry it across the road in your pocket!
Cray Chicken: Crosses faster than any other chicken, but if you don't dip it in liquid nitrogen first, it arrives on the other side fully cooked.
Quantum Logic Chicken: The chicken is distributed probabalistically on all sides of the road until you observe it on the side of your course.
Lotus Chicken: Don't you *dare* try to cross the road the same way we do!
Mac Chicken: No reasonable chicken owner would want a chicken to cross the road, so there's no way to tell it to.

Al Gore Chicken: Waiting for completion of NCI (Nation Chicken-crossing Infrastructure) and will cross as soon as it's finished, assuming he's re-elected and the Republicans don't gut the program.

COBOL Chicken: 0001-CHICKEN-CROSSING. IF NO-MORE-VEHICLES THEN PERFORM 0010-CROSS-THE-ROAD VARYING STEPS FROM 1 BY 1 UNTILON-THE-OTHER-SIDE ELSE GO TO 0001-CHICKEN-CROSSING

Top 10 Signs You're Addicted to the Net

10. You wake up at 3 a.m. to go to the bathroom and stop and check your e-mail on the way back to bed.

9. You get a tattoo that reads "This body best viewed with Netscape Navigator 1.1 or higher."

8. You name your children Eudora, Mozilla and Dotcom.

7. You turn off your modem and get this awful empty feeling, like you just pulled the plug on a loved one.

6. You spend half of the plane trip with your laptop on your lap... and your child in the overhead compartment.

5. You decide to stay in college for an additional year or two, just for the free Internet access.

4. You laugh at people with 2400-baud modems.

3. You start using smileys in your snail mail.

2. The last girl you picked up was a JPEG.

1. Your hard drive crashes. You haven't logged in for two hours. You start to twitch. You pick up the phone and manually dial your ISP's access number. You try to hum to communicate with the modem. You succeed.

Adventures From the Phone Support World...

ring *ring*

"Hello! Local ISP, how can I help you?"

Customer: "Hello? Tech-support? Uh, yes, I have service with you and... uh, well, I don't know what program I'm using, but it's not working."

Support: "Okay. What are you trying to do?"

C: "I don't know. I want the Internet."

S: "...Rrright. Are you..."

C: "Well, do I need the modem?"

S: "Yes. You need the modem. Now, are you..."

C: "And what kind of cable do I need for that? The one in the modem box should work, shouldn't it?"

S: "Yes yes, that's right. Uh, is the modem hooked up?"

C: "Yes. I think so."

S: "Okay then. Now listen, are you..."

C: "And does the modem need to be on?"

S: "...Yes, the modem needs to be on. Are you..."

C: "I don't understand why this doesn't work. I put your disks in my computer, but I don't have the Internet."

(beat)

S: "Do you have a gun?"

C: "A gun? Yes I do, right here."

S: "Good. Put the gun to your head."

C: "Is a pistol okay? I don't know what caliber it is."

S: "I'm certain it will be just fine. Is the gun to your head?"

C: "Yes."

S: "Good. Now pull the..."

C: "Wait, let me switch sides, the phone is in the way."

S: "Fine, okay. Now pull the trigger."

C: "The what?"

S: "The trigger! The hook-shaped thing in front of the handle."

BLAM

C: "Now what?"

S: "...um... I'm sorry, did you point the gun at your head?"

C: "OH! No, sorry, I was looking at the gun to find the trigger. Ha ha ha."

S: "Okay, look, point the gun at your head, then pull the trigger WHILE IT'S POINTED AT YOUR HEAD."

C: "Okay, hang on..."

click

S: "ARGH. Is the gun loaded?"

C: "Loaded?"

S: "ARE THERE BULLETS IN THE GUN?"

C: "Yes. There is one bullet."

S: "OKAY. Set the gun to fire the bullet. Put the gun to your head, then pull the trigger, okay?"

C: "I've never configured a gun before."

S: "Just turn it so that the bullet is at the top."

click

S: "Is the bullet in the gun the one you just fired?"

C: "Can't you use the same bullets? I didn't know I was going to have to buy more hardware..."

S: "Okay, forget the gun. Do you have a knife?"

C: "Yes, right here."

S: "Good good. Put the knife to your stomach."

C: "Should I open the knife first?"

S: "YES!!! Of COURSE the knife has to be open!"

C: "Well, I've never actually used this knife before. My brother gave it to me for Christmas last year and well... how about a Salad Shooter?"

S: "Okay, forget the knife. How about sleeping pills, do you have sleeping pills?"

C: "Yes, right here."

S: "GOOD. This should be easy. You'll need the whole bottle, but you want to take them in small groups so that..."

C: "I can't get the bottle open."

S: "CHRIST ON A CROSS WITH NAILS! Don't you ever use these things?!? I thought these were your sleeping pills."

C: "Well, my daughter is the one who opens the bottles. She's not home, though. She's at work."

S: "FORGET IT then. Shit... okay... how high up are you? Which floor do you live on?"

C: "We live on the 27th floor, apt. 2712 in the Murdock Building on Hampton Street in the Theater District just south of..."

S: "OKAY! That's good. Go to the window and open it."

C: "I've got Windows95. Will that work?"

S: "It's... appropriate, yes. But I want you to go to the window in your wall."

C: "Okay, I'm at the window. How do you open the..."

S: "JUST BREAK THE WINDOW! Use your computer. Throw your computer through the window."

CRASH tinkle tinkle

C: "Some glass got on the floor."

S: "That's okay, just fine, you won't need the floor when we're done. Now, want you to jump out of the window."

C: "Okay. I'm going to throw the phone out first and then ask you where I should jump."

S: "NO! WAIT!"

CRASH

S: "Hello?.,. Hello?... eeeuuurrrrrgh."

click

ring

S: "Yes... tech... support."

C: "Yes, hello, I think something's wrong with my phone."

(two beats)

S: "Do you have a gun? And do you know how to use it?"

C: "Yes, right here, I've used it many times."

S: "Good. Let's get started..."

Murphy's Technology Laws

1. You can never tell which way the train went by looking at the track.
2. Logic is a systematic method of coming to the wrong conclusion with confidence.
3. Whenever a system becomes completely defined, some damn fool discovers something which either abolishes the system or expands it beyond recognition.
4. Technology is dominated by those who manage what they do not understand.

5. If builders built buildings the way programmers wrote programs, then the first woodpecker that came along would destroy civilization.

6. The opulence of the front office decor varies inversely with the fundamental solvency of the firm.

7. The attention span of a computer is only as long as it electrical cord.

8. An expert is one who knows more and more about less and less until he knows absolutely everything about nothing.

9. Tell a man there are 300 billion stars in the universe and he'll believe you. Tell him a bench has wet paint on it and he'll have to touch to be sure.

10. All great discoveries are made by mistake.

11. Always draw your curves, then plot your reading.

12. Nothing ever gets built on schedule or within budget.

13. All's well that ends.

14. A meeting is an event at which the minutes are kept and the hours are lost.

15. The first myth of management is that it exists.

16. A failure will not appear till a unit has passed final inspection.

17. New systems generate new problems.

18. To err is human, but to really foul things up requires a computer.

19. We don't know one millionth of one percent about anything.

20. Any given program, when running, is obsolete.

21. Any sufficiently advanced technology is indistinguishable from magic.

22. A computer makes as many mistakes in two seconds as 20 men working 20 years make.

23. Nothing motivates a man more than to see his boss putting in an honest day's work.

24. Some people manage by the book, even though they don't know who wrote the book or even what book.

25. The primary function of the design engineer is to make things difficult for the fabricator and impossible for the serviceman.

26. To spot the expert, pick the one who predicts the job will take the longest and cost the most.

27. After all is said and done, a hell of a lot more is said than done.

28. Any circuit design must contain at least one part which is obsolete, two parts which are unobtainable and three parts which are still under development.

29. A complex system that works is invariably found to have evolved from a simple system that works.

30. If mathematically you end up with the incorrect answer, try multiplying by the page number.

31. Computers are unreliable, but humans are even more unreliable. Any system which depends on human reliability is unreliable.

32. Give all orders verbally. Never write anything down that might go into a "Pearl Harbor File."

33. Under the most rigorously controlled conditions of pressure, temperature, volume, humidity, and other variables the organism will do as it damn well pleases.

34. If you can't understand it, it is intuitively obvious.

35. The more cordial the buyer's secretary, the greater the odds that the competition already has the order.

36. In designing any type of construction, no overall dimension can be totalled correctly after 4:30 p.m. on Friday. The correct total will become self-evident at 8:15 a.m. on Monday.

37. Fill what's empty. Empty what's full. And scratch where it itches.

38. All things are possible except skiing through a revolving door.

39. The only perfect science is hind-sight.

40. Work smarder and not harder and be careful of yor speling.

41. If it's not in the computer, it doesn't exist.

42. If an experiment works, something has gone wrong.

43. When all else fails, read the instructions.

44. If there is a possibility of several things going wrong the one that will cause the most damage will be the one to go wrong.

45. Everything that goes up must come down.

46. Any instrument when dropped will roll into the least accessible corner.

47. Any simple theory will be worded in the most complicated way.

48. Build a system that even a fool can use and only a fool will want to use it.

49. The degree of technical competence is inversely proportional to the level of management.

[LINK] Back

Are You In the Market For a New Toaster?

• If IBM made toasters... They would want one big toaster where people bring bread to be submitted for over-night toasting. IBM would claim a worldwide market for five, maybe six toasters.
• If Microsoft made toasters... Every time you bought a loaf of bread, you would have to buy a toaster. You wouldn't have to take the toaster, but you'd still have to pay for it anyway. Toaster'95 would weigh 15000 pounds (hence requiring a reinforced steel countertop), draw enough electricity to power a small city, take up 95% of the space in your kitchen, would claim to be the first toaster that lets you control how light or dark you want your toast to be, and would secretly interrogate your other appliances to find out who made them. Everyone would hate Microsoft toasters, but nonetheless would buy them since most of the good bread only works with their toasters.
• If Apple made toasters... It would do everything the Microsoft toaster does, but 5 years earlier.
• If Xerox made toasters... You could toast one-sided or double-sided. Successive slices would get lighter and lighter. The toaster would jam your bread for you.
• If Radio Shack made toasters... The staff would sell you a toaster, but not know anything about it. Or you could buy all the parts to build your own toaster.
• If Oracle made toasters... They'd claim their toaster was compatible with all brands and styles of bread, but when you got it home you'd discover the Bagel Engine was still in development, the Croissant Extension was three years away, and that indeed the whole appliance was just blowing smoke.
• Does DEC still make toasters?... They made good toasters in the '80s, didn't they?
• If Hewlett-Packard made toasters... They would market the Reverse Polish Toaster, which takes in toast and gives you regular bread.
• If Tandem made toasters... You could make toast 24 hours a day, and if a piece got burned the toaster would automatically toast you a new one.
• If Thinking Machines made toasters... You would be able to toast 64,000 pieces of bread at the same time.
• If Cray made toasters... They would cost $16 million but would be faster than any other single-slice toaster in the world.
• If The Rand Corporation made toasters... It would be a large, perfectly smooth and seamless black cube. Every morning there would be a piece of toast on top of it. Their service department would have an unlisted phone number, and the blueprints for the box would be highly classified government documents. The X-Files would have an episode about it.
• If the NSA made toasters... Your toaster would have a secret trap door that only the NSA could access in case they needed to get at your toast for reasons of national security.
• If Sony made toasters... The ToastMan, which would be barely larger than the single piece of bread it is meant to toast, can be conveniently attached to your belt.
• If MCI made toasters... They would claim their toaster cost less per minute to run than all the other toasters only to find out later that you can only toast between the hours of 5pm to 5am to get your savings.
• If AT&T made toasters... They would advertise "True-toast" and claim that their toaster "really" toasts bread, while MCI and Sprint only makes bread "look" like its toasted.
• If Sprint made toasters... They would tell you that their toasting is so clear, you could distinctly see every gran-ule of toasted bread.
• If Sun made toasters... They would be programmable, you could get a really good cuppa Java while you waited, and the toast would be simple, object- oriented, distributed, robust, secure, architecture-neutral, portable, high-performance, multithreaded and dynamic: in other words--buzzword compliant. But actually Sun doesn't need to make toasters because "The Network is the Toaster".

Computer Industry Almanac: Unbelievable Headlines

These are headlines that could happen, have happened or are totally off the wall. Can you tell which of these are real?
o Microsoft says it will not support Java because it can cause cancer in mouse devices.
o A rash of ergonomic injuries are found to be caused by thumb twiddling while waiting for Internet data.
o IBM sells its OS/2 business to a management team funded by Netscape.
o Sun Microsystems acquires Starbucks to control copyrighted coffee names.
o Spencer F. Katt is run over by the Universal Serial Bus at a COMDEX party.

o Miss King's Kitchen in Dallas has filed suit against Yahoo to stop using its logo and name on the Internet because the cake company has sold cakes known as YA-HOO! since 1980.

o Most IRS databases are sabotaged by a group of computer terrorists called Freedatamen.

o A computer executive runs his pet dog for Congress with the slogan "Take a bit out of Congress".

o The U.S. postal service says it will install computer equipment that will track all pieces of mail at all times.

o Intel enters the birth control market with the RU-486 microprocessor.

o Windows 95 is a disappointment--it only sold 40M copies in its first 12 months.

o A survey of dating habits show a drop in the number dates due to the realism of virtual reality technology.

o America Online has sent over 100M diskettes to potential subscribers--one for every American households. If laid end-to-end, they would stretch from Vienna, VA to Redmond, WA and back.

Computer Industry Almanac: Pain in the 'Puter

The top 10 things that irritate us when we use PCs:

10. No local online access phone numbers.
9.   Email accounts that are easy to get and nearly impossible to close out.
8.   Tech support that has no humans-only on the phone menu.
7.   Tech support that says "That can't happen!" when it does.
6.   Software packaging that isn't once its opened.
5.   Software that lacks any backward compatibility.
4.   Software upward compatibility that isn't.
3.   Manuals that assume you've read everything before you've read anything.
2.   New version has added software features and the SAME OLD BUGS.
and the No. 1 reason we get irritated when we use the PC:
    JUNK EMAIL !

David Letterman: Top 10 Signs You Bought a Bad Computer

We found one of David Letterman's famous Top Ten Lists on the Internet and couldn't resist using it here.

10. Lower corner of screen has "Etch-a-sketch"
9.   Its celebrity spokesman is "Hey Vern!"
8.   You need jumper cables and car to start it
7.   It's got a floppy keyboard instead of disks
6.   You type in: "Need comedy bit for talk show"; It prints out: "Stunt doubles"
5.   Whenever you turn it on, all the dogs in your neighborhood start howling
4.   Screen frequently freezes and message comes up, "Ain't it break time, Chester?"
3.   The manual contains one sentence: "Good Luck!"
2.   The only chip inside is a Dorito
1.   It cyber-sucks!

The Internet, January 11, 1995.

Index

Symbols

E

F

I

N

O

S

W

People Index

A

C

D

H

I

J

M

O

Q

R

T

W

X

Y

The Computer Industry Almanac

By Karen Petska-Juliussen and Egil Juliussen Ph.D.

The Computer Industry Almanac is an annual reference book about the computer industry. Its 800-pages that's authored by two experienced industry observers - Karen Petska-Juliussen and Egil Juliussen. It is the most cost-effective resource book in the computer industry. The Computer Industry Almanac has thousands of facts that summarize the industry. There are databases such as:

- Computer companies - 3,200+ entries (5,000+ on Disk)
- Computer publishers - 180+
- Associations, organizations and users groups - 350+
- Testing companies - 50+
- Conference companies - 80+
- Publications - 1,150+
- Research companies - 250+
- PR & marketing communications agencies - 260+
- Conferences - 250+
- People - 10,000+

The Almanac is full of rankings and awards for companies, people and products, which have been excerpted from the business press (i.e., Forbes) and the computer press (i.e.,Computerworld, Datamation, PC Magazine and Soft•letter). One of the most popular chapters is the salary and wealth rankings of the top computer people as well as the average salaries for various computer-related occupations. It has summaries of computer market forecasts for hardware, software and peripherals. There are also estimates of the number of computers in use for over 50 industrialized countries. A technology forecast focusing on 2000 to 2002 reviews the expected advances and product capabilities.

An introductory chapter explains the structure of the computer industry and defines the computer categories from personal computers to supercomputers. Software, peripherals and service products are also categorized and defined. Additionally, there is a history of the computer, employment data, computer comedy and much, much more. The Computer Industry Almanac was compiled using PCs and desktop publishing and all products used are listed in the Computer Industry Almanac.

Availability: The Computer Industry Almanac 8th Annual is **$53** paperback, **$63** hardcover plus S&H and is available directly from the authors. The directories, for mailing list use, are available on disk in delimited ASCII format. Prices are **$250** for the Company database (includes all companies and organizations) and **$200** for the People database. **$100** each for Computer Publications; Market Research Companies; Associations and Organizations, Conferences or High-Tech Public Relations or Marketing Communications Agencies. **$50** for Computer Publishers or Testing Companies. To buy **all databases** the cost is **$400** plus S&H.

Note: Our NEW ADDRESS: Computer Industry Almanac, PO Box 600, 1639 Logan Creek Drive, Glenbrook, NV 89413-0600, USA. Tel 800/377-6810, 702/749-5053 Pacific time, fax 702/749-5864, 73543.3506@compuserve.com, cialmanac@aol.com.

To order: 800/377-6810, fax 702/749-5864. Hours: 9 a.m. to 5 p.m. Pacific Time, Monday through Friday

Order Form
Computer Industry Almanac (Book or Directories)

EIN #93-0965444

Shipping:
Name:
Title:
Co.:
Add.:
Tel #:
FAX #:

Billing:

Name:	Title:
Co.:	Add.:
Billing Tel. #	Fax #:

☞ Credit card: VISA, MasterCard or AmEx   Card#:
Exp. date:

Name on card (print or type):

Signature _____

Send _____ copies **8th Edition paperback** (avail. 4Q'96 includes) X **$53** ea. =............................$_____
Send _____ copies **8th Edition hardcover** (avail. 4Q'96) X **$63** ea. =.......................................$_____
Send Database(s) Name:_____...... Quan.: _____ copies X $_____ ea. =.... $_____
Send Database(s) Name:_____...... Quan.: _____ copies X $_____ ea. =.... $_____
Send _____ copies **1994-95 paperback** (7th edition) X **$50** ea. =...$_____
Send _____ copies **1994-95 hardcover** (7th edition) X **$60** ea. =...$_____
Send _____ copies **1994-95 CD-ROM** (DOS only) X **$60** ea. =...$_____
....Shipping (See below) = $_____
....In NV add 7% Sales Tax =.... $_____
....TOTAL = $_____

• **Put me on your <u>Mailing List</u>**:   Y   N   Checks in U.S.$; U.S. bank only

• *Availability:* Order from: Computer Industry Almanac, PO Box 600, 1639 Logan Creek Drive, Glenbrook, NV 89413-0600, U.S.; **Tel.# 800-377-6810 U.S., 702/749-5053 Pacific Time (PT)** or **Fax 702/749-5864**; cialmanac@aol.com, 73543.3506@compuserve.com. Office hours are 9 a.m.-5 p.m. Pacific Time, Monday through Friday.

• Direct Order Volume Discounts are available on request.

• **ISBN #s:** 8th Edition (1996): paperback ISBN# 0-942107-07-1, $53; hardcover ISBN# 0-942107-08-X, $63
        1994-95 (7th Edition): paperback ISBN# 0-942107-05-5, $50.00; hardcover ISBN# 0-942107-06-3, $60.00;
CD-ROM (DOS only) ISBN# 0-942107-09-8, $60.00

Shipping & Handling Charges						
Location	------ Continental USA ------			Hawaii, Alaska, Canada & Mexico		
Type of Shipping	Ground	2nd day	Overnight	Ground	2nd day	Overnight
Single Book	$6	$8	$20	$6	$15	$35
Single CD-ROM	$6	$8	$15	$6	$15	$25
Location	--------- Europe ---------			Japan & Rest of World		
Type of Shipping	Surface (3-4 weeks)	Airmail (1-2 weeks)	Express (2-4 days)	Surface (3-4 weeks)	Airmail (1-2 weeks)	Express (2-4 days)
Single Book	$10	$25	$50-$55	$10	$30	$60-$100
Single CD-ROM	$6	$10	$30-$35	$6	$10	$35-$45

Purchases include a 30-day money-back guarantee.